The SAGE Encyclopedia of Marriage, Family, and Couples Counseling

Editorial Board

Editors

Jon Carlson
Adler University

Shannon B. Dermer
Governors State University

Managing Editors

Brenna R. Frayn
Governors State University

Katie Paulson
Governors State University

Editorial Board

James Robert Bitter
East Tennessee State University

Scott Browning
Chestnut Hill College

William J. Doherty
University of Minnesota

Leslie Greenberg
York University

Katherine M. Helm
Lewis University

Alan J. Hovestadt
Western Michigan University

Jay Lebow
Northwestern University

Susan H. McDaniel
University of Rochester

Fred P. Piercy
University of Vermont

Robert L. Smith
Texas A&M–Corpus Christi

The SAGE Encyclopedia of Marriage, Family, and Couples Counseling

Volume 1

Editors

Jon Carlson
Adler University

Shannon B. Dermer
Governors State University

Los Angeles | London | New Delhi | Singapore | Washington DC | Melbourne

FOR INFORMATION:

SAGE Publications, Inc.
2455 Teller Road
Thousand Oaks, California 91320
E-mail: order@sagepub.com

SAGE Publications Ltd.
1 Oliver's Yard
55 City Road
London, EC1Y 1SP
United Kingdom

SAGE Publications India Pvt. Ltd.
B 1/I 1 Mohan Cooperative Industrial Area
Mathura Road, New Delhi 110 044
India

SAGE Publications Asia-Pacific Pte. Ltd.
3 Church Street
#10-04 Samsung Hub
Singapore 049483

Acquisitions Editor: Andrew Boney
Editorial Assistant: Jordan Enobakhare
Developmental Editor: Sanford Robinson
Production Editor: Tracy Buyan
Reference Systems Manager: Leticia Gutierrez
Copy Editors: Diane DiMura, Talia Greenberg, Megan Markanich, Terri Lee Paulsen, Gretchen Treadwell
Typesetter: C&M Digitals (P) Ltd.
Proofreaders: Lawrence W. Baker, Caryne Brown, Sarah Duffy, Scott Oney
Indexer: David Luljak
Cover Designer: Candice Harman
Marketing Manager: Leah Watson

Copyright © 2017 by SAGE Publications, Inc.

All rights reserved. No part of this book may be reproduced or utilized in any form or by any means, electronic or mechanical, including photocopying, recording, or by any information storage and retrieval system, without permission in writing from the publisher.

All trade names and trademarks recited, referenced, or reflected herein are the property of their respective owners who retain all rights thereto.

Printed in the United States of America

Library of Congress Cataloging-in-Publication Data

Names: Carlson, Jon, editor. | Dermer, Shannon B., editor.

Title: The SAGE encyclopedia of marriage, family, and couples counseling / editors, Jon Carlson, Shannon B. Dermer.

Other titles: Encyclopedia of marriage, family, and couples counseling

Description: Thousand Oaks, California : SAGE Publications, Inc., [2016] | "A SAGE Reference publication." | Includes bibliographical references and index.

Identifiers: LCCN 2016025752 | ISBN 9781483369556 (hardcover : alk. paper)

Subjects: | MESH: Psychotherapy, Group | Counseling | Interpersonal Relations | Family Relations | Encyclopedias

Classification: LCC BF636.7.G76 | NLM WM 13 | DDC 158.3/5—dc23
LC record available at https://lccn.loc.gov/2016025752

This book is printed on acid-free paper.

16 17 18 19 20 10 9 8 7 6 5 4 3 2 1

Contents

Volume 1

List of Entries   *vii*
Reader's Guide   *xv*
About the Editors   *xxv*
Contributors   *xxvi*
Introduction   *xxxix*

Entries

A	*1*	C	*187*
B	*141*	D	*411*

Volume 2

List of Entries   *vii*
Reader's Guide   *xv*

Entries

E	*487*	I	*825*
F	*589*	J	*925*
G	*707*	K	*937*
H	*759*		

(Continued)

Volume 3

	List of Entries	*vii*		
	Reader's Guide	*xv*		
	Entries			
L	*941*		P	*1191*
M	*999*		Q	*1349*
N	*1133*		R	*1361*
O	*1173*			

Volume 4

	List of Entries	*vii*		
	Reader's Guide	*xv*		
	Entries			
S	*1433*		U	*1747*
T	*1679*		V	*1753*

Appendix A. The History of Marriage, Family, and Couples Therapy   *1767*

Appendix B. Resource Guide   *1789*

Appendix C. Selected Readings   *1795*

Index   *1799*

List of Entries

Acceptance and Commitment Therapy
Acculturation
Active Parenting
Adjustment Disorder in Adolescents
Adlerian Family Therapy
Adlerian Open-Forum Family Counseling
Adolescent Behavior Disorders
Adolescent Behavior Problems
Adolescent Mental Health
Adoption
Adoption, Cross-Cultural and Interracial
Adoptive Families
Adult Attachment Assessments
Adult Development
Affect Regulation
African American Families
Aging and Caregiving
Alcohol and Substance Abuse
American Association for Marriage and Family Therapy
Anger Management
Anxiety
Anxiety Disorders in Adolescents
Asian American Families
Assertiveness
Assessment, Biopsychosocial
Assessment, Suicide
Assimilation: Immigrants and Refugees
Attachment
Attachment and Adolescents
Attachment and Health
Attachment and Romantic Love
Attachment Styles
Attachment Theory
Attachment-Based Family Therapy
Attention-Deficit and Disruptive Behavior Disorders

Attunement, Clinician
Attunement in Relationships
Authoritative Parenting
Autism and Children
Autism Spectrum Disorder
Avoidance

Behavioral Family Therapy
Beliefs and Values
Bereavement
Bereavement Counseling
Best Interests of the Child
Bibliotherapy. *See* Self-Help
Bilingual Families
Birth Control and Contraception
Blended Families. *See* Stepfamilies
Body Dysmorphic Disorder in Adolescents
Bonding
Boundaries
Bowen Family Systems Theory
Brief Adlerian Couples Therapy
Brief Family Therapy

CACREP. *See* Competency-Based Standards for Marriage, Couple, and Family Counseling; Council for Accreditation of Counseling and Related Educational Programs
Career Planning and Couples/Families
Caregivers
Certified Family Life Educator
Chaos Family Therapy
Child Behavior Problems
Child Guidance Movement
Child Maltreatment
Child Protective Services
Child-Centered Parenting
Childhood Anxiety

Childhood Obesity, Prevention and Treatment of
Childless Couples
Child–Parent Relationship Therapy
Children With Chronic Illness
Children With Special Needs in Family Therapy
Choice Theory and Reality Therapy
Chosen Families
Chronic Illness With Couples and Families
Cinematherapy
Circular Questions. *See* Questions: Open, Closed, and Circular
Circularity and Linearity
Circumplex Model
Clinical Case Conceptualization With Couples and Families
Clinical Interviews With Couples and Families
Clinical Practice
Clinical Versus Statistical Significance
Clinician-Directed, Solution-Focused Supervision
Cognitive Maps and Couples
Cognitive-Behavioral Couples Therapy
Cognitive-Behavioral Family Therapy
Cohesion
Collaborative Couples Therapy
Collaborative Language Systems
Collaborative Therapy. *See* Collaborative Language Systems
Commitment
Common Factors
Communication Disorders
Communication Errors/Problems in Couples and Families
Communication in Couples and Families
Community Programs
Compassion
Competency-Based Standards for Marriage, Couple, and Family Counseling
Complementary and Symmetrical Relationships
Compulsive Sexual Behavior
Conduct Disorder
Confidentiality
Conflict in Couples and Families
Conflict Resolution
Conflict Styles
Confrontation

Conjoint Family Therapy
Constructivism
Contextual Family Therapy
Core Competencies for Marriage and Family Therapists
Cost–Benefit Analysis
Cotherapy Team
Council for Accreditation of Counseling and Related Educational Programs
Couple and Family Forensics
Couple Development
Couples, Quality Time
Couples and Marriage Counseling
Couples Therapy Research
Court-Mandated Clients
Crisis Intervention With Couples and Families
Critical Theory
Crucible
Cultural Issues in Couples and Families
Custody Evaluations
Cutting/Self-Mutilation. *See* Self-Injury
Cybernetics

Dating Coaching
Dating Relationship Dissolution
Death, Parents of Deceased Children
Death and Dying
Debt and Financial Strain
Decision-Making
Delphi Research Method
Depression in Adolescents
Depression in Children
Depression in Couples and Families
Developmental Model of Marriage
Differentiation
Discernment Counseling
Disinhibited Social Engagement Disorder in Children
Diversity
Divorce and Separation
Divorce Therapy
Domestic Violence
Double Bind Theory
DSM and V-Codes
Dual and Multiple Relationships

Dual-Earner Families
Duty to Warn and Protect

Earned Attachment
Eating Disorders
Ecological Systems
Eco-Map
Ecosystemic Structural Family Therapy
Ecosystems Perspective
Effectiveness Research
Elder Abuse
Elimination Disorders in Children
Emotional Disengagement
Emotional Intelligence, Children
Emotional Intelligence, Families
Emotionally Focused Therapy for Couples
Empathy
Empirically Validated Models
Empowerment in Families
Enactments
Engendering Hope
Entitlement
Epistemology in Family Therapy
Equine-Assisted Family Therapy
Erectile Disorder
Ericksonian Family Therapy
Ethical Codes
Ethical Decision-Making
Ethnicity
Evidence-Based Practice With Couples and Families
Experiential Family Therapy
Externalizing Behaviors
Extramarital Affairs and Infidelity

Faith-Based Therapy
Families and Poverty
Families and Substance Abuse
Family and Medical Leave Act of 1993
Family Assessment, Models of
Family Life Cycle
Family Life Educators
Family Mediation
Family Mode Deactivation Therapy
Family Myth
Family of Origin

Family Reconstruction
Family Resilience
Family Resource Management
Family Rituals
Family Strengths
Family Stress
Family Stress Adaptation Theory
Family Values
Feedback. *See* Positive and Negative Feedback
Female Orgasmic Disorder
Female Sexual Interest/Arousal Disorder
Feminist Family Therapy
Feminization of Poverty
Fetishes
Fidelity
First-Order Change
Focal Family Therapy
Forgiveness
Foster Children
Friendship
Functional Assessment and Children
Functional Family Therapy
Functionalism
Fusion

Gambling, Compulsive
Gender- and Culture-Sensitive Therapies
Gender Dysphoria
Gender Issues
Gender Orientation, Gender Identity, and Gender Expression
Gender Roles
General Systems Theory
Genito-Pelvic Pain/Penetration Disorder
Genograms
Gestalt Family Therapy
Goals, Treatment
Gottman Method Couples Therapy
Grief Counseling
Group Family Therapy
Group Parenting Classes

Health Issues
Healthy Marriage and Responsible Fatherhood
Hierarchy
HIPAA Standards

Hispanic Healthy Marriage Initiative
Hoarding
Holism
Home-Based Therapy
Homelessness
Homelessness and Youth
Homeostasis
Homework Assignments in Therapy
Homicide
Hope-Focused Approach to Couple Enrichment in Counseling
Hospice
Human Sexual Response
Humanistic Family Therapy
Hypnosis
Hypothesis, Systemic

IAMFC. *See* International Association of Marriage and Family Counselors
Identified Patient
Imago Relationship Therapy
Immigrant Families
Incest
Individual and Family Development
Individual Family Culture
Individual Versus Family Therapy
Infertility
Informed Consent for Research
Informed Consent in Clinical Work
In-Law Relationships
Integrating Systemic and Individual Theories
Integrative Couples Therapy
Intellectual Disability and Autism
Intercultural Marriage and Family
Intergenerational Loyalty
Intergenerational Trauma
Intermittent Explosive Disorder in Adolescents
Internal Family Systems Model
International Association of Marriage and Family Counselors
International Classification of Diseases (ICD)
International Family Therapy
Interpersonal Neurobiology, Attachment and
Interpersonal Neurobiology, Couples and
Interpersonal Neurobiology, Parenting and
Interpersonal Violence
Interracial Marriages and Families

Intimacy, Specific Threats to
Isomorphism

Job Loss
Joining
Juvenile Firesetter Interventions

Kinship Care

Latino Families
Legal Issues in Parenting
LGBT Families
Licensure and Certification
Life Balance
Life Events
Life Transitions
Listening, Empathic
Live Supervision
Loneliness
Loss
Love, Physiology of
Love, Theories of
Love, Types of
Love and Rituals
Love Languages

Male Hypoactive Sexual Desire Disorder
Mandated Reporter
Marital Distress
Marital Group Therapy
Marriage, Arranged
Marriage, First and Second
Marriage and Health
Marriage Education
Marriage Encounter
Marriage Enrichment
Marriage Myths
Marriage Versus Civil Unions
Marriage-Friendly Therapy
Mate Selection
Media in Family Therapy
Medical Family Therapy
Men in Counseling
Mental Health, Systemic Perspective
Metacommunication
Metaphors
Milan Team

Military Couples and Families
Mindfulness
Mindfulness and Children
Mindfulness and Couples
Mindfulness and Sex
Miracle Question
Mood Disorders in Adolescents
Mood Disorders in Children
Moral Dimensions of Therapy
Morphogenesis
Morphostasis
Mother-Blaming
Motivational Interviewing
Multicultural Counseling Competence
Multiculturalism
Multiple Family Therapy
Multiple Relationships. *See* Dual and Multiple Relationships
Multisystemic Therapy
Muslim American Families

Narrative Therapy
National Marriage Initiative
Native American Families
Network Therapy
Neuro-Linguistic Programming
Neutrality and Curiosity
No-Harm Contracts
Non–Rapid Eye Movement Sleep Arousal Disorders in Children
Nonresidential Fathers
Nonverbal Communication
Normalizing
No-Secrets Contracts
Nuclear Family
Nudity: Beliefs and Values

Object Relations Theory
Online Dating
Open Relationships
Oppositional Defiant Disorder
Outcome Research

Paradoxes and Paradoxical Intervention
Paraphilic Disorders
Parent Effectiveness Training (P.E.T.)
Parent Management Training

Parent Study Groups
Parent–Adolescent Relations
Parental Acceptance–Rejection Theory
Parental Alienation Syndrome
Parental Stress: Effects on Children
Parent–Child Communication
Parentification and Diverse Family Systems
Parenting
Parenting Education
Parenting Styles
Patriarchy
Peer Counseling
Person of the Therapist
Play Family Therapy
Polyamory
Polygamy
Pornography
Positive and Negative Feedback
Positive Psychology
Postdoctoral Training
Postmodern Therapies
Postpartum Depression
Posttraumatic Stress Disorder in Children
Poverty and Family Development
Power Issues in Couples
Practice Management
Pregnancy
Pregnancy and Sexuality
Premarital Counseling
Premature Ejaculation
Prenuptial Agreements
PREPARE/ENRICH
Presenting Problems
Prevention Research
Primary and Secondary Emotions
Process Research
Professional Associations
Progress Notes for Couples and Families
Psychoanalytic Family Therapy
Psychobiology of Attachment
Psychoeducation
Public Health Code
Punctuation

Qualitative Research
Quantitative Research
Questions: Open, Closed, and Circular

Racial Disparities in Foster Care
Racism
Reactive Attachment Disorder in Children
Reconciliation
Recursiveness
Reflecting Team
Relational Diagnoses
Relational-Cultural Therapy
Relationship Enhancement
Release of Information for Couples and Families
Religion
Remarriage. See Marriage, First and Second; Stepfamilies
Resilience
Resistance
Respect
Restoration Therapy
Retirement
Rituals in Family Therapy
Role-Playing
Romance
Rule-Setting
Rural Families

Same-Sex Couples
Scales, Children
Scales, Couple and Marital
Scales, Family
Scaling Questions
Scapegoating
Schizophrenia and Families
Schools, Family Involvement in
Second-Order Change
Second-Order Family Therapy
Secrets
Self of the Therapist
Self-Care Practices for the Trauma-Informed Couple and Family Counselor
Self-Esteem
Self-Esteem in Children
Self-Help
Self-Injury
Sensate Focus
Sentiment Override, Positive and Negative
Sex, Definition of
Sex Positivity

Sex Researchers
Sex Therapy
Sexual Abuse
Sexual Assault and Rape
Sexual Assessment/History
Sexual Dysfunction
Sexual Enhancement, Sexual Toys
Sexual Health
Sexual History
Sexual Intimacy
Sexual Minorities
Sexual Orientation, Attraction, and Identity
Sexual Prejudice
Sexual Relationships With Clients
Sexual Toys/Sexual Aids
Sexuality and Religion
Sexuality Education
Sexually Transmitted Infections
Sibling Relationships
Single-Parent Families
Social Constructionism
Social Support
Socioeconomic Status
Solution-Focused Brief Therapy
Somatic Symptom Disorder and Related Disorders in Adolescents
Spirituality
Stages of Family Therapy
Statutory Rape
Stepfamilies
Stillbirth and Miscarriage
Strategic Family Therapy
Stress Management
Structural Determinism
Structural Family Therapy
Structural Maps
Substance Use Disorders in Adolescence
Suicide
Supervision
Supervision, Approved Supervisor in Marriage and Family Therapy
Supervision, Developmental Model
Supervision, Gatekeeping
Supervision, Individual and Group
Supervision Contract
Supervision of Supervision

Supervision Philosophy Statement
Supervision Theories
Support Groups
Symbolic Interactionism
Systemic Family Therapy
Systems, Subsystems, and Metasystems
Systems Theory

Technology and Families/Marriage
Teen Parenting
Termination
Therapeutic Alliance
Therapeutic Assessment
Therapeutic Contract
Therapeutic Impasses
Therapists' Values
TIME Program. *See* Training in Marriage Enrichment (TIME) Program
Torture Treatment
Training and Licensure

Training in Marriage Enrichment (TIME) Program
Transgender Families
Transgenerational Family Therapy
Transracial Adoption
Trauma and Children
Trauma and Families
Trauma-Focused Cognitive-Behavioral Therapy
Treatment Planning With Couples and Families
Triangulation
Trust

Urban Families

Virginia Satir Model

Women's Project, The
Work Relationships
World Association for Sexual Health
World Health Organization

Reader's Guide

Assessments
Adult Attachment Assessments
Assessment, Biopsychosocial
Assessment, Suicide
Circumplex Model
Clinical Case Conceptualization With Couples and Families
Clinical Interviews With Couples and Families
Common Factors
Custody Evaluations
DSM and V-Codes
Ecological Systems
Eco-Map
Family Assessment, Models of
Functional Assessment and Children
Genograms
Interpersonal Violence
Love, Physiology of
Love, Types of
Love Languages
Marital Distress
Marriage Education
Nonverbal Communication
Parent–Child Communication
PREPARE/ENRICH
Progress Notes for Couples and Families
Scales, Children
Scales, Couple and Marital
Scales, Family
Scaling Questions
Sentiment Override, Positive and Negative
Sexual Assessment/History
Sexual Health
Sexual History
Suicide
Therapeutic Assessment
Treatment Planning With Couples and Families

Attachment
Adult Attachment Assessments
Affect Regulation
Attachment
Attachment and Adolescents
Attachment and Health
Attachment and Romantic Love
Attachment Styles
Attachment Theory
Attachment-Based Family Therapy
Attunement in Relationships
Bonding
Child-Centered Parenting
Earned Attachment
Emotional Disengagement
Emotionally Focused Therapy for Couples
Interpersonal Neurobiology, Attachment and
Primary and Secondary Emotions
Psychobiology of Attachment

Communication
Assertiveness
Avoidance
Collaborative Language Systems
Communication Disorders
Communication Errors/Problems in Couples and Families
Communication in Couples and Families
Conflict in Couples and Families
Conflict Resolution
Conflict Styles
Confrontation
Disinhibited Social Engagement Disorder in Children
Empathy
Forgiveness

Love Languages
Metacommunication
Metaphors
Nonverbal Communication
Parent–Child Communication
Power Issues in Couples
Respect
Secrets
Social Constructionism
Symbolic Interactionism
Therapeutic Impasses
Trust

Coping

Bereavement
Children With Chronic Illness
Chronic Illness With Couples and Families
Conflict Styles
Death, Parents of Deceased Children
Empowerment in Families
Engendering Hope
Families and Substance Abuse
Family Resilience
Family Strengths
Family Stress
Family Stress Adaptation Theory
Forgiveness
Hope-Focused Approach to Couple Enrichment in Counseling
Parental Stress: Effects on Children
Reconciliation
Resilience
Self-Esteem
Self-Esteem in Children
Social Support
Stillbirth and Miscarriage
Stress Management

Couple, Marriage, Family Policy

Best Interests of the Child
Child Protective Services
Family and Medical Leave Act of 1993
Healthy Marriage and Responsible Fatherhood
Hispanic Healthy Marriage Initiative
Marriage Versus Civil Unions
National Marriage Initiative

Public Health Code
Self-Esteem in Children
Social Support

Diagnosing and Disorders

Adjustment Disorder in Adolescents
Adolescent Behavior Disorders
Adolescent Behavior Problems
Adolescent Mental Health
Alcohol and Substance Abuse
Anxiety
Anxiety Disorders in Adolescents
Attention-Deficit and Disruptive Behavior Disorders
Autism Spectrum Disorder
Child Behavior Problems
Childhood Anxiety
Childhood Obesity, Prevention and Treatment of
Compulsive Sexual Behavior
Conduct Disorder
Depression in Adolescents
Depression in Children
Depression in Couples and Families
Disinhibited Social Engagement Disorder in Children
DSM and V-Codes
Eating Disorders
Elimination Disorders in Children
Erectile Disorder
Female Orgasmic Disorder
Female Sexual Interest/Arousal Disorder
Fetishes
Functional Assessment and Children
Gambling, Compulsive
Gender Dysphoria
Genito-Pelvic Pain/Penetration Disorder
Hoarding
Intermittent Explosive Disorder in Adolescents
International Classification of Diseases (ICD)
Male Hypoactive Sexual Desire Disorder
Mood Disorders in Adolescents
Mood Disorders in Children
Non–Rapid Eye Movement Sleep Arousal Disorders in Children
Oppositional Defiant Disorder

Paraphilic Disorders
Parental Alienation Syndrome
Postpartum Depression
Posttraumatic Stress Disorder in Children
Premature Ejaculation
Reactive Attachment Disorder in Children
Relational Diagnoses
Schizophrenia and Families
Sexual Dysfunction
Sexually Transmitted Infections
Somatic Symptom Disorder and Related Disorders in Adolescents
Substance Use Disorders in Adolescence

Diversity
Acculturation
Adoption, Cross-Cultural and Interracial
Adoptive Families
African American Families
Asian American Families
Assimilation: Immigrants and Refugees
Beliefs and Values
Bilingual Families
Children With Special Needs in Family Therapy
Chosen Families
Cultural Issues in Couples and Families
Diversity
Empowerment in Families
Ethnicity
Faith-Based Therapy
Families and Substance Abuse
Family Resilience
Family Values
Feminization of Poverty
Foster Children
Gender- and Culture-Sensitive Therapies
Gender Issues
Gender Orientation, Gender Identity, and Gender Expression
Gender Roles
Immigrant Families
Individual Family Culture
Intellectual Disability and Autism
Intercultural Marriage and Family
Interracial Marriages and Families
Kinship Care

Latino Families
LGBT Families
Marriage, Arranged
Marriage Versus Civil Unions
Men in Counseling
Military Couples and Families
Mother-Blaming
Multiculturalism
Muslim American Families
Native American Families
Nudity: Beliefs and Values
Parentification and Diverse Family Systems
Patriarchy
Racial Disparities in Foster Care
Racism
Relational-Cultural Therapy
Religion
Resilience
Rural Families
Same-Sex Couples
Sexual Minorities
Sexual Orientation, Attraction, and Identity
Sexual Prejudice
Sexuality and Religion
Single-Parent Families
Socioeconomic Status
Spirituality
Stepfamilies
Therapists' Values
Transgender Families
Transracial Adoption
Urban Families
Women's Project, The

Financial Issues
Career Planning and Couples/Families
Debt and Financial Strain
Dual-Earner Families
Families and Poverty
Family Resource Management
Feminization of Poverty
Gambling, Compulsive
Hoarding
Homelessness
Homelessness and Youth
Job Loss

Life Balance
Poverty and Family Development
Prenuptial Agreements
Retirement
Socioeconomic Status
Work Relationships

Intimacy

Attachment
Attachment and Adolescents
Attachment and Health
Attachment and Romantic Love
Bonding
Cognitive Maps and Couples
Commitment
Compassion
Confrontation
Couple Development
Couples, Quality Time
Dating Coaching
Dating Relationship Dissolution
Empathy
Fidelity
Forgiveness
Friendship
In-Law Relationships
Intimacy, Specific Threats to
Loneliness
Love, Physiology of
Love, Theories of
Love, Types of
Love and Rituals
Love Languages
Marital Distress
Marriage, Arranged
Marriage, First and Second
Mate Selection
Online Dating
Open Relationships
Polyamory
Polygamy
Reconciliation
Relationship Enhancement
Romance
Secrets
Sexual Intimacy

Sibling Relationships
Trust
Work Relationships

Life Events/Transitions

Adolescent Behavior Problems
Adolescent Mental Health
Adoption
Adult Development
Aging and Caregiving
Autism and Children
Bereavement Counseling
Career Planning and Couples/Families
Caregivers
Child Behavior Problems
Childhood Anxiety
Childless Couples
Chosen Families
Chronic Illness With Couples and Families
Couple Development
Couples, Quality Time
Dating Coaching
Dating Relationship Dissolution
Death, Parents of Deceased Children
Death and Dying
Divorce and Separation
Divorce Therapy
Dual-Earner Families
Families and Poverty
Family Life Cycle
Family Reconstruction
Family Stress
Grief Counseling
Health Issues
Homelessness
Homelessness and Youth
Hospice
Individual and Family Development
Job Loss
Life Balance
Life Events
Life Transitions
Loss
Marriage, First and Second
Parent–Adolescent Relations
Parenting

Postpartum Depression
Posttraumatic Stress Disorder in Children
Poverty and Family Development
Power Issues in Couples
Prenuptial Agreements
Retirement
Rural Families
Sibling Relationships
Single-Parent Families
Spirituality
Stepfamilies
Stillbirth and Miscarriage
Suicide
Teen Parenting
Transracial Adoption
Urban Families

Major Concepts
Affect Regulation
Attachment
Attachment Styles
Attunement, Clinician
Attunement in Relationships
Boundaries
Circumplex Model
Cohesion
Complementary and Symmetrical Relationships
Crucible
Cybernetics
Differentiation
Ecological Systems
Eco-Map
Ecosystems Perspective
Emotional Disengagement
Entitlement
Epistemology in Family Therapy
Family Myth
Family of Origin
Family Rituals
Family Strengths
Family Values
First-Order Change
Fusion
Gender Roles
Hierarchy
Holism

Homeostasis
Hypothesis, Systemic
Identified Patient
Individual Family Culture
Intergenerational Loyalty
Intergenerational Trauma
Isomorphism
Kinship Care
Marriage Education
Marriage Encounter
Marriage Myths
Morphogenesis
Morphostasis
Mother-Blaming
Neutrality and Curiosity
Nuclear Family
Paradoxes and Paradoxical Intervention
Patriarchy
Person of the Therapist
Positive and Negative Feedback
Presenting Problems
Primary and Secondary Emotions
Questions: Open, Closed, and Circular
Recursiveness
Resistance
Scaling Questions
Scapegoating
Second-Order Change
Sentiment Override, Positive and Negative
Social Constructionism
Social Support
Structural Determinism
Structural Maps
Symbolic Interactionism
Systems Theory
Triangulation

Models, Interventions, Techniques
Acceptance and Commitment Therapy
Adlerian Family Therapy
Adlerian Open-Forum Family Counseling
Attachment-Based Family Therapy
Behavioral Family Therapy
Brief Adlerian Couples Therapy
Brief Family Therapy
Chaos Family Therapy

Childhood Obesity, Prevention and Treatment of
Child–Parent Relationship Therapy
Choice Theory and Reality Therapy
Cinematherapy
Circularity and Linearity
Cognitive Maps and Couples
Cognitive-Behavioral Couples Therapy
Cognitive-Behavioral Family Therapy
Collaborative Couples Therapy
Collaborative Language Systems
Community Programs
Conflict Resolution
Conjoint Family Therapy
Constructivism
Contextual Family Therapy
Couple and Family Forensics
Couples and Marriage Counseling
Crisis Intervention With Couples and Families
Discernment Counseling
Divorce Therapy
Ecosystemic Structural Family Therapy
Emotional Intelligence, Children
Emotional Intelligence, Families
Emotionally Focused Therapy for Couples
Empirically Validated Models
Enactments
Equine-Assisted Family Therapy
Ericksonian Family Therapy
Experiential Family Therapy
Externalizing Behaviors
Faith-Based Therapy
Family Mode Deactivation Therapy
Feminist Family Therapy
Focal Family Therapy
Functional Family Therapy
Gender- and Culture-Sensitive Therapies
Gestalt Family Therapy
Goals, Treatment
Gottman Method Couples Therapy
Grief Counseling
Group Family Therapy
Home-Based Therapy
Homework Assignments in Therapy
Homicide
Hope-Focused Approach to Couple Enrichment in Counseling
Humanistic Family Therapy
Hypnosis
Imago Relationship Therapy
Individual Versus Family Therapy
Integrating Systemic and Individual Theories
Integrative Couples Therapy
Internal Family Systems Model
International Family Therapy
Interpersonal Neurobiology, Attachment and
Interpersonal Neurobiology, Couples and
Interpersonal Neurobiology, Parenting and
Joining
Juvenile Firesetter Interventions
Listening, Empathic
Love and Rituals
Marital Group Therapy
Marriage Encounter
Marriage Enrichment
Marriage-Friendly Therapy
Medical Family Therapy
Metacommunication
Metaphors
Milan Team
Mindfulness
Miracle Question
Motivational Interviewing
Multiple Family Therapy
Multisystemic Therapy
Narrative Therapy
Network Therapy
Neuro-Linguistic Programming
No-Harm Contracts
Normalizing
Paradoxes and Paradoxical Intervention
Parent Effectiveness Training (P.E.T.)
Parent Management Training
Peer Counseling
Play Family Therapy
Positive Psychology
Postmodern Therapies
Premarital Counseling
Progress Notes for Couples and Families
Psychoanalytic Family Therapy
Psychobiology of Attachment
Psychoeducation
Punctuation

Questions: Open, Closed, and Circular
Reflecting Team
Relational-Cultural Therapy
Relationship Enhancement
Restoration Therapy
Rituals in Family Therapy
Role-Playing
Second-Order Family Therapy
Self-Help
Sensate Focus
Solution-Focused Brief Therapy
Stages of Family Therapy
Strategic Family Therapy
Structural Family Therapy
Support Groups
Systemic Family Therapy
Systems, Subsystems, and Metasystems
Therapeutic Alliance
Therapeutic Contract
Torture Treatment
Training in Marriage Enrichment (TIME) Program
Transgenerational Family Therapy
Trauma-Focused Cognitive-Behavioral Therapy
Triangulation
Virginia Satir Model

Organizations

American Association for Marriage and Family Therapy
Council for Accreditation of Counseling and Related Educational Programs
International Association of Marriage and Family Counselors
World Association for Sexual Health
World Health Organization

Parenting

Active Parenting
Adoption
Authoritative Parenting
Child-Centered Parenting
Child–Parent Relationship Therapy
Children With Chronic Illness
Foster Children
Group Parenting Classes
Interpersonal Neurobiology, Parenting and
Legal Issues in Parenting
LGBT Families
Nonresidential Fathers
Parent Effectiveness Training (P.E.T.)
Parent Management Training
Parent Study Groups
Parent–Adolescent Relations
Parental Alienation Syndrome
Parental Stress: Effects on Children
Parentification and Diverse Family Systems
Parenting
Parenting Education
Parenting Styles
Pregnancy
Racial Disparities in Foster Care
Rule-Setting
Teen Parenting

Professional Development and Standards

American Association for Marriage and Family Therapy
Certified Family Life Educator
Child Protective Services
Clinical Practice
Clinician-Directed, Solution-Focused Supervision
Competency-Based Standards for Marriage, Couple, and Family Counseling
Confidentiality
Core Competencies for Marriage and Family Therapists
Cotherapy Team
Council for Accreditation of Counseling and Related Educational Programs
Court-Mandated Clients
Decision-Making
Dual and Multiple Relationships
Duty to Warn and Protect
Ethical Codes
Ethical Decision-Making
Family Life Educators
HIPAA Standards
Informed Consent for Research
Informed Consent in Clinical Work
Licensure and Certification
Live Supervision

Mandated Reporter
Mental Health, Systemic Perspective
Moral Dimensions of Therapy
Multicultural Counseling Competence
No-Secrets Contracts
Postdoctoral Training
Practice Management
Professional Associations
Public Health Code
Release of Information for Couples and Families
Self of the Therapist
Self-Care Practices for the Trauma-Informed Couple and Family Counselor
Sexual Relationships With Clients
Supervision
Supervision, Approved Supervisor in Marriage and Family Therapy
Supervision, Developmental Model
Supervision, Gatekeeping
Supervision, Individual and Group
Supervision Contract
Supervision of Supervision
Supervision Philosophy Statement
Supervision Theories
Termination
Therapists' Values
Training and Licensure

Research
Clinical Versus Statistical Significance
Common Factors
Cost–Benefit Analysis
Couples Therapy Research
Delphi Research Method
Developmental Model of Marriage
Effectiveness Research
Empirically Validated Models
Evidence-Based Practice With Couples and Families
Outcome Research
Prevention Research
Process Research
Qualitative Research
Quantitative Research
Sex Researchers

Sexuality
Beliefs and Values
Birth Control and Contraception
Childless Couples
Compulsive Sexual Behavior
Erectile Disorder
Extramarital Affairs and Infidelity
Female Orgasmic Disorder
Female Sexual Interest/Arousal Disorder
Fetishes
Gender Dysphoria
Gender Orientation, Gender Identity, and Gender Expression
Genito-Pelvic Pain/Penetration Disorder
Human Sexual Response
Incest
Infertility
Male Hypoactive Sexual Desire Disorder
Mate Selection
Mindfulness and Sex
Nudity: Beliefs and Values
Open Relationships
Paraphilic Disorders
Polyamory
Polygamy
Pornography
Pregnancy and Sexuality
Premature Ejaculation
Romance
Same-Sex Couples
Sensate Focus
Sex, Definition of
Sex Positivity
Sex Researchers
Sex Therapy
Sexual Abuse
Sexual Assault and Rape
Sexual Assessment/History
Sexual Dysfunction
Sexual Enhancement, Sexual Toys
Sexual Health
Sexual History
Sexual Intimacy
Sexual Minorities
Sexual Orientation, Attraction, and Identity

Sexual Prejudice
Sexual Relationships With Clients
Sexual Toys/Sexual Aids
Sexuality and Religion
Sexuality Education
Sexually Transmitted Infections
Statutory Rape
World Association for Sexual Health

Special Topics
Body Dysmorphic Disorder
  in Adolescents
Child Guidance Movement
Children With Special Needs in
  Family Therapy
Community Programs
Family Mediation
Healthy Marriage and Responsible
  Fatherhood
Hispanic Healthy Marriage Initiative
Incest
International Family Therapy
Marriage and Health
Media in Family Therapy
Men in Counseling
Military Couples and Families
Mindfulness and Children
Mindfulness and Couples
National Marriage Initiative
Online Dating
Schizophrenia and Families
Schools, Family Involvement in
Self-Care Practices for the Trauma-Informed
  Couple and Family Counselor
Sexual Abuse
Statutory Rape
Technology and Families/Marriage
Therapeutic Impasses
Torture Treatment

Theory
Adlerian Family Therapy
Assessment, Biopsychosocial
Attachment Theory
Behavioral Family Therapy
Bowen Family Systems Theory
Chaos Family Therapy
Choice Theory and Reality Therapy
Cognitive-Behavioral Couples
  Therapy
Cognitive-Behavioral Family
  Therapy
Collaborative Language Systems
Constructivism
Contextual Family Therapy
Critical Theory
Cybernetics
Double Bind Theory
Ecosystems Perspective
Epistemology in Family Therapy
Experiential Family Therapy
Family Stress Adaptation Theory
Functionalism
General Systems Theory
Isomorphism
Love, Theories of
Object Relations Theory
Parental Acceptance–Rejection
  Theory
Psychoanalytic Family Therapy
Social Constructionism
Structural Determinism
Symbolic Interactionism
Systems Theory

Violence and Abuse
Alcohol and Substance Abuse
Anger Management
Child Maltreatment
Domestic Violence
Elder Abuse
Interpersonal Violence
Self-Injury
Sexual Assault and Rape
Trauma and Children
Trauma and Families

About the Editors

Jon Carlson, PsyD, EdD, ABPP, is the Distinguished Professor of Adlerian Psychology at Adler University in Chicago and a psychologist at the Wellness Clinic in Lake Geneva, Wisconsin. He is Emeritus Professor, Division of Psychology & Counseling at Governors State University. Dr. Carlson has published 62 books in many areas, including psychotherapy, family therapy, marital enrichment, and consultation. He has also published more than 185 articles and has produced more than 300 professional training video programs that feature the most prominent leaders in the counseling and psychotherapy field demonstrating their theories and practice in action. He has been recognized for his contributions with lifetime achievement awards by the American Psychological Association, the American Counseling Association, and other professional organizations. He also held a long-time association with our SAGE journals program, serving as the Founding Editor of *The Family Journal: Counseling & Therapy for Couples & Families*, the official journal of the International Association of Marriage & Family Counselors.

Shannon B. Dermer is currently Professor and Chair of the Division of Psychology and Counseling at Governors State University. She holds a doctorate in marriage and family therapy and has taught Marriage and Family Therapy and Counseling at both the master's and doctoral levels. She is the author of numerous journal publications, book chapters, and presentations on the topics of couples counseling, training, solution-focused therapy, sexuality, parenting, African American clients, social advocacy, and other topics. In addition, she has hosted and/or produced more than 80 training videos on various topics related to the field of counseling. She has been a site visitor/chair for the Council for Counseling and Related Educational Programs (CACREP) for more than 10 years and has coordinated accreditation reports at both the master's and doctoral levels for CACREP programs and for programs accredited by the Commission on Marriage and Family Therapy Education.

Contributors

Jahaan R. Abdullah
Governors State University

Roberto L. Abreu
University of Kentucky

Hector Y. Adames
The Chicago School of Professional Psychology

Linda Adams
Gordon Training International

Mark S. Adams
Weber State University

Portia Allie-Turco
State University of New York

Shanice N. Armstrong
Licensed Professional Counselor Intern

Rachel A. Augustus
Kayenta Therapy

Lena Axelsson
Ryokan College

Molli E. Bachenberg
Florida Gulf Coast University

Manijeh Badiee
California State University, San Bernardino

Ria Echteld Baker
Houston Graduate School of Theology

Kim M. Baldwin
Lincoln Christian University

Valerie Balog
University of North Carolina at Charlotte

Monica Paige Band
Marymount University

Tasha Leroyce Banks
Governors State University

Jessica A. Baycroft
Southern Connecticut State University

Marie-Nathalie Beaudoin
Skills for Kids, Parents & Schools (SKIPS)

Sarah Becerra
Lamar University

Natasha Bell
University of Minnesota

Zvi J. Bellin
John F. Kennedy University

Christopher K. Belous
Mercer University–Atlanta

Sara Bender
Central Washington University

Andrew S. Benesh
Florida State University

Jerica M. Berge
University of Minnesota

Stephan Berry
Troy University

Janelle Bettis
Argosy University

Christine Suniti Bhat
Ohio University

James Robert Bitter
East Tennessee State University

Andrea G. Bjornestad
South Dakota State University

Caroline Adair Black
Clemson University

Zachary D. Bloom
University of Central Florida

Thomas W. Blume
Oakland University

Peter J. Boccone
Lynchburg College

Jennifer A. Boender
Governors State University

Lynn Bohecker
Messiah College

Laurie Bonjo
State University of New York at New Paltz

Caroline S. Booth
North Carolina A&T State University

Janee Both Gragg
University of Redlands

Ryan Bowers
Duquesne University

Angela B. Bradford
Brigham Young University

Sarah N. Brant-Rajahn
University of Georgia

Imelda N. Bratton
Western Kentucky University

Sue C. Bratton
University of North Texas

Erik Braun
Northwestern State University of Louisiana

Amanda A. Brookshear
Old Dominion University

Cameron Brown
Kansas State University

Eric M. Brown
Old Dominion University

Laura Bruneau
Adams State University

Thomas K. Burdenski Jr.
Tarleton State University

Mark H. Butler
Brigham Young University

Rebekah Byrd
East Tennessee State University

Andrew M. Byrne
Ohio University

Karisse A. Callender
Texas A&M University–Corpus Christi

Joseph A. Campbell
Indiana University South Bend

Kelly Campbell
California State University, San Bernardino

Jon Carlson
Adler University

Alfreda Renae Carmichael
Argosy University

Montserrat Casado-Kehoe
Palm Beach Atlantic University

Willa J. Casstevens
North Carolina State University

Ki Byung Chae
University of North Carolina at Pembroke

Christian Derek Chan
George Washington University

Nayeli Y. Chavez-Dueñas
The Chicago School of Professional Psychology

Ruoxi Chen
University of Louisiana at Monroe

Jessica ChenFeng
California State University, Northridge

Sung Cho
Florida State University

Jacob D. Christenson
Mount Mercy University

Terri Christiansen
Governors State University

Alli Cipra
Governors State University

Diane M. Clark
Mercer University

Trevon Clow
Capella University

Adam Coffey
Private Practice

Jay Colker
Adler University

John Alie Conteh
Wright State University

Ashley R. Cosentino
The Chicago School of Professional Psychology

Sarah A. Crabtree
University of Minnesota

Jaclyn D. Cravens
Texas Tech University

Gerry Ken Crete
Argosy University

Daniel R. Cruikshanks
Aquinas College

Ming Cui
Florida State University

Eric Dafoe
University of North Texas

Heather D. Dahl
University of Alaska–Fairbanks

Randy J. Davis
Lamar University

Ryan T. Day
Columbus State University

Sabina de Vries
Texas A&M University

Carlos M. Del Rio
Bradley University

Shannon B. Dermer
Governors State University

John A. Dewell
Loyola University New Orleans

Rachel M. Diamond
University of Saint Joseph

Kristen N. Dickens
Georgia Southern University

Asha Dickerson
Argosy University–Atlanta

Eric M. Dishongh
Amridge University

Mayi Dixon
Mercer University

William J. Doherty
University of Minnesota

Kimberly A. Donovan
Southeastern Oklahoma State University

Kylie P. Dotson-Blake
East Carolina University

Abby Dougherty
Walden University

Kristin I. Douglas
Murray State University

Meredith Drew
William Paterson University

Michael B. Drew
University of Georgia

Neil E. Duchac
Capella University

Mindy Dunagan
University of Mississippi

Tracey M. Duncan
New Jersey City University

Shea M. Dunham
Governors State University

Kimberly Duris
Lewis University

Jared A. Durtschi
Kansas State University

Christine H. Ebrahim
Loyola University New Orleans

Silvia Echevarria-Doan
University of Florida

Charles C. Edwards
Brooklyn College

Lindsay L. Edwards
Northcentral University

Todd M. Edwards
University of San Diego

Lori Ellison
Marshall University

Matt Englar-Carlson
California State University, Fullerton

Kathie Erwin
Regent University

Elisabeth Esmiol Wilson
Pacific Lutheran University

Alyssa Espinoza
Governors State University

Courtney Evans-Thompson
North Carolina A&T State University

Stephanie Ines Falke
Loma Linda University

Minnah W. Farook
University of Kentucky

Daniel S. Felix
Indiana University School of Medicine

Keny Felix
Richmont Graduate University

David L. Fenell
University of Colorado Colorado Springs

Mary Alice Fernandez
Texas A&M University–Corpus Christi

Stephen T. Fife
University of Nevada, Las Vegas

Regina Finan
Georgia State University

Kerrie R. Fineran
Indiana University–Purdue University Fort Wayne

Rashida Fisher
Adler Graduate School

Lauren Fix
University of Louisiana at Monroe

Douglas Flemons
Nova Southeastern University

Louisa Foss-Kelly
Southern Connecticut State University

Shatel Francis
Mercer University

Aimee Galick
University of Louisiana at Monroe

Rashmi Gangamma
Syracuse University

Shirlyn M. Garrett-Wilson
Chicago State University

Trevor G. Gates
College at Brockport, State University of New York

Diane Gehart
California State University, Northridge

Danielle L. Geigle
Ohio University

Denise Gilstrap
University of Mississippi

Tatiana Glebova
Alliant International University

Rebecca M. Goldberg
Mississippi State University

Annabelle Michelle Goodwin
Northcentral University

Dharshini Goonetilleke
Minnesota State University, Mankato

Joseph M. Graham
University of Central Florida

Miranda Gray
Waynesburg University

Shelley Green
Nova Southeastern University

Wendy L. Greenidge
Lamar University

Catherine Griffith
University of Massachusetts Amherst

Daniel Gutierrez
University of North Carolina at Charlotte

Laura Haddock
Walden University

Helen Hamlet
Kutztown University

Tiffany Hamlett
American College of Education

Terry D. Hargrave
Fuller Theological Seminary

Laura K. Harrawood
McKendree University

Aina A. Harris
Governors State University

Shaywanna Harris
University of Central Florida

Steven M. Harris
University of Minnesota

Christina M. Hassija
California State University, San Bernardino

Tammy Hatfield
University of the Cumberlands

Katherine M. Hermann
University of Louisiana at Lafayette

Katherine M. Hertlein
University of Nevada, Las Vegas

Alyssa Hess
Clemson University

Chelsey L. Hess-Holden
Mississippi State University

Janet Froeschle Hicks
Texas Tech University

Nicole R. Hill
Syracuse University

Tara Hill
Wright State University

Tricialand Hilliard
Argosy University–Washington, D.C.

Jennifer Hodgson
East Carolina University

Courtney M. Holmes
Virginia Commonwealth University

Lisa M. Hooper
University of Louisville

Stanley C. Hoover
Messiah College

Anissa K. Howard
Gordon State College

Camille Y. Humes
Counseling with Care, Inc.

K. Michelle Hunnicutt Hollenbaugh
Texas A&M University–Corpus Christi

Quintin A. Hunt
University of Minnesota

Lidija Hurni
Indiana University–Purdue University Fort Wayne

Debra Hyatt-Burkhart
Duquesne University

Jonathan Impellizzeri
Geneva College

Joe (Jodi) Ippolito
Allina Health Systems
Metropolitan State University

Gregory Irwin
University of Illinois Springfield

Terri L. Jashinsky
Mount Mary University

Marty Jencius
Kent State University

Eric D. Jett
Henderson State University

Adrianne L. Johnson
Wright State University

Scott Johnson
Family Therapy Center of Virginia Tech (Retired)

Veronica I. Johnson
University of Montana

Adam C. Jones
Utah State University

Sarah Jones
University of Georgia

Sandra Kakacek
Adler University

Michael T. Kalkbrenner
Old Dominion University

Michael A. Keim
Columbus State University

Kathleen Hartney Kellum
Walden University

Yesim Keskin
Virginia Tech

Kyle D. Killian
Capella University

Lana Kim
Valdosta State University

Jonathan Kimmes
Kansas State University

Isabel B. Kirk
Professional Counselor Psychologist

Robert H. Kitzinger
Kean University

David Kleist
Idaho State University

Cathleen Klomes
The Chicago School of Professional Psychology

Keith Klostermann
Medaille College

Kenyon Knapp
Mercer University

Stacey Kohler
Montclair State University

Demitri Kornegay
Argosy University–Washington, D.C.

Vanieca I. Kraus
Northcentral University

Lori C. Kucharski
Serenity Counseling Center, Colorado Springs

Amanda C. La Guardia
Sam Houston State University

E. Megan Lachmar
Utah State University

Katie A. Lamberson
University of North Carolina at Charlotte

Angela Lamson
East Carolina University

Amber M. Lange
Capella University

Martha Laughlin
Valdosta State University

Christopher Lawrence
Northern Kentucky University

Lindsey Lawson
Pacific Lutheran University

Elizabeth Lewis
Clemson University

Jessica Lloyd-Hazlett
University of Texas at San Antonio

Darletta Stevenson Logan
University of Akron

Christen Tomlinson Logue
University of the Cumberlands

Cathy Longa
Keiser University

E. Joan Looby
Mississippi State University

Belinda J. Lopez
Lamar University

Sonya Lorelle
Governors State University

Barbara A. Mahaffey
Ohio University–Chillicothe

Devon Manderino
Waynesburg University

Suneetha Babu Manyam
Mercer University

Julie Martin
Martin Psychiatric Services

J. Barry Mascari
Kean University

Martha Mason
DePaul University

Kimberly Mason Peeples
Mississippi State University

Jennifer L. Matheson
Aspen Trauma Therapy Institute

Miles Matise
Troy University

Ann M. McCaughan
University of Illinois Springfield

Mary McClure
Governors State University

Angela R. McDonald
University of North Carolina at Pembroke

Kashunda McGriff
Governors State University

Tai J. Mendenhall
University of Minnesota

Carol Pfeiffer Messmore
Capella University

Grace Ann Mims
University of Nebraska at Kearney

Gena Marie Minnix
Seminary of the Southwest

Amanda J. Minor
Salve Regina University

Kristen L. B. Moran
Campbell University

Stephaney S. Morrison
Hunter College

Sarah J. Moses
Adler University

Lauren J. Moss
Kutztown University

Sarah Murphy
Governors State University

Katharine Melyssa Murphy-Edmunds
Florida State University

Robika Modak Mylroie
Lamar University

Jason K. Neill
Anderson University

Judith A. Nelson
Sam Houston State University

Matthew Nelson
Open Arms Counseling

Anita A. Neuer Colburn
Walden University

Sean Newhart
Clemson University

Sheldon Nichols
Private Practice

Tiffany Nielson
University of Illinois Springfield

Elizabeth O'Brien
University of Tennessee–Chattanooga

Megan Oka
Utah State University

Amy K. Olson
PREPARE/ENRICH

David H. Olson
University of Minnesota–St. Paul

Donald J. Olund
LifeWork Counseling

Kristie Opiola
University of North Texas

Yvonne Ortiz-Bush
California State University, Bakersfield

Leslie W. O'Ryan
Western Illinois University–QC Campus

Marte Ostvik-de Wilde
University of Saint Joseph

William Owenby
University of Akron

Delila Lashelle Owens
University of Akron

Kristin Page
University of Florida

Everett W. Painter
Walters State Community College

Sarita Palmer
Penn State Harrisburg

Emma Papagni
Medaille College

Candace N. Park
University of South Alabama

LaQuita Parker
University of Mississippi

M. L. Parker
University of Saint Joseph

Shawn P. Parmanand
Walden University

Mazna Patka
Governors State University

Jo Ellen Patterson
University of San Diego

Timothy Wayne Pedigo
Governors State University

Dilani M. Perera-Diltz
Lamar University

Caroline Perjessy
University of West Georgia

Susan N. Perkins
Northwest Nazarene University

Nathan C. D. Perron
Northwestern University

LaTea Perry
Argosy University–Washington, D.C.

Sheri Pickover
University of Detroit Mercy

Sara Polanchek
University of Montana

Corderro A. Pollard
Governors State University

Verl T. Pope
Northern Kentucky University

Salena Blackburn Potter
Turning Point Counseling Services

Veena Prasad
Texas A&M University–Corpus Christi

Keeley J. Pratt
Ohio State University

Felicia Denise Pressley
Argosy University–Washington, D.C.

Jonathan Procter
Lamar University

Kristine Ramsay
Auburn University

Janna C. Ramsey
Trevecca Nazarene University

Arden G. Rand
Southern Connecticut State University

Nicole M. Randick
Adler Graduate School

Frederick Redekop
Kutztown University

Patricia A. Robey
Governors State University

Jacqueline Robinson
Mercer University

Shanel B. Robinson
Columbus State University

W. David Robinson
Utah State University

Karen Roller
Palo Alto University

Andrew H. Rose
University of Connecticut

Elizabeth Ruiz
Governors State University

Elizabeth B. Russell
Nazareth College

Suhad Sadik
Sadik and Associates

Silvia P. Salas Pizaña
University of Wisconsin–Milwaukee

Tara C. Samples
Lincoln Christian University

Jennifer Sampson
The Hoarding Project

Blake Sandusky
Auburn University

Margery C. Saunders
College at Brockport, State University of New York

David M. Savinsky
Regent University

Christina Schnyders
Malone University

Sarah Schonian
Texas Tech University

David A. Scott
Clemson University

Ryan B. Seedall
Utah State University

Jasmine Lydia Selvaraj
Movement for the Intellectually Disabled

Priscilla Rose Selvaraj
Trinity International University

Leslie Shapiro
The Hoarding Project

Carl J. Sheperis
Lamar University

Donna S. Sheperis
Lamar University

Renee S. Sherrell
University of St. Joseph

Richard Q. Shin
University of Maryland College Park

Katherine A. Shirley
Fairleigh Dickinson University

Sharon Silverberg
Capella University

Lance Christian Smith
University of Vermont

Robert L. Smith
Texas A&M University–Corpus Christi

Shannon Smith
University of Nevada, Las Vegas

Sara Smock Jordan
Texas Tech University

Melissa K. Smothers
Mount Mary University

Joy-Del T. Snook
Lamar University

Ebony Spriggs
Adler University

Sarah M. Steelman
Virginia Tech

Mallory R. Stevens
Kutztown University

Dana J. Stone
California State University Northridge

Michael E. Sude
La Salle University

Tami Sullivan
State University of New York at Oswego

Alyssa Swan
University of North Texas

Nathan Taylor
University of Nebraska–Lincoln

Emily B. Teague-Palmieri
University of North Carolina at Charlotte

Vanessa B. Teixeira
University of North Florida

Jerry Lee Terrill
Houston Graduate School of Theology

Elizabeth Doherty Thomas
Doherty Relationship Institute

Shatavia Alexander Thomas
Northcentral University

Elizabeth Suzanne Thraen
University of South Dakota

Adrianne Trogden
Sinfonia Family Services of Louisiana

Lisa Trump
University of Minnesota

Amanda Tuttle
Clemson University

Rosaria Carlone Upchurch
University of Florida/Counselor Education

Damir S. Utržan
University of Minnesota

Vance Walker
Pattison Professional Counseling Center

John W. Wallace
Daymar College

Jennifer Wallin-Ruschman
Abraham Baldwin Agricultural College

Froma Walsh
University of Chicago

David B. Ward
Pacific Lutheran University

Deborah Watson
Governors State University

Yulia Watters
Northcentral University

Matthew T. Webb
Clemson University

Shauna Lynn Nefos Webb
Milligan College

Jane M. Webber
Kean University

Daniel J. Weigel
Southeastern Oklahoma State University

Alyssa Weiss Quittner
Nova Southeastern University

Lauren Wetzel
Adler University

Gordon Wheeler
Esalen Institute

Jason B. Whiting
Texas Tech University

Tyler Wilkinson
Mercer University

Amy E. Williams
College of William and Mary

Kirstee Williams
Lee University

Lee Williams
University of San Diego

Michael A. Williams
Lynchburg College

Richard Williams
Pattison Professional Counseling Center

Brian J. Willoughby
Brigham Young University

Angie D. Wilson
University of North Texas

Gina Wilson
Sam Houston State University

Molly Rose Wilson
University of Wyoming

Lisa A. Wines
Lamar University

Robert E. Wubbolding
Center for Reality Therapy

Janet Yeats
The Hoarding Project

Miyoung Yoon Hammer
Fuller Theological Seminary

Jolie Ziomek-Daigle
University of Georgia

Introduction

The field of marriage, family, and couples counseling/therapy seems to have grown exponentially within our lifetime. One way to introduce this encyclopedia is to tell our personal stories. We are hopeful that this introduction will provide a context that serves to show the breadth and depth of this vibrant professional specialty. We also hope to show the difference and uniqueness of this important approach to counseling and psychotherapy. It is so much more than what one of Jon's early supervisors described as "*individual psychotherapy with a few more people in the room.*"

Jon's Story

In 1970, I went to Brown County, Indiana, for a weeklong workshop on family counseling. I was completing my first doctorate at Wayne State University in Detroit, and I was an instructor teaching full time in the department. An invitation came to the department chairperson asking who from our faculty would like to learn about this new area; none of the faculty wanted to go, so I asked if I could and no one cared. They were more interested at that time in career counseling, vocational development, and the different types of assessments.

I spent the week with 30 other college professors listening to Robert Goulding, a gestalt therapist and expert in transactional analysis; Zev Wanderer, a Beverly Hills behavioral psychologist who had published many of the early self-help books; Thomas Gordon, talking about his P.E.T. program; and a woman named Virginia Satir, who had a little-known book on something called *conjoint family therapy.* We attended morning sessions as a group, with the various experts presenting individually or as a panel, and then spent the afternoons and evenings in small groups with six other participants receiving extensive training from one of the experts. I was placed with Virginia Satir. This could only be explained as propinquity or serendipity or planned happenstance or maybe just plain dumb luck. During the week Virginia would instruct us via what was to be later known as *family sculpting*. She placed each of us in the roles of various family members, where we would become those people and truly understood the various ways that dysfunction occurred in families. We would, with her guidance, become dysfunctional in that family position and then she would change a few things so we could experience the healing process. I was 24 years old and soon to be a doctor, and I had never experienced anything like this. I left after seven days a very confused and yet a very different person with several lifelong friends from the group, including Virginia. Something happened in this experience that my wife, doctoral adviser, and friends could all attest but none of us could put into words: This was the beginning of my lifelong career of training and learning about couples and families.

Over my professional career I have found myself drawn to many of the different professional organizations that are devoted to couples and families. In 1974, I became a clinical member of the American Association of Marriage and Family Counseling, which a few years later became the American Association of Marriage and Family Therapy (AAMFT). At that time it was the only organization that I knew about that was devoted to this specialty area.

Throughout graduate study at Wayne State University I was involved with studying human sexuality. I became a member of the American Association of Sex Educators, Counselors and Therapists (AASECT) and even a Certified Sex Therapist. There was a lot of interest in this topic, and I was fortunate enough to have received some training from some of the pioneers in this area. I was also able to offer trainings that were attended by counselors and psychologists, as well as obstetricians and gynecologists who were called upon by patients for help with sexual problems. When I lived in Hawaii, I became involved with Ron Pion, MD; his social worker wife, Gail; and psychologists Jack Anon and Craig Robinson, who were involved with training medical doctors in a method that they developed called PLISSIT. I was able to publish with them on this model as well as to serve as a trainer. In this clever model, it was thought that most sexual problems could be resolved by providing Permission, Limited Information, and Specific Suggestion before Intensive Therapy would be needed. The power of knowledge and psychoeducation was stressed over biological or therapeutic interventions.

A few years later a group of psychologists began to organize what eventually became the 43rd Division of the American Psychological Association (APA). It became one of my professional homes and the APA division from which I received my first fellow membership. I served as the editor of *The Family Psychologist,* the divisional bulletin, for a few years. When the American Board of Professional Psychology (ABPP) offered a diplomate in family psychology I applied and became one of the early recipients. I stayed involved with ABPP for a few years, serving as an examiner in order to assist others in demonstrating their competence in this new specialty area.

My first doctoral degree was in counseling, and I have been actively involved in what is now the American Counseling Association (ACA) since 1968. In the 1980s a few of the members created a new division of ACA, the International Association of Marriage and Family Counselors (IAMFC). I was elected the third president and grew IAMFC to the largest division of the ACA. I also created and served as the founding editor of *The Family Journal.* The journal received a Gold Circle Award in its inaugural year. We invited leaders in the couples and family field to the annual ACA World Conference and videotaped them demonstrating their approaches with local couples and families. This allowed me to meet many of the leaders and allowed the membership to learn from them even if they could not attend the meeting. I created a book series devoted to working with couples and families that produced more than 30 books between 1990 and 2017, published by the ACA and then Routledge Publishers.

I also had memberships in other groups, including the National Council of Family Relations (NCFR) and the American Family Therapy Association (AFTA). Each of these professional groups had its own focus. NCFR, for example, emphasized family growth and development while AFTA was the group for senior-level marriage and family therapists (MFTs), who were concerned with how the larger social issues seemed to impact couples and families.

I was fortunate to have had an undergraduate degree in elementary education, because in addition to teaching and instructional design there was a significant amount of training in child and human development. My mentor, Don Dinkmeyer, created the *Systematic Training for Parenting* (STEP) program, and we created the *Training in Marriage Enrichment* (TIME) and *PREP for Effective Family Living* programs. These were multimedia programs that taught couples and schoolchildren the basic relationship skills. I also conducted STEP leadership training around the world for a decade, including doing radio and television in 36 cities in North America on National Public Radio (NPR), *Good Morning America,* and *The Today Show.* These experiences helped me to realize the value of training and education. It is probably accurate to say that most couples and families need training rather than psychotherapy. I was able to extend this work by becoming a relationship expert for Chicago's WGN television *Morning Show* for several years—this included one segment where Kermit the Frog and I provided relationship advice to couples getting ready for Valentine's Day.

Along with our leader, Diane Sollee, a group of MFTs who saw the value in psychoeducation served on the advisory board and created the Smart Marriages Healthy Families Conference. This conference continued for 25 years and featured a variety of experts in the area of family and couples education. This became a professional home for professionals with very different backgrounds. Some were religious, others were self-help, and others were research based. Smart Marriages was inclusive and open to all.

During this time there were many "turf wars" in the field of couples and family therapy. One of the issues was who could provide therapy and train therapists to offer therapy to couples and families. Those trained in exclusively marriage and family training programs that were accredited by the AAMFT Commission on Accreditation believed that they were the only people who could offer services. Social workers, psychologists, mental health counselors, psychiatrists, and pastoral counselors did not agree. Several of us were even called to Washington, D.C., to testify to different bodies as to who should be the purveyor of this valuable service. The door was left open, with many professionals of varied backgrounds being allowed to practice.

I have practiced psychotherapy for more than 45 years and have closely identified as a practitioner. I also was fortunate enough to train counselors and psychologists to do marriage and couples therapy. I worked in an APA-approved clinical psychology program and then helped to create the CACREP-approved program in couples and family counseling at Governors State University. I became aware of the absence of good training videos and created a proposal. Allyn & Bacon Publishers agreed to publish 18 video-based programs with the leaders in the field, titled *Family Therapy With the Experts*. I was able to interview each of them and have them work with an actual couple or family before having a discussion with each expert. Harry Aponte, Gus Napier, Cheryl Rampage, Philip Guerin, Jill and David Scharff, Stephen Madigan, Insoo Kim Berg, Jean McClendon, Ken Hardy, Frank Pittman, Bill Doherty, James Bitter, Richard Schwartz, and Bill O'Hanlon are some of the experts who were involved. I created many other family therapy videos for the American Psychological Association's Psychotherapy Video Series. Along with the videos, I was able to create some of the textbooks that were used as well as professional books for MFTs, while maintaining close friendships with many of the pioneers in the MFT field.

There were many conferences that had programs on the various aspects of couples and family therapy. I became a regular presenter on the topic at ACA, AAMFT, APA, Family Therapy Networker and then the Psychotherapy Networker, the Evolution of Psychotherapy, and Smart Marriages Happy Families Conferences. There was a great demand for information and training on working with families and the client's context.

I began speaking at venues outside of the United States and spoke in Germany, in New Zealand, and throughout Asia and Southeast Asia. For more than 15 years I have worked in Thailand, providing psychological training for a wide variety of problems including substance abuse, crisis and trauma treatment, and the breakdown of the Thai family. As part of the training, the STEP and TIME programs were translated into Thai and professionals from all of the more than 70 provinces were trained to be leaders.

Shannon's Story

Although my coeditor, Jon Carlson, and I have had different professional paths, we both ended up working together as counselor educators and supervisors in the same CACREP-accredited program. Our paths illustrate the concept from general systems theory called *equifinality*—the idea that the same end state can be achieved through many different initial conditions. My story is different from that of the "living legend," Jon Carlson. Yet, we both ended up at Governors State University (GSU), which already had three long-standing CACREP-accredited specializations (community, marriage and family, and school) when I arrived in 2004, and we later worked to add an accredited doctoral degree in counselor education and supervision. I have not had quite as auspicious a career as Jon, but a bit of his magic has rubbed off on me and many of his colleagues. I like to think I have had an impact on both the fields of marriage and family therapy (MFT) and the field of counseling. Much of my impact is due to a symbiotic relationship with Jon.

My career path as an educator was established long ago when my mother walked into the room I shared with my fraternal twin sister and I was trying to teach her colors. "Yellow," I said slowly as I held up my Big Bird stuffed animal and pointed to it. Or so that is the story I am told by my mother. Throughout the years I enjoyed learning and sharing my knowledge with others. This was partly because I enjoyed reading, learning, connecting what seemed like unrelated topics, and sharing these ideas with others. It was also partly because of my cultural and religious heritage in which teaching is revered and, to be honest, it was partly because I came from a family of "know-it-alls." In my family intelligence and creativity were funneled in mainly two ways: become involved in artistic endeavors or get an advanced degree. My grandfather was the first person to get an advanced degree when he earned a PhD in biochemistry at a young age and went on to build his own consulting company.

I knew early on that I wanted to teach, but I was not sure in what area. My mother was not keen on me becoming a teacher based on her own short-lived experience as an art teacher in the Chicago Public School System. Although she wanted me to become a "real" doctor, she was satisfied with my choice to eventually get a PhD in marital, couples, and family therapy. My trajectory to that destination was a somewhat circuitous journey. In high school I decided that the field of psychology could encompass my enjoyment of literature, history, biology, philosophy, and the brain. So, I decided to go to Illinois State University (ISU) and major in psychology and eventually become a psychology professor (I thought).

It was never my intention to work with clients. It was not that I did not want to work with them, but I just had not thought about it. It did not really cross my mind. I graduated from high school at a relatively young age and finished my undergraduate program in 3 years. I admit that I was not ready to leave ISU yet, and so I applied to their clinical psychology program and was accepted. It was here that I found out I was expected to work with clients and where I found my passion for marital, couples, and family counseling/therapy.

I was placed at a family therapy agency for my internship. My supervisors there were approved supervisors from the American Association of Marriage and Family Therapy. They had me read about solution-focused therapy and some basic systems theory readings. While I enjoyed my psychology courses, systems theory grabbed me and it never let go. The complexity of thinking of people in terms of relatedness to each other and to their context fascinated me. Systems thinking (circularity) made sense with how I already saw and understood the world—I just never had the words to describe it before. I thoroughly enjoyed working with couples and families in addition to individuals. Based on my exposure to marital, couples, and family therapy I applied to several Commission on Accreditation for Marriage and Family Therapy Education (COAMFTE)–approved doctoral programs. I believe there were only about 12 of them at the time. Luckily, I was accepted in the program at Kansas State University and my love affair with MFT continued.

Because I switched fields of study I was required to take quite a few master's-level courses in MFT while working on my doctorate. Luckily, unlike some programs, the professors there made the master's students read some of the original articles and books on systems theory. Although the materials were sometimes difficult to read, I was enthralled with how some of the pioneers of family therapy brought together ideas from philosophy, mathematics, biology, anthropology, and other fields in order to understand open (living) systems. I would like to commend my professors for how well they trained me. As I was helping to edit this encyclopedia I realized how well they grounded me in the fundamentals of marital, couples, and family therapy and systems theory.

I was grounded in MFT and dedicated to the profession. In fact, I partially got my first job as an assistant professor in 1998 at the University of Akron because of this dedication. They already had a CACREP-accredited program at both the master's and doctoral level in counseling and wanted to add a COAMFTE accreditation to their marital, couples, and family specialization. This was my first introduction to the profession of counseling. I became their program coordinator, and I was in charge of finding out how to dually accredit these programs with both CACREP and COAMFTE, and was in charge of writing the self-study for COAMFTE accreditation. Without boring you with all of the details, it became, at the time, the only university that had both CACREP and COAMFTE accreditation at both the master's and doctoral levels. In some ways it was easy to do and in others it was difficult to balance these similar, but different professional identities. It was at this point that I became a "bi-professional," having an orientation toward both the fields of counseling and MFT.

There are different things that I like, respect, and enjoy about both fields. One of the major differences between the two professions is that marriage and family therapists conceptualize their profession as an independent profession rather than a specialization. In counseling, one's core identity is as a counselor first and then one who specializes in a particular area (e.g., marital, couple, and family counseling or clinical mental health counseling). For those graduating from a COAMFTE program, their identity is that of a marriage and family therapist first, foremost, and only. Nevertheless, there are many commonalities between the two fields—between all fields of mental health. It is usually the emphasis and history of how they emerged that is different.

The field of MFT and the field of counseling both have their strengths and benefits. My MFT background gave me intensive training in working with individuals, couples, and families in addition to a strong background in systems thinking, and specialized training in supervision. My experiences with the counseling field taught me more about advocacy, social justice, and the wellness model. Together, these fields have made me a better educator, clinician, and supervisor than either would have alone.

My time at the University of Akron began my education about the field of counseling, but my time at GSU advanced that knowledge. When I interviewed for a position in the marital, couples, and family specialization in their counseling program they were interested in my experience with writing two self-reports for my previous program. They asked me to use my accreditation skills with COAMFTE to help them write their self-report for re-accreditation of their CACREP-accredited counseling program. I led the effort to write that report and later led the effort to establish a doctoral program at GSU and accredit that program. In addition, I have served as a CACREP site visitor for the last 12 years. I served as the counseling program coordinator at GSU and as the chair of the Division of Psychology and Counseling for the last 8 years. In this role I get to use all of my backgrounds—psychology, MFT, and counseling.

Over the years I have seen many changes in both the counseling and MFT fields. Jon covered many of them in his portion of this introduction, but there is one that I have to comment on. Over the last few years there has been a push in several fields to accept only graduates of their own programs to teach in university programs. I get it, I really do. There is no way that anyone can erase my identity as a MFT even though it has been a long time since I taught in a COAMFTE program. Yet, I have contributed to the field of counseling through my scholarship, accreditation activities, and training of counselors with strong counselor identities. If I was graduating now I would never be accepted to teach in a counseling program as a core faculty member. Therefore, I am for a bifurcated system where one can have an identity as a counselor educator through graduating from a counseling doctoral program or becoming an advanced member of the counseling profession through completing extra coursework and supervised experience. There should be multiple paths in both MFT and counseling to become a core faculty member. I end my introduction where I started—*equifinality*. I do not think there is one path to becoming an MFT or counselor. I think people should have alternative opportunities to get to the same place with the training, experience, and competencies needed in order to do so. Each of us may start off in a different place, but that does not mean we cannot end up in the same place and strengthen our professions through dedication and diversity.

The Need and Rationale for an Encyclopedia

Marriage, family, and couples therapists provide preventive, developmental, educational, and therapeutic interventions. They have backgrounds in psychology, counseling, social work, MFT, and family relations. There is a wide body of literature available from a variety of disciplines. Each of the disciplines knows of its individual contributions but not those from the others. An encyclopedia is needed to accurately tell the complete or comprehensive story of working with couples, family, and marriage therapy.

Neither of us had any idea as to how to create an encyclopedia or the necessary steps to completion. We learned on the go, with SAGE professionals teaching us. Now that the encyclopedia is complete, we think we would be a lot more efficient should we tackle a similar project. We thank everyone for hanging with us while we learned.

Generally the process began with selecting an advisory board that represented leaders from counseling, psychology, family therapy, and other disciplines. With the assistance of the board and the SAGE staff we created a comprehensive list of topics to be included in the volume. We then began to contact the experts who we believed would be able to develop the best or most comprehensive entry. For the entries we did not know of anyone we did research and contacted people. When all else failed we used various electronic mailing lists, inviting professionals to contribute on the remaining topics.

Concluding Thoughts

We have been privileged to watch the field of couples, family, and marriage counseling/therapy develop and to grow along with it. We are appreciative of the pioneers who struggled to develop and communicate their creative and helpful theories and ideas. The road was often blocked and obstructed by well-meaning people who doubted the effectiveness and seemingly amazing results that were being reported. Over time they realized that was something different than counseling and therapy with more people in the room, and systemic functioning rather than individual symptoms as the target of treatment.

We both took different paths to learn how to work with the systems of our clients. Initially the complexity was mind-boggling, but over time we became comfortable with working in this fashion. The overall field of helping others through counseling and therapy has also grown in complexity (to say the least). Not only has couples, family, and marriage counseling changed, but also the population of couples and families we work with are radically different. They are mobile; they are multicultural and include more immigrants; they are more enmeshed with technology, particularly social media; as families, they are often smaller; and they are more diverse in terms of gender orientation and expression, longevity of relationships, divorce, and inclusion of nonbiological family members.

We learned how to educate people about family problems, identified patients, attachment, developmental milestones as times of problems, and so much more from parenting, to sex, to substance abuse, to immigrants and the impact of culture, the impact of gender, family stories, and transgenerational patterns. There is so much to share.

Acknowledgments

We created this encyclopedia out of social interest and caring for the profession. We were thrilled with the large number of people who wanted to participate. It was a big, arduous process that was made easier through the assistance of many people. We first and foremost want to thank SAGE for giving us this opportunity to contribute to the field. Second, we want to thank all of the contributors from all over the world and our illustrious advisory board. Third, we want to show our deepest gratitude and appreciation to the managing editors, Katie Paulson and Brenna Frayn. Their time, dedication, and organizational skills were indispensable. This project could not have been completed without their unending support and work. There isn't enough hyperbole available to convey our gratitude. Fourth, thank you to Governors State University for its support. A special thank you to the dean, Andrea Evans, for her encouragement and putting up with some crabbiness from her chair, Shannon Dermer, after spending long, late nights editing. There are many Reese's Peanut Butter Cups in your future.

There are some other special thanks we would like to highlight. Thank you to Dr. James R. Bitter for contributing the section on history. We would like to give a "shout out" to Jim Brace-Thompson and Sanford Robinson for their patience and guidance in completing this project. In addition, no acknowledgment would be complete without commending friends, families, and colleagues.

Dr. Carlson would like to give a special thanks to his wife and children. Dr. Dermer would like to give special thanks to her sister Jennifer for taking on extra caretaker responsibilities with their mother during this project; to Javier, her partner in crime and all things good for the "you can do it Ms. Noodle" during late nights; to her friend and colleague Shea Dunham for her support and taking care of Shannon's dog during long editing sessions when she couldn't make it home and Riley could no longer cross her legs; and to her former student and current friend and colleague Molli Bachenberg for her patience when she was completing her dissertation and letting Shannon sit beside her (each on their own computer) and "advise" while simultaneously editing the encyclopedia.

Overall, thank you to all of the many professionals, friends, colleagues, family members, and pets who helped make this happen.

Jon Carlson

Lake Geneva, Wisconsin, and Chicago, Illinois

Shannon B. Dermer

University Park, Illinois

SAGE was founded in 1965 by Sara Miller McCune to support the dissemination of usable knowledge by publishing innovative and high-quality research and teaching content. Today, we publish over 900 journals, including those of more than 400 learned societies, more than 800 new books per year, and a growing range of library products including archives, data, case studies, reports, and video. SAGE remains majority-owned by our founder, and after Sara's lifetime will become owned by a charitable trust that secures our continued independence.

Los Angeles | London | New Delhi | Singapore | Washington DC | Melbourne

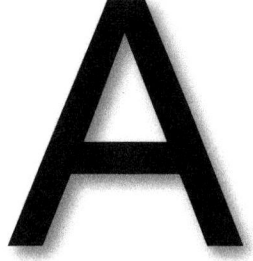

Acceptance and Commitment Therapy

Acceptance and commitment therapy (ACT) is an empirically based form of behavioral and cognitive treatment developed by psychologist Steven C. Hayes. ACT was originally developed to assist with the treatment of anxiety-based disorders but has been applied to numerous behavioral health issues since its conception. ACT is part of what has been called the third wave of behavioral and cognitive therapy, with its focus on mindfulness, acceptance, and values-based living. Since the development of ACT, it has been applied to a wide variety of clinical issues, including couples counseling. This entry provides an overview of the main tenets of this theory, discusses how these tenets are applied in treating couples, and describes the role of an ACT couples counselor.

Relational Frame Theory

ACT challenges the cultural norms that have dominated the behavioral and cognitive theory world. The three main tenets of this theory are mindfulness, acceptance, and values-based living. Rather than a focus on symptom reduction, ACT focuses on teaching clients how to live with their symptoms, not how to get rid of their struggles. This is the basis of the acceptance-based approach of this theory. Hayes posited that rather than happiness being the norm for a person's lived experience, pain, or at least some level of discomfort, is the dominant experience of human existence. This approach, based in part on the theory of how normal language process in humans develops, and grounded in relational frame theory (RFT), emphasizes the need for greater psychological flexibility compared with traditional methods of treatment commonly found in cognitive-behavioral therapy (CBT). The use of the concept of psychological flexibility in couples therapy helps the individuals in the couple focus on their current thinking patterns and notice instances of rigidity that may be complicating the relationship. By applying a more flexible pattern of thinking, each partner in the relationship is able to stop and think about their current thoughts and emotions as well as notice if their current behavior is connected to a past event or an unhealthy way of behaving. Once the person has given thought to their current behavior, the goal would be to identify what is the best response rather than what their automatic reaction might be.

RFT focused on the development of human language, which ACT used as the basis of how people become fused with their own internal experiences. The basis of RFT is that human behavior tends to be governed by a network of relational frames that make up the core of human language. These relations help to make connections in the environment without one's having to directly experience a situation. For example, a person can know that a pot of boiling water is hot by just being told that it is hot; they do not need to actually touch the pot of boiling water to know that it is hot. People make further relations arbitrarily in their environment based upon their thoughts, feelings, and behavioral predispositions toward those objects. These arbitrary relations, once established, can result in distressing thoughts and emotions, which in turn can create suffering. Examples of relational frames include *same, similar, like; before/after, if/then, cause of; better than, faster than; I/you, here/there;* and *near/far.*

Applying RFT to couples therapy involves the use of examining each person's use of language. It is necessary to identify what negative relations have been developed—whether from past relationships or each person's family history—that are lending to the current negative thoughts or emotions that one partner is experiencing toward the other partner. It is possible that a negative frame has been developed in one or both of the partners that is contributing to current fights in the relationship. Often, people in a relationship are unaware of the automatic responses that they are experiencing. Helping the couple identify the sources of their automatic responses is one of the steps in helping them to stop and notice how they are reacting in the moment.

Mindfulness

The first step in exploring ACT is to understand the concept of mindfulness. Mindfulness is a way of observing one's experience. It is commonly practiced in Eastern philosophies through different forms of meditation. Western psychology has proven mindfulness's ability to produce positive psychological benefits since its introduction to the behavioral health field. Mindfulness is a way to view one's thoughts differently. Rather than continuing to move through one's day without awareness while multitasking and continually judging one's thoughts and emotions, mindfulness teaches clients how to have contact with their present experience, observe and notice their thoughts and emotions, and respond nonjudgmentally to those thoughts and emotions. Clients are taught how to bring their attention back to the present moment when they become distracted.

Mindfulness is an important skill that each person in the relationship needs to learn how to do. The ACT therapist would begin by explaining what mindfulness is and then have the couple practice the skill in the session. Homework is given for each person to practice their own mindfulness exercises outside of therapy. After the couple has practiced using mindfulness in nondistressing situations outside of therapy, the couple is introduced to using mindfulness skills in the moment with their partner. This would include being aware of their thoughts, emotions, and urges to respond during distressing situations with their partner. Then, rather than acting on any unhealthy urges, the person would be able to make an effective decision on how to respond mindfully in the moment rather than automatically in a way that would make the situation worse. The therapist would also have the couple practice using mindfulness in the session with their partner.

Acceptance

Acceptance, as defined by ACT, refers to the ability to be fully involved in one's psychological experiences while behaving effectively at the same time. This requires the ability to view one's experiences without judgment, without defense, and being able to respond to the experience in a way that works, rather than doing what one would normally prefer to do. Acceptance does not mean passively submitting to an experience that one would otherwise rather not have; instead, it refers to the willingness to experience life events and respond to them in a way that does not make the situation worse. Rather than avoiding a painful experience, acceptance would be used to teach a client how to live with that painful experience. This lends to the ability to become psychologically flexible. Psychological flexibility is the ability to be fully present in the moment and to change or continue a behavior in order to be consistent with chosen values. According to ACT principles, people tend to be psychologically inflexible, which furthers their inability to defuse from their current internal experiences of pain. Acceptance is also used in other forms of therapy that utilize mindfulness-based strategies, such as dialectical behavior therapy (DBT), developed by therapist and researcher Marsha M. Linehan.

Utilizing the concept of acceptance, ACT separates pain from suffering. Rather than attempting to rid oneself of distressing thoughts, ACT proposes learning how to deal with those distressing experiences in order to move forward in life. The goal becomes how to live with one's experience (acceptance) rather than trying to rid oneself of all pain. According to ACT, the goal of getting rid of one's painful experiences actually increases the pain, leading to suffering. When acceptance is applied to distressing experiences, the person learns how to live their life with those experiences being present, instead of pushing one's life aside until the pain goes away. Acceptance is the metaphoric "letting go of the ropes" in order to end a game of tug-of-war. It is not uncommon for the couple to be demonstrating patterns of tug-of-war in the relationship without awareness of what the core motivations for the war really are.

The therapist assesses how each person in the relationship is currently managing internal and external negative experiences within the relationship. By identifying potentially negative responses to distress, the therapist is able to help each person identify ways to just be with the distressing situation and not have to respond in avoiding or destructive patterns. The opposite behavior of acceptance would be the use of substance abuse to deal with fights within the relationship, storming out of the room or leaving during a disagreement, avoiding bringing up concerns to the partner, or pretending that everything is fine when the partner is upset.

Values-Based Living

Values-based living is based on a set of questions that help to determine if each person in the relationship is living their life according to what they value. The following questions may be asked: Are you living the life you want to live right now? Is your life focused on what is most meaningful to you? Is the way you live your life characterized by vitality and engagement, or by the weight of your problems? People tend to put their life on hold while they are waiting for things to get better. This often leads to not living one's life according to what one values. There tends to be a viewpoint that one cannot have the life that they want to live until certain conditions are present. ACT works to help couples understand how they can live their life according to their values and dreams in the present, rather than continuing to experience barrier after barrier to living a value-added life.

Values are an indication of one's life direction. They tend to be consistent in life and are not simply about goals that a person wants to attain. In other words, values are something that a person "does," not something that a person "has." Furthermore, values are not judgments; they are choices that a person makes. The therapy process helps guide couples through the process of choosing the values that they want to live their life by and identifying goals to help them live according to those values.

One technique for using values in couples therapy would be to have each partner separately identify their individual values. This can be done through an open-ended discussion where the partner states their values or through an exercise where the therapist gives the most common values on a piece of paper, with a couple of blank spots to write in values, and asks each partner to rank-order the stated values. Once the values have been identified and ranked, the therapist engages the couple in a discussion of how their current actions are either leading them in the direction of their values or away from their values. By connecting values to the relationship, the couple is better able to recognize where there are similarities and differences between the partners' stated values. By exploring the values in connection with the current dynamics in the relationship, the couple can reflect on their behavior in comparison to their stated values. This would also include the exploration of what is stopping each partner from being the type of partner that they want to be, in keeping with what they value.

Acceptance and Commitment Therapy Principles

When mindfulness, acceptance, and values are combined, a person is able to fully experience negative life events without the need to put their life on hold until the negative experience passes. More importantly, each partner in the relationship learns how to live with pain rather than trying to avoid pain, which only leads to suffering. There are numerous concepts that assist in guiding each partner toward this psychological flexibility.

A primary concept in ACT is that pain is normal, important, and everyone has it. Psychological pain cannot be avoided and attempts to avoid it only make it worse. Pain and suffering are not the same thing. Suffering is often experienced in one's attempt to rid oneself of pain. ACT uses many metaphors to illustrate its concepts. The metaphor used to illustrate the concept of suffering is *psychological quicksand*. This refers to the tendency to engage in behaviors to eliminate suffering that actually make their suffering worse. When a person struggles to get out of the quicksand, they just sink deeper. When the person stops struggling and makes contact with the surface, then they can work at getting out of the quicksand. When partners are able to accept that pain is a part of their lived experience in the relationship, then each person is on the path toward getting rid of suffering. ACT asserts that a client can live a life of value by learning to "get out of your mind and into your life" (which is also the title of one of Hayes's books).

The language that a partner uses can create their suffering. It is common for one partner to try and suppress their thoughts as a way of fixing them. "If I just pretend that I don't think or feel this way, then I will feel better." However, ACT believes that this thought suppression only serves to make the distressing experience worse, adding to problems in the relationship. Not only is the partner disallowing themselves to think or feel something but now they have to avoid thinking about what they are suppressing. The worry will only grow larger. The suffering that is created by language leads to experiential avoidance. Experiential avoidance results in a person missing out on their life events. When one partner is not willing to have an internal experience, they will have it anyway. The more the partner tries to avoid it, the more pain they experience.

The concept of acceptance is tied to the concept of *willingness*. Willingness is a synonym for acceptance. When a person is willing to feel their emotions, to think their thoughts, then they are able to learn how to live with those experiences. To be willing means to make space in one's life for living, not just space for avoiding pain. According to ACT, this is done by letting go of trying to control your thoughts and feelings. The goal of willingness is not to feel better but to be able to experience the moment fully and move forward based upon one's chosen values.

Another concept is *cognitive defusion*. Traditionally, people tend to be fused with their thoughts. This refers to one's thoughts dominating how a person is able to respond. When a person is fused with their thoughts, the thoughts are perceived as facts. Cognitive defusion works to separate a person from their thoughts, no longer having to view the thoughts as factual. In therapy, the couple is taught to look *at* their thoughts rather than looking *from* their thoughts. This concept is demonstrated by the metaphor of living outside a war zone rather than living inside a war zone. The couple learns how to label their private experiences with the preface "I am having the thought that . . ." or "I am having the feeling of . . ." rather than being fused together with the thought or feeling. The couple practices stepping back from the argument—noticing the story that they are telling themselves about the situation—and their partner in that moment. Often, couples are thought to create "smog" in their relationship. This refers to the fusion to mental activities that creates damage to the relationship—such as thoughts, attitudes, memories, predictions, and judgments. The therapist helps the couple to explore patterns of resentment, fear, worry, of "I'm right" and "you're wrong" in the relationship, that are connected to fusion patterns of behavior.

Clinical Interventions

As for clinical interventions attached to this theory, there are none. ACT is not a set of prescribed techniques to implement with a client at specific stages of treatment. Hayes views technology-focused approaches as ineffective, stating that they lend to rule following, which is inflexible and insensitive to the needs of the client. Instead, the counselor is taught to use himself or herself in the treatment process. This is done with an emphasis on counselor compassion for the couple. The counselor is encouraged to speak to the couple as an equal, show genuineness and vulnerability, and avoid judgments. Additionally, the counselor demonstrates creativity and flexibility in how to tailor the language of the theory to fit the couple's needs. The counselor models a stance of acceptance and willingness to the couple. This is demonstrated by managing contradictory ideas, feelings, and memories without a need to resolve them for or with the client. The focus during sessions is on the couple's experiences; accordingly, the counselor avoids providing his or her own personal opinions to the client regarding the experiences that are shared. This includes refraining from any use of arguing, persuading, or attempting to convince the couple of anything. Furthermore, the counselor does not provide explanations for any of the concepts or metaphors used in the treatment. Insight is to be achieved by the couple, not given to the couple by the counselor. And finally, the counselor is allowed to self-disclose about any personal issues that would assist in illustrating a therapeutic point.

Kimberly Duris

See also Anxiety; Beliefs and Values; Clinical Practice; Commitment; Metaphors; Mindfulness

Further Readings

Bach, P., & Moran, D. (2008). *ACT in practice: Case conceptualization in acceptance and commitment therapy*. Oakland, CA: New Harbinger.

Harris, R. (2009a). *ACT made simple: An easy-to-read primer on acceptance and commitment therapy*. Oakland, CA: New Harbinger.

Harris, R. (2009b). *Act with love*. Oakland, CA: New Harbinger.

Hayes, S. C. (2004). Acceptance and commitment therapy and the new behavior therapies: Mindfulness, acceptance and relationship. In S. C. Hayes, V. M. Follette, & M. Linehan (Eds.), *Mindfulness and acceptance: Expanding the cognitive behavioral tradition* (pp. 1–29). New York, NY: Guilford Press.

Hayes, S. C., Luoma, J., Bond, F., Masuda, A., & Lillis, J. (2006). Acceptance and commitment therapy: Model, processes, and outcomes. *Behaviour Research and Therapy, 44*(1), 1–25.

Hayes, S. C., & Strosahl, K. D. (Eds.). (2004). *A practical guide to acceptance and commitment therapy*. New York, NY: Springer-Verlag.

Luoma, J. B., Hayes, S. C., & Walser, R. D. (2007). *Learning ACT: An acceptance & commitment therapy skills-training manual for therapists*. Oakland, CA: New Harbinger.

Törneke, N. (2010). *Learning RFT: An introduction to relational frame theory and its clinical applications*. Oakland, CA: New Harbinger.

ACCULTURATION

The term *acculturation* refers to the process of transformation that occurs when two or more individuals or groups from different cultures come into contact, resulting in the adoption, adaptation, or rejection of values, beliefs, and practices by one or all groups. While acculturation includes changes in the receiving community as a result of contact with a foreign group, the term is most often used to describe the process many immigrants or minorities go through when establishing themselves in a new culture or environment. The process of acculturation may differ from group to group and may vary also depending on the characteristics of the host or majority culture. This entry provides an overview of the acculturation process among immigrants living in the United States.

Levels of Acculturation

From the early settlers to the present day, individuals come to America each year from across the world. Annually, nearly 1.1 million immigrants and refugees legally enter the United States. Although California, New York, and Florida may attract the highest numbers of foreigners settling in the United States, immigrants establish themselves throughout the nation. Another 800,000 to 1.2 million individuals enter the United States illegally each year. While there are many similarities, the acculturation process can vary greatly between legal and illegal immigrants. Legal immigrants may be more open to embracing the host culture and the opportunities it affords. Contrarily, the fear of being discovered and deported may lead illegal immigrants to live more within communities similar to their culture of origin, allowing them to blend in with other individuals. Today, one of every five individuals in the United States is a first- or second-generation immigrant.

Acculturation has been described as a unidimensional and bidimensional process. As a unidimensional process, immigrants in a host country adopt the values, behaviors, and beliefs of the host culture and simultaneously discard those of their culture of origin. The unidimensional process can be described as linear. The bidimensional process, however, reflects varying levels of host-culture acquisition and heritage-culture retention, as described in John Berry's model of acculturation. Berry identified four categories of acculturation: *Assimilation* occurs when individuals acquire the values, beliefs, and practices of the host culture while discarding their culture of origin. *Separation* occurs when individuals remain separate, rejecting the host culture while retaining their culture of origin. *Integration* occurs when individuals integrate, acquiring the values and norms of the host culture while retaining their heritage culture. Lastly, *marginalization* occurs when individuals reject both the host culture and their heritage culture.

These categories are based on the assumption that members of the immigrant or minority group are free to choose how they want to acculturate. However, when forced to remain among one's own group, the term *segregation* is more applicable. Immigrants can be forced to remain separate from other groups by a larger society. Likewise, immigrants or members of a minority group may be forced to assimilate into a larger society by the dominant group in order to survive. While such an aggregate society may be viewed as a melting pot, immigrant groups can experience significant pressure to reject their cultural identity and embrace the majority group culture.

Acculturation and Cultural Identity

The degree to which a person accepts or rejects the host culture or their culture of origin informs their cultural identity. Various factors contribute to cultural identity, including language, family structure, religion, socioeconomic status, and community expectations. There are various models of cultural and racial identity, including some specific to different minority groups. The racial/cultural identity development model by Derald Wing Sue and David Sue is applicable to different populations, including immigrants and minority groups in the United States.

Individuals can be at any of the following stages of cultural identity development: *conformity, dissonance, resistance and immersion, introspection,* and *integrative awareness*. At the conformity stage, individuals have a preference for the values, beliefs, and practices of the dominant culture. They maintain an overall positive outlook toward the dominant culture while holding a negative view of self and their culture of origin. At the dissonance stage, individuals question their positive view of the dominant culture and alternate between appreciating and depreciating aspects of their heritage culture. At the resistance and immersion stage, individuals rigidly embrace their heritage culture and reject the values, beliefs, and practices associated with the dominant culture. At the introspection stage, individuals tend to experience conflict between their personal autonomy and allegiance to their heritage culture and group. They begin to question their rigid stance and begin to see variation among all groups of individuals. At the *integrative awareness* stage, individuals develop an inner sense of security about their identity and are able to accept and reject various aspects of the dominant culture. The integrative awareness stage is viewed as the most accepting of one's culture and other cultures and allows individuals to navigate well in a multicultural society.

Acculturative Stress

While immigrants may initially experience a honeymoon phase upon arrival in the United States, the process of acculturation comes with many challenges for those adapting to life in America. Housing, transportation, education, health care, employment, legal assistance, and the need for supportive relationships can be a source of significant acculturative stress. Moreover, the reason for migration to the United States or the host country is an important factor that can impact the acculturation process upon arrival. Individuals emigrate to the United States for various reasons. Some come to seek education, professional advancement, or economic opportunities to improve their quality of life. Others may be escaping war-torn countries, persecution, or political unrest. Immigrants also come with different intentions in regards to how long they will stay in the United States. While the possibility of returning home for some is nonexistent owing to disasters, violence, or persecution, some may come to America with the intent to eventually return to their country of origin after a time period. The latter group is less likely to adopt American cultural values. Even when the intent is to stay, there can be varying degrees of host culture acquisition and heritage culture retention.

The stress of adapting to life in the United States often includes a deep sense of loss as it relates to culture, language, and status. Many immigrants face the challenge of extended separation from family and close friends. They can be overwhelmed by grief or the concern for the safety and health of those left back home, particularly those who remain in war-torn, violent, or impoverished areas. Despite the economic struggle that may be experienced in adapting to life in the United States, many immigrants face the added pressure of providing financially for family left back home.

The challenge of adapting to life in a new country and community can be even greater for those whose dislocation was rapid due to traumatic events such as natural disaster, war, or persecution. Acculturative stress is reflected in the high rates of depression, acute stress disorder (ASD), posttraumatic stress disorder (PTSD), and anxiety in immigrant populations, particularly among refugees exposed to war and violence. For immigrants who entered the United States illegally, acculturative stress can be exacerbated by the constant threat of detention and deportation as well as the trauma experienced through abrupt departures and dangerous travel to enter the United States.

Discrimination also contributes to acculturative stress. Newly arrived immigrants often face the challenge of being discriminated against by the majority and other ethnic minority groups. Stress resulting from discrimination can be less among immigrants who settle within immigrant communities that reflect their native language, norms, and values. The need to adapt to the host culture as a mean of survival is thus reduced. Moreover, immigrants who settle in large immigrant communities have less need for contact with majority group members or other ethnic minority groups. They are frequently able to find and utilize services needed to survive in a new land as these services are offered by members of their own ethnic community.

Acculturation Gap

When immigrant parents and children adapt to their new environment differently, they experience acculturation gap. Children are often immediately immersed into their new cultural context by attending school. School facilitates the process of language acquisition and allows children to learn the values of their new community. Children from non–English speaking countries tend to acquire the English language faster than their parents. This gives them a social advantage over their parents when it comes to adapting to life in a new setting.

With the presence of an acculturation gap, many immigrant families face the challenge of hierarchical inversions as children become the cultural interpreters for their parents struggling to adapt. Moreover, the added pressure to fit it in with peers may lead children to discard their culture of origin as they embrace the positive and negative values and practices of their new community. This often counters parents' effort to preserve as much of the heritage culture as possible and maintain a sense of cultural and family identity while adapting to a new life in America.

Over time, children can learn to be bicultural and navigate between the host culture and heritage culture. Some maintain their native language and norms while also learning the new language and customs of the host culture. A strong sense of cultural or ethnic identity contributes to positive self-esteem, decreasing the likelihood of problematic behaviors while increasing school performance, positive peer interaction, and well-being. Children can also be marginalized, not fitting in with their culture of origin or the host culture. They can be caught between two cultural paradigms. These children often experience significant acculturative stress as they lack support within their new communities. The challenges can lead to increased behavioral or psychiatric disorders. At a time when maintaining strong family ties is needed to adapt well in a foreign land, acculturative stress can have a significant negative impact on family well-being.

Mental Health

Many immigrants successfully navigate through the challenges they experience in adapting to life in the United States. Nevertheless, depression, anxiety, and other mental disorders are experienced by many immigrants during the acculturation process. Mental health clinicians can play a significant role in assisting immigrants in need of services. However, in order to appropriately respond to the diverse needs of immigrants and their families, mental health clinicians working with individuals at various stages of the acculturation process should first be aware of their own cultural biases that can negatively impact the individuals served. Clinicians should also learn about the immigrant's story, including factors leading to the individual's arrival in the United States and the migration process. Understanding the specific cultural context of immigrants is critical to delivering culturally competent services. Behaviors and symptoms can easily be misunderstood if viewed outside of a cultural context.

Because many immigrants arrive in the United States traumatized by their experiences, clinicians should assess for trauma and loss and respond accordingly. Furthermore, since immigrant populations underutilize mental health services in the United States, clinicians should form alliances with other service providers and community leaders and centers to help bridge the gap and facilitate the delivery of mental health services to those in need. With the continued flow of immigrants arriving in the United States each year, the need for culturally competent mental health services to assist immigrants through the acculturation process will remain.

Keny Felix

See also Asian American Families; Assimilation: Immigrants and Refugees; Bilingual Families; Immigrant Families; Latino Families

Further Readings

Berry, J. W. (1997). Immigration, acculturation, and adaptation. *Applied Psychology: An International Review*, 46(1), 5–68.

Buckingham, S. L., & Brodsky, A. E. (2015). "Our differences don't separate us": Immigrant families navigate through intrafamilial acculturation gaps through diverse resilience processes. *Journal of Latina/o Psychology*, 3(3), 143–159.

Jadalla, A. A., Hattar, M. H., & Schubert, C. (2015). Acculturation as a predictor of health promoting and lifestyle practices of Arab Americans: A descriptive study. *Journal of Cultural Diversity*, 22(1), 15–22.

Schwartz, S., Unger, J. B., Zamboanga, B. L., & Szapocznik, J. (2010). Rethinking the concept of acculturation. *American Psychologist, 64*(4), 237–251.

Sue, D. W., & Sue, D. (2013). *Counseling the culturally diverse: Theory and practice.* Hoboken, NJ: Wiley.

ACTIVE PARENTING

Active Parenting is a parent education program that has been in use since 1983 and is based on the extensive work of psychologists Alfred Adler and Rudolf Dreikurs. Some of the Adlerian concepts that are incorporated into the Active Parenting programs include goal-directed behavior; the importance of relationships; the parent–child relationship; an understanding of each child's unique perspectives and needs relevant to the whole child; mutual respect for others and their differences; and personal choice and responsibility. In addition, the communication theories of Carl Rogers and Robert Carkhuff inform important foundational concepts in the Active Parenting programs. Active Parenting is a proactive approach to rearing children and incorporates the authoritative approach to parenting rather than the autocratic or permissive approaches.

Description of Active Parenting

Active Parenting is an approach to help children learn appropriate behavior. Children have the task of learning how to get along in the world, and the Active Parenting approach involves the parents' constant teaching of appropriate behaviors, values, and morals to help children accomplish this. The parents' role is that of a teacher of life skills. It is critical that children learn life skills, but they do not have to be punished into learning them. Children can learn appropriate behaviors by experiencing natural consequences, both positive and negative, for their choices. Parents simply need to make sure that instruction for appropriate and desired behaviors are consistent, that consequences are immediate and given without anger, that clear instructions are provided, and that giving choices allows for children's individual differences. Active Parenting incorporates these essentials into the parent training process.

History of Active Parenting

Active Parenting first appeared in 1983 in parent training groups when the Active Parenting Discussion Program was utilized. The original program was the first video-based delivery system applied to the field of parent education. It targeted parents (TPs) of 2- to 17-year-olds in a six-session, two-hour format. Today, Active Parenting includes a range of programs suited to the needs of diverse families. Some examples include *Active Parenting*, 4th edition, for 5- to 12-year-olds, including a Spanish-language version; *Christian Active Parenting; Active Parenting of Teens*, 3rd edition; *1, 2, 3, 4 Parents!: Parenting Children Ages 1 to 4*; and *Active Parenting for Stepfamilies.* Additionally, many of the Active Parenting programs are offered in online groups for convenience.

Application of Active Parenting

Leaders who have been trained in the model facilitate Active Parenting. Often, leaders of Active Parenting programs are school counselors, social workers, and professional counselors working in agencies or private practices; health care professionals; and religious leaders. Training is available in face-to-face classes that meet in a prescribed time frame (7 hours), as well as online classes, which can be self-paced. Trainees can be trained in any of the Active Parenting programs. Training includes the information on how to use the video-based program modules, how to recruit parents for the parent programs, and how to address the specific needs of a particular group. To become certified as a leader, a person who has been trained simply needs to conduct his or her first parent group and send the evaluations from the group to the home office. Once those steps have been completed, the new leader can advertise as a certified leader in Active Parenting. For those who desire more training, a leader can become a trainer of trainers, which requires a 3-day workshop led by experts from the Active Parenting program. Leaders of the Active Parenting program can provide a useful service to their communities by assisting families to rear children and maintain healthy family relations.

Benefits and Cautions for Active Parenting

Active Parenting is one of a variety of evidence-based parenting programs. In more than 20 years of studies, researchers have demonstrated the efficacy of the Active Parenting programs. Results ranged from showing positive changes in parent and child behaviors to better problem-solving skills, generally more satisfying parent–child relationships, and overall better family functioning. Additionally, some studies showed that parents became more aware of their roles in preventing drug and alcohol use among their teens. Participants in the Active Parenting programs have reported satisfaction with the course and how they and their children had benefited. Many organizations that have used Active Parenting in their programming have consulted with professional researchers to conduct studies regarding the outcomes of using the program with positive results. With evidence such as these researchers have produced, a strong pattern of success for the Active Parenting parent education programs is apparent.

Three of the most popular Active Parenting programs have been listed on the National Registry of Evidence-based Programs and Practices (NREPP): *Active Parenting Now, Active Parenting of Teens,* and *Families in Action.* The registry is part of the national government organization Substance Abuse and Mental Health Services Administration (SAMHSA), and inclusion in the registry is a well-respected standard for programs and practices that effectively reduce risky behaviors. Many organizations are required to use NREPP-listed programs, and now these organizations can report that their Active Parenting educational programs qualify as evidence-based resources for parents.

Although Active Parenting has many strengths, compared to some other evidence-based parenting programs it has some drawbacks. First, the program involves extra training for facilitators beyond just ordering and studying materials and can be more costly than some other evidence-based programs. Second, although there are many outcome studies to support the program, they tend to be single-group, pre- and posttest designs. Experimental designs would help increase the research base for empirical effectiveness.

Lisa A. Wines and Judith A. Nelson

See also Group Parenting Classes; Parent Management Training; Parental Stress: Effects on Children

Further Readings

Abbey, A., Pilgrim, C., Hendrickson, P., & Lorenz, S. (1998). Implementation and impact of a family-based substance abuse prevention program in rural communities. *The Journal of Primary Prevention, 18*(3).

Bernino, J., & Rourke, J. (2003) Obesity prevention in pre-school Native-American children: A pilot study using home visiting. *Obesity Research, 11,* 606–611,

Boccella, E. (1987). *Effects of the Active Parenting program on attitudinal change of parents, parent perceived behavioral change of children, and parent perceived change in family environment* (Doctoral dissertation, Temple University).

Fashimpar, G. (1992). *An evaluation of three parent training programs* (Doctoral dissertation, University of Texas at Arlington).

Fashimpar, G. (2000). Problems of parenting: Solutions of science. *Journal of Family Social Work, 5*(2).

Leonardson, G. (1991). *Active Parenting of Teens project* (Draft report). Watertown, SD: Northeastern Drug and Alcohol Prevention Resource Center.

Mullis, F. (1999). Active Parenting: An evaluation of two Adlerian parent education programs. *The Journal of Individual Psychology, 55*(2).

Pindar, C. (1994). *Effects of the Active Parenting program on children's interpersonal behavior as observed in a playroom setting.* Unpublished manuscript.

Popkin, M. (1983). *The original Active Parenting Discussion Program.* Atlanta, GA: Active Parenting Publishers.

Sprague, J. (1990). *The impact of the Active Parenting program on the moral development and parenting skills of parents* (Doctoral dissertation, North Carolina State University).

Urban, T. A. (1991). A case study on the effects of an Adlerian parent education program on parental attitudes and child rearing techniques. *Dissertation Abstracts International, 52*, A4218.

Adjustment Disorder in Adolescents

Adjustment disorder is found in the category of trauma- and stressor-related disorders in the fifth edition of the *Diagnostic and Statistical Manual of Mental Disorders* (DSM-5) with the common criterion of a significant stressor. The disorder is frequently diagnosed in adolescents experiencing reactions to a specific identifiable stressor or event typically in school, home, or work and with friends or family members. This entry describes the criteria for adjustment disorder, differential diagnosis, and issues and treatment with adolescents.

Formerly called transient situational disturbance prior to the publication of DSM-III-R, adjustment disorder focuses on emotional or behavioral symptoms as a reaction to a specific stressor within 3 months of the stressor's onset that typically end within 6 months of the termination of the stressor. Thus, when the individual is removed from the proximity of the stressor, the symptoms should decrease. The closer the client is to the stressor or trigger and the severity of the reaction, the greater the evidence for a diagnosis of adjustment disorder. Adjustment disorder is a self-limiting exclusion diagnosis that is often changed when the threshold for another diagnosis is met, such as major depressive disorder.

While adjustment disorder has been considered a subthreshold diagnosis, current evaluations support it as a distinct diagnosis with severe symptoms. Lack of response to psychopharmacological treatment (e.g., antidepressants) provides greater support for a diagnosis of adjustment disorder. Reactions are clinically significant, severe, and disproportionate to what the stressor warrants, resulting in serious occupational or social functional impairment. Individuals impacted by a situation or event may be sad, depressed, or anxious; however, the emotional reactions are insufficient to meet the criteria for anxiety, depressive or other disorders, or normal grieving. Some adolescents also respond with risky or irresponsible behaviors that appear as possible symptoms of conduct disorder (CD).

Adjustment disorder is found across ages and cultures and is a common diagnosis in primary care. In psychiatric hospital settings, adjustment disorder is the most common diagnosis, with 36% to 50% of the diagnoses made, while the prevalence of adjustment disorder in outpatient mental health is 5% to 20%. In emergency room patients with self-harm, about 32% are diagnosed with adjustment disorder compared to about 20% with major depression disorder. Adolescents living in distressed environments frequently have multiple stressors and may also be affected by intergenerational family stressors. Furthermore, the cultural context must also be considered in determining whether symptoms are considered normal or maladaptive. Demonstrations of adjustment distress are normative in some cultures but viewed as pathological in others. Adults generally have a good prognosis, while the prognosis for adolescents is poor with a higher rate of developing other disorders, especially without treatment or coping skills. Results of recent studies also indicated that adjustment disorder continues beyond 6 months in some populations.

According to the DSM-5, adjustment disorder is characterized by six subtypes based on depression, anxiety, or behavior. While the most common specifier in adults is with depressed mood, the most common specifiers for children and adolescents with adjustment disorder are with disturbance of conduct or with mixed disturbance of emotions and conduct. Other specifiers are anxiety, mixed anxiety and depressed mood, and unspecified. The identified stressor may be a single event (e.g., an auto accident) or multiple events (e.g., family illness, job loss, move to another location, new school) and may affect one person, a family, a group, or a community. Stressors may be continuous (e.g., living in an unsafe environment, a long-term or lifelong illness) or recurrent (e.g., domestic violence or a family's moving seasonally to find work).

Differential diagnosis is a lengthy process that includes consideration of most disorders in the DSM-5. Normal grief or bereavement is not a criterion of adjustment disorder, although adjustment disorder may be diagnosed with excessive bereavement or grief reactions where the bereavement and impaired functioning may be longer and are still considered adaptive rather than maladaptive. Persistent complex bereavement disorder is listed in the conditions for further study in the DSM-5 with prevalence higher in females and persistent symptoms continue for more than 1 year. Although study results identified comorbidity between adjustment disorder and major depressive disorder in almost 50% of the subjects, significant comorbidity between adjustment and complicated grief was not found.

Adolescents and Adjustment Disorder Symptoms

Diagnosing adjustment disorder in adolescents can be challenging because their reactions frequently reflect the developmental ups and downs of teenagers' daily lives and their impact on the stage of developmental functioning. The *International Classification of Diseases* (ICD-10) by the World Health Organization (WHO) requires both impairment in functioning and excessive symptoms, and together, these symptoms identify the criteria more clearly. Adolescents experience common school, athletic, and social events that could also result in disappointments, failures, and rejections. Many events reflect developmental milestones that teenagers achieve (or do not achieve) such as teams, dating, friendships, prom, driver's license, college admission, jobs, and graduation, and this diagnosis might be used to medicalize teenagers' typical negative experiences or stressful events. Family issues also affect teenagers, including parents' separation or divorce, illness, job loss, moving, or the death of a pet. Serious personal events could negatively affect adolescents' behavioral and emotional reactions (e.g., pregnancy, injury, relationship breakup, hazing, ostracism, or bullying).

Researchers suggest the major factor contributing to the development of adjustment disorder is the individual's vulnerability. One teenager may perceive a stressor as deeply upsetting, while another views it as a fleeting irritation or an uncomfortable situation. Other factors to be considered are type of stressor, family and support systems in the environment, autonomy, coping skills, and past experiences. Assessment of current functioning also includes stage of development, level of dependence upon parents, developmental disorders, learning disabilities, and cultural norms for behavior. In children and adolescents, adjustment disorder has a poor prognosis and often develops into a more serious disorder over time.

The situational stressor cannot be the worsening of a preexisting mental health disorder or medical illness; however, a severe behavioral or emotional reaction to medical illness or a change in the seriousness of a medical disorder can be diagnosed as adjustment disorder. For example, adjustment disorder is the most common diagnosis after a new onset of insulin-dependent diabetes mellitus in children and adolescents. Adolescents with adjustment disorder who use drugs for symptom relief may be diagnosed later with substance abuse as the primary diagnosis. Adolescents with adjustment disorder exhibit symptoms such as depressed mood, crying, hopelessness, feeling isolated or cut off, anxiety, worry, and nervousness, or they demonstrate both anxiety and depression as well as conduct disturbances. Behavioral symptoms include poor concentration, lower academic performance, failing grades, or insomnia.

Adolescents may respond with sadness, distress, or turmoil disproportionate to the actual event even when cultural factors are taken into consideration. Younger teens are more likely to experience irritable mood rather than withdrawn mood, and suicide ideation and attempts are common. Thus, differentiating between pathological reactions and normal responses to stressful situations in adolescents is difficult. Lower preadmission rates and shorter hospitalization stays are more evident in adolescents with adjustment disorder than with major depressive disorder. After acute events, onset of symptoms can begin immediately or within a few days, and the behavioral reaction can be severe with suicide ideation, enactment, or completion. Between 20% and 25% of adolescents diagnosed engage in suicide behavior, and in one study about 33% who died by suicide had been diagnosed with adjustment disorder. Suicide ideation and behavior including suicide completion occur earlier and with fewer prior behavioral or emotion problems in adolescents diagnosed with adjustment disorder than with major depressive disorder.

Adjustment disorder differs from traumatic disorders in this category such as acute stress disorder (ASD) and posttraumatic stress disorder (PTSD), which are characterized by more intense stressors after a life-threatening event. In the immediate aftermath of a disaster or mass traumatic event, symptoms are generally considered a normal reaction to an abnormal event; thus, individuals may adjust to the impact of the stressor event in a few days or weeks and then return to the previous level of functioning. Responses are generally normative stress reactions that are not more excessive than expected for most individuals affected. Although adjustment disorder, ASD, and PTSD share common symptoms, adjustment disorder is considered the appropriate diagnosis when an individual shows symptoms of ASD or PTSD after a traumatic event but does not meet the full criteria. Adjustment disorder differs from ASD, which must occur between 3 days and 1 month of the stressor, and PTSD with symptoms persisting more than 1 month following a life-threatening stressor. In addition, an individual who has not experienced a traumatic event but meets all the symptoms of ASD or PTSD is generally diagnosed with adjustment disorder. In the aftermath of a community or family disaster, psychological first aid (PFA) and crisis counseling help to ameliorate immediate distressing reactions. PFA also provides psychoeducation and information to family members and identifies community resources available should symptoms continue or worsen.

Treatment

After a comprehensive evaluation and mental status examination, treatment decisions are made using interviews, clinical judgment, and consultation or liaison, with low agreement among these methods. The process of clinical decision-making guides the treatment of adjustment disorder generally, including counseling, psychoeducation, coping skills, and family and school supports. Brief counseling with cognitive-behavioral therapy (CBT), solution-focused therapy, or family therapy focuses on short-term goals, with the counselor's and client's expectations moving toward recovery. Supportive counseling addresses identifying and strengthening positive relationships with family, school counselors, teachers, and coaches, and participating in formal support groups in school or in the community. Adolescents may also find online support groups comfortable, engaging, and less public. With the knowledge that symptom duration is generally short, students with adjustment disorder may be more likely to contribute to a positive plan and hope for future remission.

Family members, especially siblings, are affected by an adolescent's behavioral and emotional reactions after a significant stressor. Consultation with parents or guardians regarding treatment is essential and family counseling sessions are recommended so all members understand the stressor, its duration, and its symptoms. In family sessions, impact of the stressor on each member can be discussed and reframed, with coping skills taught to the entire family. Furthermore, consultation with the adolescent's school counselor can result in a shared understanding of what the student can accomplish academically and socially while also coping with the stressor. If the student is on home instruction, a gradual return to a half-day and then to a full school day is an effective strategy.

CBT is recommended to reduce the stressor's immediate impact and to facilitate dialogue about the importance and meaning of the stressor to the adolescent. Counseling objectives address identifying the stressor and how the teenager reacts to it, expressing feelings, understanding and reframing the meaning of the stressor for the adolescent, and eliminating or avoiding the stressor. Further, the teenager can identify and strengthen coping skills, learning additional coping strategies if the stressor cannot be reduced or eliminated. Psychoeducation with adolescents and their families helps them understand the stressor and its impact on the family; develop coping skills such as breathing and emotion regulation; and reduce tension, maladaptive coping, and substance abuse. Teenagers perceive stressors in uniquely personal ways and often have different reactions to the same event, with some demonstrating serious maladaptive reactions and others coping in more adaptive ways. Stressor-specific support groups can empower adolescents, helping them recognize that they are not alone and that others experience similar feelings and reactions. Pharmacotherapy can address depressed or anxious mood, sleep issues, or panic attacks with the goal of eliminating symptoms while the client and therapist work on reducing the impact of the stressor in counseling.

Mental health professionals frequently find that symptoms of adjustment disorder overlap with other disorders. The diagnosis is typically changed when symptoms increase, thus meeting criteria for another disorder such as depression or anxiety. Adjustment disorder has also been considered as a pragmatic diagnosis when criteria for another diagnosis are not fully met, or when treatment is needed and differential diagnosis is inconclusive. Following a crisis or disaster (e.g., traffic accident, hurricane, flood, violence), when there is a great demand for services and staff members have little time to triage patients, adjustment disorder may be coded without a comprehensive differential diagnosis even when observable symptoms do not reach full criteria for another disorder.

Jane M. Webber and J. Barry Mascari

See also Adolescent Behavior Problems; Adolescent Mental Health; Health Issues; Parent–Adolescent Relations

Further Readings

Casey, P. (2009). Adjustment disorder: Epidemiology, diagnosis, and treatment. *CNS Drugs, 23*(11), 927–938. doi:10.2165/11311000

Casey, P., & Bailey, S. (2011). Adjustment disorders: The state of the art. *World Psychiatry, 10*(1), 11–18.

Friedberg, R. D., & McClure, J. M. (2015). *Clinical practice of cognitive therapy with children and adolescents: The nuts and bolts* (2nd ed.). New York, NY: Guilford Press.

Luthar, S. S., Jacob A., Burack, J. A., Cicchetti. D., & Weisz, J. R. (1997). *Developmental psychopathology: Perspectives on adjustment, risk, and disorder.* Cambridge, England: Cambridge University Press.

Newcorn, J. H., & Strain, J. (1992). Adjustment disorder in children and adolescents. *Journal of the American Academy of Child and Adolescent Psychiatry, 31*(2), 318–326.

Pelkonen, M., Mattunen, M., Henriksson, M., & Lonnqvist, J. (2005). Suicidality in adjustment disorder-clinical characteristics of adolescent outpatients. *European Child & Adolescent Psychiatry, 14*(3), 174–180.

Ponizovsky, A. M., Levov, K., Schultz, Y., & Radomislensky, I. (2011). Attachment insecurity and psychological resources associated with adjustment disorders. *American Journal of Orthopsychiatry, 81*(2), 265–276.

Portzky, G., Audenaert, K., & van Heeringen, K. (2005). Adjustment disorder and the course of the suicidal process in adolescents. *Journal of Affective Disorders, 87*(2–3), 265–270.

Semprini, E., Fava, G. A., & Sonino, N. (2010). The spectrum of adjustment disorders: Too broad to be clinically helpful. *CNS Spectrums, 15*(6), 382–388.

Steiner, H., & Hall, R. E. (2015). *Treating adolescents* (2nd ed.). New York, NY: Wiley.

Strain, J. J., & Diefenbacher, A. (2008). The adjustment disorders: the conundrums of the diagnoses. *Comprehensive Psychiatry, 49*(2), 121–130.

Adlerian Family Therapy

The term *Adlerian family therapy* refers to a systems-based intervention process with families that is informed by individual psychology as originated by

Alfred Adler and by its applications as developed by Rudolf Dreikurs and his associates. Adlerian family therapy covers a multitude of family interventions, ranging from lifestyle restructuring when parents are extremely dysfunctional to open-forum family counseling, family education centers, and the psychoeducational models used in parent study groups. This entry describes the origins of this model of therapy, its foundation in Adler's individual psychology, and its systematic development by Rudolf Dreikurs. The structure of the model is presented from the formation of a therapeutic relationship through assessment of relational patterns within families and psychological disclosure to reorientation of family processes. Open-forum family counseling and parent study groups are addressed elsewhere in this encyclopedia.

Alfred Adler and the Development of Individual Psychology as a Systemic Model

Alfred Adler was the first psychiatrist to do family therapy. Long before systems theory gained prominence in the evolution of psychotherapy, Adler's model was holistically systemic. Even his work with individual clients relied heavily on the interpretations that people gave to their experiences of family life, school, culture, and society.

Adler described the foundation for individual patterns in life as a movement from feelings of inferiority through a striving for superiority or success toward a self-defined goal of perfection and actualization. Indeed, the formulation of a life goal unifies the personality and orients every thought, feeling, conviction, belief, and behavior toward the desired end. In this sense, the starting point of inferiority feelings is both normal and necessary for all human beings. Inferiority feelings and striving for a better place in the world are two sides of the same coin: One immediately follows and stimulates the other. Only when inferiority feelings become exaggerated (and form what Adler called a *complex*) is the individual's growth and development hampered or constrained.

Three types of children tend to develop an inferiority complex or otherwise become ill prepared for the challenges of life. Because the origin of the species was based in part on the survival of the fittest and civilized cultures prize healthy people with fully developed organs, children who are born with, or who later suffer from, *physical deficiencies* are more likely to develop an inferiority complex, a more or less fixed feeling of inadequacy. The same could be said for those who are not part of the dominant culture.

Indeed, Adler noted that severe obstacles in a child's life—from organ inferiorities to homelessness to the problems of an economic, social, or racial nature or even gender discrimination—often result in the stunting or distortion of social connectedness. Even among families from the dominant culture of any country, however, children who are *pampered* or *spoiled* and children who are *hated* also develop exaggerated feelings of inferiority, leading to behaviors that were considered problems in school or in the community.

After World War I, Adler and his associates established more than 30 Child Guidance Clinics in Vienna, where they conducted family therapy sessions and teacher consultations in front of other parents, teachers, and members of the local community. By 1934, one year after Adolf Hitler's appointment as chancellor of Germany, the Nazi Party had eliminated all of these community clinics. Rudolf Dreikurs, Adler's close associate and student in Vienna, emigrated in 1937 to the United States, where he would systematize Adler's family approach and make it available to whole communities in the form of family education centers. Dreikurs extended Adler's early work with family constellation and purposeful behavior, more clearly defining the goals of children's misbehavior and developing an interview and goal-disclosure process that became the foundation for Adlerian family interventions.

Adlerian Family Therapy: Initial Consideration

In too many families, what starts out as a nurturing relationship between parent and child deteriorates into repetitive, negative interactions. Sometimes, these negative interactions result from the common human experience of repeating parenting styles that were part of the adult's upbringing—that is, negative interactions and patterns that reflect the autocratic or permissive dialectic that has permeated much of the European American social heritage. Sometimes, these negative engagements result from personal or relational dysfunctions in the parents that signal a level of self-absorption that constrains effective parenting and sets up a troubled and negative *family atmosphere*. Certainly, abusive relationships fall into this category but so do some clinically disordered people suffering from, say, depression, anxiety, psychotic disorders, and/or substance abuse problems.

At the beginning of therapy, Adlerian family therapists start by determining whether the leaders of the family are *functional* or *dysfunctional*. Dysfunctional families include families where the children are in charge and the adults have given up on effective parenting; families with attachment issues; psychologically troubled or disordered families; or violent families, among others. Therapy with more disturbing families usually takes longer, and the development of a positive working alliance must be tended more carefully. In essence, what distinguishes *counseling* with functional families from *therapy* with difficult families is not so much the therapeutic process as the severity of the problems presented.

Adlerians recognize that families tend to bring an "identified patient" or problem person to therapy in an effort to get that member "fixed" but hoping to leave the rest of the family alone. Still, a personality-disordered and quite impaired individual seldom comes to therapy with all other family members functioning effectively. Disorders affect the whole system. In this sense, the "personality-disordered family" is a better designation.

Therapeutic Process and Assessments in Adlerian Family Therapy

All forms of Adlerian therapy place an emphasis on a strong therapeutic alliance with individuals, couples, families, and groups. This alliance is based on the therapist's ability to be fully present with clients, to approach them from a position of mutual respect and cooperation, and to engage people empathically.

Dreikurs divided therapeutic interviews into two orientations: the subjective and the objective. Subjective orientations were characterized by careful listening, empathy, and asking questions that facilitated the development of client stories, the expression of personal and family concerns, and outcomes and goals that are sought in therapy. In contrast, the objective interview tended to focus on informational areas designed to identify family patterns, relational processes, styles of living, and mistaken notions or goals. The objective interview with families most often focuses on the family atmosphere, the family constellation, mistaken goals of children and adults, a typical day, and even the individual styles of living that establish or maintain negative interactions and patterns.

Family Atmosphere

Family relationships are always recursive, with each member influencing and being influenced by every other member. Family atmosphere is the climate created by the relational interactions in which various family members engage. It is the summation of family forces that characterize the patterns of daily life. Because the family is a system, individual families develop an atmosphere or climate that characterizes the quality of interactions and relational processes within the system. Autocratic and permissive atmospheres are common in Western European and American cultures; often, these become incorporated in family life as a need for power and control.

Parental or spousal relationships are often the clearest indication of the climate that constitutes the family atmosphere. In families headed by heterosexual parents, the adults model how one gender relates to the other, how boys and girls work and participate in the world, and how children should get along with other people. Such models may create an atmosphere that is joyful or angry; loving or frightening; strict or easygoing; engaged or distant; indulgent, protective, overprotective, or permissive; nurturing, challenging, or respectful, to name a few. Same-sex parents still provide models and atmospheres based on their relational styles, but gender modeling may require close friends or extended family members to be part of the children's lives.

Values that both parents maintain and support are called *family values;* they are values that cannot be ignored and that require each child to take a stand. When parents share common beliefs with regard to religion, morality, politics, education, how to handle money, or the importance of achievement, to name a few, these convictions form the background against which children construct their own personal views. Having shared beliefs does not guarantee that children will adopt those beliefs, but having strong beliefs of any kind often leads to children who when reaching adulthood have strong beliefs of their own.

In the end, family atmosphere is often detected in the tone of how family members communicate with each other. Noting who speaks to whom and who sits next to whom may suggest alliances or coalitions. Atmosphere is created in tones that may be hostile, tense, critical, commanding, competitive, preoccupied or distant; or conversely, the atmosphere may be characterized by cooperation, warmth, love, patience, or caring. Communications may be direct or indirect (sarcastic, or double-edged) or clear and useful; problem-solving may be in the hands of one person or negotiated as a group. Differing atmospheres will signal either closed or open systems with the former signifying a need for protection and safeguarding and the latter being more flexible in the face of challenge.

Clinically disturbed families often fail to meet the needs of one or more family members, increase stress and dysfunctional behaviors around transition periods in the family life cycle, and exhibit poor decision-making and extreme conflict often resulting in explosive anger and the imposition of wills. The processes within the family will often alternate between enforced rigidity and disorienting inconsistencies. In these cases, Adlerian family therapists start with a focus on restoring stability within the parent subsystem, creating cooperative processes, and emphasizing the importance of parental leadership.

The Family Constellation and the Influence of Birth Order

Adler's phrase for the family system is *the family constellation.* In addition to focusing on the importance of parental lifestyles and relationships, Adler was the first to note the power of birth order in the development of individuals and families. He identified five birth positions: *only, oldest, second-of-only-two, middle,* and *youngest.* For Adler, the power of birth order was not in the ordinal position, itself, but rather in the phenomenological *interpretation* that each person gave to his or her position. Still, some of the common characteristics of each position serve as a starting point for understanding something about how families develop.

Parents have their strongest influence on only children and oldest children; children in these positions have the full attention of their parents—at least for a short period of time—and early development is centered in parental contact. Because of this, only and oldest children tend to have high achievement drives, even if they never actually achieve much. Children in both positions tend to absorb the family values more completely. Only children, however, are never dethroned by the birth of another sibling. They remain the center of the adult world and develop adult language sooner than other birth positions. For only children, secure attachments often foretell success while pampering or overprotection can spoil the child.

Oldest children are often impressed with being "first" or "on top," and they will act in ways that maintain that position. Because they arrive first, many oldest children are dependable, reliable, responsible, "good" individuals who seek adult approval. They can adopt perfectionism in expected activities, and parents often expect them to "be a model child" for their siblings: Younger children may think of them as bossy.

The second-of-only-two will be highly focused on the oldest. In most cases, the second-of-only-two becomes the opposite of whatever the firstborn is perceived to be. Second-born children often feel that they are in a race, trying to catch up, or in competition with the first. That at which the oldest excels, the second child avoids—and vice versa.

With the birth of a third child, second children become middle children. They may feel squeezed between the oldest and the youngest child. Life seems unfair to many middle children, especially if the oldest and youngest align against the middle child. Given the difficulty of the position, middle children may be sensitive to criticism or easily angered when bossed around. Peers may be more important to them than family.

Youngest children are never dethroned. As the baby of the family, youngest children may use helplessness and dependency to put others in their service. On the other hand, they may be good observers and develop in ways that no other sibling has attempted. Indeed, it is not uncommon for them to outshine all other siblings in an area of perceived strength.

Birth positions are vantage points from which children view the world; it is the interpretation the child gives the position that counts. Adler's emphasis on *phenomenological* interpretation of family position places an emphasis on psychological position rather than ordinal position determination as is often associated with Walter Toman and later adopted by Murray Bowen. Toman disregarded phenomenological interpretation. For him, the position, itself, was determining: In his approach, an oldest child with sibling of the other sex should ideally marry the youngest child with siblings of the other sex. These people would have their power and gender issues worked out before marriage. The worst pairing would be two oldest children with no siblings of the other sex. Toman used divorce records to prove his point: The divorce rate is higher for two oldest children. What Adlerians note is that the absence of divorce is not the same as a happy marriage, and good pairings do exist between two oldest children: It is the interpretation of the position that counts, not the position itself.

A number of other variables affect the individual's development of a birth position: the number of years between the siblings; whether a child is the only boy or girl; the effects of being special (e.g., being twins; being the favorite child or grandchild; being ill or facing death; being talented or beautiful). *Family structure* (a single-parent home, a blended family, or being raised by same-sex parent) can also make a difference in family development. The actions and interactions in the family and the interpretations that each member assigns to these give initial meaning to children's lives and to the family as a whole.

A typical investigation of a family constellation may start by asking the parents to describe each of the children. Such descriptions indicate both the effects of birth order and the ways that each child adapts behaviors to engage or challenge what is important to the parents. As in many other approaches to family therapy, Adlerians use genograms to develop a graphic picture of the family system. We start by asking parents—and then children—to give us three adjectives to describe each other. For Adler, these descriptions revealed more about the describer than the person described. Each adjective is really a relational sentence. When a person says, "My mother was loving," she or he means that the mother was loving with *me*. When a father is described as aloof, angry, and distant, it is clear that to the describer, the parent, was unknowable and unpredictable.

Descriptions of parents tend to reflect the describer's sense of belonging. Adjectives for siblings, however, can only be understood within the context of birth order. When a child's sister is "happy, achieving, and pleasing," it is only useful if it is clear that the describer is either similar to or the opposite of this sister. For Adlerians, a genogram is a structural diagram only until clients communicate the meaning they attach to it.

Mistaken Goals: An Interactional View

Adler adopted a teleological perspective for his psychology, because he wanted to focus on the motivation that accounted for an individual's *movement* through life, the person's *style of living*. As noted previously, this movement is ordered and unified by the development of goals and purposeful behavior, and specifically by a life goal. His focus on purposes extended to every part of human activity, to ways of thinking, emotions, behaviors, physical and mental symptoms, interactions, gender identity, and psychopathology. With children, however, he often emphasized more immediate and concrete goals as opposed to a life goal.

Dreikurs's original publication of children's mistaken goals was less than auspicious, but his four goals became over time the foundation for his writings on parenting, family education, and family therapy. The four goals are *attention-getting, power struggle, revenge,* and a *demonstration of inadequacy* (also called an *assumed disability*). As presented by Dreikurs, they are largely unconscious in children. His typology acts as shorthand explanations or descriptions for consistent patterns of misbehavior in children. Further, Dreikurs developed a process for goal recognition that, when properly revealed to children, would result in a *recognition* reflex, a slight smile on the face and a twinkle in the eyes.

Goal identification in children relied on (a) descriptions of the child's misbehavior, (b) the parents' emotional reactions to the misbehavior, and (c) the child's reaction to the parents' attempts at correction.

- Children seeking *undue attention* would often quit after being corrected, if only for a short period of time, and parents would report feeling annoyed or irritated.
- Children seeking *power* would tend to continue misbehaviors, maybe intensify them, and parents would report feeling angry, challenged, or defeated.
- Children seeking *revenge* would engage in intensified, mean behaviors when corrected, and parents would report feeling hurt.
- The most discouraged child would adopt *positions of inadequacy,* and parents would simply want to give up on the child.

Within this goal identification process, the most important questions for parents were as follows: "What did the child actually do?" "What did you do in return, and then what did the child do after that?" "In the midst of the problem interaction, how were you feeling?" The answers to these questions provided the therapist with a guess about the goals for a child's misbehavior. In Adlerian family therapy, they are suggested to the child tentatively.

"Do you know why you . . . [name the behavior or interaction]?"

"I have an idea. Would you like to hear it?"

"Could it be . . . [suggesting one or more of the four goals in language the child can understand]?"

In addition to delineating the mistaken goals of children, several Adlerian writers have suggested interactional, mistaken goal patterns between adults and children. Nicoll starts with the basic Adlerian position—that actions and emotions always serve an interactional *purpose* or *function*. Using systemic language, he goes on to assert that these purposes and functions emerge out of *rules of interaction* the child or adult uses to maintain a sense of personal and psychological survival. Rules of interaction are perceptual—part of a person's *private logic*. A change in interaction, therefore, starts with an understanding of the private logic used by each family member. A child's private logic tends to support very concrete goals. By late adolescence or early adulthood, private logic often functions in support of larger life goals that motivate the individual's style of living.

Bitter suggests that the goals that are a part of parent–child interactions will become complementary and will create a pattern for mutual reinforcement. For example, a depressive parent will often have at least one quiet child who uses avoidance; an anxious parent will have one child who tries to never worry the parent while another child gives the parent something real to worry about. In almost every family with a schizophrenic individual, there is a supernormal person who could remain calm in the midst of war. This is also true in severely chaotic families where functional structures are not available or maintained.

Interactive goal patterns provide an explanation for both children's behaviors and the parental reactions reported in family process. Goal recognition and disclosure is a foundation for change and for family reorientation.

Typical Day

Adlerians often use a *typical day* to assess family atmosphere and family interactional patterns. Asking about a typical day will reveal repeated patterns of interaction and the ways in which children meet their immediate goals. The various constructions of a family's typical day suggest what the family values and rules of interaction are expected and supported. An investigation of a typical day is especially useful when parents are unable to present specific incidents of concern.

Each of these more objective, formal assessments taken together should infuse the material from the subjective interview with an understanding of purpose and process. In sharing and disclosing this understanding, the family is invited to consider how they would like their relationships to develop in the future. Adlerians refer to this process as *reorientation* or as a facilitation of change.

Reorientation

When one or both parents are psychologically or relationally disordered, the leadership team is impaired. The first level of intervention may be to work individually with the parent(s) to help them gain enough functionality to fully engage in raising their children. At the same time, it is important to help the children understand in the most human of terms what goes on in their families—why mistaken interactions occur and that difficult changes may need to take place. Even when the parents are functional, the first step is to unlock, unpack, and interrupt the interactional patterns in the family that have failed to produce desired outcomes. There is a strong teaching component to Adlerian reorientation, including teaching new ways to communicate, how to set limits, and how to redirect children through encouragement and natural and logical consequences.

James Robert Bitter and Rebekah Byrd

See also Adlerian Open-Forum Family Counseling; Brief Adlerian Couples Therapy; Genograms; Parent Study Groups; Systems Theory

Further Readings

Adler, A. (1927). *Understanding human nature.* New York, NY: Greenberg.

Bitter, J. R. (1988). Family mapping and family constellation: Satir in Adlerian context. *Individual Psychology, 44*(1), 106–111.

Bitter, J. R. (1991). Conscious motivations: An enhancement of Dreikurs' goals of children's misbehavior. *Individual Psychology, 47*(2), 210–221.

Bitter, J. R. (2009). The mistaken notions of adults with children. *Journal of Individual Psychology, 65*(4), 135–155.

Bitter, J. R., Roberts, A., & Sonstegard, M. A. (2002). Adlerian family therapy. In J. Carlson & D. Kios (Eds.), *Theories and strategies of family therapy* (pp. 41–79). Boston, MA: Allyn & Bacon.

Carlson, J., & Robey, P. A. (2011). An integrative Adlerian approach to family counseling. *Journal of Individual Psychology, 67*(3), 233–244.

Christensen, O. C. (Ed.). (2004). *Adlerian family counseling* (3rd ed.). Minneapolis, MN: American Guidance Service.

Dreikurs, R., & Soltz, V. (1964). *Children: The challenge.* New York, NY: Hawthorn.

Sherman, R., & Dinkmeyer, D. (Eds.). (1987). *Systems of family therapy: An Adlerian integration.* New York, NY: Brunner/Mazel.

Sperry, L. (2011). Family therapy with personality-disordered individuals and families: Understanding and treating the borderline family. *Journal of Individual Psychology, 67*(3), 222–231.

ADLERIAN OPEN-FORUM FAMILY COUNSELING

Open-forum family counseling, sometimes called demonstration family counseling or demonstration therapy, began with the work of Alfred Adler and his associates in Vienna. Following the Great War, Adler established more than 30 child guidance centers in Vienna, where he and his associates would put the concept of a *community feeling* into practical applications. In front of often large community and professional audiences, Adler would interview the parents and teachers of troubled or "troubling" children. It was common for Adler to ask where the child came in the family constellation, what common misbehaviors were, and what the parents or teachers had tried to do about it. From this information, Adler would formulate a hypothesis about the purpose or motivation for the child's misbehavior. His hypotheses often included a prediction about how the child would behave when she or he entered the room in which the session was being conducted, a prediction that was almost always immediately confirmed as the child advanced to the front of the room.

History

These open-forum events occurred on a weekly basis through the 1920s and early 1930s. Their power was in enlisting the understanding and participation of those in the community who might most effectively redirect the mistaken behaviors of children. By 1934, however, the Nazi Party had taken over, and all of Adler's centers were closed.

Rudolf Dreikurs, one of Adler's associates, brought the process to the United States, where he would demonstrate lifestyle assessments as well as couple and family counseling in classes he taught, in family education centers he established, in schools, and at professional meetings. Starting in the summer of 1947 and continuing for five years, Dreikurs taught a summer course at Northwestern University in Evanston, Illinois, on child development that centered on demonstrations of family counseling. Dreikurs had already conceptualized his four goals of children's misbehavior as well as a systematic process for interviewing families in front of other families and professionals. His approach included an investigation of the family system or family constellation and the effect of birth order in the family, an objective investigation of mistaken family interactions and patterns of interaction in a typical day, a process for goal disclosure with children that produced a *recognition reflex* in children, and recommendations based on encouragement and natural and logical consequences. In the summer of 1950, both Ray Lowe and Manford Sonstegard took Dreikurs's course. These two men would eventually wind up in the western and eastern United States, respectively, and from their initial efforts, Adlerian family education centers would take hold in the United States.

For years, Lowe would conduct demonstration family counseling every Saturday morning at the University of Oregon. In what was often called the "family circus," Lowe used graduate students from the helping professions to run parent study groups, recruit families who would be the focus of the demonstration, and set up the forum for the public. Sonstegard opened a similar set of centers in the public schools in Iowa before moving to West Virginia University. From his home base in West Virginia, Sonstegard would help to open family education centers in Pennsylvania, Delaware, Washington, D.C., and Virginia Beach, to name a few. In 1959, Lowe and Sonstegard collaborated with Dreikurs and another Adlerian colleague named Ray Corsini to write the first manual on Adlerian family counseling and the establishment of open-forum family counseling centers.

One of Lowe's early colleagues was Oscar Christensen. Christensen had studied with Dreikurs too, and when he moved to the University of Arizona, he became the dean of Open-Forum Family Counseling. Christensen extended family education centers across the United States and Canada, and he brought the model to multiple sites throughout Europe, the Middle East, and the Asia. Most importantly, he trained doctoral students to use this approach to family counseling in their courses and in the communities that they would eventually serve. In 1983, Christensen and Tom Schramski edited the first comprehensive manual on Adlerian open-forum family counseling with chapters on basic principles, processes and techniques, special issues, program implementation, evaluation, and research written by many of Christensen's former students and colleagues.

Structure of Open-Forum Therapy

In any form of demonstration counseling, the therapist has two clients: the person or family in focus and the audience. A typical family session might start with the counselor listing the names and ages of the children on a board at the front of the room. In a family education center, the children would be in a playroom, initially separated from the parents and supported by observers and facilitators trained in early childhood education, play or art therapy, or child development. The parents are introduced as coeducators in this psychoeducational experience. The audience, sitting in a semicircle facing the counselor and the parents, would be asked to guess what each of the children might be like.

Because there is more similarity between the oldest children of two families than between the oldest two children of one family, the audience is generally able to describe the general characteristic of birth order using their own families as a guide. Audience guesses are often therapeutic, normalizing the experience of the family in focus and letting family members know that they are not alone.

Stages of Open-Forum Therapy

Next, parents are asked to describe something they would like to see going better with the children at home or in school. By seeking a concrete example of problem behavior, the counselor is able to investigate the goal(s) that may be motivating problem behaviors. A behavior that stops for a while when the child is corrected and that merely irritates or annoys the parents suggests the goal of undue *attention-getting*. Misbehaviors that continue after correction and lead to anger or the feeling of defeat in parents indicate a *power struggle*. If misbehaviors intensify and elicit hurt from parents, the goal is most likely *revenge*. And finally, when parents want to give up on the misbehaving child, this approach suggests that the child is *demonstrating inadequacy* in an effort to be left alone. A pattern of mistaken interactions between parent and child can also be investigated through a description of *typical day*. As additional problems are described, the motivational patterns become more apparent as well as the often-unconscious ways in which adults contribute to or reinforce negative interactions. While this discussion of possible goals is conducted with the family in focus, the audience can also connect one or more of the goals to the mistaken behaviors in their homes. Over the years, many parents have noted that their family concerns were addressed just by their having been part of the audience.

The movement from attention-getting through a power struggle and revenge to a demonstration of inadequacy indicates that a child is becoming increasingly discouraged. A central part of demonstration family counseling is a discussion with the children about the problems raised by the parents. In this part of the process, the parents are asked to leave the room, and the child or children take center stage. The possible goals of misbehavior are suggested in a tentative way, usually starting with a question such as, Do you know why the two of you fight?

No? I have an idea. Would you like to hear it?

Could it be . . . [suggesting the goal(s) in language the child(ren) can understand]?

Successful goal disclosures tend to result in what Dreikurs called a *recognition reflex*. This reflex comes as a quick smile across the child's face and a twinkle in the eyes. It is a look that many children might have when they are caught with their hands in the cookie jar.

Because both the family in focus and the audience have been helped to understand the motivations involved in misbehavior or mistaken adult–child interactions, both can participate in designing parental responses that redirect misbehaviors and create more harmonious relationships. Audience members' suggestions of corrective processes that make sense to the demonstration family are more likely to be followed and implemented than those that come from the professional counselor or therapist. Whether coming from the counselor or the audience, ideas that involve encouragement and the use of natural or logical consequences tend to bring about family harmony more effectively.

Family education centers and open-forum family counseling seemed to peak in the 1970s and early 1980s, but this model is still in practice in multiple parts of North America. In 1985, Jeff Zeig and associates at the Milton H. Erickson Institute in Phoenix, Arizona, produced the first Evolution of Psychotherapy conference. At that conference and all subsequent ones, demonstrations of counseling and therapy in front of thousands of participants have become a mainstay of the conference program. Erving Polster, a master Gestalt therapist on the faculty at this conference, has noted that some of his best work occurs in these public forums. Just the presence of the audience adds a community support for change that is missing in private sessions.

Limitations of Open-Forum Therapy

In any form of demonstration counseling, the client and the audience trade in confidentiality for accountability. As in any group process, confidentiality cannot be guaranteed, which is why many early analysts and therapists decried its use. Still, what is lost in privacy is perhaps more than matched by what is gained in community support. Literally, the therapist cannot take any position with the client that is not affirmed, acknowledged, and contained within the common sense of those present. An intervention that goes against community norms or cultural expectations is immediately challenged. Similarly, an intervention that is accepted as useful carries with both community support and a sense of commitment that individual or family has made to sometimes thousands of other humans.

James Robert Bitter and Rebekah Byrd

See also Adlerian Family Therapy; Brief Adlerian Couples Therapy; Group Family Therapy

Further Readings

Adler, A. (1963). *The problem child*. New York, NY: Capricorn Books.

Bitter, J. R. (2011). *Contributions to Adlerian psychology*. Bloomington, IN: Xlibris.

Christensen, O. C. (2004). *Adlerian family counseling* (3rd ed.). Minneapolis, MN: Educational Media Corp.

Christensen, O. C., & Schramski, T. G. (Eds.). (1983). *Adlerian family counseling*. Minneapolis, MN: Educational Media Corp.

Dreikurs, R. (1940a, November). The importance of group life. *Camping Magazine, 27*, 3–4.

Dreikurs, R. (1940b, December). The child in the group. *Camping Magazine*, 7–9.

Dreikurs, R. (1950). The immediate purpose of children's misbehavior, its recognition and correction. *Internationale Zeitschrift für Individual-Psychologie, 19*, 70–87.

Dreikurs, R., Corsini, R., Lowe, R., & Sonstegard, M. (1959). *Adlerian family counseling: A manual for counseling centers*. Eugene: University of Oregon Press.

Dreikurs, R., & Soltz, V. (1964). *Children: The challenge*. New York, NY: Hawthorn.

Platt, J. M. (1991). *Life in the family zoo* (3rd ed.). Elk Grove, CA: John Platt Seminars.

Sweeney, T. J. (2009). *Adlerian counseling and psychotherapy: A practitioner's approach* (5th ed.). New York, NY: Routledge.

Adolescent Behavior Disorders

Adolescent behavior disorders are mental disorders (significant cognitive, emotional, behavioral, and/or physiological impairments) that either first present during adolescence (ages 13 to 18) or are prevalent within this age group. Common adolescent behavioral disorders include anxiety disorders, mood disorders, disruptive disorders, eating disorders, and psychotic disorders. Because adolescents are undergoing significant physical, cognitive, social, and emotional changes, the presentation of disorders and their subsequent treatment can differ considerably from similar disorders in children and adults. This entry provides an overview of the common behavioral disorders in adolescence; general guidelines for assessment and diagnosis; treatment strategies; and other considerations for health professionals and practitioners who work with affected adolescents, families, and schools.

Anxiety Disorders

Anxiety disorders are among the most frequently encountered disorders for adolescents, with 8% to 11% prevalence in the United States. Adolescents are most likely to experience specific phobias, social anxiety disorder, and posttraumatic stress disorder (PTSD). Social phobias of adolescents tend to be focused on fear of animals; injuries and medical procedures; and situational phenomenon such as driving, flying, or being in confined spaces. Social anxiety disorder in adolescents is characterized by intense anxiety surrounding social situations. Adolescents experiencing social anxiety disorder often attempt to avoid social situations, which may manifest as refusal to attend school, feigned illnesses, or isolation from peers. As in adults, PTSD in adolescence is characterized by intense and intrusive thoughts and flashbacks relating to a prior traumatic event. In addition to these trauma symptoms, adolescents experiencing PTSD may present as unusually irritable, unfocused, or withdrawn from friends and family. Adolescents experiencing these disorders may be more likely to engage in drug and alcohol use and risky sexual behaviors.

Treatment of adolescent anxiety disorders often incorporates both individual and family therapy. Cognitive-behavioral therapy (CBT) is the most widely used treatment for these disorders and typically involves helping adolescents learn to identify stressors and triggers, apply emotional self-regulation techniques, and practice alternative behaviors in response. Parents and siblings may be invited to participate in treatment in order to receive psychoeducation about the adolescent's disorder, to learn skills to support the adolescent's recovery, and to address family dynamics that affect or are affected by the adolescent's symptoms. Family involvement is particularly important in the treatment of PTSD, as traumatic events are likely to affect all members of the family. Evaluation of the adolescent by a physician is strongly recommended to rule out physical illnesses that may produce symptoms and to assess whether psychiatric medication may assist with treatment.

Mood Disorders

Major depression, mania, and bipolar disorder all may occur in adolescence. However, these disorders are often unrecognized within this age group, due to both their unique presentations in this population and misinterpretation of symptoms by parents and clinicians. In particular, symptoms such as withdrawal, rapid changes in mood, irritability, and variations in sleep and appetite are often overlooked as normal developmental changes. Clinicians should attend carefully to whether such symptoms represent normal occasional difficulties, or if they are persistent indicators of a mood disorder. In addition to these symptoms, depressed adolescents are likely to experience drops in academic performance, difficulty concentrating and making decisions, lack of motivation, physical symptoms such as fatigue or headaches, and self-harmful or suicidal thoughts and behaviors. Manic symptoms, such as increased energy and lack of need for sleep, promiscuity and hypersexuality, grandiosity, excessive talking, risk taking, and intense goal-driven behaviors are often more difficult for parents and adolescents to recognize as problematic. Psychotic symptoms may also present as part of adolescent mood disorders and should be assessed for.

Treatment of adolescent mood disorders should also involve both individual and family therapy. Individual therapy for the adolescent could involve evidence-based treatments, including CBT or dialectical behavior therapy (DBT). These approaches can help adolescents learn to identify mood disorder episodes and apply emotional regulation techniques. Family therapy often focuses on identifying and defusing stressors within the family context, which may contribute to the adolescent's mood disorder; providing psychoeducation to the family; and identifying ways the family can support recovery. For adolescents experiencing manic or psychotic symptoms, family therapy can address management of expressed emotion within the household and strategies for helping the adolescent with grounding or reality testing. Safety planning should be conducted in a family context and address both direct threats (such as suicide or self-harm) and indirect threats (such as impulsive behaviors and risk taking).

Disruptive Disorders

Disruptive disorders are often the most easily identified disorders of adolescence. This category includes attention-deficit hyperactivity disorder (ADHD), oppositional defiant disorder (ODD), and conduct disorder (CD). These three disorders are characterized by cognitive and behavioral patterns that interfere with social functioning and daily activities.

ADHD is characterized by persistent and pervasive difficulty holding attention and restraining impulses as well as hyperactivity. Although ADHD is commonly diagnosed before the age of 7, symptoms may not become problematic enough to seek treatment until adolescence. Symptoms of ADHD are most commonly observed in the academic environment, where adolescents may struggle to attend to lessons and comply with classroom rules but are also observed in the home and community environments. As a result of their symptoms, adolescents with ADHD often have difficulty forming and maintaining relationships with others, complying with adult requests, and achieving academically. ODD is characterized by a pattern of anger, irritability, and defiant behavior toward parents, teachers, and other authority figures. Adolescents experiencing ODD may refuse to comply with instructions at home and school, may respond to disciplinary sanctions or perceived slights with disproportionate anger, and may engage in arbitrary argumentative or vindictive behaviors. In contrast, CD is characterized by a pattern of intentionally violating laws, rules, social norms, and the rights of others. Adolescents experiencing CD may initiate fights with peers or adults, steal from others, destroy property, engage in sexual offenses, set fires, and torture animals or younger children. For all three disorders, when adolescents have episodes of intense or dangerous behavior at school or at home, they are often referred to therapy if they have not responded to typical disciplinary measures. Often these adolescents are at risk for suspension or expulsion at school, juvenile probation or incarceration, or surrender of parental rights. Adolescents who experience CD and ODD have increased risk for abuse and victimization, so parents and therapists should carefully evaluate for related issues.

Treatment of ADHD is typically achieved through a combination of medication management but is best supplemented with individual therapy or family therapy. Individual therapy typically focuses on enhancing cognitive self-regulation through mindfulness, social skills training, and impulse control management. Family treatment is generally organized around building consistent behavioral expectations and parenting practices and helping parents support their adolescent's social skills and self-regulation. Treatment for ODD and CD will vary considerably in accordance with the severity of the presenting behavior and the involvement of the education and justice systems. Most often, treatment will involve individual, family, and multisystemic treatment interventions. Individual therapy is used to address emotional regulation skills (often with a focus on anger management), cognitive distortions, and social skills. Family therapies, such as structural family therapy (SFT) or behavioral family therapy, are used to establish strong and consistent expectations at home, create effective and enforceable consequences, enhance relationships with parents and siblings, and establish safety for the adolescent and the family. Multisystemic interventions, such as functional family therapy (FFT), multisystemic family therapy, multidimensional treatment foster care, and ecosystemic family therapy, are used to coordinate care between the family, the schools, and the legal system, and to apply consistent treatment programs across these contexts. Interventions based on intimidation tactics, such as Scared Straight programs, are often appealing to parents of adolescents with ODD or

CD. Research has shown, however, that these programs are ineffective and harmful, and on that basis, the Office of Juvenile Justice and Delinquency Prevention does not support them. Accordingly, therapists should discourage parents from pursuing these treatments.

Eating Disorders

The onset of anorexia nervosa, bulimia nervosa, and other eating disorders typically occurs during early or middle adolescence. Although they have a low prevalence in the general population (1%–2%), these disorders can cause immense physical harm and have lifelong health consequences. These disorders most often affect adolescent females, but rates of diagnosis in adolescent males are increasing. Anorexia nervosa is characterized by an extreme focus on weight loss and distorted body image. Adolescents experiencing anorexia nervosa may engage in excessively restrictive diets; aggressively monitor their calorie intake; exercise exhaustively; use over-the-counter laxatives, stimulants, and diet pills; and obsess over their physical appearance. These behaviors may result in dramatic loss of body fat, amenorrhea, hair loss, bone loss, and heart damage. If unaddressed, these symptoms may lead to death. In contrast, bulimia nervosa is characterized by a pattern of binge eating followed by purging through vomiting or laxative abuse. Adolescents with bulimia nervosa often feel they are unable to control their eating behaviors and often feel great shame and anxiety relating to these activities. Adolescents experiencing bulimia nervosa may experience anemia, heart damage, deterioration of the esophagus and teeth, bloody vomit, stomach ulcers, rapid weight gain, and life-threatening dehydration due to purging. Adolescents with eating disorders may present as depressed, anxious, or irritable to others due to preoccupation with eating behaviors and lack of adequate nutrition; comorbid mood and anxiety disorders are extremely common. Adolescents with eating disorders often make great efforts to hide or mask their eating behaviors from others and may avoid meals with friends or family, immediately visit the restroom after meals, or hide food wrappers and other evidence of bingeing behaviors. Some adolescents may also participate in "pro-ana" communities, where they exchange tips and strategies for hiding and maintaining their eating disorders. Therapists and parents should be aware that although these disorders are often focused on weight loss or gain, the present weight of the adolescent is not a diagnostic indicator for these disorders, regardless of current weight.

Treatment of eating disorders in adolescents should include considerations for both individual and family therapy. Individual therapy for the adolescent should focus on cognitive and emotional patterns surrounding body image and eating behaviors. Individual therapy should also include a strong psychoeducational component as adolescents often have misconceptions about the health risks involved with eating disorders, particularly if they have participated in pro-ana groups. Some proponents of individual therapy for eating disorders believe strongly that family involvement may adversely affect recovery and attribute the etiology of these disorders to family issues. However, family therapies for eating disorders, such as the Maudsley approach, are also evidence based. In family therapy, the parents are considered an integral part of the treatment process, and the family works together to change patterns surrounding eating. Autonomous control over eating is gradually restored to the adolescent, and treatment culminates with the parents supporting the adolescent's independence.

Psychotic Disorders

Schizophrenia commonly first appears in late adolescence or early adulthood. Schizophrenia is characterized by a combination of negative (subtractive) symptoms, such as flat affect; fatigue; loss of pleasure; and positive (additive) symptoms such as hallucinations, delusions, dysfunctional thoughts, and abnormal movements. These symptoms often escalate during periods of intense stress and may cause the adolescent to become isolated from family and peers.

Treatment of schizophrenia and related psychotic disorders should involve medication management, individual therapy, and family therapy. Individual therapy should focus on anxiety management, reality testing, and grounding skills. Family therapy should focus on expressed emotion within the home, as elevated levels of expressed emotion are associated with increased symptom severity.

Additional Considerations

As with adults, evaluation of adolescents by physicians is strongly recommended to rule out physical illnesses that may produce symptoms. Such evaluations are also essential if psychiatric medication is to be used during treatments. Therapists should also consider that substance abuse often coexists with disruptive disorders or mood disorders among adolescents.

Because adolescent behavior disorders often manifest symptoms in the school context, it is recommended for therapists to coordinate care with teachers and school counselors. These relationships can provide valuable information about how the adolescent is functioning cognitively, socially, and academically. By working with the school, therapists can help develop plans for managing disruptive or problematic behaviors without placing the adolescent in a more restrictive academic environment.

*Andrew S. Benesh,
Sung Cho, and Ming Cui*

See also Adolescent Behavior Problems; Eating Disorders; Parent–Adolescent Relations; Schizophrenia and Families

Further Readings

Carr, A. (Ed.). (2013). *What works with children and adolescents?: A critical review of psychological interventions with children, adolescents and their families.* New York, NY: Routledge.

Fonagy, P., Cottrell, D., Phillips, J., Bevington, D., Glaser, D., & Allison, E. (2014). *What works for whom?: A critical review of treatments for children and adolescents.* New York, NY: Guilford Press.

Merikangas, K. R., He, J. P., Burstein, M., Swanson, S. A., Avenevoli, S., Cui, L., & Swendsen, J. (2010). Lifetime prevalence of mental disorders in US adolescents: Results from the National Comorbidity Survey Replication–Adolescent Supplement (NCS-A). *Journal of the American Academy of Child and Adolescent Psychiatry, 49,* 980–989.

U.S. Department of Health and Human Services. (2013). *Health, United States, 2013, with special feature on prescription drugs.* Retrieved from http://www.cdc.gov/nchs/data/hus/hus13.pdf

Adolescent Behavior Problems

Adolescent behavior problems are defined as behaviors that have negative consequences for the adolescent and the environment. Externalized behaviors can include aggression, defiance, delinquency, and other behaviors of conduct and discipline. The onset of these behaviors may be a result of poor adjustment to stressors, such as faulty parenting, lack of resources, and past trauma. They can also be a result of increased pressures during adolescence, including negative peer relationships, faulty parenting, and poverty. The short- and long-term effects and costs of these behaviors to the adolescent, families, and society can be devastating. It is crucial to understand the etiology of adolescent behavior problems, as well as the signs and symptoms, in order to guide prevention and treatment interventions that lead to prosocial behaviors. The purpose of this entry is to provide an overview of adolescent behavior problems; the developmental variables that impact behavior; the current brain research that supports the connection between brain function, development, and behavior; and the prevention and intervention methods for the promotion of prosocial behavior.

Although the onset of puberty can be viewed as a time of increased rebellion and stress, this, by itself, is not a cause of behavior problems. In fact, most adolescents emerge into adulthood with a healthy self-identity, prosocial behaviors, and a sense of purpose and belonging. Adolescents do, however, have many added concerns in their lives, including the search for identity, religion, cultural issues, and need for autonomy. These concerns compounded with added pressures, such as poverty, past trauma, or family conflict, can emerge into negative acting-out behaviors and internal conflict. Behavior problems can be a sign of reaching out for help. Behaviors that start causing harm are most often a sign that something is wrong—possibly biologically, psychologically, or socially. Behaviors that are externalized are much easier to recognize, but sometimes an adolescent's problems are turned inward, causing an internal struggle of emotional and psychological turmoil.

Externalizing behaviors are behaviors that are turned outward, often in the form of aggressive behaviors (e.g., fighting, yelling) and a lack of self-control (e.g., being impulsive, stealing, breaking the rules). These behaviors are often linked to a lack of emotional and behavioral self-regulation during childhood and are often a sign that something is wrong. Acting-out behavior can manifest as a coping mechanism if a child's environment is too stressful, punitive, or controlling, or if there is an insecure attachment with a caregiver. These acting-out behaviors can become risky during the adolescent years, such as sexual promiscuity, substance abuse, criminal activity, and gang involvement. According to the fifth edition of the *Diagnostic and Statistical Manual of Mental Disorders* (DSM-5; American Psychiatric Association [APA]), externalizing behaviors can also be a sign of a mental illness. For example, conduct disorder (CD), oppositional defiant disorder (ODD), and attention-deficit/hyperactivity disorder (ADHD) all have externalizing behavior criteria.

Adolescents who exhibit externalizing behavior problems often are suffering internally. Internalizing behaviors are those behaviors that are turned inward, such as anxiety and depression. Adolescents with anxiety and depression have a high risk for suicidal ideation, substance use, and eating disorders (e.g., anorexia nervosa, bulimia nervosa) as a way to relieve emotional distress (e.g., poor self-image, low self-esteem).

Early Influences on Behavior Development

Adolescent development is at the root of understanding the importance of early experiences and influences on adolescent behavior. The tasks within the adolescent years are greatly different from childhood, where there is a need for dependence and life is more predictable. Some children can overcome childhood obstacles and stressors, such as trauma, abuse, and neglect to develop prosocial behaviors and a strong sense of identity. On the other hand, there are other children who do not overcome such obstacles and become ill prepared for the tasks within the adolescent and adult years. For example, childhood trauma has been linked to adolescent delinquency and adult health problems. Erik Erikson, Jean Piaget, and Albert Bandura are well-known theorists who addressed the developmental tasks of adolescence.

Erik Erikson's Theory of Identity Formation

In his theory of psychosocial development, Erik Erikson coined the adolescent stage *identity vs. role confusion*. In this stage, adolescents begin to explore their identity and their future. According to Erikson, adolescence is a time where the need for autonomy outweighs the need for dependence from caregivers. If given the opportunity to explore different roles and situations with independence and trust, then positive identity formation and behaviors will develop. Failing to accomplish this task through unhealthy striving, too much parental involvement, or a lack of prosocial independent exploration can have negative effects on development, identity, and future choices. Mastery of this stage provides adolescents with a clear vision of how they view themselves, others, and society as well as their role in the future. Through interactions with others, the adolescent begins to develop a sense of identity as well as understand the behaviors that can lead to positive and negative consequences.

Jean Piaget's Theory of Cognitive Development

Jean Piaget's theory of development focused on the importance of environmental influences on cognitive development. His theory was comprised of four successive stages in which we learn to understand our world and adapt our behaviors to this understanding. As we mature, our understanding of the world becomes more abstract. In addition, biological changes (e.g., puberty) and environmental demands (e.g., peer pressure, parents) add more challenges for the developing adolescent. In the *formal operational* stage, adolescents develop the ability to think more abstractly, make observations about the environment in terms of what is desirable and what is not, make inferences about the future, and problem solve more logically. These advanced cognitive processes provide the adolescent the ability to make reasonable decisions. If the demands of the environment are too great, reason and good decision-making can become challenged.

Albert Bandura and Social Learning Theory

Albert Bandura is known for his model of learning in which behavior, personal factors, cognitive factors, and environment are all interrelated. Personal factors include several variables including, but not limited to, intelligence, skills, and self-control. Bandura concluded that much of what we learn throughout life is due to observing others. As such, our environment influences our thoughts and behaviors. For example, negative environmental influences can impact cognitive processes, possibly leading to negative thoughts that can then lead to negative behaviors. In the case of observing an encouraging environment, one may develop prosocial skills and strategies that foster positive behavior. Thus, adolescent behavior problems can be viewed within the context of interrelated influences including cognition, personal factors, and environment.

Variables Affecting Behavior

Not all adolescent behavior problems start in adolescence. Behavioral problems are often first seen in childhood and can escalate in early adolescence; however, there are also adolescents with behavior problems that did not have an onset in childhood but developed in adolescence. An adolescent's environment, including family, peers, and community, combined with the genetic and biological makeup of the adolescent, have a direct impact on the development of behavior. First, we will look at how brain development influences behavior.

Biology and the Brain

The onset of puberty is a catalyst for increased risk-taking behavior, which may include substance abuse, gang involvement, eating disorders, sexual promiscuity, and juvenile delinquency. The adolescent years can also signify the peak of physical and mental ability. This puzzling contradiction can be explained by research in brain development. New technological advances (e.g., functional magnetic brain imagining) have enabled researchers to study the growth of the brain, brain structure, and the influence of neural connections on brain function, development, and behavior. Due to this research we now know that the amygdala, the emotional center of the brain, is well developed in early adolescence. This can explain adolescent behavior characteristics such as impulsivity, irrationality, poor decision-making, and risky behavior. The frontal lobe, the last section of the brain to mature, is the center where logic, organization, and judgment are developed, hence making these functions more difficult for the early adolescent to master. In later adolescence, pruning of the synaptic connections in the frontal lobe assist the brain to process information more effectively, creating a more refined, mature brain. This reconstructive process is needed to assist the adolescent with advanced thinking and reasoning skills, decreasing the emotional influence of the amygdala.

Family System

Families can play an important part in the development of an adolescent's ability to solve conflicts, make good decisions, and establish healthy relationships. Many children who grow up with high levels of stress often develop behavior problems as adolescents. Some early family risk factors for behavior problems include prenatal risks, such as birth complications and maternal substance use, and family characteristics, such as divorce, poverty, teen pregnancy, parental education level, and family conflict. Having a family member with a mental illness can be a genetic factor in developing behavior problems. Additional family variables include abuse, neglect, trauma, drugs in the home, and a lack of resources. Parents of adolescents who are too judgmental, discouraging, and controlling hinder motivation and identity formation of the adolescent. In addition, there is a higher risk for acting-out behaviors if there is a pattern of criminal activity within the family system.

School and Community System

Peers, other adults, and schools have been found to be a major source of support and influence outside the family system, especially the modeling of socially acceptable behaviors. These support systems have also been identified as negative influences if there is a lack of resources (e.g., jobs, health care, community centers, mental health services), lack of positive adult influences, gangs, drugs, and poorly performing schools. Problem behaviors within the school and community setting may include a lack of academic achievement, truancy, acting out, school refusal, early pregnancy, crime, and substance abuse. Schools that promote positive behavior through a positive school climate often foster good student–teacher relationships and prosocial behaviors. If an adolescent lacks a sense of acceptance or accomplishment within the school and community setting, he or she often has lower academic performance, which can lead to behavior problems.

Prevention and Intervention

Adolescent behavior problems have a negative social and economic impact on families and communities. Such problems can often be overlooked as stereotypical adolescent behavior, but often these behaviors are a sign of a more significant problem biologically, psychologically, or socially. It is important to recognize the signs and symptoms of behaviors that may possibly be associated with more complex psychological problems. Prevention and intervention programs designed to promote healthy adjustment and functioning in the developmental tasks associated with adolescence can help strengthen prosocial behaviors. Promoting good relationships with family and friends, participating in prosocial activities, achieving academic success, and developing a strong sense of identity can reinforce and strengthen an adolescent's self-esteem. Providing opportunities for positive interactions and encouraging prosocial behaviors reduce the risk factors associated with faulty coping strategies.

Nicole M. Randick

See also Adolescent Behavior Disorders; Adolescent Mental Health

Further Readings

Blakemore, S. J., & Choudhury, S. (2006). Development of the adolescent brain: Implications for executive function and social cognition. *Journal of Child Psychology and Psychiatry, 47*(3–4), 296–312.

Dahl, R. E. (2004). Adolescent brain development: A period of vulnerabilities and opportunities. Keynote address. *Annals of the New York Academy of Sciences, 1021*(1), 1–22.

Edwards, R. C., & Hans, S. L. (2015). Infant risk factors associated with internalizing, externalizing, and co-occurring behavior problems in young children. *Developmental Psychology, 51*(4), 489–499.

Jaspers, M., de Winter, A. F., Huisman, M., Verhulst, F. C., Ormel, J., Stewart, R. E., & Reijneveld, S. A. (2012). Trajectories of psychosocial problems in adolescents predicted by findings from early well-child assessments. *Journal of Adolescent Health, 51*, 475–483.

Lecompte, V., & Moss, E. (2014). Disorganized and controlling patterns of attachment, role reversal, and caregiving helplessness: Links to adolescents' externalizing problems. *American Journal of Orthopsychiatry, 84*(5), 581–589.

McLeod, J. D., Uemura, R., & Rohrman, S. (2012). Adolescent mental health, behavior problems, and academic achievement. *Journal of Health and Social Behavior, 53*(4), 482–497.

White, R., & Renk, K. (2012). Externalizing behavior problems during adolescence: An ecological perspective. *Journal of Child and Family Studies, 21*(1), 158–171.

ADOLESCENT MENTAL HEALTH

Adolescent mental health is defined as positive adaptive functioning that can lead to healthy growth and well-being in addition to the negative adaptive functioning that can lead to mental illness. Since many mental health problems emerge in adolescence, it is essential to understand what variables lead to healthy adjustment and well-being. The purpose of this entry is to provide a definition of *adolescence*; an overview of adolescent mental health; the current brain research that supports the connection between brain function, development, and behavior; the environmental challenges that impact healthy and unhealthy adjustment; an overview of adolescent mental disorders; healthy mental health habits; and prevention and treatment methods for the promotion of healthy functioning.

Adolescence

Adolescence is the transitional stage of human development, representing the time between early childhood and adulthood. This critical period is often characterized by changes that occur physically, socially, mentally, and emotionally as immaturity is replaced by maturity and dependence is replaced by autonomy. The onset of puberty is a catalyst for increased risk-taking behavior, which may include substance abuse, poor decision-making, sexual promiscuity, high school dropout, and juvenile delinquency. Biological changes may be compounded by conflicting environmental expectations and demands from family, peers, school, and society. In addition, the adolescent brain is undergoing significant developmental changes that can impact healthy functioning that will last into adulthood. Poor adaptation to these changes and challenges can lead to unhealthy mental health development.

Storm and Stress

The turn of the 20th century brought an increased interest in the scientific study of adolescent mental health. Changes in work and school legislation resulted in increased school attendance and jobs that required advanced skills. In 1904, G. Stanley Hall published a seminal book that emphasized adolescence as a time of extreme stress and turmoil that yielded unruly behavior (e.g., criminal activity, substance abuse) as a result of trying to manage outward conflict. He defined this as a storm-and-stress view of adolescence. His perspective of adolescent psychological development focused on the interaction of genetically predetermined variables with environmental influences.

Through the decades, new research began to emerge to debunk the stereotypical adolescent years as full of turmoil, stress, and incompetence. One such researcher, Daniel Offer, found that the majority of adolescents, although faced with challenges, were not experiencing extreme emotional turmoil and stress. On the contrary, they were competent, adaptable, and appeared to be moving toward adulthood with optimism. Despite this finding, adolescence is still a time with increased rates of mental health problems, including depression, anxiety, substance abuse, and eating disorders. Adolescent mental health is subject to influences including the environment, genetics, and social experiences. Research has revealed that all these variables act in context with the developing brain.

The Adolescent Brain

The interaction of the adolescent's developing brain, hormonal changes, and environmental stressors increases vulnerability to mental health problems. Although the adolescent years can signify the peak of physical and mental ability, it also represents a time of poor decision-making, impulsive acts, risky behavior, and emotional upheaval. This puzzling contradiction can be explained by research in brain development. New technological advances (e.g., functional magnetic brain imagining) have enabled researchers to study the growth of the brain; brain structure; and the influence of neural connections on brain function, development, and behavior. For example, researchers have found that genes can influence brain development and specific genes have been linked to the onset of major depression and schizophrenia. Schizophrenia is characterized by symptoms including hearing voices and seeing objects that are not present.

The early adolescent brain functions from the well-developed amygdala, the emotional center of the brain. This can explain adolescent behavior characteristics such as impulsivity, irrationality, poor decision-making, and risky behavior. Changes in neural connections in later adolescence assist the brain to process information more effectively. The frontal lobe, the center where logic, organization, and judgment are developed, is the last section of the brain to mature. In late adolescence, synaptic connections go through a pruning process that results in a more refined mature brain. Synapses that are reinforced are strengthened, and synapses that are no longer needed are pruned away. Myelin develops in the nerve cells, providing an insulating layer that facilitates effective communication. The result is a significant reduction in gray matter, which makes up the outer layer of the brain cortex where thought and memory are located. This reconstructive pruning process is needed to assist the adolescent transition into adulthood with advanced thinking and reasoning skills.

Environmental Context

The positive and negative interactions with family, peers, school, and society, combined with the genetic and biological makeup of the adolescent have a direct impact on mental health development. Mastery of family conflicts and healthy parental role modeling helps adolescents to develop the skills needed for identity formation, autonomy, well-being, and a successful transition into adulthood. However, the onset of puberty has been found to increase family discord and put a strain on parent child relationships. A parent's controlling, abusive, or rejecting behavior can negatively influence mental health, spiraling the developing adolescent toward mental health problems.

Peer groups, school, and other adults have been found to be a major source of influence and support outside the family system. Researchers once believed that the school system had little impact on mental health; however, schools are seen as the main source of intellectual, social, and vocational development. Schools can be a source of accomplishment or a source of emotional distress. Challenges within this context include forming a sense of belonging; dating; being accepted; and dealing with peer pressure. Mastering these challenges help to form an adolescent's status and sense of relational achievement. Negative peer relations can lead to social problems and at-risk behavior. If these influences are abusive or neglectful, it can have detrimental effects to mental health development.

Rejection, trauma, abuse (e.g., physical, emotional, sexual), and neglect are all risk factors for the development of mental disorders. For example, trauma in childhood affects the stress response systems in the brain, leading to risk of anxiety or mood disorders in adolescence. Other risk factors include poverty; family violence; a severely or chronically ill or substance-abusing parent; racism; and, according to some researchers, the single-parent household. These environmental stressors, in combination with one's biological and genetic makeup, can put adolescents at risk to develop a mental illness.

Adolescent Mental Disorders

Nearly 10% of adolescents have a diagnosable mental illness. According to *Mental Health: A Report of the Surgeon General*, *mental illness* is defined as having a mental disorder that causes distressful or impaired adaptations in thinking, mood, or behavior (concurrently or separately). Common mental disorders in adolescence include depression, anxiety, substance use, and eating disorders. Behavioral symptoms of a mental disorder may be overlooked as stereotypical normal adolescent behavior. Depression, with symptoms ranging from low academic performance, anger, and substance use, to hopelessness and thoughts of suicide, is the most commonly diagnosed disorder during the adolescent years. Major depression, a chronic form of depression, is characterized by severe symptoms that affect one's ability to function. Bipolar disorder, a rapid cycling of extreme lows (e.g., major depression) and extreme highs (e.g., mania) has been linked to high suicide rates. Anxiety, often caused by a triggering event or object, can be a disabling condition with symptoms that include excessive worrying, extreme fear, obsessive thoughts, and sleeplessness. Examples of anxiety disorders include generalized anxiety disorder (GAD), obsessive-compulsive disorder (OCD; repetitive thoughts and actions), and post-traumatic stress disorder (PTSD; symptoms triggered by a traumatic event).

Many adolescent mental health disorders often coexist with other disorders, including attention-deficit/hyperactivity disorder (ADHD), oppositional defiant disorder (ODD; disorder of conduct), and substance abuse disorder. For example, adolescents with depression or anxiety often also have substance use problems, alcohol being the most widely abused. It is also common for adolescents with bipolar disorder to also have ADHD, ODD, or an anxiety disorder. Eating disorders (e.g., anorexia nervosa, bulimia nervosa, and binge eating disorder) also commonly exist with other disorders. Eating disorders affect one's eating and weight control and are characterized by a distorted body image and low self-esteem. The result of untreated symptoms and unhealthy behavior that emerge in adolescence may lead to mental health impairment and physical illness later in life. With the proper care, nutrition, prevention, and treatment, many mental health problems can be managed.

Healthy Mental Health Habits

According to the World Health Organization (WHO), mental health is a fundamental component of the health of adolescents and cannot be seen as separate from overall healthy functioning. The health of an individual includes the complete physical, mental, and social well-being of a person and not just the absence of mental illness. Adolescents who learn healthy habits engage positively in society and are physically healthier. Healthy habits include proper diet, physical activity, stress management, relational skills, and conflict resolution as well as having a positive self-concept.

Healthy adjustment and functioning in the developmental tasks associated with adolescence increases good mental health and prevents future problems. Tasks within the adolescent years include developing good relationships with family and friends, participating in prosocial activities, achieving academic success, and developing a strong sense of identity. Caregivers and other adults can reinforce an adolescent's positive attributes, talents, strengths, and interests, thus strengthening self-esteem and self-confidence. Implementing prevention programs provide adolescents with the tools needed to handle challenging situations that may trigger emotional distress. Teaching problem-solving and coping skills builds resiliency, the ability to overcome life's challenges. Providing opportunities for positive interactions and encouraging healthy habits reduce the risk factors associated with mental illness.

Mental Health Treatment

The sheer number of adolescents with mental health problems continues to increase through the years, having significant effects on society, families, and individuals. Recognizing when problems arise and seeking treatment can help to reduce the impact on an adolescent's emotional and social well-being. Unfortunately, the stigma surrounding mental illness sometimes prevents people from seeking out treatment. For example, various cultures treat mental health differently, preventing the early recognition of symptoms or opting out of treatment. Schools, health care physicians, and community-based agencies can all assist in ensuring proper referrals are made for the most effective treatment. The type of treatment received depends on an individual's unique needs, resources available, and early recognition of symptoms. Psychotherapy combined with medication and psychoeducation provides a preventive and educational approach to mental health. Common psychotherapy models include cognitive therapy, behavioral therapy, dialectical behavior therapy (DBT), family therapy, and interpersonal therapy. Research in brain development and function has been extremely helpful to practitioners in understanding the impact biology, genetics, environment, and society have on the mental health of adolescents.

Nicole M. Randick

See also Adolescent Behavior Disorders; Adolescent Behavior Problems; Mental Health, Systemic Perspective; Resilience

Further Readings

Blakemore, S. J., & Choudhury, S. (2006). Development of the adolescent brain: Implications for executive function and social cognition. *Journal of Child Psychology and Psychiatry*, 47(3–4), 296–312.

Dahl, R. E. (2004). Adolescent brain development: A period of vulnerabilities and opportunities. Keynote address. *Annals of the New York Academy of Sciences*, 1021(1), 1–22.

Evans, D. L., Foa, E. B., Gur, R. E., Hendin, H. E., O'Brien, C. P., Seligman, M. E., & Walsh, T. E. (2005). *Treating and preventing adolescent mental health disorders: What we know and what we don't know: A research agenda for improving the mental health of our youth*. New York, NY: Oxford University Press.

Knopf, D., Park M. J., & Mulye T. (2008). *The mental health of adolescents: A national profile*. San Francisco, CA: National Adolescent Health Information Center, Author.

McLeod, J. D., Uemura, R., & Rohrman, S. (2012). Adolescent mental health, behavior problems, and academic achievement. *Journal of Health and Social Behavior*, 53(4), 482–497.

Powers, S. I., Hauser, S. T., & Kilner, L. A. (1989). Adolescent mental health. *American Psychologist*, 44(2), 200.

Resnick, M. D. (2000). Protective factors, resiliency, and healthy youth development. *Adolescent Medicine: State of the Art Reviews*, 11(1), 157–164.

U.S. Department of Health and Human Services. (1999). *Mental health: A report of the surgeon general*. Rockville, MD: Office of the Surgeon General, U.S. Public Health Service.

World Health Organization. (2004). *Promoting mental health: Concepts, emerging evidence, practice (summary report)*. Geneva, Switzerland: Department of Mental Health and Substance Abuse, Author.

ADOPTION

Adoption is, by definition, the act of legally taking on responsibility for the parenting of another person's child. Upon adoption, the adopter(s) and adoptee take on all the legal rights and obligation of biological parenthood, which may include inheritance rights, parental decisions, and legal responsibility. An understanding of the history and different types of adoption is essential to marriage, family, and couples counselors in conceptualizing the family system, including the potential emotional and psychological effects of adoption. In addition, informed practitioners can better aid couples and families preparing to adopt as well as help to ease the transition of adoption.

History of Adoption

The first U.S. adoption laws and sanctioned practices originated in the mid-19th century and were focused on relocating the children of impoverished families to more affluent homes, in part because of the efforts of a movement to place such children in families as opposed to institutions (i.e., orphanages). During that era, the so-called orphan train was one practice by which large scores of adoptable children (by some estimates a quarter of a million children in total) were transported from cities on the Eastern Seaboard to families in the Midwest. Potential adoptive families would visit the train stations to see the children who were available for adoption. Interestingly, despite the lack of communication technology in that era compared with the present day, it has been noted that a majority of those children eventually reunited with their families of origin through their own or their families' efforts; thus, the adoptions were more of a temporary arrangement than a permanent change.

In the adoption practices of that period, children were often involuntarily removed from homes or placed for adoption by parents in straitened circumstances out of concern for the children's welfare. Eventually, in response to human rights concerns, policies were set in place whereby placing a child up for adoption was not to be based on poverty alone. The early foster care practices were one answer to this dilemma—providing for children to be intentionally placed temporarily with families (again as opposed to orphanages), under the supervision of assigned case workers, and giving parents opportunities to remedy concerns related to the care of their children.

Types of Adoption

The approximately 135,000 adoptions that occur annually in the United States comprise several categories. Of the adoptions that are nonstepparent adoptions, over half (59%) are of children in the welfare or foster care system. Roughly one quarter are international adoptions, and the remainder are voluntarily relinquished infant adoptions. Adoptions in any of those categories can remain open or closed.

Open Adoptions

In an open adoption, some form of communication is left open between the biological parent(s) and the adoptive parent(s) and possibly the child. This may range from agreeing to share pictures, milestones, and other information through an intermediary (such as a lawyer or adoption agency); some direct communication between biological and adoptive parent(s); direct communication between biological parent(s) and both the adoptive parents and child; or actual visitation between the biological parent(s) and the child. The degree to which the identities or locations of each party may vary, according to the type of arrangement that is agreed upon.

Open adoption is more common for older children, who often have had an ongoing relationship with the biological parent(s) and for whom termination of that relationship would be detrimental. Some open adoptions arise as the biological and adoptive parents are previously known to one another; in fact, the adoption might have arisen out of this previous relationship. Some adoptions are initially closed and become open due to contact later being made by one or more of the parties. Adoption by relatives may also occur more frequently by open adoptions.

Closed Adoptions

In closed adoptions, there is no contact between birth parents and adoptive parents. All details of the adoption are handled by an intermediary such as a lawyer, adoption agency, personal agent, or government–social service agency. These are often also referred to as "traditional" adoptions, and there has been a decrease in their frequency as open adoptions have increased.

International Adoptions

International adoptions describe the adoption of a child who is located in a different country; thus, the culture of parent and child may differ. Historically, many of these adoptions have been of children who are living in orphanages, though some private adoptions (arrangements between birth parents and intermediary or adoptive parents) can occur. In recent years, several countries have eliminated international adoption of their citizens, citing, for example, concerns surrounding child trafficking; increased attempts to promote domestic adoptions; and nationalist sentiments.

Other Forms of Adoptions

Foster care adoption occurs when a child placed in foster care becomes eligible for adoption. In 2011, more than 50% of youth in foster care were adopted by their foster parents.

Special-needs adoptions are often more quickly executed than other types of adoption, as these children can be more difficult to place because of those needs. These include children with mental, physical, emotional, and social disabilities. Special-needs adoptions may also be less expensive than other types, and adoptive parents may be provided with financial assistance, post-adoption, to help meet the child's unique needs.

Adoption of stepchildren has its unique complications. Although one birth parent (i.e., the one the stepparent is married to) may be open to this, the other biological parent must have had their rights terminated or be willing to give up parental rights. In giving up parental rights, the biological parent is also relieved of financial and legal responsibility for the child. For birth parents who are uninvolved in the child's life, this may be an attractive option. Where both birth parents are actively involved in the child's life, stepparent adoption is less feasible. Where the other birth parent is deceased, stepparent adoption is often relatively straightforward and less time-intensive than other adoptions.

Familial adoptions may be given preference to closed or open nonfamilial adoptions, depending on the family members wishing to adopt and the perceived impact on the well-being of the child. Considerations weighed include the ability of the relatives to support the child immediately and over the long term versus those of other potential adoptive parents. If parental rights have been terminated against the parent's will, the likelihood of the birth parent(s) being involved in the child's life is diminished, especially if not supported by the courts or child welfare agencies.

Preparing to Adopt and Adjusting to Adoption

There are myriad motivations for individuals, couples, and families who wish to adopt. For those who are unable to bear their own children, adoption becomes the most feasible option for parenthood. Others may already have biological children and wish to expand their family while providing a home for a child who needs one. Some couples choose adoption over biological parenthood for personal reasons, including, for example, social consciousness, physical limitations, or a desire for children who are past the stage of infancy. For intrafamily adoptions, desire to keep the children within the family structure may serve as a motivation as well.

With the exception of the placement of children with special needs, potential parents may be faced with a wait. This is especially true for those who only wish to adopt infants. Regardless of the type of adoption, adoptive parents should expect a home visit or visits and follow-up on the placement. Besides a physical examination of the home, a thorough background history may be taken on immediate (and in some cases distant) family members and acquaintances who will be in the direct presence of the child; this can include criminal or legal, financial, educational, physical and mental health, and social background and can vary greatly depending on the practices of the agency, state governmental regulations, and in some cases the conditions set by the birth parent(s).

As with the addition of any member to the family, adopting a child results in a change to the family structure and dynamics. Whenever possible, preparing any other children that may be in the home can help to ease the transition. For the adoptee, this is of course a major change that requires ample time for adjustment. Working with a family counselor can be especially useful in helping all parties to adjust to the new system.

While not all adopted children have attachment-related concerns, some children—especially those who experienced ruptures to secure attachments or those who never had the chance to securely attach (i.e., those raised in orphanages or foster care with frequent relocation)—may be at increased risk for attachment-related disorders. Educating new or potential adoptive parents about these disorders and risks will help them to make an informed decision and provide a supportive environment as they go through the adoption process.

Adoptive parents should also be educated on what to expect in regards to the child's general adjustment to a new place. Very young children may adjust more quickly than older children, though this is not always the case. Children may miss their birth parents and other family members, and educating adoptive parents on how to respond to the child's concerns is essential. At times, the child's difficulty in adjusting to the adoptive home may be met with outright resistance, and preparing the adoptive parents for this possibility will help them to handle any feelings of rejection that may arise.

Finally, while not all children who are adopted will seek to find or reunite with their birth parents, this may be the case for some. In addition, despite terminating parental rights, some birth parents may seek to find children whom they voluntarily or involuntarily gave up. With the rise of social media, reconnecting with family members has become increasingly feasible. Preparing adoptive parents as to how will they will approach that possibility, should it arise, may be helpful.

Despite the seemingly clear-cut definition of adoption, there are many different rationales for adoptive parents in pursuing that option. In addition, the reasons why children become available for adoption can vary—parental rights may be voluntarily or involuntarily terminated for a number of reasons, or the birth parent(s) may be deceased. Knowledge of those factors, together with an understanding of developmental and attachment concerns, as well as family systems, will help practitioners in conceptualizing and treating this population.

Ann M. McCaughan

See also Adoption, Cross-Cultural and Interracial; Attachment Styles; Foster Children; Systems Theory

Further Readings

Brodzinsky, D. (2015). *The modern adoptive families study: An introduction*. New York, NY: Donaldson Adoption Institute. Retrieved from http://adoptioninstitute.org

Carnes-Holt, K. (2012). Child-parent relationship therapy for adoptive families. *Family Journal: Counseling and Therapy for Couples and Families, 20*(4), 419–426.

Malott, K. M., & Schmidt, C. D. (2012). Counseling families formed by transracial adoption: Bridging the gap in the multicultural counseling competencies. *The Family Journal, 20*(4), 384–391.

McWey, L. M., Henderson, T. L., & Tice, S. N. (2006). Mental health issues and the foster care system: An examination of the impact of the adoption and Safe Families Act. *Journal of Marital and Family Therapy, 32*(2), 195–214.

Schwartz, A. E., Cody, P. A., Ayers-Lopez, S. J., McRoy, R. G., & Fong, R. (2014). Postadoption support groups: Strategies for addressing marital issues. *Adoption Quarterly, 17*(2), 85–111.

Smith, S., & Donaldson Institute Staff. (2014). *Facilitating adoptions from care: A compendium of effective and promising practices*. London, England: British Association for Adoption and Fostering.

Adoption, Cross-Cultural and Interracial

Cross-cultural adoption is one in which the child is from a different culture than that of the adoptive parents. Many cross-cultural adoptions are also interracial, and subsequently, the child has a racial *and* cultural background that varies from those of the adoptive parents. In the professional literature, the terms *cross-cultural* and *interracial* are often used interchangeably with the terms *transcultural* and *transracial* respectively. Moreover, it is important to note that cross-cultural and interracial adoptions may occur domestically and internationally.

Although it is not always the case, cross-cultural and interracial adoptions are frequently characterized by Whites who create families with children of a different cultural or racial group by birth.

Because the practice is embedded with complex clinical, social, legal, and political implications, cross-cultural and interracial adoption has been the subject of intense debate, especially with regard to the domestic adoption of biracial or African American children and, to a lesser degree, in relation to international adoptions of Asian or Latina/o children. This entry will address the historical context surrounding cross-cultural and transracial adoption as well as the prominent themes in the professional literature, which include cultural socialization, racial and cultural identity development, and clinical implications for practice.

Historical Context

One of the original examples of cross-cultural and interracial adoption involved the Indian Adoption Project that spanned from 1958 to 1967. The project was a collaborative effort between the U.S. Bureau of Indian Affairs and the Child Welfare League of America (CWLA) that focused on placing American Indian children living on reservations in adoptive homes to support their assimilation into mainstream U.S. culture. During that same time frame, the CWLA also stated that African American children were the leading group in need of adoptive families. To address such concerns, adoption agencies accelerated efforts to place African American children by electing to recruit more relatives, foster parents, and single females in the group of potential adoptive parents. As considerations expanded to cross racial lines and place children in interracial or cross-cultural families, racial–ethnic minority communities expressed strong concerns. The National Association of Black Social Workers (NABSW) expressed serious apprehensions about children in interracial and cross-cultural placements being at risk for racial identity issues and a disengagement from their cultural backgrounds. The NABSW organization passed a resolution in 1972 appealing for a termination of interracial adoption of African American children. Similarly, the Indian Child Welfare Act (ICWA) of 1978 led to the dissolution of the Indian Adoption Project, owing to Native American opposition.

In the 1990s, concerns were again raised regarding the time span that African American children were in foster care due to extended waits for adoption by African American parents. The Multiethnic Placement Act (MEPA) of 1994 was signed into law with the intent to decrease the length of time that children waited to be placed with adoptive families; to concentrate on recruitment and retention of foster parents who could serve the unique needs of children awaiting adoption; and to abolish discrimination based on race, color, or national origin. Although MEPA prohibited delaying or refusing placement of a child based on the race, color, or national origin of the child or of the foster or adoptive parent, it contained a condition that racial heritage could still be pondered in placement decisions. In 1996, the Interethnic Adoption Provisions Act (also known as MEPA II) was passed into law and this version excluded race from adoption guidelines. MEPA II stipulated that race could only factor into adoption decisions when racial issues were a consideration related to the best interests of a particular child.

Presently, opinion polls and surveys continue to reflect mixed attitudes and opinions regarding cross-cultural and interracial adoption among Blacks and Whites. Very little is known about the feelings of Asian American, Native Americans, and Latina/o/s regarding cross-cultural and interracial adoption. Although research findings generally support positive outcomes for adjustment and self-esteem among interracial and cross-cultural adoptees, there is a definite need for further development of theory and research relating to the area.

Research Findings

The Evan B. Donaldson Adoption Institute released findings in a 2008 report called *Finding Families for African American Children: The Role of Race & Law in Adoption From Foster Care*. This report details the results of 35 years of research on transracial adoption to address disparities and concerns related to cross-cultural and transracial adoption practices. In essence, there were three key findings. The first was that interracial and cross-cultural adoption in itself does not produce psychological or social maladjustment problems in children. Another conclusion was that interracially adopted children and their families face a host of challenges by which children's development is enhanced or hindered by the means through which parents handle them. Finally, it was established that children in foster care carry a multitude of risk factors that establish potential obstacles for healthy development, even after adoption.

The report also acknowledged the issue of limited research on cross-cultural and interracial adoptions but detailed several key issues common to children in transracial homes. One concern noted was that interracially adopted children face challenges in handling the sense of being "different." Another topic indicated by the report was that interracially adopted children may grapple with developing a positive racial–ethnic identity. The final point in the report was that the life skill of coping with discrimination is essential. As such, the report noted that research clearly highlights the critical need for adoptive placements with parents who can attend to their individual needs and support their development to its fullest potential.

A literature review was conducted by Richard Lee and published in 2003. Although he called for additional theory and research to identify individual elements that affect cultural socialization, psychological adjustment, and racial–ethnic identity development, he noted those areas revealed that (a) cross-cultural and interracial adoptees and their families engaged in a number of cultural socialization coping mechanisms to address discrepancies between how they see themselves and how they are perceived by others, (b) variability was exhibited in racial identity development similar to that of same-race adoptees and nonadoptees, and (c) cross-cultural and interracial adoptees on the whole were well adjusted.

Cultural Socialization

The term *socialization* refers to the lifelong and highly influential learning process that involves inheriting and disseminating norms, customs, and ideologies. Its function is to provide individuals with the skills and habits essential for participating in their culture. As such, cultural socialization refers to child-rearing practices designed to teach children about their racial history and instill a sense of pride in their heritage. In the case of cross-cultural or interracial adoption, the cultural socialization becomes exponentially more complex.

Early studies found that the cultural socialization of cross-cultural or interracial adoptees involved cultural assimilation, which is essentially acculturation of the child in the majority culture. This cultural socialization tendency tended to be characterized by a "color-blind" racial attitude on the part of the adoptive parents in which racial and cultural differences were downplayed or rejected. Cultural assimilation is occasionally identified as a passive process in that it occurs with minimal parental effort because interracially or cross-culturally adopted children are immersed in the majority culture. As such, adoptees are likely to internalize their adoptive parents' cultural worldview and their identity is unlikely to reflect their ethnic culture.

An area that is readily highlighted in the professional literature notes the importance of adoptive parents' personal awareness of the roles that race and culture play in the daily experiences of others outside their respective racial or cultural group. In addition, experts highlight the need for adoptive parents to recognize the undercurrents of racism, oppression, and other forms of discrimination. Several authors have pointed out the need for cross-cultural and interracial adoptive parents to have the capacity to openly acknowledge that their child's race or culture is separate from their own rather than to deny it or minimize the implications of race. In fact, more recent research reveals a growing trend toward enculturation as the preferred style of cultural socialization. In this regard, parents make a deliberate effort to teach children about their birth cultures and heritage through child and parent participation in educational, social, and cultural opportunities to instill ethnic awareness, knowledge, pride, values, and behaviors. Research suggests that parents who are intentional in their involvement in their children's birth culture are more likely to have children who are engaged and secure in their culture of birth.

Racial inculcation involves the teaching of coping skills to successfully navigate the social realities of racism and discrimination. Although the importance of racial inculcation is widely discussed in the cross-cultural and interracial adoption literature, there is limited empirical research on this facet of cultural socialization. Concerns have tended to center around the notion that White parents who have had limited experience with racism directed toward them may be poorly prepared to teach functional coping strategies to counteract racism (e.g., rehearsing responses to thoughtless or prejudiced comments from others, talking openly about race and racism, and displaying a lack of tolerance for racially or culturally biased comments). In the absence of definitive research on specific strategies related to personalities and situations, it is emphasized that children of color ideally are taught to externalize (rather than internalize) racism. By parents acknowledging that their families are interracial and visibly different from most others, it is thought that they can begin to more effectively recognize prejudice, positive and negative stereotypes, and covert and overt racism directed toward themselves or their children.

Racial and Cultural Identity Development

Racial identity refers to one's self-perception and sense of belonging to a particular group, including how one differentiates oneself from members of other racial groups. Although cultural identity is related to racial identity, it is separate from racial identity; it is shaped by the specific society to which the individual belongs and encompasses values, beliefs, rituals, and forms of acceptable behavior. The difference between racial and cultural identity is occasionally indistinguishable in the adoption outcome conclusions. Nevertheless, findings indicate that this is an identifiable area of difficulty for interracial and cross-cultural adoptees. There are many studies depicting interracial adoptees who are distressed with their appearance, are embarrassed by their racial or ethnic background, or distance themselves from peers of the same cultural or racial backgrounds. Although there is an obvious need for more thorough study in this area, at this time it appears that cross-cultural and interracial adoptees are challenged to integrate an identity that includes acceptance of their outward appearance, their birth culture, and the culture of their upbringing.

According to some studies, racial identity begins to form at around age 6 and advances with development. In 1980, William Cross developed an influential model of Black identity development. He delineated a series of stages in the process of forming a racial identity. In the *pre-encounter stage*, individuals identify predominantly with the majority culture. When individuals experience prejudice, they enter the *encounter stage*, and they begin to be aware of their association with their racial group. In the subsequent *immersion stage*, racially and culturally different people immerse themselves in the norms, beliefs, and values of their racial group and disparage the norms of the majority culture. Lastly, in the *internalization stage*, individuals become able to value themselves and others as unique beings, regardless of race. Other models follow a similar progression over the course of the life span that involves moving from denial to a personal awareness (noticing others from the same culture or race) and identification, to acceptance, and finally to the integration of one's race into their broader identity.

While early models of racial and cultural identity development were an important starting point, it was apparent that they failed to fully account for variations in courses of development and variables that may be related to such deviations. As adoption agencies and professionals have become aware of the complexity of racial and cultural identity development, they have initiated a variety of approaches to support the development of racial and cultural identity in interracial and cross-cultural adoptions. These initiatives have ranged from passive educational strategies such as discussing the need for sensitivity to the adoptee's culture to offering and encouraging family participation in cultural activity programs designed to educating the family and child about their cultural roots. Although strategies vary widely, there is an increased awareness and understanding by professionals involved in interracial adoption that racial awareness is essential because parents from the dominant culture often don't grasp the need for multicultural planning and survival skills.

Clinical Implications

It is essential that mental health professionals secure cultural competency in order to work effectively in service delivery to families involved in cross-cultural and interracial adoption. As part of that process, counselors must engage in self-evaluation surrounding their personal attitudes, beliefs, and biases surrounding race and specifically about cross-cultural and interracial adoption. Without a sound understanding of one's personal prejudices and biases, a mental health professional can be impaired in their effectiveness at best or cause considerable harm at worst.

The development of a knowledge base surrounding cross-cultural and interracial adoption is also essential. In addition to understanding the history and key issues of contention, clinicians must become familiar with the psychological and cultural issues surrounding such adoptions (e.g, experiences that shape racial–cultural identity development or attempts made by parents and children alike to resolve difficulties and successfully create a bicultural family). It is important to recognize that families may differ in their levels of cultural awareness and expectations relating to cultural socialization on topics such as racial awareness, multicultural planning and engagement, and survival skills related to ignorance and prejudice. Identification of such differences and the resulting conflict and potential for alienation that may occur is necessary to support such families.

On a similar but different note, it is important to avoid tendencies to overaccentuate group differences, given the variability in psychological adjustment and racial–cultural identity development of adoptees based on the current literature base. Only by establishing cultural competency can a mental health provider effectively serve as a cultural negotiator who truly helps interracial and cross-cultural adoptees and their adoptive families identify and resolve key differences.

Finally, clinicians working with adoptive families and their children can support them by identifying useful and key resources in the adoptive and racial–ethnic minority communities that will empower adoptees and their families to receive relevant information and support. Such resources might include key articles, book, or videos. In addition, facilitated discussion groups, online affinity groups, conferences, and regional family gatherings are often phenomenal sources of information and support for families.

Terri Christiansen

See also Acculturation; Adoptive Families; Attachment; Beliefs and Values; Best Interests of the Child; Bonding; Cultural Issues in Couples and Families; Diversity; Ethnicity; Foster Children; Gender- and Culture-Sensitive Therapies; Intercultural Marriage and Family; Interracial Marriages and Families; Multicultural Counseling Competence; Multiculturalism; Racism; Transracial Adoption

Further Readings

Fogg-Davis, H. (2002). *The ethics of transracial adoption.* Ithaca, NY: Cornell University Press.

Gaber, I., & Aldridge, J. (1994). *In the best interests of the child: Culture, identity, and transracial adoption.* London, England: Free Association Books.

Gill, O., & Jackson, B. (1983). *Adoption and race: Black, Asian and mixed race children in White families.* New York, NY: St. Martin's Press.

Grow, L. (1975). *Transracial adoption today: Views of adoptive parents and social workers: Report of a study funded by grant OCD-CB-59 from the Children's Bureau, Office of Child Development, United States Department of Health, Education and Welfare.* New York, NY: Research Center, Child Welfare League of America.

Hoopes, J. L. (1990). Adoption and identity formation. In D. K. Brodzinsky & M. D. Schechter (Eds.), *The psychology of adoption* (pp. 144–166). New York, NY: Oxford University Press.

Lee, R. M. (2003). The transracial adoption paradox: History, research, and counseling implications of cultural socialization. *The Counseling Psychologist, 31*(6), 711–744.

McCoy, R. G. (1983). *Transracial and international adoptees: The adolescent years.* Springfield, IL: Charles C Thomas.

Simon, R. J., & Alstein, H. (1977). *Transracial adoption.* New York, NY: Wiley.

Simon, R. J., Alstein, H., & Melli, M. S. (1994). *The case for transracial adoption.* Washington, DC: American University Press.

Smith, S., McRoy, R., Freundlich, M., & Kroll, J. (2008). *Finding families for African American children: The role of race & law in adoption from foster care.* New York, NY: Evan B. Donaldson Adoption Institute.

Young, L., & Scully, A. (1993). *International and transracial adoptions: A mental health perspective.* Brookfield, VT: Ashgate.

Adoptive Families

Adoptive families are made up of individuals who choose to parent non–biologically related children for the purpose of offering them a permanent home and family. Adoption serves as a vital solution in response to society's need for safe and nurturing placement of children whose parents are not able to care for them. This entry will review general statistical information about adoptive families, the impact that different adoption choices (e.g., open, closed, international, domestic, transracial) have on families, the process of becoming an adoptive family, family processes and issues specific to adoptive families, and available resources for the development and well-being of adoptive families.

General Information About Adoptive Families

Adoptive families form a legally based union and are bound together by their belief in adoption, their will, and their love for each other. The adoption community often refers to adoptive families as families by choice, forever families, or families from the heart, based on the deliberate intent to make adopted children part of their family. Under most circumstances, adoptive families are just like other biologically related families in terms of form, structure, organization, and function. They face most of the same challenges that nonadoptive families face with the exception of those associated with unique aspects of adoption itself. Some added challenges may have to do with societal views and biases about adoption (e.g., the minimized role or lack of significance as parents when birth parents are consistently referred to as the "real" parents). Public scrutiny and questions are also part of the challenge when adoptive family members differ in appearance or traits. Other adjustment issues specific to the adoptive family experience are discussed later in this entry.

Adoptive Children in the United States

The 2000 census was the first to account for the number of adopted children in the United States. Findings showed that there were 1.5 million adopted children under the age of 18 in the United States, which made up 2.5% of all children in that age range. The breakdown in terms of types of adoption was 38% resulting from private domestic adoptions, 37% from foster care adoptions, and 25% from international adoptions. Data regarding family structure indicated that over 70.2% of the adoptions occurred in homes with married parents, 22.7% took place in homes of single mothers, single-father homes accounted for 5.5%, and unmarried couple homes came in at 1.6%. In terms of cost, 93% of international adoptions cost families over $10,000, in contrast to a much lower percentage in the case of private adoptions (33% paid over $10,000) and foster care (56% at no cost and 29% costing under $5,000). Despite the costs and time associated with the adoption process, 87% of adoptive parents said they would definitely make the same decision to adopt, knowing what they knew about their child at the time of the survey.

Types of Adoptive Families

The 2000 census also included percentage breakdowns of adoptive family types based on the legal nature of the adoption (i.e., private domestic adoptions 38%, foster care adoptions 37%, and international adoptions 25%). The census did not include any specifics about another distinct difference in types of adoption, open versus closed adoptions. Adoptive families who choose to go through open adoptions generally wish to maintain contact with their child's birth family. Contact may range from open contact to sharing of pictures, letters, or phone calls at agreed-upon times, which may occur directly between adoptive and birth families or be mediated through a third party (usually legal or agency personnel). Closed adoptions occur when there is no information known or shared about the birth family and there is no contact between families. Although closed adoptions can occur in both domestic and international adoption cases, they differ based on whether information is even known about the birth family (as in the case of adoptions from China) versus the practice of sealed records that occurs in domestic adoptions (when the identity of birth parents is known but deliberately sealed). In some cases, depending on the law, records may be available to the adopted child at age 18.

The adoption process involves several different stages from the time adoptive parents first think of adopting through years of living together as a family. Transitions and adjustment issues are related to the unique circumstances characteristic of each family's adoption.

Transitioning Through the Adoptive Process

The decision to adopt is both complicated and challenging. In the case of couples, it is important that they make the decision together. However, it is not uncommon for one partner to be ready to adopt before the other. Moving forward with the decision will require patience and open dialogue and may take a long time before the couple reaches consensus. There are various reasons why individuals choose to adopt. One common reason is infertility. Once couples find out that they are unable to conceive or bear their own biological children, adoption becomes an option to consider. Other related reasons for choosing to adopt are tied to the desire to provide a permanent home for a child, the wish to expand the family, or the yearning for siblings for another child in the family. Once the decision is made, the questions begin regarding how best to proceed.

There are several major decisions that prospective adoptive parents need to make once they decide to adopt. One is whether to adopt domestically within the United States or internationally from another country. Each of these options presents its own set of challenges and hurdles. If the prospective parents decide for domestic adoption, they can do so privately (with an attorney) or through an agency. Domestic adoption may also be the choice for those who would like to have better chances at adopting a newborn or who may be leaning toward an open adoption. If having the birth family's medical history is important, then domestic (open) adoptions would be a viable choice.

International adoption may be preferred by individuals and couples who deliberately want to add diversity to their families or who may have preferences for a particular country. In some cases, applying for adoption from a specific country through a particular international adoption agency simply boils down to the matching of requirements set by both of these. Additionally, parents who may want some distance between themselves and the child's birth family, or who prefer complete anonymity, may also opt for international adoption. Those who value humanitarian reasons for adoption, as is sometimes the case in adopting babies of a different race, may choose transracial adoptions (also true for international adoptions). Transracial adoptions may also apply in cases where prospective adoptive parents want to go through a more expedited approval process (that is also true with older, medically involved, or special-needs children).

In addition to the decision-making that takes place, there is the application process itself, which involves a great deal of paperwork, interviews, appointments, and scrutiny regarding one's medical and social history, finances, emotional stability, motives, and ability to parent. Then there is the wait for the highly anticipated call regarding the prospective child. The waiting period for this call varies greatly, based on the immediacy of the child's availability. This is followed by the actual meeting of the adoptive parents and the child, for which the wait can be a matter of days (as in some private adoption cases) or even years (as in some international adoptions). Once the child is turned over to the parents, there may still be other required legal proceedings and steps to finalize the actual adoption of the child, depending on the type of adoption. Despite the hurdles and challenges, it is noteworthy that according to the 2000 census, almost 90% of adoptive parents would do it over again if they had to.

Adoptive Family Processes and Issues

An adoptive family's developmental process includes all of the same family life cycle transitions, stages, and emotional tasks experienced by other families in general. However, adoptive families face some particular challenges that may compromise the viability of the parent–child bond. These issues can be related to attachment and bonding experiences that may occur between adoptive parents and children; pertinent grief issues experienced by adoptees as well as adoptive parents; the inadequacies, uncertainties, and doubts experienced by adoptive parents; and dealings with the birth family (in reality or fantasy, depending on how much contact exists).

Attachment and Bonding Issues

Attachment refers to bonds of affection that promote a sense of comfort and security. They are typically characteristic of close relationships like that of parent and child. The disruption that occurs for children who go through adoption because of the loss of their birth mother and family can present greater risk of compromised or negative attachment behaviors (e.g., negative reactions to being held) that also make the role of adoptive parents more difficult. As a result, the adoptive parents' own insecurities can also interfere with the bonding process. Signs of secure attachment are evident when adoptive parents are able to recognize and respond to their child's needs and when adopted children are willing to move away from their parents while also being able to return if stressed. This type of interaction between parent and child promotes the child's confidence and helps him or her build trusting emotional relationships later in life.

Grief Issues

David Brodzinsky and Marshall Schechter point out how adopted children experience loss in ways that are quite different from other experiences of loss like death or divorce. Their description of an adoptee's loss revolves around questions about why they were put up for adoption, and they believe that this form of loss is less socially recognized, pervasive, and more profound. Therefore, in many cases this type of grief experienced by adoptees goes unnoticed or unaccounted for based on fears they have about offending or threatening their adoptive parents as well as the relationship they have with them. Parents' awareness and openness to discussions at different points in time when the adopted child is willing can ameliorate and help relieve some of the emotional difficulties this can lead to in the future. While dealing with their child's grief, adoptive parents may also experience grief that is unique to their experience and identified losses. These may include the loss of not being able to conceive, carry, or bear his or her own biological child as well as the loss of not having a healthy child (i.e., in the case of special-needs adoptions).

Birth Family Issues

Issues regarding the adopted child's birth family can vary based on the birth family's proximity and level of involvement. In open adoption situations, monitoring of contact needs to be responsive to the needs of adoption and birth family members alike. In cases where there is limited or no contact, families might have to deal with curiosity about origins that may lead to information seeking on the part of the adoptee. Lack of information about the child's birth origin can also lead to fantasies about the birth family that can cause friction between adoptive parents and children. For instance, it might lead to confusion and ambivalence about identity for the adopted child especially as it relates to themes surrounding sameness and difference shared among family members.

Adoptive Family Resources

There are a number of resources that can help adoptive families navigate their way through many of the aforementioned transitions. Besides therapists who specialize in adoption, there are supportive networks and groups that adoptive families may join (both online and face-to-face). Many of these social networks and supportive services were created and designed by members of specific subgroups or populations within different adoptive communities. These range by groups available for particular developmental concerns or disorders (e.g., attachment disorder) to countries where children were adopted (e.g., Families With Children From China). There are also multipurpose websites like Adoptive Families (www.adoptivefamiles.com) that can provide a wealth of information on adoption-related topics and offer extensive sources of support.

Silvia Echevarria-Doan

See also Adoption; Childless Couples; Chosen Families; Single-Parent Families; Support Groups; Urban Families

Further Readings

Brodzinsky, D. M., & Schechter, M. D. (1990). *The psychology of adoption.* New York, NY: Oxford University Press.

Pavao, J. (2005). *The family of adoption* (Rev. ed.). Boston, MA: Beacon Press.

Rampage, C., Eovali, M., Ma, C., & Weigel-Foy, C. (2003). Adoptive families. In F. Walsh (Ed.), *Normal family processes: Growing diversity and complexity* (3rd ed.). New York, NY: Guilford Press.

Adult Attachment Assessments

Attachment theory, the study of the importance of a secure bond to loved ones, originally focused on the bond between parents and children. Later the theory of attachment was used to study adult relationships. An increased interest in the study of adult attachment has led to numerous studies over the past 20 years. These studies have explored different attachment styles and how each of these attachment styles shapes individuals' behavior in different relationships. Given the increased interest in adult attachment assessments, a series of measures have been developed and revised. This entry provides an overview of three of the most commonly used measures to assess for adult attachment: (1) the Adult Attachment Scale (AAS), (2) the Adult Attachment Interview (AAI), and (3) the Current Relationship Interview (CRI). The entry highlights how each of these instruments has measured and conceptualized different attachment styles.

Adult Attachment Scale

The AAS has been explored and studied by multiple researchers and, therefore, there are several conceptualizations of this scale. Overall, the AAS measures different adult attachment styles relating to feelings about the self in relationships, especially romantic relationships. Individuals are classified as one of three attachment styles: (1) secure, (2) avoidant, and (3) ambivalent or anxious. The secure style describes individuals who are comfortable with intimacy, dependency, and reciprocity in relationships and have low levels of anxiety about loss. The avoidant style is characterized as lack of trust and discomfort with intimacy and dependency. Individuals who are avoidant are nervous about getting close to others and perceive that partners want them to be more intimate than they feel comfortable with. Furthermore, the ambivalent or anxious style describes a desire to be close to others, anxiety about rejection, and a desire to be intimate to a degree greater than most people.

The AAS has been modified over the years with the intention of improving how to best measure attachment styles among adults. For example, Jeffrey A. Simpson created a 13-item measure using the original AAS version, and Nancy L. Collins and Stephen J. Read developed their own version of the AAS by adding items regarding availability of attachment figures and response to separation. Although years of research using the AAS have concluded that individuals' attachment style does not vary greatly with time, some researchers have found that attachment is not as stable and permanent as previously thought. For example, some individuals who have been identified as having a secure attachment during a relationship have been identified as having a form of insecure attachment as a result of a significantly negative experience with a partner. Therefore, one must be careful in making generalizations about an individual's attachment style and consult revised versions of the AAS for more up-to-date and accurate results.

Adult Attachment Interview

The AAI is a narrative measure that uses a semistructured interview to explore how childhood attachment relationships with parents shape current experiences and relationships with others. This attachment assessment measures both the conscious and unconscious elements of attachments. The AAI takes into account (a) descriptions of childhood experiences, (b) language and terminology during the interview, and (c) the ability to give thorough analysis of one's experiences and their meaning. The language used by participants during the interview is considered to reflect the participants' perception of attachment.

Scores are used to assign an individual to one of these major classifications: (a) secure or (b) insecure (dismissing, preoccupied, or unresolved). Individuals who are classified as secure report a positive view of early relationship with parents and view and value different attachment relationships as influential in their development. On the other hand, adults who are classified as insecure fail to integrate memories of experiences with assessments of the meaning of experiences. More specifically, adults who are classified as insecure (dismissing type) fail to see the value and impact of early attachment relationships (including those with parents), have difficulty recalling specific events with others, and describe a childhood of rejecting experiences. Furthermore, adults who are classified as insecure (preoccupied type) are often confused about childhood experiences and display either anger or passive behavior in current relationships, including with parents. According to AAI, an unresolved classification is considered to be an insecure form of attachment. Unresolved adults report traumas of loss and/or abuse as a result of attachment that has not been addressed.

Not all adults fall under the classifications that have just been described. Some individuals cannot be classified as either one of these categories. These adults show elements that are rarely seen together in an interview—for example, when a participant has strong opposite feelings for their mother and their father.

Current Relationship Interview

The CRI is a narrative measure that aims to investigate how adults view their adult partnerships by examining descriptions of the attachment behavior of the self and partner. Similar to the scoring system used by AAI, CRI assesses the experiences with one's partner and takes into account: (a) the perceived behavior of the partner; (b) one's behavior; and (c) one's style of communication, such as anger, idealization, and fear of loss.

Individuals are classified as one of three major patterns: (1) secure, (2) dismissing, or (3) preoccupied. Individuals classified as secure describe genuine and clear positive or negative behaviors by the partner, such as feeling loved or unloved by partner, and are able to find worth in their relationship. These individuals are able to provide rich narratives of an adult relationship that provides support for the individual and for the development of the relationship overall. For example, a secure individual is easily able to communicate with their partner, is aware of the partner's needs, and enjoys spending time nurturing the relationship. The dismissing classification is used when there is little or no evidence that an individual finds support and/or comfort within the relationship. These individuals often deny or minimize the strengths and/or limitations of their partners and place the primary focus on specific events in an attempt not to think or explain their attachment to their partner and how this affects the relationship. Furthermore, the preoccupied classification is given when an individual expresses strong dependency or a need to control the partner. These individuals often express dissatisfaction with the relationship or are anxious about the partner's ability to fulfill their needs and idealize love but do not perceive their partner as being able to fulfill what they perceive to be the ideal relationship. Also, these individual subjects express ambivalence about the relationship, the partner, and/or the self.

*Minnah W. Farook
and Roberto L. Abreu*

See also Attachment and Adolescents; Attachment and Health; Attachment and Romantic Love; Attachment Styles; Attachment Theory

Further Readings

Bartholomew, K., & Horowitz, L. M. (1991). Attachment styles among young adults: A test of a four-category model. *Journal of Personality & Social Psychology, 61*, 226–244.

Hazan, C., & Shaver, P. (1987). Romantic love conceptualized as an attachment process. *Journal of Personality and Social Psychology, 52*, 511–524. doi:10.1037/0022-3514.52.3.511

Sochos, A. (2013). The defining constituents of adult attachment and their assessment. *Journal of Adult Development, 20*, 87–99. doi:10.1007/s10804-013-9159-5

Adult Development

While human development is a process that occurs over the life span, adult development refers to the specific changes in biological, psychological, and interpersonal realms from the end of adolescence until the end of life. Some characteristics noted in adult development are not solely present during adulthood; however, the aspects highlighted in association with adult development seem to suggest that certain dimensions are most distinct during the adult years as compared to other ages and stages of life. This entry examines the various aspects and components associated with adult development, including adult development paradigms, stages of development, and various life tasks associated with adulthood.

Theories of Adult Development

Adult development can be conceptualized in several ways. Some prefer to categorize adult development based upon age or stage of life while others focus on tasks more than timelines. In addition, some models focus on social changes throughout adulthood.

Psychologist Daniel Levinson created a theory of adult development that describes growth based upon age and stage of life. This theory is often referred to as the "seasons of life" theory, and it asserts that people experience seven progressive stages in adulthood: early adult transition (ages 17 to 22), entering the adult world (ages 22 to 28), age 30 transitions (ages 28 to 33), settling down (ages 33 to 40), midlife transition (ages 40 to 45), entering middle adulthood (ages 45 to 50), and late adulthood (ages 50 and above). Within each stage of life, adults experience two phases: a stable period, in which the elements of that particular stage are lived and experienced, and a transitional period, in which a person prepares to leave that stage and enter the next developmental stage.

In contrast to a stage-oriented theory, George Vaillant, a psychoanalyst and research psychologist, identified six life tasks that are to be accomplished over the course of adulthood. These life tasks include identity development, experiencing intimacy, finding a career, generativity (or the selfless task of giving to others), becoming keeper of the meaning (identifying traditions and meaningful elements of life that can be passed along to the next generation), and achieving integrity (feeling at peace with oneself and one's place in the world). Instead of isolating these tasks to specific age and/or stages in life, the idea is that these tasks can be pursued simultaneously over the course of adult life.

Bernice Neugarten acknowledged both time and social influences in her theory on adult development, which is referred to as the social clock theory. The idea behind this theory is that there are social expectations for certain behaviors based upon age, such as getting married, having children, settling into a career, and even retiring. A person can be considered on time with such events by engaging in the life event at a time that aligns with the norm, or a person can be off time by not fulfilling the norm or expectation for a given life event at the expected time. Whether a person is on or off time can impact self-perception and feelings of worth. Since normed times for events may vary based upon culture, it is important to acknowledge the ways that culture can shape norms and expectations.

Psychosocial stage theory was created by the developmental psychologist and psychoanalyst Erik Erikson to describe the continuity of development that occurs throughout the life span. Within psychosocial stage theory, it is posited that people pursue various psychosocial tasks from birth to death. These tasks are all presented in the form of challenges or crises that are experienced on the basis of one's age and associated life experiences, and these stages are experienced in a set order. However, it is possible to revisit stages and find new relevance in previous stages of psychosocial development throughout the life span.

Within psychosocial theory, two response options are provided for each stage of development. Should an individual achieve success in a developmental stage, that sense of mastery allows a person to move forward in his or her development.

However, if a person fails to master the developmental task at hand, regression can occur. Eight stages have been outlined within psychosocial theory, and three stages apply specifically to adult development: intimacy versus isolation (young adulthood), generativity versus stagnation (middle age), and integrity versus despair (late adulthood).

Phases of Adulthood

Adult development has been viewed from a multitude of perspectives, and each perspective seems to shape what is observed and what is expected during adulthood. Nevertheless, adulthood has conventionally been viewed in three parts based upon differential experiences and characteristics associated with age and stage of life: early adulthood, middle adulthood, and late adulthood. Early adulthood has been understood as the period of time between the late teenage years through age 30 or an age somewhere in the mid-30s; however, increased focus on the transition to adulthood as a distinct phase of development has shifted the age range a bit: emerging adulthood is considered between the ages of 18 and 29, which pushes back early or young adulthood to the late 20s through the mid-30s. Middle adulthood describes an age somewhere between the 30s to late 50s or early 60s. Late adulthood extends from approximately sixty years of age until death. Within each of these phases, various personal and interpersonal aspects lead to distinctions in developmental and psychosocial tasks.

Transition Into Adulthood

Emerging adulthood has been understood as a distinct phase between adolescence and young adulthood, which occurs in industrialized countries worldwide. The age range for emerging adulthood is understood to be from the age of 18 through 29 years of age. Experiences associated with emerging adults seem to include both positive elements and perceived challenges. According to psychologist Jeffrey Jensen Arnett's theory, emerging adulthood consists of five distinct characteristics: identity exploration, time of possibilities, instability, self-focus, and feeling in-between (conceptualizing oneself as not fully an adolescent and yet not fully an adult). As emerging adults progress through this stage of development, they seem to settle into a greater sense of personal identity, build more secure relationships, and pursue a steady career path. It is at this point that an individual is seen to transition into young adulthood.

Young Adulthood

Upon transitioning from emerging adulthood, young adults work to gain a sense of independence while continuing to build stable relationships. Identity formation is a significant element of this life stage, and much emphasis is placed upon answering the question, Who am I? An additional focus of young adulthood is relationship-building with a romantic partner, which can also lead to the exploration and pursuit of marriage or cohabitation. Adjustment to being in a committed relationship is another aspect of this life stage. Building a family and learning to be a parent can be an important aspect of young adulthood. This can also create changes as individuals learn to be both romantic partners and parents. The demise of relationships may also impact this life stage.

Those in the early phase of adulthood value career stability and economic independence, and they explore options for occupations in an effort to work toward a specific career trajectory. Establishing healthy work relationships is also an important task of young adulthood. In young adulthood, developing the self is often pursued in tandem with career development and relational development, and this is a time when the pace of life may experience shifts due to the various demands a person experiences. Thus, balancing relationships with career pursuits can be an important aspect of this life phase.

The psychosocial task or crisis for young adults is intimacy versus isolation. Between emerging adulthood and young adulthood, the desire and need for intimate relationships is paramount. To be in a relationship with others creates a sense of enrichment and fulfillment. While intimacy is often contextualized to romantic relationships, this psychosocial task can also involve deepening intimacy in relation to family and friends. Failure to achieve intimacy can lead to isolation, which may be caused by an unwillingness or inability to engage in meaningful relationships. An overarching element that can enhance relational growth during this life stage is boundary-setting. Learning to have clear boundaries can allow individuals to experience intimacy along with a sense of independence, thereby preventing enmeshment or disengagement from taking place in relationships.

Middle Adulthood

During middle adulthood, individuals shift attention toward expanding and deepening personal relationships. Often, this phase involves greater social awareness and responsibility while also learning to identify and pursue aspects of life that seem to be fulfilling, which often includes child-rearing. For some, relational shifts during this stage may include breakups or divorces as well as recoupling or remarriage. Blended families can also result during this life phase. Learning how to parent children at different ages and stages brings forth additional modifications within relationships. Caregiving may increase as those in middle adulthood offer support to aging parents or other family members.

A primary focus during middle adulthood is career management. This phase of life allows individuals to engage in skill-building and gaining insight as to how to advance (whether by gaining further experience and expertise or switching one's career path due to a desire for increased life satisfaction). Losing a job or quitting a job to care for family members can also impact one's sense of morale or identity. Shifts in physical and mental abilities may begin to surface during this phase, which can have an impact on career choices as well. One's sense of timing and perspective on life can cause individuals in this phase to evaluate successes and disappointments, which can lead to a crisis experience if life has not turned out as one had hoped or planned.

Regarding psychosocial tasks, generativity versus stagnation is the critical point for those in middle adulthood. During this phase of life, there is a need and desire to expand focus and efforts beyond self-interest. Identity development is expanded by living in meaningful ways and demonstrating productivity through motivation and action. This sense of generativity can be displayed in one's family interactions, particularly through child-rearing, but can also be seen through a commitment to and investment in community endeavors. This phase of life can also highlight the degree to which one's plans and/or aspirations are being pursued or achieved. Failure to achieve generativity can lead to a sense of stagnation or lack of perceived growth. This can result in preoccupation with worry and a perceived lack of fulfillment in relationships.

Late Adulthood

As individuals transition to late adulthood, they typically experience a variety of shifts due to biological, economic, career, and relational changes. Physically, individuals may experience decreases in health, including memory loss or and illness, which can in turn lead to a loss of independence as people need care and help from others. Coping with physical and mental changes can be an important aspect of this life phase. Additionally, late adulthood may include the loss of relationships due to spouses, partners, or friends who die. However, becoming a grandparent is often viewed as a positive relational shift that is experienced in late adulthood. Retirement provides a significant life shift during this phase, which can offer the benefit of more time to pursue enjoyable tasks and activities.

Life satisfaction becomes a point of focus during late adulthood. Because goals are no longer aimed at career advancement, individuals must find different aspects of life for enjoyment and enrichment. Finding meaningful hobbies or leisure activities can help those in late adulthood continue to enjoy life and connect with others. The reality of death becomes an important aspect of this life phase, and the ways in which individuals perceive life and death also contribute to life satisfaction.

Integrity versus despair is the psychosocial task of late adulthood. During this life phase, individuals have the opportunity to look back on their lives in order to assess the degree to which life was fulfilling and worthwhile. One who displays integrity believes that his or her life goals were pursued and achieved, which creates a sense of ego integrity. In contrast, those who possess many regrets may experience a variety of negative emotions and sentiments, including bitterness, despair, resentment, and even self-loathing. The reality of impending death can encourage the integrity-versus-despair stage, because it allows the individual to focus upon how one has lived and whether or not expectations and hopes were meaningfully achieved.

Future Research

While various theories have been explored regarding adult development, further research is needed to understand the process and outcomes associated with adulthood. Specifically, studies exploring the impact of cultural dynamics on adult development can help bring insight regarding individual differences among adults as they age. In addition, studies that explore the transition to adulthood can help clarify distinctions between adolescents, emerging adults, and young adults. Additional research will assist individuals in understanding the dynamics that impact adults at various places in the life span, which in turn can impact the ways that adults are empowered and assisted throughout each stage or phase of life.

Christina Schnyders

See also Individual and Family Development; Life Transitions

Further Readings

Arnett, J. J. (2004). *Emerging adulthood: The winding road from the late teens through the twenties.* New York, NY: Oxford University Press.

Bengston, V. L. (1996). *Adulthood and aging: Research on continuities and discontinuities*. New York, NY: Springer.

Erikson, E. H. (1994). *Identity and the life cycle*. New York, NY: W. W. Norton.

Levinson, D. J. (1986). A conceptualization of adult development. *American Psychologist, 41*(1), 3–13.

Newman, B. M., & Newman, P. R. (2015). *Development through life: A psychosocial approach* (12th ed.). Stamford, CT: Cengage.

Santrock, J. W. (1985). *Adult development and aging*. Dubuque, IA: Wm. C. Brown.

Vaillant, G. E. (2002). *Aging well: Surprising guideposts to a happier life from the landmark Harvard study of adult development*. Boston, MA: Little, Brown.

AFFECT REGULATION

Affect is a clinical term used to describe emotions (inner feelings) and one's demeanor (external facial expressions and body language). Affect regulation is an individual's level of ability to monitor and control his or her own behaviors as related to his or her own emotional state. This entry examines how thoughts, feelings, and behaviors are related to affect regulation; how societal expectations and norms play a role in affect regulation; and how affect regulation is related to risk management, stabilization of, and prevention of emotional escalation that leads to crises. The entry concludes with a brief discussion of different techniques and models used to assist individuals in developing affect regulation skills.

Affect Regulation Defined

Affect regulation involves more than just emotion. It is the combined effort of multiple, fluid processes in the mind and body. Physical aspects such as hormones, heart rate, blood pressure, and illness influence one's ability to regulate one's affect. Positive or negative thoughts or cognitions likewise impact how quickly and regularly one can self-regulate. An individual wishing to learn skills to regulate their affect may have to make significant health changes. Nutrition, exercise, amount of sleep, medication or substance use, support systems, and coping skills all play a part in affect regulation. For example, an individual who is ill, not receiving the quality or quantity of sleep or food needed, or is experiencing loneliness, grief, or trauma may have a more difficult time monitoring their body language, temper, and impulses.

Affect regulation is necessary for an individual to be able to handle everyday living, with its stressors and duties. When an individual is unable to do so, it is called *affect dysregulation*. Affect dysregulation can lead to maladaptive or even harmful behaviors, such as the breakdown of relationships, loss of employment, addictions, impulsive behaviors, or self-harm.

Affect regulation requires that the individual maintain a degree of psychological flexibility. Those who are too rigid or too chaotic will not adequately be able to manage their emotional responses to environmental or relational triggers. In order to regulate emotionally, one must first be able to adapt to change. An individual must be able to accept influence from others (e.g., redirection to completion of a task or paying attention) in order to behave in accordance with fundamental social norms. Those who cannot regulate their emotions tend to stray from socially appropriate behaviors, frequently experiencing emotional outbursts, relational conflict, defensiveness and/or guardedness, confusion about oneself, or attacks and accusations directed toward another person. Frequent misperceptions or misrecollections of events are not uncommon. Inner rage and lack of confidence or self-esteem can lead to affect dysregulation.

Affect regulation is necessary not only for socially appropriate behaviors but for risk management as well. Individuals who experience suicidal or homicidal thoughts may require the assistance of a professional in learning and utilizing affect regulation skills. Without affect regulation skills, it is much more difficult not to act on impulses to harm oneself or others.

Researchers in affect regulation recognize a link between a person's attachment style, which is formed early in life (beginning with how an infant connects to his or her primary caregivers), and his or her ability to self-regulate. Researchers continue to investigate how parenting styles shape an individual's affect regulation or dysregulation. For example, if one had a parent who was easily emotionally disrupted and therefore became disruptive toward family members, a child in this family may adopt the same behaviors as the disruptive parent or may take the opposite extreme of never expressing emotion in order to avoid being like his or her parent. Either extreme has the potential to be equally damaging to the child's own well-being, as the child has lacked the opportunity to learn the balance of affect regulation from the parent.

Research in Affect Regulation

Process Model

James J. Gross, a psychologist at Stanford University, created the process model of emotional regulation to explain how one can alter their emotional responses to a problem or experience. His model consists of five stages: situational selection, situational modulation, attentional deployment, cognitive change, and response modulation. Situational selection is determining which situations an individual wishes to place himself or herself in; situational modulation is then determining how one wishes to behave in the chosen situation; attentional deployment is deciding what one will pay attention to and how one will choose to perceive it; cognitive change involves determining how one will think about the situation (often changing negative or pessimistic thoughts into more realistic, balanced, or neutral thoughts); and response modulation involves determining if one took the best course of action and/or needs to alter one's thoughts, feelings, or behaviors in response to a situation or experience. In the process model of emotional regulation, the goal is not to ignore an emotion or invalidate one's circumstances but, rather, to control impulses to act on said emotions.

Regulation Theory

Allan N. Schore, a professor at UCLA, combines research in attachment theory with current research into neurobiology and refers to the combination as regulation theory. Regulation theory posits that between the first and second years of an individual's life, multiple changes are happening in the brain, especially around attachment, that indicate whether an individual will self-regulate. A direct correlation exists between a parent's attachment style and one's ability to regulate one's own affect, recognizing that communication skills such as empathy, validation, respect, and compassion from primary figures in childhood lead to increased ability to regulate one's affect throughout the life span. Traditional mental health diagnoses related to personality disorders or psychosis in which affect regulation is difficult or nearly impossible may be related to a lack of, or disruption in, attachment.

Schore's work describes how the left and right hemispheres of the brain play a role in self-regulation. The autonomic nervous system, which includes the sympathetic and parasympathetic nervous systems, is necessary in affect regulation. The sympathetic nervous system, often called the fight-or-flight system, involves a series of processes that are quickly mobilized in times of fear or stress; unfortunately, for an individual who struggles to self-regulate, this system may always feel "on," and the parasympathetic nervous system, which is intended to deactivate the sympathetic nervous system once actual or perceived danger has passed, may feel as if it is always turned off. It is necessary for a child, adolescent, or adult to learn and use the skills to enable one's affect regulation if blocks or breaches in attachment prevented these skills from being learned or modeled early in life. Practices such as yoga have also been shown to assist in affect regulation.

Dialectical Behavior Therapy

Marsha Linehan, who teaches at the University of Washington, teaches strategies for tolerance of intense emotions through her therapy model, dialectical behavior therapy (DBT), an empirically based treatment modality, whose components are *mindfulness, interpersonal effectiveness, distress tolerance*, and *emotional regulation*. DBT assists an individual in learning affect regulation skills by helping him or her manage impulses toward self-harm (e.g., sabotaging of relationships, inability to maintain employment) and replace self-harming traits with those that are socially acceptable and healthy. DBT assists individuals in learning how to display appropriate facial expressions and respond accordingly and neutrally to others. DBT teaches effective techniques in which one may monitor and control one's behaviors, thoughts, and feelings.

In DBT, all modules assist an individual in learning and using skills to balance their logic and reason with their emotionality. Mindfulness is not a practice isolated to DBT. Certain religious traditions cultivate mindfulness as part of their spiritual practice, though it may be referred to as meditation, prayer, or centering. The mindfulness module consists of skills that help an individual learn how to stay in the present moment rather than fearing or fantasizing about the future or dwelling in the past. The interpersonal effectiveness module assists individuals in determining how to assess their needs in a situation and to react proactively to situations at hand in order to meet their goals. The distress tolerance module teaches skills in tolerating difficult feelings, emotions, and circumstances, whether one's own or another individual's. The emotional regulation module teaches skills that help individuals learn how to change their thinking in order to change their feelings. While DBT addresses thoughts, feelings, and behaviors, it recognizes that by changing behaviors first, one can begin to retrain their thoughts and feelings into different, more adaptive, healthy patterns.

Cognitive-Behavioral Therapy

DBT is not the only evidence-based treatment modality to increase affect regulation. Cognitive-behavioral therapy (CBT) is also regularly used by practitioners to assist individuals in regulating thoughts and behaviors in order to influence affect regulation. These forms of treatment have also been shown to be effective in couples and family therapy. CBT assists individuals in examining their irrational, or negative, automatic thoughts, with the goal of replacing negative thoughts with healthier, more adaptive positive thoughts. By changing thoughts and behaviors, one can experience more positive feelings and increase one's ability to regulate one's own affect.

Eye Movement Desensitization and Reprocessing

Eye movement desensitization and reprocessing (EMDR), a form of therapy originated by psychologist Francine Shapiro, is widely used to assist individuals in decreasing affect dysregulation and increasing regulation. This therapy has been found effective for treatment of individuals who are struggling with stress, anxiety, and posttraumatic stress disorder (PTSD). Often, practitioners utilize DBT as a treatment modality to increase stabilization and affect regulation as individuals begin the EMDR eight-step process. Similar to CBT and DBT, EMDR assists individuals in recognizing automatic, negative thoughts that are pervasive to a self-concept and promotes the reprocessing of traumatic events, sensations, and beliefs in order to allow oneself to believe more adaptive, healthful thoughts about oneself. EMDR assists individuals in overcoming their past, learning skills to manage and thrive in the present, in order to look forward to the future with skills of how to handle different situations as they may arise.

Biofeedback

Biofeedback has also been well researched and shown to assist in affect regulation. It assists individuals in utilizing controlled breathing and, at times, imagery in the management of troubling thoughts and feelings. Often utilizing a heart rate monitor connected to a computer or handheld device, biofeedback with the support of programming allows individuals to synchronize their breathing to their heart rate, increasing healthy blood flow to the brain and allowing individuals to self-calm.

General Techniques

Regardless of the therapy module, all of the aforementioned theories encourage individuals to use techniques such as grounding (or centering or mindfulness), deep breathing, guided imagery, and structured relaxation to increase affect regulation. Sometimes it is necessary to see a psychiatric care provider who can prescribe medication to assist in affect regulation. As mentioned, a proper balance of sleep, nutrition, and exercise is beneficial; a nutritional professional may recommend dietary supplements to assist as well.

Lori C. Kucharski

See also Anger Management; Boundaries; Bowen Family Systems Theory; Individual and Family Development; Interpersonal Neurobiology, Attachment and; Life Events; Mindfulness; Primary and Secondary Emotions; Self-Esteem

Further Readings

Fonagy, P., Gergely, G., Jurist, E., & Target, M. (2005). *Affect regulation, mentalization, and the development of the self.* New York, NY: Other Press.

Gross, J. J. (Ed.) (2014). *Handbook of emotion regulation* (2nd ed.). New York, NY: Guilford Press.

Hill, D. (2015). *Affect regulation theory: A clinical model.* New York, NY: W. W. Norton.

Klonsky, E. D. (2009). The functions of self-injury in young adults who cut themselves: Clarifying the evidence for affect regulation. *Psychiatric Research, 166*(2–3), 260–268.

Kohn, N., Eickhoff, S. B., Scheller, M., Laird, A. R., Fox, P. T., & Habel, U. (2014). Neural network of cognitive emotion regulation—An ALE meta-analysis and MACM analysis. *NeuroImage, 87,* 345–355.

Mikulincer, M., Shaver, P. R., & Pelreg, D. (2003). Attachment theory and affect regulation: The dynamics, development, and cognitive consequences of attachment-related strategies. *Motivation and Emotion, 27*(2), 77–102.

Schore, A. N. (1994). *Affect regulation and the origin of the self: The neurobiology of emotional development.* Hillsdale, NJ: Erlbaum.

Schore, A. N. (2003a). *Affect dysregulation and disorders of the self.* New York, NY: W. W. Norton.

Schore, A. N. (2003b). *Affect regulation and the repair of the self.* New York, NY: W. W. Norton.

African American Families

Slavery, racism, disparity and oppression, Jim Crow laws and decades of marginalization, segregation, intentional and unintentional racism, and poverty are only some of the many challenges that have characterized the lives of African American families. Although there are different ethnic groups of Black Americans, this article refers to African American families whose ancestors were born in Africa. African American families constitute the second largest minority group in the United States and have played an important part in its history as well as its economic and political structure.

Previously, studies on African American families have been replete with ideas of the pathology of the family. Recently, however, scholars are recognizing that a deficit view of the African American family is problematic when working with this population. Instead, scholars suggest that when counselors work with African American families, they need to consider the many individual and collective strengths that have enabled African American families to survive against enormous odds.

At the same time, because all of us operate out of the cultural perspectives, beliefs, and value systems we absorbed early in life, it is important for counselors to acknowledge that received notions and attitudes, including racial bias and cultural stereotypes, may continue to influence their own thinking. Such influences, if allowed to remain unrecognized and unexamined, could create barriers to forming positive and productive relationships with African American families.

This entry discusses some of the sources of strengths exhibited by African American families such as resilience, kinship bonds, religion and spirituality, educational attainment, effective parenting, and racial socialization. Counselors are encouraged to consider these strengths as protective factors that define the essence of African American families and as valuable resources within the therapeutic setting

Background

The statistics for African Americans related to income, jobs, and education are all unfavorable compared with those of the general population. According to the 2010 census, the African American population, about 38.9 million, accounted for 13% of the total U.S. population. Further, the U.S. Census Bureau stated that the poverty rate for African American families accounted for 23.5% of all African American families compared with 13% of the general population who are in poverty. According to the U.S. Department of Labor, the unemployment rate was 13.6% for African Americans, compared with 7.4% of the general population. The Associated Press (May 21, 2006) reported that of African American males in the age group 25 to 29, 12% were imprisoned compared with 1.7% of White males. Moreover, Richard Fry, in a 2010 report by the Pew Research Center, found that approximately 23% of African American adults did not receive a high school diploma. Despite these statistics, it is important to note that there are other elements of the African American community that are positive. The African American culture is diverse in terms of socioeconomic status, educational level, cultural identity, family structure, and reactions to racism. In addition, many middle- and upper-middle-class African Americans strongly value hard work and believe that they can achieve the American dream.

Strengths of African American Families

Although African American families' strengths are similar to those found in other ethnic groups, it is important to note that African American families exist within a specific contextual framework. Moreover, counselors who are aware of the strengths of African American families are encouraged to integrate effective care strategies based on these culturally specific protective factors.

Resilience

Despite their many struggles, African American families have shown great resilience and hope, which is a legacy that has been transmitted from generation to generation. *Resilience* is the capacity to recover from or to adapt to difficult and challenging life circumstances. Some of the challenges that African American families have had to overcome or adapt to include living in low-income households and life in poverty besieged by joblessness, crime, violence, and drugs. Scholars have noted that families living in poverty are more likely to be resilient when they seek, receive, and give support as a way to build interconnectedness. In addition, as part of their resilience, African Americans tend to hold beliefs about themselves or the spiritual world that nourish them. Resilience has been the driving force behind African American families' courage over the years.

Because of the courage and strength that African American families have and continue to exhibit, this is a good place for counselors to begin when working with African American families. For decades it has been noted that African Americans are hesitant in seeking mental health services because of negative experiences with, and negative perspectives of, the predominantly White theorists who have created the therapeutic models all counselors are trained in. Counselors must understand that African American families exist within a collective network; therefore, family members may define themselves collectively rather than individually. Accordingly, family members going through counseling may prefer to discuss how their decisions, change, failures, or success impact their family unit instead of just focusing on individual needs. Resilience is encouraged within a broader family network, where African Americans gain strength from each other.

Kinship Bonds

Strong kinship relationships with extended family members provide an important source of strength for many African American families. As counselors work with African American families, it is important to note that kinship networks for some African American families may extend beyond traditional blood ties and include people who are not directly related to the family. Traditionally, a strong kinship network has been the foundation for many African Americans as they navigate living in a historically oppressive society. In African American families, roles and functions are carried out within the extended families and shared by all. For example, a strong bond in the family includes fostering the children of family members who are not able to provide adequate care. Informal foster care in African American families refers to an informal social service network that has been an integral part of the community since the days of slavery. It began as, and still is, a practice in African American families to informally adopt the children of relatives and friends and take care of them when their parents are unable to provide for their needs. Counselors must understand that for many African American families, this extended network serves as a major source of stability. It functions to provide day care for children, support for unwed mothers, and the willingness to accept foster children as family members. This is important to understand when counselors work with African American families.

Strong Religious and Spiritual Commitment

A major aspect of African American lives is spirituality or religion, which has been dominant since the era of slavery. Today, religion and spirituality continue to serve numerous functions in the lives of African Americans. Religion has traditionally provided a source of socialization, education, and social support. Prayer, faith in God, meditation, and religious belief are reported as key coping strategies for African American families. In working with African American families, counselors must be sensitive to the role that religion and spirituality play in the lives of individual and how religion impacts the decisions that they make in their lives. African American religious and spiritual belief entails an awareness and commitment to a spiritual lifestyle that provides a sense of power and purpose greater than the self. Further, while all African Americans may not subscribe to organized religion or churches, they may have been raised with and have internalized a sense of spirituality. Rather than being a systemized set of religious beliefs or practices, the African sense of spirituality is woven into the very fabric of society and is a central characteristic of the African psyche. The roles of spirituality or religion are survival and coping mechanisms used to overcome many adversities in the African American family.

In providing services to African American families, counselors need to understand the significance of religion and spirituality in their lives. Moreover, various counseling associations have noted that a strong spiritual base can enhance resiliency in the family. Furthermore, the values promoted by counselors are similar to, and compatible with, African American families' typical spiritual values, including sensitivity for others, personal responsibility, personal fulfillment and satisfaction, forgiveness of others, self-discipline, a sense of purpose, and a healthy sexual life.

Educational Advancement

Self-improvement and achievement are important in the lives of many African American families. These attributes are not only for individual gains but the collective advancement of the entire family. Historically, education within the African American community, as for many other minority groups, was revered as an avenue for upward social and economic mobility. Many writers have emphasized that African Americans think of education and hard work as critical to their success and as one way to overcome societal oppression. Although many African Americans hold more than one job, African Americans continue to have less desirable jobs, receive lower pay, and are more likely to be underemployed than their non–African American counterparts. Despite adversities and challenges faced, however, African Americans continue to strive for academic excellence, upward social mobility, and occupational achievement.

Parenting and Racial Socialization of Children

African American families play a critical role in teaching their children how to become part of a racial group. Racial socialization is the process by which explicit and implicit messages are transmitted regarding the meaning of race and ethnicity. Racial socialization is an important process because of its importance as a protective factor. There is evidence that suggests racial socialization helps to foster the adjustment of children in the face of race-related adversity and serves to protect youth from negative mental health consequences. Raising African American children in the United States is a challenging task. Though all children progress through similar stages of development and all children need nurturance and sensitive guidance, African American children and their parents face special problems as a result of America's history of racism and discrimination. Parents of African American children face special challenges in terms of helping their children cope with racism and helping them maintain a positive cultural identity. This is the case whether they are raising their children in affluent suburbs or inner-city, low-income communities.

Stephaney S. Morrison

See also Beliefs and Values; Bonding; Empowerment in Families; Family Values; Kinship Care

Further Readings

Associated Press. (2006, May 21). *U.S. report: 2.2 million now in prison, jails*. Retrieved from http://www.msnbc.msn.com/id/12901873

Benard, B. (2004). *Resiliency: What we have learned*. San Francisco, CA: WestEd.

Boyd-Franklin, N. (2010). Incorporating spirituality and religion into the treatment of African American clients. *Counseling Psychologist, 38*(7), 976–1000.

Carter, D. (2008). Cultivating a critical race consciousness for African American school success. *Educational Foundations, 22*(1–2), 11–28.

Centers for Disease Control and Prevention. (2006). *National vital statistics reports: Health United States, 2006*. Washington, DC: U.S. Government Printing Office.

Fry, R. (2010). *Hispanics, high school dropouts and the GED*. Retrieved from http://pewhispanic.org/reports/report.php?ReportID=122

Hall, J. C. (2007). Kinship ties: Attachment relationships that promote resilience in African American adult children of alcoholics. *Advances in Social Work, 8*(1), 130–140.

Hollingsworth, L. D. (2013). Resilience in Black families. In D. S. Becvar (Ed.), *Handbook of family resilience* (pp. 229–243). New York, NY: Springer Science + Business Media.

Mandara, J. (2013). Discrimination concerns and expectations as explanations for gendered socialization in African American families. *Child Development, 84*(3).

Pew Research Center. (2011). *Wealth gaps rise to record highs between Whites, Blacks and Hispanics*. Retrieved from http://www.pewresearch.org/daily-number/wealth-gaps-rise-to-record-highs-between-whites-blacks-and-hispanics

Purham, T. A. (2002). *Counseling persons of African descent*. Thousand Oaks, CA: Sage.

Sheridan, M. J., Burley, J., Hendricks, D. E., & Rose, T. (2014). "Caring for one's own": Variation in the lived experience of African-American caregivers of elders. *Journal of Ethnic & Cultural Diversity in Social Work: Innovation in Theory, Research & Practice, 23*(1), 1–19.

Sue, D. W., & Sue, D. (2013). *Counseling the culturally diverse: Theory and practice*. Hoboken, NJ: Wiley.

U.S. Census Bureau. (2015). *About poverty*. Retrieved from http://www.census.gov/hhes/www/poverty/about/overview/index.html

U.S. Department of Labor. (2012). *Employment status of the civilian population by race, sex, and age*. Retrieved from http://www.bls.gov/news.release/empsit.t02.htm

AGING AND CAREGIVING

Over the course of a lifetime, individuals will be challenged with many mental, physical, and emotional health–related changes and challenges as they age. When one is young, aging is associated with growth, development, and discovery; many abilities peak near the age of 30, while others continue to grow and develop across an individual's life span. Regardless of the degree to which a person's body changes as he or she ages, individuals can be aided by the support of others who act as caregivers. Caregivers play a valuable role as they lend their eyes, ears, hands, and hearts to helping elderly people and/or people with disabilities face the challenges of aging with dignity, security, and grace. This entry examines the concepts of aging and caregiving, rates of growth, and cross-cultural issues surrounding aging and caregiving.

Aging

The aging process represents the universal and biological changes that everyone experiences with age, which are affected by disease and environmental influences. For example, the functional capacity of an individual's biological system increases during the first years of life, reaches its peak in early adulthood, and then naturally declines. It is important to note that the aging process is unavoidable and may be impacted by a progressive functional decline of organs and tissues. The rate of aging, however, varies for everyone and may be influenced by factors such as heredity, lifestyle, environmental toxins, and accessibility to health care. Engaging in exercise and maintaining a healthy weight while avoiding smoking, drugs, and alcohol as well as other environmental toxins may help people function well and avoid diseases that lead to premature aging. In addition to physical losses, social and emotional changes are part of the aging process as well and should not be overlooked. For example, relationships with people will evolve or end as the result of aging and/or death. Whether an individual experiences physical or emotional distress, the aging process may facilitate the need for assistance with everyday tasks in an effort to enhance one's overall functionality.

Benefits of Aging

Not all changes aging individuals experience are negative or harmful. Along with one's thinning gray hair and/or sagging skin comes the benefit of increased brainpower. Neuroscientists have found that the middle-aged brain actually has surprising talents. For example, it has developed a multitude of brain maps that help individuals to recognize and respond to similar circumstances when they come upon them repeatedly. These powerful systems can cut through the intricacies of complex problems to find concrete answers and begin reacting less to negative input; they are pulled more toward the positive. What this means is that as the result of being able to tap into a toolbox of social and emotional instincts that they have developed over time through experience, elderly people, in general, are better able to handle conflicts, feel happier, are more secure when compared to younger generations, and experience less stress.

Caregiving

According to the World Health Organization (WHO), approximately 20% of the workforce is estimated to be involved in caregiving. Consequently, as the number of elderly Americans increases, so does the number of employed caregivers and associated health care costs. Caregivers provide assistance as well as company and emotional support to someone who is, in some degree, incapacitated and needs help. For example, a caregiver might shop for food; cook; clean the house; give medicine; pay bills; and/or help the person bathe, dress, and eat. Caregivers, whether formal or informal, are typically "on call" 24 hours a day, 7 days a week. Formal caregivers are paid for their services and have had training and education in providing care. This may include services from home health agencies and other trained professionals. On the other hand, social, economic, and technological changes in the world of health care have shifted more responsibility for medical care into the hands of informal caregivers who are typically the patient's family members or friends and are often asked to play an active role in managing care, performing medical interventions, and dispensing medications, despite a usual lack of knowledge, skills, and awareness.

Rates of Growth

According to the 2012 national projections, between the years 2012 and 2050, the United States will experience considerable growth within its elderly population. For example, there is data showing that when all of the post–World War II baby boom generation reach at least 65 years old, there will be approximately 71 million members of this group who will not be able to care for themselves. As a result, programs such as Social Security and Medicare will become strained, which will in turn affect the families, health care providers, and the incomes belonging to elderly people. For instance, unlike other cultures, older Americans often allow and/or rely on their children and their health care providers to care for them. Additionally, even after successful careers in earlier years, elderly people are rarely asked to assume responsible roles in the community due to the assumption that they have lost their ability to think clearly, to learn new things, and are generally incapable of any physical activity other than walking or sitting. Typically, elderly people are viewed as less valuable when compared to younger adults.

Aging and Caregiving Across Cultures

As the United States ages over the next several decades, the elderly population will become more racially, ethnically, and culturally diverse. And because cultural perspectives differ across ethnic groups and may impact caregiver experiences in several domains such as one's perception of the caregiving role and the utilization of support services, it is vital for professionals and/or researchers to understand the latest information about the critical issues being faced by elderly people in today's society. With this knowledge, professionals or researchers will be better able to enhance practices and policies as they relate to members of this population. It is equally important for caregivers to be aware of cultural differences among clients and their families and tailor expectations and behaviors with respect to ethnic beliefs and values.

Across the past decade, much has been studied and learned about the aging and caregiving processes in regard to gender, race and ethnicity, sexual orientation, and disability. For example, when considering gender, despite the fact that caregiving is beginning to be recognized as a coordinated team effort, females tend to provide more care for elderly people and/or disabled than males. Additionally, more female caregivers than males are faced with the challenge of balancing work and caregiving responsibilities.

In regard to ethnicity, the proportion of older adults from ethnic and racial minority groups is projected to increase exponentially by 2050, with the largest growth rates among Hispanics, followed by Asians and Pacific Islanders, American Indians, and African Americans. This is important to note as researchers have indicated that ethnic minority caregivers provide more care for elderly people and disabled than do their White counterparts and report having more health problems than White caregivers as well. On the other hand, other researchers have found that African American caregivers experience less stress and depression from their efforts than White caregivers, whereas Hispanic and Asian American caregivers exhibit more signs of depression than White caregivers.

According to the Administration on Aging, an agency of the U.S. Department of Health and Human Services (HHS), there are currently an estimated 1.75 million to 4 million older adults who identify as lesbian, gay, bisexual, or transgender (LGBT), with about one in three of those individuals living alone (as compared to one in five non-LGBT individuals). When considering the availability of familial or spiritual support, approximately 40% of LGBT older individuals say that their support networks have become smaller over time, with African American LGBT individuals being 3 times as likely as White or Hispanic LGBT adults to say that people from their churches or faith are part of their support systems. Many supports currently in place for the aging within the United States do not cater to the aging or caregiving needs of LGBT elderly people. As a result, these older adults are also more likely to face poverty or economic difficulty and deal with more physical and/or mental health concerns when compared to non-LGBT individuals.

When considering the aging process for individuals with disabilities, until the 1970s the life expectancy rate for this population was lower than that of individuals without disabilities. Although the prevalence rate of aging with disability is unknown, the best estimates indicate that about 12 million Americans who acquired a disability in youth or midlife are presently aging with a disability. This is a number that will continue to increase as those with disabilities experience the benefits of increased longevity. Unfortunately though, with the longer life expectancy for these individuals comes the fact that they are also facing new challenges associated with their quality of life and well-being. For example, when the process of aging is coupled with a disability, it can be difficult to separate out changes associated with aging from those associated with disability. Age-related health conditions are chronic conditions and diseases associated with aging and often occur more frequently, more severely, and at an earlier age for individuals with physical disabilities then those without. Additionally, these same individuals are also at risk for developing what is known as secondary health conditions, which may create additional impairments, functional limitations, or disabilities that occur as a result of having a primary disability.

There are varying degrees of mobility associated with physical disabilities. For example, some adults with disabilities are able to address many of their needs with minimal support, while others require constant supervision and a significant amount of assistance to complete daily routines. As a result, caregivers for members of this population must be especially sensitive to their clients' abilities so they can provide the appropriate level of care necessary for each person. On the other hand, when help from a caregiver is not available or if the caregiver is unable to meet the needs of the individual with the disability, caregivers may wish to seek help from agencies where a wide range of help for both the individual with the disability and the caregiver may be available. Despite these seemingly negative cultural differences, there are some positive aspects of caregiving that have been discussed in the literature as well. For instance, a recent survey by the National Opinion Research Center found that 83% of caregivers viewed it as being a positive experience via enhancing one's well-being and mood specifically for members of the African American population, as the act of helping a loved one provides them with an intrinsic reward and feelings of altruism. Additionally, while considering the process of aging and development across one's life span, Roberto and Jarrott noted that the emerging literature on caregiver growth demonstrates a clear, positive impact of caregiving, including improvements in problem-solving abilities, increased self-understanding, and a growing sense of competence.

Joy-Del T. Snook

See also Empowerment in Families; Family Values; Hospice; Kinship Care; Respect; Support Groups

Further Readings

Administration on Aging. (2010). *Diversity*. Retrieved from http://www.aoa.acl.gov/AoA_Programs/Tools_Resources/diversity.aspx

Kemp B. J., & Mosqueda L. (Eds.). (2004). *Aging with a disability: What the clinician needs to know.* Baltimore, MD: Johns Hopkins University Press.

Lansing, A. I. (1951). Some physiological aspects of ageing. *Physiological Reviews, 3,* 274–284.

Lehman, D. (2009). 21st century caregivers: Diversity in culture. *Aging Well, 2,* 26.

McCann, J. J., Hebert, L. E., Beckett, L. A., Morris, M. C., Scherr, P. A., & Evans, D. A. (2000). Comparison of informal caregiving by Black and White older adults in a community population. *Journal of the American Geriatrics Society, 48,* 1612–1617.

Roberto, K. A., & Jarrott, S. E. (2008). Family caregivers of older adults: A life span perspective. *Family Relations, 57,* 100–111.

Services and Advocacy for GLBT Elders. (2014). *Out and visible: The experiences and attitudes of lesbian, gay, bisexual and transgender (LGBT) older adults, ages, 45*–*75*. Retrieved from http://www.sageusa.org/resources/publications.cfm

Silverstein, M., Gans, D., & Yang, F. M. (2006). Intergenerational support to aging parents: The role of norms and needs. *Journal of Family Issues, 27,* 1068–1084.

ALCOHOL AND SUBSTANCE ABUSE

An estimated 24.6 million people in the United States, according to the Substance Abuse and Mental Health Services Administration (SAMHSA), struggle with substance abuse–related problems. Substance abuse may include alcohol, illegal drugs, or prescription medications. Those affected belong to families whose other members may also be affected directly or indirectly; substance abuse may change the nature of the family relationship permanently. Because substance abuse is so prevalent, it is important that family counselors are able to assess families for substance abuse and related issues, are aware of the specific dynamics that arise when working with families with substance abuse issues, and can assess the family's readiness for change. Family counselors play an important role in treating substance abuse because treatment may help families as a whole and may also help individuals seeking help to understand their addiction from a family systems perspective. The focus of counseling sessions should be on relationships, family patterns, the safety of small children, and understanding the level of individuals' motivation for change. Individual level of change is a key predictor in how successful the family counselor will be in assisting the family with treatment. This entry discusses the importance of identifying and understanding family dynamics related to substance abuse: family assessment in determining readiness for change within the system, which includes determining the difference between substance abuse and substance dependence; family dynamics and patterns that may hinder productivity; and the effect that substance abuse has on relationships (couple or parent–child relationships).

Family Assessment

Family assessment is performed for several reasons, such as determining the level of safety for all members, especially minor children. Performing such an assessment is useful in determining whether further action will need to be taken, such as removing children from a volatile or dangerous situation. In addition, a family assessment may provide family counselors with needed information regarding the severity of substance abuse or use, the type of treatment that may be utilized, and the family's level of willingness to commit to treatment.

Among the various assessment tools used to assess families, one of the simplest is to engage the family in an intake interview. The intake interview should ask family members various questions regarding the following: their current living situation, financial status, prior treatment, homicidal or suicidal ideation, motivation for seeking treatment, family history of interpersonal (physical, emotional) abuse, history of substance abuse, prior attempts to seek treatment, and mental health history. The assessment interview may be completed in several sessions, including at least one with the entire family as well as sessions with individual members if the counselor senses that certain family members are not being allotted the opportunity to participate or if the counselor thinks that an individual is at risk of harming self or others. This allows each family member to have the opportunity to express his or her needs and desires for the family and the ability to speak freely. The family assessment should be completed at the beginning of service and should be repeated at a later date once treatment has begun so that family counselors can assess whether the treatment plan will need to be adjusted. The family assessment may also include the family counselor's helping the family to identify goals that will address core family problems, such as communication.

Stages of Change

During the family assessment, it is important to determine the family's readiness for change. One way of assessing readiness for change is by assessing the family with Prochaska and DiClemente's Stages of Change (*precontemplation, contemplation, preparation, action,* and *maintenance*). During the precontemplation stage, individuals are defensive and may only consider treatment because friends and family members have pressured them into doing so. The contemplation stage develops when individuals begin to consider treatment for their substance use but are not fully committed to treatment. When individuals have made the decision to seek treatment, they are considered to be in the preparation stage; they have decided to commit and prepare for treatment. During the action stage, individuals have affirmed their decision to change and have implemented behavior change to match their decision. Lastly, during the maintenance stage, the individual works hard to maintain the aforementioned changes and implements proactive planning to sustain sobriety long term.

Illegal Drug Use Reporting

During the family assessment, family counselors have to be aware of reportable offenses such as illegal drug use (visible) when there are children in the home as well as abuse and neglect issues concerning children and elderly people. Each family counselor should research the reporting laws of his or her respective state in which they practice. These issues are important because they will affect whether or not the family will be available for treatment; if a report has to be filed with child protective services or adult protective services, then counseling may be delayed. Some families may not have current drug use problems but may suffer from previous drug abuse. It is important that family counselors are able to distinguish between current and past drug abuse behaviors.

Substance Abuse and Dependence

When family counselors assess families, they have to make a distinction between substance abuse and substance dependence. The fifth edition of the *Diagnostic and Statistical Manual of Mental Disorders* (DSM-5; American Psychiatric Association [APA]) combines substance abuse and dependence as being on a continuum from mild to severe. Dependence may include the inability to stop use accompanied by physical symptoms when use stops or decreases, whereas substance abuse is overuse of substances in a negligent manner. It is important for family counselors to know the difference because the level of abuse will dictate the type and length of treatment for the family. An individual who is dependent on a drug may not be coherent enough to withstand treatment. As such, individuals who abuse drugs may not be as resistant as someone who is dependent; therefore, treatment may be longer in duration because they are not in full dependence. Those individuals who are dependent upon a drug may first have to receive medical assistance before committing to family treatment.

Family Dynamics and Patterns

Families who suffer from addiction and or abuse may exhibit certain patterns of family dysfunction, such as poor communication, detachment, and avoidance. Individuals who suffer from substance abuse may not communicate directly with family members because of the family's focus on their substance use. One of the reasons that drug use becomes a problem is that it comes to be viewed as more important than family, friends, and work responsibilities. Family counselors should be able to identify maladaptive family patterns, being mindful that family members will sustain negative communication and behavioral patterns in order to maintain the family's normal processes or homeostasis. Although the patterns are maladaptive, family members are accustomed to such behaviors and will find it difficult to move beyond those patterns.

Another maladaptive family pattern is detachment, which is when family members decide that they no longer want to participate emotionally with family members who engage in drug use. This act of detachment may include not talking to family members, viewing the addicted individual as nondependable and reckless, and looking to others outside of the family to meet emotional needs. Avoidance, similar to detachment, occurs when family members withdraw and avoid contact with the substance-abusing family member. Avoidance is usually accompanied by anger and frustration.

Effects on Relationships

Many relationships are changed by the course of substance abuse and addiction. Some of the core relationships that may be affected are most notably the couple relationship (parents), the parent–child relationship, and the sibling relationship. Quite often, family members will separate themselves into what Murray Bowen referred to as triangles. *Triangling* occurs when two individuals having a conflict bring a third party into the conflict in order for the third member to side with one of the original members of the conflict and lend support. With addicted families, triangling is a common occurrence.

Couples within an addicted family may experience relationship strain that manifests in lack of trust, poor communication, and financial distress. When one member of the spousal dyad is suffering from addiction, he or she may or may not be able to maintain employment. If they have maintained employment, a large portion of the family's money may be used to support and maintain the addiction. Financial stress can add to family conflict and affect engagement in treatment.

If one or both parents are addicted, then parental responsibilities may suffer, leaving children neglected and possibly abused. Children within this situation often become the *parentified child,* or a child that has a leadership or caretaker role because the parents are unable or unwilling to fulfill parental duties. These types of children may cook their own meals, wake themselves up for school, and become the caregiver of younger siblings. When children are placed in the role of parent, they develop faster and experience resentment toward their parents for relinquishing their duties. This resentment may last into adulthood.

Some children may see the lack of parenting as an opportunity to act out (misbehave) and may exhibit some or all of the negative behaviors modeled by addicted parents. Many may begin to abuse substances, not attend school, and commit crimes. Without intervention, these children are susceptible to repeating the same path of substance abuse that their parents exhibited.

The sibling relationship may also be affected by the family addiction. Siblings will have to band together for survival, taking care of one another and at times forming coalitions against the parents. Children will often exhibit anger, feel torn between family members, work diligently to bring peace to the family, and they may think that they are at fault for the family's dysfunction. All of these responsibilities and roles may cause confusion, resentment, shame, and anger amongst children. Family counselors may consider providing children with individual treatment along with family treatment to address all pertinent issues.

Mayi Dixon

See also Adlerian Family Therapy; Communication in Couples and Families; Family Assessment, Models of

Further Readings

Connors, G. J., DiClemente, C. C., Velasquez, M. M., & Donovan, D. M. (2013). *Substance abuse treatment and the stages of change selecting and planning interventions.* New York, NY: Guilford Press.

Perkinson, R. R., & Jongsma, A. E. (2014). *The addiction treatment planner.* Hoboken, NJ: Wiley.

Treadway, D. C. (1989). *Before it's too late. Working with substance abuse in the family.* New York, NY: W. W. Norton.

AMERICAN ASSOCIATION FOR MARRIAGE AND FAMILY THERAPY

The American Association for Marriage and Family Therapy (AAMFT) is the professional organization for the field of marriage and family therapy. Founded for the purpose of providing training, resources, and research to practitioners and the community, AAMFT has maintained a focus on high standards of practice since its inception in 1942. AAMFT serves the profession of marriage and family therapy through professional development opportunities, promotion of ethical practices, and standardization of training requirements. Affiliation with AAMFT signifies a commitment to the high standards of practice expected in the field of marriage and family therapy and can be demonstrated through official membership in the association. AAMFT has been important to the field of marital, couple, and family therapy through its credentialing of therapists and supervisors; its contributions to the field of marital, couple, and family therapy; its code of ethics; and its association with accrediting training programs.

Membership

The AAMFT offers six membership options for individuals interested in joining the association. The first membership option is the *clinical fellow member*, intended for independently licensed marriage and family therapists (MFTs). The second type of membership is the *preclinical fellow* for graduates working toward independent licensure. The third type of membership, simply titled *member*, is designated for clinicians licensed in a mental health field other than marriage and family therapy. The fourth type of membership, the *associate member*, is for those completing their clinical hours toward independent licensure in a mental health field other than marriage and family therapy. The fifth membership option, the *student member*, is for students enrolled in a graduate-level marriage and family therapy program or other accepted mental-health graduate training program. The sixth, and final, AAMFT membership option is the *affiliate member*. Any individual interested in the field of marriage and family therapy who is not currently enrolled in a graduate program, not independently licensed, and not currently working toward licensure in an accepted mental health field is eligible to apply for affiliate membership. To date, there are over 50,000 members of AAMFT spanning from across the United States, Canada, and abroad. Membership in AAMFT comes with many benefits; AAMFT is recognized for the support given to its members and the contributions made to the field of marriage and family therapy. Both at the member level and the professional level, AAMFT upholds high standards of excellence, which are endorsed through the provision of professional resources and support, the establishment of an ethical code of conduct, and the standardization of marriage and family therapy training requirements.

Professional Resources and Benefits

The AAMFT provides professional resources and support to its members through several means. One resource provided by AAMFT is member access to scholarly publications. Scholarly publications provide current marriage and family therapy–related research findings, which support members' continued professional development. In particular, one notable publication provided through AAMFT membership is the *Journal of Marital and Family Therapy*. Access to this journal is a significant benefit members of AAMFT receive, as the *Journal of Marital and Family Therapy* is a peer-reviewed, highly regarded resource utilized across all the mental health disciplines. In addition to the *Journal of Marital and Family Therapy*, AAMFT members are also provided professional resources such as web-based information outlets, an online job connection area, and professional trainings. Professional trainings are offered through multiple platforms including continuing education courses, annual conferences, supervision trainings, and web-based seminars, all of which contribute to the AAMFT goal of developing highly trained practitioners who provide quality services to the clients they serve.

A second benefit of AAMFT membership, beyond access to professional resources, is the provision of professional support, which is offered through several avenues. One avenue of support is through peer consultation. To participate in peer consultation, members register for an open online forum in which participants share concerns, ideas, and findings related to their clinical work. The purpose of peer consultation is for AAMFT members to collaborate in sharing knowledge and ideas to support one another's clinical practice. A second avenue for professional support is through the AAMFT legal consultation team. The legal team consists of AAMFT attorneys qualified to provide legal advice and guidance about members' clinical practices. The third avenue for professional support is the AAMFT ethical advisory team. Consultation with the ethical advisory team is free of charge to AAMFT members for the purpose of supporting members in making ethically sound decisions. The advisory team is highly versed in the field's ethical codes of conduct and they work to ensure that high standards of ethical behavior are followed.

Additional Professional Contributions

Through the provision of professional resources and support, AAMFT demonstrates its commitment to upholding the expectation for high standards of practice for its members. The upholding of standards has also been demonstrated by AAMFT through additional professional contributions. One such contribution is the development of the AAMFT *Code of Ethics*, by which all AAMFT members are bound. This professional code of ethics consists of nine standards related to (1) responsibility to clients, (2) confidentiality, (3) professional competence and integrity, (4) responsibility to students and supervisees, (5) research and publication, (6) technology-assisted professional services, (7) professional evaluations, (8) financial arrangements, and (9) advertising. AAMFT has also contributed to the upholding of high standards of practice through the creation of a programmatic accrediting body that aids in the standardization of marriage and family therapy training curriculum.

The AAMFT is the parent organization for the Commission on Accreditation for Marriage and Family Therapy Education (COAMFTE), which is the accrediting agency for educational training programs in the field of marriage and family therapy. The Council for Higher Education Accreditation (CHEA), an organization that oversees the legitimacy and quality of accrediting bodies, recognizes COAMFTE as a valid accrediting agency. Programs accredited by COAMFTE have been recognized to use best practices in their teaching and training and meet accreditation standards in the required areas of (a) outcome-based education, (b) commitment to diversity and inclusion, (c) infrastructure and environmental supports, (d) curriculum, and (e) program effectiveness and improvement. COAMFTE accreditation offers the public, prospective students, and future employers assurance that graduates from accredited programs are well prepared to work in the field of marriage and family therapy. The establishment of COAMFTE accreditation exemplifies the AAMFT commitment to high standards of excellence in the field of marriage and family therapy. Through their regulation of training standards, establishment of a professional code of ethics, and provision of professional resources, the AAMFT fulfills its purpose of promoting high standards of practice in the field of marriage and family therapy.

Jennifer A. Boender

See also Core Competencies for Marriage and Family Therapists; Council for Accreditation of Counseling and Related Educational Programs; Licensure and Certification

Further Readings

American Association for Marriage and Family Therapy: http://www.aamft.org

American Association for Marriage and Family Therapy. (2014). *Accreditation resources*. Retrieved from https://www.aamft.org/iMIS15/AAMFT/Content/COAMFTE/Accreditation_Resources.aspx

American Association for Marriage and Family Therapy. (2015). *Code of ethics*. Retrieved from http://www.aamft.org/imis15/Documents/Legal%20Ethics/AAMFT-code-of-ethics.pdf

ANGER MANAGEMENT

Anger is a normal human emotion that is experienced across the life span, functioning on a continuum from mild irritation to intense fury and rage. Anger is a natural response to those situations where individuals feel threatened, believe harm will come to them, or believe that another person has unnecessarily wronged them. Individuals may also become angry when they feel another person, such as a child or other family member, is being threatened or harmed. In addition, anger may result from frustration when needs, desires, and goals are not being met. When individuals become angry, they may lose patience and act impulsively, aggressively, or violently. This entry provides an overview of anger and responses to anger, its effect on relationships, anger management therapy models, and complications.

How anger is managed may have a variety of outcomes both positive and negative, particularly impacting work, intimate relationships, and overall quality of life. Anger is an emotion that also has physical effects on the body and triggers an increase in heart rate, blood pressure, and levels of adrenaline and noradrenaline. Anger can range in intensity from mild irritation to extreme rage. Anger has many survival benefits—specifically it is part of our *fight or flight* brain response to a perceived threat or harm. Anger commonly becomes the predominant feeling and takes over our behavior, cognition, and physiology when confronted with a perceived threat. In many cases, humans and other animals express anger by making loud sounds, baring teeth, staring, and adopting aggressive postures meant to warn perceived aggressors to stop their threatening behaviors. These types of behaviors often occur prior to any types of physical attack and may serve as a warning of imminent physical aggression. Anger instinctively surges to protect territory, offspring, and family members; prevent loss of possessions or food; and ward off many other perceived threats. Most experts agree that anger is one of the most basic human emotions and has primitive, instinctual roots. It is a primary, natural emotion with functional survival value, which all humans experience from time to time. The raised heart rate, blood pressure, and release of hormones prepare us physically for action against perceived threats—which is either fight or flight.

A less primitive form of anger, called "underlying anger," is typically caused by a perceived loss of control over factors affecting important values. The values may be related to—for example—pride, love, money, or justice, which can motivate an individual to stand up for what they believe is right. Conversely, anger can cause irreparable damage to relationships, physical health, mental health, and overall quality of life.

Common factors that cause individuals to become angry include grief, sexual frustration, rudeness, tiredness, hunger, pain, withdrawal from prescription medications, physical illness, mental illness, alcohol abuse, illicit drug abuse, injustice, humiliation, embarrassment, deadlines, traffic jams, disappointment, sloppy service, failure, infidelity, burglary, and financial problems as well as being teased or bullied or being told one has a serious illness.

Anger in Relationships

Anger as a defensive reaction to fear is a natural reaction, but anger that leads to emotional outbursts, blowups, fury, and rage is often destructive in a relationship.

The mismanagement of anger is a major cause of conflict in personal and professional relationships. Although anger is a universal emotion, uncontrolled anger can be dangerous. Anger that leads to behaviors involving breaking or hitting things, name-calling, intimidation, threat of violence, or physical aggression are signs of uncontrolled anger.

Individuals with uncontrolled anger often have anger reactions that are more frequent, intense, and enduring. They also tend to report more physical aggression, negative verbal responses, drug use, and negative consequences of their anger. In general, their anger negatively affects their relationships, their health, and their jobs.

Anger expressed inappropriately has several payoffs within relationships, including the ability to manipulate and control others through aggressive and intimidating behavior. Others may comply with the angry individual's demands due to fear of verbal threats or violence. Another payoff is the release of tension that an individual experiences when they lose their temper and act aggressively. The individual feels better after that release but may cause significant damage to those around them who experienced the outburst.

On the contrary, anger can also galvanize individuals into action, motivating them to seek change within themselves and their environment. Social and societal change is often brought about by anger over injustices within society. Anger related to interpersonal challenges can also motivate internal change and, therefore, improve interpersonal relationships.

Anger Management Therapy Models

The most common and widely accepted anger management therapy model is cognitive-behavioral therapy (CBT), blending the therapeutic approaches of Albert Ellis and Aaron T. Beck and focusing primarily on behavior modification and cognitive therapy. Many CBT-based workbooks have been developed for anger management, walking the therapist and client through identifying environmental and cognitive cues of anger, acquisition of emotional self-regulation skills as well as behavioral interventions, and rehearsal of skills in anger-provoking situations. A meta-analysis on the effectiveness of CBT anger management interventions found that persons receiving CBT treatment were 76% more successful in anger reduction versus untreated persons (Beck & Fernandez, 1988). CBT is a versatile model and can be used in individual, couple, family, and group therapy sessions. Although CBT has been heavily studied over the years, its research outcomes have been called into question due to study results not being able to be reproduced (Tolin, 2010). CBT therapists argue that conducting double-blind research studies for psychotherapeutic approaches are virtually impossible and therefore study results are difficult to reproduce making this claim an irrelevant argument.

A second, more directed anger management model is rational emotive behavior therapy (REBT). Developed by Albert Ellis in the 1950s, REBT is a form of CBT based on the premise that the beliefs people hold about an event taking place are what upset them and cause them to become enraged, depressed, anxious, and so on—not the event itself. Therefore, REBT focuses on the ABC model of cognitive-behavioral analysis where A is the activating event, B is a person's beliefs about the activating event, and C is the emotional and behavioral responses to his or her beliefs. REBT therapy involves disputing irrational beliefs and converting them to more rational beliefs, managing behavioral consequences of beliefs, and developing an acceptance of reality. Research done by Daniel David suggests a specific pattern of irrational beliefs around anger such as low frustration tolerance and demandingness that can be initial areas of focus for therapists using REBT. As one of the more heavily researched models, REBT has overwhelmingly positive therapeutic outcomes (David et al., 2005). REBT can also be used with an individual, couple, family, and group counseling sessions. A major criticism of REBT is that it is too rational and doesn't deal sufficiently with emotions. Therapists using REBT regularly refute this critique by emphasizing that REBT focused on the interrelationship between thinking, feeling, and behaving and therefore dealing sufficiently with emotions through the feeling component of the model. Additionally, REBT has come under fire for its perceived confrontational style as demonstrated by its founder, Albert Ellis, who used humor and had a confrontational interpersonal style in therapy sessions. Adherents, however, have pointed out that a confrontational style is not itself a necessary element of REBT.

Emotionally focused therapy (EFT), developed by Leslie Greenberg and Sue Johnson in the 1980s, has also been utilized as an evidence-based model of assisting clients, couples, and families manage anger and other emotions. EFT combines experiential and systemic perspectives as well as attachment style that focus on the client's present experience, how that experience is processed, and how it affects the client's partner or other family members' behavior and response to the client. EFT is a relatively short but emotionally intense therapy conducted over the course of 8 to 20 sessions typically. The therapist walks the client, couple, or family through a series of therapeutic tasks or steps that are designed to identify and acknowledge emotions; regulate and reflect emotions; and finally, transform emotional experience through a more attuned relationship with others. EFT has been heavily studied as well and has consistently strong support of positive treatment outcomes. It is typically used in individual, couple, or family therapy sessions. EFT has been criticized for its humanistic underpinnings by some Christian counselors who feel its worldview is in contrast with a Christian worldview; however, others have translated EFT into the Christian psychology context to bridge the theoretical gap.

Alternative anger management interventions with positive outcomes but less empirical data to support effectiveness include yoga, mind-focused psychoanalysis, and reiki.

Anger Management and Complications

Anger management is the process of learning the skills to recognize when one is becoming angry and to implement strategies to deal with anger in a positive manner. It teaches an individual early recognition of frustrations and how to settle those frustrations in a way that expresses the needs of the individual while allowing them to remaining calm and controlled. Common anger management strategies include relaxation techniques, cognitive therapy, and skill development. Relaxation techniques may include progressive relaxation, visualization exercises, breathing techniques, and mindfulness-based interventions. Cognitive therapy explores negative thought patterns and challenges the individual to recognize and change those patterns in order to change unwanted behaviors. Skill development may include the following: using trigger identification, responding in a nonaggressive way to triggers, learning and utilizing specific skills to manage anger triggers, identifying and refuting of irrational thoughts, using de-escalation during surging anger, and utilizing assertive communication skills.

Anger management is complicated by alcohol or drug use, physical illness, and mental illness. Researchers agree that violent outbursts are often fueled by drugs and alcohol. Alcohol in particular alters an individual's brain chemistry and increases aggressiveness, which is a leading cause of domestic violence incidents. Physical and mental illness may also increase impulsivity related to anger responses and lead to increased incidence of physical aggression. Specifically, posttraumatic stress disorder (PTSD) and traumatic brain injury (TBI) may account for increased impulsive anger responses that can complicate typical therapeutic interventions due to neurobiological functions being impaired.

Many community agencies offer anger management classes, typically structured around the use of a workbook in a group setting over a period of several consecutive weeks. Anger management counseling may also be done within the context of individual, couple, or family counseling.

Adrianne Trogden

See also Affect Regulation; Conflict Resolution; Conflict Styles; Domestic Violence; Power Issues in Couples; Stress Management

Further Readings

Beck, R., & Fernandez, E. (1998). Cognitive behavioral therapy in the treatment of anger. A meta-analysis. *Cognitive Therapy and Research*, 22(1), 63–74.

David, D., Szentagotai, A., Eva, K., & Macavei, B. (2005). A synopsis of rational emotive behavior therapy (REBT); fundamental and applied research. *Journal of Rational-Emotive & Cognitive-Behavior Therapy*, 23(3), 175–221.

Deffenbacher, J. L. (in press). Psychosocial interventions: Anger disorders. In E. F. Coccaro (Ed.), *Aggression: Assessment and treatment.* New York, NY: Marcel Dekker.

DiGiuseppe, R., & Tafrate, R. C. (2003). Anger treatment for adults: A meta-analytic view. *Clinical Psychology: Science and Practice*, 10(1).

Enright, R. D. (2001). *Forgiveness is a choice: A step-by-step process for resolving anger and restoring hope.* Washington, DC: American Psychological Association.

Johnson, S. M., & Greenberg, L. S. (1987). Emotionally focused marital therapy: An overview. *Psychotherapy: Theory, Research, Practice, Training, 24*(3S), 552–560.

Kassinove, H., & Tafrate, R. C. (2002). *Anger management: The complete treatment guidebook for practitioners.* Atascadero, CA: Impact.

Tolin, D. F. (2010). Is cognitive-behavioral therapy more effective than other therapies? A meta-analytic review. *Clinical Psychology Review, 30*(6), 710–720.

ANXIETY

Anxiety can be described as a basic human emotion that involves nervousness, worry, or fear of uncertainty toward a real or perceived event. It can be viewed on a continuum from being mild to severe. If severe enough, anxiety can also develop into a diagnosable mental health disorder if it begins to affect a person's day-to-day functioning. This entry reviews the concept of anxiety, including symptoms, causes and risk factors, types of anxiety disorders, and treatment. The first section will explain the difference between regular anxiety and anxiety disorders.

Anxiety Versus Anxiety Disorder

Feelings of anxiety are often experienced in response to a specific stressor. Examples may include taking a test, traveling by airplane, or speaking publicly. A mild level of anxiety may cause a person to be more motivated and focused on the event or activity. A person experiencing this basic level of anxiety only feels minor distress for a brief period of time. A severe level of anxiety can result in a lack of focus or concentration and/or physical symptoms. It is when anxiety impairs functioning that it can be considered an anxiety disorder. It involves excessive worrying that extends for a long period of time and can affect school, work, and/or relationships. An anxiety disorder can involve a single symptom or multiple symptoms and can be extremely uncomfortable for the person experiencing it.

Symptoms of Anxiety

Anxiety can manifest itself in a variety of ways, including physical and emotional symptoms. Common physical symptoms may include sweating, nausea, stomach cramps, shortness of breath, muscle tension, headaches, rapid heart rate, dizziness, hyperventilation, and/or insomnia. Emotional symptoms can include a lack of ability to focus, catastrophic thinking, fear of losing control, intense and sudden feelings of panic, and/or restlessness. Symptoms vary from individual to individual, and those mentioned here are not all-inclusive. Most people who suffer from anxiety experience a combination of both physical and emotional symptoms, but it is possible to experience one and not the other.

Causes and Risk Factors of Anxiety

Although it is still unknown why certain people are more prone than others to anxiety and anxiety disorders, it is generally recognized that anxiety can be caused by a variety of factors in one's life. These factors can include genetics, medical conditions or medications, the environment, and brain chemicals. Some research has shown that there is a clear genetic component to the development of anxiety and more specifically to an anxiety disorder. People with a relative who has an anxiety disorder are more likely to develop an anxiety disorder as well. Medical conditions that can be associated with anxiety include irritable bowel syndrome, diabetes, heart conditions, and asthma, among others. Anxiety can also be one of many side effects of certain medications. Environmental factors can also play a part in the development of anxiety. These factors can include experiencing stress in close relationships or related to financial concerns. It can also include stress related to school or work or experiencing a traumatic event. Lastly, people diagnosed with an anxiety disorder can have varying abnormal levels of certain neurotransmitters in their brain. These abnormal levels can cause a person to react inappropriately in certain situations.

In addition to these causes, there are several additional risk factors that are related to the development of anxiety. A person's gender is one factor; research has shown that women are more likely to develop anxiety disorders than men. It is also believed that certain personality types (so-called Type A personalities) are more apt to develop anxiety. In addition, those who have other diagnosable mental health disorders and/or who use and abuse substances are more likely also to suffer from anxiety.

Types of Anxiety Disorders

According to the fifth edition of the *Diagnostic and Statistical Manual of Mental Disorders* (DSM-5; American Psychiatric Association [APA]), there are seven main types of anxiety disorders. Each disorder is briefly described next.

Separation Anxiety Disorder. This disorder involves intense worry and distress experienced by a person who is separated from a parent, guardian, or primary caregiver. It is typically experienced in young children but can also be experienced by adolescents and adults. Separation anxiety disorder can include refusal to go to school or other places, unwillingness to be alone, and/or repeated nightmares.

Selective Mutism. This disorder is mostly experienced by children and is characterized by the inability to speak or communicate in uncomfortable settings (e.g., school) despite being able to physically talk. The person may only talk to certain people, may only whisper, or could be entirely mute.

Specific Phobia. Specific phobias include irrational fears of common objects, events, or places. Examples of specific phobias include a fear of heights, thunder, driving, flying, spiders, germs, or seeing blood. People who are suffering from a specific phobia do realize that the fear is irrational but can experience anxiety through mere thoughts as well as experiences. These phobias can also cause the person to intentionally avoid the specific object, event, or place.

Social Anxiety Disorder. A person with this disorder experiences unreasonable fears of, and avoidance of, social situations. This avoidance may include all social situations or specific situations, such as having to speak to strangers. This disorder usually involves an excessive worry over other people judging, watching, or criticizing the person with the disorder. Social anxiety disorder can make it difficult for people with this disorder to develop and maintain relationships.

Panic Disorder. This disorder includes abrupt and repeated attacks of distress and fear. These attacks are called panic attacks and can resemble having a heart attack. Panic attacks often include varying somatic symptoms, such as a racing heart, nausea, sweating, trembling, stomach cramps, and more. There is also a sense of a loss of control for someone experiencing an attack. Panic attacks can occur randomly and many times those suffering from panic disorder worry about the possibility of having another panic attack.

Agoraphobia. This disorder involves a person avoiding certain places or situations that may cause them to have symptoms of panic and of feeling trapped. These can include using public transportation, being in open or enclosed spaces, being involved in a crowd, or being alone. The person fears an inability to leave the situation or to get help. This disorder is very closely related to panic disorder since there is a concern of experiencing panic-like symptoms or full panic attacks.

Generalized Anxiety Disorder. Generalized anxiety disorder, also known as GAD, involves chronic, extreme worry that affects a person's day-to-day experiences. Anxiety may be experienced by the person just thinking about getting through their normal day. In fact, with GAD it can be difficult to identify the actual source of the anxiety. This disorder is different from the others in that a person suffering with this does not typically avoid certain situations or places, but it still can be incapacitating, causing the person to be unproductive.

Treatment of Anxiety

Medication

Although medication cannot cure anxiety, it can help treat the symptoms. It does not treat the core issues of the anxiety problems. The four main types of medications used in the treatment of anxiety are listed next, including the names of some specific drugs in each category, with representative brand-name drugs in parentheses:

Selective serotonin reuptake inhibitors (SSRIs): fluoxetine (Prozac), sertraline (Zoloft), paroxetine (Paxil), citalopram (Celexa)

Serotonin–norepinephrine reuptake inhibitors (SNRIs): venlafaxine (Effexor), duloxetine (Cymbalta)

Benzodiazepines: alprazolam (Xanax), clonazapam (Klonopin), diazepam (Valium), lorazepam (Ativan)

Tricyclic antidepressants: nortriptyline (Pamelor), amitriptyline (Elavil), imipramine (Tofranil)

Concerns with the use of medication are the significant, sometimes hazardous, side effects that can be experienced. These side effects can include nervousness, weight gain, stomach problems, confusion, dizziness, headaches, and sleepiness. Also, certain types of medications can potentially be addictive. Medication is typically recommended to be used in conjunction with therapy.

Psychotherapy and Complementary Treatments

Cognitive-behavioral therapy (CBT) is a therapeutic approach most commonly used in the treatment of anxiety. As the title of this therapy states, this therapy pulls from both the cognitive and behavior schools of thought. This type of therapy believes that our thoughts have an impact on our feelings. It is a person's perception that influences their view of a situation, not the situation itself. Therapy involves working through the distorted thoughts by first identifying the negative thoughts, then challenging these thoughts, and finally replacing these negative thoughts with more accurate choices.

Systematic desensitization is also used in the treatment of anxiety. It is a method of overcoming one's fears that can contribute to anxiety. This process involves gradually exposing a person to the feared object or situation. Once they have identified the anxiety-producing stimulus, the person is taught ways to relax and cope within that situation. Once they are comfortable with the skills they have developed, the person is then gradually, progressively exposed to the stimulus through a developed hierarchy of fear. They use the skills they have learned to overcome their fear one step at a time.

A variety of complementary treatments have been shown to be of value in helping persons suffering from anxiety. Regular exercise is one of these treatments, as it is known to help reduce stress when properly performed. (Note: Before embarking on *any* program of exercise, it is imperative to obtain and follow the advice of one's primary health care provider.) Numerous studies have concluded that the regular practice of yoga, under qualified supervision, can be beneficial for reducing anxious symptoms. Relaxation exercises can also be beneficial for relief of anxiety. These can include progressive muscle relaxation, mindfulness, and visualization. Lastly, hypnosis, administered by a qualified specialist, can be used in conjunction with CBT to assist in looking at situations differently and in a more positive manner.

Kristen L. B. Moran

See also Childhood Anxiety; DSM and V-Codes; Life Transitions; Mindfulness

Further Readings

American Psychiatric Association. (2013). *Diagnostic and statistical manual of mental disorders* (5th ed.). Washington, DC: Author.

Bourne, E. J. (2011). *The anxiety and phobia workbook* (5th ed.). Oakland, CA: New Harbinger Publications.

Drake, K. L., & Ginsburg, G. S. (2012). Family factors in the development, treatment, and prevention of childhood anxiety disorders. *Clinical Child and Family Psychology Review, 15*(2), 144–162.

Hofman, S. G., Sawyer, A. T., Witt, A. A., & Oh, D. (2010). The effect of mindfulness-based therapy on anxiety and depression: A meta-analytic review. *Journal of Consulting and Clinical Psychology, 78*(2), 169–183.

McLean, C. P., Asnaani, A., Litz, B. T., & Hoffman, S. G. (2011). Gender differences in anxiety disorders: Prevalence, course of illness, comorbidity and burden of illness. *Journal of Psychiatric Illness, 45,* 1027–1035.

Priest, J. B. (2013). Emotionally focused therapy as treatment for couples with generalized anxiety disorder and relationship distress. *Journal of Couple and Relationship Therapy, 12,* 22–37.

Zaider, T. I., Heimberg, R. G., & Iida, M. (2010). Anxiety disorders and intimate relationships: A study of daily processes in couples. *Journal of Abnormal Psychology, 119,* 163–173.

Anxiety Disorders in Adolescents

Social anxiety disorder, panic disorder, and specific phobia are anxiety disorders frequently diagnosed in adolescents and are found in the category that addresses disorders where anxiety is the primary symptom. This entry examines symptoms and treatment of various anxiety disorders and explains the impact of anxiety on adolescents, their families, and friends.

Anxiety and fear are ubiquitous across cultures and essential to human adaptation and survival. Some anxiety is necessary and normal; however, when anxiety is excessive, it leads to dysfunctional behavior, and adolescents may continue to feel anxious even when there is no apparent reason or trigger. Response to a distressing event can result in fight-or-flight reactions and accompanying physical symptoms such as cardiac irregularities and breathing problems. Understanding the neurobiological basis of fear and anxiety helps to differentiate developmentally appropriate reactions from responses that show clinically significant anxiety with severe physical symptoms, panic attacks, and phobias. The two primary symptoms for anxiety-related disorders are persistent excessive fear and resultant intense worry, with the perceived degree of fear disproportionate to the actual danger. This anxiety is accompanied by physical and cognitive symptoms that cause functional impairment or serious disruption to the adolescent's life.

Panic attacks often accompany anxiety disorders with two criteria. First, a panic attack is a sudden unanticipated experience of intense fear accompanied by at least four of the following symptoms: shortness of breath, palpitations, chest pain, dizziness or light-headedness, trembling, sweating, heat or chills, choking, tingling or numbing feelings, nausea, depersonalization or feeling crazy, and fear of dying or losing control. Second, one or more attacks are followed with at least 1 month of persistent anxiety about subsequent attacks and/or serious maladaptive behavioral change to avoid attacks.

Panic Disorder

Panic disorder is a chronic condition in adolescents and adults, often coexisting with several anxiety and other disorders, but it is not the result of substance use, medical condition, or other mental disorder. Panic disorder is characterized by repeated uncued (unexpected) panic attacks accompanied by persistent worrying and dread about subsequent attacks, with a duration of 1 month or more. Although panic attacks have occurred in children as young as 12 years old, onset is most common between 22 and 24 years of age. The prevalence of panic disorder is twice as high in females. Adolescents often appear less concerned than adults about panic attacks and are often unwilling to disclose the attacks.

Because suicide is the third leading cause of death in adolescents, the association of panic disorder with higher rates of suicide ideation and suicide attempts is a serious psychiatric concern.

Specific Phobia

Specific phobia is diagnosed when intense, excessive fear or avoidance is irrational and disproportionate to the real risk of the phobic stimulus.

Panic attacks can be random and unexpected or expected in response to a feared situation or object. Adolescents who experience panic attacks have a greater fear response when closer to the specific stimulus and use active avoidance to prevent contact with the phobic stimulus.

According to the fifth edition of the *Diagnostic and Statistical Manual of Mental Disorders* (DSM-5; American Psychiatric Association [APA]), sympathetic nervous system arousal is common with specific objects or feared situations such as animals (snakes, insects, dogs, spiders), the natural environment (thunderstorms, bodies of water, high places), blood injection injury (drawing blood, seeing blood or needles, receiving an injection or an intravenous line, undergoing certain medical procedures), situational diagnosis (elevators, jets, enclosed spaces), or other diagnosis (costumed clowns or other figures, loud noises, situations with nausea or choking). Adolescents with blood-injection-injury phobias have a vasovagal response with fainting or near fainting, equally prevalent in females and males. Adolescents and adults specified with blood-injection-injury phobia rarely seek medical assistance even with a medical problem.

Duration is 6 months or more, often extending for several years with prevalence higher in adolescents (16%) than in children (5%) and twice as likely in females than males. Specific phobias typically develop between 7 and 11 with a mean age of 10. Multiple fears are typical, and each diagnosis is coded separately. Those diagnosed with specific phobias that coexist with other disorders are 60% more likely to attempt suicide.

Social Anxiety Disorder

The central focus of social anxiety (social phobia) is intense fear of social situations where adolescents worry they will be judged by others and humiliated if they make a mistake in public. Social anxiety disorder can be specific (with one event) or general (with many events or situations).

An adolescent fearing embarrassment and classmates' laughter for mispronouncing a word or appearing awkward will often stay home from school to avoid an oral presentation. Adolescents with social anxiety disorder avoid public situations where they may become nervous about making mistakes or those that require interaction with unfamiliar or insensitive students (e.g., eating in the cafeteria, choking on food, spilling a drink). They also avoid competitive sports and physical education class where they might be called out and humiliated for a misstep. High school students may fail classes or lose credit for poor attendance because of their avoiding anticipated humiliation and are reluctant to explain fears to counselors or administrators. Fear of performing or speaking in public is common, and adolescents freeze or become unable to continue to perform; in diagnosis, this is specified as *performance only*.

The duration of social anxiety is at least 6 months, and the disorder causes serious impairment in social, educational, or work areas. Onset is between 8 and 15 years, with a median age of 13; annual prevalence for children, adolescents, or adults is 7% of the general population and more common in females than males, especially in adolescents and young adults. Symptoms are not the result of substances, medical conditions, or other disorders; however, there is a relationship between social anxiety disorder, mood disorders, and suicide ideation.

Agoraphobia

Agoraphobia focuses on serious fear of certain situations from which escape or exit seems difficult or embarrassing. The situations always induce extreme anxiety and fear disproportionate to the real danger of the situation. According to the DSM-5, feared situations include public transportation, open spaces (bridge, parking lot, open-air market), enclosed places (tunnel, movie theater, indoor stadium), crowds or queues, or being alone outside the home. This intense fear persists for 6 months or more, where the situation is intentionally avoided or contact requires extreme endurance or assistance of a helper, and over one third of individuals with agoraphobia become disabled and homebound.

Both agoraphobia and a coexisting disorder are diagnosed if criteria are fully met for each, and symptoms are not better described by another disorder. Agoraphobia is not diagnosed with symptoms resulting from a medical condition except when symptoms are excessive. The risk for agoraphobia is high in late adolescence with 17 as the mean age of onset and prevalence in females twice that of males. Agoraphobia has the strongest genetic factor (61%) of specific phobias.

Generalized Anxiety Disorder

Generalized anxiety disorder (GAD) is distinguished by extreme apprehension and anxiety with three or more symptoms: restlessness and feeling on edge, irritability, sleep problems, mental disturbance (concentration problems or blank mind), fatigue, or muscle tension. According to the DSM-5, prevalence is 0.9% among adolescents and 2.9% among adults over a 12-month period. Although onset is typically after age 30, the core risk phase for the development of GAD is during childhood and adolescence, when children and teens worry excessively about developmentally appropriate school, social, and athletic situations as well as have overzealous concerns about academic assignments, punctuality, personal health, and negative world events such as natural disasters or war. This chronic distress is disproportionate to the actual event, resulting in serious dysfunction in school, work, social, and family situations. Adolescents may seek continual reassurance from teachers and family members, or they may avoid contact and not disclose their anxiety. GAD is not better explained by the use of substances or medications, a medical condition, or another mental disorder or coexisting disorder, such as social anxiety disorder, separation anxiety disorder, or obsessive-compulsive disorder (OCD).

Separation Anxiety Disorder

The focus of separation anxiety is persistent anxiety and developmentally disproportionate fear about separation from an important attachment figure (e.g., parent, guardian, grandparent, caregiver). Although more prevalent in children, separation anxiety is also found in adolescents and adults. Symptoms may follow a major stressor (e.g., accident, death of family member, going away to college, disaster, or injury). Duration is 1 month or more in adolescents with prevalence greater in females, except in clinical settings where prevalence is equal in females and males.

Adolescents with separation anxiety are often absent from school and rarely attend activities outside the home without a significant adult. The adolescent's needs limit parents' social activities and privacy, and parents may be unable to go out without facing extreme distress from the teenager. A parent or guardian diagnosed with separation anxiety also responds with extreme anxiety when family members are separated even for a few hours and may follow them, texting or calling repeatedly to track the children.

According to the DSM-5, three of eight symptoms must be met related to persistent recurring fears, refusal, or reluctance about separation: (1) being or expecting to be separated from home or attachment figure; (2) potential injury or death to attachment figures and the need to connect with them; (3) unexpected events such as illness or accidents; (4) going to school away from home or being in a separate room or hotel room; (5) being alone without the attachment figure; (6) sleeping away from home or not sleeping close to the attachment figure; (7) nightmares about separation, disasters, deaths, or monsters; or (8) somatic symptoms when separated or expecting to be separated. Fainting, dizziness, or heart palpitations are more common in adolescents.

Cultural traditions regarding the age of separation from home may influence separation issues and expectations for certain adolescents and young adults to remain at home. Comorbidity is high in adolescents with GAD and phobias, and differential diagnosis with adolescents is important with illness anxiety disorder, agoraphobia, autism spectrum disorder (ASD), or psychotic disorders.

Other Anxiety Disorders

Adolescents with substance- or medication-induced anxiety disorder experience anxiety, panic attacks, or shortness of breath resulting from a medical condition or substance use. The symptoms are not better identified by another mental disorder and do not occur only in a delirium. Adolescents with this disorder have significant educational, work, and social impairment such as high absenteeism in school, sports and activities, and part-time jobs.

Other specified anxiety disorder is diagnosed when impairment or distress results from symptoms of an anxiety disorder but where all criteria are not met. The reason for diagnosis may be specified as insufficient days of occurrence, limited symptoms, or cultural expressions including attack of the nerves (*ataque de nervios*) or wind attack (*khyal* or *trung gio*). When impairment results from symptoms of an anxiety disorder that have insufficient information, the diagnosis *unspecified anxiety disorder* is used.

Children with selective mutism consistently refuse to speak in selective settings where they are expected to speak, such as school, resulting in significant impairment in functioning in education and with peer relationships. Onset is typically before age 5, and the disorder is rare especially in adolescents and adults.

Treatment of Anxiety Disorders

Family counseling is an important part of the treatment plan for adolescents diagnosed with anxiety disorders to help the family understand the disorder and the adolescent's impact on each member. Through psychoeducation sessions, the family can be educated about the nature and course of the disorder and how the adolescent's maladaptive responses and behaviors affect the family.

Cognitive-behavioral therapy (CBT), systematic desensitization, and eye movement desensitization and reprocessing (EMDR) are evidence-based approaches to treat most anxiety disorders. Somatic and emotion regulation, bilateral stimulation, diaphragmatic breathing, and relaxation training are integrated into treatment to reduce muscle tension, overwhelming reactions, emotional dysregulation, and excessive worrying to learn self-help strategies.

The experience of a panic attack is frightening both to the adolescent and to individuals who are present. Learning simple emotion regulation techniques will help the adolescent, teachers, and family members present, such as providing calm and support, and using breathing techniques including breathing into a paper bag or through a cocktail straw to slow exhalation. Family members also need to understand the differences in responses to specific phobias and how to provide support or interventions to help the adolescent return to a parasympathetic response—or in the case of blood-injection-injury phobias—to recognize signs of fainting and how the family should act. Psychoeducation with adolescents helps them understand somatic symptoms and reactions, and the role of fear and anxiety when they experience situations that provoke maladaptive responses; in addition, psychoeducation provides self-help strategies.

Jane M. Webber and J. Barry Mascari

See also Adolescent Behavior Problems; Adolescent Mental Health; Health Issues; Parent–Adolescent Relations

Further Readings

Alfano, C. A., & Beidel, D. C. (Eds.). (2011). *Social anxiety in adolescents and young adults: Translating developmental science into practice*. Washington, DC: American Psychological Association.

Beauchaine, T. P., & Hinshaw. S. P. (2013). *Child and adolescent psychopathology* (2nd ed.). New York, NY: Wiley.

Beck, A., Emery, H., & Greenberg, R. (2005). *Anxiety disorders and phobias: A cognitive perspective* (15th ed.). New York, NY: Basic Books.

Beesdo, K., Knapp, S., & Pine, D. S. (2009). Anxiety and anxiety disorders in children and adolescents: Developmental issues and implications for DSM-5. *The Psychiatric Clinics of North American, 32*(3), 483–524. Retrieved from http://doi.org/10.1016/j/psc.2009.06.002

Beidel, D. C., Morris, T. L., & Turner, M. W. (2004). Social phobia. In T. L. Morris & J. S. March (Eds.), *Anxiety disorders in children and adolescents* (2nd ed., pp. 141–163). New York, NY: Guilford Press.

Hube, T. J. (2012). *Anxiety and depression in children and adolescents: Assessment, intervention, and prevention.* New York, NY: Springer.

Morris, T. L., & March, J. S. (Eds.). (2004). *Anxiety disorders in children and adolescents* (2nd ed.). New York, NY: Guilford Press.

Ollendick, T. H., Birmaher, B., & Mattis, S. G. (2004). Panic disorder. In T. L. Morris & J. S. March (Eds.), *Anxiety disorders in children and adolescents* (2nd ed., pp. 189–211). New York, NY: Guilford Press.

Ollendick, T. H., & Hirscheld-Becker, D. R. (2002). The developmental psychopathology of social anxiety disorder. *Biological Psychiatry, 51*(1), 44–58.

Ranta, K., La Greca, A. M., Garcia-Lopez, L.-J., & Marttunen, M. (Eds.). (2015). *Social anxiety and phobia in adolescents: Development, manifestation, and intervention strategies.* New York, NY: Springer.

Rao, P. A., Beidel, D. C., Turner, S. M., Ammerman, L. E., Crosby, L. E., & Sallee, F. R. (2007). Social anxiety disorder in childhood and adolescence: Descriptive psychopathology. *Behaviour Research and Therapy, 45*(6), 1181–1191.

Asian American Families

There are generally three subgroups of Asian American families: (1) families from Southeast Asian countries (Philippines, Malaysia, Burma, Cambodia, Thailand, Vietnam, Brunei, Singapore, Laos), (2) families from South Asian countries (India, Bhutan, Pakistan, Nepal, Bangladesh), and (3) families from East Asian countries (China, Korea, Japan, Taiwan, Mongolia). Though there may be similarities within each of these subgroups due to shared histories and cultural values, many factors shape the unique dynamics of each Asian American family. Since Asian Americans are the fastest growing racial group in the United States, it is of great importance to have awareness about these families so that marriage, family, and couples counselors can best serve them. This entry will discuss information and research significant to understanding the Asian American family: diversity of families, immigration, acculturation and intergenerational relationships, family values, the myth of model minority, and help-seeking behavior and mental health.

Diversity of Asian American Families

Asian American families represent a diverse group of cultures with a history of immigration to the United States from various Asian countries and live in communities all across the United States. Because of the rapidly changing demographics of Asian Americans, there is often a lot of misconception about these families, since what it means to be an Asian American family means something different today than it did a few years ago. Though there may be stereotypical ideas and images of the Asian American family, it is important to recognize how much diversity is represented across countries of origin, cultural values, socioeconomic status, educational background, language, and much more. This entry is meant to give a general overview of Asian American families while at the same time remind the reader of how any one Asian American family can have its own different experience around the issues presented.

Immigration

It is important to understand the immigration of Asian Americans and know where they emigrated from and immigrated to, as well as the context surrounding immigration and how this significantly shapes each family's experience in the United States. In the mid- to late 19th century, Chinese came in large numbers to Hawaii and the West Coast as contracted laborers for the plantations, the gold rush, and transcontinental railroads. The Japanese were the next group to come in large numbers as replacements to the Chinese workers in Hawaii. Both of these groups encountered discriminatory laws and regulations that restricted their right to become citizens and to own land.

There were then decades of restrictive immigration policies in the United States until 1965, when the Immigration and Nationality Act (INA) allowed immigrants from Mexico, Latin America, and Asia to enter the United States. Some Asian families immigrate to the United States because they see it as an opportunity for a better future for their children and have the ability to make this choice. This was the case for some families during this point in history, such as families from Taiwan and Hong Kong. In the immigration process, such families may experience downward mobility, which means that they lose some degree of social status due to skills they can no longer utilize because of language and access barriers. For example, a father who worked as a medical doctor in Taiwan may have to learn to cook and run a Chinese restaurant after immigrating because his medical license cannot be used and his English-speaking abilities are poor.

Some Asian families come from home countries where education and family closeness is highly valued. These cultural strengths allow their children to achieve academic success in America and to have an opportunity to move up in socioeconomic status. In more recent decades, Asian families have come to the United States because they are refugees and are leaving countries devastated by war, often having been forced out of their home countries. Such circumstances lead to a very different family life in America because of the history of trauma and significant loss.

Where Asian families end up settling in the United States impacts their postimmigration lives. Families who settle in communities with few other Asian or minority families have the experience of feeling very different and may try to "not be Asian" or hide their culture in order to fit in. There may be more areas for stress such as not being able to communicate in English to meet their day-to-day needs or encountering overt discrimination. Over time, this has significant impact, often negative, on family relationships and on health. Families that settle in Asian ethnic enclaves have greater opportunity to connect to others who share their culture, language, food, and religion. This can serve to protect the family by helping members to stay connected to their cultural identities and to each other.

Regardless of the reason families emigrate or where they immigrate to, all Asian American families experience layers of loss and grief in the process of immigration, whether it is leaving other family behind, grieving over changes in their cultural identities, or facing family disconnect due to challenges after immigration. The losses and changes that take place postimmigration will be further discussed in the following section.

Acculturation and Intergenerational Relationships

Acculturation has typically been defined as the process of adopting the values and mores of the new host culture. In this discussion, it is how Asian American families grow to become more assimilated into American culture. There are a number of challenges that arise for Asian American families in this process. The first-generation parents immigrate to the United States with their more traditional Asian values and mind-set, but the second-generation (term for the generation that is born in the United States) children grow up in a drastically different American context, with pressures and expectations from home and the new larger context that may pull them in different directions. Naturally, the cultural disconnect and differences between the generations lead to challenges in family relationships.

The intergenerational strains increase the frequency of intergenerational conflict and research shows that this has a significant impact on second-generation young adults' well-being and adjustment. Parents and children can also have very different expectations of what it means to communicate. Congruent with Asian values, parents often expect children to listen to them obediently without making challenges or talking back. This can be difficult for children who are comparing their parents to Western American ways of parenting observed with peers or seen in the media. Additionally, the second-generation children often function as translators for their parents and are put into positions making household decisions because they speak English and their parents cannot. The structure of the family is then flipped upside down, with parents feeling as though they cannot sufficiently care for their families because they must rely on their children.

Though a large portion of research has focused on these intergenerational challenges, more studies highlight the strengths of Asian American families. For example, family strengths between Asian American parents and children include (a) parents providing practical help, (b) open communication, (c) recreational activities and time spent together, (d) respect for children's autonomy, (e) comparisons with other Asian American families, and (f) parents' sacrificial love. The strengths inherent in the Asian American family system have allowed them to have resilience through the immigration process.

Family Values

The Asian American values scale provides a general idea of values important to Asian Americans. B. K. Kim, L. C. Li, and G. F. Ng developed this scale that assesses six Asian cultural value dimensions: *collectivism, conformity to norms, emotional self-control, family recognition through achievement, filial piety,* and *humility*. Collectivism is the emphasis on considering the group's needs before one's own needs; it means seeing one's own achievement as equivalent to the family's achievement. Conformity to norms means conforming to social expectations such as those that are significant to the family and fulfilling expected gender roles.

Emotional self-control is valued because it means having the capacity to control emotions; one is expected to have the internal resources to resolve emotional issues and have unspoken understanding about emotional needs. Family recognition through achievement is the importance of avoiding shaming the family by being successful in academic and occupational endeavors.

Filial piety refers to a deep respect of parents or elders as having greater wisdom than those younger as well as taking care of parents' needs when they are older. It means refraining from talking back to parents or expressing disagreement. Humility is the emphasis on holding onto modesty and refraining from being boastful. These values can contribute to protective factors and to challenges experienced by the Asian American family.

Model Minority: A Myth

Perhaps these Asian American values have allowed some Asian Americans to succeed in America. Asian Americans have been labeled the "model minority" because they have achieved a higher degree of success than other racial minorities academically (higher educational attainment), financially (higher median household incomes), and socially (lower crime rates). This stereotype misinforms the general population about the actual experiences of these families. This label, which was introduced in the 1960s, does not take into consideration a number of important variables. Though some East Asian Americans have succeeded in graduating from high school and have pursued higher education, most Southeast Asian Americans have high school graduation rates that are lower than other racial minority groups. Asian American families also have higher median household incomes because more family members work, but the median personal income is still much lower. Because some Asian American families have achieved the American dream does not mean that all Asian American families have.

This model minority stereotype has had a negative impact on the Asian American family by minimizing actual experiences of discrimination in the academic or workplace environments. Asian Americans earn less money than their White counterparts with the same level of education or experience. Asian Americans feel the pressure to live up to this stereotype and thus further perpetuate their silence and fear of speaking up about problems they may experience.

Help-Seeking Behavior and Mental Health

The model minority stereotype contributes to low help-seeking behavior among Asian Americans. As a whole, mental health services are both underutilized and difficult to access for Asian Americans. Asian cultural norms and expectations make it difficult to seek help as stigma and shame are associated with doing so. There are practical barriers such as treatment costs, knowing how to access care, and language challenges. Though most Asian Americans will go to family, friends, and their religious community first to seek help, the majority do not discuss emotional challenges with anyone at all.

Asian Americans tend to go to medical providers first because there is less stigma about having physical ailments treated. Additionally, there are higher rates of somatization of symptoms. Research has shown that Asian Americans have at least the same if not higher rates of depression, posttraumatic stress, and suicidal ideation as White Americans.

Asian American families have multiple cultural identities and generational differences to navigate within the larger American society around them. Research and training that are culturally sensitive and congruent with Asian American populations are increasing and are very much needed in order to best serve Asian American families.

Jessica ChenFeng

See also Acculturation; Assimilation: Immigrants and Refugees; Bilingual Families; Diversity; Ethnicity; Immigrant Families

Further Readings

Han, A., & Hsu, J. (2004). *Asian American X: An intersection of twenty-first century Asian American voices*. Ann Arbor: University of Michigan Press.

Kim, B. K., Li, L. C., & Ng, G. F. (2005). The Asian American values scale—multidimensional: Development, reliability, and validity. *Cultural Diversity and Ethnic Minority Psychology, 11*(3), 187–201.

Lee, R. M., Su, J., & Yoshida, E. (2005). Coping with intergenerational family conflict among Asian American college students. *Journal of Counseling Psychology, 52*(3), 389–399.

Lee, S., Juon, H.-S., Martinez, G., Hsu, C. E., Robinson, E. S., Bawa, J., & Ma, G. X. (2009). Model minority at risk: Expressed needs of mental health by Asian American young adults. *Journal of Community Health: The Publication for Health Promotion and Disease Prevention, 34*(2), 144–152.

Leong, F. T. L., Kim, H. H. W., & Gupta, A. (2011). Attitudes toward professional counseling among Asian-American college students: Acculturation, conceptions of mental illness, and loss of face. *Asian American Journal of Psychology, 2*(2), 140–153.

Min, Z., & Yang Sao, X. (2005). The multifaceted American experiences of the children of Asian immigrants: Lessons for segmented assimilation. *Ethnic & Racial Studies, 28*(6), 1119–1152.

Su Yeong, K., Gonzales, N. A., Stroh, K., & Wang, J. J.-L. (2006). Parent-child cultural marginalization and depressive symptoms in Asian American family members. *Journal of Community Psychology, 34*(2), 167–182.

Wong, A., Wong, Y. J., & Obeng, C. S. (2012). An untold story: A qualitative study of Asian American family strengths. *Asian American Journal of Psychology, 3*(4), 286–298.

Yong, S. P., Yuying, T., & Vo, L. P. (2009). Family affection as a protective factor against the negative effects of perceived Asian values gap on the parent-child relationship for Asian American male and female college students. *Cultural Diversity & Ethnic Minority Psychology, 15*(1), 18–26.

ASSERTIVENESS

Assertiveness is a component of communication, often taught in conjunction with social skills training, which is used to encourage healthy and honest communication with others. The use of assertiveness can be a helpful tool when engaging in couples and family systems, particularly when conflicts arise, because it provides each individual with skills to discuss points and perspectives while also maintaining value for others. This entry examines the components of assertiveness, the history of assertiveness in mental health theory, and skills associated with assertiveness training as well as assertiveness techniques.

Definition and Explanation

Assertiveness involves the honest articulation of wants, needs, and perspectives without hurting others or infringing on their rights. Verbal and nonverbal communication can assist individuals in being assertive. While words are typically used to state one's desires or viewpoints, the use of eye contact, vocal tone, posture, fluency, and timing can also suggest a sense of personal value and worth when communicating with others.

Verbal assertions can come in a variety of forms. Empathic assertions seek to communicate that the perspective of someone else is being acknowledged. Consequence-oriented assertions outline the consequences of a person behaving or not behaving in a certain way. Discrepancy assertions identify a discrepancy between what was agreed upon in a given situation and what is actually happening. Negative feelings assertions identify one's reaction to a situation or behavior. When using verbal assertions, it is important to use *I* language so as to acknowledge and own one's reaction or perspective. This empowers the individual to identify how a situation or behavior is creating a personal impact rather than to maintain a primary focus upon others.

To better understand assertiveness, it is helpful to contrast this construct with passive and aggressive approaches to communication. Passive communication is a response to anxiety that is often based upon a stance of devaluing oneself; thus, behaviors associated with this form of communication are often self-deprecating in nature. This generally results in an individual being nonresponsive emotionally and can lead to limited physical reactions to people and/or situations. For some, passive responses are situation-based, whereas others respond in a passive manner in virtually all situations.

In contrast to assertiveness and passivity, aggressiveness typically involves pursuit of one's wants and needs without taking into account the wants and needs of others. Interestingly, aggression is also a response to anxiety but instead of turning toward self-deprecation, the aggressor places his or her needs above the needs of others. Such individuals may demonstrate a volatile nature and can be prone to emotional outbursts to express their views, emotions, and behaviors. As with passivity, aggressiveness can be situational or global in nature.

History and Relevance to Mental Health

Assertiveness became a therapeutically relevant concept and practice as part of behavior therapy. Joseph Wolpe and Arnold Lazarus noted assertiveness as a behavior therapy technique, which brought attention to this concept and its relevance to clinical sessions. In addition, the emphasis upon humanism in the 1960s and 1970s made room for focusing on personal growth and positive change, which allowed assertiveness training to be viewed as an effective method for valuing oneself and enhancing personal relationships. Since its inception, assertiveness has found application in counseling theory and clinical practice.

Cognitive-Behavioral Therapy

Within cognitive-behavioral therapy (CBT), assertiveness is often taught as a psychotherapeutic tool under the umbrella of social skills training. As such, assertiveness skills are used to help individuals identify and express thoughts and feelings. Individuals are educated to recognize that people have the ability and the right to express themselves, and time is spent practicing ways to be effectively assertive while also encouraging assertiveness on the part of others. Effort is spent on recognizing the ways that specific beliefs have led one to devalue oneself, thereby leading to self-defeating behaviors. By understanding the role that thoughts and feelings have on behaviors, cognitive-behavioral therapists educate clients how to engage in cognitive restructuring, thereby identifying and changing mistaken thoughts and core beliefs. In so doing, individuals can replace mistaken thoughts with new core beliefs that demonstrate personal value, and assertiveness skills can be used to reflect this shift in personal value.

Feminist Therapy

Another clinical approach that values assertiveness training is feminist therapy. Within this approach, individuals who have experienced some form of oppression become educated and aware of their own value as cultural beings. As such, individuals gain knowledge and insight into the ways that recognizing one's value and worth can influence and shift personal power. As part of the therapeutic process, the client learns when and how to be assertive in ways that influence the self while also potentially making a systemic or even societal impact. Although the feminist approach may initially have emerged in the context of its use by women, men also can engage in this form of therapy by identifying and acknowledging aspects of power imbalances present in their lives. Because of this, assertiveness training can be appropriately used by both men and women as part of a feminist therapeutic approach.

Clinical Applications

The implementation of assertiveness skills and training has been used for a wide range of therapeutic concerns. When counseling couples and/or families, assertiveness training allows each person to identify and articulate wants and needs. At the same time, each family member is also given the opportunity to listen to the wants and needs of significant others, thus increasing relational awareness and interpersonal sensitivity. In situations where power and control have been used to coerce others, assertiveness training allows for each person to have a valued and validated voice in the relationship or family system.

Assertiveness Training

Assertiveness training is considered a form of social skills training that helps teach and empower individuals to properly assert themselves in various social situations. A preliminary step is to help individuals recognize that they have opportunities to be assertive, which can be followed up by consciously choosing to engage in assertive behaviors. This approach also involves educating people to the differences between passive, aggressive, and assertive behaviors. Typically, assertiveness training is taught and modeled so that the desired responses and behaviors can be observed before they are practiced. Within a clinical setting, individuals learn to practice assertiveness by watching a demonstration of the skills or engaging in a role-play with a therapist. As clients learn about assertiveness and practice the skills within the therapeutic relationship, they can receive feedback that can be implemented when using assertiveness skills in everyday interactions outside of a clinical setting.

While assertiveness training can occur on an individual level, it can also be taught to groups, thereby allowing for the concepts of assertiveness training to be applicable when working with couples and families. When offering group instruction on assertiveness, instructions and demonstrations are offered to a group collectively, and then individuals have the opportunity to practice what they have learned by rehearsing the skills through role-playing scenarios. Upon completion of the various role-plays, participants receive feedback that highlights the strengths of their skills while also discussing aspects that could be refined or changed in order to better demonstrate assertiveness. These rehearsals continue until participants have gained a solid ability to utilize assertiveness skills.

An important element to consider regarding assertiveness is its cultural relevance and significance. Generally speaking, the value placed on assertiveness and assertiveness training reflects a Western mind-set. Because of this, it is important to understand how cultural differences may inform the degree to which one does or does not find merit in these ideas and corresponding behaviors.

Assertiveness Techniques

Various skills have been identified to assist individuals in becoming more assertive. Manuel Smith identified seven assertiveness techniques that can be implemented to enforce one's assertive rights. By practicing and integrating these skills, people gain the ability to overcome the manipulation of others and to change others' behavior by changing one's own communication patterns.

The broken-record technique reinforces one's ability to repeat what he or she wants without responding in anger or irritation. This teaches individuals to be persistent without needing to be loud to get one's perspective or point across. The aim of this approach is to affirm and encourage persistence as well as encourage self-respect, which is a foundational motivator for assertiveness.

Free information is another assertiveness technique that allows an individual to take note of information offered by others in order to follow up on it through further dialogue. Acting upon free information allows an individual to show assertiveness by engaging in conversation, and it also shows that information offered by others is valued. By recognizing elements that seem to be important to others, a person can demonstrate assertiveness through their recognition and discussion of things that seem to be important to others.

Communication is also enhanced by self-disclosure. This involves the task of sharing information about oneself, including thoughts, feelings, and/or behaviors, and can be understood as a complementary skill to free information. When free information is used in conjunction with self-disclosure, communication can be mutual rather than one-sided. Self-disclosure also demonstrates that aspects of oneself are valued enough to be discussed, which again affirms the sense of personal rights and values that are demonstrated through the use of assertiveness skills.

Fogging is an assertiveness technique that allows an individual faced with criticism to refrain from reacting or responding. Instead, the person is empowered to agree with any elements of truth or basic principles that are suggested or stated in the midst of the critical statements made by others. Fogging requires individuals to truly listen to the person who is being critical rather than reacting out of emotion to the criticizer's ideas or sentiments. It also empowers an individual to hear criticism without embracing feelings of anxiety or insecurity about oneself, which allows self-worth to be maintained throughout the experience of receiving criticism.

When confronted with situations in which a person has made a mistake, typical reactions can include feeling anxious or guilty or outright denial of the error. In contrast, negative assertion is an assertiveness skill that helps individuals cope with imperfections by accepting aspects of oneself that are flawed. The idea is that by changing the belief that imperfections are unacceptable, the associated negative emotions can also change, and the ability to accept oneself in light of imperfections becomes possible and achievable.

Another option when confronted with a critical response by others is to engage in negative inquiry. This is a nondefensive approach that suggests that the point of criticism is acceptable and in fact should be explored further, which is achieved by the criticizing person outlining what elements of a person's behavior seem to be likable versus those that are frustrating. Through negative inquiry, criticism does not lead to anger or insecurity but rather enhances dialogue and understanding about situations and relational qualities that could otherwise be sources of conflict or self-defeating beliefs.

When one is confronted by another individual, a workable compromise can be used to encourage healthy communication and affirmation. A workable compromise allows give-and-take for all who are involved in a conflict. The aim of a workable compromise is to communicate value to each party without compromising one's self-respect or self-worth.

Taken collectively, then, these skills can enhance one's sense of self and inherent value while not compromising the value of others. By practicing these skills, individuals can gain a sense of confidence and competence in assertiveness. As these skills become integrated, corresponding thoughts and feelings shift to reflect personal rights that are demonstrated through verbal and nonverbal behaviors. In sum, assertiveness skills are a valuable part of healthy and honest communication, and implementation of these skills helps individuals engage in effective strategies to value self and others.

Christina Schnyders

See also Communication Errors/Problems in Couples and Families; Conflict Styles; Confrontation; Nonverbal Communication

Further Readings

Alberti, R. E., & Emmons, M. L. (2008). *Your perfect right: A guide to assertive behavior* (9th ed.). Atascadero, CA: Impact Publishers.

Corey, G. (2013). *Theory and practice of counseling and psychotherapy* (9th ed.). Belmont, CA: Brooks/Cole.

Lange, A. J., & Jakubowski, P. (1976). *Responsible assertive behavior: Cognitive/behavioral procedures for trainers.* Champaign, IL: Research Press.

Michel, F., & Fursland, D. (2008). *Assert yourself module 4: How to behave more assertively.* Retrieved from http://www.cci.health.wa.gov.au/docs/Assertmodule%204.pdf

Paterson, R. J. (2000). *The assertiveness workbook: How to express your ideas and stand up for yourself at work and in relationships.* Oakland, CA: New Harbinger.

Smith, M. J. (1975). *When I say no, I feel guilty: How to cope—using the skills of systematic assertive therapy.* New York, NY: Dial Press.

Wolpe, J. (1973). *The practice of behavior therapy.* New York, NY: Pergamon.

Assessment, Biopsychosocial

Assessment in marriage and family therapy is one of the most essential components to proper treatment. Without a full understanding of what is going on for the individuals and families, it is difficult for marriage and family therapists (MFTs) to determine a proper treatment plan. One holistic way to assess clients is through the biopsychosocial (BPS) model. The BPS model was developed by George Engle, a psychiatrist, in order to highlight key aspects of the human condition: biological, psychological, and social. Through these concepts, clinicians are able to systematically assess clients. Recently, spirituality was added to the BPS model as clinicians and researchers have recognized the importance of assessing the client's belief systems and viewpoints on existential viewpoints. The biopsychosocial-spiritual (BPSS) model, therefore, is an approach that incorporates the interconnectedness of biological, psychological, social, and spiritual aspects of the human condition. Throughout this entry, an overview of the various aspects of the BPS model will be presented and discussed.

Use of the BPSS model is one approach to holistically assess both individuals and families (see Figure 1). The BPSS model was created to allow clinicians to assess and treat individuals and families from biological, psychological, social, and spiritual perspectives. These perspectives, when conceptualized together, can be used by MFTs to make an accurate and holistic assessment of individuals, couples, and families and the biological, psychological, social, and spiritual contexts within which they reside. This information then can be used to administer appropriate multisystemic treatment. Although for clarity in writing we have divided up these sections, it must be stressed that there is a complex interaction among and between all of the four component areas. Change in one area will often have an impact in one or more of the other areas. For example, heart disease is not just a biological condition. Loss of ability and stress impacts the psychological well-being of the individual and family. It also can change roles and interactions within and outside the family (social) and often creates a spiritual or existential change (positive or negative) as they try to make sense of their experience. This complex interaction comes full circle as the psychological, social, and spiritual aspects can have a direct impact on the heart disease. Because MFTs are already trained to understand systems concepts and multiple perspectives, the BPSS model can easily be utilized to help MFTs holistically assess the individuals, couples, and families with whom they work. This entry reviews the key aspects of the biological, psychological, social, and spiritual components of a BPSS assessment.

Biological Component

It is imperative that MFTs assess the impact of family history of illness and disease, past and current history of illness and disease, and current health behaviors. While it is often accepted that medical health is only under the purview of medical professionals, family therapists can often identify health difficulties, recommend changes (i.e., diet, exercise), and/or refer their clients for the appropriate medical evaluation and treatment.

Current Health

The biological assessment begins by assessing the current health of all members of the family. The process is quite simple but is often overlooked. Clients should be asked at the beginning of treatment about the current health status of each member in their family. This can be accomplished by adding questions about health status of family members during the genogram assessment or as part of the intake paperwork. MFTs should ask about current illnesses, physical disabilities and limitations, medications, dosages, and other health treatments. It is also important to identify the key medical professionals that the family is using and get a signed release so collaboration can occur. Once the nuclear family is assessed, therapists might also ask about current health status for their extended family. A common stressor for many families is the current health status of the grandparents or other family members.

Past Health History

Another key component to a proper biological assessment is to identify the previous experiences that clients have had with illness and disability in their lives. These experiences can truly shape a

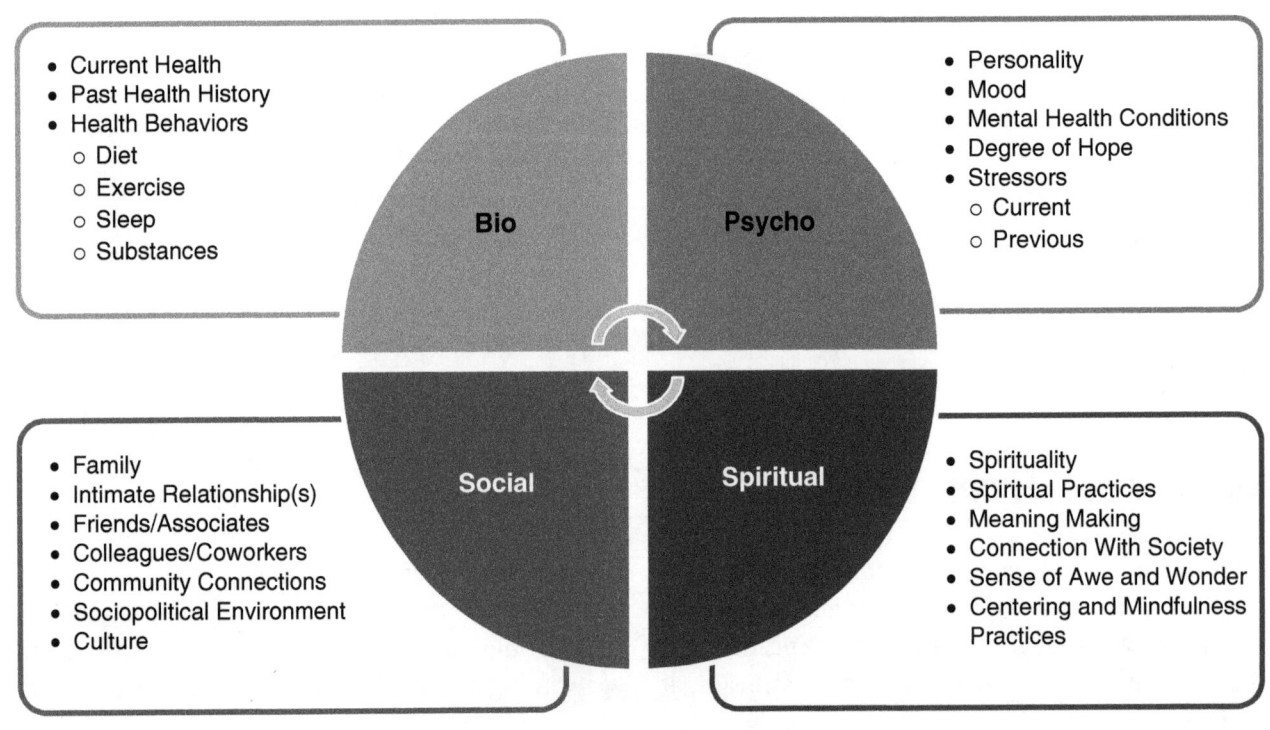

Figure 1 Component Parts of the Biopsychosocial-Spiritual Model

person's life from an early age. Strength, compassion, fear, and anxiety, along with a host of other outcomes, can be attributed to experiences with illness. Overcoming and/or dealing with illness within the family can be a significant and pivotal point of coming together or suffering in silence for many families. Some behaviors or fears can also be intergenerationally transmitted without the current client even having had any personal interaction with the individual who was ill (e.g., a mother who takes her child to the doctor every time the child coughs because her father died of an infection that was ignored). This part of the assessment can also be done during the genogram or on the intake form by asking about past history of illnesses and/or disabilities and causes of death.

Health Behaviors

Although MFTs are not medical professionals, they can play a significant role in helping clients change many health-related behaviors. There are many aspects to health behaviors that MFTs are able to assess. Diet, exercise, sleep habits, and use of substances are some of the key aspects to be considered in this part of the assessment.

Diet

It is important to first assess the family's experiences with food, their successes and struggles with their everyday diet. Most people know what the recommendations are as far as diet, so often all we need to assess is the family's and each individual's current satisfaction with their food intake. Family traditions, culture, and behaviors can play significant roles in an individual's interactions with food. Malnutrition and missing of key elements of a diet can lead to significant mental and physical difficulties. Referral for medical evaluation and/or nutritional consultations can be done if there is significant concern.

Exercise

It is important for MFTs to assess the types and levels of activity for each member in the family and the family's level of activity as a whole. Once the current exercise regimen is understood, encouragement for more movement can play a key role in improving the overall mental and physical well-being of the client. Too often, clients see exercise as a burdensome task, but by stressing the specific benefits of movement based upon a person's presenting problem, motivation can be found. Involvement of the family as a whole can make this process easier as they all learn to encourage each other and find exercise that is convenient and doable.

Sleep

Sleep can be one of the most overlooked components of assessment but has a significant impact on the physical and emotional well-being of our clients. Too much sleep (e.g., as an effect of depression) or sleep deprivation (e.g., from caring for a newborn child) can have detrimental effects. For these reasons, it is imperative that we assess the sleep patterns of our clients. Key aspects of this include time going to bed, time to fall asleep, nighttime awakenings, the duration of the wakening, snoring, dreams and types of dreams, wake-up and get up time, restorative sleep, and the role of naps.

Substance Use

A thorough assessment of the types, dosages, duration, and effects of the substances used by the client must be assessed. *Prescription drugs* are not without their negative effects on clients. For this reason, therapists should assess what drugs the person takes and their impact. For example, sexual dysfunction is not an uncommon side effect for clients taking an antidepressant. Overuse of narcotics or other types of medications is also not uncommon. *Illegal, nonprescribed, or overused drugs* can have a significant impact on the family. Unless the family is coming in specifically for substance abuse treatment, many therapists forget to collect this important biological data. Collaboration with a medical provider and possibly drug treatment and/or detox may be needed. Other behavioral addictions can also cause significant problems for individuals and their family members and should be assessed (e.g., gambling, video gaming, exercise, sex, food, computers, hobbies, and spending).

Psychological Component

The psychological assessment involves the exploration of the intrapsychic interaction of the individual, couple, and/or family system. The psychological assessment includes assessing personality, mood, mental health conditions, hope, and stressors, and is most often achieved through formal assessments, interviews, or identifying patterns. Though psychological assessment often focuses on the individual, as systemic thinkers, it is important that MFTs assess both the intrapsychic aspects of each member of the family and how these interact with one another. Through this assessment the MFT will be better able to identify how the psychological well-being of each individual impacts the couple and/or family psychological patterns.

Personality

Assessing personality is an important part of the psychological component, which includes assessing and understanding the interaction of personalities within the individual, couple, and/or family system. Areas of personality assessment include locus of control, optimism, self-esteem, personality disorder struggles, and resilience. Using circular questioning may be helpful in identifying others' perspectives on the personality interactions of the system. Through questioning, enactments, and observations, MFTs can obtain a clear understanding on the personalities of each of their clients and how these personalities interact with one another.

Mood/Affect

Another component of the psychological assessment is to understand the interactional patterns of mood within the individual, couple, and/or family system. Mood includes the feelings or state of mind experienced at any point in time. With moods frequently changing, it is essential to assess the type, frequency, and duration of moods within each individual and how those moods impact the system. Affect is the objectively observed behavior often used to describe mood. Common descriptors of mood include euthymic, euphoric, angry, anxious, apathetic, anhedonic, and dysphoric. Mood should be assessed by observing affect and exploring with the client their current experience with their mood. They should also be encouraging clients to identify, log, and track their moods over a period of time. This information can then be used to explore how couples and/or families adapt to and interact around distinct individual moods with the system.

Mental Health Conditions

An assessment of clients' and their families' previous and current mental health conditions need to be included in the psychological assessment. An examination of their family and own history of mental health can provide insight and direction to possible conditions. This can be done when completing a genogram by asking about the familial history of mental health. Mental health conditions may be manifested in the biological, social, and spiritual components, which highlight the strengths of using the BPSS model to gather a holistic view of the individual, problem, and system. Examples include personality disorders manifesting in the social component and somatic disorders being manifest in the biological component.

Degree of Hope

An assessment of hope can inform MFTs on the psychological aspects of the client and can be an influencing factor in the outcome of treatment. Hope can be assessed by asking the members of the client family system to rate on a 10-point scale the amount of hope they have that their presenting problem can be resolved or become more tolerable. Therapists should not only assess hope but also assist in instilling or increasing hope in all members of the family system. An example is instilling hope in parents of a delinquent adolescent who may have otherwise given up.

Stressors

Included in the psychological assessment is an analysis of current and previous stressors within the individual, couple, and/or family system. For both current and former stressors, it is important to assess the change in family dynamics in response to the stressor. Assessment of current stressors includes both chronic and acute stressors. Current stressors may be what prompted clients to reach out for treatment. The therapist should explore additional stressors, often other components of the BPSS model that contribute to the presenting problem. It is also important to assess how current stressors manifest themselves in the individual, couple, and/or family system. *Previous stressors* may not be discussed unless specifically asked. Previous stressors provide valuable information about the family's reactions to stressors; the personality of the clients; and what has worked previously for the individual, couple, and family system. The assessment of how families overcame previous stressors can be used to build hope and can be beneficial in eliciting individual and family strengths. This can be assessed by asking what challenges they, or their family, have faced in the past, and how the challenges were handled.

Social Component

The third component of the BPSS model is social support, which includes those inside and outside the family system that individuals, couples, and/or families turn to for support. Assessment of social support includes an exploration of family, intimate relationships, friends, colleagues or coworkers, community, sociopolitical environment, and culture. It is important to explore where each of the members of the family turn for support and guidance. Both intrafamilial and extrafamilial support systems should be assessed. Though there are several standard measurements to assess social support, it can also be measured through self-report, with genograms being a useful tool to gather necessary information.

Family

An assessment of the family should include identifying individual, couple, and/or family structures. Understanding family relationships, triangles, and boundaries are all included in assessing the family. An important consideration should also be who they consider family and who in the family would be willing to attend treatment. It is essential to assess family patterns, such as conflict, mental illness, or abuse, and how the interaction of the patterns affects the individuals, couple, or family system. Family boundaries and patterns can be assessed formally through genograms or informally by observing family interactions.

Intimate Relationship(s)

In addition to assessing family, the presence and quality of intimate relationships can be used to identify social support strengths and areas of deficit. Intimate relationships consist of physical and/or emotional intimacy. These relationships can be identified by asking clients who they are likely to turn to in times of need and with whom they share their most important thoughts and emotions. These individuals should be considered as support for treatment, whether by attending sessions or being involved outside the therapy room.

Friends/Associates

Friends and associates are not as close as intimate relationships. Association with these individuals may evolve around hobbies, friends, spouses, work, or family members. Assessment should include frequency of association, type of personal information shared, support reciprocated, and conflict. Friends and associates can provide valuable information into boundaries, as the relationships are sometimes not strong enough to warrant high degrees of emotional connection.

Colleagues or Coworkers

Colleague or coworker relationships are also important social support constructs to assess. Included in this assessment should be a work and/or school history, with questions about absenteeism, reprimands, promotions, and suspensions. In addition to assessing the relationships formed, the information from this assessment can be valuable to identify strengths and interests, such as areas of success and enjoyable subjects.

Community Connections

Community involvement can also be an important avenue of social support. The extent to which one feels connected with one's community, involvement in community activities, and value placed on community can all be asked to assess community social support. Interventions can be assigned to increase this support, such as participating in a community service project, attending a council meeting, or volunteering with a community youth group. These interventions are also beneficial for the spiritual component of the BPSS model as they provide clients meaning and being part of something greater than themselves.

Sociopolitical Environment

The sociopolitical environment is an influencing social factor that also needs to be assessed. Assessment includes how current policies may be contributing to the presenting problem, such as a same-sex couple's wishing to adopt a child when there are legal barriers to such adoptions in their state. The sociopolitical environment may also provide opportunities for solutions to the presenting problems, such as laws protecting victims of domestic abuse. When discussing legal policy, therapists must ensure they do not advise beyond their scope of competence.

Culture

The final social construct needing assessment is culture. Culture needs to be addressed with sensitivity. The assessment should begin with developing an understanding of the clients' culture. This understanding can be fostered by asking about country of origin, ethnic identification, and religious values and beliefs. Included in this discussion should be how their culture makes sense of the therapy process, specifically the family and their culture's acceptance of therapy, medication, mental illness, and their presenting problem. The assessment also includes how the individual, couple, and/or family systems cultures interact with other cultures within their system (e.g., a multicultural couple; minorities' experiences with the majority population).

Spiritual Component

The final interactional component of the BPSS model is the spiritual aspect. While not all clients declare a spiritual or religious side, it is important to assess how they make sense of the world and humanity. The key aspects of this assessment are religious practices, meaning-making, connection with society or humanity, the clients' sense of awe and wonder, and centering and mindfulness practices.

Spirituality

As a key part of the BPSS assessment, it is important to talk with clients about their current view of spirituality. It is essential that this is asked in a way that allows for a myriad of responses. Organized religion is only one part of this assessment. MFTs also need to find out in what/whom do they feel they get their strength. When they are not coping well, where do they turn? There are religious people who are not very spiritual, and there are spiritual people who are not very religious. MFTs should assess, when clients are looking outside themselves, how they make sense of their world, life, and humanity.

Spiritual Practices

The most straightforward spiritual assessment is to find out what, if any, spiritual practices clients have. This can be done by asking clients if they are participating in a specific organized religion or if they participate in activities that help connect them to a higher power, society, nature, and a host of other possibilities. There are many possible spiritual practices that play a role in providing comfort to clients. Taking nature walks, interacting with others, praying, practicing specific religious behaviors, or becoming more attuned with one's body through exercise are a few examples of spiritual practices that are common for clients.

Meaning-Making

Assessing how clients make sense of their lives and the positive and negative things that occur is the focus of meaning-making. This is often highly correlated with the psychological concepts related to attitude. Does the client believe that everything is good and everything happens for a reason? Or do they believe that they are doomed to bad things happening and are just expected to endure endless trials? The way that clients make sense of their experiences can play a significant role in how the therapeutic process is focused.

Connection With Society or Humanity

For many individuals, connection with society or humanity and working to make a difference with others is a large part of their spirituality and creates a sense of meaning. MFTs should explore this aspect of spirituality as it can often be overlooked and for most clients can be a real source of healing. This aspect of spirituality allows people to feel part of a larger system and feel as if they are not alone. For some, this may be connection with others through community service or humanitarian outreach. For others, this may be based upon community organizations such as civic office, organized religion, youth sports organizations, or a host of other formal or informal groups dedicated to serving others.

Sense of Awe and Wonder

There are many aspects of life that create a feeling of awe and wonder. Some interpret this as a higher power working in their life. Others see these as overall goodness and use this to focus on the great and wonderful things in life—for example, birth, the complexity of the human body, the beauty of the natural world, the essential goodness of people, the lives of animals, and a myriad of other options.

Centering and Mindfulness Practices

The final aspect of a spiritual assessment is to identify what, if any, centering and/or mindfulness practices the family uses. Centering and mindfulness practices are behaviors that clients engage in to monitor internal workings of the body, providing them with time to contemplate, relax, and rejuvenate. There are many of these practices that clients use. A few of these include meditation, prayer, yoga, religious texts, and fasting, along with a variety of other practices.

*W. David Robinson
and Nathan Taylor*

See also Attachment and Health; Children With Chronic Illness; Chronic Illness With Couples and Families; Health Issues; Medical Family Therapy

Further Readings

Borrell-Carrió, F., Suchman, A. L., & Epstein, R. M. (2004). The biopsychosocial model 25 years later: Principles, practice, and scientific inquiry. *The Annals of Family Medicine, 2*, 576–582. doi:10.1370/afm.245

Campbell, W. H., & Rohrbaugh, R. M. (2006). *The biopsychosocial formulation manual: A guide for mental health professionals*. New York, NY: Routledge.

Engel, G. L (1977). The need for a new medical model: A challenge for biomedicine. *Science, 196*, 129–136.

Friedman, H. S., & Silver, R. C. (2007). *Foundations of health psychology*. New York, NY: Oxford University Press.

McDaniel, S., Hepworth, J., & Doherty, W. (2014). *Medical family therapy and integrated care* (2nd ed.). Washington, DC: American Psychological Association.

Prest, L. A., & Robinson, W. D. (2006). Systemic assessment and treatment of depression and anxiety in families: The BPSS model in practice. *Journal of Systemic Therapies, 25*, 4–24. doi:10.1521/jsyt.2006.25.3.4

Rolland, J. (1994). *Families, illness, & disability.* New York, NY: Basic Books.

Wachholtz, A. B., Pearce, M. J., & Koenig, H. (2007). Exploring the relationship between spirituality, coping and pain. *Journal of Behavioral Medicine, 30,* 311–318. doi:10.1007/s10865-007-9114-7

Assessment, Suicide

The most daunting, and among the most important, of all clinical responsibilities, suicide assessment requires therapists to determine to the best of their ability whether the client in front of them is in imminent danger of making an attempt on his or her life. This entry introduces the most salient topics to address during a suicide assessment, and it offers suggestions for how best to conduct an interview devoted to determining suicidality. Assessment is inexorably linked to preventive action when clinicians conclude that the risk of death is high, so this entry also includes guidelines for making a safety decision regarding hospitalization and, when hospitalization isn't necessary, for collaborating with clients on the construction of an idiosyncratic safety plan.

Skills

The skill to sensitively and thoroughly conduct a suicide assessment is of critical importance for all psychotherapists, as research indicates that those in full-time practice average five suicidal clients per month. Researchers have determined that a significant percentage of people who die by suicide visited a mental health and/or medical professional during the last month before their death. Thus, family therapists, like their professional colleagues, are uniquely positioned to effectively distinguish those who are at greatest risk and to take responsible action to help clients safely negotiate their desperation and hopelessness.

Few therapists receive graduate training in suicidality or suicide assessment, so many feel unprepared to speak in depth with clients about their desires and intentions to die. They must also contend with the frightening possibility that they will be wrong in their determination of clients' level of suicidality. Given such hurdles, it makes sense, then, that some clinicians wish to use a paper-and-pencil assessment instrument when faced with a potentially suicidal client. However, even the best measure can be unreliable when completed in the midst of an emotional crisis, and some clients who are withdrawn, distrustful, or afraid of the mental health system are less than forthcoming about their current thoughts, emotions, and behaviors. A safer, more comprehensive alternative is to conduct the assessment as a clinical interview, which allows the therapist not only to inquire about relevant issues but also by tracking the client's engagement in the conversation to get a sense of the dependability of the information being shared.

Myths

The suicidologist Thomas Joiner has catalogued a score of myths about suicide—myths that, if clinicians mistakenly hold them to be true, can hamper the assessment process. Among the most problematic myths is the idea that suicidal individuals do not make future plans. In fact, suicidal individuals can simultaneously be thinking and talking about upcoming events and projects *and* be making preparations for a suicide attempt. It is thus important for clinicians not to be lulled into a false sense of security when their clients are able to detail what they expect to be doing next week, next month, or next year.

Another myth that Joiner has identified is the mistaken belief that suicidality is an invariable commitment to die so that once a person has made up his or her mind it is just a matter of time until the inevitable happens. The reality is that almost every person making a suicide attempt is ambivalent right up to the end, and the urge to die varies over time and in response to circumstances and the responses of others. This means that preventing a suicide attempt is not just a stopgap measure; it can be a lifesaving *and life-changing* intervention. Indeed, a long-term study of people who had been stopped from jumping from the

Golden Gate Bridge into the San Francisco Bay found that 90% did not go on to die by suicide or violent death.

Suicide Assessment

Perhaps more than any other mental health professionals, family therapists are uniquely equipped to grasp the vitally important interpersonal complexities that characterize depression, desperation, and suicidality. The risk of completed suicide is heightened when clients believe that they are a burden to others and that by dying they will actually be doing their loved ones a favor. Family therapists have the relational interviewing skills necessary to bring such beliefs into the open and to effectively engage family members in responding to them.

The strength-based orientation of many family therapists is also a benefit during suicide assessments. Given the high stakes involved, it makes sense that some clinicians would find themselves developing deficit-focused tunnel vision, anxiously and exclusively homing in on potential risk factors. Is the client hopeless? Does he or she perceive himself or herself as a burden? Does he or she have a history of trauma and previous suicide attempts? Is there easy access to weapons or other lethal means? Does the client have an intense desire for relief or an intent, a commitment, or a plan to die? All of these topics are essential to address, but for an assessment to be reliable, it must be balanced. Danger must be evaluated within the context of potential safety. Thus, it is also important for the clinician to explore the client's resilience. What are his or her beliefs? Are there any skills, any strategies that could come into play? What are past or current examples of grit and resilience? In short, what resources does the client possess, and are there any that could be put in service of survival?

The need for balance does not end there. Of course it is important to be curious about the client's interior world—the dark and frightening places as well as the exceptions, the variations, and the occasional glimmers of hope. Interpersonal context is also of crucial relevance. Thus, it becomes necessary to also explore the extent to which loved ones, close friends, and professional helpers could be contributing to the danger and the extent to which they are able to help protect against it. Sensitivity to the *context* of an individual's suicidality helps clinicians further appreciate possible dangers and possible protections.

If the issue of a client's suicidality is raised during a couple or family session, then at least part of the assessment should be conducted with the other(s) present, as the perspective(s) offered will contribute to a more complete understanding of the situation. But then at some point in the interview, the therapist will need to continue with just the suicidal individual. This frees up the client from having to shield loved ones from forthright answers to probing questions.

Also essential in helping clients to let down their guard—allowing them the opportunity to reveal deeply personal, deeply troubling truths—is the clinician's continual offering of empathy. Therapists who intersperse their questions with empathic statements help ensure not only that their clients feel heard, understood, and respected but also that they do not feel interrogated. Empathy alters the rhythm of the interaction, so clients aren't simply fielding question after question. It also allows them to determine whether the clinician has an accurate grasp of their experience when they hear statements such as these: "What a mountain of obligations! Too much to even think about, never mind do something about." "How exhausting it must be, trying to keep at bay these intrusive thoughts about shooting yourself. No wonder you're not sleeping."

It is impossible to predict the future actions of an individual, so any determination about suicidality is at best an informed guess, but therapists can draw on the results and conclusions of hundreds of excellent sociological and clinical studies to help them know what to ask during their assessment interviews. Studies indicate that suicidality is intensified by particular kinds of experiences, histories, medical and psychological conditions, beliefs, and behaviors. Clinicians thus inquire, at some point during the conversation, about the following risks:

- Overwhelming demands and obligations
- Relationship losses (through divorce, death, or emotional cutoff)
- Threat to or loss of legal, social, or financial status
- Threats to personal safety, whether through life-threatening traumatic events or abuse or bullying
- Severe suffering from physical or psychological symptoms, including chronic or acute pain, depressed or manic moods, anger or anxiety, insomnia, or hallucinations or delusions
- Conflicted identity (gender, religious, spiritual, or cultural) and/or sexual orientation
- Feeling shame and/or a burden to others
- Risky coping mechanisms, such as withdrawing, self-medicating with alcohol and/or drugs, self-harming, disordered eating, or acting impulsively or compulsively
- Personal or family history of previous suicide attempts
- Feeling desperate for relief and hopeless about the future
- Making plans for, preparing for, or rehearsing an attempt
- Seeking out and accessing the means of making an attempt

Because suicidality is buffered by various kinds of intra- and interpersonal resources, it is also essential that clinicians inquire thoroughly about resiliency, spiritual beliefs, meaningful social responsibilities, a willingness to seek personal and professional help, and the availability of empathic and supportive significant others. However, when inquiring about resources, therapists must be careful not to attempt to impose hope or to offer unsolicited encouragement. It is possible for a well-conducted suicide assessment to actually be experienced as therapeutic by clients, particularly when the clinician is adept at communicating an empathic understanding of the clients' suffering. But depressed clients recoil from naively optimistic professionals (or family or friends); they will worry whether the person trying to help is emotionally equipped to handle the extent of their despair.

At some point during a suicide assessment, the clinician must decide on a course of action. Given the current circumstances and experiences of the client, how can the suicidality best be managed? Juxtaposing the information gathered about intra- and interpersonal risks and resources, along with any impressions formed from the client's participation in the interview, the clinician either takes steps to have the person protected in a hospital or to garner the requisite client resources and support from significant others to safely manage the suicidality at home. If the former decision is made, then the clinician makes arrangements for the client to be assessed for involuntary admission. This is always a difficult decision to arrive at, as it results in the temporary removal of the client's ability to choose. However, despite the personal toll this may take on the client, as well as on therapists who strive to maintain a nonexpert, noninterventionist stance with clients, all therapists can recognize that by legally removing client choice in the short term, they secure the freedom of the client to be alive to make choices in the future.

If the clinician decides that safety is possible to maintain outside the hospital, then he or she works collaboratively with the client to complete a safety plan—a resource-based to-do list that identifies protective steps that the client and relevant significant others are willing and able to undertake. First and foremost, the plan establishes how they will restrict, or at least limit, access to the means for attempting suicide. From there, the clinician and client typically identify coping behaviors that he or she has been using to contend with the desperation (e.g., self-harming, abusing substances, engaging in impulsive or compulsive behaviors, or withdrawing from people and activities) and brainstorm temporary, safer, alternatives. They identify safe havens the client could access for a limited time if necessary (anywhere from a friend's home to voluntary admission to the hospital), and they write down contact information for family members, friends, and professionals willing to offer various forms of support. Phone numbers are included so that the client has easy access to them even at times of great distress.

Rather than uniquely constructed safety plans, some therapists rely on boilerplate no-harm or no-suicide contracts. Such legal-appearing documents ask for clients to sign a promise not to hurt or kill themselves. When first introduced in the 1970s, it was believed that a signed contract in the file would help secure a troubled client's commitment to live and lessen the clinician's legal exposure if the client were to end up completing suicide. However, research has shown that contracts do not afford the client any added protection and, when sued, clinicians who use them do not fare any better in the courtroom than those who do not.

Suicide assessments are inherently anxiety provoking and emotionally taxing, even when they go well and the client is able to safely negotiate harrowing desires, thoughts, and circumstances. Following an assessment, clinicians can benefit from securing time with colleagues to talk through how the client presented and responded, the information they were able to gather, what they decided needed to happen to ensure safety, and what they experienced throughout the process. Such postsession analysis serves as excellent preparation for the next time a suicidal client presents.

Douglas Flemons

See also Empathy; No-Harm Contracts; Resilience; Suicide; Therapeutic Assessment

Further Readings

Flemons, D., & Gralnik, L. M. (2013). *Relational suicide assessment: Risks, resources, and possibilities for safety*. New York, NY: W. W. Norton.

Jamison, K. R. (1999). *Night falls fast: Understanding suicide*. New York, NY: Vintage.

Jobes, D. A. (2006). *Managing suicidal risk: A collaborative approach*. New York, NY: Guilford Press.

Joiner, T. (2005). *Why people die by suicide*. Cambridge, MA: Harvard University Press.

Joiner, T. (2010). *Myths about suicide*. Boston, MA: Harvard University Press.

Rudd, M. D., Mandrusiak, M., & Joiner, T. E., Jr. (2006). The case against no-suicide contracts: The commitment to treatment statement as a practice alternative. *Journal of Clinical Psychology, 62*(2), 243–251. doi:10.1002/jclp.20227

Shea, S. C. (2002). *The practical art of suicide assessment: A guide for mental health professionals and substance abuse counselors*. Hoboken, NJ: Wiley.

Assimilation: Immigrants and Refugees

According to the U.S. Department of Homeland Security (DHS), almost 4,000 immigrants and 70,000 refugees are granted admission into the country every year. While integrating into the mainstream culture, immigrants can lose certain aspects of their identity as they are faced with cultural values and customs that are sometimes markedly different from what they are accustomed to. These can include expectations guiding interpersonal family functioning, gender roles (and alongside these, courtship, dating, and marital scripts), and a myriad of social norms and practices. *Assimilation* is the lifelong process of adapting or adjusting to a new society's culture. This term has been applied to immigrants and refugees insofar as the experience of migrating to a new country (voluntarily or otherwise) brings with it considerable stressors. Assimilation is an important issue for mental health professionals in the United States because increasing numbers of individuals, couples, and families are resettling here as a consequence of ongoing economic globalization and armed conflict. Understanding multiple processes of assimilation is essential to understanding the American experience and helping immigrants adjust to its mainstream (and new, to them) culture. This entry presents a brief historical overview of immigrants in the United States. A discussion regarding legal differences between immigrants and refugees, processes of resettling and assimilating, and clinical principles for working with these groups follows.

Historical Overview of Immigrants in the United States

The United States has a long-standing history of immigration. An estimated 8 million immigrants were admitted into the country between 1855 and 1890. This rate continued to increase throughout the 1900s, with an estimated 12 million immigrants arriving between 1892 and 1954. In 2013, almost 70,000 refugees and over 25,000 asylum-seekers were admitted. The terms *refugee* and *asylum-seeker* are often confused. A refugee is someone who is seeking protection from persecution and whose claim has been evaluated and granted. An asylum-seeker is someone seeking protection from persecution but whose claim for refugee status has not been evaluated or granted yet. The leading countries of origin for refugees in the United States today are Iraq, Burma, and Bhutan. The leading countries of origin for asylum-seekers are China, Egypt, and Ethiopia. In 2014, the rapidly escalating armed conflict in Syria prompted the United States to increase the number of refugees being permanently resettled on its shores from 350 to nearly 10,000 annually.

Legal Differences Between Immigrants and Refugees

The legal differences between immigrants and refugees are important to understand because they impact assimilation in considerable ways. To begin, these respective designations dictate eligibility requirements for gaining entry into a country and (then) what resources individuals, couples, and families are eligible to receive.

According to domestic legislation—which is comprised of the Immigration and Nationality Act (INA) and Refugee Act—a refugee is a person who is unable or unwilling to return to his or her country of origin because of persecution, or a well-founded fear of persecution, on the grounds of race, religion, nationality, membership in a particular social group, or political opinion.

An immigrant is any alien except one legally admitted under specific nonimmigrant categories. An undocumented immigrant (i.e., illegal alien) who enters the United States without proper documentation would be defined as an immigrant according to legislation, but they would not be eligible for legal privileges given to permanent residents (e.g., legal employment rather than under-the-table work and health insurance). Assimilation is further complicated by the process of obtaining legal residency status in the United States.

Processes of Cultural Assimilation

Theories about assimilation are complex because they take into consideration multiple factors involved within the experience. Each subsequent generation descending from immigrants and refugees becomes more assimilated than the generation before it. This uneven process consists of adapting, learning, and incorporating a new society's language, traditions, values, and behaviors. Field leaders have argued that the social distance created between the new society and immigrants and refugees (and between sequential generations of immigrants and refugees) perpetuates divides between groups and can prevent successful assimilation. The International Organization for Migration (IOM) describes adjustment as a four-stage process: arrival, reality, recovery, and balance.

Arrival

As immigrants and refugees arrive to the United States, they often hold feelings of relief and hope. Immigrants look forward to accomplishing goals related to bettering their personal and/or family well-being and typically have a social support system in place to assist them in doing so. Refugees, on the other hand, are glad to have escaped a dangerous or potentially life-threatening situation.

Reality

In the second stage, immigrants and refugees face the reality of adjusting to a new culture. Drastic changes in socioeconomic status become apparent as language barriers, for example, force immigrants and refugees who were professionals (e.g., physicians, teachers) in their homelands to now work low-skilled positions. They also struggle with being labeled as "minorities," even if they are of White European descent. This perpetuates a social divide that can sabotage assimilation.

Recovery

The third stage is characterized by efforts to assimilate to mainstream values in the United States. It typically consists of learning the English language, interacting with the community, renewing a sense of purpose, and—for college-educated immigrants—regaining professional roles and competencies. This is also where the process of working through past traumatic experiences and dealing with loss begins. As immigrants and refugees adjust to a new culture, they also face challenges associated with holding onto key components of their cultural identity. It is also important to note that women generally do this more easily (and faster) than men. The sense of emasculation that men often experience as a result of losing traditional family and community roles during migration, especially if they come from a patriarchal society, can lead to more mental health problems. Conventional stigmas related to admitting such struggles (or seeking help to allay them) can further exacerbate symptoms' severity.

Balance

In the final stage, which is lifelong and ongoing, immigrants and refugees feel a sense of belonging to the new culture while synchronously embracing selected native cultural values. While this may suggest that assimilation is "complete," it is actually an ongoing and lifelong process. It is important to note, too, that some refugees (more than immigrants) never learn English, pursue a formal education, or participate in gainful employment. The mental health differences between those who reach this fourth stage and those who do not are profound. This becomes particularly apparent in situations where traditional cultural values conflict with cultural values of the dominant society. The developmental stage of going to college, for example, can present challenges for families wherein elders presume that their children will care and provide for them in perpetuity. This can lead to considerable intergenerational conflict. As young adults pursue higher education, professional careers, and smaller families (while at the same time adopting the comparatively individualistic mores of the United States), they are often faced with difficult choices and discord vis-à-vis their parents and grandparents.

Guiding Clinical Principles for Working With Immigrants and Refugees

Both refugees and immigrants relocate to the United States in search of a better life. However, their resettlement conditions are different. As a result of fleeing persecution, refugees are typically at an increased risk for developing mental health problems (e.g., posttraumatic stress disorder [PTSD], major depression) and interpersonal or family conflict. Immigrants, on the other hand, made a personal decision to leave their native country. The mental health problems associated with willing relocation can manifest in less severe mental health problems and/or dyadic and familial conflict.

For both groups, a desire to assimilate with the mainstream culture while maintaining a sense of their own cultural heritage compounds existing mental health problems. Innovative research in working with refugees and immigrants by scholars such as Joe Giordano, Monica McGoldrick, Nydia Garcia-Preto, and Elizabeth Wieling emphasizes the importance conducting a comprehensive biopsychosocial-spiritual diagnostic assessment (BPSS-DA), clearly defining treatment goals, and honoring cultural differences.

Conducting a Comprehensive Biopsychosocial-Spiritual Diagnostic Assessment

A comprehensive assessment is informed by George Engel's early model that embraces a multidisciplinary treatment approach. It places emphasis on factors important to biological (e.g., physical, neuropsychiatric), psychological (e.g., mood, cognition, meaning-making), social (e.g., interpersonal conflict or accord in marital and family relationships, community involvement), and spiritual (e.g., religious beliefs, connection with a sense of divine, personal serenity) functioning. In developing a formulation of the presenting problem across time, clinicians should be careful to honor these and other complexities inherent to the intersections between culture and assimilation. This can be particularly useful in the consideration of formal diagnostic criteria required to be eligible for particular services (e.g., insurance coverage, case management). It can also serve to facilitate attention to individual and relational trauma histories and ongoing political and legal processes.

Clearly Defining Treatment Goals

Treatment goals should be clearly defined, achievable, and build on the clients' (individual, couple, or family) desire to assimilate into the mainstream culture. These goals, for example, may consist of attending English-language and/or citizenship classes, interacting with members of the mainstream community, or volunteering. They may also include building a sense of safety in the therapeutic relationship through mutual education about cultural nuances that contradict mainstream expectations.

Honoring Cultural Differences

The way that refugees and immigrants are treated in society is connected to their classification as a minority group. This taxonomy can uphold negative stereotypes and make disclosing sensitive information relevant to treatment difficult. In turn, this can prevent building a strong therapeutic alliance and interfere with treatment. Providers should recognize these differences in the clinical setting and openly discuss concerns during the intake and BPSS-DA processes and (actively) throughout treatment. While intervention at the arrival stage may buffer hardships associated with unexpected challenges, refugees and immigrants typically are unaware of resources in the community upon arrival. This leads to the importance of targeting clinical interventions at the recovery stage, which could help clients regain a sense of control over their lives and avoid marginalization that manifests in relationship ruptures, feelings of isolation, despair, rigidity, and helplessness. Doing all of this effectively requires moving beyond the traditional clinical approaches learned in graduate training. Mental health providers must function with an awareness of cultural nuances related to assimilation, general sequences associated with it, and skills in psychoeducation and advocacy. This means embracing the dual roles of mental health professional and human rights advocate.

Damir S. Utržan and Tai J. Mendenhall

See also Acculturation; Assessment, Biopsychosocial; Family Assessment, Models of; Immigrant Families; Systemic Family Therapy

Further Readings

Alba, R., & Nee, V. (1997). Rethinking assimilation theory for a new era of immigrants. *International Migration Review*, 31(4), 826–874. Retrieved from http://www.jstor.org/stable/2547416

Berry, J. W. (2008). Immigration, acculturation, and adaptation. *Applied Psychology*, 46(1), 5–34. doi:10.1111/j.1464-0597.1997.tb01087.x

Center for Victims of Torture. (n.d.). *Resources for health and human service providers*. Retrieved from http://www.cvt.org/resources/health-care-providers

Hays, P. A. (2007). *Addressing cultural complexities in practice: A framework for clinicians and counselors* (2nd ed.). Washington, DC: American Psychological Association.

Hoshmand, L. T. (Ed.). (2006). *Culture, psychotherapy, and counseling: Critical and integrative approaches*. Thousand Oaks, CA: Sage.

Imprint Project. (n.d.). *Immigration and professional integration*. Retrieved from http://www.imprintproject.org

McGoldrick, M., Giordano, J., & Garcia-Preto, N. (Eds.). (2005). *Ethnicity & family therapy* (3rd ed.). New York, NY: Guilford Press.

McGoldrick, M., & Hardy, K. V. (Eds.). (2008). *Re-visioning family therapy: Race, culture, & gender and clinical practice* (2nd ed.). New York, NY: Guilford Press.

Wing-Sue, D. & Sue, D. (2013). *Counseling the culturally diverse: Theory and practice* (6th ed.). Hoboken, NJ: Wiley.

ATTACHMENT

First formed in infancy, attachment is based on the emotional connection between infants and their primary caregivers and affects the models infants have of self and other as well as how they regulate their emotion when distressed. Attachment theory highlights the importance of consistency, attunement, and responsiveness in creating a secure base whereby infants can explore their environment and seek safety when needed. These same principles are applicable in adulthood and, more recently, have formed an important foundation for couple and family therapy. This entry highlights the development of attachment theory, including the contributions of John Bowlby and Mary Ainsworth. It will also highlight the role of attachment in adult relationships, how attachment change occurs, and the role of intervention in facilitating that change.

John Bowlby's Contributions

In the early part of the 20th century, there were many ideas that de-emphasized the importance of love and physical affection in close relationships. In the midst of these ideas, John Bowlby was one person who emerged to highlight the importance of the close relationships and their role in promoting health and proper development. Bowlby used an interdisciplinary theoretical approach that integrated concepts from a variety of fields (e.g., psychology, ethology) to explain the importance of early relationships in helping to form intimate bonds that are crucial for healthy development. He emphasized that unexplained and prolonged separation from caregivers brought distress and could lead to unintended negative consequences. These ideas directly called into question the nature of the parent–child bond as explained by psychoanalysts and behaviorists.

Bowlby emphasized that strong, secure emotional bonds of attachment are formed when an infant can consistently depend on an attachment figure to provide warmth, reassurance, safety, and sensitivity in regard to physical and emotional needs. He framed these attachment bonds within the individual as internal working models of self and other. These models informed whether a person felt worthy of love and also whether others could be reliably depended on to provide that love. He also discovered that when a child feels secure, they are better able to explore the world around them rather than being inhibited by a fear of being separated from their caregiver. The caregiver is then considered a secure base to which the child can return for consistent comfort and reassurance when needed while also feeling free to wander and examine the external world in order to learn and grow.

Mary Ainsworth's Contributions

Much of the empirical basis for attachment theory was developed as a result of the work of Mary Ainsworth. She collaborated with John Bowlby throughout her career and was thus greatly affected by his concepts related to separation of mothers and children and how it affected a child's development. Ainsworth used this basis when she began collecting a vast amount of naturalistic observational data of infants and caregivers, which provided a central foundation for examining mother–infant interactional patterns. Initially observing mothers and infants in Uganda; Africa; and later in Baltimore, Maryland, Ainsworth discovered important differences in the quality of infant–mother relationships. Maternal sensitivity to infant signaling was found to be a crucial factor in the attachment patterns of the infants, which was associated with crying levels and contact-seeking behavior.

Mary Ainsworth's naturalistic observational background in studying the quality of infant–caregiver relationships led to the development of the strange situation procedure (SSP). This procedure is a laboratory observational method used to examine 12- and 18-month-olds' attachment behaviors with their primary caregiver during exploration and separation. Various conditions are set up with the most pivotal being the reunion episodes, when the caregiver returns after a brief absence. Many observed behaviors during the procedure paralleled the interactions Ainsworth had seen during her naturalistic observations.

Ainsworth developed different dimensions of infant attachment patterns based on the behaviors exhibited during the SSP. *Secure attachment* is defined as an infant being able to depend on their parent for comfort and reassurance. They showed normal levels of distress when the caregiver left the room but were able to clearly signal their need for comfort upon return.

Some infants were found to exhibit avoidant strategies during the SSP (*avoidant attachment*). Although it was evident that they felt distress similar to other infants, they did not signal that distress. Ainsworth found that these infants were more likely to have their bids for closeness and comfort consistently rejected by the caregiver.

Other infants were more difficult to comfort following the SSP, demonstrating bids for closeness coupled with anger or frustration with the caregiver (*ambivalent or resistant attachment*). Caregivers of these infants were more likely to be inconsistent in their responses, oscillating between sensitive and rejecting responses. Some infants also demonstrated odd or disorganized behaviors during the SSP (*disorganized attachment*). Caregivers of these infants were more likely to demonstrate frightening or dissociative behaviors toward the infant. The odd behavior arose from the infant because the caregiver was simultaneously a source of potential comfort while also being a source of worry and distress.

Attachment in Adulthood

Although much of the original focus of attachment was on the primacy of the infant–caregiver relationship, scholars later began to examine the role of attachment in adult relationships. As with the infant–caregiver relationship, the goal in adulthood is *attachment security*, typified by a feeling of safety in relationships and a confidence that attachment figures will be available and responsive when needed.

With the added attention on romantic relationships in adulthood, the issue of measurement arose. Two distinct measurement traditions have emerged in the adult attachment literature. Both measurement traditions have been shown to be valid and useful in understanding couple relationships. However, in many respects they seem to be more different than similar, making it important not to make inferences across measurement traditions.

Within social and personality psychology, self-report is used to measure conscious representations of how people view themselves and others and their overall comfort level in close relationships. Attachment insecurity represents negative perceptions of self and/or other. More specifically, fear of abandonment points towards *attachment anxiety*, and discomfort with intimacy and disclosure typifies *attachment avoidance*. Those higher in attachment anxiety often desire connection with another person so much that they struggle when others do not reciprocate in the way they would like. Those higher in attachment avoidance tend to seek a greater physical, psychological, and/or emotional distance in their close relationships than others.

Within developmental psychology, process-focused interviews and interactions are typically used to measure unconscious representations and the function of relationships in coping with and regulating distress. Attachment insecurity represents maladaptive approaches to distress. Specifically, *preoccupied attachment* refers to those individuals who tend to feel overwhelmed by emotion and seek to have their attachment needs met by exaggerating those needs to the attachment figure. The primary problem with soliciting support in this way is that it actually pushes the other person away.

Dismissing attachment refers to those individuals who typically deflect or deny their attachment needs when they are distressed. For these individuals, seeking to have their needs met has been consistently unproductive. As a result, they stop signaling those needs to others, even though they do not stop feeling distress. In addition to these three attachment strategies (secure, preoccupied, and dismissing), there is also an added designation within the developmental psychology measurement tradition. *Unresolved attachment* refers to difficulty processing loss and/or trauma and has been linked to disruption and inconsistency in attachment relationships.

The conceptual differences between the two approaches as well as the different labels associated with each tradition can make it somewhat difficult to understand and therefore generalize to clinical work. Nonetheless, it is most important to understand that research has consistently found attachment security as defined by both approaches to be an asset in close relationships, whereas attachment insecurity has greater potential to disrupt relationships. The attachment-related challenge in close relationships is for both people to be able to signal their attachment needs clearly and also be attuned and responsive to the needs of others.

Attachment Change

Because of the potential for attachment security to provide individual and relationship benefits, a good amount of attention has been given to understanding attachment change. This is especially relevant from a therapeutic perspective. Much of the research has supported the idea that there is a decent amount of stability across the life span in a person's working models of attachment. Because attachment experiences in infancy form a blueprint for close relationships, relationship experiences after infancy are typically filtered through a preestablished lens.

However, despite the tendency toward stability, there are fluctuations that occur in terms of attachment representations and strategies. One of the more robust findings is that attachment has been shown to be negatively influenced by highly stressful life events such as loss, trauma, or serious illness. Conversely, it has been a bit more difficult to identify findings related to positive attachment change (i.e., enhancing attachment security). Although findings have been mixed, there are some indications that attachment security in one person can help increase the security of interactions, even if the other person is more insecure in his or her attachment representations.

Attachment and Intervention

Another issue of great clinical relevance is the relationship between attachment and intervention. Several early evidence-based intervention programs exist that are designed to help increase the attachment security between infants and their caregivers. Many of these are skill-based and designed to help caregivers recognize infant signals and then respond appropriately.

Within the context of therapy, the therapist–client relationship has the potential to exhibit many of the characteristics of an attachment relationship where the client feels understood and supported. Although more research is needed in this area, the process of therapy has the potential to create a useful context for positive attachment change.

Although elements of attachment theory are becoming more common in a variety of systemic treatment models, emotionally focused therapy (EFT) and attachment-based family therapy (ABFT) are two evidence-based approaches that anchor concepts and interventions in attachment theory. Within EFT, couple distress represents a disruption of the attachment bond, and the EFT therapist works to increase relationship safety so that partners can explore deeper and more vulnerable emotions in reaching out and being accessible to each other in new, relationship enhancing ways.

ABFT uses interpersonal relationships to decrease depressive symptoms in adolescents. Within ABFT, the attachment relationship between parents and children is strengthened by helping the adolescent express difficult emotions related to past relationship ruptures or traumas and facilitating availability and responsiveness in parents.

The use of attachment within EFT and ABFT not only points to its potential utility as a useful conceptual tool in therapy but it also highlights the potential for attachment concepts to guide intervention development and adaptation. Specifically, because individuals develop different attachment-based strategies for coping with distress, it may be crucial for therapists to adapt their interventions to their clients' attachment characteristics. This may be especially important in couple and family therapy, where contrasting attachment strategies in partners and family members may make it difficult for clients to identify and be responsive to each other's attachment needs.

Ryan B. Seedall and E. Megan Lachmar

See also Attachment and Romantic Love; Attachment Styles; Attachment Theory; Attachment-Based Family Therapy; Conflict in Couples and Families; Emotionally Focused Therapy for Couples; Social Support

Further Readings

Ainsworth, M. D. S., Blehar, M. C., Waters, E., & Wall, S. (1978). *Patterns of attachment: A psychological study of the strange situation.* Hillsdale, NJ: Erlbaum.

Bowlby, J. (1983, 1976, 1982). *Attachment and loss: Vols. 1–3.* New York, NY: Basic Books.

Bowlby, J. (1988). *A secure base.* New York, NY: Basic Books.

Bretherton, I. (1992). The origins of attachment theory: John Bowlby and Mary Ainsworth. *Developmental Psychology, 28,* 759–775.

Cassidy, J., & Shaver, P. R. (2008). *Handbook of attachment: Theory, research, and clinical applications* (2nd ed.). New York, NY: Guilford Press.

Diamond, G. S., Diamond, G. M., & Levy, S. A. (2013). *Attachment-based family therapy for depressed adolescents.* Washington DC: American Psychological Association.

Johnson, S. M. (2004). *The practice of emotionally focused couple therapy: Creating connection* (2nd ed.). New York, NY: Brunner-Routledge.

Karen, R. (1994). *Becoming attached: First relationships and how they shape our capacity to love.* New York, NY: Oxford University Press.

Mikulincer, M., & Shaver, P. R. (2007). *Attachment in adulthood: Structure, dynamics, and change.* New York, NY: Guilford Press.

Seedall, R. B., & Wampler, K. S. (2013). An attachment primer for couple therapists: Research and clinical implications. *Journal of Marital and Family Therapy, 39,* 427–440.

Attachment and Adolescents

Attachment styles are influenced by attachment experiences from various stages of life, including childhood, young adulthood, and adulthood. Early experiences with parenting styles and with other caregivers can shape how individuals relate to their caregiver and how they form and interact in other relationships later in life. Although attachment styles are fairly stable throughout the life span, adolescents are at a unique period of development, allowing for changes in attachment patterns through corrective experiences. This entry addresses the changes in relationships and manifestation and functioning of attachment styles during adolescence.

Adolescence is the stage of development marked by major changes, stress, and emotional turmoil. It is a time when individuals assert their independence by relying less on their primary caregivers. It is also a transformative stage when adolescents start to picture the possibility of themselves as caregivers as they transition into adulthood. Adolescents seek to develop new close and supportive relationships (such as friends and romantic partners) outside of their family and primary caregivers. Similar to how infants and children explore the world around them, adolescents use their caregiver as a secure base but return to their family for support when faced with severe stress. As we can see, at this stage of their development adolescents are not ready to become completely independent from their primary caregivers.

Peer relationships are an important part of emotional and social development. For example, by mid-adolescence, many adolescents start forming peer relationships, which are influenced by the quality of relationships they have had with their family. Peer relationships are sources of essential experiences, such as intimacy, romance, and feedback regarding appropriate social behaviors and influence. Although early attachment patterns continue to shape the adolescents' experiences, during adolescence attachments continue to develop depending on the quality of peer relationships.

Attachment relationships during adolescence can be evaluated and understood through *felt security*, *proximity-seeking*, *secure-base behavior*, and *safe-haven behavior*. Felt security is exhibited in the affect adolescents express toward their parents and peers. Proximity-seeking refers to the extent adolescents seek the support of their parents and peers under various stressors. Secure-base behavior applies to the exploration of the surrounding environment from close proximity of the parents or peers, and safe-haven behavior is returning to parents or peers when faced with extreme stress. The following sections will address how adolescents manifest each attachment style: (a) *secure*, (b) *avoidant*, (c) *resistant–ambivalent*, and (d) *disorganized*.

The capacity to manage stress, adapt to changes, and build relationships can be impacted by the attachment style adolescents developed during childhood. John Bowlby's attachment theory identified four distinct attachment styles: secure attachment, avoidant attachment, resistant–ambivalent attachment, and disorganized attachment. Adolescents who have a secure attachment style from early childhood tend to be more resilient and adaptive when faced with changes in their life and disruptions in close relationships due to their strong early foundation. When presented with an emotionally corrective experience, such as counseling or psychotherapy, adolescents are able to quickly recover from any temporary disruptions. Additionally, they tend to be successful in developing supportive relationships outside of the family that they often rely on. During this development stage, adolescents are starting to form their identities; thus, the group provides a supportive space and access to multiple sources to experiment with different facets of themselves or different versions of themselves.

Adolescents have an avoidant attachment style due to unavailable caregivers and the rejection they experienced in early childhood. They tend to be emotionally distant and have difficulties separating from their family and forming new close relationships. They often feel uncomfortable with closeness and feel more comfortable with communicating their emotions indirectly. Owing to their experience of rejection early in life, adolescents with an avoidant attachment style seek independence and self-reliance but experience difficulties when faced with adversities, as they are less likely to reach out to others for support. Helping them express their emotions and communicate their struggles, as well as validating their effort toward independence, can help them have a positive experience in a close, supportive relationship with others besides their primary caregivers.

Resistant–ambivalent attachment results from a lack of consistency in attention from caregivers during early childhood. Adolescents with an ambivalent attachment may appear disagreeable and hostile while demanding the attention they lacked from their caregivers during childhood. Also, ambivalent adolescents have difficulties building new relationships due to their strong attachment to their primary caregivers and tend to reject peers because of their focus on their primary caregivers. They are prone to seeking negative attention and have difficulty getting close to others for fear of abandonment. A relationship that emphasizes strong boundaries and support may provide an emotionally corrective experience for adolescents with this type of attachment style.

People with disorganized attachment have often experienced a traumatic childhood, where their caregiver was the source of both support and anxiety. Because of the instability individuals with disorganized attachment experienced in childhood, they may appear childlike and exhibit emotional, cognitive, and social difficulties. Their behavior is often unpredictable, as they assess safety while wanting to be in control. On the other hand, adolescents with a disorganized attachment style crave attention and closeness from others. However, they are overwhelmed by the concept of being close to someone else and are unsure of how to connect with others. This unpredictable behavior makes it difficult for others to get close to them and form a healthy relationship. Therefore, they require a highly structured, stable, and predictable environment. Adolescents with a disorganized attachment style can benefit from verbalizing their emotions and setting realistic goals that are appropriate for their level of social functioning.

In summary, the adolescent years are an essential period for individuals' social, cognitive, and emotional development. Early attachment experiences and attachment styles are predictive of how attachment relationships are manifested during adolescence. Given that adolescents are not fully developed at this stage of life, they are able to make changes in their attachment styles if provided with an emotionally corrective experience.

Minnah W. Farook and Roberto L. Abreu

See also Adolescent Behavior Problems; Adolescent Mental Health; Attachment; Attachment and Health; Attachment Styles; Attachment Theory

Further Readings

Allen, J. P., & Land, D. (1999). Attachment in adolescence. In J. Cassidy & P. R. Shaver (Eds.), *Handbook of attachment: Theory, research, and clinical applications* (pp. 319–335). New York, NY: Guilford Press.

Dover, J. (2015). The impact of early attachment patterns on adolescent development. In L. French & R. Klein (Eds.), *Therapeutic practice in schools, Volume two: The contemporary adolescent: A clinical workbook for counsellors, psychotherapists and arts therapists* (pp. 19–28). New York, NY: Routledge/Taylor & Francis.

Kobak, R., Zajac, K., Herres, J., & Ewing, E. K. (2015). Attachment based treatments for adolescents: The secure cycle as a framework for assessment, treatment and evaluation. *Attachment & Human Development*, 17, 220–239. doi:10.1080/14616734.2015.1006388

ATTACHMENT AND HEALTH

Attachment can be defined as the emotional affectionate bond created in the context of the intimate relationships formed by infants with their primary caregivers. The capacity of a secure attachment persists into adulthood and is reflected in an individual's quality of relationships with others. Researchers use attachment theory (i.e., the study of intimate bonds and their influence on a number of relationships and life factors) to understand the impact of relational quality on health-related conditions (e.g., disease, chronic illness) and mental health (e.g., mood, anxiety, deficits in self-concept). Specifically, they examine the relationship between attachment styles (i.e., secure, anxious, avoidant, or ambivalent) and the expression of acute or chronic illnesses. This entry provides an overview of the existing literature on attachment and health (including mental health), with attention to the specific attachment styles. The entry concludes with a brief discussion of how attachment styles can affect physical and mental health as well as treatment adherence.

Attachment

Research on attachment has demonstrated that early childhood parenting practices and styles can result in the formation of four different attachment systems that are evident in adult relationships: *secure* (trust in relationships), *insecure–ambivalent* (monitor their relationships and look to others to make them feel secure), *insecure–avoidant* (tend not to want to rely on others and fear being too close to people), and *disorganized* (no clear style of dealing with others; usually is the result of abuse). Attachment systems can provide important information about the patterned ways in which people cope with difficult life situations; thus, these attachment systems can assist health care providers and researchers to understand the help-seeking behaviors of individuals. Moreover, research is beginning to examine the connection between attachment and health outcomes (e.g., medically unexplained symptoms), as well as health care utilization. All of this suggests that an individual's attachment system may impact the overall health and health-seeking behaviors of an individual.

Adult Attachment and Physical Health

The use of attachment theory to understand acute and chronic illnesses suggests that insecure attachment can influence the expression and/or course of a disorder. In general, insecurely attached individuals (insecure–ambivalent and insecure–avoidant) are more susceptible to stress (i.e., perceive more stress) and may have more physiological responses to the stress. Research indicates that this may be due to the influence of certain attachment systems on coping responses to disorders. Consequently, a tendency to use external methods (e.g., increased substance use, risky sexual behaviors, poor diet, less exercise) of regulating affect may occur in both adolescents and young adults that may lead to increased health-related problems. Although research has found that individuals with insecure attachment styles also report frequent health symptoms such as headaches or digestive upsets, they are less likely than those with secure attachment styles to seek assistance and social support. On the other hand, research has found that insecure–ambivalent attachment (also known as anxious attachment) may be a predictor of increased inflammatory bowel disease, vascular accidents, heart attacks, chronic pain, high blood pressure, ulcers, and lower levels of T-cells that impact the immune system, suggesting that an individual's attachment system is correlated with physical and not just behavioral manifestations—that is, it can be expressed biologically. Moreover, attachment systems may also have an impact on an individual's overall mental health (e.g., mood, anxiety).

Adult Attachment and Mental Health

Research suggests that attachment styles may influence the progression of mental health disorders. For example, empirical research proposes that the majority of patients who are either in the initial phase of a major mental health episode or who experience chronic psychiatric disorder(s) may display insecure attachment systems. Furthermore, one study has shown that some people with a first episode of psychosis were classified as having a disorganized attachment style. These findings raise the possibility that psychopathology and insecure and disorganized systems of attachment are interrelated. Thus, the literature supports the need to understand not only how attachment systems affect physical and mental health but also their impact on patients' responses to health treatments and interventions.

Adult Attachment and Health Interventions

Various studies have explored the correlations between patients' attachment systems, interactions with health care providers, and adherence to health treatments and interventions. The findings indicate that adherence to treatment is impacted by the patient's attachment systems. For instance, researchers have suggested that treatment adherence occurs as a result of the perception and behavior of the patient in relation to their health care provider, who may become their "secure base." These findings demonstrate that in order for successful health interventions to take place, a relationship alliance must be formed. Hence, both the patient's and the provider's attachment systems need to be taken into account in the professional or healing relationship. One study postulated that securely attached patients were more likely to adhere to one-on-one interventions and insecurely attached patients showed poorer adherence. Thus, patients with an insecure–avoidant attachment style may find it difficult to engage in the therapeutic process for mental health services. Similarly, insecurely attached patients were found to experience poorer diabetes self-management (i.e., lower adherence to recommendations related to diet, exercise, and foot care) and experienced increased negative outcomes. Therefore, understanding the attachment styles of patients could help increase adherence to treatment. In regard to treatment adherence, it is also important to consider the patient's social support and how it is impacted by the patient's attachment style.

Adult Attachment and Social Support

Research has established that social support and supportive relationships are a health protective factor. Furthermore, people who lack social ties or social integration experience higher mortality rates (e.g., from cardiovascular disease or cancer). Yet attachment research has shown that more anxious (ambivalent attachment) individuals generally perceive less support or remember helpful behavior more negatively. This finding suggests that health professionals who are informed about attachment systems can aid patients in recovery and maintenance of health by encouraging them to seek the benefits of high social support. How the environment helps to shape an individual's attachment system is an additional area to consider in understanding the connections between attachment health, the patient–provider relationship, and social support.

Silvia P. Salas Pizaña, Minnah W. Farook, Nayeli Y. Chavez-Dueñas, and Hector Y. Adames

See also Attachment; Attachment Styles; Attachment Theory

Further Readings

McWilliams, L. A., & Bailey, S. J. (2010). Associations between adult attachment ratings and health conditions: Evidence from the national comorbidity survey replication. *Journal of Health Psychology, 29*(4), 446–453. doi:10.1037/a0020061

Nanjappa, S., Chambers, S., Marcenes, W., Richards, D., & Freeman, R. (2014). A theory led narrative review of one-to-one health interventions: The influence of attachment style and client-provider relationship on client adherence. *Journal of Health Education Research, 29*(5), 740–754. doi:10.1093/her/cyu029

Pietromonaco, P. R., Uchino, B., & Dunkel Schetter, C. (2013). Close relationship processes and health: Implications of attachment theory for health and disease. *Journal of Health Psychology, 32*(5), 499–513. doi:10.1037/a0029349

Staton, S. C. E., & Campbell, L. (2014). Perceived social support moderates the link between attachment anxiety and health outcomes. *PLOS ONE, 9*(4). doi:10.1371/journal.pone.0095358

Attachment and Romantic Love

One of the most primary human needs is to have a secure emotional connection, an attachment, with those who are the closest to us—our parents, children, lovers, and partners. Attachment theory helps explain how all couples, healthy or not, need to depend on each other. This theoretical perspective can shed light on why problems emerge in relationships, on why people behave the way they do in relationships, and one who is at most risk for relationship problems. The goal of all attachment relationships is felt security. Attachment theory is a systemic theory that has emerged as a tool for describing the deeper roots of close relationships. Prior to the inception of this theory, treatment with couples employed the therapy models designed for families. The trouble with applying systemic family theories to couples is that when confronted with the dependence of a partner, such dependence would be labeled as *enmeshment*, a condition of overinvolvement. Les Greenberg and Susan Johnson have used attachment theory as part of their emotionally focused couple therapy (EFCT) model to describe the couple dynamics that are commonly found in couples therapy. Couples in which the wife is anxious and the husband is avoidant are consistent with predominant sex-role stereotypes.

Attachment Theory

John Bowlby and Mary Ainsworth pioneered attachment theory studies. Bowlby concluded in these studies that the bond between infants and their parents was based on a biological drive for proximity that evolved over the process of natural selection. When danger threatens, infants who stay close to their parents are less likely to be harmed (e.g., killed by predators). Bowlby also believed that attachment provides a person with a secure base, the ability to regulate emotions, and the confidence to explore the world. When attachment is threatened, the first response is likely to be anger and protest, followed by some form of clinging, which eventually gives way to despair. If attachment figures do not respond, detachment and isolation will occur.

Ainsworth proposed that infants used their attachment figures, usually mothers, as a secure base for exploration. When an infant feels threatened, the infant will turn to the caregiver for protection and comfort. Security in the relationship with an attachment figure indicates that an infant is able to rely upon that caregiver as a source of comfort and protection. When threats arise, infants in secure relationships are able to direct attachment behavior (approaching, crying, reaching out) to their caregivers and take comfort in their reassurance. This translates to the infant feeling confident in their interaction in the world as well. Confidence is not evident in infants who have anxious attachment relationships. Bids for attention may have been met with indifference or rebuff. As a result, such infants remain anxious about the availability of caregivers.

Although the attachment system is most critical during the early years of life, Bowlby claimed it is active over the entire life span and is manifested in thoughts and behaviors related to proximity-seeking in times of need. In order to be sure that attachment needs are being met in a romantic relationship, adults monitor their partner's availability and ability to meet their needs, just as children do with their parents. Unlike caregiver–infant relationships, love relationships between two adults involve two equal partners, both of whom are somewhat threatened, frightened, or injured and in need of protection or comfort. From the standpoint of attachment theory, love is a dynamic state involving both partners' needs and capacities for attachment, caregiving, and sex. There are three relational styles that have emerged from Cindy Hazan and Phillip Shaver's study of the attachment aspects of adult relationships, which were modeled on the three major patterns of caregiver–infant attachment described by Ainsworth. Infants and adults with a secure attachment style are ones who find it relatively easy to trust others, open up emotionally, and commit themselves to a long-term intimate relationship. Those with an anxious style are uncertain that they are loved, worthy of love, and likely to be protected. This fearful uncertainty explains their excessive vigilance, reassurance seeking, frequent angry outbursts, and jealousy. Those with an avoidant style have learned that in order to feel relatively secure they have to rely heavily on themselves and not openly seek support from a partner, even when such support is necessary for survival and optimal development.

Couple Relationships and Attachment History

Attachment is an important component of romantic love and marital commitment, and meeting needs for a felt sense of security is one of the primary reasons for marriage. The way couples deal with one another reflects their attachment history. Attachment strategies will play out differently depending on the attachment characteristics of a partner. Thus, attachment style affects marital satisfaction. According to emotionally focused couples theory, emotion organizes attachment responses and serves a communicative function in relationships. When people express their vulnerability directly, they're likely to elicit a compassionate response from their partners. A healthy relationship, according to Johnson, is a secure attachment bond, characterized by emotional accessibility and responsiveness. But when an insecurely attached person fears vulnerability and shows anger instead, the response is more likely to be withdrawal rather than evoke that desired response. The person most in need of attachment may, by being afraid to expose that need, push away the loved ones he or she longs to get close to. The antidote for this dilemma in therapy is to help partners relax fears so that deeper and more genuine emotions can emerge. It may be difficult to bolster an anxious spouse's sense of security because when he or she is reminded of seemingly desirable experiences of love and closeness, negative concepts and memories related to past hurts and attachment injuries will also become active, whether consciously or unconsciously. Attachment injuries are traumatic occurrences that damage the bond between partners and, if not resolved, maintain negative cycles and attachment insecurities.

People who are securely attached tend to have long, stable, and satisfying relationships characterized by high investment, trust, and friendship. Secure people are characterized by low levels of avoidance of intimacy and low levels of anxiety about abandonment. They view themselves and their partners positively and feel worthy of love. They describe their style of love as relatively selfless and devoid of game playing. Sexually they are open to exploration but usually with a single long-term partner, and their intimate relationships are characterized more by mutual initiation of sexual activity and enjoyment of physical contact. Those insecurely attached individuals, or preoccupied people, are high in anxiety and low in avoidance and tend to become vigilant toward and preoccupied with their romantic partners and experience low relationship satisfaction and a high breakup rate. They question whether they are worthy of love and are extremely sensitive and expressive and often seek reassurance about their partners' love and availability and their own self-worth. They are more likely than secure or avoidant individuals to experience passionate love and to exhibit an obsessive, dependent style of love. People high in attachment anxiety show a greater preference for the affectionate and intimate aspects of sexuality than for the genital aspects. In comparison with secure and anxious people, predominantly avoidant individuals are less interested in romantic relationships, especially long-term, committed ones. Like anxious people, their relationships are characterized by low satisfaction and a high breakup rate, but these relationships are also characterized by relatively low intimacy. Although they idealize partners, they may also be demanding and never feel that their needs are fully met. Avoidant individuals, or dismissing people, are less likely than secure or anxious people to fall in love and their love style is characterized by game playing. Dismissing people have a relatively low need for relationships, do not care much about what others think of them, and are content being self-sufficient. Although avoidant individuals express dislike for much of sexuality, especially the affectionate and intimate aspects, they also hold more accepting attitudes toward casual sex and tend to have more one-night stands than secure and anxious people. Those who are high on both the anxiety and avoidance dimensions, also known as fearful, show some of the emotional vulnerability and pining for closeness characteristics of their preoccupied counterparts, but they also back away from closeness behaviorally. This backing away is more consciously motivated by fear of negative outcomes (rejection and abuse) than is the avoidant behavior of dismissing individuals. They also question whether they are worthy of love, are extremely worried about being rejected, and want close relationships. However, like preoccupied people, they manage their fears by avoiding intimacy in relationships. When in relationships, they may have difficulty being emotionally or physically close and may inhibit self-disclosure as well as emotions. They may not turn to partners when upset or in need of support, and they may fail to perceive or believe that partners care about them.

Attachment security influences satisfaction by promoting open expression of positive and negative emotions, high levels of facilitative disclosure, which is disclosure plus the ability to elicit disclosure from one's partner, and mutual expression and negotiation during conflicts. Attachment security is also associated with ability and willingness to give a spouse the benefit of the doubt when interpreting potentially troubling comments or behavior. In contrast, attachment insecurity is associated with destructive tracking of recent partner behaviors that might be interpreted as threatening. Avoidant husbands fail to provide the reassurance that anxious wives crave, and anxious wives are unable to accept the emotional distance desired by avoidant husbands, creating a vicious cycle in which the wife's need for reassurance and the husband's need for distance aggravate each other. Men's avoidance and women's anxiety are associated with negative ratings of a relationship by both partners, and men with highly anxious partners tend to rate their relationships as lower in love, satisfaction, and commitment. A secure partner can sometimes buffer the negative effects of an insecure partner, but, alternately, an insecure partner can sometimes erode his or her partner's sense of security.

The sexual behavior system, along with attachment and caregiving, is a central component of romantic love. Securely attached people are open to sexual exploration in the context of a stable relationship; if both partners are secure, initiation of sexual activity is mutual and physical closeness is enjoyed. Secure individuals engage in sex primarily to show love for their partners. Many anxious individuals prefer the affectionate and intimate aspects of sexuality, such as hugging and cuddling, over the genital aspects, while avoidant people tend not to get as much pleasure from sex as nonavoidant people. In Tracy's study of adolescents, anxious individuals engage in sex primarily to please their partners, feel accepted, and avoid abandonment, while avoidant adolescents have sex for reasons such as losing their virginity and generally have less sexual experience than secure or anxious adolescents. Relationship exclusivity is highly negatively correlated with attachment avoidance, suggesting that avoidant people tend to be more promiscuous and nonexclusive in their relationships.

Couple conflict is affected by attachment styles. Couples with two anxious partners functioned especially poorly, engaging in high levels of emotional manipulation and power assertion. Anxious individuals tend to feel misunderstood and underappreciated, become demanding and coercive, and focus on their own concerns at the expense of their partner's needs. Anxiety is linked to aggression only if the other partner is avoidant, establishing the pattern in which one partner's fear of abandonment and the other partner's fear of intimacy exacerbate each other. A secure partner may buffer the negative effects of insecurity by consistently encouraging openness and mutual expression, leading the insecure partner to modify maladaptive behaviors associated with insecurity. However, a couple containing at least one insecure partner can erode the sense of security of both its members. Even secure individuals can become anxious about loss and rejection in the face of emotionally distant partners.

Attachment Theory in Couples Therapy

Attachment theory is applied to clinical treatment by linking symptomatic expressions of fear and anger to disturbances in attachment relationships. Couples can be helped to understand the attachment fears and vulnerabilities behind angry and defensive interactions. Therapists can use attachment theory to illuminate current relationships by showing how a husband's avoidance may be due to ambivalent attachment or how a wife's animosity may be an expression of anxious attachment. When therapists feel drawn into a family's script, they can avoid taking over a role that's missing in the family by using attachment theory to point out family members' needs for being cared for. Instead of being recruited to comfort a distressed spouse, a therapist can hand back responsibility to the partner and encourage them to become less defensive and more supportive.

A therapist working with an anxious member of a couple should be sensitive to this person's intense need for support and affection, from both the therapist and the spouse. A therapist working with an avoidant member of a couple should be aware of this person's difficulty in providing support, especially when a partner is anxious and needy. The anxious person is likely to exaggerate threats and injuries while the avoidant person seeks to minimize them in therapy.

Julie Martin

See also Attachment; Attachment and Adolescents; Attachment and Health; Attachment Styles; Attachment Theory; Attachment-Based Family Therapy

Further Readings

Gladding, S. T. (2011). *Family therapy: History, theory, and practice.* Upper Saddle River, NJ: Pearson.

Johnson, S. M., & Whiffen, V. E. (2006). *Attachment processes in couple and family therapy.* New York, NY: Guilford Press.

Nichols, M. P. (2013). *Family therapy: Concepts and methods* (10th ed.). Boston, MA: Allyn & Bacon.

ATTACHMENT STYLES

Children form a special relationship with their caregivers. Attachment theory states that all infants have a natural desire to bond with a primary caregiver. The first 12 to 18 months are critical to the infant's ability to build a healthy and stable attachment with a primary caregiver. According to attachment theory, there are two basic attachment styles: secure and insecure. Furthermore, the insecure attachment style can manifest itself in either an *insecure–avoidant* attachment style or an *insecure–anxious* attachment style. Children with a secure attachment style have a warm, comforting, and safe relationship with a primary caregiver. Children with an insecure–anxious attachment style are worried about their connection with a caregiver and hypersensitive to any threats to the relationship. Those with an insecure–avoidant style are also worried about the attachment but cope with the insecurity by avoiding and denying the need for an emotional bond. These attachment styles are formed in childhood and the quality of this emotional bond will have significant effects on the child's emotional and relational development and his or her ability to connect with significant others later in life as an adult.

Attachment Theory

Attachment theory was derived from the work of the psychoanalyst and child psychiatrist John Bowlby in the 1950s. Bowlby was interested in the adverse effects of institutional child care, such as children who had frequent changes of mother figures. Much of his early worked examined the emotional attachments of children in institutions (e.g., hospitals, residential nurseries) whose mothers visited infrequently if at all and how these experiences shaped their personality development. Though his early work focused on the mother–child relationship, Bowlby's later research showed that the father–child relationship was also significant in the formation of the child's emotional attachment. Bowlby developed attachment theory for use in clinical counseling with disturbed patients and their families; it has since become a major theory in developmental psychology.

Mary Ainsworth, a developmental psychologist, was a major proponent of attachment theory and created an experiment in 1965 known as the "strange situation." Ainsworth had mothers bring their infants into a room filled with toys, leave them in the room for several minutes, and then return. Ainsworth and colleagues wanted to see how each infant would respond both when the mother left and when she returned. Based on the child's response both to the mother's leaving and her return, Ainsworth came up with initially three attachment styles: *secure, insecure–anxious,* and *insecure–avoidant.* In later years, researchers developed a fourth attachment style labeled *disorganized.* Whether children have a secure or insecure attachment is thought to be dependent on the quality of the parenting they have received from the primary caregiver. Securely attached infants are those whose parents were emotionally responsive to their needs, particularly when in distress. Insecurely attached infants were those whose parents may have provided the necessities of life but did not provide the consistent attention, comfort, and soothing that the child needed, or conversely, they may have smothered the child with their own need for love and affection. Since Ainsworth's original study, a number of other researchers have done long-term follow-up studies that have shown the attachment styles she designated to be enduring into adulthood.

Secure Attachment

An infant with a secure attachment has a relationship with a primary caregiver who provides the infant or child a sense of comfort, security, and the ability to be soothed by the caregiver. As a result of having a secure attachment, the child is able to leave the primary caregiver and explore the world with the security of knowing that if danger occurs they can go back to their caregiver for safety and comfort. Ainsworth found that infants with secure attachments would show some signs of distress when the mother left the room but would then go on to explore the toys; when the mother returned, the infant moved toward her and would respond favorably to the mother's comforting. Persons with secure attachments are able to create and remain in stable, safe relationships throughout their adulthood. As adults, they have a better chance of staying in a stable, caring marriage. They are also more likely to reduplicate a secure attachment with their children.

Insecure–Anxious (Ambivalent) Attachment

Infants with an insecure–anxious attachment struggle when in proximity to their primary caregiver because of insecurity and anxiety about whether the caregiver will leave or be emotionally available to comfort them. In Ainsworth's studies, infants with ambivalent attachments did not explore the toys when their mothers left but often showed signs of physical distress such as continual crying or tantrums. These infants often would not be comforted readily when the mother returned. Adults with insecure–anxious attachments will struggle in significant relationships as adults, fearing that the person they are in the relationship with does not really care for them or will not be there when they need to be comforted. A parent with an ambivalent attachment style may overwhelm their child with a desire to be emotionally close or put pressure on their children to return affection. In this way, insecure–anxious attachments are reproduced from one parent to their child.

Insecure–Avoidant (Avoidant) Attachment

Infants with an insecure–avoidant attachment failed to engage significantly with their mothers. When the mother left, the infant showed no apparent distress, and when she returned the infant did not go to her to seek comfort; at times, the infant may have even turned his or her back. Children with avoidant attachment styles appear to have no expectation of being comforted by a caregiver. As adults, those with avoidant attachment styles struggle to maintain emotionally close relationships as they often feel that when they're in distress, no one can meet their emotional needs. Likewise, they may also fail to respond empathically when significant others are seeking comfort from them. At times, those with avoidant styles are detached from their own emotional needs. Parents with an avoidant attachment can unwittingly reproduce the same in their children by not attending to their infants and small children in emotionally responsive ways when they are in distress.

Disorganized (Disoriented) Attachment

Researchers later developed the designation disorganized attachment style to describe what they saw in certain children, some who had suffered severe abuse. These children seem confused or disoriented when the mother leaves and returns. As these children develop into adulthood, they struggle with emotional regulation, and their relationships are often characterized by fear and conflict.

Persistence of Attachment Styles

Counselors and developmental psychologists who are attachment theorists agree that once a child's attachment style is developed, it tends to be pervasive throughout their adult lives. More than half of persons are thought to have a secure attachment (~60%), whereas the rest are thought to struggle with one of the three insecure attachments. Fortunately, researchers have found adults with what they have labeled "earned secure attachments"—adults who over time have developed stable and caring relationships with significant others that have allowed them to feel safe and secure in close relationships with important people in their lives.

Eric M. Brown

See also Adult Attachment Assessments; Attachment; Attachment Theory; Attachment-Based Family Therapy; Attunement in Relationships; Bonding

Further Readings

Ainsworth, M. D. S. (1989). Attachment beyond infancy. *American Psychologist, 44,* 709–716. doi:10.1037/0003-066X.44.4.709

Ainsworth, M. D. S., Blehar, M. C., Waters, E. & Wall, S. N. (2015). *Patterns of attachment: A psychological study of the strange situation.* New York, NY: Psychology Press.

Bowlby, J. (1988). *A secure base: Parent-child attachment and healthy human development* (Reprint ed.). New York, NY: Basic Books.

Bowlby, J. (2005). *The making and breaking of affectional bonds.* New York, NY: Routledge.

Cassidy, J. & Shaver, P. R. (2010). *Handbook of attachment, second edition: Theory, research, and clinical application.* New York, NY: Guilford Press.

Lowenstein, L. F. (2010). Attachment theory and parental alienation. *Journal of Divorce & Remarriage, 51*(3), 157–168. doi:10.1080/10502551003597808

Newland, L. A., & Coyl, D. D. (2010). Fathers' role as attachment figures: An interview with Sir Richard Bowlby. *Early Child Development and Care, 180* (1–2), 25–32. doi:10.1080/03004430903414679

ATTACHMENT THEORY

Attachment theory is used to describe and explain the affectional bond that is formed between infants and their caregivers and is used to understand how people trust and depend on others or avoid doing so. This emotional bond is seen as key to the survival of infants and to the emotional and relational health of infants, children, and adults. Attachment theory was created by John Bowlby, a British psychiatrist and psychoanalyst, in the 1950s and later expanded by the Canadian American psychologist Mary Ainsworth and others. The quality of the emotional bond (categorized as either secure or insecure) of child to parent influences the infant's later development of emotional regulation, social skills, and parenting skills. These skills and ability (or inability) to see people and relationships as trustworthy and a source of security is carried into adulthood. The idea of secure and insecure attachment informs work with individual children but also helps clinicians in understanding and working with couple and family relationships. In this entry, a brief introduction will be given to the creation of attachment theory, the definition of attachment styles, and the application of attachment theory to couples and family counseling or therapy.

Historical Context

John Bowlby believed that affectional bonds are essential to the survival of humans. He focused on how primary caretakers (usually the mother) serve as an attachment figure if they created an attentive, caring, warm, continuous relationship. Those who are able to monitor the needs of an infant and soothe distress effectively are said to be attuned to the infant's needs and provide security for the child. Bowlby's research and writings on emotional bonding, attachment, and attunement influenced psychology, education, child care, and parenting.

Ainsworth expanded the understanding of attachment theory by studying differences in attachment patterns (styles) using an assessment technique called the *strange situation classification*. The strange situation consisted of observing children 12 to 18 months old as (1) a mother leaves the room that is considered an unfamiliar environment, (2) the child is approached by a stranger, and (3) the mother returns and the stranger leaves. During these stages, four behaviors were measured: separation anxiety, the infant's willingness to explore the environment, stranger anxiety, and reunion behavior. Separation anxiety is the distress that an infant displays when the caregiver leaves, stranger anxiety is the infant's distress in response to the presence of a stranger, and reunion behavior is how the infant reacts when the caretaker returns.

Ainsworth classified attachment based on three different styles: secure, insecure avoidant, and insecure ambivalent. These three styles have been explored and expanded by subsequent researchers. In the stranger situation, securely attached children appeared distressed when the mother left the room, avoided the stranger when alone, appeared happy when the mother returned, and used mother as a safe base from which to explore the environment. Ambivalently attached children were intensely distressed when the mother left, avoided the stranger and were fearful, approached mother when she returned while avoiding contact with her, and cried more and explored less than children with other types of attachment. Finally, children with avoidant attachments did not show distress when mother left, were not distressed by stranger presence, and showed little interest when mother returned.

Attachment Styles

Attachment is a deep emotional bond between two people based on one person's ability to make the other feel safe, secure, and protected. In a caretaker–child relationship, attachment is from the child to the parent. It is not the child's responsibility to make the parent feel safe, secure, and protected. In adult relationships, especially romantic ones, this attachment is reciprocal. Both people are responsible for creating safety and security in the relationship. Based on whether people are securely or insecurely attached, they will tend to seek or not seek deep emotional connections with others and will have differing levels of security or anxiety attached to those relationships.

A *secure* attachment is characterized by feelings of emotional intimacy, emotional security, and physical safety in relation to an attachment figure, especially when distressed. Securely attached children are confident that attachment figures are reliable and can meet their needs. This security encourages exploration of the world with the knowledge that the attachment figure can soothe them in times of distress. These children tend to become adults who enjoy being connected to others and trust that others can and will meet their emotional needs. The securely attached person feels comfortable expressing distress and need for comfort and has confidence that the attachment figure is attuned to his or her needs. People with secure attachment styles tend to balance needs for intimacy and independence. A securely attached adult would describe himself or herself as being comfortable depending on others and being depended on. They do not tend to be worried about being abandoned by others or fear others getting too close to them.

Anxious–avoidant attachment is a type of insecure attachment where a person has learned not to be able to depend on close relationships as a source of comfort and soothing in times of distress, nor as a source of consistent support and joy in times of nondistress. Avoidantly attached children have had minimally close and emotionally expressive communication with their caregiver. They do not trust that people will be there for them during times of emotional distress. As they grow up, these children tend to be controlling of others and are distant from their own emotional needs. The yearning for interrelatedness is minimized and denied. People with avoidant attachment styles tend to undervalue the importance of relationships, withdraw in relationships, and are emotionally distant. They do not like to depend on others and often deny the need for intimacy. Adults with this type of attachment are uncomfortable being close to others and find trust difficult. They tend to find that others want them to be more intimate than they are comfortable being.

Anxious–resistant attachment is a type of insecure attachment characterized by having one's need for feelings of safety and security inconsistently and unpredictably met by an attachment figure. For children who are ambivalently attached, the need for others is amplified rather than denied. The caregiver is sometimes attentive and at other times is not; the intermittent reinforcement creates an uncertainty about the relationship so that the child becomes dependent upon parental input for a sense of security even into the adult years. People with this type of attachment may become preoccupied with feelings of mistrust and rejection in adult relationships. In response to an inconsistently responsive attachment figure, a person may exaggerate distress in order to elicit caretaking behaviors from significant others. People with anxious–resistant styles may overvalue the importance of relationships and monitor them closely. These adults worry that others do not really love them and worry about being abandoned. They monitor relationships closely and want to get very close to others, which sometimes scares people away.

Later, researchers added another style of attachment, *disorganized*, to describe attachment styles sometimes created by abusive caregivers. Disorganized attachment results from frightening experiences with a caregiver. In order to cope with these experiences, the person may dissociate from experiences and/or feelings. People with this type of attachment have extreme difficulty regulating emotions and maintaining relationships; in addition, their relationships may be characterized by fear.

Understanding Attachment

A secure attachment is created when a significant person consistently and appropriately attends to the needs of a child or partner. The attachment figure can be counted on to be available physically and emotionally available when needed. About 60% of the general population form secure attachments as children and grow up to become securely attached adults. The parent–child relationship becomes a model for expectations in other relationships; the quality of attachment to the parent is thought to predict the quality of romantic and other relationships later in life. Approximately 20% formed anxious–avoidant attachments, and approximately 20% formed anxious–resistant attachments.

Bowlby believed that the need to attach and basic attachment behaviors (behaviors that elicit soothing responses from others) are innate. Because infants are fragile at birth and need extended caregiving during infancy to survive, Bowlby believed that they are born with an innate drive to form a unique bond with a caretaker to ensure survival. In order to enhance the emotional bonding between infant and caregiver, the infant forms an intense attachment to the caregiver, and the infant behaves (e.g., crying, making eye contact, cooing, reaching for, and crawling toward) in ways that tend to elicit caretaking behaviors from the parent. Children and adults both have ways of forming attachments with others and ways of signaling their attachment figures that they need to be soothed. Adults also have variations of the infant behaviors that tend to elicit soothing from an attachment figure.

Attachment bonds have four defining features: wanting to be physically close to the attachment figure (proximity maintenance), having separation distress, being a safe haven (retreating to caregiver when sensing danger or feeling anxious), and providing a secure base (exploration of the world knowing that the attachment figure will protect the infant from danger). Attachment relationships develop over the first two years of life and beyond, but most importantly these early attachment relationships overlap with a time of significant neurological development of the brain in children. The relationship between parent and child, and the environment that parents create, can actually influence the infant's brain development and structure, which has lasting effects on the child.

The child's first attachment with the primary caregiver provides the basis for an internal working model (a cognitive map) of understanding the self, relationships, and the world. Based on the internal working model, a person evaluates the trustworthiness of others, one's own value, and the self as effective when socializing with others. Based on their internal working model, people can feel positive about relationships and worthy of love (secure attachment), feel rejected and unworthy of love (insecure–avoidant attachment), or feel angry and confused about whether they are lovable or not (insecure–avoidant attachment). Future relationships are guided by expectations based on the primary attachment and the resulting internal model.

Although changes over time can influence the attachment status of a child, there is a strong continuity between infant attachment patterns, child and adolescent patterns, and adult attachment patterns. Changes in attachment status can occur in either direction (secure to insecure, insecure to secure), and in fact, the term *earned secure* has been used to describe individuals who experience parents who are not attuned to their needs (and therefore one would expect an insecure attachment status) but form securely attached relationships with others. For the majority of individuals, however, the manner in which they learned to manage anxiety early on in life will continue unless their circumstances change or other experiences intervene.

Adult Romantic Relationships

Bowlby focused on mother–child attachment but believed that attachment influenced relationships across the life span. Cindy Hazan and Phillip Shaver were two of the first researchers to explore attachment in the context of adult, romantic relationships. They believed that the emotional bond that forms between adults is related to some of the needs that caretakers fulfill for infants. They suggested the relationship between infants and caregivers and the relationship between romantic partners are similar in the following ways: (a) proximity and responsiveness increases feelings of safety; (b) close, intimate bodily contact reinforces the bond; (c) the attachment figure is a secure base; (d) infants and romantic partners both tend to be fascinated with the attachment figure and are fascinated with one another's facial features; and (e) attachment figures engage in "baby talk." Based on the hypothesis that romantic relationships are attachment relationships, many of the same processes that make a secure attachment more likely between caretaker and child should apply to adult relationships.

Therapy Models

There are individual, couple, and family therapy models based on attachment theory. These approaches highlight the need for emotional bonding and feeling secure in a relationship, and they view emotions as a source of information about one's attachment and relationship. They see attachment and emotions not only as adaptive but also as key to optimal physical, emotional, and relational health.

Les Greenberg is one of the founders of emotion-focused therapy (EFT), an empirically based approach to creating secure attachments through emotional intelligence. The approach is based on emotion, attachment, and growth theory, and the clinician focuses on helping people become aware of emotions, reflect on them, regulate them, and learn to express them. Clients learn about these things and are also helped to experience and practice them in the safety of therapy sessions. Overall, emotions are viewed as adaptive and guide attachment as well as the tendency toward growth.

Emotionally focused couple therapy (EFCT) is an empirically based model that stems from the work of Susan Johnson and is primarily used with couples but can also be used with individuals and families. This approach is based on a conceptualization of adult love, adult attachment, and relationship distress through an experiential, person-centered, systemic approach. The goals of couples therapy are to expand and reorganize key emotional responses, create new patterns of interaction for the couple, and support the creation of a secure bond between partners.

Attachment-based family therapy (ABFT) is based on the idea that when parents are better attuned to the needs of their children, then children develop a better ability for independence and affect (emotion) regulation. When parents are not very attuned, then injuries to the attachment security occur. However, as a life span development model, attachment theory hypothesizes that these injuries are repairable. The ABFT model strengthens or rebuilds secure parent–child relationships and promotes adolescent development and autonomy.

Shea M. Dunham

See also Attachment; Attachment and Adolescents; Attachment and Health; Attachment and Romantic Love; Attachment Styles

Further Readings

Bowlby, J. (1988). *A secure base: Parent-child attachment and healthy human development. Tavistock professional book.* London, England: Routledge.

Diamond, G. M., Diamond, G. S., & Hogue, A. (2007). Attachment-based family therapy: Adherence and differentiation. *Journal of Marital and Family Therapy, 33*(2), 177–191.

Greenberg, L. S. (2004). Emotion–focused therapy. *Clinical Psychology & Psychotherapy, 11*(1), 3–16. London, England: Routledge.

Wallin, D. J. (2007). *Attachment in psychotherapy.* New York, NY: Guilford Press.

ATTACHMENT-BASED FAMILY THERAPY

Attachment-based family therapy (ABFT) is an empirically supported brief, clinical model of family therapy. It is a trust-based, emotion-focused approach, and the goal is to repair interpersonal ruptures and rebuild emotionally protective, secure-based parent–child relationships. It is based on the idea that strong family relationships buffer against risk factors for mental health problems. From this perspective, strong relationships within families can be a barrier against interpersonal problems and assist with treatment success. However, ruptures in secure attachments increase the risk for pathology. The model was first created for treatment of abused and neglected children living in foster or adoptive care and for working with depressed adolescents. However, this approach can be used with all families to create supportive communication, assist with affect regulation, and teach problem-solving skills that promote positive relationships. It is believed that damage to attachments to parents are reparable and that repairing these relationships can help children to strengthen internal and external resources that promote healthy development. For children from families that have had troubled relationships, the focus is to reestablish in families attachments that are safe and supportive. In ABFT, the belief is that unmanageable family conflict, constant and harsh disapproval, and/or abuse in any form will negatively impact attachment bonds. Overall, the model is grounded in the idea that when parents are responsive and protective, children develop a healthy sense of self, trust in others, and interdependence. In this entry, the theories informing ABFT and fundamental concepts will be reviewed.

Theory

ABFT is based on attachment theory and intersubjectivity theory. Attachment theory was first proposed by John Bowlby in the 1950s to explain the need for infants to bond with a primary caregiver (usually the mother). This theory was later expanded by others to explain different types of attachment (secure and insecure) and used to understand romantic attachments. Rather than seeing emotional attachments to others as "dependence," this theory posits emotional attachments as a necessary part of being a healthy child and adult. Infants have an instinctual need to bond with caregivers and are hardwired to activate an attachment system (a series of behaviors designed to bring an attachment figure closer) when there is a perceived physical or psychological threat. A basic assumption of Bowlby's theory is that physical or psychological treats automatically activate the attachment system. Attachment behaviors in both children and adults are designed to assure proximity to supportive others (attachment figures). Intersubjectivity theory is closely related to attachment theory and is used to explain the development of an individual within a family.

Intersubjectivity theory describes how people are both influencing and influenced by the experience of themselves and others; it describes the way in which infants learn about the self, the family, and the larger community and culture. Intersubjectivity focuses on the relationship between two people and the sharing of meaning. People coconstruct meaning through their interactions with each other and society. In ABFT, intersubjectivity is used to describe how meaning is passed down from parents to children and between them. From this point of view parents influence children and children's experiences influence the continuing development of parents.

The Importance of Safety and Security

Security is a key aspect of feeling safe in relationships and a key aspect of having a secure attachment in intimate relationships. For humans, there is an innate need to seek an attachment figure for feelings of safety and security. If infants are able to maintain closeness with significant others and those people are attentive and attuned to the needs of the infant, a sense of safety and security is created. These are also an essential part of ABFT. Therapists begin by facilitating safety in the therapy room with the therapist and then having parents facilitate safety for children. Creating safety and security for parents, and in turn parents doing so for children, is a central goal of ABFT. Therapists help parents be more aware of their children's safety needs and how those can be met. Some of these parents did not have secure attachments when they were children. It is difficult to replicate a secure attachment when someone has not experienced one. When adults are not aware of their own safety needs and/or are not getting those needs met through a secure attachment with another adult, then it is difficult for them to recognize and fulfill those needs for their children. Hence, focusing on safety, security, and secure attachments for both adults and children is imperative. It is important to note, though, that adults should seek to have their attachment needs met from other adults, not from children.

Although family therapy is interactive, the primary responsibility for repairing relationships lies with parents. The main emphasis should always be on repairing relationships. Conflict is never more important than relationships. There will always be conflict, misunderstandings, and other injuries to relationships. However, if family members know everyone is committed to relationship repair, then relationships will be more secure.

Attachment and the Brain

Neurological research, specifically on the brain, supports the connection between attachment and brain development. A child's brain is influenced by daily interactions with caregivers. Nurturing touch, responsive relationships, predictable interactions, and soothing from a caregiver when upset all help influence what someone will expect from relationships and creates a context for healthy brain development. When a child does not have these things, they face stress. Stress occurs when people are not responsive to a child's distress (e.g., hungry, uncomfortable, scared). In addition, because children monitor their attachment figure, a child will notice when that figure is stressed or tense and internalize those feelings. Constant higher levels of this stress hormone disrupt healthy development. Having unmet physical and emotional needs leads to stress, which results in higher levels of the hormone cortisol. Conversely, low levels of stress coupled with secure relationships allows the child's brain, especially in the first three years, to develop more connections in parts of the brain related to language, intellect, and sensory and motor areas. These connections become permanent when they are repeatedly stimulated through a child's environment and through relationships with significant others.

Interdependence

Although infants are dependent on their caregivers, in a secure relationship this emotional and physical dependence eventually assists children in developing and relying on their own skills. They learn to be interdependent—open to relying on others when appropriate and to also be self-reliant. As children develop, they become more self-reliant, but healthy adults are able to be self-reliant while also accepting and giving help when needed. Interdependence is viewed as healthier than being dependent or independent. The therapist emphasizes the importance of both self and relationships. One does not need to sacrifice the self for the family or the family for the self.

An excessive focus on self-reliance develops for children when the importance of attachment figures is minimized. When this happens, children (and later adults) tend to avoid attachment relationships. This type of pattern usually develops in childhood when one learns that he or she cannot rely on an attachment figure. The avoidant person tends to diminish the importance of emotions and overemphasizes a cognitive approach to decision-making. A therapist will explore the roots of avoidance patterns and help the family to explore together thoughts, emotions, and expectations that have led to these patterns. Over time, the therapist will facilitate deeper emotional intimacy without sacrificing self-reliance.

If self-reliance is minimized then a child may become overly focused on relationships and become anxious. When this happens, children (and later adults) tend to cling to attachment figures. The anxious person tends to fear losing relationships and pursues others. A therapist will explore anxious patterns and explore relationship history to help understand what relates to the fear of losing attachment figures. They will explore thoughts, emotions, and expectations that relate to these patterns in both children and parents. The therapist will create a safe environment to explore the experience of self-reliance without sacrificing the ability of being emotionally intimate.

Working Models of Self and Others

Patterns of interdependence, avoidance, or anxiety become working models of how the self and others are perceived. Based on working models, people make assumptions that influence people's inner lives, including thoughts, feelings, and memories. Inner working models affect emotional awareness and expression, boundaries between self and others, as well as someone's ability to have insight. As a consequence of inner working models, people either become confident, open, and flexible for self and in relationships, or they become rigid or chaotic because of anticipated barriers. Rigid or chaotic patterns impede opportunities for development.

PACE

The acronym PACE encompasses the primary ways in which a therapist should interact with a family: playfulness, acceptance, curiosity, and empathy. PACE is enacted through affective–reflective dialogues. This type of dialogue focuses on both positive and negative affective experiences. These types of conversations help families learn to validate new information about past and present experiences. While the therapist and family are processing these experiences and inner working models, the therapist adopts a nonjudgmental attitude. This models the same way in which parents should engage with their children.

Goal: Secure Attachment

Attachment security is created when parents are reliable, available, responsive, sensitive, and loving on a consistent basis, especially when children's attachment behaviors are activated. In other words, a secure relationship develops when parents provide comfort and support when a child is scared and vulnerable. When an attachment is unreliable or unable to provide comfort and support to assuage stresses, over time the child may learn to not rely on an attachment figure. Parents' responses to distress are an important predictor of what type of attachment will be formed.

A secure attachment helps children understand emotions and cope with them appropriately. This is particularly important for dysregulating emotions such as fear, anxiety, despair, shame, and grief. Whether children or adults, the ability to depend on others in the face of dysregulating emotions is important. It is often easier to regulate these emotions in the context of a secure relationship rather than by oneself. The therapist helps parents recognize when their children are in distress and evoke caregiving behaviors. Part of this process is engaging the family in affective–reflective dialogues about distress without people getting angry, defensive, or avoidant.

Although therapists explore relational vulnerabilities, they also focus on strengths. As relationships become more secure, they tend to enhance positive emotions such as joy, excitement, pride, and satisfaction. Highlighting movement toward more secure attachments and the resulting positive emotions helps families become more aware of thoughts, emotions, and hopes outside of problems. Secure attachments increase emotional strength, happiness, and relational satisfaction. Although the goal is to have parents be more attuned to children, as positive emotions increase and the family engages in nonjudgmental conversations, children become more interested in what their parents think, feel, and want.

When the goal is creating a more secure attachment, intersubjective communication becomes more important than focusing on behavior. In behavioral approaches, the therapist focuses on helping parents focus on children's behavior by linking behavior and consequences. From an attachment perspective, though, better behavior is a consequence of creating attachment safety and open, intersubjective communication. When this occurs, families are more flexible, open, and accepting of mutual influence. This sets the stage for effective communication about behaviors and expectations. When people have secure relationships, behavioral problems occur less often, and when they do occur, problem-solving is more effective. Overall, when families have secure attachments they are able to explore self, other, and the broader social–emotional world without fear or shame.

Shea M. Dunham

See also Adult Attachment Assessments; Attachment; Attachment Styles; Earned Attachment

Further Readings

Diamond, G. S., Diamond, G. M., & Levy, S. A. (2014). *Attachment-based family therapy for depressed adolescents*. Washington, DC: American Psychological Association.

Hughes, D. A. (2007). *Attachment-focused family therapy*. New York, NY: W. W. Norton.

Hughes, D. A. (2009). *Attachment-focused parenting: Effective strategies to care for children*. New York, NY: W. W. Norton.

Hughes, D. A. (2011). *Attachment-focused family therapy: Workbook*. New York, NY: W. W. Norton.

ATTENTION-DEFICIT AND DISRUPTIVE BEHAVIOR DISORDERS

The category of attention-deficit and disruptive behavior disorders includes attention-related disorders that feature symptoms of inattentiveness, hyperactivity, or inability to control impulsive behaviors (such as verbally interrupting others), as well as behavior-specific disorders related to conduct, defiance, and verbal aggression. In the fourth edition of the *Diagnostic and Statistical Manual of Mental Disorders* (DSM-IV-TR), behavior disorders were grouped under the classification of disorders usually diagnosed in infancy, early childhood, or adolescence. The fifth edition of the manual (DSM-5), published in 2013, includes some changes to general classifications and specific diagnoses; for example, the updated manual lists attention-deficit/hyperactivity disorder (ADHD) as a neurodevelopmental disorder, and disruptive, impulse-control, and conduct disorders (CDs) appear in a separate category.

Prevalence rates for ADHD are estimated at 5% among children and 2.5% among adults. Approximate prevalence rates for both intermittent explosive disorder and oppositional defiant disorder (ODD) are 3%, and the prevalence rate for CD is an estimated 4%. The potential for disruption in home, academic, and employment settings for individuals with attention-deficit and disruptive behavior disorders and associated disruptions in the respective lives of families, partners, friends, academic peers, or coworkers suggests the need for further study and exploration within the context of marriage, family, and couples counseling. The following sections provide an overview of diagnostic criteria or features, prevalence, and treatment options for attention-deficit and disruptive behavior disorders.

Attention-Deficit/Hyperactivity Disorder

As a neurodevelopmental disorder, symptoms of ADHD usually appear before age 7, between the ages of 3 and 6. While the earliest written descriptions of ADHD suggested an association with moral shortcoming, the disorder is now widely described as featuring a neurobiological component. Although the onset of ADHD often occurs in early development, symptoms may persist into adolescence and adulthood. The DSM-5 includes a category for adult ADHD. Males are diagnosed with ADHD more frequently than females as children, adolescents, and adults. Criteria for this disorder include symptoms related to inattention, hyperactivity, or impulsivity that interfere with regular functioning or development during a minimum of six consecutive months.

An ADHD diagnosis requires a patient presenting at least six of the nine listed symptoms (or five of nine for adolescents or adults over the age of 17) in the DSM-5 for either *inattention* or *hyperactivity/impulsivity*. Symptoms for inattention include lack of attention to details, low levels of attention in work or play, appearance of not listening, difficulty following through on instructions, and difficulty organizing or remembering daily tasks. The list of symptoms for hyperactivity and impulsivity include fidgeting, inability to quietly engage in play activities, difficulty waiting for one's turn to speak, and frequent verbal interruptions when others are speaking. In addition to the aforementioned criteria, an ADHD diagnosis also requires the presentation of some symptoms before the age of 12. Also, the symptoms interfere with work, academic, or social life and present in more than one setting—for example, both at school and work or both among friends and at home. ADHD diagnoses are specified as *combined presentation* when both the inattention and hyperactivity and impulsivity criteria are met.

Children experiencing ADHD symptoms may seem disorganized in classrooms or with homework assignments, slow to complete tasks at home, unwilling to engage in activities that require prolonged mental effort, as well as may show unrestrained emotion, interrupt others, and talk continuously. Symptoms may affect academic performance and peer relationships. Adults with self-reported ADHD symptoms may also experience difficulty in social or occupational functioning. Individuals with ADHD are more likely than the general population to have an anxiety disorder, a CD, or a substance use disorder. The previously listed symptoms and behaviors associated with ADHD may contribute to interpersonal difficulties. Family members or peers might interpret inattentiveness as lack of interest or care and hyperactivity as disrespectful. ADHD symptoms can also contribute to low frustration tolerance and anger management issues.

Medical treatment often includes the use of stimulant medication. ADHD diagnoses and prescriptions for ADHD medication in the United States have increased since 2003; however, many individuals with ADHD receive no medication or mental health counseling. Historically, behavioral interventions have been one of the most common treatment methods. School counselors are recommended to collaborate with teachers and parents or guardians on behavioral interventions.

Disruptive, Impulse-Control, and Conduct Disorders

The updated DSM-5 reorganized disruptive disorders, impulse-control disorders, and CDs into a separate classification. In the previous edition of the manual (DSM-IV-TR), CD and ODD were classified as disorders usually first diagnosed in infancy, childhood, or adolescence. Also, the fourth edition listed intermittent explosive disorder separately as an impulse-control disorder.

The disorders described in this section often have early onset in childhood and adolescence. Also, these disorders are diagnosed more often in males than females. General prevalence rates are approximately 3% for ODD, 3% for intermittent explosive disorder, and 4% for CD.

Conduct Disorder

The diagnostic criteria for CD relate to behavior toward others, property, and rules. For a justified diagnosis, the behavior associated with CD must have a significant negative impact on home, school, or work functioning. The categories include showing aggression toward people or animals, destructing property, lying, stealing, and consistently breaking the rules. Individual criteria include bullying, frequently staying out late against parental direction, and being physically cruel to others. These criteria primarily relate to impact on others—specifically in terms of others' rights and social norms. Lack of remorse for actions and lack of empathy are not necessary conditions for a CD diagnosis; however, a clinician would specify if the diagnosis included a limitation of prosocial emotions.

It is recommended that counseling professionals consider the use of Multisystemic Therapy (MST) or functional family therapy (FFT) in the treatment of youth and adolescents with CD. These approaches include family members in treatment, emphasize behavioral approaches, and aim to counter identified contributors to behavioral disorders. Both approaches focus on family systems as opposed to treating only the individual.

Intermittent Explosive Disorder

While CD focuses almost exclusively on behaviors, the diagnostic criteria for intermittent explosive disorder tend toward emotional considerations. Criteria are similar in that both disorders list physical and verbal aggression and destruction of property; however, criteria for intermittent explosive disorder also include consideration of impulsivity or angry outbursts. In typical occurrences, outbursts last less than a half-hour, and the individual responds in a manner out of proportion to the event or interaction that prompted the response. Similar to other disorders listed in this section, some symptoms and behavioral criteria of intermittent explosive disorder may occur as part of typical development; however, diagnostic criteria for intermittent explosive disorder consider degree, frequency, and disruption of either social or occupational functioning as well as financial or legal consequences related to the disorder.

Published professional research suggests that cognitive-behavioral therapy (CBT) may reduce aggression, anger, and depression; therefore, counselors are recommended to consider inclusion of CBT in therapy. Treatment may also include medication. Outbursts may surprise others, as the aggressiveness often quickly emerges. It is suggested that school counselors remain aware that the impulsive behavior often surprises even the individual with intermittent explosive disorder.

Oppositional Defiant Disorder

Diagnoses of ODD have high comorbidity with other mental health disorders and increased risk for later development of anxiety and depressive disorders. In relation to CD and intermittent explosive disorder, ODD includes both behavioral and emotional criteria. Specifically, the eight symptoms, four of which are needed to justify an ODD diagnosis, include loss of temper, purposeful annoyance of others, argumentative behavior, and angry or resentful feelings. The cluster of symptoms related to argumentative or defiant behavior focuses on relation to others, such as peers or recognized authority figures. Clinicians should specify the severity based on the presence of symptoms in one or more than one setting (such as school or home). Symptoms usually appear in more than one setting. Diagnoses of ODD are associated with increased risk of criminal behavior and academic difficulty. Rates of ODD are higher in individuals with an ADHD diagnosis compared to the general population. Symptoms often have early onset. Clinicians are recommended to include parents/guardians in counseling and education.

Pyromania and Kleptomania

Pyromania involves purposeful firesetting and is diagnosed more often in males. Kleptomania involves impulsive stealing and is diagnosed more often in females than males. The lifetime prevalence for both pyromania and kleptomania is estimated at 1% or less in the general population.

Robert H. Kitzinger

See also Anxiety; Depression in Adolescents; Depression in Children; Substance Use Disorders in Adolescence

Further Readings

American Psychiatric Association. (2000). *Diagnostic and statistical manual of mental disorders* (4th ed., text rev.). Washington, DC: Author.

American Psychiatric Association. (2013). *Diagnostic and statistical manual of mental disorders* (5th ed.). Washington, DC: Author.

Cederna-Meko, C., Koch, S., & Wall, J. (2014). Youth with oppositional defiant disorder at entry into home-based treatment, foster care, and residential treatment. *Journal of Child & Family Studies, 23*(5), 895–906.

Coccaro, E. F. (2011). Intermittent explosive disorder: Development of integrated research criteria for *Diagnostic and Statistical Manual of Mental Disorders, Fifth Edition. Comprehensive Psychiatry, 52*(2), 119–125.

Erford, B. T., Paul, L. E., Oncken, C., Kress, V. E., & Erford, M. R. (2014). Counseling outcomes for youth with oppositional behavior: A meta-analysis. *Journal of Counseling & Development, 92*(1), 13–24.

Fabiano, G. A., Pelham, W. E., Jr., Coles, E. K., Gnagy, E., Chronis-Tuscano, A., & Briannon, C. (2009). A meta-analysis of behavioral treatments for attention-deficit/hyperactivity disorder. *Clinical Psychology Review, 29*(2), 129–140.

Grothaus, T. (2013). School counselors serving students with disruptive behavior disorders. *Professional School Counseling, 16*(4), 245–255.

Harvard Mental Health Letter. (2011). Treating intermittent explosive disorder: Emerging data show medication and cognitive behavioral therapy may help patients. *Harvard Mental Health Letter, 27*(10), 6.

Henggeler, S. W., Schoenwald, S. K., Rowland, M. D., & Cunningham, P. B. (2009). *Multisystemic therapy for antisocial behavior in children and adolescents* (2nd ed.). New York, NY: Guilford Press.

Henggeler, S. W., & Sheidow, A. J. (2012). Empirically supported family-based treatments for conduct disorder and delinquency in adolescents. *Journal of Marital & Family Therapy, 38*(1), 30–58.

Karver, M. S., & Caporino, N. (2010). The use of empirically supported strategies for building a relationship with an adolescent with oppositional-defiant disorder. *Cognitive and Behavioral Practice, 17*(2), 222–232.

National Institute of Mental Health. (2012). *Attention deficit hyperactivity disorder*. Retrieved from http://www.nimh.nih.gov/health/publications/attention-deficit-hyperactivity-disorder/index.shtml

Portrie-Bethke, T. L., Hill, N. R., & Bethke, J. G. (2009). Strength-based mental health counseling for children with ADHD: An integrative model of adventure-based counseling and Adlerian play therapy. *Journal of Mental Health Counseling, 31*(4), 323–337.

Vidal, R., Castells, J., Richarte, V., Palomar, G., Garcia, M., Nicolau, R., . . . Ramos-Quiroga, J. A. (2015). Group therapy for adolescents with attention-deficit/hyperactivity disorder: A randomized controlled trial. *Journal of the American Academy of Child and Adolescent Psychiatry, 54*(4), 275–282.

Visser, S. N., Danielson, M. L., Bitsko, R. H., Holbrook, J. R., Kogan, M. D., Ghandour, R. M., . . . Blumberg, S. J. (2014). Trends in the patient-report of health care provider-diagnosed and medicated attention-deficit/hyperactivity disorder: United States, 2003–2011. *Journal of the American Academy of Child and Adolescent Psychiatry, 53*(1), 34–46.

Wadsworth, J. S., & Harper, D. C. (2007). Adults with attention-deficit/hyperactivity disorder: Assessment and treatment strategies. *Journal of Counseling & Development, 85*(1), 101–109.

Williamson, D., & Johnston, C. (2015). Gender differences in adults with attention-deficit/hyperactivity disorder: A narrative review. *Clinical Psychology Review, 40*, 15–27.

Attunement, Clinician

Clinician attunement allows clinicians to convey, verbally and nonverbally, that they are aligned with the present-moment experience of their clients. Originally, this term was used to describe parents or caretakers being attuned to the needs of infants and children. Later, this concept was applied to adult relationships, including the therapeutic relationship. From a holistic-mindfulness perspective, attunement begins with a resolve to stay connected to one's own emotions and body sensations. Therapists use their own feelings and sensations as clues to the inner experience of clients and the connections between all those in the therapy room. Attunement is when clinicians use their own internal cues to allow clients to experience a sense of being supported. This entry discusses the complexity of clinician attunement in working with couples and families, the relationship between attunement and related constructs, and what we can expect to occur when attunement is present.

Preparing for Attunement

Before a clinician can be attuned to her client, she needs to first decide to pay attention to her own emotions and body sensations that arise as she sits with her clients. For example, as one client discusses a past trauma the therapist may notice feelings of anger and sadness arising, along with tightness in her chest and throat. The clinician also observes the client and his or her family or partner's interactions for signs of emotion and bodily sensation as well. The client sharing about trauma might become tearful or adopt an erect and tense sitting position. Thus, the client's inner experience may send a ripple effect throughout the room, eliciting feelings and sensations from the other clients and the therapist herself. In couples and family work, the clinician pays attention equally to all those in the room. Staying attuned to multiple people can be confusing at times, though clinicians can always return to their own inner experience in order to reconnect with their attention to what is occurring in the session.

Attunement also involves attention to the meaning that clients hold about the stories they share. For example, the client with a history of trauma may share his experience as a story of powerlessness, or of empowerment. Attunement thus involves both affect and cognitive experiencing. Clients want to know that the clinician "gets" how something makes them feel and why it makes them feel that way. In couples and family work, clinicians have to pay attention to how family members and/or intimate partners reflect the meaning of stories that exist between multiple people.

Ability for Attunement

Attunement includes the clinician's actively tracking her own internal experience of being with clients, attending to cues that hint at the internal experiences within and between clients, and when the clinician checks in, using questions and reflections to ensure that the clients are experiencing a sense of being held. The language of being held comes from attachment theorist Donald Winnicott, who wrote about the holding environment that manifests when a primary caregiver is attuned to an infant's needs. Attunement has two active components: tracking and expression.

Tracking

Louis Cozolino, a psychologist, introduced a skill he called *shuttling,* which serves as an excellent guide to learn tracking. A clinician can shift, or shuttle, attention both internally and externally and up and down. *Internally* refers to attending to the clinician's own subjective experience, while *externally* refers to attending to the cues that reveal the clients' inner experience. While staying attuned internally, the clinician can shuttle up, attending to thinking and meaning-making, or shuttle down, attending to feelings and body sensations. Tracking is cultivated through continued experience as a clinician, and also through trainings in mindfulness, improvisation, and other body-oriented practices, such as yoga and Authentic Movement. In couples and family therapy, clinicians use their own internal cues to guide what and whom to track, moment to moment.

Expression

Expression is the second component of attunement. The clinician makes sure that clients know that she is attempting to emotionally and cognitively hold them. Writers on sociocultural attunement discuss three ways by which the clinician can express attunement to clients. By *questioning,* the clinician wonders with the clients about possible affective and cognitive interpretations of an experience. With *reflecting and validating,* the clinician can ensure that the client feels understood. Reflecting and validating can occur with verbal cues, such as paraphrasing what clients shared, or through nonverbal cues, such as emotionally reflective facial expressions. Daniel Siegel, a psychiatrist, explored how nonverbal reflection and validation also occurs on subconscious levels as pathways in the therapist's and clients' brains resonate and coregulate. Finally, attunement is expressed by *naming emotions* connected with the inner experience of clients, or feelings that are shared between the people in the therapy room, including the clinician.

Related Constructs

Clinician attunement is related to other constructs that describe the therapeutic relationship—namely, empathy, resonance, and joining. Attunement is a core component of empathy. While attunement is the moment to moment intending, tracking, and expressing of being with a client, empathy is a fuller flowering of the experience of sustained holding. When a clinician is in attunement with her clients, the couple and family relationships can be injected with empathy, which lasts beyond therapy itself, creating sustained openness and connection. Resonance is the affective by-product of attunement. When the clinician is attuned with her clients, there is a felt sense of togetherness and a lessening of separateness. Finally, *joining* is a term used by marriage and family theorists such as Salvador Minuchin, as a general first step of the therapist to find a place of alliance within the family system. Clinician attunement can create the trust needed for families to allow the clinician to join.

Positive Outcomes

The main positive outcome of clinician attunement is a robust relationship between the clinician and her clients. As already described previously, attunement creates a holding environment that is experienced as a sense of being affectively and cognitively understood. In the presence of attunement, clients will generally reveal more about their internal processes and are more likely to explore more deeply for new meanings. Attunement tends the therapeutic soil for empathy to flower, a predictor of successful therapy to occur, whatever a clinician's chosen theoretical orientation.

Zvi J. Bellin

See also Empathy; Interpersonal Neurobiology, Attachment and; Joining; Listening, Empathic; Therapeutic Alliance

Further Readings

Cozolino, L. (2004). *The making of a therapist.* New York, NY: W. W. Norton.

Davis, M., & Hadkis, D. (1994). Nonverbal aspects of therapist attunement. *Journal of Clinical Psychology, 50,* 393–405.

Pandit, M. L., Chen-Feng, J, Kang, Y. J., Knudson-Martin, C., & Huenergardt, D. (2014). Practicing sociocultural attunement: A study of couple therapists. *Contemporary Family Therapy, 36,* 518–528.

Siegel, D. J. (2007). *The mindful brain.* New York, NY: W. W. Norton.

Attunement in Relationships

Attunement is the ability for individuals in any form of relationship to be connected to and harmonious with one another. For maintaining intimacy in close relationships it is a necessity. In any interaction, an individual may recognize the thoughts, feelings, and nonverbal communication of another. This can take place between life partners, parents and children, friends, business partners, teachers and students, employers and employees, or even those in the service industry and their patrons. One party may be more attuned than another in a relationship. For example, a parent may attune to their child's hurt or fear even when the child is unwilling to talk about it. An employer may genuinely sense and understand the frustration in an employee who is upset about a business issue or a matter of protocol. Attunement is awareness in combination with empathy, compassion, and often validation. It helps diffuse stressful situations. This entry summarizes three of the primary theories of attunement in relationships and discusses how relationships thrive, survive, or fail based upon their levels of attunement. It continues with a brief explanation of the history of attunement theories and concludes with a discussion on how one may attune to others.

Historical Background

In the 1960s, researchers such as John Bowlby and Mary Ainsworth studied how infants connected to their caregivers. This was referred to as *attachment*. The research indicated that an infant's levels of trust in a caregiver's ability to meet his or her needs indicated how secure that infant would feel in the caregiver–child relationship, leading to long-term abilities to feel safe in the world and to connect to other humans. This attachment theory has developed over decades as studies have been able to follow relationships through the life span. With the need to address how attachment influences relationships of partnering and marriage, newer theories emerged that address the ability to maintain the attachment: attunement.

Modern Theories of Attunement in Relationships

Three research teams that have visibly headed the field of researching attunement in relationships are John and Julie Gottman in Washington; Sue Johnson and Les Greenberg of Ontario, Canada; and Dan Siegel in California. While the three teams have many commonalities, each has a distinctive approach.

John and Julie Gottman: The Gottman Institute

The Gottmans have been researching for over 40 years what makes relationships work, and they have consistently determined that attunement is of key importance. They define attunement as the ability to be aware and respectful of a partner's emotions and opinions, to understand one another, and to react with empathy instead of defensiveness. The Gottman approach is based chiefly on skills or behaviors that must be employed consistently in a relationship to maintain attunement. The Gottmans recognize that regression from these skills leads to lack of attunement and ultimately can lead to divorce. Focusing on the establishment and maintenance of attunement, the Gottmans strongly emphasize the need for trust.

Sue Johnson and Les Greenberg: Emotion-Focused Couples Therapy

Johnson and Greenberg's research has demonstrated how emotions create and maintain attunement, thereby contributing to the success or deterioration of relationships. By focusing on primary and secondary emotions, identifying helpful or maladaptive emotions, and addressing unmet attachment or attunement needs, Johnson and Greenberg have helped promote the field of attunement theory. Emotion-focused couples therapy focuses on the creation and maintenance of emotional safety to perpetuate attunement in relationships by focusing on unmet attachment needs, such as respect, validation, intimacy, and recognition.

Dan Siegel

Dan Siegel is a psychiatrist at the University of California, Los Angeles. His attunement theory in relationships is unique in that it is based upon findings in neuroscience. Siegel defines *attunement* as the ability to understand and experience the thoughts and feelings of another person. When this happens, a neurological shift is created, increasing feelings of connection and closeness. For children, this is necessary for their growth and emotional development. From childhood through the life span, humans require this security in relationships. This state of relational wellness is being *felt* by another person. When children are not felt as in their early and primary developmental years, it can stunt their ability to seek and engage in attuned relationships in adolescence and adulthood. Siegel teaches parents how to attune to their children and teens. He also trains mental health professionals in attuning to traumatized, hurting populations without burning out.

How to Attune in Relationships

In this age of technology, multitasking has become common and may be encouraged for productivity. This may lead some to feel that they are less able to attune to others. Because attunement is focused attention, it is important that an individual minimize and disengage from distractions in order to attune properly. Turning off electronic devices offering entertainment and social media, taking a walk, talking in the car during a drive, or making eye contact across the kitchen table are all ways that two or more people can attune to one another. Asking questions that show interest and concern and making respectful, validating statements maintain the attunement. With some individuals, proximity or touch is a way to attune. Often, a gentle hand on an energetic child's shoulder helps an authority figure attune to the child, leading to calmer behavior from the child. With others, remembering details about or desires within a person increases attunement as that individual realizes that their needs are important to the other. Generally speaking, any increase in attunement by one party increases the likelihood of reciprocity and mutuality of attunement in a relationship.

Lori C. Kucharski

See also Adult Attachment Assessments; Attachment and Romantic Love; Attachment Styles; Attachment Theory; Attachment-Based Family Therapy; Attunement, Clinician; Couple Development; Empathy

Further Readings

Gottman, J. (2011). *The science of trust: Emotional attunement for couples.* New York, NY: W. W. Norton.

Johnson, S. (2008). *Hold me tight: Seven conversations for a lifetime of love.* New York, NY: Little, Brown.

Siegel, D. (2007). *The mindful brain: Reflection and attunement in the cultivation of well-being.* New York, NY: W. W. Norton.

Authoritative Parenting

Authoritative parenting, also sometimes called "democratic" parenting, refers to a style of parenting for children and adolescents that involves high expectations couples with support and warmth. The term *authoritative parenting* was coined by Diana Baumrind approximately thirty years ago following research on parenting and children. Baumrind did research in order to identify the most effective parenting style. Three distinctly different styles of parenting emerged: authoritative, authoritarian, and permissive. A fourth parenting style prototype, neglectful, has also been developed since Baumrind's original study. As a concept, authoritative parenting has been further researched in the last three decades and been found to be the most effective style of parenting, offering a balance between behavioral control and the development of autonomy. An authoritative parenting style is correlated with a secure attachment in children and adults. This entry focuses on the authoritative style, its definition, and its importance in the parenting literature. In order to contextualize the authoritative style, additional styles of parenting, including the authoritarian, permissive, and rejecting–neglecting/disengaged are included. In addition, the research related to authoritative parenting, the effectiveness of each approach, and the messages learned by children are discussed.

Parenting and Family

Parenting is an essential component of family functioning in terms of the creation and management of the family. The parents are the developers and managers of the family environment. The family is a system and, as such, functions with the requirements and structure of a system. Urie Bronfenbrenner first introduced the concept of child development occurring within a system in the early 1970s with his bioecological model. This posits that development occurs through a reciprocal interaction of the individual with that of the persons and objects in his or her immediate environment. Growth occurs as a result of the child's interaction with the system. Others have extended this view of the individual within the family context in the development of family therapy (see Salvador Minuchin, Murray Bowen, and Virginia Satir's work). The family as a system is well known in the research literature; however, the discussion here of person and environment is limited to its connection to parenting within the family.

Parenting has often been characterized according to how adult parents view children. This can include seeing children as simple animals, "little adults," or innocent darlings. Each of these views then determines how parents will operate in response to their child's needs, demands, and expectations across the life span. In other words, these views influence how parents enact their authority with their children. *Authority* is defined as the power to make decisions or give orders to others; one who possesses parental authority refers to one who has the knowledge and power vested to make such decisions for his or her own children. Diana Baumrind's parent typologies allow for greater clarity in understanding parental authority and specifically the authoritative style, its definition, and differences from the other parenting styles.

Research on Benefits of Authoritative Parenting

Although later in this entry all four of Baumrind's parenting styles are compared and contrasted, the outcome of research has supported that authoritative parenting styles are generally associated with positive behaviors in children more so than the other styles. Each style has its costs and benefits, but the authoritative style has been shown to have the most positive correlations with outcomes that people typically want for their children. Authoritative parenting styles are about setting limits, reasoning with children, and being responsive to their emotional needs. Based on the attributes of this style, it may be easy to understand why these children tend to have higher self-esteem and self-confidence. They are more likely to be independent, self-reliant, well-behaved, and socially and academically successful. These children are less likely to experience depression and anxiety.

The balance of high expectations, high responsiveness, and warmth with firm limits means parents take an active role in their children's lives, but do not try to use methods of control that are sometimes associated with "rebellious" behavior. They tend not to try to control children through harsh punishments, arbitrary punishments, shaming, or withdrawal of love. Taking the time to reason with children and explain rules is associated with better moral reasoning skills. In addition, talking with children about thoughts and feelings and the responsiveness of authoritative parents promotes secure attachment of children to their parents. Finally, the ability of these parents to also set limits means their children are also less likely to be aggressive, more likely to have better peer relationships, less likely to engage in school delinquency, and less likely to abuse drugs. Authoritative parenting is partially so helpful to children because it balances warmth, demandingness, limit-setting, and responsiveness. The other styles may also have some of these aspects, but parents exhibit them to more of an extreme.

Baumrind's Parent Typologies

As noted previously, there are four basic styles of parenting. The first, authoritative, is a blending of high expectations for children along with support. Authoritarian parents also have high expectations but with lower levels of warmth and support. Permissive and neglectful styles of parenting both have low levels of expectation, but permissive styles combine those with warmth and support, whereas neglectful styles are low on both expectations and warmth and support.

Authoritative Parenting

Authoritative parenting is characterized by a high demand from parents coupled with high warmth and support. Parents have high expectations for children in this style, asking for achievement, problem-solving, meeting the demands of their developmental tasks, and increasing independence when necessary. However, parents also serve to support in a targeted way the goals they determine are most important for their children to reach. The authoritative parent values independence and compliance from children—balancing closeness and autonomy. They have clear expectations for children and expect them to meet them but are also willing to negotiate with children. Parents institute a reciprocal relationship with their children in establishing ways to resolve problems and serve to use discipline as a teaching tool to help children develop competency and agency in confronting challenges they face.

As children get older and enter adolescence, authoritative parents continue to develop a partnership with their teenager and negotiate to find flexible solutions to ongoing dilemmas. When the child is unable to cope or problem solve effectively, authoritative parents assist in supporting, directing, and finding solutions to these problems in order to maintain a healthy relationship between parent and child while also tasking the child with developing skills for managing the new problem. The authoritative parent views both control and power as essential to effect change with their children but does not, however, utilize power in a coercive manner. This differs from the authoritarian parent, who may use power in a coercive or controlling manner (e.g., to demand respect or adherence to an obedient mind-set). The authoritarian parent views the parental role and authority as primary in importance and the child's autonomy as secondary.

The way in which authoritative parents utilize power is a distinguishing factor from authoritarian parents. Authoritative parents use what Diana Baumrind calls *confrontive* control versus *coercive* control. Both authoritative and authoritarian parents use confrontive methods to assert control and expectation for their child's behavior; however, authoritative parents do this within the context of specified goals for such behavior and have flexibility dependent upon the child's developmental stage and capacity. Control is in the form of high expectations and is goal directed. This is quite different from authoritarian parenting, which uses coercive control in order to obtain fully obedient responses from children, including punishment, intrusiveness, and overall restriction. Generally, parents' demonstration of control and power within the family system can compel children to comply with given directives; however, the manner in which this occurs determines the child's response to such demands. In authoritative parenting, given the inherent flexibility in adjusting control to suit a child's needs, power is used judiciously.

Authoritarian Parenting

Authoritarian parenting is characterized by a high demand for children to achieve their goals, understand and develop competencies, and problem solve when dilemmas arise, while the parent's response is characterized by low warmth. In other words, high expectations are married with low assistance and warmth around working through problem-solving. Historically, this is a traditionally conservative parenting approach in that the expectation from the parent is that children solve their own problems and need limited support or direction in becoming competent in such problem-solving. A popular phrase for this parenting style is "pull yourself up by your own bootstraps." In addition, it's believed on the part of an authoritarian parent that this approach is the most effective—that children learn best when "thrown into the deep end of the pool." The parent's responsibility then in this context is to place the child or adolescent in a position to deal with life on life's terms with little to no coaching or direct support. This view of direct support or warmth is thought to be less effective as the child learns by not leaning on the parent (this might be viewed as dependent and gets in the way of learning). The power and control in the authoritarian typology is characterized by using coercive control, which tends to be restricting and punishing for the child. Thus, the development of autonomy and agency in response to situations is undermined by coercive control.

Permissive–Overprotective Parenting

This parenting style is characterized by low demand for the child's behavior coupled with high warmth and support. This approach creates less expectation for the child's behavior and rewards behavior without viewing the context of that behavior. Historically, this approach is a more liberal view of behavior and child-rearing, in which children are seen as needing consistent and ongoing love and support to develop effectively within the world. The parent in this case adopts an accepting, supporting, and nurturing attitude toward the child and allows the child to self-regulate behavior. Further, the parent may explain rules but does not emphasize conforming to external rules and expectations.

Rejecting–Neglecting/ Disengaged Parenting

The rejecting–neglecting parenting style is characterized by low demand from parents and low warmth. This parenting style is often described as not supporting or directing children at all, regardless of the child's behavior. In other words, parents do not respond to child demands and requests for assistance and do not provide direction (rejecting) or support (neglectful) for their needs. This style is also considered disengaged given that parents are disconnected from their child's needs and demands.

Parenting Style Effectiveness and Messages Learned by Children

Authoritative Parenting

The authoritative approach is considered in the literature by researchers and parenting experts as the most effective style because it combines high expectation for the child's behavior and competency while also having high expectations from the parent to assist the child in developing those competencies. Successful transition from one developmental task to the next is characterized by a partnership between parents and children in setting and meeting important developmental goals. The results of this partnership are generally more successful given that the attempts to meet goals, learn new skills, and problem solve when dilemmas arise are met with parents and children together.

Authoritarian Parenting

Authoritarian parenting, according to Diana Baumrind's research and the collective research of the past 30 years by others, has been found to be less effective than authoritative as a parenting approach. This is primarily measured in the competency and capacity developed on the part of the child. The approach dictates development and problem-solving on the part of the child without parenting direction or coaching. The effect on development is that the child, when in need of assistance to problem solve or support to understand their emotion or difficult developmental task, is met with redirection to solve the task independently. This approach does not take into account the developmental needs of the child and adjust to the different demands a child's developmental tasks bring. Further, it does not assess the actual needs the child has in terms of support or assistance; rather, it is a uniform approach by which problem-solving needs to be completed by the child without consultation with an adult or parent. It also does not teach the child ways to cope or problem solve when necessary. At times, when a problem develops, assistance from an adult may be necessary in order for the child to effectively solve problems. Children may not learn to develop effective problem-solving skills or adequate help-seeking behavior, believing all solutions must come from them internally and that compliance is more important than independence.

Permissive–Overprotective

The permissive–overprotective approach is generally considered less effective, given that children are given praise, support, and reinforcement for all behavior, rather than for specific behaviors in context. This can result in a child's overdependence on their parent as they are frequently faced with developmental tasks and challenges yet receive praise and support instead of direction. Children who frequently need assistance with multiple tasks and problems and when seeking guidance from parents often are not given a clear path on how to solve those problems. Behavior is accepted in all relevant contexts when in fact, in other environments other than home, this may not be accurate. Children are not adequately prepared for the demands of the world and outside environment, where the responses may be less supportive or rejecting of their behavior.

Rejecting–Neglecting/Disengaged

The rejecting–neglecting/disengaged parenting style is considered the least effective of the four styles as parents offer little to no assistance or support to their children. It is well understood that parents serve as the structural support for effective family functioning. The parental dyad sets rules, boundaries, and expectations for the children in the family. In this parenting style, the parents set either limited or no rules and expectations for their children and this can lead to a chaotic family structure. In many cases, the results can be catastrophic for childhood development and family functioning. Expectations may be unknown, boundaries are confused or inconsistent, and goals for behavior are not established or discussed. Neglectful parenting leads to a poor developmental outcome for children.

Children simply may not be able to meet basic developmental tasks and if able, do so without the assistance and support of their parents. In the extreme, abuse may follow or be combined with neglect given the lack of parental monitoring and response to a child's behavior. Basic needs are not met, which can include food, shelter, clothing, safety, or other developmental necessities. In addition, children are not actively protected and may be at risk for exposure to unsafe practices or developmentally inappropriate behaviors (e.g., substance abuse, sex, pornography or graphic images, television, movies). Neglectful parenting is considered ineffective given that parents are not actively engaged in the parenting process.

Relevance and Importance of Parenting Typologies

While no parent fits perfectly within one of these typologies, parenting style in responding to the needs and demands of children is relevant in determining how to understand and predict effective child development. In family systems theory (FST), this is understood to mean the need and capacity for self-determination and autonomy while maintaining affiliation with the family structure, family demands, and family community. It informs fully the child's development into a mature adult who can maintain self in context.

David M. Savinsky

See also Active Parenting; Adolescent Behavior Disorders; Child Behavior Problems; Child-Centered Parenting; Family of Origin; Group Parenting Classes; Parent–Adolescent Relations; Parent–Child Communication; Parenting Education; Parenting Styles

Further Readings

Baumrind, D. (1966). Effects of authoritative parental control on child behavior. *Child Development, 37*(4), 887–907.

Baumrind, D. (1991). The influence of parenting style on adolescent competence and substance abuse. *Journal of Early Adolescence, 11*, 56–95.

Baumrind, D. (2013). Authoritative parenting revisited: History and current status. In R. E. Larzelere, A. S. Morris, & A. W. Harrist (Eds.), *Authoritative parenting: Synthesizing nurturance and discipline for optimal child development* (pp. 11–34). Washington, DC: American Psychological Association.

Bronfenbrenner, U. (1974). Developmental research, public policy, and the ecology of childhood. *Child Development, 45*(1), 1–5.

Larzelere, R. E., Morris, A. S., & Harrist, A. W. (Eds.). (2013). *Authoritative parenting revisited: Synthesizing nurturance and discipline for optimal child development.* Washington, DC: American Psychological Association.

Nelson, J., & Lott, L. (2012). *Positive discipline: Empowering your teens and yourself through kind and firm parenting* (3rd ed.) New York, NY: Three Rivers Press.

Autism and Children

Autism is defined as a complex neurodevelopmental disorder that manifests in early childhood and is characterized by deficits in social interactions and social communication (verbal and nonverbal) in addition to restricted, repetitive, and stereotyped patterns of behavior. Moreover, these symptoms limit or impair everyday functioning. Up until the most recent revision of the *Diagnostic and Statistical Manual of Mental Disorders* (4th ed.; DSM-IV-TR; American Psychiatric Association [APA]), autism was delineated as a separate disorder within the diagnostic category of disorders usually first diagnosed in infancy, childhood, or adolescence. In the DSM-5, the diagnoses of autism, pervasive developmental disorder-not otherwise specified (PDD-NOS), and Asperger's disorder were merged under a single diagnosis now designated *autism spectrum disorder* (ASD) within the category of neurodevelopmental disorders. Although the diagnostic criteria are essentially unchanged, research findings suggested that similar symptoms were more effectively differentiated by clinical specifiers of severity and associated features.

Recent estimates in 2014 suggest that the prevalence of autism or ASD in the United States is 1 in 68 children (1 in 48 boys and 1 in 189 girls). Rates have dramatically climbed with a 30% increase over the prevalence of 1 in 88 in 2012. This steady increase in prevalence is thought to stem from changes in the broadening of the definition of autism, improvement in diagnostic efforts, and an actual increase in the disorder itself. Autism is 4 to 5 times more common in males than females, although females are more likely to have a comorbid intellectual disability. Symptoms are typically detected by 18 months of age with reliable diagnosis by 2 years of age; in instances where developmental delays are more severe, autism may be diagnosed prior to 12 months of age. Autism occurs in all racial, ethnic, and social groups.

The following sections review the clinical features, other related disorders, assessment and diagnosis, causes, pathophysiology, and treatments of autism (also known as ASD).

Clinical Features

There are a number of behavioral and developmental symptoms that suggest the presence of autism. Some of the symptoms noted in the area of social development include diminished eye contact, difficulties in turn taking, and challenges in grasping and understanding the more complex social emotions and interactions or in considering others' perspectives. Such difficulties in understanding the intentions of others are common and may impede the successful development of peer relationships. As the child progresses developmentally through adolescence and young adulthood, these social challenges may become more profound and lead to loneliness or depression.

Communication deficits are common and generally lie on a range of severity from those who acquire no functional language to those who demonstrate language that falls near normal limits. However, the continuum of echolalia is one such deviation, and it involves the repetition of sounds, words, and phrases with similar intonation. Pronoun reversal is another common feature in which the child may confuse *he* and *she* or *you* and *I*. Because communication is a socially embedded process, individuals on the autism spectrum often learn communication "intellectually." This can result in some of the language delays and deviations often observed, which include highly literal interpretation and use of language (which impede comprehension of figurative language, irony, or sarcasm), difficulty starting conversations, and challenges reading body language and nonverbal cues that make it possible to interpret whether someone is interested or uninterested. Finally, individuals on the autism spectrum may lean toward stilted and scripted language. For example, their conversation may sound monotone, obscure, and inauthentic as well as lack animation. They may also use scripted language in which they can literally recite dialogue from various sources on television, movies, or videos.

Repetitive behaviors that are routinely observed in children on the autism spectrum include stereotypy (e.g., hand flapping, teeth grinding, rocking movements, nail biting), compulsive behavior (e.g., lining up toys in very specific ways), sameness, ritualistic behavior, restricted behavior (e.g., always driving a specific route to school or only wearing long-sleeved shirts even in hot weather), and self-injury (e.g., head banging). Many of these behaviors seem to serve a sensory processing need to support upward and downward regulation.

Deficits in executive functioning, which includes skills such as using working memory, organizing, planning, sustaining attention, and inhibiting inappropriate responses, are common for individuals with autism. While some individuals may pay attention to trivial details but be unable to grasp the "bigger picture," others may have difficulty organizing their thoughts and actions to effectively carry out multistep processes. Executive functioning deficits can impact the performance of daily routines such as getting dressed or taking a bath or involve difficulty in complete school assignments, monitoring mistakes, and organizing work space.

Other symptoms that are of interest and importance for consideration include splinter skills, sensory processing disorder, unusual eating behaviors, and parental or familial stress. Splinter skills, highly task-specific abilities, may be exhibited in the areas of music, art, mechanical, or spatial skills; hyperlexia; memory; calendar calculation; mathematical calculation; computer ability; athletic performance; or sensory sensitivity. Splinter skills may reach extraordinary levels, as seen in autistic savants who display gifted levels in a specific area that are in stark contrast to the levels of functioning related to their disability.

Sensory processing disorder is a neurological condition that causes obstacles in processing information from sensory input, including the sense of movement (vestibular) or positional sense (proprioceptive). It is closely aligned with autism in that most children have challenges in this area that result in them being underreactive or overreactive to stimulation. As a result, they may have unusually high or low activity levels or fluctuate between the extremes; struggle with gross or fine motor skills; or struggle with impulsivity, distractibility, and planning.

Unusual eating behaviors, namely selective or restrictive eating in which a limited range and types of food are eaten, result in children refusing foods based on their presentation (e.g., placement on the plate) or characteristics (e.g., texture). These difficulties are thought to be the result of sensory disorders that impact the perception of smell, flavor, and texture and/or another manifestation of the insistence on sameness.

Finally, family stress is a major area of research focus. Because parents need to significantly shift their resources of time and money (estimates suggest that it costs between $17,000 and $21,000 more per year, which includes related therapies, education, health and child care, and family-coordinated services) toward providing treatment and intervention to the exclusion of other priorities, the needs of a child on the autism spectrum complicate familial relationships. Higher levels of parental stress and notable challenges to emotional well-being and family functioning are common difficulties that necessitate support.

Other Related Disorders

ASDs and intellectual disability covary at a rate of 40% to 69%. In addition, greater severity of intellectual disability carries significant impact on the expression of autism. Recent research suggests that the most common genetic form of intellectual disability and autism co-occur because of a mechanism that shuts off the gene associated with the disease. Co-occurring central nervous system disorders that occur at a concerning frequency include learning disabilities (comorbidity rates range from 25% to 75%) and epilepsy (more than 35% develop clinical seizures by adolescence). Genetic disorders are more commonly found in children with autism with approximately 10% having been diagnosed with fragile X syndrome, Down syndrome, tuberous sclerosis, or other genetic and chromosomal disorders. Also, co-occurring mental disorders include depression (4% to 58%), anxiety disorders (over 40%), attention-deficit/hyperactivity disorder (ADHD; 28%–55%), and obsessive-compulsive disorder (OCD).

Gastrointestinal disorders are one of the common medical conditions and may include gastroesophageal reflux disease (GERD), chronic constipation or diarrhea, and other irritable and inflammatory bowel conditions. Many children on the autism spectrum also have underlying metabolic conditions such as mitochondrial disease and mitochondrial dysfunction, and all of these have been associated with epilepsy in children on the autism spectrum. Aside from metabolic defects, children on the spectrum frequently present with minor physical anomalies and Tourette syndrome as well. Sleep problems including difficulty falling asleep and frequent nighttime waking were noted in 53% to 78% of children on the autism spectrum (compared to 26% to 32% of typically developing children).

Assessment and Diagnosis

Currently, the diagnosis of autism or ASD is based on behavioral and developmental indicators. Typically, a child is initially assessed through a developmental screening. This generally involves the completion of a questionnaire or screening instrument that relies on parent reports or a blend of parent and physician observations. If the developmental screening is suggestive of autism, a comprehensive diagnostic evaluation is recommended. The comprehensive evaluation is much more thorough and intensive as it frequently involves a team of specialists, which may include a developmental pediatrician, pediatric neurologist, pediatric psychiatrist, child psychologist or neuropsychologist, speech language pathologist, and/or occupational therapist. Detection is often quite good at 18 months or younger although a highly reliable diagnosis can safely be made by the age of 2 years.

A number of diagnostic instruments are routinely used in comprehensive evaluations. One frequently used instrument is the Autism Diagnostic Observation Schedule, Second Edition (ADOS-2), which is a semistructured, standardized assessment of social interaction, communication, play, and imaginative use of materials. Another instrument is the Autism Diagnostic Interview–Revised (ADI-R), which is a semistructured parent interview that is administered by a trained clinician. The Childhood Autism Rating Scale, Second Edition (CARS-2) is a brief rating scale that helps distinguish children with autism from nonautistic children with developmental delays. Finally, the Gilliam Autism Rating Scale, Third Edition (GARS-3) is a norm-referenced instrument that helps clinicians diagnose autism and its severity. Best practices in assessment dictate that multiple instruments should be used as the basis for diagnosis and there should be a minimum of two main sources of information (i.e., the parents' or caregivers' description of the child's development and a professional's observation of the child's behavior).

Causes

The term *refrigerator mother* was coined around 1940 to label mothers of children with autism and was based on the assumption that autistic behaviors stemmed from the emotional frigidity and unresponsiveness of the mother. Although the theory has long been disproven, the prejudice that autism is the result of poor parenting still exists.

Although autism is thought to be a complex disorder whose core aspects have distinct causes that often co-occur (including environmental, biological, and genetic factors), the causes of autism currently remain unknown. The genetics of autism alone are complex, owing to interactions among the environment, various genes, and epigenetic factors that do not alter DNA but influence the expression of genes and are inherited. On a related note, it is known that many genes linked to autism affect synaptic development and function. Some researchers have hypothesized that the nervous system of individuals on the autism spectrum may have a greater number of synapses due to a slowdown in the typical pruning process of synapses during development. Sometimes known as synaptic dysfunction, this excess of synapses has profound effects on how the brain functions, given that synapses are the junctions where neurons communicate with one another.

Environmental agents that have been causally linked to autism include pesticides, parental age over 40, pharmaceutical exposure in utero (including selective serotonin reuptake inhibitors [SSRIs], valproic acid, and thalidomide), freeway proximity and/or air pollution, and limited prenatal vitamin intake. Vaccinations have been disproven as a cause of autism. However, many researchers and professionals believe that it is premature to rule out a link between autism and vaccinations, particularly in a subpopulation of children who are genetically predisposed to immune, autoimmune, or inflammatory conditions.

Pathophysiology

The disordered physiological processes associated with autism include neuroanatomical abnormalities, neurotransmitters, hormones, and immunology. Research findings reveal irregularities in several regions of the brain (i.e., frontal lobes, mirror neuron system, temporal lobe, cerebellum, amygdala). However, there is no definitive pathology suggesting that the time progression of brain development may be more related to autism than the final structure. Approximately 30% of persons with ASD have increased head size and brain volume.

Abnormalities in neurotransmitter systems, including serotonin, dopamine, glutamate, and gamma-aminobutyric acid (GABA), have also been linked to autism via a hypothesized imbalance in inhibitory and excitatory signaling in the brain. In regard to immunology, high fetal testosterone levels have been linked with traits of autism in toddlers and older children. Finally, there is an increasing body of evidence concerning the link between neurological dysfunction with autism and abnormal immune function. Researchers are confident that there are multifactorial immune anomalies in children with autism, with different anomalies presenting in "classic autism" versus "regressive autism." The role of cytokines has also been a topic of recent research and suggests a relationship with altered blood–brain barrier permeability and ensuing neuroinflammation.

Treatments

There is no known cure for autism, but there are a number of treatments that research has shown to be particularly effective in remediating the challenges associated with autism. Given the diverse ways in which autism presents in children, treatment protocols should be tailored to address each individual child. Early intervention is deemed critical and results in better prognostic outcomes.

In regards to early educational intervention, children generally benefit from full-day early childhood programs. Frequently, educational programming includes speech, occupational, and social skills training and therapy to address social communication, sensory integration, fine motor, and visual-motor challenges. Social skills may include techniques such as social stories, integrated playgroups, facilitated or peer-mediated play during recess, and video modeling. Although some children are educated in a mainstream school (either in a regular education classroom or self-contained special education program), others attend private schools that target the educational needs of children with varying levels of challenges.

Behavioral intervention, specifically applied behavior analysis (ABA), targets social and language skills through the use of principles of learning and motivation inherent in behavioral analysis. Discrete trail training, verbal behavior intervention, pivotal response training, and early intensive behavioral intervention are all forms of ABA. ABA is intensive and typically involves 20 to 40 hours of therapy per week. Based on research evidence supporting ABA, it is frequently reimbursed by insurance companies through most states.

Other therapeutic techniques include (1) developmental play therapies that address core deficits in social skills and interaction through child-led, relational play; (2) structured teaching, which is a therapeutic and educational tool that targets five key areas (physical structure, scheduling, work system, routine, and visual structure) to assist children in better understanding their environment; (3) occupational therapy, in which an occupational therapist uses techniques such as sensory integration therapy and fine motor skill activities to support handwriting and to help regulate the child's reaction to external stimuli in order to support functioning in social, educational, adaptive, play, and work domains; (4) speech therapy to support communication and social skills; and (5) social skills training, which often employs social stories, comic strip conversations, social skills groups, and video modeling.

Medication is sometimes used in the treatment of specific autism-like symptoms such as ADHD, OCD, severe behavioral problems, anxiety, depression, and seizures. Research has supported the use of risperidone (Risperdal), olanzapine (Zyprexa), and other antipsychotics in alleviating irritability leading to the challenges of severe tantrums, self-injurious behavior, and aggression. Although more research is needed, the SSRIs are most often prescribed for symptoms of anxiety, depression, and OCD in children over the age of 7. To treat seizures found in one of four children with autism, anticonvulsants are used at the lowest amounts and blood levels are monitored frequently. Lastly, ADHD symptoms are treated through stimulants in higher-functioning children but may include antidepressants, mood stabilizers, and benzodiazepines.

Complementary and alternative medicine treatments are widely used, with research suggesting that 35% to 90% of children with diagnosed autism have been treated through such techniques. Because of the lack of scientifically rigorous studies surrounding such interventions, there is concern about the cost and effectiveness of many complementary and alternative medicine treatments. Some examples of more commonly used integrative treatments include melatonin, probiotics, omega-3 fatty acids, nutritional supplements such as multivitamins and methyl B12, and gluten-free/casein-free diets. Noningestible CAM treatments include massage, acupuncture, exercise, neurofeedback, animal-assisted therapy (AAT), and art and music therapy.

Family supports are crucial given that a diagnosis of autism involves profound challenges and stressors. As such, parents can benefit from parent-to-parent programs and support groups. Families of children with autism may require additional family support services such as respite and child care, in-home behavioral training, adaptive equipment and assistive technology, social and recreation activities, and other services and supports unique to each family's needs. Conferences, books, and videos can also provide excellent sources of information to support parent growth and learning on how to best support their child.

Terri Christiansen

See also Community Programs; Family and Medical Leave Act of 1993; Family Resilience; Functional Assessment and Children; Nonverbal Communication; Parenting; Parenting Education; Sibling Relationships; Single-Parent Families

Further Readings

Barbera, M., & Rasmussen, T. (2007). *The verbal behavior approach: How to teach children with autism and related disorders.* Philadelphia, PA: Jessica Kingsley.

Biel, L., & Peskey, N. (2009). *Raising a sensory smart child: The definitive handbook for helping your child with sensory processing issues.* New York, NY: Penguin.

Bock, K., & Stauth, C. (2007). *Healing the new childhood epidemics: Autism, ADHD, asthma and allergies.* New York, NY: Ballantine.

Chez, M. G. (2009). *Autism and its medical management: A guide for parents and professionals.* Philadelphia, PA: Jessica Kingsley.

Durand, V. M. (2014). *Autism spectrum disorder: A clinical guide for general practitioners.* Washington, DC: American Psychological Association.

Greenspan, S., & Weider, S. (2009). *Engaging autism: Using the floortime approach to help children relate, communicate, and think.* Philadelphia, PA: Da Capo Lifelong.

Harris, S. L., & Glasberg, B. A. (2012). *Siblings of children with autism: A guide for families.* Bethesda, MD: Woodbine House.

Leaf, R., McEachin, J., & Harsh, J. (1999). *A work in progress: Behavior management strategies and a curriculum for intensive behavioral treatment of autism.* New York, NY: DRL Books.

Matson, J. L. (2008). *Clinical assessment and intervention for autism spectrum disorders*. London, England: Academic Press.

Wright, P. D., & Wright, P. W. (2006). *Wrightslaw: From emotions to advocacy: The special education survival guide*. Hartfield, VA: Harbor House Law Press.

Autism Spectrum Disorder

Autism spectrum disorder (ASD) is a neurodevelopmental disorder that impairs a child's ability to effectively communicate with and relate to others and also results in restricted and repetitive behavior, activity, and interests. It is called a spectrum disorder because the level and type of impairment created by these symptoms varies widely by individual, such that some diagnosed with ASD experience severe dysfunction in communication and day-to-day activity while others experience milder symptoms. ASD was diagnosed in 1 out of 68 children (about 1.5%) in 2010, a level more than doubled from that in 2000. This increase may be partially explained by the change in diagnostic terminology surrounding ASD or increased awareness of the disorder but may also reflect a real increase in the prevalence rate. Specific causes of ASD are not known, though some factors that imply higher risk for the disorder have been identified. There is no cure for ASD, but interventions have proven effective in enhancing coping and compensation for symptoms of the disorder and reducing the level of dysfunction it creates. Throughout this entry, the background of ASD, symptoms, and diagnosis and treatment will be addressed.

Background of Autism Spectrum Disorder

ASD was introduced as a diagnosis in 2013 when the fifth edition of the *Diagnostic and Statistical Manual of Mental Disorders* (DSM-5; American Psychiatric Association [APA]) established this single umbrella diagnosis to reflect the family of related neurodevelopmental disorders that had been previously defined as autism, Asperger's disorder, childhood disintegrative disorder, and pervasive developmental disorder (PDD). In doing this, the APA recognized the wide range of symptoms and severity of impairments ASD reflects and the unique presentation of the disorder across individuals.

The exact causes of ASD are not known, which may not be surprising given the complexity of the disorder and the diversity of its presentation in terms of both symptoms and their severity. Ongoing research suggests that genetic predispositions toward the development of ASD may exist and that environmental factors that may act as triggers for the disorder include viral infections, pollutants, or complications during pregnancy. Much discussion has been given to the possible link between childhood vaccinations and ASD, though there has been no reliable research to validate this. It is likely that a perceived connection here may be due to the timing of ASD onset as coinciding with the age at which vaccinations are typically given.

Though causes of ASD have not been isolated, a number of factors appear to place children at higher risk of developing ASD. Gender is an issue here, as boys develop ASD at a rate 4 times higher than do girls. Family history is related to ASD in that families who have one child with ASD have a higher than average likelihood of having a second child with the disorder. Further, relatives of children with ASD are more often found to have traits similar to the symptoms of ASD. Babies born preterm earlier than 26 weeks also may be at higher risk of developing ASD. Early research indicates there may also be a connection between children born to older parents and the occurrence of ASD, though further research is needed to support this. Some recent studies have shown that the risk of autism is reduced when the mother consumes at least 600 mcg of folic acid (vitamin B9) during the months preceding and during pregnancy.

Symptoms of Autism Spectrum Disorder

Symptom criteria for ASD include onset of the disorder in the early developmental period, typically before age 2. The manifestation of the symptoms must not only be apparent but must also result in significant impairment in social or other areas of functioning. Two categories of symptoms must be present to support a diagnosis of ASD. The first involves impairments to communication and socialization skills. The second involves rigid and repetitive patterns of behavior, areas of focus, or activities. For each of these symptom areas, the diagnosis should also indicate the level of severity in terms of the level of support needed by the child given their level of functional impairment due to ASD. Individuals with ASD are found to have a high rate of comorbidity with other physical and mental health disorders; diagnosis of ASD should also give consideration to the possible existence of these coexisting conditions.

Symptoms are generally recognized at the age of 12 to 24 months, though severe symptoms may manifest before that time, and milder symptoms may not be detected until a later age. In some cases, onset of ASD is detected as a result of developmental delays in language and socialization skills. In others, typical development followed by a loss of language and socialization skills between 12 and 24 months of age presents a strong indicator of ASD as few other conditions are associated with this symptom. It would be very rare, however, for a loss of these skills after the age of 24 months to be attributable to ASD.

Deficits in social communication are present to some extent in those who have ASD, and research indicates that roughly 25% of those with ASD are nonverbal. Three areas of impairment in social interactions that must exist across multiple contexts to support a diagnosis of ASD are noted in the DSM. The first relates to the ability to maintain reciprocal social interactions, where at the most severe level there may be no initiation of or response to communications with others. Milder presentations may reflect awkwardness in social situations; failures to appropriately recognize social patterns and cues; and lack of conversational sharing of interests, emotions, etc. A second type of communication deficit relates to nonverbal communication patterns. Those with more severe ASD may not engage in eye contact or provide any typically appropriate facial expressions, gestures, or other body language. At a more moderate level, deficiencies here might reflect nonverbal communications that are limited, inappropriate, or poorly coordinated with verbal messages. Limited ability to understand, form, and maintain relationships is the third area of deficit in this category, where persons with severe presentations of ASD may display no interest in interacting with others. Less severe presentations may involve the inability to differentiate appropriate behaviors across different contexts or limited ability to share in interactive play or make friends.

The second category of ASD symptoms involves rigid and repetitive patterns of behavior, activity, and interest, where at least two of the following four criteria are met. The first of these involves engaging in repetitive movements or speech patterns. Examples of this are hand flapping, rocking, arranging objects in an exacting pattern, and repeating words or phrases. The second criterion reflects the inability to accommodate changes in routines or need to exercise inflexible rituals in various contexts. Consistency may be extremely important to those with ASD, and minor changes such as taking a different route or introduction of a new food can cause great distress. Fixation on a rigid, atypical area of interest is the third criteria in this category. Children with ASD may become preoccupied with an object such as a vacuum cleaner or toilet or develop an intense interest and depth of knowledge about a topic or activity such as trash disposal or space travel, such that their attention is difficult to redirect. Finally, those with ASD may develop an unusually high or low level of sensory awareness and sensitivity to certain stimuli. Hypersensitivity to touch may create an inability to wear clothing, for example, while hyposensitivity may create indifference in responding to extremes of temperature.

Persons with ASD tend to have difficulties in regulating their emotions, particularly when frustrated or presented with new environments that disrupt repetitive behavior patterns. This may result in behavior such as crying or temper outbursts that appear immature but may also involve aggressive behavior toward others or self-harming activity such as head banging or self-biting. It is common for those with ASD to suffer from comorbid mood and/or anxiety disorders as well as attention-deficit/hyperactivity disorder (ADHD). Those with ASD also frequently suffer from intellectual impairment. Comorbid medical conditions commonly occurring with ASD include gastrointestinal, seizure, and sleep disorders.

Diagnosis and Treatment of Autism Spectrum Disorder

Though every child follows a unique developmental path, early signs of ASD reflect situations where a child fails to meet typical developmental milestones such as where the child doesn't respond with a smile or happy expression by 6 months; doesn't mimic sounds or facial expressions by 9 months; doesn't babble or coo by 12 months; doesn't gesture, such as point or wave, by 14 months; doesn't say single words by 16 months; doesn't play make-believe or pretend by 18 months; doesn't say two-word phrases by 24 months; or loses previously acquired language or social skills at any age. A variety of information and self-evaluation checklists are available to help parents become aware of early signs of ASD. Medical and other care providers may also provide regular screenings for ASD and provide valuable insights as to when specialized assessment for ASD should be sought. Though there is no single medical test for ASD, specially trained medical and mental health care professionals provide a variety of behavioral evaluations to confirm the ASD diagnosis.

Treatment for ASD can involve medication, behavioral therapy, or both. Given the many co-occurring conditions that may exist with ASD, coordination of treatment protocols by a team of professional may be required. Medication does not address the core symptoms of ASD but is often useful in managing the comorbid mental and physical disorders such as anxiety, mood disorder, ADHD, sleep problems, gastrointestinal issues, and seizures. Behavioral therapy is the primary approach to address the primary symptoms of ASD, and early intensive intervention with behavioral therapies has been empirically proven effective in increasing socialization and learning skills. Though there are many specific approaches to behavioral therapy, these tend to have a number of common attributes. Therapy should involve coordinated efforts by a team of professionals as needed to meet the unique needs of the child and may include behavioral, speech, and physical therapists as well as medical, psychological, and educational professionals. Parents should be highly engaged in decisions regarding intervention and in the intervention itself. The preschool child should typically receive at least 25 hours per week of therapeutic intervention that focuses on the core areas affected by autism: social skills, language and communication, imitation, play skills, daily living, and motor skills. Specific objectives should be defined, and progress should be monitored and evaluated. The program should also provide the child with opportunities to interact with typically developing children of the same age. Treatment for school-age children will typically be coordinated with services provided within the school system.

A number of alternative therapies are also available to address ASD symptoms, though their effectiveness has yet to receive empirical research support. These include several diet strategies, acupuncture therapy, sensory therapies, and chelation therapy, which has been targeted at removing mercury and other heavy metals from the body. As with other therapies noted previously, there is no empirical support for use of chelation therapy. Beyond this, there is no known link between mercury and ASD, and this therapy can be dangerous or even deadly.

Families of children with ASD may be placed under tremendous stress in coping with the challenges of the disorder. Building a team of trusted professionals to care for the member with ASD is important in establishing a program of care and also in obtaining resources for learning about the disorder and connecting with networks of families who are facing the same challenges. Outcomes for children with ASD vary widely, and though symptom improvement and enhancement of social and educational skills are likely with treatment, achievement of a typical level of social interaction is rare for those with ASD. Given the range of symptoms and comorbid conditions typical for those with ASD, there is little data on the extent to which those diagnosed with ASD in childhood overcome the diagnosis in later life or become capable of living independently.

Mary McClure

See also Autism and Children; Intellectual Disability and Autism

Further Readings

American Psychiatric Association. (2013). *Diagnostic and statistical manual of mental disorders* (5th ed.). Washington, DC: Author.

Autism Speaks, Inc. (n.d.). *What is autism?* Retrieved from https://www.autismspeaks.org/what-autism

Mayo Clinic Staff. (2014). *Autism spectrum disorder.* Retrieved from http://www.mayoclinic.org/diseases-conditions/autism-spectrum-disorder/basics/risk-factors/con-20021148

Morris, B. K. (2008*). Help with autism, Asperger's syndrome, and related disorder.* Retrieved from http://www.autism-help.org/index.htm

Avoidance

Avoidance is the act or measure taken to escape or withdraw from an unwanted or unpleasant person, place, or experience. It can be either passive (e.g., ignoring) or active (e.g., walking away). Behavioral and personality theorists have parsed the concept of avoidance into two distinct theoretical perspectives. According to theories of personality, avoidance is a defense mechanism that involves withdrawing from an experience or social situation deemed emotionally painful or anxiety-provoking. According to most psychoanalytical theorists, such as Sigmund Freud, avoidance is often an automatic response to feelings or situations that evoke unconscious fears or desires. When the psyche is in danger, avoidance presents as a way out of a situation that produces intolerable feelings and thoughts. Behavioral therapists use the term *experiential avoidance* to describe this act of trying to avoid negative or distressing experiences such as thoughts, feelings, memories, and urges. Similarly, principles of learning and behavior define *avoidance* as an escape from an aversive or unpleasant situations. In behavior training or modification, avoidance learning is a conditioning technique in which the subject learns to avoid an unpleasant stimulus or situation. Moreover, in applied behavior analysis (ABA), *avoidance* is also defined as a likely function of a behavior. For example, a student might disrupt class to avoid a challenging academic task. Regardless of theoretical perspective, research suggests that avoidance as a means of escaping averse thoughts or emotions is counterproductive. The immediate benefit is that the unwanted or uncomfortable stimulus is avoided. So, conflict and distress is avoided. However, the efforts to suppress or avoid negative or unwanted feelings might actually increase or intensify the distress and result in unresolved and/or pent-up emotions, which creates even more distress. In what follows, the social and behavioral concepts of avoidance, reinforcement theory, and avoidant personality disorder (APD) are addressed in detail.

The Social and Behavioral Concepts of Avoidance

Escaping or withdrawing from social situations is a readily observable example of avoidance. Examples of avoidant behaviors might include fleeing, lying, denying, ignoring, or negating. Repressed memories are also a type of avoidance but not as readily controlled as lying or hiding. When a person displays avoidant behavior, he or she will remove himself or herself from the unpleasant situations. Avoidant behavior might be triggered by real or perceived hurt, fears, or frustrations. For example, many people fear speaking in public. The experience can create insurmountable feelings of fear. Symptoms vary, but some people may experience sweating palms, cotton mouth, racing heartbeat, and irrational or disorganized thoughts, which might leave the person feeling paralyzed. In this example, avoidant behavior might be dropping the course or skipping the class to avoid presenting.

When avoidance is impossible, escape may be used as a means of dealing with an intolerable situation. Escape behaviors occur when a person physically flees a distressing situation. For instance, if an individual is fearful of communicating with another person, she may leave the room or building to avoid or withdraw from an encounter. Partial avoidance occurs when neither avoidance nor escape are possible. Partial avoidance is also referred to as a safety behavior, which reduces or removes feelings of anxiety during social or performance situations. Using the public-speaking example, partial avoidance would be avoiding direct eye contact with the audience during a presentation. A person experiencing partial avoidance or safety behavior might also present with self-soothing behaviors such as pacing, rocking, nail biting, hand wringing, and playing with one's hair. These behaviors allow the person to confront the fearful situation but can become what's often referred to as nervous habits.

Distraction and procrastination are also forms of avoidance in social situations. Specifically, procrastination is the avoidance of a stressful or averse task or situation until the last minute. "I'll do it later" is a common utterance of a procrastinator. Distraction is readily seen in schoolchildren who are faced with an unwanted behavioral or academic demand. The student may seem hypervigilant to movements or sounds in the classroom as an effort to avoid a request or task. In this situation, the student seems to have a short attention span as evidenced by tangential comments, looking around the classroom, or focusing on irrelevant stimuli in the environment. In behavioral psychology, avoidance is classified as a negative reinforcement. As a negative reinforcement, the absence of something (e.g., unwanted task, distressing feelings) will likely increase or intensify the avoidant behavior.

Negative reinforcement involves an escape contingency. Thus, the response produces escape from the continuing or persistent presentation of a trigger. People encounter instances of escape on a daily basis. For example, when the lights in a room are so bright that vision is blurred, the common response is to turn the lights down or off. Most behavior that is caused by negative reinforcement is called *avoidance contingency*—that is, a response that stops or delays the presentation of a trigger. Thus, negative behavior may be strengthened or reinforced because the response successfully stopped the averse trigger. The negative behavior will now be maintained because of the reinforcement. These negative behaviors are adaptive and can become coping skills because the behaviors enables the person to cope, whether positively or negatively, with the environment. Hence, negative reinforcement can foster the development of maladaptive, dangerous, and/or disruptive behaviors. Lastly, escape and avoidance can be either innate or learned reactions to an aversive stimulus. And, each time the stimulus is successfully avoided, the probability of future avoidance or escape behaviors will increase.

There is an abundance of literature on the fight-or-flight response patterns to conflict. The three approach styles provide a framework to explain how most people respond to difficult situations. In the first response style, approach–avoidance, a person is presented with something desirable but s/he is afraid of obtaining it. Thus, the person is forced to choose between the two incompatible experiences of desire or fear. In the second option, avoidance–avoidance, a person is forced to choose between two undesirable choices. Lastly, in the approach–approach style, a person is forced to choose between two desirable choices or outcomes.

Several theories on relationships also address avoidant response patterns. For instance, in attachment theory, *avoidance of intimacy* refers to the act of emotionally abstaining within a relationship out of insecurity or fear. In instances of fear, a person may be reluctant to attach out of fear that the partner will not be physically or emotionally available, responsive, or attentive. As well, bonding and attachment may be avoided out of fear that feelings and affection will not be reciprocated. Additionally, the term *avoidant couples* is used to refer to the quality or state of relating. For example, avoidant couples are said to minimize conflict by avoiding each other or contentious topics.

Reinforcement Theory

The psychologist B. F. Skinner was a behaviorist and the father of operant conditioning. Skinner built upon Thorndike's law of effect and introduced the law of effect reinforcement. Simply stated, any behavior that is reinforced will be strengthened. Behavior that is not reinforced will likely weaken or cease. In his work with operant conditioning, Skinner conducted several experiments using an apparatus he called the "Skinner box." The Skinner box is very similar to Thorndike's puzzle box. By repeatedly exposing a lab rat in the Skinner box to an electric shock, Skinner's experiments provided evidence for how escape learning and avoidance learning occurs. Other studies have also demonstrated the efficacy of avoidance learning. For instance, psychologist Richard Solomon demonstrated the persistence of avoidance behavior in his shuttle box experiment. In this research, Solomon placed a dog in a large cage with a low wall that separated two chambers. When Solomon electrified the floor on one side, the dog instinctively jumped to the other side. This is an example of escape conditioning because the dog emitted the behavior of jumping after it experienced the aversive stimulus (electric shock). If Solomon electrified the floor on the other side of the cage, the dog jumped back to the original side, which was no longer electrified.

Avoidant Personality Disorder

Avoidant behaviors can also be pathological. As such, APD is a clinical disorder classified within the *Diagnostic and Statistical Manual of Mental Disorders* (DSM), characterized by pervasive and persistent patterns of social avoidance, feelings of inadequacy, and hypersensitivity to comments or feedback. Individuals with APD tend to be socially reserved and feel socially incompetent. Symptoms include avoidance of social activities, inability to initiate or engage in adequate social interactions, guardedness in intimate relationships, preoccupation with being criticized, and reluctance to take social risks. A person with APD may fantasize about having intimacy, affection, and acceptance with others but struggle to obtain such social connectedness. This disorder is marked with avoidance of work, school, and any setting or activity that requires social engagement. Thus, APD causes significant difficulties in social, emotional, and behavioral functioning. Individuals with APD are often described as shy, lonely, withdrawn, or socially inept. A person with APD might cautiously watch the expressions and movements of others in social settings, thus presenting as excessively nervous, tense, or fearful. Although characteristics of APD can be seen throughout developmental milestones, APD is typically diagnosed in early adulthood by a qualified mental health professional.

Tasha Leroyce Banks and Alyssa Espinoza

See also Conflict in Couples and Families; Conflict Resolution; Conflict Styles; Power Issues in Couples

Further Readings

American Psychiatric Association. (2002). *Diagnostic and statistical manual of mental disorders* (4th ed., text rev.). Washington, DC: Author.

Amir, N., Kuckertz, J. M., & Najmi, S. (2013). The effect of modifying automatic action tendencies on overt avoidance behaviors. *Emotion*, 13(3), 478–484.

Beesdo-Baum, K., Jenjan, E., Hofler, M., Lueken, U., Becker, E., & Hoyer, J. (2012). Avoidance, safety behavior, and reassurance seeking in generalized anxiety disorder. *Depression and Anxiety*, 29(11), 948–957. doi:10.1002/da.21955

Chance, P. (2014). *Learning and behavior* (7th ed.). Belmont, CA: Wadsworth.

Neumann, R., Lozo, L., & Kunde, W. (2014). Not all behaviors are controlled in the same way: Different mechanisms underlie manual and facial approach and avoidance responses. *Journal of Experimental Psychology: General, 143*(1), 1–8.

Nifadkar, S., Tsui, A. S., & Ashforth, B. E. (2012). The way you make me feel and behave: Supervisor-triggered newcomer affect and approach-avoidance behavior. *Academy of Management Journal, 55*(5), 1146–1168. Upper Saddle River, NJ: Prentice Hall.

Olson, M. H., & Hergenhahn, B. R. (2011). *An introduction to theories of personality* (8th ed.). Upper Saddle River, NJ: Pearson.

BEHAVIORAL FAMILY THERAPY

The intent of behavioral family therapy is to teach family members how to negotiate mutually acceptable solutions to their problems while simultaneously creating and maintaining positive relationship changes. This model of therapy is primarily concerned with adapting or changing problematic and maladaptive behavior. The roots of this approach are grounded in operant conditioning, which focuses on stimuli that increase behaviors and stimuli that decrease or extinguish behaviors. *Positive reinforcement* works by presenting motivating stimuli after a behavior in order to increase it; *negative reinforcement* works by removing aversive stimuli after a behavior in order to increase it; and *punishment* involves noxious or aversive stimuli after a behavior that results in a decrease of that behavior. Overall, the focus on observable, changeable behaviors and goals, rather than feelings and emotions, makes behavioral family therapy more understandable for clients and easier for them to accept interventions when they can see concrete change. Although originally created to work with individuals, the principles also can be applied to couples and families, and have been shown to be effective with diverse populations and a wide variety of problems and concerns. To promote an understanding of behavioral family therapy, this entry discusses its tenets and assumptions, goals, and techniques. Also discussed are the stages of family therapy, the use of the contingency contract with clients, the issue of resistance to change and intervention, and the modification of behavioral family therapy in working with socially diverse populations.

Tenets and Assumptions of Behavioral Family Therapy

Behavioral family therapy is used to identify and change maladaptive behaviors of an individual within the family unit, multiple members within the family unit, or the family as a whole. The treatment process involves specific areas of behavioral change for each member, and the changes usually involve effective communication and problem-solving skills. It is a time-limited approach that focuses on specific behavioral goals and on increasing positive behaviors. Behavioral change is best when one accelerates the favorable behaviors and decreases the unfavorable ones. Effective therapists tend to focus assessment on the present rather than the past, and do not focus on what is considered "normal development." Rather, they tend to focus on the functioning of the individual, couple, or family.

The therapist proceeds on the assumption that all behaviors (good and bad) are acquired and maintained in similar ways, according to the principles of learning. Because the behavior is learned, the therapist uses behavior-modifying techniques to change unwanted or dysfunctional behaviors to more favorable behaviors. It is assumed that if problematic behavior is learned, then it can be extinguished or unlearned by learning new patterns of behavior. A primary tenet of behavioral family therapy is that the treatment can be operationally defined. In short, this means that if variable A is manipulated, then change will result in B. In other words, for every action there is a reaction. These are regarded as simple operant conditioning measures. Behavioral treatment outcomes are determined by measurable changes in a particular family member or family member's behaviors. Because each family is assessed for its functioning related to goals, behavioral family therapy is not generic; it is tailored to the needs of each individual family.

To determine which observable and measurable behavior needs to be modified, the therapist must conduct an in-depth assessment to identify behaviors that may be maintaining undesirable interactions. This assessment is an ongoing process of treatment and drives the treatment methods in their intensity and duration. The therapist must keep accurate assessment records on the specific behaviors the family has identified as maladaptive or needing to change in order to see whether a given intervention is effective at helping couples or families reach their goals. The therapist will use these records as a tool to make adjustments and balance the treatment by accelerating or decelerating the specific identified behaviors. Overall, this process includes selecting specific behaviors to change, creating a specific plan to change behavior, and an empirical evaluation of whether the intended change is occurring or not.

Because the focus is on the current functioning of the family, behavioral family therapy is practiced in the present. Focusing on the present and on specific goals is partially what makes this a briefer therapy than some other approaches. In some instances, though, understanding the history of a problem can offer useful information about possibly related events in the present. In this way, the therapist can then use observations from the current environment to make changes that keep the problem from recurring.

Even though the therapist focuses on discrete behaviors, the therapist understands the importance of the client and their interaction with other family members, or what is sometimes called circular causality. Clients influence others with their behavior and are also influenced by others' behaviors in a circular or reciprocal manner. The therapist focuses on changes in the individual client and changes in their interactions with others in their family (and vice versa).

Goals

The goal of successful behavioral family therapy is to meet the needs of all family members. Ideally, to be effective, a modification is made to individual behaviors that influence the interconnected relationships of families. In other words, constructive changes to the patterns within the family can be realized through improvements in the individual. Although the therapist focuses on individual behaviors, the goal is an increased quality of family life. Depending on the identified need for behavioral family therapy, these improvements in the individual could include reduced incidents of self-harm, improved social skills, fewer relapses, fewer outbursts, and/or a better ability to recognize the need for help.

While behavioral change is an important aspect of this type of therapy, insight is not necessarily a goal and is considered less important than behavioral changes. Changes in individual family members constitute a change in the family system; one cannot change without the other.

Stages of Behavioral Family Therapy

In order for the therapist to facilitate the enactment of change, a systematic approach must be used to facilitate these changes. The initial family interview can be divided into five stages, or as many others as time will allow. These five initial stages are the social stage, the problem stage, the interaction stage, the goal-setting stage, and the task-setting stage.

Social Stage

The social stage is the rapport-building stage. During this stage the therapist will include as many family members and relevant people in the process as needed who will commit to the treatment. It is at this stage that the assessment begins. The therapist begins gathering information about the environment, the situation, and the individual members making up the family unit. Some of the observations the therapist will record are the overall mood of the family and how not only the family as a whole, but also how individual family members deal with stress. This includes how the parents interact with the children in the family, how the children interact with the parents, how the children interact among themselves, and how the parents and/or children interact with any additional party who is considered to be a part of the family. The therapist will compile information on the physical layout of the family environment. They will also assess the dynamics of the family, such as who is aligned with whom. There is no need for all of this assessment information to be shared with the family.

Problem Stage

During the problem stage the therapist/counselor will draw out the pertinent problems and issues the family and/or individuals in the family are experiencing by questioning and interviewing each member and the family as a whole. In this stage, the therapist will make use of active listening skills and good record-keeping. The problem is then assessed and clarified. The therapist will determine what the problem is, who is involved, and what the family thinks the therapist's role is going to be in resolving the problem. During this interview the focus will be on the present, and only on what pertains to the issues in question. The therapist will take careful note of who participates the most and the least. This could translate into who is the most invested in change and who is the least invested.

Interaction Stage

In the interaction stage, the entire family should be induced to participate by having each member comment on the problem. Interaction and communication within the family should occur. Some family members may not offer suggestions freely and thus might require more forceful prodding to participate in the dialogue.

Goal-Setting Stage

In the goal-setting stage, the contingency contract is drawn up. It needs to be absolutely clear, concise, and specific on what behavioral changes are needed to take place. All of the agreed-upon changes need to be quantifiable in terms of the specific goals as defined by resolution of the problem or dysfunction.

Task-Setting Stage

In the task-setting stage, the therapist will relegate family tasks for small, systematic changes in behavior and in the context of the social interactions and structure of the family. In subsequent sessions the counselor will perform maintenance on the goals and tasks needed for change and reinforce the positive aspects that have occurred. The counselor will also make adjustments for any noncompliance by family members and remind them of their contractual commitment to change. Any additional problems or information will be applied in the appropriate manner, whether it is beginning a new task-oriented goal, or adding to an existing behavior modification.

Techniques Used in Behavioral Family Therapy

Of the techniques used in behavioral family therapy, many are the same as, or similar to, those used in other behavior therapies. Behavioral family therapists may have discussions about coping mechanisms, encourage activities to promote focus, provide social skills training, and use positive reinforcement. Therapists in behavioral family therapy also employ role-playing, assertion training, aversion therapy, token economy, and flooding. Other successful techniques can include instruction, modeling, role rehearsal, social reinforcement, and homework tasks.

Token Economy

Use of the token economy is in effect when favorable behavior is rewarded with a representation of worth (i.e., a coin or ticket) that can be "cashed in" for an agreed-upon treat or action. For instance, a child who kept his room clean for five days received five tokens, which he traded for an extra hour of video gaming on the weekend. Other types of rewards can include (but are not limited to) food, TV time, and toys.

Modeling

Modeling is a behavioral method used to teach complex behaviors in a short amount of time. This is accomplished by having one party imitate another or learn from watching someone else. This technique is based on social learning theory, which posits that people learn through observing others' behavior and the outcomes of those behaviors.

Role-Playing and Role Reversal

Role-playing and role reversal are instances where clients act "as if." In role-playing the client or clients act as if they are ideally the person they want to be. They will act out a number of behaviors to see which work the best. In role reversal the client takes on the role opposite of what they consider normal. Through this experience, the client can experience new thoughts, feelings, and behaviors to expand their ability to empathize more with individuals who are different from themselves.

Social Reinforcement

Social reinforcement is the attention given by an individual of influence (spouse, mother, father, etc.) either verbally or nonverbally that reinforces a behavior and makes it more likely to occur. Positive social reinforcement (things that are likely to increase a behavior) includes smiles, praise, and attention. Children and adults are more likely to increase behaviors that are socially reinforced.

Assertion Training

Assertion training is designed to help people express their needs and wants in an appropriate manner. It assists the client in empowering himself or herself. Assertiveness is a reaction that seeks to maintain an appropriate balance between passivity and aggression. Assertive responses promote fairness and equality in communication, based on a positive sense of respect for self and others. Assertion training is used in behavioral family therapy to help to take control of situations within one's life and allow one to communicate their needs with ease.

Aversion Therapy

Aversion therapy is designed to help the client learn to overcome an undesirable behavior. In aversion therapy, the client is made to think of the undesirable activity they enjoy while being exposed (with their consent) to something unpleasant such as a bad taste, a foul smell, or even mild electric shocks. This is used to suppress or eliminate undesirable behavior and is usually employed as a last resort, and only with informed consent.

Flooding

Flooding is used to treat individuals with fears or phobias. Flooding involves prolonged exposure to the thing that frightens the client. The concept behind it is that by exposing the client to their fear, they will eventually see it as less fear-producing. For example, a counselor may take a person who is afraid of dogs into a kennel and expose them to a large number of dogs in a controlled situation.

Behavioral Family Contracting

Behavioral family therapy uses forms of contracting as part of the therapeutic process. This especially includes contingency contracting. Therapeutic contracting involves written agreements that stipulate the specific behavioral changes. The behavior-changing criteria should mandate caveats for development, such as: They must be positive in nature, they must be specific, they must be instances of behavior that are demonstrated daily, and they must not have been the subject of intense conflict in the recent past. This is a management strategy whereby the family or individuals within the family system enter into an agreement with themselves, their family, and the therapist to perform in a specified manner to attain prespecified goals. Contingency contracting is based on operant conditioning principles. They will invariably involve some give and take during the negotiation of the contract. The contingency contract formalizes the expectations of the family and the responsibilities of its members.

The contract will usually have specified consequences related to the goals set in the contract. This may be used as a behavior-changing strategy or as an evaluation tool. Contingency contracting consequences can be seen as a source of motivation to change, such as depositing a sum of money in an account or having an object of value attached as a consequence of the contract. The flexibility of the contract is based on the creativity of the family and the therapist.

The terms of the contract should be clear to all parties involved. The behavior aims and performance levels should be explicit. Rewards and prohibitions should also be specific, and appropriate to the contract. Commitments from all involved people should be affixed with signatures.

The effectiveness of the contract is ultimately dependent on the participants. Some families like having a formalized contract on paper, while others find it hard to follow such a rigid procedure. The therapist must adjust the contract to fit the needs of the family. The contract represents a tangible symbol for targeting positive behavioral change. It is also an opportunity for demonstrating success, accomplishment, and reward.

Resistance to Change

Sometimes, individuals outright refuse to comply with interventions, fail to follow through with interventions even after they have agreed to them, or do not fully comply with interventions. When clients do not comply with interventions, this, in some models, is called *resistance*. Although resistance can stall or interfere with change, it is a natural part of all systems and a typical consequence of request to change a family pattern. This concept of resistance to change can be used by the therapist in the family session. Resistance may occur because a family is afraid of change, the goals are incongruent with the family's wishes, or the interventions do not fit with the family (e.g., they are creative types and the therapist assigns very structured tasks).

Resistance can be addressed in various ways, but sometimes it merely needs to be discussed in order to be dissipated. The very act of acknowledging resistance to change can assist in bringing about the very change the family is resisting. This applies to "properly" or "normally" functioning families, as well as to dysfunctional families. At times families are rigid, and these nonconforming aspects may need to be identified and changed in order to make progress. A family member's resistance to change can be kept in check and the underlying issue resolved through a modification in the member's behavior.

Diversity

Behavioral family therapy can be modified to allow for cultural and gender differences. In most cases the modifications made to allow for diversity will not affect processes used in behavior family therapy. Cultural values must be taken into consideration when working with diverse populations. Male and female roles, religion, sexual orientation, age, and race are all important considerations for a behavioral family therapist.

*Kristin Page, Vance Walker,
and Richard Williams*

See also Child Behavior Problems; Cognitive-Behavioral Family Therapy; Core Competencies for Marriage and Family Therapists; Families and Substance Abuse

Further Readings

Ball, J., & Mitchell, P. (2004). A randomized controlled study of cognitive behavior therapy and behavioral family therapy for anorexia nervosa patients. *Eating Disorders, 12*(4), 303–314.

Glynn, S. M., Eth, S., Randolph, E. T., Foy, D. W., Urbaitis, M., Boxer, L., . . . & Crothers, J. (1999). A test of behavioral family therapy to augment exposure for combat-related posttraumatic stress disorder. *Journal of Consulting and Clinical Psychology, 67*(2), 243.

Gurman, A. S., & Kniskern, D. P. (Eds.). (2014). *Handbook of family therapy.* New York, NY: Routledge.

Ho, M. K., Rasheed, J. M., & Rasheed, M. N. (2003). *Family therapy with ethnic minorities.* Thousand Oaks, CA: Sage.

Krisp, B., & Knox, D. (2009). *Behavioral family therapy: An evidence based approach.* Durham, NC: Carolina Academic Press.

Lipps, A. J. (1999). Family therapy in the treatment of alcohol related problems: A review of behavioral family therapy, family systems therapy and treatment matching research. *Alcoholism Treatment Quarterly, 17*(3), 13–23.

Mueser, K. T., & Glynn, S. M. (1999). *Behavioral family therapy for psychiatric disorders.* Oakland, CA: New Harbinger Publications.

Nichols, M. P., Schwartz, R. C., & Minuchin, S. (2004). *Family therapy: Concepts and methods.* Needham Heights, MA: Allyn & Bacon.

Robin, A. L., & Foster, S. L. (2002). *Negotiating parent-adolescent conflict: A behavioral-family systems approach.* New York, NY: Guilford.

BELIEFS AND VALUES

Beliefs and values are essential constructs in understanding human social interactions. Beliefs refer to the judgments people make about themselves, others, and the world around them. Values are a person's principles or standards of behavior. Values create the foundation for judging what is important in one's life, and serve as the foundation for human action and motivation. People's thoughts and actions are constantly being impacted by their beliefs and values. Individuals, groups, social institutions, and societies can be understood in terms of their values and beliefs. These concepts impact people at all levels: interpersonal relationships and economic, social, political, and legal institutions. Human beings hold their beliefs to be true and their values to be important.

This entry focuses on the impact of beliefs and values in human social interactions, exploring these constructs in terms of their definitions and placing special importance on beliefs and values in marriage, family, and coupling relationships.

The Nature of Beliefs and Values

The concepts of beliefs and values are often paired together because of their close connection and interdependence. Writers have, however, pointed out the need to distinguish the two constructs. Beliefs are the judgments that individuals make about themselves and the world around them, and they are critical in connecting values to experiences. Beliefs can be categorized into three groups: (1) those that can be and have been validated; (2) those that can be validated, but have not been validated; and (3) those that cannot be validated. Beliefs that cannot or have not been validated tend to elicit affective and sometimes irrational responses. Hence, individuals may feel very strongly about their beliefs irrespective of their basis.

Values are the basis for human behavior and motivation; values are abstract, hierarchical, and dynamic in nature. The abstract nature of values means that they are usually a generalization and do not offer a specific way of being or doing. People may have several different values, some of which we may feel more or less strongly about. Values can also change, may be relative to other values, and depend on contexts.

Shalom H. Schwartz, in presenting his *Theory of Basic Human Values,* first identified values as a type of belief that expresses a desirable goal. He also saw values as dynamic, relative, ordered, and transcendent. The interdependent nature of beliefs and values is apparent inasmuch as statements of value often reflect beliefs and statements of beliefs reflect values.

Complexity of Beliefs and Values

The process of learning the beliefs and values associated with one culture can be complex as well as dynamic. Beliefs and value systems can change; there may also be competing systems in any given society. A child may grow up to reject some of the beliefs and values with which he or she was raised. In a complex, multicultural society there are often competing value systems that make outcomes difficult to predict. Time, context, and life experiences may result in changes in a person's beliefs and values.

The Importance of Beliefs and Values

Human history has been significantly influenced by beliefs and values. These constructs are critical to understanding simple as well as complex societies that have existed over time. What human beings have created, eaten, celebrated, worshiped, loved, and hated are indicative of their beliefs and values. Significant changes such as the French Revolution, Industrial Revolution, and British slave emancipation can be traced to changes in beliefs and values. Beliefs and values related to family and marriage in the United States, for example, continue to evolve. This evolution has often resulted in conflicts that are played out within families, communities, and the legal system. The focus on beliefs and values is therefore important in understanding of ourselves, others, and the world around us.

A study of beliefs and values can help people to better understand the past, present, and future directions of human societies. Philosophers and social scientists have long explored the impact of beliefs and values on human society. Thomas Kuhn, the American physicist and philosopher, argued in his book *The Structure of Scientific Revolutions* that beliefs and values also have significant impact on studies of the natural world. Here, Kuhn highlighted that "objective" scientific disciplines such as biology, physics, and chemistry are also impacted by beliefs and values.

Scholars study beliefs and values because these constructs are useful in understanding many aspects of social reality. References to family values, economic values, cultural values, marriage values, political values, American values, or Western values demonstrate the widespread use of these constructs to understand or describe different aspects of human society.

Understanding Behaviors Across Different Societies

Knowledge of beliefs and values can assist in our understanding of human behavior across different groups and societies. Cultural differences often correspond with differences in beliefs and values between and among different groups. While it is possible for two different groups to have shared values, it is almost impossible for all their values to be alike. A study of the beliefs and values that exist within and among groups allows social scientists to compare differences or similarities among groups. These comparisons can be made on the basis of observed behavior and practices, as well as knowledge of the groups' beliefs and values.

Motivations for human social behavior are often not obvious. For example, if a European or North American were to visit India without any prior knowledge of its culture, the visitor may be surprised or disappointed to find an absence of beef from the menu of family dinners or restaurants. The curious traveler may seek to understand why this is so. On inquiring she may learn that, for the Hindu majority, religious beliefs and values related to the sacredness of the cow require that it not be eaten. Here, it is knowledge of Indian religious beliefs and values related to the cow that provides an explanation for something a traveler may have found puzzling. Beliefs and values are therefore important in our understanding of shared practices and behaviors among groups of individuals or across societies.

Understanding Individual Behavior

By looking closely at beliefs and values, scholars can better understand an individual's behaviors and motivations. Others are often able to observe a person's actions but cannot directly observe the motivations for those actions. Being able to access a person's beliefs and values may provide important insight into the motivations for their actions. These beliefs and values are typically internalized, or learned, from the individual's culture as part of the socialization process. Thus, the individual may have learnt these values in the context of family, school, or community. We may also consider personal beliefs and values that are more specific to the individual and may have been influenced by their personal experiences. Social scientists study the personal or shared beliefs and values of an individual because it provides a better understanding of them. A family counselor may simply ask each partner to talk about their beliefs and values related to child-rearing to gain insight on the challenges they have been experiencing in this area.

Examining Personal Beliefs and Values

The study of beliefs and values may also include looking into and examining oneself. If people are able to do so effectively they may gain insight into their own behaviors and motivations. People may discover that their beliefs and values are not universally shared. By studying beliefs and values, counselors may be able to understand that values are relative, dynamic, and sometimes irrational. Counselors, educators, and other professionals who live and work in socially diverse settings are particularly interested in studying beliefs and values. Counselors often seek to gain multicultural competence—that is, the ability to provide effective help to all individuals irrespective of race, ethnicity, socioeconomic status, gender, sexual orientation, first language, religion, or ability. Effective counselors recognize that the individuals they seek to help may have beliefs and values that are influenced by their group identities, and that these beliefs and values may differ from the counselor's own. A serious interest in understanding our personal beliefs and values can support our understanding of others; this is especially important in societies that are culturally diverse.

Culture, Beliefs, and Values

Culture can be defined simply as the way of life of a group of people. This way of life may include their language, cuisine, dress, folklore, rituals, traditions, beliefs, and values. Human beings are first exposed to culture (including beliefs and values) during childhood in context of family. Other agencies of socialization such as the school, community, and communications media will later influence the process of teaching the child the culture of his or her group or society. Contained in every culture are a number of beliefs and values that are shared. Some societies, such as that of the United States, may be multicultural, with many different subcultures coexisting within their geographical borders.

When a person shares their beliefs about dating, marriage, or parenting, their response is often influenced by their cultural background as well as their personal experiences. Individuals may accept, reject, or find ways of integrating the beliefs and values with which they were raised with the present realities. Individuals and groups who migrate to other societies may adapt their original beliefs and values in order to better assimilate into the new society.

Charles C. Edwards

See also Family Values; Individual Family Culture; Trust

Further Readings

Boudon, R. (Ed.). (2001). *The origin of values: Essays in the sociology and philosophy of beliefs*. Piscataway, NJ: Transaction Publishers.

Joas, H. (2000). *The genesis of values*. Chicago, IL: University of Chicago Press.

Levy, Y. (2006). *Assessing the value of e-learning systems*. Hershey, PA: IGI Global.

Schwartz, S. H. (2012). An overview of the Schwartz Theory of Basic Values. *Online Readings in Psychology and Culture, 2*(1). Retrieved from http://dx.doi.org/10.9707/2307-0919.1116

BEREAVEMENT

Bereavement is defined as a period of grief and mourning following the death of a loved one. It is considered part of a normal reaction to loss through death. During bereavement all areas of functioning can be affected, and responses include mental, physical, social, and emotional reactions. The length and intensity of the reactions are influenced by a number of factors. These include the type and degree of attachment to the deceased, nature of the relationship to the deceased, whether the death was sudden or expected, the type of loss (e.g., natural causes, suicide, accidental), when the death occurred in the life span, how the bereaved dealt with previous loss, the internal resources of the bereaved, and the support network of the bereaved. There is some similarity among the ways individuals experience bereavement, yet individual differences can vary greatly and the impact on family functioning also can vary greatly. This entry describes the wide range of reactions an individual may experience during bereavement, provides an outline of examples of several theories of grief and loss, and concludes with a brief review of the impact of bereavement on the family.

Bereavement Reactions

Grief responses occur in the mental, physical, social, and emotional realms. Grief responses of those experiencing bereavement occur on a continuum from comforting to troubling. Mental reactions can include confusion, forgetfulness, and lack of focus and mental clarity. "Brain fog" is a term typically used to describe this set of symptoms. Depending on the circumstances of the loss, individuals may also experience intrusive thoughts. The intrusive thoughts can range from fond memories of the deceased to vivid, troubling memories. Dreams that are comforting or nightmares can also occur. Physical reactions during the time of bereavement also vary and may encompass back, neck, and general muscle pain; headaches; dry mouth; stomach pain, diarrhea, and constipation; inability to eat or overeating; weight loss or weight gain; restlessness; chills; chest pains and difficulty breathing; and crying. Social reactions during bereavement range from an overwhelming need to be with others to craving solitude. Depending on how the person who is grieving was socialized to deal with his or her grief, he or she may turn inward, isolating in order to effectively escape the pressures from others to get better or to deal with the loss in a certain way. As with the mental, physical, and social reactions, emotional reactions during bereavement are vast. Some emotional reactions include anxiety, agitation, frustration, shock, numbness, guilt, and regret. However, not all emotional reactions are troubling. Many individuals report feeling degrees of joy, happiness, pride, and hopefulness. Emotional states during bereavement vary, change quickly, and may include both positive and negative emotions simultaneously.

Theories of Grief and Mourning

Numerous theories of grief and loss have been outlined. Freud associated mourning with melancholia and noted that during bereavement the ego must accept the reality of the loss, and that grief is a long and arduous process. Others have developed stage theories, in which individuals pass through predetermined periods marked by specific grief reactions and tasks to accomplish. For example, during the 1940s Erich Lindemann identified acute grief as a syndrome and noted that there were six characteristics: somatic distress, preoccupation, guilt, hostility, loss of functioning, and assuming the traits of the lost one. These reactions could occur immediately after the loss, or they could be delayed. Additionally, there are three tasks of grief that must be accomplished for successful resolution to occur. They include emancipation or relinquishment from the attachment to the deceased, readjustment to the environment without the deceased, and finally the formation of a new environment. The new environment is where the individual returns to fully functioning.

In the late 1960s, Elisabeth Kübler-Ross presented her widely popularized stage theory. Here, Kübler-Ross proposed that individuals pass through five distinct emotional stages in a linear progression. The stages include denial, anger, bargaining, depression, and acceptance. During the first stage of denial, individuals refuse to acknowledge or recognize that the death occurred. Instead, the mourner prefers to live in a reality where the death did not occur. The second stage, anger, is marked by recognition of the loss and thoughts of life as being unfair and questions such as Why me?

In the third, or bargaining, stage, where the death has not yet occurred, people might try to negotiate for more time or for the death not to occur at all. In cases where the death has already happened, mourners might ask God to bring the deceased back in exchange for changes in the way they live their life. Stage four, depression, is noted for extreme sadness. During depression mourners may isolate themselves, shutting themselves off from the outside world. The fifth and final stage of acceptance is the time when the individual embraces the loss and takes on a sense that everything is going to be okay. At this point, the individual can look toward a future. This theory was originally developed through work with dying patients and later applied to reactions toward the death of others as well as other types of loss, including divorce. Despite Kübler-Ross's acknowledging that not everyone who experiences grief moves through these stages, others have applied the theory in this manner.

Another theory that focuses on task completion is that of William Worden. Worden proposed four tasks of mourning. First, the individual must accept the reality of the loss. Next, he or she must work through the pain of grief. The next task is to adjust to an environment where the deceased is missing. Adjustment occurs on three levels: external adjustments, internal adjustments, and spiritual adjustments. Finally, during bereavement mourners must emotionally relocate for adjustment to be successful. In other words, the emotional energy and focus that was given to the deceased must be directed elsewhere.

A final example of a stage and phase theory is that of Therese Rando. This theory is referred to as the Six "R" Process Model, and encompasses three phases and six processes. The three phases are avoidance, confrontation, and accommodation. During the avoidance phase, individuals refuse to *recognize* there is a loss. In the confrontation phase, mourners *react* to the separation by *recollecting* and *reexperiencing* the deceased and the relationship. Finally, the accommodation phase is marked by the *relinquishment* of the old attachment to the deceased, *readjustment* to daily life, and the *reinvestment* or adoption of new ways of being in the world.

Contemporary models of grief and loss have challenged some of the assumptions found in the stage and phase models. Among the assumptions being challenged is that there is a "right" way to grieve, and that stages are discrete and are not revisited. It is also implied in stage models that bereavement is time limited. Examples of contemporary models of grief and loss experienced during bereavement that challenge these assumptions include a model spearheaded by Dennis Klass, Phyllis Silverman, and Steven Nickman, called *continuing bonds,* and another theory championed by Robert Niemeyer, called *meaning reconstruction.*

The continuing bonds and meaning reconstruction theories of grief both adhere to a postmodern view of what individuals can experience during the time of bereavement. Applied to grief work, postmodernism adheres to the notion that grieving is subjective, and that it can take on any number of forms depending on the individual who is grieving. The central premise in continuing bonds theory is that the relationship to the deceased does not have to be severed, and that maintaining a connection to the deceased can be healthy. How the one who is grieving maintains that bond is highly individualized. Likewise, meaning reconstruction purports that each person's response to the loss of a loved one is unique. Here, the central focus is on what meaning he or she gives to the deceased, their relationship, the death, events after the death, and so on. Both continuing bonds and meaning reconstruction attempt to depathologize grief reactions. The theory of continuing bonds depathologizes because a continued attachment to the deceased is no longer considered unresolved grief, and meaning reconstruction sees "pathological responses" as unsuccessful attempts at meaning-making and attachment preservation.

Models of Coping

Family members can each react very differently to the loss of another member. Two models of coping that may help family members understand one another during bereavement are the *dual-process model* and *adaptive grieving styles*. The dual-process model purports that individuals oscillate between two foci. Individuals can be loss-oriented or restoration-oriented. Loss-oriented individuals focus on the deceased and death. During this time they dwell on the loss by focusing on the funeral, and reading letters from and looking at pictures of the deceased. Restoration-oriented individuals focus on secondary stressors such as paying the bills, mowing the lawn, shopping for groceries, and cleaning the house. In this model, grief work is occurring whether or not the individual is loss-oriented or restoration-oriented.

The adaptive grieving styles model includes three different styles of coping with the loss: the intuitive grieving style, the instrumental grieving style, and the blended grieving style. The intuitive grieving style is affective in nature in that the griever reacts on an emotional level and expresses what he or she is feeling. Adaptation to the loss involves exploration and expression of feelings. The instrumental grieving style is marked by the individual experiencing cognitive or physical reactions with expression of cognitions and behaviors. Adaptation to the loss for instrumental grievers involves thinking and doing. The blended grieving style is a combination of the intuitive and instrumental styles. Most people align with a blended style of grieving.

Impact on the Family During Bereavement

As with the individual, the death of a loved one can have a profound impact on family functioning. The family, membership in which is defined by its members, is a system of interlocking relationships that act and react to one another. When a family member dies, the system must realign itself to accommodate to the impact of the loss. The type of accommodation needed is mediated by the role and function the deceased played in the family, the family's structure, emotional expression, spirituality and religious beliefs, internal and external resources, and the stage of life the family is in at the time the death occurred. Also, family rules, both overt and covert, dictate how the family functions. If the family rules are rigid about how its members communicate, family members will have a limited degree of flexibility in how its members respond to one another. Research has found that families who have the ability to express emotion, have open communication, and who feel close to one another show fewer symptoms of grief over time.

Laura K. Harrawood

See also Attachment; Bereavement Counseling; Grief Counseling; Life Transitions; Loss

Further Readings

Humphrey, K. M. (2009). *Counseling strategies for loss and grief*. Alexandria, VA: American Counseling Association.

Klass, D., Silverman, P. R., & Nickman, S. L. (Eds.). (1996). *Continuing bonds*. Philadelphia, PA: Taylor & Francis.

Kübler-Ross, E. (1969). *On death and dying* (1st ed.). New York, NY: Simon and Schuster.

Lindemann, E. (1979). *Beyond grief: Studies in crisis interventions*. New York, NY: Aronson.

Martin, T. L., & Doka, K. J. (2000). *Men don't cry . . . women do: Transcending gender stereotypes of grief*. Philadelphia, PA: Brunner/Mazel.

Neimeyer, R. A. (Ed.). (2003). *Meaning reconstruction & the experience of loss*. Washington, DC: American Psychological Association.

Rando, T. A. (1993). *Treatment of complicated mourning*. Champaign, IL: Research Press.

Schoka Traylor, E., Hayslip, B., Kaminski, P. L., & York, C. (2003). Relationships between griefs and family system characteristics: A cross lagged longitudinal analysis. *Death Studies, 27*, 575–601. doi:10.1080/07481180390220780

Stroebe, M. S. (2002). Paving the way: From early attachment theory to contemporary bereavement research. *Mortality, 7*(2), 127–138. doi:10.1080/13576270220136267

Stroebe, M., & Schute, H. (1999). The dual process model of coping with bereavement: Rationale and descriptive. *Death Studies, 23*, 197–224. doi:10.2190/OM.61

Worden, J. W. (2008). *Grief counseling and grief therapy: A handbook for the mental health practitioner* (4th ed.). New York, NY: Springer.

BEREAVEMENT COUNSELING

Bereavement (grief) counseling entails a specialized skill set that requires the practitioner to be fully present in accompanying the client or clients on their unique grief journey. Theories of the progress of normal, uncomplicated grief are abundant, and no one theory can fully describe the grief experience for all individuals. Bereavement counseling must attend to both the cognitive and psychological processes of the bereaved. Although individuals can experience grief for a myriad of different reasons including loss of a relationship, divorce, loss of a career, and so on, this entry will focus on counseling those who are experiencing loss due to the death of a significant person or persons. The construct of grieving is reviewed from a multicultural perspective, from the standpoint of significant theories, and in terms of the process and goals of bereavement counseling.

Multicultural Aspects of Bereavement Counseling

In any discussion of bereavement counseling, the term *culture* needs to be considered in its broadest sense to include race, religion, ethnicity, sexual orientation, disability, and socioeconomic status. Additionally, it is important to reflect on the idea that regardless of cultural belief, grief has its own physiological and psychological response that is similar across all cultures. The difference lies in the expression of bereavement and the cultural rituals attached to expressions of grief. Therese Rando, a leading and recognized expert in the field of grief and bereavement counseling, proposes that all cultures fall into one of three groups: *death accepting, death defying,* or *death denying*. It has been suggested that Western culture is death defying in that its members tend to view death as an issue to be avoided. Contrasted to this might be the view of those who follow the Islamic faith. Muslims often welcome death as a way to paradise and a means of sacrifice to God's glorious cause. Mexican families tend to honor deceased family members and maintain a strong bond to the deceased through storytelling, dreams, and festivals. Asian families also often maintain strong bonds to the deceased, and those of the Buddhist faith continue to respect the deceased with an offering of food and incense to guide the deceased in their journey to the next level of existence. Asian people, however, are often more reticent in their grief expression than those of some other cultures. Regardless of culture, bereavement occurs for all people in the context of a series of rituals and patterns to which the counselor must be sensitive.

Conceptual Approaches to Bereavement

Although each individual grieves in his or her own way and own time, theorists have posited both stage models of grief and process-oriented suggestions for counselors to be aware of when engaging in bereavement counseling. John Bowlby, as an adjunct to his theory of attachment, suggested that grief occurs in four phases: numbing, yearning and searching, disorganization and despair, and reorganization. Of all of the theories of grief, perhaps the most famous is that of Elisabeth Kübler-Ross, who in 1965 began working with terminally ill patients in an effort to study the stages of their grief process. She narrowed her observations to five distinct stages: denial, anger, bargaining, depression, and acceptance. Many bereavement counselors look to Kübler-Ross and her stage model of grief as a way to explain client behaviors in regards to loss.

However, not all individuals fit neatly into these categories or steps as they journey through their grief. In response to the stage model of grief, Therese Rando suggested a series of phases through which the bereaved journey. The first of these is avoidance, which includes a numbing, and feelings of shock and disbelief for the bereaved. Second, there is a phase of confrontation, during which grief feelings are intensely felt and the mourner begins to feel panic and anxiety over the uncertainties of life without the deceased. Third, the bereaved client eventually enters into the reestablishment phase, during which there is a gradual decline in the intensity of the emotions being felt.

William Worden built on Rando's phases of grief and developed a model of the four tasks of grief. Worden explored the activities through which a grieving individual might engage as they look for meaning in the loss of a loved one. The first task of grief is to accept the reality of the loss. During this task, the bereaved person must come to accept that reunification with the deceased is impossible and move to intellectual and emotional acceptance. Second, the bereaved must work through the pain of the grief. Having fully experienced the pain of the loss, the client then needs to adjust to an environment in which the deceased is no longer present. Third is the task of adjusting to an environment in which the deceased is not present. Last is the task to emotionally relocate the deceased so that the bereaved person can move on with life.

In contrast to stage, phase, and task models of grief, Peggy Whiting has suggested a developmental approach to grief counseling that entails providing a safe space in which to accompany the client through the grief process but does not delineate specific steps through which the client must journey. Each of the aforementioned conceptualizations of grieving has merit and can inform the bereavement counseling process. Three that lend themselves well to the bereavement counseling process are Rando's phases of grief, Worden's tasks of grief, and Whiting's developmental response to personal loss.

Bereavement Counseling Using Rando's Phases of Grief

Rando suggested grievers need nonjudgmental acceptance, active listening, and facilitation of a review of the relationship with the lost loved one. Counselors need to allow the grieving client to integrate loss with life in the present. To do this, Rando contends that the bereavement counselor must reach out to the bereaved, make contact, and assess the state of emotional disturbance being experienced by the bereaved. The main task in the avoidance phase is to be present with the griever, both physically and emotionally. Physical contact during the initial shock and disbelief of the loss establishes that the person grieving is not alone and reorients the individual to the present. Giving the mourner permission to grieve is paramount during the counseling process because the griever often can accept the loss intellectually but cannot accept it on a more visceral level. Many times society discourages outward showing of extreme emotion, and this can suppress the grief process. Verbally and through nonjudgmental behavior, the bereavement counselor needs to show acceptance of all emotionality involved in the grieving process.

During the confrontation phase, it is important to assess the feelings that the client has about himself or herself. This is a time for angry sadness on behalf of the bereaved, and extreme emotions will be expressed. The therapist may suggest that the client write or keep a journal about his or her feelings and thoughts. Clients are encouraged to bring pictures or mementoes of the deceased to therapy, and to tell stories of the deceased. During this time bereaved clients may tell and retell the story of the final days of the deceased's life. The counselor should be making continued assessment throughout this phase of grief, evaluating for the presence of such things as illogical or magical thinking, or increased feelings of guilt and responsibility. The bereavement counselor who is working with children may see them acting out in aggressive ways during this phase. They have trouble expressing their feelings of aloneness, and child-centered play therapy is often a helpful way to get them to express their pain. Adults may begin to overidentify with the deceased, taking up their hobbies or trying to "follow in their footsteps." The task of the counselor is to keep the client focused in the present and to explore the reasons behind their behaviors. Auditory or visual hallucinations are not abnormal in the course of grieving, and the bereavement counselor should accept these without pathologizing them. The counselor should assess how these hallucinations are affecting daily functioning.

As the bereaved client moves from the confrontation phase to the reestablishment phase, there will be a gradual decline in the intensity of emotional expression. During this time the counselor can help the bereaved client identify current and potential secondary losses and resolve those in a healthy manner through active listening and caring confrontation. Helping the client to understand that they will always have reminders of their significant loss while also pointing out the client's resilient factors assists in the resolution of grief. The counselor assesses with the griever which roles and skills must be assumed and works with him or her to accomplish this. This may involve education and direct intervention with the griever. As the griever finds new energy to reinvest in life, the counselor should encourage finding rewarding new things to do and people to invest in. The counselor should beware of pushing the bereaved into new relationships before he or she is ready. Rather, the counselor offers affirmation, encouraging the gains that the griever makes in reestablishing a life without the presence of the loved one.

Bereavement Counseling Using Worden's Tasks of Grief

Worden suggested that grief counseling not begin during the first few weeks following the loss. Rather, it is important that the counselor allow the client time to come to terms with the need for counseling and to offer to simply be a presence during the first few weeks. The first task of grief is to accept the reality of the loss. During this task the counselor helps the client to come to an emotional and intellectual acceptance of the loss by encouraging the use of cultural rituals and by actively listening to the client during sessions. People who get stuck during this task will need consistent encouragement and unconditional positive regard. Counselors may see clients attempt to contact the dead person or enshrine objects that remind them of the deceased.

During the second task, working through the pain of grief, the counselor must allow the client to talk about the loss. The client should be encouraged to express their feelings about the person lost, both positive and negative, as well as the circumstances surrounding the loss. The counselor normalizes these feeling and thoughts, even helping the client to realize that the physical pain that often accompanies loss is normal. Rather than allowing a client to suppress the grief, bereavement counselors should assist in the expression of grief during this task. The use of expressive therapies (music, art, play) is often helpful in assisting clients to express deep-seated feelings.

The final tasks include adjusting to an environment in which the deceased is no longer present and moving on with life. Adjusting to life without the deceased involves the counselor empowering the client to gradually take control of both internal and external components of his or her life. During this task, the counselor educates the client in ways that the loss has strengthened him or her as a person and presents interventions that are aimed at increasing self-esteem. The final task is to emotionally relocate the deceased and to move on with life. As with Rando's final phase, the counselor and client work together to find new interests for the client while forming new attachments. As Freud suggested, during this time the counselor helps the client "detach survivors' memories and hopes from the dead."

Bereavement Counseling Using Whiting's Developmental Approach

Peggy Whiting focuses on "companioning" the bereaved on their journey of grief. She suggested that the counselor is not present to "fix" things; rather, it is the counselor's job to walk with the bereaved members and allow them to feel the pain. The counselor is tasked with soothing the fears of the survivors and to help the bereaved make some sense of the loss. This is done through listening and maintaining a nonjudgmental attitude. The counselor assists in separating truth from fantasy in regard to the circumstances of the death. While the client is searching for information or the answer to "why," the counselor must be accepting of that need to know the answers.

The counseling space becomes a safe environment for the client to express both positive and negative feelings. It is an environment where the grieving client can explore ways of making adjustments with the assistance of the counselor. The counselor can point out the strengths and resilient factors that work in the client's favor. Whiting points out that the counselor must be fully aware of his or her own losses so that the counselor does not take on the client's loss as his or her own. The counselor must be aware of the accurate facts surrounding the client's loss in order to diffuse rumors and speculation. As always, counselors should beware of blame and use questions judiciously. The empty chair technique, as well as other Gestalt exercises, can be helpful in allowing the client to express thoughts and feelings toward the deceased. According to Whiting, the most important factor is the therapeutic relationship during bereavement counseling.

Family Systems and Bereavement Counseling

It is not enough to examine bereavement counseling from the standpoint of the individual alone. Most people are part of a family system that has informed their way of interacting in the world. Many significant losses occur within the context of the family unit. The death of a family member disrupts the stability, or homeostasis, in the family and may cause the family members to behave in ways that signify a need for intervention.

A number of influences will impact how a family functions after a loss. These include stages of the family life cycle, the role of the deceased in the family, power, affection, communication, and sociocultural factors influencing the family. Family dynamics can sometimes be detrimental to grieving and must be dealt with accordingly.

An examination of family grief includes looking at family myths. Myths within a family serve in the same way that defense mechanisms protect individuals. Change occurs in the family upon the death of an individual. This is often symbolic of the death of the family as it was known, and a rebuilding phase must occur for the family to continue in a healthy manner. The trained bereavement counselor works with the family to help them express this loss in ways that are supportive of other family members. If the family does not tolerate openly expressed feelings of sadness, acting-out behaviors can ensue. These will need to be recognized by the counselor, and he or she will need to help the family accept the vulnerability that comes with outward expressions of grief.

When assessing for grief in family systems, it is first important to understand the functional role of the deceased in the family unit. If the deceased is a child, siblings and parents will act in entirely different manners. The death of a parent in the life of a young child can often bring on feelings of insecurity among the children in the family and cause further acting out and disruption of the family system. It is important that the counselor be fully aware of the importance of the deceased to the overall functioning of the family system and to help the individual members express their grief. Moreover, it will be the task of the therapist to help the family create a new balance, or rebuild a system of homeostasis, that is secure and healthy. This is done through combining family therapy with grief therapy and helping family members to express themselves in emotionally healthy ways.

Second, it is important to assess the emotional integration of the family. Less well-integrated families have difficulty expressing grief at the time of death, and the grief reaction can appear later as social misbehavior or emotional and physical symptoms. Simply helping individual family members express grief will not help the overall emotional integration of the family; rather, the counselor will need to spend time with the family using interventions that increase the overall emotional functioning of the family unit. Exercises as simple as teaching the family the use of feeling words and using feelings to express themselves is often helpful. Sometimes, a retrospective examination of the family using a family genealogy can be helpful in tracing the antecedents of a lack of emotional integration.

Last, assessing the family's ability to facilitate emotional expression will help the therapist to understand the value that the family places on emotion and the patterns of communication within the family. Some have found that in families where expression of emotion is discouraged, sadness has been equated with "craziness." Encouraging male family members not to cry over the death of a loved family member encourages gender role stereotypes and leads to repressed emotions that are then acted out in ways that are not acceptable. Families in which feelings are not openly expressed or in which they are suppressed keep individuals from resolving feelings of grief. It is the role of the counselor to bring these feelings and emotions to the forefront of the family and to help the family discuss negative feelings in a healthy manner. Communication patterns within the family can be changed with the help of a skilled family therapist, and this will assist families in expressing grief.

Families must restructure after the death of a family member. The therapist helps them do this by discussing the ways that the role left vacant by the deceased can be filled by reorganizing family roles and helping family members "try on" the new roles. Furthermore, the therapist must help the family to make meaning from the loss. By helping family members share their own unique understanding and beliefs about the loss, the counselor can help connect the family members to one another. This encourages the entire family unit to make meaning of the loss and encourages cohesion.

Those families that do well after a loss are those that are most cohesive, are able to tolerate individual differences among family members, that communicate openly about emotion and other matters, that derive support from within the family unit and outside the family unit, and that cope actively with problems.

Diane M. Clark

See also Adult Development; Anxiety; Beliefs and Values; Bereavement; Child Behavior Problems; Crisis Intervention With Couples and Families; Cultural Issues in Couples and Families; Death and Dying; Empathy; Grief Counseling; Trauma and Families; Trauma-Focused Cognitive Behavioral Therapy

Further Readings

Hease, T. J., & Johnston, N. (2012). Making meaning out of loss: A story and study of young widowhood. *Journal of Creativity in Mental Health, 7*(3), 204–221.

Irwin, H. J. (1991). The depiction of loss: Uses of clients' drawings in bereavement counseling. *Death Studies, 15*(5), 481–497.

Klass, D. (1999). Developing a cross-cultural model of grief: The state of the field. *Omega: Journal of Death and Dying, 39,* 153–178.

Kübler-Ross, E. (1965). *On death and dying.* New York, NY: Scribner.

Rando, T. A. (1984). *Grief, dying, and death: Clinical interventions for caregivers.* Champaign, IL: Research Press.

Rothaupt, J. W., & Becker, K. (2007). A literature review of Western bereavement theory: From decathecting to continuing bonds. *Omega: Journal of Death and Dying, 15,* 6–15.

Supiano, K. P., & Vaughn-Cole, B. (2011). The impact of personal loss on the experience of health professions: Graduate students in end-of-life and bereavement care. *Death Studies, 35*(1), 73–89.

Whiting, P. P. (1985). A developmental response to personal loss. *Dissertation Abstracts International, 47*(6-A), 2001.

Wilson, J. (2011). The assimilation of problematic experiences sequence: An approach to evidence-based practice in bereavement counseling. *Journal of Social Work in End of Life and Palliative Care, 7,* 350–362.

Worden, J. W. (2001). *Children and grief: When a parent dies.* New York, NY: Guilford.

Worden, J. W. (2002). *Grief counseling and grief therapy: A handbook for mental health practitioners* (3rd ed.). New York, NY: Springer.

Best Interests of the Child

The "best interests of the child" doctrine remains one of the most acclaimed, disdained, and depended-on standards in family law today. It is considered an integral part of family law because it advocates the best and highest standard; it is disdained by some because it is essentially subjective; and it is depended on because there is nothing better in place. The doctrine affects the placement and disposition of children in cases of divorce, custody, visitation, adoption, the death of a parent, illegitimacy proceedings, abuse proceedings, neglect proceedings, crime, and all forms of child protective services. And in every case, a judge must decide what is "best" for any child at any time under any particular situation, based on the presenting circumstances. Currently, family courts in the United States function on the premise that judges are capable of making finely tuned judgments about a child's best interests.

Basically, then, the role of the "best interests" standard is an attempt to provide that custody and visitation decisions are made with the ultimate goal of promoting and encouraging the child's happiness, security, mental health, and emotional development into young adulthood. It's often in the child's best interests to sustain a close and loving relationship with both parents, but the practicalities of promoting and maintaining such relationships can be the main challenge in protecting the child. However, it should be noted that as society, societal views, and family structure have changed throughout the years, the implementation of this doctrine has also attempted to adapt.

Until the 1800s the United States took the judicial definition of a child's best interest as gender based. Fathers customarily received custody of the children, as the courts and society viewed children as "property" of the father. The reasoning behind this decision was based on the fact that the father was able to support children financially. Men had access to resources allowing them to provide for their children, and women generally did not. During this time mothers were also considered the property of their husbands, and thus did not have access to develop an independent economic existence. As society changed, this belief also changed, as reflected in the introduction of the "tender years" doctrine, which gave a preference to the mother as the designated primary caregiver. Although well intended, this philosophy often failed to benefit the child. Indeed, the parent who was left out of the decision-making often felt no connection to the child, and basically abandoned any future interest.

As mothers and fathers became more mutually involved in child-rearing and financial commitments to the family, courts began to reevaluate the idea of granting custody to one or the other parent.

The idea was to try and keep both parents involved in the rearing of the child; accordingly, the concept of joint custody became more prevalent in child custody proceedings. Joint custody gave both parents the opportunity to be involved in the child's life and experiences. However, both parents needed to commit to the health and welfare of the child. Through this concept, the courts tried to encourage more collaboration between the parents and decrease the likelihood of emotional problems for the child.

The "best interests" doctrine describes the formal process accompanied by strict procedural provisions designed to determine the child's best interests for particularly important decisions affecting the child. A mature child should have the ability to participate with the decisionmakers in determining his or her future. The idea of best interest remains a subject of debate among many experts, as it requires an evaluation of the entire family situation to see what is best for everyone involved. This means that the courts need to evaluate all factors before determining the proper custody arrangement for a child. Judges and lawyers must consider: (a) disposition of the child; (b) whether the parent can meet the needs of the child; (c) any applicable and material information acquired from the child, including the articulated preferences of the child; (d) the preferences of the birthparents regarding custody; (e) the willingness and ability of each parent to encourage continuing a parent–child relationship between the child and the other parent; (f) the capability of each parent to be involved actively in the life of the child; (g) the child's adjustment to the home, school, and community environments; and (h) the amount of time that the child has lived in a stable and satisfactory environment. The court frequently considers the continuity of the environment favorably. A parent who voluntarily leaves the child's family home in order to alleviate stress in the household is also regarded positively by the court. Child custody is predicated on fostering and encouraging the happiness, safety, emotional development, mental development, and physical development of the child.

The federal government enacted the Uniform Child Custody Jurisdiction Enforcement Act to create a framework that determines what is appropriate for child custody decisions. However, the 50 states, rather than the federal government, govern family law legislation. Therefore, the act does not necessarily mean that the state will follow the provisions set forth. This requires those engaged in child custody or marriage and family practice to look at the specific state where the parents are located and familiarize themselves with the requirements of that state.

Many people have a role in the judicial proceedings dealing with the custody of children. The role of the court is to protect the child. As a result, many jurisdictions have determined that an independent lawyer needs to be appointed to represent the child to protect the child's interests during the custody proceedings. It then becomes the responsibility of the child's lawyer to include other professionals, such as a social worker, psychologist, and marriage and family therapist. These specialists should evaluate the emotional, intellectual, and financial needs of the child. In this way, the child's interests are properly presented, along with the interests of both parents. The opinion of the child should be taken into consideration if they are of an age where they can express their interests and concerns. The court should interview the child, not just the parents, to determine fully what is in the best interest of the child.

One of the roles of the courts is to investigate the home life of the child prior to making a determination. The home environment remains an important factor in evaluating the best interests of the child. This investigation should include evidence that demonstrates the absence of physical and emotional abuse among all members of the family. Keeping siblings together is another aspect the courts will consider. The reason for this is to maintain the continuous love and affection among the siblings and extended family members. The courts recognize the importance family relationships exert on a child's growth and development.

The evolving global society requires continuing reevaluation of the methods used to determine the best interests of a child. Society needs to protect its most vulnerable members from exploitation and emotional and physical abuse. Creating loving, caring, and positive environments promotes self-esteem and, eventually, productive and contributing members of society. The laws need continual review and revision to meet this objective.

Alyssa Weiss Quittner

See also Child Maltreatment; Child Protective Services; Child–Parent Relationship Therapy; Custody Evaluations; Parental Alienation Syndrome

Further Readings

Child Welfare Information Gateway. (2013). *Determining the best interests of the child.* Washington, DC: U.S. Department of Health and Human Services, Children's Bureau.

DiFonzo, J. H. (2014). From the rule of one to shared parenting: Custody presumptions in law and policy. *Family Court Review, 52*(2), 213–239.

DiFonzo, J. H., & Pruett, M. K. (2014). AFCC Think Tank Final Report: Closing the gap: Research, policy, practice and shared parenting. *Family Court Review, 52*(2), 152–174.

Howe, W. J., & McIsaac, H. (2008). Finding the balance: Ethical challenges and best practices for lawyers representing parents when the interests of children are at stake. *Family Court Review, 46,* 78–90. doi:10.1111/j.1744-1617.2007.00184.x

Kohm, L. M. (2008). Tracing the foundations of the best interests of the child standard in American jurisprudence. *Journal of Law and Family Studies, 10,* 337–375.

Schepard, A. (n.d.). *Best interests of the child.* Virginia Foundation for the Humanities Child Custody Project. Retrieved from http://childcustodyproject.org/essays/best-interests-of-the-child/

BIBLIOTHERAPY

See Self-Help

Bilingual Families

Bilingualism is the ability to communicate in two different languages. In some countries it is typical for families to learn and speak two or more languages. In the United States, English is the dominant language, and some families also speak a native or "heritage" language. In many ways, bilingualism becomes a defining characteristic for these families, having a positive effect on parenting, mealtime conversation, socialization, and general family interactions. If bilingual families choose to immigrate to a monolingual foreign nation, the families not only have to face the challenges of learning a new culture but also may encounter difficulty preserving their native language, which plays a key role in maintaining communication with people from the country of origin. However, based on the vital linguistic diversity that these families possess, it is important to understand the unique characteristics that bilingual families share. This entry explores the meaning of bilingualism; the characteristics, challenges, and benefits of bilingual families; multicultural considerations; and future implications for the helping professions.

Forms of Bilingualism

Bilingualism, in a general sense, is the ability of an individual to speak and/or understand more than one language. More specifically, there are various terms that have been ascribed to an individual's level and means of acquisition of bilingualism. *Functional bilingualism,* for example, is the frequent use of one language while being mildly proficient in another language. This is the most common tendency for individuals: to be stronger in one language than another.

In terms of childhood bilingualism, the acquisition of two languages from infancy at the same time is referred to as *simultaneous bilingualism.* For example, when a child experiences consistent exposure to, and/or immersion in, two languages from infancy, he or she may be classified as a simultaneous bilingual. Alternatively, *successive bilingualism* is the concept of an individual learning a second language only after becoming fully proficient in a primary language: for example, an English-speaking student taking a course in a foreign language (e.g., Spanish or French) at the high school or undergraduate level. Furthermore, within bilingual families individuals can be classified as *receptive bilinguals* versus *productive bilinguals*. The receptive bilingual is the family member who may be able to understand a language but cannot speak it; a productive bilingual is an individual who can both understand and speak the language. Within a bilingual family system, family members may function at differing levels of bilingualism. For example, a grandmother from an immigrant Asian American family may be a receptive bilingual, whereas her daughter living in the new country for the past five years may be a productive bilingual. Last, a *balanced bilingual* is an individual who is proficient in speaking and understanding both languages.

Characteristics of Bilingual Families

Understanding bilingual families is a journey of cultural exploration, regardless of their means of acquisition of their languages. In marital, couples, and family counseling it is important to focus on strengths in order to show respect for what the family already does well, promote the therapeutic relationship, help clients embrace positive aspects of their relationship, and create a more uplifting therapeutic environment.

To work successfully with bilingual families the clinician needs to understand the unique aspects of bilingual parenting. In conceptualizing a family, one must understand the family's means of socialization and rules for language use. These rules for language use are recognized as a major part of the process of language acquisition and maintenance. Moreover, these rules may vary for different families. For example, bilingual parents may opt for the family not to speak the language of the surrounding society at home. Rather, in the home, they may speak the language that is foreign to the surrounding society.

Also, parents may choose to speak one language only to each child at home. Parents can also opt to speak the language of the surrounding society at home primarily, while only using the language that is foreign to the surrounding community on special occasions or with a specific family member. Other parents leading bilingual families blend the use of both languages so that they become proficient in both languages. A point that is particularly important to highlight here is that bilingual parents encourage and give more significance to the diversity in socialization of speaking two languages than the style of language chosen and/or in-home communication. Even in the nature of their conversation, bilingual parents teach their children the significance of having mutual respect for cultural differences. For example, a Hispanic American immigrant parent will be proud to teach her first-generation children to treat both Spanish and English with the same respect and passion because the first is the native language and the latter is the language that her kids are more frequently exposed to outside of the home.

By nature, there is a cultural dualism within the homes of bilingual families, creating stronger socialization competence for each member. Mealtime language use is a prime example of ways that bilingual parents develop language acquisition, maintenance, and socialization tendencies in their children. During mealtimes, language use for bilingual families, especially those with small children, is determined by parents' motivation to teach what language to speak and how one should speak; that is, mealtime interactions often tend to be linked to educational issues. Here, some bilingual parents may choose to teach appropriate language use and interactions by modeling. Others may use this time to create family cohesion by returning to speaking the primary language of the family. However families choose to use mealtimes, this time with the family can definitely be a means to language acquisition and maintenance.

Benefits and Barriers for Bilingual Families

As noted earlier, bilingual families are equipped with the art of speaking and using two languages, possess linguistic diversity in the global village, and take pride in transmitting their linguistic heritage to the younger members of their families or communities. They often tend to be multiculturally sensitive to both cultures from which they acquired languages. Research also suggests that bilingual children may possess a slightly more enriched ability to think creatively than do children who speak only one language.

Some of the barriers that children from bilingual families may face concern language choice and its use in different contexts. Kids may encounter challenges and perhaps may be confused if the native language is different from the medium of instruction at school and/or that of the majority culture. There may be some challenges even with the new language acquisition. For example, a Spanish-speaking first-grader may have severe difficulty learning English (medium of instruction) if the parents and siblings at home speak mostly in Spanish. Other sets of barriers come from the individuals of a monolingual-monocultural society. For example, a bilingual child from a Russian-French-speaking family may get disapproval from their Russian or French extended family members or relatives for embracing one language or culture more than the other. This could be misperceived by monolingual extended family members as disassociating from the native language and culture of origin. Similar challenges are inevitable even from the school. For example, monolingual classmates and school administrators may not understand the benefits of bilingualism, resulting in potential exclusion or teasing by children, and misunderstandings and sometimes even discrimination by adults. In such situations, bilingual parents can support their kids more closely and serve as social and language engineers for them. Parents can do this by further encouraging their children in bilingualism through frequent use of both languages. Parents can serve as advocates for their children by educating monolingual school officials and extended family members about the benefits of dual language use. Additionally, parents can serve as social and language engineers by exposing their children to literature and media in both languages.

Through these measures children receive indirectly affirming messages from their parents about dual language use.

Multicultural Considerations

Bilingual families are very often bicultural and/or multicultural, which adds greater complexity to their family's fabric. The environment and circumstances in which these bilingual children grow are vital in shaping the type of bilingualism that these children exhibit. For instance, if the child is continually encouraged to learn both languages and receives constant reinforcement from home, school, and community to master both languages, there will be better chances of that child's becoming a balanced bilingual. Apart from the challenges related to speaking more than one language, bilingual-multiracial families have to deal with issues related to their ethnicities and cultures as well. Parents from these families need to be committed to preserving the linguistic values and cultural heritages that they follow and would like to pass on to the youngsters. At the macro level, teachers, clinicians, and policymakers should be mindful of the multiple variables impacting the lives of bilingual families and exercise multicultural sensitivity in their interactions with them.

Implications for Therapists

Monolingualism can impose limitations in many professions, including marital, couples, and family therapy. When treating a family whose primary language differs from that of the therapist, the benefits of treatment may be limited because of the communication gap. In this instance, both the clinician and the client's understanding of the issues discussed may be limited.

As the U.S. population continues to grow and become even more of a metaphorical "melting pot" of cultures, it is beneficial for therapists and counselors to begin to understand the areas of improvement needed in working with bilingual individuals. It is essential to identify bilingual family strengths like resiliency and cohesion that are vital in accomplishing treatment goals. When treatment providers are more familiar with the family's culture through personal bilingualism and/or constant exposure, then treatment will undoubtedly be more beneficial for these families. As in multicultural competency, helping professionals should be mindful of their own preconceived notions about bilingualism and hone their knowledge, skills, and best practices in working with the individuals from bilingual families regularly. They can do so by reviewing the relevant research, attending workshops, immersing themselves into these communities, learning through their personal experiences with bilingual clients, and working toward advocating for their growth and development.

*Suneetha Babu Manyam
and Jacqueline Robinson*

See also Active Parenting; Cultural Issues in Couples and Families; Family Resilience; Family Strengths; Family Values; Group Family Therapy; Immigrant Families; International Family Therapy; Interracial Marriages and Families; Latino Families; Multicultural Counseling Competence; Multiculturalism

Further Readings

Ball, J. (2011). Enhancing learning of children from diverse language backgrounds: Mother tongue–based bilingual or multilingual education in the early years. Retrieved July 19, 2013, from http://unesdoc.unesco.org/images/0021/002122/212270e.pdf

Caldas, S. (2006). *Raising bilingual-biliterate children in monolingual culture.* Clevedon, England: Multilingual Matters.

Genesee, F. (2015). Myths about early childhood bilingualism. *Canadian Psychology, 56*(1), 6–15.

Genesee, J. C. (Ed.). (1999). *Trends in bilingual acquisition* (8th ed.). International Association for the Study of Child Language. San Sebastián, Spain: John Benjamins.

Nzai, V. E., & Boleli, F. K. (2013). Challenges faced by bilingual children from mixed parents in predominantly monolingual-monocultural Spanish speaking extended families. *MEXTSOL Journal, 37*(2), 1–9.

Pitton, L. M. (2013). From language maintenence to bilingual parenting: Negotiating behavior and language choice at the dinner table in binational-bilingual families. *Multilingual, 32*(4), 507–526.

Rosenberg, M. (1996). *The Internet TESL Journal.* Retrieved April 1, 2015, from iteslj.org/Articles/Rosenberg-bilingual.html

Birth Control and Contraception

Birth control is the medical or behavioral act of attempting to prevent pregnancy either before or after sexual intercourse. The term may also apply to an actual device or medication used to prevent pregnancy. Humans have attempted to find ways to control when and if pregnancy occurs for centuries, with the effectiveness, safeness, and general acceptability of those various methods fluctuating over time. This entry reviews the history of birth control as well as related religious/moral and political issues. It also reviews various types of birth control currently available, along with possible relational issues and considerations.

History

The history of birth control dates back to seventh century BCE Chinese writings in which ancient physicians discussed types of intercourse, and sexual practices such as the withdrawal method were designed either to prevent pregnancy and/or strengthen a form of sexual/spiritual self-control. Writings on the subject date back from 1550 BCE Mesopotamia and ancient Egypt. Various herbs, plants, and other natural substances such as crocodile dung were thought to have spermicidal and/or abortive properties, and were commonly used throughout the ancient world. Some plant-based substances such as silphium became so popular that the demand surpassed the supply, which eventually led to the extinction of the plant species between the second and third centuries BCE. Crude condoms were fashioned out of animal skin in some cultures, and honey and other natural substances were used for birth control purposes in ancient civilizations such as in India.

In medieval Europe, the topic of birth control became a moral/religious issue as well as a medical/public health issue when the Catholic Church officially deemed any attempt to prevent pregnancy as immoral. However, despite the Church's disapproval, by the Victorian era birth rates had significantly declined, and birth control devices such as rubber condoms and diaphragms were widely available. The debate waxed and waned throughout this time period, with many women continuing to use crude or "natural" techniques such as the withdrawal method until the 19th century, when various medical, political, and economic activists in Great Britain and the United States began linking the availability and use of birth control to a variety of sociopolitical issues such as feminism, capitalism, and economic growth/sustainability.

In the United States, birth control had been generally legal throughout most of the 19th century until the Comstock Act was passed in the 1870s, which criminalized not only the use of contraceptives but also the dissemination of information about birth control information and/or devices. Margaret Sanger is credited with coining the term *birth control* around 1914 as she crusaded in both the United States and Europe for women's access to contraception. However, even though this movement began in the early 20th century, it was not until the 1950s that the first birth control pill was developed and later made available in the United States in the 1960s.

Many developed countries had laws in effect until the late 20th century that criminalized the use and/or possession of birth control devices. France, Ireland, and the Soviet Union, for example, all struck down or modified legislation during the 1960s, 1970s, or 1980s in order to allow women more access to birth control information and devices. In 1965 (*Griswold v. Connecticut*), the Supreme Court of the United States overruled states' ability to prohibit contraceptive use between married couples and in 1973 (*Eisenstadt v. Baird*) decriminalized the use of contraceptives among nonmarried individuals. Japan did not lift its legal ban on birth control pills until 1999. As recently as 2014, the American Congress of Obstetricians and Gynecologists recommended that oral birth control pills be converted from prescription-only access to an over-the-counter medication. To date, this recommendation has not been accepted by the U.S. Food and Drug Administration.

Religious/Moral Issues

Historically, the ability to control or prevent pregnancy has been regarded as a religious/moral issue by many people. The inextricable combination of women's sexuality, sexual behavior in general, and the issue of pregnancy has served to significantly limit women's access to and knowledge of birth control over time. Until the 1930s, birth control had been specifically banned by almost all Christian religions (Catholic and Protestant) because it was associated with promiscuity and adultery; however, after the Anglican Church officially began to allow the use of birth control, most other Protestant denominations followed. While individual Catholic subgroups and parishioners vary widely on their moral view and actual use of birth control, the official stance of the Catholic Church continues to be that the purpose of sex is procreation, and therefore any action that interferes with the natural consequences of sexual intercourse is sinful.

The combination of religious/moral issues regarding access to birth control continues to intersect with modern-day efforts to provide universal access. Based on religious convictions or moral teachings, many argue that abstinence from sexual activity is the only appropriate and effective means of birth control that should be advocated. Birth control opponents typically argue that free, easy access to birth control may increase sexual promiscuity, risky sexual behavior, and the proliferation of sexually transmitted diseases. They oppose legislation that provides free or reduced-rate birth control to various populations that might not otherwise have access, such as adolescents, individuals in lower socioeconomic classes, and racial minorities. However, while abstinence by individuals not financially, emotionally, or relationally prepared to support a pregnancy may be an ideal solution from some perspectives, abstinence is generally not the behavioral reality, regardless of whether birth control is available. During the presidency of George W. Bush, for example, federal and state funding for contraceptive services was cut, and by 2004 unplanned pregnancy among women of low socioeconomic status (SES) increased by 29%, while unplanned pregnancy among higher-income women decreased by 20%. Therefore, limiting access to birth control for low-SES women did not succeed in decreasing risky sexual behavior among that population, but instead resulted in more unplanned pregnancies. For these reasons, among others, many continue to advocate that birth control must be viewed as a political, public health, and financial issue, regardless of one's personal religious or moral convictions.

Political, Cultural, and Financial Issues

Proponents for the availability and use of birth control have long argued that access to the ability to choose when and how procreation occurs is a human-rights issue firmly rooted in equal rights for women. By providing women with knowledge of and access to safe and effective means of birth control, many argue, gender equality and the autonomy of women is also promoted. The disproportionate impact of pregnancy and child-rearing on women's bodies, time, career, health, and financial earning power makes birth control availability a crucial issue in the reduction of gender disparities. Women who find themselves with unwanted and/or unplanned pregnancies frequently experience higher rates of poverty, lower rates of education, increased risk of domestic violence/partner dependency, and/or poorer physical health. Therefore, many argue that any act to restrict such access is, in effect, gender discrimination. Others note that birth control promotes gender equality by enabling women to enjoy sexual activity on the same basis as men rather than constantly bearing the weight and fear of unplanned or unwanted pregnancy. Birth control also allows women whose health may be at risk if they conceived to engage in sexual activity.

One of the most recent sociopolitical debates regarding birth control occurred in the context of the Affordable Care Act. In 2010, President Barack Obama signed legislation that required new or substantially changed health insurance plans to provide contraceptives to patients without a co-pay. As many as 28 states previously had mandates that required health insurance companies to cover prescription contraceptives, but the federal law strengthened this provision by specifically forbidding insurance companies to charge part or all of that cost to the patient. Many religious employers with employer-sponsored health plans fought this legislation, stating that paying for birth control—specifically, medications known as morning-after-pills, which are taken to prevent pregnancy after an act of sexual intercourse has occurred, and intrauterine devices (IUDs)—violated their religious or moral convictions. Others argued that failing to provide free access to birth control (regardless of the form) through employer or marketplace-sponsored health plans was discriminatory toward women and could result in many of the social, health, or financial problems described previously. The original legislation allowed an exemption to the contraception mandate for certain religious, nonprofit employers, but in 2014, the U.S. Supreme Court ruled that religious exemptions can be claimed by certain for-profit employers as well.

Types

Birth control exists in many different forms. One of the most popular is the use of hormone-based medications. The hormones in these medications (typically either progestin and/or estrogen) are delivered through a variety of means such as pills, patches, shots, subdermal devices, vaginal rings, and intrauterine devices. Some pills are taken daily, and others, known as morning-after-pills, can be taken after unprotected sexual intercourse to prevent a pregnancy from occurring. The various delivery methods each have pros and cons related to effectiveness, ease of use, potential for side effects, and ease of reversibility. The combined estrogen/progestin pill continues to be the most commonly used form of birth control by women in the United States.

Female tubal sterilization is the second most frequently used form of birth control in the United States. Female sterilization surgery involves a procedure in which a health care provider closes or blocks a woman's fallopian tubes by tying or cutting the tubes, sealing the tubes with an instrument that utilizes an electrical current, closing the tubes with devices such as clamps, or actually removing small pieces of the tube. This form of birth control is meant to be permanent. Male sterilization, also known as a vasectomy, is an outpatient procedure in which a health care provider makes tiny cuts in, ties, or blocks the vas deferens, the two tubes that carry sperm to the penis. Men who undergo this procedure usually need to use alternative forms of birth control such as a condom for approximately three months afterward in order to ensure all sperm have been removed from the semen. This form of birth control is also designed to be permanent, but it can be reversed in some cases.

Barrier methods involve blocking the entrance of sperm into the uterus. Spermicides (substances designed to kill sperm cells) can also be used in combination with barrier methods in order to increase effectiveness rates. The spermicide serves to kill most of the sperm that enter the vagina and then the barrier blocks any remaining sperm from passing through the cervix to fertilize an egg. The male condom, female condom, diaphragm, cervical cap, and cervical shield are examples of barrier methods. One important benefit of the male and female condom is that these are the only two forms of birth control that also protect against sexually transmitted diseases.

Awareness and "natural" methods are forms of birth control that do not involve any medical, hormonal, or surgical intervention and are thus sometimes preferred by individuals who wish to avoid outside intervention due to medical, religious, or moral reasons. Women have attempted to predict fertility and thus limit or avoid sexual intercourse during days when they perceive themselves to be most fertile. The body's cycles are tracked through the use of signs such as vaginal lubrication, menstrual cycle calendars, body temperature, and perceived libido. Men may also use awareness of the body's ejaculation cycle to attempt withdrawal of the penis from the vagina before ejaculation occurs. Exclusive breast feeding is also a form of natural birth control utilized by women who are actively lactating. Because of the personalized and subjective nature of these methods, they tend to have a highly variable effectiveness rate in terms of the prevention of pregnancy and have no impact on the prevention of sexually transmitted disease.

Abortion is the act of surgically terminating an existing pregnancy. The abortion process differs widely depending on when in the pregnancy it occurs, as well as other health factors of the mother and fetus. While this controversial approach is generally not recommended as a standard form of birth control due to the physical and emotional risks involved, it continues to be utilized as a routine form of birth control for populations that do not have regular access to other forms of contraception such as teenagers, women living in poverty, and those in developing countries.

Relational Issues

The decision of whether and how to utilize birth control is an important factor in any sexual relationship. Potential areas of discussion and negotiation between sexual partners include determining who is responsible for purchasing and correctly utilizing preferred birth control methods, and selecting a method that best fits the budget, lifestyle, health concerns, and sexual preferences of both partners. When birth control preferences and expectations do not align, there is the potential for relational discord and/or unplanned pregnancy, among other issues. Sexual partners are advised to discuss birth control plans and preferences before becoming sexually active in order to avoid relational and reproductive problems in the future.

Christen Tomlinson Logue

See also Infertility; Pregnancy and Sexuality; Sexuality Education

Further Readings

Antonishak, J., Kaye, K., & Swiader, L. (2015). Impact of an online birth control support network on unintended pregnancy. *Social Marketing Quarterly, 21*(1), 23–36. doi:10.1177/1524500414566698

Crooks, R. L., & Baur, K. (2013). *Our sexuality* (12th ed.). Belmont, CA: Wadsworth, Cengage Learning.

Gordon, L. (2007). *The moral property of women: A history of birth control politics in America.* Champaign: University of Illinois Press.

Gori, A., Giannini, M., Craparo, G., Caretti, V., Nannini, I., Madathil, R., & Schuldberg, D. (2014). Assessment of the relationship between the use of birth control pill and the characteristics of mate selection. *Journal of Sexual Medicine, 11*(9), 2181–2187. doi:10.1111/jsm.12566

Hatcher, R. A., Trussell, J., Nelson, A. L., Cates, W., Stewart, F. H., & Kowal, D. (2007). *Contraceptive technology* (19th ed.). New York, NY: Ardent Media.

Hill, N. J., Siwatu, M., & Robinson, A. K. (2014). "My religion picked my birth control": The influence of religion on contraceptive use. *Journal of Religion and Health, 53*(3), 825–833. doi:10.1007/s10943-013-9678-1

Moniz, M. H., Davis, M. M., & Chang, T. (2014). Attitudes mandated coverage of birth control medication and other health benefits in a US national sample. *JAMA: Journal of the American Medical Association, 311*(24), 2539–2541. doi:10.1001/jama.2014.4766

Sanger, M. (2004). *The autobiography of Margaret Sanger.* Mineola, NY: Dover. (Originally published 1838)

Schwartz, P., & Kempner, M. (2015). *50 great myths of human sexuality.* West Sussex, England: John Wiley & Sons.

Zorea, A. W. (2012). *Birth control (health and medical issues today).* Santa Barbara, CA: Greenwood.

BLENDED FAMILIES

See Stepfamilies

BODY DYSMORPHIC DISORDER IN ADOLESCENTS

Everyone experiences concerns about their physical appearance, especially during adolescence. Some individuals, however, can become so overly distressed, anxious, and fearful about their appearance that it begins to affect their lives. These exaggerated fears, and the array of delusional thoughts and maladaptive behaviors that accompany them, may suggest the onset and development of a severe psychological condition known as body dysmorphic disorder.

Body dysmorphic disorder (BDD) is a distressing psychological condition that is often underrecognized and misunderstood, occurring chiefly in the adolescent population. BDD is characterized by a preoccupation with perceived bodily flaws and poor physical appearance. These flaws are often minimal or nonexistent. However, individuals with BDD genuinely believe that they are physically defective or deformed. As such, they tend to experience debilitating anxiety stemming from fears of deformity, inadequacy, and judgment by others.

The development and maintenance of BDD has major implications for adolescent social development, adjustment, and transitioning. Unfortunately, due to the nature of the symptomology, BDD often goes unnoticed and unrecognized among teachers, friends, family, and health care professionals alike. Given its adverse effects on adolescent psychosocial functioning, understanding the intricacies of BDD is paramount in improving awareness, acceptance, and care.

The central symptom of BDD is excessive concern with a specific facial feature or body part. Research done in the United States indicates that the features most likely to be the focus of the patient's attention are (in order of frequency) complexion flaws (acne, blemishes, scars, wrinkles), hair (on the head or the body, too much or too little), and facial features (size, shape, or lack of symmetry). The patient's concerns may, however, involve other body parts, and may shift over time from one feature to another.

Other symptoms of body dysmorphic disorder include:

- Ritualistic behavior, consisting of actions that the patient performs to manage anxiety and that take up excessive amounts of his or her time. Patients are typically upset if someone or something interferes with or interrupts their ritual. In the context of BDD, ritualistic behaviors may include exercise or makeup routines, assuming specific poses or postures in front of a mirror, etc.
- Camouflaging the "problem" feature or body part with makeup, hats, or clothing. Camouflaging appears to be the single most common symptom among patients with BDD and is widely reported.
- Abnormal behavior around mirrors, car bumpers, large windows, or similar reflecting surfaces. A majority of patients diagnosed with BDD frequently check their appearance in mirrors or spend long periods of time doing so. A minority, however, react in the opposite fashion and avoid mirrors whenever possible.
- Frequent requests for reassurance from others about their appearance.
- Frequently comparing one's appearance to others.
- Avoiding activities outside the home, including school and social events.

The loss of functioning resulting from BDD can have serious consequences for the patient's future. Adolescents with BDD often cut school and may be reluctant to participate in sports, join religious- or civic-sponsored youth groups, or hold part-time or summer jobs. Adults with muscle dysmorphia have been known to turn down job promotions in order to have more time to work out in their gym or fitness center. Economic consequences of BDD also include overspending on cosmetics, clothing, or plastic surgery.

Diagnosis

Diagnosis of BDD is often missed in clinical settings, although the disorder has been described for more than a century and increasingly studied over the past several decades. Therapists are often unfamiliar with characteristics of BDD and hence have difficulty recognizing it. Furthermore, the repetitive, compulsive, ritualistic behaviors aimed at examining, improving, or hiding the perceived "defect" may lead to a misdiagnosis of obsessive-compulsive disorder, since such symptoms are similar to the diagnostic features for that diagnosis. In addition to excessive grooming rituals, the individual with BDD typically engages in camouflaging, consisting of efforts to conceal, fix, or otherwise try to make the imagined flaw or slight defect in appearance unnoticeable. The more common methods used are baggy clothing, excessive makeup, hats, and the strategic placement of one's hair or the use of a body part such as an arm or hand over the imagined flaw.

Prevalence

BDD usually appears during early adolescence, but it can occur in childhood; clinical features in children and adolescents appear similar to those in adults. Available data indicate that the disorder is typically chronic. Some studies report an approximately equal gender ratio, whereas others report a preponderance of males or females (although referral biases are evident in some reports). A majority of adult patients with BDD have never been married, and a relatively high proportion are unemployed. The disorder's clinical features appear generally similar in women and men, although several differences are apparent.

A Range of Consequences

Patients diagnosed with BDD have problems with relationships, social life, school or work, and other aspects of their life. They tend to avoid gatherings, dating, sexual intimacy, or places with lots of mirrors, places where they feel exposed, or places with lots of people.

Those diagnosed with BDD often feel severely anxious about being viewed in social situations (i.e., parties, clubs, and reunions), where they fear that others are focused on and judging their appearance. Some who have been diagnosed with the disorder have stated that their symptomology is the cause of their social problems, or significantly contributes to them. If symptomology improves with treatment, both social functioning and relationships improve as well.

Many BDD patients seen in psychiatric settings have other co-occurring mental disorders. Most studies have found that major depression is the most common comorbid disorder, with the largest study ($n = 293$) reporting a current rate of 58% and a lifetime rate of 76%. In this study, onset of major depression most often occurred after onset of BDD, consistent with clinical impressions that depression is often although not always secondary to BDD.

Treatment

The recommended intervention for patients with a diagnosis of BDD is a combination of psychotherapy and psychotropic drug treatments. Behavioral modification therapy is highly recommended in conjunction with selective serotonin reuptake inhibitors (SSRIs, a type of antidepressant medication). Mental health approaches include systematic desensitization, exposure techniques, self-confrontational techniques, and cognitive imagery. General strategies for successful treatment are continuity of care, regularly scheduled appointments, and cognitive restructuring. According to the American Psychiatric Association, patients who are taking maintenance medications should be seen at least three to four times per year. Approximately 53% of those with BDD experience relapse within six months of discontinuance of treatment.

Shirlyn M. Garrett-Wilson

See also Anxiety; Anxiety Disorders in Adolescents; Avoidance; Eating Disorders

Further Readings

American Psychiatric Association. (2013). Obsessive-compulsive and related disorders. *Diagnostic and Statistical Manual of Mental Disorders* (5th ed.). Arlington, VA: American Psychiatric Association.

Bjornsson, A. S., Didie, E. R., & Phillips, K. A. (2010). Body dysmorphic disorder. *Dialogues in Clinical Neuroscience, 12*(2), 221–232.

Grant, J., Won Kim, S., & Crow, S. (2001). Prevalence and clinical features of body dysmorphic disorder in adolescent and adult psychiatric inpatients. *Journal of Clinical Psychiatry, 62,* 517–522.

Koran, L. M., Abujaoudee, E., Large, M. D., & Serpe, R. T. (2008, April). The prevalence of body dysmorphic disorder in the United States adult population. *CNS Spectrums, 13*(4), 316–322. doi:10.1017/S1092852900016436

National Collaborating Centre for Mental Health. (2006). *Obsessive-compulsive disorder: Core interventions in the treatment of obsessive-compulsive disorder and body dysmorphic disorder.* London, England: British Psychological Society, Royal College of Psychiatrists.

Phillips, K. A., Hollander, E., Rasmussen, S. A., Aronowitz, B. R., DeCaria, C., & Goodman, W. K. (1997). A severity rating scale for body dysmorphic disorder: Development, reliability, and validity of a modified version of the Yale–Brown obsessive-compulsive scale. *Psychopharmacology Bulletin, 33,* 17–22.

Phillips, K. A., & McElroy, S. L. (2000). Personality disorders and traits in patients with body dysmorphic disorder. *Comprehensive Psychiatry, 41,* 229–236.

Phillips, K. A., McElroy, S. L., Keck, P. E., Pope, H. G., & Hudson, J. I. (1993). Body dysmorphic disorder: 30 cases of imagined ugliness. *American Journal of Psychiatry, 150,* 302–308.

BONDING

Bonding can be understood as the process of developing a relationship or attachment between two people. One type of bonding is the creation of a caring, nurturing relationship between the primary caregiver and a child. This process can begin during pregnancy for the biological mother or after birth for the father and other caregivers. Often, the process of bonding is referred to as "falling in love" with the baby. Some parents report that the bond with their child was instantaneous; others say that the process may take days, weeks, or months. It is the quality of the relationship that makes the difference, not the amount of time it took for the relationship to develop. Notably, bonding describes a one-way connection from parent or primary caregiver to the child; the newborn infant is not yet able to respond socially to the parent or to differentiate and regulate emotions.

Attachment may be considered the emotional connection between two people that is developed through the process of bonding. For infants and parents, attachment occurs after the period of bonding and is considered in place near the end of the first year of the relationship and is reciprocal in nature; at that time the infant has developed sufficiently to respond to the parent socially and emotionally. A positive-quality parent–child bond is characterized by a mother who perceives joy in her role as a mother, holds unconditional love for the child, and finds parenting this child rewarding despite the child's temperament, appearance, or abilities. The bond with other primary caregivers may also be identified with these similar qualities.

The positive or negative quality of the primary caregiver–child relationship impacts the caregiver's and/or child's long-term mental health and relationship-building capacities. Qualities of a primary caregiver such as the consistency of engagement, responsiveness, and type of response can influence the relationship process. Research indicates that mothers who engage with their babies consistently, have appropriate developmental expectations, and initiate and respond to the infant vocally and with soft, sensitive physical touch are thereby supporting the infant's development of self-regulation strategies, which leads to the ability to cope in stressful situations. These infants develop into children who are independent, focused, curious, and able to engage socially and develop positive relationships. The mothers who are unable to consistently engage with their infants and engage in abusive and/or nonresponsive ways experience infants who develop higher levels of arousal and a lower capacity to self-regulate in stressful situations. Consequently, these infants grow into children who are more likely to have delayed development, are more difficult to soothe, and are more likely to have sleep problems, aggressive or impulsive behaviors, and difficulty calming themselves when older.

The British psychiatrist John Bowlby, widely recognized as a pioneering attachment researcher, theorized that the secure foundational relationship or bond of the parent and child establishes the path for the healthy development of attachment as the child grows, explores, and learns about the world. Research has demonstrated that the quality of the bonding relationship between primary caregiver and child impacts the child's brain development, self-regulation abilities, self-esteem, social behaviors, and the sense of trust that supports the child feeling secure and safe.

Unlike some other species, human beings are not self-sufficient at birth; consequently, newborns must have a caregiver respond to their needs, even if minimally, for survival. The parent or caregiver brings his or her own history and social experience into the caregiving process, which may have a positive or negative impact on the relationship. Counselors may want to talk with clients about and observe the caregiver–child relationship quality, as it could impact the way the adult or the child interacts with and perceives others.

Factors Impacting the Bonding Process Between Caregiver and Child

Pregnancy

Many women report that the relationship with their baby began prenatally, enhanced by feeling the movements of the baby in utero. Ultrasound technology now shows parents three-dimensional images of the unborn baby, which helps start the emotional process of visualizing their child outside of the womb. Mothers create images of their babies, the "imagined baby" by which they process what life will be like when the baby has been born. This process of imagining the baby is the start of the bonding relationship prenatally. The ultrasound images can also support the bonding process between the unborn baby and other caregivers such as the father, another mother, or extended family members who will be involved intimately in the care of the child after birth.

Childbirth and Immediate Contact After Birth

Research continues on the process of the mother–infant bond, as there is no formula for how a high-quality bond can be developed. The science of relationships has been studied, and oxytocin, a hormone created in the brain and secreted through the pituitary gland, has been found to be involved in the social and emotional acts of a relationship such as kissing, hugging, and other relationship-building behaviors. Studies have further identified that oxytocin levels play an important role in the human mother–infant bonding process. Oxytocin production is stimulated by labor and childbirth, and the release of oxytocin produces feelings of pleasure, drowsiness, euphoria, and pain relief in the mother. After birth, oxytocin release is prompted through contact between the mother and baby: the mother stroking the baby's skin, the baby suckling, and the baby being cradled by and nestling into the mother. Research tells us that mothers who are able to hold the baby immediately after childbirth are more likely to feel pleasure and calmness, and a higher rate report more positive emotions toward the infant. These mothers also feel more comfortable in their role as mothers and are able to respond to the infant's needs at a higher level than mothers who were not able to have the immediate contact and interaction with their infant.

Research has also demonstrated that promoting this immediate contact and interaction results in early discharges from the hospital, as well as less crying and more alert states in the infants. Biological mothers who breastfeed continue to have high rates of oxytocin production, which is also stimulated by lactation. Breastfeeding offers another opportunity for the mother to demonstrate care, responsiveness, and consistency to her infant, which are factors necessary for a supportive and high-quality mother–infant bond. Fathers and other primary caregivers also are encouraged to stroke the baby and hold the baby close to begin their own bonding process with the newborn.

Not all parents are able to have immediate contact, due to medical reasons or logistics such as fathers who are on military deployment at the time of delivery. Delay in the interaction or limits to the interaction do not negate the importance of this time together; however, it may take more time for the primary caregiver to develop the strong positive feelings toward the infant that are representative of the quality bonding process.

Maternal Mental Health During and After Pregnancy

The mother's mental health can have a negative impact on the development of a positive mother–child bond and further impact the child's social and emotional developmental process. Perinatal depression, postpartum depression, and other mental health issues can take the focus of the mother away from the pregnancy and the infant. She may feel overwhelmed by the thought of having to care for another human being when she is feeling challenged to care for herself. The lack of attention to the infant can result in a poor mother–infant bond, which means the foundation for attachment is unpredictable. Children who have poor bonds with their primary caregivers typically also have challenging attachment styles because they have not had the opportunity to be consistently supported and nurtured in their environment. These children do not have a trusting relationship with their primary caregiver; consequently, they do not explore or learn at the same levels as children who do have a sense of trust with their primary caregiver(s), which equates to a sense of safety and security for the child.

Bonding and the Nonbiological Caregiver

Despite the biological nature of bonding, it can happen for primary caregivers who are not the biological mother of the infant. The key aspect of developing the caregiver–infant relationship is for the caregiver to be consistent and responsive to the infant's needs. This consistency supports the infant's sense of safety, and allows the infant to feel comfortable exploring and learning because he or she understands that all that is needed is a cry or a squeal to bring the caregiver to his or her side. The consistent actions of the caregiver support the positive schema of the relationship for the infant, which is then encoded onto the baby's neural pathways and is the foundation for the attachment relationship. This attachment relationship, formed in infancy, may impact the attachment relationships that the infant forms many years later as an adult.

Carol Pfeiffer Messmore

See also Attachment; Attachment Theory; Attachment-Based Family Therapy; Postpartum Depression

Further Readings

Barrack, C. (2007). A journey of love: The influence of prenatal and perinatal psychology on parent–child bonding. *Journal of Prenatal & Perinatal Psychology & Health, 22*(1), 55–78.

Brazelton, T., & Greenspan, S. (2000). *The irreducible needs of children: What every child must have to grow, learn, and flourish.* Cambridge, MA: Perseus.

Erickson, M. F., & Kurz-Riemer, K. (1999). *Infants, toddlers, and families: A framework for support and intervention.* New York, NY: Guilford.

Giustardi, A., Stablum, M., & De Martino, A. (2011). Mother infant relationship and bonding myths and facts. *Journal of Maternal-Fetal and Neonatal Medicine, 24*(1), 59–60.

Johnson, K. (2013). Maternal–infant bonding: A review of the literature. *International Journal of Childbirth Education, 28*(3), 17–22.

Siegel, D. (1999). *The developing mind.* New York, NY: Guilford.

Tronick, E. (2007). *Neurobehavioral and social-emotional development of infants and children.* New York, NY: W. W. Norton.

Winnicott, D. W. (2002). *Winnicott on the child.* Cambridge, MA: Perseus.

Zeanah, C. (Ed.). (2009). *Handbook of infant mental health* (3rd ed.). New York, NY: Guilford.

BOUNDARIES

Boundaries are defined as invisible lines that help keep the "good" in and the "bad" out, but are also permeable enough to allow some things to pass through. When defining them in the context of relationships, they are guidelines, rules, or limits that regulate communication and contact with others. Typical boundaries include physical, mental, emotional, and sexual limits set on relationships to regulate those relationships and protect people from abuse or manipulation. Clear boundaries help develop responsibility and self-control while still helping people feel cared for, connected, and safe. This entry discusses the development of boundaries in childhood, how the idea of boundaries is utilized in structural family therapy, and concludes with recommendations for maintaining healthy boundaries.

Boundary Development

Individual boundary development is an ongoing process. The most crucial stages of individual boundary development are in the early years and can be categorized into three phases: hatching, practicing, and rapprochement. During the hatching phase, children are still dependent on their caregiver; however, if they feel safe enough they will start to explore new things and take risks. During the practicing phase, the child is trying to leave his or her caregiver behind and may feel exhilaration and energy, even an unrealistic sense of grandiosity. The next phase, rapprochement, is when the grandiosity starts to fade and the child comes back to reality. The child will return to the caregiver, but as a separate self in the relationship. In this phase, children start to realize the role of their thoughts, feelings, and behaviors in the maintenance of their relationship with self and others.

Some tools that children can use to help build boundaries during rapprochement include anger, ownership, and saying no. Anger is used to help distinguish between self and others and helps the child define their own experiences from others. Ownership, or using the word *mine,* gives children a sense of responsibility. Using the word *no* gives children the power to make choices, to separate what they do not like, and to protect themselves.

Parents can help their children through these transitions by setting realistic limits on behaviors that are firm and consistent, without spoiling their enthusiasm. Healthy boundaries allow children to grow and learn from their mistakes by creating a sense of autonomy. There may also be some instances in which healthy boundary development is interrupted and can lead to unhealthy boundaries. Some occurrences may result from overcontrol, lack of consistent limits, withdrawal of love, and trauma or abuse.

Structural Family Therapy

Structural family therapy focuses on boundaries and hierarchy in families. These therapists focus on the often unspoken rules that govern family interactions and functioning. They conceptualize families as organized by subsystems whose interactions are regulated by interpersonal boundaries. Subsystems are based on generation, gender, and/or function (e.g., parental subsystem or child subsystem) that are established through boundaries. Interpersonal boundaries can vary and range from rigid, to clear, to diffuse.

The three different boundaries lay on a continuum and range from more restrictive to less restrictive. Rigid boundaries permit little contact with internal and/or outside subsystems, and are restrictive. These boundaries often lead to disengagement (distance in relationships) or disengaged subsystems that are isolated. Disengagement limits affection or support but can foster autonomy. Disengaged parents may be unaware that their child is struggling or having difficulties until the problem is advanced. On the other end from disengagement is enmeshment (excessive closeness), caused by diffuse boundaries. Diffuse boundaries allow too much contact and interference from other subsystems. Enmeshed subsystems offer too much closeness, which can hinder initiative so that family members become too dependent on one another. For example, enmeshed parents may interfere with their child's ability to solve her own problems, which can stunt the child's development.

The goal of structural family therapy is directed at altering the family structure so as to enable the family to solve its own problems. For enmeshed families, the designs of interventions are used to strengthen boundaries and allow for more autonomy. For disengaged families, interventions are aimed at challenging conflict avoidance to break down walls between members. Some of the interventions used include highlighting and modifying interactions, challenging unproductive assumptions, boundary-making, and unbalancing (see Structural Family Therapy in this encyclopedia). In order to achieve lasting change, the rules and limits that govern the entire family structure or subsystems need to be considered.

Setting Healthy Boundaries

Setting healthy boundaries starts with good communication and knowing how one wants to change the rules of a relationship. Healthy boundaries should allow for appropriate levels of trust, flexibility for growth and development, being able to challenge those who violate boundaries, and respecting others. Maintaining healthy boundaries in relationships includes being able to clearly identify and communicate wants and needs, being able to trust in one's own decisions, and being open to being influenced by others and negotiating aspects of boundaries that meet someone else's needs (when appropriate).

Boundaries can also become a problem if they allow too much closeness, resulting in enmeshment, or keep people too distant, resulting in disengagement. Healthy boundaries are flexible, safe, and connected. Needs for closeness and distance change across the course of individual and family development. For example, a toddler naturally needs more closeness, regulation, and direction than does a young adult. Healthy boundaries help maintain an appropriate level of connectedness and autonomy across time.

Cathleen Klomes

See also Assertiveness; Communication in Couples and Families; Healthy Marriage and Responsible Fatherhood; Parent–Child Communication; Structural Family Therapy

Further Readings

Cloud, H., & Townsend, J. (1992). *Boundaries.* Grand Rapids, MI: Zondervan.

Johnson, P., & Waldo, M. (1998). Integrating Minuchin's boundary continuum and Bowen's differentiation scale: A curvilinear representation. *Contemporary Family Therapy: An International Journal, 20*(3), 403–413. doi:10.1023/A:1022429332033

Mesch, G. S. (2006). Family relations and the Internet: Exploring a family boundaries approach. *Journal of Family Communication, 6*(2), 119–138. doi:10.1207/s15327698jfc0602_2

Minuchin, S. (1974). *Families and family therapy.* Cambridge, MA: Harvard University Press.

Minuchin, S. (1982). Reflections on boundaries. *American Journal of Orthopsychiatry, 52*(4), 655–663. doi:10.1111/j.1939-0025.1982.tb01455.x

Najavits, L. (2002). *Seeking safety.* New York, NY: Guilford.

Nichols, M. P. (2013). *Family therapy: Concepts and methods* (10th ed.). Boston, MA: Pearson Education.

Perosa, S. L., & Perosa, L. M. (1993). Relationships among Minuchin's structural family model, identity achievement, and coping style. *Journal of Counseling Psychology, 40*(4), 479–489. doi:10.1037/0022-0167.40.4.479

Shiau, S. (2008). A review of boundary issues in counseling: Multiple roles and responsibilities. *Counseling and Values, 52*(2), 172–174. doi:10.1002/j.2161-007X.2008.tb00100.x

Bowen Family Systems Theory

Bowen family systems theory is a theory of human interaction that focuses on families as an emotional unit connected within and across generations. Murray Bowen, the creator of this theory, believed emotional anxiety heightens patterns of interaction in the nuclear family (family members that grew up in a household together) and throughout the interconnected web of family relationships. How well people cope with emotional anxiety and how much they are negatively influenced by the larger family is described by the concept of *differentiation of self*. This term, along with seven other major concepts and systems theory, make up the bulk of Bowen's approach. Bowen's theory has been influential in the field of marriage and family and couples therapy, and genograms, a visual assessment tool for looking at intergenerational patterns, have been used across behavioral and medical professions to understand family functioning. This entry presents the history and major concepts of Bowen family systems theory, and describes the nature of therapeutic interventions based on Bowen's principles.

Theoretical Foundations

Bowen, a psychiatrist, integrated ideas from biology, systems theory, evolution, and family research to create a comprehensive theory of family functioning. Bowen focuses on intergenerational processes and related kinship ties and social structures. Although Bowen's approach can be broken down into eight major concepts, it centers around two opposing forces: togetherness and individuality. In Bowenian terms, it can be viewed as the tension between fusion and differentiation. Fusion and differentiation are both intrapersonal and interpersonal concepts. Fusion represents the blurring of boundaries between the thinking, feeling, and emotional systems within a person and the boundaries between people. The more blurred those boundaries are, the more fusion there is and less differentiation of self. The more differentiation of self, the clearer the boundaries within a person and between people. Clear boundaries between people represent a balance of togetherness and individuality. Someone can think and act independently while still being connected to others—what is sometimes called interdependent.

Bowen extrapolated many of his ideas based on his knowledge of biology, evolution, and the brain. He utilized the idea of the triune brain as a model of evolution and functioning. This model was proposed by the physician and neuroscientist Paul D. MacLean. In this theory the human brain is seen as having three different parts: reptilian, paleomammalian, and neomammalian. The reptilian complex (reptilian brain), responsible for species-typical instinctual behaviors, tends to categorize things as all or nothing, black or white, safe or dangerous. The reptilian brain is somewhat simplistic and is often activated by anxiety or stress. When activated, this part of the brain overrides higher-order thinking and restricts a person's repertoire of responses. The second part of the brain, the paleomammalian complex (mammalian brain), is believed to have evolved later than the reptilian complex but still relatively early in brain development, and oversees many of humans' instinctual behaviors related to feeding, reproduction, and parenting. The third part of the brain, the neomammalian complex (neocortex), is a structure found in higher mammals and is involved in perception, language, and abstract thinking. While this model has fallen out of favor in explaining brain function because it is not complex enough to accurately explain them, it can be used as a simplified model of the brain. Bowen used MacLean's model to understand individuals and their connections to others.

Bowen believed individuals are influenced by three systems: emotionality (reptilian brain), feeling (mammalian brain), and thinking (neocortex). The first two parts of the brain are more instinctual in that they are reactive and do not require forethought. If an object comes hurtling toward someone's eye, the person's automatic instinct is to blink and move his or her head. There isn't forethought—it's an instinctual response. Bowen believed that family emotional systems, over time, develop their own "family instincts." These instincts are activated by emotional anxiety in relationships, and then families react based on patterns of interaction that have evolved in their families over generations. The thinking part of one's brain, unlike the first two parts, is not instinctual. This part of the brain involves forethought, intention, planning, and self-reflection. It is this part of the brain that allows people to plan for the future, think about their influence on others, learn from experiences, analyze their own behaviors, consider multiple alternatives, regulate feelings, and modify behavior. The more someone is able to access and act from his or her "thinking brain," the more differentiated one is from the influence of his or her reptilian and mammalian brain and the pull of negative family patterns—and therefore the less they are influenced to act instinctually when faced with emotional anxiety. People with higher levels of differentiation are connected to their families, but not controlled by them.

Although Bowen, in his initial view of human interaction, viewed rationality (thinking) as the most important, a more modern view is that thinking and feeling are both important and inform one another. Emotionality, in this view, is not the same as "feelings." Emotionality represents automatic reactions, whereas feelings represent sadness, joy, anger, fear, excitement, surprise, and other experiential states that serve to motivate human behavior and human bonding. Feelings give a context to decision-making and help prioritize choices.

Major Concepts

Differentiation

Anxiety is a fact of life, and Bowen's approach, rather than trying to extinguish emotional anxiety, is more about helping individuals and families to be able to act from the thinking system in the face of anxiety. Increasing one's level of differentiation means increasing what Bowen called the *basic self* and decreasing the *pseudo-self*. The basic self is the core of who someone is, regardless of influence from others, a specific context, or emotional anxiety. It is comprised of someone's principles, priorities, and thought-out ideas. The more differentiated one is, the more one makes decisions from the basic self without fear and anxiety. The pseudo-self is the part of oneself that is more open to being changed based on guilt, fear, anger, or familial expectations. Operating from the basic self does not mean that one does not take others' ideas and feelings into account; rather, it analyzes and perhaps integrates these based on its congruence with one's basic self.

Emotional Triangles

A two-person system is called a *dyad,* and a three-person system is called a *triad* or *triangle.* Dyadic relationships tend to be unstable and will sometimes draw in a third person to stabilize the system. When there is anxiety in a system, having more people in the system allows the anxiety to be spread over more people. So a two-person system may bring in a third; and a triangle, when overwhelmed by anxiety, may spread the anxiety over a series of interlocking triangles. While a triangle or interlocking triangles may temporarily reduce anxiety by having it shared by more people, it also prevents people from having direct communication, direct conflict resolution, and more intimately connected relationships. Families with lower levels of differentiation tend to use triangles as a way of addressing emotional anxiety. Families with higher levels of differentiation tend to stay connected to family members directly and resolve tension in relationships directly with one another.

Nuclear Family Emotional Process

When families have to contend with prolonged periods of tension they tend to develop one of four ways of addressing that tension: couple conflict, dysfunction in one partner, impairment in one or more of the children, and emotional distance. When one of these patterns is deployed and remains in effect for extended periods of time, symptoms are likely to occur in the family. Couple conflict causes distance between partners as they try to control each other and escape the control of the other. Dysfunction in one partner occurs when the subordinate partner accommodates the relationship so much that he or she eventually manifests psychological, medical, or social problems. When partners focus their anxiety on one or more of their children, then that child will usually experience problems; the more intense the focus, the more intense the symptoms. Finally, sometimes people utilize emotional distance to manage relational tension. When people distance themselves, they risk becoming isolated from resources. In addition, the more one family member distances from their relationships, the more pressure there is for others who are more connected to absorb relational anxiety.

Family Projection Process

Family projection process describes the ways in which parents project their emotional vulnerabilities onto children. When a child is overly focused on, then he or she is less free to explore the world and relationships free from a parent or caretaker. The child grows up being prone to relational problems that will heighten their vulnerability to the effects of chronic emotional anxiety, and they will develop lower levels of differentiation.

Multigenerational Transmission Process

The multigenerational transmission process describes how levels of differentiation are passed down from generation to generation. People pick partners at similar levels of differentiation, even if on the surface the partners look different. These partners then project their levels of differentiation onto their children. Children who are overly focused on will have a lower level of differentiation than those who are not overly focused on. This helps explain small differences in levels of differentiation between parents and children and between siblings. Over generations the level of differentiation gets magnified. The family line with slightly higher levels of differentiation will undergo a marked increase in differentiation over the generations, and the family line with a slightly lower level of differentiation will experience a marked decrease in differentiation over generations.

Emotional Cutoff

Emotional cutoff is a pattern for managing unresolved emotional anxiety. It is an extreme form of distancing whereby contact with family members is either stopped or greatly reduced. Cutting off from family members may temporarily reduce anxiety, but it does not resolve the family patterns creating the emotional anxiety. These patterns get repeated with others and put more pressure on the relationships the person has left. Emotional cutoff is not an effective long-term resolution for emotional anxiety.

Sibling Position

Bowen became convinced, on the basis of Walter Toman's research, that people born into particular sibling positions (oldest, middle, or youngest) displayed certain behavior patterns and characteristics. Oldest children tend to be in charge and leaders, youngest tend to be followers and want their needs attended to, and middle children may exhibit characteristics of both oldest and youngest children. Based on these ideas, partners work best when there are two people in complementary positions. For instance, an oldest child married to a youngest child probably works better than two oldest children marrying.

Societal Emotional Process

A family is just one level of a system. There are larger systems, such as communities and societies. Bowen believed his ideas about families can also be applied to larger systems. Bowen saw society as a large family with its own multigenerational transmission process, and society has its own ways of dealing with emotional anxiety. In times of high emotional anxiety, society can develop social problems and symptoms.

Interventions

In Bowen family systems theory the main goal of therapeutic work is to reduce emotional anxiety and help individuals and families raise their level of differentiation. Interventions are aimed at coaching family members to recognize unhelpful family patterns, act from their thinking system, de-triangle, remain connected, increase their basic self, and increase their level of differentiation. All of these goals are interconnected and influence one another and one's ability to increase differentiation. Bowen helped people to recognize and change their own part in family patterns and coached them how to break free of a family's natural propensity to bring individuals back into family patterns. In Bowen family systems theory, genograms (diagrams of family trees) are used to visually represent families, their relationships, and typical family patterns. Genograms help the therapist hypothesize about family strengths and damaging patterns, and help clients to recognize family patterns. In addition, Bowen asked questions during therapy in a way to keep emotional anxiety low and coached family members to practice in the "real world" what they learned in therapy. He approached relationships in a calm, objective way in order to keep emotional reactivity low in sessions. He wanted clients to feel cared for and connected to him within the context of low reactivity and objectivity. It was his hope to teach this same style to clients in their own dealings with relationships outside of therapy.

Shannon B. Dermer

See also Affect Regulation; Anxiety; Circumplex Model; Contextual Family Therapy; Differentiation; General Systems Theory; Genograms

Further Readings

Bowen, M. (1993). *Family therapy in clinical practice.* Lanham, MD: Rowman & Littlefield. (Original work published 1978, Northvale, NJ: Jason Aronson)

Brown, J. (1999). Bowen family systems theory and practice: Illustration and critique. *Australian and New Zealand Journal of Family Therapy, 20*(2), 94–103.

Kerr, M., & Bowen, M. (1988). *Family evaluation: An approach based on Bowen theory.* New York, NY: W. W. Norton.

McGoldrick, M., Gerson, R., & Petry, S. S. (2008). *Genograms: Assessment and intervention.* New York, NY: W. W. Norton.

Titelman, P. (1998). *Clinical applications of Bowen family systems theory.* Binghamton, NY: Haworth.

Brief Adlerian Couples Therapy

Alfred Adler is the founder of individual psychology, a theory for understanding human development and a holistic and systemic approach to psychotherapy. Through this strength-based model, Adler did not view people with symptoms as sick, but instead conceptualized them as discouraged and in need of encouragement. The concept of the individual in individual psychology is not meant to emphasize individualism. Rather, Adler suggested humans are indivisible and cannot be understood by reducing them to separated parts. He emphasized the importance of understanding people in terms of their whole complex self in the context of their social relationships and environment. These principles of understanding individuals within their systemic context are applied with couples by understanding the social dynamics and patterns of the couple, encouraging their strengths, and educating the couple on cooperation and communication skills.

Alfred Adler

Alfred Adler was born in 1870 in a suburb of Vienna. He was raised in a middle-class Jewish family, the second of six children. He had several health issues growing up. He suffered from rickets, which delayed his walking ability, and he almost died of pneumonia when he was 5 years old. His older brother was strong and athletic, which highlighted Adler's frailty. When Alfred was only 3 years old, his younger brother died, and this event, Adler later recalled, was a factor that influenced his intention to become a doctor. Although Adler performed poorly in school and was discouraged by his teachers to continue his academic studies, his father urged him to pursue his dreams of becoming a doctor. Adler completed his medical degree, despite these early challenges, at the University of Vienna.

Adler began working with Sigmund Freud at the Vienna Psychoanalytic Society; however, he soon left the organization once he recognized the fundamental differences in philosophy he held about human development compared to Freud. Freud concentrated on psychosexual development and the significant influence of the unconscious. Alternatively, Adler viewed human development through a psychosocial lens. While he believed the past may impact individuals' current patterns, he believed people were capable of choosing and making changes in their life. He founded the Society for Free Psychoanalytic Study on these humanistic principles. He wrote and taught across Europe and the United States on social and political issues, promoting social reform and equity. He educated teachers and parents on child development, parenting, and discipline methods. He also advocated for marital and premarital counseling. Sophie Lazarsfeld, Olga Knopf, Rudolf Dreikurs, and Danica Deutsch were early writers who continued Adler's work regarding the topic of couples counseling.

Basic Tenets

The principles of individual psychology, which is a holistic systems approach and assumes that individuals need to be understood in context of their social relationships, lend to understanding the system of a couple. Adler asserted that every person has an innate capacity and tendency for *social interest*. He described social interest as caring for others, being considerate and responsive to social needs above the individual's own needs, and the ability to understand what another person is experiencing. This social interest extends beyond individual relationships to the community and the sense of belonging with that community. The sense of responsibility to live cooperatively and improve the community is associated with social interest. While Adler believed social interest was innate, he suggested that it is nurtured by the social context. Marriage and forming intimate relationships are methods of exercising and developing this social interest.

Adler maintained that all behavior has purpose and is goal directed. He assumed that individuals in the couple each contribute to the system in ways that will either promote the relationship or create dissonance or conflict. For the Adlerian therapist, behavior is not viewed in terms of pathology but is assessed in how useful it is for the individuals or their relationship. The problem behaviors the couples describe are understood as creative, yet perhaps ineffective, ways the individuals have been attempting to get their needs met.

Adler also emphasized personal responsibility. He believed the past does influence current choices, but he also highlighted that in the present, the couple has the ability and is accountable to choose new behaviors and create new perceptions.

Lifestyle and Private Logic

In order to understand the intentions and goals of behaviors, Adler proposed it was necessary to understand individuals' *lifestyles*. The *lifestyle*, or *style of life*, consists of the cognitive, emotional, and behavioral patterns that make up the individuals' approach toward life, others, and their orientation to the world. It is shaped by early experiences in individuals' family of origin. These perceptions create a lens for meaning-making. Individuals with adaptive lifestyles feel courage to engage in life's tasks and strive for goals. Individuals with maladaptive and less effective lifestyles feel discouraged and may withdraw from life's tasks. Adler recognized that individuals hold *private logic* as part of this lifestyle. This private logic is the hidden cognitive assumptions, attitudes, and beliefs of the individual and shapes how they interpret situations and others' intents.

Each individual in a couple approaches the relationship from this unique lifestyle and private logic. These expectations create unspoken marital rules that are helpful or destructive for the relationship. Conflict may also arise as the couple attempts to negotiate getting their needs met from these divergent perspectives. The meaning and expectations couples ascribe to a situation are important, as they will influence their choices on how to respond. Uncovering this meaning is an important part of the work of Adlerian therapists.

Adler explored different factors that could impact a person's lifestyle and private logic. Society's messages such as "happily ever after" themes in fairy tales create unrealistic expectations for relationships. Individuals can also develop basic mistakes as part of their lifestyle. These basic mistakes can be overgeneralizations, impossible goals of security, misperceptions about life's demands, minimization of one's worth, or faulty values.

Attending to this lens and the meaning individuals make about their partner's behavior is important when working with couples.

Family Constellation and Birth Order

The family constellation consists of the members, structure, and relationship dynamics of the clients' families of origin. The purpose of assessing this information is to understand the place the clients hold in their family and the social context for behavioral patterns that were established in childhood. These early interactions and family structures can be influenced by culture, gender, and family alliances, and contribute to the development of the individuals' lifestyles by becoming a paradigm for future relationships.

Adler suggested individuals' birth order was significant in understanding the roles they played in their families of origin. These roles have significant influence on the individuals' perceptions of the world and their patterns in their current relationship. For example, first-born children are given a lot of attention when they are the only child and may feel resentment when the second child is born. First-born children tend to be responsible, respectful of rules, perfectionists, and focused on achievement. If the oldest child helped take care of younger siblings, he or she may take on a caretaker role in their adult relationships. The second child does not receive the same attention the first child received and may feel rivalry with the first sibling. They may choose different interests or behaviors from the first-born in order to avoid competition and comparison. Middle children may feel out of place in the family system and may be envious of their siblings. Middle children are often peacemakers. Youngest children recapture the special attention of the family and are often pampered by their parents. Last-born children tend to be easygoing, adventurous, and charming. Only children have similarities with first-born children, except they have never experienced being dethroned by a sibling or had to compete for attention. They also tend to be perfectionists and demanding of themselves.

Mistaken Goals

Given that Adler believed that all behavior had a purpose and intent, Rudolf Dreikurs developed four goals that describe the motivation behind children's misbehavior, including attention, power, revenge, and proving inadequacy. These intents are mistaken goals, because as children attempt to achieve attention or power through their behavior, they inadvertently decrease their social interest. These early mistaken goals can result in creating long-term patterns that influence their adult relationship dynamics later. For example, a child who had a mistaken goal of power may express intense anger in an attempt to gain power in their adult relationship. An Adlerian therapist assists couples in exploring these old patterns, becoming cognizant of how they are attempting to get their needs met, and explores alternate ways that are more effective and constructive for the relationship.

Inferiority and Superiority

Adler posited that all people have feelings of inferiority as a result of being born dependent on others and in bodies that are vulnerable. Children also evaluate themselves against others and assess a deficiency in comparison. He suggested a major goal of human behavior is to overcome feelings of inferiority by attempting to gain competence or superiority. Adler did not use the term *superiority* to mean being superior to another; rather, he saw it as a motivation for seeking perfection, mastery, and significance. While this striving for superiority is a healthy goal, it can impact relationships in an unhealthy way. For example, in order to gain superiority, a partner may assert dominance or use manipulation to gain power over the partner.

Adler identified how cultural expectations and gender roles can impact these dynamics. For example, he discussed the *masculine protest,* which is the false belief portrayed in the culture that men are superior to women. Both men and women may internalize this belief as part of their lifestyle and relate with each other from the perspective that men must be strong and women should be obedient. Adlerian therapists seek to identify these underlying beliefs and encourage the couple to relate on more equal terms and challenge these internalized beliefs about the imbalanced gender roles.

Life Tasks

Adler described three life tasks as areas where people engage in life. These tasks include work, friendship, and love. He did not view these tasks as only benefiting the individual, but saw them as a way to exercise social interest as well. For example, work tasks benefit the individual by providing a means to make money for survival. Concurrently, the role also has value for others by providing a service to the community. In the same way, marriage is not only for creating an intimate bond with another individual, but also a way that people can live and work in society and give to their community. Later Adlerian theorists added developing a sense of self, spiritual and existential efforts, and parenting to the list of life tasks. Adler believed that people with courage and a willingness to take risks will engage in these life tasks, while others may withdraw from or avoid them.

Healthy Relationships

Adlerian therapists conceptualize healthy relationships as having certain characteristics. A primary goal of therapy is to promote social interest in the relationship. Individuals in a healthy relationship are responsible for their own choices in the relationship. They do not expect their partner to give them a sense of their self-esteem. They have communication skills that allow them to seek understanding and express empathy. They resolve conflicts respectfully, cooperatively, expressing feelings honestly, and considering both partners' needs. Partners in healthy relationships also balance togetherness and closeness by honoring the dyad, yet also maintain a sense of separateness where both individuals are valued. Healthy couples are attracted to each other physically, but also engage together collaboratively in all aspects of life, including financial, intellectual, spiritual, and emotional. Regarding the power dynamics, Adlerian therapists will encourage equal power between the partners and recommend avoiding behaviors that dominate or manipulate. They encourage couples to develop a cooperative stance and build skills that are in line with this attitude.

Stages of Couples Therapy

Adlerian therapists work with couples through four stages of counseling: relationship-building, assessment, interpretation and insight, and reorientation. During the relationship-building stage, therapists explore the presenting problem and the history of the problem. Therapists want to know what brought them to counseling now. During this process there is also a focus on instilling hope, communicating empathy, and exploring resources and strengths of the couple.

The second stage begins with assessing the couple and their dynamics. This process begins before the first session, with couples filling out inventories that gather initial perceptions of the problem. During the first session, therapists ask questions about their history and the current functioning of the relationship. For example, what is currently happening in the relationship, how does each person feel about the relationship, and how is each individual approaching their life tasks? The goal is to understand the dyad's system, their patterns of relating, the individuals' lifestyles, and their strengths and assets. Therapists should ask about how the problem has developed and how it has been maintained, how each individual has contributed to the problem or helped in its resolution, and how their lives would be different if the problem did not exist. The lifestyle inventory can also be used in order to gather these dynamics.

During the interpretation and insight stage, the couple's patterns and dynamics and the purpose of the presenting problems are understood. Couples gain awareness about the unspoken marital rules and values that are impacting their behavior. They recognize underlying forces in their private logic and interactional patterns. By becoming more aware of these values and beliefs, the couple can increase their options of responding and can take the responsibility to make new choices. The counselor will use confrontations and notice discrepancies between choices the individuals make and how they hinder the relationship. The therapist will reframe the individuals' behavior in terms of their basic mistakes as attempts to get their needs met. This perspective shifts away from previously held assumptions that the individuals' behaviors are meant to hurt their partner.

During the reorientation stage, the focus is on action. The counselor teaches skills of communication, perspective-taking, encouragement, and cooperation. The therapist encourages the partners to take responsibility for their own behavior and to take the risk to implement these new skills from a perspective of respect and equality. The counselor also observes strengths and encourages the couple to notice these in each other as well.

Interventions

There are several interventions that practitioners of brief Adlerian couples therapy will use throughout the four stages of therapy.

- *Early Recollections:* Exploring early memories of childhood is a tool for recognizing the couple's individual lifestyles and private logic. By revisiting these early recollections, the therapist and couple gain clues as to what is influencing how they approach life and contributing to their current relationship patterns. Therapists explore these memories by asking the clients to recall one of their earliest memories. They also identify what was the most vivid part and the feelings associated with that aspect.
- *Individual Lifestyle Assessment:* This assessment also explores the couple's lifestyles by identifying expectations and beliefs that may hinder or encourage the relationship. Hidden attitudes about needing to be in control, be perfect, or be pleasing can impact the choices the individuals make in the relationship. The effort and price of trying to maintain these needs often come at the expense of the other partner.
- *Couple Enrichment:* Given the emphasis on education and skill-building, several couple enrichment programs have been developed using Adlerian principles. These programs are devised to build greater awareness on the part of the couple, improve the quality of their relationship, and provide instructions in a group format on topics such as expressing emotions in a respectful and clear manner. The groups emphasize identifying strengths and resources and use experiential practice. G. Hugh Allred and Thomas Graff developed the *Couple Handbook for Effective Communication* (CHEC), which uses exercises to apply Adlerian concepts in a six-week program. Clair Hawes developed the Couples Growing Together (CGT) program, which consists of eight weeks of sessions to develop awareness of the couple's interactions and their relationship system. Don Dinkmeyer and Jon Carlson developed Training in Marriage Enrichment (TIME), which focuses on taking responsibility, encouragement, building communication skills, and learning conflict resolution skills over 10 weeks.
- *Catching Oneself:* Adlerian therapists will assign homework to the couple to "catch themselves" engaging in the behavior that is not effective. By anticipating and identifying the old habits, the couple become more aware of the behavior and can make a new choice to change it.
- *Switching Roles:* The technique of switching roles asks the individuals to take their partner's opposing perspective in the discussion. While conversing in a thoughtful way from this opposite position, the partners gain insight into the other person's emotions, which in turn, builds empathy.
- *Paradoxical Interventions:* Adler discussed using paradoxical interventions with clients, which is the process of the therapist taking an unexpected position of joining the clients in their ineffective behaviors, rather than trying to encourage them to change. The counselor asks the clients to experiment by continuing the old behaviors in an amplified way. Through this process, couples will often become more aware of how unconstructive the behavior is and stop putting effort into continuing it.

Limitations

Brief Adlerian couples therapy has been criticized because of its focus on the past, and some clients may not give credence or want to make the connection between past dynamics and what is currently happening in the relationship. Brief Adlerian couples therapy is suited for people from various cultures, since it considers the whole background of the person, including the cultural and social context. The emphasis on social interest also merges well with collectivist cultures that place value on the interdependence of people and assign greater value to family and community than to oneself. Conversely, Adlerian therapists may not meet the expectations of people from cultures that desire or expect a counselor to take the expert role. These clients may benefit from education about the counseling process and the role of the therapist.

Sonya Lorelle

See also Adlerian Family Therapy; Adlerian Open-Forum Family Counseling; Family of Origin; Holism

Further Readings

Ansbacher, H. L., & Ansbacher, R. R. (Eds.). (1956). *The individual psychology of Alfred Adler: A systematic presentation in selections from his writings.* New York, NY: Harper Torchbooks.

Carlson, J., & Dinkmeyer, D. S. (1999). Couple therapy. In R. E. Watts & J. Carlson (Eds.), *Interventions and strategies in counseling and psychotherapy* (pp. 87–99). Philadelphia, PA: Accelerated Development.

Carlson, J., & Dinkmeyer, D. (2003). *Time for a better marriage.* Atascadero, CA: Impact.

Carlson, J., & Maniacci, M. (2012) *Alfred Adler revisited.* New York, NY: Routledge.

Carlson, J. D., & Slavik, S. (1997) *Techniques in Adlerian psychology.* Philadelphia, PA: Taylor and Francis.

Carlson, J. D., Watts, R. E., & Maniacci, M. (2005). *Adlerian psychotherapy.* Washington, DC: American Psychological Association.

Englar-Carlson, M., & Carlson, J. (2012). Adlerian couple's therapy: The case of the boxer's daughter and the momma's boy. In D. S. Shepard & M. Harway (Eds.), *Engaging men in couples therapy* (pp. 81–103). New York, NY: Routledge.

Hoffman, E. (1994). *The drive for self: Alfred Adler and the founding of Individual Psychology.* Reading, MA: Addison-Wesley.

Hooper, A., & Holford, J. (1998). *Adler for beginners.* New York, NY: Writers and Readers Publishing.

Mosak, H., & Maniacci, M. (1999.) *A primer of Adlerian psychology: The analytic-behavioral-cognitive psychology of Alfred Adler.* New York, NY: Brunner/Routledge.

Robey, P. A., & Carlson, J. (2011). Adlerian therapy with couples. In D. K. Carson & M. Casado-Kehoe (Eds.), *Case studies in couple's therapy: Theory-based approaches* (pp. 41–51). New York, NY: Routledge.

Slavik, S., & Carlson, J. (2005). *Readings in the theory of Adlerian psychology.* New York, NY: Routledge.

BRIEF FAMILY THERAPY

Brief family therapy, more commonly known as brief therapy, did not evolve out of an earlier, longer-term family therapy approach; rather, it was one of the originating orientations of the field. Primarily associated with the model developed at the Mental Research Institute (MRI) in Palo Alto, California, in the 1960s, brief therapy is sometimes used more encompassingly to refer also to Jay Haley's strategic therapy, Steve de Shazer and Insoo Kim Berg's solution-focused brief family therapy (SFBFT), and the work of the Milan team. This entry concentrates primarily on the contributions of the MRI clinicians, but when relevant, it explores conceptual and practice-based connections to the other brief models.

History

The beginnings of brief therapy can be traced to a research project. Between 1952 and 1962, Gregory Bateson led a research team—consisting of John Weakland and Jay Haley, with William Fry and Don Jackson as consultants—in Palo Alto that was devoted to understanding multilevel communicational complexities in a variety of phenomena, including humor, schizophrenia, play, family interaction, and hypnosis.

In 1955, two members of the team, Haley and Weakland, initiated an investigation of hypnosis by contacting Milton Erickson, a Phoenix-based psychiatrist who, at the time, was the most respected medical hypnotist in the country. Their exploration of Erickson's approach continued for several years, facilitating their incorporation of Erickson's methods in their own developing therapy practices, and inspiring Haley to write several books about Erickson's work, including *Uncommon Therapy*.

In 1958, Don Jackson, wanting to support and participate in a continuation of the Bateson group's research focus, founded the Mental Research Institute. Bateson and his wife, Lois, and Haley, Weakland, and Fry were all initially involved in different capacities, and soon Jackson brought on Virginia Satir, Richard Fisch, and Paul Watzlawick. In 1965, Fisch proposed the launching of a research project into a brief approach to family therapy. Using communicational ideas gleaned from the Bateson project and therapeutic strategies and interventions derived from Erickson's work, the brief therapy team at MRI articulated an approach to intervention that was time limited, goal directed, strategically oriented, and change focused. The therapeutic principles they established and the practices they developed, known as the MRI model, were broadly influential, and the developers of the model were personally helpful in mentoring others, including the Milan team in Italy and Steve de Shazer in Milwaukee.

Organizing Principles

The developers of the brief model articulated several foundational assumptions about the nature of communication, problems, and problem resolution that gave rise to or provided theoretical support for a variety of innovative therapeutic practices, discussed below.

Communication

Bateson asserted that "you can't not communicate." The double-negative structure of this claim underscores the fact that in any relationship, everything said and done, as well as everything not said and not done, serves to communicate something to the other(s). The attempt to negate or deny or avoid communication is inevitably just another form of communication.

Paradox

Communication is inherently multileveled. One statement can be *about* another (e.g., "When you say that, I feel sad"), and nonverbal gestures (e.g., a raised eyebrow or a rueful smile) similarly convey information *about* the verbal statements that precede or accompany them. Thus, not only do we communicate, but we also *metacommunicate*—that is, we send verbal and nonverbal messages that comment on or classify other messages.

Another way multiple levels are generated is through self-reference, which inevitably produces paradox. For example, the statement "I am lying" classifies itself. If the claim is true—that is, if the person is truly lying—then, by virtue of being true, it is false. And if it is a lie that the person is lying, then the statement is true. Which makes it false. And so on.

The MRI group took such complexities seriously, recognizing, for example, the paradoxical results of one person's demand for another to act in a spontaneous manner. Consider, for example, the effect of a person saying to his or her spouse, "I want you to tell me you love me, but not because I'm telling you to do so." Any purposeful effort on the part of the spouse to comply with such an injunction will paradoxically undermine itself; compliant or obedient spontaneity is an oxymoron. Such paradoxical dilemmas can create great suffering; indeed, the Bateson project specifically investigated how painful relationship paradoxes—what they termed *double binds*—contribute to severe mental distress. However, as will be discussed later in this entry, brief and strategic therapists have also recognized the potential of using therapeutic paradoxes or double binds for inspiring change.

Context

The context within which a communication is experienced classifies the communication and thus determines its meaning. For example, a husband's understanding of his wife's telling him "I love you" will vary tremendously, depending on whether (a) they've just had great sex; (b) they've just had disappointing sex; (c) he has just told her he's been having an affair; (d) she has just told him she's been having an affair; (e) she's pointing a gun at him; (f) she's just given birth to their baby. Bateson proposed the metaphor of *frame* as a way of characterizing the defining nature of context. Put an ordinary household item inside a frame—say, as part of an assemblage, as Pablo Picasso and the Cubists did—and put the framed item inside an art gallery, and the item takes on an entirely different meaning. It becomes, as a result of this framing, this contextualizing, an *objet trouvé*—a "found object" work of art. This recognition of the importance of contexts or frames gave rise to the therapeutic idea, which will be discussed below, that a change of frame—a *reframe*—can have reverberating effects on the way a symptom is understood and experienced.

Problems

From a communicational perspective, a problem can only be made sense of within the context(s) informing how it is being experienced. Thus, rather than defining problems in terms of the reified categories found in the American Psychiatric Association's *Diagnostic and Statistical Manual* (DSM), brief therapists attend to the interactive context within which a person suffers. What has the person and his or her significant others been doing in response to the problem? How have they been trying to alleviate, control, or eliminate it? Such a contextual approach allows the recognition that many of the symptoms that bring people to therapy begin as everyday life difficulties that escalate into intractable problems as a result of their best attempts to fix them. Thus, therapeutic interventions must address not only the problem as distinguished in language (e.g., the client's "panic attacks" or a couple's "fighting"), but also the interactive efforts to do something about it.

Patterns of Interaction

The medical model wisely directs clinicians to intervene only after they've correctly diagnosed the illness or disease afflicting the body of the patient. Medical diagnosticians are highly valued, as their ability to isolate and locate the causes of bodily distress ensures that interventions are as targeted and potent as possible. Once the practitioner correctly diagnoses, say, cancer or diabetes or Lyme disease, precise treatment protocols can follow. However, in the world of mind, where emotional and psychological problems prevail, the medical model becomes highly problematic, for it is blind to the complexities of reflexivity and interaction. A woman, for example, may not only feel anxious, but also feel anxious *about* feeling anxious. And any anxious efforts she mounts to control her mounting anxiety will of course contribute still more anxiety to the mix. It is in this way that problems tend to self-referentially escalate. More complexity is added when other people get involved in trying to help. A man, for example, will not only feel angry, but will also feel angry that his partner is angry at him for displaying his anger. He may also feel sad and desperately repentant when the partner threatens to leave in response to what the man proclaimed during their angry exchange.

Sensitive to such relational complexities, brief therapists avoid trying to establish diagnosable causes of such distress, focusing their curiosity instead on the *patterns of interaction* that play out within and between people when someone's attention is drawn to a difficulty of some kind. Whereas insight-oriented therapists try to establish the reasons *why* a symptom is present, believing that this will somehow be "curative," brief therapists attend to *how* a symptom is being maintained, directing their therapeutic interventions toward interrupting the patterns that relationally contextualize and constitute the suffering. When such patterns unravel, problems unravel.

Therapeutic Practices

Brief therapists' communicational orientation and interactional ideas inform their sensitivity to the way their clients are orienting to therapy, to the therapist, and to the possibility of change. They seek to determine early on in the first session who in a couple or family is invested in being in the therapist's office and who is not, and they assiduously avoid offering suggestions to anyone who is not a "customer" for change. Unlike those family therapists who require everyone in the family to attend every session, brief family therapists are comfortable working with only those members who decide it is important to come in. And because they don't want the clients' experience of the therapist to get in the way of their participation in therapy, they downplay their own knowledge and importance in the therapeutic enterprise, preferring instead to underscore the clients' expertise and resources. Adopting this nondefensive *one-down* position serves to help clients have an easier time of accepting and incorporating the therapist's suggestions.

Attending to Expectancy

Brief therapists don't presume to know what is best for their clients, so they work collaboratively with them to define where the clients are headed in therapy and how they will know that their goals have been reached. Many brief therapists also put an explicit cap on the total number of sessions at which they are willing to see their clients. The originators of the model at MRI put this limit at 10; others say no more than 20, and some practice single-session therapy and therefore put the cap at *one* session. HMOs prefer a session-limiting approach for cost-saving purposes; however, brief therapists take this position not out of a commitment to reduce insurance companies' health care spending but out of respect for their own and their clients' expectancy. By organizing everything that happens in terms of defined, time-limited goals, brief therapists help ensure that the sessions are efficient and more likely to produce discernable change.

Doing Something Different

Brief therapists typically adopt a minimalist approach to intervening. First establishing what the clients have been doing unsuccessfully to try to solve their problem, they take care not to contribute to more of the same. And recognizing that change depends on clients *doing something different*, they often encourage clients to conduct outside-of-session experiments (commonly called *homework assignments*). For example, a depressed man who has been failing to cheer himself up by diligently practicing positive affirmations throughout his day might be asked to find out what happens when he sets aside 15 minutes (but no more) every morning or evening (but not both) to becoming curious about and acknowledging the legitimacy of his sadness. It might be further suggested that he find a way to express his sadness in some meaningful but different way, perhaps through writing about it or painting it.

When brief therapists give such homework assignments, they take care to follow up the following week. Did the clients undertake the suggestion(s)? What happened? What differences, if any, have the clients been noticing in their experience since carrying out the experiment(s)? Such questions contribute to clients' expectations that change is possible, but they also help clients discern subtle changes that have the potential of increasing and intensifying. If what they did made a difference, then the therapist may suggest they continue with it; if it didn't make a difference or made things worse, then the therapist will explore alternative possibilities.

Reframing

Very often, clients' understanding of their problem changes as a result of their doing something different in response to it. However, sometimes a change in behavior is most easily introduced and enacted as a result of the therapist's recontextualizing or reframing the problem. For example, parents who view their son's refusal to go to school as the result of his being lazy will likely increase the intensity and frequency of their exhortations and punishments when they can't get him out the door in the morning. And when louder yelling and harsher consequences don't work, they may conclude that, in addition to being lazy, he is problematically oppositional.

If the parents bring their son to a brief therapist, he or she will likely normalize the child's truancy—commenting, perhaps, on how common it is among boys at this stage of brain and emotional development. Normalizing is a generic form of reframing that serves to depathologize the client's behavior; this would make it possible, in this case, for the parents to relax their ineffective solution attempts, and the son to relax his efforts to protect himself from their harsh reproaches. A further reframe might then be explored, with the therapist possibly determining, based on other information gathered in conversation with the family, that the son, far from being lazy, appears to be overly concerned about doing well. If this were accurate, then, afraid to fail, he might have found himself avoiding school in an effort to avoid disappointing his parents. With such a reframe in place, the parents quite easily would be able to forgo the yelling and punishments, encouraging him instead to improve his ability to "learn from mistakes." With the parents relating to him differently, and with the son not recoiling from their vociferous efforts to change him, returning to school could be accomplished painlessly.

Prescribing the Symptom

Brief therapists, along with strategic therapists, are noted for prescribing clients' symptoms as a means for helping them change. A woman who blushes excessively, worried about what people are thinking of her, might be asked to intentionally commit some public blunder that will draw previously unwanted attention. A young man who wets the bed at night might be directed to purposefully urinate on the sheets before falling asleep on them. Or a couple worried that their upcoming vacation will be marred, like many in the past, by a series of petty fights, might be asked to arrange a significant fight the first night of their trip. The therapist might add that the fight should be significant enough to require "really great make-up sex" the next morning; and with that precedent established, they should, whenever either of them feels amorous, arrange to create a spat so that another occasion for make-up sex—this time *before* the next morning—can follow. Such suggestions dramatically reframe the meaning of the fights, laying the foundation for a significant change in how the couple orients to "fighting."

Many brief therapists consider symptom prescription to be a species of paradoxical intervention, specifically what they term a "Be spontaneous!" paradox. Because symptoms, being unwanted and uncontrollable, always occur unintentionally, then, the reasoning goes, purposefully undertaking to create the symptom—blushing, wetting the bed, fighting—puts the client in a paradoxical situation, the result of which is often the nonoccurrence or disappearance of the symptom. Other brief therapists recognize the therapeutic benefits of prescribing the symptom, but they are less inclined to attribute the change to the transformative effects of paradox. Instead, they recognize that changing a strategy of effortful avoidance (trying so very hard not to blush, not to pee, not to fight) to one of effortless inclusion (encouraging blushing, peeing, fighting) meaningfully alters the pattern of interaction defining the problem. From this perspective, it is the shift in pattern that occasions the change.

Focusing on Exceptions

As the visionary behind the creation of solution-focused brief family therapy (SFBFT), Steve de Shazer made several important contributions to the field of brief family therapy. One of the most important was his recognition that therapists and clients can benefit greatly from directing their attention away from the problem and toward *exceptions to the problem*. He would have clients notice what they were doing when the problem wasn't occurring and then would direct them to do more of whatever that was. This shift in perspective is an excellent way of freeing clients up from continuing their unsuccessful attempts to solve their problem through efforts to control or expunge it.

Naive SFBFTs sometimes pridefully contrast their approach to the MRI model, claiming that whereas they themselves are concerned with solution-building, MRI therapists are, unfortunately, problem focused. In so doing, these naive therapists lump the MRI approach in with those models that espouse a thorough investigation of the etiology of a problem as a necessary precursor to any efforts at intervention. In fact, the SFBFT and MRI approaches are far more compatible than many people realize. De Shazer considered John Weakland, one of the prime architects of the MRI approach, to be an important mentor, and Weakland, an admirer of de Shazer and his innovations, endorsed the importance of attending to exceptions. Both men clearly recognized that if problems are understood in terms of interactive *patterns*, rather than as isolable entities, then variations in symptom expression will be inevitable.

Respecting Clients and the Process of Change

Brief therapists strive for a deeply empathic understanding of their clients' experience. Once they grasp how their clients are talking about and making sense of their predicament, they can offer interventions that fit the clients' language and respect their worldview. Recognizing, in keeping with the SFBFT therapist Eve Lipchik, that a "rush to be brief" can actually make therapy less efficient, they encourage clients to "take it slow," and they focus on introducing small shifts that can subsequently ramify throughout the patterns of interaction that have been keeping the problem in place.

Douglas Flemons

See also Homework Assignments in Therapy; Milan Team; Paradoxes and Paradoxical Intervention; Solution-Focused Brief Therapy; Strategic Family Therapy

Further Readings

Cade, B., & O'Hanlon, W. H. (1993). *A brief guide to brief therapy.* New York, NY: W. W. Norton.

De Shazer, S. (1982). *Patterns of brief family therapy.* New York, NY: Guilford.

Fisch, R., Ray, W. A., & Schlanger, K. (2009). *Focused problem resolution: Selected papers of the MRI Brief Therapy Center.* Phoenix, AZ: Zeig, Tucker, & Theisen.

Fisch, R., Weakland, J. H., & Segal, L. (1982). *Tactics of change: Doing therapy briefly.* New York, NY: Jossey-Bass.

Green, S. K., & Flemons, D. (Eds.). (2007). *Quickies: The handbook of brief sex therapy* (Rev. ed.). New York, NY: W. W. Norton.

Haley, J. (1963). *Strategies of psychotherapy.* New York, NY: Grune & Stratton.

Haley, J. (1986). *Uncommon therapy: The psychiatric techniques of Milton H. Erickson, M.D.* New York, NY: W. W. Norton.

Hoyt, M. F., & Talmon, M. (Eds.). (2014). *Capturing the moment: Single session therapy and walk-in services.* Bethel, CT: Crown House Publishing.

Ray, W. A., & de Shazer, S. (1999). *Evolving brief therapies.* Galena, IL: Geist & Russell.

Selvini Palazzoli, M., Boscolo, L., Cecchin, G., & Prata, G. (1978). *Paradox and counter-paradox.* New York, NY: Jason Aronson.

Slive, A., & Bobele, M. (Eds.). (2011). *When one hour is all you have: Effective therapy for walk-in clients.* Phoenix, AZ: Zeig, Tucker, & Theisen.

Watzlawick, P., Weakland, J., & Fisch, R. (1974). *Change: Principles of problem formation and problem resolution.* New York, NY: W. W. Norton.

CACREP

See Competency-Based Standards for Marriage, Couple, and Family Counseling; Council for Accreditation of Counseling and Related Educational Programs

CAREER PLANNING AND COUPLES/FAMILIES

Fundamental to career planning with couples is an understanding of the meaning of careers and the role that work has for each partner and, if they have children, for their family. Couples counselors indicate that one third of their clients report work–family stressors, and younger couples identify career issues as one of their highest concerns in counseling. Gender role socialization, gender equity, and evolving family roles have shifted career planning from individual assessment and decision-making to couple and family counseling. The purpose of this entry is to provide an overview of the career needs and work stressors of partners and families, and career planning approaches for couples.

Work Stressors and Couples Counseling

Achieving satisfactory life–work role balance for both partners impacts the stability and success of a couple's relationship, as well as their careers. Stressors such as finances, job dissatisfaction, role imbalance, child care, and lack of time together affect both relationship and work satisfaction. More than half of all married couples in the United States are dual-career couples in which each partner focuses on his or her career path; however, with the added responsibilities of parenthood career priorities of one or both partners often change. When dual-career couples have children, women still generally provide more of the household and child care duties, although men have increased their participation.

In the United States, more women are deferring marriage until they have established their careers. The majority of women with preschool- or elementary-aged children work outside the home, the majority of marriages end in divorce, and many single parents, especially women, raise children. With rapid changes in gender and social roles, more women now enter college than men, and their college majors extend to disciplines previously perceived as male choices. Women fill the majority of middle management and administrative jobs, and they earn half of the medical degrees and the majority of veterinary degrees. Women frequently step out of high-stakes career advancement paths to care for children and fear they will not be able to recover the loss in income or promotions when they reenter the workforce. Although women and men assess job opportunities using the same criteria of interests, income, and advancement, females also value relationships and altruistic values when making career decisions.

Donald Super's life career approach focuses on the personal and contextual factors of a person's roles over time as a child, student, citizen, homemaker, worker, and retiree. When partners fill multiple roles concurrently, couples often experience stress from role confusion or role conflict. Although an average workday spans 7.6 hours, time spent commuting has substantially extended the workday for many couples, reducing the quantity and quality of time with partner and family. Dual-career couples often work 12-hour days with overtime, weekend hours, and on-call shifts, and partners in the sandwich generation may also take work home to complete while caring for both children and older parents. Commuter couples may be required to work several days or weeks away from home (e.g., truck driver, regional salesperson, global manager, professional athlete, or coach). In a dual-earner family one partner typically compromises personal career plans to support the other's career advancement that is often in professional, technical, or administrative fields. The trailing partner assumes more child care responsibilities and is frequently underemployed, settling for a lower-level job that does not meet his or her level of education, experience, or training.

Couples frequently seek mental health, career, or couples counseling during a work crisis that severely impacts the family, such as a job furlough or layoff. To regain income quickly, a partner may take a job in another location or settle for employment at a much lower salary as a temporary financial solution, which could limit career change in the future. Partners also struggle with decisions about further education needed for their career advancement, job transfers, and relocation to find employment opportunities.

In couples counseling sessions, partners may present somatic and emotional problems, including exhaustion, sleep deprivation, oversleeping, smoking, tension, stress, alcohol or drug use, or loss of attention and nurturing by the partner. With the shock of sudden lifestyle and life role changes after a job loss, one or both partners often report feeling depressed, anxious, hopeless, or angry about being unable to secure a new position at an equivalent level.

Identifying current work-related stressors and family needs is an important first step in couple career planning. Partners may underestimate the impact of job responsibilities and requirements on family members when they continually take work home, work overtime, are on call, or work rotating shifts in 24/7 fields (e.g., employment in medicine, military, security, law enforcement, information technology, or aviation). In studies of police and military, researchers found job stress and work frustrations intensified couple conflicts, financial stress, and strain on extended family relationships and traditions.

Military veterans experience numerous work–life stressors when they reunite with their family and reenter civilian life through multiple personal, social, family, and career transitions and adjustments in a brief time span. A spouse's return to civilian life and resumption of the role as head of the household may upset the partner who made decisions independently and filled the roles of both parents while the spouse was deployed. The high percentage of suicides in veterans, particularly National Guard and Reserves, is cause for intensive prevention and intervention mental health services linked to career planning and job transition from military to civilian life. The Veterans Administration (VA) provides numerous services to assist veterans and their families in this transition, including support groups, individual counseling, and group psychotherapy to improve both coping and job-hunting skills.

Dual-career gay and lesbian couples report planning as a key strategy in finding GLBT-friendly work environments where both partners feel comfortable and safe from marginalization or harassment. Couples career counseling addresses the unique concerns of same-sex partners regarding each partner's role in career advancement, job relocation, workplace events, birth and education of children, salary, and choice of neighborhood. With the Supreme Court's 2015 marriage equality ruling, same-sex couples may reevaluate long-term career and retirement plans that now can include eligibility for their spouse's health and retirement benefits.

Career Construction and Transition

Planning for work and career is an integral part of couple and family counseling. Rapid global and technological changes in the world of work have led to career destabilization and rapid obsolescence of work skills. Individuals can generally anticipate changing careers multiple times and working longer and harder than the previous generation. Finding fulfillment by working in the same job until retirement is no longer a viable goal for most people, and many couples struggle to develop their own long-term plans for retirement income. Super's life span approach emphasizes the development of one's self-concept through career experiences through the life span.

Developmental approaches to career planning focus on how workers move through five maxicycles (stages): growth, exploration, establishment, maintenance, and decline. With several transitions to new careers in their lifetime, minicycles provide individuals in any stage the tools to recycle through needed stages to make new career decisions. With dual-career couples, a minicycle can be a collaborative process leading to cooperative decision-making that recognizes the career needs of each partner.

Nancy K. Schlossberg identified four types of transitions and pivotal points that affect couples and families: unanticipated events, anticipated events, chronic hassles, and nonevents. Anticipated life transitions represent positive or planned events (graduation, first job, marriage, retirement), while unanticipated transitions frequently follow sudden crises (job loss, involuntary transfer, death of a family member, military deployment, job promotion, disaster). Chronic hassles reflect persistent problems (commuting, changing work shifts, difficult supervisors, unsafe working conditions). Nonevents also impact workers who desire a change that does not occur and range from denial of an expected job promotion to the lack of financial resources to take a desired leave to stay at home to care for children. Recognizing nonevents in couple career planning facilitates moving underlying wishes and unfulfilled dreams to the career session.

John L. Holland found that when an individual's type and the work environment type are congruent, the employee feels more satisfied and successful and performs better on the job. Individuals migrate toward people like themselves, and they are happiest working with similar people in similar environments. Incongruence between the person and work environment can lead to frustration and distress, having a spillover effect on partners' level of dissatisfaction in their relationship. In addition, couples with different work styles may experience conflicts about making career decisions that affect both partners. Understanding similarities and differences in their work styles, and learning to communicate with each other about the purpose of work in their relationship, can lead to greater couple satisfaction and joint decision-making. Determining the level of congruence between the worker's satisfaction with the job and the worker's satisfactoriness to the employer is central to the work adjustment approach to career planning. Both partners must weigh how long they can persist in an unsatisfactory job and what active and reactive work strategies they will try before quitting or seeking other employment.

The Meaning of Work for Couples and Families

Career planning has shifted from a focus on occupational assessment and choice to the process of finding meaning in work for both partners and being prepared to adjust to unanticipated career changes over their lifetime. Narrative career counseling and career construction are postmodern approaches that address how partners view and interact with their world expressed through their ministories. Integrating ministories into a larger story empowers partners to understand each other's career identities, needs, and goals, and to coconstruct their future careers. Through the process of career construction, partners deconstruct past career stories that they created or others created for them, and reconstruct their career paths.

Mark Savickas's life design paradigm encourages individuals to share stories about their role models, as well as favorite television programs and stories. Couples coconstruct their career story through career narrative tools, including the occupational daydream, headlines, life–career timeline, future biography, family career genogram, and obituary. Ministories of people's work lives are integrated into a larger story or life portrait. The power of career coconstruction emerges from a shared understanding of the meaning of work as a couple or family and movement toward new career decisions. Indecision is the process of wavering back and forth on their career path as the couple moves toward finding their own meaning.

Integrating career planning into couples counseling sessions empowers partners to identify and strengthen connections among work, relationships, and family. In periods of economic downturns where there is a scarcity of jobs, long-term career paths become increasingly limited to the highly educated, affluent, or privileged. The poor, less educated, or working-class families face greater obstacles to career paths and more limited choices about work. David L. Blustein and colleagues describe how work can meet the fundamental needs for survival, relatedness, and self-determination. Cultural values and expectations affect the family's career story, and in some cultures career plans of family members reflect the interdependence and common goals of the extended family. In other cultures, a greater focus on individual career goals may emphasize competitiveness and autonomy, or may increase disagreement in coconstructing the couple's or family's future story.

Three career patterns have emerged that respond to the changing nature of work transitions: kaleidoscope, boundaryless, and protean career paths. Couples face both daily work choices and long-term occupational decisions along a *kaleidoscope* career path that reflect the metaphor of numerous colors and pieces moving and changing concurrently. This dynamic career transition style is genuine, authentic, balanced, and challenging, and illuminates how dual-career partners, especially women, transition to integrate family and child care roles with their work roles. The *boundaryless* career path is characterized by multiple transitions with complex job rotations and transfers where workers need flexibility, adaptability, and optimism. Similar to the boundaryless path, the *protean* career path focuses on self-direction and strong personal values about work saliency, reflecting frequent career and work environment changes, such as temporary and contract employment, and telecommuting.

After a sudden, unanticipated work event or when increasing frustrations from chronic hassles peak, partners and family members may seek counseling to cope with the stressors of a career transition. The career construction model developed by Savickas identifies four dimensions of career adaptability that are applicable to couples counseling: identifying concerns, increasing confidence, becoming more curious, and being in control of their life and work. These dimensions influence the stories partners tell, leading to a shared meaning of work and what matters to couples and families as they reconstruct their career story. Rather than a linear path from first job to retirement, career planning with couples and families is a cyclic journey with multiple minicycles that address changing work needs and decisions throughout their lives.

Jane M. Webber and J. Barry Mascari

See also Decision-Making; Dual-Earner Families; Job Loss; Life Balance; Military Couples and Families; Same-Sex Couples; Work Relationships

Further Readings

Beutell, N. J., & Wittig-Berman, U. (2008). Work-family conflict and work-family synergy for Generation X, baby boomers, and matures: Generational differences, predictors, and satisfaction outcomes. *Journal of Managerial Psychology, 23,* 507–523.

Blustein, D. L., Medvide, M. B., & Kozan, S. (2012). A tour of a new paradigm: Relationships and work. *Counseling Psychologist, 40*(3), 253–254.

Fider, C. O., Fox, C. A., & Wilson. C. M. (2014). Physicians in dual-career marriages: Nurturing their relationships. *The Family Journal, 22,* 364–370. doi:10.1177/1066480714547699

Gilbert, L. A., & Bingham, R. P. (2001). Career counseling with dual career heterosexual African American couples. In W. B. Walsh, R. P. Bingham, M. Brown, C. M. Ward, & S. H. Osipow (Eds.), *Career counseling for African Americans* (pp. 77–98). New York, NY: Routledge.

Holland, J. L. (1997). *Making vocational choices.* Odessa, FL: Psychological Assessment Resources.

Lent, R. W. (2013). Career-life preparedness: Revisiting career planning and adjustment in the new workplace. *The Career Development Quarterly, 61.* doi:10.1002/j.2161-0045.2013.00031

Richardson, M. S. (2012). Counseling for work and relationship. *The Counseling Psychologist, 40*(2), 190–242. doi:10.1177/0011000011406452

Ryan, L. W., & McFarland, W. P. (2010). A phenomenological exploration of the experiences of dual-career lesbian and gay couples. *Journal of Counseling and Development, 88*(1), 71–79.

Savickas, M. L. (2012). Life design: A paradigm for career intervention in the 21st century. *Journal of Counseling and Development, 90,* 13–19.

Schlossberg, N. K. (2009). *Revitalizing retirement: Reshaping your identity, relationships, and purpose.* Washington, DC: American Psychological Association.

CAREGIVERS

Caregivers are those who take responsibility for the care of another. A caregiver can be a parent providing care for young children, an adult sibling providing care for a disabled or chronically ill adult sibling, a young adult caring for a middle-aged parent with schizophrenia, or a middle-aged adult caring for a parent with dementia. Sometimes a caregiver is paid, such as a nanny or a nurse, while other times a caregiver is a member of the family who takes on the responsibility of caring for another member of the family in an unpaid position. The family member may become a full-time caregiver for another family member or may take on a role as advocate for services for a family member living in an assisted-living or memory care facility. This entry discusses the transition from being the recipient of parental care to being the provider of care, caregiver stressors, and cultural considerations in caregiving. It concludes with considerations for marriage and family therapists working with those impacted by the caregiving role.

Transition From Recipient of Care to Provider of Care

In attachment theory, the term *caregiver* is typically used to refer to a person caring for an infant or a small child. The care of the child by the attachment figure or figures, typically a parent or both parents, continues as the child ages, with the general expectation that the care lasts until the child is at the age of 18. Often financial support is required past the age of 18, as children may continue to reside with their parents in their early twenties or thirties and sometimes beyond. As young adults transition into adulthood, they may have their own children and become caregivers to those children. During middle age, many parents find that they are not only caring for and/or supporting their own children but also transitioning into providing care for their own parents.

Caregiver Stressors

Caregivers are faced with stressors, including but not limited to those of an emotional and/or financial nature. These stressors could have an impact on the well-being and physical health of the caregiver. Many caregivers report a negative affect, including symptoms of depression. Caregivers may find themselves ignoring their own health needs, as they focus on the health needs of a sick sibling, disabled spouse, aging parent, or other recipients of their care. They may feel burdened with the extra responsibility of managing the finances of the person receiving care, while attempting to balance their own financial responsibilities. Caring for an aging parent who is experiencing Alzheimer's disease or another form of dementia may increase the stress levels of the caregivers. The stress may be tied to both the emotions surrounding the parent's symptoms and to the areas of life in which the caregiver is spending less and less time, such as their other relationships, personal care, occupation, and leisure activities. It should be noted, however, that although many caregivers report feeling emotional and physical exhaustion, many report feelings of joy and satisfaction. End-of-life issues may invoke sadness but may bring families closer together.

Cultural Considerations

Cultural considerations are important to consider, including the expectations to care for an aging parent, as well as gender norms. For example, some cultures may not recognize the labeling of someone as a caregiver because the care of another is inherently established in the values of the culture. Gender roles and expectations for women often dictate that women should be caregivers, and therefore the responsibility of women to provide care may be felt strongly. Cultural norms regarding living in proximity or remaining emotionally connected to one's family of origin may influence expectations. For example, women typically remain emotionally closer to their family of origin in adulthood and therefore are more likely to assume the role of caregiver. These factors may contribute to enhanced stress levels.

Considerations for Marriage and Family Therapists

The burdens of caregiving can bring stressors on the entire family system, sometimes in both the family of origin and the marriage of the caregiver. Within the family of origin, siblings may experience increased conflict as the caregiver consults with them about decisions regarding an aging parent. New roles may develop within the family, as the caregiver may become the family member responsible for organizing the connections between the siblings and other members of the family, a role that was originally undertaken by the parent. As the caregiver transitions into the role, sibling rivalry established in early childhood and somewhat dormant as siblings each established their own families may be brought to the spotlight again, as competition over the parent(s) and resources becomes an area of focus.

Marriage relationships may become strained as caregivers begin to spend more time with the aging parent and less time with their spouse. There may have been an expectation that once the children left the house, there would be time to focus on the couple, or on individual goals. Plans for retirement and leisure activities such as vacations are put on hold as the caregiver takes on the responsibility of caring for an aging parent. This can lead to feelings of resentment and strain the marriage.

Sarah J. Moses

See also Aging and Caregiving; Debt and Financial Strain; Family Stress; Life Transitions; Sibling Relationships

Further Readings

Gottlieb, B. H., & Gignac, M. A. (1996). Content and domain specificity of coping among family caregivers of persons with dementia. *Journal of Aging Studies, 10*(2), 137–155.

Igarashi, H., Hooker, K., Coehlo, D. P., & Manoogian, M. M. (2013). "My nest is full": Intergenerational relationships at midlife. *Journal of Aging Studies, 27*(2), 102–112.

Rabin, C., Bressler, Y., & Prager, E. (1993). Caregiver burden and personal authority: Differentiation and connecting in caring for an elderly parent. *American Journal of Family Therapy, 21*(1), 27–39.

Sheehan, N. W., & Nuttall, P. (1988). Conflict, emotion, and personal strain among family caregivers. *Family Relations, 37*(1), 92–98.

Certified Family Life Educator

Family life education and family life educators (FLE) focus on providing preventive strategies to promote healthy family functioning within a family systems perspective. In order to gain a greater level of recognition and acceptance from other helping professions, family life educators have worked during the last 35 years to establish standards and practices that align with and complement other professionals who help families. The National Council on Family Relations (NCFR) was instrumental in the professionalization of this occupation, and in 1984 initiated a task force of nationally recognized experts to draft the first curricular standards for a Certified Family Life Educator (CFLE). Once approved, this certification program was launched in 1985 and provided 10 content areas in which CFLEs must be proficient in order to obtain their certification. Since that time, CFLE curriculum guidelines have been through several revisions, of which the most recent was completed in 2014. This entry briefly describes the main tenets of family life education along with pertinent historical information, educational and certification requirements, the CFLE ethics code, as well as information on employment opportunities and research in the field.

Purpose of Family Life Education

Certified Family Life Educators typically deliver information to families in a classroom setting and/or with educational materials. As stated previously, CFLE can be complementary to other helping professionals who are responsible for intervening with families that may be experiencing developmental crises or societal problems, such as substance abuse, domestic violence, debt, or unemployment. CFLEs complete this task by working with families to increase their knowledge and develop their skill sets so that they can work toward better or more optimal functioning. Because CFLEs focus on strengths-based interventions, families are engaged to capitalize on skills they may already have. CFLEs typically work with families in a variety of settings, such as community-based youth and elder care programs, in military family support services, in faith-based family education programs, in drug and alcohol rehabilitation programs, and in consumer protection agencies.

History of Family Life Education

The professionalization of the CFLE emerged from the NCFR, an organization that was founded in 1938 by Paul Sayre, Ernest Burgess, and Rabbi Sidney E. Goldstein. This nonpartisan, nonprofit organization was the only one of its kind that focused specifically on family research, policies, and best practices. Since its inception, NCFR has extended its professional membership to include individuals from the areas of social research, teaching, policy analysis, and human services. Forty-six years later, NCFR was instrumental in creating the CFLE credential and continues to be the national body that regulates this credential worldwide. More recently, the organization has made a concerted effort toward expanding relevant services to diverse populations both in the United States and worldwide. Currently, the NCFR supports these initiatives by hosting an annual conference, supporting 10 interest networks within the parent organization, and publishing three scholarly, peer-reviewed journals. These annual meetings and publications are designed to serve a multidisciplinary group of providers as well as supporting the growth and development of CFLE through scholarships and fellowships for students and emerging leaders and researchers in the field.

Certification Requirements

NCFR has determined that, in order to become a CFLE, candidates must demonstrate working knowledge and skills in the following curricular content areas:

1. Families and Individuals in Societal Contexts: Understanding families in relationship to social institutions;

2. Internal Dynamics of Families: Understanding family strengths, weaknesses, and interpersonal relationships;

3. Human Growth and Development Across the Life Span: Knowledge of typical and atypical development from birth to death in aspects of functioning;

4. Human Sexuality: Understanding aspects of sexual development and healthy sexuality across the life span;

5. Interpersonal Relationships: Understanding and maintaining healthy relationships;

6. Family Resource Management: Understanding and appropriately allocating resources (such as money, time);

7. Parent Education and Guidance: Parental responsibilities in educating and maintaining relationships with their children throughout the life span;

8. Family Law and Public Policy: Understanding legal issues and public policies that affect the family;

9. Professional Ethics and Practice: Understanding ethical issues as they relate to CFLE professional practice; and

10. Family Life Education Methodology: Understanding pedagogy, including delivery and evaluation of educational content.

Most individuals can obtain the aforementioned competencies by completing bachelor's level course work in an NCFR-approved family program. Upon completion of degree work, candidates can apply for either provisional or full certification. Provisional certification can be obtained by individuals with a bachelor's, master's, or PhD degree who are able to demonstrate knowledge of the 10 content areas as measured by a passing score on the CFLE exam. Those with bachelor's degrees who wish to obtain full certification must complete the exam as well as complete 3,200 hours of FLE work in the field. Individuals with a master's or PhD in a family degree program must complete 1,600 hours of FLE work experience. In either case, FLE employers must complete candidates' field certification forms to verify work experience and corroborate competency in the 10 CFLE content areas. It should be noted that individuals who matriculate from non-NCFR family programs or hold non-family degrees can apply for certification, but they may need to obtain additional course work or field work experiences to qualify for provisional and/or full CFLE status.

Maintaining CFLE status is dependent upon individuals remitting the annual renewal fee and applying for recertification every five years. Recertification can be obtained by submitting proof of continuing education (CE) experiences every five years. CFLE are required to complete 100 CEs every five years, experiences that can include academic course work, conference session attendance, and work experiences in the field that are new and have not been previously documented in previous certifications/renewals. Individuals with lapsed certifications may be able to apply for recertification if they meet requirements and/or complete trainings required by the national office.

Employment

Because of the diverse content areas of CFLE training, individuals with this certification may have opportunities to work in a variety of settings. Settings can include (but are not limited to)

- consumer and family resource centers, such as consumer protection services and vocational guidance centers;
- community-based social services, such as 4-H youth development and adult day care centers;
- education, such as college student life programs and public schools;
- family intervention, such as divorce mediations and victim/witness support services;
- faith-based organizations, such as youth programs and marriage/relationship programming;
- early childhood education, such as preschools and Head Start programs;

- government and public policy, such as family court and juvenile justice;
- health care and family wellness, such as nutrition, wellness, sexuality education, and hospice;
- international education and development, such as Peace Corps and international human rights advocacy;
- research, such as grant proposal writing and program evaluation and assessment; and
- writing and communication, such as curriculum development, blogging, and social media campaigns.

Although the preceding list is not exhaustive, it is important to consider that a CFLE credential could be complementary to a variety of bachelor's and other degree programs, depending on an individual's interest and specific ability level. For example, a political science major who is interested in family issues may benefit from this type of training so that he or she is able to incorporate CFLE-specific knowledge into a future career as a political advocate or policy maker. In a brief search of NCFR's careers website, employment opportunities range from a research technologist at a military family help center to tenure-track faculty positions at large research institutions in the United States. This range implies that there is a need for CFLE and that there are career opportunities for individuals with a variety of educational attainment levels. Moreover, CFLE training can be applied to a variety of settings and constituents, from metropolitan areas to rural settings. However, all positions delineate the effort to strengthen families and individuals throughout the course of their life span.

As mentioned previously, CFLEs typically engage in an educational modality when working with their constituents. Therefore, these individuals can be instrumental in helping organizations either procure relevant curricula or develop curricula that are appropriate for the individuals and families that they serve. CFLEs are also responsible for measuring the efficacy of their interventions, and are often involved in examining data regarding the outcomes of their various interventions.

Perhaps the most important role of the CFLE is working with individuals and families on a personal level. In this role, CFLEs must be sensitive to the individual differences of the families they are working with, tailor education and interventions to the ability levels of these families, and maintain ethical and professional comportment while engaging in these helping relationships.

Code of Ethics

Similar to many human service providers, CFLEs must abide by a specific code of ethics when they engage in their professional practice. Although most individuals enter into human service professions with good intentions, many professionals can be faced with issues that can challenge their decision-making processes. Ethics codes can provide some parameters for practices and are typically determined in conjunction with professionals engaged in the field and a professional organization. As with other human service providers' codes of ethics, interpretation can be challenging and multifaceted, and professionals must attempt to balance the ethical principles of autonomy, benefits, nonmaleficence, fidelity, justice, and veracity. It is recommended that individuals consult with other professionals when faced with ethical dilemmas that require difficult decisions.

When CFLEs apply for their initial application for training and examination, they must review and sign the ethical codes and submit them to the NCFR. These ethical codes serve as standards of conduct for professionals and are intended to guide educators in their work with diverse individuals and families. There are four overarching ethical categories, with a total of 36 ethical codes that CFLEs should endeavor to follow. The four broader ethical categories are as follows: (1) Relationships with Parents and Families, (2) Relationships with Children and Youth, (3) Relationships with Colleagues and the Profession, and (4) Relationships with Community/Society. As with most ethical codes, the behavior set forth in these guidelines is aspirational, and practitioners may not always be able to follow these codes due to specific governmental laws and/or agency policies. Moreover, there is not a clear understanding of how violations of ethics codes are handled within the NCFR organization, by individual agencies, and/or through legal regulations.

Research

The world has changed a great deal since the initial professionalization of FLE and CFLE, and although the core competencies remain largely intact, research within the profession is focused on meeting the needs of the present-day population. Current research on FLE is centered on issues related to diversity and how to best serve families from a global perspective, best practices in online FLE service delivery, and continuing to develop the professional identity of CFLE. As the world's population continues to grow and diverse populations increase in numbers, it is imperative that CFLEs be multiculturally aware of the needs of their constituents. This becomes particularly important as current data from NCFR.org shows that the majority of CFLEs are female, have higher educational attainment, and are predominantly Caucasian. Moreover, while face-to-face interactions are highly desirable where new skills and information are concerned, the current generations are more digitally aware and may have certain expectations that information be available to them at any time and in an online forum. Finally, as FLEs and CFLEs engage with other professionals in the field, they continue to establish how they fit into the multidisciplinary team treatment models that are so often found when working with families in need.

Elizabeth O'Brien

See also Adlerian Open-Forum Family Counseling; Family Life Educators; Individual Family Culture; Psychoeducation

Further Readings

Darling, C. A., & Cassidy, D. (2014). *Family life education: Working with families across the lifespan* (3rd ed.). Long Grove, IL: Waveland Press.

Galvin, K. M., Braithwaite, D. O., & Bylund, C. L. (2014). *Family communication: Cohesion and change* (9th ed.). New York, NY: Routledge.

Goldsmith, E. G. (2012). *Resource management for individuals and families* (5th ed.). Upper Saddle River, NJ: Prentice Hall.

Nakkula, M. J., & Toshalis, E. (2006). *Understanding youth: Adolescent development for educators.* Boston, MA: Harvard Education Press.

National Council on Family Relations. (2015). *What is family life education?* Retrieved from https://www.ncfr.org/cfle-certification/what-family-life-education

Chaos Family Therapy

The term *chaos* often is seen as having something to do with tumult and disarray. But this common use of the term belies its scientific meaning and fails to appreciate the implications for understanding complex systems afforded by chaos theory. Chaos theory provides a way of understanding complex, nonlinear systems that often seem to behave randomly. Although many associate the term chaos with randomness, chaos theory actually describes the kind of order found in the complex, seemingly random behavior of all kinds of systems. At its core, chaos theory is a branch of mathematics involved with understanding behavior in systems whereby seemingly insignificant actions can ripple outward, ultimately leading to highly complex behavior. This includes the idea of the "butterfly effect," which suggests that the disturbance caused by the flapping of a butterfly's wings in Golden Gate Park affects the system such that eventually there might be a cyclone in Australia. In chaos theory, systems evolve in response to feedback to or within the system. The principles found in this theory offer several conceptual principles that provide a way of understanding the complex behaviors associated with family systems. Families can be seen as life forms that first emerge and then, in response to ongoing feedback, evolve—that is, they change over time in response to events. The purpose of this entry is to provide an overview of the application of chaos theory to family therapy.

As a relatively new scientific construct that emerged from a number of unrelated disciplines, chaos theory has no universally agreed-upon, unified definition. Chaos theory is a model that provides a way to understand complex nonlinear systems. What is meant by nonlinear? Traditionally, Western science attempted to break things down into predictable, linear behavior. For example, think of a linear regression where all of the data points are plotted and a line is drawn that offers the "best fit" for the data. Chaos theory is nonlinear. Each data point has the potential to interact with the rest of the system, affecting the overall behavior of the system in unpredictable ways. In other words, systems evolve in response to events within the system as well as to events that happen to the system. Thus, even seemingly simple systems, such as a pendulum, can evolve complex behavior.

Chaotic Systems

All interpersonal systems, including family systems, are chaotic systems. Because of the complexity of these systems, however, it will be easier to understand chaotic systems with a simple example. Think of a pendulum. Start a pendulum swinging, and it will swing back and forth predictably while gradually rotating either clockwise or counterclockwise depending on its location relative to the Earth's equator. Although the pendulum follows roughly the same path every time it is set in motion, it will never follow the *exact* same path: its apparently simple behavior is actually complex. Moreover, if a magnet is placed near the metal plumb of the pendulum, its behavior will change dramatically in response to this new force. In this case, the magnet becomes a "strange attractor," a force acting on the system and affecting its behavior in unusual ways.

The Discovery of Chaos

Not long ago, efforts to predict the weather were all but futile. The joke was "whatever the news weather person predicts for tomorrow, expect the opposite!" But why was this so? Weather is an incredibly complex system, and in order to predict weather effectively, an extraordinary amount of data is needed on what the weather is doing at a given moment. In the early 1960s, Edward Lorenz began working with early computers, attempting to model weather. Using just 12 rules about the relationships between temperature, pressure, wind speed, and direction, Lorenz would start his computer model and watch what happened. At first the patterns that emerged made sense and seemed to simulate global weather patterns reasonably well. However, when rerunning the model using the numbers generated by the computer in the previous run as the starting point, patterns that should have repeated themselves instead changed dramatically. Lorenz would start the model at the same place, but with each run it came up with new and different predictions. It was as if he were starting the model with randomly selected conditions. Eventually, Lorenz solved the problem and discovered one of the most important concepts in nonlinear dynamics: the butterfly effect.

Sensitive Dependence on Initial Conditions

The butterfly effect, more technically known as *sensitive dependence on initial conditions,* is the phenomenon in which tiny variations in the conditions of a system can have ripple effects that lead to major effects later on: thus, the flapping of the butterfly's wings as an event compounding eventually to cause a cyclone in Australia. As Lorenz struggled to understand the unpredictable weather outcomes his computer model was generating, he thought he was dealing with a programming error. He solved the problem when he realized that the output he used as input for his next run included only three decimals (e.g., 0.207) while his program was set for six decimals (i.e., 0.207346). When it comes to complex systems like the weather, such tiny differences eventually can have huge effects over time. Lorenz realized that attempting to describe the initial conditions of a system means that measurements can never be absolutely accurate. Whether involving temperature and pressure for a weather model or mood and stress in a family model, even our best measurements are imprecise. Even small perturbations of a complex system will ripple out and affect the system over time in completely unpredictable ways.

Attractors and Strange Attractors

Perhaps the easiest way to see chaos is to pour cream into a cup of coffee and observe the interaction between the two fluids. The complex interaction between the two is a form of chaos called *turbulence*—an extremely complex interaction between two fluids as they resolve their differences. This dynamic system contains an almost infinite number of variables with an almost infinite number of possible behaviors in which all of the variables are in a constant state of motion. Predicting these complex changes is impossible.

By the early 1970s, efforts to understand turbulence led to the introduction of the term *strange attractor*. In physics, the term *attractor* is used to describe a system either in a steady state or a state in which it continuously repeats itself. This can be understood as a fixed point around which behavior cycles or repeats. When a pendulum is swung, the central point of the system is the attractor, the point at which the pendulum eventually reaches a steady state when it comes to rest. The most important feature of attractors is the property of stability. Regardless of how the system is perturbed, it will return to its stable state (rest).

Strange attractors are different. Systems governed by strange attractors are characterized by the appearance of seemingly random behavior, like turbulence. Over time, from this seeming randomness emerge patterns of repetition, patterns of behavior that seem to follow some kind of rule while never quite repeating exactly. Patterns of behavior may follow the same path closely, but they never repeat exactly. Strange attractors are organizing principles or rules that govern the behavior of systems resulting in complex, nonrepeating, but similar patterns of behavior.

Figure 1 A Lorenz Strange Attractor Illustrating the Butterfly Effect

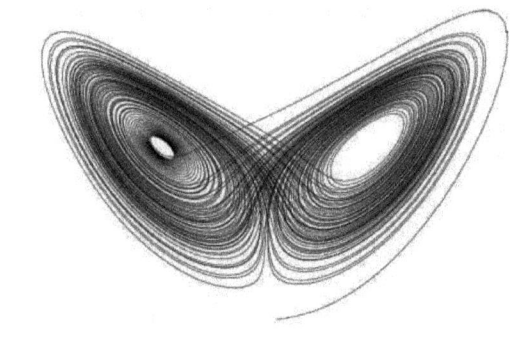

Source: Daniel R. Cruikshanks.

As a general rule, most people start their day at roughly the same time and begin a set of predictable behaviors. They get out of bed, use the bathroom, move to the kitchen where they might prepare some coffee or tea, and get something to eat. They get dressed, and if it is a work/school day, they make their way to work or to class, and so on until bedtime. People follow schedules that regulate their behavior and determine what they are doing at any given time. No two days are exactly alike, yet every day tends to be remarkably similar. In this case, the strange attractor can be thought of as "routine." Routine is a guiding set of rules that structure time and determine what people are likely to be doing at any given time. Everyone has a routine, and that routine tends to be similar for everyone.

There are many other strange attractors that further affect behavior. For example, some people live in close-knit families with certain expectations about when and how to spend time together. When a new member is introduced, that person represents a new attractor. This new attractor is a new force that will act on the system by interacting with all other elements in the family system. The family's implicit rules affect when and how new members are introduced and received. Some families accept new members with love an acceptance while others with suspicion and hostility. A family's culture, values, beliefs, and relationships all will provide a structure affecting behaviors and becoming strange attractors. Thus the new member of the family becomes a source of feedback to the system. In this way, either the family system will evolve in response to the structural change, or the system will enter crisis, becoming stuck in a maladaptive and disruptive pattern of behavior. When family therapists are sought for assistance, they become a new strange attractor acting on the system and providing feedback that facilitates evolution of the system.

Battered Person Syndrome: Maya's Case

Maya, a 38-year-old mother of two teens, presented for counseling initially complaining of severe depression. She was clearly distressed. She complained of feeling exhausted, sad, and hopeless. She reported feelings of guilt as she felt responsible for the poor state of her marriage and her husband's dissatisfaction. She appeared worn out and much older than her stated age. A stay-at-home mom, she reported that she had been suffering from depression for years but complained that things were getting much worse now as her kids increasingly seemed to need her less. Despite her long history, she had never sought treatment before.

Maya described her family as "wonderful, loving and supportive." She reported that her problems seem to have always been there despite her loving family. As her problems had gotten worse, she had become an increasing burden on them. Maya reported that there was a history of depression in her family, particularly on her mother's side. Perhaps this was purely biological?

At the request of the counselor, Maya brought in her spouse in an effort to understand her problem fully. Maya's spouse presented as a concerned and caring man who was mystified by her long history of depression. He reported being there for her throughout, but that nothing he did seemed to help. He offered to help in whatever way he could, though he said that coming to regular counseling sessions would be impossible for him because of work demands.

After several sessions, Maya presented with a noticeable bruise on the side of her face. Reluctantly, she acknowledged that her husband had hit her during an argument. Maya had been complaining to her husband about the heavy demands of his work and his lack of availability to the family. The argument escalated as she "nagged" him unrelentingly until he lost control and hit her. Overcome by guilt and remorse, he claimed only to have hit her after she had "pushed" him beyond his limits until he lost control. Maya took full responsibility for the incident, and she begged the counselor to help her learn to control her behavior so as not push her husband in this way.

Maya revealed that this was a recurring pattern that went back to the earliest days of their marriage. She had been shocked and stunned by the first incident of this behavior from her husband. Each time, he cried and apologized, telling her that she pushed him "over the edge." Maya always accepted responsibility and tried never to push him like this again. Despite her best efforts, however, Maya seemed unable to avoid regularly pushing him over the edge. At first, it was months between violent episodes, but over time the incidences increased in frequency until eventually he would hit her at least once a week. Maya reported working hard to accommodate him, but no matter how hard she tried, she failed. She felt increasingly helpless and that she was a failure. Maya had developed battered person syndrome.

Battered person syndrome is characterized by a recurrent and escalating cycle of violence and abuse in a relationship that is typically perpetrated by one person against the other. Typically, the abused is unable or unwilling to place responsibility for the abuse on the abuser and often blames herself or himself self for the violence. The abused typically sees the abuser as perfect, faultless, and even omnipotent. To outside observers, these relationships are characterized by a simple solution paradox—why doesn't she or he just leave? What is more, if and when victims of battered person syndrome finally do escape the relationship, why is it that they often find themselves in the same situation when they enter a new relationship? It is almost as if they are seeking relationships with batterers, when in fact, nothing could be further from the truth.

Maya's Chaos

Battered person syndrome provides an excellent vehicle for illustrating the value of chaos theory in understanding family systems and the application of chaos family therapy. Here, the most obvious strange attractor is the recurring cycle of battery. Time and time again, Maya's husband follows his beatings with tears of apparent remorse saying that his explosive rage was forced by her needling, and time and time again, she stays. After many years in this cycle of abuse Maya seemed completely stuck in her relationship, and this is what makes strange attractors so "strange" and so powerful.

By all reports, Maya had been perfectly normal when she first met her "Prince Charming." Early in their courtship, he represented a powerful attractor. He was well on his way to a successful career. He was smart, charming, and a perfect gentleman. Unlike so many men she had dated, he did not push her for sex (indeed, he felt that it was important to wait until after they were married). He always paid for everything, he brought her flowers, and he took her on special trips. He treated her as if she were the most important thing in the world. In short, he knocked her socks off! He convinced her that they were "meant to be" and asked her to marry him after only three weeks of dating. Despite concerns from friends and family, of course, she said "Yes!"

Almost immediately, everything changed. To Maya, it seemed as if her Prince Charming had slipped away becoming a shimmering mirage on the horizon, always just out of her reach. Now, instead of Prince Charming, he was like Dr. Jekyll and Mr. Hyde. One moment he would be fine, but then suddenly, he would become a monster. He demanded sex with her daily and punished her if she tried to refuse. Moreover, for him sex was always about satisfying his needs, and he showed no interest in her pleasure. He became demanding in other ways, too. Dinner had to be ready and on the table promptly when he got home (though she was never quite sure when that would be). Then he expected uninterrupted quiet while he watched TV and enjoyed some drinks. Then, when he decided he was ready, it was off to bed for sex. Maya would have liked to work, but he refused to allow it. Once there were children, the pressures were greater. The kids made noise and messes and interfered with his expectations for sex. Maya believed that she was failing him, but she believed that if she just worked harder, she would be able to make him happy, and her "Prince Charming" would return to her.

With each new union, a new set of strange attractors emerge. Strange attractors are neither good nor bad; rather, they are natural by-products of interaction (think about the cream in the coffee). With interaction comes new feedback in the system, resulting in strange attractors. When a new couple is formed, the dynamics of both families of origin change. Each family has a new member, and a new larger family emerges. Family cultures, values, beliefs, rituals, and traditions all must adjust or be adjusted to. The inevitable strange attractors that emerge cannot be anticipated. Mental illness, substance abuse, medical problems, legal problems, occupational problems, and children all will change the dynamics of the system in complex and unexpected ways.

For Maya, the dominant strange attractor that emerged forced her to isolate herself from friends and family so as not to upset her spouse. Much of her energy was invested in trying to make her husband happy, but nothing she did ever worked. Over time Maya learned that she was helpless, but she also remained convinced that she could make him happy and find happiness herself. Helplessness resulted in depression, and this made her husband more disappointed in her.

Application of Chaos Theory in Family Therapy

Maya was stuck, and she had been for many years. As with a car stuck in snow, the more she tried to get unstuck, the deeper the rut. According to chaos theory, variability (adaptation and evolution) is indicative of a healthy system. Family systems can get "stuck" in ways that are unhealthy when they get locked into stagnant or destructive patterns of behavior. Strange attractors are natural sets of rules that drive patterns of behaviors in complex systems. Maya found herself stuck in a kind of feedback loop. Her husband's ever-increasing demands caused her to invest more and more energy into trying to satisfy him in a desperate effort to find her "Prince Charming" again. "Prince Charming" never hit her, never demanded sex from her, and always treated her like a princess. This was a very powerful and destructive strange attractor.

So how does a family counselor effect change in this system? Should Maya be forcibly removed from this violent system with the hope that she realizes the futility of her plight? Unfortunately, whether done by family, friends, or family counselors, forced separation rarely succeeds and usually makes the problem worse. It is important to remember that these systems develop over time and, like a feedback loop, the forces that keep them going are incredibly strong.

Family Systems and the Butterfly Effect

The concept of the butterfly effect in chaos theory is valuable to family counselors. Counselors who adopt chaos theory understand that they are sources of feedback in the system. Because of the butterfly effect, even small interventions (feedback) can ripple out to have large, unpredictable effects. Counselors practicing chaos therapy also understand that it is difficult to predict which feedback interventions will be effective in a given system. Each system is unique. Sometimes there is one salient piece of feedback that perturbs the system, while other times a series of perturbations will accumulate to have significant effects. In Maya's case, the counselor ultimately will need to find a way to help her discover that she is not responsible for her abuse and to empower her to behave differently in response to her husband. While trying to convince her of this may be difficult, the counselor might help her discover small ways to exert power in her relationship that will alter the dynamics of the system. For example, she might be encouraged to withhold sex until he behaves better toward her. Although the family counselor cannot predict specific changes, she or he can be assured that there will be change if Maya in this case chooses to withhold sex.

Families are complex systems, but they are not systems in isolation. Family systems are composed of individuals, and each individual is also a complex system that includes a personality (a system of preferences and characteristics), a brain, a heart and circulatory system, and so on. This complex set of systems exists in a larger system of peers, communities, culture, society, and so on. Ultimately, every single system is part of the largest known system, the universe. Every system interacts with other systems. When an individual, couple, or family seeks counseling, the counselor joins the client's system. Just as the cream added to coffee results in turbulence, the addition of counselor feedback into the system will lead to turbulence and the emergence of new strange attractors. The goal of counseling is to understand the problem within the various systems that define the family and its individual members and to identify the strange attractors that are regulating the problem patterns of behavior. Once the strange attractors are identified, then efforts can be made to make adjustments to effect change in the systems. Counselors must remember, however, that one need not overpower the system. Subtle perturbations can lead to larger effects over time. The principle of the butterfly effect means that even small actions can have large effects, and there is no way to know which actions will be the ones that matter most.

Daniel R. Cruikshanks

See also Clinical Case Conceptualization With Couples and Families; Clinical Practice; Couples and Marriage Counseling; Domestic Violence; Homeostasis; Sexual Assault and Rape; Systems Theory

Further Readings

Butz, M. R., Carlson, J. M., & Carlson, J. (1998). Chaos theory: Self organization and symbolic representation in family systems. *The Family Journal, 6*(6), 106–115.

Butz, M. R., Chamberlain, L. L., & McCown, W. G. (1997). *Strange attractors: Chaos, complexity, and the art of family therapy.* New York, NY: John Wiley.

Gleick, J. (1987). *Chaos: The making of a new science.* New York, NY: Penguin.

Heiby, E. M. (1995). Chaos theory, nonlinear dynamical models, and psychological assessment. *Psychological Assessment, 7*(1), 5–9.

Stevens, B. A. (1991). Chaos: A challenge to refine systems theory. *American Journal of Family Therapy, 12*(1), 23–26.

Child Behavior Problems

Children's behavior generally falls within a range that is considered "normal" for their age, developmental level, personality type, and sociocultural background. A necessary developmental task for children is to learn how to manage and regulate feelings and behaviors, but this practice does not always come easily or automatically. Children who lack the skills, modeling, and support to develop healthy coping skills may develop behavior problems. Child behavior problems can be defined as a pattern of emotional or behavioral dysregulation that is disproportionate to a triggering event (or lacking a triggering event); inappropriate for the child's developmental age; prolonged (e.g., temper tantrums longer than 10 minutes in duration); severe (e.g., violent, threatening to self or others, or destructive to property); disruptive to the child's individual, familial, or social functioning; and culturally inappropriate. It is common for adults to expect children to be compliant, respectful, nonaggressive, and show self-control in most situations. When children act outside of these expectations, or have behavior problems, it can be a cause for concern, or an indication that it is time for the parents to realign their expectations to match their child's developmental age. The entry explores the various types of child behavior problems, discusses how this varies from culture to culture, indicates specific risk factors, and suggests potential treatments.

Child behavior problems may result from depression, anxiety, and social withdrawal or isolation. Related symptoms include somatic complaints, food refusal or overeating, insomnia or hypersomnia, low mood, anhedonia, suicidality, fearfulness, disrupted thought patterns (e.g., obsessions), avoidance behaviors (e.g., school refusal), and interpersonal and communication issues (e.g., selective mutism, separation anxiety). Older children may also use alcohol and drugs as a form of internalizing behavior. Externalized behaviors are related to an overt display of emotions (e.g., irritability, verbal aggression) or acting-out behaviors (e.g., disruptiveness, defiance, physical aggression, relational aggression or harassment, property damage, violating the rights of others). At times, attention-deficit/hyperactivity disorder (ADHD)—which is characterized by inattention, hyperactivity, or both—may appear to be a behavioral problem, but it should be considered a separate neurodevelopmental disorder, although it can be comorbid with behavioral problems.

All children will exhibit behavior problems from time to time as a natural process of learning and development. However, internalizing or externalizing behavior that exceeds normal developmental expectations can be indicative of a more serious problem. Behavior problems fall on a continuum from mild to severe. Behaviors that are more severe and persistent can be disruptive to the child's functioning in one or multiple domains (emotional, educational, familial, social, self-sufficiency). Extreme or ongoing behavior problems that are left untreated can lead to one or more mental health diagnoses, delinquency problems in adolescence, and antisocial behavior in adulthood. There are also indirect societal effects related to child behavior problems, due to the overuse of health services (both physical and mental). Fortunately, there is often an identifiable trigger, or a reason why children's behavior changes, which may frequently be identified and treated before the onset of mental illness, delinquency, or serious consequences. In some cases, child behavior problems are situational or environmental, so that once certain conditions are removed, problematic behavior largely resolves.

For example, children raised in a neighborhood with gang violence who exhibit behavior problems may show improvement if the gangs are removed or otherwise neutralized and the environment becomes safer and less anxiety-provoking. The way in which the support system responds to a child's behavior can moderate the outcomes for children with behavior problems, as well. For example, children are more likely to respond positively to adults who openly address boundaries and behavioral expectations than they are to adults who ignore or allow behavior problems.

Risk Factors

Risk factors for child behavior problems may be present before a child is even born, as current research indicates that babies in the womb are affected by their mothers' anxiety and depression, suggesting a possible epigenetic basis for later behavior problems. In general, parental behavior does play a large part in children's behavior throughout the life span. Parents who are unable to provide an emotionally warm household with a consistent parenting style may put their children at risk for behavior problems due to unclear boundaries and expectations for appropriate behavior. Parenting inconsistencies have been linked to high parental stress and family conflict, as well as parental mental illness and substance use. Child maltreatment, including substantiated child abuse and neglect (and especially repeated or ongoing maltreatment), is also a significant risk factor for the development of child behavior problems. Children with other mental health challenges or diagnoses may also be at increased risk for behavior problems. In addition, a child's social environment, including the immediate neighborhood and community, may influence behavior problems, especially if the area is violent and impoverished.

It is important to note that not all children who have experienced inconsistent parenting, mental illness, or community violence will necessarily develop behavior problems. Children who have positive temperaments and who are characterized as having resiliency may naturally be able to develop healthy coping and self-control skills, and may avoid patterns of maladaptive behavior. Children seem to thrive with parenting that is warm, consistent, and responsive. Parents who can proactively anticipate children's needs and implement appropriate treatment are more likely to have children who are able to self-regulate emotions and behaviors. Additional protective factors include higher socioeconomic status, higher parental education levels, safe communities, and strong social and environmental supports.

Treatment

There are a number of possible ways to treat behavioral problems, but as with any successful intervention, all begin with proper assessment.

Behavior Assessment

To assess causes of child behavior problems, it is important to observe a child's behavior immediately before, during, and after a problem behavior. All behaviors generally have a related purpose or intended outcome that a child may or may not be completely aware of or may not even be capable of understanding. Four main variables that tend to motivate child behavior are attention (which can include positive or negative attention from peers or adults), rewards (e.g., physical items such as candy or toys, or intangibles, such as more time to play before bedtime), escape (e.g., to avoid having to complete a chore or schoolwork, or physically being allowed to leave a classroom or other undesirable situation), and sensory stimulation (e.g., receiving a hug, or simply receiving physical comfort or release from moving around, making loud noises). Understanding the function of the child's behavior will allow adults to appropriately intervene. If the function is still not able to be determined or the problem is unable to be resolved, adults should seek professional counseling to address an ongoing child behavior problem.

As a part of a broad evaluation of child behavior problems, counselors should consider collaborating with a treatment team consisting of all the important stakeholders in the child's life, which may include parents, siblings, extended family members, teachers, school counselors, child study teams, coaches, medical doctors, and religious leaders. Multiple evaluators can help to identify the behavioral problem as occurring in a single setting or across settings. Counselors also need to be aware of cultural factors that may influence child behavior problems and people's perceptions of such. Social and cultural norms affect the perception of children's behavior as acceptable or unacceptable, and may vary widely. There are racial and socioeconomic disparities for non-majority-status children to be labeled as having behavioral "problems," when such behaviors may in fact be culturally relevant or acceptable within the minority culture, or cultures, of which the child is a member. There is also a great deal of stigma from the general population to children with behavior problems and their families, which is not often addressed. Parents of children with behavior problems are often shamed, which may limit their desire to seek help. Once a problem has been identified, there are multiple strategies for reducing child behavior problems.

Behavior Modification

Behavior modification is a system for reducing child behavior problems that is based on principles of conditioning, specifically that acceptable behaviors are reinforced and strengthened, and unacceptable behaviors are ignored or given a negative consequence. Target behaviors are identified collaboratively with the child, and should be directly measurable, attainable, positive, and specific. The target behaviors are then paired with a motivating reward, such as praise, stickers, toys, outings, or special privileges. When the child meets the target behavior a certain number of times within a specific time frame, he or she is given a reward. The key to effective behavior modification is consistency in monitoring for target behaviors and applying the reward. Eventually, positive behavior should become habitual and behavior problems should decrease.

Family Systems Approaches

Nearly all authors seem to agree that parents and caregivers need to be included as an essential component of therapeutic interventions for child behavior problems. With family systems approaches, based on family systems theory, children with behavior problems are viewed in the context of the family unit as a whole. Negative behaviors are seen as the outcome of family dysfunction and complex interactions between family members that support or contribute to a child's acting out. By working together, families identify common goals, learn to effectively communicate expectations, reduce scapegoating, increase empathy and respect for others, and learn to solve problems collaboratively. Unfortunately, there are sometimes challenges in engaging parents in their child's counseling, in cases where the parents are sharing the same risk factors that contributed to the child's behavior problems in the first place (i.e., parental mental health and substance abuse issues, poor parenting skills, inconsistency), as well as low socioeconomic status and related issues, such as needing to be at work, and an inability to find child care for additional children. Treatment costs may also be prohibitive to increased family engagement.

Pharmacological Interventions

Counselors should also seek consultation from a psychiatrist in relation to possible psychopharmacology, when child behavior problems significantly impact a child's ability to function or persist for a long period of time or when counseling interventions alone are less than optimally effective. Psychotropic medications are designed to target symptoms that lead to behavior problems—not the specific problematic behaviors. For example, stimulant medications (e.g., methylphenidate; brand name Ritalin) are commonly used for treating inattention and hyperactivity; antidepressants (e.g., sertraline; brand name Zoloft) are commonly used to treat anxiety, depression, and obsessive-compulsive behavior; and tranquilizers (e.g., risperidone; brand name Risperdal) are used for mood stabilization and psychosis. It is well known that counseling and medication interventions combined are often more effective than counseling or medication interventions alone.

Natural and Logical Consequences

Another approach to child behavior problem treatment is to promote natural and logical consequences and responses to behavior. Natural consequences occur without specific planning but are allowed by adults to happen. For example, if a child throws food in the lunchroom at school, peers may not want to sit near them again. This unintended natural consequence may decrease future food throwing because the child would like to sit with peers during lunch. Logical consequences do take some planning and adult intervention to impose related and appropriate social learning, as it might occur in adult contexts. For example, the student who throws food might be encouraged to sit alone at lunch for the remainder of the week and write an apology letter to the affected peers. This student will learn that relationships may have to be repaired after a wrongdoing. All logical consequences must be reasonably related to the problematic behavior and should not be confused with punishment (e.g., yelling; forcing the child to throw away lunch; school suspension).

Professional counseling literature suggests that interventions for child behavior problems should be implemented as early as possible in the child's life, in order to promote healthy behavioral changes. Outcomes for children who receive early services are quite favorable, as child behavior problems generally subside after adolescence, and relatively few individuals continue to have significant behavior problems into adulthood.

Katherine A. Shirley

See also Active Parenting; Adolescent Behavior Problems; Behavioral Family Therapy; Conduct Disorder; Depression in Children; Functional Assessment and Children; Oppositional Defiant Disorder; Parental Stress: Effects on Children

Further Readings

Kauffman, J. M., & Landrum, T. J. (2012). *Characteristics of emotional and behavioral disorders of children and youth* (10th ed.). Boston, MA: Pearson/Merrill.

Mash, E. J., & Barkley, R. A. (Eds.) (2014). *Child psychopathology* (3rd ed.). New York, NY: Guilford Press.

McClure, F. H., & Teyber, E. (2003). *Casebook in child and adolescent treatment: Cultural and familial contexts.* Pacific Grove, CA: Brooks/Cole.

Schroeder, C. S., & Gordon, B. N. (2002). *Assessment and treatment of childhood problems* (2nd ed.). New York, NY: Guilford Press.

Vernon, A. (2009). *Counseling children and adolescents* (4th ed.). Denver, CO: Love Publishing.

CHILD GUIDANCE MOVEMENT

From the 1920s through the mid-1940s, the child guidance movement implemented progressive social reforms under the foundational belief that changes in society could be directed and controlled by management of the moral, psychological, and physical development of its children. This view reflected a significant contrast to the conventional wisdom of the time in two areas. First, it elevated the understanding of children and childhood development to be important and worthy of research attention, a departure from common belief that the study of children lacked value or purpose. Second, philanthropic and social service attitudes shifted from the paternalism of providing charity to that of seeking to initiate and direct social change through knowledge and empowerment. This progressive reform movement reflected confidence in and reliance upon scientific research findings and development of systematic programs to utilize them. This entry addresses the influences from juvenile justice reform, research in child development, and child guidance clinics.

The child guidance movement initiated extensive scientific study of child development and welfare as well as providing a foundation for sweeping changes in mental and physical health services, educational standards, parenting knowledge, and recreational and other programs related to children.

Child guidance movement efforts were accomplished by a variety of organizations, including private charitable foundations, governmental services, and both researchers and practitioners in the medical and mental health professions. Where private funding tended to shoulder the research efforts and draw conclusions from theoretical findings as to the best approaches to managing child welfare efforts, governmental agencies were more involved in administering organizations designed to carry out this work once proven strategies were developed.

Earlier work in the area of juvenile justice reform was carried over into the child guidance movement's initial focus on prevention of delinquency as the key to diminishing future antisocial behavior. Later efforts departed from this preventive theme and focused on delinquents, shifting toward work with typical children and toward early detection of mental illness and treatment of behavioral and emotional problems. Education and training within the community were also emphasized as the movement continued to mature.

Influences From Juvenile Justice Reform

The ideology of the emerging child guidance movement was influenced by sweeping revisions in the juvenile justice system during the prior two decades. The first juvenile court was established in Chicago in 1899, and by 1920 only three U.S. states did not have them. These reforms created separate court and detention facilities for youth to segregate them from adult criminal populations, and emphasized rehabilitation rather than punishment of adolescent offenders. Family and community resources were involved in this rehabilitation, and the concept of probation was introduced to facilitate reentry into the community. Toward this end, court processes for juveniles were informal and targeted toward diagnosis of conditions that might be addressed in the rehabilitation process. The first psychiatric clinic was established within the juvenile court system in Chicago in 1909 to research juvenile delinquency and develop approaches for diagnosis and treatment of offenders. Though experts differed as to whether the causes of delinquency were primarily biological, psychological, or sociological, the establishment of these clinics created a framework that served as a foundation for future child guidance movement activity. It also established the psychiatrist's role in directing care for juveniles, expanding the scope of this profession beyond the historical focus in asylum care for insane adults.

Research in Child Development

Given the leadership role of psychiatry in juvenile justice clinics, the field of psychiatry was foremost among professions responding to the need for increased knowledge of all aspects of child development. Mental health wards were established in general hospitals to allow psychiatric treatment of less disabling, and more curable, conditions than those typical in asylums. These hospital settings were used as bases for theoretical research and development of treatment protocols for mental health conditions with much broader social applicability than traditionally existed for the profession. Psychologists, social workers, counselors, and educators also received private and public funding to study child development and related issues. Whereas only a handful of researchers were dedicated to study of children in 1918, there were more than 600 by 1930. Although research findings were shared among disciplines, work emphasis varied by profession according to their respective philosophies and approaches to intervention. For example, where psychiatrists focused more on individual biological and psychological factors impacting child development, social work and education specialists looked more toward social and environmental causes of maladaptation and delinquency; optimal child rearing and development standards; and prevention, identification, and remediation of childhood mental health issues within the community. This collective research informed the direction taken in establishing community-based clinics to provide services related to child development issues.

Child Guidance Clinics

The child guidance movement is perhaps best known for the Child Guidance Clinics, established to provide a variety of direct and indirect services aimed at enhancing child development within the community. The Commonwealth Fund, a private charitable organization, was instrumental in establishing an initial eight clinics in 1922, and 60 clinics by 1942. A number of other private and public funding sources also established clinics or adopted the practices they endorsed. The clinics generally followed the organization established in the juvenile justice reform movement, employing teams of psychiatrists, psychologists, and social workers who operated in conjunction with existing medical, educational, and social welfare services in the community. In addition to providing direct mental health services to typical children experiencing behavioral or emotional problems, the early "demonstration" clinics were designed to deliver education and training in new child development knowledge and practices to professionals and parents. Although the Community Fund opened a training institute for child guidance professionals and became less engaged in management of clinics until it withdrew in 1945, many of the clinics founded within the child guidance movement continue to operate and provide community and child services to the present day.

Mary McClure

See also Community Programs; Parenting Education; Prevention Research

Further Readings

Horn, M. (1989). *Before it's too late: The child guidance movement in the United States 1922–1945.* Philadelphia, PA: Temple University Press.

Richardson, T. R. (1989). *The century of the child: The mental hygiene movement and social policy in the United States and Canada.* Albany: State University of New York Press.

CHILD MALTREATMENT

Child maltreatment is abuse and neglect that occurs to people under 18 years of age and is an ongoing problem across the world. In the United States it is a national public health problem consistently documented over time. Globally, the World Health Organization (WHO) reported almost a quarter of adults state they experienced physical abuse as a child, and one in five women and one in 13 men reported experiencing sexual abuse. Results of child maltreatment can cause serious lifelong consequences. Current research helps to identify potential causes of child maltreatment, which can be used to create awareness, increase knowledge, and develop prevention and intervention programs. All states have laws addressing childhood abuse and neglect. Additionally, there are mandated reporters, such as doctors, teachers, counselors, and social workers, who are required to report any suspicions of abuse and neglect to child protective agencies. Over the past decade an increasing focus on child maltreatment has led to greater awareness and advocacy; however, child maltreatment remains a serious issue. This entry provides an overview of the federal laws and definition of child maltreatment, and an introduction to the risk factors for child maltreatment.

The Children's Bureau

Over the past 50 years, there has been an increase in research dedicated to the study of maltreatment experienced by children. The Children's Bureau, a federal agency, was created in 1912 under the administration of President William Howard Taft to investigate issues relating to the well-being of children. However, state laws requiring the reporting of child maltreatment were not legislated until 1967. The most current data from the National Child Abuse and Neglect Data System identified approximately 679,000 children as victims of abuse and neglect in 2013. Roughly 25% were under 3 years of age, and 20% were 3 to 5 years of age. Children under 1 year of age had the highest victimization rate, indicating this age group is more at risk. Over 79% of the total victims included circumstances of neglect.

Federal Laws and Definition of Child Maltreatment

On January 31, 1974, President Richard Nixon signed into law the Child Abuse Prevention and Treatment Act (CAPTA). Senator Walter Mondale (D-MN) and Representative John Brademas (D-IN) were instrumental in the legislative efforts of CAPTA. Even though all states had child abuse reporting laws before CAPTA was passed, primary concerns of Mondale and Brademas were the deficiency of training received by Child Protective Services (CPS) employees and a lack of significant coordination in the child abuse reporting process. CAPTA was established to provide financial support to prevent, identify, and treat child abuse and neglect. Additionally, government research was authorized to develop strategies for reducing and treating victims of child abuse and neglect. The National Center on Child Abuse and Neglect (NCCAN) was established in the Department of Health, Education, and Welfare, which later became the Department of Health and Human Services (HHS).

Since CAPTA was established, there have been several amendments to improve and expand services covered under the original law, most notably the 1990 Stewart B. McKinney Homeless Assistance Act Amendments and the 2010 CAPTA Reauthorization Act. The McKinney Act addressed several issues relating to homelessness, and also included provisions for children who were homeless or at risk of becoming homeless. Furthermore, the CAPTA Reauthorization Act of 2010 addressed adoption of children in foster care and provided a clear description of child abuse and neglect. Each amendment to the original CAPTA law created additional legal safeguards for children in conditions that could produce an abusive or neglectful situation.

The establishment of CAPTA emphasized the prevention and response to child maltreatment. Because this is a federal law, funding is provided to states and nonprofit organizations that meet basic criteria. States that accept federal funding are required to create programs that have child abuse reporting laws; investigate reports of abuse and neglect; provide awareness and education of abuse and neglect; provide a guardian ad litem (GAL), which is an advocate for a child who is in the process of an abuse or neglect court proceeding; and maintain records of reports and investigations of child abuse or neglect. Unsubstantiated accusations or false reports of abuse and neglect are expunged from public records. CAPTA sets national standards for what child abuse means, and each state has the freedom to set its own specifications in order to satisfy the state's own needs. Each state provides its own definitions of abuse and neglect within civil and criminal statutes. Federal law requires that states accepting CAPTA funding must define child abuse and neglect by identifying a minimum set of actions or behaviors. Currently all 50 U.S. states, Washington, D.C., and Puerto Rico receive the federal grant.

The Centers for Disease Control and Prevention and WHO defined child maltreatment as acts of commission (physical, sexual, or emotional abuse) and acts of omission (neglect). Child maltreatment may include one or more of the following types of abuse or neglect. While each state establishes its own law regarding child maltreatment, there is consensus regarding the following definitions.

Physical Abuse

Physical abuse includes injuries resulting from physical force, either intentional or unintentional. Injuries may be caused by hitting, kicking, burning, shaking, throwing, choking, or use of other force against a child. Inappropriate discipline, such as injurious spanking and hitting with a hand or belt or other object, is also included as physical abuse. Even though the intent may not be to cause harm, if it leaves fractures, bruises, or minor marks, it can be considered as physical abuse. Physical abuse can occur through a single instance or ongoing long-term abuse. Some cultural practices, such as "coining," which is the practice of forcibly rubbing a coin on the skin, may not be considered abuse, but may cause physical harm.

Sexual Abuse

Sexual abuse includes any type of sexual behaviors, exploitation, pornography, prostitution, or sexual acts involving children. This may include rape; penetration that is oral, anal, or genital; or genital contact. Fondling of the breasts, buttocks, or genital area and indecent exposure are included. Sexual abuse can be through physical contact of the child or by exposing the child to sexual material. The lack of or inadequate parental supervision of a child's voluntary sexual behavior is considered sexual abuse.

Emotional Abuse

Emotional abuse, also known as psychological abuse, involves behaviors that diminish a child's self-concept, self-worth, or emotional well-being. Emotional abuse may not leave physical effects on a child; however, the pain is still as real as, or more destructive than, physical harm. Emotional abuse is a pattern of behavior by parents or caregivers that may include chronic verbal hostility, ignoring the presence of a child, rejecting a child by not touching or providing attention, verbally terrorizing or bullying a child, or exploiting or corrupting a child by forcing him or her to engage in or perform illegal activities.

Neglect

The most common form of child maltreatment is neglect. Neglect is the omission of care or failure of a parent or caregiver to meet the basic needs of a child. The intent of neglect may not be to harm a child; however, it can be equally as harmful as acts of commission (abuse). Neglect encompasses a broad spectrum that includes physical, emotional, medical and dental, educational negligence, inadequate supervision, and exposure to violent environments. Physical neglect is the eviction of a child from the home without providing alternative placement or refusal to provide shelter for a child, such as when a runaway returns home. Abandonment occurs when a child is left to take care of himself or herself, without any assistance or support from the parent or caregiver. Additionally, physical neglect includes the lack or delay of medical or dental treatment needed for medical issues, such as illness, impairment, or injury. Failure to provide basic nutritional needs such as food and water, or a safe living environment free from hazards, is also considered physical neglect.

Emotional neglect is defined as the lack of providing emotional support or security necessary for positive growth. Educational neglect occurs when a parent does not enroll a child in school or does not ensure that a child receives an education or experiences that are needed for growth and development. Inadequate supervision is the lack of supervising a child, such as a child left at home alone, or the lack of appropriate supervision, such as allowing a minor to have sexual relationships while the parent or caregiver is present. Exposure to violent environments can include threatening a child with violence or reckless disregard for the safety of a child. Moreover, a child witnessing or being present during intimate partner violence (IPV) situations, which are repeated physical, sexual, or emotional violence by a partner, can have just as much impact as the child's directly receiving the abuse.

Risk Factors of Child Maltreatment

Because child maltreatment is a serious social problem, many researchers have tried to identify potential risk factors. Risk factors are qualities of a parent or situation that increase the probability of child maltreatment. Findings indicate that the mother's previous experience with child maltreatment, IPV, substance abuse, and stress have a significant association with a child's potential for experiencing child maltreatment. It is important to point out that there is not one specific cause, but rather factors that may be associated with child maltreatment.

Families are most at risk of child maltreatment when the mother has had previous experience of abuse. Child maltreatment can have a lasting impact across the life span. Negative childhood experiences are more likely to cause posttraumatic stress disorder (PTSD), anxiety, and depression in individuals. When mothers have prolonged emotional concerns, it can be difficult to attend to the demands that are common with children. Females who experience child maltreatment in their family of origin may have less confidence as parents, lack the skill to set appropriate boundaries, and develop poor-quality parent–child relationships. These mental health issues can impact parent–child relationships as the mother may be more self-focused than child-focused. Strong parent–child relationships provide feelings of nurturing, promoting a positive relationship and decreasing the likelihood of child maltreatment.

In addition, adults with previous experience of child maltreatment may select partners who tend to be aggressive or violent. The parent with a history of maltreatment may indirectly expose the children to maltreatment, as it could originate from the other parent or partner. Women with negative childhood experiences such as maltreatment may believe that abuse is to be expected, or that they do not have any control over abusive situations, such as IPV relationships. Less supportive relationships, in which a partner is directly or indirectly forceful, can create a violent environment. Partners who are violent tend to have an authoritarian discipline style in which physical force is used as discipline. Authoritarian parents are rigid and lack flexibility, which may perpetuate a violent atmosphere. Children raised in an authoritarian-style home are often resentful of the harsh discipline and physical force, rather than discussion and explanations, that follow when the child misbehaves.

A high majority of families investigated by Child Protective Services also had substance abuse issues. Substance abuse by a parent or caretaker can have a negative impact on a child's well-being. Drug or alcohol abuse can impact safety in the home. The severity of substance abuse also has a direct impact on a child. Lack of supervision, an increase in anger, inability to control emotions, and lack of nurturing are common results of substance abuse. Furthermore, money that may be intended for household payments may be used instead to pay for illegal or legal substances, which can be very expensive. Individuals who are addicted to illegal or legal substances can spend considerable time obtaining money to buy them, leaving less time available to spend with a child. Some parents or caretakers become violent or withdrawn while using substances, which can directly impact the well-being of a child.

Another risk factor for child maltreatment may include families experiencing elevated levels of stress. Single-parent families, and those with low socioeconomic status and low levels of education, may be under an increased level of stress. These demographic elements may indicate a lower level of material resources or social support. Lack of resources tends to exacerbate the amount of stress experienced by families if they are not able to meet the needs of their children.

Although annual reports of maltreatment are fairly high, an unknown number of maltreatment events go unreported. Adult survivors have described experiencing maltreatment as children in incidents that were not reported to CPS. Previous research indicates many survivors of sexual abuse did not disclose the abuse until years after the abuse occurred, often only after they had reached adulthood. Lack of reporting may have resulted from the child's wanting to protect a parent or family member, inability to identify their situation as maltreatment, embarrassment, fear, or the child's need to pretend the maltreatment did not occur. Furthermore, even though most states have mandated reporters, these agents may not have enough knowledge of what constitutes maltreatment or are unable to recognize maltreatment and ultimately fail to report.

Imelda N. Bratton and John W. Wallace

See also Authoritative Parenting; Child Behavior Problems; Child Protective Services; Conflict in Couples and Families; Domestic Violence; Emotional Disengagement; Families and Substance Abuse; Parental Stress: Effects on Children; Sexual Abuse

Further Readings

CAPTA Reauthorization Act of 2010. Retrieved from http://www.gpo.gov/fdsys/pkg/PLAW-111publ320/pdf/PLAW-111publ320.pdf

Child Maltreatment. (2013). United States Department of Health and Human Services. (Washington DC: Government Printing Office). Available at http://www.acf.hhs.gov/sites/default/files/cb/cm2013.pdf#page=31

Holmes, M. M. (2000). *A terrible thing happened: A story for children who have witnessed violence or trauma*. Washington, DC: Magination Press.

Lang, A. J., Gartstein, M. A., Rodgers, C. S., & Lebeck, M. M. (2010). The impact of maternal childhood abuse on parenting and infant temperament. *Journal of Child and Adolescent Psychiatric Nursing, 23*(2), 100–110.

Leeb, R. T., Paulozzi, L., Melanson, C., Simon, T., & Arias, I. (2008). *Child maltreatment surveillance: Uniform definitions for public health and recommended data elements*, version 1.0. Atlanta, GA: Centers for Disease Control and Prevention, National Center for Injury Prevention and Control.

Pinto, R. J., & Maia, A. C. (2013). A comparison study between official records and self-reports of childhood adversity. *Child Abuse Review, 22,* 354–366.

Shaffer, A., Huston, L., & Egeland, B. (2008). Identification of child maltreatment using prospective and self-report methodologies: A comparison of maltreatment incidence and relation to later psychopathology. *Child Abuse & Neglect, 32,* 682–692. doi:10.1016/j.chiabu.2007.09.010

Thompson, R. (2006). Exploring the link between maternal history of childhood victimization and child risk of maltreatment. *Journal of Trauma Practice, 5*(2), 57–72.

Child Parent Relationship Therapy

Child parent relationship therapy (CPRT) is a play-based family therapy model with a strong empirical foundation demonstrating its effectiveness for a broad range of issues that bring families with young children to counseling. CPRT is based on the filial therapy model introduced by Bernard and Louise Guerney in the mid-1960s, who promoted teaching child-centered play therapy principles and skills to parents to use during supervised parent–child play sessions. The CPRT model, a more structured and condensed version of the Guerneys' model, was developed by Garry Landreth in the late 1980s and later formalized with a protocol and published treatment manual.

At the heart of CPRT is the premise that a secure parent–child relationship is essential for children's well-being. The focus on promoting secure familial attachment relationships makes CPRT particularly effective for adoptive families. In a supportive, small-group environment, parents learn play-based skills to respond more effectively to their children's emotional and behavioral needs, and improve overall family functioning. In turn, children learn that they can count on their parents to reliably and consistently meet their needs for love, acceptance, safety, and security. The purpose of this entry is to provide an overview of CPRT, including the underlying principles that contribute to its success, particularly for adoptive families struggling to connect. A brief overview of the structure, format, and content of the CPRT model is also presented.

CPRT is grounded on the principles of attachment theory, child-centered play therapy, and child development. The primary objective of CPRT is to promote secure parent–child attachment relationships and increase parent responsiveness. A parent's ability to communicate empathy, understanding, and acceptance promotes an attuned parent–child relationship, which is essential to the development of secure attachment. CPRT is a strengths-based approach based on the principles of child-centered play therapy, and as such, the relationship between parent and child is viewed as the vehicle for change. By teaching parents basic play therapy principles, attitudes, and skills to practice in weekly, supervised parent–child playtimes, parents learn to convey empathic understanding and acceptance to their child. Whereas most popular parenting models are problem focused and teach parents strategies for changing the child's behavior, in CPRT the focus is on helping parents understand their child's needs and increasing parental efficacy. Parents are taught to nurture the development of their child's internal resources and coping abilities with working toward the long-term objective of facilitating their child's self-regulation, self-control, self-motivation, and self-direction. Finally, CPRT is grounded in a developmental understanding of children and focuses on special, weekly parent–child playtimes. Play is acknowledged as the primary means that children use to communicate, express their worries, and make sense of their world. Thus, in CPRT, play is utilized as the means of enhancing the parent–child relationship and provides a lens through which parents and caregivers can become more sensitive and attuned to their child's needs and better understand their child's experiences and worldview.

Current research, including findings from research based on neuroscience, strongly supports a focus on the parent–child relationship as the optimal treatment for adoptive families struggling to connect. CPRT has an extensive research base and meta-analytic findings to support its efficacy with diverse populations and presenting concerns, including adoptive families and families in which children have experienced interpersonal trauma. CPRT has also been recognized as having robust research support for use with foster families. Across multiple studies, CPRT has been shown to be especially effective in increasing parental empathy and acceptance, reducing stress in the parent–child relationship, and reducing child behavior problems.

CPRT's focus on promoting secure familial relationships is particularly suited to families with adopted children who have experienced multiple or significant breaks in their attachment experience. Attachment disruptions can significantly impair young children's capacity to develop a bond with their adoptive parents, which can be confusing to parents who are eager to form an attachment to their new child. Consequently, adoptive parents may feel discouraged and believe that they are failing as parents. In CPRT, adoptive parents learn developmentally responsive skills that promote attuned and responsive parenting, which over time can help the child trust that parents will consistently meet needs for safety, nurturance, and love. As parents learn new skills and feel better equipped to parent their adopted child, parents' confidence and joy in parenting their child grows, which subsequently can enhance the child's experience of feeling prized and unconditionally loved. Through this reciprocal experience, the child–parent bond is strengthened and has the potential to continue to deepen long after the intervention ends.

CPRT utilizes a closed-group format of six to eight parents who typically meet 2 hours weekly for 10 weeks. The small-group format includes a balance of supportive group experiences and didactic activities. Initial objectives include creating a group climate of safety, acceptance, and encouragement, while helping parents normalize their experiences though sharing with other group members. Parents are given information about child development and child-centered play therapy principles, attitudes, and skills that positively influence the parent–child relationship. Skills include reflecting the child's verbalizations as well as nonverbal expression, reflecting the child's feelings and experiences, building self-esteem, encouraging the child's effort, limit setting, and choice giving. Equipped with developmentally responsive ways of communicating, parents are able to strengthen their relationship with their children.

Arguably the most critical element of the CPRT model is the supervision component in which parents video-record required weekly 30-minute playtimes with their children and receive feedback from the therapist and the group members. Promoting secure attachment relationships between parents and children through the weekly play sessions is central to the success of CPRT.

During these weekly child-led playtimes, parents apply CRPT attitudes and skills aimed at fostering a more attuned and empathic child–parent relationship. Sensitive support of parents' emotional needs and struggles as they apply the new skills is particularly crucial to the supervision process. Throughout the 10-session program the

CPRT therapist models genuineness, empathy, warmth, attunement to parents' emotional world, and unconditional positive regard based on the belief that parents' self-acceptance and sense of self-efficacy is vital to their success in learning and integrating attitudes, principles, and skills taught in CPRT.

Sue C. Bratton, Kristie Opiola, Eric Dafoe, and Alyssa Swan

See also Adoptive Families; Attachment-Based Family Therapy; Child-Centered Parenting; Interpersonal Neurobiology, Attachment and; Play Family Therapy

Further Readings

Bratton, S. C., Landreth, G. L., Kellam, T., & Blackard, S. R. (2006). *Child parent relationship therapy (CPRT) treatment manual: A 10-session filial therapy model for training parents.* New York, NY: Routledge.

Guerney, L., & Ryan, V. (2013). *Group filial therapy: The complete guide to teaching parents to play therapeutically with their children.* London, England: Jessica Kingsley.

Landreth, G. L., & Bratton, S. C. (2006). *Child parent relationship therapy (CPRT): A 10-session filial therapy model.* New York, NY: Routledge.

Siegel, D., & Hartzell, M. (2004). *Parenting from the inside-out: How a deeper self-understanding can help you raise children who thrive.* New York, NY: Jeremy P. Tarcher/Putnam.

VanFleet, R. (2003). Filial therapy for adoptive children and parents. In R. VanFleet & L. Guerney (Eds.), *Casebook of filial therapy* (pp. 259–278). Boiling Springs, PA: Play Therapy Press.

CHILD PROTECTIVE SERVICES

The Latin term *parens patriae* roughly translates as parent of the country. As a legal concept, *parens patriae* authorizes the government to protect individuals who are legally unable to safeguard themselves. In the United States, *parens patriae* has had its greatest impact on the treatment and protection of children. It asserts that government has an active responsibility to intervene and protect children when parents fail. As a result, states have been empowered with the authority to act to ensure the best interest of a child and to prevent further incidents of harm. Through federal legislation and local laws, Child Protective Services (CPS) is a government-sponsored initiative to investigate, intervene, prosecute, and prevent child abuse.

Historical Underpinnings

The maltreatment of children extends throughout the course of American history. During the 17th and 18th centuries women had limited rights. Consequently, children were considered the property of their fathers. So, children could be treated with mercy or malice without reproach. As early settlers explored the American frontiers, efforts were made to safeguard children and adolescents. Orphanages in America grew out of the need to care for orphaned children and were pioneered largely by religious charities. And, unfortunately, the country experienced a growing need for them. The first orphanage was opened and operated by Catholic nuns in Natchez, Mississippi, in 1729. The nuns provided shelter to the children of early settlers killed by Native Americans during settlement by people of European descent.

Before government-sponsored child welfare initiatives, orphans were traditionally cared for by tribes, clans, or extended families. Not only was kinship care the primary resource for abandoned or orphaned children, but it also had strong cultural and religious roots. For example, early Christian and Jewish traditions required the care of dependent children as a duty under law. In addition, many immigrants from Asia and Europe imported the practice of caring for children in the absence of birth parents. Today, many Latino, Native American, and African American families continue the tradition of relative care when biological parents are unable to provide adequate support.

When kinship care was not an option, parentless children had two choices: institutions/orphanages or indentured servitude. Up until the late 1870s orphans were placed in orphanages or institutions. In asylums and institutions, these children typically lived alongside mentally ill or disabled adults. The other option was indentured servitude. As an alternative to institutions, orphans were placed with artisans who could provide training, room, and board in exchange for work. Children typically worked for six to seven years as indentured servants.

Between the 1850s and the 1930s, approximately 200,000 children were transported from Eastern cities by trains to farming families in the Midwest. This movement, referred to as the *orphan trains,* shipped thousands of poor and orphaned children from large cities like Boston, Baltimore, and Philadelphia, and even smaller cities like Watertown, New York, to the heart of the homeland. Children whose parents could not afford to take care of them and orphans living on the streets or in orphanages could arrive in agriculturally rich states like Iowa, Missouri, and Texas within a week. Upon their arrival to the Midwest, farming families could choose the child(ren) they wanted. As with any other child welfare program, some children found loving homes. Some never felt connected to their new families, and others were mistreated.

During the 1870s the country was galvanized by the story of 9-year-old Mary Ellen Wilson, who endured daily beatings at the hand of her foster mother, Mary McCormack Connolly. Wilson ended up in Connolly's care after her father died and her mother was no longer able to financially care for her. Wilson's mother boarded the child, but eventually 2-year-old Wilson was placed with a surrogate family by the New York City's Department of Charities when Wilson's biological mother missed visits and could no longer make the boarding payments. For years Wilson suffered a lack of affection and daily physical abuse and neglect. It was neighbors, hearing Wilson's cries, who solicited help for the child. At that time, there was no formal child welfare organizations to intercede. A Methodist missionary worker, Etta Wheeler, and an attorney for the American Society for the Prevention of Cruelty to Animals (ASPCA) came to Wilson's rescue. Attorney Henry Bergh took on Wilson's child abuse case as a private citizen. However, it was his ties to ASPCA, the legal system, and the press that gave the case credence. Bergh, president of ASPCA, was instrumental in having Wilson removed from her abusive home. The case was won with a guilty verdict; Wilson's foster mother was sentenced to one year of hard labor in the penitentiary for felony assault and battery. This case sparked national outrage and inspired public awareness of child abuse. More important, Wilson's case also gave birth to the country's child welfare movement. Additionally, Wilson's case inspired the nation's first child welfare organization, the New York Society for the Prevention of Cruelty to Children.

Out of concern for adolescents in adult jails, the country's first juvenile court was established in Chicago in 1899. Although the purpose of juvenile court was primarily delinquent behavior, the court was charged with intervening in child abuse and neglect cases from inception. By 1919, the vast majority of states had juvenile courts. Before long the remaining states followed suit. Today, juvenile court plays a central role in protecting children.

In 1909 the White House Conference on the Care of Dependent Children was convened by President Theodore Roosevelt. In 1912, the federal government established the Children's Bureau to direct funding to needy families and to support state-run child welfare programs. Child welfare initiatives blossomed over the next 10 years. The 1920s brought the emergence of more than 250 humane societies aiming to protect battered children and to generate resources for families. In 1935 Congress passed the Social Security Act (SSA) as part of President Franklin D. Roosevelt's New Deal in response to the economic ruin caused by the Great Depression. In addition to pensions, unemployment insurance, and vocational services, SSA provided funding and authorized the Children's Bureau to collaborate with state public welfare agencies for the care and protection of homeless, dependent, neglected, and delinquent youth. It was this stipulation, tucked deep within the new law, that furthered the country's child protection initiatives.

The country was captivated once again with issues of battered children in 1962 when an article appeared in the *Journal of the American Medical Association*. According to the journal article, child abuse was medically diagnosable. The article proceeded to outline signs and symptoms of abuse. Within 10 years every state had enacted mandatory reporting laws with the inception of the National Child Abuse Prevention and Treatment Act of 1974 (CAPTA).

It was the enactment of CAPTA that centralized the nation's efforts to define, investigate, and respond to child abuse, neglect, and maltreatment. Consequently, this legislation was key in conceptualizing the current system of Child Protective Services. According to CAPTA, the problem of child abuse and neglect requires a comprehensive approach. Thus, the federal government facilitated the movement to safeguard children by providing states and communities with funding for grants, multidisciplinary collaboration, and technical resources aimed at the implementation and development of strategies that provide adequate protection for children. Furthermore, CAPTA provides funding to states, public agencies, and nonprofit organizations for activities such as prevention, training, prosecution, and treatment. These federal resources fueled the evolution of Child Protective Services in each state. Although the definition of abuse, procedure for reporting abuse, and specifics about mandatory reporting can vary from state to state, each state uses CAPTA as a guideline to secure federal funding. Thus, the fundamental provisions and protections are universal across states.

The Investigation Process

Parents have the right to raise their children, and a responsibility to ensure their child's safety and security. However, when parents fail to safeguard their children, states have the power and authority to act and protect the child from harm. Thus, CPS is charged with protecting children from abuse, neglect, and maltreatment when parents are unwilling or unable to care for their children. Each state has policies and procedures for reporting, investigating, intervening in, and prosecuting cases of child abuse. However, each state's CPS programs stem from the provisions of CAPTA. Therefore, despite variations from state to state, core components are the same. The CPS process entails several steps, including receiving a report of abuse, investigating the allegation, and ensuring the child's safety.

CPS investigations are typically initiated via a written or oral report of suspected abuse by a mandated reporter, neighbor, family member, friend, or a concerned citizen. Once a report is made it is assigned to a CPS investigator. Reports of abuse are categorized by the severity of the suspected abuse. Thus, the response time for a CPS investigator to arrive to the scene or home of the child is usually determined by the imminence of risk. Some reports require an immediate response. Thus, CPS investigators will likely respond within three hours. Reports depicting moderate risk might have a longer response time, such as 24 hours and up to 2 or 3 days. In addition to the severity of the allegation, response times also vary by agency. Next, a CPS investigator arrives on the scene (e.g., school, hospital) or home of the child to investigate the allegation and conduct the initial screening. For CPS investigators data collection includes interviewing the child suspected of being abused as well as each family member, including the suspected abuser. In addition to observations and interviews, the CPS investigator conducts a risk assessment to determine whether a child is at moderate to severe risk of harm. If the CPS investigator deems that a child is at imminent risk of harm, the investigator will petition the court for temporary custody of the child to ensure safety and to prevent further harm.

Within 48 to 72 hours of a case being assigned to a CPS investigator, a temporary custody hearing is held to determine whether the state needs to take temporary custody of the child to ensure the child's safety. In addition to working with the family, the CPS investigator gathers other information for the investigation. This might include gathering and reviewing evidence such as medical or educational records, photographs, police reports, or witness statements. A family assessment is conducted as part of the investigation to determine the family's general functioning. Accordingly, CPS investigators use sound clinical skills to collect pertinent information about the family, including familial dynamics and interactions, strengths and resources, social adjustment, risk factors, employment and educational history, physical and mental health history, substance use and abuse, and any other relevant knowledge.

A family group conference (FGC) is facilitated by the CPS investigator to address risk concerns and to plan for safety. The FGC is a decision-making process that encourages family involvement and responsibility for the safety of the child and the preservation of the family. Dispositional hearings are conducted by the court to create court-sanctioned case planning for the child. Because the goal is the safety and well-being of the child, each member of the team (e.g., the parent, CPS investigator, child's attorney, state's attorney) leaves the disposition with action items. Most CPS agencies employ concurrent planning approaches. Thus, two plans are created and implemented at once to ensure safety and permanency for the child. For example, as the parent(s) is working on one plan to reduce risk factors and to improve the stability of the home environment, CPS may be enacting a separate plan in the event that returning home is not a safe option for the child. The initial service plan, and subsequent service plans, will likely include concurrent planning for the child. Family engagement and case planning continue until the risk of harm is nominal and the child is returned home or until an alternative permanency plan is achieved (e.g., long-term foster care, relative placement, adoption, emancipation).

There are three likely outcomes of an investigation of suspected child abuse. A finding of *unfounded* indicates that, as a result of the investigation, the allegation of abuse did not or could not have occurred. A finding of *unsubstantiated* indicates that there is no direct evidence or not enough evidence to support the allegation of abuse. It does not imply that the allegation is false, only that there is not enough information to make a determination or that the information collected during the investigation was conflicting or inconclusive. When an investigation is *founded,* it indicates that the evidence collected during the investigation confirms or substantiates the allegation of abuse.

Tasha Leroyce Banks

See also Best Interests of the Child; Confidentiality; Elder Abuse; Ethical Codes; Ethical Decision-Making; Informed Consent in Clinical Work; Mandated Reporter; Therapeutic Alliance; Trust; Work Relationships

Further Readings

Child Welfare Information Gateway. (2011). *About CAPTA: A legislative history.* Washington, DC: U.S. Department of Health and Human Services, Children's Bureau.

Brittain, C. R., & Hunt, D. E. (Eds.). (2004). *Helping in child protective services: A competency–based casework handbook* (2nd ed.). New York, NY: Oxford University Press.

Illinois Department of Children and Family Services. (2009). *Parent resources for information, development and education: Foster PRIDE/Adopt PRIDE.* Arlington, VA: Author.

Myers, J. E. B. (2008, Fall). A short history of child protection in America. *Family Law Quarterly, 42*(3). Retrieved from http://www.americanbar.org/content/dam/aba/publishing/insights_law_society/ChildProtectionHistory.authcheckdam.pdf

Warren, A. (1996). *Orphan train rider: One boy's true story.* New York, NY: Houghton Mifflin. http://www.acf.hhs.gov/sites/default/files/cb/capta2003.pdf

CHILD-CENTERED PARENTING

Both experts and parents agree that raising children is one of life's hardest, most challenging, and demanding jobs. It takes patience to raise children, but it can be extremely rewarding and fulfilling for parents to see their children attain maturity, having developed their own personalities, values, and ideas. In the parenting literature, several different styles of parenting are discussed as more prevalent in U.S. culture, and for counselors who may be working with parents or families, it is important to be aware of different parenting styles and the benefits and drawbacks of each. This entry briefly reviews popular parenting styles, including authoritarian, authoritative, permissive, and uninvolved parenting. Next, the entry focuses on the child-centered parenting approach, which gives autonomy to the child to be the decision-maker and to take a more active role in his or her own learning and development. The final section discusses the benefits and drawbacks of this approach.

Authoritarian Parenting Style

Parents who are authoritarian establish rules for their children without any conversation or input from the child about the rules or consequences. The expectation of the parents is that their child follows the rules set by them, without question, and if the child does challenge the rule or asks why a particular rule must be followed, the answer tends to be "Because I said so." According to experts, a child who grows up with this type of parent may lack self-confidence and self-esteem, as well as the necessary problem-solving skills needed later in life because they have had no opportunity to negotiate or talk about household rules with their parents. Such a child may grow up to be a "blind" rule follower, which could result in his or her being overly submissive and being taken advantage of. They could also enter into relationships where they ultimately exert control over others. On the other hand, this parenting style could encourage a child to be more achievement oriented and successful. Still, this feeling of lack of control could cause children to become angry with their parents and rebel as they get older.

Permissive Parenting Style

Permissive parenting is the opposite of authoritarian parenting; permissive parents tend to establish either unclear rules or have no rules at all. As a result, there is very little structure or discipline. If a child breaks the rules, permissive parents often do not follow through on implementing consequences. Permissive parents tend to take on more of a "friend" role than the role of a parent. Children who grow up with permissive parents tend to either not respect authority or be self-centered; they could also be overly generous and accommodating. Since they are not accustomed to obeying or following rules, they may feel stifled by having limits and be unprepared to deal with life's inevitable expectations and disappointments.

Authoritative Parenting Style

Authoritative parenting could be considered a proper balance between permissive and authoritarian parenting. Authoritative parents establish rules for their children but encourage some input from them about rules and limits. Parents explain the rationale for their rules and, although there are some rules on which they may not bend, they are able to see things from their child's perspective and allow for some exceptions to some of their rules. Authoritative parents often use a reward system to encourage positive behavior and instead of using punishment, children are often given consequences. Parents follow through on giving consequences, but in a respectful, warm, and loving way. This style of parenting is considered to be the healthiest, and children tend to grow up being better adjusted, independent, able to make beneficial decisions, and feeling comfortable sharing their opinions with others.

Uninvolved Parenting Style

Uninvolved parents tend to be absent from their children's lives and are often considered neglectful; they provide insufficient support for their children. Parents who practice this type of parenting style often leave their children to raise themselves or have an older sibling care for the younger children; they have a hard time establishing rules or enforcing consequences for bad behavior. Uninvolved parents may not be present in their children's lives either by choice or for reasons they cannot control. Reasons parents may be uninvolved include mental health impairments, drug or alcohol addiction, or because career or professional obligations take them away from home. These parents may also disengage because they feel overwhelmed by either job or household obligations, or they simply have never had positive roles models to follow. Children who grow up in these types of households tend to have significant behavior issues and lack discipline; they may not respect authority or rules because they have never had any. On the other hand, children of uninvolved parents may become emotionally "clingy" and look for attention in any way they can get it.

Child-Centered Parenting Style

The term *child-centered* is often used in relation to child development and in the context of education and counseling approaches used with children. Child-centered parenting refers to the way in which parents teach, treat, and parent children by making the child's needs and wishes their highest priority. They do this by creating a safe and respectful environment in which children are allowed and encouraged to make their own choices. It is through having the ability to make their own decisions, not just simply following the directions or "rules" of their parents, that children learn the necessary skills to make favorable and sound decisions throughout their lifetime. By having been encouraged and allowed to make their own choices, children who grow up in child-centered households learn to analyze problems, develop ways to solve the problem, and learn how to evaluate the outcome. They tend to grow up to be happy and confident, feel empowered, be accountable, and develop the resources to solve problems on their own.

Beginning in Infancy

What does child-centered parenting look like in infancy? A child-centered parent recognizes that when their infant cries, he or she is communicating any of a number of needs, including a need for food, sleep, stimulation, or physical contact. Parents learn to decipher what their infant needs and give it to him or her right away. For instance, instead of feeding on a parent schedule or putting their children down for naps or bedtime on a schedule that suits them, child-centered parents take the lead of their baby and put the perceived needs of their baby above their own. Beginning in infancy, child-centered parents give their undivided attention to their children.

Acknowledging Feelings and Emotions

When children get either physically hurt (e.g., fall and skin a knee) or emotionally hurt (hurt feelings or embarrassment), child-centered parents are empathic and do not trivialize or ignore their children's feelings or emotions. Instead of saying "Oh, you're OK" or "You'll be fine," they listen to their children and allow them to express themselves fully. They do not try to stop the crying (this action sends the message to the child that crying is not okay) or diminish or ease the emotional pain; instead, child-centered parents encourage their children to express, however they would like, what they are feeling. Child-centered parents ensure that their child feels supported, loved, and understood by validating the child's feelings.

Respecting Opinions

Child-centered parents create a peaceful and safe living environment and encourage their children to reflect on their own viewpoints and opinions. Parents respect and value the original viewpoints and opinions of their children and ask questions or make observations to encourage their children to share. Parents also recognize and appreciate that children have their own realities and refrain from pushing their own realities, or imposing their own opinions or prejudices, onto their children. Child-centered parents understand that when they push their opinions or agendas onto their children, the children either do not get the opportunity to develop the skills needed to foster their own opinions or, if they have differing opinions, will stop sharing these with their parents in order to not risk disappointing them. These actions ultimately can compromise the level of open communication between children and their parents.

Discipline

Child-centered parents do not use physical punishment and often use no form of punishment at all. The word "no" is not used unless absolutely necessary. In fact, the word "yes" is used as long as there is no risk of serious physical injury to the child. If a child is not behaving in a way that is acceptable to the parents, child-centered parents examine whether or not what they are asking from the child is age appropriate. They do not take their child's negative behavior as a personal attack. They do not give consequences or punishments, but look at this as an opportunity to use undesirable behavior as a teachable moment.

Parents as Positive Role Models

Child-centered parents act as positive role models for their children from very early on. They create a warm and nurturing environment and treat their children and others with dignity and respect. Some people view this as the means by which child-centered parents teach their children positive behavior. Parents, through modeling appropriate social interactions with others, using good manners, and showing empathy, teach their children ways to interact and treat others appropriately. By focusing on the feelings that their child exhibits when he or she really wants something, parents model empathy, and children learn naturally how to share with others; instead of being told to share, they learn how to empathize with others and share at their own pace.

Criticisms of Child-Centered Parenting

People who criticize child-centered parenting express several concerns about this style of parenting. One of the greatest concerns is that this style of parenting creates and perpetuates selfishness in children. Children get accustomed to continually having their way, and this gives children the false idea that the world revolves around them. When children are used to being able to make their own decisions about everything (what to eat, what to wear, what rules to follow) they do not know how to handle disappointments and they become upset when things do not go their way. Critics argue that children need to know that life is not always fair and that school, work, and friendships certainly do not always revolve around them.

Critics of child-centered parenting also argue that this style of parenting negatively affects the relationship between the child's parents. When so much time and energy is spent catering to the wishes and desires of their children, parents sometimes do not have the time to care for themselves or each other. Marriages suffer when they put the children's wants first (a child who wants to sleep in the bed between his or her parents is allowed to do it) and do not focus on the marriage as a priority.

Child-centered parents refrain from setting limits, and critics argue that children need and want limits. Having boundaries and having limits enforced is how children know they are loved and cared for. Young children especially are not emotionally equipped to regulate themselves and do not have the skills to be able to function in a world without limits. Again, critics argue that the "real world" is full of limits and rules, and by not having them and teaching children how to work within them, parents set children up to deal with an unrealistic future.

Finally, it seems that the foremost argument child-centered parenting critics have is that the overall life of the family is centered on the perceived desired of the child. For example, the children are allowed to make decisions about such things as when or where the family eats out, or how they spend their Saturday afternoons. Critics argue that for a family to function properly and efficiently, there must be balance; although children can surely give opinions about where they want to get takeout food, or what movie the family should see during movie night, having a child make all the decisions for the household is unnatural and unhealthy.

Christine H. Ebrahim

See also Parenting; Parenting Styles; Self-Esteem in Children; Single-Parent Families; Systemic Family Therapy

Further Readings

Csikszentmihalyi, M. (2014). *Applications of flow in human development and education.* New York, NY: Springer.

Durgel, E., Vijver, F., & Yagmurlu, B. (2013). Self-reported maternal expectations and child-rearing practices. *International Journal of Behavioral Development, 37*(1), 35–43.

Hans, S., Thullen, M., Henson, L., Lee, H., Edwards, R., & Bernstein, V. (2013). Promoting positive mother–infant relationships: A randomized trial of community doula support for young mothers. *Infant Mental Health Journal, 34*(5), 446–457.

Saldinger, A., Porterfield, K., & Cain, A. (2004). Meeting the needs of parentally bereaved children: A framework for child-centered parenting. *Psychiatry, 67*(4), 331–352.

CHILDHOOD ANXIETY

Concern or worrying is a part of life and can lead to physical responses caused by an increase of adrenalin (epinephrine) and other hormones that produce a fight-or-flight response to escape from danger. Our body's natural alert signal helps us become physically, emotionally, and cognitively prepared for an actual threat or potential threat. Normal developmental fears are distinguished from other emotions at around 6 to 12 months of age.

During early childhood, toddlers and preschoolers generally show fear of various individuals and actions. Young children can become distressed when a stranger or unfamiliar individual is near. This response can begin around 9 or 10 months of age and is commonly referred to as "stranger danger." This may continue later in childhood, but it decreases as children begin to explore their world and interact with more individuals. Around the age of 2 to 3 years, children may become frightened by loud sounds such as thunder. Children around the age of 4 or 5 begin to experience fear of real or imaginary situations. As children develop their imagination, they may begin to fear the monster under their bed or the dark of night. These types of fears are typical of childhood and are not generally indicative of an anxiety disorder. As children mature and cognitive skills increase, they are able to distinguish between the real and the imaginary, and their fear fades. Most children experience some or all of the types of fears just described.

Childhood anxiety evolves into a disorder when it begins to negatively affect normal development. Children can begin to have maladaptive thoughts and misunderstandings of typical events, and begin to catastrophize. They may also begin to avoid situations or events, procrastinate, lack self-confidence, become hypersensitive to criticism, cry, develop shyness, or require continuous attention. Anxiety is the most common issue impacting childhood; however, unless the behavior is extreme, many children do not receive professional treatment. Children suffering from an anxiety disorder have constant worry, fear, tension, and other symptoms. These symptoms negatively affect learning, behavior, and emotional development, and can continue into adulthood. This entry discusses childhood anxiety disorders found in children and adolescents, their criteria for diagnosis, and how they are treated.

Types of Anxiety Disorders in Children and Adolescents

Separation anxiety disorder is more common in childhood than adolescence. Developmentally, infants up to 30 months of age frequently experience some anxiety when separated from parents or caregivers. Separation anxiety typically diminishes between 3 to 5 years of age. As children develop and mature, they are cognitively able to understand that the separation is temporary. Children experiencing separation anxiety disorder have intense anxiety and fear of harm when leaving or thinking about leaving parents. They usually want parents or caretakers to be in constant sight as they may have a fear of being alone. Other fears include refusing to attend school or day care, refusing to go to sleep alone, and fear of sleeping away from home. Children may have physical complaints such as stomachache, nausea, vomiting, or headaches. Additionally, apathy, social withdrawal, or fears such as death or harm to their parent or themselves may develop. Excessive distress when separation occurs may cause children to be clingy when parents or caregivers begin to leave. A unique characteristic of separation anxiety disorder is that the anxiety subsides when the child is in the presence of the parent or caregiver. For children and adolescents, anxiety or fear of being away from parents or caregivers must occur for at least four weeks, have an impact on daily functioning, and be inappropriate for the developmental stage to meet the *Diagnostic and Statistical Manual,* Fifth Edition (DSM-5), criteria for separation anxiety disorder.

Social anxiety disorder (SAD), previously referred to as social phobia, is an anxious, fearful, or uncomfortable feeling when in social or performance situations with peers and adults. The discomfort originates from a fear of behaving in an embarrassing way or being judged by others. Participating in sports or extracurricular activities, speaking in front of others, interacting with peers, being in public places, and meeting new people are commonly feared social situations. Children attempt to avoid situations where their fear escalates. The anxiety or fear intensifies, and children may respond by clingy behavior, refusing to participate, crying, freezing, or being unable to think (blanking out). These symptoms must be persistent, typically occurring for 6 months or more, to meet the criteria in the DSM-5. Fear or anxiety dissipates or reduces when children are in their home environment where they are comfortable and have minimal stressors. Children may have poor social skills and low peer acceptance, which can be due to their avoidance of social situations.

Selective mutism is a failure to speak in specific social situations. Children with selective mutism have the knowledge and ability to speak, although they do not speak when they are in situations where they experience anxiety. They may speak in their home while parents or immediate family members are present. Selective mutism occurs when children feel scared of social interactions, have increased shyness, and attempt to avoid embarrassment. Children frequently have social isolation and withdraw from peers or other adults. Additionally, compulsivity, clingy behavior, mild oppositional behavior, and temper tantrums usually occur. Children may use sounds such as grunting or body language to communicate with others, and they may be willing to participate in activities that do not require speaking. Symptoms must occur for at least 1 month (not limited to the first month of school) to meet the DSM-5 criteria for selective mutism. Selective mutism can develop in childhood, adolescence, or adulthood.

Specific phobia (SP), also known as simple phobia, is the excessive fear of a certain situation or object that leads to avoidance or distress. The fear, anxiety, or avoidance is persistent, typically lasting for at least 6 months. A specific fear can evolve into a specific phobia when children persistently have extreme distress or intense anxiety that is not appropriate to the situation or developmental stage. Children can have phobias relating to the natural environment, animal(s), or situations. One or more specific phobias may be experienced by children concurrently. The reaction to a specific phobia may include a physical reaction of sweating, muscle trembling, elevated heart rate, and heightened arousal. A response to an environmental or situational phobia may produce thoughts such as "I am crazy." Children experiencing a blood-injection-injury phobia may have a slowing heart rate or fainting reaction. Specific phobias usually originate in childhood; however, they are not typically evaluated until adulthood.

Generalized anxiety disorder (GAD) is characterized by excessive worry and anxiety related to such areas as family, friends, social interactions, school, grades, health, physical appearance, natural disasters, and so on. These worries must be chronic and excessive and have an impact on daily functioning for at least 6 months to meet the criteria for DSM-5. Parents or caregivers are able to recognize the inflated worrying as children have difficulty controlling their worries. An associated symptom such as restlessness, inability to concentrate, muscle tension, difficulty sleeping, or irritability must be present to meet the DSM-5 criteria of GAD. Children with GAD may also experience physical complaints such as headaches, fatigue, stomachaches, or hyperstimulation. The anxious response can cause distress in children, and they may try to manage their response by becoming focused on perfectionism, have an increased desire for approval of others, require more assurance, and be overly conforming. Onset typically occurs during early adolescence; however, symptoms of anxiety and worry may be seen in early childhood and referred to as an anxious personality.

Panic disorder (PD) is the occurrence of continual spontaneous panic attacks. Panic attacks are instances of intense discomfort or fear that transpires within minutes. Panic attacks may be expected or unexpected. During the attack, a minimum of four symptoms must appear to meet the DSM-5 criteria of PD: sweating, muscle trembling, difficulty breathing, pain or discomfort in chest, pounding heart, nausea, dizziness, fainting, sensations of chills or heat, tingling, fear of dying or losing control, or feelings of not being in reality. Following panic attacks, children begin to worry or have a high concern about future attacks. The worry and concern causes a substantial change in behavior, such as avoiding situations to avoid further attacks. Onset typically appears during middle childhood or adolescence, although panic attacks can develop in early childhood. Panic disorder commonly happens with other anxiety or psychiatric disorders.

Treatment of Childhood Anxiety Disorders

Child anxiety disorders can cause many issues, including problems in academic learning, family and peer relationships, and even negative impacts on the child's self-esteem. It is helpful to begin treatment as early as possible so that children and parents can learn positive skills to help during times of anxiety and to decrease future anxiety. Anxiety disorders can be assessed and diagnosed by a pediatrician, psychiatrist, or licensed mental health provider (clinical mental health counselor, psychologist, or social worker). Assessment typically involves gathering information from parents, teachers, and the child (depending on the age).

Anxiety can be treated using an individual, group counseling, or family therapy approach. Therapists use a variety of developmentally appropriate treatment approaches for the treatment of children. For early childhood, play therapy is recommended as the therapist uses toys to work with children. As young children do not have the cognitive abilities required for talk therapy, play therapy is helpful for entering the world of children in a nonthreatening way and helping them express their fears and emotions through the toys. Play therapy can be used with children as young as 3 years of age, and many techniques are successfully used with adolescents and adults. Expressive arts are different techniques that use mediums such as art, journaling, music, dance, or a sand tray. In expressive arts, creativity is used to help children work through thoughts or feelings. Children can express and communicate their issues through the action of creating. Creating can divert attention away from the anxiety so children may become calm. It can also be used in a nonverbal way where children can represent their thoughts and fears through the object they are creating. The object can be a work of art, written words or poetry, a song or musical sounds, a dance, or figurines placed in the sand tray to represent their thoughts, emotions, or fears.

Any therapeutic approach works best when parents or caregivers are involved in the process. This may require parent consultations, family therapy, or participation in parent training. In addition to therapy, medication such as selective serotonin reuptake inhibitors (SSRIs) may be helpful for children exhibiting a moderate to severe level of anxiety.

Imelda N. Bratton

See also Attention-Deficit and Disruptive Behavior Disorders; Autism Spectrum Disorder; Avoidance; Child Behavior Problems; Depression in Children; Mood Disorders in Children

Further Readings

Beidel, D., & Turner, S. (2005). *Childhood anxiety disorders: A guide to research and treatment.* New York, NY: Routledge.

Bernstein, G. A., Bernat, D. H., Davis, A. A., & Layne, A. E. (2008). Symptom presentation and classroom functioning in a nonclinical sample of children with social phobia. *Depression and Anxiety, 25*(9), 752–760.

In-Albon, T., & Schneider, S. (2010). Does the vigilance-avoidance gazing behavior in children separation anxiety disorder change after cognitive-behavioral therapy? *Journal of Abnormal Child Psychology, 38*(2), 225–235.

Layne, A. E., Bernat, D. H., & Victor, A. M. (2009). Generalized anxiety disorder in a nonclinical sample of children: Symptom presentation and predictors of impairment. *Journal of Anxiety Disorders, 23,* 283–289.

Lester, P., Peterson, K., Reeves, J., Knauss, L., Glover, D., Mogil, C., . . . Beardslee, W. (2010). The long war and parental combat deployment: Effects on military children and at-home spouses. *Journal of the American Academy of Child and Adolescent Psychiatry, 49*(4), 310–320.

Manassis, K., & Hood, J. (1998). Individual and familial predictors of impairment in childhood anxiety disorders. *Journal of Academic Child Adolescent Psychiatry, 37.*

McCurry, C. (2009). *Parenting your anxious child with mindfulness and acceptance: A powerful new approach to overcoming fear, panic, and worry using acceptance and commitment therapy.* Oakland, CA: New Harbinger.

Oler, J. A., Fox, A. S., Shelton, S. E., Rogers, J., Dyer, T. D., Davidson, R. J., . . . Kalin, N. H. (2010). Amygdalar and hippocampal substrates of anxious temperament differ in their heritability. *Nature, 466*(7308), 864–868.

Rapee, R. M., Kennedy, S. J., Ingram, M., Edwards, S. L., & Sweeney, L. (2010). Parental intervention alters children's anxiety trajectory. *American Journal of Psychiatry, 167*(12).

CHILDHOOD OBESITY, PREVENTION AND TREATMENT OF

Childhood obesity can have both immediate and long-term consequences. In the short term, children with obesity have a higher likelihood of having (a) high blood pressure and cholesterol, which are risk factors for cardiovascular disease (CVD); (b) increased risk of impaired glucose tolerance, insulin resistance, and type 2 diabetes; (c) breathing problems, such as sleep apnea, and asthma; (d) joint problems and musculoskeletal discomfort; (e) fatty liver disease, gallstones, and gastro-esophageal reflux (i.e., heartburn); and (f) psychosocial problems, such as weight stigma/discrimination and poor self-esteem.

Long term, children who are obese are more likely to become obese adults. Adult obesity is associated with many serious health conditions, including heart disease, diabetes, and cancer. Thus, addressing childhood obesity prevention and/or treatment as part of family therapy is important. Beginning with a brief review of the prevalence of childhood obesity in the United States, this entry continues with an explanation of how overweight and obesity are defined and measured. Next, the findings of an interdisciplinary panel on obesity prevention are outlined. A discussion of the perspective of family systems theory on obesity follows, and the entry concludes with an overview of medical family therapy.

Prevalence of Childhood Obesity

Childhood obesity prevalence in the United States has tripled over the last two decades. According to the Centers for Disease Control and Prevention (CDC), 17% of children between the ages of 2 and 19 are obese, and 33% are overweight. Among 2- to 5-year-olds specifically, obesity has declined slightly based on CDC's National Health and Nutrition Examination Survey (NHANES) data in 2012. However, there are large disparities in childhood overweight and obesity for racially/ethnically and socioeconomically diverse children. For example, in 2011–2012, obesity prevalence was higher among Hispanic (22.4%) and non-Hispanic black youth (20.2%) than non-Hispanic white youth (14.1%).

How Is Childhood Overweight and Obesity Measured?

A child's weight status is determined using an age- and sex-specific percentile for body mass index (BMI) rather than the BMI categories used for adults because children's body composition varies as they age and by sex. BMI is calculated using a child's weight and height. BMI does not measure body fat directly, but it is a reasonable and cost-effective indicator of body fatness (or adiposity) for most children and teens. CDC Growth Charts are used to determine the corresponding BMI for age and sex percentile. For children and adolescents (age 2–19):

- *Overweight* is defined as a BMI at or above the 85th percentile and lower than the 95th percentile for children of the same age and sex.
- *Obesity* is defined as a BMI at or above the 95th percentile for children of the same age and sex.

Prevention and Treatment

Intervening to keep children from becoming overweight or obese is the main goal of childhood obesity prevention. Intervening to reduce weight status once a child is already overweight or obese is the main goal of childhood obesity treatment. In 2007, the American Medical Association (AMA), CDC, and Health Resources and Services Administration (HRSA) formed an interdisciplinary panel of established childhood obesity practitioners and researchers to produce a set of clinical guidelines for practitioners' use titled *Expert Committee Recommendations Regarding the Prevention, Assessment, and Treatment of Child and Adolescent Overweight and Obesity*. These recommendations detailed four stages of pediatric obesity management, from prevention to surgical approaches. Providers are instructed to address families based on the chronological age of the referred child. For families with a young child, parents should be the primary focus of the encounter. School-aged children and parents should be equally addressed. In families with an adolescent, the adolescent should be the focus of the encounter, with the parent/guardian providing an optimal home environment for behavior change (e.g., healthy foods in the home, transportation to an exercise facility). Stages 1 and 2 are aimed at obesity prevention, whereas stages 3 and 4 increase in behavioral treatment and intensity.

Stage 1, Prevention Plus, commonly takes place in a primary care office during an annual well-child visit or physical examination. A child and his/her parent or guardian are told what weight category the child occupies (underweight, healthy weight, overweight, obese), and preventive messages are delivered by the provider around dietary and physical activity behaviors.

In a stage 2, Structured Weight Management, encounter, there is the added support of a health care provider with specific training in weight management, most commonly a dietitian. Visits in a stage 2 encounter provide greater structure around dietary and physical activity goal setting and accountability, ideally on a monthly basis.

Stage 3, Comprehensive Multidisciplinary Care, utilizes a multidisciplinary treatment team to address behavioral, dietary, physical activity, and social/community factors. Families are seen weekly for 8 to 12 weeks in primary care or specialty care settings, with additional follow-up services as needed. A behavioral or mental health clinician (e.g., medical family therapist, psychologist, social worker) commonly works with the family to aid in goal setting, social support, mental health diagnoses, and challenging family dynamics.

The most intensive stage is Tertiary Care Intervention, which is reserved for severely obese youth (> 97th BMI percentile). This fourth stage relies on behavioral treatment and utilizes additional aggressive treatments such as medication (e.g., orlistat), very low-calorie or liquid diets, or weight-loss surgery. Tertiary Care Intervention usually takes place at a specialty clinic.

Family Systems and Childhood Obesity Prevention and Treatment

According to family systems theory, the interactions related to health behaviors that occur within the family are reciprocal. That is, each family member is shaping and being shaped by each other family member's health behaviors, which ultimately contribute to the development and maintenance of dietary and physical activity behaviors that influence weight status over time. These mutually influencing patterns can model and support healthful behaviors, downplay the importance of them, or may even serve to sabotage one member's efforts at becoming healthy.

Family systems theory can be used as a framework for understanding the hypotheses and research findings to date regarding the links between the family environment and childhood obesity. Specifically, parenting style (i.e., authoritative), noncontrolling parent feeding practices (i.e., not using restriction or pressure-to-eat practices), family support and encouragement (i.e., not engaging in weight teasing), behavior modeling by parents, and healthful resources available in the home (e.g., healthy foods available and accessible to eat; no sugar-sweetened beverages available) have been shown to be important mechanisms through which families promote, or discourage, physical activity and healthful eating in children.

Additionally, key target areas identified in the literature and endorsed by the American Academy of Pediatrics to reduce childhood obesity patterns include reduced intake of sugar-sweetened beverages, reduced servings of energy-dense (i.e., high-calorie/high-fat) snacks, appropriate child portion sizes, attending to satiety cues (i.e., stop eating when full), reduced hours of television and computer time, increased hours of physical activity, increased frequency of family meals, and increased servings of fruits and vegetables. As mentioned above, parents and other family members can influence these key behaviors through modeling (e.g., eating fruits and vegetables for snacks, engaging in > 2 hours of television and computer time per day), providing support (i.e., not enforcing a "clean-your-plate rule" at family meals), making resources available to increase these healthy behaviors in the home (i.e., doing family-level physical activity together), and engaging in positive parenting feeding practices and parenting styles (i.e., parent is responsible for what food is brought in to the home/put on the table, child is responsible for saying how much they eat/responding to satiety cues) to promote health behaviors in the home.

Medical Family Therapy and Obesity Prevention and Treatment With Families With Children Who Are Overweight or Obese

Medical family therapy settings are an ideal place to address childhood overweight and obesity. For example, medical family therapists can be involved with addressing childhood obesity through direct therapy with the child and family, via collaborating with primary care or pediatric providers, or through group-based care delivered in primary care and pediatric settings.

First, direct therapy allows for medical family therapists (MedFTs) to address family-level behavior, as well as individual and dyadic contributions to dietary and physical activity patterns in the home environment. Topics addressed are grounded in evidence-based best practices from the childhood obesity literature mentioned earlier. Therapy modalities commonly used in these sessions include solution-focused therapy, cognitive and behavioral therapy, motivational interviewing techniques, narrative therapy, and strengths-based approaches. These visits usually include setting SMART goals (i.e., *s*pecific, *m*easurable, *a*ttainable, *r*ealistic, *t*imebound) around key behaviors and then following up on goal progress in future sessions. Additionally, MedFTs work with family members on being accountable for the SMART goals they set, and negotiate how each family member will remind and/or reinforce the goals set within the family. Family therapy sessions also allow for addressing underlying issues that may have reinforced behaviors that led to, or have sustained, childhood overweight or obesity, such as parent feeding practices, parenting style, life stressors, depression, emotional eating, weight stigma/teasing, and other psychosocial issues or family dynamics. Addressing both behavior-change strategies and underlying psychological and relational issues contributing to overweight and obesity allows for increasing parent and child capabilities to promote behavior change within the household that is more likely to be sustainable.

Second, collaborating with primary care or pediatric providers is another pathway to intervene for prevention or treatment of childhood obesity. This model typically uses a medical provider and a behavioral provider (MedFT) in a joint visit with the parent and child. Usually these interactions occur during well-child visits where the medical and MedFT provider collaboratively educate and intervene with the parent/child dyad around lifestyle behavior change. A typical intervention would include a discussion of baseline health behaviors the child is currently engaging in, such as hours of sedentary behavior (e.g., screen time) per week, hours of physical activity per week, servings of fruits and vegetables per week, and frequency of family meals per week. The parent/child dyad and the medical/behavioral dyad then discuss goals for improving lifestyle behavior in the home and identify follow-up time points to check in about goal progress. A SMART goal framework is typically used, and both the MedFT and medical provider have been trained in motivational interviewing techniques in order to increase the likelihood of behavior change. Having the MedFT in the visit allows for catching other underlying issues that may interfere with health behavior change (i.e., controlling parent feeding practices, depression). The MedFT also inquires about additional systems the child is consistently involved in that could help or hinder progress and SMART goals, including schools, religious/spiritual organizations, and other community settings. If underlying issues are identified, the parent/child dyad may be referred for further resources such as family therapy to address these underlying issues. These collaborative visits are highly useful for population-level prevention of childhood obesity because they capture a large audience and can potentially intervene before overweight/obesity issues become a problem.

Third, group-based care is another way in which MedFTs work to prevent or treat childhood obesity. These visits typically occur in either primary care or pediatric clinics in which team-based group visits operate as part of the overall health care delivery system. For example, parent/child dyads are invited to attend group visits with other families experiencing similar health issues such as asthma or diabetes. Childhood obesity is yet another type of group-based care option that can be provided. In these activities, parents and children attend groups in which an interdisciplinary group of providers (i.e., medical, behavioral [typically MedFT], nutritional) facilitate the group. The topics discussed include evidence-based best practices from the childhood obesity literature, as noted earlier. In this model, it is expected not only that parents will receive high-quality care because multiple providers with interdisciplinary expertise are working together but also that parents and children will receive support and encouragement from other families who are experiencing the same issues they are.

Jerica M. Berge and Keeley J. Pratt

See also Medical Family Therapy; Motivational Interviewing; Narrative Therapy; Solution-Focused Brief Therapy

Further Readings

Barlow, S. E., and the Expert Committee. (2007, December). Expert committee recommendations regarding the prevention, assessment, and treatment of child and adolescent overweight and obesity: Summary report. *Pediatrics, 120*(Supplement 4), S164–S192.

Berge, J. M. (2009). A review of familial correlates of child and adolescent obesity: What has the 21st century taught us so far? *International Journal of Adolescent Medicine and Health, 21*(4), 457–483.

Berge, J., Wall, M., Bauer, K., & Neumark-Sztainer, D. (2009). Parenting characteristics in the home environment and adolescent overweight. *Obesity, 17*, 1–8.

Pratt, K., Lamson, A., Swanson, M., Lazorick, S., & Collier, D. (2012). The importance of assessing for depression with HRQOL in treatment seeking obese youth and their caregivers. *Quality of Life Research, 21*(8), 1367–1377.

Pratt, K., Lazorick, S., Lamson, A., Ivanescu, A., & Collier, D. (2013). Quality of life and BMI changes in youth participating in an integrated pediatric obesity treatment program. *Health & Quality of Life Outcomes, 11*, 116–125.

CHILDLESS COUPLES

Couples who do not have children can be placed into two categories: those who choose not to have children, or are voluntarily childless, and those who would like to become parents but are unable to, and are involuntarily childless. Having a baby can change the relationship between partners in positive and/or negative ways. Likewise, being unable to have a baby because of infertility can also change a couple's relationship. The extent to which positive and/or negative emotions affect the relationship depends on the self-esteem of the individual partners and the couple's ability to cope. Voluntarily deciding not to have children can affect couples as well. Societal and familial pressures may weigh on couples emotionally. This entry discusses the effects on couples of being unable to have children or deciding not to have children, and the methods used by couples who want children and are infertile. It also discusses the particular issues that can arise for same-sex couples who want to have children.

Involuntarily Childless Couples

In general, a couple is considered infertile if they are unable to conceive after 1 year of unprotected sex. Some are able to conceive after fertility treatments, but others exhaust all avenues to have a child and are considered involuntarily childless. There are several emotional factors to consider for counselors working with this group. If one partner is infertile, the other partner may blame that person for the couple's inability to have a child. The person who is infertile may have his or her own emotional responses trying to cope with this issue. Marital satisfaction may decrease. Couples must work on nurturing their relationship and coping with the infertility. This can be increasingly difficult if methods used to get pregnant are unsuccessful.

Infertility Treatments for Involuntarily Childless Couples

Treatment for infertility depends on the reasons for infertility. The most commonly known treatment is in vitro fertilization (IVF), but there are other treatments that may be used instead of or prior to IVF. Infertility that is a result of a woman's inability to ovulate because of a condition such as polycystic ovary syndrome may be managed by prescribing medication. These oral treatments may be relatively inexpensive but could cost several hundred dollars for a woman without insurance.

Surgery may be performed if the woman has blocked or damaged fallopian tubes or, in the case of a woman with endometriosis, to remove endometrial tissue growth. If the doctor is unsure of the reason for infertility, treatment may include clomiphene, which is used to stimulate ovulation; hormone injections; or artificial insemination. Depending on the treatment, it can cost thousands of dollars.

IVF involves collecting a woman's eggs from her ovaries and fertilizing them with sperm in a laboratory, then transferring the resulting embryos to the woman's uterus. The average cost of an IVF cycle in the United States is $12,400, according to the American Society for Reproductive Medicine. Many couples go through multiple IVF cycles. There is a higher likelihood of multiple births with IVF because several embryos are transferred to the uterus.

Other Options for Involuntarily Childless Couples

Some options for couples who wish to have children do not involve the woman getting pregnant. Some couples use gestational carriers or surrogates, in which an embryo is created in a laboratory and carried by another woman, although paid surrogacy is banned in some states. Adoption is another possibility for many couples, though there are exceptions for some couples depending on the state in which they live. For instance, if an individual has served any jail time in certain states, he or she is not eligible to adopt. For those who are eligible to adopt, the adoption process can take several months to several years and cost thousands of dollars. Some couples who want children may be unable or unwilling to bear the cost and go through the time-consuming process of adoption.

Impact on Family Life Cycle

Becoming a parent, and eventually a grandparent, is considered part of the family life cycle, or the emotional and intellectual stages that individuals go through in their lives. For couples who want children and are unable to have them, not fulfilling these developmental roles may have a negative impact on their emotional health and well-being. Some couples may feel a sense of hopelessness or even depression. Members of a couple's extended family are also affected by infertility as their roles may not be met—they will not be grandparents, aunts, or uncles, for example. These extended family members may also need help to work through the stress of infertility as they may feel at a loss to help their children or may put undue pressure on them. Any negativity from family members can result in further difficulties for the couple.

Voluntarily Childless Couples

Couples who choose not to have children do so for many reasons. Some couples may decide not to have children because both partners want to further their careers and believe they cannot do this with a child or children. One or both partners may feel they would not be good parents because of their own personalities. They may feel they do not want to lose a sense of independence or believe that having children may have a negative effect on their marital satisfaction.

Couples who choose not to have children may find that others have a negative view of this choice. Others may view these couples as selfish or uncaring and make remarks that are inappropriate or unkind. This can cause marital insecurities, where the couple begins to question their choice not to have children. Another issue that may cause problems within the marriage is that as the couple grows older, one or both partners may feel lonely and regret their past decision not to have children.

Financial Impact

Couples who choose not to have children may be more financially stable as long as they are sensible with finances. For a middle-income couple, the financial cost of raising a child from birth through 18 years of age has been estimated at several hundred thousand dollars. Although parents can make certain choices to save money, such as relying on second-hand children's furniture and clothes, childless couples do not face these expenses at all.

Societal Pressures

Voluntarily childless couples face a number of societal pressures. Many people may not understand why a couple chooses not to have children. Many television shows and movies present love stories that show couples falling in love, getting married, and having children. Not until recently have movies and television shows ventured to show some of the difficulties of having children.

Couples who do not have children may feel left out of conversations among friends who do have children. Couples with children may not see their childless friends as often as they did before they had children, either because of schedules or because they believe their childless friends wouldn't understand their lives. Women especially may feel pressure from society to have children.

Familial Pressures

Family members may put pressure on voluntarily childless couples because these family members want to be grandparents, aunts, and uncles. Those from earlier generations are especially likely to put pressure on couples because they grew up at a time when people were less likely to choose not to have children. Parents of childless couples may not want to see their genetic line end with their children. Children can also be a status symbol for some families. Not having grandchildren or nieces or nephews can hurt a family member's status.

Same-Sex Couples

Same-sex couples who want to have children together may choose a medical procedure such as artificial insemination or may use a surrogate. Adoption is also an option for couples living in states that allow same-sex adoption. However, despite the U.S. Supreme Court ruling in 2015 that made same-sex marriage legal nationwide, there are still restrictions on same-sex adoption in some states. Second-parent adoption, when the biological parent's child is adopted by the parent's partner, is allowed for same-sex couples in some states but not others.

For same-sex couples, it can be devastating if they want to become parents but are not allowed to do so. The same emotional issues can occur as with heterosexual couples as the stress of not having children becomes more prominent. Same-sex couples may also struggle with infertility problems when using procedures such as artificial insemination and, while fertility treatments are available, they can be expensive and cause the same stress and strain on the relationship as they would with a heterosexual couple. Same-sex couples may choose not to have children for the same reasons as heterosexual couples, although research on same-sex couples who remain voluntarily childless is limited.

Robika Modak Mylroie

See also Adoption; Adoptive Families; Depression in Couples and Families; Family Life Cycle; Infertility; Same-Sex Couples

Further Readings

Lawrence, E., Cobb, R. J., Rothman, A. D., Rothman, M. T., & Bradbury, T. N. (2008). Marital satisfaction across the transition to parenthood. *Journal of Family Psychology, 22,* 41–50.

Pelton, S. I., & Hertlein, K. M. (2011). A proposed life cycle for voluntary childfree couples. *Journal of Feminist Family Therapy, 23,* 39–53.

Sabatelli, R. M., Meth, R. L., & Gavazzi, S. M. (1988). Factors mediating the adjustment to involuntary childlessness. *Family Relations, 37,* 338–343.

Shaw, R. L. (2011). Women's experiential journey toward voluntary childlessness: An interpretive phenomenological analysis. *Journal of Community and Applied Social Psychology, 21,* 151–163.

Stammer, H., Wischmann, T., & Verres, R. (2002). Counseling and couple therapy for infertile couples. *Family Process, 41,* 111–122.

CHILDREN WITH CHRONIC ILLNESS

Childhood chronic illness is the presence of a health condition, in an individual under the age of 18, that has a measureable negative affect on the child's functioning, and that is not expected to improve or be cured over an extended period of time. This entry discusses the characteristics and implications of childhood chronic illness, with particular attention to the reciprocal relationship between the course of the illness and family functioning. The entry concludes with an overview of some of the considerations that should be undertaken when providing family therapy to this population.

Chronic Illnesses

Chronic illness, in general, affects children from all social and economic strata and does not discriminate by race, creed, or nationality. Although the estimates vary, many analyses have shown that approximately one out of every 10 children does suffer or will suffer from a chronic illness before the age of 18. By far the most common chronic childhood illness is asthma, a lung condition that results in inflammation and narrows the individual's airways. Other illnesses and diseases, though not as common, are just as likely to create impairment in functioning and remain a part of the child's life for a considerable amount of time. Among these are diabetes, juvenile rheumatoid arthritis, congenital heart disease, cystic fibrosis, hemophilia, and sickle cell anemia. Also, a growing health concern that has arisen within the last few decades has been childhood obesity.

The causes of chronic childhood illnesses fall within two categories: genetic or environmental. Hemophilia, a disease that prevents normal blood clotting, is an example of a genetic disorder that is passed on to the child through the parents' genes. Conversely, some childhood cancers can be attributed to exposure to carcinogens in the environment in which the child is raised. More common, though, is a combination of genetic and environmental risk factors that contribute to the development of a condition or illness. A good example of this can be seen in the case of asthma. Although genetic risk factors have been identified for acquiring asthma (e.g., a family history of the illness), it is also very common for environmental factors, such as air pollution and allergens common in homes, to create the context for the exacerbation of symptoms.

Given the demands these individuals face, there is often a significant psychological and developmental impact on children living with a chronic illness. Children with a chronic illness may be ostracized by their peers for being "different," or struggle with not being able to engage in behaviors that are typical for their age, and in which their peers participate without any issues. Rejection and isolation from peers can lead to a delay in social skills development and impaired relationship functioning. Children who acquire the illness as an infant or a toddler may struggle to understand what they are going through and grow to resent their dependence on their parents during times when they are growing and trying to increase their autonomy. Additionally, the psychological strain imposed on children by chronic illness can lead to poor adjustment and the development of mental illness. Internalizing behaviors frequently observed among this population include depression and anxiety, while common externalizing behaviors include rebellion and aggression. Despite the negative effects of chronic illness on mental health that can sometimes be manifest, many children with chronic illness also show exceptional resilience and adaptation.

Childhood Chronic Illness and the Family

When a family is confronted with a childhood illness there is an acute phase that occurs during, and shortly after, the time of the diagnosis. During this phase, families are required to be highly flexible and adaptable. They are often required to mobilize quickly, gather information, and coordinate an active and comprehensive response to the illness. Families that are flexible and cohesive tend to do well during this phase of the illness. The acute phase of the illness is followed by a phase of prolonged response, during which the family's fiscal and coping resources are tested. During the chronic phase, parents may become frustrated with each other because of different approaches to handling the day-to-day needs of the child, or find themselves in conflict over dwindling financial resources. This is often complicated by the competing needs of treating the illness and the developmental needs of the child. For example, a mother might be concerned about sending her asthmatic daughter on a field trip, while the father wants the child to have a "normal" experience and be able to spend time making and associating with friends.

The example above highlights one of the core issues in adapting to life with a child who has a chronic illness. What often occurs is that the family becomes organized around the illness, and they filter many important decisions through this lens. Decisions about family vacations, which foods to eat, what activities to participate in, what employment opportunities to pursue, and more can become subject to the demands of the illness. The time and attention paid to the ill child can lead to siblings feeling ignored and resentful, which in turn may lead to increased conflict, jealousy, and rejection within this important subsystem. Putting the illness in its place frequently becomes one of the core challenges families confront.

Some of the struggles these families face, and the unhealthy behaviors they engage in, can exert a negative influence even on the course or the outcome of the illness. One common example of this can be seen in the relationship between diabetic control and parent–adolescent relationships when a child has diabetes mellitus. An often-used illustration is that of an adolescent who is struggling to develop himself or herself as an autonomous individual, while also having parents who are heavily involved in his or her treatment. When the adolescent is not diligent in maintaining blood sugar levels within a healthy range, the parents may be likely to exert more control to make sure that the adolescent is appropriately monitoring his or her health. This effort of the parents to exert control in turn creates conflict with the adolescent's desire for independence, which leads to rebellion and less diligence in making sure that blood sugar levels stay in a healthy range. The conflict between the developmental needs of the adolescent, the concerns of the parents, and the deteriorating health of the adolescent all combine to create a vicious amplifying cycle, which can in turn have a significant negative effect on the course or outcome of the illness and lead to serious health consequences.

Additionally, a substantial body of evidence suggests that parental discord can have a negative effect on the physiology of their children. Most often, this is through the cumulative effects of stress children experience when confronted with parental conflict. Prolonged exposure to stress has been shown to have a negative effect on various physiological processes. Triangulation is another process that has the potential to result in harm. Sometimes this might be one parent aligning with the child against the other parent. Also common is a coalition formed between a member of the health care team and a parent or the child against another member of the family. These types of coalitions have the effect of causing disruption in the family's response to the illness and decreasing adherence to treatment recommendations. The likelihood of triangulation occurring with the health care team is increased because of how frequently these families are required to interact with health care professionals.

Treatment Considerations

Susan H. McDaniel and her associates have come up with a set of significant treatment issues for providers to consider when working with childhood chronic illness. Among these issues are helping the parents to accept the child's illness, putting the illness in its place, fostering healthy and open communication, and helping family members work effectively with the health care team. Accepting the child's illness can be a difficult task for families, since it runs counter to the assumptive reality they have formed for their child's health and future life. Instead of facing the illness, families may retreat into denial or disillusionment, which has the effect of creating a poor response to meeting the demands of the illness. Therapists working with these families can expect to be faced with the challenge of helping families to grieve and adapt to the new reality they are facing.

As highlighted above, one of the greatest challenges families with chronic illness face is putting the illness in its place. While those who have difficulty accepting the illness may tend to respond in an overly detached manner, families who fail to put the illness in its place respond in a way that allows the illness to dominate their lives. In the process, relationships are damaged and individual progress may be hampered. One example of this is the tendency for mothers to become heavily involved in the care of the ill child, thereby leaving little time for their spouse or partner. The lack of time available for attending to the spousal subsystem can further unbalance the entire system. The task of the family therapist in this regard is to help the family balance the needs of the illness with the needs of the other family members and promote balance in the approaches they use to address each of these.

Therapists working with these families will also be challenged to help the family communicate openly regarding their beliefs, feelings, and concerns about the illness. Open communication about the illness can promote healing and cooperation, though it is not at all uncommon to see a family communicate very little about the illness itself, preferring instead to avoid the topic. By facilitating open communication, the therapist is able to help the family better respond to the illness and heal ruptures that may have occurred as a result of this tendency to shut down open dialogue. A final consideration is how the therapist can promote effective collaboration between the family and health care professionals. Misunderstanding between health care professionals and the people they treat can create the context for poor treatment adherence and resistance on the part of the family. McDaniel and her associates suggest that therapists can help the family learn to communicate effectively with health care professionals, ask appropriate questions, make legitimate requests for changes in the treatment plan, and seek a second opinion when necessary. When a therapist helps the family address the challenges inherent in responding to a chronic illness, they have the potential to positively influence the course and sometimes the outcome of the illness.

Jacob D. Christenson

See also Adolescent Behavior Problems; Adolescent Mental Health; Child Behavior Problems; Childhood Anxiety; Chronic Illness With Couples and Families; Conflict in Couples and Families; Family Resilience; Family Stress; Health Issues; Medical Family Therapy; Parent–Adolescent Relations; Parental Stress: Effects on Children; Parent–Child Communication; Self-Esteem in Children; Sibling Relationships; Stress Management

Further Readings

Atwood, J. D., & Gallo, C. (2009). *Family therapy and chronic illness.* Piscataway, NJ: Aldine Transaction Piscataway.

Barlow, J. H., & Ellard, D. R. (2004). Psycho-educational interventions for children with chronic disease, parents and siblings: An overview of the research evidence base. *Child: Care, Health and Development, 30*(6), 637–645.

Coffey, J. S. (2006). Parenting a child with chronic illness: A metasynthesis. *Pediatric Nursing, 32*(1), 51–60.

Drotar, D. (2006). *Psychological interventions in childhood chronic illness.* Washington, DC: American Psychological Association.

Herzer, M., Godiwala, N., Hommel, K. A., Driscoll, K., Mitchell, M., Crosby, L. E., . . . Modi, A. C. (2010). Family functioning in the context of pediatric chronic conditions. *Journal of Developmental and Behavioral Pediatrics, 31*(1), 26–34.

McDaniel, S. H., Doherty, W. J., & Hepworth, J. (2014). *Medical family therapy and integrated care.* Washington, DC: American Psychological Association.

Perrin, J. M., Bloom, S. R., & Gortmaker, S. L. (2007). The increase of childhood chronic conditions in the United States. *Journal of the American Medical Association, 297*(24), 2755–2759.

Rolland, J. S., & Walsh, F. (2006). Facilitating family resilience with childhood illness and disability. *Current Opinion in Pediatrics, 18*(5), 527–538.

Children With Special Needs in Family Therapy

With the advances in diagnostic sciences over the past three decades, there has been an unprecedented increase in the number of identified families who have children with special needs. Family has been defined in a multitude of ways. For the purpose of this entry, *family* is defined as a nuclear unit containing one or more parents (biological or stepparents) with or without children other than the child or children with special needs. *Special needs* is presently defined as diagnosed limitations in physical, mental, and/or social abilities as a result of a medical condition, injury, or genetic anomaly—including affiliated behavioral issues. The term *special needs* is often used interchangeably with *disabled*. Some have advocated the use of the term *differently abled,* but others, including some people with disabilities and some advocacy organizations, object to the use of this term.

Families of children with special needs are just as diverse as the general population, and any attempt to capture all elements inclusive of this diversity would fill a volume on its own. This entry discusses the most prevalent reasons these families seek help through counseling. The challenges these families face include emotional challenges, social challenges, and challenges with the administration of services. Accordingly, counseling, which may help empower these families, must recognize these challenges and be as unique as the individual families themselves.

Types of Families With Children Who Have Special Needs

Mainly, there are two types of families that have children with special needs. These families are heretofore recognized as the *unsuspecting* and *suspecting* families. The unsuspecting family will have a child born with a congenital anomaly, or defect created from the birth process. These families are often caught off guard and must rapidly adjust to the infant's needs. There are two types of *suspecting* families. The first type are those who receive a prenatal diagnosis of a potential disability. The second type of *suspecting* family recognizes over a period of time the failure of the infant/child to reach milestones in a timely manner. Because both types of suspecting families have some information, or suspicion that there may be a problem, they are, if only slightly, prepared. Although both types of families (unsuspecting and suspecting) will have similar experiences, it is important for the counselor to be aware of the differences in their experiences.

Emotional Challenges

There are many emotional themes presented by families who have a child with special needs. Most all families will experience a time of grief upon diagnosis of a child with a disability. For the suspecting family, the grieving process may begin as early as the first recognition of a problem and culminate at the time of diagnosis. This can occur in a matter of weeks, or over a period of several months or years. For the unsuspecting family, the time of grief is immediate and usually comes with much more intensity since these families have had no time to become emotionally prepared.

The period of adjustment as the family traverses the grieving process and gradually adjusts to their life with a special needs member necessitates changes in several areas. The special needs child with health issues will require two to three times as much medical care, doctors' appointments, and often surgeries, as those medically unaffected. This requires more parental involvement in child care, which can disrupt work schedules, family income, and time spent with other family members.

Common themes among parents with a chronically ill special needs child are uncertainty, fear of not making the right decisions, a lack of control, always wondering how much time they have left (if the child is terminal), and sadness for the suffering their child must endure. A common theme for both suspecting and unsuspecting parents of children with all types of special needs is the stress of constantly having to adapt to this new "normal." This is frequently compounded by a chronic state of anxiety as parents face a society that is often reticent to accept individuals who are unique.

Social Challenges

Parents of children with special needs, like most parents, take pride in their children. Still, this sense of pride can be frustrated by a societal tendency to struggle with accepting those outside the norm. Some common themes of parents with a child who has special needs are fear of the child acting out in public or breaching a social boundary, feeling closed off and worried about reintegration, and sadness over long-term family members and friends who fall away after the child is born or diagnosed.

Although societal pressure may be difficult for both types of families, for the suspecting family who has a child who has been diagnosed with autism spectrum disorder or selective mutism, the societal struggles appear to be more difficult than for families who have a child with a genetic anomaly. This stems from the differences in physical appearances, for the most part. Society has been generally conditioned to recognize a child with certain anatomical features that accompany a genetic anomaly such as Down syndrome, or a child who suffered an injury at birth that resulted in cerebral palsy. These children are expected to act differently, and these characteristic behaviors are more acknowledged by the populace. Conversely, children who look ordinary and act differently are vulnerable to being more harshly judged, as are their parents. Therefore, the suspecting parents may struggle with the societal pressure to teach these children to conform. Unfortunately for these families, the pressure to conform to societal norms can leave some feeling as if they should limit contact with the outside world.

Limiting participation in the community can result in a family reducing their involvement with social ties and in other areas that would typically provide additional support resources. Without a good support system, the family will struggle with establishing or maintaining a sense of stability needed, and perhaps miss out on additional opportunities that may be beneficial for the ideal development of their child. It is crucial that any counselor who works with families with special needs help them develop and depend upon their family, friends, and other advocates as resources to stabilize the family.

Administrative Challenges

For the most part, when a child is born with a diagnosable disability, the parents are given the resources to establish early contact with a local government agency, organization, or school district that will provide them with a starting point. This starting point, which varies according to state laws, involves a home visit once the infant arrives in his or her new home. The home visit is conducted by a social service worker or a representative of the local agency to which the family has been assigned. The infant will then undergo numerous evaluations to determine his or her needs and this results in an individualized family service plan (IFSP), which activates the therapeutic services the infant needs, such as speech, physical, and occupational therapy. If there is a failure in the administration of these responsibilities, the parents are forced to look into the administrative system in order to determine if they have additional options. Since these services are federally mandated but are provided by various local agencies, the process rarely works as smoothly as these families hope, and the lack of available therapy providers can be a frustrating experience.

The same federal law that provides services for infants, the Individuals with Disabilities Education Act (IDEA), also guarantees that the needs of children with physical and mental disabilities be met in the public school system. Adherence to the law and the availability of the needed services are largely dependent on the state, the school system, and the administration.

The educational system, although governed by the IDEA for these children, does not uniformly enforce the law's provisions. IDEA mandates that once the child reaches school age, a team of school officials and the child's parents develop an individualized education program (IEP) that addresses the special educational needs (goals and objectives) of the child. The IEP is updated twice per year according to the child's progress, and per any additional desires the parent(s) may have. Many parents agree that the IEP is helpful in providing the educators guidelines that address learning and developmental deficiencies. Yet many parents struggle with school administrators on where their children receive this education.

In public school systems across the United States, there are two ways in which children with special needs receive their education: self-contained and inclusive. Self-contained classrooms are those where the child spends more than 50% of his or her school day in one classroom setting with one or more teachers and teacher's assistants. This classroom comprises other children with special needs, but no children without special needs. Inclusive education provides the child with special developmental needs the opportunity to spend the majority of class time with unaffected peers. For many children, this is possible with the assistance of a designated aide who guides the children in their daily classroom activities.

Since it is beneficial for children with special needs to socialize with their unaffected peers, many parents desire inclusive education. Nevertheless, for public school systems to provide each child with special needs a single designated aide is costly, and many school systems are unwilling to pay the price when they can insist on self-contained education for a portion of the expense.

Counseling Considerations

Although there is no empirically established therapy model for this specific population, emotional, social, and administrative challenges can be addressed in a supportive effort. Counseling should consider helping the family manage the initial grief and deal with the emotions related to having a child with special needs. The struggle with grief in the early period of diagnosis is highly important as this plays a role in overall family dynamics—including the marital relationship. Parents deal with grief in numerous ways. Many parents respond well when receiving psychoeducation or the encouragement to keep a journal. Others quickly learn to master their grief by becoming involved with other families who have children with a similar diagnosis in group activities. Still, some parents may need to adjust to their perceived loss by being present with their newborn or recently diagnosed child in counseling and by allowing the counselor to help them recognize the advantages they may have overlooked.

Another area that needs to be considered is the element of empowering these families. This includes looking at their past successes in a similar challenge, or in one single challenge they have had with their child. How were they able to master the transition of bringing their child with special needs home from the hospital with success? How did they manage to keep their infant on a feeding schedule? If there is a medical issue involved, what was their greatest success as a family when it came to managing the child's surgery and recuperation? How did they manage their child's last outburst in a social area with success? These are all possible questions that can be posed to help the parents and family realize they have internal resources on which they can draw in times of anxiety or stress.

All too often, parents of a child with special needs feel they are on the outside of society. Encouraging them to use the resources they have and build upon these resources will serve them well. Managing day-to-day life with an infant or child with special needs can be difficult within a family. Thus, including other individuals in the family circle can provide a wealth of assets. Family members, friends, social contacts, and the like can become "part of the family" as they provide the needed care that will give the nuclear family some time to relax and adjust. Furthermore, these resources will provide a rich environment for the child with special needs that he or she may not have received in a nuclear family.

Salena Blackburn Potter

See also Acculturation; Best Interests of the Child; Children With Chronic Illness; Empowerment in Families; Family Resilience; General Systems Theory; Social Support

Further Readings

Aron, L., & Loprest, P. (2012). Disability and the education system. *The Future of Children, 22*(1), 97–122.

Brody, D. (2008). *The elephant in the playroom: Ordinary parents write intimately and honestly about raising kids with special needs.* New York, NY: Plume/Penguin.

Gallagher, C., & Konjoian, P. (2010). *Shut up about your perfect kid: A survival guide for ordinary parents of special children.* New York, NY: Crown.

Halfon, N., Houtrow, A., Larson, K., & Newacheck, P. W. (2012). The changing landscape of disability in childhood. *The Future of Children, 22*(1), 13–42.

Individuals with Disabilities Education Act, P. L. 108-446 (2004), 20 U.S.C. § 1400 et seq.

Kilic, D., Gencdogan, B., Bag, B., & Arican, D. (2013). Psychosocial problems and marital adjustments of families caring for a child with intellectual disability. *Sexuality and Disability, 31*(3), 287–296.

Choice Theory and Reality Therapy

Choice theory offers an explanation of human behavior and motivation. With its emphasis on the importance of satisfying relationships, choice theory provides a format for understanding why all human beings have a need for interpersonal connections and alliance with others and why people have difficulty maintaining these connections. Reality therapy is the process in which this understanding is put into action. In counseling, the integration of choice theory and reality therapy helps couples and families change their ineffective thinking and actions and create new behaviors that lead to healthy and happy connections with others. This entry provides an overview of choice theory and reality therapy and how these ideas help guide the therapeutic process in couple and family counseling.

Effective and Ineffective Relationship Habits

An axiom of choice theory is that most psychological problems are based on relationship problems. Unhappy relationships result from the use of behaviors that attempt to coerce, control, or change others. These behaviors are developed as a result of the mistaken belief that if people are unhappy it is because of other people or things that are out of their control. Instead of taking responsibility for what people can control, they attempt to change others with the belief that if others or things outside themselves will change, their misery will be eliminated. Among these ineffective, coercive, and controlling behaviors are (a) *criticizing*, (b) *blaming*, (c) *complaining*, (d) *nagging*, (e) *threatening*, (f) *punishing*, and (g) *bribing or rewarding to control*. Other behaviors that people find to be relationship killers are guilting, manipulating, cheating, or withholding sex. The list is unlimited, and people usually have no difficulty in identifying the painful behaviors that others are using to control them.

Choice theory teaches that people can control only themselves. If they are unhappy in their relationships, they must focus on what they can do to improve it, not on what someone else must do. When people change their own behavior, the system tends to change as well. The way people influence change is through the use of effective relationship skills. These skills include (a) *listening*, (b) *supporting*, (c) *encouraging*, (d) *trusting*, (e) *respecting*, (f) *accepting*, and (g) *negotiating differences*.

Choice Theory

Choice theory postulates that all human beings are motivated by basic needs of survival, love and belonging, power, freedom, and fun. People constantly strive to get their needs met; therefore, the motivation for all human behavior is considered to be purposeful, and behavior is chosen to fulfill basic needs. Because basic needs are genetically based, they are not considered to be hierarchical and are not the same for every individual. Evidence to support the theory that there is a link between genetics and basic needs can be offered by parents who have more than one child. When their children are born, parents can see that their children are different from each other in what they need, in spite of sharing the same parents. For example, some children may be hungry for personal contact and connection, while others are content to play by themselves in their crib.

Survival

The need for survival, or self-preservation, is at its most fundamental the need to continue living. The survival need is also manifest in the psychological desire to feel safe and secure. People with a low need for survival enjoy taking risks, live for the moment, and easily adapt to change. People with high need for survival are aware of threats to safety and security. They are motivated to protect themselves and the important people in their lives. They don't accommodate to change easily. Conflicts in couple and family relationships occur when members have different levels of survival needs, and behavior is intended to control others' behavior to meet the level of safety and survival desired.

Love and Belonging

All humans have a need for love and belonging and affiliation with others. This need is met through friendship, family, intimacy, romance, and involvement with groups. Relationships in which the members have similar needs for belonging are usually the most cohesive. People who have a high need for belonging desire a great deal of time and interaction with their partners, children, and other significant people in their lives. They want to be both physically and emotionally close and desire a high level of intimacy. Conversely, people with a low level of need for belonging don't have the same desire for this type of connection and don't understand why increased intimacy is important.

Power

For many people, the word *power* implies control, domination, and exploitation. From a choice theory perspective, power refers to the desire for personal achievement, accomplishment, self-esteem, or inner control. People with a very high need for power often are perfectionistic. They have little tolerance for others who do not share their aspirations. They tend to be ambitious and are often focused on success at work rather than family or relationships. They want to be recognized and respected. People with a low need for power are usually content to take a secondary role or to act as a support to others or a project.

There are several challenges for relationships because of power needs. Relationship difficulties occur when both partners have high power needs and are in competition with one another. Another power-based problem results when one person in a couple or family relationship uses power to coerce or control others. The most effective balance of power needs in relationships occurs when one partner has a high need for power and others have a low need, or when both partners have low or moderate power needs. In any case, it is obvious that a choice of power over behaviors in any relationship results in disconnection and unhappiness.

Freedom

The need for freedom manifests itself in the drive for independence and autonomy, the desire to make choices, to function without restriction, and to have time away from the demands of relationships with others. High-freedom people are often considered to be selfish because they seem to do what they want without regard for others. People with a high need for freedom dislike the control that comes with rules or constraints. They like to work alone and have difficulty admitting that they need help. Challenges to relationships occur when members have conflicting needs for freedom. People with high needs for belonging often struggle with those who have high needs to be free.

Fun

People who have a high need for fun enjoy life. The need for fun can be met in many ways, but people with a high need for fun are often seen laughing, playing, or engaging in activities that stimulate learning. The ability to share fun, laughter, and learning makes a strong foundation for successful long-term relationships. Unfortunately, when problems arise in relationships, fun is often one of the first things to be eliminated.

Quality World

All people have basic needs, but the ways they get their needs met are unique to each person. As a result of life experiences, people develop very specific pictures or wants that satisfy one or more of their basic needs. These pictures include (a) the people we want in our lives, (b) the things we think will increase our pleasure, and (c) the ideas, values, or beliefs that guide our behavior. These unique, ideal, and specific pictures of what people want are stored in what William Glasser referred to as the *quality world*. Difficulties occur in relationships when the pictures in the members' quality worlds are unrealistic or incompatible. The painful perception that what people have is not what they want results in a sense of feeling emotionally out of balance and stimulates motivation to take action that will end in getting wants and needs met more effectively.

Total Behavior

Unique to choice theory is the concept of total behavior, which includes the observable component of actions, but also includes cognition, emotions, and physiological functioning. When people perceive that they are not getting their quality world wants and their basic needs met, they feel an urge to take action. Therefore, all total behavior is purposeful. People choose behavior so they can get what they want, which satisfies one or more of their basic needs. People have direct control over actions and cognition. Making changes to actions and cognition will indirectly change emotions and physiology.

Reality Therapy

Couples and families often have many conflicting and unfulfilled wants and needs. When they come to counseling, what they are most aware of is what is wrong with their relationships. Typically, clients point to others as the source of the problems. The task of the reality therapist is to collapse the conflict by helping clients recognize what is happening, their part in the conflict, and what they can control. After establishing a therapeutic relationship and empathically listening to the clients' perceptions of events, the therapist guides the clients from their focus on the problem to discussion of what they can all agree upon, that what they want is a happier, healthier relationship.

Reality therapy is an optimistic, action-oriented, client-focused approach to couple and family counseling. Clients are helped to recognize that they are more than just individuals in counseling; they are members of a larger entity—the couple or family system. In due course, clients not only work toward individual need fulfillment, but will also work to create need fulfillment for all members of the system. Clients identify the strengths of the relationship and look for times when the problem is absent or minimized. The therapist aids clients in changing their perception of the relationship from hopeless to hopeful.

As part of the reality therapy process, clients are taught choice theory concepts. Clients are helped to understand that if their relationship is to become need-satisfying they will have to come to agreement about what they want and how they perceive the world and their relationship system. Once this agreement has been made, the therapist will ask the clients what they have been doing to get what they want for their relationship. This self-evaluation of the effectiveness of clients' current behavior is an important part of counseling with reality therapy. Self-evaluation creates a sense of internal dissonance that stimulates a desire for something to be different and creates motivation for change. Clients evaluate whether the continued use of their current behavior is likely to bring them closer to the important people in their lives or if the behavior is likely to bring more harm and unhappiness to their relationships.

When the evaluation has been made, the therapist guides the clients in generating options for alternative behavior. Clients are asked to take personal responsibility for their own behavior and to make a commitment to putting their part of the plan into action. Clients leave each session with concrete, behavioral-specific, attainable, and measurable plans for change that are likely to move the entire system into more effective functioning.

Patricia A. Robey

See also Beliefs and Values; Brief Family Therapy; Parenting

Further Readings

Bellows, J. T. (2007). *Happiness in the family: Using choice theory to eliminate hostility in the family.* Lincoln, NE: iUniverse.

Buck, N. S. (2000). *Peaceful parenting.* San Diego, CA: Black Forest Press.

Buck, N. S. (2009). *Why do kids act that way? The instruction manual parents need to understand children at every age.* Denver, CO: Peaceful Parenting Inc.

Glasser, W. (1998). *Choice theory*. New York, NY: HarperCollins.

Glasser, W. (2000). *Reality therapy in action*. New York, NY: HarperCollins.

Glasser, W. (2011). *Take charge of your life: How to get what you need with choice theory psychology*. Bloomington, IN: iUniverse.

Glasser W., & Glasser, C. (2000). *Getting together and staying together*. New York, NY: HarperCollins.

Olver, K. (2011). *Secrets of happy couples: Loving yourself, your partner, and your life*. Chicago, IL: InsideOut Press.

Robey, P. A., Wubbolding, R. E., & Carlson, J. (Eds.). (2012). *Contemporary issues in couples counseling: A choice theory and reality therapy approach*. New York, NY: Routledge.

Wubbolding, R. (2000). *Reality therapy for the 21st century*. Philadelphia, PA: Brunner Routledge.

Wubbolding, R. (2010). *Reality therapy: Theories of psychotherapy series*. Washington, DC: American Psychological Association.

CHOSEN FAMILIES

Chosen families are nonbiological kinship bonds, whether legally recognized or not, deliberately chosen for the purpose of mutual support and love. The nuclear family unit was historically believed to include a husband, wife, and children. However, modern definitions of family have become more expansive and may include any configuration of individuals who provide support for one another. Chosen families have often been embraced within lesbian, gay, bisexual, and transgender (LGBT) communities. Practitioners engaged in marriage, couples, and family counseling provide services to individuals in a variety of family configurations, some of which are chosen families. The purpose of this entry is to explore the social context in which chosen families have emerged, particularly the emergence of chosen families as a response to LGBT stigma and as a vehicle for LGBT parenting. Additionally, the influence of LGBT chosen families on broader cultural definitions of family, including implications for practitioners engaged in marriage, couples, and family counseling, is explored.

Chosen Families as a Response to LGBT Stigma

Anthropologist Kath Weston provided one of the first succinct accounts of the influence of modern LGBT life on definitions of chosen family in the United States during the 20th century. In her seminal work *Families We Choose*, Weston described chosen family as deliberately chosen networks of support in LGBT communities, consisting of friends, partners and ex-partners, biological and nonbiological children, and others who provide kinship support. Chosen families may live together in a single household, or they may be spread through a larger community.

Chosen families are not uniform in the type of support they may provide to one another. The support of a chosen family can wax and wane throughout life, similar to traditional support from families of origin. For example, chosen families may play a strong role in the life of a young person and then play a less prominent role as the young person ages and identifies a partner of her or his own. Older adults, when no longer able to live alone, may rely upon chosen families for support. In some cases, the support is financial and may involve sharing of household expenses. In other cases, emotional care and support are the common currency.

Chosen families emerged in LGBT communities at least in part due to necessity. Prior to the declassification of homosexuality in the 1973 edition of the American Psychiatric Association's *Diagnostic and Statistical Manual for Mental Disorders*, same-sex desire was considered to be a pathological, developmental disturbance requiring psychiatric intervention. Psychiatric intervention for homosexuality was primarily in the form of aversion therapy. Aversion therapy was a behavioral conditioning approach whereby the patient was subject to chemical or electrical aversion upon being stimulated. For example, a gay male patient may be exposed to gay male pornography and then administered an electrical shock. The American Psychiatric Association later condemned the practice as unethical and ineffective.

Treatment for homosexuality, however, has not been uncommon. Many LGBT people grew up in families that either entirely ignored LGBT identity or were openly hostile toward it. Some LGBT people sought counseling to cure their illness, while others fully embraced their LGBT identity. Others sought a spiritual solution to their problem, as many mainline Christian denominations once condemned homosexuality as a violation of human and spiritual law. Fortunately, hostility toward LGBT people has diminished, and more people, including the psychiatric community, have begun to see LGBT identities as falling on the normal spectrum of human experience. These beliefs have not always been widely adopted within families of origin.

Until approximately the turn of the 21st century, societal stigma against LGBT people was commonplace and widely sanctioned by the U.S. government. LGBT people could be dismissed from their jobs or evicted from their apartments or houses solely due to sexual orientation or gender identity. Homosexuality was believed to be incompatible with military service. Federal employees who were LGBT were routinely believed to be a security risk, as it was believed that homosexuality was such an objectionable illness that it could be readily used for blackmailing those with a security clearance.

Crimes motivated by hatred or fear were either ignored or not prosecuted to the full extent of the law. Violent hate crimes against a person solely because of her or his sexual orientation or gender identity were not classified as such. In some cases, the police themselves were the ones harassing or otherwise victimizing LGBT people. Thus, even if hate crime laws had existed, it is unlikely that these crimes would have been prosecuted, as this would entail the risk of exposing oneself to further violence from the police and/or coming out to loved ones.

Societal sanctioning of stigma by the government also affected family relationships. This led some not to disclose their sexual orientation to family (what some refer to as "staying in the closet") and to remain invisible, fearing that coming out to their families might result in rejection. Other rejection within families was implicit. For example, family members might presume that their family members are heterosexual, asking questions like, "When are you going to bring a girlfriend home?" or "When are you getting married?" These factors, coupled with societal stigma toward LGBT people, kept many LGBT people from disclosing their sexual orientation. Others who lived open and honest lives did so at great personal and professional risk.

Risk or rejection drove many LGBT people away from their families and communities of origin. Especially in large cities where LGBT communities were more visible and robust, LGBT people began to seek alternative forms of support. In some cases LGBT people sought out large metropolitan areas such as Chicago, New York, San Francisco, and the District of Columbia because they perceived a greater social tolerance for LGBT people in these cities. Within the major cities, social and community organizations, which often had the activist component of fighting for LGBT liberation, emerged as a ready source of forming alternative family kinship bonds. These relationships would be particularly beneficial to the LGBT communities during times of great struggle. One period of great struggle was the HIV/AIDS pandemic that emerged in the 1980s, which profoundly impacted LGBT communities. Gay and bisexual men were, at first, among the most visibly affected by HIV/AIDS, as initially the disease was called Gay-Related Immunodeficiency Syndrome. Because of a lack of information about how the disease was spread, panic occurred in some communities. Some families feared that the disease could be communicable by sharing a toilet or drinking from the same cup as an infected person, though this turned out to be an unfounded fear.

LGBT chosen families were often called upon to care for the sick as well as survivors of the disease. Social service organizations emerged in larger cities, tasked with caring for vulnerable members of the communities by meeting their social welfare needs. Each of these organizations emerged, in part, due to HIV/AIDS/LGBT stigma and due to a perceived need for providing services that were culturally relevant and sensitive.

During the beginning of the pandemic, chosen families sometimes housed the sick until their death. After it became clear that the disease could be effectively treated and prevented, chosen families were the primary source of education about the disease because LGBT young people often could not rely upon their families of origin or communities for providing LGBT-sensitive sexual health education.

Chosen Families as a Vehicle for LGBT Parenting

Driven at least in part by the HIV/AIDS pandemic and the desire for greater social acceptance of LGBT identities, the quest for respectability became a new social norm within certain LGBT communities. While LGBT activism of the 1960s and 1970s was characterized by sexual freedom and resistance of heteronormativity (seeing heterosexuality and marriage as the most normal and healthy lifestyle), sexual responsibility is now the new social norm for dominant LGBT communities. An agenda that included the rights to same-sex marriage and to families became the goal of mainstream LGBT activism.

LGBT couples seeking to have biological children often looked to their chosen families for assistance in making their dreams of family a reality. In some cases, gay men were sperm donors for lesbian friends seeking to have biological children. In other cases, lesbian friends were used as surrogates for gay male couples. Different types of parenting bonds emerged from these arrangements, ranging from donor-only relationships with no further parental involvement to full co-parenting involving two couples and four parents. In other instances, the donor parent did not actively parent the resulting child but maintained a "special" aunt/uncle role. While these arrangements were often not without complication, chosen families often provided a great deal of support for biological childbearing.

When biological childbearing was not possible or desirable, LGBT couples sought other ways to realize their dreams of parenting. Some jurisdictions in the United States began expanding family and child welfare laws, making it possible for same-sex couples to foster and/or adopt eligible children. Second-parent adoptions enabled some LGBT partners to adopt their partner's biological child from a previous heterosexual relationship. At the time of this writing, LGBT adoption is not universally available in all states. However, a number of jurisdictions have widened LGBT adoption opportunities, acknowledging the empirical evidence that suggests children do just as well or better with same-sex parents as they do with opposite-sex parents. These factors are likely to even further widen the development of chosen families.

Implications of LGBT Chosen Families on Broader Cultural Definitions of Family

Expanded definitions of kinship within broader society have been influenced by the emergence of LGBT chosen families. The nuclear family of husband, wife, and children is no longer the social norm in the United States. According to the American Association of Retired Persons, nearly 8 million children live with and/or are cared for by grandparents or other relatives. High parental divorce rates make it likely that children will live with only one biological parent. Additionally, an unknown number of children live either temporarily or permanently with other people within their communities, bound by informal bonds of kinship based on cultural identity, shared faith, or other factors.

At the same time, negative views toward LGBT communities still exist in the United States. Much of the negative rhetoric around LGBT people centers on the argument that LGBT people are a threat to the traditional family. Much LGBT bias is motivated by religion. However, these arguments that LGBT people are anti-family stand in contrast to available evidence. LGBT people have indeed changed the traditional family by broadening the definition of family. Chosen families have expanded family bonds, not threatened them.

Practitioners engaged in marriage, couples, and family counseling increasingly recognize the importance of chosen families when providing services. Families can provide significant emotional and other tangible support during times of need. Because bonds of kinship are formed in a variety of ways, only some of which are bound by blood ties or legal arrangements, practitioners can effectively intervene with the family only once the practitioner has an understanding of how identified clients define family. As clients take the lead in defining family, practitioners are increasingly coming to respect how family is uniquely defined, even when that definition of family falls outside the practitioner's own definition of family.

Further, more and more practitioners are advocating expanded protections for chosen families. Failure to recognize differing bonds of kinship is often rooted in homophobia (fear of homosexuality) and heterosexism (a bias toward opposite sexuality and relationships), and results in the privileging of the nuclear family as the ideal form of family relationships. However, the nuclear family has increasingly become less common and is more of an anomaly than not in some communities. When clinically appropriate, practitioners should help chosen families recognize how heterosexism, homophobia, and other inequalities may be impacting current family functioning, and provide strategies for overcoming these social problems.

Trevor G. Gates

See also LGBT Families; Sexual Orientation, Attraction, and Identity; Sexual Prejudice

Further Readings

American Association of Retired Persons. (2015). *Grandfacts: State fact sheets for grandparents and other relatives raising children*. Retrieved from http://www.aarp.org/relationships/friends-family/grandfacts-sheets/

D'Emilio, J. (1998). *Sexual politics, sexual communities*. Chicago, IL: University of Chicago Press.

Gates, T. G., & Kelly, B. L. (2013). LGB cultural phenomena and the social work research enterprise: Toward a strengths-based, culturally anchored methodology. *Journal of Homosexuality, 60*(1), 69–82.

Weston, K. (1991). *Families we choose: Lesbians, gays, kinship*. New York, NY: Columbia University Press.

Chronic Illness With Couples and Families

The impact(s) of chronic illness—characterized as *any incurable and ongoing disease or condition*—can be both profound and far-reaching. This is an important issue for mental health providers serving in contemporary health care systems, insofar as individuals, couples, and families can bear significant medical, emotional, relational, and social burdens when facing it. Approximately half of all adults in the United States—more than 117 million people—currently live with at least one chronic health condition, and 25% report two or more. This already widespread prevalence is increasing fast, too, as technological advances and improved quality of care facilitate the aging of the population. Most training programs across disciplines (e.g., psychology, counseling, family therapy) do not equip new professionals to work effectively with patients who are living with a condition that is both permanent and likely, in the long run, fatal. This entry continues with a brief discussion regarding the complex ways that couples experience chronic illness, explains why using a biopsychosocial/spiritual approach in therapy is thereby indicated, and offers clinical guidelines for those working with couples who live with chronic illness.

Responses to Chronic Illness

There is considerable variability in how people respond to their chronic illness. Some act proactively and seek care as soon as the illness is recognized, while others deny or avoid receiving a diagnosis and initiating treatment. Alongside these initial responses, there are a myriad of emotions, both fleeting and long-lasting, that contribute to how a chronic condition is experienced. For example, patients frequently report feeling sadness, anger, confusion, and fear. Others find acceptance, renewal, and courage. Significant others and families span the emotional gamut, as well, ranging from despair and uncertainty to an increased sense of closeness with each other and/or the patient.

While common factors unite couples coping with chronic illness, there is variability in the illness onset, course, and outcome. For many couples, the illness becomes an intrusive and demanding part of their lives, even going as far as infiltrating their couple identity. Due to its unpredictability, such as frequent changes in the patient's energy level, couples can become more defined by the illness than by their previously established dyadic or family goals and values. They no longer make plans for future events; they instead live day to day according to the patient's health status.

Consistent with the biopsychosocial/spiritual approach advanced by George Engel and other scholars like Kerr White, Franklin Williams, and Bernard Greenberg, the fields of marriage and family therapy (MFT) and medical family therapy (MedFT) have begun to adapt their treatment approaches to chronic illness in ways that capture a holistic understanding of chronic illness on a dyadic level. As research has continued to reveal the significant impacts, both detrimental and potentially beneficial, of chronic illness on the dyad, the need for working with and treating couples with chronic illness from a systemic perspective has become even more compelling.

Clinical Guidelines for Working With Couples Who Live With Chronic Illness

Working clinically with couples who are coping with one or more chronic illnesses can be very challenging, both professionally and personally. Clinicians can experience both joy and pain when walking alongside couples through their experiences of chronic illness. Field leaders, including Susan McDaniel, William Doherty, Jeri Hepworth, and others, have identified several sets of guidelines for clinicians engaged in these efforts; the following is a distillation of these: (a) eliciting the couple's illness narrative; (b) attending to affect; (c) facilitating communication between partners, family members, and medical providers; (d) shifting focus from "your" illness to "our" illness; and (e) maintaining an empathic and resilience-focused presence.

Eliciting the Couple's Illness Narrative

Given the high prevalence rates of chronic illness in the United States, most people have encountered it in some way(s), either personally or within their families or social circles. The experiences surrounding chronic illness can differ significantly from one person to the next, however, thereby influencing unique understandings about and meanings connected to chronic illness. For example, one person may have experienced chronic illness within his/her family as a challenge that everyone rose up to and conquered, while another experienced chronic illness as something that tore his/her family apart. And to be sure, any person's experiences with chronic illness in the past will influence the way he or she sees it in the present or future. When two individuals (each with their own narrative) are united in a couple, these different perspectives may or may not be in accord.

Clinicians, then, must gather information about couples' illness narratives. By making partners' respective meanings and expectations explicit, and acknowledging similarities and differences among them, a space is created in which the partners learn about each other. This enables them to jointly define shared expectations for the current illness. While not all differences can be negotiated easily or quickly, the clinician can address both partners' beliefs and values underlying their different views. This can free the couple to develop new solutions rather than feel as if they have to fight for their individual beliefs to be recognized and understood.

Attending to Affect

It is understandable that partners would experience a variety of emotions as they progress through different phases (e.g., diagnosis, initial adjustment, long-term lifestyle changes) of their illness. However, for many, it is less expected that there might also be feelings (e.g., blame and guilt) that may be considered less acceptable reactions. For example, the partner of someone who recently received a chronic illness diagnosis may feel sadness regarding the loss of the ability to partake in certain activities, may feel anger and blame the partner for making bad health decisions that caused this disruption in their lives, and may feel guilty about being healthy. The role of the clinician here is to normalize feelings that may feel unacceptable but are normal.

Family therapists are uniquely trained to navigate these difficult terrains and can validate and normalize complex emotions and facilitate tenderness between partners. Without having a space that feels safe for partners to address their authentic feelings, emotions may become misplaced and revealed in unexpected and potentially hurtful ways. Only after some of these difficult emotions are explored can couples move forward with a better understanding of the other's experiences and find comfort.

Facilitating Communication Between Partners, Family Members, and Medical Providers

Chronic illness often becomes the unspoken presence in the room for couples and families. They feel it and are constantly thinking about it, but it remains difficult to talk about explicitly. For many, there are questions about what language to use. Do you refer to an illness by its medical name (e.g., "diabetes" or "cancer"), or do you refer to it more vaguely (e.g., "the illness" or "the sickness")? Many are fearful of being insensitive in how they approach these conversations, so they avoid talking about the chronic illness altogether. For patients, partners, and family members, this can impose difficulty because it may create a sense of disconnection between them. For patients, this may also make them feel isolated as others are not asking how they are doing or openly communicating support regarding the challenges they are living with.

Therapists must facilitate this conversation in a way that feels genuine and comfortable. By doing so, partners and families are provided with permission to ask questions and learn how to talk about the illness from a curious stance. Clinicians can also address the void between couples and families and the medical providers treating them. Specifically, they can provide psychoeducation about the illness and facilitate new understanding(s) about symptoms, treatment, and realistic expectations for illness progression. They can help families navigate the complex terrains of the medical culture, acting as a liaison, translator, advocate, and guide, and as a connector between multiple providers, payers, and patient/family/social communities of support.

Shifting Focus From "Your" Illness to "Our" Illness

In the same ways that partners can manage work-related stress differently, so too can they manage illness-related stress differently. For example, one partner may find a sense of peace from gaining as much knowledge as he or she can about a condition, whereas his or her partner may find more comfort from doing activities that distract attention away from the problem. Researchers Cynthia Berg and Renn Upchurch discussed the importance of shared coping that shifts the discussion about illness from something that solely impacts the patient to being something that is experienced as the couple's illness. There is a dramatic difference in coping when the couple approaches the illness as "our" challenge, and thereby shares the process of managing and adjusting to the condition as a joint venture. This works to capitalize on the strength of the relationship and unites partners together in facing a tremendously difficult experience. This approach helps couples regain their sense of agency. It takes power away from the illness and places it back in the couple.

Therapists can begin to facilitate this transition by using language that explicitly discusses the illness in a way that positions it as a dyadic experience. This may also act to shift parts of couples' identities back to their dyadic goals and values. The clinician can help the couple determine what is realistic for them, and then support the partners as they enlist their resources en route to this goal(s).

Maintaining an Empathic and Resilience-Focused Presence

Throughout the clinical course of working with couples living with chronic illness, whether early on (e.g., at the time of diagnosis) or in later phases (e.g., discussing end-of-life care and family-based decision-making), it is important for clinicians to maintain a therapeutic presence that is both empathic (e.g., compassionate, affectively attuned, supportive) and strengths-based. This is essential in creating and maintaining an environment in which difficult topics can be discussed with a sense of caring and safety, and strategies and solutions can be created in a manner that honors the resiliency of the unique partners and the union they share. Conducting therapy in this way facilitates and encourages couples to foster a sense of communion together as a relational team, while synchronously advancing agency toward the challenge(s) they face together.

Further Development of Chronic Illness in Couples and Families

As medical care and technology continues to improve and advance, and as the population grows older, the prevalence of chronic illness in clinics and across the country will continue to rise. And contrary to the vignettes put forth in conventional clinical training and textbooks (i.e., those that conclude with a clear "happy ending" or resolution after the clinician does and says all the right things), couples and families who seek care are living with something that will not go away. As clinicians work with them through their journey in adapting—and often adapting again and again with a disease's natural progression—they must endeavor to create safe spaces where they can make sense of where they have been, unite in the challenge(s) that face them, and navigate together where they are going. And along the way, it is the couple who does most of the work while clinicians, of course, continue trying to provide support.

Lisa Trump and Tai J. Mendenhall

See also Children With Chronic Illness; Grief Counseling; Health Issues; Medical Family Therapy

Further Readings

Berg, C., & Upchurch, R. (2007). A developmental-contextual model of couples coping with chronic illness across the adult life span. *Psychological Bulletin, 133,* 920–954. doi:10.1037/0033-2909.133.6.920

Engel, G. (1981). The clinical application of the biopsychosocial model. *Journal of Medicine and Philosophy, 6,* 101–124. doi:10.1093/jmp/6.2.101

Hodgson, J., Lamson, A., Mendenhall, T., & Crane, R. (Eds.). (2014). *Medical family therapy: Advanced applications.* New York, NY: Springer.

McDaniel, S. H., Doherty, W. J., & Hepworth, J. (Eds.). (2014). *Medical family therapy and integrated care* (2nd ed.). Washington, DC: American Psychological Association.

Ward, B. W., Schiller, J. S., & Goodman, R. A. (2014). Multiple chronic conditions among US adults: A 2012 update. *Preventing Chronic Disease, 11,* 130389–130393. doi:10.5888/pcd11.130389

White, K., Williams, T., & Greenberg, B. (1996). The ecology of medical care. *Bulletin of the New York Academy of Medicine, 73,* 187–212.

CINEMATHERAPY

Cinematherapy is the use of motion pictures, within a therapeutic setting, to help clients gain insight, evoke emotion, create a therapeutic metaphor, give a couple or family a common story about which to communicate, and/or educate clients. Movies can be a catalyst for insight, emotion, and inspiration—they affect people at both conscious and unconscious levels. The characters, how the movie is filmed, the storyline, music, and imagery can influence viewers. They can change the way people think and feel and provide a common ground for discussion in therapy. In cinematherapy, movies are carefully selected and assigned to match the client's and the clinician's goals. The movie selections are viewed by the client and discussed in therapy sessions with the idea that the movie contributes in some manner to the growth and development of the client. One of the goals of most uses of cinematherapy is that clients will identify with a character and be able to explore their own emotions through identification with a character and their storyline. This entry provides a brief history of cinematherapy, the benefits of its use, and a discussion of the process.

History

Movies have the benefit of being able to tell a story in a captivating way in a relatively short amount of time. Since the inception of motion pictures in the late 19th century, people have been fascinated by them. Movies have evolved over the years, from the early silent films to the inclusion of human voice in the late 1920s to ongoing developments in visual effects, with different therapeutic benefits being noted. Like poetry, painting, and music, movies can elicit emotions, provide a different worldview, and be cathartic. It generally takes less time to watch a movie than to read a book, and movies can be watched by multiple people at once. Individuals can identify with different characters, and each person in a couple or family can share what each gained from watching the movie. Movies gain the attention of clients through the storyline, cinematography, and sound. Movies engage people through multiple senses.

Benefits of Cinematherapy

Cinematherapy has many positive features as a therapeutic intervention. Online video streaming and online descriptions of movies have made selecting and viewing movies easier for many people. Additionally, given the increased diversity that is presented in movies, people have an easier time selecting characters with whom they can identify. Viewing movies is a pleasurable, easy way to engage in activity that can have considerable therapeutic value. The same movie can appeal to people of different ages and developmental levels.

The utilization of movies within a therapeutic setting offers several benefits to the client and counselor. The movie may instill in the client a sense of hope or offer encouragement to the client through an emotional identification with the characters. Additionally, movies are often selected that will aid the client in deepening emotions or providing a role model for the client. Further, many movies depict personal strengths that clients possess but do not recognize in themselves, or depict personal strengths clients would like to attain. Movies also can help enhance communication between clients in a couple or family, and between clients and the therapist. Clients can discuss similarities and differences between themselves and the characters in order to help others to know the clients better. Lastly, movies may help clients examine their values and prioritize or re-prioritize what they consider to be important.

The Process of Cinematherapy

Movies allow clients to see the complexity of information and experiences from a more objective perspective. Clients can discuss the characters, rather than themselves, which may reduce clients' defensiveness and allow them to have frank discussions with each other and the therapist. Through a discussion of a movie between a therapist and a client, topics are broached that may have been more difficult had the movie not been utilized. Further, most movies and therapy have some climax of activity or emotion and end with a resolution. Therapeutically, this resolution often results in hope or enhanced coping skills for the client.

Matching the Movie to the Person and Problem

In order for cinematherapy to be advantageous, the client should be of at least moderate functioning.

Movie characters can model desired behavior, but more often movies are used as a metaphor for client problems. Metaphors allow for creative comparisons and provide imagery to capture client thoughts and emotions in a language that is meaningful to the client. Because a metaphor needs to be meaningful to a client, the therapist should assess what types of movies and stories might be most impactful. Additionally, when selecting a movie, the therapist should pay attention to any trauma or violence depicted in the movie. One would not want to recommend a movie that could inadvertently retraumatize a client. Finally, those who have trouble differentiating between fantasy and reality are not good candidates for cinematherapy.

Therapists should assess other aspects in order to effectively utilize cinematherapy. For example, the timing of an intervention is important. The therapist should assign a movie when the clients have enough insight and knowledge to understand some of the themes of the movie and yet be challenged enough to grow and learn something new. The goal is to use cinematherapy to accelerate the therapeutic process, but not overwhelm clients.

Neil E. Duchac

See also Couples, Quality Time; Couples and Marriage Counseling; Couples Therapy Research; Experiential Family Therapy; Strategic Family Therapy

Further Readings

Dollarhide, C. T. (2003). Cinematherapy: Making media work. *ASCA School Counselor, 42*(6), 16–17.

Hesley, J. W., & Hesley, J. G. (2001). *Rent two movies and call me in the morning: Using popular movies in psychotherapy* (2nd ed.). New York, NY: Wiley.

Wedding, D., & Niemic, R. M. (2014). *Movies and mental illness* (4th ed.). Boston, MA: Hogrefe.

CIRCULAR QUESTIONS

See Questions: Open, Closed, and Circular

CIRCULARITY AND LINEARITY

Circularity and linearity are two essential terms in the theory and practice of couples and family therapy. Understanding the distinctions between circularity and linearity as well as their clinical applications opens the door to exploring important historical shifts that helped birth and later improve the couples and family therapy field. This entry first defines circularity and linearity, discusses the implications of circularity, and gives examples of circularity. It then discusses feminist critiques of circularity and describes the both/and approach that incorporates circularity and linearity. Finally, it explores how circularity and linearity apply to couples and family therapy.

Defining Circularity and Linearity

At its simplest, circularity and linearity describe different types of patterns or relationships. Specifically, linearity describes a pattern that moves from *a* to *b* to *c*, in essence a pattern that depicts a straight line. Thinking in terms of causality, linearity describes a causal relationship in which *a* causes *b* which causes *c*. For example, if you drop a fragile glass bowl over a tile floor, the bowl will fall, and on hitting the floor it will probably break. In such a linear relationship, each action causes a new action or reaction.

In contrast, circularity describes a pattern of interaction involving a recurring sequence of behavior or exchanged messages. For example, a circular pattern moves from *a* to *b* to *c* and then back to *a* again and repeats regardless of new content. In terms of causality, circularity suggests a relationship of *circular causality* in which cause is also circular. However, circular causality is more about the effects of behavior than the pure causal effects of *a* on *b* on *a*. In the simplest relationship, circular causality is at work when *a*'s behavior effects *b*'s behavior, and *b*'s behavior effects *a*'s behavior. In this way, circularity highlights that all parts are simultaneously impacting each other.

General Systems Theory and the Implications of Circularity

Circularity is one of the core concepts in general systems theory, the foundation of family therapy. Ludwig von Bertalanffy, an Italian biologist, helped develop general systems theory in the 1950s and 1960s. Systems theory gave birth to the field of couples and family therapy, as thinkers such as anthropologist Gregory Bateson and clinicians such as Murray Bowen and Nathan Ackerman began applying such concepts as circularity to family therapy. At the time, linearity and a linear causality of cause and effect were foundational to traditional experimental science, which deeply influenced psychotherapy. Systems theory offered a new perspective by introducing concepts such as circularity. The following six important implications of circularity changed how clinicians thought about and worked with families.

Emphasizing Effect Over Cause

Circular causality applied to family therapy emphasized the relational and reciprocal effects of behavior instead of a pure linear cause and effect. Systems thinkers Paul Watzlawick, Janet Beavin, and Don Jackson applied the black box concept to family therapy to emphasize cause over effect. They stated that although what happens in the box (i.e., in the human mind) cannot be observed, such observation is not necessary. Instead they urged family clinicians to observe input and output from the box (i.e., communication between people). This was an important clinical shift, from focusing on the intrapsychic or what was inside someone's mind to focusing on the interpersonal and the dynamics between individuals. Additionally, family therapists shifted from the classic psychoanalytic question of *why* (which is about cause) and began asking *how* and *what* (which are about effect). For example, "Why did she say that and why is he doing that?" is about cause and what is happening inside the box. Questions such as "How did her behavior impact him and what happened after he responded?" focus on observable interactions going in and out of the box. Circularity helped define this pivotal shift toward observing behavioral effects of communication patterns, foundational to family therapy.

Diagnosing Whole Systems

Another important implication of circularity and circular causality was a shift in understanding the process of diagnosis. As issues of how versus why became more important, family therapists were less prone to diagnose one member in a family and thus "blame" the issue on a single person. Instead, family therapists saw unhelpful patterns of communication as a product of the larger family system and a dynamic created by all family members. This led to a more nonpathologizing approach to treatment in which the identified patient actually became the family as a whole.

Working With Whole Families

The implications of circularity also impacted how family therapists understood and worked with families. Traditional psychoanalysis analyzed individuals. But as family therapists focused on circularity and the circular patterns occurring between family members, they began understanding families as a meaningful whole, in which the whole is larger than the sum of its parts (i.e., nonsummativity). Circularity played a significant role in this important shift toward working therapeutically with multiple family members.

Considering Multiple Perspectives and Systems Within System

Implications of circularity led to considering the perspective of every family member. Attending to multiple perspectives gave family therapists a different and arguably more complex understanding of family systems. Circularity also supported the idea of circular connections not only within systems but also between systems. Appling developmental psychologist Urie Bronfenbrenner's ecological systems theory to family therapy helped recognize circular influences between family systems and larger systems such as extended family, friends, work, school, religious systems, and legal systems.

Understanding Context

Circularity also influenced the concept of context in family therapy. Context is everything that influences, impacts, and gives meaning to a particular situation or person, and arguably context is boundless. For example, as one's context changes and expands (e.g., growing up and learning about reproduction), so does one's understanding and the meaning one attributes to an experience (e.g., babies come from reproductive fertilization, not flying storks). Finally, a circular relationship exists between context and meaning, in an ever-expanding pattern of greater understanding and possibly greater compassion.

Defining the Rules of Systems

Circularity helped define the rules for how systems of communication operate. Along with general systems theory, Bateson and colleagues used cybernetics, or the study of self-regulating systems, to deeply influence family therapy. One of the rules of self-regulating systems is that they tend toward a state of equilibrium or homeostasis. Such systems rely on negative feedback that helps perpetuate these homeostatic patterns in a circular pattern. Families are a prime example of self-regulating systems and operate under the rules of cybernetics, tending toward homeostasis as members interact in negative feedback loops of circular communication patterns. As family therapists studied these interactional patterns, they observed different examples of how circularity impacts families.

Relational Examples of Circularity

Circularity is also referred to as nonlinearity in family therapy literature, emphasizing the opposite of a linear relationship in circular patterns. In exploring relational examples of circularity, two basic types of circular patterns emerged: symmetrical and complementary relationships.

Symmetrical Relationships

Symmetrical relationships emphasize equality and tend to minimize difference, in contrast to complementary patterns that maximize difference. The following two examples demonstrate that symmetrical patterns can help or potentially hinder the relational connection.

Helpful Symmetrical Patterns

Reciprocal generosity and helpfulness are examples of symmetrical patterns. O. Henry's classic tale, *The Gift of the Magi,* tells the story of a poor young husband and wife who each sell their most precious possession to give the other a gift. In this case we see difference minimized, as both partners are equally willing to give up what they most hold dear to show their love for the other. Imagine these two partners continue to interact throughout their marriage in a recurring sequence of generous, gift-giving behaviors. The circularity of this symmetrical pattern is evident as the husband's generosity, *a,* effects the wife's generosity, *b,* which again effects the husband's generosity, *a.* Such patterns minimize difference and often escalate these reciprocal and repeating behaviors.

Unhelpful Symmetrical Patterns

Competing, bragging, and boasting are examples of potentially unhelpful symmetrical patterns. Kisha and Tyson are two adolescent siblings competing for family resources. Kisha wants to borrow the family car to see friends, but Tyson says he needs the car to go to work. Kisha states that seeing her friends is more important because they are studying for an exam together, but Tyson says using the car for work is more important because he is making money. Kisha argues that passing her exam will help her get into college and make more money. Finally, a parent then tells them to stop fighting and that neither can use the car, but a little while later the siblings begin competing again. In this symmetrical pattern, each sibling minimizes the difference to promote his or her own case as more important.

Complementary Relationships

Complementary relationships maximize difference in a circular pattern as *a* takes a one-up position, which leads to *b* taking a one-down position, further enforcing *a*'s one-up position. Like symmetrical patterns, complementary patterns can either help or hinder relational connection. Classic complementary patterns include the pursuer and withdrawer, the over-compensator and the under-compensator, and the caregiver and care-receiver.

Helpful Complementary Patterns

In a complementary relationship between mother and infant, the infant wakes up crying and the mother picks up and feeds the infant. The infant stops crying, eventually starts yawning, and the mother rocks the infant to sleep. Later the infant wakes up crying again, and the cycle repeats. A clear circular relationship is at work in which both the infant's crying and yawning leads to the mother's soothing and feeding behavior while the mother's holding and feeding similarly affect the infant's behavior of being soothed and comforted. Differences are maximized and relational connection is fostered as mother cares and infant receives care in an ongoing circular pattern of mutually reinforcing one-up and one-down roles.

Unhelpful Complementary Patterns

Maximizing difference can hurt relationships when patterns become too rigid. For example, Yvette complains to her husband, Francisco, about their children fighting, and he remains quiet and walks away. When she pursues Francisco to tell him he needs to discipline the children more, he asks to talk about it later. Yvette complains they need to talk now but drops the conversation until the children fight again. Circular causality suggests that Yvette's pursuing, nagging behavior affects Francisco's withdrawing, while his withdrawing similarly affects her pursuits.

Feminist Critiques of Circularity

Feminist critiques in the late 1980s challenged general systems theory and family therapy's understanding of circularity and circular causality. They argued that impact is not equal. For example, with Yvette and Francisco, circular causality assumed his withdrawing behavior impacts her pursuing as much as her pursuing impacts his withdrawing. Yet feminist family therapists critiqued such circular conceptualizations and highlighted the influence of gendered power: As Yvette pursues and Francisco withdraws, he holds a male-privileged, one-up position to her one-down position as he determines the end of their conversation and she remains unable to influence him and gain his support.

The feminist critique exposed the error of applying circular causality to situations of domestic violence. Specifically, the critique challenged the following traditional systemic assumptions based on circularity and circular causality: (1) all family members in a system have equal influence on each other and on the system; (2) in cases of domestic violence, abuse serves the function of maintaining homeostasis; and (3) all family members are equally responsible for maintaining and perpetuating abusive cycles, even the person being abused.

The field of family therapy responded by recognizing the existence of gendered power and important ways that all power dynamics limit, restrict, and even silence family members at home and in the larger society. Family therapists began to see the limits of traditional circular causality not only in domestic violence cases but also in all family therapy work. As a field, family therapy began to acknowledge that power inequities impact all families, systems, and relationships. The feminist critique also helped family therapists understand that causality and linearity do not need to be mutually exclusive.

A Both/And Approach to Circularity and Linearity

Arguably, one of the most important results of the feminist critique of circularity was the shift in couples and family therapy toward embracing both linearity and circularity. Clinicians began to understand that power dynamics significantly impact human relationships and that every person in an interactional pattern does not have the same power. Initially this awareness exposed gendered power, including male privilege and the subjugation of women. However, in time power began to be understood much more broadly as involving many social identities and the intersection of these identities including gender, class, education, race, ethnicity, culture, sexual orientation, religion, nationality, age, and ability.

A Case Example

Clinically speaking, what does it look like to simultaneously hold both circularity and linearity in one's approach to practicing therapy? Imagine the same mother and infant discussed earlier, yet now the mother suffers from postpartum depression. When the infant wakes up crying, the mother immediately feels severely anxious and overwhelmed. The mother tries to rock the infant but struggles to soothe the infant and starts feeling intensely irritated. The mother has difficulty feeling close to her infant and feels worthless and ashamed. She puts the crying infant down, feeling excessively fatigued. As the infant continues crying, the cycle repeats. Using only linearity or circularity to understand this mother and infant would not sufficiently explain the situation.

Limits of Linearity

The concept of linearity alone might lead to seeing the postpartum depression, *a*, as causing the mother, *b*, to be depressed and unable to provide the necessary infant care, causing the infant, *c*, to continually cry. From this linear understanding one might simply treat the mother's postpartum depression with antidepressants, which may be necessary. However, one might be missing important contributions to the system, such as a recent move away from family support, the infant's colic, the father's recent unemployment, understanding the couple's Hispanic culture, and understanding their lack of consistent primary health care.

Limits of Circularity

Using the concept of circularity suggests a more complex circular relationship that considers the larger system and all relevant factors including their culture, their move, his unemployment, their inconsistent health care, their lack of family support, the crying infant, her postpartum depression, and the couple relationship. Yet an early understanding of circular causality might still incorrectly suggest each factor affects the others with an equal weight of influence. Simplified examples might be that the crying, colicky infant is causing the mother's anxiety as much as the mother's anxiety is causing the infant to cry, or that the father's unemployment is impacting the mother as much as her depression is impacting the father. Yet the feminist critique argues circularity alone does not account for the gendered power dynamics and dominant societal discourses impacting this family.

Integrating Circularity and Linearity

While the colicky infant certainly impacts the mother's anxiety, a feminist critique would examine linear influences of dominant discourses and cultural expectations. For example, does this mother feel an unequal burden to take care of her infant and her unemployed husband? What are the expected gendered divisions of labor? Gendered expectations may assume she should carry the larger responsibility for the infant's needs, for the well-being of the couple's relationship, and for staying attuned to her husband's needs as he tries to find a new job. How are issues of marginalization impacting the family's health care and the father's unemployment? What is the impact of societal and cultural expectations on the father to provide for his family? His failure to meet such expectations may lead to feelings of inadequacy, compounded by real experiences of marginalization and limited work options. Linearity highlights that these effects are different as power dynamics are not equal or equitable, sometimes operating in a more linear than circular relationship. Circularity highlights the recurring interactional patterns and the effects, even if different, of all parts on each other. Finally, a feminist-informed integration of circularity and linearity provides family therapists with a unique lens that honors the complexity of family relationships in the larger context of overlapping systems with oppressive and unequal power distributions.

Circularity and Linearity Applied to Couples and Family Therapy

A feminist-informed integration of circularity and linearity directly impacts how family therapists assess and treat individuals, couples, and families. The following four commonly practiced clinical interventions demonstrate this practical integration of circularity and linearity in family therapy.

Mapping Patterns of Interaction

From its inception, couples and family therapy, and in particular early strategic family therapists such as Jay Haley and his colleagues in Palo Alto, were interested in interactional patterns. Conceptualized as a repeating circle of interactions, a simple visual map of the competing adolescents discussed earlier might be as follows: Kisha states a need → Tyson states a more pressing need → Kisha argues her need is more pressing → Tyson argues his is more pressing → Parent tells them to stop → Kisha states a need. Family therapists still use circular maps during assessment and treatment phases of therapy and can attend to feminist critiques by highlighting discrepancies in power and which voice or voices are privileged.

Genograms

Genograms, developed in the 1980s by Monica McGoldrick, Randy Gerson, and their colleagues, are a specific graphic way of drawing family members to depict relationships between and across multiple generations. Concepts of circularity are inherent in the genogram and in the symbols used to denote family relational patterns and degree of connection. Today genograms are also used to highlight larger cultural and contextual issues including race, ethnicity, religion, and medical history.

Circular Questions

Circular questions emerged out of the Milan family therapy group and are based on circularity and circular assumptions about patterns of interaction. The purpose of circular questions is to discover and understand the patterns, connections, and relationships in a system. Circular questions often begin with *how, what,* or *who,* for example: "How does Tyson usually respond to Kisha needing something?" "What typically happens after Tyson tries to one-up Kisha?" "Who sees their competing?" and "How do Kisha's and Tyson's parents respond?" Such questions help family therapists construct a family's interactional pattern. Following the feminist critique, post-Milan approaches to circular questions encouraged attention to therapist biases and to dominant and subjugated cultural discourses.

Contextual Issues and Societal Discourses

Circularity supports seeing connections within and between systems. Yet the feminist critique along with postmodern influences challenged family therapists to acknowledge the impact of power discrepancies within and across systems. Integrating circularity and linearity encourages family therapists to consider how power disparities impact individuals, systems, and the meanings people make. Holding a both/and approach to circularity and linearity supports family therapists in exploring larger contextual issues, including the impact of dominant societal discourses and socially constructed power inequities, attending to subjugated societal discourses, and listening to marginalized and oppressed voices.

*Lynn Bohecker
and David Kleist*

See also Complementary and Symmetrical Relationships; General Systems Theory; Genograms; Systems Theory

Further Readings

Brown, J. M. (2010). The Milan principles of hypothesizing, circularity and neutrality in dialogical family therapy: Extinction, evolution, eviction . . . or emergence? *The Australian and New Zealand Journal of Family Therapy, 31*(3), 248–265.

Cottone, R. R., & Greenwell, R. J. (1992). Beyond linearity and circularity: Deconstructing social systems theory. *Journal of Marital and Family Therapy, 18*(2), 167–177.

McConaghy, J. S., & Cottone, R. R. (1998). The systemic view of violence: An ethical perspective. *Family Process, 37*(1), 51–63.

Smith-Acuna, S. (2011). *Systems theory in action: Applications to individual, couples, and family therapy.* Hoboken, NJ: Wiley.

Watzlawick, P., Beavin, J. H., & Jackson, D. D. (1967). *Pragmatics of human communication: A study of interactional patterns, pathologies, and paradoxes.* New York, NY: Norton.

CIRCUMPLEX MODEL

When working with families, clinicians use a framework to conceptualize, assess, and intervene in order to help the family to function in a way that supports people as individuals and the group as a family. The circumplex model of marital and family systems was developed to help create a seamless flow between research, theory, and practice. It is based on three concepts that have repeatedly emerged as important in family theory models and approaches: cohesion (togetherness), flexibility, and communication. The model was created to help clinicians diagnose family patterns and classify family patterns along a continuum of unbalanced–disconnected, balanced, and unbalanced–overly connected. This entry reviews the development of the circumplex model, the structure and components of the model, and how it has been used in research and clinical applications.

The Model and Its Components

First developed in 1979 by David Olson, Douglas Sprenkle, and Candyce Russell, the circumplex model was proposed in response to a noticeable gap between research in family systems and application of research in working with couples and families. In addition to noticing this gap, the developers of this model also noted that there were consistencies in the research that had been done. Notably, several theorists and researchers had reported, independently, that three components had surfaced when researching successful families. These three dimensions are cohesion, flexibility, and communication. Although these components were not always referred to by these labels, the developers of the circumplex model observed consistency in the appearance of these components throughout the literature regarding couples and families.

The general hypothesis of the circumplex model is that couples/families with balanced cohesion and adaptability will generally function better across the family life cycle than will those at the extremes of these dimensions. This hypothesis relies a great deal on the first two components of the model and less on the component of communication. As discussed later in this entry, this hypothesis is what is most frequently tested in research applications of the instruments most commonly associated with the model. Communication is not viewed as part of the hypothesis because it is considered to be a component that is used to facilitate the others.

Cohesion

Cohesion is the degree to which family members are connected via shared interests and experiences. Cohesion is also represented by synonyms such as affiliation, affective involvement, and coordination. The idea of balance is central to optimal functioning. Balance between involvement with one another and each member's independence within the family structure is viewed, according to the model, as essential. Cohesion is best viewed as a spectrum, with too much togetherness (enmeshment) at one end of the spectrum and too little cohesion (disengagement) at the other. Both extremes may have negative repercussions. According to the model, individuals and families experiencing difficulty are expected to be found with levels of cohesion near the polar ends of such a spectrum. The goal of the model in regard to cohesion would be to restore balance within the spectrum. The level of balance needed for optimal functioning is unique to each relationship and its stage of family development.

Flexibility

The second component of the circumplex model is flexibility. Flexibility is the family's ability to adapt to change within the family's structure with regard to rules, roles, and leadership. Like cohesion, flexibility is best experienced when in balance. Families that are categorized as rigid have an excess of structure, whereas families that are classified as chaotic lack a sufficient amount of structure.

Couples and families that are balanced in the areas of flexibility tend to be more stable over the duration of the relationship. In a balanced relationship, roles are flexible and often shared. The leadership of the structured relationship will exhibit characteristics that are more egalitarian in nature, receiving input from all members of the family. Of course, these attributes become less rigid the more flexible a family is, with many decisions being made with an increasing amount of input from members, including children.

Relationships that are at either end of the spectrum possess negative attributes that are consistent with the particular form of unbalance. In other words, the more chaotic or rigid a family is, the more problems will arise as a manifestation of the unbalance. In contrast, families that lie more toward the middle of the flexibility spectrum will be more likely to function in a way that is stable and adaptable to changes as these arise. As is true with cohesion, there is no single level that is best for all families. The uniqueness of each individual family or relationship brings with it factors that influence the ability to find balance.

Communication

The third and final component of the circumplex model is communication. This component is considered by researchers to be the "facilitation dimension," since communication plays an essential role in facilitating change in the other two areas of the model. Both sides of communication, speaking and listening, are often the focus of treatment when developing communication skills. Focusing on the communication skills of the family as a group is often the selected course of action. These skills include, but are not necessarily limited to, listening and speaking skills, clarification, and respect. Speaking skills focus on speaking for oneself and not for others. Listening skills emphasize empathy and paying attention to what other family members are saying. Staying on topic is also considered to be a valuable communication skill. Respectful communication is focused on problem solving and understanding one another. As with the other components of cohesion and flexibility, communication is balanced when there is an equal distribution of communication skills, whereas unbalanced family relationships possess poor or few communication skills.

Application of the Model in Research

The use of the circumplex model in research is extensive and is not limited exclusively to the field of mental health. Multiple studies in a variety of fields have shown positive correlation between one or more of the components of the model. Most of the research utilizes assessments created based on the model. These instruments are collectively known as Family Adaptability and Cohesion Evaluation scales (FACES). The FACES Instrument, which is in the fourth version at the time of this publication, consists of six family scales. Additionally, FACES IV includes the Family Communication scale and Family Satisfaction scale, all of which consist of 62 items total.

There is extensive documentation of studies utilizing the model and the corresponding instrumentation. The variety of these topics include family relations and dynamics, marriage and divorce, types of families, physical health, stages within the family life cycle, reproduction and sexuality, the family and society, development of individuals, families with special problems, family counseling and education, and research and theory regarding family. It should be noted that this list of topics is not comprehensive and does not speak directly to the many subtopics discussed within each.

All of the versions of FACES and their respective instruments have been validated in studies spanning a variety of populations, from children aged 12 and older to older adults. Additionally, FACES has been translated and validated into multiple languages. The reliability of FACES has been tested, and reliability is strong. Overall, FACES, in all of its versions, is considered to be suitable for researching the intersection of family relationships with a variety of matters. Historically, about half of the research conducted using FACES is in the field of psychology, where medicine, including psychiatry, constitutes about 21% of all studies. The remaining studies have taken place in the fields of gerontology, sociology, family law, human relations, education, and other health care.

Although the model has been researched by using versions of FACES and related instrumentation, in a variety of contexts, the vast majority of research using the model typically falls into three main categories. These categories are stages in the family life cycle, satisfaction with marriage, and child and adolescent development. The original hypothesis of the model holds that families and couples who are in balance tend to be more adaptable over the life span of the family than families and couples who lie on the ends or unbalanced parts of the spectrum. Thus, focusing on the stages that families and couples pass through during the course of the family life cycle is a useful way of examining the validity, reliability, and applicability of the model and the related instruments. The results of the independent studies have varied depending on the subject of the investigation. However, studies have consistently shown that the hypothesis of the model is correct. That is to say, couples and families that are balanced between cohesion and flexibility tend to navigate the family life cycle more successfully.

Clinical Application of the Model

Application of the model in clinical settings is primarily accomplished via assessment. The combination of self-reported scales and the observations of the clinical profession provide a multimethod assessment, which combines perspectives from both inside and outside the relationship. Both of these perspectives are considered important sources of useful information. In addition to the clinical use of several approaches to assessment, using several family members provides a variety of viewpoints. Considering one person's perspective on a family system is considered to be limited according to the family systems approach. A more comprehensive view can be constructed when as many members of the family as possible are involved in the assessment process. A multi-trait assessment considers all three components of the model. Thus, not one component, cohesion, flexibility, or communication is considered more than any other. According to the model, when the examination of these three is combined, results will be comprehensive, and a picture of the family system and how it functions will become clear. Assessing the family system from a multisystem approach allows the examination of the subsystems within a family, such as a marital system within a nuclear family structure. Likewise, there are extended family systems that may be considered part of the overall family system by some members but not by others. Examining how individual members of a family view the limits and boundaries of the family system as a whole may expose the differences and similarities in what makes up the "real" family system. This approach is especially important given the current complexities and diversity often found in today's families.

Goals of using the circumplex model in the treatment of families tend to be centered on strengthening one component, usually the component that is least balanced. It has been observed, by those who follow the model, that movement in one component affects the other components. When applied to couples, treatment should focus on both members of the couple, understanding the expectations of the other in regard to cohesion: how much separateness or togetherness does each partner desire within the relationship?

Michael A. Williams

See also Communication Errors/Problems in Couples and Families; Communication in Couples and Families; Couples Therapy Research; Parent–Child Communication; Therapeutic Assessment

Further Readings

Kouneski, E. F. (2000). *The family circumplex model, FACES II, and FACES III: Overview of research and applications.* Retrieved from http://www.facesiv.com/pdf/faces_and_circumplex.pdf

Kouneski, E. F. (2000). *Studies using FACES and the circumplex model.* Retrieved from https://www.prepare-enrich.com/public/Studies_using_FACES.pdf

Maynard, P. E., & Olson, D. H. (1987). Circumplex model of family systems: A treatment tool in family counseling. *Journal of Counseling & Development, 65*(9), 502–504.

Olson, D. H. (2000). Circumplex Model of Marital and Family Systems. *Journal of Family Therapy, 22*(2), 144–167.

Olson, D. H., & Gorall, D. M. (2003). Circumplex model of marital and family systems. In F. Walsh (Ed.), *Normal family processes: Growing diversity and complexity* (3rd ed., pp. 514–548). New York, NY: Guilford.

Olson, D. H., Sprenkle, D. H., & Russell, C. S. (1979). Circumplex model of marital and family systems: I. Cohesion and adaptability dimensions, family types, and clinical applications. *Family Process, 18*(1), 3–28.

Sanders, C., & Bell, J. (2011). The Olson circumplex model: A systematic approach to couple and family relationships. *InPsych, 33*(1).

White, J. M. (2008). *Family theories.* Thousand Oaks, CA: Sage.

Clinical Case Conceptualization With Couples and Families

Case conceptualization refers to how a therapist thinks about, or conceptualizes, the client's concerns. These conceptualizations inform all aspects of treatment, including who should attend sessions, the type of therapeutic relationship, the therapist's theoretical orientation, and therapeutic interventions. Each theoretical model has a unique approach to developing a case conceptualization. Arguably, the primary distinction between theories is how each conceptualizes client problems. For example, humanistic family therapists focus on the emotional dynamics and communication in a family system, whereas an intergenerational family therapist would conceptualize the same presenting problems by focusing on cross-generational patterns, triangulation (bringing a third person into relationships), family projection processes (how family patterns are passed from parents to children), and differentiation (the ability to balance closeness and togetherness and balance feelings and thinking). Case conceptualization often involves a process in which the therapist gathers theory-specific information necessary to make an assessment. For example, in structural family therapy, the therapist listens to clients describe their concerns, and then asks additional questions as necessary to assess boundaries (how much interaction there is between groups within the family and outside the family), subsystems (small groups within the family), hierarchy (power structure), and other areas of focus for structural intervention. This entry discusses the main aspects of case conceptualization: relational patterns, theory, diversity, and diagnosis.

Conceptualizing Relational Interaction Patterns With Couples and Families

Although each theoretical model has its own particular approach to conceptualization, virtually all approaches developed for working with couples and families involve some form of assessment of *relational interaction patterns* within the system. Specifically, therapists focus on identifying the problem interaction cycle around the presenting problem. Typically, couples and families have one or two basic patterns of interaction that characterize the presenting problem. When conceptualizing interaction cycles, family therapists view these from a neutral perspective, with no single person as "the cause" or "to blame." Instead, these cycles are understood to emerge as properties of the system, with each person's response mutually shaping the other's response. However, those within the system typically experience these interactions very differently. A classic example is the nag/withdraw pattern seen in couples: one partner claims, "I withdraw because the other nags," while the other complains, "I nag because the other withdraws." Neither partner sees the mutually reinforcing pattern or, if they do, it is seen as "caused" by the other. Problem interaction cycles are unique to each relational system, but all follow this basic structure:

Homeostasis/Normal: Behaviors are within the acceptable range, and the relationship is experienced as "normal" or "okay."

Rise in Tension: Behaviors and emotions are becoming more outside the acceptable range of behavior, and the members of the system are experiencing tension and stress, either internally or externally in the form of bickering or other mild conflict. In cybernetic theory, this is referred to as *positive feedback*, meaning there is a "change" in the homeostasis.

Symptom/Problem: The primary symptom or problem occurs, which is often a fight for couples or families, but it can also be tense silence or isolation.

Return to Homeostasis: Finally, action is taken by one or more parties to bring the system back to homeostasis. This may involve apologies, "talking it out," or simply pretending that nothing happened.

Problem interaction patterns can be traced in various ways. For example, in the systemic approach developed at the Mental Research Institute in Palo Alto, California, and in strategic family therapy, the therapist focuses on behavioral descriptions of the interaction. In contrast, experiential approaches focus on the emotional processes in addition to the behaviors. In emotionally focused couples therapy, the therapist may start with describing the cycle in behavioral terms, and then go back to trace the secondary, more surface-level emotions and the primary emotions (attachment-based needs). In solution-focused therapy, the therapist would first track the behaviors using video-talk, and then go through and track the interpretations the couple or family is making about the interaction. In all cases, the therapist obtains a detailed description of the interactional sequence.

Example of conceptualizing a couple's interactional cycle using behavioral descriptions:

Normal: Couple able to talk without tension.

Rise in Tension: Wife makes request; husband ignores her. This repeats several times over 2 or 3 days.

Symptom: Finally, one of them (typically the wife for this couple) makes a hostile comment that leads to a major argument. Couples verbally fights for 30 or more minutes until husband leaves room or otherwise removes self from argument. Couple has cold silence and distance for remainder of day.

Return to Normal: Next morning both partners wake up and pretend nothing has happened; both ignore the topic that was argued about and do not resolve disagreement.

Theory-Specific Case Conceptualization in Couples and Family Therapy

Each couples and family therapy approach has a distinct, theory-specific approach to conceptualizing relational concerns that define the approach. Additionally, family therapists can use a cross-theoretical case conceptualization approach, drawing from multiple systemic models to inform their work. Some of the more common elements of case conceptualization in couples and family therapy include the following:

Systemic and Strategic Approaches

Problem Interaction Cycle: Track problem interaction cycle using behavioral descriptions.

More-of-the-Same Solutions: Identify the general logic of the solutions attempted by the couple/family thus far (e.g., using harsher and harsher punishments).

Communication, Metacommunication, and Double Binds: Attend to verbal and nonverbal communication patterns.

Complementary Patterns: Recognize exaggerated patterns (e.g., good/bad parent; emotional/logical one).

Hypothesizing: Identify potential role of presenting problem in maintaining homeostasis.

Structural Family Therapy Case Conceptualization

Subsystems: Identify couple, parent, sibling, and other significant subsystems in family.

Boundaries: Assess for enmeshed and diffuse boundaries between various subsystems.

Hierarchy: Consider hierarchy between parents/children and various subsystems.

Family Life Cycle: Identify developmental needs of individuals and family system as a whole.

Coalitions: Detect problematic cross-generational or other coalitions.

Complementary Patterns: Recognize exaggerated patterns (e.g., good/bad parent; emotional/logical one).

Satir's Human Growth Model

Survival Stances: Identify each family member's survival stance: placating, blaming, superreasonable, or irrelevant.

Family Roles: Assess each person's role in the family system.

Role of Symptom: Identify the role of the presenting problem in maintaining family homeostasis.

Self-worth: Consider each family member's sense of self-worth and how it relates to family dynamics.

Communication: Examine the various levels of communications within the system: behavioral, interpretation, feelings, rules for commenting, and so forth.

Family life chronology: Use a timeline to map out key events in family history.

Bowen Intergenerational Therapy

Multigenerational Patterns: Identify significant patterns across three or more generations.

Differentiation: Assess each member's level of differentiation from the system.

Emotional Triangles: Detect triangles and coalitions that have developed to stabilize dyadic relationships.

Emotional Cutoff: Examine patterns of emotional cutoff across generations.

Sibling Position: Consider the possible effect of sibling position within the system.

Family Projection Process: Recognize patterns in which parents are projecting their anxieties onto children across each generation.

Cognitive-Behavioral Couples and Family Therapy

Problem Definition: Define problem in measurable, behavioral terms (e.g., son is noncompliant with parental requests 50% of time).

Baseline Assessment: Carefully track actual frequency of behaviors, along with antecedents and consequences.

Functional Analysis: Use systemic theory to identify how the problem is mutually reinforced within the family system (e.g., assess problem interaction cycle).

Family Schemata and Core Beliefs: Detect cognitive schemata and core beliefs that relate to presenting problem (e.g., overgeneralizations, dichotomous thinking, etc.).

Relational Cognition Patterns: Consider specific cognitions that organize rules for relating within the system (e.g., expectations, assumptions, standards).

Solution-Focused Therapy

Strengths and Resources: Identify individual and relational strengths and resources.

Exceptions and What Works: Notice the times when the problem is a lesser problem and what solutions do seem to help.

Miracle Question: Define preferred solution using client's response to the miracle question and description of what life would look like without the presenting problem.

Motivation: Consider client's level of motivation to determine how to best engage client.

Functional Family Therapy

Relational Function: Notice the relational function of the presenting symptoms in maintaining the family homeostasis.

Relational Connection: Identify the family's pattern for balancing interdependence and independence.

Relational Hierarchy: Consider how control and influence are expressed in the family.

Risk and Protective Factors: Track individual, family, peer/school, and community risk and protective factors.

Multisystem Assessment: Examine the interaction of all systems in the child's or family's life, including extended family, neighborhood, school, peers, employment, human service agencies, cultural groups, and religious affiliations.

Diversity and Case Conceptualization

In addition to theoretical models of conceptualization, competent therapists consider client diversity factors when developing a case conceptualization and use this to modify their theory-based assessments. Diversity factors may include race, ethnicity, sexual/gender orientation, ability, socioeconomic class, religion/spirituality, age, gender, immigration status, language, and education. Each client has diversity factors that need to be considered. The fifth edition of the American Psychiatric Association's *Diagnostic and Statistical Manual* (DSM-5) includes an approach to cross-cultural formulation that can be used to help clinicians consider diversity issues as part of their case conceptualization. This model includes the following:

Cultural identity of the individual: Identify important aspects of the client's identity, including race, ethnicity, religious affiliation, socioeconomic status, sexual orientation, migrant status, and so on.

Cultural conceptualization of distress: Consider how the presenting problem is conceptualized—including the origins and possible solutions—from within the client's cultural and relevant social reference groups.

Psychosocial stressors and cultural features of vulnerability and resilience: Consider unique psychosocial stressors and resources related to diversity factors, such as religious limits and supports, local community networks, extended family, and so on.

Cultural features of the relationship between the individual and the clinician: Finally, the clinician should consider the interaction between his or her own sociocultural location and that of the client and how this may impact the therapeutic process.

Additionally, therapists need to adapt constructs from theoretical models to cultural norms. For example, healthy family boundaries typically look quite different in the context of individualistic cultures than they do in communal cultures. Thus, therapists need to adapt their assessment of boundaries to account for how closeness and distance are typically communicated within a given culture, between genders, and across generations.

Diagnosis and Case Conceptualization With Couples and Families

Historically, family therapists have not relied heavily on clinical diagnosis of an individual client to conceptualize couple and family dynamics. An individual's symptoms, such as depression and anxiety, are often viewed as part of the larger family dynamics and homeostasis. For example, a child's conduct issues may be viewed as serving the function of uniting two parents whose marriage is faltering. Similarly, one partner's severe depression may elicit caretaking behaviors from the other, creating a strong bond and a sense of meaning for one and sense of being valued for the other. Family therapists carefully attend to the relational effects of alleviating individual clinical symptoms; it is not uncommon for a reduction of psychiatric symptoms in one member to lead to new symptoms in another. For example, if symptoms in a child identified as the "problem child" subside, often the former "good child" sibling will suddenly develop new symptoms; systemically this serves to keep parents united. When such a pattern is observed, a family therapist will then focus on improving the parental relationship, which generally results in resolving the children's concerns.

Case Conceptualization in Practice

In practice, case conceptualization is one of the most frequently used clinical skills. In some practice contexts, formal case conceptualizations are written and presented to treatment teams for discussion. In other contexts, case conceptualization is more an informal element of practice, which is used to inform treatment planning and intervention. For all therapists, the ability to carefully think through and conceptualize clients' concerns is critical to navigating the complex problems and interaction patterns that clients present. When working with couples and families, case conceptualization is particularly important in helping the therapist quickly identify complex and multilayered dynamics as they unfold in relational sessions. Once a therapist has a solid and clear conceptualization of a couple or family, developing a treatment plan, identifying appropriate interventions, and responding to the unexpected become far easier and often appear effortless.

Diane Gehart

See also Boundaries; Family Life Cycle; Genograms; Systems, Subsystems, and Metasystems; Systems Theory; Treatment Planning With Couples and Families; Triangulation

Further Readings

Gehart, D. (2015). *Theory and treatment planning in family therapy: A competencies-based approach.* Pacific Grove, CA: Brooks/Cole.

Haley, J. (1976). *Problem-solving therapy: New strategies for effective family therapy.* San Francisco, CA: Jossey-Bass.

Johnson, S. M. (2004). *The practice of emotionally focused marital therapy: Creating connection* (2nd ed.). New York, NY: Brunner-Routledge.

Minuchin, S., & Fishman, H. C. (1981). *Family therapy techniques.* Cambridge, MA: Harvard University Press.

Neufeldt, S. A., Pinterits, E. J., Moleiro, C. M., Lee, T. E., Yang, P. H., Brodie, R. E., & Orliss, M. J. (2006). How do graduate student therapists incorporate diversity factors in case conceptualization? *Psychotherapy: Theory, Research, Practice, Training, 43*(4), 464–479. doi:10.1037/0033-3204.43.4.464

Satir, V., Banmen, J., Gerber, J., & Gomori, M. (1991). *The Satir model: Family therapy and beyond.* Palo Alto, CA: Science and Behavior Books.

Tomm, K., St. George, S., Wulff, D., & Strong, T. (Eds.). (2014). *Patterns in interpersonal interactions: Inviting relational understandings for therapeutic change.* New York, NY: Routledge.

Watzlawick, P., Weakland, J., & Fisch, R. (1974). *Change: Principles of problem formation and problem resolution.* New York, NY: Norton.

CLINICAL INTERVIEWS WITH COUPLES AND FAMILIES

A clinical interview is an assessment process that begins with the first contact between counselor and clients. Clinical interviewing with couples and families is by far the most important process in providing counseling services to multiple individuals. For the counselor to assess and identify the problem, a clinical interview must occur. During this process, a dialogue between the counselor and a couple or family takes place to help the counselor evaluate and determine the course of action and plan for treatment. This entry discusses important concepts in clinical interviewing, the counselor's theoretical orientation, and when assessment begins. The entry concludes with a presentation of typical clinical interviewing questions.

Key Concepts

When the counselor first begins to develop a conceptualization of the family's narrative, it is important to keep in mind three concepts related to family dynamics: the content of the narrative, the therapeutic process, and the guiding role of theory. Often counselors look for the content of the story first to develop an understanding of the family's background, its history both public and private. Identifying significant events in the family story is key to understanding the connections between members, the strength of those relationships, and the basis of conflict in both the past and the present. For example, the death of a matriarch or patriarch, those who have shaped the family story over a long period of time and who have served as the repositories of the oral history of the family, may sever links to that family history and continuity. These figures often serve as the structure around which generations of the family are gathered, and their loss may lead to significant turmoil and redevelopment of roles within the family. Other catalysts for change within the family structure may include children moving out of the home (i.e., "empty nest syndrome"), marriages, and significant career successes or setbacks. Change may also occur within the family due to births that have a significant impact on the roles of members, as well as their responsibilities and position within that family.

It is also important to focus on how the content of the narrative is expressed; that is, the process of expression. When counselors focus on this process, they can identify the patterns of communication used within the family. The family's narrative about the problem gives insight into hierarchies and interconnectedness within the family system and the roles that each member plays. It provides information as to how miscommunication may lead to misunderstandings, maladaptive cognitive patterns by individuals, and the nature of conflicts within the unit. It can also give insight into the nature of certain behaviors by individuals or the family as a whole in context, such as how they have adapted to that system. This information further provides the means for counselors to help improve the way members relate to one another and work through issues together.

Theoretical Considerations

When developing a conceptualization of the family dynamic, it is important to consider what theoretical basis the counselor will use to understand the family and provide for successful treatment planning. In general, these theoretical approaches tend to focus on belief systems and patterns of behavior. A few of the most widely used theories include structural, cognitive-behavioral, strategic, solution-focused, and narrative family therapies.

Structural Family Therapy

The main premise of this theory, as posed by Salvador Minuchin, was that the reason for the behavior of the individual can be observed only during interactions with the family. Since the family is operating under a series of unwritten rules or demands that are known only to the family, this structure can be observed only when it is in play. As such, the structure can influence a family positively or negatively. Therefore, it is the work of the counselor to assist the family in restructuring the family to interact in less dysfunctional ways.

Cognitive-Behavioral Family Therapy

In cognitive-behavioral approaches working with families or couples, the counselor focuses not only on the emotions and behaviors of the members but also on their thoughts, or cognitions. There are cognitions that promote growth and harmony in the relationship while others may exacerbate distrust, distress, or conflict. Members may also hold irrational beliefs about themselves, their partners, or about relationships in general. From this perspective, a counselor works to address these maladaptive cognitions and to promote growth in the relationship through a variety of techniques including education, coaching, and contracting, to name a few.

Strategic Family Therapy

Linked with the noted practitioners Chloe Madanes and Jay Haley, strategic family therapy has been associated with brief therapies in that they tend to provide clarity, or brevity, to what should be changed. This approach is goal oriented and problem focused, and based on the premise that members must change the way they act toward one another first, followed by changes in emotions and perceptions of others. The role of the counselor is to assist the family to strategize, or plan, how they will go about making these changes in behavior within the family context.

Solution-Focused Family Therapy

Based on social constructivist theories, solution-focused family therapy posits that the family must be understood in its sociocultural context and that that reality is socially constructed by its members. This approach focuses on what families believe should be changed, drawing on their collective and individual strengths, and constructs solutions in collaboration with the family members. Assisting clients to free themselves from dysfunctional interactions, from being "stuck" in the same patterns, the counselor uses techniques that are appropriate in the context of the family's behavior.

Although there are numerous theoretical contributions to this field, other significant theoretical approaches to working with families and couples should be considered. Suggested couples and family theories include psychodynamic/Bowenian family therapy, experiential family therapy, narrative family therapy, MRI brief therapy, structural family therapy, functional family therapy, and Milan systemic family therapy.

Telephone Interview

Clinical interviewing begins with the initial telephone contact. When someone is looking to receive couples or family counseling, the first contact is via telephone. The telephone interview is the first opportunity where the relationship between counselor and client begins. The client has the opportunity via telephone to request information regarding the counselor's style and clinical approach. In addition, the counselor will schedule the initial counseling session date and time, and briefly discuss methods used in assisting individuals in overcoming problems and issues. The telephone interview also allows the counselor to obtain necessary information and evaluate as to the reason the client is in need of services. The initial telephone consultation can last between 10 and 20 minutes. Usually, it is the assumption that the person calling is the identified client. However, in most cases of couples and family therapy the person calling is looking for help for someone else or the entire family. Counselors must be careful not to take in too much information via telephone, because other family members are not present. Further details and information gathering should take place during the initial counseling session.

Initial Counseling Session

The initial counseling session consists of all family members present—for example a couple, or the nuclear family—and may include extended family members. The process of clinical interviewing happens during the initial counseling session and starts with an overview of the presenting problem. Then the interview will further explore the history and duration of the problems or conflicts, and the impact of various physical, emotional, and mental symptoms of each family member. In some cases, it may be appropriate to conduct a mental status exam prior to the initial clinical interview with families to assess the mental and psychological functioning of each member. Assessing mental status helps to eliminate any contributing presenting problems that directly relate to any mental illness and its associated presenting symptoms. Nonetheless, asking open-ended questions can be more effective when interviewing couples and families than directly asking closed-ended (yes or no) questions. Utilizing open-ended, probing questions helps the counselor efficiently assess the extent of family dysfunction, healthy and unhealthy relationship patterns, and emotional functioning. The initial counseling session can last between 60 and 90 minutes. The more time spent interviewing and working with a family, the stronger the counselor–client relationship should become. More important, counselors must be aware that clinical interviewing is an ongoing process throughout the course of couples and family therapy. In addition, a clinical interview occurs almost in every counseling session and is necessary to address and further resolve the presenting problem. Throughout the process of clinical interviewing, the counselor must refrain from taking sides in disputes, becoming emotionally engaged within the family problems, or overly sympathetic with one member and angry at others. The counselor approach to clinical interviewing with a family must be objective in nature, unbiased and nonjudgmental, and interested in all family members' narratives about the problem. This task can often be challenging and overwhelming at times. However, counselors can overcome clinical interviewing challenges when their presence is engaging, authentic, empathic, and their attitude remains positive even in crisis or hostile situations.

Clinical Application

When conducting a clinical interview with couples and families, it is the responsibility of the counselor to create a safe and calm environment for the clients to be able to discuss their problems and issues openly. Counselors must first build trust and establish rapport with the family by asking surface-level questions (e.g., Where does your family live? What do you like most about living here? What are some activities that you like to do for fun?). Counselors may also use the opportunity to say why they enjoy working with families or why they have a passion for couples and family therapy, and so on. Prior to starting the clinical interview, it is important to discuss the importance of confidentiality and its limitations for breaking it in therapy. Family members have to be reminded that the information disclosed will not be shared unless there is an immediate (i.e., suicidal or homicidal) danger to the client or someone else, any report of child or elderly abuse, and if a judge subpoenas the counselor. To summarize, building a safe and calm environment in the clinical interview helps the counselor build trust and allow the clients to be honest in the therapeutic process.

List of Clinical Interview Questions

Once the counselor has established rapport with the clients and discussed confidentiality, now it is appropriate for the counselor to ask open-ended, probing questions that examine the presenting symptoms and evaluate any family dysfunction. Listed below are some questions to consider when interviewing couples and families:

- What are some concerns or issues that you would like to discuss in therapy?
- What are some of the biggest stressors? Describe them.
- Can you list any triggers that cause tension in your relationship?
- When do you become aware that things have escalated?
- Describe a time when things were normal. When do you remember things changed?
- What are the relationship interactions like at home versus when not at home?
- How often does the problem happen?
- How long does it take for you all to calm down or to open up again?
- What discussions or situations are hot topics?
- Are things different when certain family members are not present?
- In your family, who do you feel more close to and why?
- If you could resolve your issue(s) and get along better, what would be different for you that is not happening now?

One of the most effective techniques used to facilitate the process of clinical interviewing is the use of circular questioning. This process involves asking each member of the family probing questions that address a difference or define a relationship between two other family members. Circular questioning can also be implemented by asking each family member the same question, but to address the differences between one family member's narrative compared to others. The purpose of this technique is to draw various conclusions of the presenting problem based on the multiple perceptions held by family members. Circular questions intentionally expose any dysfunctional family patterns and seek to reveal a clearer picture of the problem. The counselor then takes the feedback and information learned from the investigation to determine the root of the problem. Once this process has begun, the clinical interview is an ongoing process and happens at every stage of working with couples and families. If it is to evaluate family interactions, rituals, roles, life dreams, goals, or to search for meaning, the clinical interview provides the counselor with the tools and resources to investigate these aspects.

Ryan T. Day and Michael A. Keim

See also Assessment, Biopsychosocial; Genograms; Scales, Children; Scales, Couple and Marital; Scales, Family

Further Readings

Gehart, D. (2013). *Mastering competencies in family therapy: A practical approach to theories and clinical case documentation* (2nd ed.). Belmont, CA: Brooks/Cole.

Gladding, S. T. (2010). *Family therapy: History, theory, and practice* (5th ed.). Upper Saddle River, NJ: Pearson.

Goldenberg, H., & Goldenberg, I. (2013). *Family therapy: An overview* (8th ed.). Belmont, CA: Brooks/Cole.

Gottman, J. M. (1999). *The marriage clinic: A scientifically based marital therapy*. New York, NY: Norton.

Paratore, J. B., & Nichols, M. (1998). *Family therapy: Historical overview*. Retrieved from http://www.abacon.com/famtherapy/history.html

Sommers-Flanagan, J., & Sommers-Flanagan, R. (2012). *Clinical interviewing* (4th ed.). Hoboken, NJ: Wiley.

CLINICAL PRACTICE

Clinical practice in marriage, couples, and family therapy can be defined as the professional application of therapeutic and family systems theories and techniques in the delivery of services to families, couples, and individuals. Services include the assessment, diagnosis, and treatment of a wide variety of serious and developmental mental, emotional, cognitive, and behavioral disorders and issues. Clinical issues in practice can include depression, anxiety, premarital counseling, marital problems, divorce, child and parent issues, addictions, and much more. Additionally, clinical practice includes referrals to and collaboration with health care and other professionals when appropriate. This entry presents an overview of clinical practice in marriage, couples, and family therapy, beginning with an outline of the history and development of clinical practice, including major concepts and theories. The entry continues with a discussion of professional issues, including education and licensure, and concludes with a brief account of clinical practice, including assessment, diagnosis, and the therapy process.

History and Development

Although there is a long history in the formation and thinking involved in marriage, couples, and family therapy, a significant breakthrough was achieved in the 1950s by scientists and counselors who were studying communication and discovered that certain schizophrenia symptoms made sense within the context of the family's communication style. This suggested that individuals with schizophrenia were not "crazy" in a meaningless way, but rather that what appeared to be odd behavior had a purpose in the context of their families. Research observations were made on how mothers and their schizophrenic children cycle through closeness and distances. Research on clients with schizophrenia launched the family therapy movement. Once "the client" was conceptualized as "a family," there was a need for new ways to think about peoples' issues. This process introduced the idea of a systems perspective.

In the United States, family therapy began growing independently in four places with different individuals: with John Bell at Clark University, Murray Bowen at the Menninger Clinic, Nathan Ackerman in New York, and Don Jackson and Hay Haley in Palo Alto. Each of these founders had distinct and different backgrounds and theoretical orientations, and the family therapy approaches they developed were also different. This diversity is part of the marriage, couples, and family therapy profession today.

Major Concepts and Theories

Marriage, couples, and family therapists have a variety of concepts and theories that inform clinical practice. This section briefly describes some of the major concepts, theories, and techniques. Different systems theories (e.g., structural family therapy, strategic family therapy, psychodynamic) offer marriage, couples, and family counselors guiding principles about family and relational dynamics and techniques to promote growth, development, and change. One major concept in the clinical practice of couples, marriage, and family therapy is considering client issues from a systems perspective. Such a perspective helps clinicians and researchers understand how family members are in constant interaction and mutually impact one another. Thus, a change in one member of the family system will have an effect on all the other members. Families balance stability and change. To stabilize and maintain the current level of functioning, systems use negative feedback loops; to promote change, systems use positive feedback loops. Other major concepts in thinking about client issues from a systems perspective in clinical practice include family rules, triangles, and roles (discussed elsewhere in this encyclopedia).

Beyond key concepts in marriage, couples, and family therapy, therapists use theory and techniques in order to help provide interpretation and explanations of family functioning and the ways to promote change. While there are many theories and techniques used in clinical practice, following is a brief note on the specific theories developed by pioneering marriage, family, and couples therapists. Psychodynamic family therapy was pioneered by Nathan Ackerman and focused on dream analysis, transference, focusing on strengths, and life history. Murray Bowen created another family therapy theory that introduced a common therapy assessment tool: genograms. A genogram is a visual representation of an individual's family tree and includes mental health, career, divorce, health, and other factors that are a focus of treatment and exploration. Experiential family therapy came from the work of Virginia Satir and Carl Whitaker and focused on family roles and reconstruction, using "I" messages, play therapy, touch, and humor. Structural family therapy, created by Salvador Minuchin, highlights the structure and boundaries of families in which the therapist joins with the family and creates disequilibrium and reframes issues. Last is strategic (Jay Haley) and systemic (Milan) family therapy (Mara Selvini Palazzoli). Techniques from these theories, used in clinical practice, can include reframing (i.e., express ideas and issues differently), paradox (i.e., a complex concept asking clients to engage in the very issue that clients want to work on), circular questioning (i.e., information seeking about differences before and after an issue began), and rituals (i.e., behaviors or activities that involve most/all members of a system, have value and meaning to the system, and are carried on in the future).

Professional Issues

Education and Licensure

To be a marriage, couples, and family therapist and engage in clinical practice, one must first have at least a master's degree in marriage, couples, and family therapy and become licensed. As part of the academic program leading to a degree, the trainee will practice therapy while under supervision in practicum and internship. This type of supervision continues beyond obtaining a master's degree for a specific number of hours or years. In the United

States, licensure as a marriage and family therapist is granted by each state; most states require an accredited graduate degree, a specific number of supervision and client contact hours before and after obtaining a degree, as well as an examination, application, and fee.

Ethical Practice

Ethical clinical practice is a critical issue in marriage, couples, and family therapy. Depending on the type of education, program accreditation, and other factors, a clinician is expected to follow the code of ethics of the organization that outlines clinical practice. The American Association for Marriage and Family Therapy (AAMFT), the International Association of Marriage and Family Counselors (IAMFC), the American Counseling Association (ACA), other professional associations, and state licensing boards all have ethical codes. The multiple ethical codes can overlap in content, but generally address the following issues related to clinical practice: therapists' responsibility to clients and the profession; confidentiality and informed consent; professional competence and integrity; financial arrangements and private practice; diagnosis and assessment; advertising; and supervision and research. Therapists must be aware of and follow the codes of ethics that apply to their clinical practice.

Elements of Clinical Practice

Assessment and Diagnosis

Clinical practice in marriage, couples, and family counseling includes a variety of assessment and helping behaviors. First, a marriage, couples, and family counselor will assess the family, using tools such as diagnostic interviews, genograms, family mapping, symptom inventories, and personality assessments. The diagnostic process includes differential diagnosis and the use of the current diagnostic classification systems, the *Diagnostic and Statistical Manual of Mental Disorders* (DSM) and the *International Classification of Diseases* (ICD).

Marriage, couples, and family counselors examine and work with families to explore the effect of human sexuality on the couple and family functioning, aging and generational influences on family concerns, and the impact of crisis and trauma on marriages, couples, and families. Additionally, issues related to addiction, interpersonal violence, and employment concerns are explored for potential impacts on the marriage, couple, or family.

In addition to assessment and evaluation, marriage, couples, and family therapists engage in case management services from a systems perspective. There is a focus on family wellness and not just the pathology of problems. In clinical practice, there is a need to keep records, get reimbursed for treatment provided from insurance and other third parties, and engagement with, and strategies for working within, the legal system.

Therapy Process

Overall, clinical practice is the therapist offering services to a couple or family. Initial contact between a client and a therapist could be a phone call, referral by an agency or legal system, or response to advertising online or in the phone directory. This can be a time to gather information about the family or couple, hear about the caller's perception of the problem, identify members of the system who might be involved, and schedule the first appointment, taking notice of who should attend. Next is the first interview or session, and the goal of this meeting is to build a relationship with the family, conceptualize what is maintaining the presenting problem, and gather information. One way to gather additional information and assess relationships and generational influences is by using a genogram. As noted earlier, a genogram is a diagram that shows how individuals in the system are connected and how the family system is connected generationally to other family members.

During sessions with the family, couple, or system, two ideas are important for therapists to consider: content and process. Generally, *content* refers to what is being said and *process* to how it is said. For example, if a family calls and wants to help a shy family member make friends, the family therapist is trying to figure out why the family hasn't been able to solve the stated problem and what it is about the way they've been trying to increase the person's friendships that isn't working. The therapist listens as much to the process of the discussion (e.g., who speaks to whom, in what tone, the covert or unconscious message being sent) as to the content of what is being said (e.g., my daughter struggles to make friends). In the early phase of family treatment, the therapist is refining the conceptualization of the issues and the work needed to help resolve them. During this time, a therapist might confront, challenge ideas, and encourage change. Some major tasks during this phase of treatment include identifying major conflicts and bringing them into session, developing and refining a hypothesis about how the family is failing to resolve the issue, focusing on primary concerns and the interpersonal conditions supporting them, assigning homework to address problems and structures that maintain the issue, challenging system members to see the role they play in the issue, and pushing for change.

In the middle phase of treatment, problems have been identified and responsibility is taken by individuals and members of the system. The next stage of the therapy process is the working stage, which creates opportunities for the family to learn to rely on their own resources to solve issues rather than depend on the therapist, make sure that efforts to improve relationships have a positive impact on the issue, and be creative with techniques and discussion to continue to move the system to wellness. The final phase of therapy is termination, where the family and therapist process how the presenting issue has improved. They collaboratively review the new tools and skills to address issues in the future, discuss and process what it means to have the issue resolved, and determine new ways of communicating that are responsive to the system's needs. This final phase, termination, happens in a variety of ways. There are instances where a family or couple will not return for additional treatment, times where the therapist and system discuss and agree on a termination plan, or situations when treatment goals are met and treatment is no longer necessary.

Joseph A. Campbell

See also Assessment, Biopsychosocial; DSM and V-Codes; Ethical Codes; Informed Consent in Clinical Work; Clinical Case Conceptualization With Couples and Families; Clinical Interviews With Couples and Families; Licensure and Certification; Progress Notes for Couples and Families

Further Readings

Bowen, M. (1985). *Family therapy in clinical practice.* Lanham, MD: Rowman & Littlefield.

Carr, A. (2000). Evidence-based practice in family therapy and systemic consultation II. *Journal of Family Therapy, 22,* 273–295. doi:10.1111/1467-6427.00152

Johnson, S., & Lebow, J. (2000). The "coming of age" of couple therapy: A decade review. *Journal of Marital and Family Therapy, 26,* 23–38. doi:10.1111/j.1752-0606.2000.tb00273.x

Northey, W. F. (2002). Characteristics and clinical practices of marriage and family therapists: A national survey. *Journal of Marital and Family Therapy, 28,* 487–494. doi:10.1111/j.1752-0606.2002.tb00373.x

Pinsof, W. M., & Wynne, L. C. (2000). Toward progress research: Closing the gap between family therapy practice and research. *Journal of Marital and Family Therapy, 26,* 1–8. doi:10.1111/j.1752-0606.2000.tb00270.x

Walsh, F. (2003). Family resilience: A framework for clinical practice. *Family Process, 42,* 1–18. doi:10.1111/j.1545-5300.2003.00001.x

CLINICAL VERSUS STATISTICAL SIGNIFICANCE

Research methods and statistical analysis have become a vital part of studying treatment effectiveness in the field of mental health and psychotherapy. As a specialty within the mental health field, marriage and family therapy desires to understand what is most effective in treating couples and families. As a broad profession, psychotherapy has a responsibility to numerous stakeholders, including clients. Clients, the general public, various payees, and practitioners alike all want to know with a degree of certainty whether treatment is helping clients. Why should people pay large sums of money to engage in a process if there is no certainty that this process delivers the desired outcomes? Specifically, does counseling help clients resolve their difficulties? Also, most stakeholders want to know what is the most efficient and effective therapy for their problem. In this age of questioning and accountability, the field has had to turn to other fields to prove to the public that psychotherapy does work. Practicing clinicians want to know that they are helping and not harming their clients. In addition, clinicians want to figure out which therapy seems to be the most effective for a specific client with a specific concern at a specific time. To answer these questions, people look to research that shows a statistical difference between two groups.

Statistical significance is determined by a set of data that shows there is a difference between two groups and that this difference is not likely due to chance. However, just because there is a statistical difference between two groups does not mean that the difference has any clinical value. In addition, just because there is no statistical difference between two groups does not mean there is no value to the treatment being studied. It may be that the groups were too small to detect statistical significance. In this entry, statistical and clinical significance are defined in greater detail, and the strengths and weaknesses of each are reviewed from the perspective of research related to marital, couples, and family counseling.

Psychotherapy as a Science

As a helpful adjunct to answering questions about research, the field of psychotherapy has turned to the field of science, specifically of research methodology and statistics. There are many who argue that human behavior cannot be reduced to a set of behaviors and data; that there is an art, or intuitive element, to psychotherapy. Others argue, however, that the risks of building a profession on "going with your gut," intuition, or operating solely on the basis of nonscientific knowledge is a risky proposition. Therefore, research and statistics comprise an important aspect of the programs of all mental health training, including marriage and family counseling. Nevertheless, beginning students and the lay public generally have anxieties surrounding the use and interpretation of research and statistics.

Indeed, the domain of research methods and statistics can appear confusing and perhaps overwhelming to many people who are not engaged in the study or have only minimal training; however, it is still important for those considering a career in counseling to understand the basics of these fields. Just as there are many different ways to scientifically study the effectiveness of therapy, so are there multiple research methods and multiple tools of statistical analysis that guide the process of research. Space limitations do not permit a detailed discussion of these topics here, which are addressed elsewhere in this encyclopedia.

Types of Statistical Significance Analysis Predominantly Used in Effectiveness Research

Historically, researchers want to understand the variables that impact the complexities involved in the counseling process. In examining the effectiveness of counseling, there are multiple questions regarding the effective practice of counseling that require answering certain general and specific questions. Thus, researchers measure the outcomes of counseling in general and then specific treatments for specific people and problems addressed in counseling.

The most basic question becomes: Is the process of counseling a mere product of chance, or is what clinicians do actually effective in helping the client? A second question is typically: What is most helpful to what person, with what problem, at what point in time? Historically, three types of statistics have typically been used to examine these questions and others in the quest for counseling effectiveness, as well as types of therapies used in treatment outcomes within psychotherapy. These three most common statistical analyses are used in and reported in quantitative research studies to examine the statistical means of (1) differences among the members of a given treatment group, (2) differences between two separate treatment groups, and (3) the size of that difference (effect size) and clinical significance as it relates to a particular client. Each type of statistical analysis is important in measuring the degree of change that is not due just to chance alone. However, each statistical analysis only contributes a piece of information to the knowledge base of treatment effectiveness research. To date, most research studies have focused primarily on within- and between-group and effect size statistical analysis, but the use of clinical significance analysis has lagged behind in the research.

Each statistical analysis used within research is important and examines one aspect of treatment effectiveness, but it does not provide all of the important elements a clinician may need to know as he or she is working with a specific client. For instance, using within- and/or between-group statistical analysis may show the average or mean difference with specific treatment protocols within a group and between groups. Then, effect size statistics may provide the degree of difference regarding the changes of a group or groups of clients. However, neither of those two statistics explains the reasons two different clients may respond so differently to the same treatment that has been shown to be the most effective. For instance, a clinician may know that using one intervention has been shown to be effective for a certain issue; however, the clinician has two clients that respond totally differently to that intervention. The field needs further research information to help give science-based clues on the client level. It is important to know the research and statistics that explain individual change as another tool for evaluating effective treatment.

History and Importance of Clinical Significance

There is a need to look further into clinical significance, which is based on a different set of methodologies aimed at studying individual change within the course of treatment. This means that a micro-level analysis might give more weight or power to looking at smaller-group studies as well as examining individual client change across a treatment protocol. The problem is that, to date, there is no single agreed-upon statistical method for analyzing clinical significance. The actual development of methods and statistical analysis, to some degree, is still in its infancy in comparison to the other types of research methods and analysis.

Michael Lambert and Benjamin Ogles traced the history of clinical significance, pointing to its emergence in the 1970s with two separate tracks used to analyze the data. The most prominent track individually tracked a client's progress on the goals set at the beginning of counseling; this has been the predominant form of analysis. However, there is another track in looking at clinical significance, that of using clinical statistical analysis. This second track has rarely been seen in the reporting of research. One of the studies using a type of clinical statistical analysis in the early 1980s examined distressed couples' self-reports as they went through treatment. Since then, there has been a slow but steady increase of analysis, methods, and research focusing on client response to treatment; this line of research has been termed *patient-focused research*.

Work Needed to Refine Aspects of Clinical Significance

Even as the use of clinical significance methodologies and studies has advanced, there still remain problems and concerns regarding the use of clinical significance analysis within research.

As Lambert and Ogles have noted, much work remains to be done before this area of analysis gains a reputable and usable foothold in the psychotherapy research. According to Lambert and Ogles, one area of concern is that there is no agreed-upon method to calculate clinical significance. Several analyses have been used, but the field does not have one agreed-upon analysis as the best standard. To complicate matters, each analysis raises questions about the practical consequences of the outcome of the analysis. It goes back to the primary question regarding how this helps with a specific client. Lambert and Ogles note other concerns, such as a lack of normative data, suitability for various populations, defining parameters, and validity concerns. Many of these concerns go back to understanding the basics of research methodology and statistics.

Given the confusion and concern that arise in the work of clinical significance, Lambert and Ogles have issued a call for the field to move toward using one single analysis of clinical significance. This would facilitate comparisons of research studies across time and treatments. In addition, it might push the field to do more work in the areas needed, such as looking at setting parameters and amassing more data on validity in this field of clinical significance.

Analysis of clinical significance within research has the promise of helping clinicians in several ways. Lambert and Ogles list how this type of research analysis could assist clinicians in predicting client treatment failure, signal negative concerns to both client and clinician, as well as provide problem-solving strategies for specific clients. However, client-focused research, which relies on clinically significant methods and analysis, requires more development in order to be helpful for clinical practitioners.

Kathleen Hartney Kellum

See also Effectiveness Research; Evidence-Based Practice With Couples and Families; Outcome Research; Process Research; Qualitative Research; Quantitative Research

Further Readings

Davis, S. F., & Smith, R. A. (2004). *Introduction to statistics and research methods: Becoming a psychological detective*. Upper Saddle River, NJ: Pearson.

Heppner, P. P., Wampold, B. E., & Kivlighan, D. M., Jr. (2007). *Research design in counseling* (3rd ed.). Belmont, CA: Brooks/Cole.

Lambert, M. J., & Ogles, B. M. (2009). Using clinical significance in psychotherapy outcome research: The need for a common procedure and validity data. *Psychotherapy Research, 19*(4–5), 493–501.

Lick, J. (1973). Statistical vs. clinical significance in research on the outcome of psychotherapy. *International Journal of Mental Health, 2,* 26–37.

Ogles, B. M., Lunnen, K. M., & Bonesteel, K. (2001). Clinical significance: History, application, and current practice. *Clinical Psychology Review, 21,* 421–446.

Speer, D. C., & Greenbaum, P. E. (1995). Five methods for computing significant individual client change and improvement rates: Support for an individual growth curve approach. *Journal of Consulting and Clinical Psychology, 63,* 1044–1048.

Tingey, R. C., Lambert, M. J., Burlingame, G. M., & Hansen, N. B. (1996). Assessing clinical significance: Proposed extensions to method. *Psychotherapy Research, 6,* 109–123.

CLINICIAN-DIRECTED, SOLUTION-FOCUSED SUPERVISION

Some seasoned professionals in the field of marriage and family therapy elect to serve as supervisors, helping clinicians on the path to licensure. Supervision often includes watching sessions live through closed-circuit recording equipment, observing through one-way mirrors, sitting in on sessions, listening to audio recordings, or discussion of clinical cases (often called case consultation). This supervision can also take place within individual dyads (up to two clinicians and the supervisor)—or with groups of up to six associate-level (before being fully licensed) or student therapists.

Supervisors are trained professionals who are required to be fully licensed and often approved by national certifying boards as having the qualifications to provide services as a supervisor. For example, the American Association for Marriage and Family Therapy (AAMFT), the leading national organization for couples and family therapists, has a qualification credential called Approved Supervisor that requires a clinician to accomplish several steps before they can achieve it. In order to be an approved supervisor, a clinician must be fully licensed (for at least 18 months) and take a required didactic and experiential learning course, followed by a period of time in which they supervise other therapists while they are in turn being supervised by even more seasoned supervisors.

As part of the application process, AAMFT requires that a supervisor develop a philosophy of supervision paper, similar to the way in which therapists develop a theory of change. There are several methods and models of supervision, most of which are directly correlated with the models of therapy in couples and family therapy. This push toward being able to discuss what approach is used in supervision has spurred the development and further validation of many theories of supervision. One model that has been developed is the clinician-directed, solution-focused supervision (CDSF) model. This entry discusses the development of the CDSF model and the process of CDSF supervision.

The CDSF model came out of emerging literature that focuses on collaborative and strengths-based relationships between the supervisor and the beginning clinician. This was added to the work of Insoo Kim Berg, who was one of the founders of solution-focused brief therapy with Steve de Shazer. With the addition and integration of common factors through a constructivist, feminist-informed practice, the process of CDSF supervision was developed as a method to incorporate and privilege the clinician-directed paradigm. In addition to the theoretical basis, many scholars have researched what therapists believe effective supervision entails, finding that clinicians think collaborative, therapist-centered, respectful, positive and affirming, deconstructive, and analytical, solution-oriented and future-focused supervision is the best, most helpful to participate in.

CDSF supervision is rooted in both what the clinicians have stated is the most effective types of supervision, as well as the traditional roots of the postmodern solution-focused therapy work of Berg and de Shazer. The relationship between the supervisor and the clinician is a cornerstone of the work, combined with collaboration, empathy, genuineness, and positivity. The work is strengths-based and focused on what the clinician needs. This process requires that clinicians have the ability for insightful introspective self-examination of how they are providing therapy and can recognize the strengths and weaknesses of their approach.

Process of Doing Clinician-Directed, Solution-Focused Supervision

Clinician-directed, solution-focused supervision comprises six main components: clinician needs, strengths-based approach, collaboration, supervision process, deconstructive meaning-making, and an overarching goal of self-supervision. These six components break down into the process by which the supervision is provided, as well as the way in which the supervisor and clinician interact. This method of providing supervision is suitable for all clinicians, as it is based on clinician needs.

Clinician Needs

The first component of the model, clinician needs, is a representation of the influence of the clinician on the process. Clinicians under supervision must come prepared and ready to ask for advice, feedback, and direction on what they need for their clients—thus being "client directed." If they are not fully prepared, this process can look like an exploration of the current state of progress with their clients, facilitated by the supervisor. In practice, this is done by requesting that therapists bring in a "cheat sheet" of all of their current clients, with a brief rating scale on which they rate their overall impression of the progression of the case. For those cases that are rated lower on the scale than others, or decrease in rating over time, the supervisor can lead a conversation exploring what is needed and what can be used to advance the case. For those cases that are consistently rated highly over time, a conversation can be had about the appropriateness of continuing therapy.

Strengths-Based Approach and Collaboration

A core component of CDSF that connects directly to the theoretical development stemming from solution-focused brief therapy is the focus on strengths and collaboration between supervisor and clinician. This looks more like a conversation among colleagues, in which the supervisor asks for thoughts and ideas from the supervisee and any fellow therapists. This process privileges the abilities and experiences of the supervisees, and deconstructs the hierarchy of supervisor as expert; the supervisor is seen as more of a knowledgeable facilitator than an all-knowing guru. By asking the clinician to take on this responsibility, the process of self-supervision is promoted, as formal supervision must end at some point; clinicians must learn to be able to handle difficult cases on their own in the future, by gaining confidence and trust in their abilities. As part of the deconstruction of this hierarchy and facilitation of deeper thought, the supervisor challenges the therapist on matters of social justice and encourages creative thinking. This process is called "leading from one step behind."

A pivotal component to the process of CDSF is the usage of feedback in supervision. This can be easily incorporated with objective brief measures, such as the Leeds Alliance in Supervision Scale (LASS), developed by Nigel Wainwright. This scale is a three-item measure that uses "visual analogue rating scales"—a simple measured line on which respondents place a mark—to exemplify the supervisory alliance and effectiveness. The three items deal with the approach (was the session focused?), the relationship (did the supervisor and supervisee understand each other?), and a question on meeting the needs of the supervisee (was the supervision helpful to the supervisee?). The supervisee places a hash mark on a line with dichotomous statements at either end, with the mark placed closer to the side they agree with the most. The actual LASS instrument can be downloaded free of charge through many libraries.

Beyond traditional objective scales, there are many ways to gather feedback directly from supervisees as to how the supervision session went. Many CDSF supervisors will ask verbal and direct questions about how the supervision process is going, and what can be done to improve the experience. This feedback should be reviewed with the clinician at the earliest opportunity, either at the beginning of the session or directly after the feedback is given, with a brief, nondefensive conversation on how supervision can be improved to be more helpful. In addition, this information can be tracked over time to show effectiveness of supervision in a process known as *feedbacking*.

Supervision Process

The supervision process itself looks similar to many supervisions that are completed with other theories and models. In a confidential setting, case files are reviewed, suggestions are given, and client data are reviewed (through case consultation or live video or audio feedback). At the start of a CDSF supervision session, a supervisor would be expected to start with an open-ended question, such as, "What do you need from supervision today?" This statement fits easily and well with the collaborative idea of constructing a sense of what is important to the clinician, as well as what would be needed to make the supervision session more helpful for that person. By asking this question, only what the clinician needs will be covered that day, and not anything that is not needed. Typically, at the start of the supervision relationship the supervisor and clinician will determine the frequency and length of time that they will meet, according to needs and legal and ethical requirements.

Deconstructive Meaning-Making

Clinicians are not immune from stress, bias, and influence. Through the careful and respectful examination of beliefs, values, and automatic thoughts the supervisor can help to guide the clinician through a process of self-growth by deconstructing the clinician's and supervisor's automatic and instinctual beliefs or biases. This is usually accomplished through gentle challenges to "all-or-nothing" statements, the examination of self of the therapist issues, and the highlighting of potential biases or polarizing statements within sessions and about clients, groups, or cultural influences. Encouraging the clinician to be responsive to issues of diversity and contexts of the human experience is an important component that can be achieved through this process.

Self-Supervision

This process continues indefinitely until either full licensure is obtained (thus ending the supervision process), or the clinician no longer wishes to engage in the supervisory relationship—referring back to the first part of the model, being clinician directed. The end goal and the overall constant in this model is the guiding purpose of achieving self-supervision. Self-supervision is defined as having confidence and knowledge to be able to handle most cases through an introspective process of self-talk in which a clinician can work out solutions. Through deconstructive meaning-making and collaborative strengths-based solution work with the clinician, the clinician is consistently challenged to build up awareness of personal attributes and capabilities—a process called "taking a step back."

Probably one of the more difficult things for any supervisor to do is to believe that a beginning clinician has the answers to clinical questions already. This is because there is a pervasive belief in the developmental approach to supervision, based in assumptions of "expert" abilities being achieved at an arbitrarily decided level of experience—most often achieved with the legal requirements set forth for full licensure. This approach works toward the deconstruction of this belief, and attempts to build a sense of accomplishment that continues to be improved over time, without delimited hierarchies of ability. In addition, in recent work with colleagues, this approach has shown effectiveness and promise in peer supervision groups as well. Taking a strengths-based collaborative approach such as this one will achieve a greater level of competence in the field of mental health, and provides the foundation for ongoing feedback groups that mimic the supervisory experience throughout a clinician's career.

Christopher K. Belous

See also Solution-Focused Brief Family Therapy; Supervision; Supervision, Approved Supervisor in Marriage and Family Therapy; Supervision, Developmental Model; Supervision, Gatekeeping; Supervision, Individual and Group; Supervision Contract; Supervision of Supervision; Supervision Philosophy Statement; Supervision Theories

Further Readings

American Association for Marriage and Family Therapy. (2000). *Readings in family therapy supervision*. Alexandria, VA: Author.

American Association for Marriage and Family Therapy. (2014). *AAMFT approved supervisor designation: Standards handbook*. Alexandria, VA: Author.

Koob, J. J. (2003). The effects of solution-focused supervision on the perceived self-efficacy of therapists in training. *The Clinical Supervisor, 21*(2), 161–183. doi:10.1300/J001v21n02_11

Marek, L. I., Sandifer, D. M., Beach, A., Coward, R. L., & Protinksy, H. O. (1994). Supervision without the problem: A model of solution-focused supervision. *Journal of Family Psychotherapy, 5*(2), 57–64.

Morrissette, P. J. (2002). *Self-supervision: A primer for counselors and helping professionals*. New York, NY: Routledge.

O'Connell, B., & Jones, C. (1997, November). Solution focused supervision. *Counselling, 8*, 289–292.

Selekman, M. D., & Todd, T. C. (1995). Co-creating a context for change in the supervisory system: The solution-focused supervision model. *Journal of Systemic Therapies, 14*(3), 21–33.

Thomas, F. N. (2013). *Solution-focused supervision: A resource-oriented approach to developing clinical expertise*. New York, NY: Springer.

Todd, T. C., & Storm, C. L. (Eds.). (2014). *The complete systemic supervisor: Context, philosophy, and pragmatics*. Malden, MA: Wiley-Blackwell.

Wainwright, N. A. (2010). *The development of the Leeds Alliance in Supervision Scale*. (Unpublished doctoral dissertation). University of Leeds, England.

Waskett, C. (2006). The pluses of solution-focused supervision. *Healthcare Counselling & Psychotherapy Journal, 6*(1), 9–11.

Wetchler, J. L. (1990). Solution-focused supervision. *Family Therapy, 17*(2), 129–138.

Cognitive Maps and Couples

Cognitive maps are mental representations of our emotions and behaviors that inform how we navigate situations within our environment, whether the situations concern moving through physical space or engaging in interpersonal interactions. In the context of a couple relationship, cognitive maps are representations of each partner's internal thoughts and feelings that inform the way they engage in relationships. Albert Brok is a psychodynamic therapist who uses cognitive maps to help partners construct and articulate what he refers to as their "internal vision" of the other and the couple relationship. The restoration therapy (RT) model, developed by Terry Hargrave, is a family systems approach that uses cognitive maps as a tool to help partners identify their internal processes of reactivity and to understand how these processes impact the couple relationship. The focus of this entry is to describe the use of cognitive maps in the RT model and its value in raising awareness of destructive patterns of interaction and developing agency toward healthy ones. First, a brief explanation of cognitive maps and its relationship to cognitive neuroscience is provided, followed by a description of the use of cognitive maps in the RT model.

Cognitive Maps and Neuroscience

The concept of cognitive maps was first developed by the psychologist Edward Tolman, who studied rats in mazes and claimed that like rats, humans create cognitive maps by accumulating and connecting information about places, situations, or relationships. Eventually the connected points of information become a map embedded with meaningful knowledge that informs how the person interacts with the world. Exposure to different experiences results in broader and more comprehensive maps, which increase adaptability to new and unfamiliar situations.

In the field of cognitive neuroscience, a concept that complements the cognitive map framework is how the brain is understood to be both stable and adaptable. The brain's neocortical system holds stable information such as beliefs and norms, while the hippocampal system of the brain processes new and unfamiliar information. When new information/experience is repeated, the brain moves that information into the neocortical system and essentially incorporates the now-familiar information into a stable landscape of knowledge. Cognitive maps are developed and embedded in the neocortical system of the brain. Cognitive maps can be adaptive or maladaptive and can be developed at an unconscious or conscious level. This understanding of the brain's plasticity offers interesting possibilities regarding sustainable change in the therapeutic process, particularly when dealing with deeply embedded experiences, such as trauma and pain, which result in developing maladaptive cognitive maps.

The Cognitive Map of Pain and Peace

All humans experience psychological pain. According to the RT model, such pain results from violations of one's identity (one's sense of value, worth, being known, etc.) and/or one's safety (one's feelings about people or the world being safe and trustworthy). These violations occur in all types of relationship contexts and can occur through the delivery of words and actions over time or in one significant or traumatic event. Most often, the violations that define the initial template of one's cognitive map of pain occur within the context of the primary caregiver relationship during childhood. Violations such as abuse, discrimination, and betrayal become perceived messages about the person's identity and/or safety. For example, imagine that a young child is constantly criticized and nagged at by his parents about how he fails to measure up in school or at home. This child experiences a violation of identity—*you are not good enough*—and at an unconscious and perhaps a conscious level, begins to identify himself as being inadequate. This is not simply a feeling of inadequacy but rather a core belief about his identity that can remain with him into adulthood. These violations are the roots of pain expressed through primary emotions that trigger a fight-or-flight response to cope with the pain. The four major categories of reactive coping are shaming, blaming, controlling, and escaping. The shaming and escaping behaviors are flight responses, whereas the blaming and controlling behaviors are fight responses. Thus, when the same person described above feels inadequate, he might cope by blaming others (fight) or withdrawing and isolating himself (flight), establishing a pattern of coping that continues into adulthood. This internal pattern of pain to reactivity is referred to as the *pain cycle*. As the pain cycle is repeated over time, a cognitive pain map is constructed in the brain and becomes the template for relating to others in unhealthy ways when pain is triggered.

During the initial stages of therapy the primary therapeutic tasks are to understand the client's pain and to identify his or her pain cycles. The pain cycle is drawn out as a visual illustration of the cognitive pain map. The illustration is displayed during every session and referenced whenever the client describes situations when reacting to pain. Through repeated references to their pain cycle, clients gain an awareness of their cognitive pain maps and eventually are able to quickly recognize when they are in their pain cycles and are able to articulate their primary emotion and related reactivity.

When it is evident that clients understand their pain cycles, the therapist begins to move toward developing an alternative internal pattern called the *peace cycle*. The peace cycle is based on truths about the client's identity and/or safety. Restoring one's truth can be done using therapeutic techniques such as finding exceptions to the narrative of pain or re-parenting using guided imagery. For example, if asked to identify a time when he did not feel inadequate, the client described above might talk about a person who believed in him or an experience when he measured up, defying the core belief that he is an inadequate person. The client would identify the truth that he is good enough and consequently begin to develop a new message about his identity. After truth is identified the client is asked to describe how he acts when he is functioning from his truth. If the client were to say that when he feels good enough as a person he tends to stay engaged, then the alternative pattern can be established: When he knows he is good enough, he stays engaged. This new pattern connecting truth to nonreactive response is the *peace cycle* that becomes an entrée into a construction of an alternative map, the cognitive peace map.

Current understanding of neuroplasticity and the brain's capacity to alter even the most deeply embedded information, such as painful experiences and their unconscious effects, is significant in regard to working with clients at both the relational and neurological levels. Clients construct and reinforce the template of their cognitive peace map by learning a simple yet powerful emotional-regulating intervention, called the Four Steps, that embeds the alternative map into the brain. The Four Steps are as follows:

1. When I feel _____

2. I usually do _____

3. But the truth is _____

4. Knowing the truth, instead I will _____

The first two steps are the articulation of the cognitive pain map. The third and fourth steps are the articulation of the peace cycle, which eventually becomes the new cognitive peace map. The Four Steps for the client described above would be: *When I feel inadequate I usually withdraw. But the truth is, I am good enough and so instead I will stay engaged.* The Four Steps serve as a self-regulating tool that interrupts the cycle of reactivity and orients the client to having more open and responsive interactions. With repetition, the Four Steps help embed the cognitive peace map into the brain, and as clients are able to self-regulate, their sense of agency increases, and ultimately clients understand that they can choose to live from their truth instead of their pain.

Cognitive Maps in Couples Therapy

When two people enter into a couple relationship, they inevitably bring their respective pain cycles into their dynamics of interaction. At the time couples enter therapy, they are often entrenched in their destructive interactions and are so entangled in their reactivity that they struggle to identify the root cause and meaning of their distress. What most often proves to be true is that couples have one argument that takes on a multitude of issues shaped by context. That one argument is the interaction of their pain cycles, leaving both partners stuck in their pain and at an impasse in their relationship. Therapists lose valuable time and energy by chasing down the content of each argument when, in fact, it is the process of the couple interaction that should be the focus of couples therapy. It is important for therapists to remember that although a partner's cognitive pain map may have developed in the context of the couple relationship, very often each partner has a cognitive pain map that he or she brings into the couple relationship. Thus, the focus of couples therapy is for both partners to understand their cognitive pain maps that are fraught with reactivity, and to realize the impact their reactivity has on the relationship.

The use of cognitive maps with couples helps ground the therapeutic process because they help organize internal patterns as well as sequences of interpersonal interactions. Each partner has pain and peace cycles separately constructed, and for the most part, the use of cognitive maps as described above is similar with couples and an individual client. However, the therapist additionally visually illustrates the interactive pain and peace cycles that correspond with each partner's cycles. Although each partner has his or her own cognitive map, there is always the possibility that each partner can give input to and engage the other's story. For example, when exploring truths, partners can be a source of truth during the process of identifying and reinforcing truth if it is appropriate to do so. When partners participate in identifying cognitive maps of pain and constructing new cognitive maps of peace with one another, that aspect of the therapeutic process can contribute to relational repair. Similarly, when partners practice the Four Steps together in session, they are more likely to apply the intervention when conflict arises outside of the session.

Working with both partners in the room is particularly beneficial because it allows the therapist to work directly with the relationship in distress, and it allows each partner to be meaningfully involved in making sustainable change for the individuals and for the relational system. When working with couples, the therapist is able to witness the interaction of the cognitive maps as well as work directly with the relational system in which the interaction is embedded. Furthermore, as partners listen to each other's stories of pain, they are invited to enlarge their empathy toward one another and to develop new lenses for seeing each other.

*Miyoung Yoon Hammer
and Terry D. Hargrave*

See also Clinical Case Conceptualization With Couples and Families; Clinical Practice; Couple Development; Restoration Therapy

Further Readings

Brok, A. (2011). Working with couples from a psychodynamic perspective using cognitive maps. In D. K. Carson & M. Casado-Kehoe (Eds.), *Case studies in couples therapy: Theory-based approaches* (pp. 53–63). New York, NY: Routledge.

Hargrave, T. D. (2000). *The essential humility of marriage: Honoring the third identity in couple therapy.* Phoenix, AZ: Zeig, Tucker, & Thiesen.

Hargrave, T. D., & Pfitzer, F. (2011). *Restoration therapy: Understanding and guiding healing in marriage and family therapy.* New York, NY: Routledge.

Hargrave, T. D., & Yoon Hammer, M. (2011). Forgiveness and trauma: Working with love, justice, and power for healing. *Psyche en Geloof, 22,* 102–111.

COGNITIVE-BEHAVIORAL COUPLES THERAPY

Cognitive-behavioral couples therapy (CBCT) is a common therapeutic approach used by clinicians who work with couples and families. It emphasizes cognitive, behavioral, and emotional factors and focuses on how thoughts, behaviors, and feelings interact in individuals and between the members of a couple. It is grounded on the premise that altering distorted cognitive appraisals about a relationship event will result in positive changes in behavior and emotions. This will eventually lead to an increase in relationship satisfaction. Cognitive-behavioral couples therapy has strong empirical support for its effectiveness in reducing couple distress and is also applicable to a wide range of other relationship issues that couples may present with. Although CBCT has endured some criticism, it is still considered to be the most popular approach among couples and family therapists. Cognitive-behavioral couples therapies are evidence-based approaches and possess wide applicability. This entry highlights the main tenets of cognitive-behavioral couples therapy, discusses its strengths, and provides examples of its use in therapy.

History

Cognitive-behavioral couples therapy evolved from the initial models used by pioneers such as Neil Jacobson and Gayla Margolin, and also from Richard Stuart's work, which described the benefits of treating distressed couples using a social learning framework. Social cognition research as well as the work of cognitive therapists such as Aaron Beck led to the emergence of focusing on partners' cognitions about each other in clinical treatment. Results from empirical research demonstrate that behavioral interventions that include behavior change contracts and communication and problem-solving skills training yield significant improvement in the way couples interact with each other as well as increased relationship satisfaction.

Applications of CBT

Cognitive-behavioral therapies emerged in an effort to better understand and treat problems such as depression, anxiety, unassertiveness, and impulsive behaviors, but increasingly have also been useful in treating issues in interpersonal relationships. CBCT emerged from the popularity of behavioral couples therapy (BCT), which focuses on the behaviors displayed by each member of the dyad, identifies maladaptive behaviors, and replaces these with more adaptive and functional ones. CBCT differs from behavioral couples therapy as it also addresses cognitive distortions and emotions in addition to maladaptive behaviors that may be negatively impacting the relationship. It is a therapeutic model that examines the impact that one's thoughts have on feelings, moods, and behaviors. As in individual cognitive behavioral therapy, CBCT also includes skill-building sessions coupled with homework assignments.

The goal is to assist couples in identifying the impact of distorted cognitions and faulty behaviors on the relationship. CBCT operates under the premise that when a couple is experiencing relationship distress, their problems all have behavioral, cognitive, and affective influences, and treatment strategies should include interventions that focus on both changing behaviors and modifying dysfunctional patterns in the relationship. Consequently, in CBCT, cognitive, behavioral, and emotional components are all the focus of treatment. Another major premise of CBCT is that a partner's behavioral and emotional responses are a result of his or her cognitions about the relationship event. In distressed couples, these cognitions are either unrealistic or distorted. CBCT seeks to assist couples in being aware of faulty cognitions as well as their assumptions and expectations of their relationship. CBCT identifies two different stresses in relationships: primary distress and secondary distress. Primary distress is a result of unmet needs such as intimacy, security, and autonomy. Secondary distress develops when the partner with unmet needs employs maladaptive behaviors when attempting to communicate his displeasure. The role of the therapist is to assist the couple by teaching skills and directing behavioral, cognitive, and affective change.

CBCT is also theoretically rooted in social learning and social exchange theories. Social learning theory posits that behavior is learned from the environment through observation. Individuals learn by observing others' behaviors, attitudes, and the outcomes of these. According to social learning theory, human behavior entails a continuous interaction between behavioral, cognitive, and environmental influences. Social exchange theory argues that social behavior is the result of an exchange process in which individuals weigh the anticipated benefits against the anticipated risks of social relationships. Relationships are formed and maintained when the anticipated rewards from being in the relationship are maximized and the costs or risks are minimized.

Another premise of CBCT is that couples often evaluate their relationship and partners according to unrealistic expectations and cognitive distortions. These distorted cognitions may result in maladaptive behaviors and psychological disorders. If these beliefs and expectations are altered, it will lead to positive changes in the individual's behavior and emotions. Cognitive distortions are irrational, faulty thoughts or beliefs that distort one's perception of reality. These faulty beliefs often have negative consequences. Some irrational beliefs include the belief that one must be loved and approved of by everyone, or the idea that happiness is a result of external factors and one has little or no influence on one's own happiness. Other examples of irrational beliefs include the idea that it is catastrophic if things don't go as one planned or expected, or the belief that one should be excelling in all areas in order to be considered worthy. As a result, CBCT therapists collaborate with their clients to identify distorted cognitions and unproductive beliefs, and replace these with more rational thinking.

The following are some common examples of cognitive distortions. *All-or-nothing thinking* involves viewing situations in absolute terms. This dichotomous thinking pattern involves seeing things as either/or, very black-and-white thinking. *Overgeneralization* is defined as perceiving a single negative event or situation as a never-ending pattern of defeat. *Mental filter* occurs when the individual focuses only on the negative and ignores the positive. *Magnification or minimization* occurs when things are blown out of proportion or, conversely, their importance is reduced. *"Should" statements* involve thoughts that include "should," "must," or "ought." These distortions often result in feelings of shame or guilt. *"Should" statements* often extend to others as well. For instance, "She should have known that I needed help."

Labeling occurs when one labels someone or something based on just one experience or event. *Catastrophizing* occurs when an individual views an unpleasant situation as the worst possible outcome. *Jumping to conclusions* involves thinking negatively about someone or something without any supporting evidence. There are two main types of this cognitive distortion: (1) *Mind-reading*—thinking that someone is thinking negatively about you despite having no evidence to support this claim, and (2) *The fortune teller*—one genuinely believes he or she knows what will occur in the future without having any evidence.

Emotional reasoning causes an individual to think that one's feelings can be accepted as reality. For instance, if an individual *feels* unworthy of love then he thinks that he is actually unworthy of love. *Personalization* occurs when one takes things personally, even those things that are outside of his or her control. Personalization also includes taking blame for other people's behaviors. *Blaming* can be perceived as the exact opposite of personalization. Instead of viewing everything as his or her fault, the individual assigns all blame to others.

CBCT is also aimed at the interpersonal relationship between partners, and assists in resolution of these problems. It provides the couple with targeted behavioral techniques to help resolve current and future issues. The main goal of CBCT is twofold: First, it aims to provide the couple with problem-solving skills and, second, it provides the couple with strategies for confronting future problems. Two common types of cognitive-behavioral couples therapy include the classic cognitive-behavioral therapy and integrative behavioral therapy.

Integrative behavioral couples therapy (IBCT) emphasizes acceptance and change as major goals of couples therapy and assists couples in better understanding each other's emotions. However, acceptance is at the foundation of treatment with couples. IBCT also utilizes a variety of therapeutic interventions within a behavioral theoretical framework. There are two major phases in IBCT: an evaluation and feedback phase, and an active treatment phase. The focus of treatment is on current issues and situations affecting the couple.

The Process of Cognitive-Behavioral Couples Therapy

During the assessment phase of treatment, the CBCT therapist focuses on gathering information from the couple to determine the cognitive, behavioral, and emotional factors that are related to the couple's presenting concerns. The therapist also determines whether this mode of treatment is suited to the couple.

Once the initial assessment is complete, the goal-setting stage begins. The therapist typically meets with the couple to provide feedback. During this session, the therapist verbalizes what he or she perceives the problem to be and seeks feedback from the couple. The therapist also collaborates with the couple to establish therapeutic goals for therapy. The typical length of CBCT is between eight and 25 sessions, with sessions two and three reserved for assessment and goal formation. Treatment is terminated when the couple attains their goals and the therapist has assessed the couple's readiness to move from reliance on the counselor to being able to maintain progress on their own. Treatment may also be terminated if the couple is noncompliant or no progress is being made.

In cognitive-behavioral couples therapy, assessments are used to assist the therapist in identifying behavioral and cognitive patterns that may be contributing to the couple's presenting issues. During the initial sessions and assessment periods, another focus is building trust in the couple and establishing a safe and therapeutic environment that will facilitate change. Typically a contract for therapy is created after the couple understands the process of therapy, expectations, and requirements.

Some behaviors that are the focus of CBCT include communication skills, problem-solving skills, unhealthy patterns of behavioral exchanges between partners, and behavior modification. These interventions are aimed at skills training as well as increasing positive behavior exchanges between couples. In treatment, couples learn to reinforce desirable behaviors in each other and are encouraged to avoid punishing unwanted behaviors. Couples are taught basic communication skills and problem-solving skills as an aid in successfully resolving current and future issues.

CBCT focuses on five interrelated parts of cognitions: perceptions, attributions, expectancies, assumptions, and standards/beliefs. Distortions in these areas may result in dysfunctional relationships insofar as individuals have a distorted view of reality. Cognitive restructuring is used to replace distorted cognitions that may lead to destructive behaviors and dysfunctional emotions. Some intervention strategies used to address this include teaching couples to be aware of their cognitive processing and distortions, how to test the validity of these cognitions, and how to modify distorted cognitions. Some common CBCT techniques used for disputing and replacing cognitive distortions include role-playing, countering arguments, and perceptual shifting. Perceptual shifting involves countering arguments but goes further by having the client generate and rehearse evidence that supports the counterargument.

CBCT also focuses on the couple's ability to identify and describe their emotions, the degree of overall positive and negative emotional experiences, and how emotions are expressed and may be negatively affecting the functioning of the relationship. Some common emotions that often accompany impaired relationships include jealousy, depression, anger, and anxiety. CBCT interventions are aimed at changing dysfunctional emotions by focusing on understanding and recognizing emotions and learning to express emotions in healthy and positive ways. Emotional expressiveness training (EET) is one technique used in CBCT to teach couples how to express emotions in healthy ways. Some of the skills couples learn through EET include how to appropriately express both negative and positive emotions, empathic listening skills, how to reflect on each other's feelings, and how to effectively manage anger, jealousy, depression, and anxiety.

The Role of the Therapist

The CBCT therapist remains flexible throughout treatment and may assume multiple roles based on what is needed by the couple. The therapist may play the role of a director, facilitator, advocate, teacher, and model, among many others. In the early stages of treatment, the CBCT therapist also assumes an active and directive role. In CBCT, the therapist is actively engaged in three relationships: one with each individual partner and one with the couple as a whole. The therapist provides guidance and support in each relationship as the couple works to attain their goals.

Commonly Used Interventions

CBCT offers a plethora of interventions and techniques that the therapist may use with couples. Some common examples of interventions used in cognitive-behavioral couples therapy include *guided behavior change,* which is used to describe techniques aimed at changing behavior but do not include a skills component. An example of a line of questioning that the therapist may use in this case is "Think about how you might behave differently if you were behaving like the partner that you would like to be." *Skills-based interventions* are also very commonly used in CBCT. When using these interventions, the therapist provides the couple with information and resources aimed at behavioral change. Some common skills addressed in these sessions are communication and decision-making skills, and anger management.

Socratic questioning is another intervention and is aimed at changing distorted cognitions and beliefs. The therapist presents the couple with a series of questions aimed at helping the clients to reevaluate the logic of their thinking. These questions also assist clients with discovering and understanding any underlying issues and concerns that have not been presented. *Guided discovery* utilizes several techniques that allow the therapist to create experiences for a couple that lead them to reevaluate their faulty cognitions and work on substituting these with more realistic ones. These techniques may include generating a list of pros and cons, and role-playing. *Restricted or minimized emotions* is another commonly used intervention and is used to assist one or both partners with becoming more comfortable with specific emotions and refrain from avoiding or stifling them.

An Example of Cognitive-Behavioral Couples Therapy

Clinical psychologist Arthur Freeman offers one example of how CBCT can be implemented in couples therapy. His approach focuses on the present but first evaluates past experiences to identify strategies for improving the interpersonal relationship. Freeman motivates couples remain in the relationship and helps them substitute distorted cognitions and maladaptive behaviors with healthy ways of thinking and behaving.

Freeman employs skill-building and skill-using techniques in his sessions. Successful relationships involve communication and negotiation skills. Partners are also able to unconditionally accept each other even during times when they do not agree. One of the roles of the therapist is to assist the couple in identifying the values, beliefs, behaviors, or emotions that are nonnegotiable. His approach utilizes the following five steps:

1. Identify positives in the relationship
2. Identify difficulties in the relationship
3. Meet with each member individually to talk confidentially
4. Identify directions for the therapy; what the couple is able and willing to change
5. Recommend a plan that will be implemented over the next 10 sessions

Limitations of Cognitive-Behavioral Couples Therapy

While CBCT has been proven to be highly effective in working with couples in distress, there are a few limitations to this approach. Other theorists have argued that while this approach focuses on a couple's cognitive appraisals, communication styles, and the manner in which partners relate behaviorally with each other, it fails to account for the influences of one's personality and other individual characteristics on relationship events. Second, the influence of environmental factors on couple functioning is ignored. External and environmental stressors can also influence a couple's level of functioning. Third, although CBCT also addresses one's emotions, this comes in secondary to cognitions and behaviors and is seen as a direct result of the two. Fourth, with the emphasis on distorted cognitions and maladaptive behaviors, highlighting and emphasizing the couple's strengths takes a back seat.

Wendy L. Greenidge

See also Cognitive Maps and Couples; Communication Errors/Problems in Couples and Families; Communication in Couples and Families; Conflict in Couples and Families; Couples and Marriage Counseling

Further Readings

Baucom, D., Epstein, N., & LaTaillade, J. (2002). Cognitive-behavioral couple therapy. In *Clinical handbook of couple therapy* (3rd ed., pp. 26–58). New York, NY: Guilford Press.

Bernstein, A. C. (2000). Remarriage: Redesigning couplehood. In *Couples on the fault line: New directions for therapists.* New York, NY: Guilford Press.

Datilio, F. M. (2010). *Cognitive-behavioral therapy with couples and families: A comprehensive guide for clinicians.* New York, NY: Guilford Press.

Freeman, A. (2006). *Cognitive behavioral couples therapy.* American Psychological Association. Retrieved from http://www.apa.org/pubs/videos/4310765.aspx?tab=2

Gladding, S. (2015). *Family therapy: History, theory and practice* (6th ed.). Boston, MA: Pearson Education.

Helping couples deal with medical challenges: Various types of couples therapy offer different approaches and coping strategies. (2010). *Harvard Mental Health Letter, 27*(5), 4–5.

Simpson, L. E., Gattis, K. S., Christensen, A., Berg-Cross, L., Morales, M., Moore, C., . . . Juffer, F. (n.d.). *Therapy—Couple relationships, family relationships, parent-child relationships.* Retrieved from http://family.jrank.org/pages/1694/Therapy.html

COGNITIVE-BEHAVIORAL FAMILY THERAPY

Cognitive-behavioral family therapy (CBFT) was developed by a diverse group of therapists who integrated cognitive approaches and interventions to use with couples and families. CBFT can be defined as a family systems approach based on the premise that the thoughts and behaviors that influence one family member have the potential to simultaneously influence other family members as a whole. The thoughts and behaviors of one family member can drastically continue the cycle of family dysfunction or prohibit change within the family system. CBFT techniques are used to assist family members and groups of people with resolving marital distress, family conflict, and other areas that have led to family dysfunction and problems within the family system. CBFT therapists are often seen as teachers or coaches in the process of treatment. They are active within the counseling relationship and directive in their approach to facilitating change within the family system. This entry seeks to provide readers with a basic foundation and overview of CBFT treatment, assessment, interventions, and the role of the therapist.

Early Developmental Considerations

The early applications of cognitive-behavioral family therapy can be traced back over 50 years ago through the work of Albert Ellis, who studied and researched the role of cognitions and their impact on marital problems. During the 1960s and early 1970s, family therapists started to see the need to integrate behavioral approaches with family systems approaches to treating the problems and issues stemming from family dysfunction. Since then, CBFT has become one of the contemporary theoretical approaches used by family therapists worldwide. CBFT was derived from the framework and theoretical foundation of cognitive therapy (CT) and cognitive-behavioral therapy (CBT). Cognitive therapy originated in the 1960s and was developed by psychiatrist Aaron T. Beck. Beck's advancement of cognitive therapy started in session when he observed that clients often spontaneously expressed negative and irrational thoughts about themselves and others, and that their worldview and perceptions were significantly distorted. Using this rationale, Beck coined the term "automatic thoughts," the cognitions that go on to affect the client's feelings and behaviors. By identifying one's automatic thoughts, clients are able to pinpoint specific thoughts and impractical feelings that are preventing them from overcoming challenges. Beck postulated that automatic thoughts began in childhood. Children who were rewarded or punished for different behaviors or attributes would form automatic thoughts, which would emerge randomly, causing irrational thoughts to resurface. By exploring these thoughts in session, clients could learn to be more pragmatic, allowing them to function better both physically and emotionally.

Beck later referred to cognitive therapy as cognitive-behavioral therapy (CBT). The principles of CBT focus on changing the way one views the world as it applies to one's life. Also key to CBT is the goal of modifying one's behaviors to promote a more desirable system of cognition. Many clinical tests and research experiments have subsequently confirmed its effectiveness in treating a wide range of mental disorders. Relaxation and exposure techniques developed in Beck's research have been introduced as clinical aids to promoting favorable changes in behavior. CBT interventions are widely used to assist clients with identifying irrational thinking patterns, finding alternatives to these beliefs, and altering the associated behaviors. CBT has been used to treat an array of issues, including marriage and family conflicts, parent–child relational issues, and trauma-related problems, as well as mental health diagnoses such as anxiety, schizophrenia, depression, and substance-related disorders.

Key Concepts

Like most approaches to family therapy, cognitive-behavioral family therapy (CBFT) attempts to assist families and couples in resolving relationship difficulties and challenges. Each member of the family brings his or her life experiences to the relationship; their different perceptions help to shape behaviors and communication styles, emotional well-being, and patterns of thought within the family system. In CBFT, it is believed that dysfunction within the family is driven by negative patterns of thought that have become internalized habits within that system. Although, for example, what each member of a couple brings to the relationship from their respective families of origin is essential in understanding that couple's functioning, CBFT is focused mainly on current interactions within the family system and how these perceptions and expectations play out within that system and society at large.

Through counseling, family members become aware of their cognitions and how those thoughts and patterns of thought (schemata) affect behaviors with others within the family. These automatic thoughts are deeply ingrained over time, and once negative thought processes are developed, they impact individual functioning that in turn affects the family as a whole. By changing the schemata of each member, the dynamics of the family may change. This process allows for more open communication and a greater possibility for improved decision-making, sustained positive relational change, and growth as a family or couple.

During treatment with individuals using a CBFT approach, the counselor creates situations for clients that challenge negative schemata and cognitive distortions to bring about change. In applying this approach to family therapy, the counselor challenges each member to examine his or her schemata regarding family relationships as well as collective schemata that govern interactions with other family members. The counselor then works with the family as a whole to facilitate change and promote more efficient communication by modifying or eliminating cognitive distortions. Such distortions often include differing perceptions of past events in the relationship, biases pertaining to the causes of events, erroneous expectations of future events, unrealistic standards for the relationship, and inaccurate assumptions about relationships in general.

Treatment Process Overview

The overview of CBFT treatment listed below was adopted from the work of marriage and family therapist Diane R. Gehart. The therapy process for most CBFTs includes the following steps:

- *Step 1. Assessment:* Obtain a detailed behavioral and cognitive assessment of baseline functioning, including the frequency, duration, and context of problem behaviors and thoughts.
- *Step 2. Target Behaviors and Thoughts for Change:* Cognitive-behavioral therapists identify *specific* behaviors and thoughts for intervention (e.g., rather than using the general goal of "improve communication," the therapist targets tantrum frequency, name-calling, curfew compliance, and other problem behaviors).
- *Step 3. Educate:* Therapists educate clients on their irrational thoughts and dysfunctional patterns.
- *Step 4. Replace and Retrain:* Interventions are designed to replace dysfunctional behaviors and thoughts with more productive ones.

Assessment Methods

In cognitive-behavioral family therapy, assessment is an essential and ongoing process, measuring the degree of the problems encountered by the family or couple and monitoring progress. The assessment process is the most important process in CBFT because it provides the necessary information used to evaluate the family problems, conflicts, strengths, areas for improvement, irrational thoughts and beliefs, and sources of family dysfunction. Also, this process helps support contentions and perceptions held by some within the family and helps set goals that guide treatment planning. CBFT uses personality tests, genograms, family inventories, standardized questionnaires, problem analysis, and assessment of baseline functioning to gain insight into the daily interactions and dysfunctional behavior patterns of the couple or family. The assessment process starts at the beginning of family therapy but continues throughout the course of therapy. It is important to conduct ongoing assessments because the information provided by the family at the beginning may turn out not to be the real or authentic issue within the family. As therapy progresses, the therapeutic relationship becomes stronger and provides the therapist with an opportunity to explore further the various levels of family dysfunction that may emerge. These are the problems and issues that the family has kept secret and not disclosed in therapy. It is also common for CBFT therapists to conduct individual interviews with each family member in the group after the first initial assessment. This process may help to gather the information that a family member may not have been comfortable sharing with the other family members present. Individual interviews give the clinician an opportunity to evaluate different problems that may negatively impact the family system and to assess critical issues that are disrupting family interactions. The CBFT therapist must identify the schemata and core beliefs within the family system. Frank Dattilio defined family schemata as beliefs about one's own family, and core beliefs are the beliefs the family has about families in general. These are the statements that family members make among one another and in therapy. These statements should not be disregarded but taken into careful consideration, as they may provide insight into the irrational thoughts and adverse decisions within the family system.

Goals and Treatment Planning

Individual family members who have been diagnosed with a mental health disorder may have a severe impact on the overall functioning of the family. Family members may not understand how to respond appropriately to a parent or sibling, and this can in turn lead to negative thoughts and maladaptive patterns of interaction, creating destabilization within the family. Treatment goals are identified from the information gathered during the assessment process. Goals are then developed in behavioral and measurable terms, such as "family will decrease arguments at home from twice a week to no more than twice monthly." All goals developed and added to the family treatment plan must be mutually agreed upon by all family members. General goals for counselors working within a CBFT framework include trying to help family members learn to accept themselves and others unconditionally. Additionally, CBFT attempts to change dysfunctional behavior patterns by assisting family members to become aware of and purposely alter maladaptive thought processes. During treatment planning, family members work together to determine which behaviors they would like to change. Within a CBFT framework, family members set goals with each other, and, if achieved, they will bring about change not only for the individual but also for the interactions of the family members as a whole.

Techniques and Interventions

The framework and origin of many of the techniques used in CBFT are derived from cognitive-behavioral therapy. Prior to using these interventions in treatment, the therapist must first teach clients the basis of the cognitive-behavioral model of treatment. The premise of this model is that the way we perceive situations influences how we feel, and that these perceived thoughts affect not only how we feel but also how we behave. Listed below are some of the main techniques and interventions used in CBFT:

- *Psychoeducation:* This involves teaching about and providing information to the family regarding mental health conditions, relational strategies, coping skills, and alternative methods used to deal with current problems and dysfunctions.
- *Problem-Solving Strategies:* This consists of a set of guidelines that can be used to define the problem in specific behavioral terms, generate solutions to resolving the conflict, and evaluate its effectiveness. This process may also incorporate out-of-session homework assignments to assist with implementing the chosen solution outside of therapy.
- *Contingency Contracts:* This technique consists of a written contract that can be used to foster positive behaviors and empower alternative behavioral responses. When the individual exhibits the new behavior, only then can he or she receive the desired reward, instead of the undesirable or disruptive response that is leading to problems.
- *Behavioral Exchange Agreements:* These written agreements, like contracts, are used to facilitate mutual behavior exchanges between the family and are used to reduce family tensions. The goal of this intervention is for each family member to identify and enact a specific behavior that would evoke self-growth and improvement among family members and develop a positive set of negotiated relational rules.
- *Assertiveness Training:* The goal of this technique is to assist shy and intimidated family members in expressing their needs and wants rather than avoiding conflict and not speaking up for themselves. This process has family members practice nonassertive, assertive, and aggressive response styles with each other, with the intent of gaining insight and awareness regarding the benefits of being assertive.
- *Communication Training:* This intervention consists of family members developing skills for expressing thoughts and feelings, as well as learning active listening skills with one another. This process may include the skills of assertiveness training along with active listening

skills used to increase effective communication among family members. The therapist facilitates this process by teaching this approach during the session and models this approach by having one family member play the role of the speaker and the others act as the listeners.
- *Dysfunctional Thought Record:* This is a type of structured journaling or record-keeping activity that seeks to ask clients to confront their irrational thinking and problem behaviors. This usually takes place outside of therapy in the form of assigned homework. Completed assignments are brought to the next session to be discussed.

The Role of the CBFT Therapist

The CBFT therapist serves as a guide to help the family through the steps of the treatment process. The course of treatment depends on the levels of dysfunction that exist within the family. The CBFT therapist repeats the steps as many times as needed to resolve the presenting issues and assist the family with moving past the problematic stimuli. When major conflicts arise within the therapeutic relationship, the response of the CBFT therapist includes an effort to restore an atmosphere of empathy and warmth to create and sustain a healthy and active connection with the family. It is essential for CBFT therapists to demonstrate and model empathy, caring, and understanding during family sessions. This is where the family may have an opportunity to learn directly from the therapist and process these interactions during the session. This process also helps to ensure that the therapeutic alliance between the therapist and family is strong and collaborative. The CBFT therapist should not be seen as manipulative or demanding. The decisions made in therapy should be mutually agreed upon by all parties represented in therapy. One of the key resources that assist therapists with this process is to elicit feedback at the end of the session to evaluate the progress of the therapy session. Some clients report feeling that their therapist does not understand them or the therapist did not listen to what they had to say. The CBFT therapist strives to build rapport with the client first before engaging in intense treatment interventions or asking confrontational questions that may cause the client to shut down emotionally or become withdrawn. CBFT therapists are aware that in order for therapy to be effective in addressing a history of dysfunctional family problems, the therapeutic relationship must be collaborative, and the therapist must be engaged throughout the process of therapy.

Working With Diverse Populations

CBFT is valued in working with various populations because of its approach in understanding that each individual is different in his or her own right. CBFT focuses on the essential aspects of clients and their particular needs, not on the grounds of a particular theoretical approach, but rather on the symptoms and concerns specified by the client. Therapists must be careful in understanding and defining behavioral norms, recognizing that family values and relational interaction expectations differ from culture to culture. CBFT places an emphasis on recognizing that all clients have strengths and weaknesses and takes into account that not all client issues should be treated the same way.

CBFT provides clients with the power to begin to control their thoughts and actions, making them their own support system when challenging situations arise. This approach helps clients learn how to manage their thoughts and emotions based on specific events in their lives. CBFT challenges the client to be in control of the therapeutic process, so differences in cultures are welcomed rather than overlooked. Other multicultural strengths include CBFT's ability to allow clients to assess where they believe they are in therapy, again placing the control with the client. CBFT can be particularly effective in working with clients whose primary language differs from that of the therapist because its fundamental concepts can be presented clearly and understandably to diverse populations.

Ryan T. Day, Michael A. Keim, and Shanel B. Robinson

See also Cognitive-Behavioral Couples Therapy; Functional Assessment and Children; Goals, Treatment; Homework Assignments in Therapy; Scales, Children; Scales, Family

Further Readings

Dattilio, F. M. (2010). *Cognitive-behavior therapy with couples and families: A comprehensive guide for clinicians.* New York, NY: Guilford Press.

Dattilio, F. M., & Epstein, N. B. (2003). Cognitive-behavior couple and family therapy. In T. L. Sexton, G. R. Weeks, & M. S. Robbins (Eds.), *Handbook of family therapy* (pp. 147–173). New York, NY: Brunner-Routledge.

Gehart, D. (2013). *Mastering competencies in family therapy: A practical approach to theories and clinical case documentation* (2nd ed.). Belmont, CA: Brooks/Cole.

Gladding, S. T. (2010). *Family therapy: History, theory, and practice* (5th ed.). Upper Saddle River, NJ: Pearson.

Goldenberg, H., & Goldenberg, I. (2013). *Family therapy: An overview* (8th ed.). Belmont, CA: Brooks/Cole.

Hays, P. (1994). Multicultural applications of cognitive-behavior therapy. *Professional Psychology: Research and Practice, 26*(3), 309–315.

Herbert, J. D., & Forman, E. M. (2012). *The evolution of cognitive behavior therapy: The rise of psychological acceptance and mindfulness.* Retrieved from http://www.researchgate.net/profile/Evan_Forman/publication/230531871_The_Evolution_of_Cognitive_Behavior_Therapy_The_Rise_of_Psychological_Acceptance_and_Mindfulness/links/0fcfd503fbf1040cbc000000.pdf

Judith, B. (n.d.). *History of cognitive therapy.* Retrieved from Beck Institute for Cognitive Behavior Therapy website: http://www.beckinstitute.org/history-of-cbt/

Sexton, T. L., Weeks, G. R., & Robbins, M. S. (Eds.). (2003). *The family therapy handbook* (pp. 147–175). New York, NY: Routledge.

COHESION

Cohesion is the level of emotional connectedness between members of a system. In marital, couples, and family therapy, cohesion is an important concept used to capture the level of connectedness or separateness of family. Being overly connected stifles individuality and is called *enmeshment;* not being connected enough may leave important emotional, relational, and/or physical needs unmet and is called *disengaged.* Cohesion plays an important role within a system and also when people join a system. Research has demonstrated that cohesion plays an important role in an individual's ability to develop secondary family relationships. All who enter into a family system other than that of their family of origin bring with them the attitudes, beliefs, and expectations associated with their experience of the level of cohesiveness in their family of origin. These do not always align with those levels of cohesiveness brought into the relationship by the partner or by other members of that family system. Being able to negotiate these differences and come to an agreement as to what levels are ideal for the new relationship or family system is essential to the success of the relationship and the system that may develop from it. The ability to be flexible or adapt, as learned or experienced in one's family of origin, will have a direct influence on how a person is able to adapt to what the other family members will bring into the "new," secondary family relationship. The following sections of this entry take a closer look at the concept of cohesion, its purpose in understanding relationships, how it is applied in therapy, and how it is assessed.

Defining Cohesion

Cohesion can perhaps be best understood from a family systems perspective. Viewed in this way, the family constitutes a system whose individual members behave in ways that support its functions as a unit or those of various internal groups. Within these groups every member holds one or more roles that support the function of the family or of various members of it. Each of these groups, or subsystems, falls along a continuum from close to distant—within the subsystems and between subsystems. Cohesion is a concept that is commonly understood when viewed on a continuum of disengaged to enmeshed, with separateness and connectedness more toward the middle of the continuum. Couples and families that have a balance between connectedness and separateness tend to be more functional compared to those who are unbalanced (toward the extreme ends of the continuum). Couples and families that seek therapy often fall into the unbalanced areas.

Enmeshment

Relationships are describes as enmeshed when members of a family system are overly involved in one another's personal lives. Members of family systems that are enmeshed appear so closely joined with other members of the family that it is difficult for each individual member to develop personal identities that are separate from one another. Fidelity is not only expected but also enforced through the social structure of the tight-knit family. Members are dependent upon one another, and involvement with people outside of the family system is discouraged. Because of this strong tie, members of enmeshed families often have difficulty maintaining relationships with individuals who are not part of, or will not conform to, the family system.

Disengaged

When family members are disengaged they are disconnected with each other to the extent that there is little or no relationship structure. Members of these family systems are expected to have their needs met by people other than those in the family system. High levels of autonomy in these families prohibit the formation of healthy interpersonal relationships.

Separateness and Connectedness

Between enmeshed and disengaged are the states of separateness and connectedness. In the state of separateness, members of the system experience a sense of togetherness but enjoy emotional independence. Time apart from one another is valued, with support being a secondary consideration. Relationships with people outside of the family system are more common for family systems that fall on this side of the spectrum. In regard to connectedness, there is a strong sense of emotional togetherness and fidelity with less, but still some, emphasis placed on individuality. Time spent with other members of the family system is valued more highly than time spent by oneself. Relationships outside of the family system are more often shared with other members of the family system.

Compared with members of family systems that are either enmeshed or disengaged, members of family systems that are either connected or separated are better able to find balance in their roles with one another and have their needs met successfully while they work to meet the needs of other members of the family system. These family systems tend to function well when it comes to adapting to the other aspects of family life. Family systems at the extreme ends (enmeshed or disengaged) of the cohesion spectrum are more likely to experience difficulty throughout the overall life cycle.

Circumplex Model

Although the concept of cohesion has been examined and explained by many psychological researchers and theorists, the concept is most recently and most frequently understood as part of a model known as the *circumplex model* of marital and family systems. According to this model, the level of cohesion experienced by a family system is maintained and altered as needed via the facilitative process of communication. As the family shifts in structure, size, and function and adapts to life experiences and stressors, cohesion is maintained, strengthened, and weakened from time to time.

The second part of this model is that of flexibility. Flexibility is the ability of the family system to adapt to change and stressors experienced through the family life cycle: typically, these include having and raising children, the shrinking of the family, and changes in the roles of the members of the family system. Adaptability of the family system is viewed as important due to the inherent nature of change that comes with family developmental events such as death, marriage, childbirth or adoption, and other events. The level of cohesion experienced by a family has a direct influence on the level of flexibility that the family is able to experience and vice versa. Families and their individual members who are balanced or nearer the center of the spectrum are more likely to be able to adapt when faced with changes and challenges during the life of the family system.

According to the circumplex model, communication serves a facilitative function, which allows movement in the other domains. Cohesion is reinforced, gained, or diminished by either progressing or regressing in the frequency or quality of communication. By increasing the quality of communication within the family system, clinicians are able to assist the family in strengthening bonds and relationships. As noted previously, growth in cohesion should have a positive effect on the family's ability to adapt to challenges including difficulties in communicating. Thus progress in one area of the circumplex model has a direct effect on the others.

An Alternative View

Not all models view cohesion and enmeshment as polar opposites on a spectrum. Some theorists have viewed both concepts as being very different from one another to the point that they are not to be viewed as relative to each other. According to this viewpoint, cohesion is not an indicator of the degree to which families are enmeshed but rather an indicator of how much the family provides or receives support from and toward its members. Cohesion includes the extent to which family members are concerned and committed to the family and the degree to which family members are supportive and helpful to each other. Cohesion serves the purpose of building unity and strength in order to address the negative issues that arise throughout the course of the family life cycle. This is done by providing a sense of support and togetherness, which each member of the family system sees as a resource to be used in order to have his or her needs met. According to these models, cohesion is positively associated with individual members of family systems developing autonomy and positive relationships with members of the primary and secondary family systems in which they are, and may become, engaged. Cohesion is viewed as being empowering of the individual members of the family system.

Conversely, the concept of enmeshment is not a result of an elevated level of cohesion but is an agent of psychological control or dependency. This point of view holds that enmeshment, a separate concept entirely, is often associated with problems within the family and is not a resource that benefits the family system or its members. Examples of the problems enmeshment are associated with include, but are not limited to, aggression and delinquency in adolescents, anxiety and depression, and withdrawal from family members and social relationships. In such models, enmeshment is not an excess of cohesion but rather a separate concept that reflects the amount of control that the family system, or members of it, have over the individual members. Enmeshment maintains the status quo of the system without providing any benefit to the individual members of the system. Enmeshment-related behaviors may serve individual needs of few members of the family system either intentionally or as a result of unhealthy development.

As mentioned previously, other theorists and researchers have examined cohesion in family systems and relationships. The construct has been examined in connection with a wide variety of issues related to marital and family therapy. These include, but are not limited to, satisfaction with family functioning, family structure, social support, depressive symptoms in adolescents, adjustment to college and other life changes, self-esteem, the differences in perceptions of family cohesion among adolescents and their parents, the relationship between cohesion and the mobility of families, and the changes in trends related to cohesion among adolescents.

Michael A. Williams

See also Circumplex Model; Communication in Couples and Families; Communication Errors/Problems in Couples and Families; Conflict in Couples and Families; Family Resilience

Further Readings

Barber, B. K., & Buehler, C. (1996). Family cohesion and enmeshment: Different constructs, different effects. *Journal of Marriage and the Family, 58,* 433–441.

Cooper, J. E., Holman, J., & Braithwaite, V. A. (1983). Self-esteem and family cohesion: The child's perspective and adjustment. *Journal of Marriage and the Family,* 153–159.

Cumsille, P. E., & Epstein, N. (1994). Family cohesion, family adaptability, social support, and adolescent depressive symptoms in outpatient clinic families. *Journal of Family Psychology, 8*(2), 202.

Galvin, K. M., Bylund, C. L., & Brommel, B. J. (2012). *Family communication: Cohesion and change* (8th ed.). Boston, MA: Allyn & Bacon.

Litwak, E. (1960). Geographic mobility and extended family cohesion. *American Sociological Review, 25,* 385–394.

Noller, P., & Callan, V. J. (1986). Adolescent and parent perceptions of family cohesion and adaptability. *Journal of Adolescence, 9*(1), 97–106.

Olson, D. H. (2000). Circumplex model of marital and family systems. *Journal of Family Therapy, 22*(2), 144–167.

Olson, D. H., & Gorall, D. M. (2003). Circumplex model of marital and family systems. In F. Walsh (Ed.), *Normal family processes* (pp. 514–547). New York, NY: Guilford Press.

Olson, D. H., Sprenkle, D. H., & Russell, C. S. (1979). Circumplex model of marital and family systems: I. Cohesion and adaptability dimensions, family types, and clinical applications. *Family Process, 18*(1), 3–28.

Rice, K. G., Cole, D. A., & Lapsley, D. K. (1990). Separation-individuation, family cohesion, and adjustment to college: Measurement validation and test of a theoretical model. *Journal of Counseling Psychology, 37*(2), 195.

COLLABORATIVE COUPLES THERAPY

Collaborative couples therapy (CCT) is a form of counseling that was created by Daniel B. Wile. The focus of CCT is to help both people in the counseling session find their voices in the face of arguments or times of stress. While most forms of couples therapy focus on the communication patterns found within a partnership, in collaborative couples therapy the therapist works as a clarifier to help each of the partners better hear what is being said in the moment. Collaborative methods focus on the here and now: The focus is on the immediate problem and using language between the partners that can be taken out of the therapeutic setting. During this form of therapy, the therapist will listen intently to the couples who are communicating about a problem and help them speak in a more intimate way, where both partners feel empowered to work together in a collaborative way to solve problems, rather than in a destructive way that reinforces negative communicative patterns.

Wile describes the first step of CCT as working toward understanding the problem at hand, rather than trying to solve the problem. This allows the therapist to have freedom to truly listen to the clients' overt and covert messages, rather than listening for an answer to solve the problem. For the couple in the therapeutic setting to learn to communicate on an intimate level, there is a need to keep the conversation in the immediate, present moment, rather than focusing on past issues or the prediction of future issues. When the partners focus on their immediate feelings, they are able to create this more intimate conversation, which can encourage the partners to work through the problems on their own.

To engage effectively in collaborative couples therapy, it is helpful for the therapist to understand the postmodern constructivist views on clinical relationships, which encourage collaboration. In more traditional orientations of therapy, the therapist is viewed as the expert. Collaborating therapists, on the other hand, view themselves as equals to the couples seeking treatment. The therapist feels that the partners are the experts and the therapist can enter into a collaborative relationship only when he or she can communicate equally with the couple. When the collaborative couples therapist is able to enter into the relationship in a collaborative way with the couple, he or she can then work to keep the couple's conflicts in the moment. The couple's focus will be centered on the partners' dynamic feelings about the conflict, in the moment. The therapeutic goal is for the couple to communicate on a more intimate level to help produce empathy toward each other. Empathy is defined as feeling the emotion of the other person in the conversation. This is different from sympathy, which is where the partners only understand the issue but do not have an emotional connection.

While the couple is trying to get to a more intimate level of communication, there might be some old communication habits that re-enter the conversation. Wile speaks about couples' communication as either withdrawing or becoming adversarial in nature, which can lead to disintegration of the empathetic listening needed for effective collaborative couples therapy. Adversarial communication is a negative communication style where the couple become hostile toward each other, whereas withdrawing occurs when one person avoids or moves away from the conversation to avoid being in the moment.

There are ways the therapist might intervene in the conversation to help facilitate the collaborative communication. The therapist might help the couple to speak one at a time, rather than speaking out of order. When the couple is able to speak in turn with each other, the partner who is not speaking will have the opportunity to hear what the other partner is saying. The therapist might also try to help the couple to understand the point of view of each of the partners. When the partners are able to state their individual points of view, in the present moment, the collaborative process can begin. Turning the avoidance or adversarial stance into a collaborative conversation will create the intimate situation for the couple to resolve their problems on their own.

CCT is a contemporary approach to working with couples in a therapeutic setting that allows for communication skill-building, while allowing the partners in the relationship to share their voices with each other. In more traditional therapies, the therapist takes the formal role of being the expert and identifying pathological issues that might be causing problems within the relationship. In collaborative couples therapy, the partners are able take control of their therapy and have a professional therapist stay alongside as they explore their intimate communication issues. CCT borrows some of the tenets of postmodern therapies such as narrative therapy, in which the therapist takes a nonpathologizing stance. This means that the therapist in not concerned with giving an accurate diagnosis on the basis of a prescribed set of interventions aimed at fixing the problems in the relationship. The CCT approach allows the partners to define the problem and create their own interventions to overcome their problems without having to be concerned about a medical or psychological diagnosis. The CCT method also allows for the use of other interventions from other theoretical orientations. This allows therapists to tailor the therapeutic experience for the individual couple. More traditional forms of couples therapy may incorporate prescribed methods for working with clients. The CCT method allows for individuation of treatment with couples to ensure a positive therapeutic experience and positive clinical outcomes.

Ryan Bowers

See also Brief Family Therapy; Communication in Couples and Families; Couples and Marriage Counseling; Narrative Therapy; Postmodern Therapies

Further Readings

Anderson, H. (2006). *Collaborative therapy: Relationships and conversations that make a difference.* New York, NY: Routledge.

Morgan, A. (2000). *What is narrative therapy?* Retrieved from http://www.dulwichcentre.com.au/what-is-narrative-therapy.html

Wile, D. (1981). *Couples therapy: A nontraditional approach.* Hoboken, NJ: Wiley.

Wile, D. (1993). *After the fight: Using your disagreements to build a stronger relationship.* New York, NY: Guilford Press.

Wile, D. (2008). *After the honeymoon: How conflict can improve your relationship* (Rev. ed.). Oakland, CA: Collaborative Couple Therapy Books.

Collaborative Language Systems

Collaborative language systems involve a collaborative relationship between therapist and client. This type of approach (also referred to as collaborative therapy) encourages and promotes a process that helps the client find solutions through a mutual, rather than hierarchical, relationship between the therapist and the client. The relationship involves mutual understanding and respect for the client's situation.

Collaborative therapists believe that knowledge and language are interdependent and interact in constantly evolving, dynamic processes through the exchange of information and ideas. The collaborative language systems approach involves a reciprocal relationship through which the client works through clinical problems in dialogue with the therapist. Harlene Anderson and Harry Goolishian developed the theory and therapeutic approach of collaborative language systems in the 1980s. The theory is based on the idea that meaning is given to situations through narration and dialogue. This entry provides an overview of the collaborative language systems approach and the concepts behind it. It then further discusses the process of therapy and the therapist's role in the collaborative language systems approach, and describes some of the situations in which this approach is used.

Overview and Concepts

The theory of collaborative language systems is rooted in social constructionist theory and hermeneutics, which is the methodology of interpretation. In collaborative language systems, hermeneutics plays a role in understanding and assessing the language clients use and formally establishing a conversation between the therapist and client, which is critical to therapy.

Social Constructionism

Social constructionism explains the dynamics of human relationships within a philosophical and spiritual context. The therapeutic framework in a collaborative language systems approach is based on the idea, central to social constructionism, that knowledge is a product of social interaction. Social constructionism finds meanings in conversations. In the collaborative language systems approach, therapeutic intervention takes the form of active conversation between the therapist and the client. People give meaning and organization to their realities through the collaborative use of language. Language helps to define cultures and civilizations and give people their identity.

Meaning-Making

There are six main assumptions in collaborative therapy. They are as follows:

1. Human systems and relationships are formed through language and finding meaning.

2. Social context gives reality to collaborative therapy.

3. One's thoughts are composed in relation to oneself and one's social settings.

4. One's reality, meaning, and experiences are created through conversations and interactions between them.

5. Language is the soul of life, and it is the key that unlocks one to the outside world.

6. One acquires knowledge through interaction with others, communication, and experiences.

In short, a client's experiences set the tone of therapy.

Therapists contribute to meaning-making in therapy. The client and therapist are partners in a conversation and together share a common inquiry. The client is the expert about his or her particular situation, but the therapist has to facilitate a productive conversation that may lead to a change. Language is a common thread for human beings to form bonds, communicate, and understand each other. It is also a way to express feelings and emotions.

Process of Therapy

The process of therapy using a collaborative language systems approach is a therapeutic conversation in which the client discusses problems that cause discomfort in the client's life. The therapist becomes a participant in cocreating the definition of the client's problem and helping the client resolve it through dialogue. Therapeutic conversations provide ways to create new meanings through dynamic interaction between the therapist and the client. As the therapist reflects on the client's situation, the therapist encourages the client to reflect on the situation, thereby facilitating a therapeutic relationship. There is no formal assessment in collaborative language systems therapy. The assessment is done by the therapist interviewing the client about the problem.

Therapist's Role

In collaborative language systems, therapists create a space to facilitate a therapeutic process. This space feels safe to the client and allows the client to feel comfortable facilitating a change in the perceived problematic situation. The therapist does not intervene but merely participates in creating therapeutic reality. The therapist invites the client to a mutual, shared inquiry about the client's current situation. The therapist enters this relationship as a learner, and the client becomes the teacher. That there is no hierarchy in the process helps the client discover new meaning in his or her situation.

Collaborative therapy involves a mutual, participatory process of conversation. It values, invites, and incorporates the client's perspectives of what is important in daily life. The therapist is nonjudgmental, listens, and asks questions. Collaborative therapists recognize that the client is the expert regarding knowledge of the client's life experiences. Collaborative therapists respect the client's agency, working with the client's resiliency and desire for healthy, successful relationships and quality of life. The therapist facilitates an opportunity for new aspects of the client's meaning system to emerge, thus shifting behaviors and views.

The therapist does not take on the role of a narrative editor, referee, or an interventionist. Inquiry occurs within the parameters of the problem as described by the client. Multiple and contradictory ideas are encouraged. Cooperative language is encouraged. The therapist takes time to understand the problem so the client gets time to see the situation in a different light.

Uses of Collaborative Language Systems

The collaborative language systems approach has been used in family therapy. This approach focuses on the clients and their subjective views of reality, rather than on the structure and role of the family as a social system. The therapist questions the individual family members about the situation that is seen as a problem so they can see the problem in a different light. Therapists facilitate conversation and encourage the individual or individuals in the family to resolve the problem situation.

The collaborative language systems approach is well suited to settings in which the client and the therapist belong to different cultures and have different social norms. A therapeutic alliance is facilitated through language and meaning generated in response to the client's situation. Collaborative language systems therapists are able to facilitate intercultural communication because of their role as active listeners. Collaborative language therapists work with clients to help them communicate their social preferences and norms to reduce misinterpretations in intercultural communication.

The collaborative language systems approach has been used as a model for supervision in family therapy. The collaborative stance involves an understanding that the supervisor and the supervisee bring different levels of experiences. Experiences and subjective realities are valued in the individual's personal and interpersonal framework. Many supervision models separate the role of the supervisor and the supervisee based on their positions, which can make a supervisee vulnerable and less likely to share anxieties about supervision. The collaborative language systems approach enhances the importance of mutual respect for supervisee and supervisor, and this relationship facilitates learning in a positive atmosphere. In this relationship, the supervisor focuses on generating possibilities and relies on the supervisee to be creative and contribute to their own learning process. The supervisor empowers the supervisee by letting the supervisee know that knowledge is an evolving process.

Veena Prasad

See also Collaborative Couples Therapy; Multiculturalism; Narrative Therapy; Supervision

Further Readings

Anderson, H. (1997). *Conversation, language, and possibilities: A postmodern approach to therapy.* New York, NY: Basic Books.

Anderson, H. (2007). Dialogue: People creating meaning with each other and finding ways to go on. In H. Anderson & D. Gehart (Eds.), *Collaborative therapy: Relationships and conversations that make a difference* (pp. 33–41). New York, NY: Routledge.

Anderson, H. (2007). The heart and spirit of collaborative therapy: The philosophical stance—"A way of being" in relationship and conversation. In H. Anderson & D. Gehart (Eds.), *Collaborative therapy: Relationships and conversations that make a difference* (pp. 43–59). New York, NY: Routledge.

Anderson, H. (2007). A postmodern umbrella: Language and knowledge as relational and generative, and inherently transforming. In H. Anderson & D. Gehart (Eds.), *Collaborative therapy: Relationships and conversations that make a difference* (pp. 7–20). New York, NY: Taylor & Francis.

Anderson H., & Goolishian, H. A. (1986) Problem determined systems: Towards transformation in family therapy. *Journal of Strategic & Systemic Therapist,* 5(4), 1–13.

Mackay, L. and Brown, J. (2013). Collaborative approaches to family systems supervision: Differentiation of self. *Australian and New Zealand Journal of Family Therapy,* 34, 325–337. doi:10.1002/anzf.1036

COLLABORATIVE THERAPY

See Collaborative Language Systems

COMMITMENT

Commitment refers to a state of perceived dependence on a relationship. Dependence results from believing that one's partner provides better relationship rewards than any alternative partner. Commitment causes people to hold a long-term orientation toward their relationship and engage in thoughts and behaviors that will uphold it. This topic is relevant to marriage, families, and counseling because commitment is the bond that holds relationships together. This entry first reviews social exchange, the predominant framework used to explain commitment. Next presented are two well-known paradigms of commitment, the investment model and commitment framework, followed by a list of behaviors that are commonly enacted by committed partners. The entry concludes with a discussion of the advantages of commitment.

Theoretical Background

According to social exchange theory, people seek to maximize rewards and minimize costs in intimate relationships. *Rewards* are the benefits obtained from a partnership that fulfills one's needs and provides enjoyment. Costs are expenditures, or rewards that are forgone, due to being in a relationship. Needs and benefits are subjectively evaluated and vary depending on the person. One person might prioritize sexual satisfaction, whereas another may emphasize financial security. When a person successfully meets a partner's needs, his or her partner will feel dependent on the relationship. If both partners are responsible for the rewarding outcomes experienced by the other, a state of interdependence exists. Satisfying or profitable relationships are ones in which the rewards exceed the costs.

A person determines relationship expectations through comparisons with other relationships, including prior involvements and the romantic relationships of family members and friends. People who obtained high profit in their previous relationships and who are aware of others with high profit will have a high comparison level (CL) and be harder to satisfy. Individuals who have been involved in few profitable relationships, and who are unaware of others in profitable relationships, will have a low CL and be easier to satisfy. When the outcomes of a given relationship fall below the CL, individuals will feel dissatisfied and may consider alternative partners.

Comparison level for alternatives (CL-alt) is a standard for evaluating other relationship options. CL-alt involves comparing the profit obtained from one's current relationship to the perceived profit available from another partner. If profit in the current relationship is high, the individual is more likely to remain with a partner. However, if the individual perceives there to be a more profitable alternative available, he or she may leave the current partner to pursue the other relationship. When few profitable alternatives exist, a person will be more dependent on the relationship.

Investment Model

The investment model is the most widely used conceptualization of commitment. According to the model, commitment can be predicted by considering the collective influence of relationship satisfaction, quality of alternatives, and relationship investments. As mentioned, satisfaction results from having a partner who exceeds one's expectations in terms of need fulfillment. Alternatives refer to options outside the relationship that can fulfill needs better than a current partner. Investments refer to the amount of irretrievable resources put into a relationship. These can include time, money, disclosures, and linking one's personal identity to a relationship. Investments strengthen commitment because they increase the costs of terminating a partnership. Accordingly, a committed partner will perceive high levels of satisfaction and investments, and low-quality alternatives to the relationship.

Commitment Framework

The commitment framework provides a competing conceptualization of commitment. According to this perspective, people remain committed to a partner for personal, constraint, and/or moral reasons. Personal commitment involves choosing to be in a relationship because it is personally gratifying. With constraint commitment, people believe they have to remain in a relationship for reasons such as financial dependence or social pressure. Moral commitment involves feeling that one ought to persist in a relationship for ethical or religious reasons. People who commit for moral reasons are likely to stay together even if they are not personally satisfied. A majority of North American relationships are based on personal commitment, which is one reason for their relative stability. With satisfaction as the relationship foundation, partners are more likely to break up when satisfaction declines or disappears.

Commitment Behaviors

Partners with high levels of commitment use cognitive and behavioral strategies to maintain their relationships. They perceive their relationship as better than other people's relationships and tend to derogate alternative partners. When a problem emerges, they use constructive problem-solving and are likely to be empathetic toward their partner. They also own responsibility for relationship issues and provide their partner with positive feedback. They tend to compromise, sacrifice, and not reciprocate negative behaviors, a practice that is termed *accommodation*. The more often partners engage in these maintenance behaviors, the more likely they are to be satisfied and committed to their relationship. Therefore, the association between maintenance strategies and commitment is bidirectional.

Conclusion

Committed relationships are important for people's health and well-being. Individuals with high-quality intimate partnerships experience better immune system functioning and quality of life, whereas those without them are more susceptible to depression and disease. Considering the influence of couple relationships on health and happiness, an understanding of the factors that make for a high-quality, committed partnership is essential.

Kelly Campbell

See also Bonding; Cost–Benefit Analysis; Dating Relationship Dissolution; Divorce and Separation

Further Readings

Johnson, M. P. (1999). Personal, moral, and structural commitment to relationships: Experiences of choice and constraint. In J. M. Adams & W. H. Jones (Eds.), *Handbook on interpersonal commitment and relationship stability* (pp. 73–87). New York, NY: Kluwer Academic/Plenum.

Le, B., & Agnew, C. R. (2003). Commitment and its theorized determinants: A meta-analysis of the investment model. *Personal Relationships, 10*, 37–57.

Nye, F. I. (1979). Choice, exchange, and the family. In W. R. Burr, R. Hill, F. I. Nye, & I. Reiss (Eds.), *Contemporary theories about the family* (Vol. 2, pp. 1–41). New York, NY: Free Press.

Rusbult, C. E., Olsen, N., Davis, J., & Hannon, P. A. (2001). Commitment and relationship maintenance mechanisms. In J. Harvey & A. Wenzel (Eds.), *Close romantic relationships: Maintenance and enhancement* (pp. 87–113). Mahwah, NJ: Erlbaum.

Common Factors

The term *psychotherapy* can be broadly defined as a deliberate attempt to apply psychological principles in an interpersonal setting to help modify an individual's behavior that is interfering with daily functioning. Within that framework, the field has evolved from a hierarchical stance (with the therapist considered the expert) to a more egalitarian approach (client and therapist are partners), to a more client-directed stance in which the client is considered the expert concerning his or her life. Consistent with this shift toward a more client-directed approach to therapy, researchers and clinicians alike began to examine the factors that seemed to account for success in therapy. Given the hundreds of models of treatment, coupled with the recognition that all seemed to work to varying degrees, the common factors (CF) movement arose. CF refers to the characteristics associated with the client–therapist interaction that are believed to account for change, regardless of models or techniques employed. In this entry, a history of common factors and common factors models are briefly reviewed.

The common factors position provides another way to conceptualize the therapeutic process and the factors that seem to account for change. According to this approach, the factors believed to account for change in therapy are a function of conditions that transcend models and techniques. In other words, proponents of the CF approach argue that the effectiveness of therapy is not due to differences in counseling approaches, but to elements that are shared among major therapeutic approaches. Saul Rosenzweig first introduced the notion of common factors in psychotherapy in 1936 when he described the "dodo bird hypothesis" (alluding to an incident in Lewis Carroll's *Alice in Wonderland* in which a dodo bird declares all the contestants in a race to be winners). Rosenzweig was referring to the observation that no one psychotherapy approach was superior to another—they all seemed to work.

The CF model centers on factors that are necessary for change, which include but are not limited to: (a) an emotional bond between therapist and patient, (b) a healing setting where the therapy takes place, (c) a therapist who provides a psychologically and culturally driven explanation of distress, (d) an adaptive explanation that is accepted by the patient, and (e) a set of procedures that leads the client to a positive, helpful, or adaptive experience. Consequently, from a CF vantage point, the technique or theory is just one aspect of many common factors that also contribute to behavior change. Therapeutic factors common to all therapies include the development of a strong therapeutic bond, hope, and empowerment. The degree to which these variables contribute to therapy outcome varies depending on the client's presenting issues or concerns.

Jerome Frank, whose work influenced current CF research, divided common factors into common features (observable components of behavior) and common functions (what therapy does to a client that is different from his or her daily life) of psychotherapy.

Frank identified four common features: a helping relationship, a healing setting, a rationale explaining the client's distress, and a "ritual" implied by the rationale believed to help solve the issue. He proposed six common functions, which include emotional arousal, expectations of improvement, decrease in alienation through the therapeutic relationship, providing new learning experiences, providing opportunities for practice, and enhancing a sense of self-efficacy and mastery. Even though Frank's factors were published over 50 years ago, his work marked a shift away from focusing exclusively on models and techniques as the mechanism of change and sparked interest in identifying, explaining, and exploring common therapeutic factors across different orientations. Frank posited that treatments had more in common than what made them different.

More recently, Michael Lambert has made significant contributions to the CF literature. Lambert identified four factors that seem to account for change: (1) extratherapeutic events (clients' strengths and resources—40%), (2) the therapeutic alliance (agreement on the goals and tasks of therapy—30%), (3) hope and expectancy (15%), and (4) model and technique (15%). Along with client factors, the therapeutic alliance has been heavily investigated and is the subject of over 1,000 empirical findings. The alliance is often defined as the bond between therapist and client, agreement on treatment goals, and agreement on tasks during treatment. In fact, it is believed that the client's perception of the alliance is the most consistent predictor of improvement. In 1996, researchers Sidney J. Blatt and colleagues analyzed client perceptions of the therapeutic relationship and found improvement was largely based on client-rated quality of relationship.

As noted above, placebo, hope, and expectancy have also been found to account for 15% of psychotherapy outcomes. *Expectancy* refers to both the therapist's and client's beliefs that the treatments are restorative. Furthermore, rituals or shared characteristics of healing procedures inspire hope and a positive expectation by conveying that the user possesses a special set of skills for healing.

Lambert's work had important implications for clinicians in terms of the way they conceptualized the therapy process and the amount of emphasis that was given to each of these areas, especially in light of the implications on outcomes. For example, hitherto the emphasis for many clinicians was on adhering to and competently delivering the model or techniques; Lambert's findings challenged therapists to also consider how best to incorporate clients' existing strengths and resources into the therapeutic context and operationalize the ingredients that comprised a strong therapeutic alliance.

At present, not only are both the effectiveness and efficacy of psychotherapy well established, but also its effectiveness in real-world clinical settings. Evidence supports the hypothesis that people treated with psychotherapy are better off than those on wait lists or untreated. Variations in outcome are more influenced by symptom severity than by a diagnosis; furthermore, patient characteristics and clinician and contextual factors seem to play a larger role in outcome than any particular diagnosis or specific treatment. The CF approach represents a shift from a one-size-fits-all approach to psychotherapy, to privileging the client's contributions to the therapy process and outcome; simply stated, the client is the single most powerful contributor to outcome in psychotherapy. Factors such as persistence, faith, optimism, openness, and a supportive family member may all play a critical role in the therapy process, and the ability to access these resources may increase the likelihood of a successful outcome.

*Keith Klostermann
and Emma Papagni*

See also Constructivism; Effectiveness Research; Outcome Research; Social Constructionism

Further Readings

Blatt, S. J., Sanislow, C. A., III, Zuroff, D. C., & Pilkonis, P. A. (1996). Characteristics of effective therapists: Further analyses of data from the National Institute of Mental Health treatment of depression collaboration research program. *Journal of Consulting and Clinical Psychology, 64*(6), 1276–1284. http://dx.doi.org/10.1037/0022-006X.64.6.127

Grencavage, L. M., & Norcross, J. C. (1990). Where are the commonalities among the therapeutic common factors? *Professional Psychology: Research and Practice, 21,* 372–378. doi:10.1037/0735-7028.21.5.372

Hubble, M. A., Duncan, B. L., Miller, S. D., & Wampold, B. E. (2010). Introduction. In B. L. Duncan, S. D. Miller, B. E. Wampold, & M. A. Hubble (Eds.), *The heart and soul of change: Delivering what works in therapy* (2nd ed., pp. 23–46). Washington, DC: American Psychological Association.

Lambert, M. J. (1992). Psychotherapy outcome research: Implications for integrative and eclectic therapists. In J. C. Norcross & M. R. Goldfried (Eds.), *Handbook of psychotherapy integration* (pp. 94–129). New York, NY: Basic Books.

Wampold, B. E. (2001). *The great psychotherapy debate: Models, methods and findings.* Mahwah, NJ: Erlbaum.

Communication Disorders

Communication disorders involve deficits in speech, language, and other verbal or nonverbal communication behavior. Disruptions in prenatal brain development are thought to cause many communication disorders, but the causes for these disruptions are not fully understood. In addition, research has linked problems with the production of language to recurrent ear infections, which can affect hearing and reduce input to the developing brain. Researchers have drawn connections between communication disorders, poor academic achievement, and mental health issues. Schools play a vital role in the diagnosis of communication disorders and in early intervention. Children can make significant progress in overcoming many communication disorders through working with speech-language pathologists. By working with parents and teachers, counselors can ensure that children receive assistance to improve their communication skills and increase social interaction. The remainder of this entry discusses each of the communication disorders listed in the *Diagnostic and Statistical Manual of Mental Disorders.*

Forms of Communication Disorders

Many forms of communication disorders have been identified. Those listed in the *Diagnostic and Statistical Manual of Mental Disorders,* Fifth Edition (DSM-5), are language disorder, speech sound disorder, childhood-onset fluency disorder, and social (pragmatic) communication disorder. The DSM-5 also includes a diagnosis of unspecified communication disorder, which is diagnosed in people who have symptoms of a communication disorder but do not meet all the criteria for a communication disorder or another neurodevelopmental disorder, and whose symptoms cause distress or impairment.

Language Disorder

Language disorder involves difficulties in learning and using language that include having a limited vocabulary, trouble forming sentences, and an impaired ability to carry on a conversation. Language abilities in the disorder are well below what would be expected for the person's age, interfering with effective communication, social interaction, academic performance, and/or performance on the job. Symptoms of language disorder develop in early childhood, but because of normal variations in children's development of language, it is difficult to make a diagnosis before age 4. Language disorder is considered to have a genetic component. Language disorder may involve impairment in expressive ability (the production of language), receptive ability (receiving and comprehending language), or both. Impairments in expressive language often are found together with speech sound disorder.

Speech Sound Disorder

Speech sound disorder (SSD) involves ongoing difficulty with producing speech sounds, resulting in speech that is unintelligible or that does not allow for communication of one's message.

Symptoms of the disorder begin in early childhood. Social participation, academic achievement, and/or occupational performance are impacted by the disorder.

Although speech sound disorder is a single diagnosis in the DSM-5, speech and language specialists often discuss speech sound disorders that can be categorized into two separate disorders: articulation disorder and phonological disorder. Articulation disorder involves problems with particular consonants or vowels, while phonological disorder involves problems with phonemes.

Childhood-Onset Fluency Disorder

Childhood-onset fluency disorder is also called stuttering. It involves problems with the fluency and rhythm of speech and is characterized by the repetition of sounds or syllables. These difficulties interfere with social interaction and/or with performance at school or work. The disturbances in speech tend to be more severe in situations when there is more pressure to communicate, such as during a job interview.

Fluency disorder can lead to severe social anxiety. Many studies have shown that people with fluency disorder can benefit from cognitive-behavioral therapy. Speaking at a slow pace, paying attention to the conversation instead of paying attention to stuttering, and creating a tension-free atmosphere can greatly reduce stuttering.

Social (Pragmatic) Communication Disorder

Social (pragmatic) communication disorder involves problems in the use of verbal and nonverbal communication in ways that are appropriate for the context. These deficits must be severe enough to limit the ability to communicate effectively, develop social relationships, and/or perform in school or on the job. The disorder may be diagnosed in children as young as 4, but less severe forms of the disorder may show up during adolescence, when language and social interactions are more complex. Autism spectrum disorder (ASD) may be present in those with social communication deficits; communication disorder may be differentiated from ASD by the absence of restricted or repetitive patterns of behavior, interests, or activities that is found in ASD.

Veena Prasad

See also Autism Spectrum Disorder; Communication in Couples and Families; Social Support

Further Readings

American Psychiatric Association. (2000). *Diagnostic and statistical manual of mental disorders: DSM-IV-TR*. Washington, DC: American Psychiatric Association.

American Psychiatric Association. (2013). *Diagnostic and statistical manual of mental disorders* (5th ed.). Washington, DC: Author.

Cirrin, F. M., & Gillam, R. B. (2008). Language intervention practices for school-age children with spoken language disorders: A systematic review. *Language, Speech, and Hearing Services in Schools, 39*(1), S110–S137.

Gleason, J. B. (2001). *The development of language*. Boston, MA: Allyn & Bacon.

Lewis, B. A., Avrich, A. A., & Freebairn, L. A., et al. (2011). Literacy outcomes of children with early childhood speech sound disorders: Impact of endophenotypes. *Journal of Speech, Language, and Hearing Research, 54*(6), 1628–1643. doi:10.1044/1092-4388(2011/10–0124)

Liégeois, F., Mayes, A., & Morgan, A. (2014). Neural correlates of developmental speech and language disorders: Evidence from neuroimaging. *Current Developmental Disorders Reports, 1*(3), 215–227.

Lonigan, C. J., Fischel, J. E., Whitehurst, G. J., Arnold, D. S., & Valdez-Menchaca, M. C. (1992). The role of otitis media in the development of expressive language disorder. *Developmental Psychology, 28*(3), 430.

Mash, E., & Wolf, D. (2005). Assessment, diagnosis and treatment. *Abnormal Child Psychology*, 73–107.

Norbury, C. F., Paul, R., Thapar, A., Pine, D. S., Leckman, J. F., Scott, S., & Taylor, E. (2013). Disorders of speech, language, and communication. *Rutter's Child and Adolescent Psychiatry*, 683–701.

Communication Errors/Problems in Couples and Families

Communication errors often lead to conflicts in couples and families, or they can exacerbate existing conflicts. Conflict management, or the ways in which family members deal with conflict, can be negatively impacted by communication errors and problems that impede possibilities for conflict resolution and relationship repair. Relationship outcomes for romantic partnerships are consistently linked with the ways in which the couple communicate with one another. Specifically, as it relates to conflict, communication between romantic partners predicts the satisfaction and stability of the relationship. This is particularly important when couples have children, as they learn communication from their families of origin. What this means is that children learn how to communicate on the basis of observing and interacting with family members; generally, the way that parents communicate will be replicated by their children. Spouses who engage in communication that is marked by errors and problems are, in effect, likely teaching their children how to repeat the same patterns of poor communication. Couples counselors and family therapists need to intervene when this occurs, teaching the family new, more effective means of communication. This entry provides an overview of communication errors, both verbal and nonverbal; specific approaches to intervention, including those of John Gottman and Virginia Satir, are also be presented.

Communication errors and problems often exist when there are gaps in between intentions and perceptions. What this means is that when an individual communicates with another, he or she *intends* for a certain message to be conveyed. However, the way that message is *perceived* depends on the other family member engaged in the conversation. When there is a difference between the intention of a message and its perceived meaning, communication errors occur. Communication errors also occur when family members fail to empathize with one another, meaning that they are not taking into account other family members' perspective and worldview; instead they focus solely on the self. Communication problems also happen when family members have different ways or methods of communicating with one another. Couples counselors and marriage and family therapists should never assume that all members of one family engage in similar means of communication. This is especially true in the case of blended families. Spouses may come from varying backgrounds, cultures, religions, or ethnicities, and family members are likely to have different personalities and levels of development, which will affect how they communicate. For example, the individual who is introverted and focuses on emotions will probably communicate differently than the individual who is extroverted and focuses on cognitions and reasoning. When one person communicates from a state of feeling and another communicates from a state of cognition or behavior, it is as if they are speaking two different languages. Couples counselors and marriage and family therapists have to do their best to act as translators. Additionally, children communicate differently from adults because they are in different stages of life span development. Accordingly, children should not be treated as little adults; family therapists must adapt their approaches to understanding and addressing communication errors and problems among children within client families.

Communication errors do not only result from different ways of communicating; rather, the topic of discussion itself can promote problems in communication. Topics considered to be of significant importance may include finances, issues balancing work and family, marital infidelity, parenting styles, relationships with in-laws, or quality of the spousal sexual relationship. These topics are likely to escalate from simple discussions to blowout arguments with certain couples or family members. Discussion surrounding topics that carry more weight are more likely to provide stimulus and opportunity for poor communication behaviors to occur. When this happens, couples counselors and marriage and family therapists often act as referees, mediating the situation and encouraging healthier communication patterns among family members.

Communication errors and problems can be verbal or nonverbal in nature; this entry discusses both types. Included in the section on nonverbal communication errors are attending skills, facial expressions, paralanguage, body language, and eye contact. This entry does not, however, include information regarding domestic and intimate partner violence, as those behaviors go beyond the scope of typical communication errors and problems in couples and families and must be addressed differently by couples counselors and marriage and family therapists.

Verbal Communication Errors

The simplest verbal communication error is *not* using one's verbal communication skills clearly during times of conflict. Clamming up and not addressing an issue of concern with a loved family member can breed contempt and lead to breakdown of the quality of the relationship. Couples counselors and marriage and family therapists encourage client families to openly communicate their wants and needs with one another, whether they are experiencing conflict or not. Simply closing the lines of communication will not lead to conflict resolution or relationship repair. Another error in verbal communication occurs when individuals think that by using "I" statements, they have carte blanche with the content of their messages (e.g., "I feel like you are a jerk."). Putting an "I" statement into a sentence does not mitigate a harsh message. Verbal communication, when overused, can also result in problems. When family members speak over one another, interrupt, and try to talk at the same time, functional communication will not occur.

Gottman's Categories of Flawed Communication

John Gottman established four categories of flawed communication patterns in romantic partnerships: criticism, defensiveness, contempt, and stonewalling. He found that these four styles of communicating ("Four Horsemen of the Apocalypse") are toxic to romantic partnerships, leading to relationship dissatisfaction and dissolution. Criticism occurs when one partner blames the other for a negative situation (or attributes its cause to characteristics internal to the partner) instead of blaming oneself, the situation itself, or a factor external to the partner or relationship. Criticism also involves putting down one's partner, effectively disempowering him or her by listing negative comments or making accusatory statements. Defensiveness, the second of the four horsemen, is a common reaction to criticism. Defensiveness manifests as self-protection, counterattacking one's partner, making excuses for one's behavior, and denying responsibility for relationship conflict. Contempt occurs when one partner expresses disgust for the other partner, with the aim of causing psychological pain. Contempt may be experienced when one partner feels nagged by the other partner, or that the other partner is putting too many demands upon her or him. Contempt can occur through both verbal (e.g., name calling, mockery, insulting one's partner) and nonverbal (e.g., rolling one's eyes, making rude hand gestures, making faces) means and usually signifies a lack of respect for one's romantic partner. Stonewalling, the fourth horseman, occurs when one partner withdraws from the other, either physically, emotionally, or both. Stonewalling can include withholding of expressing thoughts, feelings, and behaviors from one's partner in both positive and negative areas. The partner who physically leaves the residence in response to a conflict is stonewalling, as is the partner who emotionally withdraws from a conflict without first reaching a solution.

Satir's Communication Stances

Virginia Satir distinguished types of communication stances that people tend to adopt under stress and during times of conflict that are problematic: placating, blaming, distraction, and "the computer" (i.e., super reasonable). The family member who placates is a people-pleaser and mediates family conflict, typically putting other family members first and often blaming oneself for family problems. Out of fear of rejection the placater does not disagree with other family members but instead, seeking approval, always agrees with them. The family member who blames will put the onus for problems on other family members but will usually take responsibility when there is success in the family. A fault-finder tries to control others through showing dominance; the blamer disagrees with others indiscriminately, acts critically toward them, and is likely to feel superior when compared with the rest of the family. The blamer will do whatever is necessary to preserve feelings of self-worth and does not like being challenged. The family member who is the distraction pretends that the stress is not there and may engage in tangential refocusing (i.e., doing things to take the focus off the family conflict). The distractor acts in ways and speaks about things irrelevant to the situation. The distractor's role is to provide the family with comfort during uncomfortable situations (such as conflict) and shift the family's focus to something less stressful and painful. The family member who is the computer is super reasonable and will bypass affect and go straight to reason and logic, seemingly unaffected by, or uninvolved in, the family conflict. The computer may lack emotion if she or he is cut off from feelings, socially distances or isolates himself or herself, and is likely to minimize reactions to family conflict. The hyper-reasonable individual works to control his or her emotions and place conflict into a manageable context.

Nonverbal Communication Errors

Communication errors and problems can occur when family members do not use simple attending skills with one another (e.g., active listening, making eye contact); these are often taught or modeled appropriately by the couples counselor and marriage and family therapist. When family members do not attend to one another, they are usually not being sensitive or responsive, often appearing uninterested in the conversation. Inappropriate use of nonverbal communication creates problems as well. When a family member is annoyed with another individual, calmly explaining one's feelings is preferred to negative facial expressions (e.g., overtly rolling one's eyes and sticking out one's tongue) in an effort to mock the other family member. The improper use of paralanguage, or vocal qualities, can also negatively impact family communication, causing problems to exist. Raising the volume of one's voice or changing one's vocal tone to that of disdain can drastically impact the direction of a conversation. It is worth noting that conflict does not necessarily have to escalate to the point of yelling; conflict can be discussed calmly and at a quiet volume. Also, consider how impactful body language is in communication errors and problems: The individual who chooses to loom over another family member, arms crossed and pointing his/her forefinger, is communicating a more threatening message than the individual who communicates while sitting and maintaining an open posture and using neutral (or positive) gestures. Eye contact is indicative of engagement; lack of eye contact during family communication shows possible lack of involvement in the discussion. Also, misusing eye contact is a communication problem (e.g., staring down a family member in order to intimidate). One's general behavior is also highly indicative of communication problems in couples and families. For example, if a parent requests a change in his or her child's behavior, failure to comply with that request indicates the existence of some kind of communication problem.

Rebecca M. Goldberg

See also Boundaries; Conflict Styles; Decision-Making; Gottman Method Couples Therapy; Metacommunication; Nonverbal Communication; Scapegoating

Further Readings

Bitter, J. R. (1993). Communication styles, personality priorities, and social interest: Strategies for helping couples build a life together. *Individual Psychology: Journal of Adlerian Theory, Research, and Practice, 49*(3–4), 330–350.

Fowler, C., & Dillow, M. R. (2011). Attachment dimensions and the four horsemen of the apocalypse. *Communication Research Reports, 28*(1), 16–26. doi: 10.1080/08824096.2010.518910

Gottman, J. M. (1999). *The marriage clinic: A scientifically based marital therapy.* New York, NY: Norton.

Heatherington, L., Escudero, V., & Friedlander, M. L. (2005). Couple interaction during problem discussions: Toward an integrative methodology. *Journal of Family Communication, 5*(3), 191–207. doi:10.1207/s15327698jfc0503_2

Satir, V. (1972). *Peoplemaking.* Palo Alto, CA: Science and Behavior Books.

Vangelisti, A. L. (1994). Couples' communication problems: The counselor's perspective. *Journal of Applied Communication Research, 22*(2), 106–126.

Williamson, H. C., Hanna, M. A., Lavner, J. A., Bradbury, T. N., & Karney, B. R. (2013). Discussion topic and observed behavior in couples' problem-solving conversations: Do problem severity and topic choice matter? *Journal of Family Psychology, 27*(2), 330–335. doi:10.1037/a0031534

Communication in Couples and Families

Communication is the process of exchanging or imparting information, feelings, ideas, and concepts. Effective communication among couples and families is often regarded as tantamount to the success of such relationships. This entry addresses what communication is and how the process of communication is developed and agreed upon, and provides an example of a framework that is suitable for understanding how effective communication supports and strengthens family systems. Also discussed are variables affecting communication in family systems. Lastly, this entry addresses how communication processes change over the course of the family life cycle.

Types of Communication

Communication is commonly expressed in two ways, verbally and nonverbally. Both forms utilize a series of symbols to express the ideas, emotions, and other information they represent. Verbal communication is the use of symbols in the form of spoken words in order to convey information needed to express ideas and feelings. Verbal communication is modified by volume, rate, frequency, and other mechanical factors. The meaning of these modifications depends on the context in which they are expressed. For example, in some contexts speaking loudly is a means of expressing urgency or frustration, and in other contexts loudness may convey anger or aggression.

Nonverbal communication is how people communicate with each other by not using formal language. This is done through a variety of actions (e.g., tone of voice, facial expressions, body movements). When people roll their eyes, stand close or far away from another person while talking to them, or position themselves by sitting upright or slouching, they are communicating nonverbally. All of these behaviors demonstrate a level of feeling, thought, or emotion that the person is experiencing. People interpret these behaviors as they communicate with others. Nonverbal communication often adds emphasis to verbal communications, which results in clarity to the person who is being spoken or communicated to. For example, a movement of the hand(s) during a conversation of intense emotion may emphasize that the person speaking feels very passionate about the topic.

In either form, both the speaker and the listener must mutually understand these symbols. This perspective is viewed as being "transactional" in nature, where there is an exchange of not only ideas, through communication, but an understanding of those ideas by each person involved in the communication. If this is not the case, then the meaning of the communication is lost and the process is frustrated. Lack of clarity may result in confusion, misunderstanding, and in many cases harm to the relationship.

The nature of the transactional perspective is congruent with a family systems perspective. The family systems perspective holds that the family is a "system" wherein the members operate in a way that functions as a team or unit; every member has one or more roles that support the function of the family or members of the system. Both concepts, the transactional perspective of communication and the family systems perspective, are centered on the relationship between two or more individuals, in this case, family members. A systems perspective of communication highlights the idea that each person, through various types of communication, both influence the system and are influenced by the system.

Differences in Communication

From the early days of a person's life, communication is essential in order to have one's needs met. From birth people begin to communicate—through crying, moving, sucking, various noises, and later more complex forms of verbal and nonverbal communication. However, in most cases, another person is trying to interpret that communication, and the meaning may not be shared or may not be clear to the person trying to interpret it. The meaning of communication is a reflection of a person's view, attitudes, feelings, or beliefs.

Within one's family of origin, individuals are taught the means, patterns, and styles of communication from an early age. Meaning and the understanding of meaning are developed through a process whereby members of a family system come to understand the way that words and actions are interpreted by each individual according to his or her worldview. Common meanings for communication behaviors are eventually agreed upon through an evolving process involving the family system or other social structure. The origins of these meanings are commonly outside of the immediate family. How meaning is applied to communication as well as the other aspects of communication patterns are influenced heavily by multigenerational experiences with communications. For example, the communication behaviors of parents are commonly passed to their children and onto grandchildren and so forth. Likewise, the communication patterns of a partner in a couple are also influenced by those behaviors established by his or her family of origin. As couples come from different families, each having its own method of making meaning, it is important that communication between the members of the couple be understood and developed.

How Effective Communication Supports and Strengthens Family Systems: A Framework

A well-known model that describes the role of communication's facilitative process is the circumplex model of marital and family systems. This model, developed beginning in 1979, argues that effective communication is part of a three-point structure. These three components are cohesion, flexibility, and communication. Cohesion is the level of emotional connectedness between members of a system. Flexibility is the ability of the family system to adapt to change and stressors. The model views both of these constructs as existing along a continuum. For the cohesion component, one end of the spectrum is enmeshment, which is an excess of cohesion, and the other is disengagement, which is a lack of cohesion. In regard to the continuum of flexibility, the ends are represented as rigidity on one end and chaotic on the other. Family systems that are successful in navigating the family life cycle are balanced in both respects. However, when families, according to the model, exist on either end of the spectrum, then they are viewed as being unbalanced.

Communication serves as a facilitative function wherein families are able to strengthen bonds and adapt in order to meet each other's needs and achieve balance in cohesion and flexibility. Communication often serves as the means by which the family relationships are regulated, negotiated, and adjusted in order to function successfully. When considering communication as a process, one is able to understand that communication is constantly changing and adapting in order to meet the needs of those who are communicating. For example, a couple or family without children has far different needs from one with children. Therefore, the methods and content of the communication within the family should develop over time and adapt to meet the changing needs of the family. As the family expands and contracts over the course of the life span of the family, the means, frequency, style, and content of the communication should continue to adapt in order to meet the needs of the family or couple.

Variables That Affect Communication in Family Systems

In regard to the family system itself, there are multiple considerations, which can and often do have influence on the way that communication is used. Understanding the role of these variables is key to effective communication. One of these variables is the family system type. In Western culture, families tend to fall into several common categories. There is the intact type, which most resembles what is commonly referred to as a nuclear family; divorced families; and blended families. Additionally, there are families that include members from a diverse set of ethnic or cultural backgrounds, as well as extended families, which include members of the families outside of the typical "nuclear" arrangement.

Communication in intact families is influenced by the established communication patterns of the couple from which it originated. The children in this family system typically communicate in ways that are similar to the ways the parents communicate. Families of this type work to develop a social agreement on acceptable and mutually understood communication behaviors. Intact families also reach this understanding of acceptable communication behaviors through a process called conformity. Conformity in intact families is indicated by the degree to which all members of the family share the same values, beliefs, and attitudes as expressed similarly via communication behaviors.

Communication in divorced families, as in other family types, is heavily influenced by the nature of the relationship between the members of the family system. As in intact families, this influence tends to originate from the parents in the family system. The way that the divorced couple chooses to communicate has influence not only on the functioning of the family system overall, but also over the individual relationships within the family system. These relationships include the relationship between former spouses, the co-parenting relationship, and the parent–child relationships. As the system changes throughout the process of divorce and the time thereafter, shifts in communication styles will be inevitable. The most successful navigation of this transition includes communication behaviors that are facilitative and cooperative. As in intact families, communication behaviors in divorced families are learned, maintained, and transmitted generationally.

As in other family system types, it is equally important that blended family systems develop an agreed-upon understanding of how communication actions are understood and interpreted. Studies have shown that communication plays an important role in assisting blended families in their efforts to adapt to the variation between the two parts of the "new" system. There is a need to negotiate contradictions between the "old" and "new" family systems. Creating new family rituals (patterned ways of marking life transitions and celebrating important moments in a family's life) has been shown to assist in this blending process. The establishment of new patterns allows for the old family meanings to remain intact, all the while developing new behaviors that facilitate the growth and development of the "new" system.

Cultural Influences

It is necessary to consider the implications of culture when discussing or understanding communication behaviors of individuals. As past generations of families influence the communication behaviors of individuals, so too are those behaviors influenced by such things as cultural context. This goes beyond simply using different symbols to express ideas and feelings. The expressions of such things are more or less appropriate depending on the cultural context that is applied. In some cases, certain words or patterns are used when talking to older adults rather than peers. Looking an adult in the eye is acceptable for youth in some cultural contexts while in others it is not. It is important for members of family systems that include individuals with backgrounds different from other members (such as when someone brings a new partner or spouse into the system) to be aware of these influences and how they affect the nature of communication, as well as how they serve as a way to facilitate family satisfaction.

Communication Over the Course of the Family Life Cycle

During the natural course of the life cycle (how it develops over time) of a family, roles of individuals change and adapt to new people and needs. Communication behaviors are closely related to these changes. The stages typically encountered during the typical life cycle range from being a couple, to being a parent of young children, to midlife, to the later years of life. The ideas, feelings, attitudes, and needs encountered during these different periods tend to vary. Therefore, it is no surprise that communication will need to vary in order to ensure that the family system remains effective while negotiating changes such as changes in employment of family members, relocation, the birth of children, divorce, and the death of family members. In effective families, all members involved at each stage cooperate in developing the accepted communication behaviors appropriate for the stage in the life cycle.

Michael A. Williams

See also Circumplex Model; Cohesion; Communication Errors/Problems in Couples and Families; Conflict in Couples and Families; Family Resilience

Further Readings

Anderson, S. A., & Sabatelli, R. M. (2003). *Family interaction: A multigenerational development perspective.* Boston, MA: Allyn & Bacon.

Braithwaite, D. O., Baxter, L. A., & Harper, A. M. (1998). The role of rituals in the management of the dialectical tension of "old" and "new" in blended families. *Communication Studies, 49*(2), 101–120.

Galvin, K. M., Bylund, C. L., & Brommel, B. J. (2012). *Family communication: Cohesion and change* (8th ed.). Boston, MA: Allyn & Bacon.

Olson, D. H., & Gorall, D. M. (2003). Circumplex model of marital and family systems. *Normal Family Processes, 22,* 514–547.

Segrin, C., & Flora, J. (2014). *Family communication.* New York, NY: Routledge.

Thompson, T. L., Parrott, R., & Nussbaum, J. F. (Eds.). (2011). *Routledge handbook of health communication.* New York, NY: Routledge.

Vangelisti, A. L. (Ed.). (2003). *Handbook of family communication.* New York, NY: Routledge.

COMMUNITY PROGRAMS

Community programs take on a variety of forms. In mental health, among the most significant are community mental health centers, which offer a variety of services and take a public health approach to the prevention and treatment of mental health problems. Community mental health centers received a boost on October 31, 1963, when President John F. Kennedy signed into law the Community Mental Health Act. This legislation provided the funding for more than 2,000 community mental health centers in the United States. However, the breadth of community programs far exceeds community mental health centers. This entry discusses the rationale for community programs and details a variety of types of community programs, including 12-step, health, school, and development programs. Some of the issues addressed through these programs, such as economic development, may seem removed from marriage and family therapy. However, numerous studies have demonstrated how financial stress and poverty contribute to mental health struggles such as anxiety.

Rationale

As medical, social, mental health, and other problems present themselves, state and national leaders look for solutions. Problems such as childhood obesity, drug addiction, homelessness, and dropping out of high school may be best addressed on the local level. Centralized, geographically limited, top-down assistance often does not reach all those in need. Often new programs are tried in one region and are then either marketed to larger areas, or spread spontaneously due to the critical acclaim they receive. Community programs discussed in this entry include those funded by the federal government and run by organizations at the local level, as well as programs developed at the local level and funded mainly through donations.

Types of Community Programs

Healthy Marriage Community Programs

There are many programs in the United States designed to support healthy marriage. According to the California Healthy Marriages Coalition, successful marriages are connected to better physical and mental health, children's success in school, and better parent and child relationships, among other benefits. In recent years, states and the federal government have provided funding for organizations to offer marriage education and relationship skills classes. The government promotion of marriage has caused some controversy. There are also questions about the effectiveness of these programs, but researchers have found positive outcomes for participants in some of the programs.

12-Step Community Programs

One of the most common types of community programs worldwide are 12-step groups for addictions. These programs are almost always run by volunteers who are themselves in recovery from addiction (i.e., they are abstaining from a behavior or substance). Various websites suggest that millions of Americans attend 12-step groups each week, although due to their loose associations and confidentiality, exact numbers are hard to verify. The beginnings of the 12-step movement trace back to the early 1900s to the Oxford Group, a Christian movement in the United States and Europe. The movement grew quickly after Alcoholics Anonymous (AA) was founded in 1935. In subsequent years, the model of AA was applied to other substances and behaviors, and dozens of other 12-step groups were formed. Most 12-step groups are only for adults, although some groups also allow teenagers, as addictive behaviors often start in the teen years. The exact number of different 12-step organizations is unknown, but they can largely be grouped into the following categories:

Alcohol-Related 12-Step Groups

The most widely known group is Alcoholics Anonymous, with groups in 90 countries around the world, and millions of people who attend weekly. However, Adult Children of Alcoholics (ACoA) and Al-Anon/Alateen, for friends and family members of alcoholics, also have members worldwide. Some professionals in the mental health field have been skeptical as to the efficacy of these groups, but recent research shows some promising outcomes.

All 12-step groups follow roughly the same 12 steps, which include admitting to being powerless over alcohol (or another addiction), surrendering control to God (or a higher power), and making amends to those whom the participant has wronged. Participants in these groups have varying degrees of comfort and/or agreement with various aspects of these steps, particularly the references to God. Most 12-step groups have the phrase "as we understand Him" after the reference to God, so as to be more inclusive. Although this still causes discomfort for some, many people in 12-step groups also assert that if it were not for God being in the recovery process, they would not have succeeded as they have.

Substance Abuse 12-Step Groups

The most widely known substance abuse 12-step group is Narcotics Anonymous (NA), although there are groups specific to cocaine, crystal methamphetamine, marijuana, nicotine, and a few others. Narcotics Anonymous has been active for almost 100 years, and has groups in 29 U.S. states. These support groups assist participants in overcoming their addictions to various substances through the 12-step treatment model, accountability, and encouragement. An element of accountability is for the participant to have a sponsor who checks on him or her frequently and offers encouragement and guidance in the 12-step process.

Process Addiction 12-Step Groups

Some people in the mental health community have questioned the validity of so-called process addictions, also called behavioral addictions, such as addictions to gambling, sex, or shopping. However, some research has indicated that these addictions, like addictions to substances, can alter brain chemistry and neurological pathways. The 12-step groups for process addictions include Gamblers Anonymous, Sex Addicts Anonymous, Sex and Love Addicts Anonymous, and Shopaholics Anonymous.

Food-Related 12-Step Groups

Eating disorders are growing in prevalence around the world, with particularly high rates in China, India, and the United States. These disorders, though treatable, have a high rate of mortality, as many people with these conditions do not seek treatment or do not continue treatment as needed.

According to the National Association of Anorexia Nervosa and Associated Disorders, eating disorders have the highest mortality rate of any mental illness. An estimated 4% to 5% of people with eating disorders will die from the condition. The more Westernized a culture is, the more likely people are to struggle with eating disorders. This may be due to the emphasis in Western society on youthfulness, beauty, and slim and toned bodies. As globalization occurs and Western versions of beauty are projected onto the rest of the world, Western struggles such as eating-disordered mind-sets are also exported. The 12-step groups for food issues and eating disorders include Anorexics and Bulimics Anonymous, Compulsive Eaters Anonymous, Eating Addictions Anonymous, and Overeaters Anonymous.

Emotional Issues 12-Step Groups

The variety of groups related to emotional issues is quite extensive also, and includes groups such as Emotions Anonymous, Survivors of Incest Anonymous, and Co-Anon (for family and friends of addicts).

Community Development and Economic Development Programs

Community development and economic development programs span many different areas. Those funded by the federal government include assistance for small business development, economic education, housing assistance, and programs to redevelop foreclosed and abandoned homes. There are also faith-based organizations that work toward some of the same goals, such as the Christian Community Development Association and Habitat for Humanity.

Health-Related Community Programs

Health-related community programs work to improve the health status of the community. Colleen Flattum and colleagues describe one example, a community program for increasing healthy family meals and exercise and preventing obesity, through group sessions and phone calls.

The Centers for Disease Control and Prevention (CDC) operates a program in the Division of Community Health called Partnerships to Improve Community Health (PICH). In 2014, PICH awarded $49.3 million to 39 awardees to deal with four health issues: tobacco use and exposure, poor nutrition, physical inactivity, and lack of access to opportunities for chronic disease prevention, risk reduction, and disease management.

In addition to government-funded initiatives, private organizations have led efforts to improve community health. In Atlanta, a pediatric hospital called Children's Healthcare of Atlanta (CHOA) began the Strong4Life program, which battles childhood obesity through children's programs and an information campaign about foods to eat or avoid, exercise, and guidelines for electronic screen time for children. Strong4Life is promoted to the thousands of families who use CHOA's health facilities every year.

School-Based Community Programs

Julia Bryan and Lynette Henry describe how community programs can collaborate with schools and detail one program that worked to empower low-income minority students. Additionally, the U.S. Department of Education has provided funding for comprehensive academic, social, and health services through its Full-Service Community Schools Program. Other schools have offered a range of services through a community school model, providing such things as free meals, career guidance for parents, and programs that blend academic and health education.

Community Programs for At-Risk Youth

There is a constant need for programs to assist at-risk youth, as well as their parents and guardians. Some communities use informal approaches and volunteer mentors to provide guidance in assisting youth and their parents or guardians. One well-known program with a documented record of success is Big Brothers Big Sisters. Youth assigned an adult mentor through the program have been documented to have improved behavior with family and at school, and are less likely to skip school, or use drugs or alcohol. An estimated 240,000 American adults serve as Big Brothers or Big Sisters in the program each year, resulting in a long-term positive impact on the community.

Community Programs for Older Adults

Due to advances in medical care, Americans are living longer, and the related programmatic needs have dramatically increased and have broadened. Community programs for older adults are related to physical fitness, healthy behavior promotion, care for those with cognitive impairments such as dementia, respite care for caregivers of elders, aging in place (home care), transportation needs for low-mobility senior citizens, grief and loss support, food security, assistance with medication management, predatory lending prevention, chronic illness management, and end-of-life/hospice care.

Support for community social services for older people at the federal level was enacted into federal law in 1965 with the Older Americans Act (OAA). The U.S. Department of Health and Human Services' Administration for Community Living provides services through a national network that includes 56 state agencies on aging, 629 area agencies on aging, and nearly 20,000 service providers. These agencies and providers either deliver or support programs addressing such areas as oral health, diabetes self-management, falls prevention, behavioral health, and chronic disease self-management. Other programs such as Meals on Wheels are also supported by this agency. Meals on Wheels delivers meals to 2.5 million American seniors every year, which helps many seniors stay longer in their homes instead of needing nursing home care.

Kenyon Knapp

See also Alcohol and Substance Abuse; Health Issues; Marriage and Health; Schools, Family Involvement in; Socioeconomic Status

Further Readings

Bryan, J., & Henry, L. (2008). Strengths-based partnerships: A school-family-community partnership approach to empowering students. *Professional School Counseling, 12*(2), 149–156.

California Healthy Marriages Coalition. (n.d.). *Why marriage matters* [Flyer]. Retrieved November 15, 2015, from http://www.smartmarriages.com/index.html

Flattum, C., Draxten, M., Horning, M., Fulkerson, J. A., Neumark-Sztainer, D., Garwick, A., . . . Story, M. (2015). HOME Plus: Program design and implementation of a family-focused, community-based intervention to promote the frequency and healthfulness of family meals, reduce children's sedentary behavior, and prevent obesity. *International Journal of Behavioral Nutrition & Physical Activity, 12*(1), 1–9. doi:10.1186/s12966-015-0211-7

National Association of Anorexia Nervosa and Associated Disorders: http://www.anad.org

National Association of Anorexia Nervosa and Associated Disorders. (n.d.). *Eating disorder statistics.* Retrieved November 6, 2015, from http://www.anad.org/get-information/about-eating-disorders/eating-disorders-statistics/

Struthers, W. M. (2009). *Wired for intimacy: How pornography hijacks the male brain.* Westmont, IL: Intervarsity Press Books.

12Step.com. (n.d.). *12 step program.* http://www.12step.com/12stepprograms

U.S. Department of Health and Human Services. Administration for Community Living. (n.d.). *Administration on Aging: Older Americans Act.* Retrieved November 10, 2015, from http://www.aoa.gov/AOA_programs/OAA/

U.S. Department of Housing and Urban Development. (n.d.). *Community Development Block Program—CDBG.* http://portal.hud.gov/hudportal/HUD?src=/program_offices/comm_planning/communitydevelopment/programs

Wilson, G. (2015). *Your brain on porn: Internet pornography and the emerging science of addiction.* Margate, Kent, England: Commonwealth Publishing.

COMPASSION

Compassion is a state of mind that an individual experiences by gaining awareness of another person's existence, and intentionally thinking about and desiring his or her well-being, which may lead to pertinent action. To be compassionate is an innate ability of human beings and a characteristic of being human. When an individual, family member, or a friend is in distress, one naturally gravitates toward assisting that person. When someone does see other individuals in pain and responds, takes action to assist them in alleviating that pain, provides a kind word to make them feel better, assists them in reducing that grief, takes action to increase their quality of life, or helps them in gaining better circumstances of living, it is recognized that this person has compassion toward others.

Most of us are capable of experiencing compassion. By gaining awareness of others around us and intentionally thinking about and desiring their well-being, one tries to understand the pain and sufferings of their existence. The desire to alleviate that pain and increase their well-being is the mark of a compassionate person. This recognition may lead one to take action to alleviate that distress of another and increase the quality of life for that individual.

Being compassionate can come in many forms: sensitive and kind words, taking physical action, listening wholeheartedly, and being deeply present. Generally, compassion is not limited to taking action to help people, yet it includes understanding of all beings' suffering and taking action to assist them as well. This includes all animals and creatures, our rivals, people whom we know and do not know, and beings that are living and those that are yet to be born. Being compassionate could happen in a fraction of a moment, spontaneously, or it could have been planned and strategically carried out because of a previous thought. For those who practice being compassionate on a daily basis, it is very likely that this is innately driven—a way of life for these individuals.

It is also a skill that one can develop. As one realizes and recognizes another's pain and suffering a shift of perspectives may lead to being compassionate, thus leading to compassion-driven action aimed at alleviating the other individual's pain. The more one feels and thinks from a compassionate framework, the more one's worldview is likely to focus on others' well-being or existence, continuing to strengthen compassion as a characteristic of that individual.

Compassion comes through the realization of, or an effort to understand, what the other person is going through. To be compassionate does not require one to have gone through a similar experience previously. It simply requires one to be aware of, and recognize, the distress the other individual is going through.

Compassion often may encourage and even compel one to be altruistic. Being altruistic naturally calls for making sacrifices of one's own (e.g., time, money, personal possessions) in order to act for the betterment of others. Thus, an individual has to set aside his or her own needs, a sense of self in the moment, and thoughts or intentions of selfishness while responding for the sake of others' well-being.

Understanding Distress

If individuals are submerged in their own worries and distress, that may put them in a state of mind where it is difficult for them to see or be aware of another's distress, because they are overwhelmed and shadowed by their own grief and pain. An individual going through a painful experience may disconnect or dissociate. If they are capable of compassion they can put aside their own feelings for the time being in order to be of assistance to the person who needs their compassion and kindness. Also, people who are open to their own pain may be more reflective and use their pain to become more understanding of the other person's pain, to be more aware of the universal quality of suffering and pain, and to develop more compassion for others.

A sincerely compassionate person must be careful not to lose compassion for his or her own self during this process. Having compassion for oneself is essential to developing compassion for others. If a person displays compassion from a point where they place everyone else before themselves, and feel or believe that they are undeserving or unworthy, what they experience for themselves is aversion—the opposite of being compassionate.

If an individual experiences less compassion for himself or herself, it will likely be difficult for that person to experience compassion for another person. Individuals who are aware of their own distress, grief, and pain—and are truly open to reflecting, exploring, and understanding that pain—are better candidates for delivering compassion for others. Individuals who are more in touch with their own feelings, grief, and pain are aware of how they may contribute to or cause pain in others. This provides them with better insight into the roots of suffering and distress.

Also, when individuals develop a mind-set to be compassionate for themselves, the skill is strengthened and can be used as a transferable skill for others who warrant compassion. What becomes an inner voice becomes habitual, easily spilling over into our day-to-day lives, and if individuals use an inner voice that emits compassion to themselves, this is easily transferred to another person. They are more capable of being aware of another's pain and are more emotionally and cognitively capable of responding effectively and acting on alleviating the other person's pain.

Mindfulness and Compassion

Mindfulness can be defined and understood as our ability to be in the moment and be aware of what is really happening. Mindfulness plays a significant role in understanding another person in distress and being compassionate. Mindful people can open their heart, open their mind, and be more aware of what surrounds them; consequently, one becomes more sensitive to one's own distress and pain and that of others. Like nurturing oneself to be compassionate, cultivating mindfulness is a skill. Thus, mindfulness naturally will aid in fostering a compassionate demeanor. Most important, being mindful will allow one to be more insightful along with being compassionate, and to maintain a harmonious balance between the two.

Compassion and Insight

Having compassion without insight could be dangerous and detrimental to oneself or to others. For example, if a compassionate person were assisting a friend in need at the cost of his or her own well-being, this would not be wise or insightful. The result would be a loss of self-compassion in the process.

On the other hand, having insight without compassion could also be damaging and harmful to oneself or others. Consider an individual who is possessed with a certain insight, who understands that everyone is subject to dying or losing someone, and that this is a natural phenomenon. If this individual is incapable of displaying compassion toward someone who has lost a dear one or a family member, and only uses insight to understand the situation, he or she would be insensitive to the other person's pain and distress. Thus, having a harmonious balance between compassion and insight is vital. Being mindful can contribute to having this desired harmony between compassion and insight.

Compassion and Empathy

Being compassionate goes hand in hand with being empathic and complementary to displaying empathy. Feeling empathy for a person could lead to taking compassionate action. An empathetic person tries to imagine what another person is experiencing by hypothetically placing himself or herself in the same situation, and attempting to feel the way the other person is feeling. An empathetic person must be constantly aware of the separation of himself or herself and the other and remember that it is the other person's pain, not one's own, that is important.

Being compassionate toward oneself can also foster empathy for others. When one is feeling empathy, the situation does not necessarily have to be painful; it could be joyous as well. When one is experiencing compassion the distinction is (in contrast to feeling empathic) that there exists an unfortunate situation or circumstance that is causing pain and distress. This feeling may lead an individual to desire to alleviate the pain of another, and increase the other's comfort and happiness.

The Opposite of Compassion

Eastern philosophers have their own understanding of compassion. As the philosopher Bhikku Narada states, wickedness or maliciousness is the opposite of compassion. Another Eastern philosopher, Bhante Gunarathana, states that aversion is the opposite of compassion. When a person has a desire to be malicious—to hurt, trigger pain, and cause harm to another being—it appears that this person is malicious or has aversion. This desire will lead that person to behave in a manner that causes harm and pain to another person. Similarly, one could also maintain this attitude toward oneself, thinking of harming oneself, and inflicting intentional pain on oneself. This is understood as the failure to be compassionate toward the self.

The Compassionate Counselor

Having compassion for oneself as the therapist, as well as for one's clients, is extremely important to the process of facilitating healing. A counselor's compassion plays a vital role in providing effective therapeutic services. When counselors are compassionate toward their clients, they strive to find ways to alleviate their clients' pain. As Thomas Bien notes, though counselors are not responsible for the realities of the client and the life they have built around themselves, they are responsible for resolving the issues of their clients. Bien observes that a compassionate counselor will join the client in finding solutions to the client's issues. By taking a client-centered approach, the counselor will guide the client compassionately in exploring his or her life circumstances. The compassionate counselor will assist clients in gaining better insight into themselves and find answers to issues and questions that they may have.

Thus, by being compassionate in the relationship, the counselor is able to strengthen the client's trust and convey the sense that the counselor has the best of intentions in the relationship. The client may feel that the counselor has acknowledged the client's pain and suffering, thus feeling genuinely listened to and heard. Being compassionate gives a counselor the opportunity to be congruent in the relationship, thus resulting in counselor authenticity, which will help facilitate further client healing.

Some counselors can be innately compassionate and bring that quality to the healing relationship. Others may have to learn to be compassionate. If trainee counselors are guided to be compassionate early in their training, they are very likely to develop this mind-set and strengthen it throughout their professional life. Though being compassionate is introduced as a skill, trainees must be encouraged to make compassion a lifestyle, so being compassionate spills over from their own lives to their clients' lives with greater ease. Addressing the importance of training counselors to be compassionate, Paul Fulton asserts that mindfulness is the most potent way to cultivate compassion and foster empathy in clinicians without fostering those qualities as simply objective skills.

Moreover, the compassionate counselor will assist clients in taking a compassionate stance toward people in their lives. In many families, members are often blinded by their own distress and pain, and unable to see and understand the other members' pain and distress, which could contribute to having an unhealthy or unhappy relationship. Therefore, when working with families and couples, encouraging compassion for family members will help the client to understand the family members' pain and suffering. This will alleviate some pain for clients, thus help them in gaining better insight into their own behavior and how it can cause pain and suffering to themselves as well as for other family members.

Compassion Fatigue

Compassion fatigue is a common occurrence with counselors after working in the field for some undermined time period. Thus, counselors who work in facilities that serve clients who have experienced significant trauma such as sexual and physical abuse may be more susceptible to compassion fatigue given the intense nature of their clients' issues. Charles Figley notes that compassion fatigue is a state of tension and preoccupation with the traumatized patients from imaginatively re-experiencing the traumatic events, and avoiding and numbing of reminders of the trauma, resulting in a persistent state of arousal that is associated with the trauma the patient experienced. Compassion fatigue is the result of being a witness to the suffering of others, and turning one's feelings into those of one's clients. The tragedy overwhelms the counselor, who in turn feels a misplaced sense of empathy for the clients. As time passes, these feelings accumulate and remain unresolved, often resulting in mental exhaustion and burnout. The alternative is the practice of compassion with insight.

Persons who are sincerely compassionate will take action to continue to be compassionate toward themselves as well as their clients. Such an understanding will assist counselors in recognizing when they need to separate from their clients' realities and take steps to maintain or enhance their own mental health.

Dharshini Goonetilleke

See also Empathy; Mindfulness

Further Readings

Bien, T. (2006). *Mindful therapy: A guide for therapists and helping professionals.* Somerville, MA: Wisdom Publications.

Gilbert, P. (Ed.). (2005). *Compassion: Conceptualisations, research and use in psychotherapy.* New York, NY: Routledge.

Gilbert, P. (2007). Evolved minds and compassion in the therapeutic relationship. In P. Gilbert & R. I. Leahy (Eds.), *The therapeutic relationship in the cognitive behavioral psychotherapies* (pp. 106–142). London, England: Routledge

Gilbert, P. (2009). *The compassionate mind.* London, England: Constable & Roberson.

Gunaratana, H. (2001). *Eight mindful steps to happiness: Walking the Buddha's path.* Somerville, MA: Wisdom Publications.

Patsiopoulos, A. T., & Buchanan, M. J. (2011). The practice of self-compassion in counseling: A narrative inquiry. *Professional Psychology: Research and Practice, 42*(4), 301–307. doi:http://dx.doi.org/10.1037/a0024482

Competency-Based Standards for Marriage, Couple, and Family Counseling

The Council for Accreditation for Counseling and Related Educational Programs (CACREP) Marriage, Couple, and Family Counseling (MCFC) competency-based standards refers to the organization that accredits MCFC educational master's degree programs and the standards used to determine whether a program meets accreditation requirements. This entry provides an overview of CACREP MCFC accreditation and explains CACREP accreditation within a larger context.

A Brief History of CACREP

Accrediting bodies exist to accredit educational programs, business organizations, and even individual service providers; they serve the main purpose of quality control. Internationally, the government agency that regulates education may oversee or even administer accrediting standards. In the United States, accrediting bodies are often connected to professional associations, but they may also be independently established; they typically base accreditation standards on a profession's ethical codes, best practices in the profession, professional literature, values of that profession, experts' perception of upcoming opportunities and challenges in the profession, and practitioners' input. Accreditation standards are updated regularly. Accreditation involves a process in which organizations choose to meet the standards established by an accrediting body. The process of accreditation begins when an organization applies for accreditation to the accrediting body and demonstrates how it meets each standard. The accrediting body then evaluates the organization and determines whether it meets the standards to the degree expected. If the standards are met, accreditation will be granted. The educational program, organization, or individual may then advertise that it is accredited by this particular accrediting body, which demonstrates a high-quality program.

Accreditation is usually optional, but it is expected in some professions. Accreditation of counseling programs is not mandated, but in the United States a few states' laws now mandate that licensure applicants have a counseling degree from a CACREP-accredited program. Because of this licensure requirement, a program may continue to exist, but its graduates may not be eligible for counseling licensure in some states. This requirement will be phased in over a few years, allowing time for programs and licensure applicants to prepare. The National Board of Certified Counselors (NBCC) intends to promote CACREP accreditation as a licensure requirement in all states.

Being accredited can benefit an organization in several ways: accreditation can document the quality of the organization; accreditation can make an organization more competitive; and in some situations accreditation is required for benefits such as licensure or payment for services. Accreditation is seen by many to benefit a profession because it establishes a baseline of quality and provides a clear definition of what it means to be in that profession. For example, the term "counselor" is used in many generic ways in society, but the more pervasive accreditation becomes, the easier it is to point to what, or who, *is* and *is not* a counselor because the standards are better known and broadly applied.

In the counseling profession, CACREP is the main accrediting organization. CACREP was established in 1981 when leaders from the Association for Counselor Education and Supervision (ACES) asked the American Personnel and Guidance Association (APGA) to consider working together to develop an accreditation process for counseling programs. At that point, CACREP was organized under the APGA, which developed into the American Association of Counseling and Development and became the American Counseling Association (ACA) in 1992. Although for a time CACREP was under the ACA, they later separated. Subsequently, NBCC became the parent organization for CACREP. In July 2015, CACREP and the Council on Rehabilitation Education (CORE) announced a plan to merge.

As an accrediting body for counseling programs, CACREP develops standards for the education of counselors at the master's and doctoral level. Counseling programs may choose to apply for CACREP accreditation if they want to demonstrate that they have met the requirements of CACREP. CACREP updates accreditation standards approximately every 7 years, with the most recent versions being the 2016 and the 2009 standards. While CACREP accredits counseling programs throughout the world, in 2016 only one program outside of the United States was accredited by CACREP.

Other Accreditation Options for MCFC Programs

Regional accrediting bodies may include counseling programs in a university's regional accreditation. No other accrediting body specifically accredits marriage, couple, and family counseling master's degree programs, though competitors of

CACREP occasionally attempt to establish themselves by offering alternative accreditation options for counseling programs. Additionally, marriage and family therapy programs may be accredited by the Commission on Accreditation for Marriage and Family Therapy Education (COAMFTE), which is a subset of the American Association for Marriage and Family Therapy (AAMFT).

CACREP and Marriage, Couple, and Family Counseling Programs

CACREP endorses the ACA's definition of counseling as "a professional relationship that empowers diverse individuals, families, and groups to accomplish mental health, wellness, education, and career goals." Based on this definition of counseling, CACREP views all counselors as having the same core competencies and applying the counseling philosophy and skills through specialty areas in counseling professions. A variety of specialty areas have developed over the history of CACREP. CACREP's approval of the addition of accreditation standards for marriage and family counseling/therapy was finalized by the board of directors of the Council on Postsecondary Accreditation in 1992. Over time, the title of this specialty has changed slightly, and the 2009 CACREP standards introduced the current title: Marriage, Couple, and Family Counseling. The 2016 CACREP standards included accreditation standards for specializations in (a) Addiction Counseling, (b) Career Counseling, (c) Clinical Mental Health Counseling, (d) Clinical Rehabilitation Counseling, (e) College Counseling and Student Affairs, (f) Marriage, Couple, and Family Counseling, and (g) School Counseling.

All counseling programs are required to fulfill core standards as well as specialization-specific standards. This is congruent with the counseling philosophy that all applications of counseling have core similarities and work from one philosophy, which then is applied through specialized training. According to CACREP's website, in 2016, 43 marriage, couple, and family counseling degree programs were accredited by CACREP.

CACREP Standards for MCFC Tracks

CACREP's 2016 standards include five core areas that must be met by all programs. A sixth area focuses on doctoral standards, which does not emphasize marriage and family counseling training. The five core areas include

1. The learning environment,
2. Professional counseling identity,
3. Professional practice,
4. Evaluation in the program, and
5. Entry-level specialty areas.

The first four of these areas apply to all programs, and include 154 standards, with many standards involving multiple components. These areas contain university expectations; eight core content areas; requirements for practicum and internship sites and hours; faculty, staff, and supervision qualifications; and evaluation and assessment practices and use. The eight core content areas are

1. Professional counseling orientation and ethical practice,
2. Social and cultural diversity,
3. Human growth and development,
4. Career development,
5. Counseling and helping relationships,
6. Group counseling and group work,
7. Assessment and testing, and
8. Research and program evaluation.

The 27 standards in the 2016 CACREP standards that are specific to marriage, couple, and family counseling require programs to demonstration that students develop knowledge and skills in areas related to (a) foundations, (b) contextual dimensions, and (c) practice of couple and family counseling. The foundations section includes history, theories, and models of marriage and family counseling, with focus on systems theory, sociology, assessment, and case conceptualization. The contextual dimension section comprises couple and family assessments and diagnoses, a variety of topics in the marriage, couple, and family counseling field (e.g., human sexuality, aging, crisis and trauma, addiction, interpersonal violence, employment difficulties, mental health), and professional awareness such as limitations of practice, ethics and laws, and practical practice logistics. The practice section focuses on application of marriage and family counseling skills, including prevention, assessment, case management, conceptualization, and intervention skills in a variety of professional contexts. The importance of systems theory is woven through all sections of the marriage, couple, and family counseling accreditation standards.

The process of becoming accredited by CACREP involves the program stating its intention to apply for accreditation, paying applicable fees throughout the process, writing a self-study that documents how every CACREP standard is met, hosting an evaluative site visit by a CACREP team, and responding to any standards that are not met. Accreditation may be denied, given conditionally for 1 to 2 years, or awarded for up to 8 years, at which point accreditation expires. Programs wishing to remain accredited must renew their accreditation prior to the expiration date.

Comparing Accreditation, Certification, and Licensure

Accreditation, certification, and *licensure* may be easily confused. Accreditation allows an educational program, organization, or individual to claim that it has met a specific set of basic professional standards. The term *accreditation-equivalent* is used by some educational programs that have not gone through the process of accreditation. It seems to be used to indicate that the program includes the same basic topics in training as are required by the accrediting organization. However, because of the number of standards, the intensity of the application process, and the scrutiny involved when accrediting body representatives evaluate a program, it is impossible for a program to know whether it is actually equivalent to an accredited program.

Certification is a less formal process in which training programs, organizations, conferences, and other groups may offer certification for organizations or people who complete a specified course of training. Certification is typically not required by the state, but it may be required by an organization before a person can claim that he or she offers that organization's service, such as a specific counseling approach.

Licensure occurs when the government issues permission to an individual to practice a profession that is regulated by the government. When a license is required for a particular profession, it is illegal to practice that profession without a license. Licensure and certifications required for practicing as a counselor differ across the world, with some countries having very stringent requirements and others only minimally monitoring the work of counselors. In the United States of America, all 50 states have laws that require that a person have a license from that state to practice counseling in that state. As of 2011, all 50 states regulate the professions of counseling and marriage and family therapy by requiring licensure to practice as a counselor or as a marriage and family therapist. The laws outlining the requirements for licensure differ in each state, but all include an educational component and a supervised practice component. Graduates of CACREP–accredited marriage, couple, and family counseling programs may be eligible to apply for state licensure as a counselor or as a marriage and family therapist, depending on the specific components of the program and the licensure requirements of particular states.

Susan N. Perkins

See also Certified Family Life Educator; Couples and Marriage Counseling

Further Readings

American Counseling Association. (2014). *20/20: Consensus definition of counseling.* Retrieved

January 5, 2015, from http://www.counseling.org/knowledge-center/20-20-a-vision-for-the-future-of-counseling/consensus-definition-of-counseling

Bobbie, C. L. (1993, Winter). News and views: COPA officially recognizes CACREP's inclusion of marriage and family counseling/therapy programs. *CACREP Connection* [Online]. Retrieved February 1, 2015, from http://www.cacrep.org/wp-content/uploads/2013/03/Winter-1993.pdf

CACREP. (2015). *2016 CACREP standards*. Retrieved August 16, 2015, from http://www.cacrep.org/wp-content/uploads/2012/10/2016-CACREP-Standards.pdf

CACREP. (2015). *About CACREP*. Retrieved January 3, 2015, from http://www.cacrep.org/about-cacrep/

Lee, C. C. (2013). The CACREP site visit process. *Journal of Counseling & Development, 91*, 50–54.

Levitt, D. H. (2004). Ethical responsibilities in training marriage and family counselors. *The Family Journal, 12*, 43–46. doi:10.1177/1066480703258704

Nassar-McMillan, S. C., & Niles, S. G. (2011). *Developing your identity as a professional counselor: Standards, settings, and specialties*. Belmont, CA: Brooks/Cole.

Urofsky, R. I. (2013). The Council for Accreditation of Counseling and Related Educational Programs: Promoting quality in counselor education. *Journal of Counseling & Development, 91*, 6–14.

Complementary and Symmetrical Relationships

Complementarity and symmetry are two terms that can be used to explain people's characteristics in a relationship and the patterned ways people tend to interact. Complementary relationships comprise two or more people who tend to have different characteristics that together make a "whole." Their characteristics balance each other out. One may be more extraverted and one more introverted. In a symmetrical relationship two people are similar in their styles. Having similarities can have advantages, but it can also lead to competitiveness. While these terms are most often used to classify romantic partnerships, they can also be seen in a variety of person-to-person relationships, such as family dyads and counseling relationships. This entry provides an overview of complementary and symmetrical relationships, highlighting findings on both the strengths and challenges of these types of relationships.

The individuals in a complementary relationship tend to have opposite or contrasting characteristics, which are seen as polar opposites. For example, if one person in the relationship is seen as a dominant personality type, then the opposite personality type, submissive, would be the complementary personality style. Minimal differences in people's styles might not cause problems; however, large differences, or feeling stuck in these different styles, can cause relationship problems. When people are polar opposites and feel stuck in those roles or relationships, anxiety increases, people may become more and more different, and the relationship is referred to as polarized. For example, one parent becomes more of a disciplinarian because he or she thinks the other parent is too easy, and the "easy" parent becomes more protective of the child to offset the increasing discipline of the other parent. Unchecked, people in complementary relationships can become more and more opposite.

In contrast to a complementary relationship, a symmetrical relationship is based on similarities of the two individuals in the relationship. Characteristics are similar and therefore work in conjunction with each other, applying the same strengths and an egalitarian point of view. For example, if there are two individuals with a submissive personality type, then each individual works in conjunction with the other's strengths and weaknesses because they are similar to their own. In the case of symmetrical relationships, the similarity of characteristics is the main basis of the relationship. However, sometimes symmetrical relationships can become competitive because each person wants similar things.

Although personality characteristics are one way to characterize the differences and similarities in the two relationship types, many cultural characteristics can contribute to a relationship being either complementary or symmetrical in nature. For example, a relationship would be complementary if a man was expected to take care of financial responsibilities and a woman was expected to take care of the home. Together they cover the responsibilities of the relationship, but they are each pressured to take certain responsibilities based on gendered expectations from society (rather than based on which individual would actually be better at different responsibilities). A relationship being classified as complementary or symmetrical is not an indicator of the functionality of the relationship, as both come with strengths and weaknesses. In a complementary relationship, too many opposite characteristics may result in fundamental differences in the perspectives from which life is viewed. In a symmetrical relationship, there may be too many similarities, which could lead to the weaknesses of each of the two individuals' personality characteristics to be more prevalent without the balance of someone who is more opposite in their line of thinking.

Complementary and symmetrical relationships can also occur in many settings. While romantic relationships are the most commonly discussed dyad, family dyads can be complementary and symmetrical in nature. For example, if a father and daughter have similar personality characteristics, that may lead them to form a symmetrical relationship in the family structure. For the counselor, this leads to multiple implications for the family's dynamics when working with clients in a family counseling setting. For example, people with symmetrical relationships can sometimes form coalitions against people in the family who do not share those symmetrical traits.

Further, the counseling relationship itself can include complementary and symmetrical relationships. In a couples counseling setting, a dyad can form between a therapist and one or both clients, which can have an influence on the way the counseling sessions move along. In this case, it's important for the counselor to be aware of what type of relationship is forming, and how to work effectively within those relationships so that the counselor is not seen as siding with or competitive with a particular client. Overall, complementary and symmetrical relationships are present in multiple relationship dyads across formal relationships and are neither a positive or negative attribute in a relationship; rather, understanding relationship styles helps further understanding of the people with whom one is working.

Heather D. Dahl

See also Couples and Marriage Counseling

Further Readings

Bengtson, V., Giarrusso, J., Mabry, B., & Silverstein, M. (2004). Solidarity, conflict, and ambivalence: complementary or competing perspectives on intergenerational relationships? *Journal of Marriage and Family Therapy, 64,* 568–576.

Miller, F. E., & Rogers, L. E. (1987). Relational dimensions of interpersonal dynamics. In M. E. Roloff & G. R. Miller (Eds.), *Interpersonal processes: New directions in communication research* (pp. 117–139). Thousand Oaks, CA: Sage.

Tyndall, L. W., & Lichtenberg, J. W. (2007). Spouses' cognitive styles and marital interaction patterns. *Journal of Marital and Family Therapy, 11,* 193–202.

COMPULSIVE SEXUAL BEHAVIOR

Compulsive sexual behavior, which may also be described as sexual compulsivity, hypersexuality, or sex addiction, involves frequent sexual behavior that is excessive in nature and leads to significant difficulty or impairment in life functioning. Compulsive sexual behavior may include conventional sexual behaviors, referred to as nonparaphilic sexual behaviors (e.g., masturbation), that have become compulsive. Compulsive sexual behavior may also include more deviant sexual activities, referred to as paraphilic sexual behaviors, which become compulsive, such as frequently exposing one's genitalia in public for the purpose of sexual arousal. Individuals may also engage in compulsive sexual behavior via the Internet. These behaviors may include excessive viewing of pornography or frequent participation in fantasy chat rooms. With the increase in Internet accessibility and utilization over the past two decades, Internet sexual behavior has increased and is expected to continue as a common way of engaging in compulsive sexual behavior. Compulsive sexual behavior negatively affects individuals' lives and usually has a negative impact on their loved ones' lives and functioning. People who have concerns related to compulsive sexual behavior often have difficulty in relationships and experience significant relationship strain. Those engaging in compulsive sexual behavior, as well as their families and loved ones, often experience shame, embarrassment, and emotional distress as a result of the sexual compulsivity. This entry discusses common characteristics and features of compulsive sexual behavior, diagnostic considerations related to sexual compulsivity, assessment of compulsive sexual behavior, and treatment implications for those who experience compulsive sexual behavior.

Characteristics and Features

Compulsive sexual behavior is generally categorized in addiction literature as a behavioral addiction, along with such concerns as pathological gambling and compulsive Internet gaming, as well as various other addictive behaviors. However, pathological gambling is the only behavioral addiction that is accepted as a diagnosable addictive disorder in the diagnostic manual used by mental health practitioners and researchers; the diagnostic term for pathological gambling is Gambling Disorder.

Behavioral addictions are viewed like substance addictions, the primary difference being that behavioral addictions involve a focus on behavior whereas substance addictions also involve use of psychoactive substances. There is evidence suggesting that various compulsive behaviors impact the neurological pathways and reward center of the brain in a manner similar to that of psychoactive substances. While there is a possibility that some individuals may be more vulnerable to developing addictions, such as those with a family or personal history of addiction or those who have experienced trauma, there is substantial evidence to support the contention that anyone may become addicted to a substance or behavior, regardless of their personality characteristics, background, mental health, or family history.

Determining whether sexual behavior is compulsive can be difficult. There are some common indicators that suggest compulsive sexual behavior. The first indicator includes frequent, excessive engagement in a sexual activity. For example, someone may spend many hours a day watching pornography, including times when it may not be appropriate, such as during work hours, when with family, or while driving. Compulsive sexual behavior involves more than the sexual activities in which one engages; obsessive thought patterns related to the sexual behavior are an additional indicator of compulsive sexual behavior. For example, individuals may find themselves thinking about sex so frequently and intensely that they are unable to be productive at their jobs or they may have difficulty sleeping at night because they cannot stop thinking about their next sexual encounter. Another common indicator of sexual compulsivity is continued engagement in the sexual activity despite significant negative consequences related to the behavior. These negative consequences may include physical consequences, such as injury to genitals or contraction of a sexually transmitted infection; vocational consequences, such as loss of job or loss of a colleague's respect; family or relationship consequences, such as dissolution of a marriage/partnership or loss of a loved one's trust; emotional consequences, such as hopelessness or depression; social consequences, such as loss of friendships due to inappropriate sexual comments or regularly canceling plans with friends in order to engage in sexual behavior; and spiritual consequences, such as feelings of disconnect from self, others, and/or a higher power. Often, continued engagement in compulsive sexual behaviors despite these substantial negative consequences leads to significant feelings of loss of control over the sexual thoughts, urges, or behaviors.

Diagnosis and Treatment

There is some controversy and disagreement in the mental health field related to compulsive sexual behavior and whether or not it should be understood as a mental health disorder. While professionals understand compulsive sexual behavior as an addiction, similar to a substance addiction, other professionals conceptualize sexual compulsivity as an impulse control disorder, a psychosexual disorder, or an obsessive-compulsive disorder. There are some researchers and professionals who have concern that a diagnosis of sexual compulsivity may be misused to pathologize or cast moral judgment on sexual behaviors that are unusual or uncommon according to mainstream society. There are others who have concern that a diagnosis of compulsive sexual behavior may be used as an excuse when one engages in behavior that is viewed as immoral or aberrant, or when one faces legal consequences resulting from sexual behaviors.

The current diagnostic system used by mental health providers in the United States, the *Diagnostic and Statistical Manual of Mental Disorders, Fifth Edition* (DSM-5), does not include a diagnosis specific to compulsive sexual behavior. At the time of the DSM-5's publication, there was not sufficient empirical literature to include a diagnosis specific to sexual compulsivity. However, there is a growing body of literature focusing on compulsive sexual behavior that is leading to better understanding of sexual compulsivity, as well as ways in which to support and treat those who seek professional help for compulsive sexual behavior.

Patrick Carnes is considered a leader in conceptualizing sexual compulsivity as a mental health concern, specifically as a behavioral addiction. Carnes's early work has contributed greatly to the current understanding of sexual compulsivity, including definitions, development, common features, and ways to address sexual compulsivity. He described sexual compulsivity as being an addictive cycle that involves preoccupation, ritualization, compulsivity, and despair. Carnes conceptualized sexual compulsivity as ranging from common, culturally acceptable sexual behaviors that become excessive, to compulsive sexual activities in which significant boundaries are violated. As regards substance addictions, Carnes described compulsive sexual behavior as something that may be experienced by people of all racial, ethnic, gender, and economic backgrounds. He developed recommendations for treatment to help those with sexual compulsivity that guides many current sexual addiction treatment programs. In addition, he identified successful treatment and recovery from sexual compulsivity as involving a supportive, caring community of peers; professional support to address thinking and behavior that contributes to sexual compulsivity; and building and rebuilding trusting, healthy relationships with others.

Most often, behaviors are understood as being compulsive if the behavior presents similarly to some or all of the established diagnostic criteria for addictions described in the DSM-5. In the context of compulsive sexual behavior, these criteria may be understood as

- engaging in the compulsive sexual behavior for longer periods of time than intended;
- unsuccessful attempts to reduce or control the sexual behavior;
- significant time or energy spent engaging in, preparing for, or recovering from the compulsive sexual behavior;
- cravings or intense urges to engage in the sexual behavior;
- difficulty managing life responsibilities
- (e.g., work, family) due to the sexual behavior;
- continued engagement in the compulsive sexual behavior despite significant problems in relationships due to the behavior;
- reducing or giving up social activities because of the sexual behavior;
- continued engagement in the sexual behavior despite risk or danger involved in the activity;
- continued engagement in the sexual behavior despite physical or psychological concerns being caused by or made worse by the sexual behavior;
- needing to engage more and more in the sexual activity in order to experience the desired effects of the sexual behavior (tolerance); and
- experiencing symptoms of withdrawal, either physical or psychological, when not engaging in the sexually compulsive behavior.

Addressing compulsive sexual behavior in a mental health setting often involves obtaining an extensive sexual health history, including exploration of the development of the compulsive sexual behavior(s), as well as the severity and intensity of thoughts, behaviors, and feelings associated with the sexual compulsivity. Certain assessments or screening tools may also be used to better understand the compulsive sexual behavior. The Sexual Addiction Screening Test (SAST), developed by Carnes, is a measure used to assist clinicians in determining the severity of compulsive sexual behavior and better understand the ways in which a respondent is affected by sexual compulsive behaviors. The screening tool has a series of questions to which the respondent indicates "yes" or "no" in response. Items on the SAST include efforts to quit problematic sexual behavior, feeling guilt or depression after engaging in sexual activity, and feeling preoccupied with sexual thoughts. Severity of sexual compulsivity and a profile of specific concerns may be derived from the results of the SAST. The SAST is not a diagnostic measure, but rather a screening tool to assist clinicians in better understanding sexual compulsivity concerns. Various other tools exist to assist professionals in screening or assessing for sexual compulsivity.

While some addictive behaviors, such as pathological gambling, are addressed by encouraging abstinence from the behavior, recovery from compulsive sexual behavior does not usually involve complete abstinence from sexual activity. Some period of abstinence from sexual activity may be recommended, but most often people with sexual compulsivity focus on learning how to engage in healthy sexual relationships, as well as learning to participate in healthy nonsexual activities. Individuals with compulsive sexual behavior may also benefit from involvement in mutual support groups focused on sexual compulsivity, similar to the way in which Alcoholics Anonymous may be a beneficial support network for those with alcohol use disorders.

Similar to other behaviors and concerns that are addictive in nature, individuals with compulsive sexual behavior often benefit from therapy and counseling to address these concerns. Most people with sexually compulsive behavior will respond best to interventions that are individualized to meet a person's unique needs and that focus on a whole-person, strengths-based approach to care. Some common types of therapeutic approaches that may be valuable for individuals with compulsive sexual behavior include 12-step-based interventions, motivational enhancement, psychodynamic therapy, cognitive approaches, behavioral strategies, and, at times, pharmacological agents. Cognitive approaches aim at exploring thinking patterns related to the sexual compulsivity, and learning ways to stop these thought processes or experience such thoughts without acting on them. Behavioral strategies to address sexual compulsivity involve identifying actions to prevent one from acting on sexually compulsive urges and learning healthy activities, including healthy sexual behaviors. Psychodynamic therapy involves increasing awareness of unconscious thoughts, along with working toward resolving conflicts. Depending on the nature and severity of the compulsive sexual behavior, these interventions may be provided on an inpatient or outpatient basis, and may be presented in individual, family, or group therapy formats. Prescription medications, such as selective serotonin reuptake inhibitors (SSRIs), may assist in treating compulsive sexual behavior, though these medication treatments are often most effective when combined with mental health therapy and counseling interventions.

Terri L. Jashinsky

See also Alcohol and Substance Abuse; Fetishes; Pornography; Sex, Definition of; Sexual Assessment/History

Further Readings

American Psychiatric Association. (2013). *Diagnostic and statistical manual of mental disorders* (5th ed.). Washington, DC: Author.

Carnes, P. (2001). *Out of the shadows: Understanding sexual addiction* (2nd ed.). Center City, MN: Hazelden.

Garcia, F. D., & Thibaut, F. (2010). Sexual addictions. *American Journal of Drug and Alcohol Abuse, 36*, 254–260.

Grant, J. E., Potenza, M. N., Weinstein, A., & Gorelick, D. A. (2010). Introduction to behavioral addictions.

American Journal of Drug and Alcohol Abuse, 36(5), 233–241.

Rosenberg, K. P., O'Connor, S., & Carnes, P. (2014). Sex addiction: An overview. In K. P. Rosenberg & L. Curtiss Feder (Eds.), *Behavior addictions: Criteria, evidence, and treatment* (pp. 215–236). San Diego, CA: Academic Press.

Shaffer, H. J. (Ed.). (2012). *APA addiction syndrome handbook*. Washington, DC: American Psychological Association.

Conduct Disorder

Conduct disorder is a mental health diagnosis characterized by deviant behaviors among children and adolescents, classified as one of the disruptive behavior disorders. Also described as juvenile delinquency, conduct disorder is marked by cruelty and deprivation of others' rights. This entry provides a description of conduct disorder and how it is diagnosed and manifested, outlines risk factors for the disorder, and concludes with a discussion of some of the various treatments currently in use.

Description

At first glance, the consistent rule-breaking behaviors represented by conduct disorder are arguably similar to those of oppositional defiant disorder (ODD). Both conduct disorder and ODD feature trouble with authority figures and deviation from prescribed rules. In fact, disruption and impulsive behavior are common among adolescents with other mood, impulse, and developmental disorders such as depressive disorder, adjustment disorder, autism spectrum disorder, or attention-deficit disorder. These types of behaviors go beyond the usual developmentally normative mischief that children may get into, and are identified clinically because of their frequency and pattern. Conduct disorder is sometimes referred to as the under-18 version of antisocial personality disorder, which includes similar social deviancy, cruelty, and deprivation of others' rights without remorse. It is important to note that antisocial behavior is completely different from introversion or shyness—it is a criminal disposition. Reassuringly, most children with conduct disorder do not grow up to engage in criminal or antisocial behavior in adulthood.

Diagnosis

The *Diagnostic and Statistical Manual of Mental Disorders,* Fifth Edition (DSM-5), and the World Health Organization *International Classification of Diseases* (ICD-10) are used to classify and categorize mental health diagnoses, including conduct disorder. It is diagnosed on the basis of a pattern of behaviors—for example, bullying, fighting, cruelty to people or animals, stealing, and avoidance of home, school, or authority. The DSM-5 requires behaviors meeting three criteria over the course of a year, with one in the most recent six months preceding the diagnosis. An example of a child meeting the diagnostic criteria for conduct disorder in either the DSM-5 or ICD-10 would be one who has recently brought a knife to school with the intent to injure, spray-painted graffiti on a neighbor's house, and skipped school.

Manifestation

Children with conduct disorder tend to have general social difficulty, even among peer friendships, but also with parents and teachers as well as strangers. The earlier in childhood conduct disorder manifests itself, the greater the risks for severity and later adulthood-based antisocial disorder. Aggression could include animal cruelty, interpersonal violence, and sex offenses. Theft can include forceful robbery or just taking things secretly. Other disregard for rules and societal norms are also common, such as running away from home and being disobedient in general. Because crime and family custody and dependency issues are so often a part of conduct disorder, children and adolescents are sometimes ordered out of the home via court order and placed in foster care, juvenile detention, or other treatment programs.

Conduct disorder shares some of its traits with other diagnoses. Oppositional defiant disorder, or ODD, for instance, features similar difficulties with authority. Children with ODD, however, do not engage in cruelty. A child cannot have both ODD and conduct disorder, although it is possible for one to transition from one to the other when defiance crosses into criminal deviance. Mood disorders such as depression, or developmental disorders such as autism spectrum disorder and intellectual disabilities, may share anger, deviation from social norms, and are not necessarily exclusive of conduct disorder; a child may have conduct disorder along with another disability. Substance use disorders often tend to coexist with conduct disorder. Conduct disorder may interfere with developmentally notable milestones in learning due to attendance or refusal to engage in school, and sometimes leads to later specific learning disorders. The key for differentiating conduct disorder is to seek a pattern, not a single occurrence, of cruelty and criminal behavior.

Children with conduct disorder tend to exhibit impulsivity, both in social situations and when alone. They demonstrate defiance and disruption, particularly when faced with authority, and little regard for others' feelings, interests, or rights. They tend to externalize responsibility for their actions, and deviate from instructions and directives. In adolescence, conduct disorder is often accompanied by substance abuse and manipulative relationships. Most notably, a child with conduct disorder acts cruelly toward others.

Risk Factors

Conduct disorder has a number of risk factors associated with it, although many of the risks have not been proven to necessarily cause conduct disorder, nor do they always indicate that conduct disorder will be present. It is more prevalent in males than in females. Most of the risk factors are associated with family, including parents and siblings. Children of parents who also have/had conduct disorder, substance use, personality disorders, and mood disorders are at greater risk. Some of the family-related risks for conduct disorder are genetic, but some of the risks are also environmental. Oftentimes, conduct disorder is preceded by a lack of consistency and structure in the home, such as neglect, poverty, and frequent violence or abuse. Siblings with conduct disorder can be another warning sign that younger siblings may enact similar behaviors.

Treatments

Most of the treatments for conduct disorder focus on family interaction, problem-solving, and behavior modification techniques. Treatment can take place in outpatient and inpatient settings, with the latter typically pursued when the former is repeatedly not successful, or when there are drugs or unsafe conditions in the home.

Outpatient therapies are often focused on family interactions and seek to improve parent–child relationships as well as to train the parent in behavior management, and also to assist the child in gaining more control over emotions and behaviors. Family interactions may include closing gaps in emotional as well as physical aspects of the household, where neglect may have contributed to the maladaptive behaviors.

Family Interaction

Parents and/or caregivers are an integral point for conduct disorder treatment interventions, in that they can be trained in identifying behavior transactions through which the child behaves negatively. Behavior management includes varied efforts to influence a person to behave in a desired way. Two common techniques used to manage behavior include person-centered therapies and behavior therapies.

Person-Centered Therapy

Person-centered therapy seeks to use empathy, acceptance, and congruence as tools to foster positive decisions by the child. The originator of person-centered therapy, Carl Rogers, believed that people have a natural tendency to self-improve, or actualize; this happens when people feel positively about themselves and experience positivity from others. This therapy is not directive in nature, and it does not include confronting the child; rather, it focuses on acceptance. Often referred to as a relational model, this type of treatment ultimately seeks to strengthen the bonds between parent/caregiver and child. Behavior change in this model is only encouraged, or welcomed, and is couched in high levels of empathy, rapport, and child autonomy.

Behavior Modification

Behavior modification is based on a learning theory in which each behavior has an antecedent, or something that happens prior to a behavior; then comes the child's behavior choice, or a reaction that the child chooses; and then a consequence. Consequences can be natural or artificial. Natural consequences occur as a result of behaviors, without intervention. Artificial consequences are incurred intentionally as a response to a behavior. In either case, the consequence can serve to reinforce positive or negative behaviors, depending on the nature of the consequence. Positive reinforcement and negative reinforcement are behavior modification interventions used to encourage or discourage a behavior.

For example, a child refuses to complete math homework. The child's parent is made aware of the situation and decides to confine the child to the house every time the homework is not turned in at school. The parent explains to the child that the confinement, sometimes referred to as being grounded, will be lifted when the child follows through and turns in completed homework. Taking the confinement away in response to a desirable behavior like homework completion is an example of what is termed *negative reinforcement*. It is important to note that negative reinforcement is often wrongly referred to as punishment, like a spanking—but in reality, negative reinforcement is when a component is removed, or subtracted, from the situation. Another option is for the parent to reward the child when homework is turned in.

The reward, which is added as a consequence, is thus a *positive reinforcement*. How youths process the effects after they make choices that work in their favor or not in their favor is dependent on a consistent environment and intentional follow-up. The more a consequence can be associated with, or experienced through, natural and nonmanipulated means, the more likely this will connect logically with the youth's grasp of self-direction or locus of control.

Problem-Solving

Inextricable from the antecedent, behavior, and consequence schema is problem-solving. Another area of treatment for conduct disorder focuses on the antecedent as a problem, using experiential learning. Group and individual programmed experiences where hypothetical or analogical problems are introduced for learning purposes have shown high potential for adolescents with conduct disorder. While younger children are less developmentally likely to respond to analogies, adolescents and teens have greater potential to learn through techniques such as psychodrama and adventure-based learning. In these settings, a problem or antecedent is introduced, and the activity becomes a laboratory where the youth can try various responses to hypothesize on the potential outcome or consequence. Such techniques draw upon Gestalt techniques, where participants are encouraged to focus on the here and now, and then to apply that experience to future decisions.

Cognitive-Behavioral Therapy

Cognitive-behavioral therapy, or CBT, is related closely to problem-solving behavioral interventions, and is one of the most efficacious treatments in terms of frequency and effects documented in scholarly literature. CBT focuses on consciously working through the thoughts that lead to behaviors by emphasizing that those behaviors are not automatic, but fully within the youth's control. CBT addresses faulty notions by encouraging the child to question each automatic thought pattern critically. For example, a young person has been insulted by a peer, who spoke derogatorily about her mother. The teen lashes out, and retaliates with punches thrown. The insulted party's violent response results in a consequence that includes suspension from school and punishment from a parent. Furthermore, she also injures her hand in the altercation. A CBT intervention might include taking an inventory of the consequences that were desirable and weighing this against the consequences that were undesirable. The teen claims that there was no choice: A fight had to occur. The therapist would process the true results of the altercation and assist the youth in evaluating the violence in terms of whether it solved the problem created by the insult. Focus may intensify on the sensations the teen felt when she heard the insult, including the feelings that she felt were automatic, whether those feelings necessitated the behavior response, and whether the outcome was the best possible one. CBT is sometimes criticized for seeming overly prescriptive, so care is ideally taken by therapists not to judge the client's thought patterns, but rather to create space where the client can evaluate her own thoughts and behaviors. Greater self-control with consideration toward the desired outcome is a central feature of CBT, and it lends itself well to patterns of disregard and deviance enacted by youth with conduct disorder.

Inpatient Treatment

The above treatments are only some of many choices. Interventions such as these and others may also take place through inpatient treatment. Inpatient treatment, through which the child is removed from the home, tends to be a last resort, and does not preclude further work with the family, as well as home visits or gradual transitions through which the child slowly reintegrates into the home in order to practice interventions and problem-solving skills undertaken through out-of-home placement. Options for inpatient interventions include foster care, group homes, treatment agencies, psychiatric hospitalization, and juvenile detention centers. Inpatient treatment may be initiated by a parent or caregiver, but it is more often ordered through a judge. Such cases can involve myriad professional personnel, including child advocates, social workers, therapists, juvenile probation officers, attorneys, case managers, and parents/caregivers. Once the out-of-home placement takes temporary custody of the child, the point of intervention is the environment itself—which includes the staff or foster parents, as well as the systems or protocols used to modify behaviors, whether relational, behavioral, or a combination thereof. Children in these environments are often encouraged through problem-solving, community living and chores among other peers, participation in education, and other therapeutic interventions as necessary.

Inpatient treatment, versus outpatient treatment, is regarded as controversial depending on the circumstances. While inpatient treatment is a last resort, an argument put forth by advocates for its increased use relates to substance use among adolescents. Brain cells, particularly the myelin sheath structures that protect neurons, continue to develop well into early adulthood. Alcohol and some drugs have been found to potentially contribute to abnormalities in brain tissue, so if there are drugs and/or alcohol in a child's home and the child is using those substances, simply curbing access to drugs and alcohol to allow the brain to more fully develop would be advisable. On the other hand, there is also considerable literature on the potential damages inherent in removing a child from the home and family, including cautions that focusing on the child and not enough on the family as a whole will not improve conditions for when the child is released back into the family environment. Due to family risk factors that include other problem areas such as neglect, or parental or sibling impairment, the newest interventions view the family as a system that precipitates problems in child behavior, rather than focusing on a so-called problem child.

Treatment is likely to be successful in situations where parents act early, as soon as the onset of conduct disorder traits occurs. Intentional efforts to address risk factors can have a significant impact on the disordered behavior. For instance, abusive responses to defiance on the part of a parent, caregiver, or counselor can be replaced with behavior management and logical consequences, leading to a greater sense of self-control. A parent, caregiver, or counselor who intentionally focuses on relational, empathic interactions may help reinforce a sense of empathy and morality in a young person treated for conduct disorder. While persistent cruelty through adolescence indicates a greater risk for adulthood antisocial disorder and prolonged criminal justice involvement, the prognosis for conduct disorder is considerably better when therapeutic interventions are employed.

Andrew M. Byrne

See also Adolescent Behavior Disorders; Adolescent Mental Health, Anxiety Disorders in Adolescents; Bereavement; DSM and V-Codes; Juvenile Firesetter Interventions; Loss; Mood Disorders in Adolescents; Oppositional Defiant Disorder; Substance Use Disorders in Adolescence; Suicide

Further Readings

American Psychiatric Association. (2013). *Diagnostic and statistical manual of mental disorders* (5th ed.). Arlington, VA: Author.

Beck, J. S. (2011). *Cognitive behavior therapy: Basics and beyond* (2nd ed.). New York, NY: Guilford Press.

Buitelaar, J. K., Smeets, K. C., Herpers, P., Scheepers, F., Glennon, J., & Rommelse, N. J. (2013). Conduct disorders. *European Child Adolescent Psychiatry, 22,* S49–S54. doi:10.1007/s00787-012-0361-y

Eyberg, S. M., Nelson, M. M., & Boggs, S. R. (2008). Evidence-based psychosocial treatments for children and adolescents with disruptive behavior. *Journal of Clinical Child and Adolescent Psychology: The Official Journal for the Society of Clinical Child and Adolescent Psychology, American Psychological Association, Division 53, 37*(1), 215–237. doi:10.1080/15374410701820117

Gass, M. A., Gillis, L., & Russell, K. C. (2012). *Adventure therapy: Theory, research, and practice.* New York, NY: Routledge.

Jongsma, A. E., Peterson, L. M., McInnis, W. P., & Bruce, T. J. (2014). *The adolescent psychotherapy treatment planner* (5th ed.). Hoboken, NJ: Wiley.

Lahey, B. B., & Waldman, I. D. (2011). Annual research review: Phenotypic and causal structure of conduct disorder in the broader context of prevalent forms of psychopathology. *Journal of Child Psychology and Psychiatry, 53,* 536–557. doi:10.1111/j.1469-7610.2011.02509.x

Phelan, J. (2009). Activities of daily living and controls from within. *Reclaiming Child and Youth, 17,* 46–51.

CONFIDENTIALITY

Clinicians have a professional obligation to respect and protect the information learned within their working relationships with clients. Confidentiality is the term used to refer to that covenanted communication between a client and a counselor. By definition, confidentiality means spoken or written in confidence. Clinicians are entrusted with intimate details and secrets about the personal and professional lives of the clients they serve and must keep that information confidential. Although confidentiality is an essential component of any therapeutic relationship, confidentiality is not as easy to maintain as some may think. Confidentiality can be a complex, multifaceted practice. For example, confidentiality with adults is practiced differently than confidentiality with children. Undoubtedly, it is easier to ensure confidentiality in individual sessions than in group settings. As a result, clinicians must be aware and intentional in their efforts to maintain their clients' confidences in the various and unique instances for which treatment exists (e.g., individual, group, couple, and family sessions). In addition, clinicians must understand the parameters for releasing information and the limitations to confidentiality. Following a brief discussion of the scope and purpose of confidentiality between counselor and clients, the entry notes the conditions under which exceptions to confidentiality are permitted. Next explored are issues of confidentiality in couples and family counseling, special considerations in counseling minors, and confidentiality in the context of research. The entry concludes with a discussion of confidentiality in the documentation of treatment sessions and progress notes.

What Is Considered Confidential?

Confidential information includes data that can identify a client as well as any information (e.g., written, oral) about the client's life, dealings, and associations obtained during the therapeutic relationship. This can include knowledge of and information about family members, dwellings, health, finances, employment, affiliations, and business associates. Anything the clinician came to know through the counselor–client relationship is considered confidential. As part of their professional obligation, clinicians should assume that the client does not want any data or details about his or her life released without prior permission, no matter how seemingly insignificant.

Confidentiality is both a legal and ethical obligation. According to the American Counseling Association 2014 Code of Ethics, counselors must protect the confidential information of prospective, current, and previous clients. Within a professional relationship, confidentiality is an ethical decision not to disclose what a client reveals or discusses during a therapy session. Confidentiality is the core of the working relationship. It is an essential component of building rapport and establishing a therapeutic foundation of trust, genuineness, openness, and mutual respect. Without this therapeutic condition, clients are less likely to disclose their true thoughts, feelings, and behaviors, which can significantly hinder the helping process. Confidentially becomes a legal issue when protected information is released without prior authorization. Clinicians can be held civilly liable under state laws for breaches of confidentiality. Thus, clinicians should disclose confidential information only with written consent or with sound legal or ethical justification.

Exceptions to Confidentiality

There are some limitations to confidentiality that must be discussed with clients at the outset of the therapeutic relationship. These exceptions include instances of abuse, imminent risk of harm to self or others, and when the therapist is compelled by a court of law to testify. For instance, clinicians can divulge confidential information only in those situations in which failure to disclose would result in imminent danger to the client or others, such as allegations of child abuse, abuse of an elderly or disabled person, and suicidal or homicidal ideations. In addition, clinicians may be compelled to disclose confidential information when subpoenaed to appear in court on an issue involving the client.

In 1976, the case of *Tarasoff v. Board of Regents of the University of California* further expanded the limitations on confidentiality. Prosenjit Poddar, a college student at the University of California, Berkeley, participated voluntarily in psychological services via the student health center. Within the confines of the therapeutic relationship with a university psychologist, Poddar reported that he intended to kill his ex-girlfriend, Tatiana Tarasoff. The psychologist notified campus police; Poddar was detained and questioned but released because he appeared rational and denied any intent to harm his ex-girlfriend. Poddar refused further treatment by the psychologist, and no additional actions were taken to ensure Tarasoff's safety. Unfortunately, Poddar killed Tarasoff 2 months later, and her family sued the university for failing to notify the victim of the threat on her life. In this case, the California Supreme Court ruled that the clinician's obligation to maintain the client's confidentiality was outweighed by the clinician's duty to protect the public. This landmark case became known as the clinician's *duty to warn*. In these instances (e.g., abuse, imminent danger), confidentiality can be breached and entrusted information can be shared with appropriate individuals or authorities *without* the client's consent. Sound counselors reiterate these limitations periodically throughout the therapeutic relationship. Furthermore, counselors working with terminally ill clients and/or clients with communicable, life-threatening illnesses face additional issues with confidentiality, imminent risk of harm, and legal mandates. For instance, terminally ill clients may seek to end their lives. Clients with communicable, life-threatening diseases such as HIV/AIDS may be placing a third party at imminent and foreseeable risk of harm. In such situations, counselors must assess the risk, seek consultation or supervision, including legal advice, and adhere to state laws regarding breaching confidentiality.

Sharing Confidential Information

Frequently, clinicians consult and collaborate with others (e.g., collateral service providers, medical personnel, educators, lawyers) to be advocates for and to support their clients. Thus, written consent for the release of information must be obtained from the client prior to the clinician sharing any privileged communication. This written consent must specifically include what information will be disclosed, to whom, the purpose of the disclosure, and the date the consent will expire. The American Counseling Association 2014 Code of Ethics suggests that counselors should engage in ongoing discussions with clients about when, how, and with whom information will be shared.

Often, colleagues mingle in public places such as hallways, reception areas, restrooms, or restaurants. Openly discussing clients can lead to breaches of confidentiality that strain the therapeutic relationship and place the clinician in an ethical or legal conundrum. Thus, clinicians must also guard against unintentional breaches of confidentiality. For example, because therapeutic relationships exist within the context of a larger community, it is not uncommon for clinicians to encounter clients in public places such as grocery stores and restaurants. Simply acknowledging how the clinician knows the client to a third party is a breach of confidentiality. Voicemail messages, files left on desks, documents left on fax or copying machines, and even greeting neighbors during a home visit all create dilemmas for protecting a client's confidences. Thus, counselors should take precautions to guard against dual relationships and accidental disclosures of the client's identity and/or any knowledge learned from within the therapeutic process.

Many counselor–client relationships occur within the confines of a larger context such as a residential treatment facility, correctional facility, rehabilitation center, hospital, or educational system. It is not uncommon for a teacher to refer a student for counseling or a court to mandate counseling as a measure to facilitate safety and stability. Even when counseling occurs in an open context, such as a school or a court of law, maintaining confidentiality is still a priority. Although judges, probation officers, teachers, and principals may know that the client is seeing a clinician for counseling, the clinician has an obligation to ensure the client's confidences and share information only on a need-to-know basis.

Society is constantly making technological advances; needless to say, technology has infiltrated the field of counseling. Computers are used for billing, scheduling, assessments, record keeping, and even to administer and score psychological tests. Keeping client information confidential and restricting access to databases that store client information are of paramount importance for a legally and ethically sound practitioner. Simply walking away from a computer that is logged into client billing or progress notes can create a potential breach in confidentiality. Additionally, confidentiality is an enormous concern in telephonic and online counseling, which are heavily dependent on exchanges via cell phones, e-mail, the Internet, instant messaging, and webcams. Continually monitoring and added precautions are needed to safeguard clients in such treatment modalities.

Confidentiality in Couples and Family Counseling

Helping couples and families explore presenting problems, build communication skills, and disagree effectively can be challenging enough. The added issues of confidentiality in couples and family therapy further complicates the work. Although the family is in treatment as a unit, clinicians must respect and protect each member's confidences. It is not uncommon for warring families and couples in the midst of conflict to present with individual needs and competing interests. Thus, many therapists create policies and guidelines as preventive measures for managing issues of confidentiality when working with couples and families. At the outset of treatment, sound clinicians clearly define the client (e.g., the family as a unit), how secrets are managed, and whether individual counseling sessions will be permissible when treating the couple or family.

There are two opposing positions for how secrets are to be managed in couples and family therapy. The first approach is absolute confidentiality. Thus, the clinician will keep each family member's confidence much as in individual counseling. In this approach, information about one family member will not be disclosed to any other family members without permission. Clinicians may work with the family member to encourage and facilitate disclosure to the uninformed family members. However, regardless of whether the family member shares the secret, confidentiality is upheld. Some counselors might even encourage individual sessions to facilitate the divulging of secrets. Bringing secrets to the forefront can help the clinician to better understand the couple or familial dynamics, and also help the clinician to learn of issues at the core of familial dissension. The second approach is a "no secrets" policy. Specifically, some counselors may adopt a policy of not keeping any secrets in couples and family treatment. In this approach, clinicians might even refuse to engage family members separately to avoid secrets and untherapeutic alliances. The therapist must (1) pick an approach compatible with his or her treatment style, theoretical framework, and clinical practice for conducting family treatment and (2) explain the policy to the couple or family at the onset of treatment. Regardless of the approach, it becomes the role of the clinician to balance the familial conflict, competing interests, and dual relationships to achieve therapeutic outcomes for the family.

Limits of confidentiality, subpoenas, and releases of information are even more perplexing in couples and family treatment. For instance, can one member of a family consent to the release of information for the whole family? Can a therapist be called to testify in a divorce proceeding after providing counseling to the couple or the family? Would it be a breach of confidentiality if a clinician confirms that the wife is a part of the treatment unit when releasing information to the husband's probation officer? In an effort to lay the foundation for respect and guarding confidences in therapeutic relationships involving more than one person, the American Association of Marriage and Family Therapy (AAMFT) offers guidelines for how clinicians can respond respectfully, responsibly, and competently to issues of confidentiality. The AAMFT requires a "secrets" policy of its members and also outlines what is best clinical practice in regard to confidentiality. For example, it is recommended that a clinician seek the authorization of all members in treatment before the release of records or any confidential information. In addition, clinicians may also invoke therapist–patient privilege on behalf of the patient (i.e., family unit) if subpoenaed for records or testimony.

Confidentiality in Group Settings

In addition to being an efficient therapeutic approach, group counseling provides opportunities for vicarious learning, behavioral rehearsals, and a variety of viewpoints and feedback. Despite its advantages, confidentiality in group settings can be quite challenging. Groups work best when members feel safe and safety is grounded in confidentiality. Although confidentiality is an essential component of group counseling and therapy, it is not guaranteed. In a group setting, members must be taught about confidentiality, and it is the role of the group leader to clearly define and explain its importance, and to provide examples. However, there is no way to ensure confidentiality in a group setting. Although the group leader has a professional obligation to maintain confidentiality, the members do not. Thus, the screening and initial stages of a group should be used to build rapport and cohesion, and to emphasize the importance of "what's said in the group, stays in the group."

When creating group norms and expectations, confidentiality should always be a group rule. When members suspect that confidentiality has been breached, it should be dealt with as swiftly and therapeutically as possible. Letting the suspected breach or betrayal of the group's confidence go unresolved will likely fester and shake the foundation of the therapeutic process. Once a group no longer feels like a safe place, group cohesion, trust, and mutual respect falter, thereby rendering the group process untherapeutic.

Confidentiality With Minors

When counselors work with children or individuals who cannot give informed consent, parents and guardians may be included in the counseling process. However, counselors must consistently act in the best interest of the identified client (e.g., the child) and take measures to ensure confidentiality. For instance, the initial interview for family counseling and/or counseling with a minor should include an earnest and frank conversation with the child and the caregiver(s) about confidentiality and how/what information will be shared. Clinicians must explain to the parents how/why confidentiality is key to establishing and maintaining the trust needed in a therapeutic relationship. Furthermore, clinicians must seek parental agreement that no disclosure will occur that could hinder the working relationship. However, parents and caregivers should be informed promptly in situations where safety is an issue.

Confidentiality in Research

Counseling, like other fields of study, has an ongoing need for progressive research. Research informs and improves our practice. Therefore, many social service and mental health agencies, much like universities, spearhead studies. These studies typically provide evidence of treatment efficacy, validate services, develop new interventions, and test theories. Consequently, there is a need to protect subjects when doing such research. Participants in studies have a right to confidentiality. Participants must be assured that identifying information will be concealed and that responses shared during the study will not be released carelessly or flagrantly. Just as in individual therapy or group counseling, information should not be released without the subject's consent. Undoubtedly, researchers bear the responsibility to safeguard the subject's identity and data from careless, damaging, and unauthorized releases.

Confidentiality in Progress Notes

How records are kept in group, couples, and family therapy is another area where clinicians must be cognizant of confidentiality. For example, in group treatment, clinicians have the option of writing one progress note per group session or writing individual progress notes for each group member. It is very easy and efficient to write one note for a group. However, if one progress note is written to capture the group process, then it is likely that confidential information about members may be detailed in one document. This poses a significant problem if records are requested, subpoenaed, or reviewed by one of the clients. Individual progress notes with global group and treatment information is ideal for ensuring confidentiality. However, if individual progress notes are written for each group member, then the issue of how to document client interactions arises. In individual progress notes, some clinicians refer to other group members vaguely, by initials, or use a system for coding names to protect identities and to promote confidentiality. It is also a best practice that clinicians keep separate progress notes on each family member in couples or family therapy. Information that pertains to the entire treatment unit can be copied and placed in each member's file. That way, if records are requested, subpoenaed, or reviewed by a family member, the files can be readily separated and confidences kept. Because therapy progress notes are subject to review by the client(s), subpoenaed, or requested by a third party, progress notes should be written as a clear, concise record of the facts, observations, and interventions to account for such releases. It is not uncommon for clinicians to keep two sets of books (e.g., the client's treatment record and the therapy notes). The therapy notes provide more subjective information and observations about the client(s) and the therapy process and are meant solely to aid the clinician. Even the Health Insurance Portability and Accountability Act (HIPAA) of 1996 makes a distinction between therapy notes and the client's treatment record.

Tasha Leroyce Banks

See also Best Interests of the Child; Court-Mandated Clients; Dual and Multiple Relationships; Duty to Warn and Protect; Elder Abuse; Ethical Codes; Ethical Decision-Making; HIPAA Standards; Informed Consent for Research; Informed Consent in Clinical Work; Legal Issues in Parenting; Mandated Reporter; No-Harm Contracts; No-Secrets Contracts; Release of Information for Couples and Families; Suicide; Therapeutic Alliance; Trust; Work Relationships

Further Readings

American Association of Marriage and Family Therapy. (n.d.). *Code of ethics.* Available at https://www.aamft.org/iMIS15/AAMFT/Content/legal_ethics/code_of_ethics.aspx

American Counseling Association. (n.d.). *2014 ACA code of ethics.* Available at https://www.counseling.org/resources/aca-code-of-ethics.pdf

Appelbaum, P. S., & Gutheil, T. G. (2006). *A clinical handbook of psychiatry and the law* (4th ed.). Baltimore, MD: Lippincott Williams & Wilkins.

Barsky, A. E. (2010). *Values and ethics in social work: An integrated approach from a comprehensive curriculum.* New York, NY: Oxford University Press.

Corey, G., Corey, M. S., & Callanan, P. (1998). *Issues and ethics in the helping profession* (5th ed.). Pacific Grove, CA: Brooks/Cole.

Hecker, L. (2010). *Ethics and professional issues in couple and family therapy.* New York, NY: Routledge.

Jacob, S., & Hartshorne, T. S. (2007). *Ethics and law for school psychologists* (5th ed.). Hoboken, NJ: Wiley.

Margolin, G. (1982, July). Ethical and legal considerations in marital and family therapy. *American Psychologist, 37*(7), 788–801.

Conflict in Couples and Families

Conflict in relationships involves serious disagreements or arguments and is typically a result of incompatible expectations, hopes, and/or goals. Conflicts are normal in relationships and, depending on how they are resolved, their resolution can help people become closer or can cause damage to relationships. Sometimes fundamental differences in views cannot be resolved, and so a couple or family instead sets goals to respect differences and agree to disagree. If conflict is experienced as a personal attack, rather than as differences, disputes may escalate and become entrenched in the relationship. Numerous theoretical premises have added to the understanding of conflict in couples and families. This entry discusses how family dynamics can contribute to conflict and some models for understanding what causes conflict in couples and families and how to resolve it.

Family Dynamics

Individuals learn from their families how to negotiate, resolve problems, and share emotions. The structure of the family, including family rules, forms the basis of learned patterns that often are the underlying factors in conflict for adult couples. In addition, conflict can arise in relationships in which two or more family members are overly close, a process Salvador Minuchin refers to as enmeshment. Richard Schwartz describes the unspoken or unresolved issues in relational patterns as one of the prime areas of conflict. Individuals carry into a new relationship or new family preconceived prior rules, roles, and patterns of communication. When conflict arises, using what they know from their past may or may not be healthy in the new relationship.

Starting a new relationship, individuals tend to not have much conflict and ignore or deny any problematic issues. However, once the couple evolves past the initial relationship phase, conflict may become pronounced. The next stage is how the couple works through the conflict. Dealing with family members of each partner often is a point of contention. Although there is a sense of loyalty to the partner, when disagreements arise, the well-known patterns learned as a child surface.

The entrance of a new member into an existing family creates a new beginning as roles and rules need to be reassessed. Thus, the family returns to the "forming stage" again. Norming occurs in time, and this will also establish the rules of how the family operates, including how conflict is managed. The ultimate goal of a family is to perform or work well as a unit. Self-differentiation, or forming the partnership by establishing a working system apart from each other's family from childhood, does occur and is seen as healthy.

Conflict and Transitions

The transitional stages of family life are often the times conflict occurs: birth, infancy, childhood, school, adolescence, leaving home, finding a partner, being a parent, being a grandparent, and dealing with old age. Transitions also include life situations that are sometimes out of one's control, including financial losses, chronic illnesses, and death. Conflicts in couples and families often occur due to miscommunication. Transition points are times when rules and relationships may need to change in order to meet the needs of individuals, the couple, and/or the family. For example, different rules may be needed for an adolescent who is going to high school and still in the home than for an adolescent who is leaving for college. Different views on how to renegotiate these rules and relationships may lead to conflict. Another example of a transition point is when a couple decides to move in together. They may have different ideas about roles, responsibilities, and how to manage outside relationships. Transition points may bring to the forefront topics about which people did not realize they disagreed.

Models for Understanding and Resolving Conflict

Gottman Method

Researchers such as John Gottman are providing knowledge about conflict and how clinicians can help couples and families understand conflict. For Gottman, the goal is helping clients learn to manage conflict rather than eliminating it. His research supports that approximately 65% of conflict in couples is unsolvable (cannot be completely resolved). Methods for working with couples and families to have successful relationships identify some agents of conflicts such as (1) criticism, (2) defensiveness, (3) contempt, and (4) stonewalling (ignoring attempts to resolve issues).

Each of these patterns is harmful to a relationship over long periods of time, but contempt is the most damaging, even over the short term. Criticism is a complaint about a partner with a comment about their personality. A simple complaint, without criticism, is considered appropriate feedback to another person. However, criticism in disagreements results in one feeling not good enough and generally rejected by the partner. Critical remarks point out what the other person is doing incorrectly and typically begin with the word "you never" or "you should" and/or attach an insult, such as "you are lazy." Defensiveness results from interactions whereby one protects the self by not accepting responsibility for one's actions. Even if a situation is not an individual's fault, the individual can accept his or her part in the interaction or at least acknowledge the other person's feelings. Contempt is expressed through verbal and nonverbal actions that convey that the other person is not as worthy as the person being contemptuous. Contempt can be conveyed through name calling, insinuating that someone is "less than" the partner (e.g. not as smart, not as competent, not as good of a person), or through nonverbal actions such as sneering. The behavior seemingly escalates and becomes more hurtful to the relationship. Lastly, stonewalling is when one partner has literally "checked out" of the conversation or is minimally present, both verbally and nonverbally.

Object Relations and Internal Objects

Another view of communication problems with couples and families is based on object relations theory. In this approach, people's goals and expectations of one another are formed by early experiences. Later in life the goal is to find a partner who can fulfill what was missing in earlier relationships. People look for in a partner what was most missed in relationships within families, such as belonging, being taken care of, or safety. This leads to individuals seeking fulfillment outside themselves rather than looking to their inner resources. As a result, an individual may expect and demand that a partner meet his or her needs. Expecting a partner to meet unmet emotional needs often leads to conflict in the relationship.

Bowenian Genograms

Murray Bowen believed patterns for handling emotional anxiety are passed down through generations. The lower one's level of differentiation (ability to balance closeness and distance; ability to separate intellect and emotion), the more likely one is to have conflict and not handle it well. Bowen used a genogram (a pictorial representation of family relationships across at least three generations) to do an honest appraisal of how themes and messages were passed down generations. His goal was to help people become more differentiated, to have an understanding of intergenerational patterns, and to communicate with others directly.

Long and Young Developmental Stages of Conflict

According to Lynn Long and Mark Young, conflict is likely to occur between couples at specific stages of a couple's development. The stages occur whether the partners are in a legal relationship or not. Being aware of typical developmental stages for a couple can help couples prepare to negotiate conflicts and assist both the couple and clinician in assessing the severity of conflict. The clinician can utilize his or her knowledge of the stages to design interventions for the couple.

Long and Young list four developmental stages of conflict: (1) early disagreement, (2) repeated conflict, (3) severe conflict, and (4) severed couple's relationship. The first stage is early disagreement and occurs when the duration of the relationship is six months or less. Anger is not entrenched in the couple's patterns, and they tend to have an easier time communicating. Thus, couples can repair the conflict, and change can occur. Stage two is repeated conflict in a relationship lasting more than six months. The couple still has open communication; however, blame and triangulation (pulling a third party into disagreements) become more pronounced. Stage three is severe conflict and is characterized by stress and anxiety. This stage also is marked by severe anger, and a lack of communication and trust. Stage four, severed relationship, is characterized by very poor or little communication, severe criticism and blame, and power struggles. Discussion is minimal. Separation or dissolution of the relationship is likely at this stage and, if the partners have children together, conflict may arise involving who the children will live with after the couple splits up.

Adlerian Birth Order

Alfred Adler believed some conflict may be due to personality characteristics related to one's birth order (oldest, middle child, or youngest). The oldest child tends to have characteristics of being in control and being organized. The middle child may attempt to be in charge and tries to find his or her own place in the family. The youngest child is often the negotiator or problem solver for conflicts and uses pleasing behaviors so siblings all are acknowledged.

Adler professed that our place within our families can be recognized and identified by our birth order. This idea can help to make sense of people's behavior in a relationship. For example, a partner who makes all the decisions and is rigid with rules may understand that the oldest in a family must be the leader. The awareness of birth order may help reduce conflict by adding a new dimension of self-awareness and provide information when a couple is in conflict. Adler also professed that the self has a need to belong. Understanding and communicating internal needs is positive communication and can lead to change.

Haley and Language of Change

Many issues couples and families identify as presenting problems have long been attributed to basic issues with financial stress, in-laws, children, and/or sex. Problems in these areas may occur due to a lack of meaningful communication. Creating a meaningful relationship is dependent on communication. Taking time to listen and ask appropriate questions of one another is time-consuming and often awkward. Jay Haley's work on language and how to create dialogues to indicate needs, wants, and desires sets the stage for change to occur. The premise is relationships are based on behaviors that follow rules. Thus, conflicts are issues with broken rules or changes that result in symptomatology. The problem a partner may express about the relationship may not be the core issue; for instance, an individual may complain about a partner forgetting to take out the garbage, when the underlying problem is that the individual feels the partner doesn't care about household responsibilities.

Disagreements about presenting problems are the core of many conflicts. Each partner may view the handling of the presenting problem from a different perspective. Each brings his or her own experiences to the relationship. Partners enter counseling often talking about what are perceived as here-and-now issues, but unresolved issues tend to surface quickly. Often the blame is on lack of communication or perceived inaccurate understandings.

Solution-Focused Communication Strategies

Solution-focused therapy, as Steve de Shazer has discussed, focuses on (1) what is the presenting issue, (2) when it has not been present, (3) presupposing what it would be like if it were not present (miracle question), and (4) practicing new behaviors.

One intervention of solution-focused therapy for presenting problems is working on clear communication with couples, families, and people in general. Using simple "I" statements, and thus owning one's feelings, is a pattern change and may lead partners away from blaming one another. Although conflict may still be present, the result is clearer communication.

Acknowledging that fear and anger coexist is an important tool for deconstructing miscommunication. Helping the couple and family use a genogram of "anger" can help look at where the themes and messages of anger or fear of communicating needs, wants, and desires has derived.

Assessing when the problem was not happening may also lead to looking at the positives. This is called reframing. Reframing is a powerful technique that can alter the seemingly harsh actions of a couple or family so they are manageable. For example, viewing "nagging" as a desire to be helpful can deescalate issues to formulate a new action plan or open up the possibility for change to occur. Another powerful set of tools using reframing is derived from a set of specific questions that is aimed at finding solutions based on what has worked in the past. Solution-focused therapy utilizes the "miracle question" as a way to look at what would be happening in the future if the complaint were no longer present, as well as searching for times when the complaint was not present.

Sandra Kakacek

See also Affect Regulation; Assertiveness; Communication in Couples and Families; Conflict Resolution; Conflict Styles; Confrontation; Interpersonal Violence; Marital Distress

Further Readings

Bandler, R., & Grinder, J. (1982). *Reframing: Neurolinguistic programming and the transformation of meaning.* Cupertino, CA: Real People Press.

de Shazer, S. (1985). *Keys to solution in brief therapy.* New York, NY: Norton.

Gottman, J. (1999). *The marriage clinic.* New York, NY: Norton.

Haley, J., & Richeport-Haley, M. (2007). *Directive family therapy.* New York, NY: Haworth.

Long, L. L., & Young, M. E. (2007). *Counseling and therapy for couples* (2nd ed.). Belmont, CA: Brooks/Cole.

Minuchin, S. (1974). *Families and family therapy.* Cambridge, MA: Harvard University Press.

Nichols, M. P. (2013). *Family therapy. Concepts and methods* (10th ed.). Boston, MA: Pearson.

Satir, V. (1972). *Peoplemaking.* Palo Alto, CA: Science and Behavioral Books.

Scharff, D. E., & Scharff, J. S. (1991). *Object relations couple therapy.* Northvale, NJ: Aronson.

Sweeney, T. J. (2009). *Adlerian counseling and psychotherapy* (5th ed.). New York, NY: Routledge.

Yalom, I. (1995). *The theory and practice of group psychotherapy.* New York, NY: Basic Books.

Conflict Resolution

Conflict resolution refers to the process by which a peaceful termination of conflict is realized. Relationship conflicts can be critical and defining events, and approaches to conflict management can either support or undermine a relationship. Although resolution implies the ending of a conflict, the concept of conflict resolution needs to embrace the idea that conflict is not only unavoidable, but also a critical, recurring, and defining part of most relationships. Understanding sources of conflict, and then emphasizing appropriate approaches and tools to deal with conflict, supports outcomes that deepen understanding and strengthen connections between people. This does not involve avoiding conflict, but rather approaching its resolution with a "softer edge" that supports a less polarized, more productive outcome. This entry describes sources of conflict in relationships, why conflict is so commonplace, the varying types of couple conflict styles, and intrapersonal and interpersonal methods for managing conflict.

Sources of Conflict

Conflict occurs when the wishes or desires of one individual differ from those of another. Because no two people are exactly alike, differences in what one individual wants or needs in comparison to the wants and needs of his or her partner are inevitable. Any wish, big or small, that cannot be realized is cause for conflict. Relational dialectics are one cause of conflict. Dialectics, the opposing tensions that exist between two people, include (for example) autonomy and connection, and openness and closeness. Mismatched needs for connection or independence in any given moment or on any given day can easily result in conflict. Similarly, individually defined needs for boundaries and privacy can lead to tension in a relationship. Importantly, these boundaries are diffuse and easily influenced by moment-to-moment variations in our physical and mental health. Lack of sleep, illness, anxiety, hunger, and stress are all examples of factors that may contribute to the development of conflict. The relationship tensions and conflicts resulting from both dialectics and our naturally fluctuating state of being deeply influence our connections to each other, and indeed, make us human. Understanding sources of conflict, and embracing these tensions as a natural part of our humanness, informs productive approaches to conflict management and resolution.

Work by researchers Julie Schwartz Gottman and John Gottman further supports the idea that the pursuit of resolution inside a conflict is often an unrealistic and misguided goal. They found that 69% of relationship conflict cannot be resolved. Focusing strictly on resolution to all conflict can lead to gridlock—a state of frustration and angst that is neither productive nor conducive to relationship building. For example, two individuals with different fundamental ideologies may never find a "solution" to their differences. The perpetual nature of this "unresolvable" conflict could easily become a divisive factor in the relationship. However, if these same individuals approach their ideologically based conflicts through a lens of compassion and understanding, they create opportunities to deepen connection and strengthen the relationship.

Conflict Styles

Regardless of the desired outcome for conflict, most individuals display consistent patterns in the way in which they approach conflict. Conflict and the styles individuals employ when approaching conflict have been studied for decades, resulting in a myriad of models and style categories. John Gottman has identified four styles in his work, three of which are considered functional (more likely to lead to successful relationship outcomes) and one dysfunctional (more likely to result in relationship instability). The three styles in the functional category are avoidant, volatile, and validating. Avoidant couples tend to minimize conflict by accepting differences and "agreeing to disagree." Volatile couples argue with passion and fervor and expend extensive energy trying to persuade each other.

Although this style might appear dysfunctional to some, the key to its functionality is that couples maintain more positive than negative interactions even in the midst of their strife. Validators are more careful and polite. They address conflict by making sure each other is understood, and they seek collaboration in their resolutions.

Conversely, hostile couples fail to maintain more positives than negatives in their conflict. Further, they employ contempt—name-calling and ill-spirited remarks that come from a place of superiority—in their arguments. A hostile style of conflict is often destructive and undermines relationship stability. Further, another destructive but common pattern is referred to as the *demand/withdraw* pattern. In this dynamic, one partner (the demander) is critical and makes "demands" on the other. The other partner "withdraws" in an attempt to avoid unpleasant confrontation. This avoidance, in turn, leads the demander to become more intent and thus leads to increased resistance from the withdrawer; a cyclical pattern that often escalates with destructive outcomes. One antidote to the demand/withdraw pattern is for the withdrawer to let his or her pursuer know that he or she needs a break. If the withdrawer can reassure his or her partner that he or she will indeed return after his or her defined reprieve, the pattern can be interrupted and the course has a chance to follow a more productive trajectory.

Conflict styles are undoubtedly important to consider as a way of understanding and predicting the way that partners will engage in conflict. Beyond prediction, however, are specific skills that can assist in the effective management, and sometimes resolution, of conflict. Both intrapersonal skills (those that an individual cultivates from within) and interpersonal skills (those that help to diffuse tension and foster effective communication between partners) emerge.

Intrapersonal Skills

Most of the time when we consider conflict resolution, we think of what visibly happens between two people, or what is observable. There is an intricate series of events that occur intrapersonally, however, before the observed conflict ever happens. The skills described here influence the ensuing conflict, and can sometimes prevent it from happening altogether. At the very least, practicing some of these skills can assist couples in creating a culture where conflict leads to deeper understanding, connection, and sometimes, resolution.

Humans have an inherent tendency toward assuming the worst of others and the best of themselves, termed a self-serving bias. When a self-serving bias appears in a relationship, one partner might attribute the behavior of the other to something negative—"he is late, he must have forgotten," "she is quiet, she must be angry at me," for example. Taking the positive perspective, or a relationship-serving perspective, gives the partner the benefit of the doubt. Instead of assigning blame or fault to a partner, the approach or attribution one makes is of concern and compassion. Committing to a relationship-serving bias, or positive perspective, as opposed to a self-serving bias, can take practice, but when done consistently partners feel more connected, understood, and validated. Research in the area of couple relationships suggests that a ratio of at least five positive interactions to every one negative interaction is necessary for maintaining relationship satisfaction. Negative events and interactions are so impactful in a relationship, that it takes at least five positive events or interactions (ideally more than five) to maintain a positive perspective, termed positive sentiment override. If this minimum ratio (5:1) is not met, the relationship is often riddled with what John Gottman calls *negative sentiment override.*

Even when positive sentiment override is present in a relationship, there will still be times when, during conflict, one or both partners become so physiologically aroused, or "flooded," that conflict resolution is difficult. During heated conflict, one or both partners can employ tools to soothe themselves and avoid *diffuse physiological arousal*—a state that occurs when emotional triggers are such that an individual's heart rate exceeds its average by 20 beats per minute or more. In this state, an individual typically finds it much more difficult to access solid reasoning abilities and to tap into compassion and humor, all known factors in higher functioning, productive styles of conflict.

Individuals can learn simple mindfulness techniques that will prevent them from moving into a diffuse state in the course of conflict. Mindfulness is a form of emotional regulation that involves focused attention on the present moment, and judgment-free acceptance of thoughts and feelings. Mindfulness-based practices are increasingly being utilized to address anxiety and depression. Moreover, mindfulness has been found to be very effective in reducing physiological arousal, a critical variable in the pursuit of conflict management and resolution. Further, individuals can practice mindfulness as a way of developing an awareness of idiosyncratic triggers and how these triggers lead to negative emotions that can be found physically in the body. Such awareness is a productive first step toward conflict-moderating behaviors and away from conflict-fueling behaviors. Participants in multiple research studies who practiced mindfulness techniques for only 5 minutes per day reported more positive relations with others (in addition to multiple other benefits) in just three weeks. Although there seem to be endless techniques available in the pursuit of mindfulness, studies have found that slowing the breath—a count of 4 on both inhale and exhale—is a simple and effective beginning exercise that can be done to moderate overall life stress (a contributor to conflict) as well as the physiological response that accompanies conflict.

Some couples counselors recommend owning a pair of pulse oximeters that partners wear during sessions that measure heart rate. When the heart rate reaches 100 beats per minute, the oximeter signals that the person is "flooded," at which point the session pauses and the therapist leads the person through a relaxation exercise that serves to bring the heart rate down and allow the person to re-engage in the session. Learning how to identify signs of flooding can facilitate productive conflict. Couples can learn to take a break from the conflict, practice self-soothing techniques such as deep breathing, and remain engaged in conversation that does not become escalated.

Accepting influence from one's partner, especially for men, is another intrapersonal skill that contributes significantly to relationship satisfaction and successful conflict resolution and management. Research shows that the most successful and fulfilling relationships demonstrate equality in gender roles, with both partners accepting influence from the other. An important component of conflict resolution is compromise. Couples who are skilled in the art of compromise value the perspective of their partner, and work together toward a solution that serves both partners. Accepting influence does not mean that one partner fully succumbs to the other's perspective, but that he or she can honor his or her beliefs and values, while also understanding the partner's perspective—a type of relationship empathy.

Interpersonal Skills

The intrapersonal skills outlined above are important to practice and integrate into a person's approach to conflict. Successfully taking the positive perspective, self-soothing and practicing mindfulness, and accepting influence will greatly improve a couple's ability to learn and implement the more concrete interpersonal skills described here.

The way that couples approach a conflict is predictive of the outcome; harsh beginnings ("you always," "you never," for example) lead to poor outcomes—blame, criticism, often accompanied by stonewalling, defensiveness, and so on. An important skill for couples to master when approaching conflict is a gentle "startup." The Gottmans propose that the first 3 minutes of a conversation predicts how well the discussion and the overall relationship will go—emphasizing how important this skill is to master. Guidelines for a gentle startup are as follows:

- Avoid blaming the partner by beginning statements with "I" instead of "you."
- Be specific about what is happening without assigning blame to the partner.
- Express what is needed in positive terms—say what *is* wanted instead of what *is not* wanted.

- Be polite.
- Notice what the partner does well, and tell him or her about it.
- The statement should follow the proceeding formula—"I feel _____ about _____. I need _____."

Learning to practice softened startups is integral to the next skill, which could perhaps be the most important skill that couples can learn for managing conflict—a form of active listening commonly referred to in the counseling literature as the speaker-listener technique, or the Gottman-Rapoport exercise. The exercise outlines specific roles that each partner is instructed to take during conflict. The couple first practices in session with a counselor's guidance, with the intention that the couple will integrate this style of dialogue into their conflicts at home. Before launching into a conflict, the couple's goal is to create a climate of understanding, compassion, and acceptance. With regard to the positive perspective described previously, when partners catch themselves attributing a positive trait to themselves, they should make an effort to make the same attribution toward their partner, and vice versa—when they notice a negative trait in their partner, make an effort to see the trait also within themselves—this fosters positive sentiment override, and also encourages taking responsibility for at least a part of the conflict. Before the conflict dialogue begins, each partner agrees to a role: the speaker or the listener. The rules for the speaker are as follows:

- Do not blame or criticize.
- Begin statements with "I" instead of "you."
- Express feelings.
- Be specific—avoid generalizations such as "always" or "never."
- Be clear about what is needed, in positive terms.

After the speaker has fully expressed his or her issue, the listener has an opportunity to respond, which entails only a reflection of understanding, not a rebuttal. The rules for the listener are as follows:

- Listen only to understand the partner's perspective, and focus on repeating the content of the message to display understanding.
- Listen for and reflect the feelings expressed in the speaker's message.
- Validate the speaker's message—"it makes sense to me that . . ." or "I understand that you feel that way because . . ."
- Ask questions only to deepen understanding of the speaker's perspective.

Both partners are encouraged to employ self-soothing practices during this exercise, as needed, and work to accept influence from each other throughout the process. Once the speaker feels heard and understood by the listener, the partners switch roles so that both get an equal chance to express their perspective, be heard, and feel understood. Only when these conditions are met can effective dialogue around a conflict issue occur.

While the skills discussed previously make a conflict encounter more successful, there will undoubtedly be times when partners behave badly toward each other and say things that hurt the other. When this happens, effective repair of the injury is an essential component of reconciliation. Specific practices that can assist in repairing a rupture that occurred during a conflict are as follows: share feelings, understand that each partner experienced the interaction from his or her own subjective reality—share that reality, identify anything that occurred during the conflict that triggered past injuries as a way of deepening the partner's understanding of the hurt, take responsibility for at least a part of the conflict, and finally, make plans as to how to behave differently next time. A productive conversation about a conflict that ended poorly gives the couple another chance at conflict resolution, and an opportunity to gain empathy for the other's experience after the conflict has subsided and both have had a chance to "cool down."

De-escalation is a set of interpersonal skills, and is an extension of the self-soothing techniques discussed earlier as an intrapersonal skill. Intimate partners become quite skilled at "pushing buttons" in their partners—couples know exactly what to do to "get a rise" out of their partners during conflict. What couples are less practiced at is calming each other during conflict to avoid escalation. The skills discussed previously (gentle startup and the speaker-listener technique) both serve to limit escalation, as well as maintain a positive perspective in most interactions. Just as it is important to notice flooding within oneself, partners can help notice flooding within each other and suggest that they take a break from the conflict, or pause to practice deep breathing together before continuing a conflict discussion. De-escalation is a set of skills that most people can benefit from learning and practicing, and the importance of employing these skills in an intimate relationship conflict cannot be understated.

Compromise, revisited here, is the last critical interpersonal skill discussed that can aid in conflict resolution. When it comes to conflict, most problems cannot be solved. As previously stated, only one third of all conflicts that occur between intimate partners are resolvable. Effective compromise allows couples a way to dialogue about perpetual problems that surface in their relationship. While the conflict will remain, productive dialogue around the issue will last for years, reduce the hurt around the issue, and allow each partner to hold onto what is most meaningful to them around the conflict. Compromise forces us to give something up, but allows us to keep what is most treasured and rooted in our beliefs and values. The major components of compromise that couples must consider in order to be effective are to (1) each reflect on areas of flexibility—where is each partner willing to bend, and what areas are absolutely inflexible; (2) explore what they agree about; (3) identify any common goals the couple can work toward; (4) work together to accomplish shared goals; (5) identify a temporary compromise; (6) identify feelings that the couple share; and (7) determine how each partner can help the other meet the deeper need present within the conflict.

It is essential that couples possess certain skills that will assist them in managing and resolving the inevitable conflicts that will occur throughout their relationship. Beyond the scope of this discussion, however, are relationship-enhancing techniques and ways of being that "prime" the relationship for successful conflict management. Maintaining closeness and intimacy, making time for fun, mutual respect and admiration, and responding to each other's needs for attention and affection are but a sampling of the ways that couples can prevent really detrimental conflicts from occurring. When it comes to conflict between intimate partners, it is not about win or lose.

Veronica I. Johnson and Sara Polanchek

See also Conflict in Couples and Families; Conflict Styles; Gottman Method Couples Therapy; Mindfulness and Couples

Further Readings

Erbert, L. A. (2000). Conflict and dialectics: Perceptions of dialectical contradictions in marital conflict. *Journal of Social and Personal Relationships, 17*(4–5), 638–659.

Gehart, D. R. (2012). *Mindfulness and acceptance in couple and family therapy.* New York, NY: Springer Science & Business Media.

Gottman, J., & Silver, N. (2015). *The seven principles for making marriage work: A practical guide from the country's foremost relationship expert.* New York, NY: Harmony.

Holman, T. B., & Jarvis, M. O. (2003). Hostile, volatile, avoiding, and validating couple-conflict types: An investigation of Gottman's couple-conflict types. *Personal Relationships, 10*(2), 267–282.

Ladd, P. D. (2007). *Relationships and patterns of conflict resolution: A reference book for couples counseling.* Lanham, MD: University Press.

Conflict Styles

Conflict is part of life because people are all different and discrepancies in values and expectations are typical. Conflict involves disagreement between people and can exist in any situation where there is a difference of opinions, feelings, or needs. People have different ways to deal with conflict depending of their life histories and personalities. In the 1970s, Kenneth Thomas and Ralph Kilmann identified five main styles of dealing with conflict. The Myers-Briggs Type Indicator is a personality assessment that has been used to understand conflict style differences. This entry discusses the conflict that occurs in adult, intimate relationships, with a focus on how attachment theory explains the different behaviors that partners exhibit during conflicts and steps that people can take to change the behavior patterns associated with their attachment style.

Conflict occurs regularly in most relationships. Some people seem to be inclined to resolve conflict easily while for others that is not the case. During conflicts some people bicker, argue, or become insistent about their point of view while others become silent and withdrawn. Some try to convince the other party that their way is best by ignoring or demeaning the other's perspective; others always accommodate or give in to keep the peace. Conflict, however, does not have to be destructive to an intimate relationship. When people have the appropriate skills, conflict may even facilitate the development and maintenance of intimacy and satisfaction in a relationship. Without these skills, conflict can increase distress and create negative cycles that people can't break by themselves.

Using Attachment Theory to Understand Conflict

Attachment theory provides an explanation of human bonding and can be used to explain why people behave the way they do in conflict. It provides reasons why certain people navigate conflict and grow from it and others get hurt and stuck in it. According to attachment theory there are four types of attachment styles that help to explain and predict people's thoughts, feelings, and behavior in conflict situations. An attachment style is not a diagnosis or a mental illness, but identifying a person's attachment style can help explain that person's conflict style and how it relates to a positive or negative outcome to a conflict.

Overview of Attachment Styles

Research on adult attachment is influenced by the idea that there is a link between the emotional bond that develops between a child and parent or primary caregiver during childhood and that between adults later in life. There are different types of attachment depending on the quality of main relationships throughout life: the secure or optimally healthy attachment and various types of insecure attachment (anxious/ambivalent, avoidant/dismissive, and fearful/disorganized). Each attachment style involves different ways of manifesting and relating. People with different attachment styles perceive situations in different and often opposing manners: They pay attention to diverse aspects of situations, and they interpret them differently. Even their brain activity is often remarkably different.

Attachment style influences the ability to build or maintain successful relationships and to be healthy, happy, and balanced in life. In conflict resolution, attachment style is responsible for the ability to maintain emotional balance and the ability to take care of others and oneself. It has been estimated that just over 50% of people have a secure attachment style; the remainder have attachment styles that make it more difficult to deal successfully with conflict. In a study by Cindy Hazan and Phillip Shaver in 1987, 56% of respondents identified themselves as secure, while 25% identified as avoidant and 19% as ambivalent/anxious.

Attachment in early relationships influences brain development. It helps shape affect regulation, problem-solving skills, capacity for closeness and separation, empathy, and communication skills. When in conflict, securely attached people tend to promote communication and closeness while still allowing for separation times. Because they are in tune with their own feelings and needs, they can also acknowledge and validate the other party's, and are able to compromise in ways that benefit the relationship without losing themselves.

People with an insecure attachment style tend to have a more restricted ability to deal with conflict. They get stuck in patterns that tend to create more distance in their relationship over time. Insecure attachment styles are associated in general with poorer conflict resolution skills. Those with an anxious style tend to worry about the relationship and monitor it too closely. They want a close relationship, but they are afraid of losing it; they tend to pursue others when there are perceived problems in a relationship. People with avoidant styles tend to minimize the need for relationships and are afraid of being too close to others; they tend to distance themselves from others when there are perceived problems in a relationship. Disorganized style is a result of abuse and trauma, and it is not discussed further in this entry. Couples with insecure attachment styles will often include one who has an anxious style and one who has an avoidant style. These styles may manifest in a pursuer/distance pattern, which causes relational problems.

Manifestations of Anxious and Avoidant Styles

When couples experience conflict they tend to automatically function from their attachment style. The problem with having one person with an anxious style and one with an avoidant style is that they tend to antagonize one another. When they go into protection mode, the partner with the anxious style will focus more on intimacy and the partner with the avoidant style will focus more on independence, leaving little room for negotiation. When in conflict, people with anxious style tend to feel intense feelings of abandonment, anxiety, and anger with a propensity to externalize them. People with avoidant style tend to have more intense feelings of numbness and disconnection, with an inclination to internalize them and take an offended position. In terms of specific behaviors, anxious style manifests by pursuing, coercing, and manipulating the partner into displaying whatever thoughts, feelings, or behaviors they need to experience intimacy or reconnection. People with anxious style tend to focus on feelings and values (maximization of feelings). Avoidant style, on the other hand, manifests in behaviors such as withdrawing, lack of warmth and support, and excessive judgment. People with avoidant style tend to focus on facts and logic (minimization of feelings).

When coping with stress, anxious individuals tend to use emotions as their main tool and tend to sustain them or even exaggerate them. They tend to overemphasize feelings of helplessness and vulnerability, which usually interferes with their ability to problem-solve and increases the experience of negative emotions about themselves and the world. Anxious individuals have a poor ability to suppress separation-related thoughts and tend to ruminate and catastrophize, or fixate on the worst-possible outcome, behaviors that often become detrimental to the individual and the relationship. However, they also tend to be more intuitive and able to detect subtle information. They tend to be more empathic and supportive of the other person's distress.

In contrast, avoidant individuals in a stressful situation tend to detach and rely on distancing, which is also problematic for the individual and the relationship. The person tends to lose a sense of connectedness, which can make it more difficult to achieve emotional regulation. Moreover, avoidant people tend to view emotions in a negative way and see expression of weakness or vulnerability as incompatible with their desire for self-reliance. In their effort to maintain a deactivated attachment system, they tend to promote problem-solving and disregard emotions. In this way, they refuse to care for and support the other party, which usually elicits more anger in the anxious person. However, they may also be able to remain more steady during troubled times and can be effective at problem-solving.

Anxious people tend to retrieve more painful memories from childhood and overreact to situations that might not be a threat, but are perceived in their cognitive structure as such. Avoidant people tend to block painful memories or record fairly shallow ones. They present low levels of self-reported anger while having high levels of physiological arousal and facial expressions.

Changing Patterns in Relationships

Attachment theory, although it initially developed as a theory to understand the relationship between children and their parents or early caretakers, can be used to understand the development of attachment in adult, intimate relationships. While there is some correlation between the attachment style to one's parents and one's style of attachment to a partner, people can change their way of relating. Research has indicated that whether people who had an insecure attachment with their parents as children can go on to develop what psychologists call "earned secure attachment" depends largely on their understanding of their early experiences. People with an anxious or avoidant style can learn to recognize their patterns and work to change them. There are certain patterns that people with an avoidant or anxious attachment style tend to default to when in conflict. There are also changes they can make so they do not fall into a cycle of pursuing and distancing.

Some typical reactions from people with an avoidant style include the following:

- Brushes off a partner's emotional needs.
- Makes the other person feel needy, inadequate, or foolish.
- Responds to the other person only factually and doesn't take emotions into consideration.
- Cannot get in touch with what is really bothering them.

People with avoidant style can try to keep emotionally present, be empathic, and restrain from offering immediate logical or practical solutions.

Some typical reactions from people with an anxious style include the following:

- Becomes flooded with emotions.
- Thinks in terms of black and white.
- Attacks partner.
- Wants to solve conflict immediately.

People with an anxious style can restrain from attacking or manipulative behavior. They can take time to calm down and assess the situation in a more realistic manner in order to regulate emotions and engage in productive dialogue.

Isabel B. Kirk

See also Communication Errors/Problems in Couples and Families; Conflict in Couples and Families; Confrontation; Family Stress; Intimacy, Specific Threats to; Nonverbal Communication; Stress Management

Further Readings

Becker-Phelps, L. (2014). *Insecure in love: How anxious attachment can make you feel jealous, needy, and worried and what you can do about it.* Oakland, CA: New Harbinger.

Cassidy, J., & Shaver, P. R. (2010). *Handbook of attachment, Second Edition: Theory, research, and clinical applications.* New York, NY: Guilford Press.

Eaker, B. W. (2010). *Make up, don't break up.* Avon, MA: Adams Media.

Johnson, S. (2013). *Love sense: The revolutionary new science of romantic relationships.* New York, NY: Little, Brown.

Levine, A., & Heller, R. (2010). *Attached: The new science of adult attachment and how it can help you find and keep love.* New York, NY: Penguin.

Lewis, T., Amini, F., & Lannon, R. (2001). *General theory of love.* New York, NY: Vintage.

Siegel, D. J. (2012). *The developing mind: How relationships and the brain interact to share who we are.* New York, NY: Guilford Press.

Sroufe, L. A. (1997). *Emotional development: The organization of emotional life in the early years.* New York, NY: Cambridge University Press.

Tatkin, S. (2012). *Wired for love: How understanding your partner's brain and attachment style can help you defuse conflict and build a secure relationship.* Oakland, CA: New Harbinger Publications.

Weinhold, J. B., & Weinhold, B. K. (2008). *Counterdependency: The flight from intimacy.* Novato, CA: New World Library.

Confrontation

Confrontation refers to challenging an individual's, couple's, or group's behaviors or thoughts. In therapy, confrontation often includes the therapist asking clients to identify self-defeating patterns of thoughts or behaviors that may negatively impact interpersonal relationships or personal safety. Confrontation also includes feedback to the clients about their impact on the therapist. It is important for therapists to be able to confront clients at times in order to help clients and therapy progress. This entry describes confrontation as it relates to the interaction between client and therapist, ways to confront, and the impact on relationships.

The Importance of Confrontation

Confrontation is important because it is used to identify inconsistencies in beliefs, actions, or words. For example, a couple says they want to increase intimacy but they refuse to spend time alone with each other. The therapist may point out this inconsistency in an attempt to help the couple recognize that their behavior is not consistent with their desired goal. It is important for the therapist to use caution when confronting clients to prevent possible criticism, shame, or judgment. Confrontation helps individuals separate who they are from what they think they should be; therefore, the individual's reality is separated from expectations. Since confrontation can be recursive, both clients and therapist can experience confrontation; that is, the therapist may confront the client and the client may confront the therapist.

Clients may not always be aware of their inconsistencies, so when confrontation takes place, they are provided an opportunity to recognize manipulations and unhealthy communication patterns in their relationships. To identify contradictions and effectively increase awareness of the clients, the therapist can engage in gentle confrontation. Confrontation helps clients recognize consequences of disruptive behavior and take personal ownership of feelings and actions. Although confrontation can enhance the therapeutic alliance (relationship), they are not directly related to each other.

While it is important for the therapist to engage in confrontation soon after the client demonstrates maladaptive behavior, the therapist must be careful with the timing of confrontation. Establishing rapport is essential for clients to be receptive to confrontation and should be avoided during initial stages of therapy (e.g., during the intake session). The decision to use confrontation should be based on the therapeutic process and the relationship between therapist and client. Confrontation that is untimely may elicit feelings of anger and defensiveness in clients. For example, when clients demonstrate strong defenses, appear unwilling to confront their issues, or are behaving in highly maladaptive ways, the therapist should avoid engaging in confrontation.

Common Discrepancies

Clients may experience a variety of conflicts and discrepancies about their views of the world, past experiences, internal messages, and behaviors. First, incongruence may occur between verbal and nonverbal messages. Clients may be willing to verbalize a plan of action but lack the necessary skills to make their nonverbal messages congruent. For example, when a son is discussing his sexual orientation, he may laugh while explaining how painful it is to have an open discussion with his parents and siblings. Second, couples and families may encounter discrepancies between what they say and what is actually done. Clients may be able to come up with ideas, plans, and ways to correct behavior while talking with the therapist. However, there may be some challenge when it comes to actual implementation. For example, a couple may state that their goal is to improve intimacy but they never complete homework assignments of setting time aside each week to spend time alone with each other.

Another discrepancy occurs when clients share beliefs that conflict with experiences. Couples and family members may share core values and beliefs about their lives and how their experiences match these beliefs. However, beliefs are not always congruent with experiences, and this may negatively impact the therapeutic progress. For example, parents may express their belief in sobriety but have a glass of wine every night at dinner with their children.

A fourth example of discrepancy is between personal experiences and future plans. Clients may experience conflict between what they experience and how they intend to continue living their lives. For example, distress may arise between a couple due to financial concerns; however, during therapy they mention current plans to take a cruise for relaxation and purchase a time-share in another country.

Process of Confronting

When a therapist identifies discrepancies to confront, there are steps to consider when offering this to clients. First, it is important to listen carefully to the issue being presented, gain some understanding of the situation, and be sure of having rapport. A therapist must consider whether it is the appropriate time to confront and how it may impact the therapeutic relationship. The second point of consideration is how to present the confrontation to clients so they are receptive to it. The therapist can use open-ended questions (e.g., "Help me understand what you mean when you say you feel conflicted"), reflect feeling (e.g., "If I heard you right, you feel frustrated because you don't think you are able to communicate effectively and this brings on feelings of rejection and inadequacy because your partner complains a lot about your behavior"), paraphrase (e.g., "Life seems to be very complicated at this time because you have increased responsibilities but you still want free time to socialize with friends"), and reflect meaning (e.g., "It sounds as if the ability to voice your own opinion means you will be rejected").

After considering the timing of the confrontation and presenting it to clients, the next step is to observe their response. Clients may accept or reject the confrontation based on their readiness to accept their current situation. When clients accept the confrontation, the therapist should gradually encourage them to consider alternative thoughts and behaviors. If clients reject the confrontation, the therapist should not force the point but instead acknowledge the resistance and make another attempt in a gentle and caring manner.

Finally, the therapist should follow up with the clients after confrontation has occurred. The therapist may engage in further exploration of the topic, clarification of any questions or concerns, and process new insight gained by the client. Follow-up should be done whether the client accepts or rejects the confrontation.

Using Immediacy

Immediacy involves directly addressing feelings, thoughts, attitudes, and behaviors demonstrated in therapy. The most effective way to integrate immediacy in confrontation is to conduct it in the present moment, the here and now in the session. Immediacy also involves being in the moment with clients and dealing with what therapist and client are experiencing in that moment. For example, the therapist may say, "I notice you slouched your shoulders when you started to talk about your relationship with your mother. Would you like to tell me what you feel right now?" Another example from a therapist's perspective may be, "I'm wondering if you are telling me this because you think it is what I expect to hear, or if this is truly what you are experiencing in this moment."

Immediacy can be useful in situations where the therapy session is stagnant or when there is apparent tension between clients or between clients and therapist. Immediacy may also be effective in dealing with transference and countertransference issues, and when there is incongruence between words and actions in session. The therapist may also use immediacy to discuss the client–therapist relationship.

Using immediacy helps remove roadblocks hat may potentially harm the therapy process. Immediacy may also help clients gain insight into how their discrepancies impact their lives. Confrontation and immediacy teach clients how to become more aware of the dangers of maladaptive behaviors and how to address them accordingly. Through the use of appropriate immediacy in session, the therapist can model interpersonal interactions that clients can use outside of the therapeutic relationship.

Setting Boundaries

For confrontation to be effective and beneficial, the client and therapist should establish boundaries to protect themselves. Boundaries may include identifying a time and place for discussion, persons to be involved, and how long each person should speak. Setting boundaries may also define what will not be tolerated. This may be an agreement that there be no obscene language, no shouting, no physical abuse, and no interruption while the other person is speaking.

Boundaries can be set for physical, emotional, spiritual, environmental, financial, and sexual needs. Because our boundaries help keep us safe, it is important to remember their value when engaging in confrontation. Boundaries are not set to punish others, and establishing them is not considered a selfish act; instead, it is a way to increase feelings of self-worth and self-respect, create opportunities for healthy communication, and practice healthy assertiveness. Boundary-setting can be taught in session with the therapist in order to give clients additional skills for improving interpersonal relationships outside of therapy sessions.

Resistance in Therapy

Couples and families seeking treatment usually lack some skills necessary for a healthy, balanced life. Clients seek help from their therapist to deal with problems and to find solutions for a better way of living. Sometimes, clients are unsure about the process of change and may have doubts about their abilities to change, or the abilities of their partner and family members. The experience of resistance in therapy can become the coping mechanism for clients as the anxiety over the change process may prevent them from following through with the treatment plan or therapeutic goals.

For this resistance to be confronted, the therapist must seek to understand what the clients are experiencing. A key factor in removing obstacles to treatment is the clients' willingness to facilitate change and be open to suggestions. This change can be behavioral, cognitive, or affective, and these changes can be made individually or as part of a system. Occasional signs of resistance with treatment goals can be expected as clients engage in a shifting of norms and behaviors.

When examining resistance, it is useful to consider not only the circumstances of the clients but also the execution of the therapeutic approach by the therapist. Clients may demonstrate resistance by refusing to complete homework assignments or other between-session assignments, unwillingness to actively engage in therapeutic goals, and reluctance to gain independence outside of the therapeutic sessions. When the therapist engages in confrontation in these situations, consideration should be given to the function that the resistance serves for the clients, the fears that support the resistance, possible discrepancies, and the client's ability to process and engage in the change process.

Ethical Considerations

Working with couples and families can involve volatile situations, and therapists must ensure that they conduct themselves in a professional and ethical manner. The purpose of confrontation should not be for the therapist to vent personal frustrations, as the needs of the client are always the higher priority. Cultural, religious, and spiritual aspects of the client must be considered before confrontation is attempted. It is also crucial for therapists to understand that they should avoid using confrontation techniques they are unfamiliar with or have no training in. If the therapist has doubts or challenges, a supervisor should be consulted.

Karisse A. Callender

See also Anger Management; Boundaries; Conflict Resolution; Conflict in Couples and Families; Homework Assignments in Therapy; Therapeutic Alliance; Triangulation

Further Readings

Adler, G., & Myerson, P. G. (1973). *Confrontation in psychotherapy.* New York, NY: Science House.

Kiesler, D. J. (2001). Therapist countertransference: In search of common themes and empirical references. *Journal of Clinical Psychology, In Session: Psychotherapy in Practice, 57,* 1053–1063.

Leavitt, J. P. (2010). *Common dilemmas in couple therapy.* New York, NY: Routledge.

Newman, C. F. (1994). Understanding client resistance: Methods for enhancing motivation to change. *Cognitive and Behavioral Practice, 1,* 47–69.

Patterson, J., Williams, L., Grauf-Grounds, C., & Chamow, L. (1998). *Essential skills in family therapy: From the first interview to termination.* New York, NY: Guilford Press.

Safran, J. D., Crocker, P., McMain, S., & Murray, P. (1990). Therapeutic alliance rupture as a therapy event for empirical investigation. *Psychotherapy, 27,* 154–165.

Sanford, K. (2014). A latent change score model of conflict resolution in couples: Are negative behaviors bad, benign, or beneficial? *Journal of Social and Personal Relationships, 31,* 1068–1088.

Young, M. E. (2013). *Learning the art of helping: Building blocks and techniques* (5th ed.). Boston, MA: Pearson.

Conjoint Family Therapy

Therapy can be done with individuals, couples, and/or families. When a clinician sees one family in therapy it is called *conjoint family therapy.* Including families as a part of therapy is a core part of most family therapy approaches. Family therapy is based on systems theory, which is the idea that one must look at parts of a system (in this case a family) in relation to the whole. Therefore, an individual behavior, perceptions, and feelings are inseparable from the interactions of functioning of the family system. If one holds the idea that an individual is inseparable from his or her family, then it makes sense to see the whole family in session. In this entry, a brief review of conjoint family therapy and how it is a core part of family therapy are discussed.

History

The term *conjoint family therapy* was coined in 1959 by Don D. Jackson, the founding director of the Mental Research Institute in Palo Alto, California. In 1959, Jackson published an article titled "Family Interaction, Family Homeostasis and Some Implications for Conjoint Family Psychotherapy." Jackson, and others, believed that there was a relationship between mental illness and family interaction. They hypothesized that families caused and/or held the key to resolution of an individual's problems. Therefore, he thought that it was helpful to see an identified patient (the person referred to therapy) in the context of family, which is the functioning natural group the patient lives and/or interacts in. In conjoint family therapy a therapist would approach a family as a unit (doing therapy with all the family members present) to resolve problems and work with the family using psychoeducational conversations, demonstrations, and interactions, rather than seeing a patient/client individually.

Along with Jackson, Virginia S. Satir, who was trained in social work and was instrumental in conducting family therapy research at the Mental Research Institute (MRI), participated in several family therapy projects with the purpose of researching ways to help ameliorate family issues. Her initial title at the MRI was director of Training, Family Project. After years of listening to family calls about a symptomatic family member, Satir wrote that she decided to research how the family influences individual client issues. The term *conjoint family therapy* was defined by Satir to denote the therapist actively directing a conversation with the family and involving every member in a therapeutic manner in treatment sessions with the intention to provide symptom relief for an identified patient. Her underlying belief that patients could be better served if the entire family participated in therapy was considered novel and innovative for its time. In addition to writing books to detail the philosophy and techniques of conjoint family therapy, Satir traveled throughout the United States and internationally to demonstrate family therapy practices using volunteer families.

Satir's three books detailing the strategies and evolution of the conjoint family therapy approaches were written to teach students and therapists how to take an active role in sessions by using exercises and directive techniques. She referred to this therapy as "larger systems" approach, in which a therapist would engage an entire family in treatment to provide support for change in the family system. This approach focused on assisting an identified patient as a person in the family rather than seeing a patient or client in individual sessions with an isolated problem. In their respective writings, both Jackson and Satir identified conjoint family therapy as a "conceptual frame" that encouraged utilizing families and their interactions in therapy.

Conjoint Family Therapy as a Part of Family Therapy

Doing conjoint family therapy is a hallmark of many family therapy approaches. Family therapists tend to find it useful to observe and intervene in family patterns in session rather than having an individual recount family interaction in session. For example, in structural family therapy, the therapist assesses family structure (family rules, boundaries, hierarchy, and interactions) through observing how families interact in session. The therapist also has them "enact" specific family interactions in session and then intervenes in those interactions in order to alter some aspect of their family structure. Another example is in experiential family therapy, where the therapist has the family interact and identify and express their feelings in the moment. The therapist assists the family in session to learn to be vulnerable with one another and make it safe to express one's feelings, wants, and desires. Regardless of the particular family therapy model, all share in common the idea that it is useful to have a family in session. The family is the system in which an identified patient is most immediately embedded. Each individual both influences and is influenced by the family system. This recursive influence can sometimes be the source of maintaining problems and the source of possible solutions. Even if an individual changes, going back to the same family interactions and family rules tends to make long-lasting change more challenging. In order to make change more viable, from a family systems perspective, means including families in therapy.

Barbara A. Mahaffey

See also Systems Theory; Virginia Satir Model

Further Readings

Bodin, A. M. (1968). Conjoint family therapy. In W. E. Vinacke (Ed.), *Readings in general psychology*. New York, NY: American Book Company.

Satir, V. S. (1967). *Conjoint family therapy: A guide to theory and technique.* Palo Alto, CA: Science and Behavior Books.

Satir, V. S. (1972). *Peoplemaking*. Palo Alto, CA: Science and Behavior Books.

Satir, V. S. (1983). *Conjoint family therapy*. Palo Alto, CA: Science and Behavior Books.

Satir, V. S. (1988). *The new peoplemaking*. Mountain View, CA: Science and Behavior Books.

Virginia Satir Global Network: http://www.satirglobal.org

CONSTRUCTIVISM

We live in an interpreted world. Constructivism is a theory of knowledge that postulates human beings construct new knowledge rather than receive it. This knowledge construction occurs within a social context. New knowledge and meaning are generated by the interaction of an individual's experience, ideas, and relationships with others. Constructivism has gained traction in the postmodern era and has influenced many disciplines. Constructivist roots may be found in Western philosophies (e.g., the work of Immanuel Kant), Asian philosophies (Buddhism), education (the work of John Dewey, Paulo Freire), 20th-century psychology (Alfred Adler, Jean Piaget, Lev Vygotsky, George Kelly), contemporary psychology (Michael Mahoney, Robert Neimeyer), and in other disciplines such as cultural anthropology. The assumptions of a constructivist approach may offer many opportunities relative to therapeutic work with clients. This approach is inherently positive, developmental, collaborative, and flexible. It recognizes that we are resilient and capable of growth. Such qualities make it particularly well suited for working with couples and families, where consideration of narrative and context is needed.

The Foundations of Constructivism

Constructivist ideas may be found throughout history across many different schools of thought. For example, in synthesizing rationalism and empiricism the philosopher Immanuel Kant (1724–1804) noted we do not have a direct way of knowing an external reality; rather, we use internal cognitive processes to understand experiences. Therefore, perception becomes critical in how we process outside stimuli. Siddhartha Gautama (c. 560–480 B.C.E.), known as the Buddha (meaning "awakened one" or "enlightened one), also emphasized cognitive processes in addition to already possessed knowledge throughout his teachings. Ideas such as these point to the necessity of a person's internal state, and their perception of events, as important contributors to the process of understanding the world.

John Dewey (1859–1952) was an American philosopher, psychologist, and education reformer. His writings on education contributed to an early foundation for constructivist thinking. He believed teachers should not simply impart information to students but use their position as people with greater knowledge to help guide students and create new experiences for them. These experiences with other people help form the space in which growth may take place. Dewey took a pragmatic approach in his work and called for something greater than what he termed the "spectator view" of learning, whereby the acquisition of knowledge is akin to a spectator sport: People learn by watching. Dewey recognized that this was a passive approach and that the individual watching has no impact on the outcome. Therefore, he asserted that people should be active participants in the game. In doing so we assume a specific role and also learn while utilizing knowledge we already possess. The process of learning becomes interactive and more highly enriched. He believed this approach results in becoming more proficient at a task while achieving a greater understanding of it as well.

Jean Piaget (1896–1980), a Swiss developmental psychologist, is generally credited with formalizing the "theory" of constructivism and is often referred to as its founder. He studied the play of children and refuted earlier views that regarded play as unimportant. His major contributing concept is the process of accommodation and assimilation as a means for constructing knowledge from experiences. Through assimilation a person takes in new information and integrates it with his or her knowledge base; new information is incorporated within an existing framework without changing that framework. In contrast, accommodation forces an individual to change their knowledge structure. If a person has an experience that does not fit into existing knowledge, he or she experiences incongruence and must change the framework so the new information can be integrated. Thus, through the process of accommodating or reframing that new experience, people learn and grow. Similarly, Piaget discussed the importance of schemata. A *schema* is a cognitive framework that helps individuals perceive and make sense of what is happening around them. An example of a schema is the *just world hypothesis*, "good things happen to good people, bad things happen to bad people." When something happens that contradicts this framework, a person must have a way to make sense of it. The disruption results in accommodation and the changing of the particular schema in question. This process is under constant revision as people interact with the world and establish practice and complexity with knowledge creation.

Lev Vygotsky (1896–1934) was a Russian psychologist and contemporary of Piaget. He shared many of Piaget's assumptions and was also interested in how children learned. His best-known construct is the *zone of proximal development*, an idea that is still very much in use within modern elementary education. This idea refers to the gap that exists between what people can do without help and what they can do with it. Support is needed from an adult with greater information in order to get the student to reach for knowledge just outside of what the student already knows. The coaching or scaffolding that takes place during such exchanges illustrates the importance of interpersonal interaction for learning within a social context; scaffolding involves the inclusion of enough information and support early on so that the learner is equipped with the knowledge once they are on their own. It also magnifies the importance of adults in creating an environment suited to development and transmission of cultural understanding.

Paulo Freire (1921–1997), a Brazilian educator, worked with literacy programs and was concerned about the systemic nature of education and its ability to inadvertently lead to oppression. His pedagogical views were informed by and further promoted constructivism. Freire focused on the role of experience in learning. In *Pedagogy of the Oppressed*, he explained that education requires an interaction between people and their world. Like Dewey, he asserted experience plays an integral role in the construction of knowledge. His approach emphasized critical thinking and the promotion of problem-posing rather than a banking approach. He believed this form of traditional education, in which students are viewed as essentially empty containers into which educators "deposit" knowledge, tends to diminish critical thinking and knowledge ownership, eventually reinforcing oppression. In such a system educators are the authority. Students are passive and ultimately adapt to the world as presented to them.

His alternative of problem-posing recognizes the role of students' prior knowledge as they are encouraged to address problems utilizing internal resources. This approach creates and promotes dialogue between teacher and student. In such a system, the learner becomes an active participant and knowledge is not simply provided but is created through a shared, collaborative process.

Theoretical Assumptions

Since much of the aforementioned foundation stems from education, constructivism is often mistakenly thought of as a pedagogic approach. However, it is more a theory that describes how learning and growth take place. In fact, a major criticism of constructivism relates to its philosophical nature and the difficulty of measuring associated outcomes. How does one determine more correct or better ways of behaving, for example? At the same time, constructivism provides a means for exploring these very questions.

Constructivism posits that reality and truth are constructed by each individual within a social context. In such a framework there is not one "truth" to be discovered or taught. Rather, many truths are generated. In a sense, information is invented, and learning is an extension of that construction. There is a continual reworking and re-imagining of information.

This means knowledge is understood as subjective. There is also a rejection of absolutes. Perception is more important than an objective reality. The belief that objectivity can explain everything is discarded. Knowledge from this perspective is self-organized. This also means that information and knowledge must remain tentative. Everything is open to interpretation based on further experience, and there is not one single or correct way. Ongoing revision of knowledge becomes a rule.

As mentioned earlier, learning becomes an active process rather than a passive one. The individual is no longer an empty container or spectator. Collaboration is necessary in order to achieve a complex understanding of the world and where we fit into it. This understanding is relational and requires interaction with our surroundings.

This approach respects multiple perspectives and ill-defined problems. Individual processes in concert with a person's social-cultural surroundings are needed to acquire knowledge. This interplay is also necessary for the construction of meaning. This meaning-making allows for the generation of unique answers to complex problems.

Constructivism and Counseling

George Kelly (1905–1967) was instrumental in bridging the gap between constructivist practice in education and its use within a psychotherapeutic context. Kelly was a psychologist and is best known for his *Personal Construct Psychology*. He was interested in how we perceive the world around us. The roles of cognitive processes were emphasized due to the belief that our expectations may alter how we feel and act. His therapeutic approach aimed to help clients uncover how they view the world. The creation of personal constructs relative to what we choose to pay attention to may provide insights into our attitudes, beliefs, and personality. He developed these ideas during the mid-20th century, although it took decades before they were widely considered. Currently, constructivism is receiving increased attention in the psychotherapeutic community.

Constructivism can be thought of philosophically or as a state of mind. However, there are several natural connections with the humanistic, cognitive, and existential approaches. Additionally, the constructivist framework is well suited to the counseling environment, where participants deal with multiple perspectives, diverse worldviews, and ill-defined problems. Within therapeutic work, individuals construct their own selves through the interpretations they make and the actions they take.

An interesting aspect of constructivism relative to counseling is that many practitioners already utilize parts without even realizing it. Many theoretical approaches embody ideals common to constructivist thinking. For example, drawing from education, we know that working from this approach means that we do not "deposit" information into an empty container (the aforementioned banking approach). Rather, the teacher recognizes the unique knowledge and gifts that each student already possesses. The current knowledge and interests of the students become part of the dialogue that takes place during learning, and they are encouraged to take an active role as knowledge is constructed in collaboration with the teacher. Similarly, counselors in most nondirective psychotherapies take the position of a facilitator. The client is viewed as possessing active human agency as well as being the expert about his or her own life. Counselors from this perspective work to form a beneficial therapeutic relationship in which advice is generally not given, but where clients may have the best opportunity to explore issues and ultimately make the decisions and choose their directions.

This approach recognizes that we are resilient, adaptable, and capable of growth. Such an orientation moves away from an objectivist framework and pathological views of behavior. This is an important distinction. Constructivism in a therapeutic context takes a holistic, flexible, and forward-moving posture. It is inherently positive and developmental and thereby meshes well with mental health fields that are focused on growth and wellness.

This approach respects the individual differences of clients. Counselors have an ethical mandate to be culturally competent and sensitive practitioners in working with clients from a variety of backgrounds. Constructivism is inherently suited to working with these multiple perspectives. It encourages counselors to take a step back from a position as the expert or authority and to consider how the client's perspectives are related to the issues being explored and how those perspectives contribute to meaning-making. Counselors take on a facilitative stance. Not only is a consideration of the client's cultural context necessary for this type of work, it could be said the approach creates work that becomes culture-centered. Engagement in such a way signals to clients that counselors respectfully value and celebrate the varied heritages they, the clients, bring into the therapeutic space.

Given this orientation, constructivism can be a useful guide for framing therapeutic perspectives and ensuring collaborative processes where the client is valued and becomes an active agent of meaning-making. However, as this approach is less concrete in nature, it can sometimes be difficult to understand how precisely to put it into practical use.

Clinical Techniques

In practice, it is somewhat of a paradox to try to create specific interventions from the constructivist approach. After all, flexibility and openness occupy so many of its theoretical assumptions. Nevertheless, searching for ways in which these assumptions may be expressed in a practical, applied manner may result in effective and rewarding working alliances. Constructivism provides for a unique opportunity to put theory into practice. The client is viewed as an active participant, and techniques utilized should generally encourage self-analysis, reflection, and awareness.

Given the philosophical position of constructivism, a technique toolbox is unavailable. However, several of its principles allow for the borrowing of ideas from a variety of therapeutic approaches. For example, the Adlerian perspective rests comfortable alongside constructivism in its recognition of active human agency and the important role cognitive processes play in our ability to self-author or construct our own personal psychology. And the narratives or stories that we create for ourselves undergo constant revision as we interact with and try to make sense of the world around us. The complementary aspects of these approaches begin with a strong, collaborative working alliance. The therapeutic relationship forms the basis needed to explore, gain insight, and make changes. The counselor does not impart knowledge but facilitates a respectful environment where clients are encouraged to make meaning. Additionally, both perspectives discard pathological explanations for problems in favor of a forward-looking, positive outlook. Thus, counselors position their feedback to clients in a manner that reflects a belief in the client's ability to change, thereby instilling the facilitative power of possibility and hope. Finally, Adlerians emphasize focusing on a client's strengths, which corresponds with the constructivist notion that we are not empty containers. Counselors are therefore encouraged to explore what resources a client might already possess that can be brought to bear on the current issues at hand. Such activities also uncover strategies that can be used by clients once the therapeutic relationship has ended.

Counselors working from this perspective tend to be less directive. This is congruent with moving away from the aforementioned banking orientation and placing the client in an active, determinative role. Counselor and client work together to produce change from within.

The use of metaphors within a therapeutic context is well known. Metaphors can be powerful in that they help the client to make connections, visualize, and evoke emotions in unique and novel ways. Using metaphors as a technique is congruent with constructivism as they encourage contemplation and reflection.

Dialogue is important in terms of constructing new knowledge. Therefore, questioning is a necessary component of this approach. It is important, however, that questions not be delivered in an interrogative manner. The goal is the establishment of narrative. Questioning should be conducted in an open, tentative, and curious way in order to create a context where the client is free to explore new ideas and possibilities, not provide a definite answer to something. It can sometimes be helpful to make the ongoing narrative more concrete. One way to do this is through the use of mapping, where the client sketches out elements of a particular problem on a piece of paper. The visual can be helpful in making connections, examining all elements of a situation, and beginning to chart a solution.

Just as counselors must come to understand the worldview of their clients, so is reflection necessary for clients to understand their own attitudes, values, and beliefs. It is also important to the process of change. Examining our assumptions allows us to modify our worldviews, gain new insights, and focus on holistic development. These are all consistent with a constructivist perspective. This reflexivity is crucial today as people interact with a world that presents increasing ambiguity and uncertainty. People need to continually seek active and creative ways to navigate crooked pathways. Journal writing may be a useful resource that allows the client to reflect on his or her experiences. Reflective writing establishes a context for critical thinking and insight development relative to assumptions and decision-making. Journaling also provides reflective continuity throughout therapeutic work to help understand underlying daily decisions and actions.

Constructivist counseling may be particularly useful within a marriage and family context. A relationship or family system does not exist in a vacuum. This approach is empowering for clients as it allows them to work with and understand problems within their social context. Such work allows clients to gain more control over their environment as well as themselves, leading to more engaged connection with their life. Examination of assumptions is critical in attempting to understand interpersonal conflict. In this approach, values and meaning are more important than the behavioral processes that normally take center stage in working with families. Finally, the process of meaning-making is inherently supportive of problem solving, for which the construction of new solutions is essential. The ability to make meaning, construct knowledge, and actively change ourselves signals that our biography, to date, is not destiny.

Everett W. Painter

See also Adlerian Family Therapy; Beliefs and Values; Cognitive Maps and Couples; Cultural Issues in Couples and Families; Family Strengths; Holism; Metacommunication; Narrative Therapy; Social Construction; Therapeutic Alliance

Further Readings

Dean, R. G. (1993). Teaching a constructivist approach to clinical practice. *Journal of Teaching Social Work, 8*(1), 55–75.

Guterman, J. T. (2013). *Mastering the art of solution-focused counseling* (2nd ed.). Alexandria, VA: American Counseling Association.

Hansen, J. T. (2006), Counseling theories within a postmodernist epistemology: New roles for theories in counseling practice. *Journal of Counseling & Development, 84,* 291–297.

Mahoney, M., & Granvold, D. (2005). Constructivism and psychotherapy. *World Psychiatry, 4*(2), 74–77.

McAuliffe, G., & Eriksen, K. (2000). *Preparing counselors and therapists: Creating constructivist and developmental programs.* Virginia Beach, VA: Donning.

Neimeyer, R. A. (2009). *Constructivist psychotherapy.* New York, NY: Routledge.

Neimeyer, R. A., & Raskin, J. D. (Eds.). (2000). *Constructions of disorder: Meaning-making frameworks for psychotherapy.* Washington, DC: American Psychological Association.

Contextual Family Therapy

Contextual therapy with its emphasis on relational ethics remains a unique contribution to the field of family therapy. Its integrative approach incorporates ideas from psychiatry, philosophy, psychoanalysis, and family systems theories, offering a comprehensive framework for counseling that has been widely endorsed by clinicians around the world. This entry provides an overview of development, basic theoretical constructs, clinical conceptualization, and interventions of contextual therapy, concluding with contemporary applications of the model.

Foundations

Contextual therapy was founded by Ivan Boszormenyi-Nagy in the 1960s and further refined by Geraldine Spark, Barbara Krasner, Catherine Ducommun-Nagy, and others. Boszormenyi-Nagy grew up and was educated as a psychiatrist in Hungary. He immigrated to the United States after World War II in the midst of political oppression. Contextual therapy was developed as a comprehensive approach to treating mental illnesses. Its main assumption is our existential interdependence, our interconnectedness as a fundamental aspect of being. It posits that an individual's self develops and evolves within a context of relationships. The relational context is rich and broad and includes current close relationships and their dynamics as well as previous and subsequent generations. Thus, contextual therapy is an intergenerational model encompassing the past and the future. It is also a strengths-based model viewing relationships as resources rather than sources of pathology. The approach is integrative as it aims to capture the complexity of human life and relationships. Contextual therapy was one of the first theories to integrate individual psychotherapeutic approaches with family systems by providing a framework for changing family relational processes while emphasizing the individual's role and accountability in relationships.

The landmark idea of the theory is in the realm of relational ethics. Ethics here does not refer to moral judgments, but rather to the idea of a subjective sense of relational fairness where our actions and inactions have consequences in relationships. Contextual theory views the balance of fairness or relational justice as the guiding principle of close relationships. We need to consider both our own and others' needs to establish a fair balance of "give and take" in relationships. Violation of relational fairness may lead to dysfunctional consequences for current and future relationships. A just or fair relationship is one where those involved are able to give and receive freely. A mutual process of giving and receiving care is essential not just for the satisfaction of individual needs but also for the promotion of health in families. Mental health symptoms such as anxiety, depression, substance abuse, and relationship distress are indicators of an imbalance in give and take or unfairness in relationships. The balance of give and take is dynamic and changes across the life span and stages. There are two types of relationships in regard to that balance: symmetrical and asymmetrical. Symmetrical relationships exist between partners or friends and are based on expectations of equitable give and take. The caregiver–child relationship, in contrast, is inherently asymmetrical, with the caregiver expected to give more to the child than vice versa.

Conceptualization and Major Constructs

The complexity of reality and human behaviors is reflected in the multidimensional conceptualization within contextual theory. Its early developers proposed four dimensions for better understanding and alleviating symptoms: (1) facts, (2) individual psychology, (3) transactions, and (4) relational ethics. A fifth, ontic, dimension was added later. These dimensions are interrelated and converge at the idea of importance of justice and fair relating in family systems.

Facts refer to biological and historical determinants as well as events that occur during the course of one's life, such as age, sex at birth, national origin, race/ethnicity, and so on. Medical or psychiatric diagnoses can also be included here with the understanding that the diagnosis is not the sole identity of the individual. For instance, a diagnosis of terminal illness in a parent is a fact that could impact how the family functions. One of the children may have to step up and become an "adult" in order to take care of certain roles in the family. This change in the organization of the family may impact how each individual perceives fairness in relation to what they give and receive.

Individual psychology refers to cognitions, affect, perceptions, and experiences that vary from one individual to another. It is possible to incorporate concepts from other psychotherapy theories here for a more comprehensive understanding of the relational system. For instance, in a couple relationship one partner may have a tendency to withdraw in the face of conflict, while the other person may have a tendency to pursue. These differences could be their individual coping mechanisms; however, they impact how the couple perceives the balance of fairness. In this example, the partner who pursues may believe that he or she does more in the relationship and thus it is unfair toward him or her.

Transactions refer to patterns of interactions between members of a relationship. Concepts from family systems theory such as hierarchies, boundaries, roles, rules, and triangles are used to better understand relationships and formulate interventions. For instance, a situation in which a daughter is caught in a conflictual relationship with her parents could be regarded as an instance of loyalty conflict (relational ethics dimension, explained below). As part of understanding the process of loyalty conflict, contextual therapists would also regard this relational pattern between the daughter and parents as a triangle with unhealthy boundaries. The therapist may work to reduce loyalty conflict for the daughter by attempting to establish clearer and healthier family boundaries.

Relational ethics is the hallmark feature of the contextual approach. This dimension merges concepts from individual psychology and family systems theory in the realm of ethics. It refers to concepts of trust, loyalty, and entitlement, which influence justice and fairness in relationships, and are transmitted through generations. *Trust* is the primary relational resource from which we learn how to interact with others. While the notion of importance of trust in relationships is not unique, contextual theory highlights the importance of trustworthiness in impacting individuals' ability to engage in fair give and take with others. For example, if you have a partner who constantly shows irresponsible behaviors, at some point, even if you are a very trusting individual, your trust will erode. Trustworthiness is based on actions and accountability.

We learn to trust and be trustworthy through our early life experiences. A trusting relationship with one's caregivers lays the foundation for continued trustworthy interactions with others. If, on the other hand, early experiences involved a lack of trustworthiness of caretakers or exploitation, the individual may have difficulties building trust in other relationships. Growing up in an abusive environment, an individual may not have the resources to be trustworthy in a partner relationship. It is possible that the individual would demand more of the partner as a compensation for something she or he did not receive in earlier relationships, which may contribute to an imbalanced relationship.

Loyalty

Loyalty refers to a deep sense of commitment that exists between people related to each other either biologically (parents, siblings, etc.) or through a mutually caring relationship (partners, peers). Loyalty between parent and child involves two legacies of parental accountability (i.e., what parents/caregivers are expected to do to nurture their children) and filial indebtedness (i.e., the indebtedness children feel toward their parents/caregivers for the nurturance received). Loyalty also refers to the commitment between partners in a mutually caring relationship. Contextual therapists emphasize action as being part of loyalty; that is, loyalty is not just an emotional experience. Our actions denote our loyalties or struggles with loyalty. According to this view, we are bound by filial loyalty (i.e., loyalty toward parents and/or caregivers) even if we are cut off from our family of origin. The extent and expression of loyalty may depend on the quality of our relationship with our caregivers. Children who experience their parents as trustworthy may easily express their bond with them. However, violations of trust in the parent–child relationship may foster struggle in the expression of loyalty. Two manifestations of this struggle are noted in the theory: One, children may experience *split loyalty*, where they are forced to choose between two competing sides. A child may experience being torn between the parents engaged in a divorce fight. Two, they may remain loyal to their parents or family-of-origin patterns without realizing it. This is called *invisible loyalty* because individuals are not typically aware of the pull of loyalty. Invisible loyalty is regarded as an indirect expression of loyalty when its direct expression is blocked. For instance, a mother may unintentionally attempt parenting practices used by a parent with whom she had a conflictual relationship, or a teenager may start abusing alcohol at around the same age that her or his estranged father began abusing alcohol. For a contextual therapist, emotional cut-offs from the family of origin provide clues to invisible loyalties and relational stagnation. Loyalty conflicts in the form of split and invisible loyalties are considered major deterrents in interpersonal fairness and the health of individuals and relationships.

In some instances, the legacy of filial loyalty and existential debt to parents could set the stage for "parentification" of the child. Parentification occurs when an individual is expected to take on adult roles prior to the appropriate developmental stage. For instance, when a 9-year-old child is expected to take care of his 2-year-old sister, the 9-year-old has been cast in a role that is developmentally inappropriate. However, parentification may not always be unhealthy; sometimes, it may be needed for a family system in crisis. It may have unhealthy consequences, though, if other aspects of relational ethics are damaged. In the example above, if the 9-year-old's parentification is temporary (that is, the developmentally inappropriate tasks do not extend to other stages), and if his contribution is duly acknowledged and credited by significant others in his life, it may not create imbalance in his relationships. If, on the other hand, this parentification is prolonged, and the contributions go unacknowledged, it could set the stage for imbalances in later relationships. The parentified child may then expect to receive more in their relationships with others. They may also not be forthcoming with validating others' hurt and suffering (because no one validated theirs). These relational patterns are not intentional, that is, the parentified child may not explicitly decide to expect more in relationships. Rather, parentification and subsequent invalidation may have depleted their capacity to give in relationships. These patterns of imbalance are related to destructive entitlement in relationships.

Entitlement

Entitlement refers to the sense of what one is owed in relationships. For instance, an individual may earn the entitlement to receive more care in a relationship by actually caring for another. While merit earned on the basis of self-validation leads to the development of constructive entitlement (where one's actions do not perpetuate injustice), individuals could also earn the "right" to be destructive. Destructive entitlement, often a result of experiencing imbalanced relationships, predisposes individuals to engaging in repetitive and harmful behaviors toward themselves or others. When individuals act on this sense of entitlement, the cycle of unjust relationships is perpetuated.

A fifth dimension was later articulated by Catherine Ducommun-Nagy. According to her, Boszormenyi-Nagy had been developing this dimension in his later works. The *ontic* dimension conveys the idea that the self exists in relationships. This relational self strives for meaningful connections with others. Genuine or meaningful connections are possible when people engage in what the philosopher Martin Buber called the "I-Thou" dialogue. Such a dialogue occurs when people are able to "see" the other for who they are and not as projections of unresolved issues. For instance, a meaningful connection between partners could develop if they are able to see each other and connect with each other genuinely, and not if they see each other as projections of their parents or others. An I-Thou stance is free of exploitation; it is one where an individual is able to state one's own stance as well as to receive another's.

Interventions

Clinical practice shows that many clients present their issues in terms of fairness and trust: "it is unfair," "I don't trust her/him anymore," and so on. Contextual therapy makes discussions of those issues explicit. Its goal is to facilitate a dialogue within a family to express individual needs and to make claims as well as to consider needs of other family members. Thus, it aims to move clients to a place of accountability where they can adopt the I-Thou stance in their relationships. Contextual therapy is action-oriented, with the ultimate goal of changing future relational patterns by understanding the past and working on the present.

Contextual therapy interventions and techniques are closely related to its theoretical principles. Since relational context of interdependence and consequences is the foundation of health, therapeutic interventions impact not only those who are present in therapy but the entire client system as well. Contextual therapists strive to be accountable to everybody who may be potentially affected by therapeutic interventions. This is achieved through *multidirected partiality*, the principal and unique method of contextual therapy. It requires the therapist to see a situation from the perspectives of each of the individuals who are likely to be affected by the course of therapy. The therapist does not adopt a neutral position in this approach; she or he takes sides with an intention of taking each side equally. The therapist must consider each participant's previous experiences, especially those that involve unfair relational injury, along with their current needs. The therapist needs to balance her or his partiality by "lending weight" to those who need it most at the given moment. In the case of family therapy, the therapist can support the person who is less powerful or more vulnerable, for instance, a child. Multidirected partiality is based on empathic understanding of each family member's situation. Its integral components are *crediting* and *acknowledging*. To build trust between family members, the therapist initiates and supports the process of mutual crediting among them. Uncovering family resources for giving and receiving that can increase trustworthiness in the family is an important goal of contextual treatment. Contextual therapists believe that trustworthiness increases when one person is able to acknowledge the positive intentions of another. There are two forms of acknowledgment. The first involves giving credit to another person for considerate actions. The second involves acknowledging the unfairness that has occurred in another's life. The latter includes the process of exonerating those who have been unfair. Exoneration, while resembling forgiveness, is different. For example, an adult child may start seeing her parent's own victimization and limited choices that led to her unfair treatment. This makes it possible to restore trust and fair relating in the family, thus unblocking relational resources. Through exoneration people can break a cycle of blaming and destructive entitlement. The exonerating person earns merit and constructive entitlement, which leads to greater self-respect, integrity, and freedom.

The *therapist's self* is an important tool in the contextual approach. The practice of contextual therapy requires understanding of issues related to fair give and take in the therapist's own experiences. Boszormenyi-Nagy and Krasner, in their seminal book on the theory, suggest that therapists' firm conviction in the importance of justice and fairness in relationships and a willingness to examine them in their lives is essential, as is the belief that there are multiple, valid perspectives of any situation. This requires that therapists examine their own entitlements in relationships and be prepared to work toward balanced relationships in their lives.

Contemporary Applications

Some scholars note that while contextual therapy theory is widely used by therapists, there is little empirical evidence in the form of clinical research studies. Clinical developments include, but are not limited to, the practical clinical guide by Peter Goldenthal, applications to couples by Janet Hibbs, and work on forgiveness by Terry Hargrave. Also, one of the earlier codevelopers, Barbara Krasner continues to practice and train therapists in the United States and abroad. There are several training and clinical centers guided by the principles of contextual therapy in the United States and in European countries such as the Netherlands and Belgium.

Hargrave and others also developed the Relational Ethics Scale, which has been used in several studies testing the theory in clinical and nonclinical settings. One of the challenges of conducting empirical research on the effectiveness of contextual therapy is the measurement of constructs and the training of therapists. Work in this area continues, and clinical research using contextual therapy is still in its early stages.

The integrative, strengths-based approach has much to offer in clinical practice with individuals, couples, and families. Many therapists and family therapy students are drawn to contextual therapy because of its emphasis on relational ethics and its unique way of comprehensive and systemic treatment of relationship problems.

Tatiana Glebova and Rashmi Gangamma

See also Bowen Family Systems Theory; Entitlement; Intergenerational Loyalty; Parentification and Diverse Family Systems; Trust

Further Readings

Boszormenyi-Nagy, I. (1996). Relational ethics in contextual therapy: Commitment to our common future. In M. Friedman (Ed.), *Martin Buber and the human sciences* (pp. 371–382). New York: State University of New York Press.

Boszormenyi-Nagy, I., & Krasner, B. (1986). *Between give and take: A clinical guide to contextual therapy.* New York, NY: Brunner/Mazel:

Boszormenyi-Nagy, I., & Sparks, G. (1973). *Invisible loyalties.* New York, NY: Brunner/Mazel.

Ducommun-Nagy, C. (2002). Contextual therapy. In F. W. Kaslow & R. F. Massey (Eds.), *Comprehensive handbook of psychotherapy: Volume 3* (pp. 463–488). New York, NY: Wiley.

Gangamma, R., Bartle-Haring, S., & Glebova, T. (2012). A study of contextual therapy theory's relational ethics in couples in therapy. *Family Relations, 61,* 825–835.

Goldenthal, P. (1996). *Doing contextual therapy: An integrated model for working with individuals, couples, and families.* New York, NY: Norton.

Grame, A. H., Miller, B. R., Robinson, W. D., Higgins, J. D., & Hinton, J. W. (2008). A test of contextual theory: The relationship among relational ethics, marital satisfaction, health problems, and depression. *Contemporary Family Therapy, 30,* 183–198.

Hargrave, T. D., Jennings, G., & Anderson, W. (1991). The development of a relational ethics scale. *Journal of Marital and Family Therapy, 17,* 145–158.

Hargrave, T. D., & Pfitzer, F. (2004). *The new contextual therapy: Guiding the power of give and take.* New York, NY: Routledge.

Hibbs, B. J., & Getzen, K. J. (2009). *Try to see it my way: Being fair in love and marriage.* New York, NY: Avery.

Core Competencies for Marriage and Family Therapists

Marriage and family therapists work with individuals, couples, and families who seek professional help in resolving conflicts arising from various circumstances. Marriage and family counselors work in private practices, nonprofit agencies, for-profit agencies, mental health clinics, hospitals, and other settings. Each of these settings requires different approaches, and each individual, couple, and family requires different techniques; however, there is a need for a set standard of practice for certain aspects of marriage and family therapy. Core competencies for marriage and family therapy are the standards that provide this clear definition of what it means to provide marriage and family therapy and how to properly meet the needs of those seeking services from those who distinguish themselves as marriage and family therapists. This entry examines the six core competencies that guide marriage and family therapy: admission to treatment; clinical assessment and diagnosis; treatment planning and case management; therapeutic interventions; legal issues, ethics, and standards; and research and program evaluation.

The American Association for Marriage and Family Therapy's Six Core Competencies

In marriage and family therapy, the unit that is being treated is the family, and any individual work is done in the context of the family. The counseling may aim to educate the family concerning the patterns that exist in their relationships that are contributing to stress and the need for counseling. The core competencies are the basic knowledge and skills needed to effectively practice as a couple and family counselor/therapist. There are six core competencies as established by the American Association for Marriage and Family Therapy. Each of these core competencies contributes to the foundation of quality service to individuals, couples, and families. Understanding of the importance of these core areas assists the counselor in providing the therapeutic needs of families that they work with. Marriage and family therapists cannot only be knowledgeable of the core competencies; they must be proficient in each conceptual, perceptual, executive, evaluative, and professional aspect of each competency in order to provide marriage and family service.

The counselor must also be able to demonstrate knowledge of relevant counseling theories and techniques that serve as a foundation for marriage and family therapy. This includes systems concepts as well as the common risks and benefits of a family participating in couples, marriage, or family counseling as opposed to individual or group counseling. In the context of family therapy, problems with an individual are seen as symptoms of family dysfunction. Part of admission to treatment therefore involves determining whether an individual, couple, or entire family will be seen for treatment and determining if additional therapists are needed in order to address singular needs or specialized issues that may present during an intake process.

Core Competency 1: Admission to Treatment

Admission to treatment is the work that is done before working with a family that has not yet been assigned client status. Counselors must assess whether or not they possesses the education needed to work with families. This includes having a thorough knowledge of counseling theories as well as techniques for working with individuals, in addition to knowledge of counseling theories and techniques that are specifically proven to work in the field of family counseling. Admission to treatment should only begin once a thorough assessment has been completed. This assessment requires an understanding of an individual family's dynamics and issues as reported by the family.

Core competency 1, admission to treatment, is the first step to providing quality marriage and family therapy. As with any area in the counseling field, some of the other components of this first step include becoming cognizant of any metal health diagnoses, physical health issues, participation in other therapeutic services, and whether counseling is mandated or expected to have any effect in a legal case. This information will likely be gathered during an intake process and further explored during an initial assessment if necessary. Gathering and considering preliminary information also includes recognition of cultural influences in counseling. The family and family members' ages, ethnicity, religion, sexual orientation, socioeconomic status, and other cultural factors will determine the importance and relevance of issues to be addressed in sessions.

Once counseling has begun, the counselor must be aware of each member's involvement in the counseling and assist with determining which people should be involved in the counseling. These beginning sessions must also include obtaining consent forms in conjunction with setting standards, and acknowledging rules, rights, fees, and responsibilities of the family and the counselor. This is the time when confidentiality, duty to warn, and other components of informed consent are reviewed. Although expectations are stated in the beginning, rules and expectations must continually and consistently be reviewed and evaluated through collaboration with the family and continually building on the relationship with the client. This forming of a therapeutic relationship assists with session management and quality interaction throughout the counselor's time with a family.

Ultimately, admission to treatment comprises many steps of preparation. The core competency is concerned with whether or not the counselor is prepared to provide counseling and is equipped with enough information to provide quality services to their clients. This core competency also requires remaining cognizant of ethical and legal standards regarding providing couples and family counseling to adults and children.

Core Competency 2: Clinical Assessment and Diagnosis

The second core competency includes activities that assist with identifying issues that will be addressed during the counseling. There is a thorough need to understand human development, psychopathology, sexuality, and the implications and clinical needs of each of these areas. Numerous assessment tools can be used to get a better understanding of issues that plague the family, including identification of various mental illnesses.

Although initial assessment is done when addressing the first core competency, there is a need for more in-depth assessment and diagnosis if applicable. In order to be competent, the counselor must fully understand mental health diagnoses and symptoms of each along with the implications, effective treatments, and prognosis. There must then be an understanding of how certain behavioral health disorders manifest themselves within families and how they affect overall family functioning.

Myriad assessment instruments are available for assessment of marriages, couples, families, and individual family members. Similarly, assessment instruments assist with diagnosis of substance use and other mental health disorders. Once a diagnosis is made, it then has to be taken into account throughout treatment.

Conceptually, the counselor should understand basic human and family development, behavioral health disorders, psychopharmacology, and treatment modalities. Perceptually, the counselor must assess client engagement while considering relationships outside the family and emotional and physical issues. Much of this is done through integration of reports and hypothesis development.

Core Competency 3: Treatment Planning and Case Management

There must be a plan in order for counseling to flow properly. There must be a goal and purpose for meeting with clients. Conceptually, there is a need for the counselor to be familiar with models and techniques for treatment planning and case management, as well as the effects that various medications may have on clients and their treatment. In addition, there must be an understanding of the requirements of third-party payees, including the codes that are needed for reimbursement and the liabilities associated with billing said third parties.

Part of treatment planning often involves connecting the family to other outside resources and/or activities. This may include recovery referrals, classes for specialized issues, and medical services. There must be measurable steps that show progress or lack of progress associated with counseling, pairs with realistic goals, and steps for meeting those goals. The plan serves as an evaluative tool.

Core Competency 4: Therapeutic Interventions

Once treatment planning and basic interviewing have been completed, the therapeutic process begins. The counselor must be able to discern which interventions are most appropriate based on the strengths and limitations of each intervention considered along with the risks associated.

The fourth core competency also involves determination of which techniques and interventions have the greatest potential to assist the family in their goals. The counselor must then correctly utilize the techniques and interventions that are deemed culturally appropriate and relevant while engaging family members when and where appropriate. Periodically, it may be determined that an intervention is not effective and that modification is necessary. Need for modification is determined by recurrent evaluation of family progress, outcomes, and reaction. This is a collaborative and ongoing process that includes the counselor, family members, and relevant supervisors.

Core Competency 5: Legal Issues, Ethics, and Standards

Family laws are created by state legislative branches and provide governing standards that ensure legal and moral justice. Counselors are mandated to follow laws, ethical codes, and standards that govern counseling in order to practice. However, many laws differ from state to state, and counselors must be aware of both federal and state laws of each state in which they practice. Specifically, the counselor needs to be aware of all aspects of family law, including marriage, divorce, and child custody. Even when possessing some legal knowledge, marriage and family therapists must be able to recognize when legal consultation from an attorney is necessary.

Various codes of ethics may be followed by various counselors depending upon their membership in professional organizations and possession of certain licenses and certifications. Ethics are normative in nature, and ethical codes serve as guidelines for what counselors can and cannot do.

Each situation is unique, however, and the code must often be interpreted.

Depending on the practice setting, there may also be policies and procedures of an agency, organization, or practice of which to be cognizant. Policies and procedures give direct and specific directions for how certain situations must be handled in accordance with the organization's stated goals and objectives. These are rules and guidelines that define appropriate operations to ensure consistency in practice within said organization.

Counselors must execute laws, ethical codes, policies, and procedures accordingly and take appropriate action when problems arise as required by each. One should obtain the necessary licenses and other credentials relevant to practicing marriage and family therapy and always evaluate his or her own personal issues, attitudes, and well-being in an attempt to prevent susceptibility to misconduct. Proper maintenance of and adequate notes in client files will also assist in the event that ethical or legal complaints arise, and continuing education and professional development are necessary in order to stay abreast of changing laws as well as to reiterate current legal issues, ethics, and standards.

Core Competency 6: Research and Program Evaluation

Counselors must be able to understand both qualitative and quantitative research as well as program evaluation methods in order to be competent as a marriage and family counselor. In order to stay well informed concerning evidence-based practices in marriage and family therapy and mental health services, frequent reading of existent marriage and family literature and research is key. Program evaluation refers to the process of collecting and properly analyzing information concerning the effectiveness or lack of effectiveness of interventions and techniques utilized in a specific program and the impact that those interventions have had on those being served by them.

Counselors can also participate in the body of research available by conducting research if possible and participating in various research studies when the opportunities present themselves. Beyond evaluation of current clinical literature and knowledge, marriage and family therapists should contribute to the development of new knowledge to advance the profession.

Asha Dickerson

See also Clinical Case Conceptualization With Couples and Families; Ethical Codes; Process Research; Quantitative Research; Therapeutic Assessment; Treatment Planning With Couples and Families

Further Readings

American Association for Marriage and Family Therapy. (2004). *Marriage and family therapy core competencies.* Alexandria, VA. Author.

Capuzzi, D., & Stauffer, M. D. (2015). *Foundations of couples, marriage, and family counseling.* Hoboken, NJ: Wiley.

Gehart, D. (2010). *Mastering competencies in family therapy: A practical approach to theory and clinical case documentation.* Pacific Grove, CA: Brooks/Cole.

Miller, J. K., Todahi, J. L., & Platt, J. J. (2009). The core competency movement in marriage and family therapy: Key considerations from other disciplines. *Journal of Marital and Family Therapy, 36*(1), 59–70.

Sperry, L. (2010). *Core competencies in counseling and psychotherapy: Becoming a highly competent and effective therapist.* New York, NY: Routledge.

Cost–Benefit Analysis

Cost–benefit analysis is a research method used to analyze the economic impact of interventions and treatment programs. Cost–benefit analysis in its complete form requires the measurement of all costs associated with the delivery of specific interventions and all the benefits that occur as a result of the treatment. While cost–benefit analysis is considered to be the gold standard in cost analyses, it also shares features with cost allocation and cost-effectiveness. This entry presents some of these basic methods for analyzing intervention, treatment, and program costs, and continues with a discussion of full cost–benefit analysis.

Cost Allocation

All cost analysis is based on the assumption that the treatment produces a benefit to the recipient and is an effective means of intervention. If the treatment is not effective then it cannot be justified, regardless of how inexpensive or cost-efficient the methods might be. Accordingly, cost analysis is not typically employed until after a treatment or intervention has been found to be clinically effective in a number of previous studies. Before conducting a cost analysis, studies demonstrating effectiveness are evaluated and reviewed to determine if the study possessed sufficient internal validity (i.e., the study was well designed and rigorous). Studies that possess low internal validity are more likely to draw false conclusions about the effectiveness of the intervention and are therefore excluded from cost analyses. A well-written cost analysis will include information on how studies were selected and what methods were used to evaluate the internal validity of each as part of the methods section.

Once clinical effectiveness is determined through a review of studies, a wide range of options for evaluating costs becomes available, the most simple of which is cost allocation. Cost allocation is used to determine the gross cost of providing the particular intervention or treatment program. In cost allocation all possible costs are quantified by the researcher. For a typical treatment program, at the most basic level, this would include costs associated with things like therapist salaries, cost of printing and reproducing materials used by clients, support staff compensation and wages, and therapist and staff training. These are the direct costs that are realized up front, are easy to recognize, and are more simple to quantify monetarily. However, for a more comprehensive delineation of costs the research would also include costs associated with administrative overhead, rent or mortgage for the space used to deliver the treatment, utilities such as gas and electricity, parking fees, security for the premises, and so on. The only two requirements for what type of costs can be included are that they be associated with the provision of the treatment and that they can be quantified as a dollar amount. Cost allocation is a straightforward method for determining the fiscal impact of a program and provides a basis for comparing the costs of competing interventions.

Cost-Effectiveness

Cost-effectiveness extends cost allocation by also including the outcome of the intervention in the calculations. Whereas cost allocation is simply concerned with the total costs of an intervention or treatment program, cost-effectiveness examines the cost for each unit of a particular outcome. In order to compare two different interventions or treatment programs a common outcome must be available for review and analysis. The outcome is what links the two programs and allows for a direct comparison of costs. It would not be possible, for example, to compare the cost-effectiveness of two interventions for depression if the only information for one study was scores on a depression scale and the other study only measured number of days absent from work. However, one way to get around this problem and create a common unit for analysis, even when the outcome measures are different, is to use effect sizes.

One of the simplest methods for conducting a cost-effectiveness analysis is to take two treatments with very similar outcomes (e.g., similar effect sizes) and compare the costs of the two. Whichever has the lower cost would be considered the more cost-effective treatment. The issue with this, of course, is that treatment programs do not always have similar outcomes. For interventions and programs where there are disparate outcomes, the Incremental Cost-Effectiveness Ratio can be used. The formula for this ratio is the cost of Treatment A minus Treatment B, divided by the Outcome from Treatment A minus the Outcome from Treatment B. As an example, consider two treatments for relationship problems that measure the number of days without a conflict over 12 months as the outcome. First is a new treatment, Treatment A, which costs $9,000 and produces 150 days free of conflict over the year after treatment is completed. The second treatment, Treatment B, costs $3,000 and produces 75 days free of conflict. Applying the formula described above produces a result of $80, which means that the extra conflict-free days produced by Treatment A were created at a cost of $80 each. Conversely, if Treatment A cost $3,000 and Treatment B costs $9,000, the result would be −$80, which would show that there is actually a savings associated with the new treatment. The results of this type of analysis provide a basis for stakeholders to make decisions about which treatment provides the best results for the money spent. However, cost-effectiveness analysis is still limited in that it shows only what is being directly obtained in exchange for each dollar spent. Missing are the many indirect benefits associated with mental health treatment.

Components of Cost–Benefit Analysis

Cost–benefit analysis encompasses cost allocation and cost-effectiveness, and addresses the weaknesses of these methods by monetizing the benefits of the outcomes. The benefits defined in cost–benefit analysis might be tangible (e.g., increase earning potential) or intangible (e.g., prevented criminal activity or reduced medical expenses), though they are always based on quantifiable economic data available to the researcher. Often the benefits are defined in terms of increased productivity or avoided costs. For example, if a person receives treatment for alcohol dependence and works 20 more days in the year after treatment than in the year before, the wages earned for those 20 days would be considered a benefit and factored into the calculations. Furthermore, if possible the researcher could also quantify the benefit to the company that comes with the increased productivity and consider that as a benefit as well. Avoided costs could include things such as avoided court fees, hospitalization costs, and medical treatment. For example, a study on schizophrenia might measure the reduction in hospitalizations following treatment and monetize the associated savings.

Once all costs and potential benefits are calculated, the information is entered into a formula to calculate the Cost–Benefit Ratio. In this formula the total benefits are divided by the total costs. A value over 1.0 indicates that the benefits are greater than the costs of the program. The next step is to calculate the Net Present Value of the intervention or treatment program. In this formula the monetary value of a benefit of the program is multiplied by number of the benefits produced, after which the cost of the program is subtracted. Continuing with the example for the $9,000/150 conflict-free days of treatment outlined above, if the value of a conflict-free day was quantified as $200, the net present value of the treatment program would be approximately $21,000. This shows that even though the program cost $9,000 to implement, it was associated with an overall saving of $21,000 after factoring in the benefits. These annual savings can be projected into the future for as many years as the benefit is expected to last, though this requires the use of a discount rate to adjust for the value of money not yet spent, since in theory money gains value over time. By calculating the Net Present Value of two competing treatments, researchers are able to show which produces the greatest overall benefit. This can be especially important when a new treatment costs more than treatment as usual. Using cost-benefit analysis it is possible to show that even though the cost of treatment is higher for the new treatment, the overall benefits far outweigh treatment as usual. This method has been used successfully to argue for coverage of treatment programs that cost more than treatment as usual. One of the most notable instances of this is seen with multisystemic therapy, as developed by Scott Henggeler and his colleagues.

Uses and Criticisms

As highlighted above, cost–benefit analysis is used to argue for the provision of treatment programs and services. Decision-makers in the health care market are concerned with the value of treatment programs and whether the overall impact is positive. Cost–benefit analysis provides a means for researchers and practitioners to demonstrate to stakeholders the value of the services they offer. This has become increasingly important as consumers rely heavily on third-party payers and become more and more separated from direct payment for services. Marriage and family therapy research has been behind the curve compared to other professions when it comes to understanding the importance of cost analysis. Results from cost–benefit analysis can be used to argue for the implementation and use of underutilized services that have been found to be clinically effective, like marriage and family therapy. Given the position of marriage and family therapy in the health care market, it is not uncommon to hear pleas for more cost analyses in journals and other scholarly publications. Finally, cost–benefit analysis is especially important when seeking government funding since proposals and reports often require the application of this methodology.

Despite the widespread use of cost–benefit analysis to determine the fiscal impact of programs, it is not without its detractors. Among the criticisms is that cost–benefit analyses do not take into consideration the quality of the clinical intervention being offered and focuses exclusively on the monetary impact. Those who offer these criticisms see cost–benefit analysis as a method primarily used to justify funding cuts and limiting access to services. As noted above, however, this is not always the case, and in fact sometimes cost–benefit analysis can actually be used to expand services. A final criticism is that cost–benefit studies may lack internal validity and use metrics that are inaccurate, which would have the effect of overestimating or underestimating the values used to calculate the results. It can be difficult for the average researcher to monetize benefits, especially when it comes to the intangible benefits of a particular treatment or intervention. For this reason it is not uncommon for research teams to contract with an economist to help them make decisions concerning costs and benefits.

Jacob D. Christenson

See also Clinical Versus Statistical Significance; Effectiveness Research; Outcome Research; Quantitative Research

Further Readings

Boardman, A., Greenberg, D., Vining, A., & Weimer, D. (2010). *Cost-benefit analysis* (4th ed.). Upper Saddle River, NJ: Prentice Hall.

Christenson, J. D., & Crane, D. R. (2014). Integrating costs into marriage and family therapy research. In R. B. Miller & L. Johnson (Eds.), *Advanced research methods in family therapy research: A focus on validity and change* (pp. 420–436). New York, NY: Taylor and Francis.

Fals-Stewart, W., Yates, B. T., & Klostermann, K. (2005). Assessing the costs, benefits, cost–benefit ratio, and cost-effectiveness of marital and family treatments: Why we should and how we can. *Journal of Family Psychology, 19,* 28–39. doi:10.1037/0893-3200.19.1.28

Gold, M. R., Siegel, J. E., Russell, L. B., & Weinstein, M. C. (1996). *Cost-effectiveness in health and medicine.* New York, NY: Oxford University Press.

Hargreaves, W. A., Shumway, M., Hu, T., & Cuffell, B. (1996). *Cost-outcomes methods for mental health.* San Diego, CA: Academic Press.

Lazar, S. G. (Ed.). (2010). *Psychotherapy is worth it: A comprehensive review of its cost-effectiveness.* Washington, DC: American Psychiatric Association.

Lee, S., & Aos, S. (2011). Using cost-benefit analysis to understand the value of social interventions. *Research on Social Work Practice, 21*(6), 682–688. doi:10.1177/1049731511410551

Yates, B. T. (1994). Toward the incorporation of costs, cost-effectiveness analysis, and cost-benefit analysis into clinical research. *Journal of Consulting and Clinical Psychology, 62,* 729–736. doi:10.1037/0022-006X.62.4.729

Yates, B. T. (1996). *Analyzing costs, procedures, processes, and outcomes in human services.* Thousand Oaks, CA: Sage.

COTHERAPY TEAM

Cotherapy refers to any therapy session—individual, couple, family, or group—in which more than one therapist conducts a therapy session at the same time. When all practitioners are not present simultaneously, the treatment provided is concurrent therapy; one therapist working with an adolescent child and another therapist working with a parent demonstrates concurrent therapy. Another common example of concurrent treatment would be a case in which an individual seeks pharmacotherapy from one provider and psychotherapy from another.

Cotherapy is common in training situations, both in early training phases of therapy education and also when more experienced therapists learn the protocol for a treatment that involves a specified series of steps—as commonly occurs in many clinical trials. Outside of these more controlled environments, cotherapy is less common but still has valid justification as an approach. Clients typically report a positive experience with cotherapy. Many clients feel they get more "bang for their buck" with two or more therapists. When more than one therapist is involved it is more likely that the clients will have someone to join with positively, which is a common factor of success in therapy. This entry discusses the reasons for using cotherapy, challenges experienced by cotherapists, and effective techniques used in cotherapy.

Reasons for Cotherapy

There is often concern with the gender of therapist when working with clients who have a history of abuse. In these cases there is research that supports a female and male cotherapy team. There is also research evidence supporting gender-matching cotherapy teams when a couple is being treated. If a heterosexual couple is being treated by cotherapists, then the team would consist of one male and one female. When a heterosexual couple is treated by either two men or two women, it is more common that one of the partners would feel ignored or placed in a defensive position.

The benefits of cotherapy include a sharing of responsibilities and increased pool of resources for the therapists to draw from, and a greater sense of confidence in the therapists' experience on the part of both the therapists and clients. Cotherapy teams are also recommended when a therapist feels stuck, as a method of training less experienced therapists and as a way of preparing a client for the eventual departure of a therapist. In the case of a therapist's pending departure, cotherapy can allow therapeutic progress to continue with greater ease than starting from the beginning with a new therapist. It is also recommended that a therapist utilize a cotherapy team when there is concern that a client may take legal action against the therapist. In many cases, malpractice lawsuits are brought because of poor communication or a misunderstanding, which may be resolved with the assistance of a cotherapist. Research on cotherapy suggests that other advantages include an increase in the range of roles for the therapists, greater freedom in expressing emotions, and increased confidence in therapeutic direction.

Challenges in Cotherapy

A major challenge in cotherapy is that the literature on how to conduct cotherapy is very limited. Therefore, training is often experiential, with cotherapists learning the process as they go. This can be difficult because there are inevitably difficulties within the cotherapy process involving perspective-taking, power, and alliances. Some of the underlying relationship issues that clients bring into session are a lack of perspective-taking or positive regard. This problem of awareness is also a common challenge in cotherapy. When cotherapists fail to consider each other, it is not uncommon that cotherapy does not work well. For cotherapy to be effective, the therapists involved must communicate effectively before, during, and after each session in order to understand the client's situation and then execute planned treatment.

It is essential that the therapy team presents themselves to the clients together as a united team. The development of a productive and safe therapeutic team can be one of the biggest challenges in cotherapy. In some cases issues of power arise, and therapists battle each other over the direction of therapy. However, while some directions may be more relevant or more important, rarely is a direction wrong. There will be times when cotherapists have differing views on how treatment would best proceed—rarely is one right and the other wrong.

Another common challenge occurs when one therapist joins more closely with the clients than another. While this is not uncommon, when it is not recognized it is likely to marginalize one therapist and has potential to create a coalition between the client(s) and one therapist against the other. It is important that each therapist in a cotherapy team avoid the assumption that the other has malicious intent—called the assumption of malintent. The assumption of malintent is one of the most common problems seen in couples therapy. This assumption can turn just about any harmless interaction into a purposeful and planned attack meant to hurt and demean.

Cotherapy is more complex than treatment provided by one provider. It requires therapists to approach the treatment planning, implementation, and closure process differently than when providing therapy alone. Most challenges cotherapists experience that are a result of the modality rather than the presenting problem are based in the unwillingness of one or both providers to treat each other as competent colleagues and teammates. This unwillingness may result from an assumption of malintent, or it may be because of laziness or even insecurity on the part of one of the cotherapists.

Another common problem with teamwork occurs when therapists take an approach that cotherapy consists of two different types of therapy occurring in the same room. One treatment approach will be led by therapist A and another by therapist B. When therapist A is engaged in treatment, therapist B may take a backseat and assume the role of "observer." While an observer can be a valid and meaningful role in cotherapy, it requires paying close attention rather than listening to the discussion only in order to respond to it. When a cotherapist pays only cursory attention, the treatment process is deprived of the power that comes from two therapists who are engaged in the treatment process.

Effective Techniques in Cotherapy

Cotherapists will inevitably have different ideas. Effective cotherapists will develop a pattern of communication throughout the treatment process that allows them to conceptualize the case and develop a treatment plan. This allows the therapists to hash out differences of opinion outside of the therapy room, allowing them to appear as a team and united when with the clients.

In session, it is important to respect a cotherapist's opinions and style and help the cotherapist explore ideas that may differ. When each cotherapist helps the other to further a train of thought or exploration, the therapeutic team also acts as a model and example for clients in how to act in interpersonal relationships appropriately. This style of cotherapy maximizes the experiential potential that exists within the often-conflicted relationship of cotherapists.

It is also important to maintain systemic thought while conducting cotherapy. If a cotherapist cannot effectively follow the other's train of thought, it is possible that the client cannot either. Rather than blaming a failed segue on the cotherapist, it is more beneficial to approach a conflict situation as a learning opportunity.

Essential to success as cotherapists is the ability to disagree with one another and to continue being on the same therapeutic team. Essentially this is the same task therapists ask their clients to attempt. Ultimately, it does not really matter who was right, but how the process occurred does matter. Some issues should be addressed in private away from the clients; however, most differences of opinion or alternate thoughts can be expressed and shared in session to further develop a therapeutic strategy. When cotherapists are able to work in tandem, neither partner feels inadequate or unheard. Each cotherapist brings important and valuable skill to the team.

A common challenge for new and experienced therapists is to find a way to challenge and push their clients while also maintaining a warm, supportive, and safe relationship in which feelings can be freely expressed and emotions processed. Cotherapy can make this process easier. One therapist can adopt a role that is more challenging and the other a role that is more supportive. Cotherapy can provide both clients and cotherapists with more exposure to treatment styles and approaches. When one therapist's approach does not quite fit, the cotherapist can refine and redirect the direction of therapy. Cotherapy can be a transformative experience for not only the clients involved but also the therapists involved—if they allow themselves to open to the process of working with another person and the possibility of being challenged.

*Quintin A. Hunt
and Rachel A. Augustus*

See also Common Factors; Communication Errors/Problems in Couples and Families; Conflict Resolution; Strategic Family Therapy; Systems Theory

Further Readings

Barnard, C. P., & Miller, B. (1987). Cotherapy: A means of training with the family. *Australian and New Zealand Journal of Family Therapy, 8*(3), 137–142. doi:10.1002/j.1467-8438.1987.tb01218.x

Berger, M. (2002). Envy and generosity between co-therapists. *Group, 26*(1), 107–121. doi:10.1023/A:1015430913790

Crowther, D. (1991). Cotherapists: Learning to work together. *Perspectives in Psychiatric Care, 27*(4), 18-23–25. doi:10.1111/j.1744-6163.1991.tb00346.x

Friedman, R., & Handel, O. (2002). Facilitating individuation processes in supervision groups comprised of co-therapists conducting group therapy with bereaved parents. *Group, 26*(1), 95–105. doi:10.1023/A:1015478829720

Hendrix, C. C., Fournier, D. G., & Briggs, K. (2001). Impact of co-therapy teams on client outcomes and therapist training in marriage and family therapy. *Contemporary Family Therapy, 23*(1), 63–82. doi:10.1023/A:1007824216363

Hoffman, S., & Laub, B. (2004). Dialectical cotherapy. *Israel Journal of Psychiatry and Related Sciences, 41*(3), 191–196.

Perl, E. (1997). Treatment team in conflict: The wishes for and risks of consensus. *Psychiatry, 60*(2), 182–195.

Roesler, T. A., & Lillie, B. K. (1995). Slaying the dragon: The use of male/female co-therapists for adult survivor group therapy. *Journal of Child Sexual Abuse, 4*(2), 1–17. doi:10.1300/J070v04n02_01

Steinberg, E., Gedzior, J., Mervis, P., & Lulof, P. (2013). Group cotherapy in a training clinic. *Group, 37*(3), 229–237.

Weinberg, H., & Ditroi, A. (2007). Concurrent therapy, countertransference, and the analytic third. *Group, 31*(1–2), 47–62.

COUNCIL FOR ACCREDITATION OF COUNSELING AND RELATED EDUCATIONAL PROGRAMS

The Council for Accreditation of Counseling and Related Educational Programs (CACREP) is the accrediting agency for counselor training programs in the United States and across the world. CACREP aims to promote the counseling profession through the establishment of standards that guide program development and ensure quality counselor education. CACREP accredits master's level counseling programs in the specialty areas of (a) addiction counseling; (b) career counseling; (c) clinical mental health counseling; (d) marriage, couple, and family counseling; (e) school counseling; and (f) student affairs and college counseling. In addition, CACREP is the accrediting agency for the doctoral-level counselor education and supervision program. There are currently more than 680 master's level and doctoral-level counseling programs accredited by CACREP. Of the currently accredited programs, 42 are in the specialty area of marriage, couple, and family (MCF) counseling. Program accreditation, like CACREP, provides assurance of program quality to prospective students, employers, insurance companies (or other sources that reimburse for counseling services), and clients.

Accreditation Standards

Accreditation is a voluntary process, in which academic programs choose to come under review by trained, outside evaluators. During review, the evaluators assess the program against professional standards. Counselor training programs seeking accreditation must go through CACREP, as CACREP is the only acknowledged accrediting agency for the field of counseling by the Council for Higher Education Accreditation (CHEA). CHEA is an association of degree-granting colleges and universities that scrutinizes accrediting agencies and ensures their legitimacy. To date there are 60 accrediting organizations recognized by CHEA, of which CACREP is one.

CACREP was established in 1981 through a collaboration of the Association of Counselor Education and Supervision and the American Personnel and Guidance Association (now known as American Counseling Association). CACREP has been recognized by CHEA as an accrediting agency since 1987. CACREP's quality assurance of counselor preparation is accomplished through the evaluation of programs on three categories of standards (i.e., learning environment, professional counseling identity, professional practice) for the 2009 standards, and a fourth category was added in the 2016 standards (Evaluation in the Program).

Learning Environment

The first category of evaluation is the environment in which counseling students learn. Included in this area is the evaluation of institutional support, program structure, faculty/staff qualification, and program assessment plans. According to the standards in this category, institutions that house a CACREP-accredited counseling program must demonstrate support of the program through provision of appropriate resources including, but not limited to, student support services, monies, appropriate technologies, and physical space. Marriage, couples, and family counseling programs are required to provide 60 semester hours (90 quarter hours) in their training program and maintain a student to faculty ratio of 10 to 1. Faculty members are required to demonstrate a counselor identity and remain active members in the counseling profession through scholarly research, activities, and discourse. CACREP-accredited programs are also required to have an evaluation process in place so that feedback on student learning, faculty teaching, and supervision can be collected and used to inform future program decisions. All of these standards, along with additional requirements not mentioned, but specified in CACREP standards, make up the evaluation area of student learning environments. In addition to this category of standards, CACREP has established standards around student knowledge.

Professional Counseling Identity

Student competency is the second category of CACREP evaluation. Students in CACREP-accredited counseling programs are expected to develop a counselor identity evidenced by participation in professional organizations and supported by faculty members' use of current research in their instruction. It is expected students in CACREP-accredited training programs will develop a strong knowledge base in the eight core competency areas of (1) professional orientation and ethical practice; (2) social and cultural diversity; (3) human growth and development; (4) career development; (5) helping relationships; (6) group work; (7) assessment; and (8) research and program evaluation. Each of the counseling specialties has domains under the eight competencies that are specific to their area of counseling. For example, students enrolled in MCF programs must know not only general development theories but also development theories specific to marriages, couples, and families. The specialty-specific domains ensure that students gain a knowledge base specific to their chosen area of counseling expertise. Student knowledge in the eight areas of competency is developed through classroom-based learning and cultivated through professional practice.

Professional Practice

Professional practice is the third category of CACREP standards. Professional practice includes the clinical classes of practicum and internship. During these classes, students have an opportunity to apply their knowledge and skills in a supervised counseling setting. According to CACREP standards, counselors in training must complete 100 hours of practicum experience (at least 40 of which are in direct client service). Practicum is the first training experience students have working with clients from the community. In addition to a practicum experience, students must complete a 600-hour internship experience (240 of which need to be in the provision of direct client service). Internship is the culminating experience, completed at the end of a student's training, involving a more extensive provision of counseling services to community members. CACREP standards provide clear guidelines around these clinical experiences to ensure that supervision from an appropriately credentialed person is provided, liability insurance is obtained, and essential clinical skills are practiced. Through evaluation and review of the three categories of standards, CACREP accreditation provides assurance of quality counselor training.

Evaluation in the Program

In the past, accreditation standards tended to be input based (did the program teach required material?), but have become more output based (did students demonstrate learning in required areas?). The addition of a whole category on evaluation in the 2016 accreditation standards reflects some of this shift in emphasis. The evaluation category includes standards related to faculty comprehensively evaluating the overall effectiveness of the counseling program and specialties, evaluating student progress, and evaluation of faculty and supervisors. Programs must have a systematic plan for how the program, students, faculty, and supervisors will be evaluated, which must include a plan for (a) what data will be collected, (b) method of data collection, (c) analyzing data, (d) utilizing data for program modifications, and (e) disseminating data.

Benefits of Accreditation

Students seeking to study MCF counseling benefit from enrollment in a CACREP-accredited program for several reasons. Because CACREP accreditation is a quality indicator, employers prefer applicants from CACREP-accredited training programs over non–CACREP accredited programs. As a result, students in CACREP-accredited programs are more likely to secure employment postgraduation than students from non-CACREP counseling programs. CACREP accreditation is also beneficial for counselors in training because of its implications on licensure eligibility. While professional licensing requirements vary by state, CACREP-accredited programs meet most states' educational requirements for licensure. In addition, a degree from a CACREP-accredited program provides graduates immediate eligibility for national certification from the National Board of Certified Counselors (NBCC). Beginning January 1, 2022, NBCC will require students seeking national board certification to have an advanced degree from a CACREP-accredited counseling program, or they will not be eligible for certification. Graduating from a CACREP-accredited counseling program also has implications for a graduate's ability to bill for counseling services, since some insurance providers (such as TRICARE) will pay only for services rendered by a licensed counselor trained in a CACREP-accredited program. Prospective students pursuing a career in MCF counseling should strongly consider the benefits of training in a CACREP-accredited counseling program. CACREP is recognized in the field of counseling as a quality indicator, and thus there are many professional benefits students gain by graduating from a program accredited by the Council for Accreditation of Counseling and Related Educational Programs.

Jennifer A. Boender

See also American Association for Marriage and Family Therapy; Competency-Based Standards for Marriage, Couple, and Family Counseling; Licensure and Certification; Training and Licensure

Further Readings

American Association of State Counseling Boards: http://www.aascb.org

American Counseling Association: http://www.counseling.org

Council for Accreditation of Counseling & Related Educational Programs: http://www.cacrep.org/

Council for Higher Education Accreditation: http://www.chea.org/

National Board for Certified Counselors: http://nbcc.org/

COUPLE AND FAMILY FORENSICS

Clinical records and assessments are not only used by therapists to assist in the treatment of their clientele, but they also can be used by various court systems and attorneys to attempt to sway the decisions of judges and juries. Practitioners may become involved in legal matters especially if there have been prior mental health services provided to the client. Counselors whose practice involves couple and family forensics will likely be called in as expert witnesses, to make treatment recommendations, to provide various therapeutic services, and/or to provide any other information that is requested by judges and other legal representatives. Because there are legal and ethical obligations associated with counseling couples and families, counselors involved in couple and family forensics must be familiar with laws and legal terms, and must also be able to communicate mental health terms and principles into language that court and legal officials can understand. Without proper knowledge of the legal and court systems, counselors may risk losing credibility in their community and among other professionals. This entry describes the nature of couple and family forensics; the circumstances in which therapists may be called on to provide information and testimony within the court system; the legal and ethical responsibilities of counselors in matters of family law such as divorce, child custody, and domestic violence; and the need for therapists to be cognizant of both professional codes of ethics governing confidentiality and the laws of the particular state in which they are practicing.

Individuals may be referred or begin to seek services because of pending or potential legal cases, and the criminal justice system is a major source of referrals, especially among families with low incomes who may not otherwise be able to afford counseling services. Counselors must be wary of testifying for their clients rather than about their clients. Part of the counseling process is the building of a therapeutic relationship, but feelings of being an agent of protection must not undermine a counselor's ethical obligations to correctly report clinical information. When testifying in court, the professional must be aware that providing false information will also be a legal issue.

Involvement in couple and family forensics requires each counselor to be cognizant of family law and be willing to stay abreast of various changes to those laws. In some instances, couples and families have previous involvement with a counselor after voluntarily seeking services or on the advice of schools, child protective service agencies, employers, and other groups that the couple or family have associated themselves with. Upon involvement with a court system, counselors are often nonbiased parties who have had enough engagement with the family to be able to testify on topics including the family's mental health, parental fitness, and treatment prognosis. Counselors have power to state their professional opinions in court based on information gathered during time working with a couple or family.

External coercion can complicate an assessment or counseling, and institutional leverage can affect the counseling process. Mandated counseling by court order or any other situation where a client is forced to participate or face an unwanted consequence affects the therapeutic process and validity of information acquired during an assessment. Therefore, couple and family forensics requires attentiveness to details, reports, and the situation that resulted in the mandated meeting(s). In forensics, there will also be limitations on what issues the counselor can address and report on.

Forming a therapeutic alliance with a family is commonly part of the counseling process and yet providing forensic services complicates this process. Knowing that what is said to a counselor is reportable or will be considered in a court case may in part determine what information is disclosed during meetings, since individuals will want their reports to be favorable. This dynamic creates difficulty in forming relationships with family members and establishing trust in order to create an environment where family members will be willing to disclose sensitive information when appropriate.

The counselor must disclose initially and remind the family repeatedly, of his or her role in couple and family forensics and make the family members aware of the obligations associated with the position as well as limitations and stipulations put in place by third-party payers and legal entities.

Divorce

Some U.S. states require that couples go to counseling before they can be granted a divorce. This is usually in an effort to encourage reconciliation and effective communication. If divorce still ensues following mandated counseling, the counselor can be called to testify to their professional opinions of the cause for divorce and the dividing of family resources and custody of children.

Husbands and wives will often initially attempt to prove that the other party is mentally unstable or incapable of caring for children in the event that custody becomes a subject that they no longer agree upon. During these times, a party may attempt to have past conversations misinterpreted and ultimately attempt to tarnish the reputation of the other parent. Counselors who have previously worked with the family may be required to give their professional opinion on the stability of each parent as well as outline all of the issues that the couple previously tried to work on. In other situations, one party may seek a counselor to help deal with the stresses and life changes surrounding divorce, only for the other party to attempt to establish in court that such use of a counselor is evidence that the individual is not mentally stable. In these instances, the role of advocacy for the client and for the counseling profession comes into play. People seeking mental health services are not to be penalized for seeking help. Rather, the awareness of potential stress and the decision to address this should be viewed as strengths.

Counselors may also be requested to provide psychosocial interviews to assist with determining the best fit for placement of children. It is important to note that a counselor who is requested specifically to complete any sort of assessment should not later on serve as an individual counselor to either of the parties in a case.

Child Custody

An important part of divorce and separation where there are children involved concerns where the children will reside and what part of their time will be spent with each parent. This can be an extremely emotional ordeal for all parties involved. Unfortunately, many custody disputes involve allegations about the safety of a child made by one or both parents against the other. There may be allegations of various forms of abuse, mental unfitness, mental illness, substance use, and lack of proper decision-making skills. Those seeking custody may even attempt to coerce the child in question to make statements to support such allegations.

In an ideal arrangement for forensic evaluation, the counselor will be appointed by the court rather than hired by either party so that neither parent believes that the counselor will serve as his or her personal advocate. It is often necessary to substantiate or disprove allegations. The counselor performing couple and family forensics is least biased when appointed as an evaluator by the court rather than as an expert hired by an individual attorney. Although various tests may be used, the assessments completed by the counselor usually include interviews of each guardian and child and often additional interviews of other caretakers. This series of interviews should cover general topics and also give each parent the opportunity to discuss concerns and the reasons behind the concerns. In addition to interviews, observation of parents and guardians with the children in question is helpful, as is gathering information from collateral sources. If there has been police or child protective services involvement in the past, that should be taken into consideration. Any past psychological and behavioral testing to assess a child's emotional functioning and parenting relationships may be necessary according to the age and development of the child(ren).

Coparenting

In the last few decades, some couple and family forensics has involved coparent coordination. This is an alternative dispute resolution process that involves assessment, case management, education, and where necessary, conflict resolution and decision-making when compromise cannot be attained. Both parties and the judge must approve the decision-making aspect before the coparenting begins. Although a mutually agreed-upon parenting plan is ideal, in most situations where parents continue to have disputes over issues concerning their child or children, the coparenting coordinator may also be brought in by the legal system to enforce provisions that are already in place concerning children. Overall, the purpose of a coparenting coordinator is to determine and facilitate an arrangement that is deemed to be in the best interest of the children involved and minimize conflict that may otherwise be witnessed by or affect the children.

Abuse Cases

Occasionally, the counselor may determine that involving certain individuals in a family counseling session would be counterproductive because of safety issues or questions of the appropriateness of said involvement. Family counseling may be ruled out because of safety issues or due to legal restrictions. Perpetrators of domestic violence (DV) may seek to exploit the co-parenting process and attempt to intimidate and control the victim through requests made in court. DV perpetrators often seek to control their victims not only through abuse but also through intimidation and other forms of control. A perpetrator with large amounts of money may frequently file complaints against his or her victim(s) in an effort to drain them financially and provoke them.

Couple and family forensics in these cases involve not only protecting innocent family members but also assessing risk of involvement of DV perpetrators in sessions and in co-parent coordination. The counselor may also serve as an advocate for the victims of DV and assist with guarding against any further manipulation and identifying valid parenting concerns versus utilization of the court system as a weapon against custodial parents or divorcees.

The same rules apply for children who have been physically or sexually abused. Family counseling that involves the child and the perpetrator is counterproductive to the mental health of the child. Couple and family forensics in these cases will involve assessment of child safety and investigation into whether alleged abuse has occurred, along with the extent of said abuse. Counselors make recommendations for the placement and duration of ongoing counseling with the child and family, keeping in mind the appropriateness and likelihood of progress to be achieved from those services.

Legal and Ethical Considerations

There are numerous legal and ethical considerations for the counselor when doing couple and family forensics. Counselors must frequently consult the code(s) of ethics for professional organizations to which they belong and those codes that are associated with all credentials that the counselor holds. Those practicing couples and family counseling should take advantage of legal and consultative services provided by professional organizations before considering providing forensic services. Specialized training is recommended whenever possible in order to protect oneself and stay in compliance with all relevant laws and ethical codes.

Different regulations also affect the family counseling field, including regulations by government agencies and third-party payees, as well as licensing and certification entities. Federal regulations are designed to guarantee confidentiality for people who participate in work with a counselor, even if the services are mandated. Counselors must be familiar with regulations in their state that affect clients' court proceedings while also being cognizant of how they must follow the ethical mandates associated with state licensure.

In many instances, rules for confidentiality for couple and family forensics and therapy are considered less clear-cut. Some state laws restrict a counselor's right to divulge information obtained in meeting with minors and their parents or guardians unless the minor signs a release. In such cases the counselor must ensure that said release is properly worded. The laws concerning couple and family forensics differ from state to state, including what a counselor is permitted and/or required to report or share with guardians or with courts and law enforcement agencies.

Overall, couple and family forensics involves a blended knowledge of mental health and relevant laws. Although the traditional counseling role requires empathy and progress toward goals set with and by the couples and families involved, in couple and family forensics the goals are set forth by the legal system and the counselor must be able to comply with those laws and their own codes of ethics simultaneously.

Asha Dickerson

See also Court-Mandated Clients; Custody Evaluations; Legal Issues in Parenting

Further Readings

Kaslow, F. W. (2000). *Handbook of couples and family forensic issues: A sourcebook for mental health and legal professionals.* New York, NY: Wiley.

Snyder, C. M., & Anderson, S. A. (2009). An examination of mandated versus voluntary referral as a determinant of clinical outcome. *Journal of Marital and Family Therapy, 35,* 278–292.

Vairo, E. (2010). Social worker attitudes toward court-mandated substance-abusing clients. *Journal of Social Work Practice in the Addictions, 10,* 81–98.

Watson, A. (2015). Self-determination within the context of legally mandated treatment. In P. Corrigan (Ed.), *Person-centered care for mental illness: The evolution of adherence and self-determination* (pp. 173–189). Washington, DC: American Psychological Association.

COUPLE DEVELOPMENT

Couple development is the incremental progression of committed partners through relationship intimacy stages. When two people come together in an intimate, committed relationship, they will experience multiple stages of love as their relationship progresses over time. Knowledge of couple development is pertinent to the practice of marriage, family, and couples counseling because it aids in case conceptualization and the provision of effective treatment. According to therapist and researcher Patricia (Pat) Love, if partners stay committed to their relationship long enough they will progress through four successive stages of love. Knowing the characteristics and common experiences associated with each stage provides a framework for helping clients find satisfaction in their intimate relationships.

Infatuation

The first stage of love is the infatuation stage. Infatuation builds from the initial attraction first experienced by the couple, which is theorized to be determined by a combination of genetic and environmental factors. Attraction alone is limited in its function; although it promotes survival of the species by bringing two people together, it does not ensure relationship sustainability. In order for couples to develop satisfying, long-term relationships, they must work through the stages of love, beginning with infatuation.

Infatuation perpetuates the attraction goal of meeting, mating, and procreating, and it adds a level of commitment not experienced during the time of initial attraction. During the infatuation stage partners are consumed with one another; while attraction can be felt toward multiple people at the same time, infatuation can be directed toward only one person at a time because of the intensity of focus it involves. The infatuation stage is often compared to a drug-induced state or to "runner's high"; during infatuation couples experience such things as an enhanced sense of well-being, heightened libido, and increased energy, which is correlated with increased levels of neurohormonal activity. The mix of these neurotransmitters, which Patricia Love refers to as the "love cocktail," induces euphoria. Couples naturally put positive energy into their relationship by making their relationship a priority, showing affection, encouraging one another, and having fun together. These behaviors contribute to the evolutionary purpose of furthering the human species through the connecting of two people, but the behaviors of the infatuation stage also contribute to feelings of life enhancement. Infatuation, however, is a time-limited state lasting only about six months. At the end of infatuation, neurotransmitters return to their normal, baseline levels, causing partners to come down from the high of the love cocktail. When the sense of euphoria starts to fade, some couples mistakenly associate it with falling out of love, when in fact the change in chemistry is a sign that the couple is moving into the second stage of love.

Post-Rapture

Post-rapture, according to Patricia Love, is the second stage of love. During this stage couples are no longer as strongly under the influence of the love cocktail, and are tasked with deciding whether or not to continue in the relationship without the euphoric feelings that were experienced during infatuation. The transition from infatuation to post-rapture is gradual and marked by less time together, questioning of the relationship, and the surfacing of unmet relationship needs. During this stage, couples no longer see each other as perfect beings, but instead begin to notice things they do not like about one another. This is the time when tension develops between the partners as needs and expectations go unmet. During the post-rapture stage, partners must shift from the effortlessness of the infatuation stage to the intentional work necessary for the sustainability of long-term love.

Some common areas of conflict during the post-rapture stage include sex, priorities, and values. In facing these conflicts, couples often exhibit a "dance of intimacy," a metaphorical pushing and pulling between the partners that signifies a behavioral attempt at getting one's relationship needs met. In the dance of intimacy, one partner becomes the pursuer, wanting more time and attention from the relationship, while the other partner becomes the distancer, wanting more time away from the relationship. The pursuer's behaviors result out of a fear of rejection and a need for more relationship closeness. The distancer's behaviors result from a fear of being controlled and a need for relationship distance. These roles sometimes reverse, depending on the situation. For example, a partner may be the pursuer in the bedroom but a distancer when it comes to financial planning. The labeling of roles is not as important as the recognition that the dance of intimacy is present. The dance of intimacy is hazardous because of the vicious cycle it can create: the more the pursuer tries to pursue, the more the distancer will try to avoid, and the more the distancer tries to avoid, the more the pursuer will try to pursue. This cycle prevents partners from learning each other's underlying needs and places them in danger of dissolving their relationship if they do not begin to compromise. The pursuer/distancer behaviors indicate that the partners are focused on their own needs instead of what is best for the relationship. While during infatuation, partners naturally did what cemented the relationship; during the post-rapture stage, partners begin to focus more on their own personal needs. If the partners want the relationship to continue they must be willing to compromise and make choices based on what is best for the relationship. Couples who stay focused on their individual needs will lose relationship momentum and be unsatisfied with the relationship. Couples who choose to do what is best for the relationship are more likely to progress through the post-rapture stage and move into the discovery stage of love, where they deepen their connection through learning more about each other.

Discovery

The discovery stage is the time in a relationship when partners come to know each other more deeply. At this point in the relationship, partners must commit to continued learning, both about themselves and their partner. Through the continual seeking of information couples gain knowledge to help them make informed decisions about what is best for the relationship. Similar to the post-rapture stage, the discovery stage includes disagreements, misunderstandings, unmet expectations, and changing relationship needs. Flexibility in adapting to each other's changing needs is vital to the relationship's survival. Long-term, committed partners who describe being happy and satisfied in their relationship report the same number of challenges as people who describe being unsatisfied in their relationship. According to Patricia Love, the difference between the two is not the number of problems experienced, but the flexibility exercised in the midst of the struggles. Partners who are willing to compromise and adapt, putting the needs of the relationship first, experience greater happiness in their relationship than partners who stay cemented in their position and remain closed to influence.

During the discovery stage of couple development, common causes of conflict are the unmet expectations that result from things such as role responsibilities and differing definitions of love. Partners enter a relationship with preconceived expectations about each partner's role; for partners who are living together, these often include the issues of who is responsible for specific household chores and how the finances are divided. Each partner comes into the relationship with differing role expectations based on family norms, religious values, societal messages, and past experiences. Often couples assume their partner has the same expectations as they do, but they come to find out through moments of conflict that their partner views roles and responsibilities differently. Unmet expectations also occur around the partners' definitions of love. In general, there are three components to a loving relationship: chemistry, commitment, and compatibility. While all three are important to relationship sustainability, partners tend to hold these components in differing orders of priority. As a result, partners find themselves disappointed when their priority does receive as much attention from their partner as desired as a result of their partner having a different love priority. Identifying each partner's expectations, adapting to meet each other's expectations, and most important, developing shared expectations promotes partner satisfaction as the couple comes to operate in a mutually agreed-upon way.

When expectations are met, the trust between the partners strengthens. Trust is a foundational component needed for couples to progress to the next stage of love. Without trust, couples lack a security net for when their relationship is challenged. Trust needs to be cultivated, and the discovery stage is when this happens. There are several ways trust is built, namely through honesty, consistency, reliability, and fidelity. Fidelity involves the avoidance of any secrecy or deception. During the discovery stage, as couples work on knowing more about each other, fidelity in all things including sex, finances, and friendships provides transparency within the relationship, thus creating a sense of security whereby the partners are able to be vulnerable with each other and build upon their connection.

Connection

The final stage of couple development is the connection stage. During the connection stage partners continue to focus on what is best for the relationship and start to build a shared experience. Their sense of safety and security in the relationship strengthens during this stage, allowing them to know each other more deeply and intimately than before. In order for couples to experience this deeper level of connection they must continue to make their relationship a priority. For couples at this stage of development, one of the major threats to their relationship is time. As the demands of life compete for each partner's attention, couples must be intentional about putting energy toward their relationship. This is accomplished through spending time together, making time for sexual intimacy, supporting one another, and creating a shared life.

A shared life is experienced when partners continue to involve one another in the day-to-day happenings of their lives. It is easy for couples to get caught up in life's demands and find themselves living parallel lives, where they co-exist but lack connection. Couples who make it through the discovery stage and into the connection stage accept that love does not exist on its own and acknowledge personal responsibility in making the relationship last. Couples in the connection stage of love dedicate themselves to the relationship as evidenced by the way they think, act, and prioritize their lives. The relationship of a connected couple goes beyond friendship; they serve as each other's confidants, financial partners, lovers, cheerleaders, roommates, health caretakers, and more. Their words and deeds communicate that the relationship is a priority, and they find joy in the love they share with one another. While some couples commit to staying together in observance of religious or family values, such relationships based on an acceptance of normative constraints are not examples of couples in the connection stage of love. True love, a descriptor of the connection stage, can only be associated with partners who continually choose each other out of genuine desire for the relationship.

While the experience of true love is the goal of couples in a committed partnership, the stages of couple development must be acknowledged. Clinicians can help couples conceptualize their relationship challenges through a development lens that normalizes their experiences and provides them a framework for moving forward. By understanding couple development, clinicians can guide their clients through the relationship stages, promoting choices that are beneficial to the relationship and cultivating a sense of intimate connection.

Jennifer A. Boender

See also Development Model of Marriage; Love, Physiology of; Love, Theories of; Love, Types of; Marriage, Arranged; Mate Selection

Further Readings

Fisher, H. (2004). *Why we love: The nature and chemistry of romantic love*. New York, NY: Owl Books.

Gottman, J., & Silver, N. (2015). *The seven principles for making marriage work: A practical guide from the country's foremost relationship expert*. New York, NY: Harmony Books.

Johnson, S. (2008). *Hold me tight: Seven conversations for a lifetime of love*. New York, NY: Hachette Book Group.

Love, P. (2001). *The truth about love: The highs, the lows, and how you can make it last forever*. New York, NY: Fireside/Simon & Schuster.

Sternberg, R. (1986). A triangular theory of love. *Psychological Review, 93*, 119–135.

Sternberg, R., & Weis, K. (Eds.). (2008). *The new psychology of love*. New Haven, CT: Yale University Press.

Tatkin, S. (2012). *Wired for love: How understanding your partner's brain and attachment style can help you defuse conflict and build a secure relationship*. Oakdale, CA: New Harbinger Publications.

COUPLES, QUALITY TIME

Quality time (QT) is a technical phrase referring to the use of time that couples and families choose to spend together so that they can focus on conversations and activities that strengthen their relationships. During this time the individuals choose a mutually agreed-upon activity. It should be one that satisfies their internal motivators as described in choice theory (the theory informing reality therapy, a therapeutic model used with individuals, couples, and families): belonging, inner control, freedom, and fun. When couples report that they are not getting along (i.e., cannot communicate empathically; argue, blame, and criticize each other as well as fail to solve their problems) they invariably have failed to spend pleasant moments together. They add that their enjoyable times together are in the past. When their relationship was a happy one, they scheduled quality time even though they probably did not think of it as significant. And yet, it is the foundation necessary for a thriving and mutually satisfying relationship. This entry discusses the theoretical basis for QT, the significance of QT, and the characteristic effects of QT.

Theoretical Validation of Quality Time

The theoretical justification for the use of QT is rooted in principles of choice theory formulated by the psychiatrist William Glasser (1925–2013). This theory consists in an explanation of human behavior and posits that behavioral choices spring from five universal needs or motivators: self-preservation, love and belonging, inner control or power, freedom or independence, and fun or enjoyment. Emerging from the five needs of all human beings are specific strivings, desires, or aims called *wants*. The inner world of wants sends signals to the behavioral system to generate actions, cognitions, emotions, and physiological behaviors. All behaviors are made up of these four components. Thus the phrase *total behavior* describes this grouping and is sometimes known as a suitcase of behavior. Behaviors are purposeful and are an attempt to impact the world so as to gain input; that is, perceptions. The perceptual system contains three lenses or levels. At the *low* level of perception human beings simply recognize the world around them. *Middle*-level perceptions mean that the person perceives and understands relationships. Favorable or unfavorable judgments take place at what is called the *high* level of perception.

The delivery system for choice theory from a counseling perspective is reality therapy. Summarized by the acronym WDEP, it provides a flexible but structured format for therapeutic interventions made by mental health professionals. It also serves as a system with interlocking parts for couples to utilize for improving their time together, their communication skills, and their problem-solving techniques. Emphasized here is the use of the WDEP system as a communication model used during QT. The characteristics of quality time provide the context for couples' conversations.

The WDEP System of Reality Therapy

Each letter in the acronym WDEP represents a cluster of ideas useful for couples in their discussions. W stands for interacting about each person's specific wants related to five needs. The dialogue includes interactions about each person's worldview or perceptions. Avoided, however, are arguments about painful topics. Reality therapists advise couples to emphasize comments about *Doing* that includes actions, thinking, emotions, and physiology. The couple keeps in mind that the discussion focuses on topics seen from a low level of perception. If a couple chooses to walk in the neighborhood or in a park and discuss what they see in their surroundings with as few judgments as necessary, they find areas for agreement. The agreements rooted in such conversations might seem trivial, but they provide a solid groundwork for more intense communication and compromises that are necessary in any relationship. This experience often proves to be new for individuals and allows them to attend not only to the other person but also to their own inner mental life. Moreover, the findings of neuroscience indicate that experiences such as these help to establish new neural pathways and enhance the brain's physical structures. Thus, advances in the study of neuroplasticity provide a scientific basis that highlights the significance of quality time. As practicing quality time becomes habitual, it is easily integrated into the levels of more effective communication and problem-solving. In the beginning of the developmental process of QT, counselors urge clients to "keep it simple" by discussing what appears to be inconsequential topics of negligible importance. As the couple develop a greater sense of need satisfaction, especially belonging and enjoyment or fun, they can then more effectively focus on controversial topics without mutual criticism or interpersonal turmoil. At that point they help each other self-evaluate their choices as well as make plans for more effective future choices.

The WDEP system of reality therapy constitutes a communication model that can be integrated into the concept of quality time and its characteristics. It also serves as a flexible system for individual, couples, and family counseling. Effective users of reality therapy enjoy the option of instructing clients on the use of QT and its value. It also provides a tool for addressing the pain often experienced by couples and families. Its limitation lies mainly in the misunderstanding that it seems to have little to do with the problems presented to counselors. However, using QT is an application of the Ericksonian principle that sometimes the solution seems to have nothing to do with the problem. And yet, when explained properly to couples, the use of QT surrounds the problem and reduces the difficulty in managing it.

Significance and Characteristics of Quality Time

When couples choose to make the effort to spend time with each other, and with their interactions guided by the characteristics of quality time described below, they benefit in a variety of ways. They gain practice in the art of communicating in a constructive and enjoyable way. They also build up a storehouse of fond memories and perceptions about each other and their relationship. These two results serve as the foundation for more effective communication that necessarily involves disagreements and tense moments. It also makes compromise easier than it would have been if their conversations had been limited to painful discussions.

The characteristics of QT help couples pour the foundation of the structure of their relationship. Communication about delicate subjects is rendered easier. Respect for the other person's feelings increases. Both people gain an updated sense and clarification of each other's thinking process. The key to successful QT is that each person remains nonjudgmental and accepting of the other person's wants, hopes, and dreams; vulnerabilities; total behavior (actions, thinking, and feelings) as well as perceptions of the world around them. In short, they increase their deep appreciation of each other as well as their relationship. For maximum mutual benefit, their time together has the following qualities: (a) requires effort, (b) reflects mutually agreed-upon values, and (c) includes awareness of the other person. Activities are (d) performed repetitively, and (e) performed for a limited amount of time. During QT the couple (f) discuss safe topics; (g) avoid criticism, complaining, and condemning; and (h) avoid discussion of past misery. Finally, (i) the activity is enjoyable.

Requires Effort

Activities that build strength in a relationship are not passive; they require some effort. It is not about just being in the same place at the same time. For example, watching television requires little effort, yet interaction about the content of the television show can be somewhat effortful. By expending energy, the couple—and this is the result counseling aims for—may come to believe that they have done something worthwhile together.

Reflects Mutually Agreed-Upon Values

These values are defined on an individual basis according to the perceptions of the couple. If one person values athletics and attends sports events while the other person has little regard for sports but prefers attending Mozart symphonies, the selection of one or the other of these events would not be quality time due to the lack of enjoyment experienced by the other party. Although it may be nice for one partner to offer to do this for another, it is not defined as quality time. Quality time is sharing something that reflects both partners' values.

Includes Awareness of the Other Person

Activities that enhance a relationship are best performed together such as walking, hiking, or any activity that requires or is enhanced by the presence of more than one person. But to be of maximal benefit to the relationship, both persons need to choose to do the activity together. An effective counselor helps couples recall past activities that they found mutually satisfying. The couples then describe at least one behavior that had helped them in that it bonded them together and still provides happy memories. They evaluate what worked for them and what did not work for them without engaging in criticism. Infused throughout the discussions with couples is the theme of self-evaluation, a necessary prerequisite of relationship enhancement.

Performed Repetitively

Just as human beings eat, sleep, and exercise regularly, couples with strong relationships choose to spend quality time with each other on a regular basis. Once a week is better than once a month. Once a day is better than once a week. Spending quality time together should be part of their routine.

Performed for a Limited Amount of Time

The activity is confined to a narrow time frame. Though it is best performed often, it need not be excessively time-consuming. A few minutes a day often suffices to create a bonding experience. A 10-minute walk in the neighborhood on a regular basis creates a new experience, and as mentioned earlier, there are benefits to the brain and the relationship as couples process new experiences with one another.

Discuss Safe Topics

During QT couples avoid focusing on controversial topics that serve to create tension. While these topics need not be avoided overall in a relationship, during quality time conversations should be light. For instance, parents who have a "problem child" are often consumed with discussions about the child. Arguments can ensue. Blame and criticism can result from a conversation originally intended to be helpful. In the language of choice theory, the theoretical basis for QT and for reality therapy, topics for discussion should be limited to the low level of perception. This level of perception excludes judgments, or at least minimizes them. On the other hand, topics that connect with a high level of perception often involve emotion-laden judgments about the content of the discussion. For some couples limiting the discussion to low-level perceptions is difficult to implement. Often counselors can help them formulate topics for discussion that are mutually satisfying.

Avoid Criticism, Complaining, and Condemning

Avoidance of criticism, complaining, and condemning is an extension of the characteristics described above. The conversation should focus on positive messages rather than attacks aimed at the other person. Complaining about other people can diminish the strength in the relationship. Extending complaints to the level of condemnation can lower the positive energy existing between two people. While there can be many reasons to complain about world conditions and behaviors that deserve rejection, during QT these discussions are out of bounds.

Avoid Discussion of Past Misery

During QT couples should avoid discussing unhappy events from the past. The conversation should focus on current choices, behaviors, events, and ideas. Discussions of past misery serve only to bring them into the present. Of course, memories of past events that are pleasant remain legitimate topics.

The Activity Is Enjoyable

The best activity is fun for both parties. As the late comedian Victor Borge stated, "Laughter is the shortest distance between two people." Laughter, though it can occur alone, when used with other people can strengthen the relationship.

Robert E. Wubbolding

See also Choice Theory and Reality Therapy; Conflict in Couples and Families; Marriage Enrichment; Relationship Enhancement

Further Readings

Glasser, W. (1998). *The quality school teacher.* New York, NY: HarperCollins.

Glasser, W. (2011). *Take charge of your life.* Bloomington, IN: iUniverse.

Siegel, D. J. (2012). *Pocket guide to interpersonal neurobiology.* New York, NY: Norton.

Siegel, D. J. (2013). *Brainstorm.* New York, NY: Tarcher.

Wubbolding, R. E. (2000). *Reality therapy for the 21st century.* Philadelphia, PA: Brunner-Routledge.

Wubbolding, R. E. (2011). *Reality therapy: Theories of psychotherapy series.* Washington, DC: American Psychological Association.

Wubbolding, R. E. (2016). Reality therapy. In H. E. A. Tinsley, S. H. Lease, & N. S. Giffin Wiersma (Eds.), *Contemporary theory and practice in counseling and psychotherapy.* Thousand Oaks, CA: Sage.

COUPLES AND MARRIAGE COUNSELING

Individuals do not exist in isolation; they are influenced by their relationships from the cradle to the present, none more so than familial relationships. The field of marriage and couples counseling emerged from individual and family theories of psychology, many of which acknowledged the influence of the family on the person but did not focus on working with the couples in particular. The key difference between individual counseling and marital and couples counseling is the focus on the relationship dynamics as the client, not the individual. In other words, while each individual is very important in counseling, how indviduals relate and impact each other is the focus in couples work.

Key Concepts

While there are multiple theoretical orientations to couples counseling with their own key terms, there are a few overall concepts to keep in mind with regard to thinking from a family systems perspective with a couple. A *family systems* perspective takes the notion that when one piece of the couple and family is changed, there is a change in the whole. This is because, as mentioned before, individuals do not live in isolation and relationships are made up of individuals. Therefore, one piece cannot change without altering the overall structure of a relationship. In couples and family counseling, *structure* refers to the dynamics of the overall relationship, or what a couple looks like in who makes the rules, if someone is being labeled as "the problem," and who makes up the couple and family system. A couple and family system has multiple layers to account for, including each individual, *dyads* (or individual relationships between two members of a family, such as a couple or a parent–child dyad), and how each individual and dyad affect the whole system. It is important to always keep the relationship and the dynamics at play in the couple and family relationship at the fore.

Defining Couple and Marriage Relationships

Traditional couples counseling has historically studied a narrow view of what a couple looks like, focusing on Western married heterosexual couples. However, this narrow definition of couples is not accurate for all the populations served. Heterosexual couples represent only one view of couple relationships and most likely do not accurately inform the gender norms of a same-sex couple who may be equally committed. A committed couple does not have to be married, and a married couple is not always committed. With this in mind, a counselor must assess the level of commitment of a couple to the relationship in order to facilitate couples counseling, since the commitment to the relationship is the foundational principle in any couples counseling. While couples may hold many different values and definitions of commitment, research has shown that monogamous couples are overwhelmingly more committed to enhancing their relationship through couples counseling and report higher rates of relationship satisfaction in several realms. From a couples counseling perspective, a couple is defined as two consenting adults committed to a loving relationship.

Multicultural Considerations

In couples and marriage counseling, a crucial component to the dynamics in the room are multicultural aspects that impact who each individual is, how differing cultural factors impact the relationship between family members, with the counselor, and with the world. In considering multiculturalism, a helpful tool in assessing multiple dimensions of cultural identity is Pamela Hays's "ADRESSING" model. ADRESSING is an acronym for *a*ge, *d*evelopmental and acquired disabilities, *r*ace, *e*thnicity, *s*ocioeconomic status, *s*exual orientation, *i*ndigenous heritage, *n*ational origin, and *g*ender. Each of these is important to consider in couples and families, and may also need to be considered multigenerationally as well. For instance, a couple may have very different views of what being an American is like due to past generations' history of immigration, acculturation, and socioeconomic status, despite having many current cultural similarities. In a heterosexual couple dynamic, the male may be unintentionally playing out roles of being head of the household and holding power based on past generations' cultural gender norms, which may or may not be working in the current couple relationship. In addition to the ADRESSING model, another added culture of importance for couples may be their work and school cultures. Some couples may be equally career oriented, while in others one partner may view work as a paying job, and not a piece of her or his identity. These are just a few considerations the couple and marriage counselor must be aware of.

Couple and Family Counselor Traits

When working with couples and families, the counselor has many dynamics to honor, including an empathetic and nonjudgmental understanding of each individual in the relationship, the relationship between each dyad, and how each piece of the relationship puzzle is affecting the overall dynamic of the family system. The couple and family counselor must be careful to not fall into traps of aligning with certain members of the family, which is easy to do unintentionally by spending too much time focusing on one partner or family member more than another, or even aligning body postures with one more than others. When the couple and family counselor spend focused time on an individual, the rationale must be thoughtful, intentional, and empathetically handled with other family members.

Attitudes Toward Sexuality and Intimacy

The couples counselor must maintain a level of self-comfort and maturity around specific topics that may feel uncomfortable or biased to some based on societal messages, such as with sexuality and intimacy. Psychologist Robert Sternberg posited that in order for love to exist, physical passion, emotional intimacy, and commitment to the relationship must all three exist. If a couples counselor is uncomfortable discussing sex with a couple, the counselor is missing out on a huge component of the couple relationship. In addition, the couple's counselor must recognize that sexuality and intimacy are not one and the same, however frequently they go together. Intimacy is the overall experience of affection, autonomy, and understanding (to mention a few components) among couples. Sex may be a part of a couple's experience of intimacy, but intimacy is so much more, and physical sex is not always emotionally intimate between couples. In working toward becoming ethical and competent, couples counselors complete should complete coursework and training to have a clear understanding and skill regarding sexuality and intimacy with couples.

Professionalism in Couples Counseling

All licensed counselors in any U.S. state must have a master's degree in counseling or a related field, such as clinical social work or clinical psychology. It is highly encouraged that anyone seeking a graduate program in working toward becoming a couples counselor attend a program that is accredited to ensure that requirements through programmatic training is geared toward competent and ethical, evidence-based training. In addition to the completion of a graduate degree, licensed counselors must complete clinical internships and clinical supervision while in school as well as afterward. Hourly requirements for post-master's degree clinical supervision vary from state to state, requiring the hopeful couple's counselor candidate to investigate a state's requirements for licensure. In addition to the initial clinical training through a graduate program and post-master's supervision, an ethical and competent couples counselor will seek out continuing education trainings and certifications to stay in line with best practices and create a clinical community of appropriate referral and consultant sources to meet the needs of the couples seen.

Determining Suitability for Couples Counseling

Although couples can present with numerous issues and levels of severity, certain factors determine whether a couple is appropriate to work with a counselor together in couples counseling. The primary and most important ongoing requirement for a couple to engage in couples counseling is safety. Couples counseling is by nature hard work for clients, as clients expose vulnerable emotions and information in counseling more than they do in other areas of life. In couples counseling, the potential for vulnerability may be even higher as clients work in couples counseling to increase insight, awareness, and vulnerabilities with one another.

Screening for Intimate Partner Violence

Couples who cannot feel safe and trust their partner enough to remain safe will not be able to effectively participate in couples counseling. In fact, if not assessed, a couple could hide ongoing violence (*intimate partner violence*), and the encouragement from the couples counselor to heighten emotional expression or sharing vulnerable information with the partner could potentially escalate the violence in the home and pose a high, even deadly, risk to a client. Therefore, it is of the utmost importance that couples counselors engage in ethical, careful screening for intimate partner violence prior to engaging in couples counseling. While there are many schools of thought for what appropriate intimate partner violence screening looks like, most (if not all) counselors would agree that potential for violence in the relationship cannot be accurately or ethically assessed with both partners present. This means that ethical intimate partner violence screening should include making time to see each member of the couple relationship individually. Due to the potential for an aggressor to become dangerously curious about a partner's answers to questions in individual sessions if aware that violence is being assessed for—as well as research on heterosexual couples indicating that the male partner is much more likely to be the aggressor (and with higher levels of lethality when violent)—couples counselors may ethically ask the female in the relationship only about potential violence in the relationship. Screening for intimate partner violence, as well as how to ethically proceed in helping a victim or couple experiencing intimate partner violence is an advanced skill, requiring specialized training for couples counselors to be competent providers. Understanding the warning signs, ethical screening for intimate partner violence with all couples (even if there is no suspicion), and working with couples who have struggled, or are currently struggling, with intimate partner violence are absolute necessities for any counselor working with couples.

Screening for Severe and Persistent Mental Illness

As noted earlier, couples counseling is insight-oriented, geared toward greater awareness and emotional vulnerability, as well as improved communication skills between partners. Untreated persistent mental health issues, such as mood disorders (e.g., depression or bipolar disorder), anxiety disorders (e.g., obsessive compulsive disorder or posttraumatic stress disorder), or a psychotic disorder (e.g., schizophrenia) could be a barrier in healthy communication and reaching goals. While it is not the job of the couples counselor to provide mental health diagnoses to clients, it is appropriate to have a strong clinical understanding of how various persistent mental health issues present and how these could be affecting the couple relationship. If a couples counselor suspects one or both of the partners to be struggling with untreated mental health issues, it may be appropriate for the couples counselor to suggest that the couple have a physical checkup with their physician (to ensure there is not a non–mental health physical issue affecting emotional regulation) and refer them to see an individual counselor prior to (or concurrently in some cases) engaging in couples counseling.

Screening for Substance Abuse

Similar in rationale to screening for mental health issues in a couple is the importance for the couples counselor to assess for substance abuse in a couple relationship. One or both partners could be actively using drugs or alcohol in ways that affect the presenting concerns of a couple. If addiction is a part of the couple's history, it is healthy and important to discuss the current supports the couple has gotten in treatment in the past and what current supports remain. Just as intimate partner violence and mental health screening are important areas of training for a couples counselor to be familiar and competent about (including knowing when referrals are needed as treatment, for those specific concerns may be beyond the scope of the couples counselor's practice or inappropriate due to seeing the couple), screening for and treatment of substance abuse are a complex issue and requires training.

Theories and Models of Couples Counseling

Couples and marriage counselors may devote their counseling orientation to a purist perspective, following one chosen theoretical orientation, while others integrate various theoretical orientations for an eclectic style of counseling. Regardless of which school of thought is chosen by the couples and marriage counselor, it is highly important for the counselor to have a strong understanding of multiple evidence-based theoretical perspectives for best practice. Other entries in this encyclopedia delve more deeply into specific theories and models of couples and family counseling. The following sections provide an introduction to several historically and currently significant theories and models of couples and family counseling; these are discussed in greater detail elsewhere in this encyclopedia (see specific topics).

Psychodynamic, Object Relations, and Attachment Theories

In Vienna in the early 1900s, the psychiatrist Sigmund Freud developed his psychoanalytic theory, which saw human relationships as a reaction to individual needs in childhood and familial relationships (particularly with the mother). Freud had many students who went on to develop their own theories, including Melanie Klein, who expanded Freud's concepts of the id, ego, and superego complexes into internal parts that need to be soothed and made whole. In James Framo's application of object relations theory to couples, it is suggested that individuals tend to unsuccessfully seek that soothing wholeness from outside of themselves through relationships, which can lead to couple distress. Another theory that addresses this issue is John Bowlby's attachment theory, suggesting that humans have an innate need to attach to others in a secure manner and experience belonging. According to attachment theory, attachment styles are formed in earliest infancy with caregivers, and the relationship with childhood parents informs how one relates to others and to the world through emotional experiences and behaviors throughout life. It is suggested that while attachment styles are shaped at birth and through childhood, adult attachment can shift through relational experiences with self and others.

Bowenian Multigenerational Theory

Murray Bowen (1913–1990), an American psychiatrist, is foundational in family therapy for his introduction of the concept of *differentiation,* or in casual terms, understanding where one partner ends and the other begins in a relationship and understanding that one partner's experience does not have to define the experience of the others. In working with couples and families, Bowen believed that the counselor would see best results if working more in the room with the more differentiated partner, as awareness and boundaries with higher levels of differentiation tended to be higher as well, allowing for productive counseling. Bowenian therapy is seen as one of the most influential multigenerational models of family counseling, as the presenting couple or family is not conceptualized solely in the moment, but as a product of each members' family of origin, and their families' histories. Bowenian therapy suggests the use of a tool called the *genogram,* which serves as a generational map of family members, important facts about who each person is, what type of relationship each of them have, and how those relationships could be informing the current issues facing the couple or family.

Cognitive-Behavioral Therapy

Behavioral therapy arose with the work of Russian psychologist Ivan Pavlov (1849–1936) and his theory that humans are conditioned, or trained, to behave in ways that lead to positive rewards and avoid negative consequences. This behavioral theory was expanded to pose that behavior is also informed by learned thinking patterns and strategies that extend to how people view themselves and function in the world within themselves and with others. Cognitive-behavioral theorists believe that thoughts, behaviors, and feelings all generate one another in a cycle. In couples counseling from a cognitive-behavioral perspective, the couple relationship is informed by these individual patterns, which then generate an overall pattern of functioning in the couple. In other words, the couple has learned to be who they are with each other based on their own individual experience as well as their experience with their partner.

Gottman Method

The Gottman method arose out of approximately 40 years of clinical research with couples based on more than 3,000 participants. One of the most astonishing products of John Gottman's research is the ability to predict relationship success based on behavioral and verbal expressions of couples in relation to one another, organized into themes he calls "The Four Horsemen of the Marital Apocalypse," consisting of contempt, criticism, defensiveness, and stonewalling. While every couple will display some of the four horsemen from time to time, the frequency and combination of the four horsemen have been analyzed and calculated to specific ratios that predict divorce. Through this research in measuring elements of couple interactions, Gottman was able to operationalize and empirically compare common patterns in couples who are functioning in a healthy manner versus an unhealthy manner, as well as the continuum range in between. These findings have been applied to numerous theoretical approaches to couples work and inform the ongoing assessment of couples counselors. The Gottman method is one that is strongly tied with cognitive-behavioral theory as well as emotionally focused therapy and suggests many practical assessments and activities for couples counselors to use. Overall, Gottman suggests using a framework called "The Sound House," which consists of seven principles: building love maps, sharing fondness and admiration, turning toward rather than away from each other, be open to influence from a partner, solve solvable problems, understand each other's dreams and hopes to overcome gridlock, and create shared meaning.

Emotionally Focused Therapy

Emotionally focused therapy (EFT) is a more recent, empirically validated method of couples counseling, formulated by Susan Johnson, that integrates several counseling theories. Since its initial development, this framework for working with couples has continued to be studied and proven to be effective for many couples. One of the reasons that EFT has been studied (and therefore empirically validated) is the clear framework of nine steps along three stages, with clear descriptions of what a couple's problem, or *emotional dance*, is, as well as the counselor's role in supporting the couple. EFT is strongly rooted in Bowlby's attachment theory, discussed earlier, as the attachment style of each member of the couple relationship is understood to inform the person how to react to emotionally vulnerable situations. When the attachment needs of each member of the family are honored, insight tends to improve for each person and, with high emotions de-escalated in the safety of the counseling relationship over time, and partners can begin to ask for their emotional needs to be met in more healthy interactive ways. The EFT counselor must have strong person-centered skills in order to serve as a nonjudgmental, curious consultant, reflecting the concerns and feelings of the clients they work with, all while maintaining unconditional positive regard and "catching the bullet" of harmful verbal jabs that family members throw at each other in stressful moments.

Integrative Model of Couples Counseling

Many couples counseling theories overlap, and many have tools and techniques valuable in addressing various areas of a couple's relationship. While remaining pure to a theory could be valuable, a purist approach could miss out on a realm of a couple's life that another theory may have addressed in more detail. In an effort to create a consistent and ethical comprehensive approach to counseling, providing the opportunity for the counselor to tailor the approach to the specific couple, Mark Young and Lynn Long developed the *integrative model of couples counseling*, which provides an overall systematic guideline for working with couples from a variety of theoretical frameworks. This model is grounded in evidence-based application of theory that has been and continues to be researched.

Research in Couples Counseling

While Gottman, through his institute, works to generate research on couple dynamics and tendencies, there are also many other research institutes with ongoing intervention-based studies in working with couples, informing the couples counseling process and encouraging a high standard of practice among professionals. Marriage and relationship education programs tend to be highly structured in the way couples are taught to improve communication styles through specific activities, allowing these programs to be studied with more ease than some other modes of couples counseling. In addition, marriage preparatory programs allow for new couples to enrich their relationship through preventive strategies that utilize a structured format, which lends to ease of research that may provide evidence of effectiveness. There is a call to produce additional evidence-based research for other theoretical approaches to couples counseling; however, less-regimented approaches that tend to be more intuitive in application are inherently more difficult to regulate or shape into a scientific model for study.

Couples counseling is highly informed by individual and family counseling approaches, with the important difference of the client being the *relationship* rather than the individuals it comprises. Couples are unique in identity and present from a variety of cultural, historical, and familial backgrounds, all of which could be informing the current dynamics at play in the couple's relationship. The multiple layers of background and influence, as well as potential concerns with couples, require additional and ongoing training for couples counselors to practice in ethical, competent, and evidence-based ways. Those interested in a career in couples counseling are encouraged to view the foundational and popular theories and models presented here as only the tip of the iceberg, an invitation to invest time and energy in training and education to gain an in-depth knowledge of these and many other worthy modalities of couples counseling practice.

Emily B. Teague-Palmieri

See also Attachment; Bowen Family Systems Theory; Cognitive-Behavioral Couples Therapy; Communication Errors/ Problems in Couples and Families; Conflict in Couples and Families; Emotionally Focused Therapy for Couples; Genograms; Gottman Method Couples Therapy; Integrative Couples Therapy; Marriage Education; Object Relations Theory; Sexual Intimacy; Systems Theory

Further Readings

Bowlby, J. (1969). *Attachment and loss.* New York, NY: Basic Books.

Gottman, J. M. (2000). *The seven principles for making marriage work: A practical guide from the country's foremost relationship expert.* New York, NY: Rivers Press.

Johnson, S. M. (2004). *The practice of emotionally focused therapy* (2nd ed.). New York, NY: Brunner-Routledge.

Long, L., & Young, M. (2007). *Counseling and therapy for couples* (2nd ed.). Pacific Grove, CA: Brooks/Cole.

Scharch, D. (2009). *Passionate marriage: Keeping love and intimacy alive in committed relationships.* New York, NY: Norton.

Couples Therapy Research

Couples therapy refers to a type of psychotherapy that addresses relationship distress experienced by individuals, couples, or families. While there are a number of different treatment modalities to address couple concerns, the focus of this entry will be on research addressing couples treatment in which a clinician meets conjointly with both parties in the relationship. Couples therapy research is an important contribution to the field of marriage, family, and couples counseling because it demonstrates the efficacy and progression of therapeutic interventions with relational dyads. Couples therapy research informs clinical training and practice, which directly benefits families and society as a whole, and also provides direction for future research that will address present and predict future societal concerns. This entry includes a brief historical overview of couples therapy research, its expansion and progression in recent years, treatment efficacy and outcomes, and a review of several treatment modalities with the strongest empirical support.

Brief Historical Overview

While relational and systemic theories have gained momentum and support in literature and practice over the past few decades, family therapies have not yet become as mainstream as individual therapies. Within the broad field of family therapy, couples therapy has not been given as much attention in empirical research as other forms of therapy and is often considered to be a younger field with less established tradition than both family therapy and individual psychotherapy. One reason that may account for less representation in the literature may be the lack of clear distinction between family therapy and couples therapy—many prominent systemic theorists desired to holistically include couples therapy within family therapy rather than distinguish them as separate types of therapy. Though it was relegated and unpopular within the broad practice of family therapy, in the past two decades couples therapy has become a common practice among mental health providers and is now the most popular form of clinical practice within the umbrella of systemic therapies.

Couples Therapy and Culture

Couples therapy, or couple therapy, has become the preferred term for both clinical practice and research purposes to address what has historically been referred to as marriage therapy. In previous years, couple therapy was used to distinguish working with unmarried couples, while marriage therapy was used only to address traditionally married individuals. Current literature and research accepts the term *couple therapy* as comprehensive to more accurately describe committed romantic relationships between two individuals without placing the assumption of a cultural norm or value upon the couple. Couple therapy can address the concerns of many types of both traditional and nontraditional couples, as well as gender and culture concerns in current society. Couple therapy has evolved along with society to address blended families, those who have experienced a divorce, couples in older adulthood, infertility or parenting concerns, and sexual dysfunction.

Although much emphasis is now being placed upon diversity within the clinical practice of couple therapy, research has not yet satisfactorily explored how treatment may be different for lesbian, gay, bisexual, or transgendered (LGBT) individuals. Research has not been able to stay abreast with the steady movements of society, and very few studies include LGBT couples in representative numbers or generalizable samples. There is no universally accepted research indicating specific differences in the application of couple therapy to LGBT couples, and further research will continue to explore how to best meet the needs of these couples and other couples who may not fit into the category of traditional relationships and marriages.

Research Expansion and Progression

Because couple difficulties are not included as an official disorder in the *Diagnostic and Statistical Manual of Mental Disorders,* Fifth Edition (DSM-5), or in previous editions of this manual, couples therapy research has not received as much funding and attention as research investigating treatments addressing specific disorders. However, recent years have shown tremendous growth in the prevalence of couples therapy, and the research base has expanded along with clinical practice. In the early decades of couples therapy, clinical work and research focused upon treating relational conflict and distress; the focus was placed upon relationship dissatisfaction and enhancement, communication, conflict resolution, intimate partner violence, and family discord. The past three decades of couples therapy research has steadily expanded to address not only these difficulties but also more comprehensive treatment enhancing both members' psychological and physical health.

Couples therapy is now considered a viable option for addressing depression, anxiety, and other mental illnesses that were once believed to need individual treatment separate from treatment for couple concerns. Research shows how these treatments can now effectively be combined to provide a therapy that may be more comprehensive than individual treatment for couples in distress. Research suggests that significant relationship distress may place individuals at higher risk for psychological disorders and that recovery from mental illnesses and addictions are aided by the presence and support of one's romantic partner during treatment. Couples therapy offers a way for couples to better learn how to be supportive and understanding of themselves and their partners, as well as the impact that symptomology can have on their systemic relationships.

Because couples therapy has successfully been expanding to include many common adult mental disorders, the mental health field has seen significant advancement in couples therapy's usefulness and applicability. Couple interventions have been found to help couples more effectively manage the mental or physical illness of one spouse. Couples therapy has been shown to have positive outcomes with many prevalent individual diagnoses, including anxiety, depression and other mood disorders, PTSD from childhood trauma, substance use, and alcoholism.

Treatment Efficacy

Literature from the past several decades indicates that couples therapy is a consistently and universally efficacious treatment. Outcome studies demonstrate positive outcomes in around two thirds of couples who are treated and that the average couple after treatment is better off than around 75% of couples who have not attended therapy. These results mirror what is found in individual psychotherapy research and further validate the use of dyadic therapy, showing that the expanded use of couples therapy is appropriate and effective and should continue to be considered for a broad range of adult mental illness treatment.

There has been some discussion over the years as to whether couple therapy research is effectively informing clinical practice of working with couples because of the lack of empirically supported approaches and the rapid expansion of clinical work with couples. In light of this, researchers and scholars have pondered how to help bridge the gap between literature and practice. There is no definitive evidence indicating what mechanisms of change are most effective in couple therapy. There is also no conclusive evidence that one model of couple therapy is superior to others. While more research is clearly needed in these areas, current literature indicates through randomized controlled trials that theories and modalities that have been researched do not show significantly different outcomes from one another. Some of the most heavily researched theories are discussed in the following sections.

Emotionally Focused Therapy

Emotionally focused therapy (EFT) with couples is an experiential-humanistic model based on attachment bonds and the way that insecure partner attachment influences conflict and distress within relationships. The purpose of this three-stage, nine-step therapy is to help both partners understand their own attachment needs as well as their partner's attachment needs to eliminate threatening behaviors, reprocess experiences, and create a more secure attachment between the partners. Emotion is used as the primary instrument of change. The therapist helps the couple to express and reciprocate needs and emotions in order to create an emotionally safe environment for both partners.

Couples treated with EFT have been found to have significant levels of improvement in their levels of relational distress and to be more emotionally engaged with one another; these results remain stable over time. EFT has been found to be highly effective with trauma survivors, including those who have posttraumatic stress disorder (PTSD), have experienced a major betrayal, have experienced severe marital distress due to medical diagnoses, or have been chronically sexually abused. It is also considered highly effective treatment for couples who have significant trust difficulties, high levels of conflict, attachment injuries, and where one or both parties have experienced depression or other mood disorders.

Behavioral Couple Therapy

Behavioral couple therapy (BCT) is also commonly known as traditional behavioral couple therapy (TBCT) and is based on behavioral principles of reciprocity and mutual reinforcement. In BCT, the clinician works with the clients to maximize benefits and minimize costs within the couple's relationship. Therapy is a process in which couples learn important skills, including effective problem-solving, more expressive and positive communication, and reciprocity. Change is fostered by first creating a more positive environment through behavior transactions, followed by negotiations that make the relationship more satisfying and gratifying for both parties. While this therapy as a whole has been found by extensive research to be highly effective for many couples, there are researchers and clinicians who have suggested that BCT may not be the most appropriate treatment for couples who are severely distressed. One result of this criticism was the expansion of BCT into the following treatment model.

Integrative Behavioral Couple Therapy

The most popular variation of BCT is integrative behavioral couple therapy (IBCT). While many principles are shared with BCT, the significant difference that is represented in the name change to IBCT is the additional emphasis on acceptance and less focus placed directly upon change. The integration of change and acceptance adds an additional layer that works with the couple on changing not only the way that they interact with one another but also the way that they accept the behavior of the other party. In addition to this, the therapeutic process includes a functional analysis recognizing that circumstances and context help explain relational interactions and that behavior serves a purpose. Acknowledging and addressing this purpose is believed to help contribute to more beneficial outcomes for the couple. This theory also considers that what works well for one couple may or may not work for another couple; each couple has to determine what behaviors and interactions are appropriate for their needs.

IBCT has been found to increase intimacy among couples. It has been found to be effective in treating couples where one or both parties have problematic alcohol use, in couples who have experienced infidelity, and in heterosexual couples with a depressed woman. Noted outcomes from completed IBCT are higher relationship and sexual satisfaction, lower divorce rates, and having fewer conflicts and problems within couple relationships.

Theory Comparisons

There have not been any conclusive differences found between the efficacy of BCT and IBCT. The outcome trajectories are different in that couples receiving TBCT typically seem to improve quickly and then slow down, whereas couples receiving IBCT seem to improve more gradually and steadily throughout therapy. Both therapies maintain couple satisfaction at fairly equivalent rates and show similar levels of significant improvement among couples who have completed therapy, with some research showing slightly higher levels of lasting effects for IBCT. Both therapies show significant improvement in couples ranging from minimally to severely and chronically distressed. Though EFT has very different theoretical influences and methods from behavioral couple therapies, studies have not been able to conclusively determine that one method is more effective than the other.

According to many researchers in this area, there are several other couple therapies (e.g., structural-strategic, MRI-style, and affective-reconstructive) that are not well represented in the literature and have not formally completed enough randomized controlled trials to be considered empirically supported couple models. Because these underresearched theories and others are used in clinical practice, it is imperative for couples therapy research to continue to seek information that can be used to encourage the use of empirically supported methods. It is also important for research to continue expanding to include successful treatment application to nontraditional couples. Finally, though current literature strongly suggests that couples therapy is effective, couples therapy research should expand to answer questions of why and how it is effective.

*Chelsey L. Hess-Holden,
Kimberly Mason-Peeples, and E. Joan Looby*

See also Cognitive-Behavioral Couples Therapy; Collaborative Couples Therapy; Evidence-Based Practice With Couples and Families; Gottman Method Couples Therapy; Integrative Couples Therapy

Further Readings

Greenman, P. S., & Johnson, S. M. (2013). Process research on emotionally focused therapy for couples: Linking theory to practice. *Family Process, 52,* 46–61.

Gurman, A. S. (2011). Couple therapy research and the practice of couple therapy: Can we talk? *Family Process, 50,* 280–292.

Gurman, A. S. (2013). Behavioral couple therapy: Building a secure base for therapeutic integration. *Family Process, 52,* 115–138.

Gurman, A. S., & Fraenkel, P. (2002). The history of couple therapy: A millennial review. *Family Process, 41,* 199–260.

Johnson, S., & Lebow, J. (2000). The "coming of age" of couple therapy: A decade review. *Journal of Marital and Family Therapy, 26,* 23–28.

Lebow, J. L., Chambers, A. L., Christensen, A., & Johnson, S. M. (2012). Research on the treatment of couple distress. *Journal of Marital and Family Therapy, 38,* 145–168.

Mairal, J. B. (2015). Integrative behavioral couple therapy (IBCT) as a third-wave therapy. *Psicothema, 27,* 13–18.

Snyder, D. K., & Halford, W. K. (2012). Evidence-based couple therapy: Current status and future directions. *Journal of Family Therapy, 34,* 229–249.

Court-Mandated Clients

Court-mandated clients, also referred to as "involuntary clients," are individuals who are required by the courts to attend counseling. These individuals have legally sanctioned relationships with counselors, case managers, social workers, and other individuals providing services within the spectrum of human services, individual, family, and marriage counseling. Court-mandated clients can have legal sanctions with the criminal justice, child welfare, and mental health systems and can be adults, children, or adolescents. The mandates are imposed by the human service agency involved with the individual and may result in heightened client resistance. Several studies have suggested that mandated clients are more resistant to treatment than voluntary clients. Psychologist Carlos DiClemente suggested that resistance in treatment is the result of client reluctance, rebellion, resignation, and rationalization. Mandated treatment for adults can impact an individual's family life, employment, mental health, and education. For children and adolescents, court-ordered stipulations can impose restrictions on leisure activities, education, employment, and future encounters with the agency providing oversight. Examples of services that are often court-mandated include assessments, personal/social development programs (i.e., anger management, parenting), and treatment (e.g., substance abuse). This entry provides a brief overview of the family preservation era of United States history and explains the various settings in which clients may be mandated for services. The entry continues with a discussion of ethical considerations for rendering court-mandated services and concludes with a discussion of client rights and the manner in which these rights impact the delivery of mandated services and corresponding interventions.

Best practices for working effectively with compulsory populations are regarded as a challenging and complex aspect of human service delivery and marriage and family therapy. The underlying supposition for court-mandated services suggests that court mandates can encourage individuals to change and perhaps facilitate appropriate conditions for change to occur. Court-mandated clients are often faced with limited time frames and also require assistance with navigating bureaucratic processes and procedures. In marriage and family therapy, court-mandated services typically require that a therapist have some working knowledge of processes, procedures, reporting requirements, and strategies for effective practice with court-mandated clients. Such efforts on the part of a marriage and family therapist would also necessitate knowledge of ethical considerations regarding disclosure to third parties.

A Brief History of Family Preservation and Child Welfare

The trajectory of human service delivery for families in the United States has been heavily impacted by social-cultural values as enacted in policies and legislation. One example of this dynamic is the family preservation era, which has had a lasting impact on the development and implementation of social welfare policy in the United States. The family preservation era began in the late 1800s and lasted well into the mid-1960s. During this time, welfare policy emphasized stabilizing poor families and enhancing child general welfare. Examples of services provided include material support, supportive counseling, parental education, financial support, and targeted housing. The underlying premise during this era was that families could remain intact if they were able to establish access to local community organizations and state and local resources to garner needed supports.

Child maltreatment can be perpetrated in a number of ways, which includes acts of commission (e.g., physical abuse, sexual abuse, and psychological abuse) and/or acts of omission (e.g., physical neglect, emotional neglect, medical/dental neglect, inadequate supervision). In operating from a family preservation framework, families without proper resources and support are more likely to have incidences of child maltreatment and are also more likely to live in poverty. Research studies suggest that relationships exist between economic hardship, poverty, and increased risk of neglect and physical abuse to families. By garnering supports, families could become more self-sufficient and better able to prevent child maltreatment and poverty. In preventing or successfully addressing issues related to child maltreatment, families could avoid further involvement with child welfare services.

An applied example of the family preservation model is noted in the ecological systems-informed model of risk for out-of-home placement during services. This model, which is influenced by psychologist Urie Bronfenbrenner's bio-ecological model, posits that specific environmental factors (e.g., financial need) influence family outcomes through factors that are more immediate (e.g., caretaker mental health) to the family unit. There are four "blocks" of variables that encompass environment/resources, agency factors, family factors, and individual/caretaker factors. Issues that may arise in either of the domains can ultimately influence family outcomes and may jeopardize the family's preservation. When parents of families are accused of child maltreatment, such accusations warrant involvement with various human services agencies such as the criminal justice system, departments of mental health, and child welfare agencies. More often than not, such involvement typically entails oversight by one or more of the human services agencies where the individual is deemed in compliance with such sanctions when set requirements are met by the client's efforts. Failure to meet previously established stipulations could result in fines, incarceration, and other restrictions that may impact other areas of the client's life.

Substance Abuse, Domestic Violence, and Mandated Clients

Juveniles with substance abuse problems may be mandated to either inpatient or outpatient treatment facilities depending on the severity and chronicity of the issues. Availability of such programs in the youth's community further hinders treatment mandates. When substance abuse treatment is available for mandated youth, cooperation and compliance on the part of the parent or guardian is necessitated. While attending substance abuse treatment, juveniles must undergo substance assessments to capture substance use history and individual, group, and/or family therapy. Mandates regarding substance abuse treatment may originate from probation officers, judges, and child welfare agencies and may take the form of referrals to approved providers. Failure to comply typically results in restrictive sanctions, fines, community service, or jail time.

Coercion for treatment for alcohol and drug problems was a by-product of a reform movement that swept the United States during the 1800s. During this time, alcoholics were involuntarily committed for treatment. Mandated substance abuse treatment for adults can look slightly different from those provided to juveniles, for such services are contingent upon the circumstances that warrant mandated treatment. Several states have implemented family drug treatment courts to address parental substance use for parents involved with child welfare service agencies. Parental substance use is a risk factor that can increase the likelihood of child maltreatment occurring within a household. Parents who misuse or abuse substances are often reported to child welfare agencies for abuse and neglect. In the event that reunification is warranted, children of parents who misuse or abuse substances are least likely to return to the custody of their parents. Chronic substance use complicates the course of treatment and can decrease the likelihood of reunification. When parents are involved with child welfare agencies, a contingency of their case plan completion is for the parent to address substance abuse problems while simultaneously addressing other issues of concern that could potentially increase risk of child maltreatment. Practitioners who provide these services may do so in the comfort of the individual's home or may provide these services in an office setting. An example of in-home services includes Homestead or Wrap-Around services, where the provider is required to regularly communicate the client's progress, compliance, and attendance to the case manager.

Adults who are not involved with child welfare agencies often have involvement with the criminal justice system. Involvement with the criminal justice system for substance abuse and misuse usually requires mandated services related to the infraction. Multiple arrests for possession of drugs or misconduct related to drugs typically results in mandated services such as substance abuse treatment and individual, group, and/or family therapy. Practitioners who render these services are typically required to report the individual's progress to a judge, attorney, or probation officer. Perpetrators of domestic violence tend to enter therapy either at the insistence of a mate or by court order. Concerns related to the attendance and completion of domestic violence programs are significant for those who are mandated to complete these services. Outcomes for domestic violence programs are more favorable for individuals who complete the programs. Furthermore, when treatments are backed by active court interventions, mandated clients are more likely to be compliant and are also more likely to complete their mandated programs and treatments.

In current service contexts for individuals with serious mental health disturbances, institutional and legal controls may strongly impact the treatment relationship. In the case of psychotherapy, the quality of the relationship between the client and therapist most often predicts the outcome of psychotherapy; however, in mandated relationships involving mental health, such outcomes may not be enjoyed. Compared with voluntary relationships, mandated relationships in mental health often display greater therapist control and less autonomy on the part of the mandated client. Individuals with mental illnesses who are mandated to court services often have co-occurring substance abuse problems that may prevent them from following treatment recommendations. Other key issues of concern include client resistance and motivation to change.

Ethics: Client Rights, Self-Determination, and Informed Consent

A controversial topic related to court-mandated services concerns the adherence to specific legal and ethical principles concerning a worker's relationship with a court-mandated client. The worker's ability to adhere to specific ethical considerations is often secondary to that of legal principles that usually define the worker's role and obligations for fulfilling the role in the mandated relationship. Inherent to every human services worker–client relationship is the concept of *authority*. The obligations for fulfilling such roles are conceptually akin to the duties ascribed to those vested with the responsibility of fulfilling societal, institutional, and professional sanctions. The authority vested in human services practitioners is typically founded on rational, formal grounds and is the basis of the mandated client–practitioner relationship.

In addition to social and legal senses, mandated clients encounter authority in psychological senses. According to Samuel Mencher, a historian of social welfare policy, psychological authority derives from several sources, including fear of punishment, respect for the authority figure as a holder of wisdom or expertise, and expectation of reward from the authority figure. Both psychological and sociological components of authority have the potential to influence mandated relationships, for mandated relationships are often characterized by high levels of formal authority as monitored and vested by the agency mandating services. Specific agencies, such as those employing social workers, often employ a greater degree of social control over individuals' lives and can further complicate the mandated relationship.

Several studies point to the influence that human services workers, social workers, therapists, and counselors have on the behavior and ultimately the success of clients. Ethically sound and effective service delivery to a client's mandated services typically requires adherence to the best interest of the client while also adhering to specific boundaries and the avoidance of role conflicts. The democratic values and individual rights culture that is fostered in American society warrants further considerations on the use of coercion in human services delivery, since protecting the rights and autonomy of individuals involved with human services agencies is of central importance to treatment outcomes. A client's right to self-determination is often thought of as being the contrary of coercion in human services delivery. Self-determination gives the client an opportunity to participate in decision-making processes that will affect them. Informed consent provides a means by which individuals can assert self-determination.

Anissa K. Howard

See also Families and Substance Abuse; Home-Based Therapy; Substance Use Disorders in Adolescence

Further Readings

Brodsky, S. L., & Titcomb, C. (2013). Treating reluctant and involuntary clients. In G. P. Koocher, J. Norcross, & B. Greene (Eds.), *Psychologist's desk reference* (3rd ed., pp. 197–202). New York, NY: Oxford University Press.

Huang, Y., Duffee, D. E., Steinke, C., & Larkin, H. (2011). Youth engagement and service dosage in a mandated setting: A study of residential treatment centers. *Children and Youth Services Review, 33,* 1515–1526.

Hutchison, E. D. (1987). Use of authority in direct social work practice with mandated clients. *Social Service Review, 61,* 581–598.

Regehr, C., & Antle, B. (1997). Coercive influences: Informed consent in court-mandated social work practice. *Social Work, 42,* 300–306.

Snyder, C. M., & Anderson, S. A. (2009). An examination of mandated versus voluntary referral as a determinant of clinical outcome. *Journal of Marital and Family Therapy, 35,* 278–292.

Vairo, E. (2010). Social worker attitudes toward court-mandated substance-abusing clients. *Journal of Social Work Practice, 10,* 81–98.

Watson, A. (2015). Self-determination within the context of legally mandated treatment. In P. Corrigan (Ed.), *Person-centered care for mental illness: The evolution of adherence and self-determination* (pp. 173–189). Washington, DC: American Psychological Association.

CRISIS INTERVENTION WITH COUPLES AND FAMILIES

Crisis intervention is an urgent, brief, and intense level of treatment conducted in the event of a crisis to stabilize the situation, alleviate stress, improve coping and adaptive skills, and restore the individual or family's homeostasis. Crisis intervention with couples and families focuses on the unit and not just a single individual. Couples, marriages, and families are unique units bonded by kinship, love, values, and/or shared experiences. Thus, a crisis or traumatic event that affects any member of the unit will likely affect the other family members but not always in the same way. Specifically, a crisis is a stressful life event that becomes overwhelmingly unbearable and impairs a person's ability to cope effectively with the traumatic event or experience. The stress caused by a crisis creates psychological distress that alters baseline functioning (e.g., thinking, feeling, and/or behaving) for the individual, couple, or family. Some examples of a crisis might include a natural disaster, fire, rape, abuse, domestic violence, death of a loved one or friend, suicide or suicide attempt, depressive or psychotic episode, medical illness, accident (e.g., car accident, airplane crash, train derailment, or personal injury), unwanted pregnancy, loss of a job or financial resource, legal trouble, robbery, financial strains, and/or lack of resources (e.g., access to adequate community services or health care). In each of the aforementioned examples, individuals are faced with significant stress and problems that are likely perceived to be insurmountable. Thus, the traumatic event suddenly disrupts normal functioning and propels the individual, couple, or family immediately into a state of shock and disarray. As a result, people may seek counseling or therapy to help cope with the aftermath of a crisis. In marriage and family therapy, crisis intervention takes a systemic approach. For example, a crisis situation with a spouse, parent, or child will have ripple effects throughout the family unit. Thus, crisis management involves the unit (e.g., the couple or the family) because of the cohesion and interdependence of the family system. Although a crisis is a unique event that presents danger, it also provides opportunities. The presence of both danger and opportunity renders families susceptible to changes in roles, boundaries, communication, bonds, values, and overall functioning. In addition, unresolved crises can ultimately lead to familial dysfunction or breakdown. Thus, treatment should target the couple or family as a unit. Simply focusing on any one individual within a couple or family does not address the crisis being experienced by the unit. In this entry, the definition, outcome, history, and models of crisis intervention with couples and families will be reviewed.

Crisis and Outcomes

A crisis is defined more by the change or distress it creates rather than by the actual event. Thus, what a crisis is or is not can be idiosyncratic. Small events can be experienced as traumatic. For example, a car accident, or a family member in a drunken stupor, might be a crisis for one family and merely a bad day for another. As well, a crisis can emerge as the result of challenges within a developmental stage (e.g., midlife crisis, adolescent identity crisis) or as the result of challenges to a person's fundamental religious beliefs or personal values. The duration and intensity of an event can also thrust an individual or family into a state of crisis.

Regardless of the event creating the distress, there are three possible outcomes of a crisis situation: (1) individual and/or familial functioning or relationships get worse (decompensation); (2) individual and/or familial functioning or relationships stay the same (return to pre-crisis state), or (3) individual and/or familial functioning or relationships get better (growth). The ultimate goal of any traumatic event is for the global functioning, coping, and relations of the individuals experiencing the crisis to improve after the crisis. A crisis is a change agent and has therapeutic potential.

Ideally, as a crisis is resolved, the individuals should experience an increased sense of mastery of their domain, improvement in intimacy and caring attachments, and new revelations about self. For couples and families, sharing in the experience of the traumatic and stressful event can improve familial support and bonding. Ideally, crises create an opportunity to build familial cohesion, trust, and interdependence. Further, a crisis is an opportunity to better understand oneself and the other members of the family. However, skills such as communication, problem-solving, resiliency, decision-making, self-awareness, adaptability, and ability to accept help are key variables involved in how a crisis is managed. Therapeutically, it is never the goal to have things (e.g., relationships, communication, functioning) get worse or stay the same.

A person's response to a traumatic experience or event starts in the brain. In addition to thoughts, feelings, and emotions being affected and guided by the crisis, a crisis can alter the brain. And some couples and families exist in a constant state of chaos and crises. Research suggests that chronic exposure to trauma (e.g., abuse, violence) can impair connectivity in the brain and cause stress-induced structural changes in the hippocampus, amygdala, and prefrontal cortex. These neurobiological changes in the brain's stress-response system can impair psychological, behavioral, and physiological responses, making it more difficult for the person to solve problems effectively, and can hinder how the person responds to future crisis-like situations.

What Is Crisis Intervention?

Because of the stigma and stereotypes surrounding counseling and related services, it usually takes a crisis for individuals, couples, and families to seek treatment. Since a crisis hinders baseline functioning, it is likely that the person or family's usual coping behaviors and resources have failed to reestablish homeostasis. In the midst of the crisis, most individuals or families realize that they have exhausted all options for achieving stability and resolving the problem on their own. It is the realization and search for a solution that lead individuals and families to seek professional help. The help typically sought in a crisis situation is an immediate and acute intervention referred to as crisis intervention.

History of Crisis Intervention

Some might argue that the first crisis within a couple or family began with Adam and Eve in the Garden of Eden when, according to the biblical book of Genesis, the couple grappled over eating from the forbidden tree of the knowledge of good and evil. However, it was the suicidal hotline established in San Francisco, California, in 1902 that gave rise to our modern system of providing emergency psychological care. Subsequently, the concept of crisis management was advanced by the work of the military in its response to soldiers re-experiencing battle trauma after combat. Psychological first aid began during World War I when psychiatrists began treating war veterans for symptoms of crying, screaming, memory loss, fatigue, and lack of responsiveness. The work of Thomas W. Salmon in World War I and the work of Abram Kardiner and Herbert Spiegel during World War II created fundamental concepts for crisis work. Kardiner and Spiegel are best known for their work with wartime neuroses, which laid the groundwork for managing traumatic stress. Throughout his career, Salmon was an advocate for mental hygiene. During the war, Salmon served as a chief consultant in psychiatry to the military. He devised a system to screen recruits for mental health problems, organized the military's neuropsychological services, and helped to develop new treatment procedures. Also noteworthy are the studies on grief conducted by Erich Lindemann following the aftermath of a fire in a nightclub in the mid-1940s.

Theoretical Models of Crisis Interventions With Couples and Families

According to Kardiner and Spiegel, there are three core principles of crisis work: (1) the immediacy of the interventions, (2) the proximity to the occurrence of the event, and (3) the expectancy that the individual or family will regain stability and resume an adequate level of functioning. Since World War II, several models of crisis intervention have developed, including crisis incident stress management (CISM); Myers's detect, direct, protect, and connect framework; and Roberts's seven-stage crisis intervention model (R-SSCIM). Cognitive-behavioral therapy (CBT), solution-focused therapy, and behavior therapy have all been adapted to serve and support couples and families in crisis. Integrative or eclectic approaches also have been employed. The community systems (CS) model and multiple impact therapy (MIT) are two approaches commonly employed by clinicians intervening with couples and families in crisis.

The CS approach to family crisis intervention shifts the focus from pathology to the client's interaction with the environment. In this systems-centered approach, service coordination and linkage to community resources and services are deemed the most effective strategies for stabilizing a crisis. Thus, crisis workers guide couples and families in crisis toward accessing and utilizing community resources. Efforts are coordinated with agencies and organizations that can provide medical, legal, housing, education, employment, mental health, religious, advocacy, and social service support. Thus, crisis workers are more likely to accompany the family to an appointment rather than simply providing the family with a phone number to facilitate community connectedness.

Multiple impact therapy (MIT) is also rooted in consultation, collaboration of service providers, and strong relationships with community service systems. However, MIT uses multiple clinicians, one assigned to each family member, for assessment, crisis intervention, and long-term treatment. The clinicians assigned to each family member can be students, volunteers, counselors with general training, or clinicians with specialized training such as behavior management, substance abuse, sexual abuse, gender identity issues, or eating disorders. In this treatment modality, each family member meets individually with their assigned clinician. Then, sessions are facilitated with the entire family and with each clinician. Family members are asked to observe as the clinicians role-play other members of the family from their client's perspective. Each clinician expresses the client's needs and wants within the family portrayal. Time-outs are called to address misrepresentations.

Because of the diversity in cultures and familial constellations, no single model will work with every family or even every time with any one family. Thus, crisis workers must be flexible and willing to seek knowledge in an effort to meet the various needs of couples and families. Regardless of the model, the goals of crisis intervention are universal. In a crisis, the role of the clinician is to intervene immediately to facilitate healing and recovery. For example, a marriage and family therapist must interrupt the crisis, prevent maladaptive coping, promote stability, and help restore order in a confusing, overwhelming, and possibly chaotic situation. Whatever theoretical framework the counselor employs, immediate steps might include a risk assessment, ensuring safety (e.g., contracting for safety, facilitating psychiatric hospitalizations, coordinating respite care for children or disabled family members), hearing the client's story, emphasizing strengths, connecting to resources (e.g., shelters, food banks), instilling hope, and creating a plan to follow up.

The Impact of Crises on Families

Supporting an individual through a crisis can be complex work. Supporting a couple or family through a crisis is even more challenging. Unresolved crises can create myriad difficulties and dysfunction. Couples and families present with different rates of emotional growth, varying expectations and coping styles, as well as unconscious fears and anxieties that have to be successfully navigated in a crisis situation. These factors help create the danger potential that exists in familial crises. Undoubtedly, a familial crisis can damage bonds that connect the family, cause role reversals, hinder feelings of gratification or self-esteem, force autonomy, hinder communication, create residential or financial instability, alter daily living patterns, interrupt interpersonal reward systems (e.g., unconditional love, intimacy, nurturance, affection), and change core values.

Marriage and family therapists play an intricate role in supporting, mediating, and repairing during a crisis. Initially, marriage and family therapists are charged with problem identification, managing initial anxieties, identifying protective factors and resources, providing information and support, facilitating familial communication, and performing needs assessments. Ultimately, alternatives are explored and an action plan is generated. Marriage and family therapists support couples and families through plan implementation and follow up as needed to ensure balance is restored.

Tasha Leroyce Banks and Aina A. Harris

See also Family Resilience; Family Strengths; Family Stress Adaptation Theory

Further Readings

Cisney, J. S., & Ellers, K. L. (2009). *The first 48 hours: Spiritual caregivers as first responders.* Nashville, TN: Abingdon.

Flannery, R. B., Jr., & Everly, G. S., Jr., (2000). Crisis intervention: A review. *International Journal of Emergency Mental Health, 2*(2), 119–125.

Gentry, C. E. (1994). *Crisis intervention in child abuse and neglect.* Washington, DC: U.S. Department of Health and Human Services.

McEwen, B. S. (2007, July). Physiology and neurobiology of stress and adaptation: Central role of the brain. *Physiological Reviews, 87*(3), 873–904.

Myers, D. G., & Vee, D. F. (2005). *Disaster mental health services: A primer for practitioners.* New York, NY: Brunner-Routledge.

Myer, R. A., Williams, R. C., Haley, M., Brownfield, J. N., McNicols, K. B., & Pribozie, N. (2014). Crisis intervention with families: Assessing changes in family characteristics. *Family Journal: Counseling and Therapy for Couples and Families, 22*(2), 179–185.

Critical Theory

Critical theory refers to a diverse family of theories focused on improving the human condition through the exploration of asymmetrical power distributions and the social construction of human behaviors, emotions, and interactions that undergird oppression in society. Critical theory is particularly relevant to marriage, family, and couples counseling due to the impact of societal context on individual identity, family relationships, and the intersection of the individual and family developmental trajectory with societal and contextual stressors. In order to operate from a transformational, critical theory framework for practice, counselors must have an understanding of the historical development of critical theory and its subtheories, the philosophies that undergird the theory, the research methods that support professional scholarship, and how the family of theories is utilized in clinical practice. This entry will address these topics.

Definition and Historical Development

In counseling and therapy, theories are used to order human behavior, thoughts, emotions, and relationships into structures and systems to allow for professional description and understanding. Critical theory, a term typically used to describe a larger family of critical theories, goes a step further, delving into the societal, cultural, and economic factors impacting human development, interactions, and relationships while also oppressing and marginalizing some groups in society. Critical theory and its subtheories operate from the perspective that oppressive ideologies are pervasive throughout institutional structures and societal practices. Critical theory and its subtheories assert that these ideologies and practices are normal, not anomalies, and shape the belief systems and functioning of individuals within society. Furthermore, these institutional and societal practices lead to imbalances of power that allow the dominant group holding the power to maintain a societal system and structures that disempower other groups while granting power to the dominant group. An additional fundamental component of critical theory is a focus on empowerment and action to improve the human condition and encourage a more equitable balance of power.

Critical theory emerged from the work of theorists at the Institute for Social Research in Frankfurt, Germany, in the 1920s and 1930s. Theodor Adorno, Max Horkheimer, Herbert Marcuse, and their colleagues led the initial development of the theory in an effort to better understand how injustice and oppression shaped the world and human interactions. But when the Nazi party took power after Adolf Hitler became chancellor of Germany in 1933, all Jewish academics were dismissed from their university positions, liberal institutions such as the Institute for Social Research were ordered closed, and people of Jewish ancestry were barred from participating in the intellectual and cultural life of Germany. The lives and professional work of these theorists, and others, were heavily impacted by their subsequent emigration to the United States as they sought to evade the social marginalization and increasing threats to personal safety facing the Jewish population and other minorities in the German-speaking world. After arriving in the United States and becoming immersed in U.S. culture, they were intrigued by the complex dichotomy between open discussions of equality in American society and the contrasting societal realities of highly prevalent racial and class discrimination and oppression. From their life experiences and professional study, these theorists developed a theory that viewed the social construction of experience as fundamental to understanding human behaviors, emotions, and relationships. Their theory highlighted that understanding as the key to unfettering humans from oppressive societal structures.

Philosophical Underpinnings

Critical theory and the subtheories that have developed from critical theory fit within an overarching paradigm of critical humanism. At the heart of critical humanism is the acknowledgment of individual consciousness as a tool of empowerment and transformation. By raising individual awareness, critical humanism asserts that social transformation can be promoted and groups may be liberated from oppressive social processes. Within the paradigm of critical humanism, critical theory and its offshoots evolved to focus specifically on understanding the role of power, politics, and social structures on the perpetuation of oppression and marginalization of specific groups within society. The family of critical theories holds as a foundational philosophy that we must, as a society, seek to identify institutionalized norms and values that perpetuate the subordination of minority populations and work to eradicate these oppressive conditions. By understanding the societal structures and processes that oppress the equitable participation of certain groups within society, critical theories posit that as a society we will all better understand how these structures and the resulting oppression and discrimination limit the success of all of us. In order to address the multifaceted nature of oppression and discrimination within U.S. society, a family of subtheories has evolved from the parent theory, critical theory. These include critical race theory, feminist critical theory, queer critical theory, Latina/o critical theory (LatCrit), critical social theory, and others developed within specific disciplines to address prevalent issues of marginalization, discrimination, and oppression.

Contrasting Critical Theory and Deficit Theory

For a fuller understanding of critical theory, one must understand the contrasting deficiency theory. Deficiency theories have been used throughout history to situate the cause of a minority population's marginalization in deficiencies held within the minority population's biological makeup, culture, or social structure. According to deficiency theories, culturally bound characteristics, including interdependency rather than autonomy, language, and an internal present-focus rather than future-focus, are deficiencies that manifest as academic failure, career impediments, and/or individual struggles with relationships and interactions within society. Further, out of deficiency theory has grown the deficit hypothesis, which espouses that individuals are evaluated by the characteristics that they do not have rather than by the strengths that they possess. The population is accused of not making greater efforts to be able to overcome challenges and succeed in society, and society accepts no responsibility for the contextual challenges facing the minority population. Critical theory stands in stark contrast to deficiency theories in its efforts to analyze the experiences of minority populations through an exploration of the impact of society, social perceptions, and socioeconomic resources on individual and family development and wellness. Additionally, from the perspective of critical theory it is not enough to simply explore issues and relationships with a cool, professional detachment; rather, it is essential that professionals be willing to be engaged and working to address oppression and marginalization. This essential intersection of theory and practice is termed *praxis*. For counselors and therapists, this praxis is achieved through empowerment of the client. Empowerment is achieved, in part, by making space for the voice of the lived experiences of minority populations. The voice and empowerment component of critical theory is an essential element of the theory.

Role of Voice in Critical Theories

Voice is a highly important component of critical theories. Voice has been highlighted by researchers within the field of critical theory as a vital factor necessary for emancipation and empowerment of the individual. Critical theory and its associated subtheories assert that making a space for the voice of the marginalized and the oppressed is fundamental for healthy identity expression, a well-functioning society, and the full representation of culture throughout that society. Critical race theory, feminist theory, queer theory, Latina/o critical theory, critical social theory, and other critical theories challenge one to view the feelings and perceptions of marginalized populations as legitimate and important. Through the inclusion of the voices of disenfranchised and marginalized populations, critical theories believe that dialogue is able to be transformed into a tool for empowerment and emancipation.

Research Strategies Within the Critical Paradigm

Praxis is fundamental to critical theories, which espouse that it is not enough to simply understand theoretically issues of oppression and marginalization within society, but that one must also strive to address these issues. Professionals aligned with the field of critical theory believe that societal transformation requires dialogue, the inclusion of all voices, research, and efforts to change oppressive structures and processes within disciplines and society. Consequently, specific research methods have evolved to promote the integration of critical theory into professional scholarly investigation. Critical ethnography, referred to by Concha Delgado-Gaitan and Henry T. Trueba as *ethnography of empowerment,* is one such research strategy that integrates critical theory, research methods, social action, and empowerment. In ethnography of empowerment, change occurs through the sharing by research participants of their own experiences with others who have had similar struggles. The sharing of these personal experiences fosters the development of a collective consciousness among participants, which leads to a community of empowerment. Other critical research strategies rely heavily on the importance of knowledge gained through the experiences of participants, utilizing narratives, counterstories, testimonies, and oral histories. Critical theory research views experiential knowledge as personally individual but foundationally connected to the institutions and populations within society. Research within the critical paradigm requires that researchers move from the production of knowledge into the transformation of knowledge, and this transformation involves the recognition of research as a tool for social change.

Implications for Counseling

Critical theory, through a critical examination of societal institutions, challenges dominant ideologies that perpetuate oppression. Counselors utilizing a critical theoretical framework for practice strive to create a space where marginalized voices can be heard. These counselors seek to explore the intersections of political, social, and economic influences on the identity development, interpersonal relationships, and wellness of clients. Counselors operating within a critical theoretical framework also engage in intense self-reflection exploring their own cultural, gender, and racial biases. These counselors recognize that when one's lens is colored by intersecting and implicitly accepted oppressive beliefs, one's internal views and understanding are projected upon clients and clients' presenting concerns, and thus further perpetuate oppression.

At its core, critical theory holds the ideal that to examine comprehensively the experiences of minority groups, one must do so with the understanding that what at first appear to be gender, cultural, or race-neutral policies and structures in society actually contribute to a larger structure that oppresses and disempowers some while granting power to others. Critical theory includes a call to action to remedy the inequalities perpetuated by oppressive ideology. The call to action is answered by counselors seeking to create a space for the voice of minority clients to share their experiences and contribute to empowered dialogue that transforms knowledge and societal structures leading to social change. Critical theory has deep historical roots and is focused on broad social change, but at the heart of this theory and all of the theories within the family of critical theory is the power of the individual. The promotion of consciousness of contradictions and oppressive structures within social, political, and economic forces is essential to empowering individuals. Fostering insight and awareness and empowering individuals to use this awareness to act against oppression is, according to critical theory, the vehicle to improving the human condition.

Kylie P. Dotson-Blake
and Angela R. McDonald

See also Cultural Issues in Couples and Families; Diversity; Empowerment in Families; Gender- and Culture-Sensitive Therapies; Racism; Social Constructionism

Further Readings

Agger, B. (1991). Critical theory, poststructuralism, postmodernism: Their sociological relevance. *Annual Review of Sociology, 17,* 105–131.

Bronner, S. E. (2002). *Of critical theory and its theorists* (2nd ed.). New York, NY: Routledge.

Delgado-Gaitan, C., & Trueba, H. (1991). *Crossing cultural borders: Education for immigrant families in America.* New York, NY: Falmer Press.

Kincheloe, J. L., & McLaren, P. (2000). Rethinking critical theory and qualitative research. In N. K. Denzin & Y. S. Lincoln (Eds.), *Handbook of qualitative research* (pp. 138–157). Thousand Oaks, CA: Sage.

Ladson-Billings, G., & Tate, W. F. (1995). Toward a critical race theory of education. *Teachers College Record, 97,* 47–68.

Roithmayr, D. (1999). Introduction to critical race theory in educational research and praxis. In L. Parker, D. Deyhl, & S. Villenas (Eds.), *Race is . . . Race isn't* (pp. 1–6). Boulder, CO: Westview.

Solorzano, D., & Yosso, T. (2001). Critical race and LatCrit theory and method: Counter-storytelling. *Qualitative Studies in Education, 14*(4), 471–495.

Valdes, F. (2000). Outsider scholars, legal theory and outcrit perspectivity: Postsubordination vision as jurisprudential method. *DePaul Law Review, 49,* 3–31.

Villenas, S., & Dehyle, S. (1999). *Race is . . . race isn't.* Boulder, CO: Westview.

CRUCIBLE

A crucible is defined as a container in which substances, such as metal, may be melted or subjected to very high temperatures. A crucible is also an occasion of severe test or trial, as well as a situation in which different elements interact to produce something new. In counseling, the word *crucible* has been used to describe the intense experience of family therapy. The process of family therapy is like a crucible—helping contain the intense experiences of the family and helping them create newer, more functional ways of relating with one another. The book titled *The Family Crucible* was written by Augustus Napier with Carl Whitaker, and was based on Whitaker's experiential-symbolic approach. This approach to family therapy focused on the experience of the family in the here and now, with the symbolic element representing the meanings families hold and how those are enacted in their relationships, behavior, and communication.

Carl Whitaker and Augustus Napier

Carl Whitaker was a family therapist and professor of psychiatry at the University of Wisconsin. Augustus Napier studied with Whitaker for several years through his Ph.D. clinical hours and in a postdoctoral fellowship. Whitaker and Napier would work together as a team, counseling families in recognition of and as a balance to the power within families. As a co-counseling team, they also were able to use symbolic meanings to model effective communications and behaviors for the families with whom they worked.

The Process of Therapy

The heart of the crucible in family therapy is not something the family "does." It is also not something the therapist "does," although the family may nurture the hope that the therapist will be able to magically fix everything that is wrong in the family. The therapeutic moment, when a change in the family occurs, is the product of particularly complex forces that occur within the whole therapy group. Like the high heat to which the crucible is subjected, the emotional heat of the family and the intensity of the therapist's responses become exaggerated and strengthen the process of change. As a result, a transformation of how people understand and relate to each other produces something new. This therapeutic moment cannot be planned, and the therapist waits for a dramatic pivotal moment. Carl Whitaker's methods were often described as confrontational and dramatic.

The premise of this view of change is that the family tries to pull the therapist into their system and do to the therapist what they do to each other. At the same time, the therapist projects his or her own family system onto the family he or she is treating. This is a key "push" element in the crucible. The family is pulling and the therapist is pushing. Without the emotional involvement of the therapist, the event remains merely a technical exercise. Alternatively, if the therapist becomes overinvolved, he or she loses the status of a professional and becomes ineffective. The ideal formula has a rapidly generated intensity from the chemistry of the family's pull with the therapist's push. The escalating and impending therapeutic opportunity contains elements of danger and excitement. It's a balance of professionalism and emotion, of pushing and pulling, and of the therapist being part of the family system without getting drawn into ineffective ways of communicating and relating.

To avoid becoming too involved, a therapist initially maintains a professional relationship and outsider's perspective through the use of boundaries, rules, procedures, and focusing on reframing problems as family predicaments. The family listens attentively and generally has a strong desire to change; however, trying is not enough. The family maintains layers of denial and avoidance that can be permeated only by the personal power of the therapist. This happens because the therapist allows himself or herself to become emotionally concerned, invested, and ultimately involved that moves him or her beyond the psychological borders and deep into the family. The therapist identifies with one of the family members and becomes intensely involved through this countertransference. Clients often transfer emotions they have for others onto the therapist and, in turn, therapists sometime transfer their own emotions and expectations about relationships back onto the clients. The countertransference with one of the family members provides an opportunity for the therapist to parent the way he or she wishes to have been parented when a child. The therapist is able to provide the family with a new model for intimacy. It is also the belief that family counseling takes place both on the intrapersonal (individual) level and at the same time the interpersonal (between the individual members) level. Therefore, the therapist crosses the emotional boundary into the intrapersonal conflict of an individual in order to provide the family with an interpersonal model for intimacy.

This approach has been controversial because of the therapist's becoming personally involved and jeopardizing conventional, competent professionalism; however, cotherapy can help balance between professionalism and emotional intensity. Napier and Whitaker believed having two therapists present provides the stability that makes this type of personal involvement possible. As one therapist engages in the family struggle, the other therapist remains silent, more objective, and ready to take initiative when the active therapist becomes tired or confused because of overinvolvement. The in-and-out movement of the therapists is a pattern that may vary but is an essential component for the therapists to be both personal and professional.

There is a strong focus on the present moment and on current relationships within the family in the counseling sessions. Regardless of the presenting problem of any individual, the crucible of the family system is deemed to be always the best approach, and the more family members involved, the better. Expanding this further, the family is influenced by the contexts in which it exists. Additional elements that are added to the crucible are the social, cultural, governmental, school, and work systems that all influence and exert power over families.

The success of this form of therapy is dependent on the self of the therapist involved. Therapists must have the ability to turn up, and withstand, the emotional heat in a family, and become a catalyst for therapeutic moments. The crucible approach to counseling has benefited families; however, there may be an equal benefit to the therapists. Ongoing personal counseling for the therapists is crucial, and maintaining awareness is paramount for jumping into a family to engage at just the right moment.

Lynn Bohecker

See also Boundaries; Conflict in Couples and Families; Cotherapy Team; Experiential Family Therapy; Self of the Therapist

Further Readings

Napier, A. Y., & Whitaker, C. (1978). *The family crucible: The intense experience of therapy.* New York, NY: HarperCollins.

Whitaker, C. A. (1977). The technique of family therapy. In G. P. Sholevar (Ed.), *Changing sexual values and the family.* Springfield, IL: Charles C Thomas.

Whitaker, C. A., & Bumberry, W. A. (1988). *Dancing with the family: A symbolic-experiential approach.* New York, NY: Brunner/Mazel.

Cultural Issues in Couples and Families

This entry explains how issues involving culture and cultural identities surface in couples and families, and discusses the implications for counselors. To understand how cultural issues operate in couples and families, it is important to become familiar with some commonly used terms. The word *culture* refers to the attitudes, beliefs, behaviors, and values of a particular social group or community. An individual's *cultural identity* is shaped by that person's membership in these various social communities. Cultural communities, or groups, include but are not limited to people who share attributes based on geographic location, level of education, gender, socioeconomic status, religion, age, political affiliation, disability status, sexual identity, ethnicity, and race. Thus, a person's cultural identity is an intersection of multiple memberships in a range of cultural communities.

The term *intersectionality* refers to the idea that an individual's identity comprises membership in more than one cultural group. This means that the individual does not reflect one single culture, but rather several cultures. For example, a person may have grown up in Philadelphia but currently lives in New York. The person may feel that having lived in each city has imprinted certain characteristics that have become a part of his or her identity. This person could culturally identify with both places or may feel that one of those two places is more or less representative of "who I am." The same person's cultural identity would also be shaped by other factors. Perhaps the person is woman–identified and is educated at the graduate level. Perhaps she was raised in a working-class family that was Italian American and Catholic and she later became middle class and Buddhist. She may culturally identify with all of those communities or only some of them. To further complicate matters, this person could marry someone with a similar background, or she could partner with a person whose background is substantially different from hers in any number of ways. In this case, the individuals in the couple are members of some cultural communities together and are members of other cultural communities on their own. Thus, the couple's dynamics would be informed by their cultural similarities as well as their differences.

The preceding example demonstrates how cultural influences in couple and family relationships can be quite complex. A number of terms are used to help sort out the various configurations of cultural issues that potentially manifest in couples and families. To begin with, when issues arise in couples and families between individuals who are members of the same culture, these issues are referred to as *intracultural*. Similarly, issues that are contained within a family are considered *intrafamilial*. A family may come to therapy to work on issues that are both *intracultural* and *intrafamilial*. One example of an issue that is both *intracultural* and *intrafamilial* is a family experiencing conflict between some family members who practice a more conservative form of a particular religion and other family members who practice a more liberal form of the same religion. The conflict exists within the family (intrafamilial) and between people who share a religious identity (intracultural).

By contrast, an issue can be both *intercultural* and *intrafamilial*. *Intercultural* is a term that refers to those interactions involving members of distinct cultural communities. When two people from different cultures form a couple, the couple can be referred to as intercultural. The extended family would be an intercultural family. One partner may come from a family that strongly values personal achievement and is therefore highly individualistic, while the other partner may come from a background that values collaboration within the family and is therefore highly collectivistic. The differing worldviews come from different cultural vantage points (intercultural) but are contained within the family (intrafamilial); thus the couple and family may experience issues that are both *intercultural* and *intrafamilial*. Each of the preceding examples has involved individuals who are within the family, but there are also opportunities for culture to become a factor in relationships that exist outside of the family.

Cultural issues that are *extrafamilial* arise between the family and individuals or groups outside of the family unit. As with *intrafamilial* cultural issues, *extrafamilial* issues may be either *intracultural* or *intercultural*. An issue that would be characterized as both *extrafamilial* and *intracultural* would be a conflict occurring between a family and a cultural community to which the family holds membership. An example of this type of conflict could arise around gender roles. A family who belongs to a cultural community that typically reinforces rigid gender roles may experience conflict with the cultural community if the family dynamics include many nontraditional gender roles. The family may receive messages from the *extrafamilial* cultural community about the ways that the family's dynamics do not fulfill cultural expectations. Thus, this situation shows how cultural issues may be both *extrafamilial* and *intracultural*. Relatedly, cultural issues can also manifest in configurations that are both *intercultural* and *extrafamilial*. This means that the issue arises between the family and people outside of the family who are members of a cultural community to which the family does not belong. Examples of this type of configuration could involve a couple or family living and working in a neighborhood where most of the people around them are members of a noticeably different cultural community. For instance, a family that strongly values formal education may experience a sense of cognitive dissonance living in a community that places a high value on informal education. Likewise, a family that places a high value on "street smarts" may experience cognitive dissonance in a community where formal education is emphasized. These situations represent cultural issues that develop between the family and cultural communities.

In addition to issues that can exist within the family or with people outside of the family, there is the potential for cultural issues to exist between the clinician and the family. As in the previous instances, these can be classified as *intracultural* and *intercultural*. *Intracultural* issues may arise when the family and the clinician share a cultural identity, whereas intercultural issues may be present when the family and the clinician occupy different cultural statuses. In either of these situations, there is potential for the clinician to make assumptions about the family and vice versa. *Intracultural* interactions pose potential risks for the family to make assumptions based on the clinician's perceived sameness with the family (transference) and for the clinician to make assumptions based on the family's perceived sameness with the clinician (countertransference). Likewise, when a clinician and a family come from different cultures, *intercultural* issues may manifest. For example, the family may question whether lack of cultural sameness will inhibit the clinician's ability to understand and connect with the family. Conversely, the clinician may make assumptions about a family's openness to working with a clinician from a different culture. Thus, both *intracultural* issues and *intercultural* issues have the potential to impact the relationship between the clinician and the family.

Finally, when treatment and intervention strategies are not culturally congruent with the family, there is potential for negative outcomes in therapy. Historically, theories, treatments, and interventions have been founded on research conducted with population samples that represent the dominant culture. This results in research that supports social trends that occur in the dominant population but leaves out information that can be applied to nondominant groups. For example, existing research supports verbal communication and training in problem-solving as valuable clinical practices, but these strategies may not be culturally congruent for some families.

Clinicians must pay careful attention to the embeddedness of cultural assumptions in various approaches to treatment. Applying treatment that is culturally incompatible with the family could lead to treatment failure and has the potential to do more harm than good. An example of how a lack of cultural congruence could impact the efficacy of treatment strategies involves a couple who discloses they did not complete the homework assigned to them by the clinician in a previous session. There are many ways that the clinician may respond to this disclosure. Without taking culture into account, the clinician might assume that the partners simply forgot the assignment or might assume that they are lazy. Alternatively, the clinician could explore the possibility that the assignment was not culturally congruent with the couple. The clinician may learn in follow-up assessment that in accordance with their cultural identity the couple does not place a high value on direct confrontation, which was a major focus of the assignment. This example shows how lack of cultural congruence can slow or halt the family's progress in therapy. Clinicians must be flexible in applying treatment strategies and be on the alert for when interventions do not seem culturally congruent.

Self-Awareness, Knowledge, and Skills

Clinicians who work with couples and families need to be reflective concerning their own perspectives and biases regarding various cultural factors. Does the clinician agree or disagree with characteristics they associate with the cultural identities represented by the family? Does the clinician have any knowledge about the cultural identities represented by the family? In order to work effectively with culturally diverse couples and families, clinicians need to have an understanding of their personal perspectives about their own cultural identity as well as how their cultural identity may impact the decisions they make, the treatments they provide, and the interventions they use. Further, culturally competent couple and family counselors reflect on what values they hold regarding intimate relationships. This awareness helps the counselor become more cognizant of how the values that he or she possesses about relationships may impact decisions made, treatment employed, and interventions used. For example, does the counselor value staying together? What are the clinician's personal beliefs about gender roles, the relative importance of children, or relationship fidelity?

Clinicians who are unaware of their culturally embedded values, beliefs, and attitudes may inadvertently impact the direction of the therapy provided to couples and families who are struggling with these issues. Clinicians who are aware of their personal beliefs may avoid blindly assuming there is a "right" way to proceed and may instead focus on discovering and evaluating the couple's preferences. Counselors who work with diverse couples and families frequently consider many potential hypotheses about possible cultural or noncultural factors and reflect on whether cultural knowledge actually applies to the couple or family in question. Further, counselors working with couples and families make space in therapy for open discussion of cultural issues. Creating an environment wherein the family is comfortable sharing cultural information is an important safeguard in assuring that the clinician does not make unconscious application of cultural assumptions and stereotypes.

Culturally competent counselors who work with couples and families make efforts to develop a wide background of cultural knowledge and know how to seek such knowledge out in order to be helpful with diverse clients. For example, a clinician from a primarily individualistic culture who is working with a couple from a primarily collectivistic culture learns that the couple would like to include extended family in decision-making processes. In this case, the clinician would best serve the couple by developing knowledge about the possible cultural appropriateness of this intervention. Culturally competent counselors who work with couples and families bring cultural issues into the therapeutic discourse to reinforce trust and understanding. Clinicians who model a process of open communication and consideration about cultural issues help clients develop these skills while also encouraging a similar process between partners and family members.

To effectively work with diverse couples and families, clinicians must be able to talk about cultural influences. This being said, it is important to recognize that not all cultural differences are problematic, and not all differences are about culture only. Culturally competent clinicians work to understand couples from the dominant cultural view, such as from one's theoretical orientation, as well as from an emic, or within-group, view. This requires that the clinician conduct an expansive analysis of contexts, including how class, gender, race, religion, and socioeconomic status affect the family. Becoming aware of common characteristics associated with a range of cultural groups may be necessary, but at the same time clinicians must be aware that this practice has the potential to reinforce stereotypes that overgeneralize the diversity that is present within each culture. Rather than focusing on acquiring adequate in-depth knowledge about every possible minority group, clinicians should focus on developing skills in learning about unfamiliar cultures.

Laurie Bonjo

See also Diversity; Interracial Marriages and Families; Multicultural Counseling Competence; Multiculturalism

Further Readings

Bigner, J. J., & Wetchler, J. L. (2012). *Handbook of LGBT-affirmative couple and family therapy*. New York, NY: Routledge.

Bobes, T., & Bobes, N. S. (2005). *The couple is telling you what you need to know: Couple-directed therapy in a multicultural context*. New York, NY: Norton.

Carson, D. K., & Casado-Kehoe, M. (2011). *Case studies in couples therapy: Theory-based approaches*. New York, NY: Routledge.

Dworkin, S. H., & Pope, M. (2012). *Casebook for counseling lesbian, gay, bisexual, and transgender persons and their families*. Alexandria, VA: American Counseling Association.

Hays, P. A. (2008). *Addressing cultural complexities in practice: Assessment, diagnosis, and therapy*. Washington, DC: American Psychological Association.

Lamanna, M. A., Riedmann, A., & Stewart, S. (2014). *Marriages, families, and relationships: Making choices in a diverse society*. Stamford, CT: Cengage Learning.

Pope-Davis, D. B., & Coleman, H. L. K. (2001). *The intersection of race, class, and gender in multicultural counseling*. Thousand Oaks, CA: Sage.

Rastogi, M., & Thomas, V. (2009). *Multicultural couple therapy*. Thousand Oaks, CA: Sage.

CUSTODY EVALUATIONS

The high rate of divorce in the United States means that many children will not live full time with both parents. These divorces will have a direct impact on the children's psychological and social functioning. Children will experience the separation of family in a much different manner from that of their parents. How children respond to the demands of a changing system will depend largely on the child and how the parents handle the process of divorce and shared custody. Sometimes parents cannot amicably decide on a custody arrangement, or one parent is considered a possible danger to the children. A custody evaluation is a court-ordered process in which a mental health professional assesses a family to assist in establishing custody of the minor children. This entry discusses the mental health of children during a divorce, outlines the process of a custody evaluation, and presents related considerations.

Acting-Out Behavior and Attachment Theory

The purpose of a custody evaluation is to determine what type of custody arrangement will be in the best interests of children and their parents. Sometimes parents, social services, or the court may request a custody evaluation because children are distressed. Mental health distress may come in the form of "attention-seeking" behaviors such as aggressive acting out, distress, impulsivity, depressive symptoms, and feelings of abandonment and insecurity. These behaviors can be displayed in a host of environments. In school environments in particular, these behaviors may result in adverse reactions and consequences. Furthermore, it can be difficult for parents to affirm the emotions and feelings of children if they themselves are adversarial. Thus, the negative emotions of children are exacerbated when parents are in conflict.

The level of attachment that the child has to each parent will also affect the child's overall adjustment after a divorce. A familiarity with attachment theory can provide valuable insights into a child's psychological functioning. During times of change and stress it is common for human beings to attach to someone for comfort. There are two key theories of attachment that help demonstrate how children connect with others to meet their basic needs for love and belonging. The first theory of attachment holds that children are born with an innate ability to attach to parents. The attachment style developed will be largely formed by parents and how they respond. The attachment style that the child develops in infancy will set the stage for all subsequent relationships and shape the child's view of self. There are four primary attachment styles that children develop to their parents: secure (positive), avoidant (positive self/negative other), ambivalent (negative self/positive other), and disorganized (negative self/negative other).

It is important for the evaluator to assess the level of attachment children have to each parent. In addition, it is extremely important for the evaluator to consider cultural variables in the evaluation and assessment of family functioning.

Purpose of an Evaluation

The custody evaluation process has many components and is usually ordered by a family court judge. Custody evaluations are important because they are used to determine who will be the child's primary caregiver and thus have the right to make critical decisions about the child. Once a marriage involving children is dissolved, a petition is filed with the local family court. There is a retainer fee involved. The purpose of the hearing is to determine what is in the "best interest" of the minor child or children. This may involve decisions regarding the child's primary residence, parental visitations, and parents' legal rights. In order for a judge to make such a difficult decision, it may be necessary to enlist the expertise of a mental health professional who will be charged with completing an assessment to assist the judge in determining the least restrictive environment in which to place a child. It is expected that the mental health professional completing the assessment be familiar with the courts, laws, and jurisdiction and have expertise working with divorced families. The evaluation should be conducted by a licensed mental health professional who has a good understanding of the legal process related to the ways in which custody or visitation can be arranged and one who is culturally sensitive. Evaluators must become aware of their own unintended biases in order to provide the least biased assessments during the evaluation process.

Who Does an Evaluation?

A *custody evaluation* is usually conducted by a licensed mental health professional, who makes conclusions and recommendations concerning custody and time-sharing. The evaluation is the most widely used tool to assist the family court system when deciding a minor child's best interest. The conclusion from the evaluation report is typically given to the parents' respective attorneys or the attorneys of records. A parent may also proceed with a custody evaluation *pro se,* which means that parents have no legal representation and will be representing themselves.

The professional evaluator should have highly developed skills in the areas of child psychological assessments, mental health disorders, and family systems, as well as parenting skills and cultural dynamics of diverse families. A full, professional evaluation involves multiple methods of data-gathering, including psychological testing, clinical interviews, and behavioral observation. The evaluation process includes interviewing the children and both parents. Other sources may be consulted, such as teachers, health care providers, agencies, or child care providers. Relatives in the extended family, friends, and other collateral sources may be contacted if significant. The custody evaluation should be timely, comprehensive, and fair to both parties and should include interviews, collateral contacts, and observations.

Types of Custody

Custody hearings determine both sole and joint custody. Sole custody designates one party as the residential parent and legal custodian of the children. On the other hand, joint custody, also referred to as "shared parenting," allows both parents to contribute equally in the decision-making process for the minor children. The other parent will have scheduled visitations agreed upon by the parties, or in accordance with a local visitation statute.

Ethical Considerations

There are many ethical considerations in conducting a custody evaluation. Caution with dual relationships (having more than one relationship with a client) is important for evaluators involved with issues of child custody. For example, an evaluator cannot be someone who has also done therapy with either of the parents or with the children. The evaluator must ensure that he or she does not interview others who will speak negatively of the opposing parent. A custody evaluator looks at the overall functioning of the children and parents in order to gather information to determine "best interest" of the children. Issues related to confidentiality become a concern as there is no protected "right" in a custody evaluation as is normally expected in the therapeutic process. Establishing the limitations is important and requires a clear understanding of the situation.

Proceedings

Preparation for an evaluation can be unnerving yet critical in that parents have to be ready to demonstrate why they believe they are the most suitable parent and why the minor children should reside with them and not the other party. The custody evaluation can be extensive and include detailed interviews with each parent, children, stepparents (or new significant others in either/both parent's lives currently, and possibly with extended family members. Both parents will receive psychological testing that could extend to stepparents (or significant others) of either or both parents. The evaluator will make observations of the interactions between the children and each parent in a neutral setting using various techniques. More often than not, the technique of choice for evaluators will involve some sort of play time with the children. There may be joint sessions to witness how the "disputing" parents interact with one another in a controlled setting. Home visits at each parent's residence will also be a part of the evaluation. Finally, there will be a review of pertinent court documents and materials related to the case. School-age children can expect a review of report cards, attendance records, and behavioral records.

Cooperation is a key component in assisting the evaluator to better understand a parent's disposition. Accordingly, parents should observe several principles throughout the evaluation process: do not speak poorly of your spouse or the spouse's family; avoid threatening comments about your spouse; refrain from making harassing calls to the evaluator or stopping by his or her office unannounced; and if there are new spouses or significant others, keep them away from the proceedings. The interviewee should consider making the best impression possible by being well organized, timely, dressing appropriately, and answering questions honestly with self-assurance.

Other Considerations

Collaborative divorce is an alternative technique used to dispute resolution in family law. Essentially, it is a method of practicing law in which the lawyers for the involved parties agree to help the clients solve disagreements by utilizing collaborative strategies rather than oppositional tactics and litigation. A crucial component of a collaborative divorce is that the lawyers pledge to manage the discord, emotional concerns, and relationship issues resourcefully. Collaborative law is intended to replace legal action yet achieve a settlement, but it may fall short of intent. In this case, there may be additional expenses due to the need to hire an attorney who would pursue a resolution through the court system.

Collaborative divorce does not have a universal application. It requires a commitment of working with, and not against, the other person in order to obtain a favorable outcome. Individuals who are committed to the resolution process, able to accept their situation, and maintain a vested interest in the well-being of the other party involved are the best candidates for collaboration. The parties should be understanding of the long-term goals and demonstrate a willingness to uphold the relationship with the other party in order to improve the overall well-being of everyone involved.

*Delila Lashelle Owens
and Darletta Stevenson Logan*

See also Best Interests of the Child; Divorce and Separation; Divorce Therapy; Legal Issues in Parenting

Further Readings

American Psychological Association. (2010). Guidelines for child custody evaluations in family law proceedings. *American Psychologist, 65,* 863–867.

Artis, J. E. (2004). Judging the best interests of the child: Judges' accounts of the tender years doctrine. *Law and Society Review, 38,* 769–806.

Bala, N. (2005). Tippins and Wittman asked the wrong questions: Evaluators may not be "experts," but they can express best interests opinions. *Family Court Review, 43*(4), 554–562.

Bowlby, J. (1969). *Attachment and loss.* New York, NY: Basic Books.

Tippins, T. M., & Wittman, J. P. (2005). Empirical and ethical problems with custody recommendations: A call for clinical humility and judicial vigilance. *Family Court Review, 43,* 193–222.

CUTTING/SELF-MUTILATION

See Self-Injury

CYBERNETICS

Cybernetics is a construct that is the basis for many theories of relational interaction in family therapy. It is often credited to the mathematician Norbert Wiener (1894–1964), and originally referred to an understanding of how machines maintained their functioning. Gregory Bateson, an anthropologist involved with the development of family therapy, was one of the first to apply cybernetics to family interactions (family systems). Cybernetics refers to ways that systems are organized and maintained through circular feedback (the output of a system becomes information to the system and influences the functioning of the system). It most often is associated with traditional, first-order models of family therapy, such as Bowen, structural, strategic, Mental Health Research Institute (MRI), and others, which are focused on observable patterns of interaction in relational systems. This entry explores two concepts central to understanding cybernetics: circular causality and feedback loops. It contains several examples of the concepts to illustrate how they work in couple and family systems.

Circular Causality

One of the main concepts in cybernetics is circular causality, a systemic concept that challenges some of the traditional, linear thinking that is common to many fields of psychology. Linear thinking implies that there is a direct cause-and-effect relationship that can be identified to explain an outcome. One can imagine a straight arrow with a beginning and end, where A leads to B. For example, childhood trauma leads to psychological symptoms, or alcoholism is caused by genetics.

In family therapy, relational interactions are often understood through circular causality. Circular causality is the idea that A leads to B and B leads back to A, leading back to B, and back to A. In circular causality, there is no clear beginning or end point because there is no beginning or end to a circle. The common question, "Which came first, the chicken or the egg?" exemplifies circular causality. If one cannot identify the beginning or end, then it is circular.

Circular causality can be found in relational systems with two or more members, and the first example will involve a dyad (two-member system). When examining a circular pattern of interaction, couples and family therapists are more interested in "how" the interactions play out as opposed to "why" each partner prefers more closeness or distance. In other words, understanding the "how" is often considered more important in helping the couple change their patterns of interactions as opposed to seeking to understand "why" they act in the ways that they do.

Individuals in couple relationships have needs for both closeness and distance, but often at varying levels. Susan Johnson and John Gottman have stressed that in almost all couple relationships there is a pursue–distance pattern. In the case of an opposite-gender couple where one partner pursues (often the female partner) and the other distances (often the male partner), circular causality is an appropriate framework for understanding their pattern of interaction. For the couple, when he distances, she may feel more alone and an increased need for connection with him. Thus, she pursues. When she pursues, he may feel emotionally overwhelmed and thus distances to feel more comfortable. His distancing only amplifies her loneliness and need to pursue, and her increased pursuit only amplifies his discomfort and need to distance. They are both responsible for the pattern of relating to each other, and this shared (but not necessarily equal) responsibility is referred to as recursion. It is futile to argue over who "started" or initiated the sequence of interaction because there is no clear beginning or end to the circular pattern. In other words, each partner's behaviors exist in direct response to the other's actions, and thus their actions are contextually dependent on each other's. It is important to note that people do not necessarily act the same way in all relationships. For example, it is possible that the female partner may be more of the distancer in her relationship with her mother, where her mother is more the pursuer.

In addition to understanding patterns in dyads, circular causality can explain patterns in families with more than two members. In the example of a stepfamily household with a child who is having behavioral problems at home, a circular lens will focus on how each family member is maintaining the child's behavior. When the child misbehaves, she receives attention from her mother in the way of concern and comfort. When the mother expresses concern and comforts, the stepfather gets anxious about his role as a parent and feels a need to discipline the child and balance the parenting. When the stepfather attempts to discipline the child's behavior, the child is hurt because she does not yet trust the stepfather's love as a parent figure. This amplifies the child's need for her mother's comfort and concern, and her reliable way of receiving it is to misbehave. In response to the discipline, the child misbehaves again and lashes out at the stepfather, leading the mother to act more concerned and try to comfort her, leading the stepfather to act more anxious about his role and discipline more, leading back to the child seeking even more comfort from her mother by misbehaving. Again, it is a circular loop of behavior where A leads to B, B leads to C, and C leads back to A. Further, it is again not important to try to identify who started the sequence of interaction. What is important is to understand that the child's need for concern and comfort, the mother's need to provide comfort, and the stepfather's need to establish his parental role all produce actions that maintain the child's undesired behaviors.

Positive and Negative Feedback Loops

Circular causality explains interactions that occur from a systemic perspective. Circular patterns can also be described as feedback loops, and feedback loops can be positive or negative. It is important to understand that negative and positive feedback loops do not refer to value judgments. In other words, "negative" does not equal "bad" or "undesired," and "positive" does not equal "good" or "desired." Positive and negative feedback loops differ by how the circular interactions lead to stability or change. In short, negative feedback loops maintain stability, and positive feedback loops lead to change.

Negative feedback loops maintain homeostasis, or systemic stability. A common example of a negative feedback loop is a thermostat used to control a heating system. A thermostat is set to maintain a specific temperature. When the temperature drops a certain amount below the set temperature, the heat turns on to stabilize the system and bring the space back to the desired temperature. This is a self-regulating system for maintaining the status quo, and for a machine such as a heating system (and mostly any other machine), a negative feedback loop is desired to keep it functioning properly.

In relationships, negative feedback loops exist to maintain relational status quo. In the example of a couple that does not discuss their sex life, one partner may state "I would like to discuss our sex life," and the other may respond with a statement such as "We're not having this conversation." If the result is that the interaction ends at this point, it can be labeled a negative feedback loop that maintains the status quo. They are still a couple and still not discussing their sex life.

However, consider what could happen if the partner who opened the conversation continued to attempt to engage in the discussion. It could look like the following:

Partner 1: "I would like to discuss our sex life."

Partner 2: "We're not having this conversation."

Partner 1: "This is important to me and I need you to talk with me about this."

Partner 2: "I already told you that we're not having this conversation."

Partner 1: "You never want to talk about it and I am getting tired of doing this your way."

Partner 2: "So, what does that mean?"

Partner 1: "That means that if you care about me, you will at least listen when I tell you that something is important to me."

At this point, the conversation could lead to Partner 2 agreeing to have a conversation about their sex life, or continuing to dig in and refuse to engage. If they begin a conversation, this would characterize a positive feedback loop because a change has occurred from their normal patterns of relating to each other. They used to be a couple that did not discuss their sex life, and now they are a couple that is discussing it. Further, if Partner 2 still refused to engage in the conversation, Partner 1 could state that she is leaving the relationship because she does not feel valued. This outcome would also characterize a positive feedback loop, because although they would not engage in a conversation about their sex life, they would no longer be a couple.

Clearly, whether discussing their sex life or ending the relationship had a "positive" value or impact on the partners likely depends on who is asked. It is possible that each partner would give a different answer to the question of either positive feedback loop being a "positive" experience. What is important is that the interaction led to a change in the relationship, and that is what makes it positive feedback. As illustrated in the example of the couple, positive feedback loops are often characterized by escalating responses that lead to the change in the relational system.

Many family systems theorists support the idea that both positive and negative feedback loops are necessary for systems to function. In other words, there needs to be ways to maintain stability so that family members can count on some level of predictability and reliability, and there also needs to be room for flexibility and change so that the system can grow and adapt as needed. The terms *morphostasis* (stability in the context of change through a negative feedback loop) and *morphogenesis* (adaptation to change through a positive feedback loop) refer to ways that systems cope with and adapt to change, and both are often necessary for the system's survival over time.

For example, in a parent–child relationship, change is inevitable due to the passage of time because the child (and parent) will age and grow. There will likely need to be rules that maintain homeostasis (such as a bedtime, curfew, expectations for doing chores), and those rules will need to be flexible to accommodate the child's development. Parent–child relationships will likely endure escalating struggles that lead to positive feedback loops or changes in the relationships. If a parent and child argue over a bedtime, it is likely that the bedtime will change as the child grows. When the child reaches adolescence, the struggles may lead to the parents no longer monitoring a bedtime, and instead leaving that decision to the teen. The positive feedback loops that help the system grow and change will lead to a new state of normal, or equilibrium, that will then be maintained through negative feedback loops that keep the system stable until the next developmental struggle occurs.

Michael E. Sude

See also General Systems Theory; Homeostasis; Morphogenesis; Morphostasis; Systems Theory

Further Readings

Becvar, D. S., & Becvar, R. J. (1998). *Systems theory and family therapy: A primer* (2nd ed.). Lanham, MD: University Press of America.

Gottman, J. M. (1999). *The marriage clinic: A scientifically based marital therapy.* New York, NY: Norton.

Hoffman, L. (1981). *Foundations of family therapy.* New York, NY: Basic Books.

Nichols, M. P. (2013). *Family therapy: Concepts and methods* (10th ed.). Boston, MA: Pearson.

Smith-Acuña, S. (2010). *Systems theory in action: Applications to individual, couple, and family therapy.* Hoboken, NJ: Wiley.

Stone Fish, L. (2000). Hierarchical relationship development: Parents and children. *Journal of Marital and Family Therapy, 26,* 501–510. doi:10.1111/j.1752-0606.2000.tb00319.x

Winek, J. (2010). *Systemic family therapy: From theory to practice.* Thousand Oaks, CA: Sage.

Dating Coaching

Over the last decade, dating coaching has developed as a way to enhance the personal approach one has to dating and offer strategies to improve the success experienced in the search for a suitable partner. Dating coaching includes teaching interpersonal skills and offering related products and services to help improve the likelihood of a client's finding people to date and maintaining a successful relationship.

Dating coaching has always had its respective place, but seemingly it has become more relevant due to the nontraditional approaches or failures experienced in recent years. In fact, marriage and family counselors are beginning to rethink their roles in working with couple systems due to major changes in how people couple in the 21st century. According to the Pew Research Center, a record number of Americans have never married and marriage is declining in all groups of people in the United States. In 2010, the Pew Research Center reported that in 1960, two thirds (68%) of those in their 20s were married, but in 2008, just 26% were. Thus, marriage and family counselors might be better named couples coaches or systems coaches to more accurately describe who they serve. With coupling being more complex due to technology, education and work demands, longevity, and mobility, it seems reasonable that marriage and family counselors will spend more time coaching individuals on how to couple and what to do in the event of a breakup than in how to get married and stay married. Individuals seeking relationships not only have the daily option of randomly meeting people, but there are also options of meeting potential partners through organized approaches, such as "eferrals," hookups, blind dates, speed dating, or dating services for professionals. Now, in the 21st century, initiating new romantic relationships has taken new shape with the increased use of communications technology and social media. The possibility of locating a potential mate is now available through various applications ("apps") on computers, tablets, and cell phones. Individuals can go online and access many websites such as www.match.com or www.plentyoffish.com. There are websites designed to market to specific groups of people, such as Christians of various denominations, African Americans, sexual minorities, or those interested in interracial dating. According to a 2013 Pew Research Center report, one tenth of American adults have used online dating sites or mobile applications.

The following sections provide information on the components of dating coaching, the nature and appropriateness of various services, and their potential benefits to clients. Also discussed are delivery methods for counselors practicing dating coaching, and the importance for clients of choosing wisely among the options available for coaching services.

Components of Dating Coaching

The process of dating coaching largely involves affective, behavioral, and cognitive components, which inspire enhancement of confidence, congruent communication, and one's ability to connect with others. Affective components are the feelings and emotions a person experiences. Behavioral factors entail both the observable, such as body language, and reported actions of a person (or offering a personal anecdote). Cognitive factors consist of thoughts and beliefs, all of which impact the preferred outcome of dating experiences.

Dating coaching assists individuals in aligning who they are (personality, values, and morals) with their successes and failures in relationships, inclusive of specific phase of life and future goals. This form of transparency gives clients permission to make favorable relationship choices and refines their ability to discriminate among the options. Unlike other options for dating, when people seek out dating coaching as a service, they should be most interested in obtaining a quality relationship with an individual of like mind, without immediate gratification.

Appropriateness of Dating Coaching

Individuals may be curious as to whether or not a dating coach is an appropriate service for them. Some may seek out the services of a dating coach and may deem it necessary depending on their personal circumstances. For example, a person may have historically been very committed in relationships, whereas their selected partners did not have the same standards of fidelity and honesty. Some people have not been afforded the opportunity to gain experience dating for a multitude of reasons. One rationale could be because they married early and divorced, and now they find themselves in a stage of life that warrants a new beginning. Another explanation could be simply a lack of knowledge and the desire to know more relative to dating. During adolescence and early adulthood, some individuals may have struggled with their self-esteem, identity, or perceptions of attractiveness, which kept them from having the courage to engage in dating. Some people may simply be extremely shy and possibly harbor fears of rejection but actually would like a relationship or feel that it is the appropriate step to take at their developmental stage of life. A further motivation for seeking the services of a dating coach is the lack of opportunity to observe the interactions of those participating in dating cultures. Another reason may be that an individual spent their younger years in a parentified state or condition, meaning that there was no opportunity to be youthful and participate in the natural experiences of most adolescents. These individuals may have lived early on as caretakers to their parents, who were unable to fulfill their parental role due, for example, to alcoholism or unforeseen illness. For all these reasons, not knowing how to meet people or how to approach someone as a potential partner, some people may find a dating coach helpful.

Benefits to Dating Coaching

Dating coaching takes a self-efficacious, positive, empowering, and strengths-based approach. Individuals who receive this form of coaching may benefit from an introspective process that encourages authenticity, transparency, hope, and inspiration, along with opportunity to harness past experiences and ways to learn from the failures within those experiences. Additionally, dating coaching connects values to aspirations, while reducing the inclination to self-sabotage or the tendency to fear rejection. Within the process, attempts are made to reduce negative communication patterns and ignite replacement behaviors indicative of conflict resolution, making a person's dispositions conducive to handle situations more favorably.

There are other benefits to receiving dating coaching. The process augments assertiveness, as distinguished from arrogance. Some perceive it as a personal investment, with foci of healthy living and intrapersonal intimacy. It promotes stronger partnerships in couples and enhances commitment within relationships. High value is placed on clarity, especially with respect to role changes, responsibilities, and expectations of the partner. Ultimately, dating coaching allows self-confidence to develop; a willingness to meet new people regularly can be strengthened through the process of coaching.

Skills and Topics Offered in Dating Coaching

The role of a dating coach is to expand and nurture competence in a process that otherwise tends to lack strategy and concentrated effort. A dating coach teaches the skills needed to achieve one's desired outcomes through discussion, modeling, role-play, and real-world practice. These skills may include approaching individuals, introducing oneself, starting a conversation, knowing how to find out about another's interests and life experiences, asking for a casual date, being honest yet positive about oneself in conversation, and so forth. Individuals are encouraged to become resourceful, using what is present as a tool to enact change. Individuality is embraced, and personable or favorable qualities are celebrated with the client.

A dating coach may have the desire to understand the client's relationship goals and the outcome expectancy for them. How one presents himself or herself in person or online and the content of online profiles becomes significant in evaluating whether or not someone may be a good match for the individual. More specifically, it is relevant to determine whether or not the person in question has similar interests, background, and life goals as the client. Understanding the qualities clients are seeking in a prospective partner becomes relevant. Other topics broached may include interpersonal relationships, flirting techniques, fashion recommendations, self-esteem identifiers, and social activities.

Methods of Delivery for Dating Coaching

There are several methods to deliver dating coaching to interested clients. Some clients feel more secure in a face-to-face meeting with their coach. Some individual coaches or agencies conduct boot camps, seminars, or workshops that interested clients can attend. A convenient and personal modality for some is the option of a home study program that allows individuals to move at their own pace. Coaches may also offer their support online through instant messaging or blogging techniques. Finally, some dating coaches are available by telephone to address the client's specific needs, and may follow up with electronic newsletters or other literature for use after the telephone discussion. In order for these methods to be effective, clients must be receptive to the information being presented and willing to integrate the information obtained into their daily lives.

Stigmas Associated With Dating Coaching Services

There are associated stigmas that accompany an individual's decision to receive dating coaching. Some believe that teaching romance and ways to properly date is somehow inappropriate. People may feel embarrassed by this service, which can elicit feelings of social isolation and inhibitions toward allowing others to support them through this process. Others may believe that individuals with deeply rooted psychosocial issues cannot successfully be coached, being deeply rooted. Additionally, people also have a tendency to think that associated fees for dating coaching are costly, especially when there is doubt regarding the quality or the effectiveness of the services being rendered. Dating coaches often lack credentials and, therefore, their abilities and qualifications to assist anyone in dating endeavors become questionable. Finally, some may believe that coaches embellish or exaggerate their own experiences and their ability to be of assistance.

Real-Life Stories

Some dating coaches and dating Internet sites provide helpful and informative tips for finding relationship satisfaction. These coaches do not just help people find dates, but rather help them determine the nature of healthy relationships. They use a personal growth model that may be useful throughout a person's lifetime. One coach actually watched his client approach women in a nightclub.

After he was "shut down" several times, the coach gave the client some sound advice mostly about body language, self-perception, and tonality. As the evening proceeded, the client became successful at landing coffee dates with two women who showed interest in him.

Hiring a dating coach is not for everyone. For example, Marge, a 30-year-old professional who had not dated in over a year, used the services of a dating coach for a few weeks. The coach gave Marge specific directives that seemed rather silly, but Marge followed through with all of them. The coach also sent messages to potential online dating candidates as if she herself were Marge. Marge did not feel good about this and was put off by the failure of the coach to follow through with promises to call Marge to see how things were going. Eventually Marge decided to end the relationship with the coach and felt that she could indeed find her "one true love" on her own.

In some instances, male dating coaches have been accused of teaching men to "pick up" women and even seduce them. Such was the case with a coach in California who presented his information in the form of lucrative seminars. Although he had not broken any laws, feminist groups and several journalists investigated his tactics; a major broadcast news organization quoted one critic as accusing him of "fostering a culture of rape."

The take-away from these experiences is that potential clients of dating coaches should do their homework before actually hiring a coach. Simply reading Internet advertisements is not a sufficient basis to make a decision about a coach that someone intends to hire. In general, these advertisements promise "true love" and "finding the love of your life." A legitimate dating coach should be willing to meet with a potential client initially to see if the relationship seems to be a good fit. Potential clients are entitled to expect a certain level of professionalism. Questions should include the following:

- Is there a contract that spells out the expectations of both the client and the coach including payment plans and times and length of meetings?
- How long will the relationship last?
- What type of training and education does the coach have and how can the client verify this information?
- How will the client contact the coach? Is texting permissible?
- Where will face-to-face meetings be held? Does the coach have an office?

If possible, the potential client should find out what other clients have to say about their experiences with this particular coach.

In our fast-paced world, some people who want a partner but do not feel that they can find one on their own may turn to dating coaching as a legitimate way to succeed in the pursuit of a satisfying relationship. Clients must be willing to learn the skills that dating coaches can teach them and then actually use these skills as they search for a dating partner.

Lisa A. Wines and Judith A. Nelson

See also Hope-Focused Approach to Couple Enrichment in Counseling; Romance; Self-Help

Further Readings

Anderson, J. L. (2007). From engineering geek to dating coach. *Kiplinger's Personal Finance, 61*(7), 96.

Finkel, E. J., Eastwick, P. W., Karney, B. R., Reis, H. T., & Sprecher, S. (2012). Online dating: A critical analysis from the perspective of psychological science. *Psychological Science in the Public Interest, 13*(1), 3–66.

Oesch, N., & Miklousic, I. (2010). The dating mind: Evolutionary psychology and the emerging science of human courtship. *Evolutionary Psychology, 10*(5), 899–909.

Dating Relationship Dissolution

In cultures where dating is a societal norm, dating relationship dissolution is a commonplace human experience that entails the ending of a couple's relationship. Other terms used for dating relationship dissolution include *breakup, nonmarital relationship dissolution, relational disengagement,* or *relational dissolution.* Dating relationship dissolution is not only an event; it is a process, and the experience has been described as multilayered. This entry discusses the process and its dynamics, its connection to adult attachment style, and the cognitive and behavioral approaches to dating relationship dissolution.

Process for Dating Relationship Dissolution

The process of ending or dissolving a relationship can involve complex, even contradictory states of mind. The partners may feel disbelief that the relationship has ended and pain at the loss of a significant other. Some have described the dissolution of a relationship as similar to death—permanent, irreversible, and leaving one with only memories of the partner. In addition, one or both of the partners may feel loss related to hope for the relationship and for the life they thought they were going to build together. Although both partners may feel pain and loss, typically one person decides to end the relationship and that person may experience less distress at the ending of the relationship.

A couple may agree to end their relationship because they have grown apart and want to remain friends, they have changed as individuals, or life circumstances have changed. The partner who chose to terminate the relationship may experience relief, happiness, freedom, or simply the notion of having a chance at a new beginning (transitional). Even when the end of a relationship can be perceived as "good," such as in the case of social, emotional, physical, or financial injury, partners may still grieve the loss of the relationship. The grieving process may be complicated by the fear of retribution by the abusive partner; a person may both miss the relationship and fear an ex-partner. The dissolution of any relationship can have a range of feelings and results, some of which may be predictable and others not. Sometimes people feel indecisive and contemplate reestablishing the relationship. Avoidance, withdrawal, or devastation may be experienced. Questions typically arise from former partners seeking to know how long it will take to overcome the emotional effects of the breakup or, in some cases, to understand their initial decision to enter the relationship with that partner. This process for some individuals can become quite dysfunctional or even emotionally dysregulating (ED), and result in attempts to self-harm, stalk or torment the other partner, throw or break objects, self-medicate, or demonstrate forms of verbal and physical aggression. While these emotions and behaviors might be unwanted, individuals who believe they have been betrayed often feel out of control and in need of support that will assist in stabilizing feelings and actions. Even after seeking support, and as with other losses in life, individuals may find that certain times of the year, music being played, or places revisited may result in overwhelming feelings that were thought to have been put to rest. Follow-up visits to a mental health provider can be helpful during these times.

Other considerations may be health related and manifest physiologically. Social rejection hurts both emotionally and physically. Heartache can literally equate with physical pain, which can be debilitating. Examples of health-related concerns such as chronic stress, a weakened immune system, digestive problems, and weight loss or gain are often immediate considerations. In addition, relationship dissolution has effects on the brain. Both emotional pain from a breakup and physical pain activate the same parts of the brain and share the same neural pathways. When people are in love, the release of hormones related to feeling happy, like dopamine and oxytocin, increases. When people break up, levels of these hormones decrease and stress hormones such as cortisol and epinephrine are released.

Dynamics Conducive to Dating Relationship Dissolution

Sometimes people enter a relationship under conditions that make it likely that the relationship will not be successful. For example, they may enter a relationship where one or both of the partners do not want to define it as a long-term relationship, where one person is already in a committed relationship, selecting someone who has a history of unsuccessful relationships, or selecting someone whose relationship history includes a series of infidelities or episodes of abuse. In addition, sometimes people pick someone whom they know is not a good match, but is attractive physically or financially.

People enter these types of relationships for various reasons. Sometimes people enter into these relationships with hopeful attitudes, somehow believing they can change the other person. Another scenario is the example of the couple who agree they have no interest in commitment or are just looking for a casual sexual relationship. These types of agreements can seem attractive to a person just coming out of a previous relationship or afraid of being hurt. Some people believe they only need sexual gratification, and therefore, using the partner as an outlet for sexual activity seems appropriate. An additional scenario may be that a couple agrees that their relationship is a matter of convenience, and having something more stable is not a viable option. Nevertheless, even when someone enters a relationship that is likely to fail, it does not necessarily prevent the heartaches, hurt, and discomfort that generally ensue from other types of breakups.

Approaches to Dating Relationship Dissolution

People who decide to end a relationship have a rationale for doing so. A study conducted by Vicki L. Loyer-Carlson and Alex J. Walker examined the reasons people ended their relationships and, based on their research, they found three types of rationales for ending a dating relationship: (1) independence, (2) disposition, and (3) relationship problems. Independence was explained as the individual perceiving continued involvement in the relationship as too much of an investment. Disposition breakups were when people wanted a relationship, but found the disposition (e.g., egotistical, disorganized, irresponsible) of a partner undesirable. Relationship problems included differences between the couple on larger issues (e.g., religion, education, culture) that caused relational problems and conflicts in everyday interactions. Sometimes people break up directly and sometimes they enact disengagement strategies to "force" the other person to end the relationship.

Cognitive and Behavioral Approaches to Dating Relationship Dissolution

The dissolution of dating relationships usually encompasses intersection of both cognitive and behavioral approaches. These approaches are also known as disengagement strategies. Cognitive efforts to disengage may consist of the individual having internal dialogue and external conversations with others that provide rationales and justifications for ending the relationship. Another cognitive approach may be to choose self-help resources (e.g., clergy or literature) to help support reasons to break up and to justify ones' own actions, desires, and needs. This helps to provide clarity and often substantiates differences in healthy versus nonhealthy relationships for the seeker. Other cognitive tasks that assist in the process of dissolving relationships may be to keep a journal of thoughts and feelings, perhaps charting the pros and cons of the other partner, as a way to be reflective, track, and recall unfavorable or hurtful experiences.

People engage in behaviors that are often precursors to ending a relationship. For example, someone may no longer make a partner a priority, spend less time with a partner, and engage in social activities that exclude the partner. In essence, the partner is no longer consistently available to a partner. One partner may send confusing or mixed messages, contradictory in nature, and may exude unfriendliness, intolerance, or be impatient. Often, the partner becomes less involved, which subsequently results in infrequent conversations, less intimacy, less attentiveness, which is also known as relationship distancing. In a time when a person is feeling dissatisfied with self and discontented with his or her partner, dissolving the relationship becomes more of a tenable option.

Lisa A. Wines and Judith A. Nelson

See also Divorce and Separation; Intimacy, Specific Threats to; Reconciliation; Relationship Enhancement

Further Readings

Hess, J. A. (2002). Distance regulation in personal relationships: The development of a conceptual model and test of representational validity. *Journal of Social and Personal Relationships, 19,* 663–683.

Hess, J. A. (2003). Measuring distance in personal relationships: The relational distance index. *Personal Relationships, 10,* 197–215.

Lambert, A. N., & Hughes, P. C. (2010). The influence of goodwill, secure attachment, and positively toned disengagement strategy on reports of communication satisfaction in non-marital post-dissolution relations. *Communication Research Reports, 27*(2), 171–183.

Madey, S. F., & Jilek, L. (2012). Attachment style and dissolution of romantic relationship: Breaking up is hard to do, or is it? *Individual Differences Research 10*(4), 202–210.

Sbarra, D. A., & Emery, R. E. (2005). The emotional sequelae of nonmarital relationship dissolution: Analysis of change and intraindividual variability over time. *Personal Relationships, 12,* 214–232.

DEATH, PARENTS OF DECEASED CHILDREN

Traversing the long road of mourning and grief at the death of a parent, spouse, friend, or associate is a meandering trail. It involves detours, side roads, reversals, and seemingly impassable barriers. This seemingly interminable journey often means taking a few steps forward, many steps backward, and frequently includes a sense of being frozen in time and space. These obstacles are worsened by an internal sense of loss accompanied in many instances by virtually every emotion known to humankind.

The death of a child of any age intensifies the pain of loss and the accompanying feelings. It also brings its own unique agony. The death of a child turns upside down the expected cycle of life and death. Almost without exception parents experience an exponential increase in feelings of guilt, regret, anger, rage, helplessness, shame, shock, blame, apathy, numbness, and dozens of other emotions. Additionally, parents report physical responses such as sleepless nights, loss of appetite, excessive drinking, and dulling of the senses. The cognitive responses accompanying such feelings and physiology include virtually every self-talk statement imaginable, including the following: "This is not fair." "I should have seen it coming." "I was negligent in my parenting of this child and I am worthless as a human being." "How could God allow this to happen?" "It's all your fault." "I told you not to allow . . ." "I thought I was a good parent, but I am the worst parent on earth." "Why didn't I exercise more care and vigilance?" "If only I had been there." Action responses are often characterized by withdrawal from relationships, apathy toward professional and family responsibilities, and quick trigger reactions to comments and remarks made by other people. Sudden and unpredicted expressions of sadness such as tears, sobbing, crying, wailing, and uncontrollable lamentations occur both publicly and privately.

Oftentimes parents are inconsolable because of what they believe is their incurable broken-heartedness and hopelessness. The mere passage of time can prove to be unhelpful in spite of others' repeated attempts to console them by saying that things will get better in the future. And yet their lives can become better with the passage of time—with caring, sharing, support, and friendship, grieving parents can regain a sense of purpose and can even come to realize that in spite of the death of their child they can achieve at least some peace of mind. The death might even come to have a singular meaning to them and to others. This entry explores why pain is especially intense in the case of the death of a child and provides models for working with parents who have suffered such a loss.

Why the Pain?

The death of a child constitutes a direct attack on parents at the deepest level of their being. According to Abraham Maslow, universal human needs lie at the basis of human nature. These include belonging, knowledge, self-esteem, and self-actualization. The loss of a child violates the human need for belonging in an incomparable way. Because human beings have a need for knowledge they want to know why this loss has occurred. When they suffer the loss of a child, parents frequently and relentlessly ask themselves and demand of their higher power an acceptable explanation. Yet they believe there is no explanation that will satisfy them. The death of a child is also an attack on self-esteem and self-respect resulting in feelings of guilt. The need for self-actualization means that parents desire to be everything they can be in their parenting even though their parenting skills might be imperfect. As a result of a child's death parents feel helpless and hopeless. Without understanding psychological terminology such as self-actualization they frequently believe they can never feel worthwhile again. They often feel shame about what they believe to be negligence. Their self-criticism can shroud them thereby making effective choices unavailable and impossible. They are tempted to believe that their lives have little or no value.

According to William Glasser, the founder of reality therapy, human beings also have genetic inclinations to satisfy their needs for belonging, inner control or power, freedom, choices or independence, and enjoyment or fun. The death of a child permanently severs the parents' earthly relationship with the child. The loss is a direct attack on the parents' sense of being in charge of their lives. They feel out of control. They feel at the mercy of fate and therefore feel a lack of independence or freedom. They are deprived of the ability to make choices necessary for raising the child and to enjoy life with their child. Consequently, the death of a child is a direct attack on their entire need system. Viktor Frankl, founder of logotherapy, tags meaning and purpose as the most basic human need. Giving meaning to one's life is an inexorable drive that helps human beings make sense of the world and of themselves as part of the world. Parents find meaning and purpose, belonging, inner control, knowledge, self-actualization, freedom, and intense enjoyment in planning and raising a family. All of these motivators, human needs, and drives are written into the fabric of human nature. Consequently, parents who lose a child feel a deep dread that seems incurable.

Working With Parents Who Have Suffered the Loss of a Child

Counseling and even informal conversations with parents of deceased children can be a daunting endeavor. The following guidelines can ease the fear and reluctance of counselors and friends surrounding these conversations. First, no one can appreciate the pain that the parents have felt. Friends intend to be helpful but they often say things that are irrelevant or even hurtful. In support groups, parents of deceased children often encounter comments such as "Your child is in a better place," "God doesn't give you anything you can't cope with," or "I know what you're going through." An empathic and appropriate comment preferred by parents is, "I cannot begin to understand or comprehend the agony that you must be feeling. I wish I could say something that would take away some of your suffering." Likewise, one might say, "There is nothing I can say that will be very helpful to you at this time." Parents report that sharing one's own inadequacy is one of the most supportive statements that counselors and friends can make.

Second, parents often want to talk about their child, and they do not want friends and family to avoid such discussions. This can be difficult because sometimes people fear that parents of deceased children will become out of control with expressions of grief. They don't want to exacerbate the pain felt by the parents and so they steer conversations to other topics. And yet, a counselor or a friend can be of help by asking the parents to describe the child to them. What is their favorite memory of the child? What were they doing when they enjoyed the child's company? If the child was an adult and killed in a war, what thoughts led the child to enlist and to serve his or her country? Brief comments about the child's bravery and deep commitment can be helpful. Parents attending support groups sometimes bring pictures of their son or daughter for other members to see, and they seem to experience a slight momentary lessening of the pain of loss. They state that the support group members are the only people who *want* to hear about their child. The listener need not feel any obligation to say something profound or insightful. The axiom "listening is doing" is useful at this time. The listener is doing something and is providing help whether or not the parents express gratitude to the listener.

Third, there is no answer to the question "why." Often the relentless search for an answer to this question is based on the inability to accept the tragic event. Parents appreciate friends and counselors who respond with empathy for the underlying feelings of powerlessness, guilt, and often anger at the perpetrator, society, government, and even God. At this point the listener and counselor are well advised to help parents identify the underlying emotion. Even labeling emotions can lessen their intensity. The axiom "name it to tame it" applies in full force.

Fourth, pain lessens with the passage of time. While the mere march of time does not completely inoculate the family from pain and turmoil, it does allow for parents to make choices that give them at least moments of relief.

Fifth, as the death of the child recedes into the past, parents can eventually make plans to assist other people. A way to benefit oneself is to be of assistance to another person. Members of support groups find that consoling others, talking to them at meetings, and visiting with them between meetings reaps a fruitful reward for them and for the persons they are helping. Everyone involved experiences at least a few minutes of improvement. One parent stated that she felt not good but less bad. At an appropriate time, counselors can encourage parents to look to need-satisfying activities and thereby replace the burdensome sense of loss for a limited amount of time. Consequently, parents can learn that attempting to *overcome* their grief might be a futile and even a counterproductive effort. Rather, they restructure their thinking from overcoming to *replacing* or at least lessening the agony and other debilitating feelings. Counselors teach them to replace their self-talk from self-condemning statements to more realistic and nonjudgmental statements. "I'm being treated unfairly" can become "I will work on accepting the unfair event as best I can." Their self-talk does not cure or eliminate pain but it can make it more manageable and "less bad."

Grieving over the loss of a parent, friend, or associate of any kind is a difficult journey. And yet, grief over the death of a child of any age is perhaps even more intense. The consensus of many individuals and families who have lost a child is that the pain of loss is chronic. Even after the passage of many years, the sadness continues. It is like the waves of the ocean. They come at various times, sometimes more devastating than at other times. Persons who have attended one support group for several years suggest that parents who have lost a child begin to attend the meetings several months after the loss of their child. They state that grief and pain are like a shadow by which they are constantly surrounded.

Sixth, counselors can suggest that parents deepen their relationship with each other or with another person. Conversations can be helpful but also spending time with a family member or a friend can be very therapeutic. This time is most beneficial if the parties involved avoid the ABCs: arguing, blaming, and criticizing. The phrase "quality time" describes these valuable moments together. It should be for a limited amount of time, perhaps 10 minutes a day.

Seventh, counselors and friends can gently encourage parents to realize that all their thoughts and feelings are normal. Ruminating and playing the same internal tape over and over again is normal.

Eighth, even though feelings tend to linger for days, weeks, months, and longer, the power to choose remains. Human beings have a choice to nurse their feelings, to make them worse, or to fight them. There is also another choice: to embrace the emotions and say to themselves, "I am going to feel upset for now." Paradoxically, choosing the feeling helps to lessen its intensity. A person gains at least some control rather than being victimized by the emotion.

Above all, counselors and friends of grieving parents can serve as part of an effective support system by realizing that each person grieves in a way different from other individuals. These differences take on a myriad of expressions. The process of grieving is gradual and involves steps forward and steps backward. In helping parents deal with the death of a child it is crucial to recognize that parents are often not ready or able to hear some of the previous suggestions too soon after the death of their child. As they begin to feel better or more accurately less bad, they become more open to such suggestions. They also are willing to accept the motives of other people who make unacceptable statements to them. They come to realize that friends and acquaintances wish to console them even if their comments appear clumsy and at times unhelpful. In counseling families or couples who have experienced the death of a child, the counselor can be there for them and encourage them to be there for each other.

The death of a child creates intense and long-lasting pain for parents, yet a skilled and empathic counselor, compassionate friends, and support groups can provide moments of peace. These moments of respite can become steps leading clients to at least some sense of rehabilitation, peace of mind, and an appreciation of their own lives.

Robert E. Wubbolding

See also Choice Theory and Reality Therapy; Death and Dying; Depression in Couples and Families; Loss; Mental Health, Systemic Perspective

Further Readings

Center for Reality Therapy: http://www.realitytherapywub.com

Frankl, V. (1984). *Man's search for meaning*. New York, NY: Washington Square Press.

Glasser, W. (1998). *Choice theory*. New York, NY: HarperCollins.

Glasser, W. (2011). *Take charge of your life*. Bloomington, IN: iUniverse.

Siegel, D. J. (2013). *Brainstorm*. New York, NY: Tarcher.

U.S. Department of Health and Human Services, Health Resources and Services Administration. (2005). *The death of a child—The grief of the parents: A lifetime journey* (Revised). Retrieved from https://www.ndhealth.gov/sids/Publications/TheGrief%20of%20the%20Parents%20ALifetimeJourney.pdf

Wubbolding, R. (2000). *Reality therapy for the 21st century*. Philadelphia, PA: Brunner Routledge.

Wubbolding, R. (2011). *Reality therapy: Theories of psychotherapy series*. Washington, DC: American Psychological Association.

DEATH AND DYING

It has been said that the two things a person can never look directly at are the sun and one's own death. Despite an inability to look directly at death, death has been an integral part of religions, myths, and sciences. Dying is the one certain thing that all human beings will experience. Although cognitively people know that everyone will someday die, people are very hesitant to think of their own deaths; death is one of people's greatest fears. Prior to the 20th century, death was not a mystery in the average household in the United States. Most people lived on farms, where death was a part of life. Death and the bereavement processes, however, have been standardized by laws and regulations and the societal shift to death occurring largely in hospitals or nursing homes rather than at home. Grief and bereavement do not solely occur after death—they are also integral parts of the process of approaching death. This entry examines the shift from home to institutional deaths, psychiatrist Elisabeth Kübler-Ross's model of the five stages of dying, death and dying in the context of family, and the role of family therapy in this process.

The Changing Context of Death

In centuries past, mourning largely occurred at home. In today's world it has moved into hospitals and funeral parlors; laws that regulate the role of funeral directors and employees greatly influence how our society mourns and have created an environment in which society sets limits on grief. Many constraints on behavior and time have been imposed by workplaces and governmental institutions attempting to impose social uniformity on the bereavement process. While these movements have standardized expectations and beliefs about bereavement, they have also dehumanized one of the deepest and most human experiences—to grieve the loss of life. Though grief is universal, mourning and bereavement vary greatly between cultures and even within a single culture.

Every human being will suffer loss and bereavement. Recovery may take several years and may have a profound and lasting impact on the remainder of their life. Accordingly, it is important to enable everyone—children and adults—to regain meaning in life, alleviate enduring distress, and maintain spiritual, personal, and psychological integrity.

Kübler-Ross and the Stages of Dying

In the 1960s Elisabeth Kübler-Ross developed her model of the five stages of grief while she was working with terminally ill patients dying from cancer. Since then, the model has come to be understood by many as applicable not only to the grief of accepting one's impending death but also to the bereavement felt after the death of a loved one, and to the process of dealing with loss in general. According to Kübler-Ross, the five stages of dying are denial, anger, depression, bargaining, and acceptance. Denial is observed when people fail to face the reality of impending loss. The person attempts to disprove the severity and permanence of the loss that is coming. After it is realized that denying the severity of the situation will not alter the course of death and dying, it is common that people begin to be angry. They experience anger with themselves, at those who will survive them, at God, and typically at the people who are closest to them. It is common for people to ask, "Why me?" when experiencing anger about the impending death. In bargaining, there is hope that something can change the course and possibility of death. There is often an effort to negotiate a stay of death in exchange for living a healthier or better life; people often bargain with God or a greater power in an attempt to compromise. In depression, people start to grasp that death really is coming. They are still unable to deal with the impending death. The reality of our lack of power over death is very prominent in this depression stage. Acceptance is the final stage and perhaps the most misunderstood. It is often described as a stage when people are finally okay and able to function normally again; it is not about life returning to normal—it never will. Acceptance is about beginning to understand the reality and the permanence of death. It is more appropriately the stage when people divert their effort from trying to avoid death and begin to prepare for it. It is in acceptance that people are able to speak with their families and spend quality time with loved ones before their death.

Although this five-stage model has been contested and there is a lack of empirical support for claims of its universality, the model has become widely accepted among the general public. Subsequent research indicates, however, that the sequence of stages can be experienced in any order and a feeling may reoccur after one has apparently "passed through" the stage. Critics have also pointed out that although there is some similarity between the experience of dying and the experience of grief after a loss, there are also many profound differences.

Death and Dying in Family Context

The mental health professions have mostly failed to address the impact that death and loss can have on family systems; there is a significant amount of literature on grief and bereavement, but it is focused mostly on individual experience. Even John Bowlby—who pioneered attachment theory, which is a powerful systemic notion—restricted the study of death and loss to an experience within a dyad. Murray Bowen, the pioneer of intergenerational family therapy, is commonly thought to have said that death is society's most taboo subject. He proposed two processes occurring around death: first, an intrapsychic process in which people deny death; and second, a closed system in which people cannot communicate their thoughts on death because they fear upsetting their families. One of the most important lessons to be learned from Bowen's thoughts on death and dying is that families and family processes are profoundly influenced by how death or the fear of death is understood and talked about—or rather, not talked about.

The way death is ignored and not talked about often means that people are not talking about how they want to die or how they want to be remembered. Many people die without any sort of will or instruction left for how their material possessions should be dispersed among survivors. While wills certainly have the use, the most important part of this process is not the material possessions but how families experience death. For a topic that is talked about so little, death is the focus of significant rituals with profound implications for families. Some cultures place importance on sharing a review of life experiences, both good and bad, with the family member who is dying, as part of saying goodbye. Other rituals around death include traditions that create bonds across generations, as they all feel different aspects of the same loss. Many cultures create understanding in the family around death and dying through their spiritual beliefs. Some families believe a physical death is a temporary experience and await a later reunion; others believe death brings an end to their connection. It is essential to understand what meaning death has to help a person and family prepare for and deal with it.

Family Therapy Around Death and Dying

Therapy addressing the subjects of death, dying, and bereavement can be challenging. One of the reasons addressing these issues is so difficult is their inevitability and permanence. No matter how skilled the clinician or how great the effort on the part of a client, death cannot be reversed. Working with families who are dealing with death requires that we achieve a degree of comfort with a topic that evokes discomfort. It is not easy to talk about dying—but not talking about it will only increase feelings of isolation, loneliness, and distress. Families will often need assistance in learning how to talk with each other about dying. Both the dying person and the families of the dying can find it difficult to talk about what is happening. There are frequently fears about saying the wrong thing, fears of loss, fears of one's own mortality, guilt or shame about the past, and denial about the truth of what is coming—each of these topics can be addressed in therapy. Once families are able to stop hoping for a past or present that is impossible, they can begin to have a realistic possibility of having hope.

When the sadness families experience surrounding death is normalized and given voice, it allows for interventions that build hope and remembrance. One of the goals of therapy around death and dying is to accept the reality of the situation but also to find new ways to experience hope; the life that existed previously cannot be returned. Ambiguous loss is experienced when there is a psychological absence but physical presence (as in dementia) or psychological presence but physical absence (as in missing persons). This ambiguity, discussed perhaps most notably by Pauline Boss, is often experienced in families dealing with aging members, especially when Alzheimer's disease or other forms of dementia are present.

Our culture highly values self-mastery and problem-solving; death seems to contradict both of these values. It is very common that when anticipating a death, families cling more closely to their loved ones but push them away at the same time. This push-and-pull pattern is not unique to experiences around death and is deeply rooted in the history of family therapy. Family therapy is particularly well suited to address these family patterns and expectations—both explicit and implicit. Family therapy is a place to help families talk about things they do not otherwise want to face and to practice new skills to do so; family discussions about death and dying are a necessity when death is approaching but are best and rarely done preemptively. Family therapists—with advisement to consult other professionals when needed—can also help families start discussions about the following topics: advanced care directives or living wills, estate planning, a traditional will, family legacy, genealogy or family history, durable power of attorney, medical power of attorney, guardians for dependent children, long-term care insurance, and preplanning a funeral or talking about desires for how a memorial service should be conducted.

Quintin A. Hunt

See also Bereavement; Grief Counseling; Life Events; Life Transitions; Loss; Religion; Rituals in Family Therapy; Support Groups; Therapists' Values

Further Readings

Becvar, D. S. (2003). The impact on the family therapist of a focus on death, dying, and bereavement. *Journal of Marriage and Family Therapy, 29*, 469–477. doi:10.1111/j.1752-0606.2003.tb01689.x

Boss, P. (1999). *Ambiguous loss*. Cambridge, MA: Harvard University Press.

Bowen, M. (2004). *Family therapy in clinical practice*. Lanham, MD: Rowman & Littlefield.

Hedtke, L. (2014). Creating stories of hope: A narrative approach to illness, death and grief. *Australian & New Zealand Journal of Family Therapy, 35*, 4–19. doi:10.1002/anzf.1040

Isaacs, D. (2015). Death and dying. *Journal of Pediatrics and Child Health, 6*, 569–570. doi:10.1111/jpc.12864

Kübler-Ross, E. (1970). *On death and dying*. New York, NY: Simon & Schuster/Collier Books.

Marco, C. A., & Lint, V. R. (2013). Death and dying. In A. Chanmugam, P. Triplett, & G. Kelen (Eds.), *Emergency psychiatry* (pp. 267–277). New York, NY: Cambridge University Press.

Neimeyer, R. A., Harris, D. L., Winokuer, H. R., & Thornton, G. F. (2011). *Grief and bereavement in contemporary society: Bridging research and practice*. New York, NY: Routledge.

Sesame Workshop. (2010). *When families grieve: A special guide for parents and caregivers*. Retrieved from http://www.sesamestreet.org/grief

Wright, K. (2003). Relationships with death: The terminally ill talk about dying. *Journal of Marital and Family Therapy, 29*, 439–454. doi:10.1111/j.1752-0606.2003.tb01687.x

DEBT AND FINANCIAL STRAIN

Debt and financial strain occur when a person or family does not have the financial means to pay their bills, and when this inability to pay bills continues to result in higher bills. The condition of being in debt might be caused by an unexpected illness or accident that comes with astronomically high medical expenses, or an unpaid student loan, or frivolous spending habits, or coming into a marriage with a high degree of personal debt, or unemployment/underemployment, just to name a few. Just as there are multiple reasons people could find themselves in debt, there are a variety of emotional and behavioral responses people have when faced with debt and financial strain. Beginning with a discussion of responses from individuals and couples, this entry continues with an examination of the impact of debt and financial strain on the broader system. The entry closes with a scenario of a family facing debt and financial strain.

Individual Reponses

The intensity of individual responses to debt and financial strain usually correlates with the magnitude of debt they are carrying and the current financial pressures they may be under, along with their basic personality traits before going into debt. The state of being aware that one is regularly spending more than one is earning has commonly been associated with higher levels of stress. Additional emotional responses may include denial, anxiety, shame, resentment, and depression.

People experiencing denial may engage in such behaviors as not opening their bills, or not answering the phone when they suspect a bill collector might be calling. Additionally, they might not make any changes in their current spending habits, which could, in turn, exacerbate the problem. They might hide bank statements and late notices in a junk drawer, refusing to see the additional finance charges and late fees being added to already-high balances due. These denial behaviors could simply be linked to an initial shock response, or they might also be linked to growing feelings of anxiety. Some people who are in debt are constantly worrying about money—how they can get more and how they'll ever be able to "put a dent" in the mounting pile of bills. Individuals might become so overwhelmed that they do not see a resolution in sight, which could lead to real feelings of fear: fear of losing a car or a home, or even fear of losing a relationship. Panic can set in, causing people to make ineffective decisions and engage in behaviors such as lying, cheating, or stealing.

Additionally, people who are in debt tend to feel some degree of embarrassment about their situation, and report that they don't want others to know and they don't like talking about it. They feel ashamed that they don't make enough money, or that they are poor managers of their money, or that something financially devastating happened to them—they might feel that they have failed. The shame often leads to anger and resentment. People can become angry with themselves, or with those to whom they owe money, or they may direct their anger toward their partner or another member of the family.

The tangible and ambiguous losses associated with high debt lead to disenfranchised grief and constant stress. This experience, together with the shame, fear, anger, or self-imposed isolation, might lead people to choose unhealthy coping mechanisms (e.g., drinking, drug-taking, or gambling). Worse yet, they can become clinically depressed the deeper they go into a failure cycle. Depression is a dangerous illness that can lead to broken relationships and even suicide or homicide. Depression can be treated, but the management of the debt or financial strain would also have to be changed to alleviate depressive symptoms.

Love and Money

Studies have shown that couples with more money and less debt often report higher overall marital satisfaction, while couples with more debt and less money tend to spend less time together, have more arguments about money, and report lower marital satisfaction. Many people grow up with social and multigenerational norms that discourage conversation about money, and being poor or being unable to pay one's bills is often stigmatized in society. Couples are reported to be more comfortable talking about sex or even infidelity than managing the household budget or brainstorming ways to get ahead financially. Money has also traditionally been associated with power, and can influence hierarchy in the couple's relationship and in the family in general. Ideas about money are also linked with gender roles in the family. The presence or absence of money may be tied to each partner's individual perceptions of identity (as both self and mate). The changing world of work, with women sometimes being paid more than men, more men staying home to raise children, and increasing options to work remotely, are beginning to change attitudes about money and individual power in relationships. Nonetheless, dealing with the topic of money is necessary for any couple planning a life together.

Partners argue about money more frequently when they have different values and approaches toward money management, or when one partner comes into the marriage with much higher debt than the other. Interestingly, both of these conditions are more common than most realize, as research suggests that people gravitate toward their opposite, in terms of spending tendencies, when choosing a mate. At the same time, we also know that this complementary attraction leads to higher frequencies of financial arguments, which predict both marital dissatisfaction and divorce. Affluent couples may not feel the pressure to discuss matters related to money. However, couples facing debt and financial strain are compelled to navigate these differences and find enough common ground if they are to build a satisfying personal relationship.

Impact on the Family

Given the context of individual and partner responses to economic stress, the impact of debt and financial strain on families with dependent children, or families who are supporting aging parents, can be especially complex. Stressors related to money impact individuals within the family, as well as the relationships among and between family members. The addition of children to the family unit adds both predictable and unpredictable costs to the household budget, leading to higher expenditures and higher, more quickly accumulated debt. Even parents with greater financial resources experience this as a challenge, and parents living near or below the poverty line have consistently difficult choices to make in terms of providing the basics of food, clothing, and shelter for the family versus paying down on credit card debt or trying to keep up with the other financial needs associated with school-aged children (including school supplies, fees for sports teams and field trips, and trying to keep up socially by having the "right" things). Furthermore, carrying a high debt-to-limit balance on credit cards can lower one's credit score, increasing interest rates and making it more difficult to borrow money (e.g., for necessities, or for a more efficient home or a better car) in the future.

Children might be individually negatively impacted in a variety of ways. Aside from simply having less, and having access to fewer opportunities, they might pick up on the unhealthy example of living beyond their means, extending the problem of debt to the next generation. Conversely, they could also decide to stop the cycle and commit themselves to healthy money management strategies as adults. In the presence of financial strain, parents might be so preoccupied with dealing with money and bills that they overlook opportunities to bond with their children in positive ways. Parents in low-income families have been found to exhibit less positive parenting behaviors than their higher-income counterparts, but when the number or intensity of stressors can be minimized, even families with high financial strain can show remarkable resilience. Children of poverty are often not as physically or mentally healthy as their counterparts in higher-income families, and when they enter the important stage of adolescence, they are at higher risk for participating in unhealthy or dangerous behaviors.

Family Scenario

Let's consider the example of Joe and Harry, who met and fell in love during their time in college, and who are now trying to adopt a child. Joe came from a family of limited means, but qualified for several scholarships, which ended up covering only about 45% of his expenses. He took out student loans to cover the balance. Harry came from a wealthy family and was proud to romance Joe by paying for most of their dates when they first met. Things were easy, and they never really talked about money. However, Joe had to quit school when his father became sick, so he could help provide care and also work to make money to pay for uninsured medical expenses. He quickly maxed out the credit cards that had been given to him while he was a college student. In the meantime, Harry graduated and secured a well-paying job. Joe is now trying to support his mother, having to repay the student loans, trying to pay off the high-interest-rate credit cards, and having difficulty finding professional employment. He loves Harry and wants more than anything for the two of them to become parents together. Joe manages to keep most of his debt "under wraps" until the adoption agency runs a credit check as part of their screening process for prospective parents. The report is shared with the couple together at the adoption agency office, and now Joe and Harry are faced with multiple crises, including the probability of not being approved as adoptive parents, the betrayal that Harry might feel, the guilt and shame that Joe might feel, and serious questions about their future together, on top of the obvious financial issue.

These crises might be just the beginning for Joe and Harry as they try to begin a life together. Their ability to navigate and resolve the issues will be dependent on their ability to empathize with each other, communicate effectively, compromise, and reconnect emotionally. The initial crises will be followed by a period of debt and financial strain as the couple attempts to stabilize both their bank account and their relationship. This scenario demonstrates how easily people can fall into debt, how innocently they might deal with it in terms of hiding it from their partner, and how high the stakes might be in terms of learning to navigate financial strain together.

Anita A. Neuer Colburn

See also Chronic Illness With Couples and Families; Conflict in Couples and Families; Depression in Couples and Families; Family Resilience; Family Stress; Family Stress Adaptation Theory; Job Loss; Life Balance; Resilience; Stress Management

Further Readings

Atwood, J. D. (2012). Couples and money: The last taboo. *American Journal of Family Therapy, 40*, 1–19. doi:10.1080/01926187.2011.600674

Dew, J. (2008). Debt change and marital satisfaction change in recently married couples. *Family Relations, 57*, 60–71.

Herrmann, A. F. (2011). "Losing things was nothing new": A family's stories of foreclosure. *Journal of Loss and Trauma, 16*, 497–510. doi:10.1080/15325024.2011.576982

McCloud, L., & Dwyer, R. E. (2011). The fragile American: Hardship and financial troubles in the 21st century. *Sociological Quarterly, 52*, 13–35.

Ponnet, K. (2014). Financial stress, parent functioning and adolescent problem behavior: An actor-partner interdependence approach to family stress processes in low-, middle-, and high-income families. *Journal of Youth and Adolescence, 43*, 1752–1769. doi:10.1007/s10964-014-0159-y

Rick, S. I., Small, D. A., & Finkel, E. J. (2011, April). Fatal (fiscal) attraction: Spendthrifts and tightwads in marriage. *Journal of Marketing Research, 48*, 228–237.

DECISION-MAKING

Decision-making can be defined as a process that draws on the cognitive, emotional, and motivational components of an individual and results in selecting a behavior, belief, or course of action from among many alternatives and possibilities. The process results in the selection of a final choice that may or may not require action. Although decision-making happens constantly in relationships, there are instances where a couple or family cannot agree on a direction. Questions and decision-making are integral to relationships: intimate, friendly, or other. This entry discusses decision-making models in families and couples, important factors in decision-making, including the role of stress, values, a general decision-making process, how changes in gender roles have impacted decision-making, and decision-making in connection with career and ethical issues.

Theories

There are several theories that can help to understand decision-making in families and couples and the factors that sometimes pose problems in the process. One theory used in understanding the dynamics of decision-making is resource theory. According to resource theory, the power a partner has in the decision-making process varies according to the economic resources that the partner contributes. The second theory used to understand the decision-making process is social exchange theory, which has become widely used as a framework in assessment of family power and decision-making. An assumption of social exchange theory is that individuals act, react, and initiate action and are not just passively responding to environmental factors. Additionally, people tend to act in a way that will maximize rewards and minimize costs, and decisions can be negotiated. The third theory, role theory, notes that family decision-making is structured, family members know and accept roles (e.g., parent, mother, child) and there is little or no negotiation. The fourth theory is the process-oriented model. This model focuses on analyzing (e.g., observation and self-report measures) the joint decision-making partner dyad, the nature of sex roles, and their impact on the decision-making process.

Stress

Stress, as an effect of change, is inevitable and normal. Individuals are constantly in a state of change and these changes can create stress within partnerships, marriages, and families. The amount of stress change generates depends on the parties' perception of the demands they face and resources they have available to them. Some strategies to reduce the perceived demands are to talk about and share perceptions, thoughts, and feelings with one another and make decisions together. How couples and families resolve stressful situations depends on their day-to-day interactions and patterns of communication. Early in relationships, individuals can be influenced by how their family of origin negotiated stressful situations and decision-making.

Stress in relationships and families can be controlled or can continue to be an issue. When problems arise in the relationship or family, there are many points to consider. First, do the couple or family support each other and consider each person's viewpoint, consider every alternative, seek outside counseling, or talk about it? Individuals can have a variety of reactions to stress that will impact the processes of communication and decision-making. The level of stress an individual can tolerate and the coping strategies used will influence individual reactions. Some people are able to tolerate higher levels of stress than others. What might cause stress for one person will not for another. How well individuals cope with stressful situations also impacts the decision-making process. Someone who has a low tolerance for stress and limited coping strategies might stop talking and withdraw. Other individuals might react by yelling or by simply ignoring the issue. Coping strategies to deal effectively with stress and make decisions include talking about the issue and being physically active (e.g., running, yoga, swimming) to reduce stress levels. Other reactions can include taking sides, scapegoating, holding a grudge, increased substance use, and aggression or sarcasm, which are less likely to have a positive effect on the decision-making process.

Values

Values and motivation have an influence on decision-making. Values are ideas and beliefs that are significant and important to an individual, and they play a role in how stress is handled, factors related to personality, and preferences. For example, if a couple is deciding where to go on vacation and one partner values the opportunity to rest and relax, that individual might prefer going to a resort, while the other partner, who values adventure and activity on vacation, might suggest wilderness hiking and whitewater rafting. These different preferences in how to spend vacation time potentially create stress in the relationship and require a decision-making process.

Values play a significant role in levels of stress in relationships. There are many decisions that are related to values. For example, some individuals want children, while others do not. That issue can create enough stress to require a decision about continuing the relationship. Values surrounding financial issues—saving, spending, and investing money—can create a situation where a couple or family needs to define the issue, explore and brainstorm alternatives, and bring cognitive, emotional, and motivational processes to arriving at a final decision.

John Gottman discusses the concept of gridlocked problems, which he sees as an outcome of incongruent values, expectations, and dreams for one's life and relationships. Gridlocked issues in a relationship happen when partners in a couple have hopes, aspirations, or wishes that are not being respected or realized in the relationship. For example, one partner wants a big family with many children because this represents joy and the partner was raised with love, support, and ample resources, while the other partner was raised in a family that struggled to provide basic needs, and thus children could represent a threat to this partner's comfort and security. With these dynamics at play in the relationship, the decision-making process to have children could be a gridlocked problem. To overcome a gridlocked problem, couples need to understand the importance of supporting each other's hopes, aspirations, and wishes. That does not mean either partner is expected to give up on their dreams and hopes, but instead share goals and wishes together and decide how to fulfill them.

Gender Roles

Research over the past few decades has explored how gender roles and societal changes have played a role in decision-making in couples and families. Profound changes began happening in families and couples in the 1970s. Since then some individuals have made decisions to not get married and still be parents, the divorce rate has increased, and the category once occupied by the traditional nuclear family now includes a far greater number of blended families and stepfamilies. These changes influence family decision-making by taking a shift away from a commanding nature in decision-making to a negation approach. Additionally, decision-making in families and couples has changed due to the idea of two-income families, which has not only increased the income and status of the family, but provided additional options for women and generated the ability to negotiate gender roles and responsibilities.

There are many areas in which a couple needs to make decisions, and some research indicates that in the American family, as a result of dual earner relationships, increased status, and education, women have gained more influence in most decision-making, particularly the initial and final stages of the decision-making process. Although women have gained more influence in decision-making in opposite-sex relationships, some data suggest that men and women may still have different degrees of influence depending on the decision being made. Research on decision-making in families suggests that men are perceived as more dominant when deciding issues related to automobiles, family savings, and life insurance. Women are perceived to be more dominant in decision-making related to issues of furniture, food, and general family decisions about money management. Areas of shared decisions include vacations and purchases of major appliances. In general, research suggests that husbands, more than wives, perceive children to be more influential in family decision-making.

Process

Some research on decision-making is focused on individual processes, other research is from a systems perspective, and some research relates to specific life moments (career decision-making, mate selection decision-making, etc.). Regardless of which partner is most influential in particular decisions or what the decision is about, there is a general process that most decisions follow: collect facts, information, and data related to the issue or problem; listen and pay attention to each other's point of view; brainstorm ideas and alternatives and come up with a plan that everyone can accept; summarize areas agreed upon and implement the decision; and reflect on the decision and outcome. In addition to this process, couples and families can implement the following strategies:

1. Define feelings, needs, wishes, and wants.
2. Remain calm and engaged in the process; stay positive and optimistic.
3. Respect a partner and family's feelings and wishes.
4. Ask open-ended questions with a nonjudgmental attitude.
5. Discover common interests and reinforce possible positive positions.
6. Negotiate conflict but do not let it become a fight.
7. Try out a plan, and practice and reevaluate the plan and action after a few weeks to see if any adjustments need to be made.

Special Topics in Counseling

A considerable amount of research in counseling has been about career decision-making and ethical decision-making. Particularly in career decision-making, research has focused on skills and abilities, values, discrimination, and education. Young people often struggle with identifying a career or vocation. Counseling in the area of career issues helps individuals explore what they value in a career choice (e.g., independent work environment versus extensive supervision), the requisite skills and interests (e.g., listening skills, empathy, artistic ability, etc.), and how discrimination can impact what individuals see as options for their career.

In addition to career decision-making, clinicians need to be mindful of ethical issues in counseling relationships and develop a process for making sound ethical decisions. There are various ethical decision-making models for counselors. One of the principles found in most models is the idea of autonomy. Clients should be free to make individual choices. However, in practice, this is not simple for a counselor because there are exceptions to total autonomy for clients. For example, counselors are required to intervene if a client poses an immediate physical threat to himself or herself or others (e.g., suicide, homicide, sexual abuse, child abuse). In addition, counselors may have to help clients understand the impact of decisions on others, not just the impact on oneself.

Joseph A. Campbell

See also Career Planning in Couples/Families; Communication in Couples and Families; Conflict in Couples and Families; Conflict Resolution; Conflict Styles; Dual-Earner Families; Family Values; Gender Roles

Further Readings

Blood, R. O., Jr., & Wolde, D. M. (1960). *Husbands and wives: The dynamics of married living.* Glencoe, IL: Free Press.

Cottone, R. R., & Claus, R. E. (2000). Ethical decision-making models: A review of the literature. *Journal of Counseling & Development, 78,* 275–283. doi:10.1002/j.1556-6676.2000.tb01908.x

Davis, H. (1976). Decision-making within the household. *Journal of Consumer Research, 3,* 241–260.

Garcia, J. G., Cartwright, B., Winston, S. M., & Borzuchowska, B. (2003). A transcultural integrative model for ethical decision-making in counseling. *Journal of Counseling & Development, 81,* 268–277. doi:10.1002/j.1556-6678.2003.tb00253.x

Gladding, S. T. (1995). *Family therapy: History, theory and practice.* Englewood Cliffs, NJ: Merrill.

Gottman, J., Notarius, C., Markman, H., Bank, S., Yoppi, B., & Rubin, M. E. (1976). Behavior exchange theory and marital decision-making. *Journal of Personality and Social Psychology, 34*(1), 14–23. doi:10.1037/0022-3514.34.1.14

Hill, W., & Scanzoni, J. (1982). An approach for assessing marital decision-making processes. *Journal of Marriage and the Family, 11,* 927–941.

McDonald, G. (1980). Family power: The assessment of a decade of theory and research. *Journal of Marriage and the Family, 11,* 460–467.

DELPHI RESEARCH METHOD

The Delphi research method is used to better understand a topic by building a consensus of thought from people considered to be most knowledgeable about it. The method was introduced in the 1950s by the RAND Corporation as a forecasting tool, and has been used and modified in numerous research applications since that time. Though Delphi methodology has not historically played a significant role in marriage and family therapy research, there is ongoing interest in this technique to better appreciate and define existing concepts in the field, as well as to build a sense of future direction. This entry discusses the typical structure used in the Delphi research method, as well as some of the benefits and challenges it presents.

Delphi is considered a mixed-method research approach, as it uses elements of qualitative research in gathering and analyzing participants' subjective beliefs and comments, but also uses quantitative research techniques in describing and ranking the different ideas appearing in these responses. Although the exact procedures used in Delphi studies will vary to meet the specific needs of a research project, the process typically involves the following stages: (a) initializing steps to define the research question, establish procedures, and engage participants considered to have expert knowledge on the topic; (b) circulating initial questionnaires and analyzing responses to identify conceptual themes; (c) soliciting and aggregating participant evaluations of themes identified; and (d) obtaining and summarizing participant feedback of final item rankings or consensus achieved. Three rounds of participant feedback and data analysis is typical in identifying areas of consensus, and possibly of conflict, relative to the research topic. Additional rounds, if used, typically involve repetition of requests for participant reevaluation and reranking of themes based upon review of other participant feedback.

Design of a Delphi study begins with the research question, which might seek to identify issues that are relevant to working with a problem or situation, obtain perspectives on future opportunities and challenges in an area, or explore the meaning given to constructs that are often used but lack precise definition. Once the research topic has been defined, the researcher must identify participant characteristics necessary to be considered highly knowledgeable or expert in the area. Such things as years of academic or clinical experience, level of participation in professional organizations, or extent of professional presentations and published research may become criteria for selection. A Delphi study does not require a set number of participants, though there should be a sufficient quantity and diversity to ensure all perspectives on the topic are represented. Participants should be informed of research study goals, processes, schedule, and realistic estimates of time commitments to help ensure their engagement throughout the study. Delphi study communications are typically done in written electronic form, rather than in face-to-face individual or group formats. This is advantageous because participant initial responses are not influenced by the opinions of other study members, participants can work at their own pace and schedule, and the cost of participants meeting at a single location and time is avoided.

The initial round of data collection is prompted by an open-ended questionnaire designed to solicit a broad range of thought relevant to the research topic. The questions may include some direction or outline to prompt and structure participant responses, though this may increase the risk of biasing or limiting response scope. A suggested limit to the number of response items submitted for each question may also be included to direct participant focus toward their most critical items and also to control the overall level of data. Analysis of initial responses involves identification of themes supported by one or more direct participant comments, using participants' exact wording to the extent feasible to best ensure their precise meaning is retained. The data analysis process should be planned and documented so that decisions made in creating themes from raw data can be examined. Once all themes are articulated and listed by initial questionnaire categories, this information is provided to participants for their evaluation in the second round of feedback. Results are validated by participant review and comment.

By listing themes from all respondents, the second questionnaire allows participants to broaden their perspective on the research topic as they review and evaluate themes they may not have originally considered. In this round, participants are typically asked to rate each theme on a visual, graduated, Likert-type scale. For example, responses might be provided on a scale of 1 to 7, where 1 indicates the item has very low importance and 7 indicates it has very high importance. Participants are also asked to verify that their original responses are appropriately reflected, and to provide any additional comments on the themes presented. Researchers aggregate participant ratings for each theme to generate a measure of its most central or average score, typically a median or mean. A measure of score variability for each theme is also developed, typically an interquartile range or standard deviation.

The third questionnaire typically presents the average score and variability for each item evaluated in the prior round of feedback, as well as the participant's own rating of items. Participants are provided the opportunity to rerate items based on further consideration of aggregate ranking results, and may also provide comments on study findings given the rating data. This step may be repeated many times as the researchers see ratings move toward consensus with additional rounds of participant input. It may be difficult to define what consensus means in a Delphi study. When iterations are completed, the study design may allow for elimination of items that have average scores below a predefined target level, reasoning that participants have not achieved consensus supporting these. Items with average scores below this level, however, might also be given additional scrutiny to determine whether they have been consistently rated in midrange by participants, or whether high variability in scores may indicate conflicting views regarding the item.

In the final questionnaire, researchers share the final item ratings and study conclusions regarding consensus on research questions. Participants are invited to share their critiques of study results for inclusion in the final research report, as well as their perspectives on the experience of participating in the study. Insights gained from experts in a Delphi study may often suggest directions for further research.

Mary McClure

See also Couples Therapy Research; Effectiveness Research; Outcome Research; Qualitative Research; Quantitative Research

Further Readings

Dawson, M. D., & Brucker, P. S. (2001). The utility of the Delphi method in MFT research. *American Journal of Family Therapy, 29*(2), 125–140.

Skulmoski, G. J., Hartman, F. T., & Krahn, J. (2007). The Delphi method for graduate research. *Journal of Information Technology Education, 6*, 1–21.

Stone Fish, L., & Busby, D. M. (2005). The Delphi method. In D. H. Sprenkle & F. P. Piercy (Eds.), *Research methods in family therapy* (2nd ed., pp. 238–253). New York, NY: Guilford Press.

West, A. (2011). Using the Delphi technique: Experience from the world of counseling and psychotherapy. *Counseling & Psychotherapy Research, 11*(3), 237–242.

Depression in Adolescents

Major (also called clinical) depression is a mood disorder that causes persistent feelings of sadness and may interfere with work or school, eating, and the ability to enjoy life. Depression among adolescents impacts millions of young people and their families each year. When family members suspect that an adolescent has the symptoms of depression, assistance should be sought from a medical or mental health professional. The earlier an adolescent can receive assistance, the better. In addition, other issues may present with depression, such as anxiety, posttraumatic stress disorder, or substance abuse. This entry discusses the prevalence of depression in adolescents, diagnostic criteria, risk factors, developmental factors influencing depression, and prevention and intervention.

Description

Depression in adolescents is one of the most prevalent mental health issues to affect families in the United States. The National Institute of Mental Health reported a high prevalence of adolescents who have experienced a major depressive episode, approximately 5% among males and 16% among females (a combined estimation of nearly 11% of the overall population of adolescents between 12 and 17). This frequency of depression warrants careful attention by families and providers who work closely with them.

Depression is also an important issue to note because it poses the risk of progressing into suicidal thinking. Suicide has been described by the U.S. Centers for Disease Control and Prevention (CDC) as a key concern for adolescents because it remains the third leading cause of death for young people between the ages of 10 to 24 in the United States. According to the World Health Organization (WHO), it is also the second leading cause of death in the 10- to 24-years age group throughout the world. WHO made suicide a top priority issue in 2014, reporting that every year over 800,000 people die from suicide, corresponding roughly to one death every 40 seconds. These figures do not include suicide attempts, which can be many times more frequent than completed suicide (10, 20, or more times according to some studies).

Diagnosis of Depression

The American Psychiatric Association defines the diagnostic criteria for major depressive disorder (MDD). The symptoms characterizing depression among adolescents may include having a sad or depressed mood, reduced interest in general activities that may have been enjoyable in the past, alterations in weight (either higher or lower), psychomotor agitation or retardation, increased tiredness, inappropriate feelings of intense guilt, challenges with concentration, or recurrent thoughts of death or suicide. These symptoms are expected to exist for a period of 2 weeks or longer. In addition to MDD, other depressive disorders include persistent depressive disorder (PDD, formerly dysthymia), disruptive mood dysregulation disorder (DMDD), and premenstrual dysphoric disorder. From a family standpoint, adolescents experiencing a depressive episode may appear less engaged and sad much of the time. There may be some attempts by the adolescent to fake happiness, possibly with exaggerated expressions of joy and laughter. Adolescents who are depressed may spend more time in their room away from the rest of the family, showing sudden changes in patterns of eating, sleeping, tiredness, and observed hopelessness. Parents who observe these behaviors are encouraged to express concern with the adolescent directly and seek help from a professional counselor to explore the young person's goals. Depression that remains unaddressed and untreated results in greater potential for adolescents to develop chronic mental illness or to attempt suicide.

Risk Factors

Identifying risk factors can help families identify depression among adolescents early. Adolescents have a much greater likelihood for experiencing serious depression when they have low self-esteem related to a variety of factors such as obesity, academic problems, bullying, socioeconomic status, and others. They also have a greater risk for depression when they have been the victim of violence or a witness to violence, such as physical or sexual abuse. Having co-occurring conditions such as anxiety disorders, autism spectrum disorder, attention-deficit/hyperactivity disorder, and others can pose higher risks for depression, along with chronic medical illnesses such as cancer, AIDS, diabetes, or others. Parents and families may want to explore further when adolescents have very few friends and personal supportive relationships, and if they display various problematic personality traits, such as overdependence, self-critical thoughts, and low self-esteem. Additional risk factors include substance use such as alcohol, drugs, and nicotine; being female, among whom depression occurs more frequently; and identifying as lesbian, gay, bisexual, or transgender. Adolescents with family histories of depression, bipolar disorder, or alcoholism show greater risk, along with having a family member who has committed suicide, having dysfunctional family engagement and conflict resolution, and the previous experience of significant traumatic experiences or losses.

Developmental Influences

Parents and families may blame themselves when their adolescents are experiencing depression. While all parents could likely benefit from some changes, the majority of parents are simply experiencing the typical challenges of adolescent development. Much has been written regarding human development, and adolescence is frequently depicted as one of the most rapid and formative times of change for young people as they progress toward adulthood. Adolescent development generally occurs between the ages of 11 and 18, though this range may differ among individual young people and in various cultures. These changes occur with regard to changes in the self and the emotional, physical, social, and spiritual makeup of young people.

Self

Adolescents' perceptions of themselves undergo transformation during this period of development. Erik Erikson described this period as a time when adolescents will either successfully form an identity or experience role confusion. In many ways adolescents engage in this process with an increased sense of autonomy. This leads to greater potential for an increase or decrease in self-esteem. Adolescents begin experiencing a change from identifying with caregivers to defining their own identity, which may include more focus on their peer group. This search for identity also becomes focused on the future, considering future careers and specific areas of interest in which to invest time and energy. Sexual identity is facilitated as adolescents strive to make sense of their new sexual development and influences from the culture around them. Self-development also poses a challenge as young people may experience dissonance with competing values. Moral reasoning and choices may impact identity formation as adolescents move from accepting rules and standards expressed by others to adopting principles or beliefs for themselves. Erikson's description of role confusion suggests depression potentially results from discontent or uncertainty related to establishing a clear sense of self.

Mental

Mental development and logical reasoning in adolescence includes a number of changes related to the increase of abstract thought. Young people are able to engage in reflective processes and consider different opinions and perceptions in different circumstances. Young people are increasingly able to experience and express empathy, showing an increase in their ability to engage critical thinking to solve problems. The fluctuation of mental changes can contribute to depression, especially when accompanied by an inability to conceptualize any hope or help for improvement in the future. Thoughts of the future emerge as never before, considering hypothetical scenarios of future ambitions, vocations, and relationships.

Emotional

Adolescent development may produce heightened emotional reactions and mood swings. This is often associated with the hormonal changes that are physically occurring during this time, yet this period of development also has potential for learning adaptive ways for expressing emotion. This is frequently a period when young people encounter emotionally charged disagreements and conflicts with parents as they exercise abstract reasoning. Emotional development gives rise to the potential for increased loneliness if there is a perception of disconnection from peers or dissatisfaction with oneself. Depression and anxiety increase substantially during this period of development, with adolescents posing a higher risk for suicide and self-harm behavior as a result of intense emotional reactions. The impulsive nature of emotional reactions poses a risk not only for suicide, but for other risky or self-harm behaviors.

Physical

Physical development during adolescence is more rapid than at any other time, with the exception of infancy. After a relatively stable and gradual period of growth through childhood, adolescents experience a time of substantial growth called puberty. This change includes sexual development, body and muscle changes, hair growth, and brain functionality. Sexual changes are characterized by modifications with sexual organs and hormones. For many youths, sexual development impacts their self-image and relations with their peers. Young people perceived as experiencing puberty earlier have been found to enjoy greater popularity among their peers. Adolescent girls experience breast and muscle growth, initiation of the menstrual cycle, hormonal increases of estrogen, internal development of the ovaries, hair growth in the pubic area, armpits, arms, and legs, and modifications to a more mature voice. Male adolescents experience growth of the penis and testicles; capability for ejaculation; muscle and body growth; hair growth on the face, pubic area, armpits, arms, and legs; and male voices become modified to a deeper, more mature voice. Depression has also been attributed to biological factors, so increased hormone changes may serve as a catalyst for depression to emerge among adolescents who are predisposed, that is, with family histories of depression or other mental illnesses. Poor body image can play a significant role in depression among adolescents, and can lead to comorbid conditions such as a variety of eating disorders, risky sexual activity, and other problems.

Social

A significant shift occurs among adolescents, whereby the focus of social self-identity frequently shifts from parents and family to a peer group. Young people begin experiencing greater autonomy in their own perspectives and in the levels of responsibility they may be given. In general, adolescents begin to seek out relationships that are more intimate over time, which exhibits new levels of loyalty and commitment that were previously assumed within family roles. Young people may begin enhancing their connections with others through an increased understanding of their own interests and preferences. A lack of connection with a social peer group may result in an increase of depressive features overall. Issues such as teasing and bullying by peers have shown greater likelihood that adolescents will experience low self-esteem and hopelessness that can lead to depression and suicide.

Spiritual

Spiritual changes also occur at a rapid pace through this time of development. With increased ability to think abstractly and theoretically, young people begin to question prior beliefs, traditions, and practices taught by families, communities, and cultures. The expanded ability to think beyond their own experiences may lead adolescents to questions of the existential meaning and the teleological direction of life. The search for purpose and direction provides not only the opportunity for increased doubt and confusion, but also the potential for increased confirmation and commitment to firmly held beliefs. Young people may develop greater understanding and rationale for maintaining prior beliefs. A spiritual identity can become more defined with early foundational experiences or with newly discovered beliefs that shape current perspectives. Adolescents have the potential to experience depression in times when spiritual conflict arises. Experiencing tension in one's spiritual beliefs for the first time can create a significant disequilibrium that results in confusion and disconnect from prior sources of support. This confusion may lead to spiritual guilt that influences a young person's ability to properly align with a spiritual identity.

Family Engagement

Families may have difficulty differentiating between the sometimes turbulent development of adolescence and signs of depression. They can begin with watching for risk factors that have the potential to contribute toward depression, and by remembering to contextualize behavior within the typical development adolescents encounter during this time of rapid change. Parents and families can ease the difficulties of adolescents with high risk for depression by considering elements of prevention and intervention.

Prevention

Although some young people will experience depression as a biological dysfunction regardless of the support and love offered in the home setting, parents and caregivers can help prevent depression as much as possible by fostering an atmosphere of openness and warmth. Such an approach can be approached with modeling behaviors of openness and acceptance, even in cases where disagreement occurs. Parents have the opportunity to emphasize the importance of ongoing involvement even when adolescents display tension as a normal reaction in their struggle toward autonomy and self-identity.

Parents and caregivers benefit from approaching adolescent struggles through a combination of love and limits. Such support may be demonstrated through a model called the parenting four Cs: choices, consequences, consistency, and care. Families support growth by demonstrating that choices result in consequences all the time, for both positive and negative behavior. Parents also support the development of moral reasoning and stability through ongoing consistency in their words and actions. Each of the previous Cs offers further opportunity to emphasize the foundation of care from which parental actions must proceed. Providing a setting of encouragement and unconditional love will offer room for mistakes by both the young person and the parent. In this way adolescents may be empowered to adopt strategies for overcoming depression.

Intervention

Families can engage adolescents in a number of ways that offer the opportunity to overcome depressive features. Supportive atmospheres will not always prevent the occurrence of depression. Even before symptoms become severe, families will benefit from understanding options for intervention and treatment. The National Alliance on Mental Illness (NAMI) describes the many avenues available to adolescents with depression, including counseling and psychotherapy, exercise, light therapy, psychoeducation and self-awareness, alternative natural approaches, mindfulness or contemplative worship, behavior contracts and other cognitive-behavioral therapies, medications, and use of brain stimulation. In cases when young people find themselves suicidal or unable to remain safe on their own, hospitalization may be required until the young person stabilizes and returns to the family in safety. Seeking professional advice in light of the symptoms displayed by any adolescent will assist families in understanding what steps are the best to take in various circumstances.

Nathan C. D. Perron

See also Adjustment Disorder in Adolescents; Adolescent Mental Health; Depression in Children; Parent–Adolescent Relations; Parent–Child Communication

Further Readings

American Psychiatric Association. (2013). *Diagnostic and statistical manual of mental disorders* (5th ed.). Arlington, VA: Author.

Centers for Disease Control and Prevention. (2012, August 1). *Child maltreatment*. Retrieved from http://www.cdc.gov/ViolencePrevention/childmaltreatment

Henderson, D. A., & Thompson, C. L. (2016). *Counseling children* (9th ed.). Belmont, CA: Brooks/Cole.

James, R. K. (2008). *Crisis intervention strategies* (6th ed.). Belmont, CA: Thomson/Brooks/Cole.

Mayo Clinic. (2015). *Teen depression risk factors*. Retrieved from http://www.mayoclinic.org/diseases-conditions/teen-depression/basics/risk-factors/con-20035222

National Alliance on Mental Illness. (2015). *Depression*. Retrieved from https://www.nami.org/Learn-More/Mental-Health-Conditions/Depression

National Institute of Mental Health. (2015). *Major depression among adolescents*. Retrieved from http://www.nimh.nih.gov/health/statistics/prevalence/major-depression-among-adolescents.shtml

Perron, N. C. D., & Pender, D. A. (2015). Meeting the need: Applying concepts for assessment and planning with child and adolescent trauma. *Journal of Child and Adolescent Counseling, 1*(1), 37–49. doi:10.1080/23727810.2015.1023607

Vernon, A., & Clemente, R. (2005). *Assessment and intervention with children and adolescents: Developmental and multicutural approaches* (2nd ed.). Alexandria, VA: American Counseling Association.

World Health Organization. (2015). *Mental health: Suicide data*. Retrieved from http://www.who.int/mental_health/prevention/suicide/suicideprevent/en/

DEPRESSION IN CHILDREN

Depression in children, not unlike depression in adults, is defined by symptoms that include but are not limited to a marked period of sadness, loss of interest in activities, and mood changes. Typically, these symptoms are not a result of a recent experience, although depressive symptoms can mirror those associated with grief and loss. There is some debate among professionals about whether or not children should be diagnosed with depression (or any other mood disorder), because they are still in the early stages of development. Research shows, however, that children, like adults, can experience symptoms of depression that can be clinically treated. Depression is often undiagnosed in childhood and may have implications throughout the life span. This entry provides an overview of the symptoms, causes, and treatment of childhood depression, specifically for children between ages 8 and 18 years.

Symptoms of Depression in Children

As with any disorder, symptoms can vary from one individual to another. Environmental, biological, and cultural factors, for example, must be taken into consideration before diagnosing children with depression. The following list of symptoms is not exhaustive but it is representative of the most common symptoms present in children who suffer from depression.

Sadness

Although children may experience sadness for many reasons and many times throughout the earlier stages of development, sadness in children who are depressed is marked by duration, frequency, or intensity of symptoms. Children who are sad for a longer period of time than is normal for them may be suffering from depression, especially if their sadness is inconsolable. For example, children who are sad may go through brief periods of pouting or crying. Children who are depressed may be sad for several hours or over a period of days, long after any known trigger. Similarly, children who are depressed may experience sadness more frequently than other children in their age group. Feelings of sadness may become more of the norm for children who are depressed, presenting more often than any expression of happiness or excitement. While the intensity of sadness is difficult to measure, children who are depressed will express sadness in ways that are beyond their normal level. For example, children who are sad may cry or limit contact with others. Children who are depressed might yell, scream, or become completely withdrawn. What is important to note when distinguishing between children who are sad versus depressed is that sadness, like any emotion, is a temporary expression. Depression is a mental health condition that, if untreated, can have lasting effects on the social and emotional development of children.

Change in Appetite or Sleep

Children who are not depressed typically follow a regular eating and sleeping pattern. Changes in appetite could include eating less, eating more often, or refusing to eat. Similarly, changes in sleep could include sleeping less, more often, or not sleeping for days at a time. When either an eating or sleeping pattern changes, particularly in the absence of an illness or some other medical cause, it can be reason for concern. Life events such as the birth of a sibling, loss of a parent, or change in environment can impact children's daily routines without the diagnosis of depression. However, when these life events are followed by a consistent disruption in the eating and sleeping pattern of children, it could be symptomatic of a depressive disorder.

Reduced Activity

Children who are depressed may show a diminished interest in their regular activities. Their level of activity may decline or even cease for a period of time. It is important to note that, for children who are depressed, a decrease or change of interest in normal activities would not be due to interest in new activities. Reduced activity in children who are depressed is of particular concern because it is sometimes the precursor to suicidal ideation.

Suicidal Ideation or Attempts

It is more common for children who are depressed to have suicidal ideation or attempts than adults who are depressed. Although the number of children who attempt suicide every year has increased, these attempts are often unsuccessful. Researchers have noted that children who are depressed say that their attempts at suicide are a cry for help, often a desperate effort to get the attention of adults. Also noted is that children who suffer from depression are likely to consider or attempt suicide because they are not able to manage the physical, social, and emotional changes that are inherent to the developmental stages of childhood.

Causes of Depression in Children

There is no single cause of depression in children. Although there are many factors that can contribute to depression, research does not support the idea that children who are depressed must have experiences, education, or their cultural background in common. However, what research does suggest is that there are several indicators for the diagnosis of depression in children.

Biology

Biological factors that may cause depression in children include those that are medical as well as genetic. When children have certain medical diagnoses, abuse drugs, or take certain prescription medications, symptoms of depression may be a side effect. When medical issues contribute to the onset of depression in children, managing symptoms can be challenging. The modification of medication, for example, could exacerbate the medical diagnosis. Children may then be subject to enduring symptoms of depression because their medical condition requires that they take certain medication. Children who abuse drugs may experience withdrawal and a subsequent depression when drug use ceases. Children with depression due to medical factors often struggle to balance their physical health with their social and emotional health and well-being.

Genetic factors, such as prenatal exposure to drugs or having a parent with a history of depression, can also cause depression in children. Similar to medical factors, genetic factors that lead to depression can be a challenge to manage. When children have been exposed to drugs prenatally, the effects on their social and emotional development can be immediate and long-lasting. Consequently, children who suffer from depression may not have the capacity to manage their feelings and emotions. Additionally, their symptoms may not be prompted by any specific triggers. Research indicates that when parents have suffered from depression, their children are more likely to be diagnosed. Those children, according to the research, may also experience depressive symptoms as a result of parent mood (and subsequent parenting capacity). Genetic factors that contribute to depression in children may be difficult to manage, but they can be the highest predictors. It is therefore imperative that children who have been exposed to drugs or whose parents have been diagnosed with depression be screened and treated in early childhood.

Environment

Poverty can have a profound impact on children and families. When children live in an environment that is not conducive to meeting their basic needs, depression can become pervasive. Children who do not get proper health care, nutrition, and social support can present with symptoms of depression that are not typically attributed to environmental stressors. A change in appetite, for example, may be due a lack of food and not due to preexisting depressive symptoms. These symptoms should not be mistaken for those that many experience after major life events, such as the loss of a loved one. Children who live in poverty are often caught in a cycle of oppression that is not conducive to ensuring that they are socially and emotionally healthy. Access to a quality education may be limited. Health issues may impact school attendance and academic performance. Depression may become more evident as children struggle to cope with the challenges that environmental stressors cause. Those challenges, similar to major life events, can create emotional problems for children. For children who suffer from depression due to environmental stressors, treatment can be a challenge until those stressors are eliminated.

Treatment of Depression in Children

The decision about which treatment is most appropriate for a child may be based on several factors, including medical history, cost of treatment, cultural beliefs, and the accessibility of treatment options. Regardless of the treatment option chosen, individual differences and preferences must be considered.

Medication

In order to rule out underlying medical causes of depressive symptoms in children, a complete physical examination should be conducted. Though medication management is typically an accepted method of treatment for adults, medicating children for depression continues to be controversial. There are some who argue that children who experience symptoms of depression will outgrow the feelings that they are experiencing. Physical, social, and emotional development in childhood has a noted effect on mood and behavior. Those who are opposed to medicating children contend that medication could alter some of the normal stages of development in childhood, thereby causing additional complications. Clinical research, however, indicates that appropriate use of medication can be an effective treatment option for depression in childhood, especially when combined with other treatments.

Counseling

Counseling is one of the methods of treatment for depression in children that has proven to be effective. When children are depressed, counseling can provide an opportunity to better understand the cause of presenting symptoms. Once the cause of depression is determined, children and their families can learn strategies to either minimize or eliminate symptoms. Psychoeducation, a common component of counseling, can also help children to learn alternative ways to managing stressors. When genetic or biological factors are the cause of depression in children, counseling can help balance the support that medication management provides. When all of the factors that can contribute to depression in children are considered as part of the counseling process, a treatment plan can be developed to help address those factors. Counseling is considered to be successful for children who are depressed when symptoms are managed, the need for services decreases, and the likelihood that the children will be emotionally healthy adults increases.

Depression in children continues to be a topic of research. Though the diagnosis of depression in children remains controversial, the number of children diagnosed each year is increasing. Symptoms such as sadness, changes in appetite, loss of interest in activities, suicidal ideation or attempts, and changes in mood are common in children with the diagnosis. While there is not a single cause of depression in children, it is well known that biology, environment, and life events can contribute to depressive symptoms. Depression in children, if left untreated, can have implications throughout the lifespan. Medication and counseling are the most widely used and effective methods of treatment. Consideration of individual differences such as culture, education, and medical history is critical to determining how best to support children who suffer from depression.

Camille Y. Humes

See also Depression in Couples and Families; Mindfulness and Children; Mood Disorders in Children; Parental Stress: Effects on Children; Posttraumatic Stress Disorder in Children; Trauma and Children

Further Readings

Bostic, J. Q., Rubin, D. H., Prince, J., & Schlozman, S. (2005). Treatment of depression in children and adolescents. *Journal of Psychiatric Practice, 11*(3), 141–154.

Erford, B. T., Erford, B. M., Lattanzi, G., Weller, J., Schein, H., Wolf, E., . . . Peacock, E. (2011). Counseling outcomes from 1990 to 2008 for school-age youth with depression: A meta-analysis. *Journal of Counseling and Development, 89*(4), 439–457.

Hooper, L. M., & Britnell, H. B. (2012). Mental health research in K–12 schools: Translating a systems approach to university-school partnerships. *Journal of Counseling and Development, 90*(1), 81–90.

Mitchell, J., McCauley, E., Burke, P. M., & Moss, S. J. (1988). Phenomenology of depression in children and adolescents. *Journal of the American Academy of Children and Adolescent Psychiatry, 27*(1), 12–20.

Muller, B. E., & Erford, B. T. (2012). Choosing assessment instruments for depression outcome research with school-age youth. *Journal of Counseling and Development, 90*(2), 208–220.

Son, S. E., & Kirchner, J. T. (2000). Depression in children and adolescents. *American Family Physician, 62*(10), 2297–2311.

Depression in Couples and Families

Depression is one of the most commonly diagnosed disorders in clinical settings. As many as 10% of individuals in the United States suffer from this mood disorder. The impact of depression is widespread and leads to economic, health, family, and societal difficulties. This entry focuses on explaining the systemic impact of depression on individuals, couples, and families. After identifying the various forms of depression, the entry discusses various contributing factors to the onset, maintenance, and management of depression. An overview of approaches and considerations for systemic treatment of depression concludes the entry.

Types of Depression

There are various forms of depression and depressive symptoms. It is important for therapists to identify the specific type so that the appropriate treatment can be given. These conditions are as follows:

- Major depressive disorder (MDD)
- Persistent depressive disorder (PDD)
- Premenstrual dysphoric disorder
- Depressive disorder due to a general medical condition or treatment
- Substance-induced depressive disorder
- Depressive disorder with postpartum onset
- Depressive disorder with seasonal pattern
- Adjustment disorders with depressed mood
- Grief/bereavement

There seem to be three common scenarios that are essential for marriage and family therapists (MFTs) to assess in the onset of depressive symptoms. They are (1) biologically or personality-based depression affecting the entire family system, (2) relationally stressed individual (couple relationship/family dynamics) developing depression, and (3) a combination of biologically or personality-based depression combined with long-standing relationship stressors.

Impact of Depression on Couples

Depression occurring within the context of a dating or married relationship is not uncommon. Reports of depression are often coupled with relational strain, outside stressors, or trauma. Examining the effects of depression through a systemic lens creates the opportunity to expand the conceptualization of its symptoms, causes, and effects in order to provide greater opportunities for healing.

While depression is often portrayed as a women's health issue, it is common in both genders. Women, however, are more than twice as likely to report symptoms of depression and to seek professional help. These depressive symptoms are most commonly experienced from the ages of 45 to 64, some of which may be explained by the changes in family development stages and common hormonal changes.

While men may report depressive symptoms less commonly than women, they are also very likely to experience depressive symptoms in their lifetime. These depressive symptoms often go unreported and are often unrecognized and undiagnosed. The key difference in this disparity between male and female reports of depression may be due to different ways that males and females manifest depressive symptoms. When men show signs of depression it is often misconstrued for normal male behavior. Studies have also shown that depression may have a greater influence on negative perceptions of interpersonal relationships for women than for men.

The vast majority of depression reports include at least one type of relational component in the diagnosis. The most commonly reported relational problem is having a strained relationship within dating or married couples. The challenge for clinicians is to understand the complex interaction between the depression and relational distress. In other words, an individual's depression may be the catalyst for relational problems just as relational distress may initiate the onset of depression within an individual.

Depression as the Cause of Relational Distress

Depressive symptoms within one partner commonly lead to confusion and frustration on the part of the nondepressed partner. The onset of depressive symptoms is often associated with symptoms such as fatigue, lack of sleep, fluctuations in weight, diminished or absent sex drive, and unstable moods. To the nondepressed partner, these changes are often difficult and this partner may find himself or herself frustrated because they lack the ability to help the depressed partner and they also struggle to cope with the symptoms.

It is very common for a nondepressed partner to feel overwhelmed and powerless, leading him or her to blame, shame, or even withdraw from the depressed partner. One of the biggest struggles that couples face, when one partner is dealing with depression, is recognizing whether the changes are due to depression and not due to a relationship problem. It is common for these nondepressed partners to see these symptoms as personal attacks or evidence of a lack of love or affection. As a part of this interaction, it is common for both partners, depressed and nondepressed, to report a lack of intimacy, decreased communication, sexual dissatisfaction, and poorer relationship quality.

Couple relationships may further be affected by depression due to unhealthy and risky behaviors that may be used in an effort to cope with the illness. Addictions to alcohol, drugs, gambling, or other activities and substances may deepen the depression and put further strain on the relationship.

Relational Distress as the Cause of Depression

When diagnosing depression, one common contributing factor is that of preexisting relational problems. Unknowingly, one partner may maintain or be a significant factor in the other's depression. Dysfunctional interactional patterns, significant power differentials, enmeshed or rigid boundaries, or intimate partner violence within relationships are all common factors that lead to an individual's depression. The dissolution of a relationship is another common cause of depression. Breakups, separations, and divorces commonly send individuals into depressive states that may require professional assistance.

Reciprocity Between Relational Distress and Depression

Sometimes there is no clear identification of which came first, depression or relationship problems. Some individuals come into the relationship with a long history of depression. In addition, there are many common causes of relational dysfunction. Therefore, a couple's poor relationship and the depression of one or both individuals can deepen the depression and worsen the relationship in a reciprocal fashion. Depression may be best conceptualized in this relational context, yet it is often the most overlooked. Being sure to be sensitive to relational components, clinicians and other interested parties begin to see that nondepressed partners can cause, enable, maintain, or be part of the solution with a partner's depression.

Impact of Depression on Family Relationships

As with depression and couple relationship playing key roles with one another, other family relationships can have a huge reciprocal impact on the depression. Other stressors in family systems can also create significant stress that can initiate depressive symptoms.

Children and Adolescents With Depression

Depression may begin to develop in children as young as 3 years of age. Unfortunately, children with depression often go undiagnosed for a number of different reasons. Diagnosing symptoms of depression in children may be especially difficult as mood swings, sadness, despair, and hopelessness may be passed off as personality traits or as developmentally appropriate behaviors. Diagnosing depression in children is done best by assessing negative behaviors in conjunction with the surrounding context of the child's family relationships. If a child has a family history of depression, has witnessed intimate partner violence, has uneducated parents, or is aware of family stressors, he or she is a likely candidate for a depression diagnosis when paired with behavioral problems.

Assessing depression in adolescents is easier to observe and diagnose. One of the greatest contributing factors of adolescent depression is connected to parenting styles. Receiving harsh verbal discipline or different types of abuse increase the likelihood of adolescent depression.

The Effect of Children's Depression on Parent–Child Relationship

Children and adolescents who deal with depression usually have more difficulty building interpersonal relationships, especially familial relationships. The child's relationship with his or her mother is the most commonly strained relationship within the family. When children have a negative self-view brought on by depression, they are more likely to view parents and other authority figures as controlling or rejecting.

When children develop depression due to factors unrelated to the family interactions (e.g., trauma or school bullying), family relationships may also be affected negatively. Parents may misinterpret the depressive symptoms as laziness or character flaws in their children. Parents commonly feel overwhelmed and frustrated by their child's depression, not knowing how to best help. In turn, the child may interpret this frustration as shame and rejection on the part of the parent, potentially exacerbating the child's depression. It also is not uncommon for a parent to struggle emotionally from his or her child's depression to the point that the parent also develops depression.

Numerous studies have begun to show that depression in children is connected to maladaptive relational patterns later in life. These negative outcomes include attachment disorders, proclivity toward child maltreatment and intimate partner violence, poor communication skills, and ineffective conflict resolution abilities. Positive parenting styles are among the most influential factors in improving the bond between parents and depressed children and developing healthy family coping skills for the child's depression.

Depression in Parents

Parenthood brings with it a number of stressors that may lead to acute or chronic depression. When a parent deals with depression, the ability of the parent to manage everyday tasks is decreased. With depression, roles, rules, and responsibilities in the family shift, and the demands on other family members increase. If this adjustment is not handled well, it is common for family members to become frustrated and distant.

Nondepressed partners may often become overwhelmed, feeling they have the greatest share of domestic responsibility on their shoulders. Children of depressed parents are often neglected and parentified, being required to perform caretaking responsibilities above their appropriate developmental age level. In each of these cases, the family system compensates for depressed individual ways that put added strain on the relationships. Parents may deal with depression at any age or development stage; however, most commonly, new parents or "empty-nesters" are at greatest risk for developing depression.

Effect of Parent's Depression on Parent–Child Relationship

When one parent suffers from depression, it usually has a more adverse effect on family functioning than a depressed child. When a depressed parent communicates depressed feelings to a child, the child is at a markedly greater risk for developing depressive traits or other psychiatric illnesses.

The effects of parental depression on child outcomes may also differ according to the gender of the parent. When mothers are depressed, they are significantly less involved in parenting and are also more likely to engage in dangerous and abusive parent behaviors. These mothers are also less sensitive to a child's developmentally appropriate behaviors, which has an adverse effect on children's self-esteem and emotional regulation. When fathers suffer from depression they are commonly less involved in family interactions. This isolation has been shown to lead to negative outcomes on children's social competencies.

On average, 75% of children are aware of their parent's depression. When the parent–child bonding is negatively affected, it may lead to negative relational outcomes, decreased educational capabilities, and an increase in risky behaviors later in life. Research has begun to show that decreasing marital conflict through marital therapy may mediate the effects of these negative outcomes. Receiving treatment for conflict management may help mitigate the effects of the depression on child outcomes.

Reciprocity Between Parent and Child Depression

Numerous studies have shown that depression in either a parent or a child may negatively affect the entire family system. Just as in couples, family members may unconsciously be enabling, causing, or maintaining an individual's depression. Each family member (children and partners) plays an important role in finding solutions to the family member's depression.

Systemic Treatment of Depression in Couples and Families

Numerous studies have shown that the most effective treatment for an individual with depression is psychotherapy combined with an antidepressant medicine. However, there is a considerable emerging body of literature that suggests systemic treatment of couples and families may be equally, if not more, effective in treating depression in individuals.

The responsibility falls on the therapist to know when systemic treatment is appropriate in treating depression. Systemic treatment usually aims to increase healthy communication patterns within the family system while treating the depressive symptoms.

The most effective systemic treatments should be guided by understanding which of the two important components (relational distress or depression) precedes the other. If relational distress precedes the depression, a focus on relational problems (and not the depression) is most effective. When depression precedes the relational distress, focusing couples treatment on the depressive symptoms is most effective. In each case, including the nondepressed partner or family member is more effective in decreasing depressive symptoms.

Treatment of Couples When One or Both Partners Are Depressed

There is burgeoning empirical support for the systemic treatment of couples when one or more partners are suffering from depression. Studies have shown that clients most commonly report that the involvement of a spouse and the relationship with the therapist were the two most influential parts of treatment. Directional studies are inconclusive to show if relational distress causes depression, or if depression is what leads to relational distress; however, the interpersonal interactions within couples are highly predictive of how couples manage depressive symptoms as well as the probability of relapse.

While couples therapy is effective in treating depressed couples, its benefits may be more substantial in terms of cost-effectiveness. Couples treatment has been shown to reach the same outcomes in less amount of time. Recent studies have shown that female depressive symptoms as well as male psychological distress and depression-specific burden are reduced in fewer sessions. Relationship satisfaction and empathic communication also increase in both partners and negative attitudes toward depression decrease. In short, individuals being treated in a couple context for depression leave treatment with both stronger mental and relational states at a more affordable price.

In general, the guiding principle for systemic interventions of couples is to use interventions that aim to increase social support, improve interpersonal relationships, reduce the impact of stressors, and change the patient's perception of the depressive symptoms. These treatment goals have shown to have the greatest results in systemic treatments. Relational treatment may also be useful because the depressed partner often misinterprets the nondepressed partner's support. The nondepressed partner may also be confused and feel overwhelmed and unequipped to appropriately help his or her partner. The treatment may help develop healthy couple coping by helping each spouse communicate more effectively.

The systemic treatment with the strongest empirical support in helping reduce depression in couples is emotion-focused therapy (EFT). EFT focuses on helping partners recognize repressed primary emotions that drive negative interactions between spouses. The process helps rebuild emotional attachment through sincere emotional expression.

Cognitive-behavioral therapy (CBT) also provides effective treatment for depression with solid empirical support. CBT focuses less on emotions and concentrates mostly on the connection between thoughts and behaviors. By helping couples identify the negative thought patterns and behavioral reactions within themselves and their relationships, empathic communication increases and perceptions of the depressive symptoms also change.

Treatment of Children and Adolescents With Depression

When treating depressed children, systemic approaches that address negative perceptions and that target familial relationships are most effective. Given that the onset of childhood depression is often influenced by family interactions, these approaches have a strong focus on helping parents know how to cope with their child's depression and to promote healthy interactions within the family.

Couples treatment for the parents or parenting courses have also been proven effective when dealing with a depressed child. Often external trauma or other outside factors bring on a child's depression, and parents feel incapable of helping their young ones. These options help educate parents on how to reduce dyadic conflict, increase the parent–child bond, and build resiliency in their children.

Attachment-based family therapy (ABFT) is one of the few family therapy models with empirical support that is designed to treat adolescent depression. ABFT focuses on developing secure attachments in parent–child relationships. Techniques of ABFT focus on changing negative environments that inhibit the normal development for children by a number of different therapeutic tasks. These tasks include changing the family perception of the problem from the adolescent to focusing on the family relationships, increasing the parent's empathy toward the child, creating a safe space for adolescent expression, increasing the attachment bond between parent and child, and developing these interactions within the home.

Building a healthy foundation of attachment is the first step in changing risky and unhealthy behaviors in adolescents. Allowing depressed adolescents to express vulnerable emotions in a safe environment is crucial to developing healthy family coping. Therapists trained in ABFT can effectively treat adolescent depression while helping the family develop positive family interactions.

Treatment of Parents With Depression

In treating a parent with depressive symptoms, it is important to assess for significant life changes (i.e., childbirth) or relational stressors. While still developing, there is a small amount of literature being devoted to understanding the best approach to treating parents with different mood disorders. Most commonly, children are not included in treatment. However, more research has begun to show that systemic treatment of children with their depressed parents is effective in reducing the child's likelihood of developing a depressive disorder. Targeting parenting skills and teaching children to cope with the parent's illness significantly reduces the child's risk of MDD or other psychiatric illnesses.

These family treatments with depressed parents and their children help promote mother–child or father–child relationships. While many of the findings are still preliminary, limited evidence shows that targeting the parent–child and couple's relationships reduces the depressive symptoms in the parents. Evidence is also growing to support the very important role fathers and children play in the treatment of postpartum depression. Similar to treating a child with depression, attachment-based treatments build parent–child and partner relationships and develop healthy family coping in cases of postpartum depression.

Adam C. Jones and W. David Robinson

See also Anxiety; Depression in Adolescents; Depression in Children; Depression in Couples and Families; Postpartum Depression; Systemic Family Therapy

Further Readings

Beach, S. R., Sandeen, E., & O'Leary, K. D. (1990). *Depression in marriage: A model for etiology and treatment.* New York, NY: Guilford Press.

Bodenmann, G., & Randall, A. (2013). Marital therapy for dealing with depression. In M. Power (Ed.), *The Wiley-Blackwell handbook of mood disorders* (2nd ed., pp. 215–227). New York, NY: Wiley-Blackwell.

Carr, A. (2014). The evidence base for family therapy and systemic interventions for child-focused problems. *Journal of Family Therapy, 36*(2), 107–157.

Jones, E., & Asen, E. (2000). *Systemic couple therapy and depression.* London, England: Karnac Books.

MacFarlane, M. M. (2003). Systemic treatment of depression: An integrative approach. *Journal of Family Psychotherapy, 14*(1), 43–61.

Whisman, M. A., Whiffen, V. E., & Whiteford, N. (2009). Couples therapy for depression. In J. H. Bray & M. Stanton (Eds.), *The Wiley-Blackwell handbook of family psychology* (pp. 650–660). New York, NY: Wiley-Blackwell.

Developmental Model of Marriage

Developmental models are conceptual frameworks devised to assist in understanding people or things across time and transitions. Marriages follow a developmental trajectory, and understanding stages of the marital developmental cycle can help preempt and address problems arising in marriages. Developmental models are used to help understand the evolution of a relationship, identify possible problem transition areas and typical problem times, normalize changes in relationships over time, and help assess the viability of relationships. By studying marriage as a developmental process it has been possible for social and behavioral scientists to come up with developmental models that show distinct stages and predictable crises in marriages. This entry reviews the commonalities of the developmental models of marriage, their functioning and steps, as well as their application in family therapy.

Developmental Models

All developmental models are characterized by five markers. The first marker is an identifiable state that demarcates the levels or stages of the process. Developmental models consist of stages that are characterized by qualitative differences. For example, they might be in an infatuation stage marked by high amounts of affection and low amounts of disagreement and later be in a companionate state where shared values are more important. By identifying the current state a marriage is in, the counselor and clients are able to discuss what typically happens in that stage. The second marker identifies the qualities of change in the process; the change can, for instance, be described as being sudden, progressive, recurrent, or abrupt. The third marker of developmental models is the patterns of development, including linear, oscillating, or spiral patterns. The fourth marker identifies the motivation or forces responsible for changes or for a move in the stages of development. For example, stress or a drive for self-actualization may motivate an individual or couple to change. The fifth marker of the developmental models is the environmental or genetic possibility for growth (potentiality). Potentiality is what ultimately constrains development. The creation of a developmental model of marriage, therefore, is undertaken in order to understand marriage, aid in making proper diagnosis of marital difficulties, and assist in the creation of a prognosis to help couples make changes in thoughts, behaviors, or emotions to increase the likelihood of a lasting, happy marriage.

Assumptions

A developmental model of marriage takes into account several assumptions that are critical to the model's usefulness. First, there is the assumption that relationships evolve through a number of stages. These stages are predictable and can be inferred in any marriage relationship since they are a sequence of typical developmental stages. The model also structures these stages to resemble those in Margaret Mahler's stages in her model of early childhood development. These stages are enumerated as symbiosis, differentiation, practicing individuation, rapprochement, and mutual interdependence. In the Bowenian model and psychodynamic model of family therapy, the developmental model of marriage presupposes that the developmental issues the partners had from childhood will surface in their marriages. In other words, the past is influencing the present and change will occur as the individuals in the family system proceed in the process of individuation.

The Etiology of a Developmental Model of Marriage

Developmental models of marriage borrow heavily from Margaret Mahler's stages of separation and individuation in her separation-individuation theory of child development. Like a parent–child bond, a couple goes through different stages of dependence, independence, and interdependence. The separation-individuation theory of child development posits that after the child is born, it spends the first few weeks barely conscious and unaware. After that period passes, the child moves on to the first phase, known as the normal-symbiotic phase, where the child perceives itself as being one with his or her mother in the context of the larger environment. The second phase is the separation-individuation phase in which the child begins to see himself or herself as separate from the mother and begins to explore his or her environment. Finally, the rapprochement stage indicates where the child gets close to the mother again, but is now more aware of them being distinct from one another. Similar to the developmental stages of a marriage, one could say there is an "in love" stage where the two individuals in the marriage are symbiotically attached. Eventually, as their love matures, they move into a separation-individuation stage where the individuals realize and assert their individuality, while maintaining their union with one another.

These developmental stages of the child–mother relationship greatly influenced the creation of a developmental model of marriage, since they closely mirror the developmental milestones of most marital relationships. The issues arising between couples are similar to those of childhood and they are progressive in their development over the course of the couple's marital life cycle. These issues between couples begin with basic trust issues where the individuals establish basic trust for their partners. The second developmental issue to arise is the problem in self–other differentiation. The third issue is the couple's formation of avoidant or anxious attachment patterns. The fourth developmental issue for the couples is separation anxiety. The fifth problem faced is the inability to self-soothe and the final developmental stage problems are difficulties when disappointed or angry.

Developmental Stage Model of Marriage

Marriages do not conform to a linear model that can be applied wholesale to all of them. The explanation for issues in one marriage may not fit the next one but they all have similarities that can be identified to fit into the different stages of the model. A developmental model must have an invariable order of steps in the development cycle. A developmental model must also possess a clear notion that no stage in the cycle can be avoided or skipped and that every step becomes more complex than the preceding one as each step evolves into a new form after transforming from the form of the previous step. Each step must also be based on the preceding one and be in preparation of the step to come after it. In this case, a developmental stage model of marriage also fulfills these requirements as each of its stages cannot be skipped and there are an invariable number of steps to proceed through.

Developmental models of marriage have steps that develop and transform into more complex forms; each step is reliant on the successful completion of the previous step and acts as the basis for the step ahead of it. The first stage involves the couple engaging in passionate and exciting interactions and powerful feelings of affection and love toward each other. Feelings of desire for each other and of physical well-being are strongest during the first stage more than at any other time. During this stage, annoying things that may come up are quickly brushed aside. The strong feelings of excitement stimulate the production of chemicals in the body that promote happiness, energy, feelings of goodwill for each other, and heightened sexuality and sensuality. It is during this stage of euphoria that the couple decides to commit to each other for life and get married. This first stage is known as the symbiosis stage and in this stage both partners explore the possibilities of committing to each other and sharing a life together as a couple. The couple establishes a bond of togetherness and common identity through similarities during this stage.

It is common to overlook differences during this stage and there is little demand for change. Both partners engage in a mutual give-and-take where both parties are considerate of each other and both work to nurture the relationship. During this period, when one partner feels that the other partner has nurtured him or her well enough, this partner is able to smoothly transition to the next stage of the developmental model. However, problems can arise here because at this level of the relationship, there are a lot of expectations about each other that are based on fantasy and projection. When individuals engage in a relationship to cover their anxiety of remaining alone or to "fix previous wounds," there is the risk that they may fail to look beyond the symbiotic fantasy, therefore missing signs of incompatibility, which may prevent resolution of pending personal issues. These shortcomings can then prevent a transition into the next stage of the developmental model. Enmeshment occurs as a problem when the couple fails to move on to the differentiation stage and instead tries to hold on to the symbiosis fantasy. In the first instance, a couple may try to avoid conflict by trying to anticipate the other's needs and moods. This type of enmeshment is also characterized by fear of separation and of not meeting one's own or the partner's needs. Enmeshment can also take on the hostile and dependent form where there is constant arguing and bickering.

Differentiation is the second stage of the model and it entails both partners becoming aware of and acknowledging their differences. At this point, disappointment may occur as reality kicks in and the fantasy of the symbiotic phase fades away. It is during this stage that the couple begins to spend their lives together by living together and conflict starts to arise. During this stage, the partners focus on their differences from each other. The partners develop their self-definition within the relationship by recognizing their uniqueness. At this stage, the partners need to develop skills to negotiate their differences, as this is vital to successfully fulfilling the needs of this stage. Coming to terms with the individual differences and supporting each other despite not always agreeing is the biggest challenge here. At this point the disillusionment and conflict may make one partner or both choose to leave the relationship, ending the marriage as they go off in pursuit of another symbiotic fantasy.

Practicing is the title of the third stage, and here the successfully differentiated couples have laid a firm foundation in their relationship and can now each individually focus on their self-development and individual pursuits. In this stage, each individual focuses on his or her own personal activities, career, separate friends, school, and generally on one's self. The couple uses their relationship as their secure base to which they retreat after returning from the outside world. The challenge in this step of the relationship is for the partners to maintain their relationship bond while also learning how to support each other's individual pursuits. Problems at this stage arise when one partner feels threatened by separation. When that happens, the partner may try to control the other partner's activities and individual pursuits. The partners may then find themselves in a situation where one partner is focused on the relationship and the other wants more separateness. At this stage, one partner could be trying to pull the other to regress back to symbiosis, leading to conflict as the other partner resists. It is common for affairs to develop at this stage.

The next stage is referred to as the rapprochement stage, and it involves a rekindling of the intimacy between the couple. After both individuals have established strong individual identities and a well-developed sense of themselves, they are ready to establish intimacy between them again. At this point, the couple has a well-developed sense of balance in the relationship with a better-structured connection and separation between them. There is a lessening of the fear of getting engulfed in the symbiosis since there is a well-developed sense of individuation within the relationship. This confidence allows for the individuals to be more vulnerable, and childhood issues can be better resolved here since the partners perceive more safety to be themselves. Problems can arise at this stage if one partner is still in the practicing phase and wishes to remain independent. However, conflict at this stage is easier to handle because both parties have developed their own way of resolving conflict. This is the case since they have already learned how to negotiate their differences in an earlier stage.

The final stage is the mutual interdependence stage. In this stage, a strong foundation exists for the relationship and the couple has reconciled fantasy with reality. Couples in this stage of development base their relationship on helping each other's growth rather than needs. The strong foundation provides the couple with a sense of constancy which is very comforting. There is little conflict in this stage of development and the couple can easily deal with arising conflict due to the skills learned over the stages and the strong foundation their relationship is based on.

Application of Developmental Model in Therapy

Overall, different couples face different challenges that depend on their personalities, circumstances that arise leading to a reaction from the individuals in the relationship toward each other, and childhood issues. Generally, problems arise when couples fail to move on from one stage to the next or when they skip stages in the developmental process of growth in the relationship. Having a clear understanding of the model allows therapists to identify the stages at which their clients may have developed their problems and provides a guideline for them to diagnose and develop beneficial interventions to help the couple.

Miles Matise

See also Individual and Family Development; Psychoanalytic Family Therapy; Stages of Family Therapy; Strategic Family Therapy; Systemic Family Therapy

Further Readings

Bader, E., & Pearson, P. (1983). The developmental stages of couplehood. *Transactional Analysis Journal, 13*(1), 28–32.

Bader, E., & Pearson, P. (2013). *In quest of the mythical mate: A developmental approach to diagnosis and treatment in couples therapy*. New York, NY: Routledge.

Bradbury, T. N., & Weiss, R. L. (Eds.). (2006). *The developmental course of marital dysfunction*. Cambridge, UK: Cambridge University Press.

Carlson, J., & Sperry, L. (Eds.). (2013). *Intimate couple*. New York, NY: Routledge.

Casado-Kehoe, M., & Parker, D. K. (2015). Key issues and interventions in couples counseling. In D. Capuzzi & M. D. Stauffer (Eds.), *Foundations of couples, marriage, and family counseling* (pp. 289–316). New York, NY: Wiley.

Harris, N. (2010). Tell me no lies: How to stop lying to your partner and yourself in the 4 stages of marriage [book review]. *Psychotherapy in Australia, 16*(2), 71.

Sharpe, S. A. (2004). *The ways we love: A developmental approach to treating couples*. New York, NY: Guilford Press.

Differentiation

The concept of differentiation derives from psychiatrist Murray Bowen's family systems theory, also known as Bowen theory or Bowenian theory. Bowen (1913–1990) observed that the mothers of adult children with schizophrenia, a severe mental disorder, often had a symbiotic relationship with them, as if both parent and child were dependent on each other in ways that tended to reinforce the schizophrenic's dysfunction. This intense emotional fusion between parent and child was the result of a multigenerational process that would be evident in the dysfunction of family members in other generations.

Subsequently, in the course of formulating his family systems theory, Bowen developed the concept of differentiation, which refers to a people's ability to distinguish between their emotional and thought processes. Persons who are less differentiated are less able to make this distinction between their thoughts and feelings and therefore are often overrun by their emotions. Those who are highly differentiated are better able to regulate themselves emotionally by thinking clearly and charting a course of action that is based more on their directed goals than on how they feel in the moment. Persons who are less differentiated spend more energy concerned with what others think or feel about them. This results in either an automatic conformity to the thoughts or opinions of others or automatic rebellion. The conformity or rebellion of the less differentiated is a result of their being highly emotionally reactive to others.

One's level of differentiation denotes their ability to relate to their family of origin (primarily their parents and siblings) as an individual while still being connected emotionally. Differentiation allows a person to have an opinion or belief that is self-developed by principled thinking, not developed in reaction to or in conformity with others. A differentiated person can be influenced by others but only as a result of reasoned decision, not out of conformity or rebellion due to emotional anxiety. Mature differentiation gives the ability to be guided by one's thought processes and not the emotional climate of the family or relational context. Fundamentally a person's level of differentiation is determined by their parents' level of differentiation from their own families of origin. If one's parents are still emotionally fused with their respective families of origin, then the child will be parented within that same level of emotional charge that creates less differentiation.

Differentiation Scale

Bowen created a theoretical scale of differentiation, not based on research but for conceptual purposes. The scale went from 0 to 100, and Bowen denoted four categories: 0–25, 25–50, 50–75, 75–100. What determines whether a person is seen as belonging to one category or another is the ability to distinguish between one's emotional and intellectual processes. People in the 0 to 25 range are at the lowest end of differentiation, often suffering from chronic mental health issues. These persons live in a world controlled by their emotions, almost devoid of any ability to distinguish between their thoughts and feelings. These persons are highly emotionally reactive, their lives often being derailed by their tendency to fuse themselves in the destructive emotions of others. People on the lowest end of this range are often institutionalized; schizophrenia would be a common diagnosis for people in the 0 to 10 range.

People in the 25 to 50 range are able to distinguish somewhat between their thoughts and feelings but are still overwhelmingly influenced by the thoughts and opinions of others. These persons can appear to be ideological chameleons, quickly adapting to whatever is the prevailing view of the persons who are close to them. On the other hand, they may be constantly rebelling against the prevailing views of others more out of emotional reactivity than an intentional and decisive process of thinking for themselves. Unlike persons in the 0 to 25 range, people in this category have an ability to raise their level of differentiation to a degree that can improve their functioning. Parents in this range will likely have children who are just as emotionally reactive as they are and will therefore suffer from conformity or rebellion due to the level of emotional reactivity in the home.

People who fall on the 50 to 75 range are more aware of the difference between their feelings and intellectual processes, though under times of high stress they will still tend to fall into emotional fusion with others. At this range the person, under less stressful conditions, is able to choose a course of action in relating to others based on principle. In other words, this person can decide whether to relate to another in the moment based on their emotions or their intellect. In this regard they have more flexibility in relating to others than is the case for those lower on the scale. During times of high stress, persons in this range can suffer from emotional, physical, or social symptoms though they tend to recover faster than those lower on the scale and are able to calm themselves after the initial crisis.

Bowen believed that most people do not function at the 75 to 100 range, that it is rare for anyone to reach 85 to 95, and that no one reaches 95 to 100. People who are between 75 and 100 are remarkably free from the stressors and symptoms of relationships that most people live with. These are persons who are able to state an "I" position without feeling the need to coerce others to think like them or conforming to the opinions of others thoughtlessly. These individuals are not preoccupied with the thoughts and opinions of others about themselves and are able to live a thoughtful and principle-directed life while engaging in their emotions in ways they believe are helpful and appropriate. These are the persons with the most stable and happiest marriages and they tend to raise very well-adjusted children.

Eric M. Brown

See also Boundaries; Bowen Family Systems Theory; Communication Errors/Problems in Couples and Families; Triangulation

Further Readings

Bowen, M. (1965). Family psychotherapy with schizophrenia in the hospital and in private practice. In I. Boszormenyi-Nagy & J. T. Framo (Eds.), *Intensive family therapy* (pp. 213–243). Hagerstown, MD: Harper & Row.

Bowen, M. (1976). Theory in the practice of psychotherapy. In P. J. Guerin Jr. (Ed.), *Family therapy: Theory and practice* (pp. 42–90). New York, NY: Gardner.

Bowen, M. (1978). *Family therapy in clinical practice.* New York, NY: Jason Aronson.

Chung, H., & Gale, J. (2009). Family functioning and self-differentiation: A cross-cultural examination. *Contemporary Family Therapy, 31*, 19–33.

Holman, T. B., & Busby, D. M. (2011). Family-of-origin, differentiation of self and partner, and adult romantic relationship quality. *Journal of Couple & Relationship Therapy, 10*, 3–19.

Jankowski, P. J., & Hooper, L. M. (2012). Differentiation of self: A validation study of the Bowen theory construct. *Couple and Family Psychology: Research and Practice, 1*(3), 226–243.

Kerr, M. E., & Bowen, M. (1988). *Family evaluation: An approach based on Bowen theory.* New York, NY: W. W. Norton.

Discernment Counseling

Not all couples that enter couple or marital therapy agree that the therapeutic agenda for change should focus on improving the relationship. In fact, in as many as 30% of couples that show up for couple therapy, one member is likely ambivalent about being in the relationship at all. William (Bill) Doherty and colleagues with the Minnesota Couples on the Brink Project at the University of Minnesota refer to these clients as "mixed-agenda" couples in which one partner is leaning into the relationship and wants it to be healthy, and the other partner is ambivalent or even leaning out of the relationship and has difficulty with the thought of staying together. Traditional couple therapy efforts to improve these relationships are often fruitless when one of the partners is unsure if she or he is interested in remaining in the relationship at all. Discernment counseling is a therapeutic intervention tailored specifically for the mixed-agenda couple.

Traditional goals for couple or marital therapy often include improving communication, strengthening conflict management skills, helping couples resolve relational impasses, and deepening emotional connection. In contrast, the goal of discernment counseling is for couples to gain greater clarity and confidence in their decision-making about the future of their marriage, based on a deeper understanding of their relationship, including what got them to the place where divorce is a possibility and each person's role in that relational pattern. The model is short-term and oriented toward "counseling" as opposed to therapy. As such, the discernment counselor plays an active and directive role in helping the couple understand how the marriage got to where it is and helps each partner understand and assume responsibility for the ways in which they have contributed to the current state of their marriage. Discernment counseling can last anywhere from one to five sessions, and the sessions are typically an hour and a half long with the first session lasting up to two hours.

During the initial session, and in front of each other, both partners are asked to share their perspectives on (1) the divorce narrative, which is how it came to be that divorce is a plausible option; (2) the repair narrative, which is what either one has done to try to fix the problems they identified; and (3) the degree to which (if any) their children factor into their decision-making. Finally, each partner is asked to recall a time in the relationship when things were going very well. As the protocol is designed for mixed-agenda couples, there is no assumption of consensus between the two partners in their responses to these questions. The discernment counselor's job is to ensure both parties are heard and respected. One of the main tasks for the discernment counselor is to help the couple become aware of their interactional patterns, which often prevent couples from successfully resolving conflict and are largely outside their awareness (e.g., pursuer/distancer or withdraw/withdraw). For many couples, seeing their pattern for the first time provides a new way of understanding the context and process of their conflict, and this awareness can provide them with hope that change might be possible.

A Choice of Paths

The discernment counselor shares with the couple that there are three paths in front of them, and that the discernment process will focus on and be informed by these paths. In Path 1, or the status quo path, couples make a decision to maintain the relationship in its current state. In Path 2, the path of separation or divorce, one or both partners may choose to dissolve the relationship. Most couples that come to discernment counseling are already heading in this direction. Path 3, the possible reconciliation path, entails intentionally working toward getting the couple's relationship to a healthier place, including taking divorce off the table for a period of 6 months to work on the relationship with good couple therapy and other resources. Couples are informed that at the end of this 6-month period they can then decide whether or not they have done sufficient work to notice healthier patterns of interaction and connection or whether they think their efforts have not resulted in a healthier relationship. When a couple chooses Path 3, they do not commit to stay married or avoid divorce at all costs for the rest of their lives. Rather, they both agree to work on the relationship for a period of 6 months and decide how to proceed with the future of their marriage only after making a significant effort to improve their relationship.

After introducing the three paths, the discernment counselor meets alone with each partner to discuss the paths in greater detail. Objectives for the time with each partner are related to whether the partner has a leaning-out or leaning-in position regarding the future of the marriage. The discernment counselor helps the leaning-out partner discern the paths, what each would entail, and the potential impact of each path on self, partner, and the couple's children (if applicable) and other stakeholders (e.g., extended family and social networks). This is done so that a decision on how to proceed in the relationship is marked by clarity and confidence. Additionally, leaning-out partners are encouraged to consider the efforts they have made to change the relationship thus far; they are offered a new perspective on the marital patterns and are encouraged to consider what the relationship might look like if each made a concerted effort to make changes in self along key domains. With the leaning-in partner, the conversation focuses on how to demonstrate to the leaning-out partner an understanding of the concerns raised and a realization that they will need to make certain changes in themselves regardless of the path their partner chooses. Leaning-in partners are also encouraged to read Michele Weiner Davis's book, *The Divorce Remedy*, which speaks directly to leaning-in partners who have recently discovered that their spouse wants a divorce. At the end of each individual conversation, each partner shares with the other what she or he will take from their individual conversation with the discernment counselor. The counselor plays an active role in helping each individual identify what it is they might say to their partner and to craft the delivery of that message. Attention is paid to helping each individual disclose only what will help the couple productively express understanding of one's self in the context of the relationship and how each person is thinking of the three paths.

Future discernment counseling sessions are an hour and a half in length and begin with a brief couple check-in. The purpose of this check-in is to inquire about each partner's process of gaining greater clarity and confidence in their decision-making. The rest of the time is spent in individual conversations with each partner using the three paths as a framework to guide the discussion. Following the individual meetings, both partners then share with their spouse what they have learned about themselves or where they are in the discernment process. Finally, in each individual session, the counselor asks if each person would like to continue to meet for an additional session. Valuing the autonomy of each partner is of the utmost importance with this model, as neither should feel forced to attend any discernment session.

Once a path is chosen, the discernment counseling is concluded and couples are referred to appropriate resources based on the selected path. Couples that select Path 1, the status quo path, discontinue sessions with the discernment counselor. The invitation remains open for these couples to return at a later time should they wish to reengage the discernment process. While a small minority of couples choose this path, it can be helpful when a couple, together, agrees that the present time is not right to make such a life-changing decision.

When a couple or individual selects Path 2, the divorce/separation path, they receive a referral to a collaborative family law attorney who can help the couple proceed with the legal aspects of divorce. The discernment counselor can also facilitate additional conversations between the partners about how they want to see the divorce proceed. In these conversations, partners can identify the principles that they'd like to see guide their separation and divorce process. For example, they might both agree that they want what is best for the kids or that they want to treat each other civilly despite the decision to divorce.

Couples that select Path 3, the reconciliation path, sign a reconciliation agreement that outlines principles each will follow during the 6 months they commit to working on their relationship. These principles often include agreements to be generous with their time and effort to restore their relationship to a healthier place, engage in appropriate services as the discernment counselor recommends, and raise a voice of warning if at any point they believe changes are not happening in the relationship, rather than remain silent and plan an exit. Finally, each partner meets with the discernment counselor to identify a personal agenda for change. This consists of personal changes each partner agrees to make to help give the relationship the best chance of getting to a healthier place. For example, one partner might agree to an alcohol evaluation and to follow through on its recommendations while the other partner may have identified a need to work through unresolved grief issues that have made it difficult to be fully present in the relationship. Both partners and the discernment counselor agree upon these personal agendas for change.

The key to the success of Path 3 is the "personal agenda for change" and both partners taking responsibility to do what they told their partner they would do in the discernment counseling. Without the personal agenda for change, discernment counseling could result in each partner sharing a personal wish list of changes desired in the other person, which typically results in resentment and disconnection between partners. Instead, each partner is asked to identify and follow through on changes in himself or herself. At the end of 6 months, the couple can then review with their couple therapist the progress they have made. Some couples may even put the issue of divorce back on the table as a plausible option, should they so choose. Theoretically, each partner will be in a place marked with greater clarity and confidence to either continue with the commitment to the relationship, or move toward separation based on an assessment of the relative health of the relationship and whether or not the couple believes their current relationship trajectory will continue to lead toward healthier interactions.

Application and Outcomes

Discernment counseling is a divorce decision-making protocol that can be applied by those who have received training in the model, and it could be considered an appropriate pretherapy assessment protocol. There are also versions of the model specifically designed for lawyers, family law professionals, and clergy, as each of these groups often interacts with couples on the brink of divorce.

A review of the first 100 consecutive cases of discernment counseling revealed that approximately 12% of the couples chose Path 1 (status quo) with 41% choosing Path 2 (divorce) and 47% choosing Path 3 (reconciliation). Colleagues at the Minnesota Couples on the Brink Project, housed at the University of Minnesota, continue to conduct program evaluation and outcome research on this protocol and continue to develop the model.

Steven M. Harris and Sarah A. Crabtree

See also Dating Relationship Dissolution; Divorce and Separation; Premarital Counseling; PREPARE/ENRICH; Relationship Enhancement

Further Readings

American Psychological Association (Producer). (2007). *Working with couples considering divorce, with William J. Doherty, PhD* (video). American Psychological Association Video Series IV: Relationships. Washington, DC: Author. Available from http://www.apa.org/pubs/videos/4310754.aspx

Doherty, W. J. (2006). Couples on the brink: Stopping the marriage-go-round. *Psychotherapy Networker*, March/April, 30–39, 70.

Doherty, W. J. (2011). In or out: Treating the mixed agenda couple. *Psychotherapy Networker*, November-December, 45–50, 58, 60. Available at http://www.drbilldoherty.org

Harris, S. M. (2013, December 31). Feeling ambivalent about your marriage? So is everyone else. Retrieved from http://family-studies.org/feeling-ambivalent-about-your-marriage-so-is-everyone-else/

Harris, S. M., & Doherty, W. J. (2015, February 17). *Are all divorces necessary?* Retrieved from http://family-studies.org/are-all-divorces-necessary/

Hawkins, A. J., Fackrell, T. A., & Harris, S. M. (2013). *Should I try to work it out? A guidebook for individual and couples at the crossroads of divorce.* Provo, UT: Author.

DISINHIBITED SOCIAL ENGAGEMENT DISORDER IN CHILDREN

Disinhibited social engagement disorder (DSED) is a disorder of attachment and social relationships, often initiated by traumas or stressors in early childhood. As a result of these traumas, children lack opportunity to develop positive attachment to a caregiver and they have difficulty relating to others. Their behavior with unfamiliar adults is often overly friendly, indiscriminate, and inappropriate. Children often do not make distinctions between parental figures and strangers and may be excessively familiar with strangers, both verbally and physically. These children often show no reluctance or concern about leaving with strangers and may not check back with adult caregivers when with unfamiliar people or in unfamiliar settings. This behavior is not due to inattention or impulsivity (such as in attention-deficit/hyperactivity disorder [ADHD]); instead, it may be an attempt to control the situation or gain approval from adults. Interestingly, the indiscriminate and overly friendly behavior may not be as indiscriminate or as friendly as it first seems. Children with DSED do show a preference for caregivers with whom they are familiar, but they will also be excessively familiar with strangers. Even as attachment improves with caregivers, the children may continue to seek out shallow relationships indiscriminately.

In order for DSED to be diagnosed the child must have a developmental age of at least 9 months and there must be evidence that the child has experienced a pattern of insufficient care. For example, this could occur with frequent changes in the primary caregiver or lack of caregiving interaction opportunities such as in institutions that lack an adequate number or quality of adult caregivers. Insufficient care may also be the result of perpetual lack of having basic needs met. Children who are not regularly provided with adequate comfort, stimulation, and affection from a caregiver may be at risk. The reaction of being excessively affectionate may be an adaptive response because it allows the child to attract much needed attention and emotional connections.

Early Childhood Attachment

Attachment theory, first formulated by John Bowlby, propounds that infants naturally seek proximity to their caregiver. The caregiver's response to the child's needs creates either a secure or insecure attachment. A caregiver who is sensitive and responsive to the child's needs helps the child develop a secure attachment. Young children with secure attachments generally will engage with others in the presence of their caregiver and show a degree of distress when the caregiver leaves. Securely attached children will unreservedly explore their environment, occasionally returning to their caregiver for attention.

Reactive Attachment Disorder and DSED

Until recently, children with disorders of attachment may have been diagnosed with reactive attachment disorder (RAD). Disinhibited social engagement disorder was considered to be a disinhibited form of reactive attachment disorder. In the fifth edition of the American Psychiatric Association's *Diagnostic and Statistical Manual of Mental Disorders* (DSM-5) these disorders have been separated to more clearly identify the key distinctions between the two due to the significant differences in behavior. Both RAD and DSED are related to stress or trauma in early childhood. These stresses and traumas may include physical or emotional neglect, abuse, or lack of stable attachment to a caregiver. Disinhibited social engagement shares its origins with RAD because children with both disorders have experienced neglect and deprivation. With DSED, however, children do not distinguish between loving caregivers and strangers. These children are verbally and physically overly familiar with adults and seek the attention of adults indiscriminately.

Children with RAD have difficulty responding appropriately to others socially and emotionally and may appear to be resistant to interacting with others. They may be withdrawn and sad, even when experiencing positive interactions with adults. These children tend to appear emotionally subdued and rarely seek comfort when distressing events occur. The justification for splitting RAD into inhibited and disinhibited types is based primarily on research surrounding children raised in Romanian orphanages in which it was found that some children react to lack of attachment by avoiding social and emotional interactions (RAD), while other children react to lack of attachment by indiscriminately seeking relationship with others (DSED). Additional research found that children with DSED tend to persist in arbitrary attachments even after being placed in a secure setting and having developed an attachment to a new caregiver. This is unlike the inhibited type of RAD which tends to have a more promising outcome when children are placed in a caregiving situation that allows them to form a more normative attachment. The developmental differences in outcome between RAD and DSED led to the distinction between the two disorders.

Differential Diagnoses

Clinicians must be careful when diagnosing DSED as it implies a history and pathology that may not be present. Children who have ADHD often have similar characteristics to children with DSED; therefore, ADHD must be ruled out as a diagnosis. Children with ADHD may also be overly familiar with strangers but, in this case, it is due to impulsivity and deficiencies in attention. Care must be taken to determine if the child's indiscriminate friendliness is a result of a pattern of insufficient care or if it is a result of hyperactivity and/or inattention.

Williams syndrome, a genetic disorder affecting approximately 1 in 10,000 people, must also be ruled out. Williams syndrome is present at birth and causes a myriad of medical issues and learning disabilities. As with DSED, children with Williams syndrome are very sociable and friendly and may indiscriminately seek adult attention. Their excessively social personality and lack of fear around strangers may be confused with DSED.

Risk Factors

The risk factors for DSED include traumatic childhood events and stressors, which may impact the child's ability to form healthy attachments to adult caregivers. Parents who are actively present, caring, and responsive tend to elicit healthy attachments with their children. Children who are in institutions with multiple caregivers may not be provided the relational stability necessary to create strong attachment. Other risk factors include abuse, neglect, parental drug use, and parental mental health issues.

Treatment

The goal of therapy with children experiencing DSED is to repair the damage caused by insufficient caregiving and to process and heal the child's fears of abandonment and loss. Children with DSED quickly create very shallow relationships with others but rarely enter a deep relationship out of fear of being rejected or abandoned. Therapy with both the child and caregiver focuses on working through the fear and creating a deep, meaningful attachment. In order to accomplish this, the caregiver may need education services, parenting training, social work support, and personal or family therapy.

Play therapy is a highly effective form of therapy often used in the treatment of children with DSED. Play therapy uses the therapeutic capacity of play to provide a safe, caring environment in which the child can express his or her thoughts, feelings, and experiences. Play therapists observe the child as he or she plays in order to understand the underlying impulses that drive the child's behavior. Children are allowed to have unstructured play time in order to work through their issues. Caregivers may be included in the play therapy sessions as the therapist models and encourage positive interactions with the child.

Janna C. Ramsey

See also Adoption; Attachment; Bonding; Child–Parent Relationship Therapy; Foster Children; Parent–Child Communication; Play Family Therapy; Reactive Attachment Disorder in Children

Further Readings

Cassidy, J., & Shaver, P. (Eds.). (1999). *Handbook of attachment: Theory, research, and clinical applications.* New York, NY: Guilford Press.

Gleason, M. M., Fox, N. A., Drury, S., Smyke, A., Egger, H. L., Nelson, C. A., . . . Zeanah, C. H. (2011). Validity of evidence-derived criteria for reactive attachment disorder: Indiscriminately social/disinhibited and emotionally withdrawn/inhibited types. *Journal of the American Academy of Child & Adolescent Psychiatry, 50*(3), 216–231.

Hornor, G. (2008). Reactive attachment disorder. *Journal of Pediatric Health Care, 22*(4), 234–239.

Lawler, J. M., Hostinar, C. E., Mliner, S. B., & Gunnar, M. R. (2014). Disinhibited social engagement in postinstitutionalized children: Differentiating normal from atypical behavior. *Development and Psychopathology, 26*(2), 451.

Zeanah, C. H., & Gleason, M. M. (2010). *Reactive attachment disorder: A review for DSM-5.* Washington, DC: American Psychiatric Association.

DIVERSITY

Diversity in the context of the counseling profession and counseling-related research is usually described as "multiculturalism" or "cultural diversity." Diversity is typically thought of as the various identities and characteristics of an individual, group, or population. From a humanistic perspective, diversity is what makes us distinct from one another. Categories such as gender identity, sexual orientation, ethnicity, race, and spirituality are put in place to conceptualize people's life experiences. From a research perspective, diversity within a sample size may increase the generalizability of the findings. However, racial and ethnic diversity remains a common concern with respect to assessments and interventions that were originally conducted with homogeneous samples. In regard to ethical conduct, mental health professionals have a responsibility to facilitate effective psychotherapeutic interventions that take into account diversity, or in other words, a multicultural perspective. In this entry, important aspects of diversity are discussed as well as the multicultural competencies needed to be an ethical and effective therapist.

Mental health professionals have an ethical responsibility to facilitate effective psychotherapeutic interventions for all clients; this necessarily entails accounting for and being sensitive to human diversity. Although mental health professionals would not intentionally mistreat clients from diverse multicultural backgrounds, inadequate cultural knowledge or awareness may result in unintentional harm to the client. For example, when a clinician misunderstands a client's cultural worldviews, lifestyles, and experiences, the mental health needs of the client may remain unrecognized and unmet.

To prevent this type of situation, scholars have suggested that therapists gather information from a sociocultural perspective. A sociocultural perspective of diversity acknowledges the influence social systems have on an individual or marginalized group. Traditionally, diversity from a sociocultural perspective can be conceptualized as struggles between groups: Those who are in the majority are thereby privileged and thus hold power over the minority or marginalized group, which experiences oppression. However, considering the multiple cultures and identities one could experience and identify with, it is common that there may be internal conflict between a person's identities that are more privileged and those that are not. For example, an individual may identify as a White male, which is a generally privileged identity in Western culture. However, he may also identify as homosexual, which is a culture that is traditionally oppressed by mainstream Western culture. Again, an individual may identify with many cultural groups, so the personal balance between these privileged and oppressed factors becomes important information when providing culturally diverse, ethical counseling services. Diversity is typically thought of as the various identities and characteristics of an individual, group, or population. Categories such as gender identity, sexual orientation, ethnicity, race, and spirituality are put in place to conceptualize people's life experiences.

Multicultural Competences

To honor the diversity of others in an ethical manner, the broad concept of multicultural counseling competence (MCC) has been operationalized in terms of multicultural counseling competencies (MCCs), which are most often described as therapists' awareness, knowledge, and skills in working with diverse clients. The potential benefits to diverse clients of having therapists who are aware, knowledgeable, and skillful in handling multicultural issues may be so obvious that perhaps some scholars immersed in multicultural psychology have taken them for granted. Despite wide acknowledgment of MCCs and attempts to evaluate them across more than three decades, scholars in multicultural psychology actually have limited data about how these competencies affect clients' perspectives and experiences in therapy.

Some of the difficulties associated with evaluating MCCs may be due in part to the methods traditionally used to measure these constructs. Self-report measures have long been used to determine clinicians' multicultural case conceptualization abilities, but self-report measures overestimate abilities compared with expert ratings. The inherent confounds associated with self-evaluation raise serious questions about the validity of self-report measures of MCCs (e.g., overconfidence, social desirability). For example, research suggests a positive correlation between MCC self-report measures and a general index of social desirability: After the researchers had controlled for social desirability, none of the self-report scales were significantly related to a clinician's MCC conceptualization ability. Thus, many research questions should be asked about therapists' MCC. Most notably, to what degree do MCCs increase the effectiveness of therapeutic services provided to culturally diverse clients, reduce clients' premature discontinuation of therapy, and enhance clients' experiences in therapy? It would not be an exaggeration to say that the MCC construct is the most fundamental concept in applied multicultural psychology, which is based on the premise that therapeutic services received by culturally diverse clients are more effective when therapists skillfully attend to specific cultural variables. Without the concept of MCC, multicultural psychology informs mental health treatment but does not prescribe specific actions.

Domains of Aspirational Competences

In 2015, the MCCs were revised to include a social justice aspect, aptly named the Multicultural and Social Justice Counseling Competencies (MSJCC). The merger of these competencies acknowledges an intersection of identities and the dynamics of power, privilege, and oppression that influence the counseling relationship.

Counselor Awareness

Therapists who are keenly aware of their own cultural values, beliefs, and worldviews should be able to more accurately discern and interpret the cultural values, beliefs, and worldviews of their clients than those who are not. Therapists lacking cultural awareness risk misunderstanding clients' actions and comments, perhaps assuming that their clients' values are the same as their own. Or they may fail to account for their own implicit biases. For instance, a middle-class male therapist who fails to account for his own insecurity over his socioeconomic status may falsely conclude that because his affluent female client was "born into money," she does not appreciate the value of work. This preconceived notion could subtly (or perhaps not so subtly) affect the approach of the therapist and the relationship between the therapist and client.

Cultural Knowledge

Therapists with cultural knowledge can ascertain both differences and similarities across various domains, such as race and ethnicity, gender, sexual orientation, and religion. They are able to put into context and accurately interpret the meaning of the actions and perceptions of others. For instance, a psychologist familiar with the traditional Latin American value of *familismo* ("family first") may welcome a client's request that family be included in the therapy process, rather than interpreting this request as a form of enmeshment. Examples of multicultural knowledge include the following, based on Patricia Arredondo's work: (a) knowledge of the impact that culture and history have had on psychological theory, inquiry methods, and professional practice; (b) knowledge of specific contexts of oppression, discrimination, and prejudice that many culturally diverse clients have encountered and experienced; and (c) knowledge of cultural attitudes about mental health and mental health services.

Multicultural Interventions

Multiculturally skilled therapists apply their awareness and knowledge to engage effectively with others and to use culturally appropriate strategies in therapy. They avoid overgeneralizing or overindividualizing treatment by accounting for cultural contexts as they meet the needs of the client. For instance, a therapist who learns of an African immigrant's strong beliefs regarding gender roles (knowledge) that differ from those of the therapist (awareness) will appropriately seek common ground with the client in other areas to strengthen the therapeutic alliance (skills) before exploring how gender roles relate to the client's presenting concern. The following are examples of multicultural skills: (a) ability to look beyond color, culture, religion, sexual orientation, accent, and so forth, and see individuals in a holistic way, thus viewing the client in the context of his or her historical, sociopolitical, and economic background; (b) initiative to seek out educational and consultative experiences to increase the therapist's own effectiveness in working across cultural differences; and (c) ability to modify assessment and treatment methods to better match the needs of multicultural clientele.

Since the 1970s, a growing body of literature has addressed cultural and cross-cultural issues, culturally specific groups, and multiple concepts that have given multidimensionality to the multicultural domain. Initially, the literature had greater focus on issues of acculturation, ethnic identity, language, and the cultural differences between therapist and client. These topics have not disappeared, but attention to other dimensions of identity and intersectionality affecting mental well-being is increasing. For example, multicultural competency is discussed in relation to religion and spirituality, counseling internationally, family counseling, and so forth. The concept of social justice has been claimed and integrated as a rationale for multicultural competencies.

Since the mid-1990s, there has been an emergence of ethnic/racial minority–specific readers, texts, and handbooks with a focus on knowledge building and application of knowledge to customized cultural practices for people of African, American Indian, Asian, Latino, Pacific Islander, and European descent. Specific ethnic groups also addressed in the MCC literature are Arabs, Filipinos, Jews, Koreans, Mexican Americans and Chicanas/os, Muslims, and South Asians. The list of groups is exhaustive. In emic-oriented publications, the emphasis is on knowledge-building about the specific group's cultural worldview and culturally appropriate interventions. Cross-cutting themes generally include a focus on group history, cultural identity, religion, spirituality, family ethos, gender socialization, beliefs about mental health, and indigenous therapy beliefs and practices. MCC continues to transform the counseling and psychology professions. MCC reflects an increase in multicultural counseling outcome research; advancements in the measurement of counselors' multicultural competence; an increased focus on counselor education, training, and supervision; and the development of specialty and culture-specific competences or guidelines.

Monica Paige Band

See also Ethical Codes; Gender- and Culture-Sensitive Therapies; Multicultural Counseling Competence; Multiculturalism

Further Readings

American Psychological Association. (2003). Guidelines on multicultural education, training, research, practice, and organizational change for psychologists. *American Psychologist, 58,* 377–402.

Bronstein, P. A., & Quina, K. (Eds.). (1988). *Teaching a psychology of people: Resources for gender and sociocultural awareness.* Washington, DC: American Psychological Association. doi:10.1037/10066-000

Carter, R. T. (2007). Racism and psychological and emotional injury: Recognizing and assessing race-based traumatic stress. *Counseling Psychologist, 35*(1), 13–105. doi:10.1177/0011000006292033

D'Andrea, M., & Heckman, E. F. (2008). A 40-year review of multicultural counseling outcome research: Outlining a future research agenda for the multicultural counseling movement. *Journal of Counseling & Development, 86*(3), 356–363. doi:10.1002/j.1556-6678.2008.tb00520.x

Fong, R. (Ed.). (2004). *Social work practice with children and families: Culturally competent practice with immigrant and refugee children and families.* New York, NY: Guilford Press.

Fouad, N. A., & Arredondo, P. (2007). *Becoming culturally oriented: Practical advice for psychologists and educators*. Washington, DC: American Psychological Association. doi:10.1037/11483-000

Kenney, K. R. (2002). Counseling interracial couples and multiracial individuals: Applying a multicultural counseling competency framework. *Counseling and Human Development, 35*, 1–12.

Kenney, K. R. (2006). Counseling multiracial individuals and families. In C. C. Lee (Ed.), *Multicultural issues in counseling: New approaches to diversity* (3rd ed., pp. 251–266). Alexandria, VA: American Counseling Association.

McLean, R. (2003). Deconstructing Black gay shame: A multicultural perspective on the quest for a healthy ethnic and sexual identity. In G. Roysircar, D. S. Sandhu, & V. E. Bibbins Sr. (Eds.), *Multicultural competencies: A guidebook of practices* (pp. 109–118). Alexandria, VA: Association for Multicultural Counseling & Development.

Miller, J., & Garran, A. M. (2008). *Racism in the United States: Implications for the helping professions*. Belmont, CA: Thomson Brooks/Cole.

Nassar-McMillan, S. C., & Hakim-Larson, J. (2003). Counseling considerations among Arab Americans. *Journal of Counseling & Development, 81*(2), 150–159. doi:10.1002/j.1556-6678.2003.tb00236.x

Sue, D. W. (1995). Multicultural organizational development: Implications for the counseling profession. In J. G. Ponterotto, J. M. Casas, L. A. Suzuki, & C. M. Alexander (Eds.), *Handbook of multicultural counseling* (pp. 474–492). Thousand Oaks, CA: Sage.

Sue, D. W. (2004). Whiteness and ethnocentric monoculturalism: Making the "invisible" visible. *American Psychologist, 59*(8), 761–769. doi:10.1037/0003-066X.59.8.761

DIVORCE AND SEPARATION

The marriage rate in this country is 6.8 per 1,000 and is accentuated by the rate of divorce reaching 3.6 per 1,000. Statistics indicate 50% of first marriages end in divorce. The reasons for divorce are varied. The most frequently reported causes include infidelity, indifference, financial issues, sexual problems, and familial issues. Regardless of the precipitating factor(s), poor or absent communication underlies discontinued relationships. Some couples opt for separating, and often the purposes are not congruent between partners. Generally, one wants to resolve the issues and remain together, while the other is ready to end the marriage. For couples who choose to separate, the outcome is divorce in 79% of cases. Counseling a couple who are exchanging mixed messages raises the necessity to process with the couples what stage they are at in terms of the relationship. Beginning with an assessment of the stages a couple may be experiencing when they enter treatment, this entry discusses prime factors of separation, divorce, and the resulting experience of grief and loss. Throughout this entry, interventions appropriate to each stage of the separation and divorce are discussed.

Assessing Stages

Counseling a couple begins with assessing their purpose and goal for treatment. Generally, couples enter a session with great trepidation and a wide array of emotions. The counselor, while remaining neutral and unbiased, attempts to ascertain if the couple is there to work on the relationship or separate in a positive manner. Regardless of the purpose or who proverbially "has their foot out the door," communication is most likely at a standstill or embedded with anger, frustration, and unsaid and unmet wants, desires, and needs. The counselor can prepare by recognizing five general kinds of characteristic patterns in relationships and note which one may be present with the couple. These characteristic patterns include the following:

1. Pursuer–distancer relationships occur when one partner wants to confront and discuss problems, while the other person avoids the discussions.

2. Disengaged relationships are those in which there is little commonality, a lack of emotions, and little engagement.

3. Operatic relationships are very loud, vocal, and emotionally expressive; they can also be passionately physical.

4. Cohesive-individuated relationships are balanced emotionally.
5. Traditional relationships are those in which one partner provides and the other takes care of the home.

The therapist uses these relationship patterns to help assess and formulate a treatment plan. This is especially useful to begin to develop interventions to improve communication and identify the stages of divorce.

Stages of Pending Separation and Divorce

There are numerous models that describe the typical stages of divorce and separation; however, the commonality is that the movements throughout the processes are not linear. Much like the stages of grief and loss when encountering death, each person will cycle and sometimes recycle through the stages.

Stages of separation are directly correlated with stages of grief and loss. The stages include (1) disbelief and denial; (2) anger and blame; (3) sadness and depression; and (4) acceptance. The stages are not necessarily sequential and individuals may invariably be in more than one stage at any given time. For example, individuals within the same sentence may emote disbelief and at the same time express anger. The therapist needs to be mindful of the stage and normalize emotions and thoughts.

Stages, Impact on Couples

Separation can occur in the decision-making stage of divorce. Some reasons for separating rather than divorcing may be an attempt to renew the relationship, financial uncertainty, and lack of emotional resources. Often one partner wants to work on fixing the relationship, while the other does not. Sometimes the one who does not want to fix the relationship suggests disengaging (separating) as a kinder method to move forward. However, studies do indicate that 79% of separations end in divorce within a year or two.

Intervention

There does need to be an intervention in therapy with the pending separation. The most helpful intervention is to develop a contract of who is exiting and the timeline to reassess. Additionally, discussions of finance, handling of home issues, and parental roles need to be included in the contract. Couples need to continue in therapy to address and continually reassess goals.

Stages of Divorce

One model that discusses the stages of divorce is based on emotionality and has three stages: (1) decision-making about whether to stay in the relationship, (2) restructuring living conditions, and (3) starting anew.

Decision-Making Impact

Stage 1 is replete with emotions and incongruence. The issues that bring couples to therapy are generally the pinnacle of what the primary causality factors are and thus, many mixed language messages may arise. One primary issue that is noted in dissatisfaction in couples is the difficulty of sustaining love. For example, the dialogue may take the form of statements such as, "if only she would" or "I am the only one trying" or "he never cares," and so forth. Additionally, at this stage, the therapist's role is to assist the couple in discussing the many components of a divorce, which include emotional, financial, family, and children.

Interventions

The primary purpose of this stage is for the therapist to create a safe environment whereby couples may emote in a productive communication style that is collaborative in nature. The difficulty of this initial stage, as within the next stage, is often the presence of anger by one member of the couple and its resulting blame on the other member of the couple. At this stage, the couple's communication provides a glimpse into their dysfunction. Processing with each partner to understand what expectations each had for the relationship can begin to unpack the issues and begin to look at each one's vulnerability. One primary issue that is noted is the difficulty of sustaining love. Partners conceptualize what "love" is for them in terms of sensory experiences. No two people have the same pattern or nominalization of the concept of love. Thus, when disagreements unfold, or disappointments, it tends to be a lack of communicating needs, wants, and desires.

Addressing the "shoulds, oughts, and nevers" is one way to focus on decision-making. This focus helps to normalize modal operator words and, at the same time, point out the schemas that have arisen in each person throughout the relationship. Additionally, Irving Gottman's tenets of the five horsemen (criticism, defensiveness, contempt, stonewalling, and belligerence) as predictors of divorce are useful to discuss with the couple as an intervention to recognize their pattern of unhelpful communication.

Contracts

Finally, another intervention is having each member of a couple prepare a decision-making contract assessing whether their needs can be met within their marriage. The two separate contracts are then used in the session. Keeping the language focused using "I" statements for setting the boundaries of the contract helps each take responsibility for their needs, wants, and desires.

Therapist Demeanor

Counseling a couple in their decision-making can be quite daunting. Ethically the therapist needs to maintain a stance of impartiality. Sometimes the nuances of the interactions impact the therapists' ability to maintain neutrality. For example, the therapist may respond in a tonality that is not objective. Additionally, the therapist may nonverbally respond with a judgmental stance. Couples often seek to place the therapist in the role of referring or siding with one partner over the other. As a result, working with couples is challenging. Achieving a collaborative working environment for the couple may take time to establish. The goal is for the decision to be unilateral and prepare the couple for the next stage, which is restructuring.

Restructuring

Restructuring is composed of the nuts and bolts of the ramifications of the pending divorce. At this stage, legal, financial, parenting, emotional, social, and family issues come into full view. Stress levels are noted to be high at this time due to all the pending changes. The mere pragmatics of resettling can be quite frightening and time-consuming for each partner. Although each partner may have already begun a list literally or figuratively of what to take or leave behind physically, the process can be a source of great disillusionment as it represents the metaphor of breaking apart a relationship.

Interventions

Separating material goods and finances is often one of the most difficult restructuring issues with families. Often the extended family members become enmeshed not only with the separation emotionally, but also with physical property. The goal in therapy is to discuss how the divorce will impact others and at the same time set realistic goals to move through the restructuring. Social relationships often are thought of as family as well and are typically marred by a sense of having to choose one partner over the other. The change of a couple dissolving will alter the dynamics of people socially connected.

Mediation

This stage is also where mediation takes place. Mediators are trained professionals who specifically work with pending divorces and discuss financial and parental obligations. Joint custody is often pursued through mediation. No-fault divorce, present in many states, is another component of mediation. The goal of restructuring is to help the couple prepare and negotiate while hopefully continuing to have productive communication. The outcome, then, is starting anew.

Starting Anew

The final stage of divorce is the beginning of individuation. The therapist now works with the individual. Therapists may or may not be comfortable seeing each member of the couple individually. If the choice is to do so, the therapy must focus on the individual's future and not that of the other individual who once was part of the couple. Therefore, seeing each is generally not the case at this stage.

Interventions

The goal is to help the individual grow and develop while also addressing emotional and cognitive paradigms. The individual is encouraged to attend divorce support groups as well, thus providing a format of commonality. This is also a crucial time for the individual to develop new resources and rekindle those at the present time.

The stage also needs to address the children who by nature will most likely have a full myriad of emotions, including a sense of self-blame. Family therapy is the protocol and the sessions may or may not include both partners. The goal is to help the children share their feelings about how the divorce impacts them in their home, with extended family, and with friends. The parent(s) goal is to be able to hear and understand the children's needs both emotionally and physically. Negotiations about visits, as well as simply talking about how the children have mixed feelings, is paramount to helping all cope.

Remarriage

Starting anew may include new relationships and the prospects of "being a family again." Remarriage rates are approximately 55% for men and 46% for women. The divorce rate of remarriage is 12% for both. Therapists need to help the individuals prepare for expectations of the new family and how this is implicated in the extended families.

Interventions

Work with a remarriage couple needs to take into account the new family system and address the reorganization of roles and patterns with stepfamilies. Studies indicate that often the remarried couple and stepfamily assume all to be a cohesive transition. However, issues arise quickly. For example, children's adaptations to the stepparent roles and responsibilities as a parent may be not accepted. Additionally, for the remarried, it is essential to understand what their perceptions are of a healthy relationship. Any preconceived myths and ideas about "this time the marriage will be perfect" should be discussed.

Therapeutic Goals

The goal of therapy in the renewal stage overall is to help the individual take account of their behaviors and emotions and accept the new phase of life in a positive vein. Some people do indeed use the struggles and pain to strengthen themselves for the future while others do not. Divorces can be devastating and very involved with trauma, abuse, and neglect to name a few. It is imperative to continually assess the client for wellness. Some may require much more in-depth work. Therapy needs to help assess the client for depressive symptoms, which is quite common, as well as discussing the sense of belonging, that has been altered. Combined with this is the client discovery of resources. Recalling that family and social disruptions have occurred, it is imperative for clients to develop new resources.

Grief and Loss

Changes

The results of divorce may be a powerful positive change agent for some. For example, consider a client who has experienced severe trauma with physical and verbal abuse. Therapy with the couple will not be conducted. However, the individual will still need to work through a maze of emotions to begin anew. The stages of grief and loss are ongoing. It is important to help clients cope and prepare for backlashes of feelings.

Interventions

Couple and family rituals often remind the individual of the loss. One important intervention is to establish new rituals. For example, changing the position of the furniture in the home, such as the bed, and repainting can begin a small new beginning. Changing the rituals of how holidays are experienced, such as locations, chosen day, and so forth can develop new rituals.

Metaphor

Therapists help process the changes and in fact the metaphor of doing so can become a new source of strength for the individual. Grief and loss will continue, less pronounced, and at times as though the divorce just occurred. Counselors need to encourage clients to be patient and engage in self-care.

Sandra Kakacek

See also Conflict in Couples and Families; Couples and Marriage Counseling; Divorce Therapy; Grief Counseling; Stepfamilies

Further Readings

Bandler, R., & Grinder, J. (1982). *Reframing: Neurolinguistic programming and the transformation of meaning*. Cupertino, CA: Real People Press.

Carlson, J., & Sperry, L. (Eds.). (1998). *The disordered couple*. Bristol, PA: Brunner/Mazel.

Conway, M. B., & Christensen, T. M. (2001). Adult children of divorce and relationships: A review of the literature. *The Family Journal, 9*(3), 289–294.

Conway, M. B., Christensen, T. M., & Herlihy, B. (2003). Adult children of divorce and relationships: Implications for counseling. *The Family Journal, 11*(4), 364–373.

Gottman, J. (1999). *The marriage clinic*. New York, NY: W. W. Norton.

Haley, J., & Richeport-Haley, M. (2007). *Directive family therapy*. New York, NY: Haworth.

Harway, M. (Ed.). (2005). *Handbook of couples therapy*. Hoboken, NJ: Wiley.

Long, L. L., & Young, M. E. (2007). *Counseling and therapy for couples* (2nd ed.). Belmont, CA: Brooks/Cole.

Minuchin, S. (1974). *Families and family therapy*. Cambridge, MA: Harvard University Press.

Piercy, F. P., & Sprenkle, D. H. (1986). *Family therapy sourcebook*. New York, NY: Guilford Press.

Piercy, F. P., Sprenkle, D. H., & Wetchler, J. L. (1996). *Family therapy sourcebook*. New York, NY: Guilford Press.

Rice, J. K., & Rice, D. G. (1986). *Living through divorce: A developmental approach to divorce therapy*. New York, NY: Guilford Press.

Wetchler, J. L. (Ed.). (2011). *Handbook of clinical issues in couple therapy*. New York, NY: Routledge.

Divorce Therapy

Divorce therapy refers to a therapeutic encounter that specifically deals with a couple seeking to dissolve their marital relationship. This is unlike marriage therapy that seeks to enrich, help, or even save the marriage. The couple has often begun the divorce process by seeking out advice from their family, coworkers, friends, and possibly an attorney. They are searching for help because their family law attorney or the judge has strongly encouraged them to engage in counseling before the divorce is made final. Attorneys and friends will often encourage a couple to consider therapeutic guidance to expedite a divorce. This allows for the opportunity to create a divorce that is more amicable and equitable. This entry describes divorce and divorce therapy, divorce recovery groups, and continues with discussions of spirituality and divorce, discernment therapy, children and divorce, and resources related to divorce, including collaborative divorce and divorce mediation.

Divorce and Divorce Therapy

Divorce is not a spontaneous event. It normally occurs after a period of weeks, months, or even years of contemplation. Many individuals who feel trapped in a marriage see divorce as the only way out. Sometimes divorce occurs because the marital partners live parallel lives and have "grown apart." At other times the termination of the marriage can be the result of major dysfunctional issues and problems. These may include addictive behaviors, spousal or child abuse, or incest. Trauma, be it personal or familial, may create an emotional imbalance that disrupts the essential holistic character of the marriage partnership.

Divorce

Existentially, separation or divorce therapy provides a safe place to consider the impact, the closure, and the unseen opportunities of moving on with life. Divorce or separation therapy becomes a time for reflection that provides a haven of rest from the stress and pressures that are a part of separation and divorce. Every attempt is made to engage in a "conscious uncoupling" from their "significant ex." Separation or divorce therapy seeks to create an atmosphere that creates a peaceful, cooperative, and nondestructive collaborative divorce. The Honorable Anne Kass, a district judge in the Second Judicial District, State of New Mexico, believes that divorce counseling is a good idea for nearly everyone who is getting a divorce. Counseling is strongly recommended for couples with children. She believes that divorce counseling is intentionally aimed at dissolving a marriage. Judge Kass posits that divorce therapy provides an opportunity to end the marriage with dignity and respect.

Divorce Therapy

Divorce therapy often has two different phases: predivorce counseling and postdivorce counseling. In the first phase, a couple will work through the reasons for the dissolution of the marriage, providing an opportunity to learn to communicate effectively and civilly regarding the "point of no return" in the marital relationship. It provides a forum for each partner to be heard.

This phase of therapy will discuss each individual's personal metacognition regarding the divorce process. It may commence with the couple's functional strategy to deal with family members' perception of the imminent dissolution of the family. Topics that might be included are responsibilities and rights of each partner, when and how to break the news to the children, and joint custody issues. Subconscious preliminary emotional issues will often begin to surface such as anger at a partner, resentment, bargaining, and feelings of abandonment, bereavement, and grief issues. A divorce is the death of the marriage, since things will never be the same. When children are part of the process, there will be school events, games, recitals, graduations, marriages, and numerous other family events at which both former spouses will want to be in attendance. This can cause much stress and anxiety among the family members.

Predivorce therapy provides an opportunity for the partners to begin to get a grasp on how they will deal with this new reality and how they may cope. They are in a time of crisis as they are part of a life-altering event. The breakup of a committed long-term relationship will require a restructuring for the individual, couple, and family.

Postdivorce counseling takes place when the divorce is legally over and may include the former spouses seeking to deal with unresolved issues, or one or both former spouses seeking help and guidance for themselves as individuals. According to the Virginia Longitudinal Study of Divorce and Remarriage, during the first year after the divorce men were more likely to have a more difficult time coping with the reality of the divorce than women. The men experienced more severe symptoms that included health problems, depression, low self-esteem, and alcohol or drug abuse. Women typically experienced less severe problems in the first year after the divorce, but tended to experience higher levels of distress and depression than men in the years that followed. Their distress seemed more related to the consequences of divorce, rather than to the divorce itself. Postdivorce and recovery clients may ask, "When will I be OK?" There is no one answer for all, but 18 months is considered a very early transformation, and it is not unusual for many individuals to experience the postdivorce effects for 3 to 4 years.

Divorce recovery may include elements of Elisabeth Kübler-Ross's five-stage theory of loss and grief.

1. *Denial:* "This is not happening to me," or "She will come to her senses," or "this is just a bad dream; when I wake up it will be gone." Shock and disbelief may cause withdrawal from society, family, and friends, and these "psychological runners" may produce major depressive episodes.

2. *Anger:* Resentment plays a major role in the development of anger. "I wouldn't be in this mess if he had not initiated this divorce" or "He/she left me for another woman or man." Anger can be healthy because it will move one from a state of denial, to begin moving forward to the creation of a new life. It can also have negative consequences; such as excessive drinking or drug use, or seeking "love in all the wrong places." Children and adolescents may experience anger, resentment, or pain and hurt that may be acted out in behavioral ways. These may be seen in tantrums in public places or problems in the home, at school, or at other social settings.

3. *Bargaining:* One may reach a state where anything may be said or done, such as bargaining with God or lashing out with pain, guilt, or shame. The feelings may be overwhelming. In desperation one may try to do whatever may restore peace, harmony, and make things like they used to be in the "good old days."

4. *Depression:* This is a normal part of the dissolution of a marriage. One feels sad and unproductive, experiences anhedonia (a lack of pleasure), has trouble concentrating on normal activities, and has sleep issues (such as having trouble getting to sleep, or experiencing early morning awaking). It is recommended to therapists to conduct an assessment for suicidality of individuals who experience a loss of hope and meaning in their life.

5. *Acceptance:* This is when divorce becomes real, and it is time to move forward to a new beginning, or a "new normal." The divorcees need to be encouraged to live in the present, as they will never forget their former spouse, who was a significant part of their life. They will need to make a concerted effort to move on to new friends and acquaintances, and new opportunities and experiences that are theirs alone. They will begin to experience more good days than bad days. As they live in the here-and-now, they may look forward with eager anticipation to what a new tomorrow brings.

Divorce Recovery Groups

Divorce recovery (DR) groups allow individuals to achieve closure in a group setting. This gives individuals the opportunity to grow emotionally, spiritually, and psychologically in a support group. The DR groups offer classes in self-help in a supportive group setting of men and women who have experienced the raw trauma of a divorce. Various churches and synagogues have in-house programs to assist newly divorced individuals. It is not uncommon for individuals to repeat the class to experience the full depth of the program. Divorce Care is a national divorce recovery group with thousands of chapters across the nation and world. Divorce Care groups cover many topics, including self-awareness and individual identity, anger, depression, loneliness, dating, children, sexuality, finances, forgiveness of self, and topics related to the former spouse and partner.

Spirituality and Divorce

Many individuals will turn to God and their religious affiliation for help during divorce or after the divorce. Being a part of a religious institution, taking part in worship, praying, and being with other congregants may create a sense of connection with a community or opportunities for moments of peace and serenity. Others may blame God, feel punished by God, or question why this misfortune has come upon them. Spirituality and religious faith are no guarantee that God will perform a miracle and "save" the "holy matrimony." However, there is a positive correlation between religious faith and coping with loss. Faith and spirituality provide the opportunity to begin the process of forgiveness. Spirituality may also provide beneficial growth in the adjustment to post-traumatic stressors. Most important, religious faith or spiritual beliefs may increase psychological health and physical well-being.

Discernment Therapy

Discernment counseling is a new therapeutic theory and process that has in recent years offered help to couples who want one more opportunity to determine whether they want to continue their marriage relationship or proceed to a divorce. Discernment therapy is often the last chance for reconciliation. A divorce is one of the most difficult traumas to experience in life. It often brings about feelings of failure, with thoughts such as "I am a failure," "we are a failure," and "what went wrong?"

Discernment counseling began under the leadership of William Doherty at the University of Minnesota. The project was named the Minnesota Couples on the Brink Project. During this process, a couple comes in seeking counseling and agrees to meet for one to five sessions. The first session normally lasts 2 hours and future meetings run for 1.5 hours. The assigned counselor will work with the couple together and as separate individuals. The counselor investigates the presenting problem by asking questions such as the following: What has gone wrong? Who have they spoken to about this problem? Was anyone able to help? Did they experience any resolution? If they were to consider a future life together, what might positively contribute to bringing this about? Discernment counseling helps two individuals "discern" what would create a positive outcome for their marriage, or end in a collaborative agreed-upon divorce.

Discernment counseling does not work for everyone but does help transform an ambivalent relationship into an opportunity for personal and couple growth. Often, one partner wants out of the marriage while their partner is seeking to desperately save the marriage. This is referred to as leaning out of the marriage or leaning into the marriage. The Couples on the Brink Project was created specifically for these couples, referred to as "mixed agenda couples." The couples are then separated for individual sessions. This allows the individuals to grow and to develop their self-awareness. It provides clarity and confidence in the individual's decision-making process. If the couple chooses to work on their marriage, they will begin an intensive 6-month reconciliation process. If the couple's decision is to divorce, the counselor will help them discover divorce professionals in the community for a fair and often mediated divorce.

Divorce and Children

Children of divorce deal with the consequence of two parents choosing to end their relationship. This is not always a bad thing. However, for most children, a divorce will have immediate and life-long consequences; nothing will ever be the same. Many children and siblings react with behavior that is radically different from their past childhood or adolescent history. This might involve a sense of a lack of support, aloneness, and meaninglessness. Many times their behavior will reflect their sadness, resentment at the loss of a parent, or anger at a new and different parental authority creating a binuclear family. Children and adolescents at times may engage in self-destructive behaviors such as lying, stealing, experimenting with illegal substances, and suicide attempts. Problems at school may be reflected in a decline in grades, disengagement with extracurricular activities (e.g., sports), or displays of anger directed toward teachers. Younger children may experience enuresis, fearful nightmares, and engage in self-blame for the loss of a beloved mother or father.

Divorce therapy for the family may be indicated to assure the children that they are not the cause of the problem and that both parents are still committed to loving them. The parents will continue providing them with their time, financial support, and presence for a satisfying compassionate relationship. With both divorcing parents involved in the counseling process, they provide a role model for the children. The children will come to understand that people may agree to disagree but can mediate, cooperate, and come to a peaceful settlement even in the face of conflict.

Resources Related to Divorce

This section presents a number of resources, approaches, and programs intended to help couples and families in obtaining a more benevolent, noncontested divorce.

Association of Family and Conciliation Courts

This is primarily an association for attorneys who specialize in family law and divorce cases. It also publishes a journal, *Family Court Review,* which features interdisciplinary articles. It is published in cooperation with the Center for Children, Families and the Law at Hofstra University School of Law. This group offers numerous pamphlets and publications that deal with divorce, separation, child custody issues, and even a pamphlet on what the children are experiencing as their parents are seeking a divorce. They also produce material on what the divorce mediation process involves. They have numerous Web resources for families.

Collaborative Divorce

Collaborative divorces occur when both parties agree to collaboratively seek a resolution to their marriage out of court. The couple agrees to not go before a judge or magistrate and to work with a collaborative team of lawyers, mental health professionals, and financial advisors. This helps a couple negotiate a settlement or agreement that is financially less costly and preserves the dignity and worth of each individual.

Divorce Mediation

Mediation is another less costly approach to the divorce process, conflict resolution, or reconciliation. Mediation is confidential, allowing both parties the opportunity to be open and honest without the fear of their honesty being used against them in a court room. This allows each spouse the freedom to work with a neutral party, a mediator, who works to discover and negotiate a settlement that is fair and equitable to both parties. Mediation attempts to move disputes from a "win-lose" to a "win-win." It is a natural process for the resolution of child custody or visitation, child or spousal maintenance and support, distribution of property, insurance, taxes, and other pressing issues. Mediation may not be right or possibly even harmful in cases dealing with domestic violence, or major substance abuse issues in the relationship.

A neutral mediator will help the couple identify key issues, discover issues of disagreement, and seek out and assist in the development of major areas of agreement. Mediators will help the couple focus on troublesome disputes which hinder the couple from moving forward to a settled agreement. This may involve a "caucus" where the mediator moves between both parties, speaking in private while seeking to develop a consensus to move forward to an agreement.

The mediator will help the couple learn to communicate effectively. This in turn creates future harmony and agreement in order to help the couple avoid future conflicts. A mediator cannot give advice, but seeks to move the couple forward to accomplishing a joint resolution that is flexible and agreeable to both parties. This joint resolution is created with the new communication skills the couple has cultivated. Mediation is voluntary, allowing the couple to be in charge or control of the process.

Although a mediator might be an attorney, he or she does not act in mediation as a lawyer for either party. Often a mediator is licensed and certified by the state. Many individuals from the mental health professions become a trained mediator as part of their therapeutic expertise to help couples move forward to a healthy closure.

Mediation can be a very useful, nonthreatening therapeutic technique to help couples come to an agreement. Couples do need to be open to compromise and willing to negotiate. Mediation may be accomplished in as little as one session, often in four to five sessions, sometimes longer. In the end, a written agreement will be drawn up by the mediator and signed by both parties. This agreement will be presented to a judge for the final divorce settlement and the court's approval.

Conclusion

The therapeutic process of divorce therapy or counseling provides a process and procedure for two people to come to terms with the collapse of an intimate partnership. It offers the freedom to explore differences and how these differences resulted in the two individuals in question falling out of love. It also offers both parties an opportunity to consider how to move forward. By focusing on the needs and desires of both parties and the needs of their children, progress can be made. Ideally, divorce therapy and counseling serves as a testing ground for future negotiations and increased communication skills. It allows for the growth of both individuals to move beyond their pain, anger, and sorrow to a new and better future as whole and complete individuals. Paradoxically, divorce therapy provides hope in the present and for the future.

Jerry Lee Terrill and Ria Echteld Baker

See also Conflict in Couples and Families; Court-Mandated Clients; Divorce and Separation

Further Readings

Academy of Professional Family Mediators: http://apfmnet.org/

Association of Family and Conciliation Courts: http://www.afccnet.org/

Certified Divorce Financial Analyst: The Institute for Divorce Financial analysts (IDFA): https://www.institutedfa.com/

Clark-Stewart, A., & Brentano, C. (2006). *Divorce: Causes and consequences (Current Perspectives in Psychology)*. New Haven, CT: Yale University Press.

DivorceNet: http://www.divorcenet.com/

Family Court Review: http://onlinelibrary.wiley.com/journal/10.1111/%28ISSN%291744-1617

Gadoua, S. (2008). *Contemplating divorce: A step by step guide to deciding whether to stay or go*. Oakland, CA: New Harbinger.

International Academy of Collaborative Professionals: https://www.collaborativepractice.com/

Jacobs, J. (2005). *All you need is love and other lies about marriage*. New York, NY: HarperCollins/Perennial.

Krumrei, E. J., Mahoney, A., & Pargament, K. I. (2011). Spiritual stress and coping model of divorce: A longitudinal study. *Journal of Family Psychology*, 25(6), 973–985.

McWade, M. (1999). *Getting up, getting over, getting on: A 12-step guide to divorce and divorce recovery*. New York, NY: Random House.

Paul, P. (2003). *The starter marriage and the future of matrimony*. New York, NY: HarperCollins.

University of Minnesota, Minnesota Couples on the Brink Project. (2013). *Counseling for couples: Discernment counseling*. Retrieved from http://www.cehd.umn.edu/fsos/projects/mcb/couples.asp

Domestic Violence

As relationship specialists, family counselors and therapists should understand and be prepared to address domestic violence. Domestic violence includes patterns of physical or verbal behavior that threaten or hurt an intimate partner. It is common, damaging, and often hidden. Despite the frequency of violence in relationships and the serious costs it has for individuals and families, many professionals struggle to effectively treat violence. This entry describes the nature of domestic violence, outlines the risk factors for it, the prevalence and costs of violence, and discusses the critical issues for family therapists to understand when encountering it.

What Is Domestic Violence?

Domestic violence, also called intimate partner violence, is more than just physical assault. It can include abusive behaviors and psychological abuse used to gain control over a partner. It can also occur when emotional escalation becomes physical. The endless ways that partners may hurt, threaten, and manipulate each other make domestic violence difficult to define. However, one important issue is that the underlying intent of a violent action is to hurt or control. Many couples are psychologically hurtful to each other, but the term *domestic violence* usually refers to physical actions that may include not only verbal abuse but also pushing, slapping, hitting, choking, or sexual assault.

The complexity of violence makes it difficult to determine exact prevalence rates, but most surveys suggest that about one in four women in the United States will experience at least one incident of physical violence in their lifetime. It is estimated that about a quarter of romantic relationships have had some violence, and of these, about half were reciprocally violent. Surveys also suggest that most incidents of partner violence are not reported to the police. World Health Organization researchers found that domestic violence exists in most countries at rates between 30% and 60%. The pervasiveness of this social issue means that family professionals will inevitably come in contact with couples and individuals experiencing violence. Violence is not only found in married and cohabiting couples. It occurs with similar frequencies in dating relationships, and women aged 20 to 24 are at the highest risk of being victims of violence.

Types and Patterns

Domestic violence is multifaceted, multicausal, and complicated. Abusive behavior occurs in many types of intimate relationships, and these behaviors will vary in intensity and risk. For example, some violence has a clear perpetrator and victim, with the violent and controlling partner dominating the other. This, according to one empirically based typology, is called intimate terrorism. Intimate terrorism is characterized by a coercive and threatening partner, who is usually male. He uses physical violence as well as other controlling tactics to monitor, punish, isolate, and wear down an intimate partner. This is the type of violence most often reported to authorities, and these victims are more likely to seek social and health services as well as legal protections. This kind of violence is psychologically abusive, and is likely to include sexual assault as a form of domination and control.

The other common type of violence is called situational couple violence. Situational couple violence is not characterized by domination and control, and is less likely to result in serious injury. It is more often bidirectional and tends to occur when an argument escalates into verbal and physical aggression. Men and women are equally likely to be situationally violent, and research suggests that up to half of all couples presenting for therapy have had some situational violence in their history.

In virtually every case of physical violence there also exists psychological abuse (sometimes referred to as emotional or verbal abuse). This includes shaming, contempt, sarcasm, and other demeaning speech that communicates that a partner is unlovable, worthless, or unwanted. It can range from harsh, degrading words to more subtle forms of criticizing and disrespect, all of which destroy confidence and self-worth. Victims of violence will often say that emotional and verbal abuse is more damaging than physical assault. Psychological abuse and control can also occur in relationships that have no physical aggression, but these relationships still may fit the pattern of intimate terrorism.

Risk Factors and Damage of Domestic Violence

Violence is found in all sectors of society, affecting all kinds of couples: gay, straight, married, cohabiting, dating, rich, poor, and of all ethnic and cultural backgrounds. However, researchers have identified some risk factors that are associated with an increased likelihood of violence. These include substance abuse (alcohol abuse predicts violence perpetration, and two thirds of incidents of violence involve alcohol), male partner isolation, economic stress, witnessing or experiencing violence in one's family of origin, unemployment, beliefs about gender inequality, and psychopathology. Although these are contributing factors, it is important to recognize that these contextual issues are not causal, and that these factors exist in many relationships that are free of abuse and violence.

Considerations of Gender

Both women and men can be violent, and both can be victims. However, in heterosexual couples, women are at far greater danger for physical and emotional trauma than are men. Also, men cause more injury to women than the reverse, and female victims express more fear than do male victims. The physical differences between the sexes usually put women at a higher safety risk when aggression occurs. Although some women are the aggressors, it is much less common for a man to be terrorized and dominated by his female partner in the same way that occurs in a typical intimate terrorist relationship where the man is the batterer. Also, some violence from women occurs in response to male domination and control, and is therefore of a different nature (called violent resistance) than that which comes from a controlling and violent perpetrator. Although it is not currently clear why, there is evidence that when violence is happening from both partners there is the most potential for injury.

Costs of Violence

Violence damages relationships, leads to emotional and physical disorders, is traumatizing for children who witness it, and has heavy costs for society (in lost work time, legal fees, police and mental health intervention, and hospitalization). These costs are disproportionately borne by women. Abuse is emotionally and psychologically damaging for victims. Females who are hurt are more likely to have symptoms of posttraumatic stress disorder, depression, stress, low self-esteem, substance abuse, low social support, and limited material resources. Abuse is also associated with health problems for female victims, such as chronic pain, arthritis, disability, migraines, frequent headaches, ulcers, and other illnesses.

Treatment Issues With Domestic Violence

In assessing for violence, several factors are important for therapists to consider. First, violence is common but often hidden. Even in therapy, many couples will not disclose violence unless asked specifically about it. Additionally, therapists often feel inadequate in dealing with a couple who have been violent, and therapists vary widely in their screening processes of couples. However, since around half of the couples who come for therapy have been violent, therapists need to be assertive when assessing for violence.

Denial and Deception

One of the reasons it is difficult to assess for violence is because a natural reaction to violence is to minimize it or deny that it exists, and therapists often get caught in this dynamic. If therapists are uncomfortable or unequipped to address violence if it is found, they may collude (i.e., all parties ignore or minimize the violence) with a couple who are reluctant to bring it up. This kind of denial is common and is usually operating at other levels. For instance, intimate terrorists minimize the abuse and downplay their responsibility for violence. They may blame the victim ("You knew what would happen"), justify the violence ("I couldn't help it after so much stress"), distort the facts, blame an outside factor ("I was drunk"), or lie about the events. This can have the effect of causing the victim to doubt his or her own reality and to self-blame. Because they are traumatized, victims of violence may use denial or minimization as coping mechanisms. A victimized woman may minimize the abuse out of fear that she will not be believed, or because she has been systematically recruited by her partner to accept blame. She also may downplay because she fears retribution on her children or herself if she seeks help, or she may lack faith in the system's ability to help her at all. Sometimes family or friends ignore warning signs for the same reasons that society does: It may be easier to turn away than engage and address it.

Assessment and Treatment Decisions

Assessing for violence should be done with care, but also with persistence. For example, it is useful to do paper-and-pencil assessments as part of an intake process, and then proceed to specific interview questions. These questions can be part of a typical therapeutic interview, but should include direct inquiries about escalation in intimate relationships. For example, it is better to ask "What happens when you become angry and fight?" than it is to ask "Are you violent?" If violence is discovered, there are many possible treatment options, including referring for specialized services, or addressing the violence in therapy.

The traditional paradigm for treating violent couples has been to separate them and assign the male (if he is the offender) to a batterer intervention program (BIP), while female victims are sent to a support group or a shelter. Batterer intervention programs are often psychoeducational in nature, where groups of mandated men are taught anger management skills, gender equality, and coping skills. The historical rationale behind treating couples separately is that treating a violent couple together can provoke further abuse (if difficult issues are brought up) and that conjoint therapy may imply equal responsibility for the violence.

However, in recent years evidence has accumulated that suggests that this type of one-size approach does not fit all violence, and that while batterer intervention for perpetrators and support groups for victims may be the best fit for intimate terrorist patterns of violence, they may not work well for situational couple violence. Several programs have confirmed that for milder types of violence that are not controlling it can be beneficial and safe to treat couples conjointly.

There are several reasons that this may be possible. First, some couples who experience violence do not occupy permanent respective roles of perpetrator and victim, but have back-and-forth physical altercations. Second, in these situations there is not one partner who is controlled and fears for their safety. Third, many of these couples do not want to separate but do want the escalation and violence to stop. Fourth, conjoint treatment can help violent individuals recognize things that trigger their violence and having a partner in session helps the therapist avoid getting caught in the minimization or one-sided nature of many partners' stories. Conjoint work should help each partner take responsibility for their actions, as well as remove themselves from provocative situations. This does not imply that in these situations the violence is free from risks or should not be taken seriously. Safety is always the highest priority when working with individuals or couples.

In order for conjoint work to be feasible, several factors must be present. First, both spouses must agree to participate in therapy, and the violent member must take full responsibility for any violence (or if the violence is mutual, the male is willing to acknowledge his greater threat or physical power). In addition, the violence must have been minor and infrequent, and not based on intimidation or control. The therapist should ensure that there are no risk factors for lethality. This means that there are no red flags like active substance abuse, coercive control (such as the presence of intimate terrorism), violent crimes, threats, denial of responsibility, or fear of retaliation following therapy. In couples work, there should be frequent checking in (including separately) of both partners to ensure that partners are being safe and honest.

Although violence is a common and serious issue, it can be effectively addressed through clinical intervention or appropriate referrals. Family therapists who understand domestic violence and are prepared to work with it can make a difference in preventing, slowing, and even stopping violence. This can change the lives of the individuals and couples who are harmed by it.

Jason B. Whiting

See also Anger Management; Couples and Marriage Counseling; Crisis Intervention With Couples and Families; Gender Issues; Patriarchy; Power Issues in Couples; Stress Management

Further Readings

Garcia-Monroe, C., Jansen, H., Ellsberg, M., Heise, L., & Watts, C. H. (2006). Prevalence of intimate partner violence: Findings from the WHO multi-country study on women's health and domestic violence. *Lancet, 368,* 1260–1269.

Heyman, R. E., & Slep, A. M. S. (Eds.). (2007). *Therapeutic treatment approaches to violent behavior.* New York, NY: Cambridge University Press.

Jenkins, A. (2009). *Becoming ethical: A parallel, political journey with men who have abused.* Dorset, England: Russell House.

Johnson, M. (2008). *A typology of domestic violence: Intimate terrorism, violent resistance, and situational couple violence*. Boston, MA: Northeastern University Press.

Logan, T. K., Walker, R., Jordan, C., & Leukefield, C. G. (2006). *Women and victimization: Contributing factors, interventions, and implications*. Washington, DC: American Psychological Association.

Stith, S. M., McCollum, E. E., & Rosen, K. H. (2011). *Couples therapy for domestic violence: Finding safe solutions*. Washington, DC: American Psychological Association.

Double Bind Theory

Strategic family therapy was introduced in the 1950s by two influential sources, one of which is Gregory Bateson, who studied family communication patterns using the science of cybernetics. In 1956, Bateson and his colleagues (including Don D. Jackson, Jay Haley, and John H. Weakland) studied the family communication patterns of individuals diagnosed with schizophrenia in an attempt to unearth the source of their symptoms. They were of the belief that psychotic behavior in a family member may be best understood within the context of pathological family communication. In their report, "Toward a Theory of Schizophrenia," they went further to hypothesize that the psychotic symptoms in a family member might be a direct result of a specific and complex pattern of communicating—a pattern they termed *the double bind*. This challenged the prevailing conceptualization of schizophrenia, which was largely based on biological phenomena. Bateson's team described the double bind process as having three common traits. The double bind theory was instrumental in helping to shape the field of family therapy and continues to be of value to marriage and family counselors today. This entry highlights the main characteristics of the double bind theory and describes how it is used to conceptualize psychopathology and dysfunctional relationships.

In recent times, the term *double bind* has frequently been misused to describe a contradictory message. However, the original researchers were describing much more complex interactions. The main premise of the theory is that the individual who displays psychotic symptoms finds himself or herself in a communication matrix. In this matrix, the individual receives contradictory messages, the contradiction cannot be communicated, and the victim perceives himself or herself as being unable to leave the interaction.

Bateson offered three common traits of the double bind interaction: (1) the relationship is important and regarded as intense; (2) the sender of the message expresses two messages where one contradicts the other; (3) the receiver of the message is not allowed to comment, point it out, or try to correct the confusion.

Michal Nichols and Richard Schwartz articulated the following six basic characteristics and examples of a double bind:

1. The communication involves two or more people who have an important emotional relationship.

2. The pattern of communication is repeated. The situation is not a single event but rather a repetitive activity from which an expectation develops.

3. The communication involves a primary negative injunction or a command not to do something on threat of punishment. It may take one of two forms: (1) Do not do __ or I will punish you or (2) If you do not do __, I will punish you.

4. There is a second abstract injunction also under threat of punishment that contradicts the primary injunction. As with the primary negative injunction, it is enforced by punishment or perceived threats to survival. This is frequently communicated via one's tone, posture, and messages such as "Ignore the contradiction between my claim to love you and my willingness to withdraw my love from you."

5. A third or tertiary negative injunction demands a response and prevents escape, effectively binding the recipient of the demand. Examples of this type of injunction may include suicide threats and promises to be better.

6. The recipient eventually becomes conditioned to respond, and as a result, no longer needs the entire sequence to maintain the symptom.

In marital therapy, this may play out in the following way:

Primary negative injunction: I won't stop cheating if you stay. (That is: Do not stay.)

Secondary negative injunction: I'll kill myself if you leave me. (That is: Do not leave me.)

Tertiary negative injunction: Be my guest. Leave! Unlike me, you are a quitter and unwilling to work on our issues. (That is: Do not leave the field.)

To further illustrate this concept, Bateson's group offered the case of a patient with schizophrenia who was recovering really well and received a visit in the hospital by his mother. He was elated to see her and immediately demonstrated his excitement by putting his arms around her in an embrace. The mother immediately stiffened and as a result he withdrew his arms. She then asked if he didn't love her anymore. The patient only blushed to which the mother responded by admonishing that he should not be so easily embarrassed and avoidant of feelings. The patient later relapsed and had another psychotic episode.

The double bind theory introduced an interactional perspective to the field of counseling. This hypothesis highlighted the possibility that psychiatric symptoms and disorders can be conceptualized as being a consequence of maladaptive external interactions. It also paved the way for family therapy in identifying pathological interactions that could lead to psychiatric illness. The theory also offered a deeper understanding of psychoanalytic concepts such as projection, splitting, denial, and projective identification.

Bateson and his colleagues introduced the notion that symptoms of schizophrenia developed as adaptive responses to maladaptive or unhealthy interactions. Although nearly 60 years has passed since Bateson presented the double bind hypothesis, it has survived because it provided practical value in the diagnosis and treatment of mental disorders and became useful in family therapy.

Wendy L. Greenidge

See also Communication Errors/Problems in Couples and Families; Communication in Couples and Families; Conflict in Couples and Families; Couples and Marriage Counseling; Cybernetics

Further Readings

Bateson, G., Jackson, D., Haley, J., & Weakland, J. (1956). Towards a theory of schizophrenia. *Behavioral Science, 1*(4), 251–264.

Cronen, V., Johnson, K., & Lannamann, J. (1982). Paradoxes, double binds, and reflexive loops: An alternative theoretical perspective. *Family Process, 21*(1), 91–112.

Dush, D. M., & Brodsky, M. (1981). Effects and implications of the experimental double bind. *Psychological Reports, 48*, 895–900.

Gibney, P. (2006). The double bind theory: Still crazy-making after all these years. *Psychotherapy in Australia, 12*(3), 48–55.

Nichols, M. P., & Schwartz, R. C. (1998). *Family therapy: Concepts and methods.* Needham Heights, MA: Allyn & Bacon.

Poster, M. (1988). Family therapy and communication theory. *Critical Theory of the Family.* Retrieved from http://www.hnet.uci.edu/mposter/CTF/chapter5.html

Zuk, G., & Zuk, C. (1998). When more is better than less: Three theories of psychosis—projection, double bind and possession. *Contemporary Family Therapy, 20*(1), 3–13.

DSM AND V-CODES

The *Diagnostic and Statistical Manual of Mental Disorders* (DSM) is a diagnostic system and handbook published by the American Psychiatric Association, which is used by mental health professionals for understanding and categorizing the different classifications of mental health disorders. V-codes are not mental disorders, but are descriptors for reasons clients may seek therapeutic treatment; they are also known as "Other Conditions that may be a Focus of Clinical Attention." They may be topics like academic, occupational, or relational issues. All licensed clinicians should know how to utilize the DSM, but some mental health fields are wary of the stigmatizing effect that diagnosing someone with a mental disorder may have. The V-codes have been particularly important to relational counselors and therapists because they lend themselves to a more systemic view of issues rather than seeing problems as only individual in nature. In this entry, the history, development, uses, and criticism of the DSM are reviewed.

History and Development of the DSM

The DSM-5 is the seventh revision of the original manual; some revisions did not contain significant changes in diagnostic criteria, but included modifications and additions to narrative material. Early versions typically included only narrative descriptions of disorders, offered perspectives from a specific theoretical viewpoint, and/or failed to attend appropriately to cultural variations in experience and behavior. Recent revisions of the DSM have included specific attention to empirical support for criteria sets, the use of the manual for clinical work, and alignment with the International Classification of Diseases (ICD).

Relationship to ICD

The ICD is a diagnostic tool used for all health purposes. Since 1948, it has been published by the World Health Organization, and is updated on a regular basis every few years. The ICD is used for coding, tracking, reimbursement, collection and classification of mortality data, and resource allocation purposes. All countries that are members of the World Health Organization use the ICD. The ICD is currently in its 10th version and is expected to be revised again in 2017. The DSM-5 includes ICD 10 codes, where previous versions of the manual have had a different coding structure. This is helpful to many therapists because the Health Insurance and Portability and Accountability Act (HIPAA) requires ICD codes for coding and billing purposes, and now the diagnostic criteria and the alpha and numeric codes can be found in one manual.

Understanding the Components of the DSM

The DSM-5 is made up of three sections and various appendices. Section I serves as an introduction and guide to the use of the manual and Section III outlines additional information that may be helpful such as emerging disorders for further study, cultural considerations, and various assessments like the 2.0 version of the World Health Organization Disability Assessment Scale (WHODAS). Section II has 21 chapters of biologically based disorders including the following disorders and those related to them: neurodevelopmental, schizophrenia spectrum and other psychotic, bipolar, depressive, anxiety, obsessive-compulsive, trauma and stressor related, dissociative, somatic, feeding and eating, elimination, sleep-wake, sexual dysfunctions, gender dysphoria, disruptive, impulse-control, conduct, substance-related and addictive, neurocognitive, personality, paraphilic, medication-induced, and other. It also includes a section for other conditions that may be a focus of clinical attention (see V-Codes below).

The manual attempts a developmental life span approach with disorders that are more often diagnosed in childhood primarily seen at the beginning of the book and disorders diagnosed late in life seen toward the end. There are several section headings within the DSM that are revisited within each chapter. Thus, one can expect to find information about diagnostic criteria and descriptors for each diagnosis as well as information on the following topics:

- *Subtypes and specifiers*—used to either define subgroups of individuals with the disorder or describe features about the subgroup
- *Diagnostic features*—a listing of common or typical symptoms seen in individuals diagnosed with the disorder

- *Associated features supporting diagnosis*—symptoms that also may be associated with the disorder
- *Prevalence*—percentage of occurrence in general population as well as sample populations
- *Development and course*—age of onset with developmental trajectory
- *Risk and prognostic factors*—list of common risk factors and likely outcome of disorder
- *Culture-related diagnostic issues*—issues related to race or culture
- *Gender-related diagnostic issues*—issues related to gender
- *Functional consequences*—impact on activities of daily living
- *Suicide risk*—notes potential for suicide risk and need for assessment
- *Differential diagnosis*—ruling out other diagnoses based on presenting and qualifying symptoms
- *Comorbidity*—the presence of another disease or disorder

V-Codes

Other conditions that may be a focus of clinical attention are called V-codes and in the ICD 10 are now classified as Z-codes. V/Z-codes describe problems that warrant clinical attention, but that are not mental disorders (i.e., child physical abuse, adjustment, domestic violence). Ninety-two V-codes are listed on pages 873–876 in the DSM-5. Many times these types of problems have an impact on a primary diagnosis and are used as a secondary or tertiary diagnosis. Part of using these codes in a secondary or tertiary way is to be able to provide accurate documentation and further explanation of the client's presenting problems.

V/Z-codes also can be used as primary diagnoses. For example, if a clinician were to assess a client and establish that he or she presented symptoms that were not rooted in any biologically based disorders, but were instead due to the experience of going through a divorce from his or her spouse, then the clinician may consider a diagnosis of V.61.03 (Z63.5), disruption of family by separation or divorce. V/Z-codes typically describe many of the experiential and developmental problems that marriage and family therapists (MFTs) and other clinicians see in practice, and are often the best fit to describe constellations of symptoms. Assigning these codes can be problematic, however, because without a diagnosis of a mental disorder, many managed care/insurance companies may deny payment for services.

Diagnostic Process

Many professionals in various helping fields may diagnose mental health disorders including medical professionals, researchers, and clinicians. Psychiatrists are medical doctors who specialize in the diagnosis and treatment of mental health disorders. As medical doctors, they are able to prescribe medications, and psychiatrists in particular work to develop accurate mental health diagnoses in order to inform the prescription of psychoactive drugs. Psychologists typically have doctoral degrees, but with varied foci. For example, some psychologists focus on conducting social science research, whereas others focus on clinical work with clients. Psychologists often have significant training in the use of various assessment procedures, and the diagnosis of mental health disorders is often one of these. MFTs, counselors, and clinical social workers inhabit a field in which the terminal clinical degree is a master's-level degree (doctorates in these fields are often degrees that focus on research or teaching in higher education). These professionals often have extensive training in working with clients individually, in families, and in groups, and in most states are required to have training in the assessment and diagnosis of mental health disorders. These professionals often use diagnosis to inform clinical treatment planning and for research purposes. It is important to note that other professionals may also diagnose, including some nurses, physician's assistants, and student interns under the supervision of licensed professionals.

Risks and Benefits of Diagnosis

Diagnosis is often a controversial topic, especially when one considers the often far-reaching implications and consequences of a diagnostic label related to mental health disorders.

Benefits of Diagnosis

First, the DSM provides a structured framework for identifying and describing the complex symptomology of many mental health disorders. This structure helps to increase understanding of the symptoms and their relationship to one another, which then, in turn, assists therapists in client conceptualization, enables the development of treatment plans, selection of evidence-based interventions and appropriate adjunct assessments or standardized inventories, and provides a foundation for the evaluation of therapy effectiveness. The DSM provides an agreed-upon "diagnostic language" that helps to facilitate communication among professionals (and therefore, continuity of care), managed care/insurance reimbursement for services, the consumption of and development of mental health research, and decreases in the risk of malpractice. One of the most significant benefits of having a system for diagnosis is that it helps to reduce the subjective bias of the clinician in assessing client symptomology. In terms of direct benefits to clients, the diagnosis may help to promote self-awareness and self-acceptance, and may help both clients and related others to externalize experiences as a problem coming from an "identified external enemy" rather than from within the person, in a characterological sense.

Risks

As with almost any scientific system, the DSM has limitations, and in many cases, these may be significant. First, the criteria for mental health disorders often place the problem within the individual, rather than on a problematic system. This causes some problems, particularly for systemically based MFTs and the theories and models used in treating couples and families. Therapists may fail to view clients holistically by narrowing their focus strictly to diagnostic labels, fail to recognize that criteria are often based on social constructions of "normal" and "abnormal" behavior that are often based in traditional Western perspectives and values, understand that the criteria themselves may be biased and some have less empirical support than others, be swayed by popular trends in diagnosis, and not fully accept that although the DSM provides a description, it does not necessarily promote understanding of pathology. For the client, an assignment of a diagnosis may be stigmatizing, be discouraging, lead to a "self-fulfilling prophecy," or move the client from an internal understanding of self to one that is externally imposed. Once a diagnosis is assigned, it often follows the client for life, through both treatment charts and managed care organizations.

Process of Diagnosing and Differential Diagnosis

Therapists begin the diagnostic process by collecting information. This is often done through interviewing clients, but may also include information from assessment measures, behavioral observation, and informants (such as family members and physicians). It is important that diagnoses only be assigned after a thorough assessment process, and that treatment plans then be informed by the diagnosis. Completing a differential diagnosis involves the process of ruling out disorders. When diagnosing, it is important for MFTs to routinely rule out malingering, substance use, and disorders related to general medical conditions (GMCs). A differential diagnosis typically compares diagnoses that are often characterized by similar symptomology such as acute stress disorder and posttraumatic stress disorder, or bipolar 1 and bipolar 2 disorders. One way to conduct the process of diagnosis is to follow steps such as these:

- Identify all reported and observed symptoms, including data from assessments.
- Identify all the disorders that could explain those constellations of symptoms.

- Consider the impact of confounding issues such as substance use, GMCs, and malingering.
- Compare the symptoms with the criteria sets associated with each disorder for best fit.
- Consider provisional, differed, unspecified, and no diagnoses.
- Consider comorbidity (multiple diagnoses).
- Assign the diagnosis or diagnoses that are the best fit for the client's presenting symptomology, while working to avoid over- or underdiagnosis and diagnostic bias.
- Ensure that all associated specifiers (additional information that may be required or optional depending on the diagnosis, such as *in early remission* that may be assigned to a substance use disorder) are included and accurate.
- Dedicate oneself to ongoing assessment and evaluation of the accuracy of the diagnoses, updating diagnoses as necessary.

Kerrie R. Fineran and Amber M. Lange

See also International Classification of Diseases (ICD); Licensure and Certification; Presenting Problems; Professional Associations; Relational Diagnoses

Further Readings

American Psychiatric Association. (2013). *Diagnostic and statistical manual of mental disorders* (5th ed.). Washington, DC: Author.

Barnhill, J. W. (2013). *DSM-5 clinical cases.* Washington, DC: American Psychiatric Association.

Braun, S. A., & Cox, J. A. (2005). Managed mental health care: Intentional misdiagnosis of mental disorders. *Journal of Counseling & Development, 83,* 425–433.

Dailey, S. F., Gill, C. S., Karl, S. L., & Barrio Minton, C. A. (2014). *DSM-5 learning companion for counselors.* Alexandria, VA: American Counseling Association.

First, M. B. (2013). *DSM-5 handbook of differential diagnosis.* Washington, DC: American Psychiatric Association.

Francis, A. (2013). *Essentials of psychiatric diagnosis, revised edition: Responding to the challenge of the DSM-5.* New York, NY: Guilford Press.

Seligman, L., & Reichenberg, L. W. (2014). *Selecting effective treatments: A comprehensive, systemic guide to treating mental health disorders* (4th ed.). San Francisco, CA: Wiley.

World Health Organization. (n.d.). *The ICD-10 classification of mental and behavioral disorders: Clinical descriptions and diagnostic guidelines.* Geneva, Switzerland: Author.

Dual and Multiple Relationships

With regard to marital, couple, and family counseling, the term *multiple relationship* is often used interchangeably with the term *dual relationship* or even *nonprofessional relationship*. Regardless of the terminology used, when referring to clinical practice, the term is used to describe any relationship or relationships between the therapist and client in addition to or separate from the therapeutic relationship. The term can also be used in regard to relationships in additional supervisor or supervisee relationships. These relationships can either be simultaneous or sequential, meaning that the additional relationships could occur at the same time as the primary professional relationship or the additional relationship could occur either before or after the primary professional relationship. Such additional relationships can be of varying degrees and natures, including but not limited to multiple relationships that are social, collegial, or even sexual. For example, a therapist might be approached to provide services to someone he or she works with or someone with whom he or she has daily contact in the community, such as a bank teller or business proprietor. Other examples might include being asked to provide services to a previous acquaintance, or even a friend. The following discussion focuses on several factors relative to nonsexual multiple relationships including but not limited to the various types of multiple relationships, ethical concerns regarding multiple relationships, as well as factors contributing to decisions around multiple relationships. This discussion is significant to the field given that multiple relationships of various kinds and degrees are prominent in many areas of practice including but not limited to rural, congregational, and educational settings.

Various Types of Multiple Relationships

Dual or multiple relationships can be either sexual or nonsexual in nature. In other words, the additional relationship may be a romantic or physical relationship, or it may be simply platonic in nature. Sexual multiple relationships, however, are addressed separately in the codes of ethics pertaining to marital, couple, and family counselors. These codes carry their own clear timelines and restrictions, often prohibiting sexual relationships with clients not only for the duration of a counseling relationship but also for a period of time after the counseling relationship has ended. Given these distinct differences, for the purpose of this discussion, nonsexual dual or multiple relationships will be the specific focus of this discussion and will be referred to as multiple relationships.

Furthermore, although the term is commonly used to refer to additional relationships in the clinical realm, marital, couple, and family counselors may encounter multiple relationships in several aspects of their professional careers, including supervision, research, and academic settings. As with clinical work described previously, these multiple relationships can occur concurrently or sequentially and refer to any relationship in addition to the primary professional relationship. For example, in academic settings a marriage and family counselor may serve as both clinical supervisor and teacher for the same student. Furthermore, a marriage and family counselor who is conducting research may include an acquaintance, friend, or family member as a research subject.

The frequency and nature of multiple relationships marriage and family counselors encounter may be influenced by their practice setting, area of specialization, or geographic location. Clinicians in more rural practice settings may encounter multiple relationships more frequently. With regard to rural practice, the frequency increases relative to the smaller number of people per therapist. For example, a clinician might find that one of his or her clients is also his or her mail carrier, dentist, or child's teacher. Each of these additional relationships may influence the therapeutic relationship in unique ways; in the same way, each of these relationships may be impacted by the therapeutic relationship. Furthermore, multiple relationships may be a factor when clients seeking services must choose between seeing a therapist they have an additional relationship with or being unable to access appropriate services relative to their location. In other words, the potential client and therapist may have to contend with the fact that the only therapeutic services feasibly available for the client will involve a multiple relationship. For the client this can mean that needs go unmet; for the therapist this can mean contending with the potential ethical dilemma of not providing services to a potential client.

In addition to rural settings, clinicians working with certain populations or within certain organizations, such as the military, law enforcement, religious organizations, or within specific communities such as certain cultural or ethnic communities, may find that these settings are somewhat similar to rural settings. Although they may differ from rural settings in that clients may have more than one therapist to choose from and the general area may be more populated, these settings are similar in that clients may prefer to seek services from people they believe to be like-minded. Clinicians working in these types of settings often face similar challenges as those clinicians in rural practice. Therefore, they may experience multiple relationships more frequently as well. While some clients may prefer the anonymity of a therapist they do not know or have additional contact with, other clients may specifically choose their therapist based on a previous relationship or cultural, ethnic, or religious similarities. These types of potential multiple relationships may impact the therapist and the client on a personal level, as well as impact the therapeutic process.

With these factors in mind, some clinicians suggest that experiencing multiple relationships while in the practice settings described here is simply unavoidable; however, not all practicing clinicians share this view. Regardless of the stance taken regarding this matter, it is clear that there are many ethical factors surrounding the topic of multiple relationships.

Ethical Gray Area

Given the variety of potential dual or multiple relationships listed in the preceding section, in that not all multiple relationships are problematic, and although there are certain clear statutes regarding specific types of multiple relationships as mentioned previously with regard to sexual multiple relationships, multiple relationships in general represent an ethical gray area for many clinicians. For example, codes of ethics pertaining to marriage and family counselors prohibit sexual multiple relationships with clients as well as prohibit counselors engaging in behaviors that may contribute to conflicts of interest. With regard to dual or multiple relationships in marital, couple, and family counseling, conflicts of interest involve situations in which the therapist's interest in helping and at least not harming the client is in conflict with other interests that may be present in the therapist's relationship with the client. For example, a therapist who receives gifts from a client might be tempted to extend or prolong the therapeutic relationship in order to continue to receive gifts from the client, which represents personal gain.

While many ethical codes warn clinicians about potential conflicts of interest and explicitly prohibit multiple relationships that are sexual in nature, the final decisions regarding nonsexual multiple relationships are left to individual clinicians. Perhaps this is because unlike sexual multiple relationships or conflicts of interest, not all multiple relationships are problematic. In other words, given the wide variety of potential multiple relationships such as the ones described, ethical codes seem to point more to the clinician than to specific prohibitions as in the case of conflicts of interest or sexual multiple relationships. This includes such decisions around whether or not to engage in multiple relationships in general or which types of multiple relationships do not represent conflicts of interest.

Given this latitude, the marital, couple, and family counselor may take into account certain risks and benefits associated with multiple relationships.

Risks

Although certainly some multiple relationships are more risky than others and not all multiple relationships constitute a risk for the therapist, client, or therapy process, there are certain types of multiple relationships that constitute a risk to one or both parties. Major themes surrounding these risks deal with varying types of conflicts of interest. Specific risks include certain conflicts of interest that may impact the counselor's judgment with regard to clinical practice. Such conflicts of interest might stem from a variety of multiple relationships such as doing additional business with a client, engaging in superfluous self-disclosure, or accepting gifts from clients. For example, if the multiple relationship is one with a friend, business associate, or authority figure, the therapist's maneuverability may be impacted by the nature of the various additional relationships. That is, the therapist may not feel the freedom to ask certain questions or focus on specific topics that may not be appropriate topics in the additional relationship, but that are essential to the therapy process. Furthermore, the therapist may find that choosing to discuss the topics that are essential to the therapy process might hinder his or her additional relationship with the client. This could impact not only the therapist's clinical practice but also his or her life outside of the therapy room. Such conflicts of interest may negatively impact the client, the therapy process, or even the clinician.

Benefits

Some marital, couple, and family counselors are proponents of multiple relationships and present arguments pertaining to their beneficial nature. Some major themes of these arguments surround the accelerated joining process and the comfort level of clients who prefer to see someone they know.

Proponents of multiple relationships maintain that such additional interactions with clients allow them additional insight into the client's life and story, accelerating the process of the therapeutic alliance. Furthermore, proponents suggest that surface-level issues could be surpassed more quickly to address the client's most pressing, if most intimate, issues. Additionally, certain clients may prefer to seek treatment from a clinician that they already know for similar reasons, perhaps feeling uncomfortable sharing their personal lives with strangers. For example, a potential client might select a particular therapist that has a similar belief system, cultural or ethnic background, or even someone with whom they have an existing relationship in hopes that this connection will benefit the therapeutic experience.

Factors to Consider

Therefore, as in other areas of clinical practice, when engaging in multiple relationships, clinicians might consider such factors as the following: all appropriate legal and ethical statutes relevant to their practice, how their particular theory of change may influence a multiple relationship, their own abilities to remain objective when involved in multiple relationships, how the client or therapeutic progress might be impacted, how to structure appropriate informed consent when multiple relationships are involved, as well as how the multiple relationship will be documented in the case file. It might also be fruitful for clinicians to take into account certain important works on the topics of dual or multiple relationships, including but not limited to those listed subsequently. Furthermore, given the various risks and benefits, as well as the many factors that may be involved in decisions around multiple relationships, clinicians might choose to seek supervision or consultation appropriate to their level of practice. Such precautions could be helpful in maintaining the marital, couple, and family counselor's professional responsibility to do no harm.

Lauren Fix

See also Boundaries; Decision-Making; Ethical Codes; Ethical Decision-Making

Further Readings

Aducci, C. J., & Cole, C. L. (2011). Multiple relationships: Perspectives from training family therapists and clients. *Journal of Systemic Therapies, 30,* 48–63.

Herlihy, B., & Corey, G. (2006). *Boundary issues in counseling multiple roles and responsibilities* (2nd ed.). Alexandria, VA: American Counseling Association.

Kitchener, K. S. (1988). Dual relationships: What makes them so problematic? *Journal of Counseling and Development, 67,* 217–221.

Lazarus, A. A., & Zur, O. (2002). *Dual relationships and psychotherapy.* New York, NY: Springer.

Mamalakis, P. M. (2000). *Ethical issues of nonsexual dual relationships: A modified Delphi study* (Doctoral dissertation). Retrieved from ProQuest Dissertations and Theses. (275868289)

Pope, K. S. (1988). Dual relationships: A source of ethical, legal, and clinical problems. *Independent Practitioner, 8*(1), 17–25.

Pope, K. S. (1991). Dual relationships in psychotherapy. *Ethics & Behavior, 1,* 21–34.

Welfel, E. R. (2013). *Ethics in counseling and psychotherapy: Standards, research and emerging issues* (5th ed.). Belmont, CA: Cengage.

DUAL-EARNER FAMILIES

In contemporary U.S. society, it is common for both parents to work outside the home to provide for the financial needs of the family. The term *dual-earner family* describes such households. When working with dual-earner families, therapists should not make assumptions regarding why both individuals work, because the reasons vary. Regardless of the reasons associated with working outside the home, doing so can influence how the family unit operates. A number of individual and family-related concerns emerge when both parents work outside the home. Knowing the historical context of dual-earner families, as well as some of the struggles these families experience, will assist the therapist in helping the family function effectively and overcome the challenges they face.

Development of Dual-Earner Families

Before industrialization, many families functioned as an insular unit that worked to survive off the land. Work centered on the home and involved the effort of the whole family. Men and women assumed different roles in running the household. Historically, the expected role for women within the family was to bear children, assume the daily operations of the household, and work within the home setting. Mothers assumed the role of primary caregiver, and remained in the home to raise children and handle the domestic chores. The role of men was to provide for the family through labor and paid employment.

As society was transformed by industrialization, jobs were created. These jobs contributed to population growth within the cities where jobs were located. Simultaneously, opportunities for women to work outside of the home increased. From the 1940s until the present there has been an increase in the percentage of families where both parents are gainfully employed. According to the U.S. Bureau of the Census, by the early 2000s over 70% the nation's families were dual-earner households.

Reasons for Work Outside the Home

The reasons why both parents work outside of the home vary, but in many cases it is a matter of economic necessity. The increased cost of living and the pursuit of material benefits lead both parents to obtain gainful employment outside of the home. Families of lower socioeconomic status often require more than one income to cover basic necessities such as housing, food, transportation, and health care. However, not all dual-earner families are such because of financial circumstances.

As U.S. society accepted the notion of equal rights for women, opportunities for women to work in different occupational settings expanded. Women may choose to work outside the home because they enjoy the experience and have skills that are suited for employment in numerous occupations and industries. At the same time, it has been widely noted that inequality with men regarding professional advancement and pay continues to characterize many workplaces.

Concerns of Dual-Earner Families

A variety of concerns can emerge when both parents work outside of the home. Individuals and the family system experience stressors as well as conflict. Additionally, the influence of the work environment, expectations for performance, and relationships with bosses and coworkers can affect how the home life functions. In fact, work outside the home may influence the overall family culture, which includes shifting of roles, values, and habits.

Influence on Family Relationships

The category of dual-earner families applies to situations where both adults work full-time, when one adult works full-time and one works part-time, and when both adults work part-time. While all of the above employment statuses are considered dual-earner families, the number of hours worked influences the relationships between family members. Some studies have indicated that both parents working full-time has a negative influence on the development of children and adolescents, particularly if there are times when children are unsupervised. Lack of supervision can lead to increased likelihood of substance abuse or other psychological concerns. Additionally, the relationships children have with each parent may be affected. How children respond to the parents' working may range from indifference to anger and increased conflict. Additionally, with both parents spending time at jobs, children may be required to take on more responsibility in the home. This is particularly true as children age and become more responsible. The increase in responsibility may also result in conflict. However, parents who remain attentive and connected to their children can mitigate the negative effects.

When both adults work, their marital relationship may also be affected. Finding opportunities to spend quality time together can be a challenge. Additionally, the increase in stress from both work and family responsibilities can cause tension between the couple.

Furthermore, the relationships that children have with each other may change. Older siblings may take on caregiving duties while parents are at work. This change in roles may cause conflict between siblings. The increase in responsibility may also cause undue stress in trying to balance the multiple roles of child, sibling, student, caregiver, and friend, among others.

Influence of Gender

In studying the conflicts individuals experience between work and family within a dual-earner family, Tammy Allen and Lisa Finkelstein found differences between the conflicts men and women face. Family roles and expectations intruded into the work world of women more often than it did for men. However, men noted more instances of work interference with home life. Furthermore, the family's stage of development influenced the amount of conflict each parent experienced between work and family life. Men experienced relatively little change in the extent to which work interfered with family until the children had left home (the "empty-nest" stage of family life). Women experienced the most interference when the youngest child was in early and middle childhood. Other studies confirmed differences based on gender, including what causes conflict and how individuals cope with the conflict between home and work.

As noted, both compensation for paid employment and professional advancement opportunities differ between males and females. Additionally, some employers do not view male and female employees equally. Often supervisors expect women not only to meet job expectations, but also to excel in job performance. These beliefs are not always conscious but, rather, rooted in the socialization process that occurs within every society. However, the influence of gender does not just affect working adults.

Depending on gender, children have different views of their parents' working. Generally, girls experience the dual-earner household more positively than do boys. A study by Ann Crouter and Susan McHale noted that, when compared with girls from single-earner families, girls observing both parents working led to increases in confidence and high career aspirations. For boys, the experience may not be as positive. When compared with boys from single earner families, boys from dual-earner homes tend to have increased conflict with both mothers and siblings.

Child Care

Not all dual-earner families include children; however, many do or will in the future. As such, child care can require additional planning and schedule management. Women may experience a range of emotion when working while their children are in day care or after-school programs. Some women report feeling guilty while others are relieved to be able to maintain careers. Men, on the other hand, may not experience the same emotions regarding child care. While it could be a source of conflict between parents, fathers are usually socialized to believe child care responsibilities are chiefly in the realm of the mother.

Dual-Earner Families With Same-Sex Couples

The concept of family is rapidly expanding. With progress in granting equal rights for lesbian, gay, bisexual, transgender, queer/questioning (LGBTQ) individuals, many same-sex couples are building families. However, same-sex couples in dual-earner families have different challenges to manage. Researcher Kristin Perrone investigated same-sex, dual-earner couples, and explored the differences these couples experienced. The differences included work stability, availability of work benefits, and social connectedness to other families. A possible advantage for same-sex couples is the tendency to have more egalitarian relationships when compared with heterosexual couples.

Therapy With Dual-Earner Families

When dual-earner families experience trouble, marriage and family therapy is a valuable resource.

Therapists working with dual-earner families need to recognize how the work environments add to the complexity of the family system. Work can increase stress for the parents, which influences the home life. Therapists can help families recognize areas of conflict and help increase communication between family members. Additionally, therapists can help identify goals and strategies that increase the functioning of the entire family system.

Shauna Lynn Nefos Webb

See also Family Stress Adaptation Theory; Individual Family Culture; Parenting; Socioeconomic Status; Work Relationships

Further Readings

Allen, T. D., & Finkelstein, L. M. (2014). Work–family conflict among members of full-time dual-earner couples: An examination of family life stage, gender, and age. *Journal of Occupational Health Psychology, 19*(3), 376–384. doi:10.1037/a0036941

Crouter, A. C., & McHale, S. M. (2005). The long arm of the job revisited: Parenting in dual-earner families. In T. Luster & L. Okagaki (Eds.), *Parenting: An ecological perspective* (2nd ed., pp. 275–296). Mahwah, NJ: Erlbaum.

Perrone, K. M. (2005). Work-family interface for same-sex, dual-earner couples: Implications for counselors. *Career Development Quarterly, 53*(4), 317–324.

Schneider, B., & Waite, L. J. (2005). *Being together, working apart: Dual-career families and the work-life balance.* New York, NY: Cambridge University Press.

U.S. Bureau of the Census. (2012). *Statistical abstract of the United States: 2012.* Washington, DC: Author.

Duty to Warn and Protect

Intimate partner violence (IPV) is a significant public health concern requiring a concerted and coordinated effort among mental health and criminal justice professionals. A large percentage of victims of IPV are injured (i.e., 40% of females, 20% of males). In addition to the physical consequences of IPV, the emotional and economic costs of IPV on victims and perpetrators, as well as those around them (e.g., family members, friends, and members of the community at large) have been well documented. As a result, clinical and criminal justice settings are placing a greater emphasis on not only investigating and treating IPV, but also prevention activities that may reduce the likelihood of victimization. Practice in law and social sciences is intertwined when determining the appropriate response to these phenomena. Given the data indicating the prevalence of violence among couples, this information has important implications for marriage and family therapists regarding their professional obligation and mandate to warn potential victims. According to the American Association for Marriage and Family Therapy, the duty to warn refers to the therapist's obligation to take reasonable precautions to provide protection from violent behavior expressed by clients. The client shall only be discharged by the marriage and family therapist once reasonable efforts have been made to communicate the threat to the victim or victims and to a law enforcement agency. However, as recently noted, 76% of psychologists were misinformed about their state laws, believing that they had a legal responsibility to warn when they didn't or assuming that warning was their only legal option when other choices did not require a breach of confidentiality. Throughout this entry an overview of important court cases, limits to confidentiality, and the impact of the duty to warn on marriage and family therapists will be presented and explored.

Overview of the *Tarasoff* Rulings

The importance and complexity of the issues surrounding therapist disclosure of intent to harm is best exemplified in the landmark case of *Tarasoff v. Regents of the University of California*. The rulings in these cases (i.e., *Tarasoff* 1974; *Tarasoff* 1976) have had a tremendous impact on state and federal laws regarding privilege and confidentiality, therapist liability, and professional standards for practice. The California Supreme Court, in two rulings, established a precedent in that state that counselors and other mental health professionals have an obligation to warn and protect third parties. In 1969, Prosenjit Poddar, a student at the University of California, Berkeley, disclosed to his therapist at the university counseling center that he intended to kill his former girlfriend, Tatiana Tarasoff. Upon hearing this information, the therapist contacted the campus police (both verbally and in writing) about his client's intentions and consulted with his supervisor. Campus police interviewed Poddar about this threat, but ultimately released him, deciding there was not enough information to act upon. Poddar did not return to counseling and the therapist did not follow up with him or inform Tarasoff (or her family) of these threats. Two months later Poddar murdered Tarasoff, upon her return from a trip to Brazil. Tarasoff's family filed a lawsuit against the University of California for failing to warn Tarasoff of imminent danger. The case was eventually heard by the California Supreme Court (1974), which ruled the treating therapist has a responsibility to warn third parties of foreseeable danger; it also noted that privilege ends where public peril begins. In response to this ruling, the defendants successfully petitioned the court for a rehearing. The case eventually ended up back in California Supreme Court (1976). In its second decision, the court expanded on its previous ruling to include a duty to protect the intended victim against danger using various steps including warning the intended victim, notifying the police, or any steps necessary under the circumstances.

The ruling in each of these cases set the standards for privacy rights in the counseling process and extended the responsibilities of therapists to third parties (i.e., nonclients). Simply stated, in 1974, the court ruled that therapists have a duty to warn, while in 1976, the court ruled that mental health practitioners had a duty to protect and use reasonable care to protect the intended victim. Interestingly, the first Tarasoff case is often mistakenly believed to contain the core ethic (i.e., the duty to warn); however, it is the ruling in the second case (i.e., duty to protect) that serves as the clinical guideline. These cases are important because they mark the first time mental health professionals were deemed to have a professional duty to someone other than a client.

Breaching Confidentiality

Confidentiality is critical to the marriage and family therapy process and is an ancient concept in the medical field. It is through this protection that clients can feel safe disclosing embarrassing, damaging, and sensitive information in treatment. The implications of the *Tarasoff* cases can be found in the number of U.S. states that enacted legislation to define the duty to protect (or warn) in law. The court ruled that public peril superseded the client's protective privilege. This decision resulted in the therapist's legal duty to warn the intended victim. However, given that states differ in their interpretation of the mandated reporting and confidentiality, therapists must be aware of their responsibilities according to the law of the state in which they practice.

In potential cases of third-party victimization, the therapist faces a difficult clinical and ethical dilemma: Breach confidentiality or possibly face legal consequences. However, a client's threat to a third party may not always be clear and thus places the therapist in a precarious situation.

Therapists' Values and the Decision to Break Confidentiality

While a number of studies have examined the confidentiality process, there is a dearth of information examining therapists' knowledge of their duty to protect third-party victims and even less exploring the factors that influence a therapist's decision to breach confidentiality to warn a third party. Researchers explored the differences among therapists from a variety of backgrounds including professional organizations, work settings, and personal characteristics about their beliefs, experiences, and behaviors in handling confidentiality with clients. Participants ($N = 114$) were randomly selected from the American Psychological Association, American School Counselor Association, and

American Mental Health Counselor Association, and a survey was mailed along with a return address envelope. The Therapy with Clients Survey Measure was used to assess therapists' views of the way they manage confidentiality issues in therapy. Results revealed differences in therapist behavior in terms of how they handled confidentiality issues with clients of diverse ages. More specifically, findings revealed differences in the ways of obtaining informed consent, approach to discussing confidentiality, information shared with parents or guardians, and the influence of client-specific factors on the management of confidentiality.

Bardia Monshi and Verena Zieglmayer describe the results of an ethnographic study of patient–healer relationships in Sri Lanka. Results indicated that participants' view of privacy differed greatly from Western views and that the privacy protections used in the study created discomfort among participants. The study took place at the University of Human Sciences in the Principality of Liechtenstein. According to Monshi and Zieglmayer, the study was pluralistic and integrative; in particular, results from quantitative, qualitative, and introspective procedures were used to allow the investigators to assess a participant from different perspectives. The sample consisted of 47 Sri Lankans and 9 Germans. Data collection methods included semistructured interviews, behavioral observation, qualitative experiments, diaries, and continual conversations between the researchers and the interpreter. The authors conclude that any definition of privacy must take into account the cultural variations in defining and understanding this concept. The study has important implications for practitioners, who may be working with a very diverse caseload, yet applying confidentiality as a one-size-fits-all approach.

Implications for Marriage and Family Therapists

As a result of the *Tarasoff* ruling, many states have enacted laws outlining the responsibilities of mental health professionals to third parties who may be at risk for violence. Yet there is a great deal of variability among states in terms of how to handle these situations. For example, some states have established that therapists and other mental health professionals have a specific duty to warn, other states mandate the responsibility is to protect, still others permit (but do not require) a breach of confidentiality, and a few states have not ruled on the issue. More specifically, at the time of writing, 23 states have enacted legislation requiring either a duty to warn or duty to protect, 13 states permit a breach of confidentiality, and 7 states have not ruled on the issue. Perhaps complicating matters further, in California, the duty to protect has further broadened to include situations in which the therapist receives third-party information about the actual dangerousness of the client.

Given the variability interpreting these statutes among states, coupled with the fact that no two states approach this issue identically, it is imperative that marriage and family therapists keep up with the laws and standards regarding professional responsibilities to third parties in order to ensure competent clinical practice. In fact, as argued, general principles regarding the decision to breach confidentiality should not serve as a substitute for consulting with a competent and knowledgeable attorney in this area and should be examined on a case-by-case basis and interpreted within the context of the jurisdiction within which the situation falls. Along these lines, an improper breach of confidentiality may leave the therapist open to potential civil liability. As recently noted, 22 states with a duty to warn provide protections against civil liability, but only when the breach of confidentiality meets the standards for doing so.

While the duty to protect a third party from harm is discretionary in many states, there may be consequences for failure to do so. Further complicating this matter is the fact that warning third parties of potential danger from the client does not guarantee safety; the person warned may disbelieve the client, become panicked to the point of not being able to care for themselves, or become violent against the client. In addition to legal and ethical obligations, the counselor's decision to warn a third party of potential danger will often be influenced by personal and religious values as well.

Because of the multiple people involved, confidentiality can be very complicated in marital and family therapy. The American Psychological Association (APA) and American Association of Marriage and Family Therapy (AAMFT) recommend that policies concerning confidentiality be discussed at the beginning of therapy. There are four conceptually distinct variations of confidentiality that could be used with couples or families: (1) treat information disclosed individually as confidential; (2) inform each client that no information is confidential; (3) allow certain information to be confidential as a matter of personal privacy; or (4) agree to allow certain information to be temporarily kept confidential, but it must be disclosed at a later time. Deciding which of these approaches to use is not a mere academic exercise; it may have very serious implications depending on the client (or family, couple) scenario. For example, a therapist treating a couple is informed by one of the partners that he or she is having an affair. The type of confidentiality approach chosen at the onset of treatment will dictate how the therapist proceeds. In cases of couples or family treatment, the therapist should outline the rules of treatment, defining who the patients are, as well as confidentiality and the limitations to it.

Keith Klostermann and Emma Papagni

See also Confidentiality; Domestic Violence; Elder Abuse

Further Readings

Gutman, A. R., & Sadoff, R. L. (2014). Patient privilege and dangerousness: Should duty to warn affect confidentiality? *Journal of the American Academy of Psychiatry and the Law, 42*(2), 245–247.

Johnson, R., Persad, G., & Sisti, D. (2014). The *Tarasoff* rule: The implications of interstate variation and gaps in professional training. *Journal of the American Academy of Psychiatry and the Law, 42*(4), 469–477.

Monshi, B., & Zieglmayer, V. (2004). The problem of privacy in transcultural research: Reflections on an ethnographic study in Sri Lanka. *Ethics and Behavior, 14*(4), 305–312. doi:10.1207/s15327019eb1404_2

Sonne, J. L. (2012). Duty to protect: Reporting client threat of harm to another. In J. L. Sonne (Ed.), *PsycEssentials: A pocket resource for mental health practitioners* (pp. 151–161). Washington, DC: American Psychological Association.

The SAGE Encyclopedia of Marriage, Family, and Couples Counseling

Editorial Board

Editors
Jon Carlson
Adler University

Shannon B. Dermer
Governors State University

Managing Editors
Brenna R. Frayn
Governors State University

Katie Paulson
Governors State University

Editorial Board

James Robert Bitter
East Tennessee State University

Scott Browning
Chestnut Hill College

William J. Doherty
University of Minnesota

Leslie Greenberg
York University

Katherine M. Helm
Lewis University

Alan J. Hovestadt
Western Michigan University

Jay Lebow
Northwestern University

Susan H. McDaniel
University of Rochester

Fred P. Piercy
University of Vermont

Robert L. Smith
Texas A&M–Corpus Christi

The SAGE Encyclopedia of Marriage, Family, and Couples Counseling

Volume 2

Editors

Jon Carlson
Adler University

Shannon B. Dermer
Governors State University

Los Angeles | London | New Delhi | Singapore | Washington DC | Melbourne

FOR INFORMATION:

SAGE Publications, Inc.
2455 Teller Road
Thousand Oaks, California 91320
E-mail: order@sagepub.com

SAGE Publications Ltd.
1 Oliver's Yard
55 City Road
London, EC1Y 1SP
United Kingdom

SAGE Publications India Pvt. Ltd.
B 1/I 1 Mohan Cooperative Industrial Area
Mathura Road, New Delhi 110 044
India

SAGE Publications Asia-Pacific Pte. Ltd.
3 Church Street
#10-04 Samsung Hub
Singapore 049483

Acquisitions Editor: Andrew Boney
Editorial Assistant: Jordan Enobakhare
Developmental Editor: Sanford Robinson
Production Editor: Tracy Buyan
Reference Systems Manager: Leticia Gutierrez
Copy Editors: Diane DiMura, Talia Greenberg, Megan Markanich, Terri Lee Paulsen, Gretchen Treadwell
Typesetter: C&M Digitals (P) Ltd.
Proofreaders: Lawrence W. Baker, Caryne Brown, Sarah Duffy, Scott Oney
Indexer: David Luljak
Cover Designer: Candice Harman
Marketing Manager: Leah Watson

Copyright © 2017 by SAGE Publications, Inc.

All rights reserved. No part of this book may be reproduced or utilized in any form or by any means, electronic or mechanical, including photocopying, recording, or by any information storage and retrieval system, without permission in writing from the publisher.

All trade names and trademarks recited, referenced, or reflected herein are the property of their respective owners who retain all rights thereto.

Printed in the United States of America

Library of Congress Cataloging-in-Publication Data

Names: Carlson, Jon, editor. | Dermer, Shannon B., editor.

Title: The SAGE encyclopedia of marriage, family, and couples counseling / editors, Jon Carlson, Shannon B. Dermer.

Other titles: Encyclopedia of marriage, family, and couples counseling

Description: Thousand Oaks, California : SAGE Publications, Inc., [2016] | "A SAGE Reference publication." | Includes bibliographical references and index.

Identifiers: LCCN 2016025752 | ISBN 9781483369556 (hardcover : alk. paper)

Subjects: | MESH: Psychotherapy, Group | Counseling | Interpersonal Relations | Family Relations | Encyclopedias

Classification: LCC BF636.7.G76 | NLM WM 13 | DDC 158.3/5—dc23
LC record available at https://lccn.loc.gov/2016025752

This book is printed on acid-free paper.

16 17 18 19 20 10 9 8 7 6 5 4 3 2 1

Contents

Volume 2

List of Entries *vii*

Reader's Guide *xv*

Entries

E	487	I	825
F	589	J	925
G	707	K	937
H	759		

List of Entries

Acceptance and Commitment Therapy
Acculturation
Active Parenting
Adjustment Disorder in Adolescents
Adlerian Family Therapy
Adlerian Open-Forum Family Counseling
Adolescent Behavior Disorders
Adolescent Behavior Problems
Adolescent Mental Health
Adoption
Adoption, Cross-Cultural and Interracial
Adoptive Families
Adult Attachment Assessments
Adult Development
Affect Regulation
African American Families
Aging and Caregiving
Alcohol and Substance Abuse
American Association for Marriage and Family Therapy
Anger Management
Anxiety
Anxiety Disorders in Adolescents
Asian American Families
Assertiveness
Assessment, Biopsychosocial
Assessment, Suicide
Assimilation: Immigrants and Refugees
Attachment
Attachment and Adolescents
Attachment and Health
Attachment and Romantic Love
Attachment Styles
Attachment Theory
Attachment-Based Family Therapy
Attention-Deficit and Disruptive Behavior Disorders

Attunement, Clinician
Attunement in Relationships
Authoritative Parenting
Autism and Children
Autism Spectrum Disorder
Avoidance

Behavioral Family Therapy
Beliefs and Values
Bereavement
Bereavement Counseling
Best Interests of the Child
Bibliotherapy. *See* Self-Help
Bilingual Families
Birth Control and Contraception
Blended Families. *See* Stepfamilies
Body Dysmorphic Disorder in Adolescents
Bonding
Boundaries
Bowen Family Systems Theory
Brief Adlerian Couples Therapy
Brief Family Therapy

CACREP. *See* Competency-Based Standards for Marriage, Couple, and Family Counseling; Council for Accreditation of Counseling and Related Educational Programs
Career Planning and Couples/Families
Caregivers
Certified Family Life Educator
Chaos Family Therapy
Child Behavior Problems
Child Guidance Movement
Child Maltreatment
Child Protective Services
Child-Centered Parenting
Childhood Anxiety

Childhood Obesity, Prevention and Treatment of
Childless Couples
Child–Parent Relationship Therapy
Children With Chronic Illness
Children With Special Needs in Family Therapy
Choice Theory and Reality Therapy
Chosen Families
Chronic Illness With Couples and Families
Cinematherapy
Circular Questions. See Questions: Open, Closed, and Circular
Circularity and Linearity
Circumplex Model
Clinical Case Conceptualization With Couples and Families
Clinical Interviews With Couples and Families
Clinical Practice
Clinical Versus Statistical Significance
Clinician-Directed, Solution-Focused Supervision
Cognitive Maps and Couples
Cognitive-Behavioral Couples Therapy
Cognitive-Behavioral Family Therapy
Cohesion
Collaborative Couples Therapy
Collaborative Language Systems
Collaborative Therapy. See Collaborative Language Systems
Commitment
Common Factors
Communication Disorders
Communication Errors/Problems in Couples and Families
Communication in Couples and Families
Community Programs
Compassion
Competency-Based Standards for Marriage, Couple, and Family Counseling
Complementary and Symmetrical Relationships
Compulsive Sexual Behavior
Conduct Disorder
Confidentiality
Conflict in Couples and Families
Conflict Resolution
Conflict Styles
Confrontation

Conjoint Family Therapy
Constructivism
Contextual Family Therapy
Core Competencies for Marriage and Family Therapists
Cost–Benefit Analysis
Cotherapy Team
Council for Accreditation of Counseling and Related Educational Programs
Couple and Family Forensics
Couple Development
Couples, Quality Time
Couples and Marriage Counseling
Couples Therapy Research
Court-Mandated Clients
Crisis Intervention With Couples and Families
Critical Theory
Crucible
Cultural Issues in Couples and Families
Custody Evaluations
Cutting/Self-Mutilation. See Self-Injury
Cybernetics

Dating Coaching
Dating Relationship Dissolution
Death, Parents of Deceased Children
Death and Dying
Debt and Financial Strain
Decision-Making
Delphi Research Method
Depression in Adolescents
Depression in Children
Depression in Couples and Families
Developmental Model of Marriage
Differentiation
Discernment Counseling
Disinhibited Social Engagement Disorder in Children
Diversity
Divorce and Separation
Divorce Therapy
Domestic Violence
Double Bind Theory
DSM and V-Codes
Dual and Multiple Relationships

Dual-Earner Families
Duty to Warn and Protect

Earned Attachment
Eating Disorders
Ecological Systems
Eco-Map
Ecosystemic Structural Family Therapy
Ecosystems Perspective
Effectiveness Research
Elder Abuse
Elimination Disorders in Children
Emotional Disengagement
Emotional Intelligence, Children
Emotional Intelligence, Families
Emotionally Focused Therapy for Couples
Empathy
Empirically Validated Models
Empowerment in Families
Enactments
Engendering Hope
Entitlement
Epistemology in Family Therapy
Equine-Assisted Family Therapy
Erectile Disorder
Ericksonian Family Therapy
Ethical Codes
Ethical Decision-Making
Ethnicity
Evidence-Based Practice With Couples and Families
Experiential Family Therapy
Externalizing Behaviors
Extramarital Affairs and Infidelity

Faith-Based Therapy
Families and Poverty
Families and Substance Abuse
Family and Medical Leave Act of 1993
Family Assessment, Models of
Family Life Cycle
Family Life Educators
Family Mediation
Family Mode Deactivation Therapy
Family Myth
Family of Origin

Family Reconstruction
Family Resilience
Family Resource Management
Family Rituals
Family Strengths
Family Stress
Family Stress Adaptation Theory
Family Values
Feedback. *See* Positive and Negative Feedback
Female Orgasmic Disorder
Female Sexual Interest/Arousal Disorder
Feminist Family Therapy
Feminization of Poverty
Fetishes
Fidelity
First-Order Change
Focal Family Therapy
Forgiveness
Foster Children
Friendship
Functional Assessment and Children
Functional Family Therapy
Functionalism
Fusion

Gambling, Compulsive
Gender- and Culture-Sensitive Therapies
Gender Dysphoria
Gender Issues
Gender Orientation, Gender Identity, and Gender Expression
Gender Roles
General Systems Theory
Genito-Pelvic Pain/Penetration Disorder
Genograms
Gestalt Family Therapy
Goals, Treatment
Gottman Method Couples Therapy
Grief Counseling
Group Family Therapy
Group Parenting Classes

Health Issues
Healthy Marriage and Responsible Fatherhood
Hierarchy
HIPAA Standards

Hispanic Healthy Marriage Initiative
Hoarding
Holism
Home-Based Therapy
Homelessness
Homelessness and Youth
Homeostasis
Homework Assignments in Therapy
Homicide
Hope-Focused Approach to Couple Enrichment in Counseling
Hospice
Human Sexual Response
Humanistic Family Therapy
Hypnosis
Hypothesis, Systemic

IAMFC. *See* International Association of Marriage and Family Counselors
Identified Patient
Imago Relationship Therapy
Immigrant Families
Incest
Individual and Family Development
Individual Family Culture
Individual Versus Family Therapy
Infertility
Informed Consent for Research
Informed Consent in Clinical Work
In-Law Relationships
Integrating Systemic and Individual Theories
Integrative Couples Therapy
Intellectual Disability and Autism
Intercultural Marriage and Family
Intergenerational Loyalty
Intergenerational Trauma
Intermittent Explosive Disorder in Adolescents
Internal Family Systems Model
International Association of Marriage and Family Counselors
International Classification of Diseases (ICD)
International Family Therapy
Interpersonal Neurobiology, Attachment and
Interpersonal Neurobiology, Couples and
Interpersonal Neurobiology, Parenting and
Interpersonal Violence
Interracial Marriages and Families

Intimacy, Specific Threats to
Isomorphism

Job Loss
Joining
Juvenile Firesetter Interventions

Kinship Care

Latino Families
Legal Issues in Parenting
LGBT Families
Licensure and Certification
Life Balance
Life Events
Life Transitions
Listening, Empathic
Live Supervision
Loneliness
Loss
Love, Physiology of
Love, Theories of
Love, Types of
Love and Rituals
Love Languages

Male Hypoactive Sexual Desire Disorder
Mandated Reporter
Marital Distress
Marital Group Therapy
Marriage, Arranged
Marriage, First and Second
Marriage and Health
Marriage Education
Marriage Encounter
Marriage Enrichment
Marriage Myths
Marriage Versus Civil Unions
Marriage-Friendly Therapy
Mate Selection
Media in Family Therapy
Medical Family Therapy
Men in Counseling
Mental Health, Systemic Perspective
Metacommunication
Metaphors
Milan Team

Military Couples and Families
Mindfulness
Mindfulness and Children
Mindfulness and Couples
Mindfulness and Sex
Miracle Question
Mood Disorders in Adolescents
Mood Disorders in Children
Moral Dimensions of Therapy
Morphogenesis
Morphostasis
Mother-Blaming
Motivational Interviewing
Multicultural Counseling Competence
Multiculturalism
Multiple Family Therapy
Multiple Relationships. See Dual and Multiple Relationships
Multisystemic Therapy
Muslim American Families

Narrative Therapy
National Marriage Initiative
Native American Families
Network Therapy
Neuro-Linguistic Programming
Neutrality and Curiosity
No-Harm Contracts
Non–Rapid Eye Movement Sleep Arousal Disorders in Children
Nonresidential Fathers
Nonverbal Communication
Normalizing
No-Secrets Contracts
Nuclear Family
Nudity: Beliefs and Values

Object Relations Theory
Online Dating
Open Relationships
Oppositional Defiant Disorder
Outcome Research

Paradoxes and Paradoxical Intervention
Paraphilic Disorders
Parent Effectiveness Training (P.E.T.)
Parent Management Training

Parent Study Groups
Parent–Adolescent Relations
Parental Acceptance–Rejection Theory
Parental Alienation Syndrome
Parental Stress: Effects on Children
Parent–Child Communication
Parentification and Diverse Family Systems
Parenting
Parenting Education
Parenting Styles
Patriarchy
Peer Counseling
Person of the Therapist
Play Family Therapy
Polyamory
Polygamy
Pornography
Positive and Negative Feedback
Positive Psychology
Postdoctoral Training
Postmodern Therapies
Postpartum Depression
Posttraumatic Stress Disorder in Children
Poverty and Family Development
Power Issues in Couples
Practice Management
Pregnancy
Pregnancy and Sexuality
Premarital Counseling
Premature Ejaculation
Prenuptial Agreements
PREPARE/ENRICH
Presenting Problems
Prevention Research
Primary and Secondary Emotions
Process Research
Professional Associations
Progress Notes for Couples and Families
Psychoanalytic Family Therapy
Psychobiology of Attachment
Psychoeducation
Public Health Code
Punctuation

Qualitative Research
Quantitative Research
Questions: Open, Closed, and Circular

Racial Disparities in Foster Care
Racism
Reactive Attachment Disorder in Children
Reconciliation
Recursiveness
Reflecting Team
Relational Diagnoses
Relational-Cultural Therapy
Relationship Enhancement
Release of Information for Couples and Families
Religion
Remarriage. *See* Marriage, First and Second; Stepfamilies
Resilience
Resistance
Respect
Restoration Therapy
Retirement
Rituals in Family Therapy
Role-Playing
Romance
Rule-Setting
Rural Families

Same-Sex Couples
Scales, Children
Scales, Couple and Marital
Scales, Family
Scaling Questions
Scapegoating
Schizophrenia and Families
Schools, Family Involvement in
Second-Order Change
Second-Order Family Therapy
Secrets
Self of the Therapist
Self-Care Practices for the Trauma-Informed Couple and Family Counselor
Self-Esteem
Self-Esteem in Children
Self-Help
Self-Injury
Sensate Focus
Sentiment Override, Positive and Negative
Sex, Definition of
Sex Positivity

Sex Researchers
Sex Therapy
Sexual Abuse
Sexual Assault and Rape
Sexual Assessment/History
Sexual Dysfunction
Sexual Enhancement, Sexual Toys
Sexual Health
Sexual History
Sexual Intimacy
Sexual Minorities
Sexual Orientation, Attraction, and Identity
Sexual Prejudice
Sexual Relationships With Clients
Sexual Toys/Sexual Aids
Sexuality and Religion
Sexuality Education
Sexually Transmitted Infections
Sibling Relationships
Single-Parent Families
Social Constructionism
Social Support
Socioeconomic Status
Solution-Focused Brief Therapy
Somatic Symptom Disorder and Related Disorders in Adolescents
Spirituality
Stages of Family Therapy
Statutory Rape
Stepfamilies
Stillbirth and Miscarriage
Strategic Family Therapy
Stress Management
Structural Determinism
Structural Family Therapy
Structural Maps
Substance Use Disorders in Adolescence
Suicide
Supervision
Supervision, Approved Supervisor in Marriage and Family Therapy
Supervision, Developmental Model
Supervision, Gatekeeping
Supervision, Individual and Group
Supervision Contract
Supervision of Supervision

Supervision Philosophy Statement
Supervision Theories
Support Groups
Symbolic Interactionism
Systemic Family Therapy
Systems, Subsystems, and Metasystems
Systems Theory

Technology and Families/Marriage
Teen Parenting
Termination
Therapeutic Alliance
Therapeutic Assessment
Therapeutic Contract
Therapeutic Impasses
Therapists' Values
TIME Program. *See* Training in Marriage Enrichment (TIME) Program
Torture Treatment
Training and Licensure

Training in Marriage Enrichment (TIME) Program
Transgender Families
Transgenerational Family Therapy
Transracial Adoption
Trauma and Children
Trauma and Families
Trauma-Focused Cognitive-Behavioral Therapy
Treatment Planning With Couples and Families
Triangulation
Trust

Urban Families

Virginia Satir Model

Women's Project, The
Work Relationships
World Association for Sexual Health
World Health Organization

Reader's Guide

Assessments
Adult Attachment Assessments
Assessment, Biopsychosocial
Assessment, Suicide
Circumplex Model
Clinical Case Conceptualization With Couples and Families
Clinical Interviews With Couples and Families
Common Factors
Custody Evaluations
DSM and V-Codes
Ecological Systems
Eco-Map
Family Assessment, Models of
Functional Assessment and Children
Genograms
Interpersonal Violence
Love, Physiology of
Love, Types of
Love Languages
Marital Distress
Marriage Education
Nonverbal Communication
Parent–Child Communication
PREPARE/ENRICH
Progress Notes for Couples and Families
Scales, Children
Scales, Couple and Marital
Scales, Family
Scaling Questions
Sentiment Override, Positive and Negative
Sexual Assessment/History
Sexual Health
Sexual History
Suicide
Therapeutic Assessment
Treatment Planning With Couples and Families

Attachment
Adult Attachment Assessments
Affect Regulation
Attachment
Attachment and Adolescents
Attachment and Health
Attachment and Romantic Love
Attachment Styles
Attachment Theory
Attachment-Based Family Therapy
Attunement in Relationships
Bonding
Child-Centered Parenting
Earned Attachment
Emotional Disengagement
Emotionally Focused Therapy for Couples
Interpersonal Neurobiology, Attachment and
Primary and Secondary Emotions
Psychobiology of Attachment

Communication
Assertiveness
Avoidance
Collaborative Language Systems
Communication Disorders
Communication Errors/Problems in Couples and Families
Communication in Couples and Families
Conflict in Couples and Families
Conflict Resolution
Conflict Styles
Confrontation
Disinhibited Social Engagement Disorder in Children
Empathy
Forgiveness

Love Languages
Metacommunication
Metaphors
Nonverbal Communication
Parent–Child Communication
Power Issues in Couples
Respect
Secrets
Social Constructionism
Symbolic Interactionism
Therapeutic Impasses
Trust

Coping

Bereavement
Children With Chronic Illness
Chronic Illness With Couples and Families
Conflict Styles
Death, Parents of Deceased Children
Empowerment in Families
Engendering Hope
Families and Substance Abuse
Family Resilience
Family Strengths
Family Stress
Family Stress Adaptation Theory
Forgiveness
Hope-Focused Approach to Couple Enrichment in Counseling
Parental Stress: Effects on Children
Reconciliation
Resilience
Self-Esteem
Self-Esteem in Children
Social Support
Stillbirth and Miscarriage
Stress Management

Couple, Marriage, Family Policy

Best Interests of the Child
Child Protective Services
Family and Medical Leave Act of 1993
Healthy Marriage and Responsible Fatherhood
Hispanic Healthy Marriage Initiative
Marriage Versus Civil Unions
National Marriage Initiative

Public Health Code
Self-Esteem in Children
Social Support

Diagnosing and Disorders

Adjustment Disorder in Adolescents
Adolescent Behavior Disorders
Adolescent Behavior Problems
Adolescent Mental Health
Alcohol and Substance Abuse
Anxiety
Anxiety Disorders in Adolescents
Attention-Deficit and Disruptive Behavior Disorders
Autism Spectrum Disorder
Child Behavior Problems
Childhood Anxiety
Childhood Obesity, Prevention and Treatment of
Compulsive Sexual Behavior
Conduct Disorder
Depression in Adolescents
Depression in Children
Depression in Couples and Families
Disinhibited Social Engagement Disorder in Children
DSM and V-Codes
Eating Disorders
Elimination Disorders in Children
Erectile Disorder
Female Orgasmic Disorder
Female Sexual Interest/Arousal Disorder
Fetishes
Functional Assessment and Children
Gambling, Compulsive
Gender Dysphoria
Genito-Pelvic Pain/Penetration Disorder
Hoarding
Intermittent Explosive Disorder in Adolescents
International Classification of Diseases (ICD)
Male Hypoactive Sexual Desire Disorder
Mood Disorders in Adolescents
Mood Disorders in Children
Non–Rapid Eye Movement Sleep Arousal Disorders in Children
Oppositional Defiant Disorder

Paraphilic Disorders
Parental Alienation Syndrome
Postpartum Depression
Posttraumatic Stress Disorder in Children
Premature Ejaculation
Reactive Attachment Disorder in Children
Relational Diagnoses
Schizophrenia and Families
Sexual Dysfunction
Sexually Transmitted Infections
Somatic Symptom Disorder and Related Disorders in Adolescents
Substance Use Disorders in Adolescence

Diversity
Acculturation
Adoption, Cross-Cultural and Interracial
Adoptive Families
African American Families
Asian American Families
Assimilation: Immigrants and Refugees
Beliefs and Values
Bilingual Families
Children With Special Needs in Family Therapy
Chosen Families
Cultural Issues in Couples and Families
Diversity
Empowerment in Families
Ethnicity
Faith-Based Therapy
Families and Substance Abuse
Family Resilience
Family Values
Feminization of Poverty
Foster Children
Gender- and Culture-Sensitive Therapies
Gender Issues
Gender Orientation, Gender Identity, and Gender Expression
Gender Roles
Immigrant Families
Individual Family Culture
Intellectual Disability and Autism
Intercultural Marriage and Family
Interracial Marriages and Families
Kinship Care

Latino Families
LGBT Families
Marriage, Arranged
Marriage Versus Civil Unions
Men in Counseling
Military Couples and Families
Mother-Blaming
Multiculturalism
Muslim American Families
Native American Families
Nudity: Beliefs and Values
Parentification and Diverse Family Systems
Patriarchy
Racial Disparities in Foster Care
Racism
Relational-Cultural Therapy
Religion
Resilience
Rural Families
Same-Sex Couples
Sexual Minorities
Sexual Orientation, Attraction, and Identity
Sexual Prejudice
Sexuality and Religion
Single-Parent Families
Socioeconomic Status
Spirituality
Stepfamilies
Therapists' Values
Transgender Families
Transracial Adoption
Urban Families
Women's Project, The

Financial Issues
Career Planning and Couples/Families
Debt and Financial Strain
Dual-Earner Families
Families and Poverty
Family Resource Management
Feminization of Poverty
Gambling, Compulsive
Hoarding
Homelessness
Homelessness and Youth
Job Loss

Life Balance
Poverty and Family Development
Prenuptial Agreements
Retirement
Socioeconomic Status
Work Relationships

Intimacy
Attachment
Attachment and Adolescents
Attachment and Health
Attachment and Romantic Love
Bonding
Cognitive Maps and Couples
Commitment
Compassion
Confrontation
Couple Development
Couples, Quality Time
Dating Coaching
Dating Relationship Dissolution
Empathy
Fidelity
Forgiveness
Friendship
In-Law Relationships
Intimacy, Specific Threats to
Loneliness
Love, Physiology of
Love, Theories of
Love, Types of
Love and Rituals
Love Languages
Marital Distress
Marriage, Arranged
Marriage, First and Second
Mate Selection
Online Dating
Open Relationships
Polyamory
Polygamy
Reconciliation
Relationship Enhancement
Romance
Secrets
Sexual Intimacy

Sibling Relationships
Trust
Work Relationships

Life Events/Transitions
Adolescent Behavior Problems
Adolescent Mental Health
Adoption
Adult Development
Aging and Caregiving
Autism and Children
Bereavement Counseling
Career Planning and Couples/Families
Caregivers
Child Behavior Problems
Childhood Anxiety
Childless Couples
Chosen Families
Chronic Illness With Couples and Families
Couple Development
Couples, Quality Time
Dating Coaching
Dating Relationship Dissolution
Death, Parents of Deceased Children
Death and Dying
Divorce and Separation
Divorce Therapy
Dual-Earner Families
Families and Poverty
Family Life Cycle
Family Reconstruction
Family Stress
Grief Counseling
Health Issues
Homelessness
Homelessness and Youth
Hospice
Individual and Family Development
Job Loss
Life Balance
Life Events
Life Transitions
Loss
Marriage, First and Second
Parent–Adolescent Relations
Parenting

Postpartum Depression
Posttraumatic Stress Disorder in Children
Poverty and Family Development
Power Issues in Couples
Prenuptial Agreements
Retirement
Rural Families
Sibling Relationships
Single-Parent Families
Spirituality
Stepfamilies
Stillbirth and Miscarriage
Suicide
Teen Parenting
Transracial Adoption
Urban Families

Major Concepts
Affect Regulation
Attachment
Attachment Styles
Attunement, Clinician
Attunement in Relationships
Boundaries
Circumplex Model
Cohesion
Complementary and Symmetrical Relationships
Crucible
Cybernetics
Differentiation
Ecological Systems
Eco-Map
Ecosystems Perspective
Emotional Disengagement
Entitlement
Epistemology in Family Therapy
Family Myth
Family of Origin
Family Rituals
Family Strengths
Family Values
First-Order Change
Fusion
Gender Roles
Hierarchy
Holism

Homeostasis
Hypothesis, Systemic
Identified Patient
Individual Family Culture
Intergenerational Loyalty
Intergenerational Trauma
Isomorphism
Kinship Care
Marriage Education
Marriage Encounter
Marriage Myths
Morphogenesis
Morphostasis
Mother-Blaming
Neutrality and Curiosity
Nuclear Family
Paradoxes and Paradoxical Intervention
Patriarchy
Person of the Therapist
Positive and Negative Feedback
Presenting Problems
Primary and Secondary Emotions
Questions: Open, Closed, and Circular
Recursiveness
Resistance
Scaling Questions
Scapegoating
Second-Order Change
Sentiment Override, Positive and Negative
Social Constructionism
Social Support
Structural Determinism
Structural Maps
Symbolic Interactionism
Systems Theory
Triangulation

Models, Interventions, Techniques
Acceptance and Commitment Therapy
Adlerian Family Therapy
Adlerian Open-Forum Family Counseling
Attachment-Based Family Therapy
Behavioral Family Therapy
Brief Adlerian Couples Therapy
Brief Family Therapy
Chaos Family Therapy

Childhood Obesity, Prevention and Treatment of
Child–Parent Relationship Therapy
Choice Theory and Reality Therapy
Cinematherapy
Circularity and Linearity
Cognitive Maps and Couples
Cognitive-Behavioral Couples Therapy
Cognitive-Behavioral Family Therapy
Collaborative Couples Therapy
Collaborative Language Systems
Community Programs
Conflict Resolution
Conjoint Family Therapy
Constructivism
Contextual Family Therapy
Couple and Family Forensics
Couples and Marriage Counseling
Crisis Intervention With Couples and Families
Discernment Counseling
Divorce Therapy
Ecosystemic Structural Family Therapy
Emotional Intelligence, Children
Emotional Intelligence, Families
Emotionally Focused Therapy for Couples
Empirically Validated Models
Enactments
Equine-Assisted Family Therapy
Ericksonian Family Therapy
Experiential Family Therapy
Externalizing Behaviors
Faith-Based Therapy
Family Mode Deactivation Therapy
Feminist Family Therapy
Focal Family Therapy
Functional Family Therapy
Gender- and Culture-Sensitive Therapies
Gestalt Family Therapy
Goals, Treatment
Gottman Method Couples Therapy
Grief Counseling
Group Family Therapy
Home-Based Therapy
Homework Assignments in Therapy
Homicide
Hope-Focused Approach to Couple Enrichment in Counseling
Humanistic Family Therapy
Hypnosis
Imago Relationship Therapy
Individual Versus Family Therapy
Integrating Systemic and Individual Theories
Integrative Couples Therapy
Internal Family Systems Model
International Family Therapy
Interpersonal Neurobiology, Attachment and
Interpersonal Neurobiology, Couples and
Interpersonal Neurobiology, Parenting and
Joining
Juvenile Firesetter Interventions
Listening, Empathic
Love and Rituals
Marital Group Therapy
Marriage Encounter
Marriage Enrichment
Marriage-Friendly Therapy
Medical Family Therapy
Metacommunication
Metaphors
Milan Team
Mindfulness
Miracle Question
Motivational Interviewing
Multiple Family Therapy
Multisystemic Therapy
Narrative Therapy
Network Therapy
Neuro-Linguistic Programming
No-Harm Contracts
Normalizing
Paradoxes and Paradoxical Intervention
Parent Effectiveness Training (P.E.T.)
Parent Management Training
Peer Counseling
Play Family Therapy
Positive Psychology
Postmodern Therapies
Premarital Counseling
Progress Notes for Couples and Families
Psychoanalytic Family Therapy
Psychobiology of Attachment
Psychoeducation
Punctuation

Questions: Open, Closed, and Circular
Reflecting Team
Relational-Cultural Therapy
Relationship Enhancement
Restoration Therapy
Rituals in Family Therapy
Role-Playing
Second-Order Family Therapy
Self-Help
Sensate Focus
Solution-Focused Brief Therapy
Stages of Family Therapy
Strategic Family Therapy
Structural Family Therapy
Support Groups
Systemic Family Therapy
Systems, Subsystems, and Metasystems
Therapeutic Alliance
Therapeutic Contract
Torture Treatment
Training in Marriage Enrichment (TIME) Program
Transgenerational Family Therapy
Trauma-Focused Cognitive-Behavioral Therapy
Triangulation
Virginia Satir Model

Organizations

American Association for Marriage and Family Therapy
Council for Accreditation of Counseling and Related Educational Programs
International Association of Marriage and Family Counselors
World Association for Sexual Health
World Health Organization

Parenting

Active Parenting
Adoption
Authoritative Parenting
Child-Centered Parenting
Child–Parent Relationship Therapy
Children With Chronic Illness
Foster Children
Group Parenting Classes
Interpersonal Neurobiology, Parenting and
Legal Issues in Parenting
LGBT Families
Nonresidential Fathers
Parent Effectiveness Training (P.E.T.)
Parent Management Training
Parent Study Groups
Parent–Adolescent Relations
Parental Alienation Syndrome
Parental Stress: Effects on Children
Parentification and Diverse Family Systems
Parenting
Parenting Education
Parenting Styles
Pregnancy
Racial Disparities in Foster Care
Rule-Setting
Teen Parenting

Professional Development and Standards

American Association for Marriage and Family Therapy
Certified Family Life Educator
Child Protective Services
Clinical Practice
Clinician-Directed, Solution-Focused Supervision
Competency-Based Standards for Marriage, Couple, and Family Counseling
Confidentiality
Core Competencies for Marriage and Family Therapists
Cotherapy Team
Council for Accreditation of Counseling and Related Educational Programs
Court-Mandated Clients
Decision-Making
Dual and Multiple Relationships
Duty to Warn and Protect
Ethical Codes
Ethical Decision-Making
Family Life Educators
HIPAA Standards
Informed Consent for Research
Informed Consent in Clinical Work
Licensure and Certification
Live Supervision

Mandated Reporter
Mental Health, Systemic Perspective
Moral Dimensions of Therapy
Multicultural Counseling Competence
No-Secrets Contracts
Postdoctoral Training
Practice Management
Professional Associations
Public Health Code
Release of Information for Couples and Families
Self of the Therapist
Self-Care Practices for the Trauma-Informed Couple and Family Counselor
Sexual Relationships With Clients
Supervision
Supervision, Approved Supervisor in Marriage and Family Therapy
Supervision, Developmental Model
Supervision, Gatekeeping
Supervision, Individual and Group
Supervision Contract
Supervision of Supervision
Supervision Philosophy Statement
Supervision Theories
Termination
Therapists' Values
Training and Licensure

Research

Clinical Versus Statistical Significance
Common Factors
Cost–Benefit Analysis
Couples Therapy Research
Delphi Research Method
Developmental Model of Marriage
Effectiveness Research
Empirically Validated Models
Evidence-Based Practice With Couples and Families
Outcome Research
Prevention Research
Process Research
Qualitative Research
Quantitative Research
Sex Researchers

Sexuality

Beliefs and Values
Birth Control and Contraception
Childless Couples
Compulsive Sexual Behavior
Erectile Disorder
Extramarital Affairs and Infidelity
Female Orgasmic Disorder
Female Sexual Interest/Arousal Disorder
Fetishes
Gender Dysphoria
Gender Orientation, Gender Identity, and Gender Expression
Genito-Pelvic Pain/Penetration Disorder
Human Sexual Response
Incest
Infertility
Male Hypoactive Sexual Desire Disorder
Mate Selection
Mindfulness and Sex
Nudity: Beliefs and Values
Open Relationships
Paraphilic Disorders
Polyamory
Polygamy
Pornography
Pregnancy and Sexuality
Premature Ejaculation
Romance
Same-Sex Couples
Sensate Focus
Sex, Definition of
Sex Positivity
Sex Researchers
Sex Therapy
Sexual Abuse
Sexual Assault and Rape
Sexual Assessment/History
Sexual Dysfunction
Sexual Enhancement, Sexual Toys
Sexual Health
Sexual History
Sexual Intimacy
Sexual Minorities
Sexual Orientation, Attraction, and Identity

Sexual Prejudice
Sexual Relationships With Clients
Sexual Toys/Sexual Aids
Sexuality and Religion
Sexuality Education
Sexually Transmitted Infections
Statutory Rape
World Association for Sexual Health

Special Topics
Body Dysmorphic Disorder
  in Adolescents
Child Guidance Movement
Children With Special Needs in
  Family Therapy
Community Programs
Family Mediation
Healthy Marriage and Responsible
  Fatherhood
Hispanic Healthy Marriage Initiative
Incest
International Family Therapy
Marriage and Health
Media in Family Therapy
Men in Counseling
Military Couples and Families
Mindfulness and Children
Mindfulness and Couples
National Marriage Initiative
Online Dating
Schizophrenia and Families
Schools, Family Involvement in
Self-Care Practices for the Trauma-Informed
  Couple and Family Counselor
Sexual Abuse
Statutory Rape
Technology and Families/Marriage
Therapeutic Impasses
Torture Treatment

Theory
Adlerian Family Therapy
Assessment, Biopsychosocial

Attachment Theory
Behavioral Family Therapy
Bowen Family Systems Theory
Chaos Family Therapy
Choice Theory and Reality Therapy
Cognitive-Behavioral Couples
  Therapy
Cognitive-Behavioral Family
  Therapy
Collaborative Language Systems
Constructivism
Contextual Family Therapy
Critical Theory
Cybernetics
Double Bind Theory
Ecosystems Perspective
Epistemology in Family Therapy
Experiential Family Therapy
Family Stress Adaptation Theory
Functionalism
General Systems Theory
Isomorphism
Love, Theories of
Object Relations Theory
Parental Acceptance–Rejection
  Theory
Psychoanalytic Family Therapy
Social Constructionism
Structural Determinism
Symbolic Interactionism
Systems Theory

Violence and Abuse
Alcohol and Substance Abuse
Anger Management
Child Maltreatment
Domestic Violence
Elder Abuse
Interpersonal Violence
Self-Injury
Sexual Assault and Rape
Trauma and Children
Trauma and Families

EARNED ATTACHMENT

According to John Bowlby's attachment theory, human beings are compelled to form connections with caregivers for physical, emotional, relational, and developmental support. It is not enough just to have an infant's basic physical needs met; infants also need to feel emotionally secure and bonded to a caregiver. When caregivers are not responsive to the needs of a child (both physically and emotionally), the child develops an insecure, rather than secure, attachment to the caregiver. Having an insecure attachment is associated with less healthy relationships as an adult. *Earned secure attachment* describes people who had insecure attachments with their parents but have found ways to overcome the insecure attachment and are assessed as securely attached later in life. Therefore, the early negative life experiences do not always dictate that the child will grow up with an insecure attachment in relationships. This entry discusses the connection between earned secure attachment and the family dynamics of developing relationships with parents, siblings, friends, and significant others.

Attachment and Parenting

Childhood experiences with caretakers form children's style of attachment and their internal working model (representation of self and representation of self in relation to others). Based on these internal working models, children and adults develop expectations about themselves and relationships. Parents are the first teachers to their children about love, acceptance, and responsiveness and what to expect overall in loving relationships. Therefore, parents help children learn how to act, react, think, and feel about themselves and their presence in the world.

Those children who learn that they cannot (or not consistently) depend on parents to protect them, make them feel safe, and make them feel loved become insecure about relationships—either overmonitoring relationships out of fear of losing them, avoiding needing others, or vacillating between being afraid of losing relationships and avoiding needing others. Consequently, children who do not form a secure connection to parents tend to have difficulty in relationships with family members, friends, and romantic partners. Children who have insecure relationships often grow up to be adults who have the inability to maintain or sustain secure, interpersonal relationships.

Attachment Across Time

Although there tends to be continuity between one's attachment style in childhood and in adulthood, attachment styles can change from secure to insecure and from insecure to secure. When a person had a secure relationship as a child and they continue to have a secure attachment as an adult, it is referred to as continuous security.

When positive experiences and positive relationships help people move from an insecure style to a secure style, they are said to have moved to an earned secure attachment. Those who have earned secure attachment can recollect hurtful experiences as a child, but they are able to make some sense of their insecure attachment with parents, recount those experiences with coherence, and show some insight into how their life has changed with an earned secure attachment.

Working to create earned secure attachment is important for an individual, for his or her adult relationships, and for parenting. People with insecure attachments are more likely to have relational and psychological issues. In addition, those with insecure attachments are less likely to be attuned with the needs of their own children. However, those with earned secure attachment can show similar strengths in parenting and their relationship with their children as continuous secure attachment.

Attachment and Counseling

Attachment can be assessed when doing individual, couple, or family counseling. There are therapeutic models based on attachment theory that clinicians can use to work with clients. Developing a thorough intake assessment to address and review with the client their psychosocial development from birth until adulthood can assist the therapist with identifying attachment issues. Helping people develop earned secure attachment will help improve themselves and their relationships.

Felicia Denise Pressley

See also Attachment Styles; Attachment Theory; Couples Therapy Research; Genograms

Further Readings

Booth-LaForce, C., Groh, A. M., Burchinal, M. R., Roisman, G. I., Owen, M. T., & Cox, M. J. (2014). Caregiving and contextual sources of continuity and change in attachment security from infancy to late adolescence. *Monographs of the Society for Research in Child Development*, 79(14), 67–84.

Bourne, K., Berry, K., & Jones, L. (2014). The relationship between psychological mindedness, parental bonding and adult attachment. *Psychology and Psychotherapy: Theory, Research and Practice*, 87, 167–177.

McCarthy, G., & Maughan, B. (2010). Negative childhood experiences and adult love relationships: The role of the internal working models of attachment. *Attachment & Human Development*, 12(5), 446–461.

Roisman, G., Padron, E., Sroufe, L. A., & Egeland, B. (2002). Earned-secure attachment status in retrospect and prospect. *Child Development*, 73(4), 1204–1219.

Shibue, Y., & Kasai, M. (2014). Relations between attachment, resilience, and earned security in Japanese university students. *Psychological Reports*, 115(1), 279–295.

Venta, A., Sharp, C., Shmueli-Goetz, Y., & Newlin, E. (2015). An evaluation of the construct of earned security in adolescents: Evidence from an inpatient sample. *Bulletin of the Menninger Clinic*, 79(1), 41–69. doi:10.1521/bumc.2015.79.1.41

Eating Disorders

Eating disorders in the United States continue to be a problem for millions of women and men. Eating disorders include various psychological disorders involving food intake and choices. The category includes anorexia nervosa, bulimia nervosa, and binge eating disorder. According to the National Eating Disorder Association in the United States, 20 million women and 10 million men suffer from a clinically significant eating disorder at some time during their life. However, there are many individuals in the United States who have not been diagnosed with an eating disorder but have disordered eating and binge eating behavioral patterns. Eating disorders continue to have the highest mortality rate of mental disorders, which increases the urgency to provide effective treatment modalities, including family therapy. This entry provides a history of eating disorders, explains the different types of eating disorders, and offers an introduction to the effective treatment of eating disorders.

History of Eating Disorders

Although eating disorders have been characterized as encompassing several psychological disorders, the concept of eating disturbances is nothing new. Eating disorders—in particular, forms of self-starvation—have been around since Ancient Greece and were also reported during medieval times. In many religions, fasting or abstaining from meat was part of one's spiritual quest. People who starved themselves were held in a higher regard and were believed to be closer to God. Under Catholicism, Saint Catherine of Siena (1347–1380) was said to have suffered from anorexia. In *Fasting Girls: The History of Anorexia Nervosa*, Joan Jacobs Brumberg reports that some women were even burned at the stake when thought to be anorexic, since the condition was once believed to be common among witches. In some Eastern religions, believers were known to fast for prolonged periods, sometimes dying as a result. However, these psychological conditions were not called eating disorders until Sir Richard Morton, an English physician, discussed two cases in his research of what he called a "wasting disease" in 1689. The two cases described a female adolescent and a male adolescent that exhibited symptoms of "wasting away" and nervous consumption due to experiencing emotional distress. This wasting disease would later be coined *anorexia nervosa* by Sir William Gull, Queen Victoria of England's physician, and French physician Charles Lasègue in 1874. There were other physicians who expanded on the works of Sir Richard Morton, including Giorgio Baglivi and Robert Whytt in the 1700s and Louis-Victor Marcé in 1860.

In the 19th century, anorexia nervosa became a medical diagnosis for the first time. Gull and Lasègue described anorexia nervosa as being a "nervous" condition that also entailed starvation, specifically self-starvation. The term *anorexia nervosa* continued to gain a wider audience and was translated to mean "nervous loss of appetite." As Gull continued to conduct research and publish on anorexia nervosa, the diagnosis gained wider acceptance. In the 1930s, German-born psychoanalyst Hilde Bruch immigrated to the United States and began working at a pediatric hospital where she continued her earlier work in childhood obesity. This helped to foster her interest in eating disorders. In 1964, after working nearly three decades in hospitals in New York and Baltimore, she became a professor of psychiatry at the Baylor College of Medicine. In 1973, she published *Eating Disorders: Obesity, Anorexia Nervosa, and the Person Within*. In her book, Bruch wrote about the steady rise of eating disorders and the emotional aspects of those plagued by eating disorders and body image distortion.

In regard to the origins of bingeing and binge eating, British psychiatrist Gerald Russell is credited for coining the term *bulimia nervosa* in 1979. Both anorexia nervosa and binge eating were first introduced as a clinical diagnosis in the third edition of the *Diagnostic and Statistical Manual of Mental Disorders* (DSM-III) in 1980. In 1987, a revised edition adapted binge eating to the term *bulimia nervosa*. Anorexia nervosa and bulimia nervosa hold similarities, but bulimia nervosa is considered distinct from anorexia nervosa since those afflicted with bulimia use diuretics, laxatives, excessive exercise, and purging (e.g., vomiting following binge eating) rather than self-starvation. In ancient Egypt, purging was practiced as a part of one's overall health. During the times of the Roman Empire, there were even "vomitoriums," which provided wealthy Romans with a place to go vomit and purge themselves after eating.

In the updated 2013 *Diagnostic and Statistical Manual of Mental Disorders* (DSM-5), a new term was added—*binge eating disorder*. This eating disorder was first introduced by psychiatrist Albert Stunkard as "night-eating syndrome" in 1959. The term was changed to include specific binge eating behaviors and not only those that occur at night. Binge eating disorder is currently the most prevalent eating disorder among adults. Additional research is needed on this specific disorder, since most scientists and researchers have heavily focused on anorexia nervosa and bulimia nervosa. However, all three eating disorders continue to affect people across all backgrounds.

Types of Eating Disorders

Anorexia Nervosa

Anorexia nervosa is characterized by an intense fear of gaining weight and inability to maintain normal body weight, which can ultimately require medical treatment. Exercising and dieting are implemented in order not to gain weight, oftentimes to the point of starvation and death. Some people with anorexia nervosa also binge and purge by using laxatives and various methods to induce vomiting. Their body image is often distorted, and they see themselves as overweight when in fact they are often severely underweight. Over time, obsession with counting calories and restrictive eating is also prevalent (e.g., eating only an apple for breakfast or a small cup of applesauce). Anorexia often develops in late adolescence, with the average age being 19.

The Mayo Clinic's 2015 report on eating disorders describes the following behaviors and symptoms in relation to anorexia nervosa:

- Losing a considerable amount of weight
- Wearing bulky clothes in order to hide weight loss
- Being preoccupied with counting calories, food, and dieting
- Refusing to eat certain foods (e.g., any foods with fats)
- Avoiding mealtimes or eating in front of others
- Preparing elaborate meals for others, but refusing to eat them
- Overexercising
- No longer menstruating although of premenopausal age
- Having gastrointestinal problems such as upset stomach or constipation
- Denying that extreme thinness is a problem

Bulimia Nervosa

Bulimia nervosa can be characterized by binge eating large quantities of food in a short period of time despite a fear of gaining weight. However, unlike people with anorexia nervosa, in the case of bulimia nervosa, a normal weight is often sustained. In addition, people with this disorder experience body image distortion and view themselves as "overweight" and "fat" and want to lose weight. In order to avoid gaining weight, unhealthful methods are used to prevent weight gain (i.e., induced vomiting, the use of diuretics and laxatives, and extreme dieting). With bulimia nervosa, there is often intense shame and guilt for bingeing and purging. A common physical sign of bulimia nervosa is knuckle scarring and loss of tooth enamel due to vomiting.

Binge Eating Disorder

Binge eating disorder is characterized by recurrent episodes of binge eating (and cravings), especially on large amounts of food, excluding purging behaviors. It is similar to bulimia in that people with binge eating disorder have a sense of shame and guilt and feelings of being out of control. It is part of an unhealthy cycle of bingeing, but in most cases, people with binge eating disorder are overweight or obese, unlike those with bulimia (normal weight) or anorexia (underweight). Binge eating disorder affects both men and women at about the same rate. In addition, the National Institute of Mental Health (NIMH) statistics show that the average onset is 25 for binge eating disorder, and it is more prevalent among people under age 60.

Anorexia nervosa, bulimia nervosa, and binge eating disorder are the three primary eating disorders that affect people. They are also the primary eating disorders researched and encountered by therapists in a clinical setting.

Treatment of Eating Disorders

There are several treatment options for treating eating disorders, depending on the client and the specific eating disorder diagnosed. It is not uncommon for comorbid conditions to be prevalent along with an eating disorder (i.e., depression and binge eating disorder, or anxiety and anorexia nervosa). In addition, there are several factors that cause eating disorders; the Mayo Clinic published a report in 2015 that details genetics (biological) as well as social, psychological, and emotional factors (i.e., poor self-image, low self-esteem, impulsivity, and perfectionism) that contribute to eating disorder development.

For anorexia nervosa, bulimia nervosa, and binge eating, treatment such as behavior therapy, cognitive-behavioral therapy (CBT), dialectical behavior therapy (DBT), interpersonal therapy, family therapy, group therapy, and medication to minimize anxiety or depression symptoms are effective treatment options. However, CBT has been the most widely used therapy in the treatment of eating disorders. Psychiatrist Aaron T. Beck is credited with developing CBT in the early 1960s, and psychologist Marsha Linehan is credited with developing DBT in the 1970s. DBT was influenced by CBT and was originally developed for the treatment of borderline personality disorder. Ideally, a treatment team is formulated to assist in anorexia nervosa recovery. This would include a registered dietician, primary care provider (essential to help monitor weight), psychiatrist, and mental health therapist (licensed professional). An individualized treatment plan is also necessary, since each case is different. In addition, those suffering from an eating disorder often need more intensive treatment, such as intensive outpatient treatments or an inpatient stay for 1 to 3 months or longer in an eating disorder treatment center.

Eating Disorders and Family Therapy

Eating disorders impact not only the person who has been diagnosed but also their family; this is especially true when the diagnosed person is a child or adolescent. Families can be instrumental in helping in the recovery of clients with eating disorders. This was not always the case, however, since historically families were frequently seen as part of the problem and a hindrance to the recovery process.

Families in therapy gain insight into how they communicate, handle negative emotions, and manage conflict, which in turn can help their family member in eating disorder recovery. For children and adolescents, having families be part of treatment can also help to resolve family challenges, and family therapy can help to foster a strong parental alliance. Additionally, family therapy helps families to better understand the role the eating disorder has played within their family, what factors may be maintaining the disorder, and how to differentiate between their family member and their family member's psychological disorder.

In the 1970s, family therapist Salvador Minuchin and his colleagues developed the first family approach to anorexia nervosa with structural family therapy (SFT). Through his work and research, this approach demonstrated how family involvement in therapy was helpful. Other family-based approaches for anorexia nervosa were soon created, specifically Maudsley family therapy, which was developed in London at the Maudsley Hospital by Christopher Dare and his associates in the late 1970s. This is both an evidence-based and family-based approach that was developed in order to empower and support families in minimizing anorexia nervosa in their children.

Daniel Le Grange and James Lock are credited for bringing the Maudsley approach to the United States, after Le Grange received training in 1986 in the Maudsley approach. Le Grange and Lock expanded on this family-based approach by improving treatment outcomes for adolescents with both anorexia nervosa and bulimia nervosa. The Maudsley approach is an intensive outpatient treatment, in which parents play a vital role in helping their child or adolescent recover from their eating disorder. Weight restoration is essential, as is empowering the adolescent in treatment to have more control over their eating.

Sarita Palmer

See also Behavioral Family Therapy; Body Dysmorphic Disorder in Adolescents; Elimination Disorders in Children; Mood Disorders in Adolescents; Mood Disorders in Children

Further Readings

Bemporad, J. R. (1996). Self-starvation through the ages: Reflections on the pre-history of anorexia nervosa. *International Journal of Eating Disorders, 19,* 217–237.

Brumberg, J. J. (2000). *Fasting girls: The history of anorexia nervosa.* New York, NY: Vintage Books.

Dare, C., & Eisler I. (1997). Family therapy for anorexia nervosa. In D. M. Garner & P. Garfinkel (Eds.), *Handbook of treatment for eating disorders* (pp. 307–324). New York, NY: Guilford Press.

Eisler, I. (2005). The empirical and theoretical base of family therapy and multiple family day therapy for adolescent anorexia nervosa. *Journal of Family Therapy, 27*, 104–131.

Fairborn, C. G., & Brownell, K. D. (2002). *Eating disorders and obesity: A comprehensive handbook.* New York, NY: Guilford Press.

Keel, P. (2006). *Eating disorders.* New York, NY: Chelsea House.

Le Grange, D., & Lock, J. (2007). *Treating bulimia in adolescents: A family-based approach.* New York, NY: Guilford Press.

Lock, J., & Le Grange, D. (2001). Can family-based treatment of anorexia nervosa be manualized? *Journal of Psychotherapy Practice and Research, 10*, 253–261.

Lock, J., Le Grange, D., Agras, W. S., & Dare, C. (2002). *Treatment manual for anorexia nervosa: A family-based approach.* New York, NY: Guilford Press.

Mayo Clinic. (2015, February 14). *Diseases and conditions: Eating disorders.* Retrieved March 7, 2015, from http://www.mayoclinic.org/diseases-conditions/eating-disorders/basics/definition/con-20033575

National Eating Disorders Association. (n.d.). *Get the facts on eating disorders.* Retrieved January 5, 2015, from http://www.nationaleatingdisorders.org/get-facts-eating-disorders

Ecological Systems

The central premise of ecological systems theory is the view of development as emerging from the interaction of individual and environment. Urie Bronfenbrenner, known as the developer of this theory, focused his research on the interrelationship of different processes and the importance of context on human development. Central to ecological systems theory is that development does not occur in isolation but rather in relation to one's family, home, community, culture, and society. These ever-changing and multilevel environments, as well as one's interactions within them, are central to development. First proposed by Bronfenbrenner in 1979, the theory underwent significant revisions and adaptations in application to different developmental processes and interventions, until his death in 2005. It is now a widely accepted framework for grounding research and interventions in life span development, family therapy, social problems, and mental health.

With the increasing emphasis on the active role of the individual in relation to his or her environment, the contemporary form of this theory is that of bioecological systems theory. Bronfenbrenner referred to the individual's capacities to transform genotypic characteristics into phenotypic expression, where genetic potential is actualized, as proximal processes. The use of bioecological systems theory in the practice of marriage and family therapy broadens a contextual understanding of the interconnections and interactions of the individual and family with various social domains, institutions, and cultures. Clinicians working with individuals and families intervene at multiple levels of these interrelated contexts. This entry presents a description of the history of bioecological systems theory, the theoretical underpinnings, its major concepts, and concludes with a brief discussion of its applications to marriage and family therapy.

Historical Context

Bronfenbrenner first proposed ecological systems theory in a series of groundbreaking publications in the 1970s and 1980s. Bronfenbrenner's viewpoints are phenomenological in orientation and broke from the common thinking of the time that development was largely an individual construct. Human behavior, he posited, is multiply determined by a series of dynamic interactions between social systems. The first known writings on person–environment interrelatedness can be traced to German researchers Schwabe and Bartholomai in the 1870s. Since then, other writers who were not considered to represent the mainstream of psychology have contributed to the study of contextualism in development. It was not until the 1970s, when Bronfenbrenner underscored the interdependence and multilevel systemic influence on individual development, that the idea took hold in developmental psychology.

Bronfenbrenner's work was largely influenced by Lev Vygotsky and Kurt Lewin. Vygotsky's sociocultural theory (1934) stresses the fundamental role of social interaction and culture in the development of cognition. His work emphasizes the role that community plays in fostering meaning-making in children's development. Kurt Lewin (1935) is credited as one of the first theorists to recognize the importance of interactions between person and environment in describing human behavior. Lewin formulated a basic representation of human development in which one's behavior is considered an interaction between the person and the environment. At the time of Bronfenbrenner's seminal publication *The Ecology of Human Development: Experiments by Nature and Design* in 1979, the majority of child development studies researched narrow aspects of a child's world and without explicit reference to the environment. Beyond his academic writings, Bronfenbrenner is widely recognized for his social activism in support of children and family; he was cofounder of the Head Start Program, a program designed to prepare young children for school success in the United States.

Theoretical Underpinnings

The term *ecology* refers to a system of interacting organisms that form physical ecosystems, such as rivers, forests, and deserts. Bronfenbrenner expanded this idea to describe individual development within a set of interacting social systems. Development takes place in a complex system of dynamic interactions between the individual and multilayered systems. In addition to defining the ecological systems in which development takes place, a critical dimension of bioecological systems theory is the emphasis of context, process, time, and the personal attributes of the developing individual. The construct of development is defined within the multisystemic layers of the environment that influence an individual's development. Most importantly, these processes are viewed as multilayered and dynamic.

Major Concepts

Bronfenbrenner used the metaphor of a set of Russian matryoshka dolls to portray his model of development as a set of concentric circles. The developing individual is located at the center of a series of concentric circles that represent multiple layers of systems that become progressively more distal. Connecting these systems are multiple bidirectional arrows that represent the intrinsic linkages of contexts within and between systems. Development is represented as taking place through a series of increasingly more complex reciprocal interaction between the individual and their environment. Bronfenbrenner identifies four ecologies where development takes place through processes of progressively more complex reciprocal social interaction: the *microsystem, mesosystem, exosystem,* and *macrosystem* framed within historical time.

The most prominent and significant sphere in ecological systems is the microsystem. The microsystem refers to all the settings in which the individual interacts and is influenced. Contained in the microsystem are those objects and persons in the immediate setting that encompass the individual's pattern of activities, roles, and interpersonal relations. The developing person will have many microsystems, such as family, school, peer group, workplace, and church. Bronfenbrenner refers to these different settings as subsystems. Each subsystem can be viewed within itself as a system. Subsystems vary in the length of influence on the individual; some last throughout one's development, such as a family, and others come and go regularly, such as teams, clubs, and peer groups. It is in these subsystems that the individual has the most direct relationships and interactions. The individual is not passive within this context; interactions between the individual and family members, teachers, peers, and others can mutually influence one another. Individual characteristics and temperament impact the perception or interpretation of the activities, roles, and interpersonal relations that occur in the microsystems. Different roles are played within each of the subsystems, and thus, the individual is impacted by their perception or interpretation of their activities, roles, and interpersonal relations.

The interrelations among the microsystems in which the developing person actively participates is termed the *mesosystem*. Bronfenbrenner considered the mesosystem to be a system of microsystems. Individuals develop in the context of others or the social environment. Social environments can exert both negative and positive potentials on one's developmental trajectories. Depending on the quality of linkages between the relationships of the microsystems, the impact on development can be quite powerful. The pattern of interrelationships among microsystems for an individual can influence his or her perceptions and behavior within any of the settings where he or she is presently located. For example, a child's ability to achieve academic success is influenced not only by the competence of the teacher but also by the quality of the relationship between the school and home. If relationships are strained, the child is more likely not to orient herself or himself positively toward school. Developing individuals may also experience multiple influences of the family system as they encounter different interactions and experiences within the family subsystems that impact development, health, and well-being.

The exosystem is composed of settings to which the developing person is exposed but in which the person is not directly involved as an active participant. Contexts and events that can remain outside one's influence that can still have a dramatically long-term impact albeit indirect effect include new laws, government reform, school policy, social unrest, and financial upheaval. Influences from the exosystem can trickle down through relationships and experiences, directly impacting the individual's immediate environment. By the way of illustration, a parent's work environment, pay, and benefits impact the quality of their children's lives. A parent's work travel requirements may increase, requiring more time away from home, less flexibility, and more stress—all of which could impact the child–parent relationship and home life. These dynamic exchanges between an individual and larger contextual systems where no direct interaction occurs deeply influence an individual's developmental trajectory.

The broadest ecology in the concentric circle model is the macrosystem. The macrosystem is the overarching network of embedded systems that exert an indirect influence on the individual. Mediated by those with whom the developing person comes in contact, the effects of the macrosystem include ideologies, lifestyles and options, patterns of social interchange, social expectations, and legal and moral perspectives. At the cultural level, macrosystemic influences on development encompass views about race, social class, ethnicity, religion, sex, class, and age, which may alter ways the individual views self and others. From an individual's lived experience, the macrosystem provides a lens through which appraisals and interpretations of experiences are made. Each culture establishes values and beliefs that govern the priorities of educational, political, and social systems. While most remote from an individual's immediate experience, macrosystemic shifts in social paradigms can subconsciously affect values, attitudes, and behaviors. While public policy occurs within the exosystem, it is deeply influenced by the belief framework of the macrosystem. Ideological influences in the macrosystem can change public policy. For instance, the U.S. Supreme Court's 2015 ruling that legalized same-sex marriage nationwide represented a profound cultural shift in the social climate. Public forms of acceptance for same-sex marriages have led to decreasing the social stigma for sexual minorities. This array of attitudes, practices, and convictions shared throughout society has the potential to change the cultural milieu to positively impact the psychological well-being of many same-sex couples, representing new dimensions of freedom.

Lastly, the *chronosystem* adds the dimension of time to the ecological systems theory. The chronosystem provides a way to comprehend the impact of historical time on individuals and families. The chronosystem represents how the historical and cultural milieu of individuals can be perceived and experienced differently. The timing of an event, the length of time of events, and the number of events all impact how one perceives the events and experiences the transitions that occur over time.

Bioecological Systems Therapeutic Applications

Historically, clinical work with families is rich with an understanding of context. Bioecological systems theory provides a broad conceptual framework for therapeutic work. Ecological interventions may target all four levels in the concentric nested systems and gives particular attention to the interrelationships that exist within and between them. Ecosystemic approaches are frequently applied to family and school-based interventions, preventive efforts and social policy change where child, family, school, neighborhood, and community variables are targeted in order to achieve desired outcomes. A widely recognized approach to addressing youth conduct problems that focuses on the family's social context is Multisystemic Therapy (MST), developed by Scott W. Henggeler and colleagues in the 1990s. MST provides an efficacious framework for addressing the manner in which youth conduct problems develop and are maintained within the multilayered systems. Ecologically based family therapy (EBFT) originated from work with substance-abusing runaway youth. Interventions are directed toward assessing the multiple influences that maintain dysfunctional behavior and directing therapeutic efforts so that change is supported throughout all systems affecting and maintaining the youth's problem behavior. Therapeutic techniques that are ecologically informed broaden the scope of interventions through an integration with multiple environmental contexts.

Tami Sullivan

See also Ecosystemic Structural Family Therapy; Ecosystems Perspective; General Systems Theory; Multisystemic Therapy

Further Readings

Bronfenbrenner, U. (1979). *The ecology of human development: Experiments by nature and design.* Cambridge, MA: Harvard University Press.

Bronfenbrenner, U. (1986). Ecology of the family as a context for human development: Research perspectives. *Developmental Psychology, 22*(6), 723–742.

Bronfenbrenner, U. (1988). Foreword. In A. R. Pence (Ed.), *Ecological research with children and families: From concepts to methodology* (pp. ix–xix). New York, NY: Teachers College Press.

Bronfenbrenner, U. (1995). The bioecological model from a life course perspective: Reflections of a participant observer. In P. Moen, G. H. Elder, & K. Luscher (Eds.), *Examining lives in context: Perspectives on the ecology of human development* (pp. 599–618). Washington, DC: American Psychological Association.

Bronfenbrenner, U. (2005). On the nature of bioecological theory and research. In U. Bronfenbrenner (Ed.), *Making human beings human: Bioecological perspectives on human development* (pp. 1–15). Thousand Oaks, CA: Sage.

Bronfenbrenner, U., & Ceci, S. J. (1994). Nature-nurture reconceptualized in developmental perspective: A bio-ecological model. *Psychological Review, 101*(4), 568–586.

Hawe, P., Shiell, A., & Riley, T. (2009). Theorising interventions as events in systems. *American Journal of Community Psychology, 43*, 267–276. doi:10.1007/s10464-009-9229-9

Henggeler, S. W., & Borduin, C. M. (1990). *Family therapy and beyond: A multisystemic approach to treating the behavioral problems of children and adolescents.* Pacific Grove, CA: Brooks/Cole.

Slesnick, N., & Prestopnik, J. J. (2005). Ecologically based family therapy outcome with substance-abusing runaway adolescents. *Journal of Adolescence, 28*(2), 277–298.

Steinberg, L., Darling, N. E., & Fletcher, A. C. (1995). Authoritative parenting and adolescent adjustment: An ecological journey. In P. Moen, G. H. Elder, & K. Luscher (Eds.), *Examining lives in context: Perspectives on the ecology of human development* (pp. 423–466). Washington, DC: American Psychological Association.

Tudge, J. R. H., Mokrova, I. L., Hatfield, B. E., & Karnik, R. B. (2009). Uses and misuses of Bronfenbrenner's bioecological theory of human development. *Journal of Family Theory and Review, 1*, 198–210.

Eco-Map

An eco-map is a paper-and-pencil assessment that produces a pictorial representation of the interconnections between the individual and family and other related systems (e.g., schools, religion, social services, and hospitals). It is used to diagram and assess personal and social relationships within someone's environment. The eco-map is typically depicted by drawing the individual or family within a large circle and then drawing smaller circles, representing people or groups, around the larger circle. Different lines are used to draw the nature of the relationship of the individual or family to those smaller circles. Relationships can be strong, stressful, or tenuous. This map can then be used as an assessment tool and as a component of treatment planning. This entry explains the theoretical underpinnings of systems theory and the ecosystemic approach that is also known as ecological systems theory; describes the four broad interlocking systems that are included in the eco-map, including the microsystem, mesosystem, exosystem, and macrosystem; and outlines the use of eco-maps in assessment and treatment planning in individual and family counseling. The entry concludes with a short discussion of current research on eco-maps.

Systems Theory and the Ecosystemic Approach

Before conceptualizing the eco-map, it is important to have a basic understanding of systems theory and the ecosystemic approach. Systems theory is based on a number of constructs, one of which is circular causality. Circular causality is the notion that causality is not linear but instead is relational and results in a web of interlocking loops. The loops encompass actions and reactions that can be both a cause and an effect. Systems theory, therefore, focuses on the interlocking loops or the relationship between components rather than the components themselves.

The ecosystemic approach recognizes that not only does circular causality occur within the system but it also occurs between systems. In other words, the interlocking loops are also created when systems interact with one another. The ecosystem approach recognizes that the individual and family system acts and reacts to other systems (e.g., school, work, health care, church, welfare, and the legal system), and it is mitigated by broad cultural influences. The degree to which the family system interprets other systems as supportive can range from very supportive to not at all supportive. When there is difficulty between systems, system theory postulates that neither system is the cause of the problem. Instead, the systems interact in such a way as to create and maintain the problem.

Elements of the Eco-Map

As previously mentioned, the eco-map consists of four circles. The inner circle is called the microsystem; working outward, there is the mesosystem, the exosystem, and the macrosystem. These circles each represent systems at various levels. Beginning in the center, the circle representing the microsystem refers to the immediate system and includes the individual, family, school, and work. These are the systems that individuals interact with on a daily basis. The microsystem is embedded within the mesosystem and represents the relationships in which the members of the microsystem take part. The relationships can be healthy and marked by clear and open communication, or they can be less than optimal with communication that is masked and misunderstood.

The mesosystem is also called the interface because it connects the microsystem to the two outer levels: exosystem and macrosystem. The exosystem includes larger systems that are not as immediate as those in the microsystem. This level includes extra-school activities or organizations, neighbors, extra-school peers, nuclear family, extended family, religious community, social and mental health agencies, legal services, volunteer support services, government agencies, universities and private educational facilities, community health and welfare, citizen advocacy or citizen interest groups, and professional associations. The outside level of the eco-map represents the macrosystem, which are the broad social and cultural forces that impact the family. These forces include class, region, cultural attitudes and ideologies, gender, race, and ethnicity. Although not included in the eco-map, the theory of origin, known as ecological systems theory, included a fifth level called the *chronosystem*, which addressed the influence of life span transitions. A counselor operating from an ecosystemic perspective believes that an intervention at any of the four levels of the eco-map described here can bring about positive change in family functioning.

Relational lines and color coding are also used to provide additional interpretation of the multisystemic interactions. Lines with arrows on the eco-map denote the direction of movement. Bidirectional arrows extend through the three outside levels while lines are also drawn within the mesosystem to denote movement between and within relationships. Additional lines can be drawn between specific systems on the eco-map. Dual-direction arrows indicate that energy is flowing in both directions. Single-direction arrows denote energy that is flowing in one direction. A curved line between systems indicates that there is a disconnected relationship, while no line at all signifies no relationship between the systems. A different color can be utilized for each level of the eco-map as well as different colors denoting separate but similar social systems.

Assessment and Treatment Planning Using the Eco-Map

When an individual or family presents for counseling, the eco-map can provide a pictorial representation of the specific systems for which the individual or family is intertwined. The individual or family's affiliated systems can be plotted on the eco-map. An assessment of the concerns and the complexity of the problem is outlined. The following is a case example of how a family counselor might utilize the eco-map when working with a client.

Charlotte is a family counselor who has recently begun to work with Ruth, who is seeking services because she had her children placed in the state foster care system. Charlotte begins the intake assessment by utilizing the eco-map to conceptualize the systems in which Ruth is involved, the relationships she has with the other systems, and the broad social influences that shape Ruth's experience. Charlotte first discovers that Ruth has two adolescent boys: Emilio who is 15 years old and Marco who is 12 years old. Both boys have missed a number of days at school because their home life is chaotic. Ruth has been unable to care adequately for the boys due to the domestic violence she has experienced from her current boyfriend who has recently moved out of their shared apartment. Ruth also has not been able to secure more than 10 hours a week of work at her minimum-wage job (microsystem). Ruth reported that her relationships with others are marked by distrust. She stated that the principal at her son's school has always been "out to get" her, her parents and siblings do not understand her, and she has few friends with whom she keeps in touch. However, she does have one sister with whom she confides (mesosystem). Next, Ruth reported that she recently had her children placed in foster care, that she has been meeting with a foster care caseworker, and that her next court date was in 2 weeks. Meanwhile, both of her boys, Emilio and Marco, blame Ruth for allowing protective services to take them away. Ruth also stated that she missed her appointment at the public aid office and will not be getting the food stamps she needs this month. Ruth commented that when she and her children were living in the domestic violence shelter, meals were provided for them. Ruth declares that going to church is a great source of support, and at times, her religion is all that she has to hang on to (exosystem). As the intake assessment concludes, Charlotte discovers that when she was a small child Ruth and her family, who identify as Hispanic, came to the Midwest to work in the area orchards as migrant workers. While in school, Ruth often felt like an outcast, and she believed that others were looking down on her. As a female, she tried to be a strong role model for her children like her mother was for her, but she feels as though she has never been able to measure up (macrosystem).

After conducting the initial assessment through the use of the eco-map, Charlotte can now decide what course of action would be helpful for Ruth. Charlotte is aware that an intervention at any level on the eco-map could bring about an improvement in Ruth's family functioning. Additionally, in this case study, there are a number of interventions that could be carried out on each level of the eco-map. Potential areas of focus are to (a) improve the relationship between Ruth and her children (microsystem); (b) help Ruth build trusting relationships with her parents and siblings (mesosystem); (c) educate Ruth on how to appropriately advocate for herself with her children's school administrators; and (d) have Ruth volunteer in the community to give educational talks on the impact of domestic violence on the family (macrosystem) (see Figure 1).

Finally, in regard to assessment and treatment planning, the eco-map can also be used to illustrate the interconnection between systems as well as the client's resources. Ruth is involved in a number of systems including the children's school, the foster care and court system, the domestic violence shelter, the extended family, and the religious community. Charlotte and Ruth could discuss Ruth's involvement in each system and how the systems are connected. It may be helpful for Ruth to recognize how her involvement in one system influences her involvement in another. In relation to Ruth's strengths, Charlotte and Ruth can discuss how her religious community and the relationship with the sister with whom Ruth confides can continue to be a source of support as well as resources to assist Ruth in the development of additional healthy relationships.

Current Research on Eco-Maps

The eco-map described previously or some variation of it has been used with children and adults to address a wide range of mental health problems and social concerns. Current research in mental health and social concerns includes spirituality,

Figure 1 Eco-Map as Applied to Ruth

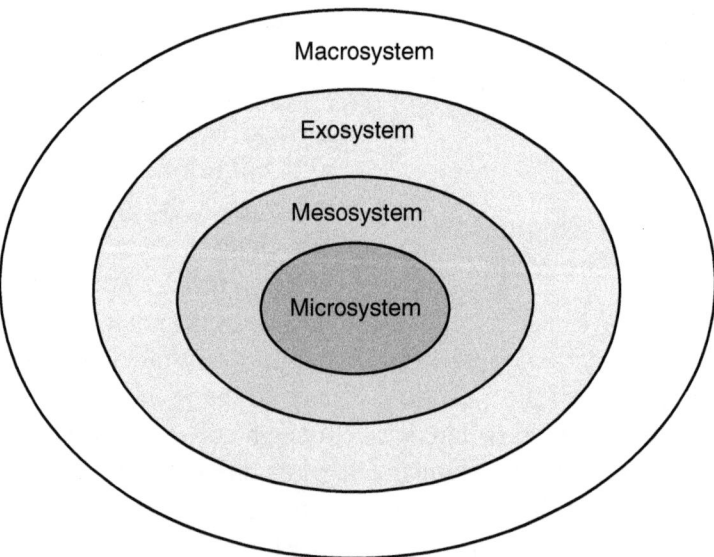

Microsystem: Ruth, Emilio, and Marco; minimum-wage job; school
Mesosystem: interface, relationships with parents and siblings, distrust
Exosystem: mental health system, foster care system, court system, public aid, domestic violence shelter, extended family including sister, church
Macrosystem: Hispanic, female, impact of culture of violence, low socioeconomic status, influence of religion

children's social support networks, foster and adoptive families, the social network of alcohol users undergoing treatment in a mental health service, sex offenders, stereotyping in children, family strengths and resources, parenting, adult survivors of incest, feminist theory, and family relations to name a few. Some research has involved diverse groups including Native American, Chinese American, African American, and Ghanaian women. Although the research is not as extensive, the eco-map has also been applied in the fields of medicine and education. In the medical field, the eco-map has been used to guide the treatment of cancer and used in genetic counseling. In the educational field, the eco-map has been used to assess risks and protective factors in program completion, teach family ecology, and train social workers.

Laura K. Harrawood

See also Boundaries; Circularity and Linearity; Ecological Systems; Ecosystems Perspective; General Systems Theory

Further Readings

Baumgartner, J. J., & Buchanan, T. K. (2010). "I have HUGE stereo-types": Using eco-maps to understand children and families. *Journal of Early Childhood Teacher Education*, 31, 173–184. doi:10.1080/10901021003781270

Baumgartner, J., Burnett, L., DiCarlo, C. F., & Buchanan, T. (2012). An inquiry of children's social support networks using eco-maps. *Child Youth Care Forum*, 41, 357–369. doi:10.1007/s10566-011-9166-2

Bertalanffy, L. von. (1968). *General systems theory.* New York, NY: Braziller.

Bronfenbrenner, U. (1986). Ecology of the family as a context for human development: Research perspectives. *Developmental Psychology*, 22(6), 723–742. doi:10.1037/00121649.22.6.723

Goldenberg, H., & Goldenberg, I. (2013). *Family therapy: An overview* (8th ed.). Belmont, CA: Cengage.

Imber-Black, R. (1988). *Families and larger systems: A family therapist's guide through the labyrinth.* New York, NY: Guilford Press.

McCormick, K. M., Stricklin, S., Nowak, T. M., & Rous, B. (2008). Using eco-mapping to understand family strengths and resources. *Young Exceptional Children*, 11(2), 17–28. doi.org/10.1177/1096250607311932

Robbins, M. S., Mayorga, B. A., & Szapocznick, J. (2003). The ecosystemic "lens" to understanding family functioning. In T. S. Sexton, G. R. Wells, & M. S. Robbins (Eds.), *Handbook of family therapy, The science and practice of working with families and couples.* New York, NY: Brunner-Routledge.

Souza de, J., Kantorsk, L. P., Vasters, G. P., & Luis, M. A. V. (2011). *Revista Latino-Americana de Enfermagem*, 19(1), 140–147.

Ecosystemic Structural Family Therapy

Ecosystemic structural family therapy (ESFT) is an empirically supported, strength-based, trauma-informed model of family therapy developed by Marion Lindblad-Goldberg. The theory is based on the assumption that the functioning of a family and its members is influenced by and is inseparable from their environmental context. The model draws from systems theory and is an evolutionary adaptation of Salvador Minuchin's structural family therapy (SFT). It is based on the idea that the child, parental, and marital functioning are interrelated and fundamental to family functioning. ESFT is important to family counseling and therapy because it was designed to help children and adolescents with moderate to severe emotional and behavioral problems and prevent them from being removed from their homes. The model can be utilized in outpatient or in-home settings. ESFT has been practiced extensively in the state of Pennsylvania for over two decades. There, it is a team-delivered, intensive service with between 2 and 10 hours of direct service provided per week. The service is generally limited to 32 weeks of treatment. As one of a number of practice-based evidence (PBE) models, ESFT fits in well with the movement toward empirically based, time-limited approaches favored by managed care. In this entry, the basic constructs of ESFT are reviewed, and a brief overview of its application is provided.

Ecosystemic Constructs

ESFT is comprised of five interrelated constructs. The first is the *family structure*, which includes the distribution of power, hierarchy, and patterns of interaction that develop in families as they navigate everyday routines and tasks. Within this structure, clinicians examine the intergenerational dynamics that characterize family relationships and explore the family rules, roles, and boundaries that organize the subsystems.

The second construct is *affective proximity*, which is the individuals' inner and subjective understanding of the emotional attachment and connections within the family system. Individuals who experience their familial relationships as secure tend to feel a closeness that promotes intimacy, open communication, and security, which enables the system to effectively accommodate and change in response to stressors. In families where individuals experience their relationships as distant, stressors to the system may be particularly destabilizing to family functioning and impede the system's ability to adapt.

The third construct of ESFT is *family and individual emotional regulation* and refers to how the system and its members make meaning of and cope with emotional or affective experiences. All individuals have different capacities for and tolerance of emotional expression. ESFT looks at the ways in which a family develops rules or predictable patterns that regulate and minimize the discomfort and chaos that can result from emotional reactivity. Exposure to stressors can create trouble in the organization of the system that may be disruptive to families with poor adaptability. In such systems, coping strategies to manage circumstances may involve unspoken rules about what emotions may be expressed, the intensity with which an emotion can be expressed, and how others in the system are to respond to such expression. These rules often restrict emotional development and negatively influence the security of attachment. In more adaptive families, emotional expression is able to be endured and family members experience a greater sense of safety and support. In adaptive families, children learn how to express and respond to emotion, which is a key in the development of positive and satisfying relationships. The affective proximity of a family system is a significant area of focus for the ESFT clinician as it provides an entry point for examining and intervening in the most fundamental organizational process of a family.

The fourth construct, *individual differences*, refers to individual preferences, strengths, growth areas, needs, and characteristics. Although family therapy approaches tend to focus on the interpersonal, intrapersonal (individual) factors are also important to assess and address in successful family therapy. Interventions are created to help families as a whole, but they must also benefit individuals' needs and promote positive growth and development. Structural family therapy—and other early family therapy models—focused primarily on family transactions. However, it is also important to look at individual differences. In particular, psychologically based differences (e.g., depression, anxiety, emotional styles) may need special consideration in addition to larger family patterns.

The fifth construct in ESFT is *family development*. ESFT clinicians view the family through a developmental, life cycle perspective. By considering the developmental stage and major tasks with which a family is faced, clinicians may contextualize the family's experience. As ESFT clinicians do not believe that there is one hierarchy or organizational structure that is inherently better or more functional than another, the context of the family becomes crucial in planning interventions.

The Process of Change

ESFT is similar to SFT in its conceptualization of the process by which change occurs, but the importance and sequencing of common factors between the two models varies. Primary to the process of change in ESFT is the integrity and viability of the therapeutic relationship between the family, its members, and the counselor. It is the counselor's ability to establish a safe, trusting, and hopeful environment that is paramount to successful intervention.

The second key part of the process of change in ESFT is the counselor's ability to involve in treatment all relevant stakeholders who play an impactful part in the family system. It is not just the nuclear family that participates in counseling. Community partners, peers, schools, and anyone whom the family identifies as significant to their functioning are all desired partners in treatment.

Third, the ESFT process entails helping families to view their issues from a relational standpoint. Here, clinicians help family members to identify and understand how they influence and impact one another. This new perspective is then used to promote better problem-solving. ESFT is an action-based approach where clinicians assist the family to practice different ways of interacting and relating in order to promote healthier patterns. Sessions are interactive, dynamic times in which families can experiment with new skills in a real way.

Finally, ESFT focuses on enhancing the emotional regulation of families and their members. Again, in an action-oriented way, clinicians strive to help families to resolve their presenting concerns and improve their interactions in the hopes that the family can increase emotional regulation, develop a growth focus, and engage appropriate resources that will support their change.

The Therapeutic Process

The therapeutic process of ESFT can be conceptualized as occurring in a four-stage sequence. The stages are overlapping and recursive. Each stage serves as a building block for the next, while the tasks of each previous stage remain vital through the entirety of treatment.

The first stage is the development of the therapeutic system. In this stage, the clinician is tasked with establishing a therapeutic alliance (a secure, safe, supportive relationship) with the family, each individual, and each distinct subsystem. This joining process is crucial to the treatment process and is the foundation of all work that will occur. Through an exploration of each of the family members' perceptions of problems, relationships, and potential goals for treatment, the clinician creates a partnership with the members. Such partnering provides the family members with a sense of agency within the process, which enhances the potential for positive outcomes.

The second stage is the development of a focus for interventions that is contextually grounded in experiences of the family and its members. During this assessment phase, the clinician seeks to gather information about the bidirectional influences of the family's presenting issues with respect to their major social contexts (e.g., school, community, peers). This focus can expose the hurdles with which the family is confronted and the methods that they employ to address them. This information is used to assist in the formulation of a hypothesis, or an inductively derived guess, about what keeps the family functioning in the way that it is. This hypothesis then leads to a targeted plan for intervention designed to meet the family's goals for change. Of particular import in this assessment is a focus on inherent family strengths and the resources, both tapped and untapped, that the family can bring to bear upon their concern. Once interventions have been undertaken, reassessment occurs, a new hypothesis is generated based upon this new information, and another set of interventions is developed. This recursive approach continues throughout treatment as assessment and hypothesis generating are an integral part of intervention in this model. The process also relies heavily upon the therapeutic alliance that has been established between the clinician and the family. Members need to be secure in the relationship, be in agreement about the goals of therapy, be committed to these goals, and feel as if they are allied with the clinician in the therapeutic process in order for productive work to occur.

The third stage is the creation of growth-promoting experiences. In this stage, the goal is to help the family alter the unproductive or negative patterns of interaction that prevent them from changing or growing. There is a focus on strengthening the parental hierarchy (executive system), creating positive alliances between caregivers, increasing positive emotional regulation and distress tolerance among the family members, and enhancing positive emotional bonds between them. All therapeutic goals are developed in collaboration with the family based upon their views of the presenting concerns. The focus is upon what enables the problems to continue and how the problem impacts the members of the system.

The fourth stage is solidifying change and moving to termination. The goal of this stage is to help families understand the changes that they have made and how those changes have helped them to attain their desired goal. With a significant focus on cementing change so it can be maintained in the future, the clinician works to transfer the orchestration of therapeutic change to the family members themselves. The aim is for the family to generalize the positive changes they have made beyond issues addressed during treatment to new challenges with which they may be faced.

Assessment Tools

During assessment, ESFT clinicians use a variety of tools that are designed to promote their own and the family's understanding of the structure, boundaries, rules, roles, and processes of the system. Many of these tools are drawn from SFT. These tools can also be used by clinicians in other theoretical approaches but are central to the work of ESFT.

Genograms and time lines are used to look at the family's history. Genograms help to identify generational patterns. They provide a visual representation of relationships between family members. In a sense, this is a therapeutically focused "family tree" that helps family members understand the ways in which they are connected.

Time lines provide a chronological account of significant family life events. The clinician and the family are able to identify themes that recur and events that have had a significant impact upon the family. It is important to promote the inclusion of "positive" life events in a time line. People under stress often focus solely on negative or stressful life events. Exploring times when a family has experienced health and happiness dramatically assist the process of developing a strength-based approach to intervention.

There are also several other pictorial interventions to understand family processes. Mapping is used to provide further pictorial representation of how the family is functioning. Eco-maps address the ways in which outside systems impact the family and its members. Structural maps show the perceived family hierarchy or power structure and who has what type of emotional access to whom. Maps of negative interaction patterns display how family members relate to each other. In combination with the clinician's and family's observations that are derived from therapeutic interviews, a complete, circular view of the family's functioning can be developed. This comprehensive and systematic assessment continues throughout the course of treatment with tools being revised and revisited to punctuate the changes that are being made.

Techniques

Intervention techniques common to ESFT are also adapted from SFT. Clinicians are active during sessions and work to help the family develop new ways of interacting. Probably the most characteristic technique of ESFT is an enactment. Enactments are authentic interactions between family members directed by the clinician. These enactments can be spontaneous or invited but provide the clinician with a real-world experience of patterns of interaction. The clinician can then intervene to help alter those patterns and improve functioning. ESFT clinicians also use unbalancing (e.g., the intentional upsetting of normal, hierarchical functioning), reframing (e.g., helping families reconceptualize weaknesses as strengths), and punctuating change that is observed during sessions as tools to effect change within the family system. Essential to the use of these tools remains the therapeutic relationship between the family and the clinician.

Debra Hyatt-Burkhart

See also Boundaries; Hierarchy; Structural Family Therapy

Further Readings

Jones, W., & Lindblad-Goldberg, M. (2008). Ecosystemic structural family therapy: A primer. In K. Jordan (Ed.), *The quick theory reference guide* (pp. 331–347). New York, NY: Nova Science.

Lindblad-Goldberg, M., Dore, M., & Stern, L. (1998). *Creating competence from chaos: A comprehensive guide to home-based services.* New York, NY: W. W. Norton.

Lindblad-Goldberg, M., Igle, E., & Simms, S. (2011). Ecosystemic structural family therapy with couples. In D. Carson & M. Casado-Kehoe (Eds.), *Case studies in couple's therapy: Theory based approaches* (pp. 121–131). New York, NY: Routledge.

Lindblad-Goldberg, M., & Northey, W., Jr. (2013). Ecosystemic structural family therapy: Theoretical and clinical foundations. *Contemporary Family Therapy, 35,* 147–160.

Ecosystems Perspective

The ecosystems perspective is widely accepted in the professions of family therapy, social work, and developmental psychology. Central to the ecosystems perspective is the dynamic interaction between the person and the environment with an emphasis on the person's active participation with their environment. The person and the environment are seen in terms of their relationship, in which each continually influences the other within a particular context. Families interact with their environment to form an ecosystem. The use of an ecosystems perspective to understand individual and family functioning broadens the context of understanding through considering the multiple systems with which the family interacts. In family therapy, the ecosystems perspective is based on the reciprocal relations within the family and relationships outside its boundaries among individuals, families, and communities. Primarily used as a heuristic aid, the ecosystems perspective provides clinical guidance in the multiple interacting elements that exist in a system, and it is a perspective that honors the transactional realities of individuals, couples, and families, providing a multidimensional view for understanding the interdependence of family and its interactions with multiple contexts. In this entry, attention is given to the historical contexts of the development of the ecosystems approach and its major concepts. Implications for practice are discussed, including innovative applications of the ecosystems perspective that enhance understanding of the intersectionalities of the family and its environment.

Historical Factors

The ecosystem perspective emerged in the 1970s from two bodies of scientific theory: ecological theory and general systems theory. The late 19th century is recognized as a period of growth in natural sciences and a period that marked the beginning of many social science disciplines. The origins of the concept of ecology (derived from *oekologie,* from the Greek word *oikos,* meaning house) can be credited to German zoologist and evolutionist Ernest Haeckel. In 1869, Haeckel proposed ecology as a new science to study the interrelationships between organisms and the environment. The writings of Ellen Swallow Richards, an American scientist and the first female MIT graduate, became the foundation of human ecological theory in the 1890s. Richards applied ecological concepts to the family and is credited with developing the field of home economics. It was not until early in the 20th century that the incorporation of ecology into the scientific traditions began, which in turn ushered in an era of experimental models in botany and biology. In 1935, botanist Arthur Tansley was the first to introduce the term *ecosystem* as a distinct level of analysis of the flow of energy in, through, and out of biological systems.

The new epistemological approaches of Ludwig von Bertalanffy's general systems theory in the late 1920s and cybernetic concepts in 1948 established ecosystem ecology's credibility in scientific circles.

These theories united the natural sciences with the diversity of the social sciences. Ecosystemic ideas denote the transactional processes that exist in nature and are representative of human relatedness. Human ecosystems are interactive and interdependent and involve interrelationships of the individual with the environment, achieve stability through self-regulation and feedback, and seek equilibrium but are equally dynamic and ever-changing. With the integration of ecosystem ecology and general systems theory, early family therapists began using systems concepts that emphasized transactional processes for understanding a family's interactions among the individual members and the surrounding cultural community. Attention is given to the function the family plays as an energy transformation system, the relationship between elements, and the production of human capital through the building of individual competencies. These competencies are necessary for successful interaction with the multitude of systems in the environment.

Over time, the conceptual framework of the ecosystems perspective was elaborated and refined. Developmental psychologist Urie Bronfenbrenner, whose research focused on the interrelationship of human-environment interaction, developed ecological systems theory between 1979 and his death in 2005. Central to ecological systems theory is the premise that human development has to go beyond the immediate behavior setting. According to Bronfenbrenner, development does not occur in isolation but rather in relation to one's family, home, community, culture, and society. Each of these ever-changing and multilevel environments, as well as one's interaction among them, are central to development. Bronfenbrenner advocated for the ecological validity of developmental research, emphasizing the assessment and study of children in their natural settings. Bronfenbrenner proposed the conceptual framework of concentric circles to represent the ecological environment where development takes place through processes of progressively more complex reciprocal social interaction, which represent factors farther and farther from individual control: the microsystem, mesosystem, exosystem, and macrosystem, framed within the chronosystem. The foci of the microsystem is on one's immediate interactions and contexts, the links and interrelations among the microsystems make up the mesosystem, the exosystem is composed of settings with which one does not have direct involvement yet affect the individual, the macrosystem is the overarching network of embedded systems that exert an indirect influence on the individual, and the chronosystem represents the dimension of historical time.

Major Concepts

In the ecosystems perspective, biological, social, and physical aspects of the individual, couples, and families are considered within the context of their environments. These environments may be the natural world, reality as constructed by members of a particular system, and/or the social and cultural milieu in which they live. Major concepts of the ecosystems perspective follow a general ecological model that views individuals interacting with their environment. The ecosystem contains levels of systems of varying complexity.

The Human Ecosystem

The human ecosystem includes interactions with the total environment in three organizing levels: human-environment level, environment level, and the interactive level between the two. The human-environment level is comprised of individuals and family. For the individual, the therapist will assess and intervene on cognitive, behavioral, and affective components. At the family level, clinical attention is given to family development issues, system function issues, and communication as well as relational and interactional issues. Environments are defined as the physical, biological, social, economic, political, aesthetic, and structural surroundings for individuals and families. The distinct but interrelated environments are natural, formed by nature with space-time, physical and biological components; human-constructed, altered or created by humans; and human-behavioral, essential for meeting physical, biological, psychological needs for love, relationships, communication, knowledge, and self-fulfillment. The third organizing concept of an ecosystem is the reciprocal interaction between and among the system components, which occur simultaneously. Interactions between and among the individual, family, and the environment are critically important for health and well-being. Rather than viewing individual functioning in isolation, therapeutic interventions should be targeted at multiple levels to improve family functioning.

Larger Systems

Families interact with larger societal systems, schools, health care, religious institutions, work, welfare, community, and the legal system. For illustrative purposes, school or work and community will be discussed. School and work have considerable influence on individuals and families. Areas for therapeutic work are school or work climate, teacher–student/worker–colleague relationship, and parent–teacher/supervisor–worker cooperation as well as discipline and morale. Finally, the community level constitutes the highest level of complexity and involves cultural, social, and institutional issues including contact with social agencies, social networks, economic and social status, employment opportunity, and crime and violence.

Transactional Importance

The ecosystem perspective takes a transactional focus, in which all systemic relationships are considered bidirectional and cyclic between the individual, family, and environment. In essence, individual and environment are adaptive to one another and thus contribute to adjustment and development. The family therapist does not view the individual and family apart from their environment; the environment contributes to their reality, which in turn creates unique responses with the environment. In essence, individuals, family, and their environments are adaptive to each other. Through the concept of transaction, the therapist can be expected to intervene at multiple levels of the entire transactional field, which could involve a case management approach involving interventions with the larger social ecology (e.g., advocacy, linkages with community resources, school consultation, and/or legal referrals).

Ecosystems Perspective Applied

Practice principles derived from the ecosystem perspective are aimed at promoting individual and family health, growth, and satisfying social functioning. Therapeutic efforts that focus on multisystemic levels, including the individual, family, community, and society, are the most effective. Problems may be addressed at the microlevel (e.g., by focusing on individual functioning or on improving relationships between family members); the meso level (e.g., by adopting a consulting approach that takes into account the interaction between the two systems impacting the individual or family); the ecosystem level (e.g., by addressing challenges by connecting to community resources, such as Alcoholics Anonymous, legal services, or spiritual communities); or at the macrosystem level (e.g., by participating in advocacy or social justice efforts).

Eco-Map

A family's connection to larger social systems can be pictorialized as an eco-map, which is a graphic device for drawing a family's social environment. An eco-map is a common tool used by social workers and therapists to assess the interconnections and multilayered realities of a family so that they may understand the uniqueness and complexities of the systems in which the family is embedded. An eco-map guides the clinician to see the connectedness of the family with their environment; identify transactional problems, intrapersonal issues, resources, support; and obtain deeper insights into the complex dynamics of a family's ecosystem. Complex environments, roots, and interactions are depicted as a matrix. The eco-map lays out multiple transactional realities, enabling the clinician to coordinate helping sources, organize supports, and identify stressors and protective factors in the family's network to coordinate professional action.

The Ecosystemic Structural Family Therapy Model

The ecosystemic structural family therapy (ESFT) model is an evidence-based practice (EBP) model developed by Marion Lindblad-Goldberg in the 1970s. ESFT has been implemented in clinical, home, and community settings for youth with severe emotional and behavioral disturbances and their families. The foundations of ESFT are structural family therapy (SFT) and attachment theory and utilizing family attachment and emotional processes as focal areas of treatment. Professional assistance is directed toward assessing multiple influences and directing therapeutic efforts so that change is supported throughout all systems affecting problem behaviors. The model has three program components: individual and family therapy, case management, and emergency crisis intervention. Interventions are targeted at family structure; family and individual emotional regulation; individual differences that include historical, biological, cultural, and developmental factors; affective proximity; and family development. ESFT has been demonstrated to be an efficacious alternative to more restrictive linear practice models in behavioral health settings, and for the most part, it is offered in the least restrictive environments (e.g., a family home or community setting). An ecosystemically oriented therapist takes into consideration all of the systems in which the family interacts, working from as many directions and at as many levels as possible.

Tami Sullivan

See also Ecological Systems; Eco-Map; Ecosystemic Structural Family Therapy; General Systems Theory; Structural Family Therapy

Further Readings

Allen-Meares, P., & Lane, B. (1987). Grounding social work practice in theory: Ecosystems. *Social Casework*, 68, 515–521.

Bubolz, M. M., & Sontag, M. S. (1993). Human ecology theory. In P. G. Boss, W. J. Doherty, R. LaRossa, W. R. Schumm, & S. K. Steinmetz (Eds.), *Sourcebook of family theories and methods: A contextual approach* (pp. 419–448). New York, NY: Plenum Press.

Compton, B. R., & Galaway, B. (1999). *Social work processes* (6th ed.). Pacific Grove, CA: Brooks/Cole.

Henggeler, S. W., & Borduin, C. M. (1990). *Family therapy and beyond: A multisystemic approach to treating the behavioral problems of children and adolescents*. Pacific Grove, CA: Brooks/Cole.

Henggeler, S. W., & Cunningham, P. B. (2006). School-related interventions and outcomes for multisystemic therapy (MST). *Family Psychologist*, 22(1), 4–5, 28–29.

Jones, C. W., & Lindblad-Goldberg, M. (2002). Ecosystemic structural family therapy: Elaborations of theory and practice. In F. Kaslow (Series Ed.), R. Massey (Vol. Ed.), & S. Massey (Vol. Ed.), *Comprehensive handbook of psychotherapy: Vol. III. Interpersonal, humanistic and existential models*. New York, NY: Wiley.

Lindblad-Goldberg, M., Jones, C. W., & Dore, M. (2004). *Effective family based mental health services for children with severe emotional disturbances in Pennsylvania: The ecosystemic structural family therapy model*. Harrisburg, PA: CAASP Training and Technical Institute.

Lindblad-Goldberg, M., & Northey, W. F., Jr. (2013). Ecosystemic structural family therapy: Theoretical and clinical foundations. *Journal of Contemporary Family Therapy*, 35, 147–160.

Robbins, M. S., Mayorga, B. A., & Szapocznik, J. (2003). The ecosystemic "lens" for understanding family functioning. In T. L. Sexton, G. R. Weeks, & M. S. Robbins (Eds.), *Handbook of family therapy: The science and practice of working with families and couples*. New York, NY: Brunner-Routledge.

Stormshak, E. A., & Dishion, T. J. (2002). An ecological approach to child and family clinical and counseling psychology. *Clinical Child and Family Psychology Review*, 5(3), 197–215.

EFFECTIVENESS RESEARCH

Effectiveness research emerged from medical and pharmaceutical research. This method seeks to determine the effectiveness of specific interventions, devices, or medications for treatment of diseases or disorders. Inherent in this type of research is an assumption that results lead to a positive or therapeutic outcome. As disciplines move in the direction of using evidence to guide practice, effectiveness research has gained more attention as a way of determining which specific therapeutic interventions promote positive outcomes. Effectiveness research in marriage and family therapy involves the application of family therapy models and is designed to give more information on the efficacy of an intervention under ordinary situations. The purpose of effectiveness research in these settings is to implement the intervention under less controlled circumstances and evaluate the "effectiveness" or "efficacy" of the intervention under normal or usual situations. Prior to conducting effectiveness research, a study that tested the intervention has usually been completed. Effectiveness research provides conclusions that lead to EBP derived from the integration of best research evidence conducted by practitioners and scholars engaged in family therapy. This entry offers an overview of effectiveness research in the field of marriage and family therapy.

Effectiveness research emerged out of the "hard" sciences such as medicine, biological sciences, and chemistry. Randomized clinical trials (RCTs) are the most common methodology used in these fields. In this methodology, participants in the study are randomly assigned to either an experimental group, which receives the treatment, or a control group, which does not receive the treatment. Although most "hard" sciences have the ability to develop RCTs, not all social science research lends itself to this methodology. However, social scientists still engage in research with the goal of determining which therapeutic interventions promote positive patient–client outcomes.

Family therapy research is a method of systematic inquiry with the goal of developing knowledge about issues of importance to the profession. This research approach seeks to determine which interventions offer the best evidence leading to positive client outcomes. In the field of family therapy theories, models and research provide the necessary foundation for practice. A reciprocal relationship exists between practice and research in that practice provides the source of questions for research. Practice also acts as the testing ground for models and their associated interventions and therefore is the place where effectiveness research occurs.

Effectiveness research conducted within the discipline of family therapy encompasses the following: (a) the model or therapeutic approach; (b) the client and/or family problem; and (c) the interventions. For example, research regarding clients who have an eating disorder would discuss a specific therapeutic approach, such as narrative therapy. The interventions aligned with that approach include deconstruction, externalization, and reauthoring. The researcher would then evaluate the effectiveness of these interventions when using this approach with clients who have eating disorders. The hope would be that these specific interventions would lead to positive outcomes for these types of client problems.

Until recently, family therapy research has focused on publishing the results of individual studies. It is important to remember that one or two studies about a specific intervention may indicate that the intervention shows applicability to practice; however, these results suggest a need for more research that continues to test the intervention in order to generalize its applicability to larger populations. With the move to EBP, family therapy researchers have started to realize the need to analyze and synthesize previously conducted research interventions to determine their overall effectiveness in clinical practice. Considering the number of models and the different therapeutic results associated with each model, engaging in effectiveness or outcomes research is a daunting task.

The best method for evaluating effectiveness or outcomes research is to access databases, such as the Cochrane database, that provide systematic reviews of treatment interventions for specific client and/or family problems. These reviews compare several family therapy models and their accompanying interventions and provide evidence on which to base practice. From this base, the discipline finds itself in a position to develop EBP guidelines for therapists to follow and apply within the practice setting.

Research evidence may be ranked according to a hierarchy. The evidence hierarchy allows family therapists to determine if the evidence is strong enough to indicate practice changes. The best evidence comes from RCTs. The lowest form of evidence is that of expert opinions. However, expert opinion creates a basis for asking the research question that guides a study or studies that in turn provide evidence of the effectiveness of the interventions.

Since a deficiency of systematic reviews exist within the profession of family therapy, scholars and practitioners may need to evaluate existing research. A review of research articles can also provide evidence on which to base practice approaches. Guides for appraising a study are available in a number of research texts. Using these guides helps to determine the rigor of the study. A therapist who conducts a review of research to determine the effectiveness of an intervention should attempt to publish his or her findings as a systematic review of current research in order to add to the body of knowledge of the discipline. For example, a review of several therapeutic approaches for the treatment of eating disorders in adolescents showed that systemic family therapy leads to positive outcomes in this population. This review compared 10 studies conducted over a period of years from 1985 to 2000, including follow-up studies. The researchers analyzed and synthesized the results on the effectiveness of the interventions associated with these models. This review provided the basis for EBP interventions. In addition, outcome research in schizophrenia demonstrated that family intervention significantly decreased the number of relapses of the schizophrenic family member at both 12 and 24 months. The research also showed that patients in families who received intervention remained more compliant with their medication regimens.

Alyssa Weiss Quittner

See also Outcome Research; Prevention Research; Process Research

Further Readings

Gingerich, W. J., & Eisengart, S. (2000). Solution-focused brief therapy: A review of the outcome research. *Family Process, 39*(4), 477–498.

Gurman, A. S., & Kniskern, D. P. (Eds.). (2013). *Handbook of family therapy* (Vol. 1). New York, NY: Routledge.

O'Farrell, T. J., & Clements, K. (2012). Review of outcome research on marital and family therapy in treatment for alcoholism. *Journal of Marital and Family Therapy, 38*(1), 122–144.

Sprenkle, D. H. (2002). *Effectiveness research in marriage and family therapy*. Alexandria, VA: American Association for Marriage and Family Therapy.

ELDER ABUSE

Elder abuse is both a crime and a hidden tragedy that affects an estimated 1 in 10 adults over the age of 60 in the United States each year. Understanding what actions constitute elder abuse and exploitation are necessary for mental health professionals to recognize and proactively assist victims. Because the victims are often isolated, helpless, and fearful, the actual extent of elder abuse is likely much larger than the numbers of cases reported to law enforcement. Elder abuse can be any type of active harm or passive neglect that is intended to intimidate, control, or cause physical harm to an elderly person. The insidious nature of elder abuse is that it is perpetrated by a caregiver, family member, or other person on whom the elder depends and trusts. This entry examines the prevalence of elder abuse and types of elder abuse. This entry also discusses society's obligation to respond to elder abuse and some of the efforts being made to do so.

The Prevalence of Elder Abuse

The Centers for Disease Control and Prevention (CDC) further clarified the nature of elder abuse as actions within six categories: physical abuse, sexual abuse, emotional abuse, financial abuse, neglect, and abandonment. The lines become blurred when the abuse is between elder adult couples. What distinguishes this from domestic violence? In terms of relationship violence between a married or committed couple, the distinction may be drawn by law. Typically, the domestic abuse between partners may be considered elder abuse when the victim is an older adult who falls under the definition of state statutes addressing elder abuse. In situations where there has been no domestic violence during earlier years of the relationship, the later life relationship violence that occurs may be part of caregiving frustration or anger over draining financial resources for medical or disability care.

Elderly women are at higher risk for abuse and exploitation than elderly men; however, the oldest old are particularly vulnerable and least likely to report abuse or neglect. Because victims are often isolated and intimidated, investigators look first at the people on whom the elders depend for care and support. Sadly, 90% of the abusers are family members, including spouses, partners, adult children, and relatives. This estimate is based on what is found nationally in reported elder abuse cases.

For older adults with a disability or dementia, the risk of being abused, neglected, or exploited rises dramatically. As with other types of abuse, older women are at higher risk. Among the disabled or cognitively impaired older adults, physical abuse and sexual abuse are most common toward older women while physical abuse and financial exploitation are more common toward older men. Older adults with memory impairment or dementia are easy prey for abuse and exploitation because they lack the capacity to recall details of the abuse and are confused when questioned. This problem is magnified by Alzheimer's disease, which impacts 11% of adults over 65 and among whom a majority (82%) are age 75 or older.

Types of Elder Abuse

Obvious types of physical abuse are hitting, pushing, shaking, kicking, or intimidating from a person who is physically stronger or more agile. Physical abuse may also be subtle such as inadequately caring for wounds, failing to provide assistive devices (walker, cane, wheelchair, hearing aid, eyeglasses), or excessively medicating as a tool of control. Intimate partner violence may use any of these methods as well as restricting food, refusing to provide clean clothing, or failing to get medical attention for injuries caused by the abusive partner toward the victim.

Emotional or psychological abuse is difficult to detect. Threats, insults, ethnic slurs, and demeaning comments about the mental or physical disability of elders occurs in family homes as well as in nursing homes. A family caregiver may resort to isolating the elder from relatives or friends. Nursing home caregivers may refuse to allow the older adult to have telephone contact with family to exert control or as punishment. Other nursing home staff that observe or overhear these abuses and do not report share guilt in their failure to protect elderly patients. Another less apparent type of emotional abuse by family or paid caregivers is refusal to allow religious symbols in the elder's room or to respect the elder's desire to speak about spirituality and read spiritual books. Other treasured personal items like photographs, jewelry, or other memorabilia may be destroyed or used as a behavioral inducement. Pets may be harmed or given away to punish the older adult for noncompliance. Like a kidnap victim, the older adult may become hypervigilant, withdrawn, and depressed as well as exhibit other noncharacteristic behaviors. What can appear as paranoia may be a real expression of fear. The abusers typically explain the elder's pleas for help as delusional, which may or may not be accurate. Health care professionals must be careful to listen and ask for investigation if uncertain. The abuser may also drug the older adult so that efforts to tell another person about the mistreatment sound like confused ramblings.

Sexual abuse of disabled and cognitively impaired elderly people is a horrific violation that may include intimate touching, kissing with sexual intent, molestation, object penetration, or intercourse. Such abuse involves assault or sexual acts with a person who is not mentally competent to give consent. Older women in long-term care facilities are most often the victims of sexual abuse. Signs of possible sexual abuse may be unexplained bruises, bleeding, genital or anal pain, stained clothing, or a sexually transmitted disease. In this digital age of camera phones and easy uploading, abusive caregivers may circulate photos of older adults nude in the shower or arrange a drugged or sleeping person in a sexually exposed position.

Financial abuse involves stealing the older adult's Social Security payments, pensions, savings, or other assets. The unscrupulous caregiver or guardian may sell heirloom jewelry, collectibles, or property by tricking the older adult into signing approval or by misusing a power of attorney. Online and telephone scams get headlines; however, most financial exploitation is done by family members, caregivers, lawyers, and professional advisers. A caregiver, family member, or financial adviser who secures a guardianship over the older adult can literally wipe out savings before the misdeeds are revealed. Even if prosecuted for the theft, the money is usually not recoverable.

Neglect is a passive yet equally harmful type of elder abuse. The caregiver fails to provide the basic needs of food, clothing, shelter, hygiene, social support, medication, or access to health care. Whether due to stress or other factors, the caregivers (family in home or facility staff) ignore or dismiss the older adult's pleas for assistance. In the most heinous situations, the caregiver may willfully neglect the medical or safety needs of the older adult, hoping to hasten death and gain inheritance. Some families may assume that once the older adult is in a professional care setting, there is no risk of mistreatment and cease to monitor the care.

Abandonment is another form of neglect whether the older adult lives alone, without family support, lives with relatives, or is dropped at the nursing home. The purposely neglectful attitudes of family members toward the elder are not merely related to the caregiving burden but may come from prior family resentments. Family members may consistently be unavailable for support or move away from the older relative to avoid caregiving responsibilities. Only a few states have laws specifically detailing what constitutes abandonment of elderly people. In other family care situations, the caregiver may have become ill, disabled, depressed, frustrated, or discover that the care needs exceed his or her training and ability to manage on a daily basis with little or no relief.

Self-neglect, formerly known as Diogenes syndrome, occurs when an older adult refuses basic self-care, nutrition, health care, or a clean and safe home. Factors consistent with self-neglect may include dementia, social alienation, mental disorders, psychotic disorders, substance abuse, or personality disorders. An individual who neglects self-care to the point of harm has a condition also referred to as social disengagement. The older adult is not necessarily incapable of interacting with others but persistently chooses not to engage in social interactions. In such cases, it can take a long time to determine whether or not the older adult is mentally competent to care for self or others.

Ageism: Social Attitudes That Sustain Elder Abuse

Ageism is an accepted social stigma that ranges from indifference to intentional mistreatment. Psychiatrist and gerontology pioneer Robert Butler coined the term *ageism*, which he defined in his Pulitzer Prize–winning nonfiction book *Why Survive? Being Old in America*. Ageism is an ongoing process of discrimination toward older adults because of their advanced age. Ageism is reinforced by stereotypes of older adults as slow, inept, nonproductive, demanding, and wasting resources. Age discrimination cuts across ethnic, cultural, gender, and socioeconomic lines. Butler warns about how ageism is transmitted to younger generations and causes them to lose connection with older adults. As this attitude becomes culturally accepted, it is reinforced by actions and words that dehumanize older adults. When young adults lose respect for the older generation and view them as a burden or obstacle, that prejudice supports abusive actions. While frail elderly people at home or in long-term care seem to be the most vulnerable, community-dwelling elders are no less at risk.

Other factors that can lead to elder abuse include the presence of younger family members who resent spending resources or time on older relatives. The demands of caring for older adults with Alzheimer's disease or other long-term illnesses often also leads to burnout. While caregiver stress is a genuine problem, unscrupulous relatives or facility staff may hide behind this as an excuse to conceal their reprehensible motives. The inconsistencies among state legal definitions for elder abuse and the fear of reporting the caregivers on whom victims depend perpetuates a system that unwittingly protects perpetrators at the expense of older adult victims.

Duty to Protect

Professional staff caregivers, nurses, counselors, psychologists, and physicians have a duty to protect older adults from abuse by family, staff, or other residents. Those who are mandatory reporters by state law are required to report signs of abuse to law enforcement for investigation. While friends and neighbors do not have a legal or professional obligation to report suspected elder abuse, those who hear, see, or have a genuine concern need to accept a social obligation to be the voice for the older adult and seek help.

Ageism is sometimes viewed as the last prejudice that seems to be unnoticed or easily dismissed. Challenging ageism with the vigor that has been shown against racism and sexism will be a significant step forward in dismantling the damaging impact of ageism and the elder mistreatment that is shielded behind this generational prejudice. As ageism continues virtually unchecked in American society, the warning that Butler gave 40 years ago is perhaps more prevalent than ever before. As Butler observed at the time, we are becoming a society that is uncaring, even hostile, toward anyone who is older. Elder abuse is a substantial part of the tragedy of growing old in the United States.

Learning to recognize signs of possible elder abuse is key to stopping this crime and protecting the rights of vulnerable older adults.

Kathie Erwin

See also Aging and Caregiving; Conflict in Couples and Families; Domestic Violence

Further Readings

Pavlou, M. P., & Lachs, M. S. (2006). Could self-neglect in older adults be a geriatric syndrome? *Journal of the American Geriatrics Society, 54*, 831–842.

Payne, B. K. (2011). *Crime and elder abuse: An integrated perspective.* Springfield, IL: Charles C Thomas.

Sandell, D. S., & Hudson, L. (2010). *Ending elder abuse: A family guide.* Fort Bragg, CA: Cypress House.

Shenoy, C. (2015). *Elder abuse prevention and intervention: A guide to dealing with nursing home abuse and other elderly abuse issues.* Seattle, WA: CreateSpace Independent Publishing Platform.

Wiglesworth, A., Mosqueda, L., Mulnard, R., Liao, S., Gibbs, L., & Fitzgerald, W. (2010). Screening for abuse and neglect of people with dementia. *Journal of the American Geriatrics Society, 58*(3), 493–500.

Zimnisky Pickering, C. E., & Phillips, L. R. (2014). Development of a causal model for elder mistreatment. *Public Health Nursing, 31*(4), 363–372.

ELIMINATION DISORDERS IN CHILDREN

Elimination disorders are defined by the inappropriate release of feces or urine from the body and are typically categorized as encopresis (fecal incontinence) and enuresis (urinary incontinence). Elimination disorders may be triggered by a physical condition or a psychiatric condition; therefore, it is critical for medical issues or medication side effects to be ruled out as a cause of the disorder. This entry examines encopresis, enuresis, and evidence-based treatments of both.

Encopresis

Encopresis, also referred to as fecal incontinence, is characterized by repeated bowel movements in inappropriate places such as in clothing or on the floor. The behavior may or may not be purposeful. This should not be confused with toileting accidents, which are frequent for young children. Instead, encopresis should be considered only when the behavior occurs frequently for a period of time longer than 3 months and the child is 4 years or older. Encopresis is reported in approximately 3% of pediatric referrals and is more common in boys. Negative interactions with parents, peers, and teachers regarding the issue can potentially impact the behavioral and psychological aspects of the disorder.

Encopresis can often be traced to a chronic constipation, which may lead to fear of toileting. Compaction of feces in the colon causes the colon to stretch, which produces a disruption in the nerve signals that indicate when it is necessary to use the toilet. When compaction occurs and the colon is overly full, leaking of fluids or soft stool ensues, and the child is unable to control the leakage. Encopresis has many possible sources including a lack of fiber in the diet, milk allergies, medication side effects, lack of proper fluid intake, fear of toileting, stress, or not toileting because of not wanting to interrupt playtime. Left untreated, encopresis can have potentially serious medical and social–emotional implications.

Evidence-Based Treatments

A biopsychosocial (BPS) model is often used, combining both medical treatment and psychotherapy. A behavioral treatment plan may include the following:

1. Referral to a physician for laxative therapy and disimpaction as necessary.
2. Psychoeducation for parents and children to rectify feelings of guilt and shame in the child as well as negative judgments by the parents ("He's just being lazy," "He's doing this on purpose," etc.).
3. Modeling provided by the parents.
4. Desensitization to the toilet by rewarding incremental approaches to the toilet such as going into the bathroom, standing close to the toilet, sitting on the toilet with the lid down, sitting on the toilet fully clothed with the lid open, and sitting on the toilet with the lid open and pants down.
5. Eliminating all punishment, focusing primarily on a reward system and praise for appropriate toileting.
6. Creating a toileting schedule.
7. Instituting dietary changes to include more fiber and fluids.
8. The utilization of research-based online programs such as U-Can-Poop-Too.

Enuresis

Enuresis refers to the passing of urine in inappropriate places such as in clothing or bedding. As with encopresis, this may or may not be intentional behavior. The term *enuresis* can be further defined as being nocturnal (occurring at night, as is the case for bed-wetting), which is the most common form, diurnal (occurring during waking hours), or both. To be considered clinically significant, enuresis must occur in an individual older than age 5 a minimum of twice weekly for 3 months or more. As with encopresis, medical causes for the incontinence should be ruled out. Typically, diurnal enuresis is more commonly found in girls whereas nocturnal enuresis is more commonly found in boys. As children mature, episodes of enuresis tend to decline.

Enuresis can have a significant impact on the social and emotional well-being of both the parents and the child. Children affected by the disorder may experience depression and poor sleep quality, particularly as they grow older. Mothers of children with enuresis may experience anxiety and depression as well.

The causes of enuresis are complex. Medically speaking, enuresis can be a product of an underlying physical abnormality such as an undersized bladder. Psychologically, there are possible emotional components as well. Stress, separation from a parental figure, developmental delays, and attention-deficit/hyperactivity disorder (ADHD) are all potential factors.

Evidence-Based Treatments

Bladder training can be used for either diurnal or nocturnal enuresis. Often, children and parents want to cut back on fluids to try to avoid bedwetting; however, this is counterproductive because the bladder adjusts to the change and holds less fluid resulting in more frequently needing to urinate. With bladder training, children are encouraged to increase the amount of fluids taken in during the day in order to increase bladder capacity. In addition, this method establishes a toileting routine in which the child uses the toilet every hour and then increases the intervals over a period of time. Combining these two techniques increases bladder capacity. The third part of this method is ensuring that the bladder is completely emptied when the child uses the toilet. This can be accomplished by counting slowly to 10 after urinating.

Conditioning therapy paired with medication to decrease urine production is the most commonly utilized form of therapy for nocturnal enuresis. Conditioning therapy consists of using an alarm system, which alerts the child when the bedding gets wet. This trains the child to become more aware of bladder fullness during sleep. This type of therapy is considered to be the most effective with the lowest rate of relapse.

In recent years, researchers have begun studying alternative methods for treating nocturnal enuresis and have found acupuncture to be a promising treatment. Specific acupuncture points are selected that lessen bladder contractions and suppress muscle activity prominent in enuresis. Acupuncture, particularly electroacupuncture, in conjunction with traditional Chinese medicine has been shown to have more positive results than the use of a nighttime bed-wetting alarm. This and other alternative forms of treatment have potential, but more research needs to be conducted.

Janna C. Ramsey

See also Attention-Deficit and Disruptive Behavior Disorders; Childhood Anxiety; Depression in Children; Parental Stress: Effects on Children

Further Readings

Bower, W. F., & Diao, M. (2010). Acupuncture as a treatment for nocturnal enuresis [Electronic version]. *Autonomic Neuroscience, 157*(1–2), 63–70. doi:10.1016/j.autneu.2010.07.003

Freeman, K. A., Riley, A., Duke, D., & Fu, R. (2014). Systematic review (and meta-analysis) of behavioral interventions for fecal incontinence with constipation. *Journal of Pediatric Psychology, 39,* 887–902. doi:10.1093/jpepsy/jsu039

Friman, P. C., Hofstadter, K. L., & Jones, K. M. (2006). A biobehavioral approach to the treatment of functional encopresis in children. *Journal of Early and Intensive Behavior Intervention, 3*(3), 263–272.

McGrath, M. L., Mellon, M. W., & Murphy, L. (2000). Empirically supported treatments in pediatric psychology: Constipation and encopresis. *Journal of Pediatric Psychology, 25*(2), 225–254.

Moser, N. L., Plante, W. A., LeLeiko, N. S., & Lobato, D. J. (2014). Integrating behavioral health services into pediatric gastroenterology: A model of an integrated health care program. *Clinical Practice in Pediatric Psychology, 2*(1), 1–12.

UCanPoopToo. Retrieved from http://www.ucanpooptoo.com

Wassom, M. C., & Christophersen, E. R. (2014). A clinical application of evidence-based treatments in pediatric functional constipation and incontinence. *Clinical Practice in Pediatric Psychology, 2014*(3), 294–311.

EMOTIONAL DISENGAGEMENT

Emotional disengagement is a pattern of response, typically to negative emotional experience, that attempts to deny, suppress, or mask those resulting negative feelings. It can be manifested in a number of behaviors, but the goal is to remove oneself from the unpleasantness of those emotions, regardless of the consequences. This entry examines emotional disengagement, its associated behaviors, and their consequences.

Emotion

When one discusses emotion, sometimes referred to as affect, the first difficulty in understanding it is to find an appropriate definition. This can be a challenge as there are many ways to describe what emotion is and not all of them align. Adding to the challenge is the qualitative classification of emotions as "good" or "bad," which is also highly subjective. It seems that when searching for a definition of emotion, only one thing can be agreed upon—emotion is a psychological, physiological, and behavioral response to an event. As such, different emotions may be best explained in relation to combinations of these three components.

Emotional Socialization and Dysregulation

Most people are relatively adept at identifying emotions, both within themselves and in others around them. Even infants are capable of recognizing different emotions in their parents' faces. What typically occurs as a part of a child's socialization growing up is that they are taught to identify some emotions as positive (e.g., happy, content, and excited) and others as negative (e.g., sad, angry, and depressed). Parents will usually send their children either verbal or nonverbal messages about which emotions are acceptable and which are not. They may also focus particularly on the child's behaviors associated with those emotions (e.g., hitting when angry). How much parents focus on these behaviors and how they respond to them will depend largely on two things: (1) the ways in which they have interpreted the value of certain emotions and (2) how well they are able to regulate their own emotions. For example, if parents see anger as a negative emotion, and if it is, perhaps, one with which they have difficulty, they may attempt to discount or discourage its expression in the home, even if it is expressed appropriately. It could be that they are unable to recognize appropriate expressions of emotion themselves and therefore are unable to teach a child how to do so as well.

In some cases, especially in situations where parents may have some difficulty with the ability to regulate their own emotions appropriately, parents may inadvertently pass on some of that dysfunction to their children through their own, albeit poor, example. This is particularly true for those emotions that are deemed negative. In such cases, it is not uncommon to see difficulties with affect regulation in both parents and children. For example, if a mother or father is emotionally disengaged from the family, the likelihood that one or more of the children will also become emotionally disengaged is much stronger. The connection between emotional expression and attachment styles also can be used to explain maladaptive attachment between parents and their children.

Categorization of Emotion

Some researchers argue that emotion, in and of itself, is neutral but that the associated categorization of positive or negative is a socially imposed norm. However, the actual experience of many emotions suggests that there are noticeable differences in how one experiences feelings and how these experiences are categorized isn't always intuitive (e.g., is it positive or negative?). For example, feeling happy generally is a positive psychological experience, lifting the person up and producing good feelings, but some may feel guilt for feeling happy in certain circumstances. So is that positive or negative? Likewise, feeling sad or angry may elicit an undesirable state or experience that may even perpetuate the original feeling response (with more sadness or anger). In another case, that sadness or anger might be justified so there may also be a sense of vindication or contentment. The question becomes whether the emotional classification stems from the visceral, the intellectual, or a social norm. Perhaps there are components of all three, but regardless of the source, the interpretation of emotions being positive or negative is significant to the individual who experiences the emotion. This categorization can influence the choices and actions that lead to emotional disengagement.

Components of Emotion

The Psychological Component

The psychological component of emotion, some will argue, is the individual's appraisal of the event in question. The individual must recognize the event and, in some way, interpret the event with regard to whether it might pose a threat, present a dilemma, or bring a positive and/or desirable outcome. Some researchers have stated that there is a question whether there truly is a conscious appraisal of emotion or, because of the short amount of time that is necessary to elicit an emotional response, whether it might be an automatic brain response. Others have stated that without meaning assigned to an event, there is no need for emotional response. Certainly these all have their values, but there appears to be no definitive answer to which is correct. Perhaps it is not the means of appraisal but rather its result that is most important in the psychological component of emotion.

The Physiological Component

The physiological component of emotion can be found in responses to an event that trigger arousal in some way. The body will produce sweat or tears and perhaps goosebumps, flushing, or muscle tension among other reactions. Many of these responses are associated with certain emotions (i.e., fear often produces muscle tension, sweat, and perhaps tears). However, the confusion comes when those same responses can also be associated with more than one emotion. For example, sweat may be associated with fear, arousal, or anger. As a result, physiological responses may indicate a particular emotional state and signify other emotional states at the same time. This can be confusing and unpleasant and may even lead to a desire to disengage from the emotional process altogether.

The Behavioral Component

The third component, the behavioral response to emotion, may be the best predictor or identifier for emotional disengagement but is also not a completely reliable measure. Behaviors that stem from emotion are usually termed as expressions of emotion and are usually deemed appropriate or inappropriate. These may be aggressive types of behaviors, or avoidant behaviors, or they may be neutral behaviors but may also be associated with emotions in some context. For example, an angry child might lash out at a peer or family member (aggressive), a sad event may cause a person to withdraw from those around them (avoidant), or a happy event may cause a person to jump up and down in excitement (neutral). The concept of avoidance, which is primarily associated with emotional disengagement, is also part of the behavioral component.

Disengagement

To disengage is to move away from something or to detach oneself. In this case, one avoids an experience with the hope that the experience will subsequently cease to exist. However, this course can have both interpersonal and intrapersonal costs. For example, when an unpleasant event occurs, such as a death in the family, an emotionally disengaged person may be determined not to be involved in the funeral arrangements or perhaps not even attend the funeral in order to eradicate the idea that a painful loss has occurred. It is this pushing away or suppressing the distressing emotion that is the key. They may be completely oblivious to the consequences and detrimental effects the resulting actions (or inactions) may have on others around them. And their own lack of acknowledgment of the loss could prevent them from ever reaching a sense of closure with the grief process. If carried through, the process would lead to growth. What is often not understood is that such avoidance can further perpetuate one's dysfunction and even prolong the pain one is trying to avoid. Although emotional disengagement is most often understood as a behavioral component of emotion, in therapy, psychological and physiological components also need to be taken into account.

As noted previously, the need to disengage, or retreat, from one's emotions is born of the discomfort that one feels in the experience of negative emotion. Psychoanalytic theory traces the use of defenses to avoid unpleasant emotions and circumstances. The avoidance of negative feelings is a strong motivator for behavior. With disengagement, however, it goes a step beyond mere avoidance. Whatever must be done to divert attention and energy away from the negative is what one will choose over the healthier option of just facing something and dealing with it. The ways in which this may happen vary. Disengagement can begin with simple denial, but typically it is much further advanced. It may involve deliberate distraction or rumination on some unrelated topic to keep the mind occupied elsewhere. It will often involve whatever one sees as a potential way to relieve the anxiety that the negative emotional experience may present. Emotional disengagement will seek to deny or even suppress those emotions to get the experience completely out of the mind so as not to have to deal with those negative emotions. It is almost an "out of sight, out of mind" proposition. While, to the average person, that may sound like a perfectly legitimate way to deal with negativity, there can be some serious consequences to the one who has disengaged.

Consequences of Emotional Disengagement

When one is emotionally disengaged, they are essentially cut off from their emotional experience. They have a very difficult time connecting with their own emotions as they are very nearly incapable of allowing themselves to feel anything at all, particularly so when it is deemed a negative emotional experience. When that happens, one is deprived of key communication tools that allow them to relate to those around them including significant others and family. For example, without the ability to acknowledge, let alone share, one's emotional experience, it will be very difficult for them to enter into the emotional experience of their significant other and thus block the potential for intimacy. A shared emotional connection is the foundation for an intimate relationship. For the emotionally disengaged partner, this will seriously impede attempts to connect and to remain connected with a significant other.

Likewise, intergenerational consequences can occur with an emotionally disengaged parent and his or her children. Many of these parent–child dyads will spawn dysfunctional interaction patterns that may continually perpetuate a pattern of emotional disengagement in the children from as early as infancy and into adulthood. As stated previously, the pattern is easily passed on from parent to child via behavior modeling. In addition, there is also some evidence that there may be a genetic propensity to engage in this type of emotional avoidance. In such a case, the individual would need to learn strong behavioral skills to overcome that propensity toward disengagement.

And still a third consequence is the physiological effects of disengagement. The experience of emotion, as stated previously, has a physiological component. When that aspect is ignored or suppressed, there is a physiological change that occurs. There can be substantial change in the ability of the brain to regulate arousal, thus making it more difficult for a psychotherapeutic intervention to be of help. There are significant cardiovascular and immune system effects, which can lead to serious physical illness if left unchecked. And there are several mental health diagnoses for which the person will become more vulnerable. There is a stronger propensity toward mood disorders, anxiety disorders, binge eating, and substance and food addictions. All of these diagnoses can present serious challenges to a person's well-being, their relationships, and their livelihood without appropriate treatment.

Emotional disengagement, to summarize, serves a purpose. It is a means of coping with stressful or painful situations that some people adopt in order to avoid rather than address difficult situations. Some researchers maintain that people who consistently choose emotional disengagement do so due to the genetic and/or behavioral example they were given in their family of origin. However, there can be both the desired results (e.g., the temporary avoidance of situational pain) and, as discussed throughout this entry, a number of more permanent undesired results.

Lori Ellison

See also Affect Regulation; Attachment; Avoidance; Conflict Styles; Parent–Child Communication

Further Readings

Campos, J. J., Frankel, C. B., & Camras, L. (2004). On the nature of emotion regulation. *Child Development*, 75, 377–394. doi:10.1111/j.1467-8624.2004.00681.x

Cumberland-Li, A., Eisenberg, N., Champion, C., Gershoff, E., & Fabes, R. A. (2003). The relation of parental emotionality and related dispositional traits to parental expression of emotion and children's social functioning. *Motivation and Emotion*, 27, 27–56.

Eisenberg, N., Champion, C., & Ma, Y. (2004). Emotion-related regulation: An emerging construct. *Merrill-Palmer Quarterly*, 50, 236–259.

Eisenberg, N., Cumberland, A., & Spinrad, T. L. (1998). Parental socialization of emotion. *Psychological Inquiry*, 9, 241–273.

Gross, J. (1998). The emerging field of emotion regulation: An integrative review. *Review of General Psychology*, 2, 271–299.

Hill, D. (2015). *Affect regulation theory: A clinical model*. New York, NY: W. W. Norton.

Rice, J. A., Levine, L. J., & Pizarro, D. A. (2007). "Just stop thinking about it": Effects of emotional disengagement on children's memory for educational material. *Emotion*, 7, 812–823. doi:10.1037/1528-3542.7.4.812

Weeks, G. R., & Treat, S. R. (2001). *Couples in treatment: Techniques and approaches for effective practice*. New York, NY: Brunner-Routledge.

Emotional Intelligence, Children

Intelligence is a term people often associate with one's cognitive abilities. However, there are multiple forms of intelligence, including emotional intelligence. Emotional intelligence is a multifaceted term used to describe people's emotional abilities and skills related to cognitive abilities and disposition. For example, it is used to describe an individual's ability to exercise good judgment and guide their thinking and behaviors based on emotions and further used to describe the ability to correctly identify other people's emotions. An additional component of emotional intelligence is the individual's ability to register and understand conflicting emotions, such as feeling excited and scared at the same time. The ability to differentiate and label various emotions appropriately demonstrates the intersection of the cognitive and emotional systems. These systems create the entirety of emotional intelligence. Though the term is applicable to all individuals, it is especially relevant in the discussion of children and their developmental process. This entry briefly introduces emotional intelligence as an ability and as a trait. In addition, two theories of child development and their relationship to emotional intelligence are discussed. Finally, the influence of attachment and parenting styles on emotional intelligence is reviewed.

Background

The idea of emotional intelligence can be traced back to E. L. Thorndike's construct of emotional intelligence in the 1920s; Howard Gardner's work on personal intelligence (intrapersonal and interpersonal); Peter Salovey and John D. Mayer's model of emotional intelligence in the 1990s; and Daniel Goleman's perspective, which he introduced in his 1995 best-selling book and subsequent work. In addition, there is a foundation of research that points to the importance of emotional intelligence in learning, decision-making, creativity, relationships, and health. Over time, it has been concluded that emotional intelligence contains three central ideas: (1) perceiving emotions of self and others, (2) understanding emotions, and (3) managing emotions. If people are able to perceive their emotions and understand them, they are also better able to manage emotions.

Trait Emotional Intelligence

Emotional intelligence can be viewed as a cognitive-emotional ability or as emotional self-efficacy. This latter type of emotional intelligence is called *trait emotional intelligence* and is a constellation of self-perceptions and dispositions linked to the child's emotions that affect the individual's personality. For example, emotional regulation, assertiveness, self-esteem, and stress management are all areas believed to be controlled within the context of trait emotional intelligence. It is believed that the weaker a child's trait emotional intelligence is, the more somatic complaints, such as stomachaches or headaches, a child may have in relation to stressful or upsetting situations. This is related to an inability to emotionally regulate during stressful times causing the child to experience physical reactions to the environmental stressors. However, a strong correlation exists in parenting styles and the increased development of trait emotional intelligence. Parents who spend quality time with their children doing educational activities appear to have a stronger influence on their children's trait emotional intelligence development. This indicates a relationship between trained emotional intelligence and other cognitive development, showing the importance of parents teaching problem-solving skills to their children.

Dynamic Systems Theory

Dynamic systems theory is a modern theoretical lens that is considered broad by nature and encompasses all developmental theories. The theory creates an observation for all possible factors that are in action during a developmental stage. According to this theoretical orientation, development occurs on many levels and throughout an individual's life. Development is a consistent, fluid, and multidetermined process. Dynamic systems theory is a framework that emphasizes emotional intelligence as important to the social and physical context of a child's development. It recognizes that a child begins to understand that certain emotions can be expressed at certain times (e.g., it is okay to cry when you are sad, and people laugh when they are happy).

Looking at emotional intelligence in children, dynamic systems theory brings into consideration the many variables and factors that occur to reach emotional intelligence, such as family dynamics, educational settings, and life experiences. A child's emotional development can be observed through the theoretical lens of dynamical systems, which seek to understand how the child interacts and exists in dynamic family structure. Through this lens, the child develops emotionally through expressive behaviors, patterning emotions after observing others, identifying social and physical contexts, and identifying action tendencies of self and others. These items change over time as the child ages and impact areas of psychosocial development.

Emotional intelligence also goes through stages of development as a child ages and can be identified as mile markers in the child's emotional development when considered from the dynamical theory. Emotional intelligence shows how the child changes and becomes more aware of their emotions and begins to become more aware of the emotions of others. Research has indicated that children between the ages of 0 and 12 months can perceive the emotions of others; however, the child may lack the capability to understand the meaning of those emotions outside of contextual understandings for survival. As a child ages and begins to develop cognitively, it is assumed that the child will also begin to develop a stronger sense of emotional intelligence by understanding more in-depth emotional diversity. By the age of 5, it is indicated that children, through the use of patterning emotions after observing others, begin to not only perceive but also understand basic emotions such as sad, angry, and happy. As children begin to reach the age of 7, emotional intelligence becomes more concrete, and children begin to make choices based on the perception and understanding that they have of emotions (e.g., Mom is angry, so I should pick up my toys).

Functionalist Theory

Functionalist theory, also known as functionalism, is a theoretical perspective that is based on how social order is possible. The theory creates a foundation to interpret society in terms of how it contributes to the stability of the whole society. In functionalism, society is considered to be more than the sum of its parts. In other words, a single aspect of society is vital or functional for the stability of the entire society. Functionalism has been used throughout research to look at the role emotional intelligence has in adults and children. This is due to the fact that emotional intelligence is made up of multiple parts that create the whole.

Functionalist theory allows the individual to look at emotional intelligence as an adaptive set of regulatory skills. The regulatory skills are similar to the single aspects of society, each being vital to the functioning and development of emotional intelligence. These skills emerge over time, in the construct of the social setting and what the child observes according to functionalism. As the child observes adults around them regulating emotions and demonstrating skills of being able to make decisions based on their emotions, they begin to mirror these observations. This increases the child's emotional intelligence and helps them gain a greater perception and understanding of making decisions based on emotional reactions. From a functionalist theory, the development of emotional intelligence may be delayed for various reasons. If the child observes adults who struggle with emotional regulation and demonstrate poor decision-making based on emotions, then the child himself or herself may also demonstrate these behaviors showing low emotional intelligence. Functionalist theory, however, identifies in its framework that cognitive development and temperament influence emotional intelligence, so children who have cognitive developmental delays may have a lower state of emotional intelligence. This would indicate that children with lower emotional intelligence might struggle perceiving others emotions, or identifying their own emotional feelings.

Measurement of Emotional Intelligence

Emotional intelligence is often measured using self-reporting measures or more standardized assessments where individuals are asked to solve a series of emotionally related problems. Assessments such as the Genos Emotional Intelligence Inventory provide an assessment of how often individuals display emotionally intelligent behaviors. The Trait Emotional Intelligence Questionnaire (TEIQue) is a self-reporting inventory that covers 153 items, measuring 15 distinct facets of emotional intelligence. The Emotional and Social Competence Inventory provides an overview of the behaviors required to measure emotional intelligence in professionals and leaders. However, the assessment of emotional intelligence in children has proven challenging. Most assessments used to measure emotional intelligence are normed for individuals 17 years of age or older, leaving a gap in assessments for those who are 16 years of age and younger.

Research on children has indicated that emotional intelligence is best measured through the assessment and understanding of attachment styles between the child and their parent. The four basic attachment styles—(1) secure, (2) preoccupied, (3) dismissive, and (4) fearful—can be a strong indication of a child's emotional intelligence. Children with lower emotional intelligence may demonstrate less or more chaotic attachment to guardians, such as ignoring the fact that a parent is in the room or becoming emotionally distressed when a parent leaves even when they know the parent will return. This is due to a lack of perception and understanding of emotions, causing difficulties in emotionally regulating their own feelings and attaching to others. Research indicates that these may be children who have a fearful attachment style or dismissive or preoccupied attachment to their parents.

A child who has a stronger link to emotional intelligence, however, holds a secure understanding of the emotions others have as well as their own. This may lead the child to demonstrate stronger and healthier attachment styles to their parents and others around them. A healthy style may be indicative of a child who does not get upset when their parent steps out of the room because they know their mom or dad will soon return. This is due to being able to understand how others feel and being able to more easily express their own emotions in a way that is socially acceptable. The secure attachment a child has also demonstrates the child's ability to access the emotional regulation skills needed to remain calm or to self-soothe during stressful situations, demonstrating that perception and understanding of emotions is also linked to regulation.

Parenting Style

Parenting styles are also a strong indicator of how a child will develop emotional intelligence. Researchers have found that appropriate parenting styles are one of the strongest influences to helping a child develop emotional intelligence. More importantly, the time parents spend with their children has been linked to a child's ability to develop emotional intelligence. Consistent and frequent time spent between parents and children is especially beneficial. First, interacting with their children, parents model emotional regulation, which encourages children to regulate their emotions through observation. Second, parents reinforce the child's attempts to regulate emotions and improve self-regulatory strategies as the child ages. Modeling and reinforcement are vital roles for parents since both assist in emotional intelligence development.

Expectations, modeling, and the amount and type of interaction parents have with children are categorized by several parenting styles: authoritarian, indulgent (or permissive), neglectful, and authoritative. The authoritarian parent is more demanding and less responsive to the child and may impact the development of emotional intelligence in the child by decreasing the child's social competence and decreasing the individuality of the child. The indulgent parenting style may also have negative effects of the development of emotional intelligence. Children raised by the indulgent parent are seen to struggle with impulse control and struggle to make positive judgments based on their emotions. The neglectful parenting style leaves the parent to be neither demanding nor responsive, being only a figure in the child's life. This leaves nothing in regard to role modeling emotional regulation and leaves the child alone to figure out emotional meanings and how to regulate feelings. However, the authoritative parenting style creates an environment where the parent is both demanding and responsive. Known as propagative parenting, authoritative parenting has expectations of maturity and allows the parent to set clear standards for their children through the use of modeling emotional regulation. The authoritative parenting style also encourages the child to develop autonomy and maintain age-appropriate behaviors based on age-appropriate understanding of emotions. How a parent chooses to approach their child affects not only emotional intelligence during childhood development but also emotional intelligence well into adult hood.

Eric D. Jett

See also Attachment Styles; Attachment Theory; Emotional Disengagement; Emotional Intelligence, Families; Self-Esteem in Children; Social Constructionism

Further Readings

Alegre, A. (2012). The relation between the time mothers and children spent together and the children's trait emotional intelligence. *Child & Youth Care Forum*, 41(5), 493–508. doi:10.1007/s10566-012-9180-z

Jellesma, F. C., Rieffe, C., Terwogt, M. M., & Westenberg, P. M. (2011). Children's sense of coherence and trait emotional intelligence: A longitudinal study exploring the development of somatic complaints. *Psychology & Health*, 26(3), 307–320. doi:10.1080/08870440903411021

Keefer, K. V., Holden, R. R., & Parker, J. A. (2013). Longitudinal assessment of trait emotional intelligence: Measurement invariance and construct continuity from late childhood to adolescence. *Psychological Assessment*, 25(4), 1255–1272. doi:10.1037/a0033903

Emotional Intelligence, Families

Emotional intelligence is a multifaceted term that is used to describe an individual's ability to base their judgment and guide their thinking and behaviors on their emotions. A measurement of how an individual recognizes their emotions, emotional intelligence also is reflective of how an individual identifies other people's emotions. An additional component of emotional intelligence is the individual's ability to register and understand conflicting emotions, such as feeling excited and scared at the same time. The ability to differentiate and label various emotions appropriately demonstrates the intersection of the cognitive and emotional systems. These systems create the entirety of emotional intelligence.

Initially introduced in the early 1960s, the term *emotional intelligence* gained more currency during the 1980s when research identified emotional intelligence as a construct that is separate from other forms of intelligences, such as auditory intelligence or visuospatial abilities. Over time, it has been concluded that emotional intelligence contains three central ideas: (1) perceiving emotions of self and others, (2) understanding emotions, and (3) managing emotions. If people are able to perceive their emotions and understand them, then emotional intelligence leads to the ability to manage those emotions based on the first two ideas. Emotional intelligence has been applied primarily to individuals; however, emotional intelligence is also applicable to families and to understanding family dynamics. This entry briefly introduces emotional intelligence as it relates to families and discusses two theories that adopt the concept of emotional intelligence: conservation of resources theory and dynamical systems theory.

Conservation of Resources Theory

Conservation of resources theory provides an understanding of how individuals accumulate the resources needed for survival. These resources can be used to accommodate, withstand, and overcome life threats. In the diversity of conservation of resources theory, resources might include such things as self-esteem, material resources, and social support. If stressful or traumatic events occur, resources can be consumed offsetting the impact of the situation. When looking at resources, such as reputation, it is believed that the more secure the resource or favorable in a positive light, the more prone the resource is to be used to obtain other resources. Conservation of resources theory is often used to understand the role emotional intelligence has in families. Each member of the family has their own emotional intelligence that meets their developmental level; however, as a whole, the individual's emotional intelligence is a resource for the family. A stronger or more developed individual emotional intelligence is a greater resource for the family. However, the persistence of actual or anticipatory stress in the family can create conflict and burnout. Emotional exhaustion from conflict and burnout can deplete the resources associated with emotional intelligence from the family and decline the capacity of the family to perform effectively. High emotional intelligence helps families be more capable of preventing burnout or emotional exhaustion within the family. This is seen by family members working together to identify the perception of the emotions each family member has about the current situation, understand why the emotion is present, and then create a plan for change if desired. In the family dynamics of emotional intelligence, the conservation of resource theory also identifies the transference of resources and emotional development from one generation to the next. Parents hold a strong developmental role in helping their children also develop a high level of emotional intelligence. While children initially do not have a strong understanding of emotional intelligence, parents hold enough emotional resources to assist their children in emotional regulation and their emotional development. However, parents who struggle with their own emotional regulation may cause developmental delays in regard to emotional intelligence with their children. Adults in a family setting with low emotional intelligence may also see a higher rate of work–family conflict depleting emotional resources even further.

Dynamical Systems Theory

Dynamical systems theory is a modern theoretical lens that is considered broad by nature and encompasses all developmental theories. The theory attempts to account for all the possible factors that are in motion during each developmental stage. Dynamical systems theory recognizes that development occurs on many levels and throughout an individual's life cycle. Development is a consistent, fluid, and multidetermined process. Looking at emotional intelligence in families, dynamical systems theory brings into consideration the many variables and factors that occur to reach emotional intelligence, such as life experiences in family dynamics. Through this lens, the family develops emotionally through expressive behaviors, patterning emotions after each other, identifying social and physical contexts, and identifying action tendencies of self and others. These items change over time as the family members interact. Emotional intelligence also goes through stages of development as a family changes. Emotional intelligence shows how families change as well as become more aware of their emotions and become more aware of the emotions of others. Research has indicated that family members can perceive the emotions of others; however, the more cohesive the family, the more contextual understanding of emotions that family members will have of each other. As a family grows and changes, it is assumed that the family will also begin to develop a different level of emotional intelligence by understanding more in-depth emotional diversity based on variables that have impacted the family on both positive and negative levels. As with children, emotional intelligence in families occurs through the use of patterning emotions after observing others. Family members begin to not only perceive but also understand emotions of others within the family as a way to gauge their own emotional reactions. Dynamical systems theory emphasizes that emotional intelligence is important to the social and physical context of a family's development since it helps family members understand that certain emotions can be expressed at certain times. Dynamical systems theory also provides a framework that identifies how emotional intelligence in the family changes as family dynamics change (e.g., as children grow up and move out of the home, parents may come to rely more on each other's emotional intelligence).

Eric D. Jett

See also Affect Regulation; Attachment-Based Family Therapy; Conflict in Couples and Families; Contextual Family Therapy; Emotional Disengagement; Emotional Intelligence, Children; Social Constructionism

Further Readings

Cheung, F. Y., & Tang, C. S. (2012). The effect of emotional dissonance and emotional intelligence on work-family interference. *Canadian Journal of Behavioural Science/Revue Canadienne Des Sciences Du Comportement*, 44(1), 50–58. doi:10.1037/a0025798

Gao, Y., Shi, J., Niu, Q., & Wang, L. (2013). Work-family conflict and job satisfaction: Emotional intelligence as a moderator. *Stress and Health: Journal of the International Society for the Investigation of Stress*, 29(3), 222–228.

Lenaghan, J. A., Buda, R., & Eisner, A. B. (2007). An examination of the role of emotional intelligence in work and family conflict. *Journal of Managerial Issues*, 19(1), 76–94.

Emotionally Focused Therapy for Couples

In the field of couples therapy, there has been a need for research on models that impact marital distress and satisfaction. Emotionally focused therapy (EFT) for couples has emerged as a short-term (8 to 20 sessions), empirically based model and framework used to work with couples. The approach was originally developed by Susan Johnson and Les Greenberg. Emotion-focused work with couples is based on attachment theory, which highlights consistent, safe, and secure relationships with significant people as the crux of healthy lives and relationships. EFT clinicians enact these ideas by using experiential and family systems models. Experiential family therapy focuses on processing in-the-moment experiences through identification of emotion and honest expression of emotion. Openness, sincerity, and candid communication about feelings are hallmarks of this approach. If each person in the couple or family can correctly identify his or her own emotions; honestly express emotions, needs, and wants; and is accepting of others doing the same, then the couple or family system is more likely to be healthy. EFT also builds on concepts from attachment theory and experiential family therapy and the idea of mutual influence from family systems to help couples manage distress and build a safer, more secure relationship to buffer them from future distress. In this entry, the theories and models upon which EFT is based are discussed as well as the process of EFT.

Experiential and Attachment Theory

EFT is an experiential approach to working with couples based on a theory of love grounded in attachment theory. Experiential therapists help clients focus on in-the-moment experiences and discover their own possibilities and potentials. The goal is to help clients live their lives as congruently as possible with who they want to be and live an authentic life. This is done by helping people fully experience their lives and their emotions. The therapist helps clients to attend to their own physical sensations and emotions and to be able to communicate clearly with others about their wants, needs, and desires. In addition to helping people be their authentic selves, clients are helped to accept others being their authentic selves. The idea is that if each person is able to be in-the-moment, be authentic, accept other people being authentic, and communicate honestly, then everyone will be more healthy—as individuals and as couples or families. There is true intimacy when people can be accepted and accept people for exactly who they are.

Being attuned to one's emotions and using them as a compass for direction in one's relationship is a fundamental part of EFT. In attachment theory, emotion is seen as data about the well-being of important relationships. It is a healthy, secure attachment to a primary person that allows people to be free to experience and explore life and relationships. A major principle held by EFT is that emotion and attachment are the bases of human existence. However, emotion and the information it provides can become distorted when people try to protect themselves from experiencing their emotions because of damaging relationship events or what Johnson calls attachment injuries. Attachment injuries occur when a partner fails to respond in times of urgent need, and these times are seen as abandonments or betrayals.

In EFT, attachment theory is used to understand love, relationship distress, and trauma. Attachment theory accentuates the tendency for individuals to create and maintain impactful emotional relationships with significant others. At first, significant others are parents or caretakers; later in life, significant others are romantic partners. One can also form attachments to friends, siblings, mentors, and others. The difference with adult relationships is that the attachment goes both ways rather than just from child to caretaker. Both people in an adult relationship (especially a romantic one) must attend to one's own attachment needs and the attachment needs of the other. They are both guardians of the relationship. The security of the relationship is the conduit through which attachment needs are met. Couples that are securely attached engage in relationship behaviors that provide mutual closeness and security.

These ideas were adapted from John Bowlby's and Mary Ainsworth's observations of children and the importance of a loving, secure relationship with a caretaker. Children, and later adults, monitor their relationship with significant others. Being attached to someone and knowing that person will be there to support, protect, and love creates a feeling of safety and soothes anxieties. When someone does not have a secure attachment, it is said to be an insecure attachment. Various theorists and researchers have classified insecure relationships differently, but they are all variations or combinations of either an anxious style or an avoidant style. People with an anxious attachment monitor others for signs that they love them and can be trusted. They want a loving relationship but wonder whether or not they are lovable. People with an avoidant style tend to believe that they do not need others and do not think they can count on others. When in distress, people with an anxious attachment style tend to pursue, and people with an avoidant style tend to withdraw.

Emotion plays an important role in attachment. People are born with the innate ability to express certain universal emotions such as anger, joy, sadness, fear, shame, and surprise. These "primary" emotions serve an adaptive and motivational function. They prompt action, when needed, and they are adaptive when they indicate a need for contact with others and support. The need for others is seen as instinctual and healthy from an attachment perspective.

Secondary emotions are emotional responses that one learns over time. These emotional responses tend to be culturally based and reactive. They are a reaction to a reaction (a primary emotion happens first, and then the secondary emotion follows) and are used to protect one from getting hurt emotionally and to cover primary emotions. In the short term, responding from secondary emotions may help someone feel protected from being vulnerable, but in the long term it keeps people from having close, honest, sincere relationships.

Emotionally focused couples therapists see the way people regulate their emotions as an attempt to engage or deflect a partner. If they are able to express and accept expressions of primary emotion, then the quality of their relationship will be better. However, if a couple is afraid to express and/or accept expressions of primary emotions, then they will likely misread a partner's attempt to evoke support and closeness. Emotional expressions, whether primary or secondary, are an attempt to signal a partner to enter into an interaction when someone is distressed. The action of one partner evokes movement from the other partner and vice versa. The mutual influence each has over the other and the pattern this creates over time is referred to as the couple's "dance." In essence, attachment theory is a theory of emotional regulation, and each person has an attachment system. The attachment system motivates someone to behave in ways that are intended to motivate attachment figures to come closer when needed. The attachment system helps a person monitor whether an attachment figure is likely to be responsive to one's needs and if that figure is likely to be available when someone needs that person the most.

If a partner proves to be available and responsive over time, then distress and the accompanying emotions are regulated more easily. If the partner is unavailable and unresponsive in times of need, then the partner learns that his or her distress does not result in comfort and soothing from the significant other. Each partner will form preferred ways of coping with emotional distress in the relationship and form expectations about what to expect from self and others. This is called an *internal working model*. Often one's way of coping with emotional stress creates more relationship distress and pushes partners farther apart rather than bringing them closer together. When the attachment system goes into action in a secure relationship, the attachment behaviors bring partners closer together; in an insecure relationship, there may be the opposite effect.

Stages and Steps to Emotionally Focused Therapy

The goal of EFT is to help partners create a secure relationship and effectively engage one another as support when distressed. In order to do this, the therapist guides the couple through a series of stages and steps. According to Susan Johnson, there are three stages and nine steps.

Steps 1 and 2

Stage 1 focuses on the couples' interactions and de-escalation of their negative (problematic) cycles. This stage has four steps. In the first step, the clinician assesses the couple and outlines their patterned ways of interacting with and influencing one another, which Johnson refers to as "the dance." In this step, the clinician is creating a therapeutic alliance with the couple in which they feel understood, supported, and safe. In addition, the clinician begins identifying issues of conflict and core attachment issues. These attachment issues may be relationship injuries from the past in other relationships and relationship injuries in the current relationship. In step 2, the negative interactional patterns between the couple are identified, explored, and acknowledged. Negative interactional patterns are patterns of interacting that have become part of the couple's relational dance and keep them from establishing or maintaining a secure bond.

Steps 1 and 2 create a foundation for the rest of therapy. It is important to create a safe environment for the couple to identify and explore the injuries in their relationship. These injuries, if left unhealed, fester and get in the way of having a healthy relationship. It can be difficult for the couple to go over past hurts in their relationship. The purpose is not to "dig up" all past hurts but to identify ones that are still not healed and that impact the couple in their current relationship.

Table 1 Three Stages and Nine Steps of Johnson's Emotionally Focused Therapy

Stage	Step
1: Assessment and Cycle De-Escalation	
	1: Showing alliance and assessing
	2: Identifying the negative interactional cycle
	3: Accessing previously unacknowledged attachment-related emotions that support the behavioral reactive stance of the couple
	4: Reframing the problem in terms of the negative cycle, underlying feelings, and attachment needs
2: Changing Interactional Positions Creating New Bonding Events	
	5: Promoting identification with disowned needs and aspects of self and integrating these into relationship interactions
	6: Promoting acceptance of the partner's experience and being responsive to the partner's new behavior in the interaction
	7: Facilitating the deeper expression of attachment emotions and needs, creating new interactional patterns as a result of this sharing
3: Consolidation and Integration	
	8: Facilitating the emergence of new solutions to old relationship patterns of disconnection
	9: Consolidating new positions and new cycles of closeness and safe attachment

During these steps, the clinician will go slowly and guide the couple at a pace that feels safe for them. During this time, the couple is also learning about the process of EFT and the goals for therapy. In addition, going slowly during these steps allows the clinician enough time and information to assess the couple's appropriateness for EFT. Since safety is a major hallmark of this approach, if there is violence in the relationship EFT would not be used. The goal of EFT is to have emotional safety in order for the couple to meet each other's attachment needs. This is not possible if there is physical violence. There may be other issues that may also not make it safe to continue with EFT.

Once the clinician and clients decide they want to proceed, the clinician continues to identify intrapsychic and interpersonal indicators that influence the couple's relationship. Intrapsychic indicators are related to emotional stories within one's self. The indicators of the story are shown when people are talking about their past or present and there is either a strong emotional response or a stark lack of emotion. It is important to acknowledge verbal indicators of emotion and nonverbal indicators of emotions (e.g., crying, clenching one's fist, looking away) as a way of showing that the clinician is attuned to the clients and making clients feel safe to share their stories.

Furthermore, the therapist is listening to stories and paying attention to behaviors associated with relationship distress in order to ascertain what role someone tends to play when attachment systems are activated due to a perceived threat. For example, one member of the couple tends to be a pursuer and one tends to be a withdrawer. The task here is for the clinician to observe how the couple reaches for one another and what the results are of that reach.

Once the therapist has a clear understanding of the roles each person takes in the couple's dance and the negative indicators of emotion, the therapist explains the couple's dance to them. In session, the therapist may use several interventions such as the following:

1. Reflecting (paraphrasing and restating) each partner's emotional experiences and interaction to make each person feel understood and to help each partner understand.

2. Validating and legitimizing each partner's emotional responses not as an excuse but as a way for their partner to see that their partner is not out to hurt them purposefully but that their resolution to the problem is the best they have to offer.

3. Utilizing evocative reflections and questions to clarify each partner's perception of the problem and their partner's perception of them in relation to their relationship. Evocative reflections and questions use words, stories, or metaphors to evoke and reinforce emotion.

4. Tracking and reflecting interactions (the most behavioral focus of the model), the therapist focuses on the action tendencies (how they tend to behave in the face of relationship distress) of the couple. Here, the narrative is explored and the couple provides concrete examples of their story or dance.

5. Reframing the problem in a manner that the couple can see how they individually play a role in their cycle impacts the building of a securely attached relationship.

The main goals of the therapist in steps 1 and 2 are to acknowledge and encourage the process.

Steps 3 and 4

The main goal of the therapist in steps 3 and 4 is changing the couple's "music" to their dance. Here, attachment injuries materialize and are then made clear for the couple. The couple and therapist investigate issues and patterns that prevent an emotional connection. They will begin to face their real fears of disclosing their true selves to their partner.

In step 3, the therapist isolates emotions not acknowledged in the past. When tapping into emotions, it is important for the therapist to reengage withdrawn partners in a way in which they can find strength to express themselves. The accusing or blaming partner will learn to express emotional distress in a less aggressive manner. It is important to note that in step 3 the therapist is not focusing on past emotional experiences but rather actively engaged in the here and now with regard to emotional experience and reprocessing those experiences. Even if they are discussing an event from the past, the point is to focus on how discussing that event evokes emotion in the moment.

In step 4, the therapist is reframing the conflict in terms of the negative cycle. Here, the couple can start the process of coming together and see the negative cycle as the relationship's enemy. The interventions used in steps 3 and 4 include interventions utilized in steps 1 and 2.

Steps 5, 6, and 7

Steps 5, 6, and 7 comprise stage 2 and focus on identifying unacknowledged attachment needs, promoting partner acceptance, and encouraging the couple to express their needs and wants in a way that creates emotional bonding and secure attachment. The therapist helps by tracking and reflecting on the cycle with the aim of helping to deepen the couple's emotional engagement. In stage 2, the main goal of the therapist is for the partners to own their experiences and to see their partner in a more positive light as the partner demonstrates more engaging behaviors. At this stage, the withdrawn partner has returned and the critical partner has softened. Both partners are willing to allow access to their emotional experiences by communicating their attachment needs directly.

Steps 8 and 9

In stage 3, the final stage (steps 8 and 9), the couple is practicing new, attachment-enhancing cycles to create new solutions to old problems. In step 8, the couple begins to have more self-awareness and is able to own their role when conflict arises in the relationship. The couple begins to have a different dialogue when processing ongoing problems. Now the couple actively chooses to come closer during this process as they strengthen their attachment bonds. In step 9, the couple is consolidating their new relationship dance. They have new ways of interacting and letting each other know they are in need of support and validation. The couple nears the end of therapy when they are able to identify when their dance gets off track and their interactions get in the way of enhancing their attachment bonds. In stage 3, the main goal of the therapist is for the couple to be involved emotionally and to use the relationship to regulate negative affect, be responsive toward one another in session and out, and change how they perceive their mate. When couples are able to consistently express love and move toward each other even in times of distress, it is time to terminate counseling.

Shea M. Dunham

See also Attachment and Romantic Love; Attachment Styles; Attachment Theory; Earned Attachment; Experiential Family Therapy; Systems Theory

Further Readings

Johnson, S. M. (2004). *Creating connection: The practice of emotionally focused marital therapy* (2nd ed.). New York, NY: Brunner/Mazel.

Johnson, S. M. (2008). *Hold me tight: Seven conversations for a lifetime of love.* New York, NY: Little, Brown.

Johnson, S. M. (2013). *Love sense: The revolutionary science of romantic relationships.* New York, NY: Little, Brown.

EMPATHY

The concept of empathy continues to intrigue researchers and psychologists because it remains a common, cross-cultural thread that connects humanity. Edward B. Titchener, a British psychologist who studied under Wilhelm Wundt, is credited with having coined the term *empathy* from a German translation in 1909. Sometimes we feel emotions because something has directly happened to us. Other times, we experience emotions because something happens to someone else. The term *empathy* is commonly used to refer to a different phenomenon that is related to emotion sharing. Empathy is a vicarious response of emotions. In some situations, people may feel the same emotion that the other person feels. In addition to feeling the same emotion, someone may understand another person's condition and perspective. Having empathy is not limited to a physical person; it can be experienced from fictional or salient beings. Empathy is a motivator for altruistic behavior. The development of empathy can be conceptualized through many theories based in psychological, behavioral, and neuroscientific research. In this entry, several conceptualizations of empathy are presented and discussed.

Developmental Perspective

Developmental psychologist Martin L. Hoffman theorized the development of morality as a comprehensive way to view empathy. Hoffman's theory includes five mechanisms to explain how someone becomes distressed after observing another's distress. These five mechanisms include (1) mimicry, (2) classical conditioning, (3) direct association, (4) mediated association, and (5) role-taking. During the first three mechanisms (mimicry, classical conditioning, and direct association), an observer perceives another's emotional experience directly. These experiences are considered to be a primitive and involuntary reaction that is automatic. Mimicry involves a two-stage process. First, the observer automatically imitates the other's emotional facial, postural, or vocal expressions. Second, sensory feedback from the immediate reaction becomes associated with the emotional state in the observer. Situations that make us feel emotional even if we have never experienced them before are the beginnings of classical conditioning. For example, you may feel scared the first time a bee stings you. After you experience this emotional situation, you learn cues that are indicative of the situation happening again. As a result, you start to feel emotional when you perceive those cues. You may hear the sound of a bee's buzz, and you begin to feel scared. In classical conditioning, the bee sting is an unconditioned stimulus that causes you to feel afraid as an unconditioned response. The bee's buzz is the neutral stimulus that is paired with the bee sting, but it is often enough to become a conditioned stimulus that causes you to feel scared as a conditioned response.

Behavioral Perspective

Classical conditioning can be related to empathy in that the features of others' emotional experiences can become the cues that trigger a conditioned emotional response. One interpretation of classically conditioned empathy is that during conditioning we experience emotional situations with others who are expressing emotions. The pairing of the situation with another's emotional expressions causes the emotional expressions to become cues that a similar situation is about to occur. For example, you witness someone looking scared right before he or she is stung by a bee, and you feel afraid. In the future, when you see others expressing fear, you will feel afraid again. In another version of classically conditioned empathy, the conditioned stimuli are not others' emotions; rather, they are perceived features of the situation. For instance, you may hear a bee buzzing right before it stings you, and you feel afraid. In the future, when you hear a bee buzz before it stings someone else, you feel afraid. In the first interpretation, the other person's emotional expression causes empathetic emotions, whereas in the second version features of the other person's emotional situation cause an empathic response.

Direct association refers to when one person, the observer, sees another's emotional expression or situation; it reminds the person of their past emotional experiences. As a result, the observer feels the emotions that they felt during the original experience. For example, you see a bee sting another person, then you may remember a time when a bee stung you. You experience the original fear from the memory. Mediated association and role-taking are considered to involve more advanced cognitive abilities. In regard to mediated association, the observers learn about the others' emotional experiences through words. When the observers imagine the others' emotional expressions and mimic them, they remember their own past experiences and/or feel the emotions from the memories. Mediated association is similar to mimicry or direct association, except the one does not have to witness another's experience directly. For example, if someone else tells you that they were stung by a bee earlier in the day, you may remember a time when you were stung and feel afraid because of your memory. Role-taking occurs when someone either imagines himself or herself in another's situation or imagines how he or she may feel. Not unlike mediated association, observers might mimic imagined emotional expressions or might feel emotions by using their own emotional memories to imagine another's situation. Role-taking requires active attempts to understand another's perspective by bringing emotional memories or imagined emotional expressions to mind. In contrast, mediated associations involve a more automatic response of emotional memories or imagery. For example, if you learn that someone else was stung by a bee, you might try to actively imagine how they felt, recall a time when you were stung by a bee, and feel afraid from the memory.

Hoffman explains mimicry, direct association, mediation association, and role-taking as separate mechanisms for empathy even though they largely overlap. All of the mechanisms are similar in that the observer's vicarious emotional experience comes from imitating emotional expressions or recalling emotional memories. The differences are whether the observer must witness another's emotion or situation directly (i.e., mimicry and direct association) or can infer them indirectly (mediated association and role-taking) and whether the observer actively puts effort into empathizing (i.e., role-taking) or not (i.e., mimicry, direct association, and mediation association). Also, during the role-taking mechanism, the observers can imagine another's emotional situation so vividly that they feel the same emotion. This is the only case in which empathy might not rely on prior experience or a history of conditioning and/or memories.

Neuropsychological Perspective

Contemporary research on empathy largely centers on neuroscience, particularly after the discovery of mirror neurons in the 1990s. Mirror neurons were first discovered in the F5 region on the premotor cortex in macaque monkeys. These neurons discharge during the performance and observation of goal-oriented actions. For example, mirror neurons discharged when a monkey grasped food and also when a monkey watched an experimenter grasp food. This suggested that a mechanism by which two seemingly different systems, the perceptual and motor systems, could be linked. Based on these findings, some researchers argue that mirror neurons help organisms understand and imitate actions of others.

Other researchers have argued that mirror neurons are responsible for vicarious sensations, emotions, and actions. In other words, whenever an observer perceives another's emotion, the mirror neurons of the observer, which are responsible for the experience of that emotion, are automatically discharged. As a result, the observer feels the emotion and experiences empathy. For example, if you see a bee sting another person and you perceive that the person is scared, the neurons that are involved in your own experiences of fear automatically discharge, so you feel scared too.

Stephanie D. Preston and Frans B. M. de Waal's perception–action model of empathy is similar to the mirror neuron theory. Similar to mirror neurons, perception–action models were developed to address how perceptual information turns into motor action. Based on the common-coding account, perception and action share some underlying process so that perceptual information automatically prepares action without the need for any intervening cognitive process. The mirror neuron and perception–action theories of empathy are similar to Hoffman's mechanisms of mimicry and association. Instead of mimicking observable behaviors of emotion, mirror neurons mimic the brain activity. Instead of the perception of another's state or situation activating the observer's emotional memories, the perception of another's state activates the observer's representation of the same state. The mirror neuron theory of empathy continues to draw debate and the majority of neuroscientific experiments on empathy examine vicarious experiences of physical pain rather than emotional experiences.

Social Learning Perspective

Emotional matching or emotion sharing is an essential process in how empathy is developed. The experience of empathy is based on the observer's past experiences, so an observer can only feel vicarious emotions for events like those that they have experienced. Classical conditioning theory relies on the observer's past experience by the observer having a conditioned history for any empathetic emotion. Additionally, with direct and indirect association, the observer must have relevant emotional memories that they can actively recall. With role-taking, the observer mimics the imagined emotional expressions of another. Similarly, with the perception–action model, the observer's representation of the other's emotional state could be activated without any one specific emotional memory if the observer has experienced the emotional state in the past. In comparison, mimicry and mirror neurons do not rely on the observer's past experiences and the observer can mimic or mirror any expressed emotions. In addition, researchers studying emotion sometimes ask participants to recall previous emotional experiences to make them feel specific emotions. Overall, it appears that past experience most likely plays a role in empathy.

In addition to the observer having previous experience with anther's emotional state, all the theories of empathy require the observer to perceive another's emotional state or situation. Some theories require the observer to view another's emotional expression or situation directly (i.e., direct perception) and others allow the observer to imagine the other's emotional expression or situation or to learn about them through language (i.e., indirect perception). Less attention has been raised regarding the absence of empathy or the unemotional observer. The phenomenon of not feeling empathy or "empathy failures" can be explained through the process of nonmatching. Nonmatching could mean that the observer reacts unemotionally to another's emotional experience. An observer's unemotional response poses a challenge to any theory or process that claims that empathy happens automatically. One explanation is that empathy occurs automatically, but it requires some minimal conditions. These conditions include the observer attending to another's emotional state or situation. So if the observer never notices the other person or attention is diverted away from the situation, then there will be no empathy. Another condition relates to experience, in which if the observer lacks relevant experience then there will be no empathy. Another explanation for an unemotional observer may be that empathy occurs automatically, but the observer can regulate or inhibit it. For example, research shows that physicians and acupuncture practitioners do not show empathetic neural responses to needle pricks. This may be because they have more experience than others with regulating their vicarious pain response and because they need to inhibit their empathetic reactions to their patients. The dominant perspective in empathy research favors a late appraisal model, which means that the observer begins to automatically match another's emotion but then can regulate and/or inhibit the empathetic emotion. However, a late appraisal model cannot explain why an observer would feel something for another who does not seem to feel anything or who seems to feel something else.

Appraisal theory of emotion would argue that current empathy mechanisms are limited in their ability to explain nonmatching because they focus on another's emotional state as the primary cause of empathy. However, if someone does not display emotions, then the observer will feel no vicarious emotions. Adam Smith's theory of moral sentiments argues that empathetic emotions are not based on how we perceive the other's state but rather they are based on how we interpret the other's situation. If Smith's theory is true, then nonmatching emotional responses are no longer problematic and the observer's emotion is not limited to what the other feels, but instead it can be any emotion that the observer interpreted based on the other's situation. Similar to Smith's argument that our empathetic emotions are based on how we interpret another's situation, appraisal theories generally argue that firsthand emotions are based on how we interpret our own situations; thus, previous experience is required to experience empathy. Appraisal theories add that emotional experience is based on evaluative interpretations of the situation (i.e., appraisals).

The phenomenon of empathy is often described by researchers as a way to explain emotional matching. Other theories, such as an appraisal theory of empathy, describe empathy as just one possible outcome of a general emotional process. Several theoretical perspectives on empathy emphasize that the observer must maintain a sense of self as distinct from the other person for emotional matching to become true empathy and not become a firsthand emotional experience. Empathy is the ability to feel what another person feels. In research, it is treated as a special phenomenon, separate from firsthand emotional experience.

Monica Paige Band

See also Affect Regulation; Emotional Intelligence, Children; Emotional Intelligence, Families; Emotionally Focused Therapy for Couples

Further Readings

Brodley, B. T., & Brody, A. F. (1990, August). *Understanding client-centered therapy through interviews conducted by Carl Rogers.* Paper presented at the annual meeting of the American Psychological Association, Boston, MA.

Caracena, P. F., & Vicory, J. R. (1969). Correlates of phenomenological and judged empathy. *Journal of Counseling Psychology, 16,* 510–515. doi:10.1037/h0028437

Cartwright, R. D., & Lerner, B. (1963). Empathy, need to change, and improvement with psychotherapy. *Journal of Consulting Psychology, 27,* 138–144. doi:10.1037/h0048827

de Vignemont, F., & Singer, T. (2006). The empathic brain: How, when and why? *Trends in Cognitive Sciences, 10,* 435–441. doi:10.1016/j.tics.2006.08.008

Decety, J., & Ickes, W. (Eds.). (2009). *The social neuroscience of empathy.* Cambridge, MA: MIT Press. doi:9780262012973.001.0001

Decety, J., & Jackson, P. L. (2004). The functional architecture of human empathy. *Behavioral and Cognitive Neuroscience Reviews, 3,* 71–100. doi:10.1177/1534582304267187

DeSteno, D., Gross, J. J., & Kubzansky, L. (2013). Affective science and health: The importance of emotion and emotion regulation. *Health Psychology, 32,* 474–486. doi:10.1037/a0030259

Dowell, N. M., & Berman, J. S. (2013). Therapist nonverbal behavior and perceptions of empathy, alliance, and treatment credibility. *Journal of Psychotherapy Integration, 23,* 158–165. doi:10.1037/a0031421

Jordan, J. V. (1997). Relational development through mutual empathy. In A. C. Bohart & L. S. Greenberg (Eds.), *Empathy reconsidered: New directions in psychotherapy* (pp. 343–351). Washington, DC: American Psychological Association. doi:10.1037/10226-015

Keil, W. (1996). Hermeneutic empathy in client-centered therapy. In U. Esser, H. Pabst, & G. Speirer (Eds.), *The power of the person-centered approach: New challenges, perspectives and answers.* Cologne, Germany: GwG-Verlag.

EMPIRICALLY VALIDATED MODELS

More than ever, couples and families are seeking the help of professional therapists in order to cope with mental health, marriage, family, and couples problems. It is important that effective treatments are offered to these frequently distressed individuals, but there are a great number of marriage, family, and couples therapy models from which to choose. The humanist Rollo May once concluded that there are over 300 different models of therapy; however, it appears that a large number of these models are not backed by empirical research. Empirically validated models are those that have been researched utilizing scientific methods and were found to be effective in treating marriage, family, and couples concerns. This entry provides an overview of empirical research, evidence-based practice (EBP), and empirically validated therapies. It also discusses specific effective marriage, family, and couples therapy models. Common factors are also addressed.

Empirical Research

In more recent times, there have been calls for empirical validation of such interventions in terms of their effectiveness in treating marriage, family, and couples concerns. Empirical research uses scientific methods and holds that all knowledge comes from direct or indirect observation. To this end, data can be collected in numerical or narrative form. Numerical data, also referred to as quantitative data, is collected using statistical methods whereas narrative or qualitative data is frequently collected by conducting interviews and eliciting people's stories. Some research approaches such as mixed-method designs and sometimes action research collect both forms of data, nevertheless most empirical effectiveness research is based on quantitative methodology. Some quantitative research methods include true experimental designs, quasiexperimental designs, and correlational designs. True experimental designs are conducted under tightly controlled conditions, such as those suggested by W. M. Pinsof and L. C. Wynne, which include the following six characteristics of adequate research pertaining to marriage, family, and couples research:

1. It occurs in controlled laboratory settings.
2. The focus is specific mental health concerns.
3. At a minimum, two groups or conditions are compared.
4. Assignment of participants to treatment or control group is random.
5. Treatment is specified in detail, and therapists are monitored during the research process as to their adherence to the treatment manual.
6. Participants are assessed pre- and posttreatment or control condition.

It must be pointed out that frequently social science research is based on correlational and quasiexperimental designs. These designs cannot establish causality; this can be achieved only through true experimental research. Correlational and quasiexperimental designs can tell us only that a connection exists between variables, but they cannot establish that changes in one variable *cause* changes in another. It is possible that other factors not accounted for in the research could be the reason for the study outcome. An often-cited example of correlation not equating to causation are study findings indicating there is correlation between an increase in ice cream sales and crime rates. This of course is far fetched. Rather, a third variable is at play—namely summertime. Ice cream sales and crime rates greatly increase during the warmer summer months. People are out more, there is no school, tempers flare, and people consume more ice cream.

Attempts have been made to assess the efficacy of marriage, family, and couples counseling approaches through empirical research. The findings of such research are commonly published in peer-reviewed journals such as the *Journal of Marriage and Family* and *Marriage Review*, to name just two. The effectiveness of specific counseling models can be determined based on the accumulation of evidence through a number of research studies. In addition, effectiveness studies are frequently based on meta-analyses, which attempt to summarize findings of several quantitative research studies on a specific topic.

Evidence-Based Practice and Empirically Validated Therapies

J. C. Norcross reported that from empiricism arose EBP, which had its origins in the 1990s in the United Kingdom. Through its wider introduction in Canada and the United States, it is now being utilized worldwide. Empirically validated therapies are not synonymous with EBP; however, these two concepts are closely related. The American Psychological Association (APA) Task Force on Evidence-Based Practices in Psychology has defined *EBP* as the "integration of the best available research with clinical expertise in the context of patient characteristics, culture, and preferences" (p. 273). EBP started out as a medical endeavor. The goal was to find a more scientific way to inform medical practice. This concept was borrowed by a number of social sciences, including marriage, family, and couples therapy, in part due to pressure from managed care organizations to provide evidence of effectiveness of therapeutic approaches utilized in working with couples and families. The goal of managed care organizations is to cut costs and provide only what is deemed medically necessary including mental health care. This led to the development of the manualized treatment movement. Exact steps were developed for treatment approaches in order to create a uniform manner of applying therapeutic interventions with the goal achieving similar results. Some have questioned their effectiveness since human beings are multidimensional and problems can be quite complex.

Effective Marriage, Family, and Couples Therapy Models

Thorough systematic evaluations of marriage, family, and couples therapy models are still somewhat lacking, but attempts have been made to obtain empirical support. For example, Baucom, Shoham, Mueser, Daiuto, and Stickle found that behavioral marital therapy (BMT) is the most widely researched marriage and family intervention, and studies show that BMT is an effective marital intervention. Emotionally focused therapy (EFT) is also considered to be effective. Cognitive-behavioral therapy (CBT) and insight-oriented therapy have also been found to be possibly effective. Emotionally focused and insight-oriented therapies are both rooted in psychodynamic perspectives with EFT also drawing from attachment theory. In addition, A. S. Lebow and J. L. Gurman reported that Milan systemic approaches (a set of therapeutic approaches that focus on altering family belief systems to bring about positive changes) as well as structural, strategic, and systemic approaches showed effectiveness.

In terms of specific marriage and family concerns, D. H. Baucom and colleagues found that several partner-assisted or family-assisted modalities were effective. These interventions sometimes include partners or family members as surrogate therapists in aiding a struggling family member. In terms of anxiety disorders, several possibly effective treatments were found. Family-assisted exposure and partner-assisted exposure seem to be effective in treating obsessive-compulsive disorder (OCD). CBT and partner-assisted exposure appear to be effective in treating agoraphobia. In terms of depression, BMT is deemed to be possibly effective. There is empirical support that sexual skills training, Masters and Johnson for female orgasmic disorders, BMT, and orgasm consistency training are possibly effective in treating female sexual dysfunction. The community reinforcement approach, which constitutes a behavioral intervention, and BMT are possibly effective in treating alcohol abuse and dependence. In general, it seems that partner and family engagement in the treatment of alcoholism is preferable. In terms of significant mental health diagnosis, long-term family therapy for the treatment of schizophrenia seems to be effective. Specifically, behavioral, supportive, and family systems approaches were found effective in helping individuals suffering from schizophrenia.

According to Pinsof and Wynne, several conclusions can be drawn pertaining to effectiveness of marriage, family, and couples interventions. In many instances, marriage, family, and couples therapies are more effective than those not including a family member in treating adults and adolescents diagnosed with a host of mental health conditions. Marriage, family, and couples therapy is also more effective than no treatment at all in treating a great number of mental health concerns.

It has not been shown that marriage, family, and couples therapy has any type of negative effect on clients, and no specific interventions have been shown to be superior. In terms of clients diagnosed with schizophrenia or bipolar disorder or adolescents diagnosed with conduct disorder (CD) it has been shown that marriage, family, and couples therapy is more cost-effective than hospital or residential treatment respectively. It has also been established that marriage, family, and couples therapy is not sufficient by itself in treating some of the more severe mental health concerns. On the other hand, these interventions have been shown to greatly enhance individual treatment outcomes in family members who have been diagnosed with a significant mental health condition.

Common Factors

Using the scientific model to drive counseling practice is not without controversy. Some find empirically validated therapy approaches, EBP, and manualized treatment endeavors too simplistic for often-complex marriage, family, and couples issues. For example, B. E. Wampold suggests that in terms of therapy effectiveness, 6% to 9% of client outcomes are due to therapist attributes as opposed to specific therapeutic approaches or techniques. It was also found that only 8% of client improvement is due to specific therapeutic models or interventions. It has also been established that receiving therapy is greatly more effective than not receiving therapy. Research also showed that 22% of the counseling outcome is due to client-specific factors. On the other hand, it has been established that 70% of favorable client changes are due to common factors such as the quality of the therapeutic relationship as opposed to specific factors of the interventions used. Common factors are those that are common to most therapeutic approaches as opposed to at time vastly different techniques inherent to various counseling approaches. In short, common factors are those that virtually all counseling approaches have in common. Research has shown that these common factors are at the root of positive changes in those seeking psychological or therapeutic help. Some common factors are individual client characteristics, specific qualities of the therapist, and the quality or strength of the counseling relationship.

Another critique of the empirically validated treatment model approach is that it is based on the medical model. This model may not readily transfer to counseling matters, which are frequently quite complex. Also, some marriage, family, and couples therapy approaches lend themselves to being empirically researched more readily than others. For example, cognitive-behavioral and behavioral approaches are easier to validate through research than psychodynamic approaches in which clients' inner experiences, unconscious conflicts, and self-perception cross paths with the task of relating to others. These deep, internal dimensions are not as easily observed or measured as behaviors and conscious thought patterns that are the focus of behavioral and cognitive-behavioral approaches. Also, cognitive-behavioral and behavioral therapeutic interventions are relatively brief in comparison to psychodynamic approaches, meaning it can be more costly to seek out the latter. Considering that health management organizations are the driving force in the health care marketplace, it is not surprising that psychodynamic approaches are less utilized, less researched, and less supported since they are viewed as being more costly. This is not to say that psychodynamic approaches are not effective—as we have seen, emotionally focused couple therapy (EFCT) as well as insight-oriented therapy have a psychodynamic background and have been established as effective interventions. Overall, there seems to be a consensus that most marriage, family, and couple approaches are effective to some extent and preferable to no treatment.

Sabina de Vries

See also Common Factors; Couples Therapy Research; Effectiveness Research; Emotionally Focused Therapy for Couples; Evidence-Based Practice With Couples and Families; Outcome Research; Quantitative Research; Schizophrenia and Families

Further Readings

APA Task Force on Evidence-Based Practice. (2006). Evidence-based practice in psychology. *American Psychologist, 61*, 271–285.

Baucom, D. H., Shoham, V., Mueser, K. T., Daiuto, A. D., & Stickle, T. R. (1998). Empirically supported couple and family interventions for marital distress and adult mental health problems. *Journal of Consulting and Clinical Psychology, 66*(1), 53–88.

Lebow, J. L., & Gurman, A. S. (1995). Research assessing couple and family therapy. *Annual Review of Psychology, 46*(1), 27–57.

Norcross, J. C., Hogan, T. P., & Koocher, G. P. (2008). *Clinician's guide to evidence-based practices: Mental health and the additions.* New York, NY: Oxford University Press.

Pinsof, W. M., & Wynne, L. C. (2000). Toward progress research: Closing the gap between family therapy practice and research. *Journal of Marital and Family Therapy, 26*(1), 1–8.

Wampold, B. E. (2001). *The great psychotherapy debate: Models, methods, and findings.* Mahwah, NJ: Erlbaum.

EMPOWERMENT IN FAMILIES

Empowerment in families is often used to refer to the facilitative and collaborative efforts of marriage and family therapy professionals and families when working to help families establish self-sufficiency and resiliency and identify counseling and social service supports within the community. Empowerment, in a general sense, has many definitions but is often used to refer to a process whereby individuals gain influence or power over circumstances that impact their lives. Empowerment, in a psychological sense, can include both intrapersonal and interactional components that influence a person's ability to exert greater control and efficacy in a therapeutic setting. Empowerment involves mutual respect, empathy, and intentionality toward the end of helping individuals and families gain greater access and control over resources needed. Other definitions of empowerment encompass the sociopolitical environment and participation in the community, which is suggestive of an ecologically based representation of the construct. This entry provides a brief overview of empowerment theory as represented by the construct of psychological empowerment. This entry will also explore the family support movement in the United States, which captures the sociocultural implications of empowerment theory. The entry concludes by exploring the implications for empowerment in individuals and families in various marriage and family therapy subcontexts and discusses various measures of empowerment.

Family Systems and Empowerment

The basic underlying notion of family-centered systems of care and family empowerment in general reflects a conceptual focus on strengths-based approaches to service delivery. The strengths-based approach views families as having the capacity to make informed choices if given (a) sufficient support from professionals who work with families and (b) access to resources necessary for solving problems in the future. Ideally, with such sufficient supports, families are able to see themselves as active contributors to the positive changes in their lives. Empowerment-based interventions are widely used in the human services field and are useful in helping families establish a greater sense of agency.

Families work with marriage and family therapy professionals to utilize services and supports that address the unique needs of the family. Efforts toward family empowerment can often be categorized in three primary domains: family preservation; parent empowerment; and child abuse prevention, intervention, and treatment. Family empowerment can best be understood in relation to trends in family-centered social policies and university-based intervention programs. Theoretical and empirical evidence exists which supports and clarifies the relationship between practices used by professionals who support families in various capacities.

Empowerment Theory

Empowerment theory in human services reflects ideas that relate to individual and collective behaviors of individuals and groups that focus on shaping the environment within a socioemotional context. Families are units where such changes can occur. Empowerment-based interventions have been used frequently in social work, human services, and counseling settings. When considering social cohesion, one component of empowerment, individuals and families endow trust in their marriage and family therapists (MFTs) who work to establish a sense of connectedness that helps the family resolve issues.

Marc A. Zimmerman and colleagues are well known for their work with identifying and analyzing empowerment at the individual level. Zimmerman states that empowerment at the individual level encompasses three components that include intrapersonal, interactional, and behavioral aspects. The intrapersonal component considers the way in which a person perceives control, competence, and is motivated to control. The intrapersonal component also considers self-efficacy, which is a term proposed by Albert Bandura and used to describe the degree of confidence a person has in their ability to achieve a goal and desired outcomes. In the most general sense, the intrapersonal context examines a person's capacity to influence social and political systems that impact their lives. Charles H. Kieffer, on the basis of his research in the 1980s, stated that four conditions must exist in order for empowerment to occur. These conditions include a sense of self that promotes social involvement, a knowledge or ability to critically analyze social and political systems that impact one's personal life, an ability to develop strategies while also cultivating resources to help one achieve their goals, and the ability to act with others to define and achieve goals for the group.

According to Zimmerman and colleagues, the interactional component considers the communications between individuals and environments that allow an individual to enjoy success in social and political arenas. This component also looks at the various resources that a person can utilize to achieve goals while also considering an individual's awareness of their environment, contributing factors, and the development of both problem-solving and decision-making skills, which are deemed essential for engagement within the environment. The final component, behavioral, refers to actions taken by the individual to assert influence on the social and political environment by way of involvement in community organizations and activities. All three components represent significant aspects of psychological empowerment and are representative of the researchers' attempt to specify and empirically test the constructs of psychological empowerment. Peterson and colleagues expanded upon the intrapersonal and interactional components to consider social cohesion, which encompasses reciprocity and shared emotional commitment.

Another important component of empowerment involves social cohesion. Social cohesion frames the participation of individuals and members of groups in various aspects of treatment in a larger context. Specifically, social cohesion considers the level of engagement and trust shared among members of a specific group or population. Although this concept can be considered with regard to family cohesion, this term is different in that it looks at group behaviors that may impact families disproportionately. Cohesion, as proposed by several scholars, also considers how social cohesion is impacted by wealth disparity within certain populations and how such disparities lead to negative health outcomes. In accordance with Emile Durkheim's theory of the individual and society, the social framework of society is impacted when inequality is rampant. Such distrust leads to an unraveling of the social fabric and, consequently, greater social isolation.

Empowerment theory provides a mechanism from which MFTs can elect to enhance service provision to the individuals and families they serve. There are currently several instruments used to measure empowerment in the health and education fields. Assessment tools range from qualitative to quantitative measures of various constructs defined as being intricately related to the construct of empowerment. Such measures, however, can differ considering that empowerment is defined in several different ways in various resources across the disciplines. Two examples of such assessment tools include the Family Empowerment Scale and the empowerment evaluation.

The Family Empowerment Scale, as developed by Paul E. Koren, Neal DeChillo, and Barbara J. Friesen, was created to measure nine constructs from a two-dimensional framework. The framework for this assessment measure involves family empowerment level and the expression of empowerment. The levels under which empowerment can occur include family, a service system, and the community. The second dimension of the framework for the Family Empowerment Scale examines empowerment expression in knowledge, attitudes, and behaviors. The instrument contains 34 items.

The empowerment evaluation strategy was introduced as a by-product of action research. The empowerment evaluation strategy has been used by several researchers involved in substance abuse prevention projects. The underlying principles of this framework include 10 principles that include social justice, participation, community knowledge, and community ownership to name a few. The ultimate goal of empowerment evaluation is to bring about change in power as the very basic premise underlying the method involves those who are most likely to be impacted by such changes. In order to understand how the tenets of empowerment theory can apply to service provision with families and individuals, it is important to explore the family support movement in the United States.

The Family Support Movement in America

Environmental, social, and economic changes over several decades have contributed heavily to the patterns of family life in the United States. Several social support programs have been created for the purpose of building on family strengths within the social services system. The rationale for the creation of family support programs was centered on a deficit-based approach. Social service programs were ill equipped at addressing the various needs of families, which in turn left a void in social service delivery. Families are arguably more likely to experience hardships if social supports, or informal support networks, do not exist. From this line of thought stemmed many federal- and state-funded efforts, such as the War on Poverty in the 1960s, to help improve the well-being of families. This ideology was the foundation for understanding empowerment in families.

Empowerment and Families

When considering families, it is important to acknowledge how families are embedded within larger sociopolitical systems in order to facilitate the process of change. Empowerment within families considers the relationships between professionals and families and the identification of various indicators that can give insights into the quality of relationships between the families and professionals. In family therapy, professionals often work to help families and individuals by employing a systemic perspective in addressing the social realities that relate to the intersectionality of gender, class, sexual orientation, and race. Although many systemic approaches do not address such constructs directly at the core of the development, family therapy does help to create a complete explanation within the therapeutic process.

The family empowerment perspective generally encompasses several underlying assumptions. In the mental health field, family empowerment involves the empowerment of parents, or parental self-efficacy, which increases parental knowledge, skills, and competencies as well as the ability to advocate for their children in the various systems that they encounter. The basic premise of such efforts is to ultimately increase the parents' ability to control aspects of their lives and the lives of their children.

When considering domestic violence, also referred to as intimate partner violence, empowerment is also a key construct, because it is the empowerment of survivors that remains a central goal of marriage and family therapy professionals who work with survivors. By restoring power, victims of intimate partner violence can regain a voice and control over aspects of their lives that may have been controlled by the abuser. Regardless of its importance with regard to the domestic violence context, empowerment is both an outcome and a process that can be used to assess both immediate and long-term outcomes.

There are other instances where empowerment impacts the family. This includes providing long-term care for family members with disabilities and advocacy for individuals who suffer from various mental health conditions. The unique needs of individuals in both circumstances require not only that family members have access to the resources needed but that MFTs working with these families are aware of the resources available to support these families.

Anissa K. Howard

See also Communication in Couples and Families; Decision-Making; Family Resource Management

Further Readings

Bayes, J. (2015). *Empowerment: Understanding the theory behind empowerment*. Bryan, TX: Dunamis.

Cunningham, P. B., Henggeler, S. W., Brondino, M. J., & Pickrel, S. D. (1999). Testing underlying assumptions of the family empowerment perspective. *Journal of Child and Family Studies, 8*, 437–449.

Graves, K. N., & Shelton, T. L. (2007). Family empowerment as a mediator between family-centered systems of care and changes in child functioning: Identifying an important mechanism of change. *Journal of Child & Family Studies, 16*(4), 556–566. doi:10.2007/s10826-006-9106-1

Guitierrez, L., Parsons, R. J., & Cox, E. (1998). *Empowerment in social work practice: A sourcebook*. Pacific Grove, CA: Brooks/Cole.

Kieffer, C. H. (1984). Citizen empowerment: A developmental perspective. *Prevention in Human Services, 3*(2–3), 9–36. doi:10.1300/J293v03n02_03

Kirst-Ashman, K., & Hull, G. H., Jr. (2015). *Understanding generalist practice* (7th ed.). Stamford, CT: Cengage.

Shulman, L. (2015). *Empowerment series: The skills of helping individuals, families, groups, and communities* (8th ed.). Belmont, CA: Brooks/Cole.

Zastrow, C. H., & Kirst-Ashman, K. K. (2016). *Understanding human behavior and the social environment* (10th ed.). Boston, MA: Cengage.

Zimmerman, M. A. (1990). Taking aim on empowerment research: On the distinction between individual and psychological conceptions. *American Journal of Community Psychology, 18*, 169–177.

ENACTMENTS

One of the important mechanisms for change in therapy is the therapeutic relationship between a therapist and client, which provides an important healing context. In all forms of psychotherapy, the relationship between the therapist and client is crucial to the change process because at its best it provides a secure, supportive, and trustworthy relationship. Although the therapeutic alliance remains an important part of relational therapies, working with more than one client in the room means that there are additional relationships to engage in order to bring about both relational and individual change. One way to engage those additional relationships is through an enactment. In their most basic form, enactments are opportunities for clients to interact directly with one another during the therapeutic process and recreate their family patterns inside the therapy room. Having clients enact their patterns allows the therapist to assess patterns and intervene in unhelpful interactions. This entry examines how enactments vary across several different approaches, each of which highlights some important potential uses of enactments that can be useful in understanding the theory of enactments and their implementation within the context of relational therapy. This entry further examines the use of enactment from several perspectives: structural family therapy (SFT); behavioral, skills-based models; and emotionally focused therapy (EFT). This entry concludes with an overview of the developmental model and core elements of successful enactments.

Rationale for Enacting Relationship Healing

The presumption behind reliance on enactments in relational therapy is that the couple and/or family relationships are primary; it is a breakdown in these relationships that brings couples or families into therapy, and the couple or family relationships ought to be what receives direct support and intervention. Overreliance on having clients interact with the therapist ultimately disserves the couple or family because they need to interact more successfully with each other. The goal of using enactments is to assess and alter couple or family interaction patterns or process. Use of enactments stems from the presumption that what trips couples and families up is not the problem itself but their process, the way they engage and interact around the problem.

In individual therapy the primary, therapeutic (healing) relationship is between the therapist and client, but in relational therapy the focus is on the couple or family relationships in the room. Therefore, the goal is to help the clients enact their processes in the therapy room and directly facilitate and coach new, healthier interactions. The relational therapist assists clients in altering their interactions so that they are developmentally appropriate and support secure attachments among family members. In this view, the ideal relational therapy is couple-centered or family-centered, with the therapist maneuvering, facilitating, and coaching from the periphery and with the couple or family (not the therapist) as the provider of security.

Structural Family Therapy

Salvador Minuchin was one of the first in marriage and family therapy to highlight the potential use of enactments in relational therapy. In structural therapy, there are various purposes and stages of enactments, which build upon the other to ultimately change roles and interactions. One of the more common purposes of enactments in structural therapy is assessment. Enactments help the therapist disengage from the family system and let common interaction patterns and family rules emerge. Although the couple or family might initially make conscious attempts to positively portray themselves, eventually the clients' natural and unconscious patterns will emerge, allowing the therapist to observe and examine both constructive and destructive patterns of interaction. In this manner, enactments are useful to observe relationship process in vivo rather than only verbally exploring content or talking about interaction patterns.

After using enactments to understand family interaction patterns, structural therapists might use enactments to highlight specific family patterns and roles, especially those that are particularly well entrenched in the interactional process but may be unconscious to the couple or family. A therapist may come up with a scenario or even use one that has occurred naturally in therapy and ask the clients the goal of the interaction. Clients will often have a pretty definite idea of what they would like to get from an interaction, but they sometimes struggle with knowing how to get there. At this point, the enactment does not focus on changing the interaction but rather serves to highlight the mechanisms that may be making it difficult for the couple or family to accomplish its goals.

Enactments may also be used in the context of structural therapy as an intervention to help the couple or family develop alternative ways of interacting. The therapist directs the interaction from the periphery and provides only the structure and prompts that are minimally necessary for the couple or family to enact new roles in their relationships and accomplish their interactional goals. This introduces a positive feedback mechanism that the therapist can help the couple or family introduce into their relationships. Enactments as an intervention in structural therapy can be designed by the therapist, but it can be useful for the therapist to facilitate enactments that occur spontaneously in the course of the therapy session.

Behavioral, Skill-Based Models

Behavioral enactments focused on skill-building are common in working with couples within a communication-based framework. There are a wide variety of these models, each with its own nuanced theory and skills, and some do not use the term *enactment*. However, they all share the common goal of using direct couple interaction to help couples develop the skills necessary to interact more effectively. In addition, the general process by which enactments are used to facilitate direct couple interaction in these models is also fairly standard.

According to these models, couples struggle in their interactions in large part because they move too quickly in their interactions and become reactive because they feel misunderstood by one another. From a communication standpoint, the message that is given is not always the message that is received, and both partners end up making a wide array of interpretations without checking them with the other person. Within these models, the interaction patterns and processes are viewed as the root of problems, not any particular content or problem itself. As a result, one of the primary goals of skill-building enactments is to facilitate and coach traditional communication skills by slowing down the interaction between partners, even if sometimes the highly structured format leads to the interaction feeling somewhat artificial. During these enactments, the therapist supervises the interaction and works to ensure that both partners follow the format of the interaction, thereby lessening the chance that partners will misunderstand each other's messages and become reactive.

A focus on concrete communication-based principles and skills is another method for slowing down the interaction. Speaker-based skills highlight the importance of sending very clear messages that are framed accurately but also in a way that does not alienate the listener or invite defensiveness. Listening-based skills focus on the listener understanding the message and helping the speaker feel heard by ensuring that the message received was the same as what was intended. For example, before responding, the therapist might have the listener summarize the message that she or he heard from the speaker. The speaker then has the opportunity to confirm or clarify the message. It is also important for the listener to then respond appropriately to the speaker through standard relationship-building techniques such as empathy, validation, and so on. One final skill that is common in these models is metacommunication (i.e., communication about communication). In other words, it is built into the interactional process that couples pause discussion of the content to address process issues, such as how they are feeling and whether adjustments in how they are talking about things need to be made. Enacting couple communication in the presence of a therapist whose primary attention is to process, not content, enables the couple or family to develop meta-awareness of their communication experience.

Emotionally Focused Therapy

The goal of enactments in EFT is to foster a new client interactive experience where both partners experience each other as available and responsive. Within EFT, enactments have an important place and are implemented gradually, typically after containing and decreasing reactivity. Although much of the interaction in EFT is filtered through the therapist, the direct interaction fostered by enactments places temporary focus on the client relationship in an effort to lessen distress and increase the security partners feel with one another. Within EFT, enactments are not designed to facilitate fully self-reliant couple or family interaction. Rather, enactments in EFT are relatively brief but powerful, designed to highlight and heighten brief snippets of attachment-related relationship dynamics that can be useful in lessening distress and bringing about change. The therapist adds structure to the enactment by asking one partner to express a particular phrase or idea to the other person. Enactments may be used at a variety of points within EFT, including in the early stages to assess the relationship or to help accustom partners to interacting directly with one another in a therapeutic context. The first function of enactments in EFT is to highlight important themes or dynamics related to emotional closeness and availability. As the therapist processes one partner's emotional experience and uncovers certain attachment fears, threats, or longings, it can be useful to have that person express those directly to his or her partner. For example, one partner may be expressing a great deal of anger, but beneath that is a strong desire for connection and a fear that the other person will not be available. The therapist might encourage the person to express the vulnerability in softer, more vulnerable emotions rather than more volatile secondary emotions in order to more likely receive a softened response (e.g., "Can you tell him that you are scared that he won't be there when you most need him?"). Direct couple interaction heightens authenticity, producing powerful change moments and interaction. This process evokes powerful emotions that can be further explored and deepened.

The second potential function of enactments in EFT is to heighten and expand upon rarely occurring positive expressions. In the course of therapeutic interactions, there are occasional, spontaneous softened and conciliatory comments made by clients toward one another. However, outside of the context of enactments, these are filtered through the therapist. Although these can still be useful and help produce change moments when being filtered through the therapist, there is an added emotional dimension that occurs when clients express those ideas directly to one another. Again, firsthand direct interaction adds powerfully to the authenticity and impact of attachment messaging and experience. As a result, there are times when a therapist might point out that something the client said was really powerful and ask him or her to tell that directly to the other person (e.g., "I really like what you just said about her being the most important part of your life. Can you tell her directly?"). The expression and processing of these novel moments can lead to new interactions between partners.

Developmental Model

Although enactments are commonly associated with the previously mentioned models, a developmental approach to enactments has been proposed in recent years as an overlay to a therapist's primary approach. The developmental model was developed, in part, to highlight the broad utility of enactments in a variety of therapeutic contexts and that they were not being utilized enough. In other words, therapists (especially beginning therapists)—sometimes in an effort to curtail potential escalation and maintain control over the content and tone of the session—overstructure the therapy process by limiting interactions between clients. Although this can be appropriate at times, it also risks precluding the potential for positive interactions between clients to occur that can lead to powerful change moments that occur only through authentic, direct interaction.

The developmental model was also developed in response to the fact that when enactments were being used they were not always facilitated effectively, primarily because they were not being structured according to the specific interactional needs of clients. In other words, some therapists were too laissez-faire in their approach to enactments, allowing interaction that was counterproductive and destructive and predictive of poorer overall outcomes. From a developmental perspective, it is crucial that the therapist provide clients with the appropriate amount of interactional structure during enactments based on their presenting condition and readiness for direct interaction. More specifically, because couples and families vary greatly across the course of therapy in terms of their levels of relationship distress, emotional reactivity, and interactional volatility, enactment process and structure need to be adapted accordingly in order be successful. The developmental model of enactments proposes structure and process interventions that allow for successful enactments across the entire course of therapy, always providing adequate interactional supports that the couple or family need. The developmental model consists of five stages. One of the primary mechanisms of the developmental model is adapting the process and interactional structure of the enactment by the amount and type of therapist involvement. In contrast to the high process structure of skill-based enactments, enactments within the developmental model keep the process fluid and focus on interactional structure by adjusting how much the therapist is involved in the interactions between clients based upon their volatility and reactivity. When couples are more volatile and reactive, more of the interaction is filtered through the therapist. The therapist focuses on modeling appropriate ways of interaction. As reactivity decreases, the interactional focus gradually shifts from the therapist to the clients, allowing them to interact directly while the therapist highlights positive moments and coaches them through more difficult interactional moments. During later stages when the clients are more interactionally self-reliant, the therapist shifts further to the periphery and provides prompts only as needed.

A clear understanding of the development model of enactments, with its focus on developmental sequencing, can be a very useful starting point for training, even while it is recognized that in process of time a therapist's natural use of enactments will become more fluid, spontaneous, and creative. Operationally detailed training in enactments can enable therapists to become confident in their ability to regulate couple or family interaction—not have it "get away from them"—and facilitate successful, authentic experiences of mutual caring, attachment assurance, and problem-solving.

Core Elements of Successful Enactments

Although there are theoretical and stylistic differences in how enactments are executed across various models, there are several core elements to successful enactments. These include an introduction to the enactment, the delivery of the enactment intervention where the couple or family talks directly to each other, and the processing or evaluation of the enactment. Although the content and process of these three phases will likely vary based on the type of enactment and on the familiarity of the clients to the enactment process, all successful enactments involve at least some extent of these three phases.

In introducing the enactment, it is important for the therapist to monitor therapeutic and relational factors to ensure that the context and timing have sufficiently "set the stage" for the use of enactments. Once that has occurred, the therapist then introduces the enactments in some way. No matter the extent of the introduction, it is important for the couple to have some understanding of the enactment's purpose as well as their role in the enactment. The topic and structure are also developed during this initial phase.

The second phase consists of the enactment intervention where clients interact directly with one another. Having set up the interaction in the initial stage, the therapist shifts the focus to the couple and monitors the interaction to ensure its success. It is crucial for the therapist to facilitate a constructive enactment. To accomplish this, the therapist helps sustain the interaction by commending and promoting healthy expression and responding, curtailing destructive negativity, and coaching the couple through potentially difficult interactional points.

The third phase involves processing the enactment. This can be easily forgotten by therapists but is an important component of successful enactments. Whether processing progress toward previously defined skills or goals or each partner's experience of engaging the relationship through the enactment, it is important for the therapist to help clients explore their experiences. This can include validating and heightening their experiences, highlighting positive change moments, or identifying interactional elements to improve. Regardless, the processing phase sets the stage for additional positive experiences with enactments.

*Ryan B. Seedall
and Mark H. Butler*

See also Behavioral Family Therapy; Ecosystemic Structural Family Therapy; Emotionally Focused Therapy for Couples; Individual and Family Development; Structural Family Therapy

Further Readings

Andersson, L. G., Butler, M. H., & Seedall, R. B. (2006). Couples' experience of enactments and softening in marital therapy. *American Journal of Family Therapy, 34,* 301–315.

Butler, M. H., Davis, S. D., & Seedall, R. S. (2008). Common pitfalls of beginning therapists utilizing enactments. *Journal of Marital and Family Therapy*, 34, 329–352.

Butler, M. H., & Gardner, B. C. (2003). Adapting enactments to couple reactivity: Five developmental stages. *Journal of Marital and Family Therapy*, 29, 311–327.

Davis, S. D., & Butler, M. H. (2004). Enacting relationships in marriage and family therapy: A conceptual and operational definition of an enactment. *Journal of Marital and Family Therapy*, 30, 319–333.

Gottman, J. M., & Gottman, J. S. (2008). Gottman method couple therapy. In A. S. Gurman (Ed.), *Clinical handbook of couple therapy* (4th ed., pp. 138–164). New York, NY: Guilford Press.

Nichols, M. P., & Fellenberg, S. (2000). The effective use of enactments in family therapy: A discovery-oriented process study. *Journal of Marital and Family Therapy*, 26, 143–152.

Seedall, R. B., & Butler, M. H. (2006). The effect of proxy-voice intervention on couple softening in the context of enactments. *Journal of Marital and Family Therapy*, 32, 421–437.

Tilley, D., & Palmer, G. (2013). Enactments in emotionally focused couple therapy: Shaping moments of contact and change. *Journal of Marital and Family Therapy*, 39, 299–313.

Woolley, S. R., Wampler, K. S., & Davis, S. D. (2012). Enactments in couple therapy: Identifying therapist interventions associated with positive change. *Journal of Family Therapy*, 34, 284–305.

ENGENDERING HOPE

Engendering hope is a critical element of effective individual, couple, and family counseling. Without hope, individuals, couples, and families will struggle to find the motivation needed to make the changes necessary to achieve individual and relational satisfaction. Hope is a concept that is at the core of human existence and has application to all of life's endeavors, including counseling. It has been said that to live without hope is not to live at all because when hope ceases to exist, despair enters and action ceases.

In relation to individual, couple, and family counseling, hope has been identified as a key component of effective therapeutic work that must be present within clients and therapists in order for clients to accomplish their personal and counseling goals. This entry reviews two prominent theories of hope (namely, Richard Snyder's theory and David B. Ward's theory) and provides specific strategies that can be used within the therapy room to engender hope.

The Concept of Hope

While various theories related to the construct of hope exist within different fields of study, Richard Snyder's theory of hope within the field of psychology and David B. Ward's emerging theory of hope within the field of marriage and family therapy are two significant frameworks that provide clarity regarding the concept of hope.

Snyder's Theory of Hope

Snyder conceptualizes hope as being anchored in goals that are at least of moderate importance and intermediate in their attainment (i.e., not too easy to obtain and not too hard as to promote hopelessness). Snyder divides this goal-directed behavior into two components of hope: pathways (way) and agency (will) thinking. Pathways thinking represents an individual's perception that they can generate effective routes to achieve desired goals. Agency thinking represents the individual's thoughts about their capacity to use the pathways. In other words, it is the mental energy to say, "I can do this" and "I will get this done." Within this theory, emotions are acknowledged but only as a consequence of successful or unsuccessful goal pursuit. In addition, Snyder sees goals, agency, and pathways as reciprocally and causally related so that any increase in one will lead to increases in the others. For example, the hope of individuals who are interested in becoming less depressed will increase as they develop goals and develop steps to carry out those goals. Generating these goals will increase their sense that they can overcome their depression (will), which will lead to carrying out the pathways behavior (way). The increase in pathways behavior will in turn increase their sense that they can accomplish their goal (will), which will in turn increase their ability to develop further pathways. Thus, an increase in goals, pathways, or agency will likely result in an increase in the other factors.

Ward's Theory of Hope

In response to the lack of information about hope from within the field of marriage and family therapy, Ward developed a theory of hope grounded in interviews with active marriage and family therapists (MFTs). Ward's theory defines hope as a belief and a feeling that a desired outcome is possible and identifies four foundations of hope that, taken together, determine an individual's hope for a particular outcome: *options, action, evidence,* and *connection*. The options foundation suggests that hope is dependent upon the belief and feeling that a person has options to choose from in order to achieve their desired outcome. This foundation is similar to Snyder's concept of pathways. The action property represents the idea that a person's level of hope is influenced by the belief and feeling that one is *able* to and *willing* to act in order to reach desired outcomes. This foundation is similar to Snyder's concept of agency but adds the concept of willingness to what influences hope. The evidence property suggests that a person's level of hope is partly determined by evidence that the desired outcome is likely to occur. Although hope may exist without any evidence that the desired outcome is possible, in the long term, in order for hope to continue, it must eventually be backed up by some evidence. Finally, the connection property represents an important relational component of hope. It is the idea that connection with other human beings, with a higher power, or some other intimate connection provides a sense of hope that the desired outcome is possible. Increased connection leads to increased hope.

To demonstrate these foundations, one might imagine a yet unachieved desired outcome in one's life. As one thinks about how much hope they have for achieving that outcome, they will notice that their hope is partly based on a belief and feeling that they have options to choose from to achieve that outcome. The greater the number of options that one perceives they have, the more likely they are to feel hopeful. Second, one's hope is sustained (or diminished) by one's belief and feeling that they are both willing and able to *act* on those options. Third, one's hope is influenced by the evidence they have that the desired outcome is possible. For example, if one has accomplished a similar task, or seen others like oneself achieve such a goal, they are more likely to feel hopeful that they too can achieve the goal. Finally, one's hope is related to one's feeling of connection to others who can support or help one to achieve the desired outcome. Stronger relationships with others surrounding one's goal also build hope.

Strategies for Engendering Hope

Although some individuals, couples, and families enter counseling with a clear hope that they can make improvements, clinical experience suggests that most clients enter treatment after having tried a variety of strategies on their own and, finding themselves in the midst of a continual struggle, reach out to a counselor. Thus, the first strategy of any effective therapy is to engender hope in the possibility of achieving goals. The four foundations of hope provide insight into early steps that can assist in this process. From the foundation of options, counselors help the client discover options that can be pursued in order to achieve their goal. If counselors lack specific options for pursuing the desired goals after the first session, it is important to instill a belief that having pursued the option of counseling will likely contribute to finding additional options. A common phrase that communicates this idea is "Coming to counseling is an important step in your process of seeking change, and I believe that our work together is an option that can lead to increased strategies for you to achieve your goals." As seen in this phrase, a counselor's own confidence in their work is a key component of the options foundation. Clients must see the counselor as a key "partner" who can help them bring about change.

From the foundation of action, counselors should provide clients with specific actions that are easily within the capacity of clients to accomplish when they leave the session. These actions often connect to a therapist's preferred theory of treatment. For example, therapists practicing from a systemic perspective with a couple in distress might assign the couple to share positive feelings for each other on at least three occasions before the next session, regardless of how negative they might be feeling toward each other. Counselors practicing from a cognitive-behavioral perspective might ask an individual who is struggling with depression to track their thoughts and identify alternative, strengths-based ways of thinking. Thus, our preferred theories provide direction on the actions we should ask clients to take to achieve their goals. In addition, counselors should find ways to communicate confidence in the client's ability to act in these ways.

From the foundation of evidence, counselors can increase hope by normalizing presenting complaints and providing evidence that others have experienced similar types of challenges and have found solutions to those challenges. Problems that lead people to enter counseling often lead to isolation and shame. Thus, therapists who can share a larger vision of the reality that others, in similar circumstances, experience similar challenges *and* have found solutions provide evidence to the client that they too can achieve their desired goals. A phrase that communicates this idea is "I have worked with others who are experiencing [presenting complaint]. It makes sense that you'd be [presenting complaint] given all that is going on, and I believe that, similar to others that I've worked with, you too can find solutions to your challenges."

Finally, from the foundation of connection, counselors must create strong relationships between themselves and their clients and, when working with couples and families, create experiences that promote great connection among each other. Hope is inherently increased as people feel connected to others (as opposed to alone and isolated) in their journey to achieve their desired goals. Clearly, this is related to the counselors' ability to join effectively and to create the foundations for a strong therapeutic alliance. In addition, given the diversity of clients, cultural preferences related to joining and relationship satisfaction are particularly relevant to this foundation of hope. A one-size-fits-all model of joining will certainly not work for clients whose views, experiences, and backgrounds differ significantly. Thus, it is critical that counselors both learn about and are sensitive to the preferred ways of connecting among a variety of cultural groups.

David B. Ward

See also Clinical Practice; Common Factors; Goals, Treatment; Hope-Focused Approach to Couple Enrichment in Counseling; Normalizing; Therapeutic Alliance

Further Readings

Hubble, M. A., Duncan, B. L., & Miller, S. D. (Eds.). (1999). *The heart and soul of change: What works in therapy.* Washington, DC: American Psychological Association.

Lopez, S. J., Snyder, C. R., & Pedrotti, J. T. (2003). Hope: Many definitions, many measures. In S. J. Lopez & C. R. Snyder (Eds.), *Positive psychological assessment: Handbook of models and measures* (pp. 91–107). Washington, DC: American Psychological Association.

Snyder, C. R., & Taylor, J. D. (2000). Hope as a common factor across psychotherapy approaches: A lesson from the dodo's verdict. In C. R. Snyder (Ed.), *Handbook of hope: Theory, measures, and applications* (pp. 89–108). San Diego, CA: Academic Press.

Sprenkle, D. H., & Blow, A. J. (2004). Common factors and our sacred models. *Journal of Marital and Family Therapy, 30,* 113–129.

Ward, D. B., & Wampler, K. W. (2010). Moving up the continuum of hope: Developing a theory of hope and understanding its influence in couples therapy. *Journal of Marital and Family Therapy, 36,* 212–228.

Entitlement

Entitlement generally has a negative connotation. Individuals who are labeled as "entitled" are often described as greedy, demanding, and/or overprivileged. Entitlement has a different connotation in couple and family therapy and is most commonly used within the model of contextual family therapy (CFT) developed by Ivan Boszormenyi-Nagy. It most often refers to what one is deserving of or owed in significant relationships, and it can be relationally constructive or destructive. This entry begins with a discussion of how entitlement differs in horizontal and vertical relationships. It then defines *constructive* and *destructive entitlement* and explores both concepts through examples.

Horizontal and Vertical Relationships

The structure of significant relationships helps to determine what one is entitled to. In CFT, it is ideal when significant relationships are balanced. Balance means that each individual is giving what she or he owes and is receiving what she or he is entitled to. This is often referred to as give-and-take, and it is important to note that giving and receiving does not always need to be equal at all times for relationships to be balanced. Further, expectations for balanced give-and-take are not the same for all types of relationships.

In CFT, there are two different types of significant relationships. Horizontal relationships theoretically lack hierarchy and thus have equal power distribution. Siblings, colleagues, classmates, and romantic partners are all examples of horizontal relationships. It is important to note that contextual power differences could exist in these relationships due to differences in sociocultural privileges based on gender, race, socioeconomic class, religion, sexual orientation, age, and physical or cognitive ability among other factors. Further, siblings could have differences in relational power due to birth order.

In horizontal relationships, the balance of give-and-take should be relatively equal over time. In the example of a couple, each partner could provide the other with love, emotional support, and understanding. The levels of giving and receiving in horizontal relationships are usually relatively symmetrical. In other words, individuals in horizontal relationships take care of each other. Although there may be times when one individual is giving more than the other (e.g., when one is ill, grieving, injured, or overwhelmed), the hope is that both individuals are generally getting their most important needs met over time. If this occurs, then the relationship is considered balanced.

Vertical relationships work much differently than horizontal ones. Vertical relationships exist where there are power differences due to hierarchy. These power differences do not necessarily extend to social power differences based on privileged or marginalized sociocultural identities, but like horizontal relationships, these can exist as well. Power differences in vertical relationships are due to hierarchy in the systems in which they reside. For instance, parent–child, teacher–student, and supervisor–employee are all examples of vertical relationships.

In vertical relationships, the balance of give-and-take is skewed, not symmetrical. The individual with more hierarchical power owes more, and the individual with less hierarchical power is entitled to more. In the example of a parent and child, the child is entitled to love, nurturance, emotional support, understanding, curiosity, and financial support (e.g., food, clothing, and shelter). The parents, however, are not owed any of these things from their young children. Thus, they do not take care of each other as in horizontal relationships like couples or friends. In a parent–child relationship, the child is entitled to being taken care of by the parent(s), but the parents are not entitled to the same caretaking from the child. Understanding the expectations in both types of relationships is vital to understanding the differences between constructive and destructive entitlement.

Constructive Entitlement

Constructive entitlement is the positive form of entitlement. It is "earned" when individuals reliably give to others in significant relationships (e.g., family, romantic partners, or close friends) in fair, considerate, loving, and trustworthy ways. There is no perfect formula for reliable giving, but reliability exists when loving and caring actions can be counted on and are much more the rule than the exception. When people give reliably to others, they earn constructive entitlement and are justly owed or entitled to receiving love and trust in those relationships. Constructive entitlement is a natural consequence of acting loving and trustworthy in significant relationships.

As already stated, children are entitled to loving and trustworthy behaviors from their parents. Parents are obligated to physically and emotionally nurture their children to the best of their ability and are entitled to expect their children to act similarly in the future when they are in positions of hierarchical power. They are not entitled to receive the same level of nurturing of the relationship as their children, and these expectations could extend to other forms of hierarchical relationships (e.g., teacher–student, therapist–client, or supervisor–employee).

A good example of constructive entitlement is found in the book *Teens Who Hurt* by Ken Hardy and Tracey Laszloffy. The authors introduce the "PTA rule," which states that parents, teachers, therapists, and other adults must always respond in healthy ways to adolescents' behaviors. In other words, no matter how offensive teenagers' behaviors may be, they are still entitled to respectful and healthy responses from significant adults in their lives. Adults have more contextual power as compared to teens; thus, teens are entitled to expect adults to take on more relational responsibility.

Related to children growing into adolescents, families need to adapt to growing children. Children are able to be more responsible as they grow into adolescents and are entitled to expect their parents to adapt to their growth. These adaptations could include teens having opportunities to set their own bedtime, complete homework on their own schedule, go out with peers albeit with curfew, and use the family car. If teens are able to meet these expectations at a reasonably reliable rate, trust increases in the relationships with their parents. The parents learn to trust the children to take on more responsibility, and the children learn to trust that their parents are respecting their growth. The children learn to trust themselves to do more as well. In sum, growing children are entitled to be trusted with more responsibility, and parents are entitled to expect that their children can take on more.

Destructive Entitlement

Destructive entitlement, the opposite of constructive entitlement, occurs when an individual acts relationally destructive. Destructive behaviors usually include some sort of violations of love and trust such as punishment, abuse, physical or emotional neglect, lying, and so on. The premise of destructive entitlement is that individuals do not have the right to be relationally destructive no matter how they are treated by others. Individuals are assumed to always have some choices about how to act, respond, and/or behave toward others.

Destructive entitlement can occur in any relationship but most often occurs in one of two ways. The first is when an individual has been harmed in a relationship and looks to retaliate and get revenge. For example, in a couple where one partner was unfaithful, the infidelity is a form of destructive entitlement. The partner who was cheated on does not deserve the violations of love and trust caused by the infidelity and could respond in many ways. Some ways would also be forms of destructive entitlement including cheating themselves, physical aggression, passive-aggressiveness (e.g., not speaking to the partner), and any other form of behavior that is destructive to love or trust. Although the partner who was cheated on is entitled to better treatment, the circumstances do not entitle her or him to retaliate or seek retribution.

The second common form of destructive entitlement occurs when one was "cheated" out of love and/or trust in one relationship and acts similarly in another relationship. A common example is someone who was sexually abused as a child and then becomes a perpetrator of sexual abuse to other children. Although the child who was abused was entitled to better treatment, this does not entitle her or him to hurt others in similar ways. Another example is when someone is emotionally neglected as a child and then is emotionally absent with her or his children as an adult. The thinking behind this type of behavior is similar to the thinking behind organized hazing that occurs in youth or collegiate sports teams, fraternities, and sororities. In other words, "I was treated like this, so you have to suffer through it too."

In both types of destructive entitlement, it is presumed that the individual acting destructively is in some sort of emotional pain. In CFT, individuals who act destructively are hypothesized to be victims of destructive entitlement themselves and then become perpetrators of similar relationally destructive behavior. When parents act destructively with children because of their relational pain from their own childhoods, the cycle of destructive entitlement is passed from one generation to the next. In CFT, this pattern is referred to as the "revolving slate." A common example of this is parentification, or putting children in positions where they need to physically and/or emotionally care for their parents in unreasonable ways. Again, it is the primary responsibility of the parent to care for the child, not for the child to care for the parent.

In addition to directly hurting others, destructive entitlement also includes refusing to receive that to which one is entitled. Failing to receive prevents others from being able to earn constructive entitlement through giving. This could look like someone who will not let others give compliments or gifts, or do favors or chores. In the example of an opposite-gender couple, the man could do most of the household chores. From the outside, his behavior could look thoughtful and even altruistic. However, if his female partner says that she will do the dishes after he cooked and he does not allow her to, he is being more selfish than altruistic. He feels good when he gives to her and earns constructive entitlement in the process, but she never has the opportunity to earn constructive entitlement with him. It creates a situation where she will constantly feel like she owes him but never has the opportunity to give.

Finally, destructive entitlement can also extend to sociocultural issues in broader social systems. Boszormenyi-Nagy states that White individuals in the United States who are unaccountable for how they have benefited from the slavery of African Americans are acting with destructive entitlement. This is not to say that every White individual is responsible for things that happened over 150 years ago, but it is to say that every White individual reaps the benefits of an unjust system that still exists today, albeit to a lesser degree. As Boszormenyi-Nagy acknowledges, people are entitled to equal treatment, and when someone is treated unfairly on the basis of their race, gender, religion, ethnicity, sexual orientation, or social class, that individual is entitled to reparation for the unjust treatment.

Michael E. Sude

See also Contextual Family Therapy; Intergenerational Loyalty; Intergenerational Trauma; Parentification and Diverse Family Systems; Trust

Further Readings

Boszormenyi-Nagy, I., & Krasner, B. R. (1986). *Between give and take: A clinical guide to contextual therapy*. New York, NY: Brunner/Mazel.

Boszormenyi-Nagy, I., & Spark, G. M. (1984). *Invisible loyalties*. New York, NY: Brunner/Mazel.

Goldenthal, P. (1996). *Doing contextual therapy*. New York, NY: W. W. Norton.

Hardy, K. V., & Laszloffy, T. A. (2005). *Teens who hurt*. New York, NY: Guilford Press.

Hargrave, T. D., & Pfitzer, F. (2003). *The new contextual therapy: Guiding the power of give and take*. New York, NY: Brunner-Routledge.

Krasner, B. R., & Joyce, A. J. (1995). *Truth, trust, and relationships: Healing interventions in contextual therapy*. New York, NY: Brunner/Mazel.

Stone Fish, L. (2000). Hierarchical relationship development: Parents and children. *Journal of Marital and Family Therapy, 26,* 501–510. doi:10.1111/j.1752-0606.2000.tb00319.x

Sude, M. E. (2015). The acknowledgment, naming, and giving (ANG) activity: A systemic self of the therapist training exercise. *Journal of Systemic Therapies, 34*(1), 1–15. doi:10.1521/jsyt.2015.34.1.1

Epistemology in Family Therapy

Epistemology is the philosophical study of how one comes to know and believe things about the world in which they live. The word is rooted in *episteme* from the Greek word for "knowledge" and *logos,* meaning "the study of." Epistemology explores what individuals believe about knowledge and how they draw conclusions about the environment in which they live. Epistemology in family therapy is important because the underlying beliefs individuals hold about knowledge dictate the rules used to create understanding of experiences and to influence the descriptive language used to describe these experiences. Counselors who work with families need to understand their assumptions regarding how they can come to know something about another individual. Gregory Bateson is credited for bringing thoughts about epistemology into the field of family therapy by introducing to it the concept of *cybernetics* (a term coined by Norbert Wiener, referring to the study of systems), which he considered a specific type of epistemology. This epistemological view is rooted in what is now known as *systems theory.* The emergence of systems theory in family therapy was influenced by shifts in counselors' understanding of how they can come to know a client's reality toward an epistemological view that is influenced by processes and patterns of information. Individuals are not subject to linear chains of causality; rather, they are part of complex systems of communication, feedback, structure, and relationships. This entry discusses three different views within epistemology: empiricism, rationalism, and constructivism. Next, epistemology in family therapy is discussed within a historical context.

Epistemological Views

Epistemology deals with ways in which people acquire knowledge to better understand reality. Counselors' epistemological view influences the theoretical approach they utilize in therapy because at the root of most counseling theories is a stance regarding how one can come to know and believe things about their clients. Individuals' epistemological view is essentially the theory one holds about the nature of reality. An epistemological view will influence how counselors understand the presenting concerns of individuals and which interventions bring about change. Shifts in different epistemological views have influenced shifts in counseling theories over time. For example, the emergence of behavioral theories was partly influenced by an empirical epistemological view that holds that knowledge is derived through sensory data, such as the reliability and validity of observations. Family therapy is traditionally characterized by a certain epistemological framework that separates this therapeutic modality from other common counseling approaches. Recent research has suggested that individuals tend to have a dominant epistemological view and one's preference theoretically in clinical practice is influenced by one's epistemological leanings. Though many different thoughts exist regarding epistemological views, three that seem to directly influence family therapy are discussed in what follows.

Empiricism

Empirical views of epistemology hold that knowledge is constructed out of sensory data. All human knowledge is only derived a posteriori (based upon experience). One can only know about reality through what can be sensed, touched, and measured. Direct observations of experiences lead one to use inductive reasoning to arrive at knowledge. The empirical mind-set is what drives the scientific method. Hypotheses are developed and then compared with observations from the natural world. Utilizing validity and reliability procedures, knowledge is determined based upon the evidence of the observation.

One quality of empiricism is that there exists an essential feature to reality in which direct observations can discover knowledge. Essentialism is the doctrine that knowledge exists as an objective, discoverable thing, which individuals can find through the use of the scientific method.

Counselors who work from an empirical epistemological view will often utilize therapies in which theories can be tested against observations from the natural world. Behavioral therapy and some medical models of treatment have been associated with this epistemological view in the literature.

Rationalism

Rationalism is an epistemological view that appeals to intellectual and deductive reason. Rational views of epistemology state that knowledge comes from pure reasoning. Knowledge is derived from that which is logically consistent rather than experienced through the senses. Any sensory experience or outside teaching is opposed to the rationalist position. Intuition holds high esteem in rationalism, and the underlying principle is that all individuals are rational beings who can use deductive reasoning to arrive at knowledge. As such, rationalists argue that there exists a single, stable reality whereby thoughts are placed as superior to experiences.

Counselors operating from a rationalist view tend to find themselves in the role of helping clients to think in a more logically consistent manner. They tend to operate in a more directive, analytical way to help instruct clients into creating thought patterns that are more logically consistent as a way of determining reality. According to some observers, cognitively oriented theories can be associated with this epistemological view.

Constructivism

As opposed to the previous two views of epistemology, constructivism adheres to the belief that knowledge is constructed in human perception and social exchange. Constructivism is commonly understood to be consistent with postmodernism, whose proponents maintain that knowledge is not inherent in the world and merely awaiting discovery; rather, knowledge is created through our interactions with the world. In this view, reality is personal and mutable rather than fixed, and individuals construct their bases of knowledge from their personal learning histories, external experience, and their own personal constructive processes. Family therapy allows for many different theoretical approaches; however, the field is often characterized by a distinct epistemological view that is influenced by cybernetics, consideration of systemic influences, and constructivist epistemological views.

For some, a source of debate regarding the epistemological view of constructivism has to do with difference. Relativism, as a product of constructivism, maintains that individuals' conception of reality is relative to their own historical and contextual experiences. Knowledge is derived from the meaning individuals make of their experiences. As such, no objective reality exists, so how can one particular view of reality be determined useful as compared to a differing view? Neopragmatism, also known as postmodern pragmatism, has emerged to address potential issues that arise from relativism. Neopragmatism asserts that the best interpretation of reality is the one that has the greatest utility and is workable in a given situation.

Constructivism may encourage individuals to be proactive in their own reality creation. On this view, individuals are responsible for the way they make meaning of the situations in which they find themselves and how they change in response to them. Postmodern, systemic, and narrative approaches of treatment have been associated with this epistemological paradigm.

Epistemology, Systems Theory, and Family Therapy

Many researchers credit the emergence of family therapy as a distinct model of treatment to have its genesis in the 1950s. It was at this time that various theorists (e.g., Nathan Ackerman and Gregory Bateson) were proposing new approaches to treatment that were rooted in a constructivist epistemological view. Prior to this shift, many of the theories driving clinical work were rooted in psychoanalytic and behavioral paradigms. More importantly, the focus of treatment in a clinical setting was on the individual. The emergence of family systems theory (FST) shifted the perspective away from individuals' linear behavior patterns and toward a focus on the family system and patterns of interaction. The emergence of this perspective presented an epistemological shift in the field of counseling.

The new epistemological view, perhaps partly in response to constructivism, moved the focus from individuals' intrapsychic patterns and problematic behaviors to interpersonal, transactional patterns. Increasingly, individuals were seen as existing inside complex family, relational, and community systems. Early research studies after World War II explored the relationship between mother and child as it relates to the development of schizophrenia. Researchers such as Frieda Fromm-Reichmann and Gregory Bateson began postulating concepts that schizophrenia could be related to communication sequences in families. These early theorists helped emphasize a focus on the entire family system rather than just the individual. Over the years, the field of family therapy began to root itself in an epistemological view of knowledge as being influenced by the systems and patterns of communication in which people find themselves. This led to the ongoing development of FST, which views individuals as existing inside a family system with complex rules, relationships, hierarchies, and communication patterns.

In a family systems paradigm, the counselor adopts a specific epistemological view regarding how knowledge is to be understood in the context of complex relationships and systems. When multiple family members share their unique perspective of the presenting problem, the counselor's epistemological view will shape how they are understanding each member's view of reality. In family counseling, the focus becomes on *what* is occurring, *how* it is occurring, *when* it is occurring, and *the process* by which it is occurring. This focus on the process rather than on the content keeps counselors from getting dragged into "epistemological battles" in which the members of the family fight for their own version of reality to be acknowledged. An additional task of many family counselors is to develop a skill set in which to educate the *identified patient* and the other family members regarding their view of how one can understand problems to exist inside a family system. Holding to a constructivist view is often taught in family therapy so as to help the clinician focus on the process of the relationships and to minimize having to pick one individual's view of reality over the other competing views.

The epistemological view in systems theory, whereby problems are viewed as occurring inside a system, made way for clinicians to begin providing treatment to the entire family rather than to single individuals, consistent with the understanding that each family is a system. Accordingly, early family counselors began conducting treatment with the entire family unit. Nathan Ackerman is usually credited with being the first individual to start seeing families; however, many other prominent figures, such as Carl Whitaker, seemed to spontaneously emerge doing similar work although at the time, these clinicians had no knowledge of each other. This new treatment orientation is a result of a shift in epistemology.

In programs where individuals are being trained to work with couples and families, students are often exposed to one or multiple classes on systems theory. Not all mental health clinicians are willing to work with entire families, and this could be due to differences in their epistemological views. If individuals do not agree with the paradigm that problems can be understood in the framework of a family system, in which each member's understanding of the problem may be constructed through the interaction of other family members, then they will probably tend to operate from a different framework.

To summarize, family therapy emerged as a result of certain individuals allowing their research and clinical work to be shaped by their epistemological views. Family therapy is typically rooted in a systemic framework that is influenced by the epistemological views of the clinicians, theorists, and researchers that helped bring these theories to the field. These epistemological idiosyncrasies help separate family therapy as a practice from other therapeutic interventions that exist.

Tyler Wilkinson

See also Cybernetics; Identified Patient; Schizophrenia and Families; Systems, Subsystems, and Metasystems; Systems Theory

Further Readings

Arthur, A. (2000). The personality and cognitive-epistemological traits of cognitive-behavioral and psychoanalytic psychotherapists. *British Journal of Medical Psychology, 73,* 243–257.

Gladding, S. T. (2015). *Family therapy: History, theory, and practice* (6th ed.). Boston, MA: Pearson.

Goldenberg, H., & Goldenberg, I. (2013). *Family therapy: An overview* (8th ed.). Belmont, CA: Brooks/Cole.

Hansen, J. (2006). Counseling theories within a postmodern epistemology: New roles for theories in counseling practice. *Journal of Counseling and Development, 84,* 291–297.

Hansen, J. (2014). *Philosophical issues in counseling and psychotherapy: Encounters with four questions about knowing, effectiveness, and truth.* Lanham, MD: Rowman & Littlefield.

Lee, J. A., Neimeyer, G. J., & Rice, K. (2013). The relationship between therapist epistemology, therapy style, working alliance, and intervention use. *American Journal of Psychotherapy, 67*(4), 323–345.

EQUINE-ASSISTED FAMILY THERAPY

The field of animal-assisted therapy (AAT) has been growing exponentially in recent years, with research and clinical practice demonstrating the benefits of the human–animal bond for physical health, improvement of medical conditions, alleviation of grief and suffering, management of anxiety and depression, and a host of other issues. AAT encompasses clinical work incorporating dogs, cats, dolphins, turtles, elephants, and other animals, often as companion or service animals that aid humans in specific, task-oriented ways. As an outgrowth of AAT, equine-assisted psychotherapy was developed with an awareness of the specific physical and mental health benefits that contact with horses offers humans. While therapeutic riding and hippotherapy (physical, occupational, or speech therapy using horses) have long been acknowledged as therapeutic for individuals with physical limitations, incorporating horses into the mental health context reflects the field's growing emphasis on innovative, nontraditional methods of providing clinical services. Equine-assisted psychotherapies, including equine-assisted counseling and family therapy approaches, have grown and developed rapidly over the past 20 years. This entry examines equine-assisted psychotherapies in terms of their theoretical and applied focus, relevance and utility within counseling approaches, and application with diverse populations and presenting problems.

An experiential approach, equine-assisted psychotherapy approaches offer an alternative context for clinical work, taking the client out of the traditional office setting and incorporating the beneficial and often unpredictable effects of nature. Typically provided by a team consisting of both a mental health and an equine professional, equine-assisted sessions offer the opportunity for clients to engage in structured activities with horses while the clinical team observes and determines how best to utilize their observations therapeutically. While some equine-assisted approaches incorporate riding, the majority of this work is unmounted, with the focus on direct observation of the clients' process as they attempt to build trust and cooperation with a large and potentially intimidating animal.

Advantages of Using Horses in Animal-Assisted Therapy

As prey animals, horses are attuned to their environment, allowing them to offer a unique response to humans that distinguishes equine-assisted psychotherapy from other animal-assisted approaches. Because of this sensitivity to their surroundings, horses respond immediately and directly to any change in their environment. When humans approach, they react with caution, inquisitiveness, and a readiness to flee if anything seems to indicate imminent risk. They can thus provide immediate feedback about clients' efforts to establish a relationship, build trust and cooperation, and accomplish a task. If they feel threatened, they will not engage, and they will not maintain proximity; this alone can increase clients' awareness of how they may be approaching their relationships with others in their lives, allowing them to try something new and potentially create more positive outcomes.

Typical Session

In a typical session, the clinical team may have the clients spend time simply observing the horses and describing what they see. Informed by the theoretical assumptions of the therapist, these descriptions and observations will shape the process of therapy, serving as a template for understanding the clients' subsequent encounters with the horses. As the session progresses, the client will likely be asked to accomplish a simple task, such as grooming, haltering, leading, or asking the horse to cross a small obstacle.

As this process unfolds, the therapist observes and comments on how the client engages with the horse, building a metaphoric understanding of how the client may approach challenging experiences in daily life. As clients connect with the horse, gaining cooperation and attempting new skills, they find ways to effectively manage their anxiety regarding unpredictability or uncertainty, to take charge and accomplish goals, and to see their own behaviors reflected in the reactions of the horses. Through this process, clients may work on relationship building, confidence, assertiveness, or self-esteem and also may experience the richness of nonverbal communication as a component of experiential work. This feedback is often less intimidating and more palatable than similar feedback from individuals who are important in their lives. The therapist monitors and processes these interactions with the horses, creating a reflective, experiential context for change.

Presenting Concerns

Many equine-assisted programs have been developed for working with at-risk adolescents, providing them the opportunity to care for, groom, and ride horses; benefits have included reduction in high-risk behaviors and increases in self-esteem, responsibility, and accountability. Other, more clinically focused programs utilize licensed mental health professionals and target a wide range of presenting issues, including trauma and posttraumatic stress disorder (PTSD), eating disorders, substance abuse and addictions, domestic violence, anxiety and depression, and grief and loss. Perhaps most notable in recent years has been the integration of therapeutic riding with equine-assisted mental health approaches to treat PTSD and traumatic brain injury (TBI) in veterans returning from Iraq and Afghanistan. The power of these animals to connect with veterans who have experienced physical and emotional trauma has been well documented. As prey animals, horses offer a unique connection with veterans who, traumatized by their experiences in a war zone, have learned to remain hypervigilant and immediately responsive to perceived threats and who must reintegrate to civilian society. Research, while growing, has lagged behind practice, and the impact of this dynamic approach is just beginning to be widely acknowledged in the scientific community.

Organizations

Several national and international organizations have developed as the field has grown, offering education, training, and in some cases, certification for professionals. These include the Equine Assisted Growth and Learning Association (EAGALA) and the Professional Association for Therapeutic Riding, International (PATH Intl.), among others. Additionally, coursework is being developed at the college and university level to prepare both equine and mental health professionals to conduct this work.

As this innovative field continues to expand, career opportunities for counselors and family therapists interested in creative, nontraditional approaches to mental health practice will expand as well. The power of the human and horse bond is a resource that can enrich and inspire clinical work, changing lives in the process.

Shelley Green

See also Brief Family Therapy; Clinical Practice; Crisis Intervention With Couples and Families; Experiential Family Therapy; Metaphors; Military Couples and Families; Systemic Family Therapy

Further Readings

Chandler, C. (2012). Equine assisted counseling. In C. Chandler (Ed.), *Animal assisted therapy in counseling* (2nd ed., pp. 205–228). New York, NY: Routledge.

Green, S. (2012). Horses and families: Bringing equine assisted approaches to family therapy. In A. Rambo, T. Boyd, A. Schooley, & C. West (Eds.), *Family therapy review: Contrasting contemporary models*. New York, NY: Taylor & Francis.

Green, S. (2014). Horse sense: Equine assisted single session consultations. In M. Hoyt & M. Talmon (Eds.), *Capture the moment: Single session therapy and walk-in service*. Williston, VT: Crown House.

Pichot, T., & Coulter, M. (2006). *Animal-assisted brief therapy: A solution-focused approach*. New York, NY: Routledge.

Trotter, K. (2011). *Harnessing the power of equine assisted counseling: Adding animal assisted therapy to your practice*. New York, NY: Routledge.

ERECTILE DISORDER

Erectile disorder (ED), often referred to as impotence, is the inability to attain or maintain an erection sufficient for intercourse the majority of the time. Inability to achieve an erection occurs due to limited blood flow to the penis that could be caused by several factors: exhaustion; medication or alcohol use; heart disease; chronic illnesses; or emotional, social, or psychological factors. Because ED affects sexual health and satisfaction, couple intimacy, work, and social interaction and can also have a psychological component, it is often discussed in counseling sessions. This entry discusses the diagnosis and description of ED as well as the diagnosis with regard to the typical male sexual cycle. In addition, this entry details the causes, psychological and relationship issues, consequences, and common treatments for the disorder.

Diagnosis and Description

Most men experience the inability to achieve an erection at some point during their lifetime, and odds of this occurring increase with age. While occasional difficulty achieving erection is not cause for concern, difficulty maintaining erection most of the time is considered abnormal. This is true regardless of a man's age. For this reason, ED is diagnosed only if the problem occurs more often than not over an extended period of time. To completely understand the diagnosis and manifestation of ED, counselors can read specific diagnostic criteria found in the fifth edition of the *Diagnostic and Statistical Manual of Mental Disorders* (DSM-5; American Psychiatric Association [APA]). It is also helpful to learn more about the typical male sexual cycle.

The Male Sexual Cycle

Typically, exposure to sexual thoughts, fantasies, or images causes the male brain to transmit signals to the vascular system (also called the circulatory system and includes veins and arteries throughout the body). These signals result in vasocongestion, a condition where more blood flows into than out of the penis. This additional blood flow results in rigidity of the penis, an increase in testicular size, elevation of the scrotum, flushing of the skin, heightened nerve sensitivity, and increases in heart rate and blood pressure. There are different physiological responses that occur throughout the sexual response cycle, which includes the following phases: excitement, plateau, orgasmic, and resolution. With continued sexual excitement, the aforementioned excitement stage transitions to the plateau stage. The plateau stage is evidenced by a further increase in the size of the penis. For men with ED, an interruption occurs in this process resulting in the inability to achieve or maintain erection prior to orgasm.

Causes

Disruptions in the male sexual response occur as a result of psychological and/or biological processes. A man's medical, psychological, relational, and sexual history should be considered when assessing ED.

Physical Issues

Physical issues such as heart disease, blocked blood vessels (atherosclerosis), high blood pressure and/or cholesterol, and obesity are known culprits of ED as are diseases such as Parkinson's, multiple sclerosis, Peyronie's disease (scar tissue inside the penis), sleep disorders, metabolic syndrome (lowered metabolism accompanied by increased blood pressure, high insulin and cholesterol levels, and body fat in the midsection), and obesity. Substance use can also influence ED. For example, tobacco, alcohol, specific prescription medications, and other drugs may block vessels that supply blood needed to achieve erection. Surgeries involving the spinal or pelvic area may also be culprits. Essentially any biological component that blocks nerve signals and blood supply such as the brain, spinal cord, hormones, nerves, muscles, and blood vessels all affect the ability to achieve erection.

Psychological and Relationship Issues

Psychological factors such as stress, anxiety, depression, anger, intimacy, and relationship problems can disrupt the sexual cycle. Thoughts, mood, and self-esteem as well as social and cultural cues interrupt the brain's sexual signals and, consequently, physical responses. For example, social teachings inferring the immorality of sex may produce feelings of guilt, which, in turn, interrupt sexual stimulation. Work-related stressors and relationship issues such as poor communication, inability to resolve issues, lack of intimacy, and infidelity may also impede sexual responsiveness by blocking stimulation. Furthermore, mood disorders with symptoms such as anxiety and depression may also alter sexual libido. Not only is libido impaired due to the mood itself but medications prescribed to improve mood block blood flow or block nerves, resulting in lowered ability to achieve erection. Counselors may have difficulty distinguishing between ED as well as social, cultural, medical, and substance-related disorders. The DSM-5 helps counselors distinguish between these disorders so proper diagnosis and treatment occurs.

Risk Factors

A number of factors contribute to a man's chances of experiencing ED. Some of these risk factors are controllable. For example, factors such as prolonged bicycling, using drugs and alcohol, and being obese can be avoided or controlled. Other conditions, however, are not so easily controlled. For example, aging, certain medical conditions, injuries, medical treatments, and psychological conditions may not be avoidable. In order to avoid ED, a man may wish to avoid injuries or conditions that compress nerves in the pelvis; practice health habits that contribute to a healthy cardiovascular system; and only take drugs or medications or receive medical treatments that are absolutely necessary. In addition, relationship problems, anxiety about sexual performance, values and beliefs about sexuality, and sexual history may cause and/or contribute to erectile difficulties. Both physical and psychological risk factors should be assessed.

Consequences of Erectile Disorder

ED affects a man's relationships, work, and social life. A man who is unable to complete the sex act often suffers negative feelings such as low self-esteem, embarrassment, depression, shame, an unsatisfactory sex life, lowered partner intimacy, and emasculation due to the inability to father children. A man with ED may withdraw from intimacy due to frustration and humiliation. As a result, the sexual partner may feel unattractive and unwanted. These issues along with lowered self-confidence and fear of sexual intercourse via failure are often faced in counseling.

Impotence may also be a symptom of deeper emotional or relationship problems. Couples who experience a lack of communication, infidelity, distrust, mood and anxiety disorders, and other nonsexual mental disorders may contribute to erectile problems. While these issues are not diagnosed as ED, consequences include not only those associated with the primary diagnosis but also problems mentioned above resulting from the symptoms.

Finally, work and social relationships may be affected via eroded confidence that often accompanies ED. When a man is unable to sexually perform, he may lose enjoyment in life and motivation at work. On the flip side, work and social problems may also affect a man's libido. Lack of respect from peers or failure at work can affect sexual performance due to feelings of failure.

Treatment Considerations

Medical treatments and/or counseling offer help to men experiencing the phenomenon as well as to couples wanting a more fulfilling sex life. Physicians, sex therapists, couples counselors, and clinical mental health counselors each offer unique treatments and assistance for men suffering from ED. The following sections discuss medical treatments, sex therapy, and ways in which counseling can improve the conditions and accompanying symptoms.

Medical Treatments

First, men who smoke, drink alcohol, or take other nonmedical drugs are encouraged to stop. Since heart health is linked with ED, preventive actions that improve cardiovascular health such as weight reduction, stress management, and exercise are suggested. Prescription medications known to contribute to ED may be reduced or replaced with another drug. Men with ED should also avoid prolonged bicycling or other activities that impair nerves within the groin area.

Prior to treatment, physicians may conduct a number of tests to determine underlying conditions. Tests such as a physical examination, blood tests, and urine tests (urinalysis) help determine overall health. Next, an ultrasound may be given to view penile blood vessels. This helps the physician determine if problems exist in blood flow. Finally, an overnight erection test and psychological examination are administered. The overnight erection test determines whether erections spontaneously occur during sleep. This helps determine whether erectile issues are biologically or psychologically influenced. If physical causes are eliminated, a psychological test can help diagnose mood disorders, anxiety, and stressors that might be influencing sexual functioning.

Specific medical treatments are available to assist men suffering from physically influenced ED. A number of medications such as sildenafil (Viagra), tadalafil (Cialis), vardenafil hydrochloride (Levitra), and avanafil (Stendra) have shown promise. These medications (called phosphodiesterase type 5 [PDE5] inhibitors) work by loosening the penile muscles so blood flow increases. When the aforementioned oral medications are ineffective, other medical treatments such as penile injections and suppositories may be used. A medication called alprostadil (Caverject or Muse) can be injected directly into the center of the penis (intracavernosal injection therapy) or as a suppository inserted into the tip of the penis to increase penile blood flow.

Vacuum devices and prosthetics are also available for men with ED. Vacuum devices work by placing a cylinder over the penis and pumping air out, which increases blood flow temporarily. Penile implants or prosthetics may be surgically inserted into the penis to create erections. An inflatable cylinder is placed inside the penis and is connected to a reservoir of saline solution. To attain erection, a man squeezes the pump and inflates the cylinder, which creates an erection.

Finally, men testing with low testosterone may be given hormone replacement therapy. While not typically a cause of ED, those with lowered hormonal levels often experience erectile improvement once levels are restored. Hormones are given through application of gels, injections, or patches. Since each medical intervention has risks, patients must weigh benefits and consequences of treatment with help from their physician.

Sex Therapy

Counseling and sex therapy show promise in helping restore sexuality and improving emotional issues among men suffering with erectile difficulties. The American Association of Sexuality Educators, Counselors and Therapists trains counselors, educators, and therapists to help clients overcome psychologically and physically based sexual issues. Sex therapists help couples learn new ways to express intimacy; relax and eliminate sexual distractors; and use touch, often called sensate focus, to enhance intimacy. Couples may start with nonsexual touching and advance to more provocative sensations. Couples learn that intercourse is not required to experience intimacy and sexuality can be expressed in numerous ways. Consequently, these sessions help couples maintain sexual intimacy and enhance libido even when ED remains an issue.

Counseling

Counseling offers assistance in managing self-esteem; confidence; shame; guilt; and issues of embarrassment, frustration, and humiliation associated with ED. Further, counselors can teach men to implement stress management activities such as muscle relaxation, exercise, and meditation to manage stress and anxiety. Communication, relationship, work, and social issues that affect sexual stimulation can be explored in individual and couples' counseling sessions. Since ED is only diagnosed if a nonsexual mental disorder does not better explain the issue, counselors ensure that proper diagnosis and treatment are given to clients.

*Janet Froeschle Hicks
and Stephan Berry*

See also Male Hypoactive Sexual Desire Disorder; Sexual Health

Further Readings

American Psychiatric Association. (2013). Erectile disorder. In *Diagnostic and statistical manual of mental disorders* (5th ed.). Washington, DC: Author.

DiMeo, P. J. (2006). Psychosocial and relationship issues in men with erectile dysfunction. *Urologic Nursing, 26,* 442–446.

Masters, W. H., & Johnson, V. (1966). *Human sexual response.* New York, NY: Ishi Press.

Masters, W. H., & Johnson, V. (1970). *Human sexual inadequacy.* New York, NY: Ishi Press.

Mayo Clinic. (2015). *Erectile dysfunction.* Retrieved from http://www.mayoclinic.org/diseases-conditions/erectile-dysfunction/basics/causes/CON-20034244

U.S. National Library of Medicine. (2015). *Erectile dysfunction.* Retrieved from http://www.nlm.nih.gov/medlineplus/erectiledysfunction.html

ERICKSONIAN FAMILY THERAPY

Milton Erickson was born in Arum, Nevada, on December 5, 1901. He was raised in Wisconsin on a farm with six sisters and one brother. Erickson struggled with a number of physical and health ailments including color blindness, dyslexia, tone deafness, and polio. He came to see these issues as strengths and opportunities that fortified him with the abilities that enabled him to succeed as a psychotherapist. Of particular note, he felt that his paralysis as a result of polio gave him the opportunity to study human behavior in depth and learn about the inclinations, motivations, verbal and nonverbal messages, and nuances of the people around him. Erickson earned his master's degree in psychology, graduated from medical school, and specifically trained as a psychiatrist. He also taught himself hypnosis and became a master in this practice. His early career work was in settings as a psychiatrist and researcher. For health-related reasons, he and his family relocated to Phoenix, Arizona, where he worked out of his home as a psychotherapist. As a result of a second bout of polio, Erickson spent many of his late years in a wheelchair. He remained active as a psychotherapist until his death in 1980 at the age of 78. This entry provides an overview of Ericksonian family therapy, paying attention to the orientation and its specific application in individual and family therapies, and further examines the therapy's specific strategies and techniques. The entry concludes with criticisms and a summary of Ericksonian family therapy.

Definition or Relevance of Ericksonian Family Therapy

Family Therapy

Family therapy began to develop in the 1940s and started to become a clear professional practice in the 1950s. Early pioneers in family therapy included Nathan Ackerman, Gregory Bateson, Carl Whitaker, Murray Bowen, and Milton Erickson. In family therapy, the focus is on relationships and communication as well as on readjusting how families relate and interact as a unit. The process of family therapy can involve any configuration of the following components: individuals, couples, family units (parents and children), and communities.

Ericksonian Family Therapy

Erickson did not subscribe to any particular theoretical orientation; his approach as a psychotherapist was eclectic and integrative. Erickson didn't describe himself as a family therapist, yet he is credited as being one of the early contributors to the field. One of the reasons for this may be because his approach involved using whatever was available to him, which could include a client, the family, the community, and community resources. His influence became notable in his consultation work with Gregory Bateson, Jay Haley, and John Weakland on clients with schizophrenia and their families.

Ericksonian Orientation

As noted earlier, Milton Erickson did not hold himself to any specific theoretical orientation. He preferred to view his work through the individual needs of each client. Some basic tenets of his orientation included individualized therapy; flexibility; a focus on the importance of the unconscious mind as a positive and healing force; insight as unnecessary; pragmatism and a solutions-focused approach; information that the client provides; and consideration of life cycle transitions.

Individualized Therapy

Erickson spent much of his time carefully observing what others said, what they did not say, how they said it, how they behaved, what seemed to motivate them, what seemed to disengage them, and so forth. He realized that every single person or family is different and requires a unique interaction to be successfully engaged. In this way, he may have seen multiple families for the same issue yet treated them using completely different techniques based on what he identified as their individual and unique needs. In working with family issues, he would at times work with a family as a unit and at other times in any number of configurations. He would determine what the family needed and then configure the interactions to achieve their goals.

Flexibility

The flexibility that Erickson employed went beyond treating each client as a unique entity and taking an individualized approach. He believed that a therapist should be available to take advantage of promoting client growth whenever it could occur. In this way, he met clients at their homes, in public, day or night, multiple times during the week, and for varying durations of time. He would see just one member of a family, the entire family, or any number of configurations of the family unit.

Importance of Unconscious Mind as a Positive and Healing Force

Erickson believed in the importance of the unconscious mind as a positive and healing force in therapy, just as much as he believed in the importance of the conscious mind. While some of his approach can be seen as psychodynamic, he parted dramatically from that path in this regard. While psychodynamic therapy saw the unconscious mind as harboring negative associations, he saw it as a resource associated with the client's ability to know what they needed. Erickson frequently used hypnotic trance to tap into the unconscious in his work with individuals and families.

Insight as Unnecessary

As much as Erickson believed in the importance of the unconscious mind, he equally believed that insight was not a necessary factor for the therapeutic process. Understanding the past and the "why" of behavior was of little concern to him. From his perspective, what has already happened will not change. Erickson wanted to focus on what could be done now and in the future. However, if he felt he could use past information to motivate a family and to encourage a new pattern of behavior, he would do so.

Pragmatism and Solutions-Focused Approach

For Erickson, an important outcome of therapy was to find a new perspective, to change a behavior, or to try a different approach that would help a family to become more functional and achieve their goals. He was very pragmatic in this approach and realistic about the situation and the possible outcomes. Part of this pragmatism was the acceptance of individuals and meeting them where they are. In this approach, he identified what change a family needed to make to restore them to balance as well as what resources were available for him to use in his therapeutic process. He was realistic about any limitations.

Information That the Client Provides

Erickson was often recognized for his uncanny ability to figure out exactly what would work with his clients. In his approach, he focused intensely on each client to determine their role, strengths, weaknesses, and relationship to other family members. He observed their communication patterns, vocal inflections, use of verbal and nonverbal language, and relational positions (where they physically and psychologically placed themselves in relationship to other family members). Erickson listened to their stories, their hopes, their frustrations, and all the things in between that they did not say. All of this rich content built the rationale for how he proceeded to work with a family in therapy.

Life Cycle Transitions

For Erickson, life cycle transitions were extremely important to the psychological health of families. He viewed family issues as issues with life cycle transitions. These transitions include courtship and independence, coupling and marriage, childbirth and parenting, weaning parents and launching children, and retirement and later life. When working with a family, he would ascertain which life cycle event was most relevant. If the family could not successfully navigate through the appropriate transition phase, they could become stuck and engage in maladaptive behaviors and patterns.

Strategies and Techniques

Erickson admitted on a number of occasions that he sometimes had no idea how an intervention was going to turn out. He spent many years experimenting with a variety of strategies and techniques in a diverse array of situations and circumstances. Strategies and techniques that he primarily used include directives, double bind, encouragement of resistance, humor, hypnosis and hypnotic trance, manipulation of relationships, metaphors and storytelling, and motivational hooks as well as prescribing the symptom. It has been said that Erickson used whatever worked to promote change and well-being for his clients.

Directives

Erickson was known for being very direct with his clients. At times, he employed such unorthodox directives such as going out to dinner, going to a beautician, eating beans and expressing flatulence in the nude, taking dance lessons, and more. However, many of his directives came in the form of subtle and indirect suggestions.

Double Bind

The double bind was another frequently used technique that Erickson employed. In essence, this involved presenting a client with two unwanted options, thereby forcing them to choose the one less offensive to them. Ultimately, this strategy gives clients a choice, even if they must choose between two things they do not really want to do. An example that Erickson used in session was to ask a client if they wanted to go into a light trance or a deep trance.

Encouragement of Resistance

Erickson felt it was a mistake to fight a client's resistance. He saw resistance as a failure of the therapist to adequately build a therapeutic relationship with the client. Resistance provided an opportunity to use what the client gave him as a therapeutic tool. In this way, he would not only accept but also encourage a client's resistance. If he thought a client did not want to divulge information, he would instruct them to only share with him what they wanted to share. This provided a sense that the therapist was on their side and gave them some control in the session, which enhanced the therapeutic relationship. Eventually the client would find less and less that they wanted to keep from the therapist.

Humor

Humor was a useful tool that Erickson brought into his therapy. Again, he used anything available to him in order to promote change and growth for his clients. He found that humor could be especially useful in family therapy as a way to help diminish power dynamics and defensiveness in families. Humor can serve in other ways as well, such as decreasing tension, helping clients to feel at ease, and taking away some of the power the therapist has in the relationship.

Hypnosis and Hypnotic Trance

Hypnosis and hypnotic trance is an area for which Erickson is especially known. He was self-taught and experimented for his entire career with hypnosis. For the purpose of working with families, it is probably most relevant to focus on his concept of the hypnotic trance. He viewed this as a way of fully and intentionally communicating with the client. It was less about a deep hypnosis and more about how he met the client where they were by "pacing" with them. Pacing was his way of mirroring their breathing pattern, cadence of speech, posture, word choice, and more. This was how he connected with a client and eased them into openness to directives as well as subtle suggestions. He was able to use this technique with individuals as well as groups.

Manipulation of Relationships

Allies

In working with families, Erickson sought to use positions in families and build alliances that served to promote change and growth. When working with a couple, if he sensed resistance on the part of the husband, he might ally himself with the husband against the wife in a way that opened up the husband to be more vocal and communicative. Once that goal was achieved, he might then ally with the wife so that she could feel supported in responding to the husband's concerns. Then he could possibly place himself in opposition to the husband and wife, thereby making them allies against him.

Spacial Orientation

The positions that individuals hold in the family unit can identify interactional patterns. Erickson sought to disrupt these patterns in therapy by altering the spacial orientation of family members. He would take note of where everyone would choose to sit and how each member related to the others. Based on this, he would intentionally move them in order to change their perspectives or their ability to relate. He might do this by sending the son out of the room and asking the mother to sit in the son's seat and having the father move to the mother's seat. He would then ask the mother what she thinks of the son's relationship with the father. Then he might ask the father what he thinks about how the mother relates to the son.

Metaphors and Storytelling

Erickson frequently used this technique in his work. He believed in the effective use of language to promote change and plant ideas in a way that indirectly allowed clients to accept what he suggested, with minimal resistance. Metaphors are figures of speech that make a comparison or draw parallels between two unrelated concepts. The storytelling that Erickson used closely resembled allegories, in that they were stories meant to convey some kind of meaning or lesson. This was regarded as one of Erickson's most developed talents and most powerful tools.

Motivational Hooks

Milton Erickson was adept at identifying what was motivating a client or a family to engage in a pattern of behavior. By identifying the motivation that influenced the behavior, he could use those elements to inform his strategies to help families resolve their issues. George Sargent and Bleema Moss discussed this technique in an example of a family in mediation regarding the custody of the children. In using effective questioning, the mediator was able to isolate the father's motivation for wanting sole custody and was able to craft intentional dialogue to address the benefits of the father's continued involvement and ways it would serve both the mother and father. In identifying the mother's motivations for wanting sole custody, the mediator was able to direct an activity that addressed what the mother needed from the father.

Prescribing the Symptom

Prescribing the symptom, or paradoxical intervention, is a strategy that encourages a client to increase and intensify a behavior. This can diminish the power of the behavior and redirect an individual to adopting other ways of communicating an issue. In Erickson's use of this strategy, he would make some adjustment to the behavior. For example, in a case where a family sought him out to address the daughter's thumb sucking, Erickson separated the child from the parents and instructed her to increase the intensity and noisiness of the thumb sucking. He also indicated that she should do this for 20 minutes while her father was reading the paper and then go to the mother while she was sewing and do the same for 20 minutes. In a separate conversation with the parents, he instructed that no matter what the child did that they should not react for the duration of 4 weeks. The outcome was that gradually over the 4 weeks the thumb sucking stopped completely. In other cases, he used similar strategies to address bed-wetting, vandalizing, and even vomiting.

Criticisms

Erickson had many devoted followers and many who wrote extensively about his approach. However, he also had a number of critics who questioned his abilities and practices. A major criticism of his practice of psychotherapy was how he used hypnosis. He was not a conventional hypnotist and crafted hypnotic techniques to fit his ideals of therapy rather than conform to widely accepted practices of hypnosis. There are many critics who simply do not view hypnosis as a legitimate practice, especially in therapy. He was also criticized for being too eclectic and failing to work from a specific theoretical paradigm. Because of this, it has been said that his approach can be difficult to understand and replicate. There are also some who question his directives. One specific example involves a case when he instructed a young woman to undress in front of him and point out her genitalia, but in this case, he indicated that his wife was also present during the intervention.

Conclusion

Erickson never formalized his approach for working with families. He felt strongly that the therapist should use an individualized approach with each client that utilized what the client presented. What is clear is that Erickson valued individualized therapy, flexibility, and a focus on the importance of the unconscious mind as a positive and healing force. It is also clear that Erikson regarded insight as unnecessary, valued a pragmatic and solutions-focused approach, sought to use whatever information or resources the client provided, and recognized the importance of life cycle transitions. While by no means an exhaustive list, many strategies and techniques Erickson used include the following: directives, double bind, encouragement of resistance, humor, hypnosis and hypnotic trance, manipulation of relationships, metaphors and storytelling, and motivational hooks as well as prescribing the symptom. Erickson cultivated a large following and also had his share of critics. He ultimately has been credited with contributing to the field of family therapy as well as to the field of medical hypnosis. Erickson's approach and strategies offer salient considerations for practitioners who work with families.

Regina Finan

See also Communication in Couples and Families; Couples and Marriage Counseling; Hypnosis; Neuro-Linguistic Programming; Paradoxes and Paradoxical Intervention; Solution-Focused Brief Therapy; Strategic Family Therapy; Systemic Family Therapy

Further Readings

Battino, R., & South, T. L. (1999). *Ericksonian approaches: A comprehensive manual*. Bancyfelin, Wales: Crown House.

Feldman, J. B. (1985). The work of Milton Erickson: A multisystem model of eclectic therapy. *Psychotherapy, 22*(2), 154–162.

Gladding, S. T. (2015). *Family therapy: History, theory, and practice*. Hoboken, NJ: Pearson.

Havens, R. A. (1985). *The wisdom of Milton H. Erickson*. New York, NY: Irvington.

Hayley, J. (1973). *Uncommon therapy: The psychiatric techniques of Milton H. Erickson, M.D.* New York, NY: W. W. Norton.

Hayley, J. (1985). *Conversations with Milton H. Erickson, M.D. Volume 3: Changing children and families*. New York, NY: Triangle Press.

Jenkins, T. D., & Forrest, A. W. (1999). Ericksonian approaches to counseling: Toward an assimilated paradigm of practice for the twenty-first century. *Journal of Humanistic Counseling, Education & Development, 37*(4), 224–231.

Lankton, S. R., & Lankton, C. H. (1986). *Enchantment and intervention in family therapy: Training in Ericksonian approaches*. New York, NY: Brunner/Mazel.

Sargent, G., & Moss, B. (1986/1987). Ericksonian approaches in family therapy and mediation. *Mediation Quarterly, 14/15*, 87–100.

Scroggs, K. A. (1986). Ericksonian approaches within family hypnotherapy. *Individual Psychology: Journal of Adlerian Theory, Research & Practice, 42*(4), 506–520.

Ethical Codes

The ethical issues that a professional counselor faces in the field are as diverse and complex as the clients they serve. Personal, professional, and cultural interpretations of a given situation can have a major impact on how that issue is conceptualized and ultimately addressed. In the absence of specific guidelines, two counselors may come to two very different resolutions for the same issue. As such, ethical codes have been developed and refined over time to guide the practices of counselors and protect the welfare of the individuals they serve. Ethical codes, typically established by organizations that govern or guide a profession (e.g., American Counseling Association [ACA], American Association for Marriage and Family Therapy [AAMFT]), outline specific expectations of behavior that set the standard for appropriate practice. This entry reviews the purpose, structure, and uses of ethical codes as they exist today, with special attention given to how these codes can be utilized as well as their potential shortcomings.

The Purpose of Ethical Codes

Ethical codes can serve different purposes. In general, one could say that all codes are designed in such a way as to protect clients as well as counselors. These codes are often grounded in one or more core ethical principles such as autonomy (i.e., empowering clients to be self-directive) or fidelity (i.e., living up to commitments with clients). Although most codes are crafted in the spirit of protecting counselors and ensuring the well-being of clients, the format in which individual codes are crafted can vary significantly. This, in turn, affects the way that a counselor must adhere to a given code.

The Structure of Ethical Codes

When ethical codes are revised, there are often amendments or additions that are in response to particularly relevant issues at that moment in time (e.g., distance counseling). Given the complexity of ethical issues in the field, however, it is impossible to craft a code to address every potential dilemma a counselor may encounter. Thus, the structure of each ethical code can vary from describing concrete directives to providing general guidance on how to address a more broad range of ethical concerns. These are often described as mandatory and discretionary codes.

Mandatory Ethics

As the name suggests, mandatory ethical codes compel counselors to take certain courses of action when faced with specific ethical dilemmas. As such, these codes are often the easiest to conceptualize and presumably the easiest to comply with. Mandatory codes often take one of two forms: (1) obligatory or compulsory codes or (2) prohibitive or restrictive codes.

Obligatory codes describe actions that counselors are mandated to take when faced with specific ethical dilemmas. For example, in an effort to protect clients, counselors are often obligated to report disruptive or damaging professional policies to their employers. In this example, the conditions are relatively specific and the action counselors are obligated to take is clear.

Perhaps one of the better-known ethical obligations is the duty to warn. Should a client reveal in session that they are a danger to themselves or others, counselors are mandated to report the threat to the appropriate parties and take all necessary steps to ensure the safety of those involved. Special attention has been given to the duty-to-warn obligation when it involves individuals from particularly vulnerable populations such as minor children. It must be noted, however, that despite this concrete obligation, the debate rages on as to what constitutes a significant enough threat to require the counselor to take action. This can vary depending upon the nuances of the ethical code one is utilizing or the state in which one is practicing.

As one would expect, prohibitive or restrictive codes describe actions that counselors are prohibited from engaging in. Arguably the most well-known prohibitive codes stipulate that counselors are forbidden from engaging in a romantic or sexual relationship with current clients. There are a number of prohibited actions, however, that are not as obvious. For example, counselors are prohibited from assessing or evaluating current or former clients for forensic purposes. Consider a scenario in which a counselor is providing services to a couple that is experiencing marital difficulty and considering a divorce. If that couple eventually decided to move forward with a divorce and legal proceedings were initiated to determine custody of their child, it would be unethical for their counselor to testify as to the appropriateness of each parent. This may seem counterintuitive given the fact that the counselor likely has an in-depth understanding of each parent by virtue of his or her counseling relationship. Regardless, such an evaluation is expressly prohibited.

As stated previously, obligatory codes require counselors to report potentially dangerous policies to their employer. For example, a counselor may find that the way psychotropic medications are stored in a residential facility is insecure and presents the threat of theft. Complementary to that obligation, prohibitive codes also exist that forbid counselors from harassing a colleague or employee who reports damaging policies to the appropriate parties.

Discretionary Codes

To a certain degree, a counselor must use their discretion with almost any ethical code they utilize. It is simply not possible to address the infinite number of scenarios a counselor may encounter in the field. This was illustrated in the duty-to-warn example previously that points out that, although there is a clear ethical obligation for counselors to report potentially dangerous situations, there is not complete consensus on what constitutes a valid threat. With discretionary codes, however, counselors are merely provided with considerations to help them make an informed decision about issues that the organization that developed the code has yet to take a definitive position. One such example is the issue of accepting gifts. Codes exist that provide a variety of considerations a counselor should take into account when deciding whether or not to accept a gift from a client (e.g., monetary value of gift, cultural significance of gift giving for the client). In the end, counselors are not obligated to refuse, or prohibited from taking, gifts. They are expected to consider all the variables and make the most appropriate decision. Counselors often have to navigate these sorts of "gray" issues and will need to reexamine and debate them for the duration of their professional career.

Multiple Codes

Navigating the gray areas of counseling ethics can be a challenge in and of itself. To complicate things further, there are many ethical codes that counselors can be obligated to abide by depending on their certifications, organizational affiliations, or professional specialties. These codes are often similar and overlap in major issues that are addressed. Some are even modeled after others. Despite the similarities, however, these various codes are not identical, and differences certainly exist. In some cases, one ethical code may even disagree with another.

To illustrate, consider the example that was given regarding sexual relationships with clients. Such a relationship is strictly prohibited by most if not all professional regulators. When it comes to sexual relationships with *past* clients, however, disagreements begin to emerge. Some organizations, such as the ACA, allow for a counselor to ethically engage in a romantic relationship with an ex-client as long as the interaction occurs after treatment has been terminated for a minimum of 5 years. The American Psychological Association (APA) has similar standards but requires only a 2-year hiatus after terminating services.

The issues surrounding multiple ethical codes can be related to the question of professional identity. How you define yourself as a professional will often dictate what professional affiliations and certifications you pursue. Those affiliations will dictate what ethical standards you are obligated to abide by. In the end, counselors will inevitably face complex ethical issues and only an in-depth knowledge of all the ethical codes applicable to them will provide them with the necessary knowledge to make decisions.

Ethical Codes and Couple and Family Counseling

Couple and family counseling is unique in many ways to individual counseling. By virtue of a third party being incorporated into the therapeutic process, many standards of practice change and often become more complicated. This may include standards related to the sharing of information and confidentiality or client welfare. These standards are made more complicated due to the change in the way the counselor defines the "client." In an individual session, it goes without saying who the client is. In a couple or family counseling relationship, however, it is not as cut and dry. It is possible for one member of the family to be identified as the primary client. Often, however, the client is actually the couple or entire family unit. This should be determined during the intake process and when informed consent is being obtained.

In cases where the couple or family unit is considered the client, practices—from an ethical perspective—may need to change. Take, for example, confidentiality. Counselors are charged with maintaining confidentiality and protecting the clients' privacy in every feasible way. When multiple individuals make up the client, it becomes much more difficult to control and maintain that same level of confidentiality that can be achieved in individual sessions. Even if each member of the unit agrees to respect the privacy of the group, it is possible that someone will share information outside of sessions. This is one of the reasons why identifying the client needs to occur during the informed consent process. Each member of the unit needs to be aware that this sort of breach of confidentiality is possible and beyond the control of the counselor. Respecting the privacy of the group is just one consideration. In couple and family counseling, another consideration is maintaining confidentiality between members of the group. Suppose, for example, that you were seeing a couple for counseling and one party disclosed that they were having an extramarital affair but did not want to disclose this to their partner. What is your ethical responsibility? This is an issue that is unique to couple and family counseling, and there is no one correct answer. Again, much of the counselor's responsibility here can be traced back to the informed consent process. If a counselor creates a specific "no secrets" policy for their sessions and both parties agree, then they are obligated to live up to the agreement. If no such policy is outlined during the consent process, however, it can be much more difficult to decide.

Another unique issue in couple and family counseling relates to client welfare. Counselors are obligated at all times to protect the welfare of their clients. This process becomes much more complicated, however, when the "client" is actually a couple or family unit. Protecting the welfare of the unit may have adverse effects on specific members of the group. For example, a counselor may provide services to a couple and their child and determine that one of the parents poses a threat to the rest of the unit. It could be considered "protecting the welfare of the client" to suggest a trial separation between the couple. Although this may have a positive impact on the family as a whole, the impact on the segregated parent may have a number of negative effects. It is still possible to protect that member of the unit by providing support or offering individual services, but this is an example in which the good of the unit is the sum of the good of each member.

Peter J. Boccone

See also Confidentiality; Conflict in Couples and Families; Empowerment in Families; Ethical Decision-Making; Family Mediation; Legal Issues in Parenting

Further Readings

Ahia, C. E. (2012). *The danger-to-self-or-others exception to confidentiality* (2nd ed.). Lanham, MD: University Press of America.

American Association for Marriage and Family Therapy. (2015). *Code of ethics*. Washington, DC: Author.

American Counseling Association. (2014). *ACA code of ethics*. Alexandria, VA: Author.

American Mental Health Counselors Association. (2010). *AMHCA code of ethics*. Alexandria, VA: Author.

American Psychological Association. (2010). *Ethical principles of psychologists and code of conduct*. Washington, DC: Author.

Herlihy, B., & Dufrene, R. L. (2011). Current and emerging ethical issues in counseling: A Delphi study of expert opinions. *Counseling and Values, 56*, 10–24.

Herlihy, B., & Remley, T. P. (1995). Unified ethical standards: A challenge for professionalism. *Journal of Counseling and Development, 74*, 130–133.

Zibert, J., Engels, D. W., Kern C. W., & Durodoye, B. A. (1998). Ethical knowledge of counselors. *Counseling and Values, 43*, 34–48.

Ethical Decision-Making

In family and couples therapy, ethical decision-making refers to the actions counselors take in regard to precarious situations that occur within the therapeutic context. *Ethical decision-making* is a specific term that encompasses the various processes and considerations counselors take into account in order to manage an ethical quandary that does not have a clear solution. Decision-making processes can vary depending on the presenting ethical issue(s), the client population, and the counselor. In ethics literature, several different models of ethical decision-making are discussed, most of which include similar steps to guide the counselor working through an ethical dilemma. Given the complex nature of couples and family counseling, it is advantageous for counselors to be aware of common issues that occur within couples and family therapy. This entry briefly introduces ethical decision-making as it relates to couples and family counseling, identifies various components of the decision-making process for counselors to consider, and presents some common ethical issues that emerge in couples or family counseling. The entry concludes by discussing the importance of ethical decision-making within the context of couples and family therapy.

Ethics and Values

Ethics

The term *ethics* refers to the behaviors of counselors as they seek to make decisions in the best interests of their client(s). Ethical practices are rooted in fundamental principles that include an individual's values, morals, and priorities. There are two categories of ethics: *principle ethics* and *virtue ethics*.

Principle ethics are the set of guidelines counselors use to make choices regarding client welfare. Counselors often consider the following principle ethics when analyzing ethical dilemmas: autonomy, beneficence, nonmaleficence, justice, and fidelity. A sixth principle of veracity has been added in recent years. Autonomy is the principle that clients are self-regulating individuals with the right to make their own decisions. Beneficence is the principle of "doing good" and indicates that counselors should strive to act in ways that benefit clients. Nonmaleficence is the principle of "do no harm," meaning that counselors should behave in a manner that prevents harm from befalling clients. Justice is the principle that clients deserve to be treated fairly and equally. Fidelity is the principle that counselors uphold their commitment to their clients. Veracity is a newer principle that prompts counselors to be open and honest with their clients.

Virtue ethics refers to the character traits of a counselor and prompts them to consider what type of counselor they want to be. Counselors practicing virtue ethics consider the qualities they wish to embody in their counseling practice that are congruent with their professional goals. The four virtuous components that counselors are encouraged to practice in their work are prudence, integrity, respectfulness, and benevolence. Prudence is a virtue that encourages counselors to practice good judgment after thoughtful planning. Integrity prompts counselors to maintain their beliefs and include them into their decision-making processes. Respectfulness encourages counselors to treat others with kindness and deference. Lastly, benevolence prompts counselors to act in ways that advance the welfare of humankind.

Values

Values play an important role in ethical decision-making, as they are persistent beliefs that guide an individual's behavior. The values that counselors hold have the potential to influence how they conceptualize an ethical dilemma and inform their navigation of the issue. Counselors are encouraged to identify their values and recognize situations in which they might be triggered to make values-based decisions that favor their interests rather than uphold client welfare.

Ethical Issues in Couples and Family Therapy

There are a variety of commonly occurring ethical issues within couples and family therapy. Following is a brief presentation of a few types of issues to consider when providing couples or family therapy.

Conceptualization of the Client and Goal-Setting

Counseling couples and families poses a unique consideration as to who is the official client. In individual counseling, it is clear to the counselor that the sole individual is the client. Sometimes when counseling couples or families, one member of the unit will be identified as the "problem" and the reason why the couple or family is seeking counseling. Additionally, individuals that comprise the couple or family may have varying ideas about what constitutes the therapeutic goal(s). For example, a couple may bring their teenage daughter to therapy because of her disruptive and disrespectful demeanor toward her younger siblings. The parents' goal may be for the daughter's behavior to change, while the daughter's goal is for her parents to acknowledge her maturation and individuation. In this scenario, the counselor would take note of each family member's therapeutic goal and weigh the pros and cons of labeling one goal as primary over another. The recommended course of action is for the counselor to acknowledge the family system as the client and, as such, have each individual member identify a familial goal rather than prioritize his or her individual goal. The same recommendation can be applied to a couple or partnership system.

Confidentiality

Counselors face a unique dilemma in couples and family therapy with confidentiality, especially in relation to secrets and transitioning from individual counseling to systemic counseling. The types of couples and family secrets can vary, as can the moment at which they are revealed. For example, one partner may not want to disclose to the other partner that the reason for her distant demeanor is due to her extramarital affair. The partner may choose to disclose this information to the counselor outside of the session, thus putting the counselor in the precarious position of wondering how to address the self-disclosure. The counselor may decide to encourage the partner to disclose in session to her partner rather than do it on her behalf. Alternatively, the counselor could treat the two partners as individuals and choose not to address the infidelity disclosure in session. In situations when an individual receiving counseling adds another person to the counseling session, the counselor must be clear on what information (if any) will be shared from the individual's session. It is imperative for counselors to revisit the parameters of confidentiality and informed consent when the counseling format changes from individual to couples or family therapy and to document all clients' understanding of the changes.

Informed Consent

Counselors should take great care when discussing informed consent with all individuals participating in couples or family therapy, especially within the context of setting therapeutic goals. In particular, counselors need to explain the potential risks and benefits to each member of the unit, noting that initial changes within a system can have a ripple effect on the rest of the members for whom changes may prompt discomfort and resistance. Though it is impossible to anticipate every potential scenario, it is vital for each member to understand what the risks and benefits of therapy are for each individual in the system.

Privileged Communication

Counselors should be aware of legislation regarding privileged communication within their state. Additionally, counselors should be clear with individuals in the couple or family regarding what types of communication are protected and within what context. In cases where a couple seeks a divorce postcounseling, the counselor may be called to share counseling records pertaining to the sessions. Counselors are encouraged to seek legal counsel regarding privileged communication agreements prior to discussing them with clients.

Components of Ethical Decision-Making

Currently, a multitude of ethical decision-making models exist that address a variety of issues and some that are specifically geared toward working with certain client populations. The following presents vital components that are commonly included in multiple ethical decision-making processes.

Identifying the Problem

The first step involved in the ethical decision-making process is clearly identifying the ethical dilemma. Counselors recognize an ethical dilemma as a situation that challenges their ability to determine the "right" option that would prevent harm. Counselors may be aware an ethical issue is present; however, dilemmas pose a layer of complexity, as the counselor may truly be unsure as to which is the best course of action to take.

Reviewing Ethical Guidelines

Counselors are mandated to abide by ethical codes and laws. In this second step, counselors should refer to the American Counseling Association (ACA; 2014) *Code of Ethics* in addition to other pertinent ethical codes. Counselors consult ethical guidelines in an attempt to glean information on how best to work through the ethical dilemma at hand. Ethical codes include mandatory actions for some ethical scenarios, such as the prohibition of sexual or romantic relationships between clients and counselors. Additionally, counselors are cautioned against imposing their values onto clients, such as a counselor who refuses counseling to a same-sex couple. It is important to acknowledge that while ethical codes recommend certain courses of action, they do not address every potential ethical scenario that a counselor may encounter.

Knowing Applicable Laws

Counselors should be aware of state and national laws regarding ethical scenarios such as when mandatory reporting of an issue is required. For example, counselors are mandated reporters of child abuse and neglect. Thus, if a client discloses about known child abuse occurring, the counselor is required by law to report the incident to the proper authorities. Legal guidelines may be of particular significance when a counselor faces issues of confidentiality, privileged communication, and informed consent.

Consulting With Other Professionals

Counselors are encouraged to consult other professionals regarding their ethical quandaries in order to glean information to assist them with finding a solution. Counselors may choose to consult with supervisors, peers or colleagues, members of other mental health disciplines, lawyers, or health professionals. Discussions with other knowledgeable professionals can assist counselors with identifying multiple layers of the dilemma they have not yet considered, which may alter their initial course of action. Consultations can help counselors avoid egregious decisions that may unintentionally hurt clients or lead to potential lawsuits.

Considering Possible Actions and Consequences

Prior to making a decision as to the best course of action of solving an ethical dilemma, counselors should seriously ponder all potential choices and how the decision will affect their clients. Counselors are encouraged to generate a list of possible pros and cons of each decision. Things to consider are how the decision will affect the client in terms of the therapeutic relationship, confidentiality, self-disclosure, and potential harm to the client. Couples and family therapists are encouraged to take a systemic approach and consider how the intended course of action may impact all individuals involved.

Choosing the Most Appropriate Course of Action

After sufficiently consulting the *Code of Ethics* and applicable laws, consulting with other professionals, identifying possible courses of action, and weighing the pros and cons of each one, the counselor should be ready to make a decision in an effort to resolve the ethical dilemma. This may involve transparency on the part of the counselor to inform clients of the best course of action, including matters in which the counselor must report the issue to an authoritative party (e.g., police, child protective services). It would behoove counselors to document each stage of the decision-making process, noting specific evidence as to what led to their final decision. At multiple stages within the ethical decision-making process, counselors may consider the role of principle and virtue ethics as well as how their own personal values affect their course of action.

Kristen N. Dickens and Candace N. Park

See also Couples and Marriage Counseling; Cultural Issues in Couples and Families; Ethical Codes; Informed Consent for Research; Informed Consent in Clinical Work; Secrets

Further Readings

American Association for Marriage and Family Therapy. (2001). *AAMFT code of ethics.* Alexandria, VA: Author.

American Counseling Association. (2015). *ACA code of ethics.* Alexandria, VA: Author.

Wilcoxon, S., Remley, T., Jr., & Gladding, S. (2014). *Ethical, legal, and professional issues in the practice of marriage and family therapy* (updated 5th ed.). Upper Saddle River, NJ: Pearson.

ETHNICITY

Ethnicity forms the basis for understanding values, beliefs, and perspectives from a given cultural group based on ties to the culture in a particular nation. An individual's ethnicity can be informed by living in a particular culture, growing up in the culture, or having family influences from the culture (e.g., social influences, parents, siblings). Ethnicity often carries a sense of personal belonging with a community. There are also larger categories to define specific ethnic identities, such as European American, Asian American, and Latina/o American. However, some of these categories are too broad to distinguish the ethnic values associated with specific nationalities and heritages, such as Mexican American, Cambodian American, Filipino American, German American, and Irish American. This entry adopts a broad definition of ethnicity with the goal of describing how ethnicity shapes both individuals and families. The first part of the entry demonstrates the extensive complexity of ethnicity, race, and cultural identities. The entry then examines how identity develops, paying specific attention to Jean Phinney's research on how adolescents develop ethnic identities. Finally, this entry discusses the importance of ethnicity in couples and family counseling.

Ethnicity, Race and Cultural Identities

Understanding the role of ethnicity in family counseling is vital because ethnicity often underlies ideas about family conflict, values, and what it means to grow and change as a family within a specific cultural context. While members of a particular family might carry heritages from their own parents and context of living, multiple ethnic identities can be present within and across families. As counselors consider couples who enter a relationship or marry, they must also consider how the couple's ethnic identities are shaping the relationship and interacting with each other. For example, a Peruvian American woman could marry a Chinese American man, or a Mexican American man could marry a man with German and Irish heritage. While some of their ethnic values might appear similar, they will interact differently according to the relationship. Sometimes, the understanding of the other person's ethnic identity can help couples to interact well with each other. In other cases, the differences and similarities in ethnic identity might present a clash, which could result in more conflict.

Counselors must also consider ethnicity in the context of entire families. It is possible for families to share multiple ethnic values within a single ethnic identity and possible for families to share different ethnic identities based on stepfamilies and marriage. Couples who have children together can carry a diverse set of identities, which may influence their children to assume numerous perspectives on ethnic identity. The children of these couples can sometimes take on a multiethnic approach or identify much more with a specific ethnicity.

Cultural identity holds a strong presence within the counseling profession because individuals live in dynamic and shifting environments. Indeed, because culture is dependent on the experiences of individuals and groups as well as contextual factors, cultural identity development continually transforms. One major construct in culture is the recognition of ethnicity or ethnic identity. While a significant component of cultural identity, ethnic identity development demonstrates a strong presence in recognizing values, belief systems, communications, languages, worldviews, rules, norms, and communities. Ethnicity is one of many constructs that contribute to cultural identity development. Ethnicity is inextricably linked to other factors (e.g., race, gender identity, sexual or affectional orientation, generational status, socioeconomic status, spiritual identity). While race and ethnicity carry major linkages, the two constructs provide significantly different definitions of individuals' cultural identification. Ethnicity is also a useful construct in describing identity, as there are several histories, values, and experiences tied to particular ethnic groups. Ethnicity can account for the heterogeneity of a larger racial grouping, which identifies with diverse perspectives. For example, among Asian Americans, there are several ethnic groups (e.g., Malaysian American, South Asian, Cambodian American, Chinese American). The diversity of ethnic groups can also illustrate intersections with other cultural groupings, including socioeconomic status. For example, within Latina/o American communities, one finds members who originate from countries with a high percentage of working-class individuals and others who originate from regions with a high level of access to resources and financial wealth.

While race is an important construct in demonstrating sociopolitical issues, positions, inequalities, and marginalized groups, ethnicity adds to the construction of cultural identity in allowing for diverse personal identifications. Individuals are not relegated to the stereotypes that are imposed upon them and are able to develop meaningful personal identities as a result of the shared experiences and meanings with other individuals in their ethnic group. Race manages to demonstrate particular oppressed identities, where individuals are positioned by visible physical characteristics. Ethnicity provides more flexibility with how individuals negotiate processes of identification with diverse ethnic groups. This ethnic identity is formed through the interaction of internal processes and external forces. In considering ethnic identity, multiple ethnic identities and contact with several cultures can inform how individuals develop this personal identity.

Transmission of Ethnicity

Ethnic identity is a conglomeration of values, beliefs, perspectives, thoughts, and rituals. Ethnic identity can develop from multiple sources. However, there are two major points of socialization that provide messages about values, beliefs, and norms within a culture. Individuals can be socialized horizontally, which occurs from contact among peers, or individuals can be socialized vertically or intergenerationally, which occurs from contact with parents, guardians, and caretakers. There is also oblique socialization, which is a form of socialization that takes place within institutions and other formal contexts (e.g., schools or cultural centers).

Identity Development

While many racial identity development models have surfaced, including Janet Helms's people of color racial identity and White racial identity models, there are also identity development models for ethnic identity development. Racial identity and ethnic identity may seem similar, but they can differ in their research, constructs, and conceptualization. Race and ethnicity are also interrelated constructs in defining an individual's identity development based upon the interactions between an individual and their environment. Ethnic identity development slightly differs based on expanding a definition beyond classifications of race, which are mostly imposed by society onto individuals. Ethnic identity development also focuses on the various definitions in how individuals utilize personal interpretations to describe their own cultural identifications and create meaningful understanding in how they express themselves. When an individual captures his or her ethnicity, individuals explicate this identity through beliefs, worldviews, and value systems. There is a multiplicity of components that can capture the meaning of these belief systems, as worldviews are measured through spirituality and gender in some ethnic cultures. For example, there is widespread religiosity and spirituality within the Filipino American ethnicity, where Filipino American individuals embody the ethnicity through taking on spiritual values from Catholicism. Similarly, Native American cultures often take into account extensive histories and use of rituals that involve spirituality. While the spirituality may not be named or represent a formal construct, it can be widely integrated into ethnic cultures. In addition, some of the spiritual values that are integrated within ethnic identity are created within the language of that specific identity.

Phinney's Model of Ethnic Identity Development

A major pioneer in the area of ethnic identity development is Jean Phinney, who utilized research to gain more insight into how adolescents perceive ethnic identity. Through these perceptions, her research provided more information on how adolescents maintain a connection to their ethnic history, the values tied to parents' ethnic identities, and sense of pride with regard to ethnicity. By exploring ethnic connection, she also investigated how ethnic identity can be rooted in well-being and meaningful experiences. Her model is also rooted in how individuals grow and respond to events across the developmental life span. As a result, her studies, while often focused on adolescents, applied to the adaptation of individuals in human development. She argued that categories of race were often too limiting, as there are multiple dimensions related to ethnic identity.

Primarily, Phinney and her colleagues developed research using self-identified characteristics to seek how individuals capture ethnicity through diverse characteristics, values, and worldviews. Her theory added that individuals undergo a process that exemplifies a sense of belonging. With this aspect, Phinney's research resulted in three stages known as Phinney's model of ethnic identity development. In comparison to Janet Helms's racial identity models, Phinney's model was often regarded as a stage model due to the stages that an individual experiences throughout the course of the life span.

The first stage of Phinney's model describes individuals in a diffused, unexamined, or foreclosed stage. Individuals in this stage form their identities specifically through the messages socialized from other individuals, including family, peers, teachers, and authorities. A primary result of this socialization includes the internalization of stereotypes, where individuals begin to characterize their identities through the stereotypes they encounter. When individuals take their messages from individuals outside their own personal reflections or insight, individuals from the diffused stage either believe that there are no problems with ethnic identity in society or refrain from exploring the meaning of their ethnic values.

The second stage within Phinney's model describes individuals in a moratorium stage. In this stage, individuals demonstrate an active willingness to explore their ethnic identity. They wish to seek more understanding about their ethnic identity, but they cannot fully capture the full meaning of ethnicity or how to describe their ethnicity. Individuals often remain unsure of how to characterize their ethnicity, especially in creating associations of values specifically tied to their ethnic backgrounds.

The third stage of Phinney's model characterizes individuals in the achieved or accepted stage. Within this stage, individuals express appreciation for their ethnic values. In addition, individuals exhibit an active identification with their ethnicity and a growing confidence of how to capture values and understanding regarding their ethnic background. Individuals additionally exhibit continued exploration of ethnicity, particularly an understanding of how their own ethnic values are characterized.

Critiques of Phinney's Model

Phinney's stage model of ethnic identity development carried several intentions of attempting to explore how ethnicity is captured and how ethnicity contributes to human development. Phinney and her colleagues conducted research that opened areas of research into how ethnic identification can contribute to adaptation. As a result, ethnic identification can result in healthy development through understanding aspects of the self in relation to other individuals. In addition, ethnic identity development is often viewed as a means of optimal development. In order to research these processes, Phinney's model visualizes the process as a set of stages. However, critics of the model often note that the stage model proposes a linear perspective of development as opposed to a multidirectional process, which recognizes that individuals constantly change and adapt due to interactions with shifting contexts and environments. Individuals are shaped by their environments, which can change across the life span (e.g., relocating, employment, schools, and composition of family). Critics of the model maintain that Phinney's stages do not offer enough fluidity in demonstrating the multidirectional nature of human development. While individuals may continue moving from a diffused to accepted stage, critics argue that there is a possibility for particular events in the life span to shift individuals from the accepted stage to foreclosed stage. An additional critique is the complex nature associated with multiethnic individuals who represent several forms of ethnic identity and development. With the complex nature of several ethnicities, some individuals may not necessarily reach the moratorium stage with all sets of ethnic values. Phinney and colleagues, however, developed the basis of the model to address a variety of ethnic groups, especially considering the various ethnic groups that fall within the same racial categories. In addition, Phinney developed the model with the intention to explore the diversity of cultures within the European American identification.

Implications for Family Counseling

Ethnicity is integrated heavily into the counseling process across modalities (e.g., individual, couples, group, family). However, the representation of ethnicity in couples and family counseling remains largely significant to the counseling process. Ethnicity provides a base of understanding for counselors to work with the worldviews and values tied to their clients' identities. It can be helpful for family counselors to recognize and validate differences that exist in the counseling relationship, especially as a means to gain empathic understanding. In addition, obtaining more information about ethnicity allows for specific interpretations of culture that are important to creating a capacity for the clients to act as change agents. This act of creating the openness for agency of change within clients comes with the intention to empower, especially when clients are the targets of oppression. Furthermore, such understanding can be validating as it recognizes the challenges that exist for families who are under pressure to acculturate to a new culture. The acculturation process can shape ethnic identities, and at times, it can affect clients' well-being as they are forced to adapt to a new society while attempting to remain genuine to their ethnic values.

Christian Derek Chan

See also Cultural Issues in Couples and Families; Family Rituals; Family Values; Immigrant Families; Individual Family Culture

Further Readings

McGoldrick, M., Giordano, J., & Garcia-Prieto, N. (2005). Overview: Ethnicity and family therapy. In M. McGoldrick, J. Giordano, & N. Garcia-Prieto (Eds.), *Ethnicity and family therapy* (3rd ed., pp. 1–42). New York, NY: Guilford Press.

Moore-Thomas, C. (2010). Cultural identity development. In D. G. Hays & B. T. Erford (Eds.), *Developing multicultural counseling competence: A systems approach* (pp. 32–52). Upper Saddle River, NJ: Pearson.

Nelson, K. W., Brendel, J. M., Mize, L. K., Lad, K., Hancock, C. C., & Pinjala, A. (2001). Therapist perceptions of ethnicity issues in family therapy: A qualitative inquiry. *Journal of Marital and Family Therapy*, 27(3), 363–374. Retrieved from http://search.proquest.com/docview/220977274?accountid=11243

Phinney, J. S. (1989). Stages of ethnic identity development in minority group adolescents. *Journal of Early Adolescence*, 9(1–2), 34–49.

Phinney, J. S. (1992). The multigroup ethnic identity measure: A new scale for use with diverse groups. *Journal of Adolescent Research*, 7(2), 156–176.

Phinney, J. S. (1996). When we talk about American ethnic groups, what do we mean? *American Psychologist*, 31(9), 918–927.

Sue, D. W., & Sue, D. (2012). *Counseling the culturally diverse: Theory and practice* (6th ed.). Hoboken, NJ: Wiley.

EVIDENCE-BASED PRACTICE WITH COUPLES AND FAMILIES

Evidence-based practice (EBP) is the integration of best research evidence with clinical expertise and patient values. In recent years, an expanded definition has included consideration of the environmental and organizational context as well. In essence, when a family therapist uses EBP, she or he uses research findings to guide treatment decisions. EBP is about *using* research, not clinicians collecting data themselves. Attempts to bridge research and the practice of marital, couples, and family therapy have historically generated controversy and passionate debate. Family therapists have questioned the usefulness of research that focuses on individual therapy for treating mental health disorders, which ignores the complexity of interacting relational systems (e.g., couple or marital, parent–child, intergenerational, and larger system relationships) and families coping with multiple problems. The populations studied in research do not accurately reflect the complexity of families with multiple problems seen by family therapists and run counter to the systems-based clinical training that characterizes family therapy training. As a result, family therapists have sometimes asked, "What does research have to do with my clinical work with couples and families?" Clinicians working with couples and families can become evidence-based in the following ways: (a) employing a process to gather the necessary information to answer clinical questions and (b) learning and using established evidence-based treatment models in their work. This entry discusses the history of EBP, the key steps involved in EBP, and its application in different types of family therapy.

Background

EBP has its roots in the mid-20th century, when Archibald Cochrane, a Scottish physician, argued for funding health care that had empirical support. The principles of EBP were ultimately developed at McMaster University in Canada in the 1980s. A group of scholars wanted to discover improved methods for finding, evaluating, and applying clinical research. They had the ultimate goal of finding better ways of deciding what new information should be incorporated into their practices.

Since the 1980s, many human service professions have adopted evidence-based principles including psychology, behavioral medicine, social work, education, and others. Also, employers, insurance agencies, and other stakeholders have begun to require that clinicians use EBP. A great deal of work has been done to gather evidence through research and to create user-friendly efficient ways for the busy clinician to locate the evidence. A prime example of this process is a government agency called the Agency for Healthcare Research and Quality (AHRQ), which created a center to gather evidence on health care topics. Additionally, the AHRQ is funding Translating Research into Practice projects that evaluate how effectively research-based approaches can be successfully implemented in applied settings.

The Five As of Evidence-Based Practice

EBP follows five steps:

1. Converting the need for information into an answerable question

2. Locating the best evidence to answer the question

3. Using critical appraisal of validity, impact, and applicability of research

4. Integrating research findings with our clinical expertise, patient preferences, and clinical context

5. Evaluating the effectiveness and efficiency of chosen treatments

The process can be summarized with five As: (1) ask, (2) acquire, (3) appraise, (4) apply, and (5) analyze and adjust, which are described next.

Ask (Step 1): Create a Question That Can Be Answered by the Literature

The question needs to be narrow enough to avoid being overwhelmed by information that does not apply. However, the question also needs to be broad enough to get results. For example, a therapist might ask, "What treatments work for autism?" In this question, her or his key word is *autism*. If the therapist searches for autism, she or he will be overwhelmed with literature because the search is too broad. An example of a relevant specific question would be "What brief, family-based treatments work best for treating aggressive symptoms in a child with autism?" In this question, the therapist has significantly narrowed the search by adding key words, including *brief*, *family-based*, and *aggressive symptoms*.

Acquire (Step 2): Locate the Best Evidence to Answer the Question

Being able to effectively and efficiently locate research pertinent to one's questions requires knowledge of different databases. Some databases contain articles on specific research studies, while other databases, such as the Cochrane Library, specialize in providing reviews of the research in different areas. Databases with reviews of the research save considerable time. Some databases not only summarize findings from individual research studies but also make specific recommendations based on the data. These recommendations might even be graded on the strength or power of the supporting research. If a clinician does not have free or easy access to a database like Cochrane, some research can also be found through the Internet by using search engines like Google Scholar or PubMed, although the clinician may need to pay to access the article from the publisher. Membership in professional organizations may allow therapists to access some databases.

Appraise (Step 3): Evaluate the Literature

While many busy clinicians bypass this step by relying on summaries that review and evaluate the existing research on a topic, it is still a good idea to possess the skills necessary to evaluate the quality of primary sources. The original research will allow the therapist to evaluate how closely the clients who received the study treatment match her or his current client. If a review of the research does not exist for a particular issue, the therapist needs to evaluate the quality of a study to know how much confidence can be placed in the findings before applying them.

Apply (Step 4): Integrate Appraisal With Expertise, Client Preferences, and Context

Step 4 encourages therapists to use their personal expertise and client preferences in deciding how to best help their clients. The founders of EBP state that clinical expertise refers to a therapist's unique skills and experiences, while client preferences include the values, concerns, and expectations that clients bring to the clinical encounter. Some therapists might be reluctant to use evidence-based skills because they worry that it will lead to a "cookbook" approach to treatment especially as manualized treatments become increasingly common. They worry that EBP will displace the therapeutic relationship and the caring and concern that is at the heart of good therapy. Step 4 suggests these fears need not materialize. Information gleaned from evidence-based resources is at best a guide and is not meant to replace the human wisdom or the empathic attunement that the therapist and client can share.

Analyze and Adjust (Step 5): Evaluate the Effectiveness and Efficiency of Treatment

As EBP is incorporated into the treatment, the therapist needs to evaluate if the approach is working and meeting the clients' needs. Using a variety of tools, the therapist can evaluate the therapeutic alliance or determine if therapy is being successful. Evaluation is usually not a one-time event. Instead, the therapist must continually adjust the treatment to new circumstances or challenges. For example, a therapist might know that some behavioral treatments might help a client become less aggressive, but when the therapist sees that the client's mother is too overwhelmed to systematically and consistently deliver the behavioral treatment at home, he or she might need to amend the treatment protocol to fit the challenging life circumstances that the client faces.

Utilizing Evidence-Based Treatments in Family Therapy

In addition to employing the five As outlined in the previous section, therapists can also incorporate research into their clinical work by learning and using models that have empirical support for their effectiveness. Since 1995, the *Journal of Marital and Family Therapy* has published research reviews of family-based interventions for specific family problems, including conduct disorder (CD) and delinquency in adolescents, drug abuse, child and adolescent disorders, alcoholism, couples distress, intimate partner violence, affective disorders, and physical health problems. Here, evidence is discussed in relation to three broad categories: (1) children and adolescents as the presenting problem, (2) family-based treatments for mental disorders in adulthood, and (3) couples as the presenting problem.

Children and Adolescents as the Presenting Problem

Of all the family therapy approaches studied to date, the most impressive results have emerged from integrative models that address serious conduct- and drug-related problems in adolescence. These models include functional family therapy (FFT), brief strategic family therapy, Multisystemic Therapy (MST), and multidimensional family therapy. All four models share much in common. First, they are integrative in being attentive to multiple systems: the individual, the couple or marriage, family, and community. They borrow from multiple systemic and nonsystemic models, including structural family therapy (SFT), strategic family therapy, and cognitive-behavioral therapy (CBT). Second, they emphasize joining skills, a therapeutic alliance, and active engagement of the therapist. Therapists do not take a passive approach; they simultaneously provide support, leadership, and direction to mobilize the family toward desired changes. Third, they focus on structural change and the disruption of dysfunctional patterns, both within and outside the family, during and outside the sessions. Fourth, they emphasize the importance of looking at peers and developing a prosocial group of friends. Finally, they are adaptable; the models are tailored to what families need.

In addition to these models, additional family-based interventions have been shown to be effective for other child-related problems. Parent management training (PMT) and parent–child interaction therapy (PCIT) have both been demonstrated to be effective in addressing common problems in children, including oppositional defiant disorder (ODD), attention-deficit/hyperactivity disorder (ADHD), and CD.

Family-Based Treatments for Mental Disorders in Adulthood

Recovery from psychiatric illness is slower when family dysfunction is present. Alternatively, healthy family functioning is a key factor in better outcomes. An effective family-based treatment for severe mental illness is family psychoeducation (FPE). Many studies from around the world have shown that FPE is effective in reducing relapse and rehospitalization rates for individuals coping with severe mental illness, especially schizophrenia. Behavioral couples therapy (BCT) has been shown to be effective for adult drug abuse and alcoholism. The research has been clear that BCT is more effective than individual treatment at increasing abstinence and improving marital and family functioning.

The clinical culture of most treatment programs for severe mental illness and substance abuse focuses on the individual patient. However, the research just discussed reminds us that therapists are more effective when they engage family members in treatment for drug and alcohol abuse and severe mental illness. Engaging families doesn't mean blaming them for problem behavior. Rather, engaging families allows the therapist to address relational stress that exacerbates problems. More importantly, therapists can access a family's skills and resources to help the patient in need.

Couples as the Presenting Problem

The evidence-based models for treating couple distress include Gottman method couples therapy, emotionally focused therapy (EFT), integrative behavioral couple therapy, and cognitive-behavioral couples therapy. EFT is an experiential approach based on attachment theory that emphasizes changing interactional patterns through accessing primary emotions. The other models share much in common, including an emphasis on teaching couples communication and conflict management skills, increasing caring behaviors and positive affect, and building connection through acceptance.

Todd M. Edwards, Jo Ellen Patterson, and Lee Williams

See also Behavioral Family Therapy; Cognitive-Behavioral Couples Therapy; Cognitive-Behavioral Family Therapy; Emotionally Focused Therapy for Couples; Empirically Validated Models; Functional Family Therapy; Gottman Method Couples Therapy; Multisystemic Therapy

Further Readings

Council for Training in Evidence-Based Behavioral Practice. (2008, July). Definition and competencies for evidence-based behavioral practice (EBBP). In *Evidence-based behavioral practice*. Retrieved from http://www.ebbp.org/documents/EBBP_Competencies.pdf

Karam, E. A., & Sprenkle, D. H. (2010). The research-informed clinician: A guide to training the next-generation MFT. *Journal of Marital and Family Therapy, 36*, 307–319.

Lebow, J. (2006). *Research for the psychotherapist: From science to practice.* New York, NY: Routledge.

Patterson, J. E., Miller, R. B., Carnes, S., & Wilson, S. (2004). Evidence-based practice for marriage and family therapists. *Journal of Marital and Family Therapy, 30*, 183–195.

Sackett, D. L., Straus, S., Richardson, S. W., Rosenberg, W., & Haynes, B. R. (2000). *Evidence-based medicine: How to practice and teach EBM* (2nd ed.). New York, NY: Churchill Livingstone.

Williams, L., Patterson, J., & Edwards, T. M. (2014). *The clinician's guide to research methods in family therapy: Foundations of evidence-based practice.* New York, NY: Guilford Press.

Williams, L. M., Patterson, J., & Miller R. B. (2006). Panning for gold: A clinician's guide to using research. *Journal of Marital and Family Therapy, 32*, 17–32.

Experiential Family Therapy

Experiential family therapy is an approach to family therapy that addresses hidden and subconscious issues in the family through the use of activities, role-playing, guided imagery, props and expressive arts, and other active engagement. Experiential family therapy uses the family members' expression of emotion within a genuine, supportive, yet challenging environment. Experiential family therapy attempts to make the covert assumptions overt, unlock defenses to enhance self-esteem and individualism, and promote creativity and playfulness. The purpose is to help eliminate a climate of emotional deadness that can occur in families that are not flexible in roles and in the expression of primary emotions. Engaging family members in the expanding experience opens them up to new ways of being in the family and improves the family's functioning. Experiential family therapy assists families in developing new relationships where emotional risk is supported. These relationships can be better suited for the developmental challenges that families face. The focus of this approach is on how the family interacts and adapts new roles during the session. Experiential family therapy also has an emphasis on the genuineness of the relationship with the family. The effective therapist uses his or her own personality and is open, spontaneous, empathic, active, and willing to take risks. This entry discusses the major concepts, the major proponents of the theory, and a series of interventions typically used in the experiential therapy process. This entry concludes with the current status of experiential family therapy.

Concepts

Experiential family therapy emerged from the humanistic-existential movement in the 1960s and from the practices of client-centered therapy and Gestalt encounter groups. The concepts associated with experiential family therapy engage a family member's honest emotion and prevent the suppression of feelings. The basic concepts guide the experience that the therapist constructs for the family, helping them have freedom, choice, and self-determination.

Experience Is Primary

Experiential family therapists see a family member's experience of themselves within the family as primary to the health or the dysfunction of the family. Since experience is primary, the experiential family therapist attempts to create connecting experiences in the session, focusing on the present experience of the family versus the historic experience. For example, an experiential family therapist may ask a family member to use a family sculpting technique to elicit their current experience of being part of the family. The family member's experience of the family is what is motivating their communication pattern and assumed role.

The Person of the Therapist in the Family

The experiential family therapist joins the family not as a member but as a coach. The therapist shows the family how they might better create an environment of support, become more flexible, and take risks together to grow and individuate. In order for the family to be able to express themselves, they need to see and model the genuineness of the therapist expressing emotion and taking risks. For example, a therapist early on in the relationship with the family will encourage the open expression of ideas without editing the ideas when the family and therapist brainstorm together. As part of the family brainstorming of ideas, the therapist may have to suggest a few ideas initially rejected by the family in order to illustrate the importance of listening to every idea, independent of its quality and who provided it. In this example, the therapist is putting themselves into the family process to illustrate taking risks and supporting each other in the family to take risks.

Spontaneity of Family Interaction

Dysfunctional family interactions are guided by the rules and roles that are in place to maintain the family in a balanced, albeit alienated, system. The experiential family therapist uses their creativity as a "coach" and the growing creativity of the family to establish new flexible roles and expectations. Carl Whitaker suggested that the use of "techniques" is counterintuitive to spontaneity because techniques are planned activities, and by using them, the therapist can take away from the in-the-moment genuineness of the family.

Global Goals for the Family

The goals in experiential family therapy are seen as global improvement of functioning (such as improved awareness, increased flexibility, improved relationships) and not specific outcomes as seen in other family therapy approaches. Goals are deliberately left vague, open, and flexible, which permits the family to change them as their understanding and awareness of the family problems change.

Expression of Affect

For families to be in touch with their present experience, they must express affect. Experiential family therapists will use expressive and sometimes provocative engagement in order to elicit emotion from members. The goal is for family members to feel less alienated from each other and begin to see each other with human qualities and not as a symbolic representation.

Family Myths

Family myths are stories that are created by families to enshrine a particular understanding of the history of the family; they are the basis of the rules and practices that the family abides by. Family myths are the narrative that experiential family therapists help unveil in the family through experiential engagement. Exploring the myths provides the family the opportunity to question their impact and relevance and consider creative options and alternatives to maintaining them.

Leaders in Experiential Family Therapy

Experiential family therapy methods have emerged as an extension of individual, humanistic, and Gestalt methods. At the time of their development, they were challenged by the behaviorists who were attempting to reduce family interactions to a series of actions and reactions. Experiential family therapy approaches elevated the importance of the individual's experience and their awareness. This approach recognized that the interpretation of that experience in the context of the family was crucial to healthy family functioning. Leaders in experiential family therapy—Walter Kempler, Carl Whitaker, Virginia Satir, and Susan Johnson—provided distinct contributions on the concepts, structure, and process of experiential family therapy.

Walter Kempler

Walter Kempler was trained in the psychoanalytic tradition but gravitated toward existential issues with family therapy. He is best known for his introduction of Gestalt concepts into the family therapy arena. Kempler believed that clients must have an existential encounter that is real and reciprocal with other family members and/or the therapist. Each family member is one part of the larger whole of the family. An experiential family therapist should expand awareness in the individual and unify the parts of the family. Kempler posited that intellectualizing an experience was a way in which people and families avoid having a complete encounter. Complete encounters, which therapy can assist in creating, are key to growth toward integration of a person and a family. Incomplete encounters with others are what lead to discomfort and the inability to be whole and accept responsibility.

Kempler would encourage direct and sometimes confrontational encounters, the purpose of which was to have a genuine expression from the family. He reasoned that the therapist engaged in the process actively as a model for others and offered observations and ways to relieve the anxiety of the moment. The therapist's ability to focus on the moment added completeness to the encounter. Kempler's aim was to develop creativity and spontaneity in the encounter so the family felt a sense of freedom from other family members to express anything that in the past may have been risky.

Carl Whitaker

Carl Whitaker's work has been seen as driven by his own personality. Underlying Whitaker's approach was a conceptual framework related to existential and humanistic theory. Carl Whitaker first worked as a psychiatrist in a small diagnostic hospital and then in a child guidance clinic before joining the medical school faculty at Emory University. He saw families and evolving related members that are attempting to self-actualize as healthy families.

According to Whitaker's theory, healthy families have flexible roles that are supportive of family members' changes and growth. Dysfunctional families avoid change and risk. They also are rigid and avoid confrontation. This avoidance of change perpetuates the inability to experience and leads to interpersonal and individual member problems.

Whitaker advocated that the experiential family therapist needs to have genuine engagement with the family. He not only acknowledged transference as a phenomenon in family therapy but also encouraged it as a means for psychotherapy to work, with the caution that transference does not work unless both client and therapist participate. He felt that if the family is expected to be open and genuine, the therapist has an obligation to be open and genuine as well as take risks in the process. In this way, the therapist is also obligated to share countertransference experiences when working with the family as a genuine personal reaction to the therapy experience.

Whitaker's method has emphasized different "battles" when engaging with the family. For example, the "battle for structure" is with regard to which family members will attend a session, when, and how. In order for the family to maintain dysfunction, they will often try to control who can or will attend sessions. Whitaker would set clear expectations of who should and would attend for him to work with the family, often including members via speakerphone during sessions.

The "battle for initiative" occurs when the family resists the responsibility for the work in the session. Whitaker would assert that the experiential family therapist should be engaged with the family and provide them with expertise as a coach would; however, the family has the responsibility for creating change.

Although Whitaker was known to reject the use of stylized techniques in session, claiming that techniques and theories often got in the way of good therapy, he identified important interventions in the early part of the therapy process to test the family's commitment to becoming healthy. The list of suggestions included the following:

1. Symptoms are redefined as efforts to grow. For example, a family member's depressive symptoms are their ineffective means to have a voice in the family.

2. The therapist would model the use of a fantasy as alternatives to real-life issues. For example, the therapist might say, "If you were all living on an uninhabited island, then you wouldn't have to care about what the neighbors thought."

3. The therapist should separate what is true interpersonal stress in the family from what is their fantasy stress.

4. The therapist should be ready to test a small intervention on the family once a relationship is established.

5. The therapist should augment the despair of a family member and bring it to the forefront of the family to see how the family works on that issue.

6. The therapist should use affective confrontation.

7. The therapist should treat children like children in session instead of treating them like little adults.

Virginia Satir

Virginia Satir was a social worker whose change process model was a major contribution to experiential family therapy. Satir posited four assumptions about therapy that were the basis for the change process model. The first assumption is that people naturally move toward health. Second, people possess the resources for their own healthy development, and therapy is meant to encourage an environment where that healthy development could be realized. Third, there is a mutual influence that occurs in relationships among family members. And fourth, therapy is a process involving the relationship between the therapist and the family.

Satir organized communication stances around *placating, blaming, super-reasonable, irrelevant,* and *congruent.* Each of these communication patterns has its own distinct behavior and form of expression. Her work with families would address these patterns and the discrepancies that are created in families when these stances of communication are conflictual and ineffective. This is reflected in Satir's focus on the *primary survival triad*, both parents and the child. Each child developed their personality and relational interaction with the world based on this triad and the ways in which the triad communicated.

Satir, like Whitaker, believed that the family and the therapist must join to be able to be successful in treatment and that the therapist was a resource person and facilitator of the family interaction in session. Satir's focus was on creating healthy communication within the family. She established methods of working with families to enhance their communication and, hence, their relationships, that drew upon the use of experiential exercises. Much of what Satir did in session used affective experiences to bring out the conflicted communication patterns. She believed that these patterns could be represented not only in communication but in form and physical symptoms. To address this expression, Satir used experiential techniques and activities like *sculpting* and *family reconstruction.* The sculpting technique involves posturing family members to express (communicate) inner relationships in outward form. Similarly, family reconstruction uses psychodrama to enact the development of their primary triad by establishing a family life fact chronology. In Satir's *parts party* intervention, she has other family members—or in the case of group counseling, other group members—enact out parts of the client's personality in order to see how they operate from an externalized viewpoint. The personality parts interact with each other, and the client can see and feel the nature of their own expressed personality.

Susan Johnson

Susan Johnson is a cofounder and current proponent of emotionally focused couple therapy (EFCT). Born in England, Johnson describes her recognition of emotions in relationships beginning with her working-class English upbringing. She notes that her family owned a pub and she enjoyed watching her father interact with customers. She became accustomed to people's intense expression of emotion and the ways others chose, or did not choose, to respond. Her early influences include the attachment work of John Bowlby from whom she recognized that attachment issues are not just parent–child but continue, and are acted on, throughout a person's life span. Johnson was trained in a systems approach, with which she merged the genuineness and therapeutic safety emphasized by Carl Rogers. Through her work, she has incorporated experientially engaged sessions with procedural methods.

In developing EFCT, Johnson looked at the way in which people will hide their *primary emotions* with *secondary reactive emotions*. In using secondary reactive emotions (which are often defensive or coercive), a person sets the stage for other family members to mistrust them and develop a negative interaction pattern. Once couples and families can access their primary emotions and share them, a new method of interaction and a healthy supportive relationship environment can be established. By creating a safe environment, couples and families can interact with secondary reactive emotional sets, and the therapist can interrupt at points to explore the experience of the other members and begin discussion around what was the unexpressed primary affect.

Johnson provides a procedure for conducting EFCT that takes the idiosyncratic nature of the therapist, found in other experiential family therapies, out of the process. Steps are as follows: assess the conflicts, identify negative interactions, access unacknowledged primary affect, reframe the problem with primary affect, promote client connection with primary affect, promote others' acceptance, facilitate a restructured interaction, recognize the new solutions, and crystalize new positions in the couple or family. Each of these steps is trainable, replicable, and measurable, generating empirical support for the method.

Interventions

EFCT has a wide variety of experiential activities that can occur during the course of the treatment. The activities emerge as a natural extension of the conversation by the family. Interventions are not imposed without context but are added to the process as a meaningful experience related to the family conversation. Interventions include the therapist's use of self, role-play, sculpting, choreography, humor, puppet interviews, family drawing, and reconstructing family events, to name a few.

Current Status

Creative experiences help families get in touch with their experience but cannot be reliant on the charisma of the therapist. In his 2014 review of the current status of experiential family therapy, Michael Nichols points to two hopeful directions that the theory has taken. First, the work of Johnson continues to emphasize the replicable and measurable outcome aspect of working with clients' expressive emotions and making the process a trainable system. In addition, Nichols points to the Internal Family Systems (IFS) therapy of Richard Schwartz, who uses the intrapsychic assessment of family members and their experience of it as a method for systematic change. Schwartz's idea is that people in conflict are usually in intrapsychic conflict with themselves. The focus and study in both EFCT and IFS therapies is on the process of the interventions that produce results in session versus the larger outcomes of family therapy.

Marty Jencius

See also Humanistic Family Therapy; Self of the Therapist; Symbolic Interactionism; Therapeutic Alliance; Trust

Further Readings

Connell, G., Mitten, T., & Bumberry, W. (1998). *Reshaping family relationships: The symbolic therapy of Carl Whitaker*. London, England: Routledge.

Greenberg, L. S., & Johnson, S. M. (1988). *Emotionally focused therapy for couples*. New York, NY: Guilford Press.

Jencius, M. (2003). This thing called love: An interview with Susan Johnson. *Family Journal, 11,* 427–434.

Keith, D. (2014). *Continuing the experiential approach of Carl Whitaker: Process, practice, and magic*. Phoenix, AZ: Zeig, Tucker & Theisen.

Kempler, W. (1973). *Principles of Gestalt family therapy*. Oslo, Norway: Nordahls.

Kempler, W. (1981). *Experiential psychotherapy with families*. New York, NY: Brunner/Mazel.

Napier, A., & Whitaker, C. (1988). *The family crucible: The intense experience of family therapy*. New York, NY: Harper & Row.

Nichols, M. P. (2014). *The essentials of family therapy*. New York, NY: Pearson.

Satir, V. M. (1972). *Peoplemaking*. Palo Alto, CA: Science and Behavior Books.

Satir, V. M. (1983). *Conjoint family therapy* (3rd ed.). Palo Alto, CA: Science and Behavior Books.

Satir, V. M., & Baldwin, M. (1983). *Satir step-by-step*. Palo Alto, CA: Science and Behavior Books.

Whitaker, C. (1989). *Midnight musings of a family therapist*. New York, NY: W. W. Norton.

Whitaker, C., & Keith, D. (1982). Symbolic-experiential family therapy. In A. Gurman & D. Kniskern (Eds.), *Handbook of family therapy* (pp. 187–225). New York, NY: Brunner/Mazel.

Externalizing Behaviors

People respond to challenges in a variety of ways. Some people direct emotional problems outward into externalizing behaviors. People with *externalizing problems* express their negative reactions to life's pressures with behavior that generates discomfort and conflict in the surrounding environment. Conversely, people with *internalizing problems* direct their negative reactions to life's pressures inward in ways that cause distress. As a clinical term, *externalizing disorders* is applied to a cluster of disorders (e.g., attention-deficit/hyperactivity disorder [ADHD], oppositional defiant disorder [ODD], and conduct disorder [CD]) with prominent issues related to impulsiveness and decreased self-regulation, disruptive conduct, and substance use symptoms. Externalizing behaviors manifest as behaviors that disregard social norms, generate discomfort and distress in others, and upset the environment. Externalizing behaviors are common and reported across a range of diverse languages, ethnicities, religious backgrounds, and other social and cultural communities. This entry defines externalizing behaviors; examines how age, gender, and location affect the presentation of externalizing behaviors; and considers the importance of understanding externalizing behaviors through a developmental lens.

Definition

People with externalizing behaviors act out their emotional issues by directing anger, frustration, anxiety, or other emotional struggles into behaviors that are frequently categorized as aggressive or delinquent. Externalizing behaviors can also be categorized as hyperactive or impulsive. Many externalizing symptoms are associated with the breaking of age-appropriate social rules, including being disobedient with authority figures, failing to follow social or peer group norms (e.g., aggravating others), and violating the law. Young children may outwardly express emotional problems through a range of aggressive behaviors, including arguing, bragging, teasing, threatening, screaming, seeking attention, behaving in demanding ways, and losing their temper. Examples of externalizing problems that are typical of adolescents include lying, swearing, stealing, running away from home, being truant, being destructive, showing aggression, refusing to follow rules, threatening others, committing arson or vandalism, and being delinquent.

Externalizing behaviors are more of a concern when an individual's behavior deviates significantly from behavior that is developmentally normative. Also, these behaviors are generally considered more problematic when they are frequent, intense, lasting, and pervasive than when they occur as a single or infrequent event. Further, an externalizing behavior raises more concern when it is one component of a cluster of problems than when it is an isolated symptom.

Effects Related to Age, Gender, and Location

Cross-cultural factors such as age, gender, and location of residence have been shown to impact the presentation of symptoms. For example, externalizing behaviors can manifest across the life span. It is possible for problematic externalizing behaviors to be confined to the child or adolescent years or they may develop into antisocial behavior that is persistent across developmental stages and continues into adult life. Early childhood onset of externalizing problems indicates a greater likelihood that the problems will continue over the individual's life course. Also, unaddressed externalizing behaviors occurring in early childhood seem to amplify with age. Older adolescents exhibit a greater tendency to engage in conflicts, particularly those related to behaviors that involve rule breaking and aggression. Some studies demonstrate an inverted U-shaped curve in the appearance of externalizing behaviors, with prevalence peaking in midadolescence being followed by a subsequent decline. After the toddler years, from 2 to 10 times as many boys as girls are diagnosed with an externalizing disorder. Furthermore, boys report more aggressive and rule-breaking externalizing behaviors than girls. By contrast, no difference is found according to gender in terms of syndromes characterized by attention problems. Studies comparing the presence of externalizing problems over different countries support cross-cultural regularities with rare exceptions.

In children, the negative reactions to life stressors manifest as nonnormative behaviors that are typically characterized as hyperactive, aggressive, or poor impulse control. Of course, some amount of hyperactive, aggressive, and poor impulse-related misbehavior is expected and considered a normative, perhaps even healthy, part of growing up, and it is true that all children break rules sometimes. However, children with externalizing behaviors tend to do so at a younger age than their peers, and the rule violations in externalizing behaviors are neither normative nor insignificant. In fact, externalizing behaviors should be addressed early or the problems may continue into adulthood.

Applying a Developmental Lens to Externalizing Behaviors

Developmental context is an important consideration regarding the timing as well as the nature of disruptive behavior. Externalizing behaviors have been reported in children as young as 1 year of age. They typically become noticeable in childhood and adolescence and are the most frequent reason for referral of preschool age children to mental health services. Childhood and adolescent externalizing behaviors represent a young person's inability to manage stress in ways that conform to the expectations of parents, teachers, peers, and/or legal authorities. When children use externalizing behaviors to cope with stress, adults around them are likely to take notice because the problems manifest in the outward environment in behaviors that can be quite irritating to the people in the child's immediate surroundings. Proper responses to these cues that something is wrong are essential because externalizing behaviors have the potential to become barriers to the child's personal, social, and academic development. Further, early development of externalizing behavior problems has been shown to be predictive of other forms of psychopathology in later years.

Children and adolescents who display externalizing behaviors are often described as negative, angry, and aggressive. They may express more negative thoughts and feelings or may engage in aggressive behaviors such as bullying. They can also be hyperactive, as displayed by behaviors such as squirming, fidgeting, and being restless, which can occur even during leisure activities like watching television. Many struggle with internal direction of behavior, also known as executive functioning, which is also associated with increased levels of impulsivity. Distractibility, difficulty completing tasks, careless errors, problems with organization or effort, and general "spaciness" are other potential indicators of an attention deficit component of externalizing behaviors. It is important for clinicians and caregivers to understand that inability to sustain attention and impulsivity are not deliberate or oppositional; rather, these symptoms are present despite an apparent desire to maintain focus.

Maintaining a healthy mental state requires some ability to cope adaptively with life's stressors. It is not surprising that many studies have been centered on relating externalizing behaviors to an inadequate use of coping strategies. Another factor to consider is that during adolescence an increase in stressors typically produces a corresponding increase in all types of coping strategies. This is probably due to the fact that adolescents face numerous conflicts that generate tension and unease; therefore, they increase the use of both engagement and avoidance coping strategies.

Laurie Bonjo

See also Adolescent Behavior Disorders; Adolescent Behavior Problems; Adolescent Mental Health; Attention-Deficit and Disruptive Behavior Disorders; Child Behavior Problems

Further Readings

American Psychiatric Association. (2013). *Diagnostic and statistical manual of mental disorders* (5th ed.). Washington, DC: Author.

Chandler, L. K., & Dahlquist, C. M. (2002). *Functional assessment: Strategies to prevent and remediate challenging behavior in school settings*. Upper Saddle River, NJ: Merrill Prentice Hall.

Hann, D. M., Borek, N., & National Institute of Mental Health. (2001). *Taking stock of risk factors for child/youth externalizing behavior problems*. Bethesda, MD: Department of Health and Human Services, Public Health Service, National Institutes of Health, National Institute of Mental Health.

Macklem, G. L. (2014). *Preventive mental health at school: Evidence-based services for students*. New York, NY: Springer.

Semrud-Clikeman, M. (2007). *Social competence in children*. New York, NY: Springer.

Extramarital Affairs and Infidelity

Infidelity can be one of the most traumatic experiences for couples in committed relationships. Of all the problems that lead couples to seek professional help, there are few more challenging than infidelity. In general, infidelity is a violation of the commitment to faithfulness within a devoted relationship (i.e., being married, cohabiting, or dating). However, infidelity can take various forms including emotional, physical, and Internet infidelity, and each may lead to deep feelings of betrayal, pain, anger, insecurity, or depression. This entry will define *infidelity* and further explore different types of infidelity, their prevalence and impact, cultural and contextual factors, and common approaches to treatment.

Definition and Typology

Infidelity can be defined in a number of different ways, and therapists often find that relationship partners have different definitions of what constitutes infidelity. In marriage and other committed relationships, there is typically a stated or unstated commitment to intimate exclusivity, including both emotional and sexual fidelity to one's partner. Even in open, swinging, and polyamorous relationships, there are typically boundaries defined by the partners regarding what is acceptable and unacceptable in terms of outside relationships. With extramarital affairs and infidelity, there has been a violation of the stated or unstated contract or boundary regarding intimacy, with sexual and/or emotional intimacy being shared with someone outside of the committed relationship without the knowledge or consent of the other partner(s). Infidelity may include a wide variety of behaviors or relationships that can be placed into certain categories including emotional, physical, or Internet infidelity or some combination of the three. The behaviors or relationships are usually kept hidden from a spouse or partner, with various forms of deception being employed, including lying, denying when confronted, and minimizing the extent or nature of the contact with the other person(s).

Physical infidelity is the most commonly recognized type of infidelity and may include various sexual and nonsexual behaviors. Sexual infidelity may involve vaginal or anal intercourse, oral sex, petting, or other forms of sexual contact. Physical infidelity can also include acts of physical intimacy, such as amorous touches, massages, kissing, and hand-holding.

Emotional infidelity tends to be less acknowledged than physical infidelity. However, it occurs more frequently than physical infidelity and can be just as damaging. This type of infidelity involves the formation of emotional bonds or commitments with persons outside of the primary committed relationship and can range from friendship to feelings of love that are shared with another person. Behaviors indicative of emotional infidelity include sharing quality time, sharing intimate information, communicating extensively and frequently, or seeking as well as receiving emotional support from a person outside the committed relationship.

Internet infidelity (also known as online or cyber infidelity) has grown as computers, smartphones, tablets, and social media technologies have saturated modern society. Although the Internet can be used to strengthen connection between partners in the primary relationship, it has also become a common avenue for extradyadic relationships (relationships that extend beyond the dyad of the couple) due to its potential for secrecy, easy access, and variety of potential interactions. The effects of Internet infidelity can be as devastating as face-to-face physical or emotional affairs. Katherine Hertlein and Armeda Stevenson describe seven reasons why Internet affairs have become more prevalent: (1) anonymity, (2) affordability, (3) accessibility, (4) approximation (the capability of the Internet to approximate, or simulate, real-world experiences), (5) acceptability, (6) ambiguity (online behavior can be trickier than "real-world" behavior to define as problematic), and (7) accommodation (the Internet can accommodate the felt need to engage in rule-breaking behavior that is incompatible with one's everyday self or persona). The mobility and capabilities of computers, smartphones, and tablets—as well as nearly ubiquitous access to the Internet—allow for various interactions to be carried out in a variety of ways and during a range of times. Online infidelity can be understood as activities where one pursues or provides emotional or sexual fulfillment online by forming relationships or viewing related media. Potential offenses can include chatting, messaging, texting, sexting, gaming, video chatting, engaging in cybersex, viewing pornography, or sharing or sending personal videos or pictures, among others. Internet infidelity may occur through e-mail, text, online chat rooms, social networking sites, video chat apps or software, online gaming (e.g., *World of Warcraft*), or virtual worlds (e.g., *Second Life*). There are also websites for the purpose of facilitating affairs, with large numbers of users throughout the world.

It is important to note that whether an action is perceived as infidelity will depend on the definition held by the potentially injured partner. Relevant factors may include the nature of the action or interaction, whether the action was intentional, and whether it was kept hidden. An incident of infidelity can include aspects of one or more types. An individual can commit infidelity in more than one way simultaneously and have multiple affair partners.

Prevalence

Given the varying definitions of infidelity, sensitivity of the subject matter, and differing study designs, researchers have struggled to determine the prevalence of infidelity. Most research has been done with heterosexual couples regarding sexual infidelity. Some have looked at the lifetime prevalence; others have looked at the recent past. Studies show that approximately 22% to 25% of married men and 12% to 15% of married women in the United States have engaged in some form of sexual infidelity during their lifetimes. However, the prevalence for sexual infidelity on a yearly basis for married individuals is much lower; only 1.5% to 4% of respondents indicated that they had engaged in some form of sexual infidelity in the previous 12-month period. Studies also suggest that prevalence rates are typically higher for dating and cohabiting couples when compared with married couples. Research findings should be considered tentatively, as further information may be acquired through surveying different groups and expanding the definition to include other types of infidelity. Prevalence rates also vary across national and cultural contexts.

Impact

Infidelity can have significant effects on individual partners and the relationship. Partners may be affected both physically and emotionally. Sexual infidelity increases the chance of unfaithful partners contracting a sexually transmitted disease that may potentially be passed on to their partner. The emotional and relational impact can be divided into pre- and postdisclosure. Prior to disclosure, one or both individuals may notice a change in the relationship, manifested in diminished emotional and/or physical intimacy. For the unfaithful partner, there are stresses associated with hiding activities from one's partner and the fear of being discovered. For the betrayed partner, there may be doubt, growing mistrust, and fear of discovering unfaithfulness. The impact is even greater after the discovery of infidelity, which often brings a whirlwind of emotions. The betrayed partner is likely to experience an initial phase of shock, confusion, anger, and intense emotional reactivity. Next, they may experience a period of questioning where they seek information and try to deal emotionally with what has occurred. Accompanying this may be feelings of grief and mourning the loss of trust and the unique commitment in the relationship. Lastly, they must decide whether to move forward with their partner or terminate the relationship. Emotional reactions experienced by the betrayed partner may also include loss of one's sense of purpose and adequacy, lowered self-esteem or self-confidence, increased insecurity, and worries about physical attractiveness and sexual desirability. Symptoms of depression, anxiety, and posttraumatic stress disorder (PTSD) are also common.

The offender's experience will likely depend on whether or not they feel guilt and remorse, stop the infidelity, and desire to stay in the primary relationship. Cheating partners may feel a sense of relief that the truth is out in the open. Many partners experience guilt, self-loathing, mourning, and depression. In such cases, the unfaithful partner has been acting in a manner inconsistent with his or her own value system and recognizes the pain they have caused. In cases where the individual continues to emphasize their own needs and does not want to end the affair or work on the primary relationship, there may be a lack of empathy, patience, and interest in reconciliation.

Cultural and Contextual Factors

There are various cultural and contextual factors that influence perceptions and behaviors related to infidelity. For example, perceptions and behaviors regarding infidelity are often different between men and women. Historically and cross-culturally, there has been a double standard that supports greater sexual permissiveness in men. Men are more likely to perceive sexual relations with a person outside the primary relationship to be infidelity, whereas women are more likely to perceive an emotionally intimate relationship with another person to be infidelity. However, gay men may perceive emotional infidelity as more damaging than sexual infidelity. Additionally, men are more likely to engage in sexual-only affairs, and women are more likely to participate in emotional-only affairs.

Nearly all societies have standards regarding extramarital sexual relations, which typically arise from religious, cultural, or family values. Major world religions including Christianity, Judaism, Islam, and Buddhism have specific standards forbidding adultery. In many countries, infidelity is acceptable grounds for divorce. Although sexual attitudes and practices in many societies became more liberal during the sexual revolutions of the 1920s and 1960s, multiple studies indicate that a vast majority of individuals find it unacceptable. For example, a cross-national study from Britain, Ireland, Germany, Poland, Sweden, and the United States. found that 82% to 94% of participants disapproved of infidelity, and a study of 24 countries found that only 4% of participants believed that it is "not wrong at all." However, statistics also show a discrepancy between attitudes and behaviors, as indicated by the prevalence statistics reported previously.

There are also individual and relationship factors that influence a couple's risk of infidelity. Mental health or illness (e.g., depression), low self-esteem, permissive attitudes about infidelity, low religiosity, and low relationship satisfaction increase the risk of infidelity. Additionally, cohabiting couples are at greater risk than married couples, and couples with previously divorced spouses are at greater risk.

Treatment and Healing

In many cases, infidelity leads to divorce or the ending of the committed relationship. However, couples that desire to stay together may seek help through friends, family members, clergy, self-help books, or professional counselors.

Given the significant emotional and relationship damage that accompanies infidelity, it is important for therapists to have effective treatment models. However, the majority of existing treatment models are based on the authors' clinical experiences and expertise rather than empirical research.

Assessment

Thorough assessment is critical at the beginning of treatment. Therapists must ascertain the type of infidelity committed (whether emotional, sexual, Internet, etc.) and degree of deception, when and how long the infidelity occurred, the frequency and location of communication and/or sexual contact, the degree of emotional involvement or attachment, history of previous infidelity, the relationship of the affair partner to both partners, the degree of awareness of the betrayed partner, and the social and cultural context of the affair. Assessment should also include whether the partners want to stay together and work on their relationship.

Treatment Models

With the emotional turmoil surrounding infidelity, research suggests that couples may benefit from therapists providing a road map for what they can expect during the healing process. Research by Mark Butler, Mark Bird, and Stephen Fife on the process of healing from infidelity suggests that healing occurs as couples pass through seven stages: (1) explore emotions and thoughts surrounding the infidelity, (2) express these to their partner, (3) develop empathy, (4) soften emotions, (5) accept personal responsibility and reduction of blame, (6) establish accountability, and (7) restore trust.

Treatment usually begins with providing damage control for the couple and providing a safe environment for partners to work on relationship healing (if desired). Stephen Fife, Gerald Weeks, and Nancy Gambescia developed an integrative treatment model that addresses the individual, relational, and intergenerational factors associated with infidelity. The approach provides clinicians with a framework for helping couples seeking therapy for infidelity by focusing on five related phases: (1) utilize crisis management and assessment, (2) explore systematic considerations, (3) facilitate forgiveness, (4) treat factors that contribute to infidelity, and (5) promote intimacy through communication. Kristina Gordon, Donald Baucom, and Douglas Snyder developed a treatment model for infidelity that incorporates cognitive-behavioral and insight-oriented strategies in three stages: (1) deal with impact, (2) explore context and finding meaning, and (3) move on. Regarding the unique aspects of Internet infidelity, Katherine Hertlein and Fred Piercy summarized the seven common elements of treatment: (1) develop physical boundaries; (2) develop psychological boundaries; (3) manage accountability, trust, and feelings; (4) increase client awareness around etiology of the Internet relationship; (5) assess the couple's context and readiness for change; (6) assess the presence of unique circumstances; and (7) work toward forgiveness.

Although the negative impact of infidelity can be significant and many relationships do not survive, research and clinical experience indicate that healing is possible. Couples who commit to staying together can work on repairing the damage caused by infidelity, restoring trust, and rebuilding intimacy. Therapists can also help couples take steps to decrease risk factors and increase protective factors in order to reduce the likelihood of future infidelity.

Stephen T. Fife

See also Couples and Marriage Counseling; Extramarital Affairs and Infidelity; Fidelity; Forgiveness; Marriage and Health; Rule-Setting; Secrets; Sexual Intimacy; Technology and Families/Marriage

Further Readings

Allen, E. S., Atkins, D. C., Baucom, D. H., Snyder, D. K., Gordon, K. C., & Glass, S. P. (2005). Intrapersonal, interpersonal, and contextual factors in engaging in and responding to extramarital involvement. *Clinical Psychology*, 12(2), 101–130.

Blow, A. J., & Hartnett, K. (2005). Infidelity in committed relationships II: A substantive review. *Journal of Marital and Family Therapy, 31*(2), 217–233.

Fife, S., Weeks, G., & Gambescia, N. (2008). Treating infidelity: An integrative approach. *The Family Journal, 16*(4), 316–323.

Gordon, K., Baucom, D., & Snyder, D. (2005). Treating couples recovering from infidelity: An integrative approach. *Journal of Clinical Psychology, 61,* 1393–1405.

Hertlein, K. M., & Piercy, F. P. (2012). Essential elements of Internet infidelity treatment. *Journal of Marriage and Family Therapy, 38,* 257–270.

Peluso, P. (Ed.). (2007). *Infidelity: A practitioner's guide to working with couples in crisis.* New York, NY: Routledge.

Faith-Based Therapy

Faith can be described as confidence in someone or something. It may also refer to belief in God or a deity and/or certain religious doctrines. Addressing issues in therapy from a faith-based perspective is both compelling and complex. While there may be distinctions between faith-based therapy and so-called secular therapy, both approaches offer a means of hope. Faith-based therapy specific to theology involves integration of scripture or religious texts and practices. Sessions typically incorporate references to the Bible and conversations about the power of prayer. Faith-based therapy in the general or secular sense offers a means of facilitating clients' mental, emotional and relational well-being. Sessions include exploration of hope, motivation, and principles. Addressing issues in therapy from a faith-based perspective is both compelling and complex. While some clients seek therapy for symptom relief, others may yearn for something more. Faith-based therapy offers an opportunity to explore clients' goals related to finding meaning, discovering purpose, and gaining an overall sense of peace. Exploring clients' faith-based beliefs reveals information about their values and ideas of creation, suffering, relationships, and life after death. This entry reviews faith-based therapy from the standpoint of the therapy process, the therapeutic relationship, and religion and spirituality.

Faith in the Therapy Process

One of the essential factors related to the therapy process is hope. This principle has implications for client motivation, engagement, and participation. Clients with hope embrace the process and possess faith in the potential for positive results, even when faced with the most severe presenting problems. They keep appointments, actively participate in sessions, and demonstrate a willingness to work toward achieving goals. Faith is one of the many life forces and belief systems that clients use to make sense of their world and cope. Related principles include strength, courage, wisdom, character, and determination. Utilizing faith as a conduit, therapists offer hope to clients as a means of empowerment. This faith in the process fuels motivation and active involvement in therapy. Some have distinguished faith from hope as assurance regardless of outcome. In other words, one can *hope,* or wish for a good outcome, but one can also have *faith,* or trust in the ability to cope despite undesired outcomes.

Breaking the stigma of therapy by being willing to seek mental health services is the first step in exercising faith in the therapy process. As compared to an attitude of doubt or despair, a position of hope reflects openness to and confidence in the therapy process. Clients struggling with faith in the therapy process tend to be uncertain and ambivalent. Clients exhibiting faith in themselves and in the process of therapy define their own goals, honor their strengths, consider peer and social support, and take responsibility. Therapists honoring the process are knowledgeable about theories and skilled in case conceptualization and treatment planning. At the same time, therapists being faithful to the therapy process act ethically by remaining aware of the impact of their own values and beliefs. Whether noticing internal reactions, reflecting on therapist–client rapport, or exploring ways to directly incorporate spirituality or religion into the process, it is essential to consider the role of faith in the therapy process.

Faith in the Therapeutic Relationship

Faith in the therapeutic relationship is evidenced by strong rapport, a good working alliance, and overall attunement. In other words, a sense of trust is evident between therapist and client(s). Clients typically experience trust when they feel that therapists are respectful, reliable, dedicated, and skilled. In addition to adhering to ethical and legal guidelines, trustworthy therapists tend to express empathy, exhibit congruence, set boundaries, and address safety concerns. Therapists begin sessions with joining and paying attention to clients' language and preferences. They also demonstrate awareness of and concern for clients' emotional state, by knowing when to respond to affect and how to pace sessions. Therapists respect the uniqueness of clients, as compared to operating according to assumptions or generalizations. Faith in the therapeutic relationship is a reciprocal and ongoing process. Therapists and clients work to build and maintain trust while working together.

Research reveals that the therapist–client relationship impacts success or satisfaction more than the theoretical orientation or approach. What this means is that therapists should concentrate on connecting with clients just as much as following a treatment plan or utilizing theory-based or symptom-based techniques. When there is confidence in the process and trust in the relationship, therapists and clients tend to be more mutually engaged, connected, and committed. While clients are responsible for making the change, therapists are charged with finding ways to track and facilitate the process. This includes finding respectful ways to address an impasse. Tracking internal reactions, such as doubt or impatience, and interpersonal issues related to opposition and overall fit are important. As interrelated factors impacting the therapy process and therapeutic relationship, hope and trust are key ingredients to therapeutic change.

Religion and Spirituality

While aspects of the therapy process and therapeutic relationship entail intrapersonal factors (e.g., hope) and interpersonal factors (e.g., trust), therapists can also utilize spirituality and religion when clients express faith in something or someone greater than themselves. While religion guides norms and expectations related to behaviors and worship, spirituality informs values and virtues. Religion is an organized system of beliefs and traditions related to creation, worship, and purpose. Religious individuals customarily belong to a certain group, give deference to a higher power and leader, subscribe to a code of conduct based on morality, and participate in certain rituals. Religious clients often reference language from their respective sacred texts, which influences their self-concept, values, and interactions (e.g., a client in turmoil about her struggle to follow the mandate to forgive; a client dealing with committing an offense such as infidelity or stealing). Faith-based, religious practices in therapy include the use of scripture and prayer. These interventions have been applied to presenting problems such as infidelity, interpersonal conflict, resentment, trauma, grief, depression, eating disorders, and substance abuse, and have been shown useful in helping clients to better cope with various types of conflict and crisis.

Spirituality is more difficult to define. It is most often referred to as a subjective experience of discovering meaning or purpose, finding fulfillment, connecting with "other than self" (e.g., social connections, nature, ancestors, higher level of consciousness), and exhibiting moral virtues related to goodness and mercy. Therapists and clients alike may consider themselves "spiritual, but not religious" or "more spiritual than religious." Nonreligious-based spiritual practices include mindfulness meditation, internal cleansing, fasting, chanting, and participating in retreats. Spirituality has been noted as one of the dimensions of wellness useful for stress management and overall well-being. Like religion, it gives many people a sense of community and purpose.

Therapists may be hesitant to encourage or initiate conversations about faith due to personal discomfort or concerns about appropriateness. Because some clients hold faith and related constructs as their source of existence, it is essential for therapists to consider the role and impact of religion and spirituality in presenting problems when working with clients. Strengths of religion and spirituality include increased coping and resilience, better self-control, social support, and, as many have claimed, more satisfied and meaningful lives. While these factors are often untapped resources, they can also function as sources of pain and shame. Unfortunately, some clients have suffered from abuse by spiritual leaders or other members of their religions group. Examples of relational experiences within religious circles include humiliation, oppression, and ostracism due to factors such as race, interfaith or intercultural relationships, sexual orientation, infidelity, addiction, and divorce. Others have witnessed or been made aware of deceitful behaviors, often resulting in a general distrust for religious institutions. Instances may have involved false teachings, inappropriate behaviors, or fiscal mismanagement.

Dilemmas may arise when there are distinctions between the faith of therapists and clients, as well as when there is incongruence with values and expectations due to faith-based differences (e.g., clients of different religious backgrounds within their own family making decisions about a marriage ceremony or child-rearing practices; a Buddhist therapist seeing Muslim clients; a Christian therapist working with atheist or agnostic clients). As such, therapists must be mindful of ethical considerations, including personal triggers, self-disclosure, and cultural sensitivity. As deemed by ethical codes, therapists are not to impose their beliefs on others or attempt to indoctrinate clients based upon their own values.

Religious and spiritual resources can be an important part of therapy for some clients. Continued efforts are needed to enhance ethical use of religion and spirituality in graduate and professional programs, as many report limited training on religion and spirituality in their academic curriculum. Both novice and seasoned therapists should remain aware of the impact of their own faith and find ways to work with clients ethically and effectively. When there is a distinction between faiths or lack of familiarity with certain principles or practices, therapists must act ethically by considering the potential need of consultation, additional training, or the need to refer to other professionals. Additional recommendations include being curious about clients' beliefs and presenting spiritual or religious-based interventions as options.

Even though most view religion or spirituality as an important value in their lives, some therapists are hesitant to acknowledge and address these issues. Clinical implications for faith in therapy can be traced back to traditional models such as person-centered, existentialism, Gestalt, behavioral and cognitive-behavioral therapy, and reality therapy. They are also applicable to family systems approaches and postmodern therapy models. *Unconditional positive regard*, a term relative to humanistic models, is an attitude of acceptance with clients in therapy. This stance embodies spiritual principles of mercy. Virginia Satir exemplified this principle in offering hope, empathy, and an authentic sense of self. Experiential therapists, with their emphasis on emotional expression and congruence, use faith as a means of promoting growth and closeness. The existential approach involves helping clients face despair by searching for meaning. One might posit that faith is a prerequisite for accepting the challenge of finding purpose. Gestalt therapy focuses on freedom and responsibility, as well as how clients function and thrive in relationship to one another, including God (e.g., the I–Thou relationship as described by philosopher and theologian Martin Buber). Behavioral and cognitive-behavioral methods emphasize doing what is purposeful, moral, and rational. Cognitive behavioral family therapists assess how unrealistic expectations and faulty patterns of thinking result in problematic behaviors; therapists refer clients to respective religious texts as a guide for modeling appropriate or sensible expectations and actions. Reality therapy urges clients to choose their attitude and behavior and to consider the importance of human relationships and caring. Faith, in this instance, represents a sense of connection and shared experiences with others.

Postmodern therapists, including solution-focused, narrative, and collaborative therapists, are characterized as curious and nonjudgmental. They may also use clients' spirituality and religion as a resource, using their language to set goals reflective of client preferences and worldview. Again, this sense of faith in the process and outcome of therapy helps to empower them to make sense of their experiences and to work toward attaining therapeutic goals. Faith invokes discernment and strength. Useful questions for clients identifying faith as a spiritual resource include "What is the role of religion or spirituality in your life? How does your faith impact your perspective on life and your ability to cope?"

Solution-focused therapy empowers clients by focusing on strengths, amplifying exceptions to their problems, presenting miracle questions (questions that ask a client to identify what life would be like if their problems were no longer present), scaling progress, and asking about coping. Spiritual or religious clients may be receptive to an integrated miracle question, prompting them to exercise their faith in God or higher power. Solution-focused therapists might pose questions or prompts including the following: (a) scaling questions ("On a scale of 1 to 10, how hopeful are you that things will improve? On a scale of 1 to 10, how much faith do you have in your ability to cope with this issue?"), (b) exception questions ("Tell me about a time when you were able to rely on your faith or spiritual or religious practice to address a problem."), and (c) the miracle question ("If you woke up tomorrow and a miracle occurred, meaning your problem went away or was less intense, how would you know? What would you be doing differently? Who would notice? What would they notice?").

Another strengths-based approach, narrative therapy, separates the person from the problem, reframes problem-saturated stories, identifies unique outcomes, and helps clients reauthor their lives. Narrative therapists also consider how clients' experiences are shaped by social, political, and cultural contexts. Narrative therapists incorporate questions such as (a) deconstructing dominant discourse ("How does your faith pull you through and give you hope [as compared to others who might have given up]?"), (b) externalizing questions ("When doubt rears its ugly head and interferes with your functioning, how do you bounce back? When anger or resentment hinders your relationship with each other, how have you worked together to regain calmness and connection?"), and (c) landscaping or relative influencing questions ("How has spirituality or religion been a resource for you and your family? How has prayer affected your sense of peace? How has meditation impacted your overall health?").

Letter-writing, a common technique in narrative and solution-focused approaches, summarizes progress and documents new stories. Faith-based letter-writing includes God as author, in addition to the therapist and client. Postmodern therapists attend to language, meaning, and context; thus, borrowing from sacred texts and asking curious questions about the impact of family of origin, values, and societal norms is a natural fit.

Froma Walsh, a prolific clinician, writer, and researcher of family resilience, notes that spiritual void and religious conflict can contribute to distress. As such, therapists should be mindful of areas of conflict in clients' lives related to faith, including personal anxiety or trauma and relationship tension. Harry Aponte, a pioneer of family therapy, refers to spirituality as the heart of therapy. He notes that spirituality is significant because it is how clients define their lives. He highlights the importance of its inclusion in intake and assessment, noting that spirituality guides personal philosophies on how to deal with loss, mortality, intimacy and relational issues, parenthood, sex, diversity, and other presenting problems. Therapists including specific questions or sections in their paperwork and during initial consultation open the door to exploring clients' spiritual and religious values. Aponte urges therapists to exhibit cultural sensitivity by pondering the role of spirituality in clients' lives during sessions and to exercise ethical awareness by contemplating how their own spirituality influences their work with clients.

Faith-based practices can be employed to help clients deal with many presenting problems. Therapists working from a biblical, Christian perspective explicitly integrate prayer and scripture into sessions in order to impart God's wisdom and to affirm faith, as congruent with a client's worldview. Many clients rely on biblical texts to learn about truth and other spiritual virtues. Multiple verses emphasize how thoughts and attitudes influence feelings and behaviors. This parallels the focus of cognitive-behavioral therapy, as therapists help clients see the connection between cognitions, emotions, and actions. This focus in therapy reminds believers about how they should love, forgive, and treat one another, according to principles based upon their self-professed value system. These references can be useful for families dealing with conflict or crisis. Rational emotive behavioral therapy works with clients to minimize irrational beliefs and issues such as low frustration tolerance and self-defeating beliefs. Mindfulness and acceptance-based therapies aim at increasing awareness and compassion; moreover, they involve working with clients on both self-talk and action. Buddhist psychology suggests that clients shift their thinking about distress by embracing or befriending their suffering in order to allow it to serve as a teacher. Meditation and affirmations are used as tools for inviting peace, harmony, awareness, acceptance, and gratitude. Spiritual disciplines such as solitude and confession may also be combined with breathing techniques and imagery to bring about changes in thinking, feeling, and behaviors. Spiritual genograms (a multigenerational depiction of family history of religion or spirituality) and spiritual ecograms (images of current influence of religion or spirituality) may also be utilized to culturally assess clients' family history and personal beliefs and patterns.

Therapists working with couples from a faith-based perspective often explore the presence and meaning of compassion, patience, forgiveness, unity, and acceptance. When clients come to an impasse in their relationships or in therapy, these spiritual factors may be useful for helping them get unstuck and find a solution. Even clients not identifying as religious may agree that these values are essential in their relationships. With religious clients, faith-based therapists may refer them to scriptural texts or religious leaders to reiterate roles and rules of interaction. Depending on the personal beliefs and professional approach, a therapist might even decide to pray for or with clients. Others may assign praying as an exercise between sessions, prompting them to pray for themselves and their family members and/or to pray together as an assignment. Whether filtered through the lens of human connection or specific creeds, many opportunities exist to integrate faith and therapy. Faith-based therapy gives prominence to engendering hope, building connection, and discovering meaning.

Shatavia Alexander Thomas

See also Family Values; Hope-Focused Approach to Couple Enrichment in Counseling; Religion; Rituals in Family Therapy; Spirituality

Further Readings

Aponte, H. J. (2002). Spirituality: The heart of therapy. *Journal of Family Psychotherapy, 13*(1/2), 13–27.

Boyd-Franklin, N. (2010). Incorporating spirituality and religion into the treatment of African American clients. *The Counseling Psychologist, 38*(7), 976–1000.

Frame, M. W. (2001). The spiritual genogram in training and supervision. *Family Journal, 9*(2), 109–115.

Guterman, J. T., & Leite, N. (2006). Solution-focused counseling for clients with religious and spiritual concerns. *Counseling and Values, 51*(1), 39–52.

Hodge, D. R. (2006). Spiritually modified cognitive therapy: A review of the literature. *Social Work, 51*(2), 157–166.

Kocet, M. M., Sanabria, S., & Smith, M. R. (2011). Finding the spirit within: Religion, spirituality, and faith development in lesbian, gay, and bisexual individuals. *Journal of LGBT Issues in Counseling, 5*(3/4), 163–179.

Tan, S. (2007). Use of prayer and scripture in cognitive-behavioral therapy. *Journal of Psychology and Christianity, 26*(2), 101.

Walsh, F. (Ed.). (2008). *Spiritual resources in family therapy*. New York, NY: Guilford Press.

FAMILIES AND POVERTY

Poverty can be defined in many ways, but one way of defining family poverty is as the inability to earn a sufficient wage to participate in mainstream society. Being economically disadvantaged has a pervasive impact on all aspects of family life. Scholars have suggested that having low socioeconomic status may be one of the most underrecognized hardships that families face. There are few areas of a child's life or an adult's life that are not impacted when there are insufficient resources to meet basic needs. This entry first discusses the level of poverty, risk factors for poverty, and effects of poverty in the United States. It then discusses the intersection of poverty and contextual factors (e.g., gender and whether one lives in an urban or rural setting) and the pattern of multigenerational poverty.

Poverty in the United States

Poverty status is determined by a formula designed by the U.S. Census Bureau comparing pretax cash income against a threshold that is set at three times the cost of a minimum food diet in 1963. The threshold is updated annually taking into consideration inflation, family size, family configuration, and age of the head of household. The U.S. Census Bureau defines *family* as "a householder and one or more other people living in the same household who are related to the householder by birth, marriage or adoption" (Pemberton, 2015).

In 2014, 46.7 million Americans, or 14.8% of Americans, were reportedly living in poverty. Family structure is an important consideration in assessing the probability of poverty. In 2014, the family poverty rate in the United States was nearly 12%, with 9.5 million families living in poverty, but the poverty rate for families varies depending on the family structure. For example, 6% of families headed by married couples were considered poor, 16% of families headed by males only were deemed poor, and 31% of families headed by females only were considered poor. Not only does this information highlight the financial challenges of being a single parent, but also the continued disparity between the capacity for men to earn a living and support a family compared to that of women.

Poverty Risk Factors

There are a number of variables that put families at risk of experiencing and living in poverty. In general, research indicates that women, children, and minorities are more likely to experience the vulnerability, deprivation, and powerlessness associated with poverty than men and other groups. Specific risk factors for family poverty include low levels of parent education, single-parent family structure, and immigrant-parent households. The effects of family poverty on children are far reaching and those at most risk are people encountering poverty earlier in their development or experiencing repeated and chronic challenges associated with poverty.

Effects of Poverty

The impact of economic hardship on family, adult, and child development is well documented. There are both long- and short-term effects for the family and its individual members. Effects are often physical, emotional, and developmental.

The physical health of all family members can be significantly impacted by poverty. For example, the World Health Organization (WHO) has recognized links between tobacco consumption and production and chronic disease in impoverished people due to both increased exposure to risks and limited access to health care. In addition, poor children are more likely to die of infectious diseases, are less likely to be vaccinated, and have increased rates of asthma and anemia. Recently, there has been an increased recognition among scholars and practitioners alike that the link between physical and mental health is robust and reciprocal in nature. Therefore, family members living in poverty and experiencing health problems as a result are also at risk of experiencing psychosocial stressors that have the potential to impact their daily functioning.

The research literature has consistently shown the negative effects of poverty on early childhood development specifically. Children living in poverty, like adults, experience both long- and short-term effects. Most notable are the influences on a child's physical health. But understandably, children living in poverty also experience deficits in their emotional health. The stress of living in poverty can cause emotional withdrawal as well as feelings of anger and sadness. In addition, opportunities for academic engagement and achievement as well as overall future success in life are depleted when children do not have the economic resources required to meet their basic needs. For parents, poverty can also cause stress related to financial pressures and shortages in needed resources, increased risk of abuse or neglect of children, and increases in drug and alcohol use in the home.

Poverty and Stress

Insufficient environmental resources (e.g., food, housing, clothing) produces daily levels of family stress that can impact individual health and social emotional functioning. Researchers have demonstrated the link between poverty and the experience of stress. This *context of stress* is where variables associated with poverty including family conflict, domestic violence and lack of food, and lack of security and physical and emotional safety become ordinary life experiences. The continued exposure to heightened stress responses, like other trauma responses, has impacts on physical, cognitive, and psychological functioning. Rand Conger and his colleagues describe the adverse impact of economic stress in their family stress model. This model proposes that economic hardship leads to economic pressure (unmet financial needs), which leads to parental distress (emotional and behavioral problems, resulting in disrupted family relationships, which lead to child and adolescent adjustment problems manifesting as emotional and behavioral problems). Basically, the chronic psychological stress caused by long-term poverty affects family development overall, including the relationship between parents, the nature of parenting, and ultimately the health of children. More specifically, long-term economic poverty can lead to extensive hardship, stress, isolation, exclusion, and altered adult developmental trajectories. In addition, individuals in poverty can experience despondency, depression, anger, and aggression.

Gender and Poverty

The demonstrated relationship between violence and poverty and the effects of poverty on families and children are profound. The *feminization of poverty* was a term coined in the 1970s to describe the disproportionate percentage of women represented among the world's poor. For women, poverty is linked to the increasing frequency with which they are becoming heads of households as well as ongoing disparities in earnings. While some are critical of the concept, believing that it has been used too loosely and is conceptually ambiguous, others argue that it has value in highlighting the patriarchy, institutionalized classism, and institutional racism that perpetuate poverty among working women and women of color especially.

Historically the literature on domestic violence has neglected to acknowledge the role that poverty plays in promoting, perpetuating, and exacerbating domestic violence. Rather the focus has been primarily on the role of gender with little attention to the many other variables overlapping and intermingling with gender. For example, different forms of oppression such as unjust treatment based on sexual orientation (heterosexism), race (racism), and economic and social status (classism) influence relational dynamics and the resulting treatment of women. More recently, however, attention has been drawn to these important links and to exploring socioeconomic status as a core contextual factor within which domestic violence is frequently situated alongside numerous other oppressing dynamics playing out simultaneously in the lives of impoverished women.

Despite past beliefs, it is now commonly understood that domestic violence does not impact all women equally. In fact, most homeless women have at some point been the victim of domestic violence as have over half of those receiving public assistance. Further, the most lethal cases of domestic violence are more frequently experienced by low-income women of color. Still, scholars and clinicians recognize the highly individualized experiences of these women and the need to customize approaches to addressing domestic violence that best fit the circumstances of each woman.

Poverty Across Generations

Living in poverty and its consequences can be deeply ingrained into the fabric of family functioning and identity. Frequently, poverty affects families across generations as they are faced with traversing multiple, simultaneous inequities with minimal to no resources. Without the education and financial means needed to break away from the multigenerational patterns of survival, families frequently stay stuck in positions of socioeconomic powerlessness. The life course perspective helps explain how one's history and the influence of one's social and cultural contexts influences future decisions. This theory can be used to explore the persistence of poverty through the lens of individual life-span development and the economic responsibilities in a given phase of life.

The life course perspective or life course theory gained traction in the 1990s, but the theory's core concepts were proposed over 100 years ago by British sociologist Seebohm Rowntree. In more recent years, analysis of the theory found that several important points were still relevant to modern-day dynamics. First, the individual life-span development process has important interaction with and connections to family outcomes. For example, according to the life course perspective, the age and stage of life of an individual are associated with the level and extent of poverty experienced within a family. Second, these patterns tend to persist across generations. Finally, patterns of multigenerational poverty have the ability to be altered by social, political, and economic circumstances.

Poverty in Urban and Rural Settings

There is no one specific set of circumstances that delineates rural poverty from urban poverty. While there are certainly similarities, families are likely to experience different obstacles and require distinct resources to adequately address their economic conditions depending on their geographic location. In addition, there are more people living in poverty in rural areas than in urban areas. The International Monetary Fund (IMF) reports that poverty in rural areas accounts for 63% of those living in poverty throughout the world.

The Family Life Project is a study being conducted jointly by the University of North Carolina and Penn State, looking at children in rural counties. The study explores how growing up and living in rural communities impacts developmental trajectories for both children and their families. It is a multidisciplinary collaboration bringing together researchers from across disciplines, including education, medicine, psychology, sociology, anthropology, geography, and human development, to explore poverty in rural communities. The launching of the Family Life Project was a response to the previous trend in poverty research focusing primarily on urban poverty. In addition to contributing to the scholarly research on rural poverty, the project provides information and resources to community members, parents, and schools.

Janee Both Gragg

See also Domestic Violence; Family Stress; Feminization of Poverty; Health Issues; Homelessness; Individual and Family Development; Job Loss; Poverty and Family Development

Further Readings

Bengtson, V., & Allen, K. (1993). The life course perspective applied to families over time. In P. Boss, W. Doherty, R. LaRossa, W. Schumm, &

S. K. Steinmetz (Eds.), *Sourcebook of family theories and methods: A contextual approach* (pp. 469–504). New York, NY: Plenum.

Chant, S. 2006. Re-thinking the "feminization of poverty" in relation to gender indices. *Journal of Human Development, 7*(2), 201–220.

Conger, R. D., Song, H., Stockdale, G. D., Ferrer, E., Widaman, K. F., & Cauce, A. M. (2012). Resilience and vulnerability of Mexican origin youth and their families: A test of a culturally informed model of family economic stress. In P. K. Kerig, M. S. Schultz, & S. T. Hauser (Eds.), *Adolescence and beyond: Family processes and development* (pp. 268–286). New York, NY: Oxford University Press.

Crenshaw, K. (1994). Mapping the margins: Intersectionality, identity politics and violence against women of color. In M. A. Fineman & R. Mykitiuk (Eds.), *The public nature of private violence: The discovery of domestic abuse* (pp. 93–118). New York, NY: Routledge.

DeNavas-Walt, C., & Proctor, B. D. (2015, September). *Income and poverty in the United States: 2014 current population reports*. Washington, DC: U.S. Census Bureau. Retrieved from https://www.census.gov/content/dam/Census/library/publications/2015/demo/p60-252.pdf

Lyon, E. (1998). *Poverty, welfare and battered women: What does the research tell us?* Retrieved from http://www.vaw.umn.edu/Vawnet/welfare.htm

Mann, S. A., & Grimes, M. (2001). Common and contested ground: Marxism and race, gender and class analysis. *Race, Gender & Class, 8*(2), 3–22.

McLoyd, V. (1990). The impact of economic hardship on Black families and children: Psychological distress, parenting, and socioemotional development. *Child Development, 61*, 311–346.

Pemberton, D. (2015, January 28). Statistical definition of "family" unchanged since 1930 [Web log post]. *Random Samplings*. Retrieved from http://blogs.census.gov/2015/01/28/statistical-definition-of-family-unchanged-since-1930/

Sokoloff, N., & Dupont, I. (2005). Domestic violence at the intersections of race, class, and gender: Challenges and contributions to understanding violence against marginalized women in diverse communities. *Violence Against Women, 11*, 38–64.

U.S. Census Bureau. (n.d.). *Poverty: 2014 highlights*. Retrieved from https://www.census.gov/hhes/www/poverty/about/overview/

FAMILIES AND SUBSTANCE ABUSE

Historically, substance use disorders were considered personal problems that are best treated on an individual basis. More recently, treatment has given way to a greater acceptance and acknowledgment of the family's critical role in the development and maintenance of drug and alcohol abuse. As a result, an increasing number of treatment providers and the programs in which they work are intervening with the family. In this entry, the prevalence of substance abuse and comorbidity with family problems is emphasized, along with treatment options involving the family for clients dealing with substance abuse. In particular, the impact of drug and alcohol misuse on the family system is examined.

During the past 3 decades, the results of numerous clinical studies have demonstrated the efficacy of family-based treatment approaches for substance use disorders. Meta-analytic reviews of randomized clinical trials have concluded that partner- and family-involved treatments produce better outcomes across several domains of functioning (e.g., reduced substance use, improved marital and family functioning) compared to individual-based interventions that focus exclusively on the substance-abusing client. In response to these findings, the Joint Commission on Accreditation of Healthcare Organizations (JCAHO) standards for accrediting substance abuse treatment programs in the United States now requires that an adult family member who lives with an identified substance-abusing patient be included, at minimum, in the initial assessment of the treatment process.

Enthusiasm for understanding the role that family members may play in the development, maintenance, and treatment of alcoholism and drug abuse has not been limited to researchers or even the broader professional community; the sheer volume of texts that have appeared on the topics of codependency, adult children of alcoholics, addictive personality, enabling, and so forth is enormous. Because relationship problems and substance use disorders so frequently co-occur, it would be very difficult to find clinicians who specialize in the treatment of substance use disorders or relationship problems who have not had to address both sets of issues concurrently (either with the client individually or in the context of the client's larger family system).

Prevalence of Substance Use Disorders and Comorbidity With Family Problems

Previous studies support the assertion that substance abuse and family problems often coexist. For example, Gary O'Farrell and Timothy Birchler found that levels of relationship distress among alcoholic and drug-abusing dyads are typically high, and these couples are more likely to divorce compared to the general population. Moreover, relationship dysfunction has been found to be predictive of worse prognosis in alcohol and drug abuse treatment, and poor response to substance abuse treatment seems to be predictive of ongoing marital difficulty.

Unfortunately, as the individual's substance problem progresses, he or she may become increasingly isolated from other family members, which may make it difficult to engage them into the treatment process. Relatedly, other family members may experience a wide array of emotions (e.g., anger, guilt, fear, embarrassment) as a result of the patient's drinking or drug use and, consequently, reduce or eliminate contact altogether with the substance-abusing person. The therapeutic implications of this type of isolation are mixed; while some family approaches might consider this type of avoidance to be appropriate and therapeutic, other models might view this behavior as corrosive.

The Interplay Between Substance Use and Marital and Family Maladjustment

The interconnection between substance use and relationship distress appears to be marked by what can perhaps be best described as *reciprocal causality*. Alcoholism and drug abuse by a family member appear to contribute causally to the many relationship problems observed in these families.

Families characterized by substance abuse may experience high levels of relationship dissatisfaction, instability, conflict, sexual dissatisfaction, or psychological distress. A number of studies have also found that relationship dysfunction is strongly linked to substance use and appears to be a major contributing factor to relapse among alcoholics and drug abusers after treatment. Thus, the link between substance use and relationship problems is not unidirectional, with one consistently causing the other; rather, each can serve as a precursor to the other, creating a vicious cycle from which couples that include a partner who abuses drugs or alcohol often have difficulty escaping.

There are several family environmental antecedent conditions and reinforcing consequences of substance use. In particular, marital and family problems (e.g., poor communication and problem-solving, arguing, financial stressors) often serve as precursors to excessive drinking or drug use. Unfortunately, the resulting family response may have an unintended effect and inadvertently facilitate continued drinking or drug use once these problematic behaviors have developed. Moreover, even when recovery from the alcohol or drug problem has begun, marital and family conflicts can, and very often do, precipitate relapses.

Although the misuse of alcohol and other psychoactive substances by adults often has serious physical, emotional, behavioral, and economic consequences, the ancillary short- and long-term negative effects on those who live with these adults are often no less destructive or traumatic. In general, the deleterious environments these caregivers frequently create victimize children living with parents who abuse alcohol and other drugs. Stress and negative affect, which are comparatively high in families with an alcoholic family member, are associated with alcohol use in adolescents.

The strong interrelationship between substance use and family interaction suggests interventions that treat the dyadic or larger family systems (versus an exclusive focus on the substance-abusing patient) hold much promise for being effective. Although marital and family therapy approaches take many different forms, they share two overarching objectives that evolve from a recognition of the nature and degree of interrelationship between substance use and family member interaction: (1) harness the power of the family and dyadic system to positively support the patient's efforts to eliminate abusive drinking and drug use and, relatedly, (2) alter dyadic and family interaction patterns to promote an environment in the home that is conducive to long-term stable abstinence for the substance-abusing individual.

Foundational Frameworks of Partner- and Family-Involved Approaches for Alcoholism and Drug Abuse

Given the finding that marital and family treatments have been shown to be clinically effective for a variety of health problems, many different marital and family therapy approaches have been developed for use with substance-abusing patients including strategic family therapy, structural family therapy, cognitive-behavioral family therapy, behavioral couples therapy, and solution-focused family therapy. Of these, three theoretical perspectives have come to dominate family-based conceptualizations and are thus viewed as the foundation for the family-based treatment strategies most often used with substance-abusing clients: (1) family disease approach, (2) family systems approach, and (3) behavioral approach. Each of these frameworks is reviewed in more detail here, with an emphasis on some of the hallmark therapy techniques identified with each approach.

Family Disease Approach

The best known and most widely used paradigm is the *family disease approach*. From this vantage, alcoholism and other drug abuse are viewed as an illness of the entire family, suffered not only by the substance user, but also by the other family members. Consequently, as the term implies, alcoholism and drug abuse are thought of or viewed as a "family disease," one that affects all (or nearly all) family members. In particular, family members of substance users are viewed as suffering from the disease of "codependence," which describes the process underlying the various problems observed in the families of individuals who abuse psychoactive substances. Some argue that codependence is a disease that parallels the addiction disease process and is marked by characteristic family symptoms such as external referencing, caretaking, self-centeredness, control issues, dishonesty, frozen feelings, perfectionism, and fear. The cornerstone of codependency theory is *enabling*, which, as the term implies, is described as any set of behaviors that perpetuates the psychoactive substance use and may include activities such as making it easier for the alcoholic or drug abuser to engage in substance use or shielding the substance user from the negative consequences often resulting from substance misuse.

Given that the family disease model argues that the entire family unit is believed to be sick, the solution is for each family member to recognize that he or she has a disease, detach from the substance user, and engage in his or her own program of recovery (e.g., Al-Anon, Alateen, or Adult Children of Alcoholics [ACOA] groups). Family members are taught that there is nothing they can do to help the substance user to stop using other than to cease enabling and to detach and focus on reducing their own emotional distress and improving coping behaviors.

Family Systems Approach

The family systems model views the misuse of alcohol or other drugs as a major organizing principle for patterns of interactional behavior within the family system. A reciprocal relationship exists between family functioning and substance use, with an individual's drug and alcohol use being best understood in the context of the entire family's functioning. According to family systems theory, substance abuse in either adults or adolescents often evolves during periods in which the individual family member is having difficulty addressing an important developmental issue (e.g., leaving the home) or when the family is facing a significant crisis (e.g., job loss, marital discord). During these periods, substance abuse can serve to (a) distract family members from their central problem or (b) slow down or stop a transition to a different developmental stage that is being resisted by the family as a whole or by one of its members.

From the family systems perspective, substance use represents an unhealthy attempt to manage difficulties, one that, over time, becomes homeostatic and regulates family transactions. Because the substance use serves an important function, the therapist seeks to understand its role in the family and explain how the behavior has come about and the purpose it serves. Thus, the primary objective of treatment involves restructuring the interaction patterns associated with the substance use, thereby making the drinking or drug use unnecessary in maintaining a healthier systemic functioning.

Behavioral Approach

Behavioral family therapy models are heavily influenced by operant and social learning theories in their conceptualization of the substance user within the family context. Simply stated, behavioral approaches assume that family interactions serve to reinforce alcohol- and drug-using behavior. From this vantage, substance-using behavior is learned in the context of social interactions and reinforced by contingencies in the individual's environment. Thus, from a behavioral perspective, substance use is maintained, in part, from the antecedents and consequences that are operating in the family environment. Three general reinforcement patterns are typically observed in substance-abusing families: (1) reinforcement for substance using behavior in the form of attention or caretaking, (2) shielding the substance user from experiencing negative consequences related to his or her drinking or drug use, and (3) punishing drinking behavior.

Consistent with the tenets of operant and social learning approaches, treatment emphasizes contingency management designed to reward sobriety, reduce negative reinforcement of drinking or drug use, and increase prosocial behaviors that may be incompatible with substance use. More specifically, the substance user and involved family members are taught techniques to increase positive interactions, improve problem-solving, and enhance communication skills. Behaviorists believe that the use of these newly developed skills serves to reduce the likelihood of continued drinking or drug use by the substance-using family member.

*Keith Klostermann
and Emma Papagni*

See also Behavioral Family Therapy; Couples and Marriage Counseling

Further Readings

Halford, W. K., Price, J., Kelly, A. B., Bouma, R., & Young, R. M. (2001). Helping the female partners of men abusing alcohol: A comparison of three treatments. *Addiction, 96*, 1497–1508.

Longabaugh, R., Donovan, D. M., Karno, M. P., McCrady, B. S., Morgenstern, J., & Tonigan, J. S. (2005). Active ingredients: How and why evidence-based alcohol behavioral treatment interventions work. *Alcoholism: Clinical and Experimental Research, 29*, 235–247.

O'Farrell, T. J., & Birchlery, G. R. (1987). Marital relationships of alcoholic, conflicted, and nonconflicted couples. *Journal of Marital and Family Therapy, 13*(93), 259–274. doi:10.1111/j.1752-0606.1987.tb00705.x

Velleman, R. D. B., Templeton, L. J., & Copello, A. G. (2005). The role of the family in preventing and intervening with substance use and misuse: A comprehensive review of family interventions, with a focus on young people. *Drug and Alcohol Review, 24*, 93–109.

FAMILY AND MEDICAL LEAVE ACT OF 1993

The Family and Medical Leave Act of 1993 (FMLA) is a United States federal law that was signed into effect by President Bill Clinton on February 5, 1993. The legislation, which focuses on an employee's right to take a leave due to medical issues, speaks to the changing demographics of American families. Introduced to the House of Representatives by William Ford (D-MI), the bill was designed to reduce pressure on working parents who often have to choose job security over family member needs. This entry provides an overview of the impetus for the legislation and a description of the law.

Utilizing FMLA

Since the middle of the 20th century, when divorce rates began to climb and American women began to enter the workforce in increasing numbers, family structures have changed. The United States census data for 2013 indicated that in nearly 50% of two-parent families, both parents were employed. In single-parent households, the percentages were even higher, with 70% of single mothers working and 80% of single fathers employed outside of the home. With no traditional "stay-at-home" primary caregiver, such families experience hardships when faced with long-term medical needs, maternity, or extensive disability among family members. In the past, the choice was often to care for a family member and lose one's job or relinquish the care to another person, which can be cost prohibitive.

As mothers were working in greater numbers, the need for postpartum leave became a significant focus of the bill. Women workers have primacy in childbearing and usually in child-rearing. The bill sought to reduce workplace discrimination against mothers and protect their jobs during maternity. The legislation also recognized the importance of early care giving and bonding in the healthy development of children. As such, both mothers and fathers are afforded a protected right to spend the first few weeks of a child's life at home in a caregiving role.

Similarly, there was no legal protection for workers who needed to be absent from work to care for seriously ill parents. Also at issue were those workers who needed to have time away from work due to exigencies related to military deployment and/or the need to care for a recovering service member. The FMLA protects the employment status of individuals in these situations, thereby allowing people to attend to family members in the most stressful of times without fear of negative financial implications.

The bill also addressed the needs of workers who have long-term health problems themselves. Prior to the FMLA, workers who needed to take time off from work for ongoing medical treatments (e.g., chemotherapy) or who experienced serious illness that required protracted absence from work (e.g., recovery from a serious car accident) had no assurance that their jobs would be there for them when they were able to return. The act allows for individuals to engage in health care as needed.

Intended to help provide a balance between the demands of employers and the needs of families, the FMLA provides for 12 weeks of protected leave during a 12-month period for qualifying events. Qualifying events include the birth or adoption of a child (for both mothers and fathers); the need to provide care for a seriously ill spouse, child, or parent; and serious health conditions that prevent an employee from attending work and/or performing their required job duties. Leave may be taken in a 12-week block or intermittently (weekly, daily, hourly) based on medical necessity. Family members who are caring for a recovering service member are entitled to 26 weeks of leave. The leave does not have to be paid and employers can require that employees use accrued sick and/or vacation time toward said leave. Documentation of medical necessity may be required at the discretion of the employer.

Employers

The FMLA is very specific regarding the type of employers who must comply with the law and the types of employees who are eligible for protection. Employers covered by the law include all public agencies, federal employers, and businesses that employ 50 or more individuals. In order to qualify for protection, the worker must be a permanent, full-time employee who has performed a minimum of 1,250 hours of work within a 12-month period while employed by a covered employer. Workers who are part time, seasonal, or temporary are not covered by the law, nor are elected officials or their staff members.

The law is also specific as to what parts of employment are protected. Workers must be returned to the same position after their leave or be placed into a position that is equivalent in pay, benefits, and status. The FMLA entitles workers to be covered by the same health insurance for which they would be eligible if they were not on leave. Employees cannot be punished or retaliated against for exercising their right to use FMLA. There can be no loss of benefits that were accrued prior to the leave. Employers cannot interfere with an employee's right to use FMLA.

Changes to FMLA

Since its introduction, there have been clarifications and proposed changes to the law. In June 2010, the Department of Labor clarified that employees who assume a caregiving role to any child are entitled to leave regardless of legal or biological status. This permits same-sex parents and those in informal custody agreements the protection of the law. The striking down of the Defense of Marriage Act may bring further refinements to the law. The FMLA can provide a significant reduction in stress to families faced with serious illness or disability. For families in such circumstances and in the process of therapy, this reduction in stress can enhance the ability to make progress in treatment.

Debra Hyatt-Burkhart

See also Adoption; Chronic Illness With Couples and Families

Further Readings

Family and Medical Leave Act of 1993, 29 U.S.C. §§ 2601–2654 (2006).

Gerstel, N., & McGonagle, K. (1999). Job leaves and the limits of the Family and Medical Leave Act. *Work and Occupations*, 26(4), 510–534.

Waldfogel, J. (1999). The impact of the Family and Medical Leave Act. *Journal of Policy Analysis and Management*, 18(2), 281–302.

Family Assessment, Models of

Assessment in family counseling is an essential practice that focuses on the evaluation of the function of the entire family system or some subset of the family. As with all assessment in counseling, family assessment begins at the initial contact and continues throughout treatment. Some broad areas of formal assessment include evaluating levels of satisfaction and adjustment, communication styles, transaction patterns, strengths, and coping strategies. Additionally, assessment in family and couples can be used to screen, to create treatment plans, to predict relationship sustainability, and to evaluate therapeutic outcomes. The clinician's choice of assessment models, which can be quantitative or qualitative in nature, depends largely on his or her theoretical orientation to how systems function. This entry presents four models of family assessment that produce empirical measures and one that is qualitative by design and produces a graphic representation of the family.

Models of family assessment are based on systems theory and the notion of circular causality. Circular causality is counter to linear causality, which adheres to the notion that one event follows another. Instead, circular causality refers to the idea that events or processes have a reciprocal impact on one another. Family members act and react to each other, resulting in a mutual interaction of causes. Counter to the individual diagnosis, which is the central focus of the American Psychiatric Association's *Diagnostic and Statistical Manual* (DSM), circular causality lends itself to a relational diagnosis (DSM-5 codes) that focuses on interpersonal transactional patterns occurring within the system. The following is an overview of some of the most widely used and empirically validated models of family assessment.

The Circumplex Model of Marital and Family Systems

The circumplex model of marital and family systems focuses on three dimensions of functioning: family cohesion, flexibility, and communication.

Cohesion is the emotional bonding that couples and families have toward one another. Part of the emotional bond is the ability of the family to balance separateness and togetherness. Separateness refers to each family member's ability to be an individual, while togetherness denotes a family member's ability to see himself or herself as part of the system. Cohesion is assessed on five levels ranging from extremely low to extremely high: disengaged or disconnected, somewhat connected, connected, very connected, and enmeshed or overly connected. Within this 5-point range, the three middle levels (i.e., somewhat connected, connected, and very connected) are considered balanced, and the two extreme levels (i.e., disengaged or disconnected and enmeshed or overly connected) are seen as unbalanced. Optimal functioning is reflected in the balanced levels while the unbalanced levels denote problematic functioning. With regard to problematic functioning, disengagement is marked by high levels of emotional separateness with little to no involvement resulting in family members not being able to turn toward each other for support. Enmeshment, however, is marked by high levels of closeness whereby family members are overly dependent on one another. Overdependence results in family members being unable to make decisions independent of family involvement. Typically, families change levels of cohesion throughout the life cycle and during times of high stress.

The next dimension of the circumplex model of marital and family systems is flexibility. In this model, flexibility has to do with how the family manages stability and change with the central focus on leadership, discipline, negotiation, roles, and rules. As in the cohesion dimension, there are also five levels of flexibility that range from extremely low to extremely high. These levels, in ascending order, include rigid or inflexible, somewhat flexible, flexible, very flexible, and chaotic or overly flexible. Again, the three middle levels (i.e., somewhat flexible, flexible, and very flexible) are considered balanced and signify optimal functioning while the extremes (i.e., rigid or inflexible and chaotic or overly flexible) are unbalanced and depict problematic functioning.

The basic premise around flexibility is that families need some degree of flexibility and should be neither too rigid in their leadership and rules nor too flexible whereby leadership is erratic and rules change frequently. Within this model flexibility and cohesion are graphically depicted on the couple and family map. The figure is a square with 25 boxes. The center nine boxes represent optimum functioning with the outside inner edges noting midrange and the outer corners noting the unbalanced extremes.

The final dimension of the circumplex model of marital and family systems is communication. Communication mitigates both cohesion and flexibility. Aspects of communication include listening and speaking skills, self-disclosure, clarity, continuity tracking, and respect and regard. There are a number of components of each aspect that denote good communication. For example, listening skills include the ability to show empathy and to be attentive while listening. Good speaking skills are marked by the ability to speak for yourself and not others. High on self-disclosure involves openly sharing of oneself, including thoughts and feelings. Clarity encompasses clear and congruent messages. Continuity tracking is the ability to follow what others are saying and to respond appropriately. Finally, respect and regard are positive when family members consistently portray respectfulness toward others through verbal and nonverbal messages. Poor communication is the absence of the aforementioned components and will most likely correlate with unbalanced levels of cohesion and flexibility.

Two family-focused assessment scales that assess the dimensions of the circumplex model of marital and family systems are the Family Adaptability and Cohesion Evaluation Scales (FACES-IV) and the Clinical Rating Scale (CRS). The FACES-IV is a 42-item self-report questionnaire with six subscales: enmeshed, balanced cohesion, disengaged, chaotic, balanced flexibility, and rigid. Six family types are identified: balanced, rigidly cohesive, midrange, flexibly unbalanced, chaotically unbalanced, and unbalanced. The scores from the assessment can be plotted on the couple and family map previously described. Validity and reliability of the scale been shown to be good, with high internal consistency among the subscales.

The CRS can be completed by family counselors and researchers from observation of family members' interactions or from clinical interviews. This scale addresses all three dimensions of the circumplex model of marital and family systems: cohesion, flexibility, and communication. Observers rate families on all three dimensions in relation to specific indicators. This scale has also been found to be a valid and reliable measure.

The PREPARE/ENRICH is a widely used assessment tool and program that also encompasses the circumplex model of marital and family systems. This program can be used to assess couples' readiness for marriage, and it can also be used as a framework to help couples who are already married to enhance their relationship. The computer-based inventory generates a report that is interpreted by a trained clinician or clergy member. The assessment has a number of scales including, but not limited to, 12 that focus on the relationship including communication, conflict resolution, roles, sexuality, finances, and spiritual beliefs; five that focus on personality; four directed at the couple and family with focus on the circumplex dimensions; and four others that address relationship dynamics. There is also a parenting version of the assessment available and a workbook titled *Building a Strong Marriage*. Facilitators are required to participate in a one-day training and materials are available for purchase. Over three million couples have completed the assessment. It has been widely researched and has been found to have good reliability and validity.

The Beavers Systems Model

The Beavers systems model focuses on family functioning and includes their biology, experiences, skills, and current stressors. The two central concepts within the model are the health/competence dimension and the stylistic dimension. The health/competence dimension addresses tasks with the focus on how the family organizes and manages itself. Here adults provide the structure of the family and negotiate and share leadership while establishing clear boundaries between generations. Other elements within the health/competence dimension include members developing confidence and self-esteem, displaying clear and direct communication, presenting feelings, accepting differences, and demonstrating the ability to resolve conflict. Deficits in these areas denote less-than-optimal functioning.

The stylistic dimension in the Beavers systems model has to do with boundaries and whether or not the system is closed or open. In systems theory, boundaries are rules that govern a number of functions within the family, including who is allowed in the family and the flow of information in and out of the family. Seen on a continuum, the more closed family system is referred to as centripetal (CP) and the more open family system is denoted as centrifugal (CF). Centripetal family styles are marked by family members who look within the family for support, downplay negative emotions, are less trustful of the outside world, and in which children leave home at a later age than children from CF families. Conversely, families who have CF qualities look outside of the family for support, display a wide range of emotion, and place trust outside of the family; children in CF families leave home at an earlier age. Extremes on either end of the spectrum have been found to be problematic, with optimal functioning found in a mixed style of both CP and CF.

A conceptual figure is available that depicts all of the components of the Beavers systems model. The horizontal axis of the model outlines the health/competence dimension and includes five ranges of functioning from optimal to severely dysfunctional, which often produces sociopathic offspring. The health/competence score is on a 10-point scale with higher scores denoting dysfunction. The vertical axis of the model shows the stylistic dimension and includes three ranges of functioning including CP, mixed, and CF. The stylistic dimension is on a 5-point scale with lower scores indicating CP, which often produce schizophrenic offspring, and higher scores depicting CF. The figure also illustrates through a V-shaped notch that severely disturbed families are found on the extremes and are found not to demonstrate blended styles of behavior.

In the Beaver systems model, assessment of the family is done both through family self-report and through observation of the family's interactions. The Self-Report Family Inventory (SFI) is a 36-item, 5-point Likert scale questionnaire that produces a health/competence score and a cohesion score used to help generate an overall level of family style. Cohesion has to do with the family's degree of emotional closeness. Conflict, leadership, and expressiveness are also assessed using this scale. The SFI score can be plotted on the vertical axis of the figure described above. The SFI can be administered to individuals 11 years of age and older, has been extensively researched, and has been found to have good reliability and validity.

The health/competence and stylistic dimensions are assessed through observation using the Beavers Interactional Style Scales and the Beavers Interactional Competence Scale, respectively. The Beavers Interactional Style Scales is completed first and requires the assessor to note behaviors that align with CP or CF styles. The assessment has seven ratings and a global style rating ranging from one to five, with one indicating high CP and five being high CF. Constructs measured via subscales include meeting dependency needs, managing conflict, use of space, appearance to outsiders, professed closeness, managing assertion, and expression of feeling. Next, the Interactional Competence Scale is completed. This scale produces two subscales on a 10-point scale and a global score with higher scores denoting greater dysfunction. Subscales assess family structure, family mythology, goal-directed negotiation, autonomy, and family affect. Observation scores for this dimension can be plotted on the horizontal axis of the figure previously described. For these scales, validity with the exception of family mythology has been established and interrater reliability is high.

The McMaster Model of Family Functioning

The basic premise of the McMaster model of family functioning (MMFF) is that the family's role is to provide support for each family member so he or she can develop and maintain functioning in three areas: social, psychological, and biological. While helping to care for one another, families have three task areas to address: the basic task area, the developmental task area, and the hazardous task area. The basic task area addresses instrumental issues that are family members' fundamental needs such as food, money, and shelter. The developmental task area encompasses issues that pertain to life stages such as marriage, pregnancy, and launching children. Finally, the hazardous task area involves managing crises like illness and job loss. Optimal family functioning is the ability to adequately address all three tasks.

According to the MMFF, the three task areas are addressed through six overlapping dimensions: problem-solving, communication, roles, affective responsiveness, affective involvement, and behavior control. Problem-solving has to do with the way that families solve two types of problems: instrumental and affective. Instrumental problems are problems related to the instrumental task described above, while affective issues relate to problems surrounding emotions and feelings. Families must effectively handle instrumental problems before they can effectively deal with those that are affective in nature. Within the MMFF there is a seven-step model of effective problem-solving: identifying the problem, appropriately communicating the problem, developing a set of solutions, deciding on one solution, carrying out the action, monitoring, and evaluating the effectiveness of the choice. All families, whether they are functioning effectively or not, have problems; however, effective families have the ability to resolve their problems.

The next dimension in the MMFF is that of communication. Here, patterns of communication encompass only that which is exchanged verbally and is assessed in relation to the instrumental and affective areas that are addressed in the problem-solving domain. Communication is assessed on two continuums: clear to masked and direct to indirect. Clear communication is communication that is distinct, while masked communication is disguised and vague. Direct communication is communicating toward the appropriate person, while indirect communication is routed to other people. Communication patterns can fall into four discrete patterns: clear and direct, clear and indirect, masked and direct, masked and indirect.

Family roles are patterns of behaviors that guide how family members fulfill family functions. The MMFF includes five family functions: (1) provision of resources, (2) nurturance and support, (3) adult sexual gratification, (4) personal development, and (5) maintenance and management of the family system. Each has a number of its own tasks and functions to complete. The provision of resources is related to the tasks and functions that address the instrumental or basic needs described above. The function of nurturance and support involves the provision of comfort, warmth, and reassurance. Adult sexual satisfaction includes the ability to be satisfied and satisfying your partner with a mutually agreed-upon level of sexual activity. The personal development function assists family members in obtaining individual achievement and may include tasks related to physical, emotional, educational, and social development. Maintenance and management of the family system has a number of functions including decision-making, boundary and membership functions, implementation and adherence of behavior, household finance, and health-related functions. Two overarching aspects of family role functioning are role allocation and role accountability. Role allocation has to do with patterns of assignment roles and whether or not the family member can complete the task, while role accountability refers to the family's procedures for making sure the functions are completed.

The affective responsiveness dimension has two foci including the ability to respond to stimuli with a full range of emotion and whether or not the emotional response is in line with the precipitating event. Welfare and emergency are two types of emotions. Examples of welfare emotions are love, happiness, and joy. Conversely, examples of emergency emotions are anger, fear, and sadness. Families with healthy affective responses means that individual members have the capacity to feel and express a wide range of emotion.

Affective involvement is defined as the extent to which the family shows interests and values others' activities and interests. The MMFF has six types of interests ranging from complete lack of involvement to overinvolvement. The six types are lack of involvement, involvement devoid of feeling, narcissistic involvement, empathic involvement, overinvolvement, and symbiotic involvement. Lack of involvement depicts no interest at all. Involvement devoid of feeling is showing some interest with no emotional investment. Narcissistic involvement is showing interest to promote the self. Empathic involvement is showing interest to promote the other and is seen as optimum. Finally, overinvolvement is excessive, while symbiotic involvement is extreme and pathological and can be likened to enmeshment as described in the circumplex model. Families can exhibit some variation within the midrange and still maintain healthy functioning.

Patterns of behavior control occur in three types of situations: those that are physically dangerous, those that address meeting and expressing psychobiological needs and drives, and those involving interpersonal socializing behavior. When addressing these areas, four types of behavior control emerge: rigid, flexible, laissez-faire, and chaotic. Rigid patterns of behavior are marked by narrow responses with little variation. Flexible patterns manifest as reasonable behaviors with room for negotiation and are seen as the most effective. Laissez-faire patterns possess no set of standards for responding and are extreme and erratic. Chaotic behavior control is described as random shifting between rigid, flexible, and laissez-faire styles; family members have no way of knowing which standards apply, causing confusion.

The self-report instrument used to assess the construct found in the MMFF is the Family Assessment Device (FAD), while the McMaster Clinical Rating Scale (MCRS) is completed by a clinician from data gathered during the McMaster Structured Interview of Family Functioning (McSiff). The FAD is a 60-item assessment with items rated on a 4-point Likert scale. This scale measures the problem-solving, communication roles; affective responsiveness; affective involvement; and behavioral control dimensions, as well as general functioning. The MCRS allows the clinician to rate the family on a 7-point scale with

1 denoting severely disturbed and 7 indicating superior functioning. This scale rates the same six domains as the FAD and also provides an assessment of general functioning. There is also an observational form of assessment called the Mealtime Interaction Coding System (MICS). Areas of assessment for this device include task management, communication, roles, affect management, interpersonal involvement, and behavioral control. The reliability and validity of the FAD have been documented.

The Process Model of Family Functioning

The process model of family functioning is a model of family functioning that has some common elements of the McMaster model yet differs on areas of functioning and their reciprocal influences, integration of various theories, and integration of the greater social system and family history. In the process model of family functioning, the main goal of the family is to successfully accomplish basic, developmental, and crisis tasks. Basic tasks have to do with keeping the family safe, developmental with continued growth, and crisis with management during times of difficulty. Additionally, the model is based on the exploration of seven dimensions, all of which are vital to task accomplishment. These dimensions include task accomplishment, role performance, communication, affective expression, involvement, control, and values and norms.

The conceptual framework for the process model depicts task accomplishment, which encompasses the basic, developmental, and crisis tasks at the center of the model. Task accomplishment is attained through identification of the problem, exploration of alternative solutions, implementation of selected approaches, and evaluation of the effects of the chosen approach. The other components of the model are areas that influence task accomplishment or are areas where task accomplishment is carried out. Role performance includes the assignment of an activity, willingness to take on the role, and actually following through with the behavior. Communication assists if it is mutually understood by everyone and is clear and direct. Affective expression is a part of communication and is evaluated on the basis of content, intensity, and timing. Involvement is explained as the degree and quality of interest family members have for each other and includes five types: uninvolved, interested with no feeling, narcissistic, empathic, and enmeshed. *Control* has to do with influence and has three styles: predictable versus inconsistent, constructive versus destructive, or responsible versus irresponsible. Combinations of these styles give rise to four types of control: rigid, flexible, laissez-faire, and chaotic, whereby flexible is seen as the healthiest style of functioning. Finally, the values and norms of the family that are rooted in the family's history dictate how all processes are carried out and influence family rules, attitudes, and behaviors.

There are a number of assessments associated with the process model of family functioning. The central assessment device is the Family Assessment Measure (FAM-III). The FAM-III is a 134-item self-report instrument that has a general, a dyadic, and an individual scale, titled the self-rating scale. The general scale has 50 items and nine subscales that provide an overall rating on family functioning, seven measures relating to components of the process model of family functioning, and two other scales that address social desirability and defensiveness. Results of the social desirability and defensiveness scales allow for further interpretation of the results. The dyadic relationship scale and the self-rating scale both have 42 items and seven subscales and provide an overall rating of functioning, while the dyadic scale focuses on family pairs and the self-rating scale focuses on the individual's perception of their functioning. All responses are based on a 4-point scale ranging from agree to disagree. There is also a brief 14-item version of each scale. The FAM-III is appropriate for family members age 10 and older.

One observational rating system used with the process model of family functioning is the Iowa Family Interaction Rating Scales (IFIRS). Items are mostly rated on a 9-point scale, with 1 indicating not at all characteristic and 9 being highly characteristic. There are numerous scales found in this rating system, each having several subscales. The scales address individual characteristics, dyadic interaction, dyadic relationship, group interaction, parenting, individual problem-solving, and group problem-solving. To utilize this rating system, coders watch videos of the family engaged in discussion or activities while rating them in accordance with the scale items. Coders must undergo extensive training in order to be proficient at coding.

The Genogram as a Model of Family Functioning

The genogram is a qualitative measure that can be used as both an assessment and an intervention. When used for assessment, the gathering of family information begins at the onset of treatment when the family or individual presents for the intake interview. Clinicians map the family's structure, patterns, and transactional sequences. The completed graphical representation results in an overall view of family functioning that can range from rudimentary to complex. Because assessment is ongoing, the genogram can be revised and updated during all phases of treatment.

Before utilizing the genogram as an assessment tool, clinicians should have an understanding of Bowenian family therapy, also referred to as multigenerational family therapy. There are two basic assumptions of this systems theory. The first assumption is that an individual's problems cannot be understood without looking at the role of family, which is seen as an emotional unit. The second assumption is that in order for the individual to function optimally, he or she must address unresolved emotional fusion or attachment to the family unit. The term *emotional unit* is aligned with the concept of circular causality, in that members act and react to one another on an emotional level. Emotional fusion can be likened to enmeshment, previously discussed in the circumplex model. Individuals who are in a state of emotional fusion are highly reliant on one another to the point that independence on any level is sacrificed.

Further explanation of the basic assumptions can be found in the eight key concepts in Bowenian theory: differentiation of the self, triangles, family projection process, emotional cutoff, nuclear family emotional process, multigenerational transmission process, sibling position, and societal emotional process. Differentiation of the self is the ability of the individual family member to think and act for himself or herself while maintaining a connection to the family that is not marked by emotional reactivity. Individuals with emotional fusion are typically low in self-differentiation. Triangles can be either positive or negative and occur when one or more members of a dyad pull in a third (i.e., triangulation) to offset the pressure that is building between the two members of the dyad. An example of a negative triangle is the family projection process whereby the parents draw in a child who then often becomes the individual who is the identified person (IP) for whom the family seeks treatment to "fix." Emotional cutoff is extreme emotional distancing that can include contact or noncontact between family members, marked by conflict or silence. The nuclear family emotional process refers to a situation in which family members either engage in conflict or distance themselves from one another, resulting in a spouse who develops dysfunction to the point that he or she becomes incapacitated. The multigenerational transmission process is the process by which emotional processes such as triangulation are handed down from generation to generation. Sibling position theory is based on the work of Walter Toman and includes 12 positions (i.e., oldest brother of brothers, youngest brother of brothers, oldest brother of sisters, youngest brother of sisters, male only, twins, oldest sister of sisters, youngest sister of sisters, oldest sister of brothers, youngest sister of brothers, female only, and middle sibling) with specific traits; it adheres to the notion that siblings will seek out a mate who has a complementary level of differentiation. The societal emotional process has to do with the influence of societal pressures on the family, in that families react to outside stressors such as overpopulation, poverty, and scarcity of resources.

In order to construct the genogram, the clinician must have a basic understanding of the symbols used to identify patterns and lines used to reflect emotional connectedness. Traditionally, gender and sexual orientation are depicted by squares for heterosexual males and circles for heterosexual females, squares with triangles within for gay men and circles with triangles within for lesbian women, broken triangles within squares and circles for bisexual, and circles with squares within for transgendered males, and squares with circles within for transgendered females. The nature of relationships includes solid lines for marriage, broken lines for sexual relationships or living together, and both solid and broken lines to denote a committed relationship. Various lines through the marital line identify marital separation, reconciliation, divorce, and reconciliation after divorce. Adoption and foster children are noted by drawing a line from the family from which the child moved to the family into which he or she has been placed. Children are placed between and directly below the relational line of their biological parents with single births from a straight line and twins originating from the same point on two lines. A circle can be drawn around family members who live in the same household at the time of the genogram construction, and the IP is drawn with double lines and is placed lower than his or her siblings. To maintain clarity of the genogram, like generations in relation to the IP should be placed on the same horizontal level as the IP. Other important information that may be noted includes birth and death dates, ages, affairs and family secrets, location of residence, immigration, career, income, and pets. Addiction, physical and mental illness, and other concerns such as smoking and obesity should also be included.

The next focus of the genogram is to denote interactional patterns between family members. Lines between family members denote the nature of, and emotional connectedness within, the relationship. Relationships are described as close (double line), fused (triple line), hostile (jagged line), close-hostile (double line with jagged between), distant (broken line), and cutoff (single line interrupted). Physical, emotional, and sexual abuse are also noted by corresponding jagged lines with an arrow pointing toward the family member experiencing the abuse. Individuals involved in triangulation are connected by a triangle with arrows drawn toward the individual being pulled into the dyad. Color coding can also be utilized for ease of recognizing various patterns and transactional sequences. It is suggested that in order to adequately identify multigenerational transmission processes a minimum of three generations should be tracked. The genogram should be labeled appropriately and include a legend that explains the various symbols and emotional lines. Additionally, computer-based programs are available for the construction of the genogram.

Laura K. Harrawood

See also Attachment; Boundaries; Bowen Family Systems Theory; Circumplex Model; Clinical Case Conceptualization With Couples and Families; Clinical Interviews With Couples and Families; Complementary and Symmetrical Relationships; Genograms

Further Readings

Beavers, W. R., & Hampson, R. B. (2000). The Beavers system model of family functioning. *Journal of Family Therapy, 22,* 128–143.

Beavers, W. R., Hampson, R. B., & Hulgus, Y. F. (1985). The Beavers systems approach to family assessment. *Family Process, 24,* 398–405.

Bowen Center for the Study of the Family. (n.d.). *Theory.* Retrieved from http://www.thebowencenter.org/theory/

Epstein, N. B., Baldwin, L. M., & Bishop, D. S. (1982). *The McMaster clinical rating scales (MCRS).* Providence, RI: Brown University Family Research Program.

Epstein, N. B., Baldwin, L. M., & Bishop, D. S. (1983). The McMaster assessment device. *Journal of Marital and Family Therapy, 9*(2), 171–180.

Epstein, N. B., Bishop, D. S., & Levin, S. (1978). The McMaster model of family functioning. *Journal of Marriage and Family Counseling, 4,* 19–31.

Life Innovations. (n.d.). *FACES IV.* Retrieved from http://facesiv.com/

McGoldrick, M., Gerson, R., & Petry, S. (2008). *Genograms: Assessment and intervention* (3rd ed.). New York, NY: W. W. Norton.

Multi-Health Systems. (n.d.). *Family Assessment Measure-III*. Retrieved from http://www.mhs.com/clinical.aspx

Olson, D. (2000). Circumplex model of family systems. *Journal of Family Therapy, 22*(2), 144–167.

Olson, D. (2011). FACE IV and the circumplex model: Validation study. *Journal of Marital and Family Therapy, 3*(1), 64–80.

Skinner, H. A., Steinhauer, P. D., & Santa-Barbara, J. (1995). *Family assessment measure-III manual*. Toronto, Canada: Multi-Health Systems.

Skinner, H. A., Steinhauer, P. D., & Sitarenious, G. (2000). Family assessment measure (FAM) and process model of family functioning. *Journal of Family Therapy, 22*(2), 190–210.

Sperry, L. (2004). *Assessment of couples and families: Contemporary and cutting-edge strategies*. New York, NY: Taylor & Francis.

Steinhauer, P. D., Santa-Barbara, J., & Skinner, H. A. (1984). The process model of family functioning. *Canadian Journal of Psychiatry, 29*, 77–88.

Thomlison, B. (2007). *Family assessment handbook* (2nd ed.). Belmont, CA: Brooks/Cole.

Walsh, F. (Ed.). (2003). *Normal family processes: Growing diversity and complexity* (3rd ed.). New York, NY: Guilford Press.

Family Life Cycle

The family life cycle provides a framework for understanding the passage of families through time. Each family goes through different stages of development, with emotional, intellectual, and social changes for each member of the family. Individual changes influence the family, and changes in the family structure (e.g., births, deaths, and marriages) influence individuals. The family life cycle affords a multidimensional context for understanding individual development and the impact of broader social systems on the family unit. This entry provides a general definition of the family unit and development, describes the stages of the family life cycle with specific attention to key emotional and structural changes undergirding each developmental phase, and outlines critiques of the family life cycle model. The entry concludes with a brief discussion of the value of the family life cycle as a conceptual tool for couples, marriage, and family practitioners.

Individual and Family Development

While configurations and meaning vary widely, all individuals are in some way connected to larger family and social systems. More than a mere collection of individuals connected by blood, legal, and/or historical ties, families may be considered unique and sustained social systems. Family systems are multigenerational, multilayered, and multifaceted. Each family creates their own "culture" and family members become aware of this culture and associated expectations through spoken and unspoken rules. These rules influence family member roles, the power structure of the family, communication patterns, and strategies for negotiating and solving problems. A family life cycle approach helps professionals and families understand typical transitions and possible problems families may face.

Originally formulated in the mid-1900s, the family life cycle approach reflects efforts to summarize major developmental transitions and tasks faced by multigenerational family systems. With expanding definitions of *family* and of *normal developmental trajectories*, a certain level of oversimplification with the framework is necessary; however, these models of typical family transitions should only be used as a guideline. These models help give families and clinicians a simplified view of family life transitions within a generation and across generations. How families do or do not fit with typical life cycle models can be used to understand and assess the family.

The family life cycle outlines major marker events many families progress through regardless of structure or cultural heritage. Different stages of development are characterized by *developmental tasks*, or activities and experiences families undertake to overcome evolving conflicts and challenges. Family role expectations are largely forged through these developmental tasks toward a goal of achieving necessary *second-order changes*. Second-order changes transpire when the system restructures its governing rules and establishes a new form of homeostasis (status quo). Some developmentalists believe tasks associated with each stage of family life cycle must be resolved in order for healthy development to proceed. Achievement of developmental tasks is most often a gradual transition over a singular event.

Stages of the Family Life Cycle

In the 1980s, Betty Carter and Monica McGoldrick delineated six major stages of the family life cycle: (1) young adulthood, (2) coupling, (3) families with young children, (4) families with adolescents, (5) families at midlife, and (6) families at later life. Chief emotional tasks and second-order changes ascribed to each stage are described below. Across each stage, families may experience tensions between the need for continuity and the need for change.

Young Adulthood

Young adulthood serves as a time of preparation and cultivating readiness for subsequent phases. A chief developmental task of the *young adulthood* stage is acquiring financial and emotional responsibility for oneself. This transpires through a number of interrelated second-order changes to the family system. These include establishing a differentiated identity from one's family of origin, forging intimate peer and romantic relationships, and career and workplace exploration.

Qualitatively, young adulthood may be categorized by a certain spirit of self-involvement and idealism stemming from experimentation and clarifying one's self-identity. There is an emphasis on autonomy and separation during this stage. Additionally, similar to progression through other developmental stages, cyclical progressions are common, with movement in and out of the home, as well as in and out of relationships. Tensions may also arise, as children desire independence, but may still demonstrate financial or other types of dependence on parents.

Coupling

The second stage in the family life cycle is *coupling*. Movement within this developmental stage is marked by tendencies toward interdependence over independence and commitment within a new immediate family system. Partners may learn to rely on one another, to work together as a team, and to also make compromises that benefit the couple dyad. Individuals may also begin to prioritize the couple relationship when making decisions. Second-order changes include the formation of the marital or couple system and realignment of existing relationships with friends and family to include the partner.

Mutual commitment to the partnership is important to managing transitions associated with the coupling stage, such as establishing new relationships with one's family of origin. Partners work to create a new "we" without sacrificing the "I." As each member of the partnership comes from a unique family "culture," considerable attention is given to understanding and bridging differences. Couples work to establish relational rules (spoken and unspoken) related to finances, intimacy, power, boundaries with extended family, and divisions of labor, among others.

Families With Young Children

The third stage, *families with young children*, is described as one of the most definitive transitions of the family life cycle. Family systems are forever altered by the birth of a new family member. New generations of parents, grandparents, aunts, uncles, and so forth are also created by the birth of a new child. Key transitions during this family life cycle stage include shifts from coupledom to parenthood, the renegotiation of work and household tasks, and the redefinition of multigenerational roles and relationships.

For some families, the joy and fulfillment of welcoming a child is accompanied by difficult transitions. Issues related to child-rearing, including child care and discipline, are central during this phase of the family life cycle. Partners may also feel social pressures around decisions to have or not have children, the roles of parents, and expectations for work–life balance. Shifts toward more traditional gender and power roles can also occur following the addition of children to a family system.

Families With Adolescents

The next stage of the family life cycle, *families with adolescents,* is marked by changes to the family system to support and prepare children for entrance into the adult world. Increasing the flexibility of family boundaries is important during this stage to allow for children's growing independence. Adolescents are encountering numerous physical, sexual, emotional, and identity changes. Families also work to renegotiate rules and limits to accommodate the emerging adolescent.

Concurrent to transitions for adolescent family members themselves, other second-order changes unfold in the family as adult members focus on midlife couple and work issues. For example, a parent may choose to return to the workforce or to pursue a new career trajectory once a child gains more autonomy in his or her daily care. There may also be increasing emphasis on caring for the older generation, with "sandwiched" responsibilities for younger and older generations.

Families at Midlife

The fifth stage, *families at midlife,* entails adjusting to a series of entries and exits from the family system. Midlife represents the longest phase of the family life cycle. It is also one of significant family restructuring. A major second-order change associated with this stage is the development of adult-to-adult relationships between parents and grown children. Within the couple subsystem, partners face the task of realigning and reconceptualizing their dyadic relationship. As grown children leave the home and couple themselves, the system continues to grow and change to include in-laws, partners, and new children. Exits to the family system may also occur as families deal with disabilities, divorce, and deaths within the older generation.

Though midlife is often correlated with "empty nests" and "crises," this developmental stage is a time of flourishing for many individuals. With the launching of children, greater flexibility may exist for partners to reengage as a couple. Individuals may also choose to reenter the workplace or to have greater time and finances to participate in leisure activities. However, for some couples, the exit of children from the immediate system can bring a time of tremendous stress; midlife can bring a peak of divorces and remarriages. Separated, divorced, and remarried family systems may recycle through previous stages of the family life cycle.

Families in Later Life

The final stage of the family life cycle, *families in later life,* represents a time of challenge and opportunity as generational roles shift within families. Families encounter a number of milestones, such as retirement, grandparenthood, illness, loss, and ultimately, preparation for one's own death. Primary second-order changes include a more central role for the middle generation. Family members also consider new family and social circles.

Critiques of the Family Life Cycle Model

Since the early studies of the family life cycle in the mid-20th century, significant societal shifts have occurred. Chief among these is an increased recognition of diverse family structures and systemic processes. Critics have stated that the family life cycle model may promote normative views of the family system, as an intact, heterosexual nuclear structure comprised of members of the dominant culture. Additionally, the sequencing of the family life cycle stages suggests a stage-by-stage progression that may not account for the complexity of multigenerational family transitions. Little attention is also given in the model to what happens between stages.

Transitions across the family life cycle are inherently embedded within a larger sociocultural context. Factors such as gender, race, ethnicity, and sexual orientation play a role in how family life cycle stages are negotiated and defined. In response to criticisms of the original family life cycle model, developmentalists have made expansions to the framework to better capture the complex realities of a diverse society. For example, models of divorced, single-parent, and remarried family life cycle development have been delineated. Greater consideration of family stressors, such as addictions and chronic illness, is given in more contemporary expansions of the family life cycle framework.

Why the Family Life Cycle Is Important

Researchers and practitioners recognize the utility of the family life cycle in conceptualizing family transitions over time. The framework may also assist families in understanding their own transitions and development. The family life cycle model can serve as an important tool for contextualizing family structure. This can contribute to better case conceptualizations and treatment planning. Understanding of the family life cycle can assist families in understanding and establishing developmental momentum, increasing flexibility, and ultimately, promoting optimal development for the family system and individual members alike.

While some complexities of family life are minimized within the theoretical model, it is essential that professionals utilizing this framework not ignore these factors in practice. If applied too rigidly, the family life cycle framework may pathologize normal deviations. For example, while gay and lesbian families face many of the same normative demands as their heterosexual counterparts, these family systems must also simultaneously cope with the stresses of living in a stigmatizing society. As such, definitions of family and the timing and meaning of family life cycle phases should be constructed by families themselves.

Jessica Lloyd-Hazlett

See also Couple Development; Family of Origin; Homeostasis; Individual and Family Development; Life Transitions; Second-Order Change

Further Readings

Carter, B., & McGoldrick, M. (Eds.). (2005). *The expanded family life cycle: Individual, family, and social perspectives*. Boston, MA: Pearson.

Gehart, D. (2015). *Theory and treatment planning in family therapy: A competency-based approach*. Boston, MA: Cengage.

Goldenberg, A. E. (2010). *Lesbian and gay parents and their children: Research on the family life cycle*. Washington, DC: American Psychological Association.

Goldenberg, H., & Goldenberg, I. (2013). *Family therapy: An overview* (8th ed.). Belmont, CA: Brooks/Cole.

McGoldrick, M., & Carter, B. (2003). The family life cycle. In F. Walsh (Ed.), *Normal family processes* (3rd ed., pp. 375–398). New York, NY: Guilford Press.

McGoldrick, M., & Hardy, K. V. (Eds.). (2008). *Re-visioning family therapy: Race, culture, and gender in clinical practice*. New York, NY: Guilford Press.

FAMILY LIFE EDUCATORS

Family life educators create and implement educational interventions that are aimed at strengthening individuals and families. The National Council on Family Relations (NCFR) is the primary professional association for the understanding and strengthening of families. This membership organization offers several benefits to family life educators and also sponsors the Certified Family Life Educator (CFLE) credential. Certified family life educators have a minimum of a bachelor's degree and preparation and experience in family life education settings. CFLEs work in a variety of settings including adoption agencies, marital and premarital programs, educational settings, family law settings, caregiver and long-term care education, public policy settings, and nonprofit administration. Family life education emphasizes a preventive and educational approach and provides family members with information, skills and resources aimed at enriching their family experience. This entry highlights the work of CFLEs and describes the applicability of family life education in several contexts, including health care, educational, correctional, and corporate settings.

Objectives of Family Life Education

The main objective of family life education is to improve the quality of life and family relationships. It differs from family therapy as it primarily utilizes a prevention model to impart the knowledge, skills, and attitudes needed to improve or sustain family relationships. Likewise, rather than employ a therapeutic stance, family life educators use an educational approach. The main premise is that prevention techniques benefit both the individual family members and society: Families are not debilitated by the problems they face and this in turn results in less expense to society. Family life education has wide applicability and as a result, certified family life educators are employed in a variety of settings.

Family life educators focus on healthy family functioning, and the programs and services they provide are all aimed at equipping individuals and families with the tools needed to maintain or reestablish a healthy family environment. They practice using a family systems perspective and preventive approach and provide the skills and knowledge that are essential for healthy functioning. Among these are communication skills, decision-making skills, skills for healthy interpersonal relationships, and other topics essential for fostering stronger, healthy families.

CFLEs are qualified to be instructors, facilitators, and advisors to families who are currently or likely to be experiencing distress. They also work with families who have a desire to strengthen relationships or learn various skills and knowledge needed to avert the formation of difficulties and dysfunction within the family.

Skills and Characteristics

Effective family life educators all possess compassion for and dedication in creating and sustaining healthy, functional family relationships. As with other human service providers, a CFLE needs great listening skills and the ability to objectively evaluate information. Other skills that are essential for the work that CFLEs perform include patience and persistence, empathy, communication and interpersonal skills, and open-mindedness to be able to work free of bias and judgment. CFLEs are able to navigate and successfully work with varying personalities, manage hostility, and foster open dialogue among family members in an effort to bolster healthy, functional families.

There are several guiding principles that direct and inform the work of family life educators. Some of these include the principle of order (behavior has predictable consequences), the principle of empathy, the principle of agency (people are free to make choices), the principle of momentum (one's life is defined by the accumulation of choices), the principle of loss, the principle of integrity, and the principle of goodness.

Family life educators address societal issues, such as parenting, work–family balance, gender, sexuality, and economics, from a family systems context. They espouse the belief that societal problems such as domestic violence, substance abuse, and child sexual abuse are more effectively addressed and resolved by viewing the individual and family as part of a larger system. They provide knowledge to help prevent or minimize these at the individual, family, and societal levels. This knowledge is commonly disseminated using an educational approach.

Family life educators also facilitate a wide range of programs to meet the needs of the community, businesses, and other settings in which they are employed. Some of these programs include premarital education, marriage enrichment programs, parenting classes, and family financial planning workshops.

Family Life Educator Certification

The National Council on Family Relations focuses solely on research, policy, and practices that are aimed at strengthening families. Members include practitioners in the United States and the rest of the world and are multidisciplinary; the organization includes professionals with social research, teaching, practice, policy analysis, and human services backgrounds. The NCFR produces three scholarly journals, hosts an annual conference and offers the CFLE credential. Certified family life educator curricular requirements are integrated into degree programs at more than 120 U.S. colleges and universities.

The NCFR developed and manages the certification process for family life educators. This certification is recognized not only within the United States, but internationally as well. Certified family life educators come from a range of professions, but they have all completed required training and have experience working in family life education settings, including educational environments, research facilities, health care clinics, military family support programs, and/or community education programs. The minimum education requirement for certified family life educators is a bachelor's degree; however, many counselors hold advanced degrees. Professional counselors have the option of obtaining this additional certification, and clinical mental health counselors and family counselors may opt to integrate family life education into their counseling practice.

Family life educators may be certified through several different agencies. Generally, individuals become certified following a series of training programs and the successful completion of the certified family life educator exam. Educators are required to demonstrate a certain number of continuing education hours every 5 years in order to become recertified. These continuing education hours may be accrued by attending relevant conferences, workshops or successfully completing a course, to name a few.

CFLE Content Areas for Certification

According to the NCFR, to become certified as a family life educator, individuals are to demonstrate competency in various family life education content areas. These include the following:

1. Families and individuals in societal contexts
2. Internal dynamics of families
3. Human growth and development across the life span
4. Human sexuality
5. Interpersonal relationships
6. Family resource management
7. Parent education and guidance
8. Family law and public policy
9. Professional ethics and practice
10. Family life education methodology

The benefits of becoming a certified family life educator include boosting one's credibility as a family life educator and validating one's experience, skills, and knowledge. In addition, holding the credential endorses the value of the prevention model and also provides an avenue to network with other professionals in the field.

Career Opportunities

Family life educators are employed in a variety of settings including health care settings, educational settings, correctional and rehabilitative programs, faith-based programs, social service agencies, corporate settings, government agencies, retirement communities, and the military. More specific options include business, consumer and family resources services, community-based social services, early childhood education, family intervention, government and public policy, health care and family wellness, and international education and development. According to the NCFR, family life educators generally have the following employment options:

- Practice: this includes teaching, education, research, and program development
- Administration: this includes leadership or management positions, organizing, and coordinating

- Promotion: this includes, lobbying, public policy, advocating for system change and awareness

Family life educators provide families with the tools needed to improve or sustain relationships through prevention, education, and collaboration among professionals, families, and communities. Individuals from various professional backgrounds may become family life educators through appropriate training and experience. Generally speaking, family life educators plan, implement, and evaluate educational programs that are designed to improve the quality of family relationships. The work of family life educators is largely based on the premise that all families can benefit from education and enrichment programs and not just those currently experiencing difficulties.

Wendy L. Greenidge

See also Empowerment in Families; Marriage Education; Marriage Enrichment; Parenting Education; Relationship Enhancement; Stress Management

Further Readings

Ballard, S., & Taylor, A. (2011). *Family life education with diverse populations.* Thousand Oaks, CA: Sage.

Bredehoft, D. J., & Cassidy, D. (Eds.). (1995). *Family life education curriculum guidelines* (2nd ed.). Minneapolis, MN: National Council on Family Relations.

Bredehoft, D. J., & Walcheski, M. J. (Eds.). (2003). *Family life education: Integrating theory and practice.* Minneapolis, MN: National Council on Family Relations.

Bredehoft, D. J., & Walcheski, M. J. (Eds.). (2011). *The family life education framework poster and PowerPoint.* Minneapolis, MN: National Council on Family Relations.

Darling, C. A., & Cassidy, D. (2014). *Family life education: Working with families across the life span.* Long Grove, IL: Waveland Press.

Duncan, S., & Goddard, W. (2010). *Family life education: Principles and practices for effective outreach.* Thousand Oaks, CA: Sage.

National Council on Family Relations. (2014). *Family life education content areas: Content and practice guidelines.* Minneapolis, MN: Author.

National Council on Family Relations. (2015). *Careers in family science.* Minneapolis, MN: Author.

Powell, L. H., & Cassidy, D. (2007). *Family life education: Working with families across the life span.* Long Grove, IL: Waveland Press.

Family Mediation

Family mediation is a rapidly growing and complex field used as a method of intervention between two or more family members involving a myriad of issues. At its core, family mediation is composed of a diverse group of providers ranging from attorneys to those specialties involved in family practice and family therapy. These providers are paramount to appropriate dispute resolution and facilitation. Effective mediation can deescalate conflicts and amplify understandings. Family mediators face many challenges in managing a wide range of conflicts on family matters. This discussion on family mediation will cover the history of family mediation, basic tenets of family mediation, mediation versus counseling, types of conflict resolution involved with family mediation, and who benefits from family mediation. It will also cover different forms and the principles of mediation as well as steps for conducting family mediation and diversity and counselor competencies in family mediation.

History of Family Mediation

Mediation as it is known in the United States had its origins with the Quakers, or more correctly, the Society of Friends, founded in England by George Fox in the 17th century. Their traditional testimonies of nonaggression, social equality, integrity, and simplicity shaped the foundation of mediation. It was the absolute simplicity of its foundation and historic albeit often behind-the-scenes success that led to the adoption of the concept of mediation during the Industrial Revolution of the 18th and 19th centuries. It is often said that the Quakers were the first and oldest mediation organization in the world.

Basic Tenets of Family Mediation

The family is a system and responds to almost all conventional systems theory approaches. Like other family therapies, family mediation is used when a problem can clearly not be solved without the cooperation of an impartial outside party. Sibling rivalry, marital conflict, or intergenerational conflicts are examples of reasons for family mediation.

A family mediator uses progressive, nonconfrontational methods in an unbiased manner to intervene in situations for an agreeable outcome or behavioral change. This collaborative method of negotiation assists families and family members with improving relationships, preventing fights, and initiating respectful communications. This intervention style helps to resolve conflict by assisting family members in understanding each other's point of view. Family mediation is a client-centered approach that uses interventions that are future focused and problem-solving strategies rather than revisiting incongruent behaviors of the past.

Family mediation usually requires a series of meetings with the counselor and the family to discuss communication, conflict resolution, and any other problem areas that need to be addressed. Family mediators are trained to be able to assist family members in facilitating discussions, decision-making, outcome resolution, and any number of other problems through brainstorming, active, and attentive listening.

Due to the nature of mediation, especially family mediation, topics can be emotionally charged. Family mediators should encourage the family members to talk openly and honestly about their feelings. However, increased emotion is not a desirable goal, since the main focus of the mediation is to come to practical agreements. The mediator can recommend individual counseling to family members and provide referrals to other counselors.

Mediation Versus Counseling

Mediators in family mediation do not take sides and should always be available for all family members. Mediators do not give advice; they give information and offer guidance. If in the course of a mediation the mediator finds that there is sufficient evidence to believe a client is in need of psychological therapeutic assistance, such assistance should be found outside of the mediator's practice. Ideally, the person would see another counselor to avoid a dual relationship. This could be viewed as an impropriety. A mediator can provide referrals to a counselor if needed.

Types of Conflict Resolution

Family mediations may raise a variety of issues, including possibly mental health ones. Keep in mind mediation is designed to be used as a family-friendly method of resolving issues. Some of the most common issues found in mediation include emotional abuse, unhappy marriages, forgiving an unfaithful spouse, and letting go of anger. Family mediation also deals with financial issues, such as impulsive spending, financial realities, financial planning, and taking control of money issues. Family mediation can also be used for changing parenting styles, dealing with stepchildren, dealing with addictions, and dealing with social media use.

Who Benefits From Family Mediation?

Family mediation is beneficial for all family members but can be tailored to suit couples, siblings, sibling groups, whole families, extended family, and individual family members. Family mediation should always involve those central to the dispute. At times, other individuals may want to participate who are not central to the dispute. However, those involved in the dispute are the best ones to resolve it.

Family mediation can benefit anyone committed to resolving differences within a family, or anyone who has influence on the family. This method can also be used to resolve disputes between different families. For example, Romeo and Juliet would have benefited from family mediation. The technique would have established the positive results from nonaggressive interaction and effective communication over the negative incongruities perpetuated by learned behaviors.

Family mediation also benefits the participants by lessening the negative emotional impact by resolving disputes in a controlled environment. The mediator should create and foster an atmosphere of goal-oriented mutual resolution to make the session as stress free as possible. The collaborative effort of the parents and authority figures will also have a more favorable impression on the children of the family.

Forms of Family Mediation

Family mediation can also involve litigation. In this form, the conflicting family members work to resolve their issues with the help of the neutral third-party mediator. In this instance, the parties will come together, either through court order or voluntarily, and discuss their issues in a neutral setting that has the benefit of confidentiality, guidance, controlled environment, and mutual support. Typically, this form of family mediation is used in situations of marital separation or divorce.

Parent coordination is another aspect of family mediation. During this type of mediation, the parent and child need to resolve conflicts and disputes. Family mediation in this setting involves implementing positive parenting skills, education, and communication skills. The ultimate aim of this role is to protect and sustain healthy and meaningful parent–child relationships. Some of the tools used in this type of family mediation are developing and implementing a parenting plan, monitoring compliance, and resolution of the conflicting behaviors and situations in a meaningful and effective manner.

The Principles Used in Family Mediation

In order for successful implementation, all participants and family members must adhere to basic principles of family mediation. First of all, the mediator does not make any decisions. The family members themselves work out what applications they think will take the issues forward. The proposals will only be binding if the proper authorities (i.e., an attorney or judge) create a legally binding agreement. A second principle is that the mediator does not judge, criticize, disparage, or try to censure any other family member. Third, the mediator does not attempt to exercise power or control over any other family member through the use of anger, name calling, intimidation, influence, coercion, or manipulation. Finally, a mediator is to treat all family members with dignity and respect.

Steps for Conducting Family Mediation

Step One: Identifying Issues

The family mediator will commence with an opening statement that is adapted from informed consent documents and will include confidentiality. The mediator will also establish communication ground rules for the session. The mediator will emphasize the importance of being open-minded and honest as well as the idea that they are volunteering to be present for the entire session. At the conclusion of the opening comments, the family mediator will invite participants to say what issues and challenges need to be addressed.

The mediator will take notes throughout the mediation, including details about the specific issues being raised. This is a concerted effort to keep the mediation on track. The list is usually written in a sequential numeric order. This list can then be prioritized or discussed as listed. In some cases, the issues are written on a whiteboard or on a flip chart.

It is significant that as the list is being written, the mediator uses reflective listening as needed in order to clarify meaning. If the problems are emotionally charged, the participants may become too verbal and so the mediator should use basic skills such as reflective statements, check to see if the person feels understood, and then direct the participants back to the issues.

One method of determining the importance of the issues is to ask each member to state the issue listed that he or she thinks needs to be addressed first. The mediator will make a tick by the issue selected by participants then underscore the ones with the most ticks; this becomes the first topic for solution development.

Step Two: Creating Solutions

The mediator will then ask for possible solutions to the areas in dispute. Once again the mediator is keeping notes on what is discussed and by whom. The family member will discuss as many probable courses of action or resolutions that they can think of, without judgment or criticism. In order to increase the number of ideas, large groups can break into small groups or dyads.

Once the family or participants have concluded brainstorming, the mediator will bring everyone together to discuss the possible solutions. The mediator will guide the discussion and keep written notes on the probable resolutions.

Step Three: Reaching a Creative Agreement

The mediator, using mediation skills to come to a consensus, guides a discussion of the pros and cons of each possible solution. The family will debate and come to an amicable agreement on what should be done to resolve the dispute or issue. The mediator will then get acknowledgment that the solution is agreeable to all involved. There are many variations on this technique, but the important thing is to keep the interaction between participants civil and amenable.

Step Four: Concluding the Mediation

The mediator and the parties can choose to have something signed in writing by them or not. The mediator may write a synopsis of what the parties agreed to and have them sign. When litigation is involved, the mediator or the attorney may write an agreement that will be signed by the parties and possibly notarized. The mediator always thanks the parties for participating in the process and suggests a follow-up session if needed.

Diversity and Counselor Competencies in Family Mediation

Family mediation is just one style or technique used in family therapy. Therefore, just as with any other form of counseling, the counselor must also display a firm grasp of fundamental competencies in counseling. The counselor's in-depth understanding of the effects of diversity is of paramount importance in the family mediation process.

How the family mediator deals with an Asian family can be profoundly different from working with, say, an African American family. Cultural factors strongly influence the way families function and different cultures have different understandings of the roles of family members. Each culture may have values and norms specific to that culture.

The family mediator should consider the developmental aspects of children in the family, the gender of each person, and the ages of each person. The mediator will also have to take into consideration the overall health of the individual and the family. Another major issue that must be considered is the socioeconomic status of the family.

If values, culture, or religion is the source of the dispute in mediation, the mediator should understand that change will most likely not occur. For example, if parents believe that their son should go to church every Sunday because that is what their religion tells them, this is not a conviction they are likely to surrender. In this case, the mediator must find positive common ground between the parties and help them accept the things that will not change. In order for this to occur, the mediator must be familiar with the intricacies of the family's background, culture, and morals.

Family mediation issues and topics can vary widely. So too can styles of mediation. A mediator should keep in mind the basic tenets of mediation and its desired goals. This will help ensure a successful outcome for the parties.

Kristin Page, Vance Walker, and Richard Williams

See also Divorce and Separation; Dual and Multiple Relationships; Legal Issues in Parenting; Marriage, First and Second

Further Readings

Beck, C. J., & Sales, B. D. (2001). *Family mediation: Facts, myths, and future prospects.* Washington, DC: American Psychological Association.

Emery, R. E. (2011). *Renegotiating family relationships: Divorce, child custody, and mediation.* New York, NY: Guilford Press.

Hanson, M. J. (2006). Moving forward together: The LGBT community and the family mediation field. *Pepperdine Dispute Resolution Law Journal, 6,* 295.

Katz, E. (2007). A family therapy perspective on mediation. *Family Process, 46*(1), 93–107.

Lemmon, J. A. (2008). *Family mediation practice.* New York, NY: Simon & Schuster.

Roberts, M. M. (2014). *Mediation in family disputes: Principles of practice.* Farnham, England: Ashgate.

Family Mode Deactivation Therapy

Family mode deactivation therapy focuses on the elimination of emotional dysfunction, undesirable cognitions, and inappropriate behaviors in adolescents and their families. This form of psychotherapy utilizes systematic, goal-oriented processes in order to allow the individual to recognize and modify dysfunctional cognitive modes. Family mode deactivation therapy (FMDT) is an offshoot of mode deactivation therapy (MDT), which was originally created by psychologist Jack Apsche as a means to more effectively treat adolescents with complex issues, including conduct disorder, sexual and physical aggression, and emotional dysfunction. This entry examines the theoretical underpinnings of FMDT, its effectiveness, core concepts, and key treatment strategies.

The Theoretical Basis

FMDT is theoretically based in the cognitive theory of Aaron Beck and the rational emotive theory of Albert Ellis. Apsche's development of MDT was intended to build on the strengths of Beck's cognitive-behavioral therapy while decreasing treatment resistance. Additionally, Apsche's intention was to create a therapy that would increase effectiveness for adolescents with serious coexisting diagnoses. Cognitive-behavioral therapy (CBT) primarily focuses on irrational cognitions and is present focused rather than attempting to pinpoint underlying causes of the irrational cognitions. Apsche, however, asserted that investigating the significance of the root causes of irrational cognitions allows the client to understand that their thought processes are valid considering the experiences on which they have constructed their beliefs.

Schemas and Modes

FMDT explores the cognitive modes that develop as a result of an individual's experiences. Modes are enduring behavioral responses created when an individual's coping methods become maladaptive as a result of their irrational cognitions and schemas. Cognitive schemas allow us to interpret and react to the enormous amounts of information encountered in everyday life. Essentially, schemas provide a context that allows the individual to focus on information and ideas that substantiate preexisting beliefs. Cognitive schemas are automatic reactions to the environment, and they often group together to create cognitive modes. In other words, when individuals develop irrational cognitions based on their experiences, the cognitions merge to create cognitive modes that drive behavior. FMDT differs from CBT in the way cognitive modes are approached. CBT views dysfunctional modes as irrational; however, FMDT views dysfunctional modes as being a natural response to difficult experiences. The suggestion is that dysfunctional modes are to be understood and accepted before they can be changed. Encouraging the understanding of how these modes were developed increases rapport between therapist and client and increases client motivation in the therapeutic process.

Effectiveness of FMDT

MDT has been found to be effective in the treatment of adolescents with sexually aggressive behavior, physical aggression, conduct disorder, and recidivism. Beginning in 2006, Apsche began to integrate MDT into family therapy in order to treat the family systems of adolescents and to create a sustainable decrease in symptoms. Family mode deactivation therapy, building off of Bowenian systems theory, treats the family (rather than the individual) as the client with the understanding that the family is an emotional unit which impacts the thoughts and feelings of the unit as well as each individual within the unit. The focus of FMDT is on identifying dysfunctional emotions, cognitions, and behaviors and applying a specific, systematic goal process.

Apsche first began to incorporate MDT into family therapy with an adolescent by the name of David, a developmentally delayed 13-year-old in residential treatment for sex offenders. David began MDT and over a course of several months, he began to cultivate new belief systems using the techniques he developed in therapy. As David began to move from dichotomous to balanced thinking, he began to share his insights with his family. The family was encouraged to utilize the techniques David had learned as they noted the changes in his thought patterns and behaviors. The authors hypothesized that the methods utilized in MDT could also be used collaboratively in family therapy. Since this original hypothesis, Apsche and others have conducted multiple studies regarding the efficaciousness of FMDT.

Core Concepts

FMDT utilizes three fundamental concepts: experiential avoidance, defusion, and mindfulness. *Experiential avoidance* differs from acceptance in that individuals engaging in experiential avoidance are reluctant to delve into emotions or cognitions that may be psychologically painful. When individuals find acceptance to be problematic, the end result is often the inability to employ flexibility in response to adverse situations and difficulty in choosing appropriate behaviors. The continued use of experiential avoidance as a coping mechanism increases psychological symptoms and negative behaviors. FMDT seeks to address the issues of experiential avoidance through the individual's schemas and core beliefs, viewing the avoidance as a conflict between external demands and core beliefs resulting in the individual experiencing fear. Schemas are a way of organizing and interpreting cognitive perceptions, which help people categorize information in order to form expectations. Schemas are viewed in FMDT as being rational and sensible in light of past experiences; however, schemas must be brought into the individual's and family's awareness in order to begin the process of defusion.

The next core concept, *defusion,* builds upon and expands the definition which was first explored in acceptance and commitment therapy (ACT). The ACT definition of *defusion* focuses on neutralizing or resolving undesirable neural loops; in other words, it focuses on identifying destructive thought patterns and substituting thought patterns that are more functional. Neural loops develop when thoughts become fused with emotions leading to automatic reactions and may result in behaviors which are inappropriate for the context. For example, a child who has experienced abuse may become overly fearful or defensive when an adult expresses negative emotions. Defusing the initial thoughts is a technique that allows the individual to separate the thought from the automatic reaction by learning to accept their thoughts as literal. Based on the hypothesis that experiential avoidance encompasses a combination of thoughts and fears, FMDT builds on ACT's cognitive defusion by adding the element of emotional defusion. Emotional defusion identifies emotions connected with avoidance cognitions and pinpoints where the individual feels emotional pain in the body. Identifying and defusing both thoughts and emotions allows family members to accept those thoughts and emotions as valid parts of each individual within the family.

Mindfulness, the third core concept in FMDT, is rooted in Buddhist practices of enlightenment and meditation. Mindfulness is the purposeful focusing of awareness in the present in an accepting and nonjudgmental manner. Three specific mindfulness approaches are utilized with families: guided imagery, engagement, and short activities. Guided imagery is the practice of guiding clients through the visualization of imagery in order to increase relaxation and focus. It incorporates all of the senses and often includes the use of metaphor to engage the unconscious mind. Engagement is the process of focusing on the present moment while nonjudgmentally accepting all of one's thoughts and feelings. Although guided imagery and mindfulness practices can sometimes be time-consuming, FMDT features short activities which have been found to be as effective as more lengthy exercises.

Validation, Clarification, and Redirection

One of the key treatment strategies of FMDT is the use of VCR: validation, clarification, and redirection. The VCR strategy is unique to the mode deactivation approach and is designed to identify and create equilibrium in the individual and family belief systems. The VCR method exposes irrational cognitions deeply rooted in the family system and allows the therapist to teach family members how to rebalance their beliefs through integration of the core concepts of mindfulness, acceptance, and defusion with the strategies of validation, clarification, and redirection.

The fundamental principle of validation is the acceptance of each person's thoughts and beliefs as authentic, valid, and understandable in the context of their past and present circumstances. The therapist actively endeavors to communicate acceptance and understanding without discounting or trivializing. A technique referred to as the "grain of truth" is used by therapists when the goal is to reveal what is valid in the client's response and then amplify and reinforce that validity.

Clarification is a critical step in recognizing and altering long-held cognitive schemas of the individual and the family. Clarification bolsters rapport with the therapist and increased trust, empathy, and understanding between family members. During group sessions, the therapist leads the family in a discussion of their personal perceptions of the individual and familial experiences. The family is then guided in identifying and clarifying values and motivations for each individual and the family as a whole. In the final step of clarification, the therapist leads the family through a process of deliberating on alternative thoughts and beliefs with the intention of creating individual and family goals.

The redirection component of the VCR strategy encourages families to understand that their fundamental beliefs are valid and understandable but may not be effective or beneficial. This concept is rooted in principles of dialectical behavior therapy, which emphasizes the balancing of dichotomous thinking. Families are led through a process of brainstorming thoughts that may be incorporated as alternatives to their automatic cognitions. In the course of creating a variety of possible thoughts, family members are encouraged to note any changes, no matter how small, in their emotions, belief systems, and behaviors. This progression from thinking dichotomously to encompassing a variety of possibilities allows family members to acquire skill in identifying exceptions and positive changes. Redirection is particularly beneficial for guiding family members with differing belief systems into a new understanding of themselves and each other.

FMDT research up to this point shows promise but is somewhat limited by the number and scope of studies which have been conducted. The number of participants in the studies has been small and the research has been primarily focused on families of adolescent males. Further research with families of female adolescents and young children would be beneficial and informative. Although FMDT appears to be a promising new treatment modality, further research is needed to create a clearer picture of the effectiveness of the therapy.

Janna C. Ramsey

See also Cognitive-Behavioral Family Therapy; Conduct Disorder; Mindfulness

Further Readings

Apsche, J. A., & Bass, C. K. (2006). Family mode deactivation therapy results and implications. *International Journal of Behavioral Consultation and Therapy, 2*(3), 375–381. doi:10.1037/h0100791

Apsche, J. A., Bass, C. K., & Houston, M. (2007). Family mode deactivation therapy as a manualized cognitive behavioral therapy treatment. *International Journal of Behavioral Consultation and Therapy, 4*(2), 264–277. doi:10.1037/h0100848

Apsche, J. A., Ward, S. R., & Evile, M. M. (2003). Mode deactivation: A functionally based treatment, theoretical constructs. *The Behavior Analyst Today, 3*(4), 455–459. doi:10.1037/h0100002

Bayles, C., Blossom, P., & Apsche, J. A. (2014). A brief review and update of mode deactivation therapy. *International Journal of Behavioral Consultation and Therapy, 9*(1), 46–48. doi:10.1037/ho101016

Swart, J., & Apsche, J. A. (2014). Mindfulness, mode deactivation, and family therapy: A winning combination for treating adolescents with complex trauma and behavioral problems. *International Journal of Behavioral Consultation and Therapy, 9*(2), 9–14. doi:10.1037/h0100992

Family Myth

A family is a system of people who are connected by blood, marriage, adoption, or shared commitment to maintain a mutual relationship. The family system is the primary context of individual development. No matter the structure or the amount of time individuals spend with their families, families are one of the most powerful influences on an individual's development. A family's socialization of children begins before a child is born and is influenced by the ways in which each partner views family. As partners negotiate their roles in the family, they influence the socialization of their children. Socialization of family members is influenced by "family myths." Each family has beliefs about itself, and the stories about itself that the family constructs, which includes its beliefs, are called *family myths*. Sometimes these stories are helpful to individuals and their families and sometimes they constrain them. These stories are told over and over again and directly and/or indirectly tell family members how to behave. This entry describes the nature of myths in general and the ways in which family and family myths influence individual and familial development. The entry concludes with a discussion of the implications of family myths for counseling practice.

The task of socializing children is a primary role of families. As children are socialized within their families, family values and family myths are transmitted. The values and myths passed down to children from their parents shape their individual perspective, personality, and worldview. Therefore an individual's lifestyle is shaped by the myths to which families subscribe. A myth, in general terms, is a traditional story or legendary account of a larger-than-life hero or event; they often explain a practice, rite, or phenomenon of nature. More specifically, family myths are beliefs or a system of beliefs held by families even though they are not "true." For example, in a family where physical abuse is happening: "We just use tough love. It's strong discipline so that we have strong children." Or in a family where there are secrets: "Family loyalty is everything." Family myths influence behavior and perception and leave a space for children to connect to their parents; at the same time, however, behaviors that contradict myths are often seen as threatening.

Myths

While elements of myths may appear actual or real, myths typically contain elements of fiction. Because they are situated in both fiction and reality, some experts consider myths as the intersection of literature (fiction) and anthropology (culture). Though fictions and fabrications are known elements of myths, individuals view myths as ideals or truths and often use them as an instrument to judge and construct reality. Furthermore, myths are the cognitive structures individuals use to activate schemas and help make meaning. They capture and reflect the complex belief system of the author and embed overarching themes into sacred narratives.

It is precisely the sacredness of the narrative and implications these mythical accounts have for a community that make myths different from other family story lines. While myths vary in the amount of truth included, one professional, John Byng-Hall, described three typical types of myths and the ways they influence individuals' ability to make meaning. They include myths of the *ideal self-image, consensus role images,* and *repudiated role images.* Ideal self-image myths encompass behaviors everyone is pressured to adopt. Examples of ideal self-image myths include a traditional view of marriage, with the union of one male partner (husband) and one female partner (wife). This myth is furthered when, after marriage, the husband and wife have children, which they raise together. When individuals subscribe to the ideal self-image myth, they base their value on their role as a husband or wife and parent. While ideal self-image myths encompass the behaviors individuals are pressured to adopt, consensus role images include the myths associated with the roles individuals agree that they occupy. Examples of consensus role images include the tasks and division of labor individuals believe they must perform based on their title of wife, husband, mother, and/or father. These myths look at traditional roles of family members and may perpetuate falsehoods about the ways in which wives and husbands act. For example, a family may struggle with the myth of consensus role images if the mother works outside the home, while the father stays at home with the children. Since the actions of family members are different from the myths perpetuated by media and other social influences, family members may struggle with consensus role images.

Myths associated with repudiated role images are those related to proscribed behaviors and attitudes of the family. These myths typically involve longstanding family traditions or practices. Individuals who diverge from or reject their family's religious beliefs, for example, may struggle to find and affirm an identity outside the family status quo, whether or not they choose to affiliate with a different religious tradition. For members of a family, repudiated role images can cause anxiety and skew the meaning-making process for individuals.

Erroneous beliefs or myths held by family members, particularly children, are examples of symbolic statements that must be demythologized (explored and analyzed in order to understand their influence). Demythologization is necessary if family members are to recognize and understand the meaning of the original myth. When meanings of myths are explored and deconstructed, families have an opportunity to make meaning in different ways.

Family Myths

While counselors debate the definition of myth, most agree that family myths, like literary myths, are based on half-truths and socially constructed images. Family myths help convey the family context and, while they do not accurately account for the past, family myths are effective stories used to convey values handed down from ancestors. Family myths are deeply rooted and represent the ways families appear to each other and to those on the outside.

Traditional family myths address transitions (i.e., birth and death), separation (i.e., divorce or leaving for college), and rivalry (i.e., competition between siblings or partners). While most myths express fundamental values and act as a moral compass for future generations, family conflicts almost always revolve around interpretation and perceptions of family myths. Accordingly, close inspection of family myths can provide insight into family problems.

Transmitted from one generation to the next, family myths act as guidelines for behaviors of family members. At times, family myths aid in familial development because they provide examples of strength and perseverance through crisis. However, more often than not, family myths include societal messages that perpetuate and preserve idealized, prescriptive images of family reality, for example, the narrative that idealizes the construct of the American nuclear family as a marriage between man and woman that produces children, although there are many U.S. households that do not conform to this image. These constructs, however, often go unchallenged.

Implications for Practice

Though uncovering the myths that undergird family perception can be challenging and tedious, counselors can encourage clients to first identify the myths to which their families subscribe. Identification of myths can provide clients and counselors an opportunity to elucidate the often unspoken and previously unidentified myths that shape the perception of family life. Genograms or family diagrams are tools counselors can use to prompt the discussion of family myths. As clients map out their family history and consider the interplay of values and behaviors among generations of family members, counselors and clients can look for overarching themes that influence family myths. Genograms often provide counselors with insight into families' structures and systems. As clients talk through and examine their genograms, myths begin to surface. As the client and counselor work together to deconstruct stories of the past, myths become less psychologically compelling and mysterious to the client. As clients are better able to identify and understand the myths that undergird their family, they are more likely to understand the origin of their values and beliefs. This knowledge brings insight into the meaning-making process for families, thus creating a space for families to consider the myths that are embedded in their stories and that influence their perception of family.

The family myth represents a constructed narrative, often perpetuated through family history and media that emphasizes the importance of family tradition and maintenance of the status quo. Within family myths, outsiders are easily identified as their differences are often viewed from a deficit perspective. While most families rely on myths to outline common practices, the myths associated with each family differ depending on the influences and worldviews of each member. Deconstructing family myths leads to greater individualization and gives family members space to consider differences as acceptable, rather than as evidence of deficits.

Sarah Jones

See also Beliefs and Values; Genograms; Intergenerational Loyalty; Intergenerational Trauma

Further Readings

Byng-Hall, J. (1973). Family myths used as defense in conjoint family therapy. *British Journal of Medical Psychology, 46*(3), 239–250.

Cuskelly, M. (2009). Challenging the myths and redressing the missteps in family research. *Journal of Policy and Practice in Intellectual Disabilities, 6*(2), 86–88. doi:10.1111/j.1741-1130.2009.00211.x

Feinstein, D., & Krippner, S. (1989). Personal myths: In the family way. *Journal of Psychotherapy & the Family, 4*(3/4), 111–140.

Ferreira, A. J. (1966). Family myths. *Psychiatric Research Reports of the American Psychiatric Association, 20,* 85–90.

Holle, K. A. (2005). Myth and legend in family therapy: Maintaining the distinction between the sacred and secular in family process. *Contemporary Family Therapy, 27*(4), 507–519.

Kradin, R. (2009). The family myth: Its deconstruction and replacement with a balanced humanized narrative. *Journal of Analytical Psychology, 54*(2), 217–232.

Nicoll, W. G., & Hawes, E. C. (2013). Family lifestyle assessment: The role of family myths and values in the client's presenting issues. *Techniques in Adlerian Psychology, 41*(2), 147–160.

Pillari, V. (1986). *Pathways to family myths.* Ipswich, MA: Family & Society Studies Worldwide.

van der Hart, O., Witztum, E., & de Voogt, A. (1988). Myths and rituals: Anthropological views and their application in strategic family therapy. *Journal of Psychotherapy and the Family, 4*(3/4), 57–80.

Family of Origin

The term *family* has many different definitions but is usually used to describe a unit composed of parents, caretakers, siblings, or other individuals who played a significant role in a person's upbringing. *Family of origin,* another term referring to the immediate and extended family a person grows up in, is responsible for teaching an individual important information about who they are, how to act, and what beliefs and values to adopt. Additionally, the family of origin may also pass down cultural traditions, practices, behaviors, and genetics that contribute to the makeup of an individual. The intention of this entry is to discuss family-of-origin topics relevant to the field of marriage and family therapy. These include, but are not limited to, intergenerational transmission of relational and cultural patterns, beliefs about relationships and dating, and family therapy theories.

Family Therapy and Family of Origin

The field of marriage and family therapy assumes that individuals cannot be understood apart from others, which resulted in the need for relational models of therapy. Based on the assumptions of family systems theory, marriage and family therapists (MFTs) view families as being interconnected and interdependent and individuals cannot be understood in isolation from their families. Each member plays a role and has rules to respect within their family. Families also create boundaries and specific patterns of interaction develop within the family that create certain behaviors; these behaviors may lead to healthy stability in the family or to dysfunction. Theorists in the field have various ideas about how an individual's family of origin contributes to healthy or unhealthy interpersonal relationships, styles of communication, and coping with life's changes.

Family of origin is an important concept to the field of marriage and family therapy, and helps therapists and clients explore the ways in which families teach individuals how to act, how to communicate, and who they are. Marriage and family therapists use genograms to explore patterns or problematic behaviors that may be passed on through each generation, such as violence, substance use disorders, mental health issues, divorce, and beliefs about dating and relationships.

Assessments

In the early stages of the therapeutic process, therapists will collect information from clients to assess the nature of the presenting problem, which may include information about the presenting problem, attempted solutions to the problem, issues of harm (e.g., suicide ideation, family violence, duty to warn), and substance abuse. These assessments help the therapist create a specific treatment plan for working with the clients. Additionally, therapists may gather information about family of origin to provide insight about the problems presented in therapy.

One way that MFTs gather information about clients' family of origin is to create a genogram. A genogram is a visual map that uses standardized symbols to map out several generations of a family, specifying information, such as family structure and composition, boundaries and relationships between family members, substance use and mental health issues, spiritual and religious beliefs, and other important information about a family. The genogram is also helpful to clients, as it provides detailed information about how family patterns such as divorce or family violence may be transmitted across generations.

Intergenerational Transmission

Presenting problems in therapy may be a result of unhealthy patterns of behavior passed through generations. At times, unhealthy behaviors are normalized within a family and that cycle is adopted by future generations. Some of these unhealthy intergenerational patterns include, but are not limited to, intimate partner violence, substance abuse or dependency, mental health care issues, and divorce. Other important factors, which may be healthy or unhealthy, carried through multiple generations are cultural values, beliefs, and traditions.

Intimate Partner Violence

Communication styles and patterns are often modeled by one's family of origin. At times, these patterns do not portray healthy communication and involve anger, reactivity, and violence. For example, if a child grows up in a home where the primary caregivers communicate by yelling and escalate to physical aggression, the child may grow up believing that this is how they should behave in a relationship. The intergenerational transmission of violence is a frequently studied phenomenon, in which individuals who grow up in families where violence is present will legitimize violence and increase the likelihood that the children will perpetrate violence as adults. There is also a large body of research on what is called the cycle of violence, where a child who is victimized becomes an adult who perpetrates violence. Despite the empirical support for these phenomena, it is possible that a child who is exposed to intimate partner violence or is a childhood victim of violence may see the behavior as problematic and detrimental to the family system and work toward healthier communication patterns. It is helpful for a therapist to be aware of intergenerational patterns of family violence, as it could inform treatment and provide insight into the presenting problem.

Substance Use Disorders and Abuse

Substance use disorders (SUD) can be passed on throughout generations by normalizing the excessive use of substances, modeling an unhealthy way of coping with one's problems, and/or by genetic components related to the development of an SUD. If an individual presents to therapy with substance or behavioral addiction-related issues, it is important to know whether or not there is a familial history of addiction. Family-of-origin information will inform the therapist about genetic traits that could be inherited, traumatic experiences, or cultural ideas about substance use and addiction. The risk of an individual developing an SUD is much more likely if they are genetically predisposed, if they have experienced trauma, or if their family or culture is supportive of the consumption of a certain substance.

Mental Health

Clinicians should collect a family-of-origin mental health history from their clients in order to enhance understanding about potential genetic risks of developing or having a mental health disorder. For example, if a client presents symptoms of depression in therapy, it may be helpful to know whether or not the client has a family history of depression. It is also important for a clinician to know about a history of suicide attempts or medication that a family member was prescribed for mental health-related diagnoses. Understanding family-of-origin suicide attempts is exceptionally important because an individual who has a close family member die from suicide is considerably more likely to attempt suicide.

Divorce

Another pattern that is prevalent in today's society is divorce. When collecting family history information, it is important to understand the primary caregiver's relationship dynamics from the perspective of the client. Divorce, depending on the circumstances, can be traumatic for a child. Children have to learn coping skills to adapt to a significant family change and, depending on the client, there might be significant religious or cultural implications. Additionally, if divorce is something that is modeled for children, it may increase the likelihood of the future generation's relationships to end in divorce.

Culture and Beliefs

An integral part of any family is culture, or cultural beliefs, values, and traditions. Cultural identities are often passed through multiple generations. Those who challenge the cultural values of their family of origin tend to experience discomfort, associated with the process of change and growth, and this discomfort may motivate someone to seek professional help. Sensitivity to the unique cultural dynamics that each individual client may be a part of is paramount to therapy and appropriately connecting with clients and their unique needs. An example of why someone may struggle within their family of origin due to cultural beliefs is a client who is struggling with identifying as a sexual minority but whose family's culture believes that sexual orientation is a choice and does not support same-sex intimate relationships or marriage. This client would feel torn between his or her family's cultural beliefs and his or her sexual identity.

Because these belief systems from our family of origin are engrained in our everyday way of functioning, we may not acknowledge when they are helpful or harmful. While some may want to step away from these intergenerational patterns and beliefs, they still make up a significant part of someone's identity and one may be fearful of resistance from their family of origin for challenging ideas or beliefs. Drawing attention to these intergenerational cultural patterns, whether they have been adopted or abandoned by the individual, can be helpful during the therapeutic process.

Relationships and Dating

Marriage and family therapists are trained to look at interpersonal relationships and see one individual as a part of something larger. It is not uncommon for an individual, couple, or family to come into therapy with issues surrounding romantic relationships, intimacy, or dating. It is important for the therapist to understand a client's beliefs and expectations in a relational context in order to inform treatment. Therapists may do so by asking about family-of-origin ideas and beliefs about dating, relationships, and marriage. When a couple comes into therapy, the therapist should develop an understanding of both partners' expectations and beliefs about relationships. In couples therapy, two sets of rules or belief systems about relationships and expectations come together to develop a new set of rules in the relationship. This merging of beliefs may be conflictual at times. For example, a couple may argue over which holiday traditions are the most significant, what each partner's role is in the relationship, parenting styles, or how money is managed. Even if both partners in a relationship have similar fundamental beliefs, there are still certain ideas or communication styles that are passed on throughout generations that can create conflict. MFTs are trained to gain a richer and more culturally competent understanding of clients in order to assist them in developing a skill set that can be used to manage issues or conflicts in their relationship.

MFT and Family of Origin

There are many ways a therapist may conceptualize presenting problems in therapy and the assessment and intervention with family of origin issues can be integrated with various couple and family therapy models. Although MFTs receive similar training, therapists differ in the model of therapy used in therapy. Each model of therapy assumes the inclusion and significance of family of origin–related problems in different ways. Some theorists believe that clinicians should have a strong understanding of a client's family of origin, whereas others find it to be less significant and focus therapy on other areas, such as on the client's future or societal influences on clients, and spend less or no time on transgenerational familial patterns. The following two sections review a model of therapy that prioritizes family of origin information, Bowenian family therapy, and a model of therapy that does not focus on family of origin, solution-focused therapy.

Bowenian Family Therapy

Bowenian family therapy stresses the importance of family of origin in treatment. The goal of Bowenian family therapy is to improve the intergenerational transmission process, which is accomplished by the therapist focusing on eight interconnected major theoretical constructs: differentiation, emotional system, multigenerational transmission process, emotional triangle, nuclear family, family projection process, sibling position, and societal regression. Of these eight concepts, the core concept is differentiation, which refers to one's ability to differentiate one's self from others (being independent) and the ability to differentiate one's feelings from one's intellectual process (one's emotions do not cloud one's decisions).

Although differentiation is the ultimate goal, other constructs explain why an individual may not be a fully differentiated individual. For example, an emotional triangle occurs when there is conflict between two members of a system (e.g., the parents or primary caregivers) and they involve a child in that conflict to diffuse the anxiety beyond the dyad. Within that system, a child holds less power than the primary caregivers and feels stuck in the middle, which creates dysfunction in the family system. This involvement may prevent the child from becoming a fully differentiated individual, capable of healthy relationships, and this pattern of managing anxiety can be transmitted to the child's adult relationships. While Bowenian family therapy believes that there is a significant need to gather information about a client's family and past, other family therapy models are more future focused and do not believe that such information is as necessary to promote lasting changes.

Solution-Focused Therapy

One model of family therapy that does not believe that the family of origin is significant is solution-focused therapy (SFT). SFT is designed to be a short-term form of therapy that focuses on identifying solutions to the clients' presenting problem, is goal directed, and is future focused. This theory assumes that clients are capable of change and that each client has the skills necessary to make changes. The SFT therapist structures therapy to be focused on the present or future and does not spend time exploring a client's past, due to the assumption that past talk keeps clients in what SFT therapists refer to as "the language of problems." A focus on problems is assumed to prevent clients from seeing possible solutions and resolving their presenting problem. In this model of therapy, the therapist would explore previous solutions, exceptions to the client's problem (times when the problem was not present), and help the client do more of what is working. Thus, an exploration of family of origin dynamics is not conducted by SFT therapists, as the information is not needed to create change based on the assumptions of this model of therapy.

Sarah Schonian and Jaclyn D. Cravens

See also Clinical Practice; Conflict in Couples and Families; Family Rituals; Individual and Family Development; Presenting Problems; Systemic Family Therapy

Further Readings

Bowen, M. (1985). *Family therapy in clinical practice.* Lanham, MD: Rowman & Littlefield.

DeMaria, R., Weeks, G., & Hof, L. (2013). *Focused genograms: Intergenerational assessment of individuals, couples, and families.* New York, NY: Routledge.

Karam, E. A., Blow, A. J., Sprenkle, D. H., & Davis, S. D. (2014). Strengthening the systemic ties that bind: Integrating common factors into marriage and family therapy. *Journal of Marital and Family Therapy, 41*(2), 136–149.

McGoldrick, M., Gerson, R., & Petry, S. S. (2008). *Genograms: Assessment and intervention.* New York, NY: W. W. Norton.

FAMILY RECONSTRUCTION

Family reconstruction is a therapeutic intervention first developed by Virginia Satir in the 1960s. In its classical form, a family counselor guides a person, with family members present and participating, in dramatically reenacting significant family life events from the past. The purpose of these experiences is to gain a deeper insight into how unresolved issues from one's family of origin impact oneself and one's families in the present. The family reconstruction model assumes that people desire personal growth and that everyone has within them the inner resources needed to thrive. The model is informed by family systems theory, which asserts that every person in the larger family system affects every other person. The family reconstruction model also incorporates psychodrama or role-playing, which was first pioneered by Jacob Moreno. In this model, the therapist often uses aspects of Gestalt therapy, hypnosis, and family sculpting. The family counselor initiates, teaches, and facilitates this process but does not dictate it; the counselor encourages family members to collaborate with each other in achieving a greater sense of wellness. This is a creative process where family counselors use drama, metaphors, reframing, and humor as part of the learning experience. This entry examines the history of family reconstruction, how it assigns roles to different family members, and its relationship to both family sculpting and family mapping techniques.

History

Virginia Satir (1916–1988), an American social worker and author, conceived of family reconstruction as a transformational process where one gains a better connection with oneself by identifying and understanding the dysfunctional patterns learned from one's family of origin. In its classical form this could take many days and involve dozens or even hundreds of participants. Originally, family reconstruction involved reenacting three generations of family dynamics. A shorter version lasting 2 to 3 hours, developed in the 1980s, targeted the most significant life-changing events.

The Star

During the family reconstruction session, one person is identified as "the star," and it is this person who explores significant triumphs and tragedies throughout his or her life. The star begins by identifying and acting out the present family dynamic with family members before exploring past incidents. The process of acting out past events allows the star to make sense out of previously confusing past experiences. At the end, the star returns to the present to celebrate any new discoveries. When successfully facilitated, the star often finds peace and reconciliation with estranged family members even if those family members are not present during the reconstruction. The star resolves unfinished business from the past and is liberated from old patterns of behavior. The star learns to make better decisions in the present and takes responsibility for self. Self-esteem increases when the star learns to trust and respect himself or herself. Congruence and peace occur when the star experiences a state of harmony with the self and achieves freedom from past wounds.

In family reconstruction, the counselor is intensively engaged as a facilitator and helps family members recognize their coping patterns rather than focusing exclusively on past events or past behaviors. Through the role-plays, clients are reintegrated into their family of origin so that they can see themselves and other family members with a new and hopeful perspective. In addition, clients are encouraged to recognize their yearnings and set realistic expectations. As clients connect with their parents or other family members in the role-plays, they recognize that current negative patterns were learned but can be changed in the present. Also, clients begin to discover their own personhood apart from past negative dynamics.

The counselor helps the star find congruence between his or her outer and inner worlds. Experiential counselors encourage clients to examine their inner construction of experiences that happen in their interaction with others. These inner constructions evoke certain interactional responses between a person and important others and those interactions then influence inner constructions. Inner and outer worlds influence each other in a recursive manner. The model encourages the counselor to see the family reconstruction process like fluid and changing energy that moves the star toward healthy functioning. The star identifies his or her true self and desires in order to influence feelings, perceptions, and expectations. It is not the counselor who identifies the path; it is the star who discovers and chooses his or her own path, which leads to positive growth.

Family Sculpting

Family reconstruction often uses family sculpting. This intervention involves each family member taking a turn physically positioning other family members into various poses. Each pose or "sculpture" represents how that family member views the family. It is a nonverbal method for communicating difficult family dynamics that promotes empathy. Family members are also asked to reposition the family sculpture to represent how they would like their family to be. This creates a vision for change and mutual understanding. Family members may view their entrenched grievances in a new light through this process and recognize that change is possible. They may literally "see" their family differently and imagine new possibilities.

Family Mapping

Family reconstruction also involves family mapping, whereby information is collected on three generations. The counselor may "map" the family's historical information by diagramming it in some way on a board while the client describes it, or the client may "sculpt" the historical information in a creative way (using art, stuffed animals, action figures, actual people, etc.) in order to externalize his or her perceptions of self and others. Sometimes the family mapping and reconstruction occurs purposefully in a triadic group, which imitates the structure of father, mother, and child. Early negative childhood communication patterns are identified. The counselor then helps the client to "resculpt" or reconstruct patterns and events in an effort to create new possibilities that involve self-nurturing behaviors and cooperative rather than competitive dynamics. Essentially, the client gains the ability to experience the healthy dynamic that they needed but did not receive as a child. The process of reconstruction allows the client to take responsibility for his or her life and improves self-esteem.

Satir's family reconstruction model includes many positive themes including a belief that people can survive and thrive despite painful past traumas and tragedies. Family reconstruction promotes unconditional positive regard and each person's right to experience self-actualization. Reconstruction allows a person to discover why they stay stuck in negative coping patterns, which in turn promotes forgiveness, deeper levels of empathy, and personal transformation. Automatic survival patterns from the past that can interfere with healthy present functioning are identified. The client expresses the pain from the past in order to experience deep personal and spiritual healing. The reconstruction process itself allows for the client's inner strength to emerge, which brings about healing, change, and personal wholeness.

Gerry Ken Crete

See also Emotionally Focused Therapy for Couples; Enactments; Experiential Family Therapy; Gestalt Family Therapy; Virginia Satir Model

Further Readings

Beaudry, G. (2002). The family reconstruction process and its evolution to date: Virginia Satir's transformational process. *Contemporary Family Therapy, 24*(1), 79–91. doi:10.1023/A: 1014373605900

McLendon, J. A. (1999). The Satir system in action. In D. J. Wiener (Ed.), *Beyond talk therapy: Using movement and expressive techniques in clinical practice* (pp. 29–54). Washington, DC: American Psychological Association.

Nerin, W. (2002). Family reconstruction: The masterpiece of Virginia Satir. *Contemporary Family Therapy, 24*(1), 129–138. doi:10.1023/A:1014329823646

Satir, V. (1988). Family reconstruction: The family within—a group experience. *Journal for Specialists in Group Work, 13*(4). doi: 10.1080/ 01933928808411877

Satir, V., Banmen, J., Gerber, J., & Gomori, M. (1991). *The Satir model: Family therapy and beyond.* Palo Alto, CA: Science & Behavior Books.

FAMILY RESILIENCE

Resilience involves dynamic processes fostering positive adaptation in the context of significant adversity. The concept of resilience has come to the forefront in mental health and developmental science and practice over recent decades, largely focused on resilience in individuals. Studies of those who overcame harsh childhood conditions initially focused on personal traits or on constitutional hardiness. With expanded research, an interactive perspective emerged, recognizing that the impact of risk conditions or traumatic experiences could be outweighed by resilience-promoting variables in the family and social context. Notable for individuals' resilience is the crucial influence of supportive relationships, especially the role of models, and mentors (e.g., grandparents, coaches, or teachers) who believe in their worth and potential and encourage them to make the most of their lives.

A strengths-based family systems lens shifted focus from parental or family deficits to search for potential resources in the family relational network. Leading developers of family resilience theory, research, and practice, Hamilton McCubbin and Froma Walsh applied the concept of resilience to the family as a system. They extended models of family stress and coping and major research on well-functioning families to identify key transactional processes that facilitate the resilience of families and their members, including community, cultural, and spiritual connections. This entry examines the concept of family resilience, approaches to assessing family resilience, key factors in family resilience, and practice applications in a family resilience framework.

The Concept of Family Resilience

The concept of family resilience refers to the ability of the family as a functional system to withstand and rebound from adversity. Rather than a set of traits, it involves dynamic processes in overcoming challenges in highly stressful situations. A basic premise guiding this approach is that serious life crises and persistent adversity impact family functioning, with ripple effects to all members and their relationships. In turn, family processes influence the recovery and resilience of all members, their relationships, and the family unit. Strengthening the family's ability to master its immediate challenges also increases its resourcefulness in meeting future adversity.

Family studies find that although some families are shattered by crisis or persistent stresses, others surmount their challenges and emerge strengthened and more resourceful. For instance, the devastating death of a child heightens risks for parental divorce, yet couples that pull together in dealing with their tragedy report stronger relationships than before. Thus, the concept of resilience extends beyond coping and adaptation to recognize the enhanced personal and relational growth that can be forged out of adversity. Although there is suffering and struggle, adversity can spark a reappraisal of life priorities and investment in more meaningful relationships and pursuits. A family resilience framework, grounded in systems theory, combines ecological and developmental perspectives, viewing the family as an open system that functions in relation to its broader sociocultural context and evolves over the multigenerational life cycle.

Ecosystemic Perspective

A biopsychosocial-systems orientation views problem situations and their solutions as involving multiple recursive influences of individuals, families, communities, larger systems, and sociocultural variables. A family resilience approach assesses distress contextually, involving an interaction of individual—and family—vulnerability and strengths with the impact of risk factors, stressful life events, and challenging social contexts, from neurobiological and genetic factors to broad sociocultural influences. Family distress may be fueled by unsuccessful attempts to cope with an overwhelming situation: a crisis event, such as early parental loss, or widespread trauma experiences, such as a major disaster, war and combat, or the plight of refugees. Stresses may be related to chronic conditions, such as serious illness, or to the persistent challenges of poverty, racism, heterosexism, or other forms of discrimination.

For resilience, families are encouraged to draw on extended kin, social networks, community affiliations, and diverse cultural and spiritual resources. They actively engage with their environment, navigating and negotiating transactions with school, workplace, health care, and other larger systems that impact their lives. In collective trauma, collaborative approaches aim to strengthen both family and community resilience.

Developmental Perspective

A family resilience approach attends to adaptational processes over time, from ongoing interactions and the trajectory of stressful conditions, to family life cycle passage and multigenerational influences. How a family confronts and manages a disruptive or threatening experience, buffers stress, effectively reorganizes, and reinvests in life pursuits will influence adaptation for all members.

For instance, in risk and resilience with divorce, family transactional processes make a difference in child and family adaptation: from buffering predivorce tensions, to dealing with postdivorce financial strains, ongoing coparental conflict or cooperation, and further disruptions with residential changes, parents' repartnering, and stepfamily formation. Such research, identifying core processes that promote resilience, can inform intervention efforts.

Family functioning is assessed in the context of the multigenerational system moving forward over time. A resilience-oriented genogram (diagram of family relationships) and family time line (noting major events and stressors) are useful to organize relationship information, track system patterns, and guide intervention. Connections are noted between the timing of symptoms and stress events, such as a son's school dropout following his father's job loss and heightened family stresses. Distress frequently coincides with stressful developmental transitions or a pileup of stressors. While all families deal with predictable, normative stresses such as becoming parents, unexpected, disruptive events, such as the birth of a child with disabilities, are significantly more stressful.

Family history and patterns of relating and functioning are transmitted across the generations, influencing response to adversity and future expectations, hopes and dreams, or catastrophic fears. Strains increase exponentially when current stressors reactivate vulnerable issues from the past, especially traumatic losses. It is important to explore what can be learned from past experiences of adversity and to inquire about models and sources of resilience that might inspire current efforts in overcoming challenges. Families, especially immigrant and transnational families, are more resilient when they are able to balance intergenerational continuity and change and maintain links between their past, present, and future.

Assessing Family Resilience

Assessment of healthy family functioning is fraught with dilemmas. Postmodern perspectives have heightened awareness that clinicians and researchers bring their own assumptive maps into evaluation and intervention, embedded in cultural norms, professional orientations, and subjective personal beliefs and experiences.

Moreover, the definition of *the family* has been expanding with recent social and economic transformations, changing gender patterns, and a multiplicity of family arrangements. Abundant research reveals that well-functioning families and healthy children can be found in a variety of family structures. What matters most are family processes that support nurturing, protective, and committed bonds. Yet, over a more fluid and extended life course, children and their parents increasingly live in varied, complex family and household arrangements, requiring resilience to adapt to disruptive transitions.

Research on healthy family functioning has provided empirical grounding to identify key processes in intervention with distressed families. Unlike family typologies (a classification of families based on narrow, fixed variables) that tend to be trait based, static, and acontextual, a family resilience framework focuses on dynamic multilevel processes in response to stressful life challenges. It is assumed that no single model fits all family situations. Functioning is assessed in context: relative to cultural norms, family resources, and the adverse conditions faced. Processes for optimal functioning and members' well-being may vary over time, as challenges unfold and families evolve across the life cycle.

Key Processes in Family Resilience

The Walsh family resilience framework, widely applied in research and practice worldwide, identifies nine key processes in resilience, as outlined in Table 1. It is informed by three decades of research in the social sciences and clinical field on resilience and well-functioning family systems. Designed to provide a flexible map for clinical practice and research, it synthesizes findings in three domains (dimensions) of family functioning: family belief systems, organizational

Table 1 Key Processes in Walsh Family Resilience Framework

Belief Systems

1. Making Meaning of Adversity
   - Relational view of resilience
   - Normalize, contextualize distress
   - Sense of coherence: view crisis as meaningful, comprehensible, manageable challenge
   - Facilitative appraisal: explanatory attributions; future expectations

2. Positive Outlook
   - Hope, optimistic bias; confidence in overcoming challenges
   - Encouragement; affirm strengths, focus on potential
   - Active initiative and perseverance (can-do spirit)
   - Master the possible; accept what can't be changed; tolerate uncertainty

3. Transcendence and Spirituality
   - Larger values, purpose
   - Spirituality: faith, contemplative practices, community; connection with nature
   - Inspiration: envision possibilities, aspirations; creative expression; social action
   - Transformation: learning, change, and positive growth from adversity

Organizational Processes

4. Flexibility
   - Rebound, adaptive change to meet new challenges
   - Reorganize, restabilize: continuity, dependability, predictability
   - Strong authoritative leadership: nurture, guide, protect
   - Varied family forms: cooperative parenting/caregiving teams
   - Couple/coparent relationship: mutual respect; equal partners

5. Connectedness
   - Mutual support, teamwork, and commitment
   - Respect individual needs, differences
   - Seek reconnection and repair grievances

6. Mobilize Social and Economic Resources
   - Recruit extended kin, social, and community supports; models and mentors
   - Build financial security; navigate stressful work/family challenges
   - Transactions with larger systems: access institutional, structural supports

Communication/Problem-Solving Processes

7. Clarity
   - Clear, consistent messages, information
   - Clarify ambiguous situation; truth seeking

8. Open Emotional Sharing
   - Painful feelings: sadness, suffering, anger, fear, disappointment, remorse
   - Positive interactions: love, appreciation, gratitude, humor, fun, respite

9. Collaborative Problem-Solving
   - Creative brainstorming; resourcefulness
   - Share decision-making; negotiation and conflict repair
   - Focus on goals; concrete steps; build on success; learn from setbacks
   - Proactive stance: preparedness, planning, prevention

Source: Copyright © 2016 by Froma Walsh.

patterns, and communication processes. Some processes may be expressed differently or are more or less relevant in varied family situations and social contexts. Key processes are mutually interactive within and across domains and in transactions with their environment, with synergistic influence that boosts resilience. For instance, meaning-making facilitates and is enhanced by communication clarity. Emerging mixed-method studies can further advance our understanding of multilevel influences in family resilience for diverse populations in varied situations of adversity and sociocultural contexts.

Practice Applications of a Family Resilience Framework

A family resilience practice approach applies principles and techniques common among strengths-based systemic models with families facing crisis situations or persistent adversity. Assessment attends more centrally to the impact of highly stressful life challenges and identifies family strengths and potential resources that can be mobilized to overcome those challenges. The family resilience framework offers a flexible map to guide assessment, intervention, and prevention to target and strengthen key processes that foster recovery and positive growth. This approach is grounded in the conviction that even troubled and highly vulnerable families can forge greater resilience through collaborative teamwork and mutual support.

This family resilience framework has useful application in a wide range of adverse situations:

- Recovering from crisis, trauma, and loss (e.g., complicated family bereavement; collective trauma in major disasters, terror attacks, combat-related trauma, war-torn regions, displaced and refugee families)
- Navigating disruptive transitions (e.g., job loss; migration, separation, divorce, stepfamily formation)
- Overcoming multi-stress challenges of chronic conditions (e.g., serious illness/disability; impact of poverty, discrimination, and blighted neighborhoods for at-risk youth and vulnerable families)
- Family resilience-oriented clinical training and community-based services are increasingly being designed and implemented in a wide range of settings and contexts worldwide.

Efforts to foster family resilience benefit all family members from children to elders. Furthermore, in drawing out stories of client resilience, helping professionals experience vicarious resilience in their professional and personal lives. A systemic assessment may lead to multisystemic interventions depending on the relevance of various system levels to risk and problem reduction and for individual and family positive development. Interventions often involve collaboration and change in the community with workplace, school, health care, and other larger systems. Resilience-oriented family interventions can be adapted to a variety of formats.

- Family consultations, brief intervention, or more intensive family therapy may combine individual and conjoint sessions, including members most affected by stressors and those who can contribute to resilience.
- Psychoeducational multifamily groups provide social support and practical information, offering concrete guidelines for stress reduction, crisis management, problem-solving, and optimal functioning as families navigate through stressful periods and face future challenges.
- Brief, cost-effective periodic "check-ups" can be timed around stressful transitions or emerging challenges in long-term adaptation.

Family research, practice, and policy need to rebalance focus from how families fail to how they can succeed under stressful conditions in order to advance useful practice approaches for families facing adversity. This research-informed family resilience framework can guide clinical and community-based practice by (a) assessing family functioning on key system variables as they fit each family's values, structure, resources, and challenges and then (b) targeting interventions to strengthen family functioning as presenting problems are addressed. This collaborative approach increases family resourcefulness in meeting future challenges by strengthening relational, community, cultural, and spiritual connections as lifelines for resilience. This practice approach is grounded in a deep conviction in the human potential for recovery and positive growth forged from adversity.

Froma Walsh

See also Genograms; Individual and Family Development; Positive Psychology; Structural Family Therapy; Systems Theory

Further Readings

Becvar, D. (Ed.). (2013). *Handbook of family resilience.* New York, NY: Springer.

Masten, A., & Monn, A. R. (2015). Child and family resilience: A call for integrating science, practice, and training. *Family Relations, 64,* 5–21.

Walsh, F. (Ed.). (2012). *Normal family processes: Growing diversity and complexity* (4th ed.). New York, NY: Guilford Press.

Walsh, F. (2016). *Strengthening family resilience* (3rd ed.). New York, NY: Guilford Press.

Family Resource Management

Being part of a family requires giving time and attention to the myriad of resources shared by members of families. Although many initially think of money and financial stability when considering resources, family resource management refers to the time and energy put into the family as well as financial abilities, people outside of the family, objects, and space. Resource management is multifarious and family decisions are made after considering how each resource affects the goals of individuals in the family and the goals and comfort of the family as a whole. Family resources can even include love and all of these resources can be used positively or negatively within the family system. Family resource management is a unique component of marriage and family counseling. Arguments surrounding money and the presence and use of financial resources continue to be the number one reason for divorce in the United States. While clients may be referred to financial literacy courses, resource management skills and communication concerning family resources are necessary to sustain the well-being of families. Social and mental health can be shaken when daily management is not practiced, but by identifying needs versus wants of each individual family member and then the needs of the family as a whole, families can reduce tension. This entry discusses resource management in counseling and in relation to the specific context of single parents and blended families, addictions, and poverty.

Resource Management in Counseling

Counselors work with family members to define their ultimate goals, interests, and decision-making patterns while also identifying policies and community resources that affect the family or assist in realizing the family's goals. This is because an individual's resources are a component of family interaction and day-to-day resource allocation is part of meeting the needs of the family. This allocation of resources and determination of how resources can and will be best used can cause a great deal of stress for all family members involved.

Family resource management is fluid in that the components being managed may continue to change and management must adjust as the family does. It must evolve over the life span and is not a one-time budgeting of financial and other resources. This process also includes estate planning. Families must consider how resources will be managed after a family member passes away, what resources will be affected, and whether or not they have or will participate in estate planning if there are resources to be allocated in an attempt to lessen the financial and emotional strain produced by the death of a close loved one. The ability to adjust when necessary can also be assisted through the construction of an emergency plan.

Family resource management is not a confidential process because of the need for communication between family members involved in managing family resources and communication with other relevant parties. There is a coordination and case management component to family resource management. Families can benefit from coordinating and evaluating information from other professionals and systems involved in their lives including, but not limited to, professionals who provide physical health care, mental health care, social services, legal assistance, and education. Extended family members and significant others can also be a source of information concerning how the family manages resources, especially if these family members have ever been called to assist the family due to lack of adequate family resource management in the past. The service provider who has been tasked with assisting families in this area must also assist the family members with working out disagreements and minimizing conflict.

Committed engagement in family resource management will assist in first solving problems surrounding family resources and then avoid further issues in the future. Although some issues are ranked differently in importance for various family members, the family can compromise on sharing of all or most resources and ultimately create a family environment that supports the needs and desires of all of those involved.

Single Parents and Blended Families

Parents become single for various reasons including divorce, death, and choice and understanding the factors surrounding singlehood while also understanding that each of the scenarios involves vastly different dynamics assists the counselor in promoting healthy family resource management in the families with which they work. Divorce commonly splits resources. Families often split time and money and often must manage emotions concerning each. Being in one another's presence or even attempting communication with each other may require energy that is needed for other family members. Furthermore, this dynamic continues to be complicated if one parent does not share resources as much as the other.

The death of a parent means that the deceased parent has no choice in the diminishment of resources on their end. Even with financial benefits for survivors, there will still be the lack of time, emotional support, and other resources for the surviving parents and children paired with mourning and grief. For single parents by choice, the element of choice provides for preparation and deliberation concerning resource management. Each of these situations entails adjustment of roles and resource management.

Individual needs may be neglected, and instead focus of family resources may become geared toward a child (the presence of multiple children will require that resources be stretched further). Family resource management is the base of life adjustment. The necessity of dealing with environmental constraints and personal stress involves a period of evaluation and decision-making about what now constitutes the family and what resources are available from each parent. Other relatives may also share resources or previously shared resources may be discontinued because of strained relations between the parents. Management of mental energy when dealing with exes and their families must be evaluated alongside quality time spent with the child, cost of childhood activities, and educational necessities.

Education and economic status greatly affect adjustment for single parents. Higher income is correlated with better life adjustment, which increases as income increases. However, having the ability to manage financial resources does not provide for the assumption that emotional or other resources are also well managed. Family resource management is essential to the life adjustment of a single parent whether the status of single parent derived from divorce, widowing, unwed pregnancy, adoption, or any other reason. The presence of children creates a different dynamic in relation to prioritization, categorization, and allocation of family resources when a healthy family structure is present. Note that healthy family structure is not dependent on two parents being in the home.

Family resource management within blended families is complex. There is a unique combination of family members, family issues, family histories, and family resources. Family resource management, in this case, must be reassessed during the planning of a new marriage and, therefore, new family. There is a strong need for patience and boundary setting in these cases. Time, space, and financial resources are further stretched, combined, and/or rearranged. Roles are defined as are resources while resource sharing by other family members may be renegotiated.

Addictions

One of the biggest drainers of family resources is a family member who is suffering with some type of addiction. When in active addiction, one may steal from one's friends and family, begin to avoid those friends and family, and exhibit behaviors when in social settings that may cause others to avoid being around him or her. Addiction not only affects the individual, but also affects the family and the community.

Addicted individuals often cause a strain on their family members and may be seen as being a burden to them. This is especially true if the family member was once a large contributor to the resources and is expected to be a main provider for the family. Other family members may find themselves providing additional financial resources, devoting time to taking care of the person with the addiction, and providing other assistance that is physically or emotionally exhausting. Conversely, fear of lessening family resources by entering treatment can be a barrier to seeking needed services.

Poverty

Poor management of family resources contributes to poverty, and without the adequate instruction on family resource management, habits and practices continue to be taught to younger generations and continue to perpetuate the cycle of poverty within the family. Unquestionably, resources available to families are influenced by number of family members, education and income of the heads of the household, as well as cultural influences on allocation of resources combined with priority of family resource management.

Ultimately, families may not seek assistance from a counselor because of the associated costs or lack of time; however, studies have shown that there are cost benefits for families who seek assistance from a counselor, especially when family resources are entangled with disorders within the family, such as a family member suffering with substance use issues. There is also a relationship between family counseling and the lessened need for medical care in addition to social costs.

The socioeconomic status of a family may complicate counseling. One implication for working with a family in poverty is that methods of survival and meeting of basic needs will have to be addressed. Very little work can be done if a family is losing their housing and people will find it difficult to concentrate in family session when they have been missing meals and are hungry. The counselor may assess that family resource management is necessary and yet lack resources to counteract the need for said management. This dynamic necessitates the use of case management skills and employment of referrals to social service agencies in an attempt to assist the family with gaining initial resources to be managed.

There are common stresses to which most people have adapted, economic stresses that are determined by finances and can be acute or chronic, and there are emotional stresses that may be the result of common or economic stresses and have an effect on other areas of life. Additionally, the concept of sharing resources across various families assists in strengthening communities.

Cultural Considerations

Family resource management and family counseling as a whole is extremely applicable across various cultures. Cultural consideration must be given as values and behaviors are a part of culture. Most cultures see family as important, although this does not necessarily equate to healthy family functioning. Cultural differences contribute to the importance of specific family resources and prioritization of seeking assistance with family resource management. Some resources are more important in some cultures than in other cultures.

For this reason, the counselor engaging with a family needs to assess the degree to which the family's deviation from conventional norms is due to a distinctive cultural background rather than pathology. Cultural consideration must be given to the hierarchical arrangements of the family to determine who makes major decisions about management of resources and how communication is structured within the hierarchy.

Technology

The rapid growth of communications and information technology has shaped younger family members who learn differently, work differently, and require new and innovative techniques and devices in order to function comfortably in society. Technology can both help and hinder family resource management. A great deal of multitasking is possible through the use of recent technology advancements and some families have been able to profit from these advancements. Although technology allows for some family members to work from alternative locations and also seek out information that was not readily accessible in the past, technology has also become a way for some family members to remain disconnected from the family.

Use of technology allows people to communicate more frequently and at faster rates than conventional communication tools, such as basic telephones and postal mail. Quality time is a resource that may be diminished because of the use of technology. While budgeting resources and family assistance may be obtained via new technologies, time and financial resources can also be drained as a result of these technologies.

Committed engagement in family resource management will assist in first solving problems surrounding family resources and then avoiding further issues in the future. Although some issues are ranked differently in importance by family members, a family can compromise by sharing all or most resources and ultimately create a family environment that supports the needs and desires of all those involved.

Asha Dickerson

See also Communication in Couples and Families; Cost-Benefit Analysis; Debt and Financial Strain; Dual-Earner Families; Family Stress; Stress Management

Further Readings

Deacon, R. E., & Firebaugh, F. M. (1988). *Family resource management: Principles and applications.* Boston, MA: Allyn & Bacon.

Goldsmith, E. (2012). *Resource management for individuals and families* (5th ed.). Upper Saddle River, NJ: Prentice Hall.

Mid-State Technical College. (1992). *Low income family resource management.* Wisconsin Rapid, WI: Author.

Moore, T. J., & Asay, S. M. (2008). *Family resource management.* Thousand Oaks, CA: Sage.

FAMILY RITUALS

Rituals, broadly defined, are behaviors or series of actions that one regularly and invariably follows, as, for example, in religious ceremonies. By extension, a family ritual refers to any repeated special activity or behavior involving a family member or members that has some symbolic meaning for those involved. Family rituals often reflect cultural, religious, or ethnic practices and are usually passed down from one generation to the next. Experts agree that family rituals are important because they communicate special meaning to family members, which might include expressions of love, shared happiness, a sense of security, cohesiveness, exclusiveness, and peacefulness. This entry reviews common family rituals and the positive effects they have on participants while also outlining the differences between family rituals and family routines.

Defining Family Rituals

Family rituals are recurring acts that take on special meaning. Rituals can be quite simple and practical. For example, the simple act of reading a bedtime story to a child or praying together before meals form common rituals for many families. These rituals are intentional acts with clear purposes and expectations. While common family rituals may center around religious or cultural celebrations, they are not restricted to such themes. For example, something as simple as

Sunday dinner can quickly evolve into a regular family ritual that nuclear and extended family members come to expect and for whom special significance is created.

Religious and Cultural Rituals

Other common family rituals that center around religious or cultural celebrations might include decorating the Christmas tree on Christmas Eve, baking a cake to celebrate Rosh Hashanah, lighting a black candle together on the first day of Kwanzaa, or serving meals at a local homeless shelter on Thanksgiving Day. Often families cherish having a certain night of the week designated as a family game night, making certain "traditional" foods for a specific holiday or birthday, eating pancakes for breakfast on Saturday, going to Grandma's house for lunch on Sundays, taking a walk after dinner, taking yearly photos of the child(ren) on the first day of school, going to the pumpkin patch every year to choose a Halloween pumpkin, visiting a loved one's gravesite on the anniversary of his or her birth or death, or going to the same place every year for vacation with extended family members. In all of these and other family rituals, certain behaviors within the family are exercised, and messages are sent to family members about their importance within the family structure.

Family rituals are particularly important to children and adolescents; through these rituals, they are learning and getting messages about their identity as individuals and as members of their family. They can also begin to see how they fit into their family and how their family is similar as well as different from the sea of families that surround them. Having particular meals on certain days of the week (Friday pizza night or Taco Tuesday), a unique handshake or greeting between father and son, or a special facial expression or phrase traded between mother and daughter before she gets on the school bus in the morning are all examples of family rituals. Such ritual behavior creates a bond with family members and sends a message that they are loved, appreciated, and they belong. Of course, family rituals evolve over time. This is especially true as children grow and their wants and needs develop and change. The bedtime story or song a mother used to sing to her 3-year-old will not have the same impact when her daughter is 13. However, the child, when she grows up, may sing that same song to her own young daughter. The boy whose father reads to him every night before bed will eventually want to read to himself at night. Even though some rituals will change or even stop altogether, the effect of the ritual and its special meaning to those involved persists. Some family rituals are handed down from generation to generation while others may be formed within the confines of the new family structure. The process of creating a ritual can be as simple as a one-time act that brings sufficient joy or peace to family members that is repeated with hopes of recreating the feelings of comfort and togetherness.

How Rituals Differ From Routine

A family routine is a habitual behavior that simply exists to ensure a particular task or job is accomplished. Although a routine occurs on a regular basis, it is not unique, extraordinary, nor does it hold any symbolic meaning. These are tasks that just must be done within the family, rather than something the family *wants* to be done; once the task is completed, there is little or no thought about it until the next time it needs to be done. One way to distinguish between a family ritual and family routine is to consider how a disruption might affect the family. When a routine is disrupted, it may be a small annoyance but a disruption to a ritual is more likely to threaten the family structure and cohesiveness. An example of a family routine might be going to the grocery store after church. The family goes to the grocery store because it's on the way home from the church, more family members at the grocery store means individuals can spread out in the store and complete the task faster, and more hands are available to help take the groceries into the house and put them away; no one necessarily enjoys going to the grocery store, it holds no symbolic meaning, and family members don't necessarily bond over the experience. That's not to say that it cannot *become* a ritual one day. For instance, if a parent passes away and the rest of the family continues to go to the grocery store after church each Sunday, it may become a way for the family to remember the parent who passed away and as a result, it may bring meaning, comfort, and closeness to the remaining family members.

The Importance of Family Rituals

For many people, family rituals provide a sense of security, identity, and belonging; emotional connections are made when family members engage in these rituals. When family members sit around the dinner table and converse with each other (both children and parents put away their electronic devices) about what happened during the day, the message is that not only is each family member important but the family as a unit is also important. Each member of the family is valuable, interesting, and worthwhile.

There are several types of family rituals that actually help promote children's creativity. Take, for example, the ritual of making up stories, games, or songs before bedtime. As parents and children bounce the story, game rules, or song lyrics from one family member to the next, children not only practice their language and listening skills, but learn about themselves and others. They also must use their imaginations and creativity to help create the finished product. Some families create a garden together and part of their family ritual is to care for the garden one day a week. Giving children the freedom to choose what they will plant and how they will care for that plant cultivates their creativity. Allowing children to plan and help create the menu for their family's regular Friday night family time helps them begin to experiment with different food or ingredient combinations.

Family rituals provide structure and stability for members of the family. For family members whose ritual includes going to a grandmother's house every Sunday, they know that every Sunday they will get to see their grandmother and be able to visit with other members of their family. They know what to expect, may look forward to these interactions, and feel a sense of comfort in this routine. This type of structure is really important for children and adolescents. As children get older, their schedules tend to become more hectic with an increase in after-school activities, as well as academic and social responsibilities. Maintaining family rituals provides a way for family members, especially children and adolescents, to remain connected and enjoy being together. Rituals help create a feeling of being safe, teach family members about cultural or religious heritage, and help communicate family values as well as personal and family identity. Family rituals are associated with stronger family relationships; they help create bonds between family members and strengthen existing family ties. The example also illustrates how family rituals tend to confirm the family's priorities not only to other family members but to those outside of the family structure.

The existence of family rituals also helps in times of transitions or family crisis because such rituals can promote healing to occur in times of grief and confusion. Additionally, because there is an emotional connection or closeness created through family rituals, if family members find that they are not able to participate in one or they "outgrow" the ritual, they will often reminisce or play back those experiences in their mind to try and re-create the feelings of happiness or connection. Often for family members who are feeling pain, isolation, fear, and anxiety, remembering those family rituals or starting new rituals within their own family creates a sense of peace and belonging. Finally, couples engaging in family rituals have a higher level of marital satisfaction, and they help create valuable memories for everyone else in the family.

Christine H. Ebrahim

See also Active Parenting; Couples and Marriage Counseling; Family Stress; Family Values; Humanistic Family Therapy; Individual and Family Development; Single-Parent Families

Further Readings

Compañ, E., Moreno, J., Ruiz, M., & Pascual, E. (2002). Doing things together: Adolescent health and family rituals. *Journal of Epidemiology & Community Health, 56*(2), 89–94.

Cox, M. (2012). *The book of new family traditions: How to create great rituals for holidays and every day*. Philadelphia, PA: Running Press.

Denham, S. (2003). Relationships between family rituals, family routines, and health. *Journal of Family Nursing, 9*(3), 305–330.

Fiese, B. (2006). *Family routine and rituals*. New Haven, CT: Yale University Press.

Imber-Black, E., Roberts, J., & Whiting, R. A. (Eds.). (2003). *Rituals in families and family therapy*. New York, NY: W. W. Norton.

Spagnola, M., & Fiese, B. H. (2007). Family routines and rituals: A context for development in the lives of young children. *Infants & Young Children, 20*(4), 284–299.

Family Strengths

Family strengths are attributes or characteristics within a family that facilitate its ability to successfully overcome adversity and hardship and move forward in ways that promote growth and resilience. Identifying and promoting family strengths is an important function of advancing the survival and enrichment of families. The topic of family strengths is relevant in marriage, family, and couples counseling because it promotes the identification and utilization of positive family attributes that can greatly influence therapeutic change. This entry will present an overview of family strengths by focusing on the assumptions underlying a family strengths perspective, the unique challenges associated with strength-based practice, family research models that have contributed to knowledge about family strengths, and conceptual frameworks and therapeutic approaches that inform clinical practice.

Assumptions Underlying a Family Strengths Perspective

A number of theorists and researchers have used various terms to describe strong families. These terms include *resilient, emotionally healthy, resourceful, successful, balanced, harmonious,* or what Froma Walsh refers to as families who are able to "struggle well" and "bounce forward." A strength-based perspective requires practitioners to go beyond deficit-based thinking and minimize the tendency to pathologize clients by taking into account how they have been able to successfully deal with difficulty and crises in the past. This entails having a worldview or orientation that encourages positive aspects of family life and actively searches for what families do well despite the odds they face. The significance and recognition of family strengths in clinical practice today has been influenced by several different developments and programmatic efforts over the past four decades. Contributions originated from research-based models of family functioning, research on how families respond to stress, family enrichment and family life education programs, theoretical frameworks associated with the family life cycle and normal family processes, and various approaches that incorporate strength-based thinking and practice.

Unique Challenges in Strength-Based Practice

A strengths perspective emphasizes resilience and growth and focuses on one's ability to cope, thrive, and adapt. It requires paying attention to inner resources and protective factors even when individuals and families are faced with the most adverse of situations. In contrast, the nature of therapy is characteristically geared toward a focus on deficits, problems, and pathology based on the reasons why clients seek counseling in the first place. Families do not seek therapy because things are going well. They actively seek or are mandated to seek services because of their inability to resolve issues and problems. These are just some of the constraints and obstacles that get in the way of identifying and utilizing family strengths within the scope of current-day practice. Other obstacles that obscure family strengths, as noted in Mark Karpel's writing about family resources, include the search for pathology, the search for perfection (based on normative standards), therapists' attitudes, limits of language, and the focus on the mastery of the therapist.

Family therapists and counselors see families at their worst and lowest points, and as a result, they tend to learn more about families' dysfunctional patterns and behaviors in therapy than their strengths. A strength-oriented perspective reminds them that a family's problem-based presentation in therapy is only one aspect of who they are and what they are capable of doing.

A key assumption is that attempts to access a family's full potential are temporarily inaccessible or somehow constrained as they attempt to resolve given developmental and unexpected crises. Despite the mistakes and points of stuckness clients may have encountered, there are positives to be noted in all families from which members are able to derive connectedness, support, and growth. As practitioners, it is worth noting that the exploration of clients' previous positive experiences and resourceful moments can promote a strength-based perspective that can alter preexisting beliefs (for both clients and therapists) and lead to needed change desired by family members. This does not mean that problems are ignored in therapy. Problems are simply addressed within the context of how these very same difficulties are embedded within the full scope of clients' experiences and can serve them in ways that can eventually lead to their capacity for connection, support, and adaptability. Strength-based therapy emphasizes, promotes, and attempts to generate client resources and strengths as problems and issues are dealt with in therapy.

Family Research Models

The concept of family resources gained momentum and visibility following research in the 1970s on characteristics that make families strong. The study of successful families by researchers from a variety of disciplines, including sociology, psychiatry, psychology, and marriage and family therapy, has yielded important information that has significantly contributed to educational, therapeutic, and policy-oriented efforts to strengthen families. Of notable mention is a 1990 report compiled by Child Trends, Inc. for the U.S. Department of Health and Human Services that highlighted that across disciplines and perspectives, researchers and practitioners across the world present similar findings regarding the basic dimensions of strong and healthy families. In short, they report that communication, encouragement among individual family members, expressions of appreciation, commitment to family, religious and spiritual orientation, social connectedness, the ability to adapt, clear roles, and spending time together contribute to strong family units. Three of these programmatic research efforts are discussed below.

Nick Stinnett and John DeFrain's Family Strengths Model

The family strengths model developed by Nick Stinnett and John DeFrain grew out of their Family Strength Research Project that was conducted between the 1970s and 1980s. The model proposed six clusters of qualities of strong families that were founded upon a sense of positive emotional connection. These included appreciation and affection, commitment, positive communication, enjoyable time together, spiritual well-being, and effective management of stress and crisis situations. The findings indicated that individuals in strong families care deeply for each other and were not afraid to express their love, they prioritize time and energy with family over other responsibilities, spend time listening and talking with one another to stay connected, genuinely enjoy sharing family time, rely on spiritual beliefs and practices to carry them through hard times, and are able to manage daily stressors and difficult life crises in creative and effective ways. Other strength-based frameworks have emerged from research designed to understand how families coped with stress. Knowledge about the elements and processes that helped families cope with stress also led to clinically useful strength-based conceptualizations and interventions (e.g., the double ABCX model and the circumplex model).

Hamilton McCubbin and Joan Patterson's Double ABCX Model

The ABCX model is a research-based model focused on family adjustment and family adaptation to crisis events. Findings suggested that families who were able to deal with crisis events and adapt successfully shared both individual personal resources and family system resources. Individual resources benefit the system as a whole in times of crisis and include personal characteristics like finances, education, health, and psychological resources like self-esteem and mastery. Family system resources generally revolved around aspects of family cohesion and adaptability involving shared power, flexibility of roles, and family support. The combination of both personal and systemic resources provided key information about the importance of assessing for individual and family strengths.

David Olson's Circumplex Model

The circumplex model of marital systems was developed by David Olson and is used for clinical assessment and treatment planning with couples and families. The model's self-report assessment scale, FACES (Family Adaptability and Cohesion Scale, now in its fourth version) has contributed greatly, because of its versatile application as a research and clinical tool. This model presents a typology based on two basic dimensions, family adaptability and family cohesion, with a third dimension, communication, that serves as a facilitative dimension of the other two. Latest developments of this model matrix yield 25 possible family types based on a family's level of cohesion and adaptability. In this model, family strengths include family pride (i.e., focus on respect, trust, and loyalty within the family), family accord (i.e., involving a family's sense of competency), parent–adolescent communication, and congregational activities. Other marital strengths including communication, sexual relationship, conflict resolution, and role relationships are also noted.

Strength-Based Frameworks and Approaches

The development of conceptual frameworks like the family life cycle and normal family processes in the 1970s and 1980s also led to greater awareness of family strengths in clinical practice. Normalizing the process that families go through as they shift developmentally from one stage to the next and transition through critical and unexpected events allowed for greater awareness aligned with strength-based perspectives. As a result, practitioners were able to utilize language that contextualized and normalized a family's experiences at different stages of development and crises in ways that minimized deficit-based thinking and pathologizing of clients.

Mark Karpel's Family Resources Approach

Mark Karpel's definition of *family resources* is also useful for therapists who work with families. Karpel's definition makes a distinction between personal and relational resources, which he describes as individual and systemic characteristics among family members who promote coping and survival, limit destructive patterns, and enrich daily life. Karpel utilizes this definition to assess for resources in his assessment of families. Personal resources include self-respect, protectiveness (or caring in action), hope, tolerance, affection, and humor/playfulness. Relational resources include respect, reciprocity, reliability, repair, flexibility, family pride, and loops of interaction. His approach endorses the importance of conceptualizing, identifying, promoting, and mobilizing family resources in clinical practice.

Froma Walsh's Family Resilience Approach

Froma Walsh describes resilience as the ability to withstand and rebound (i.e., bounce forward) from disruptive life challenges. Her approach is informed by clinical and social science research and is based on a conceptual framework made up of three domains: belief systems, organizational patterns, and communication processes. The framework serves as a map to help target key family processes that can assist in the reduction of stress and vulnerability, foster healing and growth, and empower families out of high risk and adverse crisis situations. Key processes under belief systems are categorized under making meaning of adversity, positive outlook, and transcendence and spirituality. Key processes under organizational patterns are categorized under flexibility, connectedness, and social and economic resources. And key processes under communication processes are categorized under clarity, open emotional expression, and collaborative problem-solving. Some practice guidelines offered by Walsh include using respectful language to contextualize distress and decrease shame, blame, and pathologizing; viewing crises as opportunities for learning, change, and growth; and identifying and affirming strengths and courage alongside vulnerabilities and constraints among others.

Final Thoughts About Family Strengths

It is easy to lose sight of the presence of family strengths given its vagueness in definition and the problem-oriented nature of therapy itself. Client families are the first to disregard what may be going well for them, or what they may be doing well within the context of therapy. The focus on family strengths and its presence in research, practice, supervision, education, and policy addresses the need to counteract this rather long-standing bias against the lack of recognition, identification, and utilization of family strengths in counseling. Conceptual and research-based models and approaches can guide practitioners in the search for ability and success rather than pathology and failure, which in turn will add to the body of knowledge that recognizes family strengths, including endurance, cohesiveness, affection, and mutual support.

Silvia Echevarria-Doan

See also Circumplex Model; Cohesion; Family Resource Management; Family Stress Adaptation Theory; Hope-Focused Approach to Couple Enrichment in Counseling; Normalizing; Prevention Research; Solution-Focused Brief Therapy

Further Readings

Echevarria-Doan, S. (2001). Resource-based reflective consultation: Accessing client resources through interviews and dialogue. *Journal of Marital and Family Therapy, 27,* 201–212.

Karpel, M. (1986). *Family resources: The hidden partner in family therapy.* New York, NY: Guilford Press.

Krysan, M., Moore, K. A., & Zill, N. (1990). *Identifying successful families: An overview of constructs and selected measures.* Washington, DC: Child Trends.

Walsh, F. (2003). *Normal family processes: Growing diversity and complexity* (3rd ed.). New York, NY: Guilford Press.

Walsh, F. (2006). *Strengthening family resilience* (2nd ed.). New York, NY: Guilford Press.

FAMILY STRESS

Stress is the physical and psychological response to demands placed on an individual. An individual or family is considered *stressed* when their level of demands outweighs their resources. Stress produces emotional, psychological, relational, and physiological responses that are often unhealthy and harmful. Triggers of stress (i.e., stressors) have powerful effects on biological and psychological functions, and when individuals are stressed, their bodies can go into a prolonged state of heightened arousal that can be harmful. Researcher Julia Malia likens this to a car that is stuck revving the engine. Eventually, a car forced to accelerate nonstop for a prolonged period will wear down and become damaged. Likewise, human beings stuck in a state of prolonged arousal will eventually experience physical and psychological fatigue.

Stress researcher Robert Sapolsky compares the human stress response to those of animals and noted that whereas a zebra chased by a lion on the savannah will enter into a flight-or-fight mode, it will quickly descend from that heightened, stressed state after the lion is gone and no longer poses an immediate threat. Conversely, human beings can be continually stressed by a crisis long after the stressor has vanished (e.g., posttraumatic stress) or long before a stressor comes to the forefront (e.g., fear). Therefore, stress can have a long-lasting effect on an individual's health. Consequently, families experiencing high levels of stress are more prone to illness, may have difficulty communicating, may struggle with parenting, and could experience more conflict.

Family stress is more complex than individual stress. The same stress mechanisms apply in families as they do in individuals (i.e., the balancing of resources and demands); however, in families, family members must also deal with stress individually in their own personal way and on their own schedule. For example, if a family is undergoing financial crisis, the parents will experience the stress more directly, whereas the children will experience effects that are more indirect and appraise the event differently, according to their own level of understanding. Additionally, the parents will most likely encounter the stressful event earlier and have to cope with the stress for a longer period, whereas the children may never be informed of the pending threats. Thus, for a family experiencing stress there are numerous stress responses and coping strategies taking place simultaneously and on different schedules. Each family member's response to stress tends to interact and create an aggregated stress and coping response. So, if one family member is stressed, it influences others in the family system. Family stress is often characterized as pressure or a force placed on the family that distorts their state of equilibrium and fosters conflict. Therefore, it is crucial that marriage and family therapists develop an understanding of family stress and help families find effective methods for stress management.

Theories and Models of Family Stress

Several models of family stress exist. Reuben Hill created the oldest family stress model in 1949 in the aftermath of the Great Depression and World War II. Hill's model, known as the ABC-X model of family stress, posited that the stressor (A) places demands on the family's crisis-meeting resources (B) that interact with how the family appraises the stressor (C) and determines if the stressor is a crisis (X). The ABC-X model is the foundational model for family stress, and has been modified and expanded by various theorists over the years.

Some scholars argued that Hill's model was limited because it only accounted for the stress process up until the point of crisis. These researchers expanded the ABC-X model and dubbed their variation the *double ABCX model*. The double ABCX model includes the original ABC-X model with slight variations to the language. The A and the B in the double ABCX model remained the same as in the original model, except that the B was given the more general title of *existing resources* and included factors such as psychological and community resources. Additionally, whereas Hill's model ended with the crisis event (X), the double ABCX model included postcrisis variables. In essence, after the crisis, families experience a *demand pileup* that resulted from the combination of the initial stressor, the overlapping of hardships that relate to the stressor, family transitions, the outcome of family coping efforts, and the uncertainty within the family structure. Like Hill's original model, after the demand pileup, the family moves on to B—the existing resources—and combines that with C—the appraisal of the crisis, the stressor, and the existing resources. When a family is able to make a positive appraisal, it is more likely to experience healthy coping. Subsequently, coping influences how a family will adapt to the crisis. Adaptation is the final phase in the double ABCX model. Some families will adapt in a healthy manner or *bonadaptation* as evidenced by a balance between members, and others will experience increased imbalance or *maladaptation*.

Another model of family stress is the *contextual model* by researcher and theorist Pauline Boss. Boss's model extends the ABC-X model to include contextual factors, such as the structure of the family and uncontrollable factors like heredity and family culture. Each family is a unique system with a unique set of values and beliefs, and this uniqueness influences how they process stress. Specifically, two types of factors influence stress and coping: (1) internal context or factors that the family can change and (2) external context or factors that are unchangeable. Internal contexts include three dimensions: (1) family structure, such as roles and boundaries; (2) family psychology, such as the family's cognitive and emotional perception of the stressor; and (3) family philosophy or the family's beliefs and values. Unlike the internal context, external context cannot be changed by a family and includes the environment, history, genetics, heredity, and economics of the family system. In Boss's model, these contextual factors influence the stress process outcomes and result in either crisis or coping.

Some have suggested other models of stress that emphasize the role of culture and resiliency. These approaches also examine how family structure influences stress response. These models provide a more comprehensive understanding of family stress but are still in their infancy.

Stressors

Hamilton McCubbin and Joan Patterson's expansion of the ABC-X model developed from their work with Vietnam veterans. It is important to note that stressors can come from a number of places. *Vertical stressors* are stressors that occur *within* an individual family member. Vertical stressors include relational patterns, attitudes, and other internal perceptions that cause strain on the family. *Horizontal stressors* are associated with life events, such as the death of a family member, a sudden chronic medical diagnosis, or empty nest. The reality is that stress, whether vertical or horizontal, can impact the well-being of both the family members and the family system as a whole.

Stressors have also been defined as being *spillover* or *crossover* stressors. Spillover stressors are those that cause conflict within roles. The most common spillover stressor stems from the challenges of being a parent and/or partner as well as an employee. Crossover stress is the stress that impacts a relationship or interpersonal process within a specific setting. A crossover stressor may present itself in the form of anxiety that is transferred from one member of the family to another.

When working with a family in counseling, identifying the specific stressors or demands influencing the family system is essential to the development of a grounded treatment strategy. Regardless of how a family is defined, culturally or socially, there are common stressors that may bring the family into counseling. These include, but are not limited to, health concerns, employment and financial issues, developmental shifts within the family dynamic (such as transitioning from raising infants to toddlers), inclusion of extended family within the home environment, and role changes. It is also common for the family to be dealing with multiple stressors at once. For example, a dual career family may be dealing with the transition to all of the children being school age, while a parent is contemplating shifts to the family system because of increased health concerns for their aging mother or father. In this example, the new shifts to family roles as well as financial and time obligations might cause family members to have to redefine their definition of family and family life.

Stress Management Techniques and Therapies

The circumplex model of marital and family systems is considered by some as the foundation for the development of therapeutic strategies and techniques for working with a family experiencing stress. This model places family cohesion and adaptability on an axis and examines each area according to the four different levels. The levels associated with cohesion, emotional bonding, and autonomy within the family include disengaged (extremely low), separated (moderately low), connected (moderately high), and enmeshed (extremely high). Adaptability levels range from chaotic (extremely high), flexible (moderate to high), structured (low to moderate), to rigid (extremely low). A family's position on this axis reflects how a family will adjust to stressors and unexpected events. It is important to note that individuals within the family may perceive the levels of cohesion and adaptability differently and it is the counselor's responsibility to incorporate those differences into the process of goal setting and treatment planning. The counselor using this model should set short-term goals that reflect a transition from one level to the closest desired level on the axis. Moreover, the counselor must set realistic guidelines regarding the family's ability to shift from one level to the desired level. For example, a family that is highly *disengaged* will take time to transition to being *connected*. A counselor should expect them to slowly transition between these two polar opposite coordinates. Other models for stress reduction place emphasis on specific tasks that might be forgotten or minimized when stress is present in the family. Examples of these tasks include increasing communication and discussion about the stress, exploring how roles within the family are stretched because of the stress/stressors, and identifying any misconceptions that the introduction of the stress/stressor might have caused family members.

Techniques regarding stress management are commonly associated with various theoretical orientations and these will inform the techniques employed by the therapist with the family. One strategy that a therapist may introduce to the family is the incorporation of relaxation into the family's daily routine. Other examples include the incorporation of exercising as a family, integrating a plan to be intentional in scheduling family time away from the home, reexamining chores or responsibilities within the family, and making adjustments to family responsibilities or designating a family dinner night that becomes a nonnegotiable part of everyone's week. Another example would be to explore the incorporation of play into the family as a form of relaxation or a stress reliever. It is not uncommon for families who are experiencing stress or stressors to forget how to enjoy time together and to lose the ability to laugh, have fun, and associate with each other in a nonstressed way. The most important task of the counselor, when exploring potential stress relievers, is to be mindful of the differences within families and to ensure that any recommendations are respectful of the family's cultural norms and beliefs.

Daniel Gutierrez and Valerie Balog

See also Circumplex Model; Family Stress; Marital Distress; Parental Stress: Effects on Children; Posttraumatic Stress Disorder in Children; Stress Management

Further Readings

Boss, P. (2001). *Family stress management: A contextual approach*. Thousand Oaks, CA: Sage.

Landreth, G. L., & Bratton, S. C. (2006). *Child parent relationship therapy: A 10-session filial therapy model*. New York, NY: Routledge.

Malia, J. A. (2006). Basic concepts and models of family stress. *Stress, Trauma, and Crisis, 9*, 141–160.

McCubbin, H. I., & Patterson, J. M. (1983). The family stress process: The double ABCX model of adjustment and adaptation. *Marriage & Family Review, 6*, 7–37.

Sapolsky, R. M. (2004). *Why zebras don't get ulcers*. New York, NY: Henry Holt.

Weber, J. G. (2011). *Individual and family stress and crises*. Thousand Oaks, CA: Sage.

Family Stress Adaptation Theory

Stress originates from many sources including internal or individual causes (e.g., substance abuse, mental or physical illness, and personal injuries) as well as external stressors such as natural disasters, violence, and economic strain. Family stress adaptation theory seeks to explain the ways in which family systems adapt to stressors by focusing on the resources available to families, as well as families' perceptions of the stressful events. Different families can perceive, cope with, and adapt to stressors in different ways. Some families, for example, rely heavily on social support and view the stressor as an obstacle to overcome, while others view stress more negatively and/or through a deficit lens. To better understand stress in families, traditional family stress adaption theories focus on three researched phenomena: the stressful event or hardship; the outcome of the stress; and the intervening factors between the two. Reuben Hill created one of the most well-known stress adaption theories, called the ABC-X model, which is explained in this entry.

Stress

Experts posit that families' perceptions of stressors are the most accurate predictor of the level of parental and familial stress. Parents who adopt a negative attitude of stress typically define their situation as catastrophic, thus negatively impacting the ways in which they function, while those families who adopt positive coping mechanisms are more proactive and experience stress more positively. Families that adapt to stress positively typically employ positive coping mechanisms, which could include speaking to a counselor about the problem or seeking help and information about particular stressors like substance abuse or domestic violence, and are able to directly address the impact of the stress (e.g., creating a safe sensory environment for a child with autism). While some families adapt positively to stress, others adapt negatively and experience maladaption. Examples of maladaption include denying the existence of the problem, isolating oneself from resources including other family members, finding ways to escape the problem—such as substance abuse—and reacting negatively to family members by projecting feelings of frustration and anger onto others.

ABC-X Model

Reuben Hill was the first researcher to address family adaption theories. His original ABC model was later modified to include an additional element and became the ABC-X model of family stress adaption. This model has been influential for its description of the ways family systems make meaning from stressful situations. The ABC-X model explains a family's proneness to crisis, as well as the freedom families can feel while navigating the crisis. Explained in detail below, the ABC-X model addresses the following areas: area A addresses the precrisis variables of families; B identifies the family's crisis-meeting resources; C includes the family-defined definition of the event; and X identifies the crisis. In this formula, A interacts with B which interacts with C and produces X. Therefore, the precrisis variable (A) interacts with the family's resources (B). The family's experiences help them define (C) and navigate the crisis (X).

Looking at each variable independently, variable A encompasses the precipitating events/stressors the family experiences. In most instances, the family has little or no time to prepare for the crisis, such as the sudden death of a child or an automobile accident. Since families are diverse and bring a variety of worldviews to stressful situations, each family will work through, process, and view hardships differently, therefore leaving space for stressors to be seen as either positive or negative. The family's perception of the stressor, which is influenced by their worldview, impacts not only the initial crisis, but also how the family regards stress.

The second variable, B, emphasizes the resources that are available to families during their time of crisis. A family's stressor-meeting resources are the factors in family organization that impact the crisis. Families with more access to valuable resources (e.g., social services and extended family) have an easier time navigating crisis while those families with fewer resources are propelled into crisis. Resources determine the adequacy of crisis proneness of family units.

Variable C is the most subjective variable in Hill's formula. This variable focuses on the particular definition the family uses to label and identify the crisis. Interpretation of the crisis is influenced by the crisis itself, the worldviews of family members, the resources available, and the family's perception of the event. Variable C can also be considered dichotomously. While space exists between positive and negative outcomes, families with a more positive perspective identify stressors as challenges, while those using a deficit perspective often label stressors as *crisis provoking* or *crisis producing*. Variables A, B, and C all impact X, the crisis.

Double ABCX Model

The ABC-X model is the model on which most family stress adaption theories are based, and it was the starting point for Hamilton McCubbin and Joan Patterson, who created what is now called the double ABCX model. Similar to the ABC-X model, the double ABCX model adds postcrisis variables that help to explain and predict the ways families recover from crisis. The ABC-X model also uses the precrisis variables as ways to explain why some families are better able to adapt to stress than others.

Added to the ABC-X model are additional life stressors and strains; psychological, familial, and social resources; changes in the family's definition of the crisis; and family coping strategies, as well as a range of outcomes. In addition to the aforementioned variable ABC-X, the double ABCX model includes variable a, b, c, and x.

Variable a is linked to the original variable A and considers the precrisis pileup of demands. In this area, cumulative effects of stressors and strains are considered over time. In this area, for example, additional strains such as role changes, previous unresolved issues, and relationships with potential resources like extended families are considered as impactful to stress adaptation.

In the double ABCX model, variable b relates closely to variable B in the original model. In this precrisis stage, the family's adaptive resources are considered. Personal resources such as self-esteem and education, along with family support resources like cohesion and adaptability, and social resources such as a church or work community, combine to mediate the pileup of demands, thus increasing a family's ability to adapt to the stressors. Furthermore, a strong network of resources in place before a crisis occurs reduces the impact of demands on a family, thus leading to a more positive outlook and outcome.

Variable c in the double ABCX model is closely aligned with variable C in the original ABC-X model in that it addresses areas of perception and coherence. In this precrisis variable, the family's general attitude, acceptance, and understanding toward circumstances are considered. While perception matters in the overall impact of stress adaptation, this particular variable measures the impact of family coherence before the crisis. In this area, a family's perceived strengths and ability to trust outside influences shapes the meaning of crisis. Similar to the original model, variable c interacts with variables a and b to facilitate the family's adaptive power.

With variable x, the family adaptation is placed on a continuum from maladaption (negative adapation) to bonadaption (positive adaption) with bonadaption on the upper end and maladaptation on the lower end. Variable x, or the outcome, measures the response to crisis and the pileup demands. It considers the system and the amount of integrity a family can maintain. Families that fall closer to bonadaption typically experience minimal discrepancy between precrisis and crisis, while those falling closer to maladaptation experience decreased ability to maintain a functioning level.

Hill is often identified as the founder or father of stress theory because of his work with the original ABC-X formula. The ABC-X model, discussed above, is the basis for most family stress adaption models and is often used as a foundation to build alternative theories of stress adaption. While an initial critique of the original formula includes an emphasis on precrisis and crisis variables only, the double ABCX model extends the original formula to include precrisis, crisis, and postcrisis variables. While the ABC-X model began with the stressor and ended with the crisis, the double ABCX model extended the formula to include postcrisis variables. Both adaption models work to explain the reasons families cope with stressors differently, while emphasizing techniques and resources families can use to navigate stressors.

Sarah Jones

See also Family Stress; Parental Stress: Effects on Children; Stress Management

Further Readings

Hill, R. (1958). Generic features of families under stress. *Social Casework, 49,* 139–150.

Lavee, Y. (2005). Couples under stress: Studying change in dyadic closeness-distance. In V. Bengtson, A. Acock, K. Allen, P. Dilworth-Anderson, & D. Klein (Eds.), *Sourcebook of family theories and methods* (pp. 281–283). Thousand Oaks, CA: Sage.

McCubbin, H. I., & Patterson, J. M. (1983). The family stress process: The double ABCX model of adjustment and adaptation. *Marriage & Family Review, 6*(1/2), 7–37.

Pozo, P., Sarriá, E., & Brioso, A. (2014). Family quality of life and psychological well-being in parents of children with autism spectrum disorders: A double ABCX model. *Journal of Intellectual Disability Research, 58*(5), 442–458. doi:10.1111/jir.12042

Saloviita, T., Itälinna, M., & Leinonen, E. (2003). Explaining the parental stress of fathers and mothers caring for a child with intellectual disability: A double ABCX model. *Journal of Intellectual Disability Research, 47*(4/5), 300–312. doi:10.1046/j.1365-2788.2003.00492.x

Weber, J. G. (2010). *Individual and family stress and crises*. Thousand Oaks, CA: Sage.

Family Values

The term *family values* has been operationally defined for the purpose of this entry as the standards of behavior that the family, the primary socialization unit in an individual's life, upholds as important and worthy of practicing. Family values are stable and tend to endure across generations. These values are often goal directed and speak to the very foundation of a family's beliefs, attitudes, rituals, structure, and progress. Family values directly or indirectly impact roles of family members through communication patterns, conflict resolution strategies, and decision-making processes. They also tend to lay a strong foundation in the life of the individual. The difficulty in monitoring these values has largely to do with the fact that the family system is also affected by outside influences that include culture, socioeconomic status, and geographic location. These outside variables may redefine what is typically known as the traditional family. This entry will examine family values in collectivistic cultures and compare them to those of families from individualistic cultures.

Collectivistic Cultures

Collectivistic cultures are cultures in which the family as a unit is given priority over the goals of its individual family members. For example, a woman may be encouraged to postpone her career goals until her toddler goes to preschool. Collectivistic cultures emphasize the values of self-transcendence and family integrity. Although no two cultures are exactly the same and differences exist even within a given culture, a number of societies have been identified through research as collectivistic cultures upholding these values—for example, Japan, China, Korea, Taiwan, Argentina, Brazil, and India. Similarly, minority cultures in the United States like African American, Asian American, Latino, and American Indian cultures also subscribe to collectivistic values; accordingly, family members may have to deal with additional stress due to different expectations and possible microaggressions from the majority culture. Family members in collectivistic cultures are expected to protect each other and remain loyal to the in-group regardless of circumstance. Individual goals in collectivistic cultures are seen as self-serving and against the best interest of the family as a single unit. Behavior is instead directed toward what is best for the family and individual desires are subordinate, often not having the opportunity to be expressed at all. Members are expected to be obedient, conflict avoidant, respectful to elders, and charged with protecting the younger generations. This helps to ensure that the family will succeed as an entire unit, and the following generations will be provided for.

Studies of collectivistic cultures recognize family interdependence as a protective factor. The member of such a family is likely to receive the benefits of continual support, a sense of belonging, higher self-esteem, lower scores on depression and distress scales, and a sense of morality based on the concept of sacrifice for the greater good. The underlying values expressed are those of benevolence, universalism, and respect for tradition. At the same time, however, family members in collectivistic cultures are at risk for great psychological distress. For example, a recent study of Indian adolescents found that pressures from familial linkages coupled with high standards for achievement increase psychological distress and incidence of depression. High expectations were incorporated into every aspect of the adolescents' lives, including career goals, financial success, academic achievement, and family obligations. If members perceived themselves as falling short of family wishes, levels of depression rose dramatically.

Members of families with a collectivistic orientation tend to feel more secure because the family unit serves as a great support system during conflicts and crises. Family members approach the elders within the family first before seeking outside help to deal with conflict. This inclusion of family member input into decision-making emphasizes the values of loyalty, respect for tradition, deference to elders, obedience, and humility. Most of the existing research on family values has been done in individualistic cultures, which may lead the general public to believe that healthy familial standards cannot be achieved in other cultures. However, research findings infer that the family unit is considered more sacred in collectivistic cultures. In fact, many of these cultures view the family as a religious entity that is provided by a higher being for its members to protect and support each other. Other parties are not allowed to penetrate the sanctity of the family unit. Individualistic cultures, on the other hand, subscribe to alternative sets of values regarding how each family member is expected to behave, often making it easier to collect research data in these cultures. Thus, it is clear that family values in collectivistic cultures emphasize viewing family as a unit and have certain expectations from family members which may be beneficial to them but also create a level of accountability that may be perceived as stressful.

Individualistic Cultures

Individualism advocates for the self-reliance and independence of the individual. Families that subscribe to an individualistic value set prize individual success over the family. In the model of family values, one can assume that these cultures promote self-enhancement and openness to change. Goals, career choices, choice of spouse, and location of homes are based primarily on that individual's inalienable right to make progress toward his or her own satisfaction. Countries such as the United States, Germany, South Africa, and Australia all subscribe to individualistic values.

Within the United States, the majority culture, or European/Caucasian American culture, is considered to value an individualistic family orientation. Family members in these contexts are commonly seen as separate and distinct individuals whose actions do not reflect on their family of origin. In turn, individual values are promoted to the following generations and each additional generation utilizes this same value set.

Unlike collectivistic cultures, actions are not performed to please ancestors or for the greater good of the family. Instead, an individual has the opportunity to make choices based solely on one's pursuit of happiness. For instance, in individualistic cultures, if a husband and wife are unhappy, divorce is considered a perfectly reasonable option. This option allows the couple to separate their assets as they so choose, or as is decided by the judiciary system, and the members are allowed to remarry in the future. This asset division is often self-directed, representative of the value of independence. Each member of the couple seeks the assets most valuable to establish their power and entitlement. In collectivistic cultures, often divorce is not an option. Assets are combined, and the well-being of all the members of the family depends on the couple staying together. For those religiously affiliated there is also the belief that the divorce strips the individuals of their blessings or rewards from the higher power and any subsequent marriage is not considered "real." The more independent a member of the family is in individualistic culture, the more he or she is prized. Characteristics such as self-reliance, assertiveness, financial wealth, and great ambition are considered valuable attributes.

Cultural Comparisons

While research on individualism and collectivism suggests that cultural differences are bound by location, families could hold individualistic values while being in or from a collectivistic culture. Similarly, families could endorse collectivistic values while being in or from a primarily individualistic culture. Whether the family chooses one value set over the other has much to do with a dynamic interplay of factors including family of origin value set, ethnicity, income levels, and educational investment. For example, members of Hispanic families in the United States often marry and bear children at comparatively young ages, while majority-culture families delay marriage and child bearing. Although this may seem unrelated to contemporary cultural values, historically family formation in large part once had to do with combining families' assets. Cultures that still experience the need to combine assets due to economic disadvantage often get married at early ages to ensure the longevity of the family. These families also tend to endorse collectivistic values. By contrast, families that are not plagued by economic disadvantage have more opportunities available and are able to make choices based on individual desire over the values of the collective group.

Collectivism can be viewed as a protective factor; however, it is not free of limitations. Individuals from these cultures who go against the social and familial norms are often ostracized, leaving them without real or perceived support. For example, Latin American males who identify as homosexuals often are at conflict with identifying as Latino and gay simultaneously due to familial values. Therefore, sexuality and the action of choosing a partner might be affected by the family's wishes. This type of conflict could cause greater psychological distress among collectivistic families. The counseling profession is attempting to create a bridge between what is appropriate for treatment and what may be harmful to the client when considering family values versus individual desires. Counseling with an individual who subscribes to a collectivistic set of values may be difficult. Sessions may have to be conducted as a family, or with the overall well-being of the family as the treatment goal. The values instilled in individuals affect the course of development of the individual, and thus the course of treatment.

Dynamic Interplay of the Family Values

Constructs such as family values and worldview are intimately connected. The endorsement of one's family values affect whether he or she will choose early marriage, to bear children prior to pursuing secondary or postsecondary education, and even the career he or she will choose. Researchers are now considering shifting the idea of individualism and collectivism from existing on one dimension and leaning more toward the belief that they exist separately. By doing so, individuals and families exist somewhere along both values, not toward one or the other. Support for this new viewpoint comes from research regarding aggression in adolescents. In collectivistic cultures, youth are portrayed as exercising restraint, being more obedient, and having less aggressive behaviors. These qualities continue in later life as many collectivistic countries have low crime rates compared with individualistic countries. This, however, does not lead to a life completely devoid of aggression. While many collectivistic countries value the maintenance of harmony, misconduct is still present among youth. Comparing levels of misconduct among American, Australian, and Chinese youth, researchers found that Western youth (those from the United States and Australia) shared higher levels of misconduct than Chinese youth who endorsed individualistic family values. However, these variations were moderated by family environments and parental monitoring. This speaks to the dynamic interplay of factors that affect the endorsement of family values.

Stable, supportive families can exist within both cultural value sets. Therefore, the question is not whether one is superior to the other, but instead which family unit supports the individual's development in a quality manner, regardless of the endorsement of collectivistic or individualistic family values. Positive family environments allow individuals to succeed academically, financially, and psychologically. While collectivistic cultures promote teamwork and task completion, individualistic cultures promote competition and creativity. One can see how each of these qualities can be helpful at various times throughout life.

Future Research

While much of the literature available on collectivistic and individualistic family values has focused on the effects of endorsing one value set over the other, very little research has been done on what causes the initial endorsement. What causes families to adopt either collectivistic or individualistic values and how closely can we predict whether their children will subscribe to the same value set? Additionally, how do other constructs such as sexual preference, religiosity, geographic location, and proximity to family of origin moderate the endorsement? Future research should explore what factors may cause any fluctuation in endorsement situationally and across the lifespan. As stated previously, researchers suggest that collectivistic and individualistic values may be situational. However, support for this idea is limited to data collected from self-report questionnaires and generally states that individuals tend to utilize collectivist values in social interactions versus individualistic values concerning private matters. Moreover, results are often limited in their generalizability.

Suneetha Babu Manyam and Shatel Francis

See also Beliefs and Values; Family Rituals; Individual Family Culture; Therapists' Values

Further Readings

Edgar-Smith, S. E., & Wozniak, R. H. (2010). Family relational values in the parent-adolescent relationship. *Counseling and Values, 54*, 187–200.

Parkinson, P. (2013). Family structure and children's wellbeing: A reply to Lucas, Nicholson and Erbas. *Journal of Family Studies, 19*(3), 267–271.

Petts, R. J. (2014). Family, religious attendance, and trajectories of psychological well-being among youth. *Journal of Family Psychology, 28*(6), 759–768. doi:10.1037/a0036892

Schwartz, S. H. (1994). Are there universal aspects in the structure and contents of human values? *Journal of Social Issues, 50*(4), 19–45.

Sue, D. W., & Sue, D. (2012). *Counseling the culturally diverse: Theory and practice* (6th ed.). New York, NY: Wiley.

Wang, K. T., Puri, R., Slaney, R. B., Methikalam, B., & Chadha, N. (2012). Cultural validity of perfectionism among Indian students: Examining personal and family aspects through a collectivistic perspective. *Measurement and Evaluation in Counseling and Development, 45*, 32–48. doi:10.1144/0748175 611423109

FEEDBACK

See Positive and Negative Feedback

FEMALE ORGASMIC DISORDER

Female orgasmic disorder (FOD) is a clinical diagnosis characterized by problems achieving orgasm or dissatisfaction of orgasms in women during sexual activity. An *orgasm* can be defined as the climax of sexual excitement, involving a series of rhythmic muscular contractions leading to feelings of intense pleasure in the genitals. Although this disorder can be diagnosed as a medical condition, FOD is frequently diagnosed as a mental health disorder, as outlined in the *Diagnostic and Statistical Manual of Mental Disorders* (DSM-5). This entry is separated into three sections and provides an overview of symptoms, causes, and treatments associated with FOD.

Criteria for Diagnosis and Symptoms of Female Orgasmic Disorder

Categorized as a sexual dysfunction in the DSM-5, FOD requires specific criteria to be present for diagnosis. First, a woman must experience a delay in, infrequency of, and/or reduced intensity, or absence of orgasms approximately 75% to 100% of the time that she engages in sexual activity. These symptoms must be persistent for at least 6 months and must cause clinically significant distress or impairment to the woman's social, occupational, or personal functioning. Examples of distress or impairment include marital problems, lack of sleep, or severe anxiety stemming from symptoms associated with the disorder. Another criteria for diagnosis is that the symptoms experienced cannot be a result of severe distress or the effects of a substance, medication, or other medical conditions.

FOD can be lifelong or acquired, meaning that it can be present since the woman first became sexually active or after a period of relatively normal sexual function. It can also be generalized (i.e., not limited to specific types of stimulation, situations, or intimate partners) or situational (i.e., only occurring with specific types of stimulation, situations, or partners). Although the main symptom of FOD is difficulty achieving orgasm, women often report experiencing other symptoms that are associated with lack of orgasm, including painful sex, lack of lubrication, and lack of sexual desire.

Prevalence and Causes of Female Orgasmic Disorder

FOD is the second most frequently reported sexual problem in women, with prevalence rates reaching 42% at some point during the lifespan. In order to gain cultural perspective, a 2013 study found that up to 28% of women in the United States, South America, and Europe met criteria for FOD, while an alarming 46% of women in Asian countries met criteria for this disorder. The female sexual response is complex in nature and integrates sexual stimuli as well as emotional intimacy and relationship satisfaction. This means that a woman's physiological arousal to sex is largely connected to her psychological arousal, which may often impact the climax phase of sex.

For the past 50 years, numerous medical and psychological research studies have been conducted on FOD. These studies revealed that symptoms of this disorder are frequently associated with emotional and mental health issues, including relationship problems, stress, depression, and anxiety. Relationship problems can include the following: fighting or arguing with a partner; emotional, physical, or sexual abuse within the relationship; poor communication among partners; anger, resentment, and lack of trust toward a partner; and differences or lack of understanding regarding sexual intimacy, preferences, and satisfaction. These relationship issues often lead to an increase in stress, which can also inhibit climax during sexual intimacy. Other stressors like problems at work, financial burdens, medical illness, and having children may also lead to FOD. Mental health problems that inhibit healthy sexual functioning, such as depression and anxiety, may be a result of other personal issues, such as poor body image or a history of sexual abuse. Studies revealed that other factors, such as sexual experience and educational level may also contribute to FOD.

The way a woman thinks and feels about sex can severely impact her ability to enjoy sexual intimacy and reach orgasm. Psychological factors such as attitudes and beliefs about sex and religious values oftentimes influence a woman's initial and lifelong thought patterns and feelings about her sexuality. Some women receive negative messages about sex during childhood and adolescence and grow up believing that sex is dirty, should only be for the purpose of procreation, or that women should not talk about their sexual needs. Such negative thinking patterns often lead to feelings of guilt and shame regarding sexual activity, potentially resulting in sexual dysfunctions in adulthood.

Although psychological factors have been found to play a major role in FOD, some physiological factors have also been found to inhibit a woman's orgasmic response. Some of these factors include illicit drugs, such as alcohol, or prescribed medications, such as antipsychotics, antihypertensives, and antidepressants. Other physiological factors associated with this disorder include age (especially for women nearing menopause), physical illnesses, and poor physical health. Women seeking treatment should be evaluated for both physical and psychological factors in order to determine the best course of treatment.

Treatment for Female Orgasmic Disorder

While FOD is a complex sexual dysfunction in women, with numerous contributing physiological and psychological factors, treatment options are widely available and prognosis for this disorder is good. Due to the strong psychological component related to FOD, cognitive-behavioral therapy (CBT) interventions have been found to be an effective treatment option for women struggling with this disorder. CBT is a form of psychotherapy in which thinking patterns are challenged and modified in order to change unwanted behaviors or dysfunctions. Some CBT approaches that have been found to be effective with FOD include individual and couple's counseling, sex education, direct masturbation training, sensate focus, systematic desensitization treatments, and Kegel exercises.

Individuals seeking treatment for FOD benefit from meeting with a licensed professional counselor or sex therapist. Counseling sessions, which are strictly confidential, often take place in a comfortable and private setting with an individual who is experienced and educated, with master's degree or above, in providing mental health treatment services. Couples counseling is a popular and effective treatment option for women diagnosed with FOD. This form of therapy allows partners to come together and strengthen many skills that may be lacking in the relationship that could be negatively impacting the couple's sexual life. During therapy sessions, couples can work on their reflecting, listening, communication, emotional expression, and conflict resolution skills. This form of therapy can also help partners learn to discuss their fantasies, preferences, fears, and inhibitions about sex in a safe environment.

Sex education during couples or individual counseling has also been found to be a helpful treatment technique. Educating couples or individuals struggling with FOD about the usefulness of mental imagery or fantasizing during sexual intimacy has been found to facilitate orgasm. Bibliotherapy, which includes the suggestion of books and readings to learn more about sexual intimacy, is a useful tool in sex education. Sex education also challenges the unrealistic expectations individuals and society create regarding sex. These unrealistic expectations can be damaging and create stigma that many individuals feel toward sex and orgasms.

Direct masturbation training is another effective form of therapy recommended for women experiencing symptoms of FOD, with success rates of up to 90% after treatment is completed. This form of therapy typically lasts between 4 and 16 weeks and can take place in individual, couples, or group therapy settings. Direct masturbation training typically involves gradual exposure to genital stimulation, often incorporating roleplay, sexual fantasy, and sexually stimulating devices, such as a vibrator, that facilitates orgasm. Once women learn to masturbate and feel comfortable with their own touch, they can then teach their partners to touch them similarly, which can facilitate orgasm.

Sensate focus and systematic desensitization treatment therapies are similar to direct masturbation training. During sensate focus therapy, the goal is not necessarily to achieve orgasm, but to alleviate the anxiety and pressure many women feel to become sexually aroused and reach orgasm during sex. The first few steps of sensate focus involve becoming relaxed with a partner and exploring one another's bodies, using nonsexual touch in order to reduce any pressure to become sexually aroused. As partners become more comfortable and relaxed, they can take steps toward sexual touch, becoming aroused and eventually reaching orgasm. Sensate focus therapy normally takes place at home, where the couple is comfortable. It may take several weeks or months of exploring each other's bodies before the couple takes the steps toward becoming sexually aroused and reaching orgasm.

Systematic desensitization therapy is another treatment option for FOD and works best for women who experience severe anxiety regarding sex, which often inhibits the ability to reach orgasm. This treatment therapy involves exposing the woman to progressively more anxiety-provoking stimuli, such as sexual touch, while teaching her to relax when the stimuli is occurring. The first session might include showing a video or picture of sexual touch, and then teaching the woman relaxation techniques during the video. The second session might include the partner giving the woman a massage or providing nonsexual touch, followed by relaxation. Eventually, the stimuli increases, while the woman continues to stay relaxed. This form of therapy requires patience and trust from both partners.

While psychotherapy can be quite effective, there still exists some stigma associated with seeing a counselor or sex therapist. Many women prefer nonpsychotherapy treatments, which they can do at home, discretely, without much help. Kegel exercises are a fairly simple treatment technique for women suffering from FOD. These exercises can be self-taught and involve tightening and releasing of the pelvic floor muscles about 10 times a day. Strengthening the Kegel muscle can help facilitate orgasm. Some women with FOD report difficulty focusing on sex or staying in the moment while having intercourse, often leading to interference with reaching orgasm. Certain home practices that train individuals to stop and focus on the moment such as yoga, meditation, and mindfulness training can be effective treatment options for these women.

Vanessa B. Teixeira

See also Cognitive-Behavioral Couples Therapy; DSM and V-Codes; Sensate Focus; Sex Therapy; Sexual Dysfunction; Sexual Health; Sexual Toys/Sexual Aids

Further Readings

American Psychiatric Association. (2013). *Diagnostic and statistical manual of mental disorders* (5th ed.). Washington, DC: Author.

Bancroft, J. (2009). *Human sexuality and its problems* (3rd ed.). Edinburgh, Scotland: Churchill Livingston/Elsevier.

Bancroft, J., Herbenick, D., & Reynolds, M. (2003). Masturbation as a marker of sexual development. In J. Bancroft (Ed.), *Sexual development in childhood* (pp. 156–185). Bloomington: Indiana University Press.

Laan, E., Rellini, A. H., & Barnes, T. (2013). Standard operating procedures for female orgasmic disorder: Consensus of the International Society for Sexual Medicine. *Journal of Sexual Medicine.* 10(1), 74–82.

Nairne, K. D., & Hemsley, D. R. (1983). The use of directed masturbation training in the treatment of primary anorgasmia. *British Journal of Clinical Psychology,* 22(4), 283–294.

Pereira, V. M., Arias-Carrión, O., Machado, S., Nardi, A. E., & Silva, A. C. (2013). Sex therapy for female sexual dysfunction. *International Archives of Medicine,* 6(1), 37.

ter Kuile, M. M., Both, S., & van Lankveld, J. J. (2010). Cognitive behavioral therapy for sexual dysfunctions in women. *Psychiatric Clinics of North America,* 33(3), 595–610.

Witting, K., Santtila, P., Varjonen, M., Jern, P., Johansson, A., von der Pahlen, B., & Sandnabba, K. (2008). Female sexual dysfunction, sexual distress, and compatibility with partner. *Journal of Sexual Medicine,* 5, 2587–2599.

Female Sexual Interest/ Arousal Disorder

Female sexual interest/arousal disorder (FSIAD) is a clinical diagnosis characterized by significant absence of or decrease in sexual functioning and thoughts and fantasies about sex, causing substantial clinical distress. Women experiencing this problem commonly report symptoms such as lack of a sex drive and difficulty becoming lubricated or aroused during sexual activity. Categorized as a sexual dysfunction in the fifth edition of the *Diagnostic and Statistical Manual of Mental Disorders* (DSM-5), FSIAD can be highly disruptive and can occur at any stage of the sexual response cycle, including the desire, arousal, orgasm, and resolution stages. This entry provides an overview of symptoms, causes, and treatments associated with FSIAD.

Diagnosis Criteria and Symptoms of Female Sexual Interest/Arousal Disorder

FSIAD is a sexual dysfunction that requires specific criteria outlined by the DSM-5 to be present for diagnosis. First, a woman must regularly experience at least three of the following six symptoms related to sexual response: (1) absent or reduced interest in sexual activity, (2) absent or reduced thoughts or fantasies about sex, (3) lack of or reduced initiation of sexual activity as well as lack of receptiveness to partner's attempts to initiate sex, (4) absent or reduced sexual pleasure or excitement during sexual activity in approximately 75% to 100% of sexual encounters, (5) absent or reduced sexual interest or arousal to internal or external sexual cues (including written, verbal, or visual cues), and (6) absent or reduced bodily sensations during sexual activity in approximately 75% to 100% of sexual encounters.

According to the DSM-5, these symptoms must be persistent for at least 6 months and must cause clinically significant impairment or distress in social, occupational, or personal functioning. Examples of impairment or distress include sleep difficulties, relationship conflict, and anxiety resulting from symptoms associated with the disorder. Another criteria for diagnosis is that these symptoms cannot be a result of severe relationship distress, such as domestic violence, or the effects of a substance, medication, or other medical condition.

FSIAD can be lifelong, with symptoms present since the woman first became sexually active, or acquired, with symptoms beginning after a period of normal sexual functioning. Additionally, symptoms associated with FSIAD can be generalized or situational. If symptoms are generalized, they occur indiscriminately, not limited to specific types of stimulation, situations, or intimate partners. If symptoms are mostly situational, they only occur with specific types of stimulation, situations, or partners. The level of severity in clinical distress can also vary from mild or moderate to severe distress over the symptoms experienced.

Prevalence of Female Sexual Interest/Arousal Disorder

Low sexual desire has been widely reported as the most common sexual complaint among women. However, prevalence rates for FSIAD, as outlined in the DSM-5, vary and have proved difficult to determine due to cultural differences as well as different definitions of low sexual desire and arousal among women. For example, women from East Asia report lower sexual desire than women from Western societies. Additionally, the DSM-5 recently joined two separate sexual dysfunctions outlined in previous editions of the DSM. Sexual arousal disorder and hypoactive sexual desire disorder have been combined into the present FSIAD diagnosis. Although there is no widely known prevalence rate for this new combined disorder, sexual dysfunctions among women are quite common, with prevalence rates ranging from 30% to 50% of the female population in the United States.

Causes of Female Sexual Interest/Arousal Disorder

Sexual dysfunctions in women have been widely studied by researchers from a variety of disciplines, including medicine and psychology. Research suggests several factors that contribute to FSIAD, with both physiological and psychological causes. Oftentimes, these factors tend to be interrelated, with physical, psychological, and social problems playing a role in the sexual dysfunction. For example, in the case of an overweight woman who takes medications for high blood pressure, has self-image issues, and struggles with low sexual interest and arousal, medications may contribute to a reduced libido but her low sex drive may also be triggered by self-image issues related to her weight.

Physiological factors associated with FSIAD include age, levels of sex hormones, amount of blood flow to the genitals, medical illnesses, physical conditions, medications, and drugs. Age has been found to be a key factor in women suffering from FSIAD. Age largely determines other factors that contribute to this disorder, including reduced estrogen levels and decreased genital blood flow. Older women going through menopause report much higher rates of symptoms associated with FSIAD (52.4%) than younger and premenopausal women (26.7%). Estrogen plays an important role in vaginal lubrication, as it facilitates the enzyme that controls vaginal and clitoral arterial blood flow. When estrogen levels decrease, vaginal tissues become thin, dry, and less elastic. This causes difficulties with lubrication, which can cause painful intercourse and genital stimulation. Additionally, low estrogen levels have been found to reduce sexual interest and can also reduce tactile sensitivity in women by reducing tactile receptors in the genital area. Other factors, such as ovarian removal, recently giving birth, breastfeeding, and the use of hormonal contraceptives to prevent pregnancy can also reduce estrogen levels, negatively influencing sexual functioning.

Research on sexual dysfunctions suggests that certain medical illnesses and physical conditions associated with FSIAD include breast cancer, diabetes, urinary incontinence, bowel difficulties, arthritis, fatigue, headaches, coronary artery disease, autoimmune disorders, multiple sclerosis, and pregnancy. Certain medications often used to treat these conditions, such as antidepressants, anticonvulsants, blood pressure medications, antihistamines, chemotherapy drugs, and opioids have also been found to reduce sexual desire in women. Other drugs such as alcohol and nicotine (cigarettes) can severely affect sexual drive and vaginal lubrication.

While physiological problems such as age and physical conditions can severely reduce sexual interest and arousal among women, research suggests that psychological factors actually contribute more to a diagnosis of FSIAD than do biological causes. Psychological and social factors associated with this disorder can include mental illness, stress, relationship problems, cultural and religious issues, body image issues, and past negative or traumatic experiences.

Mental health disorders that negatively impact an individual's everyday functioning such as depression, anxiety, and eating disorders have been linked to low sexual interest and arousal among women. While not a diagnosable disorder, stress can severely impact a woman's sex drive. Financial, family, or work-related stress can become overwhelming and significantly decrease sexual interest. Relationship problems, such as lack of connection with a partner, unresolved conflicts, infidelity, and an inability to communicate sexual needs and preferences can also hinder sexual arousal and interest.

Cultural and religious issues can also contribute to a diagnosis of FSIAD. Negative thinking patterns about sexual intimacy derived from cultural expectations or strict religious teachings can lead to feelings of guilt and shame regarding sexuality. Similarly, body image issues can also play a role in this disorder. Women who feel uncomfortable or embarrassed about their body may experience anxiety or discomfort with sexual activity and may even completely disengage from sexual activity with a partner. Furthermore, past negative or traumatic experiences can negatively impact a women's sexual functioning. A history of sexual abuse or sexual trauma may leave a woman physically numb to genital stimuli or afraid to engage in sexual contact. Other negative sexual experiences, such as a history of pain or lack of pleasure during sex, may also contribute to this sexual dysfunction.

Treatment for Female Sexual Interest/Arousal Disorder

FSIAD presents as a multifaceted sexual dysfunction in women, with many contributing physiological and psychological factors. Generally, women with this disorder benefit from a combined and comprehensive treatment approach that addresses any presenting physiological or psychological factors. Treatment options that have been successful and effective in treating FSIAD include mental health counseling or sex therapy, hormone therapy, medication adjustments, vaginal lubricants, vaginal dilators, and pelvic floor rehabilitation. While treatment options are widely available and prognosis for this disorder is good, treatment largely depends on what is causing the sexual dysfunction.

Once the cause of FSIAD is determined, treatment options can be discussed with a physician or mental health counselor. If the cause of the disorder is primarily physiological in nature and is due to the woman's age, level of sex hormones, or amount of vaginal blood flow, the primary treatment option is hormone therapy. Since estrogen is essential for optimum sexual functioning, a medical doctor can prescribe estrogen via pill, patch, spray, gel, cream, or slow-releasing vaginal ring. Increased amounts of estrogen to the body improves vaginal tone and elasticity, increases blow flow to the genitals, and stimulates sexual arousal. If the cause of the disorder relates to other physiological problems, such as medical illnesses, physical conditions, medications, or nonprescription drugs, further treatment options are available. Medical illnesses and physical conditions should be closely monitored and treated by a physician. Medication changes and adjustments may help to reduce symptoms associated with FSIAD. Individuals addicted to drugs such as alcohol and nicotine may benefit from meeting with a mental health counselor, checking in to a rehabilitation facility, or engaging in self-help groups, such as Alcoholics Anonymous. If the disorder is indeed caused by biological factors, a physician should be involved in the treatment in order to properly manage symptoms.

Treatment options differ for women whose FSIAD diagnosis is primarily psychological in nature. If the disorder is due to factors such as mental illness, relationship problems, or negative thinking patterns, meeting with a mental health counselor for individual or couples counseling is the most effective treatment option. Mental health counselors are trained clinicians who are well versed in effective treatment approaches for individuals suffering from a host of disorders, including sexual dysfunctions. Counselors can help women struggling with FSIAD to better understand their body's sexual response and how to communicate their wants and needs effectively with intimate partners. Couples counseling can help partners better communicate and deal with relationship issues that may hinder their sexual intimacy. This form of therapy can also help women who are feeling stressed, anxious, or depressed by teaching them coping, stress management, and mindfulness skills. Furthermore, women struggling with body image issues and who have had negative sexual experiences can also benefit from talking with a counselor and resolving personal issues in an effort to increase healthy sexual functioning.

While many women suffer from symptoms associated with FSIAD, a variety of treatment options are available. Knowledge of the primary cause of the disorder helps trained professionals better understand the diagnosis and recommend the most effective treatment options. By treating the underlining cause of the sexual dysfunction, symptoms of FSIAD dissipate and healthy sexual functioning is restored.

Vanessa B. Teixeira

See also Couples and Marriage Counseling; DSM and V-Codes; Sex Therapy; Sexual Dysfunction; Sexual Health; Sexual Intimacy

Further Readings

American Psychiatric Association. (2013). *Diagnostic and statistical manual of mental disorders* (5th ed.). Washington, DC: Author.

Goldstein, A., & Brandon, M. (2009). *Reclaiming desire: 4 keys to finding your lost libido*. New York, NY: Rodale.

Hayes, R. D., Dennerstein, L., Bennett, C. M., Sidat, M., Gurrin, L. C., & Fairley, C. K. (2008). Risk factors for female sexual dysfunction in the general population: Exploring factors associated with low sexual function and sexual distress. *Journal of Sexual Medicine, 5*(7), 1681–1693.

Maass, V. S. (2006). *Facing the complexities of women's sexual desire*. New York, NY: Springer Science & Business Media.

Mintz, L. B., Balzer, A. M., Zhao, X., & Bush, H. E. (2012). Bibliotherapy for low sexual desire: Evidence for effectiveness. *Journal of Counseling Psychology, 59*(3), 471.

Rosen, R., Brown, C., Heiman, J., Leiblum, S., Meston, C., Shabsigh, R., . . . D'Agostino, R. (2000). The Female Sexual Function Index (FSFI): A multidimensional self-report instrument for the assessment of female sexual function. *Journal of Sex & Marital Therapy, 26*(2), 191–208.

Rosen, R., Shifren, J. L., Monz, B. U., Odom, D. M., Russo, P. A., & Johannes, C. B. (2009). Correlates of sexually related personal distress in women with low sexual desire. *Journal of Sexual Medicine, 6,* 1549–1560.

Shifren, J. L., Monz, B. U., Russo, P. A., Segreti, A., & Johannes, C. B. (2008). Sexual problems and distress in United States women: Prevalence and correlates. *Obstetrics & Gynecology, 112,* 970–978.

FEMINIST FAMILY THERAPY

A general assumption of feminist family therapy is that gender is an organizing construct that shapes the interactions of people and needs to be integrated into the work of a family therapist. Feminist family therapy (FFT) emerged in the 1970s when feminist theorists critiqued the field for not including gender issues in conversations pertaining to therapy. These values were fueled by social movements which urged therapists to consider how the construct of gender affected family dynamics. Feminist therapists also urged clinicians to consider their own role in the treatment of therapeutic clients and how their own views may be biased in regard to the roles, mental health, and abilities of women.

Feminist family therapy is an evolving set of ideas that inform the practice of marriage and family therapy. Feminism itself has been present within the United States for over a century and a half and there are many different kinds of feminism, but this entry will be limited to feminist family therapy although some of the major influences from outside of family therapy will be addressed. This entry provides an overview of the history of feminist family therapy, explains the connection between FFT and general system theory (GST), and concludes with a brief discussion of the literature on applying FFT.

History of Feminist Family Therapy

Rachel Hare-Mustin is credited with being the first to publish on the topic of feminism in family therapy in 1978. She was trained as a clinical psychologist and her contributions to FFT were shaped by her commitment to activism. Alongside her family, she was active in the peace movement and the civil rights movement. Her suggestions for feminist inclusion went beyond gender and advocated for others to examine history, context, power, and culture. While Hare-Mustin was the first to publish about feminism specifically in family therapy, it is important to note the interdisciplinary efforts in the social sciences that birthed this field of study. For example, in 1982 psychologist Carol Gilligan published the influential book *In a Different Voice*, which presented the importance of difference as it examined how women were virtually missing from psychological study. At the same time, women from other fields were coming together—what were once solitary voices challenging gender became supportive communities.

There are many people connected with the early days of feminist family therapy. Betty Carter, Peggy Papp, Olga Silverstein, and Marianne Walters joined together in the 1980s to form The Women's Project in Family Therapy. This group participated in the "Stonehenge" meetings, which were organized by Monica McGoldrick, Carol Anderson, and Froma Walsh, in 1984, 1986, and internationally in 1991. These were meetings where women joined together to challenge patriarchy and promote women's issues in family therapy. Through these meetings, participants made commitments for collaboration on efforts to advance feminist work. Books were planned and the *Journal of Feminist Family Therapy* (JFFT) was conceived. Lois Braverman became the founding editor of this important journal in 1988. The journal continues to be active and tackles topics from hierarchy to colonialism to resiliency. The journal spans a breadth of topics that seek to explore the relationship between feminist family therapy and traditional family therapy theory and practice. Deborah Luepnitz wrote *The Family Interpreted* in 1988. This book critiques eight popular approaches in family therapy. Luepnitz presented a historical context of the family and warned the reader from practicing therapy from a historical perspective. She noted the "mother blaming" that is rampant in mental health disciplines and also commented on the prevalence of women's assuming the primary burden for maintaining family health. Luepnitz wrote about her connection with the women's movement and the progressive social movements of the 1970s. It is noteworthy that much of the early efforts of the feminist movement in family therapy coincided with a historical context geared toward equity and justice.

In 1991, Marianne Walters, Betty Carter, Peggy Papp, and Olga Silverstein published *The Invisible Web: Gender Patterns in Family Relationships*. In this book, they used the lens of gender to examine family functioning. In 2003, another important book was published by Louise Silverstein and Thelma Jean Goodrich. *Feminist Family Therapy: Empowerment in Social Context* is a feminist family therapy sourcebook in which the authors acknowledged their own identities, including the point that they are both White women, and made a point to include voices from their sisters of color who were often not included in the same way that White scholars were.

The field of feminist family therapy experienced a boom in the late 1970s into the 1990s, yet more recent studies find that papers and presentations specifically about gender are on the decline.

Feminism has experienced several "waves," and the emergence of feminist family therapy coincided with feminism's second wave. Associated with the radical feminist movement of the 1960s and 1970s, the second wave coincides with the entrance of feminist ideals into the field of marriage and family therapy. During this time, the United States was experiencing many important political movements, including anti-Vietnam War protests, the lesbian and gay movements, and the civil rights movement. Many of the pioneering feminist family therapists note the importance of the social climate and align with the various movements of this era. Among the demands were sexual and reproductive freedom, equal pay for equal work, and breakdown of the division of labor based on gender.

By the 2010s, the influence of the third wave of feminism had become apparent in feminist family therapy. Taking issue with "universal womanhood" and embracing the importance of diversity, difference, and ambiguity, third-wave feminists are more interested in intersectionality. Intersectional feminists are particularly mindful of the fact that people's identities intersect in important ways and that feminists cannot narrow their focus to gender-based oppression. This perspective was very much informed by feminist theorists of the second-wave era, such as bell hooks, who advocated for a conceptualization of feminism that extends beyond men and women having equal access to power. The feminist agenda that includes an intersectional perspective recognizes oppression experienced because of gender, but also due to racism, colonization, classism, heterosexism, homophobia, and other factors.

Women in the United States have made important strides since the entry of feminism in the field of marriage and family therapy. More women than men are entering and graduating from college, more women are holding important professional and political positions. Generally speaking, women have more social capital today than in the early 1970s. It also holds true that the power women have is stratified, and not all women share the same access to power. For example, some people have more access to power than others (e.g., cisgender, wealthy, well-educated, heterosexual, White) while women who are from nondominant groups of society, including women of color, lesbians, and women who are differently abled have less power.

At the time of this writing, women continue to be paid less than men for equal work. Women continue to struggle with poverty more than men. Women have less access to high-powered positions, including political positions. Women are in the workforce in equal numbers compared to men, yet, in opposite-sex partnerships, they maintain responsibility for more of the household duties than men. In short, the importance of a feminist agenda is still relevant and needed.

Gender as an Organizing Construct

Traditional family therapy is heavily influenced by general systems theory (GST). Initially, feminist family therapists were encouraged by the influence of GST because unlike many earlier mental health models, GST looked for a systemic etiology of a problem, rather than locating the problem within one person (often the mother). In addition to the benefit of looking at shared responsibility, feminist therapists also had some concerns about adopting this perspective. Through this theory, families were seen as biological systems, or "natural" organisms in which family members had complementary and equal roles. During the early years of family therapy, it was quite common to picture a "normal" or "ideal" family constitution. During this era, many mothers were seen as "overinvolved" or "enmeshed," while many fathers were conceptualized as being "disengaged." These patterns were an indication of traditional gender roles, and therapists who promoted these stereotypes were seen as practicing in a way that accepted this "traditional" and restrictive way of thinking. Early feminist therapists noted that these dynamics were less representative of biological constructs and more connected to a socialized patriarchal framework where men were granted more power and favor over women and children.

Feminist family therapists noted that gender socialization had largely been overlooked in traditional family therapy. The presence of the overengaged mother and disengaged father was indicative of a process of gender socialization that had been mistaken for biological traits. In contrast, men are *socialized* to invest more time in the work world while women are socialized to maintain primary responsibility within the family and home life. Feminist family therapists critiqued the field by uncovering the idea that the roles we often see in families are connected with patriarchal gender roles and that part of our role as therapists is to uncover this dynamic.

In addition to the socialization of gender, feminist theorists also noted the importance of analyzing the power differential associated with gender: That is, power and gender are entwined. Men are socialized to embrace power while women are not. This point is not widely agreed upon or acknowledged, however, which makes this dynamic challenging to comment on. Feminist therapists have argued that men do indeed have more power than women. Thelma Jean Goodrich edited a book in 1991 titled *Women in Power: Perspectives for Family Therapy* that called attention to the disparity in power between men and women. She made the point that failing to comment on power discrepancies was colluding in oppressive practices. Before the feminist critique, family therapists were more committed to perpetuating the idea that members of a family system contribute equally to presenting problems. This idea is particularly dangerous in some instances. For example, ignoring power distribution can make it so that women are sharing responsibility for the reasons counseling is sought, including male-perpetrated violence. It was commonplace for female victims to be asked about their role in maintaining the cycle of abuse.

Similarly, feminist family therapists found that many of the terms associated with marriage and family therapy tend to trivialize or denigrate the experiences of women. As mentioned earlier, *enmeshment* is a popular way to describe the experiences of many mothers. This is also a term that was more commonly associated with women. A similar phenomenon exists with popular terms like *triangulation* and *differentiation*. In fact, there are compelling arguments that contest these concepts or ask that they be viewed through a feminist lens. In 1994, Carmen Knudson-Martin wrote the article "The Female Voice: Applications to Bowen's Family Systems Theory." In this piece, she critiqued the concepts *differentiation* and *emotional fusion*, which refer to the ability to balance thinking and feeling and the ability to balance closeness and distance to others. Knudson-Martin noted that women tend to be socialized to focus on relationships, which makes them appear more dependent on others than men appear. In this article she presented an expanded model that accounts for some of the differences in the experiences of many women.

Feminist Family Therapy Applied

There is not a standardized set of interventions associated with feminist family therapy. Feminist therapists continue to add recommendations and theory to enhance social responsibility and equity, but there is not an agreed-upon model to inform practice. Written contributions are largely theoretical while empirical contributions are primarily limited to small-sample studies.

There are texts that couple traditional model components but do so through a feminist lens. For example, Betty Carter, a social worker by training, and Monica McGoldrick wrote *The Family Life Cycle* in 1980. Other authors have applied feminist thought to important clinical concerns like anorexia, addiction, and abuse. Others have sought to understand the process of doing feminist therapy. In 1991, Leora Black and Fred Piercy developed a scale to assess how family therapists conceptualize the process of family therapy from a feminist perspective. The purpose of this instrument was to gauge the degree to which a person was using feminist-informed practice. Shelley Haddock, Toni Zimmerman, and David MacPhee built on past work to develop the Power Equity Guide in 2000. This guide promoted the need for evaluating gender-based power inequality in the practice of family therapy. This guide provides therapists with important recommendations for how to talk about the dynamic of power in therapy sessions. Lynn Parker and Rhea Almeida wrote an article in 2001 that investigated the political and personal aspects of feminist family therapy. Almeida and Pilar Hernandez wrote a piece in 2001 where they advocated for feminist family therapy training programs to attend to issues of diversity, noting that failing to do so would lead to collusive practices.

Recent literature and recommendations about feminist family therapy often include an intersectional perspective and one that promotes liberation for all people. As Thelma Jean Goodrich and Louise Silverstein wrote in 2005, in their article "Now You See It, Now You Don't: Feminist Training in Family Therapy," feminism and multiculturalism are entwined.

The field of feminist family therapy has grown as theorists shifted the focus from gender to a broader analysis. Authors continue to offer treatment recommendations from a feminist perspective. Although gender still remains at the center of feminist thinking for some, others have taken on a broader approach. This framework continues to be seen as both personal and political as proponents of feminist family therapy seek to benefit both clients and the larger social context.

Annabelle Michelle Goodwin

See also Cultural Issues in Couples and Families; Diversity; Feminization of Poverty; Gender Issues; Women's Project, The

Further Readings

Ault-Riche, M. (1986). *Women and family therapy.* Rockville, MD: Aspen Systems.

Avis, J. M. (1989). Integrating gender into the family therapy curriculum. *Journal of Feminist Family Therapy, 1,* 3–26.

Braverman, L. (1988). *A guide to feminist family therapy.* New York, NY: Harrington Park Press.

Goldner, V. (1985). Feminism and family therapy. *Family Process, 24,* 31–47.

Goodrich, T. J. (1991). *Women and power: Perspectives for family therapy.* New York, NY: W. W. Norton.

Goodrich, T. J., & Silverstein, L. B. (2005). Now you see it, now you don't: Feminist training in family therapy. *Family Process, 44*(3), 267–281.

Haddock, S. A., Zimmerman, T. S., & MacPhee, D. (2000). The power equity guide: Attending to gender in family therapy. *Journal of Marital and Family Therapy, 26*(2), 155–170.

Hare-Mustin, R. T. (1978). A feminist approach to family therapy. *Family Process, 17,* 181–194.

Luepnitz, D. (1988). *The family interpreted: Psychoanalysis, feminism, and family therapy.* New York, NY: Basic Books.

McGoldrick, M., Anderson, C., & Walsh, F. (1989). *Women in families: A framework for family therapy.* New York, NY: W. W. Norton.

Parker, L., & Almeida, R. (2001). Balance of fairness for whom? *Journal of Feminist Family Therapy, 13,* 153–168.

Silverstein, L. B., & Goodrich, T. J. (2005). *Feminist family therapy: Empowerment in social context.* Washington, DC: American Psychological Association.

Walters, M., Carter, B., Papp, P., & Silverstein, L. B. (1988). *The invisible web: Gender patterns in family relationships.* New York, NY: Guilford Press.

Feminization of Poverty

Feminization of poverty refers to the presence of poverty within female-headed households. *Feminization of poverty* is a specific term that encompasses the intersectionality of gender, class, socioeconomics, and culture to refer to the experiences and measure of how women experience poverty. This entry briefly introduces the history of the feminization of poverty, social and cultural contributions to the development of the term *feminization of poverty*, causes and risk factors that contribute to the feminization of poverty, and the feminization of poverty as a global phenomenon.

The History and Measures of the Feminization of Poverty

The term *feminization of poverty* was coined in the 1970s by Diane Pearce. The term was popularized in the 1990s by the United Nations. Typically, three indexes are used to measure the feminization of poverty: the gender empowerment measure, gender-related development index, and human poverty index. The gender empowerment measure and gender-related development index are utilized to collect data regarding gender inequality in relation to women. The gender empowerment measure considers items such as estimated male-to-female income ratio and the number of government seats filled by female constituents in an effort to gauge female income and political opportunities across countries. The gender-related development index measures deficiencies of needs related to standard of living, education, and life expectancy. The human poverty index measures non-income-related items and considers the differences between income poverty and human poverty (e.g., opportunities for social engagement, education, life span, and longevity). Early on in poverty-related research, it was assumed that household income was dispersed equally between the members of the family unit. Furthermore, researchers made the assumption that persons living in the same household shared the same income level, such as all members were considered as identically wealthy or poor. As poverty-related studies continued, researchers recognized the need to dissect the makeup of the household members, and examined the differences in internal household experiences of wellness and prosperity. This narrowed line of inquiry provided initial understanding into the various ways men and women experience poverty, and it was the first notable breakthrough in the progression of a gendered understanding of poverty.

Poverty and Inequality

In order to understand the complexity of the label *feminization of poverty*, it is important to understand the separate terms *poverty* and *feminization*. Poverty denotes a level of financial disparity, or inequality, between groups of people. Inequality exists vertically and horizontally. Vertical inequality refers to the ranking order of household income (e.g., upper-, middle-, and low-income class). Horizontal inequality refers to differentiation between groups that are marginalized due to their social and cultural identities (e.g., gender or race). Recent research on poverty has highlighted the intersection of vertical and horizontal inequalities and this in turn has led to insights on gendered poverty and to the sustained use of the term *feminization of poverty*.

The concept of poverty can be considered as both a state and a process. For example, the state of poverty refers to the hierarchical socioeconomic system where people exist within different levels, or "states," of poverty based on their income and previously amassed wealth. The process of poverty refers to socioeconomic, political, and other influences that can cause the poor to become poorer, as well as the nonpoor to become poor. Qualitative measures of poverty led to the development of multidimensional and intersectional conceptualizations of poverty. The concept of intersectionality is crucial to understanding the feminization of poverty, as it refers to the overlap of key factors of inequality (e.g., gender and class) on horizontal and vertical levels.

Social and Cultural Influences

Men and women experience poverty in distinctly different ways. Gender and cultural norms are two prominent factors that heavily influence the state of poverty for women. Poverty research from the 1980s purported the existence of a hierarchy of needs among poor persons. Further studies illuminated the significant gendered means in which the alleged hierarchy occurs. For example, it was previously assumed by researchers that poor men and women were equally more concerned about meeting basic human needs (i.e., survival needs) prior to worrying about social decorum and pride or improving their self-esteem. Additional findings from qualitative interviews questioned the pressures that societal norms have on women who would be accepted in some cultures by staying home (as opposed to seeking work to support their families) versus choosing to seek employment in order to feed their children and meet the basic survival needs of their family. The United Nations Development Fund for Women (UNIFEM; called UN Women since 2010) identified four dimensions that amplify the risk of poverty for women: temporal, spatial, employment segmentation, and valuation. The *temporal dimension* refers to the multiple responsibilities carried by women, which may include caring for children and maintaining a household, thus leaving minimal time for outside employment. It is not uncommon for women living in impoverished countries and cultures to choose between earning a living and caring for a family. The *spatial dimension* encompasses women who seek employment close to home due to the proximity of their family. The *employment segmentation dimension* refers to the gendered classification of women as "caretakers," and the stereotyped belief that women are better suited for domestic-related jobs. The *valuation dimension* refers to the unpaid domestic work completed by women that is often undervalued.

Female headship and *female-supported household* are similar terms that further denote the gender inequalities that exist within the context of poverty. The concept of female headship evolved from poverty fieldwork where it was found that female headship referred to homes being led by women, because the men were absent for a short period of time. Examples of women in this category included divorcees, widows, single mothers, and women in consensual partnerships. Female-headed households were identified in the late 1970s as a distinct poverty category, so much so that they are sometimes labeled *the poorest of the poor*. The aforementioned intersection of women and class eventually bore the term *the feminization of poverty*. Female-supported household refers to women being the primary financial supporter, whether or not there is another income provider in the home. Researchers rely on the statistics regarding the intersectionality between female headship and poverty in their effort to calculate the gender poverty gap. Female-supported households are utilized as measures of poverty across the globe.

Causes and Risk Factors

A number of factors have been identified that contribute to the feminization of poverty, such as gender, race, and family structure. Historically, poverty has affected women at a greater frequency than men. Since 1966, poverty rates have been particularly high for female-headed households with children; these households are two to three times more likely to be in poverty than other households. Higher poverty rates among women, relative to men, occur due to two main reasons. For one, women are typically not afforded the same economic resources as men. Even with the same educational achievements, women still earn less than men, and many positions filled by women do not offer such benefits as full-time employment, insurance, paid leave, or opportunities for advancement. Additionally, women are also more likely to be single, custodial parents early in adult life and to be unmarried, living alone later on in years. Households that are headed by a female are also more likely to be affected by poverty long term.

In addition to gender, racial and ethnic minority women are affected disproportionately by poverty due to their minority status, as well as the associated greater likelihood of living as a single parent. The latter is especially true for Black and Puerto Rican women living in the United States; Mexican American and other Hispanic women are more likely to share parenting responsibilities in a two-parent household, which demonstrates lower poverty rates. Black and Hispanic women are more likely to live in poverty than non-Hispanic, White women. In 2009, 28% of Black women and 27% of Hispanic women were living below the poverty line based on family income as opposed to only 11% of non-Hispanic White women. Women are affected by minority status economically in two significant ways. First, their options for marriage and remarriage are limited due to the impact of minority status on men. Second, minority status often presents limitations for women, regardless of their achievements, in the labor market.

Single Motherhood

One of the most influential determinants of poverty for women in the United States is single motherhood. Family structure and poverty are noticeably related as nearly one third of households in the United States that are headed by single mothers are affected by poverty, while only 6% of homes led by married couples fall below the poverty line. Additionally, 45% of children living without their father fall into the ranks of the poor. In 2009, 28% of households headed by single women (no husband present) with children under the age of 18 had incomes below the poverty level. Although research has not shown one to cause the other, poverty has been linked to early and high fertility and likewise, high fertility also contributes to poverty. Teen pregnancy and childrearing is related to larger family size, and both factors are correlated with poverty as well. Additionally, studies show that poverty is also cyclical. Individuals who grow up in poverty have a much greater chance of living in poverty as an adult. Social and economic deprivation during childhood has great implications lasting into adulthood. Moreover, as the time spent in poverty as a child increases, so does the likelihood of living in poverty as an adult.

Parenthood, specifically single parenthood, contributes to lower earnings for women over the lifetime due to the unpaid, caregiving responsibilities associated with the role. Time spent caring for their children takes time away from hours spent at the office and opportunities for work-related travel, which are often associated with higher paying jobs. Moreover, households headed by single women typically have only one adult earner contributing to the family income, which negatively impacts the net income for the family. The household then becomes more susceptible to large fluctuations in income due to loss of employment, time taken for illness (personal, child, or other family member), or reduced hours related to economic downturn, leaving the family more likely to be affected by poverty since there is no one else to supplement the lost income. Furthermore, many women are jobless due to the rising cost of child care, leaving many without the option to work outside of the home. Additionally, in the case of divorce, child custody is more often than not awarded to the mother. Divorced women who are awarded custody can often be left at a disadvantage if their former spouses do not provide sufficient child support or supply no child support at all.

Single, Elderly Status

Nearly one in five elderly women (age 65 and older) living alone is currently living in poverty. Although social welfare and demographic factors are the most influential conditions to impact current socioeconomic status, labor market and equalization measures played a significant role in women's lives earlier on, influencing the amount of social welfare benefits allocated later in life. For many women, loss of a spouse due to divorce or death can have lasting implications, particularly if their socioeconomic status hinges on their spouse's income. For elderly people who are willing and able to work into their prime retirement years, it is possible that more elderly women would have employment if the labor market conditions were better and the unemployment rates lower. Equal opportunity policies also play a role as many older adults are denied employment due to age discrimination.

Education

Level of education also plays a meaningful role in poverty. In recent decades, children are increasingly likely to live in impoverished conditions if their parents have not obtained a college education, even if their parents have full-time employment. Nearly three quarters of children whose parents work full time and year round live in poverty when the parents have less than a high school diploma. In the United States, 12% of children live with a mother who has not graduated from high school, and an additional 25% live with mothers who have completed no more than a high school education. As a result of lower socioeconomic status and ongoing racial segregation, many racial and ethnic minority youths receive less education than do their White counterparts.

Lower Wages

Although women and girls have made substantial academic gains over the past few decades, which can be seen across racial and ethnic groups, the earnings gap still remains as many women enter careers that produce lower incomes. Additionally, there is the issue of occupational sex segregation, which is when women are systematically excluded from higher paying employment opportunities. When women are forced into lower paying jobs, naturally they stand a greater chance at living in poverty. Furthermore, as gender and race intersect, the earnings gap continues to increase for women of color when compared to non-Hispanic White men and women.

Racial and Ethnic Differences

The aforementioned factors tend to affect minority women to a greater extent due to the intersection of gender and race. For example, Black women often have less education, enter the workforce at an earlier age, and experience more unemployment when compared to White women because of their minority status. Additionally, Black women are also more likely to have jobs that pay less and have a lower status because of a sex-segregated labor market. An additional factor that disproportionally affects minority women is residence within urban poverty areas. Black and Hispanic people are more likely than Whites to live in poor urban areas. Residence in areas of this nature can make leaving difficult due to the negative impact that stems from low socioeconomic status and racial discrimination, leaving many with few economic resources. Inadequate resources affect those living in rural areas as well. White women living in isolated and impoverished areas of the United States also lack local resources and networks, which contribute to a maintained poverty status. Similar circumstances affect Mexican Americans attributable to their concentrations in rural areas, which are associated with limited education, employment, and access to health care and other needed services.

A Global Issue

While the definition of poverty differs among countries, studies have shown that women have a tendency to be poorer than men globally. Worldwide, women make up the majority of the 1.5 million people living on $1 a day or less. Women are often deprived of education and health facilities and subjected to gender-based discrimination. Women have also been found to be considered responsible for child-rearing in all societies and, fittingly, they apply their income to their households and to their children more so than men. Because of these and similar findings, development theorists acknowledge the fundamental role women play in the development status of any society, understanding that without the emancipation of women globally, actual development cannot be attained. Contrary to the idea that all would benefit from globalization, poor women have not, and it is often the case than many have been negatively affected by the attempt to connect the world's cultural, political, and economic systems.

With globalization come certain systemic risks, often with undetermined consequences, and although globalization has brought unparalleled economic development to various parts of the world, it has not been without criticism. Notably, the process of globalization has been condemned for its limited role in the alleviation of poverty in developing countries while becoming a source of wealth accumulation in the developed world. As the economy becomes progressively more interconnected to global markets, often what is seen is a reduction in public spending and social programs, which pushes more costs onto families where it is most often the women who shoulder the added burden. Moreover, poor and marginalized women, those who have disproportionately borne the brunt of the negative impacts of globalization, have not seen the benefits, since those working in the informal sector of the economy in particular have been driven down further into the poverty cycle.

Kristen N. Dickens and Candace N. Park

See also Debt and Financial Strain; Poverty and Family Development; Single-Parent Families; Socioeconomic Status

Further Readings

Chen, M., Vanek, J., Lund, F., Heintz, J., Jhabvala, R., & Bonner, C. (2005). *Progress of the world's women 2005: Women, work and poverty.* New York, NY: United Nations Development Fund for Women.

Durbin, E. (1999). Towards a gendered human poverty measure. *Feminist Economics, 5*(2), 105–108.

Fukuda-Parr, S. (1999). What does feminization of poverty mean? It isn't just lack of income. *Feminist Economics, 5*(2), 99–103.

Goldberg, G. S. (Ed.). (2010). *Poor women in rich countries: The feminization of poverty over the life course.* New York, NY: Oxford University Press.

Harper, C., Marcus, R., & Moore, K. (2003). Enduring poverty and the conditions of childhood: Lifecourse and intergenerational poverty transmissions. *World Development, 31*(3), 535. doi:10.1016/S0305-750X(03)00010-X

Hassan, S. M., & Amad, K. (2014). Globalization: Feminization of poverty and need for gender responsive social protection in Pakistan. *Pakistan Vision, 15*(2), 58–80.

Hernandez, D. J., & Napierala, J. S. (2014). *Mother's education and children's outcomes: How dual-generation programs offer increased opportunities for America's families.* New York, NY: Foundation for Child Development. Retrieved from http://fcd-us.org/sites/default/files/Mothers%20Education%20and%20Childrens%20Outcomes%20FINAL.pdf

Kabeer, N. (2015). Gender, poverty, and inequality: A brief history of feminist contributions in the field of international development. *Gender and Development, 23*(2), 189–205.

Marcoux, A. (1998). The feminization of poverty: Claims, facts, and data needs. *Population and Development Review, 24*(1), 131–139.

Pearce, D. (1978). The feminization of poverty: Women, work, and welfare. *Urban and Social Change Review, 11*(1/2), 28–38.

Starrels, M. E., Bould, S., & Nicholas, L. J. (1994). The feminization of poverty in the United States: Gender, race, ethnicity, and family factors. *Journal of Family Issues, 15*(4), 590–607.

White House Council on Women and Girls. (2011). *Women in America: Indicators for social and economic well-being.* Washington, DC: U.S. Government Printing Office. Retrieved from https://www.whitehouse.gov/administration/eop/cwg/data-on-women#Population

FETISHES

Fetishes are defined here as an experience of intense and recurrent sexual arousal related to nonliving objects or non-genital body parts. *Fetish* is derived from a Portuguese word meaning "false power." Originally, this word was used by European conquerors to describe objects or charms that were believed by native cultures to have supernatural abilities. As a result, the term developed an association with rejection and ridicule. *Fetish* was first applied to sexual acts by a psychiatrist in the 19th century, and it was viewed as synonymous with disorders needing to be cured. Still today, the American Psychiatric Association categorizes fetishes in the *Diagnostic and Statistical Manual of Mental Disorders* (DSM-5) under the paraphilic disorders. This entry examines how fetishes have been defined and classified, their development and treatment, the relationship between fetishes and gender, and the social, legal, and relationship implications raised by fetishistic behavior.

The Classification of Fetishes

The modern definition of *fetish* is variable depending on the context. In the DSM-5, fetishes are separated from the other paraphilic disorders of voyeurism (sexual arousal from spying on others), exhibitionism (sexual arousal from exposure of one's genitals or a sexual act to an unsuspecting individual), frotteurism (sexual arousal from touching or rubbing a nonconsenting person), sexual masochism/sadism (sexual arousal from receiving or enacting pain or humiliation on another, respectively), pedophilia (sexual arousal to children), and transvestism (sexual arousal when dressing as a different gender). Sexuality researchers tend to collectively refer to fetishes as sexual arousal not only from objects, but also to particular acts, behaviors, or sensations. Some separate bondage, discipline, sadism, masochism (BDSM) and dominance/submission practices from the umbrella term of fetish while others include such acts.

Sexual fetishes can also be defined as an extreme end of sexual preference. For example, the *fetish* label would be applied when a person does not experience sexual arousal when the fetish object, behavior, or sensation is not present. For example, a person could experience higher sexual responses when they or their partner is dressed in leather but would be capable of enjoying sexual acts without leather. This person would not be identified as having a fetish. Conversely, a person with a leather fetish would not be able to achieve sexual arousal without contact with, or at least fantasy about, leather. Commonly, the label of *fetish* has been conflated to mean any form of sexual interest outside of "normal" sexual stimuli. While sexual preferences for a variety of stimuli, objects, or acts is considered a natural occurrence, this variation can become problematic, according to the DSM-5, when the associated sexual desires cause distress, or impairment in functioning. The DSM-5 also doesn't utilize a criterion of exclusivity, as explored above.

Regardless of contextual definitions, due to the original connection with disorder and continued inclusion in psychological diagnoses, fetishes remain shrouded in shame and secrecy. This shame may lead individuals to attempt to reject their sexual preferences, hide them from partners, or seek a cure. Social concepts of what is "normal" sexually also leads individuals who experience sexual fetishes to also experience higher levels of guilt and low self-esteem when they feel they must hide their sexual interests. Here, hypotheses regarding fetish development, treatment, gender variance, and social, legal, and relationship implications will be explored.

Development

Research is highly variable regarding how individuals develop a sexual fetish. Many early theorists believed that sexual "perversions" originate in early childhood. Sigmund Freud theorized that sexual fetishes are a primarily male occurrence, arising from castration fear. For Freud, the possibility of losing one's penis leads to the development of sexualizing an alternative external object. Other researchers postulate that fetishes arise in response to sexual trauma or unconscious conditioning. The belief that individuals who engage in BDSM practices are former victims of sexual assault or abuse is not significantly supported by research. Perhaps individuals engaged in some sensory activity in early life such as holding or blowing up balloons, if paired with a physiological genital response, could later lead a person to develop a balloon fetish.

Finally, some researchers discuss the possibility that sexual fetishes are related to comorbid social insecurities or mental health disorders. An individual with intense social fear may find it less anxiety provoking to initiate sex with a stuffed animal rather than risk rejection from a human partner. While individuals with fetishes frequently discuss having an attraction to their fetish behavior or object early on in life, as with many emotional and sexual issues, causality is never certain.

Treatment

Treatment of sexual fetishes is dependent on a person's functioning and perspective on their fetish. A person with a fetish may initiate counseling for a number of reasons, outside their sexual interest. If a person's sexual preference, while fetishistic, does not cause nonconsenting harm to themselves or others nor inhibit them from functioning in social, occupational, or other areas, attempts to change a person's sexual preference would be unethical. Oftentimes, a person may seek counseling more to assist in coping with social rejection or shame associated with their fetish, rather than seeking a cure. Working with couples could include assisting one partner in "coming out" to a partner, negotiating healthy sexual practices between the couple, or increasing self- or partner-acceptance regarding the fetish.

Extensive research has been conducted with the aim of repairing a person's sexual fetish. Harmful practices similar to attempts at changing a person's sexual orientation were common throughout history. Conditioning utilizing sexual arousal to a fetish object or fantasy with a "switch" to a "normative" sexual stimulus immediately before orgasm has been the most common avenue to treat sexual fetishes. For paraphilias like pedophilia (sexual attraction to children) or zoophilia (sexual attraction to animals), which include engaging in sexual practices with partners incapable of consent, using hormone treatments to drastically decrease any sexual interest is an option. Individuals intensely distraught by their sexual fetish may also regulate their sexual desire through medication utilizing a similar drug treatment regime.

Gender Variance

Research on fetishes tends to focus on individuals who identify as cisgendered and align their gender within a binary. Therefore, the following language will reflect that information. Reports on sexual fetish occurrence show that men overwhelmingly experience sexual fetishes compared to women. Similar to the development of sexual fetishes there are many theories as to why prevalence rates are higher in men than women. Social restrictions on women's sexuality may prevent them from reporting honestly regarding sexual preferences in regard to fetish behavior. Similarly, some hypothesize that male biological and social motivation to have many variable partners could also lead to more susceptibility to sexual interest outside the "norm." Additionally, the availability of pornography depicting any form of sexual preference could also play a role in higher variance in men's sexual preferences, concordant with men's higher consumption rates of pornography. A final theory is that due to the male model of medicine and therefore sexuality research, the types of fetishes that have been identified align more with masculine sexual arousal patterns. So called "female fetishes" may be underreported because they are not identified by researchers. Despite this variance, women still do report sexual fetishes. Again, research regarding individuals who identify outside the gender binary or as trans and rates of sexual fetishes is as yet underreported.

Social and Legal Implications

Cross-culturally, social standards typically reject the occurrence of sexual fetishes. While recent media depictions of BDSM practices have led to a rise in acceptance of bondage behavior, this acceptance is not translated into other sexual fetish interests. However, also due to media representations and the social connections able to be established through the internet, online fetish communities are very common. Individuals with sexual fetishes often feel isolated or rejected from broader society and these fetish communities can assist with normalizing a person's sexual preference and reduce feelings of shame related to the fetish.

Many states in the United States attempt to legally restrict behaviors associated with sexual fetishes. Although it is difficult for a law to prevent a person from being bound and flogged for sexual purposes, other laws related to sexual fetishes are in place to restrict a person from being a danger to others. For instance, laws regarding public indecency could be problematic for a person whose fetish is to expose their genitals to an unsuspecting person. However, being flashed is often a traumatic and startling event for the recipient, thus the law remains.

Relationship Implications

As stated, sexual fetishes can be isolating and problematic within the context of a relationship. Shame about one's sexual fetish may lead individuals to hide their sexual interest from a partner. Likewise, discovering a partner's sexual fetish may be shocking. While some couples establish mutual engagement in sexual preferences, it can be challenging for one partner to participate in a fetish act that only one partner desires. Feelings of objectification may arise when, for example, all the partner's sexual attention is focused on one's feet rather than one's own sexual satisfaction. Couples negotiating sexual fetishes can explore limitations, the extent of partner participation, or alternatives for fulfilling sexual fetish desires. Both (or any) partners involved maintain their right to a sexual life that fit's their desires. Some couples may face the hard decision about whether or not a romantic relationship can be maintained while the fetish object, stimulus, or behavior is necessary for sexual fulfillment.

Molly Rose Wilson

See also Couples and Marriage Counseling; Human Sexual Response; Sex Therapy; Sexual Intimacy

Further Readings

Castro, J. A. (2011). *Sex, fetish and him: How to cope with your partner's unusual sexual fetish*. Cork: BookBaby.

De Block, A., & Adriaens, P. R. (2013). Pathologizing sexual deviance: A history. *Journal of Sex Research,50*(3/4), 276–298. doi:10.1080/00224499.2012.738259

Feldman, M. P. (1966). Aversion therapy for sexual deviations: A critical review. *Psychological Bulletin, 65*(2), 65–79. doi:10.1037/h0022913

Kleinplatz, P. J. (2012). *New directions in sex therapy: Innovations and alternatives*. New York, NY: Routledge.

Marshall, G. L. (1974). A combined treatment approach to the reduction of multiple fetish-related behaviors. *Journal of Consulting and Clinical Psychology, 42*(4), 613–616. doi:10.1037/h0036727

Moser, C. (2009). When is an unusual sexual interest a disorder? *Archives of Sexual Behavior, 38,* 323–325. doi:10.1007/s10508-008-9436-8

Roughgarden, J. (2004). *Evolution's rainbow: Diversity, gender, and sexuality in nature and people*. Los Angeles: University of California Press.

Rowland, D., & Incrocci, L. (2008). *Handbook of sexual and gender identity disorders*. Hoboken, NJ: Wiley.

Wright, S. (2010). Depathologizing consensual sexual sadism, sexual masochism, transvestic fetishism, and fetishism. *Archives of Sexual Behavior, 39*(6), 1229–1230. doi:10.1007/s10508-010-9651-y

FIDELITY

When people conceptualize commitment in a relationship, they often think in terms of fidelity and infidelity. Fidelity is sometimes mistakenly equated with monogamy in a relationship and infidelity with non-monogamy, but fidelity is actually about adherence to agreements made between the couple about the parameters of their relationship. Fidelity is defined by loyalty, faithfulness, and adherence to promises made. Partners in a romantic relationship may define *fidelity* in different ways, but at its core, fidelity refers to an agreement to keep promises, trust that the partner is acting in accordance with those agreements, and commitment to sometimes sacrifice one's own needs or desires to attend to the partner's needs. Because many factors underlie fidelity and fidelity is so critical to an intimate relationship, and ultimately can determine the success or failure of a relationship, this entry describes each aspect of fidelity individually. Describing the factors provides an overview of the importance of fidelity in intimate relationships, how to maintain it, and how to heal when fidelity has been broken. At its core, fidelity means commitment, but in fact, it is also much more complex.

Loyalty

Fidelity is something that develops and evolves in relationships, much as emotional and physical closeness do. In the beginning stages of a relationship, partners may not expect complete loyalty and exclusivity, but as a relationship matures, those expectations are likely to change. Loyalty develops in relationships as well. The beginning stages of an intimate relationship are often characterized by intense passion and desire for the other—*dopaminergic* activity (dopamine is a chemical in the brain related to feelings of motivation and reward) gives the individual a sense of elation, or high, in the presence of the other. As the relationship progresses, dopamine released in the brain decreases, and, if the relationship is to endure, oxytocin is activated, commonly referred to as the cuddle hormone. Oxytocin is associated with mother–child bonding during nursing and also is essential to the feeling of emotional closeness and loyalty that exists between two people in an intimate relationship. Partners who are closely bonded to one another feel a sense of loyalty to their partner. They are devoted. The partner's needs directly affect their actions, and they feel compelled to protect, honor, and be true to their partner.

The degree of closeness in a relationship undoubtedly influences individual perceptions of loyalty, faithfulness, and adherence to promises made. While dopamine is stimulated in the early stages of an intimate relationship, partners often have to work harder before oxytocin increases. Awareness of what helps one's partner feel connected and close to the other and then acting on that facilitates oxytocin production, therefore deepening feelings of closeness and connection, deepening the partners' sense of loyalty. Everyday moments like waking, parting, reuniting, and bedtime are key times of the day when partners can make efforts to touch, kiss, talk, or otherwise acknowledge the other's presence and importance in one's life—this is a significant component of creating a culture of emotional and physical closeness in a relationship.

Expressing appreciation and gratitude for one's partner is another way of creating relational closeness. The key here is to develop awareness around what helps one's partner to feel close and connected, and to appreciate that each partner's needs may be quite different. It becomes the responsibility of each partner to express his or her needs clearly as much as it is the responsibility of the partner to pay attention to what the other's needs are. Relationships are reciprocal, and while perceptions of fidelity in a relationship may be individually based, developing closeness based on the individual needs of each partner builds on the collective perception of the couple as a faithful, loyal duo.

Faithfulness

Another critical component of fidelity, in addition to loyalty, is faithfulness. Partners who are faithful to one another enjoy an element of trust that the bond that is shared between them is sacred. Faithfulness is not exclusive to monogamous relationships; faithfulness is established based on how the partners define their relationship and their agreed-upon terms and can vary depending on cultural practices. Relationships are defined in many ways, and the partners are each responsible for establishing their (either explicit or implicit) relationship contracts, defining the parameters, or rules, of their relationship. Partners who agree to be polyamorous, or have multiple sexual partners, could still consider themselves faithful to one another if engaging in sexual relations outside of their relationship were part of the agreed-upon terms of their relationship. In essence, faithfulness does not refer to exclusivity, but to an agreement to adhere to the relationship agreement, or contract, that the partners establish with one another. If both consent to and are in agreement to be polyamorous, they can still consider themselves faithful to each other and to the promises they made to one another.

Faithfulness is often referred to in the context of a sexual relationship—partners who only have sex with each other might be considered "faithful." Faithfulness in a romantic relationship can also refer to agreements partners have regarding finances, religion, parenting practices, and leisure. Broadly, faithfulness refers to adherence to promises made. More specifically, faithfulness applies to the degree to which each partner abides by the agreements that have been made in the relationship surrounding a variety of areas. The couple decides on the level of importance of each area of their relationship, and the above are only a few examples of the areas of a relationship to which partners can apply the concept of faithfulness. In order for a relationship to grow, loyalty and faithfulness must be perceived by each partner, since they are critical elements of the overall concept of fidelity.

Attachment and Trustworthiness

Attachment refers to the way in which people connect to and engage with others in close relationships. Researchers have established that attachment develops at a very early age with primary caregivers and that attachment style is closely related to the trust that the child learns to place in others and to the type of response a child learns to expect from others. More recently, researchers have begun examining adult attachment styles in intimate relationships. The consensus is that the childhood attachment style follows the individual into adulthood and predicts the relationship style the person will exhibit in an intimate relationship.

More recent research has recategorized styles of adult attachment into a continuum that varies on dimensions of attachment avoidance and attachment anxiety, leading to four general styles of adult attachment that vary along these continua: secure, preoccupied, dismissive, and fearful. Securely attached adults will exhibit low anxiety in an intimate relationship, and low avoidance of intimacy. They will likely find it easy to trust others and feel confident in their relationships. A person who exhibits a preoccupied attachment style will express a high desire for intimacy (low avoidance), but also high levels of anxiety about the relationship, concern about the relationship's stability, and suspicion of the partner's faithfulness. Those who express a dismissive relationship style actively avoid intimate relationships, and as a result have little anxiety about relationship stability. Finally, a fearful attachment style is characterized by avoidance of intimacy as a result of high anxiety regarding abandonment by a potential partner.

It is evident how attachment style and trust can influence fidelity in a relationship. The good news is that attachment styles, while difficult to change, can shift with experience, education, and therapy. Individuals who have a secure attachment style are more likely to be trustworthy in a relationship. They are comfortable with others depending on them, and feel comfortable depending on others. They are content with intimacy and generally have low anxiety about trusting their partner. Healthy relationship partners develop interdependence with one another—the decisions they make directly affect the other and, therefore, they sometimes will sacrifice their own needs to meet the needs of the other.

Reliability

Becoming sensitive and aware of one's partner's needs are directly related to being available and reliable to receive explicit and implicit messages a partner sends. When an individual is loyal and faithful in a relationship, creates a foundation of trust and attachment security, and works to foster emotional and physical closeness, he or she has undoubtedly been reliable in recognizing the partner's needs, paying attention to cues the partner gave, and responding to attempts the partner has made for attention and affection. These attempts at gaining attention and/or affection are not always clear; often they are implicit. Partners must commit themselves to communicating their needs clearly to their partner, but often also must become keen decoders of their partner's incoming messages. When a partner can trust that bids for attention and affection will be reliably responded to in kind by his or her partner, the foundation of fidelity is strong.

The preceding discussion of factors that comprise fidelity make it clear that fidelity is multidimensional and consequently is so much more than a promise to remain exclusive and monogamous in an intimate relationship. Fidelity is a promise of trust, security, comfort, closeness, and availability. It is the assurance of having a witness to one's life, a person to build a legacy with, share tradition, and provide a buffer and support from life's inexplicable events as well as triumphs.

Fidelity and Intimacy

Relationships can achieve fidelity, but lack intimacy. Several theories of loving relationships have been proposed over the years, one of which is Robert Sternberg's triangular theory of love. On each point of the triangle exists one component of love (intimacy, passion, and commitment), which in combination form the ultimate—consummate love. When only one or two components of the triangle exist, love is still there, but will look very different depending on which components are present. Fidelity in its simplest form means commitment. When commitment exists alone, without the presence of intimacy or passion, the relationship is described as "empty love." The way in which fidelity has been portrayed here describes a combination of intimacy, passion, and commitment in conjunction or consummate with love. This is, of course, the ideal combination of relationship components, and it takes effort to achieve. Intimacy in relationships is a universal desire in both the human and animal kingdoms. We possess a need to belong that is fulfilled by engaging in close, connected relationships with others.

Overcoming Infidelity

Unfortunately, many individuals in relationships will experience infidelity. Healing from the rupture and moving on or working to repair the relationship can be challenging work, and can lead one to question many of the components previously described (e.g., loyalty, trustworthiness, and faithfulness). Many couple therapists will be faced with clients who have experienced or committed acts of infidelity, and it is critical that therapists are prepared to work with these clients.

There are several models of couple counseling that were developed specifically for couples who have experienced infidelity. A component of these models, regardless of theoretical approach, is forgiveness. Also common to these models is the reestablishment of trust, developing compassion and empathy for the betrayer, and a heartfelt apology. Some researchers contend that infidelity in an intimate relationship should be considered a crisis for the couple, and suggest employing trauma approaches to helping the couple overcome the transgression.

Almost without exception, fidelity is a component of intimate relationships that everyone has to face at some stage in one's developing intimate relationships. The presence or absence of the aforementioned factors contribute to an overall sense of relational fidelity and are part of the foundation upon which the relationship is built.

Veronica I. Johnson

See also Gottman Method Couples Therapy; Listening, Empathic; Trust

Further Readings

Fisher, H. (2015). *Anatomy of love: A natural history of mating, marriage, and why we stray.* New York, NY: W. W. Norton.

Fraley, R., & Shaver, P. (2000). Adult romantic attachment: Theoretical developments, emerging controversies, and unanswered questions. *Review of General Psychology, 4,* 132–154.

Gottman, J. M., & Silver, N. (1999). *Seven principles for making marriage work.* New York, NY: Three Rivers Press.

Johnson, S. (2008). *Hold me tight: Seven conversations for a lifetime of love.* New York, NY: Hachette Book Group.

Johnson, V. I. (2012, Fall). Forgiveness and infidelity: Overcoming betrayal in intimate relationships. *Wisconsin Counseling Journal, 26,* 39–45.

Sternberg, R. J. (2004). A triangular theory of love. In H. T. Reis & C. E. Rusbult (Eds.), *Close relationships* (pp. 213–228). New York, NY: Psychology Press.

First-Order Change

First-order change is a concept originally codified by Paul Watzlawick, John Weakland, and Richard Fisch in 1974 to understand how systems change. It refers to change that reduces symptoms, increases functioning, or alleviates a temporary stress rather than changing the systems and patterns that create and maintain symptoms. In couples and family therapy, first-order change is utilized both as a tool to identify the underlying assumptions of therapeutic work and to conceptualize the type of change systems require. This entry clarifies the concept of first-order change and describes how it differs from second-order change. Additionally, the entry reviews how first-order change can be utilized as a conceptual tool in family and couples therapy, discusses the rationale for working toward first-order change, and provides examples of what first-order change looks like in practice.

The Concept of First-Order Change

First-order change is change within a couple or family system that does not alter the underlying structure. Often this is accomplished through practical adjustments that meet the current demands of the family life cycle. For example, a couple might implement behavioral consequences as they work to effectively parent a child displaying aggressive behaviors. This sort of intervention is first order because it can reduce the child's aggressive symptoms and alleviate parental stress without changing the structure of the family system.

In contrast, second-order change focuses on addressing current problems by changing the underlying family structure. Second-order change is accomplished through altering the fundamental rules of the system to allow for a new way of interacting with the demands of the family life cycle. For example, the aforementioned couple might fundamentally change the way they interact with each other and their children when they are upset and, thereby, ultimately display more of a connection to each other, reduce the stress level of the child, and change the interactional patterns that led their child to become aggressive with others in the first place.

Another analogy utilized to clarify the difference is Jean Piaget's principle that development happens as a function of assimilation and accommodation. Piaget postulated that both assimilation and accommodation need to happen to promote development. Assimilation involves learning to adapt past practices to meet current demands. Accommodation involves developing new ways of interacting to meet current demands. First-order change is analogous to assimilation in that the change is an extension of past practices and focuses on helping the family or couple use the structures and patterns already in place to address a current stressor. This is contrasted to second-order change, which wants to do more than help the family adjust; it seeks to promote an accommodation to an entirely new way of engaging in the world.

First-order change differs from second-order change in that it is nontransformational whereas second-order change is transformational. Counselors seeking to promote first-order change are working within the current rules of the system and are helping them adjust or assimilate to a more effective manner of interacting. This is akin to the counselor changing the temperature on a faucet hotter or colder to reach the desired temperature (first order) as opposed to either boiling it or freezing it in order to change the underlying form of the water (second order).

A Conceptual Tool

As it was originally utilized, the concept of first-order change helped to conceptualize how people were thinking about change and, as a result, what sort of intervention was indicated. For example, in the aforementioned couple struggling to parent an aggressive child, a counselor may work toward a first-order change by adjusting interactions within the current system (e.g., following through with appropriate consequences). If this adjustment did not result in the desired behavioral change, the counselor may move along to other first-order changes such as helping the parents set firmer boundaries or working on helping the child cognitively control his or her aggressive behaviors. While it may be that a first-order adjustment would eventually work for this family, it may also be that the family system may not currently be structured in a way that allows for meaningful change to the aggressive behavior.

Continually working in a direction that does not lead to meaningful change is often experienced as frustrating by both the client and the counselor. Without the ability to conceptualize what is happening, counselors often find themselves continuing to implement interventions that may not match the system's needs. Using the concept of first-order change would allow the counselor to reflect on his or her conceptualization of the family's needs and to design interventions suited to address those needs. In the given example, the counselor might determine that for significant change to occur, the family needs more than another first-order intervention. In this case, the counselor would cease implementing first-order interventions and work to instigate a transformation focused on promoting a new way of interacting that opens up the possibility of new outcomes.

Thinking this way also challenges counselors to think about their underlying assumptions about how systems work. The philosophical assumption of first-order change is that human behavior progresses in a linear pattern that systematically builds upon previous structures of interacting. In this way, first-order change is a rationalist or modernist approach in that it typically involves the counselor having a more objective form of the "truth" about system change and relies heavily upon the counselor as an expert to guide what is done in session. For example, a counselor working toward first-order change might approach a family with a child who has an eating disorder with an assumption that the eating-disordered behavior is the problem and can be adulterated by adjusting what the family system is currently doing. The counselor would therefore lead the family toward changing what they have identified as leading to the problem. This is contrasted with a therapist working toward second-order change who might believe that the eating disorder symptomology may or may not be the core problem and the family's interactions might not have a linear relationship with the problem. As a result, the therapist might not see the goal of therapy as addressing the eating disorder but rather endeavor to create a new and more meaningful way of engaging that no longer has use for the eating disorder symptoms.

The way counselors think about systems has obvious implications for what they do in session. If a counselor believes that the couple or family's problem is constructed in a linear fashion, that is, the problem behavior is constructed as a result of a series of identifiable antecedents, the goal of therapy then becomes to adjust the way these antecedents add to the outcome. This way of thinking does not fit neatly with general systems theory. For this reason, second-order change is often seen as the traditional aim of couple and family counseling; however, many established modes of treatment work within a first-order mind.

On the whole, behavioral and cognitive inspired couple and family therapies work with a first-order mind. Structural and systemic approaches also can be considered to work toward first-order change, since they both have preexisting notions of what effective interactions for the system would look like. For example, a structural therapist may see the aggressive behavior of the child previously mentioned as a result of poor boundaries between the parental and child subsystem. This would result in the structural counselor directing the parents to adjust what they are already doing (a first-order change) in the hopes that the child's problematic behavior would cease. This stands in contrast with approaches such as brief solution-focused family therapy or narrative couples therapy where the counselor does not believe that they know best what should happen in session and is not primarily interested in working toward changing specific behaviors.

The Rationale for First-Order Change in Practice

Irrespective of theoretical orientation, first-order change is often the goal of treatment. When counselors view a couple or family as having a problem that requires immediate symptom relief or needing to learn skills to navigate their life, working toward a first-order change makes sense. For example, a counselor working with a couple who has recently dealt with the death of a child may begin acting upon the system in a manner designed to support and build active coping strategies in order to help them adjust to this current crisis. In fact, attempting to operate in any other way with this family may be impossible until they can adjust to the immediate stressor of the death of their child. Often, clinicians will also address long-standing distress or dysfunction in the system while doing this; however, their ultimate aim is to help the system change in an incremental linear manner to do more or less of what they are already doing, or do it with greater accuracy.

While some systems theorists believe that operating within a second-order mind is a more respectful and appropriate choice, it seems clear that many clients dwell in a first-order world. If counselors are to respond meaningfully to their concerns, they have to be able to understand it and to work within it. Many times a first-order change can be sufficient or at least provide sorely needed adjustments for clients. For example, while working with a couple on the verge of divorce, a counselor may work toward building communication skills and navigating expression of anger within the relationship to help them back down from the entrenched and hopeless positions in which they find themselves. This adjustment can deliver exactly the change the couple was hoping for and can provide enough of a movement to sustain the relationship for the immediate future.

Perhaps more common is a situation where a first-order change is needed to support a true accommodation to a new way of being. In much the same way that Piaget posited that both assimilation and accommodation were necessary for development, systems often require that a counselor be able and willing to work toward both. For example, to return to the above example, when working with a couple on the verge of divorce, it may be that an adjustment brings about a new experience in the therapy room but does not lead to any real change outside the therapy room. In this instance, the first-order change of learning how to be in relationship with each other, even when emotionally elevated, might be a necessary step in order to begin working toward accommodating to a new way of being and opening up the possibility of new outcomes.

First-order change refers to changes made within the boundaries of the couple or family system. It is a pragmatic strategy that seeks an adjustment to what the couple or family is already doing in order to change behavior or have it work with greater accuracy. First-order change is often utilized to conceptualize what the counselor sees as happening in a system and to suggest what sort of intervention is needed to make meaningful change.

John A. Dewell

See also Cybernetics; General Systems Theory; Milan Team; Second-Order Change; Second-Order Family Therapy

Further Readings

Becvar, D. S., & Becvar, R. J. (2013). *Family therapy: A systemic integration* (8th ed.). Boston, MA: Pearson.

Lyddon, W. J. (1990). First- and second-order change: Implications for rationalist and constructivist cognitive therapies. *Journal of Counseling and Development, 69*(2), 122–127.

Sperry, L., & Carlson, J. (2014). *How master therapists work: Effecting change from the first through the last session and beyond.* New York, NY: Routledge.

Watzlawick, P., Weakland, J. H., & Fisch, R. (1974). *Change: Principles of problem formation and problem resolution.* New York, NY: W. W. Norton.

Focal Family Therapy

Focal family therapy refers to a short-term family therapy aimed at the relief of a single symptom. Focal family therapy does not involve long-term therapy, but is established to address a single occurrence that is predominant in the family dynamics. Though the term *focal* is applicable to many forms of therapy, in focal family therapy the goal is to develop a "family focus" and create a brief-focal model for the family to follow in 12 to 14 sessions. This entry briefly introduces focal family therapy as it relates to theory and technique. The entry concludes with a discussion of the focal hypothesis and establishment of focal family treatment goals.

Theory

Family therapy has a psychodynamic foundation that can often take broad parameters in the length of time to conduct sessions creating a point of resolution. To establish a brief model of therapy, psychotherapists introduced three key principles to guide brief interventions: (1) establish and maintain a therapeutic relationship, (2) establish a focal theme or focal goal for the treatment, and (3) establish the separation and termination process early within the counseling sessions. The establishment of a focal model of therapy by design is to determine a treatment focus that sets modest and achievable goals in a limited number of sessions. The principles of psychodynamic therapy progressed over time to assess and identify the client's predisposition as well as specific stressors to which the individual was vulnerable. Predisposition referred to aspects of the individual's constitution that often made the individual vulnerable, while the stressors were identified as events or behavioral cycles that would interact and affect the predisposition. Over the past 20 years, the focal model of psychodynamic approaches has been translated into family therapy, and the theory has assisted family therapists to fashion the structure for focal family therapy. Similar to the theoretical underlining of psychodynamic models with individual, focal family therapy assesses the predisposition of the family and each member involved in the family therapy process. Understanding what makes each member vulnerable as well as the family vulnerable are primary observations noted during the development of the focal hypothesis. The stressors identified are linked to the vicious cycles occurring in the family dynamics that need to change, encouraging the therapist to develop a strong but brief-focal plan of action for the family. In conjunction with other brief psychodynamic models, on average, family focal therapy lasts less than 12 sessions, focusing on one disturbance among the family dynamics.

Therapeutic Relationship

Focal family therapy is meant to establish and maintain a therapeutic relationship, find a treatment focus, and assist in setting modest and achievable goals in a short amount of time. The emphasis in focal family therapy is interpersonal in nature, aimed at understanding the family's coping pattern, the breakdown in response to the current situation, developmental challenges in the family, and the development of interventions that enhance the family's healing. Maintaining an interpersonal scope, focal family therapy provides the counselor with a lens to use the latent healing power of the family to create positive change in the family dynamics. This latent healing power is established at the onset of therapeutic interventions, being discussed at the point of assessment or intake. It is understand that the relationship between the family therapist and the family is egalitarian in nature, and that all members of the family will have individual goals to work on in the best interest of the family's dynamic.

Special considerations should be given in the focal family therapy approach. The therapist plays a vital role in establishing therapeutic relationships with all family members. Focal family therapy is used in the briefest amount of time, placing the therapist in the role of establishing and maintaining order in each session. The establishment and maintenance of order in each session means allowing each member of the family to have a voice in discussing the need for changes to address the family disturbance. While egalitarian in nature, the therapist often will be placed in a mentoring role maintaining communication and civil interactions among families in strife. The therapist must model positive communication skills and be willing to explore the transactional patterns and developments that are impeding the family's skills to succeed. Being psychodynamic in nature, this exploration includes the therapist's impact on the transactional patterns and his or her own role in creating disturbances that impede the family's ability to succeed. During the brief-focal family therapy sessions, the therapist becomes a lead within the family structure who assists in creating change quickly and efficiently.

The primary goal of focal family therapy is to have a strong working alliance with all family members in order to create an atmosphere that is safe in every session. Growth and change can only occur in environments where safety is established. The therapist must maintain equality among all members of the family, even those of different ages, such as parents and children. Equality should be modeled by the counselor in an egalitarian way, with each member of the family being shown that they are taken seriously regardless of their age or placement in the family dynamics. The therapist can utilize this process as an assessment tool in focal family therapy to understand the dynamics of the family and how each family member is treated by others in the dynamics, as well as how family members react to being placed on an equal platform during therapy sessions.

The therapist must then consider the establishment of order in the sessions. With limited time being the driving force of focal family therapy, establishment of order takes precedence. Families entering family therapy can be fractured and struggle with communication, wanting to overtake what the other says in order to be heard. This weakens the focal focus of treatment and is to be addressed by the therapist by asking one member of the family to speak at a time while others listen. It is vital that all members of the family be given the opportunity to speak; however, the process must be done in a controlled and established order. As the boundaries of communication are established, family members will begin to adjust to the egalitarian thought process of working as a family pod instead of individuals within a family.

Once order is established, the therapist can assist the family in moving into the improvement of basic communication skills. Demonstrating and modeling the use of active listening, the therapist must be willing to break up old, reflexive nonlistening patterns of communication. The therapist should address the importance of positive communication styles such as mutual respect and empathy. The use of negative communication means, such as demanding and criticizing, should be actively discouraged from use. Focal family therapy should stress the use of "I" statements among family members in and out of the counseling session. The encouragement of self-revealing, open, and nonattacking communication through "I" statements shifts communication focus from anger, blaming, and externalizing processes to hearing what others feel and believe is occurring in the family dynamics. While the approach of "I" statements is an example of behavioral interventions, in focal family therapy, the focus is the discouragement of counterproductive communication.

The family therapist should look for the "failed solutions" that have been created in the family dynamics. It is assumed that a family has tried creating solutions on their own before making the decision to attend family therapy. It is valued for the therapist to look for and identify "family solutions" to help the family understand why the solution failed. Failed solutions can compound presenting problems, and identifying the family solution can assist families in setting aside past failures to create a clean slate. This process begins to establish the focal hypothesis and focal plan for the therapist and family to work by when continuing the therapeutic relationship.

Focal family therapy should also consist of the therapist looking for typical patterns and sequences of interactions during the counseling session. The focal family therapist should look for characteristic displays of problems within the family dynamics. If an argument occurs, the therapist should stop the negative behaviors and create a reproduction of what previously occurred. Family members should then be encouraged to explore the "unproductive consequences" of the events that just occurred and discuss how positive communication skills could have altered the emotional reactions and outcomes. The therapist should use techniques to link the conversation to the here and now, placing the negative event in the past. The interaction should then be discussed among family members of how it is reflective of past family interactions. The goal is to help the family achieve affective mastery of futile routines that continue to impact the family in various ways.

Method of Use

Focal family therapy was developed for brief family psychotherapy and the origin of methods used in focal family therapy should be considered. Basic details of all members participating in the family session, such as name, age, complaints and their duration, should be obtained. All known disturbances in the family's life with evidence identifying relationships and symptoms should also be recorded. A minimal focal hypothesis should be developed, identifying the primary and brief issue occurring in the family causing strife. The focal plan is created to implement as an intervention within the family therapy session, with evidence being collected as an assessment of the results of therapy. All initial disturbances are then reexamined so changes can be noted. Indicators of improvement with focal family therapy are psychodynamic in nature (e.g., identifying that family members are addressing the disturbance in a more positive manner than they were prior to the start of counseling and that disturbances, such as symptoms and vicious circles, have disappeared and been replaced by positive interactions).

Focal Hypothesis

Using psychodynamic theory as a foundation, a focal hypothesis is developed during the intake of focal family therapy that can encompass the reason for the referral and presenting symptoms. Salient facts from the family history as well as the therapist observations of family interactions should be noted and included into the focal hypothesis. The focal hypotheses serve as a reference point for therapeutic progress and should be created not only as a representation of the family as a whole but also as a representation of each family member. As the focal plan is implemented and treatment begins, new phenomena or observations might come to light that would warrant a revision of the focal hypothesis. The focal hypothesis acts as an anchor to demonstrate therapeutic growth. The therapist utilizes the focal hypothesis in focal family therapy to demonstrate the changes that occur in the family dynamics from the initial intake to the termination of family counseling sessions.

Focal Plan

After the focal hypothesis is identified, a focal plan is developed. The aim of the focal plan is to provide a road map of treatment for the therapist to follow, determining the desired changes and what steps need to occur to bring them about for the family. Duration and frequency of sessions are identified in the focal plan with an estimated number of sessions that would be considered for successful completion. The focal plan should include a generated outcome for the family as a whole, but also the individual focal plan should be individualized for each family member and how they will generate changes as they grow during the family session. Focal family therapy should not be more than 14 sessions in length at any one given time, so the focal plan should identify one disturbance to address within the family dynamics, and this should be the focus during therapy sessions based on the focal hypothesis. The techniques used to create change may vary from one therapist to the next, as focal family therapy is only a structured approach to maintain short-term family therapy processes. The therapist may choose to use techniques from cognitive behavioral therapy, solution-focused, or strength-based therapy in order to create change in a timely manner. The focal plan, detailing length of therapy, steps needed to create change, and the expected outcomes, is then drawn up as a therapeutic contract to be offered to the family.

Eric D. Jett

See also Assessment, Biopsychosocial; Behavioral Family Therapy; Brief Family Therapy; Gestalt Family Therapy; Psychoanalytic Family Therapy

Further Readings

Bentovim, A., & Kinston, W. (1978). Brief focal family therapy when the child is the referred patient: I. Clinical. *Child Psychology & Psychiatry & Allied Disciplines, 19*(1), 1–12. doi:10.111/j.1469-7610.1978.tb01746.x

Kinston, W., & Bentovim, A. (1978). Brief focal family therapy when the child is the referred patient: II. Methodology and results. *Child Psychology & Psychiatry & Allied Disciplines, 19*(2), 119–143. doi:10.1111/j.1469-7610.1978.tb00454.x

Swift, W. J. (1993). Brief psychotherapy with adolescents: Individual and family approaches. *American Journal of Psychotherapy, 47*(3), 373–386.

FORGIVENESS

Interpersonal hurts are a common focus of individual, couple, and family counseling. Clients may have suffered mistreatment at the hands of friends, family members, classmates, business associates, or strangers, leaving painful emotional and relationship wounds. Although there are various techniques designed to help ameliorate current emotional and relationship problems, many clients are burdened by unresolved bitterness and anger from past offenses. Forgiveness is the process of letting go of resentment and negative feelings, and forgiveness can be a powerful intervention to help clients heal from emotional and interpersonal pain and resolve ongoing conflicts. Therapists working with clients to resolve interpersonal conflicts and heal from past and current mistreatment may benefit from understanding the process of forgiveness and techniques that facilitate forgiveness. Although there is a greater acceptance among clinicians regarding the use of forgiveness in treatment, there is still confusion and debate on the subject. This entry will present common definitions and conceptualizations of forgiveness, the process of forgiveness, the benefits of forgiveness, and steps to facilitate forgiveness.

Definition and Conceptualization

Although forgiveness was often eschewed by therapists in the past, it is now viewed by many researchers and clinicians as both healing and empowering for the forgiver and as a powerful tool for relationship reconciliation and repair. Additionally, the therapeutic use of forgiveness is supported by a substantial body of academic literature. Forgiveness interventions may be beneficial for anger, depression, adolescent–parent relationships, alcoholism in families, family-of-origin issues, incest survivors, trauma from abuse, marital problems, infidelity, postdivorce challenges, sexual abuse, sexual compulsions, guilt, and cancer survivors. However, despite the increased acceptance of forgiveness, there is disagreement among researchers and clinicians regarding the definition of *forgiveness*. Although some scholars suggest it is a single act or event, most assert it is a process. Some believe it requires actions by both the giver and the receiver; others argue it is a free-will offering by the victim, independent of what the other party does.

Robert Enright and the Human Development Study Group provide a definition often quoted by forgiveness scholars. They state that forgiveness is a letting go of resentment, condemnation, and desire for revenge against unjust actions in concert with feelings of compassion toward the offender. This definition highlights three important aspects of forgiveness:

1. The offended person has suffered an unjust hurt or mistreatment from another.

2. The offended person willingly chooses to forgive.

3. Forgiveness includes affect (overcoming resentment and replacing it with compassion), cognition (overcoming thoughts of condemnation with respect), and behavior (overcoming the inclination toward revenge with positive actions of good will).

Forgiveness involves the ending of blame and negative thoughts or behaviors toward the offender, and the replacement of these with positive thoughts, emotions, and actions regarding the offender. Sometimes it is a process that one undertakes individually. At other times, it is a process that entails the mutual interaction of multiple parties in an effort to make recompense for past hurts, put the pain behind them, and restore the relationship.

Misunderstandings of Forgiveness

The concept of forgiveness has been around as long as there have been human relationships. Ancient ideas on forgiveness were developed by different societies and cultures, especially those with strong religious ties. For example, Buddhism, Confucianism, Judaism, Islam, and Christianity address the principles of forgiveness, mercy, and compassion. However, forgiveness received little attention in the psychotherapy literature prior to the mid-1980s. This lack of attention, as well as criticisms of forgiveness, can be traced to two sources. First, forgiveness was often associated with religion, and the field of psychotherapy generally viewed religion in a negative light until the latter part of the 20th century. Second, various misunderstandings and confusion about forgiveness led clinicians and clients to avoid or reject it as a therapeutic option. Such misunderstandings include the idea that forgiveness condones the misbehavior of others, exonerates offenders without holding them accountable, minimizes the seriousness of the offense, or empowers the abuser to repeat the offense. Others have erroneously equated forgiveness with pardoning, excusing, forgetting, and reconciliation. However, researchers and clinicians have challenged these erroneous definitions of forgiveness. For example, scholars usually distinguish forgiveness from reconciliation. A child may forgive an abusive parent, but may choose not to renew their relationship because the parent did not demonstrate signs of accountability, remorse, or discontinuing the abuse. Although reconciliation may be an outcome of forgiveness, it is not necessary for forgiveness to occur.

Pseudoforgiveness and the Implications of Not Forgiving

Some individuals struggle to work effectively or completely through the process of forgiveness. They may outwardly express forgiveness, but inwardly harbor anger, bitterness, resentment, and desires for revenge. This false form of forgiveness is sometimes referred to as *pseudoforgiveness*. This may occur if victims deny their authentic feelings regarding the offense or the offender (e.g., denying feelings of anger or hurt). Unfortunately, denial may have unintended negative consequences, such as undermining one's self-esteem and allowing negative emotions to fester inside. For the most part, forgiveness scholars argue that victims should acknowledge their feelings honestly before endeavoring to forgive. Those who are unable or unwilling to overcome these negative emotions may get stuck in the identity of a victim, thus hindering the liberating process of forgiveness. Withholding forgiveness may also give the offender additional power or control and bring prolonged suffering in the life of the injured person.

Benefits of Forgiveness

While mistreatment and interpersonal offenses may produce anger, bitterness, emotional pain, depression, and conflict, forgiveness offers the opportunity for liberation from these painful, unpleasant emotions. In contrast to those who experience prolonged suffering, true forgiveness is empowering, as it allows one to break the emotional bonds with the perpetrator and transcend the negative experiences from the past. Thus, it brings peace and relief from the emotional burden of resentment and ongoing pain. Research has demonstrated significant benefits associated with forgiveness. These studies indicate that clients participating in forgiveness interventions have shown a reduction in anger, depression, anxiety, grief, and the desire for revenge, and increases in self-esteem, hope, love, empathy, compassion, and other positive emotions. They are not held emotionally captive by events from the past but can enjoy life free from the burden of anger, anguish, pain, and suffering from the offense(s) they experienced. Forgiveness may also lead to increased sense of personal power; feelings of joy, peace, and gratitude; a discovery of new meaning in life; and increased spiritual wellbeing. In addition to personal benefits, forgiveness may have relationship benefits, such as reconciliation and increased closeness, understanding, intimacy, and trust. Research indicates that forgiveness is an essential aspect of successful marriage and family relationships, and those who are able to ask for and give forgiveness are more likely to have gratifying family relationships.

The Forgiveness Process

Although forgiveness can be understood as an event, a process, or final outcome, for more egregious offenses such as those likely to be addressed in therapy, forgiveness is best understood as a process. The process of forgiveness includes a number of behaviors or flexible stages that facilitate the cognitive, affective, and behavioral tasks that individuals undertake to free themselves from the emotional burdens associated with mistreatment by others. Enright's group suggests four stages in the forgiveness process. These stages are not sequential, and clients may move through, skip, or repeat them as necessary. In the *uncovering* stage, clients recognize the offense and their psychological and emotional response. In the *decision* stage, clients decide whether to forgive the offense—a cognitive choice to let go of resentment or hurt. In the *work* stage of forgiveness, clients attempt to reframe their view of the offender and unburden themselves of negative emotions directed toward the offender, replacing these with empathy or compassion. The final *outcome* stage focuses on the personal benefits and healing experienced by the forgiver. Forgiving does not necessarily mean forgetting, but the memories are no longer saturated with emotions of anger, bitterness, or revenge.

In some situations, forgiveness is a process undertaken individually by the person who was wronged. In such cases, the primary effort or change occurs within the forgiver and is not dependent upon the actions or change of others. Other times, forgiveness may be an interpersonal process that helps heal individual and relationship wounds. When individuals desire to reconcile, the process also includes efforts from both parties to heal damaged relationships, restore trust, and build new bonds of love and respect. This may entail remorse, apology, and restitution by the offending party.

Forgiveness Intervention

Therapists have a critical task of assisting both perpetrators and victims who have suffered mistreatment, injustice, betrayal, abuse, severe hatred, or misunderstanding. Without appropriate help, victims of mistreatment may suffer twice: once from the original offense and again from lingering bitterness or resentment toward the offender. It is important to help clients understand that although they may be the recipient of an offense and injustice, the power lies within them to find happiness once again through forgiveness. In order for forgiveness to be accepted by clients as a viable intervention, they must have an acceptable definition or rationale for it. If they misunderstand forgiveness in any of the ways described above, they may reject it in therapy. Thus, it is important to first ask about clients' understanding and values regarding forgiveness. The next step is to work on forgiveness in therapy in a way that is acceptable to clients. In some cases, this might be done by emphasizing personal benefits to the client rather than outcomes that benefit the offender. The pain may be so deep or intense for some clients that they are opposed to the term *forgiveness*. In such cases, therapists may substitute "letting go of pain and anger" or "giving up resentment."

After establishing an acceptable definition and rationale, therapists can utilize the following interventions to help facilitate forgiveness:

- Establish an environment in the therapy room where clients feel safe to share their story and emotions.
- Work with clients to reframe the offense and the offender. Clients may gain a new interpretation of the offense and new perspective of the offender by taking into account the larger context and seeking to understand the limitations and fallibility of the offender. Empathy toward the offender may grow as clients see the offender as a damaged person rather than as fundamentally bad.
- Promote forgiveness by having clients reflect on their experiences with offering and receiving forgiveness in the past. What memories do they have of being forgiven by another? How did they feel when forgiven?
- Ask clients to reflect on what they learned about forgiveness in their family of origin.
- Explore clients' religious and spiritual beliefs about forgiveness. Religious clients may respond positively to a spiritual rationale for forgiveness when it is an integral part of their belief system.
- Gently challenge misunderstandings of forgiveness.
- Model unconditional acceptance and positive regard for clients. This may invite them to develop greater empathy and let go of judgments and grievances toward the offender.
- Model forgiveness by apologizing for mistakes made during therapy and forgiving clients for offenses committed during sessions.
- If the offender participates in therapy and reconciliation is a goal, facilitating apologies can be a powerful intervention toward forgiveness. Therapists can encourage the offender to seek forgiveness by accepting responsibility for the wrongs they committed and the damage they caused and then sincerely apologizing for these.
- Healing rituals may be used to signify forgiveness, letting go, moving forward, and reconciliation.

Stephen T. Fife and Sheldon Nichols

See also Couples and Marriage Counseling; Extramarital Affairs and Infidelity; Religion; Sexual Abuse; Trust

Further Readings

DiBlasio, F. A., & Proctor, J. H. (1993). Therapists and the clinical use of forgiveness. *American Journal of Family Therapy, 21,* 175–184.

Enright, R. D., & Human Development Study Group. (1996). Counseling within the forgiveness triad: On forgiving, receiving forgiveness, and self-forgiveness. *Counseling and Values, 40,* 107–126.

Fife, S. T., Weeks, G. R., & Stellberg-Filbert, J. (2013). Facilitating forgiveness in the treatment of infidelity: An interpersonal model. *Journal of Family Therapy, 35,* 343–367.

Gordon, K. C., & Baucom, D. H. (1998). Understanding betrayals in marriage: A synthesized model of forgiveness. *Family Process, 37,* 425–449.

Hargrave, T. D. (1994). *Families and forgiveness: Healing wounds in the intergenerational family.* New York, NY: Brunner/Mazel.

Luskins, F. (2002). *Forgive for good: A proven prescription for health and happiness.* New York, NY: HarperCollins.

McCullough, M. E., & Worthington, E. L., Jr. (1994). Models of interpersonal forgiveness and their applications to counseling: Review and critique. *Counseling and Values, 39,* 2–14.

McCullough, M. E., Worthington, E. L., Jr., & Rachal, K. C. (1997). Interpersonal forgiving in close relationships. *Journal of Personality and Social Psychology, 73,* 321–336.

Sells, J. N., & Hargrave, T. D. (1998). Forgiveness: A review of the theoretical and empirical literature. *Journal of Family Therapy, 20,* 21–36.

Worthington, E. L., Jr. (1998). An empathy-humility-commitment model of forgiveness applied within family dyads. *Journal of Family Therapy, 20,* 59–76.

Foster Children

Foster care is a formal system usually run by a government or a social service agency that places at-risk minors in temporary care of nonfamilial caretakers, extended family, or group homes. The system of foster care that is experienced by children, families, and professionals will largely depend on the societal values related to the rights of children and the expectations for the families involved in care. Within the United States, fostering practices and laws vary from state to state but some processes and expectations related to foster care are guided by a handful of federal regulations meant to address the needs of children, families, and foster system participants and professionals. A child may be placed into foster care for a number of reasons, which could include juvenile delinquency (truancy, vandalism, violence, etc.) or founded reports of child abuse, neglect, or domestic violence. In the United States, a state department of child protective services is involved in removing children from their primary residence and placing them in foster care; however, a child's placement into foster care is not necessarily linked to a need for adoption or long-term placement away from the primary caregiver(s). If possible, mental health organizations, in conjunction with representatives from the state, choose to seek ways to reunite the child or adolescent with the original family placement or another family member. This entry presents statistics related to foster care, explains regulations influencing foster care, and discusses the counselor's role in working with families.

Demographics of Foster Care

According to the Children's Bureau, reunification is the most common goal and outcome for children placed into foster care and has remained so over the last 10 years, with the majority of children remaining in foster care for 1 to 11 months (35%, median 13.5 months). The Adoption and Safe Families Act of 1997 (ASFA) identifies three circumstances by which reunification is not a required goal of a state agency: (1) when a parent has seriously abused the child or children, (2) when a parent has killed another child, or (3) when a parent's rights to a sibling of the child in care have been terminated.

According to the U.S. Department of Health and Human Services the median age of children in foster care in 2013 was 8.2 years, having a median entry age of 6.4 years, with over 27,000 children aging out of the system each year. Additionally, the majority of children placed into foster care in 2013 identified as White (42%), with 24% identifying as African American, 22% identifying as Hispanic, and 9% identifying as multiracial.

Thus, for counselors, issues related to identity development as well as the psychological developmental needs and milestones of children in care will be of great importance when considering the conceptualization of treatment protocols. Additionally, the context of the intervention by child services must be considered when determining what direction to take when developing family treatment plans. Due to the complexities of issues inherent to the treatment of children in foster care, be they governmental, budgetary, systemic, or familial, a number of challenges face agencies and family counselors attempting to assist those involved in the fostering process. Family education and parenting, advocacy, and the education of system participants (including judges, guardians, and foster parents) are all critical components of quality psychological care for children in the foster system. In general, the majority of research regarding foster placement and family treatment emphasizes the need for interdisciplinary, community-based care that focus on developmental aspects associated with attachment, trauma, and the social-emotional needs of children as well as attending to the development of useful emotional regulation strategies and improving relational bonds. In order to develop family treatment and prevention processes that are useful, a clear understanding of the regulations associated with foster care, the role of counselors in the fostering system, and the accepted models for family involvement and practice is necessary.

System Challenges and Regulations

Most economically developed countries have regulations and expectations for the treatment of children placed into the care of the state, or foster care. Foster care has become a challenge for many countries, given that out-of-home placements involve interactions between a variety of legal, professional, and community systems, thus making foster care resource intensive. Early and intensive family intervention (as a preventive measure or following an out-of-home placement) has been shown to increase the long-term stability and functioning of families as well as the emotional well-being of children, reducing negative social and behavioral outcomes.

According to experts, foster care is a global issue affecting international political relationships as well as governmental policy, including in the United States. Relevant laws governing child placement and welfare within the United States include, but are not limited to, the Child Abuse and Prevention Act of 1974, the Adoption and Safe Families Act of 1997, the Promoting Safe and Stable Families Act of 2002, and most recently, the Fostering Connections to Success and Increasing Adoptions Act of 2008. These laws outline procedures for defining and addressing child abuse and neglect, procedures for placement decisions, funding initiatives for support programs and personnel, treatment expectations, and support for children and families through the fostering experience. While some regulations leave little room for interpretation, some aspects are somewhat vague, leaving discretionary decisions related to program implementation to individual states. Therefore, the nature of intervention and services received can vary by state.

Knowledge of federal and state regulations related to the placement and care of children in foster care is essential for appropriate family treatment. Laws outlining foster care requirements and resources can assist family counselors in creating treatment plans that advocate for the specific needs of children and families within the context of the situation that led to government intervention.

Two major systemic concerns related to psychological care include the use of psychotropic medication in conjunction with individual diagnosis, and appropriate placement of a child or sibling group with a foster family. After reviewing the 2007 Client/Patient Sample Survey (CPSS), experts in the field concluded that predictors of medication use with foster children receiving Medicaid differed from the predictors for children in outpatient care who resided with their primary caregivers receiving Medicaid. While children in this study received medication and were diagnosed at similar rates, results indicated that the odds of females in foster care receiving medication were highest as compared to males in foster care and outpatient care and females in outpatient care. Additionally, depressed mood, indications of suicidal ideation, and being emotionally withdrawn significantly influenced the odds of whether or not a child in foster care received medication when compared to outpatient children with similar demographic characteristics.

Contrary to this study, many other researchers have found that children in foster care are frequently diagnosed with mental health conditions and are prescribed medication at significantly higher rates than children not in foster care. Family counselors need to be aware of the unique mental health needs and systemic interventions associated with any diagnostic label in order to ensure families receive appropriate care and education. In addition to considering diagnostic issues, the culture of the family of origin as well as the child's experience with his or her family of origin may also influence placement decisions.

Hamido Megahead and Elizabeth Soliday reviewed two common models for foster placement: organizational ecology and goodness of fit. The goodness-of-fit model focuses on matching caregiver and child temperament whereas the ecology model focuses on the level of commitment of the foster care provider. In order to address common concerns and characteristics associated with foster care, the researchers recommend a model that includes crisis-based considerations that relate to an ability to cope with stress and resulting instability. The family adjustment and adaptation response (FAAR) model encourages family counselors to focus on and consistently assess the interaction between family stressors, resources, and the perceptions of individual family members in relation to the identified stressors and resources. As placement disruptions are predicted by trauma experience, risk behaviors, and age, a focus on empowering the strengths of children and attending to the resources of the family can help to mitigate placement issues. However, if resources are not readily available within the local community, difficulties in implementing community-based interventions can arise which could influence successful reunification and foster placements.

The Role of Counselors

Several practice modalities have been reviewed by researchers and practitioners in relation to the treatment of children and families experiencing the foster care system. The general consensus of the professional literature indicates that interdisciplinary teams in conjunction with community-based care initiatives are crucial to successful placement outcomes and long-term reunification with caregivers. With regard to family counseling, professionals suggest that problem-focused services (e.g., substance abuse treatment), parenting education and support, as well as individual and family counseling significantly influence successful reunification with a parent or primary caregiver. Philip Fisher, Patricia Chamberlain, and Leslie Leve offer specific suggestions for family counselors with regard to evidenced-based treatment approaches:

1. Evaluate resiliency factors through continuous assessment of problem behaviors and placement history so as to determine which children will likely respond well to regular foster care and which may need additional resources and services.

2. Advocate for enhanced services that include access to behavioral consultants, assignment of caseworkers with higher salaries and lower caseloads, and access to additional recreational and growth-oriented activities for children in care.

3. Provide support groups for specific behavioral problems for parents and foster parents (e.g., Keeping Foster and Kin Parents Trained and Supported [KEEP]), provide parenting education and support, and advocate for access to educational programs for children focusing on literacy, emotional regulation, and social-emotional competency.

4. Advocate and collaborate with other mental health professionals to provide intensive treatment for children with severe emotional and behavioral problems to include individual counseling, school-based intervention and support with a focus on attachment, emotional support, and socialization (i.e., multidimensional treatment foster care).

Further, research has found empirical support for the integrative approach, emphasizing that evidence-based, interdisciplinary approaches address risk factors associated with foster placement (disruptions in emotional and behavioral development, deficits in neurological development due to neglect or abuse, and the capacity to develop supportive social relationships with peers and caregivers). Other professionals highlight the importance of adding coursework in clinical training programs related to addressing the needs of families and children experiencing foster care. In their survey, they found that between 13% and 25% of master's-level graduates from the Council for Accreditation of Counseling and Related Educational Programs (CACREP), the Commission of Accreditation for Marriage and Family Therapy Education (COAMFTE), and the Council on Social Work Education (CSWE) programs were working directly with children and families in foster and adoptive settings, while only an average of 9.3% of respondent programs directly addressed issues related to foster and adoptive care in coursework. Given the complex nature of fostering issues, specific training may be required to improve a family counselor's ability to provide adequate services. Knowledge of crisis intervention strategies, emotionally focused interventions, family education, resource management, culturally responsive treatment, and strengths-oriented perspectives are essential elements of family counseling in foster settings.

Amanda C. La Guardia

See also Adoption; Adoption, Cross-Cultural and Interracial; Racial Disparities in Foster Care; Transracial Adoption

Further Readings

Al, C. M., Stams, G. J., Bek, M. S., Damen, E. M., Asscher, J. J., & van der Laan, P. H. (2012). A meta-analysis of intensive family preservation programs: Placement prevention and improvement of family functioning. *Children & Youth Services Review, 34*(8), 1472–1479. doi:10.1016/j.childyouth.2012.04.002

Cabrera, M. (2014, July 9). Foster care is an international issue. *Huffington Post*. Retrieved from http://www.huffingtonpost.com/marquis-cabrera/foster-care-is-an-interna_1_b_5297922.html

Chamberlain, P., Price, J., Leve, L. D., Laurent, H., Landsverk, J. A., & Reid, J. B. (2008). Prevention of behavior problems for children in foster care: Outcomes and mediation effects. *Prevention Science, 9*(1), 17–27. doi:10.1007/s11121-007-0080-7

Children's Bureau. (2015). *Numbers and trends 2015: Foster care statistics 2013*. Retrieved from https://www.childwelfare.gov/pubPDFs/foster.pdf

Fisher, P. A., Chamberlain, P., & Leve, L. D. (2009). Improving the lives of foster children through evidenced-based interventions. *Vulnerable Children & Youth Studies, 4*(2), 122–127. doi:10.1080/17450120902887368

Jones Harden, B., Morrison, C., & Clyman, R. B. (2014). Emotion labeling among young children in foster care. *Early Education and Development, 25*(8), 1180–1197.

Leve, L. D., Harold, G. T., Chamberlain, P., Landsverk, J. A., Fisher, P. A., & Vostanis, P. (2012). Practitioner review: Children in foster care—Vulnerabilities and evidence-based interventions that promote resilience processes. *Journal of Child Psychology & Psychiatry, 53*(12), 1197–1211.

McWey, L. M., Benesh, A., & Wojciak, A. S. (2015). Families with children in foster care: Clinical considerations and interventions. In S. Browning & K. Pasley (Eds.), *Contemporary families: Translating research into practice* (pp. 70–87). New York, NY: Routledge.

Megahead, H. A., & Soliday, E. (2013). Developing a conceptual framework of foster family placement. *Journal of Family Psychotherapy, 24*(1), 48–63. doi:10.1080/08975353.2013.762868

Weir, K. N., Fife, S. T., Whiting, J. B., & Blazewick, A. (2008). Clinical training of MFTs for adoption, foster care, and child development settings: A comparative survey of CACREP, COAMFTE, and CSWE accredited programs. *Journal of Family Psychotherapy, 19*(3), 277–290.

FRIENDSHIP

Human beings are social creatures, and interpersonal relationships are critical to their survival and their sense of well-being. Often, when intimate relationships are discussed, people think of romantic relationships or family relationships. However, friendships also play a pivotal role in people's lives across the lifespan. Friendship, although a complex interpersonal process, is the state of being in a relationship with others who share common interests, goals, and concerns for one another. Although the idea of friendship has varied meaning across people, it is often marked by a presence of mutual respect, common interests, and shared companionship. Research confirms that having friends is important at every stage of development, but how people develop such friendships, the ease with which they accomplish the task, and how they are affected by friends may vary across their lifespan. Friendships, in addition to family relationships and romantic relationships, provide an important source of intimacy in people's lives. This entry examines the ways in which friendship development changes as people age and the benefits derived from friendly relationships throughout the life cycle.

Early Childhood Friendship

Establishing friendships is an important developmental goal in early childhood. During this time, children's friendships are often created around a shared activity where having fun together forms a primary focus. For instance, when the teacher of young children asks the students to draw a picture or build with blocks, they are often encouraged to do this together. They share an activity, realize they have fun together, and that becomes the foundation of their new friendship. Initially such activities are better termed *parallel play*. Young children are able to act in the presence of others but further development is needed before they are able to interact. As these parallel play interactions proceed, most young children eventually learn and practice those skills that are essential to their social, cognitive, communicative, and emotional development. Overall, those who successfully build friendships in early childhood tend to adjust to new challenges in life and have an improved quality of life.

Early School Friendship

As previously noted, in the early stages of development, young children's friendships are often created by who is physically closest to them (they are at the same table) or the interest in the activity (they are doing something that the child finds interesting). As they move closer to school age, children begin to form the ability to see things from another's perspective, they become more curious about their friends, and they begin to ask questions to try to get to know associates better. These processes together help children determine which children they will select for friends and who will select them. Not surprisingly, at this stage, children also become aware of the idea of reciprocity. When they do something nice for a friend, they expect something nice to be done for them in return; when they feel friendly toward a classmate, they expect the same. When relationships are not reciprocal, feelings may get hurt and the friendship is likely to suffer, at least temporarily. Also at this stage of development, children start to develop a smaller circle of friends and may even have a "best" friend, although this best friend may change day by day or even hour to hour.

Middle School Friendship

Middle childhood brings about marked changes in the understanding of friendship; these preadolescents recognize that true friends offer companionship and are trustworthy, as well as loyal, supportive and understanding. They usually indicate an increasing appreciation of each other's feelings and intentions, and recognize that friendships can last over time, even if they are separated by distance. During this time, children tend to develop friendships with those who are most similar to themselves, and they are traditionally segregated by sex.

In middle school, the size of the friendship circle tends to increase because children are interacting with a larger number of peers during the day; they are changing classrooms and therefore come in contact with a greater number of peers and are more involved in clubs or organized after-school activities. However, this is also the time in which cliques, or small groups of close friends, begin to develop. This might be difficult for children who are already isolated and have not yet made good friendship connections. It is also worrisome, because positive friendships are important for healthy social and emotional development. Friendship also helps with empathy development and has a positive effect on self-image and school performance.

Some populations of children may have more difficulty than others in finding opportunities to create friendships. Although it is possible for children with disabilities to establish and maintain friendships, it is sometimes more challenging for them. Often building and sustaining relationships involves both verbal and nonverbal interactions, so this becomes more challenging for those children who struggle with those types of challenges. Depending on the level and extent of the disability, other children at school may shun them because they do not understand their special needs. Some school districts, educators, and even parents have developed programs for their children with special needs to give them an opportunity to socialize and make connections with not only other children with special needs but also other typically developing children. This helps with self-esteem, offers an opportunity for special needs children to socialize, and gives other children an opportunity to learn more about their classmates or neighbors from whom they differ.

Adolescent Friendship

At this stage, individuals tend to place a high value on genuine emotional closeness with friends, start to confide more thoughts and feelings with each other, and place more emphasis on trust and support. They can accept and even appreciate differences between themselves and their friends. They are also not as possessive, so they are less likely to feel threatened if their friends have other relationships. Friends may also influence academic success during this time of development. Studies have shown that adolescents who become friends with others who do well in school have increased test scores, are absent from school less frequently, and report enjoying school more.

Although bullying can happen at any stage of development, during adolescence, relational bullying tends to emerge, most commonly among girls. Though not as common as the more traditional forms of bullying like physical bullying among boys, relational bullying, also known as relational aggression, can be subtle, hurtful, and painful for victims. Clearly depicted in the 2004 film *Mean Girls*, relational bullying or aggression is emotional and can be perpetuated through spreading rumors and exclusion from social events. What makes this especially painful for the victims is that this form of bullying is being carried out by the people they consider their friends. Studies show, however, that having a supportive network of friends helps combat other forms of bullying. Having good, supportive friends can help boost self-esteem and offer both physical and emotional support when someone is being bullied.

Friendship in Young to Middle Adulthood

During young adulthood, individuals start to both emotionally and physically separate from their family of origin. They start new jobs, possibly in another city or town away from their family or college friends, and many may not yet be married or in a significant relationship. Due to this physical and emotional separation, young adults may be at a point in which they need to establish new friendships. In addition, because of the physical and emotional separation from family members, those in young and middle adulthood often turn to their friends first when they encounter crisis so those without friends are likely to feel isolated and lonely.

Many adults report having difficulties making friends or maintaining close relationships because of personal or professional responsibilities (getting a new job or receiving a promotion, being married, or raising children) or even a shift in interests. At this stage in life, individuals tend to rely more on a spouse or significant other for social support and less on friends. Although women often report a decrease in the number of friends after they get married and have children, they report having stronger relationships with other women; they feel comfortable self-disclosing and sharing personal information with others. Both men and women tend to develop stronger relationships with coworkers during this stage of development. Women's relationships tend to be more personal in nature than those commonly reported by men whose friendships often center on shared interests, such as sports. Those who are successful at establishing or maintaining good friendships report being happier, more secure, less lonely, and better adjusted than those who do not.

Friendships Among Older Adults

Experts agree that making friends and maintaining friendships continue to be important in older adults, and there are several factors that affect their friendship development and maintenance. Although the freedom of retirement and having fewer family commitments allows for more free time to devote to cultivating friendships, the increase in age also increases the likelihood of declining health and decreased mobility. Literature shows that older men have more difficulty replacing friends who are lost due to retirement, relocation, or death, and women, who tend to be more social overall, have an easier time maintaining old relationships and establishing new ones. Although engaging in casual friendships can prove to be helpful in combating the stress and depression that older adults sometimes find themselves feeling, having even just one close friend can help with symptoms. Just like in other age groups, friends provide emotional support, companionship, and acceptance, which are crucial to older adults, especially at a time in which they may be dealing with major life adjustments, such as the death of a spouse or a loved one. Having a supportive network of friends leads to higher levels of happiness and satisfaction, and protects against stress; physical, emotional, and social problems; as well as premature death.

Overall Physical and Emotional Benefits of Having Friends

There is little doubt that having friends is extremely important across all age groups. There are numerous benefits that children accrue from having friends. Friendships help create a sense of security and belonging. Children with no friends or those who have difficulty interacting with peers tend to have more emotional or behavioral problems. Having friends helps with self-confidence, self-worth, and leads to higher levels of happiness; having friends gives individuals a greater sense of purpose, increased feeling of connectedness, and ultimately lower levels of stress. As individuals grow older, friends help celebrate positive milestones and offer support. Having a supportive network of friends protects against stress and other social, emotional, and physical problems.

Christine H. Ebrahim

See also Compassion; Empathy; Loneliness; Trust

Further Readings

Bouwman, T., Aartsen, M., van Tilburg, T., & Stevens, N. (2014). Friendship matters: Effects of an online friendship intervention for older adults. *Gerontologist, 54*(2), 218–218.

Maguire, M., & Dunn, J. (1997). Friendships in early childhood, and social understanding. *International Journal of Behavioral Development, 21*(4), 669–686.

Sias, P., Drzewiecka, J., Meares, M., Bent, R., Konomi, Y., Ortega, M., & White, C. (2008). Intercultural friendship development. *Communication Reports, 21*(1), 1–13.

Wentzel, K., Barry, C., & Caldwell, K. (2004). Friendships in middle school: Influences on motivation and school adjustment. *Journal of Educational Psychology, 96*(2), 195–203.

FUNCTIONAL ASSESSMENT AND CHILDREN

A functional assessment is a method of assessment that aims to determine the reasons that an individual displays problem or challenging behaviors. Rooted in behavioral theory, this approach is used to address problematic behaviors in children. Children's problem behaviors are often maintained because they serve some purpose for the child, such as helping to avoid an undesirable task or gain a desired item. A clinician will use a functional assessment to determine the purpose (function) of the child's behavior. Effective treatment can then be outlined for that specific child to decrease the problematic behavior and replace it with more appropriate behavior. This entry reviews the theoretical underpinnings of functional assessment and outlines four basic steps to assess behavioral function in children.

Understanding Behavior and Function

A *behavior* can be defined as any action given as a response to a situation. The philosophy of a functional assessment is that the behavior has an intended purpose of communicating and attaining something desirable to the child. This purpose may not be immediately apparent, even to the individual demonstrating the behavior. Nonetheless, a functional assessment assumes that the function of the behavior is knowable through gathering information surrounding the behavioral occurrence. Behavioral theory posits children's behaviors as efforts to attain desires or needs. This is particularly true for children with limited verbal skills, who rely primarily on their behaviors to communicate preferences and needs. Behavioral therapy has proven effective for children with various developmental disabilities, most notably autism spectrum disorder and attention-deficit/hyperactivity disorder (ADHD). Behaviors are seen as a learned mechanism and, therefore, can be adapted through learning new ways of functioning. Functional assessments are present focused in that they concentrate less on the origins of a behavior and more on what is maintaining a behavior in the present.

Learning Behaviors

A core concept in behavioral theory is the relationship between antecedents, behaviors, and outcomes. Behaviorists do not see behaviors as isolated incidents but rather in relation to the context of antecedents and consequences. The antecedent, also known as the precipitating event, triggers the behavior. Antecedents can take many forms, but most often come in form of verbal commands, individuals present, activity, or sensory input. A child may engage in a behavior with only one parent or only when asked to transition from a desired activity to a less preferred task. Identification of the circumstances that trigger a behavior will begin to shed light on the function, or desired outcome, of the behavior.

In behavioral theory, outcomes are circumstances that occur following the behavior. The consequences may be both positive and negative. For example, being sent to the principal's office may appear negative, but if the function of the problematic behavior is to avoid class work, the behavior has succeeded. In this scenario, the child has learned the association between negative classroom behavior and avoidance of a nonpreferred classroom activity. The repetition of this cycle will continue to reinforce the negative classroom behavior because the behavior is successful in obtaining the desired result.

This pattern of behavioral response may be a subconscious or automatic feedback loop, with the child responding to situations without consciously processing the antecedent and desired outcome. Identification of the antecedents and outcomes elicits patterns of behavioral functions.

Behavioral Reinforcement and Extinction

A functional assessment seeks to identify the antecedents or consequences that are reinforcing the problematic behavior. The factors that maintain the problematic behavior will be modified to be less reinforcing to the child, thereby leading to a decrease in the target behavior. Operant conditioning, developed by B. F. Skinner, theorized that behaviors are modified in response to external factors known as reinforcements and punishments. *Reinforcement* is a term for something that encourages a person to do more of a behavior. Common examples of reinforcements include homework passes earned through class attendance, a weekly allowance earned through completing chores, or an ice cream cone after a good report card. Conversely, a *punishment* is a term for something that encourages a person to do less of a behavior. Examples of punishment include extra chores for not completing one's homework, losing privileges after a fight at school, or a time out after a tantrum.

The terms *positive* and *negative* are often assigned to reinforcements and punishments as a further description: Positive indicates the addition of something as punishment or reinforcement while negative indicates the removal of something as punishment or reinforcement. It is important to note that in this context, the terms *positive* and *negative* do not assign a moral value but rather refer to the action being taken: addition or removal. Using the above examples, a positive reinforcement would be a weekly allowance after completing chores, while a positive punishment would be extra chores for failing to complete homework. Negative punishment could refer to the loss of privileges, while negative reinforcement could be a homework pass that allows a child to avoid doing homework for one night. The reinforcers encourage the child to continue doing that behavior, and punishments aim to decrease the frequency of the behavior.

Often a problematic behavior is maintained despite negative consequences. A functional assessment aims to identify possible reinforcers for that problematic behavior that have encouraged the child to continue engaging in the behavior. For example, a child may continue to engage in tantrum behaviors at the grocery store because at some point, the parent gives in and buys the child the candy bar or toy they wanted. In that scenario, the possibility of the toy or candy bar is so reinforcing that the child engages in the behavior despite other potential consequences. The child will learn to stop the tantrum behavior when they no longer receive reinforcement (i.e., the candy bar or toy). Operant conditioning identifies that extinction of behaviors is not instantaneous but instead is influenced by how often the behavior was reinforced. A common term for frequency of reinforcement is the *reinforcement schedule*. A child that had received a candy bar each time they screamed will learn to stop their behavior much more quickly than a child who received a candy bar some of the times when they screamed because the second child still sees a possibility that the reward (i.e., the candy) will be provided.

Functional Assessment and Children

Children often develop negative behaviors that directly impact their ability to function in everyday life. The subconscious feedback loop of antecedent–behavior–consequence interferes with the child's ability to make effective, informed decisions. Families often become drawn into this loop by repeating the reinforcement or failing to understand the true function of the behavior. A proper functional assessment aims to illuminate the behavioral patterns so that children might learn more effective and appropriate means of functioning in their everyday lives.

While functional assessment is most often implemented and guided by a trained clinician, research has begun to examine the efficacy of training parents to conduct their own functional assessments of their children's behaviors. Proper guidance is necessary to ensure the families are able to effectively assess the behavioral patterns of the child. In addition, selection and implementation of appropriate behavioral interventions are necessary components for effective parent-guided functional assessment. An initial functional assessment directed by the clinician may serve as a model for the parents' continued behavioral interventions with their child.

Conducting a Functional Assessment

Functional assessment often serves as the initial stage in treatment. Although there are variations on the methods for conducting a functional assessment, the majority will include four elements: definition of behaviors, data collection, behavioral function hypothesis, and treatment planning/implementation. The following steps outline these individual elements.

Step 1. Identify the Behaviors

Identification of a behavior entails clearly outlining that behavior through an operational definition. The definition should be specific, objective, and measurable. A specific definition is one that details the parameters of the behavior. For example, the broad term of *aggression* may apply to a variety of behaviors including verbal threats, property destruction, hitting, slapping, and kicking. A specific definition of *aggression* will specify which behaviors are being measured as aggression in the functional assessment. Objectivity refers to the definition's universality. The functional assessment relies on the behavioral definition being understood and translated similarly across all individuals involved in the assessment process. For example, the parent of an aggressive child may label only physical acts as aggression, while the child's teacher includes verbal threats as aggression.

Therefore, it is necessary to provide a specific, objective definition of the behavior to ensure consistency across observers and informants. A measurable definition is one that is able to be counted and compared; for instance, how often the child attempted aggression in the classroom compared to attempted aggression during recess. A measurable behavior can be tracked to elicit patterns of antecedents and consequences; treatment effectiveness is also able to be monitored through the amount of change seen in the behavior.

Definitions are able to be adapted if necessary, though accuracy of results is dependent on consistent measurement of the behavior throughout data collection. It is often easier to broaden behavioral definitions into behavioral clusters rather than attempting to separate broader behaviors into smaller segments. The most common example of a behavioral cluster would be a "tantrum," which may consist of any number of behaviors that appear to serve the same function.

Step 2. Observation and Assessment

Once a target behavior is identified, the clinician will begin to gather behavioral data. This data will enable the clinician to make a hypothesis of the function of the problem behavior. Data collection can occur through key informant interviews and direct observation.

Key informants are individuals who come into contact with the child on a regular basis in a setting in which the behavior occurs. The most common informants are parents and teachers. Background information is collected from the key informants regarding the onset of behavior, when the behavior occurs most often, and outcomes of the behavior. The key informant interview can also elicit information on strategies that have been tried in the past. Key informant interview methods range from structured assessment tools to unstructured informal questioning. Assessment tools such as rating scales and forced-choice questionnaires may be provided to key informants to aid in identification of possible functions of the target behavior. The data collected about the behavior indirectly will highlight times and situations in which the child's behavior should be directly observed.

Direct observation allows real-time tracking of behaviors and possible antecedents and consequences. The clinician or appropriately trained individuals will record observations of the child throughout the day, identifying characteristics of the behaviors and events that occurred directly before or after the behavior. Each time a behavior occurs, the data collector will record any possible antecedents and consequences that corresponded with that behavioral incident. Data collection can be simple or sophisticated, depending on the range of behaviors observed and the data needed. Professionals will often provide parents or other individuals with a data collection tool along with proper instructions for observation and recording.

The most common data types for target behaviors are frequency, duration, and intensity. Frequency indicates how often a behavior happens in a given time frame, such as within 1 hour, 1 day, or one activity. Frequency may also refer to how many times a behavior occurred within one behavioral incident, such as how many times the child engaged in self-injurious behavior during one tantrum. Duration indicates how long the behavioral episode lasts. This may be helpful for tracking a behavioral cluster such as aggression and self-injurious behavior that occur simultaneously. Intensity describes the severity of the behaviors. This allows for a distinction between a mild episode and a severe outburst. The type of data collected is dependent on the characteristics of the target behavior.

While indirect methods such as key informant interviewing must consider the influence of the informant's perspective of the behavior, direct observation has the potential for error simply due to reactivity. This type of error occurs when the child changes their typical behaviors due to the presence of an observer. While most observable settings do not have the facilities to allow for unnoticed observation, the individual collecting data should take care to be as unobtrusive as possible. In consideration of reactivity, clinicians may wish to enlist the assistance of individuals who are naturally in the child's environment, such as parents or teachers. With proper instruction and clear definitions of the behaviors being monitored, these natural observers are able to record behavioral data throughout the child's normal routine. That data can then be compiled with the clinician's own observations to allow for a more balanced functional assessment.

While both key informant interviews and direct observation are valid methods of data collection, recent studies have suggested that direct, descriptive procedures were more likely to correspond with the identified function of a full functional analysis than indirect procedures such as interviews. This is an important consideration, for although it may be more convenient to conduct abbreviated functional assessments, indirect measures alone may not correctly identify a child's motivation for performing a certain behavior. The risk of insufficient data in either scenario is an ineffective treatment plan and the potential exacerbation of behavioral issues. The combined use of direct observation and key informant interviews allows for multiple perspectives of the same behavior.

The data collection process ideally will last long enough for saturation of behavioral patterns to emerge. Visual aids such as histograms and line graphs can aid in determining patterns of behavior. For example, a histogram may indicate how often a child demonstrated aggression when presented with different antecedents, while a line graph may depict what times of day the child was more likely to engage in the behavior. Following the development of functional behavior hypotheses, the assessor will likely continue some form of data collection to monitor behavioral changes in response to treatment.

Step 3. Form Hypotheses About Function of Target Behaviors

The emergence of behavioral patterns in the collected data is used to develop a prediction about the function, or purpose, that the behavior serves for the individual. This behavioral hypothesis identifies the behavior, the antecedent, and the suspected function of the behavior. Common functions include obtaining or avoidance of an object, person, or activity. A behavioral hypothesis is often written as "Given (antecedent), the child engages in (behavior) to (function)." For example, if a child attempts to hide each time the class transitions from free play to a structured activity, a hypothesis might read: "Given transition from unstructured play time, child will engage in hiding behavior to avoid the transition to nonpreferred structured activity." One behavior may result in multiple hypotheses if the behavior appears differently across environments.

The purpose of the behavioral hypothesis is to highlight the function of the behavior so that a treatment plan might be developed to address the behavioral concern. The clinician may wish to test the behavioral hypothesis to ensure accuracy. This practice must be done with caution, for the manipulation of antecedents or consequences has the potential to intensify and exacerbate the problematic behaviors.

Step 4. Create Treatment Plan

As the behaviors examined in a functional assessment are targeted to be changed, the final step in a functional assessment is to develop treatment goals related to the targeted behaviors. The identified function of each behavior indicates the goal of each behavior. To extinguish the problematic behavior, the consequences must be modified to ensure the intended function is not actualized. Proactive approaches can also be taken, where a more appropriate behavior may receive the desired reinforcer, rather than the problem behavior. Antecedent modifiers may also be introduced to help manage situations before they occur. Continued monitoring is necessary to determine success of treatment strategies and to reevaluate functions as necessary.

Functional Assessment and the Family

Functional assessment serves as a tool in addressing the behavioral component of family therapy. While it may be time-consuming, a functional assessment provides clinicians and families with the ability to identify the purpose of behaviors and a clearer understanding of the child's needs. The results of a functional assessment can empower the family to enact change and foster more positive behaviors through a strategic and informed modification of reinforcers.

Devon Manderino and Miranda Gray

See also Adolescent Behavior Problems; Autism and Children; Behavioral Family Therapy; Child Behavior Problems; Therapeutic Assessment; Treatment Planning With Couples and Families

Further Readings

Alter, P. J., Conroy, M. A., Mancil, G. R., & Haydon, T. (2008). A Comparison of functional behavior assessment methodologies with young children: Descriptive methods and functional analysis. *Journal of Behavioral Education, 17*(2), 200–219. doi: 10.1007/s10864-008-9064-3

Cooper, J. O., Heron, T. E., & Heward, W. L. (2007). *Applied behavior analysis* (2nd ed.). New York, NY: Pearson.

DuPaul, G. J., Kern, L., Volpe, R., Caskie, G. L., Sokol, N., Arbolino, L., ... Pipan, M. (2013). Comparison of parent education and functional assessment-based intervention across 24 months for young children with attention deficit hyperactivity disorder. *School Psychology Review, 42*(1), 56–75.

Fettig, A., & Barton, E. E. (2014). Parent implementation of function-based intervention to reduce children's challenging behavior: A literature review. *Topics in Early Childhood Special Education, 34*(1), 49–61.

Gable, R. A., Park, K. L., & Scott, T. M. (2014). Functional behavioral assessment and students at risk for or with emotional disabilities: Current issues and considerations. *Education & Treatment of Children, 37*(1), 111–135.

Love, J., Carr, J., & LeBlanc, L. (2009). Functional assessment of problem behavior in children with autism spectrum disorders: A summary of 32 outpatient cases. *Journal of Autism & Developmental Disorders, 39*(2), 363–372.

McCahill, J., Healy, O., Lydon, S., & Ramey, D. (2014). Training educational staff in functional behavioral assessment: A systematic review. *Journal of Developmental & Physical Disabilities, 26*(4), 479–505.

Moreno, G., Wong-Lo, M., Short, M., & Bullock, L. M. (2014). Implementing a culturally attuned functional behavioural assessment to understand and address challenging behaviours demonstrated by students from diverse backgrounds. *Emotional & Behavioural Difficulties, 19*(4), 343–355.

Stoiber, K. C., & Gettinger, M. (2011). Functional assessment and positive support strategies for promoting resilience: Effects on teachers and high-risk children. *Psychology in the Schools, 48*(7), 686–706.

Zane, T., Carlson, M., Estep, D., & Quinn, M. (2014). Using functional assessment to treat behavior problems of deaf and hard of hearing children diagnosed with autism spectrum disorder. *American Annals of the Deaf, 158*(5), 555–566.

FUNCTIONAL FAMILY THERAPY

Functional family therapy (FFT) was created by James F. Alexander in 1969 to help troubled youth (ages 10–18) and their families overcome issues related to adolescent delinquency, substance abuse, and violence. It is a brief, intensive, evidence-based family therapy appropriate for youth with behavior problems, ranging from mild to severe and chronic, with delinquency. It is used for the treatment of violent, criminal, behavioral, school, and conduct problems with youth and their families. FFT is based on family systems ideas that families may develop patterns of interacting and getting their needs met that stimulate, increase, and maintain problematic behaviors. Consequently, therapy focuses on changing familial patterns of communication, problem-solving, and the way family members get their emotional needs met. This is done through motivating families to change through tailoring interventions to a family's unique risk and protective factors. Therapy is conducted in five related phases with each having specific goals, assessments, techniques, and therapist skills in order to help the family achieve both proximal/short-term and distal/long-term goals. Adherence (fidelity) to the FFT model is ensured through a strict training model, complex Web-based monitoring system that provides a means for client assessment, tracking, monitoring, and outcome assessment. More than 40 years of research supports this evidence-based approach targeting at-risk youth. The sections that follow explain the basics of the FFT model and discuss training for its use in therapeutic practice.

What Is Functional Family Therapy?

FFT is a family-based approach that works to engage all family members and motivate them to actively engage in treatment. The target population is from preadolescence through adolescence. The therapist meets with the entire family, often in the home, to provide family therapy for 8 to 12 one-hour sessions for families with lesser problems and up to 30 sessions for families with more difficult problems. This is usually done over a 3-month to 6-month period. Sessions usually occur weekly, but can occur more often if needed. Each phase of treatment has specific assessment foci, intervention strategies, and goals. Interventions are selected based on careful assessment and matching to the family members' needs and developmental levels.

FFT is an integrative model whose major goals are accomplished through engaging and motivating families in curbing maladaptive behaviors and by developing unique strengths of the family in a culturally sensitive way. The initial form of FFT relied on the work of early communication and family systems theories and incorporated from them the idea that behavior serves to define and create interpersonal relationships and that behavior only has meaning within its relational context. Later, FFT incorporated cognitive theory, especially attribution and information-processing theories, to help explain how family meaning and emotion often manifest as blaming and negative family interactional patterns. In more recent times, FFT has included social constructionism in order to focus on meaning and the role of meaning in problems and solutions. These families often tend to be angry, blaming, and experience intense, negative experiences. The therapist works to reduce or eliminate problem behaviors accompanying problematic relational patterns. This is achieved through individualized behavior change interventions. Cognitive, attributional, and behavioral interventions are used to help create lasting change in the family.

Core Theoretical Principles of FFT

Every therapy model has core theoretical principles that create the foundation for assessment, case planning, session planning, goals, and specific interventions and strategies for how a therapist works with a family. FFT integrates into a structured framework many founding ideas of family therapy and early family therapy models. FFT is based on three core principles: (1) understanding clients; (2) understanding client problems systemically; and (3) understanding therapy and the role of the therapist as fundamentally a relational process. Although an in-depth examination of each of these core principles is beyond the scope of this entry, each will be briefly reviewed.

The first core principle, understanding clients, is a "warning" to understand clients through collecting information, but it is also about the attitude that the therapist takes with clients. FFT therapists believe clients can and will change. They also believe that every person and family has strengths that can be uncovered and/or developed. These strengths are individual, within family relationships, and in relationships between the family and larger systems. Families are not seen as "dysfunctional," rather they are seen as functioning with patterns that are not helpful.

The second core principle, understanding client problems systemically, can be understood from a multisystemic perspective. Behavior patterns of youth and their families are influenced by biological, relational, family, socioeconomic, and environmental factors. Therefore, multiple systems are assessed (e.g., family, parents, peers, school, community). FFT conceptualizes problems not in terms of "trying to change people" but in terms of risk and protective factors because these are alterable patterns of behavior. The problem is seen as serving a function in the family and the issue is not the "problem," but rather the way that the family (and other systems) tries to manage problematic behavior that creates difficulties. This is why family patterns are focused on in FFT and are an immediate focus of intervention.

The third core principle, understanding therapy and the role of the therapist as fundamentally a relational process, means seeing therapy as both systemic and purposeful while being clinically attuned and responsive to immediate client needs—being attentive to the relationship between therapist and clients. FFT is a systematic model with specific purposes and phases. The therapist is an expert on change processes and directs the process of therapy, but the family are the experts on their lives and how they are unique. Consequently, therapy is seen as a collaborative partnership between the therapist and clients. The therapeutic relationship is an alliance-based relationship and the therapist focuses on alliance-based motivation. Even though a therapist may not agree with or condone some of the family's behavior, he or she must find a way to respect, support, and connect to clients. It's important for therapists to be credible to clients and enhance or instill hope in the family.

The therapist works to engage and motivate the family, aiming to build an alliance between himself or herself and each family member and between all family members. Engagement means involving the family in the activities of sessions and become accepting of therapy. Engaging behaviors include asking questions about their lives, having "small talk," using humor, and constantly working to understand and respect family members. Motivation is created when families begin to see hope that problems can change and believe that the therapist can help create those changes. Engagement and motivation begin with the first contact and continue throughout the therapy process. Although creating a strong alliance is a major focus of the beginning phase of therapy, it is something that therapists need to attend to across phases of treatment.

Phases of Treatment

There are five interrelated phases of therapy: engagement, motivation, relational assessment, behavior change, and generalization. The goal of the engagement phase is to develop positive perceptions of the therapist and the program and facilitate the family in attending the first session. During this phase, interventions include the therapist accommodating family values and cultures and responding to initial barriers such as transportation, reluctance, or confusion. The goal of the motivation phase is to increase hope and motivation for change, reduce negativity and blaming, and address risk factors associated with treatment dropout. Examples of interventions include reframing behaviors to reduce negativity and blame and to increase motivation for change. Also, during the motivation phase, trust and alliance-building with all family members is essential. The relational assessment phase is used to identify relational functions, needs, and the hierarchy within the family. The therapist assesses the function of behaviors related to family relationships and needs. During the behavior change phase, the intention is to address family interaction patterns that maintain the presenting problems, build problem-solving and communication skills, and reduce family conflict. Examples of interventions during this phase include psychoeducational/parent training, communication training, and "homework" assignments to assist clients in generalizing these skills to the home environment. Finally, the generalization phase is used to increase family resources and extrafamilial support in order to maintain and generalize change, and to prevent relapses. Interventions help empower families and connect with both informal and formal supports. In addition, the therapist and family create a plan to minimize and overcome obstacles to maintaining changes.

Throughout therapy the goal is to reduce targeted risk behaviors and increase protective factors. These are targeted at multiple levels: family, peer, school, community, and therapy. Risk factors increase the likelihood of negative outcomes.

Protective factors are targeted for increase because they have positive influences and protect against negative outcomes. Risk factors can be categorized in terms of families (negative and blaming communication patterns, high conflict, poor parenting skills, low social support, and hopelessness), peers (poor peer relationships and association with troubled peers), and school (poor school–family relationship). Protective factors are broken down into the categories of family (positive parenting, supportive communication, family cohesion and bonding), peer (positive peer relationships), school (positive school–family relationship), community (positive family–community relationship), and therapy level (i.e., therapeutic alliance and therapy and program credibility).

Outcomes of Functional Family Therapy

The purpose of therapy is to help youth and their families achieve both proximal/short-term outcomes and distal/long-term outcomes. Research has shown that functional family therapy has been effective in the proximal and distal outcomes described in this paragraph. Proximal outcomes are impacted by the program immediately following program completion and include keeping the youth in the home, improved family functioning, reduced delinquent behavior, reductions in maternal psychiatric symptoms, reduced youth substance abuse, and having families complete treatment. Distal outcomes include reduction in criminal recidivism, reduced substance use, improved mental health, and reduction in sibling court involvement. Improved family functioning includes better communication and cohesion, and less verbal aggression, conflict, and a reduction in psychiatric symptoms for family members. Improved behavior and mental health consists of decreases in delinquent behavior and general behavior problems and a decrease in internalizing and externalizing symptoms. If there is substance abuse, then functional family therapy seeks to have fewer days of alcohol and/or drug use and fewer problems associated with substance use. Finally, the hope is that there will be greater rates of treatment completion in functional family therapy than alternatives (i.e., individual, group, other family therapies, social work services, and no treatment). Distal outcomes are impacted from months to years following program completion. Functional family therapy has shown reductions in criminal recidivism, including lower rates of court referral and arrest, less likelihood to be convicted of a criminal offense within the next 5 years, and a reduced number of offenses. Youth also had fewer days of alcohol and drug use 15 months posttreatment and fewer problems related to substance use. Finally, there were fewer psychiatric diagnoses 15 months posttreatment (compared with pretreatment) and a decrease in the likelihood of siblings being in court 2.5 to 3.5 years after the cessation of treatment, compared with other family treatment conditions.

Training Model

In order to ensure treatment fidelity, there is a structured training certification process, administered through the Functional Family Therapy training service, for agencies that would like to be authorized centers for FFT. During this process, three to eight therapists are trained. The FFT Site Certification is a three-phase process. The implementation and certification process focuses on clinical training, supervision training, and ongoing partnership. During the process of certification the FFT–Clinical Feedback System (FFT-CFS) is used to provide an assessment and feedback system. This is a Web-based system that includes a battery of assessment measures, family symptom reports, and models specific measures of client progress and case planning. In addition to many authorized sites in the United States, there are authorized sites for FFT across the world, including Belgium, Canada, Denmark, England, Ireland, Netherlands, New Zealand, Norway, Scotland, Singapore, and Sweden.

Phase 1: Clinical Training

Phase 1 is meant to create an infrastructure to support ongoing training and adherence to FFT, and to train therapists in the model. Trainees are meant to demonstrate knowledge and competence in FFT. Checking their proficiency is done through data gathered through the FFT-CFS, weekly consultations, and training activities. This phase takes between 12 to 18 months.

Phase 2: Supervision Training

The goal of Phase 2 is to help the site get greater self-sufficiency in FFT and to maintain model fidelity and competence. To ensure this, there must be competent on-site FFT supervision. The site's supervisor attends a 2-day supervisor training session and is supported in supervision through monthly phone consultations. During this yearlong process there are also other trainings, ongoing phone consultation, and reviews of the site's FFT Clinical Services System (CSS) database to measure adherence, service delivery trends, and outcomes.

Phase 3: Ongoing Partnership

The goal of the third phase of FFT implementation is to move into a partnering relationship to ensure ongoing model fidelity, as well as impacting issues of staff development, interagency linking, and program expansion. FFT reviews the CSS database for site/therapist adherence, service delivery trends, and client outcomes, and provides a 1-day on-site training for continuing education in FFT.

Shannon B. Dermer

See also Adolescent Behavior Disorders; Behavioral Family Therapy; Cognitive-Behavioral Family Therapy; Crisis Intervention With Couples and Families; Cultural Issues in Couples and Families; Families and Substance Abuse; Family Assessment, Models of; Systemic Family Therapy; Systems Theory

Further Readings

Alexander, J., & Parsons, B. (1973). Short-term behavioral intervention with delinquent families: Impact on family process and recidivism. *Journal of Abnormal Psychology, 81*(3), 219–225. doi:10.1037/h0034537

Hartnett, D., Carr, A., & Sexton, T. L. (2015). The effectiveness of functional family therapy in reducing adolescent mental health risk and family adjustment difficulties in an Irish context. *Family Process, 55*(2), 287–304. doi:10.1111/famp.12195

Sexton, T. L. (2010). *Functional family therapy in clinical practice*. New York, NY: Routledge.

Sexton, T. L. (2015). Functional family therapy: Evidence-based and clinically creative. In T. L. Sexton & J. L. Lebow (Eds.), *Handbook of family therapy* (pp. 250–270). New York, NY: Routledge.

Sexton, T. L., & Datchi, C. C. (2014). The development and evolution of family therapy research: Its impact on practice, current status, and future directions. *Family Process, 53*(3), 415–433. doi:10.1111/famp.12084

Sexton, T. L., Patterson, T., & Datchi, C. C. (2012). Technological innovations of systematic measurement and clinical feedback: A virtual leap into the future of couple and family psychology. *Couple and Family Psychology: Research & Practice, 1*, 285–293.

FUNCTIONALISM

Functionalism is the philosophical idea that mental states (beliefs, desires, pain, etc.) can only be defined by their functional role and, thereby, only be identified by what they do rather than by their makeup. Mental states are what occur between an input (some type of stimulus) and output (some behavior), and therefore many think that these states are connected to the subsequent behavior. This fairly abstract idea may seem at first like irrelevant philosophical jargon that has little applicability in the real world, but as emphasized throughout this entry, the implications of the idea take on increased significance when viewed in light of the fact that there are logical consequences to every idea. While there are various applications of the idea of functionalism (e.g., in philosophy of mind and structural functionalism), this entry aims to provide an overview of functionalism, including early theories, and to further outline types of functionalism, arguments for functionalism, and critiques of functionalism.

Defining Functionalism

In 1950, Alan. M. Turing suggested that the question "Can machines think?" should be replaced with another question—"Is it theoretically possible for a finite state digital computer, provided with a large but finite table of instructions, or program, to provide responses to questions that would fool an unknowing interrogator into thinking it is a human being?" This question, which was posed 65 years ago, was before its time, but essentially asked whether or not a form of artificial intelligence will ever convince us that it is human.

Many sources use analogies to explain ideas like functionalism, and one of the common analogies for this idea is a mousetrap. Consider a mousetrap, which is usually a small device that either catches or kills mice. The traps can be made from wood, plastic, metal, or some other material. There are many different designs. Some traps use bait and some traps use poison. However, the central defining characteristic of the device is that it captures or kills mice. This example illustrates the core idea of functionalism. Namely, just as the mouse trap is defined by its function rather than its materials, a mental state is defined by what it does rather than by its parts. Another example can be illustrated via Descartes' statement, "I think, therefore I am," which to a functionalist appears backward. A functionalist viewpoint suggests that for mental states, being *is* doing. In short, being apart from doing lacks definition or content in the functionalist perspective. A final way to understand functionalism is to consider a key. Being a key is not necessarily about being a 1.5 inch piece of metal with some edges, but rather about being something that can perform a specific action, which is to open a lock. In the same way, a lock is not necessarily a heavy steel mechanism on a door, but it does serve a distinct purpose of securing an opening. What makes a key a key or a lock a lock is the purpose or function that these objects serve.

Earlier Theories

Aristotle's theory of the soul (350 B.C.E.) is often considered an ancestor of functionalism. Aristotle argued that the human soul is the *form* of the human body, that is, the strength that lets it express its "essential whatness." Just as the form of an axe lets it chop a tree, or the form of the ear enables it to hear, the human soul is what enables people to function as living, interacting, and reasoning beings.

Another early theory that influenced functionalism can be found in philosopher Thomas Hobbes's suggestion that thinking is a kind of computation that proceeds due to mechanical principles. Essentially, he suggested that the thinking of people is mechanistic, as is all that they consider creative or original per se. Hobbes rhetorically stated, "Why may we not say that all automata (engines that move themselves by springs and wheels . . .) have an artificial life? For what is the heart but a spring; and the nerves but so many strings, and the joints but so many wheels . . . ?"

Some may find these ideas reductionist (oversimplifying a complex idea), naturalistic (only explaining phenomenon with observable data and excluding any other explanation), and deterministic (devoid of free will). And some functionalists would agree with you. However, others maintain that it is smarter to limit our explanations of phenomenon to what we can quantify through observed action (i.e., the function) of a given person.

Types of Functionalism

Over the years as functionalism has been developed and debated, a number of schools or types of functionalism have developed. The first type is often called *machine state functionalism*, meaning that any creature with a mind can be considered a machine, whose actions can be directed by a set of logical and sequential instructions. The sequence follows this model:

> If the machine is in state S-a, and receives input I-b, it will go into state S-c and produce output O-d (for a finite number of states, inputs, and outputs).

This sequence is totally predictable and describes the operation of a deterministic automaton.

A second type of functionalism to develop is called *psychofunctionalism,* which models itself after the goals and methodology of cognitive psychological theories. This type of functionalism was in contrast or opposition to the behaviorist assertion that the laws of psychology appeal only to behavioral dispositions, while cognitive psychologists asserted that the best explanations for behavior take into account a complex mix of mental states and processes. What is different about psychofunctionalism is its assertion that mental states and entities are just those entities, with just those properties. This was a critique of machine state functionalism, suggesting that mental states can be observed through careful laboratory experiments and is not limited to one input which will produce one dependent and sequential output.

A third type of functionalism is known as *analytic functionalism.* The goal of analytic functionalism is to give "topic-neutral" analyses or explanations of our regular mental states. This type has greater potential inputs than logical functionalism since it permits reference to the causal relationships that a mental state has to stimulations, behaviors, and other mental states. This means that one mental state could influence or supersede another mental state. Thus a person may go to a restaurant with a desire to purchase cheesecake for dessert, but once at the restaurant, they may experience anxiety about gaining weight and then decide to not purchase dessert, thereby demonstrating how one mental state can overpower another.

Arguments for Functionalism

There are many systems—things that interact—apart from humans, that model functionalism very well. The most famous arguments for functionalism come from the mind–brain identity theory. According to this theory, sensations are brain processes, and if mental states and brain states are identical, then there must be a one-to-one relation between these things. Every stimulus that creates sensation x must have brain state x as well. In addition, there must be a 100% correlation between these states, without any random or accidental states. Without listing all of the examples, this standard came to be recognized as insupportably high for mind–brain theory to be universally applicable, although it continues to be applied to the study of many nonhuman organisms.

Some other arguments for functionalism include what are often called optimistic and pessimistic arguments. The optimistic argument leans on the idea that it is possible to build an artificial mind. The optimistic argument suggests that even if someone discovers a creature that has mental states but differs from humans in its brain states, then certainly someone could build such a thing (although this remains highly hypothetical). Hence, the possibility of artificial intelligence seems to require the option of something like functionalism. Functionalism views the mind in the same way a watchmaker would view a watch: It is composed of elements which work together to keep time, though it can be built in many different ways.

The contrary is the pessimistic argument, which suggests that the alternatives to functionalism lack the power to meaningfully explain the mental states of other people or creatures. This arguments suggest that if two creatures function in the same way, perform in the same way, and have isomorphic internal states, then how could it be said that one creature has mental states and the other does not?

Critiques of Functionalism

Though functionalism or some type of it makes sense to many people, there have been many critiques of the philosophy, largely over the last 50 years. One critique of functionalism is that it is holistic. Functionalism seeks to make sense of a mental state phenomenon based on the similarities that these states have in the purpose they achieve with the given population. However, with every population there are outliers, those who do not share the norms of the typical individual in the group. Therefore, if you had a person from an Eastern country and a person from a Western country and asked them both a controversial question, it might be impossible for them—based on their potentially different beliefs, worldviews, or desires—to share the same mental state about that controversial question. In summary, functionalism seeks to explain things for large groups, but there may be differences within the group that make such explanations impossible. In other words, functionalism seeks to paint with a broad brush, while more accurate explanations may require more nuance.

A second critique of functionalism comes from what many refer to as the *causal exclusion problem,* which means that we often think that one mental state causes another. Essentially, when many people think about functionalism, it is assumed that the current mental state of the person is caused by some noted stimulus. Causation is assumed, since in a simplistic model of functionalism, there must be cause and effect; accordingly, observers connect a stimulus and a response and ignore any other, perhaps lesser factors that might be influencing the outcome. If other potential causes are noted, they are deemed casually irrelevant even when they may not be, thus leaving the person with an incorrect attribution.

A third critique of functionalism comes from the idea that people are capable of introspection and have thoughts, sensations, and perceptions. It seems that we instantly have noninferential beliefs about our mental states, and that cannot be true if mental states are identical with functional properties (which functionalism asserts). However, some proponents of functionalism say that it can accommodate the special features of introspective thinking, an awareness of the contents of one's mind, since it would be only one of many domains in which it is plausible to think that we can have immediate, noninferential knowledge of causation properties.

A fourth critique of functionalism asks the question whether any theory of the mind (mental states) that involves beliefs, desires, and other intentional states could be an empirical theory. Essentially, it is suggested that one cannot extract facts from values. However, this assertion, though perhaps sounding logical, assumes that what we deem to be "facts" are devoid of the influence of values. This involves the appealing delusion that total objectivity is possible.

The final critique of functionalism involves the qualitative character of experiences. Many examples of mental states lend themselves to functionalist explanations, ones which can be explained in causal terms. However, when a person experiences mental states such as perceptions, emotions, and bodily sensations, a functionalist explanation of them would only explain their function, not the feeling itself. There is a qualitative experience of many things, the "what it's like" aspect, which functionalism ignores. A full account of the arguments and counterarguments for this and the preceding critiques would exceed the space requirements for this entry, but many of these devolve to assertions that the material world is all that there is; thus, what we call "mental states" (or consciousness) are just neurochemical synaptic transfers that feel more personal to people, but they are really just illusions.

Kenyon Knapp

See also Behavioral Family Therapy; Experiential Family Therapy; Mindfulness; Neuro-Linguistic Programming

Further Readings

Levin, J. (2013, Fall). Functionalism. In E. N. Zalta (Ed.), *The Stanford encyclopedia of philosophy.* Retrieved from http://plato.stanford.edu/archives/fall2013/entries/functionalism/

Nikov, V. S. (2012, January/February). Functional psychology. *Journal of Russian and East European Psychology,* 50(1), 6–52. doi:10.2753/RPO1061-0405500101

Fusion

Fusion is a multidimensional theoretical concept developed by Murray Bowen, one of the pioneers of marriage and family therapy. As defined by Bowen, fusion is a manifestation of the lack of differentiation between self and other in interpersonal relationships, which is typified by extreme emotional (over)connection to another and a lack of differentiation between emotional and cognitive processes in the self. In this entry, fusion is discussed in the context of Bowen's family systems theory and is contrasted with the concept of *emotional cutoff*, which is another concept developed by Bowen but one reflecting the other end of the same emotional continuum. Interpersonal and intrapersonal processes related to fusion as manifestations of emotional reactivity are also explained.

In Bowen family systems theory, the role of anxiety is salient. The family is seen as an emotional system, and the degree to which anxiety is transmitted from one member to another and from one generation to the next is critical for understanding individual and relational health. In Bowen's theory, fusion is juxtaposed with differentiation of self, a concept referring to one's ability to differentiate between intellectual and emotional functioning, and to balance the interpersonal functions of individuality and togetherness in intimate relationships. Those who are more differentiated are skilled in emotional regulation and make thoughtful decisions that are less influenced by anxiety or other strong emotions. They maintain a strong sense of self in relationships and are not easily swayed by relational pressure, and they are clear about the difference between their own emotional experiences and those of others. Differentiated persons also have an ability to tolerate both separateness and intimate togetherness and are not overly anxious about either.

By contrast, those who are low in differentiation struggle to discern between their own emotional processes and those of others. They are characterized by higher levels of emotional reactivity and manage their anxiety by engaging in behaviors that could be placed on a theoretical continuum between emotional cutoff and fusion within intimate relationships. Emotional cutoff is the severing of emotional contact to establish independence and emotional distance. On the other end of this continuum is fusion, which is characterized by a seemingly compelling need for extreme closeness with others. For those who are high in fusion, interpersonal boundaries are indistinct, and they seek close proximity and agreement with others. They tend to find emotional distance or interpersonal differences to be invalidating to the self or threatening to the relationship. Instead, they strive for shared experiences and are less likely to firmly hold their own opinions and beliefs. Those high in fusion struggle to make their own decisions or develop a strong identity without validation or advice from others. They also easily absorb others' anxiety or project their own anxiety on to others.

Fusion happens not only on an interpersonal level, however. Intrapersonal fusing of thoughts and emotions also occurs, which has implications for interpersonal relationships. For those who are high in fusion, proximity-seeking in intimate relationships is not an intentional and thoughtful move toward intimacy in a way that respects interpersonal boundaries and is sensitive to difference; instead, it is an emotional response that serves to alleviate one's own anxiety about rejection and being alone. In this way, functioning is both borrowed and traded between the self and other, as emotional regulation and the development of the self is eminently dependent on others. Individuals with high levels of fusion may appear to be in close relationships, but the observable closeness more accurately serves to reduce anxiety.

Bowen suggested that one's level of differentiation initially develops in the family of origin, and problems with emotional fusion indicate that there are unresolved family of origin issues, or what he termed an *undifferentiated family ego mass*. In some families there is little tolerance for each member differentiating his or her cognitive and emotional processes from the rest of the family, and the emphasis is on a shared emotional experience. This pattern of seeking extreme closeness in the family of origin is then carried into interpersonal relationships later in life. Resolving emotional reactivity (i.e., fusion or cut off) involves relating differently within the family of origin, learning to manage one's own emotional reactivity, and increasing in overall differentiation of self.

Those familiar with family therapy theories may recognize similarities between fusion and enmeshment, a concept in Salvador Minuchin's structural family therapy. Both concepts speak to a lack of boundaries between family members and difficulty in interpersonal relationships. However, the emphasis of fusion is placed on the individual's process and emotional reactivity, and the emphasis of enmeshment is placed on the relationship. Fusion is an intrapersonal process that manifests in interpersonal relationships, and enmeshment is analyzed at the relational level and has implications for individuals. These concepts present similarly but are weighted differently in their respective theories.

Sarah A. Crabtree and Steven M. Harris

See also Boundaries; Bowen Family Systems Theory; Differentiation; Systems Theory; Triangulation

Further Readings

Friedman, E. H. (1991). Bowen theory and therapy. In A. S. Gurman & D. P. Kniskern (Eds.), *Handbook of family therapy* (Vol. 2, pp. 134–170). New York, NY: Routledge.

Kerr, M. E., & Bowen, M. (1988). *Family evaluation.* New York, NY: W. W. Norton.

Klugman, J. (1976). Enmeshment and fusion. *Family Process, 15*(3), 321–323. doi:10.1111/j.1545-5300.1976.00321.x

Skowron, E. A., & Schmitt, T. A. (2003). Assessing interpersonal fusion: Reliability and validity of a new DSI fusion with others subscale. *Journal of Marital and Family Therapy, 29*, 209–222. doi:10.1111/j.1752-0606.2003.tb01201.x

Gambling, Compulsive

The term *gambling* is understood as risking something that has value, such as money, on any sort of event that has a chance outcome. Individuals may gamble on card games, dice games, casino machines or bingo, lotteries, the stock market, animal races or sporting events, and various other betting activities for money or something else of worth. With the high frequency of Internet use in recent decades, Internet gambling has become the fastest-growing way in which to gamble.

Gambling behavior may be categorized as social gambling, which is gambling for recreation or entertainment purposes and involves the ability to maintain control over the amount of money, time, and energy spent engaging in the gambling behavior. Gambling behavior may also be categorized as compulsive gambling, also referred to as pathological gambling or gambling addiction, which involves feelings of loss of control over the gambling behavior and gambling behavior that continues despite significant difficulty or impairment in life functioning. Compulsive gambling often negatively affects individuals' lives and usually has a negative impact on their loved ones' lives and functioning as well. Those who have concerns related to compulsive gambling frequently experience difficulty in relationships due to their gambling, and as a result may face significant strain in family and partner relationships. Those participating in compulsive gambling, as well as their families and loved ones, often experience considerable shame, embarrassment, financial problems, and emotional distress due to compulsive gambling. In this entry the common characteristics and features of compulsive gambling, diagnostic criteria for gambling disorder, assessment of compulsive gambling, and treatment implications for compulsive gambling are presented.

Characteristics and Symptoms

Compulsive gambling is generally understood as being a behavioral addiction, similar to how some understand compulsive sexual behavior, compulsive Internet gaming, compulsive spending, and various other addictive behaviors. However, compulsive gambling is the only behavioral addiction that is accepted as a diagnosable addictive disorder in the diagnostic manual used by mental health practitioners and researchers; the diagnostic term for compulsive gambling is *gambling disorder*.

Behavioral addictions are viewed similarly to substance addictions, with the primary difference being that behavioral addictions involve a focus on behavior, whereas substance addictions involve use of psychoactive substances. There is evidence suggesting that various compulsive behaviors impact the neurological pathways and reward centers of the brain in a manner similar to psychoactive substances. While there is a possibility that some individuals may be more vulnerable to developing addictions, such as those with a family or personal history of addiction or those who have experienced trauma, there is substantial evidence to support the contention that anyone may become addicted to a substance or behavior, regardless of their personality characteristics, background, mental health, or family history.

Common indicators suggesting compulsive gambling may include frequent, recurrent engagement in gambling behavior. For example, someone may spend time at a casino gambling several hours a day and may lose track of time or cancel plans in order to spend more time gambling. However, compulsive gambling may occur in a more episodic and intermittent pattern. Compulsive gambling involves more than just the amount of time engaged in gambling activities; obsessive thinking about gambling is an additional indicator of compulsive gambling. For example, individuals may find themselves thinking about gambling so frequently and intensely that they are unable to be productive at their jobs or they may have difficulty sleeping at night because they cannot stop thinking about an upcoming bet or their next gambling experience.

Another common indicator of compulsive gambling is continued gambling behavior despite significant negative consequences related to gambling. These negative consequences may include difficulty sleeping; fatigue; dissolution of a marriage/partnership or loss of a loved one's trust; hopelessness, suicidal thoughts, or depression; loss of friendships due to regularly canceling plans with friends in order to gamble; significant financial problems; and feelings of disconnect from self, others, and/or a higher power. Continued engagement in compulsive gambling despite these substantial consequences can lead to significant feelings of loss of control over thoughts and urges to gamble, and loss of control over gambling behavior. Compulsive gamblers may experience substantial legal issues related to their gambling. Individuals with compulsive gambling concerns are known to have a higher suicide rate than those with other addictions, and the rate of suicide appears to be highest in those who have a substance use disorder in addition to their compulsive gambling concern.

Diagnosis and Treatment

In the past, compulsive gambling has been categorized as an impulse control disorder and was diagnostically referred to as pathological gambling. However, in the most recent diagnostic manual used by mental health clinicians and researchers, the *Diagnostic and Statistical Manual of Mental Disorders,* fifth edition (DSM-5), compulsive gambling is referred to as gambling disorder. Criteria for gambling disorder involve recurrent gambling behavior that has caused problems in one's life and leads to impairment in functioning. Gambling disorder is further indicated by several criteria, including the following: needing to gamble with increasing amounts of money in order to feel the degree of excitement desired (understood as tolerance); feelings of restlessness or irritability when not gambling or when attempting to cut down on gambling behavior (understood as withdrawal); unsuccessful attempts to cut down or control gambling behavior; preoccupation with gambling; frequent engagement in gambling when feeling distressed; returning to gambling behavior after losing money as a way of getting even; engaging in lying to hide the extent of gambling involvement; having lost or jeopardized relationships, jobs, or other educational or career opportunities due to gambling; and depending on others to relieve financially distressing situations that are caused by gambling. Gambling disorder is understood as being mild, moderate, or severe depending on the number of criteria met. The diagnosis of gambling disorder also involves determining that these criteria occur outside of the experience of a manic episode. Individuals may be specified as having either episodic or persistent gambling disorder, depending on the course and pattern of their gambling behavior.

Addressing compulsive gambling in a mental health setting often involves obtaining an extensive gambling history, including exploration of the development of the compulsive gambling behaviors, as well as the severity and intensity of thoughts, behaviors, and feelings associated with the compulsive gambling. Assessing for other addictive disorders and mental health history is also an important part of the evaluation process. Additionally, certain screening tools may be used to better understand the compulsive gambling behavior. Screening tools for compulsive gambling are not diagnostic measures, but rather tools designed to assist clinicians in better understanding compulsive gambling concerns. Various other tools exist to assist professionals in screening or assessing for compulsive gambling. Two examples of screening tools for compulsive gambling include the Lie-Bet tool and the South Oaks Gambling Screen.

The South Oaks Gambling Screen (SOGS) is a 16-item measure that assists mental health clinicians in determining possible problem gambling behavior and whether there is a need for further assessment of gambling behaviors. The SOGS explores various problems related to gambling, including financial, emotional, relational, and social, as well as types and frequency of various gambling behaviors. Based on respondents' answers to the items, they are categorized as likely having no problem with gambling, having some problems with gambling, or having probable pathological gambling concerns. The Lie-Bet tool is a two-item screening measure that assists clinicians in ruling out those without gambling problems and determining those for whom additional assessment of gambling concerns may be warranted. The two questions that comprise the Lie-Bet tool are "Have you ever felt the need to bet more and more money?" and "Have you ever had to lie to people important to you about how much you gamble?" If a respondent answers "Yes" to one or both of these questions, then further assessment of the gambling behavior is recommended. If a respondent answers "No" to both of these questions, then further assessment is likely not indicated and any additional follow-up related to gambling behavior is recommended only as needed.

Individuals with compulsive gambling concerns often benefit from abstaining from gambling behavior; thus, many gambling treatment approaches encourage abstinence from gambling as a component of an individual's recovery from compulsive gambling. Individuals with compulsive gambling behavior may also benefit from involvement in mutual support groups focused on compulsive gambling, similar to the way in which Alcoholics Anonymous may be a beneficial support network for those with alcohol use disorders. Gamblers Anonymous (GA) is a popular mutual support group for those with compulsive gambling concerns. GA is based on the 12 steps of Alcoholics Anonymous and has been tailored to fit those with gambling problems. There is also a mutual support network for families, partners, and other loved ones of gamblers that is referred to as Gam-Anon.

Similar to other behaviors and concerns that are addictive in nature, individuals with compulsive gambling behavior often benefit from therapy and counseling to address these concerns. Most people with compulsive gambling behavior will respond best to interventions that are individualized to meet a person's unique needs and that focus on a whole-person, strengths-based approach to care. Some additional types of therapeutic approaches that may be valuable for individuals with compulsive gambling concerns include 12-step-based interventions, motivational approaches, psychodynamic therapy, cognitive approaches, behavioral strategies and, at times, pharmacological agents.

Various therapeutic models focus on different aspects of compulsive gambling. For instance, cognitive approaches aim at exploring thinking patterns related to the compulsive gambling, and learning ways to stop these thought processes or experience such thoughts without acting on them. Behavioral strategies to address compulsive gambling involve identifying actions to prevent one from acting on gambling urges and learning healthy social and recreational activities. Psychodynamic therapy involves increasing awareness of unconscious thoughts, along with working toward resolving conflicts.

Depending on the nature and severity of the compulsive gambling behavior, these interventions may be provided on an inpatient or outpatient basis, and may be presented in individual, family, or group therapy formats. Family therapy is often an important component of compulsive gambling treatment, given the strain on relationships and families that often results from compulsive gambling problems. Specifically, the secrecy and financial difficulty that often accompany compulsive gambling behaviors are factors that can lead to a great deal of distrust and stress in relationships. Family and couples therapy provides professional intervention and support to families affected by compulsive gambling and help the family better understand compulsive gambling and recovery from gambling disorder.

There is some suggestion that certain prescription medications, such as selective serotonin reuptake inhibitors (SSRIs), may assist in treating some individuals with compulsive gambling problems and may reduce cravings related to gambling. However, psychiatric medication treatments are often most effective when combined with mental health therapy and counseling interventions, and the appropriateness of pharmacological interventions for compulsive gambling must be determined by a prescribing professional who specializes in treating addictions.

Terri L. Jashinsky

See also Alcohol and Substance Abuse; DSM and V-Codes; Families and Substance Abuse; Support Groups

Further Readings

American Psychiatric Association. (2013). *Diagnostic and statistical manual of mental disorders* (5th ed.). Washington, DC: Author.

Bellegarde, J., & Potenza, M. N. (2010). Neurobiology of pathological gambling. In D. Ross, H. Kincaid, D. Spurett, & P. Collins (Eds.), *What is addiction?* (pp. 27–51). Cambridge, MA: Massachusetts Institute of Technology Press.

Berman, L., & Siegel, M. (1992). *Behind the 8-ball: A guide for families of gamblers*. New York, NY: Fireside Parkside.

Grant, J. E., Odlaug, B. L., & Potenza, M. N. (2009). Pathological gambling: Clinical characteristics and treatment. In R. K. Reis, D. A. Fiellin, S. C. Miller, & R. Saitz (Eds.), *Principles of addiction medicine* (pp. 509–517). Philadelphia, PA: Lippincott Williams & Wilkins.

Grant, J. E., Potenza, M. N., Weinstein, A., & Gorelick, D. A. (2010). Introduction to behavioral addictions. *American Journal of Drug and Alcohol Abuse, 36*(5), 233–241.

McComb, J. L., Lee, B. K., & Sprenkle, D. H. (2009). Conceptualizing and treatment problem gambling as a family issue. *Journal of Marital and Family Therapy, 35*(4), 415–431.

Welte, J. W., Barnes, G. M., Tidwell, M.-C. O., & Hoffman, J. H. (2011). Gambling and problem gambling across the lifespan. *Journal of Gambling Studies, 27*, 49–61.

Gender- and Culture-Sensitive Therapies

The United States is one of the most racially, linguistically, and culturally diverse countries in the world. This diversity can influence belief systems and emotional expression, and ultimately influence the way in which one experiences distress. From a counseling perspective, the diverse nature of the United States raises issues around ethics, multiculturalism, and best treatment practices. This entry explores how cultural differences affect who seeks therapy, the therapeutic relationship, and how clients experience wellness. Moreover, it discusses types of culturally sensitive therapies, how gender differences and gender roles relate to the diagnosis and treatment of mental health conditions, and types of gender-sensitive therapies.

Cultural Differences

The American Counseling Association (ACA) has charged counselors with gaining the knowledge, skills, and awareness to provide adequate client-centered care with the specific client populations they are serving. When engaging in a therapeutic relationship with a client, it is important to be cognizant that clients bring with them their own belief systems, individual awareness of the world, and knowledge about the therapeutic process. However, as the United States becomes more diverse, gaining the knowledge, skills, and awareness needed to work with each population becomes more challenging. This knowledge, skills, and awareness can facilitate progress within the therapeutic relationship; however, culture- and gender-specific therapies can lead to better treatment outcomes.

Traditional models of counseling and psychotherapy within the Western world are Eurocentric in nature, and emphasis is often placed on individualism, assertiveness, and directive styles of communication. This emphasis on individualism can neglect the service needs of clients seeking a therapeutic relationship who have a collectivist orientation, as is often the case with African American, Native American, Asian American, and Hispanic clients. As clinicians, it cannot be assumed that the theories and techniques that were developed by White theorists will be suitable for culturally and racially diverse groups. Perhaps the first question that a counselor should ask is, "Is the client benefiting from the interventions that I am using?" Culturally competent counseling includes techniques that are reflective of cultural values, individualized customs, and individual views on wellness. The counselor should not be naïve and assume that one form of counseling or one therapeutic intervention would work for all population groups.

Cross-Cultural Mental Health

In the United States, culturally and racially diverse clients seek mental health services at a lower rate than the general population. There are a variety of reasons that have been documented within the literature, such as cultural differences, mistrust of services, socioeconomic reasons (e.g., access to available child care), and their individual perceptions of their mental health concerns. While culturally and racially diverse clients are less likely to reach out for mental health services, they are more likely than the general population to value cultural aspects within the therapeutic relationship, such as collectivism instead of self-directed goals. Because of the aforementioned potential obstacles, counselors should be aware of how to attend to the cultural needs of culturally marginalized clients who seek mental health treatment.

The topics of race, discrimination, and privilege can be challenging to address within a therapeutic relationship. However, exploring these topics can be very important with culturally diverse clients because these are salient aspects of their daily lives. Because of this, counselors should be prepared and willing to discuss these topics early within a therapeutic relationship. In fact, research has suggested that if a conversation is constructed around race, discrimination, and privilege within the first or second session, then clients will feel comfortable to continue a dialogue throughout the remaining sessions. This secure and safe environment will promote trust between the client and counselor, which can strengthen a therapeutic relationship and lead to better treatment outcomes.

Therapeutic Relationship

The therapeutic relationship is one of the greatest predictors of treatment outcomes. If an individual does not feel heard or understood within the relationship, then premature termination from services is likely. Early termination is disconcerting because the number of sessions that an individual attends is a predictor of high patient satisfaction and better treatment outcomes. For a counselor, it is vital to know what strengthens and what could potentially harm the counseling process. It is also important to realize that societal marginalization and multiple levels of oppression play an important role in the client seeking therapeutic services.

Research shows that when working with members of minority groups, being flexible, warm, open, honest, and respectful of their value systems can promote positive relationships; however, microaggressions, which include not only the words used but also body language and vocal tone, can negatively impact the therapeutic relationship. It is essential that a counselor remain cognizant of how microaggressions can irreparably harm the relationship. Some common examples of microaggressions include "You don't act like the typical African American," "You don't have a Latino accent when you speak," "Where are you really from?," and "You can really do a lot, for a girl!" In order to decrease the risk of harming the counseling process, it is important to remain conscious of individual and social attitudes around the populations being served.

Acculturation

An individual's culture plays a significant role in how they experience wellness and interact with others. This is important to keep in mind as the counselor is charged with upholding the wellness model to promote holism on the part of the client. A counselor should be mindful of acculturation and how it could potentially pose as an obstacle in the client's experience of the counseling process. Acculturation has been described as the incorporation and integration from one culture's norms to the dominant culture's norms. Acculturation has been documented to have an effect on an individual's perception of health care and the mental health system. For example, in some cultures, seeking mental health services can be stigmatizing. This stigma can cause individuals to underutilize mental health services that are available; additionally, for the individuals who do seek services, they may hold on to guilt, shame, and may experience real or perceived marginalization from their family. Because accessing mental health services can lead to "othering," it is important to ask the question, "What is coming to counseling like for you?" This question can promote dialogue and help the counselor understand the cultural framework of the client, and it can help shape the client's goals within the counseling relationship. Furthermore, it can help diminish stereotyping and labeling on the part of the counselor because beliefs and practices can vary widely within the same cultural communities.

Culturally Sensitive Therapy

Because of the salient nature of multicultural counseling competencies, the therapeutic relationship, and acculturation, practitioners and researchers are beginning to explore evidence-based practices for culturally specific treatments. While there are individual therapies that practitioners ascribe to within the counseling process, researchers agree that there are specific qualities that the modalities should possess. These include understanding that individuals present with their own lived experiences and worldviews that are culturally specific, treating the client holistically, and helping the client understand privilege, power, and oppression.

Research has also suggested that it is important to use a client's native language, when possible. The English language often cannot catch the specific nuances of the individual's first language. It is vital that counselors familiarize themselves with how norms and values are conveyed through language within the client's culture. Because idioms may not translate well, the practitioner should use culturally appropriate metaphors. If the counselor does not readily know or understand the cultural disparities, then consultation with peers and/or a supervision process should be sought.

Postmodern Therapies

Adhering to traditional rigid treatment plans may not be ideal for culturally diverse clients. Because of this, there are specific therapies that allow counselors to use and implement nontraditional approaches to diagnosis and treatment planning. Narrative, solution-focused, and constructivist therapies are modalities that help the client share their story in their own words. Approaching counseling from this context allows the psychological concern to be framed in sociocultural and political perspectives that are individual to the client. From the therapeutic approach of postmodern therapies, clients are not viewed as problems, but as separate from their problems—which can promote and facilitate change. Counselors who practice postmodern therapies do not ascribe to traditional psychopathology labels. Instead, clients are seen as change agents within their lives, and work toward a new "life story." Furthermore, postmodern counselors believe that the stories told are socially constructed and culturally important. The counselor helps the client explore the unbalanced relationship of power and privilege that exists between marginalized communities and the larger dominant culture.

Many varied techniques are used in counseling sessions to have the client convey their unique experiences. Some examples include privileged position, dominant voices, and journal writing. When using the privileged position technique, the counselor asks the client to assume the privileged role and begin to share their experiences. As the client is sharing their experiences, the counselor will pose questions that point out exceptions to the problem so the client can begin to see a new story emerge that points to a brighter future. When using the dominant voices technique, the counselor encourages the client to share how their beliefs systems about themselves and their current situation came to be. Once the client begins to learn how they adopted their ideas, they can work toward reconstructing new goals based on their new knowledge. When using journal writing, the counselor asks the client to write about their thoughts, feelings, ideas, notions, and beliefs to help the client see the larger picture and framework of their current situation. The counselor encourages the client to see these are mediated by the culture that they live within. Journal writing can be used in or in between sessions to promote the resolution of conflicts within the client's story. Due to the flexibility of postmodern therapies, counselors can easily tailor the techniques to involve family members or other culturally relevant aspects of the individual.

Relational-Cultural Therapy

Relational-cultural therapy is another culturally sensitive intervention that can be used with individuals who may be marginalized due to discrepancies in privilege and power. Relational-cultural therapy helps the client conceptualize themselves by context instead of a diagnostic label, such as bipolar disorder or borderline personality disorder. Moreover, counselors who adhere to relational-cultural therapy suggest that all humans desire connection; however, the current psychosocial environments and the dominant culture inhibit an individual's connection—which ultimately leads to isolation. This isolation, in due course, leads to an individual's behaviors (e.g., self-injurious behavior).

Because isolation is viewed as the genesis of all negative behaviors and experiences, the counselor and client work together to understand patterns that have led to the client's disconnections. Relational-cultural therapy is not technique driven; however, this should not sway the counselor from using culturally relevant material and experiences—such as music, journal writing, and psychodrama.

Gender Differences

Western cultures, including the United States, often view gender as both static and binary and directly based on biological sex: male and female. However, the concept of gender is socially constructed and culturally mediated. The socialization of gender informs our decision on how to behave in a socially acceptable manner. Because of this, gender socialization processes can influence how women and men internalize or externalize their feelings, which lead them to experience the mental health system and therapeutic relationship differently. It has been suggested that men are more likely to experience externalizing disorders, where their behavior is in response to neglected emotional pain. The disorders commonly associated with externalization include substance abuse, antisocial personality disorder, and intermittent explosive disorder. Conversely, women internalize the cultural messages they receive from a society dominated by men, which impacts their cognitive processes.

Disorders commonly associated with internalization include borderline personality disorder, panic disorder, and obsessive-compulsive disorder. From a gender socialization perspective, the presenting behaviors may be coping strategies and the dysfunctional behaviors are due to the expectations that are placed upon the client from society. Counselors must have knowledge, skills, and awareness of their ideas of how gender could potentially impact the therapeutic process, how the client's culture perceives gender, and how the larger society reinforces gender. This gender-bound perspective can have a lasting impact on the treatment process and can affect diagnosis and treatment planning.

Gender Roles

Gender role expectations can create a false sense of self and can lead to internalized oppression. Women who are from marginalized groups will often experience increased levels of trauma, violence, and stress from the dominant culture. Furthermore, these women may experience stressors from their own culture, such as women having been historically ascribed a lower status in the culture than men, which can negatively impact an individual woman's mental health. In turn, this internalized oppression can lead to diagnosable psychopathology—such as depression and anxiety. Also, the traditional expectation that women are to be accepting can cause women to tolerate the abuse perpetuated on women. It is important that the therapist remain mindful of the multiple levels of oppression faced by many women, and how this oppression can contribute to their psychopathology and suicidal ideation. Furthermore, acculturation can affect the likelihood of women adhering to prescribed gender role expectations.

Men also face gender role socialization. While there are gender role expectations within the dominant culture, men from marginalized sociocultural groups may adhere more rigidly to the prescribed roles. For example, men are told "Suck it up!," "Act like a man," and "Boys don't cry"; however, these gender stereotypes can be more salient in other cultures. Men are conditioned to avoid appearing vulnerable and effeminate, and the masculine persona does impact interpersonal relationships. For many males, the counseling relationship and talking about feelings can be viewed as being "girly." Counselors need to take masculine gender role conflicts into consideration when conducting the initial sessions and working to develop the treatment goals of the counseling process.

Gender-Sensitive Therapies

Traditionally, therapies have been androcentric in nature, where the focus is primarily on the male's perspective. In gender-sensitive therapy, counselors work to explore the client's gender-related experience, keeping in mind that psychopathology is culturally mediated. From the beginning, counselors should use the counseling relationship to model what egalitarian relationships should look like within the client's own interpersonal relationships. Furthermore, the counselor should help the client work through marginalization, power differentials, and oppressive experiences by encouraging the client to participate fully throughout the counseling process—sharing experiences and interpretations along the way. Shifting the therapeutic mindset in counselors from "What's wrong with you?" to "What happened to you?" ultimately will change the outcome of the counseling process.

Feminist Therapy

While traditionally thought of as an approach to treat only women, feminist therapy can be used with both genders. Furthermore, its efficacy has been supported with a variety of ethnic and cultural groups. During the therapeutic process, the counselor works with the clients to explore role conflicts and role strain that may be a result of the internalized oppression from gender roles. An example of role strain includes being a husband, father, employee, and student. Concerns arise when the responsibilities associated with each of these roles conflict with each other due to the societal expectations placed on each role.

During the therapeutic process, the counselor works with the client to increase knowledge around gender and its place in society and work to create mutual goals while establishing trust and understanding. Throughout the counseling sessions, the counselor raises the client's consciousness, explores alternative choices free of gender roles or stereotypes, and implements counterconditioning. Within counterconditioning, the counselor may model appropriate exchanges and encourages the client to try new skills learned within a therapeutic relationship, by implementing both empathy and empowerment. The interactions should be egalitarian and not reinforce societal and political power imbalances. The therapeutic interactions take place with the knowledge that clients themselves are political—there is an interconnectedness of both the inner and outer worlds. Some techniques used in feminist therapy include bibliotherapy (reading written material to pursue therapeutic goals), assertiveness training, power analysis, gender role intervention, and gender role analysis.

Male-Sensitive Therapy

Men are equally as affected by gender roles and gender role expectations as are women. It has been suggested that as many as 10% of men have a difficult time expressing any emotion, intimacy, or admit having any kind of mental health concern. This inability to express, talk about, or experience emotion can be based in gender role expectations. Male-sensitive therapy works to help men understand how the presenting concerns within the counseling process are correlated to the gender belief systems they may hold.

During the counseling process, the counselor works with the client to help him understand his personality development, and to help raise awareness of the gender expectations that are placed upon him by society. The counselor and client form an egalitarian relationship to create new gender role expectations (e.g., it is okay to have and show emotions to his partners). Research has suggested that group therapy may be beneficial to show the universality of gender role expectations and gender role strain.

*Jonathan Procter
and Carl J. Sheperis*

See also Cultural Issues in Couples and Families; Diversity; Feminist Family Therapy; Gender Issues; Gender Orientation, Gender Identity, and Gender Expression; Gender Roles; Postmodern Therapies

Further Readings

Balkir, N. (2013). *Cultural variations in psychopathology: From research to practice* (S. Barnow, Ed.). Boston, MA: Hogrefe.

Englar-Carlson, M., Evans, M. P., & Duffey, T. (2014). *A counselor's guide to working with men*. Alexandria, VA: American Counseling Association.

Jordan, J. V. (2009). *Relational cultural therapy*. Washington, DC: American Psychological Association.

McLeod, J. (2006). *Narrative and psychotherapy*. Thousand Oaks, CA: Sage.

Worell, J., & Refer, P. (2002). *Feminist perspectives in therapy: Empowering diverse women*. Hoboken, NJ: Wiley.

GENDER DYSPHORIA

Gender dysphoria refers to a psychiatric diagnosis listed in the fifth edition of the American Psychiatric Association's *Diagnostic and Statistical Manual of Mental Disorders* (DSM-5), which describes the condition of people whose birth sex is mismatched with their gender identity (i.e., experience of one's own self-concept of being male, female, a blend of both, or neither). People with the diagnosis of gender dysphoria experience clinically significant impairment in their psychosocial functioning. A person with gender dysphoria may or may not be living full time in her or his preferred gender and may or may not have legal recognition of the preferred gender identity. Practitioners engaged in marriage, couples, and family counseling may encounter people with clinically significant symptoms of gender dysphoria. This entry explores the diagnosis of gender dysphoria, particularly distinctions between gender dysphoria and gender nonconformity; sexual orientation issues in people diagnosed with gender dysphoria; and treatment of gender dysphoria in marriage, couples, and family counseling.

Gender Dysphoria and Gender Nonconformity

The diagnosis of gender dysphoria is not without controversy. In the previous edition of the DSM, the precursor diagnosis to gender dysphoria was called *gender identity disorder*. Gender identity disorder was characterized by a marked incongruence between a person's gender expression/experience and biological sex characteristics, and a strong desire to have the sex characteristics of the other gender. People with gender identity disorder usually also had a desire to be treated by others according to the person's self-identified gender identity and not the person's biological sexual characteristics. For example, a person who was born as a biological male might have preferred female gender pronouns and wanted to be thought of by others as a woman. A person who experienced gender identity disorder might have used both male and female pronouns, or possibly neither, depending on the social context or person with whom the person experiencing gender identity disorder is interacting.

Despite how the person with gender identity disorder identified, use of this identifier was problematic because it did not accurately characterize the experience of gender nonconforming people. Critics of the gender identity disorder diagnosis objected to the label *disorder*, stating that it unfairly stigmatizes people who did not strictly adhere to masculine and feminine stereotypes. Surely, many peoples' experiences with fluid or nonconforming gender identities did not lead to personal struggle nor was it contested within their communities. For example, in some Native American communities, what are now referred to as two-spirit people, people who embodied both male and female gender identities, were thought of as being a third sex. People in certain indigenous communities openly acknowledged and embraced two-spirit people. Two-spirit people were highly regarded prophets and healers. That certain people had two-spirit identities was thought to be part of the natural order, not an aberration. Similar examples of other people with fluid gender identities can also be found in other cultures.

While acknowledging that having a gender identity that does not necessarily match with one's biological sex characteristics can be deeply distressing for some people, for critics of the former gender identity disorder diagnosis, it was important to recognize the person's distress within the broader social environmental context. It may be that the experience of living as a gender nonconforming person within a society that does not embrace gender nonconformity is more distressing than the experience of being gender nonconforming itself. In this view, in a society without rigid stereotypes of maleness and femaleness, people could be free to identify with any gender without feeling a lack of congruence or distress, and gender nonconformity could be embraced as simply part of the diversity of nature.

Sexual Orientation in People Diagnosed With Gender Dysphoria

People who experience gender dysphoria may identify as male or female. They may also reject the binary categorizations of gender, preferring instead a more fluid sense of gender expression. However, gender identity is separate from sexual orientation identity. People with gender dysphoria may be sexually attracted to men, women, or people of both gender identities. They may have intimate partners, spouses, and significant others who have a gender identity congruent with birth sex and/or may be in relationships with other people with gender dysphoria.

Sexual orientation and identity among people with gender dysphoria can vary widely. Regardless of whether their physical bodies are congruent with their preferred gender, people with gender dysphoria may identify as heterosexual or nonheterosexual. For solidarity reasons, people with gender dysphoria who identify as part of the transgender community may also align themselves culturally and politically with the lesbian, gay, bisexual, and transgender (LGBT) community. Gender nonconforming people often share some of the experiences of LGBT people in that they have historically been subject to some of the same stigmas, stereotypes, and other forms of negative treatment within society. Others who are gender nonconforming may not align themselves with other LGBT individuals because they feel that they lack shared experience and that being gender nonconforming is fundamentally separate from being gay.

This also tends to manifest in how the gender nonconforming person identifies his or her relationships. For example, a person with gender dysphoria who was born female but is male-identified may classify a relationship with any female-identified person as heterosexual. This may occur regardless of the present physical sex characteristics of either person.

Relationship patterns for people diagnosed with gender dysphoria are individual and unique. For some people who form relationships and then later acknowledge to themselves and their partners that they are gender nonconforming, relationship dynamics may change. For instance, a person who was born a biological male and marries a person who is born a biological female may later experience discomfort if his wife subsequently acknowledges identification as a male. Sometimes, that relationship may not survive because the spouses may then consider their relationship to be akin to a gay male relationship when perhaps neither of them identifies as a gay male. In other cases, the sexual orientation and/or expression of the couple may adapt, acknowledging that the relationship dynamics have changed over time.

Treatment of Gender Dysphoria

Having a gender identity that does not conform to socially constructed ideals of maleness and femaleness can be as healthy as any other social identity. People who are gender nonconforming live normal, healthy lives and have significant relationships with partners, families, and communities. However, people diagnosed with gender dysphoria experience clinically significant impairment in their day-to-day functioning and may experience severe distress because of the incongruence between the body and self-identified gender identity. They may seek treatment in medical and/or marriage, couples, and family counseling settings.

There are a variety of treatments to help a person cope with gender dysphoria. Some people with a gender dysphoria diagnosis, in consultation with medical professionals, may choose to chemically and/or surgically modify the body to physically transition to the preferred gender. Surgical alteration of the body is commonly known as sexual reassignment surgery, though many gender nonconforming people prefer more affirming terms such as gender confirmation surgery or genital reconstruction surgery.

Chemical therapies typically involve the use of testosterone or estrogen under the care of a physician experienced in treating gender dysphoria. For example, chemical therapy for a biological male transitioning to female may increase estrogen levels while lowering testosterone levels to the range of a typical biological woman. Surgical alteration of the body nearly always includes some form of chemical therapy. However, chemical therapy may occur independent of surgery. For instance, a biological male transitioning to female may begin chemical therapy, develop breasts and other female characteristics, yet retain the penis. This decision can be entirely economic, as surgery can be expensive and may not be covered by health insurance plans. It may also simply reflect the personal preference of the gender nonconforming person. Decisions are also made, in conjunction with medical professionals, about the reversibility of surgical transitions.

Chemical and/or surgical transition typically occurs after a long period of living full time in the preferred gender. Additionally, assessment by a mental health professional, including a psychiatrist, psychologist, and/or other counseling professional, precedes chemical and surgical transition. For some people with gender dysphoria, the treatment is entirely psychosocial in nature. Marriage, couples, and family counseling can help people with gender dysphoria who do not wish to chemically or surgically transition to cope with psychosocial stressors and stigma. Marriage, couples, and family counselors may also provide support as a person with gender dysphoria makes decisions about changing her or his appearance to be consistent with her or his self-identity.

According to the Standards of Care for the Health of Transsexual, Transgender, and Gender

Nonconforming People from the World Professional Association for Transgender Health, formerly known as the Benjamin Standards of Care, professionals engaging people with gender dysphoria should focus, when possible, on helping families to develop an accepting and nurturing response. Marriage, couples, and family counselors also help people with gender dysphoria make decisions about the timing of the transition and possible psychosocial issues associated with the transition. They can also help identify any coexisting mental health issues that may be present before, during, or after surgical, chemical, or social transition.

Community-level interventions are also needed. Marriage, couples, and family counselors serve as advocates in society for people who are gender variant. Gender variant people continue to experience marginalization in society and may lack tangible protection from discrimination in housing, employment, or other public accommodation. In some jurisdictions, people who are gender variant may legally lack the ability to transition to their preferred gender identity. Marriage, couples, and family counselors should advocate within their agencies and communities for better social justice protections for gender variant people, and should call into question prevailing social mores that stigmatize people who do not conform to socially constructed ideals of maleness and femaleness.

Trevor G. Gates

See also LGBT Families; Sexual Orientation, Attraction, and Identity; Sexual Prejudice

Further Readings

American Psychiatric Association. (2013). *Diagnostic and statistical manual of mental disorders* (5th ed.). Washington, DC: Author.

Ansara, Y. G., & Hegarty, P. (2012). Cisgenderism in psychology: Pathologising and misgendering children from 1999 to 2008. *Psychology and Sexuality, 3*(2), 137–160.

Coleman, E., Bockting, W., Botzer, M., Cohen-Kettenis, P., DeCuypere, G., Feldman, J., . . . Zucker, K. (2012). Standards of care for the health of transsexual, transgender, and gender-nonconforming people, Version 7. *Journal of Transgenderism, 13*(4), 165–232.

Gates, T. G. (2010). Combating problem and pathology: A genderqueer primer for the human service educator. *Journal of Human Services, 30*(1), 54–64.

GENDER ISSUES

Historically, gender has been defined as the behavioral presentation associated with being a particular sex: male or female. This definition has been associated with a person's genitalia. For example, individuals with penises are assigned male sex and therefore a masculine gender; individuals born with a vulva are conversely assigned female sex and therefore a feminine gender. The conflation of sex and gender has led to the identification of all individuals with a penis as male and therefore masculine, identified as a "man." For women the same conflation has occurred: Born with a vulva means female, which means feminine, which means woman. In modern medical terms, individuals who, at birth, have genitalia that cannot be clearly defined as a penis or vulva are defined as intersex, and parents are typically given a choice to assign the baby a gender. This decision is sometimes accompanied with genital surgery so that there continues to be an alignment with genitalia and gender. Finally, sometimes the gender assigned to individuals at birth does not align with their personal identity or how they behaviorally present. These individuals are typically identified as transgender, which includes a variety of presentations and unique personal experiences. Overall, gender is a complicated construct even though it has been represented as a binary concept (male or female) in the past.

In recent decades, the mental health field as a whole has been attending more carefully to multicultural awareness in regard to the therapeutic process. Gender issues are one of the most recent aspects of this multicultural approach. Research related to gender issues in counseling relationships continues to grow and become an additional focus in the field. This entry focuses on the particular issues that can arise from a number of gendered interactions and how counselors can increase personal awareness to improve how they attend to gender in working with their clients.

Gender and Socialization

The definition of *gender* is transitioning to represent the purely socially defined behaviors associated with femininity or masculinity. Current definitions in mental health fields separate one's gender from a person's identified physiological makeup or genital presentation. Rather, one's gender is based on one's own identification of maleness, femaleness, or something in between. Related to this separation of gender and sex, one can conceptualize gender on a spectrum, with individuals landing somewhere along a continuum of masculine and feminine traits with gender neutrality (agender), gender duality (bi-gender), or gender fluidity (gender identity can change with time or context) located between these binary concepts.

Despite this shift in the definition of gender, socially defined roles and expectations based on gender based on genitalia persist and impact a person's life in many ways. Gender role socialization is also deeply tied to patriarchy (a system in which men hold more power), given that patriarchy values masculinity over femininity. Furthermore, gender roles play a role in heteronormativity (the view that being attracted to the opposite sex and gender is healthiest) due to the expectation that all individuals are, by default, assigned within the gender binary and as a result will be sexually and romantically attracted to a gender different from their own. Gender socialization influences many aspects of an individual's identity, behavior, interpersonal relationships, and existence in the world. Counselors and therapists are themselves situated within their own relationship to gender and, as such, gender plays a role in their interactions with clients.

Gender Identity and Gender Presentation

Similar to the separation of sex and gender, gender identity and gender presentation are also conceptually different. People's gender identity is their own understanding of where they fit on the gender spectrum; gender presentation is what people show to the world (whether that matches their own gender identity or not). Gender presentation speaks to the physical ways that society expects masculine or feminine individuals to appear. For example, clothing is typically designed and cut in a gendered way, with skirts and dresses being exclusively feminine. Makeup and facial hair are both also typically considered gendered.

Throughout a person's life, gender identity and presentation may change, sometimes multiple times. As stated previously, some people's gender identity contradicts the gender they were assigned at birth. Commonly, this results in identification as transgender with an individual progressing from one end of the gender spectrum to the other. Research indicates that awareness of being transgender initiates very early on in a person's life. As a result, some transgender individuals experience deep identity conflict from being unable to present in alignment with their gender identity. Transgender individuals also commonly express never fully being socialized for their assigned gender and instead covertly integrate their personally identified gender norms and expectations.

Women in Counseling

For those who identify with the feminine gender and/or self-identify as women, there are a number of social implications for daily life. Broadly, women are socially expected to be more connected to their emotions compared with men. As a result, a majority of both counselors and clients seeking counseling services identify as women. Women often communicate with higher levels of interpersonal connection and insight to internal processes. The pressure of gender alignment, tied to the experience of living in a patriarchal society, often leads to internalized gender conflict for many women. That is to say, women often experience guilt or shame when they have a preference for masculine-identified pursuits and/or reject the traditional feminine gender roles of mother or caregiver. Rejection of traditional gender norms causes additional stress from being policed by society at large and the subsequent risk of being socially shunned or outcast.

Men in Counseling

Masculine-identified individuals seek mental health services at a disproportionately low rate in relation to their experience of mental health strain. Socially constructed ideals for masculinity include a minimization of the feminine emotional connection. Men are often covertly, sometimes overtly, taught to suppress and disconnect from their feelings. Oftentimes, any emotional experience is expected to be expressed through anger, aggression, or violence. Furthermore, men are also socialized to be independent, both physically and psychologically. This further compounds an avoidance of seeking out mental health services to assist in resolving mental health concerns. All these gendered expectations combined are directly connected to the statistics of more masculine-identified individuals completing suicide compared to individuals who identify with other genders.

Men who seek out mental health services tend to have a difficult time acknowledging and communicating the mental health difficulties that they are experiencing. Because counseling and therapy works within a more feminine identified form of communication, counselors themselves may feel frustration when working with men in counseling. Many counselors struggle with how to work with masculine clients who are being emotionally restrictive, which is sometimes perceived as resistance to the process as a whole. Awareness of these gender issues adds to a counselor's ability to work with such clients.

Agender, Gender-Fluid, Nonbinary, and Transgender Individuals in Counseling

Similar to men and women who experience conflict regarding their gender identity and gender expression, individuals who fall outside of the gender binary experience unique challenges related to existing outside of the socially accepted gender roles of man or woman. At any point in a person's life span they may experience a conflict connected to the experience of gender. Because gender can be defined as completely separate from a person's genital composition, some individuals do not personally identify with gender expectations as a whole. Some individuals will reject behaviors and presentation of a particular gender or, conversely, move among masculine, feminine, or neutral genders at any given moment, particularly in regard to gender presentation. Social expectations dictate how to respond to an individual who does not fit the role assigned to them. Identifying outside of the gender binary is often an isolating experience fraught with rejection and devaluation of self. Persons who align with their assigned gender but don't quite live up to the ideal may feel the same conflict, but often at a less extreme level. On the other hand, for some, adapting a label and owning an identity outside of the gender binary may offer a comforting experience and a more secure sense of self.

Individuals who identify outside of the gender binary may be wary of seeking out counseling services for fear of being further rejected, "othered," or pathologized. Counselors can explore with clients the effect of social pressure to conform to gender norms and how to cope with these pressures. Therapists may need to work to utilize pronouns that align with the client's gender identity.

Attending to Gender Within Counseling

Gender issues in counseling, while unavoidable in regard to personal experience, can be minimized within the therapeutic relationship by counselor attendance and awareness. Therapists should be aware of personal assumptions and stereotypes related to gender so that they can notice gendered issues in their clients' experience and the role that gender may be playing within the therapeutic relationship.

Assumptions and Stereotypes

Existence in a gendered society that assumes heterosexuality leads to a number of assumptions regarding clients. Without awareness of gender issues, counselors may inadvertently uphold the stereotype that all clients who present as a particular gender identify with that gender, covertly restricting clients from expressing as otherwise or acknowledging conflicts that may be connected to gender. A similar assumption is that all clients who identify as a particular gender internalize the expectations for that gender. Counselors may subconsciously perceive women who do not aspire to motherhood or men who display high emotionality as abnormal.

Furthermore, therapists may assume clients to identify as heterosexual with sexual and romantic attraction occurring within a binary gender. Subsequently, many therapists assume that individuals who identify as having same-gender attraction will display or adopt more gendered traits of the conceived "opposite" gender. Under this stereotype, gay men are expected to present as more feminine and lesbians as more masculine.

Talking About Gender

As discussed earlier, gender is an invisible social force. As such, therapists and clients alike may not realize that their behavior is rooted in gender socialization. By inviting clients to have conversations about their gender identity/gendered experience, counselors can actively address the role of gender for the client and the therapeutic relationship. Counselors may wish to facilitate conversations regarding a client's extent of gender alignment, experience of gender, and any conflict therein. Conversations regarding barriers to building the therapeutic alliance are commonplace practice in therapy; gender is an important component of this dialogue.

Similar to other multicultural issues in counseling, counselor attendance to gender dynamics is critical within the therapeutic relationship. Without attending to these issues, the therapist may unwittingly perpetuate stereotypes, hinder the relationship as a whole, and, at worst, block the client from experiencing safe, nonjudgmental counseling. Through counselor awareness of gender assumptions and stereotypes and open dialogue with clients, therapists can respectfully explore issues related to gender with the client. Further, counselors can minimize the incidence of conflict related to gender within the therapeutic relationship.

Molly Rose Wilson

See also Gender Orientation, Gender Identity, and Gender Expression; Men in Counseling; Patriarchy; Therapeutic Alliance; Therapists' Values

Further Readings

Gehart, D. R., & Lyle, R. R. (2001). Client experience of gender in therapeutic relationships: An interpretive ethnography. *Family Process, 40*(4), 443–458. doi:10.1111/j.1545-5300.2001.4040100443.x

Iantaffi, A. (2015). Gender and sexual legitimacy. *Current Sexual Health Reports, 7*(2), 103–107. doi:10.1007/s11930-015-0044-z

Kierski, W., & Blazina, C. (2010). The male fear of the feminine and its effects on counseling and psychotherapy. *Journal of Men's Studies, 17*(2), 155–172.

Knudson-Martin, C., & Mahoney, A. R. (2005). Moving beyond gender: Processes that create relationship equality. *Journal of Marital and Family Therapy, 31*(2), 235–258. doi:10.1111/j.1752-0606.2005.tb01557.x

Rochlen, A. B., & Rabinowitz, F. E. (2014). *Breaking barriers in counseling men: Insights and innovations.* New York, NY: Routledge. doi:10.4324/9780203114636

Simon, L., Heatherington, L., Friedlander, M. L., & Gaul, R. (1992). Client gender and sex role: Predictors of counselors' impressions and expectations. *Journal of Counseling and Development, 71*(1), 48–52.

Werner-Wilson, R. J., Michaels, M. L., Thomas, S. G., & Thiesen, A. M. (2003). Influence of therapist behaviors on therapeutic alliance. *Contemporary Family Therapy, 25*(4), 381–390. doi:10.1023/A:1027356602191

Gender Orientation, Gender Identity, and Gender Expression

Gender orientation, gender identity, and gender expression are considered to be distinct but interrelated dimensions of gender. These are in contrast to *sex*, which is thought to include one's anatomical makeup and assigned sex at birth. Although used interchangeably by some, *gender* and *sex* are not synonymous terms, and in many ways are considered antiquated ways of referring to people's gender and sexual identities. Distinctions within the concept of gender, and the difference between the terms *gender* and *sex*, are best understood using a social constructionist lens. As such, this entry begins with a description of a social constructionist understanding of gender. Next, gender orientation, gender identity, and gender expression are defined in an effort to differentiate between the innate and the socially constructed elements of gender. The entry concludes with a brief discussion of the concepts' clinical implications.

Social Construction of Gender

Historical perspectives on gender assume that an individual's behavior and appearance are determined by genetic predisposition and that it corresponds with a person's anatomical makeup. This assumption is known as *biological determinism*, and it is considered a dated way of thinking about gender by most gender theorists. Gender theory has shifted from this essentialist perspective to a perspective grounded in social constructionism, which considers the effect of social context on identity formation. This understanding of gender challenges the assumption that gender and anatomy are analogous, and asserts that a person does not need to have a male body to express masculine characteristics or a female body to express feminine characteristics. Instead it assumes that all people can embody varying degrees of masculine and feminine traits regardless of biology. This conceptualization of gender embraces gender identities outside of the *gender binary*, which is understood to be a culturally based classification of human characteristics as either male or female.

From a social constructionist perspective, individuals internalize and then reproduce the gender binary by behaving and presenting themselves in ways that are consistent with these culturally defined masculine or feminine traits. Because an individual's embodiment of masculine and feminine characteristics is not genetically predetermined, individuals can express genders beyond the gender binary that combine masculine and feminine traits equally. According to modern gender theorists, a person's gender includes three dimensions; one's experience of oneself as a gendered being, one's internalization and identification with a socially defined group, and one's expression of socially defined cues that communicate one's gender identity.

Three Dimensions of Gender

Gender orientation refers to one's internal sense of being a particular gender. This can also be thought of as an individual's innate orientation toward femininity and masculinity. Because masculinity and femininity are not bipolar ends of a unidimensional construct but instead are two distinct concepts on two separate continuums, individuals can be oriented toward masculinity and femininity at equally high levels for both, equally low levels for both, or varying degrees of either. Again, this internal sense of self is separate from a person's biology, so it may or may not correspond with one's anatomy.

Gender identity is understood to be individuals' identification of their gender orientation within the context of socially defined categories. In essence, it is how we label ourselves in order to acknowledge and reflect our gender orientation. Our gender identity is also associated with *gender expression*, which is defined as how much we associate with and display characteristics of a socially defined group. If gender orientation is our most internal component of gender and gender identity is the link between the internal and external, then gender expression is primarily the external component of our gender. The important thing to note from this, however, is that individuals vary significantly in their internalization of and comfort level with identifying and expressing the features of different gender groups. Each of these dimensions can differ and is not necessarily aligned with each other.

The distinction between gender orientation, gender identity, and gender expression has become increasingly evident with the greater visibility of individuals who are oriented toward masculinity and femininity at similarly high levels and who may not orient toward either construct at all. These individuals self-identify as *gender nonconforming* and do not feel as though their gender identity falls within the gender binary. More specifically, individuals might have *gender-fluid, gender-queer, pangendered,* and *gender-bender* identities, which purposefully challenge a dichotomous view of gender. These identities are characterized by fluid gender expressions that may or may not match an individual's anatomy. Others might experience themselves as having two or more genders and might identify as *bi-gendered, tri-gendered,* or *two-spirited*. Individuals whose gender orientation is high on the masculinity continuum and low on the femininity continuum might experience themselves as having a male gender identity. If these individuals also have male bodies and express masculine cues, they would likely identify as a *cisgender male*. Inversely, those high on the femininity continuum, low on the masculinity continuum, with a female gender expression and a female body might identify primarily as a *cisgender female*.

It is important to note within any discussion of socially based identity formation that embedded within the differentiation of socially constructed groups are systems of oppression and dominance. Not all identities are equally privileged, and persons embodying identities that challenge biological determinism and the gender binary often experience a great deal of stigma, marginalization, and discrimination. Furthermore, identity formation occurs within larger cultural systems that include multiple intersecting facets of identity including race, ethnic identity, national affiliation, sexual orientation, social class, and both cognitive and physical abilities. Thus individuals' gender identity cannot be understood without considering their social location within other identity systems.

Implications

The information presented in this entry carries with it a number of implications for working as a counselor or family therapist. First, it is essential that clinicians not succumb to biological determinism and assume that a person's gender expression and anatomy are consistent with their gender orientation and gender identity. This requires self-reflection regarding one's own gender identity and potential areas of bias. Counselors and family therapists should be sure to use gender-neutral pronouns in conversation and have gender-neutral options for paperwork. It is also important that they seek out educational opportunities for better understanding the experiences of those whose gender orientations, gender identities, gender expressions, and anatomy vary across these elements.

Lindsay L. Edwards

See also Gender Issues; Gender Roles; Sex, Definition of; Sexual Minorities; Sexual Orientation, Attraction, and Identity; Social Construction; Transgender Families

Further Readings

Blumer, M. C., Ansara, Y. G., & Watson, C. M. (2013). Cisgenderism in family therapy: How everyday clinical practices can delegitimize people's gender self-designations. *Journal of Family Psychotherapy, 24*(4), 267–285. doi:10.1080/08975353.2013.849551

Lev, A. I. (2004). *Transgender emergence: Therapeutic guidelines for working with gender-variant people and their families*. Binghamton, NY: Haworth Clinical Practice Press.

Nagoshi, J. L., Nagoshi, C. T., Brzuzy, S., Filip-Crawford, G., Varley, A., & Hess, R. I. (2014). *Gender and sexual identity: Transcending feminist and queer theory.* New York, NY: Springer Science + Business Media. doi:10.1007/978-1-4614-8966-5

Gender Roles

Gender is a fluid concept, largely defined by the dominant culture, which serves to outline socially normative expectations for males and females. Global concepts related to the roles of men and women persist in varying forms ranging from rigid constructs to acceptance of diverse expression. Gender is a process of role definition assigned to individuals throughout the culture on the basis of biological sex. This entry discusses how gender roles are defined, how individuals form their gender identity, and the conflicts that can result from gender role expectations.

Definitions of appropriate gender-based behavior are inherently oriented to power. If one behaviorally ascribes to the normative definition provided by the dominant culture then one will experience a greater amount of societal acceptance. The roles of men and women created through gendered expectations are hierarchical in nature, in that those roles sustain cultural power structures. In turn, culturally defined roles influence family structures in that they serve to delineate expectations for men and women as partners and parents. Gender role norms are perpetuated through the family structure and reinforced by other societal systems, such as school, media, and governments.

Expectations for males and females are understood verbally, observed behaviorally, and reinforced socially. Intersectionality of experience has been described as one that begins with the dichotomy of gender based on biological sex; this dichotomy is of cultural importance in all cultures worldwide. Gender schema theory speaks to the development of gender identity as a process of intersections between societal messaging, individual cognitive development, and adherence to normative expectations based on one's biological sex or apparent biological sex.

In traditional Western societies women are typically expected to attend to service roles while men are expected to attend to leadership roles. This dichotomy presents a variety of issues for both men and women with regard to behavioral expectations. With the service role comes expectations that women serve as caregivers, are emotionally attuned to the needs of others, prioritize the needs of family above all else, and have a desire to become mothers. A woman is expected to serve in a supportive capacity to her intimate partner, being sexually submissive but a bastion of purity, sensitive, and agreeable. For men, the leadership role comes with expectations of independence, competitiveness, aggression, emotional distance, physical activity, confidence, rebelliousness, and focusing on financial contribution to a family.

These stereotypical expectations can be useful and harmful to both men and women. The roles can be useful if they are indeed authentic to one's way of being; however, if expectations are in conflict with one's own sense of one's authentic self, the roles can be overly restrictive, creating a sense of distress that can lead to relational conflicts. Additionally, these roles also intersect with power structures; thus, adherence may have additional consequences with regard to resource access, intimate partnerships, career aspirations, and wellness. For instance, if a male is perceived to display too many stereotypically female qualities, he opens himself up to being bullied, ostracized, and in some extreme cases, subjected to violence. For women, stereotypical male behaviors are considered to be aligned with hierarchical power structures, so achieving success in occupational settings may require women to take on some of these qualities, but not too many. For instance, clearly stating an opinion or position is an important quality of leadership and tends to demonstrate confidence. However, for women assertiveness can be perceived as unreasonable, malicious, or belligerent when the expectation is one of support and encouragement.

Gender Identity Formation

Gender identity is commonly identified as a state of being that is theorized to be the result of one of three possible processes. Some believe gender identity to be the result of an innate, predetermined state tied to one's biological sex (essentialist perspective), while others theorize that gender identity is acquired over time in stages and internalized based on learned expectations (developmental perspective). However, more recently a third theoretical concept concerning gender identity has emerged that views gender as a self-authored interactional process linked to both socialization and individual meaning-making resulting from experiences of self and the world. This active engagement in gender identify formation has been evaluated in school-aged children, serving to highlight the struggles children face when attempting to attain a sense of authenticity when role discrepancies occur.

Children are actively involved in their own gender identity development process. Many times counselors and educators encourage children to be authentic to themselves without fully understanding the pressures associated with conformist behavior and the possible consequences that may come with a lack of conformity to gender role expectations. Thus, when discussing issues of gender identity, it is important for children to weigh the benefits of authenticity within specific contexts. As individuals grow and move through life, decisions are made concerning gender expression and gender normative role involvement. Those decisions then lead to actions and experiences with family, friends, and the larger culture that in turn influence one's future sense of self and self-expression.

Societal messages regarding normative gender roles are prevalent. Communications media often sexualize women, having the effect of objectification, which can contribute to women's body image and male perspectives regarding women's societal worth. Additionally, exposure to the roles portrayed by women and men in movies, television, and advertising over the life span influence how one might attend to family roles and expectations for occupational pursuits. For instance, by age 3 children have typically begun to take on characteristics and preferences consistent with cultural gender role expectations through processes of reward and praise, be they intentional or unintentional. The level of influence that cultural messages have on gender role alignment depends largely on one's susceptibility to those messages. Susceptibility can be influenced by one's level of physical, cognitive, and emotional development; self-esteem; socioeconomic status; religion; experiences of oppression; and familial culture. When susceptibility is high and authenticity is low, role conflict is the inevitable result.

Gender Role Conflict

Issues concerning gender identity, expression, and roles influence individual experiences in a variety of settings. Family values related to gender roles and gender expression can influence children's career aspirations, emotional regulation, the division of household labor, and family conflict. Values related to gender roles and expression also influence the way one may treat others in relation to learned expectations for behavior. When an individual is at odds with the gender role that has been determined for her or him by society and/or by her or his family, an individual may experience gender role conflict. In Western societies women tend to be defined as caretakers: emotional, submissive, and pure of mind and body. Men in these societies are considered to be natural leaders, physically and sexually aggressive, and financially responsible for the success of the family. How one ascribes to normative role definitions influences family functioning and career choices. For example, research has demonstrated that egalitarian women are less likely to have children while egalitarian men are more likely than traditional men to want children and are less likely to divorce.

Gender role expectations are changing and thus the roles within families are changing as well. Women are working outside of the home but, on average, continue to experience the same expectations for household duties and child rearing as traditional women who work in the home. On average, according to research, men value their role as parents as much as women; however, their responsibilities and actions do not reflect equal attentiveness. Men and women are both constrained by normative gender roles and experience struggles when they do not perform as expected. For instance, men who perform child care responsibilities are often praised and provided with social assistance whereas women are expected to provide child care and thus their parenting behavior is treated as normative. If a woman does not want to have children, she may experience negative social consequences. If a man decides to be a stay-at-home father, he may also experience negative social consequences.

As a culture becomes more affirming of diversity in gender expression and gender role choices, expectations within the family begin to shift and change to allow for overlapping and egalitarian role expectations. The first steps in the process include recognizing and pointing out potentially oppressive role messages in media in relational contexts. Discussions related to how these messages may influence personal and interpersonal experience can be valuable when addressed openly and respectfully.

Amanda C. La Guardia

See also Beliefs and Values; Cultural Issues in Couples and Families; Feminist Family Therapy; Gender Issues; Gender Orientation, Gender Identity, and Gender Expression

Further Readings

Adams, G. R., Montemayor, R., & Gullotta, T. P. (1996). *Psychosocial development during adolescence: Advances in adolescent development*. Thousand Oaks, CA: Sage.

Adams, M., Blumenfeld, W., Castaneda, C., Hackman, H. W., Peters, M. L., & Zuniga, X. (Eds.). (2014). *Readings for diversity and social justice* (3rd ed.). New York, NY: Routledge.

Bem, S. L. (1983). Gender schema theory and its implications for child development: Raising gender-aschematic children in a gender-schematic society. *Signs, 8*(4), 598–616.

Bem, S. L. (1993). *The lenses of gender: Transforming the debate on sexual inequality*. New Haven, CT: Yale University Press.

Brinkman, B. G., Rabenstein, K. L., Rosén, L. A., & Zimmerman, T. S. (2014). Children's gender identity development: The dynamic negotiation process between conformity and authenticity. *Youth & Society, 46*(6), 835–852. doi:10.1177/0044118X12455025

Croft, A., Schmader, T., Block, K., & Baron, A. S. (2014). The second shift reflected in the second generation: Do parents' gender roles at home predict children's aspirations? *Psychological Science, 25*(7), 1418–1428. doi:10.1177/0956797614533968

Forste, R., & Fox, K. (2012). Household labor, gender roles, and family satisfaction: A cross-national comparison. *Journal of Comparative Family Studies, 43*(5), 613–631. http://www.jstor.org/stable/23267837

Gere, J., & Helwig, C. C. (2012). Young adults' attitudes and reasoning about gender roles in the family context. *Psychology of Women Quarterly, 36*(3), 301–313. doi:10.1177/0361684312444272

Huffman, A. H., Olson, K. J., O'Gara, T. C., & King, E. B. (2014). Gender role beliefs and fathers' work-family conflict. *Journal of Managerial Psychology, 29*(7), 774–793. doi:10.1108/JMP-11-2012-0372

Kaufman, G. (2000). Do gender role attitudes matter? Family formation and dissolution among traditional and egalitarian men and women. *Journal of Family Issues, 21*(1), 128–144. doi:10.1177/019251300021001006

Kivisto, K. L., Welsh, D. P., Darling, N., & Culpepper, C. L. (2014). Family enmeshment, adolescent emotional dysregulation, and the moderating role of gender. *Journal of Family Psychology, 29*(4), 604–613. doi:10.1037/fam0000118

Maier, C. A., & McGeorge, C. R. (2014). Positive attributes of never-married single mothers and fathers: Why gender matters and applications for family therapists. *Journal of Feminist Family Therapy, 26*, 163–190. doi:10.1080/08952833.2014.944060

Perrone-McGovern, K. M., Wright, S. L., Howell, D. S., & Barnum, E. L. (2014). Contextual influences on work and family roles: Gender, culture, and socioeconomic factors. *Career Development Quarterly, 62*, 21–28. doi:10.1002/j.2161-0045.2014.00067.x

Shaw, S., & Lee, J. (2015). *Women's voices, feminist visions: Classic and contemporary readings* (6th ed.). New York, NY: McGraw-Hill Education.

GENERAL SYSTEMS THEORY

General systems theory (GST), also known simply as systems theory, is a theoretical framework that seeks to explain the behavior of complex organized systems, from missile guidance computers to families. As early as the 1930s, social scientists began identifying and applying systems principles to fields such as anatomy and physiology, anthropology, communication, neurophysiology, philosophy, physics, psychology, sociology, and speech.

General systems theory stemmed from the mechanistic cause and effect models of physics and mathematics. These methodologies were viewed by most other scientific disciplines as being something for which to strive. GST offered a departure from the limitations presented by such models. Psychiatrists began viewing families as systems and led the way toward viewing dysfunctional family dynamics as a problem of the family and not the identified patient. This view is now part of many theories that seek to understand families as systems.

The field of marriage and family therapy (MFT) was significantly impacted by professionals evaluating and exploring areas of communication and interaction among and between various social systems including family members. Their work contributed to an understanding that relational systems are more complex and interactive than the more traditional cause-and-effect conceptualizations of relationships. This entry first further defines GST and discusses the assumptions associated with the theory. It then discusses how the GST perspective on system levels is applied in family therapy and explains the major concepts of GST.

Cybernetics and GST appear to be closely related in modern systems theory. Cybernetics represents a science of communication concerned with the transmission and control of information. Cybernetics focuses on the communication and manipulation of behavior for many kinds of systems, including physical, chemical, and biological involving families and other social systems. GST draws from cybernetics for many of its concepts, including self-regulation, homeostasis, and wholeness. Most modern family systems theories focusing on various subsystems, including the family, represent the application of GST.

GST is broader than a theory but still a generalized perspective that requires a systemic thought process. Encouraging individuals to observe the world according to interrelational dynamics (how people interacting with one another affects the system and how the system affects relationships), GST, like other theories attempting to explain behaviors within and between systems, holds a variety of assumptions.

Assumptions Associated With General Systems Theory

The first assumption associated with GST is that it has the ability to synthesize or manufacture science. The modernized form of GST was developed by Ludwig von Bertalanffy (1901–1972), who believed that the social and natural sciences could be integrated based on certain unifying principles. Systems theorists have since sought to do so through the concept of isomorphism. *Isomorphism* is primarily a mathematics term meaning equal shape that can be inverted. For the social and natural sciences to be isomorphic would mean that the principles and relationships that apply to the natural sciences are directly related to the social sciences. Systems theorists assume that whether working with a computer system or family system there are common rules and organizing principles.

Second, systems theorists identified that a system must be understood as a whole. In other words, to evaluate the individual parts does not provide an accurate or reliable representation of the entire system. There are properties and behaviors developed within the system, based on their unique arrangements and interactions that do not exist within the individual characteristics of the system. When viewed from the lens of family therapy, emergent family behaviors or properties are no longer the responsibility of any one member or identified patient. Rather, an adolescent who abuses drugs would not be viewed as "the problem" creating chaos and conflict in the family, but the entire system would be evaluated to identify what was happening within the system among all its parts *causing* the emergence of a substance-abusing adolescent.

The final core assumption of GST is that human systems are self-reflexive. This means that humans are able to examine and evaluate their own behavior. Some cybernetic systems are self-monitoring while other nonhuman systems do not require or imply self-awareness; cybernetics is an approach that views systems as a feedback loop, where one action affects the environment and said change is reflected within the system. Self-reflexology allows families to evaluate their system and create goals. In family therapy this is done primarily through the use of communication. Systems theorists understand that communication is what allows self-reflexivity to occur. Communication is a process that supports the making of meaning and the exchange of symbolic content. According to GST, family processes should be understood in relation to the system's ongoing processes. Family therapists are particularly interested in transactional patterns, and the extent to which a transactional sequence is repeated over time is the extent to which a system is engaged in a pattern of redundant behavior. For instance, a family whose behavior has inadvertently supported or been unable to resolve the substance abuse of one of their members over time indicates a pattern of behavior. The family has most likely attempted in various and specific ways to bring balance back into the family. These attempts then become sequences of behavior that often create "stuckness" as the family tries the same solutions multiple times. The focus then shifts from the substance-abusing member to the behaviors and relationships among all family members. This concept is in contradiction with the idea of cause and effect but has been helpful in the field of family therapy to understand and intervene in family processes without blaming any one family member and shifting away from pathologizing an identified patient.

System Levels and Family Therapy

According to GST, a unit smaller than the family is a subsystem. For example, a therapist treating a substance-abusing adolescent might be particularly interested in understanding what the marital subsystem looks like. The therapist may pay close attention to sibling subsystems to better understand the behavior of a substance-using adolescent. They may also identify possible motivation to change the behavior based on the relationship between subsystems. Suprasystems, on the other hand, include extended family, families of origin, community, and racial and ethnic subcultures. This allows marriage and family therapists and researchers to then place the family system in a larger context within which the family exists. It is often within these systems that family therapists are able to utilize additional support to aid the family through the treatment process.

Considering family issues from different system levels allows professionals working with and studying families to explore questions in much more detail than if the focus was merely cause and effect. These systemic explanations allow researchers to explore how family systems change. The process in GST of describing and explaining changes in the family system is known as morphogenesis. Systems approaches view change as being processed by the entire family system rather than a single family member, whether the change is initiated by one person or motivated through changes in the environment such as economic growth.

Concepts in General Systems Theory

There are several major GST concepts. Some of these include interdependence or mutual influence, hierarchy, boundaries and open/closed systems, equifinality, and feedback and control. Each of these will be described briefly and explained in the context of working with families. First, *mutual influence* is described as one part's ability to affect all the other parts. In a family this might take the form of each family member's individual response to an adolescent seeking treatment for their substance abuse. That is, a father may become motivated to seek treatment himself, leading to an increase in conflict between a mother and father, causing a sibling to feel angry and frustrated.

The second concept is *hierarchy*. Hierarchy in GST is a layering of systems, subsystems, and suprasystems. In family therapy it is the parental subsystem that would be considered at the top of the familial hierarchy. At the top of a hierarchy there is associated power, authority, and influence. Often in families one spouse will be treated by the other as being in the sibling subsystem. If the wife talks down to her husband, eliminates his choices, and treats him as one of her other children, the husband becomes part of the sibling subsystem while the wife remains head of the hierarchy.

Third, *boundaries* indicate the amount of interaction between the family and the supra- or subsystems. Defining a specific boundary can be difficult because it means depicting one system from another. Boundaries are defined by their permeability. Boundaries may allow or prohibit the flow of information and energy from inside and outside the system. All family systems are considered open because they all have contact with their environment; however, on a continuum some families will be too open and some not open enough. For example, a family's cultural beliefs may include that one does not talk to strangers about family issues. This may lead to a more closed family system compared to those who do not have this rule. Some families may find that they are talking to anyone who will listen including their coworkers, neighbors, and their children's teachers, showing a lack of boundaries.

Equifinality refers to the system's ability to achieve the same goal in various ways. For instance, a family's goal may be the prevention of drug and alcohol use by their children. The parents may use types of tough love or scare tactics to prevent substance use. They may try to shelter their children from any environment or event that may expose them to drugs and avoid talking to them about drugs, or the parents may talk openly about the dangers of drugs and educate their children on how to handle various situations involving drugs or alcohol. It is possible that through equifinality these two approaches may lead to the parents' desired result that their children remain drug-free.

Finally, *feedback and control* are concepts key to GST. A feedback loop is a pattern of movement that makes its way from one point in a system to another, eventually ending up where it began. Because of its circular nature the cybernetic system is able to regulate its own behavior as information is fed into the loop, altered based on negative or positive feedback, and entered back into the loop. Negative feedback restores or maintains homeostasis or balance. When the homeostasis of the family is threatened, the system will utilize negative feedback to try to rebalance the system. Positive feedback would affect systems differently by allowing family dynamics to become unbalanced and raising intensity within the family. The patterns of interaction within family systems are commonly associated with family dysfunction. According to GST, problems previously viewed as being the dysfunction or pathology of an individual are now seen as symptoms of dysfunctional transactional patterns in the entire system. Examples include eating disorders such as bulimia and anorexia nervosa, alcoholism, and drug addiction. Such approaches are seen clearly in the structural family therapy conducted by Salvador Minuchin. Some family practitioners have attempted to educate and treat one family member in an attempt to address family dysfunction. However, dynamics such as mutual influence and negative feedback limit the success of such approaches.

Janee Both Gragg

See also Boundaries; Bowen Family Systems Theory; Communication in Couples and Families; Cybernetics; Systemic Family Therapy; Systems, Subsystems, and Metasystems; Systems Theory

Further Readings

Bateson, G. (1971). Cybernetics of self. *Psychiatry, 34,* 1–18.

Bateson, G., Jackson, D., Haley, J., & Weakland, J. (1956). Toward a theory of schizophrenia. *Behavioral Science, 1,* 251–264.

Constantine, L. (1993). The structure of family paradigms: An analytical model of family paradigms. *Journal of Marital and Family Therapy, 19*(1).

Galvin, K., & Brommel, B. (1991). *Family communication: Cohesion and change* (3rd ed.). New York, NY: HarperCollins.

Littlejohn, S. (1989). *Theories of human communication* (3rd ed.). Belmont, CA: Wadsworth.

Maddock, J., & Lange, C. (1988). Integrating Milan therapy and the circumplex model: Ecosystemic consultation with families and their helpers. *Journal of Psychotherapy and the Family, 4,* 141–174.

Minuchin, S. (1974). *Families and family therapy.* Cambridge, MA: Harvard University Press.

Minuchin, S., Rosman, B., & Baker, L. (1978). *Psychosomatic families: Anorexia in context.* Cambridge, MA: Harvard University Press.

Parsons, T., & Bales, R. (1955). *Family, socialization and interaction process.* New York, NY: Free Press.

von Bertalanffy, L. (1968). *General systems theory.* New York, NY: George Braziller.

Watzlawick, P., Beavin, J., & Jackson, D. (1967). *Pragmatics of human communication.* New York, NY: W. W. Norton.

Weinberg, G. (1975). *An introduction to general systems thinking.* New York, NY: Wiley.

GENITO-PELVIC PAIN/ PENETRATION DISORDER

Pain during sexual intercourse can be distressing for women and impact significant relationships in their lives. Sexual pain is considered to be a significant women's health concern, with a lifetime prevalence of 12% to 15% of women experiencing pain during intercourse. Relationship dissatisfaction is recognized as having a significant role in maintenance and exacerbation of sexual dysfunctions. Treatment of genito-pelvic pain/penetration disorder includes psycho-education, goal setting, reducing anxiety, and improving relational dynamics. This entry introduces genito-pelvic pain/penetration disorder, particularly as it relates to couples and family therapy, explaining the diagnostic criteria, etiology, comorbidity, and the impact on relationships. Assessment and treatment recommendations are also discussed.

Women experience sexual pain disorders at a high rate, and if this disorder is left untreated or undiagnosed the woman places her health and sexual relationship at risk. Genito-pelvic pain/penetration disorder can create emotional and physical challenges in couples that engage in sexual activities. There are several factors that may result in genital pain, including a history of trauma, other medical concerns, and medication. Therefore, it is important that the clinician obtains a detailed history and incorporates a physical examination by a trained gynecologist. Treatment should focus on psychological, medical, and social dynamics with an emphasis on decreasing unwanted responses to penetration and increasing sexual desire and functioning.

Women seeking treatment for genito-pelvic pain/penetration disorder should be encouraged to take control of their sexual activities, and learn skills to help them relax prior to sexual stimulation. Women should be encouraged to engage in behaviors that they are fully comfortable with, and not feel a sense of pressure or rush to engage in these activities. Communication between the couple is also a very important factor in the treatment of genito-pelvic pain/penetration disorder. Women can learn to gain a healthy balance and increase their ability to control the direction of their sexual engagements.

Although genito-pelvic pain/penetration disorder can cause distress in relationships, it is possible to seek help and obtain treatment with an appropriate therapist, as this is an important interpersonal and intimate experience. Clinicians should ensure that they are familiar with information regarding genito-pelvic pain/penetration disorder and be aware of when they need to make a referral to medical staff. The goal of treatment should also be to empower the client to make healthy decisions for her life.

Diagnostic Criteria

The classification of sexual pain disorders has changed over time. The *Diagnostic and Statistical Manual of Mental Disorders, 4th Edition, Revised* (DSM-IV-TR) classified female sexual pain as two diagnostic conditions that appeared to be comorbid: *vaginismus,* in which the outer part of the vaginal outlet involuntarily closes, and *dyspareunia,* referring to difficult or painful coitus. These conditions were difficult to distinguish and as a result, the new definition included a merging of vaginismus and dyspareunia. The fifth edition of the DSM provided a new definition of female sexual pain as genito-pelvic pain/penetration disorder. To meet criteria for this diagnosis, one or more of the following should be present: (a) penetration of the vagina during intercourse; (b) during penetration attempts or vaginal intercourse there is marked vulvovaginal or pelvic pain; (c) in anticipation of, during, or as a result of vaginal penetration, there is marked fear or anxiety about vulvovaginal or pelvic pain; and (d) during attempted vaginal penetration there is tensing or tightening of the pelvic floor muscles.

When making a diagnosis, the clinician determines whether the disturbance has been present since initiation of sexual activity (lifelong) or after a period of relatively normal sexual functioning (acquired). This disorder may also be classified according to levels of distress: mild, moderate, or severe. It is also important to consider whether the symptoms cause significant clinical distress and whether symptoms have been present for at least 6 months before making a diagnosis. The sexual pain or dysfunction should not be better explained by a nonsexual mental disorder or result from relational distress, substance use, or other medical conditions.

Etiology

Genito-pelvic pain/penetration disorder has biological and psychological components that may explain some of the causes for this disorder. In order to experience pain-free sexual intercourse, the anatomy of the vagina should be healthy and functional without an imbalance. Therefore, sexual pain and dysfunction may be attributed to both biological and psychological factors.

Biological Factors

Sexual dysfunction, specifically vaginismus, may be caused by several biological factors including hysterectomy, vaginal atrophy, vaginitis, pelvic congestion, and constipation. Conditions such as endometriosis, a rigid hymen, hemorrhoids, pelvic tumors, and pelvic inflammatory disease should also be considered as contributing factors to genito-pelvic pain/penetration disorder. Infections such as human papilloma virus (HPV), herpes genitalis, and candidiasis may cause inflammation and pain especially if the infections are recurrent. Vaginal pain may also be affected by changes in hormone levels and may contribute to reduced lubrication and vaginal atrophy. Biological factors appear to be the primary source of dysfunction as these conditions affect the organs essential for sexual performance.

Psychological Factors

Psychological factors play a significant role in sexual dysfunctions, including genito-pelvic pain/penetration disorders, even if there is no formal mental health diagnosis or psychiatric disorder. Sexual activity is best when the individual is relaxed and experiencing emotions that do not distract or disrupt intimacy, sexual arousal, and intercourse. Psychological etiology of genito-pelvic pain/penetration disorder is sometimes based on classical conditioning. If the woman experiences pain during the initial attempt at intercourse, the pain may function as an unconditioned stimulus resulting in the tightening of the vaginal muscles. This action is considered self-protective against penetration.

With a diagnosis of genito-pelvic pain/penetration disorder, there is increased phobia and psychosomatic fear of sex or vaginal penetration leading to a tightening of the pelvic floor muscles during attempted penetration. Although there is limited research on the relationship between sexual pain and past trauma or abuse, it is believed that lifetime experience of trauma and abuse may impact sexual function and lead to difficulties or pain during penetration due to increased anxiety or fear. This fear of pain can reduce sexual desire and result in limited sexual initiative or interest.

Comorbidity

Genito-pelvic pain/penetration disorder appears to be commonly comorbid with other sexual difficulties. Relationship distress, including avoidance of sexual intercourse or related sexual behaviors, contributes to comorbidity as well. A higher prevalence of disorders such as vaginal infection, constipation, endometriosis, and irritable bowel syndrome are expected with a diagnosis of genito-pelvic pain/penetration disorder, since the pelvic floor is one of the main sources of discomfort in this disorder.

Impact on Relationships

Painful intercourse can significantly impact relationships, especially those of a sexual nature. Couples may seek therapy to address painful sex that leads to complications within the relationship. A partner may interpret the avoidance of sex as a negative message indicating a lack of interest or attraction. This may lead to the partner feeling upset and pressured to withdraw emotionally from the relationship. A partner that is negative in their response style may encourage the other partner to seek out therapy or even alternative sexual activities. The clinician should address the impact of genito-pelvic pain/penetration disorder on the relationship and intimacy between couples in order to create opportunities for improved interactions and understanding of each partner.

Assessment and Treatment Recommendations

Although women are diagnosed with genito-pelvic pain/penetration disorder, this condition impacts a couple's relationship. Women tend to believe that they are the source of the problem within the relationship and believe that therapy will focus on their individual needs. However, it is important when meeting with couples to respectfully explain that both partners can benefit from therapeutic interventions, as there can be greater awareness of the core problems that lead to the pain during sexual intercourse.

Since pain is one of the primary presenting complaints in genito-pelvic pain/penetration disorder, this should be the first assessment done. Essential information must be gathered in this assessment of pain and it may include the following: (a) identifying where the exact point of pain is during any attempt at intercourse, (b) identifying when the pain begins, (c) identifying if there is pain during other sexual encounters or nonsexual activities, (d) describing the pain (using a Likert-type scale response), and (e) getting an estimate of how long the pain lasts. One of the important aspects of intervention is the involvement of a gynecologist with special interest and experience in pelvic and vulvar pain. This referral should be made after the pain assessment is completed for a thorough physical examination and prescribed medication if needed. Other important information to gather includes the sexual function of the client and their partner, coping skills, and the presence of other disorders as outlined in the DSM-5.

When considering treatment options, providing education to the clients is an integral part of initial therapy. The clinician should be familiar with medications and procedures relevant to genito-pelvic pain/penetration disorder and be able to provide the client with reading material to enhance their knowledge on the disorder. Although complete resolution of genital pain may be difficult to attain, it is important to instill hope in the client while discussing realistic expectations. Goal setting should be done with the aim of reducing pain and increasing healthy sexual function in the couple's relationship.

Therapeutic interventions vary for genito-pelvic pain/penetration disorder; however, there are a few techniques that can be helpful during the initial stages of therapy. Some of these techniques include reinforcing the importance of seeking help, validating the experience of pain, demystifying the pain and anxiety, and encouraging genital self-exploration. There should be less emphasis on the act of intercourse and more focus on increasing desire, arousal, and connectedness with affection and sensuality.

Cognitive and behavioral interventions may be very useful in treating genito-pelvic pain/penetration disorder. The core beliefs about pain, sex, and relationships can be discussed and challenged. Cognitive reframing and restructuring may assist the client and the couple to address the beliefs or schema that interfere with healthy sexual functioning. The clinician should remain respectful of cultural beliefs and values at all times and refrain from imposing their own worldviews.

Interventions such as relaxation training and gradual exposure to penetration are also treatment options for genito-pelvic pain/penetration disorder. Relaxation skills may help the client to feel more in tune with her body and partner, and feel more reassured about the control she has over her body. The clinician should encourage the partner to be an active part of the treatment, if the client is in agreement, to understand the fear and pain associated with penetration that may cause damage to the genital area if not addressed appropriately.

The clinician should explore what the problem means to the woman so she can have a better understanding of how her body responds and how she creates meaning from these experiences. Appropriate homework assignments should be assigned gradually. One assignment may be having the client lubricate and insert her finger to determine when pain begins, focusing on relaxation skills to help relax the muscles to encourage penetration, then inserting more fingers once she does not experience pain. The client should be encouraged to involve her partner in the exercise as an observer or participant. It is important for the client to know that she is in charge of the progression of these activities. Homework assignments should always be given with consultation and agreement of the client.

Karisse A. Callender

See also Mindfulness and Sex; Sexual Dysfunction; Sexual Intimacy; Trauma and Families; Trauma-Focused Cognitive Behavioral Therapy

Further Readings

American Psychiatric Association. (2013). *Diagnostic and statistical manual of mental disorders* (5th ed.). Washington, DC: Author.

Balon, R. (2008). *Sexual dysfunction: The brain-body connection*. Basel, Switzerland: Karger.

Hertlein, K. M., Weeks, G. R., & Gambescia, N. (2009). *Systemic sex therapy*. New York, NY: Routledge.

Maass, V. S. (2007). *Facing the complexities of women's sexual desire*. Indianapolis, IN: Springer.

Petrak, J., & Hedge, B. (2003). *The trauma of sexual assault: Treatment, prevention and practice*. West Sussex, England: John Wiley & Sons.

Wincze, J. P., & Carey, M. P. (2001). *Sexual dysfunction: A guide for assessment and treatment* (2nd ed.). New York, NY: Guilford.

Woody, J. D. (1992). *Treating sexual distress: Integrating systems therapy*. London, England: Sage.

GENOGRAMS

A genogram is a diagram in standardized format that is used as an assessment and intervention tool in clinical settings. Similar to a family tree, the genogram visually represents family facts, complex family patterns, and relationships of at least three generations. The ability to collect, synthesize, and visualize important multigenerational family information is a powerful tool for marriage, family, and couples counselors who are charged with making sense out of the vast amounts of information collected while working with clients. After describing the origins of the genogram, this entry presents an overview of its clinical uses, briefly explains the method of constructing genograms, and concludes with a discussion of key issues to consider in incorporating the use of the genogram in therapeutic practice.

Historical Overview of Genograms

Family therapy began in the 1950s on the basis of a shift in thinking among mental health professionals who had come to recognize that efforts to understand the mental health problems of individuals required a greater understanding of the families of those individuals, since it was within the context of those families that the problems arose. This paradigm shift, in which the individual is to be viewed as part of a larger system, included the evaluation of family. It was during that time that family therapists and medical professionals began to recognize the connections between families and illness, and the impact of illness on family. Clinicians looked for efficient ways to capture complex family connections and interactions.

Drawing family relationships and emotional patterns emerged as a way to capture families in an efficient way. Family diagrams were used to record demographics, relationships, patterns, medical information, behaviors, and significant events. These family pictures, later called genograms, originated from the family diagram used in Bowen family systems therapy and the genealogical family tree or family pedigree used in family medicine. Murray Bowen is the first person in family therapy credited with using a pictorial representation of the family (which he termed a family diagram) to map family emotional processes in combination with his comprehensive theory based on the natural systems of biology.

Through the ongoing work of professionals in family therapy and family medicine, the genogram format and basic symbols became standardized during the 1980s. This standardized format has been established in family therapy as an efficient framework for understanding and exploring family dynamics across generations and their influence on present family functioning. Its use has extended beyond assessment and has expanded as an intervention, educational modality, and data collection tool in clinical and other professional settings. It is an easily understood framework that is adaptable to other psychotherapeutic models, which contributes to its wide range of clinical uses. Its clinical application is prevalent in the professions of counseling, marriage and family therapy, psychology, social work, and medicine.

Clinical Uses of Genograms

Clinical uses of diagrams range on a continuum from an atheoretical intake assessment to a comprehensive multigenerational family history combined with a strong theoretical foundation used throughout the therapeutic process. Clinical uses include, but are not limited to, an atheoretical assessment tool; a mechanism for generating tentative hypotheses; a technique for building rapport; developing awareness of problematic family patterns, beliefs, and relationships; developing awareness about culture, community, and spirituality; developing awareness of beneficial family patterns, strengths, and resiliencies; and as a means to develop interventions that enhance strengths and interrupt or stop harmful family patterns. It can also be used intermittently throughout the therapeutic process to assess client progress or other variables (e.g., anger, intimacy).

As an atheoretical assessment device, the information gathered during an assessment interview may include birth dates; death dates; health issues and age of onset; substance use; anniversary dates; careers; education levels; significant family events; biological, legal, and emotional relationships; religious and spiritual practices; and cultural information. It may also include community and world events that may have impacted the family. This information can be incorporated as a technique for generating tentative hypotheses about individual and family functioning. Information generated from the genogram helps the counselor to gain a better understanding of the client family and their familial patterns, relationships, and other circumstances that may contribute to the presenting issue. As a technique for building rapport, it is a way to get to know many aspects of the client family (couple or individual) in a nonintimidating, nonthreatening way. As an assessment and intervention, it is a process that includes an examination of the many influences and interactions that affect families (couples and individuals) and how the influences and interactions impact current functioning, thus creating opportunities for learning and further exploration (i.e., a mutual and reciprocal process of discovery).

The creation of a genogram is a collaborative process between client and clinician. It is a process that develops both parties' awareness of familial relationships (e.g., beliefs, behaviors, emotional connections) and other systemic influences (e.g., community resources, religion, legal system). It can be used in real time or other times in the past of the client that may be relevant to the presenting issues and concerns of the client. Possible areas of exploration include life-cycle transitions and family patterns of health, wellness, symptoms, power imbalances, and hierarchies. As relationships and influences are identified, a mutual process of learning occurs. During this process the client and clinician explore how various relationships are, or are not, beneficial. Family relationships and resources recognized as beneficial may be duplicated, adapted, or highlighted to strengthen specific areas that the client has identified, in an effort to enhance movement toward client and therapeutic goals. Relationships and influences that are recognized as damaging or destructive can be adapted, interrupted, or stopped in an effort to reach client goals, furthermore stopping the patterns from being transmitted to future generations. When exploring family patterns there is an assumption in family systems models that patterns do not occur in isolation.

The decision to use a genogram is taken with careful consideration and a well-defined purpose. The purpose is dependent on client goals, clinical goals, and the model or theory utilized by the clinician. When constructing a genogram with a client family (couple or individual), it is important to explain the process, the intention, and the expected outcomes so that clients understand and make sense out of the time and effort spent in creating a genogram.

Genogram Construction

A genogram is always to be created with respect, compassion, and sensitivity. The information elicited may be highly sensitive and quite possibly has never previously been discussed or shared, either inside or outside of the family. An initial genogram assessment with a client family (couple or individual) can be completed in one or two sessions. It can be drawn on paper, a whiteboard, or a chalk board, or developed on a computer with a genogram software program. Legal and biological relationships are depicted by straight vertical and horizontal lines that connect related individuals. Each individual is represented by a shape: Males are represented by squares, and females are represented by circles. Additional shapes within the circle or square represent gay, lesbian, transgender, and bisexual individuals. In heterosexual couple relationships, males are placed on the left and females are placed on the right. In same-sex relationships, the shapes include a triangle in the center. Dashed lines are used to indicate additional relationships (e.g., adoption, foster children, individuals living together, a committed relationship, or a sexual relationship). The structure starts with the oldest generations at the top and subsequent generations below. Children are placed in chronological age order, with the oldest placed to the left and younger children continuing to the right. Dates and additional information that is collected on each individual is written nearest to the left or above the individual that the information describes (see Figure 1).

One way to identify patterns with a genogram is to record the relationships by connecting individuals with what are termed *relationship lines*, which pictorially represent the emotional processes of the family. Relationship lines are diagonal, vertical, or horizontal lines of various designs that represent different types of relationships between individuals represented in the genogram. One example of a relationship that delineated on a genogram is *close*, which is represented by two lines connecting the individuals described as close. *Fusion* is a relationship that is considered overly close or emotionally connected in a way that the individuals are overly dependent on one another to the point they cannot think independently; this relationship is represented by three lines. *Hostile* is a tension-filled relationship represented by a zig-zag line. *Cut-off* (emotional or physical) is a distanced relationship with little or no emotional or physical contact. This type of relationship is

Figure 1 Basic Genogram

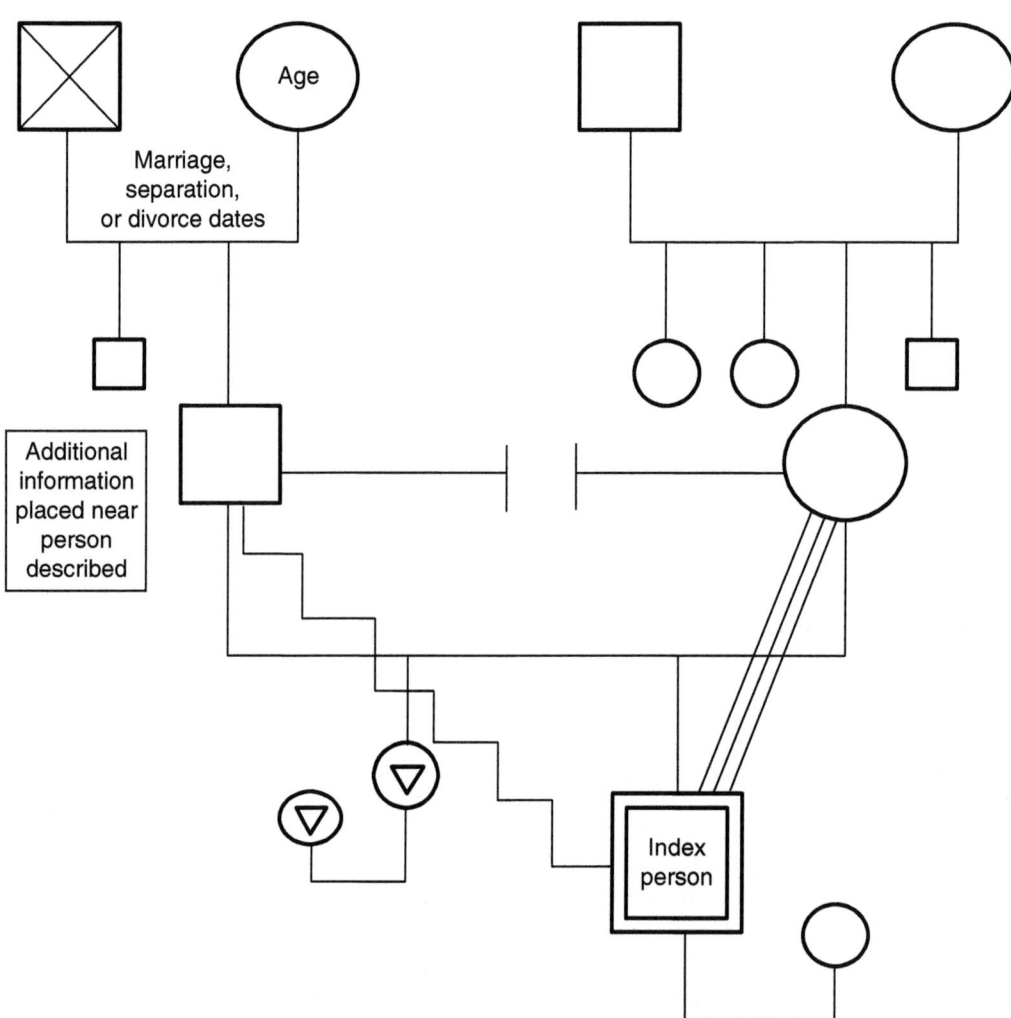

The basic genogram is constructed using standardized symbols. The top of the genogram starts with the oldest generation and moves down vertically to represent younger generations, with each generation on the same horizontal level. Males are represented by squares and placed on the left in couple relationships. Females are represented by circles and placed on the right in couple relationships. Same-sex relationships may be identified by placing a triangle in the center of the circle or square. The lines in this figure represent legal, biological, and emotional relationships. Children of couples are placed on the genogram in chronological age order. An X through a shape means that person is deceased. The client is double lined.

Source: Deborah J. Watson.

represented by a line with a space in the line that connects the cut-off relationship. To date, no single standard has emerged for relationship lines. While there are generally understood and accepted lines and concepts used to represent specific types of relationships in family systems models, there is a wide range of use and interpretation depending on the purpose of the genogram and the theoretical model chosen by the clinician.

Considerations When Using a Genogram

Although the genogram is a versatile and efficient tool for assessment and intervention, several considerations should be evaluated before creating a genogram. Informing the clients of the purpose of the genogram and how it relates to the goals of counseling is an important component of genogram construction. It can be a cumbersome process that leads to client dissatisfaction if clients do not understand how exploring the past is connected to the current issues that brought them to therapy. Proper allotment of time is necessary to address any additional issues that may be elicited during the genogram process. Exploring historical family information may stimulate painful feelings and memories. Additionally, eliciting certain family secrets or information may have negative effects on some family members. Other considerations include learning about the culture and spiritual beliefs of clients as well as knowing your own biases. Understanding what is acceptable in the cultures and spiritual lives (or religious beliefs) of clients is important. What may be suitable in some cultures or religious beliefs may be unacceptable or pathologized in other cultures. It is recommended that a therapeutic alliance is continually developed and assessed as the genogram work evolves in the therapeutic setting.

Deborah Watson

See also Bowen Family Systems Theory; Family Life Cycle; Family of Origin; Family Strengths; Fusion; Systemic Family Therapy; Therapeutic Assessment

Further Readings

Belous, C. K., Timm, T. M., Chee, G., & Whitehead, M. R. (2012). Revisiting the sexual genogram. *American Journal of Family Therapy, 40*(4), 281–296. doi:10.1080/01926187.2011.627317

DeMaria, R., Weeks, G., & Hof, L. (1999). *Focused genograms: Intergenerational assessment of individuals, couples, and families.* Philadelphia, PA: Brunner/Mazel.

Kerr, M. E., & Bowen, M. (1988). *Family evaluation: The role of the family as an emotional unit that governs individual behavior and development.* New York, NY: Norton.

Kuehl, B. P. (1996). The use of genograms with solution-based and narrative therapies. *The Family Journal, 4*(1), 5–11. doi:10.1177/1066480796041002

Magnuson, S., & Shaw, H. E. (2003). Adaptations of the multifaceted genogram in counseling, training, and supervision. *The Family Journal, 11*(1), 45–54. doi:10.1177/1066480702238472

McGoldrick, M., & Carter, B. (2001). Advances in coaching: Family therapy with one person. *Journal of Marital and Family Therapy, 27*(3), 281–300. doi:10.1111/j.1752-0606.2001.tb00325.x

McGoldrick, M., Gerson, R., & Petry, S. (2008). *Genograms: Assessment and intervention* (3rd ed.). New York, NY: W. W. Norton.

Rigazio-DiGilio, S. A., Ivey, A. E., Kunkler-Peck, K. P., & Grady, L. T. (2005). *Community genograms: Using individual, family, and cultural narratives with clients.* New York, NY: Teachers College Press.

Shellenberger, S. (2007). Use of the genogram with families for assessment and treatment. In F. Shapiro, F. W. Kaslow, & L. Maxfield (Eds.), *Handbook of EMDR and family therapy processes* (pp. 76–94). Hoboken, NJ: Wiley.

GESTALT FAMILY THERAPY

Gestalt family therapy is an application of relational Gestalt therapy, itself deriving from the basic insights of Gestalt psychology, viewing each person as a proactive, creative agent drawing on shared frames of reference and current awareness to interpret and adapt to perceived reality and challenge. These adaptations may be creative and flexible, building new creative solutions on the basis of previous experience, or they may be repetitive and "stuck," locking individuals, families, and larger systems in unsatisfying or destructive behavior and outcomes. Gestalt therapy draws on relational support to provide the safety for relaxing and exploring the emotional dynamics of these "stuck" adaptive patterns, and experimenting with new, more satisfying solutions. This entry explores how Gestalt family therapy applies these insights and methods to developmental challenges in the stresses and opportunities of family life.

Key Gestalt Principles

Gestalt family therapy rests on key Gestalt principles of contact and awareness, relationship and support, emotion and embodiment, intentionality and experiment, and a radical respect for the proactive meaning-making process of each person. The focus in Gestalt work is on present relationships and experience, as the keys to identifying and working both with current developmental challenges, and also with "stuck" or habitual patterns of interacting that are not serving the growth of each family member or the healthy process of the family as a whole. A particular strength of the Gestalt method is this "bifocal" lens, giving equal support for working with both individual development, and also the dynamic patterns of contact, support, and inhibition in their dynamic social context. Each family member is a part of coconstructing the dynamic family field, often in ways that may be long-habituated and out of awareness. The therapist's job includes slowing the family process down to heighten awareness of the separate moves, reactions, and interpreted meanings made by each family member, bringing awareness, new options and greater choice, and a greater spontaneity and flexibility of response as they enact the developing culture of the family.

Field/Relational Model

As a field/relational model, Gestalt understands experience and behavior as functions of conditions of the whole field as experienced by each particular person, or as agreed to in a particular family or other system. These field conditions will include both the "outer" perceptual field of shared events and experiences (as subjectively perceived/interpreted by each family member) and also the more private world of "inner" experience and capacities of each family member, still as organized and understood by that person. Individuals are conceived not as separate observers of a scene or system outside themselves, but as participants/observers, making sense as best they can at a given time out of the potential complexity of events as they experience them, and then reacting in ways that may look dysfunctional from the outside, but make more sense when understood from the individual's point of view. By slowing the process down, respecting each meaning made (with clear boundaries when necessary on destructive enactment of these feelings or meanings), and adding the support of seeing and attuning to each person's experience, the therapist facilitates trying out new behavioral responses that may be more nourishing, and also more solution-focused in new and desired ways.

The Role of the Therapist

Most difficult of all of course are family patterns of reaction that come out of the hyperarousal and failure of emotional self-regulation, which often characterize trauma patterns (developmental or event trauma) in and among family members. Often too, these patterns of quick "blow-up" or hyperarousal in one person are triggering post-trauma patterns in other members of the family. As an integral part of this present socially dynamic field in the here-and-now, the therapist will need to be capable of great empathy for each person, coupled with a strong presence that reassures each member of safety, and of confidence that they each will "get their turn" to have their experience opened up and understood "from the inside," often for the first time. The therapist's frequent recourse to naming emotions, identifying embodied experience, and opening up new possibilities for experiments and possible meanings—often drawing on her or his own current embodied experience—serves both to teach and to model the new empathic and experimental stance, which will serve the family better than their old entrenched contact habit. The therapist is not seen in Gestalt as an "outside expert," analyzing or advising a person or family, but rather as a dynamic part of the social field she or he is both cocreating and exploring with the client(s), using his or her expertise to offer dialogue, perspectives, possible experiments, and other interventions to understand the complex present situation in the service of the client(s).

Empathic Attunement

Thus, for example, if a mother or father or other adult caretaker says to a child, "You're making me so angry right now," the therapist might respond (if it's true), "I hear your anger, I hear the tightness in your voice—but I think I see something else on your face and in your eyes, and right in here [touching own chest] what I feel is a kind of sadness, a tight chest. When I tighten my chest like that, I know often I'm blocking something from a little farther down, right down here [touches diaphragm—again, only if this is true, now or in the past, for the therapist]. What happens for you, right now, when I say that?"

This is empathic attunement, or whole-person "presence," always the first and often the strongest intervention in all relational Gestalt work. As the therapist, one may well suppose that sadness—or hopelessness, or impotence, or grief, or something like that—is "in the field," or one wouldn't likely have "picked it up." But this supposition need not be "correct," as long as it is attuned, and self-congruent (for the therapist). If the attunement is good and the empathy is felt, then the client will likely experience some relaxation of the tightness and the apprehension of anxiety, which have kept destructive patterns in place—such as a pattern of angry response serving as a cover for more difficult, more vulnerable feelings. The therapist facilitates change by altering the old patterns through adding support for slowing down, contacting a fuller range of self-experience and awareness of others, and feeling safe enough to try new gestures, new responses that are outside our developed (and neurologically supported) habit patterns of contact and meaning-making. New support is added by "leaning in" to the client's words, feelings, embodiments, fears and longings, with authentic resonance and inquiry. The therapist's mirroring and interest in and respect for the felt experience and meaning-making of each family member (including the children) models what will likely be a new possibility for the couple or family, in how they see themselves and each other. We look for opportunities in real time to demonstrate the constructive and also experimental meanings we're making based on attention and awareness; saying, for example, "I notice you each seem to be holding yourself with a good deal of physical tension, not relaxing toward each other. Before I make up my own ideas about that, could you tell me something of whether that's true for you, and what it means to you" (which can easily lead into "imagination experiments," like "what would be bad or risky about letting some of that tension go, right now, just to try it out and see")? Or we might say, "Oh, I think I'm getting it now; you're saying that when you get that furrowed-brow look that your family interprets as angry, actually you're feeling worried, or like you're unsure about what to do next. Is that right? (and to the other family members) Did you know that?" This is the radically dialogic kind of inquiry, based on empathic resonance and also on authentic inquiry, that many families desperately need to see, feel, try out in session, and learn, if they are to turn a vicious circle of destructive communications into a beneficent circle of support and more nourishing contact all around.

These sample excerpts illustrate how therapists try to take advantage of the nourishing power of embodied, empathic attunement in every interaction—again, to offer and at times explicitly teach the missing skills that will make family communication and contact serve everyone's growth (not only the children's!). This kind of skills practice can also often serve as the material for homework for a couple or family: "So now every time you see that look (the 'hard' face, or the withdrawing, or other troubling signal), before you go off on reacting to it, the deal is you have to *comment* on it first. Just that. But do it really concretely: not 'now you're judging me,' but if you can, say 'now your brow is wrinkling.' That's all. Do you think you can add that step, and see what happens? Because when we do that here, we do find it changes what comes next, in a pretty good way."

Experiments and the Process of Making Contact

Experiment is illustrated at every turn—and with it, more and more, the idea and experience that every act of meaning-making *is an interpretation*. These "projections" (of what others might be feeling in response to me), when shared, can become invitations to greater closeness and shared self-knowledge for everybody ("I worry that that means you just don't care, or just won't try, or won't keep yourself safe," or whatever the anxiety-tinged meaning is that we have been holding so rigidly).

Each family seen, as well as each family's cultural context and meaning-making, will be unique, and needs to be understood from the inside. In Gestalt work, the goal is to learn the inner workings of a particular family's style and patterns of contact by discovering those patterns together, and opening them up together for greater understanding and the possibility of change.

In the case of the Habaneras family, their personal and cultural histories came painfully into play when their daughter Sophia was identified early on as having serious learning difficulties—a challenge that threatened the family's whole sense of safety and identity in the world. As an immigrant family who had "made good" in this country through talent and education and interpersonal skills, the Habeneras' self-concept and hopes and dreams for their daughter had been deeply shaken by the school's report that her learning difficulties were affecting not just her reading and numbers, but her social relations as well. Unfortunately, their hasty decision to address this by home-schooling Sophia had only worsened matters, transferring her school struggles to the home scene while isolating her from peers and social learning. By this time, at age 8, Sophia was constantly refusing to do her work while the parents fell into angry yelling and blaming each other for the issues with their daughter, creating a terribly painful environment of circular blaming and arguing.

The Phenomenological Stance

As is often the case, the first task of the therapist was to slow down and calm the reactivity of the family, and then to begin to understand the meaning of the intense emotions and meanings around this situation. Working from a phenomenological stance from the start of the first session, the therapist invited each family member to tell how he or she saw what was going on in the family, supporting an environment of not interrupting or correcting, instead validating each person's view of the situation, seeing it as equally valid with everyone else's no matter the age of the person. This practice would continue through the whole treatment, and gradually spread beyond therapy as well, helping the whole family to listen and validate each other's view.

Embodiment

Along with the phenomenological stance the focus on embodiment was introduced, helping each family member to become aware of sensations in their body, as the first signals that then become interpreted into emotions and meanings, thus enabling them to interact from this more aware place. In the sessions each family member was encouraged to identify their sensations and emotions, slowing down the process so as to stay in contact with themselves as they contacted the other person.

Working in the Here and Now

As the family continued the sessions, the therapist helped the family bring the "real-life" dynamics into the room, not talking so much about the previous week, but rather working on their feelings as they arose in the room, while the therapist helped the family become aware of how they made contact with each other. Mom was able to observe how she quickly started to get anxious as soon as the family started to disagree in the sessions and how quickly and rigidly she escalated to anger, expressing her felt desire to push everyone away. As she stayed with her anxiety she was able to identify a fear of abandonment: If she stood her ground with Sophia around the schoolwork, she was afraid Sophia would never love her again. With support, the mother could slow down and signal the family and therapist (and herself) when the anxiety started to increase, so they could all take a break in the process and allow the mother to de-escalate her arousal and share what was happening. As the family started this practice, Sophia soon reported feeling less like screaming and how an old familiar knot in her belly didn't come. What had been a fixed Gestalt or interactive pattern both for the individuals and the family as a whole started to become more flexible, more open to new possibilities. Gradually, over time, the family became able to put into practice at home what had begun as contact experiments and new behavioral responses in the therapy room. The resource of tutoring was added for Sophia, so that the parents could operate more effectively in their roles of first providing empathic reception for Sophia's frustrations, and then adding clear behavioral boundaries (no TV, computer, dessert, and so on until the tutor-assigned tasks—*with* a parent, in the beginning—had been completed). At the end of third grade Sophia was able to advance to the next year in school, and along with greater emotional confidence and calm, she was able to begin to have friends as well, while the whole family became able to have nourishing contact with new pleasure and closeness. Therapy ended, with the ongoing support of quarterly check-ins, to be sure the family was continuing to negotiate and apply their newly learned skills of greater emotion contact and transparency to the ever-new challenges of family life and ongoing development.

*Gordon Wheeler
and Lena Axelsson*

See also Listening, Empathic; Nonverbal Communication; Parent–Child Communication; Person of the Therapist; Self of the Therapist; Therapeutic Alliance

Further Readings

Lee, G. R. (2008). *The secret language of intimacy.* New York, NY: Routledge/Taylor & Francis.

McConville, M. (1995). *Adolescence—Psychotherapy and the emergent self.* San Francisco, CA: Jossey-Bass.

Spagnuolo Lobb, M., & Amendt-Lyon N. (Eds.). (2003). *Creative license—The art of Gestalt therapy.* New York, NY: Springer.

Ullman, D., & Wheeler, G. (Eds.). (2009). *Cocreating the field: Intention and practice in the age of complexity.* New York, NY: Routledge/Taylor & Francis.

Wheeler, G. (2000). *Beyond individualism.* Hillsdale, NJ: Analytic Press.

Wheeler, G., & Axelsson, L. (2015). *Gestalt therapy.* Washington, DC: American Psychological Association.

Goals, Treatment

In order to help any client be successful in counseling, the counselor needs to have a clear picture of what the client wants. Treatment goals operationalize (describe in achievable ways) what a client wants from counseling. Setting goals with couples and family clients may be different than setting goals with individual clients. Often the individuals in couples and family cases have different goals; it is not uncommon for each person to think another person needs to change. In couples and family counseling, the goal includes everyone who will be actively involved with treatment, and everyone needs to be willing to work toward the goal that is stated. Depending on the model of counseling, goals may be based on the counselor's perspective or the clients' professed wants and needs. In this entry goals are discussed from a collaborative approach where goals are based on what the client thinks is important. The importance of goals, establishing useful goals, and strategies for helping clients create goals are presented.

The Importance of Goals

Goals are an important part of making sure sessions stay focused on what the clients want to achieve. Goals are vital to counseling success, and are an established best practice in every helping profession. Discussing treatment goals in session helps ensure that counseling is focused on the client's goals rather than the counselor's. An exception to this general rule is if the client expresses potential for suicide or homicide, safety should be the immediate goal of counseling. In addition, if a client is not engaged in the therapy process then developing rapport is an appropriate goal for the therapist. Otherwise, treatment goals are typically determined in collaboration with clients. Overall, goal setting is also a valuable component of creating a trusting relationship (therapeutic alliance) between therapist and client.

Goals are typically established with clients during the first or second session and become a key in the case conceptualization and treatment plan. Goals should be revisited periodically because clients often become clearer about what they want as counseling progresses. Best practices guide the clinician to evaluate counseling by monitoring clients' progress toward goals, documenting progress or lack of progress in case notes, and addressing lack of progress with clients so goals can be updated or the treatment approach can be revised.

Establishing Useful Goals

Useful goals direct treatment and follow several guidelines. Most important, useful goals are focused on the *desired end result,* rather than what is *not wanted* or the *process* of achieving the goal. Additionally, useful goals are

- behavioral (able to be observed),
- measurable,
- time-limited,
- sequenced,
- specific,
- based on the person setting the goal (the client),
- realistic, and
- sufficient for resolving the problem.

See Table 1 for examples of useful treatment goals.

Different models of counseling approach goal setting differently. Some see the goal as the opposite of the presenting problem. For example, if the problem is that a couple yells and says hateful things when arguing, the goal would be for the couple to disagree respectfully. Other models emphasize helping clients identify what they *do* want, regardless of whether those goals connect with the presenting problem. For example, the arguing couple may decide their goal is to have fun together daily.

Strategies for Helping Clients Set and Evaluate Goals

Counselors must be skilled at helping clients set goals. Most clients focus on problems and struggle to describe what they want. Even clients with clear goals benefit from the guidelines listed earlier because vague goals may allow clients to continually work but never reach a goal, and without specificity, each person in the room may have a different idea of what the goal looks like.

Counselors practice strategies to collaboratively set goals with clients. Many counselors use the miracle question, which was developed by solution-focused brief therapists. In this question, the counselor asks the client to imagine that, while sleeping, a miracle happens and all problems disappear. But the client is sleeping and does not know the miracle happened. What would the client notice the next day that would help the client know things were different now? When clients talk about unrealistic changes (e.g., winning the lottery), the clinician asks questions like, "If that happened, what would you do differently? How would you treat each other? What would your partner notice was different about your attitude or actions?" These follow-up questions lead to specific, behavioral descriptions that, when combined and prioritized, can create a useful goal statement. With couples and family clients, counselors often ask each individual about his or her goals and help the family agree on common goals.

Revisiting goals routinely helps ensure that counseling continues to meet clients' needs and keeps communication open. Counselors can ask questions such as "What is your sense of your progress? Have things changed about what you want from counseling at all?" and "We started with [summary of goals], but I notice that you often talk about [topic] in session. Would it be helpful to revisit your goals?" When a client has reached his or her goals, the counselor can help the client set new goals or prepare for termination of successful counseling.

Susan N. Perkins

See also Clinical Case Conceptualization With Couples and Families; Progress Notes for Couples and Families; Therapeutic Alliance; Therapeutic Assessment; Treatment Planning With Couples and Families

Table 1 Improving Treatment Goals

Rough Goal	Problem With the Goal	Improved Goal	Explanation of Improvement
Couple will reduce conflict.	Focuses on what is *not* wanted	*Couple will engage in frequent clear, respectful communication.*	Focuses on the desired end result
Couple will work on building trust after infidelity.	Expresses the *process* of achieving the goal	*Couple will express trust in each other by sharing their plans openly.*	Focuses on the end result and includes a specific behavioral outcome
Family will be happier with each other.	Focuses on attitudes and/or feelings rather than behaviors, making it very difficult to measure; it is also very vague.	*Family members will eat dinner together three times each week and will do an activity together once a month.*	The behaviors are clearly stated, specific, and measureable—it would be simple to determine whether this goal was reached.
Couple will establish family traditions.	Open-ended—the couple could work toward this goal for years and not reach it.	*Couple will experiment with two possible traditions for five holidays this year and will decide which traditions to continue.*	This goal is time-limited and specific, making it possible for the couple to reach it.
The wife's father will honor the couple's decisions.	Not based on the client—the client cannot accomplish this goal.	*The couple will reach decisions mutually, tell others about their decisions respectfully, and consult with each other before changing a decision.*	The client can reach this goal, regardless of how the wife's father responds.

Source: Susan N. Perkins.

Further Readings

De Jong, P., & Berg, I. K. (n.d.). *Instructor's resource manual for interviewing for solutions* (4th ed.). Solution-Focused Brief Therapy Association. Retrieved from http://www.sfbta.org/trainingLinks.html

Gehart, D. (2014). *Mastering competencies in family therapy: A practical approach to theories and clinical case documentation* (2nd ed.). Belmont, CA: Brooks/Cole.

Nelson, T. S., Chenail, R. J., Alexander, J. F., Crane, D. R., Johnson, S. M., & Schwallie, L. (2007). The development of core competencies for the practice of marriage and family therapy. *Journal of Marital and Family Therapy, 33,* 417–438. doi:10.1111/j.1752-0606.2007.00042.x

Gottman Method Couples Therapy

Gottman method couples therapy (also referred to as the Gottman method) is a structured and goal-oriented model of couples counseling. Its research is based on data from over 3,000 couples in John Gottman's studies on successful, functional long-term romantic partnerships and marriages. The Gottman method includes intervention strategies designed to help partners and spouses increase their closeness with one another, aid in conflict resolution, create understanding for each other, and maintain calm during times of conflict. Specifically, the Gottman method is used to encourage romantic partnership and help negate marital or relationship dissolution, especially during times of relationship distress when repair is needed and recovery is still possible. This entry includes sections on the core triad of balance made up of three domains of human experience (interactive behavior, perception, and physiology), Gottman's "four horsemen of the apocalypse" (i.e., four relationship-harming types of interactions) and their corresponding antidotes or attempts for relationship repair, and the sound relationship house (a method for treating dysfunctional couples) including examples of interventions used in the Gottman method.

Core Triad of Balance

The Gottman method relies on data gathered from three domains of human experience: *interactive behavior, perception,* and *physiology*. These three areas are called the *core triad of balance* and are not independent concepts; rather, they are considered systemic, meaning that they affect, and are affected by, each other. Additionally, behavior, perception, and physiology contribute to a relationship's homeostasis (i.e., its stable, steady state of affairs), representing normalcy for the romantic partners or spouses. Gottman and research colleagues created a multimethod approach to assessment of marital processes, including assessing the core triad of balance. Assessing the three domains of the core triad of balance in conjunction with one another enabled Gottman and colleagues to accurately predict the longitudinal course of romantic relationships. For a relationship to survive and thrive, the stable steady state (i.e., homeostasis) must reflect more positivity than negativity in behavior and perception, and the physiological domain should remain calm and well as opposed to stressed and unwell. Each of the three domains of the core triad of balance is explained in further detail in subsequent sections.

Interactive Behavior

Measuring interactive processes between people is done by recording and observing couples' interactions in certain contexts and coding the behaviors and emotions that are exhibited by partners. Gottman uses the term *negative affect reciprocity* to explain the phenomenon whereby an individual is more likely to express negative feelings after his or her romantic partner or spouse exhibits negativity. Gottman and colleagues have also discovered that during times of conflict resolution between romantic partners in stable, happy relationships, there is a 5:1 ratio of positive to negative interactive behaviors. This means that for every one negative interaction, there are five positive interactions to counterbalance the negativity experienced. When negative affect reciprocity is experienced, Gottman method couples therapy recommends using the "four horsemen of the apocalypse" concept to understand and address the negative interactions, as explained later in this entry.

Perceptions

Perceptions of self and one's partner are assessed through questionnaires, interviews, and using video recall procedures in which recordings of their interactions are played to the couple, who are then asked to explain their perceptions of the observations. Perception is important in Gottman method couples therapy because research shows that in a happy, stable relationship, if there is a conflict, it is viewed as temporary and situational. In an unhappy, dysfunctional relationship, conflict is viewed as permanent and internally based (i.e., due to the partner's personal characteristics). Behaviors are perceived in likewise fashion. In happy, stable partnerships, when one partner does something nice for the other one, it is viewed as being a permanent, internally based function of that partner; in unhappy, dysfunctional partnerships, when one partner does something nice for the other, it is viewed as being temporary and situational. Gottman calls this phenomenon *fundamental attribution error,* whereby a romantic partner or spouse sees relationship problems as being caused by underlying flaws within his or her partner's personality or character. Perpetuating this phenomenon leads to distress-maintaining attributions of a partner's behaviors and perceptions that lie therein.

Physiology

Physiology is determined by measuring responses from the autonomic nervous system, endocrine system, and immune system and includes data on respiration, gross motor movement, electrocardiograms, and blood samples to assess standard immunology. Physiology is a key factor in the triad of core balance because it occurs beyond an individual's control and offers integral data that cannot be collected without assessing physiological functions. Heart rate reactivity and stress-related endocrine system responses are measured to assess an individual's natural response to an emergent situation (such as when one of the four horsemen is displayed). There are gender differences that exist in physiological levels of arousal when marital conflict is experienced. For example, males are more likely than females to maintain higher levels of stress after conflict with romantic partners; females are more likely to self-soothe using positive thoughts regarding their relationships after conflict.

Four Horsemen of the Apocalypse

Gottman's term "four horsemen of the apocalypse" refers to an approach for marriage and family therapists and couples counselors to identify specific communication patterns and dysfunctional behaviors that negatively impact romantic partnerships when exhibited excessively. The four horsemen include criticism, defensiveness, contempt, and stonewalling. The four horsemen, which are considered toxic and corrosive to romantic partnerships, are remedied by antidotes, or recommendations for correcting the problematic behaviors and communication. One antidote that is recommended for all four horsemen is to name them when they are expressed and inquire about them (e.g., "Things are getting critical here" or "This situation is becoming defensive—let's talk about what is really going on"). The four horsemen are explained in detail in this section, including repair attempts for healthy, stable long-term romantic relationships and marriages.

Criticism

The first horseman, criticism, occurs when one partner verbally attacks the other, globally blaming the partner personally (rather than the partner's behavior or the situation itself) for the problem. Statements that begin with "you never" and "you always" are usually considered to be criticism, not just typical complaints; adding blame to a complaint usually turns it into criticism. Complaints are not pointed at the partner, rather, the individual takes responsibility for his or her problem. Examples of complaints include, "I feel intimidated when you talk to me in that harsh voice," "It makes me feel really sad that you forget my birthday," and "I feel lonely when you go out without me." Criticism occurs when one partner ascribes negative characteristics to the other partner's personality. Examples of criticism include, "What's wrong with you?" "Why would you do that to me?" "You never listen to me," and "You always treat me like that."

The Gottman method antidote for criticism is called gentle start-up, whereby the conflict discussion starts in a more functional way; the partner's specific behavior is criticized (rather than the actual partner). Therapists using this antidote may suggest to clients that they turn complaints into requests, focusing on "I" statements. For example, a critical remark like, "You never let me know that your mother was coming to visit" can become a functional request such as, "I want to know when visitors are coming, so how do you feel about getting a family planner and writing down all visitors in advance from here on out? Is that something you will do?" Gottman and colleagues found that females are more likely than males to use criticism. A typical response to criticism is likely to be defensiveness, the second of the four horsemen.

Defensiveness

Defensiveness is the second of the four horsemen, and occurs when one partner feels criticized and takes on a position or attitude of resistance to perceived attack. Defensiveness is often exhibited as what Gottman calls the innocent victim posture whereby an individual maintains complete innocence and denies all responsibility for contributing to the problem situation (e.g., "What did I do? I didn't do anything wrong. Why are you blaming me when I did nothing?"). When one individual denies all accountability, his or her partner may interpret this as being blamed wholly for the problem situation, instead of sharing responsibility for the conflict. Some individuals exhibit defensiveness in reaction to either complaints or criticisms. A complaint such as, "I feel angry when you don't call me when you say you will" or a criticism like, "You never call me when you say you will. You don't care about me!" can be met with defensiveness, sometimes including a counter-complaint against or counter-attack on the partner to throw focus away from oneself (e.g., "What about when *you* forget to call *me*?! You obviously don't love me.").

Defensiveness usually escalates conflict, so the Gottman method antidote is designed to de-escalate the problem. The antidote for the partner who is feeling defensive is to take responsibility for one's contribution to the situation. Therapists using this antidote may suggest to clients that they make "I" statements and ask their partners for clarification in order to promote understanding between one another. For example, a partner who is feeling defensive will be encouraged to respond in a more functional, healthy manner, such as, "I hear you telling me that you think that I am not contributing enough to the relationship. Can you please clarify this for me so I understand?"

Contempt

The third horseman, contempt, enters when one partner feels negatively toward the other, and because of that, projects repulsion and condescension toward that romantic partner verbally or nonverbally. Contempt can occur in private, but is often most damaging to the relationship when exhibited in public settings or in front of friends and family. Contempt takes different forms, including use of sarcasm or cynicism, mocking or belittling one's partner, engaging in aggressive name calling, negatively exaggerating interactions and situations between partners, sneering or making faces at one's partner, aiming negative gestures at one's partner, and antagonistic humor aimed at one's partner. A commonly expressed statement of contempt is, "I could not care less" about one's partner. Gottman and colleagues found the presence of contempt to be the single best predictor for relationship dissolution or divorce; happy, stable couples do not exhibit any levels of contempt.

The Gottman method antidote for contempt is to describe one's own emotions and needs in the moment (for both the partner feeling contempt, and the other member of the romantic partnership to whom the contempt is being directed). For example, the partner feeling contempt may be encouraged to communicate that to his or her romantic partner (e.g., "I feel contempt for you right now, but I do not want that to get in the way of our ability to communicate and solve this problem"), rather than being covert or passive-aggressive. The other partner, the one to whom the contempt is being aimed, is encouraged to identify the partner's use of contempt and request that it cease (e.g., "I feel like you are belittling me right now, and I am asking you to please stop"). Contempt should not be reflected directly to one's partner if the partner is potentially explosive, abusive, or otherwise violent, as it may inflame the situation.

An additional antidote for contempt is to actively work toward appreciation for and within the relationship; this occurs when both partners lower their tolerance for acts and statements reflecting contempt within the relationship. The Gottman method teaches couples how to identify, rectify, and repair contemptuous exchanges. This is the most difficult of the four horsemen to change, but it can be done with cooperation from both partners.

Stonewalling

Stonewalling occurs when one partner withdraws from the other, effectively cutting off communication between the two. Stonewalling can take the form of the silent treatment, refusal of engagement with one's partner, general nonresponsiveness, reluctance to share thoughts and feelings, not displaying positive affect for one's romantic partner, or physically leaving the premises in order to withdraw from interaction with one's partner. Individuals who engage in stonewalling do not exhibit behaviors associated with active listening, such as maintaining eye contact, using brief assents or minimal encouragers (e.g., "mm-hmm" and "uh-huh"), head nodding, and facial movements (e.g., raising or furrowing brows, changing facial expression according to tone of interaction). Individuals who stonewall do not make eye contact; instead, they look away from their partners, often cast their eyes down, and engage only in brief glances in order to monitor situations with romantic partners or spouses. Additionally, when an individual stonewalls, she or he tends not to verbalize much and maintains neutral facial expressions regardless of the tone of the situation (e.g., keep the neck stiff, tighten the chin, and clench the jaw), the purpose of which is to control facial expressions in order to conceal emotions from one's romantic partner or spouse. Gottman and colleagues found that the majority of individuals who stonewall are male, and when females stonewall, it is highly indicative of relationship dissolution or divorce.

The Gottman method antidote for stonewalling is to compensate with physiological self-soothing, whereby individuals create differentiation between perceived threats and actual potential for danger and harm to occur. Therapists using this antidote may suggest to clients that they design conditions with their romantic partners in order to establish safe environments in which open and direct communication can occur. When romantic partners find themselves stonewalling one another, they will be encouraged to ask themselves, "What reason do I have to feel that I cannot express my thoughts and feelings? Is it safe to talk with my partner? Or is there potential risk that will result if I speak my mind?"

Repairing Criticism, Defensiveness, and Stonewalling

Gottman notes that criticism, defensiveness, and stonewalling can occur in healthy relationships in smaller doses, provided that effective repair and recovery occur. Members of happy, stable partnerships do exhibit criticism, defensiveness, and stonewalling occasionally; however, repair is what keeps the relationships healthy by promoting interest in one another, affection for each other, and humor, while lowering stress and perceived tension. (Contempt, however, cannot exist in happy, stable couplings.) Repair attempts include any efforts made by members of romantic partnerships to self-soothe or act as their own couples counselor during times of relationship conflict. Repair includes use of the aforementioned antidotes to the four horsemen, as well as any other attempts to openly communicate with one another, such as supporting and soothing one's partner, and expressing appreciation in order to use gentle start-up for a complaint. Repair attempts are successful when they decrease the level of negativity experienced among members of romantic partnerships or marriages. Repair attempts might include partners validating one another's feelings, coping with differences in opinion cooperatively, incorporating high levels of positive affect, or voicing respect for each other.

Sound Relationship House

Gottman's research shows that romantic partnerships last when the members of a partnership are friends with each other, appropriately manage conflicts, and support one another's hopes and goals for the future. The sound relationship house represents these functional, healthy romantic relationships. The Gottman method uses the sound relationship house as a method for counseling unhappy, distress-maintaining couples that do not regularly exhibit positive affect for one another or have the coping skills to limit negative affect during conflict and repair attempts. According to the Gottman method, the foundation of marital friendship lies in creating positive affect in contexts where conflict is not present. Additionally, members of healthy, happy marriages and romantic partnerships are able to regulate stress by de-escalating and resolving negative affect during times of partner conflict. Happy partners create shared meaning systems within their families; they create family philosophies, values, and morals that are upheld with consistent family rituals (e.g., holiday traditions), roles (e.g., parent, child), goals (e.g., saving money for a family vacation), and symbols (e.g., existential meanings assigned to objects such as one's home or family business).

Gottman's sound relationship house is not based on the idea that marital therapy should be crafted around how a couple resolves conflict. Perpetual problems lead to most marital conflict, so everyday marital interactions are assessed, which leads to awareness of how conflicts typically arise and are resolved. There are situations, however, whereby couples counseling is contraindicated, such as when one of the partners is engaging in extramarital affairs, there is ongoing domestic violence or intimate partner violence, or one of the partners is actively abusing substances. In these cases, individual counseling is recommended to take place before couples counseling occurs. Both members of a couple need to be in stable emotional states before they can learn how to make positive changes for the relationship. The Gottman method couples therapist is not going to soothe the clients; they need to self-soothe and soothe one another. An unstable individual is not likely to have the coping mechanisms with which to do this for himself or herself or for his or her partner.

Interventions

The Gottman method uses a wide array of interventions to address the plethora of issues that arise in couples counseling. Interventions are always selected individually and personally; there is no cookie-cutter "one size fits all" approach to use with every couple. Interventions are chosen based on the presenting complaint, whether it is dealing with blended families, dual earner households, stress management, or waning marital intimacy, for example. The Gottman method uses love maps in order to address each partner's knowledge of one another, asking questions like, "When is your partner's birthday?" and "What is your partner's major fear?" Another important intervention is called the fondness and admiration system, whereby each person lists adjectives characterizing the partner's personality that she or he appreciates about her or his partner (e.g., "I appreciate that my partner is funny"), then shares a memory of a time when the adjective was exhibited. Relaxation exercises are used when couple members have difficulty in ameliorating negative affect and stress during times of conflict. This includes physiological soothing, such as massaging one's partner or stroking his or her hair, as well as rhythmic breathing and focusing on muscle relaxation.

Rebecca M. Goldberg

See also Conflict in Couples and Families; Conflict Resolution; Conflict Styles; Couples and Marriage Counseling; Metacommunication; Nonverbal Communication; Power Issues in Couples

Further Readings

Gottman, J. M. (1979). *Marital interactions: Empirical investigations.* New York, NY: Academic Press.

Gottman, J. M. (1994). *What predicts divorce?* Hillsdale, NJ: Lawrence Erlbaum.

Gottman, J. M. (1994). *Why marriages succeed or fail.* New York, NY: Simon and Schuster.

Gottman, J. M. (1999). *The marriage clinic: A scientifically based marital therapy.* New York, NY: W. W. Norton.

Gottman, J. S. (Ed.). (2004). *The marriage clinic casebook.* New York, NY: W. W. Norton.

The Gottman Institute: http://www.gottman.com

GRIEF COUNSELING

Grief counseling is a mental health intervention for individuals, couples, or families who are exhibiting significant symptoms after the death or loss of someone or something that is important to them. These symptoms can be emotional, behavioral, physical, medical, spiritual, and relational. While the majority of people will never need or seek grief counseling after the loss of a loved one, those who do may find significant relief from symptoms and a quicker return to normal functioning. This entry first discusses theories of grief and grief counseling, the symptoms of grief, and the differences between normative and nonnormative grief. It then discusses the assessment of grief and interventions used in grief counseling.

Theories of Grief and Grief Counseling

Elisabeth Kübler-Ross's five-stage model of grief, outlined in her book *On Death and Dying* that was first published in 1969, began the modern study and practice of grief counseling. Her model indicated that most people who are grieving go through a very similar and typical pattern of emotions and behaviors, which include denial, anger, bargaining, depression, and acceptance. Kübler-Ross's concept of grief as a natural occurrence was groundbreaking, and she brought the conversation about grief into the mainstream in a way it had not been before. Arguably the most empirically validated theory of grief counseling to date, however, is William Worden's four tasks of grief. Worden's four tasks are (1) accepting the reality of the loss, (2) experiencing the pain of the loss, (3) adjusting to an environment without the deceased, and (4) withdrawing emotional energy from the deceased and reinvesting it in others. Worden believes each of these tasks, in no particular order, must be completed in order for equilibrium to be restored in a person, couple, or family.

Margaret Stroebe and Henk Schut are the developers of the dual process model of bereavement. This model poses two tasks associated with bereavement: (1) loss-oriented activities and stressors that are directly related to the death of a loved one and include crying, yearning, experiencing sadness, denial, anger, dwelling on the circumstances of the death, and avoiding restoration activities; and (2) restoration-oriented activities and stressors that are associated with secondary losses of one's lifestyle, routine, and relationships. These activities and stressors include adapting to a new role, managing changes, developing new ways of connecting with others, and cultivating a new way of life after the loss of the loved one. Stroebe and Schut suggest that people will naturally oscillate between the two tasks over time, and the process is not at all linear.

In the field of marriage and family therapy, Pauline Boss developed the theory of ambiguous loss. Boss outlines this most disturbing of all losses as either (a) the psychological presence and physical absence of a beloved person (as in a missing child), or (b) the psychological absence and physical presence of a beloved person (as in Alzheimer's disease). This model encourages grief counselors to prepare families for the traumatic, tumultuous, and often life-altering process of grief that might takes weeks, months, or years to resolve, if ever.

Regardless of the model of grief counseling employed, the most effective counselors spend the vast majority of their time simply listening to their clients without judgment or the need to change their state of being. Grief counselors elicit more details of the loss event from clients to help them not only release some of the thoughts and feelings associated with the loss, but also more deeply process some of the most difficult and confusing aspects of the loss. Grief counselors are generally not trying to fix anything for their clients, instead opting to allow the free flow of thoughts and feelings to help release some of the negative energy. Grief counselors often encourage clients to tell stories about the life or death of the loved one. Telling and retelling stories about the life and death of a loved one is one of the most effective ways to help a client feel some relief from grief symptoms.

Clients seeking grief counseling often report that they do not have people to talk to about the death of the loved one because either they do not want to burden others or they fear others are tiring from their pain and grief. Counselors can be ideal people to share stories with and to talk with about the most challenging aspects of grief. Grief counselors may educate clients about the process of grieving by helping them understand that grief is not linear nor is its course always predictable. Grief counselors often help clients understand that grief is experienced differently by everyone in their own unique way and time, so not to think that they are grieving incorrectly or that someone else is grieving correctly. In this way, grief counselors should also always be sensitive to and educated about the cultural differences among those who are grieving and tailor the interventions accordingly. Finally, grief counselors routinely assess for and suggest the person reach out to social supports such as family, friends, colleagues, or support groups. Many grieving people find symptomatic relief either when they are with others who knew the deceased or when they are with people who have also had a recent, similar, and significant loss. Most hospice organizations across the world have grief groups or grief counseling as part of their services or know those who do offer such support.

Symptoms of Grief

Grief symptoms can be experienced on a spectrum of severity, from mild to severe. Symptoms that are typical of those who are grieving include shock, anger, sadness, loneliness, depression, isolation, fear, guilt, denial, anxiety, lack of focus, longing, and hopelessness. While grief counseling is for those who are having difficulty with the loss, some may experience brief periods of relief if a loved one died after a long and painful illness. These feelings of gratitude are usually fleeting early on in the grieving process.

Marriage and family therapists and other mental health professionals may encounter clients who have as their primary presenting problem issues of grief. More likely, however, therapists will learn about past grief experiences in their clients that have not fully resolved and are still causing symptoms or problems. It is rare to identify a person who presents in therapy who has not had a grief experience in their past. Most clients do not seek grief counseling unless their grief is unusual, unbearable, or very long term.

Normative and Nonnormative Grief

Grief can be experienced as either normative or nonnormative. Normative grief includes the expected reactions to the death of a loved one such as tearfulness, sadness, mild depression, lack of focus, memory problems, intrusive thoughts of the deceased, and difficulty experiencing joy. These symptoms are temporary and mostly resolve or minimize within 6 months of the loss event. The vast majority of people experience normative grief after the loss of a loved one and notice significant symptoms in the first few weeks with significant improvement between 6 and 12 months after the loss.

A very small portion of people experience a more extreme version of grief known as nonnormative or complicated grief. The fifth edition of the *Diagnostic and Statistical Manual of Mental Disorders* (DSM-5) includes a draft of a new diagnosis for a form of complicated grief known as persistent complex bereavement disorder. While it is not yet a formal diagnosis in the DSM-5, they have included it to gather additional data to determine whether this extreme version of grief could be considered a mental illness and treated as such. There is much controversy about labeling people who are grieving as having a mental illness, even when they are experiencing grief in its most extreme form.

Complicated grief includes a number of factors and symptoms that prevent a person from healing normatively. Those can include past abuse, emotional avoidance, poor coping skills such as heavy drinking or drug use, the presence of major mental illness, and unresolved grief from earlier in life. Complicated grief is determined by the level of symptom severity and the length of time with severe grief symptoms. The symptoms of complicated grief are often the same as those for normative grief; however, a person whose grief symptoms are so pervasive and extreme that they are unable to function even in the smallest ways months or years after the death of a loved one should be assessed and treated for complicated grief. More than a year of these severe symptoms would indicate a need for assessment and treatment of complicated grief.

Assessment

The assessment of grief is an important aspect of effective grief counseling and should be done not only at the beginning of treatment but periodically throughout treatment. First, it is important to assess the type and severity of grief symptoms in a client to determine if the grief experience is normative or nonnormative. A number of questionnaires exist to measure grief symptoms and can be helpful to clinicians in assessing not only the current symptoms of grief but also for determining the effectiveness of grief counseling over time. On the other hand, a simple set of questions at intake or during a clinical interview can adequately assess the symptoms of a grief event in a client. An effective way of assessing for grief symptoms is to ask on a scale from 1 to 10, with 1 being not at all and 10 being very much, which of the following symptoms the client has been experiencing in the past week. These questions can be asked about the past month or past 6 months as well, depending on when the loss occurred and when the client is presenting for counseling. Grief counselors may assess levels of symptoms of depression, anxiety, guilt, insomnia, eating issues, tearfulness, isolation, inability to work, inability to care for self and others, ruminations, yearning, regret, and avoidance of anything that reminds the person of the loved one.

Grief Counseling Interventions

Once a person has been assessed as having symptoms that would benefit from grief counseling, the next step is to identify the best course of treatment. Thanatologists are professionals who are scholars in the study of grief and loss, and their scholarship provides an insight into the best treatment approaches. The Association for Death Education and Counseling is the professional association for grief counselors and scholars and is an important source of information to learn more about the practice of grief counseling.

Grief counseling may include an individual, a couple, or the family in the treatment and may be conducted with individuals or in groups. Interventions are best tailored to the client(s) and determined based on the type and severity of grief symptoms being treated.

Grief counseling is indicated when a person's symptoms, thoughts, and problem behaviors are unrelenting, concerning, and highly distressing. Grief counselors often use talk therapy techniques such as cognitive-behavioral therapy, narrative therapy, and psychodynamic therapy. Many forms of experiential therapies are found to be effective as well, such as play therapy, theraplay (a type of therapy focused on trust and joyful interactions), music therapy, dance therapy, art therapy, and other expressive therapies. For other clients, using Alan Wolfelt's "companioning" techniques may be most effective. Companioning the mourner involves the counselor "just being" with the person, and walking alongside him or her in a supportive, nurturing, and accepting way. The key to this technique is not trying to fix or change anything, but instead to be a companion to the person during their journey of grieving.

Finally, many grief counselors recommend adjunctive interventions during and after grief counseling. These may include exercise, journaling, reading self-help books, and good nutrition. These types of support activities are thought to supplement and enhance the effects of grief counseling. Other alternative interventions such as meditation, yoga, and massage may be added to counseling as well.

The techniques described in this section may be implemented in groups as well as with individuals, couples, or families. To be done well, group therapy for multiple grievers is best done with homogeneous groups and requires that the facilitator has some experience and training in group process. Facilitators tend to encourage members of the group to not go as deeply into personal details and content that would be better shared in individual sessions with an individual therapist.

Jennifer L. Matheson

See also Death and Dying; Trauma and Families

Further Readings

American Psychiatric Association. (2013). *Diagnostic and statistical manual of mental disorders* (5th ed.). Washington, DC: Author.

Association for Death Education and Counseling: http://www.adec.org

Boss, P. (1999). *Ambiguous loss: Learning to live with unresolved grief.* Cambridge, MA: Harvard University Press.

Ivey, A., & Gluckstern Packard, N. (2007). *Basic attending skills* (4th ed.). Amherst, MA: Microtraining Associates.

Kübler-Ross, E., & Byock, I. (2014). *On death and dying: What the dying have to teach doctors, nurses, clergy and their own families.* New York, NY: Scribners.

Stroebe, M., Schut, H., & van der Bout, J. (2012). *Complicated grief: Scientific foundations for health care professionals.* New York, NY: Routledge.

Wheeler-Roy, S., & Amyot, B. A. (2004). *Grief counseling resource guide: A field manual.* Albany: New York State Office of Mental Health, Bureau of Education & Workforce Development.

Wolfelt, A. D. (2005). *Companioning the bereaved: A soulful guide for counselors and caregivers.* Fort Collins, CO: Companion Press.

Worden, W. J. (2008). *Grief counseling and grief therapy: A handbook for the mental health practitioner* (4th ed.). New York, NY: Springer.

Group Family Therapy

Group family therapy is simply the practice of working with two or more families within a group setting. When performed by trained family counselors, group family therapy can be instrumental in assisting families with improving communication and modeling positive relational behaviors. This entry first explains the benefits of group family therapy and the similarities and differences between group therapy and group family therapy. It then gives a brief overview of group family therapy stages and group family therapy processes, discusses the counselor's role in group family therapy, and notes the ethical considerations of group family therapy.

There are many benefits of group family counseling, including a sense of altruism and the feeling that one is not alone in one's personal struggles. The group process allows individuals in the families to learn from those around them how to improve communication skills and practice new methods of interpersonal relationships. Groups allow individuals and families to practice their new skills in a safe environment before implementing the new skills within their everyday lives. Families learn in a twofold process: first, from their own family and the dynamics within, and second, from other families participating in the group process. Other benefits may include the ability of the family counselor to give all family members in different groups a voice or the ability to speak freely and express themselves in ways that may not be allowed outside of therapy. Group family therapy provides an opportunity for the family members to identify the family issues more clearly and work through them collectively in a controlled environment. Other benefits of group family therapy include educating family members about destructive group family dynamics, maladaptive communication skills, and social learning when family counselors mirror positive parenting techniques for parents.

Similarities and Differences Between Group Therapy and Group Family Therapy

In group therapy, individuals learn from each other, provide support, and challenge each other's beliefs and assumptions, whereas in group family therapy the family as a unit supports and challenges other families as well as the individuals within families. Gerald Corey noted some common goals of group therapy, such as developing compassion, learning self-trust, increasing self-confidence, increasing awareness, and developing alternative ways for handling problems. Many of these goals are similarly accomplished during group family therapy. One of the main benefits of group therapy and group family therapy is altruism, which Irvin Yalom, a prominent group therapist, discussed as the process where individuals learn from and teach each other by both receiving information from the group and providing it. For example, a client from a substance abuse group can learn how to better handle different triggers from the environment by listening to the narratives of his or her peers.

Another similarity is that both group therapy and group family therapy involve a group of three or more members; however, group family therapy may have multiple families that together include 10 or more individuals, and two or more families. In both settings, group members come together because of issues relating with others in order to work toward a common goal. Family members in the group often learn from each other by using the group as a safe place to display feelings and practice new behaviors.

The family counselor acts as a mediator as well as an extended family member and joins the system in order to help families accomplish their goals. Family members in the group can provide support to one another just as a group does by holding family members accountable for their communication and behavior inside and outside of therapy. As in group therapy, family members participating in group family therapy will have a chance to learn from each other through analogies, indirect interpretations, role modeling, and by trial and error.

Family counselors working in these settings need to understand the dynamics of different families clearly while facilitating groups of families. As family members in each group have an opportunity to continue practicing the strategies they have learned from the family group therapy sessions, the issues at hand can be worked out more effectively even when the family is at home. For example, the defiant behavior of a child in one family can be addressed with the whole family during the group family therapy session and the realigned roles and responsibilities of the child, parents, and siblings can continue to be carried out at home. As a result of that, there is a possibility of systemic change for dealing with issues or problem behavior. Group family therapy also provides an opportunity for the group members to identify the enmeshed relationships, maladaptive behaviors, dysfunctional dyads, and triangulations (situations in which two people in a conflict involve a third person to reduce anxiety or tension). With the help of a skilled family counselor, family members in either group therapy or group family therapy have a chance to work through and transform these unproductive relationships into workable alliances.

In group therapy, participants are not related to each other and they do not have emotional ties to other group members. However, in group family therapy, family members are related to each other and may have emotional ties. In group therapy, group members may be apprehensive because they do not know each other, which may hinder participation, whereas within group family therapy, members of each family may be apprehensive to participate not only because of fear of reprisal from their own family members but also because of fear of not knowing other families as well. Moreover, in the group family therapy setting, there is a distinct parental hierarchy along with the age hierarchy among siblings.

Just as the counselors have specific roles, families and their members also have crucial roles in the group family therapy setting. Sometimes, the responses of the individuals become complex and may be impacted by their own reactions toward their specific family members. In those instances, there is a good chance of projecting those unwanted behaviors on either the counselor or other families in the group. For example, a child who is disrespectful to his mother may tend to disrespect the other mother within the group or even his own female counselor. Family traditions and cultural values also play a key role in group family therapy. The family values of collectivistic cultures are significantly different from those of individualistic cultures and the counselor should be mindful of exploring these cultural values first. For example, Asian children may not actively talk in the group family session as they were taught by their family not to do so. The last major difference between group therapy and group family therapy is that when group therapy ends group members disband and may not have any further contact. However, with group family therapy, within each family the family members remain in contact and may even reside together.

Group Family Therapy Stages

When groups form they usually develop over time by working through different phases or stages. Gerald Corey, an expert in group work, identified that most groups go through the following stages: stage one, which is the formation stage; stage two, the orientation and exploration stage; and stage three, the resistance stage. Stage four is the cohesion stage, after which begins stage five, the termination stage. Families in group family therapy follow a similar format in which members learn to work together for the greater benefit of the family.

During stage one, group members or families learn the purpose of the group session, identify goals, and sometimes create rules pertaining to how sessions will be conducted. It is during this stage that group counselors communicate to group members the purpose of the group. Family counselors encourage family members in each family unit to identify problems and establish goals for their families as well as for the entire group. Setting the ground rules for the group family therapy sessions is important and should be conducted by the family members in each family unit so that they can be bound by the rules in the group session, and at home. Often groups are conceived with a prior agenda as it pertains to the population and purpose of the group in the group family therapy session. Before families are asked to participate, family counselors have identified a need, purpose, and time frame of the group. Family counselors also plan for how trust will be built within the group, how much participation the counselor will have directly with family members, clarification of expectations, and completion of necessary paperwork for each family unit in the group setting.

During stage two, formation of the group begins by exploring and establishing trust. In family sessions, although the members are related, they may still have issues with trust, perhaps more so because they have a past history, which includes conflict and sometimes trauma. It is important to remember that even when trust has been established within each group of family members that groups often backtrack, meaning that when issues or emotions arise and group work becomes difficult, members may temporarily revert back to their prior maladaptive coping mechanisms. It is the job of all group family members to assist each other with identifying negative behaviors and encouraging new ways of coping.

In stage three, group family members may experience different forms of resistance. Resistance is a type of defense mechanism, a way for family members to slow down the group process because of their own fears or anxieties. Families may show resistance by behaving in a combative manner with other members, challenging the family counselor, and creating deliberate conflict with other group family members. Family counselors may experience group members who not only challenge the counselor but also want to maintain control of the group. This could present many potential problems affecting the group cohesion process of each family unit. It is the job of the family group leader to maintain order, consistency, and balance so that all members are allowed to participate in the process.

During stage four, group family members begin the working phase, also known as the cohesion stage. It is during this stage that each family begins to work with each other as well as working within their own family and begins to trust the process of family group therapy. During this stage many defenses have been eliminated and family group culture has begun.

Termination appears in stage five of group family therapy work. During this stage families begin to evaluate their progress and hopefully have learned new positive communication skills. Families are aware that termination is next, and they may begin to plan for what should happen next. Family group leaders can offer referrals to other groups, individual counseling, or community resources. Families in group family therapy may tend to fluctuate back and forth between these stages depending upon the difficulty of the subject matter. For instance, a family may begin to work diligently during stage four but become resistant during the beginning of stage five because of fear of leaving the group or self-doubt related to whether or not they have accomplished all that they wanted to accomplish.

Group Family Therapy Processes

During group family therapy the family counselor has to make sure that families are selected based on a common goal or need, such as families desiring to improve communication. There are many group topics including, but not limited to, discipline of children, parent/child interaction, improving family parent/child boundaries, and navigating family mental health. During the group family therapy process, it is important that family counselors are comfortable with navigating the group process. It is recommended that family groups utilize a coleader model in which two family counselors work together to facilitate the group family process. Counselors may want to use a more structured approach by planning for activities such as games and art-related group projects. This structure allows family members to enhance communication by practicing boundaries, following directions, and modeling positive behaviors. Without this structure, it is common that family members in a group setting will deflect from the purpose in order to self-protect, especially during the beginning phases of group work. Therefore, family counselors need to establish ground rules early during the first stage of the group process as this will help to eliminate chaos later on.

Counselor's Role in Group Family Therapy

Working with families in a group therapy setting requires counselors to have knowledge of both group and family dynamics. It is important that group family counselors understand the emotional ties that may be apparent between family members, which may cause a strain on the entire group. It is also important that family counselors are comfortable with dealing with the issues of multiple families instead of only those of individual participants. Sometimes, family units may include as many as three generations of family members, such as mother, children, and grandchildren, which may add more complexity to the group dynamics. In those situations, family counselors have to balance attending to all members of the group or family units and should be skillful in reading nonverbal communication mechanisms of several people at any given time. In addition, family counselors need to be able to distinguish when to be an observer and when to join the group family process while helping the families transition into different phases of group family counseling.

Irvin Yalom noted some of the basic tasks of group counselors such as maintaining the group, building group culture, and encouraging the here and now. The task of maintaining the group is accomplished by helping group family members move past difficult phases within the group process. Family counselors help build the group culture by reminding group/family members about the purpose and goals of the group, and by facilitating the integrity of the group. Counselors can emphasize the here and now by reminding group/family members to focus on what is happening at the moment in an open and secure space that has already been created. In group family therapy, the counselor should educate family members on the importance of creating and maintaining boundaries, working collaboratively, and ultimately establishing the family homeostasis.

Ethical Considerations in Group Family Therapy

As in group therapy, group family therapy presents some ethical considerations. The counselor has less ability to guarantee confidentiality (e.g., keeping group information and family members' identities private) because of the presence of many members within the families and group, which increases the likelihood of members breeching the confidentiality. The need for confidentiality has to be explained to the group often to encourage them to keep information private and promote the integrity of the treatment process.

Other ethical challenges for the family counselor in group family therapy can arise from the counselor's role as a mandated reporter and other counselor responsibilities, client privileges, the need for informed consent, and conflicts among the group members' values and with the counselor's own values. If family goals conflict directly or indirectly with the counselor's ideals, then the counselor will have an ethical dilemma. For example, if the parents in the group believe in corporal punishment and the family counselor does not, then the counselor should work diligently to avoid imposing her or his personal beliefs on the family, as long as there is no indication that the child has been injured. It gets even more challenging for the counselor if the group family members express a conflict of values. Counselors in these circumstances may have to be familiar with each family member's values and should be nonjudgmental so as to be careful not to invalidate anyone's individual values.

All licensed counselors are mandated reporters, and are required to report any suspected or confirmed child abuse or neglect. When facilitating a group with various families the possibility of detecting abuse or neglect increases and the counselor may have to make a report to child protective services. The family counselor has to inform the families of this possibility and the duty to report during the first session of family therapy. This information should be in the initial paperwork signed by the family.

Additionally, other situations that a counselor may need to report to others, such as a client's self-harm or elder abuse, should also be clearly discussed during the first session of group family therapy. Counselors should strongly encourage family members not to share information with the counselor outside of the group that they are not willing to share in the group, because this will cause confusion and place the counselor in an uncomfortable situation. Lastly, family counselors should be sensitive to the multicultural issues of the diverse families within the group and should try to reiterate the need for respecting different worldviews among the group family members.

*Suneetha Babu Manyam
and Mayi Dixon*

See also Behavioral Family Therapy; Family Values; Multiple Family Therapy; Multisystemic Therapy

Further Readings

Corey, G. (2015). *Theory and practice of group counseling.* Boston, MA: Cengage Learning.

Hecker, L. (Ed.). (2010). *Ethics and professional issues in couple and family therapy.* New York, NY: Routledge.

Kilpatrick, A. C., & Holland, T. P. (2009). *Working with families: An integrative model by level of need.* Boston, MA: Pearson.

Nichols, M. P., & Schwartz, R. C. (2008). *Family therapy: Concepts and methods* (7th ed.). Boston, MA: Pearson.

Rasheed, J. M., Rasheed, M. N., & Marley, J. M. (2011). *Family therapy models and techniques.* Thousand Oaks, CA: Sage.

Yalom, I. D., with Leszcz, M. (2005). *The theory and practice of group psychotherapy* (5th ed.). New York, NY: Basic Books.

Group Parenting Classes

Group parenting classes are a type of parent education that provides parents with instrumental parenting information. The group format allows parents to learn and discuss the material with other parents in a single or specified number of group sessions. The duration of each session, number of sessions, location, and fee for service (if any) of a group parenting class program is usually dictated by the goals of the agency offering this service. Group parenting class programs are offered by various organizations such as school districts; federal, state, or local government agencies; and nonprofit groups. This entry discusses the reasons parents attend group parenting classes, the theoretical basis of these classes, and some of the types of group parenting classes offered.

Parents participate in group parenting classes for various reasons. Parents may be self-motivated to attend or may be referred to a class for a specific reason. That is, involvement may be required by a school district, child welfare agency, or family court, or participation might be completely voluntary and not mandated by any agency. The group format often facilitates the development of a supportive environment so that parents do not feel as if they are alone in their parenting concerns. Group parenting class curricula can cover various aspects of child development and parenting. While the curriculum of a group parenting class may be very similar to the information covered in a classroom-style parent education program, the synergistic combination of learning new parenting strategies and the development of universality that can occur in a group setting is beneficial to parents seeking guidance and support in their child-rearing practices.

Parent education grew in popularity in the 1970s. By that time, several notable theoretical forces had outlined key aspects of child development and learning. These included, but were not limited to, psychodynamic, behavioral, cognitive, learning, and humanistic theory. Each offered a perspective about the optimal conditions or stages for human development. Even though key theoretical concepts differed, the significance of the early years was viewed as paramount in many theoretical models. The post–civil rights era saw development of government-funded programs that lauded parental involvement. Head Start is one example of such a program.

Types of Programs

Group parenting curriculum is often guided by the developmental level of the child or specific challenges faced by a parent. For new parents, group parenting classes can provide essential information about basic caregiving needs. Normative stages of child development are also a common component of group parenting curriculum for new parents. The range of topics may include feeding, nursing, sleeping, car seat requirements, umbilical cord care, circumcision information, baby-proofing the household for safety, bathing, and attachment. First-time parents often find that participating in a group parenting class provides them a sense of relief and a baseline against which to guide their emerging parenting style.

Just as toddlers and preschool children have different developmental needs than newborn and infant children, so do their parents. Group parenting classes for these age groups are likely to cover physical, emotional, and cognitive development. Topics may include play, normative language acquisition, tantrums, limit setting, separation, and social-emotional concerns. Parents of toddlers or preschoolers with nonnormative development may also participate in group parenting classes that are both informative and supportive. Early intervention to address any developmental issues is optimal for both short-term (e.g., sleeping) and long-term (e.g., chronic illness) conditions.

Group parenting classes for parents of elementary school-aged children often focus on factors that impact the child's engagement in the learning process. This could range from school attendance and learning issues to addressing discipline and socialization concerns. Behavioral concepts such as positive reinforcement, the Premack principle, and use of token economies at home are examples of concepts that may be introduced to address common issues. Curriculum for group parenting classes at this level may be developed by the agency offering the classes. This allows the agency to address concerns specific to the topic and agency. Other schools or agencies may opt to use an evidence-based packaged group parenting program.

The Nurturing Parent and Active Parenting programs are examples of group parenting classes for this age group that have established goals and objectives and corresponding materials for both leader and parents. The Nurturing Parent (NP) program offers the children of participants correspondingly developmentally appropriate activities while their parents are attending the parenting classes. Group parenting classes meet once a week and are two and a half hours in length. This program has been utilized with teen parents who may have unique parenting needs.

Group parenting classes for parents of adolescents usually revolve around behavioral concerns. School-related issues such as truancy and completion of schoolwork are common themes of group parenting classes for parents or caretakers of junior high school and high school youth. The Parent Project is an example of a group parenting program that addresses at risk behaviors in 7th- to 12th-grade students. Group facilitators participate in a week-long training to be certified to provide this program. Research on the program's effectiveness is noted on the website.

Adolescence is a time when many mental health disorders that are seen in adulthood begin to emerge. Schools and public agencies may offer group parenting classes as a means of providing information about signs and symptoms of mental health issues. An example of this type of group parenting class is offered by the National Alliance on Mental Illness (NAMI). NAMI's 12-session Family-to-Family evidence-based education group class is designed to offer information and support to those who have a family member struggling with a mental health issue. Parents who have lived experience with the program's subject matter lead this free program.

Yvonne Ortiz-Bush

See also Active Parenting; Parenting Education; Peer Counseling

Further Readings

Barber, J. G. (1992). Evaluation parent education groups: Effects on sense of competence and social isolation. *Research on Social Work Practice, 2*(1), 28–38.

Bavolel, S. J., & Bavolek, J. D. (2002). *Nurturing parenting program.* Park City, UT: Family Development Resources.

Fry, R., Johnson, M. S., Melendez, P., & Morgan, R. (2003). *Parent Project: Changing destructive adolescent behavior.* Rancho Cucamonga, CA: Parent Project.

Mann, M. B., Pearl, P. T., & Behle, P. D. (2004). Effects of parent education on knowledge and attitudes. *Adolescence, 39*(154), 355.

Mullis, F. (1999). Active parenting: An evaluation of two Adlerian parent education programs. *Journal of Individual Psychology, 55,* 225–232.

National Alliance on Mental Illness (NAMI). (2016). *Family-to-Family.* Retrieved from http://www.nami.org/Find-Support/NAMI-Programs/NAMI-Family-to-Family

Schaefer, D. (2010). Saving children or blaming parents? Lessons from mandated parenting classes. *Columbia Journal of Gender and Law, 19,* 493.

Stolz, H. E., Vargas, L., Clifford, L. M., Gaedt, H. A., & Garcia, C. F. (2010). Evaluating "Parent Project": A multi-site inquiry. *Family Science Review, 15*(1), 1–12.

Health Issues

Health issues within the family system are common stressors for all families throughout the life span. There is an obvious systemic impact of illness on the family as the disease process often creates stress, role changes, fear for the future, sadness, and efforts to try to cope as effectively as possible. These experiences with health issues can create a *crucible effect* for the family. This crucible metaphor refers to a vessel used in the manufacture of steel. This vessel is able to withstand great heat and pressure to produce a product that is stronger than the component parts. During the creation of steel, impurities are also burnt off and discarded. When a family works effectively together during an illness, they can develop additional strengths and create a more effective family system, thus, the crucible effect. In some families, however, the opposite happens. Sometimes, the stress of the health issue, along with the family's inability to pull together, drives family members apart.

This entry reviews the common stressors associated with health issues across the life span. This entry further highlights how an understanding of the biological, psychological, social, and spiritual (BPSS) aspects of health issues can help individuals, families, and therapists explore the full impact that health has on the family system. By reviewing the impact of health issues in children and adolescence, adults, and the elderly, marriage and family therapists will be better able to identify and treat the challenges of health issues on the family system.

Health Issues in Children and Adolescence

Although serious health issues are not extremely common in children and adolescents, there are some common acute and chronic illnesses that do occur in childhood and adolescence. The following discussion outlines important treatment considerations when working with these age groups.

Acute Health Issues in Children and Adolescents

Acute illnesses are common across the life span. Many of the major infectious diseases have been effectively controlled through immunizations. Still, there are many acute illnesses that play a role with children and adolescents. Of the top 30 illnesses found in children and adolescents, over half are caused by infection. Viral, bacterial, and other infections can often create a difficult time for children/adolescents and their family members. With infants and toddlers, these infections often lead to sleepless nights for them and their parents.

It is important for parents to work effectively with their children during these difficult times. Many of these illnesses will resolve on their own but, because of the intensity of the experience, parents often seek medical attention. Some of these illnesses (and another common cause of childhood health issues: accidents) can be life threatening and involve extensive medical intervention and/or hospitalization. These experiences can create significant stress on the children and their families. It is also usually further complicated as these families with more than one child must balance the needs of all of their children.

Chronic Health Issues in Children and Adolescents

Compared with acute illness, chronic illnesses usually have a much greater impact on children and adolescents and their families. Some chronic illnesses are congenital (meaning since birth). The most common birth defects are heart defects, neural tube defects, blood disorders, and Down syndrome. These disorders cause significant distress in families since the expected outcome for new parents is a healthy child. These parents, however, have to deal with the loss of an ideally "healthy child" and try to manage and navigate important treatment decisions for their child. Other chronic health issues in children and adolescents include diabetes, asthma, obesity, attention deficit hyperactivity disorder (ADHD), depression, anxiety, epilepsy; other chronic illnesses may develop only later, in adulthood.

These medical illnesses add stress to these families as treatment regimens, doctor visits, hospital stays, and a host of other demands complicate family life. Stress, sadness, frustration, along with emotional and practical considerations need to be addressed for these families. The other huge stressor that occurs in some families is when a child or adolescent dies. These experiences often create a long-term grief experience for individual family members and the family as a whole.

Treatment for Health Issues in Children and Adolescents

Marriage and family therapists (MFTs) can play a key role in helping children and adolescents and their families with acute and chronic conditions cope with the stress of illness. One significant area of concern for most of these families is dealing with the out-of-sequence experience of illness. This is due to most people's perceptions that kids are not supposed to suffer from significant illnesses. These families may become focused or fixated on the perceived unfairness of the illness experience and be blocked from working together to manage and cope. For these and other reasons, MFTs can play a significant role in working with both significant acute and chronic illnesses. Helping the family navigate the medical world, identify support systems, process emotions, manage relationships, bond together through the grieving process, and cope with the stresses of illness are among the key ways MFTs can help these families.

Health Issues in Adults

Medical illnesses in adults also play a key role as a stressor. The younger the age at which the illness emerges, the more out of place it seems. Significant illnesses in young adults, young fathers or mothers, and during middle adulthood create stress for these families, particularly because most of the ill individuals play a variety of important roles in the family. This section addresses the impact of acute and chronic illnesses in adults on the family system.

Acute Health Issues in Adults

Acute illnesses in adults often play a significant role in heightening the stress within the individual with the illness and their family. Normal acute illnesses (e.g., minor infections, small accidents) can still play a significant role in adults as they do briefly impact the individual's ability to perform their roles. Work and family roles are often impacted during these illnesses. During adulthood, there are also significant health issues (e.g., life threatening and disabling accidents, heart attacks, depression, anxiety, strokes, significant infections) that play a huge role in the lives of these individuals and their families. Such health issues push these individuals, and often their families, to make significant changes in their lives and often require role changes within the family.

Chronic Health Issues in Adults

Chronic illnesses in adults become more prevalent as individuals age. There are many chronic illnesses that occur during this period of life. Some of these are created by acute events noted previously (e.g., long-term impact of strokes, accidents, heart attack) while others gradually emerge (e.g., type 2 diabetes, cancer, high blood pressure, heart disease, chronic pain, neurodegenerative disorders, migraines, depression, anxiety) along with the effects of normal aging. Regardless of the etiology of the medical issue, these individuals and their families encounter significant stressors and role changes as they attempt to effectively cope with the chronic medical issue. As unwanted guests to the family system, chronic illnesses often force families into lives much different than before. Families who effectively integrate and adapt tend to cope better and continue to function properly. Individuals, couples, and families with premorbid individual or relational strife not only have to deal with the addition of the chronic health issue but also the preexisting concerns.

Terminal Health Issues in Adults

Some of the acute and chronic illnesses progress and become terminal (e.g., cancer, heart disease, neurodegenerative disorders, strokes, accidents). For those individuals who are aware of their terminal illness, their families have to find a balance between preparing for death and enjoying the time that they still have. Death and loss often create profound grief and struggle within the family. Some of the illnesses have been so difficult for the individual and the family that there can also be conflicting emotions of grief and relief. Some of these families have time to prepare for the loss while other families are caught completely off guard. Both types of families eventually go through the grief process but each family member may experience it very differently based upon their personal history and personality. It is essential for MFTs to be available and allow family members to process their feelings and support one another.

Treatment for Health Issues in Adults

Key areas of MFT treatment for adults with health issues and their families involve properly assessing the impact of the health issue on the individual and her or his family. Crisis intervention, coping strategy identification for acute onset and chronic health issues, assistance with family role changes, and assisting the family as they share their unique stories and work to develop a shared meaning of illness are key aspects to effective coping. By identifying the type of health issue and how it emerged in the family, the MFT can seek to identify the common stressors usually associated with acute onset (crisis and overwhelming stress) and chronic onset (the long haul and experiences with the constant invader in the family system). These families often need assistance to deal with feelings of being overwhelmed as they navigate the health care system; having only a partial understanding of the individual's health issue can exacerbate stress and worry.

Health Issues in Older Adults

Later life is characterized by deterioration in health and functioning due to both normal, age-related changes, as well as illness. For some families, these changes create predictable demands on support and caregiving, changes in structure and roles, as well as shifts in power and responsibilities. Other families will experience crisis and dysfunction as a reaction to health-related challenges and the death of their older family members. This section addresses the impact of illnesses, grief, and death of older adults on the family system.

Acute Health Issues in Older Adults

Heart attack, stroke, and bouts of illness or injury require immediate medical attention for elderly people and often create crises for families. Older adults may face fears and uncertainties about future abilities and personal independence, which can shake the core of their identity. Family resources are called upon to shoulder physical and emotional support as caregivers and sometimes to help finance the burden of paying for medical care. Due to the sudden nature of this type of medical crisis, often a family member (typically a wife or daughter) is forced into a caregiving role whether or not she is willing or prepared to take on the role. The older adult may or may not be included in the caregiving decisions and the potential for power issues, boundary confusion, and unresolved conflicts to resurface within families can be high.

Chronic Health Issues in Older Adults

Nearly 90% of people over the age of 65 are afflicted with one or more chronic health condition(s) (e.g., arthritis, high blood pressure, diabetes, poor hearing and eyesight). Individuals who have chronic conditions can usually manage things by themselves through modifying their diets and lifestyles, taking medications, or using assistance devices (e.g., hearing aids and canes). Creativity can help older adults and their families maintain a balance between distance and connection while they adjust to the insidious health declines associated with aging and chronic illness. Changes in family structure and boundaries are usually more subtle and progressive, which can translate into changes that are not intentional or mutually agreed upon.

Grief and Loss in Older Adults

Loss is a theme of aging that can complicate the biopsychosocial-spiritual experience of illness for elders and their families. While physical healing and recovery may be possible, illness and injury in later life are usually experienced within layers of preexisting losses (e.g., physical abilities, independence, and social access). Assessing and treating grief is an essential component of working with any aging family, especially as they face the demands for change that medical illnesses present.

Terminal Illness and Death in Older Adults

The family's ability to adapt to a member's terminal illness or a death is affected by a variety of factors: the timing of the illness or death in the life cycle, the nature of the death itself, and the degree to which the loss is acknowledged. Complicating factors for families may include the centrality of the older person's role in the family or any unresolved conflict that family members may have with the dying person. Families that can access resources within and outside the family and exhibit openness, flexibility, and cohesiveness are better able to handle various death-related stressors and maintain function.

Treatment for Health Issues in Older Adults

MFTs can help families adjust and transition to the demands that illness and disability among elderly people can create. Because older age is synonymous with some degree of physical and functional decline, some of the challenges and demands associated with illness and disability can be addressed proactively. MFTs can facilitate family dialogues that are uncomfortable and untouchable, that can help give a voice to the fears, concerns, and wishes of older adults, while supporting younger generations with the expression of grief and loss. Crisis intervention skills are essential because, although some of the experiences in later life are to be expected, most families experience them as a shock and emergency. Throughout treatment, it is important for MFTs to be aware of their own beliefs and assumptions about aging.

Exploration of the biopsychosocial-spiritual aspects of health issues are key to truly understanding the impact of health issues on the individual and family system. MFTs can assist these families by helping them put the health issue in its place—in other words, not allowing it to completely take over the family system. Families that work together to develop coping strategies, shared meaning, and address the common biological, psychological, social, and spiritual aspect of health issues tend to cope most effectively. Although grief and loss is a common occurrence when dealing with health issues, families can pull together in mutual support of one another and effectively navigate difficult times. MFTs can play a key role in helping families cope with these difficult times. With this in mind, MFTs need to inform physicians and hospitals about their willingness to work with families dealing with significant health issues. Those collaborative relationships can result in improved overall health and coping for these families.

*W. David Robinson
and Mark S. Adams*

See also Adolescent Mental Health; Assessment, Biopsychosocial; Attachment and Health; Positive Psychology; Public Health Code; World Health Organization

Further Readings

Cohen, M. (1993). The unknown and the unknowable—managing sustained uncertainty. *Western Journal of Nursing Research, 15*(1), 77–96.

Hargrave, T., & Hanna, S. M. (Eds.). (1997). *The aging family: New visions in theory, practice, and reality*. New York, NY: Routledge.

McDaniel, S., Doherty, W., & Hepworth, J. (2014). *Medical family therapy and integrated care* (2nd ed.). Washington, DC: American Psychological Association.

McDaniel, S., Hepworth, J., & Doherty, W. (1997). *Shared experience of illness: Stories of patients, families, and their therapists*. New York, NY: Basic Books.

Patterson, J. M., & Garwick, A. W. (1994). Levels of meaning in family stress theory. *Family Process, 33*, 287–304.

HEALTHY MARRIAGE AND RESPONSIBLE FATHERHOOD

A healthy marriage can be defined as partners perceiving a marriage with a high degree of quality, satisfaction, and stability, and with generally low levels of hostility. Responsible fatherhood is closely linked with healthy marriage. It can be thought of as including three primary areas: accessibility (being available for the child), engagement (spending time with a child), and responsibility (being a reliable caregiver and financial provider for the child). This entry provides a brief overview of associations between healthy marriage, responsible fatherhood, and positive child outcomes in married, heterosexual households.

Marital Relationship and Responsible Fathers

Better marital quality has been linked to fathers having better well-being in the parental role, higher levels of parental involvement, and more positive parenting behaviors. Marital happiness for fathers, on average, is linked to lower levels of parenting stress. A harmonious marriage also may enhance one's enjoyment and satisfaction of being a parent. Specifically, studies show that fathers in more satisfying marital relationships tend to be more responsive, sensitive, and supportive to children; be better at setting appropriate limits for children; give more positive feedback to children; be more physically and emotionally involved in children's lives; and use less physical punishment.

Fathers' Prenatal Involvement

Prenatal involvement can be defined as a father's attitudes, behaviors, and activities with his partner during the time of pregnancy and the birth of a child. A father's feelings about the pregnancy of his partner are related to marital and child outcomes. Research shows that fathers who reported unintended births often struggle to demonstrate positive parenting behaviors to their children. These fathers also tend to report their relationships with the mother to be less stable. On the other hand, research suggests that fathers' prenatal involvement is linked with more stable and happier marital (or romantic) relationships and stronger relationship commitment. Further, fathers' prenatal involvement is linked to a higher degree of involvement with the child and reports of positive interactions ("quality time") between father and child.

Fathers and Child Gender

Father involvement often varies by child gender, and this difference in father involvement by gender can affect children and the marriage. When parenting sons compared to daughters, on average, fathers are more accessible, engage in more caregiving and play, and are more attentive and nurturing. Fathers are also more likely to discipline a son than a daughter. Perhaps due to the tendency for fathers to invest more in sons than in daughters, researchers have found that fathers generally play a stronger role in sons' cognitive and social development than in daughters' cognitive and social development. In a review of research on gender and family processes by Sara Raley and Suzanne Bianchi, fathers who have at least one son are more likely to marry the mother, have higher marital quality, and are less likely to divorce the mother, as compared with those who have daughters and no son.

Fathers' Unique Play

Fathers often differ from mothers in their unique type of play and interaction with their children. Fathers tend to spend a higher proportion of their time with their children in stimulating, playful activities. Researchers speculate that roughhousing with dad can teach children how to regulate their feelings and behaviors. Perhaps due to the more physical nature of play with fathers, two thirds of young children report preferring their fathers' form of play relative to their mothers' form of play. Fathers also tend to promote independence, achievement, and a focus on the outside world. As a result, studies find that children with an involved father are more comfortable exploring the world and demonstrate self-control and prosocial behavior.

Responsible Fatherhood and Child Outcomes

Perhaps the most commonly cited benefit in the research is the economic advantage of having a father who provides financial resources. Indeed, female-headed households with children have a poverty rate of 31.6%, as compared to a poverty rate of 5.2% of married households with children. A host of benefits come to children when they have sufficient food, housing, health care, and additional opportunities to pursue extracurricular activities. In addition to financial benefits, children can receive many advantages from having an involved, responsible, and nurturing father.

Responsible fatherhood has also been linked with advantages in intelligence, social development, higher mental health, and lower odds of engaging in delinquent behaviors. More specifically, when fathers are more involved with their children, children demonstrate more academic readiness to start school, develop better language and thinking skills, handle school stressors more readily, achieve better academically, and have higher intelligence quotient (IQ) scores. Further, these academic advantages extend into adolescence and young adulthood. Children with more involved fathers are also more likely to be securely attached to their fathers in infancy as well as more emotionally secure and sociable in early childhood. In addition, children with involved fathers tend to experience better physical and emotional health and are less likely to engage in at-risk behaviors, including lying, disruptive behavior at school, drug use, violence, delinquent behavior, and high-risk sexual activity.

Coparenting

Coparenting refers to the relationship between the mother and father in terms of the cooperation and communication in making decisions related to parenting. Not surprisingly, higher marital satisfaction has been linked with more positive coparenting. Further, research by various authors such as Eric Lindsey and Jacquelyn Mize, and Yvonne Caldera and Lindsey, have shown that positive coparenting is associated with children's greater well-being, secure attachment, and social competence. When the coparenting relationship is problematic, on the other hand, children are more likely to develop attentional difficulties, anxiety, and behavior problems.

Fathering Obstacles

Despite the many advantages of positive fathering, fathers may encounter obstacles to being an involved and responsible father, including poor examples from their own fathers, limited time, and media influences that portray fathers as inept caregivers. One particular obstacle is maternal gatekeeping, which occurs when mothers act as "gatekeepers" to a child and subsequently block or limit a father's access. Maternal gatekeeping can occur when mothers intentionally or unintentionally mock, criticize, or insult the way a father cares for his child. This can result in fathers prematurely giving up. However, some experts argue that maternal gatekeeping is just a way of blaming mothers instead of fathers and is an excuse for fathers not to continue trying to care for the child.

A responsible father contributes to a healthy marriage and improves child development. Many federal and state funded programs across the United States have been developed to increase responsible fatherhood and to strengthen healthy marriage. The efficacy of these programs has been mixed, with some studies finding improvements to families and others showing few or no positive effects.

Jared A. Durtschi, Cameron Brown, Jonathan Kimmes, and Ming Cui

See also Active Parenting; Birth Control and Contraception; Child-Centered Parenting; Developmental Model of Marriage; Hispanic Healthy Marriage Initiative; Single-Parent Families

Further Readings

Allen, S., & Daly, K. (2007). *The effects of father involvement: An updated research summary of the evidence inventory.* Guelph, ON, Canada: Centre for Families, Work & Well-Being, University of Guelph.

Caldera, Y. M., & Lindsey, E. W. (2006). Coparenting, mother-infant interaction, and infant-parent attachment relationships in two-parent families. *Journal of Family Psychology, 20,* 275–283.

Child Welfare Information Gateway. (2006). *The importance of fathers in the healthy development of children.* Washington, DC: U.S. Department of Health and Human Services, Children's Bureau.

Horn, W. F. (2006). Fatherhood, cohabitation, and marriage. *Gender Issues, 23*(4), 21–35.

Lindsey, E. W., & Mize, J. (2001). Interparental agreement, parent-child responsiveness, and children's peer competence. *Family Relations, 50,* 348–354.

Raley, S., & Bianchi, S. (2006). Sons, daughters, and family processes: Does gender of children matter. *Annual Review of Sociology, 32,* 401–421.

HIERARCHY

A family is more than a collection of related people who live together; it is perhaps best understood as a complex, interwoven system. Each family system organizes itself into smaller subsystems in order to perform necessary functions, maintain stability, and meet the developmental needs of its members. Sometimes these subsystems are organized by generation or by similar characteristics (e.g., gender, likes and dislikes, jobs in the family). How the family system organizes itself into these subsystems and the ways in which power and control are distributed and organized between parents and their children is referred to as the family hierarchy. This entry provides an overview of the origin of hierarchy as a construct within family counseling, a discussion of the types of hierarchical structures typically found in families, the importance of hierarchy as an assessment tool, and the relevance of hierarchy to the practice of family therapy.

Hierarchical Structure

Hierarchical structure is one of the primary areas for assessment and intervention in the strategic and structural schools of family therapy. In these schools, families are viewed as being composed of individual members and subsystems, which are also referred to as *holons* (e.g., parental, sibling, grandparent), whose functioning is organized around boundaries, rules, and roles that are influenced by the power structure or hierarchy of the system. Holons function both independently and interdependently. Family members may be part of multiple subsystems (e.g., adults may play multiple roles as individuals, spouses, and parents). As a family progresses through its life cycle, its organization is stressed via internal and external forces, such as financial issues, illness, the addition of new members, and community influences. Families with appropriate or functional hierarchical structures are generally able to adapt to these stressors and reorganize in ways that continue to promote healthy family and individual functioning. Families with less functional hierarchical structures have greater difficulty adapting to stressors.

Generally, a healthy family system is one in which the parental subsystem is in control of the children. This means that parents are able to give appropriate directives to their children and the children are compliant with these directives. The makeup of families can vary widely and it is important to consider the family's context when assessing the functionality of a hierarchy. Single parents may rely on the help of their older children to care for younger siblings. This may allow the older child to play a role in the parental subsystem. Such a movement between subsystems may be quite functional in this context. Intergenerational boundaries play an even more crucial role in determining functional family hierarchies.

Boundaries

Boundaries are the limits or rules regarding family member's access to or participation in different subsystems. Boundaries are an essential part of how the power structure in a family is established and maintained. There are three types of boundaries that correspond to three types of hierarchical structures: clear boundaries (effective), diffuse boundaries (insufficient), and rigid boundaries (excessive). Families with clear boundaries, where the parental subsystem is more powerful or "above" the child subsystem, create effective hierarchies. The parents are in charge of the children. Clear boundaries also mean that the parents keep adult or parental information within their system and do not share certain information with their children. Each person is able to maintain an individual identity, but close emotional contact is sufficient in the system.

Diffuse boundaries create less effective or insufficient hierarchies. In families with diffuse boundaries, the divisions between the roles of the members of the various subsystems are blurred. Parents may be too involved in their children's lives. Family members may also be overly dependent on one another. In the single-parent family described previously, if the older child who is assuming parental responsibility has access to adult information or permissions, diffuse boundaries may be present. A child who functions more in a peer role to the parent, children who dictate family rules, such as bedtime or curfew, and parents who abdicate discipline of their children to grandparents are all examples of the manifestation of diffuse boundaries. In families that are characterized by diffuse boundaries, members' individuality or autonomy is usually less well defined due to interdependence. Such a lack of autonomy leads to a greater sense of mutuality among family members that, in turn, often leads to problems of enmeshment, or codependency, in the family relationships.

Rigid or excessive boundaries are characterized by authoritative power structures in which the members have no access or ability to influence the hierarchy. In such hierarchies, the subsystems are distinct entities that are separate from one another. In families with rigid boundaries, autonomy of the members is evident and usually exists at the expense of the emotional contact and closeness that is present in families with clear or diffuse boundaries. In such families, members often become disengaged or detached from one another.

Impact of Hierarchies

A family's hierarchy can have a significant impact on the development of its individual family members. Structural and strategic family therapists, who highlight family organization as central to adaptive family functioning, assess hierarchy and often make them part of interventions. Both excessive and insufficient hierarchical structures have been shown to correlate with higher rates of substance abuse, delinquency, and attention deficit hyperactivity disorder in adolescents raised in these types of environments, as compared with those from families with effective hierarchies. Families with effective hierarchies tend to have greater success in adapting to systemic stressors and making transitions between family stages, which is where many families have difficulty. Family counselors can use the assessment and restructuring of the family hierarchy as a means to make substantive changes in the family system. However, counselors must always be mindful of the different cultural and contextual factors that influence the development of hierarchical structures when assessing and intervening with families.

Debra Hyatt-Burkhart

See also Boundaries; Ecosystemic Structural Family Therapy; Power Issues in Couples; Structural Family Therapy; Structural Maps

Further Readings

Minuchin, S. (1974). *Families and family therapy.* Cambridge, MA: Harvard University Press.

Shaw, D., Criss, M., Shonberg, M., & Beck, J. (2004). The development of family hierarchies and their relation to children's conduct problems. *Development and Psychopathology, 16,* 483–500.

Stanton, M. (1981). Strategic approaches to family therapy. In A. Gurman & D. Kniskern (Eds.), *Handbook of family therapy* (pp. 361–402). New York, NY: Brunner/Mazel.

HIPAA STANDARDS

The Health Insurance Portability and Accountability Act (HIPAA) is a federal law that was enacted in 1996 as a means of health care reform. The U.S. Department of Health and Human Services (HHS) in the Office of Civil Rights (OCR) is tasked with enforcing the HIPAA Standards. HIPAA is made up of standards, collectively known as the *Administrative Simplification,* that attempt to minimize unauthorized access and disclosure of individuals' protected health information (PHI). Through the health care system, HIPAA regulations guide the means by which health care professionals collect, store, and transmit individual PHI. Mental health professionals who work with adults and children, including those who work with couples and families, are considered health care providers and will be required to follow the guidelines set forth by HIPAA if they are considered "covered entities." Covered entities are health care providers who transmit any protected health information electronically. Because technology and electronic health records are becoming more commonplace in clinical practice, mental health clinicians need to be familiar with the rules and regulations set forth by the language in HIPAA. This entry examines three rules of HIPAA that are of particular importance to mental health providers: the Privacy Rule, Security Rule, and Enforcement Rule.

HIPAA Privacy Rule

The HIPAA Privacy Rule provides language to ensure the confidentiality and privacy of PHI in order to ensure that information is protected in the flow of health care while providing high-quality care and protecting individuals' well-being. Individual PHI includes data that relates to individuals' past, present, or future health information. This information includes basic demographic data such as names, street addresses, elements of dates (i.e., birth dates, admission dates, discharge dates), and phone numbers. It also includes information such as vehicle identifiers, Internet protocol (IP) address numbers, biometric identifiers, and photographic images. A major purpose of the Privacy Rule is to limit and define the situations in which covered entities can disclose PHI. Covered entities may only disclose PHI as permitted by the language of HIPAA or if the individual (or personal representative) provides written authorization permitting disclosure.

When working with clients as a counselor, all individuals must be provided with a "Notice of

Privacy Practices" that explain the situations in which the clinician does not need to acquire written authorization to disclose PHI. This notice must be presented to individuals at their first appointment for treatment, be displayed in a prominent location at the site of service, and be available to anyone on request. Moreover, the provider must make reasonable efforts to obtain acknowledgment of the receipt of the notice (e.g., a signature from the individual). The notice also informs individuals of their right as they relate to their care. Clinicians rely on their professional judgment and ethics in deciding when and how disclosure should be made. The situations in which authorization to release information is not needed include the following:

- *To the individual:* Individuals can be disclosed PHI in which they are the subject. In most instances, personal representatives and parents or guardians of minors are to be treated as individuals in which they could be disclosed PHI.
- *For treatment or payment:* A clinician who is covered under the language of HIPAA may use one's PHI for treatment and payment purposes. Regarding treatment, a provider may disclose PHI to consult, refer, coordinate, or manage treatment with other providers. The provider may also use necessary PHI in order to obtain reimbursement or payment for any health care services rendered to the individual.
- *Opportunities to agree or object:* Providers can seek informal permission to disclose PHI in situations such as an emergency in a manner that gives the individual an opportunity to agree or object to such disclosures.
- *Incidental to an otherwise permitted use:* The language of the Privacy Rule of HIPAA does not require that incidental disclosure of PHI must be eliminated if in the practice of another permitted use. In order to minimize risks of disclosure, the Privacy Rule clearly articulates that providers should use, except in certain circumstances as described in the law, the minimal amount of information necessary to complete the intended task so as to minimize incidental disclosure of individuals' PHI.
- *Public interest:* Disclosure of PHI is permitted without authorization as it relates to 12 areas of public interests. These 12 areas include, as required by law, public health (i.e., to control diseases), incidents regarding victims of abuse or neglect, judicial proceedings, law enforcement proceedings (i.e., to report a death or to identify a suspect), decedents, organ donation, research, threats of harm to a person to the public, essential government functions, and workers' compensation. These exceptions are discussed in detail in the Office of Civil Rights Privacy Rule Summary.
- *Limited data set:* In this case, data are limited insofar as certain identifiers have been removed (e.g., location or age) as described in the Privacy Rule. This limited data may be disclosed to organizations for research or public health purposes as long as the recipient agrees to use the data according to certain safeguards.

An individual's written authorization is required for any disclosure or use of PHI other than for treatment, payment, or health care operations. Counselors should make sure they have the procedures in place to collect such written authorization when practicing. An authorization must be in clear language and contain specific information regarding the information to be disclosed or used, the person(s) disclosing and receiving the information, expiration, right to revoke in writing, and any other necessary data.

Counselors often keep psychotherapy notes as a part of treatment. As defined by the Privacy Rule, psychotherapy notes are collected by a mental health professional in which the content of the conversations that occurred during an individual, group, joint, or family counseling session is recorded in any format and *kept separate* from the rest of the medical record. Psychotherapy notes are aspects of one's health record that are given an added level of protection under the Privacy Rule if they are *kept separate* from the rest of the individual's health record. Individuals who are the subject of the note must provide separate authorization for the use or disclosure of the psychotherapy notes. However, the Privacy Rule allows for some exceptions: (a) the provider who originated the note may use them for treatment; (b) the psychotherapy notes may be used for the covered entity's own training, and to defend itself in legal proceedings brought by the individual; (c) if HHS needs to investigate the covered entity to determine the provider's compliance with HIPAA rules; (d) if the covered entity is acting to avert a serious and imminent threat to public health or safety; (e) if the covered entity is providing them to a health oversight agency for lawful oversight of the originator of the psychotherapy notes; and (f) if it is required for the lawful activities of a coroner or a medical examiner as indicated by law. The decision to keep separate psychotherapy notes should be made in consultation with colleagues and with knowledge of state and local laws, which may supersede HIPAA laws.

HIPAA Security Rule

The HIPAA Security Rule exists to ensure that safeguards are in place at the workplace to minimize the risk of unintentional access or disclosure of individuals' PHI. Three safeguards are outlined in the Security Rule: administrative, physical, and technical.

Administrative Safeguards

Administrative safeguards exist so that covered entities can put systems in place that help ensure the protection of PHI. HIPAA language makes clear that covered entities need a set of administrative policies and procedures in place that guide the way in which the entity will meet the standards of HIPAA. Many standards exist as a part of the administrative safeguards that are designated as *required* or *addressable* (these are detailed in § 164.308 of the HIPAA standards).

The developed policies need to (1) ensure confidentiality and availability of all protected health information, (2) protect against any *reasonably* (emphasis added) anticipated threats or hazards to the security or integrity of PHI, (3) protect against any reasonably anticipated uses or disclosures of PHI, (4) ensure compliance by the workforce, and (5) provide sanctions for individuals who fail to comply with the policies. To ensure smooth implementation of these safeguards, the Security Rule requires an individual be identified as the security official who will be responsible for the oversight, training, and implementation of the policies. Ensuring confidentiality and availability means making sure that only those individuals with authorized access could and should be able to access that information that is deemed protected health information. HIPAA requires that covered entities perform a risk analysis whereby potential threats to the unauthorized disclosure or access of PHI is properly assessed so that the appropriate policies can be developed and implemented. The assessed risks will inform how providers will implement physical and technical safeguards to minimize potential data breeches.

Physical Safeguards

An important step in implementing the Security Rule is to minimize physical access to individuals' PHI. After conducting a risk analysis, potential vulnerabilities at the workplace from unauthorized intrusions or natural and environmental hazards need to be addressed. These safeguards may be thought of as the first line of defense in unauthorized access of PHI. Physical safeguards include ensuring appropriate access to facilities and workstations (e.g., door locks, locked cabinets), environmental controls to minimize loss (e.g., fire suppression equipment and fire alarms, lockdown cables on computers), and access controls to information systems (e.g., knowledge of who is physically on site during and after business hours). The Physical Safeguards also address how digital media containing PHI is to be disposed so as to minimize unintended access. For example, magnetic degaussing is a procedure used to ensure all data is removed from some hard drives.

Technical Safeguards

The implementation of the Health Information Technology for Economic and Clinical Health (HITECH) Act in 2009, which amends certain aspects of HIPAA, promotes the use of electronic health records (EHRs) whereby PHI is maintained digitally in an effort to decrease health care costs. HITECH introduced language regarding privacy and security to address the movement towards greater technology use. Technical safeguards minimize the risk of unintended access of PHI in a digital medium. For example, these safeguards attempt to minimize risks with hackers or information that is accidentally shared digitally (e.g., unsecured e-mail).

The Security Rule provides standards on controlling who has electronic access to digital media. Individuals who use PHI electronically should be given a unique user identification and passcode so their activities on the information systems are monitored and unintended access is minimized. Additionally, the use of technology requires providers to have procedures in place so that PHI can be accessed in the event of an emergency. For example, this may mean giving consideration to how data is being backed up or to having an emergency "mater password" that a designated individual holds to provide access in an emergency.

Using encryption is a way in which clinicians can render PHI unreadable. By encrypting PHI data, protected health information is rendered unusable, unreadable, or indecipherable to unauthorized persons unless they have access to the cryptic key. Encrypting PHI adds a layer of security and protection to the data. Moreover, recent amendments through HITECH allow different levels of protection from liability if an encrypted device containing PHI is stolen.

It should be noted that the language in the Security Rules is technologically neutral, meaning specific technological requirements are not specified. For example, hardware and software devices cannot be "HIPAA compliant"; individuals and entities are compliant, devices cannot be compliant. Providers should be aware of misleading claims from companies that any one device or software will make them compliant with HIPAA standards.

HIPAA Enforcement Rule

Individuals have a right at any time to file a complaint with a provider or with HHS if they believe their rights according to the language of HIPAA have been violated. The HIPAA enforcement rule establishes penalties for violating the HIPAA standards and outlines procedures for investigation. The HITECH act introduced stronger language regarding the amount of these penalties and new language about various categories of offense. Violations of HIPAA standards are classified into different categories of severity in which fines could range from $100 to $50,000 per occurrence for civil offenses and up to $250,000 and 10 years in prison for criminal offenses. Civil penalty categories range from "Did Not Know," meaning one can violate HIPAA unknowingly and still be subject to penalties, to uncorrected willful neglect. It is important for clinicians to be aware of HIPAA standards so as to ensure ethical and legal practice.

Tyler Wilkinson

See also Confidentiality; Ethical Codes; Legal Issues in Parenting; Practice Management; Progress Notes for Couples and Families; Technology and Families/Marriage

Further Readings

Amatayakul, M., Lazarus, S. S., Walsh, T., & Hartley, C. P. (2004). *Handbook for HIPAA security implementation.* Chicago, IL: American Medical Association.

Department of Health and Human Services. (2007). Basics of risk analysis and risk assessment. *HIPAA Security Series, 2*(6), 1–20.

Health Information Technology for Economic and Clinical Health (HITECH) Act, Title XIII § 13001 of Division A of the American Recovery and Reinvestment Act of 2009 (AARA), Pub. L. No. 111-5 (2009).

Health Insurance Portability and Accountability Act (HIPAA), 45 CFR §§ 160, 162, & 164 (2013). Retrieved from http://www.gpo.gov/fdsys/pkg/CFR-2013-title45-vol1/pdf/CFR-2013-title45-vol1-chapA-subchapC.pdf

Lawley, J. (2012). HIPAA, HITECH, and the practicing counselor: Electronic records and practicing guidelines. *The Professional Counselor, 2*(3), 192–200.

Letzring, T. D., & Snow, M. S. (2011). Mental health practitioners and HIPAA. *Journal of Play Therapy, 20*(3), 153–164.

National Institute of Standards and Technology. (2012). *Guide for conducting risk assessments*. SP 800-30. Gaithersburg, MD: Author.

Wheeler, A. M., & Bertram, B. (2012). *The counselor and the law: A guide to ethical and legal practice* (6th ed.). Alexandria, VA: American Counseling Association.

HISPANIC HEALTHY MARRIAGE INITIATIVE

The Hispanic Healthy Marriage Initiative is a federally funded project designed to develop and implement culturally responsive marriage and relationship programs that support and strengthen Hispanic families. The impetus for the program was to address the dearth of information about how to provide supportive relationship programming to a very diverse cultural group. While all programs developed for the Hispanic Healthy Marriage Initiative shared a central goal of strengthening Hispanic families, grantees were able to develop and implement programs that reflected their specific service populations. The project sought to address culturally specific needs that may vary based on a variety of issues. These variables, which are discussed in detail in this entry, include the spoken language, geographic region, and economic circumstances of the multifaceted and diverse Hispanic culture.

According to the United States Census, Hispanics are now the largest ethnic minority group in the country. This trend is projected to continue. In general, most social services, however, are developed to target the European-American or non-Hispanic white cultural group. In order to provide culturally relevant services to a growing Hispanic population, effective marriage and relationship education must be developed and existing programs adapted to ensure key cultural concepts are addressed. The Administration for Children and Families (ACF) and the Office of the Assistant Secretary for Planning and Evaluation (ASPE) provided the funding for this federal project. Both of these funding federal agencies are under the jurisdiction of the Department of Health and Human Services (HHS).

The Hispanic Healthy Marriage Initiative developed a series of five briefs to document the progression of this project. The information reported in this entry is based on those documents that were published over a span of 3 years, 2010 to 2013. At the beginning of the project, Hispanic Healthy Marriage Initiative grantees were screened to ensure they met four site selection criteria. These included: (1) being fully operational and not at the start-up stage, (2) having funding to support operations throughout the course of the initiative, (3) having a service population that was more than half Hispanic, and (4) consenting to provide outcome measures for study evaluation. Grantees that met the above site selection criteria were then evaluated and selected to ensure they represented different parts of the United States and their service populations were varied along several dimensions (identified country of origin, marital status and acculturation among other factors). Final grantees were also chosen for variance in their delivery of core curriculum (marriage and relationship or fatherhood focus), their method of service delivery (single or multiple sessions), and their offering of ancillary supportive services, Finally, the nine grantees had different federal funding sources. All worked with their local domestic violence organizations to ensure appropriate resources and referrals for program participants.

Hispanic Healthy Marriage Initiative Grantees

There were nine Hispanic Healthy Marriage Initiative grantees. Grantee program names and locations (in alphabetical order) were: (1) AVANCE (Houston, Texas); (2) Creciendo Unidos (Phoenix, Arizona); (3) Education Service Center 19 (El Paso, Texas); (4) Granato Group (Vienna, Virginia) (5) Holyoke/Chicopee/Springfield Head Start (Springfield, Massachusetts); (6) Meier Clinics (Chicago, Illinois); (7) New Mexico State University (Las Cruces, New Mexico); (8) Puerto Rican Family Institute (New York, New York); and (9) TELACU (Los Angeles, California). All nine programs served married and unmarried Hispanic couples. All but one, Holyoke/Chicopee/Springfield

(HCS) Head Start, provided services to Hispanic immigrants. Two programs, HCS Head Start and New Mexico State University, served migrant individuals. Almost all of the programs accommodated individuals with varying acculturation levels in their programming. Hispanic Healthy Marriage Initiative grantees' programs included participants of Mexican, Central American, South American, Puerto Rican, and Dominican origin.

The programming itself was very diverse. Five of the nine programs were created by their sponsoring organization to meet the specific cultural needs of their clientele. Most of the grantees were agencies in the southwestern region of the county, two were in the northeastern region, and one agency had sites in both the middle and mid-Atlantic regions. The shortest curriculum was 8 hours (TELACU) and the longest was 24 hours (Education Service Center 19); however, the average length of most programs was approximately 16 hours. Some programming incorporated frequent contact via weekly meetings while other programming provided information in longer sessions over fewer meeting dates. Three programs provided complimentary services to participants' children at the same time their parents were engaged in services.

Yvonne Ortiz-Bush

See also Couples and Marriage Counseling; Cultural Issues in Couples and Families; Family Mediation; Family Resilience; Healthy Marriage and Responsible Fatherhood; Latino Families; Marriage Education; Positive Psychology

Further Readings

Bouchet, S., Torres, L., & Hyra, A. (2012). *HHMI grantee implementation evaluation: Marketing, recruitment and retention strategies.* OPRE Report 2012-24. Washington, DC: Office of Planning, Research and Evaluation, Administration for Children and Families, U.S. Department of Health and Human Services.

Bouchet, S., Torres, L., & Hyra, A. (2013). *HHMI grantee implementation evaluation: Addressing domestic violence in Hispanic healthy relationship programs.* OPRE Report 2012-35. Washington, DC: Office of Planning, Research and Evaluation, Administration for Children and Families, U.S. Department of Health and Human Services.

Bouchet, S., Torres, L., & Hyra, A. (2013). *HHMI grantee implementation evaluation: Understanding Hispanic diversity: A "one size approach" to service delivery may not fit all.* OPRE Report 2012-52. Washington, DC: Office of Planning, Research and Evaluation, Administration for Children and Families, U.S. Department of Health and Human Services.

Torres, L., Hyra, A., & Bouchet, S. (2013). *HHMI grantee implementation evaluation: Hispanics and family-strengthening programs: Cultural strategies to enhance program participation.* OPRE Report 2013-19. Washington, DC: Office of Planning, Research and Evaluation, Administration for Children and Families, U.S. Department of Health and Human Services.

Hoarding

Hoarding describes the activities of a person who has difficulties getting rid of possessions, regardless of their value, and is often accompanied by excessive acquisition of particular items. Hoarding disorder was added to the fifth edition of the American Psychiatric Association's *Diagnostic and Statistical Manual of Mental Disorders* (DSM-5) as a stand-alone diagnosis. Hoarding has been defined through three criteria: (1) the acquisition of, and failure to discard, a large number of possessions; (2) clutter that precludes activities for which living spaces were designed; and (3) significant distress and impairment in functioning caused by the hoarding. The behavior has been referred to as "pathological collecting," and due to the significantly cluttered living space that can result from the behavior, it has been found to cause large amounts of distress and impairment for individuals who hoard and their family members, both living in and outside the hoarded home. Estimates project that 2% to 5% of the individuals in the United States meet standards for clinically significant problems with hoarding. Hoarding can cause problematic relationships and sometimes dangerous situations for individuals, couples, and families. This entry summarizes the definition, etiology, treatment, ethical and legal issues, and special populations relevant to this topic.

Etiology

There are various hypotheses about the etiology (cause) of hoarding. These include biological, psychological, and social factors. There may be a genetic link to hoarding, as it tends to affect multiple family members. In addition, hoarding may be impacted by psychological issues such as anxiety and depression and may be exacerbated by traumatic events across the life span.

Biological Factors

A genetic etiology of hoarding behavior has been supported through several studies. Genetic studies have found significant chromosome linkage to obsessive-compulsive disorder (OCD) in families with two or more hoarding relatives, and research has also shown hoarding behavior to affect multiple family members, with a large proportion of persons who hoard reporting at least one other first-degree relative with hoarding problems. Studies of sibling pairs have also shown that hoarding is familial.

Hoarding is generally thought to have a chronic course with early onset, with most individuals reporting symptoms that began during childhood or adolescence. The average age of reported onset is between 11 and 15, with most reporting onset before age 21; later onset (i.e., after the age of 40) is rare. Childhood hoarding behaviors are typically mild, with more severe symptoms emerging after the age of 40, suggesting that hoarding symptoms, such as clutter, take many years to develop and thus do not become severe until decades after onset.

Individuals who hoard may have neuropsychological functioning deficits related to their hoarding behaviors. Individuals with hoarding disorder may be characterized by problems related to sustained attention, impulsivity, and problem-solving, as well as possible problems of memory and the use of adaptive memory strategies. Brain differences also are thought to underlie problems of decision-making, attachment to objects, reward processing, impulse control, self-awareness, and emotion regulation in individuals who hoard.

Psychological Factors

Psychological comorbidity occurs in up to 92% of individuals who meet criteria for hoarding disorder. While hoarding has historically been considered a subtype of OCD, studies have shown that individuals with hoarding disorder are more likely to meet criteria for depression or other anxiety disorders than OCD. Major depressive disorder is the most common comorbid diagnosis associated with hoarding disorder. Other commonly associated comorbidities include anxiety disorders, attention deficit hyperactivity disorder, and other mood disorders.

The cognitive-behavioral model of hoarding argues that the manifestations of hoarding (acquisition, saving, and clutter) result in the interaction of four main factors that work together to create and maintain hoarding behavior: (1) information-processing deficits, (2) emotional attachment to objects, (3) behavioral avoidance, and (4) erroneous beliefs concerning possessions. The model offers many benefits to understanding the behaviors of an individual who hoards, which allows for multiple points of intervention for psychotherapists who are working on treating hoarding behaviors in their clients. To date, most treatment research conducted on hoarding disorder is from a cognitive-behavioral approach.

Social Factors

Hoarding behavior has been found to have a major emotional and psychological impact on family functioning. Living with an individual who hoards during childhood has been associated with elevated reports of distress and family strain. Loved ones of individuals who hoard have reported higher levels of negative relational feelings, including anger, resentment, guilt, frustration, and rejection. These negative feelings can contribute to alienation of family members and fragmentation of these relationships. Despite this, positive family relationships have been shown to serve as a protective factor against increased hoarding severity following a stressful life event, which speaks to the importance of incorporating a family focus into treatment for hoarding disorder.

Research has linked the onset and severity of hoarding behavior to the occurrence of stressful life events. Negative childhood events and experiences of trauma may act as triggering events for hoarding behavior, and higher levels of current distress related to a traumatic event has been found to be predictive of higher levels of hoarding severity. People who hoard are also significantly more likely than people who do not hoard to report a childhood history of parental psychiatric illness, home break-ins, interpersonal violence, and excessive physical discipline. People who hoard who have a later age of onset of hoarding behavior have been found to be more likely to have experienced stressful life events that occurred around the time of onset of the behaviors than those who reported an earlier age of onset.

Focusing on possessions and having trouble discarding them may also be influenced by culture. Hoarding has been found to be a problem across the Western, consumer-driven cultures in which it has been studied. To date, no studies have been conducted to understand the contribution of cultural differences to hoarding behaviors.

Treatment Approaches

The DSM-5 diagnosis for hoarding disorder involves criteria relating to difficulty discarding possessions, clutter that has accumulated to prevent the use of living spaces for their intended purposes, and resulting clinical distress or impairment that results. Excessive acquisition and level of insight are included as specifiers to the diagnosis. In addition, approximately 75% of people with hoarding disorder have mood or anxiety issues such as depression, social anxiety, and some may meet the criteria for OCD. There are several treatment approaches that may be used with hoarding disorder.

Behavioral interventions, support groups, and family therapy are all useful ways to approach hoarding. Behavioral therapy is a helpful way to address the thoughts, actions, and feelings connected to hoarding. Using interventions such as behavioral experiments and exposure techniques to introduce the client to the idea of discarding or of not acquiring is a helpful process that encourages the client to become comfortable with the discomfort. Support groups have been found to provide a safe community for people who hoard and for their family members to learn about the impact of hoarding, as well as give a space to talk freely about frustrations, concerns, and fears related to the hoarding behaviors. Family therapy can also help family members with better communication skills and even role-playing and coaching that can lead to better relationships within the family.

Helping people with hoarding disorder can involve a variety of professionals, including medical, psychological, and social workers. A task force is an organized group of professionals working toward developing a practice of coordinated response from a variety of community fields. The objectives of task forces are to provide public education about hoarding, give out service agency information, and provide support to individuals, families, and communities. There are currently no medications for the treatment of hoarding; however, medications may be helpful in managing symptoms that are related to the hoarding or co-occurring disorders. Use of medications to manage the symptoms of these diagnoses can be helpful to continue the process without undue harm to the client. In severe hoarding situations, authorities may determine that a home is unsafe for habitation and mandate an *abatement,* or clean-out intervention in which the home must be cleaned and brought into compliance, either by the homeowner or the municipality. Currently there is no research to support the effectiveness of these types of interventions as appropriate or ethical approaches for managing severe hoarding situations.

Legal and Ethical Issues

There are physical safety, health, housing, confidentiality, and ethical issues involved with assisting someone with hoarding disorder. Because of the complexity of physical, psychological, and social problems that may be present when someone hoards, multiple professionals will most likely have to be involved. In addition, the home of someone who hoards may be a danger to the person, the family, or the community.

Hoarded homes present increased risks to the physical safety and health of the person who hoards, family members, neighbors and communities, and public safety officials. Safety of a home is determined by city laws and housing codes which include, among other requirements, accessible pathways through the home, cleared entrances and exits, working smoke alarms, and nonflammable materials in the home. Hoarded homes also present a greater risk to the personal health of those impacted, including upper respiratory issues and diseases related to the improper disposal of animal and human waste. Other personal health risks may be to personal hygiene and grooming, poor attention to medical needs and finances, as well as inability to get adequate sleep. Because of the hoarding, clients may be in danger of being evicted. The Fair Housing Act of 1968 (FHA) was enacted to enforce rights of tenants against discrimination based on their race, gender, religion, national origin, familial status, or disability. Clinicians may be asked to request a reasonable accommodation based on hoarding disorder in order to allow a client more time to create an action plan to help maintain the tenant's compliance as well as allowing them to have control over how their home is going to be sorted.

Due to the delicate nature of working with a person who hoards, confidentiality and the consideration of ethical dilemmas are crucial. Collaborative relationships between a variety of professionals may require several releases of information to be signed by the client in order for a therapist to appropriately consult and coordinate client care. Obtaining a release of information document for each professional with whom one comes into contact is essential for confidentiality purposes. For documentation or assessment purposes, a therapist may also choose to obtain a photography release in order to document visual progress of client work in the home. In addition, ethical dilemmas may occur for a clinician who works with hoarding clients if there is an imminent threat of harm to any vulnerable populations, including vulnerable adults or children. Clinicians must be aware of state reporting laws and connect with protective services if they have concerns about the safety and welfare of a vulnerable person.

Special Populations

Older Adults

Hoarding tendencies are typically more dangerous for seniors as they may have physical as well as cognitive limitations. The severity of hoarding increases in age due to a variety of reasons. If the individual has never received any treatment for hoarding disorder, their hoarding tendencies may have worsened. The individual may have multiple comorbidities including anxiety and depression, coupled with a worsening cognitive state.

Children

Hoarding in children has a median age of 11 years and can be characterized with the following symptoms: an overactive acquisition of items within their possession, a failure to discard any of them when necessary, and when discard occurs there is a substantial amount of distress such as symptoms related to disruptive disorder. Items that children who hoard have been found to hoard typically involve nostalgia items, such as baby clothes, previous schoolwork, as well as nonvaluable items including broken objects. In more severe cases, trash has been hoarded, such as empty food containers or food wrappers. In addition, children who hoard can have unhealthy eating habits due to hoarding food, which may lead to obesity.

Cognitive/Developmental Disabilities

Some research has indicated that there is a difference between organic hoarding and hoarding disorder. Hoarding disorder begins during middle childhood or early adolescence. Organic hoarding occurs due to a brain injury or lesion on the brain. People who suffer from organic hoarding tend to hoard objects such as rotting food and garbage as well as bodily waste. People who suffer from this type of hoarding may have no interest in the items, or intent to use them, in contrast with those who suffer from hoarding disorder. Furthermore, those who suffer from organic hoarding appear to undergo a distinct personality change occur.

Animal Hoarding

Animal hoarding describes the actions of an individual who accumulates a quantity of animals and cannot provide basic minimum care for them, such as proper nutrition, veterinary care, adequate housing, and sanitation. Individuals who hoard animals describe themselves as animal lovers and have the intention of taking care of their pets, but given the sheer number of pets they have taken on and because they are often unemployed, they lack the means to do so. Typically the home in which they and their animals are living is squalid; unsanitary conditions may include the presence of rotting food, feces, or urine. Level of insight about behaviors is low and other psychological comorbidity is high in this population. Owing to lack of research, little is known about animal hoarding or options for treatment. People who hoard animals are typically reported by neighbors' complaints to animal care and control services, who then send officers to visit the home.

*Jennifer Sampson,
Janet Yeats, and Leslie Shapiro*

See also Cognitive-Behavioral Couples Therapy; Cognitive-Behavioral Family Therapy; Confidentiality; Conflict in Couples and Family; DSM and V-Codes

Further Readings

Bratiotis, C., Schmalish, C. S., & Steketee, G. (2011). *The Hoarding handbook: A guide for human service professionals.* New York, NY: Oxford University Press.

Frost, R. O., & Steketee, G. (2014). *The Oxford handbook of hoarding and acquiring.* New York, NY: Oxford University Press.

Muroff, J., & Underwood, P. (2014). *Group treatment for hoarding disorder: Therapist guide (treatments that work).* New York, NY: Oxford University Press.

Steketee, G., & Frost, R. O. (2013). *Treatment for hoarding disorder: Therapist guide (treatments that work).* New York, NY: Oxford University Press.

Tolin, D., Frost, R. O., & Steketee, G. (2013). *Buried in treasures: Help for compulsive acquiring, saving, and hoarding.* New York, NY: Oxford University Press.

Tompkins, M. A., & Hartl, T. L. (2015). *Clinician's guide to severe hoarding.* New York, NY: Springer-Verlag.

HOLISM

Holism is the notion that a whole organism is always much more than the sum of its parts. Coined by Jan Smuts in 1926 in his book *Holism and Evolution*, holism presented an alternate theoretical construct to reductionist and mechanistic theories. Smuts presented a theoretical position of fundamental influence—from a cellular level and extending to the entire universe—on the creation or formation of wholes. Important to his theory of holism was the idea that the essence of the whole is indeed impacted by subdivisions. This stood in contrast to established reductionist theories that maintained the whole is merely a sum of its parts and mechanistic theories that assumed the subdivision of the whole is possible with no loss of condition or quality. Further, mechanistic systems movement is not inward but rather outward while whole systems movement is inherently inward and works towards self-actualization. Holistic theory has been applied by many different thinkers to understand economic, cultural, social, and spiritual systems. This entry reviews some of these contributions and includes a discussion of how holism has impacted and continues to impact different systems, including counseling and, specifically, individual psychology. The entry begins by reviewing concepts of holism.

Concepts of Holism

The term *holism* is used to describe a theoretical position that assumes the universe and living organisms are connected and interacting wholes and as such are equal to much more than a sum of all parts and particles. Holism is an alternative to dualism, reductionism, and mechanistic theories. Over the years, different theorists have applied the concept of holism in different contexts. To name a few, holism has been applied to economics (i.e., institutional evolution), medicine (i.e., biopsychosocial model), spirituality (i.e., consciousness), and counseling (i.e., individual psychology). Some theorists have described holistic dimensions of formulation from a cellular level. For example, Charles Darwin's idea of survival of the fittest greatly impacted Thorstein Veblen's application of the concept of holism to economics. John Dewey applied the concepts of holism to systems as well and, specifically, applied them to social and cultural systems. From a counseling perspective, holism might be viewed as the unity of mind and body within an individual.

Alfred Adler fully embraced Smuts's idea of holism and it became a core tenant of individual psychology. Others have expanded the idea of holism in psychotherapy to include dimensions of spirituality. While different theorists apply holism differently, all applications seem to be based on the core concept of an attracted or drawn movement toward a higher level of functioning and self-realization.

Concepts of Holism

Early theories of holism were formed as alternatives to mechanistic and reductionist theories. Such theoretical models seemed to work very well in astronomy, chemistry, and physics. However, researchers in the social sciences, psychology, and biology also recognized the need for a holistic view—one that incorporated physical, psychological, social, and other variables that might affect an individual. A valued example of holism compares an orange to a clock. The whole clock is round and can tell time, but in parts has no value for telling time and is created or formulated from the outside in. By contrast, an orange is also round, its parts are valued as still being an orange and most important, an orange and the tree it grows on can orient themselves toward the sun. As individuals move toward holistic growth and self-awareness, their holistic orientation evolves to include concepts such as spirituality. This process of growth, from the inside out, sets holism apart from mechanistic movement. Holism is a philosophy of social science that continues to form and shape other disciplines. For example, early dualistic notions of medicine have now evolved to fit the biopsychosocial model of patient-centered practice. The *International Classification of Functioning, Disability and Health* (ICF) presents a holistic model of functioning that integrates a medical and social model. The holistic components of ICF of an individual must include body functions and structures, activity, participation, environmental factors, personal factors, and health. Parallels can be found in the mental health profession, particularly from an Adlerian perspective.

Holism and Alfred Adler's Individual Psychology

After reading Smuts's book, *Holism and Evolution,* Adler sent him a letter to share his own thoughts on holism and to indicate to him that he would be suggesting the book to his own students to better prepare them for his class. Adler integrated Smuts's holistic construct of change and movement toward higher levels of functioning into the tenants of individual psychology and further promoted the idea that humans experienced an inner striving toward wholeness. Adler chose the name individual psychology (from the Latin, *individuum* meaning indivisible), sweeping out any remaining crumbs of reductionism with his holistic approach to helping individuals achieve wellness. Adler insisted that a person cannot be known outside of their context—not as separate parts—only as a whole. Adler promoted the tenet that wellness does not come from focusing on a single area of clients' lives but rather from integrating all indivisible parts of the self.

Smuts's idea of holism beginning at the cellular level resonated strongly with Adler. He added to that notion that his idea of *Gemeinschaftsgefühl,* or sense of relatedness, also began at the cellular level. His idea of *Gemeinschaftsgefühl,* beginning at the cellular level, includes his concept of the individual's inherent need to make meaning and feel connected to others. Adler's notion of social feeling incorporated love for fellow humans into the true meaning of social interest. The true meaning of social interest carries with it compassion for others and a desire to contribute to the community in ways that enhance the well-being of others. Holistically, individuals can only be known in the contexts in which they live, through their relationships, and through their connections to other people and their own communities. Adler believed in the motivating force of the individual's need to make meaning. *Gemeinschaftsgefühl* is commonly used to denote social interest. However, Adler's true idea of *Gemeinschaftsgefühl* goes much further than simply social interest and must include community feelings or a feeling for humankind that leads to self-actualization. His holistic application of *Gemeinschaftsgefühl* is centered around community feeling or a feeling for mankind that leads to self-actualization. A holistic view of social interest includes striving for social equality and social justice and considering the full context of an individual, including family, social, and cultural relationships. Holism values the whole person and incorporates all of the parts working together as a whole. Adler's holistic approach of including mind, body, and spirit of individuals is inadvertently supported with current neuroscience research. Current evidence supports his ideas that every person holds the inner creativity needed to recognize, gain insight, and change reoccurring and self-defeating thoughts, feelings, and behaviors. The holistic movement toward positive change, self-realization, and cosmic wholeness includes a spiritual awareness that is sometimes expressed as a feeling of being connected to the whole universe.

Spirituality and Holism

In 1959, Adler provided a clear reference to spirituality by describing human beings as seeking to make cosmic and spiritual meaning to what is known in the material world. He considered spirituality as an integral part of holistic wellness. From a holistic perspective, as individuals experience change and movement toward higher functioning, integrating a spiritual dimension of self into awareness is often experienced. Further, spirituality has been shown to have positive benefits for wellness and life satisfaction. The integration of spirituality into holistic thinking has been shown to be positively associated with wellness and can provide a sense of direction, meaning, and purpose to the journey of life. Optimum levels of wellness can be arrived at by balancing spiritual understanding with physical, intellectual, social, and occupational strivings. A sense of spirituality can enhance coping skills and an ability to self-regulate in response to changing events. When applying the term holism in discussions of including an individual's spirituality as an aspect of the whole person, caution must be liberally applied. Rather than seeking to sort out different components of spirituality as applications to the whole, one must consider a perspective that encompasses the whole person. The whole person moves toward the ultimate goal (higher functioning), not just the spirituality or the psychology of the person. This notion aligns with Smuts's original idea of holism, which includes movement toward higher awareness, insight, and realization as a function of individual personality.

Why Holism Matters in Counseling

As a holistic system, a human can be defined as a physical, mental, social, spiritual, and economic entity. This definition aligns with Adlerian attributes of lifestyle, social interests, and holism inherent in individual movement towards positive outcomes. The synergy of these defining attributes creates holistic characteristics that encourage individuals to cooperate in socially acceptable and responsible ways. Research shows when individuals engage in these collaborative processes as they moved toward personal holism, higher levels of well-being are experienced. By contrast, individuals often seek counseling in relation to feelings of despair, disconnect, and loss of hope as a result of a loss in their sense of meaning and purpose in life. Researchers posit that emotions impact cognition and behavior. Holistic counselors can best help clients think more clearly, reduce irrational beliefs, and increase coping behaviors for positive change and increase overall wellness. Change or movement toward a higher level of functioning is ubiquitous in the concept of holism. To understand what one's mind, body, and spiritual needs are, one must engage in processes that contribute to enhanced self-awareness. Holistic counselors can help their clients enhance self-awareness through collaboration. Research shows that counselors generally have higher levels of wellness than individuals who are not counselors. It is important for counselors to experience the process of enhancing self-awareness in order to model the process to their clients.

Research on the relationship between mind and body shows that the human organism is holistically interdependent. Advances in brain imaging technology can now allow practitioners to view images in real time and in relation to how clients are thinking and feeling before and after an intervention. This type of neurofeedback promotes individuals' sense of self-efficacy as they learn to access their own inner creativity to successfully cope with a constantly changing environment. Adler's ideas of an individual's inner creativity for self-healing seemed to be supported by biofeedback and neurofeedback technology, suggesting that individuals can affect their own levels of wellness. Adler recognized that thinking influenced emotions and behaviors and emotions influenced behavior and thinking. His use of encouragement to help individuals access their inner creativity for positive change parallels findings in neuroscience research. Brain imaging studies show that *Gemeinschaftsgefühl* may indeed be rooted at the cellular level. In 2012, Elliot C. Brown and Martin Brüne coined the term *social brain* for the area of the brain that attends to empathy for self and others, as well as attends to feelings of unconditional positive regard. Integrating elements of feedback processes demonstrates to clients their abilities to impact their own wellness. Holism is important in counseling because *holistic counseling* promotes encouragement and hope for clients as they actively engage in the treatment process.

Research methodology that includes qualitative as well as quantitative data is important for a holistic analysis. Qualitative data enables social researchers to deepen their understanding of a participant's context and subsequently, it enhances the meaning they attach to quantitative data. As the boundaries between biological, psychological, and social systems blend and blur under the biopsychosocial umbrella of care, the importance of providing a holistic context for individuals and clients is paramount. Rather than the disease model that focuses on remediation, holistic counseling can provide educational, preventive, and positive change promoting opportunities. From this perspective it is a natural progression for counselors to focus on their clients' strengths, hopes for the future, encouragement, and advocacy for self and others. Future applications of holism in counseling must integrate concepts of equality and social justice, advocacy for self and others, and technology. When current medicine, science, and technology are combined with holistic thinking in collaboration with clients and their therapists, the possibilities for positive change are boundless.

Gina Wilson

See also Acceptance and Commitment Therapy; Affect Regulation; Assessment, Biopsychosocial; Commitment; Mindfulness; Mindfulness and Sex

Further Readings

Adler, A. (1938). *Social interest: A challenge to mankind.* London, UK: Faber & Faber.

Ansbacher, H. L. (1994). On the origin of holism. *Journal of Adlerian Theory, Research & Practice, 50*(4), 486–593.

Carlson, J., Englar-Carlson, M., & Emavardhana, T. (2011). Was Adler from Bangkok? Applying an Adlerian-Buddhist approach in Thailand. *Journal of Individual Psychology, 67*(4), 349–365.

Curlette, W. L., & Kern, R. (2010). The importance of meeting the need to belong in lifestyle. *Journal of Individual Psychology, 66,* 30–42.

Koteles, F., & Simor, P. (2014). Somatic symptoms and holistic thinking as major dimensions behind modern health worries. *International Journal of Behavioral Medicine, 21,* 869–876. doi:10.1007/s12529-013-9363-5

Linden, G. W. (1995). Holism: Classical, cautious, chaotic, and cosmic. *Individual Psychology, 51*(3), 253–267.

Mosak, H. H., & Dreikurs, R. (2000). Spirituality: The fifth life task. *Journal of Individual Psychology, 56*(3), 257–267.

Sperry, L. (2008). The psychologist station of spirituality: a compelling case for it has yet to be made. *Journal of Individual Psychology, 64*(2), 169–178.

HOME-BASED THERAPY

Home-based therapy is a treatment modality offered to individuals and families that uses the client's home as the therapeutic setting instead of a traditional office environment. There are many benefits to providing therapy and counseling services in the home. For the clients, home-based approaches offer support, services, skills building, and practical experiences in the home setting. As an alternative to working with an individual or family in an office, home-based therapy is more natural, cost-efficient, and effective. Clients may experience their home as a comfortable, familiar, or safe space. Home-based therapy can remove barriers and allow the client(s) to meet the clinician on the client's territory. Thus, providing therapy in the home can increase the therapeutic alliance (the trusting relationship between clients and counselor), improve the client's attendance, and facilitate active engagement in treatment. In addition, home-based approaches typically emphasize family preservation (keeping children from being removed from the home), are client centered and strength based, and use a multisystems approach (try to include important systems in the clients' lives). Home-based family therapy has a unique history and its own theoretical models. There are also advantages and disadvantages associated with working in the home environment. This entry examines the development of home-based therapy, approaches to home-based therapy, and its documented advantages.

Foundation of Home-Based Therapy

Existing literature indicates that the concept of home-based therapy originated in the 19th century when charitable organizations made attempts to rescue and protect children from abuse, neglect, maltreatment, and abandonment. When these conditions led to the placement of many children in foster care, juvenile courts, institutions, and adult prisons, it became evident that change was needed. Although the first initiatives for reform were to improve the foster care system through intensive training and greater compensation for services, family preservation was soon deemed a more appropriate investment. It was this shift in paradigm that allowed children to remain in the home with their birth families while receiving intensive therapy and support services to strengthen the family unit. On August 10, 1993, the Family Preservation and Support Services Program Act authorized states to use funds to create a range of family-centered services for at-risk children and families. Since then, per major provisions of this law, many programs have been successfully implemented across the nation to support and preserve the family unit. There are three core tenets of home-based family therapy. First, the family as a unit is the focus of the therapy instead of individual family members. Second, it is a strength-based approach, and as such therapy aims to identify and magnify the positive aspects of each family. As a strength-based approach, the focus is on emphasizing protective factors, such as strengths and resources, which facilitate resiliency and healthy coping. The third tenet of home-based family therapy highlights that therapy empowers families by helping to assess and meet needs, facilitates the families' access to resources for continual support, and gradually promotes the families' independence from those services.

For a clinician, home-based therapy provides a unique opportunity to observe, assess, and interpret the client in the clients' natural habitat. The clients' home as an alternative to the clinician's office is likely more therapeutic because it allows the clinician to gain knowledge and insight not available in a traditional office setting. Home-based therapy provides a first-hand look at the clients' functioning in context, familial structures (who communicates to whom, who is in charge, family rules) and dynamics, and environmental triggers for emotional and behavioral difficulties. Carefully observing an individual or family in their home can be an invaluable part of analyzing and understanding the client's reality, risk assessments, well-being checks, and progress monitoring.

Home-based therapy can be conducted with both voluntary and involuntary clients. It is a viable option for families who might experience difficulty accessing traditional in-office therapy services. There are various reasons for why in-office treatment might be problematic for some clients including, but not limited to, illness, physical or mental health disability, lack of childcare, limited finances, personal or familial crisis, issues with transportation, or scheduling conflicts. In addition, home-based therapy is often a preferred intervention approach for at-risk populations to facilitate engagement and treatment compliance.

Considering the obstacles that can complicate access to traditional in-office therapy appointments, home-based therapists aim to provide solutions and services to individuals and families that need assistance. Community mental health agencies, child welfare organizations, and juvenile justice systems are the typical providers of home-based therapy. However, some private practice therapists are beginning to recognize the need for more authentic and nontraditional approaches to treatment. Thus, there is an emergence of private practitioners who are willing to offer home-based sessions if they prove to be beneficial to their clients regardless of whether or not accessibility is an issue. Home-based therapy can also be conducted as a collaborative effort. For instance, two or more clinicians might work as a team to meet the complex needs of an individual or family.

Home-based therapists are usually master's level clinicians who provide both direct and indirect services such as service coordination, consultation, mental health assessments, crisis intervention, as well as brief and long-term counseling. A home-based therapist should be knowledgeable of various psychotherapies, child development, theories on systems and families, clinical assessments and diagnoses, community resources, as well as how to integrate this information to provide appropriate supports and services. Furthermore, home-based therapists must possess the clinical skills necessary to foster a professional working relationship with individuals and families engulfed in maladaptive behavioral patterns. A home-based therapist might provide treatment and service coordination to individuals and families around issues of juvenile delinquency, child abuse or neglect, familial conflict, parent–child relational issues, substance abuse, as well as emotional and behavioral disorders. In recent decades, home-based family therapy has been optimal for families in situations where children and adolescents are at risk for being placed outside of the home due to difficulties in school, emotional problems (including mental illness), juvenile delinquency, or abuse/neglect. In these instances, the goal of home-based therapy is twofold: (1) the prevention of outside placement by keeping children and adolescents safe and (2) restoration of homeostasis (usual functioning), wellness, and unity within families.

Home-Based Family Therapy Approaches

In response to the Family Preservation and Support Services Act of 1993, there are various extensions of home-based therapy that offer some distinctive services to children and their families. For example, functional family therapy targets adolescents between the ages of 11 and 18 who struggle with peer conflicts, school difficulties, substance abuse, and complying with rules and expectations at home. For these clients, functional family therapy facilitates the development of the essential skills needed to stabilize the family such as familial communication, problem-solving, conflict management, and relationship building. These skills allow families to reduce stress by building upon familial strengths and improving relationships within the family constellation.

Similarly, multidimensional family therapy is geared toward children between the ages of 9 and 18 who are struggling with delinquent behavior such as aggression, defiance, problematic behavior at school, and substance abuse. In this treatment model, families participate in a combination of home, clinical, and other specialized therapies to maximize treatment outcomes. Another program, called Intensive In-Home Child and Adolescent Psychiatric Services (IICAPS), targets children and adolescents between the ages of 5 and 17 who are experiencing severe emotional disorders. IICAPS provides intensive support for the child as well as the family unit. For example, when children are released from psychiatric hospitals or residential treatment facilities, IICAPS aims to reintegrate the child into the home environment by supporting stabilization and providing crisis intervention as needed. IICAPS is often an option when traditional outpatient services have proven ineffective. Treatment goals might include developing healthy coping skills such as anger management, social skills, parent coaching, familial communication, and identifying and expressing feelings appropriately.

The Child FIRST (Child and Family Interagency Resource, Support, and Training) and Integrated Family Violence (IFV) programs are other examples of home-based interventions. Child FIRST is another home-based therapy model that focuses on early intervention and is intended for the most vulnerable children and families. The vulnerabilities of these families are characterized by their at-risk living environments. Specifically, Child FIRST targets families whose environments are marked with at-risk factors such as domestic violence, substance abuse, maternal depression, and homelessness. Research has shown such tumultuous environments and exposure to chronic stress can have lasting adverse effects on the developing brain. So, the goal of the Child FIRST program is to respond early. Thus, treatment is initiated at the earliest signs of problems to reduce the likelihood of the manifestation of severe emotional disturbance, abuse, neglect, as well as delays in learning and development. Finally, the IFV program, funded by the Department of Child and Family Services (DCFS), targets children and families who are often exposed to, and negatively affected by, family violence. The goals of this home-based therapy approach are (1) to increase safety, (2) to help families develop a care plan to restore parent–child relationships, and (3) to hold batterers responsible for their actions.

Many of the aforementioned home-based therapies also collaborate with other local agencies and community organizations to create a network of supports and services for children and their families. Although these programs share some basic premises, each has a unique focus that might make one more appealing than the other. Selecting the appropriate model depends on factors such as the child's age, presenting problem, diagnosis, as well as familial strengths and structures.

The Benefits of Home-Based Therapy

There is a vast base of evidence supporting the effectiveness and benefits of home-based family therapy for a myriad of emotional, behavioral, and relational difficulties that families experience. The most obvious advantage is that home-based therapy is accessible and accommodating to families who might not access or benefit from traditional office-based therapies. Literature has also suggested that the therapist–client relationship develops faster in home-based therapies. As a result, some of the core qualities of the therapeutic relationship (e.g., rapport, trust, and mutual respect) are established more quickly, and this facilitates the helping relationship. This is due to the tendency of clients to feel more comfortable in their own homes as opposed to an unfamiliar office setting. Generally, clients who feel stronger bonds with their therapists are more likely to actively participate in the therapy process. The concept of establishing trust and building bonds is paramount throughout the entire therapeutic process; it is not limited solely to the initial stages of treatment. When the therapist–client relationship is established and solidified more readily, it can positively impact the client's progress toward treatment goals and the overall healing process. In order for family therapy to be effective, all members of the family must actively engage. Thus, attendance and engagement is another benefit of home-based therapies. Working in the family's home provides the clinician with an opportunity to ensure that each member is present, and it creates opportunities to connect, engage, and coach family members that would not be possible in an office setting.

Learning opportunities are also greater when therapy takes place in the client's home. As previously mentioned, the therapist is able to learn more about the client's global functioning when observing and interacting in a natural setting. It is also easier for the client to omit, conceal, or blatantly lie about information in an office setting. However, the realities (e.g., family dynamics, interactions between family members, condition of the home) witnessed firsthand in a person's home can speak volumes. A clinician's ability to carefully examine and consider the client's environment provides much more knowledge than the client's self-report. Additionally, the client's potential for learning is also amplified in home-based therapy approaches. Behavioral rehearsals, coaching, and modeling become more practical and applicable in a home setting.

Evidence suggests that home-based family therapy is notably more effective than individual counseling, peer groups, parent education, and multifamily interventions when used alone. One possibility is the freedom home-based therapists have to use experiential or creative "family play" approaches, instead of just talk therapy, to promote and improve involvement between family members. Interestingly, some studies have shown that creative, experiential, and play-therapy activities with families can actually help increase the retention and mastery of positive skills in treatment. Some therapists might even prefer home-based therapy over in-office sessions because of all the benefits.

Concerns and Challenges in Home-Based Therapy

For clients, their home is a private, intimate place. So, having a stranger in their home might heighten concerns about privacy, intensify feelings of vulnerability or being judged, as well as generate questions and feelings of awkwardness around etiquette and social decorum. Many of these issues will likely emerge as discussions or behaviors during treatment and can create great opportunities to deepen awareness and the therapeutic relationship if managed appropriately. However, like any other form of therapy, home-based family therapy is not without some challenges or ethical dilemmas for clinicians. Some of the ethical issues that immediately come to the forefront when working with clients in their homes include professional boundaries, confidentiality, and issues of diversity (e.g., cultural, ethnicity, religious, economical, educational). For example, some clients may take offense to a therapist not accepting food, turning down a gift given as a token of appreciation, or not sharing personal information. These instances can present problems and create challenges or strains to the professional working relationship. When a therapist enters a client's home, these rules may not be as clearly defined as in a traditional office setting. Interacting with clients in the comfort of the home can cause boundaries to become blurry. Although the therapist is in the client's home, the clinician is a professional engaging in a professional working relationship. Thus, a home-based therapist must establish boundaries at the onset of treatment and maintain boundaries throughout treatment. Another key legal and ethical challenge for home-based therapy involves confidentiality. Specifically, the added variables of extended relatives, friends, or neighbors further complicate issues of privacy and confidentiality when providing treatment in the home. Regardless of the setting, the therapist has a professional responsibility to carefully safeguard the counselor–client relationship (e.g., the power differential, boundaries) in an effort to curtail disappointments, misunderstandings, and ethical debacles.

Despite the advantages of home-based therapy, therapists should prepare to face some added challenges when providing treatment in the home. Home settings provide less structure and security than an office setting. Community violence, substance abuse, a history of family violence, psychotic or aggressive episodes, the accessibility of weapons in a home (e.g., knives), erratic or confrontational behavior developing during a session, clients or relatives making sexual advances, and jealous spouses are all variables that can pose a risk. However, safety is priority. Thus, clinicians must be respectful, cautious, hyper-vigilant, and prepared to ensure everyone's safety when in a client's home. Other concerns and considerations for home-based therapy include environmental distractions (e.g., meal time, knocks at the door, telephone ringing, boisterous pets, supervising and attending to small children), the condition of the home (e.g., clutter, lack of furniture, unclean conditions), safety concerns (e.g., community violence), as well as high rates of burnout and compassion fatigue.

Overall, home-based family therapy is an effective, accessible, and cost-effective approach for preserving and empowering families. For home-based therapy to work, families should remain engaged throughout the process, actively work toward building a working relationship with the therapist, and connect to any additional community resources that can support and strengthen the therapeutic process. Much like any other treatment modality, home-based therapy may not be suitable for every client or family. However, it can be a viable alternative to traditional office-based therapy or used when other interventions have failed. Home-based therapy should focus and build upon the family's strengths, resources, supports, and other positive qualities as opposed to emphasizing deficits, pathology, or familial chaos. It is the job of the therapist to partner with the family to build hope, foster resiliency, and to facilitate change.

Tasha Leroyce Banks and Sarah Murphy

See also Child Protective Services; Court-Mandated Clients; Domestic Violence; Functional Family Therapy; Multiple Family Therapy; Multisystemic Therapy

Further Readings

Child and Family Agency. (2014). *Home-based parent and counseling services*. Retrieved November 2, 2014, from http://www.childandfamilyagency.org/for-families-providers/home-based-parent-and-counseling-services/

In-Home Family Therapy: http://www.ndbh.com

Jordan, K., Alvarado, J., Braley, R., & Williams, L. (2001). Family preservation through home-based family therapy: An overview. *Journal of Family Psychotherapy, 12*(3), 31–44. doi:10.1300/J085v12n03_02

Scarbourough, N., Taylor, B., & Tuttle, A. (2013). Collaborative home-based therapy (CHBT): A culturally responsive model for treating children and adolescents involved in child protective service systems. *Contemporary Family Therapy: An International Journal, 35*(3), 465–477. doi:10.1007/s10591-012-9223-5

Thompson, S., Bender, K., Windsor, L. C., & Flynn, P. M. (2009). Keeping families engaged: The effects of home-based family therapy enhanced with experiential activities. *Social Work Research, 33*(2), 121–126. doi:10.1093/swr/33.2.121

Homelessness

Homelessness in the United States permeates social culture across small towns and urban cities alike. Although the scope of its impact is staggering, homelessness remains a largely invisible phenomenon. Individuals experiencing homelessness often encounter subsequent isolation, deprivation, and peril in regards to their ability to accomplish daily tasks and achieve basic fundamental needs, such as food, shelter, and safety. Individuals are unable to focus on broader goals and needs to challenge the perpetuation of the nature of homelessness in families, because daily fear and instability prevent future perspective. Interestingly, homelessness appears to affect individuals across genders, ethnicities, and spiritual beliefs, yet social culture instills pervasive bias against those who experience the traumatic occurrence. In examining the prevalence, evidence-based interventions, and advocacy needs related to homelessness, a simple fact emerges suggesting a cognitive grasp of homelessness is as uniquely complex as each individual it affects. This entry will define homelessness, present national statistics for the United States on the prevalence of homelessness, and outline intervention and advocacy efforts.

Definition of Homelessness

While always having been part of the U.S. social fabric, homelessness has gained increasing attention since the 1980s and is characterized by not having a place to live. Defined by the government in the 1987 McKinney-Vento Homelessness Assistance Act, a homeless person is one who lacks permanent nighttime housing or a person who lives in a shelter, welfare hotel, or any public or private place not intended as an overnight dwelling for humans. This definition has been criticized for its lack of inclusiveness and some suggest a definition that incorporates those at risk of becoming homeless. This would include those who must live with others despite potentially crowded conditions to avoid living on the streets. Some organizations suggest looking at the causes and types of homelessness to better define the term. Three commonly accepted types of homelessness are chronic, transitional, and episodic. The chronically homeless are persons who have experienced continuous, long-term homelessness. For this subpopulation, long-standing use of the shelter system is very common. The transitionally homeless are persons who experience typically one episode of homelessness due to a life event that leaves them temporarily between stable housing situations. The episodically homeless are persons who experience frequent episodes of homelessness that are attributed to chronic unemployment as well as medical, mental, or substance use problems. Research has identified three common causal factors in homelessness: a shortage of affordable housing options; a change in the U.S. economy, which includes the outsourcing of jobs to other nations and the recession of 2007; and the deinstitutionalization of the mentally ill since the 1970s. While research has not been able to conclusively determine which of these factors is the most significant, research suggests that each factor contributes to homelessness in the United States.

National Statistics

Differing across populations, homeless individuals vary across gender, ethnicity, age, and background. While patterns have emerged in specific demographics, no definitive predictor exists. The National Coalition for the Homelessness previously suggested that 3.5 million people experience homelessness each year while numbers from the U.S. Department of Housing and Urban Development Annual Homeless Assessment Report suggest that on any given night in January 2013, 610,042 people were homeless. Overall, a decline in homelessness has been noted with continued decreases in the veteran, chronic, and family homeless subpopulations.

According to The National Alliance to End Homelessness, the Annual Homeless Assessment Report, and the Substance Abuse and Mental Health Services Administration (SAMHSA), individual adults over the age of 25 made up a majority of the homeless population. The majority of these adults were male; however, in rural areas females were more likely to be homeless. Children under the age of 18 accounted for 23% of the homeless population and the remaining 10% of the homeless population were between the ages of 18 and 24. Although demographics do vary, minorities are generally overrepresented in the homeless population. Most research attributes this to the disproportionate percentage of minorities living in poverty, a commonly cited risk factor for homelessness. Research also cites mental illness and substance abuse problems as being a potential risk factor for homelessness. According to SAMHSA, approximately one in five homeless individuals have a serious mental illness and over one in five have a substance abuse problem. Instances of mental illness and substance abuse problems are seen more often in the chronic and veteran subpopulations.

Interventions

Intervention strategies used amongst homeless populations are often comprehensive and encompass a wide variety of modalities. The majority of strategies represent one of three primary orientations, which include the psychological, sociological, and psychosocial models. Psychological models are person centered, focusing on homelessness as individual deficits occurring within a community. Sociological models cite the scarcity of social resources as a primary cause of homelessness. Psychosocial models examine the interaction of individual and societal factors in homelessness. Across most strategies, four stages of intervention can be identified in working with the homeless population. The first is an assessment of an individual's physiological and psychological needs. Many studies have shown that the first step to successful intervention is finding reliable housing services for clients, which has led many programs to adopt a "housing first" orientation over "treatment first." The second stage of intervention involves collaborating with agencies in the community to help address an individual's needs. Data regarding mental illness, substance abuse, and co-occurring disorders among homeless individuals have led to the creation of several specialized programs to treat these individuals. The assertive community treatment model, which was originally developed by Neumiller and colleagues to serve patients with chronic psychiatric disabilities and hospitalizations, is often modified to serve the homeless with co-occurring disorders. Through the use of a multidisciplinary team, these programs attempt to provide both substance abuse and mental health treatment in order to provide the skills to function successfully in the community.

The third stage of intervention involves direct counseling services provided to the individual. Many research studies have identified common issues across this population that may be present, including social detachment, helplessness, impulsivity, and low self-efficacy. Humanistic approaches have often been identified as helping increase the perception of self-value in the homeless client while creating an environment of respect, care, and understanding. This is important, as homeless individuals may be more reluctant to trust a therapist than other clients. Specific therapeutic interventions vary according to the presenting problems of the client. For those with co-occurring disorders, motivational interviewing and cognitive-behavioral interventions are often used in conjunction. Systemic therapy has also been found to be effective in both individual and family treatment of homeless individuals. These approaches often focus on addressing emotional and relational factors in order to reclaim responsibility for the client's life. Across treatments, clients develop goals that address personal health and vocational competency in order to prevent a relapse to homelessness. The fourth stage of intervention involves advocacy, which is explored in depth in the following section.

Advocacy Efforts

Advocacy efforts related to homelessness take a multitude of forms, directing purported solutions at varying aspects of the problem. Organizations such as the National Coalition for the Homeless, the National Alliance to End Homelessness, and the Substance Abuse and Mental Health Services Administration provide information and advocacy efforts for the homeless. The first approach most commonly undertaken by community grassroots efforts, including some nonprofit organizations, seeks to provide comfort to individuals experiencing homelessness. This can include providing for basic needs like food and clothing, although neglecting to address the most significant problem at hand, lack of permanent residence. While local organizations may feel positively about providing for a need, these instantly gratifying approaches to advocacy fail to address the systemic origins of homelessness and can create a cyclical process of giving, without changing the problem. Two additional approaches stem from common language referring to homelessness policy as either a front door or back door method. Front door approaches center upon prevention of the phenomenon of homelessness and keeping individuals from ever entering into homelessness. Such approaches claim homelessness as a human rights issue, suggesting shelter is an intrinsic right deserved by all. Front door approaches may differ in the implementation of housing (e.g., while some programs offer housing only to those individuals who are willing and able to comply with specific rules, other programs offer housing without any requirements on the part of the individual). Back door approaches espouse restorative efforts, moving individuals out of homelessness as quickly and efficiently as possible. Back door approaches may include temporary shelters, group living arrangements, and job placement services. Another approach often misunderstood within the context of homelessness advocacy seeks to ban the phenomenon by implementing anti-lurking laws and ordinances, removing shantytowns and tent cities, and enforcing other equally discriminatory methods that seek to eliminate the phenomenon of homelessness by simply displacing its survivors.

One commonality exists among all approaches, suggesting the most significant shift may have less to do with understanding the homeless and more to do with understanding individuals who do not experience homelessness. Changing social perceptions of homelessness is the most fundamental component of current advocacy efforts as many challenges individuals face are related to the stigma, shame, and guilt placed on homelessness. Given the exponential growth of media coverage in recent decades, crimes committed against the homeless, as well as crimes committed by the homeless, are widely reported upon. The degree to which media portrayal seeks to understand the perspective of the homeless suggests an inherent lack of value in the story of the individual, grouping people experiencing the homelessness under a wide umbrella as either victims of homelessness or guilty participants in its continuation. Recognizing the limited understanding of homelessness by the general public, there is no question that there is a need to listen carefully to the voice of each individual experiencing homelessness and to the broader homeless population when generating advocacy efforts geared toward providing solutions to this deeply rooted social phenomenon.

David A. Scott, Caroline Adair Black, Elizabeth Lewis, and Sean Newhart

See also Homelessness and Youth; Poverty and Family Development; Socioeconomic Status

Further Readings

Burt, M., Pearson, C., & Montgomery, A. (2007). Community-wide strategies for preventing homelessness: Recent evidence. *Journal of Primary Prevention, 28,* 213–228.

Dykeman, B. (2011). Intervention strategies with the homeless population. *Journal of Instructional Psychology, 38*(1), 32–39.

Henry, M., Cortes, A., & Morris, S. (2013). *The 2013 annual homeless assessment report (AHAR) to congress.* Washington, DC: U.S. Department of Housing and Urban Development.

National Alliance to End Homelessness. (2014). *FAQs.* Retrieved from http://www.endhomelessness.org/pages/faqs

National Alliance to End Homelessness. (2014). *The state of homelessness in America.* Retrieved from http://www.endhomelessness.org/library/entry/the-state-of-homelessness-2014

National Coalition for the Homeless. (2009). *How many people experience homelessness?* Retrieved from http://www.nationalhomeless.org/factsheets/How_Many.html

National Coalition for the Homeless. (2014). *Homelessness in America.* Retrieved from http://nationalhomeless.org/about-homelessness/

Neumiller, S., Bennett-Clark, F., Young, M., Dates, B., Broner, N., Leddy, J., . . . Jong, F. (2009). Implementing assertive community treatment in diverse settings for people who are homeless with co-occurring mental and addictive disorders: A series of case studies. *Journal of Dual Diagnosis, 5,* 239–263.

Substance Abuse and Mental Health Services Administration. (2014). *Homelessness and housing.* Retrieved from http://www.samhsa.gov/homelessness-housing

Sun, A. (2012). *Helping homeless individuals with co-occurring disorders: The four components. Social Work, 57*(1), 23–37.

HOMELESSNESS AND YOUTH

Homeless youth, often called unaccompanied youth, can be described as individuals under the age of 24 years old who are lacking in parental, foster, or institutional care. These youth are often hard to identify, transient, and have difficulty seeking treatment due to lack of resources. Without intervention, homeless youth are at risk of a multitude of mental health issues, as well as academic and career concerns. Homeless youth live in both urban and rural environments. Several different factors can lead to homelessness within this population. These factors include family problems, financial issues, and lack of housing. Unfortunately, the numbers of homeless youth grow each year. The financial crisis of 2007–08 in the United States put a strain on many families struggling to pay bills and find employment. As a result, many families lost their homes or jobs and a higher percentage of youth fell into homelessness.

There are four different categorizations of homeless youth: (1) runaways, which include youths who have voluntarily left home; (2) throwaways, which include youths kicked out of their homes; (3) street youth, which include youth living on the streets in high-risk environments; and (4) systems youth, which include homeless youth who are in state custody, such as foster care or the juvenile detention system. The United States Department of Health and Human Services defines homeless youth as anyone under the age of 18 (or older if permitted by local law) who lacks a fixed, regular, and adequate nighttime residence, or sleeps in a shelter designed to provide temporary living arrangements.

National Statistics

The U.S Department of Housing and Urban Development reported that there were 199,690 children and youth that were homeless in the United States on a single night in January of 2013. Of this percentile, most homeless youth (77%) are actually still connected to their parents (i.e., they are part of a homeless family). Homeless families are more prevalent when children and youth are under the age of 18, compared to ages 18 to 24. Another part of the homeless issue is the youth who run away from home in a given year. On average, runaway youth varies from 1.6 to 2.8 million in a year.

It has been found that on average, one in seven young persons between the ages of 10 and 18 will run away (exposing themselves to possible long-term homelessness). In this population, around 75% of homeless youth are female. Studies estimate that pregnant teen females make up between 6% and 20% of homeless females in this country. Generally, studies have shown that time spent living on the streets for homeless youth ranges from 2 months to 8 years depending on situational factors. Youth who experience chronic homelessness struggle to meet basic needs such as food, water, and shelter. Homeless youth also struggle with finding and using appropriate medical and mental health services.

Homeless children and youth are at risk for poorer health, drug and sexual abuse, and even death. Homeless youth compared to their peers have higher rates of suicide, physical and sexual abuse, and psychiatric disorders. Almost 50% of youth reported being physically abused, 40% emotionally abused, and 17% sexually abused by a family or household member. It has been reported that on average each year 5,000 homeless young persons will die from assault, illness, or suicide while living on the streets. In addition, around 75% of this population have dropped out or will drop out of school. Recent studies have further shown that youth age 12 to 17 are at a greater risk of being homeless than adult populations.

Interventions

Interventions for treating homeless youth are still in their infancy. Family conflicts as well as abuse are common factors that youth have reported as a reason for leaving home. It has been reported that many youth leave home due to physical, emotional, sexual, or substance use problems by guardians or other family members. Homeless youth are more likely to engage in risky behaviors such as substance abuse, theft, and prostitution. In order to survive, many homeless youth find themselves selling drugs for money, or exchanging sexual behaviors in return for food or shelter to meet their basic needs. Many adolescents living on the streets suffer from some form of mental illness such as depression, suicidal ideation, and posttraumatic stress disorder. They are more likely to suffer from diseases or contract a serious medical condition because they lack access to health care resources. Due to the dangerous nature of being on the streets, these youth are at risk for being victimized again. It has consistently been shown that the longer youth are away from home, the more chance they have of engaging in dangerous behaviors. Interventions when youth are newly homeless offer the most promise for reducing risk.

Prevention

Prevention programs for homeless youth focus mainly on reducing risk-taking behaviors, building familial relationships to keep youth living with the family, and minimizing the chance of contracting HIV. The prevalence of HIV among homeless youth is significantly higher than any other adolescent population. Increasing relationship building, increasing social support, and increasing coping skills are important components for this population to learn. By developing these skills, it is possible to prevent dangerous behaviors that may result in harmful consequences. A key part of prevention is helping youth use community resources that will address the environmental barriers they face. An ongoing safety net serves as a structural intervention to link youth to their family, other adults, medical care, and mental health services until they are in a stable environment.

Treatment

Homeless youth are in great need of services. Several of the critical needs for these youth are adequate housing, connection to education and job opportunities, and mental and physical health programs. There has been an increase in developing treatment programs for homeless youth over the past few years although more research is needed to determine the effectiveness of the interventions. There is not one specific treatment paradigm that works with all homeless youth. Below are several examples that could be used in treatment programs.

Family-Based Treatment

Homeless youth who have contact with their parents, more specifically their mothers, are more likely to return home and get off the streets. Interventions involving youth before they become chronically homeless may offer the best chance of reducing potential harm from drug use and sexual promiscuity. Family-based treatments focus on conflict resolution as a way to reunite the adolescent and the parent(s). Norweeta Milburn's randomized controlled trial demonstrated significant reductions in risk-taking behaviors such as sexual risk behavior, alcohol use, illicit drug use, and delinquent behavior during the 12-month treatment period.

Community Reinforcement Approach

Community reinforcement approach (CRA) is a multisystemic approach that involves intrapersonal, interpersonal, and social context change. This intervention draws from an operant theoretical perspective but also integrates cognitive therapy and behavioral therapy. CRA significantly reduces substance abuse and depression while significantly increasing social stability. Treatment involves standard procedures as well as optional modules to meet the needs of the individual. Homework and role-playing are used to help the youth practice their newly acquired skills. CRA can also include additional sessions on risk assessment, skills practice, and AIDS education.

Relationship-Based Intervention

Elizabeth McCay's relationship-based intervention seeks to improve social connectedness among homeless youth to decrease the sense of hopelessness. Increasing the number of positive relationships builds strength and self-esteem as well as reduces mental health challenges. Peer and family support are essential components of recovery and have been identified by street-involved youth as playing a vital role in becoming mentally healthy. Improvement in social connectedness may lead to increased self-esteem and resilience. There is also evidence that peer-led groups have been found to increase the youth's level accountability.

Motivational Interviewing

The high-risk nature of illicit drug use and underage drinking has prompted a need for specialized substance abuse treatment for homeless youth. Brief motivational interviewing assesses the client's behavior, its consequences, and the personal and social context of use followed by personal feedback. The therapist challenges the assumptions of the youth about drug use but leaves the decision up to them. There are promising results for reducing drug use with motivational interviewing among adolescents that are engaged in treatment. Brief motivational interviewing is more effective for reducing illicit drug use than for marijuana or alcohol.

Independent Living and Supportive Housing

Independent living programs are designed as a residential treatment option for homeless youth to increase living skills. Although having marginal results, positive outcomes were found in employment and living status. Supportive housing programs provide youth with permanence and access to services such as case management. Youth in supportive housing indicate higher self-reported health and lower rates of substance use. An increase in living skills has been shown to improve family contact and life satisfaction.

Advocacy Efforts

Advocacy for homeless youth can take many forms including federal programs, peer support, psychoeducation, mentoring, and case management. Federal initiatives such as the Runaway and Homeless Youth Act and McKinney-Vento Homeless Education Assistance Act opened the door for transitional living programs, the Street Outreach Program, and the Family and Youth Services Bureau. Several states are enacting policies to combat homelessness in youth populations through the allocation of funds and by addressing educational needs. Other legislation includes prevention programs, outreach services, and counseling. On a state level, services need to be enhanced for the large number of children who age out of foster care and exit the juvenile justice system. Many times, youth transitioning out of foster care and the juvenile justice system quickly realize there are only a small number of programs available to assist them once they turn 18 years of age. Programs and legislation for helping homeless youth often rely on federal resources to operate. Showing members of Congress the impact of homelessness and homeless programs on their districts can result in more action being taken on behalf of homeless youth. Nationwide advocacy efforts have pushed the president of the United States to commit to a 16% increase in the federal budget for McKinney-Vento Homeless Education Grants in the 2016 fiscal year.

In 2013, the Department of Health and Human Services reported over 88% of youth involved in transitional living programs made a "safe exit" from the program, which means they moved into some form of stable housing (e.g., private or residential) instead of living on the street or in a homeless shelter. These are promising numbers and suggest that transitional living programs may be a treatment option for homeless youth. Furthermore, 68% of reported youth exiting transitional living programs completed further schooling over a 2-year span. Research has found these programs increased public awareness of the issues surrounding homeless youth by providing education and funding to advocates. In addition, these programs have also created services to assist in providing housing, life skills training, and financial literacy instruction.

David A. Scott, Alyssa Hess, Matthew T. Webb, and Amanda Tuttle

See also Adolescent Behavior Disorders; Alcohol and Substance Abuse; Homelessness; Substance Use Disorders in Adolescence

Further Readings

Altena, A., Brilleslijper-Kater, S., & Wolf, J. (2010). Effective interventions for homeless youth: A systematic review. *American Journal of Preventive Medicine, 38*(6), 637–645.

Arnold, E., & Rotheram-Borus, M. (2009). Comparisons of prevention programs for homeless youth. *Prevention Science, 10*, 76–86.

Aviles, A. M., & Helfrich, C. A. (2006). Homeless youth: Causes, consequences and the role of occupational therapy. *Occupational Therapy in Health Care, 20*(3/4), 99–114. doi:10.1300/1003v20n03-07

Find Youth Info: http://www.youth.gov

Henry, M., Cortes, A., & Morris, S. (2013, October 1). *The 2013 annual homeless assessment report (AHAR) to Congress*. Retrieved from U.S. Department of Housing and Urban Development, Homeless and Runaway Youth website: http://www.ncsl.org/research/human-services/homeless-and-runaway-youth.aspx

McCay, E., Quesnel, S., Langley, J., Beanlands, H., Cooper, L., Blidner, R., & Bach, K. (2011). A relationship-based intervention to improve social connectedness in street-involved youth: A pilot study. *Journal of Child and Adolescent Psychiatric Nursing, 24*, 208–215.

Milburn, N., Iribarren, F., Rice, E., Lightfoot, M., Solorio, R., Rotheram-Borus, M., & Duan, N. (2012). A family intervention to reduce sexual risk behavior, substance use, and delinquency among newly homeless youth. *Journal of Adolescent Health, 50*, 358–364.

National Alliance to End Homelessness: http://www.endhomelessness.org

National Alliance to End Homelessness. (2012). *An emerging framework for ending unaccompanied youth homelessness*. Retrieved from http://www.endhomelessness.org/library/entry/an-emerging-framework-for-ending-unaccompanied-youth-homelessness

National Association for the Education of Homeless Children and Youth: http://www.naehcy.org

Safe Horizon. (2014). *Homeless youth statistics & facts*. Retrieved December 1, 2014, from http://www.safehorizon.org/page/homeless-youth-statistics--facts-69.html

U.S. Department of Health and Human Service (DHHS). (2003). *Incidence and prevalence of homeless and runaway youth*. Washington, DC: Administration for Children and Families, Office of Family Assistance.

U.S. Department of Health and Human Service (DHHS). (2013). *Report to Congress on the runaway and homeless youth programs of the family and youth services bureau for fiscal years 2012 and 2013*. Washington, DC: Administration for Children and Families, Office of Family Assistance.

HOMEOSTASIS

Homeostasis describes an ongoing process of system-level monitoring and adjustment that occurs in systems to maintain balance and order. A system is defined as a set of smaller components that interact to form a more complex whole. A group of parents and children, for example, may form a family system. Grandparents, aunts, uncles, and cousins may reflect components connected to the immediate system and form another larger family system. Within family systems, homeostasis refers to unique behavioral, emotional, and interactional patterns developed and maintained by systems to enhance stability.

Homeostasis is not a fixed process. Instead, systems constantly use feedback, or information about the system, to monitor and self-correct. If movement beyond tolerable levels is detected, homeostatic mechanisms are activated to restore stability to the system. Homeostasis is central to system adaptability and survival. In this entry the concept of homeostasis is examined in relation to general and cybernetic systems theories (theories that look at the interrelatedness of parts of a system and how a system incorporates feedback). Positive and negative feedback and first- and second-order change are then explored as mechanisms to facilitate self-monitoring and self-correction in family systems. Broadly, positive and negative feedback refer to information that systems consider. First- and second-order changes refer to what systems do with the feedback information received. Finally, suggestions for applying principles of homeostasis into therapeutic practice and potential theoretical limitations are discussed.

General Systems Theory

General systems theory emerged from the work of biologist Ludwig von Bertalanffy in the 1920s. General systems theory emphasizes the study of system interactions in context, with specific attention to system wholeness and hierarchies between different system levels. General systems theory has been applied to biology, engineering, and psychology, among other domains. The adoption of general systems theory by early family therapists reflected a major hallmark for the profession. General systems theory was a central framework for many founders of family therapy as they sought to understand relationships among smaller family subsystems, as well as to explain the behavior of individuals in the context of the larger family systems of which they were a part. Subsystems (i.e., parental subsystem, sibling subsystems, spousal subsystems) are smaller self-contained groups within the larger system that interact with each other and are also governed by their own sets of rules, roles, and patterns.

Homeostasis is one principle from general systems theory that early family theorists applied to understanding families. Theorists observed that while an almost infinite range of possible behaviors or interactions existed, family systems tended to choose from a smaller group of known and repeated actions. In addition to tendencies toward homeostasis, theorists observed that family systems were defined by several other general principles. First, all behaviors appeared to make sense in context and should thus be considered from this perspective. For example, while a child's bed-wetting beyond a certain age may not seem developmentally appropriate, the effect that this behavior has (i.e., the child does not have to go to school on mornings following the bed-wetting) may help explain the behavior. Second, no single person is responsible for family distress or triumph. Referring back to the example of a child's bed-wetting, the roles of other members of the family in maintaining and also changing this behavior would also be considered relevant. Finally, personal characteristics of individual members dependently evolve out of the system itself. For example, it would theoretically follow that the bed-wetting behavior would influence not only the child immediately involved in this action, but also potential characteristics of parents, siblings, spouses, and others connected to the system.

Cybernetic Systems Theory

Family systems are considered to be *cybernetic,* or self-correcting. As described by Gregory Bateson in 1972, cybernetic systems are able to "steer" their own course and are not dependent on outside systems to maintain stability. Cybernetic family systems aim to "steer" their own courses by maintaining homeostasis through mutual enforcement of established rules and norms. For example, should a crisis impact a family system, rules (spoken and unspoken) will be at play that guide the family's adjustment to this crisis. Mother may take a problem-solving position, father may provide emotional nurturance, and siblings may temporarily cease fighting and form a bond that will help the family to overcome the challenge. Within therapeutic settings, *second-order cybernetics* refers to rules and norms that are established and maintained by the therapist and client alike to "steer" the course of therapy.

To maintain stability, systems tend to operate within particular ranges of norms and behaviors. Systems theorists hold a single member or entity does not control how homeostatic interactional patterns develop; rather, family systems function as a gestalt, or group larger than the sum of its part, to determine the rules, roles, and patterns of the family-system interactions that are often characterized by a *redundancy principle,* which holds family members operate within a narrow range of possible behavior open to them. For example, if a crisis strikes the family, the mother takes on a leadership role and the rest of the family system follows the mother. Redundancy fosters predictability and continuity in systems; however, if homeostatic rules are too rigid or do not adequately consider both individual and systems-level needs, conflict and dysfunction can ensue. Should the weight of the crisis be too heavy for the mother or the mother not be in a position to assume a leadership role, family rules must be flexible enough to allow change and adjustment to the way crises are normally handled by the family system.

Family systems move between homeostasis and *disequilibrium.* Disequilibrium represents imbalance in the system and can create a sense of discomfort or loss. Balance is restored through system reorganization and realignment. For example, if the mother is unable to lead the family during a crisis, the family system may temporarily feel unstable and chaotic. However, reorganization of family roles and rules to allow the father to step into this role and move the family through the crisis will help to restore homeostasis. The ability to concurrently maintain sufficient regularity and adaptability to change is critical to family functioning. Systems must provide a context of security while also promoting growth and change of members and of the system as a whole.

Negative and Positive Feedback

Family systems use feedback to monitor stability and change. *Feedback* is a process of controlling the system through reintegrating results of past performance, thereby increasing likelihood of survival. Feedback loops are circular mechanisms purposed to introduce information about a system's output back to its input so that modifications to improve functionality can be made. Feedback loops ward against excessive fluctuations and enhance system adaptability.

Systems require both negative and positive feedback. *Negative feedback* is considered attenuating, as it alerts the system to continue existing interactional patterns and norms. In contrast, *positive feedback* is considered amplifying, alerting the system to change. Identified changes may be perceived as desirable or undesirable to the family.

Using information gained through positive feedback, feedback loops are created toward either reestablishing the former homeostasis or toward creating new system norms and interactions. Emerging symptomology in families frequently signals disequilibrium, with extant interactional sequences no longer meeting the needs of the system. For example, anxiety appearing in a family member may suggest that the individual's sense of safety has been disturbed. Using this feedback, the family system may make adjustments to restore a feeling of safety. This may occur through family discussions, reinforcing family boundaries, or bringing in outside assistance (i.e., a therapist), among other responses. Positive feedback loops may adhere the following cycle:

"Normal" Homeostasis—Tension Rises—Early Positive Feedback—Symptom—Positive Feedback—Tension Subsides—Self-Correction

First- and Second-Order Change

Following the receipt of positive feedback, systems often seek to reduce disequilibrium by reestablishing the former homeostasis. *First-order change* marks a return of previously established system norms and interactional patterns. Roles may shift or reverse, but the underlying family structure remains constant. For example, within a family, a complementary or mutually beneficial relationship may exist where the parent serves as a caregiver and the child serves as someone dependent on the caregiver. However, should the family system experience chronic illness of the parent, positive feedback will be transmitted signaling potential disruptions to the system. A subsequent first-order change to the family could include the child transferring to a caregiving role for the now dependent parent. First-order change is indicated here since while roles have reversed, the basic family structure (caregiver–dependent) is preserved.

At times disruptions to the system may exceed the capabilities of the rules, roles, and behaviors shaping the current system. *Second-order change* refers to structural changes to a family system in response to positive feedback. Rules and roles that guide the system are fundamentally altered, resulting in a new form of homeostasis. For example, rather than maintaining the previously mentioned caregiver–dependent relationship, the family system would forge new ways of relating to better meet systemic needs. Potential second-order level changes here could include establishing a more equitable power hierarchy or introducing a new member to the system (i.e., grandparent, external caregiver, or spouse).

Therapeutic Application

Neither first- nor second-order change is inherently better to promote change for family systems. In determining the appropriate level of change for families, professionals should consider the client's context. Further, therapists may engage families in conversations that explore current assets and deficits within the family patterns, as well as first- and second-order changes that the family feels may be most appropriate to (re)establishing optimal functioning for individual members and the system as a whole. Systems-oriented therapists may introduce small, yet highly powerful disruptions to challenge the family's less functional homeostatic patterns of interaction. Positive feedback generated through these purposeful disturbances facilitates natural reorganization in the family in response to new information. *Reframing* is a particularly important unbalancing mechanism in family systems therapy. Reframing invites family members to considered unexamined assumptions, roles, or interactional sequences. The role of symptoms within the broader family system may also be explored, with specific attention to how undesired symptoms may unconsciously function to maintain the system-level goal of homeostasis.

Several guidelines exist for integrating principles of homeostasis into systems-minded therapy. First, homeostatic patterns provide a window into family interactional sequences. Focus should reside in the process of family exchanges over the content of interactions. To illustrate, if a parenting dyad were to describe consistent and heated stalemates regarding parenting decisions, therapeutic emphasis should be given to *how* the couple discusses and negotiates these topics versus *what* is said or decided. Second, therapists may consider the homeostatic function of the presenting problem. How does the symptom contribute to a sense of balance in the family? Does the symptom cultivate connection, power, or distance? By understanding the function of symptoms, families are optimally assisted in exploring fears or hesitance to change. Iterative therapeutic transactions occur entailing assessment and interruption of interaction sequences, scaffolding family reorganization, and evaluating outcomes and new responses. This pattern is continued until the problem is resolved, with therapist assessment and interruption informed by goals constructed by families themselves.

Critiques and Considerations

General systems theory has received some criticism related to the transferability of this metaphor to family systems. A primary area of concern is the failure of systems theorists to adequately account for power differentials in shaping homeostatic patterns. When considering family structures and patterns, it is important to account for the social, historical, economic, and political contexts in which family systems are embedded. Additionally, attention may be given to how gender and power relations in broader society are reflected in interpersonal relationships and challenges within individual family systems.

A second criticism of systems theory–oriented conceptualizations of homeostasis refer to simplistic understandings that fail to deal with change. First-order changes are described as systemic integration of positive feedback and reestablishment of homeostasis without fundamental organizational or interactional changes. However, the feasibility of returning to a former and identical state of homeostasis has been questioned. Change is a complex and at times subtle occurrence, with new states always slightly different than previous stages.

Finally, postmodern and feminist theorists challenge the idea of single "truths" in understanding social realities. These critics suggest systems metaphors (i.e., subsystems, homeostasis, feedback) are mechanical and reflect outdated modernistic views. Family systems are complex and forcing understanding of families into these "boxes" may not only be inaccurate, but also potentially harmful to families. Caution is warranted in assuming universal truths about family functioning and "normal" patterns of behavior and interaction. More than absolute truths, homeostasis and other systems principles may be more effectively viewed as conceptual tools for describing and understanding potential aspects of family functioning.

Jessica Lloyd-Hazlett

See also Complementary and Symmetrical Relationships; Cybernetics; Second-Order Change; Second-Order Family Therapy; Strategic Family Therapy; Systemic Family Therapy

Further Readings

Bateson, G. (1972). *Steps to an ecology of mind*. New York, NY: Dutton.

Bertalanffy, L. von. (1968). *General systems theory*. New York, NY: Braziller.

Carter, B., & McGoldrick, M. (Eds.). (2005). *The expanded family life cycle: Individual, family, and social perspectives*. Boston, MA: Pearson.

Gehart, D. (2015). *Theory and treatment planning in family therapy: A competency-based approach*. Boston, MA: Cengage.

Goldenberg, H., & Goldenberg, I. (2013). *Family therapy: An overview* (8th ed.). Belmont, CA: Brooks/Cole.

McGoldrick, M., & Carter, B. (2003). The family life cycle. In F. Walsh (Ed.), *Normal family processes* (3rd ed., pp. 375–398). New York, NY: Guilford Press.

McGoldrick, M., & Hardy, K. V. (Eds.). (2008). *Re-visioning family therapy: Race, culture, and gender in clinical practice*. New York, NY: Guilford Press.

Homework Assignments in Therapy

Couples and families seek therapy in order to address issues affecting their relationship with each other. With the help of the therapist, they come up with ways to effectively cope with stressors and learn new behaviors. One of the important factors in enhancing this change process is the integration of homework assignments, which are completed between sessions and discussed in therapy sessions with the therapist. Homework assignments involve completing behavioral and cognitive tasks prescribed by the therapist to cooperative couples and families. These tasks should be closely connected with the session content, connect to therapeutic goals, and be created in collaboration with the client. Therapists should be familiar with different assignments and determine appropriateness for clients. Assignments, which act as a guide in the therapeutic relationship, can include a number of activities that are customized to suit the needs of the couple or family. Assignments completed between sessions provide clients with a sense of continuity and stability, and encourage deep reflection and active demonstration of skills learned in session with the therapist. They can greatly enhance couple and family sessions and should be incorporated as often as possible to encourage personal growth and opportunities for insight development. This entry introduces homework assignments as it relates to couples and family therapy and explains the benefits of the assignments, types of assignments, implementation, and noncompliance.

Theoretical Orientation

Although clinicians with various theoretical backgrounds incorporate homework assignments (also known as between-session assignments), the primary theoretical orientation associated with homework assignments as part of the therapeutic relationship is cognitive-behavioral therapy (CBT). Originally termed "cognitive therapy," CBT was developed in the early 1960s by psychiatrist Aaron T. Beck as a short-term, structured form of psychotherapy for the treatment of depression. Beck used a variety of work from sources such as Karen Horney, Alfred Adler, Albert Ellis, and Albert Bandura to develop CBT.

Treatment is based on developing a cognitive formulation and a conceptualization or understanding of a case. In addition, an integral aspect of CBT is homework. During therapy, homework is not optional but rather used to provide clients with an additional opportunity to monitor cognitive and behavioral change during their week before returning to the next session. Cognitive-behavioral therapists working with couples and families have stressed the importance of homework assignments and consider it to be a foundational aspect of treatment.

Choosing and Implementing Homework

During the first session with couples and families, the therapist should begin thinking about introducing their clients to homework assignments. Preparing clients to engage in homework between sessions is crucial in the first session. Clients can have an open discussion about benefits and limitations, and the therapist also has the opportunity to address these concerns and provide clarification on the importance of completing homework assignments. It is imperative for the therapist to seek commitment from the couples and families to carry out the decided upon homework assignment. This also addresses any resistance the clients may have and prepare solutions to avoid self-sabotage. A commitment from each client indicates that the clients are willing to take personal responsibility for the task assigned.

Several factors must be considered when choosing homework assignments in order to provide the client with the best possible chance of success and to monitor treatment progress between sessions. Assignments should start off being small and realistic so clients learn that change is a gradual process. When choosing homework, the clients should play an active role in deciding the assignments to be completed. Therefore, the process should be as collaborative as possible in order to enhance compliance. The therapist should consider not only the quality of the assignment but also the quantity. The therapists' ability to predict possible difficulties with assignments based on client diagnosis and personality style is also beneficial as this can help determine the best possible homework that meets the needs of the clients. Assignments that have the potential to cause conflict between couples or families should not be given to complete between sessions; instead, these assignments may be beneficial to complete in session.

Homework content should be based on the sessions and not be randomly assigned. During the session, the client and therapist should work together to identify specific areas of development and change. Since one of the goals of homework assignments is to provide a successful experience for the clients, the therapist should ensure that the client demonstrates the ability to practice the assignment between sessions. Therefore, the client's mental, social, financial, spiritual, and environmental factors should also be considered when choosing homework. It is also critical that whatever homework is assigned is first demonstrated within the session so clients have a clear understanding of what is expected.

It is important to let clients know that although it is encouraged and expected that they actively engage in sessions and complete homework assignments, if an assignment is not completed, a session can still be a productive one where the therapist can obtain useful information. This reduces the possibility of clients feeling discouraged or identifying themselves as failures.

Scheduling Homework

Homework should be scheduled in a way that boosts productivity and effectiveness for the clients. The therapist should discuss with couples and families the time of day assignments would be completed as this helps the client to schedule the task while taking each person's responsibilities into consideration. The therapist should discuss the duration of time clients are expected to work on assignments, and it should not be too long or complicated. It is important to also discuss how many times during the week the task would be attempted. Clients should also discuss the possibility of having a specific place (if applicable) to complete assignments. This provides some consistency and offers an opportunity to create new spaces that are not associated with conflict or trauma.

Types of Homework

In addition to providing continuity between sessions, homework assignments help clients to turn their insights into something tangible. Selecting assignments is an important part of therapy. It should be done with care and caution as clients seek to discover what they want to change, identify the support they have in the process, and consider obstacles to be removed in order to encourage adaptive behaviors and decrease maladaptive behaviors. The therapist should also be familiar with the homework assignments and when possible, the therapist should also attempt to complete the homework in order to have a more realistic connection with the tasks assigned to the clients.

There are various types of homework assignments that can be provided to couples and families for accomplishing both long- and short-term goals, depending on the nature of the sessions. Homework can be provided to help promote awareness, provide information, and challenge attitudes and beliefs. It can also be task oriented in order to elicit behavior change either in a linear or paradoxical process.

Bibliotherapy

The purpose of assigning bibliotherapy to couples and families is to provide resources for clients to read between sessions that connect with their current presenting concerns. Couples and families with mild problems may consider reading self-help books that provide encouragement and suggestions for improving conditions. The therapist should be familiar with books that are suggested to determine whether it is appropriate and acceptable for the clients based on their goals in therapy. During sessions, the therapist should follow up by asking questions about the readings and process how the clients applied the content to their lives.

Journaling

Keeping a daily record of personal growth is a helpful way to track progress between sessions. Couples and families may complete a journal either as open-ended writing or for a more in-depth reflection of their experience, thoughts, feelings, and actions. Journal entries may also be used to document self-monitoring activities discussed in session. Journaling allows for freedom of expression and can be done in a variety of ways. Couples and families may opt for doing a collage, drawing, painting, scrapbook, paragraphs, short sentences, or select words as their journal entry. Couples and families can journal together and individually. Journaling is a way to also document new behaviors.

Thought Record

Couples and families can log their thoughts about their experience in order to assess for patterns of thinking that may help or negatively impact their current situation. Couples and families can identify trigger points that may be a source of conflict in relationships. The therapist may review thought records during sessions to determine if there are cognitive distortions impacting the relationship and help clients identify ways to challenge negative thinking. The therapist may also use thought records to teach cognitive restructuring and thought-replacement skills.

Scheduling

In order to improve relationships among family members and couples, homework assignments may involve scheduling activities together which may include: family dinners, activities with children, sex, date nights, exercise, community activities, time with other family members and friends, and social activities. Scheduling activities encourages couples and families to track time spent together and alone. This homework activity may also help couples and families to identify ways to improve time management, communication, and problem-solving skills.

Autobiography

Writing a personal story helps couples and families bond as they can identify significant events, milestone achievements, and goals for each person. It also encourages introspection and a deeper reflection of one's personal journey. Autobiographies not only create an opportunity for reconciling events from the past, but it may also provide a source of inspiration and purpose for future goals within relationships.

Worksheets

Couples and families can complete worksheets either as a combined task or individually on a variety of topics such as skill building, communication, interpersonal effectiveness, healthy confrontation, personal inventory, hobbies, daily activities, parenting, boundaries, building love maps, and relationship building activities. The therapist should review these worksheets with clients to monitor progress or identify areas of further improvement.

Out-of-Session Interaction

In order to monitor progress outside of sessions, couples and families may be encouraged to document out-of-session interactions through video or audio recordings. The therapist can review the recordings in session with the clients and elicit feedback to discuss coping strategies and the interaction demonstrated.

Benefits of Homework

Therapists use homework assignments to monitor progress of couples and families on their quest to reach therapeutic goals. Between-session assignments should allow clients the ability to master the skills learned in therapy sessions that are directed towards symptom improvement. In couple and family therapy, homework assignments create opportunities for more focus and structure within family dynamics and couple relations, resulting in progression toward therapeutic goals. Couples and families become more involved in the therapeutic process outside of the structured sessions with a therapist.

Homework assignments also give couples and families something to look forward to outside of session to keep them engaged with their therapeutic goals. Working on tasks between sessions allows couples and families to remain engaged with each other. The time spent between sessions also provides an opportunity to process content from in-session work and apply it to homework assignments for reinforcement. The ability of clients to actively engage in their therapeutic progress in between sessions is also empowering as they take personal responsibility for their growth collectively and individually.

Turmoil and dysfunction within couples and families can create a volatile environment for the clients and those around them. Homework assignments provide structure for clients, which is crucial for the therapeutic process. Without structure the therapeutic process becomes unstable and unhealthy for the couples and families. Homework assignments create an atmosphere for clients to engage in their therapeutic goals on a daily basis, with the majority of therapy occurring in between sessions in the environment where the dysfunction was created or maintained.

Implementing coping behaviors is another important benefit of homework assignments as clients have the opportunity to put into practice the coping skills and new behaviors learned in session. This increases awareness and personal responsibility for the change process. Homework assignments increase expectations that clients will follow through with these changes between sessions, which eventually leads to new learned behaviors to be practiced when therapy ends.

By adding focus and structure, couples and families can bring a sense of refreshed vitality for working towards their goals. This may result in increased motivation for change as clients have specific tasks for completion, gain insight, and develop positive coping behaviors while working at a pace that is appropriate for their progress in therapy. Couples and families are also able to elicit involvement from each other while working on assignments. This increases bonding and working relations between members and fosters a sense of trust and camaraderie as couples and families take on different roles within their environment to encourage participation. When faced with challenges, members are able to address conflict with the therapist to identify skills for dealing with resistance.

Reviewing Homework Assignments

Homework assignments should not be given in isolation to the therapeutic process. It is essential that therapists review homework assignments to monitor client progress and areas of concern for further development of skills. Couples and families take responsibility for participating in homework assignments as a way to track their progress and to remain actively involved in their therapy. If homework sessions are not reviewed, clients may be left without appropriate direction and progress made between sessions may be unrecognized or never processed. It is just as important to identify what is not working for clients between sessions since this may give the therapist a clearer conceptualization of the status of the progress of couples and families.

Before clients show up to sessions, the therapist should be familiar with the homework assignments prescribed at the last session. Therapists should begin session with a review of homework unless another matter of urgency is presented. Because homework is essential to the therapeutic process, reviewing the assignments to assess for progress is important. By doing this, clients may be further encouraged to engage in future homework assignments and be compliant in therapy. Homework may be reviewed individually or with couples and families.

Noncompliance

Compliance with any homework assignment is usually a strong indicator of commitment and can be a predictor of change for couples and families. However, clients may not always comply with homework assignments. Once the therapist is aware that clients are not completing assignments, it is important to consider the factors that contribute to noncompliance. When obstructing factors are identified, couples and families can work with the therapist to have a better understanding of what prevents active engagement in assignments.

When discussing homework assignments, it is important for the therapist to be aware of their perception of noncompliance when compared to the client's definition of noncompliance. Clients' resistance to completing homework may be as a result of a number of factors including unclear instructions, lack of motivation, and unrealistic expectations from therapist and client. Presenting symptomology, home environment, therapy goals, and clients' level of hope for change should be considered when noncompliance with homework assignments becomes an issue.

When working with couples and families, explanations for noncompliance may exist in either the individual or the interaction between members. When discussing how change can occur it is usually most effective when all members of the system are in agreement. However, when one person or persons disagree with the change process, this can result in a roadblock for completing homework assignments. Therapists should explore the meaning of change, both individually and collectively, in order to identify the core of noncompliance.

Consequences for noncompliance should be discussed in session with the therapist to encourage clients to take personal inventory of their part in achieving the therapeutic goals. When couples and families struggle to come up with a consensus on consequences, the therapist may elicit from each member their personal expectations for therapy and create a strategy to encourage clients to be more open to change.

Karisse A. Callender

See also Cognitive-Behavioral Couples Therapy; Cognitive-Behavioral Family Therapy; Confrontation; Multiple Family Therapy; Self-Help

Further Readings

Beck, J. S. (2011). *Cognitive behavior therapy: Basics and beyond* (2nd ed.). New York, NY: Guilford Press.

Cronin, T. J., Lawrence, K. A., Taylor, K., Norton, P. J., & Kazantzis, N. (2015). Integrating between-session interventions (homework) in therapy: The importance of the therapeutic relationship and cognitive case conceptualization. *Journal of Clinical Psychology: In Session, 71,* 439–450.

Dattilio, F. M., & Dickson, J. (2007). Assigning homework to couples and families. *Cognitive and Behavioral Practice, 14,* 268–277.

Dattilio, F. M., Kazantzis, N., Shinkfield, G., & Carr, A. G. (2011). A survey of homework use, experience of barriers to homework, and attitudes about the barriers to homework among couples and family therapists. *Journal of Marital & Family Therapy, 37,* 121–136.

Kazantzis, N., & Dattilio, F. M. (2010). Definitions of homework, types of homework, and ratings of the importance of homework among psychologists with cognitive behavior therapy and psychoanalytic theoretical orientations. *Journal of Clinical Psychology, 66,* 758–773.

Kazantzis, N., Deane, F. P., & Ronan, K. R. (2004). Assessing compliance with homework assignments:

Review and recommendations for clinical practice. *Journal of Clinical Psychology, 60,* 627–641.

Mausbach, B. T., Moore, R., Roesch, S., Cardenas, V., & Patterson, T. L. (2010). The relationship between homework compliance and therapy outcomes: An updated meta-analysis. *Cognitive Therapy and Research, 34,* 429–438.

Nichols, M. P. (2008). *Family therapy concepts and methods* (8th ed.). Boston, MA: Pearson.

Weeks, G. R., & Treat, S. R. (2001). *Couples in treatment: Techniques and approaches for effective practice* (2nd ed.). Philadelphia, PA: Brunner-Routledge.

Young, M. E. (2013). *Learning the art of helping: Building blocks and techniques* (5th ed.). Boston, MA: Pearson.

Homicide

Homicide is defined as one person taking the life of another person or persons. Homicide can be intentional and planned or unintentional or unplanned (e.g., cases arising out of self-defense or violence or neglect not intended to end in death). Dependent upon the details, homicide may or may not be considered a criminal act, such as in the case of self-defense. It is therefore important to separate the act of killing from any criminal definitions when conceptualizing the offense. This entry examines homicide within couples and families and considers several common risk factors. This entry pays specific attention to intimate partner homicide, familicide, and filicide.

Homicide in Couples and Families

It is imperative for marriage, couple, and family counselors to have an understanding of the risks and realities of homicide within couple and family systems. The majority of homicides are committed by individuals known to the victim(s), as opposed to by strangers; and a large portion of nonstranger homicides occur within couples and families. Women are more likely than men to be the victims of intimate partner homicide. The majority of children under the age of 5 who die by homicide were murdered by a parent, which is often referred to as *filicide*, or *infanticide*, if the children are under 1 year of age.

Intimate Partner Homicide

Intimate partner (IP) homicide refers to the killing of an intimate partner. IP homicide accounts for roughly 10% of all homicides, though comprehensive data on this can be difficult to collect due to varying definitions of intimate partners and how or if the legal system of a particular country addresses and accounts for IP homicide. Although IP homicide is considered rare, understanding the dynamics of it could help mental health professionals assess and assist those in danger. IP homicide is the only type of deadly violence in which the victims are typically female. Females are more than 3 times as likely as males to be victims of IP homicide. Conversely, males are more than 3 times as likely to be perpetrators of IP homicide. In addition, males are much more likely than females to commit suicide after IP homicide. The motives for committing IP homicide (or subsequent suicide) also differ by gender. Some literature refers to the killing of one's wife as *uxoricide* and the killing of one's husband as *mariticide*. However, some literature simply uses the term mariticide to mean the killing of a spouse. Gay male couples have the highest rate of IP homicide, followed by heterosexual couples, and then lesbian couples.

It is important to note that IP homicide is usually related to conflict between the couple that has previously occurred in a nonlethal manner. However, when a couple is faced with confounding and multiple variables, IP homicide may be the result. As mentioned previously, IP homicide may be intentional or unintentional, and the motives and risk factors for IP violence and IP homicide are similar. IP homicide can begin as IP violence but continue to escalate because of other variables, ultimately resulting in one person killing the other. The killing can be intentional and planned, intentional but not planned, unintentional and accidental (mistake), or take place as a form of self-defense in response to violence.

The motives for heterosexual males committing IP homicide typically involve infidelity (suspected or actual), jealousy, a female partner trying to leave the relationship, and discipline or consequences for a female partner who is acting too independently and without the approval of the male in the partnership. Multiple motives and risk factors, such as alcohol or separation, increase the chances of IP homicide. Motives for heterosexual females committing IP homicide are often in response to the male partner being violent, controlling, and possessive. In gay couples, the motives and risk factors may appear similar to those typically exhibited by heterosexual males or females, dependent upon the couples' relationship dynamics and roles.

Familicide

Familicide can be defined as a homicide in which there are multiple victims and where one is a spouse or intimate partner and at least one victim is a child. Familicide is overwhelmingly perpetrated by males, with males being the offenders in over 90% of the cases. That being said, it is rare that a male would kill his partner and children in the same incident. Though females do at times kill their own children, females very rarely kill their spouses and children at the same time.

In regard to motives, familicide has very much in common with uxoricides, especially when compared to filicide; indeed, familicide and filicide often have different motives. In both cases, males are the primary perpetrator and motives include infidelity, jealousy, a female partner leaving, and discipline for the female's behaviors. The obvious difference between uxoricide and familicide is the presence of children. In familicides, children can be a reminder or cue for sexual jealousy of the male. If the children are from a previous partner, they are more likely to activate the jealousy. For this reason, stepchildren have a greater chance of being killed by a stepfather than biological children do by their father (nevertheless, the killing of stepchildren happens less frequently overall than it does to genetic children, and in some studies adopted children are considered genetic children). In addition, familicides are more likely to occur in situations where older children defend the mother when she is the father's primary target. Familicides are also more likely to occur if the father uses a child to terrify and intimidate a mother who will be attacked after the child. In regard to homicide-suicide, males committing familicides are much more likely to subsequently commit suicide than in any other type of homicide. In fact, suicide by males who kill unrelated persons is quite rare.

Usually males committing familicide appear to be angry, hostile, and focused on issues of jealousy or separation. However, some cases appear to be a form of altruistic familicide, in which the killer has the perception of saving his family by killing them. The motives for altruistic familicide appear to be quite similar to altruistic filicide, though there are two obvious differences. Females almost never commit familicide in any form, though females account for a good majority of altruistic filicide. Also, in familicide, the male is being altruistic toward the entire family, including the mother, and in filicide, the other parent is not harmed or killed. Males who commit altruistic familicide are thought to be depressed and hopeless.

Filicide

Filicide is defined as the killing of a child by a parent. Though murdering a child is not common, it is a significant cause of death for children in developed countries. The term *parent* in this case encompasses biological parents, stepparents, and adoptive parents. Some literature includes foster parents, and some does not include them.

Filicide includes neonaticide and infanticide. *Neonaticide* is a term reserved for the killing of a child within the first 24 hours of her of his life. *Infanticide*, or infant homicide, refers to the killing of a child within the first year of her or his life. Filicide is devastating and obviously results in the death of a child (or children), though the motives are not always malicious or evil in nature. In fact, some motives for filicide can be seemingly altruistic. Filicide is committed by both males and females, though the method and motives can differ drastically.

Filicide is evident throughout the course of human history and within various and different cultural contexts, though attitudes and beliefs about these incidents have either changed or been controversial. One of the more well-known stories of filicide is depicted in the Bible, when the patriarch Abraham is commanded by God to kill his son Isaac (although Isaac's life is spared). Filicide also played a role in ancient Rome and Greece and is part of various mythological tales (e.g., Medea). Acts of filicide are also mentioned in African, Asian, and European histories and in the history of the Americas. Even today in some countries and cultures, children are killed after birth in order to control population numbers or select the most favorable child. For example, one-child-per-family policies implemented in China in the 1970s saw an increase of instances of female infanticide, which had been practiced for centuries in that country. It should be noted that the one-child-per-family policy in China was relaxed in 2013, but the problem still exists as preference is placed on having male offspring.

Of the types of familial homicide, filicide has the most disparity in regards to motives. Maternal filicide motives can include an unwanted pregnancy and child, denial of child and subsequent dissociation at birth, mentally ill or psychotic parent, altruistic motives, extended suicide, accidental death in relation to battered child syndrome, revenge on a partner or spouse, and even evolutionary and reproductive motives. Altruistic motives are killings that are done as a result of what the offending parent(s) report as love for the child. This could mean saving the child from a terrible and difficult existence, killing a child who has a severe and debilitating disease, or the saving of the child from a mother and family who is unable to care for it. Motives for paternal filicide are usually related to child abuse and violent tendencies. Altruistic filicide and mental illness are rarer in filicide involving a male parent. In addition, in males, altruistic familicide is more prevalent than altruistic filicide.

An important note concerning filicide is about sudden infant death syndrome (SIDS), sudden unexplained deaths in infancy (SUDI), and Munchausen syndrome; another term that has been historically used is shaken baby syndrome. As many as 20% of infant deaths from SIDS or SUDI could have occurred from nonnatural means (i.e., they may be intentional or accidental deaths that have been falsely attributed to SIDS or SUDI). It is often difficult for professionals to discern between filicide and SIDS, SUDI, or Munchausen syndrome, but actual filicide numbers may be higher than reported due to an inability to accurately assess the cause of death.

Another discussion about filicide concerns the various laws surrounding infant deaths. As it can be difficult to tell the differences between filicide, SIDS, SUDI, and Munchausen syndrome, it is also difficult to create and enforce laws in regards to them. In addition, most developed and modern societies and countries have specific laws about infanticide, which stem from the British Infanticide Act of 1922. The two countries that do not have infanticide laws are the United States and Scotland. These laws are in regards to filicide by mothers just after giving birth; as many mothers have experienced psychiatric symptoms, such as depression and dissociation, there are certain considerations under the law in other countries to account for these conditions. By contrast, mothers in the United States and Scotland can be charged with murder in the first 24 hours of a child's life, though in most other societies the maximum charge is manslaughter. Coincidentally, mothers who kill their children in the first 24 hours have a much lower rate of mental illness than mothers who kill their older children.

A final discussion surrounding filicide is the idea that many other mammals commit filicide, which leads some to believe that filicide actually has an evolutionary and reproductive purpose. Various studies have been done on filicide and other mammals; the most commonly discussed motives are sexual selection, an adaptive behavior that provides benefits to the offspring of the killers or the killers themselves, and cannibalism (which on some level does provide a benefit to the killer but is thought to be an added benefit as opposed to the primary one). Leopards, who kill roughly one third of their offspring, lead all other mammals in filicide deaths. A final note regarding mammalian filicide is that solitary animals are more likely to commit filicide, which may be important when considering the differences between rural and urban human environments.

Risk Factors

As a practitioner, it is important to consider the underlying, and sometimes indirect, risk factors for family violence and homicide. Families where domestic violence occurs are at the greatest risk for intrafamily homicide, and children are at risk whether or not they were directly victimized by the ongoing domestic violence—a factor that often goes overlooked. Women are at least 3 times more likely than men to be the victims of intimate partner homicide, and men have a much higher rate of being the offenders in family homicides. For children under 5 years of age, homicide by a parent is the most frequent type of homicide, with a similar risk of being murdered by a mother or father. Infanticides most frequently arise out of aggravated child abuse, and there is a negative correlation with the age of the parent, with younger mothers having higher risk.

Ongoing substance use, including intoxication at the time of homicide, also increases risk, with alcohol being the most frequently noted substance in familial homicide cases. Significant stressors such as separation, divorce, and custody battles can increase risk, as does extreme financial and economic distress. Violent and criminal histories are higher than for nonhomicidal counterparts, as are histories of psychiatric illness.

For male offenders, firearms are the most frequent means used to commit homicide, and access to guns coupled with other risk factors should be noted. Some offenders report that, had they not had access to a firearm, they don't believe they would have committed homicide against family members due to the difficulty of carrying out other means. Statistics on female offenders indicate a wide array of methods, with no specific method being used more frequently, though guns are one of the less frequent means.

Not all cases arise directly out of domestic violence situations or clearly volatile histories, and the motivation for intrafamily homicide can be complex, with some offenders reporting altruistic reasoning behind acts of homicide apart from relief from violent situations, such as a desire to put a family member or members out of real or imagined suffering, including illness and financial distress. In rare cases, psychiatric symptomology of a parent can result in delusional distress leading to altruistic homicide.

Additional Considerations for Practitioners

Assessing Risk/Prevention

It is the practitioner's ethical duty to report knowledge or strong suspicion of potential harm to others, and it is important to keep in mind that threats against family members may or may not be clearly made, and knowledge of risk factors and appropriate screening tools is thus all the more imperative. In addition, when working with clients who have increased risk factors and incidences of violence, it is important that the counselor attend to their own safety.

While children in homes where intimate partner domestic violence is occurring may not be directly victimized by the ongoing violence, they are nonetheless at risk if the violence should escalate, which has gone overlooked by some social service providers, and this should be considered in reporting protocols. As domestic violence reporting guidelines can vary by state, counselors should familiarize themselves with the guidelines in any states in which they practice. One preventive approach is to educate clients on specific increased risk factors they may have for victimization.

Crisis Intervention

Sometimes, preventative counseling measures fail or are never employed, and the first time a family comes into care is during a crisis. It is the practitioner's duty to first stabilize the survivors to a precrisis level of functioning as best they can, which may prove very difficult, especially if the home or family unit has been demolished due to the homicide. A working knowledge of crisis intervention strategies and referrals is imperative at this juncture and should be prioritized above long-term treatment. Early crisis intervention can help to prevent future distress.

Future Prevention

After crisis stabilization, focusing on the ongoing and long-term mental health implications for surviving relatives of family homicide becomes the focus. For instance, there is potential for grieving of multiple significant losses by both death(s) and the incarceration of the offender. Both child and adult survivors are at greater risk for posttraumatic stress disorder (PTSD), which should be initially addressed during crisis intervention, especially if they personally witnessed the homicide. Unresolved trauma surrounding the event can lead to challenges in future functioning. While immediate crisis intervention would best serve as the primary intervention, ongoing work with any surviving family members would be imperative from a preventative standpoint.

Working With Offenders

Practitioners may find themselves working with familial homicide offenders in a number of different settings. Keeping in mind that not all perpetrators of homicide are considered (or convicted) as criminal, it would be feasible to work with them in the general population. Practitioners in correctional settings could certainly find themselves working with offenders who were found guilty of criminal charges related to the homicide. As with any population, it is imperative for counselors to reflect on any biases they may have regarding work with persons who have committed homicides, in order to effectively counsel them.

The dynamics of family homicide are complex, and the act can occur in a number of ways. Understanding the relational and environmental stressors that contribute to increased risk for family violence and homicide can aid in preventing the offenses. Understanding clinical as well as legal and ethical interventions is essential as a means of prevention as well as intervention with survivors and offenders.

*Ann M. McCaughan
and Gregory Irwin*

See also Crisis Intervention With Couples and Families; Debt and Financial Strain; Domestic Violence; Duty to Warn and Protect; Loss; Poverty and Family Development

Further Readings

Balme, G. A., & Hunter, L. T. B. (2013). Why leopards commit infanticide. *Animal Behaviour, 86,* 791–799.

Bridges, F. S., Tatum, K. M., & Kunselman, J. C. (2008). Domestic violence statutes and rates of intimate partner and family homicide. *Criminal Justice Policy Review, 19*(1), 117–130.

Brown, T., Tyson, D., & Arias, P. (2014). Filicide and parental separation and divorce. *Child Abuse Review, 23*(2), 79–88.

Eke, A., Hilton, N., Harris, G., Rice, M., & Houghton, R. (2011). Intimate partner homicide: Risk assessment and prospects for prediction. *Journal of Family Violence, 26*(3), 211–216.

Hamilton, L., Jaffe, P., & Campbell, M. (2013). Assessing children's risk for homicide in the context of domestic violence. *Journal of Family Violence, 28*(2), 179–189.

Juodis, M., Starzomski, A., Porter, S., & Woodworth, M. (2014). What can be done about high-risk perpetrators of domestic violence? *Journal of Family Violence, 29*(4), 381–390.

Liem, M., & Koenraadt, F. (2008). Filicide: A comparative study of maternal versus paternal child homicide. *Criminal Behavior and Mental Health, 18,* 166–176.

Liem, M., Levin, J., Holland, C., & Fox, J. (2013). The nature and prevalence of familicide in the United States, 2000–2009. *Journal of Family Violence, 28*(4), 351–358.

Mailloux, S. (2014). Fatal families: Why children are killed in familicide occurrences. *Journal of Family Violence, 29*(8), 921–926.

Roberts, D. W. (2009). Intimate partner homicide: Relationships to alcohol and firearms. *Journal of Contemporary Criminal Justice, 25*(1), 67–88.

Weizmann-Henelius, G., Gronroos, M, Putkonen, H., Lindberg, N., & Häkkänen-Nyholm, H. (2012). Gender-specific risk factors for intimate partner homicide: A nationwide register-based study. *Journal of Interpersonal Violence, 27*(8), 1519–1539.

HOPE-FOCUSED APPROACH TO COUPLE ENRICHMENT IN COUNSELING

The hope-focused approach to marriage enrichment strives to renew marriages that are in crisis. The approach was developed in the late 1990s by Everett L. Worthington to benefit couples going through conflict. Although the approach is strongly rooted in Christian principles, the biblical language can be modified to meet the needs of non-Christian couples as well. The approach conceptualizes marriage in terms of faith, work, and love. Hope-focused approach (HFA) draws from popular secular couples therapies with a theoretical framework that supports accommodative scaffolding on the part of the practitioner. HFA provides a theoretical and skill base for practitioners working within a Christian context. In essence, it is an approach to couples therapy known as hope-focused couple therapy (HFCT) and an approach to enrichment known as hope-focused couple enrichment (HFCE). This entry defines these hope-focused approaches, discusses the development and adoption of the hope-focused approach in couple's therapy, outlines how the approach has been conceptualized, and summarizes some of its key outcomes and interventions.

Why Hope-Focused Approach and Enrichment Counseling

An estimated 50% of all marriages in the United States end in separation or divorce. Divorce and separation have an impact on the mental health and physical well-being of family members. For divorced people, the consequences include increased rates of illness, higher mortality rates, financial challenges, and downward socioeconomic mobility, particularly for women. Children, in families characterized by marital conflict or divorce, are at greater risk for behavioral and emotional problems, including oppositional behavior, aggression, and symptoms of depression and anxiety.

The hope-focused approach itself is a theory of motivation and goal attainment. Worthington and his colleagues emphasized the need to focus on factors contributing to the effectiveness of approach, namely rerouting of negative relational patterns of marriage, offering a safe space for effective bonding, and provision of hope with a positive future outcome.

Most marriages and committed relationships begin with high satisfaction and a high hope that the relationship will be enduring. Evidence from several longitudinal studies of couples suggests that communication issues and intense marital conflict are among the leading risk factors for future divorce and marital disintegration (e.g., escalation, invalidation, pursuit, withdrawal, and negative constructs). These destructive patterns undermine the marriage through the erosion of friendship, love, sexual intimacy, trust, and commitment.

Development of Hope-Focused Approach

The hope-focused marital counseling approach was developed from the clinical and research experience of Worthington. It was created as a brief intervention with couples. The hope-focused approach is faith based and rooted in biblical principles but may be used with non-Christian couples if the religious language and biblical references are translated into broader concepts. The approach can be used by both novice and experienced therapists and incorporated within the experience of couple therapists. Hope-focused counseling approach is founded on the belief that hope is at the core of the Christian experience and that a lack of hope creates a crisis of faith. Hope involves maintaining a positive motivation to change (willpower), a variety of pathways to change (waypower), and perseverance (waitpower).

In order for change to occur, partners must have (a) the will to make their marriage better, (b) access to ways of making their marriage better, and (c) the faith to wait for their marriage to improve while they actively try to improve it.

Worthington observes that marital counseling cannot completely treat the multiple difficulties that face marriages; he mentions that too often novice counselors see themselves as referees or problem solvers who believe that they should resolve every difficulty that clients present. He suggests that focusing on everything could paralyze the counselor. Jennifer S. Ripley and Worthington state that conflict is at the heart of negative cognition and when conflicts are resolved cognition becomes positive. The objective is to assess and determine which of these areas needs intervention: (1) central beliefs and values, (2) core vision, (3) confession or forgiveness, (4) communication, (5) conflict resolution, (6) cognition, (7) closeness, (8) complicating factors, or (9) commitment.

Hope-focused counseling approach disagrees with the notion that communication problems are due to misinterpretation of meaning, power differences, or even how people say things. Worthington believes that the root cause of a marriage's communication problems reflects a deficit of love and lack of valuing the partner. The partner may feel devalued, unimportant, or unloved. When partners feel insecure, threatened, or without power they want to prove that they are adequate, important and powerful, and valued and loved. The role of the counselor is to restore the couples' feeling of both being valuable and loved. Hope-focused counseling approach stresses the importance of not being a referee and rather teaching couples how to resolve their own conflicts. This approach views conflict as a lack of valuing between partners and requires the counselor to help couples value each other even when disagreeing.

Counselors support couples in their ability to challenge negative thinking and focus on the positive aspects of their relationship. Attributions of blame, which are defined as blaming the spouse for the problems in the relationship, are changed toward empathy and forgiveness. Worthington maintains that those positive expectations about the future of the marriage increase a couple's resilience to disintegration. This creates and maintains positive assumptions about the relationship. Overall, the counselor guides the couple in their effort to maintain closeness, which is a balance between distance, coactions, or events that partners engage in together, including intimacy.

The matrix of hope-focused counseling approach emphasizes repairing damaged emotional bonds by promoting forgiveness. Hope-focused couples approach recommends embedding forgiveness in counseling; the approach maintains that a lack of forgiveness for a large event, or several small events, leads to a lack of empathy, reduced motivation to use good marital skills, and negative reciprocity. Nathaniel G. Wade and Worthington describe two types of forgiveness: decisional forgiveness and emotional forgiveness. In decisional forgiveness the individual decides to control their behavior, and this involves an act of will. However, emotional unforgiveness may still be experienced in the form of resentment, bitterness, and anger. Emotional forgiveness involves replacing negative, unforgiving emotions with positive other-oriented emotions, such as empathy, sympathy, compassion, and love for the partner. Emotional forgiveness changes the heart, whereas decisional forgiveness changes the behavior.

Conceptualization

According to Patrice Turner and Jennifer Ripley, conceptualizing a hope-focused approach in counseling couples in marital conflict brings about reestablishment of values such as faith, work, and love previously overlooked in the relationship. A common conceptualization of hope in the psychotherapy literature defines it as a cognitive construct, with two essential components: pathway thinking and agency thinking. Pathway thinking represents a person's perception that they can generate effective routes to desired goals. Agency thinking represents the individual's thoughts about their capacity to use the pathways.

Hope-focused marriage counseling is characterized mostly by employing two frameworks throughout: (1) the strategy for promoting love, faith, and work and (2) the goal of building hope by increasing willpower (motivation), waypower (making changes obvious to clients through active interventions or interactive materials, like written assignment, reports, or building a physical testimony to the couple's progress) and waitpower (the patience to persevere when progress is evident).

Regarding assessment and interventions, during hope-focused therapy sessions, the therapist targets nine areas for intervention: central values, core vision, confession and forgiveness, communication, conflict resolution, cognitions, closeness, complicating problems to address, and commitment. In a study conducted by Turner and Ripley with an underlining theme of conflict resolution difficulty, counselor assessment and intervention included video feedback and conflict resolution. The first session taped 10 minutes of communication between couples and included identifying information, presenting problem, relationship strengths, areas for potential change, suggestions for improving the relationship, and an ending summary. The second session reviewed the report and set up goals. The third session focused on conflict resolution with personal rules for conflict and included reviewing the recorded first session. The study found that couples who viewed a video of a session were more able to assume an outsider's perspective in conflict resolution.

Hope-focused counseling approach differentiates between commitments that involve a contract and those involving a covenant. Contractual arrangements are interpreted as occurring between individuals on mutually agreed terms. These tend to depend on reciprocity or an equal exchange. Note that evidence indicates that contractual commitments tend to deteriorate when agreements are not fulfilled. Worthington describes that in a traditional covenant, people care for and stay committed to a partner because they have staked both their honor and their word regardless of what the other person does; this is the optimal commitment in a marriage.

Hope-Focused Counseling Research Outcomes

Over the past 20 years, a number of hope-focused approaches have emerged with outcome studies. In a review of empirically supported marital enrichment programs, Scott F. Jakubowski, Eric P. Milne, Heidi Brunner, and Richard B. Miller found 4 efficacious (including hope-focused couple enrichment), 3 possibly efficacious, and 6 empirically untested hope-focused enrichment empirically supported treatments (ESTs). In terms of the efficacious studies and their outcomes, Worthington reported that 7 were Prevention and Relationship Enhancement Program (PREP), 19 were relationship enhancement (RE), 40 were couple communication program, and 4 were strategic hope-focused enrichment. These studies were an indication of the growing popularity and empirical validity of hope-focused counseling among various client populations. Reviewers of marital therapy literature agree that marital therapy may be effective in reducing conflict and increasing marital satisfaction, at least in the short-term, when compared to nontreatment controls. Research has also shown that hope positively influences both physical and psychological health. Therapists recognize the importance of hope in the therapeutic process.

Interventions

The hope-focused counseling approach (HFCA) combines a faith, work, and love perspective with the focus on hope. The approach uses specific interventions, which are identified using the following acrostics: STEPS, TANGO, LOVE, CLEAVE, REACH, and FREE. For example, the acrostic TANGO is explained as follows in two parts: TAN and GO. In TAN, *T* stands for "Tell what happened clearly and briefly"; *A* refers to "describe how the situation *affected* you"; and *N* is a cue to provide a nurturing statement. GO is reserved for the listener. In this case, *G* refers to "Did I get it?" and *O* to "Observe the effects of the conversation and comment on them." The goal of TANGO is to teach the couple to take turns in talking, understanding how they affect each other, and listening to each other.

Hope-focused couples therapy is usually designed to be a short-term (e.g., 5- to 12-week) intervention. Beginning with a comprehensive assessment (preintervention), couples typically undergo a 2-hour assessment session, which includes written and face-to-face assessments. Couples are then scheduled for a 1-hour feedback session the following week. The therapist uses a positive, solution-focused interview to address problematic topics while also exploring those that have led the couple to stay together.

John Alie Conteh and Portia Allie-Turco

See also Acceptance and Commitment Therapy; Couples and Marriage Counseling; Humanistic Family Therapy; Positive Psychology; Relationship Enhancement; Solution-Focused Brief Therapy

Further Readings

Baucomb, D. H., & Hoffman, J. A. (1986). Effectiveness of marital therapy: Current status and application to the clinical setting. In N. S. Jacobson & A. S. Gurman (Eds.), *Clinical handbook of marital therapy* (pp. 597–620). New York, NY: Guilford Press.

Furstenberg, E. F. (1990). Divorce and the American family. *Annual review of sociology, 16*, 379–403.

Gottman, J. M. (1994). *What predicts divorce? The relationship between marital processes and marital outcomes.* Hillsdale, NJ: Lawrence Erlbaum.

Ripley, J. S., & Worthington, E. L., Jr. (2014). *Couple therapy: A new hope-focused approach.* Downers Grove, IL: InterVarsity Press.

Turner, P., & Ripley, J. S. (2006). Applying hope-focused marriage therapy to conflict resolution in marriage: Case study. *Journal of Psychology and Christianity, 26*(1), 65–67.

Wade, N. G., & Worthington, E. L., Jr. (2003). Overcoming interpersonal offenses: Is forgiveness the only way to deal with unforgiveness? *Journal of Counseling and Development, 81*, 343–353.

Worthington, E. L., Jr. (1999). *Hope-focused marriage counseling: A guide to brief therapy.* Downers Grove, IL: InterVarsity Press.

Worthington, E. L., Jr. (2005). *Hope-focused marriage counseling: A guide to brief therapy* (Expanded ed.). Downers Grove, IL: InterVarsity Press.

HOSPICE

Hospice, or palliative, care is a philosophy and type of care that focuses on the relief of physical pain and mental stress of an individual who is chronically or terminally ill. When hospice was established in the United States in 1971, an interdisciplinary approach was the hallmark of its philosophy. While most hospice care in the United States is provided in the home, the use of palliative care and hospice in institutions has risen in recent years. The National Hospice and Palliative Care Organization reports that more than 1.4 million Americans receive care from the nation's hospice providers annually. This type of care provides relief from symptoms and supports quality of life for patients with serious advanced illness and provides support to their families. Hospice professionals, including counselors, focus on the caregiving needs of the dying individual and the family, including postmortem support. They provide resources that help people through the difficulty, uncertainty, and mystery involved in approaching the end of life and the period that follows. Hospice professionals help caregivers understand patients' particular afflictions and what symptoms can be expected. Caregivers are instructed on medication administration, tracking, and anticipated effects. They are advised to notify the hospice nurse if the medications do not relieve the symptoms, especially physical pain. Often, pain can be multifaceted and severe, and complete pain relief cannot always be achieved. Hospice is a team approach to caring for the dying and has many advantages for patients and their family members over traditional approaches to care. This entry outlines the advantages of hospice care, the eligibility requirements for hospice care, the role of caregivers and counselors in hospice care, and several distinct approaches to hospice care.

Advantages of Hospice

Through a proactive approach to the natural process of dying, palliative care leads to enhanced education and communication, better quality of life, as well as lower spending and decreased length of hospital stays. The goal of hospice is not to prolong life, but to deliver services that involve focused medical care with an emphasis on pain and other symptom management and mitigation. Palliative care interventions reduce the number of tests and procedures, intensive care therapeutics, and hospital readmissions, while enhancing communication of patient and family goals of care. Hospices also provide social support and bereavement services that are not available in nursing homes. For example, social support for caregivers of institutionalized individuals with dementia is very important because depressive symptoms and anxiety are often as high in caregivers after they institutionalize their relative as when they were in-home caregivers. In hospice care, the main guardians are the family caregiver(s) and a hospice nurse who coordinates and delivers these services. Hospice professionals inform people about the voluntary services and care levels they may receive upon consent, and they are involved in their care planning. People who enter hospice are acknowledging that they are willing to stop treatments designed to cure them or to prolong their lives. They agree to receive services to control their symptoms. However, patients always have the right to reinstate traditional care at any time, for any reason. If a patient's condition improves or the disease goes into remission, he or she can be discharged from hospice and return to aggressive, curative measures. Likewise, if a discharged patient wants to return to hospice care, Medicare, Medicaid, and most private insurance companies and HMOs will allow readmission.

Eligibility for Hospice

To be considered eligible for hospice care under Medicare, a patient must be entitled to Medicare Part A and be certified as terminally ill, which is defined as having a life expectancy of 6 months or less if the illness takes the normal course. Illnesses that meet these criteria include heart failure, cancer, chronic lung disease, dementia, and other diseases. This certification must be completed by two physicians, usually the medical director of hospice or physician representing hospice and the patient's attending physician. Once patients are enrolled in hospice, their condition is evaluated after 90 days, after 180 days, and every 60 days thereafter to determine continued eligibility. Patients will not be automatically discharged from hospice if they do not die within 6 months, but in order to remain enrolled they must show persistent decline. Hospice may also initiate a patient's discharge if the patient's behavior is disruptive, abusive, or uncooperative to the extent that delivery of care is seriously impaired. Patients or their representatives can also choose to revoke their hospice services at any time. Possible reasons for revocation are the desire to seek curative or more aggressive treatment, dissatisfaction with services, sudden changes in hospice personnel, increased availability of family caregivers, and inadequate pain management. Patients who are discharged alive from hospice may decline quickly and approximately one third die within 6 months.

Caregivers

Caregivers of end-of-life patients experience disruption of normal routines leading to social isolation and profound feelings of loneliness that can impact psychosocial well-being and physical health. Informal caregivers of hospice and palliative care patients show elevated rates of emotional distress and clinical depression. Family caregivers often suffer the highest measurable levels of physical and emotional distress. Postmortem bereavement also presents considerable challenges around experiences of loss and life transition. The family, including the dying individual, is central throughout the process of continued assessment, decision-making, plan development, and care provision. Since the palliative model of care integrates bereavement into the trajectory of the care experience, family members are recognized as deserving attention even after the individual has died.

Bereavement support within the hospice generally includes a remembrance service, organized in conjunction with the organization's chaplaincy. Other aspects include family counseling with vulnerable family members, including children. Counselors dealing with those who have complex social or family situations may provide invaluable predeath support alongside that of the clinical nurse specialists. One-to-one and couples counseling are also vital areas of pre- and postdeath work. For some people, the complexity of living with a life-threatening illness or of coping with loss and grief can lead to overwhelming concerns, for which counseling can be the most appropriate support.

The Role of Counselors in Hospice

Beliefs and actions regarding dying and death are guided by cultural and spiritual values. Cultures differ considerably in providing a framework for how a person should prepare for dying and death. Differences occur in beliefs about whether or not a person should be told about the risks of disease and impending death or whether the person should be spared this information. There is also a cultural difference in the acceptance of death as a part of life, a natural process that one calmly accepts as inevitable. In Western culture, death frequently engenders fear, denial, and acute distress. People resist dealing with death and its aftermath. Information about what to expect, specific ways to address what is happening, and support from counselors can help individuals overcome these fears by providing alternative coping mechanisms that facilitate sharing, listening, and discussion. Psychosocial interventions that integrate coping skills training and cognitive-behavioral strategies have been shown to improve adaptation to stressful life events including death and dying. Basic counseling skills such as active listening and showing empathy are key components in assisting a grieving child, adult, or family across cultures and contexts.

Counseling and social support that focus on psychological, emotional, and spiritual issues are made available in hospice for the dying individual and their family. Counselors are essential members of palliative and end-of-life interdisciplinary teams and can offer many interventions that alleviate bereavement care for children, adults, families, and communities. Strengths-based, supportive interventions are used to alleviate suffering and strengthen the social network of the family during this time and also strengthen the family's coping resources and skills.

As the patient experiences the depth of the dying process, the phenomena of anticipatory grief and stages of death emerge and progress. During this process, counselors can help the patient identify and address personal content struggles (issues of health and pain), personal grief (tasks/decisions to do/make before death), as well as personal reactions (will to live, control, etc.) often in the context of the family.

Suggested Approaches

Patient-centered care is an approach that involves an informed and activated patient and family as well as an accessible and responsive health care system, and emphasizes effective communication. Concurrently, several family-systems concepts have been suggested as effective counseling tools in the hospice environment, including discussions of decision-making control, promotion of autonomy, and preferences for care.

Dignity therapy (DT) is an intervention that is designed to address these issues with the dying patient. Developed specifically for patients with advanced and terminal cancer, it is brief, flexible, and can be conducted at the bedside. Through a facilitated interview, patients have an opportunity to review their life and convey important messages and reflections for friends or relatives. The interview is transcribed, edited, and a generativity document is provided to the patient to use how they wish.

Another emerging model is the transitions and palliative care therapy model, a comprehensive systems approach that promotes collaboration through which counselors, patients, and families build coping skills and decrease bereavement-related depression, grief, and fear. This consists of a developmental, nonstep process with several components:

- *Getting ready* (preparation needed, including reviewing the medical records, interacting with the health care team members, goals set, etc.)

- *Assessing the situation* (team helps the family "tell the story of the illness," provides understanding of previous discussions with physician, and focuses on joining with the family)
- *Identifying roles* (families are organized with hierarchies and subsystems, and clarify roles for decision-making)
- *Providing information* (team assists with informed decisions, including pros and cons of treatment options and likely progression of illness)
- *Processing essentials* (symptoms of grief are identified and treated)
- *Managing conflict* (team helps identify and intervene in conflict between the clinician and patient/family, within the family, between health care staff and the clinician, and between clinicians themselves)
- *Legal and ethical issues* (team is ethically sensitive and knowledgeable of the law)
- *Follow-through* (team assesses whether the family accepts this information and is able to make decisions on appropriate goals of care and accept the impending death
- *Process issues of hospice and palliative care* (team provides assurance throughout the hospice process)

This model has a strong counseling base in providing palliative service rather than major reliance on advanced practice nurses or palliative physicians and is intended to diminish conflict, improve communication, manage time constraints, and provide knowledge.

Many practitioners suggest that this model is most effective when preceded by geriatric interdisciplinary team training (GITT). GITT is a promoted team-training approach in the field of hospice care and associated counseling approaches; this includes multidisciplinary theory of collaboration, role theory, services integration, and ecological systems theory. Additional variables that are important in team function include team structure (team task, boundaries, stability), team composition (size and disciplines), organizational influences (support from administration), team processes (communication, cohesiveness), as well as task requirements. Learning objectives are divided into three broad skills: knowledge; practice groupings, involving interdisciplinary team participation and geriatrics; and team functioning. GITT espouses the idea of an interdisciplinary model where a group of different disciplines assess and plan care in a collaborative manner and where each discipline implements its independent plan as a contributing member of the group. Leadership is determined as a function of the specific task at hand and the other professions involved, and care is then approached as interdependent, complimentary, and coordinated. The team members are committed to team process and content, and leadership functions are truly shared. Role overlap is appreciated and dialogued and members respect and solicit help from one another. This model is intended to make clinical teams function optimally and effectively, especially when paired in practice with the transitions and palliative care therapy model.

Further training in the field of hospice and palliative care counseling may be acquired with end-of-life care certificate programs. These are available in many parts of the country and online, providing counselors with in-depth study and experience in this specialty area. These programs are designed to enhance the knowledge and skills of individuals who work with dying patients and their families and caregivers by providing a multidisciplinary educational experience. This education is holistic and integrative, and it helps counselors expand their professional competencies and enhance their basic and advanced skills in the area of grief and bereavement counseling.

Adrianne L. Johnson

See also Aging and Caregiving; Bereavement; Bereavement Counseling; Chronic Illness With Couples and Families; Death and Dying

Further Readings

Edwards, A. W. (2014). Therapeutic values clarification and values development for end-of-life patients: A conceptual model. *American Journal of Hospice & Palliative Medicine, 31*(4), 414–419.

Empeño, J., Raming, N. T. J., Irwin, S. A., Nelesen, R. A., & Lloyd, L. S. (2013). The impact of additional support services on caregivers of hospice patients and hospice social workers. *OMEGA, 67*(1–2), 53–61.

Hutcheson, A. (2011). Hospice care in the United States. *Primary Care, 38*(2), 173–182.

Hyer, L., Babcock, C. W., Robinson, L. E., & Ackermann, R. (2011). Transitions model: Melding of psychotherapy and palliative care using teams. *Clinical Gerontologist, 34*, 379–398.

Lundberg, T., Olsson, M., & Furst, C. J. (2013). The perspectives of bereaved family members on their experiences of support in palliative care. *International Journal of Palliative Nursing, 19*(6), 282–288.

Lynch, T. (2012). Lessons from hospice. *Journal of Financial Service Professionals, 66*(2), 29–31.

Human Sexual Response

Human sexual response is defined, at the most basic level, as a biochemical and physiological response to sexual stimulation that occurs in men and women after puberty. The sexual response cycle refers to the sequence of physical and emotional changes that occur as a person becomes sexually aroused and participates in sexually stimulating activities, including intercourse and masturbation. Understanding physiological responses during a sexual experience can help people know how their bodies should typically respond and can help professionals identify possible physical, psychological, or relational problems that might be influencing sexual responses. In order to aid in understanding, researching, and intervening with sexual functioning, several models of human sexual response have been developed, including a four-phase model by Virginia Masters and William Johnson, a three-phase model by Helen Singer Kaplan, and a nonlinear model (phases do not happen in a set sequence) by Rosemary Basson. This entry traces the history of studying human sexual response, describes models of sexual response and the critiques of those models, and concludes with a review of the current understanding of sexual dysfunction.

History and Culture

Since the early 20th century, the conceptualization of male and female sexual functioning has been based on observing consistency from a group that is presumed to be normal. Sexual norms have been influenced by theory, empirical data, and culture. Many disciplines have contributed theories and research to improve understanding of the experiences of female and male sexuality. These disciplines include biology, psychology, sociology, anthropology, and theology; each discipline has put forward assertions and evidence concerning human sexuality. The interpretations of these theories have also been influenced by the culture, place, and social norms of the times these were applied or originated. Alfred Charles Kinsey, an American biologist and entomologist, and the author of *Sexual Behavior in the Human Male* (1948) and *Sexual Behavior in the Human Female* (1953), laid the foundation for the field of sexology. Beginning in the 1950s, researchers Masters and Johnson pioneered research into the nature of human sexual response and the diagnosis and treatment of sexual disorders and dysfunctions.

Sexual Response Models

There are several major models of human sexual response, and each has its strengths and weaknesses. One of the first models of sexual response was a four-phase model by Masters and Johnson in the 1960s. They believed sexual response occurs in four phases: excitation (E), plateau (P), orgasm (O) and resolution (R), both in women and men. This is now generally referred to as the EPOR model. Their proposed model was linear and one stage needed to be completed before someone could move to the next. Although Masters and Johnson pioneered research on human sexual response and their model has been used for many years, the linear model proposed by Masters and Johnson did not explain many confounding factors that are part of human relationship. Psychological and relational factors can influence physiology and Masters and Johnson's model lacked psychological, cognitive, and emotional components of sexual response. In addition, sexual responses do not fall into discrete stages with a linear progression.

Many newer models have been proposed since Masters and Johnson's linear model. For instance, Kaplan proposed an extension of the linear model. Kaplan's model takes into account other aspects of sexual response, besides physiological components, in order to focus on the idea of desire and to understand the various phases or stages of sexual response as interconnected. In addition, Paul Robinson argued that the four-phase model should be modified to a DEOR model, in which D represents desire, E represents excitation, O represents orgasm, and R represents resolution.

Later Basson proposed a circular model that also differentiated the human sexual response cycle based on gender. The foundation of the Basson model forwarded the idea that a woman's sexual response more commonly stems from the wish for intimacy than a need for physical sexual arousal or release, or the occurrence of spontaneous sexual desire—that a woman's sense of sexual arousal is often not correlated to objective (physiologic) sexual arousal and that a woman may be more receptive for spontaneous desire. Basson's model also proposed that orgasmic experience is highly variable. Based on this view, it was proposed that the earlier linear models described men's sexuality more accurately than women's sexuality.

Research shows that men and women may have different sexual responses. However, there seems to be correlation between sexual arousal, desire, and lubrication. Women's sexual responses are more likely to be accurately described by models emphasizing arousal and desire than by models focused on a wish for intimacy, lack of spontaneous desire, and receptive desire. The sexual response of men seems to be based on desire and sexual arousal. Men's sexual response favors both Masters and Johnson's and Kaplan's model, and both are linear. In Kaplan's model, desire is particularly mentioned as the trigger, and Kaplan's model also emphasized that arousal comes after desire; thus, for men, desire precedes arousal, and this difference can be distinguished.

There are four stages of physiological response in the sexual response model. Most researchers acknowledge these stages, even if they do make modifications to these stages in their theories. The four stages are as follows:

1. *Excitement:* In this stage there is an increase in heart and breathing rates, and a rise in blood pressure. During this phase, the penis becomes partially erect in males and in females there is swelling of the clitoris and vagina and the vaginal walls secrete fluid. In this phase, the body gets ready for action.

2. *Plateau:* This is the period of sexual excitement prior to orgasm. The phase is characterized by an increased circulation and heart rate in both sexes, increased sexual pleasure with increased stimulation, and further increased muscle tension.

3. *Orgasmic:* This phase is experienced by both male and female. It is accompanied by quick cycles of muscle contraction in the lower pelvic muscles, which surround both the anus and the primary sexual organs.

4. *Resolution:* This phase occurs after the orgasmic phase when the body comes back to its normal state.

The first phase of the sexual response cycle involves generating a desire or wanting for the particular rewards, and this may lead to reproduction. This wanting phase is partly dependent on sensory triggers and partly a learned activity. Neuroanatomy suggests that wanting is associated with the release of dopamine, and wanting is different from liking.

Sensory organs are gateways to sexual interest and arousal. Most of the literature focuses on visual stimuli, but neuroimaging techniques are now being used to study the broader effects of sensory pathways in sexual response. A growing body of research suggests that each sensory pathway has a certain effect on sexual response.

The primary sensory systems act as important triggers for initiating the human sexual response cycle. This multistage processing changes over time. The processing uses the primary sensory cortices to decode object features that are spatial and they are integrated into multimodal representations in secondary cortical regions. Some of the important features of sexual responsiveness to sensory systems are highlighted subsequently.

All of the sensory systems offer potential routes to sexual responsiveness. Visual stimuli has been studied the most. The pornography industry has made the best use of visual stimuli. All primates show robust recognition of visual cues, and this erotic content captures the brain's attention resources. Sexually salient visual features tap in to the reward circuits of motivation, which is a necessary task for procreation.

The olfactory path to human sexual responsiveness is elusive, but this path has a long history. Perfumes and perfumed oils and massages strongly exploit the erotic connotations of scent, which is driven by the biological function of sex-specific odors or pheromones. Studies have been carried out to measure the attractiveness ratings for smell depending on one's hormonal state and the hormonal state of the opposite sex; these studies show that men and women are susceptible to pheromones and rate the opposite sex as more or less attractive on this basis. Smelling pheromones also changed activity in regions beyond the hypothalamus, including the amygdala, occipital temporal cortex, and orbitofrontal cortex.

Touch is another interesting modality given the hedonic properties of particular classes of skin receptors, which seem to be abundant in the so-called erogenous zones. It has recently been demonstrated that pleasant touch in humans is served by a system of low-threshold mechano receptive tactile C-afferents (CT-afferents) that project to the insular and orbitofrontal cortices. Nipple stimulation and genital stimulation have always been part of sexual activity.

Unimodal auditory stimuli with erotic content research is in its infancy, but it has been found that auditory erotic stimulation leads to enhanced recruitment of the auditory cortices.

The effect of gustatory erotic stimuli is described in ancient literature. This effect has also been studied in some insects. Many cultures also use certain foods as aphrodisiacs (e.g., oysters). While research on this topic remains limited, aphrodisiacs have traditionally been thought to increase libido, sexual potency, and sexual pleasures.

Sexual Dysfunction

The human sexual response cycle sets the foundation for studying and categorizing sexual dysfunctions in men and women. Sexual dysfunction is another source of variability in human sexual response. Sexual dysfunction is defined as the inability to execute a sexual response in a satisfactory manner. Many sexual dysfunctions exclusively and directly affect the genital apparatus or gonadal hormone release. There is a class of sexual dysfunctions that likely originates from neurogenic or psychogenic factors. Many common sexual conditions such as hypoactive sexual desire, premature ejaculation, erectile dysfunction, anorgasmia, hypersexual desire, retarded ejaculation, and hypersexual disorder may have neurogenic and psychogenic origins.

There are four main categories of sexual dysfunction: desire disorders, arousal disorders, orgasm disorders, and sexual pain disorders. In the DSM-5, male and female arousal and desire disorders appear in separate sections. This reflects a recognition in the current literature that men readily distinguish between the sexual responses of arousal and desire while women do not. As such, DSM-5 introduced several fundamental changes for classifying female sexual dysfunction.

In women, the DSM-5 definitions of desire and arousal dysfunctions have been combined under the category of "Female Sexual Interest/Arousal Disorder." This change reflects the idea that women are unable to distinguish between arousal and desire, which builds on Basson's model. Recent research, however, also suggests that the current model of sexual response needs to be revised to better treat these dysfunctions. Some of the sexual dysfunctions can be addressed by improving self-efficacy.

The concept of self-efficacy is key to understanding general psychological health, including healthy sexual response. Self-efficacy refers to a person's perceived control over a situation in achieving a particular goal or outcome. Albert Bandura's theory of self-efficacy became popular in the 1970s. Among men, the sexual self-efficacy scale can be used to measure premature ejaculation as a biopsychosocial phenomenon. Sexual self-efficacy also has the potential to play an important role in the assessment of effective treatments for sexual problems by unifying a construct that predicts cognitive, affective, motivational, and behavioral responses.

Veena Prasad

See also Sex, Definition of; Sex Researchers; Sex Therapy; Sexual Dysfunction; Sexual Health; Sexual Intimacy

Further Readings

Basson, R. (2000). The female sexual response: A different model. *Journal of Sex and Marital Therapy, 26*, 51–65.

Berridge, K. C. (1996). Food reward: Brain substrates of wanting and liking. *Neuroscience and Biobehavioral Reviews, 20*, 1–25.

Casas-Agustench, P., Salas-Huetos, A., & Salas-Salvadó, J. (2011). Mediterranean nuts: Origins, ancient medicinal benefits and symbolism. *Public Health Nutrition, 14*(12A), 2296–2301.

Georgiadis, J. R., & Kringelbach, M. L. (2012). The human sexual response cycle: Brain imaging evidence linking sex to other pleasures. *Progress in Neurobiology, 98*(1), 49–81.

Giraldi, A., Kristensen, E., & Sand, M. (2015). Endorsement of models describing sexual response of men and women with a sexual partner: An online survey in a population sample of Danish adults ages 20–65 years. *The Journal of Sexual Medicine, 12*(1), 116–128.

Hayes, R. D. (2011). Circular and linear modeling of female sexual desire and arousal. *Journal of Sex Research, 48*(2–3), 130–141.

Kaplan, H. S. (1974). *Disorders of sexual desire.* New York, NY: Simon & Schuster.

Levin, R. J. (2008). Critically revisiting aspects of the human sexual response cycle of Masters and Johnson: Correcting errors and suggesting modifications. *Sexual and Relationship Therapy, 23*(4), 393–399.

Masters, W. H., & Johnson, V. E. (1966). *Human sexual response* (1st ed.). Boston, MA: Little, Brown.

Nicolosi, A., Moreira, E. D., Shirai, M., Tambi, M. I. B. M., & Glasser, D. B. (2003). Epidemiology of erectile dysfunction in four countries: Cross-national study of the prevalence and correlates of erectile dysfunction. *Urology, 61*(1), 201–206.

Rowland, D. L., Adamski, B. A., Neal, C. J., Myers, A. L., & Burnett, A. L. (2015). Self-efficacy as a relevant construct in understanding sexual response and dysfunction. *Journal of Sex & Marital Therapy, 41*(1), 60–71.

Sidi, H., Naing, L., Midin, M., & Nik Jaafar, N. R. (2008). The female sexual response cycle: Do Malaysian women conform to the circular model? *The Journal of Sexual Medicine, 5*(10), 2359–2366.

Humanistic Family Therapy

Humanistic family therapy is a strengths-based model of family therapy resulting from the work of Virginia Satir beginning in the 1950s. Additional prominent family counselors who are associated with the evolution of this theory include Alfred Adler, Carl Jung, Karen Horney, and Victor Frankl. Humanism, in the field of psychology, was a reaction to the predominance of behaviorism with its focus on what can be observed and was also a reaction to the roots of psychology, which emphasized the past. Humanism focuses on the here-and-now and the inner experience of people. The humanistic counselor approaches families from a philosophy that assumes people are basically good, capable, and worthy of respect. The aim is to clarify communication discrepancies between family members with a humanistic, experiential orientation toward enhancing the self-esteem and feelings of self-worth in the entire family; this in turn results in the congruence of autonomy and healthy togetherness. In this entry the core components of humanistic family therapy, the role of communication, and techniques of humanistic family therapy are reviewed.

Overview of Humanism

Humanistic theories attempt to describe the experientially constructed world of the couple or family by exploring the potential humanity of each member of the system through the individual and shared experience of values, spirituality, meaning, emotions, transcendence, and intentionality. These approaches focus on self-development, growth, and responsibilities. Humanistic therapy is often analogously conceptualized as existential theory, person-centered counseling, or transactional analysis. Each of these approaches helps individuals recognize their strengths, creativity, and choice in present circumstances.

Techniques and interventions used in humanistic therapy are framed in a perspective of respect and modeling a healthy adaptive communication style, and the counselor acknowledges the responsibility of human beings for their own destiny and recognizes that mutual interdependence is the mark of high-functioning couples. For example, if two people are to live, love, and grow together, they must know how to coexist together as individuals who can distinguish their own wants and needs from each other member in the family system with mutual respect. The counselor's approach is informed by this tenet. This is grounded in the belief that human beings are auto-regulating and self-potentiating; a healthy person does not need direction from another individual because each individual has the capability of insight into his or her own needs and how to express those needs. The humanistic therapist uses various interventions to help the family understand how to express those needs healthfully so that the family may continue to grow independently and together. This perspective offers the unique opportunity for all family members to explore the dichotomy of isolation versus relationship; all individuals are simultaneously alone and relating to others.

Satir specifically suggested that all human beings, as well as families, have the resources within themselves to flourish and grow in a healthy manner and that discrepancies of communication within the family often block individual members from healthy functioning that arrests the growth of the whole family system. These resources include the capacity for learning, changing, awareness, compassion, rationality, wisdom, hope, self-acceptance and the acceptance of others, esteem, making good choices, being cooperative, admitting and correcting mistakes, asking for what one needs, and having courage to take action. Satir viewed self-esteem and its enhancement as one of the most important family functions and firmly believed in the inherent goodness and growth potential of the individual.

Key Points

Humanistic family therapy may be conceptualized in five major key points. First, families are conceptualized as systems and as such, they will naturally seek balance to maintain homeostasis (the status quo). In an unhealthy family system, that balance is maintained through inappropriate roles, restrictive rules, and unrealistic expectations. Thus, the members' needs will not be met and dysfunction results. Second, the family of origin, including past generations, has a significant influence on people's attitudes and behaviors. Historical patterns of communication may reveal themselves in the family through unrealistic expectations based on inequalities, power imbalances, disharmony, conformity, and the loss of a sense of uniqueness and personhood. In the presence of these qualities, it is assumed that an individual will give up autonomy and personal ownership of one's own needs to accommodate the historically dominant patterns. When multiple family members bring this influence into a family system, the expectations collide, often resulting in stagnated communication styles. Third, each member of a dysfunctional family shares in common low self-esteem and defensive behavior. Low self-esteem is an expected result of a loss of a distinct sense of self within a group. Humanistic therapists assume that a basic drive of human beings is to enhance self-esteem and defend against threats to it; in an unhealthy family, these defenses are maladaptive and serve to protect an individual from further degradation of the self. Fourth, each person contains all the resources one needs for growth and healthy functioning. These resources include the capacity for learning; the ability to adapt to change; the potential for awareness and rationality, wisdom, and hope; the potential to cooperate and to accept the self and others; and having courage to take action toward healthy choices. Last, the counselor and his or her beliefs are the most important tools at his or her command. The counselor's ability to respond to the underlying messages of what is being communicated and the nonjudgmental qualities of the counselor's responses are essential; they provide new models of communication to the family.

Family Roles and Communication

Humanistic family therapy assumes that a dysfunctional family is a closed system in which there is a poor exchange of information and resources within the system. This system has communication patterns that are indirect, unclear, vague, dishonest, distorted, and incomplete. The presence of dysfunction in one family member is symptomatic of dysfunction in other family members and of the larger family system. Dysfunctional family systems are unable to cope effectively because their rules are fixed, rigid, arbitrary, and inconsistently applied. These rules may tend to maintain the status quo, or a "dysfunctional homeostasis," in which family members adopt one of four dysfunctional styles of communication: placator, blamer, super-reasonable, and irrelevant. The four dysfunctional communication stances are different ways to hide the reality of one's real feelings from oneself and from others.

The placator attempts to please others to hide feelings of low self-worth and vulnerability. These family members invest energy into pleasing others, behave in a weak and vulnerable manner, are always agreeable, and consistently apologize for their own or other's behavior. Placators are the mediators of the family system, and their primary interest is calming their own feelings of low self-esteem.

The blamer hides feelings of vulnerability by attempting to control others and by disagreeing indiscriminately, thus creating a sense of importance despite inner feelings of loneliness and failure. These individuals behave self-righteously, aspire to have the dominant position in the family, and blame others (usually the placator) for their mistakes through criticisms and verbal attacks.

The super-reasonable family member feels by distancing the self from personal feelings and emotional reactions and intellectualizing the context. They appear emotionally detached, rigid in thought, and controlled in actions, and they do not tolerate change in the family system. These individuals intellectualize hostile communications and justify actions that inhibit open communication.

The family member who takes the irrelevant stance handles family conflict and stress by ignoring it completely, or alternatively behaves as a distractor from the dysfunctional patterns. The goal of this behavior is to reduce attention from the toxic conversation happening in the moment by engaging in jokes or sarcasm; this helps create a temporary and superficial feeling of safety from exploring inner feelings.

These communication stances emerge from the concept of metacommunication (message about the message). Metacommunication conveys the sender's attitude, feelings, and intentions. There should be congruence between the communication and the metacommunication so that there are no conflicting messages; this is the aim of humanistic counseling. The humanistic counselor identifies a fifth style of communication, which is the congruent communicator. The congruent communicator models a healthy and functional style of communication. Congruency is established through the identification of verbal and nonverbal messages relayed between family members. Integration of feelings, actions, and respectful communication is the goal of examining the roles and rules. Satir believed that counselors must serve as a model for family members by immersing themselves in the family process. By doing so, the counselor behaves as a facilitator of healthy communication through practice, behaving as a mediator to demonstrate alternative communication strategies when families encounter an impasse. The counselor also educates the family on the influence of intergenerational themes and the link to current functional patterns and self-esteem.

The primary technique counselors adopt is the human validation process model, which is divided into three stages. The first stage consists of establishing contact and making an informal working contract (agreement). This is a comprehensive assessment process that is designed to invite the families to feel comfortable, reduce anxiety, and lower defenses. This is accomplished through information gathering and affirming the individual worth of each family member through family mapping, sculpture, and identifying family interaction processes. The second stage is characterized by chaos, during which the counselor intervenes in the family system and disturbs the status quo. This is the process of disrupting the initially established comfort of the family by gently encouraging family members to take risks, verbalize internal feelings, and take responsibility for their own behaviors. The third stage consists of integration of new skills learned in the therapeutic process, such as practicing new healthy communications, examining metacommunication dynamics, and maintaining congruence beyond the counseling session.

Techniques

During the human validation process, the humanistic family counselor relies on 12 basic techniques developed by Satir. Family sculpture portrays the nature of the family's relationship system in space. It is the physical arrangement of family members as determined by an individual family member's perception of the family. Family metaphor is used to help people see the similarities of their interpersonal relationships to other events, objects, or situations. Family drama allows for the metaphorical expression of interpersonal relationships that may be otherwise difficult or threatening to verbalize. Reframing is an attempt to get the family to view a family problem in a new light. Humor is used to clarify or exaggerate a dynamic, as well as to encourage movement away from defensive reactions. Communication stances are re-creations of the four dysfunctional communication stances. The *family stress ballet* is an extension of the communication stances, where participants are asked to shift incongruent positions in rapid succession, as they might in real life. The *simulated family* is a form of reverse role-play in which family members are asked to take on the role of another family member to simulate a dysfunctional interaction and increase perceptive awareness. *Ropes*, as a therapeutic tool, can be seen as a metaphor for family relationships in order to demonstrate how one part of the family system affects the rest of the family. *Anatomy of a relationship* is an extension of the family sculpting technique in which the family members are asked first to sculpt the way they see themselves in the relationship and then to sculpt the way they would like the relationship to be. *Family reconstruction* aims to guide family members to unlock dysfunctional patterns stemming from their families of origin by revealing the source of old learning, developing an awareness of the personhood of one's parents, and challenging distortions of how one views one's parents. *Touching hands* may be used in therapeutic relationships with clients to help educate them about their bodies and also to be aware of space and boundaries. This is a controversial technique and one that comes with the need for ethical caution in today's counseling settings.

The humanistic family counselor consistently strives to strengthen and enhance the coping skills of individuals in the family, which strengthens the family as a whole system. The "humanness" of the counselor is more important than expertise, and modeling is one of the most important techniques. Humanistic counselors maintain a positive feeling as they guide the family away from the identified problem and toward a new perspective of the self in relation to the family. Satir conceptualized several techniques as a means of engaging family members around a specific exercise for a particular purpose. During the process of counseling, the most important factor for the counselor to consider is the accuracy of assessment and the development of a strong therapeutic alliance and the self as a part of the process; this is the foundation for all other humanistic counseling techniques.

Adrianne L. Johnson

See also Communication in Couples and Families; Family Reconstruction; Metacommunication; Metaphors; Systems Theory

Further Readings

Angus, L., Watson, J. C., Elliott, R., Schneider, K., & Timulak, L. (2015). Humanistic psychotherapy research 1990–2015: From methodological innovation to evidence-supported treatment outcomes and beyond. *Psychotherapy Research, 25*(3), 330–347.

Schneider, K. (2012). The renewal of humanism in psychotherapy: Summary and conclusion. *Psychotherapy: Theory, Research, Practice, Training, 49*(4), 480–481.

Scholl, M. B., Perepiczka, M., & Walsh, M. (2015). Experiential and humanistic theories: Approaches and applications. In D. Capuzzi & M. D. Stauffer (Eds.), *Foundations of couples, marriage, and family counseling* (pp. 159–183). Hoboken, NJ: Wiley.

Scholl, M. B., Ray, D. C., & Brady-Amoon, P. (2014). Humanistic counseling process, outcomes, and research. *Journal of Humanistic Counseling, 53*(3), 218–239.

Volker, T., & Krum, T. (2015). Experiential approaches to family counseling. In J. Wetchler & L. L. Heckler (Eds.), *An introduction to marriage and family counseling* (2nd ed., pp. 229–258). New York, NY: Routledge/Taylor & Francis Group.

Hypnosis

Hypnosis is a state of consciousness in which someone appears to be more susceptible to suggestions. Inducing a client into a highly suggestible state can be useful in therapy for behavior modification and to explore suppressed memories. Subjects under hypnosis are sometimes able to recall memories that have not been accessible to normal waking consciousness. Although some family therapists directly employ hypnosis in their work with couples and families, it is primarily a modality of treatment for use with individuals. Nevertheless, hypnosis holds an important historical place in the development of the field, as the theoretical underpinnings and clinical techniques of the brief and strategic models of family therapy were significantly inspired and influenced by hypnosis, particularly as practiced by the leading medical hypnotist of the 20th century, Milton H. Erickson. This entry provides a theoretical understanding of what hypnosis is and how and why it can be used therapeutically to resolve symptoms that clients have been striving, but failing, to eradicate or control. It concludes with an explanation of how the principles of hypnosis are relevant to brief family therapy approaches.

Hypnosis Defined

Within a clinical setting, the term *hypnosis* is descriptive of a specialized process that clinicians use to alter their clients' experience of themselves and to facilitate changes in the clients' problem through a focused, trancelike attention. The word *hypnotic* refers to the focused, immersive quality of the experience itself. Clients commonly feel themselves to be in hypnosis or in trance when they are absorbed in the experience and are responding effortlessly, without conscious intent, to the clinician's comments and suggestions. When this happens, they find themselves able to experience one or more hypnotic phenomena such as a feeling of heaviness or inability to move; floating sensations or the seeming "independent" movement of a hand or arm; a sense that time is moving much more slowly or quickly than clock time; hallucinations, involving any of the five senses, that are either positive (perceiving something to be present that is not) or negative (failing to perceive something that is present); or alterations in perceptions of the body (e.g., numbness or loss of sensation) and in the workings of the body (e.g., blood flow or heart rate).

Many experts consider hypnotizability to be a trait within individuals that is stable across the life span and normally distributed in the general population, with approximately 10% to 15% of individuals at each end of the bell curve being classifiable as "high" or "low" "hypnotizables," respectively.

However, according to Jay Haley's theoretical writings in the 1950s, and as supported by more recent research findings, hypnotic ability is less a function of individual characteristics and more a result of the interactions between hypnotist and client, particularly as these interactions affect the client's expectations. In fact, those clients who have the least specific beliefs regarding what hypnosis is, as well as the least specific assumptions about what needs to happen for the experience to be classified as hypnosis, tend to be capable of more hypnotic phenomena. To explain the unique interactional, or relational, qualities of communication that contribute to such possibilities of hypnotic experience and hypnotherapeutic change, it helps to contrast hypnosis with everyday conscious experience.

Hypnosis as Assisted Flow

Throughout the day people perceive themselves as distinct from their surroundings, from other people, and, at times, as detached from, or unaware of, the self. This sense of detachment is an artifact of the scanning, evaluating, and choosing what one must do to successfully negotiate several distinct realms: a physical world of enticements and dangers; a social world of offers, demands, requests, and innuendos; and an internal world of pleasure, pain, fear, and longing. Whenever people scrutinize what they are encountering, they define a personal boundary, locating a sense of self in contradistinction to whatever they are noticing, judging, and deciding.

Such self-defining boundaries dissolve during the sorts of engaging activities that result in what the psychologist Mihaly Czikszentmihalyi would categorize as experiences of *flow*. When people engage in activities such as gardening, meditating, writing a poem or reading a novel, playing music or a game of chess or tennis, or having a heart-to-heart talk with a friend, they sometimes become so involved that they lose a sense of time and surroundings. Sometimes during these activities one's sense of conscious separation gives way to a feeling of effortless connection, as the awareness of being (a distinct, scrutinizing self—a something) is superseded by an involvement in doing. Athletes describe the phenomenon as being "in the zone," but a sense of flow requires neither athletic ability nor strenuous activity, only absorbed focus. This is certainly the case with the practice of mindfulness meditation, where the practitioner sits still, training his or her awareness on the movements of the breath and mind.

Hypnosis can be understood as an experience of assisted flow. Absorption is typically achieved through techniques used to induce a client into a trance-like state. Therapist-assisted induction occurs when a clinician helps a client achieve focused attention and a concomitant letting go of conscious scrutinizing and willful effort. The transition into flow makes it possible for hypnotic phenomena to naturally occur, but hypnotists heighten their clients' capacity for hypnotic responsiveness by virtue of what they say and how they say it.

Induction

Most inductions are both rhythmic and evocative. Clinicians typically speak in time with their clients' breathing, emphasizing or clustering words in sync with their exhalations. This intimate conjoining serves to blur the line of conscious differentiation that normally occurs between two people engaged in an everyday conversation. As the induction continues, the clinician's words and the client's experience become more and more entwined.

Some inductions focus on developing relaxation (e.g., "Take another deep relaxing breath in . . . and out . . . and in . . . and as you breathe out, you can allow the muscles in your face to slacken, the muscles and tendons in your neck and shoulders to loosen, your arms becoming so comfortably heavy, you can feel any remaining tension just draining away . . ."). Encouraging relaxation is an excellent means of helping clients transition into hypnosis and most people find hypnosis significantly relaxing; nevertheless, hypnosis and relaxation are not synonymous. It is possible to be relaxed and not in trance or in trance and not relaxed. Experimenters, for example, have demonstrated the ability to induce hypnosis with subjects who are riding on stationary bicycles. This finding fits with understanding hypnosis as a flow perspective, and active engagement is key.

Other inductions provide clients with a step-by-step guide for the development of trance (e.g., "As I count backwards from 10 to 1, you can find yourself going deeper and deeper into hypnosis. Ten: Readying yourself for transitioning from your waking state into hypnosis. Nine: . . ."). Still others involve the detailed description of a pleasant scene, such as a beach (e.g., a client who recently went to the coast describes what a beautiful day she had. She was sitting on a towel on the sand, soaking in the light and the sounds around her, immersed in her thoughts: "While I looked out over the water . . . the waves coming in . . . and then dispersing out across the sand and back out to sea. . . . The rhythm of that: in . . . and out, and the birds calling from above . . . catching the updrafts . . . floating . . . soaring . . . with the palm trees swaying back . . . and forth . . .").

Inductions may include elements of all three of these techniques or something else entirely; however, common to clinical hypnosis approaches is an emphasis on offering permissive possibilities. Whereas stage hypnotists are known for issuing commanding directives that require compliance (e.g., "On the count of three you will be deeply asleep, unable to open your eyes. Ready? One! . . ."), clinical hypnotists are more likely to offer opportunities for discovery (e.g., "As I count from one to three, you may notice just how quickly, just how easily, you can go into hypnosis. And when I get to three, go ahead and allow yourself the pleasant curiosity of discovering what happens when you try ever so hard to open your eyes. Really, really trying and then discovering, in a way that can surprise you, what happens next.")

More advanced clinicians vary the approach and particularities of their inductions so as to account for and accommodate any potential disruption in the developing flow of their clients' experience, whether it originates from distractions in the physical environment (e.g., bright light, intermittent or loud sounds, uncomfortable temperature or seating) or arises from clients' expectations, worries, efforts, reluctance, or behaviors (i.e., what could be classified as the client's resistance). Clinicians informed by Milton Erickson and other skilled clinical hypnotists avoid trying to stop, control, or dispense with such interruptions. Instead, they use them, making mention, for example, of outside noises, even when very loud, in a way that supports and contributes to what is unfolding in the therapy office (e.g., "Isn't it fascinating the way an emergency vehicle uses its siren to signal others to slow down, to move to the side, to safely open up space so that the vehicle and those inside can move freely and safely toward their destination, proceeding efficiently, quickly, and smoothly?").

Clinical Application in Resolution of Symptoms

The same principles used in induction can also be used in the clinical application of hypnosis in the resolution of symptoms. If a client, a woman, suffering from stomach pain is able to develop numbness in her hands, for example, the therapist may suggest that she allow one of her hands to make its way to her stomach and transfer its numbness to the afflicted area. Another woman who sees vivid colors may be invited to focus in and discover the color of her headache. Suggestions could then follow for the designated color to start shifting in some subtle way—in hue, brightness, saturation, or contrast—with the implication and dawning realization that as this or that color value starts to fluctuate, an analogous change in the headache develops. Another example could be a man, adept at hallucination and time distortion, who might be directed to gaze into an imaginary crystal ball, discovering there, in vivid, describable detail, a time in the future when the problem is no longer an issue, when he and others find themselves behaving and relating differently as a result of the change. Such an embodied recognition of the effects of the future change can then be brought back to the present and incorporated in how he now and subsequently orients to himself and his circumstances.

Implicit in such hypnotic techniques is the assumption that problems are better conceptualized and treated as patterns of interaction than as a thing. An unwanted object, an actual thing that clients dislike or disapprove of, can be locked away or discarded. However, when clients attempt to purposefully limit or eliminate an unwanted symptom, something quite different unfolds. Because a problem is not, in fact, an object existing independently of clients, but is rather woven into the fabric of their experience, then all efforts to manage it will necessarily and reflexively become a part of the problem itself. The hypnotist's task, then, is to interact with the symptom in a way that respects and uses this interconnected reality, offering possibilities that facilitate change rather than entrenchment.

Brief Family Therapies

When hypnotherapists conceive of and approach the problem as a pattern of relationship, instead of trying to do something to or against the symptom, they are freed up to join with clients to do something with it or to play with possibilities for altering different elements of its unfolding. Just as a melody (a quintessential pattern of sound) can be transformed by slightly altering one note of the whole, so too a symptom can be altered by introducing a small change somewhere in its expression. This is where hypnosis excels, but the same pattern-sensitive sensibility informs brief family therapy approaches, such as the Mental Research Institute (MRI) brief therapy model, solution-focused brief therapy, and strategic family therapy. All developed in part in an attempt to codify the hypnotherapeutic innovations of Milton Erickson in settings involving not only individuals but also couples and families.

The resolution of problems using hypnosis was traditionally understood to be the result of the therapist's persistent and persuasive efforts to "implant" suggestions in a passive recipient who, if sufficiently "suggestible," could achieve relief. Researchers and clinicians are now more likely to remark on the synergistic, mutually cooperative nature of hypnosis, in which the invention and realization of hypnotic shifts in experience and problems are the result of an active and collaborative venture, involving both hypnotist and client in an interactive, creative communication of possibilities and discoveries.

Douglas Flemons

See also Brief Family Therapy; Circularity and Linearity; Resistance; Solution-Focused Brief Therapy; Strategic Family Therapy

Further Readings

Csikszentmihalyi, M. (1990). *Flow: The psychology of optimal experience.* New York, NY: HarperPerennial.

Erickson, M. H. (1959). Further clinical techniques of hypnosis: Utilization techniques. *The American Journal of Clinical Hypnosis, 2,* 3–21.

Flemons, D. (2002). *Of one mind: The logic of hypnosis, the practice of therapy.* New York, NY: W. W. Norton.

Haley, J. (1986). *Uncommon therapy: The psychiatric techniques of Milton H. Erickson, M.D.* New York, NY: W. W. Norton.

Kirsch, I. (Ed.). (1999). *How expectancies shape experience.* Washington, DC: American Psychological Association.

Lynn, S. J., Rhue, J. W., & Kirsch, I. (2010). *Handbook of clinical hypnosis* (2nd ed.). Washington, DC: APA.

O'Hanlon, W. H., & Martin, M. (1992). *Solution-oriented hypnosis: An Ericksonian approach.* New York, NY: W. W. Norton.

Ritterman, M. (2005). *Using hypnosis in family therapy.* Phoenix, AZ: Zeig, Tucker & Theisen.

Hypothesis, Systemic

A system is a group of interacting parts that, through their interaction, form a complex whole. Couples and families are examples of living systems. Family systems theory (FST) is a means for understanding human groups through discerning patterned ways that these systems behave and interact. Assumptions about couples and families (and their patterns) can be made based on their structure (boundaries, hierarchy, overt rules, covert rules). The proposed explanation for how a particular couple or family interacts is called a *systemic hypothesis*. These hypotheses are made on the basis of general principles of systems along with observing the patterned way a particular system interacts. Systemic hypotheses help a clinician understand the functioning of a system and gain a working understanding of the influences that are maintaining or exacerbating a problem that brings the couple or family into therapy. This entry describes some of the basic elements of FST that are used to create a systemic hypothesis. Additionally, the role of empirical research and self-of-the-therapist issues are explained.

A Systemic Hypothesis Overview

A general assumption of FST is that all members of the family are interconnected, so a comprehensive understanding of a family member is only achieved by viewing this individual in the context of the whole family. While it is necessary to have a clear understanding of the core theoretical underpinnings of FST, the family therapist must consider the family's unique context when creating a working understanding of the presenting problem (i.e., mental health symptoms). Contextual considerations for family influences may include broader cultural values (e.g., stigmatizing view of psychotherapy), long-term generational patterns (e.g., substance abuse), or expected developmental transitions (e.g., adolescent identity development). Sudden stressors such as death or illness, trauma, or divorce must also be considered as an influence on the issues that clients bring to therapy. A systemic perspective maintains that presenting problems are an appropriate response to meet the changing needs of the family within its particular context. A problem is a sign to the family that it is stuck and may need to change something in the structure of the family (or change something in another related system) in order for the system to function better.

It can seem overwhelming to develop a treatment approach that is grounded in such an expansive view of the problem. However, the basic concepts of FST offer some guidelines for organizing the information that is obtained in therapy. These concepts are used to create a systemic hypothesis, or a working understanding of the influences that are maintaining or exacerbating the problem. It is important to highlight the nature of a *working* understanding as it applies to a systemic hypothesis. Family therapy is a process wherein the complexities of family relationships unfold over time, so the understanding of the presenting problem is continually evolving as more information is obtained in therapy. In other words, a single, correct, one-size-fits-all, systemic hypothesis is not the aim of family therapy. The therapist uses basic systems principles and current research to formulate a hypothesis that is reevaluated and refined over the course of treatment.

Family Systems Concepts

A systemically informed therapist is concerned with altering problem-maintaining patterns of interactions that have become maladaptive for the family. This theoretical perspective assumes the presenting problem is a result of reciprocal influences (i.e., circularity) as opposed to a cause-and-effect explanation. Sometimes families become stuck and rely on interactions that are familiar to them but are no longer helpful for growth. This maladaptive pattern, known as a positive feedback loop, is generally used to understand the presenting problem. The systemic hypothesis allows the therapist to identify the family's unique circumstances that are resulting in them becoming stuck in a pattern that is no longer working. For example, a teenager who was recently suspended from school for marijuana possession would not be seen in therapy to identify the single, underlying cause that resulted in the presenting problem. The adolescent would be seen with his or her family to gain a broader perspective on the circumstances that are affecting the family as a whole. A systemic therapy approach would be aimed at altering the cycle of interactions that are inhibiting the family's development. While basic systemic concepts are important for the foundation of a working hypothesis, updated research supplements the hypotheses with clinical findings that are relevant to the family.

Clinical Research

Theory and the therapeutic relationship play a key role in successful treatment outcomes, but research is equally necessary to integrate into the therapy approach. If family systems concepts provide a skeletal organization of a family's patterns of interaction, then empirical research could be considered the flesh that enhances the basic organization. Studies that validate the effectiveness (or ineffectiveness) of particular interventions with specific presenting problems are playing an increasing role in managed care reimbursement for mental health treatment. Empirical research is also used to identify and understand the needs of particular populations so therapy will be beneficial to a family's unique context. Socioeconomic status, race and ethnicity, culture, sexual identity, spirituality, and immigration status are some of the contextual influences that affect family interactions. Ongoing clinical research is necessary to develop treatment approaches that are appropriate and effective in meeting the needs of families in an ever-evolving society. Licensed family therapists and counselors are required to obtain hours of continuing education to stay apprised of current trends in the field. Yet, supervisors and instructors often assume responsibility for teaching students *how* to integrate research and clinical practice. Despite the necessity of clinical research, it has often been noted that many master's level clinicians do not value or see the relevance of research in their own clinical practice. Yet, theory and research serve to balance the personal attributes of the therapist, which should also be considered when developing the systemic hypothesis.

Self of the Therapist

Personal experiences, values, and beliefs, or "self-of-the-therapist" issues can either enhance or obstruct the therapy process. A systemic lens suggests that the therapist plays an instrumental role in altering the patterns of interaction that have become unhelpful to the family. In addition to systemic principles and clinical research, the self-of-the-therapist issues are also a filter that determines whether particular information is relevant or not. Therefore, the development, testing, and refinement of the systemic hypothesis are influenced by the therapist's subjective point of view. Self-awareness and ongoing personal exploration allow the therapist to gain a deeper understanding of the clients' lived experiences without pathologizing a family with different beliefs and values. Overlooking personal biases and assumptions are often a contributing factor to therapists feeling "stuck" due to a lack of therapeutic progress.

Self-of-the-therapist issues can be used to inform a systemic hypothesis that leads to helpful changes within the family when they are used with intention. On the other hand, such issues can become an obstacle when they are outside the therapist's awareness. The therapist who is working with an adolescent and his or her family would construct a systemic hypothesis that is informed by a parallel experience. If the therapist is also a parent of an adolescent who is experimenting with alcohol or drugs, it is plausible that the therapist would minimize or overlook the parents' contribution to the presenting problem in the systemic hypothesis. On the other hand, the same parallel experience could direct the therapist to ask for particular information that the family would not have otherwise offered.

M. L. Parker

See also Circularity and Linearity; Self of the Therapist; Systems Theory

Further Readings

Colapinto, J. (1991). Family systems theory and therapy. In A. S. Gurman & D. P. Kniskern (Eds.), *Handbook of family therapy* (pp. 226–266). New York, NY: Brunner/Mazel.

Gehart, D. (2013). *Mastering competencies in family therapy: A practical approach to theory and clinical case documentation* (2nd ed.). Belmont, CA: Brooks/Cole.

IAMFC

See International Association of Marriage and Family Counselors

Identified Patient

The identified patient (IP) is the individual in the family or couple whose problematic behavior triggers the family or couple's motivation to seek therapy. In a family system, this person is often a child who may be experiencing academic, behavioral, or emotional difficulties within or outside of school. The IP may also be an individual in a family or a couple who is engaging in problematic substance use or who is experiencing symptoms that indicate a mental health issue such as depression or anxiety. Within the context of couple and family therapy, the IP motivates engagement in therapy; however, he or she is not generally the sole focus of intervention. Because an individual's symptoms are both influenced by and exert influence upon the couple or family as a unit, the unit is the focus of intervention. The designation of an IP and provision of a diagnosis are typically required in order to receive health insurance reimbursements. Consideration of previous diagnoses provided by other practitioners, current ability of the couple or family therapist to provide an accurate diagnosis, benefits and risks of identifying an IP to the processes involved in couple and family therapy, and legal and ethical considerations may all impact the therapist's choice to identify an IP within the couple or family counseling context. This entry examines the benefits and limitations of identifying an IP in couples and family therapy and pays specific attention to the diagnostic, legal, and ethical considerations raised by the practice.

Benefits and Limitations of Identifying an IP in Couple or Family Work

There are benefits and limitations to identifying an IP in couple and family therapy. Benefits include the ability to provide diagnosis and treatment for an individual's mental health concerns within a family context if the symptoms indicate a specific mental health disorder. In addition, insurance companies generally require a diagnosis for an individual in order to reimburse the therapist for services. Therapists who work with couples or families who do not to provide a diagnosis for an IP may be forced to see only clients who are able to pay privately for services. Identifying the IP may also inform referrals for individual treatment for issues such as substance abuse, psychiatric disorders, or disorders of learning or development.

Limitations to identifying an IP in family or couples therapy include the discrepancy between family or couples therapy goals and identifying one individual as the focus for treatment. Specifically, couple and family therapy focuses upon impacting interactional patterns, communication patterns, emotional expression and regulation, structure, rules, and roles, and other process-based goals that help the family function more effectively. Identifying one person as the IP does not always support focusing therapeutic attention on these systemic needs. This may interfere with working toward systemic goals in favor of addressing problems experienced individually by or as a result of the IP. This focus can inadvertently communicate to both the individual identified as the IP and to the family or couple as a unit that the problems lay within one person, rather than within the system as a whole. This can negatively impact the individual who is identified as the problem as well as the system's openness to interventions that focus on the family or couple as a unit rather than focusing only on the IP.

Diagnosis of Psychiatric Disorders in Family Therapy

The diagnosis of psychiatric disorders for an IP within the context of couple or family therapy is a dilemma for the couple or family therapist. On one hand, many individuals enter couple or family therapy with a diagnosis that was previously made by another service provider. Some clients may participate in regular medical appointments to manage medications in addition to their participation in therapy. Some children presenting for family therapy may have already received a diagnosis through an assessment for eligibility for special education services within the school. These factors, coupled with the need for diagnosis as a requirement for billing medical insurance, make the provision of a diagnosis a utilitarian tool in many cases.

At the same time, a couple or family therapist's focus on the system rather than the individual puts the therapist in a difficult position if a diagnosis for one or more family members has not been made previously. Because the focus of couple or family interventions is on supporting and changing the system, the therapist may not have enough information through family-based or couple-based assessments to determine an appropriate diagnosis for an individual family member. Further, the choice to conduct an assessment for one individual in a family system for the sole purpose of providing a diagnosis may be poorly aligned with the aims of the couple or family therapist and may inadvertently impact the family's view of the problem or the family's commitment to couple or family therapy in lieu of individual therapy for the IP.

Ethical and Legal Considerations

It is important for couple and family therapists to consult the ethical codes for the professional associations of which they are a member and to also consult any relevant laws that impact identifying or diagnosing an IP in couple or family counseling. Specifically, it is unethical—and illegal if insurance is billed for services that rely upon the diagnosis as a requirement for payment—for a therapist to give a diagnosis to an individual without collecting adequate information to formulate and substantiate a valid diagnosis. Specific ethical guidelines around identification of an IP may also differ depending on one's professional affiliation. Overall, it is important to be aware of both the risks and benefits of identifying an IP in family or couple counseling and to make decisions that are in the best interest of the system as a unit.

Amy E. Williams

See also DSM and V-Codes; Ethical Decision-Making; Goals, Treatment; Individual Versus Family Therapy; Mental Health, Systemic Perspective

Further Readings

Chambless, D. L., & Miklowitz, D. J. (2012). Beyond the patient: Couple and family therapy for individual problems. *Journal of Clinical Psychology, 68*(5), 487–489. doi:10.1002/jclp.21858

Hoyt, M. F., & Gurman, A. S. (2012). Wither couple/family therapy? *The Family Journal, 20*, 13–17. doi:10.1177/1066480711420050

Imago Relationship Therapy

Often classified as a psychodynamic model, Imago Relationship Therapy (IRT) is an integrated model encompassing elements of such disciplines as cognitive, behavioral, object-relations, humanistic, developmental, existential, and depth psychology, as well as systems theory, spirituality, mindfulness, and anthropology. Developed by Harville Hendrix and Helen Hunt, IRT has a unique theoretical foundation that guides its application to couples, individuals, and families. IRT posits that people arrive at committed relationships defensive and wounded from childhood. The wounds are a central part of mate selection. The defenses create emotional distance. Through therapy, which includes learning the theory and the techniques, the couple matures and moves from a reactive relationship to a proactive one. Safety, intimacy, and relaxed joyfulness become the norm. This entry discusses the theory, model, and application of IRT in work with individuals, couples, and families.

Theoretical Underpinnings of the Model

Imago means "image" in Latin. As used in IRT, it refers to *the image that is etched in the unconscious mind of a person* from childhood and imported into intimate, committed relationships. The imago is created from all the interactions a developing child experiences with parents and caretakers, both positive and negative. Interactions that are related to unmet needs that frustrate the child cause wounds, repression, and inadequate social and psychological developmental.

The imago plays a central role in mate attraction and selection and in forming the relationship dynamic. In fact, it is their imago that leads people to choose their eventual committed partner. Through romantic attraction, and the promise that, finally, in the committed relationship, all frustrated needs from childhood will be met by the beloved, the partner is selected subconsciously. As the mental image of one's caretakers (created in childhood) and the similar traits of the potential romantic partner meet and align, the perfect setup occurs. This poises the relationship to do what it is supposed to do . . . *to finish childhood*. The person finally receives, in the present, from the committed partner, all that was not received in childhood.

It is the committed relationship context *and* the committed partner, in the present, that provide a venue for a person to reclaim the parts of the self that were lost. The person matures emotionally and moves from unconscious-reactive interactions to conscious-intentional ones. Therapy provides the frame that finally helps the couple move through and complete developmental phases of relationships (attachment, exploratory, identity, power and competence, concern, and intimacy) that are incomplete from childhood and are playing out in the present.

The Development of the Self

The concept of the self in IRT is derived in part from the philosopher and theologian Martin Buber's I-Thou concept and the idea of "the space-in-between" myself and I. The self, according to IRT, grows through evolution, psychological, and social development. Humans are made of the same material and energy as all other matter in the universe. People are pulsating energy with the ability to self-reflect and to evolve over time and space while remaining part of the fabric of the cosmos. The tripartite (consisting of three parts) structure of the human brain is atemporal and nonspatial. As such, the child enmeshes the past and future into the present and creates a symbiotic reality.

According to IRT, there are different goals for each of the parts of the brain. The mandate of the old brain (brain stem and limbic system) is to survive. For self-protection, the individual adapts a defensive mode toward perceived danger of annihilation. Much like other species in the ecosystem, the person adopts a "fight-flight-freeze" response to perceived unsafe conditions, either by constricting energy (minimizers) or exploding energy (maximizers). When the old brain engages, the person becomes reactive. When the cortex (the new brain) develops and the frontal lobes are engaged, the child–person can consciously tell the difference between real and potential danger, can reflect about thoughts, can behave with intention, and can remain individualized in the presence of others. Reality is oriented to present, past, and future with clarity.

As people develop within the context of a society, they are socialized to repress parts of the self. People express life's energy through thinking, feeling, sensing, and movement. When a child is socialized, the messages received and internalized break the natural flow of life's energy. The core of the individual is modified to include faulty beliefs, such as "don't think," "don't think that," "don't feel," and so on. As a result, the individual splits off parts of the self. The normal functions of energy are impaired. The individual blocks the ability to express energy properly and will overfunction or underfunction in thinking, feeling, sensing, or moving.

In mate selection, as IRT explains, the person will attract a complementary self where, in all four functions (thinking, feeling, sensing, and movement), the overfunctioning parts of one partner will complete the underfunctioning parts of the other. For example, if one partner is most comfortable in one's head (thinking function), the attraction might be to a partner most comfortable emoting (feeling function). Therapy helps people learn to balance the four functions.

Wounds

Wounds occur in the developing child and cannot be avoided entirely because parents and caretakers are, at best, semiconscious. They have their own repressions and wounds that they project onto the child. The child develops mechanisms that create an armor of defenses. The grown-up (a big person whose inner child is stuck at the developmental impasse and wounded) later finds himself or herself in relationships that will repeat wounding in the same fashion.

The six stages of development (attachment, exploration, identity, competence, concern, and intimacy) have the potential to meet the nurturing needs of the child or create wounds. If this pilgrimage proceeds optimally, the child emerges with strong emotional security, intact curiosity, self-definition, an internalized sense of power and ability to achieve, ability to connect and care for nonfamily members, and healthy separation from family with ability to develop satisfying sexual intimacy. Because caretakers are not perfect, they wound children by being unavailable, overprotective, possessive, underprotective, neglectful, inattentive, deflective, invasive, demanding of perfection, underinvolved, needy, controlling, and/or critical. Parents also wound by ignoring the child and withholding love and affection.

The developing child internalizes the effects of the interactions and develops related fears that play out in intimate partnerships. The child may develop fear of rejection, abandonment, absorption, separateness, being shamed, being invisible, failure, being powerful, being ostracized, being needy, being controlled, or being different from others. Depending on the stage of development and the quality of the nurturing, the child may adapt by restricting energy to avoid contact (and may be categorized as a minimizer, exhibiting tendencies of an avoider, isolator, rigid controller, compulsive competitor, loner, or rebel), or may adapt by exploding energy (and being categorized as a maximizer with the tendency to cling, pursue, become a compliant diffuser, become a manipulative compromiser, become a sacrificing caretaker, or a conformer). These tendencies especially emerge in times of conflict. In mate selection, a minimizer will be attracted to a maximizer, and vice-versa. This phenomenon, along with the complementarity of repression caused by socialization, creates the power struggle that eventually is presented at therapy.

The Three Stages of Committed Relationship

Relationships, according to IRT, are structured within three stages: (1) the romantic, (2) the power struggle, and (3) the conscious relationship. The romantic and the power struggle (reactive) stages are part of the unconscious relationship and are necessary to help the couple first become involved with each other. The triggering of each other's childhood wounds follows.

The romantic stage is activated by the imago scanning the environment for a partner who, when selected, will meet the criteria for finishing childhood. Because of romantic attraction, the self is unable to recognize negative traits in the prospective partner. The imago selects someone who will possess the characteristics of one's parents and caretakers. The blinding effects of romantic attraction create an illusion of completeness, immeasurable happiness, *unparalleled* levels of energy, and sexual attraction. The romantic stage is short lived and present until exclusive commitment is made. Soon thereafter, disillusionment occurs and the power struggle emerges.

The power struggle is the result of the two people jockeying for position in the relationship. The conflict resolution comes to an impasse as one of the following occurs in what is called "the core scene": the partner's detachment versus the partner's demands, the partner's neglect versus the partner's smothering, the partner's dominance and rigidity versus the partner's passivity and vagueness, the partner's competiveness versus the partner's manipulation, the partner's exclusion and withdrawal versus the partner's invasiveness, and the partner's rebelliousness versus the partner's control. During the power struggle, the couple may connect regarding the logistics of living but, in effect, are emotionally disconnected in an invisible divorce.

The conscious or intentional relationship is the intended destination of a committed relationship. Safety is consistently present: Anger is addressed; open dialogue is utilized; deep emotional and sexual intimacy is experienced; relationship vision is shared; stability and consistency is embraced; personal growth is encouraged; nurturing and caring is exhibited; power is shared; collaborative parenting is evident; needs and dreams are expressed; and relationship equity is prominent. Conscious couples bring energy back into the relationship space, close exits that siphon energy out, and, above all, have an agreed process for managing conflict and disagreements. Each day is lived with the intention of taking personal responsibility for oneself, for the work of the relationship, and for the commitment to the partner.

Therapy

Therapists receive extensive training. The most important therapeutic element is the establishment of total safety and trust. Couples often arrive to therapy after many failed, self-started attempts to correct the problems. The power struggle is well under way and many overwhelming issues are present. Presenting problems may include infidelity, addictions, abuse, pending separation or divorce, poor collaborative parenting, inability to blend newly formed families, and mood disturbances in one or both partners. The result is similar across the board, a severed connection and the inability to bridge the gap with productive communication and actions, causing more disconnection and loss of hope.

Case Conceptualization and Desired Outcomes

The work is conceptualized in the context of the theoretical underpinnings of IRT. Couples (or individuals) present to therapy unconsciously armed with many defense mechanisms that keep them from getting hurt, but also keep them from being loved. Conceptualizing the couple within the developmental stage in which the original wounding took place informs the therapist, and the couple, about the level of pain present, the dynamic (i.e., which form of the power struggle), the challenges the couple faces, and the timeframe necessary for the work.

The goal of therapy is always to heal and repair through improved communication, new learned behaviors, and greater safety in the relationship space. The desired outcomes of therapy are evident when the couple evolves into an emotionally mature dyad that can nurture, support, communicate openly, promote self-knowledge, and ask for what each wants and needs without fear of rejection, shame, or abandonment. Playful behavior, feelings of personal power and self-esteem, deep intimacy, good sex, strong empathy, interdependence, stability in financial and other life areas, and an overall feeling of relaxed joyfulness are present.

Therapy Process

The couple is immediately placed in what IRT calls the *Couples Dialogue*. Active listening is the key as the clients learn a new skill. As the clients become comfortable taking turns talking, listening actively, and developing the ability to validate cognitively and emotionally, they are individuating and seeing the self as separate and apart from the partner. The partners begin turn taking, becoming therapist-like toward one another as they learn to contain pain and reactions through dialoguing, while hanging onto themselves in the process.

Techniques Within the Process

The basic tool, the Couples Dialogue, also called the *Intentional Dialogue,* is used in the therapy room as well as at home. Additionally, through guided visualization, each person is led to reimage himself or herself and to reimage his or her partner as a vulnerable, wounded child who adopted certain defense mechanisms to survive. The couple learns why and how each is the other's imago match. They reromanticize the relationship; restructure frustrations, anger, and rage; show caring behaviors; and develop a common relationship vision to guide them toward their future.

The *Couples Dialogue* is designed to create safety within the relationship space. It includes three parts:

1. *Mirroring,* which consists of active listening and reflecting back to the partner all the pieces of the message the partner is sending;
2. *Validating* through active listening for feelings in the partner, affirming the sensibility of the partner's feelings and perspective within *his or her* worldview, and cognitively acknowledging the sense it makes when looked at from the partner's perspective; and
3. *Empathizing* once cognitive affirmation is made, trying to imagine how the situation might additionally make the partner feel. This deepens the connection and opens up space for more in-depth exploration of the partner's experience in the world.

Other techniques include the following:

- *The Parent–Child Dialogue*: designed to take the person to an earlier time and to have the partner sit in for the caretakers within the partner's childhood framework so that the child can have a conversation with his or her caretakers, as if in that time
- *The Holding Exercise*: when the child in one of the partners emerges and needs nurturing and holding, the partner sitting in for the loving caretakers
- *The No-Exit Exercise*: designed to allow the members of the couple to commit his or her energy back into the relationship space and close the apertures that suck the energy out
- *The Behavior Change Request*: a modified form of the couples dialogue that includes forms of the parent–child dialogue that connect the present frustration/anger to an earlier childhood wound and ends with some very specific wishes that the partner asks for
- *The Container*: designed to create safety as the couple works on resolving rage that each has held since childhood
- *Visioning*: through worksheets and intentional dialogues, the couple creating a vision of the future together
- *Positive Flooding*: the couple takes turns showering one another with the sharing of pleasure, surprises, caring, compliments, and affirmations
- *Reromanticizing*: caring days are introduced into the process as a way to structure the involvement of both partners
- *The Goodbye Exercise*: helps the couple separate or divorce more amicably
- *Guided Visualization*: the client is able to return to childhood and reexperience the positive and negative interactions he or she had with caretakers

Therapy Structure

Therapy is available in several structures. The Getting the Love You Want Workshop is a weekend-long experience where the couple joins other couples in a facilitated experience. Each couple works privately with workbooks, joins the group to learn and watch demonstrations of the techniques, and participates in visualizations. The workshop is also available as a home study, providing a way for the couple to work at their own pace.

When working with a therapist, the couple is able to fully focus on individualized work. They learn the skills necessary to be and remain safe to the partner while creating relaxed joyfulness and intimacy. Sometimes, the work is done with unattached individuals who seek to grow eventually into better partners. Both with couples and singles, working with a therapist might include individual sessions (couples are typically seen together) and/or working within a group setting. Some clients may even create and/or join imago self-help groups.

Clients may be asked to read *Getting the Love You Want,* among other books available, including associated meditation books and workbooks. Video recordings are available to assist couples and therapists with techniques.

The Self of the Therapist

The therapist is a facilitator and a coach. Because the goal of therapy is to deepen the empathic bond, diminish the symbiotic attachment, and assist the clients to grow into mature adults, the therapist facilitates connection within the couple or between parent and child. Support, encouragement, mirroring, validation, and empathy are modeled as well. A nonjudgmental stance is essential. The therapist must develop and maintain awareness, knowledge, and skills, must develop his or her own conscious way of living, and must work on healing and repairing his or her own childhood wounds. Specific training parameters are required for certifications.

Applications of IRT

Although the imago model is often associated with couples therapy, it was also developed for singles work (based on the book *Keeping the Love You Find: A Personal Guide*) and for parenting (based on the book *Giving the Love That Heals*). The intentional dialogue is useful in business, school, and friendship contexts. The imago paradigm is an integrated model of therapy applied to work with couples, singles, families, work environments, and friendships. The goal is to heal and repair wounds from childhood that play out in mate selection and in relationships in adulthood. When a person learns the skill of active listening, validating, and empathizing, he or she is empowered to create satisfying interpersonal relationships and perhaps a safer, more peaceful, loving world.

Rosaria Carlone Upchurch

See also Couples and Marriage Counseling; Couples Therapy Research; Humanistic Family Therapy; Mindfulness; Object Relations Theory; Relationship Enhancement

Further Readings

Hendrix, H. (1992). *Keeping the love you find: A personal guide.* New York, NY: Atria Books.

Hendrix, H. (2008). *Getting the love you want: A guide for couples* (20th anniv. ed.). New York, NY: Holt Paperbacks. (Original work published 1988)

Hendrix, H., & Hunt, H. L. (1997). *Giving the love that heals: A guide for parents.* New York, NY: Pocket Books.

Hendrix, H., & Hunt, H. L. (1997). *Giving the love that heals: A guide for parents: Parents' manual.* New York, NY: Imago.

Hendrix, H., & Hunt, H. L. (1999). *The parenting companion: Meditations and exercises for giving the love that heals.* New York, NY: Pocket Books.

Hendrix, H., & Hunt, H. L. (2003). *The new couples' guide: Getting the love you want workbook.* New York, NY: Atria Books.

Hendrix, H., & Hunt, H. L. (2004). *Receiving love: Transform your relationship by letting yourself be loved.* New York, NY: Atria Books.

Hendrix, H., Hunt, H. L. (2013). *Making marriage simple: 10 truths for changing the relationship you have into the one you want.* New York, NY: Harmony Books.

Hendrix, H., Hunt, H. L., Hannah, M. T., & Luquet, W. (Eds.). (2005). *Imago relationship therapy: Perspectives on theory*. San Francisco, CA: Jossey-Bass.

Imago Relationships: http://imagorelationships.org/

Luquet, W. (2006). *Short term couples therapy: The imago model in action* (2nd ed.). New York, NY: Routledge. (Original work published 1996)

Luquet, W., Hannah, M. T. (Eds.). (1998). *Healing in the relational paradigm: The imago relationship therapy casebook*. Washington, DC: Routledge.

Making Marriage Simple: http://makingmarriagesimple.com/

Nelson, T. (2008). *Getting the sex you want: Shed your inhibitions and reach new heights of passion together*. Beverly, MA: Quiver.

Immigrant Families

The term *immigrant* refers, in this entry, to individuals without U.S. citizenship at birth. Immigrants include naturalized citizens, lawful permanent residents, refugees, individuals with certain temporary visas, and those unauthorized to be in the United States. Approximately 33.5 million immigrants currently live in the United States. Almost half of all individuals who arrived in the United States since 1965 have come from Latin America and approximately 25% from Asia. Others have emigrated from Africa, Europe, the Middle East, and other parts of North America. While the positive contributions of immigrants to U.S. society can be noted over centuries, immigrant families face many stressors and challenges in adjusting to life in the United States. This entry provides an overview of characteristics of immigrant families in the United States and the challenges they face when adapting to life in their new land.

The Migration Experience

Nearly 1.1 million immigrants and refugees legally enter the United States each year and settle in different parts of the nation. The United States accepts more immigrants and refugees into its borders than any other nation. Additionally, another 800,000 to 1.2 million individuals enter the United States illegally each year. While the United States has been a nation of immigrants, until 1952, only White persons were allowed to become naturalized citizens. The majority of immigrants entering the United States until the 1960s were from Europe. The Immigration Act of 1965 finally allowed people from any nation to become naturalized citizens. Since its passage, the overwhelming majority of immigrants entering the United States have come from Third World or developing nations.

Families immigrate to the United States for various reasons. Some come to seek economic advancement or educational and professional opportunities to improve their quality of life. Others may be fleeing persecution or political unrest. Families immigrate with different dreams and ideals of how life will be in the United States. Some immigrants arrive with the intention of eventually returning to their homeland after a given period. For those uprooted by violence or persecution, settling in the United States is a permanent change as they have no possibility of return to their country of origin.

While their reasons for migration may vary, immigrants often experience a deep sense of loss of culture, language, and status in addition to prolonged separation from other family members. Those who entered illegally also experience the constant fear of detention and deportation. The migration journey for both legal and undocumented immigrants may have been laden with many dangers: sudden departures, complicated legal processes, abuse by others, or desert and ocean crossings. Refugee families can experience more acute stressors if their dislocation was sudden and involved traumatic events such as persecution, war, or disasters. High rates of depression, acute stress disorder, posttraumatic stress disorder, and anxiety have been found among refugees exposed to war. Those who resided in refugee camps prior to entering the United States may have also faced adverse conditions, including physical and sexual trauma, intimidation, and the abrupt separation from family members.

Grieving often accompanies the joy of being in a new setting with new opportunities. The natural stress of adapting to life in a new environment is augmented by concerns for those left back home. While opportunities to a better quality of life may eventually materialize, immigrant families face high levels of stressors, conflict, economic challenges, and health issues, increasing the risk of mental health problems.

Many immigrant families settle in existing immigrant communities that share their native language and customs. Throughout the United States, large immigrant populations exist within various metropolitan areas. These communities can serve as a source of support for new immigrants, helping them to cope with economic pressures, learn a new language and customs, and navigate new educational, social, and legal systems. However, support is not always available as some immigrants live away from other family members and large immigrant communities. Anti-immigrant sentiments also present a challenge. Although nativist movements have been common in the history of immigration in the United States, anti-immigrant sentiments have appeared more strongly as the majority of immigrants today are non-European. Furthermore, immigrants are more likely to experience conflict with U.S.-born ethnic minorities when living in areas experiencing economic distress with limited housing and employment.

Children in Immigrant Families

Due to financial limitations or the immigration process itself, immigrant families may experience serial migration, where members enter the United States at different times. This can lead families to endure long periods of separation. A parent may migrate first and work a number of months or years in the United States to be able to send for other family members. A child may also be sent to live first with an extended family member already in the United States ahead of the parents. Delays in the application process allowing family members to enter the United States can lead family members to migrate at different times. The experience of being separated from parents during childhood and reunited at a later stage can disrupt the parent–child bond in immigrant families, impact the child's well-being, and cause significant stress even when the family is reunited.

By being in school, children are immediately immersed into a new cultural context where they are able to learn the language and norms of their new community. Children from non-English speaking countries often learn English more rapidly than their parents. This allows children to adapt to their social context at a much faster rate than their parents. It can also lead to challenges as the family experiences a hierarchical inversion whereby children serve to interpret the new culture for their parents. The pressure to be accepted by peers in addition to the lack of a positive ethnic identity may lead children to fully adopt both the positive and negative norms and values of their new setting. This may cause additional stress within families as parents try to preserve many of the norms and values of their homeland while adapting to life in a new environment.

While children may eventually become bicultural with the ability to navigate between their culture of origin and the host culture, the adaptation process can be difficult. Immigrant children may experience intimidation and bullying in their schools, as well as violence within their neighborhoods. They may feel pressured to appear, speak, and act like other children to perhaps lose their negatively perceived immigrant status and escape negative treatment by others. However, adopting new norms can often be in direct opposition to their parents' attempts to preserve as much of their native culture as possible. As a result, children can experience a degree of marginalization, not fitting in with their American peers or members of their own ethnic community.

Immigrant Couples

Male and female immigrants may experience immigration differently. Female immigrants tend to have more legal rights and improved financial, educational, and social opportunities in the United

States compared to their country of origin. Women can more easily find employment. This may lead to conflict at times between couples as males may experience a loss of status and change in their roles at home and in the larger social structure. Immigrants who worked as professionals in their country of origin may not always enter comparable positions as they enter the U.S. labor market. Males may be unemployed or underemployed. Thus couples can often experience significant conflict as changes in the balance of power in their relationship occur, particularly if male dominance was accepted in their native cultures.

The inability to adapt to new roles and structure within the relationship increases the risk of domestic violence as males may attempt to reestablish their authority and power within the home. Isolation, economic dependence, and fear of retaliation may perpetuate a cycle of violence as victims of domestic abuse suffer in silence. Recognition that women have more protection, resources, and status can lead males to alter their behavior and treat their partner differently. Flexibility and openness to a change in gender roles from the culture of origin allow many immigrants to adapt to their new social context and establish new positive norms within their relationship.

Undocumented Immigrants

There are approximately 11.2 million undocumented immigrants in the United States. This includes many individuals who entered the country without permission and those who remained after obtaining temporary legal admission through a visa. A number of undocumented immigrants are well integrated into U.S. society. Some have children born in the United States who have never visited their parents' country of origin. While children born in the United States to undocumented immigrant parents are U.S. citizens with all the rights and privileges afforded by U.S. citizenship, their undocumented parents remain unable to access opportunities available to legal residents and citizens in the United States. Furthermore, families with undocumented members live with the constant threat of the detention or deportation of their undocumented members.

The construction, agriculture, restaurant, and hotel industries have benefited from the work of undocumented immigrants as they are more likely to accept entry-level positions to survive economically. Many undocumented immigrants pay taxes but yet only a few utilize health care, welfare, and other social services. Some fail to for fear of being exposed as undocumented immigrants and others because of the lack of knowledge about various services. Furthermore, many communities have enacted laws barring the provision of services to undocumented immigrants. The illegal status of undocumented immigrants in the United States makes them vulnerable to crimes or abuse as they are less likely to report them for fear of detention or deportation. Many are subject to unfair labor practices, inadequate housing, prejudice, and discrimination without recourse.

Mental Health

While stressors related to the immigrant experience are quite significant and place immigrants at risk of developing mental health problems, mental health services are underutilized by immigrant families, as with other ethnic minorities. Immigrants may arrive in the United States traumatized by their experiences, including sex trafficking, alcohol abuse, hunger, war, poverty, human rights violations, and other personal trauma. Depression and anxiety related problems are common to their adjustment. Various barriers to seeking mental health services exist. Some immigrants lack the knowledge about and the access to both medical and mental health services. Communication challenges and apprehension about speaking outside the home about family issues also keep many from seeking services. Others lack the resources to afford services or cannot easily make time to seek services due to work obligations. Furthermore, mental health related problems may not be recognized or may be interpreted as medical or spiritual problems. Many immigrants are also unaccustomed to counseling and therapy and are more likely to seek help from family members or a religious leader in their community.

Keny Felix

See also Acculturation; Asian American Families; Assimilation: Immigrants and Refugees; Bilingual Families; Latino Families

Further Readings

Ayón, C., Marsiglia, F. F., & Bermudez-Parsai, M. (2010). Latino family mental health: Exploring the role of discrimination and familismo. *Journal of Community Psychology*, 38(6), 742–756.

Falicov, C. J. (2007). Working with transnational immigrants: Expanding meanings of family, community, and culture. *Family Process*, 46(2), 157–171.

Kamya, H. (2005). African immigrant families. In M. McGoldrick, J. Giordano, & N. Garcia-Preto (Eds.), *Ethnicity & family therapy* (pp. 101–116). New York, NY: Guilford Press.

Maciel, J. A., Van Putten, Z., & Knudson-Martin, C. (2009). Gendered power in cultural contexts: Part I. Immigrant couples. *Family Process*, 48(1), 9–23.

Pumariega, A. J., & Rothe, E. (2010). Leaving no children or families outside: The challenges of immigration. *American Journal of Orthopsychiatry*, 80(4), 505–515.

Sue, D. W., & Sue, D. (2013). *Counseling the culturally diverse: Theory and practice.* Hoboken, NJ: Wiley.

Williams, D. R., Haile, R., Gonzalez, H. M., Neighbors, H., Baser, R., & Jackson, J. S. (2007). The mental health of Black Caribbean immigrants: Results from the national survey of American life. *American Journal of Public Health*, 97(1), 52–59.

INCEST

Incest is not a commonly researched topic in counseling literature. This lack of research may be due to the inherent taboo of the topic. Across cultures, incest is one of the most universally taboo concepts. Despite the taboo nature of incest, culturally inappropriate sexual activity still occurs within families. Marriage, couple, and family counselors may be confronted with clients who disclose childhood sexual abuse in the form of incest or may be presented with an entire family that discloses incestuous behaviors. This entry addresses the taboo nature of incest, provides an overview of current research, and discusses clinical implications for addressing incest in family therapy as well as future directions for research.

Background Information

Incest involves culturally inappropriate sexual activity or marriage between individuals who may be considered biologically related or related by kinship ties. Consequently, incest is a concept that varies in definition depending on the cultural setting. Some cultures deem it incestuous for members of the same subgroup to marry or mate regardless of biological relation or lack thereof. Thus, incest cannot be solely defined as a sexual relationship between biologically related family members. It is debated as to what led to the development of incest as a taboo but the argument boils down to the basic argument of nature or nurture. Some view the incest taboo as a biological preference for genetic diversity. That is, humans are likely to prefer individuals with whom they are unlikely to share genes. This biological aversion to inbreeding may be a result of the genetic risks associated with mutation and the evolutionary inclination for diversity. Others view the origin of the incest taboo as a socially constructed concept based on the idea that humans prefer exogamy, marrying outside of one's social group, as opposed to endogamy (marrying within one's social group). As such, individuals seek to mate with those of a different social group in hopes of forming alliances and increasing social interaction.

Edvard Westermarck theorized the origin of the incest taboo in his book *The History of Human Marriage*. Westermarck argued that individuals reared in close proximity with one another fail to develop a sexual attraction to one another. This is also known as *reverse sexual imprinting*, which may be defined as a process whereby individuals learn what not to be sexually attracted to through their experiences with those closest to them in childhood. Robin Fox later called this theory the *Westermarck effect*. This theory has itself been debated and criticized. Recently, researchers have begun to incorporate the Westermarck effect into contemporary conceptualizations of the origin of the incest taboo.

Current Research

Incest is most often regarded as an inappropriate act between a parent and child, usually a father and a daughter. Although this is very common in the incest literature, there are other forms of incest including mother–son, father–son, mother–daughter, siblings, and extended family or perceived kin. Although parent–child incest is commonly reported, the true prevalence of differing forms of incest is difficult to determine. This difficulty is due to a lack of reporting due to shame and secrecy surrounding the taboo of incest.

In cases of parental incest research, common themes arise in characteristics of abusing and nonabusing parents. Abusing parents have been shown to possess varying levels of education, social status, and income; however, research suggests that most abusing parents are male. Threats of physical harm are also common in incestuous relationships between a parent and child. It is common for an abusing parent to use their authority as the child's parent to exert power over the child and coerce the child into sexual activity. Secrecy is also a common factor as abusing parents commonly want to keep their relationships with their children a secret from other family members. The nonabusing parent in an incestuous family may be absent at the time of the acts, oblivious to the behaviors, or in denial. In cases of denial, nonabusing parents may have experienced sexual abuse in their childhood, and this could lead to a lack of willingness to believe their child. Research has shown that providing support for the nonabusing parent may be helpful not only for the parent but for the child victim of incest.

There is a definite need for more research on incest. The current literature discusses case studies and practitioner reports, but little empirical research has been conducted. As such, conducting more research on this topic would present its own obstacles as stigma, secrecy, and legal obligations prevent access to this population. With these hurdles in place, it is important for counselors—especially marriage, couple, and family counselors—to be aware of incest and its effects on family dynamics. It is also crucial for counselors to be aware of special considerations to take into account when working with this unique population.

Incest prevalence rates may be unreliable due to a lack of reporting due to stigma associated with the taboo nature of incest. As such, the research on this topic is mostly limited to case studies and practitioner clinical file reviews. As a result, this entry focuses on incest within the nuclear family; this includes research on sibling and parental incest.

Sibling incest is less researched than parental incest and is believed by some to be less harmful. Some characteristics of sibling incest include fondling, touching, sexual contact (oral, anal, and digital), inappropriate exposure to masturbation or pornography, or sexual intercourse between brother and sister or siblings of the same sex. Average offender ages range from 13 to 19 years while average victim ages range from 5 to 11 years with abuse lasting on average 22 months. Sibling sexual abuse may be categorized by situations in which a sibling takes advantage of another sibling by gaining the sibling's trust when the sibling is in a vulnerable state. This is done by acting as a nurturing and trustworthy individual during situations when there may be other forms of abuse within the family such as domestic violence between the parents. In this situation, the abusing sibling gains the trust of the vulnerable sibling and uses this trusting relationship to exploit and sexually abuse them. Additionally, a sibling may use force or threats in abusing the victim. In the case of the latter, secrecy is a common characteristic. Abusive siblings may threaten victimized siblings and exert physical force on them to keep the abuse a secret. Researchers state that sibling incest is not only just as common as or more common than parental incest, but its effects are just as harmful. Sibling incest may be overlooked or minimized within a family for multiple reasons. Research shows that family members and mental health professionals are likely to label sibling incest as childhood sexual exploration and regard it as benign or nonmalicious. This downplay of incest may be a result of a family wanting to maintain homeostasis by ignoring problematic behaviors.

Counseling Incestuous Families

When working with families that have disclosed some form of incest, it is important that counselors consider numerous factors. First, counselors may need to be aware of how the topic of incest is discussed within the family. If the family is open with the discussion, this can help assess the family's beliefs and values surrounding the behaviors and this may in turn be integral in informing the therapeutic process. Alternatively, families may be secretive about the issue and less willing to disclose. Assessment early on in therapy also allows for counselors to be intentional in the interventions and approaches to therapy. It is important for counselors to be flexible and integrative when approaching therapy with a family dealing with incest. Each family has unique needs, and a therapist's flexibility may help to address the specific needs of the family. For the sake of safety, some families may need to change treatment modality from family therapy to individual or couples therapy. Also, multiple therapists may be necessary to provide the best level of care to the family. Since most cases of incest are already involved with the criminal justice system by the time they reach a therapist, it is also important that the therapist follow any court orders regarding how the treatment should be delivered.

Another factor to consider when working with a family dealing with incest is the time of disclosure. A counselor will address a family currently experiencing incestuous behaviors much differently than a family who experienced incest in the past. If a family has experienced incest in the past and reports to therapy for other presenting concerns, it is possible that the family may not see the relevance of the past incest in the current problems. In this situation, it is important for a counselor to be willing and able to explore the past issues surrounding the incest and their relation to the presenting concern or concerns. Additionally, it is important to ensure the safety of an incest victim in a family that discloses incestuous behaviors. As such, it is imperative for counselors to be aware of local laws concerning child sexual abuse and incest and report to authorities when necessary.

Counselors should also consider their own biases and values when working with families dealing with incest. It is possible for counselors who have not addressed their own biases and values surrounding child sexual abuse and incest to do more harm than good when working with families dealing with incest. Countertransference involves feelings that arise within the therapist as a result of the client. Some of the most common feelings counselors may have when working with families dealing with incest include anger, sympathy, and rage. The types of feelings that arise may differ depending on the individual to which the feelings are attributed. With victims of incest, therapists may see their own children in the child being abused or may feel the need to rescue the child from the abuse. This countertransference may lead the therapist to blame the child's abuser and impose these negative feelings on the child. The child client may become uncomfortable with the therapist because the child may still have positive feelings toward their abuser. Therapists may also attribute positive feelings to the nonabusing parent of the victim. Therapists may assume that the nonabusing parent is psychologically mature enough to deal with the situation; however, it is common for some nonabusing parents to be victims themselves of sexual abuse, and they too may need to process their own history of abuse. It is important to assess each family member and meet the nonabusing parent where they are rather than assume they are well adjusted. When working with an offending parent or sibling, it is common for therapists to wish to punish the individual in hopes that they may not harm the victim again. This may lead to an overall fractured relationship with the offender that would need to be repaired in order for any therapeutic growth to occur. Contrastingly, some therapists may mask their feelings of anger or dislike for the offender by overcompensating with positive feelings of sympathy and false understanding. This lack of transparency is damaging to the therapeutic relationship as it prevents genuineness within the relationship and creates a nontrusting atmosphere. Thus, it is important for therapists to be aware of their feelings about each member in a family and to personally address their biases such that they will not hinder the therapeutic process.

Overall, the therapeutic alliance is at risk when therapists allow countertransference to interfere with the therapeutic process. Countertransference in these situations cannot be avoided; nevertheless, it is imperative for counselors to avoid letting it hinder the quality of treatment by addressing it. Therapists may also address countertransference by seeking counseling, participating in group supervision, completing specialized training on the topic of incest within families, and using a team-treatment approach to therapy to help with burnout and countertransference.

Shaywanna Harris

See also Child Maltreatment; Sexual Abuse; Sexual Assault and Rape; Sexual Assessment/History; Trauma and Families

Further Readings

Finkelman, B. P. (Ed.). (2013). *Treatment of child and adult survivors.* New York, NY: Routledge.

Goodwin, J. (1982). *Sexual abuse: Incest victims and their families.* Boston, MA: John Wright.

Pearlman, L. A., & Saakvitne, K. W. (1995). *Trauma and the therapist: Countertransference and vicarious traumatization in psychotherapy with incest survivors.* New York, NY: W. W. Norton.

Read, D. W. (2014). Incest taboos and kinship: A biological or a cultural story? *Reviews in Anthropology, 43*(2), 150–175.

Trepper, T. S., & Barrett, M. J. (2014). *Treating incest: A multiple systems perspective.* New York, NY: Routledge.

Westermarck, E. (1921). *The history of human marriage* (Vol. 2). New York, NY: Macmillan.

Individual and Family Development

Development denotes theoretical perspectives on how adaptive change is achieved in society. Theories of development offer models to conceptualize thinking about growth, development, and learning in human beings. Contemporary definitions characterize development as systematic changes and continuities in the individual that occur between conception and death. Development is implied to be predictable and continuous with some kind of pattern and order. Counseling is a developmental process and strength-based and the counselor aids an individual, couple, or family through normative developmental adjustments and transitions. This will focus on human development in the individual and family. Specific attention will be given to the nature of development and theories of development, including ontogenic and sociogenic theories, as well as multidimensional, holistic, and transpersonal models. The entry concludes with a discussion of Murray Bowen's theory of family development.

The Nature of Development

The developmental process occurs at the psychological, biological, and social levels. In psychological development, the perceptions of a person change, along with other mental processes. Biologically, the function of a person's body and its organs tends to decline in efficacy, while aging. The social aspect of development includes interpersonal relationships, skills, and roles played in the larger society. A developmental approach examines the interplay of environmental and individual factors on a person. Developmentally, a person is always in the process of change, influenced by the interplay of outside influences on their lives.

Development is a complex process and the result of maturation and learning. Maturation and learning are the two processes that underlie developmental change. Maturation is the biological unfolding of the individual according to the heredity of his or her parents and the passing on of genes. Learning is the process through which experience brings about changes in a person's thoughts, feelings, and behavior. Development occurs in a historical and cultural context that influences the rate and intensity of how an individual's development occurs. A broader context for discussing adult development follows by examining some early influences on the developmental perspective.

Developmental systems encompass the entire life span of the individual and offer evidence that development in a person proceeds by stages. While there are several theories of human development, which agree on some points and disagree on others, it is not so much a single theory as it is a way of looking at a person's life, in which other theories can be integrated within its framework. The shift to a life-span view of the developing individual was solidified with the developmental perspective of Erik Erikson, who sought to understand the psychosocial challenges confronting the individual at each stage of life. Building on Freud's ideas, Erikson and others broadened the developmental perspective by including psychosocial trends, as evidenced by a crisis or turning point in each stage of human development. This shift resulted in a renewed focus on issues related to the "whole" individual, including such factors as spirituality, family environment, socioeconomic considerations, and the impact of groups on the individual's developmental process.

Theories of Development

The primary tension in theories of adult development is between the *ontogenetic* perspective, which posited that developmental forces are internal and biologically based, and the *sociogenic* perspective, which argued that change in adulthood is due primarily to social influences. Ontogenetic proponents were mostly from Germany, whereas the sociogenic proponents were influenced by French sociologists such as Émile Durkheim. One such person who may be classified as part of the ontogenetic school of thought was Sigmund Freud. Influenced by the philosophers of his era (e.g., Arthur Schopenhauer and Friedrich Nietzsche), Freud saw human beings as guided by passion as well as reason. Freud went beyond the traditional Victorian views of sexuality by identifying such theories as the Oedipus complex (the legendary King of Thebes who killed his father and married his mother) and Electra complex (the mythological Greek who avenged her father's murder by killing her mother). Freud disclosed in conceptual terms what literary poets had espoused all along and stated those themes in mythopoetic terms. Even the naming of the two aforementioned theories were indicative of the passionate figures in mythology who influenced the character of Freud, as well as his own passion to become an intellectual force in his own right.

Ontogenic Models

Ontogenetic models posited that development consisted of stages that were universal, sequential, and irreversible. From this perspective, change is discontinuous and characterized by qualitative changes. Ontogenetic theorists, such as Charlotte Buhler, Erikson, Carl Jung, Daniel Levinson, and Abraham Maslow, modified Sigmund Freud's psychosexual theory to a psychosocial model. Neo-Freudians, such as Alfred Adler, suggested that siblings are significant in development. Jung claimed that adults experienced a "midlife crisis," which could lead to a liberating effect on an individual's personality in adulthood. Karen Horney challenged Freud's ideas about gender differences and Sullivan demonstrated how early relationships in life could set the stage for styles of relating in adulthood. Perhaps the person who most influenced life-span development was Erikson. Erikson concerned himself with the inner dynamics of personality and proposed that an individual's personality evolved through systematic changes. His *epigenetic* approach to human development assumed that development was the result of interacting genetic and environmental elements.

Jean Piaget believed that a person's innate intellectual development helped to adapt to his or her environment. He posited a position called *constructivism*, which claimed that a person actively constructs new understandings of the world based on his or her experiences in development. As an individual developed, he or she constructed a more accurate understanding of the world.

Sociogenic Models

Sociogenic models of adult development sought to balance a completely innate and thus predetermined perspective of human development with a perspective that a person has an influence over his or her own development and is not completely subjected to events out of his or her control, which suggest that the person is powerless. One sociogenic model is the *disengagement theory*, which suggests there is a mutual withdrawal between the individual and society as one ages. This was countered by the *activity theory*, which posited that the more active a person is as they age, the better quality of life he or she will experience. These theories were integrated by Robert Havighurst and Bernice Neugarten, who sought to demonstrate that the factor that determined the level of activity among individuals as they age was his or her personal desire. John B. Watson believed that learned associations between external stimuli and observable responses were the building blocks of human development. A basic tenet of Watson's behaviorism theory was that human development and behavior are based on observations of behavior rather than intrapsychic motives and unconscious drives. Watson stressed the importance of learning in human development, to the point that nurture was dominant and nature counted for little in human development.

A proponent of the sociogenic model was Albert Bandura and his social learning theory of development. His theory suggested that humans were cognitive beings whose processing of information from the environment had a major influence in a person's human development. *Observational learning* from other people, or models, was primarily how a person changed his or her behavior.

Multidimensional Models

Other theories recognized that individuals were active agents in the unfolding of their life course. Many theories attempted to provide some middle ground between the ontogenic and sociogenic perspectives by integrating biological, psychological, and spiritual influences on development. One such theorist was Urie Bronfenbrenner, who felt that many developmentalists assessed human development out of context. To counter this thought, he formulated the bioecological approach, which took into account *biological* and *psychological* changes in the individual, while interacting with the *environment*. From this perspective, people were not just passively subjected to outside influences, but a person shaped his or her physical and social environments, while also being shaped by the cultural environment he or she helped to create. Development was something that individuals *do*, rather than something that simply *happens* to the individual. These theories proposed an increasing liberation from social and biological conditioning of adult development.

Holistic Models

More recently, the counseling field has devoted increased attention to *wellness*, as a theoretical approach to human development. Wellness included the physical, intellectual, social, psychological, emotional, and environmental and is a way of life oriented toward optimal health and well-being in which body, mind, and spirit were integrated by the individual to live life more fully within the community. The Wheel of Wellness model was based on Adlerian theory and incorporated aspects of gender and cultural identity.

Systems theory was based on the work of biologist Ludwig von Bertalanffy. He saw the essential phenomena of life as individual entities called organisms that are parts of a larger system that interact interdependently with one another. An *organism* was defined as Bertalanffy proposed: that all living systems operate on a similar set of principles, which are internally interdependent. Proponents of systems theory conceptualized a system (i.e., individual, couple, and family) as a whole consisting of interrelated parts, each of which affects and is affected by every other part, and each of which contributes to the functioning of the whole. Development takes place simultaneously and interdependently among each member of the system, as well as affects the development of the other members.

Transpersonal Models

Mounting data about the farther reaches of human potential and experiences available to humankind exposed limitations and gaps in the humanistic models of development. As a result, a *fourth force* (originally coined by Maslow) emerged in counseling to capture a more complete perspective of the individual in development. Until recently, this approach has not received great attention. Its central themes are inclusive while still valuing diversity and unity. Pre-fourth-force theories focused on the individual's problem behaviors and cognitions. Wellness models attempted to embrace a person's differences, while facilitating a balanced way of life for an individual. More recently, developmentalists have been examining a broader perspective of development. This view of transcending human differences was an attempt at revealing what unites each person, from the subatomic level to the physical level to the spiritual level to stages of consciousness and beyond. Transpersonalism is concerned with the study of humanity's highest potential and is concerned with an individual's essential nature of *being*. This is an attempt to focus on what unifies individuals as spiritual beings, while respecting a person's biological, ethnic, religious, and other differences.

There are different theories and perspectives that seek to explain the development of individuals and family through the course of life. Understanding the development of individuals and family enables us to develop effective therapies to negate the problems affecting individuals and the family. Family therapy or counseling acknowledges that social and cultural factors in the society shape individual and family values. The factors determine what people consider normal and what people consider abnormal and socially unacceptable. According to Murray Bowen, family history sets a template that influence and shape the values and experiences of individuals and the family. Bowen's analysis of family development enables us to create effective family therapy.

Bowen's Theory of Family Development

Bowen's family development theory is integral in the understanding of the development stages of both the individual and the family. The theory enables psychologists to develop effective counseling techniques for the family. The first concept in the theory includes the differentiation of self. The concept involves the ability of individuals to separate their personal feelings from their thoughts. People who lack differentiation are unable to separate their feelings and thoughts. Such individuals often introduce their feelings in the thinking process, and this interferes with rational thinking.

Therapists introduce differentiation to individuals who are unable to differentiate their feelings and thoughts. The process involves liberating oneself from the processes set by the family and ascribing new definitions to oneself. Differentiation means that individuals can harbor opinions and values that conflict with those of their families. Despite the different opinions and values, individuals should maintain emotional connections with their families. Counseling should ensure that an individual can conflict and reflect on the conflict to enable a person to behave in a different manner in future.

Another concept that explains individual development includes triangles. Triangulation involves a coping mechanism that enables individuals to deal with difficult situations in the course of their lives. It entails the introduction of a third party in a distressing situation to provide relief. Individuals tend to triangulate a third person in a distressing situation to seek relief from them. There is a relationship between differentiation and triangulation in individuals.

Individuals who lack differentiation tend to triangulate other people or become victims of triangulation. Differentiated individuals can deal with difficult situations without triangulating other persons, and they also know how to cope with life. In counseling, therapists address the habit of triangulation in individuals. They negate the habit while reinforcing differentiation to enable individuals to cope or deal with difficult situations in the course of their life.

The concept of nuclear family emotional processes offers insight into the development of the family. According to this concept, there are emotional patterns and structures that exist in families for generations. Emotional patterns are propagated through generations of a family through family teachings and values. Families tend to adopt a distinct way of thinking that was established by previous family generations. Nuclear family emotional processes involve the propagation of emotional perspectives through the different members of a nuclear family.

The family projection process is a concept in family development that resembles the nuclear family emotional process. The process involves the introduction of triangulation on the family level. Family members tend to bond over the fact that a particular family member harbors a distinct trait or quality that does not appeal to the rest of the family. Knowledge of this negative view by the particular family member will alienate him or her further from the other family members. It also shapes the way the family member views himself or herself.

In family therapy, it is important to establish the family projections that influence the behavior of an individual. The family projections impede the ability of an individual to differentiate themselves and develop their views and personal values. Eliminating family projections through counseling enables individuals to develop their perspectives and values that do not have any influence from their family. It also enables individuals to make their choices despite the possibility of conflict with the family.

The multigenerational transmission process is also another concept in the family development theory. The process involves the propagation and sustenance of family emotional processes through the family generations. The process integrates the family projection process and encompasses the whole family. A core part of the multigenerational transmission process involves the reinforcement of the beliefs and values of a family. Current behaviors of family members are reinforced through equating them with the behaviors of past family members.

Bowen underscores the concept of sibling position or order in the family development theory. Bowen asserts that every child in a family has their place or position in the hierarchy of the family. The set positions in the family hierarchy prompt children to fit the projections that accompany the positions. According to Bowen, the oldest siblings tend to be mature and responsible while the youngest siblings are immature and lack any responsibility. The oldest siblings grow up and are attracted to other oldest siblings who are mature and responsible. The youngest siblings also grow up and pair with their counterparts who are the youngest in their families and have similar traits.

Counseling plays an integral role in changing the beliefs of individuals who are either the oldest or the youngest siblings. Such individuals have a mindset based on the position on the family hierarchy that influences their behavior and values. Therapy aims at eliminating such mindsets that force individuals to fit set projections in the family and the society. It enables individuals to differentiate themselves and establish their beliefs and values that do not originate from social projections. Counseling equips individuals and families with the necessary skills to deal with social expectations. It enables families and individuals to develop coping mechanisms to deal with social vices such as prejudice and discrimination in the society. It consequently improves the emotional health of individuals and the ability to deal with social expectations.

The normal family development concept also influences individual and family development in therapy. According to this concept, families are versatile, and there are no particular types of families in the society. The different circumstances influence the development of families and their adaptive mechanisms. Family counseling, therefore, changes the development of families to adapt to the dynamic circumstances. Bowen asserts that differentiation is integral to the optimal family development in the society. Individuals in families should be differentiated and maintain healthy emotional connections with each other.

Family development models assist individuals and families through the elimination of family disorders. Emotional fusions and family anxiety contribute to family disorders that affect the wellbeing of the entire family. Family therapy identifies the least differentiated family members who may be the cause of family problems. The kinds of problems that affect a family include vertical and horizontal problems. Vertical problems are propagated from parent to child while horizontal problems result from the family environment. Counseling contributes to the development of individuals and the family through handling the problems affecting the family.

There are several factors that affect individual and family development in the society. The various concepts in the family development theory offer insight into the role of counseling in individual and family development. Counseling contributes to individual development through emphasis on differentiation. It also deals with the various projections that limit differentiation and consequently affect family development.

Miles Matise

See also Developmental Model of Marriage; Stages of Family Therapy; Systemic Family Therapy

Further Readings

Adler, A. (1927). *Understanding human nature.* New York, NY: Greenberg.

Aldwin, C., & Gilmer, D. (2004). *Health, illness, and optimal aging: Biological and psychosocial perspectives.* Thousand Oaks, CA: Sage.

Bandura, A. (1976). *Social learning theory.* Englewood Cliffs, NJ: Prentice Hall.

Bertalanffy, L. von. (1934). *Modern theories of development: An introduction to theoretical biology.* London, England: Oxford University Press.

Bitter, J. R. (2014). *Theory and practice of family therapy and counseling* (2nd ed.). Boston, MA: Cengage.

Bowen, M. (2007). *Family therapy in clinical practice.* New York, NY: Jason Aronson.

Bowen, M., & Butler, J. (2013). *The origins of family psychotherapy: The NIMH Family Study Project.* Lanham, MD: Jason Aronson.

Bronfenbrenner, U. (1995). Developmental ecology through space and time: A future perspective. In P. Moen, G. Elder, & K. Luscher (Eds.), *Examining lives in context: Perspectives on the ecology of human development.* Washington, DC: American Psychological Association.

Buhler, C. (1968). The general structure of the human life style. In C. Buhler & F. Massarik (Eds.), *The course of human life: A study of goals in the humanistic perspective* (pp. 12–16). New York, NY: Springer.

Corey, G. (2013). *Theory and practice of counseling and psychotherapy.* Belmont, CA: Wadsworth.

Cummings, E., & Henry, W. (1961). *Growing old: The process of disengagement.* New York, NY: Basic Books.

Davis, J. (2000). We keep asking ourselves, what is transpersonal psychology? *Guidance & Counseling, 15,* 3–9.

Erikson, E. (1968). *Identity: Youth and crisis.* New York, NY: W. W. Norton.

Erikson, E. (1976). *Adulthood.* New York, NY: W. W. Norton.

Freud, S. (1977). The origin and development of psychoanalysis. In S. Freud, *Five lectures on psychoanalysis.* New York, NY: W. W. Norton. (Original work published 1910)

Gladding, S. (2004). *Counseling: A comprehensive profession* (5th ed.). Upper Saddle River, NJ: Pearson.

Gladstein, G., & Apfel, F. (1987). A theoretically based adult career counseling center. *Career Development Quarterly, 36*, 178–185.

Havighurst, R. (1961). Successful aging. *The Gerontologist, 1*, 8–13.

Horney, K. (1945). *Our inner conflicts: A constructive theory of neurosis.* New York, NY: W. W. Norton.

Jung, C. (1933). *Modern man in search of a soul.* New York, NY: Harcourt.

Kerr, M. E., & Bowen, M. (2006). *Family evaluation: An approach based on Bowen theory.* New York, NY: W. W. Norton.

Maslow, A. (1968). *Toward a psychology of being.* New York, NY: Van Nostrand.

Myers, J., Sweeney, T., & Witmer, J. (2000). The wheel of wellness: Counseling for wellness: A holistic model for treatment planning. *Journal of Counseling & Development, 78*, 251–266.

Okun, B., & Rappaport, L. (1980). *Working with families: An introduction to family therapy.* North Scituate, MA: Duxbury Press.

Piaget, J. (1950). *The psychology of intelligence.* New York, NY: Harcourt Brace & World.

Seligman, L. (2008). *Diagnosis and treatment planning in counseling.* Boston, MA: Springer.

Sigelman, C., & Rider, A. (2006). *Life-span human development* (4th ed.). New York, NY: Brooks/Cole.

Slee, P. T. (2002). *Child, adolescent, and family development.* Cambridge, England: Cambridge University Press.

Strachey, J. (1966). *Sigmund Freud: A sketch of his life and ideas.* New York, NY: W. W. Norton.

Walsh, R., & Vaughan, E. (Eds.). (1993). *Paths beyond ego: The transpersonal vision.* New York, NY: Putnam.

Watson, J. (1913). Psychology as the behaviorist views it. *Psychological Review, 20*, 158–177.

INDIVIDUAL FAMILY CULTURE

Individual family culture refers to the climate in which a family functions and organizes itself. It may include but is not limited to behaviors, rules, roles, goals, values, communication styles, activities, and cultural and spiritual practices and beliefs. Since culture is usually equated with diversity, not with family, family members may not recognize that their family is an identifiable culture with its own values, norms, traditions, practices, and thought patterns that influence their lives both consciously and unconsciously. Every family has a unique way of interacting based on a generationally prescribed, ingrained, and shared way of living. Family culture is frequently challenged by internal and external factors, developmental milestones, and sociopolitical environments. Families must develop the resiliency and skills necessary to confront these challenges. This entry discusses family organizational culture, elements of family culture, a seminal study on types of American family culture, and nurturing family culture.

Family Organizational Culture

Organizational culture shares many similarities with family culture. Corporations are referred to as families because their organizational culture models many qualities found in families such as values, norms, goals, rules, communication patterns, and traditions and rituals. Such qualities create a distinct and unique organizational culture with which individuals can readily identify. A healthy organizational culture requires continued dedication, commitment, and purposefulness. Similarly, a healthy family culture is not created overnight and requires the same dedication and purpose. Like organizational cultures, families have values which serve as the cornerstone of their existence and which impact members' behaviors and choices. Just as organizational cultures have goals that guide their vision, families set individual goals for each member as well as shared goals for the family. Like organizational cultures, families create a structure that guides their daily routines, roles, rituals, and tasks and binds them together. In both places, there are identified leaders who take charge and make necessary decisions for the benefit of everyone. As well, there are rules and norms that, if violated, can cause serious relationship ruptures. Communication patterns are also essential in shaping interactions in each entity and ascertaining whether or not members are being heard and understood. Finally, for each, traditions and rituals that provide cohesiveness and belonging are vital. The annual company picnic is as important to the organization as the yearly family reunion is to the family.

Elements of Family Culture

Families and cultures share many common elements. Four concepts that are often found in literature on the subject of multiculturalism that may also be applicable to families include values, norms, traditions, and conformity.

First, values serve as the moral compass for the family's attitudes, behaviors, actions, and choices. Values are shaped internally and are continually emphasized and positively and negatively reinforced. A family culture built on strong values can help to mitigate against members making value choices inconsistent with those of the family. Parents are paramount in insuring that values are clear and consistently practiced and expressed such that there is no room for doubts or misunderstandings. In a healthy family culture, values are explained, practiced, experienced, and connected to important family activities. Values require making choices; there are occasions when some values may be violated or rejected. These instances can provide teachable moments and generate discussions about making more appropriate choices.

A family's culture may be built on values such as hard work, loyalty, public service, compassion, communication, and respect. It may be built on negative values such as selfishness, laziness, self-gratification, and dependency. Every family culture is different, with different value sets that are shaped by demographic, cultural, and societal factors that impact their choices. For example, a strong work ethic is a value exemplified by many families. A family that values educational attainment may create a family culture where all the members obtain advanced degrees. A family that values public service may create a culture where service to others is their legacy. A family that values fun may create a culture where creativity, spontaneity, and adventure are encouraged. A family that values money may create a culture where financial acumen is emphasized. In sum, a family's values help shape its culture.

Second, norms are implicit and explicit rules of behavior often couched in shoulds and should nots that help inculcate the values of the family culture into its members. If frequently reinforced, these norms become embedded into family interactions and help to govern all aspects of behavior inside and outside the family. Norms are family values conveyed by example, inculcation, repetition, and reinforcement. Norms are necessary to set standards; sometimes they are functional, and other times they are dysfunctional. They are pervasive in creating the tone of the family's culture. In some families, norms are inflexible and rigid. In others, they are fluid and change with the prevailing circumstances. In some families, violating norms may be met with serious consequences ranging from sanctions to exclusion.

Specific family norms may include those involving communication, emotional expression, dating and marrying, gender roles, education, eating patterns, and career choices. For example, if education is strongly inculcated into the family culture, such that the males study medicine, or all family members get advanced degrees from the same university, or all the women pursue prominent careers, or grades of B are unacceptable, when a member violates this norm, it may disrupt family functioning. Similarly, if the family culture values hard work, then it may be manifested in behaviors that reinforce this norm. For example, assigning chores to children is a popular practice. By doing this, the family's cultural value of hard work gets translated into behaviors, which, if reinforced, becomes a normal family culture expectation.

Third, family traditions are occasions, events, rituals, behaviors, practices, and rites of passage, often passed down generationally, that provide families with cohesiveness, purpose, belonging, identification, and a bridge between the old and new. A family culture steeped in tradition helps to provide stabilizing rituals and symbolic connections. Family traditions can include things such as weekly dinners, movie night, yearly family reunions, midnight Mass on Christmas Eve, Thanksgiving at grandmother's house, or taking family vacations every year. They may include rites of passage such as a bar mitzvah, jumping the broom, celebrating Kwanzaa, or celebrating a quinceañera. Some traditions may continue unquestioned and others challenged. As family members enter and exit the family system, and because of societal and cultural changes, family traditions may become dysfunctional, diluted, or discarded, and replaced with new ones. Some members may not be willing to conform to the usual traditions or practices. It then becomes necessary to start new traditions and practices that will benefit the individual and the family culture.

Finally, conformity refers to how well the family culture embraces differences. Differences may range from something as simple as a family member's choosing an unexpected career path to marrying outside the family's demographic. For example, the family culture may be one in which homosexuality is not tolerated; divorce is a stigma; and maintaining friendships, dating, or marrying outside the family's race, socioeconomic status, religion, or other social demographic is not acceptable. Some family cultures embrace differences and opportunities for growth and inclusiveness. Other family cultures regard nonconformity of any kind as an attack on the family's foundations and principles. Sometimes, instead of embracing differences, families sever the relationship with the family member who chose to adopt values that differ from those of the family culture.

Types of Family Culture in America

A 3-year study by the University of Virginia's Institute for Advanced Studies in Culture identified four types of family cultures in the United States. They are identified as the faithful, the engaged progressive, the detached, and the American dreamers. The study is valuable for understanding the family cultures in which the current generation is being raised.

The faithful, who comprised 20% of the American parents included in the study, follow strict traditional religious precepts. They view humans as sinful and society as morally corrupt. They preserve their religious values by indoctrinating their children and ensuring that the values are reinforced by their church community. These parents aspire to raise children who exemplify God's purpose, as they understand it, instead of the children's purpose.

The engaged progressives made up 21% of American parents in this study and were also the wealthiest of the four types. For this type, morality is defined by freedom of choice and responsibility, with few moral absolutes. They also value honesty, religious skepticism, being politically liberal, and a morality based on individual experiences. Parental optimism is espoused, and children are given liberties at a much younger age than children of the other family types.

The detached constituted 21% of American parents in this study. In this case, parenting consists of allowing children to do as they wish and suffer the consequences. Parents are pessimistic about their children's future success. This is because the parents themselves have limited education, are in low-paying jobs, have little income, and exist in unhappy marriages. Interactions and communication between parents and children are limited, and parents have resigned themselves to losing their children to negative societal influences.

American dreamers made up 27% of the parents in this study, with half constituting Black or Hispanic families. Despite having lower income and educational attainment, their focus is on ensuring that their children have requisite material and social advantages and opportunities, protecting them from undesirable elements, and instilling strong moral character. They hold optimistic attitudes about their children's future success, feel very connected to their children, and look forward to becoming friends with their children as they reach adulthood.

The study also found that most parents want their children to be morally astute and share their values, value frequent communication and close relationships, and are optimistic but concerned about the negative influences their children constantly face.

Nurturing Individual Family Culture

Healthy families cannot exist without a healthy family culture. Family culture is shaped by the values of the larger society and the influences of the community and family into which members are raised. Family culture is the beacon individuals use to either embrace or reject morals, values, norms, traditions, attitudes, behaviors, rules, roles, and other important dynamics. Although sometimes invisible, family culture is a powerful entity for ascertaining family functioning. Understanding family culture helps those who work with families conceptualize the family's world view, understand their behaviors contextually, and devise strategies for healthy family functioning. There is no ideal family type or culture; creating a healthy family culture must become intentional. Finally, practitioners must ascertain how a family functions and the family's culture before prescribing interventions. Ultimately, the goal should be to become cognizant of each family's culture and to respect it as the family's way of functioning.

E. Joan Looby, Kimberly Mason Peeples, and Chelsey L. Hess-Holden

See also Active Parenting; Beliefs and Values; Parenting; Parenting Styles

Further Readings

Cannon, B. (2012, November). U. Va. study identifies four family cultures in America. *UVA Today*. Retrieved from http://news.virginia.edu/content/uva-study-identifies-four-family-cultures-america

Congress, E., & Gonzalez, M. (2013). *Multicultural perspectives in social work practice with families* (6th ed.). New York, NY: Springer.

Council on Foundations. (n.d.). *The effects of family culture on family foundations*. Retrieved from http://www.cfo.org/content/effects-family-culture-family-foundations

Dinkmeyer, D., Jr., McKay, G., & Dinkmeyer, D., Sr. (2007). *The parent's handbook: Systematic training for effective parenting*. Fredericksburg, VA: STEP.

McGoldrick, M., Carter, B., & Garcia-Preto, N. (2010). *The expanded family life cycle: Individual, family, and social perspectives* (4th ed.). Boston, MA: Pearson.

McKay, B., & McKay, K. (2013, July). *Fathering with intentionality. The importance of creating a family culture*. Retrieved from http://www.theartofmanliness.com

Sue, S., & Sue, D. (2012). *Counseling the culturally diverse: Theory and practice*. New York, NY: Wiley.

INDIVIDUAL VERSUS FAMILY THERAPY

Individual and family/couple therapies can be summarized in two distinct ways. Perhaps the simplest view is a *participation* perspective, which is determined by who actually attends therapy. That is, the number of client(s) participating in treatment determines whether it is individual or family therapy. Alternatively, a *theoretical* perspective assumes therapists' theoretical approach determines whether they are implementing individual or family therapy. Namely, a systemic or relational focus is considered family therapy, which can also be implemented with an individual client. Based on these definitions of *family therapy*, we will subsume couples therapy within family therapy given the great overlap in concepts and methods, although couples therapy has acquired its own identity as a form of therapy in recent decades. This entry expands on each of these perspectives and provides clinical examples as well as an overview of the recent literature comparing individual and relational therapies. The entry concludes with ethical considerations for applying each of the modalities.

Participation Perspective

From a participation perspective, individual or family therapy is determined by who is attending therapy sessions. That is, the client in treatment may either be an individual, couple, or family members (e.g., parents and children). Within individual therapies, the person presenting in treatment and the focus of treatment is with a single client. Alternatively, a participation perspective defines *family therapy* as two or more people with some significant relationship (i.e., familial, legal, and/or affiliative) attending treatment, regardless of the clinical approach. As an example, "David" may seek treatment for depressive symptoms. According to a participation perspective, if David attends therapy alone he is participating in individual therapy. Conversely, he is receiving couples therapy if David attends with his spouse, "Rebecca," for support. David and Rebecca may or may not have a treatment goal related to relational concerns. This leads to the second manner in which the two therapies are defined: the theoretical perspective.

Theoretical Perspective

A theoretical perspective of individual and family therapy may be better explained using terms such as *relational* versus *intrapsychic therapy*. A therapist informed by an intrapsychic approach emphasizes characteristics that are inherent within the individual, such as mental health symptoms, cognitive thought processes, and/or behavioral responses; thus, interventions are aimed at treating the problem *within* the person. Treatment may also include psychopharmacology in order to treat biological factors. A therapist using an intrapsychic perspective could include family members (e.g., spouse or parents) in treatment to facilitate treating the symptoms or provide psychoeducation about the presenting concerns. If we refer back to David and Rebecca, the therapist may work with David to identify particular thoughts or behaviors that make his depressive symptoms worse. Rebecca could be included in session to better understand David's depression and how she can help him manage the symptoms. Yet, such sessions would still be considered an individualized approach.

Alternatively, family therapies are informed by a systems perspective that emphasizes the *relational* processes and the effects those processes have on the individual(s). Even if only a single person presents for treatment (for one or more sessions), a relational and/or systemic focus is still assumed. To understand each person in a family, a therapist seeks to understand how each person is in relation to every other family member. Thus, with this understanding a single person can be in treatment yet be seen as participating in family therapy. If David attended therapy with a family therapist, his symptoms of depression would be conceptualized in relation to his family system (e.g., relationship distress) and other systemic variables (e.g., job dissatisfaction, family of origin). Rebecca would be included in therapy to identify and alter relational processes within their marriage. From a systems standpoint, David's depression cannot be separated from the context of his relationships. In other words, individual mental health symptoms both affect and are affected by significant relationships, which are strongly supported within the couple and family therapy research.

Research on Individual, Couple, and Family Approaches

Both individual and family therapy have a great deal of research demonstrating their efficacy and effectiveness. Furthermore, a wide body of research has been conducted to demonstrate the impact of specific approaches for individual therapy, on issues such as depression, anxiety, posttraumatic stress, and obsessive-compulsive disorder. Similarly, research has found couple and family therapies to demonstrate efficacy in the treatment of issues such as youth externalizing behaviors, substance abuse, depression, and relationship distress. Currently, research is examining when to utilize what type of therapy format (individual versus couples or family) and for what types of treatment issues. Studies have demonstrated that some disorders can be more effectively treated through couples or family interventions compared to standard and/or individual intervention. The association between personal relationships and individual mental health functioning is a common rationale for these findings.

If we again consider the example of David attending therapy due to symptoms of depression, we should consider the present state of the research and the context in which his symptoms exist. If David were a child, we would consider his symptoms within the context of his family (e.g., parents and siblings) and additional relevant systems (e.g., school, community, etc.). While the specific interventions employed in treatment would vary based on the theoretical approach, in general, family-based therapies would aim to reduce symptoms of depression by strengthening family relationships and increasing social support within the context of the family. For example, the therapist would work with the family to overcome any obstacles by utilizing the strengths the family possesses. Children and adolescents are heavily influenced by the state of family and peer relationships, so it is easy to understand why family intervention is a preferred method of treatment in this case. However, the research on the effectiveness of individual versus family psychotherapy with adults is less clear.

If David were an adult, it would be more appropriate to consider his symptoms in the context of his relationship with Rebecca, as the research closely ties individual mental health to relationship distress. To date, research supports couples-based interventions to be as effective as individual-based treatments in reducing depression and more effective than individual therapies in improving relationship distress. Marital distress can lead to poorer outcomes in the treatment of problems such as depression; thus, it becomes evident that relationship issues can have a significant impact on "individual problems" and should be considered when developing appropriate treatment strategies. If a therapist attempted to treat the symptoms of depression in isolation using an individual, intrapsychic perspective the therapist would be ignoring the context in which the symptoms are occurring and the systemic influences of depression. Even if David initially presented for therapy alone, it would be best practice for a therapist to screen for relationship distress and adapt treatment accordingly with the understanding that depression is often associated with relationship distress. Indeed, research supports the effectiveness of couples therapy as a treatment for anxiety and depression with individuals that are also experiencing relationship distress. Some such approaches include integrated behavioral couples therapy, emotionally focused couples therapy, and the Gottman method of couples therapy (i.e., sound marital house). The present approach to treatment does not reflect this practice, which highlights potential ethical concerns related to best practice.

Ethical Issues for Individual Versus CFT

Almost half of marriage and family therapists' caseloads are comprised of adults seen in individual therapy, even though couple difficulties can account for almost 60% of the most common or second most common presenting problems. Of course there are times in which couples therapy may be contraindicated, such as intimate partner violence or relationship infidelity. Overall, however, the treatment of relational issues in the context of individual therapy is problematic. If the clinical research suggests relationship distress is best treated through relational approaches, clients obtaining individual therapy are not receiving the best treatment for their presenting problem. Notably, Alan Gurman and Mark Burton specified four points of concern that interfere with best practice and pose potential risk to the client's relationship when a client is seen individually for relational issues: (1) there is a risk for inaccurate assessment and misguided interventions due to the absence of the partner, (2) empathy from the therapist toward building an alliance with the individual client may reinforce polarization within the client's relationship, (3) the therapist may unknowingly model an idealized relationship standard, and (4) the individual client in treatment may experience an excessive amount of responsibility to create change in the relationship and blame themselves for an absence of desired change. This perspective outlined here can be extended to the importance of family therapy when presenting problem(s) involve relationship issues of the family. The best course of treatment would involve family therapy rather than treating a single family member in isolation.

Given the information provided, let us finally consider the ethical ramification of David being seen in individual therapy without Rebecca for symptoms of depression. We will utilize our understanding of the context of his relationship with Rebecca by incorporating what is known in the research. As previously discussed, there is the potential that marital distress plays an important role in individuals' mental health functioning. Thus, the relational context is a necessary part of treatment for well-being that cannot be properly assessed in individual therapy. In other words, there is likely a circular pattern between David's symptoms of depression and marital distress, such that David's depression leads to increased marital distress, the increased marital distress leads to worsening symptoms of depression, and so on. Consistent with the research and a systemic framework, both David and Rebecca contribute and help maintain the symptoms of depression and marital distress through the circular pathways. In a therapist's assessment process, if Rebecca were not present, a therapist could not hear Rebecca's perspective nor obtain interactional data by seeing how David and Rebecca engage with one another.

Additionally, client progress is an important part of the therapeutic process, as it provides clients with hope and investment in ongoing change. If David attends individual treatment for his depression that is influenced by the untreated marital distress, a lack of client progress could leave both him and Rebecca feeling disheartened without the necessary investment to continue in therapy. As the "identified patient," David is assumed to be solely responsible for creating change without the full understanding of the circular pattern that includes relational distress. A therapist who is informed by a relational framework that includes Rebecca in treatment would assess the depression–marital distress pattern for targeted intervention.

Rachel M. Diamond and M. L. Parker

See also Couples and Marriage Counseling; Couples Therapy Research; Depression in Couples and Families; Systems Theory; Treatment Planning With Couples and Family

Further Readings

Gurman, A. S. (2015). The theory and practice of couple therapy: History, contemporary models, and a framework for comparative analysis. In A. S. Gurman, J. L. Lebow, & D. K. Snyder (Eds.), *Clinical handbook of couple therapy* (5th ed., pp. 1–18). New York, NY: Guilford Press.

Gurman, A. S., & Burton, M. (2014). Individual therapy for couple problems: Perspectives and pitfalls. *Journal of Marital and Family Therapy, 40*(4), 470–483. doi:10.1111/jmft.12061

Lambert, M. (2013). *Bergin and Garfields's handbook of psychotherapy and behavior change* (6th ed.). Hoboken, NJ: Wiley.

Lebow, J. L., Chambers, A., L., Christensen, A., & Johnson, S. M. (2012). Research on the treatment of couple distress. *Journal of Marital and Family Therapy, 38*(1), 145–168. doi:10.1111/j.1752-0606.2011.00249.x

Lebow, J. L., & Diamond, R. M. (in preparation). Brief history of couple and family therapy. In B. H. Fiese, K. Deater-Deckard, M. Celano, E. Jouriles, & M. Whisman (Eds.), *APA handbook of contemporary family psychology: Vol. 3. Family therapy and training*. Washington, DC: American Psychological Association.

Sexton, T. L., & Datchi, C. (2014). The development and evolution of family therapy research: Its impact on practice, current status, and future directions. *Family Process, 53*(3), 415–433. doi:10.1111/famp.12084

Snyder, D. K., & Halford, W. K. (2012). Evidence-based couple therapy: Current status and future directions. *Journal of Family Therapy, 34*(3), 229–249. doi:10.1111/j.1467-6427.2012.00599.x

Whisman, M. A., Johnson, D. P., BE, D., & Li, A. (2012). Couple-based interventions for depression. *Couple and Family Psychology: Research and Practice, 1*(3), 185–198. doi:10.1037/a0029960

INFERTILITY

Chronic medical conditions can have profound effects on people beyond just biological symptoms or physical incapacitation. These restricting conditions, such as the inability to have a child, can affect one's thoughts, moods, emotions, behaviors, relationships, families, and ability to make meaning or sense out of significant life events. Infertility, or involuntary childlessness, is a prime example of a medical condition that has whole-person influence and implications for whole-person treatment. Viewing infertility through a biopsychosocial-spiritual lens can guide those involved in the treatment of this condition toward a more complete, collaborative, and family-centered approach to care. In this entry, the biological, psychological, social, and spiritual aspects of infertility will be discussed, as well as available treatment options.

The Biology of Infertility

Definitions of *infertility* vary based on circumstance. For example, many couples cannot conceive a child without medical intervention. Others can conceive but at a rate much lower than normal. Some have already given birth to one or more children, but then for whatever reason, lose the capacity to conceive again. Others can become pregnant without medical intervention, yet repeatedly fail to carry the child to full term and miscarry. Hence, definitions of *infertility* vary. The common medical guideline for an infertility diagnosis is when a couple has not become pregnant after 12 months of unprotected sex. Although the possibility of conceiving children naturally may still be possible, medical intervention is usually recommended at this time for the male, the female, or both.

Fertility issues can be due to problems with a male and/or female partner's physiology. In one third of cases, the cause of infertility involves only the male partner's biological impairment. This can include production of impaired sperm, low or no sperm concentration, varicoceles (enlargement of the veins within the scrotum), hormone deficiencies, genetic defects, and infections. It may also be related to male sexual issues such as retrograde ejaculation (semen is directed into the bladder rather than through the urethra), erectile dysfunction, or sexually transmitted diseases. In another third of cases, infertility is related to causes involving only the female, such as fallopian tube damage or blockage, endometriosis, ovulation disorders, hormone imbalances, uterine fibroids, polycystic ovarian syndrome (PCOS), pelvic adhesions, and a variety of sexual and behavioral causes. In the remaining third of cases, infertility is due to a combination of both male and female causes, or is unexplained.

Even though male-factor and female-factor infertility occur at nearly the same rates, infertility associated with men's reproductive systems is generally less treatable than women's, with fewer successful medical interventions available. Women's treatment options generally include an array of medications and hormones to help induce or strengthen ovulation, as well as laparoscopic and other surgeries for tubal blockage, endometriosis, and other fertility-related conditions. Treatments for men most often include medications, behavioral treatments for sperm production and general sexual problems (such as erectile dysfunction or premature ejaculation), testicular surgery, or hormone treatments to increase sperm counts and motility. Both genders benefit from assisted-reproductive technologies (ART), such as in vitro fertilization (IVF), intracytoplasmic sperm injection (ICSI), and intrauterine insemination (IUI).

Psychological Aspects of Infertility

Fertility has traditionally been highly valued by most societies. For many, having children provides existential meaning, identity, and social status; and the inability to bear a desired child can have negative effects on psychosocial functioning. Negative emotional reactions to infertility frequently include anger, sadness, shame, despair, denial, powerlessness, and guilt. Some experience an overwhelming sense of loss when they discover they are unable to bear children. In addition, those couples who choose to seek medical treatment face difficult decisions and often at very high financial, emotional, and psychological costs.

Research indicates that couples who experience the stress and distress associated with infertility may be more likely to develop mood problems, including high anxiety and depression. Many variables influence the severity and incidence of depression amidst infertility. For example, when the biological cause for infertility is known, depression among women is significantly higher than among women with unexplained or undiagnosed infertility. The length of time a couple has been dealing with infertility is another example, with the highest depression scores usually seen not when couples first learn of their infertility, nor after they have gone childless for half a decade or more, but typically during years two, three, four, and five. Adjustment to new roles (e.g., a new "non-parenthood" narrative) takes time and is often a difficult path to accept and follow.

Despite the frequency of negative psychological reactions to infertility, it is important to recognize that many who face infertility do not experience significant emotional or relational distress. Coping styles, social support, financial and psychological resources, as well as other factors often mitigate the negative psychological outcomes that involuntary childlessness might otherwise have on a person or couple.

Infertility as a Social Condition

Unlike other chronic conditions, the primary symptom of infertility—childlessness—only manifests itself amid the union of two people. Certainly an individual can be considered medically infertile based on their own biological functioning, but their lack of ability to reproduce exists only in connection with another person. In fact, though medically diagnosable, we typically do not label an individual as *infertile* or recommend fertility treatment until they first desire and attempt with a partner to become a parent. Because we cannot reproduce individually, infertility may be viewed as a condition belonging to two persons. This is significant because even when one person's reproductive system is healthy and functioning normally, she or he may still suffer the biological, psychological, social, and spiritual consequences of this medical condition.

Many couples report that facing the challenge of infertility together has brought them intimately closer in terms of communication, commitment, and sexual satisfaction. These couples tend to have healthier coping styles and a higher capacity for emotional communication and connection. Other couples indicate that the inability to have children may lead to marital or relational challenges, particularly in a context of high personal and societal expectations for parenthood. In some relationships, blame and shame are placed and assumed for the inability to have children. Under traditional sociocultural expectations, women more often assume responsibility for holding their partner back from being in a "normal" family environment. Many men report that they are distressed by their female partner's emotional state as much as by their own perceived loss of a potential child.

The influence of infertility on couples can positively or negatively affect aspects of the relationship beyond just those related to childbearing expectations or parenthood roles. For example, many infertile couples report decreased sexual satisfaction, which is likely related to a change in meaning surrounding sexual intimacy. Instead of a time of sharing and closeness, sex for infertile couples can become a chore and a reminder of what is wanted but unobtainable. When romance and spontaneity gives way to ovulation calendars, pills, heightened expectations, and performance anxiety, sexual bonding and satisfaction can be diminished. In addition, women with a diagnosis of infertility are at higher risk for sexual arousal and desire problems than women with no fertility difficulties. Very little is known about whether the same is true for men.

Most societies have a parenthood narrative, or a sense of duty, authority, and privilege associated with having children. For example, from a very young age, many children look forward to parenthood, often playing with dolls, babysitting for the neighbors, and otherwise preparing for the day they will be able to do and be those things they admire in their mothers and fathers. One of the fundamental stages associated with healthy development is the transition from one's identity inside their family of origin to forming new intimate bonds through the creation of one's own family. The inability to have a desired child can significantly interfere with this developmental task.

Infertility Meaning-Making and Spirituality

Those who navigate the realities of reproduction often face deep and meaningful questions about the purposes of birth, life, death, and our participation in them. A person's spirituality informs the way they answer existential questions about such things like personal identity, family relationships, and the meaning of one's life. Significant life events, such as childlessness, can challenge meanings made and cause reevaluation of core beliefs about self and purpose. Research on the experience of infertility has shown that for many, particularly women, to be denied parenthood can mean being denied a portion of their character. Self-esteem and self-worth are often affected by the experience of being infertile. While it is true that aspects of an individual's sociocultural context (e.g., culture, race, religion, sexuality, age, and gender) do influence personal interpretations of childlessness, infertile couples of all backgrounds often ask themselves similar questions, such as "Why me?" "Am I being punished?" and "Have I done something to deserve this?"

With the increasing availability of and advancements in medical technologies, physicians today are more able to offer hope to childless couples. Although medical technology has increased the ability of some couples to conceive children, it may have also created a false sense of hope for others. This can sometimes extend the grieving, adjustment, and meaning-making process. It is often left to the couple to decide when to stop fertility treatments—when to give up—but the choice can be a source of contention between partners. The choice to end treatment, likely making permanent the end of hope for one's own biological children, can be a heart-wrenching and soul-searching one.

Collaborative Treatment for Infertility

A comprehensive treatment plan for infertility should focus on biological, psychological, social, and spiritual aspects of a person's life. While not every infertile couple will need marriage counseling, and not every infertile individual will become depressed, anxious, or have a crisis of faith, there is often an essential role for marriage and family therapists or other mental health counselors to play in treatment. Physicians, mental health counselors, family therapists, nurses, social workers, financial counselors, religious or spiritual advisors, or anyone else involved who works collaboratively can facilitate more efficient and efficacious treatment.

For example, suppose 2 weeks have passed since Marta and Matt completed their second in-vitro fertilization attempt, and they are anxious to take a pregnancy test. On a break at work, Marta enters the restroom, takes the test and discovers that all the energy and money they have invested (an IVF attempt on average costs between $12K and $15K) have again not resulted in the pregnancy they desire. Emotionally devastated, Marta calls Matt who listens anxiously. He hears her cry about how unfair this is and how she cannot possibly attend her friend's baby shower this week, yet he feels overwhelmed by her intense emotion, in addition to his own. Seeking safety through distance, he claims an urgent need has arisen at work and promises to call her back. Marta, who has already been dealing with depressive symptoms for weeks now, feels abandoned and resentful. She leaves her office wondering if God is punishing her for mistakes she made during her teenage years.

Matt and Marta are at risk for significant negative outcomes in their mental health and marital relationship, as well as in spirituality and of course, biological treatment options. However, the reason she leaves her office early this day is to attend a preplanned therapy session with their marriage and family therapist who, while hoping for the best, anticipated the worst and asked them to take the test just before their scheduled appointment. Matt arrives a few minutes later and they proceed to have a difficult but very beneficial session in which both are able to express their pain and begin to learn to appropriately turn to each other for support. During the session, the therapist refers them to a financial counselor that he knows near Matt's work. After session, with permission from Matt and Marta, the therapist calls the reproductive endocrinologist they've been working with and informs her of the emotional challenges they face. They discuss the couple's potential for becoming pregnant, and the possibility of taking a break from medical treatment with the support of the physician. As in the case of Matt and Marta, infertility is a biopsychosocial-spiritual condition. Taking a collaborative biomedical and psychosocial approach to treatment can produce the best outcomes.

Daniel S. Felix

See also Assessment, Biopsychosocial; Birth Control and Contraception; Childless Couples; Individual and Family Development; Medical Family Therapy

Further Readings

Jaffe, J., Diamond, M. O., & Diamond, D. J. (2005). *Unsung lullabies: Understanding and coping with infertility.* New York, NY: St. Martin's Griffin.

Peterson, B. D., Gold, L., & Feingold, T. (2007). The experience and influence of infertility: Considerations for couple counselors. *The Family Journal: Counseling and Therapy for Couples and Families, 15,* 251–257.

Savitz-Smith, J. (2003). Couples undergoing infertility treatment: Implications for counselors. *The Family Journal, 11*(4), 383–387.

INFORMED CONSENT FOR RESEARCH

Informed consent refers both to the process of describing clearly to research participants specific elements related to research participation and the document signed by a research participant that serves as documentation of the participant's voluntary consent to participate in research. The informed consent process used for human subjects is governed by federal law, and both national and international standards and regulations exist that protect research participants. It is important for researchers who are working with individuals, couples, or families to understand informed consent. There are laws, policies, and ethical codes governing research with human subjects and institutional review boards (IRBs), that help ensure that participants understand any potential risks and benefits of participating in research and are participating voluntarily. This entry outlines the elements of informed consent documents, the process of obtaining informed consent, and the laws and regulations pertaining to informed consent. This entry also examines the special circumstances under which additional protections apply to research subjects (e.g., research involving the participation of minors, individuals who are incarcerated, pregnant women, fetuses, and newborns, as well as participants in studies where deception has been used).

Elements of an Informed Consent Document for Research Purposes

The federal government's Office for Human Research Protections (OHRP) established laws governing informed consent for research involving human subjects in the United States. The OHRP has identified specific elements that must be included in both the informed consent document and process. These elements include clearly conveying to the potential participant that he or she is consenting to participating in research. The informed consent process includes information describing what the researcher is studying and why the topic or issue is being studied. Informed consent should clearly convey to the participant what procedures will be involved in the research study. Specific information related to any experimental procedures used in the study must also be communicated to the potential participant. The possible risks and benefits a participant may experience as a result of participation must be explained. For studies that involve the possibility of more than minimal risk, participants must be provided with information on what kind of financial compensation and/or treatment the participant may be entitled to if harm occurs.

Additionally, the informed consent process must clearly explain to the participant how collected data will be stored, including describing safeguards that will be taken during the study to protect confidentiality or provide anonymity. The potential participant must be informed that his or her participation is voluntary and that he or she may withdraw without penalty at any time during the study for any reason. Contact information for an individual who can address participant questions or concerns must also be provided within the informed consent document. The participant should be provided with a copy of the informed consent document for his or her records and the researcher conducting the study should keep the original copy.

The components of informed consent can be summarized as follows:

1. Purpose of the research

2. Procedures involved in the research

3. Alternatives to participating

5. Possible risks and discomforts associated with participation

6. Benefits of research

7. Estimated length of time to participate

8. Person to contact in case of questions, concerns, or emergencies related to the research

9. A statement that participation is voluntary, and there are no negative consequences to not participating that the participant is otherwise entitled to receive

10. The right to confidentiality and the right to withdraw from the study at any time

The Process of Obtaining Informed Consent

The informed consent process requires that participants be provided with the information described above in a manner that ensures comprehension and without undue influence to ensure full consent. Participants should be provided with a copy of the informed consent document and the researcher must provide enough time for the participant to read the document. The informed consent document and the process of obtaining informed consent should be conducted in the language that is most familiar to the participant. Technical terms or jargon should be avoided, as the informed consent process must convey information clearly and in a manner such that the participant understands what is being explained. Both verbal explanation of the contents of the informed consent document and review of the document itself by a participant are consistent with best practices in obtaining informed consent.

In cases where a written signature is the only identifying information collected from participants and obtaining signatures may negatively impact the researcher's ability to provide anonymity or confidentiality, the informed consent process may be conducted orally without obtaining a signature. In these cases, the informed consent information is described orally to the participant, and in studies that involve greater than minimal risk, the participant is given the right to decide whether he or she wishes to sign a document or to waive providing a signature.

Obtaining informed consent orally may involve the use of a shortened form of the formal informed consent document. This document summarizes the elements of the formal informed consent document and includes a statement that full informed consent information has been provided orally to the client. Both the participant and a witness to the process sign the summary; in addition, the person responsible for obtaining informed consent also signs.

In all cases, decisions about the informed consent process are made by an IRB, a panel of individuals charged with ensuring that the safety and well-being of participants is maintained in research studies involving humans. This board must approve any research being conducted on humans within the organization they are overseeing. This board is responsible for making sure that all research involving humans complies with any and all applicable laws and regulations. Any organization or institution that receives federal funding for any purpose must have an IRB to review research that involves human participants. Researchers conducting studies that involve human participants must receive IRB approval prior to initiating the study. The researchers must ensure that they adhere firmly to the research protocol approved by the IRB throughout the entirety of the study. Any deviations from the approved protocol must be submitted to the IRB for additional approval, and any unanticipated events that result in risk to participants must also be reported to the IRB for review.

Laws and Regulations

The informed consent process and the establishment of IRBs for review of research proposals involving human participants came about as a result of a series of harmful consequences of research studies conducted prior to the establishment of regulations. Laws related to research with humans first emerged in 1947, when the Nuremberg Code established the need for informed consent for human participants in experimental research. From this point on, additional national and international laws were passed over the decades that established the need to make participant welfare the top priority in studies, to charge the principal researcher with the responsibility of ensuring ethical research is being conducted, and to refine and strengthen the informed consent process and document contents to ensure participants are providing true informed consent to participate in research.

Special Cases

In some cases, federal law provides increased protections for research participants who are considered vulnerable populations. Included under these protections are minors, individuals who are incarcerated, pregnant women, fetuses, and newborns. Additional protections for these individuals are provided due to the increased risk of research participation or the difficulty or impossibility of these individuals to provide full legal and voluntary consent to participate in research.

In addition to special protections for these vulnerable groups, special protections exist for research participants who are subjected to deception during the course of a research study. In addition to ensuring that deception will not pose physical or psychological risk to the subject, the researcher must also demonstrate the necessity of deception to obtain meaningful and important results. For research that involves deception, the researcher must inform the participant of the deception directly following his or her participation. Additionally, the researcher must allow the participant to withdraw from the research study voluntarily if he or she is uncomfortable allowing the use of data collected under deceptive circumstances.

The informed consent process and document place primary importance upon the safety and well-being of individuals who choose to participate in research. Laws and regulations govern both how research with humans is conducted and how informed consent is obtained. Special populations and special circumstances require and receive additional attention and necessitate increased efforts to protect participants from harm. The IRB is charged with the task of reviewing, approving, and monitoring research involving human subjects by ensuring adherence to the laws and regulations that govern these research practices.

Amy E. Williams

See also Couples Therapy Research; Effectiveness Research; Informed Consent in Clinical Work; Outcome Research

Further Readings

Berg, J. W., Appelbaum, P. S., Lidz, C. W., & Parker. L. S. (2001). *Informed consent: Legal theory and clinical practice* (2nd ed.). Fair Lawn, NJ: Oxford University Press.

National Institutes of Health. (2014, April 2). *Timeline of laws related to the protection of human subjects*. Retrieved from http://history.nih.gov/about/timelines_laws_human.html

U.S. Department of Health and Human Services. (2014, July 8). *Informed consent checklist (1998)*. Retrieved from http://www.hhs.gov/ohrp/policy/consentckls.html

INFORMED CONSENT IN CLINICAL WORK

Informed consent is an ethical and legal concept that concerns the client's right to be aware of the counseling process and participate in decisions regarding their therapy. It is generally considered one of the most basic rights of clients in counseling. The goal is to provide information to enable the client to make a free and informed choice about whether or not to enter into the therapeutic contract. Counselors working with individuals, couples, and families must recognize the unique difficulties related to informed consent. Understanding how to address these challenges is important to protect clients' rights, support their independence, and obtain the best possible outcomes in therapy.

Components of Informed Consent

The specific information covered during the informed consent process may vary according to the setting and type of treatment. In general, counselors typically explain the purpose of therapy as well as the potential risks, benefits, and alternative treatments. Information about what can be expected from the counselor and the responsibilities of the client are also discussed. Finally, counselors present the client's rights, including the right to privacy and the limits to confidentiality. That is, counselors explain that although every effort is made to keep the client's information private, there are exceptions when ethically or legally, the counselor must disclose confidential information.

In general, there are three components to informed consent: comprehension, voluntariness, and competency. Comprehension means that the client has received enough information, presented in a way he or she can understand, so that an informed choice can be made about whether to participate in therapy. Voluntariness implies that the client is consenting to counseling without excessive influence. In other words, the client is willingly participating in therapy and is aware that he or she is free to withdraw consent and stop treatment at any time. Competency refers to the ability to make rational decisions, including the capacity to understand the potential benefits and consequences of one's choices. Counselors should take care to consider the role of diversity as it relates to the components of informed consent. For example, the client's age, developmental level, language, and cultural background may all affect his or her ability to understand and provide informed consent.

Child and Adolescent Clients

While the process of informed consent may seem relatively simple when working with adults, there are complexities when the client is a child or adolescent. Typically, it is the minor's parent or legal guardian that provides legal consent to treatment. Nevertheless, because the effectiveness of therapy relies on a trusting relationship between the therapist and client, an effort should be made to include the minor client in the informed consent process. Although a minor cannot give legal consent to participate in therapy, the client can assent. In other words, the counselor can engage the client in the consent process and ask whether he or she agrees to take part in counseling.

In considering the three elements to informed consent, working with children and adolescents present several challenges. First, depending on age and developmental level, the client may have limited understanding of the information provided. Describing the procedures in developmentally appropriate language that children can understand is important for comprehension. Second, the issue of voluntarism is complicated with minor clients. Because parents or legal guardians give informed consent, some pressure is evident in a minor being asked to assent to therapy. Some scholars have pointed out that while a child or adolescent can agree to treatment, they may be unable to refuse counseling. For that reason, counselors should be sensitive to the fact that minor clients may require extra safeguards to ensure their rights are protected. Lastly, adults are presumed to have the mental capacity to make treatment decisions unless they have been determined to be incompetent. However, children may not have the previous experiences or cognitive and emotional maturity to consider the risks and benefits and make an informed decision about participating in treatment. As adolescents develop, their ability to make independent decisions gradually increases. There is debate as to when adolescents are adequately mature to consent to their own treatment. In some states, minors can legally consent to specific types of therapy (e.g., treatment for substance abuse) without parental consent; however, these exceptions are few. Usually, the permission of a parent or legal guardian is required to begin therapy with a minor.

In addition to the minor's ability to give consent, the information presented during the informed consent process may also be different. Notably, the issue of privacy and confidentiality applies differently to minor clients. Legally, the information discussed during therapy belongs to the parent or guardian who consented to the treatment. However, the success of therapy relies on the client feeling able to talk about concerns freely. At times, minors request that counselors do not disclose the information discussed in therapy to their parents. Counselors in this difficult position must consider the client's best interests, including the principles of confidentiality while also providing important information to others who are responsible for the client's well-being. Discussing confidentiality and its limits during the informed consent process allows all parties to understand and agree to the counselor's policies at the outset of therapy in order to better navigate these complex situations.

Couples and Family Clients

Including additional participants in the counseling relationship complicates the informed consent process. Informed consent should be conducted with all individuals who participate in counseling. When counselors make the effort to obtain informed consent from all participants, they communicate that no one member is labeled as the source of all the problems. By agreeing to participate in therapy, each member of the couple or family is making a commitment to the other members and to the counselor to take responsibility for their decision to be an active participant in treatment.

The three components of informed consent also apply to working with couples and families. First, the information provided, both written and verbal, should be discussed in a way that all participants can understand. Second, the issue of voluntariness can be particularly complex when working with couples and families. It is common for some family members to be more keen to participate in counseling than others. It is also not unusual for some counselors to prefer working with the entire family and not provide services unless all family members are present. Ethically, no individual can be forced or coerced to participate in therapy either by other family members or by the counselor. In such cases, the counselor may refer the family to another professional who does not share this policy. Alternatively, counselors may encourage the hesitant family member to attend one counseling session to better understand the nature and process of therapy in order to make an informed decision about whether or not to continue to participate. Finally, all parties must be judged competent to understand and make an informed decision about their treatment. As mentioned earlier, it is important for counselors to seek the cooperation of minors who will be participating in family therapy through the informed assent process.

The information presented to couples and families during the informed consent process is similar to that of individual clients. The counselor initially provides information to each participant about the nature and purpose of therapy. Counselors also inform clients of the risks, benefits, and alternatives to treatment. The risks and benefits of family or couples therapy, however, differ from those in individual therapy. With more participants, there is less control over the results of therapy and the outcomes are less predictable. Counseling may lead to an ending that is considered undesirable by one or more participants. Divorce is one example of an outcome that may result from couples counseling that may be displeasing to one participant. It is important during the informed consent process that counselors discuss the possibility of undesirable outcomes as a result of counseling.

Also included within the informed consent process is a discussion of the rights of each participant, including the right to privacy and the limits to confidentiality. Some counselors conduct individual sessions for members of a couple or family as needed or requested by the clients. For counselors who provide individual sessions, discussing the policies on confidentiality are a particularly important part of the informed consent process. Counselors need to be explicit regarding whether the information shared during the individual session will be disclosed to the other members of the couple or family. Without discussing the specific guidelines, each member may have different assumptions about privacy. For example, one member of a couple may assume that there will be no secrets in counseling while the other member may believe that the information shared during an individual session will be kept private. Without discussing the information prior to beginning treatment, the clients have not made an informed decision about whether or not to accept the counselor's policies on confidentiality. Having clear ground rules before counseling begins can help avoid these problems.

Finally, issues related to withdrawing from treatment should also be discussed as part of informed consent. As mentioned earlier, some counselors prefer to see the entire family for therapy. Can one member of a family leave counseling while the other participants continue? Or will one member deciding to withdraw from treatment mean that all members must end treatment or transfer to another therapist? These policies vary from counselor to counselor and should be discussed in the informed consent process.

Conclusion

Informed consent is not a ritual, but a useful process that can be more complex than it appears. Counselors working with individual, couples, and families handle distinct challenges related to informed consent. Even when counselors are careful about the informed consent process at the outset of treatment, unanticipated situations may arise during the therapy requiring that informed consent be revisited. However, the more comprehensive and clear the informed consent process is, the easier it is for clients to make educated decisions about their treatment. A thorough informed consent process also allows counselors to better manage future potential problems.

Cathy Longa

See also Confidentiality; Ethical Codes; Informed Consent for Research; Therapeutic Contract

Further Readings

American Counseling Association. (2014). *Code of ethics*. Alexandria, VA: Author.

Barnett, J. (2007). Seeking an understanding of informed consent. *Professional Psychology: Research and Practice, 38*(2), 179–182.

Margolin, G. (1982). Ethical and legal considerations in marital and family therapy. *American Psychologist, 37*, 788–801.

Pope, K. S., & Vasquez, M. J. T. (2011). *Ethics in psychotherapy & counseling: A practical guide* (4th ed.). Hoboken, NJ: Wiley.

Thorp, S. R., & Fruzzeti, A. E. (2003). Ethical principles and practice in couple and family therapy. In W. O'Donohue & K. Ferguson (Eds.), *Handbook of professional ethics for psychologists* (pp. 391–406). Thousand Oaks, CA: Sage.

In-Law Relationships

At one point in history, marriages were decided based on the advantages (e.g., professional, financial, social, or otherwise) the union would bring to the partner and his or her family. In this context, it was expected that parents and their adult children would continue to maintain a close relationship even after marriage. With such involvement, in-law relationships had a strong impact on one's marriage. Traditionally, *in-laws* are defined as the family members of one's husband or wife. With relational and societal changes the definition and function of in-laws has expanded. The family of live-in opposite-sex partners or same-sex partners (whether legally married or not) may be defined and treated as in-laws, and the role of in-laws may be prominent or next to nonexistent regardless of the type of couple. Currently, with ambiguous expectations, the absence of legal ties in some situations, and the rate of divorce, in-law roles may be more transient and lack clear expectations and boundaries before, during, and sometimes after dissolution of the marriage. The hopes and expectations of couples and the in-laws can be vastly different depending on the cultural and socioeconomic influences. At times, a strong relationship, or the lack of it, with in-laws raises enough concern for couples to seek marriage and family counseling. This entry examines the role of in-laws and how these roles are affected by cultural beliefs, as well as the benefits and drawbacks of in-law relationships.

A Cultural Perspective

The relationship to in-laws may vary depending on cultural norms. The relationship of parents-in-law as well as siblings-in-law is influenced by multidimensional factors that include gender, age, generation, class, and era and are normally articulated through intergenerational expectations. A paradigm shift in some cultures contributed to the emergence of the "nuclear family," where it is believed that one must put a spouse first and foremost for a relationship to thrive. This shift also communicated the need for couples to break away from extended family to develop as a couple.

The paradigm shift did not occur or did not fully occur in all cultures around the world. In certain societies, the mother-in-law receives a privileged position where the daughter-in-law is expected to provide unconditional, unidirectional devotion to the mother-in-law. For example, historically in China, a woman became part of her husband's family and was removed from her birth family. In traditional Chinese cultures, a daughter-in-law was subordinate to her in-laws and not following their will was grounds for divorce. More recently, China has witnessed a shift in mother-in-law and daughter-in-law relationships where daughters-in-law are not completely subordinate; this has emerged with the economic and educational advancement of younger women. Another example of the subordination of daughters-in-law to mothers-in-law is in the Hindu joint family, where siblings, their spouses, and children live together and two lines of dominance intertwined. The oldest male assumes authority of the family and being the wife of the oldest male results in some power. A mother-in-law's role is running the whole family's home life. To become a mother-in-law, one must pass first the stage of daughter-in-law during which a woman subjects herself to the guidance and power of a mother-in-law.

Parents are of course not the only in-law relationship. Current siblings-in-law relationships in South Korea encompass competing Confucian (a system of ethics based on the teachings of the philosopher Confucius [551–479 BCE]) norms and egalitarian norms. In the past, age, gender, and the interaction of these two norms served as a guide to siblings-in-law relationships. Daughters-in-law were expected to disconnect from their family and serve their husband's family. Siblings-in-law, especially brothers' wives, were expected to have shared caretaking responsibility of aging parents. In essence, the oldest brother receives the most, but also has the most responsibility. The eldest brother has special responsibilities to his parents, then his brothers (oldest to youngest), then to his sons, wife, and then daughters. With changes in laws to promote equality and to remove sexual discrimination, more egalitarian norms have emerged. Although laws have changed and as a consequence some, especially women, have more flexibility (e.g., sisters can remain close, although some laws in South Korea still require women to focus their responsibilities on serving their in-laws). Family relationships are still central in Korean culture.

There are many factors to consider when considering the cultural complexities of in-law relationships, especially when a couple is from different cultural backgrounds. For instance, interracial, interfaith, and intercaste or interclass relationships may have major differences in expectations for relationships with extended family. Such differences can bring about opportunities and challenges to the couple.

Benefits of In-Law Relationships

Although managing in-law relationships can pose challenges, there are also benefits. In some cultures, in-laws provide financial, social, and emotional support to new couples so they may become established quickly with few stressors. The financial support may come in terms of gifts of land, houses, furniture, cash, and so on that may benefit the couple in beginning their life together. At times, the couple may begin their new life still living at the home of one of their parents or sharing a home with siblings. Such resources diminish the stressors of individually maintaining a household. In addition, the family may have adequate resources of transportation that the new couple does not have to purchase on their own. Financial support may even include paying for schooling for one or both partners.

Social support comes in terms of the connections in-laws can provide the couple. Such beneficial social support can lead to employment, better employment, and at times improvement in social status. In cultures where a social connection is necessary to accomplish certain tasks, such as gaining meaningful employment, attending higher education, acquiring property, and so on, in-law connections can be a powerful force of support. In-law relationships have also been instrumental in providing health care and other needed aid to some populations.

Emotional support may also come in differing forms. When young children are a part of the family, the extended family is available to guide, teach, and care for their needs. Other forms of emotional support are encouragement, advice, conflict resolution, and physical presence when needed.

When in-laws reside with a couple, as is the practice of some cultures, then the couple has financial and emotional support from these in-laws. At times, the parents may even take care of the household, completing tasks of maintaining the household, providing food, and taking care of the grandchildren. Such assistance may be welcome, but such shared households can also bring challenges.

Challenges of In-Law Relationships

In-law relationships can present challenges to the couple relationship. Indeed, there are many self-help books that explore the challenges in-laws bring to a person's relationship and how to fix them. One of the challenges of in-law relationships is the lack of privacy, especially if one lives with in-laws. The proximity of in-laws, whether parents or siblings, helps determine the level of intrusion that may occur. Those who share a dwelling with in-laws have the in-laws at all times, perhaps contributing to a lack of time for the couple to bond with each other through daily routine chores, hardships, and achievements. Similarly, where there is a dispute between the partners, there is always at least a third party present during and after the conflict, interfering in the concept of the couple as a dyad (an independent pair). At times, the dispute may arise due to in-laws residing in the same dwelling contributing to the daily functioning of the household. The presence of in-laws may influence how chores are done, as well as the nature of meal times, intimacy, and quality time. Sometimes things that a couple may typically do alone must be negotiated with a third party living in the home. When unequal power distribution based on generation, age, gender, and other multiaxial factors (i.e., class or in some cultures, caste) are considered, in-law relationships can be challenging. The couple may not have the ability to negotiate their own needs and wants. In some cultures, age is respected and venerated and therefore the parents and older siblings have more power and authority than younger adult children. Therefore, couples may be influenced to partake in parental and older sibling decisions that are not the choice of the couple.

Many of these challenges are due to expectations of filial piety or the requirement to respect one's elders. Extended family, such as grandparents, parents, uncles and aunts, and other siblings living with a couple, are a common phenomenon in some cultures. When considering age and gender factors in patriarchal cultures, the generational power hierarchy begins with the father, oldest adult son, mother, other sons, oldest son's wife, and other sons' wives. In such families, filial piety, or the devotion to one's family of origin, outweighs the conjugal ties. An older generational member, whether male or female, living with a younger couple will have more authority and control of the male partner than the wife, and the younger male is expected to listen to his elders and focus on his responsibilities toward his elders. Such a commitment expects the female partner to carry out the responsibilities assigned to the spouse. Empowerment of women and liberation laws have reduced the influence of generational, age, gender, and other multiaxial factors that challenge couples, depending on their adherence to cultural factors.

A third challenge that in-laws may bring is the disapproval of one's partner. A simple comment of disapproval may not challenge the partnership, but continuous demonstration of disapproval to the point of exclusion of a partner can bring challenges to the relationship. The disapproval can be based on many factors including personality, ethnicity, age, class, caste, gender, and so on. Disapproval can harm a partnership if partners are not mindful to work through issues as they arise.

Dilani M. Perera-Diltz

See also Conflict in Couples and Families; Cultural Issues in Couples and Families; Empowerment in Families; Multiculturalism; Nuclear Family

Further Readings

Apter, T. (2009). *What do you want from me? Learning to get along with in-laws*. New York, NY: W. W. Norton.

Du, D. Y. (2013). Living under the same roof: A genealogy of the family romance between mother-in-law and daughter-in-law in modern Chinese history. *Gender & History, 25*(1), 170–191.

Sung, M., & Lee, J. (2013). Adult sibling and sibling-in-law relationships in South Korea: Continuity and change of Confucian family norms. *Journal of Comparative Family Studies, 44*(5), 571–587.

INTEGRATING SYSTEMIC AND INDIVIDUAL THEORIES

The purpose of theory in individual, marriage, family, and couples therapy is to provide an explanation of human behavior. This explanation becomes a framework for therapists to understand what is happening with their clients and guides therapists in choosing techniques that are congruent with their therapeutic models. In training, therapists are often encouraged to choose one theoretical framework and to become proficient in the use of that approach in their work. However, many therapists find that it is useful to integrate interventions from other models to enrich their therapeutic work and to meet the personal styles and needs of their clients. Assimilative integration is a process in which therapists maintain a conceptual framework while using a considered and systematic process of integrating concepts and interventions from other theoretical approaches. This entry presents a brief overview of the differing philosophies in individual and systems theories, provides a rationale for the usefulness of integration, and offers examples of how individual theories and practices can be integrated with family systems thinking to enhance therapeutic interventions.

Individual Theory and Family Systems Theory

Individual therapy developed as a result of the assumption that the source of psychological problems was difficulty in relationships with others. The source of relationship problems was believed to be based on childhood and family experiences. Therefore, practitioners found it logical that clients should be removed from family members in order to facilitate the healing process. The belief was that healing would occur best in the privacy of the individual relationship between client and therapist.

In contrast, family systems theory was developed from the principle that the whole of the family is greater than the sum of its parts. While family members each retain their own individuality within the family system, the impact of individual behavior affects the entire system. The meaning of an individual's behavior is determined by the function of the family. The meaning attributed to behavior is based on the family's rules, values, roles, hierarchies, and subsystems. The family system regulates itself through a negative feedback process designed to restore and maintain homeostasis, or achieves heterostasis by changing the system through positive feedback.

Alfred Adler may have been the first family therapist, though he is not usually recognized for this contribution. In the 1920s, Adler rejected Freud's individualistic psychoanalytic approach and began to work with families. Adler's view of the family was as a social unit. Family behavior was seen as purposeful and interpretive and could not be understood without considering the context in which the family lived. Adler believed that dysfunction in the family occurred as a result of discouragement and the faulty logic that members used in their interactions with others.

Family therapy approaches that are more familiar to most therapists are those that originated in the 1950s through 1980s. The early pioneers in family therapy, Gregory Bateson, Jay Haley, John Weakland, and Don Jackson, noticed that the ways family members communicated had an enormous impact on the function of the family. They identified two levels of communication: the stated content of communication and the metacommunication, or the covert meaning. As more practitioners became interested in family systems work, other family theories were developed that added richness to the view of family function and dysfunction. Concepts and terms such as *birth order*, *differentiation*, *boundaries*, *structure*, *hierarchy*, and *homeostasis* have become so familiar that they are now part of the language of lay people as well as the language of therapists.

The Integrative Approach

Both individual and family therapy approaches provide theoretical constructs to help understand human behavior and motivation. Regardless of the approach to therapy, the overarching goals of therapy are to help clients overcome problems and lead happy, fulfilling lives. The difference in family and individual theories is in the foundational beliefs that drive therapy. Therapists using an individual perspective recognize the influence of the family but believe that internal forces and drives control behavior, so the focus of treatment is directed toward the individual. In contrast, family therapists believe that the family is the dominant force in clients' lives and so the focus is on changing the organization of the family. Therapy is directed to the entire family system; therefore change occurs in all members, and change is likely to continue as members maintain their influence on one another even after therapy is concluded.

Recent cultural changes have influenced the trend toward integrative therapy. For example, with the introduction of social constructionism, some therapists began to incorporate into their therapeutic approaches the belief that the way individuals think about their experiences defines their reality. Therapists are no longer considered to be the experts holding all the answers. Instead, many have added the role of facilitator or consultant to their work. As such, utilizing a variety of techniques from differing models allows therapists to meet the needs of clients and families instead of attempting to make the clients adapt their behavior to work within a theoretical model.

Another cultural influence that has impacted the integration of individual and family therapy is the limitation of services imposed by managed care and insurance providers. Brief family therapy is being recognized as cost effective because of the focus on treating more than one client at a time and because of the potential for the long-lasting change that is likely to occur when an entire system has been treated. However, therapists are now treating clients and families who are dealing with multiple issues, such as drug abuse, diagnoses of mental illness, and trauma. Specialized techniques and evidence-based treatment for these concerns are often based on individual approaches that can be incorporated into family therapy. For example, when a member of a family has been diagnosed with schizophrenia, the individual is best served by therapy and medication, while the family is provided with psychoeducation for how they can understand and cope with the schizophrenic member. The integration of individual theories with family systems thinking can provide additional therapeutic tools and interventions that can enhance the therapeutic process.

Examples of Integrative Approaches

Therapists who adopt an integrative approach to therapy differ from those who describe themselves as eclectic because they are concerned not only with what works in therapy but also with *why* something works. It may be argued that the only limitations to integrating an individual approach with family systems theory is the underlying philosophy of the theory and the creativity of therapists in adapting their thinking and modifying techniques typically used in individual work to meet the needs of a family system or couple.

The assimilative approach to integration is utilized by therapists who maintain a core theoretical belief while borrowing interventions from other approaches. For example, the genogram can be used as a tool in individual therapy to assess clients' functioning in the context of their family systems. A broader example of integration is evident when a theorist's approach to therapy becomes so widely accepted that it is considered to be a foundation for most approaches. The best example of this is Carl Rogers's core conditions for change, which are now considered to be so critical in establishing a therapeutic alliance that they are usually taught as part of basic training in counseling and psychotherapy.

Following are examples of three different therapeutic approaches that are easily integrated with family systems work: cognitive-behavioral therapy, choice theory and reality therapy, and solution-focused therapy.

Cognitive-Behavioral Theory

The cognitive-behavioral approach to therapy has its roots in behaviorism. Behaviorist principles of conditioning and reinforcement were integrated with learning theory for use in issues that influenced family functioning, such as parent training, enuresis, depression, anxiety, social inadequacy, marital discord, and sexual dysfunction. Operant conditioning is considered to be especially effective with children because parents are taught to eliminate the rewards that maintained unwanted behavior patterns and reward desired behavior.

An axiom of behavior therapy is that behavior is maintained by its consequences. This belief provides a challenge for family systems thinking because it implies linear causality. The systems view is based on circular causality, that is, the belief that events are part of ongoing feedback loops of actions and reactions. Finding the initial action is not important in changing the problem.

The inclusion of a cognitive component to behavioral therapy allows for the exploration of perceptions, beliefs, and distortions that contribute to emotional distress in individuals, couples, and families. The emphasis on cognition and behavior allows family therapists to look at patterns of thinking and interaction that maintain problems in the system. This way of working allows therapists to look at family interactions from a circular point of view; that is, the way family members think contributes to the way they behave and members influence and are influenced by one another through these patterns. The recent recognition of the importance of emotional response to cognition increases the opportunity to explore the escalation of volatile family dynamics, giving the cognitive-behavioral therapist another avenue to explore when working with families.

Cognitive-behavioral therapy (CBT) places heavy emphasis on the concepts of schemas, or core beliefs. Distorted schemas are considered to be significant contributors to dysfunction in family systems. For example, individuals have basic schemas about their families that are formed through interactions with their families throughout their lifetimes. These schemas influence how family members respond to one another, how roles are assigned, what rules are imposed, why things happen in the family, how the family is expected to function in social circles as well as in the family environment, and what consequences should occur when members fail to fulfill their responsibilities.

The therapeutic process of CBT includes both behavioral and cognitive components. Behavior is addressed through assessment of strengths and weaknesses in relationship skills. Therapists look at roles and expectations in the family and how rewards and consequences are utilized to reinforce those expectations. Specific behavioral homework activities are often assigned in the form of a written contract. Focusing on cognition occurs when therapists help family members recognize how their thinking, behavior, and emotion affect the entire family system. Therapists work with family members to examine their perceptions, beliefs, values, and behavior, and challenge members to identify, confront, and change the faulty schemas that contribute to family conflict.

Choice Theory and Reality Therapy

Like the early pioneers in family therapy, William Glasser considered cybernetic theory when attempting to explain human behavior. Glasser agreed with Norbert Wiener's assertion that the mind is a negative feedback system; when the mind perceives that something is wrong, it signals that something must be changed. Glasser integrated Wiener's theory with that of William Powers's control system theory, which explained that human behavior originates internally and that the entirety of one's experiences determines the perception of how individuals behave toward their environment. Glasser adapted these theories and developed choice theory, which emphasizes that behavior is a choice that originates from an individual's desire to meet five human needs: love and belonging, power, freedom, fun, and survival. Behavior consists of acting, thinking, feeling, and physiology. Since changes in how one acts and how one thinks directly influence how one feels and how one's physiology responds, the focus of therapy is on changing thoughts and actions.

Glasser believed that the primary cause of unhappiness and human misery is based in relationship problems. Thus, his theory and approach to therapy is easily integrated with the family systems thinking of how the impact of one's behavioral choice influences the entire system. Like Bateson and the Palo Alto group, Glasser pointed to the methods of communication that individuals use with one another as a source of disconnection in relationships. Glasser noted that difficulty in relationships stems from one's attempt to control others in an effort to get one's own needs met. This external control, while potentially effective in the short run, almost always has a devastating effect on the relationship in the long run. Choice theory teaches that all behavior is purposeful and is an effort to get needs met even in an environment of external control. Like Bateson, Glasser believed that when family members are on the receiving end of controlling behavior, their unhealthy responses may be understandable and even adaptive when considered in the family context. Chosen behaviors may serve as a function to preserve the stability of the family process and are maintained when the goal of stability is realized even as a result of behavior that appears to be dysfunctional.

Psychoeducation is part of counseling with choice theory and reality therapy. Clients are taught to recognize their own roles in their relationship conflicts. Glasser taught that people can control only themselves, and when they change their own behavior, the system changes as well. In counseling couples or families, there is no identified patient. Glasser emphasized that there is a third entity that must be considered as driving the work of the couple or family, and that entity is the relationship itself. Therefore, the needs of the entire relationship are more important than the needs of the separate individuals. Counseling is focused on what each person can control in an effort to improve the couple or family relationship.

Solution-Focused Therapy

Solution-focused therapy (SFT) was developed by Steve de Shazer as a pragmatic, goal-oriented approach that has its roots in postmodernism and social constructionism. Reality is seen as being unique to each individual, but individual reality can be shared with others and can be influenced by sharing meaning with others. The origins of SFT can be traced back to the Mental Research Institute (MRI), where the original emphasis of family therapy was problem focused and the intention of therapeutic interventions was to interrupt patterns of behavior. Therapy was brief, tailored to clients' worldviews, and emphasized resources rather than deficits. Eventually the MRI emphasis on pathology shifted to a belief that problems were maintained as a result of the inability to find effective solutions to the problems.

Families often maintain ineffective behavior with the mistaken belief that the approach taken to resolve the problem will work eventually. de Shazer shifted the emphasis of therapy away from the MRI focus on problem formation and causation. de Shazer emphasized that language is reality and that the way to make change is to change the way people talk about their problems. In family therapy, SFT keeps the focus on the future and emphasizes how the meaning attributed to language impacts the family's ability to find alternative solutions to family problems. Therefore, therapists work with family members to shift from problem-saturated stories to creating solution-oriented alternatives. Unlike other models of family therapy, SFT isn't interested in past history or family dynamics. Therapists don't insist on including all members of the family in therapy; instead, they invite any interested parties to attend the sessions.

An underlying assumption of SFT is that the family members are the experts on the family's problems and only need consultation and guidance from therapy. Therapists facilitate the change process by focusing on family strengths. Therapists are only interested in identifying the family's current complaints and helping clients identify the goals they want to accomplish as a result of treatment. Because the past cannot be changed, the focus of therapy is on the present and future, except when exploring past successes that can be capitalized on in the present. Goals are developed to resolve complaints and involve doing something different than the current behavior that is maintaining the problems. Therapists may begin this process by shifting the focus from problems to the exceptions to the problems and identification of the resources that clients already have that they can continue to utilize. Once the family begins to change their language to solutions, to identify resources, and to change behavior to what has worked in the past or will be likely to work in the future, the therapeutic goal is met.

Conclusion

This entry has presented support for the practice of theoretical integration in work with families and couples. However, it is not an exhaustive discussion and therapists who are interested in theoretical and technical integration may be interested in further reading on this topic. When evaluating approaches, therapists must consider the culture of the clients being served, the presenting problems and issues being treated, and the limits of the clinician's training and expertise. Finally, therapists should maintain an objective view of theory and practice and look at the evidence that supports the efficacy of the therapies and techniques they are exploring.

Patricia A. Robey

See also Brief Family Therapy; Choice Theory and Reality Therapy; Clinical Practice; Cybernetics; Integrative Couples Therapy; Therapeutic Alliance

Further Readings

Berg, I. K. (1994). *Family based services: A solution-focused approach.* New York, NY: W. W. Norton.

Carlson, J., & Robey, P. (2011). An integrative Adlerian approach to family counseling. *Journal of Individual Psychology, 67*(3), 232–244.

de Shazer, S. (1993) Creative misunderstanding: There is no escape from language. In S. Gilligan & R. Price (Eds.), *Therapeutic conversations* (pp. 81–90). New York, NY: W. W. Norton.

Glasser, W. (1998). *Choice theory.* New York, NY: HarperCollins.

Gurman, A. S., Lebow, J. L., & Snyder, D. K. (Eds.). (2015). *Clinical handbook of couple therapy* (5th ed.). New York, NY: Guilford Press.

Jones-Smith, E. (2012). *Theories of counseling and psychotherapy: An integrative approach.* Thousand Oaks, CA: Sage.

Minuchin, S. M., & Nichols, M. P. (1993). *Family healing: Strategies for hope and understanding.* New York, NY: Free Press.

Nichols, M. P., & Schwartz, R. C. (2012). *Family therapy: Concepts and methods* (8th ed.). Needham Heights, MA: Pearson.

Patterson, T. (2014). A cognitive behavioral systems approach to family therapy. *Journal of Family Psychotherapy, 25,* 132–144.

Snow, K., Crethar, H. C., & Carlson, J. (2005). Theories of family therapy (Part II). In R. H. Coombs (Ed.), *Family therapy review: Preparing for comprehensive and licensing examinations* (pp. 143–168). Mahwah, NJ: Erlbaum.

Snow, K., Crethar, H. C., Robey, P., & Carlson, J. (2005). Theories of family therapy (Part I). In R. H. Coombs (Ed.), *Family therapy review: Preparing for comprehensive and licensing examinations* (pp. 117–142). Mahwah, NJ: Erlbaum.

INTEGRATIVE COUPLES THERAPY

There are numerous theories that influence the work of marriage and family therapists. *Integration* is the process of combining the many techniques and perspectives from various theoretical orientations in order to produce a consistent and effective treatment strategy for a specific client. Integration has the benefit of addressing concerns and influences in couple's relationships from a multitude of theoretical orientations. There is nothing inherently wrong with guiding counseling through the lens of a single theory; however, by integrating multiple theoretical viewpoints, a couple's counselor is able to expand their perspective on the couple's presenting concern. Many relationship counselors find, at some point in their careers, that one theory or technique is insufficient to attend to all the complexity in the client's relationship, so they adopt an integrative approach. This entry presents the pros and cons of an integrative approach. Consideration is given to common concerns in couple counseling and how these concerns can be addressed through an integrative approach.

Pros and Cons

The problem with being a theoretical purist is that one may unintentionally fixate on a specific theoretical framework and miss important client, relationship, or contextual factors that could influence the course of couples counseling. There is an old adage once ascribed to psychologist Abraham Maslow that says *To a hammer, everything looks like a nail.* In keeping with Maslow's metaphor, because a counselor believes strongly that the family of origin is at the core of pathology (i.e., being a hammer), he or she may choose to only focus sessions on the client's family history (i.e., treat the client like a nail) and not on current, present-day concerns. There are many projects for which all a worker needs is a hammer, but for complex projects, one might need to employ other tools, such as a screwdriver or saw. Likewise, there are many instances when a counselor only needs a single theory, but for complex presenting concerns, he or she may need other therapeutic tools. Therefore, the chief benefit of integration is that it allows the counselor to have a larger frame of reference to work with the couple.

The challenge of integration is doing so in a manner that is ethical and effective. When counselors integrate theories, they must ensure they are making choices that are specific to their clients' needs, are ethical, and have theoretical or empirical support. Although every theoretical approach is unique and some have suggested that there are common factors that stretch across the various theories, some theories have strengths that can be more easily integrated to address a couple's needs.

Common Concerns in Couples Counseling

There are common concerns in couples counseling; however, not all theoretical orientations address these concerns with equal intensity or at all. Therefore, couples counselors often integrate various theoretical approaches in order to address these concerns as they arise in session. Discussing each of these common concerns in depth and how each couples or family counseling approach could be used to address them is beyond the scope of this entry. Nevertheless, several common issues and possible approaches are presented in the following sections.

Family

One of the common concerns that often emerges in couples counseling is the influence of the family and the family of origin. Most counselors would agree that couples are influenced by the individuals who raised them. In couples counseling, family of origin messages and the family's current involvement with the couple can be a salient part of the couple's identity. Therefore, many couples counselors utilize methods of discussing the family in session. Popular theories that address the influence of family include James Framo's object-relations approach, Sigmund Freud's psychoanalytic theories, Murray Bowen's multigenerational approach, and John Bowlby's attachment theory.

Borrowing from Bowenian theory, an integrative couples counselor may use a tool called a *genogram*, which serves as a generational map of family members. A genogram is essentially a complex clinical family tree that organizes important facts about a couple's family members. Genograms are integrated into counseling to present the type of relationships past family members have had and how those relationships influence the couple's presenting concerns. A genogram is a tool that can be used in a flexible manner to focus in on various aspects of what is going on with a couple, such as learned behavior of conflict management styles, history of substance abuse or mental health issues in generations past, positive legacies, cultural identity, or a wealth of other information. Because of the genogram's versatility, a counselor can easily integrate the genogram into couples counseling regardless of a counselor's theoretical orientation.

There are many other family issues that can be integrated into couples counseling. For example, the object-relations approach of holding a *family-of-origin conference* where identified family members join a couple's counseling session. Unfortunately, because of logistical concerns, this strategy is not often used, even though it has been shown to be an effective strategy. From a structural-strategic approach, a couples counselor could also integrate discussions on the origin of power structures and hierarchies in the couple relationship. A counselor could ask a couple to discuss how their family of origin affected their beliefs about roles in relationships. In addition, a structural strategy could be adopted to address organizations of power and hierarchies existing in the family, which may have been appropriate at one point, but are no longer healthy. The integrated couples counselor may encourage and empower that member of the couple to take more ownership and responsibility as more of an equal contributor to the family and in the relationship.

Historical Factors

When couples enter counseling, they do so with their past in tow. Many times, couples have faced traumatic experiences at various levels that may have resulted in shared despair or may have resulted in an *attachment injury* (a rupture in trust). Couples may have also struggled with past attempts to overcome smaller struggles, such as division of housework. Over time, relationship problems and failures may begin to overcome the relationship.

Whereas not all theoretical approaches focus exclusively on historical factors, some do more than others. One method of addressing a couple's history is simply to discuss it openly as part of the assessment process. A counselor could ask a couple about past trauma, relationship struggles that remain unfinished, or individual past events that shape how one partner views another. In addition, solution-focused therapy suggests that counselors ask about how past success can influence future change. A solution-focused couples counselor may ask a couple what has worked in the past and challenge the couple to use past successes to cope with present problems. These are a few examples of how historical factors can be included in couples counseling; however, not all approaches integrate a client's history. For example, a counselor using the strategic approach is more concerned with present behavioral patterns than past experiences.

Learned Behavior and Thinking Patterns

As a consequence of spending time together, couples learn ways of interacting with each other that can be either helpful or hurtful to their relationship. In other words, couples behave in ways based on learned responses and eventually form beliefs, or cognitive messages, based on these patterns of behavior and communication. These learned responses and patterns may serve a function for a part of the relationship or an individual partner but may be problematic in the overall couple dynamic. One focus of couples counseling can be to identify problematic cycles or destructive patterns in a relationship.

Learned behaviors and thinking patterns can be addressed from several different approaches. For example, from an object-relations and attachment approach, a counselor would work with partners individually to help them tolerate ambiguity and *own* areas in which they may be seeking their partner to address a personal issue that is being misunderstood as a couples issue. In solution-focused approaches, a couples counselor would discuss what the exception (or the alternative) to the problem behavior would look like and coconstruct with the couple solutions for the problem. Likewise, in the behavioral traditions, couples are asked to analyze their behavioral cycles and are encouraged to learn new behaviors that are more consistent with their goals and values. Emotionally focused therapy also integrates tools for behavioral change techniques, such as providing directive enactments, training couples to physically turn toward each other and rephrase how they speak in a way that the partner can receive and more readily accept what is said.

Affective Experiencing

Many couples also struggle to individually understand their feelings and communicate their emotions to their partner. Thus, another area of common concern in couples counseling is that of *affective* (emotional) expression and communication. Commonly, individuals will unconsciously protect their more vulnerable (primary) emotions with surface issues. The vulnerable emotion is referred to as a person's *primary emotion*. An example of a primary emotion could be fear; however, a client may unintentionally express anger toward the partner instead, as anger could feel safer to express.

Affect can be addressed from several perspectives. Bowen is foundational in family therapy for his introduction of the concept of *differentiation,* or in casual terms, understanding where one partner ends and the other begins in a relationship. Differentiation helps individuals understand that one partner's experience does not have to define the experience of the other. This is a central tendency in most, if not all, approaches in couples work, as awareness and healthy personal boundaries found with higher levels of differentiation tend to allow for more insight and therefore productive counseling. In addition, emotionally focused therapy can be used to assist clients with emotional understanding (empathy) and communication. Emotional interventions can be integrated with any approach to gently coach each individual to identify the emotion underneath a surface issue that communicates an attachment need as well as the vulnerable emotions. This is done with the goal of having partners begin to ask for their emotional needs to be met in more healthy interactive ways.

Integrated Couples Model

As previously noted, employing an integrative approach allows the helping professional to remain flexible and not restrained by a single theoretical position. However, the challenge in integrating couples counseling approaches is in developing a systematic process so that therapy is not piecemeal, haphazard, and ultimately ineffective. For this reason, Mark E. Young and Lynn Long developed an *integrative model for couples therapy* that allows helping professionals to utilize any theoretical orientation within a systematized couples counseling framework.

The integrative model for couples therapy consists of five stages: (1) assessment, (2) goal setting, (3) interventions, (4) maintenance, and (5) validation. At the center of the model is the development of a shared definition of the problem, known as the *interactive definition.* The interactive definition serves as a guide for the therapeutic process. According to the authors, if the counselor does not develop an adequate shared definition of the problem, he or she runs the risk of having the couple be noncommitted to treatment and the sessions may be ineffective.

Stage One: Assessment

Developing the interactive definition is part of the first stage of the integrative model: assessment. During the assessment phase, Young and Long recommend that couples counselors use formal assessments to screen out potential mental health issues, the possibility of violence, and learn about the client's background. Subsequently, the counselor would begin by asking the partners to describe, in each one's own words, what brings them to therapy. The goal of the assessment phase is for the couple's counselor to make every attempt to understand each partner's perspective on the problem and then reframe the problem as a shared couple's problem (i.e., the interactive definition). Thus, each partner is given about 10 minutes or so to describe their viewpoint and then the couple's counselor restates the problem as a joint solvable problem that represents the interests of each partner and ensures that the couple is committed to work on it.

The assessment phase in the integrative model is consistent with most if not all theories of couples counseling. The methods of assessment are at the discretion of the counselor and their theoretical preference. For example, some counselors choose to use genograms during the assessment phase, whereas others prefer informal methods, such as semistructured interviews. The main objective is to determine the severity of the couple's problems and assess their suitability for treatment. Additionally, the creation of a joint solvable problem gives focus to the course of counseling and strengthens the couple's commitment toward change.

Stage Two: Goal Setting

The second stage of the integrative model is goal setting. Establishing goals is an essential part of all couples counseling approaches. Goals help couples to focus on desirable outcomes rather than reverting to the negative patterns of blaming or creating conflict. Various theoretical approaches may have unique methods of goal setting, but the outcome is the same regardless of approach—to develop a workable and realistic focus of counseling sessions.

In the integrative model, counselors set goals that are consistent with the interactive definition and that have behavioral and affective components. In other words, the goals are set to include aspects that involve changing behavior that will influence emotions (e.g., a couple might decide to spend the weekend having fun together in order to achieve greater intimacy). Additionally, goal-setting in the integrative model includes externalizing the problem. *Externalizing*, a term developed in narrative approaches to couples counseling, refers to developing a goal that is separate from the couple and that they will conquer jointly. For example, if a couple argues about how each partner spends their finances, the counselor could externalize the problem by saying, "How will you two work with the money problem?" Externalizing the problem reduces blame and allows the problem to be addressed as a circular or systemic problem rather than an individual problem.

Stage Three: Interventions

The third stage of the integrative model consists of implementing interventions. Interventions are therapeutic strategies designed to help couples achieve their goals. The integrative model recommends designing interventions that make use of the couple's strengths, are approved by the couple, and are appropriate for the clients' background. At this stage of the model, counselors can integrate approaches from any theoretical system. However, Young and Long recommend that counselors match interventions directly to goals and ensure that the intervention is appropriate for the clients.

Stage Four: Maintenance

After the couple agree that they have made substantial progress toward their goal, the integrative model proceeds to its fourth stage. In this stage, the focus of each couples session is to challenge commitment and identify roadblocks. Whereas in stage three the counselor developed strategies for initiating change, stage four requires a set of strategies for maintaining gains. Regardless of therapeutic approach, couples counselors must help their clients avoid relapse so that they can continue improving. Long and Young describe stage four as fragile but crucial because even minor relapses could cause the couple to ignore or devalue any progress they have made.

During stage four, the counselor encourages the couple to discuss their commitment toward change. The counselor may pose questions like, "What is motivating you to keep this relationship growing?" or "What is keeping this positive progress going to take from each of you?" The goal of these questions is to help couples contemplate their motivation for change and encourage them to make a long-term commitment.

According to the integrative model, in order for couples to engage in a long-term commitment, they must develop a viable maintenance strategy. Consequently, Long and Young recommend asking couples to identify potential barriers to change or roadblocks. By identifying what might potentially sabotage the relationship, the couple and counselor can brainstorm strategies to avoid relationship hazards and prevent relapse. Selecting maintenance strategies is at the discretion of the counselor but could include using role-plays, engaging in cognitive-behavioral techniques, or making contracts with the couple.

Stage Five: Validation

The final stage of the integrative model is validation. During this stage, the couple and the counselor celebrate the progress made in counseling. Moreover, the couple is encouraged to identify follow-up strategies, such as coming in for sessions to check on progress and for long-term maintenance. The goal of this final stage is to encourage the couple to be invested in their success and motivated to keep progress going after sessions have terminated. Couples may be anxious at the end of treatment, feeling that things might revert after the sessions are over. By validating the couple, counselors help couples assuage doubts and engender a positive outlook.

*Daniel Gutierrez
and Emily B. Teague-Palmieri*

See also Solution-Focused Brief Therapy; Stages of Family Therapy; Strategic Family Therapy; Structural Family Therapy; Systemic Family Therapy

Further Readings

Framo, J. L. (1982). *Explorations in marital and family therapy: Selected papers of James L. Framo.* New York, NY: Springer.

Long, L., & Young, M. E. (2007). *Counseling and therapy for couples* (2nd ed.). Belmont, CA: Brooks and Cole.

Young, M. E., & Carlson, R. G. (2011). Fragile families, fragile couples [Monograph]. *Counseling and Human Development, 43,* 1–12.

INTELLECTUAL DISABILITY AND AUTISM

Developmental disability is a term used for any of several different conditions due to a physical or mental impairment. Developmental disabilities can cause difficulties in various areas of functioning such as activities of daily living (e.g., personal hygiene) or social interactions. For 2006 to 2008, the Centers for Disease Control and Prevention (CDC) reported that one in six children has one or more developmental disabilities or other developmental delays. CDC also reported in a study conducted focusing on children with developmental disabilities during the period 1997 to 2008 that the prevalence of the diagnosis has increased from 12.84% to 15.04%, about 1.8 million more children diagnosed with the disorder than a decade ago.

This entry focuses on two types of developmental disabilities: intellectual disability (ID) and autism, also known as autism spectrum disorder (ASD), highlighting the most recent changes between the diagnostic criteria in the fifth edition of the *Diagnostic and Statistical Manual of Mental Disorders* (DSM-5) and of the previous edition (DSM-IV-TR). Next, the entry explains the specific challenges experienced by individuals with ID and those with ASD, and concludes with a brief discussion of other disorders that may accompany ID or ASD and for which treatment may be required.

Intellectual Disability

Intellectual disability (ID) is manifested by cognitive deficits in mental abilities and adaptive function during childhood. Depending on severity, deficits can be observed as early as 2 or as late as 5 years of age. Causes of ID include genetic conditions, exposure to environmental toxins, problems during pregnancy or at time of birth, or substance abuse during pregnancy. Level of brain functioning determines the severity of deficits an individual will experience. Disorders commonly associated with ID are autism spectrum disorder, Down syndrome, and fragile X or fetal alcohol syndrome (FASD). Three domains of functioning—conceptual, social, and practical—are assessed in the diagnosis of intellectual disability. The conceptual domain includes language, reasoning, knowledge, and memory. The social domain includes interpersonal skills, empathy, and ability to follow rules. The practical domain includes the ability to care for self through activities of daily living (ADLs) such as personal hygiene. Some physical characteristics of an individual diagnosed with intellectual disability may include underdevelopment in physical growth, physical deformities, or delayed movement or balance. Mental characteristics may include below-average IQ, poor memory, attention, thinking, or concentration. Social and emotional characteristics may be difficulty in managing emotions, poor self-esteem, age-inappropriate responses, aggressive behavior, or other difficulties in social situations. An intellectual disability is regarded as chronic; an individual will experience deficits in various domains throughout their life span.

Changes in Diagnostic Criteria for Intellectual Disability

In earlier editions of the DSM the term *mental retardation* was used; in the revised version, DSM-5, that term has been replaced by *intellectual disability*. A vital criterion previously for a diagnosis of intellectual disability was an IQ of 70 or below. The DSM-5 highlights the importance of clinical assessment and use of standardized instruments for diagnosis rather than depending on the IQ alone. Using this approach increases the chances of a comprehensive evaluation and assessment to be completed by including clinical assessment, the three domains, and IQ. Lastly, the severity of the disorder is based on adaptive functioning rather than IQ level. The assessor determines the severity—mild, moderate, or severe, according to the individual's age and sociocultural background.

Autism Spectrum Disorder

Autism spectrum disorder (ASD) is defined as having deficits in communication, social development, and repetitive or restrictive interests or behaviors during the early developmental period. Although the cause of ASD remains unknown, research continues on suspected genetic, epigenetic, and environmental factors. CDC has reported that over the last 12 years the rate of individuals diagnosed with ASD has increased 289.5%. Deficits in social and language skills are usually noted within the first 2 years of life. Social and language deficits can include inability to (a) engage in imaginative play or making friends, (b) understand nonverbal communication behaviors such as body language or eye contact, and (c) lack of facial expression. The repetitive or restrictive interests or behaviors can include repetition of movement, inflexibility with routine, and ritualized behaviors.

Changes in Diagnostic Criteria for Autism Spectrum Disorder

Previously, the umbrella term for ASD was *pervasive developmental disorders* (PDD). Within PDD were autistic disorder, Asperger's disorder, pervasive developmental disorder not otherwise specified (NOS), and childhood disintegrative disorder. In DSM-5 the term *autism spectrum disorder* has replaced all of these: Autistic disorder, Asperger's disorder, pervasive developmental disorder NOS, and childhood disintegrative disorder have been removed; individuals are diagnosed based on a continuum from mild to severe. Severity is based on level of support needed: Level 1, 2 or 3. Level 1, *requiring support,* includes noticeable impairments in social communication and inflexibility behavior in more than one area (e.g., an individual who has difficulty making friends but can maintain a conversation, and who has difficulty transitioning between activities). Level 2, *requiring substantial support,* includes impairments in verbal and nonverbal social communication skills and inflexible coping behaviors, which can be noted by a casual observer (e.g., an individual who has minimal social interactions with others and has difficulty focusing). Level 3, *requiring very substantial support,* includes deficits in verbal and nonverbal social communication skills that interfere with functioning, and extreme difficulty coping with change (e.g., an individual who has no social interactions with others and repetitive or restricted behaviors that interfere with functioning in all areas).

Previously, a diagnosis needed to be made before the age of 3; now a diagnosis can be made after age 3, especially if an individual has developed strategies to manage their social skills but find it difficult in life to continue this pattern. Delay in language development is also no longer necessary for a diagnosis. Lastly, the criteria for social and communication skills were previously separate; in the DSM-5, they are combined.

Challenges

Early detection is extremely important for individuals with ID and ASD; those with ID struggle with mental and adaptive functioning that can cause severe impairments throughout the lifespan. From an early age, getting the appropriate services will be essential in the quality of life for the individual. Parents need to be educated about the disorder and the unique needs that their children will require to sustain a successful life. A child diagnosed with ID should have services focused on gaining the skills for adaptive living such as improving self-esteem, caring for self, and maintaining employment. Services can include speech pathology, psychiatry, counseling, and vocational rehabilitation. As the child matures, these services may need to be revisited to see if they best meet the needs of the individual. For example, a parent may need to seek services within a school that focus on developing an individualized education program (IEP) to ensure the child has the accommodations and resources to succeed in the school setting. A child with ID may need a school that has life skills and social skills built into the curriculum.

Individuals with ASD struggle with social relationships and language as well as repetitive or restrictive behaviors. Early diagnosis is important and can influence functioning throughout life. From an early age, parents may need to seek out specialists who focus on speech, language, and applied behavior analysis (ABA) or a specialized day care center that can meet the child's needs. Such needs may be met later on by the resources available at the child's school. Other forms of assistance include therapy for deficits in sensory processing, social skills groups, individual counseling, speech pathology, and neuropsychiatry. Individuals who are functioning at a higher level on the autism spectrum may require assistance to gain the skills needed to interact appropriately with others.

Comorbid Disorders

Other disorders can accompany a primary developmental disorder, such as attention-deficit/hyperactivity disorder, depression, conduct disorder or anxiety; the presence of another disorder accompanying a primary disorder is termed *comorbidity*. Studies reported that at least one such comorbid psychiatric disorder is often present in children with ID or ASD. Using the biopsychosocial model, a model based on viewing an individual's illness within the context of their biological, psychological, and social environments will be essential. For example, a child diagnosed with ISD who exhibits anxious behaviors such as pacing, panic attacks, or constant worry may suffer from an anxiety disorder. These symptoms need to be addressed along with ASD. Therapy could focus on implementing coping strategies to manage anxiety related to social interactions or group settings.

Janelle Bettis

See also Anxiety; Attention-Deficit and Disruptive Behavior Disorders; Autism and Children; Autism Spectrum Disorder; Behavioral Family Therapy; Conduct Disorder; Depression in Adolescents; Depression in Children

Further Readings

American Psychiatric Association. (2013). *Autism spectrum disorder*. Retrieved from http://www.dsm5.org/Documents/Autism%20Spectrum%20Disorder%20Fact%20Sheet.pdf

American Psychiatric Association. (2013). *Diagnostic and statistical manual of mental disorder* (5th ed.). Washington, DC: Author.

American Psychiatric Association. (2013). *Intellectual disability*. Retrieved from http://www.dsm5.org/Documents/Intellectual%20Disability%20Fact%20Sheet.pdf

The Arc. (2016). *Intellectual disability*. Washington, DC: Author. Retrieved from http://www.thearc.org/learn-about/intellectual-disability

Centers for Disease Control and Prevention. (n.d.). *Facts about intellectual disability*. Retrieved from http://www.cdc.gov/ncbddd/actearly/pdf/parents_pdfs/IntellectualDisability.pdf

Schalock, R. L., Borthwick-Duffy, S. A., Bradley, V. J., Buntinx, W. H., Coulter, D. L., Craig, E. M., . . . Yeager, M. H. (2010). *Intellectual disability: Definition, classification, and systems of supports*. Washington, DC: American Association on Intellectual and Developmental Disabilities.

INTERCULTURAL MARRIAGE AND FAMILY

Intercultural marriage is defined as the union between two people of different cultural backgrounds, which may or may not include differences in race, ethnicity, religion, and language. In this regard, the term *culture* is used to indicate meanings, beliefs, and traditions that are shared by a group as a result of a common history and experiences. Because racial differences are considered cultural differences in some societies, the term *intercultural marriage* has been applied to denote racially mixed couples. However, culture is more broadly defined and racial differences do not equate with cultural differences. In addition, because intercultural families combine members of more than one cultural group, the children share a bicultural or multicultural heritage. This entry addresses historical and legal influences on intercultural marriage, current issues pertaining to intercultural marriage, and intercultural parenting and child-rearing issues. Finally, implications for treatment and intervention will also be discussed.

Intercultural Marriage: Historical and Legal Influences

Historically, the multicultural movement has expanded our awareness of monocultural and monoracial people. While such growth in our knowledge and sensitivity to culture was an essential starting place within the realm of counseling theory and practice, the reality of multiculturalism is much more complex. Because approximately 20% of individuals living in the United States lived in another country prior to moving to the United States, these individuals are largely bicultural. Another example involves the children of intermarried couples in which they often acknowledge and embrace the cultural and racial identities of both parents.

Of the limited research that exists on intercultural marriage, there was a tendency to focus on the dynamics of Black–White couples and marriages. Furthermore, the literature was biased in a negative respect as it often approached the topic from a deficit or marginal viewpoint. Such tendencies tended to stem from historical and sociopolitical forces shaping worldviews around segregation. In fact, antimiscegenation laws prohibited interracial marriage until almost 50 years ago. While legal barriers no longer exist, intercultural marriages and families still tend to be the litmus test for prejudice within various contexts. Although intercultural couples can develop a level of strength, resilience, and increased attachment in the face of such pressures, they can experience a sense of vulnerability in the face of prejudice.

Factors that have impacted the increasing rise in the number of intercultural relationships include: (a) the civil rights movement; (b) repeal of antimiscegenation laws that forbade interracial marriage; (c) an increase of immigrants with differing perspectives on racial and cultural identity—in fact, many immigrants are multiracial and don't share a monoracial perspective (e.g., *Latino* is akin to a social category than a separation of race, Filipinos consider themselves mixed race, etc.); (d) the invalidation of section 3 of the Defense of Marriage Act (DOMA), which now allows for recognition of same-sex marriages (intercultural same-sex marriages were not legally recognized at the federal level and are now counted in intercultural marriage); and, (e) the repeal of anti-immigration and hypodescendent laws that previously forced individuals (e.g., Asian Americans, Pacific Islanders, Native Hawaiians, and Latinos) to identify themselves in a monoracial capacity up until the 1992 census when an "other" category was included. Although there have been shifts in the law, the social constructs and biases that have impacted racial and cultural identity are lingering.

Historically, a number of stereotypes of intercultural couples have been perpetuated. Some of the psychological stereotypes are that individuals comprising intercultural couples have a desire for the "exotic," harbor self-hatred, exhibit rebellion toward family, and desire to openly display liberal views of multiculturalism. The exchange theory is another bias by which intercultural couples are perceived as pursuing their relationship for social or economic mobility or to further the assimilation or dilution of distinct groups. Finally, there are pervasive sexual stereotypes in which there is a presumption of individuals in intercultural relationships preferring exotic, erotic, or unrestrained sexual exchanges.

Intercultural Marriage: Current Challenges

Stressors identified by intercultural couples are finances, juggling roles and responsibilities, parenting, employment (i.e., the number of hours worked and/or dual-career couple issues), communication related to the dynamics of the relationship, and decision-making challenges. In essence, these difficulties parallel those of monocultural couples. However, while some couples were able to create a bicultural identity that embraced and respected both individuals, other couples experienced conflict surrounding differences in values, religions/ belief systems, communication styles, child rearing, extended family roles, and conflict from societal and familial reactions to their relationship.

Intercultural gay and lesbian couples have tended to encounter higher levels of stress due to the impact of multiple oppressions. Historically, racism and bigotry were as prevalent in gay and lesbian communities as outside them. The literature suggest that due to the harmful impact of racism and classism, some couples choose not to affiliate with the gay and lesbian community, particularly if those couples resided in less diverse communities. Thus, these couples incur higher level of stress than those in intercultural relationships alone.

Issues of Parenting and Child-Rearing

The children of intercultural couples are frequently presumed to experience increased psychological and social difficulties. Rather than creating heightened sensitivity, the literature reports that such beliefs compound the challenges that parents and their children face in creating a healthy bicultural identity. While some families raise their children to identify exclusively with one aspect of their cultural heritage (often the culture that is more strongly reflected in their physical appearance), others expose their children to the values, roles, norms, attitudes, behaviors, and possibly languages of both cultures.

Multicultural families are also challenged with equipping their children to cope with racism, even within their families. This may involve instruction and discussions about what to say and how to respond in various situations. Families have also needed to develop ways to respond to social biases in response to their child's phenotype (i.e., physical appearance). Parents also noted that they were likely to talk with their children about issues of identity and focused on building strong connections to their minority culture. Other coping strategies utilized by multicultural families included providing strong options for support from extended family, "play" family, and friends; identifying strong adult role models; and, supplying identity-bolstering books, toys, and videos.

Intervention and Treatment

The increase of intercultural couples and families implies that mental health professionals have a greater likelihood of encountering and working with these individuals to support and resolve complex issues. In working with couples and families, it is vital that counselors work diligently to increase their personal awareness of personal biases and assumptions that they hold in respect to racial and cultural groups—as well as to interracial and intercultural marriage and children. In particular, two tendencies that may arise are (1) operating in a "color-blind" perspective whereby there is a passive denial that race or cultural is an issue and, conversely, (2) an overemphasis on the importance of race and culture whereby assumptions are made that the families' challenges are necessarily the result of racial or cultural differences.

In the context of counseling intercultural families, it is also vital to acquire a knowledge and understanding of each individual and the cultural values and worldview each brings to the relationship as it will impact the family's functioning and interactions with one another. In addition, there may be a need to expand the identified "client" to include extended family, which may also necessarily involve multiple cultures. In addition to typical issues facing couples (i.e., satisfaction with the relationship, effectiveness of communication, commitment and solidarity, developmental differences, occupational status, and family role expectations), cultural issues might include differences in emotional expression, expression of physical affection, beliefs of partners regarding gender roles, power distribution, cultural influences on family structure, views about parenting, and the meaning of love.

Assessment of the intercultural couple should include evaluating the racial identity development of both individuals and how well each partner understands and accepts the worldview of the other. In instances where differences exist, the counselor should help them understand each other as cultural beings and why culture is important to their dynamics. Intervention around ways to compromise and change where conflict exist will be important to their development of a bicultural identity as a couple. As a result, the counselor must learn and use strategies and skills that are culturally appropriate for each partner in order to effectively navigate the complexity of two cultural milieus.

Other issues that counselors must be prepared to address and support include the intercultural couple's acknowledgment and acceptance of racism and the role it plays in their lives. If one member of the couple is Anglo, there may be a need for them to acknowledge and identify the role of "White privilege" in their life in order to nurture their capacity for racial and cultural empathy. Counselors must also consider additional influences on the relational dynamics such as age, development, disability, religion, ethnicity, social status, educational level, sexual orientation, indigenous heritage, national origin, and gender.

The involvement of children of intercultural couples enhances the complexity of the therapeutic considerations, which include multiple cultural identities, the potential existence of competing loyalties between cultures of heritage, and the confusing messages of a racist society. Empowerment of children, families, and couples is a core feature that should be embedded in the intervention process. Knowledge of multiracial identity development models may be important to consider in assessing the children of intercultural couples. Other areas to assess include the child and family's sense of uniqueness, acceptance and belonging, the impact of physical appearance, sexuality, self-esteem, and broader identity development.

Terri Christiansen

See also Acculturation; Adoption, Cross-Cultural and Interracial; Assessment, Biopsychosocial; Assimilation: Immigrants and Refugees; Bilingual Families; Cultural Issues in Couples and Families; Diversity; Family Values; Gender- and Culture-Sensitive Therapies; Immigrant Families; Individual Family Culture; LGBT Families; Multicultural Counseling Competence; Racism

Further Readings

Gerstein, L. H., Heppner, P. P., Leung, S. A., & Norsworthy, K. L. (Eds.). (2009). *International handbook of intercultural counseling: Cultural assumptions and practices worldwide.* Thousand Oaks, CA: Sage.

Lichter, D. T., & Brown, W. A. (2009). Race, immigration, and the future of marriage. In H. E. Peters & C. K. Dush (Eds.), *Marriage and family: Perspectives and complexities* (pp. 365–381). New York, NY: Columbia University Press.

Root, M. P. (1996). *The multiracial experience: Racial borders as the new frontiers.* Thousand Oaks, CA: Sage.

Wehrly, B., Kenney, K. R., & Kenney, M. E. (1999). *Counseling multiracial families.* Thousand Oaks, CA: Sage.

INTERGENERATIONAL LOYALTY

Intergenerational loyalty refers to a sense of preferential commitment experienced between family members, particularly children and their parents.

The concept can help therapists make sense of their clients' conscious and unconscious motivations. Individuals may be driven by a loyalty to members of their family's previous generation, or a desire to restore a sense of justice or fairness to their family system. In this entry, a brief history of the term is provided, followed by a discussion of its philosophical roots and usefulness in determining family therapy goals and interventions.

Contextual Family Therapy

In contextual family therapy, Ivan Boszormenyi-Nagy described intergenerational loyalty as an indebtedness children feel in response to resources, nurturance, and values they receive from the older generation. This loyalty prompts children to reciprocate and/or pay these gifts forward to the next generation as they grow into adulthood. The balance between what is owed and what is given in a family creates a ledger of earned merit and/or indebtedness among its members. Presenting problems in therapy may be viewed as attempts by various family members to restore balance and fairness to the family system.

Philosophical Roots

The concept of intergenerational loyalty is rooted in the philosophical beliefs of Martin Buber who maintained that human beings experience a sense of self through relationships. The sense of self is first created and nurtured in the context of early family relationships. Bonds of genetic relatedness and nongenetic commitments, such as marital and adoption covenants, create a shared loyalty to the principles and symbolic value of the group or family. This sense of loyalty can operate even when family members are physically separated or cut off.

When early family relationships are fair, responsive, reciprocal, and rewarding, human beings naturally tend to gravitate toward health. This view has informed and been informed by object relations theory. Intergenerational loyalty motivates individuals to seek to attain the freedom, power, and resources necessary to reciprocate. Failure in a family to consistently meet one another's needs breeds what is called *entitlement,* or a deep, painful sense of violated trust and relational ethics. Entitlement drives individuals to seek out what they are owed from family members.

Visible and Invisible Loyalties

Visible and invisible loyalties within and between generations often express themselves in themes of justice and injustice; ledger-keeping and account-settling; and issues of abuse, exploitation, abandonment, guilt, dependency, and/or entitlement. An individual's potential involvement in subsequent new relationship commitments (e.g., marriage, parenthood, employment, etc.) must be weighed against old obligations. Loyalty conflicts serve to constantly pull the family toward symbiotic togetherness. Fulfillment of responsibilities to family of origin therefore can liberate individuals to enjoy other relationships with peers, spouse, and children.

Application in Family Therapy

Boszormenyi-Nagy maintained that therapists' most important task is to make invisible loyalties visible, thus liberating family members to make intentional choices regarding their interactions and more direct contributions to one another's well-being. Intergenerational loyalty represents a striving to balance what individuals believe they are entitled to receive with what they believe they are obligated to give. The balance of this ledger governs the actions and attitudes of family members in conscious, unconscious, and subconscious ways. The subjective balance of justice, trustworthiness, merit, and entitlement within the family constitutes a system of relational ethics.

Therapy Goals and Interventions

Awareness of intergenerational loyalty and relational ethics provides therapists with a lens to understand presenting issues and individual behavioral patterns. Injustices in early family relationships represent withdrawals taken out by parents on their child's ledger. If parents make too many withdrawals on their child's ledger, the child will be in debt, destined to make withdrawals in other relationships and/or from the next generation. What appear to be destructive and undesirable behavior patterns on the part of one individual may serve a balancing function for the overall family system.

Boszormenyi-Nagy posited that commitment, devotion, and loyalty are the most important determinants of family relationships. This conviction led him to the belief that family therapy should ideally include a three-generational family unit. Through the lens of intergenerational loyalty, the goal of therapy is to assist family members to recognize past injustices (both received and inflicted) and respond to one another with goodwill. Each act of repayment toward the debts of obligation in a family's ledger raises the level of fulfilled loyalty and trust within the family. When family members engage in ways that create a balanced ledger between give and take, entitlement and obligation, each individual's innate sense of justice is satisfied and loyalty is fulfilled.

One of the strengths of the lens of intergenerational loyalty is its optimism and impartiality toward multigenerational family members. To avoid creating a loyalty conflict for any individual, family therapists model relational ethics with all members of the family, whether present or not, through interactions based on fairness, trustworthiness, and justice. Problems in family relationships are framed as untapped resources that, when actualized, can transform injustice into fairness, anger into forgiveness, destructive entitlement into responsible giving.

Family loyalty and relational ethics provides a lens for understanding deep, multigenerational patterns of pain and hurt that keep families trapped in unfulfilling cycles. Furthermore, it does so without pathologizing individual behavior, but rather respecting each family member's efforts to restore balance and justice to the system. The perspective of intergenerational loyalty leads the therapist to expect that, when entitlements are fulfilled and justice is served, family members will naturally begin to credit one another's accounts and contribute to one another's well-being, thereby creating a new legacy for the next generation.

Gena Marie Minnix

See also Contextual Family Therapy; Differentiation; Entitlement; Family Values; Genograms; Intergenerational Trauma; Kinship Care; Transgenerational Family Therapy

Further Readings

Boszormenyi-Nagy, I., & Krasner, B. (1986). *Between give and take: A clinical guide to contextual therapy.* New York, NY: Brunner/Routledge.

Boszormenyi-Nagy, I., & Spark, G. (1984). *Invisible loyalties: Reciprocity in intergenerational families.* Levittown, PA: Brunner/Mazel.

Hargrave, T. (1994). *Families and forgiveness: Healing wounds in the intergenerational family.* New York, NY: Routledge.

Hargrave, T., & Pfitzer, F. (2003). *The new contextual therapy: Guiding the power of give and take.* New York, NY: Brunner/Routledge.

INTERGENERATIONAL TRAUMA

Intergenerational approaches demonstrate a significant need to explore the implicit and explicit effects of trauma on families. Trauma can be caused by any of a number of situations, including abuse, war, violence, and loss. While trauma has been shown to remain a presence in both research and clinical practice, histories of trauma that exist intergenerationally within families often have a much more implicit effect. Intergenerational trauma describes an interaction that is, sometimes, difficult to notice. When an individual is affected by a traumatic event (e.g., death in the family, natural disaster, war, torture, rape, assault, violence), the effects of trauma can shape the perspectives of other members within a family, a couple, or a community. Members within families and communities that do not directly experience the trauma can be targets of secondary trauma through the actions that come from individuals who have directly experienced a traumatic event. They experience the effects of trauma vicariously, as they see another family member struggling through his or her own pain with a particular trauma. As a result, a family member who experiences this traumatic effect vicariously could likely face his or her own set of symptoms, such as nightmares, anxiety, and depression. This entry examines current research on intergenerational trauma and intergenerational processes, including the dynamics between parents and children and community members.

Current Research

While the information on intergenerational approaches is rich within empirical and conceptual literature, there are a variety of systems theory constructs that elicit how other types of theoretical approaches are relevant to intergenerational trauma. In structural family therapy, for example, histories of trauma can affect how families redefine structures. When parents who have faced trauma experience psychological symptoms, their families might be restructured and children may take on more responsibility. While the research remains limited on this topic, there is a rationale for continued contributions of research and practice, considering how trauma histories can affect a variety of psychosocial developmental factors (e.g., parenting, attachment, family relationships, community relationships).

Counselors take intergenerational trauma into account through their practice with couples and families. This approach often guides how families and couples are seen as victims of the trauma. Consequently, when problems arise in the family, an initial understanding of the effects of a traumatic event should not remain limited to one family member. The information should also expand beyond noticing one family member who was directly affected by the traumatic event. Recognizing intergenerational trauma enables counselors to notice different parts of a system, including other family members, and to understand how other family members are reacting to the person or persons directly affected by the traumatic event.

While the research on intergenerational trauma is limited, current research has been disseminated to demonstrate the application of intergenerational trauma. Intergenerational trauma has played a major role in the narratives of former child soldiers, survivors of war, and war veterans. Particularly, with war veterans, research shows that individuals transmit their symptoms through other externalizing and internalizing behaviors, including violence, abuse, anger, and depression. An example of the externalizing behavior is family violence, while an example of internalizing behavior is the lack of mental presence or attention. Externalizing behaviors can also be related to substance abuse (e.g., binge drinking) and dependence issues (with withdrawal symptoms). The internalizing behaviors can also result in several psychological issues, including depression, anxiety, and withdrawal.

Intergenerational Processes and Dynamics

In the intergenerational approach, one primary perspective is to examine dynamics that occur between generations, generally in parent–child dyads and relationships. However, those dynamics can also translate to other relationships within a family system, such as sibling relationships and couple/spousal/marital relationships. Much research has been conducted specifically with parent–child relationships.

Relationships Between Parents and Children

Some research shows that the experiences of parents involved in war-related trauma and of parents who are former child soldiers can produce effects that profoundly influence intergenerational relationships. Children of these parents tend to find coping strategies to manage their parents' psychological symptoms and issues. They learn to adapt to the problems that their parents are facing. When children learn to adapt, they also assist with parents' management of the traumatic experiences. In some research studies, parents also become overly attached to their children as a result of their own traumatic history. Out of fears based on their own history, parents can become overprotective of children. Other researchers point to children creating representations of their parents as unable to be happy or as constantly sad. Parents experiencing traumatic events may also transfer anxiety, depression, withdrawal, and isolation symptoms to their children. Children can absorb these behaviors and energy as a normal life event. Specifically, with former child soldiers and war veterans, transferring traumatic events often results in higher levels of family violence. Discipline and parenting practices have been reported to be more aggressive and harsh. Children also internalize the styles of their parents in how they respond to their traumatic experiences. Often, this internalization can leave children without effective coping styles for psychosocial adaptation when they later attempt to adapt to events across the life span. Research also exhibits the significant impact of parental attachment on the attachment styles of children. When parents shift their attachment styles with children due to trauma histories, they can, in turn, affect the attachment styles of their children.

Individuals who are involved in traumatic experiences (e.g., the Holocaust and other genocidal events, civil wars in particular countries, child abuse, maltreatment) often carry high risks of revictimizing others and themselves for abuse. Consequently, the children of survivors of trauma often experience posttraumatic stress disorder (PTSD) symptoms similar to those of their parents. Parents who are survivors of child abuse also show a higher risk of perpetrating child abuse (e.g., verbal, emotional, physical, sexual) on their children. Research shows a much higher risk for individuals who are children of trauma survivors. With this intergenerational framework, patterns of abuse can occur over several generations, as the actions and revictimization are passed from generation to generation.

Community Relationships

Families who experience traumatic effects can also carry strained relationships with other members in their community or cultural groups. Many individuals experiencing trauma-related events are stigmatized within their communities. For individuals and families who adopt collectivistic values (e.g., valuing harmony and interpersonal, group relationships), this stigma can be detrimental to family processes. Families and individuals experiencing the trauma may not be able to seek help within their own community. In addition, they may face a significantly lower number of resources and refrain from seeking help.

Christian Derek Chan

See also Acculturation; Attachment Theory; Differentiation; Genograms; Intergenerational Loyalty; Interpersonal Violence; Sexual Abuse; Transgenerational Family Therapy; Trauma and Families

Further Readings

Hulette, A. C., Kaehler, L. A., & Freyd, J. J. (2011). Intergenerational associations between trauma and dissociation. *Journal of Family Violence, 26*(3), 217–225.

Iyengar, U., Kim, S., Martinez, S., Fonagy, P., & Strathearn, L. (2014). Unresolved trauma in mothers: Intergenerational effects and the role of reorganization. *Frontiers in Psychology, 5*(966), 1–9.

Kaitz, M., Levy, M., Ebstein, R., Faraone, S. V., & Mankuta, D. (2009). The intergenerational effects of trauma from terror: A real possibility. *Infant Mental Health Journal, 30*(2), 158–179.

Song, S. J., Tol, W., & de Jong, J. (2014). Indero: Intergenerational trauma and resilience between Burundian former child soldiers and their children. *Family Process, 53*(2), 239–251.

Yehuda, R., Halligan, S. L., & Grossman, R. (2001). Childhood trauma and risk for PTSD: Relationship to intergenerational effects of trauma, parental PTSD, and cortisol excretion. *Development and Psychopathology, 13*(3), 733–753.

Intermittent Explosive Disorder in Adolescents

Intermittent explosive disorder in adolescents is not what we as adults commonly think of with teenagers who become explosive when asked to complete a task or correct behavior. This disorder can be frightening for those who have witnessed the effects of someone who has been diagnosed with intermittent explosive disorder (IED). This adolescent has or performs an act of rage that is disproportionate to the triggering event. For example, the youth has been asked to clean his room and the response is to physically attack the adult requesting the task and to destroy the contents of the room. Individuals suffering from IED have described themselves as feeling as though they have lost control of their emotions and the anger just takes over. People who have been diagnosed with this disorder have reported that on occasion they have threatened animals, thrown objects, and struck other humans. Typically, individuals report that once the feelings of rage subside, they feel relief.

IED was first introduced as a diagnosis in the third edition of *Diagnostic and Statistical Manual of Mental Disorders* (DSM-III, 1980) and has since become a focus of research and clinical emphasis. The disorder consists of either high-intensity outbursts of aggression occurring several times yearly or a more treatable form with less intense outbursts several times monthly. This disorder was initially thought to be rare. There had been limited research and data until the early 2000s, and prior to this decade, IED was a little-known mental disorder marked by episodes of unwarranted anger. A recent study funded by the National Institute of Mental Health (NIMH) has found that the disorder actually has a much higher incidence.

Prevalence

IED is known to affect as many as 7.3% of U.S. adults or 11.5 million to 16 million Americans during their lifetimes. Nearly 82% of those with IED also have another diagnosable disorder, yet only 28.8% ever received treatment for their anger. About 70% of individuals with IED have at least three aggressive outbursts per year with an average of more than 27 aggressive outbursts per year.

The Diagnosis

According to the 2013 fifth edition of the DSM, a diagnosis of IED requires a history of at least three episodes of rage, or impulsive aggression, which is out of proportion to the stressor that precipitated the attack. This indicates that the reaction does not match the event; this then triggers an impulsive aggression and the response is triggered by a social threat or situation. According to the National Institute of Mental Health, the onset is usually in late childhood or adolescence. A child or adolescent with IED is unable to control his or her anger and will impulsively explode into rage with little or no apparent provocation. The object of, or witness to, the episode of intense anger may feel stunned by the force of the unexpected aggressive outburst. The pattern is often one of frequent, less severe outbursts (e.g., tantrums, tirades, arguments, or fights) that do not do physical damage. However, there are often less frequent, more severe episodes of explosiveness that that cause injury to less powerful people or animals or damage to property. IED greatly interferes with a child's family life as well as their social relationships and academic achievement.

Behavioral Description

Adolescents with IED have less ability to tolerate any annoyances or frustration than other teens. They become enraged by small situations, often becoming verbally and physically aggressive, sometimes causing property damage or even physical injury. Examples include breaking and throwing items, punching holes in walls, as well as verbal antagonistic behaviors and tirades. Road rage and getting into fights are common behaviors for people with the disorder. Adolescents with this disorder have described a feeling of becoming overcome with anger and have a feeling of being "out of control." Some others have described themselves as having an out-of-body experience in which they liken this disorder to a state of tension that continues to build up within them, but that will not be released when they act aggressively. The explosions are typically brief, less than 30 minutes, and are not previously planned or thought out but merely occur, and the event is not aimed to produce any type of desired outcome. Adolescents and young adults with IED are at a higher risk of intentionally harming themselves or committing suicide.

Aggression has been defined as behaviors intended to hurt, harm, or injure others. This includes not only physical aggression but also relational aggression such as lies, unfounded rumors, exclusionary behavior, and giving others the "silent treatment." This type of aggression can be covert or overt in nature.

Relational Aggression

Individuals with the disorder have high levels of relational aggression, behavior which is aimed at damaging interpersonal relationships. Adolescents with IED tend to show a greater degree of immature behavior and underdeveloped defense mechanisms, such as acting out and projection of their own attitudes and behavior onto others, and rationalization ("I was pushed too far and had no choice but to react the way I did"). Adolescent girls who have relational aggression tend to engage in retaliatory behaviors and spread false rumors that may encourage peers to reject a classmate. Because young girls in general are more likely to be relationally aggressive than boys, and also given that young girls' social interaction partners are most likely to be girls, girls are more likely than boys to target their relationally aggressive behaviors toward other girls.

Psychosocial Antecedents

A history of trauma in childhood has long been thought to be associated with the development of aggression in childhood and later on in adolescence. One community survey study reported a significant association between history of trauma and IED in a South African sample. In that study, a history of trauma was more common among subjects with narrowly defined IED, especially those with trauma related to being a victim of crime, trauma to a close other, or a history of multiple traumas (i.e., six or more traumatic life events).

Treatment

Further research is needed to determine risk and protective factors for the disorder, to develop strategies for screening and early detection, and to identify effective treatments. Several types of medications are currently prescribed to help control IED, including antidepressants such as fluoxetine (Prozac) and paroxetine (Paxil), at times utilized with a combination of both individual and group psychotherapy. Cognitive-behavioral therapy (CBT) is used to help people with IED identify which situations or behaviors may trigger an aggressive response. CBT also teaches people with IED how to manage their anger and control their typically inappropriate response using relaxation exercises.

Shirlyn M. Garrett-Wilson

See also Attention-Deficit and Disruptive Behavior Disorders; Conduct Disorder; Depression in Children; Depression in Couples and Families; Oppositional Defiant Disorder; Posttraumatic Stress Disorder in Children

Further Readings

American Psychiatric Association. (2013). Obsessive-compulsive and related disorders. In American Psychiatric Association, *Diagnostic and statistical manual of mental disorders* (5th ed.). Arlington, VA: Author.

Coccaro, E. F. (2011). Intermittent explosive disorder: Development of integrated research criteria for diagnostic and statistical manual of mental disorders, fifth edition. *Journal of Comparative Psychiatry, 52,* 119–125.

Coccaro, E. F., Kavoussi, R. J., Berman, M. E., & Lish, J. D. (1998). Intermittent explosive disorder-revised: Development, reliability, and validity of research criteria. *Journal of Comparative Psychiatry, 39,* 368–376.

Coccaro, E. F., Schmidt, C. A., Samuels, J. F., & Nestadt, G. (2004). Lifetime and 1-month prevalence rates of intermittent explosive disorder in a community sample. *Journal of Clinical Psychiatry, 65*, 820–824.

Dodge, K. A., Pettit, G. S., Bates, J. E., & Valente, E. (1995). Social information-processing patterns partially mediate the effects of early physical abuse on later conduct problems. *Journal of Abnormal Psychology, 109*, 632–643.

Fincham, D., Grimsrud, A., Corrigall, J., Williams, D. R., Seedat, S., Stein, D. J., & Myer, L. (2009). Intermittent explosive disorder in South Africa: Prevalence, correlates, and the role of traumatic exposures. *Psychopathology, 42*(2), 92–98.

Kessler, R. C., Coccaro, E. F., Fava, M., Jaeger, S., Jin, R., & Walters, E. (2006). The prevalence and correlates of DSM-IV intermittent explosive disorder in the National Comorbidity Survey replication. *Archives of General Psychiatry, 63*(6), 669–678.

INTERNAL FAMILY SYSTEMS MODEL

The Internal Family Systems (IFS) model was developed by Richard C. Schwartz in the 1980s and describes an integrative, nonpathological approach to psychotherapy. Schwartz was initially trained in structural family theory, which, along with many other system and individual psychotherapies, influenced the creation of IFS. The premise of IFS is that similar to the complex external family system, individuals are composed of separate and multifaceted internal parts in relationship with each other. IFS's primary focus is to work with individuals and help differentiate parts or subpersonalities in the mind. IFS is also used with couples and families to understand and explore intrapersonal dynamics that help clients better navigate interpersonal systems. This entry offers insight into the development of the internal family systems model and its key concepts. This entry also examines IFS's application in couples therapy.

The Development of the Internal Family Systems Model

Schwartz identified the concept of parts in the mind as a multiplicity. Like many theorists before him, he recognized the human psyche was not a single stagnant personality but rather something comprised of multiple elements that come together to create a whole. This concept is present in society when one makes a statement such as, "Part of me wanted to do it, but another part didn't." Despite this, the central concept of multiplicity within IFS is contradictory to the idea of a separate, autonomous person (e.g., the "I" or "me"), which has been present in much of western society for the last three to four hundred years. IFS postulates that due to life experiences such as trauma, family of origin values, and interactional patterns, the various distinctive parts within a person take on protective roles. The theory identifies three clusters of protector parts, including exiles, managers, and firefighters (each is described in detail later in this entry).

In addition to the internal system of parts identified in IFS, there is also the Self (within IFS, Schwartz specifically identifies it as a proper noun), which is the core or essence of one's being. The Self is present in all human beings; however, clients' various parts often obscure the Self. What IFS identifies as the Self is fundamentally and intrinsically whole (not wounded, injured, or crippled by experience). The Self is also replete with qualities ranging from curiosity and clarity to openheartedness, spaciousness, and compassion. Becoming aware of and living in Self-energy is the goal of IFS. Schwartz identified several qualities of Self, including calmness, clarity, curiosity, compassion, confidence, courage, creativity, and connectedness.

When one relates IFS parts to work with couples, protector parts in one partner often trigger protector parts in the other partner and vice versa, which Schwartz identifies as polarization. External systems (i.e., partners) are unable to interact with Self due to the various protector parts interfering to avoid potential pain in each member of the couple or family. This causes a breakdown in effective and authentic communication. The goal of working with couples is to first help the individuals within the system understand their different parts and then access Self-energy to be more open with each other. Once the individuals within the system learn to be aware of their parts and access the Self, the counselor can then help the couple work on being less triggered by their partner's parts. Schwartz identifies these interactions related to being in Self with your partner as courageous love.

When using IFS, it is imperative that the clinician can personally access Self and has taken the time to explore and identify their various parts. As in other theories, client parts can trigger practitioners. The ability for counselors to access Self while working with clients is essential to the success of therapy.

Parts

Schwartz first identified the concept of parts when he worked with children struggling with bulimia. These clients discussed different parts that come up as they talked with him. Initially Schwartz was concerned these parts signified pathology. However, he found if he explored the parts such as shame, fear, or the inner critic and allowed the parts to be heard instead of shunned or shamed, the clients were able to better access their Self, or their essence, and thus the need for the protective parts (shame, fear, inner critic, etc.) lessened. Within other theories, parts might be identified as defenses and can be seen as negative, one dimensional, and maladaptive; however, with IFS, an individual's parts are understood to be complex elements within a larger system. Schwartz identified these complex systems as multiplicity of the mind. Robert Assagioli, Carl Jung, and more recently neuropsychiatrist Daniel Siegel discuss similar complexities. IFS recognizes that each part serves to protect the internal system. Parts have learned through life experience how to behave and act out to protect the client. IFS identifies parts as being subpersonalities that step in or take over when there is a situation or experience they perceive as a threat to the system.

Within a person, much like an external family system, parts sometimes help each other and sometimes work against each other. For instance, the inner critic might work with or against the perfectionist part depending on the circumstance. When the parts work against each other, IFS identifies this as polarization. Polarization denotes a tug-of-war between the parts, where if either part backed down, they both might fail. This also occurs in couples when protectors are triggering each other. Within IFS, the counselor as well as the clients own Self, serve as trusted allies, and help parts talk to each other, which provides comfort and understanding for the parts. As a result, the parts become more integrated within the internal system. If one can be curious and compassionate with one's parts, an understanding about why they are afraid to change can become clearer. IFS contends that parts still carry old messages, ideas, emotions, sensations, and understanding from earlier events or episodes that define how they see themselves and the world. IFS stresses that the parts, are not something to eradicate or control. The theory suggests that all parts have a positive intent and fighting against one's parts, or a partner's parts is not helpful or therapeutic. Only when clients take time to explore their parts' various purposes and roles in a curious way will there be relief. IFS identifies this relief as unburdening or being free from the restraints of extreme emotion that once required the parts to work to protect the client.

Within IFS, much like differences between members of the same group, parts are often similar and different within unique individuals. Most individuals have parts, such as the inner critic and the intellectual. However, the ways in which these parts manifest and identify are unique to individual clients as are the ways these parts or subpersonalities interact with the different parts that make up the internal system. Schwartz and other IFS practitioners contend that exploring these parts one at a time creates an internal shift. Schwartz identified three broad categories of parts: the exiles, managers, and firefighters.

Exiles

IFS practitioners see exiles as protector parts that carry intense pain, often from childhood, and have been pushed out of the psyche. Often clients' most sensitive, intimate-seeking, open, and innocent parts take the impact of the trauma most directly. Exiled parts tend to also contain qualities that at one time were clients' most playful, spontaneous, and lively qualities. These parts tend to also be vulnerable. Exiled parts take on the memories, sensations, and emotions from traumatic events. Other elements that are exiled are feelings and behaviors that were seen as unacceptable within external systems. The elements that one categorizes as undesirable in childhood can likely become exiled parts. For example, within Western society, girls may be told "Don't make too much noise " and boys may be told "Don't be too sensitive." These don'ts are eventually exiled. Exiled parts are also stuck in the time of trauma, thus they are often childlike. Someone who is a survivor of childhood sexual abuse may fear their exiles. Clients may see the exiled parts causing them to be vulnerable, weak, sad, or dirty. IFS practitioners often find clients have done such a good job of exiling their exiles that they are not even aware of the elements they are withholding. In order to keep the exiled parts from being retraumatized or vulnerable, the psyche has managers and firefighters.

Managers

Parts that IFS identify as managers proactively arrange one's psyche, relationships, and life. Manager parts take over so individuals don't have to feel the pain of exiles. They also protect exiles from being hurt from dangers that the managers perceive as being a threat. Managers control day-to-day activities in clients' relationships and environments. The manager interprets and authors the story clients have about their personalities. For instance, managers can create a narrative that one has to be a "hard worker," "thin," or "stoic." Managers also create the stories clients tell themselves about the outside world, such as, "Men are dangerous" or "Saying no makes you a bad person." Managers take on the voice of authority; they create clients' realities. Often those ideals are from identified threats that go back to childhood and are no longer true threats, but this understanding is outside of the manager part's awareness. Individuals have many, many manager parts, such as victim, caregiver, pessimist, and isolationist. People pleasers' managers might be there so a client does not get attacked or abandoned, intellectual managers might be there to help clients avoid feeling pain by rationalization, or control managers might be present to try and control aspects of clients' lives because they are afraid of what might happen if an individual is not in control. While the jobs of the managers are to protect the exiles from retraumatization, they also blame the vulnerable exiles for initially being hurt. Often, different managers have different agendas and polarization occurs. For example, a taskmaster and an approval seeker will vie for different outcomes to protect the client.

Within ISF, managers are responsible for the job of maintaining day-to-day safety for clients. This is an exhaustive job and at times becomes impossible for manager to fulfill. When life events happen, such as feeling judged, the pain of an exile that was judged as a child can be triggered and often the protector part identified as a firefighter takes over.

Firefighter

The firefighter job is to distract individuals or rid the system of pain. Firefighters are often impulsive and do not think about the consequences. The work of a firefighter is done in the moment and is triggered when pain starts to come up for individuals. Often, individuals may not realize the pain is coming up before the firefighter protector takes over. Firefighters and managers often compromise so the actions taken are socially acceptable (e.g., work, exercise, watching television, shopping, daydreaming, or thrill-seeking behaviors). However, when these efforts don't work, the firefighters often resort to more drastic and less socially acceptable behaviors. When this occurs, social drinking becomes binge drinking. Other acts, such as using illegal drugs, suicidal thoughts or behaviors, compulsive sexual activity, or stealing, are also considered firefighter parts in action.

Schwartz identifies firefighters as good parts in bad roles. Often he has found the firefighter parts were in some ways heroes as they had taken the brunt of the insult when a person had been abused or hurt. The firefighters stayed present for the abuse while other parts were allowed to go into hiding. Much to the managers' dismay, firefighters continue to take on these roles until the exiles are healed. However, once healing has happened and the firefighters are released, they are allowed to take on more positive characteristics that were once buried by their protective instincts. This freedom can only happen when the client can access the Self.

Self

IFS counselors see the Self as the essence of one's being—something defined by pure joy and peace. Schwartz identified the Self as the seat of consciousness and identified eight attributes that he often finds when individuals are in Self-energy; these attributes include calmness, clarity, curiosity, compassion, confidence, courage, creativity, and connectedness (appropriately, they are known as the 8 Cs). Clients work with the counselor to access Self and then, the Self provides an openness and acceptance so the manager and firefighter parts feel safe to let down their protective roles and eventually the Self can interact with the exiles.

Within IFS, the Self is the agent of healing, not the therapist. In discussing the universality of the Self, Schwartz identified various religions and belief systems that incorporate the concepts of Self within their doctrine. The Self could be viewed as the soul, one's essence, or one's Buddha nature. The therapist is a coach who can help clients access Self and understand the process of self-actualization. Sometimes the therapist takes on the role of the accepting and curious Self when the client's subpersonalities are not ready to let down their guard. When active, the protective parts (exiles, managers, and firefighters) are often polarized, and it can be difficult for clients to access Self. However, when a client has worked toward a better understanding of these parts, they take on the new, more complex and satisfying personalities they prefer. In accessing the Self, a clinician works with clients to create a safe space for the self to interact with the clients' parts.

Working With Couples

While primarily an intrapersonal focus, IFS is also used when working in a system. From an IFS perspective, if an individual has an attachment injury from a relationship in childhood and thus has an exiled part, attachment reinjuries can occur when one partner reminds the other partner of the caretaker who inspired the initial attachment injury that created the exile. The reinjuries cause harm and distrust in a relationship. These interactions lead to protector and exile parts being triggered in both individuals when Self is not accessed. External interactions are also seen as a mirror for the way parts are interacting internally. Thus, a counselor or therapist gains a fair amount of information when couples interact with one another or rather, when their parts react to one another.

Initially within IFS, the counselor or therapist often works with each person's parts and has the other partner be a witness to the experience. Eventually when the individuals are able to access Self (Self-to-Self communication), Schwartz finds the interactions are more understanding and caring. Within couple-focused IFS, the individuals' parts are still present, however, when the individuals are able to be in Self, the parts are less flooded. When each client has an understanding of parts and recognizes not only the presences of their own parts but their partner's parts, healthy communication and understanding increases. The purpose of couple-focused IFS is to help each partner connect to Self and use that connection to better understand and connect to their partner. IFS labels the work one does in connecting to self and healing exiles as doing a U-turn. When the client is able to better understand their partner, this process is labeled a re-turn. Eventually, each partner is able to differentiate and better understand their partner through their better understanding of Self. Thus, clients become the caretaker of their parts instead of attempting to rely on the other to fulfill their needs and care for exiles. This leaves individuals able to interact with their partner in a differentiated, caring, and loving way.

Amanda J. Minor

See also Attachment; General Systems Theory; Individual Versus Family Therapy; Mindfulness; Object Relations Theory

Further Readings

Schwartz, R. C. (1995). *Internal family systems therapy*. New York, NY: Guilford Press.

Schwartz, R. C. (2001). *Introduction to the internalized family system model*. Oak Park, IL: Trailhead.

Schwartz, R. C. (2008). *You are the one you've been waiting for: Bringing courageous love to intimate relationships*. Oak Park, IL: Trailhead.

Schwartz, R. C. (2013). *Internal family systems therapy: New dimensions*. New York, NY: Taylor & Francis.

Siegel, D. J. (2007). *The mindful brain: Reflection and attunement in the cultivation of well-being*. New York, NY: W. W. Norton.

van der Kolt, B. (2014). *The body keeps the score: Brain, mind, and body in the healing of trauma*. New York, NY: Penguin.

International Association of Marriage and Family Counselors

The American Counseling Association (ACA) is a professional organization of counselors in the United States dedicated to the growth and enhancement of counseling. The ACA has 20 chartered divisions and the International Association of Marriage and Family Counselors (IAMFC) is one of these divisions. The divisions within ACA are specialized areas within counseling and provide leadership, information, research, and resources specific to that specialized area. IAMFC was chartered in 1989 to support professional members working with and advocating for families through prevention, education, and therapy. IAMFC's goal is to promote excellence in the practice of couples and family counseling. Marriage and family counselors practice in a variety of settings, including independent practice, community mental health agencies, managed care organizations, hospitals, employee assistance programs, and houses of worship. Included in this entry are the goals of IAMFC, membership, and certification.

Goals of IAMFC

IAMFC embraces a multicultural approach in support of the worth, dignity, potential, and uniqueness of the families served by its members. The primary goal of couples and family counselors is to promote the healthy development and evolution of family systems. They do this by understanding health, problems, and personal needs within context and from diverse perspectives. As part of this process, couples and family counselors practice clinical work based on family dynamics and systems, evaluate their own personal biases and values, and actively attempt to understand and serve clients from diverse backgrounds. In addition to serving individual couples and families, professional couples and family counselors are expected to advocate for the best interests of couples and families overall. IAMFC encourages counselors to think systemically and to advocate for the worth and dignity of all families.

IAMFC is dedicated to advancing practice, training, and research in couples and family counseling. Couples and family counselors may specialize in areas such as premarital counseling, intergenerational counseling, separation and divorce counseling, relocation counseling, custody evaluation, and parenting training. Couples and family counselors work with various populations including stepfamilies, nontraditional couples and family systems, multicultural couples and families, disadvantaged families, and dual-career couples. Members commit themselves to advocating for the healthy growth and development of the family as a whole and each member's unique needs, while advocating for the counseling profession and professionalism of counselors.

Members of IAMFC have access to two publications: *The Family Journal: Counseling and Therapy for Couples and Families* and *The Family Digest*. *The Family Journal* includes peer-reviewed articles on theory, research, and the practice of counseling with couples and families from a family systems perspective. *The Family Digest* is an electronic newsletter designed to keep IAMFC members current on activities of the organization and current on developments that affect the field of counseling.

Membership and Certification

Although associated with ACA, the membership of IAMFC includes counselors, mental health counselors, marriage and family counselors and therapists, social workers, psychologists, and psychiatrists in the United States and internationally. Members share the common bond of professional training in counseling or a closely related area, additional training in marriage and family counseling and therapy, and an interest and involvement in working directly or indirectly with couples and families. The mission of IAMFC is to be an organization that promotes excellence in the practice of couples and family therapy by creating and disseminating quality publications and media products, providing a forum for professionals to explore family-related issues, embracing diversity in its professional membership and the clientele those professionals serve, and emphasizing collaboration.

IAMFC provides national and international certification in family therapy through the National Credentialing Academy (NCA). The NCA was created in 1994 as a result of IAMFC's professional concerns and efforts in the area of credentialing. In 1994, NCA was incorporated with the primary purpose to establish and monitor a national certification system, to identify professionals who have voluntarily sought and obtained certification, and to maintain the certification process. This process grants certification to professionals who have met NCA standards in their training and experience and meet ethical standards in the field. National certification establishes national standards that can be used as a measure of training and professionalism by individuals, agencies, and health providers; promotes professional accountability, visibility, and helps establish the practice of family counseling and therapy; identifies to the public and other professionals who have met specific, recognized standards; and ensures continued professional development. Professionals are encouraged to gain licensure in states and countries that offer licensure in marital, couples, and family counseling or therapy.

The training standards for certification include a master's level degree in behavioral science plus evidence of training and supervision in marriage and family counseling or therapy. A professional's training must include courses in individual, marital, and family studies; individual, marital, and family therapy; human development; professional studies; and research. In addition, their clinical training must have included work with couples and families (either during a graduate program or in a postdegree context) under the supervision of a licensed marriage or family therapist/counselor or someone with an equivalent background.

Related professional organizations include the National Board of Certified Counselors (NBCC), the Commission on Accreditation of Counseling Education and Related Programs (CACREP), and the Commission on Accreditation for Marriage and Family Therapy Education (COAMFTE). NBCC offers national certification in counseling but does not offer any specialized certification in marital, couples, or family counseling/therapy. CACREP provides standards for training in its accredited programs in counseling. This includes training standards for marital, couples, and family counseling, which it considers a specialization under the field of counseling. In order to have an accredited specialization in marital, couples, and family counseling, a program must meet the educational and institutional standards set forth in their accreditation standards. In addition, COAMFTE accredits programs in marital, couples, and family therapy. There are commonalities between the specialized standards of CACREP and COAMFTE; however, COAMFTE sees marital, couples, and family therapy as an independent profession, and CACREP sees marital, couples, and family counseling as a specialization of counseling. Nevertheless, graduating from a COAMFTE program or CACREP program with a specialization in marital, couples, and family counseling prepares graduates for family therapy certification from NCA.

Shea M. Dunham

See also American Association for Marriage and Family Therapy; Council for Accreditation of Counseling and Related Educational Programs

Further Readings

American Counseling Association: https://www.counseling.org

Hendricks, B., Bradley, L. J., Southern, S., Oliver, M., & Birdsall, B. (2011). Ethical code for International Association of Marriage and Family Counselors. *Family Journal: Counseling and Therapy for Couples and Families, 19*(2), 217–224. doi:10.1177/1066480711400814

International Association of Marriage and Family Counselors: http://www.iamfconline.org/

INTERNATIONAL CLASSIFICATION OF DISEASES (ICD)

The *International Classification of Diseases* (ICD) is the foundational measurement of global health trends and statistics. It was founded by the Forty-Third World Health Assembly in May 1990 and implemented for use in 1994. The ICD supports ongoing research on mortality and morbidity rates, diseases, injuries, symptomatology, and other factors that influence human health. It assists the world in working together to compare and share health data with a common language for all to use and understand. Currently, 194 countries use the ICD system, with 43 translated languages; roughly 70% of the world's health expenditures use the ICD coding system for reimbursement; and it is the source of more than 20,000 research articles. These research endeavors elaborate on diseases and their patterns, as well as assist in the management and allocation of funding and resources. This entry examines the history of the ICD; ICD and its function within the *Diagnostic and Statistical Manual of Mental Disorders* (DSM); and updates, issues, and further directions of the ICD system.

Introduction to the ICD

The ICD categorizes disease into standard groupings, which provides a systematic method of storing, reporting, researching, and analyzing health information. Medical professionals, health workers, policymakers, health program managers, and mental health professionals utilize the trends, statistics, and research made possible through the system to benefit the populations they serve. The ICD is important in professional settings to apply for funding and financial reimbursement. In the United States, all health care settings are also required to utilize these diagnostic coding guidelines in order to be in compliance with the 1996 U.S. Health Insurance Portability and Accountability Act (HIPAA). Adopting the ICD enables mental health professionals an opportunity to be part of a collective approach (95% of the world's health professionals currently use the ICD) for the treatment of all society members around the globe. With one common language and diagnostic system, the ICD advances the importance of reporting and researching disease and disorder within our health care system in order to better serve and treat clients.

History of the ICD

In many early medical practices, nomenclatures were utilized in the arrangement of diseases. François Bossier de Lacroix (1706–1777) is credited with the initialization of classifying diseases systematically. His system was published under the title *Nosolgia methodica* in 1768. However, the statistical study of disease started nearly a century before Lacroix under John Graunt with his work regarding the London Bills of Mortality. Graunt's attempt to classify and measure the birth and death rates of children before reaching the age of 6 was considered pioneering. Although crude and unsystematic, his estimation provided the foundational groundwork for classifying and estimating mortality rates for a certain population.

The seminal work of Lacroix's *Nosolgia methodica* promoted the collection of mortality and disease rates in a more systematic manner and led to the advancement of preventive medicine and reporting procedures for practitioners. Founded in 1837 by William Farr (1807–1883), the General Register Office of England and Wales became a catalyst in the development of systematically defining, categorizing, and classifying diseases and mortality rates. The decision to classify diseases instead of simply reporting mortality rates was part of Lacroix's legacy. Although originally establishing five groups (epidemic, general, anatomically local, developmental, and violence diseases), it was not until after his death that the General Register Office adopted these groups for the basis of the *International List of Causes of Death*.

Over the next decades, interest increased and regions around the globe began utilizing this system of classifying and categorizing disease, starting in North America in 1898, with *The Bertillon Classification of Causes of Death* (named after Jacques Bertillon, Chief of Statistical Services of Paris). Scholars and practitioners around the world held numerous meetings with the goal of providing feedback on the development of the classification of diseases and mortality. Understanding that such information would be utilized for health care and administration, a collective approach was agreed upon in the development and revision process. Furthermore, due to the utilization in health care and fact that not all disease was related to or caused death, it was agreed that nonfatal diseases should also be introduced. This happened in 1909 under a new title, *International Classification of Causes of Sickness and Death*.

Throughout the 20th century, the *International Classification of Causes of Sickness and Death* increased in status throughout the professional world. Numerous revisions occurred, each one attempting to improve the latter in terms of diagnostic terms, classification structure, reporting procedures, and etiology. With an established presence in the development and revision process, the World Health Organization (WHO)—an agency within the United Nations (UN)—continues to have a core foundation in the ICD's presence and advancement. The title today, *International Classification of Diseases*, was changed in 1955 during the seventh revision.

Although the ICD is utilized in diagnosing and reporting in statistics of disease and used for billing reimbursement and funding opportunities, the mental health clinician is typically trained to understand and utilize the DSM. The next section will discuss the attempted parallel development of both diagnostic systems and the attempt at shared similarities for both medical and mental cohesion in diagnostic coding.

ICD and DSM

Although the ICD originated in the 1700s, numerous transitions, revisions, impairments, and challenges appeared with the development of this manual. With the introduction of the ICD-1 in the United States in 1898, the progression of disease identification and classification naturally included mental disorders. Due to the psychoanalytic wave in counseling at the time, mental health professionals required a more extensive identification and diagnostic coding system to treat patients with accuracy and a common professional language. The *Diagnostic and Statistical Manual of Mental Disorders* (DSM) was created by the American Psychiatric Association in 1952, and throughout the years, numerous revisions and editions were established. This allowed not only for the delivery of services, but also a better collective understanding of how professionals may identify and treat mental disorders in the United States.

During the early to mid-20th century, the United States had more psychologists than any other country in the world. As a result, the English language and American perspectives have historically structured understandings of presenting concerns and ultimately also guided how to categorize mental health. Over time, changing demographics within the United States and the utilization of psychological literature and counseling around the world required the field to adopt a broader perspective to diagnose, code, and categorize all forms of disease, whether mental or medical.

Both the ICD and DSM are utilized around the world and within the United States. *The International Classification of Diseases, 10th Revision, Clinical Modification* (ICD-10-CM) and the DSM are utilized to categorize and identify a disorder within a person based on presenting and reported symptoms. The DSM only tracks current mental disorders and provides criteria in order to diagnose. By comparison, the ICD-10-CM provides diagnostic coding and statistical reports of disease and mortality. Throughout each system's revisions, there have been attempts to correspond DSM and ICD-10-CM codes, starting with the DSM-IV-TR (1994) and continuing with the DSM-5 (2013). While the DSM-5 generally corresponds to the ICD-10-CM codes, DSM-5 added its own criteria, removed some disorders that are still listed within the ICD-10-CM, and added some disorders that are not listed within the ICD-10-CM. To complicate matters more, in 2015, the United States was still using the ICD-CM-9 coding system that was put into place originally in 1979 for morbidity rates, yet was using the ICD-10-CM for mortality data. This decision by the National Committee on Vital and Health Statistics was met due to the perception that no significant changes between ICD-9 and ICD-10 were identified regarding morbidity rate reporting.

Debates continue to weigh the cost-benefit analysis between revising and halting any revisions of the ICD-10-CM until the release of the ICD-11. Speculation surrounds the DSM Task Force to continue the revision process to better acclimate the DSM-5 with future ICD revisions.

Updates in the ICD

The ICD-10-CM is the official international diagnostic and reporting manual for codes and billing purposes. The Centers for Medicare and Medicaid Services recommends the use of and implementation of the ICD system within organizations, as the ICD-11 was released in October 2015. Current reports from the ICD-10-CM speculate that as many as 35% to 78% of people suffering from mental disorders do not receive proper care for their treatment, possibly due to a lack of common language or understanding for their disorder. The ICD-11 will provide a new framework to enhance the clinical applicability, usefulness, and collective language needed to treat patients on individual, cultural, and global levels.

Revisions are underway due to the ever changing process of health care, access, treatment, and reporting rates. These revisions are needed to provide better information for public health monitoring and access, client health care measurements, fraud identification, processing claims, and clinical decision-making. Current data and procedures are becoming obsolete; thus, there is a growing need for a reliable means of data collection and reporting procedures. With the advancement of technology and electronic portability, however, codes and procedures can be updated more efficiently. The projected hope of the ICD-11 is that if diagnostic coding and reporting become easier, health care will become better managed, resulting in lowered health care costs for both consumer and provider. If this change occurs, then the ability to study, analyze, and provide more concise and accurate data will advance further research endeavors.

Issues of the ICD

With any attempt to categorize, classify, and, ultimately, create a system that is user friendly and collectively understood, some challenges arise in the process. Although utilized throughout the world, the ICD system is not widely utilized among mental health practitioners. The DSM-5 attempts to correspond its diagnostic coding with the ICD coding, and many practitioners are unaware that the ICD is still utilized within billing and insurance claims behind the scenes. Due to the ever-changing nature of health care, recommendations are strongly urged for practitioners to learn more about ICD–DSM correspondence in order to better provide treatment to clients, properly bill, and efficiently report morbidity and mortality rates. However, one should anticipate correspondence challenges, since the DSM reports some diagnoses that the ICD does not report and vice versa. Furthermore, the ICD merely provides diagnostic coding of medical and mental diseases and disorders, thus creating a gap between understanding and utilization. The DSM is an attempt to clarify diagnostic procedures and treatment avenues. In the past, it lost its relationship with the ICD; however, current reporting, billing, and coding requirements have reestablished the need for coding correspondence between the DSM and ICD.

The ICD also falls short in the clinical realm for numerous reasons. In addition to only providing diagnostic coding procedures, these procedures are limiting in the sense that some mental health clients present with numerous symptoms, resulting in more than one diagnosis. Added to this complexity is the fact that not all diagnoses have a single treatment, suggesting clinical difficulties in diagnosing, billing, and the potential for differing treatment modalities. Furthermore, current challenges surrounding social, environmental, and cultural factors are minimally addressed within the current ICD. The ICD-11 is hopeful in addressing and implementing a systematic approach to biopsychosocial-cultural factors in the identification, etiology, treatment, and reporting procedures of diseases and disorders.

Future Directions

The ICD is considered a global tool, one from which all may benefit and in which all may participate. The ICD is tasked with the challenge of ongoing improvements to the classification system of disease, therefore improving diagnostic tools and clinical utility, as well as ensuring all health system technology is globally compatible. Once finalized, WHO member countries were required to implement the ICD system. Naturally, adjustments will be developed and training will occur but with this, one can also expect frustration among some clinicians and organizations due to the ever-changing coding procedures. Creating a system with the capacity to develop and update with ease is one of the many goals of the ICD-11. This will allow all providers and developers involved to adjust revisions over a shorter period of time, rather than after a decade or more. In addition to easier reporting and revising, the potential of gaining financial profit with the utilization of the ICD-11 will hopefully outweigh the costs of continuing to use outdated diagnostic coding systems. The ICD is easily accessible on paper and in its online format, free of charge to all, and absent of commercial influence. While problems may still arise, efforts to objectively and systematically report the world's health concerns will continue to assist the development of the ICD diagnostic coding system.

Delila Lashelle Owens and Bill Owenby

See also DSM and V-Codes; HIPAA Standards

Further Readings

American Psychiatric Association. (1952). *Diagnostic and statistical manual of mental disorders* (1st ed.). Washington, DC: Author.

American Psychiatric Association. (1994). *Diagnostic and statistical manual of mental disorders* (4th ed.). Washington, DC: Author.

American Psychiatric Association. (2013). *Diagnostic and statistical manual of mental disorders* (5th ed.). Washington, DC: Author.

APA Learning Center: http://www.apaeducation.org/ihtml/application/student/catalog_description_init.ihtml?course_id=17941

Goldberg, D. (2015). Psychopathology and classification in psychiatry. *Social Psychiatry Psychiatric Epidemiology, 50,* 1–5.

Goodheart, C. D. (2014). *A primer for ICD-10-CM users: Psychological and behavioral conditions.* Washington, DC: Author.

ICD-11 Beta Draft (Joint Linearization for Mortality and Morbidity Statistics): http://apps.who.int/classifications/icd11/browse/l-m/en

Jacob, K. S., & Patel, V. (2014). Classification of mental disorders: A global mental health perspective. *The*

Lancet, 383(9926), 1433–1435. doi:http://dx.doi.org/10.1016/S0140-6736(13)62382-X

Libicki, M., & Brahmakulam, I. (2004). *The costs and benefits of moving to the ICD-10 code sets.* Santa Monica, CA: RAND.

Moriyama, I. M., Loy, R. M., & Robb-Smith, A. H. T. (2011). *History of the statistical classification of disease and causes of death.* Hyattsville, MD: National Center for Health Statistics. Retrieved from http://www.cdc.gov/nchs/data/misc/classification_diseases2011.pdf

The Royal College of Physicians. (1869). *The nomenclature of diseases.* London, England: Spotteswoode.

Tyrer, P. (2014). Time to choose–DSM-5, ICD-11, or both? *Archives of Psychiatry and Psychotherapy, 3,* 5–8.

World Health Organization. (1948). *Manual of the international statistical classification of diseases, injuries, and causes of death* (6th rev.). Geneva, Switzerland: His Majesty's Stationery Office.

World Health Organization. (2015). *International Classification of Diseases (ICD) information sheet.* Retrieved from http://www.who.int/classifications/icd/factsheet/en/

World Health Organization, ICD-10 Interactive Self Learning Tool: http://apps.who.int/classifications/apps/icd/icd10training/

INTERNATIONAL FAMILY THERAPY

The development of family therapy varies widely across the globe; contextual, historical, and cultural factors all affect the status quo as well as the future of family therapy. Overall, apart from the United States, family therapy is most well developed in Australia and some parts of Europe (e.g., the UK). In societies in which family therapy has a much shorter history, a significant and increasing demand for family therapy services has resulted in the recent rapid growth of the field in many countries. This entry examines the barriers that prevent people from accessing family therapy, as well as the development of family therapy, current trends in family therapy, and future issues in the field.

Barriers

The stigma of mental illness, cultural norms, and preferences for addressing interpersonal issues (e.g., reliance on family members and communities) and a lack of trained family therapists are among the main barriers that prevent potential clients from receiving family therapy services. Though studies show that family-based interventions are increasingly sought after for treatment, in many countries, the effective delivery of such services is hindered by a lack of resources (e.g., a lack of training institutions, training materials, and supervision). Relevant regulations and licensing standards must also be established and properly implemented to ensure ethical practice. Additionally, in countries where family therapy has been introduced recently (e.g., China), family therapy services are often accessible only by those with higher education (which helps depathologize participation in therapy), greater financial resources (to afford the services, which are commonly not covered by insurance), and proximity to metropolitan areas (where more family therapists are available).

Development of Profession

Outside the United States, the developmental stages and paths of family therapy across countries are uneven. For instance, in some countries, family therapy is closely intertwined with fields such as psychiatry (e.g., in India), psychology (e.g., in Romania), social work (e.g., in Peru), and even traditional healing (e.g., in Nigeria), whereas in some other countries, clearer distinctions separate different professions. Furthermore, marked discrepancies exist regarding the standards for training and licensure among different countries. For example, as of 2014, there was no requirement for client contact hours to attain an entry-level marriage and family therapy license in China, whereas the Australian Association of Family Therapy requires a minimum of 500 hours of family therapy practice as the primary therapist for clinical membership. The introduction of different models of family therapy is also significantly uneven and largely dependent upon the orientation and background of the individuals conducting relevant training in a specific host country. Language barriers often present challenges for foreign therapists to serve local clients, for foreign experts to conduct training to local audiences, and for local therapists or students to further their knowledge about family therapy.

Trends

Despite the hurdles, there are also many encouraging trends related to the development of family therapy around the world. Cross-national collaborations of family therapy training and research play a key role in the development of family therapy worldwide. Globalization continues to promote transnational and intercultural exchanges among family therapy practitioners, researchers, and trainers from different countries. In recent years, greater numbers of Western therapists and researchers have actively participated in training family therapists in many developing countries where family therapy is still in its early stages. Some family therapy organizations, such as the International Family Therapy Association, have members internationally and regularly host international conferences to promote cross-cultural exchanges of family therapy.

Increasingly, peer-reviewed journals in the field of family therapy and related fields are beginning to promote an understanding of relationship issues in different cultural contexts, as evidenced by a growing number of publications that involve international authorships, affiliations, perspectives, and participants. These publications feature research on issues such as diversity, cultural sensitivity, applications and adaptations of various family therapy models in distinct cultural contexts, as well as the training of newer generations of international family therapists.

Many recent developments in the field of family therapy could further contribute to the progress of international family therapy. For instance, advances in conducting therapy and supervision online largely eliminate the barrier of geographic distance between therapists and clients and between supervisors and supervisees. The continuing emphasis on conducting culturally sensitive therapy also better prepares therapists in training to work with clients of diverse cultural backgrounds or to work at international locations. Additionally, as more and more international students come to the United States to pursue advanced education in marriage and family counseling (MFT), they may serve as bridges for cross-national exchanges and collaborations involving family therapy when they return to their home country or pursue research interests related to their native country or culture here in the United States. At the same time, the tremendous and growing demand of family therapy in countries with a lack of relevant resources represents rich opportunities for Western therapists. Participation in the development of family therapy in these countries may not only foster therapists' and researchers' culturally diverse experiences and perspectives but may also facilitate a wider spectrum of employment and career opportunities.

The Future

Moving forward, cross-national collaborations and exchanges in the field of family therapy are likely to expand and strengthen. To facilitate collaborations across countries and cultures, researchers have proposed, for instance, creating a platform to translate family therapy articles across languages and establishing programs to introduce new voices to the field. In promoting family therapy in different countries, it is paramount to integrate models rooted in the Western culture with the respective host cultures. For example, in collectivistic countries where filial piety is highly emphasized (i.e., China and Japan), therapists may consider interpreting and applying the concepts of differentiation and autonomy somewhat differently than in individualistic cultures (i.e., the United States and Germany).

As family therapy expands globally, it will likely follow distinctive developmental paths and assume various forms and emphases that make sense in new contexts. On the one hand, Western family scholars and therapists should be encouraged to adopt a global perspective in research and practice. On the other hand, there are urgent needs and motivations to train local researchers and therapists to better serve potential clients around the world. As our world becomes smaller, international family therapy is likely to remain a rich field for future generations of family therapy practitioners and researchers.

Ruoxi Chen

See also Cultural Issues in Couples and Families; Diversity; Multicultural Counseling Competence; Psychoeducation

Further Readings

Bacigalupe, G. (2011). Virtualizing intimacy: Information communication technologies and transnational families in therapy. *Family Process, 50,* 12–26. doi:10.1111/j.1545-5300.2010.01343.x

Ng, K. S. (Ed.). (2003). *Global perspectives in family therapy: Development, practice, trends.* New York, NY: Brunner/Routledge.

Roberts, J., Abu-Baker, K., Fernández, C. D., Garcia, N. C., Fredman, G., Kamya, H., . . . Zevallos, V. R. (2014). Up close: Family therapy challenges and innovations around the world. *Family Process, 53,* 544–576. doi:10.1111/famp.12093

Interpersonal Neurobiology, Attachment and

Interpersonal neurobiology is a field of study that looks at how the brain develops and is influenced by personal relationships. It is credited primarily to Dan Siegel, who pioneered the field of interpersonal neurobiology through his framework that unites research from various disciplines. Credit is also given to Allan Schore, who is known for his landmark research in the areas of neuroscience, attachment, and trauma. This entry begins with an overview of interpersonal neurobiology, continues with an examination of the role of attachment in relationships and brain development, and concludes with a discussion of interpersonal neurobiology and therapeutic interventions.

Background

Interpersonal neurobiology emerged as a result of the "decade of the brain." The field takes an interdisciplinary view toward understanding human development but is informed primarily from the perspective of neuroscience. The integration of ideologies from various disciplines contributes to a unique understanding of the human mind and sheds light on the underpinnings of mental health. While interpersonal neurobiology recognizes the influence of physiological and neurological processes on human development and mental health, it focuses primarily on the aspects of the brain that shape social and emotional development. It can be visualized as a framework that can be used to inform the fields of family and marriage therapy, trauma informed counseling, and mental health practices that focus on development across the life span. More specifically, interpersonal neurobiology provides a framework for understanding the neurological basis of how attachment patterns (bonding to parents, romantic partners, and others) develop and persist throughout the life span. The field also offers interventions aimed at remediating (or remedying) difficulties associated with dysfunctional childhood attachment.

Interpersonal neurobiology's main assertion is that it is through human connection that the brain develops because the basic architecture of the brain predisposes human beings to seek out and connect to other brains. The neurobiological basis of this connection is, in part, due to mirror neurons giving humans the capacity to process emotion, connect to another person's world, and develop empathy. From an attachment perspective it is empathy, as a neurological process, that allows for parental sensitivity and attunement. Through empathetic attunement, the attuned caregiver's brain is able to join with the inner world of the child's brain, and the child is able to join with the inner world of the adult's brain. It is this reciprocal experience that essentially allows an infant to have an awareness of "feeling felt" or being known by another. Those early attachment experiences lay the neurological groundwork for future psychological and emotional development that contributes to one's overall mental health and shapes the quality of interpersonal relationships.

Attachment

John Bowlby introduced the concept of attachment based on his extensive research surrounding child development where he discovered that early childhood experiences with primary caregivers play a crucial role in psychological and social development. Interpersonal neurobiology's organizational construct of internal working models of social relationships is central to the field of attachment theory. From this frame of reference, the primary caregiver works as an external system for the child's internal regulation system through nonverbal forms of communication that later become representations or patterns of behavior in relation to an understanding of oneself and others.

In essence, attachment is explained as proximity-seeking behaviors that infants and children use to bond to a primary caregiver. It is the quality of an attachment experience that is based on the type of response by the primary caregiver toward the infant. The attachment experience provides a foundation for a secure base that allows the child to experience a sense of safety and comfort needed to develop emotional affiliations throughout his or her lifetime.

Mary Ainsworth extended Bowlby's work through her discovery of different patterns of attachment determined by the way in which infants experienced their early caregiving relationships. These patterns, or styles, can best be described as a broad manner or style an individual uses to manage relationships. The four patterns of childhood attachment incorporated into the framework of interpersonal neurobiology can be described as following; secure attachments can be described as the result of consistent, attuned, and predictable caregiving that allows for neural integration that results in healthy regulatory systems. On the other hand, anxious, ambivalent, disorganized attachments based on caregiving styles that are inconsistent, neglectful, abusive, or rejecting are believed to result in dysregulated self-regulatory and impaired affective systems. Reactive attachment disorder has been identified as a disorder in the *Diagnostic and Statistical Manual of Mental Disorders* (DSM-5) and *International Classification of Diseases* (ICD) as a type of extreme attachment pattern that results from severe neglect, abuse, or trauma where infants and children create internal working models that lead to relational and behavioral difficulties throughout their lives.

Perhaps one of the most important findings in the field of neuroscience has been neuroplasticity. The plasticity of the brain allows for the generation of new neurons and the strengthening of neural pathways created from ongoing life and environmental experiences. The change of neurons and neural pathways allows the brain to reorganize in ways that cognitive, behavioral, and interpersonal attributes can be modified. What this means is that attachment patterns can be formed, reworked, or transformed throughout one's life.

Although Bowlby focused primarily on attachment patterns during early childhood development, he viewed them to be relatively consistent during the course of one's life. Cindy Hazan and Phillip Shaver have been credited with advancing Bowlby's viewpoint by conceptualizing that adult romantic relationships, parenting, and affiliated relationships are based on early attachment patterns that endure into one's adulthood. The patterns described by Hazen and Shafer include secure, anxious–preoccupied, dismissive–avoidant, and fearful–avoidant. Kim Bartholomew and Leonard Horowitz expanded Hazan and Shaver's work by adding a second style of avoidance (dismissing–avoidance). Because adult attachment styles emanate from the internal working models established during infancy and childhood, they are characterized by similar systems that can be seen in the developmental neurobiology of the early attachment experiences.

Adult attachment styles can be determined by the way each partner views him or herself and the way he or she views his or her partner. Each style is characterized by factors such as communication, emotional regulation, degree of intimacy, sexuality, anxiety, levels of insecurity, fear, and degrees of avoidance and dependency. Where adults with secure attachments experience a sense of ease within themselves and their partners with intimacy and interdependence, adults with the less healthy attachment styles of anxious–preoccupied, dismissive–avoidant, dismissing–avoidance or fearful–avoidant have working models of self and others that contribute to problematic behaviors surrounding intimacy.

Attachment and Neural Development

Early attachment experiences directly influence neural development. Early infancy is the time where rapid growth takes place in the brain. It is during this time when neural connections are developed and strengthened through use or reduced or eliminated through nonuse in a process described as "pruning." At the same time, the orbital prefrontal cortex is in a phase of buildup. This is the area of the brain that has to do with such things as emotional regulation, empathy, facial recognition, and interpersonal relating. Another part of the brain that has to do with attachment is the limbic system. The limbic system (which contains the amygdala and hippocampus, among other areas) governs motivation, emotion, learning, and memory. It is through the connections made between the orbital prefrontal cortex (which encodes social inputs), the amygdala (which identifies emotion), and the hippocampus (which records memories) that attachment figures are stored as neural representations and where relationships become internal working models that shape connections with others.

Another important activity of the fronto-limbic circuitry region of the brain is that of self-regulation (e.g., the way the mind organizes itself). Self-regulation is the ability to organize, control, and influence one's own behavior. It is linked to emotional regulation. Essential for psychological well-being, emotional regulation lays the foundation for critical life skills based on one's ability to mediate emotion. From this perspective, emotional regulation is at the heart of mental life. Emotional regulation integrates neural activity, memory, emotion and communication through interpersonal connectedness. The two hemispheres are relevant to attachment relationships because of their role in attunement and communication. Whereas the right hemisphere is responsible for actions such as registering and expressing affective facial expressions, reading emotions, visual imagery, autobiographical representations, and body image, the left hemisphere is responsible for language, logic, critical thinking, and reasoning. It is through the union of the neural processes between the left hemisphere and right hemisphere that integration occurs. Linked by the corpus callosum, the two hemispheres act in harmony to foster emotional regulation.

Emotion is at the heart of attachment. It plays a crucial role in the integration of many aspects of mental functioning. Paradoxical as it may seem, emotional processing is highly cognitive. It is emotion that essentially provides the foundation, categorizes, and regulates cognitive activity in the brain. Nonverbal communication is emotional communication. Nonverbal behaviors such as eye contact, touch, voice quality, and bodily gestures are the primary ways that emotion is communicated. From an attachment perspective, it is the communication of emotion between caregiver and infant that contributes to one's autobiographical self.

Autobiographical self and memory are closely related. From birth, an infant has a form of memory that is implicit. Later memory, or explicit memory, is what is commonly referred to as conscious memory. Attachment theory recognizes the importance of distinguishing between the two types of memories because of the role that implicit memory plays in attachment experiences. The distinction is important because most attachment memories are implicit, or not in one's awareness, and these become working models of self and others. It is the infant's schema that forms the structure of one's sense of self and self with others.

Life narratives, stories about our lives based on autobiographical memories, play a major role in the development of emotional regulation. Life stories can be coherent, in that an individual is able to make sense of their life, or they can be incoherent, in that an individual has not resolved past trauma or distress. Coherent narratives integrate both left and right hemispheres. A caregiver who is securely attached will have a coherent and integrated narrative. Through attunement, or connection to the child, the caregiver will communicate the coherent narrative, which allows the child's right hemisphere to develop a sense of self, emotion, and the memories of the experience, and the left hemisphere to hold the meaning and language. The result of the integration allows the child to develop self-regulation. On the other hand, caregivers who hold attachment styles of insecure–avoidant or insecure–anxious convey narratives that tend to be incoherent and dysregulated. That lack of integration prevents the child from incorporating a coherent narrative into their own life story.

Interpersonal Neurobiology and Therapy

It is the aforementioned types of stories, or narratives, that marriage and family therapists pay attention to in order to determine a client's attachment style. Drawing from the insights of interpersonal neurobiology, therapists integrate strategies and techniques from a variety of disciplines into their own therapeutic framework to remediate dysregulation and promote integration. From this perspective, understanding brain structure and function allows therapists to formulate specific interventions that center on stimulating neuronal activation and growth. Integrating strategies from programs such as Daniel Siegel's Mindsight Institute, therapists can draw upon research that can be used to inform their clinical work with children, adolescents, couples, and families.

Attunement is central to relational interventions that involve right-brain to right-brain connections between primary caregivers, therapists, and clients. Therapist to client attunement is similar to the sharing of a secure status by a primary caregiver. It can be viewed as a reciprocal alliance where a therapist is able to share his or her mind with the client as a means to develop greater self-regulation. Similarly, therapy with individuals, couples, or families can focus on reworking negative internal working models of self and other in order to enhance a capacity for intimacy and communication skills. Attachment difficulties that result from early life experiences such as trauma, neglect, or abuse are rectified through the use of play therapy techniques that facilitate the integration of right and left hemispheres and repair implicit attachment patterns.

Interpersonal neurobiology integrates therapy tools from various disciplines, such as psychoeducation, that provides clients with insights into the link between attachment and brain development. The field also takes a holistic approach by incorporating aspects of wellness, mindfulness, and meditation practices. As such, the blending of interpersonal neurobiology and attachment theory aims to not only solve the problems of attachment but to offer clients enhanced psychological well-being.

Leslie W. O'Ryan

See also Attachment Therapy; Interpersonal Neurobiology, Couples and; Interpersonal Neurobiology, Parenting and

Further Readings

Fishbane, M. D. (2013). *Loving with the brain in mind: Neurobiology and couple therapy*. New York, NY: W. W. Norton.

Hart, S. (2011). *The impact of attachment*. New York, NY: W. W. Norton.

Hill, D. (2015). *Affect regulation theory: A clinical model*. New York, NY: W. W. Norton.

Schore, A. N. (2015). *The science of the art of psychotherapy*. New York, NY: W. W. Norton.

Siegal, D. J. (2010). *The mindful therapist: A clinician's guide to mindsight and neural integration.* New York, NY: W. W. Norton.

Siegal, D. J. (2015). *The developing mind: How relationships and the brain interact to shape who we are* (2nd ed.). New York, NY: W. W. Norton.

INTERPERSONAL NEUROBIOLOGY, COUPLES AND

Genetic inheritance and early experiences shape human brain development and behavior. All relationships change the brain, and our interpersonal bonds impact the way we develop memories, grow feelings, and establish a sense of self-worth. Neuroimaging has shown that beginning at birth, attachments imprint on the infant brain, launching patterns of behaviors, thoughts, and self-concepts that can last a lifetime. Current research has gone on to show us that these neural transformations continue throughout life as we age and develop relationships, fall in love for the first time, and ultimately choose a mate. The body remembers how those early attachments felt, and it has direct implications as we search for adult relationships. Interpersonal neurobiology is a framework that offers counselors and the couples with whom they work an approach to promote healthy relationships. Consequently, this approach suggests that we are a product of our biology and neurodevelopmental evolution. Interpersonal neurobiology is an integrative approach that uses science to inform and assist with learning to successfully navigate the reactivity and defensiveness that are often toxic to relationships. It is important to note that neurobiology is complex; thus, an understanding of interpersonal neurobiology is needed to understand its application and viability when applied to couples.

History of Interpersonal Neurobiology

Interpersonal neurobiology (IPNB) was developed by Daniel J. Siegel and Allan Schore. IPNB uses the clinical evidence that supports continuous brain growth as its foundation. Interpersonal neurobiology integrates concepts from many different disciplines including anthropology, biology (developmental, evolution, genetics, zoology), cognitive science, computer science, developmental psychopathology, linguistics neuroscience (affective, cognitive, developmental, social), mathematics, mental health, physics, psychiatry, psychology (cognitive, developmental, evolutionary, experimental, of religion, social, attachment theory, memory), sociology, and systems theory (chaos and complexity theory). An interdisciplinary approach, IPNB provides a platform to explore the interrelationship between neurobiology and interpersonal relationships. Integrating concepts from many different disciplines, Siegel initially researched the impact of trauma on human neurological development. He discovered that relational experiences have a profound impact on a person's neurobiology and established an association between interpersonal relationships and the neurological activity of the mind. Siegel's ideas were influenced by the discovery of mirror neurons. A mirror neuron fires when a person carries out an act, as well as when observing the same action in another. Thus, the neuron mirrors the behavior of the other, as though what they are observing is what they are actually doing. For example, if one partner in a couple came home angry from work one day, the other partner's brain would register the anger, and they might start acting angrily, having observed the action in their partner. This is the brain's neurobiological mechanism for supporting an empathic attuned connection between the two partners in the couple. There is an interrelationship between the brain activity and the interpersonal actions of the couple. Thus, there is established proof that the mind develops and changes in relation to interpersonal experiences, which suggests that human beings are "wired" for growth and change.

Underlying Major Theories and Assumptions

Attachment theory and neurobiology provide the foundation for interpersonal neurobiology. Siegel first became interested in exploring similar ideas and concepts that underlie attachment theory, neurobiology, and neuroplasticity. Attachment theorists assert that infants are hardwired to seek out their attachment figures. Adult attachment is also influenced by the idea that healthy connections between couples is reflective of the quality of connection each person had with their primary caregiver. When each individual in the couple is experiencing a state of integration (balance or harmony), each has the ability to name and identify their emotional and interpersonal experiences and has the skills to communicate in a way that leads to relational attunement. In turn, the couple's connection will be secure, and their love will deepen and grow. However, as attachment theory has demonstrated, if the connection is anxious and resistant, or avoidant in nature, then the couple may need therapeutic support to learn how to promote integration and relational attunement. Neurobiology provides a lens for understanding why many couples struggle in similar dysfunctional relational cycles within their relationships. Neurobiology demonstrated that human brains are structured to produce intense states of negative emotions like anger, anxiety, or depression. The brain is structured in such a manner that when it perceives a threat, a person will lash out and fight or withdraw to avoid the stressful situation before the brain has an opportunity to respond with rationality or compassion.

An important distinction Siegel makes is the difference between "the mind" and "the brain." Siegel noted that currently there is no one definition of the mind. There are descriptions of the brain's functions and processes, but researchers do not have an absolute definition of the mind. As Siegel began to seek to understand themes and patterns across the many disciplines, he identified one central idea regarding the mind—the mind is the flow of energy and information between people. Interpersonal neurobiology rests on the assumption that the mind does not exist in a single person; rather the mind and its development are linked to the relationships among and between an individual and the minds of others.

Neuroplasticity, another concept that informs interpersonal neurobiology, is the idea that the brain is flexible and able to adjust to both internal and external stimuli. Neurobiology and neuroplasticity guide couples therapists using interpersonal neurobiology by having a framework to decide which interventions to use that will best support rewiring neural pathways, and thus help to change a couple's dysfunctional relational cycles. This will help couples to engage in difficult conversations with a sense of calmness and compassion rather than with high emotional reactivity (e.g., anger or avoidance). Siegel is a proponent of teaching couples skills to regulate their attention and emotional experience in response to sensory input. He recommends teaching couples how to use mindfulness practices to develop attention, attunement, and compassion to support integration.

Interpersonal Neurobiology With Couples

An interpersonal neurobiology approach to couples counseling draws on the basic framework of an interdisciplinary view, which combines the objective scientific domain of science with the subjective domain of human experience. We have scientific data that supports the long-held perception that interpersonal relationships influence the mind, the brain and, ultimately, the entire well-being of the individual. One aspect of relationships that has been shown consistently to be of importance is that intimate relationships can be very good for one's health. Couples who are in a healthy intimate relationship have a much greater chance of experiencing emotional and physical well-being. In contrast, couples who are in unhealthy relationships can experience depression and poor overall health and well-being.

Having some stress in one's life is a good thing. Some stress can support learning, positive growth, and development. However, too much stress can be damaging to a person's physical, emotional, and relational well-being. When couples experience a high degree of stress due to conflict or fighting, it can make it harder to work through the issues that are causing conflict. The brain will associate high stress with a high arousal state, which will keep the couple in fight or flight mode. Happy couples have disagreements, but they do not allow the fighting to continue to escalate or the avoidance to be ongoing. Thus, they train their brains to stay in a state of low physiological arousal, even when disagreements occur. With less physiological arousal, the brain has time to engage in the prefrontal cortex (an area of the brain that is responsible for bodily regulation, emotional balance and attunement, empathy, insight, moral awareness, and intuition), and the couple has an opportunity to engage in rational and compassionate dialogues.

The human brain is structured to produce powerful affective states when it perceives threats. Thus, when threatened, we become exceptionally self-protective and prone to attack or withdraw before we are able to think rationally and wisely. Using this scientific knowledge in combination with interpersonal relationship skills building allows for an approach to healing relationship dysfunction. Interventions are offered to increase skills of social and emotional intelligence, emotional regulation, the capacity to demonstrate empathy, feelings of equality, and the demonstration of partner and relationship respect. There are five primary domains, described below, that are integrated into the use of interpersonal neurobiology with couples.

Attachment

At birth, the brain starts establishing neural pathways in response to its new world. Neuroimaging provides evidence that a baby's first attachments imprint its brain. The patterns of a lifetime of behaviors, thoughts, self-regard, and choice of partners all begin with this first primary attachment. Ultimately, what we learn as a result of our attachments as infants, we take into our adult relationships. Identifying and educating couples about their attachment style is a first step toward helping them understand their relational style and how that is wired into their psychobiological nervous system.

Arousal Regulation

From the earliest moments of life, infant brains establish attachment with significant caregivers. Under favorable circumstances with positive attachments, the body remembers the feeling of oneness with the caregiver and learns healthy, positive affective regulation. However, if that process is disrupted or not healthy, the stage may be set for longtime struggles with emotional regulation. This is particularly true if an individual has established automatic and rigidly expressed affect management strategies including chronic defense mechanisms. Teaching tools of recognizing and anticipating responses can help couples learn to disrupt the automatic response of negative emotions that interfere with effective communication and disrupt healthy connection between partners. Counselors teach the couple to closely monitor the face, voice, eyes, and body of their partner for the occurrence of emotional dysregulation. Ultimately, counselors want couples to reach a point of being able to talk about any topic or do any activity together without fear.

Neurobiologic Development

The goal of work in this domain is to examine what issues the couple struggles with most (e.g., finances, sex, parenting, or time). The counselor examines the couple's ability to be a "coregulatory" team and manage each other during stressful times. It allows for an examination of how well the couple handles issues during stressful times, and whether the couple handles conflict in a secure functional manner or an insecure maladaptive manner. Ultimately, the counselor wants to help the couple move toward having the relationship come first as opposed to independent concern about each partner as an individual. This domain illuminates the couple's capacity to work as a unit.

Therapeutic Enactment

This domain is experiential in nature. The counselor promotes body awareness with each individual so they become aware of the state of their mind and the state of their body in response to particular experiences. The counselor may use psychodrama to help educate the couple on their arousal triggers and get them more fully in touch with their physiological responses instead of focusing only on cognitions.

Therapeutic Narrative

The last domain is an opportunity for the counselor to educate the couple about where they have been, the path they are currently on, and what the process looks like going forward. It creates a narrative for the couple about why they should be together. This dialog focuses on the meaning the couple is making of the experience. It assists couples in separating how they experience problems from their personal identity and creates an opportunity to access preferred experiences.

Conclusion

It is not uncommon for counselors using interpersonal neurobiology with couples to have very long sessions, sometimes upward of 2 to 4 hours in length. The therapy tends to be very interactive and experiential in nature. One strategy is that instead of talking about events, the couple enacts scenarios that allow them to make corrections to dysfunctional reactions in real time. This enables the new reactions to become part of one's procedural memory, which is what created the disruption in the first place.

The counselor must be well versed in microaggressions and have a clarity of understanding about how the brain works as well as a working knowledge of attachment theory. The use of neurobiology is complex and couples tend to be unaware of what they are doing. Our reactions are grounded in very fast subcortical processes of the brain and some primitive areas of the brain react based purely on survival instinct without regard for relationships. Thus, counselors seeking to utilize this approach need specialized training in addition to the luxury of extended session time.

Abby Dougherty and Laura Haddock

See also Communication in Couples and Families; Conflict in Couples and Families; Interpersonal Neurobiology, Parenting and; Mindfulness and Couples

Further Readings

Baderoch, B. (2008). *Being a brain-wise therapist: A practical guide to interpersonal neurobiology.* New York, NY: W. W. Norton.

Fishbane, M. D. (2013). *Loving with the brain in mind.* New York, NY: W. W. Norton.

Schore, A. N. (2003). *Affect regulation and the repair of self.* New York, NY: W. W. Norton.

Siegel, D. J. (2007). *The mindful brain: Reflection and attunement in the cultivation of well-being.* New York, NY: W. W. Norton.

Siegel, D. J. (2010). *The mindful therapist: A clinician's guide to mindsight and neural integration.* New York, NY: W. W. Norton.

Siegel, D. J. (2012). *The pocket guide to interpersonal neurobiology.* New York, NY: W. W. Norton.

INTERPERSONAL NEUROBIOLOGY, PARENTING AND

Parenting behavior critically shapes infants' behavior. The parent–infant bond provides infants with their first social experiences, creating a framework for what children can expect from others as well as how to respond to others' expectations. Much evidence exists that the physiological and mental wellness of the parents can influence the successful development of a child. Thus, unhealthy parenting can adversely influence a child's development. Interpersonal neurobiology is a framework that offers counselors and the families with whom they work an approach to promote healthy parenting and child development. To put it quite simply, this approach suggests that we are a product of our biology and neurodevelopmental evolution. Interpersonal neurobiology is an integrative approach that uses science to inform and assist with the everyday human struggle of parenting. It is important to note that neurobiology is complex; thus, an understanding of interpersonal neurobiology is needed to understand its application and viability when applied to parenting. This entry examines the history, major themes and assumptions, and the basic tenets of interpersonal neurobiology and further examines interpersonal neurobiology in relation to parenting.

History of Interpersonal Neurobiology

Interpersonal neurobiology, developed by Dan Siegel and Allan Schore, is an interdisciplinary approach that explores the interrelationship between neurobiology and interpersonal relationships. Interpersonal neurobiology integrates concepts from many different disciplines including anthropology, biology (developmental, evolution, genetics, zoology), cognitive science, computer science, developmental psychopathology, linguistics neuroscience (affective, cognitive, developmental, social), mathematics, mental health, physics, psychiatry, psychology (cognitive, developmental, evolutionary, experimental, of religion, social, attachment theory, memory), sociology, and systems theory (chaos and complexity theory).

Siegel began his research into interpersonal neurobiology by exploring how trauma impacts human neurological development. He asserted that relational experiences have a profound impact on a person's neurobiology. Siegel's ideas were influenced by the discovery of mirror neurons. A mirror neuron fires when a person carries out an act, as well as when observing the same action in another. Thus, the neuron mirrors the behavior of the other, as though what they are observing is what they are actually doing. For example, when a parent becomes very upset and begins to cry, their child may also begin to cry, mirroring their behavior. Theoretically, when the parent takes note of this act of empathy from their child, the parent's mirror neurons will reflect the child's behavior, and the parent will seek to soothe and mirror the empathy they observed in the child.

This discovery provided evidence that the human mind is developed within a relational context. Thus, there is an association between interpersonal relationships and the neurological activity of the mind. Establishing proof that the mind develops and changes in relation to a personal experience suggests that human beings are wired for growth and change. This has tremendous implications for counselors and other helping professionals who emphasize the therapeutic relationship as central to the healing of clients. Regardless of the therapeutic approach, the therapeutic relationship has been shown to be an essential component that contributes to positive therapeutic outcomes. Interpersonal neurobiology provides a lens for understanding how and why this occurs. Additionally, with numerous therapeutic modalities available, it is important for counselors to have options for guiding frameworks to integrate their theoretical approach into treatment. Interpersonal neurobiology as an interdisciplinary approach increases its utility for counselors seeking integrative models in counseling.

Underlying Major Theories and Assumptions

Interpersonal neurobiology is grounded in attachment theory and neurobiology. Siegel first became interested in exploring similar ideas and concepts that underlie attachment theory, neurobiology, and neuroplasticity. Attachment theorists assert that infants are hard wired to seek out their attachment figures. Attachment relationships are important in supporting healthy emotional and social development. Since human development is an ongoing process, it was assumed that relationships continue to influence development across the lifespan. In contrast, a number of studies have shown that an insecure attachment in childhood can lead to lifelong, chronic difficulties in relationships, with impairment in attention and the ability to understand experiences from another person's perspective. Neurobiology emphasizes our capacity to selectively direct attention toward the most important sensory inputs in any given moment. When individuals improve their capacity to focus attention, it provides a mechanism for intentionally reshaping their brains. As our brains are social in nature, relationships are an essential aspect to healthy human existence.

Finally, interpersonal neurobiology is also influenced by the concept of neuroplasticity. Neuroplasticity is the brain's capacity to be flexible and responsive to internal and environmental needs. Early research into brain functioning was based on the idea that the brain operated like a machine; it did not change or evolve, only carried out processes and functions. Further research has demonstrated that the brain is flexible and is constantly developing and altering.

Basic Tenets of Interpersonal Neurobiology

One of the basic tenets of interpersonal neurobiology is that interpersonal relationships influence the development of the brain, and simultaneously the brain develops and shapes those relationships. When exploring underlying assumptions, interpersonal neurobiology emphasizes three concepts related to brain development: mirror neurons, attention, and neuroplasticity. An important distinction Siegel makes is the difference between "the mind" and "the brain." Siegel noted that currently there is no one definition of the mind. There are descriptions of the brain's functions and processes, but researchers do not have an absolute definition of the mind. As Siegel sought to understand themes and patterns across the many disciplines, he identified one central idea regarding the mind: the mind is the flow of energy and information between people. Interpersonal neurobiology rests on the assumption that the mind does not exist in a single person; rather, the mind and its development are linked to the relationships among and between an individual and the minds of others. Counselors and researchers who use an interpersonal neurobiology framework are seeking to promote the integration of the mind, brain, body, and relational connections toward integration. Integration is characterized as a state of harmony or balance that occurs when neurobiology, consciousness, and interpersonal relationships are in harmony or balanced.

Interpersonal Neurobiology and Parenting

The quality of parenting has significant effects on the development of children. For instance, parents who employ a sensitive and responsive parenting style promote positive attachment, stable emotional and social regulation, appropriate language development, healthy cognition, and executive function development and growth. Evidence of positive parental interaction is demonstrated early on in a child's development. For example, children of mothers who breastfeed frequently demonstrate cognitive and emotional development earlier than those who do not experience close physical contact with parents. Even actions like singing or talking to an infant can stimulate development. The reverse is also true. A lack of sufficient stimulation or extended separation from primary caregivers can have damaging effects on children. Punitive, negligent, or abusive parenting can also result in higher risk for physical health problems and substance abuse, adult obesity, and chronic illness or depression. Parental caretaking is a central and innately transferred biological predisposition and parenting style and ability is undoubtedly important.

To promote integration between parents and their children, parents need to be able to develop a sense of relational attunement and an ability to be attentive. Attunement equates to a sense of connection and relational awareness. For example, parents will often remark that they know what their babies need based on how they cry. The parent has paid attention to their child's need, and thus has attuned to the need, whether for affection or food. Siegel noted that in order for this type of attunement to occur, there must be an ability to focus one's attention. Siegel is a proponent of using mindfulness practices such as meditation to develop attention and attunement. As parents have the ability to shift their attention, they also have an ability to reshape the functioning of their brains, thus facilitating healthy development within their children.

Integration is another important concept in relation to parenting. If a child is experiencing disintegration, perhaps acting out verbally or behaviorally, the child is only able to learn how to regulate his or her distress if the parent is able to do so as well. The child needs his or her parent to be present, attentive, and attuned (integrated) so that the child can reintegrate, and seek a sense of calmness, balance, and harmony. Siegel is a proponent of teaching families skills to regulate their attention and emotional experience in response to sensory input. He recommends teaching families, including children and adolescents, how to use mindfulness practices to develop attention, attunement, and compassion to support integration. Parents who struggle with tolerating difficult emotions may avoid their child, lash out in anger, or discredit their child's experience. This will ultimately affect the quality of connection or attachment the child shares with the parent. How a parent communicates with a child shapes the development of the prefrontal cortex, an area of the brain that is responsible for bodily regulation, emotional balance and attunement, empathy, insight, moral awareness, and intuition. Interpersonal neurobiology can help parents understand the importance of developing an awareness of their own emotional reactivity and receptivity and the potential negative consequences for a child's development. If parents do not learn social-emotional awareness and its impact on their parenting style, it creates the potential for multigenerational relational struggles.

There are several practical implications interpersonal neurobiology offers both parents and marriage and family counselors. Parents who are seeking to develop healthy secure attachments with their children can work to cultivate the ability to engage in collaborative communication. Engaging in communication styles that are collaborative in nature will support relational attunement. Attunement supports healthy attachment and child development. Secure attachment allows for focusing on the inner experience of each person. Parents can help their children develop an awareness of their internal states of being. When parents recognize and identify their child's internal state and then discuss the internal state with their child and give it meaning, they help the child learn attunement, empathy, and perspective taking. Siegel refers to this learning process as "mindsight."

When disagreements or verbal arguments occur, parents who respond readily to repair this relational disconnection consistently and intentionally will help their children learn healthy ways to disagree and repair attuned communication. This is important for children to learn because prolonged disconnection can lead to the child developing shame about their internal emotional experience. There are long-term negative outcomes for children's development when they experience a sense of shame about their internal affective experience. It is important for the child to see he or she can remain connected to another person, even during times of emotional duress. Additionally, children need to learn they will not be emotionally abandoned. Helping children understand and develop meaning about their internal state, engaging in attuned communication, and learning how to repair relational disconnections will help to support healthy familial attachment and child development. Finally, parents also need to develop sensitivity to their child's need for relational connection and solitude. Having an awareness of this need will also support attuned communication and healthy development for both parent and child.

Critical Remarks

Interpersonal neurobiology offers many positive insights into elements that are necessary for ongoing, healthy human growth and development. Yet, as a new and developing theory, there are few outcome studies exploring the application of interpersonal neurobiology with parenting or in marriage and family counseling. It is important to note that studies that have been conducted exploring interpersonal neurobiology in counseling settings do have positive outcomes. It is also a model not intended to be utilized on its own, but adopted to enhance the utilization of other models such as cognitive-behavioral and humanistic, as well as multicultural psychological theories. On an alternate note, Siegel has reported that this approach demonstrates positive benefits not only for clients, but for counselors as well. Family counselors may find they can more readily connect with clients, establish a more mindful connection in their work with clients, and experience a greater degree of wellness.

*Abby Dougherty
and Laura Haddock*

See also Attachment Styles; Attachment Theory; Mindfulness; Parenting

Further Readings

Schore, A. N. (2003). *Affect regulation and the repair of self*. New York, NY: W. W. Norton.

Siegel, D. J. (2001). Toward an interpersonal neurobiology of the developing mind: Attachment, "mindsight," and neural integration. *Infant Mental Health Journal, 22*, 67–94.

Siegel, D. J. (2007). *The mindful brain: Reflection and attunement in the cultivation of well-being*. New York, NY: W. W. Norton.

Siegel, D. J. (2010). *The mindful therapist: A clinician's guide to mindsight and neural integration*. New York, NY: W. W. Norton.

Siegel, D. J. (2010). *Mindsight: The new science of personal transformation*. New York, NY: Random House.

Siegel, D. J., & Hartzell, M. (2003). *Parenting from the inside out: How a deeper self-understanding can help you raise children who thrive*. New York, NY: Jeremy P. Tarcher/Penguin.

INTERPERSONAL VIOLENCE

Interpersonal violence, in its broadest terms, refers to any act of violence committed by one person or group of people toward another person or group of people. However, in the realm of marriage and family therapy, interpersonal violence typically encompasses child abuse, partner violence, elder abuse, teen violence and aggression, dating violence, rape, and stalking. These acts often occur within, but are not limited to, families and other intimate relationships. For example, cohabiting couples are more likely to be physically abusive than married couples. Additionally, rape can occur in dating or acquaintance relationships, as well as among strangers or committed partners. For the purposes of this entry, both acts that occur in families and those that do not will be considered. In discussing abuse in recent years, the word *survivor* has replaced the word *victim* to refer to those to whom abuse is occurring. The rationale for this is that the word *survivor* is thought to connote a person who is an agent and whose story is one of strength and resilience. For this reason, the word *survivor* is used throughout this entry. Specifically, this entry examines child abuse, sibling abuse, bullying, dating violence, and elder abuse.

Family Violence

Family violence is not a new phenomenon. Families, historically, have been thought of as private spheres, free from the eyes of the world. At times, women and children have been thought of as the property of men. Free from public scrutiny, family violence went unchecked for many years. However, with the increased legal rights of both women and children, a light has been shed on this as a problem. As the understanding of vulnerable populations grows, clinicians continue to expand their awareness of the abuse of those populations. More research needs to be done regarding the effects of these types of abuse, but there is considerable information regarding the scope of each type of abuse, its effects, and considerations for its treatment.

Child Abuse

Child abuse can take on many forms, including those familiar to adults: physical abuse, verbal abuse, sexual abuse, as well as neglect and witnessing domestic violence. The roots of child abuse as an issue for treatment and legal intervention go back to the 1800s, when houses of refuge were created. Unlike domestic violence, all 50 states have mandatory reporting laws for child abuse. The effects of child abuse may vary depending on the individual characteristics of both children and caregivers, as well as by the type of abuse. However, certain effects of child abuse tend to be similar regardless of the type of abuse. These include things like insecure or reactive attachment of child to parents, low self-esteem, behavior problems, social incompetence, cognitive deficits, and poor physical health. Further, the Adverse Childhood Experiences Study (ACES) examined the relationship between childhood maltreatment and abuse and adult health and well-being and demonstrated that children who experience abuse in any of its forms are more likely to have health-risk behaviors, adult social problems, and early death. Further, there appears to be an additive effect, meaning that the more of these events that a child has experienced in his or her childhood, the poorer his or her adult outcomes are likely to be. Additional effects that are unique to specific types of child abuse are discussed in the following sections.

Neglect

Neglect is the most common form of child abuse. Child protective services data estimate that neglect makes up 60% of child maltreatment cases. Neglect is typically characterized by a failure of caregivers to meet basic needs of children. While definitions of *basic needs* vary, neglect is often categorized as follows: health care (failing to take a child to see a doctor or dentist), hygiene (whether personal or household), nutritional, housing (adequate and safe shelter), supervisory, educational, and emotional. When examining parental neglect, it is important to take context into account. In many cases, various forms of neglect occur because parents live in poverty or lack resources, such as medical insurance. While there are certainly cases in which parents intentionally withhold resources and affection from their children, in most cases, treatment of neglect often means helping families get connected with governmental resources, such as housing, food stamps, and governmental health care.

Emotional/Psychological Abuse

Unlike neglect, psychological or emotional maltreatment is typically intentional on some level. Psychological maltreatment may include degrading behaviors, such as yelling, swearing at, or insulting a child. It may include rejecting or isolating behaviors, such as refusing to help a child, failing to respond to a child's emotional needs, or locking a child in a closet. It may also include corrupting or exploiting a child by encouraging or using the child for antisocial behaviors. The prevalence of psychological abuse is unclear: It is thought to be the most prevalent form of abuse to children, yet it remains the least reported. Similar to neglect cases, psychological abuse is more likely to occur in families with fewer resources. In addition to helping connect families to those resources, treatment often involves parent training programs. These programs are often built around increasing parents' knowledge and self-efficacy on child development and child-rearing best practices, as well as providing parents practical ways to decrease their own stress levels and manage their own emotions.

Witnessing Domestic Violence

While domestic violence in and of itself is not mandatory by law to be reported to child protective services, a child's witnessing of domestic violence is considered child abuse and does need to be reported. Recent estimates suggest between 10% and 14% of children have witnessed parental violence. This underscores the seriousness of domestic violence for couples with children. Moreover, it is important to understand the impact that witnessing domestic violence has on children, as either survivors or perpetrators. Children who witness domestic violence are more likely to experience domestic violence as adults. Treatment for children who witness domestic violence often starts with parent treatment, which is discussed in the partner violence section. Treatment of children may include child-centered play therapy or trauma-focused cognitive-behavioral therapy for children.

Physical Abuse

Child physical abuse is typically characterized by specific acts of violence that typically cause visible harm. While there is a small subset of physical abusers who employ tactics that more resemble torture, such as burning children, most physical abuse of children takes the form of assault (i.e., hitting, kicking, slapping, shoving, striking with an object such as a belt, etc.), and is the result of parental frustration and/or efforts to discipline a child.

When talking about child physical abuse, the line between abuse and corporal punishment is often one that gets addressed. Corporal punishment refers to physical harm to a child (i.e., spanking) in the name of discipline, and has its historical roots in both cultural and religious traditions that imply that if children are born evil, and if not beaten physically, they will grow up to be delinquents. Moreover, people who endorse corporal punishment often cite family-of-origin norms as reasons for employing it (i.e., "My parents spanked me and I turned out great."). However, research on spanking has demonstrated that it is less effective than other means of discipline, that it is linked to other forms of family violence, and that it may have negative neurobiological effects. All of that aside, it is important to note that corporal punishment typically falls into the realm of abuse only when it is accompanied by observable injuries lasting at least 48 hours, or a substantial risk for injury.

Child Sexual Abuse

Sexual abuse of children refers to the coercion of a child to participate in a sexual act, or the viewing of a sexual act, or the assistance of a sexual act. It can include sexual intercourse as well as sexual touching, and third-party activities, such as creating or viewing child pornography, child prostitution, or exposing a child to pornography. Child sexual abuse is illegal in every state, but the laws around sexual abuse typically specify an age at which a person is able to consent to sexual contact. This age varies from state to state, ranging from 14 to 18 years of age, and is based on each state's understanding of how old a person has to be in order to understand the consequences of sex and advocate for him or herself.

National incidence studies of child sexual abuse estimate that approximately 1.8 in every 1,000 children is sexually abused. Girls are more commonly abused than boys. Ages of sexual abuse survivors span a broad range, with the median ages between 12 and 14. Child sexual abuse perpetrators are much more likely to be male than female, though it should be noted that sometimes a man and woman will work together to sexually abuse a child. Most perpetrators are between the ages of 30 and 40. Perpetrators of child sexual abuse are most commonly a nonparent relative or family friend or acquaintance. Further, there is a strong relationship from being victimized as a child to being a perpetrator as an adult.

The process of child sexual abuse is unique as compared to physical and psychological abuse, in that it tends to follow a somewhat predictable pattern. First of all, perpetrators typically do not molest every child to which they have access. Rather they tend to select children who lack parental monitoring and who respond to their coercive tactics. These tactics can include threats or force, as well as manipulation and lies about what purpose the abuse serves, or a reward system. This process is known as grooming, and it tends to include progression from slight, accidental touching to more intentional or forceful contact.

Effects of child sexual abuse on survivors include reactions similar to those experienced by survivors of other types of abuse. Survivors of sexual abuse tend to feel vulnerable and may resent caregivers—particularly mothers—for not protecting them from sexual abuse. Additionally, sexual abuse survivors tend to have sexual problems. This may include having a knowledge of sexual behavior that is mature for their age's nonnormative behavior, like penetrating themselves with objects. They may act out sexually, often as children making sense of their abuse by engaging in similar acts with other children. Often, in later life, sexual abuse survivors also experience sexual dysfunction, such as low desire disorder or painful intercourse. Further, they may experience trauma symptoms or possibly posttraumatic stress disorder, which can be exacerbated by sex or other situations in which they feel physically or emotionally vulnerable.

Treatment for sexual abuse for children often involves trauma-focused cognitive-behavioral therapy (CBT) or play therapy or other individual child treatments. Often, however, child sexual abuse is not dealt with in childhood, but rather, in adulthood when trauma symptoms resurface in intimate relationships or with children or in other similar settings. Treatment for adults who experienced childhood sexual abuse has typically included helping the survivor tell her story in a therapeutic setting where the therapist can help her make sense of what happened until the trauma and power of the story lessens. A critique of this technique has to do with the way the brain's fight-or-flight mode tends to override its ability to be cognitive and rational when a person is traumatized. Critics argue that therapy must include some method of helping survivors step outside of the trauma and observe it from a distance. Such techniques can include eye movement desensitization reprocessing (EMDR), a technique that allows people to refocus their brains using their eyes, or internal family systems (IFS) therapy. IFS helps people view their internal world as a family of different parts, alternately allowing more mature, adult parts to comfort fearful child parts. Conceptualizing trauma as parts allows survivors to simultaneously acknowledge their own hurt and soothe it.

Intergenerational Transmission of Violence

One of the consequences of child abuse, including physical, sexual, psychological, and witnessing of parental domestic violence, is the link between childhood abuse and abuse in adulthood, either in a romantic relationship or a parent–child relationship. The statistics on this vary by study, but the important messages of intergenerational transmission of violence are these. First, children who experience abuse are more likely to abuse their children or to be in an abusive romantic relationship than children who do not experience abuse. Second, children who experience abuse are still less likely to abuse their children or to end up in an abusive relationship than they are to abuse their children or end up in an abusive relationship. The notion that children who are abused have the ability to change has its roots in resilience literature. Protective factors for children who have been abused may include relationships with the nonoffending parent or other healthy adults, a support system, and the child's individual temperament and intellectual functioning.

Treatment of Child Abuse

When treating child abuse, it is important to think systemically and tailor treatment to both the child survivor and the parent perpetrators and nonabusing partners. Typically, when child abuse is present in the home, child protective services will be involved in that case as well as a therapist. In cases where a parent or caregiver has mental health problems that impact the abuse, those must also be dealt with, and depending on severity of the issues (i.e., psychosis, addiction, etc.), this may be a long process. The court system will often supplement therapy with parent training, anger management, and individual trauma-focused therapy for both parents and children, and other requirements that must be completed before the family's case will be closed. However, the emotional and psychological impacts of abuse may continue long after the state's involvement with a family concludes. While family therapy with abused families may be contraindicated immediately following disclosure, family reunification is still often the goal in child protective services cases. Family therapists' tasks in working with abusing families may include repairing parent–child attachment, working on parental family of origin issues, and helping families to use their newfound skills to prevent further abuse.

Sibling Abuse

Sibling abuse is another form of interpersonal violence that has only recently come to light. Sibling abuse refers to repeated one-sided aggression from one sibling to another, often in an attempt to gain power. These behaviors are outside the realm of normal sibling fighting and would be thought of as bullying in unrelated children. Behaviors are typically physical but can also include sexual abuse. Within a family system, therapists may examine the parental subsystem under which the abuse has been maintained. There may be parental coalitions with the abusive sibling that need to be examined. Parents may need the therapist's help to support the enforcement of boundaries between themselves and their children.

Bullying

While bullying is not likely to involve members of the same family, it is an issue that may present itself in therapy. Public consciousness regarding bullying has been on the rise in recent years, and the effects of bullying can include suicide, homicide, and dating violence. Antibullying programs that schools produce have mixed results, some citing an improvement in bullying and some citing deterioration. For treatment of bullying, some therapists have turned their attention to the victims, drawing on the resilience literature that suggests that giving children better coping skills and a more effective support system can counteract the effects of bullying.

Rape and Stalking

Dating violence may also include all of the behaviors associated with partner violence in a dating situation (usually not a cohabiting relationship), but there are additional violent behaviors associated with dating violence, which have a particularly high prevalence rate on college campuses. These behaviors include date rape and stalking.

Date Rape

Rape often refers to unwanted sexual penetration, but *sexual coercion* is a broader term that refers to any sexual activity in which a person uses physical or psychological force to undermine the consent of his or her partner. Date rape itself usually refers to rape that occurs in the context of a relationship, but can also include rape between acquaintances. Having a prior relationship with one's rapist is a key contributing factor to whether or not a victim (a) recognizes the act as rape and (b) reports it. In other words, those who are raped by a date or an acquaintance are less likely to come forward and talk about the rape and, in many cases, do not even believe that rape occurred.

In addition to poor physical health outcomes as a result of rape, psychological outcomes that may manifest in therapy include anxiety and paranoia, depression, trauma symptoms, eating disorders, and suicidal thoughts. While therapists who see victims of sexual assault often concentrate on the trauma caused by the events, as well as helping victims to protect themselves, the real work of date rape intervention involves the rapists. Those who work with victims and perpetrators of sexual assault recognize that rape and related behaviors, like most forms of interpersonal violence, are more about power and control than they are about a desire for sex. While it is important to help potential victims of rape to feel empowered and protect themselves, prevention of rape must start with programs that intervene directly in the attitudes of young men regarding romantic relationships and power and control.

Stalking

Stalking is another set of violent and coercive behaviors that are often grouped in dating violence. Stalking, often thought of as unwanted pursuit or harassment, is another group of behaviors that can occur among strangers as well as acquaintances and intimates. Stalking behaviors include things like making unwanted contact, waiting or showing up at places where the victim is likely to be, leaving unwanted items for the victim, following or spying on the victim, or posting information about the victim online. While it may not be strictly physically violent, it is significantly correlated with other types of dating violence, including physical and sexual assault. It can be particularly threatening if it occurs following the termination of a violent relationship. Additionally, the effects of stalking include fear, anxiety, depression, and trauma symptoms, which are all similar to physical violence. Similar to working with victims of domestic violence, therapists who work with victims of stalking need to help clients plan for their own safety. This may mean helping clients recognize when they are in danger in order to help them prepare to leave quickly and find a safe place to which they can go.

Adult Intimate Partner Violence

Partner violence, for various reasons, is more likely to be an issue for marriage and family therapists than other types of family violence. Partner violence itself typically refers to violence that occurs between two long-term romantic partners. In examining partner violence, researchers and therapists have identified several categories to which one should attend. Generally, these categories are additive, meaning that if sexual abuse is present in a relationship, it is highly likely that physical abuse and verbal or emotional abuse is present as well. However, each of these involve a unique set of challenges and effects. For this reason, it is important for therapists to assess each of these repeatedly and to consider the impact of each in kind, as well as assessment and treatment considerations for each. When incidence and prevalence statistics are reported, it is important to recognize that however the data has been collected, incidence and prevalence rates have most likely been underreported. Both the stigma of violence and a lack of understanding about what it entails may prevent people from reporting it anywhere.

Emotional/Psychological Abuse

Emotional and psychological abuse take into account various behaviors that, while not physically damaging, are emotionally hurtful. These behaviors may include yelling and insulting a partner, but they may also include nonviolent psychological tactics, such as isolating a partner, making him or her think he or she is crazy, economic or monetary abuse (withholding funds or making it difficult for a partner to work), withholding emotional responsiveness, and using or abusing children in an effort to hurt the partner. Recent research has supported the long-held notion that emotional and psychological abuse is more internally damaging to survivors than physical abuse. Often, abusive partners use these as tactics to maintain control in the relationship. While these tactics can occur in a relationship without physical or sexual violence being present, the threat of physical violence can be used to enforce compliance to these other tactics.

Physical Abuse

Several prominent researchers in intimate partner violence have posited that there are different typologies of people who are violent in relationships. Michael Johnson and Kathleen Ferraro described situational couple violence and intimate terrorism as two types of violence that occur in intimate relationships but are fundamentally different in their execution. Situational couple violence is characterized by mutual, low-level violence between couples who have a fairly egalitarian relationship. In situational couple violence, violence tends to be infrequent, and partners tend to be very sorry when it occurs. It is more common in the general population than other types of violence. Intimate terrorism, on the other hand, tends to be more frequent, more injurious, and one sided. It is characterized by a high degree of power and control on the side of one partner, and it is more likely to be seen in relationships of people in battered women's shelters and in police reports.

Neil Jacobsen and John Gottman described similar typologies based on physiology, and Amy Holtzworth-Munroe and her colleagues also described similar differences in types of violence. Essentially, all of these researchers have suggested that there are typologies of violent people who are more amenable to treatment and others where it would be unsafe to stay in the relationship, as well as treat the relationship without the offender first undergoing intensive individual therapy. While not all of these typologies have withstood replication by outside researchers, the notion that there are different types of physically violent couples has important considerations for treatment. If there are indeed types of violent offenders who are likely to be more dangerous and less amenable to change, therapists need to be extremely cautious of how they treat those offenders.

Sexual Abuse

Researchers have suggested that anywhere between 7% and 14% of women in committed relationships are raped by a partner. Those estimates increase to approximately 87% for women who are in physically abusive relationships. Sexual abuse of a partner can include forced intercourse (oral, anal, or vaginal); forced intercourse in front of the survivor's children; penetration with a foreign object, including weapons; threatening a partner in order to get sex; refusing to wear a condom; and raping a partner while he or she is asleep. It is important to note that rape by an intimate partner or acquaintance is more common than rape by a stranger, and that rape by a partner has been shown to be more psychologically damaging to the survivor than stranger rape.

Assessment

It is important for therapists to recognize that couples who are violent may not disclose their violence in therapy. For this reason, assessment in couple therapy is paramount. Assessment should not be limited to those who seem like they could be violent. Many violence researchers have advocated, instead, that assessing for partner violence should be a routine part of the intake session for any couple.

Assessment of couple violence should take the form of both self-report measures, as well as an interview. One such self-report measure is the revised conflict tactics scale, which asks people to report on their violent behaviors (psychological, physical, and sexual) as well as their partners' violent behaviors. Additionally, therapists should interview each partner separately about the violence in their relationships. Interviews should be separate in order to maintain each partner's safety. During the course of assessment, therapists must discern whether or not couple therapy is appropriate to treat the violence, as well as assessing the safety of each partner if the relationship continues. In most states, therapists are not mandatory reporters for domestic violence, as it is often assumed that survivors of domestic violence are not a vulnerable population that needs this protection. While therapists recognize that survivors of partner violence are adults and need to have autonomy to make their own decisions, this should not stop therapists from helping their clients to recognize the serious ramifications of continuing in a violent relationship.

Treatment

There is much controversy surrounding treating couples violence in therapy. Out of concern for the safety of partners (as well as themselves), and the ethics of preserving a violent relationship, many couples therapists have refused to see violent couples together. For this reason, therapy has historically occurred with partners separated, sometimes in individual therapy, sometimes in therapy groups, under the understanding that partners had different issues they needed to work through separately, and that treating a violent couple together implicated the victim/survivor as part of the problem. For couples therapists, however, treating partners in isolation can be problematic if the therapist ignores that couples dynamics both impact and are impacted by the violence. In recent years, some therapists have posited that, if the nature of the violence is relatively minor, infrequent, and not injurious and the safety of the couple can be ensured, couples therapy can be helpful to treat some of the underlying dynamics of the partner violence.

For example, Sandra M. Stith and Eric E. McCollum have outlined a program for treating couples together, either in a traditional couples therapy setting or in multicouple groups called domestic violence-focused couple therapy. In order to ensure safety, this program, and others, begin by committing both partners to abstaining from violence during the course of therapy and beyond. It is a common practice for therapists to have a couple come up with a plan to stay safe during therapy. This plan typically includes strategies for deescalation, such as a negotiated time-out, and resources if one partner needs to leave, like a safe place to stay. The plan can also be written like a contract, with each partner agreeing not to be violent during the course of therapy. Finally, the therapist and partners should decide at the outset of therapy what the procedure will be should the partners violate the agreement and engage in violence during therapy. Therapists should assess for violence throughout therapy and continually evaluate whether or not therapy is appropriate for the couple.

As a precursor to couples work, partners receive gender-specific psychoeducation on how to handle anger and deescalate prior to engaging in violence. Following that instruction, couples begin to work on their issues. While certainly every violent couple may not be suitable for conjoint therapy, if partners can agree to safety, conjoint treatment may help partners get to the root of the conflict that escalates to violence. Work on this particular type of therapy had yielded promising results, suggesting that through therapy, violent couples can learn new skills and abstain from violence. However, couples therapy for domestic violence is far from a given, and all of the safety and treatment considerations outlined above must be present in the minds of therapists to guide their decision-making processes.

Elder Abuse

Elder abuse is another type of family violence that is relatively new to public consciousness. As medicine has advanced, people have begun to live longer in various states of health. Further, with the advent of retirement post–World War II, people now live a longer span of time from when they leave the workforce to death. These factors have combined to create a large population of vulnerable people. Elder abuse can include physical, emotional, and sexual abuse, as well as neglect, both by caregivers and by themselves. Elderly people also face other unique challenges, such as financial abuse, including scams by strangers. Because elderly people are considered a vulnerable population, therapists are mandated to report elder abuse.

Most abusers of elderly people are family members—commonly spouses or children. The reasons for this abuse may be pathology on the part of the abuser, including dementia in some cases, ignorance, intent to hurt, or caretaker fatigue. Caretaker fatigue occurs when a person is chiefly in charge of the care of another, and the burden of that caregiving is particularly stressful. Caretaker fatigue is often mediated by the quality of relationship the caretaker has with the elderly person, support from others, and the emotional well-being of the caretaker. While caretaker fatigue does not excuse abuse behavior, it does provide a systemic framework for dealing with elder abuse.

When working with an elderly person who is at risk of being abused, a therapist can help that person be a better advocate for himself or herself by connecting the client to resources like financial planners, legal aid, or government assistance programs for food or insurance. When working with someone who is at risk for abusing an elderly person, a therapist can help that person access resources as well, including alternative caretakers, respite, mindfulness, and other stress-relieving exercises. In addition, focusing on individual issues and family-of-origin issues that may impact the caretaker's relationship with the elderly person can be helpful.

Megan Oka

See also Child Protective Services; Domestic Violence; Elder Abuse; Intergenerational Trauma; Sexual Abuse; Trauma and Children

Further Readings

Barnett, O. W., Miller-Perrin, C. L., & Perrin, R. D. (2010). *Family violence across the lifespan: An introduction*. Thousand Oaks, CA: Sage.

Murray, C. E., & Graves, K. N. (2013). *Responding to family violence: A comprehensive, research-based guide for therapists*. New York, NY: Routledge.

Stith, S. M., Rosen, H., McCollum, E. E., & Thomsen, C. J. (2004). Treating intimate partner violence within intact couple relationships: Outcomes of multi-couple versus individual couple therapy. *Journal of Marital and Family Therapy, 30*(3), 305–318.

Straus, M. A., Hamby, S. L., Boney-McCoy, S., & Sugarman, D. B. (1996). The revised conflict tactics scales (CTS2) development and preliminary psychometric data. *Journal of Family Issues, 17*(3), 283–316.

van der Kolk, B. A. (1994). The body keeps the score: Memory and the evolving psychobiology of posttraumatic stress. *Harvard Review of Psychiatry, 1*(5), 253–265.

INTERRACIAL MARRIAGES AND FAMILIES

Interracial marriage is the term used to define marriage between two people of different races or ethnicities. In the United States, antimiscegenation laws outlawing interracial marriage were deemed unconstitutional in 1967 by the Supreme Court. Individuals who partner with someone outside their race and their children may have unique experiences, both positive and negative. It is important to increase awareness of these unique experiences so that clinicians may understand and serve these families better. This entry will include definitions of important terms and discuss interracial marriages, interracial families with children, the experiences of multiracial children, and important considerations for working with interracial couples and families in a counseling context.

Race and Ethnicity

Race is a sociocultural construct founded on the economic and social climates of a time and place. Within the cultural constructs of the United States, *race* is often generally defined by physical characteristics such as skin color, hair texture, and facial features; however, there is often greater variability within racial populations than there is between them. Ethnicity is influenced by skin color and the dimensions of a person's culture that may include traditions, language, religious expression, nationality, history, ancestry, and values. In general, race can contribute to ethnicity, but ethnicity is not limited to a person's race, as ethnicity tends to denote a synthesis of biology, ancestry, and cultural factors. In the United States, the terms *race* and *ethnicity* are often used interchangeably, but for the purpose of this discussion, race will account for both race and ethnicity. Racial-ethnic group categories in the United States include non-Hispanic White, Hispanic, Black, American Indian and Alaskan Native, and Asian and Pacific Islander.

Marriage

Marriage is a social and ritually recognized public union usually involving a legal contract between two people. Traditionally, in American culture, marriage referred to the legal union between a man and woman, and up until 1967, it was only allowed between individuals from the same racial groups. Today marriage is more about a commitment between any two people and may be referred to as partnering or coupling. For the purposes of this discussion, the term *marriage* will encompass two individuals committed to each other, regardless of actual legal marital status. It is most common for individuals to marry a partner who is similar to them in many ways, including racially, ethnically, religiously, and socioeconomically. Marriage between individuals who are similar is known as homogamy or monoracial. When an individual partners with someone from a different racial, ethnic, or cultural group, that partnership is referred to as interracial, interethnic, or intercultural.

Interracial Marriage

Since the 1970s, interracial unions between Whites and non-Whites in the United States have grown from approximately 233,000 to approximately 5.4 million. Interracial couples make up just under 10% of U.S. married couples. The steady growth in interracial couples over the last 45 years is often attributed to the 1967 *Loving v. Virginia* overturn of antimiscegenation laws (which outlawed marriages between Whites and non-Whites) in the United States.

While interracial marriages can include two non-White partners, much of the literature focuses on White and non-White unions. In recent American history, polls and research studies examining American attitudes about interracial couples have shown an increase in acceptance of interracial marriages, which may also explain the rise in numbers of these unions. The acceptance of interracial unions is much higher for Whites coupled with Hispanics or Asians than for White and Black interracial couples. However, because divisions still exist between races in the United States, couples who partner with someone outside their race may face resistance such as racism, discrimination, and other negative reactions from strangers who do not accept intermarriage. In addition, interracial partners may experience a lack of support or outright rejection from friends and family. For some interracial couples, their family of origin cites their major concern as the potential loss of cultural identity and heritage. Another concern expressed by both friends and family centers on the possibility of the couple's desire to have children and the challenges those children may face growing up being biracial or multiracial.

Marriage and the Family Life Cycle

According to Betty Carter and Monica McGoldrick's family life cycle model, coupling and marriage brings with it a host of celebrations, joys, and struggles. Coupling and marriage involve bringing together two people from two distinct families, each with their own unique set of beliefs, traditions, cultural values, norms, and more. When a couple decides to marry, negotiations related to how to incorporate each of their perspectives into the new family unit begin. Families of origin often have opinions and expectations about topics such as where the couple will live, with whom the couple will spend holidays, and how the couple will raise children (if they should choose to have them). When partners come from two distinct racial groups, these negotiations can become even more complicated, especially if the couple is dealing with disapproval from members in one or both families about their interracial union.

Successfully Navigating Challenges

When both individuals in an interracial couple remain open to their differences and work together to overcome conflict with the families of origin, these marriages are just as successful as homogenous marriages. In addition, interracial couples who find ways to share their histories, to directly deal with issues of difference between them, and to define for themselves what it means to be an interracial couple overcome obstacles both socially and in the family. Just as in homogenous marriages, successful interracial marriages involve open communication and mutual adaptation through the various stages of the couple's relationship and particularly when the couple decides to expand their family with the addition of children.

In addition to open communication, other protective factors for interracial couples include choosing communities and neighborhoods with multicultural families. Interracial couples also find it helpful to join organizations or groups that support mixed marriages. And finally, interracial couples may seek counseling, as a supportive measure for dealing with difficult couple negotiations, and/or challenges with family of origin.

Families With Children

Couples may become interracial families in several ways. Monoracial couples may adopt a child who differs from both parents racially or interracial couples may decide to reproduce biologically or expand their family through adoption. With the addition of children, the interracial couples will face new joys and challenges.

When interracial couples decide to have children, those children become part of a new subgroup of the population known as multiracial individuals. Exploring race and the term *multiracial* is complex. While it does not capture the language or experience of all interracial or interethnic families and children, the term *multiracial* is typically used to describe youth in interracial families who have multiple racial or ethnic heritages. As noted earlier, acceptance of interracial marriages has increased, and so too, has the acceptance of multiracial individuals. In fact, the 2000 U.S. Census was the first time in history multiracial individuals were able to select more than one racial category. In the most recent U.S. census, approximately nine million people selected two or more racial categories and of that number over 40% were under the age of 18, implicating these individuals as the fastest growing minority group among American youth. And while these youth and their families face similar developmental experiences overall, they also face struggles unique to their lived experiences.

Growth in the number of multiracial individuals has raised questions among researchers about the development of multiracial individuals and their families. Researchers have found that single race parents in interracial couples raising multiracial individuals may face some challenges. First, single race parents cannot relate to what it means for their child to belong to his or her own minority racial group. Second, multiracial persons do not fit into any one racial category, so race may be difficult to negotiate for the children and their families because of social pressure related to discrimination and racism. Children in these families may struggle with self-esteem, isolation, feelings of depression, and/or stress. Racial and ethnic socialization (group identification) is a more complex process for multiracial families than for monoracial families.

Racial Socialization Practices and Values

Researchers have noted that the lack of social support interracial couples experience socially often comes down to concerns about the children from these unions. After having children, interracial couples may have to overcome additional challenges, such as new negative reactions from strangers as well new interfamily conflicts or rejection. Interracial couples can work together in their children's racial socialization process by first discussing as a couple what it means to each of them to be a member of their own racial group. They can then communicate with each other about the messages they want to share with their children about their own racial experiences, their experiences as an interracial couple, and what it means to be an interracial family. They can complicate the messages their children receive about race and racial identity if they do not work together to teach their children about race, about what it means to the family to be interracial, and about the possibility of experiencing discrimination and bias socially. It is critical to resolve as a couple how the family will thrive in the face of discrimination or bias.

Racism and Prejudice

Interracial couples and their children may experience racism and prejudice from within the extended family. This can occur in multiple ways. First, if the family has opted to identify interracially and the children in the family identify as multiracial, extended family members may reject the multiracial identification of the child. Interracial couples and their children may also have the experience of not fitting in at family gatherings or being intentionally left out. These incidents can lead to feelings of isolation and prompt the immediate family to distance themselves from their extended family.

Socially, interracial parents and their children may also encounter bias and discrimination from society. The parent of a multiracial child may contend with stares from strangers and inappropriate questions, such as "Is he adopted?" or "Are you the nanny?" in reference to children who appear physically different than their parents and/or siblings. Such experiences may also occur for children in schools, communities, with teachers, peers, and even friends. Interracial families and children may be excluded from social groups or community events. Multiracial children may have difficulty fitting into peer groups at school or in their neighborhood. Additionally, multiracial children may not be accepted or may be criticized for their racial identity choice or for one or more of their racial heritages.

In supportive interracial family environments, discussions about race, racial identity, discrimination, and bias help bolster family members in the face of aforementioned difficulties. Many interracial families take special pride in being a part of a unique family. When families honor their identity as an interracial unit and possess a shared belief system about open communication regarding these topics, they succeed in overcoming the obstacles they face with their families of origin and in society around them. Such experiences contribute to a healthy family identity and facilitate multiracial children's resiliency.

Dana J. Stone

See also Cultural Issues in Couples and Family; Diversity; Ethnicity; Family Life Cycle; Intercultural Marriage and Family; Racism

Further Readings

Berlin, R., & Cannon, H. (2013). *Mixed blessings: A guide to multicultural and multiethnic relationships*. Seattle, WA: Mixed Blessings.

Killian, K. D. (2013). *Interracial couples, intimacy, and therapy: Crossing racial borders*. New York, NY: Columbia University Press.

Laszloffy, T. A. (2008). Therapy with mixed-race families. In M. McGoldrick & K. V. Hardy (Eds.), *Re-visioning family therapy* (pp. 275–285). New York, NY: Guilford Press.

McDowell, T., Ingoglia, L., Serizawa, T., Holland, C., Dashiell, J. W., & Stevens, C. (2005). Raising multiracial awareness in family therapy through critical conversations. *Journal of Marital and Family Therapy, 31*(4), 399–411.

McGoldrick, M., Carter, B., & Garcia-Preto, N. (2011). *The expanded family life cycle: Individual, family, and social perspectives* (4th ed.). Upper Saddle River, NJ: Pearson.

Nadal, K. L., Sriken, J., Davidoff, K. C., Wong, Y., & McLean, K. (2013). Microaggressions within families: Experiences of multiracial people. *Family Relations, 62*, 190–201.

Rockquemore, K. A., & Laszloffy, T. A. (2005). *Raising biracial children*. Lanham, MD: AltaMira.

Root, M. P. P. (2001). *Love's revolution: Interracial marriage*. Philadelphia, PA: Temple University Press.

Seshadri, G., & Knudson-Martin, C. (2013). How couples manage interracial and intercultural differences: Implications for clinical practice. *Journal of Marital and Family Therapy, 39*(1), 45–58.

INTIMACY, SPECIFIC THREATS TO

Intimacy is a multidimensional construct that can be measured in relation to the intellectual, interpersonal, affective, and physical aspects of a relationship. Couple intimacy is often understood in the context of relationship processes, communication patterns, and behavioral themes shared between partners. Discrepancies in partners' perceptions of emotional and sexual aspects of intimacy, when present, directly affect their relationship satisfaction. Perceived opportunities for increasing intimacy and closeness predict greater relationship stability, and stability is essential in achieving intimacy satisfaction between partners. Emotional and sexual aspects of intimacy in romantic relationships are two of the most important correlates of intimacy satisfaction, and these directly influence couple relationship outcomes in distinct ways. First, sexually satisfied partners may not necessarily feel emotionally close, and second, feelings of emotional closeness and connectedness do not guarantee sexual satisfaction. The factors that affect both these areas, and associated areas of partner and relationship intimacy, are diverse. When intimacy is challenged, the partners interpret these challenges as threats and respond either adaptively or react maladaptively based on interpersonal fears, including prior exposure to trauma, a lack of trust, or a perceived betrayal in a prior or in the immediate relationship. This entry examines types of intimacy and how fear, neglect, communication, commitment, and attachment impact intimacy.

Types of Intimacy

There are various forms of intimacy that provide multiple opportunities for partners to build closeness and communication. Mental intimacy involves a mutual understanding of all the important issues in the relationship; this is a cognitive awareness of issues and topics that causes conflict and an intellectual response that addresses this conflict in a way that promotes a return to homeostasis between partners, such as mutually setting goals and developing a plan to achieve them. Spiritual intimacy involves sharing and exploring religious or spiritual foundations and beliefs that contribute to intellectual, altruistic, and intrinsic growth. Emotional intimacy is an essential building block for closeness in a relationship; this involves sharing feelings, identifying and communicating needs, and working together to address various threats to intimacy in healthy, supportive ways.

Sexual intimacy is one of the most important dimensions of healthy relationship intimacy. Healthy sexual intimacy includes establishing a sexual frequency with which both partners are satisfied; engaging in sexual activities that both partners enjoy; the ability to openly talk about sex, sexual preferences, practices, expectations; and a willingness to learn with and from one another. Closeness in romantic relationships can be enhanced through both emotional and sexual communication. Sexual intimacy involves acts of physical union between relationship partners that allow them to connect interpersonally and express their passionate feelings and affection for one another. Sexual encounters that lack open communication, clear boundaries, and identifiable expectations can be a context for negative emotion and rumination. Many individuals are apprehensive to discuss sexual intimacy with their partner out of fear that the partner will react negatively to such intimate topics of conversation; this can result in injured intimacy and evasive communications when discussing these aspects of their intimate relationship.

Fear

Fears of intimacy often originate in childhood and may be related to poor individuation (becoming aware of one's own self) and/or poor attachment (bonding to key people in one's life beginning in infancy) patterns. Fear of intimacy inhibits the open expression of feelings through intellectualization, denial, or rigid beliefs of behavior and responses. And if individuals have experienced trauma in previous relationships, they may feel vulnerable and have unrealistic expectations that jeopardize healthy intimacy in the present relationship. This vulnerability also inhibits the open sharing of thoughts, beliefs, and feelings that build trust in a relationship.

Concurrently, fears of encountering anger or expressing anger are another inhibiting factor to healthy intimacy. Feelings of vulnerability and anger may be interrelated due to previous exposure to abuse, and if left unresolved, these feelings will contribute to the disintegration of intimacy. Healthy relationships include independence, interdependence, and willingness to compromise. However, if a relationship has not yet achieved a depth of intimacy built on trust and an understanding of these healthy attributes, partners may fear losing control and power in the relationship or may fear the overwhelming burden of having too much control in decision-making. This fear results in defensiveness and hypervigilance regarding the other's actions and motivations, which limits the possibility of rewarding risk-taking. One of the greatest fears that inhibits the development and maintenance of emotional and sexual intimacy is the fear of abandonment or rejection. Emotional investments in relationships may represent a greater degree of potential loss and pain should the relationship end. This may cause an individual to avoid closeness.

Neglect

Neglect is one of the most common threats to maintaining closeness and impairing intimacy between partners in a healthy relationship. Neglect can result from each partner dedicating most of their energy away from the relationship and instead concentrating on other areas of life, including children, work, stress-reduction activities, fitness, or other intimate or nonintimate relationships. Couples who fail to invest time and effort into their primary relationship on a consistent basis may create patterns of disconnectedness and perceptions of unimportance or dismissal, leaving each partner feeling less intimate with the other over a duration of time. This disparity of time investment may emerge from unrealistic expectations, which the partner inevitably fails to fulfill, resulting in a diversion of attention from the relationship which may have initially been temporary but evolves into a long-term pattern. Beliefs of entitlement, excessive demands, gender stereotyping, unfounded assumptions, overgeneralizations, and assumptions of ulterior motives are some of the consequences of unrealistic expectations that develop over time, most likely with beginnings in the family of origin. Frustration regarding neglect and related unrealistic expectations creates a chasm in communication between partners, which wears away the resolve of committed partners to creating and maintaining intimacy.

Communication

Interpersonal communication is an important factor to reducing threats to intimacy; healthy communication can facilitate intimacy and a lack of communication impedes intimacy in romantic relationships. Poor or ineffective communication patterns may pose a significant barrier to intimacy. Destructive verbal or nonverbal communication may include defensiveness, evasiveness, cycles of demand–withdrawal, conflictual problem-solving, and offering criticism instead of open feedback. One context in which indirect communication and topic avoidance can be particularly problematic is during the negotiation of sexual intimacy. People are often indirect in negotiating sexual intimacy, especially during the early stages of relationship development when ambiguity and uncertainty are high. Sexual intimacy allows partners to connect interpersonally and express their passionate feelings for one another; thus, indirect communication and sexual topic avoidance may obscure the romantic connection with a partner. Sexual topic avoidance and indirect communication about sex have negative implications for achieving sexual satisfaction. Couples who communicate openly and directly about their sexual relationship tend to be more emotionally, sexually, and ultimately relationally satisfied. This satisfaction results in relationship commitment, which provides consistent opportunities for continued intimacy and connection.

Commitment

Relationship commitment may be defined as the intention to stay with a partner in the long term based on a mutual agreement of trust, sharing, openness, and intimacy. A lack of commitment has been found to be a strong predictor of relationship dissolution. In addition to predicting the length of a relationship, commitment is related to many indicators of relationship quality. Commitment is associated with responding to a partner's negative behaviors with relationship-maintaining behaviors rather than destructive behaviors.

For example, social exchange theory suggests that relationships succeed when resources are shared with equal cost and benefit. This expectation of investment impacts the investment of intimacy by estimating each partner's commitment to exchange communication, trust, and support for the same qualities with the same effort, motivation, and commitment. When applied to the concept of intimacy, partners may perceive a lack of mutual investment as an active threat to their relationship, which will subsequently destabilize a shared trust in the relationship growth process and challenge the commitment of each partner. Commitment is a critical component in relationship stability, and many counseling theories regarding the regulation of emotional investment that are centered on social threat and social reward have been considered as frameworks for understanding commitment processes and their relationship to intimacy. Social threats refer to concerns about negative evaluation and rejection by a relationship partner and social rewards refer to opportunities for intimacy and connection. The absence of threats and the presence of rewards are both important in fulfilling relationship needs and satisfying partner expectations.

Satisfaction of belongingness needs involves both the pursuit of social reward and the avoidance of social threat. Concerns over social threats increase investment into a relationship in an effort to promote a partner's dependence on the relationship. Individuals who excessively worry that their partners see them negatively are exposed to social threats, and consequently, display doubts about their partner's positive perceptions of them resulting in emotional withdrawal from their partner. Individuals who feel inferior to their partner engage in self-sacrificing behaviors in an effort to make themselves more indispensable to their partner; this investment of one's effort into a relationship promotes higher levels of commitment to the partner. Thus, individuals concerned with social threat may not be very satisfied with their partner, but they may be highly invested in the relationship. Social threats have been theorized to play an essential role in the establishment of trust between relationship partners. When people trust their partner, they have confidence that their partner will be responsive to their needs. Trust between partners is essential in the early stages of a relationship, as it provides a sense of safety and security when opening up emotionally and sharing one's feelings with a partner.

Attachment

Adult attachment research shows that attachment security promotes compassion in a relationship, facilitates sensitive and responsive caregiving, and strengthens intimacy. In intimate relationships, attachment styles are differentiated by two types of adult avoidance of intimacy: a fearful, or anxious, style that is characterized by a conscious desire for social contact, but which is inhibited by fears of its consequences, and a dismissing style of attachment, which is characterized by a defensive denial of the need or desire for greater social contact, resulting in an undermined commitment to the relationship. Individuals who are dismissive in attachment style tend to minimize the subjective awareness of a relationship in distress and ignore or minimize the needs of their partner. This contributes to intimacy anxiety between partners, and subsequently, it negatively affects intimacy. This anxiety is exhibited in anxious avoidance. Individuals with an anxious avoidance style of relating will demonstrate strong fears of rejection or abandonment from their partner and will also see themselves as undeserving of the love, respect, and support of their partner.

These styles of attachment affect intimacy in a relationship and may be additionally impacted by an existing attachment to ex-partners. This creates a lack of commitment in current relationships, which stagnates the development of healthy intimacy. A continued desire, either consciously or unconsciously, to invest emotionally in ex-partners following the end of a relationship will promote feelings of sadness, resentment, and anger in one or both partners of the current intimate relationship. This may result in hostile communication and inhibit threat identification and effective collaborative problem-solving. A goal of relationship counseling would be to promote a healthy attachment style with attributes of forgiveness, empathy, and emotional expressiveness. These are all attributes that are present in relationships that value intimacy and demonstrate behaviors aimed at its preservation.

Partners may be differentially invested in their intimate relationship, which results in a blurred perception of real versus imagined threats to shared intimacy. This may be based in attachment style, or it may be a result of an unrealistic assessment of the ability of the couple to overcome challenges that evolve into threats to their intimacy. A strong commitment shared between partners encourages each individual to mutually discern these threats and then engage in proactive problem-solving, collaboration on adaptive solutions to threats and challenges, and negotiating communication styles to accommodate wants and needs in a stable relational style. When helping a couple assess and analyze threats to intimacy, the counselor's goal is to help them develop strong, healthy, collaborative coping skills and problem-solving capabilities, which will lead to realistic expectations, realistic appraisal of strengths, and appropriate communication skills.

Adrianne L. Johnson

See also Acceptance and Commitment Therapy; Attachment-Based Family Therapy; Sexual Intimacy; Trust

Further Readings

Gere, J., MacDonald, G., Joel, S., Spielmann, S. S., & Impett, E. A. (2013). The independent contributions of social reward and threat perceptions to romantic commitment. *Journal of Personality and Social Psychology, 105*(6), 961–977.

Spielmann, S. S., MacDonald, G., & Tackett, J. L. (2012). Social threat, social reward, and regulation of investment in romantic relationships. *Personal Relationships, 19*, 601–622.

Theiss, J. A., & Estlein, R. (2014). Antecedents and consequences of the perceived threat of sexual communication: A test of the relational turbulence model. *Western Journal of Communication, 78*(4), 404–425.

Yoo, H., Bartle-Haring, S., Day, R. D., & Gangamma, R. (2015). Couple communication, emotional and sexual intimacy, and relationship satisfaction. *Journal of Sex & Marital Therapy, 40*(4), 275–293.

Isomorphism

In family therapy and supervision, isomorphism refers to similar processes that occur at several levels of therapy (i.e., between clients in their regular lives, clients and therapists, and therapists and their supervisors). In other words, family dynamics may be replicated by families in therapy (e.g., a couple who refuses to speak to each when angry and opts instead to pass messages to each other through their child may attempt to replicate this behavior with a therapist). Isomorphism grows out of systems theory concepts, in particular the idea that systems, biological and otherwise, are similarly organized with rules, patterns, and hierarchies. Human systems, like families, are no exception. Just as a family contains an inherent structural organization in which the parents are in charge of the children, there is a hierarchy in therapy upon which clients sometimes project their family hierarchy, as in psychoanalysis.

Another explanation for this isomorphism may be that most individuals, in many ways, act the same regardless of their context. Finally, isomorphism in therapy may be a reflection of transference issues, or the supervisor–supervisee relationship mimicking a parent–child relationship in the same way that the therapist–client relationship is thought to mimic a parent–child relationship. This isomorphism can be seen in a variety of contexts from schools to workplaces to government agencies. It becomes therapeutically relevant when therapy and supervision mimic these patterns. This entry examines isomorphism and parallel process, the clinical relevance of isomorphism, isomorphism in supervision, and ethical considerations related to the concept.

Isomorphism and Parallel Process

Isomorphism has its roots in mathematics as well as the psychological concept of parallel process. Parallel process is a concept rooted in the psychoanalytic concepts of transference and countertransference. Transference involves clients' distortions of their therapists based on relationships they have had outside of therapy, while countertransference refers to therapists' distortions of their clients based on their outside relationships. Parallel process involves patterns from therapy sessions replicating themselves in supervision. Isomorphism adds that when these parallel processes occur, there are corresponding similarities for each part of the process, and that changing one of these parallel processes has an impact on another. When a process occurs in supervision that has a parallel in therapy, it typically means that there is a pattern happening, and the therapist is behaving in a manner similar to his or her clients, while the supervisor behaves similarly to the therapist in that he or she can call out the therapist's process. For example, a therapist may be working with a family that is often defensive and resistant to the therapist's ideas. When the therapist approaches his supervisor about this client, the supervisor's suggestions are met with defensiveness and resistance from the therapist.

By addressing the isomorphism and getting the therapist to be less defensive, the supervisor opens a way for the therapist to do the same with his clients. This is consistent with Howard A. Liddle's idea that the difference between isomorphism and parallel processes is that *isomorphism* as a term implies action and intervention, while *parallel processes* as a term is merely descriptive. To that end, isomorphism is often referred to as a clinical and supervisory intervention.

Clinical Relevance of Isomorphism

In therapy, these parallel processes can be both a challenge for clinicians and an important issue for their awareness. For example, if the therapist or the agency replicate the problematic patterns that bring clients into therapy, therapy will not be helpful to the clients. However, if therapists recognize that they could repeat the pattern, they have the opportunity to talk about that pattern and work on changing that pattern in the context of therapy rather than advising the clients on how to do it outside the therapy context. For example, a client might have a problem being too defensive with the other people in her life and that same pattern may also manifest itself in therapy. In such a case, the therapist may have a discussion with the client about the pattern as it occurs. The therapist can mimic people the client interacts with in his daily life and teach the client how to work through the issue in a real relationship.

In some cases, isomorphism can be positive insofar as it can help therapists work with clients on issues that are particularly relevant to why they are in therapy. In other cases, therapists may mimic the destructive patterns that reinforce the issues for which clients have come into therapy. A typical example is a client whose pattern is seeking external validation from others, rather than making an autonomous decision. A well-meaning therapist may replicate that pattern by responding when the client questions what she should do rather than helping the client increase her own autonomy by supporting her to make her own decision.

Isomorphism in Supervision

In supervision, isomorphism can be viewed as both a guiding conceptual framework and an intervention process. Conceptually, isomorphism is observed in each part of the supervisory relationship. Supervisors operate from some theory of supervision, by which they believe that knowledge and skills are transferred from them to their supervisees, similar to a therapist's theory of change. Isomorphism suggests that a supervisor's theory of supervision will be similar to his theory of change and that the processes of supervising a trainee will correspond to the processes of therapy. This provides a framework for supervision and a congruence between the therapy and supervision. Further, speaking about isomorphic patterns can take the pressure off the supervisory relationship by talking about the client–therapist relationship rather than the therapist–supervisor relationship.

There have been very few empirical studies of isomorphism. However, supervisors who were asked about isomorphism in supervision described isomorphic roles across supervision and therapy as follows: that the roles are consistent in both and are developed along a similar trajectory. Isomorphism as a supervisory intervention may involve the supervisor identifying isomorphic processes that occur in supervision and therapy and changing those processes in supervisions, where they have direct influence, in an effort to alter those same processes in therapy. The existing studies of isomorphism in supervision have found that while the majority of supervisors—including those who do not use isomorphism in their supervision—recognize isomorphism between therapy and supervision, they also recognize the limitations of isomorphism. Namely, they recognize that discussing each isomorphic interaction is impractical and that it is important to recognize that supervision and therapy are not the same thing.

Ethical Considerations

One of the important findings of research on isomorphism in supervision is supervisors' recognition of key differences between therapy and supervision. Particularly, most supervisors acknowledge that it is not their place to be their supervisees' therapists. Some supervisors may shy away from using an isomorphic lens altogether to avoid the appearance of a dual relationship. Others acknowledge that while isomorphism can be helpful in dealing with the supervisor–supervisee relationship, when supervision delves into the supervisee's personal issues, it is ethical for the supervisor to suggest that the supervisee seek his or her own therapy for those issues rather than to discuss them with their supervisors.

Megan Oka

See also Supervision; Supervision of Supervision; Supervision Theories; Training and Licensure

Further Readings

Liddle, H. A., & Saba, G. W. (1983). On context replication: The isomorphic relationship of training and therapy. *Journal of Strategic and Systemic Therapies, 2*(2), 3–11.

Liddle, H. A., & Saba, G. W. (1985). The isomorphic nature of training and therapy: Epistemologic foundation for a structural-strategic training paradigm. In J. Schwartzman (Ed.), *Families and other systems: The macrosystemic context of family therapy* (pp. 27–47). New York, NY: Guilford Press.

White, M. B., & Russell, C. S. (1997). Examining the multifaceted notion of isomorphism in marriage and family therapy supervision: A quest for conceptual clarity. *Journal of Marital and Family Therapy, 23*(3), 315–333.

JOB LOSS

Job loss is defined as the unplanned termination of employment. This may occur when an employee is terminated for cause due to perceptions of inappropriate behavior, when jobs are eliminated due to restructuring or downsizing on the part of the employer or a business closure, or when a person must resign in order to accompany a significant other in a geographical move. Job loss results in the concurrent negative effects of income loss and family stress. Family adjustment to these effects is correlated with physical and mental health, academic or professional performance, and long-term earning potential for all members of the family. This entry discusses the effects of job loss on the individual, external responses to the individual, and the family system. The entry concludes by exploring some of the potential positive impacts of job loss on the individual and family.

Impact on the Individual

Losing a job, for any reason, comes with significant emotional impact. Many people who lose a job equate the experience to the loss associated with a death. There is typically a feeling of shock when the news is first introduced, followed by sadness, or anger, or both. Losing a job might bring up other losses in a person's life—for example, when they were cut from a sports team for not being good enough. Even in situations where the individual's performance had nothing to do with the separation, feelings of self-doubt and failure can easily creep in. Employment status impacts self-perceptions of identity. For example, "What do you do?" is a common question raised when strangers first meet.

Changes in perceptions of identity are accompanied by financial concerns. Consider a young married couple in which the partner who loses a job is the primary wage earner. The other partner works part-time and stays home with their young baby. The sudden job loss first results in fear of financial loss, but as the reality sets in, the couple realizes that a short-term role reversal may be in order to ensure financial survival. This shift in roles will be new for both of them and will impact the way they see themselves and their family. The more different this is from how each of them imagined, the higher the level of stress. Consider a different kind of family in which a single mom loses her job. She will not be exempt from the grief response of losing a job and will also have to navigate a job search while still caring for her child and trying to fulfill her financial obligations. The financial strain that follows the shock of losing a job makes the grief response more difficult to manage.

The developmental stage of an individual influences the impact of job loss. Consider a new college graduate in a first professional position, terminated due to the closing of a business. She may not have developed the skills to manage the feelings of loss that come with the news. She may lean on friends, family, or counselors to help her process the loss of the dream that she had for her career, but with so much support, she has a high likelihood of finding another position, hopefully one that is similar to or perhaps even better than the first one. This is different than what might be expected from a 60-year-old man who thought he would be retiring soon but who instead is terminated due to the closing of a business. His family may be counting on his financial support, and he may be carrying built-up debt. His chances of reemployment may be reduced due to current skill level, reluctance of employers to hire older workers, his own grief response, or some combination of these factors.

Grieving the loss of a job can take time, and people may vacillate between feeling angry, sad, or even revengeful before they come to a place of acceptance and make a commitment to move forward. This process is complicated by the likelihood that the person will be pressured, from both others and themselves, to find another job as quickly as possible. However, the success of job-searching activities may be impaired by the physical and emotional strain of the grieving process. The lack of success in job searching leads to further feelings of loss and failure. The cycle can lead to depression.

Because stress and anxiety suppress the immune system, job loss survivors may be more prone to sleep disorders, colds and flu, and other illnesses. They, along with those who support them, should engage in specific efforts to monitor their physical, emotional, spiritual, and intellectual wellness. Effective job-searching skills require a keen mind and a strong sense of self in terms of presenting one's qualifications on a resume and in an interview. Since self-confidence may be lowered as a result of job loss, the person may need additional encouragement, guidance with planning, or career and personal counseling.

Influences Outside the Family

People hearing of a friend or neighbor who is suffering job loss might respond in a variety of helpful ways, like offering emotional support, recommending places that might be hiring, and making references to free job search help (e.g., in the local community). They might also respond in unhelpful ways, like ignoring the person (so they don't have to face the possibility that it could easily have been them losing the job), or worse, by talking with each other about the situation instead of talking directly to the person who lost a job.

In many communities, programs exist to help people who have suffered job loss and to help job seekers. For example, some church and nonprofit agencies offer weekly support groups to those who have suffered job loss. In these groups, the attendees might share job leads with one another and also provide emotional support during the job search process. Chambers of commerce frequently sponsor breakfast or lunch mixers, in which members and nonmembers have a chance to hear about a program and get to know each other for the purposes of helping each other in their businesses. These events can serve as worthwhile networking opportunities for job seekers who are ready to actively seek employment.

Individuals suffering job loss sometimes imagine that others think less of them, and sadly, this is sometimes true. Just as when there is a death, friends and supporters eventually feel uncomfortable about how to support the person who has lost a job, and they slowly withdraw from interacting as a way of soothing their own discomfort. For example, the person may not be invited to the monthly dinner with friends, either because the friends don't want to impose another expense on the family or because they don't want things to be awkward. Or perhaps the friends offer in advance to pay, and the job loss survivor declines the invitation, not wanting to feel like he or she is asking for a handout. This social withdrawal, regardless of how it starts, can leave survivors isolated and alone at a time when they need support.

Impact on the Family

Families are more than several individuals living under one roof. Looking through a "systems" lens, anything that upsets the way the system works causes the various parts of the system to function differently, or the entire system could be damaged. Therefore, family members must learn to adjust and adapt to any threats to the family system. Both external and internal threats to the system occur quite regularly over time, and the ability of the family to adapt is directly related to positive outcomes of those threats. Additionally, successfully navigating threats to the system increases family resiliency for navigating future threats. The negative impacts of job loss to the individual have repercussions on the entire family, and these are correlated with financial need. The higher the financial need, the more severe the negative impact. They are also correlated with the number of dependent children living in the house, with negative impact increasing with more children in the home.

Job loss typically results in an immediate need to cut back on expenses. The decision about which expenses to cut can create family conflict, and the longer this decision is delayed, the higher the stress and anxiety levels. This financial tension coupled with the pressure to find a new job can lead to a breakdown in communication, with both partners feeling misunderstood. The job loss survivor feels guilty about losing the job and perhaps defensive about his or her engagement in job search activities. The partner may begin feeling resentful with the passage of time and then guilty about the resentment.

There may be a temporary shift of power in the family until a new job is secured. The stress of the job loss impacts both partners and may be manifested in the form of less patience, more arguing, more frustration, and less intimacy. Feelings of worthlessness or powerlessness on the part of the survivor can lead to decreased sexual desire on the part of both partners and can have long-lasting effects on the dynamics of the relationship. Unsuccessful navigation of job loss can ultimately lead some couples to permanently separate.

There are also significant effects on the children living in the home. Frequently, the stress and worry of younger children is evidenced in declining academic performance or abnormal behaviors at school. Adolescents in the home may feel embarrassed about their situation and may withdraw from their own social networks, stop having friends over, or choose not to catch a ride with a parent for fear of being "found out." This response may be further exacerbated by the responses of outsiders to the family during recovery from job loss. A different form of stress may impact the family if an adult child is forced to move back into the home due to job loss.

Potential Positive Impacts

Individuals who lose a job may see an opportunity to leave a career field they do not enjoy and take time to look more deeply inside themselves and redirect their own career paths. Strong, healthy families may have a positive response to job loss. The family might enjoy much-needed quality time together, a more flexible routine, and more time for the job loss survivor to spend time with the children. The partner may appreciate more help with domestic logistics. Families can come together at the time of the termination and openly discuss their fears and needs as a way of laying the foundation to provide each other with appropriate support.

Additionally, going through a job loss experience might motivate the person and other members of the family to expand their individual and family life preparedness plans. As the world of work continues to evolve, individual employees are becoming more and more like "independent contractors" who are responsible for managing their own careers. This is in opposition to earlier times, when young people started at one company, worked hard with the expectation that the company would take care of them, and stayed there until retirement. Over the years, they might have moved up the ladder of responsibility or might simply have enjoyed the increases in their compensation that came with increased tenure. They felt secure. However, in today's world, it is anticipated that workers may pursue a variety of different careers over their life span and may work at several different jobs within each career. This phenomenon may diminish the shock and pain associated with sudden job loss.

Anita A. Neuer Colburn

See also Career Planning and Couples/Families; Dual-Earner Families; Poverty and Family Development; Support Groups; Work Relationships

Further Readings

Kalil, A. (2005, July/August). Unemployment and job displacement: The impact on families and children. *Ivey Business Journal.* Retrieved from http://iveybusinessjournal.com/publication/unemployment-and-job-displacement-the-impact-on-families-and-children/

Lent, R. W. (2013). Career-life preparedness: Revisiting career planning and adjustment in the new workplace. *Career Development Quarterly, 61,* 2–14.

Spinelli, F., & Godat, L. (2010). Midlife job search: Managing long term unemployment. *Career Planning & Adult Development Journal, 26,* 57–65.

Stevens, A. H. (2012). *Effects of job loss on individuals and families.* Lecture presented at University of California, Davis, Department of Economics. Retrieved from http://uccs.ucdavis.edu/assets/event-assets/event-presentations/a-stevens-presentation

JOINING

Joining is both a process and, in some therapy models, a technique that creates a strong bond between the clinician and clients. The therapist and family join together to form a therapeutic relationship, and that relationship governs the behavior of its members. This process is especially important in couples and family therapy because the clinician has to create a relationship with multiple people; the clinician has to be seen as on each individual's "side" and at the same time on no one's side. Clinicians must maintain a close relationship with each individual and the family system as a whole. Although joining is emphasized to some degree in all approaches, in his structural family therapy (SFT) approach, Salvador Minuchin clearly defined joining as a process and intervention used to create change in a family system. His theoretical framework seeks to alter the family structure within a family system in order to achieve individual change and typically change by the identified patient of the family system. Additionally, within this framework the members of the system also change their interactions with one another. Minuchin emphasizes the role of the therapist, using SFT as a theoretical framework, is to become part of the family system. The therapist joins the family with the goal of changing family organization in such a way that the family members' interactions with one another change, creating a change in the family structure or family system. This entry provides a general overview of joining but particularly focuses on structural therapy. Included are an overview of the history of SFT, an overview of the process of joining, and a description of joining and accommodating as a therapeutic technique. The entry concludes with a discussion of the therapist's use of self.

Different Views of Joining

Joining and Building Rapport

Milan systemic family therapy used the concepts of joining and building rapport to describe the role of the therapist. The inclusion of building rapport as a technique with the Milan systemic family therapy refers to basic counseling skills of reflective and active listening, observation of both the content and the process of what is being communicated by the family, being mindful of the therapist's body language, and other related skills.

The role of the therapist during the process of joining is to maintain a *neutral* position within the family system that does not overtly challenge or change families. Additionally, the role of the therapist is to also take a nonblaming stance by giving directives, using circular questioning, and adopting other indirect forms of intervention. Most significant in the use of joining and building rapport is the therapist's use of curiosity to help navigate reflective open-ended and circular questions asked to the family, which allow the therapist to be observant for openings. The opening opportunities, through either *what* was said or *how* it was said, create space for the therapist to help the family to see their problems in a new way.

Joining and Therapeutic Alliance

Therapeutic alliance refers to the relationship between the therapist and family. The goal for establishing a therapeutic alliance with a family is to foster a process of mutual engagement between the therapist and family and therefore predict positive changes within the family system. The process of developing a therapeutic alliance with a family begins with each family member, individually, and the natural evolution of the relationship extended to the family system as a whole.

Joining can be used to facilitate the process of developing a therapeutic alliance between the therapist and family. Joining with the family system allows the therapist an opportunity to demonstrate to the family his or her understanding of the family and commitment to working with and for them. Additionally, the process of joining (and accommodating) also helps the therapist to identify and articulate his or her understanding of the presenting problem based on the family's perspective of the problem. The use of joining also facilitates the development of the three essential components of therapeutic alliance, the agreed-upon goals and tasks of the therapy process, and the emotional bond between the therapist and family.

The development of a therapeutic alliance between the therapist and family is also compared and contrasted with the process of joining. Similar to joining, a therapist seeks to build a therapeutic alliance with a family by demonstrating nonjudgmental acceptance of the family members and family system, showing empathy toward the expressed concerns of the family and the demonstration of intentional involvement within the family system. However, a therapeutic alliance, unlike the process of joining, is a common factor used in family therapy to determine treatment outcome. It is not limited to being a technique but rather a significant component of the therapy process, despite the use of a particular family therapy model. Moreover, developing a therapeutic alliance does not require the therapist to become a member of the family or establish family membership in an effort to help the family resolve the problem.

Furthermore, the therapist must maintain, throughout the therapy process, a strong therapeutic alliance in order to allow for the ongoing development of the therapeutic relationship. Typically, the use of joining is implemented during the initial stages of the therapeutic process, and additional techniques are used during the working stages. However, there is a need to maintain an ongoing strong therapeutic alliance during the entire therapy process in order to meet treatment goals and foster change within the family system.

History of Structural Family Therapy

Minuchin is credited with being the developer of SFT. Minuchin and his associates experimented with a more active approach to therapy in which they worked with the boys and their families at the Wiltwyck School for Boys and served a population primarily from New York's inner-city communities. *Families of the Slums* was written about the Wiltwyck School experiences and is the first book to present the structural approach to family therapy. Born out of this work with low-socioeconomic-status families, SFT is an active, problem-solving approach to a dysfunctional family context.

SFT is described as a family therapy theory and technique that approaches the individual in his or her social context or family system. Structural treatment is designed to alter the organization of the family structure so that its members can better deal with their own problems. Family structure refers to the way a family is organized into subsystems whose interactions are regulated by interpersonal boundaries. The process of family interactions is like the patterns of conversation at a dinner table. The structure of the family is where family members sit in relation to one another.

Furthermore, the goal of therapy is structural change; problem-solving is a by-product. The therapeutic framework of SFT is grounded in the fundamental belief that when the structure of the family group is transformed, the positions of members in the group are altered accordingly. As a result, the structural change in the family causes individual changes within each family member, creating a healthier family functioning system and resolving the presenting problem, which often serves as the symptom of the overall problem in the family structure or family system. In other words, by adjusting boundaries and realigning subsystems, the therapist changes the behavior and experience of each family member and, as a result, opens alternative patterns of interaction that can modify family structure. Additionally, this model also tends to work with the entire family, and change is viewed as resulting from structural changes in the family, often accomplished in-session through such interventions as joining, enactments, restructuring, and reframing.

The Process of Joining

The process of joining involves the therapist creating a good rapport with family members and the family system and temporarily becoming part of the family system. The therapist joins with the presented structure of the family in order to identify with the family areas for change. This must be viewed as the therapist's approach to working with the family rather than a mere technique, which the therapist has the option to use or not use during the therapy process. The progression and the success of the therapeutic relationship and process are dependent upon the process of joining with the family. If the therapist does not succeed in joining a family system, there is no basis for additional therapy.

The therapist must first disarm defenses and ease anxiety. The therapist and family join to form a new, therapeutic relationship or system, and that relationship or system then governs the behavior of its members. The trust the family gains through the therapist's use of joining contributes to the development of an effective therapeutic relationship between a family therapist, members of the family, and the family as a whole. The therapist and family must be able to form a partnership, in order to address structural changes and transformation in the family system.

First, the family accepts the therapist more openly, making it easier for the therapist to offer assessment observations, suggest areas in need of change, and facilitate interventions to bring about change in the family system. When the therapist joins the family, the process involves the following: (a) the therapist assumes the leadership role of the therapeutic system, (b) the therapist assesses the underlying family structure, (c) the therapist develops therapeutic goals based on that assessment, and (d) the therapist intervenes in ways that facilitate changes in the family system in the direction of those goals. During this process, the therapist hears what the family members identify and discuss as the situation being experienced in the family (i.e., the problem), and the therapist also observes the way that family members relate to the therapeutic relationship and to each other.

Secondly, the therapist joining with the family is responding to events as they occur in the session and making observations and posing questions to the family. Joining allows the therapist to repair or modify the family's functioning so that it can better perform tasks. The therapist starts to point out family patterns and boundaries and discuss observations about which patterns are functional and which are dysfunctional. Based on these areas of assessment, the therapist is able to make a structural diagnosis of what needs to be changed and suggest how change might occur.

Thirdly, joining, also used as an empathic connection, opens the way for family members to begin listening to each other and establishes a bond with the therapist that enables them to accept the challenges to come. Hearing, understanding, and acknowledging each person's account of the family's problem(s) provides information and begins to release family members from the resentment of unheard feelings.

Furthermore, when the therapist joins the family, the use of accommodation must also take place as a combined therapeutic technique. Joining is used when emphasizing actions of the therapist aimed directly at relating to family members and the family system. Accommodation is used when the emphasis is on the therapist's adjustments of himself in order to achieve joining.

Joining and Accommodating

Joining and accommodating is a combined therapeutic technique used in SFT. As the therapist joins the family, there is a need to adapt to the family but also to maintain the position of leadership within the therapeutic unit. The therapist must also make attempts to adapt to (accommodate) the family system in order to be able to enter (join) the system. Joining and accommodating efforts operate to build trust with the family and an atmosphere that is conducive to client sharing of concerns within the family system. When a family feels more secure during the therapeutic process, members are more likely to explore alternative ways of interacting and organizing themselves.

The process of joining and accommodating cannot be one-sided: As the therapist accommodates to join the family, the family must also accommodate to join the therapist. Consequently, the therapist must also maintain the freedom to make interventions that challenge the family organization, forcing its members to accommodate the therapist in ways that will facilitate movement toward the therapeutic goals. The goal of the joining and accommodating therapeutic technique demonstrated by both the therapist and the family system is to create a more effective therapeutic relationship between the two. In order to effect change in the basic structure and interaction of the family, the therapist must be accepted into the family system by gaining the trust of the family. The therapist also shows respect for how the family members operate and interact with each other by accommodating the family's affective system.

One of the most significant components of the process of joining is the therapist becoming a temporary member of the family, which is considered the therapist's use of self. The family system is made up of the family members plus the therapist, and the therapist becomes personally available to the family members as an additional member of the family during the therapeutic process. There is much emphasis placed on the therapist's use of self as a temporary member of the family system.

The Therapist's Use of Self

The therapist emphasizes the aspects of his or her personality and experiences that are in harmony or consistent with the family—thereby probing and testing family structure. There are limitations to this use of self, determined by the therapist's personal characteristics and the characteristics of the family. The individual therapist is required to be mindful of not imposing upon the family system personal responses that can interfere with blending in as a temporary member of the family system. Additionally, the therapist must also understand the difference between objective responses and the responses resulting from his or her own past that are evoked by the current behavior of a member of the family or the family system. In other words, the therapist must guard against demonstrating the internal process of countertransference with the family. The therapist learns to safeguard against countertransference by developing a capacity for passive observation and also retaining the freedom to be spontaneous in experimental probes and responses.

The therapist's use of self, as a temporary family member, is to join the family culture and in so doing, modify and change aspects of the family culture. This role is complex and requires learning and the demonstration of advance skills by the family therapist. The therapist must accept the family's organization and style and blend with them. The sense of belonging to the family is more important than being a separate self. The family therapist must enter a family with open boundaries, in an effort to reach members of the family. If the therapist enters with closed boundaries, it will be very difficult to experience a sense of belonging to the family and an ability to reach family members.

Minuchin and Arthur Freeman, in their later work together, defined three positions of the therapist use of self on a continuum of emotional involvement and supportiveness of the family. The three positions are the close position, the median position, and the disengaged position.

The Close Position

First, the therapist is an active temporary member of the family system. The therapist becomes emotionally involved with the family by reflecting back the family's emotions. This position of involvement confirms the family's feelings and further enhances the ability of the therapist to join with the family.

The Median Position

Secondly, when using the median position, the therapist joins as an active, neutral listener of the family system. The therapist's use of self as an active listener demonstrates attentiveness to help individual family members and the family develop their story. The therapist, in this median position, helps the family elaborate on details of daily routines and behavioral interactions between family members. The use of this position, as an active listener, also allows the therapist to gently direct the family with exploring new behaviors as they are first provided with an opportunity to develop their story.

The Disengaged Position

In the last position, the disengaged position, the therapist plays the role of a distant family member, often referred to as the distant cousin. The therapist's use of self, as a distant family member, stays in a neutral emotional stance while directing interventions to enable change within the family. The therapist's use of self in this position provides the family system with active emotional involvement (the close position) and active listening to facilitate the process of the family exploring new behaviors (the median position). The goal of this last position is for the therapist to create new contexts for behavior and form new interactional patterns within the family system. Additionally, in this position the therapist becomes an active agent of change within the family system.

Joining With a Subsystem

A final consideration of the therapist's use of self is the therapist's option to join with a subsystem within the family system. The joining of a subsystem allows the therapist to see how the system as a whole responds. The goal of joining a subsystem, particularly as a temporary member of the family system, is to see how the other family members respond to the impact of the alliance of the therapist with another subsystem. This is an important aspect of the processing of joining and knowing the family.

Moreover, during the process of joining, which includes the therapist's use of self, the therapist is always set on implementing interventions to change the unhealthy structural patterns of the family, but the goals and strategic methods are all dependent on the effectiveness of the methods of joining with the family. Joining techniques may not always result in the family moving toward achievement of therapeutic goals, but they are successful when the use of the techniques results in the family returning for the next session.

Tracey M. Duncan

See also Structural Family Therapy; Systems, Subsystems, and Metasystems; Systems Theory; Therapeutic Alliance

Further Readings

Mahaffay, B. A., & Lewis, M. S. (2008). Therapeutic alliance directions in marriage, couple, and family counseling. In G. R. Walz, J. C. Bieuer, & R. K. Yep (Eds.), *Compelling counseling interventions: Celebrating VISTAS' fifth anniversary* (pp. 59–69). Ann Arbor, MI: Counseling Outfitters.

Minuchin, S. (1974). *Families & family therapy*. Cambridge, MA: Harvard University Press.

Minuchin, S., & Fishman, H. C. (1981). *Family therapy techniques*. Cambridge, MA: Harvard University Press.

Minuchin, S., Montalvo, B., Guerney, B. G., Rosman, B. L., & Schumer, F. (1967). *Families of the slum*. New York, NY: Basic Books.

Minuchin, S., Nichols, M. P., & Lee, W.-Y. (2007). *Assessing couples and families: From symptom to system*. Boston, MA: Allyn & Bacon.

Nichols, M. P. (2013). *Family therapy: Concepts and methods* (10th ed.). Upper Saddle River, NJ: Pearson.

Piercy, F. P., Sprenkle, D. H., Wetchler, J. L., & Associates. (1996). *Family therapy sourcebook* (2nd ed.). New York, NY: Guilford Press.

Rasheed, J. M., Rasheed, M. N., & Marley, J. A. (2011). *Family therapy: Models and techniques*. Thousand Oaks, CA: Sage.

Winek, J. L. (2010). *Systemic family therapy: From theory to practice*. Thousand Oaks, CA: Sage.

JUVENILE FIRESETTER INTERVENTIONS

Juvenile firesetting is defined as any behavior involving fire, direct or indirect, that lacks adult supervision. The importance of performing juvenile firesetting assessments and interventions cannot be overstated; it poses a threat to life, including the risk of significant burn injury to children, innocent bystanders, family, friends, neighbors, and firefighters. With so much at stake, it is imperative that marriage, family, and couples counselors include juvenile firesetting in their initial intake, screening, and assessment practices. This entry describes the motivations for juvenile firesetting; understanding these motivations is a prerequisite to providing effective therapeutic treatment in counseling. Additional factors such as treatment options and community partnerships are also discussed in this entry. Included in the following section is a basic outline of responsible treatment approaches for performing juvenile firesetting interventions along with a discussion of some of the misperceptions that surround this potentially life-threatening behavior.

What Is Juvenile Firesetting?

Juvenile firesetting is a serious family issue with the strong potential for bodily injury and the loss of life and property. Sometimes referred to as JFIRE, most firesetting incidents go unreported because children are reluctant to take responsibility for setting fires unless an injury occurs or there is a fire department response. Even when parents or guardians become aware of firesetting behavior, many will attempt to conceal this information from authorities to avoid having outside agencies involved in their private family lives.

What Motivates a Child to Set a Fire?

Juvenile firesetting threatens the safety of everyone in the home. It is imperative for family counselors to investigate the underlying motivations for firesetting before performing an intervention. One can accomplish this by communicating with family members at the fire scene, over the phone, or when making the initial appointment. The fire department having jurisdiction may also provide clues as to the nature of the incident and any relevant information such as the time of day, location of the fire, and the names of other youths involved at the fire scene. It is important to pay particular attention to fires in or near structures because these tend to be the most serious. Fires involving bedding, mattresses, and other personal belongings may indicate sexual abuse and require special attention. In such cases, a counselor may consider talking to other sources, such as school counselors, teachers, or outside agencies already involved with the family. Knowing the underlying motivations for youth-related fires will inform one's approach and development of an individualized firesetter intervention.

Misperceptions

Children want to believe that life is fair. Adults often read children stories that reinforce this master narrative of happy endings, good over evil, and right over wrong. When it comes to fire, however, counselors can counter this narrative with "Fire is not fair!" The person responsible for starting a fire is often the first person to escape, leaving family members and innocent bystanders to fend for themselves inside a burning building. Family counselors can capitalize on fictional scenarios by asking child clients to describe how it would feel if something tragic were to happen to a family member as a result of a fire. They can emphasize that unlike other mistakes, fire is very unforgiving and injuries tend to last a lifetime; broken bones return to normal, but burned skin does not. Video games have reset options, but second chances are exceedingly rare in fires. Counselors may also emphasize that the difference between a firesetter who does and does not suffer burn injuries is largely a matter of luck rather than skill.

Another misperception about juvenile firesetters is pyromania. This relatively obscure diagnosis should not be the first thing that comes to mind when counseling children involved with firesetting. As counselors, it is far more productive to investigate whether the family has adequate food, shelter, and clothing.

The Team Approach

The vast majority of juvenile firesetting goes unreported. Parents will tend to deal with the issue on their own to avoid having outside agencies involved in what they see as their personal affairs. Though understandable, this may have the unintended consequence of enabling a youth to continue playing with fire while growing more and more confident with each successive fire. Counselors can interrupt this cycle of repeated firesetting through community activism and education as a caring ally. Fire departments are encouraged to form juvenile firesetter intervention teams and recruit family counselors to assist them. Other team members can include school counselors, teachers, nurses, and parents. Emergency room personnel and ambulance attendants are also potential sources of information and referrals, given their frontline exposure to burn injuries and other behavior that might otherwise remain unreported to family counseling. Juvenile justice personnel are also helpful in mandating youths to intervention or education programs as preventive measures, especially with youths who present with overconfident, risk-taking behaviors. County mental health and social service agencies are also potential team members, proactively making youth referrals before an unfortunate fire event occurs.

Intervention

The intervention begins with the first phone call a parent makes to schedule an appointment for counseling. During this initial contact, counselors can take note of any pertinent factors leading up to the firesetting event. Once the caregivers arrive with their child for counseling, there are several different approaches to intervention, but all of them begin with developing rapport with the child. Counselors can start by inquiring into the child's favorite activities and interests such as sports, hobbies, and social groups. This information will be personally meaningful to the child later on when exploring the consequences of firesetting without the counselor raising his or her voice or casting authority.

After establishing rapport, the counselor can begin asking the youth about the firesetting event(s). This is a crucial aspect of the intervention. If the youth does not feel comfortable sharing this, it may be necessary to work harder to establish a trusting relationship. It is also helpful to use silence rather than asking additional probing questions. Once the youth begins to explain the circumstances surrounding a fire, counselors should be careful not to put words into the child's mouth and remain watchful for the underlying motivations that arise. Paying attention to the youth's general demeanor—body language, posture, tone of voice, volume, and the ability to describe the fire—yields valuable information. For the majority of youths, firesetting is an indication of curiosity or boredom, especially when left unsupervised for prolonged periods of time. If this is the case, as oftentimes it is, then the intervention involves interrupting the cycle of overconfidence surrounding firesetting by introducing stories (and graphic photos if desired) in describing other youths who have similar backgrounds, abilities, and interests who differ only in the context that they became burned or were the cause of other people's injuries. The overarching message remains: Fire is not fair.

Counselors can be creative in responding to the unique needs of these youths. Many intervention specialists use graphic photographs of burn victims the same age and gender as the client and discuss the circumstances leading up to the fire that caused the injury. They may ask clients to explain what they think the youth in the photograph would like to share with them, based on their experience with firesetting. Many youths respond well to this technique and will give heartfelt answers, demonstrative of their personal connection to the youth in the narratives or photos. This educational component may reveal that clients have never fully realized the possibility that they might contribute to the loss of life for a family member, a neighbor, or even a firefighter responding to the scene.

At this time, it may be also helpful to share the legal implications for these unintentional but very real consequences of firesetting. Counselors can share with the youth that the information in this intervention is educational, but if they leave and start another fire, the counselor will have on record that this was a family concern; notably, in such cases, the counselor may be called to testify in court, which is not something one wants to happen. As such, make sure to ask how the child gained access to matches, a lighter, or smoking material. This may reveal the need for caregivers or older siblings to make adjustments as part of the collaborative intervention strategy.

Other youths use firesetting to garner attention from peers. For this group, counselors may consider using photographs of a youth left behind by friends who escaped a fire. A counselor may also educate juvenile firesetters in the context that when it comes to fire, people will save themselves. Role-playing strategies are sometimes helpful to practice with a youth motivated by peer pressure to learn how to walk away from dangerous situations without losing face and how to report the dangerous activities to an adult. This approach can lead to discussing the difference between healthy friendships and unhealthy, dangerous friendships. Caregivers can be very helpful in reinforcing this point. It may also be useful to give caregivers an opportunity to share their feelings about certain friends who may be contributing to firesetting behaviors.

At the conclusion of the intervention, some counselors will use an informal assessment or short-answer quiz to gauge the program effectiveness. The counselor can tailor this assessment to reflect the individual age and development level of each client and intervention. The counselor can also ask the youth to explore and describe feelings associated with firesetting and any final thoughts about the intervention in a personal narrative. Family counselors may even ask the child to help create a message to share with other children who may be thinking about setting fires in hopes of preventing this.

Firesetter interventions typically last anywhere from one to two hours, depending on the individual needs of the family and their level of engagement with the counseling process. For difficult cases, referring youths to other agencies may become necessary, preferably in collaboration with caregivers. Sometimes it may be appropriate to point out that the parents or guardians have taken time from their busy schedules to attend the counseling intervention out of concern for the safety of their child. Family counselors can ask the youth to share feelings with family members about this level of commitment to family safety as a means for caring and closure. These can be meaningful dialogues that demonstrate the child's new appreciation for the consequences of firesetting and the concern of the family for their safety.

Other Considerations

Juvenile firesetting involves responsible family counseling. Never allow a parent to merely drop off and pick up a youth for an intervention, because fire poses a serious threat to everyone in the home and requires parental involvement. In addition, family counselors should ensure that caregivers have working smoke detectors with a signed promise to keep and maintain them. Some fire departments will provide smoke detectors for little or no cost, even installing them as part of their public service. Family counselors can take advantage of these local programs and services as part of case planning.

Some states have arson laws that prosecute youths involved in firesetting. It is imperative that the counselor becomes familiar with these factors as part of the educational component you provide to a family in counseling. Counselors should also be at least familiar with community fire prevention and education, easily obtained at most local fire departments or state fire academies.

Michael B. Drew

See also Assessment, Biopsychosocial; Child-Centered Parenting; Duty to Warn and Protect; No-Harm Contracts; Rule-Setting

Further Readings

Arnlund, M. (1998). *Evaluating the effectiveness of a juvenile firesetter program.* Emmitsburg, MD: National Fire Academy, U.S. Fire Administration.

Franklin, G. A., Pucci, P. S., Arbabi, S., Brandt, M. M., Wahl, W. L., & Taheri, P. A. (2002). Decreased juvenile arson and firesetting recidivism after implementation of a multidisciplinary prevention program. *Journal of Trauma and Acute Care Surgery, 53*(2), 260–266.

Grolnick, W. S., Cole, R. E., Laurenitis, L., & Schwartzman, P. (1990). Playing with fire: A development assessment of children's fire understanding and experience. *Journal of Clinical Child Psychology, 19*(2), 128–135.

Klein, J. J., Mondozzi, M. A., & Andrews, D. A. (2008). The need for a juvenile fire setting database. *Journal of Burn Care & Research, 29*(6), 955–958.

Schwartzman, P., Expert, D. T. C., Fineman, K., Mieszala, P., Gross, C., Baer, M., . . . Slavkin, M. L. (n.d.). *Juvenile Firesetter Intervention Project.* Fairport, NY: National Association of State Fire Marshals.

Schwartzman, P., Fineman, K., Slavkin, M., Mieszala, A. P., Gross, C., Spurlin, B., & Baer, M. (n.d.). *A comprehensive discussion of treatment, service delivery, and training of providers.* Fairport, NY: National Association of State Fire Marshals.

Slavkin, M. L., & Fineman, K. (2000). What every professional who works with adolescents needs to know about firesetters. *Adolescence, 35,* 759–773.

Willis, M. L. (2006). *The Juvenile Firesetter Program in the District of Columbia Fire and Emergency Medical Services Department: Leading community risk reduction.* Washington, DC: District of Columbia Fire and Emergency Medical Services.

KINSHIP CARE

Kinship care is defined as informal custodial care for children (typically grandchildren) due to parental hardship or absence. This is largely because child protection authorities increasingly favor kinship care—in particular care by grandparents—when children are considered unable to remain safely with their birth parents and because of the concerted advocacy of grandparents and the organizations representing them. Approximately 2.4 million grandparents and extended family members are raising more than 6 million children in the United States. This entry examines the typical types of kinship care and the reasons for and costs and benefits of this type of care. This entry also examines legislation related to kinship care.

Grandfamily

Grandfamily, or *grandfamilies*, are relatively new terms that have been coined to refer to families where grandparents, great-grandparents, or other relatives assume the primary role of caregiver for a child (or children) whose biological parents are unable (or unwilling) to do so. According to the U.S. Census Bureau, since 2000, the number of children living with their grandparents has increased by 50%. Five percent (or approximately 7.1 million) of all children are living in households headed by their grandparents. Eighty-two percent of these grandchildren are under the age of 18. This phenomenon is not new. In many Western contexts, grandparents have historically played a major role in the lives of their grandchildren, including as full-time caregivers during times of family crisis. In some cultures, it is even common for grandparents to play a major and continuing role in the raising of grandchildren whether or not the birth family is in crisis.

Informal and Formal Kinship Care

Terms such as *kinship care* or *kin care* refer to grandparents or other relatives providing primary care for a child or children and may also include nonblood adults (i.e., godparents or close family friends) with whom the child has a family-like relationship. In most states, there are two types of kinship care agreements: informal (private) or formal (public). In an informal, or private kinship care arrangement, grandparents or other relative caregivers have physical custody of the child or children and are the primary care providers; however, there is no legal relationship established between the grandparents or relative caregiver and the child, such as guardianship or legal custody. The majority of children living with their grandparent(s) or other relative caregivers are in informal kinship care arrangements, and these "kin" care for the child or children without involvement of the child welfare system. Thousands more grandparents are raising their grandchildren as a result of private family arrangements that may not be officially recorded with child protection authorities. The reasons for placement with relatives/kinship caregivers and with foster caregivers include substantiated orders for protection because of children's neglect and/or abuse, family violence, irretrievable breakdown in the relationship between children and parents, and the unwillingness or inability of parents to care adequately for their children, which may arise from mental illness or alcohol or drug misuse. Grandparent-headed households were one of the fastest-growing U.S. family groups in the year 2010. At the time, 5.8 million children younger than 18 were living with grandparents compared with only 4.5 million children in 2000. This phenomenon is taking place not only in the United States but in other countries as well. For example, Canada experienced a 20% increase in children living with their grandparents between 1991 and 2001.

There are certain groups of people who are disproportionately more likely to be raising their grandchildren in the United States. Nine percent of African American children and 6% of Latino children younger than 18 live with grandparents compared with 4% of non-Hispanic White children and 3.3% of American Indian or Alaska Native children. More research is needed to understand the disproportionate number of African American and Latino children being raised by grandparents. Cultural differences, economic factors, and access to social services may account for the difference.

Reasons for Kinship Care

The reasons older adults take a grandchild into the home without his or her parents varies among countries, groups, and individuals. For example, the growing number of skipped-generation homes in Kenya relates to the increasing number of orphans due to the HIV/AIDS epidemic. In the United States, studies have shown that there are various reasons for grandparent caregiving, such as biological parents' incarceration, unemployment, death, mental illness, divorce, abuse, neglect or abandonment, substance abuse, teenage pregnancy, and most recently, military involvement and obligations.

In China, the phenomenon is on the rise due to an increase in the number of people working far from home, leaving grandparents to care for grandchildren. Interestingly, this phenomenon seems to leave grandparents with increased well-being, possibly because it is seen as a status symbol to have family members earning money away from home. Nevertheless, it indicates a breakdown in the traditional family roles and the family nuclei.

Caregiving in Middle and Old Age

Several studies have been carried out that conceptualize the kinship care phenomenon from a life-span developmental perspective and seek to discover how caregiving alters the usual course of middle and old age. Research has found that as a result of taking on a parenting role later in life, caregivers experience disruptions in plans and expectations for mid or late life, a loss of control relating to retirement, and effects on their independence, financial security, privacy, leisure, and social supports. In some cases, older caregivers also experience diminished self-esteem and a lower self-image. Grandparents feel a tie to their grandchildren and usually volunteer to assume a caregiving role when the parents are no longer able to care for the children in question. In so doing, the course of their lives changes. They are caring for young children at a time when they have more health concerns and problems, and they are sacrificing what might have been their time for retirement. In addition, there are differences in the roles of traditional grandparent and parent. Grandparents caring for their grandchildren have to take on the role of both nurturer and disciplinarian (rather than just nurturer) and also may have to take on the financial responsibility of paying to care for children. Furthermore, for older grandparents there may be a deterioration in their friendships as a result of not being able to join in retirement and leisure activities that are typically enjoyed in one's elderly years.

Rewards and Benefits

Despite the hardships and sacrifices, most kin caregivers still make a commitment to raising their grandchildren. Several studies found that grandparents also derived positive rewards from the experience of caregiving. Among other benefits is the reward of feeling needed and valued, which adds meaning to one's life. Many kin caregivers reported feeling decreased anxiety once their grandchildren were with them, since they worried less about their safety and whereabouts. Grandparents described how caring for their grandchildren gave them a renewed sense of purpose for living. Other grandparents felt that being able to find meaning in the caregiving situation helped to minimize the negative effects and sacrifices they had made to raise their grandchildren. Some of the grandparents reported that their physical and emotional health actually improved after their caregiving began. Many caregivers reported taking tremendous pride in their grandchildren's accomplishments and felt that it was a measure of their own success when their grandchildren did well in school or achieved significant milestones.

Legislation

The Fostering Connections to Success and Increasing Adoptions Act was passed by the United States Congress and signed into law by President George W. Bush in October 2008. It promoted creating permanent families through relative guardianship. The act also included funding for individual states to establish kinship navigator programs to educate kin caregivers about the programs and services available in their specific communities. The central role of the kinship navigator is to provide information and referrals concerning access to legal services, child care, and financial services. They help navigate the formal support system with a specific focus on increasing awareness of services and providing assistance with clarifying eligibility procedures as stated by the Grandfamilies State Law and Policy Resource Center (Grandfamilies.org). With the 2006 Reauthorization of the Older Americans Act, grandparents and other relatives 55 years of age and older providing care to children under the age of 18 are now also eligible to receive services through the National Family Caregiver Support Program (NFCSP).

Challenges

The challenges facing grandparents who are raising their grandchildren have been the subject of much research. Financial problems have been widely documented, with many grandparent caregivers living below the poverty line. Grandparents' physical and emotional health problems have also been frequently reported in studies conducted in Australia and elsewhere. These problems include exhaustion, high levels of stress, anxiety, and depression. Housing and accommodation difficulties have also been identified as a concern, particularly if retired grandparents have moved out of the family home into smaller accommodations unsuitable for a growing family. Social isolation and inadequate support have also been frequently reported. Furthermore, there is the stress of parenting a new generation of children whose cultural norms and values have greatly changed. Finally, for many grandparents, there are the demands of caring for children who may have significant behavioral challenges as a result of their exposure to family trauma, abuse, or neglect.

Shirlyn M. Garrett-Wilson

See also Active Parenting; Adoption; Adoptive Families; African American Families; Aging and Caregiving; Family Life Cycle; Family Reconstruction; Foster Children

Further Readings

Annie E. Casey Foundation. (2012). *Kids count policy report. Stepping up for kids: What government and communities should do to support kinship families.* Retrieved from http://www.aecf.org/~/media/Pubs/Initiatives/KIDS%20COUNT/S/SteppingUpforKids2012PolicyReport/SteppingUpForKidsPolicyReport2012.pdf

Boetto, H. (2010). Kinship care: A review of issues. *Family Matters, 85,* 60–67.

Dunne, E. G., & Kettler, L. J. (2006). Social and emotional issues of children in kinship foster care and stressors on kinship carers: A review of the Australian and international literature. *Children Australia, 31*(2), 22–29.

Dunne, E. G., & Kettler, L. J. (2007). Grandparents raising grandchildren in Australia: Exploring psychological health and grandparents' experience of providing kinship care. *International Journal of Social Welfare, 17*(4), 333–345.

Farmer, E. (2009). Making kinship care work. *Adoption and Fostering, 33*(3), 15–27.

Fuller-Thompson, E., & Minkler, M. (2001). American grandparents providing extensive care to their grandchildren: Prevalence and profile. *Gerontologist, 41*(2), 201–209.

Generations United: http://www.gu.org

Gleeson, J. P., & Seryak, C. M. (2010). I made some mistakes . . . but I love them dearly: The views of parents of children in informal kinship care. *Child and Family Social Work, 15,* 87–96. doi:10.1111/j.1365-2206.2009.00646x

Goodman, C. G. (2007). Intergenerational triads in skipped-generation grandfamilies. *The International Journal of Aging and Human Development, 65*(3), 231–258.

Grandfamilies.org: http://grandfamilies.org/HOME.aspx

Grinstead, L. N., Leder, S., Jensen, S., & Bond, L. (2003). Review of research on the health of caregiving grandparents. *Journal of Advanced Nursing, 44*(3), 318–326.

Hicks-Patrick, J., & Hayslip, B. (2003). *Working with custodial grandparents.* New York, NY: Springer.

Hill, R. B. (2008). Gaps in research and public policies. *Child Welfare, 87*(2), 359–367.

Jackson, B. (2011). Grandparents raising grandchildren: CWLA launches an initiative to celebrate kinship care. *Children's Voice,* May/June, 28–32.

Koh, E., & Testa, M. F. (2008). Propensity score matching of children in kinship and nonkinship foster care: Do permanency outcomes still differ? *Social Work Research, 32*(2), 105–116.

Mackintosh, V. H., Myers, B. J., & Kennon, S. S. (2006). Children of incarcerated mothers and their caregivers: Factors affecting the quality of their relationship. *Journal of Child and Family Studies, 15*(5), 581–596. doi:10.1007/s10826-006-9030-4

Minkler, M. (1999). Intergenerational households headed by grandparents: Contexts, realities, and implications for policy. *Journal of Aging Studies, 13*(2), 199–218.

Poehlmann, J. (2003). An attachment perspective on grandparents raising their very young grandchildren: Implications for intervention and research. *Infant Mental Health Journal, 24*(2), 149–173.

Purcal, C., Brennan, D., Cass, B., & Jenkins, B. (2014). Grandparents raising grandchildren: Impacts of lifecourse stage on the experiences and costs of care. *Australian Journal of Social Issues* (Australian Social Policy Association), 49(4), 467–488.

Shakya, H. B., Usita, P. M., Eisenberg, C., Weston, J., & Liles, S. (2012). Family well-being concerns of grandparents in skipped generation families. *Journal of Gerontological Social Work, 55*(1), 39–54. doi:10.1080/01634372.2011.620072

Williams, M. N. (2011). The changing roles of grandparents raising grandchildren. *Journal of Human Behavior in the Social Environment, 21*(8), 948–962. doi:10.1080/10911359.2011.588535

Winokur, M., Holtan, A., & Valentine, D. (2009). Kinship care for the safety, permanency, and well-being of children removed from the home for maltreatment. *Campbell Systematic Reviews,* no. 1. doi:10.4073/csr.2009.1

The SAGE Encyclopedia of Marriage, Family, and Couples Counseling

Editorial Board

Editors
Jon Carlson
Adler University

Shannon B. Dermer
Governors State University

Managing Editors
Brenna R. Frayn
Governors State University

Katie Paulson
Governors State University

Editorial Board

James Robert Bitter
East Tennessee State University

Scott Browning
Chestnut Hill College

William J. Doherty
University of Minnesota

Leslie Greenberg
York University

Katherine M. Helm
Lewis University

Alan J. Hovestadt
Western Michigan University

Jay Lebow
Northwestern University

Susan H. McDaniel
University of Rochester

Fred P. Piercy
University of Vermont

Robert L. Smith
Texas A&M–Corpus Christi

The SAGE Encyclopedia of Marriage, Family, and Couples Counseling

Volume 3

Editors

Jon Carlson
Adler University

Shannon B. Dermer
Governors State University

FOR INFORMATION:

SAGE Publications, Inc.
2455 Teller Road
Thousand Oaks, California 91320
E-mail: order@sagepub.com

SAGE Publications Ltd.
1 Oliver's Yard
55 City Road
London, EC1Y 1SP
United Kingdom

SAGE Publications India Pvt. Ltd.
B 1/I 1 Mohan Cooperative Industrial Area
Mathura Road, New Delhi 110 044
India

SAGE Publications Asia-Pacific Pte. Ltd.
3 Church Street
#10-04 Samsung Hub
Singapore 049483

Acquisitions Editor: Andrew Boney
Editorial Assistant: Jordan Enobakhare
Developmental Editor: Sanford Robinson
Production Editor: Tracy Buyan
Reference Systems Manager: Leticia Gutierrez
Copy Editors: Diane DiMura, Talia Greenberg, Megan Markanich, Terri Lee Paulsen, Gretchen Treadwell
Typesetter: C&M Digitals (P) Ltd.
Proofreaders: Lawrence W. Baker, Caryne Brown, Sarah Duffy, Scott Oney
Indexer: David Luljak
Cover Designer: Candice Harman
Marketing Manager: Leah Watson

Copyright © 2017 by SAGE Publications, Inc.

All rights reserved. No part of this book may be reproduced or utilized in any form or by any means, electronic or mechanical, including photocopying, recording, or by any information storage and retrieval system, without permission in writing from the publisher.

All trade names and trademarks recited, referenced, or reflected herein are the property of their respective owners who retain all rights thereto.

Printed in the United States of America

Library of Congress Cataloging-in-Publication Data

Names: Carlson, Jon, editor. | Dermer, Shannon B., editor.

Title: The SAGE encyclopedia of marriage, family, and couples counseling / editors, Jon Carlson, Shannon B. Dermer.

Other titles: Encyclopedia of marriage, family, and couples counseling

Description: Thousand Oaks, California : SAGE Publications, Inc., [2016] | "A SAGE Reference publication." | Includes bibliographical references and index.

Identifiers: LCCN 2016025752 | ISBN 9781483369556 (hardcover : alk. paper)

Subjects: | MESH: Psychotherapy, Group | Counseling | Interpersonal Relations | Family Relations | Encyclopedias

Classification: LCC BF636.7.G76 | NLM WM 13 | DDC 158.3/5—dc23
LC record available at https://lccn.loc.gov/2016025752

This book is printed on acid-free paper.

16 17 18 19 20 10 9 8 7 6 5 4 3 2 1

Contents

Volume 3

List of Entries *vii*

Reader's Guide *xv*

Entries

L	*941*	P	*1191*
M	*999*	Q	*1349*
N	*1133*	R	*1361*
O	*1173*		

List of Entries

Acceptance and Commitment Therapy
Acculturation
Active Parenting
Adjustment Disorder in Adolescents
Adlerian Family Therapy
Adlerian Open-Forum Family Counseling
Adolescent Behavior Disorders
Adolescent Behavior Problems
Adolescent Mental Health
Adoption
Adoption, Cross-Cultural and Interracial
Adoptive Families
Adult Attachment Assessments
Adult Development
Affect Regulation
African American Families
Aging and Caregiving
Alcohol and Substance Abuse
American Association for Marriage and Family Therapy
Anger Management
Anxiety
Anxiety Disorders in Adolescents
Asian American Families
Assertiveness
Assessment, Biopsychosocial
Assessment, Suicide
Assimilation: Immigrants and Refugees
Attachment
Attachment and Adolescents
Attachment and Health
Attachment and Romantic Love
Attachment Styles
Attachment Theory
Attachment-Based Family Therapy
Attention-Deficit and Disruptive Behavior Disorders

Attunement, Clinician
Attunement in Relationships
Authoritative Parenting
Autism and Children
Autism Spectrum Disorder
Avoidance

Behavioral Family Therapy
Beliefs and Values
Bereavement
Bereavement Counseling
Best Interests of the Child
Bibliotherapy. *See* Self-Help
Bilingual Families
Birth Control and Contraception
Blended Families. *See* Stepfamilies
Body Dysmorphic Disorder in Adolescents
Bonding
Boundaries
Bowen Family Systems Theory
Brief Adlerian Couples Therapy
Brief Family Therapy

CACREP. *See* Competency-Based Standards for Marriage, Couple, and Family Counseling; Council for Accreditation of Counseling and Related Educational Programs
Career Planning and Couples/Families
Caregivers
Certified Family Life Educator
Chaos Family Therapy
Child Behavior Problems
Child Guidance Movement
Child Maltreatment
Child Protective Services
Child-Centered Parenting
Childhood Anxiety

viii   List of Entries

Childhood Obesity, Prevention and Treatment of
Childless Couples
Child–Parent Relationship Therapy
Children With Chronic Illness
Children With Special Needs in Family Therapy
Choice Theory and Reality Therapy
Chosen Families
Chronic Illness With Couples and Families
Cinematherapy
Circular Questions. *See* Questions: Open, Closed, and Circular
Circularity and Linearity
Circumplex Model
Clinical Case Conceptualization With Couples and Families
Clinical Interviews With Couples and Families
Clinical Practice
Clinical Versus Statistical Significance
Clinician-Directed, Solution-Focused Supervision
Cognitive Maps and Couples
Cognitive-Behavioral Couples Therapy
Cognitive-Behavioral Family Therapy
Cohesion
Collaborative Couples Therapy
Collaborative Language Systems
Collaborative Therapy. *See* Collaborative Language Systems
Commitment
Common Factors
Communication Disorders
Communication Errors/Problems in Couples and Families
Communication in Couples and Families
Community Programs
Compassion
Competency-Based Standards for Marriage, Couple, and Family Counseling
Complementary and Symmetrical Relationships
Compulsive Sexual Behavior
Conduct Disorder
Confidentiality
Conflict in Couples and Families
Conflict Resolution
Conflict Styles
Confrontation

Conjoint Family Therapy
Constructivism
Contextual Family Therapy
Core Competencies for Marriage and Family Therapists
Cost–Benefit Analysis
Cotherapy Team
Council for Accreditation of Counseling and Related Educational Programs
Couple and Family Forensics
Couple Development
Couples, Quality Time
Couples and Marriage Counseling
Couples Therapy Research
Court-Mandated Clients
Crisis Intervention With Couples and Families
Critical Theory
Crucible
Cultural Issues in Couples and Families
Custody Evaluations
Cutting/Self-Mutilation. *See* Self-Injury
Cybernetics

Dating Coaching
Dating Relationship Dissolution
Death, Parents of Deceased Children
Death and Dying
Debt and Financial Strain
Decision-Making
Delphi Research Method
Depression in Adolescents
Depression in Children
Depression in Couples and Families
Developmental Model of Marriage
Differentiation
Discernment Counseling
Disinhibited Social Engagement Disorder in Children
Diversity
Divorce and Separation
Divorce Therapy
Domestic Violence
Double Bind Theory
DSM and V-Codes
Dual and Multiple Relationships

Dual-Earner Families
Duty to Warn and Protect

Earned Attachment
Eating Disorders
Ecological Systems
Eco-Map
Ecosystemic Structural Family Therapy
Ecosystems Perspective
Effectiveness Research
Elder Abuse
Elimination Disorders in Children
Emotional Disengagement
Emotional Intelligence, Children
Emotional Intelligence, Families
Emotionally Focused Therapy for Couples
Empathy
Empirically Validated Models
Empowerment in Families
Enactments
Engendering Hope
Entitlement
Epistemology in Family Therapy
Equine-Assisted Family Therapy
Erectile Disorder
Ericksonian Family Therapy
Ethical Codes
Ethical Decision-Making
Ethnicity
Evidence-Based Practice With Couples and Families
Experiential Family Therapy
Externalizing Behaviors
Extramarital Affairs and Infidelity

Faith-Based Therapy
Families and Poverty
Families and Substance Abuse
Family and Medical Leave Act of 1993
Family Assessment, Models of
Family Life Cycle
Family Life Educators
Family Mediation
Family Mode Deactivation Therapy
Family Myth
Family of Origin

Family Reconstruction
Family Resilience
Family Resource Management
Family Rituals
Family Strengths
Family Stress
Family Stress Adaptation Theory
Family Values
Feedback. *See* Positive and Negative Feedback
Female Orgasmic Disorder
Female Sexual Interest/Arousal Disorder
Feminist Family Therapy
Feminization of Poverty
Fetishes
Fidelity
First-Order Change
Focal Family Therapy
Forgiveness
Foster Children
Friendship
Functional Assessment and Children
Functional Family Therapy
Functionalism
Fusion

Gambling, Compulsive
Gender- and Culture-Sensitive Therapies
Gender Dysphoria
Gender Issues
Gender Orientation, Gender Identity, and Gender Expression
Gender Roles
General Systems Theory
Genito-Pelvic Pain/Penetration Disorder
Genograms
Gestalt Family Therapy
Goals, Treatment
Gottman Method Couples Therapy
Grief Counseling
Group Family Therapy
Group Parenting Classes

Health Issues
Healthy Marriage and Responsible Fatherhood
Hierarchy
HIPAA Standards

Hispanic Healthy Marriage Initiative
Hoarding
Holism
Home-Based Therapy
Homelessness
Homelessness and Youth
Homeostasis
Homework Assignments in Therapy
Homicide
Hope-Focused Approach to Couple Enrichment in Counseling
Hospice
Human Sexual Response
Humanistic Family Therapy
Hypnosis
Hypothesis, Systemic

IAMFC. *See* International Association of Marriage and Family Counselors
Identified Patient
Imago Relationship Therapy
Immigrant Families
Incest
Individual and Family Development
Individual Family Culture
Individual Versus Family Therapy
Infertility
Informed Consent for Research
Informed Consent in Clinical Work
In-Law Relationships
Integrating Systemic and Individual Theories
Integrative Couples Therapy
Intellectual Disability and Autism
Intercultural Marriage and Family
Intergenerational Loyalty
Intergenerational Trauma
Intermittent Explosive Disorder in Adolescents
Internal Family Systems Model
International Association of Marriage and Family Counselors
International Classification of Diseases (ICD)
International Family Therapy
Interpersonal Neurobiology, Attachment and
Interpersonal Neurobiology, Couples and
Interpersonal Neurobiology, Parenting and
Interpersonal Violence
Interracial Marriages and Families

Intimacy, Specific Threats to
Isomorphism

Job Loss
Joining
Juvenile Firesetter Interventions

Kinship Care

Latino Families
Legal Issues in Parenting
LGBT Families
Licensure and Certification
Life Balance
Life Events
Life Transitions
Listening, Empathic
Live Supervision
Loneliness
Loss
Love, Physiology of
Love, Theories of
Love, Types of
Love and Rituals
Love Languages

Male Hypoactive Sexual Desire Disorder
Mandated Reporter
Marital Distress
Marital Group Therapy
Marriage, Arranged
Marriage, First and Second
Marriage and Health
Marriage Education
Marriage Encounter
Marriage Enrichment
Marriage Myths
Marriage Versus Civil Unions
Marriage-Friendly Therapy
Mate Selection
Media in Family Therapy
Medical Family Therapy
Men in Counseling
Mental Health, Systemic Perspective
Metacommunication
Metaphors
Milan Team

Military Couples and Families
Mindfulness
Mindfulness and Children
Mindfulness and Couples
Mindfulness and Sex
Miracle Question
Mood Disorders in Adolescents
Mood Disorders in Children
Moral Dimensions of Therapy
Morphogenesis
Morphostasis
Mother-Blaming
Motivational Interviewing
Multicultural Counseling Competence
Multiculturalism
Multiple Family Therapy
Multiple Relationships. *See* Dual and Multiple Relationships
Multisystemic Therapy
Muslim American Families

Narrative Therapy
National Marriage Initiative
Native American Families
Network Therapy
Neuro-Linguistic Programming
Neutrality and Curiosity
No-Harm Contracts
Non–Rapid Eye Movement Sleep Arousal Disorders in Children
Nonresidential Fathers
Nonverbal Communication
Normalizing
No-Secrets Contracts
Nuclear Family
Nudity: Beliefs and Values

Object Relations Theory
Online Dating
Open Relationships
Oppositional Defiant Disorder
Outcome Research

Paradoxes and Paradoxical Intervention
Paraphilic Disorders
Parent Effectiveness Training (P.E.T.)
Parent Management Training

Parent Study Groups
Parent–Adolescent Relations
Parental Acceptance–Rejection Theory
Parental Alienation Syndrome
Parental Stress: Effects on Children
Parent–Child Communication
Parentification and Diverse Family Systems
Parenting
Parenting Education
Parenting Styles
Patriarchy
Peer Counseling
Person of the Therapist
Play Family Therapy
Polyamory
Polygamy
Pornography
Positive and Negative Feedback
Positive Psychology
Postdoctoral Training
Postmodern Therapies
Postpartum Depression
Posttraumatic Stress Disorder in Children
Poverty and Family Development
Power Issues in Couples
Practice Management
Pregnancy
Pregnancy and Sexuality
Premarital Counseling
Premature Ejaculation
Prenuptial Agreements
PREPARE/ENRICH
Presenting Problems
Prevention Research
Primary and Secondary Emotions
Process Research
Professional Associations
Progress Notes for Couples and Families
Psychoanalytic Family Therapy
Psychobiology of Attachment
Psychoeducation
Public Health Code
Punctuation

Qualitative Research
Quantitative Research
Questions: Open, Closed, and Circular

Racial Disparities in Foster Care
Racism
Reactive Attachment Disorder in Children
Reconciliation
Recursiveness
Reflecting Team
Relational Diagnoses
Relational-Cultural Therapy
Relationship Enhancement
Release of Information for Couples and Families
Religion
Remarriage. *See* Marriage, First and Second; Stepfamilies
Resilience
Resistance
Respect
Restoration Therapy
Retirement
Rituals in Family Therapy
Role-Playing
Romance
Rule-Setting
Rural Families

Same-Sex Couples
Scales, Children
Scales, Couple and Marital
Scales, Family
Scaling Questions
Scapegoating
Schizophrenia and Families
Schools, Family Involvement in
Second-Order Change
Second-Order Family Therapy
Secrets
Self of the Therapist
Self-Care Practices for the Trauma-Informed Couple and Family Counselor
Self-Esteem
Self-Esteem in Children
Self-Help
Self-Injury
Sensate Focus
Sentiment Override, Positive and Negative
Sex, Definition of
Sex Positivity

Sex Researchers
Sex Therapy
Sexual Abuse
Sexual Assault and Rape
Sexual Assessment/History
Sexual Dysfunction
Sexual Enhancement, Sexual Toys
Sexual Health
Sexual History
Sexual Intimacy
Sexual Minorities
Sexual Orientation, Attraction, and Identity
Sexual Prejudice
Sexual Relationships With Clients
Sexual Toys/Sexual Aids
Sexuality and Religion
Sexuality Education
Sexually Transmitted Infections
Sibling Relationships
Single-Parent Families
Social Constructionism
Social Support
Socioeconomic Status
Solution-Focused Brief Therapy
Somatic Symptom Disorder and Related Disorders in Adolescents
Spirituality
Stages of Family Therapy
Statutory Rape
Stepfamilies
Stillbirth and Miscarriage
Strategic Family Therapy
Stress Management
Structural Determinism
Structural Family Therapy
Structural Maps
Substance Use Disorders in Adolescence
Suicide
Supervision
Supervision, Approved Supervisor in Marriage and Family Therapy
Supervision, Developmental Model
Supervision, Gatekeeping
Supervision, Individual and Group
Supervision Contract
Supervision of Supervision

Supervision Philosophy Statement
Supervision Theories
Support Groups
Symbolic Interactionism
Systemic Family Therapy
Systems, Subsystems, and Metasystems
Systems Theory

Technology and Families/Marriage
Teen Parenting
Termination
Therapeutic Alliance
Therapeutic Assessment
Therapeutic Contract
Therapeutic Impasses
Therapists' Values
TIME Program. *See* Training in Marriage Enrichment (TIME) Program
Torture Treatment
Training and Licensure

Training in Marriage Enrichment (TIME) Program
Transgender Families
Transgenerational Family Therapy
Transracial Adoption
Trauma and Children
Trauma and Families
Trauma-Focused Cognitive-Behavioral Therapy
Treatment Planning With Couples and Families
Triangulation
Trust

Urban Families

Virginia Satir Model

Women's Project, The
Work Relationships
World Association for Sexual Health
World Health Organization

Reader's Guide

Assessments
Adult Attachment Assessments
Assessment, Biopsychosocial
Assessment, Suicide
Circumplex Model
Clinical Case Conceptualization With Couples and Families
Clinical Interviews With Couples and Families
Common Factors
Custody Evaluations
DSM and V-Codes
Ecological Systems
Eco-Map
Family Assessment, Models of
Functional Assessment and Children
Genograms
Interpersonal Violence
Love, Physiology of
Love, Types of
Love Languages
Marital Distress
Marriage Education
Nonverbal Communication
Parent–Child Communication
PREPARE/ENRICH
Progress Notes for Couples and Families
Scales, Children
Scales, Couple and Marital
Scales, Family
Scaling Questions
Sentiment Override, Positive and Negative
Sexual Assessment/History
Sexual Health
Sexual History
Suicide
Therapeutic Assessment
Treatment Planning With Couples and Families

Attachment
Adult Attachment Assessments
Affect Regulation
Attachment
Attachment and Adolescents
Attachment and Health
Attachment and Romantic Love
Attachment Styles
Attachment Theory
Attachment-Based Family Therapy
Attunement in Relationships
Bonding
Child-Centered Parenting
Earned Attachment
Emotional Disengagement
Emotionally Focused Therapy for Couples
Interpersonal Neurobiology, Attachment and
Primary and Secondary Emotions
Psychobiology of Attachment

Communication
Assertiveness
Avoidance
Collaborative Language Systems
Communication Disorders
Communication Errors/Problems in Couples and Families
Communication in Couples and Families
Conflict in Couples and Families
Conflict Resolution
Conflict Styles
Confrontation
Disinhibited Social Engagement Disorder in Children
Empathy
Forgiveness

Love Languages
Metacommunication
Metaphors
Nonverbal Communication
Parent–Child Communication
Power Issues in Couples
Respect
Secrets
Social Constructionism
Symbolic Interactionism
Therapeutic Impasses
Trust

Coping
Bereavement
Children With Chronic Illness
Chronic Illness With Couples and Families
Conflict Styles
Death, Parents of Deceased Children
Empowerment in Families
Engendering Hope
Families and Substance Abuse
Family Resilience
Family Strengths
Family Stress
Family Stress Adaptation Theory
Forgiveness
Hope-Focused Approach to Couple Enrichment in Counseling
Parental Stress: Effects on Children
Reconciliation
Resilience
Self-Esteem
Self-Esteem in Children
Social Support
Stillbirth and Miscarriage
Stress Management

Couple, Marriage, Family Policy
Best Interests of the Child
Child Protective Services
Family and Medical Leave Act of 1993
Healthy Marriage and Responsible Fatherhood
Hispanic Healthy Marriage Initiative
Marriage Versus Civil Unions
National Marriage Initiative

Public Health Code
Self-Esteem in Children
Social Support

Diagnosing and Disorders
Adjustment Disorder in Adolescents
Adolescent Behavior Disorders
Adolescent Behavior Problems
Adolescent Mental Health
Alcohol and Substance Abuse
Anxiety
Anxiety Disorders in Adolescents
Attention-Deficit and Disruptive Behavior Disorders
Autism Spectrum Disorder
Child Behavior Problems
Childhood Anxiety
Childhood Obesity, Prevention and Treatment of
Compulsive Sexual Behavior
Conduct Disorder
Depression in Adolescents
Depression in Children
Depression in Couples and Families
Disinhibited Social Engagement Disorder in Children
DSM and V-Codes
Eating Disorders
Elimination Disorders in Children
Erectile Disorder
Female Orgasmic Disorder
Female Sexual Interest/Arousal Disorder
Fetishes
Functional Assessment and Children
Gambling, Compulsive
Gender Dysphoria
Genito-Pelvic Pain/Penetration Disorder
Hoarding
Intermittent Explosive Disorder in Adolescents
International Classification of Diseases (ICD)
Male Hypoactive Sexual Desire Disorder
Mood Disorders in Adolescents
Mood Disorders in Children
Non–Rapid Eye Movement Sleep Arousal Disorders in Children
Oppositional Defiant Disorder

Paraphilic Disorders
Parental Alienation Syndrome
Postpartum Depression
Posttraumatic Stress Disorder in Children
Premature Ejaculation
Reactive Attachment Disorder in Children
Relational Diagnoses
Schizophrenia and Families
Sexual Dysfunction
Sexually Transmitted Infections
Somatic Symptom Disorder and Related Disorders in Adolescents
Substance Use Disorders in Adolescence

Diversity
Acculturation
Adoption, Cross-Cultural and Interracial
Adoptive Families
African American Families
Asian American Families
Assimilation: Immigrants and Refugees
Beliefs and Values
Bilingual Families
Children With Special Needs in Family Therapy
Chosen Families
Cultural Issues in Couples and Families
Diversity
Empowerment in Families
Ethnicity
Faith-Based Therapy
Families and Substance Abuse
Family Resilience
Family Values
Feminization of Poverty
Foster Children
Gender- and Culture-Sensitive Therapies
Gender Issues
Gender Orientation, Gender Identity, and Gender Expression
Gender Roles
Immigrant Families
Individual Family Culture
Intellectual Disability and Autism
Intercultural Marriage and Family
Interracial Marriages and Families
Kinship Care

Latino Families
LGBT Families
Marriage, Arranged
Marriage Versus Civil Unions
Men in Counseling
Military Couples and Families
Mother-Blaming
Multiculturalism
Muslim American Families
Native American Families
Nudity: Beliefs and Values
Parentification and Diverse Family Systems
Patriarchy
Racial Disparities in Foster Care
Racism
Relational-Cultural Therapy
Religion
Resilience
Rural Families
Same-Sex Couples
Sexual Minorities
Sexual Orientation, Attraction, and Identity
Sexual Prejudice
Sexuality and Religion
Single-Parent Families
Socioeconomic Status
Spirituality
Stepfamilies
Therapists' Values
Transgender Families
Transracial Adoption
Urban Families
Women's Project, The

Financial Issues
Career Planning and Couples/Families
Debt and Financial Strain
Dual-Earner Families
Families and Poverty
Family Resource Management
Feminization of Poverty
Gambling, Compulsive
Hoarding
Homelessness
Homelessness and Youth
Job Loss

Life Balance
Poverty and Family Development
Prenuptial Agreements
Retirement
Socioeconomic Status
Work Relationships

Intimacy
Attachment
Attachment and Adolescents
Attachment and Health
Attachment and Romantic Love
Bonding
Cognitive Maps and Couples
Commitment
Compassion
Confrontation
Couple Development
Couples, Quality Time
Dating Coaching
Dating Relationship Dissolution
Empathy
Fidelity
Forgiveness
Friendship
In-Law Relationships
Intimacy, Specific Threats to
Loneliness
Love, Physiology of
Love, Theories of
Love, Types of
Love and Rituals
Love Languages
Marital Distress
Marriage, Arranged
Marriage, First and Second
Mate Selection
Online Dating
Open Relationships
Polyamory
Polygamy
Reconciliation
Relationship Enhancement
Romance
Secrets
Sexual Intimacy

Sibling Relationships
Trust
Work Relationships

Life Events/Transitions
Adolescent Behavior Problems
Adolescent Mental Health
Adoption
Adult Development
Aging and Caregiving
Autism and Children
Bereavement Counseling
Career Planning and Couples/Families
Caregivers
Child Behavior Problems
Childhood Anxiety
Childless Couples
Chosen Families
Chronic Illness With Couples and Families
Couple Development
Couples, Quality Time
Dating Coaching
Dating Relationship Dissolution
Death, Parents of Deceased Children
Death and Dying
Divorce and Separation
Divorce Therapy
Dual-Earner Families
Families and Poverty
Family Life Cycle
Family Reconstruction
Family Stress
Grief Counseling
Health Issues
Homelessness
Homelessness and Youth
Hospice
Individual and Family Development
Job Loss
Life Balance
Life Events
Life Transitions
Loss
Marriage, First and Second
Parent–Adolescent Relations
Parenting

Postpartum Depression
Posttraumatic Stress Disorder in Children
Poverty and Family Development
Power Issues in Couples
Prenuptial Agreements
Retirement
Rural Families
Sibling Relationships
Single-Parent Families
Spirituality
Stepfamilies
Stillbirth and Miscarriage
Suicide
Teen Parenting
Transracial Adoption
Urban Families

Major Concepts
Affect Regulation
Attachment
Attachment Styles
Attunement, Clinician
Attunement in Relationships
Boundaries
Circumplex Model
Cohesion
Complementary and Symmetrical Relationships
Crucible
Cybernetics
Differentiation
Ecological Systems
Eco-Map
Ecosystems Perspective
Emotional Disengagement
Entitlement
Epistemology in Family Therapy
Family Myth
Family of Origin
Family Rituals
Family Strengths
Family Values
First-Order Change
Fusion
Gender Roles
Hierarchy
Holism

Homeostasis
Hypothesis, Systemic
Identified Patient
Individual Family Culture
Intergenerational Loyalty
Intergenerational Trauma
Isomorphism
Kinship Care
Marriage Education
Marriage Encounter
Marriage Myths
Morphogenesis
Morphostasis
Mother-Blaming
Neutrality and Curiosity
Nuclear Family
Paradoxes and Paradoxical Intervention
Patriarchy
Person of the Therapist
Positive and Negative Feedback
Presenting Problems
Primary and Secondary Emotions
Questions: Open, Closed, and Circular
Recursiveness
Resistance
Scaling Questions
Scapegoating
Second-Order Change
Sentiment Override, Positive and Negative
Social Constructionism
Social Support
Structural Determinism
Structural Maps
Symbolic Interactionism
Systems Theory
Triangulation

Models, Interventions, Techniques
Acceptance and Commitment Therapy
Adlerian Family Therapy
Adlerian Open-Forum Family Counseling
Attachment-Based Family Therapy
Behavioral Family Therapy
Brief Adlerian Couples Therapy
Brief Family Therapy
Chaos Family Therapy

Childhood Obesity, Prevention and Treatment of
Child–Parent Relationship Therapy
Choice Theory and Reality Therapy
Cinematherapy
Circularity and Linearity
Cognitive Maps and Couples
Cognitive-Behavioral Couples Therapy
Cognitive-Behavioral Family Therapy
Collaborative Couples Therapy
Collaborative Language Systems
Community Programs
Conflict Resolution
Conjoint Family Therapy
Constructivism
Contextual Family Therapy
Couple and Family Forensics
Couples and Marriage Counseling
Crisis Intervention With Couples and Families
Discernment Counseling
Divorce Therapy
Ecosystemic Structural Family Therapy
Emotional Intelligence, Children
Emotional Intelligence, Families
Emotionally Focused Therapy for Couples
Empirically Validated Models
Enactments
Equine-Assisted Family Therapy
Ericksonian Family Therapy
Experiential Family Therapy
Externalizing Behaviors
Faith-Based Therapy
Family Mode Deactivation Therapy
Feminist Family Therapy
Focal Family Therapy
Functional Family Therapy
Gender- and Culture-Sensitive Therapies
Gestalt Family Therapy
Goals, Treatment
Gottman Method Couples Therapy
Grief Counseling
Group Family Therapy
Home-Based Therapy
Homework Assignments in Therapy
Homicide
Hope-Focused Approach to Couple Enrichment in Counseling
Humanistic Family Therapy
Hypnosis
Imago Relationship Therapy
Individual Versus Family Therapy
Integrating Systemic and Individual Theories
Integrative Couples Therapy
Internal Family Systems Model
International Family Therapy
Interpersonal Neurobiology, Attachment and
Interpersonal Neurobiology, Couples and
Interpersonal Neurobiology, Parenting and
Joining
Juvenile Firesetter Interventions
Listening, Empathic
Love and Rituals
Marital Group Therapy
Marriage Encounter
Marriage Enrichment
Marriage-Friendly Therapy
Medical Family Therapy
Metacommunication
Metaphors
Milan Team
Mindfulness
Miracle Question
Motivational Interviewing
Multiple Family Therapy
Multisystemic Therapy
Narrative Therapy
Network Therapy
Neuro-Linguistic Programming
No-Harm Contracts
Normalizing
Paradoxes and Paradoxical Intervention
Parent Effectiveness Training (P.E.T.)
Parent Management Training
Peer Counseling
Play Family Therapy
Positive Psychology
Postmodern Therapies
Premarital Counseling
Progress Notes for Couples and Families
Psychoanalytic Family Therapy
Psychobiology of Attachment
Psychoeducation
Punctuation

Questions: Open, Closed, and Circular
Reflecting Team
Relational-Cultural Therapy
Relationship Enhancement
Restoration Therapy
Rituals in Family Therapy
Role-Playing
Second-Order Family Therapy
Self-Help
Sensate Focus
Solution-Focused Brief Therapy
Stages of Family Therapy
Strategic Family Therapy
Structural Family Therapy
Support Groups
Systemic Family Therapy
Systems, Subsystems, and Metasystems
Therapeutic Alliance
Therapeutic Contract
Torture Treatment
Training in Marriage Enrichment (TIME) Program
Transgenerational Family Therapy
Trauma-Focused Cognitive-Behavioral Therapy
Triangulation
Virginia Satir Model

Organizations
American Association for Marriage and Family Therapy
Council for Accreditation of Counseling and Related Educational Programs
International Association of Marriage and Family Counselors
World Association for Sexual Health
World Health Organization

Parenting
Active Parenting
Adoption
Authoritative Parenting
Child-Centered Parenting
Child–Parent Relationship Therapy
Children With Chronic Illness
Foster Children
Group Parenting Classes
Interpersonal Neurobiology, Parenting and
Legal Issues in Parenting
LGBT Families
Nonresidential Fathers
Parent Effectiveness Training (P.E.T.)
Parent Management Training
Parent Study Groups
Parent–Adolescent Relations
Parental Alienation Syndrome
Parental Stress: Effects on Children
Parentification and Diverse Family Systems
Parenting
Parenting Education
Parenting Styles
Pregnancy
Racial Disparities in Foster Care
Rule-Setting
Teen Parenting

Professional Development and Standards
American Association for Marriage and Family Therapy
Certified Family Life Educator
Child Protective Services
Clinical Practice
Clinician-Directed, Solution-Focused Supervision
Competency-Based Standards for Marriage, Couple, and Family Counseling
Confidentiality
Core Competencies for Marriage and Family Therapists
Cotherapy Team
Council for Accreditation of Counseling and Related Educational Programs
Court-Mandated Clients
Decision-Making
Dual and Multiple Relationships
Duty to Warn and Protect
Ethical Codes
Ethical Decision-Making
Family Life Educators
HIPAA Standards
Informed Consent for Research
Informed Consent in Clinical Work
Licensure and Certification
Live Supervision

Mandated Reporter
Mental Health, Systemic Perspective
Moral Dimensions of Therapy
Multicultural Counseling Competence
No-Secrets Contracts
Postdoctoral Training
Practice Management
Professional Associations
Public Health Code
Release of Information for Couples and Families
Self of the Therapist
Self-Care Practices for the Trauma-Informed Couple and Family Counselor
Sexual Relationships With Clients
Supervision
Supervision, Approved Supervisor in Marriage and Family Therapy
Supervision, Developmental Model
Supervision, Gatekeeping
Supervision, Individual and Group
Supervision Contract
Supervision of Supervision
Supervision Philosophy Statement
Supervision Theories
Termination
Therapists' Values
Training and Licensure

Research

Clinical Versus Statistical Significance
Common Factors
Cost–Benefit Analysis
Couples Therapy Research
Delphi Research Method
Developmental Model of Marriage
Effectiveness Research
Empirically Validated Models
Evidence-Based Practice With Couples and Families
Outcome Research
Prevention Research
Process Research
Qualitative Research
Quantitative Research
Sex Researchers

Sexuality

Beliefs and Values
Birth Control and Contraception
Childless Couples
Compulsive Sexual Behavior
Erectile Disorder
Extramarital Affairs and Infidelity
Female Orgasmic Disorder
Female Sexual Interest/Arousal Disorder
Fetishes
Gender Dysphoria
Gender Orientation, Gender Identity, and Gender Expression
Genito-Pelvic Pain/Penetration Disorder
Human Sexual Response
Incest
Infertility
Male Hypoactive Sexual Desire Disorder
Mate Selection
Mindfulness and Sex
Nudity: Beliefs and Values
Open Relationships
Paraphilic Disorders
Polyamory
Polygamy
Pornography
Pregnancy and Sexuality
Premature Ejaculation
Romance
Same-Sex Couples
Sensate Focus
Sex, Definition of
Sex Positivity
Sex Researchers
Sex Therapy
Sexual Abuse
Sexual Assault and Rape
Sexual Assessment/History
Sexual Dysfunction
Sexual Enhancement, Sexual Toys
Sexual Health
Sexual History
Sexual Intimacy
Sexual Minorities
Sexual Orientation, Attraction, and Identity

Sexual Prejudice
Sexual Relationships With Clients
Sexual Toys/Sexual Aids
Sexuality and Religion
Sexuality Education
Sexually Transmitted Infections
Statutory Rape
World Association for Sexual Health

Special Topics

Body Dysmorphic Disorder in Adolescents
Child Guidance Movement
Children With Special Needs in Family Therapy
Community Programs
Family Mediation
Healthy Marriage and Responsible Fatherhood
Hispanic Healthy Marriage Initiative
Incest
International Family Therapy
Marriage and Health
Media in Family Therapy
Men in Counseling
Military Couples and Families
Mindfulness and Children
Mindfulness and Couples
National Marriage Initiative
Online Dating
Schizophrenia and Families
Schools, Family Involvement in
Self-Care Practices for the Trauma-Informed Couple and Family Counselor
Sexual Abuse
Statutory Rape
Technology and Families/Marriage
Therapeutic Impasses
Torture Treatment

Theory

Adlerian Family Therapy
Assessment, Biopsychosocial
Attachment Theory
Behavioral Family Therapy
Bowen Family Systems Theory
Chaos Family Therapy
Choice Theory and Reality Therapy
Cognitive-Behavioral Couples Therapy
Cognitive-Behavioral Family Therapy
Collaborative Language Systems
Constructivism
Contextual Family Therapy
Critical Theory
Cybernetics
Double Bind Theory
Ecosystems Perspective
Epistemology in Family Therapy
Experiential Family Therapy
Family Stress Adaptation Theory
Functionalism
General Systems Theory
Isomorphism
Love, Theories of
Object Relations Theory
Parental Acceptance–Rejection Theory
Psychoanalytic Family Therapy
Social Constructionism
Structural Determinism
Symbolic Interactionism
Systems Theory

Violence and Abuse

Alcohol and Substance Abuse
Anger Management
Child Maltreatment
Domestic Violence
Elder Abuse
Interpersonal Violence
Self-Injury
Sexual Assault and Rape
Trauma and Children
Trauma and Families

LATINO FAMILIES

In recent years, Latino families have become a growing segment of the U.S. population. A number of characteristics have been used to describe Latino families. Yet the changing nature of the U.S. Latino population has made attempts to categorize Latino families out of date. This entry reviews the diversity, common cultural values and scripts, and social factors that help describe today's Latino families. An overview of how these characteristics may influence family and couples counseling with Latinos is also provided.

The Diversity of Latino Families

Latino families comprised 14.7% of all households in the United States in 2013, with 62% of those being married couples. Almost 60% of Latino married couples have children under 18 years of age. In general, Latino families tend to have more children, start child-bearing earlier, and live in extended families. Yet these commonalities do not reveal recent changes in Latino family life. Latinos are now older when they marry, and a substantial number of couples divorce. Moreover, more Latinos are choosing to cohabit than ever before and more children are being born outside of marriage.

Categorizing Latinos as a whole, however, masks trends in family life that vary between different subgroups of Latino populations. Latino subgroups include Mexicans, Puerto Ricans, Cubans, Central Americans, and South Americans. Each of these subgroups differs with respect to its immigration history, settlement pattern, racial makeup, and socioeconomic situation. Mexican and Cuban families are most likely to be married, whereas Dominican and Puerto Rican families are most likely to be headed by a single female. Mexicans are less likely than other Latino subgroups to marry, cohabit, or parent with someone outside of their group.

Even within each subgroup, though, Latino families may differ based on their birth status (U.S. or foreign born) and level of acculturation, among other factors. Level of acculturation refers to the extent that a Latino family and its individual members have adopted U.S. values and customs. Taking these factors into account, Latino families whose members are foreign born and lowly acculturated may be more likely to strongly identify with traditional values and customs. By contrast, Latino families whose members are U.S. born and highly acculturated may be less traditional and identify more with U.S. values and customs. Therefore, it is important to recognize the heterogeneity of Latino families along with their commonalities.

Latino Cultural Values and Scripts

Latino families are influenced by common cultural values and scripts. These include collectivism, *simpatia* (smooth, pleasant relationships), *personalismo* (individualized self-worth or dignity), *respeto* (respect), and *familismo* (familism). These values and scripts are defined here within the context of Latino families. Collectivism involves placing the needs of the family over an individual family member's needs, even to the point of sacrificing one's own needs. *Simpatia* refers to family members' ability to maintain harmony within the family and the encouragement of positive social behaviors. *Respeto* within the family involves the expectation that children be obedient and maintain an emotional dependence on their parents. *Personalismo* underscores the importance of personal contact and social situations. *Familismo* emphasizes a strong commitment to family. It involves elements of family structure, such as family size and extended family; behaviors that encourage frequent contact and support among family members; and attitudes that foster loyalty, solidarity, and reciprocity.

In addition to these cultural values, there are three gender-specific scripts that influence Latino families. These include *marianismo* (female self-sacrifice), *hembrismo* (femaleness), and *machismo* (male self-respect and responsibility). *Marianismo* involves admiration for a mother who self-sacrifices for her children and is submissive to her husband. Because this value also involves an expectation that a woman will suppress and sublimate her sexual desires, unmarried women are expected to only socialize with men when there is the prospect of marriage. *Hembrismo* reflects the value placed on a woman's ability to fulfill her responsibilities at home and work, sometimes despite seemingly insurmountable odds and hardships. *Machismo* accentuates a father and husband's ability to protect and care for his family, rather than only describing sexist behavior, which is a more stereotypical view.

The importance of preserving the Spanish language in Latino families forms part of their traditional cultural values as well. Almost three quarters (73.9%) of Latinos in the United States reported speaking Spanish at home in 2012. Language connects family members to memories, thoughts, feelings, and places that are symbolic of their homeland. Therefore, not having the opportunity to express themselves in their native language is a loss for many. Some families pride themselves on being able to preserve the language in their families despite pressures to assimilate to U.S. culture and speak only English. Other families may learn to function in both Spanish and English, thereby adopting some level of bilingualism. More recent immigrants who speak only Spanish, however, may struggle to adapt to life in the United States.

Betty Carter and Monica McGoldrick developed a family life cycle model to describe common stages that families experience throughout the life cycle. Cultural values and scripts may influence how Latino families go through these stages. For example, families with young children or adolescents may not encourage them to become autonomous and independent. There may also be less of an expectation that adolescents become rebellious and more self-sufficient compared to other Anglo American families. Instead, Latino families may encourage their adolescents to be more mindful of their responsibilities to their families and society. Additionally, owing to *familismo*, parents may continue to live with or very near their adult children, so they may not experience the "launching" stage or "empty nest" syndrome as Anglo American families may. Furthermore, grandparents are more likely to be accorded a position of respect and may be more likely to be continuously involved in their grandchildren's lives. Therefore, it is important to consider how Latino cultural values and scripts impact the stages of the family life cycle.

Social Factors

Religious and spiritual beliefs play an important role in Latino families. The majority of Latinos (55%) are practicing or nonpracticing Roman Catholics. More recently, though, the number of Latino Catholics has decreased while the number of evangelical Protestant (22%) or unaffiliated Latinos (18%) has increased. Regardless of affiliation, however, religious and spiritual beliefs may provide a means of coping for Latino families.

Spiritual and folk beliefs may be blended with mainstream religions. Common spiritual and folk beliefs include *curanderismo* (traditional folk medicine) among Mexican families and *espiritismo* (spiritualism) and *Santeria* (religion that combines Catholic and African Yoruba beliefs) among Puerto Rican, Cuban, and some South American families. Latino families often view their churches as sources of support that provide basic needs, such as food and shelter, and other social services. Moreover, Latino families often seek emotional support and guidance from Catholic priests or *curanderos* (folk healers). Religious church rituals, including baptisms, marriages, and *quinceañeras* (a formal ball for 15-year-old Mexican females) often mark important transitions in the family life cycle.

Other social factors that impact Latino families include migration and level of acculturation. Migration experiences may differ among Latino families, depending on socioeconomic and citizenship status. Puerto Ricans are born U.S. citizens, so their migration to the mainland may be quite different from that of other Latino groups who enter the country as documented or undocumented immigrants. Regardless, migration impacts the structure, interactions, and dynamics of Latino families. Repeated separations and reunions or family cutoffs generate stresses as families adapt to losses and disruptions in family hierarchies, traditional gender roles, and community supports. Furthermore, families who have migrated often experience stress due to culture shock, discrimination, poverty, lack of health care, and alienation. Children born or raised in the United States may be more highly acculturated and may be more likely to try to adopt U.S. customs and values, leading to generational conflicts. Parents may react by becoming overly strict and overprotective. Additionally, parents may have to rely on their highly acculturated English-speaking children to navigate unfamiliar school, medical, and social systems, and to help care for younger siblings. Both generational conflict and the parentification of children may weaken the family structure.

Counseling Latino Families

Because Latino families are heterogeneous, counselors should assess the impact of traditional values and scripts and social factors to intervene in a culturally sensitive manner. Knowledge about traditional values and scripts can help counselors engage Latino families, maintain effective therapeutic relationships, establish treatment goals that are consistent with cultural values, and encourage treatment compliance. Information about social factors that impact a family can help counselors assess losses, stressors, and disruptions to family structure.

Being mindful of the role that *simpatia, personalismo,* and *respeto* play in a family can help counselors establish effective therapeutic relationships. Therefore, engaging a traditional Latino family in a warm, respectful, and personal manner can facilitate a more effective therapeutic relationship than taking a practical, task-oriented approach. Furthermore, to maintain harmony (*simpatia*) and to avoid making others uncomfortable, Latino families may use *indirectas,* or indirect forms of criticism. Counselors can maintain a therapeutic relationship by respecting this more indirect emotional expression and elicit underlying feelings in a subtle manner. Moreover, counselors may find that Latino families are hesitant to voice disagreement with them out of respect for their authority and the importance of being cooperative in Latino cultures. Counselors can encourage families to express differing opinions by offering possible alternative points of view that family members can confirm. Assessing family members' English proficiency can help counselors determine the need for a Spanish-speaking counselor. In addition, counselors can be mindful of how family dynamics are affected by differences in family members' English proficiency.

Understanding the values of collectivism and *familismo* can help counselors define treatment goals that emphasize the importance of family needs rather than the needs of individual family members. Counselors can learn to view the emphasis on family as being consistent with a family systems perspective. Furthermore, treatment goals that focus on parents' dedication to their children and their responsibility as parents can be more effective than emphasizing parenting weaknesses. To help maintain rapport and encourage treatment compliance, counselors can respect the hierarchy of the father and husband's authority over his wife and children. Couples therapy that integrates an understanding of the positive aspects of *marianismo* and *machismo* can help counselors treat traditional couples more effectively.

Social factors that may impact Latino families should also be assessed. A counselor can gain valuable information by eliciting the family's migration narrative. The losses due to separations and family cutoffs can help counselors understand how a family's structure and dynamics have been affected. The migration narrative can also reveal past and ongoing stressors. To cope with stressors, a family that holds strong religious and spiritual beliefs may seek guidance from a Catholic priest or folk healer while receiving counseling. Culturally sensitive counselors integrate religious and spiritual beliefs and practices when treating Latino families. Depending on a family's socioeconomic status, a Latino family may need help navigating resources for basic necessities and access to health care. Finally, assessing the level of acculturation for individual family members can help counselors address generational conflicts and disruptions in family structure.

Elizabeth Ruiz

See also Acculturation; Bilingual Families; Family Life Cycle; Gender Roles; Parentification and Diverse Family Systems

Further Readings

Bernal, G., & Shapiro, E. (1996). Cuban families. In M. McGoldrick, J. Giordano, & J. K. Pearce (Eds.), *Ethnicity and family therapy* (2nd ed., pp. 155–168). New York, NY: Guilford Press.

Falicov, C. J. (1996). Mexican families. In M. McGoldrick, J. Giordano, & J. K. Pearce (Eds.), *Ethnicity and family therapy* (2nd ed., pp. 169–182). New York, NY: Guilford Press.

Falicov, C.J. (1998). *Latino families in therapy: A guide to multicultural practice*. New York, NY: Guilford Press.

Garcia-Preto, N. (1996). Puerto Rican families. In M. McGoldrick, J. Giordano, & J. K. Pearce (Eds.), *Ethnicity and family therapy* (2nd ed., pp. 183–199). New York, NY: Guilford, Press.

Krogstad, J. M., & Mark, H. L. (2014, April 29). *Hispanic nativity shift: U.S. births drive population growth as immigration stalls*. Washington, DC: Pew Research Center.

Ruiz, E. (2005). Hispanic culture and relational cultural theory. *Journal of Creativity in Mental Health, 1*, 33–55.

Suarez-Orozco, M. M., & Páez, M. (2009). *Latinos: Remaking America*. Los Angeles: University of California Press.

Tienda, M., & Mitchell, F. (Eds.). (2006). *Hispanics and the future of America*. Retrieved from http://www.nap.edu/catalog/11539.html

Legal Issues in Parenting

Legal issues in parenting have become more diverse as the nature of parenthood has become more complex over time. Divorce rates remain a significant social problem. New issues such as the question of sex education in schools or the rights of a minor seeking an abortion have made the landscape of legal issues in parenting more difficult to navigate. As such, there is a greater need for counselors to educate themselves on the nature of that landscape so as to prepare for the dilemmas they will inevitably encounter in the field. This entry reviews how parenthood is generally conceptualized in the eyes of the law and the nature of parent as well as child rights.

Defining Parenthood

Historically, the typical parental unit could often be described as a man and woman, bound by marriage, dwelling in the same home, and jointly raising their biological children. Over time, however, this archetype has continued to evolve in a number of ways and for a number of different reasons. The increase in divorce rates has resulted in the introduction of the stepparent as well as single-parent homes. Nontraditional couples have led to changes in the man/woman parental paradigm. Advances in medical science have also opened a number of doors that have changed what the road to parenthood can look like.

Regardless of the circumstances, however, the roles and responsibility of a parent often look the same. Nevertheless, it is important to clarify that the nature of a parent's rights may be very different based on the specific circumstances. A stepparent does not necessarily have the same rights as a biological parent. Consider a scenario in which a married woman with the support of her consenting husband pursues artificial insemination. In this instance, assuming that the husband gives consent, typically in writing, he will be granted all the parental rights of a biological parent. On the other hand, the man who donated the semen utilized in the insemination procedure will not be considered, from a legal perspective, the parent of the conceived child. This is a prime example of how advances in medical technology have changed the landscape of parental rights. Another unique example of nontraditional conception is that of surrogate mothers. Legal conflicts may arise in cases in which the surrogate carries a child full term but has a change of heart and refuses to surrender the child upon birth. Contracts are typically drafted to ensure that all parties agree to the surrogacy, but they can be difficult to enforce.

It is important to remember that as the rights of the parent change, so do the counselor's legal obligations. The dynamics of the parental unit and their individual parental rights will have an impact on several aspects of the therapeutic process. Who is entitled to a minor client's treatment information? What parent is empowered to make decisions about the therapeutic process? The makeup of the parental system will affect how a counselor answers these questions from one client to another. As such, it is essential that the counselor have a firm grasp of these concepts in order to provide appropriate care to their clients.

Custodial Rights and Responsibilities in Parenting

Perhaps one of the most well-known and yet often misunderstood legal concepts in parenting is that of custody. The term *custody* refers generally to a responsibility for and charge over a person or thing. This does not imply ownership per se and is not necessarily associated with whom the ward resides, as it can often be misinterpreted. *Legal* custody refers to, in this context, a parent's right to make decisions about and on behalf of their child. These decisions can be related to a range of issues including lifestyle, religion, education, and so on. *Physical* custody, on the other hand, describes a parent's right to reside with their child. It is a common misconception that one having physical custody is an indication of a greater degree of parental rights in terms of legal custody. This is not necessarily the case. Likewise, a stepparent who resides with a child is not necessarily afforded the same rights as a biological parent with full legal but not physical custody.

The process of determining child custody has changed in recent years. In the past, many of the decisions related to the custody of preadolescents were made based on the idea that mothers were typically more suitable custodians. This was based on the idea that mothers were best suited to provide the necessary support and nurturing to children during what was considered their "tender years." When considering children who were adolescents or older, the courts would often opt to place the child in the custody of the parent of the same sex. These practices have somewhat been abandoned of late for an approach grounded in the idea of acting in the best interests of the child. A number of considerations are taken into account when determining the best interests of a child including, but not limited to, the wishes of the parents as well as the child, the makeup of the family unit, mental and/or physical considerations, the emotional needs of the child, and environmental considerations, such as the available school system. It should be mentioned here that it is generally advisable for counselors to avoid becoming involved in custody litigation if they have previously provided services to one of the parties involved. This may seem counterintuitive considering the fact that having previous experience with the litigants may afford the counselor unique insight into the family situation and dynamics. Serving in these dual roles, however, would create a number of ethical pitfalls that would be difficult for the counselor to avoid. As such, it is better to refuse becoming involved in a custody dispute unless otherwise ordered by the court.

It is important to mention here that the custodial landscape has gotten a bit more diverse, specifically in terms of physical custody. Often in the past, physical custody among divorced parents would consist of children residing with a specific parent the bulk of the week, in many instances Monday through Friday, and then visiting the other parent on weekends. There seems to be an increase in the number of parents who now split physical custody 50–50 with the child spending every other week with each parent. That diversity has not necessarily changed the nature of each parent's rights.

Child Rights

One of the more complex legal issues in parenting is related to the rights of minor children. From a legal perspective, minors have their rights exercised through their parents. A minor does not, for example, file a lawsuit; the parent or legal guardian files a lawsuit on behalf of the child. This legal dynamic is somewhat in conflict with the ethical perspective in counseling. Technically, when a counselor provides services to a minor child, they are actually employed by the parent or guardian. Yet a counselor is, first and foremost, committed to the well-being of their client. Although the right of the parent as it relates to a minor client is certainly a significant consideration, it does not trump the ethical obligation to the client's welfare and wishes. This can become complicated when the wishes of a minor client and their parent are in conflict. This can be as small as a client's request for the counselor to withhold information from the parent about a small youthful indiscretion. If a counselor unearths evidence of neglect or physical abuse while treating a minor client, however, the ethical and legal landscape becomes much more complex.

Peter J. Boccone

See also Best Interests of the Child; Child Maltreatment; Child-Centered Parenting; Custody Evaluations

Further Readings

Chisholm, R. (2009). The meanings of "meaningful" within the Family Law Act Amendments of 2006: A legal perspective. *Journal of Family Studies, 15,* 60–66.

Fridhandler, B., & Lehmer, M. (2014). Ethical issues in coparent counseling. *Journal of Child Custody, 11*(2), 139–158.

Garon, R., & Whitfill, J. C. (2003). A mental-health professional and judge's journey: Providing responsible parenting, giving children a voice. *Family Law Quarterly, 37*(3), 459–483.

Glosoff, H. L., & Pate, R. H., Jr. (2002). Privacy and confidentiality in school counseling. *Professional School Counseling, 6*(1), 20–27.

Gold, J. M. (2009) Stepparents and the law: Knowledge for counselors, guidelines for family members. *Family Journal, 13*(3), 272–276.

Gould, J. W., Martindale, D. A., & Eidman, M. H. (2007). Is parental sexual orientation probative in child custody advisory reports: It depends! *Journal of Forensic Psychology Practice, 7*(4), 111–124.

Handel, W. W., & Sherwyn, B. A. (1982). Surrogate parenting. *Trial, 18,* 57–77.

Harman, J. (2011). Confidentiality in family dispute resolution and family counseling: Recent cases and why they matter. *Journal of Family Studies, 17*(3), 204–212.

Kelly, J. B. (2008). Preparing for the parenting coordination role: Training needs for mental health and legal professional. *Journal of Child Custody, 5*(1/2), 140–159.

Kirkland, K. (2008). Parenting coordination (PC) laws, rules, and regulations: A jurisdictional comparison. *Journal of Child Custody, 5*(1/2), 25–52.

Kramer, D. T. (1994). *Legal rights of children* (2nd ed.). New York, NY: McGraw-Hill.

Krause, H. D., & Meyer, D. D. (2007). *Family law in a nutshell* (5th ed.). St. Paul, MN: West.

Lawrence, G., & Robinson Kirpius, S. E. (2000). Legal and ethical issues involved when counseling minors in nonschool settings. *Journal of Counseling & Development, 78*(2), 130–136.

Mnookin, R. H., & Weisberg, D. K. (2000). *Child, family and state: Problems and materials on children and the law* (4th ed.). Boston, MA: Little, Brown.

LGBT Families

In the 21st century, the typical family is far more diverse then it was 50 years ago. The idea that households largely consist of married heterosexual couples raising biological children is no longer an acceptable assumption. The legally accepted definition of family today includes anyone who plays a significant role in a person's life. This can include spouses, significant others, and either same-sex or different-sex partners. Additionally, aunts, stepchildren, grandparents, and married and/or unmarried people may also be considered part of this new family dynamic. Lesbian, gay, bisexual, and transgender (LGBT) individuals are also an integral part of this new cultural fabric. Despite this, a lack of legal protections under the law for LGBT people, couples, and families, as well as negative and inaccurate social stigmas associated with LGBT families, continue to pose psychological challenges. This entry reviews some of those challenges, provides examples of best practices believed to be useful when working with LGBT families, and offers a list of resources LGBT families can turn to for support.

Issues That Impact LGBT People and Families

Despite growing acceptance of LGBT families, the oppression, discrimination, and marginalization of gender and sexual minorities continues. These circumstances can manifest in a number of forms, such as social rejection, lack of legal protections under the law, religious persecution, housing discrimination, rejection from one's family of origin, loss of an existing spouse or partner once someone "comes out," job loss, hate crimes, and violence. Clinicians should be aware of the issues that can impact the mental, emotional, and psychological welfare of LGBT people and their families. Research shows that for many LGBT people, coping with such factors can lead to higher levels of depression, anxiety, substance abuse, and other mental health concerns. Findings show that youth who identify as LGBT are 10 times more likely to experience bullying and victimization at school and more than twice as likely to have considered suicide than their heterosexual, nontransgendered counterparts. In terms of LGBT adults, subjects reported similar forms of harassment, as well as discrimination with regard to housing, employment, education, and basic human rights.

Coming Out

The process of coming out (informing people of sexual minority identity) can be a difficult time for some LGBT people, especially those who are part of existing families and/or looking to start new ones. According to the *2013 Human Rights Campaign Foundation Resource Guide,* "coming out" is the period when an individual talks for the first time about their personal sexual orientation or gender identity with family members, friends, coworkers, classmates, and others in their life.

The process of coming out is different for everyone. Several coming-out models developed over the years loosely describe the process of gay and lesbian identity development. Of these models, the *Cass identity model* is the most widely recognized. This model outlines six discrete stages individuals go through when coming out: identity confusion, identity comparison, identity tolerance, identity acceptance, identity pride, and identity synthesis. However, researchers found that bisexuals and transgender people may experience identity development differently. For example, some bisexual-identified people may start to identify as bisexual after coming out as lesbian or gay earlier in life. Additionally, identity development for many trans-identified people may include biological as well as social identity changes.

For some individuals, coming out may mean disclosing one's identity to one's boss, a new set of acquaintances, family members, and children. Some LGBT people may experience fear and uncertainty when coming out to younger and/or adult children, because doing so may imply a change for the family, especially in cases where such a decision leads to the separation from the child's opposite-sex parent. Additionally, the process of telling younger children may also need to be repeated at various times throughout a child's developmental process. For some LGBT couples the coming-out process may re-emerge later in life if, for example, the couple decides to marry and/or have children. During situations like this, the couple may have to go through the process of disclosing this personal relationship information again to health care providers, day care workers, or extended family members.

Research suggests children respond in different ways to the process of a parent's coming out. Findings show that the way children receive this information is generally better when the parent appears confident, self-assured, and clear. Other factors that can make the process easier include disclosing in a private space where the conversation is confidential; allowing time for the conversation to continue over days, weeks, or years; explaining sexuality or gender shifts in a developmentally appropriate manner; reassuring children they are loved; and establishing connections with other LGBT families.

Marriage Equality

LGBT people have been celebrating their love in the form of same-sex unions before family, friends, and God for many years. Like their heterosexual counterparts, many LGBT families have desired legal recognition of their relationships, as well as equal protections under the law, for decades. While change occurred slowly in this regard, on June 26, 2015, the U.S. Supreme Court ruled in *Obergefell v. Hodges* that state-level bans on same-sex marriage were unconstitutional. The court further determined the denial of marriage licenses to same-sex couples and refusal to recognize those marriages performed in other jurisdictions violated the Fourteenth Amendment.

According to the Government Accountability Office (GAO), over 1,000 rights and protections are offered to U.S. citizens who are married and now, same-sex couples, are eligible for the same rights and protections. Examples of such rights include Social Security benefits, veterans' benefits, health insurance, Medicaid, hospital visitation, estate taxes, retirement savings, pensions, family leave, and immigration law.

This victory, however, did not come easily. Individuals have been campaigning for same-sex marriage equality since the early 1970s, despite pushback from conservative groups who insisted only male-female couples should benefit from legal marriage. Nevertheless, a major victory occurred in June 2013 when the Obama administration declared section 3 of the Defense of Marriage Act (DOMA) unconstitutional, thus recognizing same-sex marriage on a federal level. Prior to this, DOMA restricted federal recognition of same-sex married couples, even if the couple was legally married in a state where same-sex marriage is lawful.

A 2013 report by the Human Rights Campaign suggested a majority of Americans support the right of LGBT couples to legally marry. According to this same report, 58% of all Americans support marriage equality, and 63% of all American's support giving federal benefits to legally married, same-sex couples. Additionally, according to an online study conducted by Julie Shulman and Robert-Jay Green in 2008, having the ability to marry legally provides same-sex couples with a universal sense of security in all areas of life.

Parental Options and Child-Rearing

A common stereotype held about gays and lesbians is that they do not have children. A 2013 report released by the Williams Institute suggests otherwise and estimates more than 111,000 same-sex couples are raising an estimated 170,000 biological, step, or adopted children. Historically, most of the research done on LGBT parenting has focused on White, middle-class, lesbian families, with less attention paid to the parental patterns of bisexual people, LGB people of color, and transgender people. This, however, is changing and more inclusive and diverse studies on LGBT families are being conducted.

There are a number of parental pathways available to LGBT individuals, couples, and families today. Because many LGBT individuals and couples parent outside of established norms, there is no agreed-upon set of rules in which families form. Such parental pathways include coparenting, foster care, adoption, donor insemination, and/or surrogacy. Some LGBT parents have children while in preexisting relationships with an opposite-sex partner and continue to coparent after coming out. Additionally, others may choose to become parents or start families with a new partner after they come out.

Many LGBT parents are not fully protected under the law and may be disqualified from fostering or face additional legal restrictions when trying to adopt due to bias and discrimination. For transgender people, a lack of visible support and parenting options can cause significant distress when trying to start a family. Additionally, the court system continues to deny some LGBT parents legal rights to children because in some cases one or both parties may not be biologically related to the child.

According to the American Psychological Association (APA), children raised in LGBT households are just as psychologically fit as children raised in heterosexual households. Research shows many LGBT parents provide supportive and healthy environments for their children, suggesting that a parent's sexual orientation or gender identity does not impact a child's development and/or happiness. Children raised by LGBT parents are just as likely as those reared by heterosexual parents to thrive and grow.

Transgender Couples and Families

Gender identity and the transition process can be a defining and complex issue for many trans-identified people and families. Gender identity is a person's private sense and subjective experience of their own gender. The transition process consists of changing one's gender socially or medically in order to align one's mind and body with their internal sense of self.

Transgender people may face obstacles not encountered by gay, lesbian, and bisexual people when it comes to marriage and/or starting a family. Issues that have been known to complicate this process include how to modify documents so one can get legally married, what marriage laws apply to transgender people or not, and how to protect one's rights as a transgender parent when children are involved. Additionally, the ability to change one's gender marker on important legal documents, such as a driver's license or birth certificate, can further delay one's ability to legally marry or adopt a child. Additionally, while an increasing number of states currently permit same-sex marriage, this may not apply to trans people, who must first examine the marriage laws of the state in which they live, as well as gender-change laws, before deciding if they can get married.

Best Practices

As society becomes more aware of the existence and needs of LGBT people, couples, and families, therapists need to become more flexible in the way they help people. Approaches to treatment with LGBT couples and families must be adaptable, inclusive, and work toward incorporating different sets of values and worldviews. It is important for therapists to respect the unique experiences of LGBT couples and families, recognize the negative impact heterosexist ideologies may have on these families, and find ways to leave personal judgments at the door.

Often, LGBT couples and/or families are seeking treatment to deal with many of the same problems encountered by heterosexual couples, such as ways to improve communication and explore conflict and learn resolution skills. However, in order to approach this work from an open-minded place, therapists need to increase their overall knowledge about LGBT issues, couples, and families, and eliminate personal bias.

To do this process, therapists need to become culturally competent when working with LGBT people, couples, or families. To begin, they need to understand certain terminology, such as how the word "transgender" differs from the word "gay." Second, therapists need to spend time examining and challenging their own worldviews, morals, and attitudes in regard to gender expression, gender presentation, gender identity, and sexual orientation. Last, therapists need to attend educational trainings about the lives and experiences of LGBT people.

Newer models of family therapy used today appear to work well with LGBT couples and families. A combination of techniques, such as narrative therapy, solution-focused brief therapy, and feminist, postmodern, and multicultural perspectives, are popular alternatives to traditional models and are known to work well with LGBT couples and families. Family therapists are encouraged to look at sociocultural issues, such as how a couple's problems and beliefs are socially constructed, the need for empowerment of marginalized clients, including LGBT families, and ways to incorporate social justice measures into the therapy process. These newer models emphasize nonpathological approaches to working with LGBT couples and families, help therapists learn to respect diversity, and enforce the need to recognize the strengths found in the LGBT families they serve.

Resources and Recommendations

Since the 1990s, support and resources for LGBT individuals, couples, and families has grown both in the United States and internationally. As a result of the Internet and social media, LGBT people can now access online a growing number of resources on topics such as coming out to one's existing family, same-sex marriage, and LGBT adoption or foster care. Among other resources, therapists can refer LGBT individuals, couples, and families in need to organizations such as LGBT Families, which provides links to over 150 LGBT community centers worldwide; PFLGA, which provides support to the parents and family of LGBT individuals; and Transsexual Road Map, which provides vital information to trans-identified people, couples, and families.

Joe (Jodi) Ippolito

See also Gender- and Culture-Sensitive Therapies; Gender Issues; Gender Orientation, Gender Identity, and Gender Expression; Same-Sex Couples; Social Support; Transgender Families

Further Readings

American Psychological Association. (2011). *Practice guidelines for LGB clients.* Retrieved from http://www.apa.org/pi/lgbt/resources/guidelines.aspx

Brickley, M., & Gelnaw, A. (n.d.). *Talking to children about our families.* Retrieved from http://www.familyequality.org/resources/publications/talkingtochildren.pdf

Butler, K. (2006, March 7). Many couples must negotiate terms of "Brokeback" marriages. *New York Times.* Retrieved from http://www.nytimes.com/2006/03/07/health/07broke.html?_r=4&oref=slogin&oref=slogin&

Corley, R. (1990). *Final closet: The gay parents' guide for coming out to their children.* Miami, FL: Editech.

Devor, A. (2004). *Witnessing and mirroring a fourteen stage model of transsexual identity formation.* Retrieved from http://www.haworthpress.com/web/JGLP

Gates, G. (2013). *LGBT parenting in the United States.* Los Angeles, CA: Williams Institute.

Kosciw, J., & Diaz, E. (2008). *Involved, invisible, ignored: The experiences of lesbian, gay, bisexual and transgender parents and their children in our nation's K–12 schools.* Available from http://www.glsen.org

Shulman, J. L., Gotta, G., & Green, R. (2012). Will marriage matter? Effects of marriage anticipated by same-sex couples. *Journal of Family Issues, 33*(2), 158.

Transgender Family Law in the U.S. (2006, January 1). *A fact sheet for transgender spouses, partners, parents and youth.*

LICENSURE AND CERTIFICATION

In order to work independently as a counselor with couples or families, counselors usually need to get credentialed. Most often these credentials exist as a means to protect the public and regulate the practice of counseling. Licensure is a legal credential regulated by each state. Certification awarded by a professional organization has no bearing on the legality of practice and is most often used as a marketing tool to communicate specialized training in certain areas, though some states use evidence of certification to verify requirements indicated in their laws. In this entry, licensure and certification will be discussed, emphasizing aspects important for the practice of marriage, family, and couples counseling.

Licensure

The requirements clinicians need to meet to be licensed or certified are dictated by the entity overseeing the particular credential. Licensure is a credential that is regulated by the state, the District of Colombia, or Puerto Rico. States have established licensing boards that monitor and regulate state laws regarding the practice of various professions. For mental health professionals, the board is responsible for granting licenses to interested professionals who meet the minimum state educational, examination, and experiential requirements. Boards are also responsible for monitoring the profession by holding disciplinary hearings for licensed professionals in violation of an ethical or legal policy. Moreover, the board monitors unlawful practice of counseling. Depending on the state, a separate board can exist for different mental health professions or a composite board can exist, which represents similar groups of professionals (e.g., professional counselors or marriage and family therapists).

Individuals interested in the practice of marriage, family, and couples counseling should make themselves familiar with the licensing laws of their respective state so as to ensure ethical and legal practice. A licensed clinician is one who has been determined by the board to have met a minimum set of requirements so as to protect the public from potentially maleficent practice.

Individuals interested in doing work with couples and families can receive licensure in any of the five main mental health fields. Most states license professionals as a professional counselor, marriage and family therapist, social worker, psychologist, or psychiatrist. The Tenth Amendment to the United States Constitution allows states to develop and enforce licensing laws. As such, national licensing laws do not exist. Though some mental health groups have less disparity across states than others, it is important that individuals interested in licensure seek out the laws appropriate to the state and profession in which they want to work. It should also be noted that individuals should be aware that licensure or certification to work in the school system is typically handled by the state's Department of Education.

Title Acts

Licensing laws in different states usually have title laws that protect the way in which one can identify to the public. The laws restrict the use of a specific title to only certain individuals who have met certain educational and training requirements. For example, in many states, if someone is unlicensed, they cannot publicly use the title "licensed marriage and family therapist" without being in violation of the law. Individuals who are beginning to engage in clinical work should be mindful of state laws as to how they can identify with the public. Additionally, individuals seeking out mental health clinicians should be cautious of individuals marketing themselves with terms that are not regulated by the state (i.e., "psychotherapist"). Moreover, states have adopted different terms under which individuals can legally identify with certain professional titles; in counseling, different states use different titles to identify professional counselors (e.g., Licensed Professional Counselor [LPC], Licensed Clinical Mental Health Counselor [LCMHC], Licensed Clinical Professional Counselor [LCPC]). Some states have a multitiered licensing process denoting different levels of training. Many states will allow for individuals to hold an associate-level license if they have met the educational and examination requirements but not the experiential requirements. However, the laws for an associate-level clinician may limit the conditions under which one can practice compared to those who are fully licensed.

Practice Acts

Practice laws refer to the laws that dictate the behaviors in which one can engage without obtaining a license. For example, many states have a legal definition as to what it means to engage in the "practice of counseling." It is typically thought that practice acts provide more protection to consumers than do title laws as they regulate the practice of services rendered. Practice laws are also an area in which different mental health professional groups can find themselves in conflict where one group wants to be the exclusive profession to engage in a specific practice. For example, currently, psychologists are working to change their scope of practice in many states to allow certain psychologists with additional training to be able to prescribe certain medications. This has created some conflict with psychiatrists, who have typically been the professionals prescribing medication.

Individuals interested in the practice of marriage, couples, and family counseling should be familiar with the work in which professions are legally allowed to engage and with which groups. It may be true that the practice of counseling and/ or the practice of marriage and family therapy, for example, allows for the individual to work with families and couples.

Certain groups of professionals can be exempt from having to meet licensing requirements within either title or practice acts. Typically these professional groups include (1) professionals licensed by other statutes, (2) members of the clergy, (3) students in an education program working under supervision of a licensed professional, (4) attorneys, and (5) federal, state, or local agencies acting in an official capacity. The abilities granted for members of groups in which exceptions apply will vary from state to state. Individuals not in these groups typically need to show evidence of education, examination, and experience in order to receive a license.

Education

One key distinction between the varying mental health professions in titles adopted is often, but not always, associated with the degree held by the counselor. That is, licensed social workers typically have a degree in social work, licensed marriage and family therapists usually have a degree in marriage and family therapy, and so on. The professions of professional counselor, marriage and family therapist, and social worker often require a master's degree (e.g., MA or MS) in their respective field, though some states will recognize lower-tiered credentials with less education. A terminal degree as a psychologist is usually a doctoral degree (e.g., PhD, PsyD, EdD) in psychology. Psychiatrists are medical doctors (MD) who have gone through medical school. Each of these professions is typically affiliated with different professional organizations:

- professional counseling—American Counseling Association (ACA)
- marriage and family therapy—American Association for Marriage and Family Therapy (AAMFT)
- social work—National Association of Social Workers (NASW)
- psychology—American Psychological Association (APA)
- psychiatry—American Psychiatric Association (APA)

The respective organizations monitor the practice of each profession and lobby at the state and federal level to advocate for their respective field. State licensing boards will dictate the curriculum length and content necessary to meet the minimum requirements for licensure.

Many states are moving in the direction of expecting individuals to graduate from programs that are accredited by a specialized accrediting body that reflects high professional standards being met across the curriculum. The Commission for the Accreditation for Marriage and Family Therapy Education (COMAFTE) and the Council for Accreditation of Counseling and Related Programs (CACREP) accredit master's and doctoral degrees in marriage and family therapy and counseling, respectively.

Examination

Many states will require licensure applicants to provide evidence of successful completion of a comprehensive examination. These comprehensive examinations are designed to assess individuals' general knowledge of the practice area in which they wish to be licensed. This examination will vary from state to state and between professions. For example, professional counselors often need to provide evidence of successful completion of the National Counseling Exam (NCE), the National Clinical Mental Health Counseling Exam (NCMHCE), or both. Marriage and family therapists usually have to provide evidence of successful completion of the Association of Marital and Family Therapy Regulatory Board's (AMFTRB) examination. These are commonly accepted exams for those pursuing a career engaging in marriage, family, or couples counseling. However, some states will accept other exams in lieu of the ones listed above.

Other states will require individuals to pass a jurisprudence exam in addition to a comprehensive exam. These examinations test applicants' knowledge of licensing board rules, state law, and operating procedures that would affect the practice of clinicians in their respective state. With the myriad examinations that exist, individuals should be knowledgeable about the type of work in which they wish to engage once licensed.

A final thing individuals should consider when exploring licensure is managed care. Health insurance companies reimburse professionals at varying rates based upon the state license they hold. One trend in counseling, for example, is the requirement for clinicians to pass the National Clinical Mental Health Counseling Exam in order to meet requirements for employment at the U.S. Department of Veterans Affairs or to be eligible for reimbursement through TRICARE, the insurance of the Department of Defense. Moreover, some companies will reimburse some licensed professionals and not others. Marriage and family therapists are not recognized as providers for Medicaid in every state, for example. Licensure laws are constantly changing to reflect the sociopolitical climate and the advocacy efforts of the varying professional organizations.

Certification

Whereas licensing adheres to legal requirements monitored by the state, certification is monitored by various professional organizations or groups. The types of certifications one can obtain as a clinician are far too varied and numerous to list here, though some examples are noted below. Most certifications are designed to show specialized training with a specific therapeutic modality (e.g., Board Certified Behavior Analyst [BCBA] or Certified Emotionally Focused Therapist), a certain intervention strategy (e.g., Registered Play Therapist [RPT]), or a certain type of work (e.g., Approved Clinical Supervisor [ACS]). Most states require a license to engage in the practice of counseling or therapy, with some exceptions. Certification credentials are varied and diverse. Certifications are often managed and monitored by professional organizations. Though certification may help one get licensed, a certification typically does not allow one to use language or behaviors that would fall under a state's practice or title acts. An individual could have a certification (e.g., Nationally Certified Counselor [NCC]) but may not meet requirements for licensure. A certification is a way in which a professional can signal to the community that they have received additional training in a certain theory or subject area. Often the requirements set forth by the overseeing board of a certification are similar to those required for licensure (e.g., experience, examination, and training/education). However, some certifications may require only some of these standards to be eligible for certification. A key thing to remember is that licensure is monitored by the state whereas certification is typically monitored by a separate professional organization.

There are many certifications for those interested in couples and family counseling. These include Nationally Certified Counselor (NCC); certification as a Sex Therapist, Sex Educator, or Sexuality Counselor with the American Association for Sex Educators, Counselors, and Therapists (AASECT); Registered Play Therapist (RPT); Board Certified Art Therapist (ATR-BC); or Certified Emotionally Focused Therapist. The list of different certifications is varied. The decision to pursue any certification credential will be influenced by the educational, examination, experiential, and financial costs associated with these credentials. Certain certifications require specific training from individuals from a certain organization, whereas other certification requirements will draw on more general experience.

Licensure and certification credentialing exists so as to ensure the public that the individual providing marriage, couples, and family counseling is qualified to do so. Individuals interested in pursuing a career doing this type of clinical work should begin researching state licensure laws regarding title and practice, and become familiar with various professional organizations that provide additional training and certification in more specific areas. Individuals need to understand these legal and professional requirements in order to help make informed decisions.

Tyler Wilkinson

See also Professional Associations; Public Health Code; Training and Licensure

Further Readings

American Association for Marriage and Family Therapy: http://www.aamaft.org
American Association of Sexuality Educators, Counselors, and Therapists: http://www.aasect.org
American Counseling Association: http://www.counseling.org
American Counseling Association. (2012). *Licensure requirements for professional counselors: A state-by-state report.* Alexandria, VA: Author.
Art Therapy Credentials Board: http://www.atcb.org
Association for Play Therapy. (n.d.). *RPT and RPT-S credentials.* Retrieved from http://www.a4pt.org/?page=credentials
Center for Credentialing and Education: http://www.cce-global.org
National Board of Certified Counselors: http://www.nbcc.org

LIFE BALANCE

Life balance, sometimes referred to as work–life balance, is a concept used to help people understand how to prioritize the different components of one's everyday responsibilities and one's "lifestyle" (health, pleasure, family, leisure, spiritual). Work and family/personal obligations may leave little time for individual wants and needs. Life balance has emerged as a term used to define a balance among the various aspects of life. It can be viewed as a state of mind, a process, and a goal. As a state of mind, life balance describes a sense of meaning, contentment, satisfaction, and happiness with one's life. Viewed as a process, the term refers to actively working to effectively manage or meet the various demands of life that flow from the multiple responsibilities to one's own wants/needs and responsibilities to others. An individual's life balance, or lack of it, can positively or negatively influence his or her mental, physical, and spiritual wellness or sense of well-being. In addition, it can also influence relationships with a partner/spouse, friends, family, work, and other systems a person is connected to. Life balance becomes "unbalanced" when one aspect of one's life leads to neglect in another area. In this entry, the history of life balance as a concept will be reviewed as well as the process of life balance, the influence of gender, and life balance as a part of counseling.

Current and past research on the life balance construct is drawn from multiple disciplines and sources including mental health counseling, psychology, and the medical community. The construct of life balance is holistic and multifaceted. It is often researched, measured, or discussed in connection to individual well-being or overall wellness as mentioned. Components of life balance are broadly categorized by some as the social/relational, emotional, occupational, spiritual, physical, and intellectual domains of an individual's life.

History

An interest in life balance can be traced back to ancient times and is found in many diverse cultures and societies. An early form of the life balance construct was a central tenet for ancient Western philosophers, including Plato and Aristotle. Further evidence of the ancient origins of the concept of life balance can be found at the Delphi temple site in modern-day Greece. Inscribed on a temple wall at the archeological site is an inscription that translates to modern English as "nothing in excess," a phrase that seems to imply a need for balance in one's life. It is a reasonable assumption that this idea would include moderation not only in the consumption of food and wine, but also with respect to concepts such as work and leisure.

Members of medical communities have championed the benefits of balance and moderation in life for centuries and thus seem to have established a clear connection between the two concepts and physical well-being. In the West, examples of support of this connection can be found as early as the medieval period. In fact, there is ample evidence that early practitioners went a step further and included aspects of psychological and social balance as crucial to overall well-being. One long-held belief was that all organisms strive to achieve a state of balance. This belief is similar to the more modern idea that all organisms move from a state of simplicity to one of complexity as part of a natural process. Life balance is a complex idea in which an organism (individual, couple, or family) tries to balance relationships and responsibilities within their immediate system and relationships and responsibilities to other connected systems (e.g., work, school, extended family).

Life Balance as a Goal

Life balance, or working to achieve it, is viewed as a worthy or noble goal in several traditional belief systems, especially those that emphasize harmony and a mind–spirit–body connection. Balance in life is a fundamental belief within many Eastern philosophies and belief systems, including Buddhism and Confucianism among several others. For example, the Buddhist concept of seeking the "middle path" lends itself to the idea of moderation or balance. Similar examples can be found in the teachings of Confucius, which encourage followers to seek balance and moderation in their actions.

The restoration of balance in an individual is an essential component of indigenous healing traditions that persist to the present day. Many Native American cultures emphasize an additional element to the mind, spirit, and body triad—the environment. From this perspective, life balance can be described as a desirable condition in which the individual strives to be in harmony with the natural world. This holistic perspective on balance in life encompasses all aspects of the individual: spiritual, psychological, physiological, familial, and environmental. In this example, harmony is akin to well-being and is believed to accompany, or be a product of, the restoration or establishment of balance. For many Native American groups, this balance and harmony are essential to well-being and disruptions are harmful to the individual and indeed to the group as a whole.

Life Balance as a Process

Another aspect of the life balance construct is that realizing or sustaining a sense of life balance requires conscious effort on the part of the individual. Based on this assumption, one can infer that life balance as a process includes or calls for an element of agency. In other words, individuals must work to achieve and maintain a sense of life balance. If so, then a measure of intentionality with regard to the actions or behavior of an individual in that regard must be included in a definition of the concept of life balance. Additionally, a sense of self-efficacy or belief in one's abilities would necessarily be required to propel or motivate an individual forward in his or her quest to achieve life balance. For example, if an individual possesses the belief that life balance is both desirable and achievable through one's actions, a strong sense of self-efficacy would serve as a beneficial support and provide additional motivation toward that goal.

Life Balance as a State of Mind

There is ample evidence that an individual's perception of life balance can change over time, which indicates that the life balance construct can be viewed on a continuum. Some individuals may experience periods in which they perceive a greater sense of life balance and at other times feel or perceive a reduced sense of life balance. This may be an issue of a temporarily increased focus on a specific aspect of life, such as work or family. For example, an individual may, at a certain stage in his or her life, actively work toward career advancement and expend a higher degree of energy, attention, or resources to achieve his or her desired career goal. In doing so, the individual might spend less time on another aspect of life, such as family ties or the pursuit of leisure time. This increased focus on one aspect or another may influence or affect the individual's actual or perceived physical or mental health and thus his or her perception of the degree of life balance. Perception should never be underestimated. From some theoretical orientations or positions, perceptions held by an individual *are* reality for that individual.

Life Balance and Gender

Some researchers have posited that men and women may experience life balance differently. There may be several reasons for this difference. One such reason for this difference in experience may be related to the concept of life roles. For example, females may occupy or perform more life roles than males. In addition, it is possible that one gender may place, or is influenced by society to place, a higher value on a particular aspect of life than the other. More research is needed in this area to determine the full extent of differences in how some men and women experience life balance and the potential positive or negative influence of those differences.

Life Balance and Development

Life balance may be easier or more difficult to attain depending on one's developmental stage. For example, children in the United States tend to be skewed toward the pleasure parts of their life when they are young and add additional life roles and demands as they age. After retirement, given the financial resources available, many people move back toward the pleasure aspects of their lives. It is perhaps easy to see the struggle between many life roles during the family development phases that include partnering with someone and raising small children. People sometimes struggle with balancing obligations to work, family, and their individual wants. However, there are challenges at every individual/family phase of development. For example, an adolescent who spends or is required to spend a majority of his or her time on schoolwork may become frustrated or angry with teachers or caregivers. These emotions may result in disruptive behavior. A lack of perceived life balance may contribute to stress, impaired or decreased functioning, and other negative side effects in both adults and adolescents. Individuals in either group who perceive a lack of balance between various aspects of their lives including career, family, leisure time, and the pursuit or existence of satisfactory or fulfilling relationships may experience decreased levels of mental, emotional, or physical well-being.

Life balance can be defined in a variety of ways. Six common conceptualizations are (1) multiple roles; (2) equity across multiple roles; (3) satisfaction between multiple roles; (4) fulfilment of role salience between multiple roles; (5) a relationship between conflict and facilitation; and (6) perceived control between multiple roles. Depending on one's age, phase of development, culture, gender, socioeconomic status, and other contextual factors, one or more of these ways of conceptualizing life balance may be more salient to client(s).

Life Balance and Culture

The recognition that life balance has cultural dimensions or considerations is worthy of attention. It is reasonable to expect that an individual from one culture may interpret or perceive life balance differently than an individual from another. Although cultural groups may share certain values or place increased or decreased emphasis on one aspect of life or another, it would be a mistake to assume that the construct of life balance is itself necessarily experienced or perceived in the same way. Indeed, some cultures may place a higher value than others on life balance as a goal.

Life Balance and Wellness

The construct of life balance is clearly connected to wellness of all types, and interest in wellness has increased steadily since the 1960s in mental health and other arenas. This increase in interest may be responsible for the emergence of the life balance construct within professional literature. Mental health professionals have come to more fully understand the interconnectedness of life domains as well as the benefits of balance among those domains. These benefits include higher levels of satisfaction or happiness with life, which have been found to enhance mental well-being. However, the construct of life balance is made up of more than just satisfaction or time allocation and differs from wellness or perceived well-being alone. Much has been written about wellness, and a common metaphor used in discussing wellness is that of a wheel. Components or aspects that make up the lives of many individuals similar to those discussed herein or believed to be related to the construct of life balance such as family, career, or leisure are arranged around this wheel of wellness. It may be that the most accurate depiction of the wheel would show life balance to be in the center or axle of the wheel, with the various components arranged around it.

Life Balance and Counseling

In a number of recent studies, the concept of life balance or an individual's perception of its presence or absence was shown to be directly connected to other important concepts including mental and physical well-being. With this in mind, it is understandable that mental health counselors have come to realize that discussing the concept of life balance with clients has a definite place in the therapeutic process. Therapists have long been aware that disturbances in one or more of the aspects or components that make up a client's life can have a significant impact on psychological well-being and overall wellness. A number of researchers have indicated that assessing the perceived level of life balance or discussing the concept with a client in session may help the client to examine or realize the extent to which the aspects or domains of life are connected may be beneficial and ultimately influence decisions or behaviors in positive directions. Thus, the concept of life balance has emerged as an important construct in the area of mental health counseling and services. Although some in the mental health arena appear to question whether or not the life balance construct has yet to be fully understood or investigated, it is clear that interest in life balance has grown and continues to gain traction as an important concept in mental health counseling and other related areas including marriage, family, and couples counseling. Undoubtedly, more research would benefit both mental health workers and the medical community. A limited number of instruments designed to measure or assess levels of life balance have been created, and some have been examined for validity and reliability. Research on the construct of life balance continues apace in the United States and several countries around the world at this writing. As always, work that contributes to the promotion of positive mental health and the prevention of mental illness will remain the focus of the counseling profession.

Randy J. Davis

See also Family Values; Holism; Individual Family Culture; Mindfulness; Positive Psychology; Work Relationships

Further Readings

Christiansen, C. H., & Matuska, K. M. (2006). Lifestyle balance: A review of concepts and research. *Journal of Occupational Sciences, 13,* 49–61.

Dockett, K. H., Dudley-Grant, G. R., & Bankart, P. C. (2003). *Psychology and Buddhism: From individual to global community.* New York, NY: Kluwer Academic/Plenum.

Dunn, H. L. (1961). *High level wellness.* Arlington, VA: Beatty Press.

Grant-Vallone, E. J., & Donaldson, S. I. (2001). Consequence of work-family conflict on employee wellbeing over time. *Work and Stress, 15*(3), 214–226. doi:10.1080/02678370110066544

Greenhaus, J. H., Collins, K. M., & Shaw, J. D. (2003). The relation between work-family balance and quality of life. *Journal of Vocational Behavior, 63,* 510–531. doi:10.1016/S0001-8791(02)00042-8

Kuhnle, C., Hofer, M., & Kilian, B. (2010). The relationship of value orientations, self-control, frequency of school-leisure conflicts, and life-balance in adolescence. *Learning and Individual Differences, 20,* 251–255.

Larsen, R. (2009). The contributions of positive and negative affect to emotional well-being. *Psychological Topics, 18,* 247–266.

Leaman, O. (1999). *Key concepts in Eastern philosophy.* New York, NY: Routledge.

Myers, J. E., & Sweeney, T. J. (2005). *Counseling for wellness.* Alexandria, VA: American Counseling Association.

Myers, J. E., Sweeney, T. J., & Witmer, J. M. (2000). The wheel of wellness counseling for wellness: A holistic model of treatment planning. *Journal of Counseling & Development, 78,* 251–266.

Sheldon, K. M., Cummins, R., & Kamble, S. (2010). Life balance and wellbeing: Testing a novel conceptual and measurment approach. *Journal of Personality, 78,* 1093–1134.

Wallace, A., & Shapiro, S. (2006). Mental balance and wellbeing: Building bridges between Buddhism and Western psychology. *American Psychologist, 61,* 690–701. doi:10.1037/0003-066X.61.7.690

Yurkovich, E. E., & Lattergrass, I. (2008). Defining health and unhealthiness: Perceptions held by Native American Indians with persistent mental illness. *Mental Health, Religion & Culture, 11,* 437–459. doi:10.1080/13674670701473751

LIFE EVENTS

The term *life events* refers to any event that happens in clients' lives, including events past, present, and future. Although theories and models of counseling do not directly address life events, extra-therapeutic events can be pivotal in clients' lives. Therefore, couples and family counselors need to recognize and incorporate clients' life events into counseling. The common factors perspective offers a meta-perspective that encompasses counseling theory and life events. This is a meta-perspective because it places theories of counseling within a larger context. The common factors perspective posits that regardless of which theory is used in counseling, the same components are responsible for change. Although authors vary in which components contribute to change, the most common components are (a) client factors (e.g., personality, demographics, mental health, history, and extra-therapeutic life events); (b) therapeutic alliance; (c) theory or model of counseling (notably, which theory or model is used is less important than whether or not the counselor is skillfully using an established approach); and (d) hope or expectancy. This paradigm of change honors both theory and clients' uniqueness. This entry examines different types of life events, their complexity, and how life events can be approached in counseling.

Types of Life Events

Many events occur as part of the individual or family development cycle and can be expected by people who are looking ahead in life or are self-reflective. These events include things like graduating, getting a job, getting married, the birth of children, parental deaths, retirement, and so on.

In addition to expected life events, people experience unexpected events. Crises are the most recognized unexpected life events. Natural disasters (e.g., floods, tsunamis, earthquakes), unexpected occurrences (e.g., house fire, car accident), or events that occur because of other people or broader culture (e.g., being the victim of a crime, war, terrorist attacks, a job layoff) are unexpected life events. Others include common human experiences, but are things no one thinks will actually happen to *them.* For example, as common as divorce is, no one marries expecting *his* or *her* marriage will end in divorce. Other statistically common but often traumatic experiences include sexual or physical abuse, chronic illness, acute illness, automobile accidents, miscarriage, infertility, affairs, termination from a job, or injury. Some life events are expected, but when they happen outside of the expected time frame, they can disrupt lives. These situations include events such as parents or children dying young, acute or chronic illness, and children leaving home very young or returning home as adults.

In addition to expected and unexpected life events, transitions can be an overlooked component of life events. For example, when a couple marries, the wedding may be the event, but the transition could last more than a year. Considering the event and transition periods allows counselors to more fully understand clients' experiences.

Complexities in Understanding the Impact of Life Events on Couples and Families

Stress, Eustress, and the Importance of Adapting

People tend to categorize life events as positive or negative and call painful experiences "negative" and enjoyable experiences "positive." This oversimplifies the impact of life events in three ways. First, a similar event may be experienced very differently by different individuals. For example, one person may be delighted by the birth of a child while another is coping with an unplanned pregnancy, undesired life adjustments, and insecurity about parenting. Second, stress theory emphasizes that both stress (from "negative" events) and eustress (from "positive" events) cause strain and drain people's emotional resources as they adapt. Therefore, any significant life event, no matter how positive, can add strain to people's lives. Third, whether an event is enjoyable or not, how a person copes and adapts largely determines the ultimate impact of that event. When people adapt well, even a very painful event can lead to life improvements and increased resiliency.

Varying Individual and Systemic Impacts of Life Events

Life events may be focused on one person (e.g., a job loss), a subset of a family (e.g., changing schools), or the whole family (e.g., moving to another location). Regardless of who an event happens to, it usually impacts every family member directly and indirectly. To illustrate, consider a family in which the father is laid off from his job. Although this event happened to one person, his emotional reaction impacts relationships with other family members, which may in turn impact their functioning. Additionally, loss of income may reduce discretionary funds, which could mean children stop extracurricular activities, the family cancels vacations, possessions need to be sold, and regular social events are declined due to cost, thus changing family members' personal identity and social support. Stress may increase for all family members, who may have fewer resources to cope with this stress. Family members may change roles (e.g., the partner may feel pressure to earn more money and the father and/or children may take on more domestic responsibilities).

When a family is impacted by a life event, each member may be impacted to different degrees and in different ways. In the case of a parent's job loss, an adolescent who has to quit extracurricular activities may get a job and take on household chores and thereby be more impacted than a younger child who does not notice receiving fewer toys or new clothes. Each family member may cope with events differently and seeing others cope can be confusing. For example, couples grieving the death of a child often grieve in different ways and at different paces, and one person's coping strategies may be misinterpreted by the other as not caring, moving on too quickly, or getting too lost in grief. As family members work through the impact of life events, the way each person is coping can also impact others. In the previous example, one parent may cope with the death of a child by withdrawing and needing more personal space, which may lead to emotional distance in family relationships and neglect of domestic responsibilities.

Life Events and Mental Illness

While life events may be stressful in themselves, occasionally the event is compounded by the fact that it precipitates mental illness. For example, postpartum depression occurs after the birth of a baby, trauma may lead to PTSD, and significant events in young adulthood may trigger the onset of adult mental illnesses, such as schizophrenia. In these situations, the person has to cope with the event itself and the aftermath of that event, while also learning to manage the mental health impact.

Specific Theoretical Perspectives on Life Events

Although theories and models of couples and family counseling do not focus on clients' life events, they offer guidance for making sense of and helping clients work through difficult life events. Systems theorists explore the need for the system to *restructure* after a significant life event and emphasize that the system may need to develop rules for interacting in new, healthy ways. Theories with a strong cognitive base, such as cognitive-behavioral therapy (CBT) and rational emotive behavioral therapy, emphasize that the client's *interpretation* of a life event may be more important in determining the impact of the event than the actual event itself. CBT theories explore clients' *schemas*, which are the ways clients organize their beliefs about life. Schemas may be developed by individuals, but are often based on cultural or religious beliefs. The importance of interpretation can be illustrated by considering the death of a parent: A child who believes his parent abandoned him may struggle with grief and emotional pain for years while a child who believes his parent was relieved of pain and is watching out for him in the afterlife may find comfort and reassurance in the midst of grief. Existential models like *logotherapy* posit that people can best cope with life experiences by finding meaning or purpose.

Life Events in Counseling

One of the foundational components of systems theory, the basis of couples and family counseling, is that people function in systems, and any change in one person impacts every other person. Because of this theoretical base, couples and family counselors inquire about life events in the family and explore the systemic impact of those events.

Relationship Education

In the field of couples and family counseling, life events are most thoroughly addressed in relationship education (RE) programs. Most RE programs invite participants to reflect on significant life experiences and the impact of those experiences. RE programs help partners develop understanding and empathy for each other. These programs also often help couples predict the impact of these experiences in their future, anticipate other significant future life events, and develop plans for communication and conflict resolution. In this way, most RE programs work to build resiliency and coping mechanisms, which can buffer the negative impact of stressful life events.

Addressing Life Events in Couples and Family Counseling

Exploring life events with clients can be particularly useful because patterns are often revealed in emotionally intense situations. Because of this, how clients respond during momentous life events can help counselors assess family dynamics and provide an opportunity for counselors to help clients see their patterns play out in life. This enables clients to reflect on what they think about each person's behaviors and each person can change his or her responses in ways that help the family reach their goals.

When counselors are tuned in to cultural pressures around life events, they can better help clients navigate the impact of those events in ways that are congruent with the client's values and are not inadvertently impacted by cultural pressures. This is particularly important when clients belong to a minority group and the cultural pressures may not reflect—or may even be at odds with—the clients' values.

When counselors ignore life events, they may miss realities and challenges in clients' lives and neglect to adapt treatment appropriately. Missed life events can also lead counselors to overlook opportunities to use these events in helping clients reach treatment goals. Counselors use careful judgment when asking clients what is happening in their lives because counseling can lose focus on goals of counseling and become a "problem of the week" discussion.

When counselors incorporate life events into couples and family counseling, counselors first work from their theory and use that theory's conceptualization of life events. Then, counselors can use the following strategies in connection with their case conceptualization and treatment plan. Counselors can help family members identify life events, paying attention to both the event and transitions. Client responses to the event may be used as an example or metaphor for other aspects of treatment. Counselors can help family members individually identify ways to cope while being accepting of and gracious toward others who are impacted and coping differently. Counselors can guide family members to reflect on the effectiveness of their coping methods, evaluate what is and is not working, and adjust as needed. When the life event is a focus of counseling, the counselor can help clients develop resiliency by exploring and adapting underlying beliefs and perspectives, promoting useful coping strategies, and helping clients recognize internal and external resources. Counselors can also help clients re-evaluate the event and their understanding of the event by examining the story from a more nuanced perspective, considering the surrounding events, the impact, interpretation, and responses of others, and reinterpreting the event in more complex ways. The counselor chooses his or her strategy based on their own conceptualization of the importance of the event in relation to the presenting problem and treatment goals, and the client's preferences for treatment.

Susan N. Perkins

See also Crisis Intervention With Couples and Families; Individual and Family Development; Life Transitions; Marriage Enrichment; Resilience

Further Readings

Blow, A. J., Morrison, N. C., Tamaren, K., Wright, K., Schaafsma, M., & Nadaud, A. (2009). Change processes in couple therapy: An intensive case analysis of one couple using a common factors lens. *Journal of Marital & Family Therapy, 35*, 350–368. doi:10.1111/j.1752-0606.2009.00122.x

Bodenmann, G., & Shantinath, S. D. (2004). The Couples Coping Enhancement Training (CCET): A new approach to prevention of marital distress based upon stress and coping. *Family Relations, 53*, 477–484. doi:10.1111/j.0197-6664.2004.00056.x

Bradbury, T. N. (1995). Assessing the four fundamental domains of marriage. *Family Relations, 44*, 459–468.

Goldenberg, H., & Goldenberg, I. (2013). *Family therapy: An overview* (8th ed.). Belmont, CA: Brooks/Cole.

Randall, A. K., & Bodenmann, G. (2009). The role of stress on close relationships and marital satisfaction. *Clinical Psychology Review, 29*, 105–115. doi:10.1016/j.cpr.2008.10.004

Sprenkle, D. H., Davis, S. D., & Lebow, J. L. (2009). *Common factors in couple and family therapy: The overlooked foundation for effective practice.* New York, NY: Guilford Press.

Walsh, F. (2002). A family resilience framework: Innovative practice applications. *Family Relations, 51*, 130–137. doi:10.1111/j.1741-3729.2002.00130.x

LIFE TRANSITIONS

Life transitions can be understood as points of change resulting in the beginning of a new life phase and/or the ending of a previous phase of life. Some of these changes seem to occur universally, while others occur in specific situations. Transitions can be normative, meaning that they are experienced by all or virtually all individuals, or they can be nonnormative or distinct, suggesting that changes are unique to a specific individual, population, or culture. Traditionally, transitions were identified and understood to occur based upon developmental theories that described how individuals change between childhood and adulthood. However, later research has suggested that transitions occur into adulthood and can be identified throughout the entire life span. These transitions affect individuals, couples, and families. This entry will explore the concept of life transitions and will outline various transitions that occur throughout the life span.

Types of Life Transitions

Life transitions can hold both internal and external significance. When a transition occurs, individuals may experience a shift in self-concept, worldview, and even emotional regulation. Externally, roles and relationships can change based upon life transitions, and emotions can also be impacted on an interpersonal level. It is also important to recognize the historical impact on life transitions—cultural norms can shape how and what meaning is ascribed to various shifts that occur throughout the life span. When exploring the impact of life transitions on an individual, it is important to note the causes and effects of these transitions as well as identify which aspects seem to impact the process of transitioning throughout life.

A variety of transitions occur throughout the life span. Biologically, changes have been identified in four basic stages: infancy, childhood, adolescence, and adulthood. Within each stage, people experience specific psychological, emotional, mental, and physical aspects of development. Educationally, individuals experience changes when heading to kindergarten and also face transitions when switching schools, graduating, dropping out of school, or continuing to a different phase of education (i.e., from elementary school to middle school or from high school to college). Vocationally, transitions include starting a first or new job, promotions or demotions, job changes, job losses, and even retirement. Changes in finances, health, spirituality, and culture can also impact one's sense of self as well as one's interaction with the world around them. An overview of transitions that occur in and between each biological stage of development will be explored.

Transitions in Infancy and Childhood

A significant transition occurs when a baby is born, moving from the womb to the outside world. During infancy, which is considered to occur during the first two years of life, distinct aspects of noted growth include sensory development, motor development, the ability to communicate, emotional differentiation, and attachment formation. Increased mobility and autonomy pave the way to the first biological transition: moving from infancy to toddlerhood, the phase of development that occurs from approximately 2 through 3 years of age. Various biological changes occur during this stage, including expanded movement as well as increases in height and weight. Language and thought also expand in childhood, and imaginary or symbolic play becomes possible due to an increased capacity to pretend.

From toddlerhood, individuals are considered to be in early childhood from the ages of 4 to 6. During this stage, individuals tend to engage in gender identification and display gender preference for same-sex companionship. Cognitive ability continues to expand, and moral development is evident in early childhood in more profound ways as compared to toddlerhood. The ability to take initiative is a hallmark of early childhood as compared to previous stages.

Middle childhood describes the stage of children between the ages of 6 and 12. Social competence increases during this phase of life, and the presence of peer influence and pressure is paramount. Combined with this, self-concept development is strong during middle childhood. Skill development is a vital component of this stage, which typically occurs in school as well as through outside learning.

While biological transitions demonstrate obvious signs of transition throughout childhood, other elements have been observed as important aspects of transition among children. Lawrence Kohlberg proposed a theory of moral development, asserting that morality seems to change and develop throughout childhood based upon progressive stages that empower children to move from concrete to more abstract understanding and moral reasoning. Jean Piaget proposed a cognitive development theory, which identifies transitions in thought processes as children move from sensory experiences to language learning, discerning cause and effect, the use of logic, and finally learning to engage in both hypothetical and deductive reasoning. Erik Erikson identified psychosocial transitions or crises that occur throughout the life span. During childhood, those crises include trust versus mistrust (birth through age 2), autonomy versus shame and doubt (age 2–4), initiative versus guilt (age 4–5), and industry versus inferiority (age 5–12).

Child life stages, and thus childhood transitions, seem to be predictable in nature. They occur in a set order, and there are qualitative differences between stages. In addition, transitions in childhood allow a child's learning and development to be integrated with previous developmental gains. Typically, child development and progression through various stages is not necessarily a chosen action on the part of the child; instead, transitions are ushered in by biological or psychological influences. In contrast, adolescent and adult transitions seem to highlight the volition or will of the individual in addition to biological or psychological influences.

Transition to Adolescence

The transition to adolescence is often accompanied by various changes. Physically, individuals experience bodily changes that correspond with the onset of puberty. Relationally, adolescence includes a shift in focus from friendships to awareness and pursuit of romantic relationships. Awareness of oneself as a sexual being often increases during this stage of life. Adolescents also begin to experience emotional variability unlike that experienced in childhood, which can lead to more distinct emotional expression. While friendships were important during childhood, peer influence and the need to belong to a peer group become vital components of this life phase. Peer pressure is also an aspect that seems to greatly influence adolescent beliefs and behaviors. In terms of psychosocial development, adolescents experience the stage of identity versus role confusion, which underscores the importance of developing one's self-concept as a meaningful process prior to becoming an adult.

Transition to Adulthood

Becoming an adult also includes various transitions. Relationally, individuals tend to experience more autonomy as primary relationships shift from parents to peers. Typically, the transition to adulthood is understood to be the point at which individuals experience the psychosocial crisis of intimacy versus isolation. The focus of this life phase is the ability to create, maintain, and support meaningful relationships, and the inability to do so can lead to feelings of isolation or loneliness. Independence also increases as individuals make the transition from high school to college or make the decision to enter the work force.

Jeffrey Jensen Arnett proposed a theory of emerging adulthood, which contends that individuals who transition to adulthood are distinguished from adolescents due to a greater focus upon identity exploration, possibilities, and self-focus. In addition, emerging adults tend to feel in-between (not fully identifying as either an adolescent or an adult) and experience greater instability as compared to adolescents. As emerging adults move toward selecting a life partner, having children, and pursuing a career, they continue the journey into adulthood.

Various aspects occur during adulthood that distinguish it from previous life stages. Physically, adults have developed fully and even begin to see their physical health and well-being decline as adulthood progresses. While mental capacities continue to develop throughout adulthood, decline in cognitive ability can also occur. Competence and ability to engage in a career typify adult life for most individuals, and becoming a financial provider for oneself and other family members becomes an important aspect of this stage. The psychosocial crisis that is faced during adulthood is generativity versus stagnation, which reflects the aim to become a meaningful contributor to oneself and his or her family, the workplace, and even society. Failure to achieve this can lead to a sense of feeling unproductive or even stagnant in life.

Transition to Elderhood

As individuals continue throughout adulthood, they make the transition to elderhood during the last phase of life. Elderhood typically consists of a variety of transitions, and a primary transition occurs when individuals stop their career journey in pursuit of retirement. This vocational change brings with it a transition to new or different roles and relationships, and it can also encourage a slower pace of life. Increased hobbies and pastime activities may fill the void that was once occupied by work. Rather than focusing on productivity, elderhood affords individuals the opportunity to analyze the degree to which one's life was fulfilling and meaningful. Should an individual look back upon his or her life and determine that life was not well lived, this can be cause for feelings of hopelessness and despondency. Exploration of the degree to which one's life has held meaning is noted as the psychosocial crisis of ego integrity versus despair.

Transitions in the Family Life Cycle

Just as transitions occur within an individual throughout his or her lifetime, transitions also occur in the life of a family. An initial transition occurs when two individuals make the decision to explore a romantic relationship. This transition typically involves dating and can lead to engagement, marriage, or some form of substantial commitment. The transition from being single to part of a couple can bring a variety of emotional and mental shifts in order to make space for being part of a collective identity.

Another element of the family life cycle is the decision regarding whether or not to have children. Should children be brought into a family, individuals begin experiencing role expansion as they become not only partners to one another but also parents. Family expansion can occur through birth or adoption. In addition, blended families can be created as individuals who have children from previous marriages or relationships recouple and form a new family system. Connected with this, the separation or ending of a relationship or marriage can bring a transition to the family system as a family unit splits into two or more distinct entities. Therefore, adding to or removing a member or members of a family can deeply impact the family system, thereby influencing the ways in which the family life cycle is experienced.

Parenting approaches can change based upon the needs of a growing child or children. Parenting an infant requires sensitivity to nonverbalized needs, and the focus is often on creating healthy bonds or attachment relationships between parents and children. Parent behaviors often transition when parenting toddlers, as they desire their children to learn how to do basic tasks and explore the world around them. As children age, parents adapt to those needs while also seeking to nurture a sense of autonomy. The challenge to maintain intimacy among parents amid focusing on the development of their children can be a constant struggle, and relationship dimensions may experience change or even strains as parents learn to adapt to the needs of their children in developmentally appropriate ways. Parents not only experience their own journey through life transitions—they also have the opportunity to nurture the growth and development of their children as they experience their own life transitions.

As individuals age, they experience role shifts in the family life cycle. Parents become grandparents; individuals become aunts, uncles, or cousins; in-law relationships occur through marriage. As children leave the home and become adults themselves, couples experience a transition as they renegotiate their relationship in light of their children moving out of the home. Children who are used to being cared for by parents can shift into the role of caregiver as they seek to assist aging parents or grandparents. Each of these transitions can involve mental and emotional shifts as individuals grapple with the changes that have occurred in the family life cycle.

Life transitions occur throughout the life span and seem to have a significant impact upon the ways in which a person experiences themselves and the world around them. Further research regarding factors that influence life transitions would bring clarity on the ways that transitions are experienced. In addition, the impact of culture on life transitions is an important aspect to consider. Identifying the characteristics and corresponding impact of life transitions allows their significance and relevance within human growth and development to be observed.

Christina Schnyders

See also Adult Development; Developmental Model of Marriage

Further Readings

Arnett, J. J. (2004). *Emerging adulthood: The winding road from the late teens through the twenties.* New York, NY: Oxford University Press.

Cowan, P. A., & Hetherington, M. (Eds.). (1991). *Family transitions.* Hillsdale, NJ: Lawrence Erlbaum.

Erikson, E. H. (1994). *Identity and the life cycle.* New York, NY: W. W. Norton.

Hareven, T. K. (Ed.). (1978). *Transitions: The family and the life course in historical perspective.* New York, NY: Academic Press.

Lang, F. R., Reschke, F. S., & Neyer, F. J. (2006). Social relationships, transitions, and personality development across the life span. In D. K. Mrokzek & T. D. Little (Eds.), *Handbook of personality development* (pp. 445–466). Mahwah, NJ: Lawrence Erlbaum.

Miller, T. W. (Ed.). (2010). *Handbook of stressful transitions across the lifespan.* New York, NY: Springer.

Newman, B. M., & Newman, P. R. (2015). *Development through life: A psychosocial approach* (12th ed.). Stamford, CT: Cengage Learning.

LISTENING, EMPATHIC

Empathic listening is a way of being with a person so that the person believes and feels understood and respected without judgment. Empathic listening is often interchangeably used with active and reflective listening. Listening with empathy is more than hearing. It requires the ability to vicariously experience the world of the other through words, body language, and silence, and grasp the underlying meaning and feelings as well as the salience of what is being communicated. Empathic listening is a multidimensional construct that includes the cognitive, affective, and behavioral processes. It is part of a learned skill set expected from mental health professionals. Learning the skills is not difficult, but mastering the skills may take time. Therefore, each therapist's ability to provide empathic listening varies. This entry examines the origin of empathic listening, skills needed for empathic listening, the interplay of cultural competence and empathic listening, and the role of mindfulness in enhancing empathic listening.

The Origin of Empathic Listening in Therapy

The recognition of empathic listening finds its roots in both Carl Rogers's core conditions for counseling in his person-centered therapy and Virginia Satir's communication skills, especially mirroring, as described in conjoint family therapy. Rogers presented three conditions—empathy, unconditional positive regard, and genuineness—as necessary to create an environment conducive to change. Just to clarify terminology, empathy is the ability to vicariously experience another's experience; sympathy is the ability to feel sorry for someone else's circumstances; and apathy is the lack of concern for another. Empathy is, therefore, the ability to feel and understand a client's experience intimately. In essence, it is the ability to take the client's life journey as if it were a personal journey and destination. Empathic listening, therefore, facilitates a genuine relationship with a client, eliminates fear of being judged, and creates an environment of safety for exploration and change.

In conjoint marital therapy, Satir presents communication skills and the difficulties of understanding what a client presents as intended. During therapy, a therapist must understand the meaning of the words and the nonverbal aspects presented by a client. Mirroring, where you precisely match certain attributes of the other person's communication such as words, tone, facial expression, and body posture, nourishes a sense of familiarity and comfort and, hence, a sense of being understood.

Empathic Listening Skills

Listening with empathy is a learned skill. It requires the ability to use a specific set of skills as well as to be comfortable with silence. Adults on average spend three fourths of their time engaged in some form of communication, with about half of this time spent in listening. However, this listening may not reflect empathy. Active empathic listening can be conceptualized as a three-stage process consisting of sensing, processing, and responding. During the sensing stage, the therapist indicates to the client through both verbal and nonverbal methods that they are listening to both explicit and implicit content. For instance, the therapist can use head nodding and other encouragers to demonstrate attentiveness. A therapist may also say, "What I hear you say is . . ."; this demonstrates that they have heard the verbal content. To demonstrate understanding of the nonverbal content communicated, the therapist can reflect the feeling or the meaning underlying what is being communicated. Feeling could be identified with a phrase such as "that must be frustrating" and meaning could be illustrated by "this relationship is not meeting criteria for true friendship." In the next stage, the therapist synthesizes and conceptualizes content gathered to make meaning of it. Empathic listening is crucial in this stage as the conceptualization must be accurate for the client through their value set and not through the therapist's value set. Finally, in the response stage, the therapist asks questions for clarification while demonstrating attending. During this stage, the therapist becomes more involved verbally, clarifying feelings and meanings of what was gathered from listening to the client.

There are specific identified skills to demonstrate and communicate empathic listening. The most commonly used skills from the counseling microskills typology, also promoted as attending skills, are presented here. Questioning techniques are one form of attending skills. At times, therapists use different types of questioning to express and seek understanding of the client. While the close-ended question seeks specifics, the open-ended question is intended to expand the content being provided. One form of open-ended questions is the dangling question; this is a question that is left unfinished, hence dangling, for the client to complete. With appropriate questioning, the therapist communicates not only listening but also interest in the client. Using minimal encouragers such as "uh-huh," "mmm," and small actions like nodding is another attending skill that indicates listening while encouraging the client to continue. Paraphrasing or using the client's words to clarify key content or phrases is a third attending skill that stimulates more communication and understanding. A fourth attending skill, summarizing, involves restating client content over an extended period of time in a couple of sentences to demonstrate listening and to clarify understanding. Summarizing also helps focus the session. Reflecting meaning and feelings is yet another attending skill that indicates listening to and comprehending of both overt and covert client content. Reflection of overt and covert meaning and feelings provokes further discussion of content by indicating understanding and attentiveness. Other components classified as attending are therapist's body posture, body language, eye contact, and verbal tone. While an open body posture communicates attentiveness, comfort, and safety, mirroring body posture communicates familiarity and understanding. Similarly, for some cultures, eye contact demonstrates attentiveness while for others this is a sign of disrespect. Thus, cultural expectations and interpretations may differ and, thereby, signify cultural competence as a necessary component of empathic listening.

Cultural Competence and Empathy

Empathic listening involves grasping the cognitive and emotional content delivered by a client in the present while sequentially reconstructing the client's past in the manner intended. For such true empathic listening, the therapist must be able to hear and process information from the client's and not the therapist's worldview. To function from the client's worldview, cultural competence is required, especially when the client is culturally diverse.

Cultural competence is the level of knowledge, attitude, and skills related to a client's culture that a therapist is able to apply appropriately to the client's circumstances from gathering information, through case conceptualizing, to choosing interventions. Acquiring cultural competence is a process during which the therapist learns to arrest personal knowledge, attitudes, beliefs, and values while listening to and understanding the client through the client's set of attitudes, beliefs, and values.

Most therapists begin their intentional cultural competence journey during their formal study in a marriage and family therapy program through a course in multicultural counseling and an immersion experience. However, cultural competence is not a milestone that can be achieved by gaining a one-time wealth of knowledge, because we live in a world of rapid changes that also influences the culture of an individual. Therefore, a therapist must continuously engage in cultural exploration to develop competence. To truly progress in cultural competence, the therapist must also evaluate the attached cognitions and emotions related to each experience and how they impact the therapist's empathic listening process.

A true cultural understanding of a client's experience will facilitate the ability to experience the client's life. Empathic listening through a client's culture will shift the therapist from using a second-person explanation such as "You must have felt disappointed" to "If I am getting this right, you are feeling disappointed with the behaviors she is displaying." In addition, a culturally competent therapist using empathic listening is able to clarify not only the meaning of what the client intends to communicate but also what is slightly under the grasp of the client. In essence, the therapist is able to hear more than what the client is providing and is able to reflect this new understanding back to the client. If the therapist is able to accurately connect with a client through the client's culture, then the client will gain a clearer understanding and better control of his or her inner workings. Such achievement of empathic listening is beneficial to empowering the client to facilitate change.

Cultural competence requires that the therapist match interventions to be appropriate for the client's culture. Most commonly used therapies originate from Western culture and tend to operate from an individualistic perspective. A therapist often seeks a client's personal experience, personal meaning to events and things, and personal feelings. However, not all cultures operate from this individualist viewpoint. Inclusive cultural empathy makes a paradigm shift to a more collectivist approach by facilitating the client to evaluate who they have become as a result of their significant relationships. Inclusive cultural empathy attempts to move away from the individual-centered focus of Western societies to a more relationship-centered context by delving into the significant people and heroes that influenced the client and the client's resulting values and attitudes. Such investigation of family and kin ties may complement the client's culture better. Another perspective, relational-cultural therapy (RCT), also differs from most Western therapies that facilitate a client's movement from dependence to independence. Instead, RCT centers on identifying negative relational images and diminishing the effects of these images to help the client become more connected with others through mutual empathy. By keeping abreast of the various emerging perspectives that address cultural minorities and oppressed populations, a therapist will be able to select the best interventions for a client and find additional ways of engaging in empathic listening.

The following is an example of the interplay between empathic listening and cultural competence. The client is from an Asian culture where intergenerational ties are strong and it is common for generations to share living space and material possessions. The therapist is from a culture where individualism is valued and personal privacy is of utmost importance. The client is describing an occasion where she is at home and talking with a friend when her aunt interjects information into the conversation. Furthermore, the aunt shares the conversation she overheard with the rest of the family during their evening meal. If the therapist, whose culture upholds privacy, interjects and says,

"This must be frustrating," then the therapist would miss that the client valued this involvement by the aunt, which led to her upcoming arranged nuptial. A better option for empathic listening in this case would have been to either remain silent while encouraging the client to share or to use an open-ended question such as "How did this all work out?" Furthermore, an arranged marriage may touch on the values of a therapist who believes in individuality and finding partners based on personal preference rather than family choices that reflect social norms of compatibility. These values will trigger a thinking process, which now will propagate a stimulus to interfere with empathic listening. Mindfulness practices can be used to identify triggers of personal values and beliefs and to discipline the therapist's cognitive and emotional processes and, in turn, help the therapist engage in undivided intentional attention to a client.

The Role of Mindful Practice

Empathy requires the therapist to be able to engage in cognitive flexibility. Such flexibility is the ability to spontaneously restructure knowledge with a real-time adaptive response. Conscious restructuring increases the ability of a therapist to interpret the client's content within the client's worldview, hence engaging in empathic listening. To be able to restructure knowledge, the therapist must be aware of and be able to distinguish between meaning assigned to the content by the therapist and the client. Such awareness requires immediacy or the full presence in the moment of working with clients. Presence in the moment, which means being aware of one's internal and external processes, is mindfulness.

Mindfulness is an ancient Eastern practice that has been infused into Western therapy. Mindfulness requires one to be aware of the workings of one's internal and external functioning. This means the therapist is fully aware, using all senses, of what they are receiving from the client (i.e., words, feelings, beliefs, and values) and how they are interpreting the information. In other terms, the therapist is present and open to all possibilities that enter in that moment. The following are some examples of how the senses may hinder empathic listening. A word spoken by the client may lead to a rippling array of thoughts in the therapist, interrupting empathic listening. The client may share something that infringes on the values of the therapist, leading to a collection of feelings in the therapist that prevent complete empathic listening. A smell or a noise may interrupt the therapist's ability to fully attend to the client, moving away from empathic listening. To continuously engage in empathic listening, a therapist must be able to recognize these interruptions as they occur and refocus immediately to the present and to the client. Understandably, such mindfulness requires training and practice in being present and being attentive to a client while simultaneously able to attend to personal cognitions and emotions and discard their influence in interpretation and judgment. There are many mindfulness practices available to therapists.

Dilani M. Perera-Diltz

See also Compassion; Empathy; Experiential Family Therapy; Feminist Family Therapy; Mindfulness; Multiculturalism; Therapeutic Alliance; Therapists' Values

Further Readings

Davis, M. H. (1996). *Empathy: A social psychological approach.* Boulder, CO: Westview Press.

Drollinger, T., Comer, L. B., & Warrington, P. T. (2006). Development and validation of the active empathetic listening scale. *Psychology and Marketing, 23,* 161–180.

Greason, P. B., & Cashwell, C. S. (2009). Mindfulness and counseling self-efficacy: The mediating role of attention and empathy. *Counselor Education and Supervision, 49,* 2–19.

Jordan, J. V. (2010). *Relational-cultural therapy.* Washington, DC: American Psychological Association.

Kabat-Zinn, J. (2011). *Mindfulness for beginners: Reclaiming the present moment and your life.* Boulder, CO: Sounds True.

Kodjo, C. (2009). Cultural competence in clinician communication. *Pediatrics in Review, 30*(2), 57–64.

Langer, E. J. (2014). *Mindfulness* (2nd ed.). Philadelphia, PA: Da Capo Lifelong.

Pederson, P. (2009). Inclusive cultural empathy: A relationship-centered alternative to individualism. *South African Journal of Psychology, 39*(2), 143–156.

Rogers, C. R. (1951). *Client-centered therapy: Its current practice, implications, and theory.* Boston, MA: Houghton Mifflin.

Sando, E. K. (2012). Present moment awareness. In S. C. Hayes, K. D. Strosahl, & K. G. Wilson (Eds.), *Acceptance and commitment therapy* (pp. 201–219). New York, NY: Guilford.

Satir, V. (1983). *Conjoint family therapy* (3rd ed.). Palo Alto, CA: Science and Behavior Books.

LIVE SUPERVISION

Supervision in family therapy is the process by which an experienced clinician oversees and mentors the work of an unlicensed student or therapist in training. There are a number of different methods for conducting supervision, including case consultation, review of video recordings, and live supervision. In case consultation, supervisees and supervisors meet to share clinical impressions of a case and discuss treatment options. Video-recording supervision includes showing supervisors a segment of the actual session being discussed. Live supervision occurs when the supervisor is present during the therapy session, whether behind a one-way mirror or involved in cotherapy with the supervisee. This entry examines live supervision approaches and their related advantages and challenges. This entry also explores how to prepare for live supervisions, how to address power imbalances with the practice, and how to respond to students and therapists working at varying levels of experience.

Defining Live Supervision

Because live supervision allows for the supervisor to observe or participate in the therapy experience, it is often the preferred method for training students in family therapy. There are significant advantages to live supervision, including the opportunity for supervisors to provide immediate instruction and encouragement, as well as observe family dynamics firsthand. Live supervision can be used as a core supervision approach, or as an augmentation to case consultation or video-recording supervision. It is important for supervisors and supervisees to recognize the unique challenges and advantages of different supervision methods to select the combination that works best for those involved. Prudent implementation of the various approaches can increase the likelihood that supervision helps meet both supervisees' goals and clients' needs.

A number of family therapy pioneers, including Jay Haley, Salvador Minuchin, Carl Whitaker, Steve de Shazer, Insoo Kim Berg, Tom Andersen, Michael White, and David Epston, utilized variations of live supervision to develop their theories of practice. They elicited in-the-moment feedback from colleagues in a number of different ways, including situating teams of therapists behind a one-way mirror to observe sessions and inviting peers to join near the end of the session to provide alternative perspectives. Applied in new and innovative ways, live supervision quickly became foundational to the development of family therapy and continues to be an important component in training students today.

Live Supervision Approaches

Family therapy students are traditionally required by state law or by their training institution to have a portion of supervisory hours accrued by either reviewing videotapes or having a supervisor observe them during therapy. Different methods of live supervision reflect various types of supervisor involvement in the therapy process. For supervisors reviewing videotapes, feedback only takes place postsession, which students can then implement into their future work. When situated behind a one-way mirror, the supervisor might phone in reflections, comments, or questions to encourage students or offer direction during session. Supervisors might also ask supervisees to use a small microphone, or a "bug in the ear," by which they can provide support and guidance to the therapist in session in real time. They might also use students as messengers to provide similar feedback to clients, or ask students to take a midsession break to consult.

Reflecting teams are often used as an element of live supervision, particularly with students practicing at academic institutions. Using this approach, a team of supervisees sits with the supervisor behind the one-way mirror. Typically at the end of session, the clients are able to witness a conversation held among the therapists. Supervisees might pose hypothetical questions, reflect their observation of relationship dynamics, or compliment clients by highlighting strengths and resiliency. The supervisee benefits by hearing multiple perspectives and is often comforted by a more private debriefing in which other supervisees share countertransference experiences or provide validation.

Supervisors using cotherapy supervision vary in their degree of in-session involvement. Some take a back seat, offering little input, while others fully participate in cotherapy. Those who take a more observational stance often offer feedback toward the end of session by providing consultation to the supervisee in front of the client or by giving feedback directly to the client. Those who engage in collaborative cotherapy provide direct client intervention alongside their supervisee. Supervisor interventions build on supervisee movement, deepen the conversation, or guide the session in a more useful direction. Supervisors might periodically provide reflections or mini-consultation to supervisees during session. This serves not only to benefit the supervisee, but also to model a positive relationship for clients.

A final approach to cotherapy supervision is one in which the supervisor conducts the majority of the session. This method primarily relies on supervisee observational learning and postsession debriefing so that supervisors can share intentions behind in-session decisions. Often, supervisors using this approach compliment the supervisee in front of the client to instill hope and trust in the therapeutic process prior to the session's close.

Advantages of Live Supervision

One of the most significant advantages of live supervision is that supervisors gain a more accurate understanding of supervisees' skill level, rather than relying on supervisees' self-assessment or recollection of in-session events that might have transpired a week prior. Live supervision also provides opportunities for supervisors to give in-the-moment feedback that highlights alternative points of view or reinforces the supervisee's current movement. For supervisors doing live cotherapy, an added benefit is the opportunity to actually demonstrate interventions and be more closely connected with both the client's and supervisee's subtleties of behavior.

Live supervision might also allow supervisors and supervisees to develop a more connected professional relationship characterized by increased collegiality and mentorship that is supported by shared, lived experience. Supervisees who receive helpful, in-the-moment feedback and witness their supervisor implementing effective interventions may experience enhanced trust in the supervisory relationship. Similarly, seeing supervisees actively apply feedback may enhance the supervisor's confidence in the supervisee's ability to try new things, respond flexibly, and accept critique. Perhaps more uniquely, being privy to one another's immediate emotional responses to client circumstances either in session or in postsession debriefing may be helpful in humanizing the supervisor and enhancing feelings of camaraderie and collaboration that support strong professional relationships.

Challenges of Live Supervision

The most common potential challenge in live supervision is that students often feel pressure to perform. Supervisees in early stages of training may be less engaged in session and worried that their supervisor is analyzing each move and noting every mistake. This fear may be exacerbated when supervisors behind a one-way mirror phone into sessions too frequently, causing embarrassment or decreased confidence and derailing in-session movement. Supervisors participating in cotherapy also run the risk of undermining students when they conduct the majority of the session, rather than gently, skillfully guiding the supervisee toward asking appropriate questions and providing helpful interventions.

The duration of live supervision often runs the course of a traditional 50-minute therapy session, but also necessitates time for presession planning and debriefing. This method may require considerably more time than videotape or case consultation supervision. Related to this, if live supervision is a core supervisory method, it is important that the supervisor and supervisee be in communication about other supervisory needs, especially related to other clients who may not be seen in live supervision and might easily be overlooked. Although cotherapy supervision may help to decrease hierarchy between supervisors and supervisees, the supervisor must always maintain awareness of his or her position of power and actively elicit conversations with the supervisee about how the hierarchy inherent in the supervisory relationship is impacting the live supervision experience.

Suggestions for Practice

Preparation for Live Supervision

To aid in creating a setting for effective live supervision, both supervisors and supervisees should consider which method(s) of live supervision might best serve the client's and supervisee's needs. It is often helpful for supervisors to begin with an orientation meeting wherein they discuss the purpose of live supervision and both the supervisor and supervisee's expectations of the process. Normalizing performance anxiety, acknowledging that the supervisor's presence might initially influence therapy, and affirming supervisor commitment to supervisee growth and success can be helpful. The supervisor should also explicitly discuss differences in roles, hierarchy, and power between supervisor and supervisee so that there are clear expectations about maintaining both the professionalism of supervision and the collegial mentorship that often occurs with aspects of live supervision.

Addressing Power and Hierarchy

If live supervision is used as a core supervisory method, it may be helpful for the supervisor to set aside time for routine check-ins regarding the process of live supervision. Because of the unique advantages and challenges of this method, students may feel "exposed" in doing therapy. Given the hierarchical nature of supervision, supervisees might not willingly disclose their worries, so it is important that the supervisor gently inquire about their feelings and expectations so that students feel additionally supported in this process. Supervisors should also demonstrate openness to feedback, including inviting reflections of the supervisee's experience, perceptions, and process. Last, if cotherapy is the model of live supervision used, it may be helpful for the supervisor to invite the supervisee to initiate the session and to use careful self-monitoring to make sure that the session is not being taken over by the supervisor.

Addressing Different Levels of Experience

Live supervision may be beneficial to students with a variety of experiences and skill levels. For newer students, live supervision provides a means whereby they can enhance and understand beginning skills, particularly joining, reframing, asking for clarification, or mapping systemic process. Supervisors can guide therapy into more helpful and meaningful directions, modeling asking difficult questions, and maintaining engagement in the face of conflict. For more advanced supervisees, live supervision may be a means whereby supervisors can help them refine and strengthen higher-order skills or specific techniques, expand their theoretical base, and more strategically apply their philosophical framework after they've already mastered the ability to maintain client engagement.

Live supervision is an important aspect of family therapy training, and offers unique opportunities for growth and development. Advantages include immediate feedback from supervisors observing behind a one-way mirror and watching a more experienced clinician demonstrate helpful interventions during cotherapy. Supervisors utilizing live supervision may have a better understanding of supervisees' abilities and can address more nuanced aspects of therapy that might not otherwise be reported in supervision. Finally, the relationship between supervisors and supervisees may be enhanced, as supervisors are mentored and supported by their supervisor through shared clinical experiences.

*Lindsey Lawson
and Stephanie Ines Falke*

See also Cotherapy Team; Supervision; Supervision, Developmental Model; Supervision, Gatekeeping; Supervision Theories

Further Readings

Andersen, T. (1991). *The reflecting team: Dialogues and dialogues about the dialogues.* New York, NY: W. W. Norton.

Birchler, G. R. (1975). Live supervision and instant feedback in marriage and family therapy. *Journal of Marital and Family Therapy, 14,* 331–342.

Champe, J., & Kleist, D. M. (2003). Live supervision: A review of the research. *The Family Journal: Counseling and Therapy for Couples and Families, 11,* 268–275.

Falke, S. I., Lawson, L., Pandit, M. L., & Patrick, E. A. (2015). Participant supervision: Supervisor and supervisee experiences of cotherapy. *Journal of Marital and Family Therapy, 41,* 150–162.

Storm, C., Todd, T., Sprenkle, D. H., & Morgan, M. (2001). Gaps between MFT supervision assumptions and common practice: Suggested best practices. *Journal of Marital and Family Therapy, 27,* 227–239.

LONELINESS

Loneliness can be defined as a feeling of dissatisfaction with one's social connections with others. The feeling is often described as complex because a person who is lonely may also experience anxiety, frustration, anger, and helplessness among other emotions. Emphasis is placed on a person's subjective perception of their current relationships and their perceived need for changes or improvements. Loneliness is a common human experience. Many individuals can identify a time when they felt lonely. This entry explores the importance of loneliness in human social interactions. While marriage, family, and coupling relationships may serve as a defense against loneliness, they cannot entirely protect husbands, wives, lovers, and children from experiencing loneliness. This entry distinguishes loneliness from other related constructs and explores its manifestations, consequences, causes, and treatments. A special focus will also be placed on understanding how loneliness may impact marriage and family relationships. Families are often viewed as systems; therefore, it is understood that a single member's experience of loneliness is likely to impact functions and interactions within the entire system. Divorce, separation, death, job loss, retirement, and other life transitions can also produce emotional responses such as loneliness.

Related Constructs

Being alone, social isolation, and loneliness are related concepts; however, they should not be confused. Most individuals can identify different times throughout a given day when they are alone. Being alone refers to the condition or objective state of being by oneself. A stay-at-home dad may find himself alone after his wife leaves for work and his kids have been dropped off at school. While it is possible to experience loneliness because one is alone, this objective state does not equate to loneliness. Therefore, the stay-at-home dad who is alone may engage in a number of activities such as reading, calling friends, connecting with others on social media, or just resting. Being alone does not automatically result in him experiencing loneliness.

Social isolation refers to the absence of or limited contact with other human beings. It can also be seen as a measure of a person's social connections or proximity to other human beings. For socially isolated individuals, time spent alone significantly increases while social networks decrease. An elderly married couple whose adult children have moved away from home and whose close friends and relatives have passed may experience social isolation, since their social network does not involve frequent contact with family and friends. Similarly, the death of a lifelong partner or divorce may also result in social isolation. Social isolation is, however, not a fixed condition since individuals can make decisions that increase their connections and interactions with family and friends. While social isolation may result in loneliness, this is not always the case. The elderly couple may find new meaning and comfort in each other's company that shields them from loneliness. The human need for social connection results in most individuals choosing social connections over social isolation. The inherent need is often used to explain why human beings establish social connections such as friendships, marriages, communities, and societies. At different points in a person's life, they may subjectively assess their levels of social connections to be inadequate and this may produce feelings of loneliness. To guard against social isolation and loneliness, individuals, families, and communities establish social networks and institutions to support collective survival. Survival also relates to an individual's psychological and emotional well-being, which may be threatened by loneliness. Marriage and family are important institutions within which human beings experience social and emotional connections that may guard against social isolation, loneliness, and other undesirable states of physical or psychological being.

Studying Loneliness

Researchers of loneliness have focused on gaining a better understanding of its manifestations, consequences, causes, and treatments. Scholars have sought to understand both the individual and societal impact of loneliness. Researchers have also sought to measure the prevalence of loneliness in society.

Prevalence of Loneliness

The subjective nature of loneliness makes it difficult to determine the actual number of lonely individuals in a society. Researchers often rely on the self-report of participants in order to measure loneliness. One national survey found 25% of the American population to be lonely, while another that looked at adults 45 years and older found 35% to be lonely. The results of survey data, however, do not support the widespread belief that older adults are more susceptible to loneliness. Increasingly, researchers are looking at the presence of loneliness in various groups in society. The understanding, for example, that loneliness manifests itself across the life span has resulted in studies that look at loneliness in children, adolescents, adults, and the elderly.

Manifestations of Loneliness

Research that focuses on the psychological manifestations of loneliness attempts to describe the thought process or cognition of lonely individuals. Here, researchers are concerned with how lonely individuals process their subjective experiences of loneliness. Researchers may explore issues such as oversensitivity, inability to focus attention, vigilance, and cognitive distortions or misinterpretations related to interpersonal interactions. Researchers seek to understand how the lonely individual's thought process may help to explain their loneliness.

Scholars who look at the social manifestations of loneliness are seeking to describe how it impacts the individual's personal and social relationships to the extent that they exist. Scholars are also seeking to understand how loneliness impacts society as a whole. Sociologists who study loneliness are often concerned with its social manifestations. They emphasize the importance of social participation for society as a whole. Loneliness has therefore been described as a social problem that requires social interventions. The intersection between loneliness and other social factors such as culture, migrations, and unemployment among other factors are explored.

Researchers have described emotional, behavioral, and psychological features of loneliness. At an individual level, these manifestations are referred to as signs or symptoms of loneliness. Emotional and affective manifestations of loneliness include painful, unpleasant, dissatisfying, and stressful feeling states. Additionally, emotional states such as anger, hostility, tenseness, restlessness, misery, frustration, emptiness, and boredom have been identified. The subjective nature of loneliness allows for a number of these co-occurring negative emotional states. A wife who is dissatisfied with the level of connection with her husband may share that she feels lonely and may also experience anger, frustration, or helplessness when her effort to reach her husband fails. Human subjectivity, social, cultural, and contextual factors may influence the lonely person's emotional states. For example, an international college student within the first few weeks of the start of the semester may report feelings of loneliness. Being away from home, family, and friends, as well as experiencing a new culture, may be important social-contextual factors that impact his or her loneliness.

Attempts to describe the behavioral manifestations of loneliness have been difficult. Researchers suggest possible behavioral manifestations of loneliness such as social withdrawal, shyness, difficulty with self-disclosing, and being assertive. Affective and emotional states such as anger, tenseness, and hostility that are sometimes associated with lonely individuals may impact their relationships and behaviors with others. For example, in the context of a family, an adolescent who experiences loneliness may show signs of social withdrawal from both family and friends. His parent's struggle to understand his condition and failed efforts to re-engage him may increase his frustration. His own failed attempts at pulling himself out of loneliness may lead to feelings of hopelessness, which may lead to further social withdrawal. Despite these possible associations, conclusions regarding the behavioral manifestations of loneliness remain largely inconclusive. Therefore, it is best to seek to understand loneliness as a complex interaction of subjective, social, and contextual factors.

Consequences of Loneliness

Loneliness is often studied in terms of its negative consequences. At an individual level, concerns about loneliness may arise when it impairs social and emotional functioning. Studies of loneliness have identified its impact on human social, emotional, psychological, and physical well-being. Psychologists Letita Peplau and Daniel Perlman noted the tendency for sociologists to view too many lonely people as being bad for society. In order to function, society requires social participation, and loneliness is seen as a kind of withdrawal from society.

Psychologists Magnhild Nicolaisen and Kristin Thorsen pointed out that both health and loneliness are predictors of each other; if a person is in poor health, they are more likely to be lonely and if they are lonely, they are more likely to be in poor health. Loneliness has been associated with poor health conditions such as increased risk for cardiovascular disease and mortality, increased inflammatory response to stress, obesity, alcoholism and drug abuse, depression, and anxiety disorders among others.

Causes of Loneliness

In their attempts to identify the causes of loneliness, researchers have focused on personal, developmental, and social factors. Scholars and clinicians seek to understand recent changes in the lonely individual's life. These changes are assessed as possible antecedents to loneliness. Changes may take many forms, including life changes related to birth, death, separation, or divorce. These changes may also relate to migration, grown children moving out of the house, or close friends and families moving away. Changes may also be developmental, where an individual's needs for social connection may change as they grow older.

Researchers have also looked at personal factors that may cause loneliness. Here, the idea is that the lonely person may in some ways have contributed to their own loneliness. An examination of the lonely person's social skills, personality, perceptions, and attribution regarding social connections is often conducted with a view of identifying possible causes. Scholars also point to the possibility of a combination of social, cultural, developmental, and personal factors in causing loneliness.

Treatment of Loneliness

Researchers explore how individuals seek to deal with loneliness and how it may be treated by mental health professionals. When the subjective experience of loneliness reaches a point where the individual's social and emotional function is negatively impacted, they may seek help. Treatment may pose challenges to the extent that loneliness may coexist with other social, emotional, or mental health conditions. Some lonely individuals may also develop maladaptive responses to being lonely. Drug and alcohol abuse, for example, have been associated with loneliness. Developmental and life changes, health status, and family status among other factors can impact treatment. Peplau and Perlman outlined three clinical approaches for working with lonely individuals. These approaches included efforts to change the lonely person's social relations, efforts to change their social needs, and efforts to reduce their perception of social deficiency.

Alternative Views of Loneliness

Being alone, loneliness, and even social isolation are not always seen as negative conditions. Some scholars have focused on the benefits of loneliness. Loneliness is seen by some scholars as a mechanism that informs individuals of the need to pursue social connections. In this case, the idea is that the experience of loneliness is a call to address problems in one's social connections. Similarly, in *Loneliness and Love,* Clark E. Moustakas argues that loneliness allows for meditation and reflection, which leads to spiritual, aesthetic, and intellectual growth.

Research Directions

The impact of loneliness on individuals, families, communities, and societies as a whole is not fully understood. Despite some progress, researchers continue to grapple with the complexities associated with this phenomenon. These complexities lie in the fact that loneliness is a common, yet complex phenomenon that interconnects with individual-subjective, social, cultural, demographic, and other factors. The complex emotional and psychological states that are often associated with loneliness are not fully understood and require further research. Current research makes a continued effort to deepen the understanding of loneliness by seeking to understand its impact on specific demographic groups in society such as immigrants, adolescents, the elderly, incarcerated individuals, and users of social media technologies among others. Efforts to understand how loneliness is impacted by social and contextual factors will also improve our understanding.

Efforts to understand connections between loneliness and various mental health conditions such as depression, schizophrenia, and bipolar disorder should continue. Sociologists, psychologists, medical scientists, neuroscientists, and other disciplines will also continue to conduct research that looks at loneliness. Understanding the complex nature of the phenomenon of loneliness may be better served by a multidisciplinary approach. In the context of the family, this approach may allow for a more in-depth understanding of how an individual's experience of loneliness may affect their physical and mental well-being, as well as their relationships with family and friends.

Charles C. Edwards

See also Beliefs and Values; Divorce and Separation; Family Values; Friendship; Life Transitions

Further Readings

Cacioppo, J. T., & Patrick, W. (2008). *Loneliness: Human nature and the need for social connection.* New York, NY: W. W. Norton.

Cacioppo, S., Capitanio, J. P., & Cacioppo, J. T. (2014). Toward a neurology of loneliness. *Psychological Bulletin, 140*(6), 1464–1504.

Kasari, C., & Sterling, L. (2014). Loneliness and social isolation in children with autism spectrum disorders. In R. J. Coplan & J. C. Bowker (Eds.), *The handbook of solitude: Psychological perspectives on social isolation, social withdrawal, and being alone* (pp. 409–426). New York, NY: Wiley.

McPherson, M., Smith-Lovin, L., & Brashears, M. E. (2006). Social isolation in America: Changes in core discussion networks over two decades. *American Sociological Review, 71*(3), 353–375.

Moustakas, C. E. (1972). *Loneliness and love.* Englewood Cliffs, NJ: Prentice Hall.

Nicolaisen, M., & Thorsen, K. (2014). Loneliness among men and women: A five-year follow-up study. *Aging & Mental Health, 18*(2), 194–206.

Peplau, L. A. (1982). *Loneliness: A sourcebook of current theory, research, and therapy* (Vol. 36). New York, NY: Wiley.

Russell, D. W. (2014). Loneliness and social neuroscience. *World Psychiatry, 13*(2), 150–151.

Waite, L., & Gallagher, M. (2002). *The case for marriage: Why married people are happier, healthier and better off financially.* New York, NY: Crown/Broadway Books.

Loss

Loss is the experience of no longer having a person, thing, or experience that a person valued. This in turn leads to the experience of grieving. Loss is a normal human emotional experience that is often complex and layered. The experience of a loss can be felt on a spectrum from very mild to very extreme. These emotions and experiences of a loss may change over time and eventually dissipate, though some feel the effects of a very difficult and painful loss for the rest of their life. In the clinical professions, the term *loss* is often used synonymously with the terms *grief* and *bereavement*.

All losses are different and all people experience losses in a variety of ways. However, experts have identified symptoms that seem to be universal and common after a loss. These would generally be considered normative symptoms when they are experienced at a non-extreme level for a limited period of time. These symptoms are predictable and usual, and can be grouped as emotional, physical, relational, social, and spiritual symptoms. Specific symptoms may include shock, disbelief, sadness, anger, guilt, fear, pain, insomnia, questioning one's faith, and detaching from and being angry with others. These symptoms are also experienced on a continuum from mild to severe. Most last for a period of weeks or months. In more severe cases, they may last years. This entry highlights current knowledge about a variety of types of loss, including loss due to the death of a loved one, non-death losses, traumatic losses, and complicated losses. This entry concludes with a discussion of the ways in which people cope with loss.

Loss Due to Death

The most accepted and recognized type of loss is the loss of a loved one due to death. Everyone (except those who die very young) will experience the loss of a significant loved one at some point in their life, and most people experience many such losses. The older one becomes, the more likely he or she will have experienced many losses due to death of a loved one. After a loved one dies, survivors experience a set of symptoms known as grieving, and they enter a process known as bereavement. The severity and duration of the symptoms of the death of a loved one depends on the contextual factors of the relationship (e.g., emotional and proximal closeness or distance, interdependence, the role the person played in one's daily life) and the circumstances of the death (e.g., sudden or unexpected, timeliness, prior illness). The death of a close loved one is often accompanied by crying, disbelief, anger, sadness, disturbed eating and sleeping patterns, inability to concentrate or focus, fatigue, and a preoccupation with the deceased. It is not uncommon for survivors to look for their loved one in the hours and days after their death, and some even report that they have heard their loved one's voice or thought they saw the person in a crowd.

Another common reaction to any death-related loss is a resurgence of some of these symptoms at the anniversary date of the death. This is most common at the first anniversary, but depending on how deeply the loss is felt, it may continue to a lesser extent every year at the anniversary of their death. Commemorating the person's death date in some way is often helpful to continue the healing process after the death of a loved one. The anniversary effect can be extraordinarily difficult for others. Research indicates a higher percentage than average of older adults who die at or near the one-year anniversary date of their longtime spouse. While the anniversary of someone's death may be difficult for many years, most people find the symptoms are less disturbing each year after. Another phenomenon that is very common is that some symptoms return at major holidays such as birthdays, Mother's or Father's Day, or religious holidays. These days that represent a time to celebrate in the past may be met with feelings of resentment, sadness, and a desire not to have to face the feelings of loss again.

Non-Death Losses

All people experience losses due to something other than the death of a loved one. These non-death losses can be experienced on a spectrum from very mild to very severe. There are countless ways in which a person might experience a loss. These losses include job loss, loss of physical or mental functioning, loss of a dream, loss of a house, moving, divorce or separation, retirement, miscarriage, military deployment, loss of one's youth, and loss due to theft or other crimes, just to name a few. While death losses are accepted as legitimate and valid in society, many non-death losses are disenfranchised losses, meaning they are not readily recognized as deserving the same sympathy as other losses. This disenfranchisement can complicate the loss experience for people because they do not receive the same level of support and empathy that others rely upon.

The symptoms of non-death losses often mimic those of death losses, though they may not be as acknowledged because death losses are deemed more legitimate in our society. Still, people may notice feeling sad, depressed, angry, tearful, consumed with thoughts of the past or the future, and having trouble eating, sleeping, or concentrating. The symptoms typically last weeks or months, but depending on the impact of the loss, perhaps years.

Traumatic Loss

Most losses are troubling and sad, but they usually do not evoke triggering memories that make the person feel as though they are reliving the loss over and over again. Some losses, however, are experienced as a traumatic reaction. Traumatic losses are usually unexpected, jarring, and sometimes violent. They are usually related to near-death experiences or life-threatening situations. Traumatic losses may be caused by the death of a loved one in a terrorist attack, a plane crash, or a very violent murder. People who experience a loss that is traumatizing usually struggle to stop ruminating thoughts of the manner of death of the person and hold deep feelings of guilt about being unable to help during the death. These losses take more time and often require counseling to begin to heal, though the after-effects of these losses often last a lifetime. Beyond counseling, people who have experienced a traumatic loss may also require a doctor's assessment of the utility of anti-anxiety or antidepressant medications to help with severe post-loss symptoms.

A traumatic loss affects not only the individual but couples, families, and larger communities. According to Kathleen Gilbert, when families grieve a traumatic loss, there are tasks they should embark on to help them on their journey through grief. Some of the aspects of this process include recognizing the loss, acknowledging the grief felt by all members, reorganizing so that essential functions can be accomplished, and reinvesting the new family. Some tools Gilbert says that can be helpful include having a positive vision of each member of the family, being sensitive to each other's needs, accepting the differences in each other, having a shared purpose, engaging in rituals together, and working to have honest, open communication.

Complicated Loss

Complicated loss is the umbrella term for a loss that is unusually and persistently disturbing, either because of the incident that caused the loss itself or because of earlier or other losses and conditions that make the loss significantly more severe. These losses usually significantly impact one's short- and long-term daily functioning. Symptoms of complicated grief are usually the same as those for normative grief, but they are experienced more severely and for a longer period of time. These symptoms can include a preoccupation with the deceased, a preoccupation with the manner of death, yearning for the deceased, no longer having meaning in one's life, intense sadness, avoidance of or obsession with anything that reminds one of the deceased, severe anger, and difficulty engaging in plans or activities.

While the experience of loss is normal, there are forms of complicated grief that are so severe that the American Psychiatric Association is testing a new diagnostic category for the most extreme form of loss, which they call "persistent complex bereavement disorder." While controversial, there are some experts who believe that some forms of the most severe losses are experienced as a mental illness and require medical and/or psychological interventions for optimal recovery outcomes.

Coping

There are a number of effective ways in which people cope with losses in their life. One of the most effective coping mechanisms includes spending quality time with loved ones after a loss. People find relief from being with supportive others and talking about the circumstances of the loss, recalling memories of the person who died, and having distractions from the loss through engaging with others. In recent years, social media has become an important outlet for loss experiences and an effective way to connect with caring others during a loss. Letting people know about a loss through social media outlets can enable loss survivors to feel supported from near and far. Websites have emerged specifically for those who are experiencing a loss so that a community of grievers can come together to support each other, share information, and reminisce. These outlets are available 24 hours a day to help aid in the process of coping with various losses, whether they be the loss of a job, a relationship, or a cherished loved one.

Another coping strategy some use is positive self-care. This may include reading self-help books, getting a massage, attending religious events for spiritual encouragement, exercising, eating healthy, and expressing feelings and emotions to trusted others. If the loss is causing significant problems in the person's daily functioning, self-care may also include seeking grief or bereavement counseling. Counselors and therapists are trained to be excellent, nonjudgmental listeners and can assess whether a person's reaction to a significant loss is normative or nonnormative and may require additional interventions.

Still another way of coping that helps many people recover their daily functioning is giving back in a meaningful way that honors the person who died or the loss event. People often start foundations for loved ones after a death to honor their memory and help others who may be in a similar situation. Some build memorials to the person as a way of helping themselves and others express grief and honor the memories that people have of the person. For non-death losses, people might start a local or online support group—for example, for survivors of rape or incest, those who have struggled with a difficult divorce, those who have suffered a terrible illness or injury, or children of alcoholic parents. Support groups not only provide a place for people to express their thoughts and feelings, but they also acknowledge their pain, address their symptoms of loss, and feel they are doing something for the greater good as well. People find meaning by giving back in a genuinely caring way in the name of the person or loss event.

Jennifer L. Matheson

See also Bereavement; Death, Parents of Deceased Children; Death and Dying; Grief Counseling; Trauma and Families

Further Readings

Boss, P. (2000). *Ambiguous loss: Learning to live with unresolved grief.* Cambridge, MA: Harvard University Press.

Gilbert, K. R. (2001). *We've had the same loss, why don't we have the same grief? Family meanings and family grief.* Retrieved January 1, 2015, from http://griefnet.org/library/families.html

Holtslander, L., & Duggleby, W. (2008). An inner struggle for hope: Insights from the diaries of bereaved family caregivers. *International Journal of Palliative Nursing, 14*(10), 478–484.

Humane Society. (2013). *Coping with the death of a pet.* Retrieved January 1, 2015, from http://www.humanesociety.org/animals/resources/tips/coping_with_pet_death.html

Neimeyer, N. A. (2006). *Lessons of loss: A guide to coping.* Memphis, TN: Center for the Study of Loss and Transition.

Shupp, L. J. (2007). *Grief: Normal, complicated, traumatic.* Eau Claire, WI: Premier Publishing & Media.

Smith, M., & Segal, J. (2014). *Supporting a grieving person.* Retrieved January 1, 2015, from http://helpguide.org/articles/grief-loss/supporting-a-grieving-person.htm

U.S. Department of Veteran Affairs. (n.d.). *Reminders of trauma: Anniversaries.* Retrieved January 1, 2015, from http://www.ptsd.va.gov/public/problems/anniversary-reactions.asp

LOVE, PHYSIOLOGY OF

The physiology of love refers to the bodily events that accompany the experiences of love. There are opposing views about the human experience of love. One view would suggest that love is not a singular universal experience for all human beings. This means that how people think, speak, and define love has the power to alter the experiences of love; thus, love is not the same experience for everyone. The other view suggests that love is the same experience for all humans by virtue of their shared humanity. This means that insofar as people have bodies and these bodies include chemical, biological, and physical processes, people can be sure to find the same experiences of love in their bodies. But where does love reside? Ancient thinkers suggested that it resides in the blood, or in the heart, or in the brain. Adding to this effort to localize love, contemporary researchers, equipped with technological advances, have discovered that the experience of love is indeed physical and organic. That is to say, all systems that make up the human body are engaged in the experience of love. But the human brain seems to be the most prominent organ that maps the experience of love. This entry describes the physiological processes of love, predominant perspectives on love, how the experience of love correlates with brain activity, how the experience of love impacts self-preservation and reproduction, and what chemicals accompany the experience of love and of lovemaking.

Understanding Love

Research in neuroscience provides couples and family therapists with empirical data that indicates brain functions are associated with family relationships. This neurobiological information is crucial for practicing self-regulation, for example, when managing personal emotions while remaining available and respectful to one's partner. Evidence for neuroplasticity (the brain's ability to change and to reshape itself) indicates that through the practice of therapeutic techniques, people in relationships, and their relationships themselves, have the potential to be reshaped by means of how they interact, and this increases overall relationship satisfaction. Some of these techniques include (a) body regulation, (b) emotional balance, (c) response flexibility, (d) empathy, (e) insight or self-knowing awareness, and (f) fear modulation. Interpersonal neurobiology (focusing on relationships, emotions, and the brain) uses neuroscience to treat couples, families, groups, and individuals to better relate to one another. Essentially, the human person and love are both relational. Individuals do not exist in a vacuum, and love propels everyone toward gregariousness (seeking companionships).

The human brain is the center of bodily activity; it is the source of information that coordinates the rest of the human body or the entire human person. As such, the human brain is the center of the human person's drive toward intimacy and sociality. In turn, human relationships also influence brain development. Each human brain has the ability to self-heal and to reestablish communication paths among neurons. Understanding these brain processes provides relationship therapists and human persons with a valuable position for assessing and for enhancing the relationship aspects of living together. Studying the physiology of love is also useful for couples and family therapists and other mental health clinicians because it provides information on how some essential chemicals influence the human experience of love, including feelings and actions that follow the claim of being in love or to love someone. But what makes this truly important is the fact that the human experience of love leads people toward establishing intimate relationships with ideal partners. In essence, love is a disposition toward sociality that is intrinsic to human nature. Further, the human experience of love leads to self-preservation, to intimacy with another, and ultimately to procreation and to the preservation of life through child-rearing tasks and responsibilities. Human sexuality is the evolutionary vehicle that expresses human love in bodily intimacy.

Perspectives on Love

Experiences of love involve not only the moods that accompany a set of underlying organic processes, but most primarily they are the very chemical processes that correlate with the emotion-like experiences of love. Thus, the act of loving is a phenomenon that is highly intelligible to human beings. The physicality of love (in dualist terms) seems to have more appeal in the 21st century because it seeks to *localize* causes (the underlying chemistry) of the experience of love in neurochemical and neuroanatomical terms. Yet the very experience of love cannot be fully explicated only in terms of brain processes. Some very complex aspects of this experience include (a) the choice of a certain someone and (b) the lasting commitment to that same someone even when that very person's deficits (personal idiosyncrasies) are made manifest in daily interactions and contexts. The very complex choices a person makes toward her beloved would suggest that love (in hylomorphic terms) is more than its correlate brain events.

Mapping Brain Activity

Progress in neuroscience over recent decades has helped map the structure and functions of brain areas involved in love experiences. Available technologies include (a) electroencephalograms and (b) functional magnetic resonance imaging (fMRI), which have produced neuroimaging of lighted regions of cerebral matter when one thinks of one's beloved. These depictions are pictures of blood flow patterns, associated with a particular neurotransmitter traveling on a given region of the human brain whenever one thinks or emotes toward her beloved.

Passionate Love

Passionate love correlates with basic emotions, reward and motivation pathways, social cognition, attention, memory, mental association, and self-representation. Passionate love is an intense longing for union with one's beloved. As such, passionate love encompasses chemical, goal-directed, and reward-sensitive cognitions. If passionate love is reciprocated (through a tangible union with a desired partner), it becomes romantic love. This romantic love involves a sense of ecstasy and satisfaction from a sense of intimacy, and it carries a potential for sexual activity. People in this love experience claim to be "madly in love." During romantic love, people's brains light up in the dopaminergic subcortical systems, similar to people whose experience of euphoria and elation comes from cocaine use. Also, when romantic lovers view pictures of one another, brain areas associated with emotion and reward processes light up.

Maternal and Paternal Love

Studies using fMRIs have uncovered that mothers' brain areas light up similarly to those brain areas of romantic lovers. Additionally, however, mothers' brains light up in the periaquetactal gray matter and limbic emotional system connections, which contain high levels of vasopressin, crucial for establishing maternal and parental bonding. Vasopressin is also present in men and prepares them for child-rearing roles and responsibilities.

Unconditional Love

Unconditional love involves studies of lasting and paternal relationships, as well as of individuals with intellectual disabilities. The use of fMRI technologies has mapped the expression of encompassing love that is enduring, unselfish, and constant in individuals with intellectual disabilities. Just as maternal love, unconditional love activates the periaqueductal gray matter and higher-order cognitive brain areas that include vasopressin. This evidence of brain activity provides a means to map loyalty, relationship length, and commitment that love entails in close and intimate human relationships.

Neurohormonal Basis of Human Love

Lust

Lust is defined by the actual, physical, sexual attraction and arousal between two people. Testosterone secretions cause the strong attraction between opposite- and same-sex persons. Testosterone is the fundamental hormone for human sexual attraction.

Sexual intimacy

Oxytocin is responsible for modulating blood flow that shapes the connectivity between the posterior cingulate cortex and the brainstem. These areas are associated with the evolution of a pervasive prosocial human behavior and a marked sense of emotional and physical health. Other immediate effects of oxytocin include (a) facilitation of birth, (b) lactation, (c) maternal behavior, (d) genetic regulation that stimulates the neocortex's growth, (e) a sense of safety between lovers, (f) a proclivity toward socialization, and (g) a deep sensitivity required for raising children. Furthermore, these discoveries indicate that human love can be said to originate in the human brain.

Sociality

Vasopressin is the neuropeptide (protein-like molecules used by neurons to communicate) responsible for pair bonding and for child-rearing. It also expands the human need for social connections. As a component of the human experience of love, vasopressin supports couples' bonds and attachment styles during their relationships.

Self-Preservation and Reproduction

Beginning with the chromosomal co-participation of male (nuclear) and female (mitochondrial) deoxyribonucleic acids (DNAs), every new human organism contains the genetic blueprint toward self-preserving conduct and toward the development of procreative desires and capacities. These are indeed the essential functions of human DNA (the instructions for organic functioning, self-preservation, and reproduction), and these are the intrinsic features of human love.

Human self-preservation can be appreciated in terms of cells forming tissues that develop into organs, and organs that group together into systems that carry out nutritive and developmental functions to sustain the human organism. Ultimately, the physiological configuration of human bodies into male or female genders seems to be determined by the dominant characteristics of chromosomal pairs in each individual. This biological configuration of human bodies seems to be oriented toward sexual functions for reproduction and thus preservation of the *Homo sapiens* species.

However, the advent of reproductive technologies has supplanted the heteronormative aspect of procreation. Heterosexual coitus is only sufficient and no longer necessary in all instances for human procreation. Thus, available reproductive technologies have provided nonheterosexual couples with the ability to conceive and to raise children. Only a combination of male and female DNA is required for the transmission of new life. It is now possible for nonheterosexual couples to find (a) technical assistance, (b) surrogacy, and (c) chromosomal donors to procreate. In this sense, physiological love is the inherent-organic human capacity, regardless of sexual identity, to enter into intimate and lasting relationships that involve procreation, and the subsequent childrearing tasks and responsibilities that ensue from this evolutionary transaction of love.

Chemistry of Love

What goes on "in" the human person when she or he claims to be in love? Relevant studies have uncovered the prefrontal cortex (covering thought, attention, reasoning, and personality) and the limbic system (covering emotions, feelings of pleasure, motivation, and memories) are the two brain areas pertinent to the experience of human love. In fact, the experience of loving and being loved, which entails reciprocity at some level, has been correlated with wellness and with enhanced immune systems. These areas of the brain start developing during fetal stages.

The need to love and to be loved is intrinsic to human chemistry. And the benefits of loving and being loved provide evidence of wellness in the lives of lovers. Lovers experience happiness and satisfaction and safety. These feelings are correlated to the production of dopamine and oxytocin in the brain. These love chemicals are released most particularly when experiencing orgasms, which further lead to the development of a sense of lasting commitment among lovers. Further, prolactin enables mothers to develop a close relationship with their young, whereas vasopressin helps fathers develop a sense of care toward their children.

Studies on the covariance between brain (an organ) processes and heart (a muscle) functions have uncovered the fetal experience of the maternal heartbeat. The fetal brain perceives its maternal heartbeat. This experience during gestation is further associated with personality development and with optimal organic functioning of the fetus. Heartbeat patterns to which the fetus is exposed may be positive (state of calm) or negative (state of fright), and the neuro-experiences that ensue further shape prefrontal cortex and limbic system development in the fetus. In this sense, if the mother is under constant stress, her fetus is also affected through organic association.

Too much stress and an inability to cope positively with it, for example, leads individuals to experience negative emotions. The persistence of negative emotions from stress exposure may lead to the experience of mood disorders such as depression or anxiety. These negative reactions to love-related stress increase the likelihood for hypertension, heart disease, and anhedonia (inability to experience pleasure), a symptom of depression. For this reason it is important to prevent habitual negative interactions from shaping intimate relationships, and to take action to identify and to practice positive ways to cope with stress and to resolve conflict, which is also a dynamic of personal relationships. Relationship therapists recommend the practice of meditation and contemplation techniques (self-regulation). These practices seemingly help stimulate brain regions associated with the production of dopamine and oxytocin (neuroplasticity). As a result, positive communication skills seem also associated with relationship satisfaction.

Contrary to stressful aspects of conflict, the rewards that accompany romantic and parental love are more significant. Just as chromosomal pairs begin the development of a human being, the release of neurochemicals marks the beginning of romantic love, as we begin to fall in love with someone we find suitable. In this sense, love is an organic drive to seek for intimacy with another. Thinking about a desired beloved and being in the company of this beloved constitute pleasurable experiences that establish a motivation mechanism to seek for romantic intimacy. Usually, fMRI evidence has revealed elevated central dopamine and norepinephrine, and low central serotonin in both romantic and parental love relationships.

These love attractions cause lovers to exaggerate a beloved's positive attributes and to minimize his or her shortcomings. These attractions can be mapped by elevated dopamine and norepinephrine in the reward pathways of the brain. These chemicals fuel an increase in energy and obsessive behaviors toward a beloved. If success follows personal efforts at initial romance, a sense of attachment or lasting commitment ensues. This new sensation correlates with constant release of oxytocin and vasopressin, which further feed a motivation toward entering a commitment stage. If commitment is achieved, then lovers experience feelings of calm, security, belonging, and social comfort. But the end goal of love relationships as it were is the search for coitus with a romantic partner to complete the human species' evolutionary task: the preservation of life via procreation. This is true for heterosexual partners whose bodily configurations seem to carry out the genetic imprint to develop and to reproduce. But the motivation for intimacy and its germane sexual drive are intrinsically human processes that surpass the presumed heteronormativity of dimorphically gendered dyads. Accepting this chemical endowment makes it possible to suggest the physiology of love leads partners to engage in loyal relationships out of which they may or may not be able to have and to raise children. (Genetic fertility and to some extent solvency supersede a couple's choice to have children.) This loyalty aspect of human love is also an organic reality available to nonheterosexual and transgender partners.

Chemistry Informs Reproduction

The human physiology of love encompasses bodily (physical) configurations in terms of male and female genitalia and other secondary sexual characteristics. The development of these sexual configurations requires secretions from the endocrine system. These hormones constantly produce chemicals that prepare human bodies for reproduction. As molecules that make up each human cell come together and develop into tissues, these tissues in turn form organs with specific functions, and these larger systems make up human bodies. Constant chemical processes take place informed by DNA to repair bodies, to nourish bodies, to grow bodies. Human brains further equip persons with the intent to care for themselves and to contribute to their common good and to seek intimacy with another. This intimacy eventually leads persons to procreate and to preserve their species. This is the biological purpose of human love. As such, male testosterone prepares the individual to impregnate a mature ovum that eventually gets implanted in a uterine cavity and develops into a new human being. It is as if the whole purpose of human existence were twofold: subsistence and eventual reproduction. Furthermore, mitochondrial and nuclear DNA are the genetic foundations for transmitting human life.

Lovemaking

Outward manifestations of lovemaking include simple expressions such as hugging, holding hands, sitting together, touching, patting, caressing, and kissing. Eventual genital stimulation and orgasmic satisfaction is the goal of lovemaking. These expressions are often regulated by social mores depending on the geographic location where lovers live, but their neuronal sources remain the same for all persons. It seems this human propensity for lovemaking is the evolutionary purpose of love. It is as if every organ and physiological system within the human sexes is preparing each individual to eventually procreate. This is at core the physiological quality of human love. In the brain, when orgasmic climax is reached, oxytocin elates the couple. During sex, dopamine and oxytocin stimulate areas of the brain related to feelings of euphoria and the potential for developing strong obsessions similar to the effects from substances such as cocaine, heroin, and nicotine. The neurochemical profiles of lovers' brains are also similar to the profiles of people who suffer from obsessive-compulsive disorder. This is true because of the constant thinking and wishing to be in intimacy with one's beloved. Neurochemical releases produce hyperactivity, and perhaps even recklessness to do anything to be in the company of one's beloved. This is complicated when individuals seek to belong or to be accepted by someone else but they do not succeed. In this sense, the lover who is not loved is still experiencing the drive toward intimacy but fails to experience acceptance and contentment. These obsessive behaviors in a non-loved lover blur the picture between normalcy and psychopathology because the neuronal drive to seek a potential lover remains despite the unsuccessful attempts the non-loved lover has made.

Feeling good, however, is an essential characteristic of love. Feeling good contributes to the experiences of attraction, sexual drive, bonding, and pairing. Yet perhaps the greatest mistake is to conclude that love or loving or being loved is simply a matter of feeling. Love is not an emotion or a feeling. So when good feelings change due to relational vicissitudes, some lovers wrongly conclude that love has ended. But above and beyond euphoric feelings in dyads, lasting commitment is an evolutionary aspect of loyalty that is further cemented on an act of the human will. In fact, the cerebral cortex indicates that committed love begins with the decision to choose someone over another and over and beyond feelings. This mate selection process has preserved the human species over the basic preference for multiple partners that fails to provide a context for rearing children and for experiencing the benefits of a lasting sense of belonging and safety.

The evolutionary purpose (telos) of physiological love is the preservation of human life (through the endocrine system) and the species through the sexual activity and parental roles. Underlying these vital functions of love are the profound experiences of trust, belonging, respect, deference, and so on that are also intrinsic attributes of human love. The chemistry of organic love is too deep to be properly described in any human language or by mere neurochemistry, but it is perceptible by any human person in intimate communion with another. Thus, the physiology of love is available to all members of the human species, regardless of gender, age, culture, historical era, and any other elements of culture and diversity.

The release of norepinephrine, endorphin, dopamine, oxytocin, and other hormones and neurotransmitters that accompany sexual intimacy liken the experience to the high that endurance athletes experience. These chemicals stimulate the neuroanatomy and organic functioning of the human brain, which in turn correlate with mental processes that enable humans to self-donate their bodies to one another in intimacy and in outer social commitments.

Carlos M. Del Rio

See also Loneliness; Relational Diagnoses; Sexual Intimacy; Sexual Orientation, Attraction, and Identity; Transgender Families

Further Readings

American Physiological Society: http://www.the-aps.org/

Esch, T., & Stefano, G. B. (2005). The neurobiology of love. *Neuroendocrinology Letters, 3,* 175–192.

Fishbane, M. D. (2007). Wired to connect: Neuroscience, relationships, and therapy. *Family Process, 46,* 395–412. doi:10.1111/j.1545-5300.2007.00219.x

Fishbane, M. D. (2011). Facilitating relational empowerment in couple therapy. *Family Process, 50,* 337–352. doi:10.1111/j.1545-5300.2011.01364.x

Fisher, H. E., Aron, A., & Brown, L. L. (2006). Romantic love: A mammalian brain system for mate choice. *Philosophical Translations of the Royal Society, 361,* 2173–2186. doi:10.1098/rstb.2006.1938

Gottman Institute: http://www.gottman.com/

PhysiologyInfo.org: http://www.physiologyinfo.org/

Snyder, D. K., Castellani, A. M., & Whisman, M. A. (2006). Current status and future directions in couple therapy. *Annual Review of Psychology, 57,* 317–344. doi:10.1146/annurev.psych.56.091103.070154

LOVE, THEORIES OF

Love is a complex and important topic, thus theories of love abound. Theories are coherent and systemic descriptions of phenomena perceptible to humans, and love is a universal phenomenon of human experience. Although there are multidisciplinary attempts to describe and understand love, evidence suggests that human beings understand intuitively what love means to them. Nevertheless, love can be understood from multiple disciplinary perspectives: Law may look at love in terms of the contractual nature of individuals' relationships; philosophy may look at love in terms of its potential existence; sociology may look at love in terms of its cultural attributions over time and across regions; and psychology studies love in terms of its individual and relational attributes. Marital, couples, and family therapists tend to focus on intimate relationships and understanding love in terms of couple relationships, parenting, and family relationships. They see love as an essential tool for understanding, enhancing, and healing relationships. Providing a comprehensive review of theories from all possible disciplines is beyond the scope of this entry. Instead, the sections that follow will examine a few 20th-century theories that have become particularly relevant to familial and systemic human interactions. The entry will also consider what it means to measure love.

Measuring Love

Theories require empirical testing. The predictions about the phenomena they consider are subject to empirical scrutiny. As a result, the utility of theoretical statements rests on their validity (accuracy) and their reliability (ability to be replicated). These features in practical terms translate to the extent to which theoretical descriptions and predictions can be generalized. Usually ongoing research is needed to determine any theory's soundness (reliability and validity). Many assessment tools have emerged to test theories of love, of being in love, of loving, and of the primal need to belong. Important to seeking an appropriate tool to measure the construct of love is how the concept is defined. Most tools rest upon self-reports and these are in turn affected by the subjectivity of their respondents. In addition, clinicians are trained to make objective observations and to ask scaling questions (e.g., to better assess a person's or a couple's sense of love).

But beyond these aspects of assessment the psychometric properties of assessment tools represent their potential clinical utility or its limitations. High indexes of validity and reliability of scores on a given scale as well as an explanation of the variance or error of measurement for a given item set are very important features to comprehend before engaging in applying and interpreting an assessment tool, particularly one that relates to a multifaceted construct like love. Below, theories of love and associated assessments are briefly described.

Complementarity Theory of Love

The complementarity theory of love suggests that individuals are primarily dissatisfied with their personal characteristics. Because of this natural dissatisfaction, individuals meet someone whose attributes complement or supplant what is dissatisfying in them. In this sense, love is seen as an impulse to seek satisfaction in one's partner and as the complementary sense of satisfaction that accompanies togetherness with one's partner. Love is at the core of intimate relationships. Theodor Reik argued that individuals are attracted to partners of the opposite sex because these partners have ideal characteristics individuals lack in their own persons. Follow-up studies suggested that this quest for complementarity seems to be more prevalent in low-self-esteem individuals than in high-self-esteem individuals.

Theory of Liking and Loving

Zick Rubin described love as a romantic element of interpersonal relationships. Rubin's theory of liking and loving speculated that love comprises caring, attachment, and intimacy. These dispositional concepts are manifested by a personal desire to be with someone, to care for another and to put others' needs before one's own, and to seek for intimacy or exclusivity while being with another. This motion toward intimacy constitutes the romantic nature of love. It moves the individual into the relational context within which love makes sense relationally. Thus, the individual person is ultimately motivated to achieve intimacy with another person.

This theory contributed two measures: the loving scale and the liking scale for evaluating romantic relationships. Liking and loving conceptualized love as a forceful attraction between two unwed individuals, a romantic attraction that leads them to marriage. Of course, the heteronormativity (focus on heterosexuality as normal) of this theory is challenged by 21st-century American legal pronouncements on the meaning of marriage: It is a right for adult individuals regardless of sexual orientation. The notion of commitment through marriage is also suspect because not all committed individuals are able to marry, and not all who wish to marry are permitted to do so. An example that illustrates this challenge includes couples who have divorced and remarry civilly but not religiously, as well as those who are forbidden from marrying for dogmatic reasons.

Love Styles Theory

John Alan Lee's love styles theory describes variations of individuals' dispositions toward love relationships. Six styles include intense, passionate, and erotic attraction (eros-love); gameful loving, a series of conquests (ludus-love); compassionate affect usually evolved from friendship (storge-love); logical and practical commitment (pragma-love); obsessive and often possessive, dependent attitude (mania-love); and selfless and content sense of satisfaction that puts another before oneself (agape-love). There has been statistical corroboration to Lee's styles of love. The love attitudes scale was constructed to specifically measure the empirical validity of Lee's love styles. A short version of the love attitudes scale was constructed in 1998.

Attachment Theory

John Bowlby saw human love and bonds as central to human relationships and individual survival. He described the need for love and the bond to someone who could provide love and security as an attachment between a child and caregiver or between romantic partners. The three kinds of attachment are secure, avoidant, and anxious/ambivalent. These three inner working models, which children develop, influence their relationships' styles as they mature in life. It is predictable that one's attachment covaries either positively or negatively with loving relationships' satisfaction and duration.

Thus, attachment theory provides a life span perspective to the experience of love, one that begins early in life. Attachment in this framework manifests via personal orientation toward loving relationships with another, and the differences between levels of satisfaction and conflict while in relationship with another. Secure attachment predicts positive relationship characteristics, whereas anxious/ambivalent attachment predicts negative relationship characteristics. Avoidant lovers face difficulty forming lasting bonds.

Theory of Passionate Love

The theory of passionate love identified longing as the essence of romantic love. Elaine Hatfield and Susan Sprecher suggested that an intense longing toward union with another is the foundation of loving relationships. If the unity is established, reciprocated love ensues. If the union is dissolved or never established, unrequited love remains. These authors constructed the passionate love scale to assess the empirical validity of their constructs. Passionate love has three components. Cognitive components include intrusive thoughts to be with another. Emotive components include attraction toward another, particularly sexual attraction for another; positive feelings when good things happen and negative feelings when things go wrong; longing for reciprocity, which makes individuals desire to be loved in return; desire for a tangible and lasting union; and physiological arousal. Behavioral components include actions aimed at ascertaining the other person's feelings, providing service to the other person, and sustaining physical closeness.

Triangular Theory of Love

Robert Sternberg's triangular theory of love argued that love is a social construction necessary for cultural development. But a sense of passionate love is not required for relationship longevity. Love is defined differently across cultures yet experienced universally the same across cultures. It describes three relational aspects of love including intimacy, passion, and commitment. This triangular theory of love places focal attention on the cultural conceptions of the one who is loved, the feelings that accompany the experience of love, the thoughts that accompany love, and actions that accompany love, and the type of interactions between those who love one another. This theory makes possible the categorization of diverse experiences of love. Intimacy, passion, and commitment are the axiomatic terms of this theory. Intimacy fosters closeness and connectedness to another. Passion is the underlying motivational aspect of love, leading to a sense of affiliation and actualization when in a relationship with another. Commitment involves deliberate choice or selection of someone among others and choice to sustain personal involvement with another. The triangular love scale was created to measure the empirical validity of the triangular theory of love.

Theory of Marital Quality and Stability

Interactionist and exchange frameworks render love crucial to understanding the quality and stability of couples and their choice to marry or to enter committed, lasting relationship for individuals who abstain from or who are dogmatically prevented from marrying. Vincent Jeffries's theory of marital quality and stability depends on the dynamic structure of love as including both attraction (receiving) and virtue (giving). Love is multidimensional. It brings individuals to intimacy, and their relationship is rated in terms of their perceived quality and stability. These two aspects of intimate couples (often married) include receiving and giving. Love as receiving entails satisfaction of personal needs and desires. This sense of satisfaction generates a positive attitude toward the other partner as well as a sense of attachment. Love as giving is manifested as a personal intent to benefit the other partner and a desire to advance his or her welfare by doing what is good in general terms.

Feminization of Love

Francesca Cancian's feminization of love attempts to establish a sense of gender equality in loving relationships. Whereas women prefer expressive aspects of love including expressions of emotions and talks about feelings, men prefer the instrumental aspects of love including providing support, sharing activities, and sex. But this feminist view of relational love argues for men's incremental share in women's emotional expressions of love, and women's incremental share in men's instrumental aspects of love. As a result, an androgynous (partly female and partly male) emphasis of feminist love seeks to promote a balanced share of instrumental and expressive love by both genders. This view requires an integration of feminine and masculine aspects of love in both women (instrumental love) and men (expressive love).

Social Construction of Love

Anne Beall and Robert Sternberg's social construction of love posits that love may be understood only in terms of the cultural conceptions of the beloved, the feelings that accompany love, the thoughts that accompany love, and the actions or behaviors that accompany love toward one's beloved. These cultural, emotive, cognitive, and behavioral variables change the heretofore conception of love as simply emotive expressions between two or more individuals. In this sense, the sociocultural view of love is contextually determined and varies across geographical regions and time frames of human interaction. This framework defines love as a social construction. As such, love and its formulation varies among individuals and across cultures. The fundamental premise is that people are not passive recipients of meaning. Instead, people are active participants in making sense of the phenomena they experience. How people define love influences how people experience love, and these aspects of human experience are time and culture bound. However, this social construction of love does not negate the human capacity to experience love at some fundamental level. Love's interactional instrumentality remains at the core of social preservation. Yet a predisposition to love is based on the human socialization experience leading to contextual variability of interpretations of human phenomena of which the experience of love is one.

Carlos M. Del Rio

See also Attachment Theory; Scales, Couple and Marital; Sexual Intimacy; Sexual Orientation, Attraction, and Identity

Further Readings

Altman, L., & Taylor, D. A. (1973). *Social penetration: The development of interpersonal relationships*. New York, NY: Holt, Rinehart & Winston.

Fehr, B., Sprecher, S., & Underwood, L. G. (Eds.). (2009). *The science of compassionate love: Theory, research, and applications*. Malden, MA: Blackwell.

Partis, M. (2000). Bowlby's attachment theory: Implications for health visiting. *British Journal of Community Nursing, 10*, 499–503.

Stenberg, R. J., & Grajek, S. (1984). The nature of love. *Journal of Personality and Social Psychology, 47*, 312–329.

LOVE, TYPES OF

Usually, people fall in love with those with whom they claim to be attracted. However, there are many ways to look at love, to define it, and to experience it. For certain, love is a multifaceted construct that imbues personal experiences. It is an individualistic experience, but it takes shape only through the behavioral dynamics between persons. Types of love include not only the ways in which lovers can explain the phenomenon of love, but also the ways in which the sciences can explain what happens when people claim to be in love. This entry provides a description of types of love from both perspectives.

At its core, the experience of love is relational; it moves a person toward intimacy with another. At a personal level, love for oneself can be defined as self-preservation or an evolutionary duty to oneself. At a systemic level, love encompasses a presumed mutuality of persons, a transaction between lovers. Love is unifying, it brings people together, and it propels people toward sociality, a disposition to seek togetherness and belonging in larger groups in terms of roles and interactions. These groups include couples, marriages, families, and communities. Love extends the relational bonds of people outside blood relations to encompass acquaintances, friendships, marriages, and other familial bonds, which can generate new blood bonds when new couples come together and reproduce. This entry examines the experiences, processes, and dynamics of love.

Experiences of Love

How lovers experience love defines the types of love available to them in their own societies. Although sociologists, for example, would argue that love varies by culture and by cohort in human history, the common aspects of love remain the same for individuals of different time periods and geographical locations. Lovers' articulations of what love means to them has enabled psychologists and sociologists to identify types of love including (a) *eros* (sexual attraction toward another), (b) *storge* (affection for friends, lovers, and family), (c) *ludus* (playful interactions with multiple partners), (d) *mania* (fixation, infatuation, passion for another), (e) *pragma* (logical, and creative love in relation to another), and (f) *agapé* (selfless and encompassing love for another). These kinds of love share a systemic or relational commonality: seeking for unity with another. At this level of systemic interaction, affection, friendship, eroticism, and charity can also be discussed. Affectionate love brings a sense of togetherness. Friendship pertains to sharing disinterestedly common interests and goals beyond togetherness. Friends correct one another when needed. Erotic love encompasses embodied persons and chemical makeup and helps to find fulfillment in sexual intimacy and to propagate the human species. Erotic love encompasses passion and lust, and leads to elation when finding true companionship with another. Charity, or agapé, is the highest form of love that seeks for the good of the beloved. Then, there is magnanimity. Magnanimity is another expression of altruistic love often confused with charity. Magnanimity refers to sharing one's possessions and holdings with someone else. It is an outward manifestation of generosity. Generosity in a deeply disinterested manner is also a characteristic of charity. But charity as such is sublime love. This kind of love is similar to agape but it is more profound and often considered to be a cardinal virtue. Charity is the utmost expression of human love.

At a neurobiological level, love differs in terms of its substrates. On the one hand, there is sexual desire. This impulse to seek coitus with an attractive other seems to be a motivation to propagate the human species. The gonads produce estrogen (for women) and testosterone (for men) to motivate people to engage in sexual intimacy. But sexual desire does not necessarily lead to pair bonding through the formation of affectionate bonds. Rather the reward pathways of the human brain support attachment formation behaviors. These reward systems include *endogenous opioids, catecholamines,* and *neuropeptides* yielding a strong desire to be with a beloved. On the other hand, romantic love leads to pair bonding. It enables lovers to experience love in terms of attraction, infatuation, and companionship. These stages subject lovers to experience (a) heightened interest for a partner, and preoccupation for that same partner; (b) intense desire for physical contact and proximity with a partner; (c) resistance to separation from that partner, excitement and euphoria when receiving that same partner's attention; and (d) security, care, comfort, and belonging because of the companionship established with a partner.

Sexual desire and romantic love are inclusive but not necessarily based on the same evolutionary purposes. It is true that sexual activity accompanies and oftentimes leads to companionate love, but companionate love cannot be reduced to mere sexual activity. Sexual desire seeks to propagate the species, whereas romantic love enables partners to enter pair bonding that further prepares them to care for their offspring. It usually happens that sexual attraction and sexual satisfaction leads to companionship in adult relationships. This is the objectification of adult, consensual love. But evolutionary theorists argue that these behavioral aspects of love may have emerged for the primary purpose of establishing infant–caregiver attachment. As a result, companionate love behaviors have historically increased the survival rate of human infants. This position also suggests that the evolutionary purpose of love leads to the propagation of species because it brings together the capacity to mate (with more than one partner) and the capacity to engage in child-rearing (with one partner) as a result of coital release of neuropeptides that ensure this relational task is implemented. Thus, the patterns also experience bonding: an identification of one another as sources of security, comfort, and complementarity.

Processes of Love

What occurs when people claim to be in love with someone or to love someone serves as a vehicle to define diverse types of love in terms of relational interactions and roles. These types of love include correlated physiological processes that explain what happens when people are in love or experience love. Different types of love from a relational perspective include sexual desire, passionate love (infatuation), romantic love, committed love (attachment), parental love, and sibling love. This moves love from the personal to the relational sphere and into the creation of couples and families in the human species. At this relational and systemic level, love is further interpreted by social conventions of what is acceptable in a given place and time. For example, women are socialized to be more caring than men, and men are socialized to be independent. These attributes also serve as attraction mechanisms among potential partners.

But at the constellation level, couples and families define what works for them relationally and in terms of what love means to them. This familial understanding of love extends the ontological composition of couples and families to include nonheterosexual partners and nonblood relatives. This evolution of the familial constellation also encompasses the complexities that emerge from divorced and remarried partners and the added levels of relationships that these behaviors imply.

The use of functional magnetic resonance imaging (fMRI) has identified brain regions involved in the human experience of love. These lighted regions depict neural circuitries containing neurochemicals released when individuals experience love. Successful sexual desire that leads to coitus (physical manifestation of love) involves hormonal secretions of estrogen and testosterone. But when lovers reach orgasms they experience feelings of euphoria and elation that includes neuronal circuitries registering the presence of oxytocin, vasopressin, and dopamine. Romantic love leading to pair bonding originates in the reward pathways of the brain, instigating lovers to seek one another out. If coupling (reciprocated relationship) occurs, lovers experience neurochemicals similar to the ones accompanying coitus. Companionship (companionate love) that follows coupling denotes lasting commitment that leads to the experience of comfort and belonging. Companionship is further cemented on oxytocin and vasopressin release.

Evolutionary theorists have denoted attachment is an evolved set of behavioral activity that supports pair bonding and child care in the human species. Infants seek proximity to caregivers, and adult lovers learn to seek out comfort and security with their intimate partners. When familial systems are established, people relate to one another by the roles they are assigned. Parents are protectors and providers of children. Sons and daughters are siblings and dependent on their parents until they reach a stage of self-sustainment. Aunts and uncles are parental siblings who occasionally show support to their relatives. Families come together in times of need and to show support for one another. But families have also evolved in terms of their composition to include other figures who enter their bond. Families have also evolved in terms of their dyadic formation to include nonheterosexual partners. Single-parent households and divorced and remarried parents also increment the level of relationships and the complexity of individuals that constitute a familial constellation. These extended and diverse compositions are more and more the norm in 21st-century societies.

Dynamics of Love

But the experience of love is not always pleasant. People who experience the mutuality of love with a partner move from passionate love (intense desire to be with a beloved) to companionate love (strong affection for a significant other). This progress requires some evolutionary tasks to be completed successfully: (a) identification and selection of a mate, (b) attraction of that mate's attention and consent for pairing, and (c) organization of personal priorities and responsibilities to make room for one's mate. Upon achievement of these tasks, a more stable relationship entails other tasks: (a) raising offspring and providing for their needs, (b) competing against other sexual rivals, and (c) sustaining a status within a social group. These evolutionary tasks that lovers experience as they move from passionate love to companionate love require changes in cognition, affection, and behavior to make their experience of love last. Companionate relationships denote intimacy, caring, and trust upon which partners further engage in (a) responsiveness to each other's needs, (b) mutual provision of secure behaviors whenever needed, and (c) valuation of each individual alone and as a partner of one another. These features of companionate love are also present among siblings and best friends, thus extending the behavioral dynamics of love.

But when dyads and familial constellations are established, relational conflict also emerges. This can be seen as a side effect of loving. Conflict involves various stages of harm for the people involved: from verbal to physical instances that create pain. These sources of relational stress lead some individuals to depression and anxiety and other emotional disorders including deleterious outcomes: suicides and homicides. How individuals cope with relational sources of stress and conflict makes a difference. Some individuals may turn to addictive behaviors, whereas others simply suffer the side effects of these poor coping skills. As a result, individuals in couples and families with ongoing loving relationships experience rejection, violence, abandonment, jealousy, sexual affairs, and other behaviors that would not exist without love.

Couples and families need assistance when they create and sustain toxic environments. Individuals in these contexts suffer psychological, affective, and cognitive instances of stress. As couples and families negotiate and define what works for them, they may choose to end their relationships or to make changes that end cycles of conflict and abuse because these are intuitively counter to the evolutionary purpose of togetherness. The emotions people experience in these relationships are negative. Relational therapists use many theoretical approaches and techniques to stop cycles of abuse, and to help people enhance their relationship satisfaction. A specific application of therapy is based on the specific presenting concerns of couples and families.

Certainly much research remains to be done to uncover other dimensions of the human experiences of love. For example, from a phenomenological perspective, and as the ontology of couples and families evolves, there needs to be an exploration of love in terms of roles that include non-blood relatives and other social agents that join the familial constellation whether to provide support to or to receive benefits from that same family. From a neurobiological perspective, added studies are required to understand how brain activity relates to different types of relationships within the extended familial constellation and to changes in different stages of relationships, as well as to the differences in personality that come from the complex relationships individuals experience by remarriage, adoption, or foster parenting. A focus must be placed on uncovering a sense of normativity in these neurobiological depictions.

Carlos M. Del Rio

See also Loneliness; Same-Sex Couples; Self-Esteem; Sexual Intimacy; Sexual Orientation, Attraction, and Identity; Transgender Families

Further Readings

Barrett, L. F., Mesquita, B., Ochsner, K. N., & Gross, J. J. (2007). The experience of emotion. *Annual Review of Psychology, 58,* 373–403. doi:10.1146/annurev.psych.58.110405.085709

Berscheid, E. (2010). Love in the fourth dimension. *Annual Review of Psychology, 61,* 1–25. doi:10.1146/annurev.psych.093008.100318

Bowlby, J. (1982). *Attachment and loss: Vol. 1: Attachment* (2nd ed.). New York, NY: Basic Books.

Buss, D. M. (2005). *The handbook of evolutionary psychology.* Hoboken, NJ: Wiley.

Carter, C. S. (1998). Neuroendocrine perspectives on social attachment and love. *Psychoneuroendocrinology, 23,* 779–818.

Hatfield, E., & Rapson, R. L. (1996). *Love and sex: Cross cultural perspectives.* Boston, MA: Allyn and Bacon.

Pearlman, D., & Vangelisti, A. (2006). *Cambridge handbook of personal relationships.* New York, NY: Cambridge University Press.

Sternberg, R. J., & Barnes, M. L. (1987). *The psychology of love.* New Haven, CT: Yale University Press.

LOVE AND RITUALS

Although love rituals vary by time and culture, they help people make sense of their persistent inclination for togetherness with ideal lovers. To understand the symbolic importance of rituals while making sense of human experiences of realities that are not always tangible, such as love, this entry offers a brief history of their original uses and further reviews rituals associated with human experiences of love.

Historical Perspectives on Love Rituals

Rites, also known as rituals, originated in ancient times as prescribed behaviors to relate to the supernatural. Anthropologists, historians, and sociologists have contributed to the psychological understanding of rituals. These disciplines have uncovered evidence of rites from ancient societies including the Egyptians, Etruscans, Romans, Celts, and the Nordic peoples. For example, in ancient Rome, haruspices performed rites to discern the will of *pneumena* (spirits) of nature. These rites included sacrificing animals and looking at the shape of their entrails. Other rites involved counting birds flying in the sky, or interpreting the shape of clouds during a thunderstorm. Roman augurs practiced similarly to make sense of natural forces seemingly influencing their lives. This interpretative practice of supernatural realms was embedded into the prescribed practices of symbolic behaviors, which carried over to the religious practices of priests of the Christian church (4th century C.E.) when the Roman Emperor Theodosius sanctioned the acceptance of Christianity.

Ritual practices evolved from mythical stories that helped people understand how the universe was supposed to have come into existence. These stories led people to determine acceptable conduct to venerate and to worship the forces they considered supernatural. Stories of creation explained human dependence on an original "Creator," and how humans communicated with this supernatural order included rituals. More specific purposes of rituals included (a) to seek intercession and gifts from deities; (b) to offer sacrifice for atonement; and (c) to seek forgiveness for transgressions of what the public consciousness defined as unacceptable. Rituals usually required a qualified expert to teach or to oversee their performance.

A sense of sacredness (special purpose) imbued ritual practices, which included other human dimensions of what is considered to be highly valuable. Love is among these highly valuable experiences. Thus, humans have also practiced ritualistic behaviors around the experience of love. But the central value of rituals is the sense of connectedness they convey to those who celebrate them. It is as if a special celebration is needed to mark the experience of what lovers consider highly valued, such as their unity with their partner. Couples and family therapists consider lovers' rituals to be important to preserve a sense of togetherness. These professionals understand that rituals are culture bound. The experiences of love are also varied, and so are the rituals lovers use to verbalize or to enact their love for one another.

The human ability to love and to want to be loved is an evolutionary predisposition toward preservation of *Homo sapiens*. Rituals of love produce an ultimate sense of social cohesion. Lovers celebrate with rituals their desire to be with someone desirable and to express lasting commitment to that person. Thus, engaging in rituals of love compels people to seek someone who can tell them how to engage in this prescribed conduct and to follow instructions about what needs to be done to achieve social recognition and ultimately togetherness.

Rituals of love accompany occasions that are memorable for people including romancing someone, marrying someone, coming of age, and making lasting commitments. In this sense, the effects of rituals for lovers include symbolic actions and behaviors that convey a change in status or transformation: from single to married, from adolescent to adult, from married to divorced, from single to parent, and so on. In some societies, rituals make present the person about whom the ritual is performed. So, for example, lovers pray for protection of their lover who is in a different geographical location or perhaps facing an unsafe situation. Lovers pray this way with the assurance that the utterance of a name seeks specific intercession for the person named in the petition. In effect, rituals convey three main effects: change of status, symbolic presence by name (invocation), and social cohesion. Moreover, rituals require belief from the performers about the tradition or meaning the rituals convey. This commitment at the level of belief further ensures the social effects of rituals, harmonious interactions, and social adaptation.

Seeking Togetherness

In some societies, people who claim to be in love or who are infatuated with a desired lover may seek advice from experts on how to get attention from that same lover. The prescribed behaviors by experts may include outward signs, express formulae (spoken words), and consuming sensible objects like potions or incense. When finding a desired or potential lover, this ritualistic behavior may include shopping for special attire, dressing, applying makeup, and grooming for a date, or speaking or acting in a way that makes one look attractive.

Celebrating Togetherness

Speaking vows in public has been an acceptable manifestation of commitment for couples from time immemorial. Married couples are recognized in their communities and have historically been considered the proper context for raising a family. In some societies, betrothal ceremonies preceded marriages and linked couples' destinies. So from engagement to marriage, couples have celebrated togetherness and public recognition. Paying of dowries has also accompanied the togetherness of couples, which has traditionally created alliances between families. This financial alliance and the contribution of resources from family to family can strengthen a couple's solvency and ensure the preservation of household names in some cultures. As a result, some families' ancestries can be traced back for hundreds of years.

The sexual exclusivity of marriage has also served an evolutionary purpose for the preservation of species by creating a sense of commitment among partners toward raising their children. Fundamental religious institutions support this heteronormativity and disfavor nonheterosexual weddings. Some of these religious positions also disfavor ending marriages and declare any future marriages invalid until the first marriage is determined nonexistent by proper ritual proceedings of divorce (civil law) or annulment (canonical law). In recent centuries, the juridical aspects of marriage have expanded to include nonheterosexual couples. The main requirement is that every individual who is able to experience love and desires to celebrate unity with a reciprocating adult can do so. In essence, marriage is a public expression of love for all individuals regardless of sexual identity or gender. In societies where this new perspective has become an enforceable issue of law, couples enjoy the contractual value of their togetherness. By contrast, some societies still ban nonheterosexual unions. Their arguments carry strong religious convictions against nonheterosexual individuals.

Severing Togetherness

Severing togetherness usually accompanies another ritual proceeding that declares the couples' union finished. A bill of divorce not only ends a marriage but also generates financial and social implications for both partners. Divorces also affect the children in a given household.

Divorced partners may remarry another person. But the rituals that accompany second marriages in a given society are complex. For example, in principle religious and civil weddings may complement one another, but may not supersede one another. Both rituals have public recognition in most Western societies. Once married to an identifiable person, a person is no longer single or able to marry anyone else unless that first marriage is ended through another ritual of public recognition, such as a divorce or the death of a partner. This is true for most societies that ban polygamy (a man with multiple wives). Usually civil weddings, however, do not recognize religious weddings. Thus, people who were married religiously may opt for a civil wedding if there is no evidence of an existing civil marriage or there is evidence of a respective divorce (civil law), but cannot marry religiously until the first religious ritual is annulled (by cannon law). These ritual processes, annulment and divorce, require expert advice and formal proceedings before a tribunal or any other administrative agency with the authority to declare a prior marriage over.

Private Rituals for Togetherness

Weddings

Any wedding or marriage ritual is usually celebrated publicly. But it is only a public expression of vows and other sensible signs and behavior that express the couple's commitment to one another. The presiding minister (civil or religious) does not de facto marry the partners. By contrast, they marry each other by the vows they pronounce and the actions they perform in a public forum. This happens only because they have consented privately to do so. The presiding representative only stands in for the community and signs a certificate of public recognition, as a witness. This witness pertains to the public enactment of the private vows the partners have already expressed to one another. It could be said that the partners marry one another and the partners end their marriage when they decide what works and what does not work for them. Therapy oftentimes aids in this process by providing clarity. Therapy also serves as a means to strengthen couples' and families' interactions.

Holidays

Offering gifts is another socially acceptable ritual that people use to manifest their love for one another. Lovers offer gifts to one another to celebrate their anniversaries and their birthdays. Cakes and wines usually accompany feasts of parties that further celebrate an accomplishment of some kind. But perhaps meals are the most common rituals for celebrating lovers' milestones. From preparing a meal to actually consuming a meal, lovers, couples, and families share in daily rituals that provide them with a sense of hilarity and belonging. Sharing meals together is a ritual practice that bonds a couple or family. Perhaps meals are so important because they represent desire, hunger, and cravings that accompany human intimacy, such as in sexual encounters. In addition to meals, lovers also celebrate holidays. During holidays of religious importance, lovers find opportunity to show appreciation for one another, their children, or their friends. These celebrations include Abrahamic traditions among others: Christmas, Hanukkah, and Milad un Nabi. Some ritual actions during these holidays involve handshaking, entertaining guests, drinking, dancing, and so on.

Birth

When couples give birth to their children, the couple's friends and families usually bring gifts to show their appreciation and support. In some societies, baptizing or christening infants is a ritual that further manifests that community's recognition of a newly born member. In some societies, baptism does not happen until individuals are adults or at least until they have reached an age in which they can ask for this ritual fully aware of the belonging privileges and responsibilities that accompany this rite. Still in other societies, baptisms occur both as infants and then again as adults (or at a time when candidates have reached an acceptable age of reason).

Coming of Age

Initiation rites communicate social inclusion of lovers. For example, this change in status pertains to societies that recognize the dating eligibility of young women. The ritual involves a religious ceremony followed by a party and a dance in which the young woman is presented to society or at least to those in attendance. Other societies celebrate the development of young men and young women in more pernicious ways by circumcising them. This genital mutilation may be hygienic for men, but it has been shown to injure women. It deprives women of the capacity to enjoy sexual pleasure.

Death

When people die, their remaining loved ones assume the responsibility to dispose of their corpses. Burial rites express an aspect of love for the deceased in the way that their corpse is not left exposed to the elements but given a special ceremony by which its dignity is preserved. Some death rituals include burials, religious celebrations, memorials, and cremations.

Rituals of love encompass all symbolic and predictive conduct that helps individuals celebrate their various experiences of love. From seeking togetherness to severing togetherness and from birth to death, humans who love also engage in practices that pass down traditional mythologies and evolutionary tasks that preserve their species. The social effects of rituals related to love convey a sense of psychological belonging and social cohesion. For couples and families, rituals help them strengthen their relationships and clarify the meaning of their togetherness.

The symbolic value of rituals rests on the elements used in their performance, and these include spoken words, movements, sharing meals, exchanging vows, giving rings, kissing, burning incense, bathing in water, singing, reciting a prewritten text, and so on. These sensible elements presume the understanding of the performers when celebrating or expressing their love for one another. By implication, rituals of love are culture bound and make sense to those who practice them. The main effect of celebrating rituals of love is a twofold sense of personal belonging and social cohesion.

Carlos M. Del Rio

See also Divorce and Separation; Divorce Therapy; Rituals in Family Therapy; Same-Sex Couples; Self-Esteem; Transgender Families

Further Readings

Argyle, M. (2002). The effects of ritual. *Archive for the Psychology of Religion, 24*, 167–179.

Duran, K. (1993). Homosexuality and Islam. In A. Swidler (Ed.), *Homosexuality and world religions* (pp. 181–198). Valley Forge, PA: Trinity Press International.

Katz, S. N. (2003). *Family law in America*. New York, NY: Oxford University Press.

Marshall, D. A. (2002). Behavior, belonging, and belief: A theory of ritual practice. *Sociological Theory, 20*, 360–380.

Popp-Baier, U. (2002). Ritual studies in psychology of religion. *Archive for the Psychology of Religion, 24*, 154–166.

Smith-Rosenberg, C. (1975). The female world of love and ritual: Relations between women in nineteenth-century America. *Signs, 1*(1), 1–29.

LOVE LANGUAGES

That there are different ways to feel loved and give love is well known. Similarly, what makes one person feel loved will not always make another person feel loved. According to Gary Chapman, when people report that they do not feel loved, the problem is often that others are not speaking their love language. The concept of love languages was developed by Chapman on the basis of more than 35 years of pastoring and marriage counseling, as well as his own life experiences. Initially applied to married couples, the concept was later adapted to children, teenagers, and singles. A person's love language is based on their distinctive psychological makeup and the way significant people in their lives have expressed love to them. Chapman believes there are five love languages: words of affirmation, quality time, receiving gifts, acts of service, and physical touch.

Words of Affirmation

Words of affirmation are verbal compliments or words of appreciation. They are powerful ways to tell someone that we love them. There are different ways to use words of affirmation. Giving verbal compliments is one way to make a person feel loved, and encouragement is another way. Understanding what is important to loved ones and encouraging them shows that one empathetically understands that person's world. The way people express what they say is also important. Words themselves might convey a positive message, but unless the speaker's tone of voice and body language are consistent with those words, the listener may receive a mixed message.

For children, words of affirmation also include words of praise, affection, and encouragement. When children are praised they feel that their accomplishments have been recognized and approved. Children also need to hear words of affection. They need to hear "I love you," but they also need to hear things like "I am proud of you," "I enjoy spending time with you," and "You are special." Words of encouragement provide children with a sense of security to try something new and challenging. They also provide an inner voice for a child's self-esteem.

Quality Time

Quality time includes not only having quality conversations but also doing things together. Quality conversation is when two people share experiences, thoughts, feelings, and desires, free from interruption. Quality conversation focuses on listening. Ways to express love through quality conversation consist of maintaining eye contact, listening without doing something else at the same time, paying attention to feelings, observing body language, and not interrupting. It helps to have a set time to check in with the other person. Doing things together means giving someone complete attention. Merely being in the same room does not count; what matters more is focused attention. During the time together, each person needs to be fully present. Knowing why you are doing this is the key to being able to express love. These shared activities will provide memories for years to come.

Quality time for children means sharing moments together and being a part of their life. Actively listening to their likes, hopes, goals, and wants makes a child feel important and loved. Having a quality conversation is done by maintaining eye contact and not multitasking, listening for feelings and observing body language, not interrupting, asking reflection questions, expressing understanding, and asking permission to offer one's perspective. Quality activities are based on what the child's interests are. Children naturally seek attention; those who do not receive enough positive attention will often act out, since even negative attention is better than none. Having quality conversations with children is beneficial to their development. It helps them gain a sense of self and how to express their needs.

Receiving Gifts

Receiving gifts is another way people feel loved. A gift is a visual symbol of love. It can be purchased, found, or made. Gift giving is one of the easiest love languages to learn. Gifts do not need to be expensive or given all the time. It is more about the thought. A gift is not something that is necessarily deserved, but rather something given unconditionally. The presentation of the gift is just as important as the gift itself. If a gift is given in a hurry or as if it is no big deal, it does not make the person feel as loved as if it were given with a lot of thought. A critical factor in gift giving is an awareness of the other person's interests.

A gift does not always have to be something tangible. You can also provide a person with the gift of self. Your presence becomes a symbol of your love. Physically being there when a person needs you is as much a gift as the bestowing of an object.

This love language can be tricky in the case of children. Many people worry that if they give their children gifts they will become "spoiled." The key is to present the gift as an expression of love, so the child does not come to think of gifts as what is to be expected. The gift can also be presented in private so that the gift is something special shared between the parent and the child. It is also important not to barter by saying "If you will . . . then I will buy you . . ." This makes the gift feel like a payment, or bribe, instead of an act of love.

Acts of Service

An act of service is doing something you know your loved one would like you to do. When we request something of someone we provide direction to love, but when we demand they do something it stops the flow of love. By stating a request, you are affirming that person's worth and capabilities. Often, when a person complains about something it provides the clue to what area they need love in. The criticism just needs some clarification. Acts of service can sometimes be a struggle for married couples because of gender stereotypes of household roles.

Being a parent automatically enrolls you in the acts-of-service department. It is important to remember that routines of service are acts of love with long-term effects. As children get older, parents perform acts of service that they cannot do for themselves. If it is something the child can do, teach them how to do it. We are to serve our children, but as they grow, we show them how to serve themselves and others. Your act of service is in teaching, which helps provide them with a sense of identity and independence.

Physical Touch

Physical touch is a powerful way to communicate love. All children need to be touched, even if it is not their love language. Touch is important starting at birth. Babies and toddlers need to have daily holding/cuddling. Babies who are held, hugged, and kissed develop a healthier emotional life than those lacking physical contact. As they get older other forms of touch become just as important. Young children love hugs, kisses, wrestling, piggyback rides, and so on. The amount of touch lessens as the child gets older, but it is still needed. At the same time, parents should be aware that children may find it embarrassing, instead of loving, when their mom wants to give them a kiss goodbye in front of their friends.

Holding hands, kissing, cuddling, and touching a person's arm while talking all constitute physical touch in which people feel loved, and are not necessarily sexual. There is an appropriate time for each type of touch. Sexual touching should take place between consenting adults and in a private setting.

Learning to Speak the Language

Each language is important and appreciated to some degree by all people; however, a person will usually speak one or two preferred love languages. Love languages are not set in stone and may vary over time. When it comes to expressing love, people are inclined to speak what they want to hear. There are multiple ways to determine a person's love language. The key is to pay attention to how they express love to you and others. In general, people show love in the way they themselves want to be loved. Paying attention to what they request most often and what they complain the most about is another way to determine their needs and preferences.

Millions of people believe that learning their spouse's love languages has saved their marriages by showing them simple and practical ways to communicate their love to their partner.

People who have stronger relationships tend to express love according to their partner's preferred language. Rarely do couples have the same primary love language. The key to long-lasting, loving relationships is when couples are able to learn to speak their partner's language. Learning to speak a love language that is not our own is a true showing of selflessness. It is a fact that when we receive selfless love we are motivated to reciprocate.

Whatever language a person understands best, they need it to be expressed unconditionally. People have a need for love to be spoken to them throughout their lives. Babies' emotional health is dependent on physical touch, kind words, and tender care. The foundation of love laid early in life affects a child's ability to learn and love. As children move toward adolescence, meeting a child's need for love can become challenging. If children are not loved unconditionally, however, they learn to love only on a conditional basis. When loved unconditionally, children are likely to grow into emotionally stable adults.

Ashley R. Cosentino

See also Love, Theories of; Love, Types of; Romance

Further Readings

Chapman, G. (2007). *Now you're speaking my language: Honest communication and deeper intimacy for a stronger marriage.* Nashville, TN: BH Publishing Group.

Chapman, G. (2010). *The five love languages of teenagers.* Chicago, IL: Northfield.

Chapman, G. (2014). *The five love languages singles edition.* Chicago, IL: Northfield.

Chapman, G. (2015). *The five love languages: How to express heartfelt commitment to your mate.* Chicago, IL: Northfield.

Chapman, G. (2015). *The five love languages of men: The secret to love that lasts.* Chicago, IL: Northfield.

Chapman, G., & Campbell, R. (2012). *The five love languages of children.* Chicago, IL: Northfield.

Egbert, N., & Polk, D. (2006). Speaking the language of relational maintenance: A validity test of Chapman's (1992) Five Love Languages. *Communication Research Reports, 23*(1), 19–26. doi:10.1080/1746490500535822

The 5 Love Languages: http://www.5lovelanguages.com

Goff, B. G., Pointer, L., Jackson, G., & Goddard, H. (2007). Measures of expression of love. *Psychological Reports, 101*(2), 357–360. doi:10.2466/PR0.101.2.357-360

Male Hypoactive Sexual Desire Disorder

Male hypoactive sexual desire disorder (MHSDD) is defined by a low desire for sex and an absence of sexual thoughts or fantasies, resulting in distress or interpersonal difficulty, and the problem is not a result of medical illness, another psychological disorder, or effects of drug use. A male diagnosed with hypoactive sexual desire disorder can still function sexually. This entry discusses the current definition of MHSDD as established by the *Diagnostic and Statistical Manual of Mental Disorders*, 5th edition (DSM-5). The purpose of this entry is to give an overview of the symptoms, risk factors, causes, and treatment for MHSDD, highlighting the intrapersonal and interpersonal complexity of sexual desire. The entry concludes with a discussion of ways that counselors can be instrumental in helping individuals and couples who are struggling with this issue.

DSM-5 Definition and Diagnostic Criteria for Male Hypoactive Sexual Desire Disorder

The complexity and multifaceted nature of sexuality is reflected in the changes in the DSM criteria for sexual dysfunctions. Low sexual desire, as a disorder, first appeared in the DSM-III under the category Psychosexual Dysfunction and was termed *inhibited sexual desire*. The name of the diagnosis was changed to *hypoactive sexual desire disorder* in the DSM-III-R and the diagnosis applied to both males and females. The criterion of causing marked distress or interpersonal difficulty was later added to the DSM-IV.

The DSM-5 created gender-specific dysfunctions resulting in the diagnosis being changed to *male hypoactive sexual desire disorder* (302.71) as a new classification in the fifth edition of the *Diagnostic and Statistical Manual* (DSM-5) under the category of Sexual Dysfunctions. For women, this disorder has been named *female sexual interest/arousal disorder*. The diagnostic criteria that must be met for a diagnosis of MHSDD include (a) persistently or recurrently deficient (or absent) sexual and erotic thoughts or fantasies and desire for sexual activity, (b) symptoms must persist for a minimum of approximately six months, (c) the symptoms cause clinically significant distress in the individual, and (d) the sexual dysfunction is not better explained by a nonsexual mental disorder or as a consequence of severe relationship distress or other significant stressors and is not attributed to the effects of a substance or medication or another medical condition.

Subtypes

The DSM-5 requires more exact severity of the criteria where subtypes for sexual dysfunctions are identified. When making a diagnosis of MHSDD, the clinician will specify which of the three categories best describes the client's issue.

1. Lifelong/generalized in which the individual never had feelings of sexual desire and are not limited to certain situations or partners. Cases of lifelong or generalized MHSDD can be difficult to address since the behavior has been chronic and cannot be connected to a specific cause or event.
2. Acquired/generalized in which the individual previously had feelings of sexual desire with a current partner, but now lacks interest in sexual activity with the partner or solitarily. Cases of acquired-generalized are typically associated with a specific physiological or psychological change that can often be treated once the underlying cause is identified.
3. Acquired/situational in which the individual previously had feelings of sexual desire with a current partner, but now lacks interest in sexual activity with the partner yet has sexual desire toward solitary sexual activity or sexual activity with another partner. Cases of acquired/situational MHSDD are connected to feelings toward a specific partner. Examining the events involving the partner prior to the onset of MHSDD can help identify factors associated with the cause of the disorder.

Finally, the current level of severity is indicated based on the level of distress as a result of the symptoms; the distress level is labeled as *mild*, *moderate*, or *severe*.

Associated Features

New to the DSM-5 are criteria called associated features, subdivided into five categories: (1) partner factors (partner sexual problem, partner health status), (2) relationship factors (poor communication, discrepancies in desire for sexual activity), (3) individual factors (poor body image, history of sexual or emotional abuse), (4) psychiatric comorbidity (depression, anxiety) or stressors (job loss, bereavement), (4) cultural or religious factors (attitudes toward sexuality, sexual desire and guilt), and (5) medical factors relevant to treatment. Identifying any associated features is helpful in assessing the cause and resulting course of treatment.

Prevalence

Approximately 15% to 20% of males ages 18 to 59 will report some type of sexual dysfunction during their lifespan. Sexual problems are more frequent in older individuals and among those with chronic medical conditions and recurrent episodes of depression. Comorbidity of sexual problems is common. Men who experience other types of sexual disorders, such as erectile dysfunction, are more likely to also be diagnosed with HSDD. Consequently, HSDD is often misdiagnosed as other sexual dysfunctions. However, although men with HSDD have decreased desire, they do not always show symptoms of erectile dysfunction. The physiological responses can still function yet the psychological desire is diminished.

Elements of Sexual Desire

Views on sexual arousal demonstrate a link between sexual desire or motivation and sexual arousal, meaning the lack of desire impedes arousal. Existing models of human sexual response have been criticized for overly focusing on genital response and minimizing focus on the variety of factors that can affect arousal for both men and women. In addition, it can be difficult for men to differentiate their own experiences of desire and arousal. How the male manifests low sexual desire might be associated with this difference. Men who are experiencing low sexual desire commonly report erectile difficulties. Feeling anxious and stressed about engaging in sexual activity, or performance anxiety, can also influence level of desire.

The diagnostic categories of sexual dysfunctions in the DSM were based on the model of human sexual response proposed by researchers William H. Masters and Virginia E. Johnson. The four-stage linear model (excitement, plateau, orgasm, and resolution) was based primarily on sexual physiology, how and whether the genitalia functioned. This model was further modified by researchers who added the components of sexual desire and arousal: desire, arousal, orgasm, and resolution. Despite this addition, the model remains linear, suggesting that sexual desire is needed in order to initiate arousal. However, males experiencing HSDD do not show interest in sexual activity related to the desire stage of the model. The lack of desire may be contributed to by biological and psychological factors. Furthermore, individuals diagnosed with other sexual disorders, such as erectile dysfunction, still have the desire for sexual activity but are not able to reach other stages of the sexual response model.

Contributing Factors of MHSDD

Possible causes for MHSDD are described under two categories: biological factors; and psychological and social factors, or psychosocial factors. Biological, or medical, factors include medical conditions such as cardiovascular conditions, chronic renal failure, cancer, epilepsy, diabetes, and low levels of the hormones testosterone or estrogen; medications such as antipsychotics, antidepressants, and cardiovascular drugs; recreational drug use including heavy alcohol use prior to sex, a history of chronic alcoholism, and heavy cigarette smoking. Many of the biological factors can be attributed to physiological changes associated with aging and environmental exposure.

Studies of men with HSDD compared with control groups showed differences between the two groups in the area of the brain that controls motivation. When exposed to sexually stimulating material, typical reaction patterns of the control group demonstrated an increase of blood flow to this area of the brain, which indicates an increase in motivation. In comparison, patients with HSDD showed a steady rate of activity when exposed to sexually stimulating material, resulting in a lack of motivation, indicating a lack of sexual desire.

Psychosocial factors include rape, childhood sexual or physical abuse, poor body image, anger, fear of intimacy, low energy, sexual orientation conflicts, stress, and fatigue; relationship conflict, infidelity, poor communication, chronic illness in a partner, and anxiety about the security of the relationship; and individual religious values and cultural attitudes. Finally, psychological disorders such as major depression and anxiety are associated with sexual disorders. Loss of sex drive can be caused by depression. One of the symptoms of depression is loss of interest in activities that were previously enjoyed. Depressive symptoms or diagnosis of major depressive disorder is associated with impairment in sexual functioning. In addition, many of the antidepressant drugs prescribed are associated with development of, or worsening of, sexual difficulties.

Treatment for MHSSD

Health issues and certain medications can create symptoms of hypoactive sexual desire; accordingly, the first step in treating MHSDD is to identify any underlying medical causes through a thorough medical examination by a physician. Eliminating or treating the medical causes may help to restore normal sex drive. Physical and mental health issues, such as depression, medication use, thyroid levels, and low testosterone and androgen levels, can influence sexual desire and sexual functioning. Addressing these issues with hormone replacement therapy, drug therapy, or modification of current medications can be effective approaches to treatment. It can be difficult to provide treatment as patients might be reluctant to share issues related to sexual disorders unless prompted by a physician. Helping the patient feel comfortable with discussing sexual health is an important aspect of treatment.

Counseling Approaches to MHSSD

Male hypoactive sexual desire disorder is multidimensional, involving physical, relationship, cultural, and individual factors. Counselors need to be knowledgeable about the range of sexual desire and sexual functioning in men and be able to discuss sexual problems with clients. The lack of scientifically based evidence and research on male sexual desire leaves more reliance on a counselor's interpretation and evaluation of what is shared with them by the client. This is acknowledged in the DSM-5 criteria, that the judgment of deficiency is made by the clinician, who takes into account factors that affect sexual functioning, such as age and sociocultural contexts of the individual's life.

Counselors need to obtain a thorough assessment of the history and current symptoms in order to understand as much as possible about the nature of the problem. An initial assessment that includes a sexual history or sexual health questionnaire, such as The Sexual Desire Inventory or Male Desire Scale, is recommended. Whether out of shame, guilt, feelings of inadequacy, embarrassment, or lack of knowledge for proper terminology, clients will often not reveal aspects of sexual problems unless they are directly asked. An in-depth approach by a professional counselor may be therapeutic in itself.

It is important for the counselor to help the client or couple to determine whether the lack of desire for sexual activity is the cause for distress in their relationship. How much of the distress is a result of different libido in a relationship or from expectations from society and media messages should be discussed. Counselors also need to be aware of the cultural differences related to sexuality.

There are a variety of interventions, techniques, and approaches counselors can use when working with male clients with HSDD and their partners. Cognitive-behavioral therapy (CBT) is useful for modifying dysfunctional beliefs associated with sexual functioning, with an emphasis on homework assignments and psychoeducation. Marital therapy is helpful for its focus on relationship problems and communication skills. Intimacy exercises, such as sensate focus, which involves nonsexual to sexual touching, similar to systemic desensitization, are behavior therapy techniques designed to reduce anxiety and can be effective for clients with sexual functioning.

If childhood sexual issues are contributing to the problem, counselors can be instrumental in helping clients work though issues of the past. Eye movement desensitization and reprocessing (EMDR) techniques are recommended for trauma or stress often associated with sexual abuse.

Finally, client education through information, shedding light on myths and assumptions about sexual behavior, reassurance, and providing resources such as books on sexuality can provide relief and resolution for client and couple distress. Client education also includes a discussion with clients about the potential impact medication and recreational drug use can have on relationship and sexual functioning.

In conclusion, MHSDD is associated with a wide variety of biological and psychological factors. Men can lose sexual desire and, as a result, feel distressed about it. It is a frequent problem that is underreported, and there is no drug treatment currently available that specifically addresses MHSDD. Desire disorders and relational dynamics are intertwined, with the quality of the partner relationship contributing to distress as well as the concern about sexual desire.

Sarah Becerra
and Tiffany Hamlett

See also DSM and V-Codes; Sensate Focus; Sex Therapy; Sexual Assessment/History; Sexual Dysfunction; Sexual Health

Further Readings

American Psychiatric Association. (2013). *Diagnostic and statistical manual of mental disorders* (5th ed.). Washington, DC: Author.

Brotto, L. A. (2010). The DSM diagnostic criteria for hypoactive sexual desire disorder in men. *Journal of Sexual Medicine, 7*, 2015–2030.

DeRogatis, L., Rosen, R. C., Goldstein, I., Werneburg, B., Kempthorne-Rawson, J., & Sand, M. (2012). Characterization of hypoactive sexual desire disorder (HSDD) in men. *The Journal of Sexual Medicine, 9*(3), 812–820.

Fruhauf, S., Gregor, H., Schmidt, H. M., Munder, T., & Barth, J. (2013). Efficacy of psychological interventions for sexual dysfunction: A systemic review and meta-analysis. *Archives of Sexual Behavior, 42*, 1–19. doi:10.1007/s10508-012-0062-0

Janssen, E. (2011). Sexual arousal in men: A review and conceptual analysis. *Hormones and Behavior, 59,* 708–716.

Weeks, G. R., & Gambescia, N. (2002). *Hypoactive sexual desire: Integrating couple and sex therapy.* New York, NY: W. W. Norton.

MANDATED REPORTER

A mandated reporter is an individual with a professional responsibility to safeguard at-risk children and adults by reporting suspected cases of abuse, neglect, or maltreatment. This professional responsibility is both legal and ethical. Mandated reporters are professionals who are more likely to be aware of abuse, neglect, or maltreatment because of the nature of their work. For example, mandated reporters often work in health care facilities, schools, social service agencies, mental health clinics, residential treatment facilities, law enforcement, or nursing homes. Thus, the work of a mandated reporter usually involves support and services to at-risk populations, such as infants and children, as well as individuals who are elderly, dependent, developmentally delayed, cognitively delayed, or mentally ill. Therefore, mandated reporters must report abuse, neglect, or maltreatment of a child, an elderly person, or a dependent or disabled adult to law enforcement, Child Protective Services, or Adult Protective Services under penalty of law. Licensed counselors and therapists are part of the mandated reporter group. This entry discusses the need for reporting, the professional categories that are commonly impacted by mandatory reporting guidelines, mandates for reporting abuse, penalties for failing to do so, and the specific reporting procedures that apply to child abuse.

The Need for Reporting

There are millions of suspected cases of abuse and neglect of vulnerable adults and children each year. According to statistics from Adult Protective Services, there were 567,747 reports of abuse to elderly or vulnerable adults in 2004. However, it is suspected that a vast majority of the incidents of abuse to adults go unreported due to fear of isolation or retaliation. It is also suspected that professionals working with adults fail to recognize the signs and symptoms of abuse, which also contributes to underreporting. Per the U.S. Department of Health and Human Services, Child Protective Services agencies received an estimated 3.4 million referrals of suspected abuse and neglect involving approximately 6.3 million children in 2012. For the same year, findings from the National Child Abuse and Neglect Data System (NCANDS) reported a national estimate of 1,640 child deaths as a result of abuse and neglect. Researchers estimate that the number of reported cases of child abuse, neglect, and maltreatment represents less than half of all cases. Much like adult abuse, it is estimated that a great many more cases of child abuse go unreported each year. These statistics clearly indicate the need for mandatory reporting. Fortunately, each state has enacted laws defining who is required to report abuse.

Mandated Reporters

Mandated reporters are people who come into contact with vulnerable populations (e.g., children, dependent adults) as part of their official responsibilities as a volunteer or paid employee in both the public and private sectors. Mandated reporters include, but are not limited to,

1. Medical personnel such as medical examiners, coroners, physicians, residents, dentists, chiropractors, surgeons, podiatrists, osteopaths, nurses (e.g., registered nurses, license practical nurses, nursing assistants), nurse practitioners, physician assistants, medical social workers, emergency medical technicians (EMT), dental hygienists, medical interns, admissions and intake workers, and hospital administrators

2. School and childcare personnel, such as teachers, teacher aides, daycare and preschool teachers, principals, Head Start and early intervention providers, assistant principals, superintendents,

assistant superintendents, directors of special education services, school counselors, school social workers, school psychologists, school nurses, school occupational and physical therapists, truant officers, deans of students, secretaries, residential staff, interns, student teachers, foster parents, and personnel of institutions of higher education

3. Social service and mental health personnel in public or private agencies, such as psychiatrists, psychologists, social workers, counselors, mental health therapists, domestic violence staff, marriage and family therapists, substance abuse counselors, adult day care and nursing home staff, and interns as well as staff at state agencies (e.g., the Department of Health and Human Services, the Department of Mental Health, Veterans Affairs Administration, Department of Public Aid, and the Department of Corrections)

4. Law enforcement personnel, such as police officers, peace officers, state's attorneys, parole and probation officers, and court employees

For mandated reporters, this fiduciary responsibility transcends training, specialty, and level of education. For professionals such as lawyers and counselors who depend heavily upon privileged communication in their work with clients, confidentiality does not extend to cases of abuse, neglect, or maltreatment. Abuse, like suicidal or homicidal intentions, is one of the exceptions to confidentiality. Because educators, mental health counselors, and social services workers are mandated reporters, they are not obligated to keep client's confidences surrounding issues of abuse. Thus, a mandated reporter must report incidents or suspicion of abuse, neglect, or maltreatment if she or he observes signs of abuse, witnesses an abusive incident, or is informed of an incident of abuse by a child or adult client even if the clinician was made aware of the abuse within the confines of the counselor–client relationship. For example, if an adult client reveals that she or he is abusing a child or a disabled relative during an individual therapy session, the clinician has a legal and ethical responsibility to report the abuse to the appropriate authorities as a mandated reporter. As part of informed consent, counselors should explain this exception or limitation to confidentiality to clients at the onset of treatment or services. Failure to report abuse can have both legal and ethical ramifications.

Mandates for Reporting Abuse

Prior to the mid-1970s, efforts to prevent, recognize and respond in instances of child abuse in the United States were piecemeal at best. It was the enactment of the National Child Abuse Prevention and Treatment Act of 1974 (CAPTA) that standardized the nation's efforts in defining, reporting, and investigating child abuse. This legislation played a key role in guiding our current system of Child Protective Services (CPS). According to CAPTA, the problem of child abuse and neglect requires a comprehensive approach. Thus, the federal government spearheaded the movement by providing states and communities with the funding for grants, multidisciplinary collaborations, and technical resources needed to implement and develop strategies that provide children with adequate protection. CAPTA provides funding to states, public agencies, and nonprofit organizations for activities such as prevention, training, prosecuting, and treatment.

Beliefs about abuse can be just as varied and ambiguous as disciplinary practices. Thus, CAPTA helped to conceptualize the term by operationally defining *child abuse and neglect* as

> physical or mental injury, sexual abuse or exploitation, negligent treatment, or maltreatment of a child under the age of 18 or the age specified by the child protection law of the state in question, by a person who is responsible for the child's welfare.

Based on this federal definition of abuse, each state passed child protection laws and provisions for mandatory reporting. Congress reauthorized CAPTA in 1978, 1984, 1988, 1992, 1996, 2003, and most recently on December 20, 2010. To ensure federal funding, most states have based their child protection laws on the guidelines of CAPTA. However, there are some notable differences in mandatory reporting laws from state to state. For example, since 1989, counselors in the state of Maryland are required to report both past and present incidents of child abuse that the clinician learned about while providing therapy to an adult client. In New York, therapists must report suspected child abuse regardless of whether the clinician was informed of the abuse by the child in therapy, the abuser in therapy, or a relative. In Pennsylvania, therapists are required to report child abuse if the client, a minor child, is being abused. However, mandatory reporting laws do not apply if the client, a minor child, *is* the abuser. It is these legal variations that make it imperative for mandated reporters to stay abreast of the child protection laws in their state. As well, most states require continuing education for professionals, which addresses the essentials of assessing and reporting child abuse and neglect as a part of training for employment or renewal of a professional licensure.

Unfortunately, not every state has a mandate for reporting the abuse of an elderly or dependent adult. Since 2009, two legislative initiatives have sought to unify the protection of elderly and dependent adults under law in the United States. First, the Elder Abuse Victims Act of 2009 (EAVA) authorized a study model of state laws and funded initiatives such as grants for training, technical assistance, and multidisciplinary coordination. However, it is the health care reform bill (HR 3590), signed into law by President Barack Obama on March 23, 2010, that provides the most robust language to safeguard the elderly. The Elder Justice Act (EJA), which is a part of the health care reform bill, is a charge toward a nationally comprehensive approach for identifying, intervening, and preventing the abuse of elderly adults. It authorizes $400 million to Adult Protective Services (APS) and additional funds to the detection and prevention of elderly abuse. This new legislation is groundbreaking because individuals who are elderly need protection, not just from physical abuse and neglect but from more permeating forms of abuse, such as financial exploitation, sexual abuse, and abandonment. Until elder abuse is mandated nationwide, clinicians should seek supervision, consultation, and guidance from local authorities and professional codes of conduct to ensure the client's safety in cases where there is no state law.

Penalties for Failure to Report

Whenever a mandated reporter has reasonable cause to believe or suspect child abuse or neglect, she or he is legally required to report the incident to local authorities immediately, under penalty of fines, imprisonment, or both. Depending upon the state, penalties for mandated reporters who knowingly or willfully fail to report suspected instances of child abuse and neglect range from a misdemeanor to a felony charge, 6 months to 5 years of imprisonment, criminal fines from $500 to $5,000, and/or civil fines from $10,000 to $50,000. It is also important to note that state laws provide immunity from criminal and civil liability for having reported suspected abuse or neglect made in good faith.

What Is Reportable?

Mandated reporters are legally required to report suspected child abuse and maltreatment immediately when there is reasonable cause to suspect or believe that a child, who is known through a professional or official capacity, may be being abused, neglected, or maltreated. Each state has developed guidelines stemming from the CAPTA definition. Universally, what must be reported can be described as, but not limited to, when a parent or caregiver (a) inflicts or allows to be inflicted any physical, sexual, or psychological injury; (b) creates or allows to be created a risk of physical, sexual, or psychological injury; (c) engages in patterns of behavior that render the parent or caregiver unable to adequately care for the immediate or continual needs of the child (e.g., substance abuse);

(d) repeatedly refuses or fails to provide essential care or protection relevant to the child's age and developmental stage; (e) abandons or exploits the child; and/or (f) fails to provide adequate food, care, clothing, shelter, supervision, or medical care.

There are some factors that contribute to the likelihood of child abuse and neglect. The first variable relates to characteristics of the parent or caregiver such as age, history of abuse or substance abuse, attitude on discipline, parental stress, and/or violence in the home. Secondly, there are individual variables that might place a child at risk for abuse such as the child's age, behavior, or disability. Unfortunately, children with developmental delays or behavioral difficulties are at an increased risk for maltreatment because their care and supervision can often become frustrating and overwhelming for a caregiver. Lastly, environmental variables such as lack of resources, social isolation, and lack of support also create the perfect storm and heighten the potential that a child is abused.

Reporting Child Abuse

Mandated reporters work in an array of service-oriented roles such as health care, social services, mental health, law enforcement, and education. Thus, the work of a mandated reporter can vary from acute and brief interactions to extensive and long-term working relationships. For this reason, it is possible that a counselor, crisis worker, school psychologist, or direct care worker may not have an abundance of information for making the report. Regardless of the breadth of information a clinician may or may not have about the client, the abuser, or the extent of the abuse, a report must still be made. It is important to note that mandated reporters only need reasonable suspicion of abuse, neglect, or maltreatment to make a report. A mandated reporter does not need all the details to make a report. For example, the mandated reporter may not know the names and ages of all the children in the home or the full name of the alleged abuser. Not having the abuser's real name or the familial contact phone number is irrelevant when a bruise is present or maltreatment is suspected. The lack of information should not deter reporting. It is the role of Child Protective Services to investigate the matter.

As part of CAPTA, each state has a reporting procedure, which includes a child abuse reporting hotline. Thus, reports can be made immediately by phone or in writing depending on state statute. The following is an example of the data needed and content of a child abuse report: (a) the name, age, and address of the child suspected of being abused; (b) the names and ages of other children in the home or otherwise relevant to the report; (c) the names, address, and telephone number of any person responsible for the care of the child; (d) the nature and extent of the abuse and the child(ren)'s condition; (e) any evidence of history or a pattern of abuse, neglect, or maltreatment; (f) any evidence such as photographs, videos, x-rays, school attendance records, incident reports of behavior, or even the child's writings or drawings, which indicate abuse or maltreatment; and (g) any other relevant information.

Reporting child abuse in agencies and schools can be complex at times. Sometimes a child reports abuse to a teacher or a peer. It is always ideal that the person to whom the abuse was reported be the person who makes the report to the authorities. Often, clinicians support and assist others (e.g., teachers, administrators) with making the report. In the event that the abuse was reported to a child (e.g., sibling, classmate), the clinician should intercede, talk to the alleged victim, and make the report. Whoever witnesses or suspects the abuse should make the report. However, a clinician should not fail to report suspected abuse because she or he did not directly observe or learn of the information firsthand.

The information presented in this entry provides a framework for mandatory reporting. However, as already emphasized, laws vary from state to state. Every mandated reporter should verify the reporting laws governing their state and affecting their practice.

Tasha Leroyce Banks

See also Best Interests of the Child; Confidentiality; Duty to Warn and Protect; Elder Abuse; Ethical Codes; Ethical Decision-Making; Informed Consent for Research; Informed Consent in Clinical Work; Release of Information for Couples and Families; Therapeutic Alliance

Further Readings

Child Welfare Information Gateway. (2011). *About CAPTA: A legislative history.* Washington, DC: U.S. Department of Health and Human Services, Children's Bureau.

Illinois Department of Child and Family Services (DCFS) Children's Justice Task Force. (2015, May). *Manual for mandated reporters.* Springfield, IL: Author. Retrieved from http://www.illinois.gov/dcfs/safekids/reporting/documents/cfs_1050-21_mandated_reporter_manual.pdf

Myers, J. E. B. (2008, Fall). A short history of child protection in America. *Family Law Quarterly, 42*(3). Retrieved from https://www.americanbar.org/content/dam/aba/publishing/insights_law_society/ChildProtectionHistory.authcheckdam.pdf

MARITAL DISTRESS

Marital distress is a common occurrence characterized by emotional distress, conflict, and other difficulties within a union. The occurrence of marital distress is somewhat different from the typical highs and lows within a relationship. Although in marriages periods of distress are typical, particularly in those that are long term, distress occurs less often than the more regular disputes generally seen in relationships. Individuals who feel distressed within their marriage are unsatisfied or discontent with their marriage overall. Distress can be experienced by one or both individuals in the relationship. If one individual is experiencing feelings of distress, then marital distress has occurred. It is not essential for both people within the relationship to experience distress for marital distress to occur.

High levels of marital distress or prolonged periods of distress can have an impact on marital satisfaction. A manifestation of distress or significant unhappiness in a marriage can occur for various reasons. At times marital distress is purely based on difficulties within the relationship such as poor or ineffective communication, a lack of intimacy, financial difficulties, sexual difficulties, or infidelity. In other times, marital distress is the result of problems with one or both individuals independently, such as lack of trust, career change, substance abuse, verbal abuse, domestic violence, or unrealistic expectations from their partner. Similar forms of distress are found among those in committed relationships who are not married; this is usually called relationship distress. The remainder of this entry discusses the signs and symptoms of marital distress.

Signs and Symptoms of Marital Distress

There are numerous signs that a marriage is in distress. Many couples in distress argue frequently and are often unable to resolve their disagreements. Though not all couples quarrel, couples in late stages of distress and who are on a path to divorce may be disconnected and live parallel lives. One major contributor to distressed marriages is, according to marital researcher John Gottman, a mismatch in meta-emotional styles. This describes what people think about emotion and how much they value emotional expression. Gottman proposed three functional styles of conflict management in couple relationships: volatile, validating, or avoidant. Volatile couples express anger and frustration openly, validating couples believe in discussing big and small issues, and avoidant couples tend to not argue and tend to only discuss big issues. When there is a mismatch in styles, couples are more likely to experience marital distress.

Sometimes training in effective communication can help couples negotiate and understand different styles and expectations. With increased levels of conflict and dissension, relationships overall can deteriorate. Arguing can be considered both a sign and symptom of marital distress because individuals who possess poor communication skills often are unable to amicably resolve issues and many continue to argue or argue more frequently. A resolution of the underlying issues is no longer the focus and often individuals shift to engaging in arguments simply to win and not to rectify the issues at hand. Often people lose sight of the underlying issues in prolonged periods of marital distress, and major quarrels ensue over minor issues. Disagreements are inevitable in relationships; however, arguments often lead nowhere but to feelings of hurt, disrespect, regret, and anger.

Another sign of marital distress is an absence of physical and emotional intimacy within the relationship. When there is a lack of intimacy, either emotional, physical, or both, couples may experience marital distress. Numerous factors can contribute to a decline in intimacy within a relationship, such as stress. Physical or emotional stress, from work, school, child care, or numerous other factors, can weigh heavily on a relationship. If one or both individuals in a relationship are experiencing an increased amount of stress, more often than not there is decreased desire for intimacy. As most people experience stress at varying points throughout their life, it is considered normal for most couples to experience a decline in intimacy at some point in their relationship. Although this is normal, a significant decline in physical or emotional intimacy for an extended period of time may not be considered normal. However, a brief decline in intimacy can contribute to increased marital distress as well.

In addition to decreased levels of intimacy, sexual difficulties can also play a significant role in marital distress. Physical intimacy plays an important role in a relationship. Without it, many people do not feel close to their significant other. Sexual activity is one way people connect in relationships with their significant other. It provides one way to express feelings or emotions. When sexual activity declines, particularly over long periods of time, this can lead to marital distress.

Equally important to note when discussing sexual activity is infidelity. Infidelity is the act of being unfaithful, emotionally and/or sexually, to a significant other. Many consider emotional infidelity worse than physical infidelity although both are a common occurrence within relationships as often times they are simultaneous. There are various reasons that one might engage in infidelity, but regardless of the reason, infidelity is often a significant factor contributing to distress in relationships. Further, marital distress and infidelity can cause depression, sadness, and increased stress for one or both individuals within the relationship. Without treatment, distress can have a prolonged effect on the relationship and on others who are in close proximity, especially children. A relationship that is distressed over an extended period can have negative consequences for the mental and physical health of those involved.

Jahaan R. Abdullah

See also Developmental Model of Marriage; Marriage and Health; Marriage Enrichment; Marriage Myths; Parental Stress: Effects on Children

Further Readings

Amato, P. R., & Hohmann-Marriott, B. (2007). A comparison of high- and low-distress marriages that end in divorce. *Journal of Marriage and Family, 69*(3), 621–638. doi:10.1111/j.1741-3737.2007.00396.x

Baucom, D. H., Shoham, V., Mueser, K. T., Daiuto, A. D., & Stickle, T. R. (1998). Empirically supported couple and family interventions for marital distress and adult mental health problems. *Journal of Consulting and Clinical Psychology, 66*(1), 53–88. doi:10.1037/0022-006X.66.1.53

Bodenmann, G., Charvoz, L., Cina, A., & Widmer, K. (2001). Prevention of marital distress by enhancing the coping skills of couples: 1-year follow-up-study. *Swiss Journal of Psychology/Schweizerische Zeitschrift für Psychologie/Revue Suisse de Psychologie, 60*(1), 3–10. doi:10.1024//1421-0185.60.1.3

Markman, H. J., Renick, M. J., Floyd, F. J., Stanley, S. M., & Clements, M. (1993). Preventing marital distress through communication and conflict management training: A 4- and 5-year follow-up. *Journal of Consulting and Clinical Psychology, 61*(1), 70–77. doi:10.1037/0022-006X.61.1.70

Pihet, S., Bodenmann, G., Cina, A., Widmer, K., & Shantinath, S. (2007). Can prevention of marital distress improve well-being? A 1 year longitudinal study. *Clinical Psychology & Psychotherapy, 14*(2), 79–88. doi:10.1002/cpp.522

Rogge, R. D., Cobb, R. J., Lawrence, E., Johnson, M. D., & Bradbury, T. N. (2013). Is skills training necessary for the primary prevention of marital distress and dissolution? A 3-year experimental study of three interventions. *Journal of Consulting and Clinical Psychology, 81*(6), 949–961. doi:10.1037/a0034209

South, S. C., Krueger, R. F., & Iacono, W. G. (2011). Understanding general and specific connections between psychopathology and marital distress: A model based approach. *Journal of Abnormal Psychology, 120*(4), 935–947. doi:10.1037/a0025417

Whisman, M. A. (2007). Marital distress and DSM-IV psychiatric disorders in a population-based national survey. *Journal of Abnormal Psychology, 116*(3), 638–643. doi:10.1037/0021-843X.116.3.638

Marital Group Therapy

Marital group therapy refers to the process of counseling in which one or more practitioners meet with multiple individuals to address a common goal. Group facilitators often focus groups on a specific topic prevalent to the participating members and address topics such as career, relationships, and intrapersonal concerns. A variety of modalities for group work have been identified. Psychoeducational groups focus on educating group members about a particular topic (e.g., parenting groups). Task groups allow members to work together to accomplish a shared goal (e.g., school staff working toward improved service implementation). Self-help groups allow individuals to support one another through a shared identified issue (e.g., substance use). Finally, psychotherapy groups focus on interpersonal dynamics within the group and use *here and now* processing to address and work through these dynamics. Group therapy has been found to be beneficial for a variety of populations, including children, adolescents, college students, adults, and couples. This entry examines the benefits of group therapy and, more specifically, marital therapy groups, the criteria used to select candidates for group therapy, and phases and types of group therapy.

Benefits of Group Therapy

Individuals exist in a variety of group contexts, which allows for shared experiences, normalizing of experiences, and various perspectives and feedback. Group therapy applies this familiar experience by using a present-focused approach that provides an avenue for members to become aware of thoughts, feelings, and behaviors that are occurring within the group and using the group dynamics to process them. In this sense, the group acts as a microcosm of everyday life, as processes that occur within the group are reflective of individuals' experiences outside of the group and can provide a therapeutic outlet to manage these experiences in a safe setting.

Individuals who seek therapy often feel a sense of isolation in their experience. Group therapy allows members to feel a sense of belonging and camaraderie in knowing they are not alone in their struggles. Members with shared experiences can offer authentic guidance, support, and advice that can often be more powerful than when coming from a clinician or expert. This sense of belongingness can foster cohesion among group members. Group cohesion allows members to explore and develop social and relational skills. Relationships that are built within a supportive and cohesive environment foster intimacy, caring, and a safe place to challenge. Members can use this environment to work on changing behaviors and receive feedback on these behaviors in an empathic manner.

Being part of a group adds a level of safety to the client–counselor relationship. With multiple group members, individuals have the security of knowing they will not always be the center of attention, which can increase comfort and safety of participation. Additionally, being part of a group and the underlying notion that all members have their own personal struggles offer a sense of ease in sharing with others who may be seen as on a similar level. The giving and receiving nature of therapy groups allows members to help themselves through helping others. Members often gain significant insight into their own struggles by offering support and guidance to their peers. Also, there is a certain power in receiving similar guidance from a peer, rather than someone in what is considered an expert role. Finally, group therapy opens the door for modeling and vicarious learning. Group members benefit from seeing progress in their peers and more senior group members act as models for the positive consequences to group participation.

The Therapeutic Factors

Irvin Yalom discussed the benefits of group therapy as a complex process including what he termed the *therapeutic factors*. Although each of these factors is distinctly defined, according to Yalom, there is a constant interplay between them such that they can neither occur nor function independently. As such, clinicians who lead therapy groups must not only be familiar with each therapeutic factor but also have a comprehensive understanding of the complexity in which they interact to impact group members.

Yalom highlighted the group therapy benefit of helping others in the *altruism* factor. He also believed in the power of *cohesion*, or feeling a sense of belonging to the group. Also important to the concept of group therapy is *catharsis*, or the ability to express concerns or difficulties in the presence of others. Group therapy provides members with increased insight, or awareness and understanding of the self. This insight can be a function of other therapeutic factors, such as *interpersonal learning–input* and *guidance*. Interpersonal learning–input refers to the process of receiving feedback from others. On the other hand, guidance is direct advice or suggestions received from other members of the group. Group therapy allows for improved interpersonal skills, or *interpersonal learning–output*. The development of social skills can be an explicit goal of the group or can happen indirectly through developing and experiencing appropriate interactions with other group members.

One of the primary groups of which an individual takes part is the family group and, as such, many thoughts, feelings, and behaviors are a result of dynamics and learned behaviors or messages that exist within the family group. One of the therapeutic factors of group therapy is *recapitulation of the family*. This factor assumes that family dynamics are reexperienced within the group and resulting thoughts, feelings, and behaviors can be supported and challenged therapeutically in the group setting.

As group members begin to overcome their struggles throughout the group process, other members are encouraged by witnessing their progress. This inspiration is referred to as *instillation of hope* and is an important aspect of group therapy. As members share in the efforts of others in the group, feelings of isolation may dissipate, highlighting a sense of *universality* among group members. The realization that one is not alone in one's struggles can also lead to *identification* among group members. Identification refers to associating oneself with another member of the group, often as a result of shared experiences. Finally, *existential factors* are considered essential to group therapy. In other words, group members come to realize, through vicarious learning, truths about the world around them.

Because the dynamics of a group vary depending on each present member and group leader, no two groups are exactly alike. Despite the unique personality of therapy groups, each therapeutic factor plays a role in the group process and impacts individual and group outcomes. For this reason, group therapy is a powerful and appropriate intervention for a variety of populations and identified concerns.

Marital Therapy Groups

The benefits of group therapy for marriages began to emerge in counseling literature in the 1970s. Inspired by the work of theorists and scholars like Yalom, as well as Carl Rogers, James Framo, and

Fritz Perls, many marriage and family therapists found that group therapy offered significant advantages and unique contributions to couples in need of treatment. Alexandria Gale described her approach to marital group therapy as beginning a type of experiment that quickly proved to offer beneficial outcomes. Likewise, Framo began using couples group therapy as a method to avoid what he called the *transference/countertransference logjam*, but later described group therapy as the treatment of choice for couples at various stages.

Marital group therapy has several advantages over individual couples therapy. First, marital group sessions offer participants the opportunity to compare and contrast their relationship concerns with others. As a social microcosm, marital groups also have the potential to foster hope and a sense of universality among couples. In other words, couples can walk away from a group experience feeling less isolated and more hopeful. Additionally, Gale describes marital groups as being groups within groups that offer infinite opportunities for identification, transference, countertransference, and various other patterns of interactions. Consequently, couples may identify their relationship patterns in another couple in the group or notice their own behavior reflected in someone else's partner. By recognizing their patterns of behavior in another couple or partner, a couple may more readily find solutions and be able to process their own thoughts and feelings. Moreover, Framo noted that because couples now have a wider audience for their interactional patterns, they blame each other less and focus more on their own behavior. Marital therapy groups are also often more economical, require less time, and guard the therapist from experiencing triangulation from the couple. Further, marital groups help couples generate insight and find effective ways of communicating with each other.

Group Criteria

Not all couples may be suitable for group therapy. Framo recommends that clinicians pair couples with other couples of similar age and phase of family life. The similarities between couples can increase cohesion in the group. However, it should also be noted that heterogeneity in groups can also be used therapeutically by creating a corrective emotional experience. Additionally, couples wherein one or both partners exhibit intense emotional aggressions, are struggling with severe and persistent mental illness, or are at risk of intimate partner violence may not be appropriate for group work and should be screened out. Therapists should also be sure to thoroughly inform group participants about the nature of group therapy and help assuage some of their anxieties before they begin attending the group sessions. It is also important that group members understand that confidentiality is difficult to maintain in a group and cannot be guaranteed.

Once a group leader has identified appropriate couples for their group, scholars recommend developing a set of rules for the group to follow. Examples of group rules include having a zero tolerance policy for violence, limiting socialization outside of the group, asking participants to not speak about other couples where those not in the group can overhear them, and requiring that group members give feedback in a courteous manner. These rules are presented as examples here, but it is important to recognize that group rules are best developed in conjunction with the group and that these specific rules may not be suitable for all groups.

Phases of Group

Gale stated that marital therapy groups go through three distinct phases. Initially, the couples in the group seek connection and look for similarities in others. In this stage, the couples look toward the group facilitator as an advice-giving expert, and test the other members of the group in order to determine how much they should share about themselves and their partner. During this stage of group therapy, couples test each other's boundaries and struggle with genuineness and acceptance. Genders tend to align with each other at this initial stage, and this may foster a competition between the sexes. At this stage, the therapist should be most active.

During the middle phase of marital group therapy, couples begin to accept the group process. Thus, they begin to present topics that are more intimate and a group identity begins to emerge. At this stage, couples will begin to improve and the group ceases to be divided by gender. The therapist also begins to take less of an active role in group sessions. However, the therapist must prepare couples for termination.

In the final stage of marital group therapy, the couple begins to exhibit doubts and regresses to earlier behaviors. However, eventually the couple begins to accept the inevitable termination of the group and works more diligently toward improving their relationship. During group termination, Gale recommends that couples wanting more group experience discuss their desire with the group, and it is possible that they can be utilized as models for future groups.

Types of Groups

As with individual group therapy, there are various types of marital therapy groups. These groups range from the insight-oriented psychotherapy groups to the more directive and behavioral psychoeducational groups. The following section briefly describes a few marital group therapy types.

Psychoeducational Groups

Psychoeducational groups help share with couples information and concrete skills related to relationship enrichment. Oftentimes, these groups are most beneficial as preventative measures and for populations that typically eschew relationship counseling, such as ethnic minority groups and those with low socioeconomic status. There are numerous psychoeducational curriculums available, including PREP 7.0, PAIRS, and PREPARE/ENRICH. PREP 7.0, which is a popular and empirically supported curriculum, uses cognitive-behavioral and communication-oriented techniques to increase relationship satisfaction and reduce conflict. PREP 7.0 has several variations, including a curriculum designed for veterans, a Christian-based curriculum, and a program for singles. PAIRS, or the practical application of intimate relationship skills, is another curriculum-based psychoeducational program. PAIRS focuses specifically on enhancing three competencies: (1) developing emotional literacy, (2) building and maintaining intimacy, and (3) developing practical knowledge and attitudes associated with a positive and healthy marriage. Thus, PAIRS is more emotionally focused than PREP. Lastly, PREPARE/ENRICH is a premarital intervention based on a formal assessment of a couple's strengths and areas for growth. Some facilitators conduct PREPARE/ENRICH assessments with individual couples, but the program is also available as a group curriculum. Group members each take the PREPARE/ENRICH assessments and the facilitator uses the group to process the assessment outcomes and discuss strategies for relationship growth.

Group facilitators conduct these curricula in a workshop-style setting. Couples are given the opportunity to interact and are encouraged to share with each other, but the focus in these groups is teaching couples effective strategies for relationship enhancement. Group facilitators employ a combination of lecture and experiential activities in leading these groups. Additionally, these groups are typically closed groups with a fixed number of sessions and are by nature structured and directive.

Framo's Model for Marital Group Therapy

Framo conducted some of the earliest psychotherapy groups for couples. Unlike the psychoeducational models, his group approach was less structured and focused on generating insight rather than teaching specific skills. He facilitated the groups with a female cotherapist and recommends that facilitators conduct groups with a cotherapist of a different gender. Additionally, the groups were each 2 hours long.

During the group, he would work with three couples. He would begin by focusing all of his attention with one couple's marital concerns. Afterward, he would turn to the rest of the group and elicit feedback. After all parties had discussed the couple's situation thoroughly, he would turn his attention to the next couple. As couples terminated the group, he would invite new couples to join the group. Thus, the group remained open. His focus in each session would be how the couple interacted with each other in the presence of the group. He would highlight interactional patterns and utilize the group experience to explore each partner's family of origin with the ultimate goal of preparing them to have a session with just their family of origin apart from the group and their partners (called the *family-of-origin conference*). Framo discovered that couples behaved differently when they had the group audience, and he found that the group setting provided significant benefits to couples.

Multifamily Groups

One of the reported benefits of group therapy is the therapeutic factor of recapitulation of the family. Group therapy offers a medium in which clients can identify and address concerns that have arisen in response to their family of origin. Multifamily group therapy (MFGT) is a fusion of family and group therapy that emphasizes the unique benefits of each of these modalities by including family units as group members to more directly address these underlying familial concerns.

In multifamily groups, members have the ability to work on goals both between and within family units. Although the distinct benefits of group therapy apply to the family units involved in the groups (e.g., sense of belongingness, altruism, instillation of hope), multifamily groups have the added strength of treating the family, rather than the individual, as the identified client. In this way, each family unit that participates in the group can offer feedback, challenge, and support to each other unit in a way that identifies, explores, and treats processes that are present within the family, rather than solely focusing on an individual's thoughts, feelings, and behaviors. Furthermore, in addition to viewing family units as group members, each individual member of the group plays a unique role in the makeup of the group and the group's functioning. As such, MFGT has an added layer of therapeutic benefit in that both family and individual concerns can be addressed.

Daniel Gutierrez and
Katie A. Lamberson

See also Couples and Marriage Counseling; Group Family Therapy; Individual Versus Family Therapy

Further Readings

Bowen, M. (1971). Family therapy and family group therapy. In H. Kaplan & B. Sadok (Eds.), *Comprehensive group psychotherapy* (pp. 384–421). Baltimore, MD: Williams & Wilkins.

Framo, J. L. (1982). *Explorations in marital and family therapy: Selected papers of James L. Framo*. New York, NY: Springer.

Yalom, I. D. (1995). *The theory and practice of group psychotherapy* (4th ed.). New York, NY: Basic Books.

MARRIAGE, ARRANGED

An arranged marriage is a marital union based on two families or their agents contracting to join two individuals together. Unlike most choice marriages, where the two partners choose each other, these marriages are typically made based on compatibility of family resources or sociopolitical status. Some research has found couples in arranged marriages reporting greater satisfaction than couples in marriages of choice. While the prevalence of arranged marriage varies around the world, it is still widely practiced and in some countries is the typical way couples marry. This entry discusses how arranged marriages take place, research on satisfaction in arranged marriages, variations in how marriages are arranged, reasons for the decline in arranged marriage, and arranged marriage in the United States.

Overview of Arranged Marriage

The definition of *love* is different in every society and so is the definition of *marriage*. However, in most societies around the world, couples commit to monogamous relationships and marriage is a fundamental institution for this. Two forms of marriage occur most commonly: the love marriage and the arranged marriage. A love marriage, or choice marriage, is a process driven by individuals finding a partner based on a romantic or passionate connection. An arranged marriage is one in which family members or matchmakers select the marital partners and negotiate the marital coupling process. Arranging marriage is a widespread practice in Asia, Africa, the Middle East, and South America, as well as in other specialized communities around the globe. In fact, it is estimated that half or more of all marriages worldwide are arranged, and this custom dates back millennia. Although arranged marriages are most prevalent in certain countries and among certain religious sects as a result of international migration, both arranged marriages and choice marriages often coexist among communities all over the world.

Arranged marriages represent not only a union of two individuals, but a union of two families. As such, these partnerships are not based on love or passion, but rather on compatibility of families, economic resources, or health. The practice is typically found in cultures with a more collectivist focus rather than a focus on the individual. These families believe that young adults are not capable of making reliable partnership choices. As such, parents are better able to judge suitability and rationally evaluate prospective matches than young adults who could be too influenced by emotion. In more traditional cultures, arranged marriage can represent the practice of keeping children and adolescents separated and protected until the time of marriage. These sexually conservative societies also tend to focus on interdependence and group cohesiveness.

Arranged marital practices can vary within a country based on region, ethnicity, or religion. In some places, arranged marriage serves to support the societal structure or keep the caste system in place. Many societies with arranged marriage also have multigenerational family systems that emphasize the elders as decision-makers for the entire family. These family elders educate the next generations about marriage and socialize them to the customs, rituals, and societal expectations. They can also help with marital adjustment and provide support for these new couples, which can in turn lead to more successful marriages.

Marital Satisfaction

In contrast to romantic and passionate love, which often is the initiator of marriage in many societies, arranged marriage is not based on a love connection. However, those in an arranged marriage often report developing love and affection during the marriage in the context of the family system. These relationships can deepen over time, in contrast to many love marriages where relationship connection can decline. Higher divorce rates in Western societies are often cited as evidence of the decline in marital satisfaction in choice marriages. Empirical studies also seem to support that love matches show a gradual decline in connection and satisfaction beginning shortly after marriage, perhaps related to unmet expectations. Couples in arranged marriages often report that their parents made the right selection for them. They also report having to establish an early expectation and pattern that they will have to work at marriage since they are not as familiar with their spouse.

Proponents of arranged marriage claim these unions can strengthen families while love marriages can further individualistic pursuits. Rather than focusing on fulfilling the spouse's needs and wants, there could be a greater expectation to please and respect the spouse's parents and family. This is an example of how these unions contain complex elements not fully appreciated by many in Western societies. Additionally, it is claimed that outsiders often misunderstand the spiritual and religious components of arranged unions, which can be central to the marriage. Many family activities center on religious observances and celebrations, which serve to reinforce the spiritual and familial interrelationship.

Variations in Arranged Marriage

Different cultural groups have different practices with regard to arranged marriage. In some cases, the individuals partnered are strangers until their wedding day. However, this does not typically mean that individuals are being forced into marriage against their will. The bride's and groom's families typically agree on the individuals to be joined, the date of the marriage, and other transactional elements. At times, young children can be betrothed for arranged marriage to occur sometime in the future. In certain cases, the male's family can contribute to the costs of the female's upkeep until she is old enough to marry. These marriages are designed to protect each family's interests socially, economically, and politically.

Historically, arranged marriages did not involve the consent of the two parties involved, but this practice varies according to culture. Sometimes, the male has the power to initiate the partnership discussions with his parents based on his choice of mate, or at least has the power to agree with his parent's choice. More recently, modern arranged marriages can allow both involved parties to consent or veto the marital prospect. Dating is sometimes allowed between those selected to marry each other, but this is usually permitted only after the marriage has been agreed upon. In some contexts, families utilize the services of an external matchmaker who creates a suitable match and presents it to the family. The couple would then meet and determine whether or not they would marry.

Part of the decline in arranged marriages is attributed to shifting government policies that encourage promotion of a choice element to marriage. Incidences of suicide for individuals coerced into an arranged marriage and other negative consequences, such as child marriages, are the foundation of these changing policies. Some critics also maintain that arranged marital practices are biased against women. For instance, in some cultures women who are widows have to remain single or are remarried to one of the husband's male relatives. There is also some evidence that arranged marriage negatively impacts a woman's education and marital satisfaction more so than men's. In some societies, particularly in Africa, arranged marriages can also involve a bride price. This is the exchange of money, goods, and/or property known as a dowry, which is most often given to the groom's family. This can signify the acceptance of the bride into the groom's family and accompanying assumption of all rights and privileges. It is claimed that in these more patriarchal societies, women in arranged marriages can experience less personal power and divorce is usually not a viable option. As such, it is usually in the best interest of wives to make their arranged marriages successful.

Decline in Arranged Marriage

While the practice is still prevalent, there has been a reported decline in arranged marriages both globally and in the United States. This is attributed to multiple factors, primarily social and economic changes and governmental pressure. Worldwide modernization has expanded individualistic orientations and autonomy. Globalization has created a shift to more industrialized areas where the practice of arranging marriage is less common than in more rural locations. In some instances, due to better access to education and employment, children are now earning more than their parents, which has eroded parental influence and the reliance on historic customs. Geographic distance has also contributed to this decline since familial influence is lessened as individuals become increasingly mobile and separated. An emphasis on Western trends has also introduced alternative and more individualistic concepts of marriage into areas dominated by arranged marriage.

In areas where the practice remains widespread, there has been a shift toward greater accommodation of the individual and the individual's views in mate selection. It has been noted that increased levels of education can afford individuals greater control of the mate selection process. Couples who marry in middle age also typically have more control, or even complete control, of the process. There are also some cases of elopement where individuals secretly marry outside of familial consent.

Arranged Marriage in the United States

In the United States, there is generally a negative attitude toward arranged marriages. This is because in the United States finding a mate and falling in love are generally viewed as normative developmental tasks. But even though arranged marriages are less common in the United States than love marriages, they can often be observed with first-generation immigrant families who maintain close ties to their country of origin. These individuals often attempt to navigate both the customs of their host country and the generationally practiced customs of their home. Certain intact communities also maintain this practice, such as ultra-Orthodox Jewish communities.

Marriage and family counselors working with couples should understand that marital expectation and satisfaction are usually defined differently based on the type of marriage. Couples in choice marriages may base their definition of satisfaction on personal happiness and intimacy. In contrast, couples in arranged marriages tend to define satisfaction in more relational and social ways, with intimacy not considered a key element. Marital conflict is often viewed as a larger family issue whereby the entire family unit is disrupted. Some in an arranged marriage even view spousal conflict as an abandonment of the family in favor of personal goals and gain. Given such values, these individuals might be less likely to present to couples or family counseling.

Research has found arranged marriages to be more stable than choice marriages and to have lower divorce rates. The implications for a more stable marital system include higher overall wellness, better health, and more functional relationships across other domains. Typically, individuals in arranged marriages also subscribe to more traditional gender roles as a cultural belief and may be less likely to have individualistic pursuits. There can also be a fear that treatment of any kind can lessen a family's status and thereby reduce the potential for future generations to make beneficial marital matches.

*Caroline S. Booth and
Courtney Evans-Thompson*

See also Family Rituals; Immigrant Families; Kinship Care; Marriage and Health; Patriarchy

Further Readings

Allendorf, K. (2013). Schemas of marital change: Arranged marriages to eloping for love. *Journal of Marriage and Family, 75*(2), 453–469. doi:10.1111/jomf.12003

Bowman, J. L., & Dollahite, D. C. (2013). Why would such a person dream about heaven? *Journal of Comparative Family Studies, 43,* 207–225.

Greenberg, D., Buchinder, J. T., & Witztum, E. (2012). Arranged matches and mental illness: Therapists' dilemmas. *Psychiatry, 75*(4), 342–354. doi:10.1521/psyc.2012.75.4.342

Madathil, J., & Benshoff, J. M. (2008). Importance of marital characteristics and marital satisfaction: A comparison of Asian Indians in arranged marriages and Americans in marriages of choice. *The Family Journal, 16,* 222–230. doi:10.1177/1066480708317504

Myers, J. E., Madathil, J., & Tingle, L. (2005). Marriage satisfaction and wellness in India and the United States: A preliminary comparison of arranged marriages and marriages of choice. *Journal of Counseling and Development, 83*(2), 183–190. doi:10.1177/1066480708317504

Regan, P. C., Lakhanpal, S., & Anguiano, C. (2012). Relationship outcomes in Indian-American love-based and arranged marriages. *Psychological Reports, 110*(3), 915–924. doi:10.2466/21.02.07

Sam, M. A. (2009). Arranged marriages: Change or persistence? Illustrative cases of Nigerians in the USA. *Journal of Comparative Family Studies, 40*(5), 739–757.

Marriage, First and Second

The term *marriage* refers to the interpersonal union established in various parts of the world to form a familial bond that is recognized legally, religiously, or socially and which grants the participating partners mutual conjugal rights and responsibilities. A first marriage occurs for couples who have never been married before. A second marriage refers to the act of remarrying after an initial first marriage ends due to death or divorce. Current statistics indicate that approximately 50% of first marriages and 60% of second marriages end in divorce, prompting researchers to investigate these trends further. The purpose of this entry is to provide an overview of research on heterosexual first and second marriages, the intricacies of each relationship type, and the impact of counseling for couples in first and second marriages.

Factors Impacting First Marriages

Marital satisfaction, marital quality, personal demographics, and length of marriage are widely cited as the factors that influence the evolution of a first marriage. *Marital satisfaction* is defined as the degree to which spouses perceive that their partners meet their needs and desires. Couples who report higher levels of marital satisfaction are more likely to have a successful first marriage and better quality of life within that marriage. Conversely, couples who report lower levels of marital satisfaction are more likely to report feelings of stress and anxiety, often leading to the dissolution of a first marriage by divorce. Several factors have a significant effect on marital satisfaction: life events that cause stress for one or both of the spouses; the amount of spousal support rendered when faced with a conflict or stressful event; and similarity between the couple with respect to their needs, perceptions, and personality characteristics.

Differentiation of self is another important component of marital satisfaction. Adapted from family systems theory, differentiation of self as it applies to marriage, is the ability for a spouse to be able to balance his or her need for independence while maintaining intimacy within the marriage. A person's level of differentiation is determined by emotional reactivity, emotional cutoff, fusion with others, and the ability to take an I-position. Highly differentiated people are able to handle stress and conflict in a marriage rationally and objectively. They are also able to maintain an I-position, in which they articulate their thoughts and feelings from their point of view, without ridiculing or blaming their spouse; this is a concept very similar to that of an I-message. Couples who show high levels of differentiation communicate more effectively, experience higher levels of fusion and connectedness with their spouse, and are more likely to work on the marriage before resorting to divorce. On the other hand, couples who exhibit low levels of differentiation react to stress within the marriage emotionally, and they often have difficulty reconciling after experiencing stressful events. Lower levels of differentiation impede communication between the spouses, leading to a fractured relationship.

Personal demographics are factors and variables such as gender, perceived levels of marital quality, and age upon entering marriage. In first marriages, wives tend to report lower levels of marital quality than their husbands. Some research suggests that the quality marriage is at its highest for couples entering their first marriage between the ages of 22 and 25. Marital quality is impacted by the individual traits a person brings into a marriage. Communication patterns, desire to maintain a level of independence from a spouse, decision-making processes, and argument and conflict management style are examples of individual qualities that have an effect on a first marriage. Couples who are able to communicate, make decisions together, and resolve conflict and arguments in a productive manner report higher levels of marital satisfaction and marital quality. Moreover, couples in first marriages tend to experience higher levels of marital quality.

Length of marriage has also been found to be a factor for first marriages. In every marriage, there are times of happiness, togetherness, conflict, and discord. Also, in every marriage, there is a critical period that exists. This critical period challenges the spouses to evaluate their relationship, leading to decisions, actions, and behaviors that determine if the marriage succeeds or fails. Research indicates that such critical periods are indeed linked to marital satisfaction. In first marriages, divorce rates are highest after 3 years into the marriage, 7 years into the marriage, and when children leave for college. When examining these critical periods, the presence of children in the household may be a contributing factor to both marital satisfaction and success for first marriages. In contrast, couples who make it past these critical periods, tend to have fulfilling marriages. The rate of divorce declines continuously after the first few years of marriage, with only approximately 1% to 2% of divorces occurring after 30 years of marriage.

Factors Impacting Second Marriages

Although the United States leads the world with the highest rates of divorce, it is also the leader for rates of remarriage. Second marriages are unique because the vast majority of them are the product of a dissolution of a first marriage, as opposed to the death of a spouse. Statistics from 2013 indicate that 40% of people enter a second marriage. Twenty percent of second marriages consist of only one spouse who has been previously married and the other 20% consist of spouses who were both previously married. Additionally, current statistics indicate that both age and gender are significant factors for those individuals who are contemplating remarriage. Approximately 64% of previously married men get remarried, opposed to 54% of previously married women. Today, older adults are more likely to remarry than their younger counterparts when compared to statistics 50 years ago. Some researchers surmise that because life expectancies have increased, older adults seek companionship to enrich their lives as they navigate their golden years.

When people choose to remarry, research also suggests that people value unique and specific characteristics, and that those characteristics are more predictive of relationship outcomes than the structure of the relationship itself. Variables such as race, employment status, cohabitation patterns, the presence of children, income, education, age, gender, and religiosity all influence the likelihood that someone will decide to remarry. The need for independence and autonomy between genders also affects second marriages. Gender roles and identities have become more blended in recent years due to women becoming more financially independent and men becoming more independent domestically. By the time individuals enter a second marriage, they are often more likely to feel obligated to protect themselves both financially and emotionally. The levels of self-sufficiency and independence gained with age usually adversely impact second marriages even more than they do first marriages.

Despite the willingness to remarry, second marriages are more likely to end in divorce than first marriages. However, couples who are involved in healthy, successful second marriages report greater feelings of pride, marital satisfaction, and marital quality than their counterparts in first marriages. The key is determining what constitutes a successful marriage, and every couple is unique. It is important for individuals entering a second marriage to examine and understand why their first marriage ended. The influence of a spouse in a former marriage can have a profound effect on the second marriage. It is not uncommon for an individual in a second marriage to feel as though he is being punished for the wrongdoings of his partner's former spouse. Holding onto anger, hurt, and resentment from a previous marriage is not only unhealthy for that person but will eventually permeate the second marriage as well. A second marriage should be treated as its own entity and not compared to the first marriage. Being able to differentiate between the two will enhance intimacy, trust, resiliency in the marriage, and reinforce the bond of the newly formed couple.

The couple's bond in a second marriage is extremely important due to the complexities and structure of the new relationship. Feelings of connectedness, intimacy, trust, and respect must be nurtured from the start of the new relationship. It is equally important for each spouse to be able to recognize, understand, and reasonably accept the strengths, weaknesses, and vulnerabilities of themselves, her spouse, and the marriage. In a similar vein, couples in a second marriage must also work harder to establish a relationship style that is beneficial for both people. If marriage were easy, with a set of rules or script to follow, second marriages would not be necessary. Successful second marriages are comprised of spouses who are able to balance the need to be an individual with the necessary levels of commitment to one another to maintain the marriage.

It has been well documented that the couple's relationship is an important factor in a second marriage. The addition of stepchildren and the creation of a stepfamily also add to the complexities and dynamics of a second marriage. This is especially pertinent because in the United States, approximately one third of the population are members of a stepfamily. Sadly, the likelihood of a second divorce is higher for those families in a second marriage and more likely to occur at a quicker rate than it is for families in first marriages. It is important for everyone who is a part of the new marriage to understand and accept that, although they may not be a nuclear family, they are a family with strengths as well as vulnerabilities. Though the main focus of research dwells upon the challenges and failures of second marriages and stepfamilies, there are many second marriages that are successful. Flexibility, respect, patience, communication, and sense of humor are all factors that contribute to strong and prosperous second marriages.

Counseling Couples in First and Second Marriages

Although the utilization of premarital education and counseling is on the rise for couples in first and second marriages, couples in second marriages are less likely to seek counseling than their counterparts in first marriages. Regardless of the relationship type, many people in marriages spend a great deal of time being dissatisfied with their significant other before choosing between divorce or counseling. Research in this area has shown that once couples make the decision to work on the relationship, marital counseling is beneficial. Counseling has consistently been found to have a positive impact on marital satisfaction. In order for counseling to be beneficial, both individuals that comprise the couple must be completely invested in the process and honest with themselves and each other. There are instances in which couples may want to seek counseling to work on the issues within their marriage, but cannot do so due to financial constraints and socioeconomic status, cultural values and beliefs, religious objections, or even geographic location. These obstacles complicate situations in which people want help to make a first or second marriage work. Although counseling with a licensed, professional therapist would be an ideal form of support, alternate solutions like postmarriage workshops, relationship-oriented books, support groups, and even relevant online resources should be investigated as viable supports for couples seeking to improve their marriage.

Stacey Kohler

See also Conflict in Couples and Families; Divorce and Separation; Stepfamilies

Further Readings

Doss, B., Rhoades, G., Stanley, S., Markman, H., & Johnson, C. (2009). Differential use of premarital education in first and second marriages. *Journal of Family Psychology, 23*(2), 268–273.

Glenn, N. D., Uecker, J. E., & Love, R. W. (2010). Later first marriage and marital success. *Social Science Research, 39*, 787–800.

Jensen, T. M., Shafer, K., & Larson, J. H. (2014). Differences in relationship quality measurement and covariate influence between individuals in first and second marriages: A propensity score analysis. *Marriage & Family Review, 50*(8), 639–664.

McCarthy, B., & Ginsberg, R. (2007). Second marriages: Challenges and risks. *The Family Journal:*

Counseling and Therapy for Couples and Families, 15(2), 119–123.

Michaels, M. L. (2006). Factors that contribute to stepfamily success. *Journal of Divorce & Remarriage, 44*(3/4), 53–66.

Mirecki, R. M., Chou, J. L., Elliott, M., & Schneider, C. M. (2013). What factors influence marital satisfaction? Differences between first and second marriages. *Journal of Divorce & Remarriage, 54*(1), 78–93.

Peleg, O. (2008). The relation between differentiation of self and marital satisfaction: What can be learned from married people over the course of life? *American Journal of Family Therapy, 36*(5), 388–401.

Pew Research Center. (2013). *Four in ten couples are saying "I do," again.* Retrieved from http://www.pewsocialtrends.org/2014/11/14/four-in-ten-couples-are-saying-i-do-again/

Marriage and Health

A positive connection between marriage and health has been seen in scientific research for over a century. The idea that marriage has benefits for one's health has also been part of folk wisdom for millennia. The definition of *health* includes physical, mental, and social well-being. Although the health-related benefits of marriage are seen in many studies, the reasons for these benefits remain an area of research and debate. In the United States, marriage now includes the recognition of legal unions between people of the same sex, but the preponderance of research on marriage and health has been on opposite-sex couples. This entry examines how marriage affects physical health and mental health. It also looks at efforts to encourage marriage and increase marital satisfaction.

History

In 1858, British epidemiologist William Farr studied the mortality rates of "married," "celibate," and "widowed" French people and found data that suggested married people live far longer than single or widowed people. His research has been replicated in a number of ways, with subsequent researchers finding similar results.

Over the last hundred years, a number of meta-analyses (studies that combine and summarize the results of many other studies) have been conducted regarding the connection between marriage and health. These studies have consistently shown a positive connection between marriage and physical and mental health. In recent years, studies have examined the connection between marital quality and better health and have found greater marital quality was related to better health.

In recent years, rates of cohabitation have increased dramatically, and though research on cohabitation as compared with marriage is limited, there are some initial findings. Research has found that although those who are cohabiting fare better on psychological, financial, and health indicators than those who are unpartnered, those who are married do better still in each of these areas. Many researchers in the mental health field comment that there is a significant difference between cohabitation and marriage in that those who are married often feel a greater sense of commitment and security in their relationship than those who are cohabitating. In addition, married people are also less likely to practice many risk-taking behaviors that could damage their health.

Effects on Physical Health

While research indicates that those who are married practice more healthy behaviors, the question remains whether healthier people tend to get married or whether marriage tends to make people healthier. Some have suggested from an evolutionary perspective that healthier people may be more desirable to potential partners and therefore may be more likely to get and stay married. However, it may also be the case that people who are not unusually healthy to begin with become healthier as a byproduct of being married and having a committed spouse who helps them through any health challenges. The quality of the marriage also appears to be a factor. A person in a marriage that is undergoing significant marital strain might be more likely to experience poor health than a single person.

Although research has not provided a definitive explanation on the reasons for the health benefits of marriage, research has demonstrated that married people

- are more likely to exercise over the long term,
- have a diet that includes more fruit and vegetables,
- recover faster after surgery,
- have lower rates of heart disease,
- have longer life expectancy,
- are more likely to have health insurance,
- are more likely to have private health insurance instead of a government-run plan,
- are more likely to receive care in higher quality hospitals,
- have shorter hospital stays,
- have lower risk for hospital readmission,
- have lower health care costs, and,
- are less likely to enter a nursing home.

Research has also found that unmarried people have higher rates of alcohol consumption and binge drinking and higher rates of drug use, and are more likely to have high blood pressure.

Research studies have often found healthy behaviors increase and less healthy behaviors decrease for those who are engaged compared to those who are unmarried. It may be that being in a marriage or anticipating it creates motivation for a person to live a healthier lifestyle. Most people gain weight when they get married, but as they get older they are more likely to stay at healthier weights than unmarried people. It is common for married people to exercise less in their younger years or during the early part of their marriage; but they exercise more than unmarried persons as they grow older, resulting in more exercise overall for married persons. Most people decrease their alcohol consumption once they are married, which consequently also reduces other high-risk behaviors and problems such as drunken driving, alcohol-related accidents, and cirrhosis of the liver.

Despite the benefits of marriage, some research has found that those who were divorced or widowed have greater health problems than those who were single their entire lives. With regard to life expectancy, married men have been estimated to live about 10 years longer than single men and married women to live about 8 years longer than single women. For divorced or widowed persons, life expectancy varies depending on the age at which the person was divorced or widowed.

People who are married have many advantages when it comes to their health care. As there are two people in the relationship, if one loses his job, they are more likely to retain private health insurance than an unmarried person. Married people have been found to receive care at hospitals that are considered to be of higher quality, based on national rankings, likelihood of a residency program, and available medical technology. Spouses may prompt one another to seek regular medical screenings, such as mammograms, prostate exams, and heart-related screenings. Additionally, when a married person is in the hospital, he or she has a spouse there to help with many minor health needs, which can assist in healing and result in shorter hospital stays. That care usually continues after leaving the hospital, which lowers the chance of readmission and ultimately lowers health care costs. People who are married are more likely to follow the recommendations and directives of their physician. Finally, once people reach the later stages of their lives, those who are married are more likely to receive needed care for health care challenges, while unmarried people are less likely to have that reliable care and thus are more likely to need a nursing home.

Effects on Mental Health

Many connections have been found between mental health and marriage. First, people who have a mental health disorder in their younger years are less likely to get married than those without these disorders. However, those with a mental health disorder who do marry are more likely to receive help for their condition and function better than their unmarried counterparts. In addition, those with mental disorders prior to marriage and those who developed them after marriage are more likely to divorce than those without mental disorders.

Marriage usually has a significant impact on the mental health of a person, usually for the better. Psychologist Abraham Maslow maintained that love or belonging is a universal human need. Feeling loved and supported in marriage is a strong protective factor with regard to mental health difficulties. Marriage generally provides the person greater emotional, financial, and instrumental support. Married people have lower rates of depression, particularly those in first marriages. Research also has found a higher sense of self-worth and a later onset of psychosis in those who are married.

The research on depression related to marriage is important, as depression is connected with other issues that negatively affect people's health. Depression can be debilitating, is commonly diagnosed together with other psychiatric diagnoses, and is highly correlated with negative health care outcomes. Those with stronger social support, more often married persons, fare better with life's challenges and are less likely to suffer from depression. Some have suggested that the quality of the marriage has a significant impact on the degree to which it is a protective factor. In other words, happier marriages offer greater protection against depression.

Efforts to Support Marriage

In recent years, a number of state and federal initiatives have begun to encourage marriage and attempt to lower the divorce rate. The federal Deficit Reduction Act of 2005 allocated $150 million each year for the promotion of healthy marriage and fatherhood. Subsequent to this, the National Healthy Marriage Resource Center and the National Center for Family and Marriage Research were created.

Although research shows benefits from marriage, researchers have also found a decline in marital satisfaction since the early 1970s. The percentage of married Americans who reported their marriages were "very happy" was 60% in 2014, down from 69% in 1974. Greater preparation and support for marriages may increase marital satisfaction. Some types of premarital preparation programs have been found to increase marital satisfaction and decrease the likelihood of divorce, but only a small percentage of people getting married participate in a premarital program. These premarital programs educate, increase awareness, help the couple identify growth areas as well as strengths, and help them identify their levels of similarity. When premarital or married couples have higher levels of similarity on such factors as political views, religious beliefs, parenting desires or styles, and financial goals, they are more likely to be in long-term relationships, happier, and physically healthier.

Kenyon Knapp

See also Attachment and Health; Health Issues; Healthy Marriage and Responsible Fatherhood; Hispanic Healthy Marriage Initiative; National Marriage Initiative; World Health Organization

Further Readings

Parker-Pope, T. (2010, April 14). Is marriage good for your health? *The New York Times Magazine,* Retrieved from http://www.nytimes.com/2010/04/18/magazine/18marriage-t.html

Robles, T. F., Slatcher, R. B., Trombello, J. M., & McGinn, M. M. (2014). Marital quality and health: A meta-analytic review. *Psychological Bulletin, 140*(1), 140–187. doi:10.1037/a0031859

Smith, T. W., Son, J., & Schapiro, B. (2015, April). *General Social Survey final report: Trends in psychological well-being, 1972–2014.* Chicago, IL: NORC at the University of Chicago. Retrieved from http://www.norc.org/PDFs/GSS%20Reports/GSS_PsyWellBeing15_final_formatted.pdf

Wood, R. G., Goesling, B., & Avellar, S. (2007). The effects of marriage on health: A synthesis of current research evidence. Washington, DC: U.S. Department of Health and Human Services, Office of the Assistant Secretary for Planning and Evaluation, Office of Human Services. Retrieved from http://aspe.hhs.gov/hsp/07/marriageonhealth/index.htm

MARRIAGE EDUCATION

Marriage education (or relationship education) is an effort to increase relationship stability and satisfaction through programs for both individuals and couples. These programs are designed to intervene in potential risk factors for relationship dissatisfaction or instability by teaching important skills and principles believed to promote healthy relationships. Marriage education provides some similar benefits to therapy, but it is a nonclinical intervention distinct in several ways. This entry describes marriage education and discusses who it serves, how it is administered, its distinction from therapy, and its effectiveness in improving relationships.

Marriage Education and Who It Serves

Historically, marriage education arose from efforts within religious environments to prepare couples for marriage or enhance marital quality. The focus was to promote happiness in marriage by preparing couples and helping happy marriages remain happy. Over the years, the family psychology field adopted the approach to intervene with marriages at the educational level and developed empirically validated approaches to help transform knowledge, skills, and attitudes about marriage. The focus was to prevent relationship distress by intervening on potential risk factors. Individuals and couples attend marriage education seeking new ways to enhance relationship satisfaction or prevent future problems.

In recent years, it has become evident that many who attend marriage education are already in distressed relationships. The reasons for this are disputed, but the reality that significant numbers of distressed couples attend marriage education is unquestionable. Additionally, whereas most attendees used to be White, middle-class couples, there are now efforts to extend the reach of services to people from diverse backgrounds. These include, but are not limited to, ethnic minorities, military service members, stepfamilies, and economically disadvantaged, single-parent and divorced individuals and couples. Many programs are designed to address the unique needs of diverse couples, and continued effort is made to find what specialized groups exist and how they can best be helped in an educational context.

Content

Marriage education applies behavioral exchange and social learning theories to try to modify interactions. It usually includes two foci: (1) transferring knowledge to help improve participants' attitudes and expand their understanding about healthy relationship dynamics, and (2) teaching skills that, if regularly incorporated into the marriage, help foster a healthy relationship.

The content of marriage education programs includes diverse topic areas. Programs cover such areas as respectful listening, trust, friendship, money management, sexual intimacy, the importance of sharing experiences, expectations, and commitment. Participants learn research-based facts about these and other areas of healthy relationship functioning. For instance, a common misperception is that "opposites attract," whereas the relationship research is clear that individuals who are more like each other have healthier and more stable relationships. Marriage education provides individuals and couples with a forum in which to learn about this common myth and to encourage ways to counteract it in their relationship. Focus on similarity, rather than differences, may take the form of finding and listing similarities or engaging in shared hobbies. Some programs are focused on specific skills, such as coping or communication. Such programs teach people strategies for effectively engaging in helpful skills and giving them time to practice those skills in class. For instance, couples in a communication-based program might learn strategies for taking turns speaking and reflective listening.

How Marriage Education Is Administered

Marriage education is usually offered in a group format, with several individuals or couples attending a course together. Sometimes, however, it is offered in an individual format (one couple with one facilitator). Delivery format also varies. Most programs are offered as weekly classes, although several are taught as an intensive weekend retreat. Technological abilities have facilitated electronic delivery of some programs. And, the least structured, but often used, format is in the form of self-directed education (e.g., self-help books written by scholars for the purpose of educating and promoting healthy skills).

Trained facilitators offer marriage education classes. They may have a bachelor's level education, hold a certification in Family Life Education through the National Council on Family Relations, or hold an advanced degree. Regardless of educational background, facilitators are trained to teach the specific curriculum they are administering. Curricula vary depending on the instructor, but most curricula include relevant content and some teaching strategies.

Education Versus Therapy

Although many attending marriage education report relationship distress, it is qualitatively different from therapy. Major differences are that whereas therapy is directed toward a specific person or couple and targets a specific problem, marriage education is broad and generalized. Similarly, whereas therapy requires and is based on a treatment plan designed with specific relational problems in mind, marriage education is curriculum based and draws on educational needs of the couple. In therapy, goals are client and problem driven; in marriage education, goals are driven by research on healthy relationships and how to transmit information educationally. Additionally, whereas therapy usually addresses events and contexts from the past to help create change in the present and future, marriage education is primarily concerned with what is happening in the present and aims to produce outcomes in the future.

Effectiveness

Research has established that marriage education is effective at improving communication skills (such as positive and negative interactions between partners), relationship quality, and commitment. Indeed, changes reported by couples are quite similar to those reported by couples attending therapy. Because the research has focused largely on whether or not marriage education is effective, studies are only beginning to determine the elements associated with these improvements. For instance, preliminary evidence indicates that improvement in programs is related to having a good working relationship with the facilitator, attending programs together with a partner or spouse, and receiving a moderate dosage (i.e., 8–12 hours) of the program. Research continues to try to identify what other factors are important for change, as well as identify the mechanisms of change in marriage education (i.e., how it works).

Angela B. Bradford

See also Certified Family Life Educator; Healthy Marriage and Responsible Fatherhood; Marriage Enrichment; Psychoeducation; Relationship Enhancement

Further Readings

Berger, R., & Hannah, M. T. (Eds.). (1999). *Preventive approaches in couples therapy.* Philadelphia, PA: Brunner/Mazel.

Bradford, A. B., Hawkins, A. J., & Acker, J. (2015). If we build it, they will come: Exploring policy and practice implications of public support for couple and relationship education for lower income and relationally distressed couples. *Family Process 54*(4), 639–654. doi:10.1111/famp.12151

Hawkins, A. J., Blanchard, V. L., Baldwin, S. A., & Fawcett, E. B. (2008). Does marriage and relationship education work? A meta-analytic study. *Journal of Consulting and Clinical Psychology, 76*(5), 723–734. doi:10.1037/a0012584

Markman, H. J., & Rhoades, G. K. (2012). Relationship education research: Current status and future directions. *Journal of Marital and Family Therapy, 38*(1), 169–200. doi:10.1111/j.1752-0606.2011.00247.x

Myers-Walls, J. A., Ballard, S. M., Darling, C. A., & Myers-Bowman, K. S. (2011). Reconceptualizing the domain and boundaries of family life education. *Family Relations, 60*(4), 357–372. doi:10.1111/j.1741-3729.2011.00659.x

Marriage Encounter

Marriage encounter is a two- or three-day weekend experience designed to help married couples experience a process that may lead to change for the partners as individuals and in their marital relationships. The weekend emphasizes improvement of interpersonal communication skills within the marriage. Marriage encounter is a marriage enrichment program and is not designed to serve as a vehicle for marriage counseling for individuals with serious psychological problems. It promotes the deepening of communication and emotional intimacy in marriage and, for some, can be a mystical experience of sensing the presence of God and the sacred in one another. This entry provides a brief history of the marriage encounter movement and discusses the components of the marriage encounter weekend. It then explains the psychodynamic and theological dimensions of the marriage encounter process, lists some of the critiques of the marriage encounter approach, and discusses the influence of marriage encounter on other programs.

History of the Marriage Encounter Movement

The marriage encounter movement evolved from a series of conferences for married couples that were developed in 1952 by Gabriel Calvo, a Catholic priest in Spain. This development came at a time when the Second Vatican Council, also known as Vatican II, called for Christians to renew the world and to humanize man, starting with the family. The industrial revolution and alienation in the modern world had brought the interpersonal, subjective dimension of marriage to the forefront. Young couples increasingly needed to rely on the marriage relationship, rather than extended family, for support, protection, and comfort. Mobility of the family, the women's liberation movement, and mass media, respectively, challenged married couples' interpersonal communication skills, heightened awareness of women as people, and exposed families to diverse life styles and gender roles. Marriage encounter programs emerged as a means to address the strains on marriage relationships that resulted from these changes.

The marriage encounter conferences emphasized the importance of developing open and honest married relationships. The presentations, which eventually were offered as weekend retreats, were called "the marriage teams of Pope Pius XII" and were offered throughout Spain. The first weekend conference was held in Barcelona in 1962. In 1966, the marriage encounter weekend spread to Latin America and to Spanish-speaking couples in the United States after it was introduced by Calvo and a couple at the International Confederation of Christian Family Movements in Caracas, Venezuela. Between 1967 and 1971, the marriage encounter movement rapidly expanded to the United States and Canada under the leadership of Chuck Gallagher, a Catholic priest in New York State. Various emphases surfaced, such as the follow-up to the weekend, the weekend itself, the development of a marriage encounter community to provide support, and the renewal of the sacrament of matrimony, as a means for renewing the Catholic Church. The governing organizations, the Worldwide Marriage Encounter (WWME) and the National Marriage Encounter (NME), evolved out of the original weekend organized by Calvo. From 1971 through 2010, the marriage encounter program continued to expand to over 90 countries. Similar marriage encounter programs are now offered around the world by other religious organizations, including Lutheran, Assemblies of God, and Jewish organizations. Marriage encounter programs in the United States and Canada are offered in various languages, including English, Spanish, French, and Korean, and information about these programs and upcoming retreats can be found on their websites.

The Marriage Encounter Weekend

The marriage encounter weekend program typically extends from Friday evening through Sunday afternoon and is facilitated by one to three couples and, when sponsored by the Catholic Church, a priest. Other organizations utilize pastors, couples, or other types of individuals as facilitators, but facilitators are typically not mental health professionals. The facilitators have attended a previous marriage encounter weekend and, as a team, have had training and experience. Attendance typically consists of six to 15 couples of all ages who have been married anywhere from a few weeks to many years. The team sets the stage by offering talks on topics such as understanding of self, relationship with partner, relationship with God, relationship with children, and relationship with the world. Each individual is given time alone after the talks to write down his or her individual responses, feelings, and reflections related to the presented topics. The couple is then given time to meet alone to privately discuss their responses in an effort for the partners to understand each other better. The overall focus of the weekend is on the couples' interaction. Group therapy sessions and forced revelations of self are not included in this process.

The weekend is an emotionally intense and structured experience that often inspires hope and optimism that couples can grow closer. Some programs offer postweekend follow-up sessions.

Psychodynamic and Theological Dimensions of the Marriage Encounter Process

Three specific dynamics in the marriage encounter experience have been identified: the theory of central person, self-disclosure, and the dyadic effect. The participants identify with the couple and priest or other facilitators who function as the central persons. The team couple initiates the self-reflection exercise for the participant couples by offering a presentation on marriage, followed by an opportunity to respond to reflection questions. The partners of each couple are encouraged to dialogue, which means to reflect on one's own feelings and to participate in self-disclosure with the significant other, and to ultimately receive affirmation from the significant other. The central persons model self-awareness, self-disclosure, and affirmation of the other, which has a dyadic effect on the couple participants. The participant couples feel less guilt and anxiety when the authority figure or priest initiates the act of self-disclosure.

The partners of each couple move toward intimacy as they share their feelings and inner world with each other, first in written form and next verbally, and affirm each other with empathy and respect. When spouses disclose themselves to one another, they see their similarities and differences in thoughts, feelings, hopes, fears, and reactions to the past, and learn about each other's needs. They learn how they either satisfy or frustrate those needs and develop emotional closeness. This dialogue can also lead each individual to define his or her own identity, which moves the couple toward greater intimacy.

The theological concept of marital unity, as stated by Jesuit theologian Jared Wicks, is foundational to the marriage encounter experience. It describes the pledge of the Christian marriage as lifelong love and fidelity in which the spouses confirm themselves in a total way by taking on a new identity for each other. The pledge of love is seen as the sealing of a covenant before God. The marriage theology presented by the Catholic Worldwide Marriage Encounter or other religious denominations is presented not as a theological lecture, but as well-established principles that are fleshed out by the team couples' personal experiences in living these principles. The weekend has also been described as having two phases: the humanistic-communication phase (I–We) and the religious-theological phase (We–God, We–God–World).

Critiques of the Marriage Encounter Experience

The marriage encounter experience has been the subject of a number of critiques by behavior science professionals concerning theoretical and practical pitfalls inherent in the experience. The major concerns expressed are the following: (a) marriage encounter's theological position on unity is ill-defined and out of context; (b) marriage encounter transformed the Judeo-Christian mystical tradition of marriage ("two in one flesh" and "united like Christ in the church") into a set of norms and rules for achieving unity; (c) marriage encounter's ideology involves a collapse of individuality in marriage; (d) the structure of the weekend does not allow for discussion during the presentations; (e) couples are discouraged from interacting with each other during the weekend; (f) the presenter's attitude seems authoritarian; (g) there is a strong coercion to embrace marriage encounter's ideology and dialogue technique; (h) the weekends are male-centered; (i) the weekend may lead to temporary marital "highs," leading to a disillusioning loss of the high later; (j) the dialogue may lead to ritual dependency or a sense of guilt after the weekend; and (k) the encounter experience can divide family members from each other, into the encountered versus nonencountered.

The Influence of Marriage Encounter on Other Programs

Marriage encounter programs and curricula have influenced other marriage and family programs, such as Retrouvaille and the federal Healthy Marriage and Responsible Fatherhood initiative. Retrouvaille uses a similar curriculum as marriage encounter, but is designed for troubled marriages. Marriage encounter programs are designed for marriages that are considered to be "stale." The Coalition for Marriage, Family and Couples Education provides a website called Smart Marriages with helpful marriage and family educational resources, such as articles, books, conferences, and program offerings for couples and families. The National Healthy Marriage Resource Center provides an online listing of various marriage encounter and marriage enrichment programs in the United States.

Ria Echteld Baker and Jerry Lee Terrill

See also Empathy; Marriage Enrichment; National Marriage Initiative; Respect; Self-Help; Support Groups

Further Readings

Assemblies of God Marriage Encounter: http://ip-184-168-148-206.ip.secureserver.net/

International Lutheran Marriage Encounter: http://www.ilme.org/where.html

Jourard, S. (1964). *The transparent self*. New York, NY: Macmillan.

Marriage Encounter Weekend: http://godlovesmarriage.org/

National Healthy Marriage Resource Center: http://www.healthymarriageinfo.org/index.aspx

National Marriage Encounter: http://marriage-encounter.org/

Redl, F. (1942). Group emotion and leadership. *Psychiatry, 5*, 573–596.

Regula, R. R. (1975). Marriage encounter: What makes it work? *The Family Coordinator, 24*, 153–159.

Rubin, B. (n.d.). *Ties that bind: Program to keep marriages together*. Retrieved from http://www.smartmarriages.com/tiesthatbind.html

Smart Marriages: http://www.smartmarriages.com/index.html

Stedham, J. M. (1982). Marriage encounter: An insider's consideration of recent critiques. *Family Relations, 31*, 123–129.

World Wide Marriage Encounter: http://www.wwme.org/

Marriage Enrichment

Marriage enrichment is defined as an educational and preventive approach to enhancing or improving the functioning of marital relationships. Marriage enrichment programs teach skills needed to build more satisfying interpersonal relationships, to prevent interpersonal problems, and to resolve problems that couples may experience. These programs have historically served as a means to help fairly well-functioning couples to enhance their communication and interpersonal skills, to explore each other's feelings and thoughts, and to develop empathy and intimacy within the relationship. This entry offers a historical overview of marriage enrichment programs and discusses theoretical frameworks of the programs, the role of facilitators in the programs, the characteristics of the programs' participants, research findings on the effectiveness of the programs, and different types of marriage enrichment programs and associations.

Historical Overview of Marriage Enrichment Programs

The marriage enrichment movement has multiple origins. Preventive mental health services, the human potential movement, and organized religion's concern about the decline of marriage all contributed to the surfacing of marriage enrichment programs during the 1960s and expanding into the 2000s. Preventive mental health services emanated from the belief that prevention is more effective, humane, and less costly than intervening in problems that emerge. The human potential movement of the 1960s was formed around the concept that untapped, extraordinary potential could be cultivated in all people, enhancing their quality of life and ultimately contributing to positive social change.

Concern about the decline of marriage expressed in the Catholic Church and other religious communities also contributed to the evolution of marriage enrichment programs. The Roman Catholic Marriage Encounter program was initiated in 1962 by Father Gabriel Calvo in Spain. The group interactions in Marriage Encounter programs were primarily social and religious in nature, with limited couple-to-couple sharing of experiences. A leadership team consisting of a couple and a priest provided brief talks and supervision, and couples were given time to write down their personal reflections, leading to genuine interpersonal couple's communication. Marriage Encounter programs have continued to expand to over 90 countries and many other religious and nonreligious organizations implement this approach to enrich marriages.

Protestant church-related marriage enrichment programs, called Marriage Communication Labs, also emerged during the 1960s. This enrichment approach promoted experiential learning through exercises designed to encourage group and spousal interactions. Facilitators explained the exercises, supervised the couples, and interpreted occurrences. Marriage enrichment retreats, organized by David and Vera Mace within the Quaker tradition, also emerged at that time and were slightly different as they involved minimal organization and structure, allowing couples to establish their own goals and to focus on couple dialogue. A condition that was agreed upon at the beginning of the retreat was "communication-in-depth" about "relationship-in-depth" and emphasis was placed on voluntarily sharing and interpretation of experiences. Much of the couple dialogue took place in the presence of the other group members. David Mace founded the Association for Couples in Marriage Enrichment (ACME) in 1973, and this organization continues to promote marriage enrichment resources and programs.

Numerous other marriage enrichment programs developed from the 1970s through the 1990s, such as the Relationship Enhancement Program, L'Abate's Structured Enrichment (SE) program, the Minnesota Couples Communication program (now known as the Couple Communication Program), and Conjugal Relationship Enhancement program. In their 1981 book *Marriage Enrichment: Philosophy, Process, and Program*, Larry Hof and William Miller listed at least 50 different programs, with audiences ranging from 10 couples to more than 420,000. The programs take on different structural approaches. For example, in L'Abate's SE program, the leader gives structured information to the couples and the couples are not encouraged to interact with the other couples in attendance. The Minnesota Couples Communication program and the Conjugal Relationship Enhancement program are similar to the Marriage Encounter programs, as they provide structured information to couples within a group format and couples may discuss these topics and their insights within the group and write about them.

A review of marriage enrichment programs in the 1980s revealed the inclusion of enrichment programs for premarital, dating couples, and couples experiencing severe difficulty and dysfunction interpersonally.

Faith-based marriage enrichment programs have also expanded and a 2007 review of these programs revealed over 30 programs with various formats, foci, and nature of materials, such as video presentations; demonstration of skills and couple participation exercises; small group books and workbooks; materials written for couples to use in the privacy of their home; retreat, workshop, and group formats; and 10-week series or neighborhood study groups on marriage.

The Coalition for Marriage, Family, and Couple Education—Smart Marriages was established in 1996 and continues to provide resources, information, and a directory of national marriage enrichment programs. Diane Sollee founded this organization on the premise of preventing marriages from failing; this was also the mandate that led to the initial development of the Association of Couples for Marriage Enrichment (ACME). These organizations provide comprehensive information through their websites about marriage enrichment trainings, conferences, and resources for married couples, dating couples, cohabitating couples, premarital couples, and families.

Theoretical Framework of Marriage Enrichment Programs and Participant Skills Development

Marriage enrichment programs are guided by humanistic psychotherapy and the qualities of acceptance and nonjudgment, as described by Carl Rogers, and psychoeducational models. The Rogerian qualities of acceptance and nonjudgment help create an atmosphere in which individuals feel safe to express their feelings, learn to trust, feel accepted, and receive support from their partners. Acceptance and nonjudgment do not mean that all behaviors are approved, but that there is recognition that individuals have their own beliefs and feelings.

Many marriage enrichment programs take a psychoeducational approach and implement empirically based interventions that enhance relationships and educate families so that they may develop the skills necessary for the prevention and/or resolution of conflict and distress in the marriage and improve the quality of family life. This approach includes a structured information component and discussion component. These programs also address preparation for marriage or childbirth and provide parent effectiveness training.

Although marriage enrichment programs have ostensibly been designed for nondistressed couples, couples in the midst of crisis also benefit from participating in these programs, as they receive support from other couples and learn skills that are presented. Interpersonal learning, altruism, helper therapy, and modeling benefit all of the program participants.

The Role of the Facilitator(s)

Many marriage enrichment programs assign either couples or individual leaders to facilitate the sessions. The facilitators typically have various professional backgrounds with differing leadership styles and differ in marital status, as some are married couples and some consist of unmarried male and female teams. David and Vera Mace, founders of ACME, examined desirable qualities in marriage enrichment facilitators and the importance of proper selection and training of facilitators. They suggested that facilitators take on a modeling role by doing what they invite the other couples to do, which is to work on their marriage and to seek to develop its potential, and take on a participatory function by sharing their experiences as the other couples do and to ask the group for help.

Concerning the level of professional background training, programs are facilitated either by licensed mental health professionals or volunteer individuals or couples. The programs are typically set up to exclude people who are having serious problems coping with life, and it is therefore not necessary for the facilitators to have clinical degrees.

Potential facilitators should be warm, open, positive, flexible, and mature, have a growing relationship, and be sensitive to the needs of others. In certain programs, facilitators are required to obtain certification, which is achieved after the completion of training and demonstration of successful leadership.

Techniques that are used in the group process format of marriage enrichment programs include modeling, rehearsal of behaviors, encouragement, and reinforcement. The group facilitators model how they are working on improving their relationships. Rehearsal of behaviors is a means to help couples learn ways of communicating and responding to one another that strengthen the relationship. Encouragement and reinforcement, which are a powerful means for changing others' beliefs and behaviors, are infused throughout the sessions to stimulate self-confidence, courage, and positive behaviors in the participants.

Many programs and organizations offer workshops, conferences, and CD/DVD training materials for individuals who are interested in becoming group facilitators in various settings, such as community centers, churches, and the home. Among other organizations that offer training are Smart Marriages (the Coalition for Marriage, Family, and Couples Education), PREPARE/ENRICH, PAIRS, Family Dynamics Institute, Family Life, and the American Association of Christian Counselors.

ME Participants

Although the intent of the marriage enrichment movement was prevention, research findings on participants to various marriage enrichment programs revealed that the marital satisfaction level among participants was lower than it was for nonparticipants. Additionally, couples who participated in enrichment programs were not as discouraged as couples seeking counseling.

A study of influences on marriage enrichment participants and nonparticipant attendance decisions revealed that the following factors strongly influenced decisions to participate: (a) lower satisfaction with communication skills among participants; (b) lower self-esteem among participant wives than among nonparticipant wives; (c) participants and nonparticipants viewed the programming as primarily educational; (d) nonparticipants tended to view marriage enrichment as a therapeutic experience for couples with moderate to severe marital problems; (e) time constraints, lack of interest, and lack of information about the seminar strongly affected the nonparticipants; (f) some fear and anxiety of invasion of privacy was identified among nonparticipants; and (g) some nonparticipants cited lack of supplementary information about the facilitator and the program (i.e., information about the facilitator's race, income level, media attention, endorsements, previous experience, professional organization recognition, religious belief system, and social maturity) as a deterrent to participation. A limitation of this study was that the participants were predominantly Euro-American and middle-class samples and the participants differed in age and length of marriage. One publication suggested that marriage enrichment programs may be more appealing and beneficial to couples in earlier stages in marriage and another study found that enrichment programs were most effective with older participants with longer marriages. Another study revealed that men may be more likely than women to change after participating in a marriage enrichment program.

A 5-year intervention study, Project for Strong African American Marriages (ProSAAM), which focused on developing effective strategies to engage African American men in marriage enrichment programs, provided some helpful insights: (a) African American men were more likely to view a marriage enrichment program as legitimate and potentially useful when endorsed by a known person, such as a male religious leader in the community; (b) male recruiters to the programs had more success recruiting African American male participants; and (c) testimonials from early participants in the project were helpful in recruiting later participants.

Research Findings on the Effectiveness of Marriage Enrichment Programs

A 2004 review of 13 empirically supported marriage enrichment programs revealed that only four programs could be considered "efficacious," while three were considered "possibly efficacious." The others were untested. The programs that were considered efficacious or successful in producing the desired result were Prevention and Relationship Enhancement Program (PREP), Relationship Enhancement, Couple Communication Program, and Strategic Hope-Focused Enrichment. Each of these programs demonstrated, along with other changes, improved communication skills and self-awareness in participants. The programs that were considered possibly efficacious include the following: Couple CARE, Association for Couples in Marriage Enrichment (AMCE) programs, and Couple Coping Enhancement Training (CCET). In addition to other positive changes in the relationships, these programs demonstrated improved marital satisfaction and marital quality. Other marriage enrichment programs that were untested but often used and demonstrate positive changes in couples were the following: Structured Enrichment (SE), Marriage Encounter (ME), The Practical Application of Intimate Relationship Skills (PAIRS) program, Imago Relationship Therapy (IRT), Traits of a Happy Couple (THC), Saving Your Marriage Before It Starts (SYMBIS), Premarital Preparation and Relationship Enhancement (PREPARE), and TIME (Training in Marriage Enrichment).

Marriage Enrichment Programs

A review of marriage enrichment programs conducted in 2004 identified the programs as efficacious, possibly efficacious, and untested:

Efficacious

The Prevention and Relationship Enhancement Program (PREP) takes a skills-oriented approach and aims to teach couples better communication and conflict management strategies. PREP sessions come in an extended version and a marathon version. In the extended version, 4 to 10 couples attend a series of weekly lectures on relationship issues and skills. These sessions include exercises to learn the discussed skills. The couples are each assigned a consultant, who offers coaching and feedback to the couple as they practice new skills. The marathon version typically has an attendance of 20 to 60 couples who hear the lectures in a group during a weekend session. Couples practice skills on their own after the lectures. Video and audiotapes are also provided for study after the weekend. Topics discussed include conflict management, communication enhancement, forgiveness, religious beliefs and practices, fun and friendship desires, and maintaining commitment.

Relationship Enhancement (RE) effectively helps couples identify and express their needs through communication and behavior.

The Couple Communication Program, originally the Minnesota Couple Communication program, is a popular skills-training program and has been researched the most. It is intended to appeal to married and premarried couples and is educational rather than remedial. This program helps couples to increase self-awareness and to enhance communication skills. The communication skills are taught through a series of interventions and presentations, and homework exercises are assigned.

Strategic Hope-Focused Enrichment is focused on promoting love and faith in each other and takes a brief, eclectic approach to motivate the couple to initiate improving their relationships. Couples are trained in specific methods to achieve marital goals, as communication skills and intimacy are enhanced. The education consultants provide written feedback to the couples.

Possibly Efficacious

Couple CARE is based on the previously mentioned PREP program, as it is a skills-based, relationship education program. This program takes a flexible approach and can be accessed at home and it promotes self-directed learning. Couples communication, relationship commitment, relationship self-regulation, relationship expectations, and positive couple time are promoted through a videotape, a guidebook, and a series of phone calls with a psychologist.

Marriage enrichment programs based on ACME principles seek to improve marital relationships using a variety of enrichment activities, experiential learning, and group processes to promote strength and growth in couples. ACME has 10 principles on which these programs are based.

These principles include voluntary sharing by the individual or couple; equal partnership in the marriage; an understanding that since no advice is given, no experts are present; and a commitment to confidentiality, which is strongly encouraged in the group to build trust and promote dialogue. The programs are less structured and leaders may change the agenda and structure of the retreats to meet the need of the participants.

Couple Coping Enhancement Training (CCET) is a marital distress prevention program, which combines cognitive-behavioral therapy with theories of stress, coping, and social exchange. Communication, problem-solving, stress management, and coping skills are taught in weekend, week-long, or weekly series sessions.

Empirically Untested

Structured Enrichment (SE) offers many ways to assist couples to make positive changes and has a library of 50 programs with various theoretical and atheoretical sources. The programs contain three or more lessons and each lesson has five or six exercises that seek to help individuals change their negative reactions to each other.

Marriage Encounter takes a psychoeducational approach and helps couples improve their communication and experience each other more fully. The weekend retreats are highly structured and last up to 44 hours. A clergy and volunteer couple facilitate the retreat and offer presentations on self-discovery, dialogue, mutual trust and acceptance of each other, growth in love and union, and transcendent love. After the presentations, the couple takes time alone to write and discuss their thoughts and feelings about the topic.

The Practical Application of Intimate Relationship Skills (PAIRS) takes a psychoeducational approach and is designed to increase self-knowledge and to enhance enjoyment of intimacy in the relationship. An experiential group format, facilitated by a pair of licensed mental health professionals, takes a cognitive, affective, and behavioral approach and teach commitment, effective communication, and creative uses of conflict. The facilitator training program consists of 120 hours of training over a 4- or 5-month period.

Imago Relationship Therapy (IRT) combines education and therapy and three formats are available: (1) couples counseling with an Imago therapist, (2) a 20-hour workshop, and (3) a 7-hour home video. The emphasis is on resolving childhood issues related to parents or caregivers and matching traits exhibited in the partner with the image (imago) of one's parent or caregiver. The facilitators are licensed therapists who have attended the workshop, received 96 hours of training, received positive evaluations from program instructors, and served as a support therapist at a previous workshop.

Traits of a Happy Couple (THC) is a workshop that takes a cognitive-behavioral approach and is based on a book and study guide. Couples attend five 2-hour training sessions, complete exercises to practice concepts learned, and are given homework assignments between sessions. The topics include common sources of marital conflict, making positive requests, giving social support, providing problem-solving techniques, and building partner's self-esteem.

Saving Your Marriage Before It Starts (SYMBIS) helps couples build a successful marriage through strengthening self-differentiation. The participants complete the Premarital Preparation and Relationship Enhancement (PREPARE) assessment, attend 8 to 10 one-hour psychoeducational sessions, and maintain a year-long relationship with a marriage mentor. This program helps premarital couples to better understand each other's family of origin and to begin to identify areas where they differ in viewpoint. Couples explore the following topics: marriage expectations; communication; sexual relationship, personality differences, and financial management; attitudes regarding conflict resolution and child-rearing; preferences for how to spend leisure time; expectations about the amount of time spent with family and friends; attitudes regarding marital roles; and spiritual beliefs.

Other Programs

Pairing Enrichment Program (PEP) is a relationship enhancing program, which takes the form of weekend retreats, that is structured, couple-oriented, and a positive approach to improving the social and sexual communication in marriage. It is an action-oriented experience in communication that involves couple and group discussions, fantasy experiences, educational films, exploration of feelings and attitudes, sensory awareness, communication exercises, intimate encounter exercises and leader modeling, role playing, and discussion. A variety of evaluation questionnaires are used before and after the program and following a 3-week follow-up procedure.

Personal Growth in Marriage is a unilateral marriage enrichment program based on principles of Alfred Adler's Individual Psychology. This program was created to meet the need of couples when both partners are not able to attend the sessions together. The objectives of this program are to build self-esteem, to develop an internal locus of control, to enhance communication skills, and to teach participants how to share what they have learned in the course with the absent spouse.

Training in Marriage Enrichment (TIME) is another useful marriage enrichment program developed by Don Dinkmeyer and Jon Carlson in 1984. A pretest/posttest, treatment group/nontreatment group research study revealed that TIME had a positive effect on the treatment group's perception of the changes in their marriages.

Faith-Based or Christian Marriage Enrichment Programs

A marriage enrichment program evaluation of secular and nonsecular marriage enrichment programs that are offered by religious institutions concluded that all the most commonly used programs had strengths and limitations. The researchers encourage the use of different programs at different times in a couple's life. Programs in these settings are offered in workshop formats, small group formats, and in study guide and in-home formats.

Marriage Enrichment Organizations

The Coalition for Marriage, Family and Couples Education's (CMFCE) website provides a comprehensive list of marriage enrichment programs and marriage enrichment organizations. The Association of Couples for Marriage Enrichment (ACME) also provides guidelines for marriage enrichment programs, trains leader couples, organizes marriage enrichment events, and disseminates marriage enrichment information.

Ria Echteld Baker and Jerry Lee Terrill

See also Certified Family Life Educator; Hope-Focused Approach to Couple Enrichment in Counseling; Marriage Encounter; Self-Help; Support Groups

Further Readings

The Association for Couples in Marriage Enrichment: http://www.bettermarriages.org

Balswick, J., & Balswick, J. (2007). *Marriage enrichment program evaluation*. Retrieved from http://www.fmef.org/pages/printable_page.cfm?PAGE_ID=86

Bowling, T. K., Hill, C. M., & Jencius, M. (2005). An overview of marriage enrichment. *The Family Journal, 13,* 87–94. doi:10.1177/1066480704270229

Doherty, W. J., & Richmond, D. S. (1983). *Working with couples for marriage enrichment: A guide to developing, conducting, and evaluating programs.* San Francisco, CA: Jossey-Bass.

Jakubowski, S. F., Milne, E. P., Brunner, H., & Miller, R. B. (2004). A review of empirically supported marital enrichment programs. *Family Relations, 53,* 528–536.

Mace, D., & Mace, V. (1969). *Marriage enrichment retreats: Story of a Quaker project.* Philadelphia, PA: Friends General Conference.

Mace, D., & Mace, V. (1976). The selection, training, and certification of facilitators for marriage enrichment programs. *The Family Coordinator, 25*(2), 117–125.

Malcom, K. D. (1992). Personal growth in marriage: An Adlerian unilateral marriage enrichment program. *Individual Psychology, 48,* 488–492.

Markham, H. J., Renick, M. J., Floyd, F. J., Stanley, S. M., & Clements, M. (1993). Preventing marital distress through communication and conflict management training: A 4- and 5-year follow-up. *Journal of Consulting and Clinical Psychology, 61,* 70–77.

Powell, G. S., & Wampler, K. S. (1982). Marriage enrichment participants: Levels of marital satisfaction. *Family Relations, 31,* 389–393.

Roberts, L. C., & Morris, M. L. (1998). An evaluation of marketing factors in marriage enrichment program promotion. *Family Relations, 47,* 37–44.

Smart Marriages, The Coalition for Marriage, Family, and Couples Education: http://www.smartmarriages.com/index.html

Marriage Myths

Marriage myths are untrue beliefs and unfounded notions about marriage that tend nevertheless to persist throughout the culture. Many people believe these myths because they have been handed down from generation to generation. It is important to be aware of marriage myths because they can negatively affect the relationships of those who believe them to be true. By becoming aware of the marital myths in operation, couples can change their behavior in order to create a healthier relationship. This entry identifies and discusses some of the numerous myths that exist concerning marriage.

Partners Should Be Able to Read Each Other's Minds

Many partners believe that if their partner truly loves them that they will somehow be able to read their mind. Subscribers to this myth feel that they should not have to ask their partner to do anything, to say the "right" thing, or even give them ideas on what the perfect gift would be. The persistent belief is that if partners truly love and understand each other, then there is no need to communicate desires, because the other partner will intuitively *know* what is needed. The truth is that no matter how intimately partners know each other, they will never be able to read one another's minds. If a husband wants his wife to know that her not asking about his day at work upsets him, then he will have to tell her. His wife may understand that he is upset, but she will not know why unless he communicates. The same is true if the wife would like her husband to start putting his dirty socks in the hamper instead of on the floor. He will not be able to read her mind to know what she desires; she will need to communicate it to him. Communication is the key to a good relationship, because no matter how much partners love each other, they are not mind readers.

A Baby Will Be Able to Fix a Bad Marriage

In certain cases, having children can bring both partners of a marriage closer together. In order for this to happen, both partners need to be able to trust each other, be open to new experiences and ways of doing things, and be flexible. In all cases, having a child adds a tremendous amount of stress to both parents. For those couples who do not have a solid foundation, having a child can cause more problems. When a child enters the relationship, new issues of jealously, arguments over differing parenting styles, and the normal stresses of caring for a child put additional pressures on the couple. These pressures are especially significant in those relationships that were already experiencing difficulties. In short, having a child will not fix a bad marriage.

Having Differences Will Ruin the Marriage

Despite the adage that opposites attract, people believe that happy couples should have everything in common. Partners should have the same interests, the same values, the same opinions, and agree on everything. This is an unrealistic expectation. Partners are two different people who have grown up differently and have had different experiences. Partners may certainly be similar, but the likelihood that they are exactly alike is zero. Differences are only natural and do not necessarily portend the demise of a marriage. How couples handle their differences affects the outcome of the relationship more than the differences themselves. Differences give partners the chance to learn a new way of thinking and to expand their individual boundaries. Being curious about differences allows partners to be more themselves and feel more comfortable sharing. This does not mean that partners have to agree with everything the other says; rather, acknowledging that there are differences and appreciating those differences is healthy.

Happy Couples Do Not Fight

Couples may be afraid of fighting with each other and believe that *argument* is a dirty word. According to the myth, in order to be a healthy and successful couple, the two must never fight with each other. Arguments, however, are a natural occurrence in all relationships; even happy couples sometimes argue with each other. When two separate people decide to spend their lives together in marriage, arguments and miscommunication are likely to happen. When there are no arguments in a relationship it can mean that the partners in the relationship do not have enough trust in each other to share their real thoughts and opinions. The difference between an unhealthy relationship and a healthy one may be evident in the way that the couple argue. When healthy couples argue, they do so in an effort to squarely confront the basis for the conflict and come to a resolution. They also forgive each other following an argument and are able to move on instead of using the argument as a weapon in the future.

Happy Couples Do Everything Together

The myth that happy couples engage in all their activities together is similar to the myth that couples must be alike—for example, the wife who feels that she has to be included in her husband's guys-only poker night and the husband who thinks that he always has to go shopping with his wife. Constant togetherness can create tension in the marriage and push couples apart. It is healthier for each partner to focus on their own individual interests for a time and then come together for activities that reflect a common interest. Forcing one person into doing an activity that he or she does not enjoy can cause resentment between partners.

Marriage Ruins a Couple's Sex Life

The myth that married people have less fulfilling and passionate sex or do not have sex at all is one that is often mentioned. Many people believe that getting married means the end of passion in the bedroom. The fact is that marriage does not have to mean the end of passionate and adventurous sex. A long-term couple may not experience the intense desire that characterized the earliest phase of their relationship, but this does not mean that marital sex has to lack passion. A long-term partnership can yield a deeper level of physical and emotional intimacy.

Marital Duties Should Be Split Evenly Between Partners

In the previous century, when gender roles concerning domestic duties were more rigidly defined and prescribed, it was commonly expected that women should take care of the inside (laundry, cooking, and cleaning) and men should take care of the outside (mowing the lawn, cleaning out the gutters, and fixing the car). As marital relationships have evolved, a focus on equality and a disregard of traditional gender roles have increased. The division of household chores is no longer outside for men and inside for women. Today, many couples expect that all household chores will be divided 50/50 between partners. This expectation reflects the marital quality that many couples want, but trying to keep up a 50/50 division can actually cause more stress on the relationship. Due to life circumstances, there may be times when one partner is not able to pull his or her weight and the other partner must pick up the slack. This can cause difficulties if the partner feels that he or she is doing more than their fair share. Households may function better if the partners understand that household chores will not always be split evenly down the middle. Also, distributing tasks by what is most important to each partner could be more efficient. When a person cares more about the task, they are more likely to do it.

Partners Have to Tell Each Other Everything

It is a common misconception that married partners have to tell each other everything happening in their lives. However, sharing every detail of one's life with one's partner can create less intimacy within a relationship. Partners may begin to feel overwhelmed holding all of their partner's secrets. Also, if partners are forced into sharing all the details of their life, they may feel that there is no trust in the relationship. In a trusting and healthy relationship, partners are allowed to have their secrets and private thoughts without needing to share them with their partner.

Married Couples Have to Love Each Other Unconditionally

Some people believe that getting marriage provides a guarantee that their partner will love them unconditionally. According to this myth, partners are supposed to love each other no matter what they do and at all times. In reality, there will always be things that one person will not like about the other's behavior, and loving unconditionally can cause stagnation in a relationship, since no one has to adapt and neither partner is challenged to grow any further. In healthy relationships, partners love each other, though not unconditionally. Conditional love means that partners sometimes challenge each other to grow and change, and that there is room for this change to occur.

Marriage Can Make a Person Happy

Some people believe that once they get married all their problems will be solved and they finally will be happy. However, if a person is unhappy before they get married, they will likely be unhappy after they get married, too. There may be an initial honeymoon period that suppresses that unhappiness, but eventually this will fade and the person will become unhappy again unless the real sources of unhappiness are confronted and resolved. This also goes for a person who gets married only in order to feel less lonely. If genuine connection and intimacy are lacking, a person is likely to feel lonely even within a relationship where they are supposed to be connected.

Marriage Is a One-Time Choice

Finally, people believe that they only choose to marry a person once. In a real sense, however, a person chooses his or her partner again every day.

Ebony Spriggs and Jon Carlson

See also Commitment; Communication Errors/Problems in Couples and Families; Conflict Resolution; Marital Distress

Further Readings

Feldhahn, S., Stanley, A., & Whitehead, T. (2014). *The good news about marriage: Debunking discouraging myths about marriage and divorce.* Colorado Springs, CO: Multnomah Books.

Kaczor, C., & Kaczor, J. (2014). *The seven big myths about marriage: Wisdom from faith, philosophy, and science about happiness and love.* San Francisco, CA: Ignatius Press.

Lazarus, A. A. (2001). *Marital myths revisited: A fresh look at two dozen mistaken beliefs about marriage.* Atascadero, CA: Impact.

Marriage Versus Civil Unions

Marriage and civil unions are two different forms of legal status given to two individuals who are in a committed life partnership with one another. Marriage confers a unique legal status with a host of protections, responsibilities, and rights that are different from the protections, responsibilities, and rights afforded to people in civil unions. Civil unions were created as a way to legally recognize commitments between same-sex couples, but do not offer all of the same rights as a marriage. Until recently, marriage was a legal status provided only to opposite sex couples. Until June 2015 (when the Supreme Court of the United States made same-sex unions legal in all 50 states), practitioners engaging in marriage, couples, and family counseling may have provided services to couples in a committed, lifelong partnership who were unable to legally marry within their jurisdiction. The purpose of this entry is to discuss the history of marriage versus civil unions, political changes that have extended marriage equality to both opposite and same-sex couples, and responses of marriage, couples, and family counselors to this trend.

History of Marriage Versus Civil Unions

Whereas modern civil marriage is a unique legal status providing a host of protections, responsibilities, and rights, marriage was once considered to be primarily a religious right. In the Roman Catholic Church, the sacrament of Holy Matrimony states that the matrimonial covenant is a union between man and woman, establishing a partnership for life for the express purpose of procreation, education of offspring, and strengthening of the church community. According to the Roman Catholic Church, God Himself is the author of marriage. A baptized man and woman, unless impeded by ecclesiastical or natural law made by church leadership, should appear before a Roman Catholic priest to celebrate the sacrament of Holy Matrimony. In some cases, witness of a priest of others was not required for the church to recognize the holy matrimony. Other religious denominations sanctioned religious marriage in similar ways.

Marriage as a primarily religious right, however, changed dramatically during the 17th century. States began to claim an interest in registering and licensing marriages. Nineteen years after the settlers descended upon land that is now Massachusetts, the state of Massachusetts, in 1639, began a registry of vital records in which records of marriage, birth, and deaths were recorded. By the 19th century, most states in the United States had some sort of license that was issued to heterosexual couples wishing to marry. A duly recognized person would solemnize the marriage ceremony and register the marriage with the appropriate jurisdictional authority. Thus, the marriage ceremony, in many cases, was both a religious marriage and a civil (legal) marriage, usually solemnized by a pastor, priest, or rabbi, and then legally registered with the state.

With the legal recognition of marriage came a host of protections, responsibilities, and rights in the United States. Married spouses enjoy the benefit of filing taxes as a married couple, typically resulting in reduced tax liability. Married spouses enjoy the benefit of being designated as next of kin, which entitles each partner to certain governmental benefits in cases of disability, injury, or death. It also facilitates the disposition of a person's estate when there is no written will. In addition, married couples can sponsor one another for the purpose of immigration. Parenting relationships are strengthened through the legal recognition of marriage, particularly in that paternity is presumed to be that of the legal husband when a child is born. Though there were accompanying financial responsibilities that married partners assumed for one another, the benefits of marriage in the United States generally balanced the responsibilities for those who were in a committed life partnership. However, these benefits were extended only to heterosexual couples, as the marriage of same sex couples was not permitted by U.S. law.

Civil unions have a much shorter history in the United States than civil marriage. Civil unions were created by the state of Vermont in 2000 in order to create a legal status for committed relationships between people of the same sex in lieu of their being able to enter civil marriages. Later the states of Connecticut, New Hampshire, New Jersey, Rhode Island, Illinois, Delaware, and Hawaii also allowed civil unions.

The problem with civil unions is that they created a social distinction between relationships between opposite-sex couples and same-sex couples, and civil unions did not come with many of the privileges and protections that marriage did. Civil unions were separate and not equal. Some of the differences included a lack of portability from state to state. In addition, there is no way to end a civil union if a couple moves to a state that does not recognize civil unions. Finally, the federal government does not recognize civil unions so any legal protections and privileges are only given at the state level.

Political Trends Toward Marriage Equality

The climate of opinion surrounding civil marriage of same-sex couples changed dramatically in the United States during the 20th century. Changes in attitudes toward marriage equality occurred hand in hand with the increased visibility of the lesbian, gay, bisexual, and transgender (LGBT) communities. The origin of the modern LGBT liberation movement in the United States is often marked by the 1969 Stonewall Rebellion in Greenwich Village in New York City. The Stonewall Rebellion was a series of spontaneous demonstrations launched by LGBT people who were responding to mistreatment by the police. It has since become an icon of LGBT liberation.

Marriage was not initially the target of LGBT activism in the United States Instead, the LGBT communities focused primarily on addressing laws that criminalized same-sex sexual desire. Anti-sodomy and other anti-LGBT laws angered the LGBT communities, and the communities used initial forms of activism like the Stonewall Rebellion to call attention to their mistreatment. Coming out of the closet, out of the bars, and into the streets was believed to be a key step in challenging anti-LGBT attitudes and laws.

Some of the efforts at addressing anti-LGBT laws were more successful than others. For example, in 1986, the Supreme Court, in *Bowers v. Hardwick,* found that individuals are not afforded sexual privacy according to the Constitution. In 2003, two men were prosecuted for engaging in a consensual sexual act within a private residence, which was then in violation of Texas law. In the *Lawrence v. Texas* decision, however, the Supreme Court found that consensual intimacy between the two men was protected under the rights of privacy and due process. With this ruling, state laws that banned consensual same-sex sexual acts were no longer prosecutable. Opponents of the *Lawrence v. Texas* lamented that the decision would eventually lead to the legalization of same-sex marriage, which they considered to be a collapse of morality in society and a threat to the institution of the traditional family.

Widespread legal recognition of same-sex marriages in the United States, however, took an additional decade to be more fully realized. This was due, in part, to the Defense of Marriage Act (DOMA), which was passed by Congress and signed by President Bill Clinton in 1996. DOMA was a law that denied federal recognition of same-sex marriages and permitted states to refuse to recognize same-sex marriages performed in other states. DOMA represented a departure from the "full faith and credit" clause of the U.S. Constitution, which stated that full faith and credit should be given in each state to the acts, records, and judicial proceedings of other states. Prior to DOMA, marriages performed in other states were deemed just as valid as marriages performed within the state. A marriage legally registered in New York was generally accepted as a valid marriage in Virginia. Exceptions to full faith and credit of marriages were generally only applied to same-sex marriages. Opposite-sex marriages performed elsewhere were accepted by virtually all other jurisdictions as valid.

Despite this disappointing development in federal policy, the movement toward LGBT marriage equality emerged on a state-by-state basis. In 2000, Vermont was the first state to legally recognize civil unions. However, civil unions in Vermont were an institution separate from marriage. During this time, jurisdictions also had domestic partnerships, civil unions, and other relationship recognition laws, and some of these laws were in direct conflict with other laws of the state. For example, Chicago had a domestic partnership registry before civil unions and marriage equality were legal in the state of Illinois.

LGBT marriage equality began to gain full momentum in 2003 as a result of the Massachusetts

Supreme Judicial Court ruling in *Goodridge v. Department of Public Health,* which gave full marriage equality to same-sex couples in the state of Massachusetts. Anti-LGBT marriage laws were challenged in a host of states and eventually led to the Supreme Court decision in *United States v. Windsor,* which invalidated portions of DOMA. Support for LGBT marriage equality became a more viable option for many politicians in the United States when President Barack Obama indicated that he supported civil rights protections for LGBT people; but at first, Obama endorsed the less controversial view that a separate legal institution, like civil unions, could adequately protect LGBT citizens of the United States. Later, Obama became a more vocal ally for LGBT marriage, saying his position had "evolved" on the issue of marriage equality. Before the repeal of DOMA, the Obama administration issued a directive to the Department of Justice to discontinue defending the constitutionality of DOMA. Subsequently, Obama adopted an even more supportive stance, stating that he believes that the Equal Protection Clause of the Constitution does guarantee the right to same-sex marriage in all states.

In 2015, the Supreme Court took on the issue of same-sex marriage after accepting the case of *Obergfell v. Hodges.* The Supreme Court ruled under the Fourteenth Amendment that same-sex couples can marry nationwide. The Fourteenth Amendment provides equal rights for born or naturalized citizens. The 5–4 ruling overrode bans in 13 states against gay marriage. Same-sex marriage must now be accepted by all 50 states and is federally recognized.

Responses of Marriage, Couples, and Family Counselors

Practitioners in marriage, couples, and family counseling have generally supported LGBT marriage equality and have been at the forefront of efforts during the last century to depathologize and decriminalize homosexuality. These efforts are sometimes first linked to the removal of homosexuality from the *Diagnostic and Statistical Manual of Mental Disorders* in 1973. Since this time, homosexuality has no longer been viewed as a pathology and as a result, many practitioners in marriage, couples, and family counseling have long considered homosexuality as a normal variation of human sexuality. This change of attitude eventually spilled over to mainstream communities, and the public increasingly began to see LGBT relationships as being just as valid as heterosexual relationships. People with LGBT identities became more visible within the workplace, the media, and general public. LGBT people became less hidden in society. This increased visibility may have not been possible without depathologizing homosexuality. This development had a profound impact on the LGBT marriage equality movement.

There was not absolute consensus, however, among practitioners in marriage, couples, and family counseling. A small but vocal contingent of practitioners engage in the practice of reorientation, reparative, or ex-gay therapy, which is a controversial intervention aimed at curing same-sex sexual desire and at helping clients change their sexual orientation from homosexual to heterosexual. These interventions are often based on the now discredited hypothesis that male homosexuality is caused by a poor father–son relationship in early gender identity development.

All mainstream professional counseling organizations, including the American Association for Marriage and Family Therapy, currently have position statements that homosexuality is not a pathology or illness. Rather than focusing clinical attention on changing same-sex desire, clinical attention should focus on coping with and/or challenging negative social stigmas associated with LGBT identity. Additionally, professional organizations have called into question the ethics of reorientation therapy, stating that the therapy is ineffective at curing homosexuality at best and, at worst, actively harming vulnerable clients. Laws have been considered in several states that would ban the practice of reorientation therapy altogether.

Many practitioners in marriage, couples, and family counseling have advocated for greater legal protection of LGBT couples. Recognizing the importance of human relationships, counselors are addressing relationship issues, mental health issues within the context of family systems, and other couples-related issues from an LGBT-affirmative practice approach, while recognizing and acknowledging relationship inequity issues that still exist in the United States and elsewhere. When clinically appropriate, practitioners are helping LGBT couples and families recognize how heterosexism, homophobia, and other inequalities may be impacting current family functioning.

Trevor G. Gates

See also LGBT Families; Sexual Minorities; Sexual Orientation, Attraction, and Identity; Sexual Prejudice

Further Readings

Herek, G. M. (2006). Legal recognition of same-sex relationships in the United States: A social science perspective. *American Psychologist, 61*(6), 607–621.

Hines, J. M. (2012). Using an anti-oppressive framework in social work practice with lesbians. *Journal of Gay & Lesbian Social Services, 24*(1), 23–39.

Serovich, J. M., Craft, S. M., Toviessi, P., Gangamma, R., McDowell, T., & Grafsky, E. L. (2008). A systematic review of the research base on sexual reorientation therapies. *Journal of Marital and Family Therapy, 34*(2), 227–238.

Solomon, M. (2014). *Winning marriage: The inside story of how same-sex couples took on the politicians and pundits and won.* Lebanon, NH: University Press of New England.

Marriage-Friendly Therapy

Marriage-friendly therapy is a term coined in the early 2000s to describe an approach to counseling that affirms the value of marital commitment and lifelong marriage. In practice, the marriage-friendly therapist's first stance is to preserve and improve the relationship unless there are compelling reasons otherwise (e.g., the presence of abuse). This contrasts with the "neutral" approach, which maintains that the therapist should have no value stance about whether a client's marriage survives or ends in divorce and that what matters are clients' own values and choices for their relationship. This entry provides historical background to value orientations in the field of marriage counseling, describes relevant research, illustrates how the neutral approach also embodies value assumptions that play out in practice, and comments on the current state of marriage-friendly therapy.

Historical Background

The earliest textbooks in the field of marriage counseling in the 1950s and 1960s struggled against what the authors viewed as a popular misconception of marriage counseling as an effort to save troubled marriages no matter what the cost. But Ian Dowbiggin, the only professional historian to research the history of marriage counseling, has shown that marriage counselors historically were far from blind marriage savers. From its origins in the 1930s to its expansion in the 1970s and 1980s, the field focused mainly on marriage as a relationship promoting personal well-being, rather than marriage as a committed relationship tied to community norms about permanence. Thus, it is not that the pioneers and subsequent leaders did not value marriage, but rather that their fundamental orientation, enhanced during the social upheavals of the 1960s and 1970s, was toward marriage as a source of individual fulfillment and happiness with a de-emphasis on marriage as a lifelong bond and an important social institution. Marriage counselors, according to Dowbiggin, were influenced by cultural changes in the mid-20th century that deemphasized norms of lifelong commitment through better or worse (also known as the "we marriage") in favor of commitment as long as happiness and love last (also known as the "me marriage"). He also documents how marriage counselors enhanced these cultural trends by creating models and language that fit the new way of looking at marriage.

Against this historical backdrop, the stance of neutrality about divorce versus marital stability was a natural one for marriage counselors. If individual well-being is the main marker of a successful marriage, then individual client autonomy in decision-making about the future of the marriage becomes the values benchmark for the counselor. The counselor himself or herself should not let personal biases about commitment influence the direction people take for their marriage. Of course, as Dowbiggin points out, this stance of neutrality embodies a strong value orientation about the personal nature and purpose of marriage, and understood in historical context, this position on marriage was still new and emerging in the mid- to late 20th century. The marriage-friendly approach emerged from a critique of the individualist values of the neutral stance.

Research on Counselor Attitudes

In 1999, John Wall and his colleagues carried out a national study seeking to assess the values of marriage counselors. The study found that nearly 70% of therapists specializing in marriage and family said they were "neutral on divorce." About one third said that they were "committed to preserving marriage and avoiding divorce whenever possible." Two percent "often recommend divorce" (Wall, p. 143). These findings were supported by a poll in 2000 of divorced individuals in Minnesota, conducted as part of a random sample survey of adults in the state. When asked to think about the counseling they received, only 35% of divorced respondents believed that their therapist had a desire to help save their marriage. Forty-one percent believed that their therapist was neutral about whether or not they should stay together or to get a divorce, and 14% said that the therapist encouraged them to pursue a divorce. It appears from this limited research that at the end of the 20th century, the majority of marriage counselors embraced neutrality as a values and clinical stance.

Case Illustration of an Individualistic Approach to Marriage Counseling

Soon after her wedding, Marsha felt something was terribly wrong with her marriage. She and her husband Paul had moved across the country following a big church wedding in their hometown. Marsha was obsessed with fears that she had made a big mistake in marrying Paul. She focused on Paul's ambivalence about the Christian faith, his avoidance of personal topics of communication, and his tendency to criticize her when she expressed her worries and fears. Marsha sought help at the university student-counseling center where she and Paul were graduate students. The counselor worked with her alone for a few sessions and then invited Paul in for marital therapy. Paul, who was frustrated and angry about how distant and fretful Marsha had become, was a reluctant participant in the counseling.

In addition to the marital problems, Marsha was suffering from clinical depression: She couldn't sleep or concentrate, she felt sad all the time, and she felt like a failure. Medication began to relieve some of these symptoms, but she was still upset about the state of her marriage. After a highly charged session with this distressed wife and angry, reluctant husband, the counselor met with Marsha separately the next week. She told Marsha that she would not recover fully from her depression until she started to "trust her feelings" about the marriage. The following is how Marsha later recounted the conversation with the counselor:

Marsha: "What do you mean, trust my feelings?"

Counselor: "You know you are not happy in your marriage."

Marsha: "Yes, that's true."

Counselor: "Perhaps that you need a separation in order to figure out whether you really want this marriage."

Marsha: "But I love Paul and I am committed to him."

Counselor: "The choice is yours, but I doubt that you will begin to feel better until you start to trust your feelings and pay attention to your unhappiness."

Marsha: "Are you saying I should get a divorce?"

Counselor: "I'm just urging you to trust your feelings of unhappiness, and maybe a separation would help you sort things out."

A stunned Marsha decided to not return to that counselor, a decision the counselor no doubt perceived as reflecting Marsha's unwillingness to take responsibility for her own happiness. Yet, in this scenario, it gets even worse. Marsha talked to her priest during this crisis. The priest urged her to wait to see if her depression was causing the marital problem or if the marital problem was causing the depression—a prudent bit of advice. But a few minutes later, the priest said that if it turned out that the marital problems were causing the depression, he would help Marsha get an annulment. Marsha was even more stunned than she had been by the therapist. In the end, this couple did find a good marital therapist who helped them straighten out their marriage, Marsha's depression lifted, and the couple stayed together.

Although arguably extreme, this case illustrates how an individualistic approach, which the therapist would likely label a neutral approach, bears considerable implicit value assumptions about marital commitment. By contrast, a marriage-friendly therapist would have approached this case very differently.

Marriage-Friendly Therapy Values

Although there is no definitive statement of the value orientation of marriage-friendly therapy, the following five points cover most of the terrain.

1. *Being procommitment about marriage, not neutral.* Marriage is a relationship based on a promise of a lifetime commitment; "leaning toward" that commitment is at the core of being a good marriage counselor. In the case of Marsha and Paul, a marriage-friendly therapist would acknowledge and support Marsha's commitment to her marriage and also try to elicit Paul's own commitment, despite his frustration with the current relationship.

2. *Working with energy and dedication to help people succeed in their current relationship.* This means that the marriage-friendly therapist injects hope for demoralized couples and is not the first one in the room to give up on the relationship. Marsha was depressed, which contributed to her demoralization about the marriage. And Paul was perplexed about his wife's reactions to him. A marriage-friendly therapist would work hard to keep Paul in the therapy and to help them better understand each other and work on their problems.

3. *Helping clients pay attention to the possible consequences of their marital decisions for their children, their extended families, and their communities.* Marriage is embedded in a series of other stakeholder relationships, and decisions to stay or leave have effects on others that the therapist helps clients take into consideration. If Marsha and Paul had children, a marriage-friendly therapist would be willing to put the interests of the children on the table, especially since this was not a destructive marital relationship.

4. *Recognizing that not all marriages can or ought to be saved, especially when there is risk of harm.* This is a key to a balanced procommitment stance. Not all marriages are fit for human health and well-being, and marital stability should not be promoted blindly. If Marsha and Paul remained in therapy and, for example, Paul become violent and refused to work on his anger, a marriage-friendly therapist would support a decision by Marsha to end the marriage.

5. *If clients eventually decide to divorce, working with them to lessen the damage to everyone involved, create a viable parenting partnership if they have children, and prevent another divorce in the future.* A marriage-friendly therapist promotes healing in the divorce process. If Marsha and Paul were to divorce, a marriage-friendly therapist would actively address the importance of a constructive divorce process, and if they had children, promote the interests of the children now and in the future.

Marriage-Friendly Therapy: Core Practices

Marriage-friendly therapy is not a model of couples therapy but a values and clinical orientation that comes into play most often when a marriage is in serious distress or when one spouse is considering a divorce. In other situations when a couple comes to therapy with neither partner demoralized nor considering leaving, there is less difference in how a marriage-friendly therapist would work as compared to a neutral therapist. Both presumably would go about the work of helping a committed couple improve their relationship. The following practices of marriage-friendly therapy are most called upon when the marriage is "on the brink" either from hopelessness or active consideration of divorce.

Holding Hope

A marriage-friendly therapist maintains hope and encourages hope in couples when one or both partners enter therapy demoralized and hopeless about whether they can change enough to save their marriage. The therapist creates a holding environment for the couple's relationship until they gain traction in therapy and start to feel hopeful again.

Resisting "Fatal Flaw" Thinking

A marriage-friendly therapist avoids early judgments about whether a marriage can succeed and be restored to health. He or she actively resists a rush to judgment that a couple's relationship is doomed because of their history or the severity of their current problems, or the therapist's view that the partners are incompatible. Such judgments serve to restrain the therapist from being energetic and creative with the couple.

Encouraging Spouses to See Other Stakeholders in Their Marriage and Divorce Decisions

When spouses are not mentioning concerns for their children and others affected by a potential divorce, a marriage-friendly therapist is willing to inquire about these other people. A neutral therapist might hold back from such queries out of concern that they might unduly influence the client's decision-making process.

Encouraging "Leaning-in" Spouses

When divorce is on the table, generally one spouse is "leaning out" toward the divorce and the other is "leaning in" toward preserving the marriage. A marriage-friendly therapist encourages the leaning-in spouse to take constructive actions that create the possibility of the spouse deciding to work on the marriage. This contrasts with a neutral approach that might involve emphasizing that in a no-fault divorce state, one spouse can make the decision to end the marriage.

Challenging Leaning-Out Spouses

When the leaning-out spouse presents reasons for the divorce (other than abuse), a marriage-friendly therapist is willing to invite this person to look hard at the reasons, especially when the client has a blind spot about his or her own contributions to the problems, when the reasons seem impulsive, when there is an affair, or when the couple have not tried couples therapy.

Current State of Marriage-Friendly Therapy

Although controversial when introduced, the idea of marriage-friendly therapy has become more accepted in the field. A major review article of research behind evidence-based couples therapy models, authored by four leaders in the field, observed that these treatment approaches assume the stance of improving the relationship when feasible and take a definite promarriage view of couples therapy. In a discussion of therapists' stances toward preserving marriages with couples considering divorce, Jay Lebow, the editor of *Family Process*, reviewed two decades of controversy and concluded that there is now consensus in the field for a position that supports marriage, with the first task of the therapist being to assess the viability of the marriage while being open to other outcomes based on the stories, feelings, and commitment levels of each partner. It appears that marriage counseling is moving beyond its historic neutrality stance in the direction of marriage-friendly therapy.

William J. Doherty and Elizabeth Doherty Thomas

See also Couples and Marriage Counseling; Cultural Issues in Couples and Families; Divorce and Separation; Moral Dimensions of Therapy

Further Readings

Doherty, W. J. (1995). *Soul searching: Why psychotherapy must promote moral responsibility*. New York, NY: Harper.

Doherty, W. J. (2006, March/April). Couples on the brink: Stopping the marriage-go-round. *Psychotherapy Networker*, 30–39, 70.

Dowbiggin, I. (2014). *The search for domestic bliss: Marriage and family counseling in 20th-century America*. Lawrence: University Press of Kansas.

Lebow, J. L. (2015). Separation and divorce issues in couple therapy. In A. S. Gurman, J. L. Lebow, & D. K. Snyder (Eds.), *Clinical handbook of couple therapy* (5th ed., chap. 16). New York, NY: Guilford Press.

Lebow, J. L., Chambers, A. L., Christensen, A., & Johnson, S. M. (2012). Research on the treatment of couple distress. *Journal of Marital and Family Therapy, 38*, 145–168.

Wall, J., Needham, T., Browning, D. S., & James, S. (1999). The ethics of relationality: The moral views of therapists engaged in marital and family therapy. *Family Relations, 48*, 139–149.

Weiner-Davis, M. (2002). *The divorce remedy*. New York, NY: Simon & Schuster.

MATE SELECTION

Mate selection is a construct that refers to the process of selecting a marital, lifelong, or breeding partner. There are many different methods in which one might proceed when aiming to select a mate. Some methods of mate selection are quite traditional, while others are only made possible with cutting edge technology, or recognized legally due to advances in emerging legislation. Often, an individual's geographic location, culture, family traditions, and individual values impact how mate selection is achieved. There are a number of different historical implications, theoretical perspectives, and principles, which inform what scholars understand about mate selection. Overall, there are advantages and disadvantages in each approach to mate selection. This entry discusses the concept of mate selection, reviews historical and theoretical perspectives on the subject, and examines recent developments in mate selection.

The Concept of Mate Selection

Family formation is a cross-cultural and organic human process, yet the traditions and practices related to couple formation and mate selection vary from couple to couple, family to family, and culture to culture. Decades of research indicate that the family experience is a universally human practice that provides the foundational unit of society; therefore, all societies have a vested interest in successful mate selection and family development. In some cultures, mate selection stems from arrangements made between family members or agreements negotiated by matchmakers, while others result from individuals' free choice with minimal or no influence from others. Similarly, some individuals and cultures consider the abstract ideas of "love" or "soul mate" to be precursors to mate selection, while others believe that endearment emerges from well-matched, prearranged mate pairings.

Social scientists interested in family studies aim to understand mate selection though analysis of a variety of data sources and theoretical viewpoints. From vital statistics on a global scale (such as census data), scholars have analyzed factors that predict and influence mate selection. Overall, theorists place focus on sociocultural characteristics such as age, level of education, social class, religion, and race. Generally, the field of counseling draws perspectives of mate selection from various disciplines. For instance, anthropologists generally conceptualize mate selection through the lens of kinship structures, as they intersect with mate selection via systems of arranged marriages. Sociologists, however, tend toward a paradigm of understanding that categorizes the family as a social institution embedded within the context of the broader society and, therefore, focuses on the evolution of courtship systems, which develop parallel to societies as they modernize. Since the 1970s, scholars, such as Bernard Murstein, have reported that both cultural and historical elements affect mate selection.

Historical Perspectives

In many cultures, practical or economic gains were, and in many cases still are, considered the most important requirement for mate selection. For example, dowries, or gifts bestowed upon a groom by a bride's family, were traditionally arranged. Also, men (particularly those of lower socioeconomic classes) often aimed to find a bride who could contribute favorably to domestic tasks, child-rearing, and business pursuits.

Throughout the 1800s, genders were often divided socially, yet courtship rituals became more formal during this time period, often including engagement announcements and rings and increasingly elaborate wedding arrangements, ceremonies, and gifts. In the shadow of the Industrial Revolution in the mid-1800s, the importance of romantic love became increasingly valued. Family life became more conjugal and private throughout the Victorian era (mid-1800s through World War I), and the invention of the automobile in the late 1880s created unprecedented mobility and privacy in the following decades for couples who were—for the first time in history—"dating." During this time, love surfaced as a hallmark of mate selection, particularly for the middle and upper class, despite the formality of courtship customs.

Willard Waller, a pioneering scholar on the topic of mate selection, discussed the elements of competition and pleasure in college students in the 1930s. Mate selection scholarship punctuates the 1930s through the 1950s with the idea of "going steady" as an intermediate step between casual dating and engagement, with young adults typically marrying right after their high school or college educational obligations were completed. The feminist movement of the 1960s and 1970s yielded improved methods of birth control, increasingly empowering women to explore recreational and professional pursuits prior to selecting a mate, and offered more permissive attitudes regarding premarital sex.

By the 1980s, dating took on a much more informal tone in most parts of the Western World, with many young people socializing in groups without much emphasis on formalities before, ultimately, pairing up and selecting a mate. The idea of finding the perfect mate, or one's soul mate, extended into the 1990s and 2000s. This, along with decreased pressure to select a mate, has created the trend in recent decades to wait longer to look for a serious relationship. Yet, when modern individuals in industrialized societies are ready to select a suitable mate, they increasingly experience difficulty finding a suitable partner once they are ready to marry. This conflict has led to advances in current acceptable mate selection processes (i.e., professional matchmakers, computer match services, speed dating, and online Internet dating).

Theoretical Context

Scholars studying mate selection have given increasing attention to the marriage market. The *marriage market* refers to how exchanges based on common cultural understandings take place between individuals in contemporary mate selection processes. In this way, mate selection plays out in market-like situations impacted by "commodities" like physical appearance, earning potential, and socioeconomic status. Gender roles are significant in the marriage market exchange process. For example, men typically hold higher social and economic status (known as the *marriage gradient*) and find a mate with higher physical attractiveness and domestic skills. The tendency of women to marry "up" socioeconomically is referred to as *hypergamy*. Likewise, the trend of men to marry "down" socioeconomically is termed *hypogamy*. However, contemporary gender role developments suggest that as women gain an economic viability of their own, they are less likely to seek marriage partners. This trend underscores the ever-changing nature of the marriage market.

Individual Factors

Several theories of mate selection focus on individuals' psychological response to potential mates, such as the reinforcement model developed in 1970 by Donn Byrne and Gerald L. Clore, who postulated that individuals are attracted to potential mates who make that person feel good and/or possess similar attitudes and characteristics. Scholars from this tradition emphasize the importance of blatant characteristics (i.e., physical appearance and the expression of similar attitudes and values) on mate selection.

Researchers have conducted many experiments to glean the effects physical attractiveness has on dating and mating. Generally, findings indicate that the more attractive someone is, the more likely others will be to seek them out for dating and mating. However, scholars who study married couples or those involved in mate selection found that individuals largely pair up with mates of similar attractiveness levels. However, factors associated with value in mate selection such as wealth or intelligence have been found to compensate for attractiveness. Overall, personality characteristics and process orientation intersect more often with mate selection theories than to marriage market conditions.

Need Complementariness

Research published in 1958 by Robert Winch provided a foundation for deeper exploration of the idea that individuals of dissimilar values or personality traits would marry. This "opposites attract" idea was counter to what value theorists suggested—namely, that congruence of values and personality would lead to increased affiliation and tendency toward marriage of compatible mates. Winch's theoretical framework, however, indicates that particular trait combinations will be gratifying to the individuals involved. Specifically, Winch established 12 such paired personality traits (e.g., dominant-submissive and nurturant-receptive). Although there is a lack of empirical support for need complementariness, the concept remains of interest in the study of mate selection due to its psychological origins and subsequently developed research impulse to examine the process of mate selection on the dyadic level.

Rational Choice

Marcia Guttentag and Paul F. Secord further studied the idea of mate selection based on rational choice through analysis of the marriage squeeze concept since the 1980s. The *marriage squeeze* is a term used to describe the unequal ratio of unmarried, available women to men. According to the marriage squeeze concept, marriage and monogamy are highly valued when a scarcity of women occurs in society, yet when women of marrying age are of abundance, the converse is found to be true.

The marriage market is further defined by norms of homogamy and heterogamy, which historically play a large role in mate selection. *Homogenous* mate selection occurs when partners identify similar individual or group characteristics. In contrast, *heterogamy* is evidenced when these characteristics differ. Although homogamy continues to be strong in many societies, considerable evidence suggests that changes in social attitudes and behaviors are leading to a generally increasing heterogamous society, particularly with regard to interracial and interfaith couples.

Bossard's Law

Furthermore, endogamy, or the expectation that individuals select mates who belong to the same sociocultural groups, impacts mate selection processes. Traditionally, individuals were discouraged from entering into an *exogamous* union, or one in which partners have conflicting sociocultural groups of origin. However, exogamous unions are becoming increasingly common due to contemporary shifts in social structures, ethnic affiliations, and geographic mobility. For instance, *propinquity* (James H. S. Bossard's empirically tested theory that indicates the closer two people live to one another the more likely they are to meet, connect, and mate) has become decreasingly applicable to mate selection due to changing marriage patterns, such as delaying the age of first marriage and the degeneration of homogenous marriage markets.

Process Theories

In the 1960s and 1970s, the concept of mate selection gained interest. Accordingly, Alan Kerckoff and Keith Davis developed their *filter theory* in 1962, which empirically supported that after meeting through avenues of propinquity and endogamy, individuals go through stage progression throughout the development of the relationship. Accordingly, early in a relationship social status variables (i.e., ethnicity and social class) serve to bring a pair together. Secondly, consensus of valuing (when both individuals in the dyad assess compatibility of value orientations) determine whether or not the couple continues to the third stage, need complementariness.

Although the data presented by Kerckoff and Davis yielded weak support for need complementariness as part of the process of mate selection, it did give way to further development of *process theories* of mate selection. For example, the works by scholars in the 1970s provided several assumptions regarding the stages of dyad formation that lead to marriage, including (a) there are predictable stages of dyadic interaction that lead to mate selection; (b) the sociocultural histories of individuals provides the backdrop for a couple's interpersonal processes; (c) value similarity is a precursor to communication rapport, self-disclosure, and trust development; (d) in relational terms, an individual's assets and liabilities hold exchange values with respect to attraction and interaction; and (e) the order or duration of mate selection stages relies on conditional factors (i.e., gender, marital history, and age).

Developing Theoretical Directions

Subsequent to the development of process theories, social scientists interested in mate selection have begun to shift away from research efforts concerned about how couples end up in legally recognized marriage unions. Instead their focus has shifted toward sorting out relationship development over the life course. For instance, focus has turned toward examining the formation and development of interpersonal relationships that may move through stages of romance, cohabitation, friendship, marriage, divorce, and so forth. Emphasis on relationship quality and durability, intimacy, gender role negotiations, commitment processes, and romantic love has recently taken on increased importance in social science studies of mate selection.

Current Developments

An emerging area of research in mate selection is the LGBTQ population. Although little research has been done in this field, researchers have begun to integrate specifically gay and lesbian individuals into their studies. Findings have shown that heterosexual men prefer younger mates. Some evolutionists hypothesize this is due to younger women being better suited to bare children. Contrary to the sexual selection theory, Kyle L. Gobrogge and his colleagues found that homosexual men also prefer younger mates, which may suggest that preferring a younger mate may not be just about procreation. Some scholars believe this phenomenon may be more about similar life experiences or social interests.

Lauren J. Moss and Mallory R. Stevens

See also Gender Roles; Intimacy, Specific Threats to; Marriage and Health; Premarital Counseling; Same-Sex Couples

Further Readings

Bossard, J. H. S. (1932). Residential propinquity as a factor in marriage selection. *American Journal of Sociology, 38,* 219–224.

Byrne, D., & Clore, G. L. (1970). A reinforcement model of evaluative responses. *Personality: An International Journal, 1*(2), 103–128.

Guttentag, M., & Secord, P. (1983). *Too many women?* Thousand Oaks, CA: Sage.

Kerckoff, A., & Davis, K. (1962). Value consensus and need complementarity in mate selection. *American Sociological Review 27*, 295–303.

Murstein, B. (1974). *Love, sex, and marriage through the ages.* New York, NY: Springer.

Winch, R. (1958). *Mate selection: A study of complementary needs.* New York, NY: Harper & Row.

Media in Family Therapy

The communications media, or simply "media," are a means of delivering information to a large audience via television, Internet, print, sound recordings, movies, or radio. Therapists may be featured in print media, such as newspapers and magazines, as well as in electronic news media and documentaries. They could also be invited to work with families on daytime talk shows and reality television shows. Additional opportunities include program development, research and consultations for executives (e.g., prescreening, critical incidence debriefing and aftercare). Therapists may also utilize media in family therapy (e.g., adopting music and movies as a clinical resource). This entry summarizes the benefits and risks of therapists working with the media, as well as the use of media in family therapy as a clinical resource.

Benefits of Media Involvement

Media involvement offers therapists a chance to promote the profession and educate the public. With increased visibility, therapists in the media help to normalize help-seeking behaviors, validate human experience, and demystify the therapeutic process. At times embraced as a form of social justice, working with the media allows therapists a chance to get off of the couch and out of the room. This allows people to be reached who may never choose to see a therapist. Therapists serve as advocates, promote personal agency, reduce the stigma of seeking help, and raise awareness about mental health conditions and coping skills.

Risks of Media Involvement

Risks of media involvement include generalization of information or approach, entertainment versus education, potential exploitation, and lack of influence in editing. Media involvement has garnered critique for sensationalizing problematic behaviors, perpetuating stereotypes, and distorting reality. Likewise, some mental health professionals see media portrayals of therapy as total misrepresentations of process, violations of confidentiality, proponents of misinformation, and examples of downright exploitation. Professional reputation can also be at risk, as judgments can be made by colleagues and clients for being involved with certain types of media or working with certain types of clients on film.

In addition to potential inconsistencies when being quoted in print media or interviewed live for breaking news, there may also be concerns of engaging in social media and working on television shows. Therapists are urged to employ ethical decision-making principles, such as autonomy, nonmaleficence, beneficence, fidelity, and justice, using respective professional codes of ethics to guide decision-making. Recommendations for media involvement entails addressing informed consent, limits of confidentiality, multiple relationships, personal interests, accurate representation, and scope of practice. Therapists are advised to display professional competence, attunement, and integrity.

Social Media

Social media, often utilized for marketing and educational purposes, involves online professional profiles, business websites, and interactive networking. A growing number of mental health professionals have an online presence with profiles on Facebook, LinkedIn, Twitter, Pinterest, and Instagram. While many are cautious about social media interaction, citing unfamiliarity and boundary concerns as reasons for reluctance, others view this level of engagement as essential in building a brand and building relationships in this digital age. Therapists should also be mindful of their use of e-mail, texting, and instant messaging with clients. While some use these platforms simply for scheduling purposes, communicating general reminders, or exchanging documents, others engage in distance counseling and offer other therapeutic services online. It is important to consider a social media policy in informed consent forms in order to educate families on the purpose, benefits, and risks.

Benefits of social media include increased access, convenience, and creativity in connecting. Recent research focuses on how media and technology impact quality of relationships and presenting problems in family therapy, such as online infidelity, Internet addiction, and inappropriate use by children and adolescents (e.g., youth violence and electronic aggression).

Media as a Clinical Resource With Families

Music and movies, forms of media, serve as adjunctive interventions in family therapy. Origins of such use include depth psychology, experiential therapy, and psychodrama. As clinical resources, they augment sessions by facilitating creativity and evoking empathy. Clients experience these mediums as nonthreatening and consequently engage in personal reflection and sharing with therapists and family members. Recorded music and movies often aid in extending sessions and serve as catalysts for change in family therapy. As an alternative or supplement to bibliotherapy, films may be shown during session or assigned as homework. Similarly, reviewing lyrics to a song or listening to music may enhance critical thinking and relaxation. Clinical applications to family therapy principles include highlighting coping and resilience, demonstrating boundaries, and considering gender roles and other diversity factors. Best practices entail therapists considering the purpose and process of selecting films and songs, assessing fit based on family values, and processing experiences during family sessions. Additional research on media as a clinical resource in therapy focuses on efficacy of distance-based therapy services and electronic transfer of client information. State and federal regulations should guide practices related to liability, confidentiality, and security.

Shatavia Alexander Thomas

See also Ethical Codes; Online Dating; Social Support

Further Readings

Borczon, R. M. (2004). *Music therapy: A fieldwork primer*. Gilsum, NH: Barcelona.

Dermer, S. B., & Hutchings, J. B. (2000). Utilizing movies in family therapy: Applications for individuals, couples, and families. *American Journal of Family Therapy, 28*(2), 163–180.

Fischoff, S. (2005). Media psychology: A personal essay in definition and purview. *Journal of Media Psychology, 10*(1), 1–21.

Jordan, N. A., Russell, L., Afousi, E., Tasha, C., McVicker, M., Robertson, J., & Winek, J. L. (2013). The ethical use of social media in marriage and family therapy: Recommendations and future directions. *The Family Journal: Counseling and Therapy for Couples and Families, 22*(1), 105–112.

Luskin, B. (2012, November 30). *The media psychology effect*. Retrieved from http://www.apa.org/divisions/div46/

Rutledge, P. (2012, October). *Becoming a 21st century leader*. Retrieved from http://mprcenter.org/blog/slideshows/

Spotts-De Lazzer, A. (2013, March/April). Faceblur. *Family Therapy Magazine, 12*(2), 24–28.

Thomas, S. (2014, July/August). MFTs in the media: Personal and social responsibility. *Family Therapy Magazine, 13*(4), 59–61.

Zur, O. (2011). *To accept or not to accept? How to respond when clients send "friend request" to their psychotherapists or counselors on social networking sites*. Retrieved from http://www.zurinstitute.com/socialnetworking.html

Medical Family Therapy

Medical family therapy (MedFT) is a field in health care comprised of clinicians, researchers, educators, and policy makers who think relationally, work systemically, and honor complex biological, psychological, social, and spiritual dimensions of health. It was developed in response to several opposing forces in Western medicine that were rendering health care both inefficient and fragmented, including (a) separations between the treatment(s) of patients' minds and bodies (and concomitant disconnections between behavioral and physical health providers); (b) exclusions of the family and community contexts in which patients reside; and (c) an increasingly complex and difficult-to-navigate system of specialists, clinic procedures and care processes, rules, regulations, and payer systems. Keeping up with contemporary calls to improve health care through purposeful collaboration between and among disciplines and focused integration of behavioral and physical health care services, MedFT spans a variety of health care settings, advances patient and family agency while ensuring communion is extended from providers and the care team, facilitates healthy workplace dynamics, and functions in all roles with cultural humility. This entry describes the historical context in which MedFT evolved; outlines guiding principles for its practice; and discusses a continuum of skills and techniques for MedFT clinicians, researchers, educators, and policy makers.

MedFT in Evolution: Historical to Contemporary Contexts

Health care, including disciplines that we traditionally refer to as *medical* (i.e., those targeting physical health) and those we call *behavioral* (i.e., those targeting mental and relational health), is changing fast. Hospital and clinic systems that once provided care in silos are now getting redesigned to better facilitate collaboration among providers who represent a variety of fields and provider types. Through these changes, patients and their families are benefiting from increased access to coordinated and reciprocally informed services, while further bridging assessment, diagnoses, and treatment between the mind and body. Training sites across graduate and medical education are preparing future healers to enter more complex work environments. Moreover, former interdisciplinary tensions regarding whose field, research, or treatment is better (e.g., psychology versus social work versus family therapy) are being replaced with a new form of mutual respect for colleagues' contributions across disciplines and a recognition that the whole is more than the sum of its parts. Thus, investigators are testing rigorous and complex designs that account for dyadic relationships, complex chronic conditions, and multiple institutional review processes in order to further evidence-based research, evidence-based practice, community-based participatory research, and practice-based evidence. Policymakers, system administrators, and third-party payers are working to advance ways to financially sustain new ideas and methods of care delivery. All of this results in patients and families who are increasingly finding a stronger voice in their health care experience.

When leaders in MedFT began to purposefully initiate and advance these bridges between mental health and physical medicine more than 20 years ago, they recognized the foundational and paradigmatic orientation(s) from the field of family therapy as uniquely positioned to connect care to the multiple and complex systems that make up patients (or clients), their families, and the social contexts in which they reside. Their efforts were anchored in a renaissance of thinking in Western medicine that called upon clinicians and researchers alike to simultaneously take into account biological (e.g., disease processes, neurological structures), psychological (e.g., cognitive processes, sensation, perception), and social factors (e.g., family, peer, and community functioning). It was during this time that the term *medical family therapy* (MedFT) was first coined.

Since then, MedFT has kept up with (and, in many respects, led) the rapid evolution that we have seen and continue to see in health care. Its original biopsychosocial (BPS), and later biopsychosocial-spiritual (BPSS) frame for treating individuals and families who are dealing with medical problems, has remained stalwart while its practice has evolved to also encompass active engagement and collaboration between different professionals involved in primary, secondary, and tertiary care teams (for individual patients' and families' benefit and for the benefit of the providers serving in care teams *per se*). MedFT practitioners work to traverse the complex terrains of health care's culture and often serve as a liaison, translator, advocate, guide, ambassador, and connector between patients and families, multiple providers, payers, policy makers, researchers, and social communities of support.

MedFT case reports and emerging studies targeting a broad range of presenting problems have grown in professional literature, including but not limited to congestive heart failure, diabetes, fibromyalgia, HIV/AIDS, infertility, obesity, oncology, parenting children with health challenges, somatization disorders, trauma and disaster response teams, and emergency fieldwork among patient populations. Other studies have sought to examine compassion fatigue and burnout among providers. Next steps in research and policy are to create a shared lexicon and core competencies for MedFT techniques and manners of operationalization and to further advance knowledge and understanding (using qualitative, quantitative, and mixed-method designs) with best clinical practices, operational structures, and financial and payment models.

MedFT is quickly evolving in training programs and settings across the United States. Generally housed within sites oriented to marriage (or couple) and family therapy, as well as in primary, secondary, and tertiary care settings, credentialing is available across several levels, including post-master's certificates, master's degree specializations, master's- and doctoral-level internships, doctoral degrees, and postdoctoral fellowships.

MedFT in Practice: Guiding Clinical Principles

Pioneering and landmark texts in medical family therapy by field leaders (e.g., William Doherty, Jeri Hepworth, Jennifer Hodgson, Angela Lamson, Susan McDaniel, and Tai Mendenhall) are now mainstays in training programs across the United States. Drawing from their work and contributions, key components of what MedFT looks like in action include the following: systems theory, biopsychosocial-spiritual (BPSS) sensitivity, agency, communion, collaboration, and a three-world view of health care.

Systems Theory

By recognizing that all parts of a system are forever interacting, evolving, and adapting, MedFT clinicians are sensitive to how change in one part of a larger whole can influence change in other parts. MedFTs know that these changes can and oftentimes cannot be predicted across patients' everyday lives (generally) and/or health care sequences (specifically). They attend to the complex and reciprocal impact(s) of interventions on patients' health, relationships with significant others and/or other family members, care team members (and team functionality), and multiple facets and layers of the health care system(s) that are connected and relevant to care.

Biopsychosocial-Spiritual Sensitivity

MedFT clinicians' systemic orientation goes beyond attention to the personal and interpersonal systems in which patients reside (e.g., a couple or dyad, a family, or the neighborhood community in which a patient resides). Conceptualizing patient and family and social systems as in the middle of a larger continuum of systems, MedFT practitioners see them as influenced by (a) basic and applied tenets of psychopharmacology, pathophysiology (targeted to the specialty area(s) in which they are practicing), and medical conditions and care procedures; (b) behaviors, thoughts, and emotions that may facilitate or challenge one's ability to enact a care plan; (c) patients' care-related ecology, including clinic operations, third-party payer systems, and broad health policies that facilitate (or impede) patients' care; as well as (d) patients' sense(s) and connection(s) to cultural and religious and spiritual beliefs and/or faith communities. This holistic framework within care delivery honors the multilayered complexity of patients' and families' struggles while at the same time accesses a rich range of resources available to them.

Agency

MedFT clinicians advance clinical work in a manner that facilitates their patients' and families' active involvement in and commitment to care. This contrasts with conventional Western medical practices wherein patients and families are positioned as passive recipients of professional expertise or services. Instead, MedFT recognizes that a great resource in health care, which is often untapped, is the lived experience, wisdom, and energy of patients and families. These resources empower patients to make personal choices about, and take on personal responsibility for, managing health and illness while working with providers in the health care system. This practice advances self-efficacy, autonomy, perceived competence, and internal locus of control, insofar as patients and families mobilize to seek information, partake in care practices, and act on their own behalf in collaboration with a larger care team. Thus, it helps to increase the human tendency toward making a change, because it is the patients' and families' choice to engage in an action for their health or health-related quality of life.

Communion

Communion centers on a sense of feeling connected, loved, supported, and cared for by others, including significant others, family members, friends (old and new), and professionals. MedFT clinicians work to facilitate this in patients and families, in large part because of the well-documented influence that social and emotional connections have on health. They also encourage it to prevent the unraveling of emotional bonds and resultant isolation that illness, disability, and contact with the health care system can so easily advance if communion is left unattended. MedFT practitioners encourage patients and families, along with members of their care team and support system, to traverse illness and health care together, united in a journey they share collectively.

Collaboration

Connecting all the biopsychosocial-spiritual dots, outlined above, together, MedFT clinicians work to unite and coordinate care and resources in a way(s) that is inclusive and forward thinking. They collaborate with providers representing multiple disciplines (e.g., faith communities, primary care medicine, psychiatry, psychology, social work, nursing). They define this collaboration in accordance to C. J. Peek's integrated care lexicon, specifically as a practice team that is tailored to the needs of each patient and situation; shares a clinical population and mission; uses a systemic clinical approach supported by office practice, leadership alignment, and a business model; and engages in continuous quality improvement and measurement of effectiveness.

Three-World View of Health Care

Medical family therapists are sensitive to how training sites often prepare clinicians in a manner that is not mindful of the realities of the health care context in which they will practice. For example, MedFT practitioners believe that to provide quality clinical behavioral health and mental health care, providers must regard how other "worlds" in the larger health care system intersect and are impacted by their practice style. These worlds include the *clinical world,* which works to provide exceptional behavioral health and family therapy and care using best practices or evidence-based clinical models; the *operational world,* which works to employ efficient, well-integrated, and patient-friendly systems that maximize optimal workflow patterns; and the *financial world,* which endeavors to stay economically viable through cost-effective utilization and coordination of health care resources. MedFT clinicians, then, work to advance and/or study high-quality clinical services within a well-organized and financially sustainable clinic system. It is important to honor the three-world view because any strong therapy practice or intervention (clinical world) will ultimately not work if the clinic system in which it is situated (operational world) cannot maintain it, or if its payment and insurance structure (financial world) will not support it.

Medical Family Therapy Continuum

Some MedFT skills require minimal training, whereas others necessitate more advanced preparation and practice. The MedFT Health Care Continuum places MedFT skills across five levels of application that represent a range of both proficiency and intensity. This continuum was designed by Jennifer Hodgson, Angela Lamson, Tai Mendenhall, and Lisa Tyndall to assist clinicians, researchers, supervisors, educators, and policy makers in understanding the depth and breadth of skills possible at different levels. It also serves as an aid to determine what level of application individuals want or aspire to engage in as a MedFT. Any health care professional of any discipline can be positioned along the continuum with the appropriate training, experience, and expertise as described below.

Level 1

These MedFT practitioners have an interest in the biopsychosocial-spiritual (BPSS) approach and could have some experience or professional training in the framework. However, they rarely incorporate BPSS practice into their work. They may consult with, or be consulted by, other care professionals (e.g., mental, physical, or spiritual providers), and therein employ a relational or BPSS framework, but do so only on an "as needed" basis.

Level 2

These clinicians occasionally collaborate with health care providers or researchers from other disciplines within colocated sites or across separate locations and/or with members of patients' families or support systems (e.g., spouses, friends). Such work will periodically incorporate the viewpoints of family and support system members, health care providers from diverse disciplines, or spiritual consultants. Work reflecting the inclusion of relational or BPSS foci are evident in less than half of the clinical cases, research, or training that is done.

Level 3

Medical family therapists at this level generally undergo training in family therapy, MedFT, and/or BPSS interventions as core to the work they conduct. They regularly collaborate with multiple providers and research team members within colocated or across separate locations, patients and participants, and members of patients' support systems and community. They employ MedFT techniques and family therapy interventions in relation to aspects of health in most of their work (present in up to 75% of all interactions), and therein incorporate family and support system members into treatment planning and promotion of relational and BPSS health and well-being.

Level 4

Practitioners at this level identify themselves as MedFT professionals (clinical providers and/or researchers). They are usually positioned within health care contexts as part of a colocated or fully integrated care team. They collaborate with providers and research teams representing a range of disciplines, patients and participants, and members of patients' support systems and community. This level encompasses the use of MedFT techniques and family therapy theories, models, and interventions in relation to aspects of health, and this is evident across all traditional and integrated care visits. Clinical practice and research at this level includes relational perspectives, assessments, and/or interventions. These clinicians also attend to the professional working relationships and well-being of and among members of the health care and research team.

Level 5

Medical family therapists at this level are proficient with clinical, research, supervisory, and administration skills and situated across a diverse range of primary (e.g., family medicine, internal medicine, and pediatrics), secondary (e.g., cardiology, intensive care, and occupational therapy), and tertiary (e.g., inpatient oncology and burn units) care systems. At this level, MedFT clinicians collaborate with providers and research teams representing a range of disciplines, patients and participants, and members of patients' support systems and community in most of their work. They are proficient in the application of family therapy theories, models, and interventions, and employ MedFT techniques across both traditional and integrated care visits. They prepare treatment plans and advance care that purposefully reflects BPSS sensitivity. Attending to the working relationships among health care and research team members, these MedFT practitioners also develop curricula and/or policies to promote self-care and effective teamwork. Clinicians at this level are usually engaged in teaching, research, training, administration, policy, and/or supervision in relation to family therapy, MedFT, medicine, or health care programs and contexts.

The title or designation of medical family therapy does not rest within a specific discipline or healthcare specialization. However, the skills that characterize higher levels of this continuum—especially those pertaining to teaching, supervision, and research—tend to coincide with focused training in family therapy, MedFT, and BPSS-oriented programs. It is also important to note that these levels do not represent a desired progression in professional status (i.e., Level 5 is not an ultimate goal for all MedFTs). Again, this continuum serves to help professionals determine what is best for them, based uniquely on their own needs, preferences, training, and care contexts.

Future Directions

Contemporary health care is evolving fast, and the calls for collaborative and integrated practices are stronger now than ever before. Through its purposeful connection of care practices and providers across biological, psychological, social, and spiritual foci of patients and their families, medical family therapy is answering this call. As this happens, everybody wins. Patients and their families are better able to reclaim health or to adjust to a new health status in the effective management of an illness, trauma, disease, injury, or physical condition. Thus, they become more informed of their care options and ability to take a more active role in their health outcomes. Providers are more effective as they coordinate their respective contributions to care within a larger mosaic of expertise offered by their colleagues, thereby honoring the biopsychosocial-spiritual complexities and functioning of patients and families who seek them out.

With continued advances in research, training, practice, and policy, MedFT's place at the healthcare table will become increasingly more secure. More controlled trials, dissemination and implementation studies, and adequately powered investigations are needed to confirm MedFT's effectiveness and thus inform policies at local and national levels. With more evidence, administrators and payers will become more supportive of BPSS-informed practices, and this will further fuel efforts in the advancement of MedFT training and education. There is a hope that MedFT's scope and visibility will grow in synchrony with the health care system's evolution and that someday, MedFT will become the rule and not the exception.

Tai J. Mendenhall, Angela Lamson, and Jennifer Hodgson

See also Assessment, Biopsychosocial; Children With Chronic Illness; Family Strengths; Health Issues; Marriage and Health; Resilience

Further Readings

Engel, G. (1977). The clinical application of the biopsychosocial model: A challenge for biomedicine. *Science, 196,* 129–136.

Hodgson, J., Lamson, A., Mendenhall, T., & Crane, D. (2014). *Medical family therapy: Advanced applications.* New York, NY: Springer.

Hodgson, J., Lamson, A., Mendenhall, T., & Tyndall, L. (2014). Introduction to medical family therapy. In J. Hodgson, A. Lamson, T. Mendenhall, & D. Crane (Eds.), *Medical family therapy: Advanced applications* (pp. 1–9). New York, NY: Springer.

McDaniel, S., Doherty, W., & Hepworth, J. (2014). *Medical family therapy and integrated care.* Washington, DC: American Psychological Association.

McDaniel, S., Hepworth, J., & Doherty, W. (1992). *Medical family therapy: A biopsychosocial approach to families with health problems.* New York, NY: Basic Books.

Peek, C. (2008). Planning care in the clinical, operational, and financial worlds. In R. Kessler & D. Stafford (Eds.), *Collaborative medicine case studies* (pp. 25–38). New York, NY: Springer.

Peek, C., Cohen, D., & deGruy, F., III. (2014). Research and evaluation in the transformation of primary care. *American Psychologist, 69,* 430–442.

Wright, L., Watson, W., & Bell, J. (1996). *Beliefs: The heart of healing in families and illness.* New York, NY: Basic Books.

MEN IN COUNSELING

Though men experience the full range of mental health concerns and significant distress, men are less likely to seek help for health concerns. Understanding the gendered nature of masculinity is an important cultural competency that impacts counseling practice. To be effective with male clients, counselors must consider and appreciate the unique concerns, needs, and difficulties that men experience in life. Effective counselors are those that enhance their personal self-awareness and skills of inclusive empathy in order to build effective healing relationships with men. This entry explores themes associated with developing a gender-sensitive approach to counseling men, including understanding the presenting concerns, reviewing barriers to help seeking, and creating helpful practices for counseling men.

Masculinity and Presenting Concerns

Substantial evidence suggests that men's needs for mental health services are increasing. Men demonstrate disproportionate rates of behavioral problems (e.g., suspension and expulsion, violent crime), academic challenges (e.g., dropping out of high school), mental health issues (e.g., depression, suicide), physical health problems (e.g., cardiovascular problems, shorter mortality), public health concerns (e.g., violence, substance abuse, incarceration) and a wide variety of other quality of life issues (e.g., relational problems, family well-being). Many men face depression and anxiety-related disorders, but often it is manifested in the forms of addiction, violence, interpersonal conflict, and general irritability. Often men's own psychic pain may not be obvious to them and as a result, when they enter counseling, many male clients are not sure how to behave. They may be confused about how to enter into a relationship with a counselor and conflicted about whether or not to proceed with counseling. They may also question whether counseling can really make a difference in their life. Many men enter counseling only when they feel coerced to do so or when they are desperate about some situation in their lives.

A strong base of evidence indicates that men's adherence to traditional masculine gender norms is associated with an wide array of presenting concerns, such as depression, anxiety and substance abuse as well as interpersonal and intrapersonal health concerns. Internal psychological distress or conflict from not meeting restrictive gender norms for men has been consistently associated with the full range of men's problems. Overidentification with traditional masculine beliefs can create internal "straightjackets" that limit and restrict men's emotions and behavior.

By contrast, other research has indicated that men who are able to transcend negative gender role stereotypes report less restrictive gender role beliefs and less distress. Counselors can work with men to become aware of their definitions of masculinity and then navigate restrictive notions toward creating concepts more consistent with their life and what it means for them to be a male in an ever-changing society.

Men and Help-Seeking

A key understanding for working with men is recognizing that masculinity is both associated with a wide range of health (physical and mental) concerns and less willingness to seek help for those problems. This awareness has classically been defined as double jeopardy—those who need the most help are also the least likely to seek it out. In addition, men report higher levels of stigma concerning seeking help for mental health concerns. Men simply do not go to counseling as often as women during any given year or over their lifetime. This is true across the wide variations of masculinities and cultural identities with evidence suggesting that men from ethnic minority backgrounds seek psychological help even less frequently than those who do not identify strongly with a specific ethnic minority. Gay men, however, tend to seek help more often than heterosexual men. Men tend to hold more restrictive views of mental illness than women and have less confidence in mental health counselors. Though stark differences between men and women exist, the tendency for men to seek help less often is complex. There are many reasons why men do not seek help, such as gender socialization, structural barriers, and cultural and institutional mistrust of mental health services.

Men often believe they have plausible reasons for not going to seek help. Financial considerations, the belief that one can handle the problem without treatment, not knowing where to get help, and not having time or health insurance are avoidance factors that keep men from seeking mental health services. Though many men experience some type of distress, not all incidents lead to seeking support from others or seeking professional counseling assistance. Although those men coming to see counselors may not even represent those with the most severe distress, it can helpful for counselors to consider why seeking help is frequently difficult for men.

Counselors can understand the reluctance of many men to seeking help by recognizing the influence of masculine gender socialization. When more traditional men seek help, they are faced with a number of uncomfortable responses, including increased vulnerability, a sense of helplessness, loneliness, depression, uncertainty, and a lack of personal influence. Many of the behaviors associated with seeking help (e.g., relying on others, admitting the need for help, recognizing the influence of an emotional problem) directly conflict with the messages many men receive about being a man. If men are invested in self-reliance, being tough or strong, and maintaining emotional control, then the popular perception of counseling directly conflicts with that desire. Counselors can also work to change men's attitudes about what is considered problematic. Perception of the nature of a problem as normative also influences help-seeking attitudes and behavior. The greater the extent to which men believe a problem is normal, the more likely they are to seek and receive help for that problem.

Gender constraints may affect access to and the delivery of mental health services for men, and/or facilitate uncritical overvaluing of masculine norms and acceptance of gender stereotypes. Although there is significant public stigma in the United States with regard to seeking help for mental health, men typically report higher levels of stigma compared to women. They are more likely to underutilize health and counseling services due to not perceiving a need for them.

Engaging Men in Counseling

Though barriers to seeking help exist, many men find their way to counselors looking for assistance. Counselors can meet the needs of men more effectively by making male-friendly adjustments to their approach to fit with male socialization. This includes modifying the way counseling is conducted (e.g., addressing gender role socialization in counseling, use of more self-disclosure, use of more problem-solving, directive, and active approaches, etc.). In order to be male-friendly, counselors must first have gender competence in counseling practice. Developing that competency takes dedicated attention.

Examine Gender Bias

Men may be subjected to harmful practices include biased practices, stereotypes, and a lack of awareness and training around gender issues as applied to men. A barrier can include the counselors' own gender role expectations supporting the notion that healthy men should enact more traditional gender roles. Both men and women can simply have a negative bias toward men due to past experiences and histories that present as a failure of empathy in understanding and counseling men. This view of men may reflect lack of gender competency when working with men, or it may be connected to long standing feelings of resentment due to experiences of male privilege and social power. Regardless of the source, negative counselor bias influences work with men.

Make Masculine Friendly Adjustments

Men themselves may not fully benefit from existing and accepted models of clinical treatment. This may be due to a fundamental mismatch between the way counseling tends to be conducted and the relational styles of most men. Counseling is often a good fit for certain types of individuals, but not others. Counseling as commonly practiced rewards those able to relate in an emotionally intimate and engaging manner, those comfortable and able to talk and express their affect, and those who enjoy self-reflection. Many men are socialized to avoid the less structured, interpersonal, and exploratory activities and are geared toward the manipulation and organization of data and objects. Men may find themselves feeling out of place in traditional counseling, and therefore hampered in their attempts to get help.

Masculine-friendly adjustments can be made in order to correct for this mismatch. A guiding framework for counselors is to work from a perspective that is sensitive to the experiences of men within a larger ecological and sociocultural context. Counselors strive to find ways to adapt the context of the counseling environment for their male clients by increasing the perception of normativeness for particular problems (e.g., depression), using less jargon, being more active and directive, matching their relational style to the client's need, addressing affect in a gender congruent manner, making male-sensitive adjustments to practice, and incorporating a strength-based approach. Many of the suggestions and modifications are in line with what would be considered good counseling practice. The critical distinction here is making adjustments and modifications to one's approach focusing on male clients as gendered people.

Assessing Masculine Norms

Effective counseling with men rests upon accurate assessment of masculine norms and expectations. Though most men are influenced by traditional masculine norms, it is an error to assume that those norms necessarily comprise all men's sense of masculinity. Making that assumption can lead to miscalculating how a man sees himself and not understanding the influences and motivations that make him who he is. When the influence of masculine socialization is examined and explored openly between client and counselor, a potential bridge can be built that links a man's lifelong experience with his presenting problem.

Counselors invite men to examine their socialization experiences by linking content or process that comes up in counseling with masculine norms. Traditional masculine norms that encourage men to be tough, in control, and not showing weakness can appear in a man's reluctance to admit psychological distress and the need for assistance. Rather than viewing this as resistance to counseling, counselors can normalize these thoughts and note how it is not uncommon for men to experience expectations in Western society that make it hard to be in counseling. Further, in couples counseling, masculine norms related to being a provider can emerge in a partner's complaints about a man's unavailability due to his work schedule (e.g., the need to work late); it can be seen in the pressure a man puts on his kids to compete and succeed; and it can emerge in his complaints about not being appreciated by his partner or family for how hard he works and how stressed he is by his efforts to succeed. Norms around emotional stoicism might appear as a man recounts feeling nothing or feeling numb in the face of significant pain or loss or noting an inability to experience or share deeper feelings with others.

Men and Emotions

Because of the socialization experiences of many Western men, there is a need to be sensitive in addressing emotionality in counseling. Counseling, which has traditionally emphasized the language of feelings, disclosing vulnerability, and admitting dependency needs, can create difficulties for men who adopt or strictly adhere to traditional masculine roles. It is critical not to stereotype men as unemotional and unable to access their deep affective experiences, yet it is important not to move too quickly or deeply into affect where a man may feel overwhelmed and flooded or ashamed or judged for being too emotional. This can be a difficult task for counselors who are caught between teaching a man new skills while also trying to modify counseling to match his coping style. The caveat here is that working with men and emotions simply deserves focused attention.

Adopt a Strength-Based Perspective

The scholarly literature on men and mental health has overemphasized what is wrong with men and masculinity by focusing on pathology at the expense of highlighting aspects of men's lives that are adaptive, healthy, and prosocial. It is easy to conclude that traditional masculinity, or masculinity as a whole, is always negative. However, the critical distinction is that traditional masculinity *per se* is not always negative, but it is often associated with the rigid, restrictive, sexist enactment of traditional male roles. A strength-based perspective focuses on strengthening assets that enable men to grow and flourish, including focusing attention on resources, creativity, and building relational support networks. It is those resources (e.g., faith, optimism, persistence, or membership in supportive peer networks) that men bring with them into the counseling setting that serve as the greatest contributor to positive outcomes. Specific to men, counselors can explore aspects of a client's masculinity that he experiences as the noble, adaptive, and enhancing aspects of his identity as a model for helping him in the counseling process.

Matt Englar-Carlson

See also Cultural Issues in Couples and Families; Gender- and Culture-Sensitive Therapies; Gender Issues; Gender Roles; Multicultural Counseling Competence

Further Readings

Brooks, G. R. (2010). *Beyond the crisis of masculinity: A transtheoretical model for male-friendly therapy.* Washington, DC: APA Books.

Englar-Carlson, M., Evans, M., & Duffey, T. (Eds.). (2014). *A counselor's guide to working with men.* Alexandria, VA: American Counseling Association.

Englar-Carlson, M., & Stevens, M. (Eds.). (2006). *In the room with men: A casebook of therapeutic change.* Washington, DC: American Psychological Association.

Rochlen, A. B., & Rabinowitz, F. E. (Eds.) (2014). *Breaking barriers in counseling men: Insights and innovations.* New York, NY: Routledge.

Shepard, D. S., & Harway, M. (Eds.). (2011). *Working successfully with men in couples counseling: A gender sensitive approach.* New York, NY: Routledge.

Mental Health, Systemic Perspective

A *systemic mental health perspective* typically refers to the ability to conceive of individual mental health problems as influenced, or even created or maintained, by dysfunctional interpersonal relationships. The term itself is derived primarily from the ideas of the biologist Ludwig von Bertalanffy, who argued in his book *General System Theory* that a variety of human experiences and social and scientific problems could be thought of *as if* they were systems. It also grows, in part, out of the work of the family therapist Murray Bowen, who believed that nearly all human and animal families actually *were* systems in which the behavior of each member fundamentally shaped the behavior of the others. Bowen's and Bertalanffy's views, while largely compatible, were not identical. Bertalanffy saw a systemic perspective not as a "true" description of how human experience really was, but as a useful way of conceptualizing it. Bowen, on the other hand, thought that the systemic nature of family behavior was a biological reality, built into who humans and animals are, and not just a metaphor for how families might be conceived. This entry discusses how the systemic perspective differs from the individual perspective and how behavior is explained in the systemic perspective.

Individual Versus Systems Perspective

One distinction between the ideas of Bertalanffy and Bowen is that Bertalanffy never saw system theory—he used the singular rather than the plural in his own writing—as applying to families themselves. The "ultimate precept," he wrote, was "man as individual," not as part of larger groups. His ideas were in reaction against what he saw as the efforts of many in the mid-20th century—the Nazis and Soviets, the mass marketers of Madison Avenue, and behavioral psychologists such as B. F. Skinner, among others—to turn humans into mere cogs in larger machines—"man as robot" as he put it, or "Skinnerian rats."

Nonetheless, early pioneers in family therapy such as Jay Haley, Salvador Minuchin, Don Jackson, and others adapted Bertalanffy's concept of "system theory," adding an *s* to the word *system*, and used it as a framework for exploring family dynamics. From this grew several family therapy models such as strategic family therapy, which conceives individual functioning as governed by the way family members unconsciously reinforce or undermine particular individual behaviors within the family, and structural family therapy, which explores how family roles and structures govern individual functioning. Bowen's own theory (Bowen family systems theory), though founded on a somewhat different premise, nonetheless argues that behavioral patterns transmitted unconsciously from earlier generations play a major part in individual behavior, as does Ivan Boszormenyi-Nagy's contextual family therapy.

Behavior Within a Systemic Mental Health Perspective

A systemic mental health perspective thus is conceptually distinct from the more traditional individualistic mental health perspective, in which individual behavior is presumed to originate largely from within the person himself or herself. Bowen's systemic conception of schizophrenia, for example, looks not only at individual psychopathology, but at how the behavior of other family members either reinforces or mitigates schizophrenic behavior. Bowen in fact in his early work hospitalized whole families along with the family member under treatment so that all of them could learn better ways of relating to the sufferer and each other. His success in lowering relapse rates by this approach demonstrated convincingly that simply sending a person who had undergone successful treatment for schizophrenic symptoms back to the same relational environment would invariably bring about a recurrence, as the family continued to see the treated person as "sick," and as they related to the person in ways that reinforced rather than lessened the patient's schizophrenic behavior.

Similarly, family therapists such as Carl Whitaker, working with couples in which a partner had had an extradyadic involvement—an affair—noted that frequently the noninvolved spouse had an overinvolvement, if not with another person, then with work or with alcohol, suggesting that both parties were reluctant to be exclusively intimate with each other. Such observations led Whitaker to talk about how such couples sometimes really were engaged in "mutual affairs," rather than one being "betrayed" while the other was the "offender."

The example of the extradyadic relationships of Joseph Kennedy Sr. and his sons gives further support for the importance of adopting a systemic perspective on individual actions. It is of course well known that both Joe Sr. and his sons had numerous extradyadic involvements. Yet it is seldom noted that there was a clear transgenerational pattern to these affairs.

Joe Sr.'s father-in-law, the Boston mayor and later member of Congress John "Honey Fitz" Fitzgerald—who initially did not approve of his daughter's involvement with Joe—had an extradyadic relationship with a cigarette sales girl and hotel secretary named Elizabeth "Toodles" Ryan, an entanglement that became something of a scandal at the time. Yet as one Kennedy generation succeeded the next, the women with whom the Kennedy men became involved outside their marriages were progressively more glamorous, moving from Honey Fitz's relationship with "Toodles" to Joe Sr.'s affair with the Hollywood starlet Gloria Swanson, and culminating with John Kennedy's romance with that epitome of sex symbols, Marilyn Monroe. Thus a systemic view might see this less as simply "cheating," than each male younger generation trying to outdo their predecessors' sexual "conquests."

A systems view might also note how even for the Kennedy wives there was what is sometimes called "secondary psychological gain" in their husbands' extradyadic involvements, since the wives remained "the woman he comes home to" at the end of the day, or perhaps night. In many ways, their husbands were seen as all the more desirable for their nominally powerful libidos, while the wives themselves were often cast as "saints" or "perfect mates" for "putting up with them."

While many other systemic models have been developed since Bertalanffy and Bowen's early work, such as narrative therapy, solution-focused therapy, or emotionally focused couples therapy, a systemic perspective, in short, tries to look beyond the surface of individual actions and place them in the context of the larger relationships that, to one degree or another, govern an individual's life.

Scott Johnson

See also Integrating Systemic and Individual Theories; Systemic Family Therapy

Further Readings

Boscolo, L., Cecchi, G., Hoffman, L., & Penn, P. (1987). *Milan systemic family therapy: Conversations in theory and practice.* New York, NY: Basic Books.

Campbell, D., Draper, R., & Crutchley, E. (1991). The Milan systemic approach to family therapy. In A. S. Gruman & D. P. Kniskern (Eds.), *Handbook of family therapy* (Vol. 2, chap. 10). New York, NY: Brunner/Mazel.

Cecchin, G. (1987). Hypothesizing, circularity, and neutrality revisited: An invitation to curiosity. *Family Process, 26*(4), 405–413.

METACOMMUNICATION

Metacommunication is a type of communication other than primary verbal communication. As a secondary form of communication, metacommunication encompasses the subtleties and nuances involved in the act of communicating without the use of direct verbal interactions. Human communication is of great interest to marriage and family therapists and behavioral researchers alike. How people convey their thoughts, feelings, and ideas to others can be complex. Yet one's ability to communicate clearly and accurately is also the cornerstone to building healthy sustainable relationships.

There are a number of strategies and rules that govern how people are expected to communicate, as well as direct and indirect ways of doing so that may vary across the life span. Variances in communication are also evident across different cultures and subcultures, racial groups, genders, and religions. In short, spoken words are only a small part of what actually gets communicated to others as people try to express themselves. Body language is another way that individuals communicate with one another. In fact, people tend to express more to others with their posture, degree of eye contact, hand gestures, facial expressions, and tone and volume of voice than they do with their spoken words. Learning and managing the complexities and nuances of verbal and nonverbal communication often require engaging in metacommunication or the act of communicating about communication. This entry discusses Gregory Bateson's research on metacommunication and the application of metacommunication.

The Work of Gregory Bateson

Gregory Bateson (1904–1980) is well known for many scholarly contributions across a number of fields, including anthropology, psychiatry, psychology, and psychotherapy. Again and again, though, Bateson returned in his work to the significance of language and metacommunication. In particular, he explored the interactions and communication patterns in families with a member suffering from schizophrenia. The double bind theory evolved from this work highlighting the powerful impact that communication and more specifically, contradictory messaging within families, can have on individuals suffering from schizophrenia. The hallmarks of the double bind theory include the following: (a) contradictory messages to an individual that cannot be reconciled, (b) a pattern of conflicting or inconsistent messaging that cannot be identified and/or discussed, and (c) an individual finding themselves unable to escape the current communicational milieu. This interactional dynamic among family members was believed literally to be *crazy making*, eventually causing the psychosis observed in the schizophrenic individual.

As an extension of this work, and with special attention given to metacommunication through his understanding of human interactions, Bateson identified three relationship styles marked by their communication patterns. The first is the symmetrical relationship, which is distinguished by a process of equal initiation of relational interaction and response. In the second, the complimentary or asymmetrical relationship, relational dynamics and processes are dominated primarily by one individual while the other person is mostly responsible for responding. Finally, the metacomplementary relationship is one that from the outside appears to be complimentary in nature but leaves room to be driven at times by the less dominant partner. This may take the form of a direct request for assistance, guidance, or support and as a result, alter the nature of the relational dynamics.

Applications of Metacommunication

Essentially, it is impossible not to communicate (you can't not communicate). As humans, we constantly send signals and social cues that others must read and interpret and to which they must react. Metacommunication offers clues about how to interpret the conversational data we receive from another person in any given conversation and throughout its duration. For example, a teenager has hopes of hanging out with his friends in the evening after dinner and has looked forward to it all day. However, during dinner his parents inform him that his sister has a piano recital they will all be attending once they have finished eating. As they get up and clear the table and prepare to leave, it is clear by his facial expressions and posture that he is disappointed that his anticipated plans have changed. At the recital, he sits silently, staring straight ahead and refusing to interact with the rest of the family and to speak the rest of the evening. One might recognize by his body language that he is unhappy with how he spent his evening. In this same way, even refusing to speak (giving the silent treatment) is in and of itself communicating a strong message to his family about how he feels.

There are many observable modes and levels to communication, constructed of interactional patterns between people. Metacommunication can take on many characteristics and patterns or "pragmatic redundancies." For example, there may be a lack of congruency between verbal and nonverbal communication and these two sources of messaging may contradict one another. This mismatch between what is being said and everything else being communicated can cause miscommunications, confusion, complete communication breakdowns, and even conflict. When the metacommunication associated with an original message is altered or changed, the presenting message may be interpreted entirely differently. For example, this type of process occurs frequently as we attempt to decipher in our daily conversations with others if they may be joking or speaking sarcastically.

Individuals who are unable to master the nuances of metacommunication, picking up on subtle social cues, and responding appropriately may struggle socially in their personal and professional relationships. They may be targeted as a scapegoat or misunderstood in their families, social circles, or places of employment.

Janee Both Gragg

See also Communication Errors/Problems in Couples and Families; Complementary and Symmetrical Relationships; Cybernetics; Double Bind Theory; Schizophrenia and Families

Further Readings

Bateson, G. (1972). *Steps to an ecology of mind: Collected essays in anthropology, psychiatry, evolution, and epistemology.* Chicago, IL: University of Chicago Press.

Gibney, P. (2006). The double bind theory: Still crazy making after all these years. *Psychotherapy in Australia, 12*(3), 48–55.

Ruesch, J., & Bateson, G. (1951). *Communication: The social matrix of psychiatry.* New York, NY: W. W. Norton.

Stanislav, G. (1964). *Mind, nature, and consciousness: Gregory Bateson and the new paradigm.* Retrieved from http://www.stanislavgrof.com/wp-content/uploads/pdf/Gregory_Bateson.pdf

Watzlawick, P., Bavelas, J., & Jackson, D. (1967). *Pragmatics of human communication: A study of interactional patterns, pathologies, and paradoxes.* New York, NY: W. W. Norton.

METAPHORS

A metaphor is a figure of speech used to represent another concept or idea. In family and couples counseling, they are either verbal or visual representations of some part of the family or couple system that better describes what the members feel or think about their situations. Metaphors are able to help ease family anxiety by discussing painful, serious issues in an indirect way, and they allow the family and therapist to provide an illustration of the family process. For example, a therapist and family may discuss the complexities of relationships in the *Star Wars* movies and relate these complexities to issues represented in the family. Metaphors have a long history of use in the field of marital, couple, and family therapy. There are many types of metaphors (e.g., financial, sports, war), and they can be integrated into everyday language and multiple aspects of therapy. This entry discusses metaphoric language, the challenge of finding the right metaphor in a therapeutic context, and the use of metaphors to convey empathy. This entry further examines the use of metaphors in family therapy, types of metaphors, and the value of maintaining a metaphor throughout the treatment process.

Language

Metaphors apply to communication patterns. In other words, humans rarely speak with clear, direct communication, but instead use imagery or representations to communicate feelings and thoughts. For example, a parent might say about a child, "I wish he would get his stuff together." In this instance the parent uses the word *stuff* as a metaphor for the parent's expectations that the child has failed to meet. Family systems often exist within the world of the metaphor, and the family therapist has the task to help the family identify the metaphors, create new more functional metaphors, or work within the existing metaphor to begin to affect a change.

Many metaphors are part of our everyday language and are effective without explanation. Sayings such as "I feel like I'm stuck between a rock and hard place" or " I can't see the forest for the trees" use metaphor to describe complex feelings and emotions through use of visual imagery. These images are more effective for individuals who respond to visual stimuli and help paint a picture of their world rather than relying on amorphous constructs such as feeling frustrated or angry. By using the metaphor of "between a rock and hard place" to describe feelings of frustration, the therapist can delve deeper into the client's emotional life. For example, asking the client how large the rock is, what would make it move, or how many people are needed to move it allows the client to use a visual representation of his emotion and provide concrete plans for moving the boulder.

Finding the Right Metaphor

An effective tool in family therapy is the utilization of metaphor to engage the family, to demonstrate empathy, and to promote treatment; however, using an inaccurate metaphor that does not resonate with the family may cause treatment to be less effective. Finding the metaphor takes time and patience. Therapists sometimes have metaphors they prefer to use but these metaphors may not work for the family. In order to work with metaphors, the therapist must first hear the family's or couple's story in the way they tell it, listen to all family members, and identify their themes. This process should occur over several sessions, but at least more than one session.

Some questions that are useful to consider when determining what type metaphor might work best with a couple or family include the following: Do members talk about issues of power and inequality, or do they talk about lack of structure in the home? How do the parents and children relate to each other? What is the ongoing theme of the couple's or family's story? Is it trust, attachment, fear, transition, or something else? Other useful questions for finding the metaphor include learning more about how the family came together initially, how members enter and leave the family, and family rules.

Other types of metaphors include using existing books, movies, or music that resonate with the family. If the family has a favorite film, using the characters in the film to discuss family process works as a way to move the family, as does relying on stories with which the family is already familiar. For example, Disney films or fairy tales often work well as metaphors in a family context. A blended family might relate to Cinderella and the therapist could use the story as a way to identify with the feelings of the stepmother and stepchildren. Ultimately, ensuring that the metaphor fits the family or couple is most important.

Metaphors and Empathy

During the initial process of assessment and joining with the couple or family, utilizing metaphors can be a very effective tool for conveying empathy and can often be more effective than using descriptive feeling words. Metaphors provide a visual image for the therapist to illustrate what the family or couple is feeling and convey a deeper sense of understanding and emotion than feeling words alone. For example, working with a family who appears stressed and angry, a therapist might say, "it sounds like you are angry and frustrated." The members might agree with that statement, but if the therapist used a metaphor to paint a visual image of the family's stress, such as "it seems like you are on a ledge holding on as hard as you can," this statement provides a picture for the client and conveys the sense of despair and pain the family feels.

Use of Metaphors in Family Therapy Modalities

The use of metaphor exists in all family therapy modalities and many have the concept of metaphor built into their theoretical framework. For example, existential and experiential models of family therapy utilize the concepts of symbols, fantasies, and imagery to either help the family describe their current functioning or to enlist the therapist and family in a journey of using symbols as one tool toward achieving growth. For example, existential family therapy, developed by Carl Whitaker, specifically uses the notion of symbols within the family and draws upon images both from the family and the therapist to allow the family to grow. Existential therapists focus on the images and meanings beneath the family process, such as the backstage of a play. In this example, the therapist might explain that while the audience sees the play, it is the intricate behind-the-scenes drama that makes the play run. An existential therapist will also use his or her own personal history, thoughts, and impulses and attempt to make what is covert, overt. Virginia Satir's experiential model, the human validation process model, focuses on directly expressing emotions in order to improve self-esteem. Her initial goal of determining what price each members pays to the overall unit is an embedded metaphor, imagining the family as a system where each member's behavior has costs that end up making the member pay debts to each other.

Transgenerational models also utilize metaphor both in the explanation of family functioning and in the techniques used to elicit change. Murray Bowen's model utilizes the metaphors of fusion, differentiation, and triangles as explanations for family functioning. The transgenerational model's best use of metaphor is the creation of the genogram, a concrete representation of the family process in picture form. The genogram acts as a metaphor by allowing family members to represent their family history and family process using circles, square, lines, and other codes. A genogram then allows the family to talk about their system in metaphorical ways (i.e., who is cut off and where the triangles exist). As a result, the genogram paints a clear picture for the family.

Structural family therapy uses metaphor through the use of subsystems and boundaries. Describing families as having either permeable or rigid boundaries gives the family a metaphor for how members enter or leave the family. Similarly, using the concept of subsystem coalitions, alignment, and triangulation allows the therapist to draw visual shapes around the family process, which gives family members or couples a clear picture of how they relate to each other. The metaphors of triangulation and subsystems provide the family with a picture that can then be altered or redrawn as the family changes. During the therapeutic process, structural family therapists also utilize metaphors during an in-session reenactment of a family conflict. The reenactment is a metaphor or representation of what actually occurs in the home and provides the family an opportunity to restructure their family process in a safe setting. Structural therapists also use reframing, which is primarily a technique of using metaphor to change the meaning of an event or situation. For example, a structural therapist might reframe a depressed child as a bored child, indicating that the child needs more activities rather than focusing on his sadness.

In strategic family therapy, the technique of reframing is used to actively change or modify client metaphors. Reframing or relabeling is a primary technique in this treatment modality and again involves changing the image or perception of the family in order to improve communication. For example, a family may frame a domineering father as a "drill sergeant," but through discussion, the therapist may help the family to reframe him as a gentle giant. Seeing someone as a gentle giant rather than a drill sergeant opens up different ways of relating to someone and a different kind of relationship. Reframing occurs frequently as therapists attempt to reshape communication patterns. In this model, communication and behavior are viewed as representations of ongoing patterns that need to be altered.

Postmodern theories, specifically narrative therapy, are based on the belief that individuals and families relate to each other through metaphorical means. Narrative therapy, developed by Michael White and David Epston, purports that family interactions and functioning are socially constructed through the use of language and cultural interaction. The family members make meaning from the stories they tell each other and themselves about who they are and how they interact.

These socially constructed narratives serve as a way for ongoing interaction. In narrative therapy, the story is the metaphor and the process of therapy revolves around helping the client or family re-story the problem-saturated story with a new, less problem-focused narrative. This process focuses on changing the meaning of the story or metaphor from the first story and slowly incorporating different images and symbols until a new story, which better serves the family or individual, has been constructed. Common techniques used in narrative therapy include externalizations, seeing unique outcomes, coconstructing alternative stories, and using therapeutic letters. Externalizing lends itself to the use of metaphor by creating a visual representation of the identified problem. For example, once when treating a young woman for anxiety and anger, a therapist externalized her anger by describing it as an old chair given to her by an aunt. She cannot give it away, but she can move it into the attic and only take it out when the aunt comes to visit. This metaphor allowed the client to externalize herself from her anger and begin constructing a new story about how the anger entered her life. Generally, the therapist and clients work together to cocreate alternative stories and in the process, they assign different meanings to specific elements of a story. A narrative therapist uses therapeutic letters as a metaphorical tool to make suggestions and recommendations to the client.

Types of Metaphors

There are many types of metaphors that are useful in family and couples therapy, including metaphors that describe family functioning, metaphors that help re-create family functioning, and metaphors that help illicit feelings and empathy. Below are some common examples that might be useful in treatment.

Sport Metaphors

Sport metaphors involve using some type of sport as a representation for the family. The metaphor could be comparing the family to a team, such as a baseball or basketball team, discussing how members work together or if one member tries to win by himself. Sports metaphors might include a discussion of who is team captain or coach and who makes decision regarding plays. Sports metaphors also allow the family and therapist to talk about which members do not play well with others and which members might be playing a sport that does not require teamwork, such as tennis or ice skating. Reminding the family that no matter what sport you play there is always a team behind the athlete provides a tool for the family to discuss how to get along with each other. Other uses for the sport metaphor include a discussion of how members are traded or brought into the team (useful for new members entering or leaving the family), who gets sent to the minors (for baseball) and when they are called back up, who sits in a penalty box, who in the family plays the role of referee or umpire, and who keeps score of points in the family.

Work Metaphors

In work metaphors, the therapist compares the family to a work setting. Like the sports metaphor, the work metaphor focuses on hierarchies and coalitions within the workplace, letting the family discuss their own hierarchical intricacies in a less threatening, anxious matter. This metaphor is useful for talking about how employees are hired, fired, disciplined, and mentored to improve their productivity. Discussing what makes a good boss, a good working environment, or why employees would want to leave the workplace offers useful ways for the family to discuss their own home environment. Other uses for this metaphor include differentiating between a factory setting where someone does one thing all the time or a professional environment where members are responsible for multiple roles. Which members have assistants and who reports to whom also help illustrate the inner workings of the family.

War Metaphors

War metaphors are rather direct analogies to the fighting and conflict that occur in the family. Discussing which sides each member takes and how long the war continues can be an effective way to explain ongoing family conflict. For example, the therapist might ask questions about specific battles, the overall goal of the war, and what each side hopes to achieve. The therapist would be able to speak in terms of treaties and surrender and what constitutes peace.

Financial Metaphors

Financial metaphors use the symbolism surrounding payment and debt to describe family functioning. Using financial metaphors, the therapist compares the family process to members owing each other, being in debt, and exacting higher and higher prices. For example, framing ongoing acting out by a child as making the parent pay for a perceived injury allows the family and therapist to discuss what the debt is and when it will be paid off. This metaphor could include discussions about when a debt should go into collection, who collects the debt, when the member or family is bankrupt, and who gives out loans to each other.

Measurement Metaphors

The therapist who uses a measurement metaphor compares a family member to some type of measurement device, such as a thermometer, scale, or weight. For example, the therapist might compare a member to a thermometer and speak about who becomes hot or cold, or how the family regulates temperature in the family. If using a gas tank metaphor, the therapist might talk about the family being full or running out of gas and using the gas gauge to determine when to fill up. The therapist could also question the family about what happens when the gauge is broken and the family runs out of gas without warning.

Nature/Weather Metaphors

The therapist could utilize nature as a metaphor for family and individual member growth, transition, and death. Comparing the family to a forest allows for a discussion of how much sun each tree receives, how much water, how much food, which animals live in the trees, and what happens when trees die or autumn comes and the leaves fall. Comparing the family lifecycle to stormy weather also provides a metaphor for change and gives the family language to discuss conflict and peace. Families often struggle through transition and growth and using nature as a metaphor for the life cycle allows the family to talk about seasons and the normal process of change.

Cooking/Building Metaphors

Cooking or building metaphors are useful for discussing the process of blending families and decision-making. Discussing how to follow a recipe or having "too many cooks in the kitchen" helps the family clarify roles. Discussing the process of building a house allows the family and therapist to talk about the foundation of the family, the members working together to finish a project, and how individual tastes differ but together create a finished project.

Family Metaphors

Families often speak in their own metaphorical language and an astute family and couple therapist will utilize the language of the family to affect change. For example, a family member might describe herself as a "stage mom" and rather than shifting to another metaphor, staying in the metaphor of what a "stage mom" does and how she supports her family makes the use of metaphor more meaningful to the members.

Maintaining the Metaphor Throughout Treatment

Once the family and/or therapist have identified a metaphor that appears to work, the challenge then becomes continuing treatment in the metaphor. A therapist might be too eager to use many metaphors, or use the metaphor in one session and then not continue its use, but for the metaphor to be of most use to the client, the metaphor should be continued throughout the course of treatment, returning often to the visual imagery and even creating physical manifestations of the metaphor in order to help the family grow. For example, if the family chooses a sports metaphors, giving each member a hat with their position that they wear during treatment keeps the treatment in the metaphorical realm. The members might change hats during the course of treatment and therefore the metaphor becomes the new modality for family functioning.

Sheri Pickover

See also Clinical Interviews With Couples and Families; Collaborative Language Systems; Communication Errors/Problems in Couples and Families; Empathy; Postmodern Therapies; Power Issues in Couples

Further Readings

Burns, G. W. (2001). *101 healing stories: Using metaphors in therapy* Hoboken, NJ: Wiley.

Davies, E. W. (2013). Warriors, authors and baseball coaches: The meaning of metaphor in theories of family therapy. *Journal of Family Therapy, 35*(1), 66–88. doi:http://dx.doi.org/10.1111/j.1467-6427.2011.00537.x

Eckstein, D., & Sarnoff, D. (2007). Four Adlerian metaphors applied to couples counseling. *The Journal of Individual Psychology,63*(3), 322–338.

Legowski, T., & Brownlee, K. (2001). Working with metaphor in narrative therapy. *Journal of Family Psychotherapy, 12*(1), 19–28. doi:http://dx.doi.org/10.1300/J085v12n01_02

Mills, J. C., & Crowley, R. J. (2014). *Therapeutic metaphors for children and the child within* (2nd ed.). New York, NY: Routledge.

Pernicano, P. (2010). *Family-focused trauma intervention: Using metaphor and play with victims of abuse and neglect*. Lanham, MD: Jason Aronson.

Rattray, S. L. (2004). The use of metaphor. In J. S. Gottman (Ed.), *The marriage clinic casebook* (pp. 155–164). New York, NY: W. W. Norton.

Sween, E. (2000). Using the metaphor of teamwork in narrative couples therapy. *Journal of Systemic Therapies, 19*(3), 76–82. Retrieved from http://search.proquest.com/docview/619520314?accountid=28018

White, M., & Epston, D. (1989). *Literate means to therapeutic ends*. Adelaide, Australia: Dulwich Centre. Retrieved from http://search.proquest.com/docview/617678014?accountid=28018

MILAN TEAM

The basic process of family therapy established by Gregory Bateson and Jay Haley has become integrated into fundamental understandings of families, family dynamics, and the process of change. Some of the specifics of strategic family therapy have left lasting impressions on the field of family therapy. Family therapy concepts, such as rituals, positive connotation, and circular questioning, are identified as essential assessment techniques to understanding family dynamics that other models, such as the Milan team approach, still utilize, even if they use different terms to describe the therapeutic process.

The Milan team approach draws attention to the presenting problem in the context of the family system. Additionally, the Milan team approach built their therapeutic framework on the idea that families are self-regulated systems that function based on self-developed rules tested over time through a process of trial and error. This therapeutic framework has added to the field of marriage and family therapy because it introduced the idea that the rules of the family system determine what behaviors are allowed and not allowed in each particular family system. This entry provides a brief history of Milan systemic family therapy. Specifically, this entry examines the transition from the Milan Group to Milan systemic family therapy and offers a description of the therapy process, techniques used in therapy, and the three guidelines of therapy. The entry concludes with a description of the use of circular questioning.

History of Milan Systemic Family Therapy

In the mid-1970s, a team of Italian family therapists were the first non-American group to immerse themselves in ideas from family therapists in the

United States. This group of Italian family therapists, from Milan, engaged in the ideas derived from the roots of the Mental Research Institution and Jay Haley and Cloe Madanes's versions of strategic family therapy, which are both influenced by the work of Bateson.

In 1971, the group split and there remained four psychiatrists, Mara Selvini Palazzoli, Luigi Boscolo, Gianfranco Cecchin, and Giuliana Prata, who formed a team of family therapists, referred to as the Milan Group. They drew their inspiration from the Palo Alto group, Paul Watzlawick's 1967 publication *Pragmatics of Human Communication,* and the writings of Bateson. The Milan Group was interested in both the interactional patterns demonstrated within a family system and the therapeutic relationship that existed between the therapist and family.

This interest led to the development of a team approach to treatment. The Milan Group developed a model that incorporated a male–female team approach with a male–female cotherapist team treating the family and a male–female team behind the one-way mirror. The team would meet without the family in the middle of the session to discuss the first part of the therapy and devise an intervention for the second half of the therapy session. Additionally, the sessions were held 1 month apart to give families time to react to the interventions, and the total number of sessions was usually limited to 10. Two basic interventions, *positive connotation* and *rituals,* were used as components of the model.

In 1979, the Milan Group wrote a major paper, "Hypothesizing–Circularity–Neutrality: Three Guidelines for the Conductor of the Session." This paper focused on their transition away from paradoxical interventions and began to focus more on the interactional process between family and therapist. Their new approach to family therapy was grounded in the idea that all hypotheses were due to the interaction between the therapist and family. This idea was further explained as a feedback loop: the therapy process consisted of the therapists' questions, the family's answers, and the subsequent questions the therapist would ask the family. Their approach became known as Milan systemic family therapy because of its focus on the interactional patterns of the therapist–client relationship.

Eventually a split in the Milan team occurred; Boscolo and Cecchin's ideas had remained consistent with those initially presented in "Hypothesizing–Circularity–Neutrality" and referred to themselves as the Milan Associates. Palazzoli and Prata, however, began experimenting with the concept of an invariant prescription for treating severe psychopathology. After the split, the theoretical framework of Milan systemic family therapy was drawn from Boscolo and Cecchin's views of the family as a constantly evolving system. The role of the team is to help the family develop an alternative way of interacting by introducing new information into the family system; the new information is invited as a way to promote spontaneous change in the system. Boscolo and Cecchin's work expanded the use of circular questioning as the focus of the family therapy process.

The Therapy Process

The therapist begins working with the family from the first telephone call. Although this contact is short, the therapist is provided with information to begin formulating a hypothesis about what seems to be occurring in the family. Families were seen by a male–female dyad and observed by other team members in male–female dyads. The session was divided into five parts.

In the *presession* the therapist, and sometimes the team, comes up with an initial hypotheses. The information, typically gathered from the initial telephone call or intake session, is used to help the therapist and team develop some initial hypotheses about what may be occurring within the family system. Additionally, during this stage, four phases of the therapy process take place. Phase 1 consists of the therapist joining and building rapport with the family. Phase 2 involves the therapist working with the family to understand the presenting issues and identify the problem. Lastly, Phase 3 consists of the assessment of the family dynamics. During this phase, the therapist has an opportunity to validate, modify, and change the hypothesis. Phase 4 is the conclusion; during this phase, an intervention is delivered.

The *session* is over when the therapist begins to interact with the family to determine what the rules of the system are, and therefore, is able to form an initial hypothesis. During the session, the therapist does not make any interpretations. The session is designed for the therapist to make attempts to validate and/or modify the hypotheses developed during the *presession*.

The third part of the session is the *midsession break*. During this part of the session, the assigned therapist(s) in the room with the family takes a break and discusses what occurred with the team of therapists; the reflecting team watching from behind a one-way mirror. The discussion focuses on whether new hypotheses need to be developed and what intervention should be given to the family. During this part of the session, Phase 4 of the therapy process takes places but goals generally are not set. The therapist must trust the system to resolve itself and trust the systemic family therapy process.

The fourth part of the session is the conclusion, also referred to as termination. The therapist returns to deliver the intervention, either a positive connotation or a ritual, which is also given in the form of a paradoxical intervention. In some instances, the therapist leaves the room immediately after delivering the intervention so that family members cannot disqualify the intervention.

The final part of the session is the *postsession discussion*. The team of therapists provides an analysis of the session and formulates a plan for the next session (session to take place one month later). Additionally, the team of therapists also includes in their discussion how the family reacted to the intervention and makes some hypotheses, which will be used for the *presession* of the next month's session.

Techniques of Therapy

Paradoxical Interventions

Most notable was the group's growing disenchantment with paradoxical interventions and their evolving belief in the importance of the process of the therapy session. Paradoxical interventions are described as asking the family to do something that seems in opposition to the goals of treatment. The team conceptualized family problems as being maintained by a tendency to resist change, and therefore the team or therapist would implement a paradoxical intervention to counter this tendency of resisting changing.

Positive Connotation

Positive connotation, derived from the technique of reframing symptoms as serving a protective function, and the intervention itself share the goal of altering the way the symptom is viewed by the family. Positive connotation aims to circumvent (reframe) the patient's behavior from having a negative impact upon the family so it can serve to build resiliency within a family system. The Milan Group believed that people could not easily change under the influence of negative connotation. A negative connotation is described as diagnostic labeling or implicates the person with the diagnosis. Positive connotation, by contrast, avoids diagnostic labeling or blame by assigning a positive motive or value to each family member's behavior. However, the group also wanted there to be a clear distinction between positive connotations and reframing. Reframing can be positive or negative, and more significantly, it is directed toward one family member and ascribes meaning to a behavior. Positive connotations address every family member's part in the circular process that maintains the problematic interactions and is systemic.

Furthermore, the use of positive connotations allows the family therapist to identify the problematic behavior of one family member as preserving a healthy balance within the family. Additionally, the therapist would identify the connection between the specific problem behavior and the family system need it meets and then tell the family it ought not to change this pattern. Once this chain of behavior is identified and encouraged to continue, the strategic family therapist would employ other techniques to help the family see the destructive nature of this pattern. Moreover, the use of positive connotations is for the family to see the symptomatic or identified patient in a more favorable light (e.g., to see how the symptom may actually be something to welcome).

Rituals

Rituals are interventions that enhance a positive connotation or require the family to either exaggerate or violate family rules. This intervention was used to engage families in a series of actions in order to highlight the patterns of interaction the family may have established that maintain the identified patient. Rituals were also used to dramatize positive connotations. For example, each family member might have to express his or her gratitude each night to the patient for having a problem. The Milan Group also devised a set of rituals based on an "odd and even days" format. For example, a family in which the parents were deadlocked over parental control might be told that on "even days" of the week father should be in charge of the patient's behavior and mother should act as if she weren't there. On "odd days," the mother is in charge and the father stays out of the way. This technique of using a ritual to dramatize positive connotation is designed to interrupt the family's rigid sequences and to encourage the family to react differently to each other.

As the Milan Group became popular, they were often asked to conduct presentations of their newly developed model of the team approach to working with families. In 1978, the team wrote their first text, *Paradox and Counterparadox (Paradoxical Intervention)*, which focused on the use of paradox in the treatment of a family member who suffered from severe psychosis; the text also outlined the use of their treatment team approach.

Three Guidelines of Therapy

Hypothesizing refers to the therapist developing reasons for the family's behavior within a systemic context. The therapist is constantly generating hypotheses regarding the reason the family demonstrates certain interactional behavior as it does. Additionally, all hypotheses generated by the therapist and family are considered and treated as equally valid. Hypothesizing is the therapist's way of confirming or disconfirming necessary information regarding how the family functions and how the therapist conceptualizes their functioning. The process of hypothesizing typically begins with an initial telephone call from the family. Prior to the *session* stage of the therapy process, the therapist and reflecting team exhausts all possible hypotheses about the family's symptoms and functioning based on the telephone conversation.

Circularity has two functions. The first function is to recognize the interactional nature of families. An individual's behavior is part of a sequence of behaviors in a family. The second function refers to the interactional relationship between the therapist and each family member or family system as a whole. Circularity exists in the way the therapist conducts the session through a series of posed circular questions. Through the use of circular questions, in which one family member is asked to comment on the interactional behaviors of the others, the therapist develops a systemic picture of the family's behavior. By conducting the session in this way, new information is introduced, permitting family members to experience themselves in a new context. Additionally, the therapist's hypotheses also evolve as they receive feedback from the family as they respond to the questions. The original Milan team asserted that conducting a session, with the use of circular questions, would introduce enough new information that change could take place in the family system as family members developed a heightened awareness of their shared interactional behaviors.

Therapist neutrality is an essential component of this approach because it holds all aspects of the family process together. The therapist is free to experience the system in its entirety by avoiding issues of judgment, hierarchy, power, and most significantly, taking sides with particular family members. Milan therapists typically intervene by asking circular questions and developing hypotheses of interactional behaviors of the entire family system and providing end-of-session tasks designed to generate more information about the family in its entirety. In other words, therapists assign homework for the entire family, rather than only one particular family member in the family system. Homework is expected to be conducted within the family system with contributions from all members of the family. Additionally, another essential component of neutrality refers to the therapist's ability to be open to multiple hypotheses about family behavior, including the behaviors of individual members and the family system as a whole.

Circular Questioning

Boscolo and Cecchin eventually moved away from strategic intervening (positive connotations and rituals) toward a collaborative style of therapy. This approach grew from their conclusion that the value in the Milan model was not about the strategic interventions of positive connotations and rituals, but rather the interview process itself. Consequently, they began to use and popularized the primary technique used in strategic family therapy, *circular questioning*.

Circular questions are interview questions used to learn more about changes and differences in family relationships. This method of questioning is used to gain descriptive assessments and deliver interventions through questioning of the family members and helps to better understand family patterns within the family system. Additionally, circular questions are useful in allowing family members to begin viewing themselves as a system of individuals and the significance of working as a system to resolve the identified problem. When asked about a family member, a circular question requires the family member to answer from a relationship perspective and to try and see this relationship from an empathic standpoint.

Simply, the use of circular questions helps guide identified patients from viewing the "problem" from their perspective rather than through the perspective of their family members. This kind of reflection gives family members a more holistic view of their family and better understanding of each family member's unique perspective of the family system. The goal of this technique is to influence family shifts from seeing the identified problem as residing within a single family member to seeing the role and function of the entire family system in developing and maintaining the identified problem behavior.

Furthermore, Boscolo and Cecchin discovered that the use of circular questioning must be conducted out of the therapist's genuine curiosity in an effort to create an atmosphere in which the family could arrive at new understandings of their problem or problem behaviors. If circular questioning was used for any other reason, the responses of family members would be constrained by their sense of mistrust or discomfort with the therapeutic relationship.

Tracey M. Duncan

See also Postmodern Therapies; Questions: Open, Closed, and Circular

Further Readings

Boscolo, L., Cecchin, G., Hoffman, L., & Penn, P. (1987). *Milan systemic family therapy: Conversations in theory and practice.* New York, NY: Basic Books.

Nichols, M. P. (2013). *Family therapy: Concepts and methods* (10th ed.). Upper Saddle River, NJ: Pearson.

Piercy, F. P., Sprenkle, D. H., Wetchler, J. L., & Associates. (1996). *Family therapy sourcebook* (2nd ed.). New York, NY: Guilford Press.

Rasheed, J. M., Rasheed, M. N., & Marley, J. A. (2011). *Family therapy: Models and techniques.* Thousand Oaks, CA: Sage.

Selvini Palazzoli, M., Boscolo, L., Cecchin, G., & Prata, G. (1978). *Paradox and counterparadox.* New York, NY: Jason Aronson.

Selvini Palazzoli, M., Boscolo, L., Cecchin, G., & Prata, G. (1980). Hypothesizing–circularity–neutrality: Three guidelines for the conductor of the session. *Family Process, 19*, 3–12.

Winek, J. L. (2010). *Systemic family therapy: From theory to practice.* Thousand Oaks, CA: Sage.

Military Couples and Families

Counseling military couples, families, and their children is a subspecialty of the broader field of couple and family counseling. Military families interact in accordance with systemic principles just as civilian families do. The rules, traditions, context, and culture of the military create unique challenges for both the families and the counselor. Counselors who specialize in helping military families may provide services to a wide range of military clients. This includes U.S. service members who are currently on active duty as well as veterans of World War II, the Korean War, the Cold War, the Vietnam War, and veterans of the ongoing War on Terrorism. (For the purposes of this encyclopedia entry, the terms *service member* and *warrior* are used interchangeably.)

Role of the Family Counselor

Successful family counselors recognize that members of the military are part of a unique culture. The U.S. Army, Navy, Marine Corps, Air Force, and Coast Guard are members of the military culture, yet each has a distinct subculture. If the counselor confuses the language or traditions of the client's service branch, a polite correction will likely be forthcoming.

As in all cultures, the military has its own language, acronyms, traditions, and rituals. Family counselors should aim to acquire an understanding of the characteristics of military service and be able to communicate this understanding to their clients. For example, the grocery store on a military installation is called the *commissary* and the department store is the Post Exchange (PX), Base Exchange (BX), or Naval Exchange (NEX), depending on the branch of the military it serves.

When military families are ordered to move from one location to another, it is a PCS, or permanent change of station. The reality that military families are ordered, rather than offered the opportunity, to transfer is a significant difference between the military and civilian populations, where choice is possible. Military transfers often occur at inconvenient times for the families, uprooting children from schools they have been attending and separating them from their friends. Employed spouses of service members must resign their positions and prepare for a new search at the next duty station. Most significantly, the transfer may deploy the service member to a hostile combat zone, separating the family for prolonged periods.

Many civilian counselors are concerned that their lack of knowledge of the military will be a handicap to treatment. This is not usually the case. Military families do not expect civilian mental health providers to have a comprehensive understanding of the military culture as counseling begins. The process should proceed in a successful direction provided the counselor is open and interested in being educated by the client family about its military culture with its challenges and opportunities. Family counselors must be skilled in rapidly joining and establishing a trusting relationship with each family member. Because of the stigma associated with receiving mental health treatment, the warrior may be looking for reasons not to be in counseling. Thus forming the relationship quickly is important. The counselor joins by acknowledging the challenges that the military lifestyle presents, while at the same time validating the efforts made by each member to help the family be successful. A sure way to end counseling prematurely is for the counselor to demonstrate negative attitudes toward the military culture and fail to acknowledge the sacrifices the family makes in the defense of the nation.

Military Difficulties

The most painful, difficult, and feared reality of military life is mobilization for war. This reality was most recently realized on September 11, 2001. On that day, the World Trade Center in New York City was destroyed, with the loss of over 3000 persons, followed by the attack on the Pentagon, in Washington, D.C. This resulted in an immediate mobilization of U.S. military forces to respond to the attack. Since September 11, 2001, approximately three million deployments have been ordered, including some warriors who have deployed two, three, four, or even five times. The mobilization included the National Guard and the reserves, made up of service members who train one weekend a month to prepare for the possibility of mobilization during a national emergency. These "weekend warriors" were mobilized and ordered to leave their civilian employment and their families to support the War on Terrorism. Mobilization for war is extremely stressful for full-time military families who live with the knowledge that their purpose is to wage war when necessary. The stress is even greater for reserve and National Guard families who live primarily as civilians.

The military lifestyle presents significant challenges to families. Adapting to the culture of the military services can present difficulties for them. While the service member takes an oath to defend the Constitution of the United States and must conform to the military culture and military orders, spouses and children may not. This conflict of values can lead to marriage and child problems.

Responding successfully to multiple moves is challenging, particularly when the service member is ordered to deploy to combat. Multiple separations due to combat deployments present several problems. First and foremost, family members are worried about the safety of the deployed warrior. Will they be killed or wounded? Will the service member return with psychological wounds? Can the family sustain itself knowing that the deployments are not going to stop until U.S. participation in the War on Terrorism is concluded? All of these conditions may disturb the systemic dynamics of the military family and are best diagnosed and treated by family counselors skilled at leading discussions about these concerns.

Family counselors can be called upon to help military couples resolve relationship problems that are caused by disagreements occasioned by the requirements of the military culture. They can also be of help to families with children who develop behavioral problems due to the inconsistency in their lives resulting from frequent moves and children's anxiety about the safety of a parent deployed in combat. Counselors are also important in helping families cope with the death of the service member or, in cases of severe disability, responding to the inevitable changes of the family that will be required to accommodate the disability.

History of Military Family Counselors

The most frequent need for military family counselors since the beginning of the War on Terrorism has been to help families return to *their new normal* after dealing with combat deployments. Both the deployed warrior and the spouse who "kept the home fire burning" assume that when the deployment is over, their lives will resume as they were before the separation. This is usually an erroneous assumption and one that leads to marital conflict. Combat deployments change the service member and combat deployments change the spouse and children. Problems emerge when each spouse identifies the change in the other without recognizing the way they have changed. The common complaint goes something like this: "You have changed. You are not the same person who left the family 12 months ago." The response is: "And you are not the same person I left a year ago." The family counselor with systemic intervention skill can help the spouses recognize their interactional patterns and help them learn that each is correct because both have changed. Then the counselor helps the couple come to know each other anew, postdeployment, and develop their relationship based on the people they are at the present moment rather than the images sustained during the deployment.

For example, the wife who remained at home will have assumed new responsibilities during the deployment. She has assumed most of the duties of the deployed spouse while he is away, including budgeting, bill paying, home maintenance, and discipline of the children. She may not want to relinquish certain responsibilities when her husband returns. The service member may return with a more directive and insensitive approach to problem-solving, one that served him well in combat where orders must be instantly followed and negotiation is not an option. Upon redeployment, he quickly learns that the military approach is not effective in his home. In therapy, the counselor helps each spouse describe to his or her partner their own changes during the deployment and what they need from the spouse to move forward. The counselor is prepared to facilitate this discussion and to help the couple appreciate the sacrifices that each has made. It is important to identify how the children have changed as well. A common difficulty for the family occurs when the partner returns from combat expecting the children to rush in to his or her arms, welcoming the parent home with hugs and kisses. Children who were infants or toddlers during the deployment may not recognize the parent upon his or her return. This rebuff by the children can be difficult for both parents, but is especially painful for the returning warrior, who may try to hide disappointment with false bravado. The counselor can provide important information to the couple about this situation. First, the counselor normalizes the behavior of the children and assures the warrior that this is normal for many young children after a deployment and reassures him that it is not his fault. Furthermore, the counselor advises the partner that as the children see him show love and affection to their other parent, the children will gradually move toward him and join in the "group hug." However, if there is tension in the marriage, the children will sense the animosity toward the warrior and will ally with the stay-at-home parent, ensuring difficulty in reestablishing the warrior–child relationship. In these situations, the family counselor has more work to do with the couple and later the children to help the family restore stability and goodwill.

Posttraumatic Stress Disorder

Several studies have shown that approximately 20% of warriors return from combat affected by significant psychological problems. Posttraumatic stress disorder (PTSD) has been described as the signature wound of the War on Terrorism. PTSD occurs when an individual is involved in or witnesses a traumatic event. PTSD may also be caused by being closely associated with others who were involved in the traumatic event. The primary symptoms are flashbacks, nightmares, angry outbursts, trouble sleeping, and other unpleasant symptoms.

In order to ensure that appropriate Veterans Administration health care is available for service members discharged from the military, military mental health professionals have diagnosed PTSD symptoms broadly, sometimes providing the diagnosis even when all criteria are not met. Other professionals have suggested that the PTSD diagnosis is used too frequently and that combat stress reactions occur on a continuum ranging from mild symptoms that can be managed with traditional therapeutic interventions to severe symptoms, meeting all the criteria for PTSD that disturb normal daily functioning and include disturbed relationships with family, friends, and coworkers. Those warriors with the most severe diagnoses may need inpatient treatment with appropriate psychotropic medications. Service members with less severe cases may be best treated using a family-systems, wellness-based intervention model briefly described below.

Role of the Media

The popular press has created a narrative that identifies returning combat veterans as having significant psychological problems. This narrative is widely accepted by the general public and even by the warrior's family members. Family counselors recognize that this widespread belief about returning warriors can affect treatment. Because the media has focused on descriptions of returning warriors with the most severe psychological symptoms, it is natural that family members, friends, and coworkers are predisposed to look for problems and difficulties rather than ways that the service member is functioning adequately. When family, friends, and coworkers view the warrior as dysfunctional, it is likely they will view themselves that way as well. In other words, the service member thinks, "If the general public and my family believe there is something wrong with me, maybe there is." The family counselor knows that this narrative has to be challenged and replaced with one that supports health and improvement. Furthermore, the counselor believes that systems-based therapy including the spouse, children, friendship network, and coworkers provides the best opportunity for the warrior and family to improve.

Process of Counseling

The family counselor believes the best way to help the service member is to engage all the family and other support systems in treatment. The counselor challenges the narrative of posttraumatic *dysfunction* with a new, positive, wellness-based narrative. The new narrative that is introduced and reinforced at every opportunity is one describing the warrior having *normal reactions to the abnormal circumstances of combat*. The narrative of pathology is replaced with a narrative of normalcy.

The family counselor's first encounter should be with the returning warrior alone. The purpose of this meeting is to establish trust, develop a working relationship, and describe and gain approval for the systems-based plan for treatment that will engage the entire family and key support systems in the counseling process. During this meeting the counselor introduces the warrior to the new wellness-based narrative that is the basis for treatment. Next, and as soon as possible, the counselor meets with the warrior's spouse and children. Again trust is established and the plan for treatment is introduced, gaining the partner's acceptance of the new way of viewing the problem as normal reactions to abnormal circumstances. The spouse and children are invited to participate in sessions as they and the warrior become ready. It may take several weeks before conjoint sessions begin, or they may begin immediately, depending on the readiness of the warrior, spouse, and children. In all sessions, the counselor frequently reinforces the wellness-based narrative of the warrior's symptoms being normal reactions to abnormal circumstances. Similarly, the counselor will contact members of the warrior's friendship network and military coworkers. Again the narrative of the warrior's symptoms being normal reactions to abnormal circumstances will be introduced and reinforced. Sessions that include friends and coworkers will also be scheduled.

Change-Producing Elements

Several notable change-producing elements are embedded in this systems-based, wellness approach for treating combat stress. The first element is the trusting relationship established between the service member and competent counselor who is open to learning about military service and the warrior's current situation, both the positives and the challenges. Additionally, the counselor helps the client change her internal narrative from one of dysfunction to one of wellness: *normal reaction to abnormal combat circumstances*.

Second, the family counselor recognizes and ensures that key members of the warrior's family, friendship, and work networks are engaged in the therapy process and can frequently reinforce the wellness narrative throughout the week.

Third, the systems approach provides opportunities for the warrior to interact with family and other members of other systems under the guidance of the family counselor. Any tensions or communications difficulties that may have arisen before treatment began can be resolved within the sessions.

Fourth, individual sessions are held as needed to help the warrior identify and deal with personal issues that may be unresolved. If the issues involve other important members of the family or extended support system, conjoint sessions can be arranged as the warrior becomes ready.

While this approach is not effective for all service members with combat stress symptoms, it rejects the dysfunction-based model of PTSD and offers a model that is positive, wellness-based, and includes the important people in the warrior's life. Through this process a supportive context is built around the warrior leading to changes in the warrior, as well as all those involved in the counseling process.

Military Changes

The U.S. military services are currently undergoing significant changes that are of interest to family counselors. Personnel reductions are occurring in all services, primarily driven by severe budget cuts to the U.S. Department of Defense. This has resulted in the involuntary separations from service of thousands of service members. Family counselors may be called upon to help these families resolve the problems associated with involuntary separation and transition from the military to the civilian work force.

The role of women is changing and more opportunities are being offered to them. This is especially true in the Army and Marine Corps where studies are being conducted to determine how women will fill ground combat roles in the infantry, previously an all-male assignment. The Navy is also integrating women into the submarine fleet, previously an entirely male domain.

Moreover, military relationship work for the family counselor will be different. Homosexual unions have recently been approved. Thus, family counselors may be helping couples in same-sex marriages resolve their relationship problems related to the military lifestyle.

David L. Fenell

See also Empowerment in Families; Normalizing; Posttraumatic Stress Disorder in Children; Trauma and Families; Trauma-Focused Cognitive-Behavioral Therapy

Further Readings

Barnett, J. E., & Sherman, M. D. (Eds.). (2011). Psychological services for veterans, military service members and their families [Special edition]. *Professional Psychology: Research and Practice, 42,* (1–93).

Chan, C. S. (Ed.). (2014, December). Research on psychological issues interventions for military personnel, veterans and their families [Special edition]. *Professional Psychology: Research and Practice, 45*(6), 395–513.

Chan, C. S. (Ed.). (2015). Psychological interventions for military personnel, veterans and their families, Part II [Special section]. *Professional Psychology: Research and Practice, 46,* 81–115.

Fenell, D. L. (2008, June). A distinct culture: Applying multicultural counseling competencies to work with military clients. *Counseling Today.* Retrieved from http://ct.counseling.org/2008/06/a-distinct-culture

Fenell, D. L. (2012). Counseling military families. In D. L. Fenell, *Counseling families: An introduction to marriage and family therapy* (4th ed., pp. 389–414). Denver, CO: Love.

Fenell, D. L. (2014). Counseling stoic warriors: Providing therapy to military men. In M. Englar-Carlson, M. P. Evans, & T. Duffy (Eds.), *A counselor's guide to working with men.* Alexandria, VA: American Counseling Association.

MINDFULNESS

In today's fast-paced society, busyness and stress have become the norm. The result is an increase in reactivity and disconnection within the family and within society in general. Over the past 20 years, mindfulness practices have become popular in the West as a way to address the uncertainty, stress, and disconnection of our daily lives. *Mindfulness* is defined as the intentional awareness of the present moment with acceptance of whatever arises, within our own minds, or in the surrounding environment. By lessening our resistance to what is happening in the moment, mindfulness helps us to find peace with how life is. Mindfulness also keeps us from ruminating about the past and worrying about the future by maintaining our focus on the here and now. Mindfulness has its roots in Buddhism, a philosophy that focuses on kindness and compassion for others through the use of various types of mindfulness practice. While Buddhism has become better known in the West, the growing popularity of mindfulness in the mental health field has emerged from extensive research, particularly in the field of neuroscience. One of the primary findings of this research is that mindfulness helps to regulate emotions and improve relationships. Many marriage and family counselors use mindfulness as an important component of their counseling process because of its effectiveness in helping clients understand and manage their feelings and relationships.

The Roots of Mindfulness

While some form of meditation occurs within most spiritual traditions, the roots of mindfulness practice are in Buddhism. Appreciating the original purpose of the practice may be helpful, since mindfulness can be used in different ways depending on the intention of the individual. In the West, meditation is used primarily for the individual's own benefit, to achieve greater peace of mind and enjoyment. In Buddhism, meditation is used to settle our minds in order to transcend self-preoccupation, known as ego, so we can be with life as it is, not as we wish it to be. In fact, "clinging" to one's own ego becomes a source of greater suffering because, inevitably, ego's fantasy or delusion of reality is frustrated by the reality ego is trying to avoid. Furthermore, in Buddhist psychology, true joy and happiness come through letting go of one's agenda, flowing with or accepting life's changes, and giving for the benefit of others. Mindfulness practice is really about appreciating others as they are, outside of our ego's control or agenda. Buddhists utilize various types of meditation practices for realizing how life really is and for opening the heart.

Three Types of Mindfulness Practice

Concentration Meditation

The only constant in life is change. Yet our minds seek continuity and sameness. Our plans and hopes in life are often frustrated. As a result, our minds grow anxious and agitated. Concentration meditation is designed to stabilize our reactive and discursive minds. Sitting meditation, with a focus on breath, is the most common form of concentration practice. In this practice, the individual focuses upon feeling the breath as it arises and falls naturally. At the same time, he or she continues to be aware of the senses, smelling the scent of food cooking or hearing the furnace cycle on and off, as well as being aware of thoughts and emotions that arise. Thoughts and emotions are treated in the same way as sense phenomena: the meditator becomes aware of them but maintains primary focus on the breath. Every now and then it is common for the meditator to be overcome with thoughts or emotions, so concentration on the breath is lost. As much as possible, one gently returns to the breath without judgment, appreciating that it is normal for our minds to lose focus. By learning not to be overcome by thoughts and emotions, the nervous system gradually calms down and we abide peacefully. The process of learning to accept and relax when focus is lost during concentration meditation may take days or weeks. With persistent practice, however, the mind eventually settles down. As our minds calm, we are able to see with more clarity. We see the true nature of phenomena that arise and pass. All of our senses become more acute. Other forms of concentration practice may involve walking or eating with the same method of returning attention to the object of meditation.

Loving Kindness Meditation

Concentration meditation can lead us to relax and soften our hearts and feel a natural care and compassion for others and ourselves. Often, despite good efforts, a pattern of self-criticism persists. Loving kindness meditation is a way to help arouse compassion from the heart. We simply repeat a phrase like, "May I be free from suffering, may I find peace, may I be happy." Such a phrase is to be used first for oneself, then a loved one, then a neutral person, and finally for someone with whom one may have difficulty. The phrase is repeated silently in one's mind. It can be adapted to fit a particular issue like anxiety or depression, for example, "May I be free from anxiety, may I be calm." Repetition of a phrase is meant to generate a sense of one's common suffering with others and a sense that, ultimately, our personal suffering may be better understood as the suffering of all.

Open Space Awareness

Space awareness practice is meant to connect us more fully with nature and the world around us. Most commonly in this practice, the individual ventures out of doors to experience the open space with an appreciation of the variety of our sense perceptions. As thoughts take over, just as in concentration practice, one returns to a focus on the senses and the open space. It is in open space awareness that one can more fully experience a primal interconnectedness with all living beings. Marriage and family counselors are trained to understand that as individuals, we are all embedded in systems. Open space awareness helps to develop the individual's ability to perceive first-hand the inherent embeddedness of our very being.

Research Findings

Mindfulness meditation has been found to help with a variety of problems, including depression, anxiety, stress, addiction, posttraumatic stress, pain management, immune system protection, and more. One of the most striking findings is that, with meditation, the area of the brain related to the stress response, known as the amygdala, actually shrinks while the area that integrates emotion to the broader cortex, known as the hippocampus, actually gets bigger. Meditators have also been found to have a better balance between the left and right hemispheres of the brain. The right brain overall specializes in processing emotion, and the left brain specializes in reasoning and logical thought. Thus, instead of becoming bogged down in a conflict between emotions and rationality, meditators are able to integrate these two sets of skills. Long-term meditators have also been shown to generate more "gamma waves," which are related to whole brain synchrony, suggesting the optimal use of one's intelligence. Finally, meditators seem to manage anger and conflict in relationships better than others.

Emotional Regulation and Relationships

When we become overwhelmed by emotions, two layers of experience are involved. First, the event has an impact on us. Second, we use language and thought to interpret our experience. This second layer amplifies painful experiences so that our emotions become extreme. Individuals frequently overcorrect for extreme negative emotions by shutting down their feelings or by seeking ways to anesthetize their pain through alcohol or drugs. Mindfulness, because it helps one to disengage from the content of thoughts and bring the focus of the mind to the senses, provides a way to manage emotion without shutting down and numbing. By gaining distance from the feelings, one can become clear that the immediate perception was a distortion or an exaggeration of reality. Thus, one can defuse emotion by disbelieving an immediate interpretation. One of the major problems in relationships, especially within the family, where triggers often occur, is the distortions and projections that can cause defensiveness and either escalation or withdrawal. By being able to calm oneself and mindfully discern when projections or distortions occur, one can then implement a more productive communication process so that misunderstandings can be corrected and mutual understanding can be achieved. When the amygdala is deactivated and the hippocampus is activated, we have more access to the cerebral cortex, which stores our wisdom, and we are thus more likely to be able to resolve conflicts. Meditators may also be more able to activate "mirror neurons" located in the cerebral cortex of the brain. Mirror neurons are believed to play a role in empathy and understanding of the other, which can be missing when a family is in conflict.

The Use of Mindfulness in Marriage and Family Therapy

Marriage and family counselors can utilize mindfulness practices as a part of the counseling process in a number of ways.

Mindfulness Practice for the Counselor

When a marriage and family counselor practices mindfulness, he or she is more likely to be able to be present with clients. Awareness, attunement, and empathy are all likely to be higher. The bonding and safety these counselor qualities engender in clients are more likely to lead them in turn to be open with the counselor and other family members.

Beginning the Session With Meditation

Clients can learn how to be more relaxed and open before a session. When marriage and family counselors begin a session with a few minutes in guided meditation, clients may be able to approach the targeted conflicts in a less defended way, and the possibility of creative solution can be optimized.

Encouraging Clients to Practice Mindfulness

If clients seem open to mindfulness practice, they can develop their own practice. Improvements in emotional regulation and empathy will greatly enhance solution finding for problems that are the focus of therapy. Clients can be encouraged to use any or all of the various types of meditation depending on the client and the nature of the problem.

Pause, Breathe, and Open

During the session itself, when defensiveness arises between family members, the counselor can suggest that clients pause, take a few deep breaths, and open to what they and others are feeling. Stepping back from being fused with strong emotions can redirect an interaction. Realizing they are experiencing more vulnerable emotions can help clients feel more empathy and understanding.

Finishing the Session With Loving Kindness Meditation

Finishing the session by offering positive wishes for whatever suffering family members may be experiencing may help to stimulate compassion and empathy for the self and each other. The counselor may lead the meditation or have the clients repeat a phrase to themselves like "May we be free from anger, may we care for one another, may we be at peace with each other." In the midst of sessions focused on problems and conflict, positive feelings and intentions can be overshadowed. Loving kindness meditation allows such feelings to surface again so a sense of care can be expressed and felt.

Conclusion

Mindfulness practices offer a way to slow down and reconnect with ourselves and with each other. The original intention of mindfulness practice, which has its origins in Buddhism, is for the individual to be more concerned about benefiting others than one's self. Various types of mindfulness meditation can be used for learning to transcend the self and care for others. Since we are all embedded in larger systems, caring for others *is* caring for one's self and leads to a greater sense of joy. Research on mindfulness provides evidence of how mindfulness practices can make a difference. Marriage and family counselors can integrate mindfulness into their counseling process in a number of ways depending on the family. Mindfulness can help make counseling more effective for families and can help individuals and families affect our larger, frantic society in positive ways.

Timothy Wayne Pedigo

See also Compassion; Mindfulness and Children; Mindfulness and Couples; Mindfulness and Sex; Spirituality

Further Readings

Chodron, P. (2013). *How to meditate: A practical guide to making friends with your mind*. Boulder, CO: Sounds True.

Germer, C. K. (2009). *The mindful path to self-compassion*. New York, NY: Guilford Press.

Germer, C. K., Siegel, R. D., & Fulton, R. R. (Eds.). (2013). *Mindfulness and psychotherapy* (2nd ed.). New York, NY: Guilford Press.

Leahy, R. L., Tirch, D., & Napolitano, L. A. (2011). *Emotional regulation in psychotherapy: A practitioner's guide*. New York, NY: Guilford Press.

Love, P., & Carlson, J. (2011). *Never be lonely again: The way out of emptiness, isolation, and life unfulfilled*. Deerfield Beach, FL: Health Communications.

Siegel, D. J. (2010). *The mindful therapist*. New York, NY: W. W. Norton.

Siegel, R. D. (2010). *The mindfulness solution: Everyday practices for everyday problems*. New York, NY: Guilford Press.

Williams, M., & Penman, D. (2011). *Mindfulness: An eight-week plan for finding peace in a frantic world*. New York, NY: Rodale.

Mindfulness and Children

Mindfulness involves a person's acute awareness of their individual world. It is characterized by an intentional awareness of not just thoughts, but also emotions, sensations, and the person's environment. The focus is not on the past or the future, but what is happening in the here and now. This entry reviews the concept of mindfulness, the reported benefits of acquiring mindfulness skills, and provides examples of mindfulness practices for use with children.

Concept of Mindfulness

Although the history of mindfulness is most closely associated with the Buddhist tradition, the concept of mindfulness is not a religion or even a particular belief system. It was actually introduced as a part of the mainstream culture in the 1970s by Jon Kabat-Zinn. Kabat-Zinn created mindfulness-based stress reduction (MBSR), which is an intensive 8-week group program aimed to teach mindfulness meditation. Although the two terms *meditation* and *mindfulness* are often interchanged, they are actually different. Mindfulness is actually one type of meditation that focuses on breathing, body, senses, emotions, and awareness (thoughts). Mindfulness is considered a skill that one can learn and develop over time.

Mindful practice can be categorized as either formal or informal. Formal mindfulness practice involves intentionally setting a time to practice the skill, usually focusing on the breath, movement, or a combination of both. This type of practice actually trains the brain. Informal mindfulness is practiced during everyday life activities and events, allowing for moments of mindfulness in both personal and professional aspects.

Mindful Practices for Children

There are many mindfulness practices (both formal and informal) that can be useful for children. And many of them can be shared and discussed around the topic of the five senses. Many of the formal practices involve the breath. A first step when working with children is to have them notice their breath—feeling it go in and go out. Just this act alone allows them to be in the moment. You can even have them visualize the air going in and out of their body. Practices with the breath can include belly breathing, where the focus is making sure the breath fills up the belly. The child can watch their belly go up and go down with the breath. This forces the child to take a deep breath allowing for calmness and relaxation.

Another technique to teaching children mindfulness is through the simple act of observation. A child could pick one object in nature, such as a flower, and use her eyesight to just focus on and watch that object for a few minutes. This involves looking at the flower as if it is something you may not have seen or touched before. This may mean smelling the flower. This focus brings the child to the here and now and works with her concentration.

Mindfulness also involves a certain level of awareness, including awareness of thoughts, feelings, and more. Practicing awareness can be very beneficial. One such technique is through mindful eating. Mindful eating starts with the child deciding what he wants to eat. The act of observing whether he is hungry and what he is in the mood for allows him to be mindful. Once children choose what they are going to eat, the actual process of eating can be done in a mindful way. This involves paying attention to the different characteristics of the food, including how it feels, how it tastes, and whether or not it is cold or hot. This builds a level of awareness around the act of eating, thereby providing many benefits.

One other mindfulness practice that can be easily incorporated with children is that of gratitude and appreciation. This can easily be incorporated within normal daily activities, such as dinnertime. Each person in the family can go around the table and share one thing in his life he is thankful for that day. This again requires everyone, children included, to be in the moment.

It is important to keep in mind several considerations when working with children on mindfulness. First, keep the sessions short. Developmentally, children do not have long attention spans and therefore will become frustrated if practice is too long. Second, make mindfulness fun by using games and activities that incorporate mindfulness practice. Third, children should not be forced to practice mindfulness. Options provided during the activities allow children to progress when and how they are comfortable—for example, allowing a child to keep her eyes open rather than being required to close them during a breathing exercise.

Benefits of Mindfulness for Children

Although research is in its early stages, mindfulness has been found to provide many benefits when practiced by children. Mindfulness can assist in decreasing overall stress levels and anxiety while increasing levels of calm. It can also improve a child's impulse control by helping to improve focus and concentration. Mindfulness can help with children's emotions, by increasing the occurrence of positive emotions and allowing them to handle difficult emotions more effectively. It also allows them to build empathy toward others. This in turn can help build confidence and overall self-esteem. Mindfulness has also been found to be useful with many mental health disorders, including attention-deficit/hyperactivity disorder, anxiety, and autism. Health benefits are also associated with the practice of mindfulness, including improvements in the immune system.

Kristen L. B. Moran

See also Anxiety; Childhood Anxiety; Depression in Children; Mindfulness

Further Readings

Hanh, T. N., & Nghiem, C. C. (Eds.). (2011). *Planting seeds: Practicing mindfulness with children*. Berkeley, CA: Parallax Press.

Saltzman, A. (2014). *A still quiet place: A mindfulness program for teaching children and adolescents to ease stress and difficult emotions*. Oakland, CA: New Harbinger.

Snel, E. (2013). *Sitting still like a frog: Mindfulness exercises for kids (and their parents)*. Boulder: CO: Shambhala.

Willard, C. (2013). *Child's mind: Mindfulness practices to help our children be more focused, calm, and relaxed*. Berkeley, CA: Parallax Press.

MINDFULNESS AND COUPLES

Among recent development in couples counseling is the application of mindfulness theory and practice to couples' interactional patterns. From its roots in Buddhist and other religious and spiritual traditions, mindfulness has three main components: attention training, open awareness to the present moment, and cultivating compassion, all of which can be incorporated into the therapeutic setting. Mindfulness can be seen as an engagement with the world that is attuned to phenomena arising and passing in the present moment, with an attitude of acknowledgment and nonjudgment. Brent Atkinson's research has shown that mindfulness can aid individuals to become more attuned to their own unconscious inner experience. The intersection of mindfulness and couples suggests that by incorporating more mindfulness into a partnership, through formal and informal practice, couples can become better skilled at responding to each other in connective ways, especially during times of struggle. Mindfulness correlates with significant changes in the brain's structure and function, which may create the conditions for more satisfying relationships. The following sections discuss the three main components of mindfulness, how each can benefit a couple's interactions, and how a couple can work together to cultivate attention training, open awareness, and compassion.

Attention Training for Couples

Mindfulness within the context of a couple can be practiced in a variety of ways, both formal and informal. Individual partners can practice on their own, or couples can practice in tandem, or share in exercises together. For the first component, attention training, a fundamental practice is to sit in stillness while focusing on a chosen anchor. For example, you might choose to focus your attention on the experience of breathing in your body. Attention training occurs when your focus veers away from the breath, and then you actively return your attention to the breath. This process occurs over and over in a sitting period. Practicing in this way can be shared, as a couple can create a set time for silent sitting together in their schedule. Alternatively, the couple might take a silent walk together, each individually focusing on the pressure of their footsteps on the ground. In a more interactive format, a couple might sit facing each other with their eyes open. The goal is to use the body cues of one's partner to match the breathing pace of that partner, inhaling and exhaling together.

Attention training is beneficial for the couple as it can help a couple to be more thoughtful of how they attend to each other, especially in times of conflict. According to John and Julie Gottman, successful couples are able to attend to the positive qualities of the other in times of disagreement. Attention training can help individuals stay focused on the positive qualities of their partner, despite negative judgments of behaviors during a conflict. Attention training can also help couples stay rooted in their goal to create a particular kind of partnership, despite disagreement. Sharpening attention to one's own inner experience can provide clues to the inner experience of one's partner. Thus, knowing oneself provides greater insight into knowing the psychological needs of one's partner.

Open Monitoring for Couples

In the second component of mindfulness, open monitoring, the lens of concentration is widened, and the practitioner attends to whatever is the most prominent sensation from one moment to the next. A sensation is defined as any bodily feeling (the five senses), emotion, or thought that arises. The goal is to stay aware to the dynamic flow of experience while maintaining awareness that you are present and open. With open monitoring, the practitioner learns that sensations arise and pass on their own time, as if they have a mind of their own. Similar to attention training, open monitoring can be practiced by a couple in tandem, setting aside time to sit, walk, or eat together with the intention of staying open to whatever arises from one moment to the next. A practice called *noting* offers a way for couples to practice open monitoring in a shared experience. In noting, the couple sits together, and each person alternates sharing a one-word label for their most prominent sensation. For example, couples practicing might alternate the words *hearing*, *pressure*, *happiness*, *thinking*, *sadness*, and so on.

When an individual is emotionally primed with negative emotions, he is more likely to perpetuate a negative cycle. Open monitoring has been shown to improve a person's ability to stay emotionally flexible in the face of conflict. Thus, a couple in conflict can learn to respond to unhelpful behaviors with understanding, rather than defensiveness and retaliation. Open monitoring also adds to the skills of knowing oneself in order to know the other and increases one's ability to choose what to attend to in any interaction.

Compassion Practices for Couples

With compassion practices, mindfulness becomes a practice that leads toward the goal of cultivating greater kindness and caring. Compassion may be cultivated within the other two components, as the practitioner is mindful to recommit to a chosen anchor without blame or malice for straying. For example, when you lose your breath, or get lost in a thought, a sense of failure and frustration can arise. This is the moment for compassion, as you can use your inner voice to comfort and console while guiding yourself back to the breath or back to the next most prominent sensation. More formal compassion practices involve sitting silently with the intention of feeling love for select individuals in one's life, including oneself and one's partner. The feeling of love is generally facilitated through the use of repeated phrases and visualizations. Compassion practices can be experienced quietly together. Couples can also explore prolonged eye gazing and consensual touch as shared practices that may elicit feelings of compassion for each other.

Increasing compassion within a couple can help individuals attend to bids for affection that may usually go unnoticed. Compassion can also increase one's ability to respond favorably to these bids, especially when emerging from disagreement. Compassion for one's own shortcoming increases one's ability to accept the perceived shortcomings of one's partner.

Zvi J. Bellin

See also Affect Regulation; Attunement in Relationships; Compassion; Gottman Method Couples Therapy; Interpersonal Neurobiology, Couples and; Mindfulness and Sex

Further Readings

Atkinson, B. J. (2013). Couple and family psychology: Mindfulness training and the cultivation of secure, satisfying couple relationships. *Couple and Family Psychology: Research and Practice, 2,* 73–94. doi:10.1037/cfp0000002

Carson, J. W., Carson, K. M., Gil, K. M., & Baucom, D. H. (2004). Mindfulness-based relationship enhancement. *Behavior Therapy, 35,* 471–494. doi:10.1016/S0005-7894(04)80028-5

Gehart, D. R. (2012). *Mindfulness and acceptance in couple and family therapy.* New York, NY: Springer.

Gottman, J. M. (2011). *The science of trust: Emotional attunement for couples.* New York, NY: W. W. Norton.

MINDFULNESS AND SEX

Mindfulness can be defined as the practice of recognizing and acknowledging one's emotions and sensations, whether painful or pleasurable, in the moment and without judgment. The three key components of mindfulness are (1) a present-moment focus, (2) paying attention to one's physical and emotional feelings, and (3) approaching these with openness and acceptance (i.e., not judging or evaluating these experiences but rather acknowledging their existence). Mindfulness is a practice that has been applied for many purposes. For instance, it has been used in relaxation and meditation practices. Mindfulness is commonly associated with Buddhism, but other spiritual ideologies, especially those that practice meditation, also emphasize mindfulness. When mindfulness is discussed in the field of counseling, it is often associated with cognitive-behavioral therapy (CBT), since CBT integrates the use of meditation, intentional breathing, and other mindfulness-oriented practices into treatment. Mindfulness in the context of sexuality is of particular interest to couples counselors, since it has applications in helping sexual problems that affect relationships. When a couple's sexual activity is affected, it can lead to dissatisfaction with the relationship, or it can be an indicator of other relational issues. Though sex and intimacy can be uncomfortable for some people to discuss, they are usually necessary components for a successful relationship. This entry provides a brief overview of mindfulness techniques for treating sexual dysfunctions and concludes with some cultural considerations.

Sexual Dysfunctions and Mindfulness

Sexual activity can be affected by a number of factors, including sexual dysfunctions, such as erectile dysfunction, premature ejaculation, inability to reach orgasm, decreased sexual drive (due to medication or other factors), anxiety related to sex (e.g., performance anxiety), hyper- or hypoactive sex drive (very high or very low sexual desire), and relational difficulties that create a reluctance to become sexually intimate. Sometimes these problems are interrelated and exacerbate each other. For instance, if sexual dysfunction leads to a decrease in sexual activity, couples may become more and more reluctant to engage in sexual activity, as an absence of sexual activity becomes the norm and anxiety may increase.

Mindfulness can be used as a part of sexual interventions in order to address a variety of sexual problems and dysfunctions. Becoming more mindful during sexual interactions can help increase arousal, decrease anxiety, and increase likelihood of orgasm. In general, mindfulness is meant to help people focus on their current experience interactions. Being mindful during sexual activities involves being able to identify what one is feeling, acknowledge the emotional and physiological experiences occurring during sexual intimacy, and to be free of judgment about these emotional and physiological feelings. Being free of judgment helps keep past experiences, anxiety, relational difficulties, and other things from interfering with current sexual experiences.

Although there are many variations of mindfulness interventions that could be used with sexuality, sensate focus is a well-known technique utilized to reduce anxiety during sex. It is a three-stage process used by couples to be more in the present moment during sex. This helps them be more mindful of pleasurable feelings they are experiencing in the moment, rather than focusing on thoughts that may increase anxiety. By focusing on the experience itself, rather than on performance or the expectation of orgasm, the couple can reduce anxiety related to sex, increase enjoyment of sexual activity, and therefore, achieve a deeper intimacy and bond in the relationship. The three stages include

1. Each person takes a few minutes to touch the other person, but not the breasts or genitals during this stage. Sexual arousal is not the goal during this stage; the person being touched should be focused on the sensation of being touched and the good feelings associated with it. The person doing the touching should refrain from trying to elicit sexual arousal from their partner. Rather, their goal is to touch their partner in a way that makes them feel good.

2. The second stage is nearly identical to the first, the main difference being that touching can include the breasts and genitals, but does not have to. Again, the goal is not necessarily sexual arousal.

3. The third and final stage of sensate focus includes sexual intercourse. However, achieving orgasm is not necessarily the goal. Instead, each person focuses on the sensation and feelings they feel while engaging in intercourse.

The overall philosophy of sensate focus is to return to a focus on the pleasurable sensations during sex and reassociating sex with these positive feelings, thereby removing some of the negative associations such as performance anxiety and other thoughts that may prevent sexual pleasure.

Hypnosis and Guided Meditation in Sex Therapy

The effectiveness of hypnosis and guided meditation in clinical settings are supported by a growing body of research. Hypnosis and meditation are experiential practices related to mindfulness in that they are focused on the here and now and often encourage clients to pay attention to the physical sensations of their bodies and their emotional state. Clinicians sometimes also apply the mindfulness philosophy of encouraging the client to withhold judgment about these feelings and sensations during the experience. Hypnosis and guided meditation are similar, but the main difference is that the effects of hypnosis are often subconscious. Sometimes these effects come in the form of triggered behavioral responses, and other times they can be in the form of suggestions that can be internalized to alter one's general perspective. Hypnotherapy has been used to alter a variety of thought processes, feelings, and behaviors. Notably, hypnosis has been used with some success in helping clients quit smoking and improving self-esteem. In hypnosis, the client achieves a state of deep relaxation, similar to meditation, but the idea is that the client receives messages in her subconscious to help her alter their behavior in some positive way. The client becomes so relaxed that she may not even realize what the messages were, which certainly requires a great deal of trust.

In the context of mindfulness, hypnosis may be used to help the client internalize suggestions to be more present focused in their daily lives. For example, the clinician may give the client hypnotic suggestions while in trance to acknowledge his emotions during stressful times and apply coping skills. For clients experiencing some form of sexual dysfunction, the message may be to be more present focused during sexual interaction with one's partner.

Additionally, hypnosis is sometimes used to strengthen the sexual bond or to improve sexual performance (e.g., premature ejaculation in men). Additionally, some women have never experienced an orgasm, which is another application for hypnosis. As orgasm and sexual arousal are not simply physiological, but are also rather deeply connected to one's mind, so hypnosis can be a key contributor in helping overcome this problem. With hypnosis, emotional barriers to achieving orgasm can be removed, and the client may be able to achieve the emotional state necessary to reach climax when eventually having sexual interaction with her or his partner. Counselors sometimes apply hypnosis in session or give clients a recording. Counselors who have received the proper training have even applied hypnosis while the couple recreates the sexual dysfunction.

As one might imagine, hypnosis can be an intense experience for clients, especially when it involves sexuality. It can be powerfully helpful when appropriately applied, but it can also be damaging when not used properly. Additionally, some clients may be resistant to the idea, seeing it as "mind control," although hypnosis is only effective in altering a person in the way she or he wishes to be altered. All hypnosis is ultimately self-hypnosis and is not effective on unwilling participants. Still, counselors should seek considerable training in this area before applying hypnosis in session.

Meditation, similar in some ways to hypnosis, is often guided by the clinician and then taught to the client for his own independent practice at home between sessions. It can be used as a coping skill during stressful times and for daily use to "set the tone" for the day in a positive way. Specifically, clinicians can teach clients mindfulness meditation. Mindfulness meditation is a form of meditation in which the client silences her mind. The client focuses on an automatic bodily function such as her breathing or heartbeat. Then, rather than trying to extinguish all thoughts, the client simply notices the thoughts and feelings that arise and accepts them without judgment. Periodically, she or he returns attention to the breathing or heartbeat to reset.

The purpose of mindfulness meditation is to "be kind" to oneself and/or to forgive oneself. This concept has a number of applications for sexuality. For instance, those experiencing performance anxiety or premature ejaculation (problems based in anxiety and self-judgment) may adapt this technique to increase confidence and decrease the self-criticism that may be at the root of this problem. Specifically, she or he could begin by focusing on breathing or heartbeat as normal, then prompt themselves to think about the notion of engaging in sexual activity with her or his partner, and then note the thoughts and feelings that arise while withholding judgment. The theory behind such a technique is that these feelings can be more easily resolved when they are better understood and when one has compassion for oneself. The process may also help the client forgive her or his own perceived shortcomings and adopt a more realistic self-perception, which may lead to less anxiety during intercourse and therefore resolve the sexual dysfunction.

Another application of mindfulness meditation within the context of sexuality is related to visualization. Using this method, people experiencing anxiety-related sexual dysfunction will imagine themselves having the sexual experience that brings them anxiety and then use the mindfulness thought process (recognizing and acknowledging thoughts and feelings without judgment) to "practice" in a safe environment without the risk associated with "failure." The idea behind the technique is that the anxiety-provoking experience is emulated, but instead of having the experience as normal, the client is guided through the mindfulness thought process to get in touch with her or his own thoughts and feelings, which generally leads to having more compassion for oneself. This increased self-compassion should, in theory, lead to decreased anxiety and help begin resolving the sexual dysfunction.

Erik Braun

See also Erectile Disorder; Female Orgasmic Disorder; Female Sexual Interest Disorder/Arousal Disorder; Human Sexual Response; Hypnosis; Intimacy, Specific Threats to; Male Hypoactive Sexual Desire Disorder; Premature Ejaculation; Sensate Focus; Sex Therapy; Sexual Dysfunction

Further Readings

Araoz, D., Burte, J., & Goldin, E. (2001). Sexual hypnotherapy for couples and family counselors. *Sex Therapy, 9,* 75–81.

Brotto, L. (2008). A mindfulness-based group psychoeducational intervention targeting sexual arousal disorder in women. *International Society for Sexual Medicine, 5,* 1646–1659.

Brotto, L. (2013). Mindful sex. *Canadian Journal of Human Sexuality, 22*(2), 63–68.

De Jong, D. C. (2009). The role of attention in sexual arousal: Implications for treatment of sexual dysfunction. *Journal of Sex Research, 46,* 237–248.

Miracle Question

The miracle question is a technique created by Steve de Shazer and Insoo Kim Berg from a solution-focused brief therapy approach. The miracle question is designed to help people focus on what they want (rather than what they do not want) in order to help clients and clinicians create goals and focus on solutions, rather than focusing on problems. This technique helps the client imagine a world in which the problems they are seeking help for do not exist. Although there are variations of the basic question, Berg and de Shazer's version of the question asks, "Suppose one night, while you were asleep, there was a miracle and your problem was solved. How would you know? What would be different?" Through this question, therapists are able to help clients focus on the future rather than remain in the present or stuck in the past. In addition, the miracle question allows clients to think differently and creatively about what they want for the future. Essentially, it is a goal-setting technique that can help individuals, couples, and families clarify what they want out of therapy. This entry examines the miracle question and how it functions within solution-focused therapy, as well as potential challenges in using the technique.

The Power of the Miracle Question

The power of the miracle question lies in the process of fantasizing about a life that is no longer constrained by "real life." In addition, by explaining what their life might look like in the absence of problems, clients create a specific, behavioral plan for change. The clinician asks the client to describe minute-to-minute changes in one's day and relationships "when the problem is gone." The clinician asks questions like, "What is the first thing you notice when you wake up in the morning that tells you your problems are gone? Who is the first person to notice changes in you with your problems gone? How can they tell—what are they seeing or hearing you do differently?" Based on what someone describes in their "miracle," the clients and clinician can identify things that already occur in their real life and things that they could make happen in their real life.

The miracle question has several advantages in addition to helping people formulate goals. It helps people visualize changes, and it is easier to achieve what one can visualize. In addition, it helps people to identify exceptions to problems (parts of the miracle usually already occur in one's life). Finally, the miracle question helps clients see the impact that problems have not only on themselves, but on the perceptions and behaviors of others. Clients are constantly asked who would notice changes in the clients when their problems are gone and how that changes their relationship with those people. At times, clients share scenarios of impossible circumstances. It is important for therapists to have the client explore these details, because that information can lead to a deeper grasp of the goals for therapy.

Other Models and the Miracle Question

Even though the miracle question is grounded in the brief approaches to therapy, professionals from other areas utilize the miracle question, or a version of it, to guide people's thoughts. Solution-focused brief therapy is part of the larger postmodern approach to therapy, which recognizes the expertise of the client in understanding his or her own reality and the importance of language in influencing one's view of problems and solutions. The miracle question can work with almost any postmodern approach and/or approach that focuses on client strengths. For example, individuals working with community organizations can use the miracle question as a tool for strategic planning. Social workers may use this technique to help individuals imagine a better life. Marriage and family therapists use the miracle question to improve communication and help couples and families set goals.

Challenges Associated With Using the Miracle Question

The miracle question technique is deceptively simple. Novice therapists often mistake this technique as easy to use and may believe it leads to quick solutions for clients. However, it takes therapists a great deal of practice to learn the best ways to help their clients explore the details of a world where their problem no longer exists. Often, therapists unfamiliar with the complexity of the technique fail to engage clients in a thorough visualization process. As a result, clients initially respond that they "do not know" what the world, free of their problem, looks like. Therapists should explore how to use the miracle question effectively, and this includes using a calm tone and appropriate pauses.

Skilled therapists who use the miracle question effectively resemble the work done by hypnotherapists to bring clients into suggestive states. This connection is due to the influence of Milton Erickson, a hypnotherapist who de Shazer mentions frequently in his early text, *Keys to Solutions in Brief Therapy*. Erickson's focus on small and manageable change also influenced de Shazer's technique. However, de Shazer notes that therapists can find it challenging to direct clients away from their problems and toward a solution. It takes training, practice, and patience to engage in such work. De Shazer and his colleagues describe the miracle question, as well as proper utilization of the technique, in significant detail in *More Than Miracles: The State of the Art of Solution-focused Brief Therapy*. In their study, they emphasize that every step of how to ask the question must reflect the purposeful manner in which the therapist designs the question in order to meet the specific needs and story of the client. This allows the client to participate in the visualization process necessary to construct the world where the problem does not exist. Given the above challenges in applying this technique, researchers should continue to explore effective ways that counselors and marriage and family therapy training programs can prepare students to utilize solution-focused brief therapy and the miracle question.

Shauna Lynn Nefos Webb

See also Goals, Treatment; Hypnosis; Postmodern Therapies; Social Constructionism; Solution-Focused Brief Therapy

Further Readings

De Jong, P., & Berg, I. K. (2002). *Interviewing for solutions* (2nd ed.). Pacific Grove, CA: Brooks/Cole.

De Shazer, S. (1988). *Clues: Investigating solutions in brief therapy*. New York, NY: W. W. Norton.

De Shazer, S., Dolan, Y., Korman, H., McCollum, E., Trepper, T., & Berg, I. K. (2007). *More than miracles: The state of the art of solution-focused brief therapy*. New York, NY: Haworth Press.

Mood Disorders in Adolescents

Mood disorders are mental health disorders in which difficulties in emotional regulation cause distress and hinder activities of daily living. Mood disorders, such as depression and bipolar traits, can be common among adolescents. Because mood disorders tend to manifest by interfering with academic and social interactions, they may interfere with development and lead to other disorders such as substance use, anxiety, oppositional defiant disorder, or conduct disorder. Manifestations of mood disorders include sadness and mania. Depression is generally marked by sadness and disturbances in appetite, sleep, energy, and focus. This can include overeating, loss of appetite, or sleeping too much or not enough. Severe depression is more dramatic and features hopelessness and suicidal thoughts or attempts. Mood disorders are different from bereavement, where experiencing grief is natural. Rather, a mood disorder is clinically notable in adolescents when the behaviors interfere with activities of daily living and are outside the norms for typical adolescent development. Youth experience sadness, confusion, and anger, but when those feelings persist and manifest themselves in clinically relevant ways that impair them in school, home, or social situations at high frequencies, the disorder may be present. This entry offers a summary of the symptoms and risk factors for mood disorders and describes the mood disorder symptoms common among adolescents, including disruptive mood dysregulation disorder, major depressive disorder, persistent depressive disorder, premenstrual dysmorphic disorder, substance- and medication-induced depressive disorder, and bipolar traits. The entry concludes by briefly discussing some possible treatment concepts.

Risk Factors

Youth who live in households where parents or family have mental illness are at risk for depression, due to both the environment and genetic factors. A number of stressors in an adolescent's life may contribute to risk. Medical conditions, in both the adolescent and other family members, also increase the risk. Youth with mood disorders often attempt to treat or escape the condition through substance use, so substance use disorder is a common co-occurring diagnosis.

Mood Disorder Symptoms

Disruptive mood dysregulation disorder (DMDD) could be best characterized as extreme, chronic grumpiness with frequent temper tantrums. Irritability is one of the major markers for DMDD, punctuated with temper tantrums occurring several times per week, in varied settings, for at least a year. In addition to tantrums, the adolescent would sustain a generally irritable or disgruntled disposition most other days. A temper outburst might involve physically lashing out at others, at surrounding items, and sometimes the adolescent's self. DMDD is different from conduct disorder, as the adolescent is not lashing out at others in order to deprive them of rights, or to be cruel, but rather expressing fleeting emotional anger.

Major depressive disorder is a cluster of several depression-related symptoms measured within a given 2-week period, which may include a sad mood; lost interest in typically desirable activities; weight, sleep, and energy disturbances; and suicidal ideation or attempt. Major depression is best described as intense hopelessness. Although depressive symptoms are both culturally and developmentally normal for adolescents, those with major depressive disorder are at risk for suicide. On occasion, an adolescent will express passive suicidal ideation, which means the youth would like to die, but is not actually planning it or would be open to something external taking the adolescent's life. Traditional suicide risk assessment has tended to focus on whether the subject has a plan for suicide and the means to carry it out, which are indicative of higher risk by most suicide appraisal instruments. Often, when an adolescent expresses passive or active suicidal ideation, it is regarded by many to be a plea for attention and its veracity is questioned. However, continually neglecting suicidal ideations can lead to suicide attempts, either intended to end one's life, or to climb just to the brink of doing so without succeeding. Regardless of the motive involved in the attempt, it is treated as a dire emergency.

Persistent depressive disorder, sometimes called *dysthymia,* is a milder but lengthened form of depression, which lasts at least 1 year for a child or adolescent diagnosis (2 years for adults). It can coexist with major depressive disorder, which is more severe and acute, while persistent depressive disorder is chronic. Similar to major depression, persistent depression features a sad mood, more often than not.

Premenstrual dysphoric disorder is a set of mood disturbances, which may be experienced by adolescent females just prior to menses during most menstrual cycles over a given year. Moods may change quickly and include irritability, sadness, and anxiety. At least one of the other general depressive symptoms accompanies the mood swings, such as disturbances in focus, sleep, eating, or leisure activities; school work impairment; and physical perceptions of feeling bloated, unattractive, sore, or otherwise stressed. Sometimes these symptoms in a milder form are referred to as premenstrual syndrome. While mild versions of the symptoms of premenstrual dysphoric disorder are highly common, this disorder applies when clinically significant hindrances in relationships and activities of daily living are measurable for most of a year during menses. Menses is the period during menstruation that blood and other fluids are expelled from the uterus. This is often referred to as being on a period. Adolescent girls will begin having menstrual periods in their early teens, although some begin prior to age 10. Initial adjustment to the menstrual cycle among adolescents can be challenging, but that isolated distress is normal and would not diagnose as premenstrual dysphoric disorder.

Substance- and medication-induced depressive disorder is depression precipitated by substances or medications. It is most easily differentiated since symptoms do not exist or dissipate after discontinuing a given substance or medication. This disorder includes typical depressive traits, such as disturbances in daily life activities.

Bipolar disorder is partly a mood disorder, due to its close relationship and inclusion of depressive traits, particularly major depressive disorder, with the added feature of a manic episode. It is sometimes referred to as manic depression or manic-depressive disorder and is characterized by cycles of depression with episodes of mania. Bipolar symptoms in children and adolescents are a controversial subject because of the nature of mania, which is diagnostically significant, and its similarity to the excitement, imagination, and silliness of a child, which is not abnormal whatsoever. Mania is a form of euphoria or extreme happiness blended with unreasonably high optimism or confidence, which proves to be excessive through dangerous and erratic decisions and interactions. A manic episode may be characterized by tangential thinking with quickly changing topics and excited tones, risky aspirations, and even frustration when surrounding people do not buy in or support the thoughts or actions being expressed. The ups and downs experienced by adolescents with bipolar disorder are not like the typical mood swings that an adolescent faces; they are more drastic and cause impairment in settings like the school, family, and among peers, and they can disrupt daily life. Occasionally, an adolescent presenting with mania may simply come across as charismatic. Additionally, the delirium or grandiosity of mania is sometimes mistaken as the influence of a substance, or as another psychotic disorder, such as schizophrenia. While manic episodes must be present for bipolar disorder to be diagnosed, depression is not always necessary, although some of its traits may exist on their own. Bipolar disorder is often thought to last throughout life, although many diagnosed adults recover through the use of medication and/or a better sense of control or coping over recurring feelings that previously led to more dramatic episodes. It is most frequently diagnosed in older teens as opposed to children. Bipolar disorder often co-occurs with substance use disorders and depressive disorders.

Treatment

Models of treatment for mood disorders are numerous, but most involve medications and talk therapy.

Medication

Medications for mood disorders are typically referred to as antidepressants and are mainly categorized into selective reuptake inhibitors (SRI), monoamine oxidase inhibitors (MAOI), and tricyclics. SRIs act within the brain by blocking the reabsorption of neurotransmitters, either serotonin or norepinephrine, thereby keeping those chemicals active. The United States Food and Drug Administration warned that there is a slightly heightened risk of suicide among adolescents who take SRI medications. Despite the warning, SRIs are not easily abused and have minimal side effects compared to MAOIs and tricyclics. MAOIs also keep serotonin and norepinephrine present in the brain, as well as dopamine, another neurotransmitter. Unfortunately, MAOI side effects and risks are more frequent than those for SRIs and include blood pressure disturbances and negative interactions with other drugs and some foods. Tricyclics work similarly to SRIs and MAOIs in that they too block the absorption of serotonin, norepinephrine, and dopamine in the brain, but the medications are not consistent across all people. Overall, MAOIs and tricyclics are not often used for adolescents, as compared to SRIs. When adolescents are placed on antidepressants, they often report an immediate sense of hope or relief, but in reality the medications can take a few weeks or more before measurable effects occur. Ketamine, a very different antidepressant, which acts much faster, has gained recent support in the psychiatric community as its effects begin within hours of dosing. Ketamine's side effects are dramatic, however, and it has high potential for abuse; it is taken illegally under the street name *special K*. Bipolar disorder comes with its own set of medications, such as lithium, benzodiazepines, antipsychotics, or selected anticonvulsants. Rather than elevating mood, like the antidepressants, bipolar medications are mood stabilizers designed to address mania. The most frequent medications are lithium, an antipsychotic, and divalproex sodium (Depakote), an anticonvulsant. Medications for mental health disabilities, or psychopharmacology, can be controversial, in light of the side effects. Proponents of psychopharmaceuticals point out that while side effects abound, they tend overall to reduce behavioral risks of harm to self and others among many.

Cognitive-Behavioral Therapy

The most frequent form of talk therapy for mood disorders is cognitive-behavioral therapy (CBT). CBT is a combination of behaviorism, which seeks to teach behaviors through reinforcement, and cognitive therapy, which sees cognition as the underlying cause for behavior. CBT techniques vary considerably, but the main focus is to increase awareness about the thoughts, or cognitions, which underlie feelings and behaviors. The theory of CBT on mood disorders is that maladaptive thinking patterns are learned over time and become seemingly automatic. If the client can learn to process cognitions intentionally and evaluate whether a given thought is truly valid, says this theory, then the client can choose how to feel. For example, a client claims that he is a loser and that he never wins. His sense of hopelessness is so deep that he claims no talents. The therapist may try to engage the client in what is called a positive asset search, wherein the client considers examples of good qualities and begins to dismantle the previously firmly held automatic thought that he has no talents and always loses; sometimes the client wins. The client is encouraged to practice looking carefully at thoughts when he feels his sadness triggered and to dispute irrational thinking.

Family Therapy

Family therapy is helpful with adolescents experiencing mood disorders, in order to strengthen the immediate support system around the teen, as well as to address possible structural issues within the family unit that may underlie the depression. For instance, a depressed adolescent may be feeling emotionally neglected because another family member is considered the "problem child" or focus of concern. A family therapist would look at the child's symptoms as belonging to the family rather than just the child and look for transactional patterns within the family system that explain the depressive reactions. From this point, the therapist may try to facilitate family members' understanding of these dynamics and to teach family members communication skills appropriate to lend support to the teen or to try assignments and strategies geared toward helping the others in the family, rather than just the presenting client.

Andrew M. Byrne

See also Adolescent Behavior Disorders; Adolescent Mental Health; Anxiety Disorders in Adolescents; Bereavement; Conduct Disorder; DSM and V-Codes; Loss; Oppositional Defiant Disorder; Substance Use Disorders in Adolescence; Suicide

Further Readings

American Psychiatric Association. (2013). *Diagnostic and statistical manual of mental disorders, 5th edition* (DSM-5). Arlington VA: Author.

Angst, J. (2013). Bipolar disorders in DSM-5: Strengths, problems and perspectives. *International Journal of Bipolar Disorders, 1*, 1–3. doi:10.1186/2194-7511-1-12

Beck, J. S. (2011). *Cognitive behavior therapy: Basics and beyond* (2nd ed.). New York, NY: Guilford Press.

Burns, D. D. (2008). *Feeling good: The new mood therapy.* New York, NY: HarperCollins.

Friedman, R. A. (2012). Grief, depression and the DSM-5. *New England Journal of Medicine, 366*, 1855–1857.

Jongsma, A. E., Peterson, L. M., McInnis, W. P., & Bruce, T. J. (2014). *The adolescent psychotherapy treatment planner* (5th ed.). Hoboken, NJ: Wiley.

Tompson, M. C., McNeil, F. M., Rea, M. M., & Asarnow, J. R. (2000). Identifying and treating adolescent depression. *Evidence-Based Case Review, 172*, 172–176.

MOOD DISORDERS IN CHILDREN

Mood disorders, sometimes called *affective disorders*, are a group of mental health conditions that are characterized by instability (extreme elevations and/or lowering) of an individual's emotional state. Some of the most common mood disorders are major depression, dysthymia (a chronic, low-grade depression lasting for more than two years), bipolar (periods of depression alternating with periods of elevated mood), mood disorder related to a medical condition, and substance-induced mood disorders (related to medications, substance abuse, exposure to toxins, or other medical treatments). Mood disorders are one of the most frequently diagnosed mental health disorders in children. Children commonly demonstrate signs and symptoms of mood disorders differently than adults, and because children can struggle to express their feelings, making an accurate diagnosis can be difficult. Current research suggests that although mood disorders are one of the more frequently diagnosed mental health concerns in children, mood disorders in children remain underdiagnosed. A mood disorder diagnosis in children can also mean that the child is at a higher risk for developing substance abuse, anxiety, or behavior concerns.

What Causes Mood Disorders?

The origin of mood disorders in children is not well understood. Every individual has chemicals within the brain that are associated with positive mood, and others that regulate moods. Research suggests that mood disorders may be caused by an imbalance of these chemicals, exacerbated by stressful life events or a combination of both.

Mood disorders do demonstrate hereditary tendencies and are referred to as *multifactorially inherited*. This simply means that multiple causes can create the trait or condition, and it frequently involves a combination of genes from both parents. Interestingly, studies show that more often mothers tend to pass mood disorder traits to daughters and fathers tend to pass mood disorder traits to sons. Nevertheless, while children and adolescents who have a parent with a mood disorder might have a greater chance of developing a mood disorder, there is no certainty that this will happen.

Signs and Symptoms of Mood Disorders

Unhealthy moods or behaviors are not necessarily different from healthy moods and behavior. The key difference tends to be that unhealthy moods or behaviors occur too much, too little, or for too long. For example, it is perfectly healthful to wash one's hands before eating a meal. However, it is not healthful to wash one's hands every half hour or for a child to be so worried or preoccupied with handwashing that he or she can't get schoolwork completed or play with friends. Anyone can feel sad or depressed at times, but mood disorders are distinctly more intense and difficult to manage than normal feelings of sadness. Children who demonstrate persistent mood disruption or reactions that are disproportionate to events could have a mood disorder. The level of unhappiness, anger, or excitement feels as strong as a tsunami to the child experiencing it and kids can become stuck in these moods for days, weeks, or months. Thus, the frequency and duration of irregular moods is also an important consideration when it comes to children, emotions, and behavior.

Depending on a child's age and the type of symptoms present, each individual will exhibit distress in his or her own way. The following list represents some of the most common symptoms of mood disorders among children and adolescents:

- Chronic feelings of sadness
- Hopelessness or helplessness
- Impaired self-esteem
- Feeling inadequate
- Extreme guilt
- Diminished interest in customary activities or activities once enjoyed and/or relationships
- Trouble with interpersonal relationships
- Sleep or appetite instability or disruption (inability to achieve or maintain sleep, change in weight)
- Reduced energy
- Struggle to concentrate
- A reduction in the capacity to make decisions
- Suicidal ideation, gestures, or attempts
- Frequent physiological or illness complaints
- Running away or threats of running away from home
- Sensitivity to failure or rejection
- Irritability, antagonism, or hostility

In mood disorders, these feelings appear more extreme than what a child typically feels on a regular basis. The rate at which these feelings occur should also be considered, whether they last for extended periods or disrupt a child's interest in family, friends, or school. Any expression of thoughts of death or suicide should be evaluated immediately.

Risk Factors

There are a number of factors for counselors to be aware of when working with children suspected to have mood disorders.

Genetics

Females in the general population are 70% more likely to experience depression than males. Additionally, once a family member has been diagnosed with depression, the chances are increased for siblings to have the same diagnosis. The chance for bipolar disorder in males and females in the general population is roughly 3%. Again, once a person in the family has this diagnosis, the chance for siblings to have the same diagnosis is increased. There is evidence that early onset of depression or a mood disorder is associated with a significant risk of recurrence of depression and mood disorders later in life.

Environment

Unexpected life events and chronic life stressors can all influence the development of mood disorders in children. Stressors such as grief, poverty, living in a violent home and community, anxiety, posttraumatic stress disorder, parental substance abuse, learning disabilities, a history of being teased or bullied, and social isolation can all influence the development of mood disorders in children. It cannot be overemphasized that children are not miniature adults. Even the healthiest children do not always have the emotional resources to cope with daily life stressors and do not have the capacity for an adult perspective. Children routinely struggle with looking into the future and realizing that life will change, and this leaves them vulnerable for low moods. Combine this with the impulsivity of a child and it can be a combination that leaves children battling to cope on a daily basis.

Resilience

Since mood disorders tend to run in families, children who already have a vulnerability to mood disorders may also learn maladaptive coping mechanisms from their parents for dealing with difficult emotions or circumstances. Children learn to manage their feelings through their interactions with their family and peers. The emotional and physiological stress created from the inability to effectively deal with difficult emotions can create vulnerability leading to the development of a mood disorder. Evidence suggests that stress, grief, and suffering can place children at risk for depression or mood disorders. Thus, if a child is submerged in a stress-filled world, one may reasonably conclude that the risk increases for depression or mood disorders.

Types of Mood Disorders

There are many types of mood disorders that are experienced by children. The following list provides an overview of the most common types of mood disorders experienced by children and adolescents:

Bipolar disorder—manic episodes (periods of persistently elevated mood) that usually alternate with depressed periods

Disruptive mood dysregulation disorder—chronic irritability with frequent severe temper outbursts

Dysthymic disorder (dysthymia)—an ongoing, low, or irritable mood that lasts for at least one year

Major depression—a very low or irritable mood or a significant decrease in interest or pleasure in typical activities lasting 2 weeks or more

Mood disorder due to a general medical condition—depression that is triggered by a medical illness (examples include cancer, injuries, infections, and chronic medical illnesses)

Premenstrual dysmorphic disorder—this includes depressive symptoms, irritability, and tension before menstruation

Substance-induced mood disorder—symptoms of depression that are a result of exposure to medication or other forms of treatment, drug abuse, or toxins

Treatment Recommendations

A number of factors are typically included when determining specific interventions for mood disorders in children. For example, the child's age, overall health, and medical history; type of mood disorder (including whether the condition is thought to be chronic or time limited); and the child's cultural identity all have the potential to play a role in the decision-making process. Mood disorders are often successfully treated and effective interventions are rooted in an all-inclusive assessment process.

Assessment

It is important that mood disorders in children be diagnosed and treated as early as possible. Evaluating the seriousness of a particular emotional response or behavior can be challenging. Because developmental level, intellectual functioning, family dynamics, cultural identity, and health can all have implications for a child's experience, the assessment process is critical. One approach to the initial assessment of mood disorders is to consider the frequency and duration of presenting problems within several contexts, typically home and school. For example, a child's emotions and behaviors at home and when interacting with parents, siblings, or others in the household can offer key insight into where children are struggling. Exploring whether domestic violence, marital conflict, or abuse may be occurring in the home are also significant when considering a child's emotional and behavioral patterns. When examining a child's school experience, giving thoughtful consideration to both academics and to social functioning can facilitate understanding of each individual.

Whether the child is functioning at grade level and whether there are particular problems such as distractibility or intellectual deficits that contribute to the child's level of functioning are important. In addition, the child's interpersonal style is also of importance. For example, is the child responsive to authority figures such as parents and teachers, and does the child seem to relate to peers and/or siblings? How a child relates to his world at a particular age and level of functioning helps inform whether emotions or behaviors are typical for a particular age group or whether the emotions and/or behavior seems to fall outside of typical, developmentally appropriate norms.

Interventions

Mood disorders can be effectively treated. Children with mood disorders report feeling afraid and embarrassed by their moods or behavior. They also express unhappiness that they are not like other children and fear a future filled with these overwhelming feelings. Children may outgrow symptoms or may evolve into adults with chronic mood instability. Treatment should always be based on a comprehensive evaluation of the child and family. Treatment interventions may include individual counseling, family therapy, medication therapy, or somatic therapies. Counseling in combination with medication has been shown to be very effective in the treatment of mood disorders in children. For older children who are developmentally capable of focusing on changing distorted views of themselves and their environment, working through difficult relationships and learning skills to cope with their environment have shown success with the use of cognitive-behavioral and interpersonal therapy. Family counseling and consultation with the child's teachers have also shown success in decreasing negative symptoms of mood disorders and improving a child's positive functioning.

Prevention

While there have been advances in understanding symptom development and management, little is known about how to prevent mood disorders in children. Research suggests that early detection and intervention can significantly reduce the intensity of symptoms. Early intervention also promotes healthy growth and development and may ultimately lead to increased capacity to cope with life stressors and an overall improvement of the quality of life for children and adolescents with mood disorders.

Abby Dougherty
and Laura Haddock

See also Depression in Children; Disinhibited Social Engagement Disorder in Children; Parental Stress: Effects on Children; Reactive Attachment Disorder in Children; Self-Esteem in Children

Further Readings

Child Mind Institute. (2015). *Anxiety and mood disorders center.* Retrieved from http://www.childmind.org/

Child Mind Institute. (2015). *Disruptive mood dysregulation disorder.* Retrieved from http://www.childmind.org/en/health/disorder-guide/disruptive-mood-dysregulation-disorder

National Institute of Mental Health. (2015). *Bipolar disorder in children and teens (easy to read).* Retrieved from http://www.nimh.nih.gov/health/publications/bipolar-disorder-in-children-and-teens-easy-to-read/index.shtml

MORAL DIMENSIONS OF THERAPY

Providing a clear definition regarding *moral dimensions* in counseling is complicated because it is a term that encompasses many different aspects of the counseling profession. When counselors refer to *ethics*, it is often not clear whether they are referring to codes of ethics, moral values, legal limitations, social standards, or to some general sense of the term that encompasses any or all of these concepts. Early research regarding moral dimensions served as the foundational influence for the development of professional codes of ethics, and in today's graduate-level counseling programs, teaching students about morals in counseling is often intertwined with ethics. This is true for other non-counseling related professions as well. For example, researcher Friedrich Paulson defined *ethics* as the science of moral duty. This entry addresses moral dimensions and how they have been defined, including the relationship between morals and ethics; describes the role that moral dimensions play in the counseling process; defines moral dilemmas from both a client and counselor perspective; and finally, describes the counselor's role in assisting clients presenting with moral dilemmas (including useful skills and interventions to help clients act in accordance with their moral beliefs for the future).

Models and Theories

One of the most influential foundational models of ethics is K. S. Kitchner's model of principle ethics. While the model consists of several hierarchal levels, *the level of moral principles* include autonomy (freedom of action and choice), beneficence (doing good), nonmaleficence (do no harm), and justice (fairness). Referred to by Kitchner as an obligation that must be fulfilled, each moral principle was proposed as valid and justifiable in all aspects of counseling and psychological practice. Kitchner's work gained popularity in the fields of counseling and psychology given its applicability of ethical decision-making skills in practice. Kitchner, and others, defined ethics both behaviorally and attitudinally through four psychological criteria: moral sensitivity (interpreting the situation; awareness of how our actions affect others), moral judgment (judging which action is morally right or wrong), moral motivation (prioritizing moral values relative to other values), and moral character (having courage, persisting, overcoming distractions, implementing skills). Following this perspective, if these four criteria are met, the result is moral behavior.

In discussing the validity of moral principles, there are typically three different arguments. First, as early researchers proposed, moral principles are absolute and ought to be absolutely followed in all circumstances. A contrary argument is that they aren't valid at all. Morality is relative to the individual and therefore, no principles can guide us because morality is subjective. The third argument is that moral principles are neither absolute nor relative, but are always ethically relevant; thus, they should only be overturned when there are stronger ethical obligations. Regardless, the issue of validity of moral principles in counseling remains a complex one.

Role of Moral Dimensions in Counseling

As previously mentioned, it is difficult to differentiate moral dimensions from ethics and other similar concepts in counseling, since therapy is inherently a vehicle for moral reflection. Those who seek counseling are typically presenting uncertainties, anxieties, frustrations, and conflict surrounding underlying concerns related to personal happiness, duty to self and others, meaning and purpose of life, and identity concerns, all of which have moral aspects that are to be addressed in counseling. In other words, clients are often experiencing some level of moral dilemma, which arises when a moral principle conflicts with another moral principle. Counseling professionals also can experience a moral dilemma in working with a client, although this most often occurs when a personal moral value does not align with the professional codes of ethics. For example, while a counselor may have a personal moral value of supporting a client who is experiencing financial hardship (beneficence), this may interfere with professional codes of ethics that indicate that some types of support (e.g., providing financial assistance or gift giving) is an ethical violation and may actually cause harm to the patient (maleficence).

While many moral principles align with professional codes of ethics, sometimes they do not. In such circumstances, professional codes of ethics represent specific procedures and operations that counseling professionals must follow in practice. Codes of ethics act to serve the best interest of the client while also serving to protect the profession as a whole. Thus, professional codes of ethics (i.e., those set forth by the American Counseling

Association) always take precedence over any personal moral values (what counselors personally believe is right or wrong) in resolving an ethical dilemma. According to Kitchner (1984), it is best practice in ethical decision-making that when one ethical principle conflicts with another, the counselor carefully weigh, balance, and sift competing principles to determine which has precedence. This is still considered best practice today, as represented below in Holly Forester-Miller and Thomas Davis's ethical decision-making model:

Step 1: Identify the Problem

Step 2: Refer to Ethical Codes Pertaining to the Dilemma

Step 3: Determine the Nature and Dimensions of the Dilemma

Step 4: Generate Possible Courses of Action

Step 5: Consider the Possible Consequences of All Actions and Choose an Action

Step 6: Evaluate the Selected Course of Action

Forester-Miller and Davis thoroughly describe the actions that need to be taken at each step so as to prevent counselors from making unconscious, biased decisions toward a particular course of action in an attempt to resolve an ethical dilemma. When a counselor can demonstrate that a chosen course of action is the result of a thorough decision-making process, even if the results of the actions are not positive for the client, counselor negligence can be ruled out. Therefore, it is important that specific steps taken are well documented in the use of this approach or any decision-making process regarding ethical dilemmas. Additionally, while the model presented by Forester-Miller and Davis provides counselors with a step-by-step direction for resolving ethical dilemmas, legal aspects related to counseling (such as state and national laws regarding client confidentiality) set a more stringent guideline for counseling professionals. While professional codes of ethics often align with state laws, there have been circumstances where they do not and in such cases, state laws always supersede professional codes of ethics (as failure to follow a law could result in criminal charges). Links to state laws can generally be found on the website of the state licensing body.

Addressing Moral Dimensions in Practice

If moral dilemmas are embedded in client issues and present themselves throughout the counseling process, how can counselors not take a stance? Given inherent human nature, a counselor's initial response to complicated moral issues is strongly influenced by prevailing opinion. Although counselors may try to think clearly, neutrally, and independently about the complex moral dilemmas presented to them by clients, as humans, they will tend to rely on personal opinions, perceptions, and judgments that have formed over the course of their lives. Thus, if counselors pretend to be neutral or believe that their personal opinions, perceptions, and judgments will not affect clinical interventions, they are ultimately fooling themselves, since everything counselors say and/or do expresses a particular view that they have formed of the world. More importantly, if counselors attempt to conduct counseling in a neutral manner, they are avoiding confrontation of the client's most important issues. A counselor's neutrality may indicate to a client that what they decide does not matter. The client may also attempt to speculate what the counselor really thinks about the issue by imagining what he or she would approve or disapprove of. Having not expressed a view, the client has little opportunity to agree or disagree with the counselor's opinions, perceptions, and judgments regarding his or her moral dilemmas. This could further prevent overall progression for the clients with regard to developing their own understanding of their moral dilemma, in becoming familiar with those moral aspects they do or do not adhere to or believe in, and in gaining insight into their own prejudices, values, and opinions.

Counselors are moral agents, whether they acknowledge this or not (e.g., clients engage in counseling in order to seek assistance in helping them to resolve their moral dilemmas); as moral agents, counselors have a responsibility to learn to think about the moral dilemmas, principles, and matters of clients with some level of understanding. It is the counselor's goal to help the client find a way through a moral dilemma.

Applying Moral Decision-Making Skills

As part of her view regarding how counselors should intervene in moral dilemmas, researcher Emmy Van Deurzen proposed that moral dilemmas can never be completely or perfectly solved; thus, the best position is to have an open mind and an investigative nature. Each individual is unique, and neither the counselor nor the client will ever see quite the same dilemma again. Counselors must consider all the factors and take into consideration all the pros and cons of all sides of the dilemma, as well as provide a safe, clear space for clients to ponder and reflect upon such factors. In helping a client find a way through a moral dilemma, counselors should help clients think clearly about their contradictory feelings regarding their dilemma and further assist them in evaluating why they are feeling this particular way. Counselors should help clients evaluate their actions in the same manner, by helping them to clearly identify any actions they have taken in their dilemma that appear to be out of mere guilt, anxiety, fear, or cautiousness (and without consideration of all other related factors surrounding the dilemma). Van Deurzen proposed that although this process can be a complex struggle, it is done so for the purpose of teaching the client new things so that they will be able to find a meaningful, solid solution to their current dilemma and to help them determine their own moral course for the future.

In order to effectively assist clients in moral decision-making, counselors must strive for personal moral clarity. They need to be clear about what they personally believe and why they believe it; they must be able to think clearly about their own opinions, prejudices, and judgments and how these are helping and/or hindering client progress in working through their moral issues. As counseling professionals, finding moral clarity is done through the process of engaging in self-reflection so that they can evaluate the merit of their own opinions, perceptions, judgments, and actions as right or wrong and worthy or unworthy.

Danielle L. Geigle

See also Beliefs and Values; Decision-Making; Ethical Codes; Ethical Decision-Making; Therapists' Values

Further Readings

American Counseling Association. (2005). *ACA code of ethics*. Alexandria, VA: Author.

Forester-Miller, H., & Davis, T. (1996). *A practitioner's guide to ethical decision making*. Alexandria, VA: American Counseling Association. Retrieved from http://www.counseling.org/Counselors/Practitioners Guide.aspx

Hill, A. (2004). Ethical analysis in counseling: A case for narrative ethics, moral visions, and virtue ethics. *Counseling and Values, 48*, 131–148.

Kitchner, K. S. (1984). Intuition, critical evaluation and ethical principles: The foundation for ethical decisions in counseling psychology. *Counseling Psychologist, 12*, 43–55.

Kitchner, K. S. (1991). The foundations of ethical practice. *Journal of Mental Health Counseling, 13*, 236–246.

Rest, J. R. (1984). Reserach on moral development: Implications for training counseling pschologists. *The Counseling Psychologist, 12*, 19–29.

Sugarman, J., & Martin, J. (1995). The moral dimension: A conceptualization and empirical demonstration of the moral nature of psychotherapeutic conversations. *The Counseling Psychologist, 23*, 324–347.

Urofsky, R. I., Engels, D. W., & Engebretson, K. (2008). Kitchner's principle ethics: Implications for counseling practice and research. *Counseling and Values, 53*, 67–78.

Van Deurzen, E. (1999). Common sense or nonsense: Intervening in moral dilemmas. *British Journal of Guidance & Counselling, 27*, 581–586.

Morphogenesis

Morphogenesis is a systems theory concept that describes structural change within a family system. *Morphogenesis* means "creation or beginning of shape" and describes the process that causes an organism to develop its shape. In the family system, it describes a family's ability to grow and adapt to change while maintaining structural stability and balance. In this entry, morphogenesis is explained through the lens of systems theory. This is followed by a discussion of related family system concepts. The entry concludes with a discussion of how marriage, couple, and family counseling can be a resource for families who are struggling with changes within their family structure.

Morphogenesis and Systems Theory

Systems theory focuses on the interrelatedness between individuals and their environments as well as to their interactions with and adaptations to each other. Systems theory has its roots in two scientific schools of thought, or epistemologies: cybernetics and general systems theory. Cybernetics focuses on repeated patterns, or feedback loops, of stability and change. Feedback loops are defined information that comes out of a system and is input back into the system as information. Negative feedback tells a system to reduce change in the system and positive feedback tells a system that more change is needed.

Cybernetics, a term coined by mathematician Norbert Wiener in 1948, is the study of how communication systems are controlled by feedback loops. During World War II, Wiener examined how military missiles changed direction in response to their environment and found that they were able to self-regulate, or adjust, based on feedback loops from prior information. In systems theory, the family is viewed as the information-processing system and feedback loops are the messages that come in and out of the family system. Dysfunction in a family, for instance, is part of ongoing feedback loops that maintain the problem. Thus, cybernetics helps to explain how systems use feedback to remain stable or adapt to new circumstances.

During this same time biologist Ludwig von Bertalanffy, founder of general systems theory, emphasized the interconnections between the organism and the environment and that they cannot be understood in isolation from one another. General systems theory, much like cybernetics, focuses on the functional roles and structural rules in systems. In other words, individual problems are seen as problems within the family structure and flawed patterns of interaction.

Expanding on the patterns of interaction between individual and environment as proposed by cybernetics and general systems theory, researchers began to view families as communication systems. In the 1950s, Gregory Bateson and his colleagues studied patients diagnosed with schizophrenia, paying particular attention to the communication patterns between patients and their family members. They found communication patterns from a primary caretaker (parent) that often began during childhood and were contradictory and full of repeated conflicting messages that were difficult to process for the patients. This insight led the researchers to view the individual as a symptom of a dysfunctional family system, rather than independent from other members of their family. With the focus on the family as an information-processing and communication system, this research team was also influential in introducing the concepts of morphogenesis (how change occurs) and morphostasis (how the status quo is maintained).

Morphogenesis and the Family System

In order to understand how morphogenesis occurs, other major concepts of systems theory need to be explored, beginning with understanding the family as a system. A family is a social system with rules of behavior and communication, an organized hierarchy with roles, and shared history and values. Systems theory looks at the interconnections between parts of a whole (the family) rather than concentrating only on the parts (family members). In other words, a family is not only defined by whom it is comprised but also by how these individuals came together. Other key components of the family system include structure, subsystems, boundaries, morphostasis, and feedback. Structure in families is based on unspoken rules, or who does what, and over time form patterns in which family members interact. Structure consists of hierarchy of subsystems, formed by generation, gender, or function. Examples of subsystems are parent–child, spousal, siblings, and extended family members. Structure within a system is created by family values or the beliefs and perceptions about what is right and make sense to the family unit. Family values are developed based on past experiences that are familiar; for example, every Friday night the family goes out together for pizza, or children develop a strong work ethic by the example set by their parents. Even if the past experiences were destructive, such as alcoholism or infidelity, the patterns are familiar and stable. A family's structure is broken or challenged when one member does something differently, such as a defiant teenager or an alcoholic parent seeking sobriety.

Families try to control what is coming in and out in order to maintain stability and protect their members. They do this by forming emotional boundaries or invisible barriers that govern the amount of contact and the flow of information that a family allows with the outside environment as well as between subsystems within the family. Boundaries vary in degree of permeability and are influential in how a family reacts or adapts to changes or stresses. When boundaries are too permeable, too rigid, or ambiguous, dysfunction can arise. For example, within the family, there can be divorce, parental conflict, loss, or addictions in the parental subsystem altering the functional roles of parents. Outside influences, from the media, peer groups, and job stress to natural disasters and other environmental crises, also challenge functioning of families. Families who try to maintain their existing level of function despite the stressors tend to have rigid boundaries and are closed systems that avoid support from others claiming "it is a family matter." Open systems, characterized in healthy families, maintain their existence through the mutual interaction of its parts and are continuously open to the exchange of information from its environment, seeking outside sources for assistance, such as counseling or being open to feedback from their child's teacher at school.

Both morphogenesis and morphostasis are processes in which families try to find balance or stability in response to internal or external demands. What differentiates the two is that morphostasis is when a system tries to hold its shape in a changing environment and morphogenesis involves structural change.

Conceptualizing Change

Morphogenesis is a system that allows for growth, creativity, and change. Change is conceptualized in two ways: a change in structure, which involves morphostasis and morphogenesis, and a change in degree or level, which is described as first-order and second-order change in systems theory. First-order change is when a family responds to changes within the system in ways that are based on the same patterns. For example, in a family where an adolescent is breaking curfew, a first-order response by the parents is to set more restrictions by taking away her cell phone. On the surface, this may appear to be an appropriate response, as the parents are acting in ways that are familiar and doing more of the same. However, first-order change is usually not as effective in addressing the underlying issues of the family system and the undesirable behavior will return and may escalate to the teenager sneaking out. Second-order change, which addresses the family rules, is a response to changes in a system that leads to changes in the system's structure. Rather than setting more restrictions, the parents allow their teenager an extra hour before curfew, thus addressing the issue at a structural level and altering the rules to meet the changing developmental needs of the family.

Circular causality, or feedback loops, describes the process of information, or messages within the system indicating that change is needed. For example, a teenager who begins cutting herself is sent to treatment to address the self-harming behavior. She is set up with individual counseling sessions and soon the cutting ceases and behavior appears to be improving. However, when the girl's father comes home late after several hours drinking and her parents are fighting, the cutting starts again. From a systems perspective, the cutting behavior is sending a message or feedback to the family that there is something within the structure of the system that needs to be addressed beyond the individual symptom. When there is dysfunction in the family, the issue is viewed as shared among the entire family.

Through a better understanding of the interactions and characteristics of the family system, such as structure, boundaries, patterns, roles, values, and feedback loops, morphogenesis will occur and a second-order change in the family system will result in new patterns of behavior and ways of interacting.

Morphogenesis in Marriage, Couple, and Family Counseling

Most people go to counseling out of a desire for or a reaction to change. Counselors have different ways to identify and encourage desired morphogenesis. Life events, transitions, and crises can be opportunities for change. The counselor's role is to help individuals replace their existing problematic view of the world with one that better fits with their changing life course. Behaviors are influenced by continuous feedback from the environment. When working with a family, the counselor views the interrelationships found within the family system and identifies repeating patterns connecting each family member, even though only one member may be symptomatic. Since it is a change in the family system that has brought the individuals to counseling, the counselor's first task is in helping the family identify what is causing a sense of disequilibrium in the family.

Oftentimes the presenting problem is about an individual member of the family. For example, a couple brings their 12-year-old daughter to counseling out of concern that she might be depressed. Rather than focusing on the daughter's symptoms in isolation, the counselor views the family unit as a whole and identifies several events within the family system that are contributing to the daughter's symptoms, such as marital conflict or rigid boundaries that are restricting to the daughter's emerging age of adolescence. In order for morphogenesis to occur, improvement in an individual family member will not occur without changes in family structure and patterns of interaction.

In a system, all parts are interconnected, and what influences one member is going to affect the other. Symptomatic behavior of a family member is not seen as an individual problem, but as a reflection of the family interactions, structure, roles, and patterns. In conclusion, both change and stability are necessary for healthy family functioning. Equilibrium is off as a result of families reacting to change, such as separation, marriages, births, and deaths. The counselor works with the family to reestablish stability or homeostasis. This can be accomplished by looking at the strengths of the family, establishing goals focused on structural changes and establishing new routines, and using assessment tools such as genograms, which are visual diagrams of family structure, unspoken rules, and patterns across three generations.

Sarah Becerra

See also Boundaries; Circularity and Linearity; Cybernetics; Family Values; General Systems Theory; Homeostasis; Morphostasis; Positive and Negative Feedback; Systems Theory

Further Readings

Hanson, B. G. (1995). *General systems theory beginning with wholes.* New York, NY: Taylor & Francis.

Heylighen, F., & Joslyn, C. (2001). Cybernetics and second-order cybernetics. In R. A. Meyers (Ed.), *Encyclopedia of physical science & technology* (3rd ed., pp. 155–170). New York, NY: Academic Press.

Hoffman, L. (1981). *Foundations of family therapy: A conceptual framework for systems change*. New York, NY: Basic Books.

Kerr, M. E., & Bowen, M. (1988). *Family evaluation*. New York, NY: W. W. Norton.

Lee, C. (1988). Theories of family adaptability: Toward a synthesis of Olson's circumplex and the Beavers systems models. *Family Process, 27*(1), 73–96.

McGoldrick, M., & Gerson, R. (1985). *Genograms in family assessment*. New York, NY: W. W. Norton.

Watzalawick, P., Weakland, J., & Fisch, R. (1974). *Change: Principles of problem formation and problem resolution*. New York, NY: W. W. Norton.

MORPHOSTASIS

Morphostasis, in family systems theory, describes a static family structure. Families seek stability and predictability in order to maintain their perceived status quo or current way of functioning. While a sense of stability is an important component of healthy family functioning, resistance to change can result in stagnation and increased dysfunction. The purpose of this entry is to describe morphostasis and its relation to the other major concepts of family systems theory. This entry concludes with practical applications for counselors working with couples and families seeking to maintain a balance between stability and change.

Morphostasis and the Family System

Morphostasis is one of the core constructs of family systems theory. A branch of general systems theory, family systems theory describes the family as consisting of interrelated parts; it is always changing, self-organizing, and adapting to itself and the environment. In general systems theory, there is the principle of wholeness in that all parts of the system are interrelated and a change in one part of the system affects all other parts of the system. Relating this to families, the family unit as a whole is the system and its parts, or related elements, are the individual family members.

Feedback Loops

Morphostasis is the tendency for a system to retain stability. The way in which a family system self-regulates and communicates among members of the family is through feedback loops. This concept developed from the term *cybernetics*, coined by Norbert Wiener, as a result of his work studying the complex processes of feedback mechanisms of missiles during World War II. Wiener theorized that the missiles were able to self-regulate and maintain stability by incorporating feedback from the information they received. Cybernetics helped explain how a system uses feedback to remain stable or adapt to new situations. Feedback loops are described as either positive or negative, depending on the degree of action that results. Positive feedback produces change; the process by which systems change and evolve (genesis) is called *morphogenesis*. Negative feedback leads to self-correction and stability; the process by which a system retains stability (stasis) is called *morphostasis*. Negative feedback is also called *balancing feedback*, since it serves to help to bring a system back to its original structure and existing patterns of interaction. For example, if a teenager returns home after curfew, and his or her parents respond by grounding him or her for a week in an attempt to maintain the current structure and the teenager abides to avoid being grounded again, morphostasis has occurred as a result of negative feedback.

Conversely, morphogenesis occurs when a family member's response to a stimulus results in change and is identified as positive feedback. This is also known as amplifying feedback loops as they contribute to an increase in desired or undesired behavior. To return to the earlier example, in the case of morphogenesis, rather than ground a teenager who stays out past curfew, the parents may elect to extend the child's curfew by an hour in recognition of the adolescent's need for increased independence. Another example of positive feedback is when a wife smiles at her husband as he talks. If the husband notices this and remembers this smile is why he fell in love with his wife, he is likely to talk more, resulting in increased communication between the couple. Likewise, a child who complains of a stomach ache and stays home from school and receives extra attention from the mother may find another reason to complain about "not feeling well" in order to continue to receive special attention from the mother. Positive and negative feedback do not equate to good or bad. Rather, it is the outcome, action or no action, change or no change, that distinguishes positive and negative feedback.

Other important concepts in understanding morphostasis in a family system are boundaries, and open or closed systems. Boundaries, as discussed in family systems theory, are associated with the amount of information that is allowed to flow in and out of the family unit. A lack of boundaries, or boundaries that are too permeable, are features of chaotic families. On the contrary, a closed system, or one in which boundaries are too rigid or impermeable, are seen in families that are isolated, allowing very little to no communication from the outside in. Both boundaries and closed systems can exist with morphostasis, in an attempt to keep the family's current way of functioning within. Working too hard to retain the current state of being is the premise of morphostasis, which is form maintaining. Morphogenesis is form changing. Families who are rigid and enmeshed have strictly enforced rules, clearly defined roles, little private space or separation of self, and few outside friends. Chaotic and disengaged families have little discipline, a lack of role clarity, frequently changing rules, low interaction with one another, and are often in crisis from too much change and ambiguity. Ideally, the flow of information and change should be constant in an open system, which is a healthy system.

A concept closely related to morphostasis is homeostasis and the two are often used interchangeably. Homeostasis describes how a system self-regulates and resists change, particularly under stress, in an attempt to keep the system constant despite changing dynamics. This is not necessarily healthy family functioning, as homeostasis represents a psychological and emotional need for balance. The analogy of a thermostat in a house is often used to explain homeostasis. A thermostat set at 72 degrees is the comfortable temperature for everyone in the house. When the temperature drops below the desired 72 degrees, the furnace turns on until the temperature reaches 72 degrees, and then shuts off. The furnace operates by settings, or rules, that help regulate balance in the environment. Similarly, a family system is governed by a set of rules that maintain its structure. Families have rules about interaction, rules that govern communication, who says what, spoken and unspoken, all with the purpose of keeping homeostasis. If one member of the family changes, the system tries to change it back, like a thermostat, to maintain its internal structure and stability. Alternatively, the system will find a new homeostasis and adapt to individual behavior, in order to maintain stability. This adaptation is often seen in families where addiction is present. For example, if one parent is addicted to a substance, the other parent may be ashamed and spend more time at work and away from home in order to avoid the issue. An older sibling may in turn take on more responsibility to care for a younger sibling, allowing the parent with the addiction more time to abuse the substance. The family's behavior and patterns of action are maintained and reinforced by other members in the family system.

Finally, there is the family system concept of causality. Causality is either linear or circular, and refers to the precursor of events or behaviors that lead to dysfunction in the family system. Circular causality describes events that are related through ongoing feedback loops that facilitate movement toward morphogenesis or morphostasis. Thus, circular causality is a reciprocal process. With linear causality, there is a cause and effect that explains behavior. For example, a linear perspective for explaining why a teenager is defiant is a result of low self-esteem. Whereas, in a circular causality, a teenager's defiant behavior is an outcome of the way the family interacts based on their structure, rules, and beliefs. Rather than asking an argumentative couple how it began and what they argue about (the content), the counselor is more interested in how they argue (the process). What do you do? What do they do? How will you resolve this? These are all examples of circular questioning. Using circular questioning, the counselor seeks to understand patterns that connect perceptions and events to the given problem.

Morphostasis in Marriage, Couple, and Family Counseling

Morphostatic families go to great lengths to maintain the family system. This attribute can increase resistance to counseling intervention, yet it serves a purpose in maintaining a balanced family system and homeostasis. There is interdependence in the family system wherein family members mutually affect one another. For example, the dynamics of a sick child who suffers asthma attacks when the parents argue temporarily disrupts the conflict while the parents tend to the child, creating a sense of harmony in the family. This interplay of parental conflict, child's asthma attacks, and parental harmony are dynamic patterns that are stable and repetitive. Intervention by a counselor is to disrupt that homeostasis to achieve change.

Lifecycle transitions, unpredictable stressors, and crisis each pose additional challenges to families that struggle to adapt. Even normal developmental behavior upsets the morphostasis of a family system. For example, a teenager spending more time in his room on the computer and listening to music can be seen as rejection or defiant behavior in a family with strict rules of behavior. Rules in a family system become problematic when difficult to follow (never get angry, or always earn perfect grades in school) or when the rules are not modified according to the changing developmental needs of individuals within the family system.

When families encounter life stressors and are unable to cope without changes in family structure and patterns of interaction, they find themselves in a crisis and in need of counseling. A therapeutic model that promotes change is structural family therapy, proposed by Salvador Minuchin, which has a primary goal to create structural change in the family system. Structural family therapy focuses on family interactions in order to understand the structure and organization of the family. According to this model, a family in crisis is a result of structural problems, and structural change must occur in a family before symptoms can be addressed. In addition, the family system operates through subsystems that require boundaries that are clear and permeable. Families will try to maintain morphostasis or preferred patterns and structure of functioning for as long as possible. Dysfunction in families is a result of ineffective rules and difficulty adapting to environmental stressors. The counselor strives to maintain or reestablish stability in the family by promoting strengths, introducing role changes, clarifying patterns of communication, and reorganizing family structure. Assessment tools, such as genograms, assist to identify these strengths, as well as the family's current structure, including family rules, roles, hierarchy, boundaries, and values.

Morphostasis, or that which stays the same, was derived from theories that sought to clarify wholeness, structure, and how change does or does not occur. This approach has moved clinicians and researchers to seek ever-expanding forms of knowledge. By doing so, counselors can employ practical, effective models for helping individuals, couples, and families overcome resistance to change. In conclusion, morphostasis is the process of maintaining family structure within an ever-changing environment. Positive feedback indicates that change has occurred; negative feedback indicates that the existing condition is maintained. Morphogenesis occurs in response to the positive feedback that results in a change in family structure, usually growth or dissolution. In contrast, morphostasis occurs in response to the negative feedback loops which restore the order within a family system. Rather than adapting to change by adjusting rules and promoting change, or morphogenesis, the family keeps its same organization or structure, minimizing change, and retaining stability, or morphostasis. Stability is only temporary and it is not constant. Therefore, healthy family functioning involves both morphostasis and morphogenesis, or a balance among stability and change.

Sarah Becerra and Adam Coffey

See also Cybernetics; Family Rituals; General Systems Theory; Homeostasis; Morphogenesis; Positive and Negative Feedback; Structural Family Therapy; Systems Theory

Further Readings

Haley, J. (1968). *Techniques of family therapy.* New York, NY: Basic Books.

Imber-Black, E., Roberts, J., & Whitting, R. (1988). *Rituals in families and family therapy.* New York, NY: W. W. Norton.

Jackson, D. (1965). Family rules: Marital quid pro quo. *Archives of General Psychiatry, 12,* 589–594.

Keeney, B. (1983). *Aesthetics of change.* New York, NY: Guilford Press.

Minuchin, S. (1974). *Families & family therapy.* Cambridge, MA: Harvard University Press.

Speer, D. C. (1970). Family systems morphostasis and morphogenesis, or is "homeostasis" enough? *Family Process, 9*(1), 259–227.

von Bertalanffy, L. (1968). *General systems theory: Foundations, development, applications.* New York, NY: George Brazil.

Wiener, N. (1948). *Cybernetics: Or control and communication in the animal and the machine.* Cambridge: MIT Press.

Mother-Blaming

When an individual engages in mother-blaming, he or she is blaming the mother for a problematic behavior or pathology evidenced by the child. Throughout history, mothers have been held accountable when their child's behavior is viewed as atypical. In the United States, general health care providers, child development experts, and mental health providers, among others, have contributed to the tendency to blame mothers when a child experiences problems. This entry will provide an overview of the historical factors and review the current implications of mother-blaming.

Psychological Theory and Mother-Blaming

Refrigerator Mother Conceptualization

In the 1940s, John Hopkins University psychiatrist Leo Kanner attributed autism in children to the lack of parental warmth and particularly to emotionally cold mothers. He is credited with coining the disparaging term *refrigerator mother* to describe the cold and intellectual manner in which these mothers interacted with their children. The relationship between the mother and the child, which was theorized to result in psychological harm to the child, was identified as the primary cause of autism and this way of understanding the development of autism was widely accepted by psychiatrists and other health care providers until the 1970s. Bruno Bettelheim, a child development expert and professor at the University of Chicago in the 1960s and 1970s, is also viewed as a primary force in widespread acceptance of the refrigerator mother theory. He postulated autism to be a parenting, and more specifically, mothering disorder.

Psychoanalytic Theory

Psychoanalytic theory, as originated by Sigmund Freud and subsequently developed by many others, posits the notion that experiences very early in a child's life, particularly emotional trauma, cause unhealthy psychological development. As psychoanalysis became the favored approach to treatment of psychological problems, health care providers began to look for emotional causes for a variety of problems people experienced. By the 1940s, mothers, who were viewed as the primary caregivers of children and the most significant figure in the child's first few years of life, were being blamed by medical experts for problems such as autism and schizophrenia. The term *schizophrenogenic mother,* defined by psychiatrist Freida Fromm-Reichmann in 1948, was used in the 1940s and 1950s as a way of attributing the etiology of schizophrenia to mothers who had emotional problems and were viewed as cold and rejecting toward their offspring. Over the past few decades this conceptualization has been widely criticized and is now viewed, in the psychological community, as more myth than reality. Psychoanalytic theory has been widely criticized for mother-blaming, especially in the area of sexual violence and childhood sexual abuse.

Behavioral Theory

John B. Watson, an American behaviorist, theorized that parental behavior, particularly the mother's behavior, was responsible for the development of behavior problems in the child. He suggested that mothers' behavior directly shaped long-term child outcomes. Watson's work began to influence mainstream American society and specific behavioral strategies were recommended to produce positive outcomes in children, and when problems arose, mothers were blamed for their ineptitude in implementing what are now considered behavior plans.

Attachment Theory

John Bowlby, credited with developing attachment theory, suggested that the mother is the primary attachment figure for the child and her absence results in detrimental effects on the child's well-being and psychological health. More modern versions of attachment theory give credence to the idea that mothers and fathers, as well as other caregivers, play an instrumental role in the healthy development of a child.

Scientific Research and Mother-Blaming

Reviews of scientific literature reveal that researchers tend to focus on maternal factors that influence problems among children and focus less on paternal, family, and social factors that may influence pathology in children. Researchers Paula Caplan and Ian Hall-McCorquodale reviewed scholarly articles published in major journals focused on the science and practice of psychology and related fields during the years 1970, 1976, and 1982 and found that in 42% of articles the authors suggested a connection between the mother and the child's pathology. Their review found that mothers were mentioned more frequently than fathers in the articles. The researchers also found that when case examples were used to illustrate a problem experienced by the child, the mother was typically used as the example. Additionally, the authors found that therapists and researchers tend to target their focus on mother–child interaction. The authors noted that, in their review of these articles, published in major clinical journals, 72 problems experienced by the child were attributed to mothers.

Maternal parenting experiences have historically been viewed as more related to both child and adult outcomes than paternal parenting experiences. One area of scientific inquiry that has often focused on the role of the mother in influencing the child is the study of children's criminal behavior. A review of this research finds that conceptual models have included focus on the mothers of criminals being a victim of abuse, poor, single, having little education, or having multiple male sexual partners. Another area of research fertile with mother focus is in the area of child sexual abuse. Much research can be found that focuses on what a mother did or did not do to protect a child from abuse as well as outcome variables extending into adulthood.

Health outcome research has also tended to focus on the relationship between maternal factors and negative health outcomes. Research on maternal lifestyle has focused on the influence of maternal factors on temperament, cognitive ability, sexual orientation, heart disease, diabetes, obesity, anxiety, depression, schizophrenia, and neural development.

Current research continues the tradition of focus on maternal factors and child outcome, even throughout adulthood. It is much more common in scientific inquiry to find examples of research linking maternal factors to child and adult outcomes when compared to paternal factors. Feminist scholars would argue that research considering maternal, paternal, child, and sociocultural factors will provide us with the most balanced view of factors influencing child outcome. These often contextually based researchers suggest that multiple contributing influences to the development of the child such as maternal, paternal, and societal influences are important to study and add that the influence of fathers, racial discrimination, poverty, and access to healthy food and health care resources are now being recognized as important factors to consider in child outcomes. When balance is absent with regard to the study of factors related to child outcome in scientific research, the area of most frequent study can become the target of blame, responsibility, prevention, and intervention. Feminist scholars also suggest that the actual factors researchers choose to study are influenced by social constructions of gender, race, and class.

In addition to the actual focus of scientific research, the type of research methodology implemented influences the attributions that may be made as a result of the research. Readers and sometimes authors of research demonstrating relationships between maternal lifestyle and various mental and physical health conditions may incorrectly assume that correlation research infers causality. That is, if there is some relationship between maternal lifestyle and child pathology, maternal lifestyle is viewed as the cause of the pathology. This misinterpretation of scientific research may lead us to blame mothers and fail to search for other contributing factors influencing children's development. Reviewing research to determine whether the research method used in the study allows causal attribution is an important step in the accurate use of scientific research.

Social Context and Mother-Blaming

During a social epoch wherein contextualism may be a guiding worldview, it becomes important to consider the sociocultural context that supports the emergence of mother-blaming in societies. Gender, race, and social class are viewed as variables that influence all of us, including those who contribute to the research literature, develop psychological theories, and offer prevention and intervention programs to others. In psychological research, there has been less focus on social factors such as socioeconomic status, discrimination, oppression, and heteronormativity.

Gender and Mother-Blaming

The conceptualization of gender and the social roles assigned, based on implicit and explicit gender-based messages, are considered social factors that support the emergence of mother-blaming. When individuals are asked what it means to be a woman, responses frequently include descriptors such as nurturing, caretaking, and emotional. Mothers tend to be viewed as having a more natural or instinctual ability to care for children. There are sometimes implicit and explicit messages about what men and women should be doing, what their individual responsibilities are, with regard to their children. If a woman's role, implicitly or explicitly defined by gender-based messages, is to be nurturing and caretaking, this may set the context for women to be held accountable when something is viewed as going wrong with the nurturing and caretaking process.

Historically, women have been viewed as responsible for the primary caretaking of children. While there is some shift in caretaking roles in contemporary society, there is much evidence to support the notion that children are still viewed as primarily being a mother's responsibility. Children's problems are often defined by the circumstances and behavior of their mothers. Feminists would argue that, in the United States, common usage of the terms *unwed mother*, *super mom*, *tiger mom*, and *career-oriented mom* are examples where there is no paternal comparison. It would be uncommon to hear terms such as *unwed father* and *career-oriented father*.

Mental Health and Mother-Blaming

Psychological literature suggests that therapists more frequently gather historical information from mothers instead of fathers. Additionally, reports more frequently focus on the psychological functioning of the mother and fail to mention or exclude the father. When the father is absent, this is frequently not taken into consideration as a contributing causal factor. There is little to no research in the areas of assessment, psychological evaluation, and report writing related to children of gay couples.

History and psychological science inform us that mothers are frequently held responsible for the origin and development of problems in the child or adult who is being treated by a mental health professional. Some research suggests that mothers are often seen by mental health therapists as ineffectual. Therapists who take an expert stance with the mother may hold her accountable for therapy outcomes and for being the reason for failure of the therapy or failure of the child to change his or her behavior. When mothers are held responsible for behavior change on the part of the client and positive change does not occur, therapists may view the mother as uncooperative and consider the family to be dysfunctional rather than examining their own therapeutic practices. Mothers and the mother–child relationship are more frequently the targets of prevention and intervention. Feminist therapists assert that the tendency to focus therapy on the mother or the mother–child relationship largely ignores the father and father–child relationship and results in a tendency to mother blame.

Among therapists who self-identify as utilizing feminist therapeutic approaches, there is evidence of what may be considered more covert mother-blaming. Although therapists may use the term *parent* or *caregiver*, they may actually still be referring to the mother.

Tammy Hatfield

See also Empowerment in Families; Feminist Family Therapy; Gender Issues; Gender Roles; Therapists' Values

Further Readings

Caplan, P. J. (1990). Making mother-blaming visible: The emperor's new clothes. *Women and Therapy, 10*(1/2), 61–70.

Caplan, P. J., & Hall-McCorquodale, I. (1985). Mother-blaming in major clinical journals, *American Journal of Orthopsychiatry, 55*(3), 345–353.

Chesler, P. (1972). *Women and madness.* Garden City, NY: Doubleday.

Chodorow, N. J. (1989). *Feminism and psychoanalytic theory.* New Haven, CT: Yale University Press.

Hare-Mustin, R. T. (1989). The problem of gender in family therapy theory. In M. McGoldrick, C. Anderson, & F. Walsh (Eds.), *Women in families: A framework for family therapy* (pp. 61–77). New York, NY: W. W. Norton.

Lerner, H. G. (1988). *Women in therapy.* New York, NY: Harper & Row.

Motivational Interviewing

Motivational interviewing is a set of counseling techniques that deal with the counselor's work with clients to promote behavioral change. Motivational interviewing (MI), first described in 1983, was initially used in brief therapy related to problem drinking. Since this time, MI has been used for numerous health care issues related to behavioral change such as increasing exercise, lowering food intake, increasing medication intake, and decreasing drug use. The theoretical underpinnings of MI are outlined in William R. Miller and Stephen Rollnick's seminal work, *Motivational Interviewing: Preparing People for Change.* This entry examines the development of MI and the spirit in which MI is carried out. This entry also outlines four general and four guiding principles of MI.

The Development of Motivational Interviewing

At the heart of motivational interviewing is the belief that people change naturally and that the work of the counselor is to help facilitate this natural change in clients. Miller and Rollnick found that brief forms of counseling showed comparable results to long-term therapy when it came to facilitating behavioral change. Most significant to MI is the research finding that particular therapist characteristics, such as empathy and a noncoercive stance, are a better predictor of the likelihood of positive behavioral change by the client than the counselor's theoretical approach. In other words, when the research looked at what factors produce the greatest likelihood of the future sobriety of clients, how the counselor interacted with the client proved to be a greater predictor of the client's sobriety than the program or theoretical orientation used by the counselor. The counselor's ability to interact with clients can either increase or decrease a client's likelihood of positive behavior change a year after treatment, as compared to those who were not in treatment and those in self-help programs.

Another significant factor of client behavior change is the client's sense of self-efficacy. Research has shown that change talk is important in relation to a client's likelihood to make positive behavioral changes. How clients rate their likelihood to change at the beginning of treatment is one of the best predictors of whether or not they will make changes in the future. Similarly, resistance talk has also been shown to predict a decreased probability of behavior change occurring.

Confrontational counseling has been shown to increase resistance talk in clients who are initially resistant to behavioral change. Research has also shown that confrontational counseling correlates with higher levels of client dropout and lower levels of client retention. As a result of this research, Miller and Rollnick state that the goal of MI is to increase change talk and decrease resistance talk.

The Spirit of Motivational Interviewing

Major proponents of this intervention for behavioral change have spoken of the spirit of MI as centered in the clinician's conceptualization of the counselor–client relationship and the process of change. The key is to be able to illicit the client's own motivation to change, in contrast to the counselor's overpowering the client with logic and reason until they see the need for change. The spirit, or ethos, of the MI counseling process is summed up as being collaborative, evocative, and honoring of patient autonomy.

Collaborative

The clinician who adheres to MI recognizes that a collaborative relationship is needed with the client as it is only the client who can choose to change and sustain change over the long haul. In this regard, the counselor refuses to view himself or herself as the expert in the relationship but recognizes the client must be in charge of their treatment. The MI counselor recognizes the power dynamics that are inherent within the counselor–client relationship and seeks to create an even playing field upon which the client exercises his or her own will to change.

Evocative

Instead of the clinician viewing their role as giving clients what they do not have (e.g., insight, skill, knowledge, and wisdom), MI seeks to evoke what the clients already possess, including their own motivation and desire for positive change. The counselor seeks to evoke change in the client in contrast to persuading the client to change. Therefore, even when clients are not motivated to change their behavior initially, clients can speak to other goals and desires they have in life that will be effected by whether or not the change in behavior occurs. MI seeks to assist clients in reaching their own life goals by helping the clients make the connection between how their problematic behavior is thwarting their personal life dreams and objectives.

Honoring Patient Autonomy

The counselor who uses MI recognizes the client's autonomy to change or not. Although the clinician may care for the client and desire him or her to change, the MI-informed clinician recognizes that ultimately it is up to the client whether or not he or she will change and any pressure to do so from the clinician is likely to incite resistance from the client. Ultimately, the counselor respects the client's choice to change or not. Therefore, the counselor's own self-worth as a therapist cannot be tied to the client getting better. The clinician's main goal is not to change the client but to facilitate a therapeutic relationship that is conducive to client change.

Four General Principles of MI

In his original work, William R. Miller stated four general principles of MI practice: (1) express empathy, (2) develop discrepancy, (3) roll with resistance, and (4) support self-efficacy.

Express Empathy

MI is both a client-centered and an empathic form of counseling, which may be understood as following the same vein as Carl Rogers's work on empathy. The key understanding is unconditional acceptance of the client, which is not the same as agreeing with the client's behavior. *Empathy* is defined as not only understanding a client's feelings but also their motivations. It is through this genuine acceptance offered by the counselor that the client is given the emotional space needed to explore the possibility of change. Genuine acceptance also decreases the likelihood of resistance, as the client can trust that the clinician is generally for him and not simply trying to foster her own self-worth by getting the client to do what the clinician wants. Although the counselor desires change for the client, he or she is with the client in such a way that the client knows that his or her acceptance of them is not contingent on their changing.

Develop Discrepancy

The clinician seeks to facilitate client change by developing the discrepancy between the client's behavior and the client's stated life goals and objectives. Instead of the clinician imposing her values onto the client, the counselor seeks to understand the client's vision for his life, what he wants, what he values, and who or what he loves. The clinician then seeks to amplify the incongruence between the client's goals and his present behavior. By developing this discrepancy, the clinician seeks to increase the client's motivation to change as a result of his or her own preferred future.

Roll with Resistance

MI recognizes that resistance only occurs in reaction to the counselor's behavior. In other words, for a client to resist, she must have something or someone to resist. For this reason, MI suggests that instead of pushing against client resistance, the counselor should roll in the direction of the client's opposition to change. Resistance is a sign to the MI clinician that they need to change approaches and to step back from trying to initiate change. The counselor avoids arguing for change but invites the client to speak more about her reasons for not wanting to change, empathizing with reasons that the counselor can acknowledge as reasonable. The counselor does not cease to desire change for the client, but recognizes that it is up to the client to change. By hearing more fully and more empathically the client's reasons for resistance, the counselor can then develop a discrepancy between the client's desire not to change and her life goals.

Support Self-Efficacy

Self-efficacy refers to a client's belief in their ability to change. Since research has shown that self-efficacy is a primary predictor of behavioral change, the MI counselor seeks to bolster the client's faith and hope in his ability to change. Research has also shown that the counselor's own belief in the client's ability to change also effects client outcome, resulting in a self-fulfilling prophecy for the client.

Four Guiding Principles of MI

Following Miller's articulation of MI's general principles, Rollnick, Miller, and Christopher C. Butler further outlined another four guiding principles of motivational interviewing: (1) *r*esist the righting reflex, (2) *u*nderstand your patient's motivations, (3) *l*isten to the patient, and (4) *e*mpower the patient. These four principles make the difference between clinicians who are likely to facilitate change talk and those who unwittingly increase the client's resistance to change.

R: Resist the Righting Reflex

Clinicians often get into the field of counseling because they have a strong desire to make things right (e.g., to stop people from making bad decisions or continuing in dysfunctional ways of living). Research has shown that this righting reflex increases resistance in clients who are not yet at the point of committing to significant change. Clients who come into counseling with even a small degree of resistance are often triggered into further recalcitrance by the counselor's attempt at persuasion. If patients have two voices in their minds, one calling for change and the other saying there is no need, the counselor's call for change increases the volume of the counter voice, which manifests itself as resistance.

U: Understand Your Patient's Motivations

It is the client's motivation to change, not the clinician's, which is important since it is client motivation that will illicit and sustain long-term change. As a result of recognizing the importance of client motivation, one of the most important questions a clinician can ask the client is why she may want to make a change and what good effect may result from change. This can be done in one of the initial sessions.

L: Listen to Your Patient

This principle calls for empathic listening, which may at times require speculating about the meaning embedded in a client's statements. Although many clinicians view their role as having information that the client may need, MI recognizes that it is only by listening thoroughly to the client that the counselor can understand the patient's motivations. Deep empathy has been shown to produce positive client outcomes.

E: Empower Your Patient

This principle is in line with respecting the autonomy of the patient. One of the primary goals of counseling is to increase the self-efficacy of the clients so they will not be dependent on the clinician. The MI clinician seeks to empower the clients by respecting their knowledge of self and their ability to utilize resources for change. The client is viewed as the expert of his or her situation.

Eric M. Brown

See also Alcohol and Substance Abuse; Empathy; Empowerment in Families; Listening, Empathic; Self-Esteem; Substance Use Disorders in Adolescents

Further Readings

Arkowitz, H., Miller, W. R., & Rollnick, S. (2015). *Motivational interviewing in the treatment of psychological problems* (2nd ed.). New York, NY: Guilford Press.

Arkowitz, H., & Westra, H. A. (2004). Integrating motivational interviewing and cognitive behavioral therapy in the treatment of depression and anxiety. *Journal of Cognitive Psychotherapy, 18,* 337–350.

Hettema, J., Steele, J., & Miller, W. R. (2005). Motivational interviewing. *Annual Review of Clinical Psychology, 1,* 91–111.

Miller, W. R. (1983). Motivational interviewing with problem drinkers. *Behavioural Psychotherapy, 11,* 147–172.

Miller, W. R., & Rollnick, S. (2013). *Motivational interviewing: Helping people change* (3rd ed.). New York, NY: Guilford Press.

Miller, W. R., & Rose, G. S. (2009). Toward a theory of motivational interviewing. *American Psychology, 64,* 527–537. doi:10.1037/a0016830

Naar-King, S., & Suarez, M. (2010). *Motivational interviewing with adolescents and young adults.* New York, NY: Guilford Press.

Rollnick, S., & Miller, W. R. (1995). What is motivational interviewing? *Behavioural and Cognitive Psychotherapy, 23,* 325–334.

Rollnick, S., Miller, W. R., & Butler, C. C. (2008). *Motivational interviewing in health care: Helping patients change behavior.* New York, NY: Guilford Press.

Multicultural Counseling Competence

Multicultural counseling competence refers to the ability of counselors to acknowledge the presence of their own diverse backgrounds, attitudes, and values in conjunction with the diverse backgrounds, beliefs, and attitudes clients bring to counseling sessions. *Multicultural counseling competence* is a specific term that encompasses the various considerations counselors take into account in order to serve clients in an ethically responsible way that embraces their differences. Becoming a multiculturally competent counselor is a multiphasic and ongoing process for which a set of guidelines has been set forth. This entry briefly introduces multicultural counseling, multicultural counseling competencies, cultural differences, and the multicultural counseling process.

Defining Multicultural Counseling

Counselors come to sessions with a variety of expectations, goals, and values stemming from their individual experiences and diverse backgrounds. Part of their role is to understand how their experiences shape their learning process and effects their interactions with clients in session. It is important for counselors to consider how their notions of gender, culture, sexual and affectional orientation, religion, age, and ethnicity factor into their ability to work with diverse clients. Multicultural theory has been recognized as the fourth force in the counseling profession, and thus the need for multicultural counseling competencies emerged in response to demographic changes in the United States and need for counselors to have a knowledgeable baseline from which to address various culturally specific issues.

Courtland C. Lee identified six basic principles of multicultural counseling. The first principle, *culture*, denotes a group of people who come together due to similar identities or for a common goal. The second principle is that cultural diversity exists and can guide our interactions. The third principle is that all counseling is considered to be cross-cultural. The fourth principle emphasizes the importance and variety of human differences. The fifth principle charges counselors to increase their awareness, knowledge, and skills in order to become culturally competent beings able to address the diversity of their clients with respect. The sixth principle states that culturally competent counselors are also globally literate individuals. In conjunction with the competencies, these principles inform counselors how to effectively pursue becoming a multiculturally competent counselor.

Summarizing the Components of Multicultural Counseling Competencies

Multicultural counseling competencies can be separated into three major domains: (1) counselor awareness of own cultural assumptions, values, and biases; (2) counselor understanding the worldview of culturally diverse clients; and (3) counselor utilization of culturally appropriate intervention strategies and techniques. Originally 31 cultural competencies were identified. Each of the three aforementioned domains was discussed in terms of beliefs and attitudes, knowledge, and skills, and although the competencies were expanded upon some years later with 119 explanations, the competencies themselves remain the same today.

The first domain mentioned above, *counselor awareness of own cultural assumptions, values, and biases,* was recognized because culturally competent counselors are continually in the process of self-reflection in an attempt to become fully aware of their own values, as well as any biases, assumptions, and preconceived notions regarding individuals of different backgrounds. Culturally skilled counselors are aware of the impact that their cultural background has on themselves, as well as the impact it has on their view of psychological processes. Competent counselors are able to recognize their own limitations to multicultural counseling and their sources of discomfort within the counseling relationship that might be related to race, ethnicity, or other cultural factors. Those who are culturally skilled also have knowledge of how cultural heritage affects their decision-making in the counseling process, and they have an understanding of how oppressive forces and privilege manifest in society and effect interpersonal relationships.

Counselors who are culturally competent under the second domain, *counselor understanding the worldview of culturally diverse clients,* have an awareness of their reactions toward certain minority groups, as well as any stereotypes or preconceived notions toward individuals within these groups that might interfere with the counseling process. They have knowledge of the cultural group with which they are working and go on to learn about the specific history, cultural values, and behaviors of each individual client. To be competent, counselors learn to acknowledge the worldviews of clients with the understanding that it does not have to be shared. An understanding of the sociopolitical influences on the livelihood of minority individuals, as well as the effects that race/ethnicity, gender, and socioeconomic status among other factors may have on the many facets of a person's life, is necessary to be multiculturally competent in this area. The skilled counselor also seeks out the latest research in areas relevant to minority clients and interacts with those of different backgrounds outside the counseling setting.

Under the third domain, *counselor utilization of culturally appropriate intervention strategies and techniques*, counselors should be aware that the use of certain theories and techniques with all clients may not only be inefficient, but also discriminatory. The importance of finding techniques that are consistent with the needs of the individual client has been well documented. Certain groups may not be comfortable with talk therapy and/or self-disclosure based on cultural heritage or a sociopolitical climate that has discouraged such interactions with others. Some theoretical orientations are based on principles of the dominant culture that may not acknowledge the values of certain groups. The culturally competent counselor works to address these issues and identify appropriate intervention strategies that are consistent with the client's individual life experience. Although a counselor can attempt to understand the perspectives and experiences of minority clients, full and exact comprehension will likely not occur. However, cognitive empathy can occur if the counselor is willing to acknowledge the sociopolitical environment and its pressures that cultural minority clients must contend with daily.

For the counselor who understands the importance of multicultural competencies in counseling, the idea of social justice is also valued. Social justice is based on the concept that all individuals are entitled to equitable treatment and full participation in society regardless of gender, race, sexual and affectional orientation, age, education, religion, ethnic background, socioeconomic status, or any other characteristic that is associated with marginalized group membership. For counselors acting as agents for social change, the professional platform will be one on which all forms of discrimination and oppression are challenged. This is particularly important as many of the issues that clients bring into the counseling relationship are related to the oppressive social, economic, and cultural environments that negatively impact their growth and development. The culturally competent counselor not only acts as an agent of social change on an individual level, but does so also on a systemic level. Because social justice has become synonymous with cultural competency, it has more recently been referred to as the fifth force in the counseling field as an extension of multiculturalism.

Identifying and Understanding Cultural Differences

Understanding cultural differences goes beyond what is seen and has to begin with a thorough self-examination. Observing one's own internal dialogue can provide great insight into one's own cultural values, beliefs, and biases, but acknowledging that intrapersonal communication, which occurs when one talks or thinks to oneself, can be difficult. Intrapersonal communication begins early in life as messages are received from parents and extended family, churches, schools, media, and culture, and it shapes interpersonal communication with others in life and in the counseling session. When a counselor lacks awareness of her or his values, beliefs, and biases, the potential for unintentionally marginalizing clients grows.

Self-assessment of one's own values, beliefs, and biases can be a difficult process for a number of reasons. For one, introspection and better understanding oneself has not been an important part of socialization in the United States and other cultures that are extrinsically valuation oriented, meaning those cultures that place value on adhering to culturally expected behaviors versus identifying what is meaningful to the individual. Another reason self-assessment can be difficult is due to unconscious and implicit learning. Individuals grow and learn to adhere to a set of values within a culture before they have the ability to evaluate the impact of such values and beliefs on the formation of their view of self. The desire to hold onto one's ideal self-image can interfere with one's ability to truly evaluate the already formed values, beliefs, and biases. Additionally, in-group favoritism, which is the attribution of positive characteristics to the internal qualities of members of the group to which one belongs and negative to those of another group, can be an issue due to attribution error and social projection, leading to heightened barriers in self-assessment. However, in order to successfully implement multicultural counseling competencies, one has to overcome such barriers and address concepts and ideas that many individuals find uncomfortable.

Counselors must seek personal awareness through self-assessment in order to avoid unintentional oppressive interactions with clients that could negatively impact their welfare, even with the intention of helping. In addition to introspection, counselors must also gain an awareness of systemic oppression and privilege and internalized oppression and privilege. Recognizing such concepts enables further understanding of oppressive sociopolitical factors, such as racism, sexism, classism, heterosexism, ableism, and other "isms." Privilege often goes unseen by those who hold the privilege, just as they often overlook how societal norms often benefit them while oppressing those individuals in nondominant groups. Conversely, oppression is typically very visible to those in oppressed and marginalized groups, whether with regard to race, gender, age, class, or sexual orientation. Oppression refers to the acts displayed toward and the effects experienced by marginalized cultural groups due to the combination of power and prejudice among the dominant group in society. Counselors must understand how internalized privilege and oppression can affect a client's worldview, as well as their own.

Addressing Issues in Multicultural Counseling

In order to provide culturally appropriate treatment, a counselor must conduct therapy in a way that honors the client's worldview and culture. The counselor must see the client as a whole person with emotion and intellect, personal history, multiple cultural identities, a particular relationship to privilege and oppression, and distinct thinking patterns. The counselor must also remain compassionate, listen actively and attentively, without judgment, regardless of differences identified between the client and the counselor.

One way to address issues in multicultural counseling is for counselors to invite clients to educate them on their backgrounds, culture, attitudes, and beliefs in order to create a supportive environment for self-reflection where both parties feel empowered and encouraged to bridge cultural gaps and increase awareness of individual differences. Counselors should engage in their own introspective processes and explore how their biases, prejudices, and values could potentially affect their work with diverse client groups. A counselor's inability to reflect inward may negatively interfere with the counseling process. Furthermore, counselors are encouraged to seek opportunities to address cultural differences in sessions with clients.

*Candace N. Park
and Kristen N. Dickens*

See also Cultural Issues in Couples and Families; Diversity; Gender- and Culture-Sensitive Therapies; Multiculturalism; Therapists' Values

Further Readings

American Counseling Association. (2003). *Advocacy competencies*. Alexandria, VA: Author.

Arredondo, P., & Toporek, R. (2004). Multicultural counseling competencies = Ethical practice. *Journal of Mental Health Counseling, 26*(1), 44–55.

Arredondo, P., Toporek, R., Brown, S., Sanchez, J., Locke, D. C., Sanchez, J., & Stadler, H. (1996).

Operationalization of the multicultural counseling competencies. *Journal of Multicultural Counseling & Development, 24*(1), 42–78.

Jun, H. (2010). *Social justice, multicultural counseling, and practice: Beyond a conventional approach.* Thousand Oaks, CA: Sage.

Lee, C. C. (Ed.). (2013). *Multicultural issues in counseling: New approaches to diversity* (4th ed.). Alexandria, VA: American Counseling Association.

Ratts, M. J., Singh, A. A., Nassar-McMillan, S., Butler, S. K., & McCullough, J. R. (2015). *Multicultural and social justice counseling competencies.* Retrieved from http://www.multiculturalcounseling.org/index.php?option=com_content&view=article&id=205:amcd-endorses-multicultural-and-social-justice-counseling-competencies&catid=1:latest&Itemid=123

Robinson, T. L. (2005). *The convergence of race, ethnicity, and gender: Multiple identities in counseling* (2nd ed.). Upper Saddle River, NJ: Pearson.

Sue, D. W., Arredondo, P., & McDavis, R. J. (1992). Multicultural counseling competencies and standards: A call to the profession. *Journal of Counseling & Development, 70,* 477–483.

Sue, D. W., & Sue, D. (2008). *Counseling the culturally diverse: Theory and practice* (5th ed.). Hoboken, NJ: Wiley.

Multiculturalism

Multiculturalism is a way of thinking, being, and acting that promotes equality among different cultures and cultural groups and emphasizes a multidimensional view of the human experience. This view recognizes that one's experience is based on the intersection of the multiple contexts in which one participates and the cultural dimensions with which one identifies (e.g., race, ethnicity, gender, class, socioeconomic status, ability, sexual orientation, and spirituality or religion). The significance of multiculturalism in couple and family therapy is closely tied to socially relevant historical shifts and changing cultural landscapes in the United States. Therefore, as racial and ethnic diversity continues to increase, so does our need to be culturally responsive and competent in our clinical practice.

This entry offers an understanding of the origins of the word *multiculturalism*, examines the historical events that led to its development and to the development of multicultural theories and models, and provides definitions of terminology associated with multiculturalism and culture. This entry also provides perspectives on the significance and relationship between culture and therapy and a review of some multicultural training practices and programs.

Sociocultural History, Terminology, and Theoretical Development

Multiculturalism is a concept that, in the United States, first came into use in the mid-1960s. The roots of the word *multiculturalism* are embedded in the historical context of the 1960s when several sociopolitical movements originated in response to issues of social inequality, primarily those concerning race and gender. The significance of multiculturalism grew as different racial and ethnically identified groups (e.g., African Americans and Latina/o/s among other racial and ethnic minorities) proceeded to explore their own history and origin through the 1970s and 1980s. This cultural shift created a heightened awareness of the importance of culture-specific factors that advanced the development of multicultural theories and models of practice in various disciplines. Multiculturalism espouses the view that cultures within a society merit equal respect and scholarly interest.

As feminist and multicultural theorists responded to the need for culturally responsive practice in the 1970s and 1980s, multiculturalism became an increasingly significant force in mental health and the helping professions. Over the last several decades, the increasing diversity and cultural pluralism leading up to the 21st century reinforced the need to broaden our views of diversity beyond race and ethnicity to include other aspects like gender, education, sexual orientation, socioeconomic disadvantage, disability, religious, and spiritual belief systems. It became clear that if counselors and therapists were to have an impact as part of the changing demographics, it would require training that espoused awareness, knowledge, and skills that facilitated effective multicultural intervention.

Conceptually speaking, culture is a socially constructed system of learned meanings and behaviors that evolve over the course of generations and serve as a unifying influence for those who share cultural similarities (e.g., in terms of identity, customs, values, and traditions). Clinicians may take very different ideological positions about the relationship that exists between culture and therapy. The significance one extends to culture in theory, practice, and training can range from a peripheral or background to a more central stance. For instance, practitioners who experience themselves as cultural beings generally tend to adopt a broader definition of *culture* (i.e., see it as something we all experience as part of daily life) and therefore as something that must be central to their work with clients. By contrast, practitioners who consider cultural influences as tangential tend to view culture as just another aspect to consider in certain cases. This is true of individuals who prefer to take an ethnic-focused approach or knowledge-based view of culture, a view that is primarily concerned with characteristics of various groups, with a predominant focus on the "other." The challenge lies in one's ability to see the universal human similarities beyond specific cultural attributes, such as color, ethnicity, class, and gender while also remaining aware and respectful of culture-specific differences and in touch with self.

The historical evolution of multiculturalism in mental health professions introduced a variety of terms and related concepts as theories and clinical models were developed. Given the rather subtle distinctions shared by many of these terms, a descriptive analysis of multicultural terminology follows with the intent of providing some clarification vis-à-vis each term's meaning as part of the discourse of multiculturalism. Two of the more widely used terms associated with multiculturalism are *cultural diversity* and *cultural sensitivity*.

Cultural diversity refers to the multiplicity of cultures and cultural dimensions that pertain to a person's experience. It also implies having a multidimensional perspective of a person's place in society. Cultural sensitivity is generally associated with one's awareness and understanding of cultures, cultural principles, and practices that may be distinctly different from one's own. It involves knowing that cultural differences as well as similarities exist without value judgments (i.e., better or worse, right or wrong). Unlike cultural awareness, which is more aligned with cognition and intellect, cultural sensitivity is primarily linked to affect and emotion.

In 1991, Paul Pedersen, a well-known proponent of multicultural counseling, endorsed the development of a generic theory of multiculturalism as the "fourth theoretical force" in the field of counseling, along with the three other major traditions—psychodynamic theory, cognitive-behavioral theory, and existential-humanistic theory. Another well-known influence in counseling, Courtland Lee, described a culturally responsive professional as one who is able to view clients as unique individuals while simultaneously taking his or her common developmental and unique cultural experiences as a human being into consideration. A culturally responsive individual or professional is also one who promotes tolerance and nurtures diversity. Multicultural training generally encompasses different aspects of the practitioner's self-awareness, knowledge, and skills.

As the need for cultural responsiveness emerged in different fields and disciplines (i.e., social work, counseling psychology, family therapy, nursing, education, medicine, and even business), so did terms associated with competence and skill. The call for cultural competence initiated in the early 1980s eventually led to its pervasiveness in human service settings. This was primarily due to social directives, federal mandates, and government and professional regulations that made the inclusion of cultural competence standards mandatory for benefits tied to funding and/or professional endorsement. For instance, the National Association of Social Workers (NASW)'s Standards for Cultural Competence in Social Work Practice of 2001 defined cultural competence as "the process by which individuals and systems respond respectfully and effectively to people of all cultures, languages, classes, races, ethnic backgrounds, religions, and other diversity factors in a manner that recognizes, affirms, and values the worth of individuals, families, and communities and protects and preserves the dignity of each" (p. 11). In 2010, the American Counseling Association adopted the following definition of counseling: "Counseling is a professional relationship that empowers diverse individuals from diverse cultural backgrounds in helping relationships" (Kaplan et al., p. 368). Additionally, competencies that enable counselors to provide culturally responsive service and best practices were also developed as part of their standards. Thirdly, in 2016, the accrediting body for the American Association of Marriage and Family Therapy (AAMFT), the Commission on Accreditation for Marriage and Family Therapy Education (COAMFTE), published version 12.0 of its accreditation standards; in this document, it devotes one of five accreditation standards (Standard II) completely to diversity and inclusion. This commitment to diversity and inclusion sets expectations for accredited programs that require multiculturally informed education approaches, a climate of safety, respect, and appreciation for all learners from diverse, marginalized, and underserved populations, as well as experience with each of these populations. These training practices serve as a good example of more recent developments that place greater emphasis on social justice.

The shift in the last 10 to 15 years toward social justice is generally more aligned with active participation and advocacy work on a societal level. It is referred to by some as a natural progression and evolution of multicultural counseling with a focus on empowerment. The multicultural discourse associated with social justice goes beyond the "ism's" that were a part of the dialogue 20 years ago. Instead, it requires health providers and helping professionals to consciously reflect on how society, and its institutional beliefs, structures, and practices, have failed to provide equal access and opportunities for all. This is especially relevant in cases when clients are pathologized for many of society's ills. Active participation through client and community advocacy would be considered a likely next step to help fight oppression associated with discriminatory practices.

Multicultural Training

For several decades mental health professions have developed numerous models and frameworks and have implemented different types of multicultural training practices. Generally, training has combined aspects of self-awareness, knowledge, skill, and competence. There are varying differences associated with self-exploration and self-awareness as part of the training process. In many cases, cultural self-awareness is a prerequisite that is derived from self-exploration and understanding of one's own culture and how our experiences with other cultures influence our attitudes and beliefs about others. Knowledge generally entails learning about cultural identity development and awareness of self as a cultural being and part of the specific cultures with which one identifies. Skills and competencies are associated with the attainment of interventions that are consistent with a client's cultural identity, values, and life experiences. This aspect of training also promotes systemic change in situations when restrictive environments and cultural oppression are challenged through practice. This is especially true in situations when clients may be pathologized for culturally based differences that may not be acknowledged as such during treatment.

There are numerous examples of multicultural training programs to choose from in helping professions like psychology, counseling, nursing, social work, medicine, and family therapy. Two examples, one in medical education and one from family therapy training, are discussed here. The first, developed by Melanie Tervalon and Jann Murray-Garcia, is founded on an interesting construct referred to as *cultural humility*. Humility is considered to be a fundamental part of the students' own process of self-reflection and self-critique as lifelong learners and reflective practitioners. Essentially, cultural humility entails a role reversal of sorts, in which the medical students relinquish their role of expert to the patients in order to become their student. This means they are expected to learn about their clients by gaining awareness of their patients' agenda and perspectives (whether medical and not) while also acknowledging their patients' potential as capable partners in treatment. Training approaches include patient-focused interviewing, small group discussions, personal journals, involvement with constructive role models from representative cultural groups, videotaping, and feedback. It is one of the few training models that incorporates an active and lifelong (rather than discreet endpoint) commitment to patients, communities, colleagues, and self and includes ongoing self-evaluation and self-critique.

Another well-known multicultural model that promotes humility and collaboration between clinicians and clients is Celia Falicov's multisystemic ecological comparative approach (MECA) framework. This framework is based on the premise that clinical practice is a cultural and sociopolitical encounter between all who are part of the therapeutic system (e.g., clients, therapists, and supervisors). The MECA framework incorporates a comparative way of thinking about cultural similarities and differences across four specific domains: migration and acculturation experiences, ecological context, family organization, and family life cycle. This framework has been widely used by family therapists in clinical and research settings and is especially helpful with immigrant clients and families. The dimensions encompassed by MECA provide a useful guide to conceptualize the processes that immigrant families undergo at the level of clinical practice, pertinent to social justice and cultural diversity. Culture is central to theory and practice in MECA because it maintains that it is possible to integrate cultural awareness at every step in the process of learning to observe, conceptualize, and work therapeutically with clients. According to MECA, every clinical encounter is influenced by each participant's cultural and personal life maps (i.e., his or her ecological niche), thus making self-reflection about one's cultural and social location an instrumental part of the process. Remaining open to the discomfort often associated with multicultural training is key, especially when it entails moving away from politically correct rhetoric toward actual implementation of meaningful clinical training, practice, supervision, and research.

Silvia Echevarria-Doan

See also African American Families; Assimilation: Immigrants and Refugees; Bilingual Families; Cultural Issues in Couples and Families; Ecosystems Perspective; Ethnicity; Family Rituals; Gender- and Culture-Sensitive Therapies; Gender Issues; Gender Roles; Hispanic Healthy Marriage Initiative; Kinship Care; Native American Families; Patriarchy; Polygamy; Racial Disparities in Foster Care; Sexual Prejudice

Further Readings

Arredondo, P., & Tovar-Blank, Z. G. (2014). Multicultural competencies: A dynamic paradigm for the 21st century. In F. T. L. Leong (Ed.), *APA handbook of multicultural psychology* (Vol. 2, Applications and training; pp. 19–34). Washington, DC: American Psychological Association.

Hays, P. A. (2008). *Addressing cultural complexities in practice: Assessment, diagnosis, and therapy* (2nd ed.). Washington, DC: American Psychological Association.

Kaplan, D. M., Tarvydas, V. M., & Gladding, S. T. (2014). 20/20: A vision for the future of counseling: The new consensus definition of counseling. *Journal of Counseling and Development, 92*, 366–372.

National Association of Social Workers Board of Directors. (2001). *NASW standards for cultural competence in social work practice*. Retrieved from https://www.socialworkers.org/practice/standards/cultural_competence.asp

Sue, D. W. & Sue, D. (2013). *Counseling the culturally different: Theory and practice* (6th ed.). New York, NY: Wiley.

Multiple Family Therapy

Multiple family therapy, also referred to as multiple family group therapy and multifamily therapy, typically involves three to four families coming together to discuss common issues. With psychoeducation foundational to this approach, families simultaneously work to resolve individual and family issues. Proponents of multiple family therapy highlight family members' ability to recognize dysfunctions, accept feedback, gain perspective, and create a supportive network. Utilizing multiple family therapy can be beneficial to therapists working with clients with severe mental illness or psychological disorders. Also, it can be beneficial in a variety of settings and with a variety of issues where treating the family is a valued component of client well-being. This entry reviews the framework of multiple family therapy, including its historical underpinnings, provides a conceptual overview for the approach, and discusses models of multiple family therapy.

Conceptual Overview

Multiple family therapy originated in the 1950s in a New York hospital as a treatment for young patients with schizophrenia. This therapeutic format continued to be modified for clients with severe mental illness and eventually developed into a form of treatment for clients with various presenting issues in different settings. Similar to family therapy, the focus is on fostering healthy family relationships that positively influence the family unit and not just the client. Psychoeducation is used to highlight dysfunctions. Families are expected to gain insight and awareness, provide validation, and develop healthy communication skills. In family systems theory, emphasis is placed on understanding the family as a unit rather than as individuals within the unit. In accordance with this theory, therapists can gain insight into clients by understanding their respective family unit. For instance, Dr. H. Peter Laqueur (1909–1979), recognized as the founder of multiple family therapy, was able to better understand his clients, who were being treated for schizophrenia, by observing weekly family visits at the hospital. Multiple family therapy also grew from seeing how these families naturally interacted with each other during these weekly hospital visits, forming distinct groups and creating valued connections. Further development and structuring by Laqueur and other clinicians has presently led to the many uses of multiple family therapy.

Since multiple family therapy jointly involves family members of three to four families, knowledge in group work can be useful to the therapist. This could be advantageous for facilitating sessions, which are typically cofacilitated by two therapists. Additionally, having a theoretical knowledge in family systems theory can help therapists conceptualize families participating in multiple family therapy. This allows the therapist the ability to understand family values, patterns, and boundaries. Further, the therapist gains the capacity to understand the family norms or rules that affect behavior and communication that materializes within the family unit.

History of Multiple Family Therapy

Multiple family therapy formed as a result of families visiting patients weekly in a hospital while they were being treated for a psychological disturbance. Laqueur worked with young patients with schizophrenia in a New York city hospital who were undergoing insulin coma therapy. While their condition improved, Laqueur noticed that patients appeared worse after their first home visit. Families were then invited for informal meetings so that the staff could understand how the families function and how these behaviors or attitudes may cause patient regression. In order to increase patients' ease with these meetings, joint family meetings were implemented. Families were not only invited to visit patients but to also to aid hospital staff. When families came to visit the patients, Laqueur noticed how they interacted and formed unprompted groups. Laqueur saw these groups as therapeutic and began to theorize multiple family therapy. Due to the chaos that derived from numerous families interacting at once, the meetings were ultimately limited to no more than six families to maximize effectiveness. Multiple family therapy was seen as a treatment modality to help patients continue progress and reduce chances of rehospitalization. Additionally, multiple family therapy was viewed as an opportunity to educate families on their loved one's illness. Initially, treatment primarily involved the parents and the patient, but it was eventually expanded to include additional family members.

Laqueur noticed how different families supported each other through validation of feelings and experiences. Families focused on the patient's presenting issues as well as issues of family members. By doing this, families were able to confront challenges and support each other through this reexamination. The connection among the multiple families spontaneously formed therapeutic grouping. Working with families in therapeutic groups fostered healthy communication and empathy among members. Decreasing emphasis of the patient's psychopathology and improving functioning within family units was the primary target of multiple family therapy. Families were able to bond through shared experiences with more than one family being the focus of the group. Families also engaged in challenging each other's worldviews. Validation appeared to be a major factor influencing change within therapy sessions; families authenticated each other's experiences, sharing common feelings and challenges. Another focus was supporting the families in creating and achieving goals. Laqueur valued families working together for a common purpose as support for decreasing symptomatic behaviors of the intended primary client (client who is primarily seeking treatment for mental illness). Decreasing family discord was stressed as important for mentally ill clients.

Constructing Multiple Family Therapy

The preliminary structure involved three to four families, inclusive of extended family members (parents, siblings, partners, and children) and two therapists who cofacilitated the session. Counselor trainees may be involved in observing the family session. The sessions were also open-ended, with replacement families added to the group when necessary. Laqueur observed that randomly selecting families for participation was beneficial. Primary guidelines include disbanding the notion that the primary client is the focus or that the family is working only for the advantage of the primary client. Families are expected to address limitations that contribute to unhealthy family interactions that may also incite symptomatic behaviors of the primary client.

Strategic to multiple family therapy is understanding family structures. For example, the therapist may notice which family member is isolated from the remainder of the group. The therapist may also notice subsystems within the family, including those influenced by age gaps or separated by sex. This involves understanding which family member (or parent) operates as the head of household. The therapist should notice if any hierarchical order is present. Observing which subsystems are present can be essential to highlighting unhealthy family practices that may sustain family dysfunction and primary client regression.

Progression of Multiple Family Therapy

Following Laqueur's lead, mental health clinics and hospitals across the country began recognizing the importance of involving families in treatment, thus making multiple family therapy groups a respected treatment method. Other clinicians revised multiple family therapy to build upon Laqueur's work. For example, William McFarlane used multiple family therapy to treat patients in psychiatric hospital settings. He felt it was necessary for family members to gain insight into their respective dysfunctions that attribute to the whole family. McFarlane's goal was to integrate psychoeducation, behavioral family therapy, and multiple family therapy to create a modified approach. In doing so, he formed therapeutic elements to structure multiple family therapy. These elements include resocialization, stigma reversal, modulated disenmeshment, communication normalization, and crisis management.

Resocialization is the process of eliminating maladaptive behaviors that developed as a method of coping and replacing them with behaviors that aid the healing process. Stigma reversal is the process of reframing negative characteristics associated with particular mental illnesses or addictions. Modulated disenmeshment is a gradual reduction of negative bonds between family members while simultaneously creating new, more positive bonds and interactions. Communication normalization is the process of alleviating communication barriers and aiding the family in openly and honestly expressing their thoughts and feelings. Crisis management, within multiple family therapy, is the process of deescalating and supporting a family member experiencing overwhelming emotional reactions to their perception of an event.

In working with patients with schizophrenia, psychoeducation often became a primary component in decreasing stigma and influencing healthy communication practices. Another component in multiple family therapy is engaging in interaction outside of the group, thus extending the therapeutic setting. Today, multiple family therapy has been extended beyond treatment of patients with schizophrenia to include families with issues of substance abuse, chemical dependency, relational issues, and behaviorally and emotionally challenged children.

Components of Multiple Family Therapy

Multiple family therapy consists of several factors and components that contribute to a successful treatment process. When engaging in this process, the goals of therapy are to lessen the stress of family members, to decrease the risk of relapse of unhealthy behaviors, and to achieve the best outcome and well-being of all family members. To achieve these goals through multiple family therapy, the following principles are desired for success.

It is important to establish principles for working with families and to make sure that all members within the family are working toward the same goal. To make sure this occurs, it is vital for the therapist to restate the goals through the treatment process. Before goals are completely set, the exploration of the member's expectation of treatment is invaluable. In addition, throughout the sessions, the therapist needs to listen to the families and to treat them equally. In multiple family therapy, one family is not more important than another family and one family should not dominate sessions over other families. To keep families from dominating sessions, it is important to aid in the resolution of family conflict and to process with all the families the conflict that has arisen.

Throughout treatment, it is also important to improve communication within the family and within the group. A principle of treatment is to encourage the family to expand their social support and to also provide resources to do so. While the principles of multiple family therapy are needed, it is also important to have knowledge of the concept of the multiple family therapy.

Multiple family therapy reduces stress and burdens by sharing experiences with other families that have experienced similar types of stresses and burdens. These groups also address family issues by increasing the social support of the families by having them interact with others experiencing similar issues and challenges. Hearing from other families that have been successful instills hope within the families that are experiencing stress.

The typical intervention for multiple family therapy consists of joining, education, and problem-solving. These stages are needed for successful treatment. Many individuals and families may not be open to group treatments because they tend to be emotionally charged, which does not leave time for problem-solving and coping skills training. However, multiple family therapy addresses these concerns by engaging the families in these stages.

The first stage is joining and usually takes place within 48 hours after admission. Usually a therapist meets with each family individually to discuss the multiple family therapy process. Once the families have joined together, they share trepidations of the group therapy experience and establish rapport with one another. The education stage reduces trepidation the family members experience. It is the therapist's goal to educate each family member on a level that is needed individually. The problem-solving stage helps family members to function and cope appropriately during the sessions and after treatment is over. During this stage the families progress through six steps, which consist of defining the problem, generating possible solutions, discussing each possible solution, choosing the best solution, implementing the chosen solution, and reviewing the implementation. It is important to guide the families through the problem-solving stage so they as a family and as individuals can function outside of therapy.

Phases of Multiple Family Therapy

The phases of multiple family therapy were established by Laqueur. Phase I of multiple family therapy is initial *interest*. Within this phase, families could be relieved to participate in treatment, or they could experience drawbacks resulting from unrealistic expectations from therapy. Significant in this phase is seeing how families presently cope, which potentially provides the therapist with an idea of behaviors, worldviews, or stigmas negatively affecting the family unit. Phase II is *resistance*. Families begin to understand that the presenting problem is not the sole subject of treatment but rather includes the family unit. Families then become fearful of sharing struggles and enigmas. There may be anxiety in confronting personal issues or confronting those of other family members. Family members may also be reluctant to disrupt current patterns and relationships. This further incites fear and anxiety. However, once families are willing to take risks, they are able to emerge to Phase III. This phase is labeled *working through*. Change is welcomed and nurtured by the families. They are more open and confident as realization occurs, and they begin to explore solutions through alternate options. Families in this phase can help secure the group's foundation, providing support for other families who are working toward this phase.

Multiple Family Therapy Models

The Marlborough Model

This model was created by Marlborough Family Services in London using the principles established by Laqueur. The model is designed to create therapeutic communities by grouping six to eight families with similar problems together for an extended period of time. The families meet daily for about 12 weeks in a highly structured setting designed to help them address family problems within a therapeutic environment. This method allows families dealing with similar problems to help each other, learn from each other, and create a network of support. As the group progresses, the therapist allows the families to do most of the therapeutic work themselves; this enables the families to learn new methods of crisis management.

The Family Class Model

This model is an extension of the Marlborough Model that takes place in a school setting. The model is designed to help families and schools work collectively to address the needs of children displaying emotional, behavioral, or psychological problems. Ideally, six to eight families meet at the school once a week for 2 hours. This method allows parents to observe their child's school issues and allows teachers to observe family issues that are effecting the child's education. The group setting encourages families to share coping strategies, receive communal support, and to help their child achieve academic success.

Integrated Models

There are also models designed to address more specific problems. For example, the multidimensional family therapy model and the Johnson intervention model are designed to assist families dealing with substance abuse. In these models, the family interaction is more confrontational in an effort to engage the family member needing treatment. Integrated models combine the concepts of multiple family therapy with substance abuse treatment to find effective solutions to compound problems. There are four elements to the successful integration of multiple family therapy with substance abuse treatment: staff awareness and education, family education, family collaboration, and integration.

Staff awareness and education is the process of training staff to enhance their awareness and understanding of the influence and importance of family relationships. Family education involves opportunities to expose family members to psychoeducational information about their particular situation and the role of the family treating substance abuse. Family collaboration is the process of the family becoming actively involved in the treatment process and understanding the importance of supporting the family member in treatment. Integration is the culmination of the components of multiple family therapy and substance abuse treatment and strengths-based, family-oriented methods are operational.

Multiple Family Therapy With Children and Adolescents

Multiple family therapy has been implemented with children and adolescents due to its psychoeducational and supportive nature. Mental health clinics often implement multiple family therapy groups to address children with behavioral and severe emotional issues. Often these groups focus on parenting education and skills, as well as addressing harmful notions related to their child's behavior or emotional disorders. Just as with group therapy, families offer support and validation of each other's experiences. These psychoeducation-focused groups introduce techniques and may emphasize accountability in implementing home-based interventions.

Special Populations

Multiple family therapy can be implemented as a community approach to help families of troubled youth and juvenile offenders. Often referred to as parenting education groups, the purpose is to provide a support network for families struggling to address the delinquent behaviors of their children. Parents share common struggles and confirm each other's experiences. These groups may tend to have more structure as facilitators take a psychoeducational approach in increasing understanding of behavioral and emotional disorders affecting the primary client. Facilitators may even collaborate with families to provide behavioral-focused strategies and techniques to implement with their children. Multiple family therapy has also been used for families of children and teens who suffer from eating disorders. The supportive and psychoeducational foundation of multiple family therapy, accentuated with validation that family members receive, is believed to be supportive in helping families cope and helping the child work toward recovery.

Denise Gilstrap, LaQuita Parker, and Mindy Dunagan

See also Core Competencies for Marriage and Family Therapists; Family Values; Functional Family Therapy; Group Family Therapy; Group Parenting Classes; Multisystemic Therapy; Treatment Planning With Couples and Families

Further Readings

Asen, E. (2002). Multiple family therapy: An overview. *Journal of Family Therapy, 24*(1), 3.

Asen, E., & Scholz, M. (2010). *Multi-family therapy: Concepts and techniques.* New York, NY: Routledge.

Gehart, D. R. (2009). *Mastering competencies in family therapy.* Belmont, CA: Cengage Learning.

Hanna, S. M. (2007). *The practice of family therapy: Key elements across models* (4th ed.). Belmont, CA: Thomson Brooks/Cole.

Laqueur, H. P. (1976). Multiple family therapy. In P. J. Guerin (Ed.), *Family therapy: Theory and practice.* New York, NY: Gardner Press.

Lebow, J. L. (Ed.). (2005). *Handbook of clinical family therapy.* Hoboken, NJ: Wiley.

Leichter, E., & Schulman, G. L. (1974). Multi-family group therapy: A multidimensional approach. In G. D. Erickson & T. P. Hogan (Eds.), *Family therapy: An introduction to theory and technique.* Monterey, CA: Brooks/Cole.

McFarlane, W. R. (1994). Multiple-family groups and psychoeducation in the treatment of schizophrenia. *New Directions for Mental Health Services,* (62), 13–22.

Nichols, M. P. (1984). *Family therapy, concepts and methods.* New York, NY: Gardner Press.

Multiple Relationships

See Dual and Multiple Relationships

Multisystemic Therapy

Multisystemic Therapy (MST) is a comprehensive, multifaceted, home-based, empirical approach to conducting therapy with families that has been utilized throughout the United States and internationally. Created by Scott Henggeler, MST was initially designed to treat delinquent adolescents involved in behaviors such as skipping school, stealing, fighting, and drug use.

Henggeler received his doctorate in clinical psychology from the University of Virginia and is currently professor of psychiatry and behavioral sciences at the Medical University of South Carolina and director of the Family Services Research Center. Most significantly, MST developed out of his work with inner city youth who had been placed in residential treatment facilities, juvenile halls, and psychiatric hospitals. Historically, antisocial youth have been deemed difficult to treat using traditional therapy models and approaches resulting in limited success in reshaping behavior. One particular obstacle was the separation of the adolescent from their home environment. While positive behavioral changes were oftentimes achieved when the adolescent was in out-of-home placement, treatment gains were often short lived once the adolescent returned home to their family environment. Henggeler, like other systemically trained clinicians, understood that engaging multiple aspects of an adolescent's life into the therapeutic treatment process was likely to enhance behavioral change and ultimately improve treatment outcomes. This entry examines MST's use with diverse populations, its goals and core principles, the role of the MST therapist, therapeutic interventions and outcomes, the training of MST therapists, and some challenges and critiques to the model.

Engagement of Diverse Populations

MST stemmed from research concerned with ethnic minorities who were underutilizing mental health services. In developing MST, Henggeler was attempting to address this disparity by shifting service delivery systems to meet the deficiencies in traditional mental health care settings for various ethnic groups. Research on MST has explored the retention and engagement of primarily African American and Hispanic populations, and MST has shown favorable clinical outcomes with both of these groups. Specifically, studies found that treatment dropout rates could be improved by making services more accessible and by putting the responsibility of therapeutic engagement onto the service providers. Henggeler and his colleagues highlighted the importance of better understanding the family dynamics of various minority groups. In doing so, their work served to challenge the standard of care for delinquent adolescents. Simultaneously, they were encouraging treatment providers to more thoroughly engage diverse adolescents into the treatment process through family and community involvement.

Goals of Multisystemic Therapy

MST was designed in an effort to more effectively engage and retain delinquent adolescents in treatment in order for them to gain from therapeutic interventions. Multiple aspects of the adolescent's life including family members, school systems, peers and social groups, community members, and neighborhood resources are utilized in an effort to empower both the parents and the adolescents. MST provides parents with the skills to increase the effectiveness of their parenting and succeed in altering their child's inappropriate behavior. Adolescents are educated about the many skills they can use to cope with and manage the areas of their life that routinely influence their behavior negatively. Specifically, adolescents are supported and coached in how to best navigate their relationships with family members and peers while successfully managing the situations that routinely arise at school and in their neighborhoods.

The assessment and intervention process of MST is based on a set of nine core principles. Because interventions are chosen primarily based on the uniquely contextualized nature of individual families, their concerns and desired outcomes, operationalization of techniques, and implementation sequences have been challenging. The nine core principles were designed to help guide the process of program operationalization while preserving the responsivity required for therapists to address individual family needs and circumstances. This dynamic, a combination of operationalization while also allowing for individualized treatment planning and therapeutic decision-making, is viewed as a particular strength of the MST model in comparison to other highly scripted and highly manualized family therapy approaches.

Nine Core MST Principles

The following is a brief description of the nine guiding principles of the MST assessment and intervention processes. First, the therapist seeks to understand the presenting problem through a systemic lens. This systemic contextualization allows clinicians to place the problem within a broader social context, which assists immediately in the identification of potential allies and built-in resources. Second, therapeutic interactions are anchored in both family and individual strengths, which are then utilized to create and maintain lasting change. Third, therapeutic interventions are designed to decrease irresponsible behavior across all family members while promoting prosocial behavior that is in the best interest of the family system. Fourth, interventions are intentional and designed to address the *here and now* as opposed to past concerns or problems. That is, interventions are clearly thought through targeting issues of current concern for the family that have been equally well defined. Fifth, interventions are designed to address patterns of behavior within and across systems associated with maintaining the presenting problem. Sixth, in an attempt to increase effectiveness and receptiveness, interventions are designed with the specific developmental needs of the adolescent family members in mind. Seventh, interventions are designed with the expectation that family members will engage in routine efforts to create the desired systemic changes. Family members must be an active part of the solution moving collaboratively toward the desired outcome. Eighth, therapists are responsible for addressing the barriers that may arise during the therapeutic process. These may be identified as part of the model's regular and ongoing systemic evaluation of interventions. Finally, caregiver interventions are designed to help therapists empower family members across multiple systems in order to best support effective lasting change.

The Role of the MST Therapist

MST is a home-based therapy utilized in a larger neighborhood network. Therapists play the role of family counselor and case manager and interact with extended family, peers, the court system, and school officials. This model pays particular attention to addressing the socioecological issues of the family and believes that including significant others in the treatment process increases the therapist's effectiveness, therefore enhancing the likelihood that families will meet their desired goals. At its inception, therapists were on call at all times, twenty-four hours a day and seven days a week, through the use of pagers, and their caseloads varied between four to six families. Frequent contact with the family is foundational to MST and depending on the individual case may indicate daily therapeutic intervention and treatment typically lasting between 3 to 4 months.

Therapeutic Interventions in MST

Case conceptualization is driven by social ecological and family systems theory with explicit consideration of how treatment will lead to change for adolescents and their parents as well as improved relationships between them. Four specific interventions have been found to contribute to successful engagement with families being treated with

MST. First, *empathy* has been identified as contributing to successful engagement across psychotherapy models and is viewed in MST as an important intervention used to engage minority families in treatment. Second is what MST developers have termed *gift giving* and defined as the immediate benefits that therapists can offer families in the initial sessions. These may include the normalization of problems or emotions, reduction in anxiety or guilt, increase in sense of hope, specific skills that can assist in the alteration of behavior, and working collaboratively with a caring professional. The third intervention is *credibility*, which can either be ascribed or achieved. This means that therapists can be given credibility by their peers or it can be obtained through their own skill. According to MST, focus on the conceptualization of a problem, solutions to the problem, and the goals of treatment can help therapists gain credibility with the families they are working with. Finally, *scientific mindedness* has been identified as an intervention that promotes engagement. This describes an intellectual process by the therapist of continually analyzing family dynamics, developing hypotheses, and testing them.

MST Outcomes

According to developers, all the interventions used during the course of MST treatment are developed through research and monitored for outcome. Numerous studies over the years have successfully demonstrated the efficacy of MST for treating delinquent adolescents and their families. In addition to adolescent delinquency, the efficacy of MST has been explored with varying results for parenting, reunification, substance abuse, weight loss, transportability, quality assurance, implementation, adherence, and prevention. In general, there are numerous demonstrated positive outcomes of MST including (a) improving relationships between parents and teens, (b) decreasing delinquency and criminal behavior, (c) decreasing illicit drug use, (d) decreasing internalizing processes, (e) improving mental health, (f) increasing positive social and prosocial behavior, and (g) decreasing violent behavior. Furthermore, Henggeler's MST is "one of the few treatment models to demonstrate favorable long-term outcomes in randomized trials with youths who display serious antisocial behavior" (Henggeler, Schoenwald, & Munger, 1996, p. 427).

Both individual and systemic interventions are used in the MST treatment process. To promote change within the family system, therapists utilize strategies that are uniquely designed for each individual family's situation and needs. Another hallmark of MST's success is the crafting of interventions for adolescents who are equally personalized and developmentally appropriate. At the crux of MST is the understanding that treatment will only be effective if families attend and participate in sessions. Engagement then is crucial for exposing families to an adequate dose of the intervention required to create significant and lasting change. Signs of engagement according to the MST model include high rates of attendance, completion of homework assignments, emotional involvement in sessions, and progress toward meeting treatment goals. MST has been found to significantly improve the engagement of delinquent adolescents and their families in treatment.

In one study of 84 violent and chronic juvenile offenders who were at risk for out-of-home placement due to criminal activity, 86% completed treatment and showed a greater reduction in criminal activity than those assigned to receive the usual services provided by the Department of Juvenile Justice. In another study, MST was compared to individual therapy. The study included 200 adolescents between the ages of 12 and 17. Sixty-one percent had been incarcerated prior to the study. Seventy-three percent of adolescents and their families assigned to the MST group completed the research study. Results showed that adolescents assigned to the MST group had an increase in adaptability, cohesion, and supportiveness. There were also decreases in conflict and hostility during family discussions and parental psychiatric symptomatology. Researchers also found that these changes lasted through a 4-year follow-up. The adolescents had been arrested less often, for less serious offenses, and with lower rates of violence- and substance abuse–related offenses.

Another 3-year study of MST evaluated the treatment outcomes of engaged adolescents 11 to 17 years of age. Seventy-three percent had been in at least one out-of-home placement and 63% had committed a crime against another person. Results showed that participants in MST exhibited an increase in family functioning and decreased socialized aggression and parent symptomatology. Those receiving *usual services* deteriorated or did not make any changes in these areas.

MST Training and Supervision

Successful implementation of MST is contingent upon both thorough extensive training and then close monitoring and mentoring of therapists. Initially, the amount and intensity of supervision was so extensive that follow-up studies demonstrating MST's effectiveness required shifting these variables to more closely mirror those found in community-based service delivery models. Assessing the usefulness of MST required that researchers identify specifically what therapists are expected to do and train treatment providers to engage in those activities and interventions.

Equally important and challenging though was the next step of monitoring therapeutic interactions between treatment providers and families to determine the extent to which therapists were able to adhere to the treatment protocol. In response, researchers developed the MST Adherence Scale, a 26-item Likert scale measure designed to determine the ability of therapists to implement MST in accordance with its nine treatment principles. Training and supervision also aid in ensuring adherence to treatment protocols, which has been essential in determining the long-term effectiveness of MST in treating delinquent adolescents.

Examples of themes contained in the measure include (a) The therapist tried to understand how my family's problems all fit together; (b) My family and the therapist had similar ideas about ways to solve problems; and (c) My family and the therapist were honest and straightforward with each other. Again, given the nature of MST and its flexibility in application across families, items were not designed to determine the worth of a specific intervention. Rather, the meaure's questions were rated by the caregiver, adolescent, and therapist to determine adherence across interactions to the nine core principles of the model. Dimensions aimed at caregivers included general adherence to MST principles, nonproductive sessions, therapist–family problem-solving efforts, therapist attempts to change family interactions, lack of directions during sessions, and family-therapy consensus. Ratings for therapists included the following dimensions: (a) engagement of the family, (b) adherence to the MST principles, (c) nonproductive sessions, (d) focus on noncompliance, and (e) degree of family–therapist conflict. Finally, adolescent dimensions included therapist adherence to the MST principles, focus on noncompliance, lack of direction in the sessions, and level of productivity of the sessions.

Challenges and Critiques

Developers of MST have experienced a number of challenges in demonstrating its effectiveness. For one, it can be challenging to measure the effectiveness of interventions when they are not applied uniformly across families. Rather, MST therapy is based on nine core principles that drive the development of a unique intervention that reflects the distinctive needs of individual families. In addition, critiques have challenged research methods, including errors of logic (i.e., fidelity, site-level variations, and selective use of evidence), integrity of MST trials (i.e., inconsistent reports, missing cases and lack of transparency in the randomization process), and generalizability.

The transportability of MST results have been challenged, questioning how easily they are translated beyond the university laboratory environment to community-based clinics and agencies or to more mainstream mental health service delivery models. While training in the MST model requires a great deal of time, resources, and expense, similar engagement processes can occur naturally in community-based clinics and agencies through interventions led by master's-level trained mental health counselors and clinicians.

One research study indicated that certain therapeutic techniques closely mirroring those in MST (i.e., earning and ascribing credibility and scientific mindedness) were being used to successfully engage families with substance-using adolescents without costly specialized training. The ability to inform therapists of strategies that may be most effective in the engagement of these families without the financial investment would benefit community mental health agencies and clinics while increasing treatment outcomes for substance-using adolescents. The design of an effective engagement strategy without the time and financial expense means more effectively delivering efficacious treatments to the average community mental health agency.

The application of MST can be far reaching. For instance, the use of MST can be time consuming and costly. Indeed, its logistics and delivery differ from many other community-based approaches. This poses a number of challenges for agencies who wish to implement MST within the established context of a larger mental health service delivery system. Most professionals in academia are aware of the gap between research and practice. Unfortunately, this gap often prevents the most effective forms of treatment from reaching some of the populations most in need.

Incurred expenses in utilizing the MST model may include start-up costs, technical assistance, orientation, travel, site licensing fees, staffing, implementation fees, fidelity monitoring, and evaluation, which can total nearly one million dollars for a relatively small to moderate community of families. While professionals may naturally gravitate toward techniques that promote both engagement and efficacious intervention, continued mainstream recognition of MST is likely to support its successful implementation across diverse settings.

Janee Both Gragg

See also Ecological Systems; Empirically Validated Models; Empowerment in Families; Families and Substance Abuse; Home-Based Therapy; Outcome Research; Parent–Adolescent Relations; Parenting

Further Readings

Both Gragg, J., & Wilson, C. (2011). Mexican American family's perceptions of the multirelational influences on their adolescent's engagement in substance use treatment. *Family Journal, 19*(3), 299–306.

Cunningham, P., & Henggeler, S. W. (1999). Engaging multiproblem families in treatment: Lessons learned throughout the development of multisystemic therapy. *Family Process, 38,* 265–286.

Cunningham, P., & Randall, J. (2008). Multisystemic approaches to supervision: Tales of woe (cultural nonconnect in supervision and understanding the fit). In C. A. Falender & E. P. Shafranske (Eds.), *Casebook for clinical supervision: A competency-based approach* (pp. 181–195). Washington, DC: American Psychological Association.

Henggeler, S. W., Cunningham, P., Pickrel, S., & Schoenwald, S. (1994). Multisystemic therapy: An innovative treatment approach with serious juvenile offenders and their families. In T. Jeffers & I. M. Schwartz (Eds.), *Home-based services for serious and violent juvenile offenders*. Philadelphia, PA: Center for the Study of Youth Policy.

Henggeler, S. W., Melton, G., & Smith, L. (1992). Family preservation using multisystemic therapy: An effective alternative to incarcerating serious juvenile offenders. *Journal of Consulting and Clinical Psychology, 60,* 953–961.

Henggeler, S. W., & Schaeffer, C. (2010). Treating serious antisocial behavior using multisystemic therapy. In J. R. Weisz & A. E. Kazdin (Eds.), *Evidence-based psychotherapies for children and adolescents* (2nd ed., pp. 259–276). New York, NY: Guilford Press.

Henggeler, S. W., Schoenwald, S., & Munger, R. (1996). Families and therapists achieve clinical outcomes, systems of care mediate the process. *Journal of Child and Family Studies, 5,* 177–183.

Littell, J. H. (2005). Lessons from a systematic review of multisystemic therapy. *Children and Youth Services Review, 27,* 445–463.

Littell, J. H. (2006). The case for multisystemic therapy: Evidence or orthodoxy? *Children and Youth Services Review, 28,* 458–472.

Scherer, D., Brondino, M., Henggeler, S. W., Melton, G., & Hanley, J. (1994). Multisystemic family preservation therapy preliminary findings from a study of rural and minority serious adolescent offenders. *Journal of Emotional and Behavioral Disorders, 2,* 198–206.

Schoenwald, S. (2000). Multisystemic therapy: Monitoring treatment fidelity. *Family Process, 39*, 83–103.

Schoenwald, S., Brown, T., & Henggeler, S. W. (2000). Inside multisystemic therapy: Therapists, supervisory, and program practices. *Journal of Emotional and Behavioral Disorders, 8*, 113–127.

Tiernan, K., Foster, S., Cunningham, P., Brennan, P., & Whitmore, E. (2014). Predicting early positive change in multisystemic therapy with youth exhibiting antisocial behaviors. *Psychotherapy, 52*(1), 93–102.

Muslim American Families

Religion dictates values and beliefs, which in turn influence behaviors inside and outside the home, including help-seeking behaviors. However, little is known about Muslim American families and mental health due to the lack of research on the topic. This void in knowledge hinders effective practice with Muslim Americans and may deter Muslim Americans from seeking formalized mental health services. Little or no training on Muslim American culture among helping professionals, such as counselors, leaves them ill equipped and vulnerable to perpetuating stereotypes and discrimination. Thus, mental health professionals need to become familiar with the religious beliefs and traditions of Muslim American clients to engage in culturally sensitive practice. This entry provides a brief discussion of diversity among Muslims and further examines the formation of marital unions, spousal expectations, and the utilization of mental health services within the Muslim population. The entry concludes by providing suggestions for practice.

Diversity

It is important to note that, like Christian Americans, Muslim Americans are a diverse population representing various national cultures and denominational variations. The majority of Muslim Americans are immigrants from Arab countries and South Asia while most American-born Muslims are African American. Mainstream U.S. culture has inaccurately represented Islam. For example, cultural practices rooted within national cultures are often mistaken as religious practice. An *abaya* (also called *burqa*), a black full-length covering for the head and body of Muslim women, is often mistaken as a religious garment. In reality, modesty is conveyed through various cultural traditions. For instance, Pakistani women are not required to cover the head, but most women wear *shalwar kameez*, a tunic with loose-fitting pants and a scarf worn on the shoulders. Thus, Muslims enact their religious identity (e.g., codes of modesty) in different ways.

It should also be noted that the term *Muslim*, literally meaning "one who submits to God," is a label used by groups of varying beliefs identifying with the religion of Islam. Like Christianity, Islam is a religion with multiple denominations or sects. The majority of Muslims follow the Sunni sect of Islam, while the minority are Shi'a; both groups believe in one God and that Muhammad is God's last prophet. However, according to some, certain sub-Shi'i sects are not believed to be a part of Islam. For example, Sunnis have a spiritual allegiance to the prophet Muhammad while some Shi'i sects, like Ismailis, pledge their spiritual allegiance to the current living Prince Karim Aga Khan. The diverse and intersecting identities of Muslims must be recognized. Therefore, one must be mindful that any discussion of Muslim American families must not be viewed as a model that fits the lives of all Muslim Americans.

Marital Union Formation

Marriage is an important facet of Islamic tradition and most Muslims are expected to get married and have children. Marriage is not required for Muslims, but unmarried Muslims may be frowned upon or even experience social isolation within their community. Like their non-Muslim counterparts, Muslim Americans tend to marry in their 20s. Some but not all Muslims have arranged marriages as part of their sociocultural experiences. When Muslims practice arranged marriage, the process by which the arrangement develops varies based on cultural and familial preferences.

For families that arrange marriages, the mother typically seeks prospective partners through relatives, friends, and matchmakers. Compatibility is sought based on ethnic heritage, religious denomination, education, income, and level of religiosity. Once the mother identifies a prospective match, information about the prospective spouse is shared among one's immediate family. If the son and daughter agree to meet, then the couple may meet with their respective families or independently. After meeting on a few occasions, the potential couple decide whether they would like to get married. This decision tends to be made with one's family. For example, if a man wanted to marry a woman to whom he was introduced, he would likely discuss his wishes with his immediate family to determine the best course of action. There are variations of the above example. For instance, some couples may not see each other before their wedding, others meet each other in the presence of their families or chaperone, or they communicate through telephone or the Internet prior to their wedding.

Alternatively, some couples, like their Christian counterparts, may date prior to marriage. The initial meeting of such a couple may or may not be arranged. In some cases, one's family member, community member, or matchmaker may facilitate introductions for matrimonial purposes followed by dating to determine whether they would like to get married. In these instances, Muslim Americans may meet independent of their family and community through school, work, and other such settings.

When seeking a partner for marriage, many Muslims believe that Muslim men may marry "people of the book" (i.e., Christians and Jews), while Muslim women are limited to Muslim men. Nevertheless, like many religious issues, multiple interpretations exist of the Qur'an, the religious text of most denominations in Islam. The Qur'an states that Muslim men may marry people of the book, but it does not state anything in reference to whom women may or may not marry. Thus, some argue that Muslim women are not prohibited from marrying non-Muslims, but identifying an imam, a Muslim religious leader akin to a priest, who is willing to conduct a marriage between a Muslim woman and a non-Muslim man is a challenge.

Gender Expectations

Traditional Muslim communities are collectivistic, regardless of national origin. Familial well-being is developed through cooperation and interdependence, counter to Western values of autonomy and independence. Nevertheless, there may be a clash between what Muslim American women are learning from mainstream American culture and expectations in the Muslim community. The tension experienced by women in relation to the individual and community may be rooted within the dual cultural milieu: mainstream American society and the *ummah* (community of Muslims). The *ummah* includes one's immediate and extended family, Muslim friends, local religious leaders, and others within the general Muslim community (e.g., local teachers, businesspersons).

Some Muslim families adhere, to some degree, to a patriarchal familial structure. In some traditional Muslim families, women may be expected to stay at home to raise children and take care of the home while the husband works outside of the home to support the family financially. Such practices are not rooted within Islam, as prophet Muhammad's first wife, Khadijah, was a successful businesswoman. Islam also protects the financial freedom of women by requiring men to provide financial support for his family while women are free to spend their income as they choose. Thus, restrictions on working outside of the home may be rooted within national cultures. More specifically, it may be normative for a Kuwaiti woman to work outside of the home, but it may be shameful within Afghan culture for a woman to do so. In more traditional contexts, the expectation among men to financially support their family may be a source of tension given the current economic climate. Women may work due to financial necessity, which may be perceived as a husband's inability to fulfill his obligations as a man.

Further, many Muslim American women pursue an education and some work outside of the home, yet they are still expected to take responsibility for maintenance of the home. Some of these Muslim women may balance dual identities both in and outside of the home; outside of the home, she may be independent and assertive, but her behavior inside the home may focus on cohesion and connectedness among family. Thus, Muslim American women may struggle with the competing demands of their family and culture with their individual wants and needs.

Most of the different expectations for men and women begin at puberty. In comparison with their brothers, girls, upon reaching menarche, are expected to dress modestly and adhere to strict behavioral expectations. Modest attire for some Muslim girls may mean covering their legs (e.g., no shorts) and/or their arms. Some Muslim girls may choose to wear a *hijab* (head scarf). Islamic clergy, made up of men, prescribe *hijab*, but Muslim feminist critiques have challenged traditional Islamic interpretations of the Qur'an. The Qur'an does not state that all Muslim women must cover their head or wear a veil, but some women choose to wear a *hijab*. When freely chosen, the *hijab* can be liberating and a way for women to express cultural identity and avoid harassment and sexual objectification.

For young Muslim American girls, maneuvering between their identity as both Muslim and American may be a source of conflict. For example, within the school setting Muslim American youth may be rewarded for exercising their autonomy and sharing their opinions. While at home, however, they are expected to conform to familial norms and not speak out. At a young age, Muslims girls may be taught that violations of both cultural and religious norms will bring shame and dishonor to their family. This expectation continues into adulthood where wives are expected to care for and maintain the family structure, even at the expense of their own desires.

The tension between individual desires and behaviors and the *ummah* may cause distress for some individuals and families. This tension may be further exacerbated when maneuvering between disparate cultures and may inhibit Muslims and their families from accessing formal mental health services. Instead of seeking out services, there is a belief that the *ummah* is intended to meet the psychological needs of community members.

Utilization of Mental Health Services

Some Muslim Americans choose to live in communities with other Muslim residents, particularly those of the same ethnic group. These ethnic enclaves create literal and figurative spaces to preserve and reinforce cultural and religious beliefs and practices while also serving as a source of support. Family members and respected members of the community are sought for consultation. Therefore, Muslim Americans may not seek formal services when conflicts exist within relationships. The community serving as a source of support provides culturally appropriate responses for Muslim American couples and families, but they may also serve as a way to perpetuate culturally based inequities, particularly those experienced by women.

On the one hand, Muslim Americans may not seek formal services because of a presumed cultural tension whereby mainstream American helping professionals are not perceived as being culturally competent to work with Muslims. Muslim American families may believe that non-Muslim Americans will not understand their religious and cultural traditions. Thus, in times of need, they may not be willing to focus on teaching a non-Muslim about their religion. Additionally, Muslim Americans may also worry about non-Muslim mental health care providers preaching and attempting to impose their own value system on Muslim Americans.

On the other hand, working with a Muslim mental health care provider may pose challenges, particularly in smaller Muslim communities. Families may feel shame and may be unwilling to seek support from a professional within their community. In addition, while confidentiality is to be upheld within mental health care relationships, Muslim families may still be concerned about their challenges being shared with their community, thereby tarnishing the family name. Hence, support from trusted family members and respected members of the community is preferred because they are likely perceived to keep information private while also providing support in a culturally and religiously sensitive manner.

Suggestions for Culturally Sensitive Practice

Helping professions must be flexible and open to understanding the cultural and religious context of Muslim American families. This requires understanding different variations within Islam and within the diverse Muslim communities with which mental health care professionals work. An effective relationship will require creating a space in which Muslim Americans share experiences without judgment to create change without compromising one's religious and cultural identities. Practitioners should also be prepared to help Muslim American families negotiate the tensions they experience in the dual cultural milieu between mainstream American settings (e.g., school, work) and their Muslim American community, culture, and religion, including the specific gender expectations placed on men and women and how these may create dissonance in relationships. Professionals with a working knowledge of the religious and cultural traditions of Muslim Americans will be best suited to helping couples and families navigate these tensions.

Mazna Patka and Jennifer Wallin-Ruschman

See also African American Families; Asian American Families; Cultural Issues in Couples and Families; Immigrant Families

Further Readings

Ahmed, S., & Amer, M. M. (2011). *Counseling Muslims: Handbook of mental health issues and interventions.* New York, NY: Routledge.

Armstrong, K. (2002). *Islam: A short history.* New York, NY: Random House.

Mattu, A., & Maznavi, N. (2014). *Salaam, love: American Muslim men on love, sex, and intimacy.* Boston, MA: Beacon House.

Narrative Therapy

The history of narrative therapy rests on the work of the early family practitioners, who, operating from a systems perspective, focused on the dynamics and interconnectedness of families. These clinicians noticed the language and discourse of family members and how these conversations shaped the family unit in both negative and positive ways. This evolutionary discourse resulted in narrative therapy, created by Michael White and David Epston. Influenced by family therapist Salvador Minuchin, philosopher Michel Foucault, and the Milan school of family therapy, among others, in 1990 White and Epston published the seminal narrative therapy text, *Narrative Means to Therapeutic Ends*. Their narrative therapy centers people as the experts in their own lives and separates clients from their problems.

Narrative therapy continues to be a popular choice for treating children, families, and couples, and over the last 20 years it has increasingly received attention in family therapy journals and textbooks. This entry first provides an overview of the philosophical and etiological underpinnings of the therapy and then explores the role of the therapist in narrative therapy and how narrative therapy is used with clients. Finally, it discusses research on the effectiveness of narrative therapy.

Postmodernism

Narrative therapy falls in line with other postmodern counseling approaches, which are grounded in social constructivist theories. According to social constructivists, reality is created and maintained through language and dialogue embedded within a social cultural sphere. Through conversation and in dialogue with one another, individuals cocreate knowledge and transmit narratives that are embedded within the culture and impact how people view themselves in relation to others.

In the narrative therapy view, people's problems stem from the fact that their personal lives do not align with the social stories and dominant societal dialogue of how to live. As a result, individuals create a "problem-saturated story" that impacts the way they relate to others or themselves. They may struggle with relationship concerns, poor self-esteem, or other diagnosable mental health concerns that lead them to enter therapy. The goals of narrative therapy are to identify the problem-saturated stories, discover exceptions to these dominant narratives, and generate more preferable, alternative stories that help re-author the person's life.

In creating narrative therapy, White utilized Foucault's idea of *dominant discourse* to describe how problems remain situated within sociocultural contexts. Dominant discourses refer to culturally generated stories about what life should look like and how people should live. These stories serve to organize social groups at all levels, including couples and families, and are often foundational to how we live our lives. A result of using Foucault's ideas on power led to the idea of deconstruction within narrative therapy. Deconstruction within narrative therapy is accomplished by questioning how problems develop and are maintained; it also takes place by questioning unrecognized practices of power, and even by questioning therapeutic discourses and practices. Deconstruction provides some liberation from labels and allows the opportunity to consider multiple interpretations, discourage conflict surrounding blame, and increase feelings of agency. Those operating from a narrative perspective posit that one's self is constructed through relationships with others; thus, the focus on language, power, and dialogue often contributes to how we see and experience ourselves.

The Role of the Narrative Therapist

Narrative therapists help separate individuals from their problems by using techniques that explore how language sustains problems. In this vein, the person is not the problem, the problem is the problem. Narrative therapists pay attention to the problems people talk about in therapy, which are often part of a thin, problem-saturated story that contains few examples. The therapist points out to the client that this story is only one of many stories, and points out the times that the dominant, problem-saturated story was not evident. Whenever references to events that are not connected to the problem-saturated story are made, the therapist highlights this experience for the client by talking about it and reliving the experience; in this way, the client re-creates a new, vivid story that has a new story line. In this way, the problem-saturated story becomes one of many possible stories and, as a result, loses its power and influence over the client.

In the narrative counseling relationship, a narrative therapist is an active "coeditor" or "coauthor" who assists clients in the re-storying of their problem-saturated stories. Clients are considered the experts on their own lives; the therapist is respectful of the client, believing that problems are separate from people and assuming that the client has the skills, talents, and abilities to reduce the influence of the problem in his or her life. The therapist assumes a "not knowing," curious stance, while at the same time is aware of the social or political environment that may be influencing the client's self-worth.

Process of Narrative Counseling

The process of counseling includes helping clients discover new ways to consider themselves in relation to the problem by redefining the role of the problem in their lives. The counseling process uses structured interventions and focuses on various forms of oppression. Five stages of therapy are offered as a general guide to follow: (1) meeting the person; (2) listening; (3) separating the person from the problem; (4) enacting preferred narratives; and (5) solidifying.

An initial step in narrative therapy is to *meet the person apart from the problem,* which entails the therapist asking clients various questions about who they are as individuals: what their hobbies are, who is in their family, and other aspects related to their life. Some typical questions that determine meeting the person apart from the problem include these: "What do you do for fun? Do you have hobbies? Tell me about your family and friends. What is important to you in life?" Answers to these questions help clinicians see their clients as everyday people and can help them develop meaningful therapeutic relationships.

The next phase, *listening,* relates to listening for the effects of dominant discourses and identifying times when the client did not experience the problem. The clinician can do this by asking the client questions about the problem that help situate the problem outside of the client. In this way, the problem has a separate identity, much like the client. It is important to use the same words the client uses to help him or her relive the experience and to privilege his or her experience. These questions might help the therapist "meet" the problem: "When did the problem first enter your life?" "What were your first impressions of the problem?" "Who else has been affected by the problem?"

In separating the person from the problem, the clinician uses techniques such as *externalization,* which incorporates several dimensions and is explained in more detail later in this entry.

During the phase of *enacting preferred narratives,* the primary goal is to increase the client's sense of agency and the belief that clients can influence the direction of their lives. In working with a client on these preferred narratives, the clinician helps the client develop goals that reflect local knowledge, and attempts are made to decrease the influence of the dominant discourse (i.e., how one should live one's life according to the dominant culture).

Finally, during the *solidifying* phase, significant persons in a client's life serve as witnesses to strengthen the preferred story and identity.

Goal setting in narrative counseling is unique to each client; in a general sense, the goal of narrative counseling is to help clients enact their preferred narratives and identities. As a result, the goals for each individual client will be uniquely tied to their culture and environment. During the working phase of counseling, the targeting of immediate symptoms and presenting problems may include "Increase opportunities to interact with friends using 'confident, social' self" or "Increase instances of defiance in response to anorexia's directions not to eat."

Interventions and Techniques

One of the key interventions of narrative therapy is to *externalize* the problem. When externalizing the problem, the client or therapist names the problem or issue as a means to separate it from the individual. The use of externalizing names objectifies, and even personifies, the problem. When using externalization, the narrative therapist listens to the person's description of the problem. The therapist then renames the problem so that it is situated outside of the person, and if it is an adjective, the therapist renames it as a noun.

A more recent method to develop externalizing conversations, the statement of position map, includes four categories of inquiry that are used throughout a session and across sessions to help alter the client's relationship with the problem and discover new possibilities for action. During *inquiry category 1,* the clinician begins by defining the problem using the client's words, so, "feeling bad" is preferred to the clinical term of "depressed." During *inquiry category 2,* the clinician maps the effects of the problem by identifying how the problem affects various areas of the client's life, including home, school, work, and relationships with self and others. *Inquiry category 3* evaluates the effects of the problem's activities, where the clinician asks the client to evaluate the effects of it through questions such as this one: "Are these activities okay with you?" *Inquiry category 4* is the final phase, and is justifying the evaluation. In this phase, the clinician asks clients why they evaluated the situation the way they did. When externalizing using the previous four categories, various metaphors are used to relate to problems. Some of these include walking out on the problem, escaping from the problem, taming the problem, going on strike against the problem, and educating the problem, among others.

Relative influence questioning was the first method for externalization, and serves to both assess and intervene. There are two parts to relative influence questions: (1) mapping the influence of the problem and (2) mapping the influence of persons.

During *mapping the influence of the problem,* the therapist asks the client how the problem has affected his or her life and the lives of others. In essence, these questions relate to how the problem is affecting the client at a physical, emotional, and psychological level; the client's closest relationships with partner, children, and parents; the client's identity story and how the client conceives of his or her identity or self-worth; and the health, identity, emotions, and other relationships of important people in the client's life. It is important that the therapist follow up these series of questions with the *mapping the influence of persons* question to ensure the client does not feel worse afterward. The *mapping the influence of persons* questions involve identifying how the client has affected the life of the problem, which is in reverse to the *mapping the influence of the problem* questions. Some questions that might map the influence of the person include "When have the persons involved kept the problem from affecting their mood?" and "When have the persons involved kept the problem from impacting their work or school lives?"

Another key narrative intervention is to identify *unique outcomes*. To use unique outcomes, the therapist listens to the client's problem-saturated story and identifies events that contradict the story. A unique outcome can be a belief, thought, action, or plan. The therapist can pose questions to elicit unique outcomes, such as "How have you helped the problem from getting worse?"

When using *re-authoring conversations*, the therapist helps the client link previous unique outcomes with current unique outcomes—for example, "Tell me about another time you didn't let fear stand in your way." Conversations about these alternative story lines help *thicken* the description of these unique outcomes, which helps the client consider future problem-solving processes and identify preferred directions.

When engaging in *re-membering* conversations, the therapist helps the client identify significant others who were a part of the person's past, or who are a part of their life in the present, and help to support the alternative, emerging story. These individuals, who have memories of the client demonstrating certain skills or behaving in ways that are congruent with the preferred story, may also obtain "membership" in the client's "club of life." In being a member of the client's club of life, this person is someone who reinforces the emerging story. Clients can also dismiss individuals from their "club of life" if they do not support them in their emerging story.

Outsider witnesses are people who witness the conversation between the therapist and the person. They do not form opinions or give advice, but serve to listen to clients' "retelling" of their stories. During an interview with the therapist, they then serve to reinforce the unique outcomes during the retelling of a person's story.

The therapist asks clients if they wish to receive any *therapeutic documents,* which consist of four different types. These types of therapeutic documents are (1) letters that record emerging alternative stories; (2) documents that communicate alternative stories to others; (3) documents that record knowledge of particular skills that the person could use in times of crisis; and (4) documents that facilitate transitions or celebrate achievements. Narrative letters written by the clinician help reinforce the emerging narrative and consist of the following characteristics: (a) emphasize client agency; (b) take observer position where the clinician is observing the changes the client is making and cite specific examples whenever possible; (c) highlight temporality—the attention to time plots the emerging story and illustrates where the client was, is, and will be; and (d) encourage polysemy, where multiple meanings are considered, rather than offering single interpretations. Letters can be used early in the counseling relationship, or during, to reinforce the emerging narrative, or at the end of counseling, to summarize changes and gains made during the counseling process.

Narrative therapists use language in ways that promote a democratic counseling relationship and encourage the client to maintain a strong sense of agency when talking with the therapist. There are two specific ways they do this in narrative therapy: the use of *permission questions* and the use of *situating comments*. Permission questions are simply that—the clinician asks the client for permission to ask a question. This breaks down the power differential and empowers clients to feel comfortable not answering a question if they choose not to. Similarly, situating comments reinforce client agency by not overvaluing what the clinician says or considering it more valid or true. So a clinician who uses situating comments might share his or her perspective and the source of his or her perspective with the client, while also acknowledging that it is only one perspective among many.

Other interventions that narrative therapists use are creative approaches, such as drawing, games, and play, which can all help identify dominant narratives and create problem-solving opportunities.

Research

For a number of reasons, there is limited empirical research on the effectiveness of narrative therapy. First, the intended process of narrative therapy has not always been made clear, leaving some confusion about how the process takes place. While the techniques and interventions have been sufficiently described, the outcomes of these interventions have not always been made clear. However, several benefits to externalization have been noted, some of which include inviting people to unite in a struggle against a problem and reduce its influence; encouraging a less stressful approach to interacting with the problem; identifying new ways to reduce the influence of the problem; and decreasing unproductive conflict and blame among family members.

Michael White, in an effort to prove the systematic efforts that went into the technique of externalization, referenced Lev Vygotsky's *zone of proximal development* to describe how scaffolding assists with externalization. The zone of proximal development describes what people can learn with assistance from someone else, such as a therapist, or by themselves. If people are working independently on their own, they are operating on the initial developmental level. A proximal development level is the level of competence someone can reach with assistance. *Scaffolding* is the assistance someone receives to reach the zone of proximal development.

In recent years, more systematic efforts to understand and identify narrative practices have emerged. For example, the assessment system of narrative change (ASNC) was developed to assess specific characteristics that happen in systemic therapies. This assessment system can help clinicians diagnose and identify narrative blockages and provides a sense of how the client is progressing in therapy and how effective the therapy is proving to be. Recent research on narrative therapy reflects these efforts to systematically document the process, benefits, and potential outcome of narrative therapy.

Caroline Perjessy

See also Cultural Issues in Couples and Families; Milan Team; Postmodern Therapies; Social Constructionism; Systemic Family Therapy

Further Readings

Bruner, J. (1986). *Actual minds, possible worlds.* Cambridge, MA: Harvard University Press.

Chang, J., Combs, G., Dolan, Y., Freedman, J., Mitchell, T., & Trepper, T. S. (2013). From Ericksonian roots to postmodern futures: Part II. Shaping the future. *Journal of Systemic Therapies, 32*(2), 35–45.

Foucault, M. (1987). *Power/knowledge: Selected interviews and writings, 1972–1977* (C. Gordon, Trans.). New York: Pantheon Books.

Freedman, J., & Combs, G. (1996). *Narrative therapy: The social construction of preferred realities.* New York: W. W. Norton.

Freedman, J., & Combs, G. (2008). Narrative couple therapy. In A. Gurman (Ed.), *Clinical handbook of couple therapy* (pp. 229–258). New York: Guilford.

Geertz, C. (1973). Thick description: Toward an interpretative theory of culture. In *The interpretation of cultures* (pp. 3–30). New York: Basic Books.

Vygotsky, L. S. (1987). Thinking and speech. In R. W. Rievery & A. S. Carton (Eds.) & N. Minnick (Trans.), *The collected works of L. S. Vygotsky: Vol. 1. Problems of general psychology* (pp. 39–285). New York: Plenum Press.

White, M. (2007). *Maps of narrative practice.* New York: W. W. Norton.

White, M., & Epston, D. (1990). *Narrative means to therapeutic ends.* New York: W. W. Norton.

NATIONAL MARRIAGE INITIATIVE

The federal Healthy Marriage Initiative, which provides funding for programs that promote marriage and offer education in marriage and relationship skills, began in the early 2000s but grew out of concerns that had been expressed by political leaders for many years about declining marriage rates. This entry discusses the development of the initiative and the rationale behind it, how funding from the program is used, and the implications of the program and similar programs for counselors and educators.

Supporters of government programs to promote marriage have pointed to research indicating that children raised in single-parent homes are more likely to have emotional and behavioral problems, have lower academic achievement, use drugs, and become welfare recipients than children raised by two biological parents. Research has also found that children who did not live with both biological parents are more likely to be poor. They also have raised concerns about the growth in single parenthood; by 2010, 41% of all births were to unmarried women, up from only 7% in 1964. Critics of government programs to promote marriage have questioned whether they are effective in reducing poverty and raised concerns about stigmatizing single-parent families. In addition, some have said these programs use government money to support a religious viewpoint.

The focus on marriage at the federal level also grew out of concerns that many federal programs on which low-income people depend contain a disincentive for marriage, since a married couple receives less in benefits than do two single people together. Medicaid, Temporary Assistance to Needy Families, public housing, food stamps, and the Earned Income Tax Credit are programs geared toward single-parent families.

President Bill Clinton, in his 1996 State of the Union address, challenged the audience to take more responsibility to cherish children and strengthen families. The Personal Responsibility and Work Opportunity Reconciliation Act (PRWORA), signed into law that year by President Clinton, reformed federal welfare policy and included language that among the goals were "to encourage the formation and maintenance of two-parent families" and "to prevent and reduce the incidence of out-of-wedlock pregnancies."

President George W. Bush in 2001 proposed a national marriage initiative, which was launched in 2002 by the Administration for Children and Families (ACF), a division of the Department of Health and Human Services, as the Healthy Marriage Initiative. In 2005, under the Deficit Reduction Act, an annual amount of $150 million was designated for what was by then named the Healthy Marriage and Responsible Fatherhood Initiative. Congress reauthorized the program in 2010 and again allocated $150 million annually to fund competitive grants, with funding equally split between healthy marriage and responsible fatherhood grants. These grants are available through the Office of Family Assistance, an ACF entity, and have been awarded to state and local government agencies and private organizations. ACF provides training and technical assistance to programs that serve married and engaged individuals and individuals considering marriage.

The healthy marriage grants can be used for a variety of purposes, including public advertising campaigns on the value of marriage and skills needed for a stable marriage; education in high schools on the value of marriage, relationship skills, and budgeting; and marriage skills training for engaged couples, those who are already married, and those interested in marriage. Other activities allowed under the grants are divorce reduction programs teaching relationship skills, marriage mentoring programs where married couples serve as role models and mentors, and programs to reduce disincentives to marriage in means-tested aid programs.

Awareness of the importance of multicultural competence in working with ethnically diverse populations has led to targeted strategies within the Healthy Marriage Initiative that focus on particular populations. These include the Asian and Pacific Islander Healthy Marriage and Family Strengthening Initiative (APIHMFSI), the African American Healthy Marriage Initiative (AAHMI), the Hispanic Healthy Marriage Initiative (HHMI), and the Native American Healthy Marriage Initiative (NAHMI).

In addition to programs funded by the federal marriage initiative, state and locally funded marriage initiatives also can provide opportunities for counselors and educators to provide marital counseling and marriage education. Numerous organizations, such as the university-affiliated Cooperative Extension Service, have developed marriage and couples education programs.

Mary Alice Fernandez

See also Marriage Education; Marriage Enrichment; Relationship Enhancement

Further Readings

Administration for Children and Families. (n.d.). *Healthy marriage & responsible fatherhood*. Retrieved from https://hmrf.acf.hhs.gov/

Administration for Children and Families. (n.d.). *The healthy marriage initiative: Research*. Retrieved from http://archive.acf.hhs.gov/healthymarriage/resources/research.html#or

Bir, A., Lerman, R., Corwin, E., MacIlvain, B., Beard, A., Richburg, K., & Smith, K. (2012). *Impacts of a community healthy marriage initiative* (OPRE Report # 2012-34A). Washington, DC: Office of Planning, Research and Evaluation, Administration for Children and Families, U.S. Department of Health and Human Services.

Fincham, F. F., & Beach, S. H. (2010). Marriage in the new millennium: A decade in review. *Journal of Marriage & Family, 72,* 630–649.

Hawkins, A. J., & Ooms, T. (2012). Can marriage and relationship education be an effective policy tool to help low-income couples form and sustain healthy marriages and relationships? A review of lessons learned. *Marriage & Family Review, 48,* 524–554. doi:10.1080/01494929.2012.677751

Parke, M. (2003, May). *Are married parents really better for children? What research says about the effect of family structure on child well-being* (Couples and Marriage Research and Policy Brief No. 3). Washington, DC: Center for Law and Social Policy. Retrieved from http://www.clasp.org/resources-and-publications/states/0086.pdf

NATIVE AMERICAN FAMILIES

The United States Bureau of Indian Affairs defines a Native American as an individual with at least one-fourth native blood or whose ancestors are genealogically of Native American heritage. There are multiple terms used to describe Native Americans, including natives and American Indians. Different terms are used in different parts of North and South America, but this entry focuses on Native Americans in the United States. Native Americans are one of the most marginalized cultural groups in the United States, and it is important for marital, couples, and family counselors to be sensitive to the needs of marginalized groups. Although Native Americans have a high incidence of alcoholism, suicide, high school dropout, and unemployment, they are an underserved population in the field of mental health. In addition, there is limited research specifically addressing counseling of Native American families. This entry provides a brief history of Native Americans, discusses factors that may contribute to mistrust among Native Americans, and discusses implications for counselors in working with this population.

Brief History

There are more than 500 Indian tribes and native villages in the United States, and 252 tribal languages. The different tribes do not share standard physical characteristics. It was not until 1924 that all American Indians were granted United States citizenship. Created in 1824, the Bureau of Indian Affairs (BIA), located in Washington, DC, is responsible for relationships between the government and federally recognized tribes. Programs administered through the BIA include social services, natural resource management, and law enforcement.

The tribes are all distinctly different. Some of the largest Native American tribes in the United States are the Cherokee, Navajo, Chippewa, Pima, Pueblo, and Blackfoot. Approximately one quarter of Native Americans reside on reservations. More than half of them reside in urban areas.

Some of the states representing the largest populations of Native Americans and Alaskan Natives are Arizona, California, New York, and Oklahoma. Therapists should tailor their responses to the cultural needs of the tribal community or community in which the families reside. They must also consider levels of acculturation to the dominant culture in the United States.

Certain traditions are typical of many Native American communities. These include but are not limited to collectivism and a focus on family and respecting kinship (including fictive kin or individuals not related through blood or marriage); an appreciation and love for nature; collective child-rearing; respect for tribes and reservations; respect for the interconnection of mind, body, and spirit; and respect for the wisdom of elders. It is important for counselors to explore individuals' connection to a tribal community or reservation, which for many Native American individuals and families provides a sense of belonging. Native Americans may also hold traditional beliefs in the connection of all things in the universe, including plants, animals, and minerals.

Cultural Mistrust and Counseling

A legacy of cultural trauma exists in the Native American community. European colonization destroyed many tribal nations. Tribes were removed by bribery, threat, or a combination of both. This left many Native American tribes dislocated for years. As a result of forced relocation and a loss of their homeland, Native Americans hold adverse attitudes toward help-seeking. Furthermore, the absence of their stories and voices in the literature creates an unbalanced perspective of their reality or lived experiences. Assimilation (the process of one group's culture becoming like another's) for Native Americans in the United States was largely cultivated by Christianization. However, many Native Americans do not distinguish between Christian and Native American beliefs. Both coexist in the Native American Church (NAC).

Cultural deprivation, a concept developed by Frank Riessman in the 1962 book *The Culturally Deprived Child*, implies that people of color and the economically disadvantaged are deficient instead of culturally different. Native Americans were seen as a group whose values were divergent from the "superior," White, middle-class values. Although many counselors now may embrace egalitarian values, they may still hold biased attitudes toward Native American cultures and toward people of color in general. Research practices that were damaging to subjects and general cultural insensitivity by scholars have contributed to Native Americans' reluctance to participate in research studies. In order for racial microaggressions to be eliminated, counselors must consciously address their social and political origins. Microaggressions are defined as daily, often unconscious, verbal and behavioral insults toward an individual's race, gender, sexual orientation, or socioeconomic status.

The deleterious effects of oppression continue to be a problem in the Native American community. The ethnocentric, monocultural perspective in counseling correlates the experiences of people of color to White, middle-class, and primarily male experiences. Ethnocentric, monocultural bias (i.e., when people judge other cultures by the beliefs embedded in their own culture) is present in most institutions and can subconsciously convey the message to people of color and other marginalized groups that their values are not welcomed. Ethnocentrism is a magnification of the values and characteristics of White, Western culture. It conveys the message that one race is superior to others. Viewing Native Americans from an ethnocentric, monocultural perspective can be detrimental and thought of as a modern-day form of cultural oppression. Counselors must be mindful to respect the lived experiences of Native American clients and not assume a universal reality for their lives.

The groups in power (typically the majority) have been guilty in the past of portraying Native Americans as genetically and culturally deficient. In addition, Native Americans have been looked at as resistant for being suspicious and mistrusting of those in power in U.S. society and government. This is similar to other minority groups in the

United States who have a "healthy cultural suspicion" of the educational, governmental, and mental health systems that have labeled them in negative ways and treated them unfairly. Rather than being resistant to assistance, being "mistrusting" and "suspicious" is an outcome of their past treatment and status in society. Native American cultures have made innumerable contributions to the United States. However, these contributions have, for the most part, been devalued and ignored.

Many of the current traditions of the United States were adopted directly from Native American rituals and norms. For example, some historians believe the League of the Iroquois influenced the structure of the United States government. Activities in the Boy Scouts, Girls Scouts, Brownies, and YMCA Indian Guides (arts and crafts, outdoor camping, and other nature activities) were adopted from Native American practices.

Implications for Counselors

Native American individuals often do not separate what is occurring in the mind (mental health) from the rest of their bodies. Traditional Native American healers will treat individuals in their natural environment. Healing is not conducted in a separate or exclusive location with a specific focus uniquely on mental health. Within the Native American community there is an immense focus on wellness and nature. Counseling has historically focused on individualism and autonomy, in contrast to Native American cultural norms. Certain types of therapy may be ineffective with many Native Americans, or not seen as immediately helpful to their presenting concerns.

Counselors must make a sincere effort and commitment to acknowledge and comprehend the lived experiences of Native American individuals. There are countless strategies and techniques that counselors can use to assist Native American individuals and families. These methods include, but are not limited to, an examination of external stimuli contributing to the clients' problems, including systemic forces such as oppression and racism. In seeking to service the Native American population, counselors would be wise to identify key collaborators (usually elders) as resource persons. Counselors would want to explore levels of acculturation with Native American individuals. Goal setting would be conducted in the context of family, tribal communities, and respect for elders.

Additionally, counselors would consider the mind-body-spirit connection and how it can be manifested in goal setting. Counselors should be cognizant that in Native American cultures, loyalty and generosity are considered two of the finest personal characteristics that a human being can possess. Spirituality is seen as the center of the human being, and there is respect for harmony and nature. These ideas can be incorporated into therapy. It may be helpful in working with Native Americans to focus on the present time, rather than the past.

Racism has had, and continues to have, damaging effects on the Native American community. The behavioral components of racism can be manifested in counselor case conceptualizations and treatment goals being inconsistent with both the cultural values and the lived experiences of Native Americans. Understanding the sociopolitical effects of discrimination and how it has contributed to Native American historical mistrust for the larger society is essential. More than anything else, counselors must be mindful that cultural mistrust continues to be an issue in the Native American community.

Delila Lashelle Owens

See also Cultural Issues in Couples and Families; Ethnicity; Multicultural Counseling Competence; Racism

Further Readings

Beals, J., Manson, S. M., Mitchell, C. M., & Spicer, P. (2003). Cultural specificity and comparison in psychiatric epidemiology: Walking the tight rope in American Indian research. *Cultural Medical Psychiatry, 27,* 259–289.

Cornell, S., & Kalt, J. P. (2007). Two approaches to the development of native nations: One works, the other doesn't. In M. Jorgenson & S. Cornell (Eds.),

Rebuilding native nations: Strategies for governance and development (pp. 3–33). Tucson: University of Arizona Press.

Cross, S. L. (2005). *American Indian grandparents and their grandchildren in Michigan* [Monograph]. Michigan State University, School of Social Work.

Gray, J. S., & Rose, W. J. (2012). Cultural adaption for therapy with American Indians and Alaska Natives. *Journal of Multicultural Counseling and Development, 40,* 82–92.

Jones, D. S. (2007). The persistence of American Indian health disparities. *American Journal of Public Health, 96,* 2122–2134.

Martin, D., & Yurkovich, E. E. (2014). "Close-knit" defines a healthy Native American Indian family. *Journal of Family Nursing, 201*(1), 51–72.

Vernon, K. L., Wall, T. L., Lau, P., & Ehlers, C. L. (2006). Testing of an orthogonal measure of cultural identification with adult mission Indians. *Cultural Diversity and Ethnic Minority Psychology, 12,* 623–643.

Yurkovich, E. E., Hopkins-Lattergrass, I., & Rieke, S. (2011). Chaotic soup of politics: A Native American Indian mental health perspective. *Mental Health, Religion & Culture, 14,* 1013–1029.

Network Therapy

Network therapy is a counseling approach that utilizes clients' resources in their immediate environment, specifically their social network. Besides family, the network includes friends, relatives, neighbors, coworkers, and other significant people. The premise is that if the individual is best understood in the context of his or her family, then the family can be understood only with consideration of the social network or "tribe" to which the family belongs. A client's social relationships have a significant effect on the life of the client, including emotional support, as well as providing tangible resources (e.g., food, employment, financial support). The model brings elements of family therapy, group therapy, and community organization into a single, brief, high-impact approach. This entry discusses the background of network therapy, how the model works, and the circumstances in which it may be most effective.

The idea of network therapy first appeared in psychological literature in the early 1970s following the social upheaval of the 1960s. Ross Speck and Carolyn Attneave thought that major psychiatric disorders could be dealt with by having a meeting of the client's family, friends, relatives, neighbors, coworkers, and significant others. Up to 60 people could meet and discuss ways that they could support the client in the community and provide psychosocial support to the family.

In the early 1980s, the Massachusetts Department of Mental Health funded a project devoted to conducting network interventions at the Mount Tom Institute for Human Services in Holyoke, Massachusetts. The Network Therapy Project started to explore the kinds of network interventions that could be possible within broad populations. The project was staffed by clinical psychologists, psychiatrists, social workers, nurses, counselors, and support staff who provided crisis services 24 hours a day, as well as case management, clinical assessment, community support services, and respite services. Most of the clients who were part of the project had been recently hospitalized or were at risk for being hospitalized. The project mission was to provide services to clients in the least restrictive environment.

The process of implementing this model includes multiple steps. It begins with a home visit to the family. During this visit, the clinician assesses the client's willingness to use a network support system and the feasibility of using this system. During this initial assessment the clinician educates the family about the process, listens to the concerns about the "identified patient," and assesses the family's readiness for change. The initial home visit is designed as an education and assessment process to determine whether network therapy is a viable treatment option for the family. If so, issues of space, location, invitations, and other logistics are discussed prior to the first network session.

If network therapy is a viable treatment option for the family, three therapeutic processes must occur: (1) convening the network, (2) connecting the network members with one another, and (3) shifting the responsibility and control to the network. In addition to the process, the network experiences distinct phases, which happen in a recurring cycle and are always present. The process begins by family members contacting their network and asking members to assemble for the purpose of helping them cope with the concerns about the "identified patient" (i.e., retribalization phase). Usually, the process of gathering network members has an immediate healing effect. The second stage of connecting network members with one another begins with discussion of the issues by the facilitation team. During this phase, open and honest communication among network members encourages affective release; brings the network together, offering perspectives and viewpoints; and opens up the possibility for action (i.e., polarization phase). The final phase is facilitated by asking the network members to form committees to work on different issues (i.e., mobilization phase), asking network members to make commitments to help the family, and developing action plans to deal with problems as they arise (i.e., depression and breakthrough phases). After the three phases are complete the system concludes by experiencing the "network effect," which is a renewed sense of purpose and meaning (elation/exhaustion phase).

Unlike family therapy, which has broad support and research findings that show successful outcomes, there is limited research on, and a lack of widespread acceptance and practice of, network therapy. The limited research, though, suggests a significant decrease in service utilization by individuals who engaged in network therapy.

Families that are most appropriate for network therapy are those that are both desperate for and willing to change after other treatment interventions have not been successful. The goal of network therapy is to reestablish the client's social network so members become closer, more emotionally available and supportive, and more helpful to one another. A significant criticism of the network therapy approach is that it requires a large amount of professional time because up to three therapists conduct each meeting. Therefore, it is not considered the most cost-effective type of therapy.

Joseph A. Campbell

See also Cohesion; Group Family Therapy; Social Support; Support Groups; Systems Theory

Further Readings

Garrison, J. (1974). Network techniques: Case studies in the screening-linking-planning conference method. *Family Process, 13,* 337–351.

Helevy-Martini, J., Hemley-VanderVelden, E., Ruhf, L., & Schoenfeld, P. (1984). New developments in network therapy. *International Journal of Family Therapy, 6,* 68–81.

Rueveni, U. (1979). *Networking families in crisis.* New York: Human Services Press.

Speck, R., & Attneave, C. (1973). *Family networks.* New York: Pantheon.

NEURO-LINGUISTIC PROGRAMMING

Neuro-linguistic programming (NLP) is a view of communication, learning, and change that focuses on how the brain (neuro), language (linguistic), and behavior (programming) are connected. This approach to understanding and influencing complex human systems was developed by John Grinder and Richard Bandler in the 1970s, and their ideas have been integrated into counseling, therapy, education, creativity, business, and other fields. Bandler had a background in philosophy and psychology, and Grinder had a background in psychology and linguistics. Their interest in psychology and language led them to try to understand how people's representation of the world, the language they use to express those representations, and behavior are interrelated. They created some of the major ideas in NLP from observing master therapists such as Fritz Perls, Virginia Satir, and Milton Erickson, and later integrated the ideas of the anthropologist and systems theorist Gregory Bateson. The field of marriage and family therapy both influenced and was influenced by NLP. In this entry some of the core ideas and influences that helped create NLP are reviewed.

Core Principles and Concepts

There are two presuppositions that are the basis of NLP: (1) the map is not the territory, and (2) life and "mind" are systemic processes. Humans can know only perceptions of reality. The mind takes in information through the senses and interprets those stimuli. The mind creates a map of what it senses (but a map is not the actual land), and then people create a reality and behave on the basis of this representation. According to NLP, people's maps empower or limit them rather than "reality." This approach also takes a systemic view of individuals, their relationship with one another, and the environment. From a systemic perspective the universe is made of systems and subsystems that recursively interact with one another and influence one another. These systems and subsystems are interrelated and tend to act in patterned ways.

In addition to those two core principles, there are three main concepts pertaining to NLP: subjectivity, consciousness, and learning. NLP has similarities to radical constructivism. Radical constructivism is a postmodern theory that people create a representation of reality based on their own perceptions. In NLP the belief is that reality is subjective and is created through interpretation of information provided by a human's five senses, and this reality is conveyed through (and influenced by) language. People partially create these representations through experiences and awareness of those experiences. Consciousness, or people's awareness, is both conscious (people are directly aware of experiences) and unconscious (people are not directly aware of experiences). People can be influenced through both conscious and unconscious information. Finally, in NLP learning occurs through modeling. The term *modeling* in NLP is the codifying and reproducing of expertise in a particular area.

Development of NLP

Grinder and Bandler studied the language and behavior of some of the most influential therapists. They began their work by codifying the work of Fritz Perls, Virginia Satir, and Milton Erickson. Perls created Gestalt therapy, which is an experiential/humanistic therapy that uses creative and experiential techniques to enhance awareness, freedom, and self-direction. Major ideas in this therapy include that people cannot be fully understood apart from their context, and that context affects experience. Gestalt therapy focuses on growth and development. Similarly, Satir also focused on people's capacity for growth. She believed people learn both consciously and implicitly, and that to change behavior people need to be given motivation in a nurturing, trusting relationship. Finally, Grinder and Bandler looked at Milton Erickson's work. Erickson was a psychiatrist and psychologist who specialized in hypnosis and family therapy. He used whatever he could from the client's context to help him or her change, including their favorite words, culture, metaphors, and beliefs. He believed that the unconscious part of the mind was always listening, and that suggestions could be made in a way to resonate with the unconscious mind. He thought the unconscious mind had potential to be creative and generate solutions. Erickson, whether he hypnotized someone or not, used hypnosis techniques in his therapeutic approach.

Grinder and Bandler studied Satir and Erickson's linguistic and behavioral patterns and built formal models of them. Based on the models they built, they created concepts and interventions. They were looking to codify complex human behaviors and create a model of that human activity with associated techniques. This would allow others to learn from masters of their field. They focused on ways of gathering information to challenge clients' language and underlying thinking. Bandler and Grinder studied Satir and modeled her methods in the books *The Structure of Magic, Volumes 1 and 2,* and *Changing With Families*. From their observations of Erickson they wrote the books *Hypnotic Techniques of Milton H. Erickson: Volume 1,* and *Patterns of the Hypnotic Techniques of Milton H. Erickson: Volume 2.*

Because NLP focuses on language and how it influences one's reality and how perceptions of the world influence behavior, one can see commonalities between NLP and communication and brief therapy models in marriage and family therapy. This is not surprising, since Bandler and Grinder studied Satir and Erickson. Many of Satir and Erickson's ideas were the basis for experiential, strategic therapy models and solution-focused therapy.

Shannon B. Dermer

See also Cybernetics; Postmodern Therapies; Solution-Focused Brief Therapy; Strategic Family Therapy; Systemic Family Therapy

Further Readings

Grinder, J., & Bandler, R. (1979). *Frogs into princes: Neuro linguistic programming*. Moab, UT: Real People Press.

Grinder, J., & Pucelik, F. (Eds.). (2013). *Origins of neuro linguistic programming*. Carmarthen, Wales: Crown House.

Satir, V., Grinder, J., & Bandler, R. (1976). *Changing with families: A book about further education for being human*. Palo Alto, CA: Science and Behavior Books.

Neutrality and Curiosity

Neutrality has been defined as the tendency not to take a side in a conflict, and implies tolerance of the various perspectives despite one's own beliefs or feelings regarding the issue. A neutral stance is presented as an absence of bias, which conveys to others a sense of safety and trustworthiness. The term *curiosity* is associated with the behavior of being inquisitive and exploratory. The concepts of both neutrality and curiosity have been used in the counseling literature, often in descriptions of the counselor/therapist. The constructs of curiosity and neutrality may be seen as separate, but related. In this entry, each construct is defined separately. In addition, the entry discusses the history of each concept, including the theoretical underpinnings, and the application of each construct to family and couples counseling.

Neutrality

Historical Roots of Neutrality

The psychoanalytic tradition was the first to value therapist neutrality as a key component of psychotherapy. The main role of the psychoanalyst was to be a "blank screen" and to remain impartial in order for the client to project his or her issues onto the therapist (i.e., transference) in order for healing to occur. Within the psychoanalytic tradition, neutrality is conceived of as a positioning of the analyst equidistant from, rather than aligning with, any of the three structures of the mind (id, ego, superego) as defined by Sigmund Freud. This technical stance is seen as an ethical commitment to foster the client's growth and relative freedom rather than promoting identification with the analyst's understanding of the workings of the client's mind. As other therapeutic models developed, neutrality remained an important principle within counseling, but the definition evolved. In looking at neutrality from a systemic perspective, there are various ways in which it may be described: (1) the neutrality regarding one's own values and beliefs; (2) neutrality regarding taking sides among family members or with one partner in a couple; and (3) neutrality as to whether the family or couple decides to make changes.

Neutrality and Values

Neutrality may be considered a stance of the therapist avoiding the imposition of his or her values on a client. With the growing awareness of participant-observation effects in the social sciences, psychoanalysts began to view neutrality as its own form of participation that shapes the nature and content of what is observed. Similarly, feminist theorists in the 1970s also began to wonder whether complete neutrality is possible, and if so, desirable. The question remains whether counselors have the ability to differentiate their own (unconscious) agendas from those of their clients. Indeed, it has been recognized by both counselors and social science researchers that one is likely incapable of reaching the ideal of complete neutrality. Yet, awareness of one's own values and avoidance of imposing these values is still an important focus within the profession. Indeed, the recognition of personal values in the counseling relationship is included in the American Counseling Association's Ethics Code.

Neutrality and Technique

In an effort to avoid imposing one's own values or beliefs upon clients, neutrality may be confused with passivity and the idea that one's silence equates with objectivity. However, keeping a neutral position can be challenging at times, and necessitates thoughtful, deliberate action. It can be easy to become pulled to take one family member's side over another's, especially if there is an "identified patient," or if certain gender dynamics are present. A position of neutrality may be demonstrated by use of certain techniques in family and couples work. The Milan approach to family therapy is based on the three guidelines of hypothesizing, circularity, and neutrality. The therapist uses circular questions, which ask about the impact of an individual's behavior and response on the greater system. Circular questions allow the therapist to form hypotheses, understand the family/couple relationship in a bidirectional manner, and remain neutral toward any particular individual's perspective. A particular form of circular questioning places gender in the center of the relationship process (gendercentric questions). These questions would be used to seek understanding regarding patterns of attentiveness and who profits from certain relational patterns. They would also be asked to understand how the experiences of each partner shift when gender is considered and how each partner's response may be related to being male or female.

Neutrality in Systems Work

The concern about taking sides is specific to a systems perspective and creates numerous challenges for the therapist. At times, the therapist may have difficulty with the issue of seeing the family as the client or with certain individuals within the family system. Often, the therapist will attempt to empower and support each family member. The role of the therapist is to understand members' impact upon one another, and the therapist serves to support each member. However, at times, what might seem to be the best solution for the system (i.e., family/couple) may be unfavorable to one member. For example, when working with a couple and one partner has more power in the relationship than the other, the therapist must discern whether he or she should attempt to balance the system by empowering the individual with less authority or to remain neutral.

In addition, the therapist can be put into a precarious position regarding neutrality in a case of infidelity, divorce, or abuse. In these situations, the therapist may be challenged to decide whom to support, and if it is possible to take a neutral position. Indeed, some would say that it is necessary in such situations for the therapist to take a more instructive approach, as opposed to staying neutral. It may also be necessary to recognize the larger systems that are in place. When examining the larger systems, such as the exosystem (the larger system within which the family or couple resides), neutrality may mean not taking sides among the larger systems, but rather to appreciate and recognize the impact of these systems on the client; this would be important in working with larger systems such as work, school, or medical ecosystems.

Some have defined neutrality as relying on theory and practice that supports all individuals equally, regardless of gender, race, or sexual orientation; from this perspective neutrality may require active involvement by the therapist. The therapist would then take an active stance to address the power dynamics within the therapy room. In addition, a therapist may be neutral in a subjective manner. In bringing his or her whole person into the therapy room, the therapist may take a more egalitarian position and be less of an expert, thereby emphasizing the more human aspect of the therapist. This might look like the therapist presenting thoughts about power as hypotheses rather than facts. The therapist offers new ideas, but views the client as the one who discerns how to make sense of them. Indeed, this collaborative approach places the client's values as crucial to the work and allows the therapist to remain neutral. Some have questioned how both a neutral stance and a social justice orientation can be present within a given individual, or if these two approaches are inadvertently at odds with each other. Can a counselor remain neutral, while also recognizing injustice and inequality? Perhaps the meaning that the client makes of the situation at hand and the counselor's compassionate curiosity, as discussed in the next section, might help reconcile these seemingly disparate positions.

Curiosity

Definition of Curiosity

Similar to neutrality, the construct of curiosity in therapy started within the psychoanalytic tradition, though its relevance to depth traditions and phenomenological inquiry far preceded Sigmund Freud. Freud believed curiosity was a derivative of the sex drive that creates an interest for knowledge. Indeed, curiosity has been defined as a desire to know or learn something. Curiosity comes from the Latin root *cura,* which means to "handle with care." Curiosity has been considered a key component of psychological understanding, on the part of both the therapist and the client. In a therapeutic sense, curiosity provides an opening, a new reading or interpretation of existing assumptions. In symptomatic families, where understanding of the current distress becomes rigidified and problem saturated, curiosity may serve to highlight less privileged narratives, reframing the current distress in such a way that opens the closed system to revision.

Curiosity and Therapeutic Stance

Within the therapeutic relationship, curiosity must be paired with empathy in order for trust to develop in the process of exploration. The term *empathic curiosity* has been coined to capture this endeavor within the therapeutic relationship. Curiosity includes a willingness to enter and share in the world of a client, as well as a recognition of what is important to a client. An attitude of curiosity by the therapist can widen the client's perspective and provide opportunities for greater understanding of experiences outside of awareness. Multiple perspectives may also be considered, which replace givens and provide a place for exploration of the subjective experience of the client.

Individuals within the field have noted that curiosity is a necessary human attribute for therapist excellence. This willingness to explore potential possibilities with a client, as well as the parts of the client that may be perceived as frightening or unavailable, is a key aspect of the therapeutic endeavor. The term *benevolent curiosity* has also been utilized, as the discovery of what is unknown must be done in a compassionate manner. Indeed, when a counselor attempts to explore areas of the client's experience, curiosity must be perceived as for the client's benefit, as opposed to the therapist. Counselors might ask themselves if a certain line of inquiry will support their own curiosity or support the client's treatment goals. Keeping the best interest of the client in mind might help the counselor discern whose needs are being met when new areas are being considered.

Curiosity might include therapists opening up to their own exploration about what they believe they already know about their clients, or about their reactions to their clients. Such a stance of collaborative curiosity toward the contents of the therapist's mind might model such openness to clients, allowing the clients to become more curious about their own minds and the minds of others. To be curious is to be open to new possibilities and a desire to know more. A curious attitude is an important trait for therapists, as it can model a stance that one would like to foster within a client.

Counselors who work from a systems perspective are in an excellent position to work in a manner that is collaborative, curious, and exploratory with all of their clients. Individuals who work with families are familiar with family-centered principles, one of which is a striving for cultural curiosity. Engaging in collaborative inquiry affords a way for the therapist to enter the world of the family culture; it also allows for the possibility of meaning-making on the part of the client regarding his or her functioning.

Melissa K. Smothers

See also Ethical Codes; Feminist Family Therapy; Milan Team; Psychoanalytic Family Therapy; Systems Theory; Therapeutic Alliance; Therapists' Values

Further Readings

Cecchin, G. (1987). Hypothesizing, circularity, and neutrality revisited: An invitation to curiosity. *Family Process, 26,* 405–413.

Harrist, S., & Richardson, F. C. (2012). Disguised ideologies in counseling and social justice work. *Counseling and Values, 57*(1), 38–44.

Madsen, W. C. (2009). Collaborative helping: A practice framework for family-centered services. *Family Process, 48*(1), 103–116.

McDaniel, S. H., Lusterman, D., & Philpot, C. L. (2001). Introduction to integrative ecosystemic family therapy. *Casebook for integrating family therapy: An ecosystemic approach* (pp. 3–17). Washington, DC: American Psychological Association.

Knudson-Martin, C. (1997). The politics of gender in family therapy. *Journal of Marital and Family Therapy, 23*(4), 421–437.

Selvini-Palazzoli, M., Boscolo, L., Cecchin, G., & Prata, G. (1980). Hypothesizing-circularity-neutrality: Three guidelines for the conductor of the session. *Family Process, 19,* 3–12.

Ward, C., & Reuter, T. (2010). *Strength-centered counseling: Integrating postmodern approaches and skills with practice.* Thousand Oaks, CA: Sage.

No-Harm Contracts

No-harm contracts (NHCs) are those that document the commitment of a client not to engage in suicidal behaviors. They may also be used for other types of self- and other-injury but are most commonly associated with suicidality. Other common terms used to describe NHCs are no-suicide contracts, no-suicide agreements, contracting for safety, and suicide prevention contracts. Rather than focusing on what clients *will not do* (kill themselves), safety plans outline what a client *will do* in response to suicidal ideation. Safety plans are created jointly by the client and therapist and are intended to act as step-by-step guides for increasing client coping skills and the likelihood of staying safe in a crisis situation. Despite the lack of strong empirical evidence supporting their effectiveness, NHCs are standard practice in many mental health settings and are widely accepted as a therapeutic approach to preventing suicide.

NHCs often include statements by which clients consent not to engage in suicidal actions, to keep themselves safe, and to attend therapy. The goal is to gain commitment from clients to stay alive and to eliminate suicide. Although the individual client at risk for suicide or self-injury must agree to the contract, family members and friends may be part of the safety plan and a key part of suicide prevention. Another reason why many therapists and mental health treatment providers engage in this contracting process is to protect themselves from potential liability and legal action. However, NHCs alone do not protect clinicians from liability, but may be part of a more comprehensive intervention strategy that would include a thorough assessment and the creation of a suicide safety plan. This entry first discusses best practices and ethics in using NHCs and safety plans, and the importance of the therapeutic relationship in helping clients struggling with suicidal thoughts. It then discusses the objectives of NHCs and safety plans, how clients are assessed for the potential for suicide, the process of creating the safety plan, and special considerations.

Best Practices in Using No-Harm Contracts and Safety Plans

Safety plans are important aspects of treating clients who are at risk for self-harm, and may be done at any point in the assessment or treatment process, such as during an intake assessment, during a first counseling session, upon discharge from an inpatient stay, or during crisis hotline calls. It is important that clinicians be continually vigilant about assessing for suicide, self- and other-harm, and other associated disorders (such as mood, anxiety, substance use, and psychotic disorders) throughout the treatment process. Safety planning should occur after a thorough risk assessment using a recognized assessment strategy such as those presented later in this entry. It is important to recognize that safety planning may not be immediately appropriate depending on the level of care necessary to treat the client, such as when a client is actively or imminently suicidal. It may also not be appropriate depending on the client's ability to engage in the process for a variety of reasons, including cognitive impairment and intoxication.

Ethics

When treating suicidal clients, therapists must demonstrate that they are practicing on the basis of empirically supported methods that are considered standard practice among professionals in the field of marriage and family and couples therapy. Therapists are not evaluated on how accurately they predict suicidality but, rather, on whether or not they acted with sound clinical judgment by conducting appropriate evaluations and implementing appropriate interventions. In addition to understanding the practice guidelines when working with suicidal clients, special attention should be placed on the maintenance of client records. Part of providing ethical care and protecting against liability is carefully and accurately documenting the assessment, intervention, treatment, and follow-up processes, as well as formally documenting the safety plan if one is warranted. Clinicians should be sure to know the laws related to self- and other-harm in the states in which they practice, as well as be intimately familiar with the ethical codes guiding their work as professionals.

Importance of the Therapeutic Relationship

A strong therapeutic relationship, built on a foundation of trust and empathy, is fundamental in helping most clients, especially those who are struggling with thoughts of suicide. Therapists are tasked with creating an environment for clients where they are free to express themselves without the fear of judgment or abandonment. Creating a therapeutic alliance in which empathy and autonomy are communicated from the start is the cornerstone of building trust with a client where these issues can continuously be explored. Thus, effective intervention is a balance between completing the procedural elements necessary to ensure client safety while remaining empathetic and accepting of the client's struggles. In fact, if NHCs are pushed by clinicians before rapport is developed, they may do harm in that clients may feel misunderstood, and as if the clinician is more concerned about malpractice than their needs. Therefore, it is important to remember that the therapeutic utility of using an NHC may be directly tied to the quality of the counseling relationship.

Objectives

The purpose of developing safety plans is to provide clients with concrete guidelines to follow in the case of an emotional crisis that may lead to self-injurious behaviors. These will likely be made up of a list of coping skills, strategies, and resources that help clients to feel more autonomous and in control. Additionally, when clients work to develop plans that are unique to them, it encourages them to develop and utilize individual coping skills that can serve as both prevention tactics and interventions. Plans may include unique lists of activities that clients promise to engage in when feeling suicidal; phone numbers for emergency contacts, agencies, and hotlines; and signature lines for both clients and therapists, which act as symbolic binding contracts. In addition, family members may be brought into sessions and integrated into the contract. For example, the family members may agree that someone will always be at home with the client. Traditionally, two copies of the contract are made: One is distributed to the client, the other remains in the client file with the therapist. Depending on the situation, copies of safety plans may also be shared with family members and other treatment providers.

Assessment

Prior to developing NHCs and safety plans, therapists must take steps to determine, to the extent possible, that clients are not likely at immediate risk for suicide. There are numerous ways to assess for intended harm to self and others. This may be done in a triage or hospital setting, in schools, or by counselors and therapists seeing clients in a variety of settings. It is important to assess all clients for suicide in some way, regardless of presenting issues.

There are numerous ways to assess for suicide, including questionnaires, paper-and-pencil assessments, and interview protocols. Many clinicians make use of mnemonic devices in which each letter of a phrase is associated with a specific suicide warning sign or assessment strategy to help them to remember what to assess when they are working with suicidal individuals. There are many of these tools available, and IS PATH WARM is an easy-to-memorize mnemonic that was created by the American Association of Suicidology to help assess individuals for immediate suicide risk:

Suicide *I*deation: Ideation refers to thoughts of suicide. This may be in verbal or written form and may include direct or indirect references. The individual may have varying levels of intent or access to means by which to complete the suicide.

*S*ubstance Abuse: Use of substances is a risk factor, particularly if one has a substance use disorder, uses excessively or recklessly, or when there is a significant change in use habits.

*P*urposelessness: Often, a sense of purposelessness precedes suicidal ideation and action. This may involve an idea that there is no reason for continued living, either because one has no purpose, or due to a loss of a previously important purposeful role.

*A*nger: Strong emotions such as anger, rage, or hope of revenge against others who are perceived to have caused harm or who are at fault for one's problems may spur suicidal thoughts.

*T*rapped: Often, people feel trapped in their situations and are unable to see other ways to resolve the problem. They may believe that death would be preferable to continued living in their painful or lonely situations.

*H*opelessness: A negative sense of self, others, the world, and one's potential future (that may appear inevitable, with little chance for positive changes or outcomes) may impact suicidal ideation.

*W*ithdrawing: Isolating behaviors or desires to withdraw from family members, friends, colleagues, other significant others, or society are suicide warning signs.

*A*nxiety: Feelings of worry, ruminating on the past, and feelings of anxiety are often associated with suicidal ideation. This may be reported as physical symptoms, sleep disturbances, or being unable to relax.

*R*ecklessness: Clients may act without concern for the welfare of self and others, behave recklessly, or engage in risky activities, often without thinking or considering potential negative consequences.

*M*ood Change: Any time there is a significant mood change that is either reported or observed, there may be reason to engage in a thorough assessment. This may occur in any direction: A person who has been presenting as depressed suddenly feels great, or a person who is often happy begins to appear sullen, sad, depressed, or withdrawn.

Jason McGlothlin introduced the SIMPLE STEPS model, which is also a mnemonic that is quite thorough and serves as a more complete guide to the steps of assessment for the clinician rather than focusing fully on warning signs. The steps using the SIMPLE STEPS model (including one or more potential assessment questions for each step of the model) are as follows:

Suicidality: Clearly and directly ask clients if they are considering killing themselves/suicide. (*Are you thinking of killing yourself?*)

Ideation: Assess what clients think about when they think about suicide. (*When you think about killing yourself, tell me what you think about.*)

Method: Assess the means by which clients intend to take their lives. (*Have you thought about how you would do it? Walk me through your plan.*)

Perturbation/Pain: Assess the degree of emotional pain clients subjectively feel. A scaling question may be particularly helpful. (*On a scale from 1–10, where 1 is no pain, and 10 is the worst amount of pain you have experienced, where are you?*)

Loss: Assess recent losses clients have experienced. This may include actual losses (death, loss of job, end of relationship, physical health, etc.) that have occurred or perceived losses (what clients think they will or may lose in the near future). (*Talk to me about the loss of your partner,* or *What is missing in your life now?*)

Earlier Attempts: Assess history of prior suicidal actions, attempts, and past ideation. Previous attempts are a significant risk factor that may impact the likelihood of repeated attempts or eventual completion of suicide. (*Have you ever attempted suicide in the past?*) Assess when, what happened, and what kept them from completing.

Substance Use: Assess for use of substances including those that are legal and illegal, frequency of use, impact of use, side effects, history of substance abuse treatment, etc. (*Tell me about medications you are using . . . how much do you drink . . . any other substances you are using.*)

Troubleshooting: Assess clients' problem-solving skills, cognitive awareness, and coping skills. (*What helps you feel better?* or *What keeps you from killing yourself?*)

Emotion and Diagnosis: Assess for common emotional experiences often associated with suicidal ideation and behavior (helplessness, hopelessness, worthlessness, loneliness, depression, impulsivity) as well as any associated mental health diagnoses, treatment, or hospitalizations. (*How would you describe how you are feeling right now?* and *Have you ever been diagnosed with a mental health disorder of any kind—like depression, anxiety, schizophrenia?*)

Parent/Family History: Assess for any suicidal behavior that has occurred in the client's family. This step may also include finding out about experiences with peers and any recent experiences with suicide. (*Do you know anyone who has attempted or completed suicide? Anyone in your family?*)

Stressors: Assess current stressors that may be impacting the ideation. (*Is there anything in particular that you can identify as the source of these feelings? Anything going on that leads you to think about suicide at this particular time?*)

Developing the Safety Plan

Once the clinician has conducted a thorough assessment utilizing a model such as those just outlined and has determined that the client is not likely to be actively or imminently suicidal, a safety plan can be developed. This plan will likely include some type of language often seen in traditional NHCs in which the client agrees not to engage in suicidal behaviors and to instead implement the steps outlined in the plan.

The therapist and client work collaboratively to develop a suicide safety plan. If after conducting a suicide assessment the therapist deems the creation of a safety plan appropriate for client care, a plan should immediately be written in session. It is not enough just to document that a safety plan addressing the client's suicidal thoughts was created. Therapists should also check in with clients each session to assess suicidal ideation and the effectiveness of the safety plan. Clients can then report if and when they needed to refer to the safety plan since the previous session, and which components of the safety plan were deemed most and least useful. Each mention of the suicide safety plan or ideation in session should be documented. Maintaining a focus on continuity of care is not only an ethically sound practice, but also an essential part of suicide prevention.

Necessary Inclusions

There are a few items that are often viewed as most helpful to include in client safety plans such as agreements to remove or restrict access to means of suicide such as guns and medications; trigger identification strategies; specific coping strategies; safe contact people, agencies, and hotlines that can help in the event of a crisis; and a statement of commitment to implementing the plan. First, therapists can help clients to recognize and outline the warning signs that may precede or accompany suicidal ideation. These signs may be behavioral, emotional, cognitive, or physiological. Triggers or warning signs are specific to the individual, but may include things such as symptoms of anxiety or panic, irritation or annoyance, loneliness, sadness, feelings of boredom, negative cognitions and ruminations, fear, aggressive or isolating behaviors, and physical pain.

Once a list of high-risk situations that are associated with the client's ideation is created and discussed, the next step is typically to develop a list of potentially helpful internal coping strategies. These are things that clients can do to help or soothe themselves without contacting other people. The goal of this is to help clients to identify and use their own coping skills, distract from the suicidal impulses, prevent the escalation of ideation to action, and regulate emotions. Again, these strategies should be collaboratively developed, be unique to the individual, and be realistic things that can be done in a variety of situations. Examples include listening to a favorite song, going for a walk or engaging in exercise, getting out of the house into a social situation such as going to a shopping mall or library, spending time with a pet, cooking a meal, or watching a favorite funny movie.

The next steps in many plans involve reaching out to identified others if the internal coping strategies are not helpful. A list of names and phone numbers of trusted, safe family members and friends who could offer support or distraction from the ideation is included. Sometimes plans include simply reaching out and spending time with others, which is then followed by plans to disclose distress to others if needed. If the crisis is not mitigated after following these steps, the plan should outline names and phone numbers of the therapist, local agencies, and 24-hour hotlines (including 911) that could provide assistance.

Therapists and clients should work together to assess the reasonableness of the plan, identify potential obstacles to implementing the steps, and then adjust the plan or create alternative strategies. They should also identify ways that clients will be able to access plans when they are needed, such as keeping copies at home, at work, in a wallet or car, and with a safe person. Once a workable plan has been developed, clients will often sign with a statement that they are willing to work to implement the plan, and the counselor signs as a witness and to demonstrate willingness to support the client. Throughout this process, therapists should continue to assess for suicidal intent and be cognizant of client motivation to engage in the process. Resistance or apathy may indicate lack of sufficient therapeutic rapport or willingness to implement the plan in order to stay alive.

Special Considerations and Populations

It is important to note that the ways NHCs and safety plans are developed and used may depend on many factors, including the clinical setting; client-specific features such as age, diagnosis, access to systems of support, and functionality; and the purpose and type of plan being designed. Readers are encouraged to refer to the additional readings that follow this entry and to seek out specific best practice guidelines for a variety of other related topics such as assessment within couples and family therapy sessions, counseling minors and working in school settings, safety planning and duty to warn in cases of homicidal ideation or violence to others, and safety planning for self-injury.

Kerrie R. Fineran and Lidija Hurni

See also Assessment, Suicide; Clinical Practice; Suicide; Therapeutic Contract

Further Readings

American Association for Marriage and Family Therapy. (2015, January 15). *AAMFT code of ethics revised.* Retrieved from http://www.aamft.org/iMIS15/AAMFT/Content/Legal_Ethics/Code_of_Ethics.aspx

Feldman, S. R., Moritz, S. H., & Benjamin, G. H. (2005). Suicide and the law: A practical overview for mental health professionals. *Women & Therapy, 28*(1), 95–103.

Hyldahl, R. S., & Richardson, B. (2011). Key considerations for using no-harm contracts with clients who self-injure. *Journal of Counseling and Development, 89,* 121–127. doi:10.1002/j.1556-6678.2011.tb00069.x

Kress, V. E., Adamson, N. A., Paylo, M. J., DeMarco, C., & Bradley, N. (2012). The use of safety plans with children and adolescents living in violent families. *The Family Journal: Counseling and Therapy for Couples and Families, 20*(3), 249–255. doi:10.1177/1066480712448833

Kress, V. E., Protivnak, J. J., & Sadlak, L. (2008). Counseling clients involved with violent intimate partners: The mental health counselor's role in promoting client safety. *Journal of Mental Health Counseling, 30*(3), 200–210.

Lewis, L. M. (2007). No-harm contracts: A review of what we know. *Suicide and Life-Threatening Behavior, 37,* 50–57.

McGlothlin, J. M. (2008). *Developing clinical skills in suicide assessment, prevention, and treatment.* Alexandria, VA: American Counseling Association.

Stanley, B., & Brown, G. K. (2011). Safety planning intervention: A brief intervention to mitigate suicide risk. *Cognitive and Behavioral Practice, 19,* 256–264. doi:http://dx.doi.org/10.1016/j.cbpra.2011.01.001

Non–Rapid Eye Movement Sleep Arousal Disorders in Children

Non–rapid eye movement (NREM) sleep arousal disorders in children are defined by partial arousal during periods of sleep, typically associated with night terrors and/or sleepwalking. NREM sleep arousal is a type of parasomnia where undesired events or behaviors occur during sleep. This entry first discusses the stages of sleep and then discusses the symptoms, causes, and treatment of NREM arousal disorders. It concludes with a discussion of how counselors can help families who are struggling with this issue.

Stages of Sleep

Sleep disorders occur during different phases of sleep; therefore, it is important to be familiar with the stages of sleep to help in accurate diagnosis and treatment. There are four stages that make up one full cycle of sleep. The stages are differentiated by eye movement (nonrapid or rapid) as well as other physiological features. NREM sleep arousal disorder occurs during the first three stages of sleep. The first two stages of NREM sleep are referred to as light sleep. Stage 1, or N1, is brief—lasting about 1 to 10 minutes—and is characterized by a light sleep wherein a person is easily woken by a slight touch or sound. Stage 2, or N2, lasts longer—about 20 minutes. During this time the heart rate slows down, body temperature decreases, and the body relaxes. Stage 3, or N3, is also called deep sleep or slow-wave sleep, where brain activity slows and it is more difficult to wake a person. Children have more slow-wave sleep than adults, which could explain the higher occurrences of sleepwalking and sleep terrors in children. Stage R is rapid eye movement sleep, or REM sleep. During this stage, brain activity speeds up; and, as the name describes, the eyes are moving rapidly behind closed eyelids.

Symptoms of Non–Rapid Eye Movement Sleep Arousal Disorders

Non–rapid eye movement sleep arousal disorders are classified in the *Diagnostic and Statistical Manual of Mental Disorders, Fifth Edition* (DSM-5), as parasomnias within the broader category of sleep–wake disorders. The episodes of partial awakening occur during the first three stages of the sleep cycle and include either sleepwalking or sleep terrors.

Sleepwalking

Sleepwalking occurs when individuals arise from bed during slow-wave sleep and move around their environment. Individuals who sleepwalk will appear awake with a blank expression and will engage in activities typically done during periods of wakefulness such as going to the bathroom or getting dressed. Upon waking, children will not be able to recall the event. Sleepwalking is common in young children and typically declines as children enter into adolescence.

Sleep Terrors

Also known as night terrors, these typically occur within the first few hours of sleep and are identified by a state of partial wakefulness associated with panic and fear. During sleep terrors children will display signs of increased heart rate, sweating, and rapid breathing. The episodes usually begin with a panicky scream. During a sleep terror episode, children are nonresponsive to attempts to comfort or soothe. As during sleepwalking, children are unable to remember the incident. In addition, they do not report experiencing disturbing dreams, which distinguishes night terrors from nightmares.

Causes, Risks, and Treatment of Non–Rapid Eye Movement Sleep Disorders in Children

Sleep terrors and sleepwalking behaviors are known to run in families. Environmental factors such as medications, major life transitions, sleeping in unfamiliar settings, and physical or emotional stress can trigger the episodes. Children who experience high amounts of anxiety and stress may also have an increased rate of night terrors and sleepwalking. Often, when these variables are removed the episodes will diminish on their own. Other conditions that may be associated with sleep terrors or sleepwalking include migraines, fever, head injury, and sleep breathing disorders, such as sleep apnea. A full medical examination by the child's pediatrician or family care doctor is recommended to address or rule out any underlying medical or health problems that are triggering episodes of sleepwalking or sleep terrors.

Most cases of sleepwalking and sleep terror can be addressed at home with simple behavior and environmental modifications. Caregivers are encouraged to provide comfort to the child during the episode. Attempts to wake the child are often discouraged since they may create additional stress and fear upon waking. Caregivers should remain with their child during the episode and help the child return to sleep. In cases of sleepwalking, parents should guide the child back to bed to prevent injury. The environment should be set up to minimize risk of injury prior to sleep, such as clearing the bedroom of anything that might cause the child to fall and lock doors and windows to prevent leaving the house. Other recommendations include modifying daytime routines, promoting healthy sleep patterns, and changes in diet such as eliminating certain foods.

Addressing Non–Rapid Eye Movement Sleep Disorders in Children in Counseling

Sleep issues are often seen as secondary to, or a symptom of, mental health or behavioral problems for which children are referred for mental health counseling. In order to identify a differentiating diagnosis and develop appropriate treatment planning, it is important for counselors to properly screen for NREM and other sleep-related problems, which includes establishing a baseline of the behavior to address. It is recommended that counselors obtain a thorough history and determine the current presenting problem through an intake assessment that includes a sleep screening instrument such as the Children's Sleep Habits Questionnaire (CSHQ) or the Pediatric Sleep Questionnaire (PSQ). In addition, counselors can request that the caregiver keep a sleep log for a period of two weeks. Sleep logs help in tracking sleep patterns during the day and night, and the frequency and duration of the night terror or sleepwalking episodes, in order to identify patterns in behaviors.

Additional counselor intervention includes providing reassurance and educating parents about children's developmental needs, importance of healthy sleep patterns, and the effects of environmental stressors and ways to reduce or eliminate these stressors. Counselors will also collaborate with referral sources such as primary care doctors, psychiatrists, and school counselors and teachers when addressing NREM sleep disorders in children.

Sarah Becerra and Tiffany Hamlett

See also Childhood Anxiety; DSM and V-Codes; Family Stress; *International Classification of Diseases* (ICD); Parenting Education; Trauma and Children

Further Readings

American Academy of Sleep Medicine. (2014). *International classification of sleep disorders* (3rd ed.). Westchester, IL: Author.

American Psychiatric Association. (2013). *Diagnostic and statistical manual of mental disorders* (5th ed.). Washington, DC: Author.

Ferber, R. (2006). *Solve your child's sleep problems.* New York: Fireside.

Ferber, R., & Kryger, M. (Eds.). (1995). *Principles and practice of sleep medicine in the child.* Philadelphia, PA: W. B. Saunders.

Mindell, J. A., & Owens, J. A. (2010). *A clinical guide to pediatric sleep: Diagnosis and management of sleep problems* (2nd ed.). Philadelphia, PA: Lippincott, Williams & Wilkins.

Peterman, J. S., Carper, M. M., & Kendall, P. C. (2015). Anxiety disorders and comorbid sleep problems in school-aged youth: Review and future research directions. *Child Psychiatry and Human Development, 46*(3), 376–392. doi:10.1007/s10578-014-0478-y

Nonresidential Fathers

According to the U.S. Census Bureau, by 2009 more than one in four children did not live with their biological father. Nonresidential fathers are those men who do not live in the same household as their children. These fathers may be divorced or separated from their children's mother or may have never been married to the mother. People may assume that married fathers are present in their children's lives and divorced or unmarried fathers are absent from their children's lives, but the reality is that there is a continuum of quality of relationships between fathers and children in both residential and nonresidential arrangements. Nevertheless, it may be more difficult for nonresidential fathers to maintain quality relationships with their children, despite many children expressing a desire for a relationship with their father.

Research has demonstrated that children who do not have relationships with their father tend to be at a distinct disadvantage emotionally, academically, socially, and financially compared with those whose fathers are involved in their lives. In addition, nonresidential fathers typically want to be involved in their children's lives, and there are mental health advantages for them when they remain involved. It is important to both fathers and children to support father involvement in their children's lives. This entry first discusses how the involvement of nonresidential fathers is typically defined and details some of the myths about, and barriers to, the involvement of fathers. It then examines how children and fathers are affected by living apart from each other and the effects on children and fathers of remaining involved in each other's lives.

Definition of Involvement

Typical definitions of *involvement* when discussing nonresidential fathers include the following three components: child-support payments, frequency and length of visits, and substance of visits. While residence, financial support, and visitation are easily measured categories of paternal involvement, they do not include a father's emotional connection with his children, the amount of responsibility he takes, the sorts of activities he does with his children, his conceptualizations of fatherhood, or his paternal commitment.

More complex definitions of father involvement include engagement, accessibility, and responsibility. Engagement incorporates all methods of direct contact among fathers and children, such as care and play. It is associated with monitoring, closeness, and warmth. Accessibility includes the father's availability to children, regardless of the nature or degree of relations between father and child. Responsibility includes understanding and meeting the needs of the child by providing economic resources to the child and planning for the child's future. According to research on the father–child relationship, involvement quality is more important than the regularity of the contact. Being an actively involved father means being accessible emotionally and physically, and participating in almost every facet of a child's life.

Never-married biological fathers may be more at risk for low levels of involvement with nonresidential children than are divorced fathers. Unmarried, nonresidential fathers are even less likely than divorced fathers to be involved with children and are less likely to pay child support. Nonresidential fathers tend to stay more involved if they were married to the child's mother at the time of birth. Divorced fathers at one point lived with their children, so they had opportunities to bond emotionally with them.

Myths About and Barriers to Involvement

Some nonresidential fathers encounter barriers created by myths that can limit, or in some cases prevent, their ability to engage with their children. Commons myths about fathers include (a) fathers are not interested in being involved, (b) fathers do not have the capability to be involved, (c) fathers are harmful if they are involved, and (d) there is little to no effect if the father is not involved. Although these myths are not accurate, there are several factors that may make it more difficult for fathers to maintain quality relationships with their children. The most common ones are lack of prenatal involvement, relationship problems with the mother, inability to pay child support, lack of parenting skills and confidence, drug or alcohol abuse, unemployment, and having a low level of education.

Although divorced fathers may have some advantages over fathers who were never married to their children's mothers, divorce can be a crucial barrier to the preservation of positive father–child relationships. The amount of father involvement succeeding divorce is low. According to some estimates, nearly one third of divorced fathers have no contact with their children. For the remainder, post-divorce visitation may provide inadequate time to sustain close and psychologically meaningful relationships between fathers and children.

There are many efforts to encourage fathers, including nonresidential fathers, to take an active role in their children's lives. Culturally sensitive interventions using a holistic approach include Fathers in Training and The Fatherhood Project. Some fathers may be helped through individual counseling or attending groups where they can learn to communicate their feelings effectively.

Impact on Children

There is a positive impact for children when fathers maintain an active presence in their lives and maintain close emotional bonds with them. The relationship of children to their father is important for their well-being. Children who are close to their father tend to be happier and more well-adjusted. Studies of nonresidential fathers indicate positive correlations among father involvement, regular payment of child support, and children's overall well-being. Children of involved fathers tend to do better academically, earn more money and have greater financial stability, have lower rates of teen violence and delinquency, and have better mental health. They also are more likely to be active and involved parents when they have their own children. In addition, father involvement is related to children developing positive characteristics such as empathy, self-esteem, social competence, life skills, and being less likely to stereotype people based on their sex. When nonresidential fathers maintain parent-like contact, partake in an assortment of activities with their children, and spend holidays together, the welfare of children is sustained. Positively involved fathers reduce their children's probability of externalizing and internalizing problems, dropping out of school, and having self-image problems during puberty.

Children who grow up living with only one biological parent are worse off, on average, than children who grow up living with both biological parents; this is the case regardless of the parent's race or educational background, whether the parent was married at the time of the child's birth, or whether the parent remarries. Children growing up without a father have an increased risk of getting in trouble with the law and experiencing academic difficulties. Adolescents who lack father involvement have a greater chance of dropping out of high school and are more likely to become teenage parents. According to the research, when controlling for the low socioeconomic status of single-parent families, children raised without a father present will tend to perform poorly in school, commit more crimes, and use more drugs; they also are more likely to become pregnant as teenagers.

Impact on Fathers

In research, nonresidential fathers acknowledged that parenting was challenging and stressful, but that it was also very satisfying. Involved fathers are more likely to have secure relationships with their children, feel that they can depend on others more, and are more likely to feel more confident in their job skills, parenting skills, and social relationships. Nonresidential fathers have increased levels of emotional pain compared with resident fathers. Divorced nonresidential fathers are more likely to be depressed and struggle with adjustment problems compared with divorced custodial fathers and married fathers. Based on research, the ideal for nonresidential fathers is that they provide emotional support, financial support, and care, and that they establish legal paternity if never married to the mother.

Ashley R. Cosentino

See also Adolescent Behavior Problems; Best Interests of the Child; Child Behavior Problems; Parental Alienation Syndrome; Parent–Child Communication

Further Readings

Braver, S. L., & O'Connell, D. (1998). *Divorced dads: Shattering the myths.* New York: Penguin Putnam.

Carlson, M., McLanahan, S. S., & Brooks-Gunn, J. (2008). Coparenting and nonresidential fathers' involvement with young children after a non-marital birth. *Demography, 45*(2), 461–488.

Cheadle, J. E., Amato, P. R., & King, V. (2010). Patterns of nonresidential father contact. *Demography, 47*(1), 205–225.

Emmers-Sommer, T. M., Rhea, D., Triplett, L., & O'Neil, B. (2003). Accounts of single fatherhood: A qualitative study. *Marriage and Family Review, 35*(1/2), 99–115.

Hawkins, D. N., Amato, P. R., & King, V. (2007). Nonresidential father involvement and adolescent well-being: Father effects or child effects? *American Sociological Review, 72*(6), 990–1010.

King, V., & Sobolewski, J. M. (2006). Nonresidential fathers' contributions to adolescent well-being. *Journal of Marriage and Family, 68*(3), 537–557.

Kissman, K. (2001). Interventions to strengthen noncustodial father involvement in the lives of their children. *Journal of Divorce and Remarriage, 35*(1/2), 135.

Lin, I., & McLanahan, S. S. (2007). Parental beliefs about nonresidential fathers' obligations and rights. *Journal of Marriage and Family, 69*(2), 382–398.

Parke, R., & Brott, A. (1999). *Throwaway dads: The myths and barriers that keep men from being the father they want to be.* New York: Houghton Mifflin.

NONVERBAL COMMUNICATION

Attending behaviors are the most basic interviewing skills, but they are crucial for successful client interaction. Attending includes the ways in which the marriage and family therapist or couples counselor interacts with and responds to the client family, encouraging further communication. Attending behaviors are both verbal and nonverbal, though the former are more easily controlled than the latter. The focus of this entry is nonverbal communication, which can include body posture, hand gestures, eye contact, facial expressions, spatial distances, touch, vocal qualities, and any other means of communication that do not include words. In fact, the use of silence or the absence of speech is a powerful form of nonverbal communication.

Marriage and family therapists must be aware of their own nonverbal communication, since they are always modeling for the client family. Likewise, family therapists must observe and attend to the clients' nonverbal communications. Perhaps one of the most difficult aspects of dealing with nonverbal communication is that there is no universal set of rules that applies to all of the different facial expressions, gestures, postures, or eye movements; by and large, their meanings differ depending on the person, situation, and context. Also, similar nonverbal communications can have different meanings, depending on the identities of the message sender and receiver and their relationship. Rolling one's eyes at another may be a display of irritation and contempt for that person, or it could be a sign of feeling ennui and noninvolvement. The message being communicated is up to interpretation.

There are some nonverbal communications that are more ubiquitous in nature. Research shows that basic facial expressions (e.g., anger, happiness, fear) are displayed similarly across different cultures. Making a "V" with one's middle and forefingers is usually going to be interpreted as the peace sign, just as sticking up one's middle finger at another will be interpreted as being rude. This does not, however, account for deception or false displays of emotion. An individual can smile and others will likely interpret that they are happy; meanwhile, that person might be secretly embarrassed and trying to hide his or her true feelings. It can be very difficult to determine when certain individuals are being genuine and when they are attempting to mask their true affect; these are important observations for the couples counselor or marriage and family therapist to make. This entry discusses different types of nonverbal communication, cultural variations in patterns of nonverbal communication, and how couples counselors and marriage and family therapists use the information from nonverbal communication with client families.

Types of Nonverbal Communication

Body Language

How an individual positions his or her body speaks volumes about what that person is thinking and feeling. An individual with squared-off shoulders and an open body posture is likely having a different experience from that of the individual with rounded, hunched shoulders and closed body posture. Open posture includes uncrossed arms and minimal barriers between individuals; closed posture includes crossed legs and/or arms, as well as physical barriers placeds between individuals (e.g., sitting behind a desk, having an object on one's lap). Body language also includes gestures and body movements. Obvious obscene gestures aside, certain body movements can allow couples counselors and marriage and family therapists to investigate what their client family members are not telling them. For example, the client family member who has her legs crossed, is shaking the dangling foot, picking at her cuticles, and chewing on her lips is probably uneasy in the situation and may need the help of the family therapist to relax and feel comfortable in the counseling setting.

When individuals like one another and are comfortable communicating with one another, their body language mirrors one another's. If one spouse is crying and feeling sadness, the other spouse is likely to empathize and frown, or even cry, as a result of the partner's body language. Likewise, if one spouse is rubbing his partner's arm and, in turn, the partner begins rubbing the spouse's arm back, the phenomenon occurring is the mirroring of body language.

Eye Contact and Movement

Eye contact and visual movement are integral parts of nonverbal communication. During conversation, eye contact usually indicates engagement and active listening, that the individual is attending to the situation. Lack of eye contact can be indicative of discomfort, hidden truths, deep thinking, or even boredom. Eye movements are also nonverbal behaviors that affect communication in couples and families. Different unspoken messages are sent by rolling, darting, squinting, or shifting one's eyes. Frequently, when individuals are silent and they look up, they are thinking; when they are silent and they look down, they are feeling.

Facial Expressions

Observing clients' facial expressions provides an important clue for couples counselors and marriage and family therapists to interpret subcontext and emotions. Sometimes, the simplest answer is the most accurate one: If a client frowns, the client is probably upset; likewise, if a client laughs, he or she is apt to be in a humorous mood. The couples counselor or marriage and family therapist may simply choose to track the facial expressions of the client family by observing them and addressing them in the present moment. For example, if a client shifts his or her expression from smiling to a furrowed brow and tense lips, it may be prudent for the family therapist to call attention to the shift in client feeling (e.g., "I notice that you stopped smiling when we started talking about your in-laws. Can we address this change in mood?").

Spatial Relations

Spatial relations can vary greatly from one client family to another. Typical speaking distance between individuals depends largely on cultural norms and family traditions. Some individuals need less distance between one another when communicating, while others need more. In the United States, four zones of spatial relations are generally used: intimate space (the foot of space directly surrounding an individual; generally reserved for romantic partners), personal space (about 2 to 4 feet away from an individual; generally reserved for family and close friends), social space (about 4 to 10 feet away from an individual; generally reserved for business associates and colleagues), and public space (between 10 and 25 feet away from an individual; generally reserved for public speaking). An important note to highlight about spatial relations—and nonverbal communication as a whole—is that, again, there is no one set of guidelines with which to interpret these behaviors. There are differences in spatial relations, or proxemics, according to gender, level of authority, comfort with interpersonal interaction, familiarity, and nationality; there are numerous factors that can affect how close or how far the distance should be between two individuals communicating with one another.

Touch

Spatial relations have to be considered when addressing touch, since touch is dependent upon closer proxemics. Touch is another type of nonverbal communication that may be interpreted differently depending on the cultural norms of the individuals involved. Again, if it is culturally appropriate for there to be less spatial distance between two individuals communicating, it may also be appropriate for there to be more touch than when there is further spatial distance. When a couples counselor or marriage and family therapist uses touch with clients, it is often to signify caring. This may occur through a hug, for example, or by placing one's hand on a client's forearm and rubbing it slightly. These are comforting acts that model empathy for the client family.

Vocal Quality

Even though the words we speak are not considered nonverbal communication, the ways in which we speak are considered nonverbal communication. Vocal qualities, also called paralanguage, include the volume at which an individual speaks, the tone of his or her voice, the rate of speech used, verbally underlining or emphasizing certain words, and even the pitch the individual uses. Changes in vocal quality can indicate changes in feelings. A harsh tone delivered loudly and briskly can mean the individual is angry or otherwise upset. An individual speaking in soothing, dulcet tones at a slower pace is likely to be calm or happy.

Cultural Variations

It should be noted that cultural differences are likely to exist in nonverbal communications. This is particularly true when addressing spatial distance, as there are varying cultural norms for what is considered typical distance between individuals interacting with one another. Members from some cultures stand closer to one another when communicating, and this physical distance (or closeness) in and of itself is a form of nonverbal communication. This physical distance affects touch, another nonverbal communication type that can vary greatly depending on the client family's culture and background. For example, Orthodox Jews generally do not believe in mixed-gender touching unless the individuals are related; therefore, it would be inappropriate for a male family therapist even to shake the hand of a female Orthodox Jewish client. Eye contact is another nonverbal behavior that can drastically differ depending on the culture of the couple or client family. In the United States, eye contact is generally expected when an individual is listening; the speaker is usually less likely to make eye contact than the listener. Clients from certain backgrounds will not subscribe to this rule. For example, certain Latino and Asian families will consider eye contact from young listeners to be rude and inappropriate. Couples counselors and marriage and family therapists must be sensitive to the cultural norms of their client families, and be respectful of differences.

How Family Therapists Use Nonverbal Communication

This section gives an overview of how couples counselors and marriage and family therapists utilize their understanding of client families' nonverbal communications.

Patterns of Nonverbal Communication

Family therapists must observe and track patterns of clients' nonverbal communications. They have to be able to point out to clients when their nonverbal communications are being heard loudly and clearly. Many client family members are unaware of their nonverbal communications with one another, and may need the family therapist to shine a light on the situation. By addressing nonverbal communications when they are occurring in the moment, family therapists are better able to help clients consolidate understanding of their use of nonverbal communications, and its effect on family members. A major goal for most couples counselors and marriage and family therapists is to simultaneously maintain both family unity and personal individualism. When they point out clients' nonverbal communications, individuals learn about themselves and families learn about the members therein, meeting this goal of separate closeness.

Discrepancies

Family therapists also use nonverbal communications to notice and point out discrepancies in clients' stories, feelings, and behaviors. For example, if a client is smiling while he or she talks about something unpleasant, the client is likely trying to mask hidden pain with a false veneer. The family therapist might say, "You are talking about a horrific event in your life, yet you are smiling. Let's talk about the discrepancy between the content of your story and what you are trying to show you feel." Using the nonverbal behavior to address the inconsistency between what the client is saying and what he or she is feeling is a crucial tool for the family therapist. The same thing occurs when the therapist notices a difference between what the client is saying and what he or she is doing. For example, if a client comes to couples counseling in order to repair his or her marriage but consistently shows up late to sessions, keeping the client's partner and their couples counselor waiting, the couples counselor might say something like this: "You are telling me that you are invested in marriage counseling, yet you are showing up late to our sessions. I see a discrepancy between those two things and I want to know what you think. What's your reaction to hearing this?"

Rebecca M. Goldberg

See also Clinical Case Conceptualization With Couples and Families; Clinical Interviews With Couples and Families; Communication Errors/Problems in Couples and Families; Communication in Couples and Families; Cultural Issues in Couples and Families; Empathy; Metacommunication

Further Readings

Ekman, P. (2007). *Emotions revealed: Recognizing faces and feelings to improve communication and emotional life* (2nd ed.). New York: Holt Paperbacks.

Goldman, E. (2003). *As others see us: Body movement and the art of successful communication*. New York: Routledge.

Hagan, S. (2008). *The everything body language book: Master the art of nonverbal communication to succeed in work, love, and life*. Avon, MA: Adams Media.

Knapp, M. L., Hall, J. A., & Horgan, T. G. (2013). *Nonverbal communication in human interaction* (8th ed.). Independence, KY: Cengage Learning.

Mehrabian, A. (2007). *Nonverbal communication*. Chicago, IL: Aldine Transaction.

Riggio, R. E., & Feldman, R. S. (2005). *Applications of nonverbal communication*. New York: Psychology Press.

Weiser, A., & Latiolais-Hargrave, J. (2000). *Judge the jury: Experience the power of reading people*. Dubuque, IA: Kendall/Hun.

NORMALIZING

Normalizing may be defined as (a) acceptance of people with disabilities and (b) offering people with disabilities the same conditions that are offered to others. The normalizing principle therefore means making available to all people with disabilities conditions of everyday living that are equal to (or as close as possible to) the regular circumstances and everyday way of life of society. This includes providing to individuals with disabilities the ability to live a life with normal rhythms, including daily routines. It also includes providing to such individuals the opportunities to interact within the normal conditions of life (e.g., regular housing, schooling, employment, exercise, recreation, and independent living). The purpose of this entry is to give an overview of research on the normalizing principle, including a description of a normalizing environment in the delivery of human services.

The concept of normalizing was developed in Scandinavia during the 1960s and further operationalized in the 1970s by Wolf Wolfensberger and the National Institute on Mental Retardation (NIMR) in Toronto, Canada, as a result of individuals with disabilities being deemed "fundamentally different" and "flawed." For example, in the 1960s people with mental disorders such as mental retardation were deemed "incurable" by the medical profession. In response, individuals with disabilities were "devalued" by society and became likely to be subjected to lifelong negative experiences such as (a) being perceived as "deviant" due to their physical/functional impairments; (b) being rejected by the community, society, and even their own family members; (c) being labeled as "subhuman" or as a "burden on society"; (d) being segregated from the rest of society; and/or (e) being the victim of abuse, violence, and brutalization. Those with mental retardation, now referred to as having an intellectual disability or an intellectual developmental disorder, were often placed in residential living environments in which they were confined, sometimes for a lifetime, with little to no emphasis on improvement or rehabilitation. During the 1950s and 1960s, large public housing institutions were used as a primary means of treatment for adults with mental retardation and other disabilities in the United States, a policy referred to as institutionalization.

As society's awareness and understanding of mental disorders, including intellectual disability, increased throughout the 1970s, a new model of behavioral health care emerged that emphasized "normalization." Rather than focusing on the confinement of individuals, public housing institutes worked to provide a more structured environment designed to rehabilitate individuals with the purpose of allowing them to return to the community and live independent, productive lives. The normalized environment supports a holistic approach that incorporates private and public living spaces, dining and recreational activities, and safety and security, in order to support a continuum of socialized learning experiences.

In addition to returning people to the community and supporting them in attaining as "normal" a life as possible, normalization was intended to reduce stigma and change societal attitudes regarding individuals with disabilities. Advocates sought to broaden the category of "normal" to include *all* human beings and discontinue labeling those with intellectual disabilities as "sick," "ill," or "abnormal." More specifically, individuals with intellectual disabilities were no longer to be viewed as "incurable," but rather as people who require additional supports in life. Through this new perspective, individuals with intellectual disability can become independent and self-sufficient, two values that are central to Western society's definition of self-worth.

The normalization principle implies as much as possible the use of culturally valued means in order to enable, establish, and/or maintain valued social roles for people. Enhancing the perceived value of societal roles of an individual is called social role valorization, a principle formulated by Wolfensberger as a successor to his earlier principle of normalization. As the principle of normalization refers to individuals with disabilities maintaining valuable societal roles, it might be said that through the universal application of this principle, individuals with disabilities could be less likely to endure lifelong negative experiences. Normalization may not only help prevent bad things from happening to socially vulnerable or devalued people but also can increase the likelihood that they will experience good things in life.

The concepts of normalization and social role valorization have evolved into a guiding principle in the design and delivery of human services for individuals with disabilities. For example, the concept of providing a "normalized" environment has been supported by state laws mandating shorter patient stays at institutions and the use of evidence-based treatment, in addition to greater accountability from behavioral health professionals (e.g., psychologists, psychiatrists, counselors, social workers). Over the years the normalization principle has had wide applicability and a significant effect on the way services for individuals with disabilities have been structured throughout the United Kingdom, continental Europe, North America, Australia, and other parts of the world, and continues to do so today.

Danielle L. Geigle

See also Adult Development; Aging and Caregiving; General Systems Theory; Mental Health, Systemic Perspective; Social Support

Further Readings

Bank-Mikkelsen, N. E. (1976). *Misconceptions on the principle of normalisation.* Address to IASSMD Conference, Washington, DC.

Muirhead, K., & Treece, D. (2006). Normalizing the patient environment: Current trends in facility design aim to make inpatient psychiatric care less institutional. *Behavioral Healthcare, 26*(2), 28–30.

Nirje, B. (1969). The normalization principle and its human management implications. In R. Kugel & W. Wolfensberger (Eds.), *Changing patterns in residential services for the mentally retarded.* Washington, DC: President's Committee on Mental Retardation.

Nirje, B. (1985). The basis and logic of the normalization principle. *Australia and New Zealand Journal of Developmental Disabilities, 11*(2), 65–68.

Osburn, J. (2006). An overview of social role valorization theory. *SRV Journal, 1*(1), 4–13.

Wolfensberger, W. (1972). *The principle of normalization in human services.* Toronto, Canada: National Institute on Mental Retardation.

Wolfensberger, W., & Tullman, S. (1982). A brief outline of the principle of normalization. *Rehabilitation Psychology, 27*(3), 131–145.

No-Secrets Contracts

No-secrets contracts are confidentiality agreements designed to help define the roles of couples and families participating in therapy. These contracts are utilized to eliminate problems that may occur when a client who sees a therapist along with a partner or family members is also seeing the therapist in one-on-one sessions and discloses information that he or she wants the therapist to keep secret from the partner or one or more of the family members. No standardized contract exists to address secrets; therefore, it is advised that a therapist be proactive in creating and implementing his or her own contract. These efforts help to ensure that all those seeing the therapist together (a) are informed of the therapist's policy regarding disclosure of secrets and (b) understand the consequences of how therapy will unfold if secrets are revealed.

The Role of Confidentiality

The therapeutic relationship is predicated on an agreement of confidentiality between the client and therapist. This confidentiality allows clients to safely reveal secrets as long as the secrets are not related to harm to self or others. When a therapist agrees to enter a relationship with a couple or family, navigating secrets can become complicated because individual confidentiality may not be (a) advised, (b) permitted by the therapist, or (c) followed by the client. No-secrets contracts provide ethical and legal foundations for preventing many of the potential complications inherent when working with more than one person at a time. Some of the common client presentations whereby no-secrets contracts are useful can include infidelity, sexually transmitted infection, alcohol or drug addiction, and familial problems. It is recommended that therapists anticipate these potentially difficult situations and be prepared to address confidentiality by considering the use of a no-secrets policy.

Client Versus Client Unit

No-secrets contracts help provide definition to the question "Who is the client?" In individual therapy, the client is easily identifiable via a named individual on the intake form as well as by an insurance reimbursement for a specific person. This same identifiable client with ownership of confidentiality is not as apparent in the case of couples or family therapy. This lack of alliance to any single member occurs because the therapist is working to create an alliance with the couple or family as a single client unit. Thus, one way to differentiate between individual therapy and couples and family therapy is for the therapist to determine his or her alliance. Alliance to a client unit, as opposed to a single individual, has the potential to create confidentiality conflicts for a therapist because any member of a unit at any time can disclose secret information that he or she insists must remain secret and unknown to the other unit member(s).

Types of No-Secrets Contracts

A therapist needs to determine the type of no-secrets contract needed for his or her practice. This determination gives consideration to the client versus the client unit, confidentiality, and tolerance of the client(s) toward the therapist's perspective and desire to use the contract. Three types of policies exist: zero-tolerance-to-secrets policies, zero-tolerance-to-disclosure policies, and minimal-disclosure policies.

A zero-tolerance-to-secrets policy involves an agreement from all members of the client unit to disclose secrets to all other members of the client unit. Thus, no matter what member of the client unit is present in the therapy session, all other members of the client unit are privy to the information disclosed during that session. This type of contract protects the confidentiality of the couple or family as a unit as opposed to individual members, and places primary importance on the system as opposed to the individual.

In contrast to the zero-tolerance-to-secrets policy is a zero-tolerance-to-disclosure policy. This type of policy protects the confidentiality of each individual who is part of the client unit, with zero information shared with any other member of the client unit if the member who disclosed that information is absent from the session. This type of policy affords individual members the most confidentiality, autonomy, and freedom to disclose secrets in any given session.

A minimal-disclosure policy is a compromise between zero-tolerance-to-secrets and zero-tolerance-to-disclosure policies. A therapist, guided by clinical judgment, can define at the outset which secrets will be revealed, allowing for some secrets while not allowing for others. For example, the contract might define a list of behaviors that may interfere with therapeutic progress, and note that these secrets, such as infidelity or addiction to drugs, will be revealed. However, other behaviors, such as smoking, or a secret bank account, would not be revealed under the contract.

While all three approaches have advantages and disadvantages, it is essential that the chosen approach is clearly defined. Some factors for consideration in determining which approach will be most effective are the potential risks, potential benefits, and systemic conflicts that may result due to adherence to the policy. An ethical decision-making model is advised during the creation of the policy. An ethical decision-making model is a framework that helps therapists decide among multiple decisions in a way that is congruent with professional standards and ethics and the well-being of clients.

Content of No-Secrets Contracts

No-secrets contracts generally cover four topics: client and therapist rights and responsibilities, rationale for the chosen policy, secret navigation procedures, and contract violation procedures. It is advised that the therapist begin the contract with an explanation of each client's rights and responsibilities in therapy. The therapist needs to be clear on topics such as purpose of the contract as well as a clearly detailed discussion on autonomy, confidentiality, and disclosure. The contract should list both the rights and responsibilities of the client(s) and the therapist. The contract details what it means to maintain or waive confidentiality. Furthermore, the therapist explains the complications that can arise as a result of couples and family secrets and whether the therapy is with a single client or a client unit. The therapist explains his or her approach to dealing with secrets in understandable language that provides the client the opportunity to decide whether these parameters are acceptable. Finally, the therapist explains how the contract will be implemented, with clear steps outlining procedures if the contract is violated. The contract needs to include the process for dealing with violations, the time frame, and the potential outcomes of this process.

Ethical and Legal Implications

No specific ethical mandates regarding no-secrets contracts exist. The American Association for Marriage and Family Therapy Code of Ethics addresses both confidentiality and the therapist ensuring that clients benefit from the therapeutic relationship. These codes imply that it is the therapist's responsibility to keep client information confidential while also working to promote beneficence and forward movement toward growth. Secrets between couples and among family members may cause conflict when a secret, offered to the therapist in confidence, impairs the therapist's ability to be helpful to the couple and/or family.

An ethical dilemma arises if a no-secrets contract is not utilized in therapy, yet the therapist becomes aware of a sensitive secret. Essentially, if there is no agreed-upon policy for handling secrets, the therapist may experience a significant problem with client unit confidentiality. If no contract exists, a therapist may find it is unethical to disclose secret information while also realizing that growth potential is limited or impaired due to the kept secret. This leaves the therapist possibly triangulated with a specific client or needing to terminate the therapeutic relationship due to impaired therapeutic growth. A further complication, if termination is warranted, is the obligation of explaining why termination must happen. This situation can lead to additional unethical behaviors by the therapist, including minimizing the circumstance for termination, deceit due to an inability to release termination information, and potential abandonment of the client(s). A no-secrets contract provides an agreed-upon framework for avoiding these potentially consequential dilemmas.

If a client refuses to sign the no-secrets contract as the therapist has recommended, the therapist has a few general choices, including further clarification of roles and functions, offering individual services, and/or declining to provide services altogether. Refusal to sign the no-secrets contract may be an indication that the client needs help clarifying roles and functions of the therapist and the therapeutic hour. The therapist can use this opportunity to further educate the client(s) about the services offered. If the client continues to refuse to sign, perhaps this rejection indicates the desire for individual therapy. Finally, the therapist can decline services due to the potential ethical conflicts of treating a client unit that does not agree on the no-secrets policy.

The legal goal of a no-secrets contract is to eliminate any ambiguity related to expectations of confidentiality. If a client is seen individually, even in the context of couples therapy, it is unclear to the client if this interaction can be perceived as private and confidential. The counselor needs to state in simple and clear terms that the client legally owns the privilege to confidential communication, and that signing a no-secrets contract may waive this right.

Limitations of No-Secrets Contracts

Although clients may initially agree to any of the three types of policies, it is difficult to determine what will happen once a secret is revealed to the therapist. Individual members of the client unit may perceive the secret-keeping as an alliance with the individual and that individual's perspective on the problem (triangulation). The individual or individuals who are not informed of the secret may no longer trust the therapist and may feel betrayed upon finding out about the therapist's knowledge of the secret. Alternatively, if a therapist insists on disclosing all secrets, the secret-keeper may decide it is not safe or wise to disclose his or her secret, and this nondisclosure may inhibit progress in treatment. It is also difficult to determine how the other individual(s) will respond to a revealed secret. One or more of these individuals may become angry at the therapist for revealing something "better left unsaid." Finally, minimal-disclosure contracts leave the therapist in the position of judging which secrets can and cannot be disclosed. This therapist-as-expert model limits client autonomy and trust that client units have the necessary resources to determine their own health.

Amber M. Lange and Trevon Clow

See also Confidentiality; Conflict in Couples and Families; Ethical Decision-Making; Informed Consent in Clinical Work; Secrets

Further Readings

Adams, S. A. (2010). Who is my client? Maintaining paperwork when the client changes. *Family Journal, 18*, 70–72. doi:10.1177/1066480709357729

Bass, B. A., & Quimby, J. L. (2006). Addressing secrets in couples counseling: An alternative approach to informed consent. *Family Journal, 14*, 77–80. doi:10.1177/1066480705282060

Butler, M., Harper, J., & Seedall, R. (2009). Facilitated disclosure versus clinical accommodation of infidelity secrets: An early pivot point in couple therapy: Part 1. Couple relationship ethics, pragmatics, and attachment. *Journal of Marital & Family Therapy, 35*(1), 125–143. doi:10.1111/j.1752-0606.2008.00106.x

Butler, M., Rodriguez, M., Roper, S., & Feinauer, L. (2010). Infidelity secrets in couple therapy: Therapists' views on the collision of competing ethics around relationship-relevant secrets. *Sexual Addiction & Compulsivity, 17*(2), 82–105. doi:10.1080/10720161003772041

Butler, M., Seedall, R., & Harper, J. (2008). Facilitated disclosure versus clinical accommodation of infidelity secrets: An early pivot point in couple therapy: Part 2. Therapy ethics, pragmatics, and protocol. *American Journal of Family Therapy, 36*(4), 265–283.

Ellis, E. M. (2012). What are the confidentiality rights of collaterals in family therapy? *American Journal of Family Therapy, 40*(5), 369–384. doi:10.1080/01926187.2012.677705

Fall, K. A., & Lyons, C. (2003). Ethical considerations of family secret disclosure and post-session safety management. *Family Journal, 11*, 281–285. doi:10.1177/1066480703252339

Nuclear Family

A nuclear family is traditionally defined as consisting of a mother and father in a first-time marriage and their children. This family structure also has been referred to as the traditional American family, the elementary family, and the basic unit of society, and has often been deemed the norm for family structure. Historical trends have shown a deviation from the nuclear family, leading to an expanded definition of the family in society. For purposes of family therapy, a nuclear family is comprised of caretakers and children in one household. This entry outlines the traditional structure of the nuclear family, discusses trends leading to changes in family structure and roles, and details the expansion of the definition of the nuclear family.

Traditional Nuclear Family Structure

During the 1950s, the nuclear family archetype was dominant in American culture. This ideal was evident in media portrayals of family life that defined family roles within a more patriarchal system in a middle-class, suburban, White-dominated society. The industrial era that followed the Great Depression and World War II promoted financial security and an increase in the U.S. middle class. American suburbs grew, and the archetypal lifestyle of the nuclear family was created and supported through this time period. Job opportunities during this era made it possible for many couples to live comfortably on one income. Public policy such as tax breaks for married couples were introduced in 1948, providing financial support and benefits for those who fit within this societal norm.

In the archetype of the nuclear family during this time, the role of the father consisted of providing financially for the family through being the primary breadwinner. The father often had power in decision-making, discipline, and finances. The female role centered on her position as homemaker, which included responsibilities such as rearing the children and daily tasks around the home. The mother was expected to have complete fidelity to the husband. The children in the nuclear family system were expected to be obedient and loyal to their parents. Societal norms regarding the nuclear family system added values and expectations including love, respect, frugality, and financial security.

Research describes challenges for those who seemingly fit the nuclear family structure and those families that deviated from this norm. Terms such as the intact family, when referring to the nuclear family, led to judgment and the assumption that those families outside of the nuclear family norm, such as single-parent families, are broken. Nevertheless, the traditional nuclear family has only been emphasized in the United States for a small period of time. Before the post–World War II industrial era, families relied on close kin, community, and extended family members to fulfill financial, social, and educational needs. The emphasis on the nuclear family structure de-emphasized extended family relations and community support, with an expectation that the needs of each family member are met through the nuclear family system. The traditional nuclear family structure is viewed as a rigid, closed system that decreased family resilience.

The societal portrayal and norm of the nuclear family often created unrealistic expectations within the nuclear family on mothers, fathers, spouses, and children. Mothers were expected to fulfill the responsibility of rearing their children, which was seen as an invaluable contribution to society, yet was devalued and underappreciated. Women received messages that they were to aspire to the role of homemaker and mother, fulfill their husbands' needs, and bear responsibility for the success or failure of their children. While the men received messages regarding their gender role, it is argued that the nuclear family expectations and gender roles within this system had the most deleterious impact on women. Men additionally received messages regarding unrealistic expectations on their duty to be the primary breadwinner of the home. Literature reports a decline in parent–child relationships primarily between fathers and their children, as the nurturing role was given to women.

Couples and families became more isolated as they relied less on extended support systems. As more pressure was put on spouses to fulfill all needs of the couple and family, marriages were reported to suffer. Now all financial, household, child-rearing, and emotional fulfillment were the responsibility of the couple, with little or no help from extended support systems. These structural and gendered expectations were passed on to future generations, even though these may not be the healthiest expectations for all families. Family conflicts, secrets, and patterns often deviated from the societal norm, resulting in families hiding their problems. Transitions from the traditional nuclear family structure occurred simultaneously with changes in gender roles in society. Current literature defines the nuclear family in a more broad sense to include modern changes in family systems.

Trends Contributing to Changes in Family Structure and Roles

Historically, media portrayals of the family promoted societal norms regarding the nuclear family. It was portrayed in the 1950s as safe, secure, and happy. This is now seen as a mythologized view of the family, and the nuclear family structure itself was soon to become less prevalent. By 1970, 40% of American households were made up of married couples with children; in 2013, these families made up just 19% of households.

Beginning in the 1960s, changes in gender roles within nuclear families became more prevalent as a result of the feminist movement. Feminists advocated for gender equality and freedom from societal norms. Advancements in contraception and greater accessibility of contraception and abortion made it possible to delay or postpone childbearing for women. As more women entered the workforce they encountered what was termed the second shift; they worked yet continued to carry the homemaking responsibilities as defined within the traditional nuclear family. This gradually changed, and although working women continue to carry more responsibilities at home than their male counterparts, couples today report a desire to have an equal partnership in their marriage.

Longer life spans and couples marrying at later ages, couples having children at later ages, and fewer couples having children all have decreased the prevalence of the nuclear family in the United States. The average age of marriage in 1960 for men and women was 22 and 20, respectively; this increased in 2009 to 28 for men and 26 for women. Couples more commonly delay or refrain from having children. Cohabitation is more prevalent and common among couples than in the past and is often done in anticipation of future marriage. Divorce rates increased during the 1970s and 1980s, and remarriage rates have continued to rise since 1960, leading to an increase in blended and single-parent families. It is also becoming more prevalent for men and women to choose to become single parents, with single-parent homes more commonly found among women. There have been advances in funding support for single-parent homes, making raising families more feasible for single parents. All of these trends may be viewed as a deviation from the traditional nuclear family.

While research has found a decline in prevalence of married parents with children since the 1970s, this decline appears to be slowing. Some research attributes this to an increase in immigration among groups that may be more likely to marry and remain married, at least in the first generation. Definitions and structures of the family among certain cultures may not fit within the norms of the traditional nuclear family as it has been seen in the United States, however.

The term *nuclear family* is still used to refer to a mother, father, and biological children or children they adopt, but some use it more broadly to refer to many types of families with parents who may be stepparents, unmarried, or same-gender couples. Even with this broader definition, an emphasis on the nuclear family can marginalize single-parent homes, kinship care, and couples without children, and also minimize the role of extended family and community supports within a family system. Family systems of earlier eras incorporated larger extended family systems in defining the family. With longer life spans, grandparents, aunts, and uncles may be regaining their position in the family system. The nuclear family of the 1950s has transformed as societal norms, political policies, and media portrayals of the family all have changed.

While society is expanding the definition of the family to incorporate more types of family structure, cultural beliefs and values may continue to place an emphasis on the traditional nuclear family structure. For many social, religious, and cultural groups the traditional nuclear family continues to be established as the ideal. These values may often be connected with conservative and patriarchal belief systems regarding the sacred nature of the family. While this may be valued as the ideal for many groups, the incorporation of gender equality is becoming more prevalent, even among those who promote the traditional nuclear family.

The nuclear family ideal continues to be prevalent and privileged in society, with the transitioning definition of the nuclear family slowly gaining popularity in American culture. Policies that favor the nuclear family continue to exist, including tax breaks for couples and those with children. Same-sex marriage, while gaining support and becoming more common, continues to be challenged. Insurance policies, child-care costs, and continued gender inequality are examples of ways in which the nuclear family continues to be privileged in American society. An idealized view of the nuclear family can result in guilt for women who choose to pursue a career before, in place of, or concurrently with child-rearing. Single adults and couples without children continue to face societal pressure over not fitting within a norm. Family and individual human development models continue to include stages incorporating marriage/coupling and child-rearing as part of normal human and/or family development. While the overt messages regarding expectations of the nuclear family have diminished in the past few decades, covert stereotypes may continue to exist.

Tiffany Nielson

See also Family Life Cycle; Gender Issues; Gender Roles; Individual and Family Development; Individual Family Culture

Further Readings

Coles, R. L. (2006). *Race and family: A structural approach*. Thousand Oaks, CA: Sage.

Coontz, S. (2000). *The way we were: American families and the nostalgia trap*. New York: Basic Books.

McGoldrick, M., Gerson, R., & Petry, S. (2008). *Genograms: Assessment and intervention* (3rd ed.). New York: W. W. Norton.

Vereen, L. (2007). African American family structure: A review of the literature. *The Family Journal, 15*(3), 282–285.

Walsh, F. (Ed.). (2011). *Normal family processes: Growing diversity and complexity*. New York: Guilford Press.

NUDITY: BELIEFS AND VALUES

Nudity is defined as the act of being naked, and can include full nudity or partial nudity/being partially clothed. There are differences in familial and cultural beliefs surrounding nudity, as well as some countercultures for which nudity is a main focus. For the purposes of this discussion, those subcultures are referred to as nudists. This entry discusses nudity in the family, nudity and intimacy, and nudism.

Nudity in Family Systems

An understanding of social standards and cultural norms surrounding nudity is essential for marriage and family counselors. In addition, an awareness of their own values regarding nudity is paramount and can be impactful in regard to how the counselor may draw boundaries regarding duty to report when nudity within a family may be inappropriate. Working with couples, the counselor will ultimately encounter issues regarding intimacy and nudity.

Family Nudity in Nonnudist Families

In the early developmental years, child nudity is a necessary and frequent occurrence. For many families, during early childhood, parental nudity around children is a permissible practice. Some of this occurs out of necessity for supervising and caring for the child or children; changing, bathing, and going to the bathroom without supervising the child at the same time can be impossible when only one adult is present. For many parents, cobathing is an easy solution and also provides bonding time with the child.

There is no set guideline as to at what age naturally occurring parental/child nudity boundaries begin to change, though the late-preschool years are often a point at which opposite-sex nudity, especially father–daughter nudity, sees a decline in deemed appropriateness based on professional and social opinion. For some families, same-sex nudity may be considered normal throughout childhood, specifically regarding clothes-changing and bathing. Sibling nudity should also be considered. As the children age, same- and opposite-sex levels of comfort with nudity, and the social appropriateness of nudity, need to be addressed.

In determining appropriate boundaries surrounding nudity, it is important that the comfort level of both parent and child be assessed; does each feel their privacy is valued and respected, and is each comfortable with the behavior? For some parents, the need to supervise a child who is exhibiting demanding behavior may be such that they never have a moment of privacy, and don't confront the behavior despite discomfort. Some children may not know how to tell a parent they are uncomfortable with either the parent's or their own nudity. Thus, it is essential that the family counselor is helping the family to communicate their own boundaries as well as to educate them on what socially normative behavior is surrounding nudity. This is also true of sibling relationships, especially where there are age and gender differences among the siblings. A vastly different set of developmental concerns and physiological changes regarding nudity may be involved for each sibling.

For children who have experienced sexual abuse, additional consideration should be given to the presence of nudity within the family. The child may have poor boundaries surrounding his or her own or others' nudity, or conversely may be very uncomfortable with nudity, even surrounding routine bathing and changing. Psychoeducation for parents and caregivers of sexual abuse survivors is imperative.

While nonsexualized nudity boundaries between parents and children can be ambiguous, boundaries surrounding nudity as a component of a sexual act are much more clearly defined. Generally, engaging in sexual activity around a child is deemed appropriate in infancy and pre-toddlerhood, but not thereafter. Sexual nudity *with* a child is inappropriate at any age, and the aforementioned boundaries are regarding only those instances of nonsexual nudity in the family. It is important for parents and caregivers to be aware of the ways in which nudity may come across.

Finally, it is imperative that parents consider the ways in which boundaries surrounding familial nudity may translate to social situations. Educating children on the differences between nudity within the family and nudity outside the family will help the child to identify inappropriate acts of others' nudity in social situations, as well as to maintain social boundaries surrounding their own nudity. For instance, while it may be appropriate within a specific family for children to be partially or fully naked at home during their elementary years, their school may raise concerns with regularly removing clothes at school. Policies surrounding how to address frequent disrobing can vary among schools, and differences can be compounded by teachers' and other personnel's own values surrounding nudity.

Counselors should remain abreast of any culture-of-origin norms that may be contributing to nonnormative familial nudity, and assess, adjust, and educate themselves and clients accordingly. If a client's culture of origin does include familial nudity past what is commonly accepted in the United States, the counselor should educate the client about how familial nudity may be perceived, especially when it comes to issues of child welfare.

Nudity and Intimacy

Differing perspectives on nudity can be a source of distress in couples, and can occur during both sexually intimate and nonintimate interactions. For instance, one member of the couple may be quite comfortable being naked around the other during nonsexual interactions (i.e., when changing or bathing), while the other member of the couple may not be comfortable being naked in front of the other and even find the other partner's open nudity uncomfortable.

Differences in comfort level that might occur during intimate moments might include one member of the couple preferring to be partly clothed during sexual interactions including intercourse, having the lights off so as not to be seen naked, or immediately putting on clothing post-intercourse. Survivors of sexual abuse may have unique boundaries surrounding nudity that emerge in sexually intimate relationships.

In couples where open communication is a concern, these differences in comfort and behavior surrounding nudity are likely noted though not discussed, and could result in self- or other-shaming or blaming. Assessing the extent to which the couple is not only comfortable with nudity, but also comfortable discussing the topic, is essential to addressing concerns about nudity in counseling.

Nudism

Nudism is interchanged frequently with the term *naturism* in the United States. It is, in part, the practice of being nude in social situations, which are usually on private properties or in dedicated areas of gatherings. As a social practice, it should be noted that it differs from sexual practices or fetishes that include being physically nude.

History of Nudism

The practice of nudism is not contemporary in origin. Rather, it has historical roots that trace back to ancient Greece and Rome, where athletic training and events were practiced in the nude, as were many philosophical and intellectual gatherings. Nudism's historical roots are not unique to Greco-Roman culture; its roots can also be traced to ancient India and Egypt. In viewing practices of nudity from a historical lens, it appears that at points in history, it was a norm rather than an exception. Nudism as a lifestyle has seen a rise and fall across history in regard to social acceptance.

Nudism and Counseling

Children of social nudists who were exposed to the nudist lifestyle have been found to have higher body self-image than do nonnudist counterparts. It's important that counselors who may be working with this population assess for distress related to nudism across all domains of functioning, as children may be well adjusted or distressed by the nudist lifestyle. Discussing with parents the importance of respecting children's boundaries surrounding viewing and participating in nudism, and facilitating dialogue within the family system, will allow children to share their experiences. Social nudists have frequently been accused of engaging in child endangerment and child pornography, and this stigma has the potential to manifest in the counseling relationship.

While nudism and naturism are often used interchangeably in the United States, there are differences recognized by European followers. While nudism is simply a practice of being socially naked, naturism includes values related to whole, clean living, and symbiotic relationships with the environment and the earth. Clarification as to whether a client's identification with naturism is synonymous with social nudity or environmental naturism is recommended in conceptualizing the client's culture.

Standards of familial nudity vary greatly across nonnudist and nudist populations. With few regulations governing nudity in families, it can be difficult to assess whether specific instances of familial nudity cross into unhealthy boundaries. Determining the comfort level of all involved, especially children, is necessary in evaluating each situation. Counselors must be aware of their own opinions and values in regard to nudity and also be aware of social mores and legal restrictions that may come into play. It should be noted that the current and relevant literature surrounding nudity in families is sparse, and is seemingly dominated by nonscholarly media, such as weblogs and other websites. Counselors would benefit from consultation regarding potentially nonnormative nudity, considering the lack of research and regulation to inform them.

Ann M. McCaughan

See also Boundaries; Child Protective Services; Fetishes; Intimacy, Specific Threats to; Sexual Abuse; Sexual Intimacy

Further Readings

Friedrich, W. N. (2002). *Psychological assessment of sexually abused children and their families*. Thousand Oaks, CA: Sage.

Friedrich, W. N. (2007). *Children with sexual behavior problems: Family-based, attachment focused therapy*. Thousand Oaks, CA: Sage.

Gabb, J. (2013). Embodying risk: Managing father–child intimacy and the display of nudity in families. *Sociology, 47*(4), 639–654.

Johnson, T. C., & Hooper, R. I. (2003). Boundaries and family practices: Implications for assessing child abuse. *Assessment and Forensic Issues, 12*(3–4), 103–125.

Johnson, T. C., Huang, B. E., & Simpson, P. M. (2009). Sibling family practices: Guidelines for healthy boundaries. *Journal of Child Sexual Abuse, 18*, 339–354.

Lewis, R. J., & Janda, L. H. (1988). The relationship between adult sexual adjustment and childhood experiences regarding exposure to nudity, sleeping in the parental bed, and parental attitudes toward sexuality. *Archives of Sexual Behavior, 17*(4), 349–362.

Story, M. (1984). Comparisons of body self-concept between social nudists and nonnudists. *The Journal of Psychology: Interdisciplinary and Applied, 118*(1), 99–112.

OBJECT RELATIONS THEORY

Object relations theory is a family therapy model that blends aspects of psychoanalytic and systems theory. It is based on the idea that people form internalized images of "objects" (important relationships in one's life) and judge others based on these mental representations of significant others. Although this approach shares its roots with Sigmund Freud's psychoanalytic theory, Freud believed that humans are motivated chiefly by sexual and aggressive drives, whereas object relations theorists believe a fundamental motivation of human beings is to have satisfying relationships. Infants first form a relationship with their mother or caretaker, and it is this first, primary relationship that sets the stage for personality development. Thus, object relations theory stems from individual psychological roots and is bridged, via projective identification (the projection onto another the parts of oneself one wants either to preserve or get rid of), to systemic work. This entry pays tribute to some of the founding theorists of object relations, its key concepts (projective identification, internal objects), its usefulness within couple and family therapy (through use of containment of anxiety), and clinical implications of the theory.

Key Theorists

Ronald Fairbairn (1889–1964)

A central figure in the development of object relations theory is Ronald Fairbairn. The Scottish psychiatrist published a collection of papers entitled *Psychoanalytic Studies of Personality* in 1952. In this book, Fairbairn discussed many of his innovative concepts, including internal object relations.

Melanie Klein (1882–1960)

Considered a cofounder of the theory, Melanie Klein professed herself faithfully adherent to Freudian ideas despite questioning some of his fundamental assumptions. One of her main contributions to systemic object relational practice is projective identification that she conceptualized serving as a defense and a mode of communication.

John Bowlby (1907–1990)

While not a founding theorist, John Bowlby has contributed to deeper understandings of object relations through his work with attachment theory.

Individual Psychology

According to Fairbairn, each person is viewed as being a competent and whole self from infancy, seeking attachment through a mothering person. As with any relationship, the experience of relating is never fulfilling in every way one could need, and when the frustrations of the relations he or she is missing become intolerable, the infant begins to view the mother as rejecting. This leads the child to take in (introject) the mother as a rejecting object that is then repressed within the infant self and split off from the ideal image of the mother. Think of these introjects as cartoonish totalizing images. To stay safe, the infant would paint the rejecting mother as wholly negative and remove it from the ideal of what the infant wishes the mother to be. This object is further split into need-exciting (associated with feelings of longing) and need-rejecting (feelings of rage) aspects. Further, the infant's self in connection to this attachment becomes split from the original self and transforms the infant's personality into a few different selves: central (attached to feelings of security from the ideal internal object), craving (longingly but unsatisfyingly attached to an exciting internal object), and rejecting (angrily attached to a rejecting internal object). Splitting is ultimately done to allow freedom for an individual to continue believing contradictory things about an object—I love it and I hate it.

Two of the selves introduced—craving and rejecting—are known by a few different names. The craving self is also known as the exciting object or tantalizing object, whereas the rejecting self is generally known as the rejecting object. Internal object relationships is the process in which these two repressed and unconsciously driven systems of self relate to an object. These internal objects can then become internal saboteurs within the person's inner world. The central self becomes attached to the good or ideal object that can be loved safely, as it is detached from the frustrating elements of the original object. Taking real characteristics—of caregivers, their relation to the child, and to one another (i.e., parent to parent)—as well as distorted perceptions the child has of such relationships and characteristics, objects are created. The problematic nature of this existence is that the individual is not able to see people in his or her life as people but rather as wholly good, ignoring the bad—or wholly bad, ignoring the good.

It can be said that these early infant-stage and childhood interactions with our caregivers create the scripts by which we spend the rest of our lives seeking out others to play the parts. Thus partnerships are designed to conform to our individual scripts rather than allowing partners to cocreate a new script with roles made specifically for each to play. While everyone may have preconceived notions of what relationships *should* look like, an object-informed script would be unable to reveal the layers of a person. Think of fairy-tale princes—we know only enough about them for them to be swoon-worthy and perfect; the scripts do not allow for all aspects of their personality to enter into the picture.

Relating Partners

According to James Framo (1922–2001), with two or more relating individuals, the intrapsychic conflicts stemming from family of origin are rehashed and, eventually, processed through relationships with other intimate partners. These relationships can be romantic/sexual partnerships or among members of a family (i.e., parent–child). For ease of language, all relating individuals will be referred to as "partners," with the full meaning and intention that the term is not limited to spouses.

Projection and Projective Identification

This theory has two fundamental principles. The first of these, projection, is the act of one partner expelling a part of himself or herself that is either denied or overvalued and seeing the other partner as if imbued with these qualities. Imagine if people were colors and an individual believes he can only be blue because blue is good and he is good. If he starts to see yellow dots appear on himself, he will project this yellow onto someone who is not blue and therefore "deserves" the yellow. Projective identification (a term coined by Melanie Klein), the concept that bridges the intrapsychic and interpersonal, is the systemic process in which a person interacts with others in such a way to elicit behaviors that confirm his or her projections to be true. That is to say, if the "deserving" partner accepts the yellow being thrown at him or her, then this deserving partner was right that he or she was never blue. This process causes the partner to act as a neutralizing agent, or a container, who is able to take on these projections in order to return them as softened and more manageable interpretations. The partner can show him or her that the "bad" yellow can blend into the "good" blue to add some shading rather than needing to be taken as bright yellow spots of "bad" that stand out on an otherwise perfectly blue person.

Containment

Containment as a concept was brought about as an opposite approach to acting out, which can lead to many social consequences through one partner's attempt to escape pain through the existential expense of another. Containment is more of an equal or shared holding of the burdens pain brings with someone else being employed as container.

Accepting the role of container, the partner as a newly created object can help transform the view of their partner's self by accepting each projection, temporarily identifying with it in order to modify it, and return it in a detoxified form. A process known as introjective identification can then allow for this modified version of the partner to be taken and assimilated into his or her view of it. This partnership becomes full of mutual projective processes, with each partner going through the process of containment for the other. Maybe the yellow-carrying partner hates his or her green but the blue individual is about to see the good in green that he or she could not see in yellow? Both partners are able to help the other see the usefulness in colors they once wholly rejected.

Treatment for Couples and Families

Henry V. Dicks was the first to apply Fairbairn's concepts to couple relationships. His conceptualizations of this mutual projective relationship are useful for understanding why many seemingly antagonistic relationships can stay together yet the partners do not desire changing their relations to become less neurotic and opposing. Dicks's prediction was to describe the collusion process by each partner as being driven by a hope for integration of their lost introjects through finding them within each other.

Relational issues arise when these unconscious ways of avoiding anxiety are not mutually gratifying or when containment is not possible between the two relating partners at hand. Assessment of these dyads in treatment involves first seeing each partner as a separate individual and understanding how each individual's past relations have brought him or her to this current place. Understanding this can lead to the clinician spotting the unconscious forces infused into the couple's bond-forming processes.

Working Through Projective Identification

Many theorists have debated the differences between the projective identification process and transference. Michael Porder has suggested that projective identification contracts the therapist into a specific role that can help enable a client to reenact the past. Some, including William Meissner, have called the therapist's response to this process countertransference (a term coined by Sigmund Freud).

Despite the recruitment into these conflict-filled scene re-creations, the therapist remains neutral to the ways in which clients choose to use therapy and follow rather than lead. A main observation of the clinician is how the partners deal with him or her, as well as with one another. A few of the main tasks of an object relations therapist include remaining impartial, interpreting defenses and anxiety, listening to the unconscious, and working through all of what is uncovered.

Within the therapeutic setting, unconscious actions and relational processes need to be brought to a conscious level until their subjective meaning to each partner is clarified. This helps clinicians uncover a greater awareness of their own countertransference in their scripted roles, which can be processed and used as a way to understand what the partner might also be experiencing when on the receiving end of this identification process.

It is important for therapists to share their understanding of the clients' subjective meanings to ensure that it is correct. Once it is validated, the therapist will attempt to disengage from the partners' projective identification interaction. Once the partners stabilize after the therapist's detachment, it will be useful to draw the connections between the present situation and how it is a reenactment of the past. This newfound awareness can help block the partners from further engagements in these sequences as well as potentially serving as a catalyst to changes in relationships with other individuals in each partner's life that were cast in similar or different scripted roles.

Creating Safety

An aim of the object relations therapist is to become an object the couple can use, a representation of a person who can hold onto and become a container or cocontainer for anxiety. To do this, the therapist must have a workable capacity for tolerating anxiety.

Among the key points for an object relations therapist to remember is the great importance of creating a safe setting of acceptance and openness. The clinician should have the strength to provide protection and control that will be used as a container of emotional exchanges and unconscious drives and projections based on skewed internal objects. This can allow the couple or family to hear and be heard in new and improved ways through the safety that containment provides.

Working to help individuals heal and stop from constantly re-creating past conflicts within their current relationships can open doors for them to engage in healthy and loving interactions with one another, rather than with their projections of internalized objects.

Sarah M. Steelman

See also Attachment; Bonding; Cognitive Maps and Couples; Cognitive-Behavioral Couples Therapy; Cognitive-Behavioral Family Therapy; Psychoanalytic Family Therapy; Systems Theory

Further Readings

Dicks, H. V. (1967). *Marital tensions: Clinical studies towards a psycho-analytic theory of interaction.* London: Routledge and Kegan Paul.

Fairbairn, E. R. D. (1952). *Psychoanalytic studies of the personality.* London: Routledge and Kegan Paul.

Framo, J. L. (1992). *Family-of-origin therapy: An intergenerational approach.* New York: Brunner/Mazel.

Scharff, J., & Scharff, D. (2001). Object relations couple therapy. *American Journal of Psychotherapy, 51*(2), 141–173.

Siegel, J. (1992). Analysis of projective identification: An object-relations approach to marital treatment. *Clinical Social Work Journal, 19*(1), 71–81.

ONLINE DATING

Online dating is an Internet-based form of communication with the primary intent to establish in-person (i.e., face-to-face) friendships, or romantic or sexual relationships between consenting adults. It is estimated that 40 million adults in the United States alone have used one or more of the thousands of online dating websites or cell phone applications to meet potential partners. The popularity of online dating has grown steadily since its creation in the mid-1990s, and includes individuals from all adolescent and adult age groups. This entry explores the history of online dating and how online dating works, describes typical online daters, identifies risks associated with online dating, and provides information for counselors, including suggestions for future research.

History

Since the creation of the printed newspaper in the late 1600s, adults have created written advertisements to find a prospective spouse. With the advent of new communications technology, the format of these ads changed to include telephone and video messaging with the same intent. When the Internet became available to American households in the early 1990s, it was not long before this new form of communication—through the use of instant messaging, discussion boards, and, eventually, fully functioning dating websites—expanded dating advertisements to reach virtually the entire world. The first online dating websites, kiss.com (now defunct), and match.com (still one of the most popular and well-known online dating portals) were started in 1994 and 1995, respectively.

At its earliest stages, online dating was associated with a sense of desperation and shame. If one was to meet someone from the Internet, it suggested that they were unable to meet a partner through traditional means, such as randomly meeting in a public space (a grocery store, school, bar or club, etc.), or being introduced by a mutual friend. However, online dating has slowly gained in social acceptance; relationships that started online have been featured in Hollywood films, and social media have become widespread. As of 2015, the online dating industry was estimated to be worth approximately $2.4 billion, with various sources reporting that 20% to 33% of American marriages now originate from online dating, and the initial stigma has been significantly reduced.

How It Works

With several thousand online dating websites in the United States alone, there is a format for individuals to meet others from almost any location in the world, increasing one's opportunity to meet potential partners from one's local geographic area, or select from any location in the world. The various online dating sites cater to individuals of all relationship statuses, including single, married, divorced, widowed, polyamorous, or any other situation. There are sites designed for those who define themselves as a member of any cultural background (race, ethnicity, age, gender, socioeconomic status, profession, education level, sexual orientation, religion, and health status), and sites for seeking individuals of any cultural background. In addition, there are dating websites for almost any interest or lifestyle (politics, music, sports and physical fitness, video games, pets, reading, vegan or vegetarian diets, tattoos, sexual fetishes, and many more).

Typically, individuals become members of a website by signing up and providing at least basic identifying information about themselves. Internet service through a computer, tablet, cell phone, or other device is required. Some online dating websites are free of charge, while many others charge a monthly subscription fee to connect with other members. Monthly fees vary widely per website, but can cost $60 or more per month. To find a potential partner, individuals typically create a member profile, or a self-created online advertisement about themselves that is posted for other members to view. The typical profile minimally includes one's age, gender, location, and the type of relationship one is seeking. Depending on the format of the selected online dating portal, individuals may have the ability to independently search through profiles to find desired matches, or they will be automatically matched with others through various personality tests, answers to questionnaires, history of online browsing activity, or a uniquely designed matchmaking algorithm. Connections with matches may occur asynchronously (through messages or e-mails), synchronously (through live audio or video chatting), or in-person through the use of real-time location-based services that use GPS systems to find matches nearby to each other.

The Typical Online Dater

Anyone with Internet access can become an online dater, and as the stigma about online dating decreases, the number of individuals trying online dating increases every year. Most people who sign up for online dating are familiar with the basic operations of computer or cell phone use, and also have a higher level of comfort with social media. That being so, teens and young adults are most likely to use online dating websites, but online dating has grown in popularity with older adults as well. Most dating websites require a minimum age of 18, but since there is no age verification process, it is not uncommon for younger teens to falsify their age to participate in online dating.

Many individuals who use online dating have a firm sense of identity, and use these websites to attempt to find exactly the type of person(s) they are looking for to complement themselves. Others use online dating to explore their own identity and sexual orientation in an anonymous environment. As online daters have the freedom to present themselves in any fashion and can control the amount of information that they disclose, it can be a particularly safe way of engaging with others. For example, individuals of the lesbian, gay, bisexual, transgender, queer/questioning, and others (LGBTQ+) population can explore their sexuality by communicating with online dating members of the same or different genders, without having to publicly come out. This can be especially helpful for LGBTQ+ individuals from rural or socially isolating areas. There is also a website where married individuals can go to seek out an affair.

Both extroverts and introverts have reported a preference for online dating. Extroverts may enjoy meeting more people than they would typically encounter in their own social circles, while introverts may prefer being able to control their online dating experience by pacing the number of social interactions and sharing information and experiences at a desired speed. One group that tends to prefer online dating over others consists of those who are sensitive to feeling rejected. Online dating tends to reduce some of the burden of rejection that occurs face-to-face. At the same time, individuals may be rejected less often in an online environment because they can present more positive aspects about themselves and hide their less favorable traits.

Most online daters have the expectation that they will eventually meet their matches in a face-to-face situation and engage in the type of relationship they intend to find, whether friendship, romantic, or sexual. Transitioning an online dating relationship to a face-to-face relationship can, however, be quite challenging. Some websites provide a concierge service to introduce couples from online dating relationships, but most sites allow partners to transition the relationship at their own pace, or not at all. Although little research has been done in this area, it is thought that it is better to transition away from an online relationship early on—within a few weeks of the initial online contact—to reduce complications. Waiting to transition the relationship may inadvertently encourage partners to form idealized opinions of each other and the relationship, which may not be accurate in a face-to-face situation. Meeting a stranger from the Internet, at any stage in the relationship, has the potential for multiple risks.

Risks

All interpersonal relationships have risk that one or both parties may be emotionally or physically harmed. However, online dating relationships have the potential for unique risks, as identified in the subsequent sections.

Falsification

As mentioned previously, there is a potential in online dating for individuals to misrepresent themselves. In fact, most online daters report slightly enhanced personal characteristics in their online profiles to appear more attractive to potential matches. It is not unusual to lie slightly about age, height, weight, or other minor variables. However, because there is no way to verify the information from an individual's profile, there is a possibility that a profile may be falsified altogether. Up to 1 in 10 online dating profiles are estimated to be completely fabricated, for a variety of reasons. One form of falsification in particular is called "catfishing," which is a process of falsifying a profile in order to "catch" a partner online. Catfishing can have either negative or positive intent, but typically results in complications due to the inherent lies.

Internet Scams

Another form of falsification through online dating is to scam unsuspecting online daters. For example, con artists posing as online daters might ask their romantic partner to send money. There have also been many reported cases of identity theft, when online daters shared their home address, social security number, credit cards, and online passwords, in the name of friendship or love. In addition, some online dating websites have scammed their customers by selling personal information to other sites.

Sexually Transmitted Infections

Two thirds of online daters have reported meeting individuals face-to-face after having met on the Internet. As many of these relationships are romantic or expressly sexual in nature, there is increased risk for contracting sexually transmitted infections, especially when compounded with the potential for individuals to falsify information about themselves, their personal dating and sexual histories, and their health status.

Sexual and Relationship Violence

The risk for sexual violence and stalking when meeting strangers from the Internet is also increased. Sexual predators have used online dating websites to target unsuspecting victims. Paid websites are able to cross-reference members' official names (obtained from their credit cards) with sex offender registries to deny individuals who have been convicted of sexual crimes from becoming members, but free sites do not typically have their members' full legal names to be able to perform this same screening procedure.

Discrimination

Not all online dating websites are created equally for use by diverse members. Many websites use drop-down boxes with preselected choices that assume heteronormativity, such as forcing online daters to choose either, "man seeking woman" or "woman seeking man." In addition, some sites that screen member profiles and pictures may exclude certain individuals from becoming members for undisclosed reasons, which may include perceived attractiveness.

Information for Counselors

Counselors working with adolescent and adult clients should be aware of online dating practices and risks. While online dating can be an excellent tool for individuals to meet new partners and expand their social circles, counselors have the ethical obligation to ensure that clients are aware of potential hazards of online dating. Best practices for meeting individuals from the Internet include developing clear boundaries and relationship expectations, providing personal information at a comfortable pace, meeting face-to-face for the first time in a public place, engaging in safe sexual practices, and protecting personal financial information.

Research Directions

Because online dating has existed in its current form for only the past 20 years, longitudinal research on the relationships formed from online dating has not been possible. It is unclear if couples who initially meet through online dating websites have longer or more meaningful or satisfying relationships than couples who meet through more traditional means. Very little has been studied on the effects of mobile dating with real-time location-based GPS services. As technologies advance, research will need to progress to determine the effectiveness of online dating and its multiple modalities.

Katherine A. Shirley

See also Couple Development; Extramarital Affairs and Infidelity; Mate Selection

Further Readings

Alterovitz, S. S.-R., & Mendelsohn, G. A. (2011). Partner preferences across the life span: Online dating by older adults. *Psychology of Popular Media Culture, 1,* 89–95. doi:10.1037/2160-4134.1.S.89

Couch, D., Liamputtong, P., & Pitts, M. (2012). What are the real and perceived risks and dangers of online dating? Perspectives from online daters. *Health, Risk & Society, 14,* 697–714. Retrieved from http://dx/doi.org/10.1080/13698575.2012.720964

Pingel, E. S., Bauermeister, J. A., Johns, M. M., Eisenberg, A., & Leslie-Santana, M. (2012). "A safe way to explore": Reframing risk on the internet amidst young gay men's search for identity. *Journal of Adolescent Research, 28,* 453–478. doi:10.1177/0743558412470985

Ramirez, A., Sumner, E. M. B., Fleuriet, C., & Cole, M. (2015). When online dating partners meet offline: The effect of modality switching on relational communication between online daters. *Journal of Computer-Mediated Communication, 20,* 99–114. doi:10.1111/jcc4.12101

Smith, A., & Duggan, M. (2013, October). *Online dating & relationships.* Washington, DC: Pew Research Center. Retrieved from http://www.pewinternet.org/files/old-media//Files/Reports/2013/PIP_Online%20Dating%202013.pdf

Open Relationships

There is no agreed-upon definition for the term *open relationship,* although it could be applied to any dyadic relationship that allows for additional members, either sexually or relationally. Open relationships can be seen on a continuum, including a couple willing to have occasional sexual encounters with one or more individuals to live-in intimate relationships with additional members. One way to conceptualize an open relationship is to consider what it is not. An open relationship is not constrained by monogamy and therefore offers unlimited opportunities for relationship structure, depending on the agreement of those involved. This entry addresses the various terms describing open relationships and implications for clients and implications for therapists working with individuals in open relationships.

Important Terms

There are a variety of terms to help understand the relational configurations possible in open relationships. The different terms help define who is involved in a relationship, typical rules associated with each type of relationship, and terms related to feelings and behaviors. Monogamy and nonmonogamy are binary concepts related to whether a relationship is between two people or more than two people. Monogamy is defined as being committed to one person at a time and involving no one else either sexually or emotionally, at the same level as one's partner, in the relationship. Nonmonogamy is being in a relationship open to other relationships outside of the primary relationship. Individuals may engage in sexual relationships or intimate emotional relationships with more than one intimate partner.

If couples have a nonmongamous relationship or marriage, they may have an open relationship or group relationship. In an open marriage, the married individuals include at least one other person. That other person may be involved with only one of the partners or both. Sometimes this type of relationship is also called a *consensual nonexclusive relationship.* In a group marriage, a couple includes other couples in their relationship who define themselves as married. Relationships may be open or closed to any other outside relationships.

Following are some key terms relevant to open relationships:

Compersion—Taking delight in a partner's love for another. This delight tends to occur when there is relationship parity. Compersion can be considered the opposite of jealousy.

Friends With Benefits—A sexually intimate relationship in which there is no expectation for exclusive partnership or long-term relationship. An approach to nonmonogamy.

Polyamory—Relationships in which individuals are able to love more than one person. This term tends to define those who are in multiple relationships with a commitment toward honest, ethical, and responsible relationships. Polyamory is considered by some as an orientation, in the same way that heterosexuality is seen as an orientation. This term also may be used to describe a relationship approach to nonmonogamy.

Primary Partner—The partner in the relationship that receives the most time, attention, care, and resources. Resources such as intimacy, finances, and commitment are shared with this person. Can include a marriage or marriage-like partner.

Secondary Partner—The partner who is afforded less time and fewer resources than the primary partner. This relationship may share closeness, intimacy, and emotional support, but to a lesser degree than the relationship with the primary partner.

Swinging—Casual sex without emotional commitment. Includes parties where primary couples have sex with other individuals and return home with their partner. An approach to nonmonogamy.

Tertiary Partner—The individual in a relationship with the least amount of connection to a partner. This limited connection is due to time, emotional, and sexual constraints. Relationships are usually on-demand, infrequent, and inconsistent. This person is usually considered an occasional partner.

Implications for Clients

Opening the Relationship

Some individuals consider the relationship structure of exclusivity or monogamy to be too constrictive and incongruent with humans' natural inclinations. Agreeing to question and proceed outside the boundaries of traditional relationships tends to require a high degree of ego strength from both partners. Considerable skills in navigating communication about honesty, jealously, self-confidence, respect for one's own and others' preferences, and examination of fears, prejudices, and expectations are necessary. This is not to say that these same qualities and abilities do not exist or do not improve monogamous relationships, too. It simply means that in open relationships these topics are discussed without the notion of exclusivity toward one other person.

It is not uncommon for individuals in open relationships to assert that "It is too much to expect that one person can meet all the needs of my partner" and that "My partner has more to give than what I need. If all my needs are met and there is more to give, then it would be selfish for me to deny my partner the right to share with others as he or she is capable of doing." Some may take such a statement to mean that individuals in open relationships are simply looking to have more or additional sex, yet individuals in open relationships will cite many different reasons beyond the sexual act for opening their relationship and do not necessarily cite a deficiency with their partner as the primary reason to open the relationship ("The sex in this relationship is not good enough."). Reasons relationships are opened include both partners agreeing to explore possibilities and opportunities not afforded by the current relationship. ("What other kinds of sexually fulfilling experiences are available to us? This current relationship is fulfilling to me in certain ways; I wonder if there are other ways I can be fulfilled?")

Jealousy

Jealousy is considered a secondary emotion based on an individual's own expectations, insecurities, and fears about the relationship. In honest, open relationships, jealousy is more about the person who is feeling jealous and less about the actions and behaviors of the other partner(s). Emotionally responding, a jealous partner may try to set rules and exhibit control in the relationship. This can include mandates such as "You cannot kiss another person in front of me" as a way to settle and calm the jealous partner's insecurities.

Proponents of open relationships contend that the jealous individual needs to further assess the root cause of the jealousy and challenge those thoughts. For example, the jealous partner may actually think "I am scared my partner will reject me because my kissing is not good enough and I need to make sure that doesn't happen." In attempting to work through jealous thoughts and feelings, the jealous individual can (1) identify the feelings (for example, fear of rejection, worry about adequacies); (2) challenge those feelings with more rational thoughts (e.g., "My partner and I are honest in our needs about kissing."); and (3) trust known facts and information (e.g., "My partner values me and our relationship," or "I too can learn other ways to kiss.") Additionally, it should be noted that not all jealousy is unwarranted. If a partner has a history of secrets, lies, or betrayals, then expectations may include thoughts such as "I cannot trust my partner," or "My partner's real motives are unknown at this time." Even in these final circumstances, the jealous individual is challenged to consider what is inside and outside his or her own control.

Rule Management

There are two competing viewpoints surrounding rule-setting in an open relationship. Viewpoints include the idea that (1) rules govern relationships as opposed to the idea that (2) rules further perpetuate restrictiveness and control. There are some rules, such as mutual respect for each individual involved in the relationship, agreements about honesty, or adherence to safe-sex practices that most individuals agree are necessary. Even still, many rules tend to be seen as prescriptive, controlling, and against the philosophical bent of openness. A rule may benefit one member or even two members of the relationship while placing unreasonable constraints on another. For example, demanding that my partner not kiss Person X places restrictions on my partner while also placing restrictions on Person X. Person X may not agree or be interested in an experience without kissing and experience negative consequences due to the rule-maker's demand.

Jealousy tends to be one of the primary reasons partners establish rules to govern open relationships, although other reasons include lending structure to the relationship; creating hierarchy toward primary, secondary, or tertiary relationships; mutual understanding surrounding safe sex practices; showing respect toward the once exclusive monogamous partner; negotiating dos and don'ts in specific relationships; and circumnavigating issues of children, jobs, or living situations. Potential rules and mandates surrounding these topics seem obvious and reasonable on the surface, yet often these rules have underlying motives fueled by fear of rejection or abandonment. In their book, *More Than Two,* Franklin Veaux and Eve Rickert propose three questions partners can ask in establishing rules: (1) What is the purpose of this rule? (2) Does this rule serve the purpose? (3) Is this rule the only way to serve this purpose? These questions help to challenge preconceived notions and expectations of control over one's partner(s) while also revealing underlying jealous motives and protection to one's self-esteem, self-control, and overall self-identity.

Implications for Therapists

Therapist-Based Concerns

Therapists working with individuals in open relationships need to consider their own values and expectations about relationships. Individuals presenting with open relationship concerns can challenge and trigger a therapist's own ideas about monogamy and nonmonogamy and create countertransference toward the client(s). These triggers can lead to problems such as pathologizing the client(s) presenting issues as immoral, and misdiagnosis based on the therapist's perspective of health and dysfunction in relationships. As an alternative, it is suggested that a successful therapist will be able to listen to the client(s) and assist in identifying specific goals while also working to help the client(s) realize those goals.

Client-Based Concerns

Therapists who are able to successfully navigate their own biases around open relationships need to be prepared for client presentation to be in one of three domains, including (1) seeking information about how to broach the topic of opening the relationship, (2) negotiating boundaries and relationship parameters when individuals participate in open relationships, and (3) developing exit strategies when relationships are no longer meeting individuals' needs. Although these three domains are broad, each provides a good conceptualization of clients' presenting concerns. Additionally, the following questions can be present within any domain: who decides, with whom, under what circumstances, what type, how much, when, and how?

In order to address these concerns, therapists will need to become skilled at helping people in navigating logistics. A person-centered approach that helps the client(s) become more aware and autonomous regarding their own preferences and choices is necessary. It is expected that clients will present with areas of concern that include disagreements, expectations, and disappointments; personality styles; autonomy; intimacy; cognitive dissonance between personal beliefs and societal expectations; lack of external support; disapproval from significant others; and lack of legal protection surrounding health, children, or finances. These types of issues and transitions can be viewed as basic struggles in navigating relationships as opposed to being seen as pathological in nature.

Amber M. Lange and Tara Hill

See also Couple Development; Couples and Marriage Counseling; Extramarital Affairs and Infidelity; Polyamory; Polygamy; Sexual Intimacy

Further Readings

Barker, M., & Langdridge, D. (2010). Whatever happened to non-monogamies? Critical reflections on recent research and theory. *Sexualities, 13,* 748–772. doi:10.1177/1363460710384645

Block, J. (2008). *Open: Love, sex, and life in an open marriage.* Berkeley, CA: Seal Press.

Conley, T. D., Moors, A. C., Matsick, J. L., & Ziegler, A. (2013). The fewer the merrier? Assessing stigma surrounding consensually non-monogamous romantic relationships. *Analyses of Social Issues & Public Policy, 13*(1), 1–30. doi:10.1111/j.1530-2415.2012.01286.x

Easton, D., & Hardy, J. W. (2009). *The ethical slut: A practical guide to polyamory, open relationships and other adventures.* Berkeley, CA: Celestial Arts.

Ritchie, A., & Barker, M. (2006). There aren't words for what we do or how we feel so we have to make them up: Constructing polyamorous languages in a culture of compulsory monogamy. *Sexualities, 9,* 584–601. doi:10.1177/1363460706069987

Taormino, T. (2008). *Opening up: A guide to creating and sustaining open relationships.* San Francisco, CA: Cleis Press.

Vaillancourt, K. T., & Few-Demo, A. L. (2014). Relational dynamics of swinging relationships: An exploratory study. *The Family Journal, 22,* 311–320. doi:10.1177/1066480714529742

Veaux, F., & Rickert, E. (2014). *More than two: A practical guide to ethical polyamory.* Portland, OR: Thorntree Press.

Weitzman, G., Davidson, J., Phillips, R. A., Fleckenstein, J. R., & Morotti-Meeker, C. (2009). *What psychology professionals should know about polyamory.* Baltimore, MD: The National Coalition for Sexual Freedom Inc. Retrieved from http://instituteforsexuality.com/wp-content/uploads/2014/05/What-therapists-should-know-about-Polyamory-1.pdf

Zimmerman, K. J. (2012). Clients in sexually open relationships: Considerations for therapists. *Journal of Feminist Family Therapy, 24*(3), 272–289. doi:10.1080/08952833.2012.648143

OPPOSITIONAL DEFIANT DISORDER

Late childhood and early adolescence mark an important turning point in the lives of individuals. During this time, young people begin to rely less on their primary caretakers as they look to achieve a greater sense of self. A certain amount of noncompliance toward authority figures signifies a healthy level of identity formation; however, an overabundance of obstinate behavior may signal the presence of oppositional defiant disorder (ODD). The *International Classification of Diseases* (ICD-10) defines ODD as the consistent presence of disobedient, defiant, and provocative behavior. This behavior exceeds what would be expected from the individual based on their current stage of development. Though ODD goes beyond typical mischief or rebellion, behaviors do not present as overtly aggressive, violate the law, or infringe on the rights of others. Symptoms of ODD, differential diagnoses, case conceptualization, prevalence of ODD, causes, treatments, and future research are among the many important areas presented and discussed in this entry.

Symptoms

The onset of ODD symptoms, such as excessive irritability, can begin as early as age 3. While some irritability should be expected during this developmental stage, it should be seen to gradually reduce over time. Children who go on to be diagnosed with ODD show both higher overall levels or irritability than their peers, and a persistent or escalating level of irritability across the same developmental stage. In fact, Lourdes Ezpeleta and colleagues reported over 32% of children between the ages of 3 and 5 with high levels of irritability went on to be diagnosed with ODD in a longitudinal study of over 2,000 children.

When working with children with oppositional defiant disorder, one quickly becomes used to hearing words such as "no" and "I refuse." Youth with ODD tend to be resentful, rude, uncooperative, and easily annoyed. Furthermore, they are quick to blame others for their mistakes or difficulties. Children with ODD often initiate confrontation, especially with authority figures. Symptoms of ODD are most likely to manifest in familiar relationships, meaning defiant behaviors may not come to light during clinical interviews. Oppositional defiant disorder can dramatically interfere with both social and interpersonal relationships. This distressed level of functioning creates conflict with others, often resulting in peer rejection. The inability to create meaningful social connections can lead children with oppositional defiant disorder to experience feelings of loneliness. Extended periods of social isolation can lead to feelings of depression and anxiety, which can cause further issues at both home and school.

When defiant behaviors consistently erupt in the classroom, academic progress can stall. Teachers are often underequipped to handle students with ODD and may remove said students from the classroom in order to maintain peace for their peers. This can create a vicious cycle whereby the defiant student and overwhelmed teacher attempt to control the ever-escalating situation. When the classroom becomes a battleground, students with ODD may see no route to succeed academically. The resulting loss of motivation to try in school can lead to long-term academic struggles.

Differential Diagnosis Between ODD and CD

Though often difficult to distinguish between, oppositional defiant disorder and conduct disorder (CD) manifest in different ways. The biggest distinction between ODD and CD is the violation of the rights of others. Children diagnosed with ODD do not attempt to infringe on the rights of others; they act out to avoid being controlled. The temper tantrums, defiance toward authority, and refusal to comply keep them from feeling coerced. They lash out only in order to remain in control of their situation, not to be malicious toward others. The motive for those diagnosed with CD shift from the avoidance of being controlled to controlling others. A clear pattern of manipulation, intimidation, and aggression toward others begins to form the longer the individual goes without treatment. The ICD-10 emphasizes the lack of empathy seen in those diagnosed with CD by highlighting heightened levels of callous, unemotional traits. Research suggests ODD can slowly shift into CD when left untreated.

Case Conceptualization

Case conceptualizations are helpful in further understanding behavioral disorders. For example, a child with ODD may become defiant over a simple instruction such as turning off the TV and joining the family for dinner. Initially, the child may passively defy the authority figure by ignoring the request. When the child receives a consequence for the noncompliance, such as dessert restriction, the child will move onto more aggressive forms of defiance. Television remotes may be flung across the room, furniture may be overturned, forks may be used to gouge the kitchen table, and food may become plastered on the ceiling. Often the authority figure will become the target of screaming, cursing, insults, and back talk. Upon completing the task, the child may shift blame toward the authority figure in order to avoid taking responsibility for his or her actions. The motivations for the behaviors described here are clear; the child desired control over the situation and attempted to maintain control through the outburst. Though destructive, there was a marked absence of behaviors that violated the basic rights of others (such as theft, cruelty, bullying, assault, and destructiveness), highlighting the difference between oppositional defiant disorder and more severe conduct disorders.

Prevalence

Oppositional defiant disorder remains one of the most common psychiatric disorders in childhood, with an estimated prevalence rate between 1.8% and 16.8% in preschool-age children. The ICD-10 reports ODD to be most prevalent between the ages of 9 and 10, with prevalence rates dropping throughout middle and late adolescence. Gender and ethnicity play a role in prevalence rates, with ODD seen more in males and ethnic minorities.

Causes

At this time, most studies have not pinpointed any specific causes of oppositional defiant disorder. For example, researchers have begun to look for correlations between prenatal drug exposure and development of ODD later in the life span. Early reports suggest daily caffeine use by pregnant mothers could correlate with a higher chance of females experiencing ODD-like symptoms in early adolescence. However, results from such studies remain inconclusive due to the overwhelming number of extraneous variables in raising children. Research is now focusing on studying neurological markers that may contribute specifically to ODD. Many times, ODD is included in the research on conduct disorders, thus making it difficult to tease out specific causes for only ODD. Researchers are also examining environmental factors (e.g., parenting styles, neglect, living conditions) to determine if they play a role in the development of ODD.

Treatment and Management

Families with adolescents who are diagnosed with ODD can take comfort in knowing there are treatment modalities that can help the children improve their behaviors and thinking. As with any treatment modality, one key factor is active participation (buy-in) by the adolescent and also the legal guardian. Treatment locations for adolescents with ODD can vary, and include outpatient settings, in-home services, group home programs, juvenile detention centers, and psychiatric hospitals. Goals of treatment are to reduce oppositional and aggressive behaviors and improve overall interpersonal skills. The goals for the family will be to increase positive support, examine appropriate discipline, and understand their roles in the treatment of the adolescent. School-based treatment programs are also being explored in both traditional and specialized school settings. Traditional school settings are attempting to confront ODD by empowering teachers through intentional training and increasing chances for students to create meaningful peer relationships. Specialized schools, such as therapeutic boarding schools, have been implemented with a focus on assisting children and adolescents with behavioral issues including ODD, CD, and mood dysregulation disorders. These schools benefit from having smaller populations, enabling students to obtain more individualized care. This allows more resources, such as licensed therapists and class wide protocols, to be used to help each student.

A general guideline of treatment modalities used in working with clients diagnosed with ODD typically includes the following: (a) interpersonal skills training; (b) individual counseling; (c) behavioral programs, and (d) family counseling. Also of note, there is not a specific psychopharmacological treatment for ODD. Many times, medication is used to treat any comorbid issues that may be present (e.g., depression, ADHD, anxiety).

Comorbidity

Research by H. Walter and colleagues suggests that ODD can be seen with issues related to depression, ADHD, and substance abuse. These comorbid conditions can also be carried into adulthood if not appropriately treated.

Multicultural Perspective

Oppositional defiant disorder is diagnosed in adolescents from all races and cultures in the United States. Research by L. H. Munkvold and colleagues suggested that ODD was diagnosed more in boys than girls, but that both groups had about the same amount of comorbid mental health issues. There is also a concern that African American and Hispanic/Latino adolescents are diagnosed at higher levels of ODD and conduct disorder than White adolescents. Such data are of concern when viewed in light of the reality of disproportionate minority confinement.

Future Research

Future research is needed to examine issues related to any gender differences and the proper diagnosing of adolescents with ODD or other mental health issues (i.e., conduct disorder, ADHD). There will continue to be an exploration of finding evidence-based treatment interventions that can help the adolescent and family members. As psychopharmacological research continues to expand, there will be a continued effort to examine the usefulness of medications to help adolescents with ODD.

David A. Scott and Matthew T. Webb

See also Child Behavior Problems; Conduct Disorder; Individual Versus Family Therapy

Further Readings

Bird, H. R., Canino, G. J., Davies, M., Zhang, H., Ramirez, R., & Lahey, B. B. (2001). Prevalence and correlates of antisocial behaviors among three ethnic groups. *Journal of Abnormal Child Psychology, 29*(6), 465–478. doi:10.1023/A:1012279707372

Boylan, K., Vaillancourt, T., Boyle, M., & Szatmari, P. (2007). Comorbidity of internalizing disorders in children with oppositional defiant disorder. *European Child & Adolescent Psychiatry, 16*(8), 484–494. doi:10.1007/s00787-007-0624-1

Burke, J. D., Rowe, R., & Boylan, K. (2014). Functional outcomes of child and adolescent oppositional defiant disorder symptoms in young adult men. *Journal of Child Psychology and Psychiatry, 55*(3), 264–272. doi:10.1111/jcpp.12150

Egger, H. L., & Angold, A. (2006). Common emotional and behavioral disorders in preschool children: Presentation, nosology, and epidemiology. *Journal of Child Psychology and Psychiatry, 47*(3–4), 313–337. doi:10.1111/j.1469-7610.2006.01618.x

Ezpeleta, L., Granero, R., Osa, N., Trepat, E., & Domènech, J. (2016). Trajectories of oppositional defiant disorder irritability symptoms in preschool children. *Journal of Abnormal Child Psychology, 44*(1), 115–128. doi:10.1007/s10802-015-9972-3

Grisso, T. (2008). Adolescent offenders with mental disorders. *The Future of Children, 18*(2), 143–164. doi:10.1353/foc.0.0016

Munkvold, L. H., Lundervold, A. J., & Manger, T. (2011). Oppositional defiant disorder: Gender differences in co-occurring symptoms of mental health problems in a general population of children. *Journal of Abnormal Child Psychology, 39*, 577–587. doi:10.1007/s10802-011-9486-6

Muroff, J., Edelsohn, G. A., Joe, S., & Ford, B. C. (2008). The role of race in diagnostic and disposition decision making in a pediatric psychiatric emergency service. *General Hospital Psychiatry, 30*(3), 269–276. doi:10.1016/j.genhosppsych.2008.01.003

Niemczyk, J., Equit, M., Braun-Bither, K., Klein, A., & Gontard, A. (2015). Prevalence of incontinence, attention deficit/hyperactivity disorder and oppositional defiant disorder in preschool children. *European Child & Adolescent Psychiatry, 24*(7), 837–843. doi:10.1007/s00787-014-0628-6

Walter, H., Kernandz, P., & Kircanski, K. (2011). Oppositional defiant disorder. In M. Augustyn, B. Zuckerman, & E. Caronna (Eds.), *The Zuckerman Parker handbook of developmental and behavioral pediatrics for primary care* (3rd ed., pp. 285–287). Philadelphia: Lippincott, Williams & Wilkins.

Wichstrøm, L., Berg-Nielsen, T. S., Angold, A., Egger, H. L., Solheim, E., & Sveen, T. H. (2012). Prevalence of psychiatric disorders in preschoolers. *Journal of Child Psychology and Psychiatry and Allied Disciplines, 53*(6), 695–705. doi:10.1111/j.1469-7610.2011.02514

Winther, J., Carlsson, A., & Vance, A. (2014). A pilot study of a school-based prevention and early intervention program to reduce oppositional defiant disorder/conduct disorder. *Early Intervention in Psychiatry, 8*(2), 181–189. doi:10.1111/eip.12050

World Health Organization. (1992). *The ICD-10 classification of mental and behavioural disorders: Clinical descriptions and diagnostic guidelines*. Geneva, Switzerland: Author.

OUTCOME RESEARCH

Outcome research is defined as the investigation of the effectiveness of a psychotherapy model. The main questions examined by outcome researchers include whether psychotherapy creates a change in people's lives, whether there are differences among the therapy models with regard to their effectiveness, which factors lead to a change, and how the change occurs in psychotherapy. Outcome research findings can directly influence the improvements in clinical practice, education, supervision, and training areas of marriage, family, and couples counseling. Various researchers point out that despite the tendency for those with degrees in mental health to define themselves as researchers or clinicians, outcome research is important to both. Whether one is a researcher or client, outcome research helps the field become more informed about the effectiveness of therapeutic techniques and models, and thus both researchers and clinicians can make better and more confident decisions in their research or practice and be better advocates of the field. This entry provides an outline of the outcome research in the field of marriage, family, and couples therapy. Specifically, this entry examines common presenting problems, the major methodological issues in the marriage, family, and couples therapy outcome research field, major findings of the outcome research, and future research directions.

Overview

Psychotherapy outcome research in the field of marriage, family, and couples therapy is a relatively new yet rapidly growing field. Under the influence of the zeitgeist of experimental studies, outcome studies published in the 1980s focused on the question of whether marriage, family, and couples therapy works, and almost all studies suggest that, compared to the no treatment conditions, marriage, family, and couples therapy is effective.

In the 1990s, owing to the increased amount of research, improved analyses and synthesis techniques, and repeatedly reported high effect sizes (the magnitude of effect/change) of treatment interventions, the area of interest started to shift toward comparison studies among different constellations (individual, group and marriage, family, and couples therapy), theories, and models (psychodynamic, behavioral, cognitive, cognitive-behavioral) with differing populations or presenting problems. As the research became more complex, researchers began to discuss various aspects of the studies, including the characteristics of the sample, the design of the study, the application of the interventions, and the statistical methods being used. Thus, the outcome studies increasingly became more detailed, elaborate, and in order to eliminate the confounding factors, more standardized.

Outcomes and Presenting Problems

The effectiveness of marital, couples, and family approaches are tested with particular presenting problems. Types of problems in outcome research are often based on age groups. For example, there is a lot of outcome research on behavioral problems with children. For adolescents, externalizing problems, including delinquency and substance use disorders, as well as internalizing problems, including depression, are the most widely investigated problems by the psychotherapy outcome researchers. For adults, the presenting problems, including marital issues such as conflict and divorce, substance use problems, psychosis, and schizophrenia are the main presenting problems examined in outcome research. Furthermore, psychoeducation approaches like premarital counseling, parenting, and coparenting approaches have been investigated.

There are many examples of marital, couples, and family approaches that have been shown to be effective with particular populations or problems. For instance, multidimensional family therapy (MDFT), developed by Howard Liddle and his colleagues, is primarily used for the treatment of adolescents with substance use disorders, and there is outcome research supporting its use. Another effective approach is functional family therapy (FFT), developed by James Alexander, used for treating adolescent conduct problems. Behavioral and cognitive marriage, family, and couples therapy modalities targeting communication problems among family members and aiming for cognitive or behavioral change have demonstrated significantly effective treatment outcomes. Finally, the experiential therapy modalities, including emotion-focused therapy (EFT), developed by Susan Johnson and Leslie Greenberg, primarily targeting couples with marital problems, has produced a lot of outcome research.

Methodology

The presence of multiple family members in the session makes the application and assessment of psychotherapy models more complex and multifaceted. Because relationality, or interaction among the family members or couples, is of ultimate importance to marriage, family, and couples therapists, the methodological considerations are shaped around the goal of measuring systemic change. Most of the psychotherapy outcome research is classified as experimental and observational studies. The majority of the psychotherapy outcome studies are reported to be randomized control trials, which is a study design whereby participants are randomly assigned to either an experimental group or a control group. A smaller percentage of the studies include quasi-experimental (where participants are not randomly assigned or there is not a control group), qualitative, surveys, case studies, and mixed methods (involving both quantitative and qualitative) designs.

Randomized control trials are used to investigate the questions of whether marriage, family, and couples psychotherapy creates a change and whether there are differences among psychotherapy modalities with regard to therapy outcomes. The pretest–posttest design, with the inclusion of control group, forms the core of the psychotherapy outcome research. Quasi-experimental designs in which the interventions are tested without control groups are used in the marriage, family, and couples therapy field to study marital problems and to study behavioral problems of children and adolescents. Research has found positive outcomes, including improved communication and relationship quality.

Surveys are also used in psychotherapy outcome research. These types of assessments are self-report measures regarding thoughts, beliefs, or values. A limited number of survey studies in outcome research tend to focus on interventions targeting externalizing and internalizing behavior problems, marital conflict, and treatment quality.

Qualitative research accounts for a small portion of outcome research. This type of research tends to be used for more exploratory research than outcome research and is used to investigate in-depth meanings attributed to the phenomena of interest. In outcome research, a qualitative approach is used to assess treatment of relational and behavioral problems and the perceptions of clients about interventions and therapeutic process.

Although not used in a widespread fashion in the field of marriage, family, and couples therapy, mixed-methods designs, especially integrating qualitative research design portions into quantitative randomized control trial studies, is a rapidly growing approach. The findings revealed by the qualitative research studies are used to validate and expand the findings of the quantitative strands.

The Major Measures in Outcome Research

The most commonly used measures in marriage, family, and couples therapy outcome research include questionnaires assessing the relationship satisfaction, improvement in skills (i.e., communication, parenting, or academic achievement), and decrease in the presenting symptoms. Various researchers point out that despite the relational nature of marriage, family, and couples therapy, relational measures are used in a very limited fashion. Some researchers also examine the quality of the therapeutic relationship. The effect of the factors related to therapist, including the gender, age, years of experience, or quality of the therapeutic relationship (e.g., the quality of the working alliance), expectations from therapy, or attitudes toward receiving therapeutic help are also topics investigated by the marriage, family, and couples therapy outcome researchers.

Major Findings of Outcome Research

Although there are many studies investigating various research questions, Alan Gurman addresses three major questions enlightening the field of marriage, family, and couples therapy. These include whether marriage, family, and couples therapy is effective; whether some treatment modalities are better than the others; and whether relational therapy helps the treatment of individual problems.

For decades, outcome researchers have been repeatedly reporting that marriage, family, and couples therapy is significantly effective compared to no treatment. From the very early narrative reviews to the meta-analyses using advanced statistical methods, the studies show moderate to high effect sizes of marriage, family, and couples therapy modalities. Although there is an ongoing debate about the methodological issues with regard to treatment modality comparison studies, advanced meta-analytic study results reveal that there is no statistically significant difference among treatment modalities with regard to their effectiveness. Research shows that marriage, family, and couples therapy is effective, and no treatment modality is better than the others. In addition, a variety of researchers suggest that marriage, family, and couples therapy is effective not only for the relational problems like marital satisfaction and relationship satisfaction but also for the individual ones, including self-esteem and depressive symptoms.

Future Research Directions

Despite the fact that marriage, family, and couples therapy outcome research is a rapidly growing area, there is room for improvement in the field. One of the most essential needs is improving the amount of research with the overlooked populations, treatment modalities, and presenting problems. For instance, older adults and disability problems are generally ignored by marriage, family, and couples therapy outcome researchers. More research targeting these issues is needed. Another need is related to the standardization of the outcome research. Overall, thicker descriptions of the samples, interventions, application procedures, and methodological details are needed in order to increase the number and quality of the original research as well as the replication studies, and thus, generalizability of the findings.

As essential as the standardization and generalizability issues are, more studies focusing on the moderating and mediating factors are needed in the field in order to identify the factors related to change due to psychotherapeutic interventions. More and more researchers have been pointing out that the findings revealed by standardized outcome studies may fail to reflect the real-world effects of treatments. That is, besides efficacy studies, effectiveness studies are needed in the field.

There is also a need for better methodologies and applied research to connect researchers and clinicians. New methodologies, including dyadic research, which considers the effect of relationally in the outcomes, and process research, investigating how the change happens in treatment interventions, are needed. And there is also a need for more attention to the studies aiming to fill the scientist–practitioner gap in the field. More education, supervision, and training opportunities are needed in order to help mental health professionals be more informed about the research procedures, as well as studies "translating" the methodological density of the research findings.

Yesim Keskin

See also Couples Therapy Research; Effectiveness Research; Functional Family Therapy

Further Readings

Addison, S. M., Sandberg, J. G., Corby, J., Robila, M., & Platt, J. J. (2002). Alternative methodologies in research literature review: Links between clinical work and MFT effectiveness. *American Journal of Family Therapy, 30,* 339–371.

Gurman, A. S. (2011). Couple therapy research and the practice of couple therapy: Can we talk? *Family Process, 50,* 280–292.

Robbins, M., Sexton, T., & Weeks, G. (2004). *Handbook of family therapy: The science and practice of working with families and couples.* New York, NY: Routledge.

Sprenkle, D. H. (Ed.). (2002). *Effectiveness research in marriage and family therapy.* Alexandria, VA: American Association for Marriage and Family Therapy.

Stratton, P., Silver, E., Nascimento, N., McDonnell, L., Powell, G., & Nowotny, E. (2015). Couple and family therapy outcome research in the previous decade: What does the evidence tell us? *Contemporary Family Therapy, 37,* 1–12.

Paradoxes and Paradoxical Intervention

Paradox is a technique utilized in family therapy to disrupt a family's preferred style of interaction, coping, or problem-solving. This entry provides a definition of the concept of paradox, discusses the theoretical origins of the concept, explains when the technique is indicated and when it is contraindicated, and discusses why paradox matters. Examples of paradoxical interventions are provided within each section.

The Concept of Paradox

A therapist can expect direct suggestion to be followed only by people who have a certain commitment to change and who are motivated to cooperate with therapy. When this commitment does not exist, it is usually best for the therapist to bring about change in indirect ways. Alfred Adler is credited with being the founder of the paradoxical intervention in the 1920s. Milton Erickson is known to have employed it with his patients on occasion. Cloé Madanes and Jay Haley developed the strategic approach to family therapy to manage the power in relationships between therapist and client and within family systems. Strategies were developed to utilize this power in order to facilitate change. One effective, yet controversial, technique includes the paradoxical intervention.

The family system can be resistant to change, because it seeks to maintain the organization of the family, also referred to as homeostasis, which is viewed as normal functioning. Even if the family pattern of interaction is unstable and promotes family suffering, the family may defend their preferred method of communication, family roles and rules, and current circumstances. To disrupt a family's preferred pattern of interaction and manage the resistance to therapy, family therapists may use a paradoxical intervention.

A paradox involves providing a subtle, unexpected message counter to therapeutic goals in order to place the family in a "double bind." The double-bind message involves informing the family to change by remaining unchanged. A paradoxical intervention can be classified into three categories: (1) prescribing, (2) restraining, and (3) positioning operations.

Prescribing the symptom involves the therapist encouraging a family member to participate in the specific behavior that is to be eliminated. For example, a counselor encourages a couple that regularly argues in unproductive ways to have an argument, shifting the symptom to their conscious, voluntary control. Prescribing the symptom can also involve the utilization of pretending. By inviting the couple to pretend to have an argument, the couple is not actually arguing; therefore, the symptom is not real, which may have an effect of altering the reaction of the couple and other family members to that symptom. The couple may also be encouraged to schedule the argument for a particular time and place, other than the time and place it usually occurs. So if the argument typically occurs in the kitchen, the couple may be instructed to move the argument to the bathroom as soon as they feel an argument coming on. This weakens the power of the context to trigger the symptom and also brings the symptom under more voluntary control.

Restraining from change is an intervention that involves the therapist discouraging change due to dangers associated with improvement. For example, a mother who yells at her children is told that failure to yell might result in lack of connection and isolation within the family. The mother is encouraged to proceed with caution so that she does not sacrifice the intense connection she now has with her children. As a result, the mother may argue that she cannot wait or go slow—that she must change immediately.

Finally, paradoxical positioning involves encouraging the family member to accept and/or exaggerate the problem. For example, as parents complain about their rebellious, disobedient, and disrespectful son, the counselor agrees that he is a lost cause and suggests that the parents consider putting him up for adoption. As a result, the parents defend their son by describing many ways in which he has been a joy to have in their lives. Furthermore, the family may also be asked to increase and/or observe the symptom to learn more about how it operates with the hope that observation will paradoxically reduce the symptom.

When using a paradoxical intervention, the therapist needs to determine the family's compliance to any directive. If a family is agreeable to completing a directive, the paradoxical intervention is a compliance-based strategy. If the family rebels and is in opposition to the therapist's influence, the paradoxical intervention is a defiance-based strategy. In order to determine the family's level of compliance, it is important to understand reactance theory as it relates to the utilization of paradox.

Reactance Theory

American psychologist Jack Brehm proposed the psychological reactance theory, which describes individuals becoming motivated by a threat to or removal of a behavioral freedom. A behavioral freedom may include symptoms that a family is experiencing. Individuals may react by attempting to restore the freedom, or the individual may perceive the lost freedom as more attractive. As a result, the individual is compelled to bring back the specific freedom that was threatened or removed.

When applying reactance theory to the utilization of a paradox, the paradoxical intervention can be perceived as threatening to remove the family member's behavioral freedom, and as a result, the family member will react. Prior to implementing a paradoxical intervention, it is critical that the therapist assess the family's potential to react to the therapist's suggestions or directives as well as the family's perceptions of the "freedom" of the symptom.

A family's reactance to the therapist and view of the symptom can be assessed on a continuum of high to low reactance to assist in determining compliance and/or defiance-based paradoxical interventions. Compliance-based interventions are used when a family has low reactance and is likely to do as asked by accepting invitations or suggestions by the therapist. Compliance-based interventions may also be used when the family believes they can change and feel "free" of the symptom. Defiance-based interventions are most preferred for a family with high reactance when family members do not believe change is possible because they do not feel "free" of the symptom.

Indications and Contraindications

Controversy exists regarding the use of paradox. The controversy lies in the covert and coercive nature of paradox to achieve therapeutic goals. The hidden maneuvers by the therapist can be helpful but perhaps equally harmful. As an indirect approach, paradox allows therapists to bypass instinctive objections and to challenge client assumptions or help-rejecting tendencies without calling attention to them. Because a paradoxical intervention is indirect, it encourages more active involvement on the part of a family to become observant, find meaning, and control symptoms. However, paradox used as a sneaky, tricky, or otherwise disrespectful intervention can seldom produce lasting change and has the potential to cause a rift in the therapeutic relationship. Therefore, a skilled reactance assessment with careful and timely application is needed to reduce the risk of negative outcomes.

The paradoxical intervention should not be used as a substitute for effective understanding of the family or as a simple solution to a complex family problem. Paradoxical interventions should be undertaken only when it is safe to do so based on the reactance assessment and the nature of the symptom. It could be disastrous to suggest a client increase harmful behavior (e.g., having an eating disorder, cutting) when the client is compliant and will accept the instructions at face value with minimal opposition. Paradoxical interventions should also be used only in the context of an established, positive relationship with the therapist.

More straightforward approaches that help the family gain insight or disrupt family patterns may be more helpful in stimulating change than paradoxical techniques for several kinds of families. First, chaotic families often lack appropriate rules, roles, and boundaries that help families unite in opposition to the paradoxical intervention. Families must have sufficient cohesiveness and unity to employ paradox effectively. Second, families that express conflict in a potentially harmful manner have increased risk of social isolation or escalation of dangerous behavior. Finally, families that have already demonstrated therapeutic movement and accepted responsibility for their symptoms do not need an oppositional challenge from the therapist.

Why Paradox Matters

Paradoxical interventions offer a more discrete, indirect entrance into a closed or resistant family system. It can give therapists backdoor access to help families when the front door is closed due to high reactance. A paradoxical intervention may include asking the family to (a) change, (b) increase the symptom, (c) pretend to have a symptom, or (d) reposition the symptom. These instructions are paradoxical in that they convey symptom usefulness and meaning despite the desire to alleviate the symptom. As a result, the family is given autonomy and freedom over the symptom.

Paradoxical interventions reframe symptoms from unavoidable and involuntary to controllable. Families often feel like symptoms are happening *to* them and believe they are powerless to influence the symptoms. Embedded in each paradoxical intervention is the message that families do in fact have some control over their symptoms. When the family accepts the paradoxical intervention (e.g., increases, pretends to have, or repositions the symptom), they are clearly able to exert some voluntary control over it. If they are unsuccessful, they actually move closer to their ultimate treatment goal of alleviating the symptom.

By the time families come for help, their attempts to lessen or control the symptom have actually made the symptom worse. When clients are really stuck and have tried more transparent methods of change without success, it may be helpful to disrupt the status quo by changing course. Paradoxical interventions offer counterintuitive challenges that disrupt the pattern instantly and make it hard to maintain the symptom.

Case Example

In a specific case related to school phobia, Sean was a fifth grader who presented with anxiety related to attending school. Sean would cry and scream as his father pulled him into the middle school, and Sean would hold out his hands for his mother as she watched helplessly. Although the school counselor had been trying to help the family for the past several months, Sean continued to have stomachaches and would cry so hard that his friends would cry with him. Sean's mother revealed that when she was in fifth grade, she had also experienced extreme anxiety about school, and after her mother would drop her off at school, she would run as fast as she could, so she could beat her mother home.

The family reported that on the mornings that they knew that Sean was going to have a "bad day," the mother would call the father so he could come home to drag their son to school. Even the boy's brother, Max, would help when Sean would lock himself in the bathroom by picking the lock and dragging Sean out to their father. The family was very concerned and all agreed that these bad days needed to stop. Ironically, the more everyone in Sean's life (e.g., his parents, siblings, teachers, school counselor, principal, and friends) tried to convince him *not* to have a bad day, the more bad days he had.

The cotherapists prescribed Sean to have a bad day every other day, and even if he felt it was going to be a "good day" to pretend to have a bad day, so that the counselors could learn more about the role of each family member in the symptom. Sean was instantly crushed that the cotherapists, of all people, would want him to have a bad day. These were the first people in 6 months who had not begged, pleaded, and cajoled him into not having a bad day. Sean and his family joined together in opposition to the suggestion that having a bad day was needed and defiantly announced in the next session that no bad days had occurred. In these cases, giving permission or requiring observation rather than prohibiting the undesired interaction, pattern, thought, feeling, and/or behavior in and of itself can decrease or alleviate the problematic symptom.

Conclusion

While paradoxical interventions are most associated with strategic family therapy, they have been used in a wide range of modalities and approaches. It is crucial that the therapist understand the circumstances in which paradox can be used to most effectively help families. Even with the risks associated with paradox, it offers entrance and change when change seems impossible.

*Andrea G. Bjornestad
and Grace Ann Mims*

See also Second-Order Family Therapy; Strategic Family Therapy; Systemic Family Therapy; Therapeutic Impasses

Further Readings

Brehm, J. (1989). Psychological reactance: Theory and applications. *Advances in Consumer Research, 16,* 72–75.

Fisher, L., Anderson, A., & Jones, J. E. (1981). Types of paradoxical intervention and indications/contraindications for use in clinical practice. *Family Process, 20,* 25–35.

Foreman, D. M. (1990). The ethical use of paradoxical interventions in psychotherapy. *Journal of Medical Ethics, 16,* 200–205.

Haley, J. (1973). *Uncommon therapy: The psychiatric techniques of Milton H. Erickson, M.D.* New York, NY: W. W. Norton.

Haley, J. (1976). *Problem solving therapy: New strategies for effective family therapy.* San Francisco, CA: Jossey-Bass.

Haley, J. (1984). *Ordeal therapy: Unusual ways of changing people.* San Francisco, CA: Jossey-Bass.

Madanes, C. (1980). Protection, paradox and pretending. *Family Therapy Process, 19,* 73–85.

Madanes, C. (1981). *Strategic family therapy.* San Francisco, CA: Jossey-Bass.

Madanes, C. (1984). *Behind the one-way mirror: Advances in the practice of strategic therapy.* Eugene, OR: Wipf & Stock.

Madanes, C. (2006). *The therapist as humanist, social activist, and systemic thinker . . . and other selected papers.* Phoenix, AZ: Zieg, Tucker, Theisen.

Rohrbaugh, M., Tennen, H., Press, S., & White, L. (1981). Compliance, defiance, and therapeutic paradox: Guidelines for strategic use of paradoxical intervention. *American Journal of Orthopsychiatry, 51*(3), 454–467.

Sexton, T. L., & Montgomery, D. (1994). Ethical and therapeutic acceptability: A study of paradoxical techniques. *The Family Journal, 2*(3), 215–228.

West, J. D., & Zarski, J. J. (1983). The counselor's use of the paradoxical procedure in family therapy. *The Personnel and Guidance Journal, 62*(1), 34–37.

Paraphilic Disorders

Paraphilic disorders, also known as *paraphilias,* consist of eight clinically diagnosed disorders characterized by abnormal or unusual sexual partialities that cause significant impairment to the individual or others involved. Clinically significant distress can be experienced in the areas of work, social, or personal functioning. When paraphilic acts include illegal activities and/or the violations of others, it is not required that the individual with the paraphilic disorder experience significant clinical distress. Examples of distress or impairment can include job loss, marital difficulties, lack of sleep, or legal ramifications stemming from certain desires, fantasies, or engagement in paraphilic behaviors. Common paraphilic preferences include nonconsenting individuals, objects or nonhuman animals, and humiliation or suffering. This entry introduces and briefly explains the criteria required for each paraphilic disorder outlined in the fifth edition of the *Diagnostic and Statistical Manual of Mental Disorders* (DSM-5). These disorders are pedophilic disorder, exhibitionistic disorder, voyeuristic disorder, frotteuristic disorder, sexual masochism disorder, sexual sadism disorder, fetishistic disorder, and transvestic disorder.

Pedophilic Disorder

Pedophilic disorder, formerly known as *pedophilia*, is most commonly seen in men, with estimates of the prevalence of the disorder among men as high as 3% to 5%. The criteria for being diagnosed with this disorder include repeated intense sexual desires, fantasies, or behaviors involving sexual activity with a child who is 13 years of age or under. Additionally, the individual must experience these symptoms for at least 6 months, be at least 16 years of age, and be at least five years older than the child. Hence, a 15-year-old who has sexual fantasies or inappropriately touches a 12-year-old child cannot be diagnosed with pedophilic disorder.

An important distinction for this disorder is that the sexual desires, fantasies, or behaviors *must* cause substantial impairment or distress in work, social, or personal functioning to the individual diagnosed *or* the individual must have acted on his or her pedophilic desires (i.e., engaging in any form of sexual activity with a child 13 years of age or younger).

Behaviors characteristic of pedophilic disorders usually begin during adolescence. Most individuals exhibiting pedophilic symptoms do not actually engage in sexual penetration with children. Instead, engaging in oral sex or simply touching a child's genitals, also known as molestation, is the most common symptom exhibited. Some individuals with pedophilic disorder may be sexually attracted to adults as well as children, while others are exclusively sexually attracted to children. In addition, individuals with pedophilic disorder are usually enticed by a particular age range or sex of a child, such as a 9-year-old girl or a 12-year-old boy. A large portion of individuals with this disorder prefer female rather than male children. Use of substances, such as alcohol or other drugs also plays a major role in pedophilic behaviors, as up to 50% of diagnosed individuals drink alcohol before engaging in sexual behaviors with children. Acting on pedophilic behaviors often results in severe legal consequences such as registration on the sex offender list and prison time.

Exhibitionistic Disorder

Two criteria must be met in order for an individual to be diagnosed with exhibitionistic disorder. First, the individual *must* persistently (for at least 6 months) experience intense sexual desires, fantasies, or behaviors regarding genital self-exposure to unsuspecting strangers. Second, these desires, fantasies, and behaviors *must* cause substantial distress or impairment in the individual's life *or* the individual must have acted on such desires (i.e., self-exposure to a nonconsenting person).

Most individuals diagnosed with exhibitionistic disorder are males who expose themselves to females of any age, including children. Nearly one third of women have been victimized by exhibitionistic behaviors. These tendencies often begin before the age of 18, with individuals exposing themselves to complete strangers. Often, exhibitionistic urges are triggered by stress. Males with this disorder may expose themselves in different forms. Men may expose themselves with an erect or flaccid penis or while masturbating. Some may expose themselves hurriedly and then run away. Some individuals with exhibitionistic urges may fantasize about having sexual intercourse with their victims. However, this seldom happens. Typically, individuals diagnosed with this disorder have not been known to be dangerous and seldom try to make contact with their victims. In fact, most individuals with this disorder have successful intimate and sexual relationships, leading fairly normal lives. Nonetheless, exhibitionistic behaviors are illegal and can lead to serious mental and emotional harm to the nonconsenting person. If a person is caught performing exhibitionistic acts, legal charges can ensue.

Voyeuristic Disorder

Individuals diagnosed with voyeuristic disorder gain sexual arousal from watching unsuspecting strangers engage in intimate or private activities, such as undressing. As with exhibitionistic disorder, individuals must meet two criteria to be diagnosed with voyeuristic disorder. First, the individual *must* persistently (for at least 6 months) experience intense sexual desires, fantasies, or behaviors concerning the act of watching unsuspecting individuals who are naked or are disrobing or engaging in sexual activity. As with other paraphilic disorders, these tendencies *must* cause substantial distress or impairment in the individual's life *or* the individual has acted on such desires (e.g., watching a nonconsenting person undress).

Nearly all individuals diagnosed with voyeuristic disorder are men, with prevalence rates estimated at 12% in the male population. Voyeuristic behaviors typically begin before the age of 15, and many individuals masturbate while watching unsuspecting victims. However, it is uncommon for these individuals to ever make any contact with their victims, as they take abundant precautions to avoid being caught. Similar to individuals diagnosed with exhibitionistic disorder, individuals diagnosed with voyeuristic disorder lead fairly normal lives in the community, with successful sexual and intimate relationships. Since these behaviors are illegal and classified as a sexual offense, individuals who are caught can face legal ramifications for the violation of nonconsenting persons.

Frotteuristic Disorder

Frotteuristic disorder is characterized by gaining sexual pleasure from the act of touching or rubbing nonconsenting persons. Individuals with this disorder actually act out their paraphilic fantasies and violate the rights of others by inappropriately touching nonconsenting victims. Similar to previously outlined paraphilic disorders, individuals must meet two criteria to be diagnosed with frotteuristic disorder. First, the individual *must* persistently (for at least 6 months) experience intense sexual desires, fantasies, or behaviors involving touching and rubbing nonconsenting persons. Additionally, these tendencies *must* cause significant distress or impairment in the individual's life *or* the individual has acted on such desires (i.e., fondling a woman's breast without consent).

Almost all individuals diagnosed with frotteuristic disorder are males who violate a nonconsenting female. Individuals with this disorder may inappropriately touch a woman's breasts or genitalia with their hands or rub their own genitals against a woman's body. These acts commonly occur in public places such as a crowded street, subway, or bus. As with previously mentioned paraphilic disorders, frotteuristic acts can lead to emotional harm for the victim and legal ramifications for the perpetrator.

Sexual Masochism Disorder and Sexual Sadism Disorder

Sexual masochism disorder and sexual sadism disorder have a great deal in common (comorbidity rates of up to 30%) and are discussed together. Sexual masochism is characterized by gaining sexual pleasure from *receiving* pain or suffering, while sexual sadism is characterized by gaining sexual pleasure from *inflicting* pain or humiliation. These two disorders are vastly different from the previously discussed disorders, as engagement in masochistic or sadistic acts seldom lead to sexual offenses or legal ramifications. Diagnostic criteria for these two paraphilic disorders are similar. Both disorders require individuals to persistently (for at least 6 months) experience intense sexual desires, fantasies, or behaviors concerning real acts of receiving (sexual masochism) or inflicting (sexual sadism) psychological or physical pain. The second criterion requires that these individuals experience clinically significant distress or impairment stemming from their sexually masochistic or sadistic desires. Criteria for these diagnoses are similar to other paraphilic disorders, with one major difference: acting on the disorder is not required for a diagnosis.

Sexual masochistic and sadistic desires typically begin in childhood, are chronic, and often require an increase in the severity of behaviors to produce the same degree of sexual arousal and satisfaction. Individuals with these tendencies can participate in mild to severe forms of inflicting and/or receiving pain and humiliation. Some mild behaviors can include participating in bondage, blindfolding, spanking, and engaging in submissive behaviors such as imitating a baby or animal. More severe behaviors can include pricking, beating, choking, shocking, cutting, asphyxiating, and engaging in defecating or urinating during sexual acts. Although these behaviors may seem disturbing and dangerous, individuals with these disorders do not usually pose a danger to others. Although the prevalence of sexual sadism disorder is unknown, among civilly committed sexual offenders in the United States, fewer than 10% have sexual sadism. Additionally, many individuals who choose to engage in sexual masochism and sadism type activities emphasize the need for consent and precautions to keep themselves and their partners emotionally and physically safe.

Fetishistic Disorder

Fetishistic disorder is a paraphilic disorder defined by sexual arousal over inanimate objects or nongenital body parts. Individuals must meet two criteria to be diagnosed with this disorder. First, the individual *must* persistently (for at least 6 months) experience intense sexual desires, fantasies, or behaviors related to the use of an inanimate object or nongenital body parts. Additionally, these tendencies *must* cause significant distress or impairment in the individual's social, occupational, or personal functioning.

Almost all individuals with fetishistic disorder are men, with fetishistic interests beginning in childhood or adolescence. Fetishistic objects vary widely and can include any objects (such as balloons, cars, chairs, or pillows) or nongenital body parts (such as feet, arms, legs, or fingers). Some individuals may collect fetishistic objects and masturbate while holding, smelling, or rubbing an object. Asking a sexual partner to wear an object is also common. Although individuals with this disorder have not been known to be dangerous to themselves or others, they may eventually completely replace intimate sexual partners with their fetish.

Transvestic Disorder

Transvestic disorder is characterized by becoming sexually aroused by dressing in clothing typically associated with the opposite gender, a behavior known as cross-dressing. Similar to other paraphilic disorders, individuals *must* persistently (for at least 6 months) experience intense sexual desires, fantasies, or behaviors related to dressing as the opposite gender. Moreover, these tendencies *must* cause significant distress or impairment in the individual's social, occupational, or personal functioning.

Individuals diagnosed with this disorder normally begin experiencing symptoms prior to adolescence and may eventually replace normal sexual behaviors with cross-dressing. As with many paraphilic disorders, almost all individuals with transvestic disorder are men. Transvestic activities can vary from inconspicuously wearing undergarments of the opposite sex under work clothes to fully cross-dressing in private or public. Some individuals masturbate while cross-dressing while others have sexual intercourse in opposite-gender clothing. It is important to note that while these individuals become sexually excited by wearing the clothing of a different gender, they do not desire to change to or become that gender. Transvestic disorder should not be confused with being transgender or with gender dysphoria.

Vanessa B. Teixeira

See also Compulsive Sexual Behavior; Fetishes; Pornography; Sex, Definition of; Sexual Abuse; Sexual Assault and Rape; Sexual Health; Statutory Rape

Further Readings

American Psychiatric Association. (2013). *Diagnostic and statistical manual of mental disorders* (5th ed.). Washington, DC: Author.

Bhugra, D. (2000). Disturbances in objects of desire: Cross-cultural issues. *Sexual and Relationship Therapy, 15*(1), 67–78.

Bhugra, D., Popelyuk, D., & McMullen, I. (2010). Paraphilias across cultures: Contexts and controversies. *Journal of Sex Research, 47*(2), 249–250.

Dailey, S. F., Gill, C. S., Karl, S. L., & Minton, C. A. B. (2014). Specific behavioral disruptions: Paraphilic disorders. In *DSM-5 learning companion for counselors* (pp. 7603–7953). Alexandria, VA: American Counseling Association.

Janssen, D. F. (2014). How to "ascertain" paraphilia? An etymological hint. *Archives of Sexual Behavior, 43*(7), 1245–1246.

Långström, N., & Zucker, K. J. (2005). Transvestic fetishism in the general population: Prevalence and correlates. *Journal of Sex & Marital Therapy, 31*, 87–95. doi:10.080/00926230590477934

Laws, D. R., & O'Donohue, W. T. (Eds.). (2008). *Sexual deviance: Theory, assessment, and treatment.* New York, NY: Guilford Press.

Lee, J. K., Jackson, H. J., Pattison, P., & Ward, T. (2002). Developmental risk factors for sexual offending. *Child Abuse & Neglect, 26*(1), 73–92.

Marshall, W. L., & O'Brien, M. D. (2014). Balancing clients' strengths and deficits in sexual offender treatment: The Rockwood treatment approach. In R. C. Tafrate & D. Mitchell (Eds.), *Forensic CBT: A handbook for clinical practice* (pp. 279–301). Oxford, England: Wiley.

Parent Effectiveness Training (P.E.T.)

Parent Effectiveness Training (P.E.T.) is the name of both a book and a course that were authored by Thomas Gordon, who pioneered the idea that parents need specific knowledge and skills to be effective in their relationships with their children. P.E.T. teaches parents a set of communication and conflict resolution skills for raising their children. The course involves 24 hours of training sessions in a classroom setting with a trained and certified instructor. Since its beginning in 1962 when Gordon taught the first group of parents in a Pasadena cafeteria, this model has become popular worldwide. In addition to spreading across the United States, the course is or has been available in 45 countries around the world. In this entry, the origin, foundation, components, and core competencies of P.E.T. are presented. In addition, instructor training for the program is discussed.

Origin of Parent Effectiveness Training

In the late 1950s, Gordon was a practicing clinical psychologist in Pasadena, California. In addition to consulting with business organizations, he also had a private practice in which he counseled both adults and children. Over time, he observed that parents were bringing to him their children with whom they were having problems, hoping that he would "fix them." To him, these children seemed emotionally healthy—not "sick" or disturbed. What he realized was that they were coping with their parents' use of power over them. He saw the similarity between typical boss–subordinate relationships and those between parent and child, since both are hierarchical relationships.

He thought that if he could teach the parents the same communication skills that he had learned in graduate school and had used in his work with leaders, these children would no longer have a need to rebel against their parents, and the relationship between the parents and children would greatly improve. He had believed in the power of democratic relationships since attending graduate school at the University of Chicago where he studied and worked with Carl Rogers, the founder of client-centered therapy, or the person-centered approach. (Rogers's theory was that people have the capacity to actualize their full potential by being in a therapeutic relationship that is empathic and congruent, and in which they receive "unconditional positive regard.")

Gordon first described and explained his ideas about democratic relationships in the context of the boss–subordinate relationship in his 1955 book *Group-Centered Leadership*. In it, he described a model of leadership with the following main principles: (a) Leadership functions can be distributed among the members of the group; (b) an effective leader is one who is willing to let go of the traditional way of leading a group and have group members participate fully; (c) an effective leader creates an emotional climate in which group members feel free to express themselves and their ideas; and (d) an effective leader tends to them, listening to them empathically and conveying acceptance—that is, "Let me try to understand how you are seeing things." It was in this book that he first presented the idea that the experience of living and working in a democratic environment makes people healthy and that living in an autocratic environment makes people unhealthy.

Gordon worked to help people develop the skills necessary for creating good relationships, taking responsibility for their lives, communicating (two-way), solving problems creatively, and having peaceful conflict resolution. In recognition of his contribution to peace, Gordon was nominated for the Nobel Peace Prize three times.

The Foundation of P.E.T.

Hierarchical Versus Egalitarian Relationships

According to Gordon, traditional hierarchical relationships—the use of power, punishment and rewards, and win–lose conflict resolution—are immensely destructive both to the individuals and to relationships. He believed that the most critical barriers to healthy, happy relationships are power differentials between people and groups. He contrasted the prevailing way of thinking in favor of top-down relationships with a model that offered the idea that egalitarian relationships not only were possible but also made people healthy, both emotionally and physically. He taught a way of transitioning from the prevailing autocratic paradigm to a therapeutic egalitarian one, defined by equality, parity, and reciprocity.

Prevention, Not Treatment

Instead of seeing people with problems as neurotic or sick, Gordon thought of them as capable people in trouble. This was a shift away from the medical model to a training model—from seeing someone as a "difficult person" to seeing him or her as a "person in difficulty." He advocated education instead of treatment.

Emphasis on Learning Interpersonal Skills

Gordon believed ordinary parents could learn the same interpersonal skills that professional counselors used with their clients. He demystified psychology, took it out of the realm of academics, and offered it to the public. He converted abstract concepts into learnable skills and made them accessible to parents, teachers, youth, and others.

A Model for Relationships

Gordon's major contribution was conceptualizing a system that tied separate psychological ideas together and detailing the interpersonal skills it took to make them work. Instead of offering pat solutions to typical parent–child problems, he offered a process and a set of skills so parents and children could create their own solutions. The basis of this was the blueprint he conceptualized and developed—a visual model for handling relationship problems. He named this the *behavior rectangle* or the *behavior window*.

This model makes it possible for a person to look at a particular behavior that's causing a problem in one of his or her relationships and figure out who "owns" it—who has the unmet need. Equally important are the appropriate skills to use to deal with it.

Components of the Gordon Model

The Behavior Window and Problem Ownership

As mentioned earlier, Gordon created the behavior window and problem ownership conceptual framework to deal with relationships between people, be they parent and child, leader and member, teacher and student, spouse and spouse, or other types of relationships. As shown in Figure 1, this window contains four areas and communication skills to be used in each one depending on who owns the problem—that is, who has the unmet need. The four areas are (1) child owns a problem, (2) no problem area, (3) parent owns a problem, and (4) both own a problem.

When a problem occurs in a relationship, a parent can use this window to figure out where the problem is. Once it's clear who owns the problem, the parent then uses the communication or conflict resolution skills that she or he has learned to solve it.

Figure 1 The Behavior Window

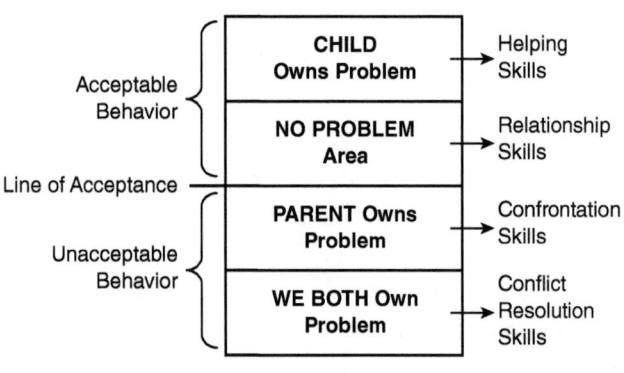

Source: Adams, L., Emmons, S., Kelly-Denslow, K., & Tyrrell, P. (2014). *Gordon Training International P.E.T. instructor guide* (p. 6-4). Solana Beach, CA: Gordon Training International.

When the Child Owns a Problem

Active listening is the skill for the parent to use when the child owns a problem. Listening in this way means that the parent puts aside his or her judgment and listens attentively, empathically, and with acceptance to understand the child's feelings and then feeds back what he or she has heard to see if he or she has understood correctly. This often results in the child's finding his or her own solution to the problem. Genuine acceptance of another person as that person is fosters a relationship in which he or she can grow, develop, make constructive changes, and learn to solve his or her own problems. Gordon learned this way of deep, empathic listening at the University of Chicago when he studied and worked with Rogers. Rogers called it "reflection of feelings."

When their child has a problem, parents want to help solve it, but often in a well-intentioned attempt to do this, they do more harm than good. Here is a list of the *12 roadblocks to communication* in P.E.T.—also referred to as the "dirty dozen"—and an example of each:

Ordering	"Stop crying!"
Warning	"You'll never make friends if . . ."
Moralizing	"You should never lie."
Advising	"What I would do if I were you is . . ."
Using Logic	"Yes, but . . ."
Judging	"If you'd done it right the first time, this wouldn't have happened."
Praising	"Well, I think you're doing a great job!"
Labeling	"That's stupid to worry about one low test grade."
Analyzing	"You're just tired."
Reassuring	"Don't worry, you'll feel better about it tomorrow."
Questioning	"Who talked you into doing such a thing?"
Avoiding	"Let's have a nice dinner and forget about it."

Instead of freeing children to say more, these responses block them from going deeper into their feelings.

Active listening is the P.E.T. skill that replaces these roadblocks. Here's a short example to show the difference between roadblocks and active listening:

Child: "Will the test be hard?"

Parent: (typical responses, or roadblocks): "Not if you study." Or "You're so smart you'll do okay." Or "Why do you ask? Haven't you prepared?"

Parent: (active listening response): "You're pretty worried about passing that test."

In *group-centered leadership*, Gordon described these as "responses that convey intent to change others." He developed this list as a part of his Ph.D. thesis based on his and other psychotherapists' clinical observations of responses used by therapists that blocked clients' communication.

No-Problem Area

These are times in the relationship when both parent and child are getting their needs met. One of the main goals of the P.E.T. skills is to keep the relationship in this area as much as possible. This can be accomplished by communicating to children in an honest, clear, authentic way that doesn't contain judgments or interpretations of them. In P.E.T., this is called an *I-message*. *Positive I-messages* convey positive feelings and describe the effects of a child's behavior: "I really appreciate that you helped your sister get dressed; it meant that we could leave on time." *Preventive I-messages* let the child know in advance about a future need so that a potential conflict may be avoided: "I need to work for a couple of hours this evening so I'd like it if we could have dinner a little earlier than usual." Gordon created the positive I-message as an alternative to praise. The preventive I-message was developed in 1976 by Gordon's wife, Linda Adams, as a part of the Effectiveness Training for Women course.

When the Parent Owns a Problem

The *confrontive I-message* is the skill that parents use when they have a problem with their child—that is, the child's behavior is interfering with the parent. The goal of an I-message is to influence the child to change his or her behavior out of consideration for the parent's need. It is an alternative to a you-message, which is usually blameful and judgmental: "You're inconsiderate."

A confrontive I-message contains three parts: (1) the parent's nonblameful description of the child's unacceptable behavior (what the child said or did), (2) a description of the concrete and tangible effects of that behavior on the parent, and (3) a description of the parent's feelings about those effects. An example of a confrontive I-message would be as follows: "When I see you text so much, I get worried that our minutes will get used up and we'll get charged more on our phone bill."

In his early P.E.T. classes, Gordon developed these messages in response to parents' asking what to do when a child's behavior caused them a problem. He referred to them as I-messages. The name was later changed to confrontive I-messages to distinguish them from the I-messages used in the no-problem area described earlier.

When Both Own a Problem

When there is a conflict in the relationship, P.E.T. offers *no-lose conflict resolution* as a way of resolving it. Gordon adapted John Dewey's well-known problem-solving model as the process for resolving conflicts by arriving at a mutually satisfying solution. For example, the family has one car; both parent and teenager need to use it at the same time. Not all conflicts involve a conflict of needs; some are values-based—that is, the behavior of the child does not tangibly affect the parent, yet she or he is bothered by it. For example, the child doesn't share the parent's religious beliefs or the child wants to get a tattoo. P.E.T. offers strategies for dealing with these values differences so the relationship is not damaged.

Parents typically use three different types of methods to cope with conflict. Method III is a nonpower, participative, six-step method for resolving problems and conflicts between parents and children in which both get their needs met—neither one loses, and both win. It contrasts with the two power-based win–lose methods: Method I (authoritarian) is when the parent uses his or her power to win at the expense of the child. Method II (permissive) is when the parent gives in and lets the child win at the expense of the parent.

P.E.T. Core Competencies

The program lists core competencies that parents are expected to achieve in the program (Gordon Training International, 2006). After participation in a P.E.T. course, it is expected that parents will have the ability to do the following:

1. Determine who "owns the problem" in a given situation.
2. Identify the 12 roadblocks to communication.
3. Distinguish between roadblocks and active listening.
4. Avoid the roadblocks that cause most helping attempts to fail.
5. Recognize when their child needs their help as skilled listeners.
6. Use silence, acknowledgments, and door-openers to help their child with a problem.
7. Actively listen to hear their child's feelings.
8. Actively listen to clarify information.
9. Distinguish between acceptable and unacceptable behavior.
10. Determine what to do when a child's behavior is interfering with the parents' meeting their child's needs.
11. Develop a three-part confrontive I-message.
12. Confront their child's unacceptable behavior with an I-message.
13. Shift gears between I-messages and active listening when appropriate.
14. Acknowledge their child's efforts with positive I-messages instead of praise.
15. Prevent problems and conflicts using preventive I-messages.
16. Recognize conflict situations.
17. Distinguish between conflicts of needs and values collisions.
18. Avoid the use of Method I.
19. Avoid the use of Method II.
20. Set the stage for Method III conflict resolution.
21. Use Method III to resolve a conflict between the parent and child.
22. Use Method III to mediate a conflict between children or others.
23. Handle values collisions.

Instructor Training

Soon after Gordon began teaching P.E.T. in 1962, others came to him saying they wanted to teach it too. As a result, he began training instructors using standardized material including a guide and a workbook for the participants. Since that time, many thousands of P.E.T. instructors have participated in workshops in countries around the world.

Linda Adams

See also Assertiveness; Conflict Resolution; Listening, Empathic; Parenting

Further Readings

Adams, L., Emmons, S., Kelly-Denslow, K., & Tyrrell, P. (2014). *Gordon Training International P.E.T. instructor guide*. Solana Beach, CA: Gordon Training International.

Dewey, J. (1916). *Democracy and education*. New York, NY: Macmillan.

Gordon, T. (1955). *Group-centered leadership*. New York, NY: Houghton Mifflin.

Gordon, T. (1989). *Discipline that works*. New York, NY: Penguin House.

Gordon, T. (2000). *Parent effectiveness training*. New York, NY: Random House. (Original work published 1970)

Gordon Training International. (2006). *P.E.T. core competencies*. Retrieved from http://www.parenting-teenagers.com/PET-Core-Competencies-brochure.pdf

Greven, P. (1990). *Spare the child*. New York, NY: Random House.

Jourard, S. (1971). *The transparent self*. New York, NY: Van Nostrand. (Original work published 1964)

Rogers, C. (1995). *Client-centered therapy*. New York, NY: Houghton Mifflin. (Original work published 1951)

Parent Management Training

Parent management training (PMT) is an evidence-based psychotherapeutic intervention originally designed to impact treatment outcomes for children and adolescents who displayed various dysfunctions in behavior where such dysfunctions cause pervasive difficulties in academic, social, and mental functioning. PMT is a comprehensive treatment protocol that has several theoretical underpinnings and unique principles that have been researched extensively over the last few decades. PMT has been used with various age-groups and populations ranging from children of incarcerated parents, stepfamilies, children with developmental disabilities, and specific ethnic minority groups. Nonetheless, treatment effects are different in different populations and often have more desirable outcomes within some populations than others. There are several variations of parent management training, which include the Incredible Years training series, parent–child interaction therapy (PCIT), and the Triple-P Positive Parenting Program. This entry briefly outlines PMT history, principles, concepts, and basics. Additionally, this entry explores and briefly defines related interventions of problem-solving skills training (PSST), Parent Management Training—Oregon Model (PMTO), the Kazdin Method, and behavioral parent training.

History of Parent Management Training

The origins of PMT date back to the 1950s and 1960s when various contextual influences were identified and deemed significant in the treatment and diagnosis of psychiatric disorders and their accompanying symptoms as they occurred in children and adults. Furthermore, the family as a source of information and possible root of clinical dysfunction began to be seen as significant in the treatment and diagnosis of disorders. It is within this framework where the primary focus of PMT stemmed from, for PMT was designed to impact the parent–child interaction as well as the child's interactions at home, at school, and in the community.

PMT was originally created to address the problem behaviors of individuals who were diagnosed with conduct disorder (CD) and was later used for children who were considered oppositional. CD, as defined in the fifth edition of the *Diagnostic and Statistical Manual of Mental Disorders* (DSM-5), encompasses a pattern of persistent and repetitive actions where an individual deliberately violates the basic rights of others or violates major age-appropriate social norms. Behavioral violations for CD are typically classified in four key domains: (1) acts of aggression toward people and animals, (2) destruction of property, (3) deceitfulness or stealing, and (4) flagrant violations of rules. Later applications of PMT, thanks to advancements in diagnostic capabilities, expanded the treatment's utility to individuals diagnosed with oppositional defiant disorder (ODD). ODD encompasses many of the problematic behaviors symptomatic of CD; however, ODD primarily encompasses negativistic and hostile behaviors that are less severe than those performed by individuals diagnosed with CD. Examples of such behaviors include willful disobedience, deliberate annoyance of others, tantrums, and active defiance of rules and requests of adults.

PMT borrows from the work of Gerald Patterson and colleagues and applied behavior analysis (ABA). PMT focuses on parent–child interactions in the home and aims to discover ways to alter this interaction as is necessary to impact problem behaviors of children who suffer from various behavioral disorders. The use of ABA allows for the alteration of behavior through the systematic means of establishing operations, reinforcements, and the functions of behaviors. At the core of PMT, however, are basic principles of behaviorism, a school of thought that emphasizes the importance of observable behaviors as measured by stimuli and responses.

Parent Management Training and Operant Conditioning: Underlying Principles and Concepts

Principles of operant conditioning, as proposed by B. F. Skinner, are central to the basic premise of PMT. At the time of the advent of operant conditioning and the extension of such principles to human behaviors, best practices in the form of therapeutic treatments were not of primary importance. B. F. Skinner's work was an expansion of Edward Thorndike's law of effect, which states that responses followed by a pleasant outcome will most likely occur again. The opposite is true for responses that produce unpleasant outcomes, for the behavior is least likely to occur again when an unpleasant outcome occurs. Operant behaviors are behaviors that are different from respondent behaviors in that operant behaviors are behaviors that become associated with consequences that may either punish or reinforce the behavior. Respondent behaviors are behaviors that are reflexive or automatic in nature and are not learned behaviors. In the case of PMT, behaviors are understood in the context of the parent–child interaction where positive reinforcers are used to help parents discourage problematic behaviors as they occur inside and outside of the home.

Operant conditioning is a type of associative learning that is influenced by the consequences of behavior. This type of learning can result in the learning of new actions as well as the elimination of old actions or undesirable actions through reinforcers and punishers. Reinforcers strengthen the likelihood of behaviors while punishers weaken the likelihood of behavior. Further distinctions can be made between positive and negative reinforcers and punishments. Positive reinforcement and negative reinforcement are used to strengthen behaviors. In using positive reinforcement, a pleasant stimulus is added or increased. When employing negative reinforcement, an unpleasant stimulus is reduced or removed in order to strengthen a behavior. Positive and negative punishments are used to weaken behaviors. Positive punishment involves adding or presenting an unpleasant stimulus while negative punishment involves reducing or removing a pleasant stimulus. In PMT, positive reinforcement is preferred as a more effective means of managing behavior than punishment. Other relevant concepts central to classical conditioning include prompting, fading, shaping, and modeling, as well as rehearsal and extinction. Classical conditioning is a form of behaviorism that aids learning through the use of associations between stimuli and respondent behaviors. Prompting and fading as well as rehearsal and extinction all involve the use of methods aimed at impacting the frequency in occurrence of a behavior. Shaping and modeling involve methods for modifying established or learned behavior. The use of contingencies in operant conditioning helps further establish the relationship between consequences and stimuli.

Much of the preliminary research using the principles of operant conditioning was first performed on animals in laboratory studies and then extended to children during the 1960s. Although much more comprehensive and complex than presented here, key principles of operant conditioning provide a means to explore the relationship between environmental events and behaviors that is essential to the foundation of PMT. The application and extension of such principles to child-rearing and parenting are contributors to the foundation of PMT. Further applications of operant conditioning principles to the behaviors of children are best exemplified in the works of Patterson and colleagues. Patterson conducted extensive research on the etiology and course of antisocial behaviors from early childhood to adolescence, and his research was pivotal to linking ineffective parenting practices to childhood CDs.

Patterson hypothesized in his early research that an understanding of chronic delinquency warranted an understanding of the developmental sequence of experiences that perpetuated such behaviors. For Patterson, several contextual variables inside and outside of the home influenced the family interaction and ultimately contributed to the persistence and chronicity of aggressive and antisocial behaviors of children and adolescents. These contextual variables include poor parenting practice, behaviors of the individual that influence academic functioning, and the individual's ability to establish connections with peers. Failures within the personal and social domains lead to the establishment of deviant peer groups, depressed moods, and a lifetime of risk for continued involvement in delinquent behaviors. Given the basic premises of PMT, it is necessary for the therapist to understand the impact of the aforementioned variables on treatment outcomes for children and adolescents.

The Basics of Parent Management Training: The Yale Program

An extension of Patterson's established notions of attuning to the parent–child interaction is the inherent belief that such attention would benefit the course of the treatment process. Several years of established research has pointed to the effects of parental stress, psychopathology, and other factions in relation to the maintenance of deviant behaviors. PMT proposes that in order to reduce antisocial behavior, attention must be given to parent and family issues that can materialize in the antisocial behaviors of children and adolescents. Other conditions related to antisocial behaviors of children and adolescents include hyperactivity and cognitive deficits and distortions. From this framework, PMT places the parent–child interaction at the heart of the therapeutic intervention, for symptoms of problematic behaviors are believed to be ingrained in the relationships that the child has with the parent, family members, and others within communities and schools.

Originally, the PMT program was created for individuals diagnosed with CD in inpatient psychiatric care at the Child Psychiatric Intensive Care Service at the University of Pittsburgh School of Medicine; however, the program was expanded to outpatient treatment, which has remained the focus of researchers at the Yale Parent Center and Child Conduct Clinic for the past two decades. The target age-group for the intervention stems from early childhood to age 14. PMT is typically used for children ages 6 and younger as a stand-alone treatment. PMT and a complementary intervention called PSST targets the rearing practices of parents, interactions between the parent and child, and contingencies that can enhance the occurrence of prosocial behaviors at home and at school. Researchers at Yale have conducted research on the combined effects of PMT and PSST and have concluded that when combined, both exert greater changes in child and parental functioning and marked changes in clinical levels of functioning.

The Yale program is comprised of a core treatment of 12 weekly sessions that last from 45 minutes to 60 minutes. Most of the content of PMT is delivered to parents who implement procedures at home once taught. Therapists do not directly intervene with children who present with the problematic behaviors. Topics of sessions include the use of positive reinforcement, prompting, shaping, mild punishment, and setting events. With the help of a therapist, parents are trained and taught specific techniques that they can practice and learn to impart changes in undesirable behaviors at home. When implemented in the home, PMT utilizes available incentives and encourages the establishment of parameters necessary for the effective implementation of the program within the home. The therapist plays a major role in the implementation of the program because the therapist models and role-plays ideal behaviors during the treatment sessions while the parent rehearses.

An additional component of the program involves the use of a token reinforcement or point system that provides the parent with a systematic, structured way of issuing reinforcements. Extensions of the program can also be applied in the school setting if the parent desires; however, teachers are usually contacted when the therapist wants to establish problem areas of concern and to generally establish a baseline for the child's academic and behavioral performance at school.

As the treatment progresses, children are invited into sessions where they can learn and practice the skills in the contexts in which the problem behaviors are occurring.

Problem-Solving Skills Training

PSST centers on cognitive processes, which are several constructs that influence how individuals with problem behaviors perceive and process social situations and experience the world. The use of this modality requires that parents receive clinical supervision in their use of various techniques. Several studies have pointed to the effectiveness of this program in reducing aggressive and antisocial child behaviors at home and school. Parents learn to routinely use contingency management techniques. When first developed, PMT and PSST were used with individuals and their parents in inpatient hospital settings. The latter treatment approach, however, was typically the favored approach for parents who either were unavailable or refused to participate in treatment. The interventions differ from one another in that the effectiveness of PSST relies on the child's perceptions, attributions, and beliefs, which may reflect deficiencies that the therapist will discover cause the behavior. PMT focuses on changes between individuals so that more effective methods for communicating across situations are developed. Most of the current work on PMT has been performed by Yale researcher Alan Kazdin.

As a learning-based procedure, PSST teaches effective problem-solving skills to children and parents that address practical problems by altering the response to interpersonal situations at home, at school, and in the community. PSST involves 12 weekly sessions with children and adolescents. The treatment's primary focus is to teach problem-solving steps that can help children and adolescents engage in thoughts and behaviors that impact future actions. Children are taught verbal prompts that include self-statements that guide actions. The first few sessions utilize games and tasks to teach the problem-solving steps. The concept underlying the verbal prompts is to facilitate a thought process that encourages contemplation of action through the generation of multiple solutions and potential outcomes. Extensive practice of the steps with the aid of the therapist allows the child an opportunity to practice skills so that prosocial skills can be developed. Role-play provides a means by which children can practice responses to multiple stimuli and conditions to help with generalization and maintenance. Over the course of the training, the therapist provides the children with concrete feedback, social reinforcements, and modeling to improve behaviors.

As the sessions are implemented, children can earn tokens that can be exchanged for small prizes after sessions. During the session, children can also lose tokens for either misuse of steps or failure to apply the steps appropriately. Other assignments, which are referred to as "super solvers," allow for further extension of knowledge of steps through these systematically programmed assignments. The super solver assignments allow further application of skills to general life situations. As treatment progresses, parents are brought into sessions to participate in super solver activities that become more complex and more closely related to problem domains that contributed to the need for therapeutic intervention.

Parent Management Training—Oregon Model

Utilizing the theoretical tenets of social interaction learning theory, PMTO is a "manualized" program (i.e., one conducted according to an instruction manual) that targets children's problem behaviors by avoiding coercive cycles of behavior that interfere with healthy relating. Like PMT, PMTO was also a by-product of the influence of Patterson and colleagues at Oregon Social Learning Center, for it was developed by Patterson and colleagues during the mid-1960s. In PMTO, parents are taught to use parenting methods that are effective toward the end of healthy child adjustment. PMTO therapists undergo approximately 18 months of training and coaching for certification. PMTO therapists must also undergo workshop seminars and coaching in the individual and group setting. Effective parenting practices as characterized in PMTO comprise the following five elements: (1) limit setting, (2) problem-solving, (3) positive involvement, (4) skill encouragement, and (5) monitoring or supervising.

Limit setting, also referred to as discipline, involves the use of appropriate and provisional use of minor sanctions such as time outs and the removal of privileges. Problem-solving involves teaching families skills that will help them use negotiation to address agreements and establish rules and consequences for violating or following rules. Positive involvement concerns interactions of loving attention between parent and child. Skill encouragement utilizes various scaffolding techniques to encourage prosocial behaviors. Prompting for appropriate behavior and utilizing praise and accompanying positive reinforcement is an example of scaffolding. Monitoring or supervising concerns tracking youth activities, known associates, hangout spots, and modes of transportation. Further information regarding the certification process is made available by Implementation Sciences International, Inc.

The Kazdin Method

A related program that is an extension of the Yale Parent Management program is that of the Kazdin Method, which was proposed by Kazdin, the director of Yale Parenting Center. Kazdin wrote a book for parents; this text was written as a jargon-free method that parents can reference for effective strategies on dealing with defiant behaviors. In this text, Kazdin expands upon a few of the concepts originally presented in the Yale Parent Management training manual. Kazdin emphasizes the elimination of unwanted behavior through replacement with positive opposites of undesirable behaviors. By replacing undesirable behaviors with strong alternative behaviors, intolerable behaviors can be addressed. Through step-by-step instructions, parents are provided with tools for defining behavior and creating opportunities for children to practice desirable behaviors.

The text also advises parents on the effective use of positive reinforcers and the application of such reinforcers in a systematic way.

Behavioral Parent Training

Behavioral parent training is an umbrella term for programs designed to change the behaviors of parents and children while utilizing the basic tenets of behaviorism and operant conditioning. Parent training typically refers to efficacious interventions used to clinically manage and prevent the disruptive behaviors of children with attention-deficit/hyperactivity disorder (ADHD) and children and adolescents diagnosed with ODD and CD. Such efficacious interventions include PMT, PSST, PMTO, and Strategies to Enhance Positive Parenting (STEPP). The primary methodology of parent training involves the supervised use of child management tactics by therapists to help parents manage problem behaviors using contingency management techniques. In times when the effects of medication may be diminished or absent, changes in parenting behavior are targeted in order to address externalizing behaviors. Ideally, changes in parenting behavior create a means by which children are able to exert more control over their own behaviors.

Anissa K. Howard

See also Active Parenting; Authoritative Parenting; Child-Centered Parenting; Group Parenting Classes; Parenting Styles

Further Readings

Hukkelberg, S. S., & Ogden, T. (2013). Working alliance and treatment fidelity as predictors of externalizing problem behaviors in parent management training. *Journal of Consulting and Clinical Psychology, 81*, 1010–1020.

Kazdin, A. E. (2005). *Parent management training.* New York, NY: Oxford University Press.

Kazdin, A. E., Whitley, M., & Marcianon, P. L. (2006). Child-therapist and parent-therapist alliance and therapeutic change in the treatment of children referred for oppositional, aggressive, and antisocial behavior. *Journal of Child Psychology and Psychiatry, 47*, 436–445.

Larson, J., & Lochman, J. E. (2002). *Helping school children cope with anger: A cognitive behavioral intervention.* New York, NY: Guilford Press.

Patterson, G. R., Reid, J. B., & Dishion, T. J. (1992). *Antisocial boys.* Eugene, OR: Castalia.

Patterson, G. R., Reid, J. B., & Eddy, J. M. (2002). A brief history of the Oregon model. In J. B. Reid, G. R. Patterson, & J. Snyder (Eds.), *Antisocial behavior in children and adolescents: A developmental analysis and model for intervention* (pp. 3–21). Washington, DC: American Psychological Association.

Shure, M. B. (1992). *I can problem solve (JCPS): An interpersonal cognitive problem solving program.* Champaign, IL: Research Press.

Sigmarsdóttir, M., & Vikar Guđmundsdóttir, E. (2013). Implementation of parent management training—Oregon Model (PMTO™) in Iceland: Building sustained fidelity. *Family Process, 52*, 216–227.

Skotarczak, L., & Lee, G. K. (2015). Effects of parent management training programs on disruptive behavior for children with a developmental disability: A meta-analysis. *Research in Developmental Disabilities, 38*, 272–287.

Spielfogel, J. E., Leathers, S. J., Christian, E., & McMeel, L. S. (2011). Parent management training, relationships with agency staff, and child mental health: Urban foster parent's perspectives. *Children and Youth Services Review, 33*, 2366–2374.

Parent Study Groups

After World War II and with the birth of the baby boom generation, an emphasis on positive parenting took hold in North America. Parent study groups were one form of training that brought together new ideas and research on child development, goals of children's misbehavior, encouragement practices, parenting styles, effective parent communication, and discipline without punishment. Initially, these groups were run by professional or paraprofessional counselors, but by the 1960s, these groups were almost always run by parents who followed published study guides and eventually integrated video-based training programs developed in the 1970s and 1980s. Even today, effective parenting skills are often taught in psychoeducational groups as an adjunct to family counseling and therapy. The information and guidance provided in these groups and programs has evolved over time as methods for effective parenting increasingly are based on empirical evidence.

The approaches used in parent study groups have psychological foundations in early 20th-century psychology—specifically those models developed by John B. Watson, Alfred Adler, B. F. Skinner, Carl Rogers, and John Bowlby—even though none of these men ever led or developed a parent study group. This entry starts with an overview of these theorists before proceeding to a description of the development and use of parent study groups, parent education, and parent training programs.

Watson, a behaviorist in the early 1900s, suggested that children be treated as if they were already adults in his book *Psychological Care of Infant and Child,* which started out as a series of articles in *McCall's Magazine.* Objectivity and aloofness were recommended for parents; mother-child bonding, cuddling, kissing, and hugging were to be avoided if not eliminated. Watson even went so far as to suggest that families were not necessarily the best place to raise children. He favored a more controlled environment in which children could be observed and developed experimentally using scientific reasoning.

By contrast, and at about the same time, Adler published his book *Understanding Human Nature* that was to become the first popular psychology book to sell more than 100,000 copies in the United States. Adler understood children to be engaged in a long growth period, one in which innate qualities such as striving for success and social interest had to be taught, guided, and developed. Adler recognized the importance of the bond between the mother and child, and his advocacy of engagement and connection on the part of parents and teachers would presage the work of Bowlby and other attachment theorists.

Adler believed that heredity and environment played a part in the development of the child, but it was the interpretation that children gave to self, others, and life that determined who they would be. Among the more significant influences in a child's life was the relationship of each parent to the other and to the child, the meaning attached to one's birth position, and the style and atmosphere in which the child was raised. Above all, Adler's approach focused on the purposes of behavior, interaction, and movement even in very young toddlers.

One of Adler's followers was Rudolf Dreikurs. Dreikurs was the first to organize an understanding of what he called children's mistaken behaviors into four goals: (1) *attention,* (2) *power struggle,* (3) *revenge,* and what he called an (4) *assumed disability* or a *demonstration of inadequacy,* really the goal of avoidance or wanting to be left alone. By 1948, Dreikurs developed a philosophy of parenting based on cooperation, democratic principles, and encouragement, a model of parenting that would later be validated by the research of Diana Baumrind.

In 1964, a registered nurse named Vicki Soltz teamed up with Dreikurs to write what would become the most used child guidance manual of all time. The book, *Children: The Challenge,* was more practical than Dreikurs's earlier books, giving precise advice for many dozens of situations that parents would face. Based on Dreikurs's belief that the fundamental need in children was to belong, *Children: The Challenge* applied Adler's principles to everyday life. The first six chapters focus on belonging, personality development, courage, and the four goals of misbehavior as well as problem-solving and teaching responsibility through the use of natural and logical consequences. Dreikurs adopted a middle ground between authoritarian and permissive parenting, which he would call *democratic parenting.* The model was suited to people living in Western countries with democratic political structures. While the first part of the book emphasizes principles, the rest of the book teaches parents and teachers how to apply the theory at home and in school.

Dreikurs had encouraged the development of parent study groups in the late 1940s, based on his 1948 book, but with the more practical advice in *Children: The Challenge,* Soltz was able to launch a large number of such groups across North America. From Eugene, Oregon, to Chicago, Illinois, to Wilmington, Delaware, family education centers and parent study groups began to spring up. In 1967, Soltz published a *Study Group Leader's Manual* through the Alfred Adler Institute in Chicago, complete with a philosophy and proven techniques for leaders, preparations for a first meeting, study guides for a 10-week group, and discussion-promoting questions for each chapter. In as little as a decade and a half, 20,000 people had participated in these groups in the United States and Canada.

In 1962, Thomas Gordon, who had been a student of Rogers, began to develop a leadership model that would later be applied to parents, teachers, and community or business leadership. Parent Effectiveness Training (P.E.T.) laid out his democratic approach that emphasized active listening, I-messages, emotional connectedness, and personal ownership of problems and their solutions. His model relied heavily on clear, authentic, and emotionally engaged communication. Gordon also developed an organization that took responsibility for training and certifying group leaders across the country.

In 1973, Don Dinkmeyer and Gary McKay, two Adlerian-trained practitioners, integrated ideas from both Dreikurs and Gordon in a book they called *Raising a Responsible Child.* The material in this book became the basis for the widely used parent-training program called Systematic Training for Effective Parenting (STEP). The first STEP kits came complete with a parent manual, posters, leadership manuals, and other program materials. Videos and leadership training opportunities were added later. After almost 40 years, an estimated 4,000,000 people have taken part in groups using the STEP approach.

In 1980, Michael Popkin introduced a video-based parenting program called Active Parenting, another approach that relied heavily on the work of Adler and Dreikurs. This parent education model has expanded over the years and has been heavily researched, with studies reporting positive changes in the behavior of parents and children. Active Parenting has video programs for parents of infants, young children, children ages 5 to 12, and adolescents; there are also special programs for parenting after divorce and parenting in stepfamilies. The videos in the Active Parenting Now series are available in both English and Spanish.

Other national parenting programs include Positive Discipline, based on Jane Nelsen's books of the same name, and the Total Transformation Program. Nelsen's approach is supported by an online training program for parent educators; her approach focuses on encouragement and solution-focused outcomes. Perhaps the most highly publicized parent training program in recent years is Total Transformation, developed by James and Janet Lehman and delivered through DVD and audio CD packages. The program melds communication practices with behavior modification principles. The Lehmans claim their approach will work with the most difficult of children, including those engaged in delinquent behavior, suffering from clinical disorders, and having special needs. Positive Discipline and Total Transformation, like STEP and Active Parenting, all claim that their approaches are supported by empirical research.

Although parent study groups run by certified leaders and parent guides peaked in the 1970s and 1980s, there are still a large number of parent education programs available in North America. One is the Parent Encouragement Program (PEP), based in Kensington, Maryland, which provides classes, events, and other educational resources to parents in the Washington, D.C., area. PEP provides training in play, learning styles, early childhood education, and effective discipline. Additional support for parents and families can be found at the National Parenting Center and the National Association of Parents.

James Robert Bitter

See also Adlerian Family Therapy; Adlerian Open-Forum Family Counseling

Further Readings

Baumrind, D. (1968). Authoritarian versus authoritative control. *Adolescence, 3*(11), 255–272.

Bettner, B. L. (2014). *The six essential pieces of the parenting puzzle.* Media, PA: Creative Press.

Bowlby, J. (1988). *A secure base: Parent/child attachment and healthy development.* New York, NY: Basic Books.

Dinkmeyer, D., McKay, D., & Dinkmeyer, D. (1997). *STEP: The parent handbook.* Circle Pines, MN: American Guidance Service.

Dreikurs, R., & Soltz, V. (1964). *Children: The challenge.* New York, NY: Hawthorn.

Gordon, T. (1970). *PET: Parent effectiveness training.* New York, NY: Peter H. Wyden.

Lehman, J. (2004). *The total transformation program.* Westbrook, ME: Legacy Publishing.

Nelsen, J. (2006). *Positive discipline.* New York, NY: Ballantine.

Popkin, M. (1993). *Active parenting today.* Atlanta, GA: Active Parenting.

PARENT–ADOLESCENT RELATIONS

When children reach adolescence, many changes occur in their relationship with their parents. This entry focuses on the developmental changes that occur within individual adolescents and the changes that occur in their relationships with parents as a result. It also discusses how the demands of parenting change during adolescence, various approaches to parenting, and theories regarding how to understand adolescent and parent relationships.

Adolescence as a Developmental Stage

The term *adolescent* can be defined in several ways: either by chronological age (e.g., ages 13 to 19); physical development, such as puberty; or by legal definitions, which refer to society's criteria for an adolescent reaching adulthood. Adolescents generally are attending middle school or high school and although they may obtain employment are understood not to be adults until the age of 18 (depending upon state recognition of adulthood).

Multiple changes occur during adolescence and its associated developmental tasks. Adolescence includes multiple developmental tasks such as the creation of identity, taking on new tasks and roles, beginning independence, autonomy, and adopting multiple roles to find one that is suitable. Further changes in adolescence include sexual maturity and beginning to experiment with teenage relationships. According to researchers on adolescent development, there are generally two areas of development: (1) adolescence and (2) later adolescence. In adolescence, the focus is primarily on the development of identity, while in later adolescence, the emphasis may be on intimacy.

Adolescence has been referred to a place "in between" childhood and adulthood given the limits placed on adolescents and their assigned responsibilities. Adolescents are exposed to multiple societal and cultural influences. Adolescents tend to attempt and participate in multiple risky behaviors, such as thrill-seeking, risk-taking, substance abuse, and sexual activity. These are some of the reasons that adolescents are at a higher risk for the development of behavioral and mental disorders, substance abuse, and delinquency.

Views of Adolescence

According to the psychoanalyst Erik Erikson and his theory of the life cycle, adolescents must work through the stage of identity versus identity diffusion (also referred to as role confusion). According to Erikson, the developmental stage of adolescence is built upon first, significant physiological changes (e.g., puberty and sexual maturation), which extends to a consolidation of social roles. Many adolescents are preoccupied and focused on the development of their own role within a social context and societal expectations. The effort to consolidate roles into identity is a gradual process of taking on multiple positions in order to find the most suitable and effective one that "fits." Erikson referred to this as the "psychological moratorium," or the frequent taking on of different roles until the suitable or final one is chosen. At the other end of the spectrum, identity diffusion refers to the difficulty in adopting or maintaining a role that is taken on perhaps unwillingly and potentially does not fit, one assigned by others (e.g., parents and/or society), and the expectation to fill out the assigned role effectively. Adolescents may respond to such societal or parental demands with varying levels of opposition, including refusal, negative moods, escaping by not being available to meet expectations, or adopting a delinquent response (e.g., breaking rules, violating social norms, and criminal behavior). This response does fit within what has been generally demonstrated by adolescents in their potential for negative behavior within society.

Much of the current work on understanding adolescents and development has been confirmatory in terms of evidence to support the known experience of teenagers struggling to develop identity and autonomy as they move toward adulthood. Given the nature of adolescent behavior and the potential for harm (e.g., impulsive behavior), there has been strong interest in understanding these behaviors and developing potential ways to manage and ultimately prevent them. Multiple family therapy and psychology researchers in the field have attempted to map the experiences of adolescents and families in the complex family system from different theoretical positions. These researchers include Betty Carter and Monica McGoldrick, who wrote on the family life cycle; Murray Bowen, who developed a systems theory of the family; John Bowlby, originator of attachment theory; and Albert Bandura, who developed social learning theory.

Theories of Family Development and Family Systems

A systems perspective on adolescent–parent relations is necessary to understand what influences the adolescent and parent relationship dynamics and conflict. Generally, family development theories focus on the continual adjustments families must make in response to transitions, which can include the addition of new members (birth), family members leaving (death), and life events that are expected (e.g., graduation, marriage, obtaining employment) or unexpected (e.g., accidents, trauma, disasters). Family systems theories (FSTs) focus primarily on the hierarchy of the family (parents, adolescents, children) and boundaries between all members in multiple contexts. The focus on adolescents in the context of the family primarily deals with the continual renegotiation of family boundaries as the adolescent develops into a mature adult. There are other background influences on adolescent–parent relations that may contribute to conflict. Adolescents are working to develop independence and form identity at the very time that parents may be managing their own aging parents while also consolidating their own careers.

Brain Development and Changes

Given the changes in technology and the insights developed from neuroimaging with adolescents, research by psychiatrist Jay Giedd and others over the past decade in brain imaging have assisted in understanding the reasons adolescents engage in different and risky behaviors. Giedd's research has demonstrated that there are distinct differences between the adolescent brain and a younger child's brain (e.g., that of an 8-year-old) and between the adolescent brain and the adult brain. The adolescent brain is still in a developmental phase of organizing and managing the development of the frontal lobe. This area of the brain is tasked with judging, organizing, planning, and "thinking about thinking," a set of mental processes and skills referred to as executive functioning. This area of the brain is not completely developed in adolescence, which can lead adolescents to struggle to follow regular expectations from parents and adults. While adolescents can do more complex tasks than a younger child, there are behaviors in which they engage that can be considered impulsive or at times dangerous. Yet adolescents can also be capable of responsible, organized, and effective behavior (e.g., attending school, completing assignments, driving, obtaining and maintaining employment, engaging in dialogue regarding substantive topics). Experiencing an adolescent's behavior is often confusing, given the distance between responsible and adult-like behavior, and strong emotional responses and unreasonable behavior.

Development Creates Conflict

The development of identity naturally leads to the potential opposition to parental rules and expectations. There is often a range of resistance between the adolescent and parent that may include many areas of conflict (e.g., values related to education, responsibility, friendship, religion, and additional areas of focus). Conflict between parents and adolescents is on a continuum, and it may range from significant and ongoing conflict to moderate or mild conflict. Even in families who are relatively healthy in their interactions and family structure, there is a period of difficulty in parents working to maintain a degree of authority while granting the adolescent some freedom to negotiate newly developed independent behavior involved in school, work, unsupervised friendships, and other relationships.

Adolescence and the Peer Group

As adolescents mature into teenage life, they begin to take more interest in and pay more attention to their peer relationships. They maintain relationships with members of their family of origin while investing in the peer group. Adolescents are moving back and forth between their family and the demands and expectations of their peer network of friendships. However, it's important to note that this peer friendship network is more powerful during adolescence than at any other time in one's life. In other words, teenagers choose the people with whom they will relate and do so independently. This is in contrast to their family of origin, which is selected for them. This process of selecting friends and important peers is considered an essential developmental task for adolescents in order to facilitate their eventual separation from their family. This task may be one of the most important tasks for a person in order to effectively separate and become an independent, healthy adult.

Parenting

Parenting Changes in Adolescence

As adolescents develop and change, so do the demands of parenting. Prior to adolescence, children have developmental goals that include the building blocks for developing identity; however, children are often hard at work accomplishing other tasks that include language development, memory development, conceptual reasoning, problem-solving and planning, and academic skills. As children reach adolescence, they begin to develop the capacity to see that there can be multiple realities in life, and they have some freedom to think more conceptually and abstractly and form personal opinions about those realities. Further, teenagers can begin to see their parents in a different light: from the simple identity of *parent* to *a person in the world* in addition to the parenting role. Adolescents are understandably critical of parents as people, given that they have changed in their potential to assess parents' behavior. This can lead to adolescents refusing to comply with their parents' demands, even when as children they typically complied. For many parents, this change can seem rapid, and they are unprepared for such a monumental change in the relationship.

Parental Tasks in Adolescence

Parents are tasked with helping assist teenagers in forming a healthy identity, which leads to the necessity of allowing for questions, difference, and challenges to parental authority and expectation. Parents need to maintain authority; however, this authority is managed through a careful observation of the adolescent developmental needs for information that they previously did not require. In other words, teenagers require explanation and rationale in order to support their understanding of decision-making and the resulting consequences. It's not enough to be told to refrain from a specific activity (e.g., "Don't touch the stove"); instead, the parents' reasons for affirming or declining requests and details of the potential outcomes of the adolescent's behavior are required. It is not uncommon for adolescents to seek out experiences and risks, given the developmental need to understand. Learning occurs on a more experiential basis, and the trust and belief in parents' superior knowledge that a younger child might have is replaced by a demand to know for themselves. Parents' goals in this type of situation may include assisting adolescents in better understanding the risks and benefits of their behavioral choices and advising them on a potentially effective course of action. In this way, parents serve as allies for their teenagers rather than serving to control their behavior overtly.

Parenting Styles and Adolescence

Research by Diana Baumrind and others has led to the classification of parenting styles into four different styles. These styles apply to the adolescent developmental stage and have distinct effects on the success of an adolescent's efforts to move to adulthood. The styles are (1) authoritarian, (2) authoritative, (3) permissive, and (4) rejecting–neglecting.

Authoritarian Parenting

The authoritarian position demonstrates a high demand for the adolescent to achieve and solve problems while offering low warmth or support from the parents. In an adolescent context, this can serve to create the potential for both cooperation and significant conflict. An authoritarian parent may expect and allow an adolescent to make multiple decisions on his or her own and have respect for the teenager's ability to do so—that is, there is harmony between adolescent and parent. However, given the tendency for an authoritarian parent to demonstrate coercive control by demanding obedience to the parent's position, there is also high potential for conflict and adolescent opposition.

Generally, a teenager's experiential learning pattern (e.g., "I need to do it myself") presents a different way of making decisions or solving problems. As long as there is agreement on the goals and likely the methods to achieve those goals, conflict is at a minimum. However, in adolescence, this agreement may often be unlikely to occur on a consistent basis. If the conflict between adolescent and parent is consistent and ongoing, due to coercive control and adolescent opposition, additional behavioral problems can result, including behavioral disorders (e.g., oppositional defiant disorder [ODD], depression and anxiety disorders, and substance abuse). Further difficulties in adulthood can be characterized by a general opposition to authority and structured direction given by others, depending upon the ongoing parent–adolescent conflict dynamics.

Authoritative Parenting

The authoritative parenting style is characterized by high demand from adolescents and high warmth or support from the parent for achieving goals and problem-solving. This style of parenting is well suited to adolescents in that it offers the potential for having limits the parent creates (e.g., rules and expectations) through confrontive control (i.e., asserting control dependent upon goals) while also allowing space for the adolescent to make decisions and create his or her own path to solving problems.

Permissive Parenting

The permissive style of parenting is characterized by low demand for adolescent behavior and high warmth from the parents. This has the potential for significant limiting in the adolescent's ability to make effective decisions and tolerate the demands others and their environment place on them. If the adolescent's developmental tasks include learning to make decisions in a more effective manner, there is balance between those decisions and the family's view of those behaviors. In the permissive parenting style, parents may offer rewards for behaviors that generally may be considered either ineffective or contrary to society's expectations. This does not adequately prepare adolescents for the world's demands and boundaries they may encounter in adulthood.

Rejecting–Neglecting Parenting

The rejecting–neglecting style is characterized by low demand for the adolescent's behavior and problem-solving and low warmth from parents. This style is the least effective of all parenting approaches. Adolescents are left to fend for themselves in managing problems that occur and in resolving crises or issues they may face. The potential for harm here is quite high in that there is little supervision or direction; teenagers have the opportunity to engage in multiple behaviors that may have high potential for consequence (e.g., sex, substance abuse, violence). Further problems that may occur in adulthood can include difficulty in forming and maintaining relationships (i.e., intimacy), potential for substance abuse, and legal problems.

David M. Savinsky

See also Active Parenting; Adolescent Behavior Disorders; Adoptive Families; Authoritative Parenting; Behavioral Family Therapy; Child Behavior Problems; DSM and V-Codes; Family of Origin; Parent–Child Communication; Stages of Family Therapy

Further Readings

Bandura, A. (1977). *Social learning theory.* New York, NY: General Learning Press.

Baumrind, D. (1991). The influence of parenting style on adolescent competence and substance abuse. *The Journal of Early Adolescence, 11,* 56–95.

Bowen, M. (1978). *Family therapy in clinical practice.* Lanham, MD: Rowman & Littlefield.

Bowlby, J. (1969). *Attachment and loss.* New York, NY: Basic Books.

Carter, E. A., & McGoldrick, M. (1989). *The changing family life cycle: A framework for family therapy.* New York, NY: Gardner Press.

Erikson, E. (1959). *Identity and the life cycle.* New York, NY: W. W. Norton.

Giedd, J. N. (2008). The teen brain: Insights from neuroimaging. *Journal of Adolescent Health, 42,* 335–343.

Giedd, J. N., Blumenthal, J., Jeffries, N. O., Castellanos, F. X., Liu, H., Zijdenbos, A., . . . Rapoport, J. L. (1999). Brain development during childhood and adolescence: A longitudinal MRI study. *Nature Neuroscience, 2,* 861–862.

Taffel, R. (2001). *The second family: How adolescent power is challenging the American family.* New York, NY: St. Martin's Press.

Taffel, R. (2009). *Childhood unbound: Saving our kids' best selves—Confident parenting in a world of change.* New York, NY: Free Press.

Wolf, A. E. (2002). *Get out of my life, but first could you drive me and Cheryl to the mall: A parent's guide to the new teenager.* New York, NY: Farrar, Straus and Giroux.

Parental Acceptance–Rejection Theory

Parents' interactions with their children have long-lasting consequences for individuals, including psychological development. Although many hypotheses about the role of parents in the healthy development of their children exist, parental acceptance–rejection theory (PARTheory) provides a comprehensive conceptualization of the influence of parental acceptance and rejection on children. Accepting parents are defined as those who demonstrate physical and verbal behaviors that make their children feel loved. Rejecting parents display hostile or neglectful behaviors toward their children, which prevent their children from feeling accepted and loved.

PARTheory is a theory of socialization that attempts to explain the causes of parental rejection and acceptance of their children and consequences for children as a result of parental acceptance or rejection. It provides insight into the psychological, environmental, and coping mechanisms present in parents' life prior to acceptance or rejection and the reasons why some children are more resilient than others when faced with parental rejection. More recently, the theory has been discussed as interpersonal acceptance–rejection theory (IPARTheory) to reflect a move away from focusing on parental acceptance and rejection to looking at acceptance and rejection in all important types of interpersonal relationships. This entry focuses on the parental acceptance–rejection aspect of the theory and looks at how the three subtheories explain the process and effects of parental acceptance and rejection. A description of how *acceptance* and *rejection* are conceptualized by this theory, or the warmth dimension of parenting, is presented first in order for the reader to understand how these terms are conceptualized.

Warmth Dimension of Parenting

The actual actions of acceptance or rejection are what make the warmth dimension of parenting. Accepting parents are defined by PARTheory as those who show their love or affection toward children physically, verbally, or both, resulting in the children feeling loved and accepted. Some examples of affection are hugging, kissing, and saying pleasant things about and to one's child, including compliments or praises. Rejecting parents are those who dislike, disapprove of, and/or resent their children. Rejection is shown in two different ways: (1) parental hostility and aggression and (2) parental indifference and/or neglect. While hostility and indifference are internal and psychological processes and feelings, aggression and neglect are external behaviors. Hostile parents are likely to be aggressive toward their children, and indifferent parents are likely to be neglectful of their children. However, parents can be both aggressive and neglectful at the same time. It is important to state that these terms are conceptualized at a physical and emotional level. For example, parents might be neglectful by refusing to bathe and feed their child but also by refusing to dedicate time to provide emotional support. Furthermore, the term *parental* refers to any person who is the main caregiver of the child and not necessarily always the biological or adoptive parent.

Acceptance and rejection constitute a continuous process—that is, children experience more or less love and affection by parents at different points of their development. Rather than classifying a parent as completely rejecting or accepting, the warmth dimension of parenting highlights a continuum process where acceptance and rejection are at opposite ends. Therefore, the quality of the bond between parent and child could vary at any given point of the parent–child relationship. In addition, parental acceptance or rejection is viewed from two different perspectives: (1) by the child (the phenomenological perspective) and/or (2) an outsider (the behavioral perspective). However, PARTheory suggests that whenever conflicting information is presented by both of these perspectives, one should trust the information provided by the phenomenological perspective. While an outsider could perceive the child to be well taken care of and loved by the parent (evidence of an accepting parent), the child might feel rejected. Therefore, according to PARTheory, parental acceptance or rejection is not a specific set of actions by parents but a belief held by the child, who is the one who experiences acceptance or rejection.

Although studies have shown that aspects of acceptance and rejection are found across cultures, the way these behaviors are manifested varies from one culture to another. For example, in Bengali culture a significant form of praise for a mother to give her daughter is to offer her a peeled and seeded orange. With this said, a cautionary note in PARTheory is that acceptance and rejection have different meanings across cultures. Therefore, one must thoroughly understand the culture and understand the child's perspective as accepted or rejected before labeling a parent's actions either way.

Besides looking at the phenomenological and behavioral aspects of acceptance and rejection, PARTheory is subdivided into three subtheories: (1) personality, (2) coping, and (3) sociocultural. The personality subtheory seeks to explore these essential questions: Do children everywhere—regardless of culture, ethnic and racial background, and gender—need parental love and affection? Do all children respond psychologically in a similar way to parental rejection and acceptance? The coping subtheory tries to explore this question: Why and how are some children and adults who have been rejected able to develop resilience? Finally, the sociocultural subtheory attempts to explore the reasons why some parents are warm and loving while others are distant, aggressive, and neglecting.

Personality Subtheory

The personality subtheory seeks to explain how children respond psychologically to acceptance and rejection. An important part of this subtheory is the *significant other*, or any person with whom the child has an emotional relationship, such as a parent, friend, or partner. However, parents are a different, and arguably a more important, type of significant other. That is, parents are primary attachment figures who provide emotional security and comfort. Such comfort and emotional security have immediate and long-lasting consequences for children and adolescents. Consistent with attachment theory, PARTheory defines an attachment figure as the secure base for the child, or the person who allows the child to explore and understand the world and is also available when the child needs love and support. Considering the influence from attachment theory in PARTheory, the term *personality* is conceptualized by this theory as the individual's stable set of predispositions to respond and actual modes of responding to various life situations and in various contexts. With this said, although predispositions and behavior are both externally and internally motivated, parental acceptance and rejection are powerful motivators of behavior in a child that influence how the child responds emotionally and behaviorally to different situations.

PARTheory posits that when children perceive they are unloved by their parents, they are likely to feel unworthy and inadequate as well as think less of themselves. These feelings create a negative global perception of how children see themselves and others, or what is referred to in PARTheory as *mental representations*. In other words, rejected children have a negative view of the world. Mental representations develop from past experiences, or the child's perception of acceptance or rejection, and influence the child's future experiences. Once mental representations have been created, individuals seek or avoid certain people and behaviors to help them operate under the mental representations they have created. Furthermore, research shows that the higher the form, frequency, severity, and duration of parental rejecting experiences, the greater the mental health issues.

Coping Subtheory

The coping subtheory attempts to explore how some rejected individuals are able to be resilient to the mental health consequence of rejection while others suffer long-lasting consequences. It is important to note that this is the least developed subtheory of PARTheory, as it is challenging to measure the process by which individuals are able to thrive under challenging circumstances. However, we know that the context where the individual is found is important to understanding coping among rejected individuals. Specifically, there are three elements that provide insight to the process of coping: (1) self, (2) other, and (3) context.

The self characteristics refer to the individuals' mental interpretation of their situation and other biological and personality characteristics. The other characteristics include how frequent and severe is the rejection from the parent and how the child interprets, internalizes, and reacts to rejecting behaviors. Additionally, context characteristics include significant others (besides the rejecting parental figure) in the life of the child and the environment where the child is placed. For example, a child whose mother is rejecting but has supportive and caring grandparents is able to create resilience more easily than a child with a rejecting parent and no contact with adults who are caring and supportive. Moreover, PARTheory posits that children who are able to differentiate themselves from the rejecting parent and be self-determined are able to cope better with rejection. That is, differentiated individuals perceive that they have control over what happens to them and are, therefore, able to use internal psychological resources to cope with rejection from parents.

It is important to point out that not every person copes the same way. PARTheory makes a distinction between affective and instrumental copers, or the difference between mentally healthy and unhealthy copers. Affective or healthy copers are individuals who, despite being exposed to rejection, are able to emotionally function well. For example, affective copers are able to form healthy emotional relationships with others. On the other hand, instrumental or unhealthy copers are able to function well when performing day-to-day tasks, such as holding a job or doing well in school, but are unable to form healthy emotional connections with others. For example, the person might form insecure attachment styles in other relationships.

Affective copers do not perform emotionally as well as individuals who come from accepting families. In other words, affective copers do better than instrumental coopers when coming from rejecting families but not as well as individuals with accepting parents. Also, PARTheory posits that as individuals transition from childhood to adulthood they have the opportunity to engage in positive experiences in order to offset the consequences of parental rejection. Therefore, individuals who come from rejecting families have the chance to experience healthy and accepting relationships and be able to form emotionally and psychologically healthy relationships with others.

Sociocultural Subtheory

As described earlier, the sociocultural subtheory attempts to explore the reasons why some parents are warm and loving while others are distant, aggressive, and neglecting. Parental acceptance or rejection takes place in a complex ecological context that includes societal institutions, family structure, economic situations, communities, and political organizations, among other institutions. Therefore, PARTheory posits that acceptance and rejection do not "just" happen; instead, antecedents are present that influence a parent's reaction. Furthermore, this subtheory goes a step further from the personality subtheory and explains that children are affected not only by their interactions and experiences with their parents but also by experiences within the different environments where they exist, the larger society, and *institutionalized expressive systems*. Institutionalized expressive systems refer to a person's internal symbolic psychological states formed over time within a specific society. Examples of institutionalized expressive systems are religious traditions and one's perception of gender socialization. It is important to note that expressive systems change, although slowly, as societal beliefs and behaviors change over time. To this end, PARTheory posits that the sociocultural subtheory strives to predict societal causes that lead parents to act in an accepting or rejecting manner. For example, research across cultures shows that in cultures where supernatural entities, such as God, are seen as negative forces, hostile, and destructive, parents act in a more rejecting manner toward their children.

Roberto L. Abreu

See also Attachment; Attachment Theory; Child-Centered Parenting; Ecological Systems; Parent–Adolescent Relations; Parenting; Parenting Education; Parenting Styles

Further Readings

Rohner, R. P. (1980). Worldwide tests of parental acceptance-rejection theory: An overview. *Behavior Science Research*, 15, 1–21.

Rohner, R. P. (1986). *The warmth dimension: Foundations of parental acceptance-rejection theory*. Beverly Hills, CA: Sage.

Rohner, R. P. (1999). Acceptance and rejection. In D. Levinson, J. Ponzetti, & P. Jorgensen (Eds.), *Encyclopedia of human emotions* (pp. 6–14). New York, NY: Macmillan Reference.

Rohner, R. P. (2004). The parental "acceptance-rejection syndrome": Universal correlates of perceived rejection. *American Psychologist*, 59, 830–840.

Rohner, R. P. (2005). Parental acceptance-rejection questionnaire (PARQ): Test manual. In R. P. Rohner & A. Khaleque (Eds.), *Handbook for the study of parental acceptance and rejection* (4th ed., pp. 43–106). Storrs, CT: Rohner Research Publications.

Rohner, R. P. (2014, September 3). *PARTheory gets a new name. Center for the Study of Parental Acceptance and Rejection*. Retrieved from http://csiar.uconn.edu/2014/09/03/partheory-gets-a-new-name

Rohner, R. P., & Khaleque, A. (2010). Testing central postulates of parental acceptance-rejection theory (PARTheory): A meta-analysis of cross-cultural studies. *Journal of Family Theory and Review*, 3, 73–87. doi:10.1111/j.1756-2589.2010.00040.x

Rohner, R. P., Khaleque, A., & Cournoyer, D. E. (2005). Parental acceptance-rejection: Theory, methods, cross-cultural evidence, and implications. *Ethos*, 33, 299–334. doi:10.1525/eth.2005.33.3.299

Parental Alienation Syndrome

Parental alienation syndrome (PAS) involves the deliberate strategies of one parent in a high-conflict divorce or child custody dispute to manipulate his or her children in such a way that they become separated and detached from the other parent in a predictably harmful fashion. It is estimated that hundreds of thousands of children and their families are affected by parental alienation in the United States and abroad. Some mental health and legal professionals believe it warranted inclusion as a distinct disorder in the *Diagnostic and Statistical Manual of Mental Disorders* (DSM) based on its prevalence and numerous harmful psychological effects on individuals, in particular children of divorce, and families. Others argue that although forms of "parental alienation" exist, referring to this systemic issue as a "syndrome" is a misnomer, claiming that PAS may then be used as a strategy in the courtroom to assist one parent in prevailing in child custody cases. Despite the controversy, the influence of PAS on children, parents, and families as well as the mental health and legal professions over the past 40 years is undeniable. This entry reviews the major premises of PAS, PAS research, PAS and the fifth edition of the *Diagnostic and Statistical Manual of Mental Disorders* (DSM-5), the surrounding controversy, the potentially damaging and lasting effects of PAS, and various suggested therapeutic and legal interventions. The role of the mental health professional in recognizing and treating parental alienation behaviors is also included.

Parental Alienation and Parental Alienation Syndrome Defined

Parental alienation is a general term that describes a child's unhealthy coalition with one parent while the child simultaneously rejects a relationship with the other parent without just cause. PAS, on the other hand, is a multifaceted condition frequently cited in mental health and legal literature in reference to a form of child abuse that can be present in high-conflict divorce and custody-related situations. The parent with whom a child has a coalition is referred to as the alienating parent. More recently, some researchers have begun to use the term *preferred parent* as opposed to the more negative or biased term *alienating parent*. This change may help professionals focus on the various forms of abuse and alienation that may occur and the inherent damages that may be caused to the child, parents, and family system as a result of the behavior.

While the behaviors associated with parental alienation have long existed, child psychiatrist Richard A. Gardner formally introduced parental alienation as a "syndrome" in the 1980s based on the earlier works of Wilhelm Reich in the 1940s and other researchers in the 1970s. According to Gardner, PAS involves the gradual and systematic destruction of the bond between a parent and one or more children by the other parent that causes varying degrees of harm to the child or children, the targeted parent (TP), and the family system as a whole. It is often present in high-conflict divorce-related child custody disputes within which the alienating parent attempts to harm the TP vicariously through the exploitation of one or more children in a custody dispute. As such, the foremost victim in such a situation is the child of PAS as he or she is actively enlisted in a carefully orchestrated ruination of his or her parent–child bond with the TP.

Through extensive research, Gardner identified a cluster of eight symptoms commonly demonstrated by children subjected to varying levels of PAS. These proposed symptoms on behalf of the indoctrinated child include (1) a campaign of denigration against the TP; (2) weak, bizarre, or unexplainable rationalizations for the deprecating behaviors engaged in by the child; (3) a binary view of the parents, wherein the child describes one parent as nearly flawless and the other parent in a very negative light; (4) an "independent thinker" phenomenon within which it is claimed that the rejections of the TP originate solely from the child and must therefore be believed and respected; (5) reflexive and unwavering support of the alienating parent; (6) a lack of empathy, guilt, or remorse with regard to the cruelty and exploitation projected onto the TP; (7) the presence of coached or mimicked derogatory phrases or litanies (usually originating from the alienating parent), which are designed to assault the character of the TP; and (8) spreading animosity, originally focused upon the TP, to friends and extended family of the TP.

Gardner and other professionals consider such behaviors to occur on a continuum of severity requiring varying interventions on behalf of mental health professionals. Further, they emphasize that for PAS to be considered, these alienating behaviors must occur in the absence of actual child abuse and/or neglect perpetrated by the TP upon the child, in which case estrangement may be expected. Additionally, normal developmental issues, such as an adolescent preferring to spend more time socializing with peers as opposed to his or her parents, should be considered as such and not automatically attributed to PAS.

Many mental health professionals consider this alienating behavior a subtle-but-extreme form of child abuse that is as much a legal issue as it is a mental health issue faced by therapists and their clients. Further, parental alienation is often found in families where domestic violence occurs, and the severity of both parental alienation and domestic violence tends to increase when separation or divorce ensues. As such, mental health professionals must recognize the various forms of abuse, including parental alienation, and thoroughly understand the cycle of domestic violence in order to effectively intervene. Understanding the cycle of power and control and the dynamics involved in such high-conflict family systems helps mental health professionals to more effectively mitigate damage and prevent future harm.

Research and Parental Alienation Syndrome

In recent years, many researchers have examined parental alienation and its effects on the family, in particular on the children and parents. Many of these studies have supported previous findings that parental alienation occurs frequently in high-conflict divorces and custody situations and damages all involved. Some parents and children suffer much more than others, depending upon the mental health status of the individual family members and the extent and severity of the alienation and abuse.

Researchers have developed various assessment methodologies to better identify and more accurately gauge the severity of past and present parental alienation and its immediate and enduring effects on children, parents, and the parent–child relationship. Over the past few decades, hundreds of published professional journal articles and several doctoral theses from around the world have examined parental alienation and its harmful effects. In 2010, William Bernet and colleagues published what perhaps is the most comprehensive bibliography on PAS, containing 630 references directly related to PAS and parental alienation.

Parental Alienation Syndrome and DSM-5

Parental alienation has never been included among the disorders listed by the American Psychiatric Association (APA) in the *Diagnostic and Statistical Manual of Mental Disorders* (DSM). PAS as a diagnostic category was submitted to the DSM-5 Child and Adolescent Disorders Work Group by a committee of invited mental health and legal professionals well-versed in the topic of parental alienation. The work group members concluded that the proposal lacked sufficient valid and reliable data to support the inclusion of PAS in the DSM-5 as a distinct disorder but noted that additional valid and reliable research findings presented by the committee to the work group in the future would be considered. Ultimately, a briefing packet published by the APA in 2013 indicated that PAS was one of four possible disorders considered but not accepted for final inclusion in the fifth edition of the DSM (i.e., the DSM-5, published in 2013).

The DSM-5 does, however, contain other sections that address many of the hallmarks of PAS. The first example is the diagnosis of parent–child relational problem, wherein hostility toward and scapegoating of one parent over the other leads to feelings of estrangement toward the TP. Second, a diagnosis of child psychological abuse, which addresses how intentional verbal or symbolic acts by one parent of a child hold reasonable potential to cause significant psychological harm to the child, may apply. Third, a diagnosis of child affected by parental relationship distress may be warranted. These conditions listed under the DSM-5 section Other Conditions That May Be a Focus of Clinical Attention all relate to the deleterious effects of PAS. Additionally, several categories mentioned in this section of the DSM-5 under the subheading Other Problems Related to Primary Support Group may apply. If working with the child alone as opposed to any subsystem within the family, other possible DSM-5 diagnoses may apply such as separation anxiety disorder or reactive attachment disorder.

Controversy Over Parental Alienation Syndrome

Critics dispute the validity of PAS primarily by pointing to what they believe is a lack of substantial and reliable research to support its existence. The evidentiary admissibility of PAS testimony in courts has also been called into question since Gardner first described the phenomenon as a formal syndrome in the 1980s.

The concept of PAS is still questioned by some mental health and legal professionals. In the past, much of the focus was on allegations of sexual abuse made by one parent against the other in order to have an "upper hand" in custody disputes. In rare instances, false claims of abuse are made by children. This can occur as a result of moderate or severe parental alienation. Such claims, regardless of their veracity, are clearly indicative of a family problem. In such a situation, either the child has been directed by a parent or another family member to make such a false claim, or the child is emotionally disturbed and in need of immediate mental health care. Regardless, reports of abuse by children should never be casually dismissed by mental health professionals, attorneys, judges, or child protection workers. Morally, ethically, and legally, all reports of suspected abuse and neglect must be properly, impartially, and thoroughly investigated. Further, all parties involved in such systems must be fully evaluated for appropriate legal decisions to be made and mental health interventions implemented as warranted. Shifting to a more objective view and having a more informed understanding of the concept of and dynamics involved in parental alienation should allow trained mental health and legal professionals to effectively advocate for their clients.

Therapeutic and Legal Interventions

Early and direct intervention is usually considered the best way to lessen, if not prevent, the damage caused by parental alienation and support the development of positive relationships between the child and both parents. Intervening on a case-by-case basis rather than applying a one-size-fits-all treatment approach is also recommended. Therapeutic remedies suggested often include, but are not limited to, the following: individual counseling for the child and each parent, individual and/or group counseling with other children of divorce for the child, play therapy, and psychoeducational groups on topics such as effective parenting practices and coping with divorce. However, in the case of severe alienation in which children may demonstrate behaviors and emotions consistent with a delusional disorder, traditional talk therapy may not be effective and could result in additional harm.

Legal interventions in cases of PAS may involve changes in custody and visitation arrangements (in the most extreme cases of alienation, a complete reversal or modification of full custody), modified or shared custody, and/or supervised visitation involving child protective services. Not allowing expert witness testimony on PAS but instead allowing the courts to focus on the alienation and abuse that may be occurring has also been suggested as a possible intervening variable. Doing so may help eliminate many of the controversies related to PAS and may allow for a more appropriate and dedicated focus on the child's welfare.

Regardless of the therapeutic and legal interventions implemented, PAS experts have recommended that mental health professionals, attorneys, and family court judges receive specialized training and continuing education to better identify and prevent child abuse in all of its forms, both subtle and direct, as well as to understand the short- and long-term effects of PAS on the children involved. High-quality education, training, knowledge, and practical experience ideally should result in adults working together to more fully protect children's best interests and their current and future well-being.

*Kimberly A. Donovan
and Daniel J. Weigel*

See also Best Interests of the Child; Child Maltreatment; Couple and Family Forensics; Custody Evaluations; Relational Diagnoses

Further Readings

American Association for Marriage and Family Therapy. (2012). *AAMFT code of ethics*. Alexandria, VA: Author.

American Counseling Association. (2014). *ACA code of ethics*. Alexandria, VA: Author.

American Psychiatric Association. (2013). *Diagnostic and statistical manual of mental disorders* (5th ed.). Washington, DC: Author.

American Psychological Association. (2010). *Ethical principles of psychologists and code of conduct*. Washington, DC: Author.

Baker, A. J. L. (2007). *Adult children of parental alienation syndrome: Breaking the ties that bind*. New York, NY: W. W. Norton.

Baker, A. J. L., & Fine, P. R. (2014). *Co-parenting with a toxic ex: What to do when your ex-spouse tries to turn the kids against you*. Oakland, CA: New Harbinger Publications.

Baker, A. J. L., & Fine, P. R. (2014). *Surviving parental alienation: A journey of hope and healing.* Lanham, MD: Rowman & Littlefield.

Bernet, W., Von Boch-Galhau, W., Baker, A. J. L., & Morrison, S. L. (2010). Parental alienation, DSM-5, and ICD-11. *The American Journal of Family Therapy, 38,* 76–187. doi:10.1080/01926180903586583

Lorandos, D., Bernet, W., & Sauber, S. R. (Eds.). (2013). *Parental alienation: The handbook for mental health and legal professionals.* Springfield, IL: Charles C Thomas.

National Association of Social Workers. (2008). *Code of ethics of the National Association of Social Workers.* Washington, DC: Author.

Nichols, A. M. (2013). Toward a child-centered approach to evaluating claims of alienation in high-conflict custody disputes. *Michigan Law Review, 112*(4), 663–688. doi:10.2307/1289212

Wheeler, A. M., & Bertram, B. (2015). *The counselor and the law: A guide to legal and ethical practice* (7th ed.). Alexandria, VA: American Counseling Association.

Parental Stress: Effects on Children

Parental stress is defined as a function of demands perceived by a parent and the parent's ability to respond to such demands. Parental stress is often influenced by mental health, medical conditions, financial and occupational status, marital relationships, cultural values, and child temperament and developmental stages. The ways in which parents manage stressful situations have major implications for their own psychological and physical well-being, their relationship with their children, and their children's ability to cope with stress. Parental stress is related to increased internalizing and externalizing symptoms in children. *Internalizing symptoms* are defined as internally directed emotions such as depression, social isolation, or anxiety. *Externalizing symptoms* are defined as externally directed emotions such as aggression. Parental stress commonly impacts children in the development of separation anxiety, depression, personality disorders, substance abuse, oppositional behavior, and attention problems. This entry presents a synopsis of parenting styles and the influence of parental stress, parent symptomatology, financial and occupational stress, marital stress, the role of culture and gender on parental stress, medical stress, child development and parental stress, and implications for clinical practice.

Parenting Styles and the Influence of Parental Stress

In her theory of parenting styles, Diana Baumrind identified four primary approaches to parenting: (1) authoritative, (2) authoritarian, (3) permissive, and (4) rejecting–neglecting. Authoritative parenting can be defined as a collaborative parenting style in which child autonomy is valued and limits are enforced with reasons that are explained and discussed. Authoritarian parenting is characterized by a restrictive parenting style valuing obedience and employing strong forms of punishment with little or no discussion. Permissive parenting can be described as a relaxed parenting style that sets very few limits and encourages children to control their own behavior and decision-making. Rejecting–neglecting parenting is understood as an uninvolved parenting style detached from emotional closeness in which the child's environment is devoid of enriching stimuli.

Research has shown that parenting styles play a significant role in child outcomes. Authoritative parenting has been linked to children's being more adaptable to changing circumstances, demonstrating more developed social skills and a greater sense of belonging in their peer group, displaying lower levels of aggression, having higher self-esteem and self-regulation, and achieving a higher level of competence. Children of permissive parents often display greater levels of impulsive behaviors, lower cognitive abilities, and more aggressive behavior. Authoritarian parents may often have children who display lower levels of self-esteem and are irritable or anxious. They may either rebel against authority or conform to authority but demonstrate poor self-regulation when not observed. They may demonstrate poor social skills and be more vulnerable to bullying. Rejecting–neglecting parenting has been associated with children who are more impulsive and demonstrate greater levels of aggression, depression, and low self-esteem.

The parenting style adopted by parents is often associated with their level of parental stress. Parental stress has been associated with authoritarian parenting, less responsive parenting, less consistent and warm parenting, and increased risk for engaging in child maltreatment.

Parent Symptomatology

Parents who are diagnosed with mental illness often experience greater levels of stress that impact not only the parent but also the parent–child relationship and the child's ability to cope with stress. Parent symptomatology has been associated with a stressful parent–child relationship, insecure attachment, abuse, neglect, or rejection. These experiences are risk factors for children that may lead to the development of pathology. These effects are consistent regardless of child age, gender, or ethnicity. Patterns of child maltreatment are often transgenerational. Many mothers who reported maltreatment in their own childhood were less sensitive to their children's needs. Parental stress mediates this relationship such that mothers who were abused in childhood are less likely to repeat this pattern of abuse with their own children when they experience lower levels of parental stress.

Parent pathology impacts children differentially, based on clinical presentation. Parents who are depressed may be less responsive and warm toward children. They may be critical of their children and emotionally insensitive. They may be less effective in enforcing disciplinary practices and attending to their child's needs. They also tend to have fewer positive interactions with their children. Anxious parents may display greater levels of overwhelming worries that something bad will happen to their children, which contribute to internalizing symptoms such as anxiety and withdrawal in children and adolescents. They may display higher levels of parental stress and are at a greater risk of abusing their children.

The impact of parent pathology is influenced by the presence or absence of other risk factors—most notably financial and occupational stress. Reports of parents in abusive households indicate that they are more commonly younger, have lower educational achievement and lower income, are unemployed, and are more likely to abuse drugs and alcohol than are parents in nonabusive homes.

Financial and Occupational Stress

The relationship between psychological health and income mediates the impact parental stress has on children. The children of mothers experiencing mental illness in low-income households were more likely to develop internalizing and externalizing symptoms than those in more financially stable homes.

Parental stress surrounding negative economic events and financial cutbacks predict child internalizing and externalizing symptoms. Children often worry about finances in their family and may experience somatic symptoms such as headaches, stomachaches, and sleeplessness due to these worries. These experiences are often not attended to by parents who are also experiencing stress related to finances. Regardless of income, parents under financial stress report feeling more fatigued and irritable as well as feeling less supported and being less likely to communicate effectively and set limits.

Work-related stressors are particularly impactful for military families. The length of parental combat-related deployments has been linked to increased parental stress and child depression and anxiety. This relationship is influenced not only by parental stress but also by long periods of parental absence, which can create marital stress.

Marital Stress

In families where marital problems are present, parents are more likely to be inconsistent in their parenting style, increase use of punitive measures, decrease use of reasoning in discipline, and offer fewer rewards. In cases of divorce or separation, single mothers are at a particularly high risk of parental stress due to financial loss and loss of support in parenting. Single mothers experience greater rates of depression and anxiety as well as reportedly use more punitive measures than single fathers.

The Role of Culture and Gender on Parental Stress

Culture and gender roles may significantly impact the level of parental stress. In both Eastern and Western cultures, mothers are expected to be more nurturing while fathers are expected to have greater authority and agency. Regardless of culture, women report greater levels of parental stress. In general, parenting values in Western cultures emphasize individual autonomy, while Eastern cultures emphasize communal values.

Cultural evolution has impacted the roles parents take on and their stress level. Authoritarian parenting increases with traditional parenting beliefs, lower individualistic self-concept, increased stress, and decreased social support. In a 2010 study by Chang Su and Michaela Hynie, European Canadian mothers demonstrated fewer overall authoritarian parenting techniques than Chinese Canadian and Mainland Chinese parents; however, they also experienced lower levels of stress. Regardless of level of stress, mainland Chinese parents used fewer authoritarian discipline techniques than Chinese Canadian parents. While studies using American samples demonstrated a mediating effect of mental health problems on the relationship between parental stress and parenting practices, Taiwanese parents, in a 2014 study by Ha-Sheng Wei and Ji-Kang Chen, demonstrated a direct relationship between financial stress and parenting practices that was not mediated by mental health problems.

While parent stress, parenting practices, and child coping share many similar associations among Western and Eastern cultures, several differences emerged among African American and European American families. In a 2011 study by Cappa and colleagues, parental stress was associated with child coping deficits in African American families but not European American families. This relationship may be impacted by other risk factors present in African American families such as disparities in income and access to community resources. Regardless of ethnicity, child coping deficits have a long-term impact on parenting stress. One factor that may contribute to coping deficits is medical stress.

Medical Stress

Parents raising a child diagnosed with a chronic medical condition, such as muscular dystrophy, may experience stress in the form of social isolation because of their child's limited mobility or behavior problems, parental grief for the loss of the healthy child they had expected, financial strain from the cost of treatment, and increased caretaking responsibilities to meet the needs of the child's disability. Parental stress under these circumstances may limit a parent's capacity to support adaptive functioning in their children, therefore exacerbating internalizing and externalizing behaviors in the ill child. Research shows that mothers of boys diagnosed with muscular dystrophy report greater stress responses to the child's externalizing behaviors than due to the physical demands of the disease.

Child Development and Parental Stress

In the formative years of development, a child's brain has greater plasticity than in later life. Neural networks are still being developed and refined; therefore, parenting behaviors and parental stress have the greatest impact. A child whose parent uses a rejecting–neglecting parenting style before the age of 6 may experience too much negative contact and have a smaller brain mass, stunted emotional expression, and poor social skills. Problem behaviors that emerge in childhood are more stable and can contribute to increased parental stress. Additionally, parental stress can influence the development of problem behaviors in young children.

Parental stress may be impacted by a lack of fit between the parent's personality and the child's innate temperament, the formative building blocks of personality that are present at birth. A parent who is more socially outgoing may experience frustration with a child who is slow to warm up to people. Particular temperaments may be more challenging for parents to manage. If a child is irritable, hard to soothe, and hard to discipline, parents may respond with greater frustration or inadequate care. This may exacerbate externalizing behaviors in children.

Adolescence is a period of development that can contribute to parental stress as children begin to explore their own autonomy and develop their identity. The influence of parenting behaviors associated with parental stress at this stage may influence the adolescent's ability to solidify personality traits. Research suggests that mothers who experience greater stress when their child is in early adolescence are more likely to engage in avoidant coping behaviors, which have been linked to adolescent depression.

Implications for Clinical Practice

Given the cyclical relationship between parental stress and child coping deficits, early intervention and prevention are of primary importance. Parent training programs have demonstrated efficacy in increasing parent-and-child coping competence. As marital support is a mediator between parental stress and child maltreatment, couples therapy serves an important role in prevention. Systemic factors can mediate the relationship between parental stress and child outcomes; therefore, case management and advocacy are important interventions aiding in reducing systemic barriers, which may reduce cyclical patterns of stress and pathology.

Lauren Wetzel and Jon Carlson

See also Caregivers; Child Maltreatment; Diversity; Families and Poverty; Family Stress; Parent–Adolescent Relations; Parent–Child Communication; Stress Management

Further Readings

Abidin, R. R. (1990). *Parenting Stress Index (PSI)*. Charlottesville, VA: Pediatric Psychology Press.

Cappa, K. A., Begle, A. M., Conger, J. C., Dumas, J. E., & Conger, A. J. (2011). Bidirectional relationships between parenting stress and child coping competence: Findings from the Pace Study. *Journal of Child and Family Studies, 20*, 334–342.

Crnic, K. A., Gaze, C., & Hoffman, C. (2005). Cumulative parenting stress across the preschool period: Relations to maternal parenting and child behaviour at age 5. *Infant and Child Development, 14*(2), 117–132.

Essex, M. J., Klein, M. H., Cho, E., & Kalin, N. H. (2002). Maternal stress beginning in infancy may sensitize children to later stress exposure: Effects on cortisol and behavior. *Biological Psychiatry, 52*(8), 776–784.

Gershoff, E. T. (2002). Corporal punishment by parents and associated child behaviors and experiences: A meta-analytic and theoretical review. *Psychological Bulletin, 128*(4), 539.

Hassall, R., Rose, J., & McDonald, J. (2005). Parenting stress in mothers of children with an intellectual disability: The effects of parental cognitions in relation to child characteristics and family support. *Journal of Intellectual Disability Research, 49*(6), 405–418.

Su, C., & Hynie, M. (2011). Effects of life stress, social support, and cultural norms on parenting styles among mainland Chinese, European Canadian, and Chinese Canadian immigrant mothers. *Journal of Cross-Cultural Psychology, 42*(6), 944–962.

Wei, H., & Chen, J. (2014). The relationships between family financial stress, mental health problems, child rearing practice, and school involvement among Taiwanese parents with school-aged children. *Journal of Child and Family Studies, 23*, 1145–1154.

Weinraub, M., & Wolf, B. M. (1983). Effects of stress and social supports on mother-child interactions in single-and two-parent families. *Child Development, 54*(5), 1297–1311.

Parent–Child Communication

The word *communication* comes from Latin, meaning "to share" or "to impart." It involves spoken words and the tone used. It also includes nonverbal communication such as body language, written language, and gestures. It is through communication that people build meaning and their worldview. People use communication to share thoughts and ideas, express needs and desires, and explain intentions. Effective communication is important in families and between parents and children as a way to express feelings and needs; impart knowledge; socialize children to expectations and rules; and create a warm, responsive relationship. Although the basics of communication are the same no matter whom one is exchanging information with, there are special considerations for parent–child communication.

Children learn words and ways to communicate through interacting with their parents. Children learn to read nonverbal forms of communication and paralanguage first. They look for facial expressions that display pleasure or displeasure, pitch, and tone of their caretaker's voice as well as touch. Children respond to these forms of communication in a like manner. For example, when the caretaker smiles, the child smiles back.

Interpersonal communication is an ongoing process, and it should be the basis for parent–child communication. As children learn words, they begin to use more verbal forms of communication and look for verbal responses in return. For this reason, parents need to be able to communicate openly and effectively with their children. It is the role of the parent to establish an open communication pattern with his or her child and be responsive. It is important for parents to notice the times their child is willing to communicate and initiate the communication. To facilitate communication, parents should (a) find time each week and engage in one-on-one activity with their child; (b) learn about their child's interests; (c) be fully present and attentive; (d) use words that are at the child's level; (e) use appropriate eye contact; and (f) sit or kneel so their bodies are physically at the child's level (e.g., if speaking to a 3-year-old, kneel so the child and adult are at the same physical height). A good way to start a conversation with a child is to share something rather than ask a question.

Good communication skills will assist children for their entire lives. Communication begins with the parents. A key action for parents to take when developing open communication with their child is to stop what they are doing and listen when the child speaks about concerns or issues. Children engage in conversation at the moment the thought occurs. This happens especially with younger children (ages 3 to 7). Parents who communicate openly and effectively will most likely discover that their child will as well. Stopping to listen conveys the message that parents respect their child and his or her concerns. Parents should avoid being intrusive and interrupting even though at times it may prove difficult to listen to the child's point of view. Parents should refrain from interrupting and allow the child to complete his or her thoughts, concerns, and ideas, even when not in agreement. An important aspect of indicating parents heard and understood what their child said is to summarize the conversation.

When engaging in unpleasant conversations, one should begin with a soft approach. Making a positive statement first keeps a child from immediately tuning out angry and/or defensive tones. Parents often express their opinion and engage in lecturing rather than conversing. They should express opinions without demeaning their child, recognize that disagreement is okay, and work with the child to resolve the conflict. Teaching negotiation is useful when possible, but not all issues are negotiable. When possible, parents should help children understand the "why" of decisions and include them in the decision-making process when appropriate. Statements such as "What do you think would happen if . . . ?" "How would you feel if I did this and something happened?" and "You are so important to me. How do you think I would feel if . . . ?" include the child and let him or her know that the parent recognizes his or her feelings. This also assists in building the child's self-esteem.

Ineffective and negative communication between parents and children can lead children to believe that they are unimportant, unnoticed, or misinterpreted. When this occurs, children are less likely to approach parents for assistance with significant issues. Maintaining a positive connection with a child opens the door to developing satisfying long-term parent–child communication. This only enhances opportunities for open communication as the child grows older and confronts more complex situations and issues.

Alyssa Weiss Quittner

See also Communication in Couples and Families; Parent–Child Communication; Postmodern Therapies

Further Readings

Brown, A. M., Fitzgerald, M. M., Shipman, K., & Schneider, R. (2007). Children's expectations of parent–child communication following interparental conflict: Do parents talk to children about conflict? *Journal of Family Violence, 22*(6), 407–412.

Hughes, A. M., & Read, V. (2012). *Building positive relationships with parents of young children: A guide to effective communication.* New York, NY: Routledge.

Rosenberg, M. B. (2004). *Raising children compassionately: Parenting the nonviolent communication way (nonviolent communication guides).* Encinitas, CA: PuddleDancer Press.

Socha, T. J., & Stamp, G. H. (Eds.). (1995). *Parents, children and communication: Frontiers of theory and research.* Mahwah, NJ: Erlbaum.

PARENTIFICATION AND DIVERSE FAMILY SYSTEMS

Parentification, whereby children take on responsibilities and fulfill family roles typically assigned to adults, is a ubiquitous phenomenon that occurs in families to varying degrees with both positive and negative consequences. A multiplicity of variables may impact the emergence and maintenance of parentification. Specifically, the empirical literature has long reported on individual-level factors that may foretell parentification. With regard to system-level factors, no other variable informs the development of parentification more than the *family structure*. The historical, accumulated, and nascent literature reveals that diverse family systems engender and maintain the parentification process, roles, relationships, and its related outcomes. For example, from the early writings put forward by Salvador Minuchin and colleagues, the criticality of the family structure was proffered as an active ingredient in the development of parentification. More recently, it appears that there are other family structures and cultural contexts wherein parentification may be commonly evidenced.

In this entry, there are two aims. First, a definition of *parentification* is provided. Second, a brief description of four family systems where parentification may commonly exist is outlined: (1) lower socioeconomic status (SES) families; (2) divorced families; (3) military families, which constitute a more recent development; and (4) U.S. families for whom English is a second language.

The Construct of Parentification

Parentification has been defined as a systems construct with outcomes and processes that happen when families have disturbances in structure, roles, boundaries, power, subsystems, responsibilities, relationships, and mental and physical functioning. It is not necessary to experience disturbances or changes in *all* of these previously mentioned domains for parentification to be evidenced. When parentification does emerge, the caregiving process typically involves a functional or emotional role reversal in which the child takes on adult responsibilities that are inappropriate for his or her developmental stage and age. The instrumental-focused responsibilities may include cooking, cleaning, and caring for siblings, and emotional-focused responsibilities may include serving as family peacemaker, confidant, and a secure base and attachment figure. As Minuchin and colleagues have long asserted, typically the parents or caregivers in the family systems where parentification exists abdicate or redirect the power, responsibilities, roles, and instrumental and emotional functions to the child or children in the family system, resulting in a family structure where the children are often in a position of power rather than the parents. Finally, and importantly, Lisa M. Hooper reminds readers in her work that the clinical, theoretical, and empirical literature shows that other terms are also used to refer to parentification and its related process. Those terms include but are not limited to *family caregivers, invisible caregivers, adultification, spousification, role reversal, adultoids, little parent,* and *mature minor.*

Parentification and Lower Socioeconomic Status Families

Linda Burton described how SES (in particular, low SES families or economically disadvantaged families) may relate to, and predict, parentification in the family system. Similar to other family systems described in this chapter, low SES families or disadvantaged families increase the opportunity for parents to depend on their children for emotional and instrumental support. Low SES can and often does push children in these family systems to grow up more quickly than their counterparts in more affluent families. For example, children in these families may be called upon to engage in daily care for their siblings, contribute to the home finances, cook and clean for family members, and forgo engaging in child-appropriate activities. In other words, children are called upon to fill in the gap in family functions—typically performed by adults—because of the dearth of human and material resources in the underresourced family structure. Whether or not parents in these systems abdicate these roles and responsibilities by choice or are forced by necessity to do so, the process is the same: Children are parentified. In addition, it is likely that families who identify as poor or of low SES have other co-occurring stressors and challenges (e.g., lack of support, lack of accessibility and access to medical and mental health care, and high levels of community and interpersonal violence) that also impact the parentification process. Taken together, these conditions and experiences (low SES and other stressors) may have an additive effect, especially if they are prolonged and chronic. In order to compensate for the minimal or insufficient financial resources, parents may be forced to spend more time out of the home to generate income for the family. This effort may negatively impact their own and family members' well-being, health, and interpersonal relationships. Like the other family systems described in this entry, the process of parentification in low SES families may not always foretell negative outcomes. For example, prolonged and chronic poverty can implicate different outcomes than those evidenced when poverty is brief and temporary. Thus, the parentified child may not encounter the lifelong deleterious outcomes often documented in the clinical, theoretical, and empirical literature. Many experts agree that the parentification process can result in both benefits and burdens for children in this family system. Although parentification may be evidenced in middle- and upper-class families, a self-identified low SES and its corollaries create a family structure where parentification is significantly and routinely prevalent.

Parentification and Divorced Families

Most professionals understand that divorce changes the structure, organization, roles, and responsibilities in families. In this context, as the parent subsystem breaks down or changes, family rules, roles, and boundaries are affected, creating a context for parentification to emerge. At an individual level, the process of divorce has been shown to relate to psychological distress, depressive symptoms, and feelings of abandonment and low self-worth in family members. Another aftereffect is that children often believe they are the cause of the divorce. Consequently, children's behaviors in the divorced family system can be an attempt to overcompensate for the missing adult-specific roles, responsibilities, and relationships in the newly organized family system. Children may be directed to take on age-inappropriate roles usually reserved for the absent parent. Children may be asked to engage in adultlike responsibilities such as caring for siblings, serve in adultlike roles such as coparenting and being a part of the executive subsystem, and in some cases serve as a confidant to either parent—that is, the parent with whom they live or the parent with whom they visit. Greg Jurkovic and colleagues discussed how individuals growing up in families where divorce was experienced often engage in greater levels of emotional parentification and perceive those responsibilities to be unfair. In their work, they found children also experience greater levels of instrumental parentification but to a lesser extent than emotional parentification. In this family system, where rules, roles, responsibilities, and relationships are lost, split, or disrupted, children may be induced to fill in for the gaps in the family structure resulting in negative outcomes evidenced at individual and system levels. Some literature points to the different effects the parent's gender may have on the parentification process in divorced families. It could be that mothers may be more inclined than fathers to parentify their children. Irrespective of which parent may be involved in the parentification process, divorced families are far more likely than nondivorced families to experience parentification and deleterious outcomes. Because of the significant structural family changes, divorced family systems serve as a risk factor for parentification for many—but not all—families.

Parentification and Military Families

Some experts have suggested that military families may be the model familial and cultural system to foster parentification. Specifically, in military families, deployments require the family structure to expand and contract quickly, unexpectedly, and frequently as parents and other family members leave and return after serving in war. As a result of the deployment process, typical supports, relationships, and tasks are absent; thus, family members must clarify who will fill the roles and carry out the duties of the members who have left for war. Consequently, family members (parent and children) are called upon to redefine and reconfigure the boundaries, structure, alliances, and power in the family system each time a family member exits and enters the family. There is no doubt that the departures, prolonged absences, and expected and unexpected returns can negatively impact the family system and individual family members. Military-impacted family systems paradoxically experience the most difficult adjustments when the parent returns from deployment. The literature suggests that the ecology in which the family system is embedded also influences coping at the individual and family levels. For example, it could be that the family resides in a community that is against war or a nonmilitary community and then creates a scenario in which the family feels isolated and disconnected from the community and related resources, forcing family members to depend only on one another for all of their needs. For children, this military-impacted system becomes an ideal context for parentification to take place. As previously mentioned, this disruption is equally problematic when the parent returns. For example, during the parent's absence, family members—including children—may develop new routines; experience increased coherence among the remaining family members; and report feelings of independence, self-efficacy, and competency as they are invited or forced to take on new roles and responsibilities in the family. Even though military families experience many of the same challenges evinced in nonmilitary families, military families face unique challenges that can result in children taking on roles, responsibilities, and relationships usually reserved for adults.

Parentification and English-as-a-Second-Language Families

As some experts have described, when English is the second language of family members, a scenario may be created wherein parents rely on their children to serve in adultlike roles such as language and cultural brokers where they translate words and customs. Specifically, Jennifer Kam describes how the strain of parents not knowing the English language and/or learning the English language at slower rates than their children can engender a power differential. Thus, the children in the family can be exposed to complex interactions with family members, and age-inappropriate interactions with people who are not family members, which may be burdensome and problematic. Specifically, children may be called upon to be involved in adultlike scenarios (translating for and attending events not appropriate for children) and consequently experience a role reversal with their parents. These mediating, negotiating, and translating roles and responsibilities that are evidenced when children are called upon to serve in the role of language broker place children in a position of power; expose children to complex situations (e.g., medical, legal, and child and family protection issues); and often, but not always, emotionally and instrumentally overwhelm children. Importantly, children may not be prepared to manage and have access to these adult difficulties, transactions, and experiences. Children who are exposed to these scenarios may feel insecure, unstable, and overly distressed. Like the other family systems described in this entry, the boundaries are often blurred when children are encouraged to serve as the translator for family members (i.e., language or cultural brokers). Although limited and recent, the accumulated literature on language brokering—a form of parentification—can have both positive and negative effects on the child's overall well-being (e.g., self-efficacy, feelings of competency, and positive intra- and interpersonal factors). There is no doubt that parent–child relationships may be impacted by language brokering. Of significance, the impact of language brokering on children and the parent–child relationship remains unclear. Research has shown (similar to parentification in other family systems) the aftereffects of language brokering can be both beneficial and burdensome. Some families have attempted to minimize the implications of language brokering and suggest it is just another "household chore" with no or minimal negative consequences. What does appear to be clear is that in a family structure when English is the second language, parentification can emerge.

Why Parentification Matters

Parentification is an important family systems construct because it often—but not always—places family members at risk for pernicious outcomes across the life span. The diverse family systems reviewed are in some ways similar because they all represent periods where the family is often in some distress. Parental loss (i.e., parenting alone) and the delegation of roles, responsibilities, and relationships typically carried out by adult family members but abdicated to child and adolescent family members places most—if not all—family members in a vulnerable position. Family members often miss out on receiving developmentally and age-appropriate emotional, physical, and psychological support needed to function well. Researchers who investigate the complex family systems from which parentification may emerge can lead to important clinical prevention, intervention, and treatment efforts. Practitioners and educators may also benefit from understanding the historical and accumulated knowledge base about parentification. Going forward, new family configurations that promote parentification or excessive family caregiving need to be explored empirically so that cultural and ecological considerations may inform why parentification remains a seminal family systems construct and *still* matters.

In all of these diverse family systems, an adult's ability to parent effectively may be compromised, and negative outcomes may be observed. Parents may be inclined to call upon their children to fill in the gaps and offer support in decision-making and other adultlike tasks during times of stress (e.g., military deployment; economic instability; inability to communicate in English; redefining of roles, responsibilities, relationships, and boundaries; newly divorced family system). In all of these diverse family systems, the adult family members are required to determine who will fill the needed family role and consider a refinement or adjustment in parent–child relationships. Often, the child is called upon to fill the needed role irrespective of its appropriateness. A constant among many of these diverse family systems is the fact that adults are often required to parent alone (e.g., low SES families, divorced families, and military families). These family configurations or structures may result in a lack of stability in the home, with parents being unavailable, experiencing increased stressors, and in need of support themselves. Also, all of these family systems require the family to contract (and expand) at different times. Thus, this regrouping process could be problematic and dysfunctional in some families, producing long-lasting effects for children and the adults they become.

Lisa M. Hooper

See also Active Parenting; Diversity; Individual Family Culture; Multicultural Counseling Competence; Parent Effectiveness Training (P.E.T.); Parenting Styles

Further Readings

Barnett, B., & Parker, G. (1998). The parentified child: Early competence or childhood deprivation? *Child Psychology & Psychiatry Review, 3,* 146–155. doi:10.1111/1475-3588.00234

Boszormenyi-Nagy, I., & Spark, G. (1973). *Invisible loyalties: Reciprocity in intergenerational family therapy.* Oxford, England: Harper & Row.

Burton, L. (2007). Childhood adultification in economically disadvantaged families: A conceptual model. *Family Relations, 56,* 329–345. doi:10.1111/j.1741-3729.2007.00463.x

Byng-Hall, J. (2008). The significance of children fulfilling parental roles: Implications for family therapy. *Journal of Family Therapy, 30,* 147–162. doi:10.1111/j.1467-6427.2008.00423.x

Chase, N. D. (1999). *Burdened children: Theory, research, and treatment of parentification.* Thousand Oaks, CA: Sage.

East, P. L. (2010). Children's provision of family caregiving: Benefit or burden? *Child Development Perspectives, 4,* 55–61. doi:10.1111/j.1750-8606.2009.00118.x

Hooper, L. M. (2007a). The application of attachment theory and family systems theory to the phenomena of parentification. *Family Journal, 15,* 217–223. doi:10.1177/1066480707301290

Hooper, L. M. (2007b). Expanding the discussion regarding parentification and its varied outcomes: Implications for mental health research and practice. *Journal of Mental Health Counseling, 29,* 322–337.

Hooper, L. M., DeCoster, J., White, N., & Voltz, M. L. (2011). Characterizing the magnitude of the relation between self-reported childhood parentification and adult psychopathology: A meta-analysis. *Journal of Clinical Psychology, 67,* 1028–1043. doi:10.1002/jclp.20807

Hooper, L. M., Marotta, S. A., & Lanthier, R. P. (2008). Predictors of growth and distress following childhood parentification: A retrospective exploratory study. *Journal of Child and Family Studies, 17*(5), 693–705.

Jurkovic, G. J. (1997). *Lost childhoods: The plight of the parentified child.* New York, NY: Brunner/Mazel.

Kam, J. A. (2011). The effects of language brokering frequency and feelings on Mexican-heritage youth's mental health and risky behaviors. *Journal of Communication, 61,* 455–475. doi:10.1111/j.1460-2466.2011.01552.x

Kerig, P. K. (Ed.). (2005). *Implications of parent–child boundary dissolution for developmental psychopathology: "Who is the parent and who is the child?"* New York, NY: Hawthorne.

McMahon, T. J., & Luthar, S. S. (2007). Defining characteristics and potential consequences of caretaking burden among children living in urban poverty. *American Journal of Orthopsychiatry, 77,* 267–281. doi:10.1037/0002-9432.77.2.267

Mmari, K., Roche, K. M., Sudhinaraset, M., & Blum, R. (2009). When a parent goes off to war: Exploring the issues faced by adolescents and their families. *Youth & Society, 40,* 455–475. doi:10.1177/0044118X08327873

PARENTING

Parenting has been described as the process of promoting and supporting the physical, emotional, social, financial, and intellectual development of children from birth to adulthood. In particular, parenting involves the methods and techniques parents use in child-rearing and all the tasks that parents do on a day-to-day basis to help children grow and mature in healthy ways. Parents offer nurturance, comfort, protection, and guidance to children at various developmental tasks and life stages. This entry looks at the various ways parenting is changing in society, the role of parenting and attachment styles, challenges in parenting, the relationship of parenting and culture, and parenting models and information for parents.

Parenting and Societal Change

The roles of parenting have changed with society's work demands and other societal changes. In the United States, there has been a significant increase over the past several decades in single-parent families and families in which both parents work. Not all couples are married when they have children, and some who are married decide not to have children or not to have them right away. Overall, there is more delayed parenthood, with many young adults focused on career development. With medical advances prolonging the years when many women can have children, women have more freedom to choose when to conceive, and both men and women are waiting longer to have children. However, as a result of delaying parenthood, many couples struggle with biological childbearing and turn to fertility treatments or adoption as alternatives.

Although the divorce rate in the United States has declined since the early 1980s, many children still grow up in divorced families, blended families, or single-parent homes. The diversity of these families and circumstances has an effect on parenting. For most children living in single-parent homes, the mother is the responsible parent. Single-parent homes are not always the result of divorce but can result from having a child without being either married or cohabitating or because of the death of a spouse or partner. In addition, there are conditionally separated families where one parent is in the military, in prison, or otherwise unavailable for long periods. Parents raising their children alone are more likely to face certain challenges, including poverty and mental health issues for both the parent and child.

With new values placed on work and changes in the economy, in two-parent families there is a much lower percentage of mothers who stay home to take care of their children. There has also been an increase in cases of fathers who are stay-at-home dads. There are also more gay and lesbian people who are in single-sex relationships and raising children.

Parenting and Attachment

From the moment an infant is conceived, attachment (or lack of attachment) to one's child begins. This dance continues to play out once the child is born. The first two years of life are critical in terms of creating emotional memories that children will carry into adult relationships. Ideally, all parents would bond with their children and provide a secure attachment. Research indicates that secure attachment impacts child development in a very positive manner. Parents who nurture and comfort children help them develop trust in the environment so they can grow and develop to the best of their potential. Ideally, parents act as a "secure base" for their children so they feel loved and have a sense of belonging. This, in turn, will impact the children's self-esteem, emotional health, and relationships with others.

Most parents tend to parent the way they were parented and are not always aware of their parenting style. Thus, making parents aware of the lessons they learned growing up can help them change and challenge their parenting style. They can evaluate how they express love to their child, attend to the child's needs, express emotions, and deal with conflict. Children have a way of tapping into parents' unresolved issues and bringing back pain from the parent's childhood. Intentional parenting requires parents to be aware of their parenting style and not simply use the same methods their own parents did. Parents can help their children by modeling healthy relationships where feelings are expressed and encouraged while uniqueness is respected and valued.

John Bowlby, who pioneered attachment theory, saw attachment as a critical survival mechanism in infants who try to gain a sense of security and safety by connecting with the caregiver in stressful situations. A secure bond with parents promotes normal, healthy emotional and social development. Based on research by Bowlby, Mary Ainsworth, and others, four attachment styles have been identified: (1) secure, (2) anxious–avoidant, (3) anxious–ambivalent, and (4) disorganized. These attachment styles are thought to affect children significantly and play a critical role in the development of mental health issues later in life. A child who feels loved, cared for, and nurtured by parents or caregivers is likely to develop a sense of secure attachment. Children learn early on in life that someone will be there for them to meet their needs.

Parenting Challenges

Every stage of infancy brings up various challenges for parents and lessons to learn. As the child moves through various developmental stages and reaches milestones, parents also develop. Early years are crucial in promoting brain development and providing enough stimulation for children to develop appropriately. Some phases are more challenging than others, such as the "terrible twos," where the child starts developing some autonomy and voices power over parents. For some parents, the challenges may arise in the middle school years when peer pressure begins to impact the parent–child relationship. For still other parents, the most challenging period will occur later in the child's adolescence when the child seeks independence from parents and the development of his or her own identity.

Parenting changes throughout the life cycle and parenting struggles can challenge the couple dyad as they try to meet the needs of their children at every stage. Parents may need to be creative in order to carve out time for themselves rather than focusing constantly on their children's needs. It is helpful for parents to have a support system, whether it be family, friends, or both.

Parenting and Culture

Culture plays a major role in parenting. Some cultures emphasize gender roles more than others, and some cultures may place a greater emphasis on attachment. Cultural differences can influence the use of child care, the type of child care used, and whether a caregiver takes on a parental role. Some parents have fewer financial resources and, as a result, the children may experience poverty in the home, which can have an effect on their stress levels, health, and development. Some parents may be more educated than others about what is necessary to raise a healthy child and to care for their children physically, psychologically, emotionally, and socially. Ultimately, the values of the culture—and in particular the values of the given family—will determine how the child is raised and the methods used in that process.

Parenting Models and Information

A wide variety of parenting models has emerged, and for some parents, it may be overwhelming to decide what parenting model to follow and what to know about healthy child development at different stages. Some models focus on parenting with consciousness while others focus on discipline. Still, others may focus on understanding brain development, attachment styles, positive parenting, nurturing, or a wide variety of other possibilities. Regardless of the model that parents may choose to follow, the ultimate goal for all approaches is to strengthen the parent–child relationship, offer support, and create a secure bond with children.

For many, parenting is the most rewarding and the most challenging work that they will undertake in their lifetime. There are many decisions to make on a day-to-day basis about what may be best for one's children. Parents turn to social media, social groups, blogs, websites, magazines, classes, television programs, and books to understand issues involving their children and to learn how to be a good parent. In addition, clinicians may provide information and advice to parents at each developmental stage that children go through. Although the wealth of information available on parenting can be helpful, parents may feel that it creates high expectations for them as parents, which can be accompanied by high levels of stress.

On the other hand, parents may find that parenthood helps them to set priorities in order to accomplish the many tasks required to raise, nurture, and support children.

Montserrat Casado-Kehoe

See also Attachment; Diversity; Parenting; Parenting Education; Parenting Styles

Further Readings

Hughes, D. A., & Baylin, J. (2012). *Brain-based parenting: The neuroscience of caregiving for healthy attachment.* New York, NY: W. W. Norton.

Medina, J. (2011). *Brain rules for baby: How to raise a smart and happy child from zero to five.* Seattle, WA: Pear Press.

Purvis, K. B., Cross, D. R., & Sunshine, W. L. (2007). *The connected child: Bring hope and healing to your adoptive family.* New York, NY: McGraw-Hill.

Siegel, D. J., & Bryson, T. P. (2011). *The whole-brain child: 12 revolutionary strategies to nurture your child's developing mind.* New York, NY: Delacorte Press.

Siegel, D. J., & Hartzell, M. (2013). *Parenting from the inside out: How a deeper self-understanding can help you raise children who thrive.* New York, NY: Jeremy P. Tarcher/Penguin.

Turner, P. H., & Welch, K. J. (2011). *Parenting in contemporary society* (5th ed.). Needham Heights, MA: Pearson.

Yerkovich, M., & Yerkovich, K. (2011). *How we love our kids.* Colorado Springs, CO: WaterBrook Press.

Parenting Education

Parenting is a process by which parents and children grow, influencing each other throughout their lives. Parenting is a complex task where it is not uncommon for parents to need help. As children change at each developmental stage, the demands of parenting also change. In recent years, there has been a growing focus on parenting education due in part to the positive psychology movement. Nick Carter and Lauren Kahn (1996) describe parenting education as "programs, support services and resources offered to parents and caregivers that are designed to support them or increase their capacity and confidence in raising healthy children." Parenting education is provided through various avenues and programs. This entry discusses the stages of parenting and the characteristics and objectives of parenting education.

Stages of Parenting

Parents move through a series of stages beginning with pregnancy, preparation for parenthood, and childbirth. Psychologist Ellen Galinsky describes how adults develop through the interaction with their children in what she calls the six stages of parenthood.

First, in the parental image stage, the mother and father begin to form an image of themselves as parents. The next stage, the nurturing stage, occurs during infancy and is when attachment forms and the roles of parents are established. The third stage, the authority stage, is when the child is between 2 and 4 years old and begins to develop independence. In this stage, the child places more demands on a parent's time. The fourth stage, the integrative stage, lasts from preschool through middle childhood and is when children develop more autonomy and social skills. The fifth stage, the independent teenage stage, is when adolescents struggle with identification, responsibility, and maturity. The final stage, the departure stage, happens at the time the adolescent leaves home. During this stage, parents evaluate their performance and prepare for their future relationship with their grown children.

Parents face many responsibilities as they are establishing their roles in the early stages of their children's lives. As young children begin to develop independence and transition from the preschool years to middle childhood, parents need to set realistic goals, communicate effectively, and establish authority. Once children reach the teenage years, there can be more conflicts between parents and children. Parents need to provide support for their adolescents while maintaining authority. Parent education can help to guide parents through their children's developmental stages.

Characteristics and Objectives of Parenting Education

Parenting education is designed to help parents learn how to improve their skills in caring for their children and to become partners in their development. The main goal of parenting education is to foster competence in parenting and family management skills. Parenting education programs can focus on a variety of topics that include childhood behaviors and development; safe and healthy practices at home in the areas of nutrition, exercise, first aid, wellness, stress, and risk management; child-rearing values and attitudes; child guidance approaches; family communication; and family resource management, as well as dealing with difficult issues such as divorce, illness, and death.

Parenting education can help to build knowledge and skills in monitoring children, showing affection, spending time together, communicating, supporting, and disciplining. When offered with appropriate quality and duration, these programs can generate greater competence in parents. Parent education programs have been found to promote well-being, strengthen families and communities, and prevent child abuse and neglect.

Parenting education programs may be general or focused on a specific stage of a child's life. Some programs are for those who are planning to have children, are pregnant, or are adopting a child. It is important that parents are provided with an opportunity to address their concerns in a parenting education program. Once parents' priorities have been acknowledged, teachers can gather resources and plan sessions to meet parents' needs.

Parenting education is provided in a variety of settings and in different ways. They usually are facilitated by resource leaders or teachers who are specialists in various aspects of parenting. Programs may involve both parents and children. According to researchers, family-focused programs are often more effective than child- or parent-only approaches. Some families benefit from more intensive programs because they need more time to develop trust, overcome dysfunctional attitudes and behaviors, and build upon the skills they have learned. Parenting education programs may be conducted in collaboration with educational or religious organizations or community agencies. Some programs link parents to services that address problems such as substance abuse, mental illness, domestic violence, unemployment, and difficulties finding child care.

Research has found that effective programs provide relevant information and give parents opportunities to practice what they learned through activities such as role-playing with other adults or with their children. Educating parents can help them to gain confidence in their ability to solve problems and know how to ask for help when they need it.

Jasmine Lydia Selvaraj and Priscilla Rose Selvaraj

See also Active Parenting; Child Guidance Movement; Communication in Couples and Families; Group Family Therapy; Group Parenting Classes; Parent Effectiveness Training (P.E.T.); Parent–Child Communication; Role-Playing; Single-Parent Families

Further Readings

Carter, N., & Kahn, L. (1996). *See how we grow: A report on the status of parenting education in the U.S.* Philadelphia, PA: Pew Charitable Trust.

Colosi, L., & Dunifon, R. (2003). *Effective parent education programs.* Retrieved from Cornell Cooperative Extension website: http://www.parenting.cit.cornell.edu/Effective%20Parent%20Education%20Programs.pdf

Galinsky, E. (1981). *Between generations: The six stages of parenting.* New York, NY: Times Books.

Huser, M., Small, S. A., & Eastman, G. (2008, July). *What research tells us about effective parenting education programs.* Retrieved from University of Wisconsin–Madison/Extension website: http://fyi.uwex.edu/whatworkswisconsin/files/2014/04/factsheet_4parentinged.pdf

Reppucci, N. D., Britner, P. A., & Woolard, J. L. (1997). *Preventing child abuse and neglect through parent education.* Baltimore, MD: Paul Brooks Publishing.

Riley, D. (1993). *Some principles for designing effective parenting education/support programs. Wisconsin Family Impact Seminars Briefing Report.* Retrieved from University of Wisconsin–Madison: Center for Excellence in Family Studies website: http://www.familyimpactseminars.org/s_wifis03c02.pdf

PARENTING STYLES

The interrelation of parental discipline techniques and parenting styles has been studied for a number of years. The effects these styles have on children are of interest to researchers, clinicians, educators, and parents alike. As with most child research, targeted intervention strategies are developed as a result of investigation into child issues. This entry reviews basic parenting styles, discipline techniques, and associated child adjustment. In addition, this entry focuses on parenting styles in the United States as they relate to ethnicity, socioeconomic status, and other considerations.

Parenting Styles and Discipline Techniques

Although a shift of discipline techniques and parenting styles may result from major changes in the home environment such as the absence of a parent because of military deployment, marital separation, or other circumstances, overall parenting styles remain consistent. These parenting practices can be thought of as established and predictable sets of behaviors in response to child demands. Further, changes in parenting practices observed after modifications in the home environment are attributed to external factors, such as financial difficulties resulting from the loss of a second caregiver. Traditionally, parenting styles are measured on the dimensions of responsiveness (sometimes referred to as warmth) and control. Additionally, various parenting styles assume differing expectations of child maturity and responsibility. As part of her extensive work on parenting styles, Diana Baumrind identified three basic parenting styles: authoritative, authoritarian, and permissive.

The authoritative parent employs moderate to high levels of control and high levels of responsiveness. These parents approach child behavior and behavioral problems from a rational perspective, encouraging the child to think through behavior and consequence in a logical manner. The authoritative parent allows for discussion and considers the position of the child but ultimately exercises discipline as an authority figure. Although seemingly contradictory, authoritative parents value both child autonomy and conformity. Explanation of disciplinary actions and consideration of child perspective are indicative of the value placed on child autonomy. However, parental control is ultimately exerted during parent–child divergence. Disciplinary measures are supportive of developing autonomy rather than punitive in nature. Expectations of child maturity are moderate. The authoritative parent generally has age-appropriate expectations for child behavior and places importance on adhering to group standards.

In contrast, the authoritarian parent employs high levels of control and lower levels of responsiveness. An authoritarian parent approaches behavioral issues in an absolute manner and highly values child conformity and parental control. At points of discipline, the authoritarian parent discourages autonomy, does not offer rationales for disciplinary decisions, and requires obedience. These parents maintain their perspective as correct and expect the child to accept demands and high levels of household responsibility without question. Disciplinary measures are inflexible and punitive, focused on instilling obedience to authority and conformity to rules. The authoritarian parent has the highest expectation of maturity and responsibility for child behavior. Often these parents expect maturity and behavior well beyond that accepted as age-appropriate, sometimes assigning responsibilities more appropriate for adults. When children inevitably do not meet these demands, punitive punishment is enforced.

The last of Baumrind's parenting styles, permissive parenting, utilizes low levels of control and high levels of responsiveness. This parent is positioned as a resource to be available whenever the child perceives a need. The permissive parent makes few demands regarding child behavior or responsibility. While this type of parent may use reason or manipulation to influence child decisions and behavior, control as an authority figure is not employed. The permissive parent is generally accepting of the child's actions and consults the child in determining household policies. Because the permissive parent has minimal expectations for child maturity or conformity to behavioral standards, discipline is rarely used. Although permissive parents rarely employ traditional disciplinary measures, when they are utilized, such practices are flexible and inconsistently enforced. Inconsistent response to child misbehavior may add to the child's continued misbehavior.

Other researchers later added a fourth category, uninvolved parenting. In the literature, the uninvolved parenting style is also referred to as disengaged, neglectful, or indifferent. Using the dimensions described previously, this parenting style employs low levels of control and low levels of responsiveness. The parent places few demands on the child and, although the child's basic needs *may* be met, the uninvolved parent has little interaction with the child and is unaware of the child's inner life. Discipline is rarely studied in this parenting style because of the limited interaction between parent and child.

Child Adjustment

While many factors influence child development, parenting practices contribute greatly to child adjustment and outcomes. In fact, several studies have linked parenting styles with social competence in small and large groups; academic competence; depression; and risk-taking behaviors such as delinquency, violence, sexual activity, and alcohol and drug use.

Authoritative Parenting and Child Adjustment

Children from authoritative homes learn to take responsibility for their actions, both good and bad. Because authoritative parents offer a supportive environment with clear but appropriate expectations, these children are more likely to perform well academically and are more flexible regarding gender roles such as sensitivity in males and autonomy in females. This flexibility contributes to high levels of social competence and emotional regulation. These children also develop higher levels of self-confidence and self-efficacy. Due to the balance between independence and social conformity impressed upon them by an authoritative home environment, these children display appropriate levels of social conformity (i.e., respect for authority) but remain largely independent. They are also less likely than their peers to engage in drug or alcohol use, delinquency, and early sexual activity and are more competent at exercising self-regulation. Additionally, children from authoritative homes have lower reported levels of depression and violence and generally happy dispositions.

Authoritarian Parenting and Child Adjustment

Children from authoritarian homes often display unhappy dispositions and are more likely than their authoritatively reared peers to be withdrawn and have anxiety. Although research is somewhat mixed regarding academic achievement and authoritarian parenting, these children are less likely to pursue higher education than their authoritatively reared peers. Because these children become accustomed to harsh discipline, they are more likely to become passive in parent–child interactions. They are also less emotionally mature and display lower levels of self-regulation in peer situations with females "giving up" and males engaging in more hostile or violent behavior. Low levels of warmth and sensitivity to child needs often result in lower levels of communication between parent and child. As such, peers especially influence children during adolescence. If these children choose peers engaged in risk-taking or delinquent behaviors, their risk for such behaviors increases significantly. Adolescent males from authoritarian homes demonstrate the highest levels of violence; are less inquisitive in intellectual endeavors; and are less autonomous, relying on direction from authority figures.

Permissive Parenting and Child Adjustment

Children from permissive homes have the most negative outcomes of all of Baumrind's categories. As a result of little to no parent-imposed boundaries, these children do not learn appropriate social behavior. Many of these children internalize rules and regulations as mutable, often attempt to manipulate authority figures, and are unlikely to accept responsibility for their actions. They are more rebellious and engage in risk-taking behaviors, including delinquency, early sexual activity, and drug and alcohol use. While authoritarian-raised children display the highest levels of violent behavior, permissively raised children demonstrate the next highest rates of violence. Self-regulation is underdeveloped, which may contribute to social difficulties in the adolescent years. Compared with Baumrind's other categories, permissively reared children have the highest rates of depression and anxiety and the lowest levels of satisfaction or happiness. Additionally, these children tend to perform poorly in school and are at an increased risk for dropping out of school.

Uninvolved Parenting and Child Adjustment

In comparison with Baumrind's parenting classifications, uninvolved or indifferent parenting receives less attention. However, this is a matter of terminology. This last parenting style is more often studied in the context of neglect, the extreme end of indifferent parenting practices. In general, neglected children have the poorest outcomes, and these outcomes are the most pervasive. Children from uninvolved homes are the least psychologically adjusted, perform more poorly in academic settings, and display limited social competence. These neglected children also demonstrate poor self-regulation and engage in a variety of antisocial behaviors. As such, there is an extensive and constantly increasing literature investigating the impact of neglect on children as well as targeted intervention strategies.

Ethnicity, Socioeconomic Status, and Other Considerations

For much of U.S. history, authoritarian parenting was the predominant style and remains so in urban neighborhoods characterized by low income levels and high crime rates. Some research suggests that in such areas authoritarian parenting may be beneficial, since children are less apt to question directions intended to ensure their safety. Therefore, in high-risk areas, authoritarian parenting may be more beneficial to child safety, academic achievement, and general development.

Research indicates that preferred parenting styles vary somewhat across ethnic groups and by socioeconomic status (SES). Although most of the parenting research initially studied middle-class European American families, studies have shown similar results for African American children of authoritative parents. African American and Hispanic families are more likely than European American families to use authoritarian parenting, whereas European American families are most likely to utilize authoritative parenting. While this suggests an ethnic split in preferred parenting styles, SES may be the more important factor. Consider that much of the research on European American families recruited middle-class samples. In contrast, much of the research on African American families utilized low-income samples. Across all ethnic groups, lower-income families are more likely than middle-class families to exercise authoritarian parenting.

A final consideration is the longevity of outcomes resulting from parenting styles. Much of the research investigating child outcomes and adjustment are limited to adolescence. Because parenting practices have significant impacts on childhood development, reason follows that parenting also shapes adult development. Many factors such as ethnicity, SES, and geographic location require further investigation. However, longitudinal analysis of adjustment in adulthood may also prove to be a rich emerging facet of research.

Alli Cipra

See also Active Parenting; Child-Centered Parenting; Parent–Child Communication; Parentification and Diverse Family Systems; Parenting

Further Readings

Borre, A., & Kliewer, W. (2014). Parental strain, mental health problems, and parenting practices: A longitudinal study. *Personality and Individual Differences, 68*, 93–97.

Jabagchourian, J., Sorkhabi, N., Quach, W., & Strage, A. (2014). Parenting styles and practices of Latino parents and Latino fifth graders' academic, cognitive, social, and behavioral outcomes. *Hispanic Journal of Behavioral Sciences, 36*(2), 175–194.

Lee, E. H., Qing, Z., Ly, J., Main, A., Tao, A., & Chen, S. H. (2014). Neighborhood characteristics, parenting styles, and children's behavioral problems in Chinese American immigrant families. *Cultural Diversity and Ethnic Minority Psychology, 20*(2), 202–212.

Nelson, L. J., Padilla-Walker, L. M., Christensen, K. J., Evans, C. A., & Carroll, J. S. (2011). Parenting in emerging adulthood: An examination of parenting clusters and correlates. *Journal of Youth and Adolescence, 40*, 730–743.

Roche, K. M., Ensminger, M. E., & Cherlin, A. J. (2007). Variations in parenting and adolescent outcomes among African American and Latino families living in low-income, urban areas. *Journal of Family Issues, 28*(7), 882–909.

Rothrauff, T. C., Cooney, T. M., & Jeong, S. A. (2009). Remembered parenting styles and adjustment in middle and late adulthood. *Journals of Gerontology Series B: Psychological Sciences and Social Sciences, 64B*(1), 137–146.

Watabe, A., & Hibbard, D. R. (2014). The influence of authoritarian and authoritative parenting on children's academic achievement motivation: A comparison between the United States and Japan. *North American Journal of Psychology, 16*(2), 359–382.

Watkins-Lewis, K., & Hamre, B. (2012). African-American parenting characteristics and their association with children's cognitive and academic school readiness. *Journal of African American Studies, 16*(3), 390–405.

Patriarchy

Patriarchy can be defined within several constructs. It may be a way to describe family, social, or political structures. Regardless of the setting, patriarchy describes a structure that favors masculine individuals or ways of being over feminine individuals or ways of being. Patriarchal structures also assume masculine forms of expression or ways of being as the "norm" or standard for all. Nearly every modern society exists within a patriarchal social and political structure. Throughout history, while some matrilineal structures have existed, where property or descendants are traced through women rather than men, a true matriarchal structure has not existed. In the modern world, patriarchal systems dominate worldwide. Living within a patriarchal structure has a significant impact on an individual's existence in the world, regardless of gender identity. There can be a detrimental effect on a person's self-concept, functioning within a family or relationship. This entry explores the impact that patriarchy has on women, men, and nonbinary gendered individuals throughout the various settings of their lives. The social and emotional implications of patriarchy are explored, particularly within the structure of counseling and therapy.

Social Implications

Gender socialization begins even before birth, and patriarchy plays a role in the way this socialization takes place. Fetuses that are identified with a penis are immediately described with masculine terms. Many parents begin conceptualizing the life of this child including being active, engaging in sports, and being high achieving and successful. Masculine children are described using adjectives related to their physicality such as *strong* or *tough*. Parents often report being less patient with a masculine baby's crying, reflecting social norms of men being perceived as less emotional.

Conversely, fetuses lacking an identifiable penis are described with feminine terms. Conceptualization of girl children typically includes a focus on emotions rather than physicality. These children are described with adjectives such as *sweet* or *precious* (*precious* also being a term connected with jewels or rare metals). And parents are quicker to comfort an infant identified as a girl than they are a boy, reinforcing early the social norm of women being passive or associated with being possessed.

Early polarization of social cues in children lays a foundation for lifelong behavior and worldviews. Under patriarchy, children receive clear messages about appropriate behavior in alignment with their genitals and therefore gender assignment. Furthermore, boys begin to reject "softer" emotions and redirect many emotions into acceptable masculine expressions of anger or isolation. Girls, on the other hand, learn to nurture and care for others, suppressing feelings of anger. Gender nonconforming children have a particularly confusing experience. For some children, their gender socialization regarding communication or play styles aligns with their developing self-concept of gender identity. For gender nonconforming children, social pressure to conform to a particular way of being conflicts with the way they are most comfortable being.

Gender socialization and patriarchal valuing of the masculine over the feminine also play a role in social acceptance of nonheterosexual sexual orientations. Because heterosexuality is assumed to be the norm, women are expected to be sexually attracted to men and men to women. Men sexually attracted to men or both men and women are perceived to be less masculine, often feminized, and therefore less valuable in social constructs. Women attracted to women or both men and women are either masculinized and therefore criticized for not aligning with their appropriate role or sexualized for masculine consumption. Within the broader LGBTQPIA (lesbian, gay, bisexual, transgender, queer/questioning, poly/pansexual, intersexual, asexual) community, the masculine gay male who is also White, able-bodied, and middle class is most represented and considered to be the norm for the gay experience. This tendency aligns with patriarchal values preferring masculinity and reinforcing masculine dominance over femininity.

Education

Regardless of gender identity, patriarchal society establishes early favoritism of masculinity over femininity. Education systems tend to reinforce this favoritism throughout a person's time in school. The gender socialization that began in childhood continues to be reinforced by teachers, with the "common knowledge" that math and science are "for boys" and social studies or arts are "for girls." Again, the genders are restricted from one another's worlds and an unspoken knowledge that masculine logical math and science are more useful in adulthood compared with feminine emotional arts. While many young girls express interest in science, technology, engineering, and math (STEM) subjects, the covert and sometimes overt messages received throughout their life often redirect them away from pursuing education in these fields.

Workplace

The workplace is one of the most obvious social arenas where patriarchy is evident. In the United States, despite decades of advocacy and proposed legislation for equal pay, women, and to a greater extent women of color, earn less for the same work than their male coworkers. Research also reflects a disparity in jobs available to women, with many women being restricted from the highest-level jobs despite time spent at a particular workplace and eligibility for the position. This is also tied to educational structures that make work associated with masculinity such as business management or technological development more valued and therefore better paid. Connected to these subliminal social messages within training for these fields, work environments tend to be at best challenging and at worst hostile for women seeking work in masculine associated fields.

On the flip side, forms of work socially perceived as "feminine," such as education or counseling, are devalued and therefore underpaid. Men who overcome the messages received early on to avoid these forms of work, in contrast to their women counterparts in masculine fields, often receive preferential treatment within so-called female-dominant fields. Regardless of this preferential treatment, however, some men experience social pressure from peers, family, or friends regarding their inability to achieve the levels they were supposed to given their masculine status. Many men in feminine work experience shame regarding their career choices.

Due to the lack of regulated, paid parental leave in the United States, women with children are particularly penalized in the workforce. Women of typical childbearing age may be overlooked for a job or promotion due to the financial risk perceived by a business or workplace of losing revenue or productivity when a woman takes leave from work to give birth or care for a newborn infant. Similarly, those who chose to leave work temporarily to give birth or care for young children find it difficult to reenter the workforce. Many workplaces expect new mothers or recent parents to immediately perform at levels similar to their performance before becoming parents. Additionally, parents are often penalized if they need to take time off work to care for children who are sick.

A patriarchal structure reinforces that women are the primary caregivers to children and restricts men from the arena of child care. This perpetuates a system where child-rearing is simultaneously undervalued as a form of work and also makes it difficult to simultaneously actively participate in the workforce and care for children. This system also penalizes fathers in that they are also not provided with an option to leave work to assist in providing early care to an infant.

Home

Patriarchy also tends to be present in family and home structures. As discussed earlier, patriarchal systems reinforce the idea that women are the primary caregivers to children. This also translates into caring for the home. The division of household labor has therefore been unequal across most historical contexts. Regardless of whether or not a woman is working outside the home, she continues to be burdened with looking after cooking, cleaning, and doing additional household chores. Many heterosexual couples struggle to find a compromise regarding the division of labor in the home. Same or similar gender relationships experience a double-edged sword of not being restricted by gender role assignment but also lacking a structure off of which to base the division of labor.

Implications for Therapy

Patriarchy is not an agreed-upon social structure nor is there a group of powerful individuals enforcing that patriarchal standards be upheld. For many, patriarchy is an unseen force that we don't realize is playing a role in our lives. Individuals who don't live up to the demands of their gender assignment experience high levels of personal conflict, shame, or guilt.

This pressure to conform restricts masculine individuals from expressing emotions in typically identified healthy ways or leads to difficulty acknowledging or noticing their internal responses as a whole. Researchers have found that men are typically less willing to seek out mental health services, struggle to maintain engagement if therapy is initiated, and have higher rates of suicide completion. Even when men seek and remain in therapy, because discussion of internal processes tends to be a focus, therapists and masculine clients may struggle with the overall counseling process.

Feminine-identified individuals also have struggles related to patriarchal pressure. Patriarchy plays a role in a feminine-identified individual's perception of being weak, objectified, passive, or less worthy. Many women struggle with independence and self-esteem, which both have an undercurrent based in patriarchy.

At its core, patriarchy awards power to masculine individuals and ways of being over all others. For therapists, attention must be paid to power dynamics within the therapeutic relationship regardless of setting or makeup of the members involved. In regard to patriarchal structures, counselors should attend to internalized patriarchal beliefs about masculine versus feminine ways of being and the value assigned therein. Because patriarchy is a subconscious force, most individuals struggle with identifying beliefs, values, behaviors, or expressions as being tied to patriarchy. In alignment with multicultural competence, privilege associated with gender identity should be explored and recognized. Masculine-identified counselors can self-monitor their expectations of their clients and be aware of the way they may unconsciously project power within therapy. Conversely, feminine-identified therapists can be aware of their own internalized sense of lower worth and deference to perceived powerful individuals, particularly within the counseling room. When working with couples, therapists can attend to the couple's replication, rejection, or struggle with belief systems tied to patriarchy that play a role in the relationship or family.

Molly Rose Wilson

See also Communication in Couples and Families; Couples and Marriage Counseling; Gender- and Culture-Sensitive Therapies; Gender Roles; Same-Sex Couples

Further Readings

Bennett, J. M. (2006). *History matters: Patriarchy and the challenge of feminism*. Philadelphia: University of Pennsylvania Press.

Chowdhury, E. H. (2015). Rethinking patriarchy, culture and masculinity: Transnational narratives of gender violence and human rights advocacy. *Journal of International Women's Studies*, 16(2), 98–114.

Crittenden, C. A., & Wright, E. M. (2013). Predicting patriarchy: Using individual and contextual factors to examine patriarchal endorsement in communities. *Journal of Interpersonal Violence*, 28(6), 1267–1288. doi:10.1177/0886260512468245

Feldhousen, E., & Baima, T. (2007). The heart of sexual trauma: Patriarchy as a centrally organizing principle for couple therapy. *Journal of Feminist Family Therapy*, 19(3), 13–36. doi:10.1300/J086v19n03_02

Knudson-Martin, C. (2015). When therapy challenges patriarchy: Undoing gendered power in heterosexual couple relationships. In C. Knudson-Martin, M. A. Wells, & S. K. Samman (Eds.), *Socio-emotional relationship therapy: Bridging emotion, societal context, and couple interaction* (pp. 15–26). Cham, Switzerland: Springer International Publishing.

Majstorović, D., Lassen, I., & Ebrary, I. (2011). *Living with patriarchy: Discursive constructions of gendered subjects across cultures*. Philadelphia, PA: John Benjamins.

Nguyen, A. (2008). Patriarchy, power, and female masculinity. *Journal of Homosexuality*, 55(4), 665–683. doi:10.1080/00918360802498625

Vogel, D., Wester, S., Hammer, J., & Downing-Matibag, T. (2014). Referring men to seek help: The influence of gender role conflict and stigma. *Psychology of Men & Masculinity*, 15(1), 60–67. doi:10.1037/a0031761

Peer Counseling

Peer counseling is a paraprofessional service that can be utilized in many different settings. This service modality is often employed as a means of supporting program goals. This entry provides an overview of the key aspects of peer counseling. These include common peer counseling training practices and examples of some of its most commonly used settings.

The use of peer counselors can be traced to the 1960s; it began to gain popularity in the self-help movement of the 1970s. *Peer counseling* is defined as a supportive service that selected members of a group provide to other members of the same group. It is also referenced in professional literature as student-to-student counseling, peer facilitation, peer mentoring, and peer education. In reality, peer counseling often encompasses a bit of each of those activities. The specific setting in which it is performed dictates the specific duties or responsibilities of the peer counselor. This paraprofessional role can be found in many different areas including academic, health care, and community settings. Much of the early research found it to be a viable service modality, especially in academic institutions. Peer counselors can range in age, developmental level, culture, ethnicity, and sexual orientation. Most commonly utilized to provide educational and supportive services, peer counseling programs can be found throughout the world.

The specific school or agency program defines the role of the peer counselor. Often, the peer counseling program is only one component of a comprehensive plan that is designed to meet the needs of the student or person served. Peer counseling is based on the premise that people respond well to those who they feel are like-minded and share similar life experiences: their peers. There may be less intimidation in approaching a peer than in relating to someone without any common point of reference or lived experience for a particular concern. For example, a person who has just experienced a miscarriage may feel more comfortable sharing his or her loss with someone who has also experienced a miscarriage. Because of the shared experience, there is a degree of relatedness that the person might not be able to get from someone who has not walked the same path. A parent of a child recently diagnosed with a developmental disability might feel more comfortable talking to a parent who has a child with the same developmental disability. While the professional may offer the same information, the peer can do so without the inherent hierarchy often associated with professionals.

The Peer Counselor

All age-groups—children, adolescents, or adults—can be trained to provide this type of service. The selection of peer counselors is aligned with the developmental level of the peer group and service they will be providing. If peer counselors are selected from a peer group (i.e., a school setting), they are often initially identified for this role because of their leadership potential. In other instances, peer counselors can volunteer for the role. For example, a senior citizen center may ask participants for a volunteer to lead a group on safety for elderly people. Once identified, peer counselors are trained to provide information and/or support to persons in their peer group. Peer counseling is usually one segment of a comprehensive intervention or service delivery model. Peer counseling is not a replacement for professional services but, with proper planning, can be an effective adjunct to many different types of systematic programming.

Training

Training and supervision by professional staff is provided to facilitate the peer counseling process. All peer counselors should receive some type of role induction training. It is important that their role in their respective system or organization be clearly defined. This is vital for legal, ethical, and practical reasons. Ethically and legally, there may be confidentiality and/or reporting mandates in regard to situations such as child abuse or elder abuse to which the peer counselor must adhere. Training also ensures peer counselors and their facilitators or supervisors know their scope of practice and have the skills necessary to perform their duties. In this manner, collaboration with other agency or program personnel is also facilitated. In a practical sense, "everyone is on the same page." Specific training in any skills peer counselors are likely to use in providing this service should also be offered.

Some evidence-based peer counseling programs may even require trainers to complete a "train the trainer" session in which standardized training procedures and standardized training materials are reviewed. Training manuals that are standardized ensure consistency by outlining specific training topics and activities that reinforce the content. Professional associations may also offer guidelines for peer counseling training.

Most peer counseling programs include training in basic listening skills, such as offering reflection of the feelings and content of what the speaker is saying, use of open and closed questions, and summarization. Peer counseling training should include an overview of each of these communication skills. Training should also include opportunities for preservice peers to practice the communication skills they have learned via role-plays that mirror the types of interactions they are likely to experience. In this manner, the preservice peer becomes familiar with his or her role and is more likely to feel efficacious. The overall goal is to help peer counselors facilitate communication and clarify what they are hearing so they can provide services to their peers.

Peer counselors may also receive training on conceptual models that might assist them in understanding the person with whom they are working. One example of a possible model that might be explored is James Prochaska and Carlo DiClemente's stages of change model. While the stages of change model may not be applicable to all peer counseling programs, those that aim to support any kind of behavior change would benefit from a review of the model's stages. It would give the paraprofessional a context for the common characteristics of behavior change and possible ways to address different stages. Training in motivational interviewing also would be beneficial to many peer counselors. It would extend training in basic listening skills as it is more goal directed. Again, although all peer counselors will not be supporting behavior change, both of these concepts may provide a peer counselor with a framework for counseling that promotes behavior change such as the establishment of study habits or smoking cessation. The developmental level of the peer counselor and peer counselee would have to be taken into consideration when utilizing either of these models.

Peer counselors should also be trained in any site- or agency-specific tasks. This might include the completion of forms, knowing what to do in an emergency, or logistical information about room reservations. Having this procedural knowledge is necessary to ensure effectiveness of service. For example, some agencies might require their peer counselors to document their services. There may be a form that briefly describes the interventions of the peer counselor so that other service providers who are working with the same person can easily coordinate services. More specifically, a peer counselor working with a student who is struggling academically could be required to document their work with the students. The student's academic adviser could in turn read this documentation that may include the fact that the peer counselor referred the student for tutoring, referred him or her to the university counseling center, or reviewed that institution's academic probation protocol. This documentation will help inform the academic adviser and influence his or her further intervention with the student. To this end, it is vital that all peer counseling training should include an overview of applicable resources and referral sources that the peer can utilize. Finally, trainees should become familiar with their program supervisor and how they can contact the supervisor if they require guidance or assistance.

Supervision

Ongoing supervision should be an inherent component of any peer counseling program. It is necessary to address any concerns or questions that might arise as peer counselors are performing their duties. This supervision can occur in either individual or group formats or a combination of these two modalities. Individual supervision would allow peer counselors to discuss issues they have encountered or questions they have. Group supervision is helpful because it creates a supportive learning environment in which the peer counselors can learn from one another. Ideally, both would be part of any peer counseling program. In general, the supervisor's role is to ensure the peer counselor is comfortable and effective in his or her role. Supervisors are also tasked with ensuring the quality of the service that is being provided.

Settings

K–12 Education

Peer counseling is utilized in a variety of educational settings. At primary, middle, and secondary school levels, peer counselors are commonly used to support guidance programming in a developmentally appropriate manner. For example, an elementary school counselor may utilize peer counselors to support character education programs. These programs often have a monthly schoolwide theme, with a particular virtue advertised throughout the school setting for the month. The virtues may be infused in academic curriculum, highlighted in highly visible locations, and reinforced in school assemblies. School guidance staff may choose a group of peers from each grade level to help plan and participate in classroom activities that highlight a particular character trait.

Peer counselors can be visible through their participation in school projects or assemblies designed to reinforce these traits.

Peer counselors are often utilized in junior high or middle school and high school programming to facilitate a positive learning environment. During adolescence, the influence of peers increases so having peers in a leadership position is consistent with the psychosocial development of this age-group. Peer counselors at this school level often help facilitate conflict mediation and bullying prevention programs. The Safe School Ambassadors program, a peer counseling program that addresses concerns about bullying and school climate, is listed on the National Registry of Evidence-based Programs and Practices (NREPP) that is provided by the federal Substance Abuse and Mental Health Services Administration (SAMHSA). The role of a peer counselor in school settings is very important as the counselor-to-student ratio in junior high or middle schools and high schools can be very high and most bullying occurs when adults are not present. Peer leaders can provide information and support to their fellow students as well as refer problems outside their scope to their adult leaders.

High school signifies the eventual launching into young adulthood. Students' choices of classes will impact the choices they have once they graduate. Most high schools have peer counseling programs that support the school's guidance program. Link Crew is an example of an orientation program that pairs high school junior and senior students with incoming freshmen to facilitate their introduction to high school, providing both parties with beneficial experiences. The freshman has a peer mentor while the more senior student receives the altruistic benefits that come with using their experience to help someone.

Higher Education

Peer counselors often serve as postsecondary resident advisers and can play a meaningful role in helping new students feel at home in their new physical environment. For many freshmen, living away from home for the first time is an experience that is both highly sought after and stressful at the same time. To this end, resident advisers can assist the recent high school graduate in acclimating to the college experience. This includes the balancing of more demanding learning standards juxtaposed with more "out of class" or free time. Peers who not long ago experienced this same transition can easily relate to the questions and concerns of program participants in a way in which adult leaders may not be able.

In addition to working in residence halls, college peer counselors take on a variety of nonteaching roles in the areas of orientation, academic advising, academic probation or retention, career exploration, learning disabilities, student recreation, student government, financial aid, and campus activity planning. Most campuses also use peer counselors in outreach programs designed to reach out to high school students who are interested in attending that school. Having a peer component in outreach programs is especially important for students from underserved populations and/or first-generation college students who may lack the support of adults who have negotiated a postsecondary academic system and may need assistance navigating the college admission and matriculation process.

Many academic advising programs use peer counselors. The peer counselors are often advanced undergraduate or graduate students who qualify for campus-based employment and may be preparing for a career in student affairs. College students who are struggling academically may feel less intimidated by talking to a peer counselor than to an administrator or faculty member. Having peer counselors participate in retention efforts is also helpful as it is likely that the peer counselors can provide more frequent contact with struggling students than their academic advisers can.

Health Care

Peer counseling is used in many programs that address a variety of health-related issues. These include but are not limited to the following topics: wellness, adolescent reproductive health, the management of chronic physical and mental health conditions, substance abuse prevention and intervention, and veterans' issues. A good example of a health-related peer counseling program is the breast-feeding peer counseling program offered through the federal Women, Infants, and Children (WIC) program. This model program utilizes a standardized manual in its training. Having a training manual ensures that all peers receive the necessary breadth of knowledge. The 13 modules in the training curriculum cover topics ranging from becoming a WIC peer counselor to concerns breast-feeding mothers may have when they are separated from their child. Each of the modules is covered during the daylong training for the program's peer counselors with the overall goal of facilitating peer-to-peer communication.

Elderly

Peer counseling can also be beneficial to elderly people who are living at home. While some peer counseling programs designed to stimulate socialization may be offered at senior centers, others may be tied to ensuring the senior citizen is receiving adequate basic care. It is vital that aging adults are able to complete their daily living tasks. This segment of the population may be more homebound than other groups due to limited mobility and economic resources. Peer counselors who provide in-home services, usually sponsored by county programming, can monitor mental and physical health status. This service is an example of a peer counseling program that fulfills a very valuable service and one that is an important adjunct to the professional health care provider. Aging adults who are living in an assisted living community or hospital setting might also benefit from the social support of a peer counselor.

Substance Abuse

Many self-help recovery programs are based on the principle that those who have sustained abstinence can offer support and guidance to those who are struggling with various types of addiction or malaise. These people are called sponsors, and this peer-to-peer contact is essential to this type of program. Alcoholics Anonymous World Services literature describes welcoming newcomers with acceptance and without judgment. The most well-known 12-step program is Alcoholics Anonymous (A.A.); however, there are also programs for various types of addictions (Cocaine Anonymous, Crystal Meth Anonymous, Marijuana Anonymous, Nicotine Anonymous) and mental health or behavioral disorders (Gamblers Anonymous, Sexual Compulsives Anonymous, Overeaters Anonymous). These types of peer counseling programs also offer services to families of those with addiction or mental health issues. These include Adult Children of Alcoholics, Al-Anon, and Alateen.

The utilization of peer counseling in substance abuse prevention on a global level is documented in a 2003 United Nations report titled *Peer to Peer: Using Peer to Peer Strategies in Drug Abuse Prevention*. The handbook offers a comprehensive overview of how to develop and implement culturally sensitive substance abuse peer programming. The handbook was developed as the result of a Global Youth Network Project meeting about drug abuse prevention with participants from several different countries and is an illustration of the inherent power of human connection and peer contact with persons across the globe.

Yvonne Ortiz-Bush

See also Group Parenting Classes; Parent Study Groups; Parenting Education; Self-Help; Social Support

Further Readings

Carns, A. W., Carns, M. R., & Wright, J. (1993). Students as paraprofessionals in four-year colleges and universities: Current practice compared to prior practice. *Journal of College Student Development, 34*, 358–363.

D'Andrea, V. J., & Salovey, P. (Eds.). (1996). *Peer counseling: Skills, ethics, and perspectives*. Palo Alto, CA: Science and Behavior Books.

Geldard, K., & Patton, W. (2007). Adolescent peer counselling: Enhancing the natural conversational helping skills of young people. *Australian Journal of Guidance & Counselling, 17*(1), 28–48.

Karcher, M. (2009). Increases in academic connectedness among high school students who serve as cross-age peer mentors. *Professional School Counseling, 12*(4), 292–299.

Newton, F. B., Ender, S. C., & Gardner, J. N. (2010). *Students helping students: A guide to peer educators on college campuses.* San Francisco, CA: Jossey-Bass.

Tindall, J. A. (2009). *Peer power, book one: Workbook: Becoming an effective peer helper and conflict mediator* (4th ed.). New York, NY: Routledge.

Tindall, J. A. (2009). *Peer power, book two: Strategies for the professional leader: Applying peer helper skills* (3rd ed.). New York, NY: Routledge.

Tindall, J. A. (2009). *Peer power, book two: Workbook: Applying peer helper skills* (3rd ed.). New York, NY: Routledge.

Tindall, J. A., & Black, D. R. (2009). *Peer programs: An in-depth look at peer programs: Planning, implementation, and administration* (2nd ed.). New York, NY: Routledge.

Walther, W. A., Abelson, S., & Malmon, A. (2014). Active minds: Creating peer to peer mental health awareness. *Journal of College Student Psychotherapy, 28,* 12–22.

PERSON OF THE THERAPIST

Clinicians bring into the therapy room their training, ethics, and their own personal history and personality. The person of the therapist is that personal part of himself or herself that every clinician brings into the client–therapist relationship. At its core, the idea of the person of the therapist, also referred to as self of the therapist, highlights that the self of each clinician is a clinical tool that can be used as part of the therapeutic process. One of the key curative factors in therapy is that in the relationship between the therapist and clients the therapist's own emotions, ideas, and vulnerabilities are as much a part of the therapeutic relationship as are the clients' presenting concerns, abilities, and background.

The importance of the person of the therapist was introduced by clinical approaches that placed a greater emphasis on the relationship between therapists and clients than on specific techniques. Various roles of the therapist range from the removed, objective stance of the therapist in psychoanalytic therapy to active participation with the clients as found in symbolic-experiential therapy. Whatever the stance, there is a general acknowledgment that the human qualities of the therapist are an essential element of clinical practice and training. The field of marriage and family therapy has highlighted the person of the therapist in certain models of therapy and supervision. This entry gives an overview of the elements of focus when discussing the person of the therapist and explains how those elements are applied in clinical practice.

Overview

The assumption that clinicians must overcome any personal issues or struggles to be skilled psychotherapists often results in a reluctance to acknowledge person-of-the-therapist issues. Therapists' personal issues must always be monitored as an ongoing area for growth. However, an expanded perspective of the person or self of the therapist proposes that difficult or painful life experiences can act as an asset or as a hindrance depending on how they are addressed. A couple and family therapy perspective assumes that the family-of-origin experiences and contextual influences affect all individuals and relationships, including the therapist. Exploration is achieved by unpacking the unique history that has informed the therapist's beliefs, values, and biases. Past experiences and ongoing contextual influences work together to affect the therapist's inner response to clients in various ways. These responses influence the therapist–client relationship, which can be used to enhance or obstruct the effectiveness of therapy.

The Self in Context

All people are influenced by the broader context (e.g., gender, culture, spirituality, race, or ethnicity) that informs the meaning they make from their life experiences. An individual's unique combination of contextual experiences and the personal meanings they draw from those experiences collectively create their view of the world. Therapists, in particular, must become aware of their own worldview, which is created by their context and personal meanings, and accept that this view will not always be shared with their clients. Identifying these contextual influences serves to make personal beliefs and values explicit for further consideration. A few examples of important areas for self-examination are culture, race, socioeconomic status (SES), religiosity, spirituality, gender, and sexual identity.

The discovery of the personal meaning that has been created by the therapist's contextual factors enhances the self of the therapist by revealing personal biases and assumptions. Values and beliefs are an inherent part of human nature; however, it is a critical part of clinical practice to continually examine assumptions. Overlooking the role of therapist biases and assumptions may become detrimental to therapy. Clients' beliefs and values that differ from those of the therapist could potentially be viewed as pathological instead of an opportunity to gain a deeper understanding of the clients' lived experiences. There is substantial evidence to suggest that therapists' awareness of their own contextual influences improves clients' experience in therapy when the client's gender and cultural as well as ethnic background differs from the therapist's.

Family of Origin and the Self

A crucial part of working effectively with families and couples is to recognize the ways in which family upbringing has influenced therapists' personal beliefs about how family members should and should not interact. The personal exploration of the therapist's relationships with parents, siblings, and extended family members, or the family of origin, is an intricate, sometimes difficult part of clinical training and practice. Unresolved issues affect the way a therapist feels about particular clients that remind the therapist of his or her own family members. Therapists' unconscious reactions to clients act as a filter for interpreting the information that is shared in therapy instead of making the best efforts to understand the perspective of the clients.

For instance, a therapist's strained relationship with parents during childhood could result in an emotional reaction to particular clients that can inhibit therapeutic progress. On the other hand, a conscious awareness of various experiences in the family of origin can provide the therapist with an inherent ability to respond to clients' needs. No one is affected by similar family experiences (e.g., alcoholism, divorce) in the same way, so an important consideration for self-of-the-therapist development is to bridge the gap between past and present experiences.

The Experience of the Inner Self

Couple and family therapists are expected to gain a deeper insight into their own family history through reflection, examination, challenge, and exploration to be effective clinicians. The therapist's emotional reactions during session can be used with intention to create a more genuine human interaction that fosters positive therapy outcomes. However, an important aspect of this process is to learn which events from the past may trigger an emotional reaction in the present. Self-of-the-therapist work includes developing a self-awareness of particular feelings and the physical reactions to those emotions as they are happening during therapy sessions. The unique emotions can be used as a tool for a deeper therapy relationship once they are identified.

Emotions such as hurt, fear, loss, or shame result in a physical reaction that is unique to each person. Over time, a pattern of emotional responses to clients' circumstances that mirror those of the therapist will begin to emerge that can provide an opportunity for personal growth and understanding. In-session emotional awareness allows the therapist to differentiate between the clients' experiences and their own reactions, which ensures the focus of therapy remains dedicated to the clients' needs. If therapists find themselves struggling with a case or a specific issue that they are not able to resolve, they are encouraged to address self-of-the-therapist concerns through supervision, with a trusted colleague, or through their own therapy.

For example, a therapist with a history of physical abuse may struggle to work with any clients that trigger a personal emotion of fear during sessions. The self of the therapist work would include learning the personal trigger (e.g., fear) that may or may not be the experience of the clients. This insight can be used as a resource for greater empathy to advocate for clients' vulnerable and fearful experiences. However, it is also the therapist's responsibility to recognize his or her own struggles with abuse victims or perpetrators and seek outside consultation to make informed decisions that are in the best interest of the clients.

Person of the Therapist in Practice

There is strong evidence to suggest that the therapist–client relationship is a foundation for effective therapy regardless of the particular approach. However, a therapist's chosen clinical approach will influence how the use of self may be used as a tool for effective therapy. The wide array of therapeutic approaches offers many different ways to view the role of self in therapy.

The Sounding Board

The therapist as an objective, removed observer is expected to resolve his or her own personal issues before practicing psychotherapy, suggesting the self of the therapist influences may be damaging to the process of therapy. Extensive training works to uncover and resolve these issues so therapy can be effective. Clinical approaches that are informed by this use of self include psychoanalysis and Bowenian family therapy.

The Coauthor

The therapist is considered a coauthor in therapy models that are informed by the assumption that each client's perspective is equally valid. These approaches emphasize a focus on the client's meaning that he or she draws from lived experiences. The therapist's contextual influences and worldview are suspended to avoid invalidating or imposing the therapist's values and beliefs onto the clients. Careful and intentional self-disclosure is used to make a different meaning of the clients' lives. Narrative therapy and feminist family therapy are two examples of such approaches.

The Human Being

The humanity of the therapist is the focus of models of therapy that emphasize new experiences for clients' growth. Experiential therapy models assume that both the therapist and the client as humans need genuine experiences in order to grow. One major assumption about the self of the therapist in experiential models is that new genuine human experiences change both clients and therapists simultaneously. Within this theoretical lens, self of the therapist work is ongoing, as genuine interactions take place and change occurs for both clients and therapists alike.

Intentionality can be a key factor in determining whether the interventions and actions therapists decide to use are in the best interest of clients or whether they are self-serving and tied to unresolved person-of-the-therapist issues. As such, therapists should continually question intentions to ensure they are not acting from a self-serving place. Continual self-examination in therapeutic practice is recommended to understand one's intentionality and rationale for therapeutic decisions. Client needs should be at the forefront of all therapeutic decision-making processes. Through the person-of-the-therapist discovery process, therapists are able to stretch themselves to grow and are better able to understand what strengths they possess. In turn, these strengths can be used to aid clients to change and overcome their unique problems.

M. L. Parker and Andrew H. Rose

See also Common Factors; Experiential Family Therapy; Family of Origin; Narrative Therapy; Psychoanalytic Family Therapy; Self of the Therapist; Therapeutic Alliance; Therapists' Values

Further Readings

Aponte, H., & Kissil, K. (2014). If I can grapple with this I can truly be of use in the therapy room: Using the therapist's own emotional struggles to facilitate effective therapy. *Journal of Marital and Family Therapy*, 40(2), 152–164.

Aponte, H., & Winter, J. (1987). The person and practice of the therapist: Treatment and training. In M. Baldwin (Ed.), *The use of self in therapy* (2nd ed., pp. 127–165). New York, NY: Haworth.

Cheon, H., & Murphy, M. J. (2007). The self-of-the-therapist awakened: Postmodern approaches to the use of self in marriage and family therapy. *Journal of Feminist Family Therapy: An International Forum*, 19(1), 1–16. doi:10.1300/J086v19n01_01

Timm, T. M., & Blow, A. J. (1999). Self-of-the-therapist work: A balance between removing restraints and identifying resources. *Contemporary Family Therapy: An International Journal*, 21(3), 331–351. doi:10.1023/A:1021960315503

Titelman, P. (1987). Chapter 1: The therapist's own family. In P. Titelman (Ed.), *The therapist's own family: Toward the differentiation of self* (pp. 3–41). Northvale, NJ: Aronson.

Play Family Therapy

Given that family therapists work with the entire family, it is important to have interventions that include children. Play therapy is an approach where children are encouraged to act out their feelings through play and other creative arts activities. Play family therapy is an effective way to engage everyone and is not only developmentally aligned with children's needs; it is also experientially therapeutic for adults. Historically, play therapists have worked primarily with children individually, and family therapists have felt unprepared for how to integrate children effectively. However, family play therapy has emerged in the field and uses play scenarios to assess family dynamics and to intervene in ways that can transform systemic functioning.

Historical Background

The idea of providing counseling to children started in the late 1920s with Anna Freud and Melanie Klein, as they discussed applying the principles of psychoanalysis to children. In the 1940s, Virginia Axline adapted Carl Rogers's person-centered theory into child-centered play therapy. In this nondirective approach, Axline suggested that by providing a warm environment and supportive relationship, the counselor could trust the children's inherent drives toward growth. Toys are used as children's words, and play is used as their language to work through their difficulties. Axline did not believe that working with the parents was necessary in order for the children to improve.

As play therapy continued to develop, various theories were adapted for play therapy. For example, Violet Oaklander developed Gestalt-based play therapy, Susan Knell applied cognitive-behavioral therapy (CBT) principles to play, and Terry Kottman created Adlerian play therapy. Play therapists often primarily worked with children individually in order to give them their own attention—though some therapists did see the benefit of including families in the process of play therapy. Bernard and Louise Guerney developed filial therapy, which is a method of teaching nondirective play therapy skills to parents in order to build a healing connection between the parents and child.

The discipline of family therapy developed separately from these strides made in play therapy. The field of family therapy began in the 1950s with several key founders. Nathan Ackerman, a child psychiatrist, recognized the systemic impact of families on individuals. He noticed the importance of the roles of family members and began seeing families alongside his individual patients from a psychodynamic perspective. Also in the 1950s, researchers began studying families that had members diagnosed with schizophrenia, looking for family patterns that were unique to these families. In the 1960s, Murray Bowen developed a theory that conceptualized problems through the dynamics of the family system and encouraged families to gain awareness of these relational patterns in therapy. He also suggested that dysfunction can be transmitted across family generations. Salvador Minuchin developed structural family therapy (SFT) and considered the family's organization, which consisted of hierarchical subsystems and boundaries, as an important part of their functioning.

There were questions as to the child's place in family therapy. Family therapists worried that children's developmental level prevented them from being able to understand or contribute to the process. There was a concern that it was not possible to balance the adults' and children's needs simultaneously. They also wanted to protect children from topics that were not developmentally appropriate. Over time, the belief developed that children are vital members to the family system and the growth process of the family, and therapists began working on integrating children into the therapeutic process with families.

Carl Whitaker and Virginia Satir were family therapists who used experiential activities with the whole family and discussed the importance of reserving play space in family therapy. While other therapists wrote about the importance of including children in family therapy, specific techniques on how to incorporate play were largely missing from the literature. Some therapists suggested allowing children to play alone while the adults talked. Others suggested using play activities such as role-plays or free play as well as coloring or encouraging the family to play games while the counselor taught and modeled new skills. In the 1990s, both Eliana Gil and Charles Schaefer began writing on how to effectively integrate play therapy techniques into family therapy.

Tenets

There are basic principles of play therapy and family therapy that are important to keep in mind in order to effectively use family play therapy interventions.

Play Therapy

When working with children, it is important to consider children's emotional and cognitive development and avoid treating them as small adults or to attempt to rush their development. Verbal communication is not always the most effective way to convey their emotional experiences. Play is a natural language for children, and it allows children a way to process feelings and can be a means of a cathartic expression. Play promotes the development of creative thinking and gives children the chance to practice new solutions. Children have naturally rich imaginations; therefore, fantasy gives children the chance to gain a sense of power and mastery in a way they don't have access to in the real world. Therapists hope that if children are given a chance to communicate their experiences through play within an accepting therapeutic relationship, the children will learn healthier ways to express emotions and more functional behaviors.

Family Therapy

Families have predictable relationship and communication patterns. These patterns result in rules by which the families function and organize. Individuals' symptoms occur as a result of dysfunctional rules. For example, the organization of the family may have problems around unbalanced subsystems and hierarchies or boundaries that are too open or too closed. Often, the family will seek equilibrium around these rules and attempt to maintain balance even if it is causing impairment. An effective family therapist wants to join the family, create insight for the family to see how the system is not working, and help adjust the dynamics. Changing parts of the relationship patterns, structure, or rules can bring about healthier functioning for the system and the individuals.

Rationale and Benefits

When seeing children as an integrative part of family therapy, the assumptions change about where the problems lie. Seeing the child individually assumes the child is primarily responsible for his or her symptoms. In play family therapy, the environment is considered important as it impacts the development of children. Therefore, the responsibility for the problem shifts to the entire family.

Rather than assuming that children do not have anything significant to add to therapy sessions, family play therapists believe that children add value. In fact, children's play is often an enactment of the family's difficulties and can be insightful. Children are less adept at disguising problems, so they can sometimes give a more accurate picture of what is happening in the family. Play is a medium through which family therapists gain this perspective in a nonthreatening way.

Play can strengthen the family's cohesion by creating a fun and spontaneous environment where family members can bond. Often, families come to counseling stressed and focused on the negatives. By introducing play, families can reconnect and be energized. Parents can also gain new perspectives by viewing the world through their children's eyes. Typically, children are compelled to enter the adults' world by being required to use language and to control their impulses of exploration. Games even ask children to play by predetermined rules. Through play, parents enter children's worlds and may understand what the child is trying to communicate, enabling them to connect in meaningful ways they have not done before.

Family play therapists believe that a lack of language skills does not have to be a disadvantage for effective therapy. Play provides an opportunity for using metaphors to express their internal world and conflicts. Children's ability to fantasize allows them to symbolically communicate about struggles. For example, children who want to feel safe or powerful may create stories with themes of strong characters versus the weak. Metaphors are effective in disarming charged topics by distancing the family from the problem. This alternative form of communication can be effective for the whole family, given that much of the family dynamics happens in nonverbal ways. Using the metaphor, the family play therapists assess these dynamics and functioning and encourage families to try new behaviors, find creative solutions, and practice problem-solving strategies.

Assessment

At the beginning of family play therapy, there is a goal for the therapist to create a safe environment where everyone can share his or her perspectives freely. The therapists should discuss ground rules to set up expectations for this openness. The therapist wants to assess the family dynamics, the symptoms they bring, the solutions they have tried, and their strengths. Using play activities, there is the opportunity to assess these areas. While the family engages in play, the therapist observes the interactions of the family. The therapist does not talk or interrupt the family during this process. By watching how parents handle setting limits and navigating conflicts, there will be clues about boundaries, the hierarchy, or how flexible or cohesive the family is. The family play therapist will also observe the family's level of enjoyment and strengths. These strengths can be shared with the family as assets they can build on for making the changes they desire.

Interventions

A variety of creative modalities such as drama, art, and specially selected toys can be used in family play therapy. There are two phases in which the therapist should engage the family: In the creation portion, the therapist gives the family a directive and allows them time to work. In the processing portion, the therapist asks questions in order to gain more insight about what was taking place internally for the family members and what they learned.

Art

Art is a versatile way to engage families in play. Colors, markers, paint, various forms of paper, and collage materials can all be made available. The helpful aspect of art in family play therapy is the process the family is involved in rather than the final product that is created.

There are several techniques that families can engage in together using art projects. For example, family play therapists could ask the family members to complete a kinetic family portrait.

The therapist gives the instructions to draw a picture of everyone in their family doing something. When the family is done drawing, the therapist will process the pictures by asking questions about who each person is in the drawing and what each one is doing. Other questions that a therapist might ask are the following: What is this person thinking? What is this person feeling? What happened just before this picture? What will happen just after this picture? Questions about the connections between family members in the pictures can also be asked, such as the following: Which of these people are most alike? Most different? Most like Mom? Most like Dad?

Evidence of family dynamics are revealed in the picture by details, omissions, or relative sizes and positions of where members are drawn. For example, if the mother and children are all depicted inside a house while the father is outside, it may suggest the family feels a disconnect with the father. Family members often gain insight into what may be concerns of individual members by viewing the differences of perspectives in their drawings.

Eliana Gil also developed an art activity called the "family aquarium." In this project, family members are asked to create a fish to represent themselves. Afterward, they are asked to make an aquarium for their fish on a large sheet of blue paper and arrange the fish inside the aquarium. Again, a variety of art supplies should be available so families can depict places to hide and play, things to eat, or dangers lurking in the environment.

Family dynamics will be revealed by observing how the family interacts during the process of assembling the aquarium and through processing it afterward. The therapist talks about the art with the family to further examine potential dynamics. Details in the picture that depict an enriched environment versus a sparse or threatening environment can point to strengths or stresses the family may have. For example, if there is food placed in the aquarium for the family, it may suggest the family has a nurturing quality. A predator may depict an unspoken danger in the family.

Sand Tray

When using sand tray techniques with families, the family play therapist needs to have a large box partially filled with sand and several different types of miniatures, which are small toys that represent a wide variety of animals, mythical or magical creatures, objects, and people in the world. Miniatures need to be carefully selected to provide a wide variety of potential symbols for families. The benefit of using miniatures is that it does not require artistic ability, so families may be more comfortable using this method. To begin, therapists can give families a variety of directives. For example, they may ask the family to create a world in the sand. They could ask the family to create an ideal world or a world that represents a solution to the problem they bring in. If the family is dealing with a change in structure or other significant life event like a divorce or death, they may ask to create a world before the change and after the change. The sand tray could also be divided into sections, and the family could build individual worlds in each section. The family then works together to create the world while the therapist observes.

During the processing, the therapist seeks to understand their world from the family's perspective using the metaphors and the symbols they selected. The therapist should ask about the world as a whole and then start inquiring about the details. As with the art and aquarium, relative position of items placed and themes of the objects selected can be further explored by noticing patterns and expanding on the metaphors present in the world they create. For example, if there is a dragon in the midst of farm animals, the therapist may ask what it is like for the animals to have a dragon in the farm. The therapist may also ask questions such as the following: What changes would you make in the world? This allows the family members to rearrange miniatures or add objects that represent solutions to issues that are present in the sand tray. This symbolic shift can then be applied to the family's real-life situation by asking questions like this: What parts of this sand tray apply to your family?

Play Genogram

The play genogram also uses the miniatures to work within metaphors. Each family member is asked to choose a miniature that represents the family members, including himself or herself. The miniatures are arranged on a piece of paper that contains a drawing of the family's genogram that the therapist completes. The therapist asks the family members to describe the symbols they chose for each member. Follow-up questions about themes and relationships among the symbols should be asked. The therapist frames all questions within the context of the metaphors. For example, the therapist would ask questions such as the following: What would the lion say to the sheep? Who is the mouse most afraid of? Who is the princess closest to? During this process, the therapist will attend to the emotional reactions of other family members during this process. The family dynamics, connections between members, and the roles they play become evident through the processing of this activity.

Puppets

The family puppet interview is a drama technique that asks the family to talk through puppets. The therapist will need a variety of types of puppets for family members to choose from. For example, there should be vulnerable, aggressive, magical, and scary puppets as well as those, such as animals, that can hide or fly away. The therapist explains that this is a fun technique that can make it easier for parents and children to talk about what has been going on. They family members decide which puppet will represent them. Insight into the family dynamics may be revealed even at this stage by seeing which one chooses first, how enthusiastic or reserved members are, and how the parents respond to the child's process of choosing a puppet. The puppets often align with the individual's role or personality in the family. For example, a timid child may choose a mouse, and an aggressive child may choose a shark.

The therapist asks the family to speak through the puppets and tell a story with a beginning, a middle, and an end. Another variation may be to ask the family to reenact a difficult situation they had just experienced so that the therapist can get a good idea of what really happened. Therapists should give the families space to come up with the story or reenact without intervening. They should observe what type of conflict was presented and how it was resolved. They should look for who takes the lead and who is left out.

During the processing part of this activity, the therapist continues talking to the family through their puppets. The therapist may focus, expand on, or ask the puppets to re-create certain parts of the story. He or she may explore alternate solutions or ask what it was like for characters to experience that scenario. For example, a quiet bunny may give advice to an angry bear about having patience. The key is to encourage the family members to interact with each other from their characters and hypothesize about the story in ways that can be translated into solutions for the family in their life at home.

Sonya Lorelle

See also Boundaries; Experiential Family Therapy; Family Assessment, Models of; Family Strengths; General Systems Theory; Genograms; Joining; Metaphors; Role-Playing; Rule-Setting; Systems Theory; Virginia Satir Model

Further Readings

Bowen, N. R. (2010). *Play therapy with families: A collaborative approach to healing.* Plymouth, England: Jason Aronson.

Gil, E. (2014). *Play in family therapy* (2nd ed.). New York, NY: Guilford Press.

Lowenstein, L., & Hertlein, K. (2012). Engaging children in family sessions: Three creative interventions. *Journal of Family Psychotherapy, 23*, 62–66.

Pereira, J. K. (2014). Can we play too? Experiential techniques for family therapists to actively include children in sessions. *The Family Journal: Counseling and Therapy for Couples and Families, 22*(4), 390–396.

Sori, C. F. (2006). *Engaging children in family therapy: Creative approaches to integrating theory and research in clinical practice.* New York, NY: Routledge.

Polyamory

Understanding various types of relationships is essential to becoming an effective, culturally sensitive family therapist. A counselor's negative biases, if left unchecked and uninformed, can result in inadvertent shaming of clients and ultimately hinder the therapeutic process. Although many people may believe that monogamy is the cornerstone of a healthy relationship, this assumption does not necessarily hold true for everyone. Consensual non-monogamy, or CNM, represents a broad range of relationships in which people agree to have multiple emotional, romantic, and/or sexual relationships with others. These relationships vary by multiple factors, such as whether sexual, emotional, or romantic aspects of connections are emphasized. One type of CNM is polyamory. Typically, polyamory consists of having more than one emotionally intimate relationship simultaneously with everyone's consent. This entry provides detailed discussion on polyamory and how it may manifest in people's lives; approaches to polyamory; whether polyamory is an orientation, practice, or identity; the historical and multicultural perspectives on polyamory; and the potential challenges and rewards of polyamory.

Defining *Polyamory*

The word *polyamory* emerges from Greek roots: *poly* meaning many and *amor* signifying love. The "love" in poly relationships indicates serious, intimate, and romantic affectionate bonds, and the stability of these bonds can vary. The connections often involve sexual activities but not necessarily in every case. The bonds may only be romantic and/or emotional. Polyamory is often used synonymously with responsible, ethical, or intentional non-monogamy, but here it is discussed as one particular form of CNM. Although there is not one single definition of polyamory, it tends to be differentiated from other relationship models by several factors. CNM, including polyamory, is distinguished from infidelity and adultery by its openness and the consent of the people involved. Unlike other types of CNM, such as swinging, polyamory often involves long-term, emotionally intimate relationships rather than strictly sexual partnerships. However, this element does not necessarily mean that polyamorous people do not have strictly sexual relationships, and their perspectives on casual sex tend to vary. Additionally, polyamory is different from relationships in which only men have access to multiple partners (i.e., polygyny). In polyamory, all genders typically have access to additional partners.

Polyamory is often associated with honesty and open communication, nonpossessiveness, egalitarianism, and community. Without honesty and a great deal of open communication, maintaining multiple relationships can be difficult to sustain. Many factors may be negotiated within polyamorous relationships, such as sexual and emotional boundaries as well as time constraints. One way to view the nonpossessiveness in polyamorous relationships is by comparing the scarcity model to the abundance model as applied to relationships. According to the scarcity model, love is finite; thus, people must compete for it, which can result in jealousy and feelings of loss. It is important to note that polyamorous individuals are not immune from jealousy but are more likely to view jealousy as something to discuss and work through rather than avoid. On the other hand, individuals who subscribe to the abundance model believe that love is a vast resource rather than a scarce commodity. People who describe themselves as polyamorous may aim to reach compersion, which can be thought of as the opposite of jealousy. Compersion reflects feelings of joy and happiness that a partner has other relationships.

Egalitarianism, or equal treatment in relationships regardless of factors such as gender and sexual orientation, is often practiced in polyamory, although it is not a necessary ingredient. Within polyamorous relationships, individuals may emphasize finding community and view larger, more complex extended families as preferable family structures to monogamy.

Approaches to Polyamory

Polyamory can be practiced in a multitude of ways, only a few of which are presented in this entry. The terms represent common definitions within polyamorous communities, but they are neither standard nor universal. It is always best to defer to people's self-descriptions.

One of the most popular forms of polyamory is polyfidelity. This type of arrangement may or may not consist of marriage. Polyfidelitous arrangements are often characterized by a group of three or more partners who consider themselves committed and/or married to everyone within the group. Boundaries are often negotiated among the group and members may or may not be sexually available to all the individuals in the group. They may live together in one home and share their resources. Polyfidelitous relationships can be closed, which means that the individuals engage in romantic and/or sexual activities only within the group. Open polyfidelitous relationships allow for emotional, romantic, and sexual relations outside the group and if marriage is involved may be referred to as open group marriages. Within such arrangements, there may be rules about the acceptable extent of sexual activity allowed outside the group.

Polyamory can consist of bonds that vary in commitment. Some individuals may choose neither to label nor to prioritize their various connections. Others may label their connections according to depth or commitment. One label set that is used with some polyamorous relationships is primary, secondary, and tertiary. Primary relationships are often described as the most intimate, closest relationship type and given the most priority and energy. These relationships may involve shared life paths, commitment to a future together, and coparenting. Secondary relationships can also be considered close but are given less time and priority than primary relationships. Thus, they may involve intimacy such as sexual activity, emotional support, and a desire for a future but may have less emphasis on shared life goals or financial involvements. Tertiary relationships are given less time and energy than secondary relationships but may still include sex and emotional support. Time devoted to tertiary partners may be sporadic rather than regular.

Polyamorous relationships may be described by the number of people involved and how they are connected. Examples include triads, which consist of three people, and quads, comprised of four individuals. The level of connection can be combined with the number of people to define the relationship. For example, within a group of three, configurations can include a triangle or vee pattern. Triangles indicate equal bonds among members whereas a vee pattern (like the letter V) implies that two of the three pairs are substantially more bonded than the third pair. Additionally, relationships can consist of combinations of relationship configurations, such as swinging and polyamory, or one partner being monogamous while the other partner engages in polyamory. Relationship configurations can evolve over time.

Is Polyamory an Orientation, Practice, or Identity?

People disagree on whether polyamory is a sexual or relationship orientation, relational practice, or identity, and each of these concepts implies certain expectations and assumptions. Thus, understanding these multiple perspectives can provide insight about the multitude of ways that clients may experience polyamory.

Some assert that polyamory is a sexual or relationship orientation with its own pattern of identity development. Within this framework, polyamory is conceptualized as similar to an LGBTQ+ (lesbian, gay, bisexual, transgender, queer/questioning, and others) sexual orientation and viewed as innate. Additionally, polyamory has been associated with being bisexual or pansexual (i.e., attracted to more than one gender); however, it is important not to assume that all bisexual or pansexual individuals are polyamorous and vice versa. Polyamory has also been described as a relationship orientation, or a tendency to enter into more than one intimate and/or sexual relationship at the same time. Sexual orientation represents an orientation to sexuality whereas relationship orientation reflects an orientation toward relationships. Scholars and activists have stated that describing polyamory as an orientation could allow for legal and societal benefits; however, others argue that this move would privilege polyamorous relationships above other forms of CNM.

Polyamory has been framed as a relational practice, which implies it is more related to behaviors and/or choices. Polyamory has also been viewed as a distinct identity. This viewpoint is supported by accounts of people not feeling fully authentic until they embraced themselves as polyamorous. Finally, feminist scholar Margaret Robinson has discussed polyamory and monogamy as strategic identities, a perspective that allows for shifts between monogamy and polyamory. This perspective implies that people may be polyamorous for various reasons that could be biological, social, behavioral, or related to identity. Robinson indicated that viewing polyamory in this way allows health care providers to more appropriately address clients' needs. Most likely, people are polyamorous due to a combination of these factors, and they vary based on the individual and his or her relationships.

Historical and Multicultural Perspectives on Polyamory

The idea of CNM is not new. Some ancestral societies were non-monogamous, and this diversity in relationships provides evidence that monogamy may not be biological or necessary for society to function. CNM has also emerged in the past few centuries. Scholars have referred to three waves of CNM in the United States: the first in the 1800s, the second in the 1960s, and the third in the 1990s. The most recent wave was shaped by (a) socioeconomic changes, (b) cultural shifts, and (c) social movements. Socioeconomic conditions allowed for women to be more economically independent. Additionally, polyamory has been considered an extension of a larger cultural transformation in society: romantic relationships based on equality, trust, and compatibility rather than tradition.

Several progressive social movements are also said to have shaped the third CNM wave, especially feminism, which challenged the notion of heterosexual monogamy as the ideal. Feminists who take this position assert that non-monogamous relationships allow people to radically alter gender dynamics, emphasize women's liberation, and create new relationship structures. They question whether societal emphasis on monogamy is an extension of male privilege over women's bodies and thus contradictory to egalitarian sexual relations. Some assert that polyamory could awaken spiritual awareness and even transform the world. Polyamorous groups, books, and neighborhoods have increased in the past few decades. It is important to note that most polyamorous works, especially of the self-help variety, have been written by women who are White, educated, and of middle socioeconomic status (SES). Thus, they do not embody the full range of sociocultural experiences of polyamory within the United States.

Challenges and Rewards of Polyamory

Polyamorous couples and families may experience a variety of challenges that lead them to therapy. One potential challenge is the societal norm of monogamy as the only appropriate type of romantic relationship. Mainstream media sources tend to exhibit any form of non-monogamy as infidelity, although that has been changing in recent years with polyamory featured in outlets such as the magazine *Newsweek*, ABC's *Nightline*, and MTV's *True Life*. The U.S. emphasis on monogamy can result in social pressure to conform to monogamy, disparaging remarks from loved ones, and feelings of isolation and shame. If people are also members of marginalized groups, such as sexual or ethnic minorities, the negative impacts can be compounded. For example, a person may be doubly stigmatized due to being both an ethnic minority and polyamorous.

Another challenge can be the complexity of multiple relationships. Within the process of polyamory, there can be a great deal of negotiation and sharing of difficult feelings such as jealousy and abandonment. Managing multiple partners can be challenging in terms of dedicating enough time to keep all parties satisfied. Despite these challenges, people often describe significant rewards from being polyamorous. The hard work of maintaining the various relationships can result in healing from difficult emotions, maturity, and satisfaction. Working through conflict may allow connections to deepen in polyamorous relationships. Indeed, one study by Todd Graham Morrison and colleagues demonstrated that polyamorous individuals experienced greater intimacy than their monogamous counterparts. When counseling polyamorous families and couples, it is important to understand polyamory while listening carefully to clients' unique experiences and insights.

Manijeh Badiee

See also Attachment and Romantic Love; Commitment; Couples and Marriage Counseling; Fidelity; Love, Theories of; Love, Types of; Love and Rituals; Open Relationships; Polygamy; Sexual Intimacy

Further Readings

Anapol, D. (2010). *Polyamory in the 21st century: Love and intimacy with multiple partners.* Lanham, MD: Rowman & Littlefield.

Anderlini-D'Onofrio, S. (2010). *Gaia and the new politics of love: Notes for a poly planet.* Berkeley, CA: North Atlantic Books.

Brandon, M. (2011). The challenge of monogamy: Bringing it out of the closet and into the treatment room. *Sexual and Relationship Therapy, 26*(3), 271–277.

Easton, D., & Hardy, J. W. (2009). *The ethical slut: A practical guide to polyamory, open relationships and other adventures* (2nd ed.). Berkeley, CA: Celestial Arts.

Morrison, T. G., Beaulieu, D., Brockman, M., & Beaglaoich, C. O. (2013). A comparison of polyamorous and monoamorous persons: Are there differences in indices of relationship well-being and sociosexuality? *Psychology & Sexuality, 4*(1), 75–91.

Noël, M. J. (2006). Progressive polyamory: Considering issues of diversity. *Sexualities, 9*(5), 602–620.

Robinson, M. (2013). Polyamory and monogamy as strategic identities. *Journal of Bisexuality, 13*, 21–38.

POLYGAMY

Polygamy refers to the practice of marriage to more than one person at the same time. A polygamous relationship can include any combination of genders but tends to have a central individual with multiple partners. Related terms are *polygyny*, referring to one male individual having multiple female partners, and *polyandry*, referring to one female individual having multiple male partners. For the most part, the social understanding of polygamy is in regard to polygyny, and the two terms are often used interchangeably. Bigamy refers to the act of marrying a person while being legally married to another and is illegal in the United States. Polygamy is accepted in many cultures and religions across the globe and is not uncommon despite many legal ramifications associated with the practice in many countries. Polygamy can be similar to polyamory, which refers to having open relationships with more than one partner at once. The primary difference is typically the religious connection to the practice of polygamy. Additionally, in polyamorous relationships, each partner may have multiple partners, while polygamy involves one central partner having several partners who are monogamous with the central partner. This entry further defines *polygamy*, discusses the relationship of polygamy and faith, reviews the portrayal of polygamy in the media, and details some of the issues involved in polygamy and counseling.

Defining *Polygamy*

The practice of polygamy is a divisive subject, with people having strong feelings favoring and other people strongly against the practice. Despite being illegal and looked down on in many societies, polygamy is not as rare as some may believe it to be. Due to social and legal consequences, in addition to strong stereotypes associated with polygamy, many individuals engaged in a polygamous relationship feel pressure to keep their relationship hidden. This secrecy may cause individuals to avoid seeking assistance from professionals to help with any emotional or relationship issues related to being in a polygamous relationship. However, some may seek counseling services despite the risk of exposure.

Non-monogamy as a relationship style has been common for centuries in many cultures. In an agricultural social structure, having many wives could allow men to have more children, which could mean having more individuals to assist with work. Supporting multiple spouses also requires a certain amount of financial stability. As a result, historically and today, participating in a polygamous relationship can be a signifier for status and accomplishment.

Polygamy and Faith

In the United States, polygamy is most strongly associated with the Church of Jesus Christ of Latter-Day Saints (LDS) or Mormon religious faith. In the mid-1800s, leaders within the LDS church incorporated plural marriage into the faith tradition. However, within 20 years of plural marriage being adopted by practicing Mormons, the U.S. government put forth regulations illegalizing marriage to more than one person. Quickly, the Mormon Church officially rejected the practice of polygamy. Although there are fundamentalist Mormon sects that practice polygamy, the LDS Church itself does not allow the practice.

Many other faith traditions include the act of polygamy. Polygamy is permitted in Islam, and it continues to be practiced in many countries with large Muslim populations in Africa, Asia, and the Middle East, although in some predominantly Muslim countries it is illegal. In some countries where polygamy is allowed, there is a limit on the number of wives a man can have. The act is often seen as an indicator both of living a religiously faithful life and of status.

Because the United States and many other countries have laws prohibiting polygamy, individuals seeking to live in alignment with their religious or personal beliefs, including polygamy, do so in secrecy. Some establish cohabitation on rural pieces of land, reducing the possibility of detection. Others establish living situations in more populated areas, often in areas where polygamy is more socially accepted. Immigrants to the United States from countries where polygamy is regularly practiced sometimes have a difficult time managing their traditional practices with the legal system of their new home.

Polygamy and the Media

Polygamy is often associated with abuse. Some Mormon fundamentalist marriages reportedly have involved girls just entering puberty. Some studies have included interviews with women who reported having left polygamous marriages where there was physical and emotional abuse. Advocates opposing polygamy also discuss the problem of forced polygamy, which refers to cases of individuals who do not desire to be in a polygamous relationship but feel they have no choice for social, cultural, economic, or other reasons. As a result, supporters of the practice of polygamy have a difficult time altering laws prohibiting plural marriage.

Modern media has presented the United States and the world with a variety of depictions of polygamy and plural marriage. The programs *Big Love* on HBO, *Sister Wives* on TLC, and *Unbreakable Kimmy Schmidt* on Netflix all depict relationships including several wives married to a central husband. These popular representations portray both positive and negative stereotypes regarding polygamy and can influence social perceptions and understandings of plural marriage.

Polygamy and Counseling

If working with an individual or individuals in a polygamous relationship, counselors must be aware of any personal biases or stereotypes held regarding polygamy. Counselors should review state laws regarding polygamy to ensure there is no professional requirement to report individuals engaged in a polygamous relationship. Counselors should assess whether emotional abuse, physical abuse, and/or coercion are present within any marriage but should be particularly attentive to the possibility when a client indicates being in a polygamous relationship. Consensual polygamous relationship structures are possible and individuals in these relationships may benefit from professional counseling to maneuver the pressures of maintaining this form of non-monogamy. Depending on the goals of those in therapy, improving communication is likely to be a focus in counseling. Common conflicts within a polygamous relationship revolve around jealousy, time management, resource division, and work divisions. As in many other relationships, sex, money, and children are often a cause of conflict.

Molly Rose Wilson

See also Couples, Quality Time; Multiple Family Therapy; Polyamory; Religion; Therapists' Values

Further Readings

Bailey, M., & Kaufman, A. J. (2010). *Polygamy in the monogamous world: Multicultural challenges for western law and policy.* Santa Barbara, CA: Praeger.

Hamdan, S., Auerbach, J., & Apter, A. (2009). Polygamy and mental health of adolescents. *European Child & Adolescent Psychiatry, 18,* 755–760.

Jacobson, C. K., & Burton, L. (2010). *Modern polygamy in the United States: Historical, cultural, and legal issues.* New York, NY: Oxford University Press.

Kleinplatz, P. J. (2012). *New directions in sex therapy: Innovations and alternatives.* New York, NY: Routledge.

Miller, A. C., & Karkazis, K. (2012). Health beliefs and practices in an isolated polygamist community of southern Utah. *Journal of Religion & Health, 48*(1).

Slonim-Nevo, V., & Al-Krenawi, A. (2006). Success and failure among polygamous families: The experience of wives, husbands, and children. *Family Process, 45*(3), 311–330. doi:10.1111/j.1545-5300.2006.00173.x

Zeitzen, M. K. (2008). *Polygamy: A cross-cultural analysis.* New York, NY: Berg.

Pornography

The definition of *pornography* continues to evolve with social norms and technology. In the broadest terms, *pornography* may be defined as materials containing sexually explicit imagery. The Internet created greater accessibility to pornographic material, and this has had adverse (and some positive) effects upon adolescents, couples, and families. The world changed drastically with the advent and widespread use of the Internet, which serves as a source of media consumption, social connection, and information-gathering. As of 2015, approximately 84% of the U.S. population report that they use the Internet. Internet pornography is now more widely used than any previous medium for pornographic material, including books, magazines, or movies. This entry discusses research on the effects of pornography on adolescents and couples, characteristics of pornography, and the implications of clients' pornography use for therapists.

As pornography became more accessible due to its affordability and ready availability, the content of pornography also changed. Researchers have identified an increase in content characterized by unaffectionate sex, male dominance, the objectification of women, and physical and sexual aggression toward women. With increased access to pornography and pornography taking on a more extreme and degrading form, the literature has established counseling implications for marriage and family therapists (MFTs) who work with clients who use pornographic media. It is important to note that the majority of current research is limited by its focus on heterosexual two-person models of relationships, which leaves other relationship models to be explored.

Pornography use impacts individuals, couples, and family systems. Because pornography exposure and use typically begin in adolescence and because adolescence is a developmentally appropriate time for individuals to begin coupling, it is necessary to discuss how adolescent pornography use impacts individuals, their families, and their future couplings. Pornography use is linked to decreased sexual inhibitions in some college-aged individuals and adults. Other researchers have reported an absence of negative impacts on pornography users and even some positive associations with pornography use. However, there is a concern that one of the primary reasons adolescents report using pornography is to learn about sexuality and that pornography is a distorted model of sexual relationships.

Pornography consumption in adolescence has been correlated with sexual preoccupation and a questioning of one's sexual beliefs and attitudes. Simultaneously, pornography consumption has been linked to hostile sexism toward women and attitudes that promote violence against women as well as viewing women as sex objects. Beyond attitudes, pornography has been correlated with potentially negative behaviors, including engaging in sexual activity earlier than those who do not view pornography, having sexual intercourse with multiple partners, and engaging in paid sex activities. Among adolescents, pornography use also has been correlated with increased likelihood of practicing unsafe sex, which may also mean adolescent pornography users have an increased risk of contracting or transmitting a sexually transmitted infection, having an unwanted pregnancy, and being involved in unwanted sex. All of these behaviors and risks impact an individual's well-being and the health of a couple or family system.

The lingering and continuing attitudinal beliefs perpetuated by increasingly violent pornographic messages manifest as problems in the context of couples. For instance, a female partner's psychological and relational well-being is impacted by her male partner's pornography use, which can negatively affect her self-esteem, sexual satisfaction, and relationship quality. One of the difficulties with pornography use in a couple is that both members of a couple have to agree about the rules of its use. Men are more likely to believe that pornography can be included in a sexual relationship than women. This discrepancy indicates the likelihood of disagreement about pornography use. While the majority of men may expect to use pornography under any circumstance, there is a nearly a 40% chance that a man's female partner will expect that he will abstain from viewing it. Therefore, the issue may be more complicated than the effects of pornography use and may involve expectations of pornography use in a couple.

There is a wide array of counseling implications associated with client pornography use. Therapists across the helping professions in general need more training to meet clients' needs related to sexuality. However, there are several steps that therapists can take to help their clients in regard to pornography use. Because of pornography's distorted modeling of sexuality, there is a call for therapists to educate clients about sex and sexuality, which would involve an emphasis on humanizing one's sexual partner(s) and encouraging a client to conceptualize sex as a cocreated experience. It is recommended that therapists familiarize themselves with the literature regarding the counseling implications associated with client pornography use and take an inventory of their own values and attitudes about pornography use, which would involve the cocreation of a working definition of pornography with clients. Further, it is suggested that counselors ask clients about their pornography use during an intake interview and on intake forms while modeling appropriate language that avoids slang or degrading verbiage.

*Zachary D. Bloom
and Joseph M. Graham*

See also Compulsive Sexual Behavior; Human Sexual Response; Sexual Enhancement, Sexual Toys; Sexual Health; Sexual Toys/Sexual Aids

Further Readings

Ayres, M. M., & Haddock, S. A. (2009). Therapists' approaches in working with heterosexual couples struggling with male partners' online sexual behavior. *Sexual Addiction & Compulsivity, 16*(1), 55–78.

Bleakley, A., Hennessy, M., & Fishbein, M. (2011). A model of adolescents' seeking of sexual content in their media choices. *Journal of Sex Research, 48*(4), 309–315. doi:10.1080/00224499.2010.497985

Bloom, Z. D., & Hagedorn, W. B. (2015). Male adolescents and contemporary pornography: Implications for marriage and family counselors. *The Family Journal, 23*(1), 82–89. doi:10.1177/1066480714555672

Flood, M. (2009). The harms of pornography exposure among children and young people. *Child Abuse Review*, *18*(6), 384–400.

Foubert, J. D., Brosi, M. W., & Bannon, R. S. (2011). Pornography viewing among fraternity men: Effects on bystander intervention, rape myth acceptance and behavioral intent to commit sexual assault. *Sexual Addiction & Compulsivity*, *18*(4), 212–231. doi:10.1080/10720162.2011.625552

Hald, G. M., Malamuth, N. M., & Yuen, C. (2010). Pornography and attitudes supporting violence against women: Revisiting the relationship in nonexperimental studies. *Aggressive Behavior*, *36*(1), 14–20. doi:10.1002/ab.2038

Manning, J. (2006). The impact of Internet pornography on marriage and the family: A review of the research. *Sexual Addiction & Compulsivity*, *13*, 131–165.

Owens, E. W., Behun, R. J., Manning, J. C., & Reid, R. C. (2012). The impact of Internet pornography on adolescents: A review of the research. *Sexual Addiction & Compulsivity*, *19*(1), 99–122. doi:10.1080/10720162.2012.660431

Stewart, D. N., & Szymanski, D. M. (2012). Young adult women's reports of their male romantic partner's pornography use as a correlate of their self-esteem, relationship quality, and sexual satisfaction. *Sex Roles*, *67*(5–6), 257–271.

Weber, M., Quiring, O., & Daschmann, G. (2012). Peers, parents and pornography: Exploring adolescents' exposure to sexually explicit material and its developmental correlates. *Sexuality & Culture: An Interdisciplinary Quarterly*, *16*(4), 408–427. doi:10.1007/s12119-012-9132-7

POSITIVE AND NEGATIVE FEEDBACK

In the field of marital, couple, and family therapy, ideas have been borrowed from other disciplines to help explain the structure and functioning of living systems such as couples and families. Cybernetics is a transdisciplinary approach used to explore and explain communication and control in nonliving and living systems. Norbert Wiener, the originator of cybernetics, examined different feedback mechanisms that would control a system by providing information about whether that system needed to de-amplify change (homeostasis) or amplify change. Feedback loops in a system represent the process of an action in a system creating change, which affects the environment, and the change in the environment is information that is fed back into the system as communication about what to do next. These feedback loops trigger change and are considered circular (they feed back into the system) and causal (they create change). Two types of feedback are positive feedback and negative feedback. Positive feedback is a message to the system to amplify change, and negative feedback is a message to a system to deamplify change. In the field of marital, couple, and family therapy, these cybernetic ideas are sometimes used to understand circular causality, communication, and change within family systems; this entry offers insight into systems theory in this context.

Systems Theory

Systems theory is an interdisciplinary approach to studying systems (interdependent parts that interact to form a whole) in order to identify patterns and principles to explain the interaction of subparts of the system and the system as a whole. In couple and family therapy, systems theory is used to understand the rules that govern the structure of a living system (e.g., couples, families, and communities) and can explain consequent behavior. For the study of couples and families, systems theory is informed by both cybernetics and general systems theory. Wiener maintained that cybernetics could be applied to both living and nonliving systems. However, one of the creators of general systems theory, Karl Ludwig von Bertalanffy, thought that not all principles that could be applied to closed systems (usually nonliving systems) could be applied to open systems (usually living systems). Nonetheless, both theories influenced systems theory as used to understand couples and families.

Cybernetics is the study of feedback mechanisms in systems. A family has a tendency to maintain stability by using information about its performance, which is known as feedback. Cybernetics systems can self-correct and steer toward homeostasis (maintaining stability). A family is a cybernetically rule-governed system. The interaction of family members typically follows organized, established patterns, based on the family structure. An upset or threatened family system initiates homeostatic mechanisms in order to reestablish equilibrium. In some families, the appearance of symptoms in a family member is a homeostatic effort to maintain or restore family balance, even if that equilibrium came at the expense of a symptomatic member becoming the identified "problem" in the family.

Don Jackson, a psychiatrist who influenced the development of family therapy, used the analogy of a home heating system with a thermostat to explain homeostasis. A furnace is set to respond if the temperature drops below the desired level of warmth and shut off if the temperature becomes too warm—maintaining a temperature within an acceptable range. Homeostasis is the tendency to resist change and keep things the way they are. In applying homeostasis to families, it is the unique set of behavioral, emotional, and interactional norms that create stability for the family. Maintaining homeostasis may sometimes entail maintaining a dysfunctional family behavior pattern. The therapist must then help the family break out of its repetitive patterns in order to attain a homeostatic balance at a new level rather than simply returning to its former ways of achieving balance and equilibrium. Symptoms in a family member may also develop when the family system is not sufficiently flexible to permit change in order to accommodate the changing developmental needs of its members. The key to maintaining stability in a system is to self-correct, which requires feedback.

Feedback Loops

At the core of cybernetics are feedback loops, which are circular mechanisms with a purpose of introducing information about a system's output back to its input in order to alter, correct, and ultimately govern the system's functioning and ensure its viability. Information transmitted may be positive or negative. The family stabilizes and maintains homeostasis by using negative feedback loops (or attenuating feedback loops), which are loops that promote a return to equilibrium. A family uses positive feedback loops (or amplifying feedback loops) to promote change. Periodic imbalance is inevitable in a family; therefore, feedback loops are meant to restore a behavior or escalate a behavior.

Negative feedback indicates that a system is straying off the mark and that corrections are needed to get it back on its course. It is the feedback process that opposes a deviation, thus maintaining the status quo by minimizing or resisting change. Negative feedback triggers the necessary changes that serve to put the system back on track and guards the system's steady state by maintaining homeostasis. Families use negative feedback to enforce rules, including behaviors such as guilt and punishment. Positive feedback is telling the system that things are changing, which is the opposite of negative feedback. The system responds to positive feedback by attempting to maintain homeostasis.

Positive feedback is a process that accepts the information about a deviation from how the system has been operating and accommodates to a change in the system by modifying its structure. If left unchecked, the reinforcing effects of positive feedback tend to compound the system's errors, leading to a runaway process, or a vicious cycle. A crisis that may be created by a positive feedback runaway, such as an escalating fight, may create an opportunity whereby the family may reexamine family rules and possibly make necessary changes. Both positive and negative feedback are self-correcting mechanisms, and both aim to maintain the stability of the system in response to new information. If it is not possible to return to normal, the new homeostasis is known as a second-order change. Times of stability and homeostasis are temporary in a family. The task of a family is to retain regularity and balance to maintain a sense of order and sameness. At the same time, it must promote change and growth within its members and the family as a whole. If there is too much permanence, the family may become stagnant; if there is too much change, the family may become chaotic. Well-functioning families are resilient and able to achieve change without forfeiting stability.

First-order change is when a system returns to its previous homeostasis after positive feedback. First-order change is characterized by its superficial nature. During first-order change, the family structure and rules remain the same. To apply this concept to family therapy, behaviors may change but the rules stay the same. An example of first-order change would be that dinner, which is usually ready at 6:00, is delayed until 8:00 to accommodate to a change in work schedule. If there were an argument surrounding the dinner, changing the time of dinner would temporarily address the issue but would not fully address the underlying source of the argument. This usually results in the issue appearing to change but basically remaining the same as when originally presented in therapy.

Second-order change is when a system restructures its homeostasis after positive feedback, and the rules of the system fundamentally shift. During second-order change, the family structure and the rules that guide behavior change, resulting in lasting changes in the system. Second-order change is much more difficult to attain in therapy because it requires the system to be willing to restructure, which it resists at its core due to the nature of systems. In the example of the argument about dinner, a second-order change would occur if the family agreed to attend family therapy in order to generate possible solutions to a family's underlying issues instead of simply voicing grievances. Family therapists who adopt a second-order cybernetic view (or cybernetics of cybernetics) see family therapy as a cocreation between themselves and family members who together construct potential changes.

Julie Martin

See also Cybernetics; First-Order Change; Milan Team; Neutrality and Curiosity; Recursiveness; Second-Order Change; Systemic Family Therapy

Further Readings

Gehart, D. (2010). *Mastering competencies in family therapy*. Belmont, CA: Brooks/Cole.

Gladding, S. T. (2011). *Family therapy: History, theory, and practice*. Englewood Cliffs, NJ: Pearson.

Goldenberg, I., & Goldenberg, H. (2004). *Family therapy: An overview* (6th ed.). Pacific Grove, CA: Brooks/Cole-Thomson Learning.

Nichols, M. P. (2013). *Family therapy: Concepts and methods* (10th ed.). Boston, MA: Allyn & Bacon.

POSITIVE PSYCHOLOGY

Positive psychology is a movement in psychology that focuses on people's strengths and virtues and on psychological factors that are thought to lead to positive outcomes. Much of the research in the field has focused on healthy relationships and families. Positive psychology investigates the elements of successful relationships such as forgiveness, compassion, gratitude, attachment, and altruism. This entry discusses significant concepts in the field of positive psychology and the conditions that allow families to flourish. In this entry, the terms *flourishing* and *happy* are used interchangeably to denote a "healthy" family.

Studies pertaining to families, marriages, and couples often explore dysfunctions and pathology, while less is known about families with regard to psychological functioning, positive resources, and well-being. Although it is important to address the needs and deficiencies of families, the failure to also study health and human strengths skews our understanding of human nature and may prevent researchers from discovering interventions that can help those who suffer. Research by Shelly Gable and colleagues indicates that an important key to understanding the strength of a relationship is to know how it works in good times, not just whether it can withstand bad times.

In recent years, there has been an increased focus on positive psychology in the fields of education, psychotherapy, and organizational behavior. Scholars of positive psychology such as Martin Seligman,

Corey Keyes, and Shane Lopez have indicated that studying human flourishing can provide a new set of tools to think about individuals, relationships, and families. Ed Diener and Seligman conducted research comparing extremely happy people with a control group of people who were not happy and found significant differences in their social lives. Happy people were characterized by close relationships and intimate friendships. Studies on resilience also have found the ability to cope with difficult circumstances among people who experienced strong social and family support.

According to the broaden-and-build theory of positive emotions developed by Barbara Fredrickson, positive emotions such as joy, interest, contentment, pride, and love can allow people to build personal resources and widen their thought–action repertoires, meaning that they become more flexible and creative in how they behave. Fredrickson's research finds that people who experience positive emotions on a regular basis develop closer connections with others, experience strengthened resilience and optimism, and are more satisfied with life compared with people who do not experience positive emotions frequently. According to Fredrickson's positivity ratio, at least three positive emotions are needed to counteract every negative emotion that brings a person down. Research has also shown that social relationships are pivotal in coping with loss and negative events and in achieving goals and maintaining wellness.

Studies by Christopher Peterson report that close interpersonal relationships of friends, coworkers, and romantic partners are significantly correlated with subjective well-being, where relationships are characterized as reciprocal, sustained, and reflecting positive emotions. Further, research indicates that the negative impact of bad friends on well-being is greater than the positive impact of good friends. These studies suggest that relationships have to be mutually supportive in order to have a positive correlation with subjective well-being.

Research has found strong effects on emotion as a result of capitalization, which occurs when an individual tells another person about a positive event and receives an active, constructive response. The benefits of telling others about positive events in one's personal life have been found to include increased positive affect and well-being that go beyond the impact of the positive event itself.

Research by Robert Emmons and Michael McCullough has highlighted the psychological benefits of being grateful. The ability to appreciate or be grateful can enable people to see beauty in their lives and in the world around them. Many studies indicate that simple exercises of gratitude yield significant improvement in feelings of satisfaction and well-being. Sonja Lyubomirsky has explored various ways to express gratitude that can be applied within families. Some practical means to express gratitude are writing a letter to someone for whom an individual is grateful, counting blessings using journals, and savoring positive experience in the moment while sharing time with family.

Whether or not partners in a relationship have positive, active, and constructive reactions to each other's good news has been found to predict the quality and endurance of the relationship. A positive response conveys enthusiasm, support, and interest. The work of David Schnarch and other researchers shows that more important than validation is the idea of *knowing and being known*. Getting to know one's partner and revealing oneself to one's partner is seen as the way to cultivate intimacy in a relationship and to increase passion in a long-term relationship. Spending time with loved ones is also seen as predictive of well-being and a way to make relationships more productive and meaningful. Healthy, flourishing families are built on a foundation of close relationships, positive attributes, and mutually shared meaningful emotions.

*Priscilla Rose Selvaraj and
Christine Suniti Bhat*

See also Family Resilience; Family Strengths; Healthy Marriage and Responsible Fatherhood; Hope-Focused Approach to Couple Enrichment in Counseling

Further Readings

Ben-Shahar, T. (2007). *Happier: Learn the secrets to daily joy and lasting fulfillment.* New York, NY: McGraw-Hill.

Fredrickson, B. L. (1998). Cultivated emotions: Parental socialization of positive emotions and self-conscious emotions. *Psychological Inquiry, 9*(4), 279–281.

Gable, S. L., Reis, H. T., Impett, E. A., & Asher, E. R. (2004). What do you do when things go right? The intrapersonal and interpersonal benefits of sharing positive events. *Journal of Personality and Social Psychology, 87*(2), 228.

Keyes, C. L. M., & Haidt, J. (Eds.). (2003). *Flourishing: Positive psychology and the life well lived.* Washington, DC: American Psychological Association.

Lyubomirsky, S., & Layous, K. (2013). How do simple positive activities increase well-being? *Current Directions in Psychological Science, 22*(1), 57–62.

Peterson, C. (2006). *A primer in positive psychology.* New York, NY: Oxford University Press.

Seligman, M. E. (2011). *Flourish: A visionary new understanding of happiness and well-being.* New York, NY: Free Press.

Postdoctoral Training

Postdoctoral training is professional preparation that occurs as part of a temporary position—typically a temporary academic position—after earning a doctorate. Although earning a doctorate in marriage and family therapy, counseling, or psychology already gives someone advanced training and a degree in that area, postdoctoral training allows someone to gain specialized experience through mentored research and/or training. In this entry, the purpose, history, and drawbacks of postdoctoral training are reviewed.

Purpose of Postdoctoral Training

Although people who want to be clinicians may enter into postdoctoral training to further training in clinical work, typically postdoctoral training is to further skills in research and/or teaching. Trainees can focus on attaining additional research skills, grant-writing skills, publishing, and experience in teaching. All of these are important skills for getting tenured (permanent) positions at universities, especially universities classified as research universities. Completing a postdoctoral fellowship provides the opportunity to address knowledge gaps in counselor training or research skills early in one's career.

History of Postdoctoral Fellowships in Mental Health Fields

Postdoctoral fellowships in mental health fields started around the late 1980s to early 1990s, and since this time, there has been some change regarding the requirements and expectations. Postdoctoral training has historically been a step in science, technology, engineering, and math (STEM) fields; however, it has not played a similar role in the social sciences, except in psychology. Since the 1980s, the American Psychological Association (APA) has set up postdoctoral fellowships around the United States and has more recently partnered with the Veterans Administration (VA). Fellows accumulate clinical hours to allow them to practice independently without constant supervision. Postdoctoral clinical fellows may seek advanced training in many fields, such as family therapy, geriatrics, and neurocounseling; many of these fields require a 2-year commitment of advanced training.

An important aspect of postdoctoral training is that students can expand their collaborative base with other researchers and professionals and develop their independent research agenda in addition to specializing in techniques and gaining in-depth knowledge in their choice of subject. Postdoctoral training provides trainees with opportunities to interact with senior researchers, get involved in grant writing, and apply their knowledge in interdisciplinary research. It strengthens their professional identity and helps them become independent researchers who are better positioned to obtain funding to further their own research programs.

As faculty jobs become increasingly competitive, postdoctoral fellowships also offer an edge for students who are looking to obtain a tenure-track position in higher education. Another advantage of postdoctoral training is that it allows junior scholars to enhance their research skills and learn grant writing without the pressures experienced by tenure track junior faculty members. In other words, a postdoctoral position can give trainees an opportunity to jump-start their research careers.

In addition, there are now increased opportunities for postdoctoral training for those graduating with a degree in counselor education and supervision and marriage and family therapy. These postdoctoral students do engage in research, but often their postdoctoral work also relates to teaching and clinical work. Most of the fellows spend time in a training clinic and once a week report to their supervisors.

Drawbacks of Postdoctoral Positions

There are a few drawbacks to postdoctoral positions. Since these are temporary positions, they may not be ideal for some as they may disrupt family life and clinical practice if the positions require one to move. In addition, salaries are relatively low. Postdoctoral training emphasizes research and presentations in meetings, and if trainees are not able to publish and present at meetings, it may harm job opportunities. The role of mentors can vary greatly; mentoring may be beneficial, but trainees may not get enough guidance from their mentors. Finally, it should be noted that there are few postdoctoral positions available to counselor educators and marriage and family therapists (MFTs), though some positions are available through the National Institutes of Health (NIH), Substance Abuse and Mental Health Services Administration (SAMHSA), and National Institute on Drug Abuse (NIDA) alongside those that arise on a one-time basis due to targeted grants.

Veena Prasad

See also Couples Therapy Research; Outcome Research; Training and Licensure

Further Readings

Association of Psychology Postdoctoral and Internship Centers. (n.d.). *Postdoctoral*. Retrieved from https://appic.org/AboutAPPIC/Postdoctoral.aspx

Bartels, S. J., Bruce, M. L., Unitize, J., & Blow, F. (2013). Developing the next generation of researchers in emerging fields: Case study of a multisite postdoctoral research training program. *Academic Psychiatry: The Journal of the American Association of Directors of Psychiatric Residency Training and the Association for Academic Psychiatry, 37*, 108.

Chen, S., McAlpine, L., & Amundsen, C. (2015). Postdoctoral positions as preparation for desired careers: A narrative approach to understanding postdoctoral experience. *Higher Education Research & Development, 34*(6), 1–14.

DeMets, D. L., Stormo, G., Boehnk, M., Louis, T. A., Taylor, J., & Dixon, D. (2006). Training for the next generation of biostatisticians: A call to action in the U.S. *Statistics in Medicine, 25*, 3415–3429.

Dunn, C. (2014, July 7). *A brief history of the humanities postdoc*. Retrieved from https://chroniclevitae.com

Jenson, J. M., Briar-Lawson, K., & Flanzer, J. P. (2008). Advances and challenges in developing research capacity in social work (Editorial). *Social Work Research, 32*, 197–200.

Khalsa, P. S., & Pearson, N. J. (2007). Financial support for research and training development in complementary and alternative medicine from the National Institutes of Health. *Journal of Manipulative and Physiological Therapeutics, 30*, 483–490.

Mendoza, N. S., Resko, S. M., De Luca, S. M., Mendenhall, A. N., & Early, T. J. (2013). Social work and postdoctoral experience. *Social Work Research, 37*(1), 76–80.

POSTMODERN THERAPIES

Postmodern theoretical constructs have been connected to theoretical approaches in research and counseling. Since postmodernism has often been tied to qualitative research, its utilization as a theoretical approach in counseling has fostered tenets that are often connected to the theoretical approach in research. Because of their adaptation for culturally competent services, postmodern therapies have seen a rise in popularity within the counseling profession. Major proponents of this theoretical approach utilize its tenets to recognize the unique worldviews of clients. Postmodern therapies emerged out of critiques that traditional counseling theories were situated generally in Western contexts. As a result, the formation of therapeutic interventions could not apply to individuals from diverse cultural groups, considering their influx into new regions. Many counterparts, including feminist theory, constructivist approaches, and narrative therapy, have defined postmodern therapies. Postmodern therapies have been translated across several forms of counseling services, including family counseling, couples counseling, mental health counseling, and career counseling. Several schools of counseling theories tend to fall within postmodern approaches, including narrative therapy, collaborative systems dialogue, and solutions-focused therapy. These approaches also emphasize strengths-based approaches that work within the perspectives and realities of their clients.

Postmodernism essentially describes how individuals tell and describe their stories differently. They utilize difficult forms of culture and language to describe their stories. When individuals meet to describe their stories, they will speak from their own cultures, their own knowledge, their own languages, and their own way of understanding. Postmodernism highlights much of this narrative reflection and highlights the stories. It also highlights the manner in how the stories are told. Postmodern therapies often relate with both solution-focused therapy approaches and narrative therapy approaches because they highlight themes of storytelling. Consequently, each approach accounts for its postmodernist concepts through featuring a focus on themes in stories, using the client as an expert and author of the story, and finding alternative ways to change the stories. A prime goal within postmodernism is to give power back to clients by allowing them to voice their stories. In sharing these stories, counselors working within the postmodernist approaches hope to work collaboratively with clients to "reauthor" the story consistent with the way clients perceive change.

A particularly special feature of this approach is the idea that most stories are grounded in the culture shaping these individuals' thoughts and feelings. There is an examination of how society carries power over some individuals, particularly when minority groups do not carry any power within a particular context. As a result, they operate only with how larger social structures (e.g., governments, society, communities) in power tell people what is important in their story. For example, a person may not describe his or her experiences with any details close to a mental illness or symptoms of a mental health diagnosis, but the person may describe ways his or her culture views feelings of sadness or anger. It may not appear to clients as depression or anxiety. This perspective demonstrates the major value in the uniqueness of a person's story.

Within marriage, couples, and family counseling, postmodernism is an important movement for how counselors work with systems of individuals, such as couples and families. Some of the major theorists in this movement include David Epston, Michael White, Steve de Shazer, Insoo Kim Berg, Harlene Anderson, and Harold (Harry) Goolishian. They have drawn attention to the postmodernist movement in family counseling in order to return power back to families and communities who did not necessarily feel safe to seek help in counseling. Their focus has been to give value and empathy to families, couples, and communities who did not see counseling as a norm. Some of these pioneers also hoped to engage more social justice perspectives by drawing attention to giving voice to the unique stories of families and communities who are often invisible in counseling. They are not given access to help or resources or validated with their unique experiences in discrimination and marginalization. This entry will cover the major theoretical tenets to describe the postmodernism movement, examples of major interventions, and a brief overview of future research directions.

Major Theoretical Tenets

Postmodern therapies tend to value flexible approaches in the matter of how clients perceive their presenting issues. These diverse perspectives are a significant notion that impacts the therapeutic relationship built between counselor and clients. This relationship can apply to several modalities (e.g., individual, couples, family, parent–child). Postmodernists often recognize the diversity in perspective that clients carry between each other and with their counselor. While counselors and clients may share similar identities and unifying experiences, their realities and narratives are constructed very differently based on their unique experiences.

Consequently, the experiences are embedded with varying themes of meaning, freedom, and change. Counselors who take on this approach often value the unique experiences of their clients in constructing those worldviews. In addition, postmodern therapies also view clients as individuals who are rooted in their contexts. This perspective means that individuals reference their cultural backgrounds to describe their stories. They use their values, which may not be as familiar to individuals outside of that culture. In addition, clients might use different types of ways to describe their stories, including images, words, key terms, body movements, and facial expressions to describe their own experiences. Some of these terms may not carry the same meaning for another person, especially a counselor who does not carry the same values and identify with the same culture. In some cases, the same words used by two different cultures might not have the same meaning. Applying this situation to counselors and client systems, they might use the same words, but they may not share the same meaning. Societal and contextual factors constantly change, which also necessitates dynamic change within individuals in those contexts.

With regard to pathology and diagnosis, the use of clinical labels and pathology remain limited in postmodern therapies, as the clinical aspects and descriptions are expressive of only one type of language. Postmodern therapies argue that there are multiple descriptions in noting the expression of particular symptoms and problems that coincide with clients' experiences. The way that a clinician may describe a clinical diagnosis may differ dramatically from how clients have perceived mental health issues and clinical problems in other cultures. Postmodern therapies also operate from approaches that see individuals as embedded within their contexts. Their issues, lived experiences, and goals often develop from the products of interactions between the individuals and their contexts. Consequently, these individuals are shaped by the contexts that carry their lived experiences. Since environments have a tendency to shift, individuals situated within these contexts also have the potential to change. Because the environments are not static, individuals are not considered static.

Language

Postmodern therapies also emphasize a strong utilization of language within the counseling process. This emphasis on language was a major direction for how the theoretical approach was distinguished and considered innovative from other theoretical approaches. The theoretical approach values the way that counselors and clients construct language, especially in how they define their problems and how they can create potential possibilities for change. The language refers to the words, the body language, and the emotions shared in describing a story. Language can include indigenous languages. With the understanding of language readily available, there are several interventions that can arise from this perspective. Counselors can help clients to externalize the issues beyond themselves, which means taking the problem out of their control. The goal is to help clients view themselves separately from their problems and see that their problems are not entirely their fault. In this manner, clients will not always be the problem; the problem can be a result of other outcomes and contextual factors that exist outside of their control.

The language that clients use becomes a tool for assessment and intervention with counselors. Counselors seek to understand how clients shape their problems and how they communicate those problems within the context of their language. Sometimes their problems are communicated through unique terms that might be indigenous to their culture. In other situations, clients might utilize body movements and facial expressions to describe their experiences, which can go unnoticed within counseling practices. Change can also be situated within the contexts of the language. Clients express themselves and their lived experiences through the language they utilize in counseling, where points of change can be situated. The dialogue between counselors and clients can create the potential for change, where the dialogue can serve as a transformative experience for both parties (counselors and clients). This transformative experience is a significant viewpoint within applications of feminist theories in the counseling process.

Individuals use particular sets of language to define their realities, but this language is also constructed with other individuals. As a result, the language is socially constructed within contexts and cultural groups. Postmodern therapies also posit that the language that can be developed from prior experiences can also form new language in the context of new experiences. Counselors can provide one form of coconstructing new ways of thinking and new ways of language with clients.

Empowerment and Social Change

Postmodern approaches also draw from the tenets of other theoretical movements within counseling, including constructivist, social constructionist, and feminist approaches. Constructivist approaches largely define an umbrella of approaches in constructing different realities for individuals. Social constructionist approaches similarly contribute in the shared meaning components, where individuals work together and construct knowledge through dialogue. Feminist approaches value equality in relationships and demonstrate an orientation toward combating social inequality embedded within particular contexts and institutions. The confluence of these approaches has contributed to postmodernist approaches' advocacy for clients and challenge of current issues. The advocacy is rooted in developing relationships that empower clients to create change of their own accord.

In these stories, clients are able to form their own meaningful visions for how change and goals in the counseling process can be achieved. Another mechanism of change in sharing these stories is the ability for clients to tell their stories. Specifically, this idea of change is extremely meaningful for groups facing oppression and marginalization, whose members have never been able to share their stories. A component of the change is the counselor's openness, nonjudgmental stance, empathic responses, and unconditional positive regard that allow clients to share these lived experiences. For those clients, the experience can often be liberating. This perspective relates to notions of recognizing unique individual experiences, even in the shared experiences that occur for persons identifying with similar cultural identities. This major tenet reinforces a strong recognition of the value of diversity.

In an empowerment role, researchers often note the collaborative relationship that exists in counseling relationships. This relationship is a primary construct within the postmodern approach, as there is an attempt to bridge the understanding of unique individual experiences. Considering how counseling imposes a power differential between counselors and clients, postmodern therapies address this issue by working toward collaborative, empathic relationships. While there is a presupposed assumption of counselors as experts and authority figures in counseling relationships, counselors taking a postmodernist approach will often work toward lessening that power differential through exacting change in a collaborative relationship. They value the perspectives of their clients as equally important. Through this relationship, counselors can serve to provide a significant effect on the meaning created within clients' experiences in the counseling process. Counselors also participate in this collaborative relationship to achieve meaning in the interaction between clients' experiences grounded in the counseling process and outside of the counseling services, such as sociocultural factors and environments (e.g., family, church, community, school). Working toward this collaborative relationship is also representative of feminist approaches' efforts toward equality in counseling relationships or acknowledgement of inequalities.

Use of Narratives

In postmodern therapies, narratives are a strong base for counselors to develop catalysts for change. Narrative therapy has a strong presence within postmodernist thought, owing to its relationships with language and differing realities. Specifically, many of narrative therapy's contributions to postmodern therapies are through its many values in counseling. These values include the role of clients as experts. They are the authors of their own stories, so they would be the best source to share the stories within their lives. Furthermore, these narrative explorations create stories that contribute to individuals' identities. Stories about communities, families, and other contextual factors affecting clients bring about a holistic perspective to develop the story expressed in the counseling process. These stories serve to inform a fuller picture of how clients are perceiving their own issues and how they can interact with their environments to enact change.

Critical Inquiry

Postmodern approaches also take a stance to hear and give voice to marginalized and oppressed groups, who are often critical of current institutional practices. With this perspective, counselors perceive their roles to create spaces for changing social inequalities, especially with individuals who have faced oppression institutionally and contextually. Seeking the interaction between individuals and context, postmodernist counselors seek to extract the stories of oppression that often result in clients' problems. These stories also bring into awareness the issues that are embedded within a society, especially social inequalities that plague marginalized and underserved groups. In the collaborative relationships built with clients, the agency to create change is relevant for both counselors and clients. Counselors recognize the need to create change within society that creates barriers for individuals, especially if that society operates on only one form of thinking. Through a collaborative dialogue with clients, counselors empower clients to also be agents of change within their own communities, especially with a recognition that clients have the ability to create contextual change independently. Within this collaboration, counselors and clients work together to examine how social inequalities impact the development of individuals and their relationships.

Meaning of Culture

Postmodern therapies were also developed as a method to address diverse cultural constructs that exist within the counseling process. As the counseling profession aims to develop professionals competent in multicultural counseling with value for diversity, there are several notions of how counseling professionals build upon those skills. While learning knowledge is valuable about specific groups, learning and gaining knowledge about cultural groups cannot necessarily build the skills and practices to work competently with persons identifying with those cultural groups. Learning the knowledge can only build broad notions about what cultural groups experience, which often come with multiple assumptions. There is also an inherent complexity in how cultural identity is constructed. Cultural identity includes but is not necessarily limited to race, ethnicity, sexual or affectional orientation, ability status, gender identity, region, and spiritual identity. Due to the intersections of several cultural factors, conceptualizing from one base of knowledge or thinking may result in a unilateral perspective, which will not provide an accurate understanding of the client.

Postmodern therapies also sought to address the issue of differing factors within groups. For example, *racial* and *ethnic groups* are often referred to as umbrella terms for individuals identifying within those groups. However, there can be extensive heterogeneity within some of the groups. For example, a person identifying as Asian American or Latino American can have several layers of identification, including their ethnic heritages (e.g., Cambodian American, Filipino American, Mexican American). In order to address the various complexities of cultural identity, postmodern therapies seek to address the diverse unique individual experiences that are tied to larger groups. While counselors and clients may share similar cultural identities, their experiences will vary due to their unique experiences and spaces in how those identities have existed.

Examples of Major Interventions

Postmodern therapies formulate many of their interventions from the techniques in narrative therapy, utilizing both language and stories to work within the constructions of clients' realities. In one method, a major narrative approach is to help separate clients from the problems, explaining that they are not necessarily the problem, but the problem stands alone. This method is often noted as externalizing the problem. This technique can assist clients with recognizing that they can have power over the problems. In addition, the technique also helps clients with the recognition that they are not at fault for their problems. This intervention, as a result, is closely related with the construct of critical consciousness. In critical consciousness, clients are not perceived as the problem; the context is the problem.

Additional techniques involve developing connections among themes within the stories of clients. Clients may have determined ways in how they tell the stories that capture connections to the problems they face or the solutions they create. Through these connections in the larger themes, they can create further meaning in how to form solutions. Another narrative technique that exists within postmodern therapies is working with clients to reauthor the story. Clients can work with diverse pathways that formulate different perspectives regarding the issues they face. This technique can provide a richer context for how clients perceive their realities and empower them with alternative solutions to create change. Counselors can also point to differences in the stories that might carry discrepancies for clients. A tool that is often used in solutions-focused therapies is the idea that this problem did not always exist. Clients have the tools and context to understand what had occurred when the problem was not occurring.

There are also strong arguments about continuing to follow up on particular points in clients' narratives that help refocus their narratives. Postmodern therapists often challenge by allowing for reflective spaces for their clients. It is possible to follow on key words and points in the stories while maintaining a demeanor that emits unconditional positive regard, empathy, and genuineness. The space provided and the stance of the counselor are significant components in the change process for postmodern therapies. The individuals involved in the counseling process are situated within the contextual forces that affect their relationship.

Future Research Directions

Because adaptations of postmodern theoretical approaches to counseling are relatively new, research utilizing postmodern theory is still emergent. There are many ways in which research can contribute to the research with postmodern therapies in marriage, couples, and family counseling. Major gaps continue to exist within the scope of both efficacy and effectiveness. Here, efficacy refers to randomized clinical trials (RCTs) that are established through control groups and intervention groups in separate conditions; effectiveness refers to whether interventions can work effectively with specific populations and communities. For postmodern therapies, the base of research is somewhat limited, but research continues to grow with these theoretical approaches. The approach is relatively new, which has not established extensive inquiries of research that search for empirically based information. Debates have also emerged over the presence of how postmodern therapies can be adapted to efficacy studies, considering the fluid nature of their constructs and interventions. This fluid nature may conflict with managing variables that exist within RCTs and settings. Effectiveness may also be plausible in showing the use of postmodern approaches within counseling settings in particular communities, such as cultural groups and regions. As a result, many researchers point toward developing practice-based evidence (PBE) that is reflective of the reality of counseling processes. This type of research is argued to depict more realistic interactions between counselors and clients as opposed to RCTs.

Researchers have also demonstrated that there is a need for inquiry in this area. Current literature shows extensive potential for developing research while some argue for the presence of postmodern therapies in research. Some researchers posit that qualitative methodology may be one manner in how to investigate effectiveness of postmodern therapies with diverse communities. Furthermore, there is a significant relationship with the contribution of postmodern approaches to counseling research. Generally, postmodern theory is utilized within qualitative research, which often creates opportunities for qualitative research in counseling.

Emerging research also highlights the presence of PBE and translational research, as the perspectives of counselor and client participants in research hold important significance in the outcomes. PBE includes counselors as part of the research design in order to address the major disparities that occur between researchers and the realities of counseling processes between counselors and clients. Furthermore, it is a result of the collaborative dialogue between counselors and clients that form knowledge of reality from several data sources. Consequently, some researchers also argue for utilizing translational research that works directly with communities, such as community-based research and participatory action research methods. In these methods, researchers seek input and communication with the community for which they intend to gather data. The major critique in research studies that do not use postmodern approaches is that they often miss innovative knowledge that is grounded in the reality of counseling processes with clients.

Christian Derek Chan

See also Constructivism; Critical Theory; Feminist Family Therapy; Multiculturalism; Narrative Therapy; Social Constructionism

Further Readings

Campbell, C., & Ungar, M. (2004). Constructing a life that works: Part 1. Blending postmodern family therapy and career counseling. *The Career Development Quarterly*, 53(1), 16–27. Retrieved from http://search.proquest.com/docview/219441460?accountid=11243

De Haene, L. (2010). Beyond division: Convergences between postmodern qualitative research and family therapy. *Journal of Marital and Family Therapy*, 36(1), 1–12. Retrieved from http://search.proquest.com/docview/220977866?accountid=11243

Jacobs, S., Kissil, K., Scott, D., & Davey, M. (2010). Creating synergy in practice: Promoting complementarity between evidence-based and postmodern approaches. *Journal of Marital and Family Therapy*, 36(2), 185–196. Retrieved from http://search.proquest.com/docview/220945160?accountid=11243

Medina Centeno, R. (2014). Introduction to critical family therapy. *Journal of Systemic Therapies*, 33(3), 50–68. doi:10.1521/jsyt.2014.33.3.50

Oliver, M., Flamez, B., & McNichols, C. (2011). Postmodern applications within Latino/a cultures. *Journal of Professional Counseling, Practice, Theory, & Research*, 38(3), 33–48. Retrieved from http://search.proquest.com/docview/888062144?accountid=11243

Paré, D., & Tarragona, M. (2006). Generous pedagogy: Teaching and learning postmodern therapies. *Journal of Systemic Therapies*, 25(4), 1–7. Retrieved from http://search.proquest.com/docview/222532865?accountid=11243

Skovlund, H. (2011). Overcoming problems of relativism in postmodern psychotherapy. *Journal of Contemporary Psychotherapy*, 41(3), 187–198. doi:10.1007/s10879-010-9166-9

St. George, S., & Wulff, D. (2006). A postmodern approach to teaching family therapy as community practice. *Journal of Systemic Therapies*, 25(4), 73–83. Retrieved from http://search.proquest.com/docview/61417201?accountid=11243

Strong, T., & Gale, J. (2013). Postmodern clinical research: In and out of the margins. *Journal of Systemic Therapies*, 32(2), 46–57. doi:101521jsyt201332246

Sutherland, O., Dienhart, A., & Turner, J. (2013). Responsive persistence: Part II. Practices of postmodern therapists. *Journal of Marital and Family Therapy*, 39(4), 488–501. Retrieved from http://search.proquest.com/docview/1460879596?accountid=11243

Postpartum Depression

Postpartum depression is a period of depression following the birth of a new child. These depressive symptoms include mood swings, feelings of guilt and shame surrounding parenthood, and disillusion with the mothering role. Recent research indicates these symptoms often occur during pregnancy so that it is often now referred to as maternal mental illness. Postpartum depression is not listed as a separate disorder in the fifth edition of the *Diagnostic and Statistical Manual of Mental Disorders* (DSM-5), but according to the DSM-5, between 3% and 6% of women experience the onset of a major depressive episode during pregnancy or in the subsequent weeks or months. About half of these cases begin during pregnancy, according to the DSM-5.

Symptoms of postpartum depression may last for a period of a few months and can emerge up to one year following the birth of a new child. The experience of depressive symptoms accompanied with the addition of a new member to a family can have a significant impact on the family system. Understanding how postpartum depression impacts individuals, couples, and families can help counselors provide help and support to families working through postpartum difficulties. This entry first discusses factors thought to play a role in postpartum depression, the symptoms of postpartum depression, postpartum depression in men, and the impact of postpartum depression on children. It then discusses treatment of postpartum depression, including antidepressants, hormone therapy, counseling, and lifestyle alterations.

Factors in Postpartum Depression

Specific causes of postpartum depression are unknown. However, some research has found the likelihood of experiencing postpartum depression increases if a mother is under the age of 20, has mixed emotions or did not want the pregnancy in the first place, or is experiencing serious financial hardship such as lack of housing or insufficient money to care for a new baby. Also, if the mother has a history of mental health disorders such as depression, anxiety, or bipolar disorder prior to or during a current or past pregnancy, the chances of having postpartum depression may increase. If a mother has experienced a significant life change during pregnancy, such as a loss of a loved one, she is at a higher risk for postpartum depression as well. Complicated pregnancies, premature delivery, birth defects, or illness in a new baby also factor into the onset of postpartum depression.

There are three types of changes in women's lives during pregnancy and after childbirth that are thought to play a role in postpartum depression. These can be categorized into three types: physical changes, lifestyle changes, and emotional changes.

Physical Changes

Women experience a myriad of physical and physiological changes prior to, during, and following childbirth. Progesterone and estrogen levels rise during pregnancy and then drop following pregnancy, which may lead to depressive symptoms. These changes in hormone levels can leave a woman feeling less energetic and less able to accomplish tasks that were once completed with relative ease. It is also not uncommon for women to experience changes in blood volume, blood pressure, and metabolism following childbirth. Pregnancy and the delivery of a child may leave permanent changes to a woman's body as well, which may be particularly difficult for some mothers to adjust to. These changes, accompanied by expectations of a return to normalcy once the baby is born, can lead to feelings of disappointment and sadness.

Lifestyle Changes

Unforeseen and unexpected lifestyle changes might increase the likelihood of postpartum depression. Difficulties such as unsuccessful attempts at breast-feeding a new baby and unmet expectations of motherhood can exacerbate the likelihood of experiencing postpartum depression. Lack of support from a significant other or extended family members may also be a culprit in the development of postpartum depression. A change in support with friends is not uncommon either, as socialization with close friends may be compromised due to the needs of a new baby. For mothers who work, the isolation from the work environment may be especially difficult. A new baby may also have inconsistent sleep patterns or difficulty sleeping altogether, leaving new mothers feeling exhausted and lethargic. Lastly, women may have less time and freedom for attending to their own specific emotional and physical needs.

Emotional Changes

It is not uncommon for women to have high expectations for the experience of motherhood. Societal and personal expectations of becoming a mother are often characterized by unabated and unending happiness. These unrealistic expectations and experiences can create a sense of guilt and shame for some new mothers who do not experience this level of joy. New mothers might be hesitant to reach out with their concerns in fear of being misunderstood or mischaracterized due to their difficulties with a new child. The perceived inability to be open and honest about struggles that often accompany early motherhood leads to further isolation for some women in fear of being deemed an unappreciative or unhappy mother. It is not uncommon for this pattern to have a downward spiraling effect, leading to further loneliness and isolation for new mothers.

Symptoms of Postpartum Depression

It is not uncommon for "baby blues" to manifest during the first few weeks of pregnancy. Baby blues refer to common effects in the first few weeks after delivery of a new child and include tearfulness, feelings of anxiety, or overall feelings of restlessness. Most often, these symptoms resolve themselves quickly and do not require additional medical or mental health treatment. Concerns arise when these baby blues do not fade over time or perhaps become even more pronounced.

Depressed mood, sadness, and lethargy are some of the most common signs of postpartum depression. Increased agitation or irritability, constant anxiety, and loss of energy and motivation are all signs of depression. Physiological changes such as decreased appetite and trouble sleeping may also be important signs to take note of. Lack of interest in activities that once provided happiness, increased disconnect from support systems, and thoughts of death and suicide are symptoms that may require immediate attention.

Postpartum Depression in Men

Most research on postpartum depression is focused on women, and the common understanding of postpartum depression is that it is experienced by women exclusively. However, research shows that many fathers can experience symptoms similar to those of women. Fears and pressures of fatherhood, a changed relationship with a significant other, new financial burdens and constraints, and a perceived loss of freedom can factor into the onset of postpartum depression-like symptoms in men. Lack of sleep leading to irritability can certainly impact new fathers as well.

The impact of postpartum depression in men may be compounded by the socialization of how men deal with mental health difficulties. Rather than talk through the difficulties associated with new fatherhood, many men are encouraged to "tough it out" and work through the newfound challenges. This may lead to dedicating more time at work, distancing oneself from family, or turning to alcohol or other substances to work through these challenges of becoming a new father.

Impact of Postpartum Depression on Children

The systematic impact of postpartum depression can impact children as well. Mothers who are experiencing postpartum depression are likely to be more distant from their children, as manifested by a reluctance to play with their children, less frequent eye contact, or avoidance of talking in a soothing or engaging voice. For older children, decreased success in school and other important systems may be a sign of their own difficulty with the transition. Depressed mothers may be more critical as well, leading some children to adopt a more negative self-image.

Treatment

There are a variety of recommendations for treating postpartum depression. Providing support for new mothers, individual psychotherapy, family therapy, and antidepressant medications have all been shown to be helpful in the treatment of postpartum depression. In addition, hormone therapy and lifestyle alterations are often included as part of treatment.

Antidepressants

Research indicates that antidepressant medication is a reliable and effective way to treat postpartum depression. However, for many women, the choice not to use antidepressants prevails. A common fear for many new mothers is that medications taken for postpartum depression will be passed to the infant through breast milk. Most often, the impact on the infant is mild, and symptoms disappear once the infant is no longer breast-feeding or the mother stops taking the medication. It is recommended that any individual experiencing postpartum depression discuss antidepressant options and side effects with her physician.

Hormone Therapy

Estrogen replacement is one method of treatment that is becoming increasingly popular. It is common for estrogen levels to drop significantly after childbirth, which is thought to increase the likelihood of postpartum depression. It is not uncommon for estrogen replacement to be used in conjunction with antidepressant medication; however, research on this method of treatment is limited. As with the use of antidepressant medications, women need to engage in conversation with their physician regarding the side effects of hormone therapy when treating postpartum depression.

Counseling

While treatment regimens vary from clinician to clinician, certain therapies and techniques have proven helpful for the treatment of postpartum depression. Many clinicians rely on cognitive-behavioral therapy (CBT), which helps mothers to understand the connections between their self-defeating thoughts and subsequent behaviors. Mental health clinicians may also teach coping strategies and tools to help new mothers avoid negative automatic thinking. Dialectical behavior therapy (DBT) is also a popular treatment option for postpartum depression. Like CBT, DBT may rely on homework and assignments in order to implement new coping strategies. However, unlike CBT, DBT focuses on mindfulness and emotional regulation. It is wise for new mothers to ask specific questions about treatment options and techniques when seeking out a new mental health professional.

Couples counseling is another treatment option for new mothers and fathers experiencing the effects of postpartum depression. It is not uncommon for relational dynamics to change after a new baby is added to a family system. Effort once placed on the relationship between mother and father is naturally placed upon the child. Opportunities for intimacy and sexual connection are often limited due to fatigue and overall busyness. Couples counseling allows couples to process their interactional patterns and identify how to alter their behaviors and communication styles in order to receive the support and hope both mother and father desire. Individual needs should be expressed during couples counseling as well as strategies to work in unison to meet the presenting concerns of the couple.

Group counseling provides multiple opportunities for support and help for postpartum depression. Most often, group counseling provides individuals with an opportunity to share their present concerns and feelings in a nonjudgmental, supportive group. Hearing similar stories of struggle can help young mothers feel less isolated and alone. Group counseling often has an element of psychoeducation as well. Group facilitators spend time discussing treatment options, causes of postpartum depression, ideas for self-care and wellness, and what is most commonly experienced in motherhood. The combination of support, education, and cathartic release can prove very helpful for mothers experiencing postpartum depression.

Other Treatment Recommendations

Alterations of lifestyle may also be important in the treatment of postpartum depression. Eating a balanced diet and getting enough sleep can prove beneficial. New mothers can also reach out to friends and family for help and support. Getting regular exercise is also an effective way to optimize healthy hormone levels and provide overall health and strength. Exercising in the sunshine helps as well, as it naturally elevates mood. Lastly, setting aside time to be alone to reenergize or participate in a meaningful activity may yield positive results. Engaging in self-care activities can reenergize the body and mind, providing more energy and enthusiasm to take care of the new baby.

Shawn P. Parmanand

See also Communication in Couples and Families; Life Events; Life Transitions; Parental Stress: Effects on Children; Pregnancy; Pregnancy and Sexuality

Further Readings

Burton, A., Patel, S., Kaminsky, L., Rosario, G. D., Young, R., Fitzsimmons, A., & Canterino, J. C. (2011). Depression in pregnancy: Time of screening and access to psychiatric care. *The Journal of Maternal-Fetal & Neonatal Medicine, 24*(11), 1321–1324.

Cohen, L. S., Wang, B., Nonacs, R., Viguera, A. C., Lemon, E. L., & Freeman, M. P. (2010). Treatment of mood disorders in pregnancy and postpartum. *Psychiatric Clinics of North America, 33*(2), 273–293.

Goodman, J. H., & Santangelo, G. (2011). Group treatment for postpartum depression: A systemic review. *Archives of Women's Mental Health, 14*(4), 277–293.

Miller, L. J., & LaRusso, E. M. (2011). Preventing postpartum depression. *Prevention in Mental Health: Lifespan Perspective, 34*(1), 53–65.

O'Hara, M. W., & McCabe, J. E. (2013). Postpartum depression: Current status and future directions. *Annual Review of Clinical Psychology, 9*, 379–407.

Pugh, N. E., Hadjistavropoulos, H. D., Hampton, A. J., Bowen, A., & Williams, J. (2015). Client experiences of guided Internet cognitive behavior therapy for postpartum depression: A qualitative study. *Archives of Women's Mental Health, 18*(2), 209–219.

Posttraumatic Stress Disorder in Children

Surviving a traumatic event or series of events is only the first step in the journey toward healing for children with posttraumatic stress disorder (PTSD). PTSD is experienced by millions of children each year as a result of personal, community, national, and global traumatic events. Trauma poses a particular concern for children because of their vulnerability and because of the risk to their development. The world generates new trauma, loss, and harm to young people on a daily basis, so caregivers must understand and respond meaningfully to children's experiences. One study of children under age 4 found that 26% had been exposed to a potentially traumatic event, with the rate of exposure higher for children living in poverty or with certain other risk factors. This entry describes PTSD, the criteria for diagnosis, the most common types of trauma that lead to PTSD, how PTSD can affect functioning and development, risk and protective factors for PTSD, how to support healing and progress among children, and some common interventions used for treating PTSD.

Diagnosis of PTSD

PTSD is one of the five main disorders that the American Psychiatric Association (APA) identifies in relation to trauma or stress-related events. PTSD is evaluated by the presence of five main criteria: (1) exposure, (2) trauma symptoms, (3) avoidance, (4) altered arousal, and (5) general qualifiers. Ruling out other possible diagnoses is very important for assuring accurate conclusions and treatment. Although PTSD can and does occur at any age, the APA makes a distinction between adults and older children compared with children 6 years old or younger. Symptoms may appear significantly different among younger children according to their developmental level.

Exposure

The onset of posttraumatic stress relies greatly upon the perceptions of the traumatic event. A child may directly experience a threat of death, injury, or sexual abuse that leads to trauma. Children may also react to a traumatic event they witnessed with someone else, particularly a caregiver. Children may take this a step further and acquire symptoms simply by learning of a past traumatic event that occurred with someone close to them. Parents and caregivers can be aware of the need to share information at a developmentally appropriate level in order to avoid exposure beyond what children can emotionally manage.

Trauma Symptoms

PTSD becomes evident among young people when intrusion symptoms occur in direct connection with a traumatic event or events. Intrusion symptoms often include disturbing memories and dreams of the event that bring renewed distress. Dissociative reactions may occur where flashbacks or thought distortions mentally bring the young person back to the traumatic event as if it were taking place in the immediate present. In the most extreme cases, this may include the youth's complete loss of awareness of his or her current surroundings. Other symptoms may include extreme reactions, such as intense distress or physiological reactions, to various activities that remind the young person of the event. Because dissociative reactions have become so prevalent among children who have experienced trauma, a young person with a PTSD diagnosis may be given specifiers for dissociative symptoms, including depersonalization (feeling mentally detached from one's body) and derealization (perceiving that experiences lack reality).

Avoidance

Avoidance is another key criterion pointing to the evidence of PTSD among children. When young people have experienced a traumatic event, they display avoidance of the stimuli and have negative changes in their thought patterns. Children may begin avoiding activities or places related to their trauma or even relational interactions they perceive to be associated with the event. They may exhibit more negative emotions than they have in the past, along with a diminished interest in their typical pleasures. This may include active avoidance of activities, people, and even emotional expression.

Altered Arousal

Responses to stimuli related to the trauma will frequently appear heightened and uncharacteristic of the child. This may be reflected in highly irritable behavior and angry outbursts toward others around them. Children may also adopt an ongoing state of hypervigilance that reflects difficulty concentrating and disturbance in sleep. The startle responses for children with PTSD may be exaggerated and swift. Parents and caregivers observing these behaviors may consider the need for immediate intervention to address the ongoing agitation that can affect overall functioning.

General Qualifiers

Other specific qualifiers are described by the APA for assuring a proper diagnosis of PTSD in children. One point references the duration of the symptoms, which must exceed one month to be considered a clinical concern. The disturbance from the symptoms must present marked evidence of disruption to relationships considered important by the child or declining behavior in school or around peers. It must also be proven that the new emotions and behaviors are not a direct result of physiological effects of substance use issues.

Ruling Out Diagnoses

The APA also describes differential diagnoses that may result from the experiences of traumatic events. Many symptoms overlap with the following diagnoses that can be attributed to children. The most closely related diagnosis to PTSD is acute stress disorder (ASD), which mainly differs in the duration of symptoms (between 3 days and 1 month). Children displaying PTSD reactions must be evaluated closely to consider whether they more properly fit the criteria for adjustment disorders, depressive disorders, obsessive-compulsive disorder (OCD), anxiety disorders, reactive-attachment disorder, psychotic disorders or features, substance-induced disorders or features, or dissociative disorders. Frequently the demonstration of a child's distress toward stimuli connected with traumatic events becomes enough evidence to suggest a PTSD diagnosis, but this must be reviewed carefully by a qualified mental health professional.

Understanding PTSD

In addition to knowing the criteria for diagnosing PTSD, it can be helpful for parents, caregivers, and others working with children to understand some of the most common types of trauma that children experience, how PTSD can impair functioning, and how it can affect development.

Types of Trauma

The National Child Traumatic Stress Network (NCTSN) has listed multiple types of trauma that are common among young people. These include *community and school violence,* where children experience an atmosphere of violence that erodes their sense of safety throughout the area in which they live and go to school. *Complex trauma* is another type of trauma that may occur and is described later in detail. *Domestic violence* affects how young people view the safety of their own homes and can raise the potential for traumatic reactions. *Early childhood trauma* can result from experiences that have occurred between the ages of 0 and 6. Because of the sensitive nature of human growth and development at this stage, such early trauma can lead to long-term consequences for the young person. Children who experience a barrage of health problems early in life may acquire *medical trauma* as a result. *Natural disasters* frequently instigate traumatic reactions. *Neglect,* or lack of care for a child's needs, is the most frequent form of trauma in children. *Physical abuse* involves causing or attempting to cause physical pain or injury. Young people who have experienced *refugee and war zone trauma* are faced with managing the emotions and memories associated with significant traumatic events.

Sexual abuse is an interaction between a child and an adult (or another child) in which the child is used for sexual stimulation, violating the personal space and safety of the child. *Terrorism* is the use of violence or the threat of violence to cause fear in pursuit of a goal, and this can affect children more intensely than adults. *Traumatic grief* is a common reaction that parents and caregivers must consider. Children may have ongoing difficulties after losing a loved one. The American Academy of Child and Adolescent Psychiatry (AACAP) lists other potentially traumatic events as including vehicular or other accidents and "other shocking, unexpected or terrifying experiences" (p. 414).

Many types of trauma and distress result from sudden and immediate changes that place the young person in harm's way. All types of trauma described by the NCTSN and the AACAP pose the risk for children to receive a PTSD diagnosis. A variety of authors distinguish two general types of trauma in describing type 1 and type 2 trauma. Type 1 trauma might be considered a sudden, distinct traumatic experience. Type 2 trauma may be recognized as more complex in nature, longstanding, and coming from repeated traumatic ordeals. Type 2 trauma also commonly is called *complex trauma* (as described earlier) and often requires greater intervention to recalibrate the mind-set and behaviors of children who have adapted to a lifestyle of trauma and abuse.

Impaired Functioning

The impact of PTSD symptoms also can be related to significant impairments in everyday functioning. John Briere described six primary impacts on psychological functioning that included (1) relational impairments, (2) heightened emotional triggers, (3) sensory reactions, (4) intrusive memories, (5) repeated thought intrusions, and (6) dysregulated emotional control. When functionality becomes clearly compromised through these reactions, care providers must explore intentional efforts to improve it.

Impaired functioning can also occur as a result of dissociative symptoms. Scott Weber called these particular symptoms a form of "protective amnesia" because they help children avoid contact with disturbing memories they may not be capable of handling in a functional way. Dissociative features may be recognized among children with inconsistent consciousness, autobiographical forgetfulness, fluctuating moods and behaviors, belief in alternative selves or imaginary friends, depersonalization, and derealization. Such features pose risks to social relationships with peers and family alike. Children who are unable to recognize their dissociative tendencies may appear to lack attention or the ability to self-manage their actions and emotions.

Studies have described altered brain functioning that occurs as a result of abuse and trauma. Clear changes in brain structure have been found with differences in brain size and changes in the structure of the brain that connects the right and left hemispheres. These alterations in brain activity signal an impairment that occurs on the psychobiological level and threaten to impact future development.

Impairments also occur in relation to spiritual or religious functioning, especially when abuse occurs in religious contexts. The disconnection of prior beliefs and convictions may cause dissonance within a child who has acquired both fond memories of religious practices and, because of the traumatic experience, a negative view of God or clergy. Confusion has been found among children in areas including the source of abuse (especially if the abuser was a religious leader), confusion about beliefs, and avoidance. These challenges pose even greater risk among young people who face rejection from their families due to beliefs that were altered after their trauma.

Developmental Considerations

In light of all the challenges associated with managing a traumatic event, parents and caregivers are encouraged to consider the impact on development. While childhood is a relatively stable and gradual progression of developmental growth (compared with infancy and adolescence), normal developmental growth may pose greater difficulty when PTSD is present. Parents and caregivers will benefit from recognizing the importance of supporting developmental growth despite multiple challenges and symptoms. Main areas of development include personal (or self), social, emotional, mental, physical, and spiritual growth. PTSD has the potential to reduce self-esteem through a variety of the symptoms previously described. Trauma symptoms may cause concrete thinking to become distorted and confused. Children may experience fluctuating emotions, physical effects such as high blood pressure and panic attacks, disconnect from relational ties, and sudden changes in previously held beliefs that brought purpose and meaning (e.g., faith in God, sense of purpose).

Risk and Protective Factors

Researchers have identified factors that are thought to increase the risk of children developing PTSD or to protect against it. Understanding the findings reported on risk factors and protective factors may help parents and caregivers offer the necessary support for overcoming the symptoms of PTSD. Communities and agencies seeking to help children thrive through traumatic events may also use an awareness of these factors to inform necessary policies and programs targeting this population.

Risk Factors

According to the AACAP, factors that seem to increase the risk of acquiring PTSD include being of the female gender, having previous trauma exposure, experiencing multiple traumas, having a preexisting psychiatric disorder, having parents dealing with mental illness, lacking social support, viewing television coverage of disaster-related events, experiencing delayed evacuation during a time of disaster, experiencing extreme panic symptoms, and having felt that one's own or one's family member's life was in danger.

Protective Factors

Factors found to predict lower levels of PTSD symptoms in children, according to the AACAP, include having parental support, observing lower levels of parental PTSD, and seeing parents successfully resolve trauma-related symptoms. These findings demonstrate how important the role of parents is to the development and progress of children who are working to overcome PTSD.

In 2012, the U.S. Centers for Disease Control and Prevention (CDC) reported that protective factors supporting healthy recovery from traumatic events included having a supportive family environment and social networks, receiving nurturing parenting, maintaining stable family relationships, having consistent household rules and child monitoring, having parents who are employed, having adequate housing, receiving access to health care and social services, and having caring adults outside the family who serve as role models or mentors.

Treatments

A variety of treatment options are available for families looking to support a child with PTSD symptoms. One of the most important aspects to remember is the need to seek a counselor or mental health professional with experience working with children with PTSD. Some of the most effective treatments that experienced clinicians have used are cognitive-behavioral therapy (CBT), play therapy, and eye movement desensitization and reprocessing (EMDR). Clinicians using CBT have used a variety of tools including flooding, relaxation skills, cognitive restructuring, and others. Play therapy is an increasingly common method of creating a safe and creative space for children to express their emotions and reactions freely through the language of play. EMDR is a technique often used in conjunction with other treatment interventions, where eye exercises are interspersed throughout the session to address symptom reduction when discomfort or intrusive memories occur.

Nathan C. D. Perron

See also Adjustment Disorder in Adolescents; Depression in Children; Parent–Child Communication

Further Readings

American Academy of Child and Adolescent Psychiatry. (2010, April). Practice parameter for the assessment and treatment of children and adolescents with posttraumatic stress disorder. *Journal of the American Academy of Child and Adolescent Psychiatry, 49*(4), 414–430.

American Psychiatric Association. (2013). *Diagnostic and statistical manual of mental disorders* (5th ed.). Washington, DC: Author.

Briere, J. (2002). Treating adult survivors of severe child abuse and neglect: Further development of an integrative model. In J. E. B. Myers, L. Berliner, J. Briere, C. T. Hendrix, T. Reid, & C. Jenny (Eds.), *The APSAC handbook on child maltreatment* (2nd ed., pp. 175–202). Thousand Oaks, CA: Sage.

Briggs-Gowan, M. J., Ford, J. D., Fraleigh, L., McCarthy, K., & Carter, A. S. (2010). Prevalence of exposure to potentially traumatic events in a healthy birth cohort of very young children in the northeastern United States. *Journal of Traumatic Stress, 23,* 725–733.

Centers for Disease Control and Prevention. (2015, November). *Child maltreatment.* Retrieved from http://www.cdc.gov/ViolencePrevention/ childmaltreatment/riskprotectivefactors.html

Cohen, J. A., Deblinger, E., & Mannarino, A. P. (2006). *Treating trauma and traumatic grief in children and adolescents: A clinician's guide.* New York, NY: Guilford Press.

James, R. K. (2008). *Crisis intervention strategies* (6th ed.). Belmont, CA: Brooks/Cole.

The National Child Traumatic Stress Network. (2015, November). *Types of traumatic stress.* Retrieved from http://www.nctsn.org/trauma-types

Perron, N. C. D., & Pender, D. A. (2015). Meeting the need: Applying concepts for assessment and planning with child and adolescent trauma. *Journal of Child and Adolescent Counseling, 1*(1), 37–49. doi:10.1080/23727810.2015.1023607

Terr, L. C. (1995). Childhood traumas: An outline and overview. In J. M. Lating & G. S. Everly (Eds.), *Psychotraumatology: Key papers and core concepts in post-traumatic stress* (pp. 301–330). New York, NY: Plenum Press.

Walker, D. F., Reese, J. B., Hughes, J. P., & Troskie, M. J. (2010). Addressing religious and spiritual issues in trauma-focused cognitive behavior therapy for children and adolescents. *Professional Psychology: Research & Practice, 41*(2), 174–180. doi:10.1037/a0017782

Weber, S. (2008). Diagnosis of trauma and abuse-related dissociative symptom disorders in children and adolescents. *Journal of Child and Adolescent Psychiatric Nursing, 21*(4), 205–212. doi:10.1111/j .1744-6171.2008.00156.x

POVERTY AND FAMILY DEVELOPMENT

Family poverty may be simply defined as the financial incapability to meet the family's basic physical needs. This simplistic definition belies its complicated and pervasive nature, as poverty is often felt in every part of family life including material, social, and emotional aspects. When finances are so strictly limited, freedom and power are thwarted in many domains of family life. Leisure time may be nonexistent, anxiety over bills is constant, and planning for the future a near impossibility. These challenges are complicated by the stigma of poverty in the United States. People living in poverty may be perceived as lazy, defective, or otherwise inferior. The daily struggle to survive alongside social oppression can harm families in significant ways. For some families, *poor* becomes a way of being and, in some cases, a stigmatized identity.

The challenge of poverty is unique for every family. Poverty may be generational in nuclear and extended families with a long-standing history of instability, or it may be situational, possibly caused by a severe life stressor such as job loss, disability, or divorce. Hopelessness and helplessness may accompany generational poverty, while shame and blame may characterize situational poverty. Increasingly, those living in poverty include full-time workers who cannot earn a living wage. However bleak poverty may seem, it is important to note that poverty is not a lifelong sentence. Rather, it is an important aspect of treating the family that must be considered in terms of its effect on multiple systems. Part of this bigger picture includes appreciation of the common struggles faced by families living in poverty and the effect of poverty on family functioning and development but also affirming the many strengths a family must possess simply to survive. This entry first discusses the common struggles of families living in poverty and how poverty affects the stages of family development. It then discusses how families living in poverty have strengths that can be drawn on in therapy to help them meet goals.

Common Struggles of Families in Poverty

In spite of the countless etiologies and wide variety of unique experiences of those living in poverty, there exist some commonalities that cut across populations. Perhaps most pervasive is the opportunity gap, or difference in educational, vocational, professional, and social opportunities afforded to those in poverty as compared with those with financial means. Many opportunities are relatively minor, such as the ability of families to send children to summer enrichment activities or the opportunity for families to mingle with others who have achieved financial success via stable and profitable employment. The cumulative effect of the opportunity gap results in limited opportunity to earn a living wage.

In contrast, a more obvious experience of poverty is life in dangerous neighborhoods where there is little access to safe recreation spaces or healthy food. Lack of transportation may mean challenges in seeking regular medical or behavioral health care, including family therapy appointments. Fatigue from long walks, long waits at bus transfers, or challenges associated with poor weather are commonplace. Further, just walking outside of one's door may be fraught with danger, including the presence of illegal drugs, gang activity, and street violence.

These families may feel trapped in a dangerous neighborhood with few resources both on a daily basis and for the long term. Indeed, depending on region, a majority of family income may be spent on housing, resulting in no savings or safety net and no money for extras, such as an outing for ice cream or books for children. Living from paycheck to paycheck, these families may alternate between paying some bills one month and others in the next in order to avoid consequences for failed payments. The result is family chaos, with ever-present anxiety about meeting basic family needs and the related loneliness and shame that can stifle positive experiences and emotional support within the family unit. As explored in the following section, life in poverty therefore impacts every stage of family development in both blatant and subtle ways.

Stages of Family Development

Individuals go through different stages in their development and so do families. The typical stages a family goes through make up the family life cycle. Poverty influences the typical stages a family experiences across time.

Forming Partnership

The formation of partnership tends to look very different for those living in poverty. Young couples may live with parents or extended family or bounce from home to home. Dating rituals may be vastly different for those with limited financial means. Debt may prohibit them from marrying or launching into independent living. Couples may postpone having children or may choose to have children prior to marriage. In general, young couples may experience a sense of differentness from mainstream culture, with the potential for a reduced sense of empowerment and control over one's future.

Child-Rearing

Concerns over basic needs take a psychological toll on parents and children alike. Impoverished families find themselves in a cycle of constant worry about family security, particularly if living in a high crime area where exposure to crime and violence is commonplace. Parents often work long hours for vital resources for their children, leaving less time to spend with their children and partner and less money for family-oriented leisure activities. These time restraints also result in limited opportunity to help children with homework or school projects. Shift work may also result in tight schedules that do not allow parents to tend to children's appointments, and child care may be unreliable or unsafe. Without any sort of financial safety net, the constant stress parents undergo can lead to frustration and anger directed toward children and partners. Likewise, children may act out in frustration, anger, or fear, or engage in other problematic behaviors. Children may also be parentified (given adult responsibilities) if they must care for siblings or elderly relatives in their home when parents work, or children may take on employment themselves thereby neglecting academic pursuits. The resulting pressure may have lasting effects on the mental health and well-being of individuals living in poverty and the long-term health and stability of families.

Launching Children

Young adulthood in poverty tends to take a far different trajectory than what would be considered the ideal, or even mythical, pattern of launching. Rather than leaving for employment, vocational training, or higher education at the age of adulthood, young adults in poverty typically do not have an option to live independently (launch) from the family. While it is becoming more commonplace in American culture for young adults to live with family members, achieving independence in one's 20s remains the normative ideal. If this milestone is not crossed, there is then a so-called failure to launch. This experience may cause feelings of shame and disappointment in both parents and their children. Young adults may feel stifled by household rules or burdensome to family members. Couples may feel robbed of the phase of life during which there is freedom from daily parenting tasks. Further, the revolving door of the household may involve children repeatedly returning to the home well into adulthood, thereby throwing family structure and patterns into disorganization. The young adult's financial struggles, such as excessive student loan debt, may transfer onto the shoulders of parents. These challenges are certain to increase stress on a partnership or on the entire family.

Middle Adulthood

Depending on the nature of the family's poverty, middle adulthood may bring expectations that the family should be out of debt or on better financial standing by this point in their lives. Again, feelings of failure, shame, and anxiety may predominate throughout the entire family. At this stage, families are more likely to struggle with medical bills or financial hardship related to the adult children. Indeed, due to financial or other constraints, parents may be required to step in as caregivers for their grandchildren, causing considerable stress. During middle adulthood, families are more likely to experience disability or divorce, both leading causes of poverty. Many families in poverty may choose to live permanently separated from a spouse rather than try to tackle the cost of seeking a divorce. Housing instability may result in limited engagement with the community.

Older Adulthood

During older adulthood, families living in poverty must face the reality that they do not have the money to sustain them through disability or health problems. The probability of retirement and the loss of dreams related to retirement must be grieved. The most challenging part of older adulthood in the United States is that it is linked to more severe poverty. Although home nursing care is on the rise, families may lack financial means to care for an older adult at home. In general, they are more likely to have limited access to health care and suitable assisted living or nursing facilities. Alongside these struggles, couples in older adulthood may experience regret for not having reached the financial goals necessary to provide assistance to their adult children or grandchildren and support themselves.

Strength and Hope

Despite the challenges faced by families living in poverty, family therapists must have hope for growth and healing when working with this population. This hope is grounded in the many ways families in poverty may be empowered. Families in poverty often have street smarts, or the survival techniques learned over the years that help them meet basic needs from day to day. For example, one might support oneself by providing a service or skill to others in the community or by bartering for necessary items. Families may be part of a religious community to which they can turn for support—either emotional or financial in nature. Neighbors who share the same struggles and lack any source of financial support may surround the family; families in such neighborhoods can work to create a kinship network by which challenges such as child care and transportation can be better addressed. These strengths may be tapped in family therapy to identify, explore, and work toward a wealth of possible solutions.

Appreciating that clients cannot grow when they are unsafe, homeless, or hungry, family therapists can remember that their work with those living in poverty cannot be limited to the therapy room. The therapist is in a good position to link clients to public services or to case management that may be helpful. Further, promoting home-based therapy and drop-in clinics can immensely help in removing barriers to treatment. Without such barriers, family therapy clients may meet therapeutic goals and even thrive in the midst of financial challenges.

Individuals and families can also benefit from a sense of the larger societal factors that impact their situation as well as the stigma they face in their world. Families that have membership in other stigmatized groups, such as those of racial, ethnic, or sexual minorities as well as underrepresented religious groups, may experience exponentially more stigma. Helping families situate their suffering in the context of societal patterns can help inspire them to find value in themselves, rather than blame themselves. Families can recognize their own strengths, resulting in empowerment and action. In other words, families can recognize that they do not have to be poor people. Rather, they may be living in poverty and therefore be able to find an identity separate from their given status in society. They are able to find hope for a better future when they believe in their own capabilities and find creative ways to meet goals, one at a time.

Louisa Foss-Kelly and Arden G. Rand

See also Debt and Financial Strain; Socioeconomic Status

Further Readings

Dakin, J., & Wampler, R. (2008). Money doesn't buy happiness, but it helps: Marital satisfaction, psychological distress, and demographic differences between low- and middle-income clinic couples. *The American Journal of Family Therapy, 36*, 300–311.

Dearing, E. (2008). Psychological costs of growing up poor. *New York Academy of Sciences, 1136*, 324–332.

Foss, L. L., & Generali, M. (2012). The CARE model for working with people in poverty. In D. C. Sturm & D. M. Gibson (Eds.), *Social class and the helping professions: A clinician's guide to navigating the landscape of class in America* (pp. 185–200). New York, NY: Routledge.

Foss, L. L., Generali, M. M., & Kress, V. E. (2011). Counseling people living in poverty: The CARE model. *Journal of Humanistic Counseling, 50*(2), 161–171.

Harper, A., Clayton, A., Bailey, M., Foss-Kelly, L., Sernyak, M. J., & Rowe, M. (2015). Financial health and mental health among clients of a community mental health center: Making the connections. *Psychiatric Services, 66*(12), 1271–1276. Retrieved from http://dx.doi.org/10.1176/appi.ps.201400438

Liu, W. M., & Estrada-Hernández, N. (2010). Counseling and advocacy for individuals living in poverty. In M. Ratts & J. Manivong (Eds.), *ACA advocacy competencies: A social justice framework for counselors* (pp. 43–53). Alexandria, VA: American Counseling Association.

Lott, B., & Bullock, H. E. (2007). *Psychology and economic injustice*. Washington, DC: American Psychological Association.

Perese, E. F. (2007). Stigma, poverty, and victimization: Roadblocks to recovery for individuals with severe mental illness. *American Psychiatric Nurses Association Journal, 13*(5), 285–296.

Smith, L. (2010). *Psychology, poverty, and the end of social exclusion: Putting our practice to work*. New York, NY: Teachers College Press.

Smith, L., Shellman, A., & Smith, R. (2013). Inequality, poverty, and counseling practice. In W. Ming Liu (Ed.), *The Oxford handbook of social class in counseling* (pp. 428–445). New York, NY: Oxford University Press.

Wadsworth, M., & Santiago, C. D. (2008). Risk and resiliency processes in ethnically diverse families in poverty. *Journal of Family Psychology, 22*(3), 399–410.

Power Issues in Couples

Power imbalances in couple relationships can cause conflict that is often not expressed verbally and that couples may not realize exists. Couples may not identify power issues when they attend therapy because they believe that their issues are due to finances, communication, intimacy, or other factors. Due to the focus on specific issues, the underlying issue of power is neglected. In addition, the dominant partner in a relationship may not see an issue with being in power, while the subordinate partner may realize that the person in power is causing issues in the relationship but may refrain from stating this to avoid conflict. This entry discusses how gender influences the power distribution in couples, how power issues interact with other issues in relationships, and how power issues can be addressed in marriage and couples counseling.

Gender and Power Issues

Differences in power distribution between men and women in couple relationships are partly due to limits on the role of women that have existed throughout much of history and to an extent still exist today even in more egalitarian societies. In the United States, as elsewhere, women have historically been viewed as being unable to fulfill certain roles and being more likely to base their opinions on emotion rather than reason. Men typically have been seen as the head of the household and have been given the right to make major decisions that affect the couple and their family. Until recently, these decisions included choosing to have sexual intercourse with a wife whenever the man wanted to, and while marital rape is now illegal throughout the United States, in some states it is still more difficult to prove or carries lesser penalties.

Gender remains a major factor in power issues in heterosexual couples. This issue has evolved as women's roles in society have changed. While in the past the primary role of married women was to be homemakers and bear children, women now may have multiple roles and may have careers while also raising children. Men are more likely than in the past to take on a significant share of household duties or even stay at home to take care of the children while their partners work outside the home. However, there can be conflict when partners disagree on their respective roles and responsibilities.

Interaction With Other Issues

Many factors influence a couple's success or failure aside from the power held by one or both partners. Power issues can promote negative beliefs or behaviors that make it difficult for couples to resolve other issues. Factors such as communication, finances, culture, and sexual intimacy each have an influence on the success of a relationship, but the power dynamic can determine a positive or negative resolution to problems in these other areas. Power is communicated unconsciously and consciously in relationships. A therapist needs to be mindful of the therapeutic techniques chosen to work with a couple because the wrong technique may support the dominant partner while confirming the subordinate role of the other partner.

Communication can be stymied by power issues because one or both partners is unable to relinquish any of their power so that a dialogue can occur. Power issues with communication include controlling the conversation, yelling, using vulgar language, or identifying the weaknesses of one's mate. Often, couples attend therapy because of problems with communication. In these situations, the subordinate partner tends to be silent when the therapist attempts to probe for answers because the subordinate partner is fearful of how the dominant partner might respond to his or her concerns.

Power issues can arise over finances when each partner does not contribute to decisions about how money is spent. Issues in couples with finance problems typically result from excessive spending and lack of budgeting, and these issues often lead to dissolution of the relationship. Power issues also can result when partners are from different cultures with different ideas and practices regarding who holds power in the relationship or how power is expressed.

Conflicts over sex can involve power issues, particularly when one partner desires sex more often than the other. In some couples, a partner may exert power through withholding sexual intercourse because of dissatisfaction over other issues. Historically, married women were expected to submit to sex with their husband at any time. Although laws in the United States no longer reflect this idea, there are some couples who base their relationship on this principle.

Power Issues and Couples Therapy

Research is limited on ways to address power issues in couples in therapy. This is mainly because during therapy power issues tend to go unnoticed or unidentified. Therapists tend to focus on the presenting concerns of the couple and related difficulties as they present themselves, in part to maintain therapeutic neutrality. To address power issues in a couple relationship, however, the therapist has to discuss topics that the couple may not have considered or that the partners are aware of but have not discussed with each other. This can include discussion of who the powerful person is in the relationship, how that person's power is affecting the relationship, and how power can be shared in a way that addresses the concerns of both partners.

Aside from individual therapy, group therapy with couples has also been identified as an effective approach for identifying power issues in couples. This approach allows for other couples to identify the issues of power for fellow group members while supporting the group members who feel powerless in their relationships.

*Kimberly Mason Peeples,
Chelsey L. Hess-Holden, and E. Joan Looby*

See also Acculturation; Couples Therapy Research

Further Readings

Cowdery, R. S., Scarborough, N., Knudson-Martin, C., Seshardri, G., Lewis, M. E., & Mahoney, A. R. (2009). Gendered power in cultural contexts: Part II. Middle class African American heterosexual couples with young children. *Family Process*, 48(1), 25–39.

Knudson-Martin, C. (2013). Why power matters: Creating a foundation of mutual support in couple relationships. *Family Process*, 52(1), 5–18.

Knudson-Martin, C., Huenergardt, D., Lafontant, K., Bishop, L., Schaepper, J., & Wells, M. (2015). Competencies for addressing gender and power in couple therapy: A socioemotional approach. *Journal of Marital and Family Therapy*, 41(2), 205–220.

Ocobock, A. (2013). The power and limits of marriage: Married gay men's family relationships. *Journal of Marriage and Family*, 75, 191–205.

Parker, L. (2009). Disrupting power and privilege in couples therapy. *Clinical Social Work Journal*, 37, 248–255. doi:10.1007/s10615-009-0211-7

Ward, A., & Knudson-Martin, C. (2012). The impact of therapist actions on the balance of power within the couple system: A qualitative analysis of therapy sessions. *Journal of Couple & Relationship Therapy*, 11, 221–237.

PRACTICE MANAGEMENT

Most training and expertise possessed by counselors involve clinical aspects of what occurs within counseling sessions with clients. However, practice management involves dynamics and strategies related to aspects of counseling that occur outside the counseling session but with the best interests of clients in mind. Practice management is of particular importance to counselors who own a private practice because, as small business owners, they are the ones responsible for the day-to-day operations of their practice. This entry addresses the legal, ethical, business, and personal aspects of managing a practice in the field of counseling.

Legal Aspects

Counselors need to be aware of the legal aspects involved in a practice. Governing boards of examiners oversee the profession of counseling in each state or region. Counselors should be aware of the laws, including scope of practice, in their geographical area. For example, a nonlicensed counselor cannot legally practice without clinical supervision and cannot charge a direct fee for service. Counselors need to consult with attorneys and certified public accountants to determine an appropriate tax status, such as sole proprietorship or limited liability company (LLC), and to ensure the payment of income taxes. Most counselors obtain an employer identification number (EIN) from the Internal Revenue Service to prevent using their Social Security number. Counselors who distribute client information electronically comply with the legal mandates of the Health Insurance Portability and Accountability Act (HIPAA). Counselors also obtain professional liability insurance on an annual basis to protect themselves in the event of a malpractice lawsuit. The insurance policy should correspond with the number of counseling hours conducted on a weekly basis and provide coverage for at minimum $1 million per occurrence and $3 million aggregate per policy year.

Ethical Aspects

In addition to the legal aspects, practice management for counselors involves ethical aspects. Counselors adhere to their relevant ethical standards published by their profession (i.e., the American Counseling Association [ACA] *Code of Ethics*). Although the following items are not exhaustive, they provide a glimpse of ethical expectations for counselors.

Continuing Education and Consultation

In order to maintain licensure, counselors must earn continuing education units in areas such as clinical practice, ethics, and diagnosis. This typically occurs via the counselor's membership in a professional counseling association. Continuing education ensures that the counselor stays abreast of current research and theories of counseling. Counselors also seek case consultation, as necessary, for difficult counseling situations.

Making Referrals

Counselors are ethically responsible for making appropriate referrals. A counselor should not continue therapy with a client who needs the help of a professional with more specialized training. Clients with severe mental illnesses should be referred for medical and/or psychiatric evaluation. The counselor carefully communicates to clients when there is a need for more specialized treatment. Counseling can result in more harm than good if the appropriate referral is not secured.

Dual Relationships

Ethical guidelines inform how counselors interact with clients outside of the therapy room. To ensure objectivity, counselors do not provide services to friends, family, or current or past sexual partners. Counselors also do not maintain virtual relationships (i.e., social media connections) with current clients.

Multicultural Environment

Multicultural training allows for the therapist to effectively treat clients from various ethnic and racial backgrounds. Specific measures can be taken by the practice to ensure a welcoming and accepting atmosphere for clients of all backgrounds, including not imposing personal values on clients. Diverse reading materials in the waiting room are also helpful.

Business Aspects

Next, counselors must implement sound business principles. Professional business skills are vital in the establishment and maintenance of a practice.

Business Plan

A business plan facilitates an organized practice from the outset and minimizes the likelihood of the practice's rapid termination. The business plan needs to be clear, brief, and logical. A business plan is the practical document of the practice that outlines pertinent information, such as the idea behind the business, a needs assessment, what makes the practice unique, start-up funds, operating costs, key milestones, and evaluation.

Marketing and Generating Referrals

Networking

Networking involves staying connected with others who will help build the practice. Generating referrals is the most important step in beginning and maintaining a practice. Referral sources include physicians, psychiatrists, nurses, physician assistants, attorneys, judges, accountants, community leaders, religious leaders, professors, dieticians, school counselors, teachers, physical therapists, professional agency leaders, and other mental health therapists. Relationships that counselors make in the community can potentially result in referrals. The options are basically unlimited; however, the key to generating referrals is to become known in the community through networking. A list of civic organizations is usually kept on file at the local chamber of commerce or clerk of court's office. Networking opportunities exist via professional counseling organizations including the ACA, the American Association of Marriage and Family Therapy (AAMFT), and corresponding state associations.

Websites and Social Media

In today's society, marketing through the Internet is a necessity. Websites need to include the services offered, unique characteristics, potential client base, why people should come, key concepts, purpose of the site, and knowledge of the market. Websites can advertise other details of the practice including therapeutic approach, photos of therapists, training and credentials, articles or blogs, hours of availability, and location including a map with directions. Counselors also have the opportunity to market their practice by creating a virtual presence on a professional level via various social media outlets.

Public Speaking

Public speaking is an effective strategy to generate referrals. Speaking engagements include businesses, schools, workshops, places of worship, and conferences. Following a presentation at a workshop or conference, counselors should follow up with new contacts. Counselors should also be prepared to make appointments from new referrals.

Business Cards

Business cards should be placed in the waiting room, carried with the counselor, and included with professional correspondence. Essential elements of the business card include the name of the counselor along with credentials and the corresponding demographic information, such as office address, telephone number, e-mail address, and website address. The back of the card could include an appointment reminder and/or directions to the practice.

Newsletters and News Releases

Newsletters are excellent modes of advertising and marketing the counseling center. Each month, the therapist can compose a newsletter containing a relevant article, description of services, and contact information. The newsletter could be e-mailed to all clients and professional contacts. Cost efficiency is a major advantage of electronic newsletters. Print newsletters, which are more costly, could be utilized once or twice a year to the surrounding community. Counselors also can send news releases to local newspapers and radio stations to introduce themselves to the community.

Office Procedures

Office Space

When selecting office space, consideration is given to accessibility, safety, and confidentiality. Some counselors share office space with other professionals to offset costs and to collaborate on services. For example, a counselor may sublease office space from a physician who will also make referrals for counseling.

Telephone and E-Mail Address

Counselors have a telephone line dedicated for the practice. A counselor will not build a client base if phone calls from prospective clients are not received or returned. Confidential voice mail services are needed to ensure privacy, and instructions are needed for clients in the event of an emergency. Counselors should receive client permission before communicating via texting or e-mailing. Counselors should be mindful of security and privacy issues when using e-mail.

Scheduling Appointments

Initial appointments are typically made at the office, by telephone, or by e-mail. After the initial counseling session, appointments are often scheduled with the counselor at the office. Reminder slips with the date and time of the next appointment should be given to the client. The 24-hour notice policy is generally accepted as standard procedure for cancellations and rescheduling of appointments.

Fees

Appropriate fees are collected to ensure the continuation of counseling services by providing income to the counselor and by covering expenses of facilitating a practice. Counselors typically have a standard fee that reflects their locality and the financial status of clients. Sliding fee scales are sometimes implemented, which allow for quality, professional services at fees dependent on economic income levels of the client. For example, a couple with a combined income of $30,000 will pay less than a couple with a combined income of $75,000. Special consideration is typically provided for families unable to pay fees, with services sometimes provided for free. For counselors who accept insurance, clients will either pay toward their deductible or make a copayment. Information concerning payment and cancellation policies should be discussed during the first session.

Forms and Documentation

Counselors are required by state licensure boards to have each client sign a declaration statement. This document outlines the expertise of the counselor, theories and techniques utilized, fees, and confidentiality issues. A section is also included for the client and counselor to sign the document. Intake forms are completed for each new client. The purpose of the intake forms is to obtain demographic information, a brief psychiatric and medical history, psychosocial concerns, family-of-origin dynamics, and presenting problems. Progress notes must also be completed for each client. Counselors are required to write case notes to facilitate effective treatment. The SOAP (subjective, objective, assessment, and plan) format of writing case notes is a popular method. Additional resources for forms such as Edward L. Zuckerman's *The Paper Office* allow the counselor to maintain essential documentation for each client.

Billing, Accounting, and Record-Keeping

Counselors have options for billing, accounting, and record-keeping. Some counselors choose to download software onto their computer while others utilize cloud-based technology. There are pros and cons for each; however, the primary concerns are client confidentiality and privacy. Also, regardless of the method utilized, counselors must understand the value of being organized. A client will typically not pay an outstanding balance without being invoiced, and an insurance company will not provide reimbursement for a claim that has not been filed.

Personal Aspects

Although counselors are mindful of the legal, ethical, and business aspects of managing a practice, focus is also needed on personal aspects. Working with clients on a daily basis can become emotionally draining and physically exhausting. Physical health must be maintained by a proper diet and regular exercise. Counselors also need to maintain personal relationships such as marriage, family, and friendships in such a way that personal problems are not explored within the context of providing counseling to clients. Counselors should seek personal counseling, as necessary. Finally, counselors need to understand the financial risk involved with a practice, especially if there are no other forms of income. If a counselor has severe personal debt or money management problems, then these fiscal tendencies tend to occur on the practice level as well. In these instances, counselors would benefit from personal finance training.

Eric M. Dishongh

See also Dual and Multiple Relationships; Ethical Codes; HIPAA Standards; Multiculturalism; Supervision

Further Readings

Dasenbrook, N. C. (2013). *The complete guide to private practice for licensed mental health practitioners.* Rockford, IL: Author.

Grodzki, L. (2015). *Building your ideal private practice: A guide for therapists and other healing professionals.* New York, NY: W. W. Norton.

Harris, S. M., Ivey, D. C., & Beam, R. A. (Eds.). (2005). *A practice that works: Strategies to complement your stand alone therapy practice.* New York, NY: Routledge.

Stout, C. (Ed.). (2012). *Getting better at private practice.* Hoboken, NJ: Wiley.

Todd, T. (2009). *Practice-building 2.0 for mental health professionals: Strategies for success in the digital age.* New York, NY: W. W. Norton.

Zuckerman, E. L. (2008). *The paper office: Forms, guidelines, and resources to make your practice work ethically, legally, and profitably.* New York, NY: Guilford Press.

PREGNANCY

Pregnancy generally results from a sperm cell traveling through the cervix into the fallopian tube to fertilize an egg cell. There are millions of sperm that are released during intercourse. If a sperm penetrates an egg, then fertilization occurs and a zygote is created, which has 46 chromosomes (23 from the male and 23 from the female), the normal complement for a human somatic cell. This is the basis for a developing person. As the zygote travels through the fallopian tube toward the uterus, the zygote continues to develop by multiplying and growing. This process can occur naturally following male ejaculation during sexual intercourse, or there may be medical intervention, such as artificial insemination or in vitro fertilization. Artificial insemination occurs when sperm is injected directly into the uterus close to the fallopian tubes, where the female egg is released during ovulation. In vitro fertilization involves the extraction of both sperm and an egg or several eggs and inserting them together into a petri dish. After a period of a few days, the resulting embryo is then transferred into the uterus to continue developing. The fetus then continues developing for a period of approximately forty weeks, if the pregnancy is viable and able to continue. This entry continues with an overview of the trimesters of pregnancy and statistics on birth and pregnancy. It then discusses abortion, teen pregnancy, and the impact of pregnancy on relationships. It closes with a discussion on postpartum depression.

Trimesters of Pregnancy

Pregnancy is divided into three trimesters that mark different phases of the fetus's development. These trimesters also mark different phases of the pregnant woman's development through the pregnancy. Typical pregnancies last 40 weeks.

First Trimester

The first trimester, which is the first thirteen weeks, is considered the most fragile time because this is when birth defects and miscarriage are most likely to occur. During this period, the brain, spinal cord, heart, and gastrointestinal tract begin to develop. Each week, the zygote continues to develop, and more body parts and organs are created and begin working. By the completion of the first trimester, the heart has begun beating and can be heard, and the jaw, lungs, nose, and palate are formed. Each part is becoming more recognizable as it further develops. The fetus weighs approximately 3 ounces, and the genitalia can be seen.

For the woman carrying the fetus, the first sign of pregnancy may be the loss of the premenstrual cycle. Then after confirmation of pregnancy, this is a time where many body changes are occurring.

Often, pregnant women feel nauseated and tired and have breast tenderness, upset stomach, and frequent urination. Some women experience mood changes and an overall change to their daily schedules (i.e., going to bed early, feeling more emotional, or being hungry throughout the day). As with many conditions, pregnant women experience different symptoms at different times of their pregnancy.

Second Trimester

The second trimester occurs between 14 weeks and 26 weeks. This phase of pregnancy is generally the most pleasant for pregnant women. Many of the unpleasant symptoms of the first trimester diminish, and women report less nausea, better sleep patterns, and an increase in energy levels. These symptoms can vary with different women and different pregnancies. As some symptoms are becoming more manageable, many women experience body changes such as their abdominal area expanding, the appearance of stretch marks, or darkening of skin and a line on the skin running from belly button to pubic hairline. There may be itching on certain parts of the body or swelling. If some of these symptoms feel uncomfortable or concerning, pregnant woman are encouraged to inform their health care provider.

The fetus is continuing to develop, and some women report being able to feel flutters of the baby early in the second trimester. The fetus has developed hair, eyelashes, and nails and continues to grow, so movement is felt more strongly by the woman later in this phase of pregnancy. The fetus's pancreas and liver have begun working, and air sacs have developed in the growing lungs. The fetus develops sleeping and waking patterns. The nervous system has developed and has some control over functions. The brain will begin to develop rapidly over the next several weeks. Toward the end of the second trimester, the fetus weighs approximately 2.5 pounds and is 14 inches in length. Generally, a fetus born at approximately twenty-four weeks would be able to survive with medical assistance.

Third Trimester

Week 27 of the pregnancy marks the beginning of the third and final trimester. This trimester lasts until approximately forty weeks (or delivery). At this phase, the fetus is continuing to develop rapidly. The fetus begins to store fat in the body, and while all the bones are formed, they are soft and delicate. The lungs are not fully functional yet but have started the process of rhythmic breathing. The eyelids finally open, having been closed since the first trimester. The baby also begins its movement toward the birth canal in preparation for birth. The movement that a pregnant woman feels at this stage decreases, since the fetus is getting larger and taking up most of the room in the uterus. Contractions may be experienced during this time that do not signal the start of labor but are a sign that the body is preparing to give birth.

This trimester brings a variety of physical symptoms to the pregnant woman, which may include back pain, sleep disturbance, urinary incontinence, hemorrhoids, and shortness of breath. These symptoms can be attributed to the increasing size of the uterus to accommodate the increasing size of the fetus. Additionally, there are many emotional responses the pregnant woman experiences at this time relating to fears, anxiety, stress, and other feelings of uncertainty in relation to the birth of the child and the anticipation of child-rearing responsibilities.

Birth and Pregnancy Statistics

There are about 6 million pregnancies annually in the United States, resulting in about 4 million live births. The remaining pregnancies are terminated or result in miscarriage or stillbirth. Couples are considered infertile if they do not conceive after 1 year despite trying. Infertility affects an estimated 2 million couples in the United States.

In 2014, almost 10% of births in the United States were preterm births, defined as the birth of an infant before 37 weeks of pregnancy, according to the National Center for Health Statistics. Major structural or genetic birth defects occur in approximately 3% of births in the United States, according to the Centers for Disease Control and Prevention (CDC). More than half of pregnancies in the United States are either mistimed (31%) or unwanted (20%), according to the Guttmacher Institute. A pregnancy is considered mistimed if the woman did not want to become pregnant at the time of the pregnancy but did want to become pregnant at some future date.

Abortion

Approximately 21% of all pregnancies (excluding those ending in miscarriage) end in abortion. Each year 1.7% of women ages 15 to 44 years old have an abortion in the United States; of these, at least half have had a previous abortion. Women in their 20s account for the majority of abortions. In 2011, the abortion rate reached its lowest level since 1973. The reasons that women decide to have an abortion include not being able to care for a baby due to caring for other children already, having concerns about relationship status, and being unable to afford a baby. In 2000, the U.S. Food and Drug Administration approved medication to terminate pregnancy, called RU-486 or mifepristone (Korlym). This has led to an increase in first-trimester abortions, which are medically the safest.

Teen Pregnancy

The teen birth rate has declined significantly since 1991, when there were 61.8 births for every 1,000 females ages 15 to 19. In 2013, there were 26.6 births per 1,000 females. Many of these births were not first-time births. In 2013, almost one in six (17%) of the births to 15- to 19-year-olds were to an adolescent who already had one or more babies. Most adolescents who give birth are 18 or older. Birth rates are higher among Hispanic and Black adolescents compared with their White counterparts. While the highest incidence of teen births occurs among Hispanics, this rate has fallen dramatically in recent years. Since 2007, the teen birth rate has dropped by 45% for Hispanics, compared with 37% for Blacks and 32% for Whites. Specific characteristics are associated with a higher likelihood for an adolescent birth. Adolescents who are engaged in learning and have positive attitudes toward learning are less likely to give birth to, or father, a baby during adolescence. Those who have lived in a household with both biological parents at age 14 also are at lower risk. Adolescents whose mothers gave birth as adolescents or whose mothers only have a high school diploma are more likely to become pregnant by age 20.

Impact on Relationships

The impact pregnancy may have on relationships varies depending on the status of the relationship (i.e., marriage, long-term commitment, short-term commitment). Evidence has been found that perceived support from a relationship has a significant positive impact on maternal well-being and the infant. Pregnancy brings a level of stress to any relationship due to the physical, mental, and emotional challenges faced by both the pregnant woman and her partner. There may be stress associated with financial concerns due to the cost of caring for a child and decisions regarding the work status of the pregnant woman. For the pregnant woman, hormonal and other physical changes and health stressors that occur during pregnancy may impact the relationship she has with her partner. Preexisting relationship problems may worsen with the arrival of a child. Some women are also at risk for postpartum depression, and this condition may add another layer to the relationship concerns.

Counseling may take place at the beginning of the pregnancy to determine if the pregnant woman is committed to keeping the pregnancy. Pregnancy counseling would be comprised of support to the pregnant woman, along with a variety of options to consider in moving forward. The pregnant woman may choose to continue with the pregnancy and keep the child, continue with the pregnancy and place the child for adoption, or terminate the pregnancy. In an adoption, the birth parents also decide whether to share identifiable information with the adoptive family and whether to have contact with the adoptive family before and after the adoption. The decision to terminate a pregnancy is time sensitive based on state laws that prevent an abortion after fetal viability (the point when a fetus can live outside the womb) or after a certain number of weeks.

Postpartum Depression

Some women experience feelings of sadness, anxiety, and depression during pregnancy and after the birth of their child. Although this has been referred to as postpartum depression, researchers now say that symptoms often begin during pregnancy and can develop any time during the first year after giving birth. These symptoms now are often referred to as maternal mental illness. Medical doctors and counseling professionals have become more aware of this concern, and increasingly, women who give birth are screened for depression before they leave the hospital and at follow-up appointments. In early 2016, a federal government panel recommended that women be screened for depression during pregnancy and after giving birth.

In rare instances, these feelings may consume women and result in a desire to harm the baby. Women who suffer from postpartum depression may also experience a lack of interest in the child and caring for the child. Treatment of postpartum depression includes therapeutic counseling, medication, and the monitoring of symptoms and behavior of the mother.

Meredith Drew

See also Adoption; Postpartum Depression; Stillbirth and Miscarriage

Further Readings

Betts, K. S., Williams, G. M., Najman, J. M., & Alati, R. A. (2014). The relationship between maternal depressive, anxious, and stress symptoms during pregnancy and adult offspring behavioral and emotional problems. *Depression and Anxiety*, 32(2), 82–90.

Divney, A. A., Sipsma, H., Gordon, D., Niccolai, L., Magriples, U., & Kershaw, T. (2012). Depression during pregnancy among young couples: The effect of personal and partner experiences of stressors and the buffering effects of social relationships. *Journal of Pediatric and Adolescent Gynecology*, 25(3), 201–207.

Guttmacher Institute. (2015, July). *Unintended pregnancy in the United States*. New York, NY: Author. Retrieved from https://www.guttmacher.org/pubs/FB-Unintended-Pregnancy-US.html

Johnson, I. (2011). Adult children of divorce and relationship education: Implications for counselors and counselor educators. *The Family Journal*, 19(1), 22–29. doi:10.1177/1066480710387494

Martin, J. A., Hamilton, B. E., & Osterman, M. J. K. (2015, September). *Births in the United States, 2014*. NCHS data brief, no. 216. Hyattsville, MD: National Center for Health Statistics. Retrieved from http://www.cdc.gov/nchs/data/databriefs/db216.htm

Ponzetti, J. J., Jr. (Ed.). (2003). *International encyclopedia of marriage and family*. New York, NY: Macmillan.

Stapleton, L. R. T., Schetter, C. D., Westling, E., Rini, C., Glynn, L. M., Hobel, C. J., & Sandman, C. A. (2012). Perceived partner support in pregnancy predicts lower maternal and infant distress. *Journal of Family Psychology*, 26(3), 453–463. Retrieved from http://dx.doi.org/10.1037/a0028332

PREGNANCY AND SEXUALITY

Pregnant individuals and their partners experience a number of changes that can have a major impact on their lives, including the nature of their sexual relationship throughout the course of pregnancy. In this entry, the physical, emotional, and social factors that play a role in how pregnancy and sexuality interact will be explored. (Note: The language throughout this section will remain nongendered given that not all cis women are able or choose to become pregnant, and conflating pregnancy with "women" excludes trans women. Conversely, trans men or nonbinary individuals may also experience pregnancy.)

Physical changes in the body during pregnancy can impact a person's sexual experience. Near the end of the first trimester, the genitals of the female begin to swell due to increased blood flow to the pelvic area, a change that continues throughout the pregnancy. This often leads to increased lubrication in the vagina. For some, this may lead to a pleasant sensation, increasing one's interest in sexual activities. Some others find that the lubrication makes intercourse less satisfying. Another result of the extra blood flow in the genitals and pelvic area is an increased responsiveness during orgasm. Individuals report both an increase in the time it takes to achieve orgasm and an increase in the perceived intensity of the orgasm. Changes in breast size and responsiveness can also play a role in a person's experience of sex during pregnancy. The increase may lead to more pleasurable responses during sexual activities or a potential need to avoid contact due to tenderness or pain.

Research indicates that many pregnant individuals know they should ask their doctors about sex during pregnancy but that a majority do not for a variety of reasons. Common issues include questions regarding whether or not it is safe to engage in intercourse or have orgasms during the pregnancy. Some couples fear that intercourse, orgasms, or ejaculation into the vagina may induce premature labor. Because the uterus contracts during orgasms, one may experience strong contractions before or after orgasms, which typically resolve after a short period of time. While many doctors consider these muscle contractions as good exercise preparing for birth, these contractions can be alarming and can lead to a fear of future sexual encounters from both partners. Another misconception about sex during pregnancy is a fear of damaging the fetus either through pressure on the vagina or from exposure to ejaculate. In reality, penetration that feels pleasurable for the receiver is not likely to harm the fetus. Furthermore, both a cervical plug that develops during pregnancy and the amniotic sac in which a fetus develops create barriers to ejaculatory fluid that makes its way into the uterus.

Overall changes in the body's appearance can also have an impact on sexuality during pregnancy. Individuals may enjoy the change in their physical appearance, feeling more beautiful. Others may find themselves unattractive and undesirable. These self-image issues can fluctuate throughout the pregnancy, and many report feeling somewhere in the middle from day to day. Depending on how people feel about their bodies can play a role in whether or not they're interested in or enjoy sexual encounters. Partners to pregnant individuals sometimes feel less confident in initiating sex. This can be related to not wanting the pregnant partner to be pressured, but it can also lead to people doubting they are still sexually attractive while pregnant.

Emotionally, pregnancy can be a tumultuous time for both the individual and his or her partner(s). Changes in hormone levels often lead to mood swings during pregnancy. At one moment, sex may seem like the only option, only to be replaced within moments by tears or fear. Again, every individual experiences pregnancy differently, typically falling somewhere on the spectrum of uninterested to extremely interested at any given point throughout the pregnancy. One positive aspect that many couples report in regard to sex during pregnancy is the relief that comes from not being able to become pregnant. While contraceptives should still be used to protect against sexually transmitted infections, the anxiety that can come from preventing (or attempting) pregnancy via condom use is temporarily relieved at this time.

Throughout pregnancy, especially for first timers, the impending life changes associated with birth and parenthood can lead to feelings of depression concurrently associated with a decreased interest in sexual activities. Many partners of pregnant individuals express feelings of pride, protectiveness, fear, and insecurity related to their partner's pregnancy. Those with penises who play a sexual role in the act of conception may experience a difficulty in achieving orgasm or issues with achieving or maintaining an erection. Often, after pregnancy is achieved, these issues are resolved and can lead the partner(s) to also have an increase in sexual confidence or interest. Another factor influencing sexuality during pregnancy is a partner's potential experience of exclusion. Some may feel as though there is no place for them in regard to pregnancy or the development of a future child, leading to feelings of strain or separation during this time. Lastly, many pregnant individuals report a dramatic increase in their need for emotional support, validation, and/or attention. Like many factors related to pregnancy, this need can become an advantage or a strain within a relationship. Pregnant individuals may worry about being a burden, while partners may experience emotional exhaustion from constantly soothing their pregnant partner's concerns.

Open communication is crucial to any relationship, especially concerning sex, particularly during pregnancy and most importantly in regard to sex during pregnancy. Pregnant individuals may find it particularly difficult to articulate their needs throughout their pregnancies, and partners may feel particularly confused regarding meeting both their own and their partners' needs. Cultural considerations regarding involvement of partners or family during pregnancy, rites related to both pregnancy and birth and the individual, couple, or family's unique stressors related to the experience should be incorporated into working with such individuals. Finally, as with many sex-related emotional issues, psychoeducation and normalizing are key to helping individuals and their partners better understand, accept, and adjust to the unique changes that pregnancy induces.

Molly Rose Wilson

See also Birth Control and Contraception; Family Life Cycle; Human Sexual Response; Parenting

Further Readings

Bartellas, E., Crane, J. M. G., Daley, M., Bennett, K. A., & Hutchens, D. (2000). Sexuality and sexual activity in pregnancy. *British Journal of Obstetrics and Gynaecology, 107*(8), 964–968.

Gałązka, I., Drosdzol-Cop, A., Naworska, B., Czajkowska, M., & Skrzypulec-Plinta, V. (2015). Changes in the sexual function during pregnancy. *The Journal of Sexual Medicine, 12*(2), 445–454. doi:10.1111/jsm.12747

Joannides, P. (2012). *Guide to getting it on!* (7th ed.). Waldport, OR: Goofy Foot Press.

Millheiser, L. (2012). Female sexual function during pregnancy and postpartum. *The Journal of Sexual Medicine, 9*(2), 635–636. doi:10.1111/j.1743-6109.2011.02637.x

Oruç, S., Esen, A., Laçin, S., Adigüzel, H., Uyar, Y., & Koyuncu, F. (1999). Sexual behaviour during pregnancy. *Australian and New Zealand Journal of Obstetrics and Gynaecology, 39*(1), 48–50. doi:10.1111/j.1479-828X.1999.tb03443.x

Sagiv-Reiss, D. M., Birnbaum, G. E., & Safir, M. P. (2012). Changes in sexual experiences and relationship quality during pregnancy. *Archives of Sexual Behavior, 41*(5), 1241–1251. doi:10.1007/s10508-011-9839-9

Soljačić Vraneš, H., Nakić Radoš, S., & Šunjić, M. (2015). Sexuality during pregnancy: What is important for sexual satisfaction in expectant fathers? *Journal of Sex & Marital Therapy, 41*(3), 282–293. doi:10.1080/0092623X.2014.889054

Woertman, L., & van den Brink, F. (2012). Body image and female sexual functioning and behavior: A review. *Journal of Sex Research, 49*(2), 184–211. doi:10.1080/00224499.2012.658586

Premarital Counseling

Humans need intimate relationships with others. Marriage is one of the most intimate relationships two people can engage in, as intimacy is provided through the physical and emotional relationships shared by partners. To ensure that a healthy level of intimacy can be developed and maintained, couples can engage in premarital counseling. Premarital counseling helps couples identify and focus on the strengths of their relationship while also allowing them to identify which components of their relationship they want to further develop. Topics covered in premarital counseling include but are not limited to expectations, communication, partner roles, sex, finances, conflict resolution, and child-rearing. In addition to discussing how these topics are addressed in premarital counseling, this entry looks at relationship education, processes of finding a premarital counselor, and establishing the goals of premarital counseling.

Expectations

Individuals have expectations for their relationships. Specifically, individuals have beliefs about how their significant other should behave, how situations or events should occur, and how their romantic relationship should appear. Often, partners do not communicate these expectations to one another, resulting in hurt feelings, misunderstandings, and arguments. These negative outcomes may be prevented by discussing expectations in such areas as communication, roles, finances, sex, intimacy, household chores, and children. Discussing expectations allows partners to engage in conversation that involves their imagined or expected fantasies and the resulting realities of marriage. Premarital counselors help couples discuss these issues in order to bring these topics to the forefront so they are not surprised by them after their marriage.

Communication

There are various styles of communication within couples, and often a couple's initial style of speaking becomes their default, or normal, way of communicating with one another. This default style of communication may continue, despite being inefficient or even damaging to the couple's relationship. Premarital counseling can help partners establish ways of speaking that allow them to feel heard and understood. A major tenet within premarital counseling is to help couples develop healthy and efficient communication patterns.

Individuals may use passive, passive-aggressive, aggressive, or assertive language when talking to a relationship partner. Individuals who are passive refrain from offering their opinion; reply to questions by saying, "I don't know" or "It doesn't matter to me"; and rarely express their wants or needs to their significant others. Because their needs are not shared, passive individuals often feel their opinion is not important and their happiness is not valued and, therefore, wind up feeling dissatisfied in their relationships. Furthermore, partners of passive individuals often struggle to get their partners to share their ideas and opinions and often feel frustrated by the lack of interaction in the relationship. Moreover, because passive individuals usually do not disclose much about themselves, it is difficult to develop intimacy within a couple. This can lead to problems within all interpersonal relationships and can attract significant others who are more controlling or aggressive, as they may be more comfortable being the dominant voice in the relationship.

Passive-aggressive communication is when individuals do not openly share their wants, needs, or expectations but, rather, choose to communicate indirectly. Passive-aggressive communicators express themselves in a roundabout manner where comments are clear enough to hurt the recipient's feelings but ambiguous enough to be denied. In addition, passive-aggressive individuals tend to view others' comments as meaning harm, engage in the silent treatment when frustrated, perceive others as underappreciating them, and mask criticism by way of compliments. Individuals who rely on this type of communication are difficult to work with, as passive-aggressiveness can be difficult to identify initially. Furthermore, passive-aggressive individuals often do not want to communicate about disagreements or their communication style, as this discussion will put them in a vulnerable position, and usually passive-aggressive individuals prefer to have the upper hand in situations. Discussing communication can cause these individuals too much discomfort, and therefore, counselors working with passive-aggressive partners may find it to be difficult and time-consuming.

Aggressive communication is often marked by bringing up past mistakes, insults, swearing, and using you-messages as a way to pass blame. Individuals who rely on aggressive communication often react spontaneously yet work to hurt the person they are speaking with. Furthermore, aggressive communicators express their needs or wants without regard for the welfare of others. They may be viewed as selfish and vengeful as well as unwilling to compromise. Discussing communication styles with aggressive communicators can be difficult because they usually resort to blaming the other person for causing them to behave in this manner.

Similar to passive-aggressive communicators, counselors may struggle to get aggressive partners to see their role in any communication problems.

Assertive communication is marked by directly expressing wants and needs while respecting the rights and welfare of others. Assertive communication involves using I-statements and refraining from passing blame onto others. Assertive communication allows partners' needs to be met while being concise, direct, and free from criticism or contempt. Counselors help partners to develop assertive communication in order to feel more comfortable with their language while also helping them to respectfully get their needs met.

In addition to discussing communication styles, counselors help premarital couples to understand that verbal communication includes both the words spoken and nonverbal signals. When communicating, partners share content (what is reported) and messages (what is conveyed nonverbally). For example, if an individual rolls her eyes when telling her partner she ran into an old friend, this could be interpreted as she ran into an old friend whom she found to be irritating. The content is usually straightforward, whereas the message can be more ambiguous.

When there is a discrepancy between the content and the message, counselors refer to it as a mixed message. Counselors help couples to examine how these mixed messages can be confusing and how, typically, partners rely on the nonverbal component of the statement when there is a mixed message. A way to help couples improve their verbal and nonverbal communication is to have partners take time to discuss their communication. Specifically, counselors work with the couple to learn about their style of speaking and how to speak honestly, listen attentively, ask for clarification if necessary, and give constructive feedback.

Partner Roles

Partner roles must be discussed during premarital counseling to ensure that individuals are aware of and comfortable with one another's views and expectations. For example, a partner may believe that one individual should do the majority of household chores, while the other individual will work outside the home and provide the primary financial support for the family. The other partner may believe that both individuals are capable and ought to share household chores and financial responsibilities. If the partners do not discuss these expectations, problems can arise. In addition, individuals usually have expectations of role-specific behaviors for themselves and their partners. For example, based on ideas about masculinity and femininity, each person in a couple may have specific beliefs about who should cook, clean, do household maintenance, and take responsibility for major parenting tasks. Often, individuals' beliefs about roles are based on their own upbringing and how caregivers modeled various roles. However, role expectations may not be discussed between partners, causing unexpected problems. Therefore, counselors can help premarital partners discuss their beliefs and expectations of each partner's role by asking questions, engaging the couple in role-plays, and exploring partners' childhood models of roles.

Sex

In the United States, the majority of couples have intercourse before marriage. Moreover, premarital relationships are often highly sexual; however, partners often avoid communication about sex. Problems can compound since men and women may differ in the importance they place on sex in their relationship; in addition, males are more likely to separate love and sex, while females are more likely to highly connect sex and love. Research suggests that the quality of a couple's sexual satisfaction relates to their overall relationship satisfaction, while the quality of their relationship can increase their sexual satisfaction. Therefore, sex is an issue that needs to be discussed to ensure that both partners have the opportunity to express their wants, needs, and expectations.

Premarital counselors work with couples to determine their attitudes toward and expectations about sexuality. Partners' views on sexuality can include their level of satisfaction on the amount of affection within the relationship, the amount of sexual interest or disinterest between partners, ability to talk about sexual issues, and ability or inability to keep their sexual relationship exciting and pleasurable. Counselors also help couples explore how to maintain their sexual satisfaction over time.

Finances

Couple satisfaction has been linked to their agreement on finances. Agreement on finances includes how the couple spends money, saves money, handles debt, and uses credit cards. Communicating about financial expectations and coming to agreements about finances serves premarital couples well, as research suggests that couples who can adequately and jointly manage their finances report a more satisfying relationship.

Financial difficulties lead to stress, and in turn, stress can take away from relationship satisfaction; therefore, premarital counselors work with couples to determine financial responsibilities within the couple. These responsibilities include decisions on who will take care of the day-to-day financial obligations, how to handle and reduce debt, and how the couple plans to live within their monetary means. Learning how to communicate about finances is an important goal within premarital counseling, as money matters often relate to partners' expectations of their married life. Being open and honest about finances helps partners remain on the same page regarding their current and future financial situation and allows trust to grow within the couple.

Conflict Resolution

As individuals engage in more communication and self-disclosure, intimacy develops. The more intimate a relationship, the more opportunities there are for disagreements; therefore, because intimacy and conflict are interconnected, premarital couples can develop a way to resolve their conflicts based on their level of intimacy. Couples can learn to benefit from their anger if they use it as a way to balance their separateness and togetherness. Ultimately, counselors guide couples in finding this balance and developing an interdependent relationship. Counselors help couples understand how too much separateness can result in a relationship with too little attention, while too much togetherness can result in feelings of suffocation and obligation.

Counselors also help couples develop effective conflict management skills that include the ability to fight fairly, resolve conflicts through a series of steps, and communicate about each partner's style of conflict resolution. Furthermore, counselors help couples examine their expectations for arguments within the relationship. A major tenet when discussing anger with couples is to remind them that anger should not be ignored or unresolved, since ignoring or burying anger often results in crises down the road.

When handling conflict, it is important for couples to abide by certain rules. These rules include avoiding ultimatums, working toward resolving the conflict rather than trying to "win" the argument, and staying away from what John Gottman refers to as the four horsemen of the apocalypse: criticism, contempt, defensiveness, and stonewalling. Although often easier said than done, couples engage in role-play arguments in their counseling session in order to practice effective conflict resolution skills that can be implemented during an actual conflict.

Child-Rearing

Parenthood is one of the most enjoyable, yet challenging, responsibilities for couples. Partners may neglect to discuss their opinions on having children, the effects of children on the marriage, and the financial burdens that accompany having children. Furthermore, couples often wait too long to discuss their personal beliefs on parenthood, including how they will discipline their children, leading to difficulties down the road. Within premarital counseling, counselors can broach these topics with couples in order for partners to communicate their expectations of children and their role within the couple's lives. Common issues to address with premarital couples regarding parenting include the choice to have children or to remain childless, the importance of agreeing on how child-rearing responsibilities will be shared, the need to focus equally on the children and the marriage, the benefit of agreeing on discipline, and ways to maintain intimacy within the marriage.

Relationship Education

Couple education programs are available to premarital couples and involve skill-building in a variety of areas as well as provide a place for couples to meet and learn from other couples engaged in similar situations. Research suggests that skill-based premarital education programs can increase relationship satisfaction and support the maintenance of effective intimate relationships among premarital couples. Similar to premarital counseling, education programs help couples to develop realistic beliefs about marriage relationships while also helping couples to identify healthy and unhealthy relationship patterns. Quality premarital education programs help couples increase their awareness of their relationships, build skills in communication and conflict management, and provide small-group discussions in which couples share their mutual struggles.

Finding a Premarital Counselor

The topics addressed in premarital counseling depend on the needs of the individuals. In addition to the topics previously mentioned, what brought the partners together and their views on and definitions of *marriage*, *aging parents*, *illness or disease*, *addiction*, and *spirituality* may also be explored. Because of the level of self-disclosure and because the topics addressed in couples counseling vary depending on the couple, it is important that couples find a counselor who fits for them and their situation. Individuals seeking premarital counseling should work to find a counselor who is trained and experienced in couples work, who is a member of professional organizations, and who makes both partners comfortable. Seeking referrals from family, friends, pastors, and/or primary care physicians may be helpful. Also, the couple should consider meeting more than one counselor to ensure they are making the best choice in counselors for them as a couple. Asking counselors about their education, training, experience, and theoretical orientation is acceptable and expected and will help the couple gain insight into who they will be working with.

Premarital couples counselors need to help individuals identify what makes their unique relationship work and use these strengths to help the couple explore their relationship more deeply. Couples should feel free to ask questions about their counseling as well as discuss any concerns they may have with their counselor. Ultimately, the relationship between the couple and the counselor will have a significant influence on the success of the counseling, so it is in the best interest of the couple to take the time to find a counselor whom they trust and with whom they feel safe.

Goals of Premarital Counseling

Counselors need to develop appropriate and effective goals with their clients. Initially, the counselor will have the couple develop what Mark Young refers to as an interactive definition of the problem; in other words, the couple will develop a new way of framing their problem that includes both partners' perspectives on the issue. Once an interactive definition of the problem is developed, the counselor will support the couple in converting these problems into positive behavioral goals reflecting how the couple would like the relationship to progress. In order for the premarital couple to feel positive about their relationship, the couple will need to state behavioral steps and feeling outcomes so that the couple and the counselor will know when they have met their goals. In other words, the couple will work with the counselor to appropriately express what they will do (behaviors) in order to feel a certain way (feelings). In addition, the counselor should consistently address these affective and behavioral goals to maintain client support for goals over time. Overall, the focus of the treatment is on getting the couple to work as a team to explore their thoughts, feelings, and behaviors in order to jointly work on their goals.

Entering a marriage as friends will increase the chances of a prosperous intimate relationship, but friendship and love are not enough to make a successful marriage. By engaging in premarital counseling, partners can learn and develop in numerous ways, including how to balance their separateness and togetherness; better communicate; effectively and safely manage conflicts; discuss sex, finances, and roles; and efficiently communicate their expectations to one another. All of these items contribute to reducing a couple's chances of divorce and improve their overall relationship. Overall, premarital counseling that focuses on couple strengths helps partners to build successful ways of relating to one another; become more aware of their relationship; develop effective and appropriate ways to solve future problems; and grow in the areas of love, intimacy, and cohesion.

Renee S. Sherrell

See also Active Parenting; Beliefs and Values; Boundaries; Communication Errors/Problems in Couples and Families; Communication in Couples and Families; Conflict Resolution; Conflict Styles

Further Readings

Britzman, M. J., & Sauerheber, J. D. (2014). Preparing couples for an enriched marriage: A model in individual psychology. *Family Journal*, 22(4), 428–436.

Carlson, R. G., Daire, A. P., Munyon, M. D., & Young, M. E. (2012). A comparison of cohabitating and non-cohabitating couples who participated in premarital counseling using the PREPARE model. *Family Journal*, 20(2), 123–130.

Casquarelli, E. J., & Fallon, K. M. (2011). Nurturing the relationships of all couples: Integrating lesbian, gay, and bisexual concerns into premarital education and counseling programs. *Journal of Humanistic Counseling*, 50(2), 149–160.

Gottman, J., & Silver, N. (1999). *The seven principles for making marriage work: A practical guide from the country's foremost relationship expert*. New York, NY: Random House.

Long, L. L., & Young, M. E. (2007). *Counseling and therapy for couples*. Belmont, CA: Brooks/Cole.

Markman, H. J., Rhoades, G. K., Stanley, S. M., Ragan, E. P., & Whitton, S. W. (2010). The premarital communication roots of marital distress and divorce: The first five years of marriage. *Journal of Family Psychology*, 24(3), 289–298.

Olson, D. H., DeFrain, J., & Skogrand, L. (2011). *Marriages and families: Intimacy, diversity, and strengths* (7th ed.). New York, NY: McGraw-Hill.

Tambling, R. B., & Glebova, T. (2013). Preferences of individuals in committed relationships about premarital counseling. *American Journal of Family Therapy*, 41(4), 330–340.

PREMATURE EJACULATION

Premature ejaculation (PE) is defined as occurring when the male ejaculates before he or his partner would like (prematurely) and causes distress. This may range from before penetration to a point just after penetration. It may leave the couple feeling unsatisfied. PE is a common sexual complaint and experienced by approximately one third of men at some point in life. If it happens infrequently, it may not be an issue for an individual or couple. PE can be primary (lifelong) or secondary (acquired). Factors influencing secondary PE include the newness of the sexual partner and the location and recent frequency of sexual activity. If recurrent, PE may become a source of individual anxiety and/or relationship tension. In this entry, causes of and treatment for PE are discussed.

Causes

PE may be caused by various factors: physical problems, learned behavior patterns, stress, and/or relational problems. A physical problem rarely causes PE; in these cases, it is usually associated with other physical symptoms, often pain. PE may be a symptom of a neurological condition, infection of the prostate gland, or urethritis (inflammation of the duct that carries urine and semen to the outside of the body). In addition, it may be related to abnormal hormone levels, abnormal levels of chemicals in the brain (neurotransmitters), thyroid problems, nerve damage, or abnormal reflexes. With the rising prevalence of substance abuse, an increasing number of cases of PE are being diagnosed in patients withdrawing from drugs, especially opioids.

Some factors relating to PE are more about behavior patterns and psychological issues. For example, as teenagers, some feel an urgency to ejaculate in order not to get caught masturbating. The male is "training" his body to ejaculate quickly. In addition, early on PE might also be about being overly excited and stimulated during early sexual experiences. When men first become sexually active, they are sometimes overstimulated and ejaculate faster than desired but with time and experience can lengthen time of maintaining an erection. The most common cause of PE seems to be psychologically based, such as performance anxiety or guilt about sexual activity.

Treatment

Preferably, therapy for PE should be conducted under the supervision of a health professional trained in sexual dysfunction. Treatment options include therapy and/or medications. Both partners may be encouraged to participate in therapeutic interventions. Treatment of PE requires patience, dedication, and commitment by both partners, and the therapist should convey this message to both. The first part of therapy often is for the couple to avoid intercourse for several weeks. This period of abstinence is helpful in relieving any troublesome performance anxiety on the part of the man that may interfere with therapy.

Behavioral techniques taught either individually, conjointly, or in groups are effective in the treatment of PE. One type of behavioral or relationship intervention is called "sensate focus" and involves the man's concentration on the process of sexual arousal and orgasm. The process involves focusing on physical pleasure and communication rather than intercourse or orgasm. The couple starts out with nongenital touch (massage) and avoids touching other erogenous zones. Eventually, the couple after several weeks moves toward touching the entire body. Eventually, the couple moves to penetration without intercourse or orgasm and when ready intercourse or orgasm. This process helps reduce anxiety, increases communication, slows down stimulation, and increases intimacy. In addition, it helps both partners become more aware of sensations and of the signals their bodies are sending. When the person with PE starts to recognize that he is getting close to ejaculation, then two techniques can be used to slow the process:

1. *The "stop and start" method.* This approach involves sexual stimulation until the man recognizes that he is about to ejaculate. At this time, the stimulation is discontinued for about thirty seconds and then resumed. This sequence of events is repeated until ejaculation is desired by both partners, with stimulus continuing until ejaculation occurs.

2. *The "squeeze" technique.* This approach involves sexual stimulation, usually by the sexual partner, until the man recognizes that he is about to ejaculate. At this time, stimulation ceases. The patient or his partner gently squeezes the end of the penis at the junction of the glans penis (tip of the penis) with the shaft. The squeezing is continued for several seconds. Sexual stimulation is withheld for about 30 seconds and then resumed. This sequence of events is repeated by the patient alone or with the assistance of his partner until ejaculation is desired. At this point, stimulation is continued until the man ejaculates.

In addition to behavioral or relational techniques, medications can be used. Certain prescription medications, especially antidepressants that produce delayed ejaculation as a side effect, may be useful as therapeutic adjuncts. Recently, the use of a class of drugs known as selective serotonin reuptake inhibitors (SSRIs) has shown promise in the treatment of PE. The SSRIs prolong the time it takes the man to ejaculate by as much as 30 minutes. The SSRIs most commonly used to treat PE are sertraline (Zoloft) and fluoxetine (Prozac), initially developed for use in treating depression and panic attacks and subsequently used with success in the management of PE.

In addition, there are other medications that may help. A physician may prescribe (or there are some over-the-counter options) anesthetic creams or sprays to reduce the sensitivity of the penis in order to delay ejaculation. Oral drugs, besides antidepressants, include some analgesics to treat pain and phosphodiesterase-5 (PDE5) inhibitors (medications used to treat erectile dysfunction). Although any of these medications may be helpful, they can have unwanted side effects and reduce sexual pleasure.

Failure to respond to treatment for PE and the complications that may result from it should encourage the patient to seek further help from a health provider trained and experienced in treating the problem. In most cases (some observers claim a 95% success rate), the patient can control ejaculation through education and practice of the techniques outlined. In chronic cases that do not respond to treatment, the PE may be related to a serious psychological or psychiatric condition, including depression or anxiety. Patients in this category may benefit from psychotherapy.

Rashida Fisher

See also Human Sexual Response; Male Hypoactive Sexual Desire Disorder; Men in Counseling; Sexual Dysfunction; Sexual History

Further Readings

Hatzimouratidis, K., Amar, E., Eardley, I., Giuliano, F., Hatzichristou, D., Montorsi, F., . . . Wespes, E. (2010). Guidelines on male sexual dysfunction: Erectile dysfunction and premature ejaculation. *European Urology, 57*(5), 804–814.

Patrick, D. L., Althof, S. E., Pryor, J. L., Rosen, R., Rowland, D. L., Ho, K. F., . . . Jamieson, C. (2005). Premature ejaculation: An observational study of men and their partners. *Journal of Sexual Medicine, 2*(3), 358–367.

Porst, H., Montorsi, F., Rosen, R. C., Gaynor, L., Grupe, S., & Alexander, J. (2007). The premature ejaculation prevalence and attitudes (PEPA) survey: Prevalence, comorbidities, and professional help-seeking. *European Urology, 51*(3), 816–824.

Symonds, T., Roblin, D., Hart, K., & Althof, S. (2003). How does premature ejaculation impact a man's life? *Journal of Sex & Marital Therapy, 29*(5), 361–370.

Waldinger, M. D. (2002). The neurobiological approach to premature ejaculation. *Journal of Urology, 168*(6), 2359–2367.

PRENUPTIAL AGREEMENTS

A *premarital contract*, also known as a prenuptial agreement (or prenup), is defined as an agreement that affirms, modifies, or waives marital rights or obligations to be adhered to during marriage, or upon dissolution of the marriage, should this occur. Most marital rights or privileges are defined to include the right to spousal support and equitable distribution at divorce. This entry offers insight into prenuptial agreements, including their advantages and disadvantages, and how counselors can support couples through prenuptial conflicts.

Components of Prenuptial Agreements

Prenuptial agreements have developed in response to the real possibility that many relationships will not endure over time despite best intentions and professed commitments. In reality, nearly half of all marriages in the United States end in divorce. Accordingly, the purpose of the prenuptial agreement is to determine and clarify financial rights before marriage and to protect individual assets.

There are key components that validate prenuptial agreements. First, the agreement must be in writing. To date, verbal prenuptial agreements are not accepted. Secondly, the prenuptial agreement must be voluntarily agreed upon and signed by both parties. Third, it must present full disclosure about the couple at the time it is executed. Fourth, the prenuptial agreement must refrain from being unconscionable, and both parties must acknowledge the agreement. The "sunset" clause (the agreement may expire after a certain time or number of years) may impact prenuptial agreements. This would require couples to renew their agreement. In the event the sunset clause is not implemented, couples may have the option to utilize the Uniform Premarital Agreement Act, which was drafted by the National Conference of Commissioners on Uniform State Laws in 1983 and subsequently adopted by 27 states.

Because marriage is seen not only as a romantic relationship but also as a practical arrangement between two partners, prenuptial agreements are gaining in popularity and are becoming more widely accepted in U.S. society.

Prenuptial Advantages and Disadvantages

Couples are increasingly choosing prenuptial agreements for a variety of reasons (i.e., prior individual wealth or inheritances needing to be preserved in case of a divorce). Adults are also delaying marriage; this results in more acquired resources being brought into the union that may need protection in case of a divorce. In addition, couples may have been exposed to divorce as children and experienced the collateral damage that can ensue. The stigma of prenuptial agreements continues to decrease as more couples adopt the practice.

A prenuptial agreement can protect a business owner so that the business is not included in a divorce settlement. In the event the couple decided that one of them would give up a lucrative career after marriage, a prenuptial agreement would ensure that individual of being compensated for his or her sacrifice if the marriage fails. If one individual had more financial debt than the other, a prenuptial agreement would protect the debt-free individual from assuming the other's financial obligations.

Prenuptial agreements reduce conflicts and possible lengthy court hearings and legal fees on division of assets and particulars. The average cost of a prenuptial agreement ranges from $2,500 to $7,000. This most likely would be considerably less costly than a divorce settlement. Another advantage of the agreement is the ability to protect the financial and mental stability of the children. Funds that have been allocated for the children can be protected with a prenuptial agreement. Primary custody of the children can be addressed within the prenuptial agreement in order to protect the children from having to choose between the parents.

However, creating a prenuptial agreement implies that the marriage may not last, and that marriage is not sacred or something to cherish. Beginning a marriage under a contractual agreement can engender a lack of trust within the relationship. Establishing a prenuptial agreement can generate unnecessary barriers and add complication. In addition, since people cannot predict every event of life or marriage, prenuptial agreements must be periodically reviewed and updated similar to wills, life insurance policies, and other binding contracts.

Prenuptial agreements are subject to the opinion of the judicial system. The justice system decides whether the prenuptial agreement meets public policy and other legal requirements in order to be deemed valid and reasonable. Even if all requirements are met, it is up to a judge to decide whether to declare the agreement legal and binding.

Counselor Involvement

A couples and family counselor will best serve his or her client regarding the subject of prenuptial agreements by considering each particular couple individually as clients. The counselor can provide uniformity, while still observing individual uniqueness, if he or she asks every couple that seeks premarital counseling if they have considered a prenuptial agreement. If the couple says yes, the counselor will listen to their concerns but only explore the prenuptial agreement as an option if and when the couple asks for more details.

Counselors who have clients who are interested in prenuptial agreements can discuss benefits and limitations of the agreement with their clients. Counselors are advised to review current codes of ethics and research how they can further assist their client within their scope. Although prenuptial agreements are not specifically stated within counselors' codes of ethics, they do provide guidelines for counselors by which to abide. Counselors are ethically bound to fully respect and acknowledge their clients' rights and expectations. Counselors have the professional responsibility to work within their trained level of competency and seek consultation as needed. In other words, counselors are to leave legal matters regarding the prenuptial agreement to the couple's attorney.

The prenuptial agreement serves as a plan of action if one or both parties decide to file for divorce. The potential spouses must remember that these are legally binding contracts and must adhere to laws and regulations of the state in which they wed. If the couple in question fully intends to approach their new relationship clearly and soberly, then consideration regarding the availability of a prenuptial agreement should be acknowledged by their premarital counselor.

Counselor Implications for Helping Couples Through Prenuptial Conflicts

In order to help a couple through conflicts that may arise as they negotiate their prenups, a counselor must encourage the couple to define the problem and then determine if it is an issue that can change. If managed properly, a conflict can bring a couple closer together as well as encourage cooperation. Ground rules must be laid during negotiations that a time-out will be called if arguments escalate during the session. This should be framed for the couple as a tool to set the tone for the session. Once the couple can agree on the defined problem and that change is necessary for their survival as a couple, then conflict negotiations and further communication interventions can ensue. Counselors should note that a further investigation of background information on the problem development may be needed in a session to explore the manifestation of the underlying issues and whether they are rooted elsewhere.

Next, the couple should interact with each other surrounding the problem. For example, using I-statements and feeling words for each partner to express themselves will allow for a better understanding of their individual concerns. The counselor must also encourage listening between the partners. For example, the counselor can ask one partner to propose a solution while the other listens and vice versa. Then the other partner can restate the solution as an active listening strategy and support technique. Several solutions can be discussed until the couple chooses one that they both agree with. The counselor can then help the couple put their plan into action and monitor their progress.

Alfreda Renae Carmichael, LeTea Perry, Demitri Kornegay, and Tricialand Hilliard

See also Family Resource Management; Marriage Education; Premarital Counseling

Further Readings

Atwood, B. A. (2012). Marital contracts and the meaning of marriage. *Arizona Law Review, 54*(1), 11–42.

Kennedy, S. (2014). Ignorance is not bliss: Why states should adopt California's independent counsel requirement for the enforceability of prenuptial agreements. *Family Court Review: An Interdisciplinary Journal, 52*(4), 709–724. doi:10.1111/fcre.12123

Ravdin, L. (2014). Premarital agreements and the migratory same-sex couple. *Family Law Quarterly, 48*(3), 397–434.

Shafer, K., Jensen, T., & Larson, J. (2014). Relationship effort, satisfaction, and stability: Differences across union type. *Journal of Marital and Family Therapy, 40*(2), 212–232.

Stevenson, B., & Wolfers, J. (2007). Marriage and divorce: Changes and their driving forces. *Journal of Economic Perspectives, 21*(2), 27–52.

Tambling, R., & Glebova, T. (2013). Preferences of individuals in committed relationships about premarital counseling. *American Journal of Family Therapy, 41*(4), 330–340. doi:10.1080/01926187.2012.701593

PREPARE/ENRICH

PREPARE/ENRICH is a customized relationship inventory and skill-building program for premarital and married couples. It is one of the most widely used programs for premarital and marital counseling and education. More than 100,000 professionals, including marriage and family therapists (MFTs), social workers, clergy, psychologists, and other counseling professionals, have been trained in and use the PREPARE/ENRICH assessment and program. PREPARE/ENRICH is an efficient, reliable, and valid assessment of a wide range of interpersonal, personality, couple, and family characteristics. More than 4 million couples have participated in the program, which includes 3.5 million couples from the United States and half a million couples from 10 other countries.

PREPARE/ENRICH contains both an assessment and a semistructured feedback process for counseling and/or education. The online couple assessment is customized to each couple on the basis of questions they answer related to their marital status, children, and other background information. As part of this feedback process, couples increase their self- and partner awareness while they are taught relationship skills such as communication and conflict management. Those who utilize PREPARE/ENRICH in their therapy or couple enrichment have the flexibility of using the assessment only or the assessment plus any or all of the 20 couple exercises available as part of the program. This program is built on extensive research and is focused on improving couples' relationships.

This entry first discusses research on the effectiveness of the assessment and program; explains its theoretical foundations, assumptions, and components; and describes the types of married couples and the couple and family map derived from the PREPARE/ENRICH assessment. It then discusses how the assessment and program can be of value to counselors and couples and how counselors are trained to use the program.

Effectiveness of PREPARE/ENRICH

PREPARE/ENRICH has high reliability, high validity, and a large national norm based on more than 100,000 couples from various backgrounds. Numerous studies have demonstrated the rigor of the assessments and its relevance to couples from a variety of ethnic groups. PREPARE/ENRICH has been found to be psychometrically sound and has been rated as one of the best instruments for premarital and marital counseling and education.

Whether used with an individual couple or in a group setting, studies have found that the PREPARE/ENRICH program helps premarital couples get their relationship off to a good start and helps married couples increase their relationship skills and satisfaction. A study by Luke Knutson and David Olson compared three levels of premarital programming; one group took the PREPARE/ENRICH assessment and received four feedback sessions (PREPARE/ENRICH feedback), the second group took only the assessment (PREPARE/ENRICH only), and the third group acted as a control group (they received PREPARE/ENRICH and feedback after the study was complete). The PREPARE/ENRICH feedback group had the most positive change with improvement on 8 of the 10 major areas, which include communication, conflict resolution, and concerns about relationships with family and friends. The PREPARE/ENRICH only group improved in 3 of the 10 major areas, and the control group made no significant change. The PREPARE/ENRICH feedback group experienced a 52% increase in the number of "vitalized" (most happy) couples and an 83% decrease in the number of "conflicted" (least happy) couples.

A study by Ted Futris, Allen Barton, Tiffiany Aholou, and Desiree Seponski compared the PREPARE/ENRICH program when delivered in an individual format (one couple and one facilitator) and a group format and found that both approaches were equally effective. It was found that couples who completed PREPARE/ENRICH in both delivery formats had gains in relationship knowledge and confidence in their relationships, had more positive conflict management behaviors, and were more satisfied with their relationship.

Theoretical Foundations, Assumptions, and Components of PREPARE/ENRICH

PREPARE/ENRICH is a comprehensive assessment that is based on a systemic model that has several important components, as shown in Figure 1. First are the 10 core scales that include the following: communication, conflict resolution, partner style and habits, financial management, sexuality, leisure activities, roles, and spiritual beliefs. Second is the SCOPE personality assessment of each person, with SCOPE standing for five scales: social, change, organized, pleasing, and emotionally steady. Third are the relationship dynamics of each person related to assertiveness, self-confidence, avoidance, and partner dominance. Fourth is the couple and family map that assesses cohesion or closeness and flexibility in the couple's relationship and in their family of origin. Lastly, the cultural context is taken into account based on the norms and expectations of different cultural groups.

One of the advantages of the PREPARE/ENRICH program is that it is compatible with many other theoretical models and therapeutic approaches. Therapists can integrate techniques and ideas from their preferred theory or integrated theory and use their preferred style of interaction. A cognitive-behavioral therapist may use a couple's results to focus on challenging thoughts and restricting beliefs while exploring the relationship between these thoughts and the emotional experiences of each person. A narrative therapist may use PREPARE/ENRICH as a foundation for discussion while still creating space for new ways of thinking about growth areas by using techniques such as externalizing and exploring unique outcomes.

The feedback component of PREPARE/ENRICH includes interventions based on the theoretical schools of psychoeducation, solution-focused, and structural approaches. It uses couple exercises to help teach the couple relationship skills that each couple needs based on the assessment results for the couple. The PREPARE/ENRICH program

Figure 1 Systemic Components of PREPARE/ENRICH

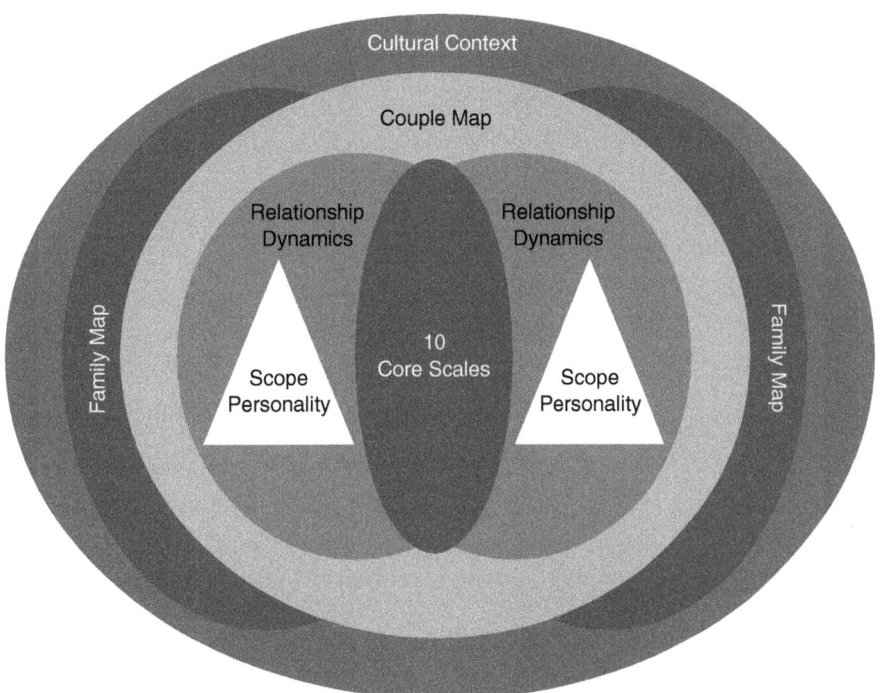

Source: PREPARE/ENRICH Training Manual (2014). Roseville, MN: PREPARE/ENRICH, Inc. (p. 2).

contains more than 20 exercises that align with the scales contained in the assessment.

The main goals of the PREPARE/ENRICH program align with couple exercises:

- Identifying and exploring relationship strength and growth areas
- Strengthening communication skills by teaching assertiveness and active listening
- Resolving conflict using a 10-step model
- Understanding their couple and family relationship on the dimensions of closeness and flexibility
- Identifying and resolving major stressors
- Understanding personality similarities and differences

There are several assumptions behind how the assessment and program were developed and how it is delivered. First, it is assumed that if a couple is taught relevant relationship skills, they will be able to deal more effectively with their current and any future problems. Second, it is assumed that the PREPARE/ENRICH couple assessment will significantly increase the effectiveness of the intervention and the couple relationship. This assumption was verified in several studies, including one completed using PREPARE/ENRICH. Third, it is assumed that the impact of the assessment and exercises are systemic so that making a positive change in any component will have an impact on the entire system. This was, in fact, found in a study by Knutson and Olson that used six couple exercises and found improvement in 10 major areas. A similar finding was reported in a study by W. Kim Halford and colleagues using the RELATE couple inventory, where skill-based training in addition to assessment and feedback resulted in the best relationship satisfaction and skill outcome. Lastly, it is assumed that the program empowers couples to take greater control over their own relationship and enables them to apply these principles to help their relationship grow.

Types of Married Couples

Five distinct types (patterns) of married relationships and four types of premarital couples were discovered when cluster analysis was used with the 10 core categories in PREPARE/ENRICH. The five basic types of married couples range from very high in marital satisfaction to very low: (1) vitalized, (2) harmonious, (3) conventional, (4) conflicted, and (5) devitalized (this last type is not a premarital type). About 15% to 20% of couples fall into each of these types that serve to describe and explain the complexity and differences between marriages. Other findings can also be linked to these types, further helping understand differences between marriages. For instance, research shows that with the happiest type—vitalized—there is very little spouse abuse, but abuse tends to be very high in the conflicted and devitalized types. (See Figure 2.)

The vitalized couples are the happiest couples, and they have the highest positive couple agreement (PCA) scores across most of the 10 core areas of PREPARE/ENRICH. These couples have the lowest divorce rate and have strengths in most areas of their relationship. Harmonious couples are also happy but at lower levels of PCA across the 10 core areas than vitalized couples. Conventional couples are more traditional and have more strengths in traditional roles and spiritual beliefs and more growth areas in communication and conflict resolution. Conflicted couples have fewer couple strengths especially in communication, conflict resolution, and partner habits and only strengths in role and spiritual beliefs. Devitalized couples have few strengths (very low PCA scores) across all 10 core areas, and both spouses tend to be very unhappy and tend to get divorced. Conflicted and devitalized couples are the ones that most typically seek marital therapy.

Couple and Family Map

PREPARE/ENRICH measures both family of origin and the couple system using the couple and family maps. These are derived from the Circumplex Model of Marital and Family Systems, originally developed by Olson, Douglas Sprenkle, and Candyce Russell. The couple and family maps use less clinical language so that they can be easily understood by the couple. The maps share the same theoretical ideas and scales as the circumplex model.

Figure 2 Five Types of Married Couples

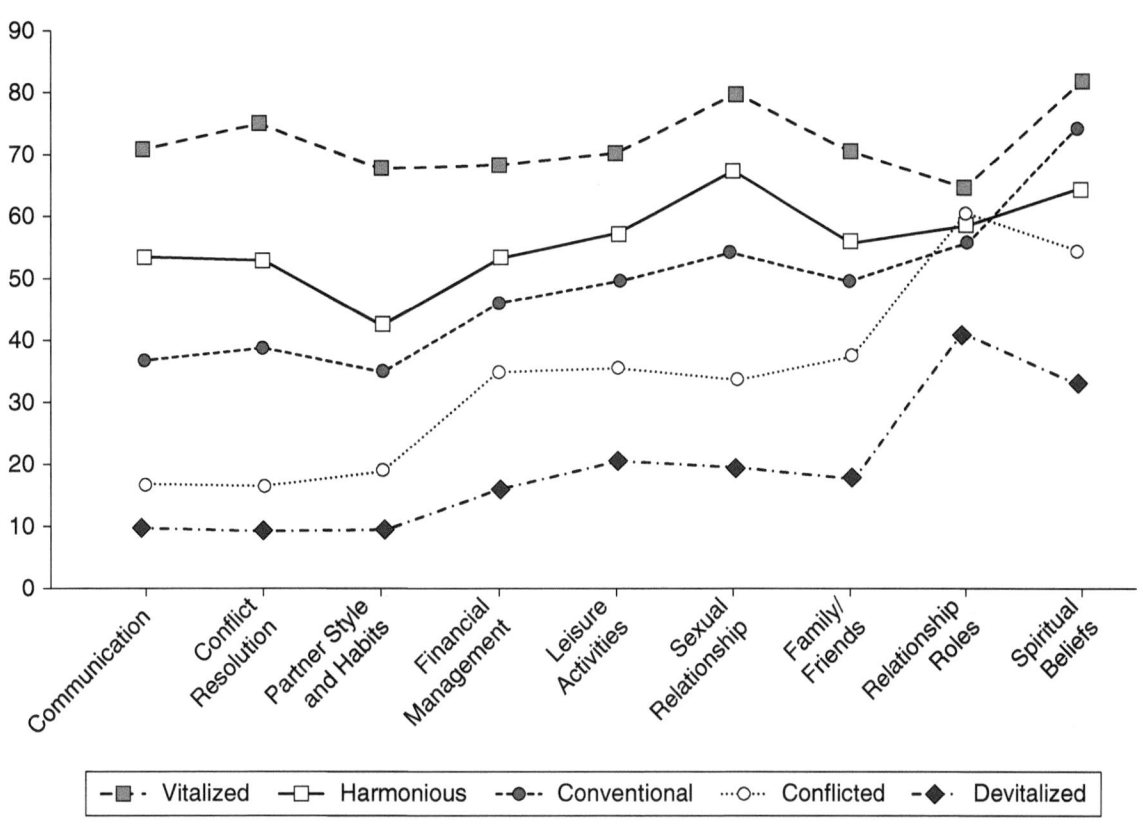

Source: PREPARE/ENRICH Training Manual (2014). Roseville, MN: PREPARE/ENRICH, Inc. (p. 11).

The maps are based on the two key dimensions of closeness and flexibility. Closeness is defined as the emotional bonding that couple and family members have toward one another and how they balance separateness versus togetherness. The indicators of closeness are the I-versus-we balance, the emotional connection, and loyalty and dependence versus independence. The couple and family maps have five levels of closeness ranging from "disconnected" to "overly connected," as shown in Figure 3. It is hypothesized that the three central or balanced levels of closeness are most functional for marriages and families.

Flexibility is the amount of change in leadership, role relationships, and relationship rules, and it focuses on how couples and families balance stability versus change. The indicators of flexibility are the amount of change, leadership, role sharing, and discipline of children. The couple and family maps have five levels of flexibility ranging from "inflexible" to "overly flexible." As with closeness, it is hypothesized that the three central or balanced levels of flexibility are more conducive to healthy couple and family functioning.

Combining the five levels of closeness and the five levels of flexibility creates 25 types of relationships. There are nine balanced types, 12 midrange types, and four unbalanced types. Theoretically, the main hypothesis is that the couples and families that are balanced on closeness and flexibility (nine central cells in the map) are most healthy and happy compared with those that fall into the unbalanced types (four corner cells). In taking the online assessment, couples respond to statements about both their families of origin and their couple relationship. These responses are plotted on the couple and family map. In the couple exercise for the couple and family map, each person is asked to reflect on what they would like to bring from their respective families of origin into their couple relationship and what they would like to intentionally leave behind.

Figure 3 Couple and Family Map

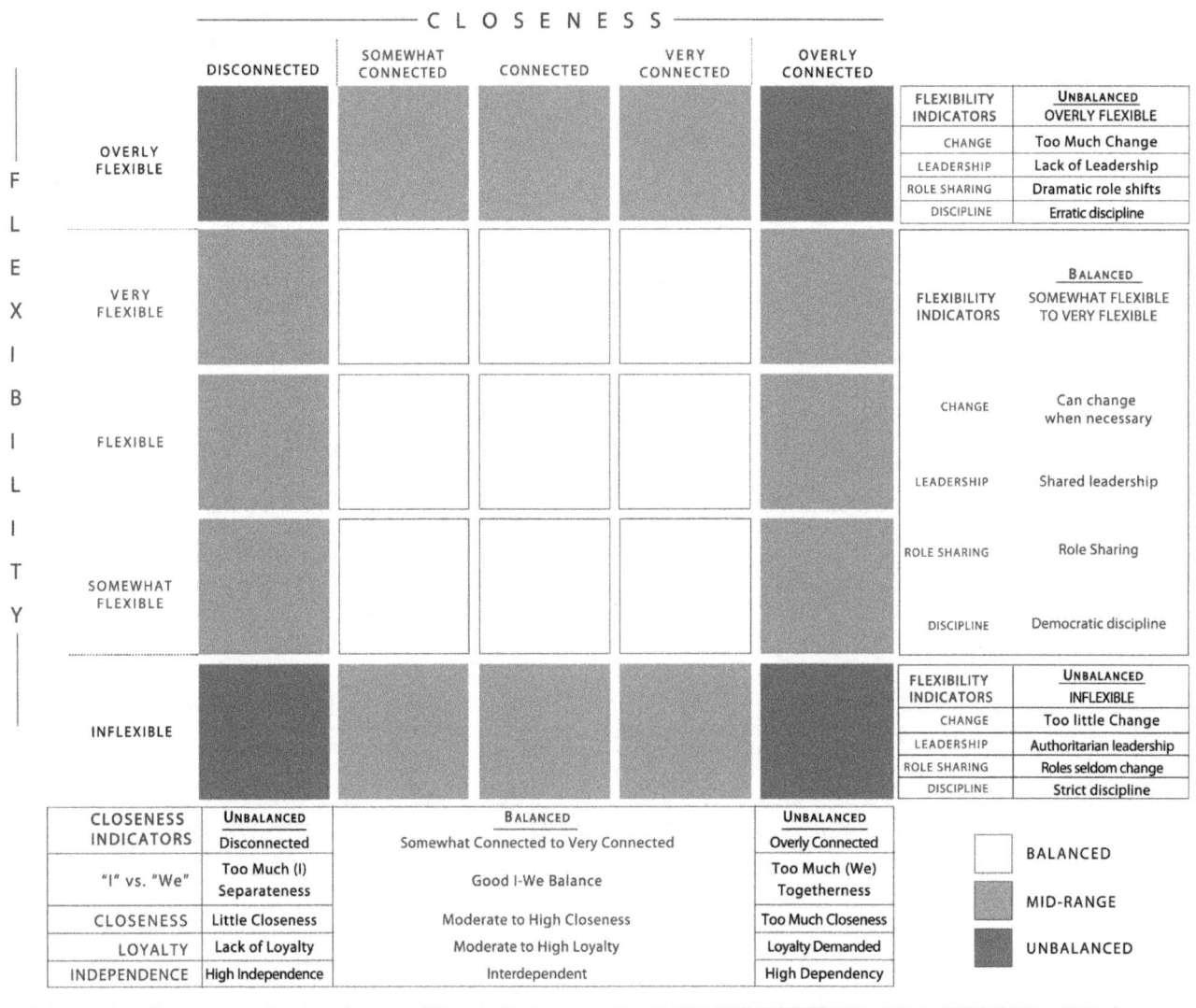

Source: PREPARE/ENRICH Training Manual (2014). Roseville, MN: PREPARE/ENRICH, Inc. (p. 28).

Value of PREPARE/ENRICH

Value for Counselors or Facilitators

Counselors can use PREPARE/ENRICH in many formats (individual, group, mentor), and specialized versions are available that deal with issues such as parenting and adoption. The program can help counselors and facilitators work with couples by doing the following:

- Providing comprehensive and objective data about the couple's relationship
- Helping identify strengths and growth areas
- Helping set relationship goals
- Teaching practical relationship skills such as communication and conflict resolution
- Allowing for additional resources and counseling skills to be integrated into the feedback process
- Empowering couples to work on their relationship

Value for Couples

Couples can benefit from taking PREPARE/ENRICH in many ways. The process of responding to the items creates curiosity about how their partner responded. In addition, the results can do the following:

- Stimulate dialogue between the partners about important relationship topics
- Increase self- and partner awareness
- Help couples apply concepts and skills most relevant to their unique relationship
- Increase couples' relationship skills and satisfaction

Becoming Trained to Use PREPARE/ENRICH

In order to be able to use PREPARE/ENRICH with couples, a person needs to attend a one-day workshop conducted by a PREPARE/ENRICH seminar director or take an online self-training program. Persons with a master's or doctoral degree in a field of professional counseling may choose to complete an online self-training option instead of a workshop. Counselors may choose to receive seven continuing education credits upon receiving a minimum score of 70% on a posttest.

Since the assessment and skill-building exercises provide a useful foundation for working with couples, many counseling training programs have integrated training on PREPARE/ENRICH into their couple programs. The semistructured approach provides clinicians with a tool to bring relevant concepts and issues to the couples with whom they work and exercises that help couples further process these concepts and issues. The objective summary of the couple that is provided by the facilitator's report is useful for diagnosis and for determining treatment planning and goal-setting. When a counselor facilitating the process is receiving clinical supervision during a training period, having a PREPARE/ENRICH facilitator's report gives the supervisor and the supervisee common ground to discuss clinical cases with less subjectivity than in a situation with only a supervisee-generated report.

David H. Olson and Amy K. Olson

See also Circumplex Model; Marital Group Therapy; Marriage Education; Premarital Counseling

Further Readings

Allen, W. D., & Olson, D. H. (2001). Five types of African-American marriages. *Journal of Marital and Family Therapy, 27*(3), 301–314.

Asai, S. G., & Olson, D. H. (2003). *Spouse abuse and marital system based on ENRICH*. Retrieved from https://www.prepare-enrich.com/pe/pdf/research/abuse.pdf

Futris, T. G., Baron, A. W., Aholou, T. M., & Seponski, D. M. (2011). The impact of PREPARE on engaged couples: Variations by delivery format. *Journal of Couple and Relationship Therapy, 10*(1), 69–86.

Halford, W. K., Wilson, K., Watson, B., Verner, T., Larson, J., Busby, D., & Holman, T. (2010). Couple relationship education at home: Does skill training enhance relationship assessment and feedback? *Journal of Family Psychology, 24*, 188–196.

Knutson, L., & Olson, D. H. (2003). Effectiveness of PREPARE program with premarital couples in a community setting. *Marriage & Family: A Christian Journal, 6*(4), 529–546.

McClurkan, J. S. (2003). *The effect of couple-to-couple mentoring on week marriage relationships* (Unpublished doctoral dissertation). Southern Baptist Theological Seminary, Louisville, KY.

Olson, D. H. (2014). *PREPARE/ENRICH facilitator's manual*. Roseville, MN: PREPARE/ENRICH, Inc.

PREPARE/ENRICH: http://www.prepare-enrich.com

PRESENTING PROBLEMS

Presenting problems can be defined as a client's chief psychological complaint or voiced concerns. When inquiring about a client's presenting problem, the counselor often begins by asking these questions: What brings you here? What is the reason for your visit? A client's presenting problem may be an ongoing pattern of symptomology consistent with a particular condition, such as depression, or the explanation of a recent event or situation that has had a psychological impact on the client, such as a crisis (e.g., attempted suicide). Presenting problems in couple and family therapy may not be as easy to understand because people may perceive different concerns as most problematic. Nonetheless, as long as people do not have mutually exclusive goals based on presenting problems, then different presenting problems are not necessarily an issue. The intention of this entry is to give an overview of the nature and purpose of gathering, understanding, and clarifying presenting problems of clients seeking counseling. The role of presenting problems in the assessment process, defining client expectations, and identifying typical presenting problems for couples and families are also discussed.

Presenting Problems in the Assessment Process

The presenting problem is generally the first source of information that is collected in the diagnostic assessment process and is used as a starting point to form an initial clinical diagnosis and to guide the treatment planning process including defining short- and long-term goals for counseling or making referrals for services (e.g., acute inpatient hospitalization, outpatient counseling, intensive or residential programming, psychiatric assessment). The type of information to be collected when inquiring about the presenting problem should always comprise the subjective, voiced concerns of the client or clients. This information should be in the client's own words, including why he or she has come or been brought in for counseling. Clients' words should be documented verbatim (using quotations as necessary) and should be recorded from each client's point of view, regardless of how bizarre or irrelevant what he or she is saying may seem. This is true for clients of all ages in all settings.

While assessing children often requires adult support and the gathering of information from other sources (such as the parents, school personnel, family physicians), researchers and clinicians have agreed that it is beneficial to hear a child's own account of his or her presenting problem as children can be competent in providing reliable and valid clinical information. Even young children can recognize and report their experiences and emotions. The incorporation of clinical interventions (such as drawing) has been found to be beneficial in adding to the amount of information received by children when asking about their presenting problems, as children may provide less information verbally than adults.

The client's point of view and perceptions surrounding the presenting issue should also be reported as part of his or her presenting problem. This may include personal feelings (e.g., feeling frustration over being anxious for a long period of time), thoughts (e.g., explanations or hypothesis as to why the client is feeling anxious), behaviors (e.g., having attempted to implement coping skills to manage anxiety), and/or overall functioning in the major areas of life as a result of the presenting issue (e.g., anxiety has been preventing the client from wanting to engage in social situations). How these aspects have evolved over time can also be investigated when gathering information on the client's presenting problem (e.g., anxiety has worsened over the past 2 weeks to the extent that the client is now experiencing panic attacks 2 to 3 times per day). Again, this information should also be documented verbatim as reported by the client or other sources who are present and/or familiar with the client (including family members, physicians, or even former medical or hospital records, which can be used as sources of information).

Many times, clients seek help as the direct result of a specific incident such as a crisis situation. In such a case, the counselor needs to explore all details surrounding the incident, including the sequential events from beginning to end (e.g., "Tell me what you did immediately following the ingestion of pills"). During the exploration of the presenting event, the counselor skillfully and persistently uses the skill of encouragement to guide the client in creating a "videotape" (an accurate picture) of what happened in the incident.

While the presenting problem is the primary and central piece of the diagnostic assessment process, information on current and past psychiatric problems; current and past medical conditions; current and past functioning; familial and social aspects of the client's life, such as his or her ability to maintain significant relationships and any family conflicts; and the client's current mental state all are also gathered and used in the assessment process in order to form a more inclusive and comprehensive clinical portrayal. Thus, while the client's chief complaint is used to develop an initial clinical diagnosis (using the *Diagnostic and Statistical Manual of Mental Disorders* [DSM] of the American Psychiatric Association [APA]), it is supported through such additional historical information. The presenting problem remains the primary source of information for establishing a diagnosis and guiding the entire treatment process.

Typical Presenting Problems for Couples and Families

In counseling, a client's presenting problems should never be assumed or generalized, which may be difficult especially when the counselor has worked with clients in the past who may have presented with similar concerns. However, there often are common presenting problems as seen by counselors, given the setting. In working with couples and partners or spouses, some of the most common presenting problems include interpersonal communication problems; issues of infidelity or marital dissatisfaction; experiences of infertility, miscarriage, or child-rearing; romantic or sexual concerns; or adult attachment issues. Counselors also work with couples as a measure to prevent future problems, as in premarital counseling or enrichment counseling. Problems that families may present with frequently include concerns such as interpersonal communication, conflict resolution, collective decision-making, agreement of parenting styles, and/or adjustment to significant changes in family dynamics (e.g., the death of a loved one). For parents specifically, agreeing upon parenting styles and/or managing the emotional, social, cognitive, or behavioral needs of children are also common themes found in presenting problems.

Client Expectations of the Assessment Process

Clients often arrive to counseling with a predetermined "fantasized" relationship with the professional in which they look to the counselor to "fix" their current problems. While there is no "magic wand" (improvement is the result of ongoing treatment), there are some actions that counselors can take in order to ease the process of coming to an agreement with the client regarding his or her expectations.

First, the counselor should consider how the client was referred. The individual or organization that makes the referral, whether it is a family member, a school, or a social agency, can influence the family's expectations and attitude toward the diagnostic assessment. Secondly, the counselor should attempt to develop rapport and explain the purpose of diagnostic assessment before directly inquiring about the client's presenting problem. When assessing children, the counselor should also keep in mind the family constellation surrounding the child. For example, in cases in which child protective services may be involved, children may be "coached" by a parent in order to meet an ulterior, personal motive (such as gaining legal custody of the child). In this example, the information verbalized by the child may not be considered "valid" or depict an accurate portrayal of the child's actual presenting concerns, yet as mentioned earlier, it should still be documented. The counselor should also maintain a nonthreatening atmosphere in the diagnostic assessment process in which each member of the family feels able to speak freely without feeling as though the counselor is "taking sides." Once the diagnostic assessment is complete, the counselor should ask the client if there are any other significant concerns or anything else that he or she would like to add. Finally, the counselor can thank the client and others present for their participation and contribution in the diagnostic assessment process.

Procedures in Assessment of the Presenting Problem

The following are procedures the counselor may use in the initial assessment of the presenting problem and examples of what the counselor might say to or ask the client in each.

Exploring and focusing (Tell me more about that . . .).

Encouraging (Was it something like . . . ?).

Making observations (You sound tense.).

Creating a timeline (What led up to this, happened after that?).

Making openings (What are you thinking/feeling?).

Accepting (Yes; Uh-huh.).

Using silence in order to give the client a chance to reflect on what he or she just said or are about to say.

Summarizing (Do I have this correct? You mentioned earlier that . . .).

Clarifying (When you say that you are in a "rage," help me understand what you mean.).

Danielle L. Geigle

See also Adult Attachment Assessments; Assessment, Biopsychosocial; Assessment, Suicide; Clinical Practice; Common Factors; DSM and V-Codes; Life Events; Therapeutic Assessment; Treatment Planning With Couples and Families

Further Readings

Billow, R. M., & Mendelsohn, R. (1990). The interviewer's "presenting problems" in the initial interview. *Bulletin of the Menninger Clinic, 54*, 391–397.

Sadock, B. J., & Sadock, V. A. (2003). Clinical examination of the psychiatric patient. In R. Cancro (Ed.), *Synopsis of psychiatry* (pp. 229–274). Philadelphia, PA: Lippincott Williams & Wilkins.

Shea, S. C. (1998). The chronological assessment of suicide events: A practical interviewing strategy for the elicitation of suicidal ideation. *Journal of Clinical Psychiatry, 59*, 58–72.

Woolford, J., Patterson, T., Macleod, E., Hobbs, L., & Hayne, H. (2015). Drawing helps children to talk about their presenting problems during a mental health assessment. *Clinical Child Psychology, 20*, 68–83.

PREVENTION RESEARCH

The term *prevention research* refers to research that directly applies to (a) identifying and assessing risk and (b) developing interventions for preventing or minimizing high-risk or harmful behaviors, disorders, or injuries. That is, prevention research aims to identify a problem, obtain epidemiological data about the problem, and identify risk and protective factors that are associated with the problem. It can then move on to develop and evaluate interventions that help prevent the problem and implement the interventions that work. Prevention research often involves public health, which promotes health and wellness for individuals, families, communities, and populations.

Sometimes called *distress prevention*, this type of work and research is becoming more important as an overall part of promoting client, couple, and family wellness. In the past, intervention, rather than prevention, was seen as the driving force in marital, couple, and family counseling. However, prevention is now seen as an important part of supporting couples and families. According to the International Association of Marriage and Family Counselors (IAMFC) Ethical Code of 2011, marriage and family counselors should both promote primary prevention and engage in research. This entry defines *prevention research*, contextualizes it globally, describes several ways to categorize prevention, and discusses areas that have been a focus of prevention research for couples and families.

Areas Prevention Research Covers

Globally, the World Health Organization (WHO) is involved with prevention research that includes different types of diseases, sexually transmitted infections, obesity, various early childhood developmental issues, mental disorders, suicide, falls, and violence. Their research on prevention of HIV transmission, child maltreatment, and violence against women is of particular interest to family practitioners. The U.S. Department of Health and Human Services (HHS) National Institutes of Health (NIH) has expanded the definition of prevention research to include research on developing and evaluating health promotion as well as public health programming. Since 1984, the U.S. Centers for Disease Control and Prevention (CDC) has sponsored

Prevention Research Centers for community-based public health/prevention research projects across the country.

Categorizing Prevention

Prevention efforts in public health can target entire populations, high-risk groups, or individuals displaying early signs of a presenting problem. When prevention focuses on an entire population, this is referred to as universal prevention. When prevention focuses on groups within a population that are at high risk, this is referred to as selective prevention. And when prevention focuses on individuals showing early signs of a problem, this is referred to as indicated prevention. The Institute of Medicine (IOM; since 2015 a division of the National Academies of Sciences, Engineering, and Medicine) adopted this universal, selective, and indicated prevention framework as part of its continuum of care model in 1994.

The IOM framework aimed to replace earlier categories of primary, secondary, and tertiary prevention, which are sometimes still used in the professional literature. Primary prevention focuses on preventing the occurrence of a disease or condition. Secondary prevention focuses on slowing or stopping disease progress or on limiting long-term disability. Tertiary prevention focuses on managing chronic, long-term conditions. These categories are included in the prevention research matrix proposed by Michael Waldo and Jonathan Schwartz and endorsed and adapted by Sally Hage, Katherine Raczynski, and others. This matrix model includes both the levels and functions of prevention research.

The Prevention Research Matrix

A matrix is an organized structure of rows and columns, and as its name implies, the prevention research matrix consists of row and column

Table I   Prevention Research Matrix

	Function		
Context (e.g., Gender, Race, Ethnicity, SES, Sexual Orientation)	*Preintervention (Epidemiology, Understanding Relationships Between Variables and Causes)*	*Preventive Intervention (Primary-Universal, Secondary-Selective/ Indicated, Tertiary-Indicated)*	*Service Delivery Systems (Dissemination, Implementation, Effectiveness, Health Economics)*
Biological development: risk and protective factors (e.g., genetics, physiology, nutrition, exercise, psychopharm)			
Psychological development: risk and protective factors (e.g., personality, locus of control, attitude, motivation)			
Sociocultural development: risk and protective factors (e.g., family, affiliations, school, work, community)			

Sources: Raczynski, Waldo, Schwartz, and Horne (2013, Table 3.2, Prevention Research Matrix); adapted from Hage, Romano, Conyne, Kenny, Matthews, Schwartz, and Waldo (2007, Table 2, Prevention Research Matrix, p. 521).

headings, as shown in Table 1. Along the left side of the matrix are row headings showing three kinds of development: (1) biological development, (2) psychological development, and (3) sociocultural development as well as the risk and protective factors associated with each. Across the top of the matrix, the three columns are titled preintervention, preventive intervention, and service delivery systems. In the upper left-hand corner of the matrix (where the rows and columns intersect) is context.

Practitioners and researchers can make use of this prevention research grid to categorize already-available studies and identify future areas for research. This latter application is particularly important, as prevention research in the area of marital, couples, and family counseling is still developing. The matrix can guide prevention research, but a particular piece of research does not need to address all of the contexts and functions in the matrix.

Prevention Research on Premarital Intervention

Premarital and relationship enhancement programs have been identified as prevention strategies for reducing potential marital distress and promoting quality relationships. Religious organizations are important contexts for prevention research in this area, as most marriages take place under religious auspices. Researchers Blaine Fowers, Kelly Montel, and David Olson have suggested using marriage and family therapy proactively as both primary prevention and secondary and tertiary prevention intervention, rather than considering it purely remedial. While marriage and family therapy can be sought after marital distress occurs, it can also be used as a premarital intervention with individuals or couples who have previously experienced divorce and view themselves as potentially at risk should they remarry. At-risk premarital couples can also be identified (e.g., through premarital inventories) so that prevention programming tailored to their needs can be offered. Finally, marriage and family therapists (MFTs) can offer primary prevention in the form of skill-building programs for couples to enrich their relationships.

Premarital and relationship enhancement programs used in the United States include the Minnesota Couples Communication Program (MCCP or CCP), Relationship Enhancement (RE), and Prevention and Relationship Enhancement Program (PREP; formerly the Premarital Relationship Enhancement Program). These educational programs focus on couples' communication and problem-solving skills. In the United States, PREP is nationally recognized as an evidence-based program on the HHS Substance Abuse and Mental Health Services Administration (SAMHSA) National Registry of Evidence-based Programs and Practices (NREPP).

Prevention Research on Distress, Divorce, and Intimate Partner Violence

More than 30 years of prevention research has contributed to PREP development, implementation, and dissemination. This educational program includes the following components: communication skill training, problem-solving training, clarification of marital expectations, and sensual or sexual education and relationship enhancement. Couples are assigned homework to complete between sessions. A major focus of the program is developing communication skills that can be used for safe and respectful problem-solving and conflict management. Research on PREP has demonstrated positive outcomes with premarital couples in the United States and other developed countries, and the program can be used with couples at all stages in their relationships. A program derived from PREP, called ePREP, is a computer-based approach that has demonstrated positive outcomes in primary prevention with married couples.

Prevention research on intimate partner violence has explored prevention programs for adults and adolescents; it appears that the more effective programs for adolescents include both an individual curriculum and community-based components. For married couples, programs that aim to prevent intimate partner violence have been developed that incorporate PREP. PREP and Stop Anger and Violence Escalation (SAVE), the violence prevention program developed for military couples, have been combined for use with couples at risk for violence.

Prevention Research Focused on Children/Youth

Prevention research on strengthening families with children is ongoing, and NREPP lists relevant programs that are considered to be evidence-based. The Early Risers "Skills for Success" program, for example, focuses on at-risk elementary school age children and is an example of selective prevention. These at-risk children began behaving aggressively at a very young age and were considered at-risk for developing CD and/or substance use issues. This multipronged, community-based approach includes a parent and family empowerment component. Initial gains were lost at the one-year follow-up, with the exception of gains in social competence.

Much of the prevention research with children and youth occurs in school or mental health settings, and some of this research has included a family component. For example, an NREPP-listed program called SAFE Children includes a group intervention developed for families who have children starting first grade in the inner city as well as a reading and tutoring program for the children. This selective prevention program showed stable parent–school contact and improved child reading scores over time for participants when compared with a control group. Parenting programs for parents of children diagnosed with attention-deficit/hyperactivity disorder (ADHD), however, are an example of indicated prevention. This is because research has shown that parents of ADHD children have difficulties with family relationships and parental functions; program participants have reported improvements in parent–child relationships. Family preservation research has also focused on juvenile justice and substance use issues. Programs studied include the Strengthening Families Program, Multisystemic Therapy (MST) for Juvenile Offenders, and Family Centered Treatment (FCT).

Prevention Research: Importance and Limitations

Historically, prevention research on couples and families has examined problem areas such as divorce, marital distress, and intimate partner violence. Destructive marital conflict and marital distress are identified as risk factors for behavior disorders in children and depressive disorders in adults, among other dysfunctions. Preventing marital distress or intimate partner violence is therefore likely to enhance relationships within family systems and may also contribute to reducing divorce rates. By contrast, prevention research involving at-risk children/youth and their families has offered somewhat ambiguous results. In part, this may be due to the limited funding available for long-term outcome studies, including prevention research. A limitation seen in much of the existing prevention research work on couples, marriage, and families is the lack of diversity among study participants, both within and across studies. This limitation can be addressed as future researchers and MFTs expand the scope of their prevention work to include intersectionality, or cumulative effects of different forms of discrimination.

Willa J. Casstevens

See also Empowerment in Families; Family Resilience; Family Stress; Hispanic Healthy Marriage Initiative; Marriage Enrichment; Military Couples and Families; National Marriage Initiative; Parental Stress: Effects on Children; Presenting Problems; Single-Parent Families

Further Readings

Bodenmann, G., Charvoz, L., Cina, A., & Widmer, K. (2001). Prevention of marital distress by enhancing the coping skills of couples: 1-year follow-up-study. *Swiss Journal of Psychology*, 60(1), 3–10.

Braithwaite, S. R., & Fincham, F. D. (2014). Computer-based prevention of intimate partner violence in marriage. *Behaviour Research and Therapy*, *54*, 12–21.

Carroll, J. S., & Doherty, W. J. (2003). Evaluating the effectiveness of premarital prevention programs: A meta-analytic review of outcome research. *Family Relations*, *52*, 105–118.

De Koker, P., Mathews, C., Zuch, M., Bastien, S., & Mason-Jones, A. J. (2014). A systematic review of interventions for preventing adolescent intimate partner violence. *Journal of Adolescent Health*, *54*, 3–13.

Fowers, B. J., Montel, K. H., & Olson, D. H. (1996). Predicting marital success for premarital couple types based on PREPARE. *Journal of Marital & Family Therapy*, *22*(1), 103–119.

Hage, S. M., Romano, J. L., Conyne, R. K., Kenny, M., Matthews, C., Schwartz, J. P., & Waldo, M. (2007). Best practice guidelines on prevention practice, research, training, and social advocacy for psychologists. *The Counseling Psychologist*, *35*(4), 493–566.

Hendricks, B., Bradley, L. J., Southern, S., Oliver, M., & Birdsall, B. (2011). Ethical code for the International Association of Marriage and Family Counselors. *The Family Journal: Counseling and Therapy for Couples and Families*, *19*(2), 217–224.

Holtzworth-Munroe, A., Markman, H., O'Leary, K. D., Neidig, P., Leber, D., Heyman, R. E., . . . Smutzler, N. (1995). The need for marital violence prevention efforts: A behavioral-cognitive secondary prevention program for engaged and newly married couples. *Applied & Preventive Psychology*, *4*, 77–88.

Murray, C. E. (2005). Prevention work: A professional responsibility for marriage and family counselors. *The Family Journal: Counseling and Therapy for Couples and Families*, *13*(1), 27–34.

Raczynski, K., Waldo, M., Schwartz, J. P., & Horne, A. M. (Eds.). (2013). *Evidence-based prevention*. Thousand Oaks, CA: Sage.

Springer, F., & Phillips, J. L. (2006). The IOM model: A tool for prevention planning and implementation. *Prevention Tactics*, *8*(13), 1–7.

Stanley, S. M., Markham, H. J., St. Peters, M., & Leber, B. D. (1995). Strengthening marriages and preventing divorce: New directions in prevention research. *Family Relations*, *44*, 392–401.

Primary and Secondary Emotions

Emotions are feelings that arise immediately and automatically in response to situations that have importance for us. They alert us that something meaningful is happening relative to our goals or values and create a predisposition for us to act in response. This emotional reaction is communicated through our body as felt experience but often will trigger rational thoughts to both inform and temper emotional reactions as we formulate a response to the situation. Emotional responses may involve external action that communicates with and changes the environment but may also involve internal processes and the way we experience and react to our emotions. Sometimes this may direct our focus away from the original emotion we felt in response to a situation, and in these cases, we may lose touch with the important information our initial genuine reaction provides. In considering this complex process, it is useful to categorize emotional experience as primary or secondary.

Primary emotions are our reflexive, immediate response to a situation. These emotions often have a biological foundation and reflect adaptive survival instincts such as fear or anger. Secondary emotions, in contrast, are learned emotional reactions we adopt in response to the primary emotion and tend to obscure or conceal the primary emotion. In this sense, a secondary emotion is a "reaction to our reaction" in a situation, as when a man might conceal sadness with anger as a more socially acceptable feeling. This entry outlines the nature and role of emotions in overall well-being, further explains the concepts of primary and secondary emotions, and relates how awareness of these emotion types can contribute to enhanced emotional functioning.

Emotional Processes

Emotions are essential to our ability to adapt in our environment and achieve our goals and interests. They provide immediate, automatic information in response to situations that signals their meaning and importance as well as the possible need for action. Emotional responses are triggered by external events but also by internal activity such as reflective thought. Remembering times with a friend, for example, might introduce tender feelings and prompt one to contact the friend. A situation can trigger multiple and possibly conflicting emotions. In these cases, we are faced with the complex task of working through a variety of feelings in deriving meaning from the situation and determining what actions might be needed in response. We retain memories of past emotional experiences, or schemes, which become the foundation of our emotional response process. These schemes include the basic elements of our experience, including beliefs, mood, motivation, behavior, what we see or sense, and how we tend to act. These schemes are stored and retrieved without our conscious awareness, triggered by current situations with similar characteristics. In this way, we use learning from past emotional experience to inform how we interpret and respond to current situations. Our emotional reactions and responses not only impact our feelings, thoughts, and actions but also communicate much about ourselves to others. Those who encounter us, in turn, will come to know us and have emotional responses based on the situations we present.

Competency in recognizing and managing emotions is critical to overall effectiveness and life satisfaction in children and adults. It is important that we be open to awareness of emotional responses and accept our genuine responses as insight into our true feelings. There are some emotions, such as jealousy or resentment, which we may be reluctant to own. It is important to accept these, however, to fully understand ourselves without judgment in evaluating a situation and the meaning it has for us. At the same time, we recognize that emotions are not the only information that should inform the actions we take. We learn to regulate our emotions, understanding that not every emotion requires an immediate or intense response.

Emotional regulation may involve intentional efforts to wait for cognitive feedback to our emotional responses prior to acting. Where emotions are experienced as feeling and stem from one part of the brain, we also need to engage our rational thinking, experienced in words from a different part of the brain, in processing the situation and determining what, if any, action to take. Putting a name to our emotions is a good step toward giving them more thought or communicating our feeling to others. With reflective consideration, we can determine whether our feeling moves us closer to or farther away from our relationships and goals and decide how our feeling can best inform our actions. In making these choices across many dimensions of behavior, individuals are motivated in complex ways. Internal factors such as needs and goals, as well as external factors such as reward systems and cultural norms, shape the way in which emotions are expressed.

Primary Emotions

As noted earlier, primary emotions are immediate, reflexive reactions to a situation. They are quick to present and also quick to fade when the circumstance changes. These primary emotions provide the clearest indicator of our genuine feeling in any moment; accordingly, it is important for our mental health to recognize and manage these. Some primary emotions are considered biological or instinctive in nature, and their expression is associated with survival, well-being, and basic communication. Responses of these core emotions such as joy, sadness, anger, and fear appear from infancy through adulthood. Other emotions, such as pride or humiliation, are socially or culturally learned. These learned emotions can also be a primary response and in many ways are derived from more basic, instinctive emotions. Primary emotions can be classified as *adaptive* or *maladaptive* in terms of facilitating our relationships and objectives.

Adaptive primary emotions represent our gut, instinctive reaction to the immediate situation. Because it is evoked in direct response to our specific current circumstances, it is most likely to be helpful in guiding us to resolution consistent with the current situation. Joy at seeing an old friend, for example, may prompt action to greet the friend warmly and invite conversation. Humiliation at interrupting a musical performance with our late arrival, for example, would likely prompt an apology as well as increased efforts to arrive at entertainment events on time. Primary adaptive emotions alert us to situations that matter to us and can facilitate responses that resolve them in a healthy, positive way. To a large extent, our communication with others consists of emotional responses so that the health of our relationships with others also depends on the authenticity of our responses.

Maladaptive primary emotions are also immediate and genuine reactions to circumstances but disrupt rather than facilitate effective functioning. These unhealthy reactions are typically schemes learned from previous, perhaps traumatic, experiences. Fearfulness in a situation, for example, may arise where we have been frightened or hurt by a state in the past. People who have been bitten by a dog, for example, may become fearful whenever they see a dog. Perhaps more commonly, however, we develop these unhealthy schemes and beliefs in a distorted view of ourselves or our past experience. Unlike adaptive primary emotions, these maladaptive emotional schemes are triggered by current circumstances yet usually offer little action orientation. These can arise from thoughts as well as from external experiences. Shame at feeling unlovable or anxiety at feeling worthless, for example, may arise and become primary and overwhelming. People tend to get stuck in these emotions and may ruminate on them in a way that perpetuates rather than relieves them. These maladaptive primary emotions may have been learned through past experience or thought yet have a destructive influence on current functioning.

Secondary Emotions

Secondary emotions follow a primary emotional response and may be a reaction to or defense against it. In this sense, they mask genuine emotions and make it difficult to be aware of our true feelings. Secondary emotions often arise when individuals have learned to believe their primary emotions are unacceptable. For example, men may feel it is not masculine to display fear, so they may become angry instead. Women, on the other hand, may feel it is not feminine to be angry and may become sad to obscure it. Secondary emotions also arise to avoid or defend against primary emotions that we feel are painful to address. For example, we may display coolness to obscure more primary, painful feelings of loneliness when not invited to an event. Secondary emotions often become troublesome and chronic indicators of primary emotions that are not dealt with. Many who feel generally depressed or anxious are living with secondary emotions without recognizing the genuine primary feelings they mask.

Instrumental emotions are another specific category of emotions that don't reflect a primary genuine emotional response to a situation but are adopted to influence the reactions of other people in a desired direction. Also called manipulative feelings, instrumental emotions may be expressed knowingly or in an unconscious habitual manner. Intentional expression of instrumental emotions to create an impression of self or evoke desired actions from others may involve a high level of skill in social and emotional interaction. Accordingly, it may be more like a personality characteristic than a spontaneous response to a given situation. Expression of instrumental emotions without awareness can pose serious relational problems as others sense efforts to manipulate and control and are driven away.

Enhancing Emotional Functioning

The information provided by primary adaptive emotional experiences is critical to effective functioning, yet people typically receive little guidance as to how to attend to and manage their emotional experiences. In fact, many are encouraged to ignore or discount them. Because of this, they are likely to struggle to deal with their own emotions and those of others around them. This may result in a low self-image, self-defeating thoughts and actions, and relational problems. Mental health professionals find that many people seeking therapy have poor emotional skills and that enhancing these can result in significant positive change for individuals as well as couples and families.

Emotionally focused therapy (EFT), developed by Leslie Greenberg and Susan Johnson, focuses on enhancement of emotional management skills in the context of the therapeutic relationship. This therapeutic process includes building awareness and skills in the processing of primary adaptive emotions during therapeutic sessions. As emotions signal that something of importance is occurring for the individual, the experiencing of emotion in session can provide therapeutic insights into the important goal, need, or desire being touched by a current situation and the action it suggests. Individuals can also be helped to develop a functional level of emotional regulation. Where some might have too little response to emotional situations, others may respond too intensely or without adequate thought as to the meaning of the emotion and consideration of possible actions and consequences. Therapeutic work here might include effort to intentionally consider the impact of various response patterns for the individual and those around him or her before taking action.

The harmful impact of faulty emotional schemes in maladaptive primary emotions and dysfunctional secondary emotions can also be recognized and addressed in therapy. Activation of faulty emotional schemes, as discussed earlier, triggers dysfunctional emotional responses such as shame, worthlessness, or feeling unlovable. As schemes exist in our memory as experiences rather than words, therapeutic intervention may involve fully walking through the scheme and putting its meaning into words. With insight development from thoughtful examination of faulty logic in these schemes, more positive schemes can be developed and introduced into our emotional response set. Similarly, examination of secondary emotional responses by walking though these reactions in session can help individuals understand their motivation for these reactions. Beyond this, it can also help them uncover and process though their authentic primary adaptive emotion in these situations.

Finally, individuals can be helped to recognize that instrumental emotions can pose serious relational problems as others sense their manipulative efforts. Therapeutic work here would be aimed at creating an awareness of the behavior and the motivation behind it as well as appreciation for how it is likely to be perceived by others. The rationale behind all of these interventions is the critical role that emotions play in our relationship with self and others and the importance of recognizing and processing our authentic primary adaptive emotions to overall mental health.

Mary McClure

See also Emotional Disengagement; Emotional Intelligence, Children; Emotional Intelligence, Families; Emotionally Focused Therapy for Couples

Further Readings

Gottman, J. (1997). *Raising an emotionally intelligent child: The heart of parenting*. New York, NY: Simon & Schuster.

Greenberg, L. (2006). Emotion-focused therapy: A synopsis. *Journal of Contemporary Psychotherapy, 36*(2), 87–93. doi:10.1007/s10879-006-9011-3

Greenberg, L. S. (2002). *Emotion-focused therapy: Coaching clients to work through their feelings*. Washington, DC: American Psychological Association.

Greenberg, L. S., & Johnson, S. J. (1988). *Emotionally focused therapy for couples*. New York, NY: Guilford Press.

Mayer, J. D., Roberts, R. D., & Barsade, S. G. (2008). Human abilities: Emotional intelligence. *Annual Review of Psychology, 59*(1), 507–536. doi:10.1146/annurev.psych.59.103006.093646

Process Research

Process research, in the context of therapy, refers to research that examines processes happening in therapy—on the part of either the clients or the therapist. It can involve observations of therapy or physiological data that capture the process of therapy. Much of the family therapy research that exists tests outcomes, such as symptomology, functioning, or satisfaction, at the end of therapy. These outcomes help answer this question: Does therapy work? While this is important information when considering whether or not a therapy model or technique is effective, it fails to answer the questions related to why or how therapy works. Process research, on the other hand, examines the mechanisms that contribute to those successful outcomes to better understand why therapy is successful. This entry first discusses how process research can help to bridge the gap between research and practice, the systems and techniques used in process research (behavioral coding systems, task analysis, and physiological data), and major findings from process research. It then discusses the clinical relevance of process research to therapists, ethical concerns raised by process research, and the limitations of process research.

The Gap Between Research and Practice

A conundrum that often exists in family therapy and other applied professions is a gap between researchers and practitioners. Often, clinicians feel that research on family therapy is not directly applicable to their practices. Outcome research is often highly controlled and follows specific steps and does not mimic conditions in most therapy settings. Process research, because it examines the processes that contribute to client change, helps clinicians decide on which behaviors and techniques to use by helping them understand how they work and with whom. When paired with outcome data, process research helps family therapists understand why their therapy is effective and what they can do to increase their effectiveness with their own clients. It can be done on an individual scale in a private practice. Additionally, it is a type of research that can be fed back into training programs to help beginning clinicians increase their efficacy by examining their own processes.

To examine therapy changes, process research often questions behaviors and phenomena that occur during therapy sessions themselves, by examining live sessions, videos, or other in-session data, such as physiology. Observational research mimics the therapist's own processes, as it most often involves data gathered by a third party observing the interaction between clients or between clients and therapists. Further, observational data gets at interactional and systemic processes that are important to family therapists. Process research may also examine physiological responses of clients and therapists during the session.

Process research has been used for years, most popularly in the field of child development. Researchers have examined such behaviors in small children as their reaction to strangers (as with the strange situation experiments done by Mary Ainsworth in the 1970s or John Gottman's research in the 1980s on how children communicate with one another). Examinations of couple dynamics are a relatively new phenomenon, but family studies researchers have examined processes related to developmental transitions, power, individual and family well-being, conflict, and problem-solving to name a few. Researchers of contemporary therapy models, such as solution-focused therapy and emotionally focused therapy (EFT), have used process research since the 1980s as a way of validating their models. Additionally, it has been used as means to examine techniques, such as enactments or questions, common to multiple therapy approaches to determine how these techniques work independent of a model.

Behavioral Coding Systems

To examine the processes of therapy, researchers often use behavioral coding. Behavioral coding involves examining behaviors that occur in therapy and assigning a code to them. While codes can simply be about the content of therapy (i.e., the issues clients and therapists discuss in therapy), process research has the ability to get deeper into the mechanics of therapy. Codes can describe a physical behavior, such as a gesture or body positioning; a manifestation of emotion, such as dysphoric affect; a verbal communication, such as a put-down; or a process, such as a person being left out of an interaction, as in couples therapy.

In many cases, codes assigned to interactions are part of a larger, predetermined coding scheme. Coding schemes are typically reflective of the research question being asked. However, some coding schemes are designed to code globally, meaning that, for the most part, each interaction that occurs in a therapy session will have some code assigned to it. These types of schemes provide codes for a wide variety of interactions, allowing multiple research questions to be asked from the same data. Additionally, behavioral coding can also be used by clinicians for assessment purposes to examine couple and family interactions at the outset of therapy to determine initial systemic functioning.

The most common of these are schemes that examine communication. These include the Marital Interaction Coding System, the Family Relational Communication Control, and the Couples Interaction Coding System. Other schemes may be used to code affect, such as the Specific Affect Coding System. Coding schemes can be categorized as micro or global. In a micro coding scheme, typically a session is divided up into segments, such as a talk turn or a time increment (10 to 30 seconds). For whatever that unit is, one or multiple codes may be assigned. These coding schemes typically have several codes, making them more difficult to code, but allow researchers to capture sequential data. Global codes tend to assign a code or a rating to an entire segment. Clients may be assigned a specific task to do, or observation of a therapy session may occur instead, depending on the research question and whether the researchers wish to capture specific interactions, such as the solving of a problem, or are more interested in the process of a routine therapy session.

Observational coding is typically done by an outside observer, thereby giving the codes more objectivity. However, there are some research questions that require clients to watch their own sessions and rate their own feelings and impressions related to their interactions. For example, a client system (i.e., individual, couple, or family) may be asked to watch a session they just participated in and report on the feelings they experienced either during the session or as they watched the recording. This can be done with individual codes or with a rating system. This kind of exercise can give researchers different insight into what is going on for clients in session than they might report on a paper-and-pencil assessment.

Task Analysis

Task analysis is a type of process research that examines events that contribute to a larger process. It differs from behavioral coding in that it requires researchers to approach the process without preconceived notions, similar to qualitative analyses such as grounded theory. The theory behind task analysis acknowledges that a prescribed coding scheme may fail to capture all of the dimensions of a therapy session. In task analysis, researchers discover events that occur in therapy that seem significant and try to map them. The mapping involves breaking the event into stages. It also means examining the processes that both clients and therapists go through and then using the data found to build a minitheory of that event. The minitheory then becomes a guideline for developing a coding scheme that can test the assumptions of the minitheory. Task analysis can be useful for further development of existing theories, to further clarify tasks germane to those theories, or to create new theories, and it provides a mechanism for empirical testing of those theories.

Physiological Data

Physiological data is another way to gather information on the process of therapy. Using physiological data for research involves measuring clients on some internal physiological process. Such data may include heart rate, cortisol levels, skin conductance, brain activity, or blood pressure. Physiological data give researchers an idea of how aroused clients are during a process and how well they are able to regulate or soothe themselves. These data have been used to draw conclusions about clients who respond in different ways and can also be used as a clinical tool to help clients learn to better regulate themselves. These studies require clients to be attached to some kind of device that measures these biological processes.

Major Research Findings

Process research studies in family therapy have yielded some important findings, particularly when coupled with outcome research. Among them is a relationship between self-reported marital discord and observed conflict. Another major finding is the presence of certain communication behaviors as predictors of divorce. Other studies have found that a person's affect changes the longer he or she is married and that couple conflict has impacts on individuals' emotional and physical functioning as well as on children's well-being.

In the realm of family therapy, process research has been used to validate change processes in various family therapy models. For EFT, it has been used to examine tasks such as blamer softening, in which a previously critical or hostile partner shows vulnerability in expressing an emotional need to his or her partner and the specific interactional behaviors that are associated with that change in a session. EFT researchers have also used process research to examine the importance of shame as a part of the forgiveness process for couples. Solution-focused therapy researchers have used it to examine the reciprocal relationships between therapist language and client responses. Process research has also been used to examine the therapeutic alliance in structural family therapy (SFT) and brief strategic therapy.

Additionally, process research has been used to examine therapist processes and techniques such as questions, proxy voice, interruptions, and softening as well as client processes such as alliances, blaming, support, and responsiveness by therapist gender that may be independent variables for future studies. Through the use of physiological data, researchers have been able to use biological processes to validate constructs such as attachment and to demonstrate physiological differences among violent men as well as between violent and nonviolent men. Further, researchers such as Gottman have been able to use physiological data to draw conclusions about couples who are able to manage conflict and couples who are not.

Clinical Relevance

Process research is a natural fit for clinicians. In addition to results from process research studies informing how clinicians do therapy, knowledge of behavioral coding may also be helpful to therapists. Understanding how various behaviors and affect states may manifest themselves in therapy can help therapists be attuned to those indicators in session and intervene as needed. Further, clinicians may become versed in a behavioral coding scheme or recognize some common behaviors and nonverbal cues among their clients.

Ethical Concerns

One of the reasons for the limited number of process research studies of family therapy has to do with the ethics of having outside coders code videotapes of sensitive therapy sessions. First, clients must agree to have their data used for these purposes. While institutions must go through the review process to determine whether or not their research practices are safe for participants, when using video data to examine processes, data can never be truly deidentified. For this reason, it is important for participants to make informed decisions and for researchers to take every precaution to keep harm to their participants at a minimum. This may include steps to make sure that videos are secure and that coders do not code information for participants they have any prior relationships with. However, as the availability and security of these technologies increase, it is assumed that research studies examining therapeutic processes with physiological and observational data will increase as well.

Limitations of Process Research

One of the main limitations of doing process research in family therapy lies in the difficulty of gathering data. Typically, observational coding is a time-intensive process and requires a great deal of training for multiple coders of the same data. In order for data to be considered reliable, the coders must be held to rigorous standards. Typically, the same video is coded independently by two coders, who then confer to make sure that they are coding the same thing with reasonable accuracy. If they are not reasonably reliable, the videos must be coded again. This can take a lot of time and often requires payment of coders. Similarly, software used for analysis of video and physiological data often requires the use of expensive equipment.

Another limitation of process research is that, like self-report research, it limits the research questions asked. For example, observational research, by itself, does not allow researchers to ask questions related to the attitudes or beliefs of therapists or clients. However, when process research is combined with outcome research, such as client self-reports, it provides multidimensional information about the why and how questions of therapeutic effectiveness.

Megan Oka

See also Couples Therapy Research; Nonverbal Communication; Outcome Research; Qualitative Research

Further Readings

Bakeman, R., & Gottman, J. M. (1997). *Observing interaction: An introduction to sequential analysis*. New York, NY: Cambridge University Press.

Bradley, B., & Johnson, S. M. (2005). Task analysis of couple and family change events. In D. H. Sprenkle & F. P. Piercy (Eds.), *Research methods in family therapy* (pp. 254–271). New York, NY: Guilford Press.

Gottman, J. M., & Notarius, C. I. (2000). Decade review: Observing marital interaction. *Journal of Marriage and Family*, 62(4), 927–947.

Wampler, K. S., & Harper, J. M. (2014). Observational research. In R. B. Miller & L. M. Johnson (Eds.), *Advanced methods in family therapy research* (pp. 230–246). New York, NY: Routledge.

Professional Associations

Professional associations are formal groups created by and for professionals to bring together likeminded individuals within specific fields of interest, creating a forum where members can grow, learn, and exchange information with peers, thereby fostering a sense of community within a given profession. For the marriage and family therapist (MFT), aligning oneself with professional associations provides many benefits both professionally and personally. It is important for MFTs in training as well as seasoned professionals to be knowledgeable about the professional associations available. Current and future MFTs are encouraged to join professional organizations in an effort to continue education and personal growth, promote advocacy, and align themselves with professional ethics and standards endorsed by the members of the association. In the field of marriage and family therapy, there are numerous professional organizations available worldwide. This entry discusses the benefits of joining professional associations, professional tools and education, ethical standards, and other considerations when selecting which professional associations to join.

MFTs are strongly encouraged to become involved in professional organizations, starting at the onset of training and continuing throughout their careers. For an MFT, membership in a given organization can impact his or her outlook on the field, educational development, and development of professional identity. There are many benefits associated with joining professional organizations for MFTs. Specifically, professional associations can assist MFTs by offering opportunities for members to build a strong professional network, an outlet to promote advocacy in the field, access to specific career enhancing tools, a multitude of additional educational resources, and a code of ethics standard for MFTs to uphold as members of the organization.

Professional Network Development

Building a professional network is essential for both current and future MFTs. Professional associations allow an opportunity for members to network with other professionals in their local and state communities as well as in national and international forums. Membership in a professional organization creates opportunities to meet others in a forum not always possible in the community at large. Networking takes place within the associations' organized meetings, conferences, and other professional development opportunities. Student members can meet other professionals in their local community and build relationships with more seasoned MFTs from whom they may seek support or mentorship. Additionally, these relationships and interactions may lead to securing a fieldwork placement or paid position with a local agency.

Professional Tools and Education

Various professional organizations for MFTs offer a myriad of resources and tools for members. Resources include information about current topics and trends in the field, continuing education opportunities, employment and scholarship opportunities, state and national licensing information, conferences, and trainings, as well as legal and ethical information relevant to MFTs. Many organizations have a monthly or bimonthly magazine, newsletter, or journal that members receive as an added benefit. Some organizations offer free continuing education credits as a member prerequisite for reading a professional article or attending an organization-sponsored webinar, followed by passing a short quiz. Additionally, organizations may provide valuable resources to assist in professional development issues, such as starting a private practice, preparing for an interview, and working with families and clients facing various challenges. Many professional organizations offer training opportunities on relevant professional topics through their websites. These training opportunities can be completed online at any time to meet states' continuing education requirements for professionals to maintain licensure status.

Ethical Standards

Professional organizations such as the American Association for Marriage and Family Therapy (AAMFT), American Counseling Association (ACA), International Association of Marriage and Family Counselors (IAMFC), American Mental Health Counselors Association (AMHCA), and the Association for Play Therapy (APT) have established codes of ethics that are intended to be endorsed by members. As a member of a professional organization with a code of ethics specific to the organization, an MFT demonstrates to others in the field and the community that he or she practices therapy while abiding by that organization's code of ethics. This is essential for students and new therapists as they will utilize the code of ethics as a guide when facing ethical issues.

Other Considerations

MFTs must navigate the professional organizations available and choose to join the organizations that best align with their professional views as well as promote codes of ethics they will endorse and be guided by throughout their careers. It will be valuable to take advantage of all of the opportunities the organizations offer to members and become involved to the extent possible to maximize the experience. Professional organizations include local, state, national, and international chapters. So involvement may look very different depending on the organizations a student or professional chooses to join. Regardless of which professional organizations an MFT chooses to join, as members students and professionals separate themselves from those who do not align with a professional organization, help promote their own knowledge base, and unify with others to promote the field as it grows and evolves.

Sharon Silverberg

See also American Association for Marriage and Family Therapy; Ethical Decision-Making; International Association of Marriage and Family Counselors; World Association for Sexual Health

Further Readings

American Association for Marriage and Family Therapy: http://www.aamft.org

American Counseling Association: http://www.counseling.org

European Family Therapy Association: http://www.europeanfamilytherapy.eu

International Association of Marriage and Family Counselors: http://www.iamfconline.org

International Family Therapy Association: http://www.ifta-familytherapy.org

International Marriage and Family Therapy Honor Society: Delta Kappa: http://www.deltakappamft.org

National Council on Family Relations: http://www.ncfr.org

Northey, W. F. (2009). The legitimization of marriage and family therapy in the United States: Implications for international recognition. *Journal of Family Psychotherapy, 20*(4), 303–318. doi:10.1080/08975350903366253

West, C., Hinton, W. J., Grames, H., & Adams, M. A. (2013). Marriage and family therapy: Examining the impact of licensure on an evolving profession. *Journal of Marital and Family Therapy, 39*(1), 112–126. doi:10.1111/jmft.12010

Progress Notes for Couples and Families

Progress notes are written or electronic notes that summarize and document the counseling treatment process. They are written after each counseling session by the mental health clinician who provided the counseling service whether that clinician is a licensed professional counselor, counseling psychologist, clinical psychologist, licensed marriage and family therapist (MFT), or licensed clinical social worker. Regardless of their specific discipline, mental health clinicians maintain and safeguard progress notes throughout and beyond the course of treatment for a couple or family. This entry further defines *progress notes*, details the information that goes into them, and discusses how progress notes relate to other information found in a client file. It then discusses why progress notes are important, how the Health Insurance Portability and Accountability Act (HIPAA) has influenced progress notes, the templates and formats used when writing progress notes, and common practices and standards related to writing and maintaining progress notes.

Format and Content of Progress Notes

Progress notes are the formal notes in a client's treatment file that officially document the treatment a client receives in counseling. They are written and maintained by the mental health clinician who provided the counseling service. Whether progress notes are handwritten or electronic, they are maintained in harmony with agency guidelines; standards set forth by mental health professional associations; and the respective codes of ethics, licensing boards, state laws, and federal laws.

Because there may be slight variations among agencies, mental health professions, and state laws, it is critical that clinicians understand the note writing policies of the agencies they work for, keep current with professional standards of practice, know their professional codes of ethics, know licensing board requirements, and understand state and federal laws pertaining to writing and maintaining progress notes. Typical progress notes contain the following information:

- Date of treatment and type of service provided
- Specific information about the length of the counseling session, including the session start and stop times
- Who attended the session
- Diagnosis and prognosis information
- Medication information
- Functional status
- Client symptom information, including any patterns and information pertaining to the severity, duration, and frequency of the symptoms experienced
- Interventions used in session and responses to these interventions

- Client progress related to specific identified goals
- Assessment, inventory, or testing results
- Treatment plan
- How crises or serious clinical situations were handled
- If applicable, billing code information (Depending on the setting, billing information may be kept in a separate administrative or billing file.)
- Clinician signature, credentials, and date signed
- If applicable, supervisor signature, credentials, and date signed

Relation of Progress Notes to Other Information in a Client's Treatment File

Treatment files are created for each client at the outset of counseling or therapy. This treatment file is often referred to as a client's chart. Since progress notes are one of many aspects of documentation that make up a larger, all-encompassing client treatment file, it is helpful for clinicians to understand how progress notes fit within the rest of a client's treatment file. Although not an all-inclusive list, common paperwork found in a client's treatment file or a client's chart includes items such as (a) client identification information, screening forms, and/or intake forms; (b) signed authorization forms such as the informed consent form, consent to record sessions (if applicable), and release of information forms; (c) intake summary; (d) assessment or testing information; (e) treatment plan; (f) contact notes; (g) progress notes; (h) other information received from health care providers such as a summary of prior treatment received; (i) a transition plan, closing note, or discharge summary; and (j) anything else deemed pertinent to the treatment received or that is required by one's place of employment, professional codes of ethics, mental health licensing boards, state laws, or federal laws. Although progress notes are just one part of documenting client care, they are a critical part of the client's file in that they provide important information regarding the counseling process, session-to-session interactions, treatment decisions, symptoms experienced, interventions used, and progress made. Clinicians should be aware of agency practices and professional practices as well as state and federal laws that could impact whether clinicians should have one treatment file per couple or family or individual treatment files for each person involved in treatment.

Importance of Progress Notes

Progress notes are important for a variety of reasons. Progress notes assist clinicians with the following:

- Providing good client care
- Documenting how crises or serious situations were handled
- Tracking progress
- Having recall and continuity of care
- Maintaining professional standards and codes of ethics in harmony with state and federal laws

Progress notes assist with providing good client care by helping clinicians reflect on their work with clients. As clinicians write their progress notes, they can take time to reflect on case conceptualization, treatment planning, and treatment recommendations. They write about the interventions utilized in session and the rationale for these interventions. They explore what worked well and what didn't and then make adjustments with treatment plans and/or treatment recommendations.

Progress notes assist with documenting crises or other serious situations. When crises or other serious situations arise (e.g., suicidal ideation, suicide attempts, child abuse and neglect), it is important for clinicians to thoroughly document the situation. Clinicians use progress notes to carefully document specific details of what happened; what clients said; how they responded as clinicians; and any other courses of action taken, including actions taken to help keep clients or other individuals safe.

As counseling unfolds, clinicians and clients typically work together to try to understand the nature of the symptoms clients are experiencing. As part of this process, they explore the patterns and triggers to the symptoms as well as possible ways to manage and/or decrease the symptoms at hand. Progress notes are a natural place to monitor and document progress clients make with counseling and managing their symptoms. Clinicians use progress notes to track information such as the severity, duration, and frequency of symptoms.

Unless clinicians have perfect recall, there is no way they can remember all details of their work with each client. Progress notes help clinicians remember details of what happened in session and therefore assist with continuity of care. Although counseling is rarely linear or sequential in nature, progress notes also serve as a step-by-step, session-to-session guide to the treatment received. This step-by-step guide to treatment received assists with continuity of care should clients need to be transferred to another clinician. Progress notes are to be written in such a manner that another clinician could easily step in, understand what has been done in counseling, and pick up where the previous clinician left off.

Mental health professionals (MFTs, professional counselors, social workers, and psychologists) are governed by professional codes of ethics and professional standards set forth by their professional associations and state licensing boards. These codes of ethics and professional standards help provide clinicians guidance regarding professional standards of care in their respective disciplines. Each mental health profession has similar but slightly different standards of care when it comes to documentation. State laws may also vary from state to state regarding documenting and writing client progress notes. It is important that clinicians are aware of professional standards of care as well as state and federal laws pertaining to keeping and maintaining client progress notes. Failure to write and maintain client progress notes goes against professional standards and each mental health profession's code of ethics.

Progress notes provide a paper trail that describes the rationale for the treatment received, counseling interventions utilized, reasons for the approaches used in session, and progress (or lack of progress) of the client. If written well, progress notes can support the reasons for the treatment method and interventions utilized in the counseling process. If a diagnosis is provided, progress notes can provide a rationale for the diagnosis given. Progress notes document steps taken and the rationale for how crises were handled—especially important if abuse is reported or if a client is suicidal, has attempted suicide, or has died by suicide while under the clinician's care.

If there were any ethical dilemmas regarding treatment, clinicians document the dilemmas involved, the ethical codes involved, and the approach they took to work through and resolve the dilemmas at hand. Progress notes also document the closure process and steps taken by clinicians to handle closure in a clinically appropriate way for the client and situation at hand. Although there are no guarantees, good documentation can help protect clinicians should a lawsuit be filed or a complaint made to a state's licensing board regarding their behavior in the counseling process. Ideally, if questioned by a client, an agency, a state licensing board, or a court of law, clinicians would be able to use their progress notes to show the quality of care given to their clients and that they acted in a manner that was in harmony with the standards of care set forth by their profession and their respective code of ethics, their licensing board, and state and federal laws.

Influence of HIPAA on Progress Notes

The Health Insurance Portability and Accountability Act of 1996, commonly referred to as HIPAA, relates to health care practices that protect private health care information; this includes client mental health care treatment information. The Privacy Rule for HIPAA has influenced and shaped how mental health clinicians view session notes and what information should (or should not) go into the notes about a client's treatment.

Prior to HIPAA, several different terms were used to reference notes that documented a client's treatment session. The term *progress notes* was often used interchangeably with the following terms: *case notes, psychotherapy notes, counseling notes, process notes, session notes,* or *therapy notes.* Although many clinicians still interchange these terms, HIPAA clarified that counseling treatment notes maintained by HIPAA-compliant clinicians are to be called progress notes and that progress notes are different from psychotherapy notes. Psychotherapy notes contain different information than progress notes and are considered the protected, private notes of the clinician so long as they are securely stored in a separate location than the progress notes.

HIPAA has specific guidelines regarding writing and maintaining progress notes. Clinicians who fall under HIPAA compliance should research and understand the difference between progress notes and psychotherapy notes. Some treatment information would be more suited for psychotherapy notes versus progress notes and vice versa. Some agencies may require individuals to maintain both progress notes and psychotherapy notes, while others may require only progress notes. Either way, mental health clinicians should follow proper guidelines and preferences set forth by their employers that are in harmony with professional and ethical standards in their specific discipline and applicable state and federal laws. Because HIPAA affects more than just writing and maintaining progress notes, it is important for mental health clinicians to learn more about HIPAA and the other ways HIPAA impacts mental health clinicians.

Templates and Formats Used When Writing Progress Notes

There are many common and acceptable formats used when writing progress notes. These formats include, but are not limited to, (a) freehand; (b) specific agency templates; and (c) standard classic formats such as DAP (data, assessment, and plan), SOAP (subjective, objective, assessment, and plan), DRAP (description, response, assessment, and plan), or BIRP (behavior, intervention, response, and plan). The format for writing progress notes will vary from agency to agency and setting to setting. Some agencies require extensive documentation with elaborate treatment plans and/or use specific templates or formats for their progress notes. Other agencies are flexible with how notes are written, and the clinicians can choose the format that makes the most sense for their style of note writing and the types of clients they are working with.

Freehand progress notes are just that—progress notes that are typically written in a free-form paragraph style. There is no specific guide to follow. Outside of the standard information that is included in progress notes, clinicians determine what information should go in the progress note and the order in which that information is to be written.

Some agencies create their own templates to use that are geared toward specific information, helping clinicians write their progress notes in a timely manner and not burdening clinicians with writing down common items over and over again for that particular setting. These template forms can easily be downloaded for clinician ease and might include lists or check boxes for items such as a client's functional status and the interventions used.

Some settings might encourage their employees to use one of several classic progress note formats such as the DAP, SOAP, DRAP, or BIRP. These standard formats for progress notes vary slightly from each other but generally ask for similar information. They are appealing for clinicians in that they apply to most work settings, have elements that are easy to remember, and have flexibility for open-ended note writing but provide more guidance than a freehand progress note.

Common Practices and Standards Related to Progress Notes

Each agency, mental health professional association, and state has its own guidelines regarding how to write notes, what information should be documented in progress notes, how to store notes, how long to store notes, and who has access to notes. It is standard practice to write progress notes within a timely manner after seeing a client. Clinicians should avoid taking too long to write their progress notes and should keep their progress notes up to date. Clinicians should be thorough, but concise, balancing how much to share and not to share.

Progress notes should be written using professional language and, ideally, in harmony with a clinician's theoretical orientation. Clinicians should avoid jargon, abbreviations, and opinions. Clinicians should be honest and accurate with their progress notes, and statements made in progress notes should be backed up with information on how clinicians made that observation. Using the phrase "as evidenced by . . ." can help clinicians clarify clinical observations or share how they know what they know. When possible, it can also help to use direct quotes from the client.

Progress notes should be written in blue or black ink and signed by the clinician the day that the clinician writes the progress note. If the clinician is under supervision, progress notes should be reviewed, signed, and dated by the supervisor. If handwriting progress notes and a mistake is made, clinicians typically draw one line through the error, initial and date it, and then continue with the notes. Clinicians should not scribble out mistakes or use correction fluid on errors. If for some reason a progress note needs to be corrected after it has been written, signed, and dated, then the clinician should write an amendment to the original progress note. This is typically done by writing a separate note, noting the changes or the additions to the original note. The clinician signs and dates this progress note and then attaches it to the original progress note.

Client progress notes should be safeguarded. Whether client files are maintained in written or electronic format, it is important that client treatment information, including progress notes, are protected from other, nonauthorized individuals viewing or having access to them. Notes should not be left out when writing them. Progress notes should be maintained and stored in secure locations according to agency practices, state and federal laws, and the clinician's professional code of ethics. It is common practice to have written records stored in locked file cabinets and behind locked doors. If electronic records are used, it is common to have additional safeguards in place to protect progress notes from unauthorized users, such as using password protected computers and software programs, writing and storing records in an encrypted manner, and storing progress notes on a secure server. Those who work for HIPAA-covered entities should work with their HIPAA compliance officer to make sure additional needed safeguards are in place that meet HIPAA compliance.

It is important for agencies to have policies regarding how clients access, view, or correct their own progress notes; what is confidential and what is not; how long their progress notes are maintained; how they are stored; and how and when they are destroyed. It is important that clients have this information up front, and it should at a minimum be included as part of the informed consent process. Clients typically have reasonable access to their files although most mental health professions' codes of ethics have important exceptions that clinicians should be aware of. As part of the informed consent process, it would also be important for clients to know if there are limitations to accessing their progress notes and what those limitations are. Clients should also be informed at the outset of treatment how progress notes would be handled should they need to be seen by a different clinician at any time. As part of this process, the clinician would also make mention to clients of who their records custodian is and what the role of the custodian is should for any reason the clinician become incapacitated or die. These items are typically discussed during the informed consent process. It is common practice to document the informed consent process in the client's progress notes.

How records are physically destroyed will also vary from agency to agency and should be in harmony with one's professional codes of ethics and applicable state laws. How long records are maintained before they are destroyed varies from state to state and agency to agency. It is not uncommon to keep records for 7 to 10 years or much longer if a minor is involved. How client progress notes are destroyed should also be included in the informed consent process.

Progress notes should not be released without properly signed written authorization. Clinicians not only safeguard a client's treatment file and the physical progress notes but also protect what information is shared or released about a client's counseling treatment process. Although what clients typically share with clinicians is confidential, there are important exceptions to confidentiality that are explained to a client up front in the informed consent process and documented in the progress notes. Some of these exceptions need signed authorization to release the information, whereas others do not.

Clinicians should be aware of what information should or should not be released pertaining to progress notes. For example, clinicians do not release documents such as progress notes or testing results received from other mental health professionals. When a signed release is obtained, it is standard practice that clinicians release only information pertaining to what the client gave permission to release and that the information meets the professional purpose of the release. It is also standard practice to release just the information from the progress notes that pertains to the client if multiple persons are involved. When in doubt of what information should or should not be released, clinicians should consult with other licensed mental health professionals, their profession's codes of ethics, state and federal laws, state licensing boards, and/or legal counsel.

Kristin I. Douglas

See also Ethical Codes; HIPAA Standards

Further Readings

American Association for Marriage and Family Therapy. (2013). *User's guide to the AAMFT code of ethics.* Alexandria, VA: Author.

American Association for Marriage and Family Therapy. (2015). *2015 AAMFT code of ethics.* Retrieved from http://www.aamft.org/iMIS15/AAMFT/Content/Legal_Ethics/Code_of_Ethics.aspx

American Counseling Association. (2014). *ACA code of ethics.* Alexandria, VA: Author. Retrieved from https://www.counseling.org/resources/aca-code-of-ethics.pdf

American Psychological Association. (2007). Record keeping guidelines. *American Psychologist, 62,* 993–1004. Retrieved from https://www.apa.org/practice/guidelines/record-keeping.pdf

American Psychological Association. (2010). *Ethical principles of psychologists and code of conduct.* Retrieved from http://www.apa.org/ethics/code/principles.pdf

Cameron, S., & Turtle-Song, I. (2002). Learning to write case notes using the SOAP format. *Journal of Counseling & Development, 80,* 286–292.

Corey, G., Corey, M. S., Corey, C., & Callanan, P. (2015). *Issues and ethics in the helping profession* (9th ed.). Stamford, CT: Cengage.

Gerhart, D. (2014). *Mastering competencies in family therapy: A practical approach to theories and clinical case documentation* (2nd ed.). Belmont, CA: Brooks/Cole.

Hendricks, B. E., Bradley, L. J., Southern, S., Oliver, M., & Birdsall, B. (2011). Ethical code for the International Association of Marriage and Family Counselors. *The Family Journal, 19,* 217–224. doi:10.1177/1066480711400814

National Association of Social Workers. (2008). *Code of ethics.* Retrieved from https://www.socialworkers.org/pubs/code/code.asp

Remley, T. P., & Herlihy, B. (2010). *Ethical, legal, and professional issues in counseling* (3rd ed.). Upper Saddle River, NJ: Pearson Merrill.

U.S. Department of Health and Human Services. (2003). *Summary of the HIPAA Privacy Rule.* Retrieved from http://www.hhs.gov/sites/default/files/privacysummary.pdf

U.S. Department of Health and Human Services. (n.d.). *HIPAA for professionals.* Retrieved from http://www.hhs.gov/hipaa/for-professionals/index.html

Welfel, E. R. (2016). *Ethics in counseling and psychotherapy: Standards, research and emerging issues* (6th ed.). Boston, MA: Cengage.

Wheeler, A. M., & Bertram, B. (2015). *The counselor and the law: A guide to legal and ethical practice* (7th ed.). Alexandria, VA: American Counseling Association.

Psychoanalytic Family Therapy

Sigmund Freud, the founder of psychoanalysis, focused on the mental processes of individuals and worked in his clinical practice with individual patients. Over the years, however, psychoanalysts developed a deep interest in the interaction between infants and children and their caretakers and how these early interactions influenced later relationships, including the therapeutic relationship. (In this entry, the terms *analytic* and *analysis* are used interchangeably with *psychoanalytic* and *psychoanalysis*.) This increasingly relational perspective in psychoanalysis coincides with the relational and interactional perspective in family therapy, helping to make it possible for a clinical practice that originated in the treatment of the individual to be applied in the treatment of couples and families.

According to Michael Nichols and Richard Schwartz, from an analytic perspective, a family and individuals in that family are motivated by deeply unconscious forces that are manifested in the individual's psyche as well as in the family's interactions. Additionally, analytic family therapists help families to become aware of these forces and work through them so that they more fully express themselves to one another and deal with one another on the basis of a more accurate picture of current reality. Furthermore, families may be ambivalent about the process of change and may express that ambivalence in resistance; families and the individuals in them may relate to each other and to the therapist in distorted ways because of their own individual and relational development histories. This entry first reviews the roots of the psychoanalytic family therapy model and its evolution and the merger of psychoanalysis and family therapy. It then discusses the important concepts of resistance, transference, and countertransference and then highlights how psychoanalysis remains relevant and useful in contemporary clinical practice.

Origins and Evolution

Freud's Drive Model

Sigmund Freud (1856–1939), a Viennese physician, neurologist, and theorist, thought that human beings struggle to balance opposing psychic forces. The "I" or ego (the more rational and reasonable part of our mental makeup) attempts to mediate between the "it" or id (our unacceptable wishes and desires); the superego (the internalized voice of our parents that is critical and demanding); and the real, external world (which is often frustrating and nongratifying). Freud believed that the infant is born with a powerful id and a weak ego and that through the first years of childhood, the developing child must learn how to gain control of his or her basic instincts, chief among them murderous rage and powerful lust.

Although Freud talked much about the internal forces that drive human beings, he devoted remarkably little space to the relational context of the foregoing struggle. In Freud's writing, parents represent objects of our lustful fantasies and of our murderous designs but do not often appear in the mundane roles of actual upbringing. Jay Greenberg and Stephen Mitchell suggest that Freud understood "objects" (people such as parents) in relation to his drive model—other people either frustrate the discharge of our drives, facilitate the discharge of our drives, or serve as the object of our drives. Nancy McWilliams suggests it is possible to infer from Freud's drive theory that good caregivers skillfully balance gratification of the child's drives (which produces pleasure and motivates the child to still further attempts to get his or her needs met) with frustration of the child's drives (which teaches the child to control his or her urges and delay gratification—skills important to successful interaction with others). Freud did occasionally discuss the upbringing of children from an analytic point of view and mentions the benefits of having parents undergo analysis so they won't repeat the mistakes that their own parents made, but he talked very little in concrete terms about the relational aspects of child development.

Object Relations

Analytic theorists following Freud explored in great detail early attachment relationships and how they impact subsequent relationships. Greenberg and Mitchell say that despite the great diversity of analytic theory, the common language is that of object relations, or the study of people's interactions with one another. Nichols and Schwartz suggest that while the work of these analytic theorists on the topic of object relations is quite complex, the essence of object relations can be clearly summarized: In our present interactions with others, we relate to them according to mental pictures of ourselves and other people that have been formed from our relational history that began in earliest infancy. Freud's drive theory has thus been modified by a very different explanatory model of human behavior—that humans are fundamentally oriented toward and motivated by their relationships with other humans. In this view, mental health increases when internal mental pictures of others and of ourselves become less distorted and more closely aligned with reality, since this enables us to be more deeply and congruently connected with others and with ourselves.

Psychoanalysis and Family Therapy

As described by numerous authors, many of the founders of family therapy were originally trained in psychoanalysis. Of these, Murray Bowen and Ivan Boszormenyi-Nagy are examined in this section to illustrate how two family therapy pioneers assimilated analysis into their theory and practice.

One key Bowenian concept that shows the process of Bowen's assimilation of Freudian terms into systemic family terms is that of differentiation. Originally, Bowen defined *differentiation* as using reason and rationality, rather than emotion, to guide one's interaction with others. As Nichols and Schwartz say, this sounds very much like Freud's description of what should occur in a person's mental life: the increasing enlargement of the control of the id by the ego. Over time, Bowen modified this definition, saying that the ideal should be a balance of reason and emotion, rather than the control of emotion by reason, and he focused on the interpersonal aspects of differentiation. Interpersonally, differentiation is the ability to be in close relationships with others while still maintaining a strong sense of one's own self. This movement, from a more intrapsychic definition to a more interpersonal definition, is consistent with Bowen's general pattern of assimilation of psychoanalytic concepts.

Bowen was less interested in fixing in-session, here-and-now interactions; Nichols and Schwartz say that working with communication may make people feel great—exhilarated even—but that in Bowen's view, this doesn't resolve underlying problems. This is similar to the classical analytic position, that symptom resolution is superficial, and lasting change will occur only as a result of addressing the underlying issues—that is, characterological reorganization, which in Bowen's case is a rational analysis of one's level of differentiation and a rational plan to increase it. At the risk of oversimplification, the point behind Bowen's approach is quite similar to that of Freud's, namely to decrease the hold of irrational emotion (id), and increase the scope of rational awareness (ego) in regard to one's own thought processes, one's relationship with one's family of origin, one's present family arrangement, and one's friends and important others. While Bowen's multigenerational approach may not often be technically classified as a form of psychoanalytic family therapy, it has been profoundly influenced by analytic concepts.

Nagy's contextual therapy is more often spoken of as a form of psychoanalytic family therapy. In essence, he explores how deeply unconscious aspects of family life become manifest. This is illustrated in two allied concepts: (1) split loyalty and (2) invisible filial loyalty. In split loyalty, children are instructed in often less-than-conscious ways that they can love either their mother or their father, but not both, which results in heavy burdens on the child. Nagy also speaks of invisible loyalty. This occurs when a child cannot or will not be loyal in direct ways to his or her family but instead expresses loyalty in hidden and indirect ways. Invisible loyalty is a clear extension of the role of the unconscious in individual and family life and can often serve to suddenly illuminate mystifying, self-destructive behavior: The child is unconsciously expressing loyalty to his or her parents. For example, a son may reject his father's crass materialism, a world in which money means everything and those who don't have money are losers. However, in rejecting this materialism, the son may go to the extreme of being so unmindful of financial matters that he ends up with no money, feeling like a loser—which confirms his father's worldview.

Another negative, unconscious aspect of family life is that of destructive entitlement, whereby a person who was wronged in the past takes it out on people who are innocent—such as current family members. A more healthy response would be for the person to give the very thing that he or she was denied and in so doing restore their his or her to avoid following destructive intergenerational patterns. Nagy describes destructive entitlement and the deep loyalties that family members have as happening at an often unconscious level and in so doing provides another example of how analytic concepts can be expressed and expanded into family systemic terms.

Resistance

Freud described resistance as the forces that impede treatment and recovery. Contemporary analysts tend to think about resistance more in terms of how it may function as a form of hidden or indirect communication. As Nichols and Schwartz say, one of the original defining concepts of family therapy was that of family homeostasis, which means that families, like a home heating system or our own bodies, attempt to maintain constancy of their functioning, and in so doing resist change to their settings. This concept, which can be seen as the systemic equivalent of Freud's ideas of resistance, helps to explain why families appear to become stuck in dysfunctional—but stable—patterns of interaction and resistance in therapy. Furthermore, family homeostasis came out of the work of the early family therapists who were concerned with family communication. These therapists thought that symptoms expressed by individual family members reinforced the family's homeostatic qualities. This aspect of homeostasis is the interpersonal and interactive corollary to the idea of resistance as disguised communication.

For example, a family entered treatment with the chief complaint being that the eldest of their three children, a boy age 14, was about to get expelled from school because he was being disruptive in class and disrespectful toward teachers. Upon further exploration, the counselor found that the boy's behavior may have served to reinforce the family's homeostasis; the boy's acting out (i.e., his symptoms) served at least in part as a way to distract everyone, including the counselor, from the father's problem with drugs and alcohol. The family's tacit agreement that the boy's behavior was the issue (and not the father's drug and alcohol use) could be seen as resistance, both in how it could impede treatment and recovery and in how his behavior was an indirect communication about his family's distress. (In this particular clinical example, the family was aware that more was going on than just the boy's behavior, and it was the boy himself who suggested that attention needed to be paid to the father's drinking. When the focus turned to the father's issues, the boy's behavior improved.)

Transference

Freud described transference as occurring when a client mixes in aspects of past relationships (often those with his father and/or mother) in his present relationship with the client; he originally thought of this as a bad thing but soon came to realize how the negative aspects of transference (e.g., that it is a distortion and non–reality based) are vastly outweighed by the positive aspects, since it can enhance the therapeutic relationship and reproduces, in real time, past relationship patterns that can be examined and worked with therapeutically. It is easy to understand that transference in this sense could be found in a family's reaction to the counselor, with children tending to treat the counselor on a par with and allied with the parental unit and with a father or mother reacting to the counselor out of his or her own relational background. In fact, the intense defensiveness of some parents to a counselor's gentle questioning of their parenting might suggest that the counselor is being reacted to as a kind of scolding superego.

Moreover, as Nichols and Schwartz observe, transference phenomena within the family itself can be further understood in light of the concept, first introduced by Melanie Klein, of projective identification, which has been taken up and developed by many theorists—family therapy theorists among them. Projective identification occurs when one is unable to tolerate aspects of one's self and locates these qualities in other people and, in a crucial interactional addition, is able to cause the object of these projections to behave in conformity with them. In the previous clinical example, the father may have been wrestling with fears of being controlled and told what to do about his drinking and projected those fears upon the boy, who then expressed them as adolescents do by telling off teachers and authority figures. It could be hypothesized that this is what the father was perhaps secretly wishing he could do—tell all the other adults in his life, "You can't make me stop drinking!" (Why would the boy allow himself to be subtly influenced to behave in ways that would get him into trouble? Through the workings of the concept previously discussed, he had invisible loyalty to his dad.)

Countertransference

Countertransference occurs when the counselor reacts to the client out of the counselor's own relational history. One can readily understand that in family and couples counseling, there would be many opportunities to do so. A counselor might identify with a teen who is struggling against a parent's heavy hand in discipline; the counselor may have had overly restrictive parents and might tend to be reactive to the teen's parent. Or a counselor might identify with the teen's father or mother either through the counselor's own experience as a parent or through unconscious identification with his or her own mother or father. A counselor might, in the course of couple treatment, identify with the male or female in opposite-sex relationships or with one of the females or males in same-sex relationships due to the counselor's own adult sexual relationship history (which, in the analytic view, has been greatly impacted by the primary caretaking relationship experienced as an infant and child).

Just as it helped with understanding transference, projective identification is also allied with and helps make sense of countertransference. Sometimes a counselor's reaction to a client might feel strange and possibly even shameful to the counselor. A counselor might, for instance, dread seeing a particular client whom she finds to be boring. Projective identification would say that this client might be deeply fearful that he is so boring and of so little value that other people experience one primary reaction to him: They dread their next encounter with him. Throughout his life, he has been quite good at getting people to confirm these fears by behaving in a dreadfully boring manner. Understanding projective identification could be helpful to the counselor; she could avoid wasting her energy on feeling guilty about her reactions and instead carefully and gently disconfirm his fears and help him to gain strategies to express the interesting and vivid parts of himself, starting in their relationship. Thus projective identification can help the practicing counselor understand countertransferential feelings and use them to help the client rather than simply rejecting them as intolerable and treatment inhibiting.

Why Psychoanalytic Family Therapy Matters

Contemporary psychoanalytic family therapy synthesizes the tradition of classical and relational analysis with the interactional perspective of family systems. It is an approach that combines a complex understanding of individuals and their past and current relationships, with a simple treatment approach by the counselor: Listen closely, think a lot, and say less rather than more. As discussed, a number of prominent family therapy approaches retain distinctive analytic influences, indicating that there is wide latitude available to the counselor in integrating analytic insights into clinical work. Psychoanalytic family therapy enables the counselor to make sense of the fundamental and hidden forces that motivate individuals and families and in the process understand sometimes puzzling and inexplicable behavior on the part of clients in their interactions within their families and in their reactions to the counselor. Finally, analytic family therapy provides resources to counselors to make sense of their own reactions to couples and families and to use them in ways that tend to enhance, rather than damage, their relationships with clients. Counselors can then provide an atmosphere in which the clients can become aware of previously repressed and unexpressed aspects of their experience and work to more fully know their family members and be known by them.

Frederick Redekop and Lauren J. Moss

See also Attachment Theory; Attachment-Based Family Therapy; Contextual Family Therapy; Homeostasis; Imago Relationship Therapy; Object Relations Theory; Resistance; Transgenerational Family Therapy

Further Readings

Boszormenyi-Nagy, I., Grunebaum, J., & Ulrich, D. (1991). Contextual therapy. In A. Gurman & D. Kniskern (Eds.), *Handbook of family therapy: Volume II* (pp. 200–238). New York, NY: Brunner/Mazel.

Bowen, M. (1985). *Family therapy in clinical practice.* New York, NY: Jason Aronson.

Gerson, M. J. (2010). *The embedded self: An integrative psychodynamic and systemic perspective on couples and family therapy.* New York, NY: Routledge.

Goldenberg, H., & Goldenberg, I. (2013). *Family therapy: An overview* (8th ed.). Belmont, CA: Thomson Brooks/Cole.

Greenberg, J. R., & Mitchell, S. A. (1983). *Object relations in psychoanalytic theory.* Cambridge, MA: Harvard.

Nichols, M. P., & Schwartz, R. C. (1998). *Family therapy: Concepts and methods* (4th ed.). Needham Heights, MA: Allyn & Bacon.

Redekop, F. (2015). *Psychoanalytic approaches for counselors.* Thousand Oaks, CA: Sage.

Sharff, D., & Sharff, J. S. (1987). *Object relations family therapy.* New York, NY: Jason Aronson.

Psychobiology of Attachment

Attachment theory is based on the work of the British psychoanalyst John Bowlby (1907–1990), who theorized that the emotional connections infants formed with their early caregivers have significant impacts on their abilities to form future adult relationships. Bowlby described two primary patterns of attachment: (1) secure and (2) insecure. Caregivers of infants who develop secure attachments have consistently met their children's needs and have shown them that it is safe and rewarding to form intimate relationships with others. These infants develop secure relationships with their caregivers and with others in their future adult relationships. In contrast, caregivers of infants who develop insecure patterns of attachment have either neglected or inconsistently met their children's needs. These infants develop ambivalent, avoidant, or disorganized–disoriented relationships with their early caregivers. As adults, they avoid establishing close relationships with others out of a fear that anyone who gets to know them will ultimately not love them and reject them. Until recently, it was believed that the roots of attachment theory were largely based in the environments and situations that infants experienced. More recently, however, research findings supporting the psychobiological roots of attachment have emerged. The purpose of this entry is to provide an overview of the psychobiological influences on attachment theory, highlighting the implications for marriage and family therapy.

The basis of attachment theory lies in the type of emotional bond that infants have with their early caregivers. Up until the mid- to late 1980s, it was believed that this emotional bond began to form only after a child was born. More recent research, however, suggests that this emotional bond begins to form prenatally. This suggests that there are both genetic and environmental influences on the development of attachment styles.

Evidence that supported the psychobiological roots of attachment theory first emerged from twin studies. Twin studies about the psychobiological influences on patterns of attachment have produced varied findings. Some research has shown that the strongest similarities between adults' patterns of attachment were found among identical twins. Other research findings have indicated that genetic inheritance has minimal if any impact on the development of one's pattern of attachment. Additional research has shown that adults with particular genetic predispositions were more likely to have secure patterns of attachment as adults. For example, individuals with higher levels of the hormone oxytocin were more likely to have secure patterns of attachment than individuals with lower levels of oxytocin. Oxytocin is a hormone that plays a role in intimacy and maternal bonding. People with higher levels of oxytocin were also more likely to maintain stable and long-term secure patterns of attachment. Future treatment modalities for insecure patterns of attachment might involve combinations of oxytocin therapy and counseling.

Other researchers have found additional genetic influences on the development of secure patterns of attachment. Dopamine is a chemical messenger in the human brain that plays a role in emotional regulation, along with a variety of other functions. Among individuals who were raised in unsupportive early childhood environments, those with higher levels of dopamine were more likely to have developed secure patterns of attachment in adulthood compared with individuals with lower levels of dopamine. These findings suggest that individuals' patterns of attachment develop from a combination of both environmental and genetic influences.

Implications for Marriage and Family Therapy

A client's pattern of attachment can have a major impact on his or her ability to participate in marriage and family therapy. Individuals who are living with insecure patterns of attachment are significantly less likely to be capable of establishing intimate relationships with their partners and family members. In both marriage and family therapy, clients with very similar early childhood environments have been found to develop different patterns of attachment. It might not be enough for a therapist to consider only the impacts of a client's early childhood environment on the development of his or her pattern of attachment. Marriage and family therapists (MFTs) should consider both the environmental and genetic factors when working with clients who are living with insecure patterns of attachment. Genetic predispositions can offer explanations for why children who grew up in the same or similar environments have developed different patterns of attachment as adults.

Attachment theory has existed for nearly 100 years; however, the etiology and prognosis of patterns of attachment are still being discovered. Until the mid- to late 1980s, it was believed that attachment styles first began to develop only after a child was born. As noted earlier, however, recent research suggests that this emotional bond begins to form prenatally. The findings from the literature are divided about whether or not biological influences directly impact the development of individuals' patterns of attachment. Patterns of attachment appear to develop from a combination of biological and environmental influences.

Further research is needed to identify new and innovative approaches to guide the practice of MFTs who are working with clients who have insecure patterns of attachment. Although still in their infancy, psychobiological treatments for insecure patterns of attachment are likely to become increasingly popular in marriage and family therapy.

Michael T. Kalkbrenner

See also Attachment and Adolescents; Attachment and Health; Attachment and Romantic Love; Attachment Theory; Attachment-Based Family Therapy

Further Readings

Constantino, J. C., Chackes, L., Wartner, U. U., Gross, M. G., Brophy, S. B., Vitale, J. J., & Heath, A. (2006). Mental representations of attachment in identical female twins with and without conduct problems. *Child Psychiatry & Human Development, 37*(1), 65–72.

Raby, K. L., Cicchetti, D., Carlson, E. A., Egeland, B., & Collins, W. A. (2013). Genetic contributions to continuity and change in attachment security: A prospective, longitudinal investigation from infancy to young adulthood. *Journal of Child Psychology and Psychiatry, 54*(11), 1223–1230.

Reiner, I., & Spangler, G. (2010). Adult attachment and gene polymorphisms of the dopamine D4 receptor and serotonin transporter (5-HTT). *Attachment & Human Development, 12*(3), 209–229.

Torgersen, A., Grova, B., & Sommerstad, R. (2007). A pilot study of attachment patterns in adult twins. *Attachment & Human Development, 9*(2), 127–138.

PSYCHOEDUCATION

Psychoeducation refers to therapeutic strategies that are largely preventive, skill-based, and educational in nature. It combines elements of psychology and education as a treatment modality emphasizing teaching and empowerment instead of therapy. Psychoeducation provides education to individuals with substance abuse, psychological disorders, or physical illnesses about their condition, etiology, symptoms, risks, clinical course, and treatment options to facilitate rehabilitation. It fosters resiliency, harnesses strengths, and helps clients gain a sense of control. The goal is to increase the client's knowledge and insight into his or her illness and treatment. In theory, this knowledge should translate into a better understanding of the diagnosis and a greater acceptance of the treatment. The assumption is that this knowledge improves coping, treatment compliance, and recovery. In addition, research suggests that psychoeducation can increase positive treatment outcomes including reducing symptoms, relapse, and treatment noncompliance. Because psychoeducation targets the development of new skills and new ways of thinking, it is a viable treatment modality for couples and family therapists.

In family counseling, psychoeducation can provide the instruction necessary for effective communication, healthy coping, and relational growth. Marriage and family therapists (MFTs) can use psychoeducation interventions across various developmental and educational levels to build skills and to empower couples and families. This entry examines the historical underpinnings of psychoeducation, its specific modality and settings, and its use in group settings. Further consideration is given to the use of psychoeducation in schools and in couples and family counseling, the difference between psychoeducation in child and adult populations, and the risks and benefits of psychoeducation.

Historical Underpinnings

A few published sources credit the military with the founding of psychoeducation because of such practices being used for debriefings and integrating soldiers back into civilian lifestyles after missions and combat. However, much more data suggests that psychoeducation derived from the pressing need to find effective treatment options for patients with serious mental illnesses such as schizophrenia.

Traditionally, individuals with chronic mental illnesses were institutionalized and isolated from mainstream society. In the 1970s, deinstitutionalization reforms shifted thousands of people with debilitating mental illnesses back into communities and families. The Mental Health Centers Act of 1963 proposed that people with chronic mental illnesses should have an opportunity for normalcy through intensive treatment and comprehensive care while residing with their families. Deinstitutionalization was presented as a more humane option for people who had historically endured maltreatment and had their rights trampled. It introduced the notion of community-based care for people with chronic mental illnesses. The deinstitutionalization movement spearheaded the frantic search to improve treatment options for patients and their families. Thus, psychoeducation evolved as a way to empower psychiatric patients and their families to better understand symptoms and to build skills and awareness, which facilitated treatment compliance.

Although medication management has been the primary treatment option for people with schizophrenia, the prognosis continues to be bleak. However, psychoeducation fostered acceptance of treatment options and a greater awareness of the diagnosis and its symptoms. This shift in thinking took an ecological perspective and emphasized the role families played in treatment, recovery, and overall stability. The approach is now used with an array of psychiatric and medical illnesses, including eating disorders, depression, bipolar disorder, obsessive compulsive behaviors, anger management, substance abuse, stress management, cancer, and diabetes.

The late 1950s saw a surge of health care professionals charged with empowering patients on good health habits. Hospitals and health insurance companies conducted health fairs, which were poorly attended and not well received. In time, health newsletters were published and made available at a low cost. These health care publications, which provided a large segment of the population with recent recommendations and current trends in health care, laid the foundations for the passive approaches to psychoeducation seen today (a passive psychoeducational intervention, by definition, is one that provides information, education materials, or advice). Such publications continue to be published by well-known medical centers like Harvard, Johns Hopkins, and the Mayo Clinic. Furthermore, the media (e.g., television, radio, Internet) has ignited the passive movement in psychoeducation. Infomercials, public service announcements, and educational websites (e.g., the Centers for Disease Control and Prevention [CDC] and National Institutes of Health [NIH]) allow millions of listeners and viewers to receive educational information with limited effort.

Modality and Settings

Psychoeducational interventions are usually presented in the form of trainings, workshops, or skill-building opportunities within counseling and therapy sessions such as anger management and stress management. Psychoeducation is a hybrid of an academic class and a counseling group. It can be conducted as a single session or across multiple sessions with therapist-driven instruction and activities to build skills and awareness related to the presenting problem. Psychoeducation interventions can be provided for a variety of ages as well as developmental and educational levels. However, psychoeducation can also be delivered in more passive approaches, such as pamphlets, e-mails, websites, public service announcements, or infomercials.

Undoubtedly, passive psychoeducational interventions are less expensive, are more readily available, reach more people, and disseminate more quickly than traditional workshops or trainings. Thus, more people can be reached faster. Both active and passive psychoeducational interventions have been implemented in various settings, including health, educational, mental health, and social services agencies (e.g., grade schools, hospitals, medical clinics, university student service centers, outpatient mental health clinics, jails, churches, group homes, and community centers). Regardless of whether the approach is active or passive, psychoeducation is aimed at empowering people in their mental and physical health care.

Psychoeducation Groups

When most people think of groups, group therapy is usually what comes to mind. However, there are various types of groups, including (a) group therapy, which helps individuals with acute or chronic mental health issues remediate psychological distress and is aimed at major changes in personality; (b) task or work groups, which are assembled to accomplish a specific task; (c) counseling groups, which help individuals address and problem-solve typical yet difficult life challenges; (d) self-help or support groups, which help members gain camaraderie and learn that others struggle and cope with the same problem; and (e) psychoeducational groups, which focus on skill-building to reduce and/or prevent maladaptive and problematic patterns of behaving.

Psychoeducation groups began as skills training for clients and caregivers. In psychoeducational groups, the group leader serves as a facilitator who sets the intervention goals, teaches new ways of thinking and behaving, and modifies the presentation of information to meet clients' needs. Psychoeducational groups may incorporate direct instruction and behavioral rehearsals to build problem-solving, decision-making, anger management, and communication and social skills. This approach is behavioral; it teaches specific skills, replacement behaviors, and coping strategies.

In psychoeducational groups, the role of the group facilitator is that of a content expert who teaches new skills, models strategies, gives specific advice, and facilitates learning experiences and activities. Psychoeducational groups tend to be more structured. Topics may vary from week to week (e.g., communication skills in week one and conflict resolution in week two). Psychoeducational groups incorporate more activities and opportunities for practice than any other group model. In addition, the duration of treatment is typically shorter, but the length of sessions is usually longer in psychoeducational groups. For instance, a psychoeducational group may run from 6 to 20 weeks with 90-minute sessions as opposed to 45-minute group counseling sessions. Psychoeducation can be used with diverse cultural and ethnic groups and can be adapted to a number of presentation formats.

Psychoeducation in Schools

Additionally, psychoeducation refers to those psychological supports, services, and interventions provided in academic settings such as high schools, elementary schools, alternative or therapeutic schools, early childhood programs, and adult transitional programs for students ages 18 to 21 with severe cognitive and developmental disabilities. School psychology is a dynamic branch of applied professional psychology concerned with students' social, emotional, behavioral, cognitive, and academic growth and development. Thus, assessments conducted by school psychologists are often called "psychoeducational evaluations" because the evaluation focuses largely on the student's functioning in an educational or vocational setting.

In school settings, psychoeducational assessments are concerned with how intellectual, social, emotional, neuropsychological, behavioral, speech/language, motor (e.g., fine, gross, visual-motor), hearing, and vision as well as the physical health and developmental functioning of a student impacts his or her learning. Overall, psychoeducational assessments measure psychological constructs such as intelligence, aptitude, achievement, emotions, and behaviors. For instance, in a school setting, if the presenting problem or reason for referral is opposition, the school psychologist or school social worker might conduct classroom observations; consult with parents and teachers; interview the student; and/or administer behavior rating scales to determine the purpose of the behavior, triggers, and reinforcers as well as mitigating or environmental factors contributing to the frequency and intensity of the behavior. School-based assessments identify strengths, giftedness, deficits, and disabilities that affect achievement and adaptive skills. This information is typically used to guide academic and behavioral interventions, train and support educators, identify appropriate resources and services, and qualify or remove students for special education services. Thus, in school settings, psychoeducation refers specifically to school-based psychological support, services, assessments, and interventions.

Family Psychoeducation

Family psychoeducation (FPE) refers to a therapeutic model where clinicians partner with clients and their respective families to treat serious mental illnesses such as schizophrenia, bipolar disorder, major depression, obsessive-compulsive disorder (OCD), and borderline personality disorder. FPE differs from traditional family therapy in that the *illness* is the focus of treatment and intervention and *not the client*.

As such, clinicians use FPE to partner with clients and families to support recovery through information and education. The essential components of FPE include the following: (a) practice information and education about the illness including symptoms and treatment options, (b) resources and referrals, (c) guidance and skills training, (d) social and emotional support, and (e) problem-solving the many complexities that arise from managing a serious mental illness.

In FPE, clients and their families learn about their illness; identify strengths and resources; and plan goals for empowerment, treatment, and recovery. The main tasks for clinicians are to build working relationships (e.g., nonjudgmental, mutual respect, trust, genuineness, active listening) and offer concrete help. The main therapeutic approaches are workshops, which may use curricula- or evidence-based practices (EBPs) to provide information and resources. FPE can be provided in a single-family or multifamily format. Additionally, FPE is not a brief treatment modality. Instead, it is recommended that FPE be implemented for at least 9 months to promote positive outcomes such as fewer relapses or hospitalizations. Other positive outcomes for the client and families include increased knowledge and awareness and decreased feelings of confusion, isolation, and stress as well as a decrease in the use of acute care for medical or psychological issues.

Psychoeducation in Couples and Family Counseling

Most MFTs would agree that intimate relationships begin to falter because of a loss: a loss of satisfaction, a loss of compassion or empathy, or a loss of dedication toward staying together. In many instances, couples and families can be helped through psychoeducation. The most popular uses of psychoeducation in family treatment center on physical or mental illnesses. For example, families who have a loved one with bipolar disorder, borderline personality disorder, schizophrenia, alcoholism, or posttraumatic stress disorder (PTSD) would participate in psychoeducation to learn about symptoms, prognosis, and treatment as well as identify resources as a sort of "survival skills workshop."

However, psychoeducation as a treatment modality has expanded beyond disease management. In less severe cases, psychoeducation provides families with the necessary information and skills to address couple interactions, parent–child relations, sibling dynamics, and overall familial well-being. Psychoeducation for distressed families and couples can help families regain control, identify resiliency factors, enhance familial relationships, improve couples communication, and build effective parenting skills. MFTs who employ psychoeducation as their primary approach or infuse it into an eclectic modality offer education and skills development directed at alleviating stress, improving positive coping skills, resolving conflicts, and promoting healthy family relations. Although FPE may not resemble traditional family therapy models, the role of the clinician is still to join the family, establish an alliance with each member, remain neutral, and assess for strengths and options for positive therapeutic outcomes.

Marriage and family psychoeducational groups are strengths-based and educationally focused. Psychoeducational groups are focused on education, acceptance, skill-building, and environmental changes. The approach is rooted in a cognitive-behavioral framework with the premise that information and instruction can change thoughts and feelings, which will ultimately improve behavioral outcomes. There is a substantial body of empirical evidence for psychoeducational groups that address domestic violence, parent training, marriage and couples enrichment, and families with members diagnosed with severe medical or mental health issues. Multifamily psychoeducational groups that center on disease management are based on several assumptions and guiding principles, including (a) the family members of a person with a serious medical or mental illness need information, assistance, and support; (b) the attitude and behavior of relatives toward the family member with a serious medical or mental health issue affect the individual's well-being and recovery; (c) a benefit in combining elements, such as education and consultation, with cognitive-behavioral strategies, problem-solving skills, and strategies for healthy coping; (d) improvement in therapeutic outcomes by addressing and involving family members; and

(e) groups being facilitated by a mental health professional. The group process includes creating a safe space for instruction, exploration, and support; normalizing and validating the family's experience; rebuffing stigmas; creating a sense of hope through shared experiences; and socializing with others outside of the family who are coping with the same issue.

Psychoeducation for Children

Psychoeducation can be a viable treatment approach for clients across demographic, developmental, and educational strata specifically because group leaders can tailor the information presented to the audience. It has been used as a treatment option for children struggling with anxiety disorders, attention-deficit/hyperactivity disorder (ADHD), eating disorders, disruptive behavior disorders, and bipolar disorder to aide with symptom management, healthy coping, resiliency, and overall treatment compliance. Psychoeducation methods include awareness and skill-building through activities such as direct instruction, educational videos, role-playing, informative readings, and/or group discussions. Because psychoeducation interventions can target both children and parents, it can improve parenting skills as well as familial communication and interactions.

Risks, Benefits, and Special Considerations

In psychoeducation, the group leader is a facilitator who provides clients and their families with illness-specific information and strategies for managing related circumstances. The leader provides information and then facilitates discussion by soliciting comments and reactions from the group. Thus, the leader must be able to educate the group as well as employ sound counseling techniques such as validating feelings, normalizing experiences, empathizing, and engaging in active listening.

Psychoeducation differs from traditional individual and group therapy; it focuses on empowerment and skill-building as a competency-based approach to family therapy, mental health stability, and/or physical rehabilitation. Psychoeducational groups target clients who are functioning relatively well but have a deficit in knowledge, skills, and awareness. Some examples of psychoeducational interventions might include a group of middle school students learning about the harmful effects of drugs, women learning assertive behaviors, teenage mothers learning parenting skills, individuals with HIV/AIDS learning about resources and medication management, supervisors of a company learning tools for human performance improvement, or people with diabetes learning about diet and nutrition.

Psychoeducation is grounded in the present reality of a condition. It is well meshed with theories such as ecological systems theory, learning theories, and cognitive-behavioral approaches. Psychoeducation can be implemented as a single session, as a series of group interventions, or within a counseling or therapy session. If the old adage that *knowledge is power* is correct, then psychoeducation is relatively harmless. However, knowledge and awareness of the etiology, clinical course, and prognosis of one's condition can also fuel depressive symptoms such as despondent moods, excessive shame and guilt, or a sense of helplessness and hopelessness that may require additional support and interventions. As well, psychoeducation addresses neither the underlying causes of maladaptive thoughts and behaviors for people who abuse drugs nor the root causes of distress for people struggling with relapse patterns or anger management.

As well, with any treatment modality, special attention and consideration should be given to the cultural, ethnic, and religious backgrounds of the clients receiving the psychoeducation intervention. A culturally competent clinician will give adequate care and consideration to the materials, information, and methods of delivery to avoid offending, stereotyping, or overlooking personal or resiliency factors important to individuals targeted by the intervention.

Tasha Leroyce Banks

See also Anger Management; Empowerment in Families; Marriage Education; Presenting Problems; Schizophrenia and Families; Stress Management; Therapeutic Alliance; Trust; Work Relationships

Further Readings

Brown, N. W. (2011). *Psychoeducational groups: Process and practices* (3rd ed.). New York, NY: Routledge.

Carlson, J., & Sperry, L. (Eds.). (1999). *The intimate couple.* Ann Arbor, MI: Edwards Brothers.

Delucia-Waack, J. L. (2006). *Leading psychoeducational groups for children and adolescents.* Thousand Oaks, CA: Sage.

Gehart, D. (2014). *Mastering competencies in family therapy: A practical approach to theories and clinical case documentation* (2nd ed.). Belmont, CA: Brooks/Cole.

Gehart, D. (2016). *Theory and treatment planning in family therapy: A competency-based approach.* Boston, MA: Cengage.

Goldenberg, H., & Goldenberg, I. (2008). *Family therapy: An overview* (8th ed.). Belmont, CA: Thomson Brooks/Cole.

Jacobs, E. E., Masson, R. L., & Harvill, R. L. (1998). *Group counseling: Strategies and skills* (3rd ed.). Pacific Grove, CA: Brooks/Cole.

Kotze, C., King, M. P., & Joubert, P. M. (2008). What do patients with psychotic and mood disorders know about their illness and medication? *South African Journal of Psychiatry, 14*(3), 84–90.

Lukens, E. P., & McFarlane, W. R. (2004). Psychoeducation as evidence-based practice: Considerations for practice, research and policy. *Brief Treatment and Crisis Intervention, 4,* 205–225. Retrieved from http://btci.edina.clockss.org/cgi/reprint/4/3/205.pdf

O'Donohue, W., & Cummings, N. A. (Eds.). (2008). *Evidence-based adjunctive treatment.* Burlington, MA: Elsevier.

Robbins, M., Sexton, T., & Weeks, G. (Eds.). (2003). *Handbook of family therapy: The science and practice of working with families and couples.* New York, NY: Brunner-Routledge.

Public Health Code

Individual states enact legislation that provides policies and procedures for each state on how to prevent and control disabilities and diseases. Such legislation is referred to collectively as the public health code or codes. Additionally, since such legislation is state driven, specific legislation provides policy on how funding is managed, any appropriations that are necessary, and sanctions for those in violation of this code. This code works in collaboration with other departmental codes such as those developed for elderly people, those with mental illness or developmental disabilities, and veterans, to name just a few. Most public health codes call for the development and running of the Department of Public Health at the state level and local levels. Additionally, they provide information about how board or cabinet members are selected and what parameters their various actions allow. Oftentimes, the public health code is looked upon by practitioners to signify elements of ethical practice and to determine what constitutes best and empirically based practices. This entry provides a brief history of public health, mental health stigma, the intersection of mental health and public health, and advocacy efforts related to public health.

Brief History of Public Health

Public health treatment in the United States dates back to the 18th century with the development of a federal network of hospitals to help sick and disabled merchant seamen. In the early 20th century, the public health service was developed. The public health service, in disseminating authority back to the states, led to the development of state and local community boards of health. With these changes came the development of the public health codes that were more specifically focused on the environment and societal problems in the given regions.

Public health in the United States started out dealing with problems related to sanitation and other environmental concerns relating to illness.

As the science of public health increased, so did the opportunities for practitioners. With this increase in knowledge came a shift in perspective focusing more on individual change that was society driven. Throughout its history, public health has evolved from utilizing a reactive perspective of dealing with disease to more of a preventive model. This preventive model of treatment is supported by the public health codes. Currently targeted prevention areas of public health include areas such as tobacco usage, HIV, vaccinations, lead poisoning, and to a somewhat lesser extent mental health though the preventive idea of mental health treatment does appear to be further evolving over time.

The development of public health has filtered down to each state calling for public health services across their states and providing needed services and coverage. The public health codes that have developed in differing states provide a sense of vision in terms of what is expected and possible. Besides these factors, the public health code has been intertwined with the code of ethics for public health, which calls for the ethical treatment and practice of public health as a profession and as a science. The 20th century was a very important period of time for public health and the further development and refinement of public health codes. Through a consolidated effort, the human life expectancy increased by more than 20 years over that of the century before. Additionally, through vaccinations, the incidences of various diseases were significantly reduced.

Mental Health Stigma

Historically, people with mental illness have long been subject to social stigma. The development of public health codes and the treatment of mental illness being recognized as a disease to some extent has helped to lessen this stigma. Additionally, bringing the concepts of mental illness, as well as the types of mental illness and methods of treatment, to the forefront has had a positive impact on public awareness and acceptance.

Mental Health and Public Health: A Unified Approach

Within the past 25 years, the divide between public health and mental health has become less obvious, and more of a concentrated approach of prevention, treatment, and advocacy has come to the forefront. The public health code has supported these efforts through funding and appropriations to mental health agencies that support prevention, treatment, and relapse in a similar fashion to public health agencies and medical maladies. It is expected that as time continues, further integration of both the public health community and the mental health community will continue with mutual support and professional respect for one another. An early example of this integration is seen in the Ticket to Work and Work Incentive Act of 1999. This act allowed for Americans with disabilities to enter the workforce without losing their Medicaid and Medicare benefits.

As the public health community expands further and engages more with the mental health community, it will be imperative for the public health codes to support the development and refinement of best practices. These practices not only help individuals but also take on the larger masses of people impacted. This may include the working of medical and mental health practitioners regularly within the same practices and having access to the same resources.

Advocacy Efforts

Taking into account the public health code and the established standards, these standards have allowed for advocacy efforts to increase as public health and mental health become further integrated. A recent example of these advocacy efforts may be seen in the Affordable Care Act, which put into place comprehensive insurance reform impacting both health and mental health care. Additionally, this connection between the public health community and the mental health community has allowed for a more positive perspective to be shared, which is more impactful because of the larger governmental agency reach and support. The more differing agencies work in collaboration and challenge each other to find better and more economical treatment modalities, the more influential the code of public health will become.

Neil E. Duchac

See also Mental Health, Systemic Perspective

Further Readings

Centers for Disease Control and Prevention. (1999). *History*. Retrieved October 3, 2013, from http://www.cdc.gov/about/history/ourstory.htm

Centers for Disease Control and Prevention. (2014, February). *Mental health overview*. Retrieved June 1, 2014, from http://www.cdc.gov/mentalhealth

World Health Organization. (2001). *The world health report 2001. Mental health: New understandings, new hope*. Geneva, Switzerland: Author.

Punctuation

Punctuation refers to a human ability to organize the continuous flow of experience into stories made up of interaction sequences with clear beginning and end points. Identified in the 1940s by Gregory Bateson during his development of a systemic description of human communication, the idea that people punctuate the same experiences differently provides both a way of making sense of misunderstandings and a basis for designing interventions. This entry offers a brief history of punctuation; distinguishes among different understandings of punctuation; and describes ways of helping couples, families, and professionals free themselves from rigid, ineffective patterns of punctuation.

Paul Watzlawick and his colleagues in the 1960s built on Bateson's foundation, describing punctuation as one of five axioms that described the most important aspect of human communication and its problems. They explained that an outsider who observes a stream of communication may not understand the participants' experience because of not knowing how they are interpreting the interaction. Participants' designations of beginning and end points in interaction sequences happen without awareness and have powerful implications.

To illustrate this process, we can look at an ongoing relationship in which a statement has been punctuated by Partner A as the beginning of a sequence—"Have you seen my keys?" At the same time, the same utterance may have been punctuated by Partner B as the midpoint of another sequence, which began with "Are you ready yet?" and involved exchanges about getting ready for an outing. If the communication sequence escalates to a crisis point, Partner B says, "Forget it, we're not going." Partner A may respond by saying, "All I did was ask about my keys." Partner B may then ask, "I was already mad because you forgot about the appointment." This might lead Partner A to say, "I was so flustered by your anger that I couldn't remember where I put my keys."

This example shows punctuation in action, as the partners move beyond the content level of conversation to what Watzlawick and colleagues referred to as metacommunication about their relationship. A particularly problematic kind of metacommunication explains some events as having been caused by other events. Family systems theorists suggest that such explanations, which they characterize as representing linear causality, are invalid when applied to human relationships. They contend that human systems are characterized instead by circular causality—one event can cause another while at the same time being caused by it. For example, couples often demonstrate the circular pattern "I withdraw because you are so critical of me" and "I criticize you because I am trying to get a response from you." Such patterns defy understanding when examined in linear terms. The partners' error of rigidly believing their competing punctuations helps to keep them stuck in their familiar positions.

Beginning in the early 1980s, the discourse in the family therapy field began to emphasize constructivist ideas introduced by Brad Keeney and others. Constructivism challenges beliefs in an objective reality and suggests that people know the world only through their representations of reality. From a constructivist perspective, then, representations do not only describe problems but become problems. Participants may utilize words and idioms that imply intentionality and/or causality, or they may use words and metaphors that exaggerate and/or alter the feelings and other impacts of interactions. But representations are often problematic in the distinctions they draw—in the ways in which they group phenomena into categories. In Keeney's usage of the word, punctuation had a broader meaning that referred to any process of drawing distinctions.

More recently, the constructivist perspective was extended by social constructionist understandings. Within this broadened perspective, illustrated in the work of Carlos Sluzki, the concept of punctuation continues to have relevance as it can describe the ways in which causal explanations of overlapping and simultaneous sequences are *socially* constructed by professionals and clients through narrative processes. Social constructionists, influenced by the work of Michel Foucault, call attention to unequal levels of power in relationships (and larger social systems) that result in some constructions being the preferred versions of a relational story. Punctuations that blame less powerful participants and elevate more powerful participants are more likely to survive, and efforts to challenge the pattern of dominance and exploitation are likely to be short-lived. This perspective has been applied to interactions among professionals and professional groups, demonstrating that they offer competing punctuations of phenomena such as anorexia, suicide, and affairs.

At the level of intervention, the original concept of punctuation can help a practitioner to gain some distance from stories as they are told. With an enhanced outsider perspective, the practitioner has the option of challenging patterns of punctuation. Such challenges can create a conversational space in which participants can imagine alternative stories that would locate cause and effect differently and allow participants to break out of their maladaptive patterns.

In its broadened usages, the concept of punctuation as describing all distinctions helps professionals normalize their clients' differences and help them step away from the goal of total agreement. A constructionist perspective suggests that many problems are exacerbated by rigid representations that are supported by cultures, languages, religions, and other social groups. With an awareness of the inevitability of different punctuations, relationships can be improved as participants adopt conversational patterns that acknowledge and value participants' different ways of understanding.

At a larger systems level, Sluzki and others have challenged family therapists to recognize distinctions and causal models embedded in their professional discourses and understand how they may participate in the oppression of groups and individuals. That recognition can provide a basis for collective efforts to directly challenge oppressive social systems.

Thomas W. Blume

See also Circularity and Linearity; Communication Errors/Problems in Couples and Families; Metacommunication; Social Constructionism; Systems Theory

Further Readings

Foucault, M. (1972). The discourse on language (R. Swyer, Trans.). In M. Foucault, *The archaeology of language and the discourse on language* (pp. 215–237). New York, NY: Pantheon.

Keeney, B. P. (1982). What is an epistemology of family therapy? *Family Process, 21*, 153–168.

Sluzki, C. E. (1992). Transformations: A blueprint for narrative changes in therapy. *Family Process, 31*, 217–230.

Watzlawick, P., Bavelas, J. B., & Jackson, D. D. (1967). *Pragmatics of human communication.* New York, NY: W. W. Norton.

Qualitative Research

Qualitative research is a form of methodology that draws its origin from various disciplines in social sciences and humanities, including philosophy, anthropology, sociology, and linguistics. These interdisciplinary influences account for multiple contexts and frameworks that provide a strong foundation for an epistemology that directs diverse methodologies classed as "qualitative." In fact, while qualitative research methods continue to evolve and change, an awareness of the origins of qualitative research is helpful for understanding its fundamental premises. This entry describes specific characteristics of the methods gathered under the umbrella of what today we call a qualitative methodology. There are commonalities between how one does marriage and family therapy and qualitative research. Finally, the entry discusses the parallels between the intent of qualitative inquiry and family therapy against the background of systems theory and postmodernism.

Here, one prominent influence is the postpositivist philosophical stance articulated by such thinkers as Karl Popper and Thomas Kuhn. On this view, researchers cannot afford to ignore such considerations as the relativity of human understanding, which rests on the principle that the facts accumulated by a researcher are never neutral, since they have been influenced by the values and beliefs of the person who accumulated the data. Thus, attention must be given to a multiplicity of viewpoints, and dialogue presents an opportunity to reach a better understanding of any particular phenomenon. Additionally, since the observer recognizes the absence of neutrality, particular consideration is given to recognizing potential biases on the part of the researcher, including an attempt to expand one's point of view through diverse interactions with others.

Such a postpositivist philosophical framework provides the foundation for diverse qualitative methodologies and for qualitative inquiry in general, which is often characterized by an emphasis on multiple perspectives and multiple voices. Hence the necessity to ensure multiple sources of data; the focus on the interpretive nature of data analysis, preferring inductive methods; the tentative nature of findings, allowing consideration of multiple meanings that might be generated by the data collected; and inclusions of concepts such as reflexivity and subjectivity, since the researcher is perceived as the main instrument for data collection and analysis.

While the postpositivist philosophical framework presents the unifying ground for qualitative inquiry, there are a variety of existing qualitative methodologies that differ in terms of research strategies and research designs. Some examples of existing approaches include those of narrative, phenomenology, grounded theory, ethnography, and case studies. Each methodology can be considered within a specific discipline. For example, ethnography has deep roots in the field of anthropology, while phenomenology is characterized by its connection to the fields of psychology and philosophy. It is important to consider various traditions supporting the methodologies, since they set the tone for the methods available within this particular approach and thereby predetermine a particular fit with a specific research question that a researcher seeks to clarify. For example, grounded theory—whose roots are in sociology—provides specific tools to generate an inductive theory based on the collected data, while narrative research—whose origins are in literature, history, and anthropology—provides a better opportunity to examine the life experience of a particular individual.

One important characteristic that applies to all forms of qualitative designs is their emergent nature. Therefore, the research process can be modified in the process of data collection to accommodate the need to learn about the phenomenon in the most accurate possible way. This "stretching" of the research methodology constitutes an important characteristic of the qualitative research design, allowing the researcher to use multiple ways to craft the research. In fact, while some researchers choose to design a specific qualitative strategy, others prefer to follow a generic perspective, guided by the general principles of qualitative methodology. Although design-informed researchers have to operate in line with the chosen theoretical and practical viewpoint, generic researchers have to be mindful to develop and maintain the coherent nature of their research process.

Independent of the chosen design, qualitative research is usually united by specific premises that guide a researcher to choose this type of inquiry:

- Based on its descriptive nature, it is often used as the first step in a better understanding of a particular phenomenon: It helps researchers generate new insights and hypotheses.
- The data are often generated in a word rather than numeric format.
- The data collection and data analysis are often completed simultaneously.
- Data trustworthiness is often built on the input from an outside reviewer—for example, peer debriefing (reviewing a study with someone who is not participating in the initial design and data collection); member checking (involving participants in the review of the collected data).

Whatever the chosen approach, some qualitative designs call for the explicit use of a particular theoretical lens that positions the scientific inquiry and helps to clarify the context of the study as well as the stance of the researcher. Such theories might include but are not limited to postmodernism or social constructionism (under the umbrella of postmodern theories), feminist theories, critical theory, queer theory, or disability theory.

Qualitative Methodology and Marriage and Family Therapy

The field of marriage and family therapy stands on the shoulders of systems-based theories that started to emerge with Paul A. Weiss and Ludwig von Bertalanffy and were further developed in the 1950s, 1960s, and 1970s through the work of researchers from various disciplines, such as chemist Ilya Prigogine, biologist Humberto Maturana, linguist Béla Bánáthy, anthropologist Gregory Bateson, and many others. One of the fundamental characteristics of systems thinking is the recognition that the whole is greater than the sum of its parts, meaning that for a better understanding of a phenomenon the emphasis should be placed on the exploration of diverse relationships among different levels of the system rather than on the ultimate outcome of the final product of this relationship. For example, in order to start understanding why one member of a family might be experiencing depression, a therapist should explore multiple interactions among various members of this family.

This fundamental premise illustrates the importance of exploring multiple perspectives of diverse individuals involved in a particular conversation and emphasizes the necessity to pay particularly close attention to the environment or the context where this situation is occurring. For example, if a particular family enters therapy, each family member will be involved in a conversation to elucidate his or her understanding of the family's particular situation. In addition, various backgrounds and specific transitional points in the family life will be accounted as indissoluble pieces of this family's life mosaic.

It is evident that a qualitative researcher adopts a similar stance: In the process of data collection the researcher seeks to engage multiple participants and explore the variety of their viewpoints. In addition, in the process of data analysis the researcher invites and accounts for multiple voices, including those of participants, researchers and coresearchers, transcribers, outside reviewers, and other contributors.

Another important connection between the foundations of family therapy and qualitative research methodology is their common evolution toward the incorporation of important tenets of postmodern approaches. Postmodernism, and more specifically social constructionism, brings forward the consideration of language as an important tool of human interaction and transformation used not to *explore* meanings, but rather to *construct* new meanings in the process of a dialogue. This conceptualization of language shifts the focus in therapy from "helping" and "treating" to "listening" and "understanding": Through appreciative and empathetic listening, accompanied with respective curiosity, the therapist hopes to create a process of change.

The whole course of therapy is also influenced by the position of a therapist vis-à-vis the clients who are attending the session. The therapist is not aiming to adopt a neutral stance or objectively observe the family; rather, he is engaging in a continuous examination of his values and biases. This therapeutic position is heavily influenced by second-order cybernetics: Not only can the observer not escape her own frame of references, but the connection between the observer and the observed is valued as an important part of a therapeutic intervention.

In the same way, qualitative research conducted in the realm of postmodern theories is consciously oriented toward a crafted ability to engage both the researcher and the participants in the shared coconstruction of meaning where the researcher is constantly looking to adopt a self-appraising stance. Adopting a not-knowing position, the researcher approaches the data collection process open not only to the possibility of defining new meanings, but even to a possibility of modifying the research design in order to accommodate the participants (often called co-investigators) and create the most trusting research atmosphere. After all, it is important to keep in mind that in the midst of a qualitative inquiry, participants often share the most intimate stories of their lives, entrusting the researcher to elucidate the most accurate representation of the phenomenon from multiple perspectives (including the viewpoints of co-investigators).

Qualitative methodologies' data collection and analysis have been organized to ensure the expansion of meanings. In this process the researcher aims to join and accommodate the participants' interviewing style; explore various perspectives by engaging multiple participants and creating open-ended questions; move forward slowly while remaining curious about each utterance; and respect silence, allowing participants to reflect on what has been shared. While analyzing the data, a qualitative researcher remains dubious about the "final" character of the research findings, often discovering new aspects with each data interaction, and finally choosing to present the most representative picture of acquired descriptions. Such an interactive aspect often comes from the fact that a qualitative researcher (similar to a family therapist) is continuously engaged in the process of self-reflection. In fact, such self-examination becomes part of the data collection and data examination, ultimately and openly influencing the end product of the study.

Because researchers are considered the main instruments of the study, they are encouraged to engage in the process of reflexivity to examine what was the thought process that led them to certain conclusions and how their historical and sociocultural backgrounds offered a particular lens though which the data were considered and interpreted. In the same way, the process of reflexivity remains important throughout a therapeutic relationship; accordingly, researchers are encouraged to remain reflective as long as they remain engaged with the data. Similarly, as different therapeutic approaches present different tools for self-retrospection and self-reflection, qualitative research methodologies offer specific methods to engage in that process (e.g., memo writing, peer debriefing, or member checking).

After examining both family therapy and qualitative research principles, it is clear that both processes can be empowering and therapeutic for participants. Despite some unique features of any research process that tends to be more descriptive, and some distinctive principles of a therapeutic approach that is designed to produce change, it can easily be seen how they are interconnected: Research can become therapeutic, and a therapeutic encounter can become part of a larger research conversation. Marriage and family therapy practitioners can gain a great advantage through the use of these research methodologies, which seem to align with many of the fundamental principles of systems-based approaches.

Yulia Watters

See also Circularity and Linearity; Collaborative Language Systems; Postmodern Therapies; Social Constructionism; Systemic Family Therapy

Further Readings

Anderson, H. (2005). Myths about not knowing. *Family Process, 44*(4), 479–504.

Becvar, D. S., & Becvar, R. J. (1999). *Systems theory and family therapy: A primer.* New York: University Press of America.

Charmaz, K. (2006). *Constructing grounded theory: A practical guide through qualitative analysis.* Thousand Oaks, CA: Sage.

Chenail, R. J. (2005). Future directions in qualitative methods. In D. H. Sprenkle & F. Piercy (Eds.), *Research methods in family therapy* (pp. 191–211). New York: Guilford.

Creswell, J. W. (2007). *Qualitative inquiry and research design: Choosing among five approaches.* Thousand Oaks, CA: Sage.

Creswell, J. W. (2009). *Research design.* Thousand Oaks, CA: Sage.

De Haene, L. (2010). Beyond division: Convergences between postmodern qualitative research and family therapy. *Journal of Marital and Family Therapy, 36*(1), 1–12.

Williams, L., Patterson, J., & Edwards, T. M. (2014). *Clinician's guide to research methods in family therapy.* New York: Guilford.

Quantitative Research

Quantitative research is systematic investigation of directly observable behavior (e.g., how much someone eats, how many cigarettes someone smokes) or indirectly assessed phenomena (e.g., intelligence, love, perceptions) using numeric data. The purpose of quantitative research is to test theories about how phenomena are related. This is accomplished by testing relationships among variables represented with numbers using statistical analysis. Quantitative research methods are based in the belief that there is an objective reality to be discovered and known. In order to investigate and know that world, researchers must remain as distant and objective as possible. Typically, numbers are assigned to participant responses or observations, and those numbers are analyzed with statistical programs like Statistical Package for the Social Sciences (SPSS). Within the field of marriage, family, and couples counseling, quantitative research helps clinicians and researchers understand many phenomena related to familial relationships, relational functioning, and counseling outcomes. With the rise of the managed care industry the need for empirically supported treatments also has increased. Quantitative research has been important in establishing and supporting the effectiveness of counseling. It is also ethical to ensure that counselors are not offering treatments that do not work or are potentially harmful. This entry provides a basic overview of quantitative research designs and briefly reviews the ways in which quantitative research is used in marriage, family, and couples counseling.

Types of Quantitative Designs

Research can be done from a quantitative or qualitative perspective; some research designs incorporate both. A quantitative perspective uses numbers to quantify the subject of study and to see if there are numerical differences between groups participating in the research. Quantitative research includes using surveys, observation, tests, and other forms of numerical data collection. Qualitative research, by contrast, tends to be more exploratory—seeking to understand phenomena in terms of ideas and concepts, rather than from a numerical perspective. Although both types of research are useful in understanding the world, this entry focuses on quantitative methods. There are many types of quantitative designs, the most typical of which are experimental, descriptive, and meta-analysis.

Experimental Research

Experimental designs examine cause-and-effect relationships. This kind of research helps counselors to examine the effects of a given type of treatment or intervention. It is useful in evaluating therapy or programs. For example, if a community counseling center offers an anger management class, it may want to evaluate how effective its program is in decreasing aggressive behavior of the participants. Experimental research is also used to compare treatment models for a particular problem, such as comparing cognitive-behavioral therapy and strategic family therapy for the treatment of couples' distress.

Experimental research can be cross-sectional or longitudinal in nature. In cross-sectional research, data are collected and analyzed from one point in time. In longitudinal research, data are collected and analyzed over multiple time points, allowing researchers to look at changes in a phenomenon over time. If researchers were examining the effectiveness of structural family therapy for the treatment of adolescent behavioral problems; collecting data before, during, and after treatment; and analyzing the data across those three time points, this would be an example of longitudinal design. Analyzing data from only one of those time points would be cross-sectional.

Descriptive Research

Descriptive research is nonexperimental in nature. Data are collected without experimental manipulation for the purpose of describing a population or a phenomenon. Descriptive research allows counselors to understand characteristics of populations and see changes in trends. For example, it may be used to understand characteristics of licensed professional counselors. Are they mostly women? Do most have a doctoral degree? What ethnicities are represented, and at what rates? Knowing about the population of counselors can help in program recruitment to increase diversity and also help in designing counselor training.

Investigating relationships among variables (correlational research) is also considered descriptive. With correlational research we can answer such questions as these: Is there a significant relationship between gender and degree level? Is there a significant relationship between age and clients who seek counseling services? Results from correlational research can also help improve many facets of counselor training, as well as services provided to clients.

Meta-Analysis

Meta-analysis is used to summarize findings across a large number of quantitative studies on the same topic (e.g., effectiveness of counseling interventions). It provides an estimate of the cumulative effect across studies, as if only one study had been conducted. Across studies main findings are converted into an effect size, which is independent of the measures used in the study and can readily be combined across studies. This is useful because most studies utilize samples with different characteristics. It also contributes to increased generalizability of findings because the more studies combined, the more closely the total sample will approximate the population being studied. Meta-analyses provide counselors with information about which clinical interventions work, and with whom. They also contribute to evidence-based practice literature.

Meta-analyses are important in integrating research on the effectiveness of therapy approaches across studies. Effect size is one way of doing that. Effect size is an indication of the size of the treatment effect. This extends beyond statistical significance, which only determines if there is a significant difference. Just knowing that a treatment had a significant effect does not tell researchers very much. If that effect was rather small, it may indicate a treatment is not as effective as one with a larger treatment effect.

Studying the Effectiveness of Therapy and Counseling

Efficacy research is the investigation of whether a treatment produces the intended effect, under ideal circumstances. It is conducted in a highly controlled environment. Once efficacy has been established, effectiveness research can be done to see if the treatment also works under real-life conditions and determine the effect size of that treatment. Treatments that produce larger effect sizes are more helpful than those with small effect sizes.

Randomized Clinical Trials

Randomized clinical trials are considered the gold standard of effectiveness research. Modeled after medical and pharmaceutical research, randomized clinical trials examine, in the most controlled manner possible, whether therapy is effective. They provide evidence for causal relationships between therapy and client outcomes. They are best utilized in conjunction with other kinds of research, such as process research. Typically, participants with some specified clinical problem (e.g., couples dysfunction) are randomly assigned to the control group (no therapy) or treatment group (therapy condition). Each group is measured pre- and postintervention on a specified outcome measure (e.g., a measure of marital satisfaction) and compared after treatment. (Here, it would be hypothesized that the treatment group would have statistically significant higher improvements in marital satisfaction.)

Quantitative Helpful Factors

The term *helpful factors* refers to research that focuses on factors that contribute to better counseling outcomes. There are quantitative and qualitative approaches to this type of research. Typically, when done quantitatively it involves counting the number of times a specific event or set of events happens in a counseling session (e.g., behaviors indicating strong therapeutic alliance), and seeing if this is significantly related to session outcomes. It can be quasi-experimental (similar to an experiment, but does not have randomized assignment of participants to an intervention group, or no intervention group), by just observing what happens in sessions without researcher intervention; or it can be experimental, in which researchers ask counselors to change the way they do therapy or something specific.

Common Factors

Quantitative research has been essential in establishing a new paradigm of thinking about how change occurs in therapy. In the traditional paradigm, change was thought to occur because of the unique contributions of models of therapy. The common-factors paradigm posits that change occurs through a set of common factors and mechanisms of change, present in most models of couples and family therapy. Meta-analyses across studies of the effectiveness of therapy have contributed to the evidence based on common factors.

Family Research

Psychometrics

Psychometrics, referring to the use of instruments for psychological measurement, are important in both quantitative research and clinical practice. Many different instruments have been developed to assist clinicians with assessment. For example, there are instruments used to measure individual constructs like depression, self-esteem, and personality. There are also instruments used to measure relational dynamics like marital satisfaction, peer relationships, and parent–child conflict. In quantitative research, variables being studied have to be measured with instruments of sufficient reliability and validity. If we are studying the effectiveness of cognitive-behavioral therapy for treating depression, we have to measure depression in a way that produces a numerical value that can be analyzed with SPSS. Instruments are designed with questions that are answered on Likert scales. Likert scales specify a continuum of responses (e.g., a range from very bad to very good), and each response is assigned a number. This allows researchers to analyze responses numerically (e.g., higher scores may be associated with more severe depression). Before this measure can be used in research studies, quantitative methods are used to establish evidence of reliability and validity of the instrument.

Dyadic Analysis

Dyadic data analysis is gaining increasing relevance in family research. While most statistical tests require independence of observations (i.e., one person's score is not related to another's), dyadic analysis takes interdependence into account. This is important when studying families, because family members' scores are interdependent by nature of their relationship. Dyadic analysis has been particularly useful in the study of couple relationships.

Evaluating Quantitative Research

Overall, quantitative research is helpful in establishing evidence for the use of counseling interventions in helping clients. Without this evidence, it is unlikely that third-party payers like insurance companies would reimburse for these services. Because quantitative research typically utilizes larger sample sizes than qualitative research, and uses random sampling techniques, findings should be generalizable to larger populations from which samples are taken. Such research also helps us understand how phenomena are related, and to test theories of family functioning and theories about how counseling is supposed to work. This information can help counselors make better clinical decisions in treatment.

Quantitative research is not without its limits. It may tell us that an intervention is effective, but not how or why it is effective. It can only summarize large amounts of information, not help us understand processes of family functioning or how counseling works in depth. Qualitative research is a helpful adjunct in this respect. Another limitation is that quantitative research can also be expensive and time-consuming. Moreover, it is often difficult to obtain truly random samples representative of the population under study.

Aimee Galick

See also Clinical Versus Statistical Significance; Common Factors; Couples Therapy Research; Effectiveness Research; Outcome Research; Prevention Research; Process Research

Further Readings

Baldwin, S. A., Christian, S., Berkeljon, A., Shadish, W. R., & Bean, R. (2012). The effects of family therapies for adolescent delinquency and substance abuse: A meta-analysis. *Journal of Marital and Family Therapy, 38*(1), 281–304.

Cooper, H. (2009). *Research synthesis and meta-analysis: A step-by-step approach.* Thousand Oaks, CA: Sage.

Creswell, J. (2013). *Research design: Qualitative, quantitative, and mixed methods approaches* (4th ed.). Thousand Oaks, CA: Sage.

Heatherington, L., Friedlander, M. L., & Greenberg, L. (2005). Change process research in couple and family therapy: Methodological challenges and opportunities. *Journal of Family Psychology, 19*(1), 18–27.

Kenny, D. A., Kashy, D., & Cook, W. (2006). *Dyadic data analysis.* New York: Guilford.

Orlinsky, D. E., Rønnestad, M. H., & Willutzki, U. (2004). Process and outcome in psychotherapy. In M. J. Lambert (Ed.), *Bergin and Garfield's handbook of psychotherapy and behavior change* (5th ed., pp. 307–389). New York: Wiley.

Sprenkle, D., Davis, S. D., & Lebow, J. L. (2013). *Common factors in couple and family therapy: The overlooked foundation for effective practice.* New York: Guilford.

Sprenkle, D., & Piercy, F. (Eds.). (2005). *Research methods in family therapy* (2nd ed.). New York: Guilford.

Trusty, J. (2011). Quantitative articles: Developing studies for publication in counseling journals. *Journal of Counseling & Development, 89*(3), 261–267.

Wester, K. L., Borders, L. D., Boul, S., & Horton, E. (2013). Research quality: Critique of quantitative articles in the *Journal of Counseling & Development. Journal of Counseling & Development, 91*(3), 280–290. doi:10.1002/j.1556-6676.2013.00096.x

QUESTIONS: OPEN, CLOSED, AND CIRCULAR

Questions are essential tools that the counselor uses to elicit information from the client; they are helpful in understanding the presenting problem and guiding the therapeutic process. Various types of question formats are used to gather different types of information, including open questions, closed questions, and circular questions. Open questions allow the client to reflect on feelings or thoughts: for example, *What were you first thinking after you heard your boss tell you that you were being let go?* Closed questions are fact-finding questions, helpful for gathering information: for example, *Were other employees let go at the same time you were?* Circular questions are helpful in gathering a relational perspective, exploring the client's understanding of himself or herself in relation to others: for example, *How do you think your boss thought you would respond to being let go?* These three question formats share certain commonalities: All have a clinical purpose or intent, all are tools for information gathering, and all are ways to clarify or direct the therapeutic conversation. The counselor must carefully balance and monitor the number and sequence of questions so as not to turn the counseling session from a dialogue into an interrogation, and must ask questions that the client understands.

Circular questions are especially useful for family counselors because they focus on learning the multiple perspectives of the problem held by the different family members involved. Before going on to explore the complexity of circular questions, the following sections first describe the communication process in counseling, including the use of open and closed questions.

Paying Attention to the Process

Counseling happens within a relationship, and communication is a vital factor in how that relationship develops. The pacing and the tone of the counselor's voice are critical, as are the ways the counselor holds his or her body and engages the client visually, as well as the words the counselor chooses. All are methods of communication that can support the development of a relationship. Not allowing space or time for the client to reflect, the counselor not showing genuineness in his or her posture, or not taking the time to be curious about the client's story, can limit the strength and supportive quality of the alliance. Research has demonstrated that successful treatment outcomes are linked to a supportive therapeutic alliance between the counselor and the client. Being curious and wanting to know more about how the client perceives the problem and what the client expects from counseling is a starting point for the development of a positive alliance. Curiosity is demonstrated through asking questions in a genuine and attentive way.

Forming Your Questions

Questions of all types, coupled with empathetic responses and validations, can support the process of gathering information through curious questioning. It is absolutely necessary to ask questions in counseling. However, the way you ask questions and which questions you ask can demonstrate either curiosity or judgment. Clients who feel their counselor is interested in their story and wants to help will engage in the therapeutic process because they feel supported. Clients who feel judged by their counselor will not allow themselves to be vulnerable enough to tell their story and therefore will not engage in the counseling process or allow the relationship to develop.

Counselors may have some questions in mind already after talking with a client on the phone to schedule the initial appointment, or after having read the client's completed intake form; these are hypothetical questions because the counselors have formulated them without first meeting the client. Counselors may also have some standard questions that they ask the client (other than their intake form) when beginning a session, such as *How can this session be helpful?* A good general rule is to develop questions based on the information that the client has just given in the discussion. This demonstrates that the counselor is listening to the client, which further develops the relationship, and allows the counselor to explore where to go in the information gathering process. Combining different question types (such as open, closed, and circular) with clinical microskills (such as attending, listening, and pacing) allows the counselor to effectively explore the client's story and assess the problem.

Open Questions

Open questions are designed to prompt clients to respond with detail about the topic of discussion and widen their perspective of the problem by asking them to think about the problem with greater specificity. These questions are typically unstructured, allowing the counselor to follow up each response with new questions or reflective statements. Open questions may start with *what, why,* or *how,* encouraging the client to consider personal feelings and thoughts about what is being discussed. The exploratory nature of the open question places the client in charge, allowing the client to be directive in the response and focus on areas that are important to him or her rather than the counselor determining the focus. The open question also allows the client to decide what and when to disclose during the counseling process, and supports the client's sense of confidence or expertise concerning his or her own story. The examples below may be considered open questions:

- What made you decide to come to counseling now?
- How did you feel when your son told you he was moving out of your house and in with his father?
- What did you think would happen when you told your husband you wanted a divorce?
- How have you been coping since your mother died?

Each question supports the client's reflection about an emotional feeling or cognitive thought related to behavior. The responses elicited from open questions offer the counselor a more substantial understanding of the client's perceptions and meanings, which can provide needed information for the treatment process. The open question can also convey genuine curiosity and demonstrate the counselor's interest in learning more about the client's story. This process supports the development of the therapeutic alliance, which in turn supports successful outcomes.

Why should be used with caution as a question prompt, as it may be considered confrontational by the client and elicit a defensive response that may not be useful and can negatively change the tone of the counseling session. The client may feel judged, as well, by the counselor, which may limit the amount of information the client decides to share in session.

Most *why* questions can be reframed into a *how* question, which gathers a richer description, offering a deeper understanding of the client's perception of the presenting issue. When a client is asked *Why did you hit your sister?* the response may be defensive: *She made me do it,* or *She hit me first.* These responses do not offer much information about the situation, and the client may feel blamed for the action being questioned. Conversely, asking *How did it make sense to hit your sister?* might bring this response: *She turned off the show I was watching and then pushed me off the couch,* or *She called me a loser because I didn't make the school basketball team.* This response offers more detail about the interaction being discussed and offers the counselor more understanding of the client's meaning of the situation; furthermore, it prompts questions such as *How do you feel about not making the school basketball team?* There are times when a *why* question can be useful and heard as a question based in curiosity rather than blame, as the examples below demonstrate:

- Why do you think your husband chose last weekend to tell you about his trip?
- Why did you decide to come into counseling now?
- You told me you used to love going to the theater. Why aren't you doing that now?
- Why do you think the kids are fighting so much?

Open questions assist the counselor in searching for the deeper meaning of the presenting problem behavior, which is a symptom of the more general problem, and to understand reasons why the behavioral symptoms are being maintained within the family system's interactions. It is critical that the questions make sense to the client and serve a clinical purpose; otherwise, the client may feel unheard, or the question may be seen as intrusive. The counselor must also pace his or her curiosity and be careful to ask one question at a time, allowing the client to reflect on the personal meaning of the question before responding. Immediately following up a client response to a question may prematurely end the client's reflection process and cut off further information or discussion about the topic at hand.

Closed Questions

Closed questions are designed as fact gathering tools for the clinician. Eliciting short responses that are not typically reflective, these questions may begin with *is, do, are, who, does, when,* or *where*. The counselor is more directive with closed questions and is able to focus the discussion toward uncovering specific information. The client does not have the ability to decide what to disclose, as when asked an open question; if the client refuses to answer the closed question, then that in itself is information and an answer to the closed question. The client is removed from feeling confident and knowledgeable because it is not a story that is unfolding; the counselor is telling the story, and the client is confirming or denying the details.

The examples below may be considered closed questions:

- Does your partner know you decided to come to counseling?
- When are you going to discuss the divorce with your children?
- Where do you work?
- Are you going to think about switching jobs?
- Is your husband going with you?

Not only can closed questions slow down the reflective process of a session, but it is important for the counselor to be conscious of the need to balance the different types of questions. Too many closed questions can turn what is meant to be a dialogue into an interrogation, so their use should be judicious. For example, the counselor may choose to use closed questions to confirm a hypothesis: *Did you leave the e-mail open in the hope that your husband might read it?* Closed questions might also be used to clarify an idea that is being discussed: *It seems that you are not sure about wanting a divorce; am I understanding you correctly?*

The counselor may find that unresponsive or anxious clients will respond more readily to closed questions than to open questions, since closed questions are easier to answer. However, asking only closed questions will limit the depth of the clinical dialogue and treatment process. The minimal responses offer only a cursory understanding of the client problem, leaving the counselor in a position of making assumptions about the meaning of the symptom behaviors. Closed questions also keep the control of the session in the hands of the counselor. The responses from the client are minimal; therefore, the counselor is able to ask more questions. Open questions, however, invite the client to offer more detail and insight to the discussion, which means that the counselor may feel as though he or she is no longer in control of the information gathering because the client is speaking.

Circular Questions

Circular questions can be understood as open questions that attend to the relational perspective of the family system. This question type can be used regardless of the number of clients sitting in the therapy room, since the counselor can ask the individual client about his or her understanding of how others in the system (family, community, culture) view the problem behavior.

Circular questions are designed to gather detailed information in the context of the relationships within the family system. Such questions are particularly useful in working with couples and families, who often enter therapy with opposing views of a problem. Initially developed in the 1970s by family therapy theorists in Milan, Italy, as an effective tool for use in interviewing families, today circular questions are used by therapists and counselors grounded in many different models.

The original work of Mara Selvini-Palazzoli, Luigi Boscolo, Gianfranco Cecchin, and Giuliana Prata—identified in family therapy literature as the Milan team—was based in efforts to understand the complexity of the family system. The Milan team realized that the counselor must understand each perspective of the family system in relation to the symptomatic behavior. Therefore, it determined that the counselor must ask each member of the system about the problem in relation to one another, which made a pattern that was recursive. The Milan team called this process *circularity*, and it was defined as the process of using feedback from the questions asked of each family member in relation to one another and to the problem. The examples below may be considered circular questions:

- When mom and dad argue, which one of the children gets most upset?
- When Tommy is crying, who notices first?
- Who works hardest to get Tommy to stop crying?
- Who gets most upset when Tommy is crying?

The unique aspect of circular questions is the feedback loop, used to understand the relationship of each system member to the symptomatic problem behavior. The responses to circular questions develop the rich context of the problem and allow the counselor to weave the different perspectives of the family members' understanding into a collaborative view of what is happening. The counselor uses each family member's response to build an understanding of what is occurring within the family system when the problem is manifesting itself. Using circular and open questions, a counselor is able to follow the system members' individual responses and explore the full context of the problem. Often, families are "stuck" when each system member conceptualizes only his or her own understanding of the problem; consequently, the family is in a recursive problem loop.

When the counselor explores the multiple perspectives of the problem by asking each family member about how other family members view the problem, the repetitive loop is interrupted. Family members hear what each thinks about how the other family member believes he or she views the problem. At that time, family members begin to "correct" what might be "misunderstandings" about their views, which adds even more context to the problem. Family members can also begin to understand how the behavior of other family members makes sense, given what has been heard. Without hearing what the other family members believe one another's perspectives to be about the problem, each family member is operating on an *assumption* of what is believed. Using assumptions about one another, the family members view the problem basically in isolation, without input from other family members. Circular questions allow each family member to become aware of how his or her involvement in the problem is impacting the other family members and can stimulate the family to do something different, which interrupts the problem feedback loop.

Other Theory-Based Questions

Important to note is that some family therapy models utilize theory-based questions unique to the model, such as solution-focused brief therapy, which includes exception-finding questions, scaling questions, coping questions, and the miracle question; narrative therapy, which includes the externalizing questions; and cognitive-behavioral family therapy, which includes thought questions, change questions, and feeling questions. There are many other examples of questions identified within theories as tools or techniques for the particular paradigm. However, all the question types share the characteristics of being open, closed, or circular.

Conclusion

Questions are basic tools for counselors to open pathways for discussion and support the development of a deeper, contextual understanding of the presenting problem. The very act of asking a question can be an intervention that supports new awareness of the problem for the client. In combination with other microskills, questions can challenge, validate, and confront clients. Furthermore, they stimulate awareness in an effort to move forward in the therapeutic process, which opens new possibilities and understandings.

Carol Pfeiffer Messmore

See also Circularity and Linearity; Clinical Interviews With Couples and Families; Cybernetics; Individual Versus Family Therapy; Milan Team

Further Readings

Anderson, H., & Goolishian, H. (1992). The client is the expert: A not-knowing approach to therapy. In S. McNamee & K. J. Gergen (Eds.), *Therapy as social construction* (pp. 25–39). London, England: Sage.

DeJong, P., & Berg, I. K. (2013). *Interviewing for solutions* (4th ed.). Belmont, CA: Brooks/Cole.

Diorinou, M., & Tseliou, E. (2014). Studying circular questioning "in situ": Discourse analysis of a first systemic family therapy session. *Journal of Marital and Family Therapy, 40*(1), 106–121.

Fleuridas, C., Nelson, T. S., & Rosenthal, D. M. (1986). The evolution of circular questions: Training family therapists. *Journal of Marital and Family Therapy, 12*(2), 113–127.

Ivey, A., Ivey, M., & Zalaquett, C. (2013). *Intentional interviewing and counseling: Facilitating client development in a multicultural society.* Boston, MA: Cengage Learning.

Lipchik, E., & de Shazer, S. (1986). The purposeful interview. *Journal of Strategic & Systemic Therapies, 5*(1), 88–89.

Penn, P. (1982). Circular questioning. *Family Process, 21*(3), 267–280.

Ryan, D., & Carr, A. (2001). A study of the differential effects of Tomm's questioning styles on therapeutic alliance. *Family Process, 40*(1), 67–77.

Seligman, L. (2009). *Fundamental skills for mental health professionals.* Upper Saddle River, NJ: Pearson.

Selvini-Palazzoli, M., Boscolo, L., Cecchin, G., & Prata, G. (1980). Hypothesizing-circularity-neutrality: Three guidelines for the conductor of the session. *Family Process, 19*, 3–12.

Sommers-Flanagan, J., & Sommers-Flanagan, R. (2009). *Clinical interviewing.* Hoboken, NJ: Wiley.

Tomm, K. (1987). Interventive interviewing: Part II. Reflexive questioning as a means to enable self-healing. *Family Process, 26*(2), 167–183.

Tomm, K. (1988). Interventive interviewing: Part III. Intending to ask lineal, circular, strategic, or reflexive questions? *Family Process, 27*(1), 1–15.

Watzlawick, P., Bavelas, J., & Jackson, D. (1967). *Pragmatics of human communication.* New York: Norton.

Williams, L., Edwards, T., Patterson, J., & Chamow, L. (2011). *Essential assessment skills for couple and family therapists.* New York: Guilford.

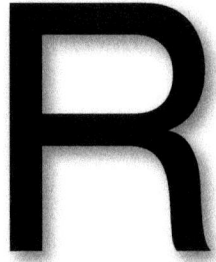

Racial Disparities in Foster Care

For decades there has been a focus on the high representation of children of color in the U.S. foster care system. Research has shown that there is a clear disparity in the rates in which children of color are reported and investigated for abuse or neglect, and the rates at which they enter and leave the system. For example, according to the U.S. Government Accountability Office, African American children made up 34% of children in foster care in 2004 but only 15% of the child population in the United States. In 2013, an estimated 42% of children in foster care were White, 24% were Black, 22% were Hispanic (of any race), and 9% were members of other races or multiracial, with the remaining 3% of unknown racial origin, according to the U.S. Department of Health and Human Services.

Based on the continued disparity and disproportionality of foster care admissions and discharges, it is vital that counselors and others who work with African American families approach their work with intentionality. Further, it is important that providers assess their biases and prejudices through the process of making decisions about children of color, especially African American children, when it comes to admittance to the foster care system and length of stay in foster care. This entry focuses on the disproportionality of African American children in foster care. Although Native Americans and, in some states, Latina/o/s have also been overrepresented in foster care, the severe racial disproportionality among African American children in foster care has been a particular focus of concern. This entry discusses factors that influence the disproportionality of African American children in foster care and the mental health issues that arise from foster care.

Contextualizing African American Children in Foster Care

Although research has documented the existence of racial disparities in foster care, there is no clear-cut understanding of the reasons for these disparities. Some scholars suggest that the disparities are the result of poverty rather than decisions about foster care based on race. Children who are subjects of initial reports of maltreatment become involved in a process in which multiple decisions are made that affect the likelihood of their entry into and exit from foster care. Decisions are multifaceted and include (a) the decision to accept the report for investigation, (b) the substantiation of allegations of maltreatment, (c) the decision to provide services, (d) the decision to place a child in an out-of-home setting, and (e) the decision to enable a child to exit out of foster care. In addition to the multiple decisions made, many different decision-makers are involved in the process, such as child welfare caseworkers, supervisors, police, judges, agency administrators, legal professionals, and policymakers. Research examining the decision-making process has indicated that disparities exist at each phase of the decision pathway. Therefore, based on this concern, it behooves those who work with African American families and children to be self-aware of the attitudes and biases that may influence their decision at each phase. Scholars have proposed some potential explanations for the disproportionate number of African American children in the nation's foster care system.

For centuries, African American families have been impacted by a history of racism and suffered low socioeconomic conditions that are associated with higher rates of contact with the child welfare system. These influence African American children's underrepresentation or overrepresentation in the system at different points in time. For example, African American children were underrepresented in the child welfare system before the civil rights movement because segregation excluded them from utilizing foster care.

The lack of political power associated with racial disparity has been raised when discussing the issue of Black children's disproportionality in the foster care system. The voices of minority groups may be silenced in the political system when their rights and needs are not well represented by politicians and politicians may garner support by targeting certain groups. Both of these issues may account for some of the racial disparity in the foster care system. Being a minority with a low socioeconomic status may prevent African Americans' demand for change in the system. In addition, racial disparity in the foster care system may reflect the political choice to investigate Black parents more often than other parents.

Bias has been apparent in social policies and in the social welfare system. For example, in a qualitative study of Michigan's child welfare system, the Center for the Study of Social Policy found that many social workers negatively characterized African American families. According to the center's report, social workers failed to properly assess African American parents' ability to care for their children. The report noted that African American parents are often described in case notes as hostile, aggressive, and angry, among other negative labels that are used to make decisions about the removal of Black children from homes and families.

Another major issue is the high rate of poverty among African American families. Blacks represent about 13% of the U.S. population, yet 26% of Blacks live in poverty, according to the U.S. Census Bureau. An analysis of census data found significant differences among racial and ethnic groups in wealth holdings, including home equity and retirement savings. The 2015 study by Demos and the Institute for Assets and Social Policy at Brandeis University found the median White household had wealth of $111,146, compared to $7,113 for Black households and $8,348 for Hispanic households. Moreover, African Americans are more likely to work in menial jobs which restrict income opportunities. These disparities may limit African American parents' ability to provide appropriate or adequate food, clothing, and shelter for their children. This economic limitation on lifestyle may lead to more investigation by social welfare agencies if, for instance, a child appears to be neglected.

African American Child-Rearing Practices

It is also important to recognize how the child welfare systems attribute deficits in Black parents' child-rearing. The deficit perspective (focusing on problems rather than looking for strengths) on African American child-rearing hides the systemic and institutional biases that devalue Black children's bond with their parents. Systemic barriers stand in the way of directing change and providing equal services for African American children.

Child maltreatment and foster care placement may also be related to poverty. Poverty may cause more stressors for a family and those in poverty may have their child-rearing practices scrutinized more than middle-class and upper-class parents. Assumptions about parents' abilities may be based on intersections of different minority identities. For example, it may be assumed that single-parent, low-income, African American women are not able to care for their children and thus poverty becomes another cause for the children to be removed from their homes. This is not to say that only (or all) low-income parents are abusing their children as this can occur in middle- and upper-class families and in families from all racial and ethnic groups.

Labeling bias by health care and human services providers, who are more likely to attribute injury in Black children to abuse, may also account for overrepresentation of African American children in the foster care system. These same providers may be more likely to believe middle- and upper-class families' explanation of an injury as a result of an accidental fall than they would be to believe a similar explanation from low-income families. It has been suggested that in cases where White families are suspected of child abuse or neglect, child welfare agencies are more likely to provide in-home services rather than removing children from their homes. In-home services are services provided by a child welfare agency, or on behalf of the agency, to children and families who have been reported to child protective services for possible child abuse or neglect. The goals of these services include ensuring children's safety and strengthening the capacity of parents to care for their children. Specific challenges faced by families, such as parents' substance abuse or depression, may be targeted in these services.

Areas That Present Risk and Vulnerability for Black Children in Foster Care

Children in foster care are vulnerable to maltreatment in the form of physical, sexual, emotional, or psychological abuse, and/or neglect. It has been reported that approximately one million cases of foster care abuse and neglect are substantiated annually. Children's mental health can be negatively affected as a result of removal from their families and abuse in foster care settings. Changes in mental health are usually marked by disruptions in emotional and behavioral development.

A report on the National Survey of Child and Adolescent Well-Being, a longitudinal survey of more than 6,200 children who had contact with the child welfare system, indicated that nearly half of the children surveyed showed signs of emotional and behavioral problems, with greater rates among children who were placed in out-of-home care. Furthermore, children with increased rates of mental health problems while in foster care still struggle with the illnesses after they are out of the foster care system. For example, 17% of children who participated in the study had been arrested in young adulthood, with arrest rates more than four times the national rate for 18 to 24 years old. Despite the widely documented and sustained mental health needs of these children, children with mental health needs in foster care typically do not receive appropriate treatment. Research has found that among youths who come into contact with the child welfare system, African Americans are even less likely to receive mental health services than non-Hispanic Whites.

Another area of vulnerability is the notion of foster children's inability to develop adaptive social relationships with caregivers and peers. Foster care children's emotional problems may interfere with their social relationships with peers, another factor influencing their ability to establish and maintain positive and healthy relationships. Similarly, children adopted from institutional settings have been shown to have poorer family and social relationships the longer the time spent in institutional care prior to adoption.

Future Direction

The foster care system has faced criticism for decades. Many scholars on racial disparity in foster care have noted the inadequate services given to racial minority children and families, especially African American families. Researchers have indicated the need for preventive measures to reduce the likelihood of children entering foster care. States have taken steps to address racial disparities in the foster care system, with 45 states having instituted cultural competency training for caseworkers at the time of a 2007 report from the U.S. Government Accountability Office (GAO). Nonetheless, state child welfare directors surveyed for the report said that bias or cultural misunderstanding and distrust between child welfare services and families contributed to the removal of children from their homes. The GAO report recommended encouraging states to track state and local data on the racial disproportionality of children in foster care and develop strategies to prevent children's entry into foster care and to help them more quickly enter permanent homes.

Stephaney S. Morrison

See also Adoption; Adoption, Cross-Cultural and Interracial; African American Families; Foster Children; Transracial Adoption

Further Readings

Children's Defense Fund. (2014, March 28). *The state of Black children in America: A portrait of continuing inequality*. Retrieved from http://www.childrensdefense.org/library/data/state-of-black-children-2014.pdf

DeNavas-Walt, C., Bernadette, D., & Proctor, B. D. (2015). *Income and poverty in the United States: 2014*. Washington, DC: U.S. Government Printing Office. Retrieved from http://www.census.gov/content/dam/Census/library/publications/2015/demo/p60-252.pdf

Dettlaff, A. J., Rivaux, S. L., Baumann, D. J., Fluke, J. D., Rycraft, J. R., & James, J. (2011). Disentangling substantiation: The influence of race, income, and risk on the substantiation decision in child welfare. *Children and Youth Services Review, 33*, 1630–1637.

Gudiño, O. G., Martinez, J. I., & Lau, A. S. (2012). Mental health service use for children in contact with child welfare: Racial disparities depend on problem type. *Psychiatric Services, 63*(10), 1004–1010. doi:10.1176/appi.ps.201100427

Horton, C. B., & Cruise, T. K. (2001). *Child abuse and neglect: The school's response*. New York, NY: Guilford Press.

Leve, L. D., Fisher, P. A., & DeGarmo, D. S. (2007). Peer relations at school entry: Sex differences in the outcomes of foster care. *Merrill-Palmer Quarterly, 53*, 557–577.

Leve, L. D., Harold, G. T., Chamberlain, P., Landsverk, J. A., Fisher, P. A., & Vostanis, P. (2012). Practitioner review: Children in foster care-vulnerabilities and evidence-based interventions that promote resilience processes. *Journal of Child Psychology Psychiatry, 53*(12), 1197–1211.

Roberts, D. E. (2012). Prison, foster care, and the systemic punishment of Black mothers. *Faculty Scholarship*. Paper 432. Retrieved from http://scholarship.law.upenn.edu/faculty_scholarship/432/

Sullivan, L., Meschede, T., Dietrich, L., Shapiro, T., Traub, A., Ruetschlin, C., & Draut, T. (2015). *The racial wealth gap: Why policy matters*. New York, NY: Demos and The Institute on Assets and Social Policy, Heller School, Brandeis University. Retrieved from http://www.demos.org/sites/default/files/publications/RacialWealthGap_1.pdf

U.S. Department of Health and Human Services, Children's Bureau. (2014). *In-home services in child welfare*. Washington, DC: Author. Retrieved from https://www.childwelfare.gov/pubPDFs/inhome_services.pdf

U.S. Department of Health and Human Services, Children's Bureau. (2015). *Foster care statistics 2013*. Washington, DC: Author. Retrieved from https://www.childwelfare.gov/pubPDFs/foster.pdf

U.S. Government Accountability Office. (2007). *African American children in foster care: Additional HHS assistance needed to help states reduce the proportion in care*. Washington, DC: Author. Retrieved from http://www.gao.gov/new.items/d07816.pdf

Racism

Racism refers to a belief that people belong to different racial groups based on their biological traits and that these differences make some races superior to others. Racism is used to justify, based on race, patterns of oppression and to allocate power to some and restrict or deny it to others. Racism is relevant to marriage, families, and couples counseling because the macrostructure of racial stratification in the United States, with White, mainly European Americans at the top and ethnic minorities below, impacts people's daily interactions and their personal and professional relationships. In this entry, the history of racial stratification in the United States is described. It is important to understand the history because it helps explain the current racial hierarchy. Next, an explanation of institutional and individual discrimination is provided and the major psychological and sociological theories of racism are discussed. The entry concludes with suggestions for counselors to consider when working with clients in therapy.

History

A majority of societies are multiethnic, which means that many racial, religious, and cultural groups reside within them. Multiethnic societies are typically stratified on the basis of race because phenotypic or visible traits provide an easy way to distinguish between groups. The United States is one of the most multiethnic countries in the world and espouses values of capitalism and competition. These defining characteristics have produced a system of social stratification whereby some people have more power than others. Power refers to having control over valued resources such as money and information. Power and race are intertwined in such a way that ethnic minority group members (e.g., those with African, Latina/o, and Native American heritage) have significantly less power on average than dominant group members (i.e., White Americans).

A major part of the history of U.S. racial stratification can be traced to the transatlantic slave trade, which involved transporting African people to the colonial Americas and other parts of the world for labor. In the early years, indentured servants, or those who worked to pay off the cost of their transport, were imported from Africa and northwestern Europe to labor in the southern United States. Through the blending of these two groups, a sizable mixed-race population emerged, which blurred racial lines. Employers preferred distinct racial groups because they could be used to stimulate competition and productivity. Laws were therefore implemented to limit interracial interactions. In 1662, Virginia legally recognized slavery as a lifelong condition that could be inherited, which solidified the foundation for a racially stratified society.

Initially, prejudiced views of Africans held the importation of slaves to a minimum. With time, however, employers developed a preference for African laborers for two reasons. First, Africans were worth more than European indentured servants because they were required to work for life, resulting in greater profits. Additionally, the southern U.S. labor demands were growing, yet fewer indentured servants were traveling to the United States from northwestern European countries. The rising per capita income in Europe combined with the high cost of travel to the United States caused low-income workers to remain in their home countries. For these reasons, employers began deliberately seeking to purchase African slaves.

At this same time, laws and practices were implemented to further divide society based on race. White Americans had legal privileges such as the right to vote, bear arms, purchase land, and testify in court, which were not extended to those with African heritage. Among the lowest classes, White workers were penalized less harshly than Africans for rule violations. They were also allowed to engage without penalty in violence toward African people. Racial stratification was therefore established through a history of slavery and the social and political customs that allocated power to White Americans and denied power to Black Americans. This racial power hierarchy, created centuries ago, has continued to influence U.S. society to the present day, even though the legal structures that supported slavery and, later, racial segregation, have long been dismantled.

Racial stratification in the United States is not limited to the Black and White racial groups. It affects every racial group. In general, those who most closely resemble members of the dominant White racial group in terms of phenotypic and cultural traits have experienced greater power and privilege than those with more distinct traits. Phenotypic traits refer to observable features such as skin color, facial structure, and hair texture. Cultural traits include socialized characteristics such as language, manner of dress, ritual practices, and food preferences. Privilege refers to the advantages people experience as a result of being White, such as their own cultural norms being the dominant societal norms. Rankings based on proximity to the dominant group's traits occur within minority groups as well. Among ethnic minorities, those who more closely resemble White Americans in terms of phenotypes and cultural traits tend to have more power than those who are dissimilar. Although dominant group resemblance is associated with greater rewards overall, members of ethnic minority groups may also face intragroup hostility due to their preferential treatment.

Discrimination

Discrimination refers to actions that are used by dominant group members to maintain power over minority group members. These actions may include purposeful avoidance, the denial of opportunities, use of verbal threats, and physical violence. Although discrimination tends to be motivated by prejudice, or dislike of a particular group, at times people discriminate even if they are not personally prejudiced. For instance, a person may engage in acts of hostility toward a minority group member in order to gain peer approval.

Discrimination occurs at two levels: individual and institutional. The former refers to an individual or a small group of people denying privileges to or causing harm to minority group members. An example of individual discrimination would be a shopkeeper who provides preferential service to White Americans while ignoring ethnic minority patrons. Institutional discrimination is more difficult to detect and isolate. This type of discrimination involves the denial of privileges through law or social custom. One example is when land is expropriated and freeways constructed through neighborhoods inhabited by a disproportionately high number of ethnic minority families. Another example involves lenders who approve fewer loans for ethnic minority group members or provide loans to them at higher interest rates. Although ethnic minorities experience discrimination more often than White Americans, dominant group members *may* experience discrimination at the individual level. A White American who lives in a predominantly Latino neighborhood, for example, may be targeted for violence because of his or her race. It is much less likely, however, for a dominant group member to experience racial discrimination at the institutional level.

Some people may believe that racism no longer affects a person's opportunities for success, yet racial disparities exist for nearly every quality-of-life indicator. In the United States, the lowest socioeconomic groups are disproportionately comprised of African, Latina/o, and Native American group members. On average, members of these groups earn 20% to 35% less income than White Americans. They are more likely to occupy unhealthy and dangerous jobs and receive an inferior education. These disparities are largely due to structural problems that disproportionately affect low-income and ethnic minority communities such as inadequate resource allocation, damaged buildings and learning materials, overcrowded classrooms, and teachers who would rather teach elsewhere. In general, ethnic minorities are more likely than White Americans to live in polluted neighborhoods, have worse health outcomes, and die at a younger age. Ethnic minority group members are typically aware of this system of racism but lack the socioeconomic and political power to change it on their own.

Theories and Clinical Applications

Theories of prejudice and discrimination focus on psychological and sociological processes. The predominant psychological theories of racism are based on the ideas of the scapegoat and the authoritarian personality. The scapegoat perspective suggests that racism occurs at the individual level when a person experiences lack of power in their own life (e.g., through poverty or abuse) and displaces their frustration on a person or group with less power. Given that the individual is unable to direct his or her aggression toward the source of oppression, he or she uses a scapegoat who is unlikely to retaliate. A similar process can occur as a result of racism. For instance, a Native

American who is unfairly passed over for promotion in favor of a White American might take out his frustration on a less powerful family member. Applied to the counseling field, therapists should examine whether institutional racial discrimination is spilling over to affect the client's interpersonal relationships. In such cases, the therapist can highlight the source(s) of frustration, suggest stress management techniques, and help the client regain a sense of personal power.

The second psychological explanation of racism is authoritarian personality theory. According to this perspective, some people are more prone to racism because they either are born with this tendency or have been socialized into it. Authoritarian people thrive within strict hierarchies. They value conformity to roles, are intolerant of change, and believe in harsh discipline for rule violations. Although this theory may help explain why certain people hold prejudiced attitudes or discriminate against others, it does not adequately explain the motivations of entire groups or societies of people. Therapists working with clients who espouse authoritarian traits can address the cause of these traits and help deconstruct the client's fears and insecurities. The client's desire for structure can be maintained by helping her set healthy personal boundaries and teaching her to respect the boundaries of other people, including those whose cultural backgrounds differ from her own.

Sociological theories address how macrolevel processes produce and maintain racism. According to these perspectives, people who are raised in prejudiced environments are more likely to hold racial biases and engage in discriminatory behavior. Often, socialization into racism is subtle rather than overt. Family members or peers are more likely to use nonverbal indicators of disapproval, such as avoiding certain ethnic groups, rather than explicit derogation. In addition to messages received from family and network members, the media provide a major source of socialization. Messages displayed on television, in the movies, and through printed material or the Internet frequently portray negative stereotypes. Therapists whose clients espouse racist views should identify the origins of their beliefs and propose alternative ways of thinking. Fears and misconceptions can be addressed and diversity resources can be recommended. In order for lasting change to occur, clients should be encouraged to foster relationships with like-minded individuals who are culturally aware and supportive of racial equality.

It is especially important for clinicians to recognize how the macro power structure impacts dynamics at the interpersonal level. Many patients experience discrimination from their own family, such as when darker complexioned individuals are devalued or lighter complexioned individuals experience resentment for their privileged social standing. Patients who are subjected to discrimination from their own family may be especially hesitant to feel safe in the therapeutic setting. Clinicians should be attentive to these issues and recognize that it may take longer than usual to build trust. Within interethnic partnerships, the partner with greater social power may be dismissive toward the partner with less social power. In such cases, it may be liberating for the therapist to point out that the couple's tensions are tied to macrolevel processes. Interethnic partners should be encouraged to learn about each other's culture and incorporate practices from each person's respective background into the relationship.

Discrimination from health care professionals continues to affect patients who seek services. It may be difficult for ethnic minorities to trust clinicians, especially if they have experienced discrimination in other contexts. The risk of racism in therapy causes some people of color to avoid getting help or to prematurely terminate services. As such, ethnic minority clients may prefer to work with a therapist who shares their cultural background. In order to minimize the risk of racial discrimination, therapists should regularly assess and challenge their own unconscious biases.

Overt, conscious discrimination is not the most common form of racism. Microaggressions, which involve dismissive or insulting behavior, are often conveyed unconsciously and devalue a person's ethnicity and experiences. A statement such as "Maybe you're thinking too much about racism;

could there be other explanations?" minimizes the client's experience and perspective. Therapists should engage in regular self-reflection and actively challenge existing and emergent biases to minimize their impact in the clinical setting.

Establishing a more equitable system involves efforts by members of all races. The challenge for people with power is to be willing to question their unearned privileges and invest themselves in becoming allies in the movement for social justice. Equal opportunity is not an ethnic minority issue; it is one that affects the entire society, so that each person has a share in the struggle to achieve social justice. Efforts in this area will need to be enduring because prejudice and discrimination continually emerge and require ongoing awareness and reflection to manage effectively for the common good.

Kelly Campbell

See also Beliefs and Values; Ethnicity; Multiculturalism; Racial Disparities in Foster Care; Socioeconomic Status

Further Readings

Adler, N. F., & Rehkoph, D. H. (2008). U.S. disparities in health: Descriptions, causes and mechanisms. *Annual Review of Public Health, 29*, 235–252.

Anderson, S. K., & Middleton, V. A. (2010). *Explorations in diversity: Examining privilege and oppression in a multicultural society*. Belmont, CA: Cengage.

Marger, M. N. (2012). *Race and ethnic relations: American and global perspectives*. Belmont, CA: Cengage.

Takaki, R. (2008). *A different mirror: A history of multicultural America*. New York, NY: Back Bay Books.

Understanding Prejudice: http://www.understandingprejudice.org/

REACTIVE ATTACHMENT DISORDER IN CHILDREN

Reactive attachment disorder (RAD) is a serious condition among children that poses the threat of impaired functionality into adolescence and adulthood. Clear descriptions of the RAD diagnosis are offered in order to capture an accurate picture of the condition. Descriptions of various risk factors that accompany the diagnosis shed light on important areas that can minimize the potential for harm, and developmental considerations offer a holistic understanding of how significantly these symptoms can affect the life of a child. Treatment approaches offer direction and hope for caregivers working to help young people manage the challenges associated with RAD.

RAD poses a tremendous challenge among families and caregivers. Because neglect and maltreatment are key to understanding RAD, it is important to consider how widespread these problems are. Over one year, states reported 678,932 victims of child abuse and neglect, the U.S. Department of Health and Human Services reported in 2015. Nearly 80% of victims were neglected, 18% were physically abused, 9% were sexually abused, and 9% were psychologically maltreated. This entry discusses how RAD is diagnosed, risk factors for RAD and impairments in development seen in children with RAD, and treatments that are used with children and caregivers in cases of RAD.

Diagnosis of Reactive Attachment Disorder

To understand ways in which families and caregivers can help young people experiencing the symptoms of RAD, a basic description of the disorder is provided. Five types of criteria signify a diagnosis of RAD based on the *Diagnostic and Statistical Manual of Mental Disorders* (DSM-5), published by the American Psychiatric Association (APA). The criteria include inhibited reactions toward caregivers, socioemotional disturbances, history of neglect and maltreatment, general qualifiers, and ruling out diagnoses.

Inhibited Reactions Toward Caregivers

The child with RAD displays patterns of behavior that appear emotionally detached or withdrawn most of the time, only rarely seeking comfort or responding to comfort when distressed. While most children experience greater comfort and satisfaction with caregivers, these children are much more likely to display indifference or even disdain for their primary caregivers. These young people have difficulty learning what their safe outlets and places of support will be. This problem also creates increased distress with caregivers striving to provide a supportive and meaningful relationship.

Socioemotional Disturbances

Families and caregivers may recognize impairments in social functionality, along with emotional regulatory abilities. Children with the disorder may have limited responses to others socially or emotionally, and they may display a positive affect on very rare occasions. Other disturbances may include emotional irritability, sadness, or fear during nonthreatening interactions with their caregivers with no clear explanation. In contrast to inhibitions with caregivers, children with RAD may conversely show fondness and affection for strangers and people whose levels of safety are unknown to the young person or caregivers.

History of Neglect and Maltreatment

An important element to remember with any RAD diagnosis is the presence of a neglect and maltreatment history. These young people experienced extremely insufficient care such as persistent neglect from caregiving adults. This condition occurred when forms of comfort, stimulation, and affection were withheld, when there were repeated changes in caregivers that resulted in a lack of stable attachments, or when the setting of child-rearing prevented opportunities for selective attachments or caregiver bonds. Many children with RAD have foster parents, adoptive parents, family members, or other caregivers who strive to pick up the pieces where biological parents left off. In some cases, biological parents, such as parents who had a history of substance abuse that resulted in child neglect, may have had to relinquish control of their children temporarily and later resume parental responsibilities after successful treatment. In these situations, the parents may encounter inhibitions characteristic of a young person reacting to poor attachment at an earlier age.

General Qualifiers

In order for a diagnosis of RAD to be made, the inhibited reactions to caregivers among children must be perceived by mental health providers as a response to their history of extremely insufficient care. A diagnosis of RAD can only be determined if the symptoms are not attributed to any other mental health conditions (e.g., medical issues, developmental delays). This can be complicated by the fact that RAD is frequently accompanied by a host of other problems and conditions that may be physical, developmental, mental, or emotional in nature. The symptoms associated with a RAD diagnosis also must become evident sometime between the ages of 9 months and 5 years old.

Ruling Out Diagnoses

Because of the presence of social-emotional neglect, other developmental delays are common, especially with cognition and language. For this reason, autism spectrum disorder may present similar features because social inhibition and disconnection from others is a key identified symptom. The absence of any historical social-emotional neglect will rule out RAD quickly, but other factors must be considered in circumstances when maltreatment is present because it may occur with both diagnoses. Depressive disorders also will result in a generally negative affect among children, although they often may respond to caregivers and be comforted.

Risk Factors

Researchers have identified a host of risk factors for RAD, many of which are associated with child maltreatment and neglect. Children may have higher risk for RAD when they live in a children's home or another institutional setting, such as the various forms of orphanages or group homes existing around the world. Children who frequently change foster homes or caregivers are also susceptible to RAD symptoms. The general instability of caregiver support can create this disconnect with children, and this instability can create severe impairments in the young person's ability to form healthy attachments.

Even when parents are present, there are some factors that place children at higher risk for experiencing RAD. Such factors may include when parents are inexperienced in raising a child and when a mother has postpartum depression or another mental health condition. Increased risk occurs when children have prolonged separation from parents or other caregivers due to hospitalization. Other children may be part of unusually large families, such that parental time is scarce or available unequally or rarely. Also, parents experiencing partner violence, substance abuse, or adolescent parenthood raise the risk for neglect and maltreatment that may result in RAD symptoms.

Developmental Considerations

As with any condition associated with children, caregivers and providers must take developmental considerations into account when determining diagnoses and needs. As mentioned earlier, young people with RAD have a tendency to experience additional co-occurring difficulties compared to the normal course of development experienced by many of their peers.

Such impairments in development can be seen across a range of areas, including self, mental, emotional, physical, social, and spiritual development. Self-development among children begins with a very egocentric focus, and children with RAD may have difficulty moving on to later stages of self-development, viewing themselves in relationship to a group of people (e.g., family, culture), viewing themselves as good or worthy of attention, or establishing a competent level of self-awareness that can aid character development in later stages. Areas of cognitive development frequently are impacted among children with RAD, resulting in poor academic performance and impaired mental processing. Emotional development may be impaired or immature, which may be seen in a limited range of emotion and inability to manage deregulated emotions.

Physical development may be interrupted in a variety of ways in relation to neglect or maltreatment, but most notable may be ongoing physical injuries, delay in physical milestones (e.g., smiling, motor skills, puberty), medical issues related to past abuse, and lack of development of neurological pathways associated with healthy attachments and relationships. Challenges associated with proper social development are the hallmark of understanding a child with RAD, as children may lack the ability to establish healthy attachments in relationships, recognize healthy forms of trust and mistrust, establish a sense of autonomy without shame and doubt, exercise initiative without guilt, offer proper responses to the support and affection from caregivers and close relationships, and show a desire to play or interact with primary caregivers. Spiritual development may become highly conflicted among young people as they may lack a sense of purpose or meaning, experience tension with their desire to connect with God and their difficulties with attachment, or struggle to establish a stable sense of moral foundation.

Treatments

Understanding how to help alleviate the symptoms of young people with RAD is important for caregivers, families, and providers. Various treatments focus on addressing the symptoms and developmental impairments that may accompany this condition. An important approach to consider with any treatment is that early prevention and intervention yield the greatest outcome.

Safety

As with any condition, the focus of any treatment begins with ensuring the safety of the child and others. This is especially important during moments of emotional dysregulation when a young person expresses threats of suicidal or homicidal behaviors. Implementing necessary procedures for evaluating and assessing the level of safety risk that exists will be important in extreme cases. Treatments always must involve enforcing necessary boundaries to maintain safe expression of intense thoughts and feelings.

Parent and Caregiver Education

Children with RAD may be raised by parents who previously perpetuated forms of neglect or maltreatment, or frequently by nonbiological caregivers who have adopted, fostered, or cared for the child. Parents and caregivers need support and resources to educate themselves on how to care for children with RAD, and to care for themselves during a difficult but meaningful task of raising the young person for success. Psychoeducational treatments may be used with caregivers to build trust, teach behavior management, create stabilizing structure and routine, and exercise various parenting skills. Parents may benefit by engaging in support groups with other parents experiencing similar challenges.

Therapeutic Skills and Awareness

Treatment for RAD often includes a focus on developing skills and awareness for managing the symptoms common with the disorder. Such treatments may involve helping the child develop positive coping skills, increase anxiety management skills, and use gradual exposure behavior techniques to break the association of fear and trauma. Young people may also be involved with social development groups, behavior contracts to help with stabilization and increase structure, and play therapy.

Trauma Recovery

Because RAD often occurs among other experiences of trauma, care must be taken to ensure such factors are managed thoroughly. Some of the most common techniques used in trauma recovery include forms of cognitive-behavioral therapy (CBT), play therapy, and eye movement desensitization and reprocessing (EMDR). Further exploratory studies with physical and medical approaches, such as a stellate ganglion block (SGB) where a local anesthetic injection is used in the spine, continue to be developed. More treatments for trauma recovery can be explored if trauma proves to be a significant factor of the child's experience.

Nathan C. D. Perron

See also Depression in Children; Parent–Child Communication; Posttraumatic Stress Disorder in Children

Further Readings

American Psychiatric Association. (2013). *Diagnostic and statistical manual of mental disorders* (5th ed.). Washington, DC: Author.

Centers for Disease Control and Prevention. (2012, August 1). *Child maltreatment*. Retrieved from http://www.cdc.gov/ViolencePrevention/childmaltreatment/

Hanson, R. F., & Spratt, E. G. (2000). Reactive attachment disorder: What we know about the disorder and implications for treatment. *Child Maltreatment, 5*(2), 137–145. doi:10.1177/1077559500005002005

Henderson, D. A., & Thompson, C. L. (2016). *Counseling children* (9th ed.). Belmont, CA: Brooks/Cole.

Lipov, E. (2015). Positive response to treatment of reactive attachment disorder (RAD) patient and pediatric post-traumatic stress disorder (PTSD) by utilizing stellate ganglion block (SGB): A case series of two patients. *Journal of Trauma Treatment, 4*(266). doi:10.4172/2167-1222.100026

Mayo Clinic. (n.d.). *Reactive attachment disorder: Risk factors*. Retrieved from http://www.mayoclinic.org/diseases-conditions/reactive-attachment-disorder/basics/risk-factors/con-20032126

Perron, N. C. D., & Pender, D. A. (2015). Meeting the need: Applying concepts for assessment and planning with child and adolescent trauma. *Journal of Child and Adolescent Counseling, 1*(1), 37–49. doi:10.1080/23727810.2015.1023607

U.S. Department of Health and Human Services, Administration for Children and Families, Administration on Children, Youth and Families, Children's Bureau. (2015). *Child maltreatment 2013*. Retrieved from http://www.acf.hhs.gov/programs/cb/research-data-technology/statistics-research/child-maltreatment

Vernon, A., & Clemente R. (2005). *Assessment and intervention with children and adolescents: Developmental and multicutural approaches* (2nd ed.). Alexandria, VA: American Counseling Association.

World Health Organization. (n.d.). *Child maltreatment*. Retrieved from http://www.who.int/mediacentre/factsheets/fs150/en/

Reconciliation

Even in the best relationships, there is sometimes damage done to the connections between two or more people. The process of reconciling a damaged relationship includes finding a way to heal and move past the hurts and conflict. Among experts there is disagreement about whether reconciliation is the same as forgiveness, whether it must end in a reunion of the parties involved in reconciliation, and whether contrition (the act of showing sorrow for one's actions and repenting) is required. When reunion and restoration of the relationship is the goal, the process of reconciliation may create a renewed sense of commitment, trust, and connection. Regardless of the specific definition of reconciliation, it is an important topic to the field of marriage and family counseling given the prevalence of disruptions in parent–child relationships, marriages, sibling relationships, and societal relationships. The role of differentiation and secure attachment in reconciliation, models of reconciliation, and the process of and barriers to reconciliation are discussed in this entry.

Role of Differentiation and Secure Attachment

Differentiation refers to the ability to balance the drives for individuality and togetherness, having a firm sense of one's thoughts and feelings, and having a low level of reactivity (making decisions from processing thoughts and feelings instead of automatically reacting). Differentiated individuals are not at the mercy of others when deciding how to respond, rather they make well-thought-out decisions. The more that someone is able to balance the drives for individuality and togetherness, discern thought from feeling, know one's own values and make decisions based on those values, and act rather than react, the higher level of differentiation he or she is said to have.

Looking through a different lens, one could describe these persons as having a secure attachment with healthy internal working models. This means that a person believes that the people to whom they are most intimately connected to (e.g., parents, partners, best friends) are trustworthy, available, caring, and responsive to their emotional needs. Secure attachment is created in an environment of responsive parenting in which the parent is attuned to the child and responds empathically. The securely attached person tends to be more empathic and has developed the ability to regulate emotions. It is not surprising that individuals who have a secure attachment stance tend to demonstrate a healthy level of differentiation.

People with a secure attachment or a healthy level of differentiation tend to be in a better position to engage in the reconciliation process. Reconciliation requires the ability to be honest. Typically trust has been broken and it must be regained. Reconciliation requires the ability to empathize. Both parties need to be able to recognize that the other person has thoughts, feelings, reactions, and histories that are separate from their own (also known as theory of mind). Then each party needs to be able to begin to feel the pain, the hurt, and the fear that the other has felt. As emotions are recognized, communicated, and experienced, the parties need to be able to regulate their emotions in such a way that they can remain engaged with each other in a safe manner. Additionally, the involved parties need to be able to tolerate ambiguity. It is seldom in life that people encounter someone who is all bad or all good. It requires skills in balancing emotions and thought to understand that a person who hurts someone may also care for that person. Lack of differentiation and insecure attachment reduce a person's ability to tolerate anxiety in relationships and create a balanced togetherness.

Models of Reconciliation

There are various approaches to the topic of reconciliation, each addressing the rationale as well as the process. For example, Frans de Waal and Jennifer Pokorny espouse a model of reconciliation based on research on nonhuman primates and from an evolutionary perspective. They see reconciliation as a behavioral mechanism that allows primates to mend social disturbances created by conflict and/or aggression. Chimpanzees have been observed to engage in behaviors to increase contact after a conflict. They showed more positive body contacts (e.g., kissing, embracing, gentle touching) between two former opponents after a conflict compared to other chimpanzees who had not been involved with the conflict. Essentially, the potential for survival is enhanced when humans (and nonhumans) experience social togetherness; therefore, processes that reduce arousal and enhance togetherness are desirable. Reconciliation is a process that helps maintain valuable social relationships by "undoing" damage to them and reducing hostility so that the participants can reunite. From this behavioral and evolutionary perspective, *reconciliation* is a term used to encompass several behaviors that serve to repair relationships and reduce tension.

Ivan Boszormenyi-Nagy introduced an interpersonal and systemic formulation of forgiveness and reconciliation that included the aggrieved person's opportunity to express the wrong and make a request for what would be needed to repair the relationship. This approach includes a chance for the perpetrator to explain possible justifications for the hurtful action. Such a systemic view recognizes the tendency for homeostasis (the tendency for things to stay the same), which works against reconciliation. Allowing the wronged person a voice and a chance to request reparation along with providing the opposite party an opportunity to explain can also be applied to larger groups of people on a societal level.

Reconciliation is included in many relational models of counseling and therapy models, whether it is formally labeled reconciliation or not. For example, Wanda Malcolm and Leslie Greenberg proposed an emotion-focused model of forgiveness that, although it does not specifically state a goal of reconciliation, does include an end product of creating a renewed narrative of those involved in the process. Everett Worthington developed a process he titled Forgiveness and Reconciliation through Experiencing Empathy (FREE). This model walks the participants through the decision about whether to reconcile, how to discuss the wrong(s), the process of assessing what other barriers stand in the way of reconciliation and moving forward, and making changes that rebuild trust. Finally, John Gottman, in his evidence-based approach to couples counseling, does not target reconciliation specifically but does address how couples might deal with unsolvable problems by creating a position of dialogue.

Process of Reconciliation

Despite the number of models of forgiveness and the dearth of models specifically addressing reconciliation, there seems to be agreement regarding components that are necessary or useful in the process of reconciliation. First, there needs to be a commitment to enter into the process of restoring the relationship. Reconciliation is hard work and should not be taken lightly. Those involved need to resist revenge and seek to understand. Second, a stance of respectful curiosity toward the other person is helpful in learning what the other person's experience has been. It is hoped that curiosity and seeking to understand will lead to empathy, a powerful catalyst for reconciliation. Third, since reestablishing trust is part of the process, honesty is crucial. Often the onus is on the person who has committed the injury to demonstrate truth and faithfulness. Fourth, throughout the process the disempowered need a chance to voice their piece of the story, which is enabled by parties taking an attitude of humility. As each person is invited to share his or her experience, emotions of hurt, pain, and shame often surface. In fact, there seems to be a consensus that if the process fails to include emotions, any change that is effected will be short lived. Fifth, in the course of learning more of each other's story, experiences, and feelings, the wrong that occurred must be acknowledged and some sort of reparation must be made. Often this is in the form of an apology, but it could also include other forms of restitution. Productive apologies include a statement of wrongdoing (it hurt you), an acknowledgment of responsibility

(I am responsible), a commitment to not repeat the offense (I won't do it again), a request for forgiveness (please forgive me), and a demonstration of sincerity. It places the apologizer in a "one-down" position to the receiver. Sixth, the offender needs to create and communicate a plan for how to prevent repeating the injury. Finally, those involved work together to make renewed meaning for their relationship out of the entire process.

Barriers to Reconciliation

Although there is a possibility of numerous barriers to reconciliation, a few that stand out include the role of memory, the tendency to retaliate, the felt need for compensation, the actor and observer bias, and the need for positive contact. All memories are recreated memories. For an item to be remembered, it must first be attended to, then stored, then retrieved. Every time a person "remembers" something, the memory is retrieved and restored, thus introducing the possibility of error in memory. To seek to have absolute agreement prior to being able to reconcile would preclude many reconciliations. Memory is also impacted by level of distress. Trauma, especially early and complex trauma, changes the way memories are processed and stored. Memories that lie dormant or below the level of awareness may still impact a person's ability to trust and may influence the person's reactions in a relationship. In addition to the impact of memory, behaviorally, people have a tendency to retaliate when wronged. This process can become cyclical, creating an increasing downward spiral.

The development of destructive entitlement (the belief that it is okay to use harmful means to make up for what someone perceives is "due" him or her) also presents a barrier. When a person is wronged, that person feels a need for compensation. This limits that person's ability to give and, at times, can influence the person to seek redress even from those who were not the ones who initially created the harm. This tendency toward a sense of entitlement is a destructive force in relationships.

Another key barrier to both forgiveness and reconciliation is the actor and observer bias. People have a propensity, especially in situations with negative outcomes, to assume that if they were the cause of a negative outcome, this was due to external circumstances. Conversely, people tend to believe that if the other person was the cause of a negative outcome, this is due to internal characteristics of that person (usually described as negative characteristics). This tendency is lessened when evaluating the source of the negative outcome with people one knows well. This may explain why reconciliation processes often include the need for positive interaction between the parties involved.

Kim M. Baldwin

See also Attachment Theory; Conflict Resolution; Divorce and Separation; Forgiveness; Homeostasis; Respect; Trauma and Families

Further Readings

Gottman, J. M. (2011). *The science of trust: Emotional attunement for couples.* New York, NY: W. W. Norton.

Johnson, S. (2013). *Love sense: The revolutionary new science of romantic relationships.* New York, NY: Little, Brown.

Kalayjian, A., & Paloutzian, R. F. (2009). *Forgiveness and reconciliation: Psychological pathways to conflict transformation and peace building.* New York, NY: Springer.

Walsh, F. (2006). *Strengthening family resilience* (2nd ed.). New York, NY: Guilford Press.

Worthington, E. L., Jr. (2006). *Forgiveness and reconciliation: Theory and application.* New York, NY: Taylor & Francis.

RECURSIVENESS

The word *recursive* is defined as relating to or constituting a pattern that can repeat itself indefinitely. In family therapy, recursiveness is a concept where relationships are viewed as interactions of communication placed into the context of each affecting and being affected by the other. This concept helps in understanding how people act in identifiable patterns that help families have stability and in understanding the mutual influence (circular causality) family members have on each other. At the same time, families can become stuck because of these recursive patterns. Recursiveness was first discussed in other fields of study, including mathematics and cybernetics, and then applied in family therapy to aid in understanding how parts of the family system are interdependent and the family system as a whole is greater than the sum of its parts. This entry provides an overview of the history of influences and the development of recursiveness within family therapy.

The Concept of Recursiveness

The general concept of recursiveness has been used mostly in geometry and computer science. For something to be considered recursive, there must always be an original example that grounds the definition, without being defined in terms of the definition itself. An example in art is the Droste effect, named after the Dutch Droste cocoa tin in the early 1900s that displayed a nurse carrying a serving tray with a cup of hot chocolate and a box with the same image. Another example is Russian Matryoshka dolls, which are a set of wooden dolls of decreasing size placed one inside another. At its root, recursiveness can be defined as relating to or involving the repeated application of a unit (as in the example of the Droste cocoa tin or the Matryoshka doll) or an activity with many successive executions.

The concept of recursiveness focuses on the interactions between parts and the patterns in larger systems. *Circularity* is a word that is often interchanged with recursiveness; however, there is a difference. Circularity involves using the term being defined as part of a definition. For example, if the word *inspiring* is defined as having the effect of inspiring someone, that would be considered a circular definition. These complex definitions highlight differences in underlying theories of knowledge and understanding (epistemology). Some theories wonder about causes and focus on the topic or content. In the examples listed earlier, a focus on the content would involve chocolate or dolls. In recursiveness, the focus is on the process of the interactions and relationships between different parts in the system. In the earlier examples, the focus would be on the pattern between the pictures of chocolate or the dolls.

Epistemological Foundations

Traditionally, Western culture has supported a scientific (also called positivistic) model of understanding the world around us. Science values objectivity, cause and effect, repeatability, reproducibility, and predictability. Information is derived (or deduced) from the five senses, and interpreted through reason and logic to form observed evidence for rules or patterns. Complex things are broken down into the smallest measurable elements, a process called *reductionism*. From this perspective, there is a belief that with precise fact-finding, the truth or reality will be found. In addition to positivism, the postpositivistic and constructivist theories of understanding view reality as influenced by human thought processes and the subjective construction of realities (or induced).

The postpositivistic view builds on science to acknowledge that the lens through which we view the observation influences what is seen. Constructivist understanding maintains that each person has a different and valid perspective of truth or reality and that scientific knowledge is formed by developing models or theories to explain our sensory experiences. These differing beliefs about how knowledge and information are gathered were instrumental in the development of another theory of knowledge called cybernetics. Rather than looking for the smallest unit to measure a linear cause and effect, in cybernetics, individual parts are viewed within the process of large, mutually interacting and interrelated complex systems.

Cybernetics

Theories about individual complex systems are not necessarily new, and early systems theorists attempted to find a general theory of universal principles that could explain all systems in all fields of science regardless of the type or nature of their elements. Initially, theories were developed that were grounded in cause and effect and viewed systems as mass and energy. However, after the Second World War, through interdisciplinary collaborations between scientists, engineers, mathematicians, and social scientists focused on the study of communications, a new theory of knowledge was developed called *cybernetics*. The term *cybernetics* is based on a Greek word relating to the use of communication channels of feedback loops (e.g., computer data cables or neurons in the brain) to organize and control the direction of a machine or organism. First-order cybernetics is focused on how parts of a system work together to communicate and control the actions that maintain stability of the system (homeostasis). In first-order cybernetics, the controller of the machine or organism was viewed as outside or separate from the system of the machine or organism being controlled. The influences of constructivist knowledge assumptions led to the development of second-order cybernetics, which applied circular causality and included the observer perspective. Circular causality refers to the maintenance of stability through mutual interactions of causes and consequences as A affects B, which then affects A. Additionally, anything or anyone attempting to observe, control, or change the system would be part of the communication channels and feedback and thus part of the system.

Gregory Bateson is credited with applying cybernetics to human communications. He thought that systems could be viewed as patterns and information that were constantly changing and evolving rather than homeostatic. Bateson developed a communication theory to explain how mental health symptoms in one family member serve to maintain the stability or homeostasis in the family system. Specifically, he hypothesized how interactions among family members contributed to the development of schizophrenic behavior in one family member and how the symptoms of schizophrenia function to maintain a homeostatic balance in the family. In this theory, stability and change are not mutually exclusive but are interdependent.

Recursiveness in Family Therapy

One of the first centers of family therapy was at the Mental Research Institute (MRI) in Palo Alto, California, where Bateson, Don Jackson, Jay Haley, and John Weakland worked. The MRI brief therapy approach viewed the therapist as an outside observer (first-order cybernetics) focused on identifying the sequence of interactions of the family system. MRI theoretical underpinnings maintained some of the same postwar thinking that moved focus from the individual to the system. Applied to human behavior, this moved the responsibility for a mental disorder from an individual patient to faulty communication patterns within the family system. A change in communication signals of one person would affect the whole family. In the MRI model, the focus of treatment was from the perspective of an outside therapist making observations and implementing interventions on family communications.

Building on the foundations of strategic family therapy, this evolutionary perspective of family functioning was incorporated into family therapy by a group of four psychiatrists at the Centro per lo Studio della Famiglia (Center for the Study of the Family) in Milan, Italy. Mara Selvini-Palazzoli, Luigi Boscolo, Gianfranco Cecchin, and Giuliana Prata were also known as the Milan team. This team produced new systemic concepts when working with families, one of which was recursiveness. They expanded on the cause-and-effect communication sequence ideas of the MRI model by viewing the therapist and family as one entity (second-order cybernetics). The focus of treatment moved from family communication patterns to the process and context of the patterns, including the idea of longer sequences evolving over generations. In 1980, Selvini-Palazzoli, Boscolo, Cecchin, and Prata published an article titled "Hypothesizing—Circularity—Neutrality: Three Guidelines for the Conductor of the Session." One of the new concepts in the family system was circular causality. An example of this circular cause and effect is when a child cries, a mother communicates with the child in a harsh tone, then the child increases the crying behavior, then the mother yells at the child, with each affecting the other.

In the Milan team, circular questioning was used by the therapist (as a part of the system) to produce more questions to develop hypotheses about universal patterns. Expanding on the previous example, the therapist will work to place the circular events into the family context. The therapist would discover that the child cries when the mother is sad, and when the child cries the husband is critical and then the wife becomes sad. The recursive pattern that occurs within the relationship between the husband and wife then creates a recursive pattern within the family system and so on.

Expanding on the previous example, the therapist would hypothesize about the communication pattern between the husband and wife. The focus of therapy would be on changing the underlying family beliefs and rules that contribute to perpetuating the occurrences through the use of recursive circular questioning. The therapist would ask questions of each family member that would elicit a perspective of the relationship between two other family members. The therapist would continue the use of recursive questions to highlight multiple perspectives. This would provide feedback to reveal how that relationship pattern is repeated recursively throughout generations in the family system. In this example, it was discovered that there was an underlying belief that the wife carries the entire responsibility for the child's behaviors at all times. Hearing the multiple perspectives of other family members would provide feedback that would modify relationship interactions, which would affect and change the family system. The recursive nature of the modification of relationships affecting one another brought recursiveness into the forefront of family systems therapy.

A further recursion specific to the Milan team is the concept that therapist as a part of the family system would affect and be affected by changes in the family. As interventions would be implemented, a family would provide feedback. The information received would be incorporated as a revision of the intervention. This would affect the therapists' interactions, which would recursively affect the Milan team. Information that changed the therapist's conceptualizations and did not fit within the team's original ideas would be feedback that would be incorporated through a modification of their theory. The Milan team would then introduce modified interventions to a family to create new interactional patterns. The recursive evolution of family systems highlighted by the Milan team was recursively modeled through the incorporation of feedback from therapy into theory and theory into therapy recursively.

Why Recursiveness Matters

Recursiveness can be seen in maintaining problems in family systems, conceptualization, and intervention, and as part of the evolutionary process of systems integrating feedback to produce change. Incorporating recursiveness into clinical formulation and patterns can facilitate awareness of the circular causality of a problem that possibly has spanned generations. The use of recursiveness in circular questioning requires the counselor to simultaneously be a part of the system and focus on the process of the system. The counselor introduces feedback to relationship interactions, behavior, and beliefs in order to correct the family system. If the therapeutic system maintains an open stance, in addition to affecting the family, feedback from counseling sessions can have an ongoing effect on counseling theory recursively.

Lynn Bohecker

See also Circularity and Linearity; Cybernetics; First-Order Change; Homeostasis; Hypothesis, Systemic; Milan Team; Questions: Open, Closed, and Circular; Second-Order Change; Strategic Family Therapy

Further Readings

Bateson, G. (1972). *Steps to an ecology of mind*. New York, NY: Ballantine Books.

Boscolo, L. (1987). *Milan systemic family therapy: Conversations in theory and practice*. New York, NY: Basic Books.

Cecchin, G. (1987). Hypothesizing, circularity, and neutrality revisited: An invitation to curiosity. *Family Process, 26*(4), 405–413.

Goldenberg, H., & Goldenberg, I. (2013). *Family therapy: An overview* (8th ed.). Belmont, CA: Brooks/Cole.

Selvini, M. P., Boscolo, L., Cecchin, G., & Prata, G. (1980). Hypothesizing—circularity—neutrality: Three guidelines for the conductor of the session. *Family process, 19*(1), 3–12.

REFLECTING TEAM

The term *reflecting* as used in this context is derived from the French-language meaning of the word. In French, *réflexion* means that something heard is internalized and thought about before a response is given. In the field of marriage and family therapy, reflecting teams are used for systemic family therapy treatment. From behind a one-way mirror, a small group of therapists observe another therapist working with a family. The process includes team members' discussion of their observations and thoughts in front of the therapist and family. The therapists and family then discuss the team's conversation among themselves.

The use of reflecting teams as a family therapy model enables families to actively engage in both conversation and reflection about their situation. Additionally, they also offer families many opportunities to revise, rethink, or reinterpret the problem rather than the team of therapists offering a single intervention. This entry provides an overview of the history of reflecting teams, highlighting the use of teams in the Mental Research Institute (MRI) and Milan team approaches and the current use of reflecting teams.

History of Reflecting Teams

In 1987, Tom Andersen created more transparency in the process of having a therapist team behind a one-way mirror through his use of reflecting teams. The reflecting team approach was conducted by a team of therapists behind a one-way screen watching and listening to an interviewer's conversation with the family members. The interviewer, with the permission of the family, then asks the team members about their perceptions of what went on in the interview. The family and the interviewer watch and listen to the team discussion. The interviewer then asks the family to comment on what they have heard. This may happen once or several times during an interview. Due to logistical difficulties in training and gathering a team, reflecting teams are most often used in training institutions and in cases where the therapist and client seem stuck at an impasse.

Andersen found the traditional strategic approaches (MRI and Milan team) were less effective because they tended to pathologize families and promoted therapist belief over family knowledge of their situation. In other words, the process was less transparent and families' thoughts and feedback about their situation were not taken into consideration as an equally valued contribution to their therapy process and an element of change in the family system. The traditional methods only took into consideration the discussion of the therapist and treatment team's impressions of the family (used with the MRI and Milan team approaches).

Additionally, the function of teams used with these traditional methods was a basic process for the assigned therapist to develop a therapeutic relationship, allowing for an effective therapeutic process with the stuck system (a family system unable to resolve its problem) while the rest of the team quietly observed behind the one-way mirror. These traditional methods did not include the observational and feedback component of allowing the family to observe the discussion between the therapist and treatment team and then discussion of the team's conversation with the assigned therapist and the family. These added components to the use of teams were implemented by Andersen and labeled as the reflecting team approach. Moreover, Andersen insisted treatment outcomes were more effective with families that had an opportunity to engage in two types of conversation: an external one in which the family actively participates in sharing their ideas with the therapist as they talk, and an internal one in which families provided thoughts with the therapist as they listened to the reflecting team.

MRI Therapy

The reflecting team approach is based in part on writings and research that came out of the Mental Research Institute in Palo Alto, California, in the mid-1970s. The MRI brief-therapy model is based on the idea that a "stuck" system, that is, a family with a problem, needed new ideas in order to broaden its perspectives and its contextual premises. The overall goal of the therapy model is to ask questions about how the presenting issue constitutes a problem by first defining the problem occurring; asking questions about who is doing what to whom and how is that a problem; taking into consideration the thoughts, feelings, and values about the problem from each family member; and lastly, working toward minimal goals for change.

The MRI approach points out the importance of sharing different versions of the same world. Learning about another person's version of the world can influence a person's own attitudes. In therapeutic settings, this means that the new versions presented to the "stuck" system move it away from the "standstill" around the problem. This integrated approach draws upon the client's strengths and abilities. In the MRI model, the interview follows the typical MRI format. After the interview, each member of a therapist team offers his or her intervention in front of the family. Rather than contriving a single intervention, the team of therapists presents several interventions.

Milan Team Therapy

The use of a team approach in the Milan model was influenced by the writings of Gregory Bateson and Humberto Maturana and observations of certain family therapists working with families. In the Milan model, the therapist team had better insight, regardless of the families' expressed insight into their situation or the process. Bateson and Maturana agreed that it is *the observer* who generates the distinctions we call "reality." Andersen further elaborated on this premise with the belief that one should think of the picture and its explanation more in terms of *both–and* or *neither–nor*, and leave out the *either/or*.

Reflecting Team Approach

In the reflecting team approach, what the family and therapist team considered were equally valued, and therefore the therapist was no longer the expert and did not have better insight into the treatment process. This shift from the Milan team approach to reflecting teams gave way to prepare for the idea of open talks (reflecting) to happen. Additionally, the MRI therapy approach to teams allowed for consideration of the use of various interventions. The team of therapists considered various interventions through their involvement with providing ongoing assessment, observation, and discussion with the assigned therapist.

The major shift from the MRI approach and the Milan approach is that team observers come out from behind the one-way mirror to discuss their impressions with the therapist and family. Andersen's technique evolved into an open and transparent process in which the client was invited to observe the treatment team, thus reducing the client's resistance. Additionally, the reflecting team is an innovation that reduces the social distance between a treatment team and the clients. This process created an open environment in which the family feels part of a team and the team feels more empathy for the family.

The therapy session is structured so that the therapist and family are observed through an observation window by the reflecting team. While the interview is happening, the treatment team listens in silence to the interview. At a point when there is a natural break, roles are reversed and the therapist and family observe the team engage in a conversation about the client family's struggle. In this conversation, open-ended questions may be asked about both the problem and the family's strengths. The team works to understand the individual members of the family in the context of their struggle without offering advice or making value judgments. When the conversation reaches another natural break, the client and therapist once again have a conversation. The therapist asks the family, "What about the conversation you just heard was helpful?" The therapist continues to listen to each family member's view of the usefulness of the team's input without being defensive, drawing a conclusion, or making a value judgment.

The assigned therapist and the family are each fully respected as autonomous systems. They talk about what they choose to talk about in the manner they prefer. Ideally the therapist is not interrupted by the team with suggestions that certain questions be asked or certain topics be considered. As the conversation unfolds, the members of the team behind the screen create their own ideas. The team of therapists respects the autonomy of every person to create his or her ideas; there is a quiet listening behind the screen.

After having followed the conversation for a while, minimally from 10 to 15 minutes, sometimes as long as 45 minutes, the team or the assigned therapist suggests the possibility of hearing the team reflect. The interviewer may ask the family, "I wonder if the team at this point has any ideas that might be helpful. May I ask them if they have?" If the family agrees, the people behind the screen switch on their sound and the family and the therapist observe the team discussion about their impressions of what has taken placed during the therapy session.

Furthermore, the reflections, which are speculative, begin by the members of the team first spontaneously presenting their ideas. Some of these ideas may be elaborated during the conversation, depending upon which ones the team members feel are more significant. These ideas should be connected to verbal or nonverbal material that emerged during the interview. As a general rule, everything that is said should be speculative: "I am not sure," "It occurred to me," "Maybe." The reflecting team has to bear in mind that its task is to create ideas even though some of those ideas may not be found interesting by the family or may even be rejected. What is important is to realize the family will select those ideas that fit. As in therapy, the team ideally tries to figure out the family's own style of reflecting, their rhythm, speed, and modes of communicating. If used for training institutions, the role of the supervisor is to ensure the reflecting team method of therapy involves the assigned therapist and a team of therapists working together with the family.

Tracey M. Duncan

See also Milan Team; Postmodern Therapies; Strategic Family Therapy

Further Readings

Andersen, T. (1987). The reflecting team: Dialogue and meta-dialogue in clinical work. *Family Process, 26,* 415–428.

Andersen, T. (1991). *The reflecting team: Dialogues and dialogues about the dialogues.* New York, NY: W. W. Norton.

Andersen, T. (1995). Reflecting processes: Acts of informing and forming: You can borrow my eyes, but you must not take them away from me! In S. Friedman (Ed.), *The reflecting team in action: Collaborative practice in family therapy* (pp. 11–37). New York, NY: Guilford Press.

Eubanks, R. A. (2002). The MRI reflecting team: An integrated approach. *Journal of Systemic Theories, 21,* 10–19.

Nichols, M. P. (2013). *Family therapy: Concepts and methods* (10th ed.). Upper Saddle River, NJ: Pearson.

Piercy, F. P., Sprenkle, D. H., Wetchler, J. L., & Associates. (1996). *Family therapy sourcebook* (2nd ed.). New York, NY: Guilford Press.

Winek, J. L. (2010). *Systemic family therapy: From theory to practice.* Thousand Oaks, CA: Sage.

RELATIONAL DIAGNOSES

Psychiatric diagnoses in the United States are made based on the *Diagnostic and Statistical Manual of Mental Disorders* (DSM-5). This manual is used to diagnose individuals and interventions are designed based on the diagnosis. However, couple and family clinicians tend to believe that individual (intrapersonal) issues influence and are influenced by interpersonal relationships and problematic relational patterns. Although the DSM-5 is primarily used to diagnose individual issues, relational diagnoses (referred to as relational problems) appear in the

DSM-5 as part of the category "other conditions that may be a focus of clinical attention." These conditions are not considered mental disorders in the DSM but may affect the diagnosis, course, prognosis, or treatment of a patient's disorder. These conditions are presented with their corresponding codes, known as V-codes or Z-codes. If the symptoms forming a condition are significantly contributing to the client's well-being and functioning, the counselor should take into consideration the condition as affecting the primary diagnosis given to a client during the assessment and intake process.

These conditions can affect a primary diagnosis and subsequent treatment, but do not meet the criteria for a mental disorder diagnosis alone and cannot be billed to insurance for coverage as such. Instead, these conditions may be used to concurrently assess for a full diagnosis and associated treatment plan. This entry explains the system of codes assigned to relational diagnoses under the International Classification of Diseases and details the various diagnoses.

V-Codes and Z-Codes

The DSM-5 is utilized in the United States, but the international system used to diagnose mental and physical health is called the International Classification of Diseases. The version approved for use in the United States beginning in 2015 is the *International Statistical Classification of Diseases and Related Health Problems* (ICD-10). The V-codes that were used in the previous edition directly correspond with analogous Z-codes used in the ICD-10. It is important to note that the ICD-10 is significantly more specific regarding the source and etiology of the code, and while the DSM-5 assigns relational diagnoses as a category of conditions, the ICD-10 assigns subcodes that definitively identify an affiliated individual, context, or explanation.

Relational Diagnoses and Counseling

All clients who are the focus of relational diagnoses are encouraged to engage in family counseling for further assessment and treatment. The focus of a relational diagnosis is on the relationship between two or more individuals within a family system, including intimate partners without children. Intimate partner relationships and family relationships, specifically caregiver and child relationships, significantly influence the health and well-being of the individuals involved in these relationships. They may promote adaptive, growth-focused autonomy, constructive feedback and communication, and an active expression of needs.

Alternatively, these relationships may feature qualities and dynamics which have a negative impact on the well-being of the individuals involved. These attributes appear as neglect, abuse, maltreatment, and consistently negative communication patterns which have measurable consequences. However, the relational problems category in the DSM-5 excludes other conditions that may be a focus of clinical attention, including those that fall under the abuse and neglect category. If abuse or neglect is suspected but not established, the counselor may want to assign a relational problems diagnosis pending further consultation. The following diagnoses listed in the DSM-5 are categorized as relational problems.

Parent–Child Relational Problem

This category is coded as V61.20 (Z62.820), parent–child relational problem. The term *parent* in this context describes a child's primary caregiver(s), who may be a biological, adoptive, or foster parent or may be another relative who fulfills a caregiving role for the child. The child in this context may be a minor or may be an adult child. The child client may present with impaired functioning in behavior, cognitive, or affective areas. In minor children, this may be exhibited by reports or observations of inadequate parental control, lacking supervision, or overprotection resulting in the restriction of heathy activities. In adult children, this may present as excessive parental pressure, escalated arguments and conflicts that result in threats of physical violence, or continued avoidant behavior resulting from either pressure or conflict without clear resolution. A counselor may assign this code if there is a possibility of a more severe diagnosis of child mental health, including attention-deficit/hyperactivity disorder (ADHD), conduct disorder, and depression.

Child Affected by Parental Relationship Distress

This category is coded as V61.29 (Z62.898), child affected by parental relationship distress. This code should be used when the focus of clinical attention is the negative effects of parental relationship stress which affects the functioning of the client or dyadic and family system. Negative effects may present as high levels of verbal conflict, emotional distress, or inferred and perceived disparagement directed toward a child (e.g., high levels of conflict, distress, or disparagement) on a child in the family, including effects on the child's mental or other medical disorders. A counselor would consider this code if the client's functioning was affected by current and past negative life events in childhood or adolescence related to the relationship of the parents within the family context. Life events that may be of consideration include frequently expressed hostility, degrading, scapegoating and triangulating, or overprotection resulting from enmeshment. This also includes the expectation that the child will "keep the family's secrets," such as the circumstances related to abuse, dyadic pairings in the family system, or the child's birth.

Sibling Relational Problem

This category is coded as V61.8 (Z62.891), sibling relational problem. Siblings in this context include full, half, step, foster, and adopted siblings. This category should be used when the focus of clinical attention is a pattern of interaction among siblings that is associated with significant impairment in an individual, or affects the functioning of the family system. The counselor may be able to assign this code when a sibling relational problem is affecting the course, prognosis, or treatment of a sibling's mental or other medical disorder. It is of particular clinical concern when the symptoms have developed in more than one of the siblings. Symptoms may present in children or adolescents as dangerous physical altercations, verbal aggression, fear or anxiety experienced by one sibling in the presence of another, depression or feelings of defeat, seemingly unprovoked outbursts of sibling-directed rage, or notable attempts by a child at triangulating a parent in the conflict. When presented in adult clients, a sibling may report unreturned attempts at healthy communication, competition for parent's attention, diminishing a sibling's achievements and successes in comparison with one's own, or ostracizing a sibling from another's created family.

Upbringing Away From Parents

This category is coded as V61.8 (Z62.29), upbringing away from parents. This category should be used when the main focus of clinical attention pertains to issues regarding a child being raised away from the parents or when this separation during upbringing affects the course, prognosis, or treatment of a mental or other medical disorder. The child could be one who is under state custody and placed in foster care, or the child could be one who is living in a nonparental relative's home or with friends, but whose out-of-home placement is not mandated or sanctioned by the courts. Problems related to a child living in a group home or orphanage are also included, but problems related to children living in boarding schools are excluded. Counselors may observe client reports of feeling rejected, empty, anxious, unable to establish stable intimate or nonintimate relationships, a persistent sense of distrust of others' motives, anxiety in the absence of environmental chaos, a restricted routine, or a history of unhealthy attachment and dependence patterns in interpersonal relationships.

Relationship Distress With Spouse or Intimate Partner

This category is coded as V61.10 (Z63.0), relationship distress with spouse or intimate partner.

Counselors may apply this category when the major focus of the clinical contact is to address the quality of the intimate (spouse or partner) relationship or when the quality of that relationship is affecting the course, prognosis, or treatment of a mental or other medical disorder. Partners can be of the same or different genders, or transitioning.

The literature linking adult intimate relationships to mental health outcomes is substantial. There are documented connections between relational processes and the etiology, maintenance, relapse, and most effective treatment of many diagnosable disorders. To diagnose accurately so that effective treatment is delivered, the counselor may assess the level of distress when meeting with clients during the intake process.

Disruption of Family by Separation or Divorce

This category is coded as V61.03 (Z63.5), disruption of family by separation or divorce. This category should be used when partners in an intimate adult couple are living apart due to relationship problems or are in the process of divorce. Clients may initially report above average levels of stress, exhaustion, depression, and sleep and eating disruptions; approximately 60% of clients who report going through a separation or divorce also describe physical ailments due to muscle tension. Additionally, parental conflict before, during, and after a divorce has observable effects on children. Following their parents' separation, children may regress in behavioral patterns; display anxiety and depressive symptoms in various circumstances; appear more irritable, demanding, and noncompliant with simple requests; and experience problems in social relationships and school performance. Parents often feel troubled by and unprepared for their children's reactions to a separation and divorce, and the separated family members are now adjusting to new, and often individualized, patterns and routines and children often feel unsupported or neglected during the establishment of these routines.

This diagnostic category may be appropriate when the levels of reported distress of the parents and children warrant immediate attention to the emergence of symptoms resulting from separation-related crisis and destabilization. Family counselors will need to attend to the relations and communication patterns within the family while considering the mental and emotional functioning of all family members, and immediate goals may be to effectively enhance coping skills, resolve conflict, and measurably improve problem-solving skills.

High Expressed Emotion Level Within Family

This category is coded as V61.8 (Z63.8), high expressed emotion level within family. Expressed emotion is a construct used as a qualitative measure of the "amount" of emotion—in particular, hostility, emotional overinvolvement, and criticism directed toward a family member who is an identified patient—displayed in the family environment. This category should be used when a family's high level of expressed emotion is the focus of clinical attention or is affecting the course, prognosis, or treatment of a family member's mental or other medical disorder.

It is essential that counselors consider culture while gathering data and seeking the identified cause of the symptoms which would indicate this code. Cultural considerations may include attention to country of origin, ethnicity, or the client's racial self-identification. For example, a client may describe elevated family tension as a trigger for anxiety or anger. Based on the level of assessed distress experienced by the client during the diagnosis process, these symptoms may be assumed to accurately represent a relational diagnosis that warrants further evaluation and possibly a concurrent or more intensive additional diagnostic code. Symptoms which are diagnostically relevant in this category are cross-cultural in context and impair functioning in the client's regular daily activities and self-care, necessitating clinical importance and consideration.

Adrianne L. Johnson

See also Attunement in Relationships; DSM and V-Codes; *International Classification of Diseases* (ICD); Parent–Adolescent Relations; Relationship Enhancement; Sibling Relationships

Further Readings

American Psychiatric Association. (2013). *Diagnostic and statistical manual of mental disorders* (5th ed.). Arlington, VA: Author.

Moore, A. M., & Crane, D. R. (2014). Relational diagnosis and psychotherapy treatment cost effectiveness. *Contemporary Family Therapy, 36*(2), 281–299.

Strong, T. (2015). Diagnoses, relational processes and resourceful dialogs: Tensions for families and family therapy. *Family Process, 54*(3), 518–532.

Wamboldt, M. Z., Cordaro, A., Jr., & Clarke, D. (2015). Parent–child relational problem: Field trial results, changes in DSM-5, and proposed changes for ICD-11. *Family Process, 54*(1), 33–47.

Wamboldt, M. Z., Kaslow, N., & Reiss, D. (2015). Description of relational processes: Recent changes in DSM-5 and proposals for ICD-11. *Family Process, 54*(1), 6–16.

RELATIONAL-CULTURAL THERAPY

Relational-cultural therapy (RCT) is a clinical therapeutic model used in individual, couples, and family counseling. The premise of RCT is that human beings are inherently interdependent and seek to connect with one another via relationships throughout their lifetime. According to the theory, humans seek reciprocal relationships in which connection, authenticity, mutual empathy, and mutual empowerment are shared. Additionally, unlike traditional theoretical models, the promotion of social justice and change through the identification and elimination of forces that create individual, cultural, and sociopolitical inequities is an important objective of this theory. In this entry, the etiology and history of RCT, its key concepts, therapeutic process, and application to working with heterosexual couples will be outlined.

Etiology and History of RCT

In 1976, psychiatrist Jean Baker Miller authored the best-selling book *Toward a New Psychology of Women*. According to Miller, traditional mental health models inaccurately labeled and excessively pathologized women as weak, vulnerable, dependent, and overly emotional. The author proposed an alternative schema for working clinically with women—one in which human connections through relationships were central to the premise. In 1978, Miller collaborated with three psychologists, Judith Jordan, Irene Stiver, and Janet Surrey. Also known as the founding scholars, the four women examined the pervasiveness with which psychodynamic theories inaccurately characterized women and their experiences. Their partnership led to the development of an original and alternative paradigm that more authentically reflected women's psychological development. The authors posited that women's sense of self and worth are intertwined in their ability to develop, participate in, and maintain healthy relationships. Originally called the Stone Center theory and self-in-relation theory, today this model is known as relational-cultural theory.

Early critiques of the model pointed out that the founding scholars were all privileged, middle-class, and White women. The founders acknowledged their lack of diversity and became intentional in their efforts to integrate voices from disenfranchised groups in the ongoing development of the theory. By 1985, RCT writings were inclusive of various multicultural and social justice contexts (e.g., race, class, sexual orientation). Today, RCT is a theory that emphasizes the necessity of healthy relationships between humans and within society. Feminist ideologies, multiculturalism, and social justice principles are incorporated in the theory and its practice. Additionally, there are essential concepts that make up RCT.

Key Concepts

The RCT clinician supports the client into deeper relational development. This occurs through the client–counselor dynamic, the reworking of past relational failures the client has experienced, as well as the integration of core RCT tenets posited to facilitate relational health. Key concepts germane to this entry include *connection, mutual empathy, mutual empowerment, mutuality,* and *disconnection.*

Connection

Connection, versus autonomy and independence, is the heart of RCT. It is defined as interpersonal communication in which mutual empathy (shared responsiveness and support) and mutual empowerment (active engagement in the relationship) are exchanged. The premise of connection is that it is the driving motivation of human beings and is paramount to healthy survival. Additionally, through connection, individuals are able to be emotionally available to one another.

Mutual Empathy and Mutual Empowerment

Mutual empathy involves an awareness and validation of each person's cognitive and affective significance on the other. Growing out of mutual empathy is the concept of mutual empowerment. This is a dynamic interpersonal interaction between participants in a relationship that fosters personal development and provides a sense of support and community. Mutual empowerment is deemed essential to psychological growth and aids in the movement toward mutuality.

Mutuality

Mutuality is characterized by an openness, vulnerability, and willingness to be influenced by the other person in the relationship. Mutuality occurs between the client and the therapist with the expectation that the client will grow to develop mutuality in other significant relationships. In couples counseling, the therapist facilitates mutuality between the couple. Conversely, in the absence of mutual empathy, mutual empowerment, mutuality, and connection, individuals disconnect and experience feelings of pain and disempowerment.

Disconnection

A disconnection is a personal isolation and withdrawal from a relationship. Disconnections derive from misunderstandings, perceived or real experiences of exclusion, invalidation, and other injuries. In the RCT model, isolation and disconnection are identified as the primary contributors of pain. Nevertheless, disconnections are ubiquitous in human relationships. Individuals disconnect at various levels ranging from acute to chronic disconnections. Acute forms of disconnection occur regularly due to minor relational failures such as a misunderstanding, and they are easily repaired. Chronic disconnections result from repeated violations of mutuality. These violations are the most painful and take the form of abuse, emotional neglect, humiliation, discrimination, marginalization, and stratified social structures that invest in one group and disempower others. These experiences impact psychological development by negatively influencing relationship dynamics between individuals, groups, and society. These disconnections require added effort to repair and are examined in therapy.

Therapeutic Process

The goals of RCT in practice are to decrease the clients' experiences of isolation and disconnection, improve their capacity to empathize for themselves and others, and reduce and/or correct cultural and relational images. The therapeutic goal is to move the clients into a growth-fostering relationship—this involves each participant mutually engaging and developing from the experience. This relationship is both modeled by and cultivated with the counselor. The positive relational experience established with the counselor facilitates the clients in safely engaging into deeper relationships with others. For couples, this deepened capacity for connection occurs between one another.

Assessment

During the assessment phase, counselors explore the clients' goals or purpose for seeking therapy as well as collect routine demographic information. Specific attention is directed at gathering information regarding significant past and present relationships to the clients. The RCT practitioner also seeks to explore the clients' capacity for self-empathy, coping skills, support systems, personal and social and cultural sources of empowerment, strengths, authentic relationships, and engaging in constructive conflict and to identify cultural and relational images clients bring into the counseling relationship.

Cultural and relational images are internalized expectations of treatment by others or society. While relational images typically involve expectations for interpersonal relationships, cultural images are beliefs held about how an individual or group will be treated within society. These behavioral expectations are typically developed during the primary years of life and frequently transferred from relationship to relationship.

Clients are also evaluated for experiences of disempowerment, discrimination, exclusion, and personal or social traumas. Additionally, it is critical for RCT practitioners to uncover their clients' strategies of disconnection. In other words, these are behaviors clients use to disengage from relationships (e.g., avoidance, preoccupation, inauthenticity, unexpected anger) to maintain feelings of safety and well-being. The counselors' awareness, acknowledgment, and respect for their clients' needs to engage in these strategies of disconnection will enhance authentic connection and help build confidence in the therapeutic relationship long term.

Working With Couples

Interpersonal conflicts are often the presenting concerns for couples that seek counseling. According to RCT theory, these disputes often result from relational roles, differing expectations, and power disparities. In patriarchal societies such as that of the United States, men intrinsically have power over women. This system of dominance creates relational expectations within intimate heterosexual relationships, can trigger psychological distress among women, and can ultimately contribute to relational disconnection.

RCT posits that acknowledging and working through gender roles, power differentials, and relationship expectations is critical to successful couples work. Specifically, when couples are able to recognize the impact of social and cultural influences on their relationship, their interactions with one another shift. In therapy, both women and men are allowed an opportunity to address their relational desires as well as explore how gender-based expectations may support or impair their needs. An objective of therapy, therefore, is to help clients identify their relational images and alter them to align more closely with their mutual relational goals. Additional therapeutic responsibilities for an RCT clinician include facilitating mutually empathetic interactions within the couple's relationship; fostering the couple's capacity for authenticity, good conflict, and respect; cultivating relational awareness and "we-ness"; promoting humor; and developing relational resilience.

Mutually Empathetic Interactions

Mutual empathy is a critical part of the therapeutic process. It facilitates change by each person's actively engaging in the relationship and being responsive to the other. The development of mutual empathy within couples plays a role in the restoration of past relational failures and assists in changing relational images that were developed in early relationships. Mutual empathy moves the couple from individual isolation and suffering toward one another and the relationship.

The teaching and practice of mutual empathy includes assisting the couple in comprehensively understanding their individual impact on one another and their mutual influence on the relationship. This occurs by helping the couple safely develop empathetic communication versus reactive communication. Couples are encouraged to carefully listen to one another and to be willing to share their experiences in a way that considers the potential impact of the information being shared. This also engages vulnerability as each participant allows the other to see and understand the impact of the exchange. It is important to note the practice of mutual empathy can be an extremely vulnerable act for some heterosexual couples due to societally prescribed gender roles and expectations. However, through trust and feelings of safety, couples can release the need to protect themselves through subscribing to gender role behaviors and practice mutual empathy and authenticity with one another.

Responsible Authenticity

Responsible authenticity is the practice of honoring truth that must be addressed in the relationship, while delivering the information in a way that encourages relational growth, support, and love. The RCT clinician plays an important role in teaching couples healthier communication styles. Counselors guide the couples through honest and caring conversations about challenges in the relationship or with one another that cause pain and suffering. An additional task of therapy is teaching couples how to participate in healthy disputes.

Good Conflict

The concept of "good conflict" is emphasized in therapy. Conflict is reframed from a negative experience that should be avoided to an opportunity to repair a disconnection. Couples are encouraged to address power dynamics that may be occurring in their relationship, explore how their differences are resolved, and evaluate how their needs are met. The role of the counselor is to assist clients in reflecting their individual needs as well as understanding the views of their partner when in conflict. An important outcome of good conflict is to help the couple negotiate a safe, authentic, and empathetic approach to addressing their concerns and challenges with one another. The RCT concept of respect is also taught and is an important goal for couples therapy.

Respect

Respect enhances relational growth and trust. It is established when couples listen to one another attentively and allow the experience of one to affect the other. Couples are also encouraged to actively listen to the desires of their partners. Through learning the concept of respect, individuals are taught to release their personal expectations for their partner. Instead, couples develop skills and practice appreciation of one another's individual qualities as well as accept the reality of their partner's role in the relationship. Through respect, couples also deepen their understanding and gratitude for one another. However, respect not only occurs at the individual level, it applies to the relationship as a whole. An additional goal of therapy is to move the couple from viewing the relationship from an individual lens to a collective one.

Cultivating Relational Awareness and We-Ness

The cultivation of "we-ness" is a critical counseling intervention. As couples learn to respect and appreciate their unique contributions to the relationship as well as the individual needs of one another, the counselor navigates them toward a collective consciousness. In other words, we-ness encompasses (a) individual and relationship awareness, (b) a willingness to be vulnerable with one another as well as to be supported, (c) accepting responsibility for the relationship and developing goals for it, and (d) prioritizing the relationship and commitment to sustaining the health of it. Counselors can guide couples into we-ness through the use of various collaborative exercises and activities, including visualization, relational assessment, and the development of a relational purpose statement.

The visualization activity can be used to assist couples with organizing their thoughts about their relationship and verbally expressing them. Participants are asked to think about their relationship and to describe its qualities to one another. An exercise that can be used to take the couple into deeper relational awareness is the relational assessment. This activity enables couples to acknowledge the overall health of the relationship by examining the strengths (connections) and weaknesses (disconnections) of it. After couples portray their view of the relationship and examine its status, counselors can help them determine their commitment to nurturing and prioritizing it. A highly reflective activity that can aid this process is the development of a personal statement.

During this exercise, the couple is instructed to collaboratively write a description of their relational intentions, uncertainties, lessons learned, and plans. A primary objective for this activity is for the couple to shift and move toward one another. Additionally, the couple learns to reprioritize their relationship, acknowledge its purpose, and focus on its success. These are a few supplemental activities that counselors can integrate into therapy to help couples process their relational awareness, capacity for connection, and commitment. Encouraging couples to intentionally inject humor into their relationship is an additional task of therapy.

Humor

The healing effects of laughter are touted in numerous adages. According to RCT theory, humor fosters connection, relational positivity, and growth. Therefore, couples are instructed to find the humor in their relationship. Specifically, they are encouraged to affectionately laugh at themselves, at one another, and together. Humor not only is essential to a healthy relationship, it also supports relational resilience.

Relational Resilience

To be in healthy connection is the ultimate RCT goal for couples in therapy. However, the process of connection is cyclical. In all relationships, disconnection is inevitable. It is especially unavoidable among couples due to misunderstandings, incongruous expectations, power imbalances, relational images, and other stressors that can cause strain on the relationship. Therefore, the paramount task for the RCT practitioner is to foster relational resilience. This begins with teaching couples about the cycle of connection. This cycle elucidates how couples connect, disconnect, repair the disconnection, and reconnect. Relational resilience is the couples' ability to move within and through the cycle of connection. The counselor aids the couple in developing strategies to repair disconnections, including the practice of mutual empathy, authenticity, good conflict, respect, we-ness, and humor. After repair, the couple moves toward the process of reconnection. Relational resilience also encompasses the openness of the couple to reach out to one another or seek professional help, when needed.

According to RCT theory, human beings are intrinsically interdependent and seek to be in relationships with one another throughout their life span. Healthy connection through relationships is a fundamental goal of RCT. This clinical model is useful for working with couples due to its emphasis on relationships.

Feminist ideologies, multiculturalism, and social justice principles are incorporated in the theory. As a result, all therapy occurs within the context of culture. In practice, the counselor pays special attention to identifying sociocultural influences on the relationship, including gender role expectations and power disparities. These oppressions are believed to have a negative impact on couples and contribute to relational distress and disconnection. In therapy, clinicians help couples explore and work through the impact of these dynamics. In addition, RCT practitioners support couples through the following tasks in therapy: develop mutually empathetic interactions; engage in responsible authenticity, practice good conflict, and respect; cultivate relational awareness and we-ness; humor; and learn strategies to support relational resilience. This final task of learning how to repair disconnections and reconnect is vital to relational fortitude among couples.

Kashunda McGriff

See also Cultural Issues in Couples and Families; Diversity; Feminist Family Therapy; Gender- and Culture-Sensitive Therapies; Multiculturalism; Power Issues in Couples

Further Readings

Bergman, S. J., & Surrey, J. L. (1997). The woman-man relationship: Impasses and possibilities. In J. V. Jordan (Ed.), *Women's growth in diversity: More writings from the Stone Center* (pp. 260–287). New York, NY: Guilford Press.

Bergman, S. J., & Surrey, J. L. (2013). Relational-cultural couple therapy: From impasse to movement.

In J. V. Jordan & J. Carlson (Eds.), *Creating connection: A relational-cultural approach with couples* (pp. 11–22). New York, NY: Routledge.

Duffey, T., & Somody, C. (2011). The role of relational-cultural theory in mental health counseling. *Journal of Mental Health Counseling, 33*(3), 223–242.

Jordan, J. V. (2010). *Relational-cultural therapy.* Washington, DC: American Psychological Association.

Jordan, J. V., & Carlson, J. (2013). Couples therapy and relational-cultural therapy (RCT). In J. V. Jordan & J. Carlson (Eds.), *Creating connection: A relational-cultural approach with couples* (pp. 1–10). New York, NY: Routledge.

Markey, R. (2013). Strangers in a strange land: Men in relational couples therapy. In J. V. Jordan & J. Carlson (Eds.), *Creating connection: A relational-cultural approach with couples* (pp. 131–148). New York, NY: Routledge.

Miller, J. B. (1986). *Toward a new psychology of women* (2nd ed.). Boston, MA: Beacon Press.

Miller, J. B., & Stiver, I. (1997). *The healing connection: How women form relationships in therapy and in life.* Boston, MA: Beacon Press.

Skerrett, K. (2013). Resilient relationships: Cultivating the healing potential of couple stories. In J. V. Jordan & J. Carlson (Eds.), *Creating connection: A relational-cultural approach with couples* (pp. 45–60). New York, NY: Routledge.

Relationship Enhancement

Romantic relationships that thrive possess specific values that provide safety and security to each partner. Partners also behave in ways that foster deep emotional connection and intimacy. The behaviors or rituals that happily committed couples engage in are considered relationship enhancement practices. Selecting a mate is a significant life task for most humans. The desires to share one's life with someone else, possibly reproduce, and grow old with someone are nearly universal. There are many opportunities online and in the popular media to either engage in or witness the pairings of single young adults. Media images penetrate the minds of individuals young and old, shaping and perhaps distorting perceptions of what lasting relationships can look like.

Relationship enhancement is an approach to developing realistic relationship expectations along with skills for maintaining long-term intimate relationships. Bernard Guerney and Louise Guerney of Penn State University developed the Center for Couples, Families, and Children in 1992, based on over 40 years of research developing relationship enhancement strategies for work with couples and families. Their Relationship Enhancement model consists of relationship education, as well as a set of core values that couples must engender: commitment to the relationship, mutual respect, acceptance, authenticity, and equity. Relationship education and the aforementioned values included in the Gurneys' Relationship Enhancement model are discussed throughout and integrated with other suggested strategies that couples can learn to practice, including reframing attributions, incorporating fun, making time for connection, and strengthening communication. These skills serve as a launch pad to reaching the ideal of a long-lasting and highly satisfying intimate relationship.

Relationship Education

Several universities across the United States have developed and taught undergraduate courses specifically targeting young adults either engaged in or pursuing intimate relationships. The overarching goals among the programs have been to teach healthy relationship skills, develop awareness of self in relationships, and foster healthy communication and conflict management skills. Components embedded in the courses that show evidence of effectiveness include experiential activities and opportunities for students to discuss reactions to material presented. These activities provide students a chance to process information that relates to their personal experience. Examples of experiential activities include in-class exercises that challenge myths and expectations about relationships, small-group work that allows students to share their perspectives with classmates, and individual relationship counseling in the form of a lab component that accompanies the in-class component of the course.

Research in relationship education has suggested that the earlier individuals are exposed to material that promotes healthy relationship skills, the more likely individuals are to incorporate learned skills into their relationships. It has been suggested that relationship education can begin as early as middle school, and there are programs around the country that are providing curriculum for this level of schooling.

The Relationship Enhancement model developed by Guerney and Guerney provides relationship education to dating, engaged, and married couples. The format is presented in a weekend intensive training for couples that teaches them specific skills that contribute to lasting and satisfying relationships. Examples of skills taught in these seminars are effective listening, communicating well, conflict management, effective problem-solving, and deepening partners' emotional connection.

Counselors who work with couples often find their clients are beyond the developmental stage of receiving preventative relationship education; instead, these clients present with significant relationship issues that are threatening their bond. Nevertheless, because relationships are so pivotal to individual life satisfaction, counselors can incorporate relationship enhancement strategies into their work with current clients, including with those who are experiencing significant relationship disturbance.

Relationship Enhancement and Couples Counseling

Attributions and Acceptance

According to several theories used in counseling, what one thinks, or how one interprets the behavior of others, formally known as attribution, has a direct impact on how one feels and as a result how one behaves. Couples often have clearly established patterns of negative attributions that have adversely affected their relationship—each partner consistently attributes negativity to the actions of the other and uses that information to define their relationship. This directly impacts the way partners feel and behave in their relationship. An example would be an individual waiting for a partner who is late to arrive at a restaurant for dinner to celebrate their anniversary. The partner sitting in the restaurant might have a series of thoughts that the other partner forgot, did not care about the anniversary, and does not make the relationship a priority. When the late partner does eventually arrive, regardless of the circumstances that caused the lateness, the waiting partner is likely to respond in a negative way as a result of the attributions he or she has made regarding the lateness. This is characterized as negative sentiment override, a concept that relationship expert John Gottman described as harmful to relationships. Negative sentiment override is defined as a sense of pessimism that clouds an individual's overall perceptions about the relationship. If the overall sentiment toward the relationship and the romantic partner is negative, an individual's actions and perceptions toward the partner are likely to be negative.

The opposite of negative sentiment override (and what couples should strive to achieve in their relationship) is positive sentiment override (PSO). PSO creates more flexibility in thinking patterns that gives the "offending" partner the benefit of the doubt during unfortunate circumstances. The principle behind PSO is that there is enough positivity "banked" in the relationship to buffer and protect it from challenging and frustrating things that happen. In the example of the individual waiting at a restaurant, if the individual is in PSO he or she might express concern and wonder what happened to cause the partner to be late and not assume that the partner does not value the relationship based on his or her lateness.

Relationship enhancement within couples counseling can begin with an assessment of the type of overall sentiment present in the relationship. If it is established that the partners frequently assign negative attributions to their partners and positive attributions to themselves—a self-serving bias—couples can learn skills that help them to restructure the attributions they make to foster more realistic, positive, and relationship-enhancing attributions.

One way to recreate the positivity that was once present in a couple relationship is to reflect on their first date, how they met, or what originally attracted the partners to one another. Through this indirect strategy, couples are reminded of what it felt like to be attracted to each other, of fun times they had together, and ways of connecting that they may have neglected or forgotten. Once positivity, or glimmers of it, are reestablished, the couple can be encouraged to use that positivity to build on their strengths. The suggested ratio of positive to negative attributions, actions, and events in a healthy relationship is 5:1.

A critical component of the Relationship Enhancement model is fostering acceptance within a couple relationship. Every relationship has strengths and weaknesses; however, the couple must accept the relationship as good in and of itself. Capitalizing on the couple's strengths and learning to accept and manage the challenging aspects of the relationship and the individuals within it can contribute to achieving a sense of PSO as described earlier.

Fun

Couples who have been together for significant time periods move through life stages together such as child-rearing, job changes, relocations, aging parents, and developmental transitions related to aging, illness, and loss. The attention paid to the relationship in its younger years may fade as responsibilities mount and life changes occur. A key component of relationship enhancement for couples is retuning the attention paid to the relationship so that it can create protection from life's stressors. The relationship needs to be strengthened so it can provide connection, satisfaction, and warmth to each partner.

Specific strategies for relationship enhancement include structured activities, such as creating a "fun deck." Couples can be instructed to each write down 10 things they would like to do with each other sometime in the next month. Guidelines such as a price limit, time allotment, and creativity (something besides dinner and a movie, for example) are encouraged to help couples place a framework around the activity. Once each partner has completed his or her list, the lists are exchanged, and each person chooses three activities he or she would be willing to plan to do with his or her partner in the next month. The couple then reconvenes with six mutually agreeable activities, from which they can choose all, or one or two, to commit to doing together. The activities should be fun, affordable, and designed for connecting and enjoying each other's company. Making time for fun is a critical component of healthy relationships, and should not be viewed as burdensome.

Commitment and Connection

Woven throughout healthy relationships and relationship enhancement is the concept of commitment. A deep sense of commitment to one's intimate partner, commitment to achieving relationship success, happiness, and connection contribute significantly to a couple's chances of long-lasting love. The practices and skills that couples learn need to be accompanied by a commitment from each partner to continue the work that it requires to achieve relationship success.

A structured activity that can deepen a couples' sense of commitment and be incorporated into the daily routine takes only 5 hours per week, divided among the 7 days of the week. Gottman calls this concept *the magic 5 hours*. The magic 5 hours are broken down into five categories of activities couples can engage in regularly throughout the week. The first activity involves partings. The couple is advised to spend 2 minutes per day, for each of 5 working days, learning something important that the partner will do during his or her day, offering affection, and saying goodbye. The second activity involves reuniting—spending about 20 minutes per day, 5 days a week, learning what happened in the partner's day, debriefing, and reconnecting. Admiration and appreciation is the third activity that comprises the magic 5 hours. Every day couples are advised to spend 5 minutes sharing a compliment or otherwise expressing appreciation for something about their partner. Likewise, couples are advised to spend 5 minutes each day, 7 days a week (more is okay) showing affection for one another—hugging, kissing, cuddling, touching. Finally, couples should set aside 2 hours per week for alone time, in the form of a date. Referring back to the "fun deck" can be helpful in guiding this activity, but it is not necessary that the couple engage in what is traditionally thought of as a date. The quality of time spent together is more important than the activity itself.

Communication and Equity

Effective communication practices are foundational to healthy relationships. Learning and practicing active listening strategies, not only when faced with conflict, leads to increased relationship satisfaction. Active listening techniques, such as reflecting what a partner has conveyed, paraphrasing a statement, or perception checking, can help partners understand each other. The power of listening cannot be understated. When a person feels heard and understood, the connection between the two individuals in the relationship is strengthened.

Learning basic active listening skills is best done around nonconflict topics. Practicing and incorporating good listening skills into one's regular style of communication can make conflict management and resolution easier. Couples are advised to develop healthy communication skills outside conflict, perhaps when discussing topics such as a dream vacation or a long-term goal so that they can learn the skills while discussing an issue that is not emotionally laden. Strong communication skills build strong relationships and serve as protective factors during conflict. Conflict within relationships can be positive if managed constructively. Good communication around conflict can help keep small issues in perspective, promote understanding and empathy for one's partner, and continue to support the positive sentiment override couples should strive to maintain in their relationships. Good communication overall supports equity in intimate relationships—both partners contribute meaningfully to the relationship, and each perspective is valued.

Revitalizing and enhancing an intimate relationship has no drawbacks. Researchers have demonstrated that being in a healthy relationship affects many areas of overall well-being. These include emotional health, psychological health, and physical health. People in healthy relationships have lower risk of heart disease, diabetes, blood pressure, and fewer mental health problems. Couples will face many problems throughout their relationship. While addressing the problems is important, attention to enhancement strategies can indirectly assist in problem-solving. As couples reconnect and enrich their relationships, problems become manageable, and collaboration can begin.

Veronica I. Johnson

See also Cognitive-Behavioral Couples Therapy; Communication in Couples and Families; Gottman Method Couples Therapy; Listening, Empathic

Further Readings

Arp, D., & Arp, C. (1997). *10 great dates to revitalize your marriage.* Grand Rapids, MI: Zondervan.

Fincham, F. D., Harold, G. T., & Gano-Phillips, S. (2000). The longitudinal association between attributions and marital satisfaction: Direction of effects and role of efficacy expectations. *Journal of Family Psychology, 14,* 267–285.

Gottman, J. M., & Silver, N. (2000). *Seven principles for making marriage work: A practical guide from the country's foremost relationship expert.* New York, NY: Three Rivers Press.

Johnson, V. I. (2011). Adult children of divorce and relationship education: Implications for counselors and counselor educators. *The Family Journal, 19*(1), 22–29.

Markman, H. J., Stanley, S. M., Blumberg, S. L., Jenkins, N. H., & Whiteley, C. (2003). *12 hours to a great marriage: A step-by-step guide for making love last.* San Francisco, CA: Wiley.

Scuka, R. (2005). *Relationship enhancement therapy: Healing through deep empathy and intimate dialogue.* New York, NY: Routledge.

Release of Information for Couples and Families

A release of information is a written document signed by a client or clients that gives permission for the therapist to share confidential information with someone outside of the therapeutic relationship. It may also be referred to as an authorization to release information. Individuals to whom information may be released include physicians, psychiatrists, school personnel, other mental health professionals, social service organizations, attorneys, court personnel, family or friends of the client, or anyone else with whom the client would like information about their treatment to be shared. In family therapy, depending on the practice setting and services provided by the therapist or agency, the release of information may need to be completed by the identified patient, by the adult guardian or guardians, or by all of the family members participating in counseling on one form.

Obtaining a release of information from a client or family member should include a clear explanation of the purpose of releasing the information, clear explanation of what will and will not be shared, identification of the dates of treatment for which information may be shared, and identification of the date when the release will no longer be valid. Adults should be asked to provide both verbal and written consent to release information. Minors, who cannot legally provide consent, should be asked to provide verbal and/or written assent whenever possible. The client or clients must provide their authorization to release information of their own free will, without coercion or fear of punishment for refusing to authorize the release of information. The need for a release of information may be suspended in cases of imminent danger to oneself or others and in cases of child or elder abuse or neglect as governed by state and federal law. This entry provides an overview of the elements of a release of information as well as the laws and regulations governing this authorization.

Elements of a Release of Information

A general release of information should be written in language that is understandable to the client or clients authorizing the release. A release document typically contains the client or clients' printed full name or names, date(s) of birth, and client identification number if the therapist provides one. The full name and position or relationship to the client for the person receiving the information should be stated on the release, as well as this person's address, phone number, and fax number if one is available. The release should specify what information is to be shared with the recipient. Typical information that may be released includes treatment summaries, diagnostic or assessment information, verbal consultation about client progress in treatment, dates of attendance, date of completion or end of counseling, case notes, treatment plans, or the entire contents of the chart. The client or clients should specify which types of information they consent to releasing to the individual receiving the information.

The release of information typically includes the date on which the release is completed, as well as the dates of service for which information can be shared. For example, if a client has been participating in therapy for several years but authorizes release of information only for the previous 12 months, only information from the previous 12 months can be released. If a client has entered therapy recently, the client may choose to authorize release of information through a future date that will allow the therapist to share information obtained in future sessions. In all cases, the start and end dates for releasing information must be stated on the written release.

In addition, the written authorization itself is only valid for a certain period. Typically, the client selects the date when the release will expire or, if no date is provided, a standard period of time that the release is valid may be stated on the release. After this date expires, a new release of information must be obtained in order to share information with individuals outside of the therapeutic relationship.

The release is considered valid only after the client or clients have signed and dated the release. In addition, a witness signature and date are also typically included on the release. The client or clients may rescind a previously completed release of information at any time. The client should do so in writing on the original release by writing *rescind* and documenting both the date and time that the release is being rescinded. The client or clients should sign and date the rescinding of the release, and the therapist should sign and date the release as a witness to the rescission.

Laws, Regulations, and Ethical Codes

Several laws and regulations govern in which circumstances a release of information must be obtained and by whom it must be authorized. The Health Insurance Portability and Accountability Act (HIPAA) of 1996 identifies regulations that must be followed to protect personally identifiable health information and describes how to protect clients' rights to privacy. HIPAA regulations apply to any agency that uses electronic means to share individual client information (including using electronic means to communicate with insurance companies). HIPAA regulations describe what kinds of information is protected, when and how authorization should be obtained to release protected health information, and under what circumstances a release of information is not needed to provide information to another individual or agency. Generally speaking, HIPAA allows adult guardians of minors to provide authorization for release of information on behalf of a minor client. HIPAA regulations also state that clients or family have a legal right to request access to or a copy of their records, which must be furnished in a timely manner. Because most agencies and therapists are HIPAA-covered entities, it is important for therapists and other service providers to be aware of this law and its implications for the release of client information to a third party.

A specific set of federal regulations governs the release of patient records when a therapist or agency is providing substance abuse treatment services in federally funded programs. This can apply to certain nonprofit agencies, clinics, schools, and programs run by or involving county or state probation agencies. The Code of Federal Regulations, Title 42, Chapter I, Subchapter A, Part 2 (42 CFR), states that information related specifically to a client's substance abuse treatment cannot be shared without client consent. In the case of minors being treated for substance abuse, the minor himself or herself must provide written authorization to release information to third parties, including to his or her family members. In a family therapy setting that falls under the auspices of 42 CFR, the client seeking substance abuse treatment services must complete a release of information authorizing verbal communication regarding treatment to family members in order for them to participate in family counseling where the client's substance use and/or substance abuse treatment will be shared. The 42 CFR provisions also protect a client's records from being subpoenaed for the purpose of using information about substance use or treatment against the client in court; the client's records may be requested by court order, however. Because this law impacts both the content and the process of obtaining a release of information from clients in federally funded substance abuse treatment settings, it is important for providers in these settings to familiarize themselves with the specific stipulations and requirements of 42 CFR.

In addition to these laws, ethical codes, such as those of the American Association for Marriage and Family Therapy (AAMFT), American Counseling Association (ACA), American Psychological Association (APA), and National Association of Social Workers (NASW), all include statements on the circumstances under which client authorization for the release of information must be obtained. The AAMFT ethical code, for example, specifies that each individual participating in couple or family counseling provide written authorization for the release; further, this ethical code states that written release be obtained from individual, couple, or family members prior to sharing information provided individually to the therapist.

Because members of a professional organization are expected to adhere to the organization's code of ethics, helping professionals should familiarize themselves with any and all ethical codes for organizations of which they are a member.

Amy E. Williams

See also Confidentiality; Duty to Warn and Protect; Ethical Codes; Identified Patient; Informed Consent in Clinical Work

Further Readings

American Association for Marriage and Family Therapy. (2015). *Code of ethics*. Retrieved from https://www.aamft.org/iMIS15/AAMFT/Content/legal_ethics/code_of_ethics.aspx

American Counseling Association. (2014). *2014 ACA code of ethics*. Retrieved from http://www.counseling.org/resources/aca-code-of-ethics.pdf

American Psychological Association. (2010). *Ethical principles of psychologists and code of conduct, including 2010 amendments*. Retrieved from http://www.apa.org/ethics/code/

National Association of Social Workers. (1996). *Code of ethics of the National Association of Social Workers*. Retrieved from http://www.socialworkers.org/pubs/code/code.asp

U.S. Department of Health and Human Services. (2007, August 13). *Health information privacy*. Retrieved from http://www.hhs.gov/ocr/privacy/hipaa/understanding/index.html

U.S. Government Publishing Office. (2015. January 29). *Electronic code of federal regulations: Title 42 Chapter I Subchapter A Part 2*. Retrieved from http://www.ecfr.gov/cgi-bin/text-idx?rgn=div5;node=42%3A1.0.1.1.2

Religion

Most people around the world identify with some form of religion. For clinicians working with families and couples, understanding clients' religious beliefs and practices can be an important and sometimes integral part of the clinical process. This entry discusses how religion is defined; research findings on its connections to health, well-being, and marital satisfaction; and how clinicians address religion in working with clients.

Defining Religion

Religion refers to a set of beliefs, practices, and views, often linked very closely to cultural practices and specific ethnic groups. Major world religions include Hinduism, Buddhism, Judaism, Christianity, Islam, Confucianism, while other religions include the Baha'i Faith, Jainism, Sikhism, Chinese folk religions, and traditional African religions. Religions often include a set of beliefs that explain or give meaning to human nature, to our purpose and role on earth, to what happens after death, and to a supernatural force or being. Religions also have associated practices or rituals, some practiced regularly on a daily or weekly basis and others tied to specific holy days. Religious practices often involve the use of sacred texts, including such works as the Qur'an in Islam, the Tanakh and Talmud in Judaism, the Vedas in Hinduism, or the Christian Bible in Christianity. Religions can fall broadly into the following categories: monotheistic religions believing in one deity, such as Judaism, Christianity, and Islam; polytheistic religions believing in multiple deities, such as Hinduism; and religions based not on a supernatural being but on teachings such as the path to enlightenment in Buddhism. A great variety of religions, and a great variety of practices and beliefs within each religious tradition, exist around the world.

Religion, Health, and Well-Being

Many studies and analyses of multiple studies have established a strong connection between religion and mental health. In order to study religion, religious behaviors are operationalized, or broken down into specific behaviors that can be measured and studied. For example, a researcher can measure how often a person reads a sacred text or how long a person prays each day. Such measurable behaviors indicate a person's degree of religiousness or religiosity. Research studies can then investigate the impact of religiosity on factors such as mental health.

An extensive amount of research indicates that religious people have fewer symptoms of depression; lower levels of drug, alcohol, and tobacco use; and lower rates of high-risk sexual practices. Similarly, religious adolescents seem more likely to engage in healthy behaviors and less likely to engage in high-risk behaviors. Among at-risk youth, religion is associated with less delinquency and fewer delinquent behaviors. However, some of the findings for religious at-risk youth are inconsistent. When researchers study the religiosity of individual at-risk youth, findings are mixed, but when at-risk youth are looked at in their peer groups, findings are more conclusive. When at-risk youth spend time in peer groups made up of mostly religious friends, then the risk of delinquent behaviors decreases. Overall, research seems to indicate that religion increases a sense of connectedness and belonging to a group and promotes positive behavior as well as physical and mental health and well-being.

Yet when looking at the impact of religion on stress and anxiety, the results appear again to be inconsistent. Religious institutions appear to be associated with both an increase and a decrease in stress. Similarly some experiences of religion appear to be associated with higher levels of anxiety. Belief in eternal life seems to help reduce some of the negative effects of stress. Yet negative religious experiences can increase anxiety and even depression. Again, the complexity of the impact of religion is apparent.

Religious Motivation and Mental Health

Religiosity can be defined as having extrinsic or intrinsic motivations. Extrinsic motivations involve the practice of religion in order to gain some specific end or to achieve a goal. Extrinsic motivations to practice religion include getting ahead in life, satisfying a deity, benefiting personal relationships or improving social standing, and earning a place in the afterlife. In contrast, intrinsic motivations involve beliefs and organizing principles that are central to a person's life, shape a person's worldview, and give meaning and purpose to life. Intrinsic motivations to practice religion include love of others, love of the divine, and compassion for those who are suffering.

These two differing types of motives for religious practice have been linked to different mental health outcomes. When examined in terms of marriage, family, and couple relationships, extrinsic religiosity can motivate responses such as duty, responsibility, and commitment as obligation. In contrast, intrinsic religiosity tends to motivate responses such as love and relational commitment as a belief and value. Research has found that extrinsic religious motivations are predictive of worsened mental health and decreased marital satisfaction. Conversely intrinsic religious motivations are predictive of improved mental health and increased marital satisfaction. Such findings seem to indicate that how religion is practiced matters, and that religious motivation can be associated with either positive or negative mental and relational health. The implications for marriage, family, and couples counselors seem significant, as clinicians may need to understand not only what religion is practiced but also how that religion is being practiced. Therapeutic outcomes may be influenced by the possible positive or negative impact religious practices are having on the individual and family members involved.

Some of the methods of study used to investigate intrinsic and extrinsic religious motivations have been critiqued. Specifically, critics have argued that what researchers are trying to investigate is not actually what researchers end up investigating. For example, trying to distinguish between intrinsic and extrinsic motivations can be difficult when people's motivations sometimes blur the line between categories. For this and other reasons, extrinsic and intrinsic religious motivations have been critiqued as poor measures of religious behavior and interactions with the divine. Instead, more researchers are turning to spirituality as an alternative and important dimension in understanding the human–divine connection.

Religion as a Factor in Marital Experience

Understanding religion as a factor in the marital experience is particularly important for clinicians practicing marriage, family, and couples counseling. The significance of religion in the United States and the link between religiosity and marital satisfaction in particular is well documented. The vast majority of the population in the United States claims that religion is either very important or fairly important in their lives.

A significant amount of research indicates that for married couples, religiosity is positively associated with relational satisfaction. Religion appears to positively impact couples in a number of significant ways, both directly and indirectly. For couples experiencing a major source grief or tragedy, such as the death of a child, religious coping strategies can be of particular support. However, that religious coping, a frequent coping strategy, can be positive or negative. Negative religious coping can lead to beliefs that a person has been abandoned or punished by God. Positive religious coping can lead to comforting beliefs, such as that a person will see their deceased loved one again.

Regularly practicing prayer also seems to support marital satisfaction, although the saying "couples who pray together stay together" may not be entirely accurate. While prayer may not predict relational longevity, studies indicate that couples who practice in-home worship activities such as prayer and scripture study have higher levels of relationship satisfaction and increased unity and trust in their partner. Also there appear to be higher levels of relationship quality among couples who share religious beliefs and participate in religious activities as a family. Greater couple satisfaction has been linked to couples in same-faith relationships who regularly attend religious services and have the same core religious values and beliefs. For partners with different faiths, relational satisfaction has been linked to sharing similar levels of religiosity. For example, a devout Catholic married to a devout Jew would tend to have higher marital satisfaction than a nominal Catholic married to a devout Jew. Additionally, couples who perceive God's influence in their marriage tend to report experiencing marital stability and unity, personal growth and motivation, happiness, and peace.

Religion, Race, and Marital Experience

Research indicates that race and ethnicity stand out as particularly important in understanding the impact of religion on individual and family identity. National origin and geography also intersect with race and ethnicity. For example, a U.S. citizen born in New York City who belongs to a Conservative Jewish congregation would be culturally and religiously different from an Orthodox Jewish Israeli citizen born in Jerusalem, despite both being ethnically Jewish and practicing Judaism. Understanding the intersectionality of religious identity with multiple other identities is essential for clinicians working with families of any religious background.

Race and ethnicity are also important in understanding the impact of religiosity on marital satisfaction. For example, researchers have struggled to understand the gap in relationship satisfaction found between non-Hispanic White couples and African American couples. Research indicates that non-Hispanic White couples tend to have significantly higher relationship satisfaction than African American couples. Yet African American couples tend to have higher levels of religiosity, which correlates with higher relationship satisfaction. The degree to which religion influences this racial gap in relationship satisfaction is extremely complex when considering issues such as discrimination, acculturation, neighborhood disorder, and poverty. In exploring this racial gap, researchers Christopher Ellison, Amy Burdette, and W. Bradford Wilcox suggest that religious faith plays a more important role among couples of color and that shared religious beliefs seem crucial in supporting minority couples' relationship satisfaction. Such findings suggest that although couple satisfaction is linked to higher levels of religiosity, a more complex relationship exists across race and ethnicity.

Religion, Gender, and Marital Experience

Research seems to indicate that gender differences also significantly impact the influence of religiosity on married couples. Religion seems to matter more for men's overall mental health than for women's, although researchers are unsure why. Also, husbands who attend religious services on a regular basis seem to experience lower levels of marital conflict and negative interactions than nonattending husbands. However, wives seem to experience similar benefits only when their husbands attend religious services with them. Gendered differences also appear to interact with racial differences among religious couples. Research suggests that among African American couples, husbands' religiosity may positively relate to both their own and their wives' level of marital satisfaction. Yet among Latino husbands, identification with Catholicism has been linked to more negative marital conflict resolution skills. These findings suggest the complexity of the link between couples' gender, their race, and their experience of religion.

Clinicians and Religious Clients

The majority of mental health clinicians do not address religion with clients. However, religious therapists are more likely than nonreligious therapists to address religion, as are marriage and family therapists compared with psychologists or psychiatrists. Research suggests that clients can benefit from having religion integrated into treatment. Research seems to suggest that as couples learn to focus on relationship strengths already present, differences in religious practice and belief and in degree of faith commitment can actually lead to more understanding and better relational outcomes. In striving for religious competency, clinicians need training in religious sensitivity, in addressing religion in therapy, and in understanding different religious traditions. Ongoing training and consultation is especially needed when approaching the complexity and uniqueness of religious cultural backgrounds.

Elisabeth Esmiol Wilson

See also Ethnicity; Gender Issues; Marriage and Health; Mental Health, Systemic Perspective; Spirituality

Further Readings

Carlson, T. D., Kirkpatrick, D., Hecker, L., & Killmer, M. (2002). Religion, spirituality, and marriage and family therapy: A study of family therapists' beliefs about the appropriateness of addressing religious and spiritual issues in therapy. *American Journal of Family Therapy, 30*(2), 157–171.

Ellison, C. G., Burdette, A. M., & Wilcox, W. B. (2010). The couple that prays together: Race and ethnicity, religion, and relationship quality among working-age adults. *Journal of Marriage and Family, 72*(4), 963–975.

Hughes, P. C., & Dickson, F. C. (2005). Communication, marital satisfaction, and religious orientation in interfaith marriages. *Journal of Family Communication, 5*(1), 25–41.

Kaslow, F., & Robinson, J. A. (1996). Long-term satisfying marriages: Perceptions of contributing factors. *American Journal of Family Therapy, 24*(2), 153–169.

Mahoney, A., Pargament, K. I., Tarakeshwar, N., & Swank, A. B. (2008). Religion in the home in the 1980s and 1990s: A meta-analytic review and conceptual analysis of links between religion, marriage, and parenting. *Psychology of Religion and Spirituality, S*(1), 63–101.

Rostosky, S. S., Otis, M. D., Riggle, E. D. B., Kelly, S., & Brodnicki, C. (2008). An exploratory study of religiosity and same-sex couple relationships. *Journal of GLBT Family Studies, 4*, 17–36.

Walker, D. F., Gorsuch, R. L., & Siang-Yang, T. (2004). Therapists' integration of religion and spirituality in counseling: A meta-analysis. *Counseling & Values, 49*(1), 69–80.

Walsh, F. (Ed.). (2008). *Spiritual resources in family therapy*. New York, NY: Guilford Press.

REMARRIAGE

See Marriage, First and Second; Stepfamilies

Resilience

Resilience is defined as the personal characteristics, resources, and processes that enable one to thrive in the face of adversity. The term *resilience* carries multiple meanings across the various disciplines and helping professions, and although it is operationalized in numerous ways, most definitions center on two major concepts: adversity and a process of positive adaptation. A common assumption is that resilient individuals are able to bounce back from adversity, reaching or surpassing a precrisis level of functioning. Resilience carries a *salutogenic orientation*, that is, a focus on factors that support health and well-being rather than on factors that cause illness. Thus, strengths, rather than deficits, are emphasized and viewed as the resources that allow individuals to overcome adversity. Principle components of resilience include a balanced perspective on life and previous experiences (equanimity), the capacity to carry on regardless of events and adverse conditions (perseverance), awareness of our own strengths and weaknesses (self-belief or self-reliance), and having goals in life (motivation and meaningfulness). This entry examines the roots of resilience, resilience in families, and vicarious resilience.

The Roots of Resilience

Resilience has roots in the field of positive psychology. A major impetus of research into the concept was a paradigm shift in the field of psychology from examination of risk factors and deficits leading to problems and pathology to the identification of strengths that might explain why some persons not only survive, but thrive, when encountering stresses, strains, and even major traumatic life events. Early studies primarily investigated characteristics such as positive self-esteem, hardiness, self-efficacy, emotional regulation, planning skills, the ability to see failure as a form of helpful feedback, and supportive social and familial environments, as contributors to resilience. Researchers have distinguished between *protective* factors that insulate or shield persons from the potential negative effects of an event, and *promotive* factors that lead to unique positive outcomes (e.g., frequent success experiences). Protective factors were the focus of research until the early 1990s, giving way to subsequent study of *processes* of resilience that include contextual and temporal considerations. A process conceptualization of resilience asserts that the effects of the protective and promotive factors vary across contexts and across a person's life span. A confluence of innovations in the fields of ecology, critical theory, sociology, systems theory, and therapy have led to a resilience framework that acknowledges the importance of multiple social contexts and relationships in resilience, and the dynamic processes involved in successful adaptation to adversity. It is acknowledged that operational definitions and indicators of resilience depend a great deal on cultural presuppositions and who has the power to decide which benchmarks are relevant or meaningful within specific populations.

Resilience can develop as people mature and gain more effective self-management skills and better understand that the ways they think influence the ways they feel about challenging circumstances. Contributors to resilience include supportive relationships with parents, peers, and others, as well as cultural beliefs and traditions that help people cope with the inevitable obstacles in life. Additional factors include a positive view of oneself and one's strengths and abilities, the ability to manage strong feelings and impulses (i.e., emotional intelligence), good problem-solving and communication skills, seeking help and resources, viewing oneself as a survivor rather than as a victim, avoiding harmful coping strategies (e.g., substance abuse), and finding positive meaning in one's life despite difficult or traumatic events. Resilient persons choose to not dwell on failures, instead acknowledging the situation, learning from their mistakes, and moving forward. Taking decisive action to address adversity as much as possible can allow persons to maintain a sense of agency. Resilient persons do not see crises as insurmountable; current circumstances that cannot be changed are accepted, allowing one to focus on other circumstances that can be altered. A hopeful, optimistic outlook permits one to anticipate good things happening in one's life and visualizing what one wants in the near future seems to be more helpful than worrying about what will be. Individual and family resilience factors do not always overlap.

Resilience in Family Systems

Sociological understandings of individuals and families, and ecologically and cybernetically informed views of family systems, have contributed to the notion of *resilience in families*. In the first wave of literature on family resilience, family stress scholars laid the foundation for family resilience through a gradual refinement of Reuben Hill's ABCX model of family stress and the proposals for the double ABCX model and the family adjustment and adaptation response model. The second wave of family resilience literature featured an increased emphasis on process, protection, and ecosystems. While individual factors in resilience have historically consisted of flexibility, self-efficacy, and self-esteem, family factors in resilience include stress management, collaborative goal-setting, and problem-solving. Family resilience involves *processes* that enable the family system to rally in times of crisis, to buffer stress, reduce the risk of dysfunction, and support optimal adaptation. A resilient family system enables members to find a sense of meaning and to regain a sense of control about their lives following adversity. Family resilience allows members to cultivate strengths in order to meet the challenges of life. Drawing on the family strengths literature, one conceptualization of resilience in family systems identifies several factors associated with resilience in families, including cohesion, connectedness, time together, commitment, communication, spirituality, and adaptability. Cohesion refers to the emotional connections among family members and is crucial to families' functioning. Too much or too little cohesion (enmeshment or detachment) tends to lead to dysfunction, but a middle region of empathic involvement tends to lead to optimal functioning. Family belief systems are also crucial to family functioning, with beliefs triggering emotional responses, informing decisions and guiding actions, and helping families make meaning of crises. Hope, positive outlook, transcendence, and spirituality are additional contributors to family resilience, as are organizational resources (flexibility and stability, connectedness and leadership, and kin and socioeconomic resources), and communication processes (clear and consistent messages, open affective expression, and collaborative problem-solving).

Resilient families are ones that facilitate their members' coping, healing, and positive growth through individual and system crises, and support these processes through familial, community, cultural, and spiritual connections. The concept of family resilience invites a shift in focus from deficits and limitations to one on strengths, resources, and potential. When stressful events occur, the family response is to facilitate the adaptation of all members through the identification of kin, social, community, and spiritual resources and to build networks and teams to support members. Resilience is relationally based, rather than relying on tropes such as the "rugged individual." A contextualization of distress can permit a decrease in blame, shame, and guilt, and shared challenges are viewed as meaningful, manageable, and comprehensible based on a family's sense of coherence. Social and economic resources represent additional sources of resilience and involve the mobilization of kin and social support and the recruitment of mentors. Professionals who carry a strong belief in the strengths and potential of all families can use language to depathologize and humanize family struggles, tamp down blaming and shaming, focus on abilities and gifts, invite clients to see crisis as an opportunity, and ground them in their ties to family, cultural, and community identity and ties.

Evidence-based resiliency programs have been developed to help military families, couples, and children. Parent-child interaction therapy is an approach designed to improve caregivers' parenting skills, reduce parents' stress levels, and ameliorate children's behavioral challenges. FOCUS (Families OverComing Under Stress) is another resiliency intervention that has been shown to be effective with military and nonmilitary families. Components include family-specific psychoeducation on issues such as traumatic brain injury, posttraumatic stress, and the impact of stress on families and child development, training in emotional awareness and regulation, goal-setting, communication, and problem-solving, and the sharing of different family members' narrative timelines and the creation of a shared family narrative from them. Formation of shared family narratives can bridge the disconnection or estrangement often experienced in families dealing with posttraumatic stress and clear up misunderstandings in these systems. Narrative therapy can facilitate the reauthoring or reframing of family members' lives and situations in more meaningful ways and help families approach adversity with a greater sense of optimism. Contemporary theories stress that family resilience is, rather than a *categorical state*, a continuum contingent on specific circumstances for specific families.

Research on resilience in children historically took a static view, with early studies employing terms such as *invulnerable* and *invincible* children. Current studies emphasize the dynamic nature of resilience, and a number of intervention programs designed to improve the resilience of impoverished and disadvantaged children have demonstrated effectiveness. Evidence-based child intervention programs include the Nurse Home Visitation Program, Carolina Abecedarian Project, Minnesota Family Investment Project, and Families and Schools Together. The most robust evidence available on individual psychological resilience is found in studies focused on children and adults. The research on resilience in families and communities is comparatively limited, with the vast majority of research on family resilience focused on possible predictors of resilient outcomes. However, there is little available research evidence on the topic of community or family resilient outcomes.

For clinical and research purposes, measures of resilience demonstrating reliability and validity include the Child and Youth Resilience Measure (CYRM), Resilience Scale, Family Solidarity Scale (a measure of family unity, mutual support, and collaborative problem-solving), Resiliency Scale, Connor-Davidson Resilience Scale, and Vicarious Resilience Scale.

Vicarious Resilience

A counterpart to resilience is vicarious resilience, a phenomenon by which trauma therapists experience personal and professional growth by being witness to and inspired by their clients' resilience and recovery processes. Specific domains of growth include (a) changes in life goals and perspectives, (b) client-inspired hope, (c) increased recognition of clients' spirituality as a therapeutic resource, (d) increased self-awareness and self-care practices, (e) increased consciousness about power and privilege relative to clients' social location, (f) increased capacity for resourcefulness, and (g) increased capacity for remaining fully present while listening to trauma narratives. Attention to vicarious resilience (VR) enriches how helping professionals who work with trauma deal with the emotional aspects of their work. Work in the area of VR points to the importance of seeing it as a process equally as significant as vicarious traumatization, since VR adds a valuable resource for empowerment rather than a measure of deficit or pathology. Trainers, supervisors, and clinicians can look to identify and decrease vicarious traumatization and identify and increase vicarious resilience by developing awareness and purposefully cultivating and expanding it. The vicarious resilience scale (VRS), developed to measure VR, correlates moderately and positively with posttraumatic growth, emotional intelligence, and compassion satisfaction and appears to measure an independent, unique construct that may explain why some helping professionals who specialize in working with survivors of severe traumas (e.g., political torture or displacement from war zones) maintain their well-being and do not succumb to compassion fatigue or burnout.

Kyle D. Killian

See also Family Resilience; Family Stress; Scales, Children; Scales, Family

Further Readings

Antonovsky, A. (1987). *Unraveling the mystery of health: How people manage stress and stay well.* San Francisco, CA: Jossey-Bass.

Bonanno, G., Romero, S., & Klein, S. (2015). The temporal elements of psychological resilience: An integrative framework for the study of individuals, families, and communities. *Psychological Inquiry, 26,* 139–169.

Fletcher, D., & Sarkar, M. (2013). Psychological resilience: A review and critique of definitions, concepts, and theory. *European Psychologist, 18,* 12–23.

Hernandez, P., Gangsei, D., & Engstrom, D. (2007). Vicarious resilience: A new concept in work with those who survive trauma. *Family Process, 46,* 226–243.

Hernandez-Wolfe, P., Killian, K. D., Engstrom, D., & Gangei, D. (2014). Vicarious resilience, vicarious trauma and awareness of equity in trauma work. *Journal of Humanistic Psychology, 55*(2), 153–172.

Luthar, S. S., Cicchetti, D., & Becker, B. (2000). The construct of resilience: A critical evaluation and guidelines for future work. *Child Development, 71,* 543–562.

Ungar, M. (2010). What is resilience across cultures and contexts? Advances to the theory of positive development among individuals and families under stress. *Journal of Family Psychotherapy, 21,* 1–16.

Wagnild, G., & Young, H. M. (1993). Development and psychometric evaluation of the Resilience Scale. *Journal of Nursing Measurement, 12,* 165–178.

Walsh, F. (2015). *Strengthening family resilience* (3rd ed.). New York, NY: Guilford Press.

Resistance

In some therapeutic models any behaviors or verbalizations that convey an unwillingness to change are labeled *resistance*. Clients may use resistance as a protective process, as they go through the stages of the therapeutic process, if they feel that they are being forced to change something they do not want to change. Even if the change is desired, clients may resist if change is happening too quickly, if it is too difficult, or if it is too scary at that particular point in time. Resistance is a common and expected part of therapeutic participation and aids in the reduction of the stress and anxiety that often accompanies therapy. A resistant client is viewed as a willing participant in the therapeutic process who at some point has become disenfranchised with the process or content of discussion. This willingness to participate is what differentiates a resistant client from one who is reluctant. Resistance may occur in any setting with any population. While not all therapeutic models utilize the concept of resistance, when implementing models that do use this concept, it is important for marriage, family, and couples counselors to recognize resistance and understand how to intervene when clients are resistant. This entry discusses how counselors recognize and treat resistance.

Recognizing Resistance

Most clients come to therapy with the intention of getting better or improving one or more aspects of their lives. In therapy, though, there are often proverbial speed bumps where the client appears less than willing to be an active participant, be heard, or share his or her story; when this happens the phenomenon of resistance is occurring. Resistance occurs at an unconscious level and is an avoidance mechanism. By being resistant, the client is avoiding or attempting to delay the expression of feelings or emotions attached to any given subject matter. Pointing out the presence of resistance and discovering the specific source leads to growth and fosters understanding and potential self-awareness. A common symptom of resistance is seen when a client shifts from an active and participatory role to one of being withdrawn, frustrated, or angry with the process. Another example may be when a client begins to miss appointments, as a way of not engaging. Resistance may be viewed as the lack of acknowledgment of a problem or the denial of the extent of a problem.

In looking at resistance, it is imperative that it be properly identified. A person who is quiet in an individual, group, or family therapy setting is not necessarily resistant. Instead, the person may be introverted, shy, or trying to process everything that is going on within the context of the setting. Silence may also be due to cultural considerations, for example, certain clients may feel that speaking about a topic with people outside of the nuclear family is a sign of weakness or brings the family some level of shame. Sometimes in attempting to determine if a behavior is resistant, it may prove beneficial to check in with the client to see where he or she is emotionally and whether or not some other distraction or influence is impacting the session.

Resistance may occur at any time in the therapeutic relationship. It may be present at the beginning of the therapeutic relationship and surface with the completion of the initial paperwork, or it may come during the middle of a series of sessions, as the intervention touches upon serious concerns or dilemmas in the client's life. Resistance may also be present toward the end of the therapeutic relationship, as the client comes to terms with the events that have transpired or begins to implement the changes that need to occur.

Treating Resistance

Resistance was a central theme in Sigmund Freud's psychoanalysis with individual clients, but it also occurs in couples and family therapy. Resistance can be more complicated because one, some, or all of the members of a system may be resistant to therapeutic progress. Clinicians may try to confront the resistance or may utilize people's resistance to bring about change. Milton Erickson was famous for utilizing interventions designed to bypass resistance or use clients' resistance to bring about change outside of the clients' awareness. In strategic therapy, therapists sometimes make use of paradoxical interventions that seem counterintuitive on the surface. Examples of paradoxical interventions include symptom prescription (continuing or expanding the symptom), restraining techniques (clients are asked not to change), or positioning techniques (exaggerating the clients' view of the problem so that they will disagree with the clinician).

Not all therapeutic models recognize resistance as part of the therapeutic process, but in general when a clinician first recognizes resistance in a therapeutic relationship, affirming its existence is important. Sometimes acknowledging the presence of resistance may soften the overall impact. Changing the subject matter briefly then returning to it is another technique that may be utilized in reducing anxiety and helping the client to be more comfortable when the topic is reintroduced into the conversation.

When working with a client who is resistant it is important to keep in mind that the client is an expert on his or her own situation and as a result wants to be heard and have his or her perceptions and opinions taken into consideration. As a therapist, it is important to take into consideration the viewpoint of the client regardless of a clinician's feelings toward the presenting situation. If a therapist disagrees with the client's perspective then it is possible that the level of resistance that the client is demonstrating may increase or solidify, thus increasing the resistance in the therapeutic relationship.

The concept of resistance extends beyond individual treatment to include group and family therapy settings. In these settings, resistance might come across as a client denying existence of the problem or indicating that another person in the setting may be responsible for the area of concern instead of personally accepting responsibility for any actions or behavior.

Resistance may occur, be worked through, and appear again all with the same client, couple, or family. Resistance may also be present as therapy concludes and the client prepares to demonstrate and implement the skills that have been used outside of the therapeutic sessions.

Neil E. Duchac

See also Anxiety; Life Transitions; Paradoxes and Paradoxical Intervention; Presenting Problems; Solution-Focused Brief Therapy; Strategic Family Therapy; Termination; Therapeutic Impasses

Further Readings

Draycott, S. (2012). Dissonance, resistance and commitment: A pilot analysis of moderated mediation relationships. *Criminal Behaviour & Mental Health, 22*(3), 181–190.

Gold, J. M. (2008). Rethinking client resistance: A narrative approach to integrating resistance into the relationship-building stage of counseling. *Journal of Humanistic Counseling, Education & Development, 47*(1), 56–70.

O'Reilly, M., & Parker, N. (2013). You can take a horse to water but you can't make it drink: Exploring children's engagement and resistance in family therapy. *Contemporary Family Therapy: An International Journal, 35*(3), 491–507.

Respect

Respect is a key indicator of health and a predictor for longevity in couple relationships. Respect for persons is addressed in philosophical and religious writings as a moral value and is included in the ethical practices of many professions, agencies, and governmental institutions that provide care for the public. Ethical considerations concerning respect include recognizing and treating people as autonomous agents and providing protection for individuals with diminished autonomy.

Research in couple relationships indicates respect plays a significant role in cohesion and satisfaction and is a predictor for stability. For nearly four decades, the Gottman Institute has conducted research in the marital relationship and has found respect as a key indicator of marital stability, particularly in the area of fondness and admiration. In 1994, John Gottman wrote of one couple that "like most couples I've worked with over the years, [they] really wanted just two things from their marriage—love and respect" (p. 18). This entry discusses types of respect, reviews information found in research on the subject, describes key elements for activation and maintenance of respect in couple relationships, and highlights the challenges and benefits of respect in couple relationships.

Types of Respect

Recognition Respect and Appraisal Respect

Research has delineated respect on two axes: *recognition* respect and *appraisal* respect. On the horizontal axis, recognition respect follows the Kantian notion of the inherent, unconditional right of an individual to exercise autonomy. This form of respect recognizes a person's right of being. On the vertical axis, appraisal respect is conditional, based on a key factor of the influence one person (object) has on another (subject). In appraisal respect, the treatment of one toward another determines the outcome.

Recognition respect is viewed as an inalienable right in social order. Within a couple relationship, it is a sentiment that honors one's personhood without interference or judgment by the other. Autonomy is understood as a basic right of an individual that should be respected by others, especially in the context of an intimate relationship. Recognition respect acknowledges the freedom of individuality. Included is the ownership and expression of one's thoughts, feelings, words, and actions in the context of the couple relationship without the threat of harm or negative appraisal. In this context, respect operates as a dynamic regulating personal boundaries, communication, and behaviors in the dyad.

Appraisal respect is based on attachment bond, where factors of trust and security are critical to the level of cohesion in the relationship. Research studies indicate that respect correlates with security of attachment. A secure bond in the couple relationship increases the level of respect between the partners. Behavior between intimate partners will have a direct effect on the dispensation of respect toward one another. Characteristics that command respect in intimate relationships include having admirable moral qualities and being considerate, accepting, truthful, trustworthy, loving, and open to influence of the partner.

The two types of respect operate differently in a couple relationship. Recognition respect suggests that a person's right to autonomy in the relationship should be honored. It is given without the need for merit. By contrast, a person shows appraisal respect to a partner based on how the partner acts toward that person. Recognition respect is about one's right to be one's own person (existence) in the relationship. Appraisal respect is about what an individual extends toward a partner based on how the individual is influenced by the partner in positive or negative ways.

Respect With Dual Focus

Respect can also be a feeling toward a partner based on traits and behaviors one exhibits toward the other. In this context, the expressions and behaviors of the object (person showing respect) generate a feeling of respect in the subject (person feeling respect). Feeling respected by a partner results in feelings of respect toward the partner. Here, the feeling of respect has a dual focus: self and other.

Key Elements in Activation and Maintenance of Respect

Research has found mutuality, reciprocity, and accommodation to be key factors in the activation and maintenance of respect in couple relationships. Mutuality can be viewed as an agreement between partners in a couple on how they will act toward each other. If respect is not mutually granted, a power differential develops in the relationship weighted on the side of the recipient, not the giver, of respect. Mutuality of respect honors each partner's individuality and freedom of self-expression. Consequently, mutual respect balances power in the relationship which increases security and cohesion in the dyad.

Reciprocity is a behavioral expression of respect in a couple relationship. It is the give-and-take process between the partners. When respect is shown to a partner, the process of reciprocity is activated where respect is returned in some form. The looping process of respectful behavior establishes a dynamic that governs the relationship. Similar to mutuality, reciprocity also balances power in the couple relationship, an effect known to increase respect.

Accommodation is a pattern of behavior that promotes the existence of individuality in a couple relationship. Flexibility of one partner to accommodate the expressed needs of another demonstrates a respectful posture. Couples who respect one another view accommodation as a means to support the autonomy of self in the relationship. A husband who supports his wife's career identity and helps with child and domestic responsibilities is an example of accommodation in a couple relationship.

A correlation between respect and personal boundaries is also found in literature on couple relationships. Studies have shown an increase in respect between intimate partners when personal boundaries are honored. Research reports a decrease in respect when intrusion or violation of personal boundaries occurs in couple relationships. Personal boundaries are associated with autonomy and self-respect. In a couple relationship, respect acknowledges and accommodates personal boundaries.

Acceptance is another key functional element of respect in couple relationships. Research in the area of family systems stresses the importance of recognizing and accepting the differences between partners within an intimate relationship. Each partner's family history includes cultural, ethnic, religious, and socioeconomic elements. Respectful couples honor and support each other's stories and mutually seek integration of personal values in the relationship.

Studies have shown communication to be another key element in the expression of respect in couple relationships. According to research, poor communication ranks high among factors contributing to divorce and relationship failure. The manner in which couples communicate is directly related to the level of respect in the relationship. Findings indicate that communication that incorporates good listening skills, conveyance of understanding, and validation increases cohesion and respect among intimate couples. Validation honors self-expression and promotes autonomy in couple relationships.

Integrating and maintaining respect as a functional dynamic in a couple relationship is beset with challenges. Studies show that the establishment of an attachment bond among intimate partners plays a key role in establishing security and trust, facilitators of respect. How couples interact in the beginning phase of the relationship determines the quality of attachment.

Honoring boundaries, promoting autonomy, and sharing power, in addition to expression of affection, are significant contributors to the strength of attachment and establishment of respect in a couple relationship. Absence of mutuality, reciprocity, and accommodation results in a power differential and contributes to a deficit of respect. A lack of respect contributes to maladaptive behavior and places the relationship at risk for dissolution.

Benefits of Respect

The establishment and maintenance of respect in a couple relationship yields many benefits. Findings indicate that couples in which the partners trust one another report higher degrees of security and cohesion. Higher levels of friendship, intimacy, and exclusivity are found in couples who exhibit mutual respect. They are less likely to worry about infidelity or other forms of betrayal. Furthermore, in couples who indicate a high level of respect, partners are more accepting of one another and accommodate each other's expressed needs within the relationship. Finally, studies also indicate that couples who indicate respect as a trait in their relationship report having fewer problems in the area of communication and conflict resolution than their counterparts who lack respect.

Donald J. Olund

See also Commitment; Communication Errors/Problems in Couples and Families; Conflict in Couples and Families; Couples, Quality Time; Couples Therapy Research

Further Readings

Frei, J. F., & Shaver, P. R. (2002). Respect in close relationships: Prototype definition, self-report assessment, and initial correlates. *Personal Relationships, 9,* 121–139.

Gottman, J. M. (1994). *Why marriages succeed or fail and how you can make yours last.* New York, NY: Simon & Schuster.

Gottman, J. M. (1999). *The marriage clinic.* New York, NY: W. W. Norton.

Olund, D. J. (2013). *Bringing respect back: Communicating without the conflict.* Hinsdale, IL: Author.

van Quaquebeke, N., Heinrich, D. C., & Eckloff, T. (2007). "It's not tolerance I'm asking for, it's respect!" A conceptual framework to differentiate between tolerance, acceptance and (two types of) respect. *Gruppendynamik und Organisationberatung, 38*(2) 185–200.

RESTORATION THERAPY

Restoration therapy is a relatively new model of marriage and family therapy developed by Terry Hargrave and Franz Pfitzer. The foundations and process of the therapeutic approach is heavily influenced by contextual family therapy, cognitive therapy, and cognitive mindfulness. In the restoration therapy (RT) approach, the therapist is careful to evaluate and assess the client in terms of identity and safety. Building on attachment theory, the RT approach is based on the idea that love and safety are basic relationship needs. The identity of the individual or family is formed through the relational experiences of love. Safety is experienced relationally through trustworthiness. The goal of restoration therapy is to restore as much of a sense of identity and safety to the individual and family as possible or feasible through the redressing of or building of love and trustworthiness.

Restoration therapists often look for healthy identity being rooted in the concepts of uniqueness, worthiness, and belongingness. Safety for an individual and relationship is often built on predictability of the relationship, the balance or justice of give and take between the individuals in the relationship, and the degree of openness in the relationship. The more secure and identifiable are these experiences of love and trustworthiness, the more the individual has a clear sense of identity and a robust sense of safety in relationships. On the other hand, the more the individual or relationship has experienced a lack of love or trustworthiness, the more likely there are to be corresponding complications in painful confusion around a sense of identity as a person and ability to maintain safety in secure relationships. RT therapists would see these violations of love and trustworthiness as the key factors driving emotional pain in individuals and their families. This entry outlines the therapeutic framework of restoration therapy.

Therapeutic Framework

There are four primary things that restoration therapists do during the process of therapy. First, the therapist helps the individual or family clearly identify emotional pain and what RT calls the *pain cycle*. Second, the therapist helps the individual or individuals in the relationship identify a self-regulating emotion that is experienced at a deep enough level to combat or dissipate the pain that is experienced from lack of identity or safety. Third, the therapist and clients develop a corresponding *peace cycle* to serve as a cognitive map for new interaction possibilities. Finally, there is a practice stage of therapy where the clients learn to regulate their own pain cycles through the practice of mindfulness.

Identifying the Pain Cycle

Restoration therapy understands the roots of pain being located in the primary emotional experience of feeling unloved (lack of identity or love) or feeling unsafe (lack of safety or trustworthiness). These primary emotions trigger fight and/or flight reactions in the individual where he or she will move to a reactive state in order to cope with the emotional pain. From a restoration therapy perspective, this reactivity produces feelings and actions that then become violating to love and trustworthiness in the experience of the individual and his or her relationships. RT therapists consistently identify four reactive frameworks that are most often used when individuals feel unloved, unsafe or both. These are (1) *blame* where the individual feels and acts angry, retaliatory, aggressive, or punishing; (2) *shame* where the individual feels and acts negative, needy, and hopeless, and is often inconsolable; (3) *control* where the individual acts in a way where he or she maintains complete power and no vulnerability in the give-and-take of relationship and may be performance driven, perfectionistic, and judgmental; and (4) *escape/chaos* where the individual feels or acts overwhelmed and avoids responsibility through leaving, anesthetizing pain, and dissociating. In understanding this reactive framework, it is helpful to realize that blame and control are fight reactions while shame and escape/chaos are flight reactions.

Typically, RT therapists listen carefully to the story of the individual or family and help identify the primary emotions related to identity and safety. These emotions (usually two to five emotions) are then placed on a chart where the clients can easily recall these feelings. Then the focus of the therapy turns to questioning what the individual or family does when these primary emotions are triggered. This reactivity may be one or any combination of the reactive frameworks driven by fight or flight, identified earlier. Usually, two to four reactive frameworks are identified per individual. These reactions are again placed on a chart where clients can easily and completely understand that when they experience the emotional trigger of primary emotion related to lack of identity or safety, they move semiautomatically into a state of reactivity.

Because of the current understanding of neuroscience, RT therapists maintain that this identified pain cycle is what is experienced most often when there is an experience of emotional disregulation or feeling an attack to identity or safety. In other words, people who often get angry (blame) because they are not given the proper consideration or respect by others (violation of love or trustworthiness) consistently disregulate over this same emotional state and get triggered over and over. In another example, people who have experienced trauma because of past relationships (violation of love or trustworthiness) and then overcontrol their circumstances by depending on no other person are likely to be triggered to perform the same disregulating behavior and make the same faulty assumptions about relationships again and again.

Drawing and illustrating this pain cycle for the client allows the therapist to make a systemic map of the interactions that lead to existing and future violations of love and trustworthiness that in turn result in insecure identity and safety. While it is easy for the therapist to understand how these emotions are triggered by history and current experiences as well as why the individual or family is reactive in destructive ways, the purpose of identifying the pain cycle is to help the client understand basic reactions and where they become harmful in relationships in similar ways to the way the client has been harmed.

Identifying and Experiencing Self-Regulating Emotions

Simply stated, RT therapists identify one of the major goals in modern psychology as regulating destructive emotions. This is certainly true when it comes to confronting the primary emotions and reactivity that become evident in the identification of the pain cycle. The key in this second phase of therapy is for the therapist to help the individual or family realize that most of what has occurred in the pain cycle has been learned from a very early age when there was no ability to understand and self-regulate emotion or these emotions have never been identified because they were, in essence, unconscious or not understood. The therapist helps empower the individual and family by commenting on the fact that no matter where these violations of love and trustworthiness came from, the person is now powerful enough to decide for himself or herself whether or not to continue to believe the affronts to identity or safety. In essence, the RT therapist is helping the individual decide what he or she will believe in terms of what the truth is regarding identity or safety.

The RT therapist has the client confront these emotions surrounding identity and safety with two techniques. The first technique is called *reparenting* where the client imagines and experiences a series of interactions with a child and working the imagery to eventually include himself or herself as he or she is now. Concentration on this imagery is intended to give the client the power to comment on what he or she wishes the message to be to himself or herself in terms of identity and safety. The second technique is called *forward looking back* where the client is asked to create an image where he or she is in the future and has accomplished all that he or she wished in the therapeutic process. Again, the focus of the imagery is to give the client the power to speak about how he or she wants to decide about the messages regarding identity or safety. When successful, identification of these "truths" about identity and safety most often carries the power to regulate the painful and disregulating emotions about being unloved or unsafe. It should be noted that helping the client to these self-regulating truths is often identified as the most difficult aspect of restoration therapy by practitioners.

Identification of the Peace Cycle

The focus of the third aspect of the therapeutic process in RT is drawing the alternative cognitive map or the peace cycle. After clients are able to regulate disruptive emotions dealing with feelings of being unloved or unsafe, they are no longer in a reactive state where they are likely to take on unloving and untrustworthy actions. Instead, they experience empowerment and freedom. This power and freedom allows them to choose actions that are based in agency. Emotionally regulated individuals, practically speaking, are able to nurture others instead of engaging in blame. Instead of engaging shame, these individuals are able to move to the agency of self-valuing. Likewise, instead of control with essentially no or very little dependence on relationships, individuals are able to engage in the agency of balanced give-and-take in relationships. Finally, instead of escape/chaos, the regulated individual is able to reliably connect with others.

In the same way the therapist drew the pain cycle for the individual or family, he or she is now able to draw the cognitive map of emotional regulation, called the *peace cycle*, where the regulating emotion or "truth" is identified and the stated goal or agency behavior is drawn on the chart. While the drawing of this map is essential, most RT therapists accomplish it in one or two sessions.

Practice of Mindfulness and the Four Steps

In the final phase of the therapeutic process, the therapist refers repeatedly to both the pain cycle and the peace cycle. The therapist uses these two cycles to help the client become mindful of how to move himself or herself from the disregulation of the pain cycle to the emotional regulation of the peace cycle. This is often referred to by RT therapists as the practice stage of therapy because it entails going over with the client the process of (a) recognizing when painful emotions get triggered in the pain cycle, (b) identifying and clarifying the reactivity that happens in the pain cycle, (c) identifying the self-regulating emotion or truth experienced by the client, and (d) moving to an empowering action of agency. This phase often requires six to ten sessions of work as the client becomes more and more proficient at moving himself or herself to an emotionally regulated state.

One of the mindfulness techniques used by RT therapists in this phase of therapy is called the four steps. The four steps are simply utilizing mindfulness techniques to help the client facilitate self-regulation by having the client (1) say what he or she feels, (2) say what he or she normally does, (3) say the truth or regulating emotion, and (4) say what he or she will do differently. The four steps walk a person through a recapitulation of the pain and peace cycles resulting in an enhanced ability to regulate emotions.

Typically, using the restoration therapy model lasts eight to 20 sessions, with an average number of sessions with an individual or family being 15. Although the therapy model is relatively new, it has shown excellent promise in improving couple relationships and interrupting damaging cycles in intergenerational issues.

*Terry D. Hargrave
and Miyoung Yoon Hammer*

See also Affect Regulation; Mindfulness; Mindfulness and Children; Mindfulness and Couples; Mindfulness and Sex

Further Readings

Hargrave, T. D., & Pfitzer, F. (2003). *The new contextual therapy: Guiding the power of give and take.* New York, NY: Brunner-Routledge.

Hargrave, T. D., & Pfitzer, F. (2011). *Restoration therapy: Understanding and guiding healing in marriage and family therapy.* New York, NY: Routledge.

Siegel, D. J. (2007). *The mindful brain: Reflection and attunement in the cultivation of well-being.* New York, NY: W. W. Norton.

RETIREMENT

The definition of *retirement* has evolved over the past several decades based on the economic landscape and related sociopolitical trends. Many people think of retirement as a time around midlife when an employee stops working at a job they held for most of their professional career which, in turn, provides them with retirement benefits. However, the use of the term *retirement* has evolved to encompass a developmental construct that considers a series of life span transitions through which individuals adjust, and readjust, as needed throughout their lives. These transitions involve people's professional occupations, identities, and activity. A thorough understanding of retirement, the process, social and family support as well as health, financial, and cultural implications will be addressed and explored. This entry further discusses conceptualizations of retirement and the idea of retirement as a process and explains some of the determinants of individuals' decisions about retirement. It then discusses counseling theories that can provide support in working with individuals at the time of retirement.

Conceptualizations of Retirement

Because early definitions of retirement and many subsequent descriptions of retirement rely on the sociopolitical context surrounding them, most lay people and professional helpers alike have historically thought of retirement as very static, permanent, and discrete. However, contemporary conceptualizations challenge this construct. A 2009 article by Frank Denton and Byron Spencer titled "What Is Retirement? A Review and Assessment of Alternative Concepts and Measures" identified eight definitions of retirement that include nonparticipation in the labor force, reduction in hours worked and/or wages, and a late-in-life career or employment change, underscoring retirement as an ever-changing concept with many contemporary meanings.

As the study of retirement developed, scholars noted that dated definitions of *retirement* continued to pose problems for conceptualizing retired individuals because they did not holistically reflect the retired population and individuals who identified as retired. Therefore, scholars and clinicians in the field of counseling began to look more closely at social definers of retirement to help conceptualize the work they were doing with retirement-age individuals and as a way to consider the idea of retirement with respect to how it impacts clients. Accordingly, the social conceptualization of retirement emphasizes the importance of each individual retiree's experience and values and requires those in the helping professions to turn to their clients for support when working to construct the most appropriate definition to anchor clinical work.

Retirement as a Process

Practitioners and academics alike have begun to conceptualize retirement as a process, rather than a specific event of career development. For example, some older workers who are at the traditional age of retirement (65) often choose to engage in *delayed retirement,* a trend that allows them to continue to work in their career, often due to fluctuating family factors or economic conditions. Similarly, *phased retirement* allows individuals to use flexible working hours and schedules to retire gradually from long-term employment. By engaging in one or a combination of benefits and strategies, phased retirement offers individuals a means of remaining in the work force while decreasing the day-to-day demands of their current professional positions. Another trend in the process of retirement is *bridge employment,* which allows individuals to transition from full-time to part-time work in one of three ways: in the same career, within the same organization, or in another field.

Determinants of Retirement

There are many factors that influence an individual's decision to retire and each person's retirement situation consists of a complex arrangement of retirement determinants. Individuals' unique life events inform their choices around retirement. For example, social skills and structure, financial profile, health status, and cultural context inform retirement choices.

Family Structure and Support

Many retirees weigh their retirement choices against their interfamilial roles and responsibilities of parent, spouse, and/or child. For example, economic factors may result in retirement-age individuals providing help to their adult children as financial support or in the form of children returning home after a period of living independently. Or retirement-age individuals may find themselves in the *sandwich generation,* a term used for individuals who are caring for their children and aging parents concurrently. Furthermore, midlife adults are often caregivers to their grandchildren. Consequently, with changing life roles, careers may not be strictly characterized by traditional paid occupations, but rather as a constellation of paid and unpaid roles. Considering one's spouse, including their interests, career, and health status, becomes important when considering retirement. *Joint retirement* is a term used to discuss the process of a couple who co-orchestrate their retirement efforts when determinants such as financial factors and health care may impact the feasibility of spouses retiring together. Some joint retirements are relatively simple to arrange whereas others can become quite complicated, depending on medical needs, financial resources, and family structure. The loss of a spouse can complicate planning strategies both emotionally and fiscally, and this complication becomes increasingly likely the older individuals are when they retire.

Social Structure and Skills

By working into the later stages in life, individuals maintain social interaction and interpersonal relationships with coworkers and colleagues. Remaining professionally engaged also offers older workers an increased sense of identity. These identities and relationships tend to spill over into individuals' nonwork lives in the form of social and relational satisfaction, decreased depressive symptoms (as compared to peers who do not work), and overall better psychological well-being. However, many older workers report a preference for work they enjoy, flexible work hours, and choice when it comes to how long and when they work without the pressure of needing to earn more money.

Health Status

In 2012, life expectancy at birth for the U.S. population reached a record high of 78.8 years, according to the Centers for Disease Control and Prevention. AARP (formerly known as the American Association of Retired Persons) estimates that by the year 2030 there will be approximately 65 million Americans over the age of 60. With advances in health care and medical science, people often reach retirement age in relatively good health with many years left to live. These phenomena have helped to increase the number of workers who elect to remain employed past the traditional retirement age of 65, even if they formally retire from a long-term career or professional position. For example, the U.S. Bureau of Labor Statistics (BLS) reported that between 1977 and 2007, there was a 101% increase of individuals 65 years old and older who were employed. In addition, it wasn't only those close to the traditional retirement age who chose to remain actively employed, but many remained employed well beyond that age. The BLS reported that workers ages 65 to 69 years of age increased by 85% from 1977 to 2007, workers ages 70 to 74 years of age increased by 98%, and workers over the age of 74 increased by 172%.

Although research points to the psychological benefits for older individuals who continue to work, the choice in favor or opposed to working often is not clear cut. For example, many aging workers require some level of accommodation to continue to perform job duties. Also, people of retirement age may feel torn between working while they are able-bodied enough to do so and using their physical abilities to engage in leisure activities. Additionally, the fact that Americans are living longer isn't necessarily indicative of the quality of life (and subsequent ability to work effectively) they experience in their older age. Yet those who are ill may need to continue to work in order to receive health benefits or extra income they apply to medical expenses.

Financial Profile

Beyond health care, aging populations experience a number of factors that may influence retirement choices. For example, the economic decline that began in 2007 served as an impetus for concern and reconsideration of retirement for many retirement-age Americans. In addition, some Americans are concerned over the sustainability of government programs such as Social Security and government medical care plans, and some companies have reduced or eliminated their pension plans or made changes in employer-supported retirement plans. So for many, the decision to remain employed may not feel like a choice, even if they enjoy remaining professionally active.

Cultural Context

Individuals from groups that have been historically marginalized, including women and members of racial and ethnic minority groups, can face increased challenges when it comes to retirement planning. These challenges can be the result of health disparities, decreased educational opportunities, and organizational and individual discrimination faced by certain groups. Although federal laws enforced by the Equal Employment Opportunity Commission serve to protect employees from discrimination in the workplace, institutionalized discrimination and intergenerational inequality often have a negative effect on wealth acquisition. For example, older White workers are almost twice as likely to be high school graduates compared with their Black and Latina/o counterparts. Women often have gaps in their work history due to taking leave to care for children and/or other family members. This ultimately impacts their accrual of benefits and salary increases, which may lead to delayed, or less fruitful, retirement. The intersection of age and other identities must be considered by counselors who work with older populations. All older workers are at risk of experiencing ageism, but those who identify as part of a historically marginalized population may experience ageism differently than someone not already affected by marginalization based on another identity.

Counseling Theories and Support

The current landscape of an active, aging workforce has pushed researchers to explore the financial and psychological benefits of delayed, phased, and bridged employment. Counselors working with this population should remain abreast of developing trends in career counseling. Addressing the career needs of this population requires knowledge of a wide variety of theoretical approaches that can account for the complexity of personal, developmental, and contextual factors.

Modern career theories, such as John Holland's theory of vocational personalities, propose understanding individuals in terms of characteristics such as interests, skills, abilities, and values that can be measured and correlated with specific jobs or career paths. Developmental theories, such as Donald Super's life-span theory, conceptualize one's career development across the life span through stages—a theme of particular relevance when considering the needs of midlife. Postmodern theories support a qualitative understanding of individual attributes and how one assigns meaning to life experience, which may help midlife individuals narratively describe their career choices and desires. Life roles and work values theory explores how life roles, work values, and belief systems mediate the career development and decision-making processes, which may help midlife adults balance work and other life roles. According to social cognitive career theory, the interplay between personal agency and contextual influences determines an individual's career interests, career choices, and how an individual persists and performs in an occupation. Constructivist theory emphasizes the interaction between personal agency and contextual factors in career development, which may support midlife adults in gaining rich insight into important events of their lives and how these events have impacted job and career decisions.

Lauren J. Moss and Helen Hamlet

See also Beliefs and Values; Community Programs; Debt and Financial Strain; Family and Medical Leave Act of 1993; Family Resource Management; Health Issues; Individual Family Culture; Life Balance; Life Events; Life Transitions; Loneliness; Social Support; Socioeconomic Status; Transgenerational Family Therapy

Further Readings

AARP. (2010). *Last decade spelled disaster for older workers*. Retrieved from http://www.aarp.org/about-aarp/press-center/info-03-2010/last_decade_spelleddiasterforolderworkers.html

Brott, P. (2005). A constructivist look at life roles. *Career Development Quarterly, 54,* 138–149.

Bureau of Labor Statistics. (2011). *Labor force statistics from the Current Population Survey*. Retrieved from http://www.bls.gob/data/#employment

Challenger, Gray & Christmas, Inc. (2010). *Despite high unemployment, older workers gain positions: Older workers join, succeed in job search*. Retrieved June 13, 2010, from http://www.challengergray.com/press/PressRelease.aspx?PressUid=135

Copeland, C. (2010). *Employment status of workers ages 55 or older, 1987–2008* (EBRI Notes No. 31).

Washington, DC: Employee Benefit Research Institute. Retrieved from http://www.ebri.org/pdf/notespdf/EBRI_Notes_03-Mar10.EmptStat.pdf

Denton, F., & Spencer, B. (2009). What is retirement? A review and assessment of alternative concepts and measures. *Canadian Journal on Aging, 28,* 63–76.

Furbish, D. (2009). Self-funded leave and life role development. *Journal of Employment Counseling, 46*(1), 38–46.

Gottfredson, G. D., & Johnstun, M. L. (2009). John Holland's contributions: A theory-ridden approach to career assistance. *Career Development Quarterly, 58*(2), 99–107.

Johnson, R. W., & Park, J. (2011). *Employment and earning among 50+ people of color* (Working Paper No. 4). Washington, DC: Urban Institute. Retrieved from http://www.urban.org/uploadedpdf/412376-employment-and-earnings.pdf

Kolb, B. R. (2012). Financial planners and baby boomer widows: Building a trusting relationship. Retrieved from http://www.fpanet.org/journal/CurrentIssue/TableofContents/FinancialPlannersandBabyBoomerWidows/

Krumboltz, J. D. (1994). Improving career development theory from a social learning perspective. In M. L. Savickas & R. L. Lent (Eds.), *Convergence in career development theories* (pp. 9–31). Palo Alto, CA: CPP Books.

Morin, R. (2009). *Most middle-aged adults are rethinking retirement plans.* Washington, DC: Pew Research Center. Retrieved from http://www.pewsocialtrends.org/2009/05/28/most-middle-aged-adults-are-rethinking-retirement-plans/

National Center for Health Statistics. (2011). *Health, United States, 2010: With special feature on death and dying.* Hyattsville, MD: National Center for Health Statistics.

National Council on Aging. (2012). *Mature workers fact sheet.* Retrieved from http://www.ncoa.org/assets/files/pdf/FactSheet_MatureWorkers.pdf

Nauta, M. M. (2010). The development, evolution, and status of Holland's theory of vocational personalities: Reflections and future directions for counseling psychology. *Journal of Counseling Psychology, 57*(1), 11–22. doi:10.1037/a0018213

Peterson, G., Sampson, J., Readron, R., & Lenz, J. (2003). *Core concepts of a cognitive approach to career development and services.* Retrieved from http://www.career.fsu.edu/documents/cognitive%20information%20processing/core%20concepts%20of%20a%20cognitive%20approach.htm

Pierrett, C. R. (2006, September). The "sandwich generation": Women caring for parents and children. *Monthly Labor Review,* pp. 3–9.

Sampson, J. (2009). Modern and postmodern career theories: The unnecessary divorce. *Career Development Quarterly, 58,* 91–96.

Savickas, M. L. (2012). Life design: A paradigm for career intervention in the 21st century. *Journal of Counseling & Development, 90,* 13–19.

Stebleton, M. (2010). Narrative-based career counseling perspectives in times of change: An analysis of strengths and limitations. *Journal of Employment Counseling, 47,* 84–78.

Super, D. E. (1990). Life-span, life-space approach to career development. In D. Brown, L. Brooks, & Associates (Eds.), *Career choice and development: Applying contemporary theories to practice* (2nd ed., pp. 197–261). San Francisco, CA: Jossey-Bass.

United States Equal Employment Opportunity Commission. (2011). *Age discrimination in Employment Act FY 1997–FY 2011.* Retrieved from http://www.eeoc.gov/eeoc/statistics/enforcement

Urban Institute Research of Record. (2012). *Unemployment statistics on older Americans.* Retrieved from http://www.urban.org/UploadedPDF/411904_unemploymentstatistics.pdf

Rituals in Family Therapy

Family rituals have been defined as behaviors or activities that have symbolic meaning and involve most or all members of the family. According to Italian psychiatrist Mara Selvini Palazzoli, rituals consist of a sequence of steps taken by the family at the appropriate moment and can encode emotional and behavioral memories in the participant with a particular, shared meaning. Family rituals have been studied as a means to understand what families do and how regular routines and practices influence the stability of families. This entry further defines rituals and discusses their purposes. It then discusses the various types of rituals in families, the assessment of family rituals, the use of rituals in family therapy, and research on the effects of family rituals.

Roy Rappaport has described six aspects of behavior that would define something as a *ritual*: repetition, action, special stylized behavior, order, evocative style, and collective social meaning. According to Evan Imber-Black, Janine Roberts, and Richard Whiting, rituals in family therapy can, but do not need to, include repetition, and rituals should allow for multiple meanings by various family members.

A distinction can be made between *family routines* and *family rituals*. In family routines, the communication is instrumental, with directions given on what needs to be done. Commitment to family routines is temporary, occurs in the moment of the routine, and involves little thought after the routine. Routines are repeated regularly over time and can be seen by outside observers to involve recognizable behavior. Family rituals, in contrast, have symbolic communication and no explicit directives. Rituals have a lasting influence on the family and have an affective component. The experience may be repeated in one's memory multiple times to reinforce the symbolism. The repetition of family rituals across generations acknowledges generational identity.

Family rituals and routines change in continuity over the life cycle of the family. When a family ages, younger generations take on more and more of the responsibility for family rituals. As new parents adjust to parenthood, rituals and family gatherings have less affect and symbolism associated with them. When children become older and can become involved in the ritual process, rituals become more regular and meaningful. As children become more responsible for their own care, routines and trials can be negotiated in the family. Children become more involved in routines and rituals as they get older, but they generally do not ascribe the depth of meaning to them that adults do until they become parents themselves.

In general, parents tend to give more meaning to rituals than their college-age children do. In interviews with adults, 80% of parents of adult children reported observing family rituals in their adult children that were rooted in the adult child's early experience. Sixty-five percent of grandparents in those same families could see the intergenerational aspects of rituals displayed by their grandchildren. Responsibility for maintaining family rituals seems to lie with the middle generation, the new adult parents, and in 85% of the cases the responsibility for rituals was with the female adult.

The Five Purposes of Rituals

Imber-Black and Roberts describe the five purposes of rituals as relating, changing, healing, believing, and celebrating. They claim that any ritual, whether it is a daily ritual, a holiday celebration, a particular family tradition, or a once-in-a-lifetime experience, will address one or more of these purposes. *Relating* is about how we handle and manage relationships in our lives. Rituals can help us see aspects of our relationship with other people and inform us on ways that we can achieve better relationships. Painful memories of childhood family rituals are tied to painful memories of childhood relationships. Conversely, new family rituals such as morning coffee around the breakfast table, an evening check-in with other family members, or family game night, can enhance relationships.

Changing represents how rituals can developmentally assist rites of passage for families throughout their life span. An individual's new marriage signifies a change in structure of their family of origin. The marriage represents a change in the individual's responsibilities, a milestone in their stage in life, and individuation into their own, new family. In remarriage situations where family traditions and rituals are brought together, changing can mean developing new rituals that are unique to the new blended family.

Healing is the process of recovery that rituals provide when members are going through loss or trauma. During a divorce, it is common to incorporate rituals into therapy. Tasks such as letter writing, burial of objects, and celebrating one's new single status are examples of healing rituals done around the experience of divorce. Examples of healing rituals extend themselves into recovery from death of a loved one, addressing prior physical and sexual abuse, and returning to the community where one was raised.

Rituals by the nature of context express what a family *believes,* and this expression is another purpose of rituals. Participating in an organized event with others is an open endorsement of what the event symbolizes, so a family meal means as members of this family we believe we should eat together. Going to religious services may have its own inherent value but it is also statement of faith to a community. *Celebrating* is the last of the five purposes of rituals. Celebrating allows us to acknowledge who we have been and who we are becoming. Graduation is a ritual that has the purpose of celebration.

Typology of Rituals in Families

Although many people describe typologies for rituals, two typologies stand out as having particular meaning in family therapy. In 1984, Steven Wolin and Linda Bennett suggested three types of family rituals: *family celebrations, family traditions,* and *family interactions.* Family celebrations are those holiday occasions that are part of the culture. This includes rites of passage (weddings, funerals, quinceañera, bar mitzvahs), religious holidays, and secular holiday celebrations. These rituals are universally symbolic and they are relatively standardized across society. Because of the importance of these celebrations, often couples and families have to negotiate an agreement as to how these celebrations will occur. Family traditions are those rituals that are less generalized across cultures but more specific to each family. They could be particular family customs, ways in which birthdays are celebrated, or ways in which vacations are handled. Family interactions are the most particular specific pattern of interaction with families. This category includes bedtime rituals for children, leisure activities, and mealtime rituals.

Imber-Black, Roberts, and Whiting extended Wolin and Bennett's family level of ritualization to establish another typology grouping based on ritual form and function. Their six typologies are the following:

1. *Underutilized*—families who neither celebrate nor make family changes or participate in societal rituals

2. *Rigidly utilized*—prescribed behaviors that must be done with each member present in certain ways

3. *Skewed ritualization*—one particular side of the family's rituals have been emphasized over the other family's side

4. *Hollow ritual*—family members celebrate without interest or engagement

5. *Ritual process interrupted*—life situations that interrupt and change the pattern of family rituals

6. *Flexibility to adapt rituals*—or how willing is the family to adapt rituals when necessary

The typologies act as a form of assessment for family therapists who wish to look at how rituals are used in client families.

Assessment of Family Rituals

Barbara Fiese and Christine Kline have developed an assessment for the prevalence and quality of family rituals. The Family Ritual Questionnaire (FRQ) is a self-report questionnaire that assesses rituals across seven settings and eight dimensions. The seven settings are dinnertime, weekends, vacations, annual celebrations, special celebrations, religious holidays, and cultural traditions. The eight dimensions are occurrence (how often), roles, routine (regularity), attendance expectations, affect (emotional investment), symbolic significance (meaning), continuation (across generations), and deliberateness (advanced planning). The FRQ was normed on middle-class Caucasian adolescents and families, but dissertation studies have been done to include Latina/o, Norwegian, Chinese, and African American families. The FRQ has adequate internal consistency, test/retest reliability, construct validity, and within-family agreement. The instrument reflects the family's level of ritual practice and can give a clinician an insight into what the family believes, what they value, and how they organize around principles.

Designing Rituals for Therapy

Family therapists may develop rituals for families to use to address particular issues that they present with in therapy. Whiting provides an organization for designing therapeutic family rituals that includes the three categories of *design elements, ritual techniques and symbolic actions,* and *other design considerations*. Major design elements take into consideration symbols, open and closed aspects of the ritual, and aspects of time and space. Symbols and symbolic action are important elements within rituals and can be words or objects. Closed and open aspects of ritual design rest on the degree to which one wants spontaneity and flexibility or specificity in the ritual. Families that are open to new changes may be ready for rituals that involve more spontaneity. Those who need to perform specific actions to resolve past developmental blocks may require some specificity to feel as if they have completed the work they need to complete.

Time and space design elements simply refer to consideration as to when the ritual will be done and where the ritual should be done. Time considerations include allowing for enough time for the family to go through the actions, as time can be distorted while members need to work through symbolic processes. Being specific about time constraints lets family members know for how long they may be engaged in something very difficult for them. Space takes into consideration whether the ritual will take place in session (with a specific role for the therapist) or out of session.

Ritual techniques and symbolic actions include techniques of letting go, utilizing differences, giving and receiving objects, ritualizing the game and prescribing the symptom, and documenting techniques. The letting-go technique is generally a process of catharsis for families as they ritually disengage from a past trauma. The technique of utilizing differences generally is used when the therapeutic situation requires one family member to address a conflict with another family member. The intervention of "odd days/even days," where family members have to agree to approach the problem one way on odd-numbered calendar days and another way on even-numbered calendar days, is an example of a utilizing difference technique. The technique of giving and receiving involves passing something symbolic between family members, between family members and the therapist, and between the therapist and the family members. The techniques of ritualizing the game and prescribing the symptom use ritual to alter typical behavior patterns through telling the client to enact the problematic behavior, often in an exaggerated way. This exaggerated behavior, done as part of a ritual, has a paradoxical effect of eliminating the undesired behavior. The documenting technique can enhance commitment by putting a desired change on paper, can establish a therapeutic contract with the family, or can be used to cocreate a document of changes the family has accomplished.

Some family rituals designed by a therapist involve alternating particular aspects of the ritual, for example, holding on and letting go of an issue on alternating days. Patterns of repetition are another additional design feature of rituals, whether it is repetition of content based on speech, writing, or playful actions. The rate of repetition and the method used in the ritual can be tied to the therapeutic needs of the family and the timeframe of recovery they are experiencing.

Application of Rituals to Family Therapy

Rituals can be used in many different types of situations in family therapy, including working with adolescents, adoption, sex therapy, remarriage, and bicultural couples. Family routines and rituals have been used in the context of working with family members who have chronic illness, are adapting to parenthood, are dealing with dramatic loss and major disaster, and are recovering from substance abuse or trauma. Ritual studies have looked at families with diverse ethnic and cultural makeup, including Jewish families and the bar mitzvah ritual.

It is clear from research that the use of rituals by families and family therapists has an impact on the well-being of children. Laurel Kiser, Linda Bennett, Jerry Heston, and Marilyn Paavola compared the use of rituals in families with an adolescent receiving psychiatric treatment and families of adolescents who were not in treatment. Among the "nonclinical families" in the study, there was greater establishment and enactment of family ritual and family rituals often included close friends or extended family members. The researchers concluded that family rituals were correlated with child well-being. Ritual and routine were seen as a predictor of the relational qualities in families. Families with established routines and rituals describe a context of successful problem-solving within the family.

Remaining Research

Research on rituals has found that families can create rituals that bring family members together as a group and help the family feel settled in place and time. Rituals were also seen as a method to provide a balance to relationships in the family. Families have described how they were able to generate and distinguish their rituals across generations.

The question remains whether family rituals and routines generally result in family mental health and well-being. A review of 50 years of research by Fiese and colleagues in 2002 did not indicate a clear relationship between family rituals and family mental health and well-being. The problem is the reliance on assessment using questionnaires, interviews, frequency checklists, or direct observation. Interview protocol varies across multiple studies, so to establish an effect is difficult. Checklists provide useful information but can restrict family responses in describing their use of ritual. Observational studies look for patterns in rituals but have problems aligning different coding methods used in different studies. The recommended approach for future studies would include direct observation of the rituals paired with self-report questionnaires. Another concern with the research done on family rituals is a lack of diversity among study participants. Further research is warranted on the direct and indirect effects of family rituals.

Marty Jencius

See also Divorce Therapy; Family Myth; Family Rituals; Family Values; Individual Family Culture; Intergenerational Trauma

Further Readings

Bossard, J., & Boll, E. (1950) *Ritual in family living.* Philadelphia: University of Pennsylvania Press.

Fiese, B. H., & Kline, C. A. (1993). Development of the family ritual questionnaire: Initial reliability and validation studies. *Journal of Family Psychology* 6(3), 290–299.

Fiese, B. H., Tomcho, T. J., Douglas, M., Josephs, K., Poltrock, S., & Baker, T. (2002). A review of 50 years of research on naturally occurring family routines and rituals: Cause for celebration? *Journal of Family Psychology,* 16(4), 381–390.

Glass, V. Q. (2014). "We are with family": Black lesbian couples negotiate rituals with extended families. *Journal of GLBT Family Studies, 10,* 79–100.

Grimes, R. (1982). *Beginnings in ritual studies.* Lanham, MD: University Press of America.

Imber-Black, E., & Roberts, J. (1998). *Rituals for our times: Celebrating, healing, and changing our lives and our relationships.* New York, NY: HarperCollins.

Imber-Black, E., Roberts, J., & Whiting, R. A. (2003). *Rituals in families and family therapy* (2nd ed). New York, NY: W. W. Norton.

Jencius, M. J., & Rotter, J. C. (1998). Bedtime rituals and their relationship to childhood sleep disturbance. *Family Journal, 6,* 94–102.

Kiser, L. J., Bennett, L., Heston, J., & Paavola, M. (2005). Family ritual and routine: Comparison of clinical and non-clinical families. *Journal of Child and Family Studies,* 14(3), 357–372.

Rappaport, R. A. (1971). Ritual sanctity and cybernetics. *American Anthropologist,* 73(1), 59–76.

Richardson, C. (2012). Witnessing life transitions with ritual and ceremony in family therapy: Three examples from a Métis therapist. *Journal of Systemic Therapies, 31*(3), 68–78.

van der Hart, O. (1983). *Rituals in psychotherapy: Transition and continuity.* New York, NY: Irvington.

van Gennep, A. (1960). *The rites of passage.* Chicago, IL: University of Chicago Press.

Whiting, R. A. (2003). Guidelines to designing therapeutic rituals. In E. Imber-Black, J. Roberts, & R. A. Whiting (Eds.), *Rituals in families and family therapy* (2nd ed.). New York, NY: W. W. Norton.

Wolin, S. J., & Bennett, L. A. (1984). Family rituals. *Family Process, 23*(3), 401–420.

Role-Playing

Role-playing is a fundamental human behavior that is naturally enacted in play, storytelling, and rituals. Role-playing helps people feel connected to each other. Examples of role-playing include children engaged in pretend play, adolescents completing graduation ceremonies, or individuals participating in religious ceremonies. Role-playing activities help people feel more connected to their communities. Role-playing can also help individuals solve difficult problems, develop complex skills, or explore new identities in a safe context. Children who "play house" or "play school," for example, might try on the role of parent or teacher. Role-playing as a therapeutic intervention occurs when a counselor guides a client to act out an unfamiliar role either as himself or herself or from the perspective of another. Therapeutic gains include reducing anxiety, instilling hope, developing a stronger sense of identity, and improving interpersonal relationships. This entry traces the history and key elements of therapeutic role-playing and then outlines how role-playing has been used with children, adolescents, and families. The entry concludes with a brief overview of several key influencers in the development of role-playing techniques in psychotherapy.

In most forms of role-playing, an individual, family, or group participates in a form of spontaneous but guided dramatized activities for the purpose of exploring some aspect of their lives. Role-playing involves imagination, action, and self-reflection to bring one's inner images into concrete physical reality. Participants are able to explore emotions, experiment with new behaviors or attitudes, and gain new insights into personal relationships. Other creative activities such as dance, music, and art can be incorporated into role-playing. Role-playing can be used in clinical, community, or educational settings as a complement to other therapeutic modalities and approaches. When used in nonclinical settings, and for the purpose of exploring professional or public relationships, psychodrama is referred to as sociodrama.

Classical Psychodrama

Jacob Moreno developed what was later called classical psychodrama as a therapeutic role-playing intervention that occurs in groups. He combined elements of his work with groups, improvisational theater, and sociometry to create psychodrama. Classical psychodrama occurs within a therapeutic group and begins with a warm-up. One member of the group is selected as the "subject" or "protagonist" and then a problem is explored through some kind of enactment, action, or role-play, which is typically referred to as a *drama* or a *scene*. The protagonist explores new ways of resolving a problem in daily life through the role-play. Group members who assume the roles of significant others in the drama are called *auxiliary egos* or *auxiliaries*. The auxiliary egos bring to life the roles in the protagonist's life, but they also support the director in the therapeutic process and have the opportunity to explore the inner life of their assigned role. Group members who observe the drama represent the world at large and they are called *the audience*. The audience often provides unconditional positive regard as well as a reality check. The drama occurs on a "stage" which is the physical space used. The stage is the place where fantasy and reality intersect and the protagonist is given flexibility and creative control to work through and resolve inner conflicts. "The director" is the therapist who guides the process. The director helps develop the dramatic action and then helps the protagonist process what is happening. This processing can take the form of empathizing, questioning, or confronting the protagonist. Afterward, the director leads the analysis and interpretation as all the group members process what occurred. Group members express how they personally connected to the protagonist's drama. This process usually takes 2 to 3 hours.

Therapeutic Role-Playing Techniques

There are many role-playing techniques that allow clients to experiment within the safety of the therapeutic setting. Clients can practice different social dynamics without fear of reprisal. They can learn new attitudes and try on new behaviors in a supportive environment.

"The soliloquy" is a technique where the protagonist is alone in the scene and is given the opportunity to share thoughts or feelings out loud. "Role reversal" is a technique where the protagonist takes on the role of another person. Acting and speaking from this new role allows the protagonist to gain new levels of empathy and understanding for others. The protagonist gains a new perspective of how others experience the world and how others experience the protagonist. "The double" is a technique where a group member acts as an auxiliary and plays the role of the protagonist's double. As the protagonist engages in a dialogue with "himself" or "herself," he or she discovers and expresses buried feelings and thoughts.

"The mirror" is a technique where the protagonist watches group members play out a scene from his or her life. One group member acts as an auxiliary and plays the role of the protagonist while other group members take on other roles in the protagonist's life. The protagonist often gains new insights into a scene that was previously overwhelming or confusing. The protagonist gains greater objectivity by engaging and dialoguing with the group members who are playing out a scene from the protagonist's life.

"The role presentation" is a technique that is often used as a warm-up. A group member announces that he or she is taking a specific role, introduces himself or herself, and shares information about the role. A role can be a person, an animal, an inanimate object, or even an abstract idea. When a person is done sharing about the role, the person "de-roles" and then becomes himself or herself again. During a "role interview" the director or other group members ask questions to the person in the role. Sometimes during other dramas, the director may freeze the scene in order to conduct a role interview with a particular person.

Role-Play in Experiential Family Therapy

There are many role-playing techniques that are specific to family therapy. Carl Whitaker, a pioneer in family psychotherapy, promoted the idea of influencing family structures by focusing on emotional processes through play and humor.

Experiential therapy researchers such as Jennifer Pereira have focused on ways to make role-play inclusive to all family members. One technique is to have the family participate in miniature genograms, similar to sand-play therapy. In this technique, miniatures are used to represent the aspects of each person's life. Miniature genograms assist in creating the therapeutic relationship between the therapist and client(s) as well as allowing the client to see a physical representation of his or her life.

Another technique used specifically for family dynamics is the family puppet story in which each member chooses a puppet, and the unit enacts or reenacts a story. It is not necessary that the story be about the family; the participants can choose any event or fictional narrative. The therapist watches for the interactions between members. He or she should note dynamics such as whether one person tended to lead the activity, whether people picked their own puppet, and how differing opinions were treated if brought up.

Experiential therapists may use a general exchange of roles approach in order to allow family members to become clearer on components such as communication styles, issues, goals, and barriers. In this technique, either the therapist can allow family members to choose who they are going to portray or the therapist carefully chooses which member is going to play another. Family members can, in different roles, work through regular problems within the family. Young children are encouraged to use puppets, and other family members should speak to the puppet for the purpose of inclusion. At the end of this technique, the therapist uses processing questions to allow the family to understand the role-play process. For example, "Dad, in telling Caleb's story, do you have a better understanding of what he is asking you as a parent?"

Experiential therapists may choose to set goals in a role-play activity through the press conference technique. In this role-play each member of the family stands at a podium in the room and presents personal and family goals for therapy. Other members portray the press corps and ask questions about the goals. At the end of the presentations, the family votes on group goals. After this technique, processing questions are used as well.

Role-Play in Adlerian Psychology

Adlerian therapists use recollections of early experiences as part of lifestyle assessments. Clients' recollections reflect current attitudes and cognitions. These recollections of early childhood experiences begin to change or can be reinterpreted as the lifestyle of the client changes during therapy.

Adlerian therapists ask about early memories, and then ask the client to recreate the scene of the memory with objects in the room. They will interview the client as if they were one of the people or objects associated with the memory. Adlerian therapists also often use Gestalt's empty chair therapy to allow the individual to view an early memory from a different perspective.

Adlerian therapists determine if the uncovered messages from these role-played memories are negative and/or affecting life today. If so, the therapist will assist the client in reconstructing the memory and messages. The therapist essentially helps replace the client's thinking processes about the early memories in order to effectively alter the client's current lifestyle.

Social and Developmental Needs of Children and Adolescents

Role-playing has been used to treat many different social and behavioral concerns in children and adolescents. Children can learn social skills through a variety of role-playing activities. When children are asked to respond to a pretend situation as if it were happening, counselors can evaluate and potentially correct negative behavior. For example, a nervous child can act out proactively engaging with others, and an impulsive child can act out how to use restraint and initiate prosocial behaviors. Role-playing has also been successful in treating adolescents with anger management issues. In this case, adolescents act out situations where they behaved inappropriately, discover their triggers, observe positive modeling, and then rehearse new appropriate behaviors.

Collaborative pretend play has been used to work with children with cognitive, academic, and social challenges. In this model, interventions are created after evaluating a child's script knowledge, meta-communication, and rule knowledge in the context of play. Children can develop skills in problem-solving, cooperative learning, and conflict resolution skills through collaborative pretend play.

Drama therapy has been used with children and adolescents to help them play out difficult emotions that may underlie their lives but go unexpressed. In particular, drama therapy can help adolescents explore their roles and envision different options and empower change. Other creative counseling strategies include using group role-playing games with gifted children in order to teach them emotional self-regulation skills or using the hero's journey and superheroes to foster inter- and intrapersonal growth.

Role-Play in Play Therapy

Play therapy recognizes that play can be used to help children process difficult feelings and develop self-efficacy. Children naturally express themselves, regulate emotions, and relieve stress through play. Play therapists may use role-reversal as a way to learn about how children see the world and how children interact with others. Play therapists can also use role-playing to help children gain a sense of control and make sense of painful and disturbing events, thoughts, and feelings. By repeatedly acting out particular scenarios or behaviors, children gain a sense of competence and accomplishment and this may relieve anxiety.

Development of Role-Playing

Along with Moreno, those who influenced the development of role-playing techniques in psychotherapy include George A. Kelly, Virginia Satir, and Adam Blatner. Their work is described in this section.

Jacob Moreno

Jacob Moreno (1889–1974) was born in Romania and graduated from the school of medicine at the University of Vienna in 1917. Moreno reacted against the neurological focus of psychiatry at the University of Vienna, where the primary concern was the classification and treatment of mental illnesses. Moreno first developed role-playing within a therapeutic context as "psychodrama." Moreno was a pioneer in the field of group counseling and psychotherapy; he invented psychodrama in the 1930s, which combines elements of improvisational theater, group work, and sociometry. Moreno's role-playing consists of experiential therapeutic interventions, methods, and techniques based on a philosophy that values creativity and egalitarianism.

Moreno also looked beyond the psychoanalytic theories of Sigmund Freud. Instead of promoting the resolution of conflicts and fantasies through introspection and verbal expression alone, Moreno believed individuals needed to act them out. He believed in working with people in their natural environments rather than solely in the confines of an office. Moreno's emphasis on living a meaningful life and improving relationships, rather than treating illnesses, would later inspire humanistic or person-centered therapies of later generations.

Moreno moved to New York City in 1925 and worked at Columbia University and the New School for Social Research. He established a sanitarium at Beacon in upstate New York in the 1930s. Moreno established the first psychodrama theater at Beacon Hill Sanitarium, where he was able to test his theories. He was the main founder of the International Association of Group Psychotherapy. In 1942, he founded the American Society of Group Psychotherapy and Psychodrama. His group work with army veterans included role-playing and was very successful and psychodrama was used in hospitals throughout the United States. He emphasized the importance of therapeutic techniques that are spontaneous and creative.

The philosophy, methods, and techniques of psychodrama and role-playing have had a lasting impact on later psychological and therapeutic theories such as family systems theory, Gestalt therapy, person-centered therapy, Virginia Satir's family reconstruction, transactional analysis, play therapy, drama therapy, and many others. He promoted mutual love and sharing in interpersonal relations. In addition to being the founder of psychodrama, Moreno's work has had a profound influence on modern social psychology and the practice of group counseling and psychotherapy.

George A. Kelly

George A. Kelly (1905–1967) was an American psychologist and author who developed personal construct psychology and fixed-role therapy. Kelly's work introduced the idea of behavior rehearsal through role-playing interventions that involve the client acting "as if" in order to modify behavior. Kelly's approach emphasized a useful social function rather than relying on spontaneity and creativity. In fixed-role therapy, the client is given a role to play out in real life. The client receives a fixed-role sketch with a description of the personality profile of someone who contrasts with their own personality but possesses desirable attributes. The client prepares for the role-play by engaging in interviews with the therapist as the new character. Then the client pretends to be the new character for 2 weeks in their real life.

Virginia Satir

Virginia Satir (1916–1988) was an American social worker and author whose work emphasized both communication strategies and experiential interventions. In her 1972 book *Peoplemaking*, she identified four dysfunctional roles or communication stances that people enact with each other: the placatory, the blamer, the super-reasonable, and the irrelevant. In 1983 with *Conjoint Family Therapy*, she identified inappropriate and unhealthy family roles. Satir's methodology included helping clients identify negative or incongruent communication patterns and then role-play new healthier behaviors within the clinical setting.

Adam Blatner

Adam Blatner (1937–) is an American psychiatrist who has written numerous texts, articles, and books on therapeutic role-playing or psychodrama. He authored the book *Acting-In*, which is a popular primer on psychodrama. He has promoted the use of role-playing as a method that can be applied in multiple settings. In 1999, he received the Jacob Moreno Award from the American Society of Group Psychotherapy and Psychodrama for lifetime service.

Gerry Ken Crete

See also Experiential Family Therapy; Family Reconstruction; Group Family Therapy; Play Family Therapy; Virginia Satir Model

Further Readings

Blatner, A. (1996). *Acting-in: Practical applications of psychodramatic methods* (3rd ed.). New York, NY: Springer.

Blatner, A. (1997). Psychodrama: The state of the art. *The Arts in Psychotherapy, 24*(1), 23–30.

Blatner, A. (2000). *Foundations of psychodrama: History, theory, and practice* (4th ed.). New York, NY: Springer.

Blatner, A. (2007). Morenean approaches: Recognizing psychodrama's many facets. *Journal of Group Psychotherapy, Psychodrama and Sociometry, 59*(4), 159–170.

Dayton, T. (2005). *The living stage: A step-by-step guide to psychodrama, sociometry and experiential group therapy*. Deerfield Beach, FL: Health Communications.

Gallo-Lopez, L. (2005). Drama therapy with adolescents. In L. Gallo-Lopez & C. E. Schaefer (Eds.), *Play therapy with adolescents* (pp. 81–95). Lanham, MD: Jason Aronson.

Hendler Lederer, S. (2002). Collaborative pretend play: From theory to therapy. *Child Language Teaching & Therapy, 18*(3), 233–255. doi:10.1191/0265659002ct237oa

Kipper, D. A. (1996). The emergence of role playing as a form of psychotherapy. *Journal of Group Psychotherapy, Psychodrama and Sociometry, 49*(3), 99.

Landy, R. J. (1991). The dramatic basis of role theory. *The Arts in Psychotherapy, 18*(1), 29–41.

Levenson, R. L., & Herman, J. (1991). The use of role playing as a technique in the psychotherapy of children. *Psychotherapy: Theory, Research, Practice, Training, 28*(4), 660–666. doi:10.1037/0033-3204.28.4.660

Leveton, E. (2001). *A clinician's guide to psychodrama* (3rd ed.). New York, NY: Springer.

Moreno, J. L. (1985). *Psychodrama: Vol. 1* (7th ed.). Ambler, PA: Beacon House.

Rosselet, J. G., & Stauffer, S. D. (2013). Using group role-playing games with gifted children and adolescents: A psychosocial intervention model. *International Journal of Play Therapy, 22*(4), 173–192.

Rubin, L. C. (2009). Our heroic adventure: Creating a personal mythology. *Journal of Creativity in Mental Health, 4*(3), 262–271.

Romance

Most people probably have their own idea of romance or what is romantic, but there is not one agreed-upon definition in counseling literature or research. A general definition of romance is that it is a state that involves expressing and appreciating demonstrations of emotional and sexual love and attraction in relationships. These expressions can be behaviors, words, time, gifts, or emotions. Romantic gestures are associated with *eros*, one of four types of love referred to in ancient Greece. Eros is a sexual type of love, *storge* is familial love, *philia* is a friendship type of love, and *agapé* refers to selfless love. Although adult, committed relationships and marriages can include all of these types of love, eros is associated with sexual and emotional attraction to a partner or potential partner. Romance can be part of attracting and maintaining intimate relationships, but the importance of romance and how it is expressed may be different depending on one's culture, family, and individual differences. Romance can be a source of strength for a couple or a source of strife. This entry provides a general view of the concept of romance and a look at romance in relationships. Theories associated with love and romance and an understanding of the importance of romance in relationships are also discussed.

The Concept of Romance

Humans, and many animals, have a predisposition toward forming long-term bonds with others. When humans are young they are compelled to attach to a caregiver. As people develop, they are also likely to bond with friends, dating partners, and marital or cohabiting partners. Partners who bond with each other are sometimes referred to as romantic partners. The behaviors associated with attracting romantic partners and maintaining romantic partnerships are referred to as romance or romantic.

Here *romance* is defined as the expression of feelings and thoughts that derive from an emotional and sexual attraction toward another person and is associated with feelings of desire or love. Although the act of being romantic varies from person to person, it is generally understood to be intimate and special. Verbal expressions of love and desire, physical gestures, and body language all play a role in delivering a message unlike what one would find in a platonic (friendly) relationship.

Romantic relationships are often differentiated from platonic relationships by sexual intercourse (or the desire for sex) coupled with commitment (or the desire for commitment). Romance is seen as a way to communicate or demonstrate a desire to connect. Commonly seen with romance is a preoccupation with the person who is the object of romantic desire. Obsessive thinking, displays of affection, and gestures such as sending cards, writing letters and poems, and giving flowers and other gifts are all common features of feelings and displays of romance. Romance, however, is not limited to these demonstrations, as some individuals may have preferences for certain displays of romance not listed here and some individuals may have a preference for certain displays of romance over others. For example, some individuals find it difficult to express their feelings out loud and prefer to communicate romantic feelings in writing. Some individuals find it difficult to be physically affectionate, but are comfortable with gift giving or writing cards. Some individuals are not comfortable with public displays of affection but find it suitable to be affectionate in private.

Views of romance can vary according to gender. For example, it is commonly thought that women highly value romance, while men do not value romance or do value it, but not that highly. Romance is often observed in the process of courting, which is the process of formal dating. Romance can also vary depending on how long partners have been dating, in a relationship, or married. For example, individuals who are newly dating might give cards and flowers and engage in frequent dinners out, whereas a couple who has been married for a significant period of time might invest in a getaway weekend. This weekend might consist of time without children to enjoy some extended time away from others, to reconnect emotionally and romantically with one another.

Major Theories Associated With Romance and Romantic Love

Theories associated with romance provide an understanding of foundations for romantic bonding. Commitment, intimacy, passion, and trust have been associated with the longevity of romantic relationships. Among the more widely noted theories of romantic love are attachment theory, triangular theory of love, and George Levinger's relationship stage theory. Although there are noted differences among these theories, familiar ideas are shared among them, including the idea that romance and love develop through stages that occur over time.

Attachment Theory

Attachment theory, developed by John Bowlby and Mary Ainsworth, posits that early interactions with significant others instill expectations and beliefs that subsequently shape social perceptions and behavior regarding what relationships and relationship partners should be like during adulthood. This evolutionary theory proposes that attachment is a lasting emotional connection between two people that develops and persists over time. Moreover, attachment orientation is the foundation people develop in childhood to form a basis for the way they interact and bond in adult relationships.

The attachment process begins in infancy with a caregiver providing safety and security for the child and through this attachment begins to form. There are three main attachment orientations: secure attachment, anxious attachment, and avoidant attachment. Children who hold a secure attachment to their parents or caregivers feel safe to freely travel and explore their surroundings unaccompanied and later return to the secure base from which they came. Children who hold an anxious attachment have a fear of independent exploration and constantly look for reassurance and a secure attachment base. Children who have an avoidant attachment are unsure of how to get their emotional needs met because they hold a fear of being hurt or abandoned.

In adulthood these attachments manifest similarly. Adults who formed secure attachments as a child generally hold similarly secure relationships as adults in their friendships and romantic partnerships. They are able to feel connected to a partner while still allowing independence for both individuals in the relationship. Adults with a secure attachment style are often in more satisfying and rewarding relationships. Individuals with an anxious attachment style often seek bonds that are not based on real love and trust within relationships. Many of these individuals search for relationships in an effort to feel secure and safe, yet often these individuals drive their significant others away with undesirable behaviors. Adults with an anxious attachment style often display needy, attention-seeking behavior and many times need a significant amount of reassurance. Adults with an avoidant attachment style are uncertain and fearful of getting too close to others because they believe they will inevitably get hurt. Individuals with an avoidant attachment style can present as dismissive, emotionally distant, and with a false sense of independence.

The Triangular Theory of Love

Developed by Robert Sternberg, the triangular theory of love posits that love has three main components: commitment, intimacy, and passion. Commitment is taking the necessary steps to maintain one's relationship. Intimacy is the feelings of affection and closeness. Passion is physical arousal or the occurrence of strong sexual desire or love. It is theorized that the different combinations derived from the three components create multiple types of love. The seven types of love are liking or friendship, infatuation or limerence, empty love, romantic love, companionate love, fatuous love, and consummate love. Liking in this sense is considered to be intimate and is characterized by true friendship. Here a bonding occurs with feelings of closeness and warmth toward another person. However, there are no intense feelings, passion, or a long-term romantic commitment.

Infatuation or limerence is what people know as "love at first sight." This infatuated form of love can dissolve quickly when not attached to the commitment and intimacy components of love. Empty love is where commitment remains, but intimacy or passion is no longer seen within the relationship. Some relationships start out in this phase and move into other components of love. One example of this is an arranged marriage. Another example of empty love is those who have committed to stay together for the sake of their children although they no longer feel the same type of love that moved them to marry. Romantic love consists of the components of liking and passion, creating a bond that produces arousal. Companionate love is a love that does not involve passion, but a great deal of affection and commitment persists in the relationship. Companionate love could be seen in a long-term relationship or marriage that no longer possesses the passion that is often seen in recently developed relationships. This love is considered stronger than friendship. Fatuous love involves a commitment prompted mostly by passion but where there is little to no intimacy within the relationship. An example of this would be individuals deciding to marry or live together mainly because of the passion they feel for one another and not because an intense, emotionally intimate connection has been made. Finally, consummate love is considered to be a whole and complete love. This is considered the ideal relationship that many people attempt to attain yet few actually achieve. Reaching this level of love is difficult; however, to preserve this love can be even tougher. This theory discusses love from the perspective that love changes over time. Although consummate love is the ideal love, many people lose passion and consummate love then becomes companionate love. Change often happens in every type of love proposed in this theory.

Levinger's Relationship Stage Theory

In the relationship stage theory developed by Levinger, also known as the ABCDE model, relationships are seen as developing, maturing, and decaying in stages over time. The first stage is acquaintance/attraction, in which people meet and form an initial attraction, frequently based on desirable physical attributes or likeness. The second stage is build-up, when individuals build emotional connection and then disclose more about private aspects of themselves about which many others don't know. The third stage is continuation/consolidation, when deep-rooted and lasting commitments are made. The fourth stage is deterioration, when many relationships have begun to deteriorate. This deterioration can be due to one or multiple factors. The final stage is ending. When the relationship is ending, both individuals in the relationship have decided to separate, or one partner has made a decision to terminate their involvement in the relationship.

The Importance of Romance

Romance is an important form of expressed communication and enhances relationships. Many view romance as the fuel to the fire in a bond between two people. Romance helps both individuals and couples. For individuals, romance can aid in the expression of new feelings or desires that are emerging. For couples, romance can help to maintain or reintroduce passion into long-standing relationships. As time passes, for those in committed relationships, it becomes easier for dullness, a lack of excitement, and routine to set in. Romance keeps things interesting and brings the spark back to the relationship if the fire is dimming and things have become routine. Romance is needed to enhance intimacy in relationships and to support feelings of love in romantic connections. When a person has a perception of being special, they are less likely to feel neglected, lonely, or unloved. Romantic behaviors such as those previously mentioned help support initial commitments in newly dating couples, and in relationships that are already formed these behaviors support longevity and satisfaction. Romance aids in initiating and reinforcing commitment, trust, and honesty between two people.

Jahaan R. Abdullah

See also Love, Physiology of; Love, Theories of; Love and Rituals; Love Languages; Sexual Intimacy

Further Readings

Braden, N. (2008). *The psychology of romantic love: Romantic love in an anti-romantic age*. New York, NY: Penguin.

Bretherton, I. (1992). The origins of attachment theory: John Bowlby and Mary Ainsworth. *Developmental Psychology, 28*(5), 759–775. doi:10.1037/0012-1649.28.5.759

Fehr, B., Harasymchuk, C., & Sprecher, S. (2014). Compassionate love in romantic relationships: A review and some new findings. *Journal of Social and Personal Relationships, 31*(5), 575–600. doi:10.1177/0265407514533768

Fletcher, G. O., & Kerr, P. G. (2010). Through the eyes of love: Reality and illusion in intimate relationships. *Psychological Bulletin, 136*(4), 627–658. doi:10.1037/a0019792

Galperin, A., & Haselton, M. (2010). Predictors of how often and when people fall in love. *Evolutionary Psychology, 8*(1), 5–28.

Harley, W. (2011). *His needs, her needs*. Grand Rapids, MI: Baker.

Levinger, G. (1980). Toward the analysis of close relationships. *Journal of Experimental Social Psychology, 16*(6), 510–544. doi:10.1016/0022-1031(80)90056-6

Sternberg, R. J. (2004). A triangular theory of love. In H. T. Reis & C. E. Rusbult (Eds.), *Close relationships: Key readings* (pp. 213–227). Philadelphia, PA: Taylor & Francis.

RULE-SETTING

Children's socially acceptable and unacceptable behaviors and continuation of problem behaviors can be seen as a systematic product of their environment. This environment is dictated by the rules that are formulated, set in place, and enforced by parents and guardians. Rules are explicit or implicit regulations governing the conduct of a particular activity, person, subsystem, or system. This entry explores types of rules, their specific application and enforcement, and how rule-setting directly impacts and facilitates certain behavioral outcomes in children.

The Home

It is important to consider the home environment and expectations of parents when analyzing rules and their effects on children. Rules provide structure and an understanding of consequences. Environmental influences, particularly the home surroundings, play an important role in the development of a child. Children are affected, to a high degree, by the emotional setting that exists in the home. Caretakers' abilities to effectively set and enforce rules may be influenced by individual and relational problems. Children are sensitive to situations when parents are suffering from emotionally based issues. For example, a parent who is suffering from depression may not feel up to the task of interacting with their children or may overreact when dealing with them. Problem behaviors can arise from children feeling neglected and confused by their parent's erratic behavior. These situations can be mediated by having a strong and cohesive family unit.

Marital unity and strength are important when setting rules and fostering an environment that produces positive outcomes for children. A couple will not always agree on everything, but when they argue in front of the children it not only models negative behavior, but also can cause significant harm. Depression, anxiety, and aggression may develop in children who witness high-intensity, high-frequency marital conflict. This can be a vicious cycle as the role of parenting can be stressful and lead to the many problematic behaviors that are found in marital conflict. For this reason, it is important for parents to formulate rules early and to set them together. Agreeing upon which rules should dictate the child's behavior will help when it comes time to enforce these rules. The manner in which they are to be enforced should also be agreed upon. Parents should agree about what punishment and repercussions a child would face when violations of the rules do occur.

Parental self-awareness is important to facilitate an effective rule-setting paradigm. Parents should also have set expectations for rules that they put into place. Rarely will one system of parenting work perfectly, so the expectations should be realistic and not set overly high standards either for themselves (as the parents) or for the children.

Rule-Setting and Administration

There are many ways that parents can implement rules for their children. Some ways are more effective than others. Effective rule-setting and implementation include clarity, conciseness, consistency, and caring. First, parents should make clear, explicit rules about the behaviors that are most important to them. Parents should explicitly state the rules and consequences instead of assuming children know them. Second, making simple, short rules will help younger children to be compliant. Third, the enforcement of rules should be consistent. Fourth, rules are set in order to ensure the safety and healthy development of children and should be set and enforced in a caring way. Helping children learn rules does not always have to be done through negative consequences. It can be done by redirecting children when they start to break a rule, reinforcing them when they follow the rules, and gently guiding them on how to do the correct behavior when they break a rule.

Rule-setting and enforcement can also be done in ineffective ways. For instance, a parent may give too many instructions or attempt to enforce too many rules at once. The friction going back and forth about rules may become tiring for the parent and the child and may create an environment for the child to have more opportunity to disobey the instructions. The more rules that are given, the more opportunities the child has to be noncompliant. An overabundance of rules may also make the child feel as though he or she is being picked on, providing less incentive for compliance. By administering a multitude of instructions and rules within a very short period of time, a parent can make it difficult for the child to comprehend every rule and leave the child feeling overwhelmed.

Also, a child's attention may simply begin to wander, which removes the opportunity to effectively attend to the instructions. An important point of consideration is the complexity of the rules and instructions. Asking a child to do something that is beyond his or her range of ability can lead to confusion and frustration. Parents should be aware of the complexity of instructions given, but also should not underestimate their children. There is a balance that must be struck in order to optimize the rule-giving relationship between parent and child. This starts with knowledge and understanding of the tasks at hand, as well as an understanding of the individual differences of the child involved and of specific parenting issues.

Parenting Issues When Setting Rules

Parents need to conceptualize their own roles in the familial unit and how challenges they face may contribute to their child's behavior. For instance, parents may deal with their children's behavior through emotionally charged, negative responses such as yelling, criticizing, arguing, and threatening. Over time, this can lead to resentment from the child toward the parent and may result in a continuation of problem behaviors or the development of new ones, and to future antagonistic rule-setting reprimands. This pattern should be recognized and avoided. It is important to remember that no child or parenting style is perfect. When the goal of rule-setting is to formulate the perfect child in the perfect relationship and the child continues to disobey, a plethora of negative feelings may begin to consume the parent. Parents may become discouraged, feel like a failure, and could even begin to ignore all negative behaviors entirely as a way to avoid future disappointment. This does not offer the child any reinforcement for good behavior and likely will not reduce problem behaviors. Reinforcement of positive behaviors (following and completion of set rules) is as important as setting rules in the first place.

Reinforcement

In the theory of behaviorism, reinforcement refers to the process of adding or removing a stimulus to strengthen behavior. Reinforcement that is contingent upon proper adherence to the set rules is crucial to the continued success and efficacy of instructions already in place, as well as future ones. Reinforcement can come in many forms. When reinforcement is administered inconsistently, rule-breaking behaviors are likely to increase in frequency and intensity. For instance, if a parent and a child are in the grocery store and the child sees candy and wants it, the parent may refuse to buy the candy. However, if the child begins to cry or continues to ask for it, the parent may go ahead and purchase the candy so that the child will cease the negative behavior. When this happens, the parent has unknowingly reinforced that problem behavior. The next time in the grocery store, the child will be more likely to ask for candy, and the intensity of the problem behavior is likely to increase (i.e., there will be louder crying for a longer period of time).

Another classic example of unintentional reinforcement is a parent removing a child from a situation because of misbehavior. For example, if a child misbehaves at a dinner party (likely because they don't want to be there) and thus does not follow the rules the parent(s) have laid out, then the parents may excuse themselves from the party and leave with the child. This removal from the party acts as a reward for the child's misbehavior and disregard for the rules. The child now is more likely not to adhere to set standards in environments that he or she wishes to escape, in hopes of achieving the same goal as the previous time. Often misbehavior is an attempt to seek attention. When parents discipline or interact with the child, then they could be reinforcing the behavior. This is a tricky situation because it is often hard to tell the exact intention of a behavior. However, it is important to try to understand the function of a rule-breaking behavior so that the proper steps toward reconciling that problem can be taken without accidentally rewarding the child.

Punishment

In behaviorism, punishment refers to adding or removing a stimulus to weaken behavior. Attempts at punishment are not always successful. Punishment is likely to be ineffective when it is harsh or inconsistent. When rules are not regularly upheld, then they are not learned, and the difference between children's behavior and what parents perceive as acceptable behavior is widened. It's unreasonable to think that parents can be perfectly consistent all of the time, but problem behaviors are likely to reoccur when the punishment is inconsistent. Parents are models for their children, so when the parents behave in an inconsistent manner, so do the children. When punishment is threatened but not followed through, it can also promote negative behaviors. It may also promote a situation that causes the child to test the veracity of the claim, resulting in more problem behaviors.

When the punishment is especially harsh, involving yelling, aggressive fits, and/or a physical component (hitting), then this models behavior for the child and likely will increase problem behavior frequency as the child learns to imitate such displays. Another problem that harsh punishment brings is the possibility of children learning to avoid punishment by engaging in other negative behaviors such as lying.

Enforcing the Rules

Proper enforcement of the rules plays an important role in producing positive behaviors and reducing the frequency of negative ones. It is important to try to understand the function of a behavior when possible. This will allow for a more accurate assessment of the environment, which can lead to instructions and rules that are given efficiently and in a way to which the child can adhere. When redirecting and giving instructions, parents should strive to do this as quickly as possible after the problem behavior has occurred. This will allow children to better understand the relationship between their actions and the consequences of these actions. If instructions are given too long after the behavior occurs, the child may not be able to connect the behavior to the punishment.

Also, these rules should be given in a way that the child is able to comprehend them. This may involve giving less detail when telling a 2-year-old to put something in the trash than it would when instructing a 10-year-old about the duties of cleaning a room. This also raises the point that a standard of completion should be in place and be understood between the parents and the children. Cleaning a room can look different to different people. A child who makes the bed and puts a few clothes away may very well think that he or she has followed the rules and cleaned the room. However, if a parent expects the child to pick everything up off of the floor and to vacuum in addition, this miscommunication could cause unneeded frustration and conflict. A clear goal for each set of instructions and confirmation of comprehension is important.

It is also important to consider when the instructions are given. Parents should gauge what their child is currently doing before asking the child to do something else or enforcing rules. If a parent could offer ample warning that a task is coming, this may also help to improve the likelihood that a child is to comply without incident with full task completion. When the child does follow the rules, reward and reinforcement are crucial for the continuation of such behavior. Positive reinforcement doesn't have to be elaborate and can be as simple as a pat on the back and a "thank you."

Suhad Sadik

See also Adolescent Behavior Disorders; Adolescent Behavior Problems; Attention-Deficit and Disruptive Behavior Disorders; Authoritative Parenting; Child Behavior Problems; Parenting

Further Readings

Call, N. A., & Mevers, J. L. (2014). The relative influence of motivating operations for positive and negative reinforcement on problem behavior during demands. *Behavioral Interventions, 29*(1), 4–20.

Kuhn, E. S., Phan, J. M., & Laird, R. D. (2014). Compliance with parents' rules: Between-person and within-person predictions. *Journal of Youth and Adolescence, 43*(2), 245–256.

O'Leary, S. G., & Vidair, H. B. (2005). Marital adjustment, child-rearing disagreements, and overreactive parenting: Predicting child behavior problems. *Journal of Family Psychology, 19*(2), 208–216.

Patterson, G. R. (1982). *Coercive family processes.* Eugene, OR: Castalia.

Sanders, M. R. (1992). *Every parent: A positive approach to children's behaviour.* Sydney, Australia: Addison-Wesley.

Shaffer, A., Kotchick, B. A., Dorsey, S., & Forehand, R. (2001). The past, present, and future of behavioral parent training: Interventions for child and adolescent problem behavior. *Behavior Analyst Today, 2*(2), 91–105.

RURAL FAMILIES

Rural families are a diverse group of families living in less developed areas of the United States. Geographically, these areas vary from mountain regions to farming communities to the Western frontier areas. Although families living in these regions have unique experiences and ethnic heritages based on their environment and cultural background, there are some commonalities facing this population. Understanding the key attributes of rural families, including well-being, quality of life, education, employment, economics, family composition, and family values, is important to providing effective marriage and family counseling for this population.

Understanding Rural Families in America

Where a family chooses to live has a direct impact on their quality of life. It is estimated that 20% to 25% of the U.S. population lives in a rural setting. There is no consistent definition of the term *rural*, but it is generally agreed that these are less inhabited areas located outside of cities. While there is great diversity among populations of rural families, particularly when examined from a regional perspective, some common traits emerge that are shared by many across the country.

Well-Being and Quality of Life

The thought of rural areas may conjure images of pastoral countryside, healthy living, and harmony. Many believe that families living in these areas usually do so by choice out of a preference for rural life and simple living. In actuality, some of these notions are accurate. Research suggests that people in rural areas experience less stress and that they feel a sense of connectedness with one another. This connectedness is partially attributed to the fact that many people in rural communities know one another and readily provide support in times of need. This support can be in the form of goods and services or emotional in nature. However, despite this supportive environment, overall quality of life is not necessarily improved for families when compared to those in urban locations.

While families living in more rural settings often experience the benefits of lower cost housing and lower taxes, their housing can also be substandard as many rural homes are older, with fewer amenities. Examples of this are homes that do not contain indoor plumbing or air conditioning. At times, changing economic conditions can also jeopardize these lower cost housing options. In many cases, local industry or recreational tourist attractions can bring in new residents who unintentionally inflate the cost of property. This inflation can ultimately increase the cost of living, causing increased economic strain to rural families.

There is also less access to goods and services that are commonly found in more metropolitan areas. There is a more limited selection of items to purchase and a lack of specialty merchants to meet the specific product needs of families. While this can be inconvenient, goods can be purchased online by those with Internet access or obtained through longer distance travel, which is a strategy utilized by those fortunate enough to have reliable transportation. However, services such as formal child care and public transportation that are widely available in cities may be unavailable in rural areas and may cause disruptions to family functioning. While faith-based and other local groups work to fill this service provider gap, the quantity of services available to families is diminished. To compensate for this, rural families often utilize an extended kin and friendship network to help meet the need for services such as child care and elder care. Families also come together to provide basic needs such as food and shelter through an extensive bartering system. Meals shared by multiple families or shared housing are examples of how these support exchange networks function. Not only does this practice help families make the best use of scarce resources, but it also serves to reinforce family and friendship connections.

Education, Employment, and Poverty

Educational opportunities in rural areas are very limited when compared to urban centers. Not only is there limited physical access to university, community college, and vocational training programs, but there can be a lack of awareness related to the existence of these opportunities. This is partly due to the marked decline in economic stability and limited perceived opportunity in rural areas. There has been steady erosion in agriculture-related employment, and growth is often isolated to small pockets of industry and service occupations. This has left many rural individuals in lower paying jobs with fewer benefits. This economic instability impacts all aspects of the lived experience of rural families. Many find employment in more high-risk occupations (e.g., mining, lumber), with high rates of work-related injury and death. The physical isolation of rural communities also means that workers in rural families often have to travel farther to secure employment. Because of this isolation and lack of economic opportunity, many rural families struggle financially and can find themselves living in poverty.

Poverty rates in rural areas are similar to rates seen in inner cities. Some estimate that one third of the nation's poor live in rural locations. Households headed by women experience higher poverty rates, with up to two of every five female-headed families living in poverty. African American families in rural areas are also more likely to be poorer than their White rural counterparts. Families living in poverty have higher rates of specific negative physical health indicators such as infant mortality, chronic disease, accidental death, and potential violence. In addition, poor families are less likely to have good nutrition, exercise, or receive preventive health care such as screening tests, all of which negatively influence overall physical health. Poverty, coupled with the isolation of rural living, can also impact individual and family mental health through behaviors such as alcohol abuse, illicit substance use, and failing to seek help for mental health problems. In certain rural areas, concentrations of poverty have persisted for generations. In other locations, new pockets of poverty have been created as immigrant populations have moved in, creating largely segregated populations within established communities.

Family Composition, Roles, and Values

Rural areas and the families within them have been significantly understudied. However, many believe that rural families more often exhibit values oriented toward family and home. Independence and self-sufficiency have been documented as core values within rural communities. Rural families also tend to exhibit more traditional gender roles. Many rural women report motherhood as a paramount life role. As such, it is not uncommon to see early marriage and childbearing. In lower income rural families, research suggests there may be repeated partnering, childbearing, cohabitation, and relationship termination. These types of transitions are at least partially responsible for creating more unstable family networks with role and boundary ambiguity. This can cause families to experience higher levels of stress and lower levels of resilience. Caretaking of the young, old, and chronically ill can also place an added strain on families both emotionally and psychologically and decrease overall family well-being.

Another relevant factor in rural families is the changing economic roles of women. In response to decreased occupational opportunities for men, more rural women and mothers are working outside of the home. This is causing a shift in gender roles within the family unit as women transition to the breadwinner role. Children in rural families also face their own unique challenges affected by the family systems in which they live. Research evidence shows a higher prevalence of obesity and accidental injury in rural families. Children and adolescents in rural families also often have less access to extracurricular activities and reproductive services and the teen birth rate is higher in rural areas of the United States than in more populous areas. Some have suggested that rural adolescents frequently begin their own families at a young age at least partially because of limited awareness of alternative life options.

Marriage and Family Counseling With Rural Families

Reliance on extended social networks in rural families can be both a barrier and a support to counseling treatment. Families tend to utilize informal support from family and friends to address mental health and relationship conflict. This reliance is partly due to the lingering stigma attached to formal treatment by qualified mental health or marriage and family professionals. Some rural residents lack knowledge of when seeking professional help might be appropriate. Others have a distrust of certain types of service providers.

There is disagreement over whether rural populations experience higher levels of individual and family dysfunction when compared with their metropolitan counterparts. Some researchers have reported that prevalence rates for drug abuse, alcohol addiction, family violence, and suicide are higher in rural areas, while other researchers have reported rates as high in rural areas as in more urban areas. What is agreed upon is that these social and mental health issues are present but they may not be as visible as in rural areas. The issues can also manifest differently in rural areas, with studies finding higher rates of certain types of substance abuse such as abuse of prescription drugs among rural adolescents than among urban adolescents.

Those families who do seek outside treatment can expect to find a limited number of providers, and physical access to these providers can be compromised by distance, poor roads, and residents not knowing how or where to access services. Another significant access issue relates to cost and insurance coverage for services related to mental health and marriage and family counseling. A move away from government-backed services and toward privatization of these rural counseling services has also complicated service delivery for consumer families. In addition, the preponderance of counseling models were developed using urban subjects and the resulting models and theories of practice often do not fit for rural communities. For instance, in most rural areas dual relationships, or multiple roles between a counselor and client, are unavoidable and auxiliary services are either limited or nonexistent. Rural health advocates have long recommended marriage and family counseling models for rural environments, but to date, there has been limited research and theoretical development in this area.

Professional practice with families in rural areas can be characterized by independence, flexibility, and creativity. Practitioners providing marriage and family counseling services might experience feelings of mistrust and concern from some clients that the treatment might not be fair. However, if the practitioner can integrate and join with the community, then the community and its social and government institutions can serve as partners and assets. Marriage and family counselors practicing in rural communities are encouraged to understand and appreciate these communities and become involved in service and volunteerism.

It is also an ethical imperative for counselors to understand how rural families connect, relate, and develop in their rural context. Even though these families share some qualities with their urban and suburban counterparts, the rural environment shapes these families in a unique and meaningful way. Counselors can frequently overlook the relevance of families' geographical context, despite the fact that it can affect a family's lived experience over generations.

*Caroline S. Booth
and Courtney Evans-Thompson*

See also Families and Substance Abuse; Job Loss; Poverty and Family Development

Further Readings

Beeson, P. G., Britain, C., Howell, M. L., Kirwan, D., & Sawyer, D. A. (1998). Rural mental health at the millennium. In R. W. Mandersheid & M. J. Henderson (Eds.), *Mental health United States, 1998* (DHHS Publication No. [SMA]99-3285, pp. 82–98). Washington, DC: U.S. Government Printing Office.

Hovestadt, A. J., Fenell, D. L., & Canfield, B. S. (2002). Characteristics of effective providers of marital and family therapy in rural mental health settings. *Journal of Marital and Family Therapy, 28*(2), 225–231. doi:10.1111/j.1752-0606.2002.tb00359.x

Morris, J. (2006). Rural marriage and family therapists: A pilot study. *Contemporary Family Therapy, 28*(1), 53–60. doi:10.1007/s10591-006-9694-3

Roberts, L. W., Battaglia, J., & Epstein, R. (1999). Frontier ethics: Mental health care needs and ethical dilemmas in rural communities. *Psychiatric Services, 50*(4), 497–503.

Weigel, D. J., & Baker, B. G. (2002). Unique issues in rural couple and family counseling. *The Family Journal, 10*, 61–69. doi:10.1177/1066480702101010

The SAGE Encyclopedia of Marriage, Family, and Couples Counseling

Editorial Board

Editors
Jon Carlson
Adler University

Shannon B. Dermer
Governors State University

Managing Editors
Brenna R. Frayn
Governors State University

Katie Paulson
Governors State University

Editorial Board

James Robert Bitter
East Tennessee State University

Scott Browning
Chestnut Hill College

William J. Doherty
University of Minnesota

Leslie Greenberg
York University

Katherine M. Helm
Lewis University

Alan J. Hovestadt
Western Michigan University

Jay Lebow
Northwestern University

Susan H. McDaniel
University of Rochester

Fred P. Piercy
University of Vermont

Robert L. Smith
Texas A&M–Corpus Christi

The SAGE Encyclopedia of Marriage, Family, and Couples Counseling

Volume 4

Editors

Jon Carlson
Adler University

Shannon B. Dermer
Governors State University

FOR INFORMATION:

SAGE Publications, Inc.
2455 Teller Road
Thousand Oaks, California 91320
E-mail: order@sagepub.com

SAGE Publications Ltd.
1 Oliver's Yard
55 City Road
London, EC1Y 1SP
United Kingdom

SAGE Publications India Pvt. Ltd.
B 1/I 1 Mohan Cooperative Industrial Area
Mathura Road, New Delhi 110 044
India

SAGE Publications Asia-Pacific Pte. Ltd.
3 Church Street
#10-04 Samsung Hub
Singapore 049483

Copyright © 2017 by SAGE Publications, Inc.

All rights reserved. No part of this book may be reproduced or utilized in any form or by any means, electronic or mechanical, including photocopying, recording, or by any information storage and retrieval system, without permission in writing from the publisher.

All trade names and trademarks recited, referenced, or reflected herein are the property of their respective owners who retain all rights thereto.

Printed in the United States of America

Library of Congress Cataloging-in-Publication Data

Names: Carlson, Jon, editor. | Dermer, Shannon B., editor.

Title: The SAGE encyclopedia of marriage, family, and couples counseling / editors, Jon Carlson, Shannon B. Dermer.

Other titles: Encyclopedia of marriage, family, and couples counseling

Description: Thousand Oaks, California : SAGE Publications, Inc., [2016] | "A SAGE Reference publication." | Includes bibliographical references and index.

Identifiers: LCCN 2016025752 | ISBN 9781483369556 (hardcover : alk. paper)

Subjects: | MESH: Psychotherapy, Group | Counseling | Interpersonal Relations | Family Relations | Encyclopedias

Classification: LCC BF636.7.G76 | NLM WM 13 | DDC 158.3/5—dc23
LC record available at https://lccn.loc.gov/2016025752

Acquisitions Editor: Andrew Boney
Editorial Assistant: Jordan Enobakhare
Developmental Editor: Sanford Robinson
Production Editor: Tracy Buyan
Reference Systems Manager: Leticia Gutierrez
Copy Editors: Diane DiMura, Talia Greenberg, Megan Markanich, Terri Lee Paulsen, Gretchen Treadwell
Typesetter: C&M Digitals (P) Ltd.
Proofreaders: Lawrence W. Baker, Caryne Brown, Sarah Duffy, Scott Oney
Indexer: David Luljak
Cover Designer: Candice Harman
Marketing Manager: Leah Watson

This book is printed on acid-free paper.

16 17 18 19 20 10 9 8 7 6 5 4 3 2 1

Contents

Volume 4

List of Entries *vii*

Reader's Guide *xv*

Entries

S	*1433*	U	*1747*
T	*1679*	V	*1753*

Appendix A. The History of Marriage, Family, and Couples Therapy *1767*

Appendix B. Resource Guide *1789*

Appendix C. Selected Readings *1795*

Index *1799*

List of Entries

Acceptance and Commitment Therapy
Acculturation
Active Parenting
Adjustment Disorder in Adolescents
Adlerian Family Therapy
Adlerian Open-Forum Family Counseling
Adolescent Behavior Disorders
Adolescent Behavior Problems
Adolescent Mental Health
Adoption
Adoption, Cross-Cultural and Interracial
Adoptive Families
Adult Attachment Assessments
Adult Development
Affect Regulation
African American Families
Aging and Caregiving
Alcohol and Substance Abuse
American Association for Marriage and Family Therapy
Anger Management
Anxiety
Anxiety Disorders in Adolescents
Asian American Families
Assertiveness
Assessment, Biopsychosocial
Assessment, Suicide
Assimilation: Immigrants and Refugees
Attachment
Attachment and Adolescents
Attachment and Health
Attachment and Romantic Love
Attachment Styles
Attachment Theory
Attachment-Based Family Therapy
Attention-Deficit and Disruptive Behavior Disorders

Attunement, Clinician
Attunement in Relationships
Authoritative Parenting
Autism and Children
Autism Spectrum Disorder
Avoidance

Behavioral Family Therapy
Beliefs and Values
Bereavement
Bereavement Counseling
Best Interests of the Child
Bibliotherapy. *See* Self-Help
Bilingual Families
Birth Control and Contraception
Blended Families. *See* Stepfamilies
Body Dysmorphic Disorder in Adolescents
Bonding
Boundaries
Bowen Family Systems Theory
Brief Adlerian Couples Therapy
Brief Family Therapy

CACREP. *See* Competency-Based Standards for Marriage, Couple, and Family Counseling; Council for Accreditation of Counseling and Related Educational Programs
Career Planning and Couples/Families
Caregivers
Certified Family Life Educator
Chaos Family Therapy
Child Behavior Problems
Child Guidance Movement
Child Maltreatment
Child Protective Services
Child-Centered Parenting
Childhood Anxiety

Childhood Obesity, Prevention and Treatment of
Childless Couples
Child–Parent Relationship Therapy
Children With Chronic Illness
Children With Special Needs in Family Therapy
Choice Theory and Reality Therapy
Chosen Families
Chronic Illness With Couples and Families
Cinematherapy
Circular Questions. *See* Questions: Open, Closed, and Circular
Circularity and Linearity
Circumplex Model
Clinical Case Conceptualization With Couples and Families
Clinical Interviews With Couples and Families
Clinical Practice
Clinical Versus Statistical Significance
Clinician-Directed, Solution-Focused Supervision
Cognitive Maps and Couples
Cognitive-Behavioral Couples Therapy
Cognitive-Behavioral Family Therapy
Cohesion
Collaborative Couples Therapy
Collaborative Language Systems
Collaborative Therapy. *See* Collaborative Language Systems
Commitment
Common Factors
Communication Disorders
Communication Errors/Problems in Couples and Families
Communication in Couples and Families
Community Programs
Compassion
Competency-Based Standards for Marriage, Couple, and Family Counseling
Complementary and Symmetrical Relationships
Compulsive Sexual Behavior
Conduct Disorder
Confidentiality
Conflict in Couples and Families
Conflict Resolution
Conflict Styles
Confrontation

Conjoint Family Therapy
Constructivism
Contextual Family Therapy
Core Competencies for Marriage and Family Therapists
Cost–Benefit Analysis
Cotherapy Team
Council for Accreditation of Counseling and Related Educational Programs
Couple and Family Forensics
Couple Development
Couples, Quality Time
Couples and Marriage Counseling
Couples Therapy Research
Court-Mandated Clients
Crisis Intervention With Couples and Families
Critical Theory
Crucible
Cultural Issues in Couples and Families
Custody Evaluations
Cutting/Self-Mutilation. *See* Self-Injury
Cybernetics

Dating Coaching
Dating Relationship Dissolution
Death, Parents of Deceased Children
Death and Dying
Debt and Financial Strain
Decision-Making
Delphi Research Method
Depression in Adolescents
Depression in Children
Depression in Couples and Families
Developmental Model of Marriage
Differentiation
Discernment Counseling
Disinhibited Social Engagement Disorder in Children
Diversity
Divorce and Separation
Divorce Therapy
Domestic Violence
Double Bind Theory
DSM and V-Codes
Dual and Multiple Relationships

Dual-Earner Families
Duty to Warn and Protect

Earned Attachment
Eating Disorders
Ecological Systems
Eco-Map
Ecosystemic Structural Family Therapy
Ecosystems Perspective
Effectiveness Research
Elder Abuse
Elimination Disorders in Children
Emotional Disengagement
Emotional Intelligence, Children
Emotional Intelligence, Families
Emotionally Focused Therapy for Couples
Empathy
Empirically Validated Models
Empowerment in Families
Enactments
Engendering Hope
Entitlement
Epistemology in Family Therapy
Equine-Assisted Family Therapy
Erectile Disorder
Ericksonian Family Therapy
Ethical Codes
Ethical Decision-Making
Ethnicity
Evidence-Based Practice With Couples and Families
Experiential Family Therapy
Externalizing Behaviors
Extramarital Affairs and Infidelity

Faith-Based Therapy
Families and Poverty
Families and Substance Abuse
Family and Medical Leave Act of 1993
Family Assessment, Models of
Family Life Cycle
Family Life Educators
Family Mediation
Family Mode Deactivation Therapy
Family Myth
Family of Origin

Family Reconstruction
Family Resilience
Family Resource Management
Family Rituals
Family Strengths
Family Stress
Family Stress Adaptation Theory
Family Values
Feedback. *See* Positive and Negative Feedback
Female Orgasmic Disorder
Female Sexual Interest/Arousal Disorder
Feminist Family Therapy
Feminization of Poverty
Fetishes
Fidelity
First-Order Change
Focal Family Therapy
Forgiveness
Foster Children
Friendship
Functional Assessment and Children
Functional Family Therapy
Functionalism
Fusion

Gambling, Compulsive
Gender- and Culture-Sensitive Therapies
Gender Dysphoria
Gender Issues
Gender Orientation, Gender Identity, and Gender Expression
Gender Roles
General Systems Theory
Genito-Pelvic Pain/Penetration Disorder
Genograms
Gestalt Family Therapy
Goals, Treatment
Gottman Method Couples Therapy
Grief Counseling
Group Family Therapy
Group Parenting Classes

Health Issues
Healthy Marriage and Responsible Fatherhood
Hierarchy
HIPAA Standards

Hispanic Healthy Marriage Initiative
Hoarding
Holism
Home-Based Therapy
Homelessness
Homelessness and Youth
Homeostasis
Homework Assignments in Therapy
Homicide
Hope-Focused Approach to Couple Enrichment in Counseling
Hospice
Human Sexual Response
Humanistic Family Therapy
Hypnosis
Hypothesis, Systemic

IAMFC. *See* International Association of Marriage and Family Counselors
Identified Patient
Imago Relationship Therapy
Immigrant Families
Incest
Individual and Family Development
Individual Family Culture
Individual Versus Family Therapy
Infertility
Informed Consent for Research
Informed Consent in Clinical Work
In-Law Relationships
Integrating Systemic and Individual Theories
Integrative Couples Therapy
Intellectual Disability and Autism
Intercultural Marriage and Family
Intergenerational Loyalty
Intergenerational Trauma
Intermittent Explosive Disorder in Adolescents
Internal Family Systems Model
International Association of Marriage and Family Counselors
International Classification of Diseases (ICD)
International Family Therapy
Interpersonal Neurobiology, Attachment and
Interpersonal Neurobiology, Couples and
Interpersonal Neurobiology, Parenting and
Interpersonal Violence
Interracial Marriages and Families

Intimacy, Specific Threats to
Isomorphism

Job Loss
Joining
Juvenile Firesetter Interventions

Kinship Care

Latino Families
Legal Issues in Parenting
LGBT Families
Licensure and Certification
Life Balance
Life Events
Life Transitions
Listening, Empathic
Live Supervision
Loneliness
Loss
Love, Physiology of
Love, Theories of
Love, Types of
Love and Rituals
Love Languages

Male Hypoactive Sexual Desire Disorder
Mandated Reporter
Marital Distress
Marital Group Therapy
Marriage, Arranged
Marriage, First and Second
Marriage and Health
Marriage Education
Marriage Encounter
Marriage Enrichment
Marriage Myths
Marriage Versus Civil Unions
Marriage-Friendly Therapy
Mate Selection
Media in Family Therapy
Medical Family Therapy
Men in Counseling
Mental Health, Systemic Perspective
Metacommunication
Metaphors
Milan Team

List of Entries   xi

Military Couples and Families
Mindfulness
Mindfulness and Children
Mindfulness and Couples
Mindfulness and Sex
Miracle Question
Mood Disorders in Adolescents
Mood Disorders in Children
Moral Dimensions of Therapy
Morphogenesis
Morphostasis
Mother-Blaming
Motivational Interviewing
Multicultural Counseling Competence
Multiculturalism
Multiple Family Therapy
Multiple Relationships. *See* Dual and Multiple Relationships
Multisystemic Therapy
Muslim American Families

Narrative Therapy
National Marriage Initiative
Native American Families
Network Therapy
Neuro-Linguistic Programming
Neutrality and Curiosity
No-Harm Contracts
Non–Rapid Eye Movement Sleep Arousal Disorders in Children
Nonresidential Fathers
Nonverbal Communication
Normalizing
No-Secrets Contracts
Nuclear Family
Nudity: Beliefs and Values

Object Relations Theory
Online Dating
Open Relationships
Oppositional Defiant Disorder
Outcome Research

Paradoxes and Paradoxical Intervention
Paraphilic Disorders
Parent Effectiveness Training (P.E.T.)
Parent Management Training

Parent Study Groups
Parent–Adolescent Relations
Parental Acceptance–Rejection Theory
Parental Alienation Syndrome
Parental Stress: Effects on Children
Parent–Child Communication
Parentification and Diverse Family Systems
Parenting
Parenting Education
Parenting Styles
Patriarchy
Peer Counseling
Person of the Therapist
Play Family Therapy
Polyamory
Polygamy
Pornography
Positive and Negative Feedback
Positive Psychology
Postdoctoral Training
Postmodern Therapies
Postpartum Depression
Posttraumatic Stress Disorder in Children
Poverty and Family Development
Power Issues in Couples
Practice Management
Pregnancy
Pregnancy and Sexuality
Premarital Counseling
Premature Ejaculation
Prenuptial Agreements
PREPARE/ENRICH
Presenting Problems
Prevention Research
Primary and Secondary Emotions
Process Research
Professional Associations
Progress Notes for Couples and Families
Psychoanalytic Family Therapy
Psychobiology of Attachment
Psychoeducation
Public Health Code
Punctuation

Qualitative Research
Quantitative Research
Questions: Open, Closed, and Circular

Racial Disparities in Foster Care
Racism
Reactive Attachment Disorder in Children
Reconciliation
Recursiveness
Reflecting Team
Relational Diagnoses
Relational-Cultural Therapy
Relationship Enhancement
Release of Information for Couples and Families
Religion
Remarriage. See Marriage, First and Second; Stepfamilies
Resilience
Resistance
Respect
Restoration Therapy
Retirement
Rituals in Family Therapy
Role-Playing
Romance
Rule-Setting
Rural Families

Same-Sex Couples
Scales, Children
Scales, Couple and Marital
Scales, Family
Scaling Questions
Scapegoating
Schizophrenia and Families
Schools, Family Involvement in
Second-Order Change
Second-Order Family Therapy
Secrets
Self of the Therapist
Self-Care Practices for the Trauma-Informed Couple and Family Counselor
Self-Esteem
Self-Esteem in Children
Self-Help
Self-Injury
Sensate Focus
Sentiment Override, Positive and Negative
Sex, Definition of
Sex Positivity

Sex Researchers
Sex Therapy
Sexual Abuse
Sexual Assault and Rape
Sexual Assessment/History
Sexual Dysfunction
Sexual Enhancement, Sexual Toys
Sexual Health
Sexual History
Sexual Intimacy
Sexual Minorities
Sexual Orientation, Attraction, and Identity
Sexual Prejudice
Sexual Relationships With Clients
Sexual Toys/Sexual Aids
Sexuality and Religion
Sexuality Education
Sexually Transmitted Infections
Sibling Relationships
Single-Parent Families
Social Constructionism
Social Support
Socioeconomic Status
Solution-Focused Brief Therapy
Somatic Symptom Disorder and Related Disorders in Adolescents
Spirituality
Stages of Family Therapy
Statutory Rape
Stepfamilies
Stillbirth and Miscarriage
Strategic Family Therapy
Stress Management
Structural Determinism
Structural Family Therapy
Structural Maps
Substance Use Disorders in Adolescence
Suicide
Supervision
Supervision, Approved Supervisor in Marriage and Family Therapy
Supervision, Developmental Model
Supervision, Gatekeeping
Supervision, Individual and Group
Supervision Contract
Supervision of Supervision

Supervision Philosophy Statement
Supervision Theories
Support Groups
Symbolic Interactionism
Systemic Family Therapy
Systems, Subsystems, and Metasystems
Systems Theory

Technology and Families/Marriage
Teen Parenting
Termination
Therapeutic Alliance
Therapeutic Assessment
Therapeutic Contract
Therapeutic Impasses
Therapists' Values
TIME Program. *See* Training in Marriage Enrichment (TIME) Program
Torture Treatment
Training and Licensure

Training in Marriage Enrichment (TIME) Program
Transgender Families
Transgenerational Family Therapy
Transracial Adoption
Trauma and Children
Trauma and Families
Trauma-Focused Cognitive-Behavioral Therapy
Treatment Planning With Couples and Families
Triangulation
Trust

Urban Families

Virginia Satir Model

Women's Project, The
Work Relationships
World Association for Sexual Health
World Health Organization

Reader's Guide

Assessments
Adult Attachment Assessments
Assessment, Biopsychosocial
Assessment, Suicide
Circumplex Model
Clinical Case Conceptualization With Couples and Families
Clinical Interviews With Couples and Families
Common Factors
Custody Evaluations
DSM and V-Codes
Ecological Systems
Eco-Map
Family Assessment, Models of
Functional Assessment and Children
Genograms
Interpersonal Violence
Love, Physiology of
Love, Types of
Love Languages
Marital Distress
Marriage Education
Nonverbal Communication
Parent–Child Communication
PREPARE/ENRICH
Progress Notes for Couples and Families
Scales, Children
Scales, Couple and Marital
Scales, Family
Scaling Questions
Sentiment Override, Positive and Negative
Sexual Assessment/History
Sexual Health
Sexual History
Suicide
Therapeutic Assessment
Treatment Planning With Couples and Families

Attachment
Adult Attachment Assessments
Affect Regulation
Attachment
Attachment and Adolescents
Attachment and Health
Attachment and Romantic Love
Attachment Styles
Attachment Theory
Attachment-Based Family Therapy
Attunement in Relationships
Bonding
Child-Centered Parenting
Earned Attachment
Emotional Disengagement
Emotionally Focused Therapy for Couples
Interpersonal Neurobiology, Attachment and
Primary and Secondary Emotions
Psychobiology of Attachment

Communication
Assertiveness
Avoidance
Collaborative Language Systems
Communication Disorders
Communication Errors/Problems in Couples and Families
Communication in Couples and Families
Conflict in Couples and Families
Conflict Resolution
Conflict Styles
Confrontation
Disinhibited Social Engagement Disorder in Children
Empathy
Forgiveness

Love Languages
Metacommunication
Metaphors
Nonverbal Communication
Parent–Child Communication
Power Issues in Couples
Respect
Secrets
Social Constructionism
Symbolic Interactionism
Therapeutic Impasses
Trust

Coping
Bereavement
Children With Chronic Illness
Chronic Illness With Couples and Families
Conflict Styles
Death, Parents of Deceased Children
Empowerment in Families
Engendering Hope
Families and Substance Abuse
Family Resilience
Family Strengths
Family Stress
Family Stress Adaptation Theory
Forgiveness
Hope-Focused Approach to Couple Enrichment in Counseling
Parental Stress: Effects on Children
Reconciliation
Resilience
Self-Esteem
Self-Esteem in Children
Social Support
Stillbirth and Miscarriage
Stress Management

Couple, Marriage, Family Policy
Best Interests of the Child
Child Protective Services
Family and Medical Leave Act of 1993
Healthy Marriage and Responsible Fatherhood
Hispanic Healthy Marriage Initiative
Marriage Versus Civil Unions
National Marriage Initiative

Public Health Code
Self-Esteem in Children
Social Support

Diagnosing and Disorders
Adjustment Disorder in Adolescents
Adolescent Behavior Disorders
Adolescent Behavior Problems
Adolescent Mental Health
Alcohol and Substance Abuse
Anxiety
Anxiety Disorders in Adolescents
Attention-Deficit and Disruptive Behavior Disorders
Autism Spectrum Disorder
Child Behavior Problems
Childhood Anxiety
Childhood Obesity, Prevention and Treatment of
Compulsive Sexual Behavior
Conduct Disorder
Depression in Adolescents
Depression in Children
Depression in Couples and Families
Disinhibited Social Engagement Disorder in Children
DSM and V-Codes
Eating Disorders
Elimination Disorders in Children
Erectile Disorder
Female Orgasmic Disorder
Female Sexual Interest/Arousal Disorder
Fetishes
Functional Assessment and Children
Gambling, Compulsive
Gender Dysphoria
Genito-Pelvic Pain/Penetration Disorder
Hoarding
Intermittent Explosive Disorder in Adolescents
International Classification of Diseases (ICD)
Male Hypoactive Sexual Desire Disorder
Mood Disorders in Adolescents
Mood Disorders in Children
Non–Rapid Eye Movement Sleep Arousal Disorders in Children
Oppositional Defiant Disorder

Paraphilic Disorders
Parental Alienation Syndrome
Postpartum Depression
Posttraumatic Stress Disorder in Children
Premature Ejaculation
Reactive Attachment Disorder in Children
Relational Diagnoses
Schizophrenia and Families
Sexual Dysfunction
Sexually Transmitted Infections
Somatic Symptom Disorder and Related Disorders in Adolescents
Substance Use Disorders in Adolescence

Diversity
Acculturation
Adoption, Cross-Cultural and Interracial
Adoptive Families
African American Families
Asian American Families
Assimilation: Immigrants and Refugees
Beliefs and Values
Bilingual Families
Children With Special Needs in Family Therapy
Chosen Families
Cultural Issues in Couples and Families
Diversity
Empowerment in Families
Ethnicity
Faith-Based Therapy
Families and Substance Abuse
Family Resilience
Family Values
Feminization of Poverty
Foster Children
Gender- and Culture-Sensitive Therapies
Gender Issues
Gender Orientation, Gender Identity, and Gender Expression
Gender Roles
Immigrant Families
Individual Family Culture
Intellectual Disability and Autism
Intercultural Marriage and Family
Interracial Marriages and Families
Kinship Care

Latino Families
LGBT Families
Marriage, Arranged
Marriage Versus Civil Unions
Men in Counseling
Military Couples and Families
Mother-Blaming
Multiculturalism
Muslim American Families
Native American Families
Nudity: Beliefs and Values
Parentification and Diverse Family Systems
Patriarchy
Racial Disparities in Foster Care
Racism
Relational-Cultural Therapy
Religion
Resilience
Rural Families
Same-Sex Couples
Sexual Minorities
Sexual Orientation, Attraction, and Identity
Sexual Prejudice
Sexuality and Religion
Single-Parent Families
Socioeconomic Status
Spirituality
Stepfamilies
Therapists' Values
Transgender Families
Transracial Adoption
Urban Families
Women's Project, The

Financial Issues
Career Planning and Couples/Families
Debt and Financial Strain
Dual-Earner Families
Families and Poverty
Family Resource Management
Feminization of Poverty
Gambling, Compulsive
Hoarding
Homelessness
Homelessness and Youth
Job Loss

Life Balance
Poverty and Family Development
Prenuptial Agreements
Retirement
Socioeconomic Status
Work Relationships

Intimacy
Attachment
Attachment and Adolescents
Attachment and Health
Attachment and Romantic Love
Bonding
Cognitive Maps and Couples
Commitment
Compassion
Confrontation
Couple Development
Couples, Quality Time
Dating Coaching
Dating Relationship Dissolution
Empathy
Fidelity
Forgiveness
Friendship
In-Law Relationships
Intimacy, Specific Threats to
Loneliness
Love, Physiology of
Love, Theories of
Love, Types of
Love and Rituals
Love Languages
Marital Distress
Marriage, Arranged
Marriage, First and Second
Mate Selection
Online Dating
Open Relationships
Polyamory
Polygamy
Reconciliation
Relationship Enhancement
Romance
Secrets
Sexual Intimacy

Sibling Relationships
Trust
Work Relationships

Life Events/Transitions
Adolescent Behavior Problems
Adolescent Mental Health
Adoption
Adult Development
Aging and Caregiving
Autism and Children
Bereavement Counseling
Career Planning and Couples/Families
Caregivers
Child Behavior Problems
Childhood Anxiety
Childless Couples
Chosen Families
Chronic Illness With Couples and Families
Couple Development
Couples, Quality Time
Dating Coaching
Dating Relationship Dissolution
Death, Parents of Deceased Children
Death and Dying
Divorce and Separation
Divorce Therapy
Dual-Earner Families
Families and Poverty
Family Life Cycle
Family Reconstruction
Family Stress
Grief Counseling
Health Issues
Homelessness
Homelessness and Youth
Hospice
Individual and Family Development
Job Loss
Life Balance
Life Events
Life Transitions
Loss
Marriage, First and Second
Parent–Adolescent Relations
Parenting

Postpartum Depression
Posttraumatic Stress Disorder in Children
Poverty and Family Development
Power Issues in Couples
Prenuptial Agreements
Retirement
Rural Families
Sibling Relationships
Single-Parent Families
Spirituality
Stepfamilies
Stillbirth and Miscarriage
Suicide
Teen Parenting
Transracial Adoption
Urban Families

Major Concepts
Affect Regulation
Attachment
Attachment Styles
Attunement, Clinician
Attunement in Relationships
Boundaries
Circumplex Model
Cohesion
Complementary and Symmetrical Relationships
Crucible
Cybernetics
Differentiation
Ecological Systems
Eco-Map
Ecosystems Perspective
Emotional Disengagement
Entitlement
Epistemology in Family Therapy
Family Myth
Family of Origin
Family Rituals
Family Strengths
Family Values
First-Order Change
Fusion
Gender Roles
Hierarchy
Holism

Homeostasis
Hypothesis, Systemic
Identified Patient
Individual Family Culture
Intergenerational Loyalty
Intergenerational Trauma
Isomorphism
Kinship Care
Marriage Education
Marriage Encounter
Marriage Myths
Morphogenesis
Morphostasis
Mother-Blaming
Neutrality and Curiosity
Nuclear Family
Paradoxes and Paradoxical Intervention
Patriarchy
Person of the Therapist
Positive and Negative Feedback
Presenting Problems
Primary and Secondary Emotions
Questions: Open, Closed, and Circular
Recursiveness
Resistance
Scaling Questions
Scapegoating
Second-Order Change
Sentiment Override, Positive and Negative
Social Constructionism
Social Support
Structural Determinism
Structural Maps
Symbolic Interactionism
Systems Theory
Triangulation

Models, Interventions, Techniques
Acceptance and Commitment Therapy
Adlerian Family Therapy
Adlerian Open-Forum Family Counseling
Attachment-Based Family Therapy
Behavioral Family Therapy
Brief Adlerian Couples Therapy
Brief Family Therapy
Chaos Family Therapy

Childhood Obesity, Prevention and Treatment of
Child–Parent Relationship Therapy
Choice Theory and Reality Therapy
Cinematherapy
Circularity and Linearity
Cognitive Maps and Couples
Cognitive-Behavioral Couples Therapy
Cognitive-Behavioral Family Therapy
Collaborative Couples Therapy
Collaborative Language Systems
Community Programs
Conflict Resolution
Conjoint Family Therapy
Constructivism
Contextual Family Therapy
Couple and Family Forensics
Couples and Marriage Counseling
Crisis Intervention With Couples and Families
Discernment Counseling
Divorce Therapy
Ecosystemic Structural Family Therapy
Emotional Intelligence, Children
Emotional Intelligence, Families
Emotionally Focused Therapy for Couples
Empirically Validated Models
Enactments
Equine-Assisted Family Therapy
Ericksonian Family Therapy
Experiential Family Therapy
Externalizing Behaviors
Faith-Based Therapy
Family Mode Deactivation Therapy
Feminist Family Therapy
Focal Family Therapy
Functional Family Therapy
Gender- and Culture-Sensitive Therapies
Gestalt Family Therapy
Goals, Treatment
Gottman Method Couples Therapy
Grief Counseling
Group Family Therapy
Home-Based Therapy
Homework Assignments in Therapy
Homicide
Hope-Focused Approach to Couple Enrichment in Counseling

Humanistic Family Therapy
Hypnosis
Imago Relationship Therapy
Individual Versus Family Therapy
Integrating Systemic and Individual Theories
Integrative Couples Therapy
Internal Family Systems Model
International Family Therapy
Interpersonal Neurobiology, Attachment and
Interpersonal Neurobiology, Couples and
Interpersonal Neurobiology, Parenting and
Joining
Juvenile Firesetter Interventions
Listening, Empathic
Love and Rituals
Marital Group Therapy
Marriage Encounter
Marriage Enrichment
Marriage-Friendly Therapy
Medical Family Therapy
Metacommunication
Metaphors
Milan Team
Mindfulness
Miracle Question
Motivational Interviewing
Multiple Family Therapy
Multisystemic Therapy
Narrative Therapy
Network Therapy
Neuro-Linguistic Programming
No-Harm Contracts
Normalizing
Paradoxes and Paradoxical Intervention
Parent Effectiveness Training (P.E.T.)
Parent Management Training
Peer Counseling
Play Family Therapy
Positive Psychology
Postmodern Therapies
Premarital Counseling
Progress Notes for Couples and Families
Psychoanalytic Family Therapy
Psychobiology of Attachment
Psychoeducation
Punctuation

Questions: Open, Closed, and Circular
Reflecting Team
Relational-Cultural Therapy
Relationship Enhancement
Restoration Therapy
Rituals in Family Therapy
Role-Playing
Second-Order Family Therapy
Self-Help
Sensate Focus
Solution-Focused Brief Therapy
Stages of Family Therapy
Strategic Family Therapy
Structural Family Therapy
Support Groups
Systemic Family Therapy
Systems, Subsystems, and Metasystems
Therapeutic Alliance
Therapeutic Contract
Torture Treatment
Training in Marriage Enrichment (TIME) Program
Transgenerational Family Therapy
Trauma-Focused Cognitive-Behavioral Therapy
Triangulation
Virginia Satir Model

Organizations

American Association for Marriage and Family Therapy
Council for Accreditation of Counseling and Related Educational Programs
International Association of Marriage and Family Counselors
World Association for Sexual Health
World Health Organization

Parenting

Active Parenting
Adoption
Authoritative Parenting
Child-Centered Parenting
Child–Parent Relationship Therapy
Children With Chronic Illness
Foster Children
Group Parenting Classes
Interpersonal Neurobiology, Parenting and
Legal Issues in Parenting
LGBT Families
Nonresidential Fathers
Parent Effectiveness Training (P.E.T.)
Parent Management Training
Parent Study Groups
Parent–Adolescent Relations
Parental Alienation Syndrome
Parental Stress: Effects on Children
Parentification and Diverse Family Systems
Parenting
Parenting Education
Parenting Styles
Pregnancy
Racial Disparities in Foster Care
Rule-Setting
Teen Parenting

Professional Development and Standards

American Association for Marriage and Family Therapy
Certified Family Life Educator
Child Protective Services
Clinical Practice
Clinician-Directed, Solution-Focused Supervision
Competency-Based Standards for Marriage, Couple, and Family Counseling
Confidentiality
Core Competencies for Marriage and Family Therapists
Cotherapy Team
Council for Accreditation of Counseling and Related Educational Programs
Court-Mandated Clients
Decision-Making
Dual and Multiple Relationships
Duty to Warn and Protect
Ethical Codes
Ethical Decision-Making
Family Life Educators
HIPAA Standards
Informed Consent for Research
Informed Consent in Clinical Work
Licensure and Certification
Live Supervision

Mandated Reporter
Mental Health, Systemic Perspective
Moral Dimensions of Therapy
Multicultural Counseling Competence
No-Secrets Contracts
Postdoctoral Training
Practice Management
Professional Associations
Public Health Code
Release of Information for Couples and Families
Self of the Therapist
Self-Care Practices for the Trauma-Informed Couple and Family Counselor
Sexual Relationships With Clients
Supervision
Supervision, Approved Supervisor in Marriage and Family Therapy
Supervision, Developmental Model
Supervision, Gatekeeping
Supervision, Individual and Group
Supervision Contract
Supervision of Supervision
Supervision Philosophy Statement
Supervision Theories
Termination
Therapists' Values
Training and Licensure

Research

Clinical Versus Statistical Significance
Common Factors
Cost–Benefit Analysis
Couples Therapy Research
Delphi Research Method
Developmental Model of Marriage
Effectiveness Research
Empirically Validated Models
Evidence-Based Practice With Couples and Families
Outcome Research
Prevention Research
Process Research
Qualitative Research
Quantitative Research
Sex Researchers

Sexuality

Beliefs and Values
Birth Control and Contraception
Childless Couples
Compulsive Sexual Behavior
Erectile Disorder
Extramarital Affairs and Infidelity
Female Orgasmic Disorder
Female Sexual Interest/Arousal Disorder
Fetishes
Gender Dysphoria
Gender Orientation, Gender Identity, and Gender Expression
Genito-Pelvic Pain/Penetration Disorder
Human Sexual Response
Incest
Infertility
Male Hypoactive Sexual Desire Disorder
Mate Selection
Mindfulness and Sex
Nudity: Beliefs and Values
Open Relationships
Paraphilic Disorders
Polyamory
Polygamy
Pornography
Pregnancy and Sexuality
Premature Ejaculation
Romance
Same-Sex Couples
Sensate Focus
Sex, Definition of
Sex Positivity
Sex Researchers
Sex Therapy
Sexual Abuse
Sexual Assault and Rape
Sexual Assessment/History
Sexual Dysfunction
Sexual Enhancement, Sexual Toys
Sexual Health
Sexual History
Sexual Intimacy
Sexual Minorities
Sexual Orientation, Attraction, and Identity

Sexual Prejudice
Sexual Relationships With Clients
Sexual Toys/Sexual Aids
Sexuality and Religion
Sexuality Education
Sexually Transmitted Infections
Statutory Rape
World Association for Sexual Health

Special Topics

Body Dysmorphic Disorder in Adolescents
Child Guidance Movement
Children With Special Needs in Family Therapy
Community Programs
Family Mediation
Healthy Marriage and Responsible Fatherhood
Hispanic Healthy Marriage Initiative
Incest
International Family Therapy
Marriage and Health
Media in Family Therapy
Men in Counseling
Military Couples and Families
Mindfulness and Children
Mindfulness and Couples
National Marriage Initiative
Online Dating
Schizophrenia and Families
Schools, Family Involvement in
Self-Care Practices for the Trauma-Informed Couple and Family Counselor
Sexual Abuse
Statutory Rape
Technology and Families/Marriage
Therapeutic Impasses
Torture Treatment

Theory

Adlerian Family Therapy
Assessment, Biopsychosocial
Attachment Theory
Behavioral Family Therapy
Bowen Family Systems Theory
Chaos Family Therapy
Choice Theory and Reality Therapy
Cognitive-Behavioral Couples Therapy
Cognitive-Behavioral Family Therapy
Collaborative Language Systems
Constructivism
Contextual Family Therapy
Critical Theory
Cybernetics
Double Bind Theory
Ecosystems Perspective
Epistemology in Family Therapy
Experiential Family Therapy
Family Stress Adaptation Theory
Functionalism
General Systems Theory
Isomorphism
Love, Theories of
Object Relations Theory
Parental Acceptance–Rejection Theory
Psychoanalytic Family Therapy
Social Constructionism
Structural Determinism
Symbolic Interactionism
Systems Theory

Violence and Abuse

Alcohol and Substance Abuse
Anger Management
Child Maltreatment
Domestic Violence
Elder Abuse
Interpersonal Violence
Self-Injury
Sexual Assault and Rape
Trauma and Children
Trauma and Families

Same-Sex Couples

Same-sex couples are defined as intimate partnerships in which both members of the couple identify as the same sex as one another. These may also be referred to as homosexual couples, gay couples (which usually means both members are male, though "gay" can be used for women as well), and lesbian couples. According to the 2010 United States Census, approximately 1% of all couple households identified as same-sex relationships, with roughly 20% of those households indicating they had children, compared to roughly 40% of heterosexual households indicating they were raising children. Statistics on noncohabitating same-sex couples remain relatively unknown; however, roughly 4% of the U.S. population identifies as gay or lesbian. The 2010 census reports also indicate that accurately measuring the population is difficult due to a reluctance to disclose sexual orientation out of fear of discrimination. Understanding the history, rights, challenges, and couple processes for same-sex couples is important to providing affirmative therapy services. This entry first provides an overview of the history of same-sex partnerships, trends in same-sex partnerships, and gender roles in same-sex partnerships. It then discusses intimate partner violence within same-sex relationships and the rights of lesbian, gay, bisexual, and transgender (LGBT) people, including the right of same-sex couples to marry. Finally, the entry closes with a discussion of affirmative therapy for LGBT people.

History of Same-Sex Partnerships

Same-sex partnerships are not a new phenomenon: There is historical documentation of same-sex relationships, including marriages, as far back in history as ancient Rome and Egypt. In addition, there is evidence of homosexual relationships throughout the animal kingdom. Despite a long history of existence in human and animal relationships, same-sex partnerships have long been condemned, and legal and public policy has often supported this condemnation. The first applications for same-sex marriage in the United States were denied in the 1970s, beginning a more than 30-year battle over denial of same-sex unions throughout the nation, until, in 2004, Massachusetts became the first state to legalize same-sex marriages. While in the early 2000s the nation saw a rise in the number of jurisdictions (and in some cases, entire states) that recognized varying degrees of same-sex partnerships, including marriages, there was also a rise in the number of states that deemed same-sex marriage unconstitutional, with a recorded high of 31 states in 2012.

While many of the categories of same-sex partnership recognized the intimate relationship between the couple, the majority of them still failed to provide the rights and privileges afforded by marriage; for instance, issues of survivorship and inheritance, insurance coverage, child custody, and more, continued to be denied to same-sex partnerships. This noted inequality served, in part, as the argument for the legalization of same-sex marriage across the nation. Specifically, the argument was that not legalizing same-sex marriage violated the 14th Amendment by denying liberty (i.e., the right to choose whom one shall marry) without due process and that under the 14th Amendment, no person shall be denied equal protection under the law. Legal and public policy are not the only arenas that have historically marginalized those with same-sex attraction; in fact, the *Diagnostic and Statistical Manual of Mental Disorders* (DSM) of the American Psychiatric Association pathologized homosexuality directly until 1973, and indirectly under other classifications until 1987.

Trends in Same-Sex Partnerships

The 2010 census reported a number of trends in regard to same-sex couple households, including a significantly higher median income for same-sex couples than for their heterosexual counterparts; a higher rate of college education (nearly half of people in same-sex couples have a college degree, compared to less than one third of people in heterosexual relationships); and a lower "divorce" rate than do heterosexuals (it should be noted that divorce rates can be difficult to track due to the lack of recognition of gay marriages; the term *divorce* may be used to represent multiple forms of separation).

Gender Roles in Same-Sex Partnerships

Research has shown that men in gay partnerships experience gender roles differently than do men in heterosexual relationships. Egalitarian division of roles and responsibilities is more common in gay partnerships, and gender role conflicts are lower for gay men in relationships than for gay men who are not in relationships. It should be noted that the majority of studies have been conducted with educated, White males, and this limits the generalizability of the research to gay men with different cultural backgrounds. It should also be of note to counselors that gay couples are more likely to seek relational counseling.

Egalitarianism in regard to gender roles and responsibilities is even more evident in lesbian partnerships. Generally, lesbian couples do not tend to divide in terms of traditionally male and female responsibilities; in fact, the notion that one member of the couple is traditionally more masculine, or "butch," while the other more feminine, or "femme," has not been statistically supported in the relevant research. Gender-traditional role division does seem to occur more frequently with child-rearing couples, with the birth mother taking on more traditional mothering, or female roles, and the nonbirth mother adopting more fatherly, or male roles, in regard to parenting and household duties.

Intimate Partner Violence

Individuals in same-sex relationships have a much higher incidence of being subjected to domestic violence than do their heterosexual peers, though the incidents are vastly underreported. This discrepancy is due, in part, to the fear of being outed or discriminated against; in fact the fear of being outed may provide the perpetrator of the abuse with more control over the victim. In regard to lesbian intimate partner violence, both members are more likely to be arrested (i.e., the violence is viewed as mutual violence), than in cases of heterosexual intimate partner violence.

Laws regarding the treatment of same-sex intimate partner violence have historically differed by state, with some states having no legal avenues to protect members of same-sex relationships, and other states' statutes viewing the violence in the same light, legally, as heterosexual intimate partner violence.

While not all same-sex relationships take on roles that look similar to heterosexual gender roles in which one member of the couple is more dominant, and often takes on more "masculine" duties, while the other is subservient, often taking responsibility for more "female" tasks, there seems to be a higher rate of violence perpetrated by the more dominant member of the couple in those partnerships that do adopt traditional roles.

LGBT Rights and Marriage Equality

Individuals who identify as lesbian, gay, or allies have been engaged in civil and political advocacy to secure equality for LGBT people. For civil advocacy, the focus is on disrupting homophobia, heteronormativity, and binary constructs of gender. By challenging these constructions, advocates hope to enhance the acceptance of LGBT people and issues within the broader society. Advocacy in the political domain focuses on creating new or changing existent laws and policies to ensure safety, access, employment security, parental rights, marriage rights, and nondiscrimination.

One of the most controversial and publicized human rights issues championed by same-sex couples is the right to legally marry. The first legal marriage in the world was performed in the Netherlands in 2001. Since then, same-sex marriage has been legally recognized in Argentina, Belgium, Brazil, Canada, Denmark, France, Iceland, Israel, Mexico, New Zealand, Norway, Portugal, South Africa, Spain, Sweden, the United States, and Uruguay.

Within the United States, the first legal same-sex marriage was performed in 2004 in Massachusetts. By 2015, 37 states and the District of Columbia had legalized same-sex marriage. For the remaining states, same-sex marriage was explicitly banned, thereby making marriage equality an ongoing and controversial issue. On June 26, 2015, the Supreme Court of the United States ruled that the Constitution does provide same-sex couples with the right to marry. In the case of *Obergefell v. Hodges*, the Justices voted 5 to 4 to rule that same-sex couples have a constitutional right to marry, based on the due process and equal protection clauses of the 14th Amendment. In the majority opinion, Justice Anthony Kennedy asserted that the notion of personal dignity was fundamental to understanding the due process clause of the 14th Amendment and that the due process clause protected the liberties to exercise certain personal choices. For the four justices who offered dissenting opinions, their arguments tended to focus on the need to have state governments exercise decision-making control over the marriage equality question, and on the view that the majority opinion was a misinterpretation of the Constitution.

Despite the legalization of same-sex marriage in the United States, strong opposition to it has continued. The American Baptist Churches, Catholic Church, Church of Jesus Christ of the Latter Day Saints, National Association of Evangelicals, Southern Baptist Convention, and United Methodist Church have explicitly endorsed a stance opposing same-sex marriage. In different parts of the world, the response to same-sex marriage ranges from acceptance to lack of acknowledgment to imprisonment and the death penalty.

LGBT Affirmative Therapy

Effectively providing therapy to same-sex couples requires a high level of therapeutic competence, knowledge, and self-awareness. LGBT affirmative therapy developed in response to the unmet psychological needs of same-sex couples. As noted earlier, it was not until the early 1970s that homosexuality was removed from the DSM. Since that time, there have continued to be therapists who approach same-sex couples as dysfunctional and needing to be treated for their identification as lesbians or gay men. Many professional associations, such as the American Counseling Association, American Psychological Association, American Psychiatric Association, and National Association of Social Workers, have condemned conversion and reparative therapy as harmful and unethical. With approximately half of all therapists working consistently with lesbian or gay clients, it is imperative that training and research is conducted to develop LGBT affirmative therapy.

LGBT affirming therapy is broadly defined as an approach that synthesizes the unique development and cultural identities of LGBT individuals, the therapist's own awareness and identity, and the knowledge of effective interventions. Such an approach endorses a nonpathological view of homosexuality, includes a therapeutic commitment to dismantling oppression, requires an awareness of heterosexist privilege, challenges homophobia, and involves advocacy to eradicate discrimination. In LGBT affirmative therapy, therapists must actively and explicitly affirm the same-sex couple as a mechanism to counteract the pervasive impact of heterosexism and heteronormativity.

Ann M. McCaughan and Nicole R. Hill

See also Couples and Marriage Counseling; Gender Roles; LGBT Families

Further Readings

Bigner, J. J., & Wetchler, J. L. (2012). *Handbook of LGBT-affirmative couple and family therapy.* New York: Routledge.

Johnson, S. D. (2012). Gay affirmative psychotherapy with lesbian, gay, and bisexual individuals: Implications for contemporary psychotherapy research. *American Journal of Orthopsychiatry, 82,* 516–522. doi:10.1111/j.1939-0025.2012.01180.x

Knudson-Martin, C., Huenergardt, D., Lafontant, K., Bishop, L., Schaepper, J., & Wells, M. (2015). Competencies for addressing gender and power in couple therapy: A socio emotional approach. *Journal of Marital and Family Therapy, 41,* 205–220. doi:10.1111/jmft.12068

Love, M. M., Smith, A. E., Lyall, S. E., Mullins, J. L., & Cohn, T. J. (2015). Exploring the relationship between gay affirmative practice and empathy among mental health professionals. *Journal of Multicultural Counseling and Development, 43,* 83–96. doi:10.1002/j.2161-1912.2015.00066.x

McGeorge, C., & Carlson, T. S. (2009). Deconstructing heterosexism: Becoming an LGB affirmative heterosexual couple and family therapist. *Journal of Marital and Family Therapy, 37,* 14–26. doi:10.1111/j.1752-0606.2009.00149.x

Obergefell et al. v. Hodges et al., No. 14-556 (U.S. Supreme Court, 2015).

O'Connell, M., Lofquist, D., Simmons, T., & Lugaila, T. (2010). *New estimates of same sex couple households from the American Community Survey.* Retrieved from https://www.census.gov/hhes/samesex/files/SS_new-estimates.pdf

Otis, M. D., Rotosky, S. S., Riggle, E., Hamrin, R. (2006). Stress and relationship quality in same-sex couples. *Journal of Social and Personal Relationships 23,* 81–99. doi:10.1177/0265407506060179.x

U.S. Census Bureau. (2010). *Households and families: 2010.* Retrieved from http://www.census.gov/prod/cen2010/briefs/c2010br-14.pdf

SCALES, CHILDREN

Scales for children are psychological and behavioral measurements used for diagnosis and treatment planning of individuals typically below the age of 18. Scales, also referred to as tests or assessments, are designed to recognize deficits or impairments in functioning. While many child-based scales have been modified from adult versions, there are those created specifically for children. Assessments may be performed by clinicians or based on parent observation. Whether working with children in schools, hospitals, or community mental health settings, clinicians can benefit from having knowledge of various child-based psychological measures. This entry provides a historical overview of scales for children, as well as information regarding clinical use and categories and types of scales.

Historical Overview

Psychological testing, assessments, and scales began to flourish in the mid-1800s in Germany and then spread to other countries. While assessments for army personnel and adults were the first assessments used for personality and psychological purposes, it was not until the late 1800s when assessments and scales were considered for children. Since the late 1800s assessments for children have continued to progress and change throughout time to better assess children.

Alfred Binet was one of the first psychologists to have research interests pertaining to children. He focused on children's fears, children's memory capabilities, and children with disabilities. He also assumed that intelligence grows with age throughout typical child development. Binet was a part of the Society for the Study of the Child and began to study the needs of children within schools. The majority of the children he studied tended to have learning problems. It was not long before Binet became an advocate for these children and eventually stated that students should not be removed from the classroom if suspected of a learning disability until they were psychologically assessed.

In 1905, after 15 years of research, Binet published the first intelligence scale for children. The scale consisted of 30 items, which were in order of difficulty. The scale has been revised several times, and some of the original items are still included in current versions. Since Binet, other psychologists have added to the research and scales available for children.

In the 1930s David Wechsler also began to focus on assessments for children. He was hoping to obtain clinical information from administering his assessments to individuals. Binet's research on scales significantly influenced Weschler's work. Wechsler believed that human intelligence was complex, involving a variety of skills. Wechsler divided intelligence into two major types of skills—verbal and performance. In 1949, Wechsler's first version of the Wechsler Intelligence Scale for Children (WISC) was published. Wechsler also developed the Wechsler Adult Intelligence Scale (WAIS) and the Wechsler Preschool and Primary Scale of Intelligence (WPPSI). The most recent version of the WISC was revised in 2014 and is the fifth edition (WISC-5).

Clinical Use of Child Scales

Scales and measurements provide a framework for diagnosing clients' presenting issues. Information obtained from the measurement typically is used to support a client's diagnosis. Clinicians also use this information to generate a treatment plan. The same measures used to assess adults may not be beneficial in assessing young children. Adults functioning on an appropriate cognitive level are able to describe behaviors to clinicians. They are able to answer questions and respond to statements about their feelings and behaviors. Unlike adults, children may not have the cognitive level of functioning that enables them to fully and accurately self-report feelings and behaviors. This may not be true for older adolescents and teens who have mature communication skills. Conversely, young children typically lack the developmental maturity to communicate limitations in a manner acceptable for adult scales. Therefore, clinicians who treat children and adolescents can benefit from scales that are designed for assessing this population.

Clinicians working with children can benefit from knowledge of psychological assessments for children. Scales assist mental health professionals in diagnosis and treatment planning. In community mental health clinics, psychological assessments are used to diagnose clients, providing a framework for implementing intervention. Accuracy of diagnosis is essential for providing services in community mental health settings. This highlights the importance of clinical knowledge of child-based scales.

Child scales are advantageous due to their developmentally appropriate design. For question-and-answer or I-statement formatted measurements, language is written in a manner suitable for children. Children are able to understand and respond to the information, giving clinicians a clear idea of presenting issues. Some measurements are designed for the clinician to observe behaviors of children and may involve a checklist or scale. Parents are often seen as a source of information. Child scales may be designed for parents to complete, providing clinicians a more accurate view of the child.

Involving families in the assessment of children can be advantageous for clinicians. Parents may have more intimate knowledge of their children, which may be the driving reason for seeking therapeutic services. Parents have the ability to notice behavioral and emotional changes in multiple environments. Disclosure of such information can assist clinicians in completing assessments. Information is usually gathered from parents during the initial intake assessment. Following this step, clinicians may have a better understanding of the child's presenting issues and can create a plan to initiate appropriate assessment techniques.

Categories and Types of Scales

A clinical interview is often conducted before administering formal assessments. A clinical interview or intake assessment is a method of collecting pertinent background information, such as family data, mental health history, and medical concerns. The information collected is useful in selecting the appropriate scales and for interpreting the results. When selecting scales for children, it is vital that developmentally appropriate scales be used to accurately assess the current functioning of the child. It is also important to review the reliability and validity of the scale. Reliability is the extent to which scales are consistent, and validity refers to whether or not a scale measures what it is supposed to measure. Although scales that have high reliability and validity are strongly encouraged, scale selection should be primarily based on the needs of the child.

There are four common categories of formal assessments for children: developmental, behavioral, intellectual, and personality. Developmental scales collect information about a child's level of growth. Developmental scales assess physical, social, cognitive, and emotional functioning in children. The results are beneficial in identifying possible developmental delays and designing proper interventions if needed. Commonly used developmental scales include Parents' Evaluation of Developmental Status (PEDS) and Bayley Scales of Infant and Toddler Development (Bayley-3). Behavioral scales collect information about a child's level of adaptive functioning and assess whether a child's behavior is age appropriate. The results are beneficial in identifying why a child exhibits specific behaviors and developing a behavioral intervention plan if needed. Commonly used behavioral scales include Behavior Assessment System for Children (BASC) and Child Behavior Checklist (CBCL).

Intellectual scales collect information about a child's general intelligence or capacity to learn and assess reasoning and problem-solving abilities. The results are beneficial in identifying both children who are above average learners and children who have learning difficulties. Commonly used intellectual scales include Reynolds Intellectual Assessment Scales (RIAS) and WISC-5. Personality scales collect information about a child's individual personality and assess traits that have developed over the years. The results are beneficial in identifying healthy personality traits or dysfunctional characteristics in children. Commonly used personality scales include Draw-a-Person (DAP) and Personality Inventory for Children, Second Edition (PIC-2).

There are additional comprehensive, evidence-based scales appropriate for use in clinical and school settings. For example, the Reiss Motivation Profile for Children was modified from its original design to measure the intrinsic motivation of children ages 4 through 11. Psychosocial assessments for children emphasize a holistic approach to evaluation. Clinicians observe developmental, social, psychological, and environmental factors that may contribute to diagnosis of a child client. Typically, assessment for children involves using a combination of scales from more than one category. For example, a psychologist may administer a developmental scale to assist in determining an appropriate behavioral scale. Multiple assessments may also be used to collect information directly from the child and information from parents and teachers. Having information from multiple sources can strengthen interventions and treatment plans for children.

Assessment and Diagnosis Using Play Therapy

Play therapy is a developmentally appropriate way to provide counseling to children and can be used in conjunction with scales and parent observations to both assess and intervene with children. Play therapy is also empirically supported through extensive research measuring its effectiveness. Through therapy, clinicians can meet children on their level by allowing them to act, communicate, express, and react in methods that are natural and comfortable for the child. Since play therapy allows children to simply be themselves, it provides a natural environment for clinicians to gather information for assessment and diagnosis. Play-based assessments involve evaluating children in a play setting where they are allowed to naturally express and communicate in ways that are comfortable for the child. An anticipated advantage in play-based assessment is clinicians' ability to assess children over time through multiple sessions. Clinicians are provided not just merely a snapshot but rather a comprehensive conceptualization of the child.

An extension of play-based assessment is therapeutic assessment (TA) using play. This may involve longer periods of observation. Parents are involved in the process as observers. Parents are also able to ask questions conducive to the assessment process. While parents observe the session, therapists check in with the parent to discuss their observations. Therapists follow up with parents after the session to summarize and discuss the session. This process is repeated with both child and parents. The summary of the session is presented to the child in a story-like manner. The process is carried out until the assessment is complete. Throughout the assessment process, therapists work with parents to implement interventions aimed at promoting positive change.

Accessing Child Scales and Measurements

When determining an assessment to use, clinicians should ensure proper access to the specific measurement. Acquiring access may mean subscribing to databases where multiple assessments are present or even contacting a publisher for purchase. Additionally, different assessments are accessible online without paid or subscribed purchase.

Use of Diagnostic Criteria

Diagnostic criteria for mental disorders are specified in the *Diagnostic and Statistical Manual of Mental Disorders*. If assessment is implemented specifically for securing a diagnosis, then ideally the child scales or measures should align with the diagnostic criteria for that specific disorder. Psychological tests may be revised to meet the standards of updated criteria. Additionally, clinicians should adhere to the ethical and clinical guidelines of their respective professional organizations in diagnosis and treatment planning.

Importance of Child Scales

Using assessments provides a foundation for developing target goals during treatment planning. In working with children, using child scales can enable a clinician to determine needs and areas for growth to improve the child's level of functioning. Implementing scales throughout therapy as a reassessment measure can also aid the clinician in reevaluating treatment goals, which can be essential to the child's progress.

Denise Gilstrap, Mindy Dunagan, and Laquita Parker

See also Play Family Therapy; Scales, Family; Therapeutic Assessment

Further Readings

Booney Vance, H. (Ed.). (1997). *Psychological assessment of children: Best practices for school and clinical settings.* New York: Wiley.

Freeman, A., Christner, R., Nigro, C. J., & Sardar, T. (2010). *Guide to early psychological evaluation: Children and adolescents.* New York: W. W. Norton.

Gregory, R. J. (2004). *Psychological testing: History, principles, and applications.* Needham Heights, MA: Allyn & Bacon.

Mercer, B. L. (2011). Psychological assessment of children in a community mental health clinic. *Journal of Personality Assessment, 93*(1), 1–6.

Stagnitt, K., Cooper, R., & Whiteford, G. (2009). *Play as therapy: Assessment and therapeutic interventions.* Philadelphia, PA: Jessica Kingsley.

Tharinger, D. J., Finn, S. E., Arora, P., Judd-Glossy, L., Ihorn, S. M., & Wan, J. T. (2012). Therapeutic assessment with children: Intervening with parents "Behind the mirror." *Journal of Personality Assessment, 94*(2), 111–123.

Wolf, T. H. (1973). *Alfred Binet.* Chicago, IL: University of Chicago Press.

Scales, Couple and Marital

Assessment is used in couples and marital counseling to gather information about the couple and can be done through interviews, observation, or formal tests. Couple and marital scales are formal, standardized assessments that are used in marriage and couples counseling to provide information about particular aspects of a relationship. These aspects include the quality of the relationship (often termed satisfaction, or adjustment), communication and conflict, and specific issues, including substance use and sexual problems. Individual personality assessments can also help the clinician and the couple understand relationship dynamics. This entry reviews the considerations for using couple and marital scales, and the basic types of scales used with couples in counseling.

Special Considerations When Working With Couple and Marital Scales

Formalized assessments are often used in the beginning of the counseling relationship; however, it is also important to use standardized scales throughout the counseling process to measure progress and goal attainment. As with all standardized assessments, clinicians need to consider the psychometric properties of the assessment, including the reliability, validity, and norming groups. A valid measure assesses the concept it is intended to assess, and when it is reliable it produces similar results with multiple administrations. In addition, the results of the scale are more useful when the scale has been created and tested based on a large, representative group. A major issue with couple and marital scales is the lack of diversity in norming groups used to validate scales. In addition, counselors need to consider the user qualifications of the assessment and whether the administration and interpretation of the scale require the counselor to have specialized training. Further, using assessments with couples is more complicated than using assessments with individuals, as the clinician must consider the dynamics of how both individuals work together to create the system.

Types of Couple and Marital Scales

There are many types of couple and marital scales. There are hundreds of scales, but not all have been used repeatedly in research. Some scales have been used more widely in research, and clinicians and researchers can be more confident in the validity, reliability, and generalizability of these scales. Some of the more well-known scales are presented in the following sections.

Premarital

Premarital assessments are used specifically to assess the relationship characteristics of couples before they are married. The most popular premarital scale is the PREPARE/ENRICH program. The purpose of this assessment is to identify aspects of the relationship that could eventually lead to problems after the couple has married, and, the researchers hope, to reduce the risk of divorce in the future and increase marital satisfaction. The PREPARE premarital assessment involves several scales of measurement, including communication, conflict resolution, family of origin, finances, and goals, as these are all considered important aspects that could cause the couple problems in the future. Once the couple has completed the initial assessment, the PREPARE/ENRICH program includes several activities and interventions to help increase the likelihood of a successful future marriage.

Relationship Quality

Several scales measure relationship quality, and they focus on measuring relationship satisfaction and relationship adjustment. Some researchers use the terms synonymously; however, others still contend relationship adjustment is a different construct from relationship satisfaction, and should not be considered equal. For example, the Dyadic Adjustment Scale measures adjustment by considering a combination of several aspects, including satisfaction, cohesion, and communication. The assessment also includes a scale that measures how much couples agree on matters considered important to the relationship. Similarly, the circumplex model of marital and family systems includes three aspects in its related scales: cohesion, flexibility, and communicating. The researchers emphasize the importance of the curvilinear nature of the constructs, and that too much cohesion and flexibility, or too little, can cause relational problems. The circumplex model is the foundation for several assessments, most notably the Clinical Rating Scale (CRS), which is based on family observations conducted by the therapist, and the Family Adaptability and Cohesion Evaluation Scale (FACES).

The Marital Satisfaction Inventory, Revised (MSI-R) includes 150 questions and 14 scales—global distress, affective communication, problem-solving communication, aggression, time together, disagreement about finances, sexual dissatisfaction, role orientation, family history of distress, dissatisfaction with children, conflict over child rearing, inconsistency, and conventionalization. However, as with all psychometric assessments, length does not always mean the scale is better for use in treatment—the Locke-Wallace Marital Adjustment Test (MAT) includes only 15 questions, and even though it was developed in the 1950s, it remains popular today due to its brevity.

Communication and Conflict

Communication style and conflict are both important considerations when working with couples. For example, the Kansas Marital Conflict Scale (KMCS) was developed to measure conflict the researchers claim the assessment accurately differentiates between distressed and nondistressed couples. The KMCS is based on the theory that there are three phases of marital conflict: agenda building, arguing, and negotiation. The developers believe that identifying the specific phases where the couple is having difficulties will help the clinician focus treatment goals and objectives. Similarly, the Beier-Sternberg Discord Questionnaire measures level of disagreement on 10 items that are considered factors that cause conflict in relationships, including children, money, sex, politics, and religion. Finally, the Primary Communication Inventory includes 25 questions and measures both verbal and nonverbal communication between members of a couple. This scale measures not only the individual's perception of his or her communication patterns but also his or her partner's perceptions of those patterns.

Domestic Violence

There are several scales that measure violence and aggression in relationships. It can be important to use an assessment regarding this issue specifically, as it is often difficult for the clinician to determine whether a partner is being abused. The individual may feel uncomfortable disclosing this information due to fear of the consequences from the abusing partner. Clinicians should be careful to ensure the abused partner's confidentiality when addressing abuse between the couple, which may include meeting with both partners individually if the clinician believes there may be abuse taking place in the relationship. One popular scale, the Revised Conflict Tactics Scale, includes five subscales that assess emotional as well as physical abuse, and includes questions related to the individual completing the assessment, as well as his or her partner.

Sexual Issues

Intimacy and sexual activity are an important facet of couple and marital relationships. There are numerous assessments surrounding sexual behaviors of couples, including individual preferences and the specific interactions between couples. For example, one popular assessment, the Derogatis Interview for Sexual Functioning, is a short assessment that can be self-administered as well as administered via interview, and includes scales related to sexual cognition/fantasy, sexual arousal, sexual behavior/experience, orgasm, and drive/relationship. Similarly, the Hendrick Sexual Attitude Scale does not focus on sexual dysfunction, and instead measures attitudes about sexuality. This assessment includes 43 items divided into four subscales: permissiveness, sexual practices, communion in the relationship, and instrumentality.

Individual Scales Used With Couples

There are several scales for individuals that can also be helpful when working with couples. By gaining a better understanding of each partner as an individual, the counselor can then address the related conflict and dysfunction within the system. Though a variety of individual assessments can be used for this purpose, the two main types used in couple and marital counseling are personality and substance use scales.

Personality Assessments

There are many assessments of personality traits, and they vary widely. Clinicians use personality tests in couples counseling by administering the assessment to both partners, and then discussing the results with them in the context of how their personality similarities and differences can influence their relationship. For example, the Myers-Briggs Type Indicator (MBTI) yields a four letter personality type based on the individual's responses to 70 forced-item questions. Each letter stands for a different dichotomous trait: extroversion-introversion, sensing-intuition, thinking-feeling, and judging-perceiving. By examining the preferences and attitudes of each trait, partners can better understand each other and decrease conflict. Similarly, the Minnesota Multiphasic Personality Inventory-2 (MMPI-2), an extremely popular assessment, gives a comprehensive view of the individual's personality, and there is a significant amount of research regarding the scores on different subscales and how they can contribute to relationship dysfunction. As a result of this research, two additional scales have been added that specifically address family problems and marital distress.

Substance Use

When one partner is using drugs or alcohol, it can have a deleterious impact on the relationship. However, it may be difficult to discern how frequently the partner is using, or if he or she is using at all. By administering a substance use assessment, the clinician may be able to clarify some of these issues. The Substance Abuse Subtle Screening Inventory-3 (SASSI-3) is a popular assessment of substance use, and includes questions that are considered *subtle* because they do not directly ask about drug use, but instead about symptoms of drug use, for example, questions about sleep patterns and memory problems. The SASSI-3 also includes validity subscales, which can help the clinician decipher whether the respondent is being truthful or not. By applying a standardized assessment of substance use, the clinician will be better suited to tailoring interventions to the needs of the couple and providing outside referrals as necessary.

Though there are numerous assessments available for clinicians to use in couples and marital counseling, they are frequently overlooked and underused by clinicians in the field. By carefully selecting standardized scales to use in treatment, clinicians can greatly increase their ability to successfully identify goals and objectives of therapy, as well as continue to measure treatment progress throughout the therapeutic relationship.

K. Michelle Hunnicutt Hollenbaugh

See also Circumplex Model; Couples and Marriage Counseling; Domestic Violence; Marriage Enrichment; Family Assessment, Models of; Scales, Children; Scales, Family; Marriage Enrichment; Premarital Counseling; Sexual Dysfunction

Further Readings

American Educational Research Association, American Psychological Association, & National Council on Measurement in Education. (2014). *Standards for educational and psychological testing.* Washington, DC: American Educational Research Association.

Cierpka, M, Thomas, V., & Sprenkle, D. H. (2005). *Family assessment: Integrating multiple perspectives.* Cambridge, MA: Hogrefe & Huber.

Corcoran, K., & Fischer, J. (2013). *Measures for clinical practice and research, Vol. 1: Couples, family and children.* New York: Oxford University Press.

Gehart, D. (2010). *Mastering competencies in family therapy: A practical approach to theories and clinical case documentation* (5th ed.). Belmont, CA: Brooks/Cole.

Myers, I. B., McCaulley, J. H., Quenk, N. L., & Hammer, A. L. (1998). *MBTI manual: A guide to the development and use of the Myers-Briggs Type Indicator.* Palo Alto, CA: CPP, Inc.

Olson, D. H., Olson, A. K., & Larson, P. J. (2012). PREPARE-ENRICH Program: Overview and new discoveries about couples. *Journal of Family and Community Ministries, 25,* 30–44.

Sperry, L. (2012). *Family assessment: Contemporary and cutting-edge strategies.* New York: Routledge.

Ward, P. J., Lundberg, N. R., Zabriskie, R. B., & Berrett, K. (2009). Measuring marital satisfaction: A comparison of the Revised Dyadic Adjustment Scale and the Satisfaction with Married Life Scale. *Marriage & Family Review, 45*(4), 412–429.

SCALES, FAMILY

Family scales are assessment tools that rely on family members' self-reports, and occasionally on clinical observations, to examine the general, dyadic, or triadic relationships among family members, as well as the overall functioning level of the family. Dyadic relationships are the interactions between two people in the family, and triadic relationships are the interactions among three people in the family. This entry discusses three of the most widely used models of assessing family relationships and functioning, all of them based on empirical research: the Beavers systems model, the circumplex model, and the McMaster model of family functioning. Each description of the model and its scales briefly includes the background of the model or scale, as well as instructions on how practitioners use, score, and plot the scales. The three models discussed emerged during the 1970s and 1980s as family therapy was becoming more widely researched and practiced.

The Beavers Systems Model

Psychiatrist W. Robert Beavers, in his research on family dynamics, created multiple scales for use in assessing family competency and family style. The Beavers systems model scales that are used for families with any age of child include the Beavers Interactional Competence Scale (BICS), the Beavers Interactional Style Scale (BISS), and the Self-Report Family Inventory (SFI).

The Self-Report Family Inventory, which is generally used with family members older than 10 years, is a 36-question inventory that has family members respond to statements about family dynamics by giving each a score of 1 to 5. An answer of 1 means the statement is highly likely for the family or applicable to the family, an answer of 3 means it is somewhat likely for or applicable to the family, and a rating of 5 means that it is highly unlikely for or applicable to the family. The lower the score, the greater the likelihood of overall family wellness and functioning. The scale's questions fall into the categories of cohesion, expressiveness, conflict, leadership, and health/competence. These five categories give two overall scores: one for "competency," and one for "stylistic dimension," as shown in Figure 1.

Competency is measured on a continuum ranging from optimal to severely dysfunctional based on how flexible and adaptive the family's boundaries are. The family's stylistic dimension is measured on a continuum ranging from centripetal to centrifugal and reflects how a family handles conflict or disagreement. When scores of both competency and stylistic dimension are plotted on a graph, they are combined to display the overall, potential symptomology in the family and the likelihood of need for clinical intervention.

Centripetal families relate satisfaction in family relationships to extreme closeness in interactions within the family. In centrifugal families, relationships outside of the family are viewed as more satisfying and promising. According to the Beavers systems model, either extreme is unhealthy, resulting in either enmeshment in the family (centripetal) or disengagement from the family (centrifugal); however, it is natural for families to display more centripetal behaviors when children are young and to gradually become more centrifugal as children reach adolescence, with the goal being to always remain overall in midrange through the life span.

The SFI plots and takes scores from both continuums (competency and style) and places families

Figure 1 The Beavers Systems Model of Family Functioning

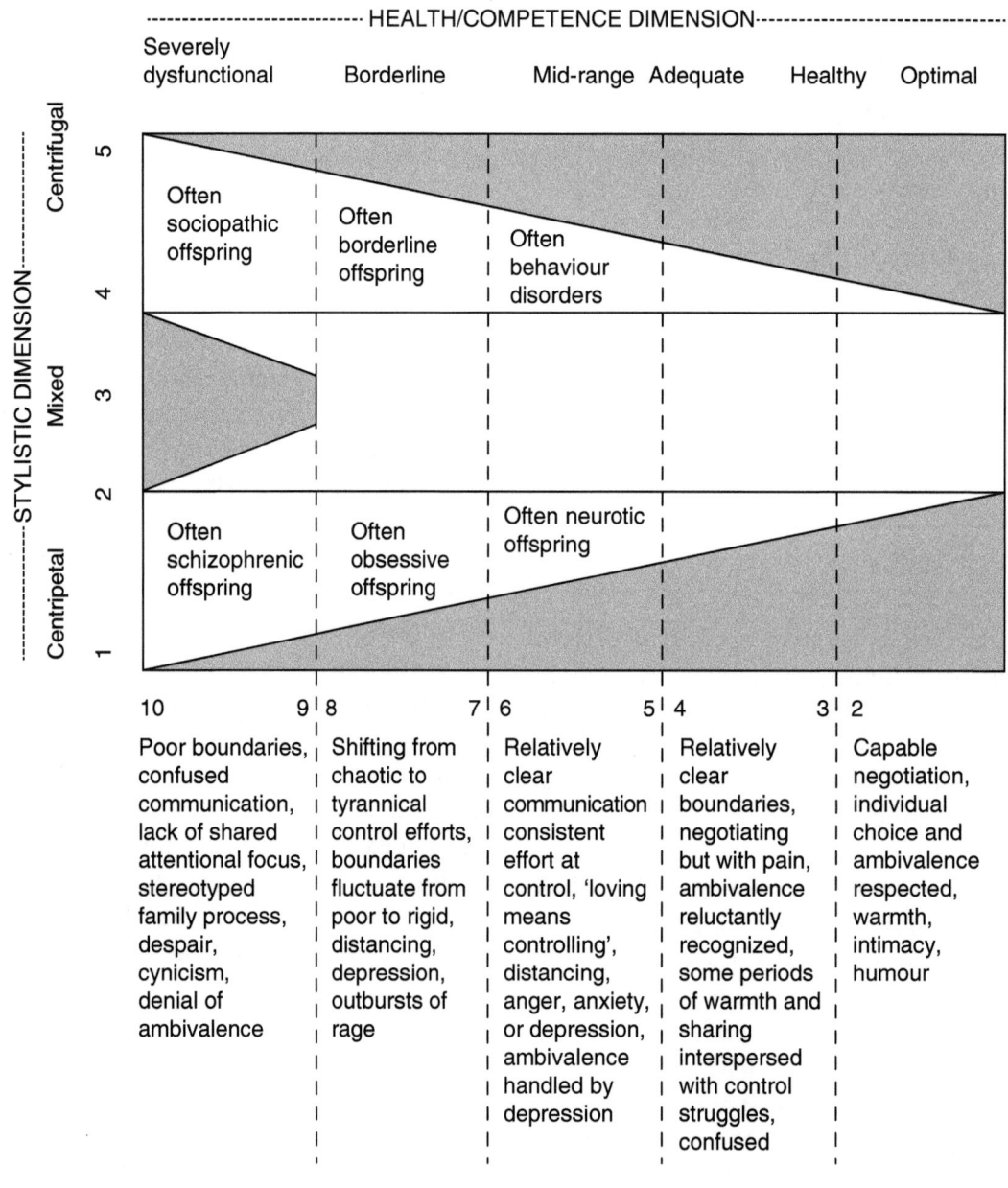

Source: Beavers, R., & Hampson, R. B. (2000). The Beavers system model of family functioning. *Journal of Family Therapy, 22,* 128–143 (figure 1).

into one of nine groups, depending on their overall score. Group 1, or optimal families, display high levels of respect, intimacy, boundaries, problem-solving, and individuation. In Group 2, or adequate families, the family structure may display slightly more controlling, intimidating, or forceful behaviors at times, potentially reducing autonomy, trust, and respect in the family. According to the Beavers systems model, power struggles, lack of communication, chaos, or rigidity manifest more strongly the higher the group number. Groups 3, 4, and 5 consist of midrange families, Groups 6 and 7 consist of what Beavers calls borderline families, and Groups 8 and 9 consist of severely dysfunctional families.

Two other scales that have emerged from the Beavers systems model, the BICS and the BISS, require specially trained evaluators to administer. The BICS looks solely at competency, while the BISS solely evaluates stylistic dimension, and both may be used with the SFI for more in-depth evaluation. All three of these scales combined (the SFI, the BISS, and the BICS) make up the Beavers Interactional Scales, sometimes referred to as BIS.

The Circumplex Model

The circumplex model (occasionally referred to as the Olson model) was developed by David Olson and focuses on the assessment and treatment of flexibility and cohesion within a family. The scale used to assess and define these areas is called the Family Adaptability and Cohesion Evaluation Scale IV (FACES IV) scale (as there have been three revisions of the original scale). The circumplex model also includes the Family Satisfaction Scale, designed to assess a family's contentment at their level of functioning. Olson also is one of the developers of the PREPARE/ENRICH, assessments and curriculum for use in premarital and couples counseling, which can be used in conjunction with FACES IV and the Family Satisfaction Scale.

The circumplex model defines cohesion as emotional bonding among family members and how family members balance autonomy and independence versus togetherness. Flexibility is defined as the ability to change and adapt among family relationships, family roles, and expectations. The FACES IV scale rates cohesion and flexibility on an x-y axis, as shown in Figure 2. The cohesion score, plotted on the x-axis, indicates the family's level of enmeshment to disengagement on a continuum with connection in the midrange as optimal. Too high levels of cohesion indicate lack of autonomy among family members, and too low levels of cohesion indicate that members of the family may be lacking attachment or may have a singular mentality.

Flexibility, plotted on the y-axis, identifies the family on a continuum ranging from chaotic to rigid, with balance in the midrange as optimal. Flexibility focuses on the need for both structure and adaptability toward change. Structure can be viewed as a parental democracy with some involvement from children in decision-making; firm, consistent rules; and stable roles among family members. Adaptability can be viewed as egalitarian leadership, negotiation, changing rules as appropriate, and fluidity among roles. Chaotic relationships appear on the scale as flexibility to an extreme, with shifting or lack of leadership, unclear roles, and inconsistent rules and consequences. Rigid relationships among family members appear on the scale as autocratic with one authority figure who has ultimate decision-making power; strict, unyielding rules; and little-to-no negotiation among family members. The cohesion and flexibility scales demonstrate that the healthiest scores range in the center of the x-y axis.

As the circumplex model measures overall relational functioning, it can also help define potential for relational success. Families that score in moderate ranges tend to function better overall than families that score in high ranges, and while circumstances or environmental factors may lead to a family functioning at a highly enmeshed or separated level for a period of time, families that stay in the high zones are more likely to have problems and disruption over time. Olson described the circumplex model as three-dimensional in that it can also illustrate the family's ability to adapt to change during or after a stressor, such as a car accident, or an event, such as the birth of a new baby. Crisis may lead to the family scoring in different domains as they adjust to the trauma; for example, a life-threatening illness or accident may shift a family's functioning from separated or disengaged to enmeshed, and as the family adjusts, functioning may become more connected and balanced. Balanced families will be able to adapt to the change, but unbalanced families will remain stuck in their dysfunction and unable to harmonize around the new situation.

Communication is evaluated in both domains, and the questions are designed to evaluate the family's speaking skills and listening skills. Examples of speaking skills include self-disclosing appropriately, using clarity and respect, and tracking the conversation. Examples of listening skills include

Figure 2 Circumplex Model: Couple and Family Map

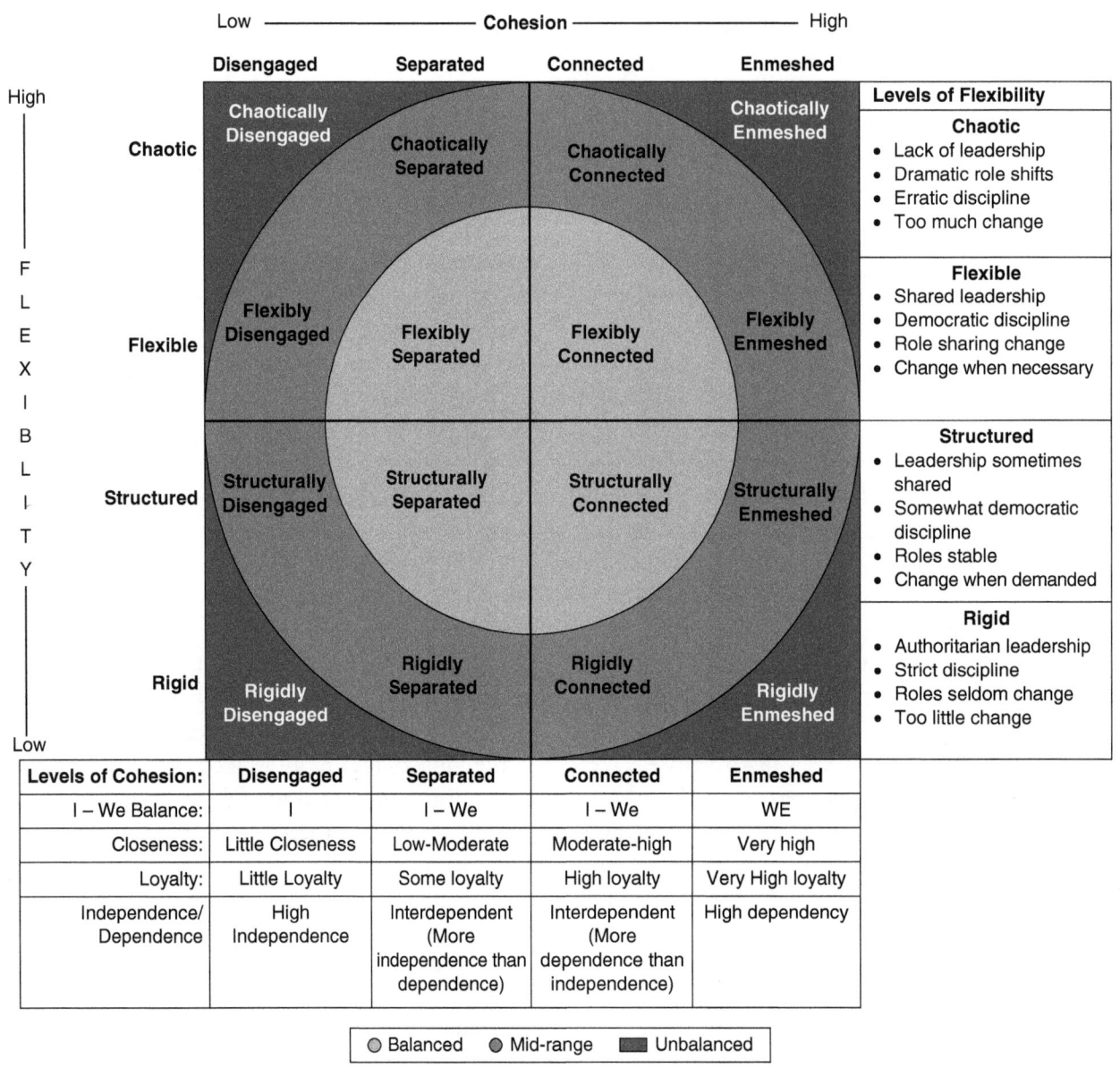

Source: Olson, D. H. (2000). Circumplex model of marital and family systems. *Journal of Family Therapy, 22,* 144–167 (figure 1, p. 148).

paying attention and displaying empathy. The more balanced the family, the healthier the communication, listening, and speaking skills.

McMaster Model of Family Functioning

Nathan Epstein and his research team developed the McMaster model of family functioning, named for McMaster University in Ontario, Canada, where some of the work on this approach occurred. As Epstein trained under Nathan Ackerman, a psychodynamic child psychiatrist who significantly contributed to the field of family therapy, Epstein's model is also rooted in psychodynamic theory, assessment, and treatment of the family. From this model came two scales: the Family Assessment Device (FAD) and the McMaster Clinical Rating Scale (MCRS).

The FAD is a 60-question self-inventory in which members of the family who are over the age of 12 years respond with strongly agree (SA), agree (A), disagree (D), or strongly disagree (SD) to each item. The facilitator of the inventory then scores each item with a number of points based on the family members' answers, with a score of 1 indicating best functioning level and score of 4 indicating worst functioning level. The inventory assesses in the domains of problem-solving, communication, roles, affective responsiveness, affective involvement, behavior control, and general functioning. As each domain is tallied, the facilitator then uses the scores to assist the family in making the necessary changes needed for each domain.

The MCRS is a seven-question scale used by facilitators who have received 5 hours of training in the administration and scoring of the MCRS. This inventory is based upon the facilitator's observation of the family dynamics, rather than family members' self-reports, and addresses the same domains as the FAD. Scores on this inventory range from 1 to 7, with 1 as the most impaired functioning level, and 7 as the highest functioning level. The scores are addressed at three different levels called anchor points: severely disturbed (a score of 1), non-clinical (a score of 5), or superior (a score of 7). An example of a severely disturbed rating in the problem-solving domain would be an indicator such as, "The family does not recognize that problems exist." An example of a non-clinical rating is, "When a family member identifies a problem, she or he communicates it to the others." An example of a superior rating would be, "After acting, the family regularly evaluated its success." The assessor also monitors communication and classifies communication style as clear or masked and as direct or indirect.

Limitations

While the McMaster model and the Beavers model scales have been well-researched and are widely used in clinical practice and taught in graduate studies institutions, both models recognize that limitations include the need for more cross-cultural scaling. The McMaster model includes recognition of potential limitations for non-English-speaking populations, as normative scoring may differ from primarily English-speaking populations. The McMaster model also indicates that, true to family systems theory, the domains are not independent of one another, and are therefore not truly separate dimensions.

The circumplex model allows for cross-cultural scaling by recognizing that what may be seen as unbalanced or enmeshed may be a cultural norm; the circumplex model states that as long as all family members are supportive of this level of functioning, the scoring may not be viewed as unbalanced. To address this potential cultural dynamic, the FACES IV scale may be taken in conjunction with the Family Satisfaction Scale to further evaluate the family's level of satisfaction with their level functioning.

Lori C. Kucharski

See also Adult Attachment Assessments; Circumplex Model; Differentiation; Family Assessment, Models of; Family Stress Adaption Theories; Homeostasis; Listening, Empathic; PREPARE/ENRICH

Further Readings

Beavers, R., & Hampson, R. B. (2000). The Beavers system model of family functioning. *Journal of Family Therapy, 22,* 128–143.

Epstein, N., Baldwin, L., & Bishop, D. (1983). The McMaster family assessment device. *Journal of Marriage and Family Therapy, 9*(2), 171–180.

Hampson, R., Beavers, W., & Hulgus, Y. (1989). Insiders' and outsiders' views of family: The assessment of family competence and style. *Journal of Family Psychology, 3*(2), 118–136.

Miller, I., Ryan, C., Keitnor, G., Bishop, D., & Epstein, N. (2000). The McMaster approach to families: Theory, assessment, treatment, and research. *Journal of Family Therapy, 22,* 168–189.

Olson, D. H. (2000). Circumplex model of marital and family systems. *Journal of Family Therapy, 22,* 144–167.

Olson, D. H. (2011). FACES-IV and the Circumplex model: Validation study. *Journal of Marital and Family Therapy, 37*(1), 64–80.

Ryan, C., Epstein, N., Keitnor, G., Miller, I., & Bishop, D. (2005). *Evaluating and treating families: The McMaster approach.* New York: Routledge.

SCALING QUESTIONS

Anyone who has received medical treatment and been asked to rate his or her pain on a scale from 1 to 10 has encountered scaling questions. Scaling questions are a tool that allows individuals to appraise their experiences and quantify progress toward goals. These questions provide marriage and family therapists with a way to gather data about the client's subjective experience. Through scaling questions, therapists help clients notice their feelings as well as see the progress they are making. These questions can assist therapists in gauging not only the client's progress and current experiences, but also the client's level of motivation in regard to change. Additionally, scaling questions allow clients to visualize and explore what higher levels of achievement look like.

Types of Scaling Questions

While the term *scaling questions* often refers to the solution-focused approach to therapy, other approaches to therapy and other professions use scaling questions to indicate current location and progress toward change. For example, managers may use scaling questions during employee evaluations to review and discuss performance. Also, marketing firms may use these types of questions to gauge whether an advertising campaign is effective. In the helping professions, several popular client rating systems exist.

Developed by Joseph Wolpe, the Subjective Units of Distress Scale (SUDS) measures the degree of psychological distress a client is experiencing. A client uses the SUDS to self-assess, and therapists rely on that rating to guide treatment. Behavioral and cognitive-behavioral therapists use SUDS in treatment of a variety of psychological concerns including anxiety and phobias.

Goal attainment scaling (GAS) uses individualized client goals, established before treatment, and scores progress in a manner that allows for statistical analysis. Ratings range from most unfavorable outcome to best anticipated outcome. Researchers developed GAS to assess the effectiveness of community mental health services, but because the structure of the instrument was seen to be compatible with the development of client-specific scales, other disciplines adopted GAS for client assessment. Psychologist Hadley Cantril created the self-anchoring striving scale. This scaling questions method is the foundation for a number of surveys and assessment used in multiple disciplines. Furthermore, Cantril's scale is the foundation for today's solution-focused scaling questions.

Scaling Questions in Solution-Focused Brief Therapy

Solution-focused brief therapists Steve de Shazer and Insoo Kim Berg adapted Cantril's technique to assess difficult-to-observe progress or feelings, such as motivation. Additionally, in solution-focused brief therapy (SFBT), scaling questions assist clients in describing their situations or current location within the problem they are experiencing. Notably, according to the assumptions of SFBT, clients do not have to fully explore or understand the problem to progress toward solving it.

Using Scaling Questions

Although the language used for scaling questions differs according to type, Coert Visser outlined six basic steps for using this tool generally, across a variety of specific applications. First, the therapist explains the scale to the client using the highest number of the scale to represent the client's desired reality or ideal situation and the lowest number to represent no progress. Next, the therapist asks the client to indicate his or her current location on the scale. Once the client notes the current position, the therapist focuses questions on the established resources and strengths of the client that allowed him or her to reach the position indicated. The client and therapist then explore circumstances and experiences when the client was at a higher position. The therapist asks the client to visualize and describe what characterized that level. Last, the client is directed to describe a small step that would allow movement toward the ideal reality. It is through making small changes that larger and more complex problems are overcome.

Other ways therapists use scaling questions are in tandem with the "miracle question" (another solution-focused brief therapy technique), and to explore exceptions to the presenting problem. Within the solution-focused brief therapy approach to counseling, it is important for clients to recognize when a given problem is *not* present in their current world. This is referred to as *exception talk*, and it helps the therapist move the client's thinking away from problems to solutions. Some therapists even ask clients to respond to scaling questions related to each completed session to gauge the effectiveness of treatment and strength of the client–counselor relationship.

Challenges to Using Scaling Questions

Although the use of scaling questions may seem simple and straightforward, their effectiveness depends on the therapist's attention to tone, word choice, and other linguistic clues. Effective use of scaling questions requires more complex interaction during client–therapist dialog than simply asking a set of scripted questions. Accordingly, it is important for therapists to continually hone their communication skills.

Shauna Lynn Nefos Webb

See also Miracle Question; Postmodern Therapies; Social Constructionism; Solution-Focused Brief Therapy; Therapeutic Assessment

Further Readings

Berg, I. K., & de Shazer, S. (1993). Making numbers talk: Language in therapy. In S. Friendman (Ed.), *The new language of change* (pp. 5–24). New York: Guilford Press.

Cantril, H. (1965). *The pattern of human concerns*. New Brunswick, NJ: Rutgers University Press.

Gillaspy, J. J., & Murphy, J. J. (2012). Incorporating outcome and session rating scales in solution-focused brief therapy. In C. Franklin, T. S. Trepper, W. J. Gingerich, & E. E. McCollum (Eds.), *Solution-focused brief therapy: A handbook of evidence-based practice* (pp. 73–91). New York: Oxford University Press.

Kiresuk, T. J., & Sherman, R. E. (1968). Goal attainment scaling: A general method for evaluating comprehensive community mental health programs. *Community Mental Health Journal, 4*(6), 443–453.

Strong, T. O., Pyle, N. R., & Sutherland, O. (2009). Scaling questions: Asking and answering them in counselling. *Counselling Psychology Quarterly, 22*(2), 171–185.

Visser, C. (2012, July). The scaling question. *Progress-Focused Approach*. Retrieved from http://www.progressfocusedapproach.com/the-scaling-question/

Wolpe, J. (1969). *The practice of behavior therapy*. New York: Pergamon.

SCAPEGOATING

The term *scapegoating* comes from the Hebraic tradition of the Day of Atonement. The patriarch Moses would take a goat and curse it with the sins of the people of Israel. This would then be followed by sending the goat, laden with the sins of the people, into the wilderness alone to die for them. The goat's symbolic sacrifice was a way of removing the year's evil thoughts and behavior from the people and transferring them to the innocent goat so that the people could move forward in a new way.

In family therapy, the concept of scapegoating has a similar origin, and potentially a similar effect, both for the family and the scapegoat.

Typically, the family will target, though not intentionally, at least not at first, one member of the family to become the focus or cause of all of the problems of the family. The result for the family is a means of deflecting attention from the real conflict. The real conflict that spawns this act of scapegoating can be anything, for example, alcoholism, chronic illness, marital discontent. The family will feel relief, but the scapegoat will feel angry and alone. The goal of the family is not to deal with and resolve the issues, but, rather, to cover them up. This effect, though seemingly beneficial, is actually an unfortunate outcome of this targeting. It does not absolve the family of their contributions to the dysfunction. Rather, it exacerbates the dysfunction and can have serious consequences for the scapegoat. The idea of scapegoating can be applied to understand families and other groups, is used within several models of family therapy, and is a typical process with certain presenting problems. This entry first discusses scapegoating and group dynamics. It then discusses scapegoating in families, including the involvement of homeostasis and triangulation of roles, and how the concept of the scapegoat comes into play in Salvador Minuchin's structural family therapy and the roles of an alcoholic family as conceptualized by Sharon Wegscheider.

Scapegoating and Groups

In group dynamics, scapegoating occurs when a group finds a common enemy on whom to focus all of its negative energy. Sports teams, school groups, political organizations, and even religious groups can see this phenomenon in the groups or "causes" they often oppose. In addition to scapegoating an outside group, this process sometimes happens within groups. The group has a conflict internally and chooses a "subject" to blame. It could be the boss, or a coworker, or a weaker member of the group. "If it hadn't been for so and so, we would have won that game." Similarly, in nuclear and extended families, this happens when the family finds one person who becomes the "problem" for the whole group. The presence of a scapegoat can become a uniting force for the rest of the family to rally around as the effect of the true dysfunction of the family remains unchecked. Often when the family presents for therapy, this person is the identified patient, or the reason the family finds for needing therapy.

Scapegoating and Families

Family members all take on various roles that enact certain functions in the family. Some will promote healthy interactions, while others might be more conducive to perpetuating conflicts. Roles can shift between family members, and each family member may have different roles in the different subsystems to which they belong. For example, a father may be head of the household and hold authority over the child subsystem, but also be the neediest among the family due to a chronic illness and weakest among the executive subsystem (those in charge of the family, typically the parents).

In the early years of family therapy, the identified patient, the scapegoat, was often the focus of therapy. They were the problem. More often than not, this scapegoat was a child, sometimes an emotionally disturbed child on whom the family typically placed a lot of blame for problems that the child actually had little to do with. Parental shortcomings, marital conflicts, extended family or multigenerational conflicts, and sibling conflicts were often the real problems behind the scenes. The therapist would often focus on the "problem child" in the hope that the issue would be addressed. As research in family therapy has progressed, the focus has shifted off of only examining the scapegoated family member to assessing and addressing the family as a whole. The larger, systemic issues become the focus of the therapy rather than trying to "fix" the behavior of one family member.

Homeostasis

One contributing factor to the maintenance of a scapegoat in the family relates to the concept of homeostasis. Homeostasis is the tendency to keep things in the family system just the way that they are, even if change would make interactions improve. Scapegoats make it easier to maintain that homeostasis because there remains someone to blame rather than changing dysfunctional interaction patterns. Change is an uncomfortable process, even when it is change for the good of the family. The family will have to make a choice to address the real issues before the scapegoat is allowed "off the hook." Unfortunately, before that happens, the process of scapegoating may have seriously harmed the child who has been the target. Emotional disturbance and emotional distancing (disengagement) may result for the scapegoat.

Minuchin's Structural Family Therapy

In Minuchin's structural family therapy, the scapegoat is notably the result of many family issues. Typically, the scapegoat's role is to relieve the tension others are feeling due to underlying conflicts in the family subsystems. One family he writes about, the Gordens, exemplified the scapegoat in that the identified patient, a child who set fires, emerged as the scapegoat when her preference for the ex-husband's permissive parenting style was made known. The unresolved conflict between the parents, together with the behavior of the girl's older brother, who was acting as though he was a parent, were part of a larger issue related to the girl's acting out. The family chose to focus on her acting out rather than address the tensions already found in the parental subsystem (mother and oldest son) and in the sibling subsystem (oldest son and three younger sisters).

The role of scapegoat is assigned, albeit covertly, by the family. There is little that the child can do about it. The parent who scapegoats the child was frequently the scapegoat for his or her own family of origin. The parent lacks the awareness and the skill to understand or prevent the process from happening all over again. Therapy can help to show the parent(s) a new, better way to respond to the conflicts and tensions in the home. The therapist will need to assess the subsystems in the family and help the scapegoated child to reintegrate into those subsystems to which he or she should belong. Boundaries will need to be reformed so that the child is both protected and supported. The family will need to be reeducated to focus on the problem where it lies, and not on the child. They will need to be prepared to avoid returning to previous role behaviors when stressful times come.

Triangulation of Roles

When family relationships have conflict, there is frequently an effort by one member of a dyad to pull in a third person to help ease the tension. This is called triangulation. When this happens the relationships shift to a two-on-one partnership against the third. As the conflict progresses, the dyads can shift so that the odd man out changes. Scapegoats often find themselves in such triangles, often as the odd man out. This takes the focus off the tensions in the dyad and onto the problem that the scapegoat represents. An example would be a parental dyad at odds about the family finances, who then focus the conflict onto the teen scapegoat's asking to get a driver's license. The blame for the conflict about money shifts to the teen's request, which will potentially cost more money.

Wegscheider's Alcoholic Family Roles

In the late 1970s and early 1980s Wegscheider wrote a book detailing her thoughts on roles found within alcoholic families. She outlined six basic roles that family members filled: the dependent, the enabler, the hero, the scapegoat, the lost child, and the mascot. The dependent is the alcoholic in the family. The enabler is the person closest to the dependent who does the most to perpetuate the addiction (buying the alcohol, covering for the alcoholic on a hangover, etc.). The hero is the one in the family who does everything right in order to hide the family secret. Usually this is the eldest child; he or she will do everything possible to keep up the facade of everything being just fine in the family and in the eldest's own life. The lost child is the one who tends to fade into the wallpaper in order not to be noticed. This family member tries to disappear from the pain that rocks the family but that no one will fully acknowledge. The mascot is typically the baby of the family and often brings laughter or the spotlight wherever he or she lands.

The scapegoat in Wegscheider's theory is a complicated soul. He or she is often the second born, perhaps third depending on how many children are in the family. For every role the hero fulfills to protect the family image, the scapegoat does so in the opposite direction. Scapegoats seek to draw attention to themselves, but in almost exclusively negative ways. They act out to get attention, any attention, from the parents. Up until their advent, the hero has gleaned it all. After their arrival, the stark truth becomes clear that the hero will continue to get the attention no matter what the scapegoat tries. So now the scapegoat will try to get attention by whatever means available. Usually it involves trouble at school, insolent attitudes, sullenness, and often slipping into the same substance abuse patterns exhibited by the dependent.

The cost of playing this role is great. The self-respect that hero can boast through accomplishments may be the only true crown he or she has, and the scapegoats are even robbed of that. Scapegoats see the shortcomings of the family and the shortcomings of their own lives and seethe with anger at themselves and everyone else around them. While heroes can remain blissfully ignorant of their empty family and their inability to really love, scapegoats are fully aware of this and must learn, somehow, to work through it to find their own identity. While the potential for growth and change is there, scapegoats are particularly resistant to therapy. They often feel it is a waste of time. Trust in the family's ability to change is all but lost.

Lori Ellison

See also Boundaries; Homeostasis; Identified Patient; Structural Family Therapy; Systems, Subsystems, and Metasystems; Triangulation

Further Readings

Gladding, S. T. (2014) *Family therapy: History, theory, and practice* (5th ed.). Upper Saddle River, NJ: Pearson.

Hollingsworth, J., Glass, J., & Heisler, K. W. (2008). Empathy deficits in siblings of severely scapegoated children. *Journal of Emotional Abuse, 7*, 69–88.

Minuchin, S. (1974). *Families & family therapy.* Cambridge, MA: Harvard University Press.

Murphy, J. P. (1984). Substance abuse and the family. *Journal for Specialists in Group Work, 9*, 106–112.

Pepper, R. S. (2013). Stirring the pot: Some clinical and ethical implications of blurred boundaries. *Group, 37*, 135–146.

Verdiano, D. L. (1986). *Family roles: An integration of theory, research, and practice.* ProQuest Digital Dissertations.

Vogel, E. F., & Bell, N. W. (1968). The emotionally disturbed child as the family scapegoat. In E. F. Vogel & N. W. Bell (Eds.), *A modern introduction to the family* (pp. 412–427). New York: Free Press.

Wegscheider, S. (1981). *Another chance: Hope and health for the alcoholic family.* Palo Alto, CA: Science and Behavior Books.

SCHIZOPHRENIA AND FAMILIES

The topic of families and schizophrenia is important because families are increasingly asked to be the long-term primary caregivers for clients. This causes unique stresses and affects both the client and the family system. This entry addresses the relevance of family in the treatment of schizophrenia, including a focus on the constructs of expressed emotion and family cohesion. The entry begins with a brief overview of schizophrenia.

Overview of Schizophrenia

There are three types of symptoms that, in combination, may result in a diagnosis of schizophrenia. These are positive, negative, and cognitive symptoms. Positive, or psychotic, symptoms include delusions and hallucinations. Positive symptoms refer to those that are viewed as an excess or distortion of a client's normal functioning and occur when an individual loses touch with reality. Negative symptoms include emotional flatness or lack of expression, an inability to start or finish activities, and lack of pleasure or interest in life. Negative does not refer to a person's attitude, but a lack of characteristics that should exist. Negative symptoms can resemble those of depression. Cognitive symptoms involve impairment of thinking processes, such as prioritizing tasks, organizing thoughts, and certain kinds of memory functions.

There are also challenges that arise from a life span development viewpoint. Schizophrenia is usually diagnosed at the beginning of adulthood when individuals are in school, entering the workforce, beginning families, or making other formative choices. It has life-changing consequences, which can include lost or damaged relationships, disability, academic failure, unemployment, dependency, isolation, physical illnesses, jail or prison, and homelessness.

The impact of this loss on a client's sense of worth and self-esteem can be devastating to both clients and their families. Family members are often frightened and confused as they see changes in the person they love; they can feel isolated and alone if social relationships are affected. Families also feel loss regarding the dreams they had for the future; additional stress includes possible financial difficulty and feelings of guilt.

Family Involvement in Treatment and Recovery

Before the 1950s, mentally ill individuals were cared for by psychiatric hospitals. In many cases, the client remained in the hospital for many years, if not a lifetime, enduring treatments that rarely were successful. Families had little contact with the client and were told to expect little change. Families understood that the client might never return home. Visiting was also discouraged for several reasons. Among these reasons was the belief that families often caused the client to become agitated. Families tended to be viewed as part of the problem rather than the solution, which caused feelings of guilt and blame for their loved ones' illness.

The advent of psychotropic medications in the 1950s and deinstitutionalizations of the 1960s have each had a large impact on the lives of clients and their families. Many discharged clients returned to live with their families, who went on to play an integral role in caring for their mentally ill loved ones. Many families uphold this practice today, and some of these family responsibilities include creating an environment that balances their needs with those of the mentally ill individual, learning to cope with symptoms, and locating appropriate services. Conflict and role overload often increase this burden. Families of racial and ethnic minorities may experience compounded strain due to discrimination, acculturation issues, language issues, lack of information regarding resources, economic hardship, and beliefs and practices that may differ from the mainstream. Families often undergo feelings of stress and stigma related to their loved ones' illness that may result in less than ideal attitudes regarding their role.

Despite the understandable development of distressing feelings, family members' attitude and feedback toward clients experiencing mental illness influences relapse, and therefore is crucial to positive treatment outcomes and recovery. With support and increased knowledge, families can have a more positive experience, and relationships with loved ones can be maintained. Some family members have reported increased feelings of hope and love, increased compassion, a sense of purpose and strength, and an appreciation for the courage of their loved one. Some family members even find an increased commitment to social justice issues and lend involvement to organizations that focus on issues of mental health care.

Family members can make a tremendous difference in clients' lives. As they listen to disclosures and see the personal pain, they can believe, can encourage, can provide hope, and can act with respect and dignity—thereby helping the recovery process begin and continue. Family interventions that aid in treatment and recovery for clients diagnosed with schizophrenia, and other mental illnesses, have been demonstrated to have effectiveness and efficacy. The primary intervention for families is psychoeducation. Family-based interventions, derived from behavioral and systemic ideas, were adapted for families with a member having psychosis following research that found that family environments altered the course of schizophrenia. Further research specifically demonstrated that the construct of expressed emotion within a family environment could predict relapse.

Expressed Emotion

Expressed emotion (EE) refers to a construct reflective of important relationship elements and can be defined as a measure of emotionally overinvolved, critical, or hostile attitudes expressed by an individual toward a mentally ill relative; EE also accounts for positive comments and warmth. High EE and low EE family members have different perceptions of their affected family member's agency, which are predictive of the course of schizophrenia. Low EE relatives have greater acceptance and understanding of their family member's symptoms. Acceptance demands less overt change through greater awareness and understanding, which then may lead to more problem-solving capability. When high EE caregivers push for change and respond with criticism and hostility, it creates more distress for the client, which exacerbates symptoms. This can be cyclical; therefore, greater understanding and acceptance may ultimately lead to more progress toward recovery.

Regaining a sense of agency is a crucial component of clients' recovery process. Clients often feel a lack of control over their own symptoms and actions, yet studies have shown that family members with high EE often perceive symptoms of schizophrenia to be under the control of the client. In fact, human agency involves a process of meaning making that involves both the individual and the audience. The individual determines the appropriate actions to complete a desired task, and the audience determines what meaning or goal the individual was attempting to convey based on the individual's actions. Since meaning making takes mutual understanding, this process can be assumed to have a cultural context. When individuals feel a lack of agency, they draw from known models within their worlds in order to create meaning and a coherent sense of self. These models are mainly their family members. Narratives from family members can be a powerful socializing device, and clients may draw heavily upon the information embedded in narratives when defining their sense of self. Family members' perception of the clients' agency affects the narratives they tell about the client. This is demonstrated by EE and affects the client's own sense of agency and self, thus contributing to relapse or recovery. Self-esteem and the client's own self-evaluation in schizophrenia have also been shown to be dependent on family attitudes regarding clients' agency.

Family Cohesion

Family cohesion is another construct of the family relationship, but has not been researched as often as EE. Family cohesion refers to individuals' perception of their family as supportive, cooperative, and interconnected. Family cohesion is positively related to decreased symptoms in clients and more emotional well-being for clients and relatives. Studies have found that high family cohesion was related to decreased symptoms and better adjustment. The attention to family factors, including EE and cohesion, is linked to the development of family interventions that have been shown to reduce the risk for relapse. The dominant family intervention used with families of clients diagnosed with schizophrenia is psychoeducation.

Psychoeducation for Families

Families are a valuable source of support to clients in their recovery, and the role of the counseling professional is to help the family in their efforts to support the client. As previously discussed, one of the reasons families are so important to clients' recovery is because of the effects family attitudes and feedback have on the clients' perception of themselves, their sense of agency, and the severity of their symptoms. Family interactions are meaningful to clients in recovery, and if family members are perceived to be coercive, intrusive, or unsympathetic, stress may accumulate, and stress increases for all involved. Families with a member who has schizophrenia may experience confusion and limited awareness regarding the illness and symptoms, compounded by the strain of the unpredictability of the behaviors and symptoms, which can affect the attitudes and perceptions of the client.

Psychoeducation comprises systemic, didactic psychotherapeutic interventions aimed at informing clients and their relatives about the illness and its treatment, facilitating greater understanding of the illness and family members' sense of personal responsibility to remain supportive. Family education programs provide information about schizophrenia to help overcome stereotypes and to teach patients and family members what they can do to help themselves, including creating and maintaining a more relaxed family environment. Studies have demonstrated clear superiority of psychoeducational family interventions when used in combination with standard treatments in schizophrenia compared to standard treatments such as medication being used alone. After participating in a comprehensive family education program, relatives' mental health and functional knowledge about schizophrenia increased, as did communications between the family members and the patient; high EE was reduced; and unreasonable expectations were lowered. There were also improvements in patients' personal functioning and social adjustment. While not successful for all families, family-based psychoeducational programs have produced enough evidence to warrant recommendations by several guidelines.

Educating the family about schizophrenia through information is the purpose of all psychoeducation models. It also includes providing helpful resources to clients' families so they can receive support if desired. Psychoeducation programs typically involve one to eight sessions, which are generally 1 to 2 hours in length. The information provided usually includes easy-to-read pamphlets that summarize the information presented, and lists of available resources. Providing such information has the effect of decreasing relatives' reported levels of burden, self-blame, distress, and anxiety.

The psychoeducation approach recognizes that families have a significant impact on their relatives' recovery. It also recognizes that a family's sense of mastery in helping their family member is associated with a decrease in fear and confusion about the illness. This decrease in confusion frees up energies that could better be used for coping with the illness. Psychoeducation also serves to normalize symptoms and relapse, and depathologize the client. This requires balancing, or finding the common denominator, between the objective knowledge regarding information about the illness and exploring the client's subjective experience. Thus, this approach focuses on educating and persuading families that how they interact with their family members can help or hinder recovery. The approach acts as an interpreter of sorts, helping families increase comprehension of the illness by translating complicated psychiatric concepts into information that can more easily be understood. This increase in comprehension, in turn, helps families become more confident in being an active part of treatment and recovery.

As evidenced by multiple family surveys, families of clients with schizophrenia and similar disorders need more information about the disorder and how to manage it more effectively. Past research on EE strongly supports psychoeducation interventions with these families. The idea that families cause schizophrenia in their relatives has been discredited, and family members are instead viewed as invaluable partners in treatment and recovery efforts. Mental health professionals have aimed for families being helpers in trying to increase clients' treatment compliance. Family interventions such as psychoeducation were therefore developed. Psychoeducation has been demonstrated to have numerous benefits, including decreased EE and family burden, increased understanding and knowledge about schizophrenia, better client and family adjustment, increased compliance, improved quality of life, and reduced cost for society.

Martha Mason

See also Mental Health, Systemic Perspective; Positive Psychology; Psychoeducation; Systems Theory

Further Readings

Anderson, C., Reiss, D., & Hogarty, G. (1986). *Schizophrenia and the family.* New York: Guilford Press.

Barrowclough, C., Tarrier, N., Humphreys, L., Ward, J., Gregg, L., & Andrews, B. (2003). Self-esteem in schizophrenia: Relationships between self-evaluation, family attitudes, and symptomatology. *Journal of Abnormal Psychology, 112*(1), 92–99.

DeSousa, A., Kurvey, A., & Sonavane, S. (2012). Family psychoeducation for schizophrenia: A clinical review. *Malaysian Journal of Psychiatry, 21*(2).

Falloon, I. (2003). Family interventions for mental disorders: Efficacy and effectiveness, *World Psychiatry, 2,* 20–28.

Hooley, J. (2007). Expressed emotion and relapse of psychopathology. *Annual Review of Clinical Psychology, 3,* 329–352.

Kuipers, E. (2006). Family interventions in schizophrenia: Evidence for efficacy and proposed mechanisms of change. *Journal of Family Therapy, 28*(1), 73–80.

McFarlane, W., Dixon, L., Lukens, E., & Lucksted, A. (2003). Family psychoeducation and schizophrenia: A review of the literature. *Journal of Mental and Family Therapy, 29*(2), 223–245.

Miklowitz, D. (2004). The role of family systems in severe and recurrent psychiatric disorders: A developmental psychopathology view. *Developmental Psychopathology, 16*(3), 667–688.

Pitschel-Walz, G., Leucht, S., Bauml, I., Kissling, W., & Engel, R. (2001). The effect of family interventions in relapse and rehospitalization in schizophrenia. *Schizophrenia Bulletin, 27*(1), 73–92.

Schools, Family Involvement in

Three systems that influence the lives of children are interrelated—schools, families, and communities. These three systems can exist in synchronicity but can also come into conflict and work against each other. National counseling codes of ethics indicate that school counselors work with families on behalf of students to achieve optimal academic and social-emotional development. Counselor preparation programs are increasingly focused on helping counselors become familiar with working with families because it moves the focus from the individual and from a deficit model to an approach that is collaborative, systems focused, and strengths based. Counselors in schools often are involved in engagement, outreach, inclusive strategies, and counseling practices for involving families in the academic and social-emotional success of K–12 students. This entry first discusses research indicating the positive influence families can have on student success, the challenges counselors experience when working with families in school settings, and family systems theory and techniques applicable to school settings. It then discusses the role and practices of the school counselor in creating sustainable school–family–community partnerships, and discusses a type of family-centered intervention for students with emotional or behavioral disabilities or other mental health issues.

Family Systems Perspective in Schools

As previously stated, families are greatly influential in children's academic and social-emotional development. This is especially relevant for elementary school age children who are solely dependent on their parents and family for basic needs. Several outcomes of parent and family involvement in the schools have been presented in the literature. The research outcomes related to student success include increased school attendance, higher grades and test scores, higher school completion rates, increased attendance at postsecondary institutions, more positive behavior, and access to health care and community resources. Additionally, parents who are actively engaged in schools have children who perform well but also increase their own social capital, social competency, and support networks support.

Counselors who involve and engage families see the value of approaching problems from a systems, strengths-based perspective rather than focusing on the individual person and possible deficits. Advocacy on behalf of students and families is also a core practice for counselors who view student issues through an ecological lens. Counselors who aim to resolve student academic and social-emotional challenges within just the school setting and school day have a very narrow scope of practice that excludes multilevel and macrosystemic influences. School counseling research supports school–family–community partnerships, as these partnerships increase collaboration with parents and community stakeholders and remain vital in implementing successful comprehensive school counselor programs.

Challenges of Including Family Work in the Schools

School counselor preparation programs often do not require courses in family counseling. Training programs often cover content on collaboration with families but do not include coursework that integrates a family systems perspective. Collaboration and family work are essential elements in comprehensive school counseling programs. Implementing strategies that include family engagement and effective partnerships can be difficult in the schools, especially for new counselors. Counselors are often overwhelmed with ratios of 1 counselor for 400 to 800 students, and many counselors may not want to expand their work to building partnerships with families and the community. Additionally, educators at schools have assumed several new roles, such as family engagement specialists and behavior coaches, and counselors may be unclear about each individual's duties. It can be difficult to meet with families during school hours because parents are often working. Sufficient office space is also necessary, and students may need to be released from class time and lose academic learning.

Family Theories Applicable for the School Setting

School counselors should be knowledgeable about three basic family system theoretical foundations: Murray Bowen's natural systems theory, Salvador Minuchin's structural approach, and Steve de Shazer's solution-focused approach. These approaches provide school counselors with skills to competently work and consult with families. Further, school counselors can share this knowledge with teachers and administrators to enhance their interactions with students and parents.

Bowen's approach emphasizes transgenerational influence and relationships with the immediate and extended subsystems of families. The use of genograms is a strategy for helping understand influences, structures, and people who are present in how the family functions. Minuchin's structural approach in family theory focuses on structures, subsystems, and boundaries. Patterns of interactions are explored and reveal how families are involved, resolve conflict, and arrange hierarchy. Finally, de Shazer's solution-focused approach promotes change and new ways of interacting rather than examining the roots of behavior. Counselors extending this approach to work with families in the schools may pose the miracle question and ask scaling questions to keep family members focused on change and movement forward. Family systems theory clearly acknowledges the interrelatedness of family members and that the experiences of one family member can invariably impact others within the unit.

School–Family–Community Partnerships

School–family–community partnerships are collaborative efforts between school staff, parents, and community members aimed at improving academic outcomes for students. Research studies indicate that school–family–community partnerships increase student academic achievement, improve school climate, enhance relationships between families and schools, and provide families with networks of community support. School–family–community partnerships help close educational gaps among students of color and low economic status by engaging parents as the central unit of support. School–family–community partnerships also align with comprehensive school counseling programs and with approaches to supporting students such as response to intervention and positive behavioral interventions and support. Developing effective school–family–community partnerships bridges the school with existing community resources and removes barriers to access to health care, mental health services, housing, transportation, child care, and employment.

In order to implement successful school–family–community partnerships, school counselors must step out of their traditional roles and engage with parents and stakeholders in the community. Occasional visits to local small business meetings, chamber of commerce meetings, places of worship, libraries, and social service agencies increase the visibility of the counselor and also help build engagement and trust. Counselors should remain mindful that establishing successful partnerships can be time-consuming. However, long-term results of these strong bonds with parents and community stakeholders will benefit the students, staff, school, and community. Administrative support is also needed to maintain school–family–community partnerships with school administration. Presenting current research to administrators and teachers and providing anecdotal information can help to garner sustained support. Although barriers do exist, such as time, role ambiguity, and geographic location, counselors are able to build ongoing relationships with parents and community stakeholders, over time, into transformational partnerships.

School–family–community partnerships can build resiliency in students, families, and communities. The partnerships allow parents and community stakeholders to interact with each other and the school administration and staff. These partnerships allow participants to collaborate and discuss the mission, vision, and goals of their partnership, decide on outreach programs and initiatives, and develop accountability measures. The issues the partnership chooses to address would be rooted in the needs of the school and community. It has been reported that two types of partnerships have been successful in increasing the academic readiness of students and providing necessary resources for children and families: family-centered partnerships, and extracurricular enrichment partnership programs. Family-centered partnerships encourage parental involvement in the classroom and on school boards. Family centers may be created at schools and schools may hire family liaisons directly to provide outreach to families. Extracurricular enrichment partnership programs provide mentoring and tutoring to struggling students either after school, on the weekends, and during the summer. Community agencies and local organizations such as the Boys and Girls Club, places of worship, service groups, and universities are often involved in this outreach.

It has been suggested that counselors should spend 1 day per week to work on strengthening the school–family–community partnership, increase parent engagement, and identify prevention interventions. By closely working with families and community entities, counselors may provide less individual and reactive/crisis counseling and increase activities, services, and resources that are community based. Forming these partnerships and outreach efforts is also a form of collaboration, which is one of the main function areas for school counselors.

Parents have reported developing positive relationships with school counselors when approaches and interactions are grounded in cultural competence, respect, and nonjudgmental listening. Relationships between parents and their children have also improved when school counselors have intervened and provided brief counseling or support when any academic or personal issues have arose. Parents have also discussed counselors' emotional support during challenging situations and that this, in turn, allowed them to better support their children in solving any personal or academic problems. The power of building strong parent–counselor relationships can lead to an improvement in chronic absenteeism and academic performance.

Wraparound Plans for Youth in Need of Services

An example of a family oriented, highly tailored intervention for struggling youth is a wraparound plan. Implementing wraparound plans in the schools is a process often led by counselors for a small percentage of students who have severe emotional or behavioral disabilities or other mental health issues. Wraparound is conceptualized as a team-based service, planning and coordination process, and is a treatment plan that blends home, school, and community interventions. The approach is rooted in cultural competency, is strengths based, values family voice and choice, and addresses the complex needs of this student population rather than focusing attention on one individualized problem such as chronic absenteeism or problematic behavior. The process, which is holistic and rooted in prevention, offers a systems framework to address multiple areas in a child's life and actively involves family and community entities. Wraparound has been widely used in implementing systems of care models by designing individualized and flexible services and interventions for youth and families.

The wraparound approach can be effective for students with complex emotional and behavioral problems, and schools are ideal settings for interagency collaboration and individualized care. Positive outcomes of the wraparound approach include improvement in living situations, health care access, academic progress, mental health, resiliency, and juvenile justice–related outcomes. Using the wraparound approach is especially relevant with youth ages 17 to 25, sometimes referred to as transitional-age youth because they are at the age when youth "age out" of foster care and juvenile justice programming and move from youth to adult social services. The high prevalence and severity rates of psychiatric and substance use disorders in this age group underscore the need for early intervention for this vulnerable population and for collaboration among counselors, parents, and social agencies.

Jolie Ziomek-Daigle

See also Adolescent Mental Health; Authoritative Parenting; Career Planning and Couples/Families; Child Behavior Problems; Parenting

Further Readings

American School Counselor Association. (2010). *The professional school counselor and school–family–community partnerships.* Retrieved from https://www.schoolcounselor.org/asca/media/asca/home/position%20statements/Partnerships.pdf

Bower, H. A., & Griffin, D. (2011). Can the Epstein model of parental involvement work in a high minority, high poverty elementary school? A case study. *Professional School Counseling, 15*(2), 77–87.

Davis, K. M., & Lambie, G. W. (2005). Family engagement: A collaborative systemic approach for middle school counselors. *Professional School Counseling, 9*(2), 144–151.

Deslandes, R., & Bertrand, R. (2005). Motivation of parent involvement in secondary-level schooling. *Journal of Educational Research, 98*, 164–175.

Eber, L., & Nelson, C. M. (1997). School-based wraparound planning: Integrating services for students with emotional and behavioral needs. *American Journal of Orthopsychiatry, 67*, 385–395.

Epstein, J. L. (1995). School-family-community partnerships. *Phi Delta Kappan, 76*, 701–712.

Epstein, J. L., & Van Voorhis, F. L. (2010). School counselors' roles in developing partnerships with families and communities for student success. *Professional School Counseling, 14*(1), 1–14.

Griffin, D., & Steen, S. (2010). School–family–community partnerships: Applying Epstein's theory of the six types of involvement to school counselor practice. *Professional School Counseling, 13*(4), 218–226.

Paylo, M. J. (2011). Preparing school counseling students to aid families: Integrating a family systems perspective. *Family Journal, 19*(2), 140–146.

West-Olatunji, C., Frazer, K. N., & Kelley, E. (2011). Wraparound counseling: An ecosystemic approach to working with economically disadvantaged students in urban school settings. *Journal of Humanistic Counseling, 50*(2), 222–237.

Second-Order Change

Many family counseling theories were derived from the family systems framework. Second-order change is a central concept in family systems theory, defined as fundamental changes within a system's function and organization that lead to permanent changes in its interaction patterns. Generally, second-order change involves a change in the structure of the system. A family counselor using a second-order change framework will go beyond working to remove the problematic symptom by attempting to understand the family's systemic interaction patterns in order to encourage change in these areas. A family counselor can facilitate change to the rules and structure of a family system and assist family members in disregarding the old system and learning to adjust to the new system in order to develop a healthier way of functioning. This entry addresses the definition of second-order change, major theoretical contributors to the concept of second-order change, and implications for marriage, family, and couples counseling.

First- Versus Second-Order Change

The principles of second-order change were developed from general systems theory. First-order changes are superficial changes within a system that are not intended to promote change to the overall level of functioning or organization of the system itself. In counseling, first-order change usually focuses on symptom reduction in the individual. First-order changes are unlikely to alter the structure and rules of the system itself in order to promote more enduring change. In family counseling, second-order change implies that the counselor is not only focused on improving the outcome by removing the symptoms (first-order change) but also helping the family change its systemic interactive patterns (second-order change). For example, a family counselor might help decrease arguments among family members by working on changing the rules or communication patterns that govern interactions among family members. Instead of focusing on reducing or increasing the targeted behavior, the family counselor uses strategies or interventions (i.e., prescribing the symptoms and positioning) to alter family interaction patterns. Even if the targeted behavior remains unchanged, the process itself can lead to fundamental changes in interactive or communication patterns. In other words, the family counselor promotes second-order change by strategically placing emphasis on reorganizing the family system to create a new way of functioning.

Second-order change, depending on the client's situation, is not always necessary in treatment. Families and even counselors might prefer solutions at the level of first-order change because second-order change involves the introduction of new rules into an existing system, which can be uncomfortable and difficult. Sometimes in a counseling session the distinction between first- and second-order changes can be hard due to the fact that changes in behavior or level of functioning occur in small shifts. However, the framework of first- and second-order change enables the counselor to ask whether roles have merely shifted or whether there has been a fundamental change in the ability to negotiate more intense intimacy and tolerate greater independence.

Second-order change has not been accurately defined, operationalized, or tested due to its complexity and lack of attention from researchers and practitioners. It has been suggested that second-order change is a process that alters the patterns of interactions in a family to the extent that the problem does not recur, and that it represents a shift in the actual structure of the system, allowing for an alteration to be made to the core structure of a relationship that will lead to fundamental changes in the way the relationship functions overall.

Major Contributors

The terms *first-order change* and *second-order change* were defined in the 1974 book *Change: Principles of Problem Formation and Problem Resolution* by Paul Watzlawick, John Weakland,

and Richard Fisch. The authors based their conclusions on set theory and the theory of logical types. They stated that first-order change focuses on alleviating immediate symptoms without changing any of the underlying patterns responsible for generating the symptoms themselves. These first-order changes are likely to be short-lived, as even if the symptom is removed, the underlying rules governing the patterns responsible for the symptoms remain unchanged, making it likely that the symptom will recur once the individual encounters new challenges. First-order change treats the most pressing issues, but is unlikely to create a stable system over time. It is important to note that although second-order change can produce the same kind of reductions in symptoms as first-order change, second-order change is much more likely to produce lasting stability in the system.

Second-order change implies a fundamental modification of the system's structure and function. This form of change involves not only removing the problematic symptom, but also modifying the systemic interaction pattern by changing the rules of the family system and subsequently reorganizing the system so that it reaches a different level of functioning. If the treatment is successful, the previous rules or ways of functioning become ineffective and then are discarded. This transition might cause the family to become temporarily confused or unstable, but then the family will attempt to reconstruct itself in a new way.

A dramatic instance of personal change is sometimes referred to as second-order change, and is achieved when an individual's structure of experience changes radically. This is in contrast with first-order change, which involves incremental changes within the existing structure. Although second-order change can be a valid form of change, making it the sole goal of counseling may interrupt the client's natural growth process.

In counseling, the concept of second-order change needs to be linked to the client's experience of change to avoid using the concept as a theoretical ideal that is not solidly rooted in what people experience in their daily lives. Enlarging an individual's belief and value system to include second-order change requires that the counselor focus on respecting the client's belief and value system. Maintaining a relationship that values the client for who he or she is at the moment is vital. Creating a context for second-order change may simply involve the basic tenets of skilled counseling, the foundation of which is built upon compassionate action in which both client and counselor facilitate each other's trusting and risking.

Later authors added additional levels of change. According to the 2014 book *How Master Therapists Work: Effecting Change from the First Through the Last Session and Beyond* by Len Sperry and Jon Carlson, there are four orders of change. Zero-order change happens when an unskilled counselor does not assist a client in making any changes. According to the authors, this usually happens when a trainee or otherwise inexperienced counselor focuses on factual questions instead of addressing problem cognitions and behaviors due to the counselor's own anxiety about the practice of counseling. First-order change occurs when the counselor focuses on reducing symptoms, making small changes, and stabilizing the client. While this kind of change may help in the short term, underlying issues within the client have not been resolved, and the problems addressed in counseling are likely to recur. Second-order change occurs when the counselor helps the client address the underlying pattern that is the root of the presenting concerns. The goal of this process is to reduce and eventually eliminate an old, maladaptive pattern for a new pattern that is more adaptive for the client. This process produces lasting change and prevents the recurrence of the client's presenting concerns. Third-order change happens when the counselor teaches the client how to identify and change maladaptive patterns on his or her own. The client effectively self-counsels and is empowered to make his or her own second-order changes.

Implications in Marriage, Family, and Couples Counseling

Second-order change techniques can be a valuable tool in marriage, family, and couples counseling for making lasting changes to the family system. Second-order change is related to identifying and changing maladaptive interaction patterns and structures. In practice, this involves three steps: minimizing the frequency and severity of a maladaptive pattern; developing a new, adaptive pattern and increasing its frequency; and maintaining the new, adaptive pattern. Because family systems are inherently complex, however, there is no single approach to effecting second-order change in a family system. The counselor must be aware of what techniques or interventions best fit the family unit and what they have experienced before.

There are several counseling techniques or interventions that promote second-order changes in family systems. Blocking and acceptance strategies are designed to stop clients from engaging in solutions that are ineffective or exacerbate the issue. A reversal technique is an approach that asks clients to try a strategy that is the opposite of what they are currently trying. Restraining change involves preventing clients from moving too fast or discouraging them from achieving their desired goal. The process of normalizing puts clients at ease by portraying their reactions as normal given their context. Framing, reframing, and deframing strategies involve placing a problem in a specific context, shifting how that problem is classified, or deconstructing a classification that is unhelpful to the client. For example, a counselor working with an unhappy couple might not simply focus on increasing marital satisfaction, but create a goal to fundamentally reconstruct their understanding of marital satisfaction.

Positioning involves taking a position that is counter to the client's expectations and designed to facilitate change. Prescribing symptoms invites clients to deliberately engage in the problem behavior or a behavior similar to it. In predicting or prescribing difficulties or relapse techniques, clients are informed of setbacks that may occur in the future and are invited to see those challenges as part of the change process. Adopting a goal-oriented future position moves clients away from a problem-oriented present–past focus and toward describing the hope for the future.

Family counselors may find the distinction between first- and second-order changes a useful framework to employ in their work with families. In particular, the levels of change framework may serve as an important guide during the assessment and goal formulation process. Second-order change may be necessary when family members exhibit a history or pattern of difficulty in addressing some developmental life challenges. In these instances, current family structure is no longer functional, and their presenting problems may seem more pervasive. One difficulty for problems that may require a fundamental shift in the family system is that second-order change tends to be a relatively unpredictable therapeutic process regarding the way it occurs and the amount of time it takes.

Ki Byung Chae

See also Communications in Couples and Families, Cybernetics; Paradoxes and Paradoxical Intervention; Second-Order Family Therapy; Strategic Family Therapy; Systems Theory

Further Readings

Davey, M., Duncan, T., Kissil, K., Davey, A., & Fish, L. S. (2011). Second-order change in marriage and family therapy: A web-based modified Delphi study. *American Journal of Family Therapy, 39,* 100–111.

Davey, M. P., Davey, A., Tubbs, C., Savla, J., & Anderson, S. (2012). Second-order change and evidence-based practice. *Journal of Family Therapy, 34,* 72–90.

Fraser, J. S., & Solovey, A. D. (2007). *Second-order change in psychotherapy: The golden thread that unifies effective treatments.* Washington, DC: American Psychological Association.

Good, G. E., & Beitman, B. D. (2006). *Counseling and psychotherapy essentials: Integrating theories, skills, and practices.* New York: W. W. Norton.

Sperry, L., & Carlson, J. (2014). *How master therapists work: Effecting change from the first through the last session and beyond.* New York: Routledge.

Watzlawick, P., Weakland, J. H., & Fisch, R. (1974). *Change: Principles of problem formation and problem resolution.* New York: W. W. Norton.

SECOND-ORDER FAMILY THERAPY

Family therapy is distinct from other psychotherapy modalities in that the presenting problems of the family are seen as a result of interactional patterns; therefore, problems are addressed relationally rather than individually. The problem is seen as created by what is happening interpersonally in the family system, rather than created from within or intrapersonally. First-order family therapy developed in the 1950s as a linear process that allowed for an understanding of what is "healthy" or "normal" behavior. These boundaries aligned with the practice of therapy. The therapist was able to function outside of the family system as an observer, determine the "problems" within the system, and act as an expert.

Second-order family therapy, which was influenced by postmodern thinking, emerged in the 1980s and challenged the political and social landscape of family therapy. Postmodernism asserted that the practice of family therapy included the language of meaning, socially constructed realities, and circular causality. Therapy became a collaborative process between the client and counselor, with the counselor taking a nonexpert stance and questioning what "normal" and "healthy" behavior really is. Change happens when the client and counselor deconstruct the meaning of the presenting problem and reconstruct it as the desired change. This entry further defines first-order family therapy and its relationship to cybernetics, then discusses the transition from first-order family therapy to second-order family therapy and the distinctions between first-order family therapy and second-order family therapy. The entry concludes with a discussion of the concept of circular causality and the practice of second-order family therapy.

First-Order Family Therapy

First-order family therapy was influenced greatly by the concepts and theories that emerged from the Macy conferences. These conferences, held during the 1950s, brought together mathematicians, physicists, and engineers who theorized about a mechanical understanding of the human brain and how it functions. Norbert Wiener, a mathematician, coined the term *cybernetics* to refer to the study of control and communication in animals and machines. He theorized that information loops provided constant feedback to self-maintaining systems. This idea has been applied to multiple systems, including the family system. Using the feedback, the system could make adaptations to maintain the process, improve the process, or diminish the process. The system uses the feedback to regulate and self-correct.

Gregory Bateson, an anthropologist in attendance at the Macy conferences, conjectured that there was a relationship between the cybernetic loop and human interaction and communication. Bateson was also studying the ideas of Ludwig von Bertalanffy, a biologist, who speculated that we must understand what is happening between the individual system members in order to understand the process of the system as a whole. Consequently, von Bertalanffy also theorized that the "whole is greater than the sum of its parts," which means that a family acting as a whole is greater than the family members acting individually, supporting the use of family therapy methods. Bateson formed the Palo Alto Group to further study communication theory. The group worked out of the Mental Research Institute (MRI) in Palo Alto, California, in the 1950s and 1960s. Other members of the Palo Alto Group included notable theorists and clinicians such as John Weakland, Jay Haley, Paul Watzlawick and Don Jackson. MRI continues to provide clinical services, training, and research around systems thinking.

As a basis of first-order family therapy, cybernetics can be understood as a theory positing that human systems seek homeostasis or stability. Feedback loops (behaviors) maintain the homeostasis and in doing so can maintain problem behavior. Change happens when the loops are interrupted and new patterns are formed. First-order family therapy is seen as a linear process of cause and effect; typically change is limited to one part of the system or symptom reduction. The feedback loops are seen as the communication process within the family system and could be observed on the level of verbal or nonverbal communication.

Further study moved to thinking about how communication happens verbally and nonverbally and how simple messages can convey multiple meanings. For example, a person may state to another person, "I want you to come with me" and then leave without telling the other person. The verbal communication indicated a positive emotional connection and action; however, the nonverbal communication indicated a contrary emotional connection and message. Therefore, communication can be seen as having multiple levels, and because of these multiple levels misunderstanding or problems develop within a system.

The Transition: First-Order to Second-Order Family Therapy

First-order cybernetic thinking theorized that the counselor was an observer of the family system and able to work from an expert stance knowing how a "healthy" family system interacted. Models that use first-order family therapy ideas include structural family therapy, which employs normative concepts of boundaries and subsystem structure to understand family interaction. Contextual family therapy, which uses ideas about loyalties or obligations across generations to make sense of system patterns, also incorporated first-order change process. These models are seen as being influenced by psychodynamic thinking and the idea that the behavior of an individual member of the system is involved with the problem in a cause-and-effect manner.

The linear function of first-order family therapy was seen as change moving in only one direction with limited impact and, consequently, limited influence on the family system. The linear concept of cause and effect did not take into consideration all of the other factors that influence behavior or the social experiences of the system members. The "expert" counselor was able to identify the cause of the family problem and manipulate the family to change in the way that the counselor determined appropriate.

In second-order family therapy, the counselor is seen as a part of the system and because of that relationship needs to be a collaborator of change with the family rather than the designer of change. Reality is also seen as socially created, with the understanding that what is "normal" for one context might not be "normal" in another context. Counselors use second-order family therapy methods to take a stance of curiosity rather than that of an expert on the client family system. The clinical process of second-order family therapy uses the supposition that change happens through shifts in the rules of system, which in turn causes a structural change. Second-order change is mutual in nature—when one part of the system changes, other parts of the system change—and alters the way the system is structured.

Models that incorporate second-order change include solution-focused brief therapy, which is based on a concept that exceptions to the problem, or times when things are better, are already happening. The counselor works with the family to do more of "what works" and less of "what doesn't work." The "problem" is not discussed as such, but rather the preferred future is detailed in the therapeutic conversation. Change happens through the client's not understanding the problem as a problem any longer. Narrative therapy is also a second-order family therapy model. In narrative therapy, language and societal knowledge shape the problem story of the client, which is changed through the counselor and client collaborating on a new story as the client desires.

Second-order family therapy can be seen as divergent from first-order family therapy in that the therapeutic system includes the therapist as a collaborator rather than in the hierarchical role of an observer. Goals are set and change occurs through a collective process with a nonjudgmental view of the presenting problem or pathology. First-order change is linear and applied individually within the system. In first-order change, the structure stays consistent.

Second-Order Family Therapy as Distinct From First-Order Family Therapy

First-order change looks to change behaviors or the frequency of behaviors within a system. Second-order change looks to change the rules of the system, which will result in changing the behaviors and frequencies of interactions in the system. First-order change is seen as a temporary fix to a problem, whereas the more complex second-order change is seen as bringing longer lasting change to a system. A family might come into therapy with 12-year-old and 14-year-old children. The presenting issue that the 12-year-old child is not following the family rules and is "acting out." The parents state that the goals of therapy are for the younger child to do his chores and not talk back.

In this situation, a first-order change, which looks just at a singular interaction within the family system, identifies linear causality of an interactional pattern. Interrupting that linear pattern will change that singular interaction; however, it will not impact the system as a whole, and the same behavioral problem can recur within another context. A first-order change would have the counselor working with the parents to discipline the child when he does not do his chores or when he talks back, and perhaps use a reward chart to keep track of when the child follows rules and acts appropriately. This may or may not decrease the presenting problem behavior. If the behavior does decrease, other unwanted behavior might begin, or the decrease in problem behavior will be temporary because the problem is not the behavior, as the behavior is a symptom of a problem that is not being addressed. In this situation, there is a reason the child is "acting out" that has not been thought about yet.

The counselor working for a second-order change would be interested in what else is happening in the family system. The therapist might find out from the child that he feels as if he has no choice in any decisions that are made about what he does, where he goes, and what he can do. The parents may feel frustrated that the older sibling feels that the younger sibling doesn't help out and that he does more chores than the younger child. At the same time, the parents want to allow the younger child to be childlike, not wanting to see that he is growing up and perhaps no longer needs the close attention of the parents. This information allows for reframing the "acting out" as the younger child's efforts to communicate that he wants more responsibility, which includes making some choices and being more like the older sibling. The counselor and family can decide together about the decisions and activities for which the children are responsible. Perhaps both children could choose from a weekly list of chores, the younger child could pick out his own clothes in the morning as his older brother does, and the younger child could decide whether to do his homework before dinner or after dinner.

These changes affect the way the family is structured and thinks about the individual members. The younger child is no longer "the baby" who acts irresponsibly as he did when the family came into counseling. The child will complete his chores, which was the goal of the frustrated parents, and he will do as much work as his older brother, which was the goal of the brother. The younger child also will be seen as more responsible and able to make some of his own age-appropriate decisions, leading to a different understanding of the child's role in the system and the way the parents interact with him. This is a change in the system rules, since previously the parents made all decisions.

First-order change is a reduction of the symptoms; however, the rules of the system remain the same, and therefore the problem can resurface in another context. Second-order change involves changing the rules of the system along with a reduction of the problem. The change in the rules prevents the same dysfunctional pattern from reemerging. The focus is on changing the way the system is organized rather than simply changing the frequency of an interaction.

Circular Causality

The concept of circular causality emerged with second-order change and is key to understanding the process of how this second-order change happens within a system. Linear causality is the belief that one event causes another; therefore, a problem can be linked to an isolated cause. However, from a second-order perspective, multiple events are responsible for the problem because each system member has a unique perspective of the problem and is to be understood in the context of the system. The second-order family therapist must hold a postmodern posture that reality is socially created and unique for each individual and each system. These multiple realities are the foundation of circular causality when conceptualizing the family system therapeutically.

This idea can be illustrated when thinking about the interactional cycle of the family discussed previously. An interactional cycle might start with the child placing his dinner plate in the sink and the parent responding in an annoyed tone, telling the child to put the plate in the dishwasher. The child also responds in an annoyed tone, which then shifts the parent to an angry answer, which in turn also shifts the child to anger and causes him to storm out of the room. The interaction can be looked at as having linear causality focused on the subsystem of the child and parent. However, when looking at the entire family system through a lens of circular causality, it is also noticed that the older sibling pointed out to the parent that the 12-year-old was not loading the dishwasher and complained that the younger child never helps out in the kitchen. When the interaction started, the other parent in the room left, stating he did not want to be a part of the verbal interchange. The parent who remained with the child then became angry and reported feeling like "the enforcer parent" because the other parent "always leaves when family rules must be enforced." Consequently, there were many more causes for the angry interaction, and they involved more system members than just the younger child and the one parent.

Circular causality exposes that there is no one reason for any one behavior. Therefore, applying a linear concept of first-order change will not bring long lasting change to this family system because it is so much more involved than A causing B, which causes C. The second-order family therapist supports all family members to present their perspective of the problem and deconstruct the interactional cycle as it existed. Through the deconstructing and reframing of the behaviors and meanings of the interactions, family members understand different intents of each other's behavior and how each made sense in context. This larger view of the "problem," or the reframing of the meaning of the behaviors, brings about system realignment as a result of the redefinition of the problem. The circular causality supports the increase in functional interaction, and the change in meaning creates a rule or system change.

The Practice of Second-Order Family Therapy

Second-order family therapy practice is a collaborative interaction between the therapist and the clients, with the therapist assuming a nondirective and neutral role as a member of the system. The therapy process can be understood as a therapeutic conversation, with the therapist being curious about the client story and listening without judgment. Families come into the therapy with each holding a singular "truth" or understanding of the problem happening within the system. The second-order family therapist works with the family to explore the multiple perspectives of the problem held by the system members. Through the discussion of the perspectives, the problem story or the singular truths are deconstructed, and the family members reframe and reorganize their understanding of the problem. The reorganization of the meaning of the behaviors supports the system members in engaging in a changed pattern of interaction. The therapist must consciously be aware of the circular causality of the system during the deconstruction as a way of highlighting the impact of each system member on each other and on the problem. The reverse is also true; circular causality supports the development of the new, more functional interaction cycle of the family system. Change in second-order family therapy happens through altering meaning and understanding of the problem, which results in a change in the system interactions.

The second-order family counselor embraces postmodern thought, understanding that there is no absolute truth in reality, and serves as a collaborator with the family. Therefore, the therapist becomes a part of the system rather than an observer of the system who might act as a director or expert. The second-order family therapist posits a nonexpert or "not knowing" stance. Language and meaning are used as tools of intervention rather than using assessments or techniques that may formulate normative ideas and linear causality.

Carol Pfeiffer Messmore

See also Circularity and Linearity; Cybernetics; Epistemology in Family Therapy; First-Order Change; Narrative Therapy; Postmodern Therapies; Second-Order Change; Solution-Focused Brief Therapy

Further Readings

Atkinson, B., & Heath, T. (1990). Further thoughts on second-order family therapy—This time it's personal. *Family Process, 29,* 145–155.

Bateson, G. (1972). *Steps to an ecology of mind.* New York: Ballantine.

Becvar, D. S., & Becvar, R. J. (2013). *Family therapy: A systemic integration* (8th ed.). Upper Saddle River, NJ: Pearson.

Bertalanffy, L. von. (1968). *General systems theory: Foundation, development, applications.* New York: Braziller.

Fisch, R., Weakland, J., & Segal, L. (1982). *The tactics of change.* San Francisco: Jossey-Bass.

Hoffman, L. (1985). Beyond power and control: Toward a "second order" family systems therapy. *Family Systems and Medicine, 3,* 381–396.

Hoffman, L. (1990). Constructing reality: An art of lenses. *Family Process, 29*(1), 1–12.

Keeney, B., & Sprenkle, D. (1982). Ecosystemic epistemology: Critical implications for the aesthetics and pragmatics of family therapy. *Family Process, 21,* 11–19.

Mills, S. D., & Sprenkle, D. H. (1995). Family therapy in the postmodern era. *Family Relations, 44*(4), 368–376.

Watzlawick, P., Weakland, J. H., & Fisch, R. (1974). *Change: Principles of problem formation and problem resolution.* New York: W. W. Norton.

SECRETS

Secrets refer to material that is intentionally withheld from others. Privacy is a related concept that also involves withholding information; however, the two are distinguished by relational norms. If the norms of a relationship state that information should be shared (e.g., discussing health concerns with a spouse) and a person elects not to share, the content is considered secret. Conversely, if there is no expectation of sharing (e.g., discussing health concerns with a coworker), and the individual elects not to share, the content would be private. Secrets are relevant to marriage, families, and counseling because they impact intrapersonal (within oneself) and interpersonal (between people) functioning. This entry addresses factors that influence secrecy in couple relationships, including personality, shame, attachment style, and relationship dynamics. The most common types of secrets and the outcomes of secret-keeping are also described. How to avoid secret-keeping and the benefits of disclosures in romantic relationships are also discussed.

Type of Secrets

Many partners agree that certain topics are private and not to be shared with each other. It is unrealistic to expect complete relational openness, and in fact, some degree of privacy is beneficial for partnerships. The most common topic partners avoid discussing is the relationship itself. Although people generally want to know the status of their relationship, they worry about receiving negative feedback and prefer to avoid the conversation. In terms of secrecy (i.e., withholding information that a partner expects to be revealed), the most common topic is infidelity. Relationship norms generally dictate that such information be divulged, but partners keep it concealed to avoid relationship dissolution. Following infidelity, the next most common types of secrets are about past partners and prior sexual experiences.

In addition to these topics, partners may conceal information pertaining to rule violations or conventional norm disruptions. Rule violations involve actions that defy the agreed-upon guidelines of a relationship. For instance, if a partner is responsible for managing the couple's finances and uses the money for gambling, he or she is likely to keep the information secret. Conventional norm disruptions involve withholding information that is culturally prescribed as too personal to share based on a relationship's intimacy level. For example, a person will likely not discuss his or her history of incest upon first meeting a prospective romantic partner.

Reasons for Secret-Keeping

In order to avoid secret-keeping, individuals should understand how internalized schemata (cognitive frameworks that help a person organize and interpret information) from their family of origin might be impacting their present-day relationships. Given that most patterns are socialized rather than biologically based, individuals can replace maladaptive schemata with healthier alternatives. Many people who have experienced a significant amount of dysfunction benefit from seeking professional help. Making self-improvements can help people avoid critical partners and opt for secure and supportive relationships. Boundaries should also be established and discussed. It is important to be aware of each person's expectations regarding information that is to be shared and not shared so that secret-keeping can be prevented.

In romantic relationships, mutual self-disclosures are common and expected. People have an innate desire to gain approval from and be validated by others. Self-disclosures promote feelings of acceptance, support, and trust. The healthy functioning of a relationship therefore relies on the open sharing of information. In the early stages of a partnership, it is important to avoid private and taboo topics such as previous sexual experiences. Such information is sometimes inappropriate to share in even established relationships. It is also important that partners disclose reciprocally and over time, rather than all at once. Ultimately, the sharing of information helps partners build intimacy, which lays the foundation for a satisfying, long-term partnership. Even though sharing with each other can increase intimacy, there are many reasons people keep secrets. These reasons are discussed in more detail in the remainder of this section.

Personality

Evidence suggests that personality traits are partially based in biology and remain relatively stable over time. Different theoretical models of personality exist. One paradigm that is relevant to secret-keeping is the extent to which people are motivated by reward seeking (i.e., approach motivation) or risk evasion (i.e., avoidance motivation). Although each person is motivated by some degree of each, one orientation tends to be most dominant. People who are motivated by approach seek experiences and relationships with the potential for fulfillment. These individuals are more likely than those who are approach avoidant to engage in risky acts such as drug use and infidelity. Those with an avoidance orientation dissociate from situations with potentially unpleasant or detrimental outcomes.

In romantic relationships, secret-keeping may be influenced by a person's dominant motivation. Those with an approach style, who are more likely to engage in risky behaviors, tend to have experiences deemed worthy of concealment. In their view, withholding information about relationship-threatening activities may keep conflict to a minimum and offer maximum reward. Given that approach-oriented people are comfortable taking risks, they may also be willing to risk losing the relationship if their thrill-seeking activities are discovered. Those with an avoidant orientation are not likely to engage in precarious behaviors, but they are similarly motivated to conceal information that may negatively impact the relationship. These individuals are more likely to hide perceived character flaws, their personal or relationship history, or anything else with the potential to threaten the partnership.

Shame

Unlike personality, which is at least partly based in biology, shame is learned through socialization. Shame emerges from a discipline method that condemns a child's character rather than addresses specific problem behaviors. Common forms of shaming include using insults and drawing comparisons to other children (e.g., age-based or gender-based expectations). Parents believe shaming is effective because children alter their behavior after it is used. However, shaming is harmful to children, results in low self-esteem, and fails to teach moral reasoning, empathy, or relationship skills. People who have been shamed develop an enduring pattern of secret-keeping as they attempt to avoid negative judgment.

Shamed individuals are attracted to critical partners because they are accustomed to being negatively evaluated. Critical partners reconfirm their undesirable views of self and are therefore perceived as honest. Supportive partners, by contrast, are perceived as undesirable because a shamed person interprets their compassion as insincere and dishonest. Those involved with critical partners are more likely to keep secrets in order to avoid negative appraisals. The shamed person's tendency to withhold information reinforces his or her perception that the material is worth concealing. This pattern of selecting a belittling partner, concealing information to avoid his or her criticism, and then continuing to believe the information is dishonorable results in a cycle of secrecy that is difficult to disrupt.

Attachment Style

Attachment style is another socialized quality that is developed through early socialization with a primary caregiver. Attachment style refers to a global orientation toward relationships. Researchers have identified three distinct styles: secure, anxious-ambivalent (insecure), and avoidant (insecure). People who are raised with responsive, sensitive, and warm care develop a secure style. The parents of securely attached children respond quickly and competently during times of need. People who receive this type of care learn that others can be trusted and relied on. The securely attached tend not to keep secrets from romantic partners because they expect to receive support. If a partner does not respond as expected, a secure individual will likely express his or her concerns and expect improvement. If a partner continues to be unsupportive, secure individuals will generally terminate the relationship in favor of a more satisfying union.

Individuals with an anxious-ambivalent (insecure) style received inconsistent or inadequate care as children. Sometimes their caregivers responded to their needs, and other times they did not, or if caregivers provided reliable attention, the quality of support was poor. As a result, those with an anxious-ambivalent style learn that others are intermittently available for need fulfillment. These individuals strongly desire closeness yet are uncomfortable depending on others; they constantly fear abandonment. People with this style are more likely than those with a secure style to keep secrets from a partner. They worry about disclosing information that may cause a partner to leave and use secret-keeping as a way to maintain the relationship.

The second type of insecure attachment is avoidant. People develop this style when their caregivers are neglectful, harsh, or absent. These children learn that people cannot be relied upon for need fulfillment. Accordingly, they begin to meet their own needs and depend on no one but themselves. They feel uncomfortable with closeness and may avoid intimate relationships altogether. In terms of secrets, they are unlikely to disclose information to others because they have difficulty establishing trust. Although they can trust themselves, they are unsure about the dependability of others.

Relationship Dynamics

Relationship dynamics differ from the previously reviewed motivations for secret-keeping in that they pertain to qualities of the relationship, rather than the individual. A person may not necessarily be prone to secret-keeping upon entering a union for intrapersonal reasons, but qualities of the partnership may elicit concealment. Given that shame and attachment styles are learned, unhealthy adult relationships may elicit shame or cause a person to switch from a secure to insecure attachment style. In such cases, an individual may begin concealing information to avoid negative evaluations. Other relationship qualities, such as high conflict or low intimacy, may also lead to secret-keeping. In the former case, concealment may be used to avoid greater conflict, and in the latter, partners may have grown apart and feel uncomfortable sharing information with each other.

Outcomes of Secret-Keeping

Secret-keeping is associated with intrapersonal and interpersonal problems. First, the keeper must actively suppress thoughts in order to ensure concealment, which causes preoccupation with the information. The heightened psychological stress negatively impacts health and can lead to hypertension, ulcers, headaches, and depression. The keeper may also build resentment toward the partner for having to regularly monitor his or her thoughts and behaviors. At the same time, the partner may notice a difference in the keeper's behavior and become suspicious. When a secret is discovered, the partner may question the keeper's reason(s) for withholding information as well as the keeper's commitment to the relationship. The partner may then distance himself or herself from the relationship and develop feelings of sadness, anger, insecurity, and betrayal.

In addition to intrapersonal outcomes, secrets have deleterious effects on the relationship. The interpersonal consequences of secret-keeping tend to vary based on the perceived severity of the information withheld. The most serious secrets generally relate to infidelity. Secrets typically lead to greater relational conflict and adversely affect levels of trust and satisfaction. The number of secrets in a relationship is inversely related to couple satisfaction. That is, the more secrets partners keep, the greater their unhappiness within the relationship. One exception is when partners have both agreed to avoid particular topics in order to protect the relationship. As noted earlier, this practice is generally associated with positive outcomes.

Kelly Campbell

See also Attachment; Extramarital Affairs and Infidelity; Family of Origin; Intimacy, Specific Threats to; Trust

Further Readings

Affifi, W. (2010). Uncertainty and information management in interpersonal relationships. In S. Smith & S. Wilson (Eds.), *New directions in interpersonal communication research* (pp. 94–114). Thousand Oaks, CA: Sage.

Carver, C. S., & White, T. L. (1994). Behavioral inhibition, behavioral activation, and affective responses to impending reward and punishment: The BIS/BAS scales. *Journal of Personality and Social Psychology, 67*(2), 319–333. doi:10.1037/0022-3514.67.2.319

Caughlin, J. P., Afifi, W. A., Carpenter-Theune, K. E., & Miller, L. E. (2005). Reasons for, and consequences of, revealing personal secrets in close relationships: A longitudinal study. *Personal Relationships, 12,* 43–59.

Mikulincer, M., Shaver, P. R., & Pereg, D. (2003). Attachment theory and affect regulation: The dynamics, development, and cognitive consequences of attachment-related strategies. *Motivation and Emotion 27,* 77–102.

Uysal, A., Lin, H. L., & Bush, A. L. (2012). The reciprocal cycle of self-concealment and trust in romantic relationships. *European Journal of Social Psychology, 42,* 844–851.

SELF OF THE THERAPIST

It is generally recognized and understood that the therapist, himself or herself, influences the process of therapy, and the personality, beliefs, and charisma of the therapist can be a tool in the therapeutic process. The therapist is the medium through which the theories, methods, and interventions of psychotherapy are filtered, expressed, and delivered to clients. It represents the marriage of the technical with the unique experiences of the individual, including his or her culture, gender, social class, personal values, emotional struggles, and spirituality. The purpose of this entry is to provide a history of the self of the therapist in the helping professions, obstacles to developing the self of therapists, and current strategies for developing therapists' use of self.

The Role of the Self

There is a growing sense in the helping professions that the self of the therapist can be both an asset and a liability. One's personal experiences can be an asset when one has successfully navigated through life experiences such as childhood trauma, serious illness, divorce, or the death of a loved one. Perhaps no other profession makes use of the self more extensively than psychotherapy, because it is the relationship itself that heals, and it is impossible to not make use of one's self when interacting with others. Indeed, psychotherapy outcome research in recent years has confirmed that the therapeutic relationship has more influence on therapeutic outcomes than theoretical orientation or technique. The self of the therapist is also critical to training and developing therapists because without awareness of what one brings to the therapeutic process and relationship, one cannot take responsibility for it, and it may become a liability.

To meet the demands of caring for the psychological needs of others, it is critical for therapists to actively care for themselves and to practice competently and ethically. Those who stray from sound practice often do so because they get lost in their own issues, stresses, relationship problems, and unwillingness to sit in the client's chair. All of these factors make them vulnerable to exercising flawed judgments and making poor decisions that can result in harm to clients or themselves.

Historical Background

Pioneering psychoanalyst Sigmund Freud's view of human nature led him to acknowledge the danger of analysts harming patients with their own issues, so he emphasized protecting patients by requiring analysts in training to undergo extensive analysis themselves to address their own issues. He also required therapists to sit out of view of the patient so that the patient would not be unduly influenced by the persona of the therapist. This concern of unduly influencing the patient with the analyst's personality led to an emphasis on maintaining neutrality and maintaining personal distance from patients and not revealing themselves lest they violate the neutrality principle. By contrast, psychologist Carl Rogers focused on creating a warm relationship between therapist and clients. He was the first to shift the terminology from patient to client, and he concentrated much more on the person of the client as the focus of the treatment rather than the analyst's interpretations and role as expert.

The family therapy movement began in the 1960s in reaction to the prevailing treatment models that focused on the individual and gave short shrift to relational, contextual, systemic, and cultural influences on the individual. Cybernetics and systems theory (theories used to explain the interactions between parts of a system and the system as a whole) were the original catalysts, and these models were developed to give the fledgling field scientific and academic validity. From these influences, family models such as the Mental Research Institute's brief therapy, Salvador Minuchin's structural family therapy, and the Milan school model developed.

Perhaps as a reaction, in part, to the objective emphasis on cybernetics and general systems theory, the experiential models of Virginia Satir and Carl Whitaker and the transgenerational approach of Murray Bowen emerged. These models emphasized subjective approaches, such as accessing unexpressed feelings, authentic communication, total joining of the therapist with the family, and giving family members a new and different experience of relating to one another, over the objective emphasis on theoretical constructs.

Satir emphasized the value of becoming a more integrated self to make a more positive personal impact on couples and families in treatment. To facilitate the use of the self, Satir engaged in psychodrama exercises that helped clients explore their families of origin so they could face and resolve their own family issues. Whitaker promoted the idea that therapists should access and use themselves with families and to do so encouraged them to explore and understand their own thoughts. Bowen emphasized listening and observing the family at least partly outside the emotional field of the family to avoid getting triggered by the family's dynamics and to model healthy individuation.

Minuchin practiced structural family therapy, a very active form of family therapy that embraced the person of the therapist, one's personality, and how one relates to the family of origin as integral to the success of the therapeutic interaction with families. He staged conversations between family members called "enactments," which brought entrenched emotional patterns immediately to life. He was masterful in the use of self with families, which he called "the central tool." Most of these early family therapy pioneers underscored the premise that self-exploration and positive growth in the self of the therapist led to a more competent therapist, and that the growth and development of the therapist can limit his or her effectiveness. This is all in the spirit that a therapist cannot take a family any further on a journey of growth than that therapist has personally traveled.

Obstacles to Developing the Self of the Therapist

While traditionally mental health was viewed as treating the whole person, the advent of managed care has focused attention on symptoms that can be systematically categorized and diagnosed, and the amelioration of symptoms using evidence-based treatments. This has placed heavy emphasis on expediency and efficiency with assessment, treatment planning, and intervention and less emphasis on treating the client as a whole person with spiritual, physical, emotional, and psychological needs that can't be reduced to a set of measurable symptoms.

Another challenge to the continued focus on the self of the therapist is related to the subjective nature of the self. Scientific inquiry is by its nature reductionistic, and the influence of the therapist's self on the self of the client is fraught with ambiguity and uncertainty. Science searches for clear linkages between cause and effect that can be isolated and re-created when the self is by its nature both ambiguous and imprecise.

Perhaps the biggest barrier to attending to the self of the therapist is self-imposed. If the effectiveness of the therapeutic process is contingent upon the relationship between the therapist and the client, this means that the therapist must fully embrace his or her own brokenness, imperfection, and limitations. It is only through being deeply attuned to one's inner self that the therapist can listen with both mind and heart and therefore attune to the client's experience with both wisdom and compassion, unencumbered by distortions caused by unresolved conflicts in the therapist's past.

Training Therapists to Develop the Self

Already burdened with meeting the professional training standards of their respective state licensing boards and national professional accreditation standards, few graduate training programs have emphasized the training of the self. This implies that it is only the client who needs to be open and vulnerable in the therapy process. Another challenge of training students in the use of self is that it requires substantial time, the use of experiential teaching methods, and outcomes that are difficult to measure and standardize.

The Therapist Use-of-Self Orientations Questionnaire (TUSO-Q) has been developed to help counselors-in-training and their supervisors clarify their use-of-self orientation. Researchers identified three styles with distinctive therapist–client boundaries. In the transpersonal orientation, the boundary between the therapist and client becomes more permeable and in some cases disappears altogether, since the emphasis is on the therapist becoming so empathically connected to the client that he or she can live the client's experience, not just know it. The recent emphasis on mindfulness and spirituality is evidence of this growing movement.

In the contextual orientation, social systems and processes such as sexism, racism, and classism that lie beyond the individual and family are the lens through which the client's experiences are understood. Often, these oppressive systems and practices are challenged as part of the treatment planning. The contextual orientation focuses attention on social justice, advocacy for marginalized voices, and challenging institutionalized oppression.

The instrumental orientation views clients as having deficits that need to be remediated and therapy as largely an attempt to reduce the role of these deficits by replacing them with skills imparted by the therapist through skills training. The boundary is most clear in this orientation as the therapist takes responsibility for clarifying the problem and formulating an appropriate intervention. This orientation is manifest in the practice of evidence-based or manualized treatments and in a focus on therapist competencies. The TUSO-Q can be used to assess the degree of alignment with each of the three orientations to raise self-awareness about one's theory of change, to assess how well matched a given therapist is with the training program's goals and philosophy, and to measure shifts in self-of-therapist orientation as the trainee gains new experiences.

Person-of-the-Therapist Training Model (POTT)

Drexel University's Couple and Family Therapy Department developed a course on Harry Aponte's person-of-the-therapist training model (POTT) for students in their master's program. The program encourages trainees to not only become aware of their race, gender, culture, values, life experience, and personal struggles and vulnerabilities, but to put this self-knowledge to work with clients as well. The model emphasizes the full person or self of therapists and their frailties. It is through identifying and transforming these frailties and vulnerabilities that effective therapists engage their clients in the change process most powerfully.

The POTT model is grounded in the notion of the "wounded healer" by Henri Nouwen, who asserted that woundedness is fundamental to human nature and that it can serve as a source of strength and healing when counseling others. Aponte believes that rather than being a liability, one's flawed humanity empowers therapists to understand and deeply attune with clients and their personal struggles. It is through their shared humanity that therapists can relate to and connect with clients, however different they may be with regard to gender, ethnicity, social class, educational level, or spiritually. It is because of the therapist's own encounters with the challenges of life that he or she has the insight it takes to face problems, address them, overcome them, and to grow and change in the process.

The POTT model assumes that by helping trainees identify their signature themes, such as fear of vulnerability, distrust of others, and fear of abandonment, they will not only increase personal awareness of their frailties and flaws, but also learn how to use them purposefully in their therapeutic interactions with clients. The POTT training model embraces three goals: first, therapists must know their own history of personal challenges as well as their current status with resolving these life themes; second, they must be able to self-observe, monitor, and exercise judgment with the memories, emotions, and behaviors that get triggered in the heat of a therapeutic relationship with clients; and third, they must subdue the psychological, cultural, and spiritual forces operating in them and focus on being helpful to the client.

The last goal points to the ability to use one's past experiences and the emotions they stir up to remain joined with the client and at the same time differentiate from the client's emotional experience. This means being so familiar and accepting of their own psychological journey that they are able to track clients' journeys while consciously connecting to their own journey; they do not embroil themselves in their client's emotional rumblings to the point that they lose the perspective needed to see and help clients address and change their perceived reality while relying on the therapist's emotional support.

A qualitative study of 54 marriage and family therapy students completing a 9-month POTT course revealed six dominant themes that were congruent with the training goals, including increased self-awareness, greater ease with their emotions, improved clinical work and clinical identity, deeper acceptance of their humanity and woundedness, greater ability to observe themselves, and a greater sense of how their personal themes influenced their clinical work. While limited, preliminary research suggests that graduate training programs can help their students to identify, accept, and use their core personal struggles or themes, and this process can have positive benefits on students' professional development. Further studies are needed to determine if POTT-trained therapists produce bigger effects on clinical outcomes for clients than therapy delivered by therapists without POTT training. It would also be useful to assess students before and after POTT training to examine how this training impacts their clinical skill development and self-awareness over a period of time. Direct observations of therapy sessions by supervisors after POTT and comparing participants to a group that does not receive self-of-therapist training would be ideal.

Thomas K. Burdenski

See also Attunement, Clinician; Boundaries; Common Factors; Life Balance; Therapists' Values; Therapeutic Alliance

Further Readings

Anderson, S. A., Sanderson, J., & Kosutic, I. (2011). Therapist Use-of-Self Questionnaire: A reliability and validity study. *Contemporary Family Therapy, 33,* 364–383.

Aponte, H. J. (2016). *The person of the therapist training model: Mastering the use of self.* New York: Routledge.

Aponte, H. J., & Kissil, K. (2014). "If I can grapple with this I can truly be of use in the therapy room": Using the therapist's own emotional struggles to facilitate effective therapy. *Journal of Marital and Family Therapy, 40,* 152–164.

Aponte, H. J., Powell, F. D., Brooks, S., Watson, M. F., Litzke, C., Lawless, J., et al. (2009). Training the person of the therapist in an academic setting. *Journal of Marital and Family Therapy, 35,* 381–394.

Baldwin, M. (Ed.). (2013). *The use of self in therapy* (3rd ed.). New York: Routledge.

Bean, R. A., Davis, S. D., & Davey, M. P. (Eds.). (2014). *Clinical supervision activities for increasing competence and self-awareness.* New York: Wiley.

Minuchin, S., Reiter, M., & Borda, C. (2013). *The craft of family therapy: Challenging certainties.* New York: Routledge.

Nouwen, H. J. M. (1979). *The wounded healer: Ministry in contemporary society.* New York: Doubleday.

Timm, T. M., & Blow, A. J. (1999). Self-of-the-therapist work: A balance between removing restraints and identifying resources. *Contemporary Family Therapy, 21,* 331–350.

SELF-CARE PRACTICES FOR THE TRAUMA-INFORMED COUPLE AND FAMILY COUNSELOR

Professional codes of ethics for clinicians require that clinicians monitor themselves for signs of impairment in their physical, emotional, and mental health that may impact services to clients. Monitoring for impairment and self-care are especially important when people are working with client trauma. Self-care means being aware of one's own needs (e.g., physical, physiological, relational, emotional, mental, and spiritual) and taking action to appropriately fulfill those needs in good timing, such that others are not negatively impacted by one's own needs. Trauma-informed couple and family therapists are practitioners who view human suffering through the lens of unresolved trauma. Trauma has been described by Peter Levine as the body's natural response to an overwhelming situation. All counselors should be aware of self-care, but it is especially important for those working with couples and families who have experienced trauma. The counselor is hearing and managing multiple stories and experiences, and managing interactions between distressed clients. In this entry the basics of self-care, trauma-informed couple and family counselors, and different kinds of trauma are discussed.

Self-Care

Self-care practices keep one physically and emotionally regulated, or in homeostasis, so that one may apply attention to the task at hand without being unduly distracted by sensation, feeling, or thought. Self-care practices for therapists include an ongoing psychospiritual embodiment practice (movement that organizes mind-body-spirit toward a sense of well-being), healthy diet and avoidance of substance abuse, healthy personal relationships, healthy emotional boundaries, maintenance of personal interests and hobbies, and personal therapy to proactively address emotional needs with a healthy role model. When employed regularly, self-care practices help the practitioner maintain emotional resilience to daily stressors, and preserve joy and gratitude across the life span. One who engages in this approach may experience acute pain, but not hurt others with their own suffering, by paying intense attention to the sensations, feelings, and thoughts the pain evokes.

Trauma

Traumatology literature outlines how trauma impacts the developing and mature nervous system and brain, mental processes, defense mechanisms, relational capacity, and self-regulation capacity. Earlier and more egregious traumas overwhelm a developing individual more than later and less intense traumas; those with early unresolved trauma are more susceptible to subsequent trauma and more likely to develop posttraumatic stress disorder, personality disorders, and less acute, yet still pervasive, reduced quality of life due to impact of trauma symptoms. Trauma-informed couple and family therapists require an understanding of the effects of Judith Herman's type 1 trauma—unpredictable, single incident shock trauma (i.e., car accidents and dog bites) and type 2 trauma—predictable yet unavoidable (more pervasive) shock trauma (i.e., attachment disruptions between child and caregiver; in-utero substance exposure; verbal, emotional, physical, and sexual abuse; domestic violence; oppression; racism; gang violence; and war conflict).

Traumatology literature suggests that trauma is a universal human experience, though the degree of exposure varies widely between individuals, families, and cultures. Due to its universal nature, mental health practitioners are understood to often have their own *primary traumatic stress*, or personal experience with trauma that requires resolution through physiological discharge of "overwhelm" from the nervous system and emotional forgiveness of pain. Practitioners who resolve their primary traumatic stress reduce their risk of *secondary traumatic stress,* or activation of personal wounds through empathic identification with clients' similar wounds.

Self-Care and Couple and Family Therapists

Couple and family therapists must regularly employ self-care, because they must be able to self-soothe and self-regulate much more effectively than practitioners who focus on individuals, due to the exponentially complex emotional regulation demands of managing stressful interactional patterns of relationships between distressed members and their alliances with the clinician. This requires that therapists discharge distress and resolve stored emotions on a regular basis, especially those that may get activated by the distress of clients. Such real-time self-regulation is possible only when practitioners are committed to ongoing self-care practices throughout their careers.

Clinicians who manage sessions wherein multiple people comprise the identified client are called upon to down-regulate their autonomic nervous system more efficiently during stressful interactions in order to maintain a safe therapeutic container for all parties, and model effective stress management for functional problem-solving and conflict resolution. The ease of validating, normalizing, and empathizing with a single individual in session while supporting that individual's treatment plan is not sufficient experience or training to facilitate the greater demands of working with multiple distressed people acting to get their needs met through strategies that are often in conflict. Effective self-regulation is even more critical when working with clients' trauma history and when aiming to resolve trauma within couples and among families. Clients with unresolved trauma will naturally enact their distress in subsequent relationships, looking to resolve their overwhelming emotions; trauma-informed couple and family therapists recognize their role in facilitating the attunement necessary to discharge overwhelming emotions and foster emotional regulation between client members.

Compassion Fatigue

Compassion fatigue literature acknowledges that the clinician's own primary traumatic stress, if not resolved sufficiently, is likely to be activated by the secondary traumatic stress of working to resolve client trauma. As emphasized in a growing body of traumatology literature that seeks to understand how broad and pervasive developmental and relational trauma tends to be in clinical populations, clinicians are advised to proactively integrate a holistic self-care plan for primary trauma resolution in order to reduce their risk of experiencing secondary traumatic stress in their efforts to resolve client trauma in couples and families. When trauma is present and there are multiple people in session, the attentional demands on the clinician leave them at greater risk for becoming overwhelmed and dysregulated. Left unaddressed, this pattern leads to burnout and compassion fatigue, which is a harm to the clinician and clients.

Vicarious Trauma

Vicarious trauma, also known as secondary trauma or trauma exposure response, appears to be a leading cause of counselor burnout and compassion fatigue. The risks for vicarious trauma are highest among practitioners with the least training in trauma resolution and the least follow-through on self-care practices. Some indicators of the unresolved trauma exposure response are feeling helpless and hopeless, a sense one can never do enough, hypervigilance, diminished creativity, inability to embrace complexity, minimizing, chronic exhaustion, somatic complaints, inability to listen, dissociative moments, sense of persecution, guilt, fear, anger and cynicism, inability to empathize/numbing, addictions, and grandiosity. Any subset of these concerns could result in counselor impairment, and thus, they merit an organized plan for protection of client and counselor.

Trauma Resolution

Essential common factors derived from various trauma resolution techniques can be integrated into current counseling practices by most counselors with appropriate supervision; this in turn improves client outcomes and quality of life, as well as reduces relapse rates for many presenting problems, while increasing counselor protection from the work-related hazard of vicarious trauma. A beginning list of common factors in trauma includes

- the universal nature of overwhelm unexpectedly occurring throughout our development and often at the hands of those we count on for caregiving;
- the unjust fact of trauma occurring more in systematic oppression of marginalized populations;
- the body-based experience of trauma impacting brain and emotional development and functioning, especially when left unresolved;
- the depletion of positive affect and felt safety in relationships;
- the specific impact of relational trauma, which is more difficult to resolve due to the broken trust that relational trauma invariably brings about (notably, this means that counselors must be trauma-trained in order to do no further harm and increase the efficacy of the treatment).

A beginning list of common factors in trauma resolution counseling for couples and families may include

- skillfully assessing and accessing client-specific capacity for recovery and resilience in response to overwhelming trauma via trust-based therapeutic rapport;
- awareness of the neurodevelopmental impacts of in-utero and early childhood trauma;
- leveraging interpersonal neurobiology to coregulate the clients' nervous systems through left-eye to left-eye contact;
- following the clients' pacing unless the clients accelerate into distress, which is retraumatizing;
- slowing the clients and session down when trauma is being processed;
- referencing the clients' bodies as a resource for soothing, regulating, and discharging overwhelm as part of the corrective emotional experience;
- following the bodies' cues for discharge of stored survival energy as evidenced by trembling, especially in the legs as the fight/flight/freeze response is released from the body;
- following the bodies' cues for discharge of emotional overwhelm as evidenced by patterns in movement (e.g., protective and defensive postures, attempts to regain balance and control, changes in breath; micorexpressions of shock, terror);
- reducing verbal processing to minimum, concrete, here-and-now awareness, talking "through" pain, not "about" pain;
- the value of accurate empathy and normalization in supporting the bodies' natural discharge of overwhelm.

Trauma Versus Resolution Models

Some trauma resolution models for couple and family therapists in practice today include accelerated experiential-dynamic psychotherapy, accelerated recovery program, acceptance and commitment therapy, dialectical behavior therapy, emotion-focused therapy; eye movement desensitization and reprogramming, Hakomi, mindfulness-based stress reduction, the neuroaffective relational model, neurogenic yoga, the neurosequential model of therapeutics, occupational therapy, sensory awareness, somatic experiencing, Theraplay, trauma-focused cognitive-behavioral therapy, and trauma releasing exercises. Given the variance in evidence collected to date on this short list, counselors are encouraged to obtain training and supervision while expanding their scope of competence. Overeager application of a technique without proper theoretical understanding and skills integration can do more harm than good.

Concerns About the Effects of Trauma on Clinicians

Compassion fatigue and limited reflexive self-awareness and preventive self-care are evident in many mental health agency settings and in practitioners. Such tendencies may occur in part because counselor education does not sufficiently prepare and train students for the number and variety of traumas they will encounter in their clients over the course of their careers. In addition, clinical supervision training does not adequately prepare supervisors to empathically and ethically monitor their supervisees with regard to trauma resolution.

In an age of managed care, when high caseloads and mass trauma affect so many communities, it is important for therapists to organize to take care of those who aim to take care of others and be embodied role models for the clients they serve. This is particularly pressing when entering into distressed client relationships as agents of change, and thereby becoming responsible for embodying a healing presence in order to resolve relational trauma. Trauma-informed couple and family therapists practice holistic self-care for the benefit of all concerned and therefore appreciate the "righteousness of selfishness," regularly emptying themselves of that which is not for their highest good and filling themselves with ease, peace, contentment, and joy, manifested in a regulated nervous system.

Karen Roller

See also Self of the Therapist; Therapists' Values; Trauma and Children; Trauma and Families

Further Readings

Aronson, E., & Pines, A. (1988). *Career burnout: Causes and cures*. New York: Free Press.

Ayala, K., & Groves, T. (2015). Implementing the neurosequential model of therapeutics. *Foster Family-Based Treatment Association, 21*(2), 1–4.

Baker, W., Blakely, T., Perry, B., Pollard, R., & Vigilante, D. (1995). Childhood trauma, the neurobiology of adaptation and "use-dependent" development of the brain: How "states" become "traits." *Infant Mental Health Journal, 16* (4), 271–291.

Bates, M., Brown, D., Money, N., & Moore, M. (2011). *Mind-body skills for regulating the autonomic nervous system, Version 2*. Arlington, VA: Defense Centers of Excellence for Psychological Health and Traumatic Brain Injury.

Belcher, H., Hunt, K., & Martens, P. (2011). Risky business: Trauma exposure and rate of posttraumatic stress disorder in African American children and adolescents. *Journal of Traumatic Stress, (24)*3, 365–369.

Berceli, D. (2008). *Transcend your toughest times*. Berkeley, CA: Namaste Publishing.

Briere, J., & Scott, C. (2012). *Principles of trauma therapy: A guide to symptoms, evaluation, and treatment* (2nd ed.). Thousand Oaks, CA: Sage.

Briere, J., Follette, V. M., Hopper, J. W., Rome, D. I., & Rozelle, D. (Eds.). (2015). *Mindfulness-oriented interventions for trauma*. New York: Guilford.

Burk, C., & van Dernoot-Lipsky, L. (2009). *Trauma stewardship*. San Francisco, CA: Berrett-Koehler.

Dobson, C., & Perry, B. D. (2010). The role of healthy relational interactions in buffering the impact of childhood trauma. In E. Gil (Ed.), *Working with children to heal interpersonal trauma: The power of play* (pp. 26–43). New York: Guilford Press.

Figley, C. R. (1993). Compassion fatigue and social work practice: Distinguishing burnout from secondary traumatic stress. *Newsletter of the NASW Florida Chapter*, June, 1–2.

Figley, C. R. (Ed.). (1995). *Compassion fatigue: Coping with secondary traumatic stress disorder in those who treat the traumatized*. New York: Brunner/Mazel.

MacFarlane, A. C., van der Kolk, B. A., Weisaeth, L. (Eds.). (1996). *Traumatic stress: The effects of overwhelming experience on mind, body, and society*. New York: Guilford Press.

Panos, A. (2007). *Promoting resiliency in trauma workers*. Poster presented at the 9th World Congress on Stress, Trauma, and Coping, Baltimore, MD.

Perry, B. D. (1999). Bonding and attachment in maltreated children: Consequences of emotional neglect in childhood. *CTA Parent and Caregiver Education Series, (1)*3. Retrieved from https://childtrauma.org/wp-content/uploads/2014/01/Bonding-and-Attachment.pdf

Perry, B. D. (2014). The cost of caring: Understanding and preventing secondary traumatic stress when working with traumatized and maltreated children. *CTA Parent and Caregiver Education Series, (2)*7. Retrieved from https://childtrauma.org/wp-content/uploads/2014/01/Cost_of_Caring_Secondary_Traumatic_Stress_Perry_s.pdf

Schnur, S., & Sori, C. F. (2013). Integrating a neurosequential approach in the treatment of traumatized children: An interview with Eliana Gil, Part II. *Family Journal: Counseling and Therapy for Couples and Families, 22*(2), 251–257. doi:10.1177/1066480713514945

Siegel, D. J., & Solomon, M. (2003). *Healing trauma*. New York: W. W. Norton.

Self-Esteem

Many people would describe self-esteem simply as the way one feels about oneself. Although this is a core definition, self-esteem is much more complex and multifaceted. It includes having a positive self-regard, a sense of dignity (self-respect), and a concern for self. Self-esteem is a summative or global evaluation of self. It is these personal opinions or appraisals that shape self-identity and self-worth (e.g., who a person is, what a person is). There are numerous influences on self-esteem. However, life experiences as well as family (e.g., spouse, parents, siblings) are fundamental in helping to shape one's self-esteem. Experienced marriage and couples counselors have a keen understanding of this psychological construct and are aware of the role of self-esteem throughout the life span and in treatment. This entry defines self-esteem, outlines prominent theories on self-esteem, and discusses the influence of family on self-esteem. Finally, self-esteem in dating and self-esteem in treatment are addressed.

Definition of Self-Esteem

Self-esteem is a psychological construct that includes the personal and emotional judgments one makes about self. However, it is not absolute; self-esteem exists on a continuum from poor to grandiose. Thus, self-esteem can change throughout one's life. A young adult who is exploring, asserting, and growing in self-identity may have a flourishing self-esteem, whereas an elderly adult who is losing control over physical and mental faculties as well as experiencing perpetual grief from loss of loved ones, employment, and financial resources may falter in self-esteem. However, low self-esteem is different from feeling low (e.g., discouraged, sad, grief-stricken). Self-esteem is grounded in liking self, self-acceptance, and one's internal dialogues.

It is not unusual for one's self-esteem to embody perceptions that do not match reality. Grandiosity is described as exaggerated, distorted, or grossly inflated perceptions of self. High self-esteem might include self-acceptance and realistic perceptions of a person's worth, abilities, and accomplishments. Although separate constructs, terms such as *self-worth, self-respect,* and *self-image* are often mistakenly used interchangeably for self-esteem.

Self-esteem plays a large role in a person's professional and personal attitude. It has been positively correlated to numerous social skills essential for adaptation, healthy coping, and effective decision-making. A person's ability to take risks, chase dreams, and improve his or her life's circumstances rather than remaining stagnated or feeling unfulfilled are all motivated by self-esteem. Professional and interpersonal life choices are predicated on feeling worthy, capable, hopeful, and self-assured. Self-esteem is also an essential factor in daily functioning. How individuals feel about themselves might determine the level of their confidence to approach a love interest or their motivation to apply for a promotion. The way a person responds to people, places, and events stems from feelings of self. Thus, self-esteem affects how an individual interacts at work, school, home, in public, and with others.

Self-esteem is a key feature in success or failure. Feeling worthy and capable is deeply embedded in high or positive self-esteem. When people feel good about themselves, they are more likely to guard against danger. By contrast, low or no self-esteem, whether based on accurate or distorted perceptions of self, is the root of feelings such as worthlessness, inferiority, insecurity, and self-hatred. Having nominal self-esteem might render someone socially and emotionally paralyzed with feelings of inadequacy and self-doubt. In addition to social and emotional ramifications, low self-esteem can be clinically profound and even dangerous. For instance, persistent emotional states such as feeling empty, lost (e.g., lacking identity, fulfillment, and/or direction), desperate, despairing, or inadequate may fuel mental health issues such as depression, anxiety, fear of intimacy, inferiority complexes, suicidal thoughts, substance abuse, and reckless or risk-taking behaviors.

By no means does having high or low self-esteem determine whether a person is good or bad. Similarly, having high self-esteem does not preclude a person from committing a crime, being abused, or using illegal drugs. However, cognitive-behavioral therapists assert that thinking affects emotions, which ultimately affect behavior. Thus, the premise is that people who feel weak and vulnerable are more likely to act weak and vulnerable. Although high self-esteem is a worthy goal, it is important to note that overindulging self can be just as damaging as low or no self-esteem.

There is no playbook or universal intervention for growing self-esteem. Largely, self-esteem develops from living consciously, which includes awareness and understanding of self, learning to accept personal realities, everyday experiences that cultivate confidence, and a sense of capability as well as challenges that hone coping skills and teach self-reliance. Because self-esteem is not an innate quality, it can also be fostered through nurture. The concept of nurture implies that a person's environment plays a role in how he or she thinks and feels about himself or herself. So, one's learning history, including subjective experiences, responses from the environment (e.g., compliments, criticisms, consequences), and vicarious learning are factors in self-esteem.

Theories of Self-Esteem

Several prominent theorists have postulated about self-esteem and its impact. Theorist and psychotherapist Nathaniel Branden proposed a framework for conceptualizing self-esteem that included six pillars: self-responsibility, self-assertiveness, self-acceptance, living consciously or practicing mindfulness, personal integrity, and living with purpose. According to Branden, having balance among the six pillars resulted in increased levels of positive self-esteem.

There is no shortage of personality theories that seek to explain how people view and define themselves, including those developed by Carl Rogers, Carl Gustav Jung, Karen Horney, Albert Ellis, and others. Theorists have postulated that self-esteem begins in early childhood. According to developmental theorist Erik Erikson, even toddlers (ages 1 to 3) actively seek opportunities to assert themselves and to build a sense of capability during the autonomy versus shame and doubt psychosocial developmental stage. Small children begin to explore their environment and quickly learn that they have control over their behavior. During this developmental stage, children begin to act independently. Parents and caregivers will frequently hear a toddler exclaim, "I can do it. I can do it," as the child attempts or even takes over a task. Mastery of tasks such as using the toilet, pouring cereal into a bowl, hanging a jacket in a cubby, and picking up toys begins to build a sense of self and capability that lay the foundation for how the child feels about self. According to Erikson, when children are restrained or harshly punished, shame and self-doubt grow. The response from the environment (e.g., caregiver, failure) helps to determine how the child feels and perceives self. Small successes, feeling capable, responses from people in their environment (e.g., parents, peers), and experiencing some control over one's domain are the beginnings of self-esteem. In addition to how people tend to reward or punish themselves (e.g., worrying, irrational thinking, positive or negative self-talk), it is fair to say that self-esteem can also be shaped by the responses adults and children receive from people and the environment.

Theorist Alfred Adler postulated that small children develop cognitive maps that assist "little me" with coping with the "big world," which fosters a sense of security and individual convictions. These convictions are divided into four categories: (1) convictions about who a person is (self-concept), (2) convictions about who an individual should be (self-ideal), (3) convictions about the world and its demands, and (4) convictions about what is right or wrong. According to Adler, when there is a discrepancy between actual self and ideal self, feelings of inferiority build. Congruency between convictions about self (e.g., actual, ideal) can promote healthy self-esteem.

According to Virginia Satir's family therapy model, self-esteem is one of the most fundamental functions of families. Satir describes a healthy family as one in which members can ask for what they need, individual needs are met, and individuality is allowed to grow. By contrast, dysfunctional families do not permit individuality, and their members lack a sense of self-worth. Members of healthy families respond to each other in ways that foster and build each other's self-esteem. Satir further asserts that self-esteem can affect familial communication and coping skills. Low self-esteem can cause people to respond to family members in unhealthy and maladaptive ways. For instance, a person with low self-esteem might cope with interpersonal conflict by communicating dysfunction (e.g., "I will do anything to please you, just please don't leave me."). However, a person with high self-esteem might communicate from a more stable sense of self and convey a message that his or her emotional survival is not contingent upon the relationship. Satir also suggests that people with low self-esteem tend to marry and create an environment with generational consequences; Satir asserts that parents with low self-esteem are more likely to rear children who struggle with low self-esteem.

The Effects of Family on Self-Esteem

Although the full range of influences on self-esteem cannot be covered here, self-esteem is shaped by the responses one receives from people (e.g., compliments, criticism) and from the environment (e.g., microsystem, macrosystem). However, the largest imprints on self-esteem come from the core people in a person's life including parents, siblings, spouses, and children. Parents are children's first teachers. In addition to changing diapers and preparing bottles, parents lay the initial groundwork for how a person perceives himself or herself. Through parenting, a person receives messages about whether he or she is valued, worthy, lovable, and capable. These interactions begin to shape the way a person feels and thinks about self. For example, parenting that is harsh, critical, or belittling might sow a seed of self-doubt. An overindulgent parent can hinder the growth of positive self-esteem in a child by not fostering confidence, autonomy, or a sense of capability. A child who fails to thrive because affection or basic needs are often neglected might learn that he or she is not significant. The opposite is also likely true. Parents who sow seeds of love, nurturance, and acceptance can help build the foundation children need for self-love, self-acceptance, and self-esteem.

A family's ability to maintain healthy functioning can facilitate resiliency factors in children, including fostering healthy self-esteem, while familial dysfunction has an adverse impact on a child's self-esteem. Financial strains, marital discord, domestic violence, and the presence of a chronic physical, mental health, or substance abuse disorder can create risk factors that ultimately strain parent–child relationships. Specifically, children have a tendency to internalize expressions of negative emotions. Thus, a caregiver's stress, frustrations, depression, and anxieties are reflected in the psychological development of the child.

Around age 12, children confront competing roles and beliefs as they face the challenges of adolescence, including those involved with sex, romance, and education. During this developmental stage, peers overtake parents as the most influential forces in young lives. Friendships, or the lack of friendships, contribute to and help define a person's sense of self. Henceforward, peers, including siblings, friends, and colleagues, are defining factors in self-esteem.

Although the parent–child relationship actively contributes to the growth and maintenance of self-esteem throughout the life span, other family members, such as siblings, aunts, uncles, cousins, grandparents, and extended relatives, also play a role in the development of self-esteem. However, the nature and extent of these relationships can vary significantly from person to person. As with the parent–child relationship, siblings represent yet another enduring relationship with lasting imprints on one's self-esteem. Sibling relationships provide an opportunity for individuals to explore and experience their sense of self through the unique love, warmth, guidance, conflict, and rivalry that exists within those relationships. With siblings, a person gains experience with acceptance as well as with socialization. Thus, siblings contribute to a person's concept of self through experiential as well as social observational learning. Because of their availability and close proximity, siblings offer an individual numerous opportunities to practice social skills and form comparisons. Sibling rivalry and comparisons can cause negative feelings that undermine confidence and a positive sense of self. Undoubtedly, the quality of the sibling relationship can determine a sibling's influence on one's self-esteem. However, high levels of warmth and positive engagement coupled with low levels of conflict and rivalry are more likely to foster positive self-esteem.

Dating and Self-Esteem

Self-esteem is a factor in mate selection. Social psychologists assert that humans are social beings. Relationships (e.g., friendships, dating) reflect how a person likes or defines self. Self-esteem can affect whom a person is attracted to, relationship satisfaction, relationship quality, and interdependence (the degree to which partners are emotionally or economically reliant on and responsible to each other). Some research indicates that people with low self-esteem are more likely to report less satisfaction within relationships. Low self-esteem can fuel damaging and self-defeating relational behaviors such as sabotaging, negativity, self-fulfilling fallacies, and a readiness to feel hurt. Low self-esteem might also drive a tendency to self-protect, avoid true intimacy, and perpetuate conflict. A person with high or positive self-esteem might be drawn to a partner who is complementary or an equal, which can facilitate appreciation, bonding, and the success of a healthy relationship. The influence of either high self-esteem or low self-esteem on mate selection, dating, and relationship sustainability can be complex, reciprocal, and grossly intertwined. Self-esteem is clearly related to relationship outcomes, whether positive or negative.

Self-Esteem in Treatment

Self-esteem can change across one's life depending on multiple external variables such as family, friends, abuse, accomplishments, and one's environment. Without an understanding of the numerous variables (especially the impact of family), marriage and family therapists might underestimate the significance of self-esteem throughout the life span, and the role of self-esteem in family therapy. Experienced marriage and couples counselors are aware of the role of self-esteem in treatment. In counseling, parents and spouses often disclose failures, shortcomings, and personal weaknesses that can evoke feelings of shame, guilt, personal disappointments, and inadequacies. These feelings after disclosures can render the spouse or parent emotionally vulnerable and make a family constellation unstable. The positive regard, authority, and respect for the parent or spouse is in jeopardy. It becomes an essential task of the clinician to facilitate resiliency and the emotional recuperation of the parent or spouse so that self-esteem remains intact during the therapeutic process. A skilled clinician is careful to maintain family solidarity. In addition, skilled clinicians assist family members with adopting an empathetic and forgiving frame of reference.

Tasha Leroyce Banks and Corderro A. Pollard

See also Coping; Decision-Making; Domestic Violence; Parenting; Parenting Styles; Resilience; Respect; Self-Esteem in Children; Self-Injury

Further Readings

Branden, N. (1969). *The psychology of self-esteem.* New York: John Wiley & Sons.

Branden, N. (1987). *How to raise your self-esteem.* New York: Bantam Books.

Branden, N. (1994). *The six pillars of self-esteem.* New York: Bantam Books.

Corsini, R. J., & Wedding, D. (Eds.). (2008). *Current psychotherapies* (8th ed.). Belmont, CA: Thomson Brooks/Cole.

Goldenberg, H., & Goldberg, I. (2013). *Family therapy: An overview* (8th ed.). Belmont, CA: Brooks/Cole.

Haley, J. (1971). *Changing families.* New York: Grune & Stratton.

Horrocks, E., & Betts, L. R. (2014). The role of siblings for children's self-esteem. *Handbook on the psychology of self-esteem.* New York: Nova Science Publishers.

Rasheed, J. M., Rasheed, M. N., & Marley, J. A. (2011). *Family therapy: Models and techniques.* Thousand Oaks, CA: Sage.

Santrock, J. W. (2008). *Life-span development* (11th ed.). New York: McGraw-Hill.

SELF-ESTEEM IN CHILDREN

Self-esteem is a general experience of oneself as being congruent with personal, familial, relational, or cultural values. It is based on a person's own evaluation of and feelings about his or her overall worthiness in a certain sociocultural context. Although the popular notion of self-esteem refers to a single, stable, fixed, and coherent experience, a more complete definition of the concept recognizes that self-esteem is: (a) constituted by one's *average* experience of self in a variety of contexts and therefore represents the integration of multiple ways of being; or (b) associated with one's *specific*, complex, and dominant preferred way of being in the world. For example, a child may feel competent about himself on average in athletic, academic, and relational arenas of life; or a young person may be raised in a religious or collectivistic cultural environment where the one value that matters above everything else is being helpful to others.

Self-esteem is rooted in subjective experiences, and it may or may not match "reality" or fit with others' views, especially in children. A young child may be convinced that he is an incredible swimmer when he barely knows how to dog-paddle. A teenager may feel deeply inadequate even when she is adored by all. Self-esteem encourages people to generally appreciate themselves, trust their skills, forgive themselves for mistakes, and more readily overcome challenges. It provides a foundation for experiences of agency. Family, caregivers, and other significant people in a child's life have a significant impact on development of self-esteem. The following sections summarize the body of literature on the importance of self-esteem, its developmental trajectory throughout childhood, key factors influencing its quality, methods used to enhance its presence, and the limitations of the concept.

Importance of Self-Esteem

In Western cultures, self-esteem or self-worth is considered an essential component of well-being; the more stable the self-esteem, the less likely one will be destabilized by the common ups and downs of life. The growing interest for this concept in the last few decades has led to the creation of a number of legislative task forces organized to research, examine, and foster its development in children in a number of countries, including the United States.

Self-worth is assumed to affect a child's functioning at the cognitive, affective, and relational level. At the cognitive level, children with reasonable self-esteem are more likely to persevere even when tasks are challenging, and have a better outlook on life. They tend to be more engaged in important areas of their lives, such as academic or athletic performances. On an affective level, they feel more in control of their inner experiences and are less likely to succumb to disregulated emotions when facing mistakes or failures. Self-esteem has been found to buffer the effects of anxiety. On a relational level, children with higher self-esteem tend to be more popular, confident, and better equipped to handle peer pressure.

Developmental Perspective

Because of their developing brains, children's experiences of self-esteem, or self-worth, rely at first solely on significant adults' view of them. Most young children (raised in moderately supportive environments) tend to have an overinflated sense of their abilities not necessarily grounded in reality. They will marvel at what their growing bodies can do, saying for example: "Look at me, look how fast I can run! I'm faster than our car!" These self-perceptions tend to be dichotomous with children seeing themselves as either "good" or "bad" at an activity. Between 5 and 10 years old, young people grow increasingly capable of observing their performances in more factual ways, but may struggle in sorting out conflicting images of themselves and finding the vocabulary to describe their experiences. Middle childhood is therefore a time when attributes mentioned by their broader community or discovered through self-observation become slowly incorporated into their self-concept.

As their cognitive abilities rise around adolescence, young people increasingly internalize peers' comments and sociocultural standards such as gender specifications. They become more involved in noticing, describing, comparing, and defining their identity based on the feedback they are given and their own self-critical assessment of their fit with the normative standards privileged in their environment. This is a period where girls, for example, can become increasingly pressured to adhere to dominant and narrow standards of beauty even if it means sacrificing their health. The process of scrutinizing their appearance and comparing it to extreme and idealized body shapes (often not even physically attainable), leaves girls vulnerable to the plight of body image issues and an impoverished sense of worth that is overly dependent on one variable: appearance.

Factors Affecting Self-Esteem in Young People

Research has shown that caregivers' acknowledgments and attitudes have a significant impact on young people's development of self-esteem. When parents or teachers respond in overly critical ways to children's mistakes, or misunderstand behaviors that are developmentally appropriate and personalize them as deficiencies, young people progressively develop a sense of being unworthy or flawed. Common examples of these developmental misunderstandings are adults' problematic perception of boys as being overly excited, hyperactive, or talkative when their energy level is simply average for a child, or parents' lack of knowledge around brain maturation and its related impact on a child's memory.

Children's developing sense of self-worth is vulnerable to significant adults' perception and criticism of them. Young children, in particular, tend to simply accept adults' negative judgments of them without having the mental capacity to question or defend inaccurate conclusions until much later. Common examples of this process include accusing a boy of "not being a very good big brother" because he struggles with sharing toys, a common developmental challenge, or telling a girl that she'll never be good in sports when her physical education performance is hampered by inappropriate shoes or lack of practice. Children grow up internalizing and believing in their lack of abilities, not having the life experience and mental capacity to realize the multiple contributors to the problem.

Methods of Enhancing Self-Esteem

Self-esteem can be enhanced by helping children experience themselves as lovable, worthy, and skilled. Given children's developing frontal lobe and cognitive abilities, they often benefit from adults' help in noticing, understanding, and articulating big-picture aspects of their growing sense of themselves, including aspects of their worthiness. Such a sense of worthiness can be boosted when: (a) a person feels "seen," connected to, and appreciated by significant others such as family members, or important people, such as a teacher, and (b) a person understands accomplishments as being the result of effort and perseverance rather than any fixed qualities (see the "fluid mind-set" research). Since these two factors can lead to an internalized sense of worthiness, they will now be explored in greater detail.

Children see themselves through others' eyes. Throughout most of their childhood, they like to contribute to others' well-being, and take great pride in having pleased their primary caregivers. A child may rejoice in drawing a love note, or making a surprise breakfast for her parent. Being with someone whom they feel deeply values them and accepts them unconditionally is profoundly shaping of people's sense of worthiness, regardless of their age. Bringing forth these meaningful relational experiences and their implications can have a transformative and lasting effect on children's sense of worth since the worthiness is based on lived experience of connections, which are complex and powerful. Of the many schools of therapy and large number of authors who have proposed methods to do this and enhance self-esteem, the work of Michael White stands out because of its unique way of treating clients as competent in their own lives.

Throughout his career, White developed conversational methods to bring forth clients' knowledge, wisdom, and skills, no matter what their problems were, and connect them with their deeply held values in a way that would meaningfully revamp their view of themselves. For example, White would explore a child's connection with a caring neighbor who offered support and comfort at a time when the child's parents were abusive or fighting over a divorce. Beyond what the neighbor contributed to the child, the young client would also be asked why the neighbor chose to spend time with the child, what he or she valued or saw in the child, and what the child's presence contributed to the neighbor's existence. The exploration of the reciprocal contribution to each other's lives would shift the young clients' experience of themselves from one where they were a powerless recipient of help to one where they were also a worthy contributor to others' lives. People don't necessarily see clearly what they contribute to others' lives unless they are invited into this exploration.

Carol Dweck, a psychology professor at Stanford University, has conducted a number of longitudinal studies on the "fixed" rather than "fluid" mind-set and its relationship to self-esteem. She found that the process of praising and complimenting children for "being good" in an activity actually reduced their self-esteem. More specifically, these children tended to develop a fixed mind-set where they believed that a person either had or didn't have an inborn talent. As a result, they took fewer risks and were afraid of making mistakes since this implied that they were not so good after all. These children also asked fewer questions and dropped out of college significantly more often as they believed that their poor performance reflected failure and lack of intelligence. In contrast, children who are brought up to value practice and those appreciated for the effort they invested in learning persevered and studied more when faced with a poor grade or feedback. Their sense of self-worth was higher and less vulnerable since they believed they could accomplish anything given the right amount of practice and effort.

The work of both of these authors contrasts with the common lay process of giving compliments to children struggling with low self-esteem. Compliments often have a limited, if any, therapeutic effect, since they arise out of an external person's evaluation, are typically superficial, and can easily be rejected. In fact, the lower the self-esteem, the greater the likelihood the compliment will be rejected. This is often visible with teenagers who may have a small moment of joy receiving the compliment but will quickly revert to not really believing it. In addition to these limitations, compliments leave young people still dependent on others for evaluating their worth as opposed to developing their own internal compass for such determination.

Limitations of the Construct

The construct of self-esteem and the various instruments to measure it have been heavily criticized. Self-esteem is an elusive and difficult construct to measure accurately. This is in part due to its tendency to fluctuate depending on the relational and sociocultural context in which participants evolve. It is also due to the fact that current psychological measures tend to take a snapshot of a subject's mental state at a specific moment in time. For example, a teenager who feels deeply inadequate could counteract his feelings of unworthiness by engaging in high-risk behaviors giving him the impression of being "cool." Or, a young woman who feels profoundly unlovable may compensate for her painfully low self-esteem by making sure she's always involved in a romantic relationship, which when she does, gives her a temporary sense of worthiness. In both of these examples, the participants may perform well on self-esteem tests during certain periods of their lives even if their experience of worthiness is fragile and contingent on external factors. Self-esteem also assumes the existence of a "self" which is an individualistic concept and therefore not suitable in all cultures. Some collectivistic cultures, for example, do not give individual names to people but label them as "first born" or "second born" of a family lineage. The concept of a "self" that should be "esteemed" by oneself can be very foreign.

In Western cultures, if the instability of self-esteem makes it a difficult concept to research, it in turn offers the advantage of being very malleable in psychotherapy. Take for example, a child who has been bullied for a long time and never retaliated. The child may feel down on himself until his specific value for nonviolence and the courage embedded in resisting retaliation is made visible in a skillful conversation, and connected to the legacy of family values. This child's feelings of self-worth would therefore be significantly improved.

Marie-Nathalie Beaudoin

See also Assertiveness; Attachment; Authoritative Parenting; Bonding; Narrative Therapy; Self-Esteem; Trust; Virginia Satir Model

Further Readings

Beaudoin, M.-N. (2014). *Boosting ALL children's social and emotional brain power: Life transforming activities*. Thousand Oaks, CA: Corwin.

Beaudoin, M.-N. (2010). *The SKiLL-ionaire in every child: Boosting children's socio-emotional skills using the latest in brain research*. San Francisco: Goshawk Publications.

Dweck, C. (Dec. 2007-Jan. 2008). The secret to raising smart kids. *Scientific American Mind, 43*, 365–373.

Ellis, A. (2005). *The myth of self-esteem*. Amherst, NY: Prometheus.

Greenberg, J. (2008). Understanding the vital human quest for self-esteem. *Perspectives on Psychological Science, 3*(1), 48–54.

White, M. (2007). *Narrative maps*. New York: W. W. Norton.

SELF-HELP

The term *self-help* has many connotations. Generally, self-help can be described as a way of improving oneself without the help of another. Self-help also refers to self-improvement strategies, such as when a person gains insight and solves problems through reading a self-help book, although self-help materials can also include workshops and support groups. When focusing solely on the reading process, self-help books typically are general advice books, inspirational books, books of programmed instruction, or autobiographies. This genre can be easily accessed in various locations for the general public, including bookstores, libraries, and Internet-based retailers. For the purpose of this entry, a self-help book is defined as a work of fiction or nonfiction that is widely available to the general public. As a high quality self-help book has the potential to complement or even replace traditional counseling and psychotherapy, this topic warrants attention by counselors. This entry reviews the advantages and disadvantages of self-help books through the lens of marriage, family, and couples counseling and discusses how to best use self-help books in counseling and psychotherapy practice.

The Market for Self-Help Books

By some estimates, the self-improvement industry in the United States is worth $10 billion or more, including books and other products and services. Self-help books are commonplace within U.S. society, with approximately 2,000 books published each year that are marketed in the self-help category. A more expansive definition of self-help books can be divided into four categories: (1) general advice or inspirational books for life issues, such as relationships and parenting; (2) books of programmed instruction for a particular problem, such as depression or remarriage; (3) autobiographies written by a person who has suffered from a mental health disorder or life problem; and (4) inadvertent self-help reading, such as works of fiction, poetry, magazine or newspaper articles, and information from the Internet.

Self-help books typically provide prescriptive suggestions for a variety of personal and interpersonal issues and life situations that may cause stress for a person, including abuse, alcohol and drug use, adult development, aging, anger, anxiety, assertiveness, attention-deficit/hyperactivity disorder, bipolar disorder, career development, infant development, child development, teenagers and parenting, communication and people skills, death and grieving, depression, divorce, eating disorders, families and stepfamilies, gender issues, love and intimacy, marriage, pregnancy, schizophrenia, self-management and self-enhancement, sexuality, spiritual and existential concerns, stress management and relaxation, suicide, and weight management. Many of these books are best sellers, with some reaching more than 1 million readers. In particular, John Gray's book *Men Are From Mars, Women Are From Venus* was the highest-ranked nonfiction book of the 1990s and has now sold more than 50 million copies.

Publishers have a considerable impact on the market of self-help books as publishers invest in marketing what is likely to sell. Establishing a best seller often relies on having a well-known author with a well-developed platform. Publishers have an undeniable interest in selling self-help books because of their popularity, but the books most likely to sell are not necessarily those that will be most effective in helping people solve their problems. Generally, self-help books are marketed with unsubstantiated claims by the publishers as being solutions for a variety of problems and concerns.

The Social Context of Self-Help Books

Self-help books are described as a postmodern phenomenon, highly influencing how the general public understands and makes sense of psychology and emotional well-being. The very nature of the self-help genre reflects the social and cultural context of a given time in history. For instance, the events of September 11, 2001, resulted in an increase in self-help books related to trauma, grief, and anxiety. American society idealizes free will, self-responsibility, and practicality, and the self-improvement industry is consistent with this message. The very concept of self-help is based on the American dream of being self-reliant or self-made. However, self-help books reinforce personal solutions rather than focusing on systemic social problems. This aspect of self-help reading is especially apparent in the marriage- and relationship-based self-help literature and is reviewed in more depth later in this entry.

Self-help reading can also be viewed as a solution to the demands of an expanding health care economy. As professionals cannot provide services to every person who needs psychological assistance, self-help books can reduce the potential numbers who need care. Self-help reading may be useful to integrate within stepped-care models of mental health services. Stepped-care models recommend that professionals provide the most effective, yet least restrictive treatment in order to serve the high volume of individuals who need mental health services.

Advantages of Self-Help Books

The act of reading has potential benefits for the reader. Within a mental health setting, professionals report several benefits of self-help reading for the client. This is also known as *bibliotherapy*. First, reading can provide a new source of information and can accelerate the learning process. As reading also addresses problems outside the focus of counseling, the process may increase client responsibility for their own learning and personal growth. Finally, reading also stimulates discussions between client and practitioner and thus can improve counselor–client engagement.

Outside of the mental health setting, benefits of self-help books for the general reader are also evident. Reading self-help books can (a) normalize feelings and problems, (b) increase insight and awareness of self and others, (c) increase knowledge about a topic or situation, (d) provide potential solutions to problems, and (e) increase coping skills for troublesome symptoms. In lieu of participating in traditional counseling and psychotherapy, reading self-help books may provide several advantages. First, because self-help books are easily and quickly accessible, the reader has more flexibility in when he or she receives care. A self-help book may be easier for readers who live in rural, isolated areas to access. Self-help books may also offer a wider range of interventions for readers. Readers with varying learning styles may also benefit as persons learn and need support in different ways. Self-help readers can also self-pace their learning. Finally, a self-help book may cost as little as $20, so self-help reading may also be more cost effective than traditional counseling and psychotherapy.

Reading provides the unique option of returning to the book's pages for additional information or comfort. Readers can return to the work at any time, at no extra cost. Self-help reading also obviates the potential stigma of receiving mental health treatment, since readers maintain anonymity. Finally, readers can feel empowered as self-help books often provide a message of hope and potentiality.

General Cautions With Self-Help Books

The marketing of self-help books builds on the expectations of potential readers. Self-help books often promise an easy solution to problems and present the author as an expert or teacher. Accordingly, readers may expect a positive effect or benefit from reading a book and be disappointed when they do not achieve desired results. It is unclear how many readers return to self-help books even when these prior reading experiences do not meet their expectations. For example, many self-help readers are described as repeat customers despite not gaining the benefits they initially desired. Critics of the self-help genre believe that readers have become overly reliant and dependent on self-help books. This of course raises the question of whether readers are actually helping themselves with self-help literature.

Research findings suggest that self-help books are best used by certain types of people. Motivation to learn independently and having an internal locus of control and high levels of self-efficacy improve the likelihood of a positive outcome from self-help reading. In contrast, readers with poor concentration and learning disabilities may experience frustration with self-help reading. Considering diversity and cultural issues, the content may not be appropriate for all populations. For example, self-help books are used more frequently by female clients, those with a high school education or higher, and clients with average or above average intellectual ability.

Within a mental health setting, authors recommend that self-help books be used with clients who enjoy reading or with those who request reading as homework. Ideally, materials should match or fit the reader's interest and need. Self-help reading may be most useful for persons with mild to moderate problems rather than for persons with severe problems, which require more extensive, specialized treatment. For clients who present with mild symptoms and life issues, self-help may be a suitable treatment approach.

Bibliotherapy

Professionals routinely use self-help books with clients in counseling and psychotherapy. When self-help reading is used as a part of the therapeutic process, bibliotherapy is a more befitting term. Bibliotherapy is the process of using literature to enhance emotional well-being. There are three interactive elements when using bibliotherapy: the counselor, the client, and the literature. Bibliotherapy includes a wide spectrum of written text and media, including fiction and nonfiction books; poetry, plays, and short stories; magazine articles; film, audiovisual recorded material; and Web pages.

Grounded in the psychodynamic approach, bibliotherapy provides readers with an opportunity to (a) experience connection with others, (b) feel deep emotions, (c) gain insight, and (d) develop solutions to potential problems. In 1950, Caroline Shrodes suggested that readers move through distinct phases in the bibliotherapy process. First, clients identify with characters, plots, or information. For example, a client may connect with the author's story. As a result of this identification, readers experience catharsis, or emotional release. Readers may find themselves feeling a sense of relief in knowing they are not the only ones who have experienced this issue or problem. This is also referred to as universalization. Finally, readers develop insight, or understand their unique thoughts, feelings, and behaviors. For example, clients may better understand their feelings as a result of reading the book. Some authors have proposed a final stage, projection, which allows readers to consider their future while providing a framework to piece together experiences. For example, the reader can gain a new perspective on his or her life situation and make a plan for moving forward accordingly.

The book can be read in or out of counseling sessions. After the client has viewed the material, the counselor focuses on the readers' experience with the reading process, specifically following up on insights gained. There are four steps to this process including: (1) recognition, or having clients experience a sense of connection to the material; (2) examination, or having readers look at issues in the material and feelings evoked through this process; (3) juxtaposition, or gaining insight through the interactive discussion with counselors regarding the reading process; and (4) self-application, or integrating insights gained from the process. When discussing the book, counselors ideally focus on situations or characters in the book. The counselor may ask questions such as "How are you like the people mentioned in the book?" or "How would you change the situation for the people in the book?" By asking readers to make sense of the characters' experiences, the counselor provides a safe venue for the client to explore his or her life situation and to consider new possibilities. In summary, clients should be encouraged to compare their life situation to the reading material through the discussion process.

Research findings support the use of bibliotherapy. Meta-analyses, which examine relationships across different research studies, indicate a moderate effect size for bibliotherapy. In other words, the outcome of using bibliotherapy is comparable to traditional counseling and psychotherapy for the same type of problem. Reading a self-help book may mirror the counseling process. How the process works is still under debate. Some theorists believe that identifying with the book or having a connection to the characters or story is the key benefit. Other theorists believe that the reading process is a medium for self-change; for example, reading provides an opportunity to move from contemplation to action. Finally, some theorists argue that self-help books are written in such a way to maximize on the common factors of counseling, for instance, generating hope that the book will be helpful, having a collaborative framework, giving feedback, and being responsive.

Feminist Analysis of Self-Help Books

This entry would be remiss without attention to the feminist analysis of popular self-help books for heterosexual couples. Discussion of this particular genre of self-help literature has been highly contentious. However, research findings indicate that couples typically first seek help through relationship-based books, or self-help books. Those couples who choose to read a book also tend to have higher levels of negative communication and to report physical violence in the relationship. Therefore, a discussion of the quality of self-help books for couples is warranted.

One title that has been extensively critiqued is the best seller mentioned previously, *Men Are From Mars, Women Are From Venus*. Although the popularity of this book has declined since the 1990s, the book is still used by couples who are attempting to improve their relationships and who seek professional help. The essential critique of this particular self-help book is that it perpetuates traditional gender-based stereotypes and therefore maintains the status quo. The author suggests that men and women are inherently different (e.g., depicting men as emotionally closed and women as irrational) and that readers cannot change. Furthermore, Gray's theory of men and women is primarily based on observation, opinion, and cultural conceptions of gender rather than on empirical research. In contrast, John Gottman's theory on the seven principles for making marriages work is based on extensive research and supports the practice of feminist family therapy. Within the past decade, there have been an increasing number of relationship-based books published that also support feminist principles. However, practitioners need to critically analyze each self-help title to determine if the book will be an appropriate match for the particular client.

Family Counseling and Self-Help Books

Self-help books can benefit families in and out of the counseling and psychotherapy process. For example, parent training programs can improve parenting skills. These programs are grounded in the idea that parenting practices contribute to the development and continuation of behavior problems in children. Two of the more popular parent training programs are parent effectiveness training by Thomas Gordon and systematic training for effective parenting by Don Dinkmeyer and Gary McKay. Overall, research findings support the effectiveness of parent training programs. These programs typically address critical issues in parent-child dynamics such as (a) improving problem-solving skills; (b) teaching parents to support the child's cognitive, emotional, and social skills; (c) promoting positive parent–child interactions; (d) improving parenting consistency; and (e) increasing strategies for responding to behavior problems.

Self-help books also have value when counseling stepfamilies. Approximately 10% of all children residing in the United States live with a stepfamily, and the number of self-help book titles on this topic has increased over the last 20 years. Practitioners working with this population have many self-help book options to choose from—overall, it is relatively easy for counselors to locate and access quality self-help books on stepfamilies. One area that needs more attention within the research literature, however, is the use of self-help books for gay and lesbian stepfamilies.

In conclusion, the self-improvement industry is booming and continually expanding, mainly due to the rise of Internet-based retailers. Within the helping professions, there is a need to better understand couples' marital and relationship help-seeking behaviors. Marriage, couples, and family counselors need to recognize the potential of self-help reading and can do so by (a) valuing self-help as a useful modality, (b) encouraging self-directed change and self-learning, (c) integrating self-help reading into counseling and psychotherapy, and (d) conducting more research on its benefit and applicability in marriage, family, and couples counseling.

Laura Bruneau

See also Communication in Couples and Families; Feminist Family Therapy; Gender Roles; Gottman Method Couples Therapy; Homework Assignments in Therapy

Further Readings

Bruneau, L., Bubenzer, D. L., & McGlothlin, J. M. (2010). Revisioning the self: A phenomenological investigation into self-help reading. *The Journal of Humanistic Counseling, Education and Development, 49,* 217–230.

Cohen, L. J. (1993). Bibliotherapy: The experience of therapeutic reading from the perspective of the adult reader. *Dissertation Abstracts International, 53*(8-B).

Coleman, M., & Nickleberry, L. (2009). An evaluation of the remarriage and stepfamily self-help literature. *Family Relations, 58,* 549–561.

Dinkmeyer, D., McKay, G. D., & Dinkmeyer, D. (2007). *The parent's handbook: Systematic training for effective parenting.* Fredericksburg, VA: STEP Publishers.

Doss, B. D., Rhoads, G. K., Stanley, S. M., & Markman, H. J. (2009). Marital therapy, retreats, and books: The who, what, when, and why and relationship help-seeking. *Journal of Marital and Family Therapy, 35,* 18–29.

Gottman, J. M., & Silver, N. (1999). *The seven principles for making marriage work.* New York: Random House.

Jack, S. J., & Ronan, K. R. (2008). Bibliotherapy: Practice and research. *School Psychology International, 29,* 161–182.

Kaminski, J. W., Valle, L. A., Filene, J. H., & Boyle, C. L. (2008). A meta-analytic review of components associated with parent training program effectiveness. *Journal of Abnormal Child Psychology, 36,* 567–589.

Norcross, J. C. (2006). Integrating self-help into psychotherapy: 16 practical suggestions. *Professional Psychology: Research and Practice, 37,* 683–693.

Shrodes C. (1950). *Bibliotherapy: A theoretical and clinical-experimental study.* Dissertation, University of California, Berkeley.

Starker, S. (1989). *Oracle at the supermarket: The American preoccupation with self-help books.* New Brunswick, NJ: Transaction Books.

Zimmerman, T. S., Holm, K. E., & Starrels, M. E. (2001). A feminist analysis of self-help bestsellers for improving relationships: A decade review. *Journal of Marital and Family Therapy, 27,* 165–175.

Self-Injury

Self-injury is the act of intentionally harming oneself. The harm is often in the form of cutting oneself, but can also be burning or any other form of superficial wounding of oneself. Self-injurious behavior is often directly related to a person's emotional state; for this reason, it is a topic that is best discussed with a mental health provider. Self-injury is also related to a person's upbringing and nuclear family. Family therapists must not only be aware of the practice of self-injury but also the best therapeutic strategies to use with an individual who engages in the practice, as well as with his or her family or partners. This entry describes the causes and types of self-injury and characteristics found in individuals who self-injure. The therapeutic implications for working with individuals who self-injure are also discussed.

Self-injury is a practice used to cope with trauma and emotional pain or to gain control over oneself or one's environment. There is evidence of people engaging in self-injurious behavior throughout history. Research seeking to understand this practice has grown significantly in the last few decades, leading to a much better understanding of self-injury. Mental health professionals now know more about who may practice it, what may cause it, and how to treat it. Self-harm, self-mutilation (SM), and self-injury (SI) are all clinical terms used to describe the practice. Many individuals who engage in this behavior call it cutting; those who use the behavior are sometimes referred to as cutters.

Forms of Self-Injury

There are three different types of self-injury; mental health professionals should treat each form differently. First, major self-mutilation is an extreme action of self-harm, such as removing genitals, gouging of an eye, or cutting off an appendage, that cannot heal without major medical intervention. This type of behavior is extremely dangerous and is best addressed by medical professionals immediately, with mental health treatment being secondary. The motivations behind this type of behavior are often religious or due to strong personal convictions.

The second form of self-mutilation is stereotypic self-mutilation. This type of behavior is often practiced by children or individuals with intellectual or developmental disabilities and is repetitive in nature, such as head banging or hitting oneself repeatedly. This type of behavior is addressed through treatment of other medical and mental health conditions or diagnoses. This behavior often subsides with age, and treatment during childhood focuses on ensuring that children do not seriously harm themselves.

The third form of self-injury, superficial self-mutilation or nonsuicidal self-injury, is the focus of this entry. This form of self-injury has emotional or psychological roots and is the form mental health professionals most commonly treat. It is used as a coping mechanism, similar to overeating or recreational drug use.

Superficial Self-Injury

Superficial self-injury is controlled, episodic, and compulsive. Individuals who practice this form of self-injury tend to use the behavior in an attempt to relieve tension or emotional pain. It may not be planned over the long term but is methodical in nature; for example, an individual may have a bad morning and then anticipate self-harming that evening when alone. Individuals often enter a trance-like state, which can cause them not to fully remember the actual self-injury episode, but rather to remember it as if it were a dream. They may not feel pain while cutting, but rather experience an intense feeling of relief, followed quickly by remorse and guilt. Individuals who engage in self-injurious behavior sometimes say that it helps them to feel more alive.

This behavior is often identified as highly compulsive, but not as compulsive as obsessive-compulsive disorder or trichotillomania (hair pulling). It is common for self-injurious individuals to harm themselves on the wrists, arms, and legs; however, people who have engaged in this behavior for longer or who desire to keep it private may use the chest, thighs, stomach, or genitals. For this reason, it is always recommended not to assume individuals have not harmed themselves because cuts are not seen.

It is important to understand that people who self-injure do not use their scars or marks to elicit attention; individuals who engage in this behavior often desire that their cutting remain a secret, often because there is deep shame in their action. It is counterproductive for therapists working with this population to check for evidence of recent cutting. This often results in individuals learning to better hide their scars. It is also important that therapists working with this population not shame an individual or make him or her feel guilty because of this behavior. It is imperative that professionals use an empathic and judgment-free tone and attitude with discussing this behavior.

The fifth edition of the *Diagnostic and Statistical Manual of Mental Disorders* (DSM-5) refers to this behavior as nonsuicidal self-injury, which it lists as one of several conditions lacking in sufficient evidence to include as mental disorder diagnoses but which warrant further study. The discussion of nonsuicidal self-injury for possible inclusion in the DSM as a mental disorder is one reason for the increase in research and clinical conversations regarding this behavior and coping mechanism. There has been confusion regarding this behavior and its relationship to suicidal ideation. It is now believed that superficial self-injury is not directly related to suicide, but is a reason to further assess a person's risk of suicide.

When Superficial Self-Injury Starts

Self-injury often begins in early adolescence, between ages 10 and 12. The individual may begin to engage in self-injurious behavior after an accidental injury leads to the calming results often reported by self-injurious individuals. Although individuals may have this experience at an early age, they may not begin to practice self-injury until years later, when they encounter stress that feels unbearable. Although this behavior is often associated with adolescence or early adulthood, it is not limited to one life stage; there have been cases of older adult self-injury as well as lifelong self-injury.

Self-injury is regularly seen in people with attachment disorders. It has been reported that approximately 50% of the people who engage in this behavior have a history of sexual abuse, while approximately 62% report physical abuse. The act of self-injury may help individuals who feel as though they have lost control of their body as a result of sexual or physical abuse once again feel in control of their body.

Who Self-Injures

When discussing superficial self-injury, it is valuable to know that there are instances of self-injury within the animal kingdom, including monkey and birds, often as a result of stress, sadness, and anxiety. Descriptions of people who self-injure are not all encompassing; there is not necessarily a typical self-injurious individual. In addition, descriptions of those who engage in self-injurious behavior in research literature are often drawn from those who engage in treatment, so that they may not be representative of all of those who engage in self-injurious behavior. However, researchers have found some attributes that tend to be more common in those who report engaging in self-injurious behavior. A majority are female. They tend to be high-achieving or perfectionistic individuals who seek to be above reproach in various areas of life. They tend to be well-liked or even popular, but feel like outsiders who are not truly understood. This feeling of being misunderstood may first be experienced in a person's nuclear family and then subsequently experienced in other relationships and settings. They have often learned not to trust, which can make it difficult for mental health professionals to establish a therapeutic alliance.

Individuals who engage in self-injury have likely experienced something that precipitated their feelings of not belonging and lack of trust. It is important that a therapist seek to understand a client's perception regarding the cause of the desire to cut. Initially the causes that the client gives may be specific to current events or experience; however, after further rapport is established, there is often a point during the therapeutic process in which the individual will begin to discuss past experiences and feelings that may be related to the desire to self-injure.

Individuals who self-injure may have anxious or depressive symptoms, which may be the reason therapeutic treatment was initially sought. These individuals may be scared to disappoint those around them, especially because they may feel inadequate or unworthy. They tend to be fearful of punishment and would often like to be unnoticed.

People who self-injure tend to be emotionally inarticulate. These individuals often lack the ability to express their thoughts and feelings, often because they have received negative feedback in the past about their thoughts or feelings. They have learned to shut down feelings that could be perceived as negative. It has been observed that they may not feel a strong attachment to many people, even to parents or family members. When working with people who self-injure, therapists may find it beneficial to provide emotional education related to feeling words as well as self-expression strategies.

It is also important to note that the tendency to seek control predisposes people to other behavioral issues as well, including eating disorders. People who self-injure have been diagnosed with posttraumatic stress disorder (PTSD), mood disorders, and anxiety disorders.

Cycles of Superficial Self-Injury

The cycle of self-injury is similar to the addiction cycle. People can have a triggering event, such as an argument with a loved one, which leads them to feel as though they have lost control. During this time people tend to be unable to analyze their feelings and the situation. In order to gain control of their thoughts, feelings, and world around them, these individuals dissociate and injure themselves. This is typically followed by a feeling of calmness, rest, and a sense of relief in taking back power, after which the individuals begin to feel guilt or remorse. People around them who are aware of their self-injury and the individuals' fear of disappointing those people can exacerbate this guilt. Studies have shown that people who self-injure can have decreased serotonin levels that lead to negative feelings and poor emotional regulation (for this reason selective serotonin reuptake inhibitors may be prescribed). The act of self-injury can temporarily increase the release of neurotransmitters such as serotonin, which helps them feel more alive. These individuals are likely not aware of the hormonal and biological factors of this behavior and will often benefit from education about this, which can lead them to feel empowered in understanding how their body is responding to different stimuli and how to break the self-injury cycle.

Amanda A. Brookshear

See also Attachment Theory; Eating Disorders; Posttraumatic Stress Disorder in Children;

Further Readings

Conterio, K., Lader, W., & Bloom, J. K. (1999). *Bodily harm: The breakthrough healing program for self-injurers.* New York: Hyperion.

Hollander, M. (2008). *Helping teens who cut: Understanding and ending self-injury.* New York: Guilford Press.

Strong, M. (1998). *A bright red scream: Self-mutilation and the language of pain.* New York: Penguin.

Sensate Focus

Sensate focus refers to a technique therapists and counselors employ to help couples experiencing certain types of sexual dysfunction build trust and reduce their anxiety. It involves nondemand touch (touch that is not meant to be sexual or produce orgasm). Many people struggling with sexual issues in their relationship will have experienced numerous failed sexual experiences over time, and each of these creates anxiety. Such anxiety can interfere with the sexual relationship and the ability to become aroused or achieve orgasm. Sensate focus exercises are meant to pair touch, and eventually sexual behaviors, with relaxation rather than anxiety. The exercise involves couples taking turns touching and massaging each other, without having the pressure of being sexual or having an orgasm. In the beginning stages they are not allowed to touch breasts or genitals, and the goal is to relax and communicate to the partner what feels good or does not feel good. Over time the couple builds up to more sexual touch.

The aim of sensate focus is to build trust between couples, allowing them to explore giving and receiving pleasure. The emphasis is on positive emotions, feelings, and sensations while reducing any negative responses. The technique allows for feedback from each person in the couple and allows for a great deal of flexibility in how it is presented and when a couple moves through the various stages. The stages themselves can be modified as needed to adapt to the needs of each couple. In the sections that follow, the history and rationale for sensate focus, the process of sensate focus, and possible challenges are discussed. The entry concludes with a discussion of the elements necessary for success in sensate focus and the benefits of the technique.

Origin of Sensate Focus

The sensate focus technique originated from work by William Masters and Virginia Johnson in the 1960s and 1970s. Their technique was further refined by Helen Singer Kaplan, a sex therapist and professor of psychiatry who held doctorates in both medicine and psychology. Over time this process has evolved and has become a standard practice for those practicing sex therapy. Originally Masters and Johnson would focus on the individual patient who was presenting with the sexual dysfunction and using the partner as a type of cotherapist at home to process the dysfunction. Systemically it is helpful to work with both partners equally, as both are influenced by problems in the sexual relationship and the other partner may have developed behaviors and beliefs that feed into sexual problems.

The Concept of Sensate Focus

The idea behind sensate focus is that underlying anxiety prevents couples from experiencing arousal and orgasm with one another. Basically, anxiety interferes with sexual functioning and sexual pleasure with a partner. It is not uncommon that partners experiencing these sexual difficulties will have little problem performing or enjoying sexual experiences either alone or outside of the marriage—but by no means is this always the case. The purpose of sensate focus is to help couples enjoy touching one another without the anxiety response that has been conditioned into their pattern and interferes with their sex life. Sensate focus is commonly used to treat issues of deficient sexual desire, difficulty in achieving sexual arousal or erectile dysfunction, and difficulty in reaching orgasm.

Therapeutic Use of Sensate Focus

Many therapists enjoy assigning homework, but for homework to be successful it should make sense to the couple and be clearly explained. If poorly explained and executed, the incorporation of sensate focus into couples' treatment can appear as a pointless assignment or do harm to the couple's relationship. Poorly preparing and assigning sensate focus to clients may reinforce the conditioned anxiety. Clients typically respond well when the purpose and point of sensate focus are explained to them. The purpose is to enjoy touching one another, *not* orgasm. Once couples enjoy touching and being touched by one another, the orgasm will occur in later stages.

There is no one right way to introduce or to implement sensate focus. Some clients will move through the steps with ease, while others will have anxiety triggered by the mere thought or discussion of sensate focus exercises. Generally, there are two major sections of this process: sensual and sexual. The assignments, however, should be gradual and require satisfactory completion of each step before moving to the next step. This helps to ensure the clients' comfort level and allows the clinician to assess for sexual anxiety.

Pressure and anxiety are two roadblocks to successful sexual encounters for many couples. The process of sensate focus should allow those feelings to be lowered, and an atmosphere of comfort and trust should be created. The point of the exercise is not to have sexual orgasm as the goal; it is to be aware of sensations that occur when being touched. Not infrequently couples report failing the assignment as they proceeded to intercourse or orgasm rather than waiting. Each of these responses, as well as any others, can be used to further understand and focus further treatment.

Typically, couples are encouraged to participate in the activities two to three times a week as time permits. Each sensate focus session should include uninterrupted time that is disconnected from electronics, pets, children, or other distractions. Each partner should have equal time as the partner touching and the partner being touched. The amount of time is dependent on how much time is available but should be somewhere between 10 minutes and 1 hour, based on availability of each partner. At the start of each turn a timer should be set so that there is no subjective interpretation of how much time has passed.

The couple take turns touching and caressing one another; they can alternate who initiates the touch. The couple should have a space that is pleasantly lighted and at a comfortable temperature, as the clients will remove as much clothing as they feel comfortable with. Here is another area where flexibility is important, as some individuals may have body image issues that they are working to overcome. Alcohol and recreational drugs should be avoided before and during the activity because they are likely to interfere with the process of feeling sensations. In general, there are five stages to sensate focus practice:

1. Touching and caressing with no breast touching
2. Touching and caressing including breasts but no genitals
3. Touching and caressing including genitals
4. Mutual touching including insertion (fingers or toys) but no intercourse
5. Intercourse but not orgasm

The clinician explains at the onset of the intervention that sexual intercourse and sexual activity should be avoided. The rationale is that by removing sexual activity performance, pressure is removed, and a nondemand atmosphere is created, and each person can feel more relaxed. The pressure to have sex can deter from the process and is often the root of much of the anxiety experienced. The initial stage has the couple find a comfortable place to engage in the touch exercise. They avoid touching the breasts and genitals and focus on the feeling, pressure, and temperature. This touching should be done by the hands and fingers only, with no kissing or full body contact. All areas of the body, except those off limits, should be explored. The focus should be on the sensations of touch, pressure, and temperature. If anxiety arises, the individual should refocus on the touch sensations and move on to a new part of the body. The touch should be long enough that the awkwardness is overcome but short enough that the partners do not get bored or tired. Each partner takes turns throughout the session performing both roles of toucher and being touched. If the one being touched feels physically uncomfortable, he or she can redirect the partner away nonverbally or by placing a hand over or under the partner's hand and guiding to a new area.

Steps one through three focus on the sensual nature of touch, while the last two gear more toward sexual touch. It is important to remember through each step that sexual intercourse and orgasm are not the goal; rather the goal is to increase understanding and awareness of one's own body and sensations.

How to Have Success With Sensate Focus

The important keys of having success with sensate focus revolve around the level of comfort the couple are able to experience. The more that the clinician is able to explain the process and allow the clients to feel comfortable, the more likely success will happen. The clinician also needs to be aware of the level of readiness of the clients. A thorough assessment of the couple's skills and levels of communication will be helpful, as any perceived failure with sensate focus will impact the couple's level of marital satisfaction. As part of the exercise, it can be helpful for the clients to have sofa sessions. These consist of a debriefing of sorts for the couple to share their experiences and to listen to their partner's experiences. The clients expand their communication about what they are feeling and respond to their partner.

It is essential that each partner have equal time in each role. When being touched, the partner being touched should focus on the experience and being mindful of how things feel. The partner being touched is not in control of the experience but is encouraged to express what is enjoyed. A prepared list of basic expressions can be provided to the couple to assist in directing the touching partner: yes, no, harder, softer. These expressions are best delivered after completing the activity in the debriefing time. This allows for questions in a nonjudgmental way. The strength of sensate focus lies with the openness of the concept. Clients are able to stretch their comfort zones and learn to explore pleasure in a nonperformance demanding way. In the later stages as the couple has progressed, the clinician may suggest adding lotion or other objects to change the touch dynamics. A few of these might include feathers, ice cubes, or soft fabrics. This is dependent upon the couple's level of comfort and the ultimate goal of the relationship.

Benefits of Sensate Focus

Sensate focus is a directly applicable intervention that can help couples reduce their anxiety with one another and help couples learn to communicate about their wants and desires in a nondemanding way. The patterns of communication in failed sexual experiences are extremely predictive of the patterns of communication that couples experience when in distress.

Sensate focus can be used as a diagnostic tool to determine a couple's readiness to commit to therapy and their levels of communication outside the therapy room. Many people are uncomfortable saying what they want or like from their partner, both in and out of the bedroom. Sensate focus helps the couple learn reciprocal connection that is focused on pleasing each other. These skills can directly be applied to much more than just the bedroom, but like sensate focus, they work well only when each partner works to please the other. Sensate focus is not just an intervention used by couples that are struggling to enjoy sensual and sexual experience with one another, it can also teach couples how to do foreplay. Sex is not simply a matter of getting to orgasm as quickly as possible; it can also be about pleasure and enjoying being pleasured sensually and sexually.

Quintin A. Hunt and Matthew Nelson

See also Anxiety; Couples and Marriage Counseling; Homework Assignments in Therapy; Mindfulness; Sex Therapy; Sexual Enhancement, Sexual Toys; Sexual Intimacy; Sexuality Education

Further Readings

Coren, C. M., Nath, S. R., & Prout, M. (2009). Computer-assisted sensate focus: Integrating technology with sex therapy practice. *Journal of Technology in Human Services, 27*(4), 273–286. doi:10.1080/15228830903329823

De Villers, L. (2014). Getting in touch with touch: A use of caressing exercises to enrich sensual connection and evoke ecstatic experience in couples. *Sexual and Relationship Therapy, 29*(1), 87–97. doi:10.1080/14681994.2013.870336

Gupta, P., Banerjee, G., & Nandi, D. N. (1989). Modified Masters Johnson technique in the treatment of sexual inadequacy in males. *Indian Journal of Psychiatry, 31*(1), 63–69.

Joanning, H., & Keoughan, P. (2005). Enhancing marital sexuality. *The Family Journal, 13*(3), 351–355. doi:10.1177/1066480705276194

Kaplan, H. S. (1974). *The new sex therapy.* New York: Brunner/Mazel.

Masters, W. H., & Johnson, V. (1970). *Human sexual inadequacy.* Boston: Little, Brown.

McAnulty, R. D., & Kazdin, A. E. (2000). Sex therapy. In *Encyclopedia of psychology* (Vol. 7, pp. 328–241). New York: Oxford University Press.

Regev, L. G., & Schmidt, J. (2008). Sensate focus. In W. T. O'Donohue & J. E. Fisher (Eds.), *Cognitive behavior therapy: Applying empirically supported techniques in your practice* (pp. 486–492). Hoboken, NJ: Wiley.

Van Hasselt, V. B., & Hersen, M. (1996). *Sourcebook of psychological treatment manuals for adult disorders.* New York: Plenum Press.

Weeks, G. R., & Gambescia, N. (2009). A systemic approach to sensate focus. In K. M. Hertlein, G. R. Weeks, & N. Gamescia (Eds.), *Systemic sex therapy* (pp. 341–362). New York: Routledge.

Weiner, L., & Avery-Clark, C. (2014). Sensate focus: Clarifying the Masters and Johnson's model. *Sexual and Relationship Therapy, 29*(3), 307–319. doi:10.1080/14681994.2014.892920

Wiederman, M. W. (2001). "Don't look now": The role of self-focus in sexual dysfunction. *The Family Journal, 9*(2), 210–214. doi:10.1177/1066480701092020

Sentiment Override, Positive and Negative

Sentiment override is a construct introduced by Robert Weiss and developed further by John Gottman. Sentiment override refers to how individuals interpret messages from their romantic partners, and individuals can either exhibit positive or negative sentiment override. The construct was developed through studies where researchers observed and coded couples' interactions, and has been examined for how it contributes to a variety of couple relationships. Sentiment override is an important construct for understanding couples' interactions. It develops out of nonconflict interactions, and can influence couples' abilities to regulate and repair conflict in their relationships. This entry defines negative and positive sentiment override and explores them further through examples. It also includes a discussion of how sentiment override relates to other elements in couple relationships.

Negative Sentiment Override (NSO)

Negative sentiment override (NSO) occurs when one partner expresses something neutral (as rated by external observers), and the other responds negatively. The receiver makes negative meaning of the message sent and responds accordingly. For example, in a same-gender, female couple, one partner may state, "I'm concerned about our finances because this has been a really difficult year." The woman's partner may respond, "Oh, so now I don't contribute enough to this relationship. Anything else you want to throw at me? Thanks a lot!" In this example, the receiver perceives that her partner's comment is critical about her abilities to contribute financially, and reacts with defensiveness. The receiver does not perceive or read any concern from her partner, but instead perceives negative intent. It is as if the partner in NSO has just heard her partner say, "You've made my life miserable because you are awful with finances, you idiot!"

Gottman has referred to individuals in NSO as having a bias toward negativity. The individual in NSO is primed and ready to respond with negativity, and could likely find many ways to perceive and interpret statements or questions negatively. In short, the individual in NSO is almost looking for a fight, and has her or his radar finely tuned to detect any hint of negativity from her or his partner.

Positive Sentiment Override (PSO)

Positive sentiment override (PSO), in contrast, occurs when one partner expresses something neutral (as rated by external observers), and the other responds positively. To take the same example of the same-gender, female couple, the receiver could respond differently to the statement, "I'm concerned about our finances because this has been a really difficult year." A PSO response could include the following: "Oh, I didn't know you were so concerned. Thank you for letting me in and telling me. Let's talk about this." It is as if the partner in PSO has just heard her partner say, "I'm concerned about something, and I want to share it with you because I care about you."

An individual in PSO is able to perceive the positive intentions of the sender and not take neutral comments as personal attacks. In contrast with NSO, the individual in PSO does not feel criticized, and thus has no need to act defensive. If there is no perceived attack or threat, there is no need to defend. One interesting thing about PSO is that it can be accomplished even if the sender of the original message conveys the neutral statement with negative affect, such as anger. Individuals in PSO can see through the negative emotion and still respond to their partners positively.

The Development of Sentiment Override and Role of Perception

Weiss introduced the concept of sentiment override to attempt to explain why unhappy couples consistently interpreted their partners' behaviors negatively. Weiss hypothesized that PSO existed more in the early stages of romantic relationship development because higher levels of relationship satisfaction are common early on. This hypothesis was based on the idea that partners were more likely to wear "rose-colored glasses" early in the relationship as compared with couples that had been together longer.

Although this early stage of couple relationships that Weiss referenced is often called the "honeymoon phase," Gottman found no empirical support for a honeymoon phase in couple relationships. Instead, Gottman discovered that patterns developed early in relationships often remained consistent as relationships developed. In other words, a couple's pattern of relating to each other often does not change, but how partners perceive those same patterns changes.

One way that Gottman explained this change in perception was through a concept that he called the "marital poop detector." The marital poop detector refers to the level of negativity (or "poop") that partners are willing to tolerate in the relationship. Gottman reported that newlyweds, especially wives, set their thresholds for negativity quite high. This is similar to what Weiss hypothesized as the rose-colored glasses that newly partnered couples often wear when looking at the relationship. Gottman discovered that newlyweds often failed to address this negativity until it built up over time and was extreme. Gottman also discovered that couples that addressed negativity as it surfaced had more long-term success. As a result, couples who were in distress because of tolerating extreme levels of negativity needed to have their marital poop detectors reset to lower levels so that they were more likely to address and repair negative interactions as they occurred. Many older, stable couples report that they "don't go to bed angry," and research has shown that PSO and higher levels of relationship satisfaction exist more in older couples.

Gottman emphasizes the importance of perception, and as one can tell from the examples, perception is essential to sentiment override. However, researchers discovered that sentiment override is more determined by global perceptions of the relationship than by the moment of interaction where the response characterized by PSO or NSO occurs. In short, PSO or NSO is better predicted by one's overall feelings about the relationship than one's feelings about the words spoken in that particular interaction. This is why it is easier for happy couples to exhibit PSO and dismiss negative emotion that comes with neutral statements. Happy couples are not bothered as much by expressions of negative affect if they are generally happy in the relationship. Conversely, this is also why unhappy couples are more likely to exhibit NSO and automatically experience neutral comments as negative, whether they are accompanied by negative emotion or not. Unhappy partners are much more likely to anticipate a negative message from their partners if they feel negative about the relationship overall.

The Sound Relationship House (SRH)

Sentiment override is the fourth level of Gottman's sound relationship house (SRH). The SRH is a theoretical model for how couples can nurture happy, stable relationships based on Gottman's years of studying couples' interactions. It contains seven "levels" or constructs, including elements of the couple's friendship, how couples manage solvable and perpetual conflict, their abilities to support each other's life goals, and how they develop shared rituals and meaning for their relationship. Sentiment override, specifically, is based on the strength of the couple's friendship and helps to determine the success of repair attempts during conflict.

Gottman believed that overall feelings about the relationship that lead to PSO or NSO are a reflection of the amount of stored positive emotion in the "emotional bank account." The metaphorical "account" is the result of couples' positive, nonconflict experiences or interactions, and Gottman discovered that happy couples have at least a 5 to 1, positive-to-negative interaction ratio. In other words, stable couples have *at least* five positive interactions for every one negative interaction. In contrast, unstable couples have about equal numbers of positive and negative interactions.

The "deposits" made into the emotional bank account are mainly a reflection of the couple's friendship. The couple's friendship is the base of the SRH, and similar to a physical house, the foundation of the relationship must be solid in order to build on top of it. In the foundation of the SRH, friendship consists of three components: love maps (i.e., how much partners cognitively know about each other), fondness and admiration (i.e., how much partners appreciate and respect each other), and turning toward versus turning away (i.e., the frequency of moments that partners are emotionally responsive and "there for" each other in times of need). Individuals in happy, stable relationships generally know their partners, respect and appreciate things about their partners, and are generally emotionally present for (turn toward) their partners when needed. Each of these actions makes a metaphorical deposit into their emotional bank account, and it is important to note that turning toward is particularly important. For individuals in unhappy, unstable relationships, these components of friendship are not working as well, and they make far fewer deposits.

This emotional bank account serves as a reservoir of trust in each other's intentions, and therefore is vital for sentiment override. The larger the emotional bank account, the more positive energy the couple has to draw on when neutral statements are made. Even when negative emotion is present with those neutral statements, a couple with a larger reservoir of positive experiences is more easily able to dismiss the negativity and exhibit PSO. Couples with smaller emotional bank accounts have little to draw on in terms of positive emotional experiences, and are therefore much more likely to interpret neutral messages as negative, with or without attached negative emotion.

For couples therapists, it is important to know that working with delivery (timing, wording, tone, etc.) of a particular comment is likely to have little success as compared to working with overall satisfaction with the relationship. This is similar to what Gottman found in researching what repairs couples' conflicts. Gottman discovered that the delivery of a repair attempt was not predictive of its success. The success of repair attempts depends on the overall feelings about the relationship much more than the words spoken in a particular interaction. Thus, sentiment override is an excellent indicator of a couple's abilities to regulate and repair conflict.

Conflict regulation and repair are the fifth level of the SRH, and PSO is vital for couples to regulate and repair damage from conflict. Gottman discovered that most conflict in couples is not solvable, so it is a couple's ability to self-soothe and regulate their emotion during conflict, as well as repair damage from conflict, that helps couples remain stable. Gottman studied conflict extensively and found that the elements of regulation and repair are two of the most important elements in couple relationships for long-term stability.

The Four Horsemen of the Apocalypse

There are particular elements in couple relationships that may be in most need of repair. Gottman adopted the term the "four horsemen of the apocalypse" to refer to four particularly corrosive elements in couple relationships: criticism, defensiveness, contempt, and stonewalling. As illustrated in the first example shared earlier, individuals in NSO are much more likely to respond with one of the four horsemen. These responses could include defensiveness (i.e., failing to take responsibility for any part of the issue and possibly acting like a victim) as shown in the first example, or could sound more like criticism (i.e., making negative global statements about a person's character as opposed to situational complaints). For example, the receiver could say in response to the original comment ("I'm concerned about our finances because this has been a really difficult year"), "Well, maybe that is because you're so disorganized and have no clue how to manage money." The receiver could also respond with contempt (i.e., statements that mock or put oneself above the other), such as, "Oh, you're concerned about that? Can't you handle anything at all without whining about it? You're pathetic." Finally, NSO could include stonewalling (i.e., physical and/or emotional withdrawal due to feeling "flooded" or emotionally overwhelmed). Stonewalling in this case could look like the receiver sighing, shaking her head, and walking away. Stonewalling could also look like having no visible response at all.

Michael E. Sude

See also Conflict in Couples and Families; Couples Therapy Research; Gottman Method Couples Therapy; Healthy Marriage and Responsible Fatherhood

Further Readings

Gottman, J. M. (1999). *The marriage clinic: a scientifically based marital therapy*. New York: W. W. Norton.

Gottman, J. M. (2011). *The science of trust: Emotional attunement for couples*. New York: W. W. Norton.

Hawkins, M. W., Carrère, S., & Gottman, J. M. (2002). Marital sentiment override: Does it influence couples' perceptions? *Journal of Marriage & Family, 64,* 193–201. doi:10.1111/j.1741-3737.2002.00193.x

Story, T. N., Berg, C. A., Smith, T. W., Beveridge, R., Henry, N. J. M., & Pearce, G. (2007). Age, marital satisfaction, and optimism as predictors of positive sentiment override in middle-aged and older married couples. *Psychology and Aging, 22,* 719–727. doi:10.1037/0882-7974.22.4.719

Rockinson-Szpakiw, A. J., Spaulding, L. S., & Knight, A. (2015). Protecting the marriage relationship during the doctoral journey: Strategies for students and partners based on the strong marital house concept. *The Family Journal: Counseling and Therapy for Couples and Families, 23,* 141–146. doi:10.1177/1066480714565106

SEX, DEFINITION OF

If someone asks the question, "What is sex?" the answer may be surprising. The term *sex* is a biological term, as well as a socially constructed term that varies by culture, time, and place in history. Among the definitions of the term *sex* are: (1) a person's biological sex of being male or female by referencing their reproductive organs (with the possibility of being born with both characteristics, a relatively rare occurrence commonly known as intersex or androgyny); (2) sex as an activity, or sexual behaviors; and (3) sex as it refers to the genitals. These three definitions are discussed in this entry. It is important for individuals, couples, and families to consider the definition of sex, know which definition they are using when they use the word *sex*, and to understand the difference between sex, sexuality, and sexual health.

Biological Sex

A person's biological sex is how a human is classified on the basis of their reproductive organs or functions, thus male or female. Approximately 1 out of every 1,500 to 2,000 births results in an individual who is intersex. *Intersex* is a general term for any individual who is born with sexual and reproductive anatomy that does not fit the typical male or female categorization. Indicators of biological sex include sex chromosomes, gonads, internal reproductive organs, and external genitalia.

Biological sex is usually one of the first questions a person asks when a child is born or in utero. People want to be able to place others into categories to better understand gender expectations and norms. Different socially constructed traits, norms, values, beliefs, and expectations are applied to people based on their biological sex. The constructed traits typically associated with one sex are referred to as *gender*. Current scholarship on sexuality and gender recognizes that gender identity is not a simple binary but exists along a continuum, with conventional notions of what constitutes male and female at opposite ends of the spectrum.

Certain behavioral traits are compatible with cultural expectations within a given community, culture, and society. If a person's behaviors are not compatible with cultural and societal expectations, a person is considered gender nonconforming. To summarize, the terms *male* and *female* are sex categories, and the terms *masculine* and *feminine* are gender categories. While some may use these terms interchangeably, they do not mean the same thing for all individuals. Aspects of gender vary among different human societies, but aspects of sex will not. For example, adult women's breasts are capable of lactating and men's are not, men have testicles, and women have the capacity to menstruate and become pregnant. Gender characteristics in some societies may include heterosexual women staying at home raising children while their male partner works outside the home; men may have more legal rights than women in some parts of the world; women must cover certain parts of their body with clothing while men do not; and women often do more housework than men, just to give a few gender specific characteristics that may exist in a society.

While most individuals define themselves as male or female by their reproductive capabilities and appearance of genitalia, scientifically there are many other factors that are assessed in order to assign a male or female categorization. Males are born with two distinct sex chromosomes, referred to as an XY genotype, while females have two of the same sex chromosomes, or an XX genotype. These XX or XY genotypes are also known as an individual's chromosomal or genetic sex. Individuals may also be categorized by their endocrinological (hormones) sex in which the phenotypic manifestations of an individual's biological sex are determined by endocrine influences, including the development of breasts and genital organs. Men produce the sex hormone testosterone in the testes, and in females the main sex hormones that are produced by the ovaries are estrogens and progesterone. These hormones affect an individual's secondary sex characteristics, such as the shape of the body, body hair, and the pitch of a voice. An individual's gonadal sex is determined by the presence of gonadal tissue present in the body (testicular or ovarian).

Sex as Activity

Often the terms *sex*, *sexuality*, and *sexual health* are used interchangeably, but they are in fact three separate entities. The World Health Organization (WHO) provides mental health clinicians, therapists, and educators with working definitions of these three that allow for distinction among terms. It is important to note that all of the definitions provided by WHO are considered working definitions because they need to be assessed within the context of time and place within history, and can change. These categories are all socially constructed and are subjective in nature.

According to WHO, *sex* refers to the biological characteristics that define humans as female or male. One's biological sex and the act of sex are important factors in an individual's sexuality and sexual health. Sexuality is a core characteristic of being human that includes a person's biological sex, gender roles, identities, and pleasure and is expressed through a variety of ways, including attitudes, behaviors, roles, pleasure, and orientation. Sexuality is influenced by the interaction of an individual's biological, psychological, social, economic, political, cultural, legal, historical, religious, and spiritual factors. The interaction of all these factors influences a person's sexual health.

Sexual health cannot truly be understood without understanding a multitude of factors about an individual including their sex, sexuality, health status, sexual identity, and sexual rights. Individuals express their sexual health through relationships but also through their own being such as their sexual identity, preferences, and fantasies. Sexual health is a positive approach to the complete wellbeing of a person in relation to sexuality. It includes absence from disease, but also one's positive outlook and the desire or need for intimacy. It allows for individuals to voluntarily participate in sexual activity free from discrimination, coercion, or harm while maintaining the sexual rights of all people.

Sexual activity can mean a variety of actions and differs from person to person. Therefore, *sex* is not an exact term. Research indicates that an overwhelming majority of people believe that sex often equates to intercourse (most often between a man and woman) through penile–vaginal penetration, yet do not consider oral sex (vaginal–mouth; penile–mouth; anal–mouth) to be sex. It is impossible for a therapist to know without asking what acts a person considers to be sex. Thus, a therapist must ask specific questions about how a person defines sex and must not be afraid to gather specific information.

Sexual activity is a part of sexual health and includes the behaviors and actions in which an individual participates. This can include sexual activity with the self, a partner, or several partners. An important aspect of therapy includes not only assessing one's biological sex, but also one's overall sexual health. While sex as an activity includes behaviors, there are also consequences that may arise, such as issues of contraception, sexually transmitted infections, reproduction, and sexual rights of an individual. Sexual health includes not only avoiding unwanted or negative outcomes from sex, but also positive outcomes such as feeling desire and pleasure.

In order to address sex with clients in a competent and effective manner, therapists must also understand that sexual health cannot not be achieved without understanding human rights, specifically those that affect one's sexual being. WHO has has performed research and produced literature that may assist in the understanding of sexual rights.

In general, human rights in regard to sex must be respected, protected, and fulfilled. Individuals have the right to nondiscrimination based on sex, have rights to privacy, choice, and education, and have the right to be free from coercion or harm, to name a few. Sexual rights allow each individual to pursue and express their sexual choices and sexual health while respecting the rights of others against discrimination.

Sex as Genitals

While sexual activity has historically been a taboo subject for many, there has been a large increase in the amount of research and literature on sexual activity available worldwide. The term *genitals* refers to the organs of the reproductive system, especially the external genital organs, and are most often part of the discussion of sexual activity. Questions on counseling and therapy assessment forms usually ask questions about sexual activity, who is having sex with whom, and what body parts (i.e., genitals) are being used in the acts. It is important to assist clients in understanding that the act of sex involves more than one's genitals. Sex as an activity includes people's capacity for cognition, fantasy, desire, and how a person feels about their body as a whole. Exploration of how clients think and feel about their body in relation to their sex, sexual activity, and sexual identity is paramount in effective treatment.

Conclusion

When working with a client, a therapist must ask what sex means to the client, how he or she learned about it, and the messages that were received about it growing up, and gather specific sexual assessment information in order to work effectively with a client in a treatment setting. An individual's sex, sexuality, and sexual health are all closely tied together and can adversely affect a client if not addressed openly and honestly.

Elizabeth B. Russell

See also Communication in Couples and Families; Marriage, First and Second; Pregnancy and Sexuality; Sex Positivity; Sex Researchers; Sexual Assessment/History; Sexual Intimacy; Sexuality Education; Sexually Transmitted Infections

Further Readings

American Psychiatric Association. (2014). *Diagnostic and statistical manual of mental disorders* (5th ed., text rev.). Washington, DC: Author.

American Psychological Association. (2006). *Answers to your questions about individuals with intersex conditions.* Washington, DC: Author.

American Psychological Association. (n.d.). *Answers to your questions about transgender people, sexual identity and gender expression.* Retrieved from http://www.apa.org/topics/lgbt/transgender.aspx

Barratt, B., & Rand, M. A. (2009). Sexual health assessment for mental health and medical practitioners: Teaching Notes. *American Journal of Sexuality Education, 4,* 16–27.

Hutchinson, E. D. (2007). *Dimensions of human behavior* (3rd ed.). Thousand Oaks, CA: Sage.

Levine, S. B. (Ed.), Risen, C. B., & Althof, S. E. (Assoc. Eds.). (2010). *Handbook of clinical sexuality for mental health professionals* (2nd ed.). New York: Routledge.

World Health Organization (WHO). (2006). *Working definitions of sex.* Geneva, Switzerland: WHO. Retrieved from http://www.who.org

Sex Positivity

Sex and sexuality are often uncomfortable topics of discussion despite frequent sexualized images and sexual undertones in the media. Sex positivity is encouraged in many health-related fields, such as psychology, social work, and public health, to counteract the negative impact sex-negative approaches have on well-being. Although sex positivity is encouraged, research in health-related fields tends to focus on disease, risks, and pathology related to sex and sexuality. Sex positivity refers to the conceptualization of sex and sexuality as a wide range of sexual and gender expression, behaviors, identities, and orientations that can be influenced by an individual's biology, psychology, and intersecting identities, such as culture, religion, spiritual beliefs, socioeconomic background, political, and social affiliations, among others. This entry focuses on discussing how sex negativity can impact an individual's well-being, defining sex positivity, and describing how a sex-positive approach can aid in well-being.

The Impact of Sex Negativity

Sex-negative conceptualization of sex and sexuality can impact social discourse and the well-being of individuals. Sex negativity associates sex with risky sexual behaviors, disease, and shame, and encourages abstinence. Many societies, including the United States, reinforce a sex-negative approach through sex education. For example, in some regions of the United States, sex education tends to focus on abstinence, where abstinence is presented as the preferred or only option for young people. This sex-negative approach limits access to accurate information about sex and contraception and often provides inaccurate information. Furthermore, there is concern about the inclusion of overt or subtle prejudicial information in sex education in the United States. As of 2016, only 8 states require that sex education programs provide instruction that is appropriate for a student's cultural background and not biased against any race, sex, or ethnicity, and only 13 states require programs to provide medically accurate information, according to the Guttmacher Institute. Research indicates that societies that take a sex-negative approach to sex and sexuality are associated with higher incidence of marginalization of segments of the population through racism, sexism, heterosexism, ageism, and prejudices related to certain sexual practices.

Sex negativity can have a negative impact on social and political discourse, and infringe on the rights of individuals. Politicians and the media frequently debate women's reproductive rights, access to abortion, and insurance coverage of birth control. Additionally, the promotion of sex for the purpose of procreation within marriage excludes large segments of society, such as lesbian, gay, bisexual, transgender, and queer (LGBTQ) and unmarried individuals. Sexual repression is encouraged in sex-negative societies, as evidenced by the negative portrayals of sexual expression of women, people of color, and LGBTQ individuals as immoral. Historically, laws and policies were enacted to prohibit sexual activities or marriage between people of color and White individuals, and between same-sex individuals. Prejudice and discrimination against individuals whose sexual activities are legislated against or seen as immoral can have a negative effect on their mental health and well-being.

Reframing Sex and Sexuality

Historically, sex and sexuality have been associated with marriage and procreation. Sex positivity promotes the separation of sex from strict traditional values and allows for sex to be associated with pleasure and health, and seen as a normative aspect of development across the life span. Also, sexual health is seen as encompassing more than the avoidance of disease and other unwanted consequences that can result from engaging in sexual activities. Sex positivity permits an open, nonjudgmental discussion about sex and sexuality that is inclusive of diverse populations, and works against sexist, heterosexist, racist, ageist, and other prejudicial undertones in discussions on sex and sexuality.

The Impact of Sex Positivity

A sex-positive approach is an inclusive and healthy way to conceptualize sex and sexuality that could reduce stigma associated with sexual expressions, identities, and orientations that are different from those of the dominant group. It can also help create healthier self-image and self-esteem by not questioning an individual's normality or morality. Advocates of sex positivity do not promote having sex frequently or abstaining from sex; they emphasize choice, freedom of sexual expression, and sexual health.

Sex positivity can change the way people conceptualize and talk about sex and sexuality. Nonjudgmental discussions about sex and a departure from the focus on sexual purity might empower people and encourage reporting sexual assaults and violence. Researchers assert that children who are comfortable talking about their bodies are more likely to report sexual abuse and may not be as likely to be targeted by sex offenders. Sex positivity also promotes sexual agency, or the ability to communicate and negotiate sexual desires and preferences, and to protest unwanted sexual activity.

Sex education from a sex-positive approach offers nonjudgmental and medically accurate information that includes safety, health, birth control methods, and the various choices related to sex and sexual activities. There are indications that this approach produces positive outcomes. Research in the Netherlands, where sex education puts an emphasis on young people's rights and responsibilities, has found that teenagers there have a positive outlook on sex, and sexually active teenagers there are more likely to use birth control than U.S. teenagers. The Netherlands has one of the lowest teen birth rates in the world, and the country's rates of sexually transmitted infection among teenagers are exceptionally low (one study found that Dutch adolescents were 75 times less likely than U.S. adolescents to contract gonorrhea). Furthermore, although most studies on adolescent sexual behavior have focused on potentially negative outcomes, some research has found that adolescent sex is associated with higher self-esteem, better self-concept, better stress management, and positive affect.

Minnah W. Farook and Roberto L. Abreu

See also Sex, Definition of; Sexual Health; Sexual Intimacy; Sexuality Education;

Further Readings

Glickman, C. (2000). The language of sex positivity. *Electronic Journal of Human Sexuality, 3*. Retrieved from http://www.ejhs.org/volume3/sexpositive.htm

Guttmacher Institute. (2016, February 1). *State policies in brief: Sex and HIV education*. Retrieved from http://www.guttmacher.org/statecenter/spibs/spib_SE.pdf

Harden, K. P. (2014). A sex-positive framework for research on adolescent sexuality. *Perspectives On Psychological Science, 9*, 455–469. doi:10.1177/1745691614535934

Williams, D. J., Prior, E., & Wegner, J. (2013). Resolving social problems associated with sexuality: Can a "sex-positive" approach help? *Social Work, 58*, 273–276. doi:10.1093/sw/swt024

SEX RESEARCHERS

Sex researchers, also known as sexologists, study human sexual behavior. The formal study of human sexuality began in the 19th century when scientists began exploring, through different methodologies, sex as a research subject. This entry discusses the work of sex researchers who are considered pioneers in the field, associations and academic journals involved in sex research today, and how counselors can make use of research into sex and sexuality.

Pioneers of Sex Research

The published works of Sigmund Freud, Henry Havelock Ellis, Alfred Kinsey, and William Masters and Virginia Johnson challenged literary, philosophical, and religious ideas by approaching the study of sexuality as a science. The following brief descriptions highlight the major contributions of these scientists along with other prominent individuals in the field of sex research.

Sigmund Freud

Freud is considered one of the founding fathers of sexology. Freud was a Viennese physician who emphasized the importance of sexuality in human behavior and motivations. In his practice as a neurologist, Freud encountered patients who presented with illnesses in which no physical cause could be found. He interviewed these men and women extensively and eventually concluded that their suffering was somehow related to early painful childhood experiences. Freud theorized that sexual energy, or libido, moved through distinct areas of the body at different ages. Freud developed psychoanalysis as a means of treating the unconscious sexual motivations. Although Freud contributed a great deal to society's understanding of human sexuality, his theories also led to some major misunderstandings, particularly regarding the nature of female sexuality.

Henry Havelock Ellis

Ellis was another influential sex researcher and practicing English physician who lived during the same time as Freud. Ellis's interest in sexual research began from his own experiences in trying to understand the nature of nocturnal emissions; at the time, some theorists believed that such emissions would lead to gonorrhea, insanity, blindness, or death. Accordingly, Ellis started keeping a diary to document the potential fate of his future. He soon realized that this fate wasn't occurring, which represented a discrepancy from what some medical theorists had taught him. Consequently, Ellis devoted his time to sex research in order to educate others. Between the years 1896 and 1928, Ellis published a series of volumes called *Studies in the Psychology of Sex*. His tolerant views of sexuality, including that masturbation and homosexuality should be considered normal, influenced many future researchers.

Alfred Charles Kinsey

Kinsey pioneered the use of case histories to study human sexuality. Kinsey created a 7-point scale that placed people on a continuum of sexual activity, from exclusively homosexual to exclusively heterosexual. It was his viewpoint that one or a few same-sex experiences did not automatically classify a person as homosexual. Rather than putting individuals into strictly dualistic categories of heterosexuality or homosexuality, he naturalized humans as somewhere in between these extremes and posited that orientation could change over the developmental life span.

Kinsey is also known for his survey research in the 1940s and 1950s. This research increased awareness of human sexuality as a scientific study; additionally, he suggested that sexual disorders could be treated in psychiatry and medicine. After a decade of gathering data on sexual behavior, Alfred Kinsey and his colleagues, including Wardell Pomeroy, Clyde Martin, and Paul Gebhard, achieved major advances in the understanding of human sexuality, which were published in his books *Sexual Behavior in the Human Male* and *Sexual Behavior in the Human Female*. Kinsey's method of data collection was through questionnaires, and in his largest sampling, he interviewed 6,000 White females in the United States. Kinsey's in-depth exploratory study of the female sexual response opened the doors for future researchers.

As a result of his contributions to knowledge about human sexuality, Kinsey is often considered the most influential American sex researcher of the 20th century. In 1947, he founded the Kinsey Institute at Indiana University, which contains one of the largest collections of archival data, photographs, and artifacts for the study of human sexuality. The Kinsey Institute remains fully operational and continues to study and publish scientific research on human sexuality.

William Masters and Virginia Johnson

The research team of Masters and Johnson formed at a time when social views and behaviors toward sex were becoming more tolerant. This tolerance can be partly understood by the discovery of penicillin and sulfa medications to treat diseases of syphilis and gonorrhea, thus rendering them less likely to be fatal.

Rather than interviewing people about their sexual behavior, as the Kinsey group had done, the data-collection approach Masters and Johnson used involved observation. They were the first researchers to directly observe and record the physiological responses of human sexual activity in a laboratory setting. In 1965, they opened the Masters and Johnson Institute in St. Louis, a sex therapy clinic. Their first published book, *Human Sexual Response,* was a textbook on the physiology and anatomy of sexual functioning. In 1970, their book entitled *Human Sexual Inadequacy* offered a model for describing the human sexual response cycle in four stages. Both of these groundbreaking books provided new insights and discredited many myths about sexual behavior. Masters and Johnson used a medical model in their research approach, thus expanding the study of sexuality to other disciplines, including counseling.

Other Researchers

The sex researchers just described made significant contributions to our current understanding of human sexuality. But other figures in the history of sex research are worth mentioning, as they laid the groundwork for those that followed. For example, German physician Magnus Hirschfeld published one of the earliest textbooks on sexology. The research of Ira Reiss focused on a sociological perspective explaining the way society influences human sexuality. Reiss explored sexual problems that are social concerns, such as teen pregnancy, rape, child sexual abuse, AIDS, and extramarital sexual behavior.

The preceding information is hardly exhaustive, but it is an overview of the main influential sex research pioneers who have crossed societal barriers and opened new opportunities for generations of researchers.

Modern Sex Research

Research in human sexuality continues to grow, as evidenced by the many research centers, associations, disciplines of study across universities, and professional journals. Technology has allowed the works of early sex researchers to sustain their influence and helped present-day researchers to conduct research and disseminate research findings to audiences beyond readers of academic journals. For example, the Kinsey Reporter app allows users to participate in research.

Today, there are many organizations with a focus on promoting continued science-based research in human sexuality, sexual health, and sexual behavior. Some examples of major organizations in sexology are the American Association of Sexuality Educators Counselors and Therapists (AASECT), the Society for the Scientific Study of Sexuality (SSSS), and the Society for Sex Therapy and Research (SSTAR).

Some organizations that focus on public policy, public education, sexual research, and reproductive health are the Guttmacher Institute, the Sexuality Information and Education Council of the United States (SIECUS), the Planned Parenthood Federation of America (PPFA), the International Academy of Sex Research, and the National Council on Family Relations (NCFR), which offers certification in family life education.

In addition to the sexuality resource organizations, there are many scholarly, academic journals. Some of the national and internationally recognized peer-reviewed professional journals that focus on sex research are *Archives of Sexual Behavior, The Journal of Sex Research, Journal of Marriage and Family, Journal of Family Theory & Review, Journal of Marital and Family Therapy, International Journal of Sexual Health, American Journal of Sexuality Education, Perspectives on Sexual and Reproductive Health, Sexual and Relationship Therapy, Journal of Sexual Medicine, Journal of Sex & Marital Therapy, Journal of Homosexuality, Sex Roles, Sex Education: Sexuality, Society, and Learning,* and *Sexuality and Disability.*

The associations, organizations, and journals noted here are just a snapshot of resources available today for the study of sexuality. The field of sex research reflects the complexity of sexuality and how it is interconnected with interpersonal relationships and human development. The scientific study of sexuality is important in addressing social and public health concerns, such as teenage pregnancy, welfare services, HIV, sexually transmitted infections, sex education in schools, sexual harassment, and rape. Additionally, modern sex researchers have studied the influence of substances and prescription medication on human sexuality, sexual desire, and relationships. These are some of the areas researched and published in the academic journals.

Sex Research and Marriage, Couples, and Family Counseling

Sexuality is an integral part of most romantic relationships. Most people will, at some point in their lives, encounter a sexual problem in their romantic relationships. Sex researchers' writings have informed many psychotherapeutic models, including those specifically designed to attend to relational challenges. When such challenges include sexuality, experienced clinicians use their preferred models to encourage disclosure, as talking about sexuality is difficult for many people.

Couples often have sexual problems stemming from different expectations about sex, including sex frequency and preferred sexual activities. Sometimes such expectation differences are based on each partner's preferred sexual experiences, or what sexologist John Money refers to as their lovemaps. At other times, partners' different expectations have emerged related to dynamic (and sometimes chronic) distress. For example, some couples find themselves in sexless relationships or marriages, defined as less than 10 sexual encounters a year. When meeting such a couple, a therapist is obliged to properly assess the onset, duration, variations, and other features of their presenting problem, which are critical in promoting a desired outcome. Masters and Johnson were known for obtaining extensive client sex histories, and this technique is still used today in counseling.

Other common concerns of couples involve communicating preferences, low libido, compromised sexual functioning, and a partner's history of sexual abuse or assault. When working with clients who present with issues regarding sexuality, effective counselors communicate facts and avoid myths. Staying up-to-date with sexuality research can help counselors avoid misconceptions. Effective counselors often stay apprised of current issues, cultural and societal influences, developmental changes, and gender in working with their clients. Clients can bring into their sexual relationships a complex history of experience, fantasies, knowledge, expectations, or misinformation.

Clients with sexual concerns generally experience the most benefit from counselors aware of and implementing best practices/competencies. Scientifically based research in human sexuality is one way to provide counselors with more accurate measures of sexual behavior and circumstances surrounding sexual relationships, identity, and health. By using an evidence-based approach, clinicians often can determine the most appropriate treatment approach to fit a client's specific needs. Evaluating the evidence that researchers in the field of sexuality have provided can ensure effective and successful treatment outcomes for clients.

Counselors need to be aware of their own values, assumptions, and personal biases regarding sexuality. An example of the need for this would be when a young adult male client presents for counseling and is struggling with intimate relationships. For a counselor to ask "Where do you go to meet women?" is an example of heterosexism and reveals a sexual-orientation bias. The social stigma against nonheterosexual individuals can be a factor in client mental health and well-being.

Counselors also can play a role in guiding clients through an examination of their beliefs and values, as sometimes societal expectations, even those that aren't valid, can contribute to relationship problems. For example, some people feel ashamed to ask for what they want from their partners, or they may have been discouraged, by various contexts, from being able to identify their sexual preferences. Finally, counselors who work with families can help educate parents to more effectively communicate with children and avoid misinformation.

Sarah Becerra

See also Beliefs and Values; Birth Control and Contraception; Certified Family Life Educator; Couples and Marriage Counseling; Human Sexual Response; Prevention Research; Sex Therapy; Sexual Assessment/History

Further Readings

Berg, P., & Snyder, D. (1981). Differential diagnosis of marital and sexual distress: A multidimensional approach. *Journal of Sex & Marital Therapy, 7,* 290–295.

Brecher, E. M. (1979). *The sex researchers.* New York: New American Library.

Bullough, V. L. (1995). *Science in the bedroom: A history of sex research.* New York: Basic Books.

Davis, O. M., Yarber, W. L., Bauserman, R., Schreer, & Davis, S. L. (Eds.). (1998). *Handbook of sexuality-related measures.* Thousand Oaks, CA: Sage.

Feray, J. C., & Herzer, M. (1990). Homosexual studies and politics in the 19th century: Karl Maria Kertbeny. *Journal of Homosexuality, 19*(1), 23–47.

Francoeur, R. T. (1995). *The complete dictionary of sexology.* New York: Continuum.

Frayser, S. G., & Whitby, T. J. (1995). *Studies in human sexuality: A selected guide* (2nd ed.). Englewood, CO: Libraries Unlimited.

Leiblum, S., & Rosen, R. (1988). *Sexual desire disorders.* New York: Guilford Press.

LoPiccolo, J., & LoPiccolo, L. (Eds.). (1978). *Handbook of sex therapy.* New York: Plenum.

Reiss, I. R. (2006). *An insider's view of sexual science since Kinsey.* Lanham, MD: Rowman & Littlefield.

Verhulst, J., & Heiman, J. (1979). An interactional approach to sexual dysfunctions. *American Journal of Family Therapy, 7*(4), 19–36.

Sex Therapy

Sex therapy refers to the mental health treatment of physical and emotional concerns related to sexuality and sexual behavior. Although use of the specific designation *sex therapist* requires specialized training and certification through the American Association of Sexuality Educators, Counselors and Therapists (AASECT), marriage and family therapists (MFTs) are legally able and, with appropriate training, clinically well-prepared to attend to the sexual issues of their clients, even without certification. This entry provides a discussion of the various issues addressed during sex therapy, and it details some of the orienting ideas, interventions, and treatment goals of different sex therapy approaches. It concludes with a list of recommendations for when MFTs should make referrals to medical professionals.

Issues Addressed in Sex Therapy

Many sexual problems are addressed within the sex therapy context. Some sex therapists organize their clinical work around diagnoses found in the fifth edition of the *Diagnostic and Statistical Manual of Mental Disorders* (DSM-5), such as erectile disorder, premature ejaculation, delayed ejaculation, hypoactive sexual desire disorder, orgasmic disorder, and genitopelvic pain/penetration disorder (pain with intercourse). However, many family therapists, particularly those working within the brief therapy or postmodern traditions, avoid conceptualizing client concerns about sexuality from a pathology-based framework, instead addressing symptoms from a relational, contextual perspective. Sex therapy is also conducted with clients presenting with concerns about sexual orientation or gender identity; past or current sexual trauma; sexual desire discrepancies between partners; issues of intimacy, anxiety, or shame around sexual performance or desires; body image distress; fetishes or compulsive sexual behaviors (often characterized as addictions); sexual difficulties associated with aging, illness, or disability; and problems related to cybersex, pornography, infidelity, and sexually transmitted infections (STIs).

Approaches to Sex Therapy

William Masters and Virginia Johnson are generally considered to have pioneered the field of sex therapy. Their groundbreaking research on sexual behavior, conducted during the 1950s and 1960s, opened the door to new interventions for assisting clients with sexual issues. Subsequently criticized for medicalizing sexuality and for incorporating cultural biases and assumptions based on gender stereotypes, their behavioral approach nevertheless broke new ground, challenging the existing psychoanalytic and psychoeducational approaches of the time.

Their most noteworthy innovation was the sensate focus technique, which helps couples to unhook themselves from the goal of orgasm, substituting instead a commitment to experiencing the intimacy of touch. Couples experiencing issues with orgasm are given specific directions for conducting a series of "touching" sessions with each other. In the initial sessions, only one partner touches the other at a time, and, although both members of the couple may be disrobed, the person doing the touching avoids contact with the other's genitals and breasts or chest. The couple is directed in subsequent sessions to gradually move toward mutual touching, still avoiding erogenous zones. Later, they are given permission to engage in touching that includes the genitals and breasts or chest as long as they avoid orgasm-focused arousal. Eventually, the couple, if heterosexual, is directed to move to penetration.

Since Masters and Johnson, clinicians from many different therapeutic modalities have made contributions to the theory and practice of sex therapy, including those working within the traditions of behavioral therapy, cognitive-behavioral therapy, multimodal therapy, psychodynamic therapy, Bowenian family therapy, object relations, contextual family therapy, systemic family therapy, research-influenced couples therapy, attachment-informed therapy, and brief therapy.

Licensed marriage and family therapists can practice sex therapy, but cannot advertise themselves as sex therapists per se. Given that many clients are anxious and uncomfortable talking about their bodies and their problems with performance or intimacy, therapists must be able to create a respectful, professional, and comfortable context for conversation regarding varied sexual practices and difficulties. Therapists must also be aware of and sensitive to cultural expectations and values that can inform clients' sexual choices and challenges. Given that clients may present with concerns regarding sexual orientation and gender identity, therapists must also avoid heterosexism and be cautious about applying conventional assumptions regarding gender identity.

Family therapists can draw on their own therapeutic models to guide their work with clients. More modernist approaches (e.g., Bowenian and attachment-based models) take a normative position with regard to defining what constitutes a healthy versus a problematic sexual relationship, whereas postmodern models (e.g., narrative, solution-focused brief therapy) are much less inclined to specify any qualities or characteristics that could be used to judge the appropriateness or quality of a sexual relationship. Instead, postmodern therapists rely on their clients to define relevant thresholds and values for themselves. The following are select illustrations of the ways some family therapists have applied their therapeutic orientation to working with clients who present with sexual issues.

A Bowenian approach to sex therapy, as described by David Schnarch, underscores the importance of differentiation of self in the construction and enhancement of an intimate sexual relationship. Differentiation is deemed to be central to an individual's successfully managing the complementary challenges in any relationship—how to not lose individuality while experiencing the thrill and challenges of meaningful togetherness. Rather than organize therapy in terms of treating pathology and reducing couple conflict, Bowen-informed therapists look for opportunities to help couples move from projecting their needs and fears onto the other person (something that happens when there is low differentiation of self), to taking responsibility for their own experience and learning to recognize, accept, and respect the partner's differences. This model allows not just for the resolution of sexual difficulties, but also for using sex therapy as a vehicle for helping couples learn how to achieve true intimacy (a living, dynamic balance of individuality and togetherness) in all aspects of their relationship.

Attachment-informed sex therapy, like the Bowenian model, attends to the active balance of engagement and disengagement in any intimate relationship. The therapist considers blockages in the relationship to be a function of an attachment injury of some kind. Safe attachment makes possible sex that is emotionally satisfying, intimate, and adventurous. In contrast to those who espouse separation as a necessary ingredient for sexual desire and arousal, attachment-based therapists underscore the importance of focused, body-based engagement. To facilitate improved relationships, the therapist brings together the needs and complexities of both attachment and sex.

From a narrative perspective, therapists helping clients with sexual concerns need to be particularly sensitive to cultural discourses that privilege or prescribe specific sexual behaviors and interactions, such as an exclusive focus on sexual performance, orgasm, or penetration. Narrative therapists seek to liberate clients from such limiting discourses, exploring "unique outcomes"—times when clients are able to move beyond limiting cultural messages or avoid the negative effects of sexual difficulties. As with most postmodern therapies, a narrative approach is concerned with avoiding the pathologizing effects of DSM diagnoses, focusing instead on exploring the larger cultural context in which problems are described and experienced. Client problems are discussed in terms of "preferred" rather than "prescribed" realities, thus opening clients to possibilities they may not have otherwise considered.

Solution-focused therapists prioritize client solutions rather than attempting to understand problem construction, maintenance, or causality. Identifying and amplifying client strengths, therapists practicing from this model seek to increase client awareness of times when the problem is not occurring (exceptions), as well as what will be happening when the problem is no longer a problem. Approaching sexual concerns from this framework allows therapists to avoid being organized by DSM diagnoses and to simply explore what is working when the problem is not central. Thus, clients experiencing challenges with maintaining erections or achieving orgasms can investigate varied ways to experience sexual desire and satisfaction; the specific pathway to these goals may or may not include an erect penis or an orgasm, and the cause of the problem will not become a focus of therapy. Once the clients begin to experience exceptions in terms of desire and satisfaction, the therapist will explore ways to build on those exceptions and thus enhance the couple's sexual satisfaction.

Similarly, possibility therapy, as identified by Bill O'Hanlon, shares an emphasis on promoting client strengths and resources, offering a nonpathologizing, nonnormative approach to resolving clients' sexual dilemmas. This model normalizes, validates, and gives permission for all client sexual thoughts, desires, and fantasies; however, it distinguishes thoughts and images about sexual behaviors from the behaviors themselves, some of which, due to their illegal or nonconsensual nature, cannot be accepted or validated. Acknowledging that sometimes clients' understanding of their current dilemmas perpetuates a problematic behavior, possibility therapy promotes clients' abilities to make significant changes in either their sexual expression or ways of viewing their expression.

Ethics

Because of the intimate nature of clinical discussions regarding sexuality, clinicians must be highly attuned to the ethical imperative to avoid sexualizing the clinical relationship. Whereas sexual surrogacy (therapeutic sexual contact with clients for specific clinical purposes) was considered a legitimate approach in 1970s and 1980s in some states, this is no longer the case. The 2015 *American Association for Marriage and Family Therapy (AAMFT) Code of Ethics* expressly forbids any sexual contact between therapists and their clients:

> 1.4 Sexual Intimacy with Current Clients and Others.
>
> Sexual intimacy with current clients or with known members of the client's family system is prohibited.

> 1.5 Sexual Intimacy with Former Clients and Others.
>
> Sexual intimacy with former clients or with known members of the client's family system is prohibited.

Anyone committing such a breach would be subject to a revocation of his or her license and clinical membership in AAMFT.

When to Refer

All therapists treating sexual concerns must remain sensitive to the complex interactions of mind and body, recognizing the need at times to make timely referrals to medical colleagues. For example, an inability to achieve or maintain an erection could reflect a man's fraught relationship with his partner, his anxious attempts to solve the difficulty by trying to get better conscious control of his body, questions of sexual identity, or cultural or personal expectancy regarding how he "should" be performing. Alternatively, it could be an indicator of a serious cardiovascular problem in need of medical attention or a side effect of one or more medications, such as an antidepressant or a drug that regulates blood pressure. Similarly, a woman's experience of painful intercourse could reflect prior sexual assault, anxiety, or shame regarding sexual activity, or emotional distance from or lack of safety with her partner. However, it could also be caused by insufficient lubrication (from decreased estrogen, lack of arousal, infection, or inflammation), by female genital mutilation, or by a structural problem—all of which should be confirmed or ruled out by a urologist or gynecologist.

Some clinicians are comfortable recommending the use of prescription drugs such as Viagra and Cialis for the treatment of erectile dysfunction; however, they need to always consider the relational ramifications of any such chemical intervention. In addition to the potential side effects of the drugs themselves, family therapists recognize that the couple's dynamics may be positively or negatively affected by medical solutions to sexual problems.

Such sensitivity to the relational complexities of mind, body, and relationship can be found in all family therapy approaches to sex therapy. Regardless of model, therapists recognize that sex-focused treatment can go far beyond simply addressing the quality or duration of sexual experiences. Although improvement of sex is a worthy and sufficient goal for many therapists and clients, sex therapy can also provide entry into the immediacy and meaning of intimacy, vulnerability, trust, and respect—in all aspects of a couple's life together.

Douglas Flemons and Shelley Green

See also Compulsive Sexual Behavior; Human Sexual Response; Sensate Focus; Sexual Intimacy; Sexual Relationships With Clients

Further Readings

American Association of Sexuality Educators Counselors & Therapists (AASECT): http://www.aasect.org

American Association of Marriage and Family Therapy (AAMFT). (2015). *AAMFT code of ethics.* Washington, DC: Author. Retrieved from http://www.aamft.org/iMIS15/AAMFT/Content/legal_ethics/code_of_ethics.aspx

Binik, Y. M., & Hall, K. S. (Eds.). (2014). *Principles and practice of sex therapy* (5th ed.). New York: Guilford Press.

Green, S., & Flemons, D. (Eds.). (2007). *Quickies: The handbook of brief sex therapy* (rev. ed.). New York: W. W. Norton.

Johnson, S., & Zuccarini, D. (2010). Integrating sex and attachment in emotionally focused couple therapy. *Journal of Marital and Family Therapy, 36*(4), 431–445. doi: 10.1111/j.1752-0606.2009.00155.x

Kleinplatz, P. J. (Ed.). (2012). *New directions in sex therapy* (2nd ed.). New York: Brunner-Routledge.

Perel, E. (2007). *Mating in captivity.* New York: HarperPerennial.

Schnarch, D. M. (1991). *Constructing the sexual crucible.* New York: W. W. Norton.

Tiefer, L. (2004). *Sex is not a natural act & other essays* (2nd ed.). Boulder, CO: Westview Press.

Sexual Abuse

Sexual abuse is the experience of unwanted sexual touch, sexual assault, or sexual harassment perpetrated by an individual or group of individuals. Sexual touch can include intercourse, attempted intercourse, fondling directly or through clothes, oral–genital contact, exhibitionism, or exposing children to inappropriate sexual material such as pornography or adult sexual behavior. Sexual abuse can occur as a one-time event or may be an ongoing experience. Estimates range from 16% to 25% of women and from 6% to 20% of men will experience some form of sexual abuse during their lifetime. In communities where sexual abuse is used as a weapon of war or occupation those estimates may be higher.

The effects of both childhood sexual abuse and adult sexual abuse impact psychological, physical, sexual, relational, and spiritual functioning. A range of trauma spectrum disorders may develop in victims of abuse as well as other members of their family, including spouses and parents. Trauma spectrum disorders among this population of clients may include depression, anxiety, posttraumatic stress, panic disorder, substance abuse disorders, and problematic relational patterns. Due to the high prevalence of sexual abuse among the general population of counseling clients, family and couples therapists should be skilled in assessment, treatment, and education about sexual abuse when working with survivors of abuse as well as their partners and family members. This entry first defines the terms used when discussing unwanted sexual activity and outlines the therapeutic steps necessary when sexual abuse is disclosed. It then discusses research findings on childhood sexual abuse and the use of family therapy with sexual abuse survivors and family members.

The terms *sexual abuse, sexual assault,* and *rape* are used in different ways, and legal definitions vary depending on the state. Sexual assault is generally used to refer to unwanted sexual touching, fondling, and/or penetration. The terms *sexual assault* and *rape* are sometimes used interchangeably, although the term *sexual assault* incorporates a wider range of abusive behaviors than the term *rape*. The term *rape* generally refers to an act of sexual intercourse that involves force or coercion, or when the victim cannot give consent. In most states sexual activity with a person who is incapacitated due to alcohol or substance use, or who is unconscious, is considered to be rape or sexual assault. The terms *date rape* or *marital rape* are often used when the victim and perpetrator are involved in a romantic relationship. The most common perpetrator of sexual assault is an individual who is known to the victim prior to the assault, which accounts for an estimated 75% to 85% of sexual assaults. Sexual assault can involve forced interaction or the use of a weapon; however, most sexual assaults do not involve the use of a weapon.

Sexual assault can occur at any age (childhood through geriatric years) but is most common in late adolescence and emerging adulthood. Sexual assault and rape are often thought of as crimes of male perpetrators against female victims, but male children, adolescents, and adults can be victimized by both male and female perpetrators. Male victims of sexual assault are often less forthcoming due to societal norms regarding sexual assault. Similar to survivors of childhood sexual abuse, adolescent and adults who experience sexual assault are at higher risk than peers for mood, anxiety, substance abuse, and stress disorders. Following an assault, victims may develop symptoms of guilt, shame, embarrassment, and safety concerns. Victims of sexual assault are at higher risk of suicide attempts than same-age peers. Victims of sexual assault have rates of posttraumatic stress disorder comparable to rates experienced by combat veterans.

Disclosure of Sexual Abuse

One aspect of treatment that is important in addressing the needs of sexual abuse survivors and their families is providing therapeutic support during the phase of initial disclosure. Therapists should be sensitive to assessment of sexual abuse. The initial inquiry of abuse must be done sensitively with careful awareness of word choice. The literature suggests that clients are more likely to respond to an inquiry about "unwanted sexual behavior" than about "rape" or "sexual assault." When working with a client with vague memories of possible abuse, counselors must be careful not to lead the client to a revelation or suggest abuse, which has been associated with the development of false memories of sexual abuse.

Once a disclosure of abuse has occurred, therapists must be attentive to the cognitive, emotional, and relational consequences of such a revelation. In addition to the relational and emotional impact of abuse disclosure, initial disclosure can heighten feelings of shame, guilt, and safety concerns for both the victim and other family members. Disclosure is an emotionally difficult process made more difficult if the individual victimized and his or her family members have a close relationship with the perpetrator. While there is increasing societal recognition of incidence of sexual abuse leading to increasing attention to childhood disclosures of abuse, initial disclosures of sexual abuse are more common in adulthood than in childhood. Disclosures that occur years after the abuse are often very difficult for family members who also may experience shame and guilt regarding the inability to protect the victim from the perpetrator. Furthermore, in cases of familial abuse, disclosure of abuse by one family member may result in disclosures by other family members.

Research on Childhood Sexual Abuse

A substantial amount of the sexual abuse literature focuses on incidents of childhood sexual abuse. Childhood sexual abuse occurs when minor children experience unwanted or developmentally inappropriate sexual touch, assault, harassment, or exposure to inappropriate sexual material by another individual or group of individuals. Perpetrators of childhood sexual abuse may be family members, relatives, trusted adults or older minor children, or strangers. The most common perpetrator of childhood sexual abuse is a close relative or close family friend. Both male and female children experience childhood sexual abuse; however, most victims of childhood sexual abuse are female. Abuse is most commonly perpetrated by family members or other trusted adults. A substantial body of clinical and legal literature has demonstrated that the risk for sexual abuse, especially for female children, increases with incidence of parental divorce and subsequent remarriage or cohabitation. Father–daughter incest is the most commonly studied form of incestuous childhood abuse, although some studies suggest that sibling incest is a more common form of family-involved sexual abuse.

Treatment processes and goals of childhood sexual abuse are influenced by the developmental maturity of the affected child as well as legal and child protective services involvement. When disclosures of childhood sexual abuse occur prior to adulthood, the treating counselor (according to applicable ethical and legal standards) may be required to report the abuse to local child protection or legal authorities. The requirements to report can be a deterrent for the individual child or family members' willingness to participate in therapy.

Another therapeutic factor may be that clinical notes may be required as evidence in legal proceedings, which may complicate the willingness of a survivor to reveal information in therapy. When sexual abuse is disclosed during childhood, the strength of attachment bonding with primary caregivers and appropriate reactions of trusted adults are an integral part of restoring safety and security. Childhood sexual abuse has been linked to several mental health and relational risk factors throughout the life span. Victims of childhood sexual abuse are at higher risk for developing mood, anxiety, and substance abuse disorders than peers without abuse history. Victims of childhood sexual abuse have higher rates of suicide attempts than peers and also have increasing risk for sexual difficulties in dating and marital relationships.

Family Therapy and Sexual Abuse

The provision of family therapy for sexual abuse requires therapeutic care for both the victim and impacted family members. Psychological and sexual consequences of past abuse may be prominent in couples work, as victims of abuse may have adapted cognitive and affective coping styles, including dissociation, anxiety responses, safety, and trust concerns in addition to any difficulties in physical and emotional intimacy. When disclosure of abuse implicates close friends or relatives, relational patterns for multiple family members may be impacted. When childhood sexual abuse is revealed, parents may also struggle with depression, anxiety, trust, anger, and safety concerns. Impacted siblings and extended family may be involved in the provision of family therapy services. The goal of family therapy is to restore safety, intimacy, and trust among family members and to promote positive adjustment for both the victim and the impacted family members.

As is true in other fields of couples and family therapy, there is increasing attention to the importance of implementing evidence-based practices when providing care for those impacted by sexual abuse. For families who experience the abuse of a child, trauma-focused cognitive-behavioral therapy is an evidenced-based structured therapy that incorporates family education, coping skill development, and narrative processing of the traumatic experience for both children and their families. Several individual-focused, evidence-based treatments include cognitive-processing therapy, eye movement desensitization and reprocessing therapy, and exposure therapy; these have demonstrated effectiveness in reducing traumatic responses among those who have experienced sexual abuse. However, these therapies have been designed for individual or group-based application. A survivor of abuse may attend individual therapy along with couples or family therapy, or may wish to receive treatment in a family setting. There are currently no evidence-based treatments designed specifically for processing sexual abuse in a family setting. However, emotion-focused couples therapy and solution-focused brief therapy have been demonstrated to be efficacious in aiding couples who are working on concerns such as trust and intimacy following revelations of sexual abuse.

Tara C. Samples

See also Evidence-Based Practice With Couples and Families; Incest; Trauma and Children; Trauma and Families

Further Readings

Foster, J. M. (2014). Supporting child victims of sexual abuse implementation of a trauma narrative family intervention. *The Family Journal, 22*(3). doi:1066480714529746.

Hershkowitz, I., Lanes, O., & Lamb, M. E. (2007). Exploring the disclosure of child sexual abuse with alleged victims and their parents. *Child Abuse & Neglect, 31*(2), 111–123.

Hunter, S. V. (2006). Understanding the complexity of child sexual abuse: A review of the literature with implications for family counseling. *The Family Journal, 14*(4), 349–358.

Kessler, M. R. H., Nelson, B. S., Jurich, A. P., & White, M. B. (2004). Clinical decision-making strategies of marriage and family therapists in the treatment of adult childhood sexual abuse survivors. *The American Journal of Family Therapy, 32*(1), 1–10.

MacIntosh, H. B., & Johnson, S. (2008). Emotionally focused therapy for couples and childhood sexual abuse survivors. *Journal of Marital and Family Therapy, 34*(3), 298–315.

SEXUAL ASSAULT AND RAPE

Sexual assault is defined by the U.S. Department of Justice's Office on Violence Against Women as any type of sexual contact or behavior that occurs without the explicit consent of the recipient. Falling under the definition of sexual assault are sexual activities such as forced sexual intercourse, forcible sodomy, child molestation, incest, fondling, and attempted rape. The perpetrator of sexual assault may be a stranger, acquaintance, friend, family member, or intimate partner. Findings from the *National Intimate Partner and Sexual Violence Survey 2010 Summary Report* indicate that the majority of men and women who experience rape knew their perpetrators, and the majority of women reported that at least one perpetrator was a current or former intimate partner or acquaintance. Sexual assault is a significant societal concern with an unfortunately high rate of occurrence that can have significant implications for an individual's mental and physical health. Fortunately, a number of important resilience factors have been identified within the larger sexual assault literature and evidence-based interventions to alleviate assault-related distress.

Estimates of Sexual Assault in the United States

Findings from the *National Intimate Partner and Sexual Violence Survey Summary Report* indicate that 1 in 5 women (18.3%) have experienced rape, with the most common form of sexual victimization being forced penetration (12.3%). Additionally, a significant number of women (44.6%) report having experienced some other form of sexual violence at some point in their lives. Rates among men in the United States are lower, with approximately 1 in 71 (1.4%) having reported experiencing rape and 5.6% reporting exposure to some other form of sexual violence in his lifetime. However, prevalence estimates among men are less reliable given the tendency for men to underreport assault experiences. The estimated prevalence of women experiencing rape in their lifetime by ethnic/racial background are as follows: 22% Black and 18.8% White non-Hispanic, 14.6% Hispanic, 26.9% American Indian or Alaska Native, and 33.5% multiracial non-Hispanic. The 2010 report did not include information on lifetime prevalence rates of rape for men in most racial and ethnic categories, because the number reporting rape was too small to calculate a reliable estimate. For White non-Hispanic men, the report estimated that 1.7% experienced rape over their lifetime. Another population at high risk for sexual assault is college women, with prevalence estimates indicating that approximately 20% of female undergraduates will experience sexual assault at some point during their college careers.

Mental Health Consequences of Sexual Assault

Sexual assault has been associated with a range of deleterious mental health sequelae. One common mental health consequence of sexual assault is posttraumatic stress disorder (PTSD). Estimates of PTSD stemming from sexual assault range from 17% to 65% among women. According to the American Psychiatric Association's *Diagnostic and Statistical Manual of Mental Disorders, Fifth Edition,* PTSD is the collection of persistent symptoms of reexperiencing (e.g., intrusive recollections or nightmares of the event); avoidance of internal (i.e., assault-related thoughts and feelings) and external (trauma-reminiscent people, places, or situations) trauma-related stimuli; negative alterations in cognitions and mood (e.g., persistent negative beliefs and expectations about oneself or the world, distorted perceptions of blame, persistent negative trauma-related emotions, anhedonia, feelings of detachment from others, and difficulty experiencing positive emotions); and hyperarousal (e.g., irritability, engagement in self-destructive behavior, exaggerated startle response, hypervigilance) following exposure to a traumatic event. Type of trauma has been implicated as a conditional risk factor for developing PTSD, with sexual assault, along with other forms of interpersonal violence, being more likely to result in PTSD.

A number of additional psychological difficulties often emanate from sexual victimization aside from or in addition to PTSD. Specifically, high rates of depression (13% to 51%), generalized anxiety (12% to 40%), alcohol misuse (12% to 49%) and misuse of other illicit substances (28% to 61%), and suicidality (23% to 44%) have been documented among survivors of sexual assault. Additionally, sexual assault survivors often experience secondary trauma reactions, such as self-blame, guilt, shame, and interpersonal/social conflicts. However, it is important to note that most individuals who experience traumatic events, including sexual assault, do not go on to develop PTSD or other chronic mental health conditions. An individual's risk of developing debilitating mental health conditions depends on a number of individual, environmental, and assault-related factors.

Factors Influencing Mental Health Outcomes

An increased likelihood of developing PTSD and other mental health conditions following sexual assault has been linked to a variety of vulnerability factors, such as a prior psychiatric history, previous exposure to a traumatic event, trauma severity, level of social support, and a family history of psychiatric illness. Additionally, a number of individual postassault factors have been associated with poorer psychological adjustment, such as an individual's use of coping behaviors, disclosure, and cognitive appraisals.

The use and success of coping strategies implemented in response to postassault distress may play an important role in survivors' psychological health. Generally, the use of avoidant variants of coping, such as denial, self-distraction, social withdrawal, and behavioral disengagement, have been associated with increased distress, whereas the reliance on approach oriented coping styles, such as support-seeking and emotional expression, have been linked to improved outcomes following sexual assault.

Disclosure of an assault to social networks has been associated with reduced psychological distress. While most women who experience sexual victimization tell at least one person about the assault, it can be a difficult decision for women to decide whether or not to disclose their sexual trauma. According to the National College Women Sexual Victimization Study, approximately 88% of college women disclosed experiences of sexual victimization to peers, 10% disclosed to family members, and 8.3% to a romantic partner. In regard to disclosure to formal sources of support, only 4% of college women reported their assault to a campus authority and only 2.1% to a police agency, and 1% disclosed to a counseling service. Disclosure can be a positive and adaptive response; however, the potential benefits of disclosure may be mitigated depending on the quality of social reactions received upon disclosure of a stigmatized experience, such as sexual assault. Research suggests that sexual assault survivors receive a mix of positive and negative reactions upon disclosure. Negative social reactions, such as being blamed, disbelieved, and treated differently, have been associated with poorer postassault adjustment, and may lead survivors to refrain from talking about the assault, encourage social withdrawal, or perpetuate or confirm maladaptive perceptions of blame.

Cognitive appraisals, particularly causal attributions offered by a sexual assault survivor to explain the cause of the assault experience, have significant implications for posttraumatic adjustment. Self-blame, a sexual assault survivor's notion of causality, whereby she or he views herself or himself as responsible for the assault, has been routinely associated with poorer adjustment. Further, increased assault-related distress has been associated with the acquisition of global negative beliefs about oneself, other people, or the future. Maladaptive cognitive appraisals may result in harsh self-criticism and low evaluations of self-worth, thereby perpetuating negative emotions, such as guilt or shame, and contributing to the development and maintenance of mental health conditions, such as PTSD and depression.

Impact on Physical Health and Health-Risk Behaviors

Sexual assault has been associated with a range of physical health conditions as well as greater engagement in health-risk behaviors. Findings from the *National Intimate Partner and Sexual Violence Survey 2010 Summary Report* suggest that women sexual assault survivors may be at greater risk for physical health problems as compared to males. Specifically, higher rates of asthma, irritable bowel syndrome, diabetes, headaches, chronic pain, difficulty sleeping, and activity limitations have been documented among women sexual assault survivors. Men with a history of interpersonal and/or sexual victimization have a higher prevalence of headaches, chronic pain, impaired sleep, and activity limitations. An additional potential physical health consequence of sexual assault is sexual health problems. Although this is an understudied area, findings from a national probability sample indicate that 40% of American women experience sexual dysfunction and that such difficulties are strongly related to prior sexual victimization for women. Specifically, exposure to variants of sexual violence has been positively associated with sexual dysfunction (e.g., lack of sexual desire, lack of orgasm) and other gynecological problems.

Sexual assault has also been associated with increased engagement in a number of health-risk behaviors. One aspect of health-risk behavior to receive considerable attention within the area of sexual assault is substance misuse. Specifically, high rates of alcohol and illicit substance dependence and abuse have been documented among sexual assault survivors. The positive association between sexual victimization and substance abuse has been interpreted in a few ways, and findings regarding the precise nature of this relationship have been mixed. Some have proposed that engagement in substance misuse, as well as other health-risk behaviors, may precede the sexual assault experience, placing individuals at greater risk for victimization. The alternate explanation accounting for this association, which has received strong empirical support, is the self-medication hypothesis, which proposes that survivors of sexual assault may engage in the use of substances, such as alcohol, in order to alleviate negative distress resulting from their assault. Additionally, increased engagement in sexual risk-taking behaviors, such as engaging in casual sex, sex with multiple partners or while under the influence of alcohol or drugs, and inconsistent use of contraception, has been documented among sexual assault survivors, particularly among college populations. The positive association between sexual victimization and sexual risk taking is of great importance, as engagement in these risky behaviors can lead to additional negative consequences, such as sexually transmitted infections, unintended pregnancies, and increased risk for sexual revictimization.

Promising Interventions for Sexual Assault-Related Distress

Fortunately, a number of evidence-based treatments exist to alleviate PTSD and associated forms of psychological distress emanating from sexual assault. Cognitive-behavioral therapies such as prolonged exposure and cognitive processing therapy have garnered substantial empirical support and are often regarded as perhaps the most effective interventions for PTSD. The primary objective of prolonged exposure is to facilitate the gradual confrontation of typically avoided assault-related memories, images, objects, and situations. During treatment, clients engage in imaginal exposure exercises, which involve recounting their traumatic experience and then reviewing their account between sessions for homework. Treatment also includes in vivo exposure exercises, which require the confrontation of objectively safe, real-life feared situations, objects, or people. Repeated exposure through either imaginal or in vivo exposure exercises to event-related phenomena is thought to facilitate the extinction of conditioned fear responses and allow for the incorporation of newly learned safety information.

The goal of cognitive processing therapy, originally developed specifically for sexual assault populations, is to target and modify distorted beliefs and cognitions about the meaning and implications of the traumatic event. This is achieved through in session dialogue and written exercises between sessions. This treatment approach also contains an exposure component; however, the primary focus of therapy is to produce cognitive change in harmful PTSD-related cognitions, such as self-blame and other trauma-generated maladaptive beliefs about the self, world, and others. Cognitive processing therapy specifically focuses on five domains commonly affected by assault survivors: safety, trust, power/control, esteem, and intimacy.

Other potentially useful interventions include those focusing on enhancing adaptive coping responses, couples therapies, and solution-oriented interventions that promote survivors' strengths and sense of empowerment. Mental health providers should also be properly educated and trained on sexual assault and be informed of appropriate legal, mental health, and other resources and services in order to effectively meet the needs of sexual assault survivors.

Christina M. Hassija

See also Anxiety; Alcohol and Substance Abuse; Coping; Sexual Abuse

Further Readings

Black, M., Basile, K., Breiding, M., Smith, S., Walters, M., Merrick, M., & Stevens, M. (2011). *The national intimate partner and sexual violence survey (NISVS): 2010 summary report.* Atlanta, GA: National Center for Injury Prevention and Control, Centers for Disease Control and Prevention.

Campbell, R., Dworkin, E., & Cabral, G. (2009). An ecological model of the impact of sexual assault on women's mental health. *Trauma, Violence, & Abuse, 10,* 225–246. doi:10.1177/1524838009334456

Fisher, B. S., & Cullen, F. T. (1999). *Violence against college women: Results from a national level study.* Washington, DC: U.S. Department of Justice, Bureau of Justice Statistics.

National Sexual Violence Resource Center: http://www.nsvrc.org/

National Center for Victims of Crime: http://www.victimsofcrime.org/home

Rape, Abuse & Incest National Network: https://www.rainn.org/get-information/types-of-sexual-assault/sexual-assault

U.S. Department of Justice: http://www.justice.gov/ovw/sexual-assault

Sexual Assessment/History

Individuals and couples sometimes experience sexual difficulties. When a therapist works with clients about sexual issues, it is important to do a sexual assessment and gather information on their sexual history. Sexual assessments are done in order to diagnose a sexual problem and/or create a treatment plan to intervene with sexual issues. Although there are specific models of sexual assessment, in general clinicians collect information about the sexual history, sexual functioning, values, and expectations of clients. The information can be collected through interviews, questionnaires, or tests. In addition, sexual assessment and history taking can be done from an individual perspective or a relational perspective. From an individual perspective the focus is on individual sexual development, sexual experiences, sexual partners, medical issues related to sexual functioning, and satisfaction with one's sexual life. From a relational perspective, information is gathered from both members of a couple related to any sexual problems one or both partners are experiencing, satisfaction with the relationship, influences from families of origin on the sexual values of each partner, and possibly some exploration of the individual sexual history of each partner. In this entry the focus is on sexual assessment from a relational perspective. Discussed in the following sections are models of assessment, the intersystem approach to sexual assessment, when to do an assessment, and the importance of clinician comfort with the topic of sexuality.

Models of Assessment

Clinicians need a framework to help guide the type of information they gather from clients. There are different types of models, or frameworks, to guide clinicians in in doing sexual assessments. Some examples of models of assessment are the biopsychosocial approach; the permission, limited information, specific suggestions, and intensive therapy (PLISSIT) model; and the intersystem model. The biopsychosocial approach looks at biological/physiological factors (e.g., menopause, cardiovascular issues, back problems), psychological issues (e.g., depression, trauma, alcoholism), and relationship and social environment factors (e.g., relationship satisfaction, communication, sexual values). The PLISSIT model, when used for the assessment portion of therapy, guides the work of the clinician and reminds the clinician about *how* assessment should be done, rather than just the information to gather. It reminds the clinician to first ask the clients for permission to ask about sex and that sometimes a sexual assessment should be limited rather than comprehensive. Sometimes individuals or couples just have a few, simple sexual questions they want answered.

Based on their work with individuals and couples, Gerald Weeks and Nancy Gambescia suggest using an intersystem approach. This approach has five domains for assessment: individual biological issues, individual psychological factors, couple (relational) dynamics, intergenerational (family-of-origin) influences, and environmental considerations (e.g. society, culture, history, religion).

Individual Biological Domain

Biological and physiological factors can affect sexual functioning and satisfaction. Clinicians should assess each person's current health and any past medical issues that may affect one's current sexual life. This assessment should include any medications and nonprescription drugs the couple take. Physical health can affect a couple's enjoyment of their sexual life in many ways. For example, back pain or being overweight can affect the types of positions that are comfortable during sexual activity. Changes in hormones can influence desire in both men and women and, among other things, can affect lubrication in women and erections in men. Cardiovascular health can have many effects on sexual activity and pleasure, and for men can directly correlate with erectile difficulties. In addition, medications can affect one's desire for sex, the ability to get excited during sexual activity, and the ability to orgasm. All of these are important issues to asses and consider in relation to sexual problems and sexual satisfaction. It is always a good idea to suggest to clients that they get a medical checkup to make sure there aren't any unknown medical issues affecting their sex lives.

Individual Psychological Domain

Sometimes personal issues, experiences, sexual development, sexual and gender orientation, sexual preferences, or mental health issues can influence people's sexuality in both positive and negative ways. Although this domain is called the "individual psychological domain," the individual is influenced by a partner and family, and in return an individual influences a partner and family. Although people are of course individuals, they do not function in isolation from others. Some of the topics that may be assessed in this area include emotional styles, attachment styles, sexual trauma, undisclosed sexual secrets (e.g., infidelity, sexually transmitted infections, trauma, sexual orientation), and mental health problems. It is important to understand each individual because this is important to understanding the couple's functioning, which is discussed in the next domain.

Couple Relationship Domain

The couple relationship domain is focused on the current relationship between partners. In this domain the clinician assesses couple communication, their current sex life, their views of eroticism and sexual pleasure, the meaning that they ascribe to sex and any sexual problems, how they would like their sex life to be, capacity for intimacy, their relationship styles, conflict resolution styles, and their strengths as a couple. From a relationship perspective there are multiple systems in the room to be assessed—each individual client, the couple's relationship, and the relationship between the clinician and the clients (e.g., their comfort with discussing sexual issues with the clinician, how much each person trusts the clinician, how effective the clients believe the clinician can be with their presenting problem(s)/goals). The relationship between the couple is seen as integral to increasing their sexual satisfaction and happiness. Their overall relationship satisfaction and their sexual satisfaction are important parts of the couple assessment. Sexual problems can influence relationship satisfaction, and relationship satisfaction can influence sexual satisfaction.

Intergenerational Domain

People learn about sexuality and sexual values in both intentional and unintentional ways from their families of origin (the family they grew up with). Families send messages about intimacy in many ways: the way they express all forms of intimacy, the way they engage in their own relationships, through formal education and the family's discussions of that education (e.g., parents explicitly explaining their views on sexuality, religious views on sexuality, and sexuality education in school), through how they talk about the sexuality of others, and through what they choose not to talk about. Some of the information people get from their families are positive and affirming of affection, intimacy, and sexuality. However, often messages are either intentionally or unintentionally negative. Some refer to one's general disposition toward sexuality as either sex negative or sex positive. In reality these ideas are on a continuum. Sex positivity means being accepting and encouraging of a variety of sexualities and sexual activities. This includes being accepting of engaging or not engaging in sexual behaviors, embracing a continuum of sexual and gender orientations, including eroticism and sexual pleasure in one's view of sexuality, and being accepting of diverse sexual activities (whether one chooses to engage in those behaviors or not).

Environmental Domain

The last domain, the environmental domain, includes the idea that culture influences people's sexual values and beliefs. This domain includes society, culture, history, and religion. People internalize messages about sexuality from their families, friends, media, education, laws and policies, ethnic groups, and other entities. Sexual values and beliefs are also influenced by racism, sexism, heterosexism, and other negative messages and experiences. Again, as in the intergenerational domain, these messages from the environment can be positive or negative, formal (e.g., laws, policies, religious restrictions) or informal, and intentional or unintentional. Clinicians should explore these areas and possibly adjust their approach based on these considerations. For example, a technique often suggested for those having trouble reaching orgasm is to masturbate to find out what feels good, increases their excitement, and help them reach orgasm. However, if clients' religion strictly forbids masturbation, then this would not be an appropriate area of in-depth assessment and intervention.

When to Conduct Sexual Assessment

In couple, family, and marriage counseling, basic sexual histories can be taken as part of the intake process (an interview and/or paperwork time before the first therapy session), but some clinicians suggest that more in-depth assessment of sexuality take place after the clients build rapport with the clinician. In addition, some suggest that the clinician actually ask permission to talk about sexual issues or at least introduce it as a topic that will be discussed. Couples sometimes seek therapy specifically for sexual issues and overtly state they want to work on sexual issues; however, they often do not reveal sexual issues until asked by the clinician. A clinician can ask a couple if they would like to discuss sexuality, or the clinician can state, "When I work with couples I typically cover the subjects of communication, conflict resolution, how power is divided in the relationship, parenting issues (if they have children), relationships with friends and family, nonsexual intimacy, and sexual intimacy. Which topic would you like to discuss first?"

In addition, when working with couples the clinician has to decide whether to do sexual assessments with each individual alone, with the couple, or do both individual and couple assessments. Many clinicians do a combination of both individual sessions and couple sessions for sexual assessment. Sometimes people are more honest when their partner is not in the room. However, doing individual assessments with only one partner can put a clinician in an awkward position if the client reveals a secret that affects the partner, but the client does not want the partner to know. Some clinicians have a "secrets" policy that they discuss with clients. The therapist will let the clients know if he or she will or will not keep secrets from individual sessions. It is usually suggested that clinicians do not keep secrets because at best it sometimes makes couple sessions more difficult and less effective, and at worst it can put the clinician in an ethical dilemma.

Comfort With Sexuality

Clinicians should appear comfortable about any topic they are discussing with clients. This can be more difficult when a taboo topic, such as sexuality, is being discussed. Although people may assume and expect that clinicians are comfortable discussing sexual issues, research does not support this. Many health professionals (both medical and nonmedical) report that they are not comfortable discussing sexuality with patients/clients, and that they feel they are not adequately prepared to do so. Even when they have the knowledge to discuss sexuality, they will be less likely to discuss, assess, or intervene with sexual issues if they are not comfortable with the topic. The more anxiety a topic produces, the more the clinician's self-efficacy is challenged.

Some believe that working with sexual issues is different from working with nonsexual issues, and that special training is needed to increase clinicians' sexual self-efficacy. Increasing a person's sexual self-efficacy increases his or her comfort level and makes it more likely a client will discuss sexual topics in a respectful, affirming, and open-minded way. In addition, clinicians should take a sex-positive approach to sexuality, which is not always easy for all clinicians to do. Like clients, they internalize messages about sexuality that are both positive and negative. Special training may also make it more likely that clinicians will adopt a sex-positive approach.

Kristin Page, Shannon B. Dermer, and Molli E. Bachenberg

See also Sexual Abuse; Sexual Assault and Rape; Sexual Dysfunction; Sexual Enhancement, Sexual Toys; Sexual History; Sexual Intimacy; Sexual Orientation, Attraction, and Identity; Sexually Transmitted Infections

Further Readings

Buehler, S. (2013). *What every mental health professional needs to know about sex.* New York: Springer.

Byers, E. S. (2005). Relationship satisfaction and sexual satisfaction: A longitudinal study of individuals in long-term relationships. *Journal of Sex Research, 42*(2), 113–118.

Crowe, M., & Ridley, J. (2008). *Therapy with couples: A behavioural-systems approach to couple relationship and sexual problems.* New York: Wiley.

Dermer, S., & Bachenberg, M. (2015). The importance of training marital, couple, and family therapists in sexual health. *Australian and New Zealand Journal of Family Therapy, 36,* 492–503. doi:10.1002/anzf.1122

Leiblum, S. R. (Ed.). (2006). *Principles and practice of sex therapy.* New York: Guilford Press.

McCarthy, B. (2015). *Sex made simple: Clinical strategies for sexual issues in therapy.* Eau Claire, WI: PESI Publishing & Media.

Weeks, G., & Gambescia, N. (2015). Couple therapy and sexual problems. In A. Gurman, J. Lebow, & D. Snyder (Eds.), *Clinical Handbook of Couple Therapy* (5th ed., pp. 635–658). New York: Guilford Press.

Weeks, G., Gambescia, N., & Hertlein, K., (2016). *A clinician's guide to systemic sex therapy* (2nd ed.). New York: Routledge.

Williams, B. K., Sawyer, S. C., & Wahlstrom, C. M. (2012). *Marriages, families, and intimate relationships.* Boston: Pearson.

Sexual Dysfunction

Couples who experience mutually satisfying sexual experiences typically report higher levels of intimacy and overall relationship satisfaction. A relationship can become strained when one or both partners are experiencing sexual dysfunction. In marriage and couples therapy, sexual dysfunction refers to emotional and relational distress experienced by one or both partners that was caused by unsatisfying experiences during sexual intercourse. Approximately one third of Americans experience sexual dysfunction at some point in their lives. There are a variety of negative consequences for couples when one or both partners are experiencing sexual dysfunction, including anxiety, depression, relationship stress, emotional disconnect between partners, and separation. The majority of individuals who are living with sexual dysfunction do not seek treatment. This entry provides an overview of the causes of sexual dysfunction and discusses treatment options in the context of couples and family therapy.

Causes of Sexual Dysfunction

Sexual dysfunction is typically caused by a combination of genetic and environmental influences. Common genetic factors that increase the chances that one will experience sexual dysfunction include congenital illnesses, anatomical deformities, and predispositions to cardiovascular disorders. The following are common environmental or precipitating factors for sexual dysfunction: increases in levels of daily stress, problematic attachments, restrictive upbringing, and abusing alcohol or other substances. Mental disorders, including but not limited to anxiety and depression, also place one at an increased risk for developing sexual dysfunction. Additionally, individuals who have experienced verbal, physical, or sexual abuse are at increased risk for developing sexual dysfunction.

Sexual Dysfunction in Men and Women

Both men and women experience sexual dysfunction. Approximately 40% of men and 35% of women experience sexual dysfunction at some time in their lives. The two most common types of sexual dysfunction in men are erectile dysfunction (ED) and premature ejaculation (PE). Erectile dysfunction involves a man's inability to obtain an erection despite the presence of sexual arousal and the desire to engage in sexual intercourse. Premature ejaculation involves a man who consistently ejaculates before he or his partner would like.

The most common type of sexual dysfunction among women is hypoactive sexual desire disorder (HSDD). Hypoactive sexual desire disorder is characterized by a consistent lack of sexual desire that causes significant relational distress. In the fifth edition of the *Diagnostic and Statistical Manual of Mental Health Disorders* (DSM-5) sexual desire and arousal disorders have been combined into one disorder: female sexual interest/arousal disorder. Orgasmic disorders also impact women and involve a consistent inability to reach orgasm in spite of adequate sexual stimulation. Women have also been found to experience sexual dysfunctions that involve experiencing displeasure or pain during sexual activity.

Treatment Options

Documented treatment methods for sexual dysfunction date back to ancient Greece and Rome. In this time sexual dysfunctions were thought to be caused by genetic, religious, and metaphysical influences. As a result, early treatments for sexual dysfunction were herbological. Common forms of early treatment approaches for sexual dysfunction involved consuming an herb or beverage.

Up until the mid-19th and early 20th centuries, sexual dysfunctions were thought to be caused by external factors, and the treatments were also external. The psychological causes of sexual dysfunctions were discovered in the late 1800s and early 1900s, and more holistic treatments for sexual dysfunctions emerged. In this era, a more integrative approach was taken to understanding and treating sexual dysfunction.

Psychoanalytic and Cognitive-Behavioral Treatment Approaches

Sigmund Freud, a Viennese neurologist who developed the field of psychoanalysis in the late 1800s and early 1900s, created a psychoanalytic approach to treating sexual dysfunction and other mental disorders. Freud's approach revolutionized treatment modalities as he emphasized the psychological and unconscious causes of sexual dysfunction. Freud's work revolutionized our understanding and treatment approaches for sexual dysfunction and for a variety of other conditions by highlighting the psychological origins of these aliments. The work of Freud and others set the foundation for the now widely accepted belief that sexual dysfunctions are caused by a combination of genetic and environmental forces. However, research findings did not support the efficacy of psychoanalytic treatments alone for sexual dysfunction.

In the late 1950s cognitive-behavioral models and treatment approaches for sexual dysfunction emerged. These approaches highlighted how an individual's thoughts and conditioned behavioral responses impacted his or her sexuality. Treatment techniques and approaches involved therapists working with clients to help them recondition problematic thoughts and behaviors that were related to sexual dysfunction. For example, the following treatment approaches and techniques were utilized to treat ED: sex education, systematic desensitization, talk therapy, sensate focus, sexual skills trainings, and self-stimulation exercises. In addition, a variety of behavioral treatment approaches for PE arose, including the stop-start technique and the squeeze technique. Clients described the most success in recovering from sexual dysfunction when combinations of the previously described cognitive-behavioral techniques were implemented by therapists. By the end of the 20th century, treatment approaches began to shift toward biomedical interventions due to the development of medications for treating sexual dysfunction.

Biomedical Treatment Approaches

In the 1980s, biomedical approaches for treating sexual dysfunction started to become increasingly dominant. A variety of biomedical approaches emerged, including hormone replacement therapies, penile implant surgeries, hormone injection therapies, and the use of medications to treat sexual dysfunction. Antidepressant medications were prescribed to treat premature ejaculation in clients. For erectile dysfunction, a new class of drugs called phosphodiesterase-5 (PDE5) inhibitors were created. PDE5 inhibitors, for example, sildenafil citrate (Viagra), work by increasing the blood flow to the penis when one is experiencing sexual arousal. This increased blood flow greatly increases the chances than a man will achieve an erection.

The increasing popularity of biomedical treatments have fallen under scrutiny as critics argue that biomedical approaches are a threat to more comprehensive biopsychosocial approaches for treating sexual dysfunction. It is widely accepted that that the causes of sexual dysfunction are both biological and psychological. As a result, researchers argue that treatments for sexual dysfunctions should have both biomedical and psychological components. There is a growing concern among some researchers that biomedical treatment approaches are being used as a quick and easy fix and neglect treating the psychological causes of sexual dysfunction. These researchers do not deny the effectiveness of biomedical treatment approaches. Instead, some argue that the most effective treatments for sexual dysfunction involve an integration of biomedical and psychological components.

Integrated Biomedical and Psychological Treatment for Sexual Dysfunction

To offer an integrated treatment approach for sexual dysfunction that incorporates biomedical and psychological components, marriage and couples therapists need to work closely with a medical provider. The three main forms of therapy for sexual dysfunction are individual therapy, conjoint couples therapy, or a mixed-mode approach. Individual therapy involves the therapist working one-on-one with a client who is living with sexual dysfunction. In conjoint therapy, therapists work with both partners to provide treatment for sexual dysfunction. The mixed-mode approach involves a combination of individual and conjoint therapy sessions. Research has found the most positive treatment outcomes among clients who received a mixed mode approach consisting of both individual and couples therapy.

Barriers to Seeking Treatment

The majority of people who are experiencing sexual dysfunction will either wait years to seek treatment or will not seek any form of treatment. A variety of barriers reduce the chances that an individual will seek treatment for sexual dysfunction. Particularly among men, a social stigma is attached to sexual dysfunction. In Western culture, social norms send the message that men are supposed to be ready and eager to engage in sexual activity at all times. Although this social norm is unsupported by research, many men feel ashamed and embarrassed about acknowledging their experiences of sexual dysfunction. These feelings of shame and embarrassment about experiencing sexual dysfunction are two common reasons that many men do not seek treatment.

Sexual abuse has been found to be an especially strong precipitating factor for the future onset of sexual dysfunction in women. A woman's relationship to the perpetrator and the frequency of abuse were related to the future onset of sexual dysfunction. More specifically, women were at increased risk for developing sexual dysfunction when the perpetrator was someone close to them, for example a parent or relative. Women were also found to be especially vulnerable to developing sexual dysfunction when they suffered multiple occurrences of sexual abuse compared to women who experienced sexual abuse on one occasion.

The cost of attending therapy sessions is another barrier for some clients. Services for sexual dysfunction might not be covered by an individual's health care plan. The cost of treatment for sexual dysfunction can also vary among different providers. Treatment for sexual dysfunctions provided by mental health practitioners who identified as psychologists have been found to be more expensive than treatments provided by practitioners with master's degrees who identified as social workers, professional counselors, or marriage and family therapists.

Michael T. Kalkbrenner

See also Sex Positivity; Sex Therapy; Sexual Health; Sexual Intimacy; Sexuality Education

Further Readings

Berry, M. D. (2013). Historical revolutions in sex therapy: A critical examination of men's sexual dysfunctions and their treatment. *Journal of Sex & Marital Therapy, 39*(1), 21–39. doi:10.1080/0092623X.2011.611218

Fawcett, D., & Crane, D. R. (2013). The influence of profession and therapy type on the treatment of sexual dysfunctions. *Journal of Sex & Marital Therapy, 39*(5), 453–465. doi:10.1080/0092623X.2012.665814

McCabe, M., Althof, S. E., Assalian, P., Chevret-Measson, M., Leiblum, S. R., Simonelli, C., & Wylie, K. (2010). Psychological and interpersonal dimensions of sexual function and dysfunction. *Journal of Sexual Medicine, 7*(1), 327–336. doi:10.1111/j.1743-6109.2009.01618

Weeks, R. G., & Gambesicia, N. (2000). *Erectile dysfunction: Integrating couple therapy, sex therapy, and medical treatment.* New York: W. W. Norton.

Sexual Enhancement, Sexual Toys

Sexual enhancement products (i.e., sexual toys or "sex toys") are items that are used to stimulate sexual arousal and erotic play. Broadly defined, sexual enhancement includes erotica, sexy clothing, sensual fragrances and oils, but the term most commonly refers to items used in or on the body to enhance sexual pleasure, such as dildos, vibrators, vaginal balls (aka Ben Wa balls or Kegel balls); anal toys, penis rings, pumps, and sleeves; bondage, domination, and sadomasochism (BDSM) gear (e.g., bondage cuffs and spanking implements); sex furniture (e.g., slings); and erotic electrostimulation (electricity for sexual stimulation). The term *sex toy* does not apply to birth control or condoms, though condoms are recommended for protection against sexually transmitted infections or unwanted pregnancy when sex toys are used. Sex toys are most commonly sold online or at specialty sex shops. This entry reviews the various types of sexual enhancement products, how they are used, and how they enhance sexual pleasure of those in the general population, as well as those dealing with sexual dysfunctions and physical limitations.

Sexual Enhancement Products and Their Use

From the time of Hippocrates until the 1920s, massaging female patients to orgasm was common to the practice of Western physicians in the treatment of "hysteria," an ailment once considered both common and chronic in women. Hysteria, a complex neurosis in which psychological conflict is turned into physical symptoms, such as amnesia, blindness, and paralysis, that have no underlying cause, was the focus of Sigmund Freud's early career. Doctors loathed this time-consuming procedure and for centuries relied on midwives. Later, they substituted the efficiency of mechanical devices, including the electric vibrator, to provide vulval or clitoral massage, leading to "hysterical paroxyism" (orgasm) that evoked at least temporary relief of symptoms. The vibrator was invented in the 1880s, and it was used until it fell into disrepute as a legitimate medical device in the 1920s.

While waning in medical use, the electric powered vibrator soon became recognized as a very effective device for women seeking to achieve orgasm, and many women have attained their first climax using a vibrator to stimulate the clitoris or surrounding area. Personal use of sexual enhancement products has increased dramatically over the past 20 years. Research in the 1990s indicated that about 2% of women had used vibrators, while a 2010 survey by the Kinsey Institute indicated that 53% of women and 45% of men have used a vibrator. A lesser known use is to stimulate the nerve endings around the penile corona in men and the anus in both men and women. The penile ring and some penile sleeves are also used in conjunction with a vibrator.

Dildos can be designed to look like a penis, but they also appear in a wide variety of shapes, sizes, and materials used to make them—they can be used for either vaginal or anal insertion and pleasure seeking. Many dildos and vibrators are made with a distinctive curve which makes them easier to stimulate particularly sensitive erogenous areas, like the so called G-spot in women and the prostate in men.

Sexual enhancement products facilitate masturbation and self-pleasuring. Vibrators stimulate and provoke arousal and orgasm. Dildos and other insertion devices like anal plugs simulate penetration and allow the user to adjust the motion, fullness, and pressure to his or her individual preferences. Sex toys also allow for experimentation and learning to explore one's own body, which can help the individual learn what sensations are most desirable with a partner. Sex toys also provide outlets for pleasure to those who do not have or want sex partners.

On the other hand, some devices are designed for use by couples during intercourse, such as the Ida and the WeVibe. Both of these items are U-shaped vibrators that stimulate both the vagina and clitoris while still allowing penile penetration, given their narrow profile. Penis rings are designed to supplement clitoral stimulation during penetration. Dildos can be be used either in one's hand for solo sex or in a harness to provide penetration for a partner. Anal sexual enhancement products can be used as a hands-free supplement during masturbation with solo sex or during sex with a partner while engaging in oral, vaginal, or manual stimulation. BDSM products such as spanking devices and bondage gear are typically used with a partner using role-play accompanied by intense sensation.

Erotic electro-stimulation refers to the use of electricity for sexual stimulation, and its use dates back to the middle of the 18th century. By the 1970s, medical transcutaneous electrical nerve stimulation (TENS) machines were widely available. The TENS machines work by stimulating nerve endings with electricity and sending signals of stimulation to the brain. Electro-stimulation follows this same principle—when the brain receives a signal of stimulation from the genitals, pleasure hormones are released. Electro-stimulation is typically added to the more conventional "butt plugs" and "cock rings," and tends to be used by more sexually adventurous individuals.

Safer Sex

Sexual enhancement products can be an effective means of experiencing sexual pleasure without risking sexually transmitted infections (STIs), sexually transmitted diseases (STDs), or the risk of pregnancy brought on by penile or vaginal penetration. STIs can be transmitted through sex toys, however. To lower risk, any device used in or on the body should be covered by a condom or another barrier unless the device is "fluid bonded" to that individual or couple. Fluid bonded means that the device was used only by that individual or couple. The condom or barrier should then be changed and replaced if passed off to another individual or couple or used in a different orifice by the same couple.

There is no evidence that sexual enhancement products in and of themselves cause health risks or pose other physical risks to those who use them. There are some general guidelines for safely using them, however. Any item used to stroke the body or insert into the body should be relatively smooth, cleanable, and not breakable. Using a poor quality sexual enhancement product or a household object may not be safe enough for all activities. Anal insertion should always be done with water or silicone-based lubrication and with an item that is not rough or scratchy with a flange at the base to prevent it from slipping up inside the rectum, which can easily happen without one. It is far less likely for an item to be lost after insertion into the vagina, mouth, or urethra, but it is still best to make sure any object inserted into an orifice has a wide base.

Some people may be sensitive to the lubricants used on toys or chemicals used in the manufacture of sex toys themselves. While most manufacturers use approved and safe materials, some are made unsafely and with questionable durability. Phthalates are esters of phthalic acid used in plastics to increase their flexibility, transparency, and longevity. These chemical compounds have been banned in many jurisdictions for use in children's toys, yet some sexual enhancement product manufacturers still use them. Some suspect that this chemical may be toxic, and sex toys made with phthalates are harder to clean. Therefore, it is best to always thoroughly clean sex toys and use them with a condom. Body-friendly, easy to clean medical grade silicone is now the rule rather than the exception with the manufacture of dildos in the medium and higher price range, and this material is widely accepted as safe.

Sexual Dysfunctions

Anorgasmia, or the inability to experience an orgasm, and difficulty with sexual arousal are probably the two most frequent conditions treated with sexual enhancement products. Anal toys may also provide a role in prostate health. Perimenopausal (the transitional time between regular cycles and full-on menopause) and postmenopausal women may find that hormonal changes alter responsiveness to vaginal and clitoral stimulation and that sexual enhancement products, coupled with an increased use of lubrication, facilitate arousal by helping them get reacquainted with their bodies and experiment with new forms of stimulation that may build arousal in new or different ways. Males with erectile difficulties may find that sex toys heighten arousal. Erectile difficulties can be addressed with a penis–pump ring combination or with a prescription-only vacuum erection device. Men considering the use of either a penis–pump ring or a vacuum erection device should consult with their physician for a medical exam to ensure that these devices pose no health risks for them.

Sex Toys and Persons With Disabilities

Sex therapists working with persons with disabilities (PWD) find that sex toys or props, along with attention to sexual positioning, preparing the PWD for sexual experiences, and coaching them with self-stimulation and how to seek relationships, can all help them to more comfortably engage in satisfying sexual activities. Several variables are relevant to treatment planning: functional or physical limitations, the individual's comfort level and desire to try a certain sexual enhancement product, and whether or not assistance would be needed to make use of that product. Personal assistant services (PAS) can be used to help the PWD move into the proper position, assist with inserting a dildo, rectal plug, or other device, or position a vibrator or sexual pillow or cushion. When PAS are not available, sexual enhancement devices can lessen or alter the need for assistance by providing more privacy (i.e., privacy pillows with pockets for erotica or sex toys). Many PWDs find that the liberal use of lubricants, vibrators, dildos, and other sex toys stimulate nerve sensations and promote sexual desire with less effort than relying on manual manipulation alone. As with able-bodied sex therapy clients, PWDs may need assistance with getting familiar and comfortable with sexual enhancement products and how to keep them clean and use them safely. They may also need sensitivity with expressing and processing their underlying concerns and fears about experimenting with sexual enhancement products, which can be exacerbated by fears of injury due to physical and functional limitations.

These limitations may necessitate careful planning around bowel and bladder functioning, timing, and hygiene, and carefully positioning one's body around catheters and other assistive medical equipment. Since pain levels vary according to time of day, the scheduling of medical treatments and other interventions, it is also important to consider these variables when planning sexual activity. To enhance the likelihood of positive outcomes, the PWD may need coaching with communication and assertiveness skills to help communicate with the sex therapist, the PAS, or his or her partner about both pain levels and positively stimulating behaviors. Assertive communication can also help with experimenting with sensual and erotic activities that do not involve intercourse or penetration, such as promoting skin-on-skin contact and kissing that can maximize pleasure and reduce the likelihood of pain. To maximize positive outcomes, the sex therapist should focus on talking through the progression of sexual steps, planning ahead for potential challenges, and preparing the environment in advance.

Cautions

All adults who desire to explore the sensations and experiences of sexual enhancement products should feel free to do so without shame. By the same token, if an individual is not interested in or open to exploring the use of sexual enhancement products, he or she should not be coerced into doing so by a more adventurous partner or an enthusiastic couples or sex therapist. Sexual exploration needs to be negotiated like any other activity that couples mutually engage in, and, given the many possibilities, not every option will be desirable to every individual or couple. As with any other aspect of a healthy relationship, when one individual is more adventurous or "sex-toy positive," it behooves the relationship to sit down and talk about the perceived benefits to the individual and to the couple. Individuals who feel threatened by their partner's sexual enhancement product use or interest in the same should discuss these feelings with the partner to get at the underlying feelings, concerns, or fears that are making them uncomfortable. It may turn out that exploring more adventurously will enhance the personal pleasure of both persons in the long run.

Thomas K. Burdenski Jr.

See also Pornography; Sex Therapy; Sexual Dysfunction; Sexual Toys/Sexual Aids; Sexually Transmitted Infections

Further Readings

Herbenick, D., Reece, M., Sanders, S. A., Dodge, B., Ghassemi, A., & Fortenberry, J. D. (2010). Women's vibrator use in sexual partnerships: Results from a nationally representative survey in the United States. *Journal of Sex & Marital Therapy, 36*(1), 49–65. doi:10.1080/00926230903375677

Jannini, E. A., Limoncin, E., Ciocca, G., Buehler, S., & Krychman, M. (2012). Ethical aspects of sexual medicine. Internet, vibrators, and other sex aids: Toys or therapeutic instruments? *Journal of Sexual Medicine, 9,* 2994–3001. doi:10.1111/jsm.12018

Kaufman, M., Silverberg, C., & Odette, F. (2003). *The ultimate guide to sex and disability.* San Francisco: Cleis Press.

Leung, I. (2009). The cultural production of sex machines and the contemporary technosexual practices. In J. Grenzfurthner, G. Freisinger, D. Fabry, & T. Ballhausen (Eds.), *Do androids sleep with electric sheep? Critical perspectives on sexuality and pornography in science and social fiction* (pp. 16–35). San Francisco: Re/Search Publications.

Maines, R. P. (1998). *The technology of orgasm.* Baltimore, MD: Johns Hopkins University Press.

Mona, L. R. (2003). Sexual options for people with disabilities: Using personal assistant services for sexual expression. *Women & Therapy, 26*(3–4). doi:10.1300/J015v26n03_03

Striar, S., & Bartlik, B. (1999). Stimulation of the libido: The use of erotica in sex therapy. *Psychiatric Annals, 29*(1), 60–62.

Warkentin, K. M., Gray, R. E., & Wassersug, R. J. (2006). Restoration of satisfying sex for a castrated cancer patient with complete impotence: A case study. *Journal of Sex & Marital Therapy, 32,* 389–399. doi:10.1080/00926220600835346

Sexual Health

Sexual health is a broad term describing a person's physical and mental well-being with regard to sexual functioning. A range of factors affect sexual health, including physical health, hormonal issues, reproductive processes, sexually transmitted diseases, disorders affecting sexual functioning or libido, psychological state, and relationship issues. Because sexual health is an important component within relationships and contributes to intimacy levels, problems with sexual health are sometimes a precursor to counseling. This entry discusses each of the factors that affect sexual health and the relationship of each factor to counseling. It concludes with a discussion on preventive and reactive treatments.

Physical Health

Sexual health and physical health affect one another through cardiovascular functioning, hormonal levels, reproductive processes, and sexually transmitted diseases. Specific diseases such as cardiovascular disease, diabetes, thyroid, kidney and liver failure, neurological disorders, alcoholism, and drug abuse impact sexual health by altering physical sexual responses. For example, atherosclerosis, often referred to as hardening of the arteries, reduces blood flow to the penis and contributes to erectile dysfunction. Side effects of medications prescribed to treat health issues as well as alcohol and drug abuse can also affect cardiovascular and hormonal processes that contribute to sexual functioning.

Hormones

Hormonal levels influence libido (sexual desire), the ability to experience orgasm, fertility levels, and the ability achieve erection in males. In males, primary pituitary hormones affect fertility and are transported through the bloodstream to the testicles. Once in the testicles, these primary pituitary hormones stimulate testosterone and sperm production. Adequate levels of testosterone result in sexual stimulation and arousal. In females, these same primary pituitary hormones signal the ovaries to produce estradiol (estrogenic hormone) and progesterone. Progesterone triggers an increase in the lining of the uterus and, therefore, prepares the body for pregnancy. Additional surges of the pituitary hormone, luteinizing hormone (LH), occur on the 14th day of the menstrual cycle. This influx of LH causes ovarian follicle maturation, ovulation, and increased libido. After ovulation, a fertilized egg embeds itself in the uterus, whereas an unfertilized egg is shed along with the uterine lining. This shedding is triggered by progesterone, secreted by a corpus luteum (the by-product of a ruptured follicle). These hormonal influences and biological functioning are crucial in maintaining sexual health, libido, and satisfaction in both sexes. Any disruption or deficiency in these hormonal levels impacts the sexual response cycle, sexual functioning, and mental and physical health.

Sexually Transmitted Infections

Sexually transmitted infections (STIs) affect a growing number of people each year and cause an immediate threat to sexual health and well-being. STIs affect a person's ability to reproduce, may cause major physical health problems, are spread through sexual contact, and often exhibit as asymptomatic. The most common STIs include chlamydia, gonorrhea, hepatitis B, herpes simplex, human immunodeficiency virus (HIV), human papillomavirus (HPV), syphilis, and trichomoniasis.

Most bacterial STIs (e.g. chlamydia, gonorrhea, syphilis, and trichomoniasis) are treatable with antibiotics. Even though bacterial STIs are curable, however, many individuals demonstrate no symptoms. This lack of symptoms increases spread of the disease through carriers who unknowingly continue to participate in sexual activity without precautions. Further, many previously curable bacterial strains of gonorrhea and chlamydia have become resistant to antibiotics, making them more difficult to treat.

Many viral STIs (e.g., hepatitis B, herpes, HIV, and HPV) are not curable, although symptoms can often be managed with medications. Some viral STIs can be fatal. For example, HIV leads to acquired immune deficiency syndrome (AIDS), leaves a person's immune system ineffective, and eventually results in death. HPV, the most common STI, presents with genital warts when symptoms are present and can cause cervical, anal, and, in rare cases, penile cancer.

Sexual Dysfunction

A number of sexual disorders are categorized in the *Diagnostic and Statistical Manual of Mental Disorders* (DSM-5). These disorders affect a person's sexual functioning by disrupting the sexual response cycle: excitement, plateau, orgasm, and resolution. Disruptions primarily occur due to lowered libido; inability to orgasm; premature ejaculation; erectile dysfunction; painful intercourse; side effects of medications or physical conditions; emotional, relationship, or cultural factors; or elevated levels of stress. Characteristics that influence diagnosis and treatment include whether or not the dysfunction occurs at all times or situationally. Sexual dysfunction that occurs situationally is more apt to be caused by psychological, cultural, or relationship issues.

Psychological and Relationship Issues

Typically, sexual signals are received and processed by the brain, resulting in physical sexual responses. Thoughts, experiences, mood, self-esteem, relationship satisfaction, and social and cultural cues can interfere with these normal physical responses. Anxiety, depression, guilt, shame, fear, and other emotions or mood disorders can be caused by these cultural and societal exposures. Previous trauma, religious experiences, abuse, body image issues, lack of emotional intimacy, infidelity, and poor communication within relationships are specific psychological and relationship issues that impede sexual responsiveness. Sex therapy has shown promise when helping clients improve sexual functioning. Training and certification in sex therapy are available through the American Association of Sexuality Educators, Counselors, and Therapists.

Treatment Considerations

Treatments involving sexual health are both preventive and reactive. Prevention includes exercise to prevent heart problems leading to erectile dysfunction, use of condoms to decrease the chances of contracting an STI, avoiding unnecessary drug and alcohol intake, reduction of stress and behaviors that perpetuate psychological and relationship issues, and counseling to improve relationship intimacy. Reactive treatments include hormone replacement therapy; erectile implants; sex therapy; medications to both improve sexual functioning and treat or manage STIs; and personal, couples, and family counseling. Because physical and sexual health are interrelated, treatments that improve overall health often improve sexual health. Heart health is linked with erectile dysfunction; therefore, cardiovascular interventions also improve sexual health and functioning.

Janet Froeschle Hicks and Stephan Berry

See also Erectile Disorder; Female Orgasmic Disorder; Female Sexual Interest/Arousal Disorder; Genito-Pelvic Pain/Penetration Disorder; Male Hypoactive Sexual Desire Disorder

Further Readings

American Psychiatric Association. (2013). *Diagnostic and statistical manual of mental disorders* (5th ed.). (2013). Washington, DC: Author.

Centers for Disease Control and Prevention. (n.d.). *Sexually transmitted diseases.* Retrieved from http://www.cdc.gov/std/default.htm

Hedges, L. E. (2011). *Sex in psychotherapy.* New York: Taylor & Francis.

Public Health Reports. (2013). Supplement 1: Understanding sexual health. *Public Health Reports, 128.* Retrieved from http://www.publichealthreports.org/issuecontents.cfm?volume=128&issue=7

Sexual History

Sexual history refers to either an individual's history of sexual partners and sexual experiences across multiple partners or the history of sex within a given relationship. The history of one's sexual experience with a partner is an important element of understanding the development of the romantic relationship, as it offers insight into when and how couples decided to become physically intimate and also often offers insight into how sexual attitudes intersect with other important value systems within the couple (such as religious values). The previous sexual history of both partners often gives additional clinical insight into many aspects of an individual's personality and relational skills.

While relational scholars and practitioners often focus on the dynamics, strengths, and weaknesses of the current couple relationship when attempting to understand or improve relationship or sexual functioning, individual sexual history is an important element that should be considered in both research and practice. Sexual intimacy, in general, has been strongly associated with relationship health. Specifically, increased sexual frequency and desire are associated with stronger reports of relationship satisfaction and healthier couple dynamics. Therefore, evaluating the sexual history of both partners in a relationship can offer a clinician important insights into a vitally important element of couple functioning. This entry focuses on how sexual histories become important markers of relationship development, current insights into why sexual histories may be important elements of relationship functioning, and how clinicians might best utilize sexual histories in their assessments and practices.

Sexual History, Current Research, and Relationship Development

Every relationship has a sexual history, and most people have a history of sexual partners they bring into their current relationship. Even if someone has not engaged in sexual intercourse in the past, they have often engaged in intimate and sexual behaviors of some nature with previous partners. Even the absence of any sexual behaviors in one's past is a sexual history for that individual. Several generations ago, it was generally common to see adults report one or perhaps two lifetime sexual partners, often withholding sexual intimacy until after marriage. However, sexual behaviors within relationships have shifted dramatically in the last 100 years. Sexual intimacy in any form is often found in relationships at early stages. A growing body of research suggests that many couples are now beginning their relationship with a sexual encounter or engaging in sexual intimacy shortly after forming a relationship. Furthermore, "hooking up" with noncommitted romantic partners and entering into ongoing sexual relationships with peers (i.e., "friends with benefits") are becoming more prevalent, especially among young adults. More generally, the vast majority of individuals and couples have engaged in some form of nonmarital sexual intimacy at some point in their life, and most couples moving toward marriage have engaged in sex prior to that marriage. This growing body of scholarship has made one conclusion very clear: Most couples are freely engaging in sexual activity of some form, and the establishment of sexual intimacy is happening sooner among younger couples. These trends also suggest that many people are entering into new romantic relationships throughout their young adult and adult years with sexual experience across multiple previous partners.

These trends have raised interesting questions for scholars and clinicians interested in understanding if such nonmarital and premarital sexual engagement has positive or negative influences on relationship development. Scholars and clinicians have increasingly become interested in understanding if such diverse sexual histories impact individual and relational functioning. Whereas past generations have largely held to strong cultural norms regarding sexual activity, modern day sexual histories likely vary widely from person to person and from couple to couple.

Sexual history influences one's desirability as a potential dating and marital partner as well as how people evaluate other potential partners. Individuals understand that someone's sexual history can offer insight into what kind of person they are. Many people are prone to making broad judgments about partners based on their sexual histories. Generally, people tend to prefer individuals with more sexual experience when considering them as dating partners and little sexual experience when considering them as marital partners. This effect appears to be gendered, as men, more so than women, prefer women with few sexual partners as potential spouses. Such findings tend to mean that people enjoy sexual variety while dating but prefer to not "share" a spouse with many previous sexual partners. Such findings raise an interesting paradox for many, whereby good dating partners are different from good marital partners, and many people by their own definition would make poor spouses based on their sexual histories.

The idea that sexual history can provide insight into a person's background and fit as a romantic partner may have some valid empirical evidence behind it. Several scholars have noted that sexual history is likely a marker of underlying personality traits that provide information on who we are as relational partners. For example, Anthony Paik found evidence in a 2010 study that relationships that began with a sexual encounter before a committed relationship was established had poorer relational quality, but he also found evidence of selection effects where such associations were largely due to underlying individual factors. Others have suggested that certain types of people may be more likely to both decide to hook up or have early sex in relationships and engage in unhealthy relationship processes.

Other scholars have suggested that sexual history provides insight into personal sexual ethic or how an individual conceptualizes sexuality and its general role in relationships. The sexual behaviors people engage in during past relationships provide an outward expression of internal beliefs and values regarding sexual intimacy in relationships. Many people view sexual relationships in different ways. For some, sexual behavior is about emotional closeness and bonding within a relationship. For others, sexual behavior is about physical pleasure. Some people view sexual behavior as simply about having fun. Regardless of what an individual's sexual ethic might be, the individual's previous experience and history with sexual relationships likely provide some insights into their perceptions.

While interesting, this research on perceptions and personality traits does not speak to whether sexual history has a more objective influence on relationships and individuals. Other studies have focused more explicitly on the impact of having multiple sexual partners across the life course. This scholarship has generally shown that increased sexual experience with multiple partners may have a negative association with relationship outcomes across several types of relationships and may also be associated with higher depression. Perhaps this is clearest in the area of divorce prediction and marital outcome research. Several studies have now shown that having multiple sexual partners prior to marriage among women is associated with an increased risk of divorce. Other studies have likewise shown that having multiple lifetime sexual partners may be linked to diminished sexual quality within a marriage. Results for dating or cohabiting couples are less clear. To date, little research has explored whether such links found for married couples are also found for dating couples.

This research runs counter to many people's assumption that engaging in sexual intimacy with multiple partners may be beneficial, as it both helps educate individuals regarding their own sexual likes and dislikes while also helping get sex "out of one's system" so they are able to settle down into a long-term and monogamous sexual relationship. Research does not support this belief, however. Rather, it may suggest that engaging in a long history of sexual behavior with many partners gets sex "into one's system." In this view, as individuals engage in a variety of sexual behavior with many partners they may begin to focus on sexual intimacy as a key aspect of relationship satisfaction and individual happiness with the relationship. This focus may become problematic in long-term marriages as sexual behaviors naturally decrease with age or as the couple experiences transitions, such as pregnancy or health issues, that interfere with normal sexual functioning.

Why Would Sexual History Matter?

Why would sexual histories impact relationship functioning and be an important element of clinical intervention and assessment? There are generally two schools of thought when it comes to individual and couple sexual history and why such factors would affect relational development. Generally, sexual intimacy is seen as an important element of relational decision-making, as it serves as an important data point in determining how intimacy was developed across time in a given relationship. Such decisions can also be a source of contention for some couples, and each partner brings into the relationship certain perspectives and opinions about the role of sexual intimacy in the relationship. These perspectives are influenced heavily by one's previous sexual history and the overall value individuals place on sex.

Dean Busby and several other scholars have noted that individuals and couples often make these sexual decisions based on two competing beliefs regarding the role of sexual intimacy. On the one hand, many people hold what is referred to as a compatibility model of sexual intimacy. In this model, engagement in sexual intimacy with a romantic partner prior to committing to that partner through marriage is a needed and important element of partner evaluation. This mind-set holds that sexual compatibility is a central aspect of healthy marriages and relationships and that couples must determine this compatibility prior to commitment. Specifically, couples must determine whether sex is mutually pleasurable, whether frequency patterns are acceptable, and whether partners have similar preferences in terms of specific sexual behaviors, or what some people refer to as "sexual chemistry." Individuals with this compatibility mind-set will often have sexual histories that include multiple partners and a quicker engagement with sex in their current relationship.

Conversely, some individuals may hold an opposing viewpoint of sexual experience called a restraint model. In this model, the individual believes that sexual experience should be delayed to avoid early entanglements where couples develop deeper emotional bonds through sexual intimacy prior to establishing healthy relational processes or making an explicit decision to commit to a partner. Engaging in sex too early may get in the way of developing other, more important elements of the relationship. Individuals who view sex through this restraint model often have fewer previous sexual partners and often move more slowly in their current relationship toward sex.

In testing these models empirically, scholars have found that married couples who engaged in premarital sex generally report poorer relational outcomes and sexual quality compared to couples who waited until marriage to have sex. Other research has likewise suggested a restraint model of sexuality may be associated with more positive couple outcomes. Scholars have noted that this may be because a compatibility model would lead individuals toward sexual engagement early in a relationship, which may keep partners together who otherwise might have realized they should dissolve the relationship. Scholars call this phenomenon premature entanglement.

Sexual History in Clinical Settings

So what does all this mean for clinicians working with couples? Clinicians should consider several aspects of sexual history, in terms of both assessment and potential points of intervention. First, scholars have suggested that sexual history is an important point of assessment for individuals and couples who enter therapeutic settings. As noted earlier, sexual histories both within a person's personal background across relationships and within their current relationship may serve as an important indicator of underlying sexual beliefs and ethics and potentially give insights into current relationship functioning. In addition, assessment of sexual histories may allow clinicians to identify differing sexual patterns and beliefs across partners that may be important points of discussion and potential disagreements. For couples presenting with specific conflicts or problems related to sexual intimacy, differing sexual histories may suggest different patterns or sexual ethics for how partners approach sexual intimacy within relationships that clinicians can work to overcome.

In addition, based on research suggesting that more sexual partners and quicker sexual transitions are linked to poorer relational outcomes, clinicians may wish to use information regarding sexual histories to explore the meaning and function of sexual intimacy for couples they see. Sexual histories that involve multiple partners may suggest that such individuals are placing a large importance on the physical aspects of their relationships. Clinicians can work with such individuals to help them also appreciate ways in which they can emotionally or cognitively connect with their partners and to diminish obsessive thinking about sex.

Brian J. Willoughby

See also Intimacy, Specific Threats to; Sexual Assessment/History; Sexual Dysfunction; Sexual Intimacy; Sexual Assessment/History

Further Readings

Busby, D. M., Carroll, J. S., & Willoughby, B. J. (2010). Compatibility or restraint: The effects of sexual timing on marriage relationships. *Journal of Family Psychology, 24,* 766–774.

Busby, D. M., Willoughby, B. J., & Carroll, J. S. (2013). Sowing wild oats: Does it produce valuable experience or a field full of weeds? *Personal Relationships, 20,* 706–718.

Paik, A. (2011). Adolescent sexuality and the risk of marital dissolution. *Journal of Marriage and Family, 73,* 472–485.

Teachman, J. (2003). Premarital sex, premarital cohabitation, and the risk of subsequent marital dissolution among women. *Journal of Marriage and Family, 65,* 444–455.

Willoughby, B. J., Busby, D. M., & Carroll, J. S. (2014). Differing relationship outcomes when sex happens before, on, or after first dates. *Journal of Sex Research, 51,* 52–61.

Sexual Intimacy

There may be no other experience that eclipses intimacy for promoting well-being and finding meaning and purpose in human existence. Intimacy is a heightened state of emotional closeness brought about by sharing the most private and inner aspects of one's self. It is the basis of a healthy, thriving couple relationship that facilitates the emotional and physical well-being of both partners. This entry reviews motivations for sexual intimacy, the roles of gender, attachment style, and the experience of sexual flow, and controversial views on the relationship between sexual desire and emotional intimacy. This entry begins by narrowing the definition of sexual intimacy, which is separate from emotional, spiritual, and physical intimacy.

Defining Sexual Intimacy

Intimacy may be verbal, such as sharing one's innermost thoughts, feelings, values, and beliefs, or it may be nonverbally expressed through sustained eye contact, longing glances, physical affection, and sexual contact. Sexual relations can include visual, verbal, and nonverbal disclosures, including sharing one's naked body, expressing what feels stimulating, disclosing sexual fantasies, and reaching climax in the presence of one's partner, so sexual relations are by their nature one of the most intimate encounters one can have with a partner. Sharing on so many levels can result in deep understanding and connection because these experiences require lowering one's defenses and sharing vulnerabilities freely.

Motivations for Sexual Intimacy

In their "good enough sex" model, Michael Metz and Barry McCarthy identified five purposes of sex that are apparent among sexually satisfied couples. These purposes include the following: (1) sensual enjoyment and pleasure; (2) reduction of anxiety and tension; (3) confidence, pride, and self-esteem that result from identifying as a sexual person; (4) relationship closeness and satisfaction (i.e., emotional intimacy); and (5) reproduction. Metz and McCarthy assert that in sexually satisfied couples, no one purpose dominates for very long and that flexibility is the norm. In contrast, dysfunctional sexual relationships are characterized by manipulation, power and control, proving something to one's self or one's partner, hurtfulness and revenge, or habitually seeking sex for a single purpose, such as for stress relief, or for reassurance of an emotional connection. Healthy partners are also flexible in terms of which of these purposes for sex are most salient at any given time, and partners do not need to match one another in terms of goals. For instance, a male partner may seek relief from work-related stress or pressure, and a female partner may seek self-esteem for effectively pleasing her partner or satisfying her need for emotional closeness.

Sexual Flow

Flow, or the full involvement of the total self, refers to the mindful capacity to be fully present with one's partner, one's self, and the interaction without distraction. The more one can tap into one's feelings, thoughts, and reactions in the moment that they occur, the more one can also attune to the partner in that moment and fully receive and respond to all of the verbal and nonverbal signals. When the fully engaged self participates in sexual experience without defenses, spontaneity emerges, and one can have an accurate and unfiltered experience of one's partner and deep sexual gratification. Couples therapists describe observing a focused and sustained sexual playfulness that allows depth and meaning to arise from sexual contact in highly gratified couples. Verbal intimacy during and after sexual contact serves to deepen the experience of intimacy by enabling each partner to verbalize the experience and share the transformational process.

This process of making the implicit sexual experience more explicit allows partners to elaborate the experience more than they would if only thinking about it themselves privately, and therefore the experience becomes more mentally organized and consolidated. Moreover, the listening partner can offer his or her reactions to the partner's disclosures and become actively involved in incorporating the experience into the partner's self-concept in positive ways (i.e., encourage the disclosing partner to frame experiences as normal, realistic, understandable, perceptive, and wise) and affirm the discloser's transformed self-concept as valuable, lovable, worthwhile, and interesting. Because the partner is included in both the content and process of making meaning from shared sexual experiences, there is less tendency to become overly familiar with one another and slip into dull, predictable, and routine sexual contact unless one or both partners are overly defended or closed off to new sexual experiences. With openness and curiosity, the couple can attain deeper levels of intimate connection as a result of sharing new experiences and cocreating meaning from one another's experiences and disclosures.

Gender and Sexual Intimacy

Preference for emotional versus sexual intimacy appears to vary by gender in the United States. It is common for young married men, for example, to prefer physical sexual contact over intimate emotional contact with their partners. This may be a by-product of social conditioning as to what defines "adequate masculinity." Highly traditional males who view openly sharing one's needs, desires, and feelings as unmanly or soft will likely seek sexual intimacy and neglect emotional intimacy. Women are more likely to favor emotional intimacy over sexual intimacy. A positive self-view of one's body as meeting societal ideals is beneficial to both men and women because it provides protection from anxiety and shame that may arise in stressful sexual encounters. For those with negative self-views of the body or one's sexuality, exposing many private aspects of the self is likely to interfere with satisfying sexual relations.

Arousal patterns also vary by gender. Sexual confidence in men is often derived from sexual performance, whereas with women it is more likely to be cultivated through an experience of security, trust, and caring. The traditional behavioral approaches to treatment of sexual problems advanced originally by William Masters and Virginia Johnson strongly emphasized physiological functioning, but newer models, such as attachment-based models and Rosemary Basson's responsive-desire model, emphasize psychological influences. Basson asserts that women and men differ markedly in terms of desire, with men on the whole having strong initiatory desire and women playing a more receptive role. Basson's model of sexual desire suggests that as intimacy in couples increases, sexual desire follows. She also downplays the role of sexual fantasy with building sexual desire and passion in women.

Attachment and Sexual Intimacy

John Bowlby conceptualized the emotional attachment between child and caregiver as fundamental to well-being and healthy human development. The most common terminology for the various attachment styles are as follows: (a) secure (low avoidance and low anxiety), (b) fearful-avoidant (high avoidance and high anxiety), (c) preoccupied (low avoidance and high anxiety), and (d) dismissive (high avoidance and low anxiety). Within the last decade, attachment researchers have begun to examine the role of attachment style on sexual function in adults. For example, while men overall express more concern about sexual affairs in their partners and women overall are more concerned about emotional affairs undertaken by their male partners, preoccupied (anxiously attached) men were more likely to be concerned about emotional affairs, and fearful-avoidant women were more threatened by sexual affairs in their male partners.

Susan Johnson, the founder of emotionally focused therapy (EFT) for couples, and Dino Zuccarini, reviewed studies on the relationship between attachment and sexuality and developed an integrated "theory of love" that emphasizes caregiving as an adult form of parent–child attachment between two adults whose attachment is mutual and reciprocal instead of directional, as from the adult to the child. This mutual caregiving is combined with meeting those attachment needs and providing sexual gratification through touching, emotionally connecting, and soothing behaviors. From this view, erotic experience is heightened when sexual contact occurs in a context of emotional openness, responsiveness, a secure bond, and tender touch. The emphasis is on emotional safety rather than sexual release.

In a review of attachment studies and sexuality, it was noted that attachment styles influence why couples have sex. Securely attached couples engaged in sex to enhance emotional closeness, while preoccupied individuals desire sex to feel reassured or to avoid feelings of rejection. Preoccupied partners were also highly sensitive to any signs of not measuring up to their partner's expectations. Fearful-avoidant partners tended to focus on their own sexual gratification and underemphasized the emotional connection between themselves and their partners. Fearful-avoidant partners also disliked affection. Given their asexual stance and lower likelihood to engage in sexual relations, there is little empirical research on how dismissive partners engage sexually.

Controversies About Intimacy and Sexual Satisfaction

While the need for intimacy and the need for autonomy need not conflict with one another, there is evidence that the most satisfied couples experience both to some degree. There is disagreement in the couples therapy field, however, about how emotional intimacy influences sexual desire. Some experts assert that a strong, loving, safe, and secure attachment bond between two individuals fosters the natural mammalian desire for sexual connection. They see emotional intimacy and erotic passion as two sides of the same coin. They cite research demonstrating that secure, loving bonds foster sexual satisfaction and engagement, whereas high levels of avoidance and anxiety are associated with lower sexual satisfaction. Since the regulation of emotion plays such a big role with facilitating desire, arousal, and sexual satisfaction in couples, the EFT model, for example, emphasizes teaching couples strategies to better regulate their emotions with one another, especially under duress.

On the other hand, experts such as Esther Perel counter the traditional view that emotional intimacy is the foundation of sexual satisfaction. She noted substantial experience with loving couples whose sexual relations were nonarousing or nonexistent, and couples whose communication and emotional intimacy increased greatly as a result of couples therapy yet had sexual relations that remained stagnant. She contends that emotional intimacy actually sabotages and interferes with sexual desire because it can make partners overly familiar to one another and desexualizes their erotic passion for one another. The challenge in long-term marriages is to keep sex vibrant and alive. A view like Perel's seems to support Murray Bowen's paradoxical view formulated in the early 1970s maintaining that true closeness can occur only when family members experience a healthy distance from one another. He defined this process as differentiation.

In the 1990s, David Schnarch applied Bowen's insights directly to sexual problems in couples. He maintained that deep intimacy and erotic arousal are contingent upon being able to relate to a partner who exists separately in terms of one's identity and needs. Markers of healthy individuation include the following: (a) not expecting the partner to allay all of one's fears and anxieties and learning to self-soothe, (b) learning to tolerate frustration and discomfort as important ingredients of personal and relational growth, and (c) not getting swept up in one another's emotions and reacting to them.

Others suggest that the notion of finding one's soul mate is the modern equivalent of a fairy tale—that it is unrealistic to meet all of one's needs for erotic pleasure, emotional intimacy, and companionship in one person. This position asserts that there is an inherent conflict, even in healthy marriages, between the desire for safety, security, and familiarity and the need for novelty and eroticism in relationships. Perel points to changing social and cultural expectations over the past couple of generations. Whereas our grandparents derived their sense of happiness and life satisfaction from many sources, such as family, church, community, siblings, and a large network of friends, our current generation tends to look toward committed partners to meet our needs for safety, security, and stability as well as mystery, adventure, novelty, romance, and excitement, yet this is an overly tall order for most partners to meet. It is probably inherently unfair as well, since we are looking for one person to provide what an entire community provided in previous generations.

"Love is about having and desire is about wanting" is one of the major guiding principles of Perel's work with couples who struggle with loss of sexual desire. She considers a lack of desire to be a normal and even predictable rut for long-term committed couples and further maintains that desire problems do not always reflect a problematic relationship. Perel challenges the traditional view by taking an opposite stance on how to foster intimacy in couples. Specifically, she recommends that couples first improve sexual passion, and an improved relationship will follow. The way to do this is to cultivate more mystery and learn to tolerate separateness and individuality.

Thomas K. Burdenski Jr.

See also Attachment Styles; Differentiation; Emotionally Focused Therapy for Couples; Love, Physiology of; Sex Therapy; Sexual Intimacy

Further Readings

Basson, R. (2002). A model of women's sexual arousal. *Journal of Sex & Marital Therapy, 28,* 1–10.

Basson, R. (2010). Low sexual desire, sexual avoidance, and sexual aversion. In S. B. Levine, C. B. Risen, & S. E. Althof, *Handbook of clinical sexuality for mental health professionals* (2nd ed., pp. 159–179). New York: Routledge.

Hertlein, K. M., Weeks, G. R., & Gambescia, N. (Eds.). (2015). *Systemic sex therapy* (2nd ed.). New York: Routledge.

Johnson, S. M., & Zuccarini, D. (2010). Integrating sex and attachment in emotionally focused couple therapy. *Journal of Marital & Family Therapy, 36*(4), 431–445.

Metz, M. E., & McCarthy, B. W. (2012). The good enough sex (GES) model. In P. J. Kleinplatz (Ed.), *New directions in sex therapy: Innovations and alternatives* (2nd ed., pp. 213–229). New York: Routledge.

Peplau, L. A., Hill, C. T., & Rubin, Z. (1993). Sex-role attitudes in dating and marriage: A 15-year follow-up of the Boston couples study. *Journal of Social Issues, 40,* 31–52.

Perel, E. (2006). *Mating in captivity: Unlocking erotic intelligence*. New York: HarperCollins.

Perel, E. (2010). The double flame: Reconciling intimacy and sexuality, reviving desire. In S. R. Leiblum (Ed.), *Treating sexual desire disorders: A clinical casebook* (pp. 23–43). New York: Guilford Press.

Prager, K. J., & Roberts, L. J. (2004). Deep intimate connection: Self and intimacy in couple relationships. In D. J. Mashek & A. P. Aron (Eds.), *The handbook of closeness and intimacy* (pp. 43–60). Mahwah, NJ: Erlbaum.

Schnarch, D. (1991). *Constructing the sexual crucible: An integration of sexual and marital therapy.* New York: W. W. Norton.

Vohs, K. D., & Baumeister, R. F. (2004). Sexual passion, intimacy, and gender. In D. J. Mashek & A. P. Aron (Eds.), *The handbook of closeness and intimacy* (pp. 189–199). Mahwah, NJ: Erlbaum.

SEXUAL MINORITIES

The term *sexual minorities* refers to a population of individuals whose sexual orientation is different from the heterosexual orientation shared by the majority of society and who therefore have unique needs in therapeutic settings. Sexual orientation broadly refers to one's feelings, identity, and practices of sexual arousal, sexual desire and/or romantic desire toward another person or persons. These feelings may be based on gender, appearance, or personality traits, among other attributes. Types of sexual orientations within the sexual minority umbrella include, but are not limited to asexual, bisexual, gay, lesbian, pansexual, queer, and questioning. This entry describes these orientations and discusses the concept of sexual minorities.

Asexuality is the term applied to individuals who generally do not experience sexual attraction. This innate lack of sexual desire contrasts with celibacy (a personal choice to remain sexually inactive). Some asexual individuals feel attracted to others, yet feel no desire to act on their attractions. Asexual individuals who experience attraction may identify as lesbian, gay, bisexual, or heterosexual/straight. The Asexual Visibility Education Network (AVEN) emphasizes that just as people rarely and unexpectedly go from being straight to gay, asexual people rarely and unexpectedly become sexual.

Bisexuality typically refers to one's attraction toward males and females. While attraction may be equivalent in degree and type among the two genders, a bisexual individual may experience more overall attraction toward one gender than the other or experience a greater amount of romantic attraction than sexual attraction to a particular gender (e.g., a bisexual man may be more romantically attracted to women yet more sexually attracted to men).

Gay sexual orientation refers to same-gender attractions. Typically, gay identity refers to men who are primarily attracted other men. However, females primarily attracted to females may also identify as gay. Often, and incorrectly, the word *gay* is used as a "catch all" to encompass those who identify as lesbian, gay, bisexual, transgender, queer, and questioning, among other sexual orientation and gender identities. Historically, "gay" was referred to as "homosexual," and to that point, homosexuality was listed as a mental disorder in earlier editions of the *Diagnostic and Statistical Manual of Mental Disorders*. The word *homosexual* is now viewed as stigmatizing and is no longer used within daily vernacular.

Lesbian sexual orientation refers to same-gender attraction but pertains only to those who self-identify as females. However, some female individuals who are attracted primarily to women may also identify as gay.

Pansexuality refers to attractions not based on notions of gender identity, sexual orientation, or biological sex. A person who self-identifies as pansexual may be attracted to androgynous, female, gender queer, intersex, male, and transgender individuals, among others. Thus, while bisexual individuals typically are attracted to males and females, pansexual individuals are attracted to people along the entire gender continuum.

Individuals who identify as *queer* may feel as if they do not fit into a societally sanctioned sexual orientation label (e.g., gay, lesbian, bisexual, or pansexual) and/or reject the notion of labeling their sexual orientation. Furthermore, the word can be used to describe sexual minority individuals holistically, much like "LGBTQ+" (discussed in more detail subsequently). Since the 1980s, *queer* has gained popularity as an empowering term, even though the term was historically used as a derogatory term for lesbian, gay, bisexual, transgender, queer/questioning (LGBTQ) individuals. *Queer* is also a word used to describe those who feel their gender is fluid or reject the notion of labeling their gender identity or gender expression.

Furthermore, *questioning* individuals may feel unsure how to label their sexual orientation and thus, may take time to explore, discover, and reflect on their own sexual identity. This can be an anxiety provoking time for individuals given the stigma surrounding sexual orientation labels and sexuality in general. Questioning can also refer to one questioning his or her gender identity or ways in which to express gender identity.

There is a growing understanding that sexual orientation is fluid and on a spectrum rather than confined to specific categories. Furthermore, the etiology of sexual orientation remains subject to debate, with some people maintaining that it is biological and others arguing that it is based on one's environment. Several studies have found that those who believe same-sex orientation is due to environmental factors are less supportive of policies pertaining to marriage equality and adoption for sexual minorities. Due to stigma surrounding sexual minority status in many parts of the world, including the United States, individuals are often assumed to be heterosexual until they "come out" or express their other sexual orientation publicly.

Sexual orientations and gender identities other than heterosexual and cisgender are often referred to as LGBTQ+. The plus symbol signifies the acronym's inclusiveness to other sexual orientations and gender identities. To that point, one's gender identity (e.g., gender queer, female, male, or transgender) or gender expression (e.g., the way in which one expresses feelings of gender by means of behavior, appearance, mannerisms) does not naturally concord with one's sexual orientation, despite false societal assumptions. Nevertheless, the gender variant minority population is often considered to be within the broader sexual minority community.

Sexual minority orientation is a complex topic that carries stigma within the dominant culture. Emotional and physical violence toward LGBTQ+ individuals remains common. While there has been progress and increased policies to protect LGBTQ+ individuals from discrimination and homophobia, violence remains a critical issue. It is crucial that within daily conversation, the correct terminologies within the broad term *sexual orientation* be used. Additionally, therapists who use the correct terminologies with LGBTQ+ clients may promote greater trust from clients and in turn, promote more productive and effective therapy sessions.

Catherine Griffith

See also Love, Types of; Multiculturalism; Same-Sex Couples; Sexual Prejudice

Further Readings

Better, A., & Simula, B. L. (2015). How and for whom does gender matter? Rethinking the concept of sexual orientation. *Sexualities, 18*(5–6), 665–680.

Herek, G. M., Gillis, J. R., & Cogan, J. C. (2009). Internalized stigma among sexual minority adults: Insights from a social psychological perspective. *Journal of Counseling Psychology, 56,* 32–43.

Mayer, K. H., Bradford, J. B., Makadon, H. J., Stall, R., Goldhammer, H., & Landers, S. (2008). Sexual and gender minority health: What we know and what needs to be done. *American Journal of Public Health, 98,* 989–995.

Sexual Orientation, Attraction, and Identity

Sexual orientation, attraction/desire, and identity are ever-evolving and complicated contextual factors in a person's life. Traditionally, sexual orientation referred to a person's preferred romantic partner (irrespective of gender identity), while sexual attraction/desire were defined as the sexual thoughts and desires of the person, which sometimes does not line up with one's sexual orientation. *Sexual identity* is now the preferred label used to describe oneself in terms of sexual orientation and/or attraction and desire. However, rarely does a person's sexuality, attraction template, or context of identification remain the same throughout his or her life. Since a person's sexual attractions and desires can be flexible, some would argue that "sexual orientation" is a misnomer in the idea that an "orientation" implies that a person's preference for sexually intimate interaction is based on a location within a physical set of continuum (i.e., a location or placement) and is therefore unchangeable. Many researchers now use the term *sexual attraction* to be able to identify a person's specific sexual preferences. This allows for a degree of fluidity when describing someone's specific sexual expression rather than a fixed point on a continuum. In this entry, the term *sexual orientation/attraction* will be used in that it is a more accepting and open idiom that encompasses both points of view.

To begin to identify what sexual orientation/attractions and identities are currently dominant in our social discourse, it is important to first clarify that sexuality is different from gender. One may notice that the *T* (transgender) component of the commonly used acronym "LGBT" is not discussed in this entry. That is purposeful in that the transgender community is often wrongfully lumped in with the overall sexual orientation and identity community. In fact, a transgender identity is a gender identity, not a sexual orientation, and these are separate components of a person's overall human identity. Gender expression is different from sexual expression—the two are not as intertwined as once thought. Thus, for the purposes of this entry, gender identities have been excluded from the discussion. Instead, the focus will be specifically on sexual orientations, attractions, and identities. These include lesbian, gay, bisexual, asexual, pansexual, and queer identities, as well as various expressions of the identity within these groups.

There are several overarching identities that have been given the label of "orientations." According to the Williams Institute, a composite estimate of around 6.9% of the overall population in the United States identifies as lesbian, gay, or bisexual. Within each orientation, there are a plethora of connected cultures that express their sexuality in different ways. Specifically, this entry examines male and female sexual orientations/attractions, gender fluid orientations/attractions, and sexual activity–specific orientations and identities.

Female Associated Sexual Orientation/Attractions

Lesbian

Typically, a lesbian is a female-identified individual who is attracted primarily to female-identified individuals. Estimates suggest that 1.1% of the total population of the United States identifies as lesbian. The lesbian culture has developed a series of evolving subcultures over time that include groupings of people who share similar traits within the overarching lesbian identity. Some of the more common groups have given themselves (or been given by other members) specific labels to identify their unique characteristics.

Butch Lesbians

Women who identify as a butch lesbian typically have what is considered a more "masculine" appearance. This may include the clothes they wear, the way in which they style their hair, or how they do not participate in stereotypical feminine roles or prefer more stereotypically masculine activities.

Femme Lesbians

A femme lesbian usually refers to a lesbian who displays a typically feminine appearance, which may include wearing makeup, wearing "girly" clothes, or participating in activities that are stereotypically feminine.

Other Subcultures

In addition to the above categories, the lesbian community has developed various derivations, including dyke, gold star lesbian, lone star lesbian, lipstick or chapstick lesbian, blue jean lesbian, pillow queen, stone butch, soft butch, sport lesbian, stem, futch, boi, power dyke, diesel dyke, baby dyke, and stud. Many of these definitions reflect geographically based cultural variations. For example, a lipstick lesbian is often confused with a femme lesbian in many parts of the country, since they have the same or similar characteristics. In each lesbian community, there may be other subgroups who identify in different ways.

Male Associated Sexual Orientation/Attractions

Gay

In typical usage, gay is applied to a male-identified individual who is sexually and romantically attracted primarily to male-identified individuals. However, in common vernacular this term has come to signify an overarching thematic identity for individuals outside of heterosexuality. Estimates suggest 2.2% of the overall United States population identifies as gay.

Bear

A gay man who identifies as a bear is someone who is typically more burly in appearance, sometimes older, and maintains body hair. This can include facial hair, chest hair, and hair in other places (i.e., on the back or legs). Bears were given their nickname due to their furry appearance and general cuddly personas; however, within the bear identity, there are those who engage in the more aggressive characteristics of bears (e.g., engaging in bondage, domination, sadism, and masochism [BDSM] and leather practices). There are also muscle bears who are larger because of muscle mass, polar bears who are older bears with graying or white hair, sugar bears who are more effeminate men who have the physical characteristics of a bear, and cubs who are younger men with extensive body or facial hair (this category may include the muscle and sugar subcategories).

Twink

A twink is usually a younger, clean-shaven, and well-defined man. The term is a derivative of the snack Twinkies and is sometimes used pejoratively to identify someone who is "yellow or light on the outside" and is "stuffed with cream" on the inside, which alludes to the fact that many twinks "bottom" or are the receiving partner in sexual activities.

Other Subcultures

Just as with their lesbian counterparts, the gay male community has created a large set of subcultures that identify smaller segments of the overall gay population, based on specific characteristics. These include otters, wolves, chubs, superchubs, chasers, pups, bulls, gym bunnies and gym rats, jocks, gay-listers, show queens, and circuit boys.

Men-Who-Have-Sex-With-Men

A person who identifies as a man-who-has-sex-with-men is an individual who does not align with a gay identity, but still engages in sexual relationships with other men. Most often a person who identifies in this way has significant romantic relationships with women, but continues to have sexual relationships with other men "on the down-low." This is particularly common in cultures and communities where being a gay or bisexual man is socially unacceptable.

Both Gender/Gender Fluid or Nonspecific Orientation/Attraction

Heterosexual

While often taken for granted (as the majority), heterosexuality is also a sexual orientation/attraction. A person who identifies as heterosexual is primarily interested in, and seeks out, relationships with someone who identifies as the opposite gender.

Bisexual

A person who identifies as bisexual will typically first identify as either male or female, and be sexually attracted to both males and females. Usually a bisexual person will have an equal attraction to both genders, but may have a preference for one gender or the other for specific activities. For example, a bisexual male may be primarily interested in women for relationships, but will engage in frequent impersonal sexual relationships with other men.

Bisexuals are actually the largest percentage of lesbian, gay, bisexual (LGB) individuals, with approximately 3.6% of the country (52% of all LGB individuals) identifying as such. Women represent a majority of people identifying as bisexual, with recent estimates suggesting that up to 77% of bisexually identified individuals are women.

Asexual

An asexual person will typically identify as male or female, but does not have interest in sexual intimacy with any gender expression. Someone who is asexual may have an intimate relationship with another person, but has no desire to engage in sexual relations. Due to this, they are often nonpartnered.

Pansexual

One of the more confusing sexual orientation/attraction/identities, pansexual people do not fit in any particular box or categorical label. Pansexuals can identify as either male or female, but may also identify as gender fluid, queer, or agender. Further, they are not attracted to any specific gender or gender(s), but are attracted to all people regardless of expressions of gender or identity. This is different from the bisexual identity in that pansexual people are attracted simply to other people, their personalities and unique expressions of self.

Queer

The term *queer* gained currency in the 1980s and is often used by activists. The overall nonheterosexual community reclaimed the term in an effort to stop its negative connotation and use it as a term of empowerment. Queer is a term/identity used frequently in a political fashion rather than simply as an identification. However, some people choose to use the term for their sexual identities; for these people, it is very similar to pansexual. Queer is an in-group term that many people continue to find offensive, and so until a person identifies, or gives permission to use the term, it should not be automatically assumed acceptable.

Sexual Activity Specific Orientations and Identities

Top

Top refers to a person who can embody several different characteristics during sexual activity (most often with a partner). In male-male relationships a top refers to the insertive partner in sexual activity. In other types of sexual activity, a top can also refer to any person who is more aggressive in their sexual expressions. A power top is someone who refuses to bottom regardless of partner or situation.

Bottom

Similar to a top, bottom can have several meanings. In most relationships, a bottom is someone who is the receptive partner for sexual activity or is the submissive partner. A person can also be a power bottom, referring to someone who will only bottom and aggressively pursues opportunities to bottom.

Versatile

Versatile men and women are sexually versatile in that they will "top" or "bottom" when they feel like it, or when their partner requests it. It is estimated that even though most commonly referred to as a top or bottom, a majority of sexually active individuals in same-gender relationships are versatile in their sexual activities.

It is important to note that however much research one does, labels and identities that are constantly evolving are constantly evolving in the lesbian, gay, and bisexual communities. Vocabulary and usage of terms, especially in counseling and therapy contexts, should always be reserved for identification by the client or individual themselves. In the field of sex therapy, this concept is called "never assume and always assume." The concept provides a welcoming atmosphere of acceptance and openness that is often empowering for clients.

Christopher K. Belous

See also Gender- and Culture-Sensitive Therapies; Gender Orientation, Gender Identity, and Gender Expression; LGBT Families; Same-Sex Couples; Sexual Minorities; Sexuality and Religion

Further Readings

Bigner, J. J., & Wetchler, J. L. (2012). *Handbook of LGBT-affirmative couple and family therapy.* New York: Routledge.

Chernin, J. N., & Johnson, M. R. (2003). *Affirmative psychotherapy and counseling for lesbians and gay men.* Thousand Oaks, CA: Sage.

Dawson, J. (2015). *This book is gay.* Naperville, IL: Sourcebooks.

Gates, G. J. (2011). *How many people are lesbian, gay, bisexual, or transgender?* Los Angeles: Williams Institute, UCLA School of Law.

Gates, G. J. (2014). *LGB/T Demographics: Comparisons among population-based surveys.* Los Angeles: Williams Institute, UCLA School of Law.

Gibson, M. A., Alexander, J., & Meem, D. T. (2013). *Finding out: An introduction to LGBT studies* (2nd ed.). Thousand Oaks, CA: Sage.

Hogan, S., & Hudson, L. (1998). *Completely queer: The gay and lesbian encyclopedia.* New York: Henry Holt.

Huegel, K. (2011). *GLBTQ: The survival guide for gay, lesbian, bisexual, transgender, and questioning teens.* Minneapolis, MN: Free Spirit Publishing.

Jennings, K., & Shapiro, P. (2003). *Always my child: A parent's guide to understanding your gay, lesbian, bisexual, transgendered or questioning son or daughter.* New York: Simon & Schuster.

Underwood, S. G. (2003). *Gay men and anal eroticism: Tops, bottoms, and versatiles.* Binghamton, NY: Harrington Park Press.

Wright, L. (Ed.). (1997). *The bear book: Readings in the history and evolution of a gay male subculture.* New York: Springer.

SEXUAL PREJUDICE

Sexual prejudice refers to negative attitudes and behaviors toward an individual based on his or her sexual orientation identity. Practitioners engaged in marriage, family, and couples counseling may encounter or display sexual prejudice when providing services. Although sexual minorities are more often affected by sexual prejudice than heterosexuals, targets of sexual prejudice may be of any sexual orientation. The purpose of this entry is to give an overview of the history of sexual prejudice, to discuss practice interventions that address sexual prejudice, and to outline the empirical evidence about the highly contextual nature of sexual prejudice.

Defining Sexual Prejudice

The term *sexual prejudice* was coined by American social psychologist Gregory Herek. In spite of much social and political change, sexual prejudice against lesbian, gay, bisexual, and queer (LGBQ) people is still a pervasive social norm in many communities. Herek and other proponents of the term sought to expand on previous conceptualizations of LGBQ bias, including heterosexism, the pervasive social norm that privileges heterosexuality over other forms of sexual orientation identity;

and homophobia, the irrational fear or dislike of LGBQ people, by introducing a term that captured negative attitudes about LGBQ people without making a judgment of whether those attitudes were rational or not. Transgender, gender-queer, and other people of noncisgender expression are frequently targets of sexual prejudice based upon negative attitudes towards LGBQ communities. However, transgender people may identify as either LGBQ or non-LGBQ.

Developments in Combating Sexual Prejudice

During the last decade, significant gains have been made in combating sexual prejudice in North America and many other parts of the world. In 1973, homosexuality was declassified as a mental illness from the *Diagnostic and Statistical Manual of Mental Disorders*. Most consensual sexual and affectional attractions between same-gender and opposite-gender people are seen to fall on the normal spectrum of sexuality. Sexual orientation identity, even if outside the mainstream, is no longer viewed as inherently pathological or deviant. Some practitioners in marriage, family, and couples counseling do not hold this view, and engage in reparative or ex-gay therapy, defined as counseling that aims to change homosexual behaviors into heterosexual behaviors. However, these efforts typically have limited success and, in some cases, cause significant harm. These practices tend to be informed by spiritual beliefs or sexual prejudice rather than empirical evidence showing that identity change is possible. Accordingly, major professional organizations have condemned sexual orientation change efforts. The U.S. Supreme Court refused to hear an appeal of California's ban on gay conversation therapies with minors, and other states have passed similar measures.

Nearly all major professional organizations, including the American Counseling Association, National Association of Social Workers, and American Association for Marriage and Family Therapy, have called upon practitioners to engage in sensitive and affirmative practice with sexual minorities. Homosexuality is not a disorder. Practitioners engaging in marriage, family, and couples counseling should instead focus on helping people to make meaning of sexual orientation identity and to cope with negative societal attitudes toward sexual minorities. Members of sexual minorities come to marriage, family, and couples counseling with psychosocial issues similar to the issues of heterosexuals. For example, sexual minorities may seek services when their relationship ends or when they have difficulty communicating with their children. The reasons sexual minorities seek services may be totally unrelated to their sexual orientation identity. Yet their shared experience of sexual prejudice may color how they interact with practitioners and others in the social environment. Understanding of sexual prejudice provides an important context for the problems that sexual minorities may bring to marriage, family, and couples counseling.

Whereas sexual prejudice was once a tolerated social norm in many communities throughout the world, there is evidence that tolerance for sexual prejudice is on the decline in some parts of North America and other places. Homosexual acts are still harshly criminalized in some parts of the world, yet an encouraging number of states offer some basic civil and human rights protections for sexual minorities. Corporate policies that prohibit discrimination based on sexual orientation identity are becoming commonplace at most Fortune 500 companies. Antidiscrimination laws in employment, housing, public service, and other forms of public accommodation, while once the exception, are now the norm in many parts of North America. Crimes that are motivated by hatred toward sexual minority communities are starting to carry harsh criminal penalties. Proactive civil and human rights laws have passed or are being considered in a number of jurisdictions. Relationship equality laws are becoming much more common. Registered domestic partnerships, civil unions, and marriage equality offer to sexual minority families the responsibilities and protections afforded to other families. Although these civil and human rights protections alone are not absolute evidence that tolerance for sexual prejudice has decreased in society, they are a promising example of improvement in attitudes and beliefs toward sexual minorities within some communities.

Research

Research suggests that there are considerable contextual factors influencing the nature and consequences of sexual prejudice. Associations have been found among several social and environmental factors and prejudicial attitudes toward sexual minorities. At the individual level, contact between members of sexual minorities and heterosexuals tends to lead to less prejudicial attitudes toward sexual minorities. Within organizations, tolerance for prejudicial attitudes and behaviors has been correlated with a decrease in the self-reported well-being of sexual minorities as well as other proxies of job well-being, including the number of sick days used and employee leaving intentions. Within organizations that tolerate prejudicial attitudes and behaviors toward sexual minorities, there is some evidence that observing tolerance for prejudice toward another group of people also negatively affects workers who do not belong to the target group. In these organizations, there may be a perception that, if sexual prejudice is tolerated, other forms of prejudice may also be tolerated. When providing services, practitioners in marriage, family, and couples counseling should consider the multiple contextual factors influencing experiences of sexual prejudice in order to develop an intervention strategy that best meets the needs of the client group seeking services. Practitioners and counseling organizations should take steps to decrease any sexual prejudice in the services offered and find ways to make services both welcoming and culturally competent.

Trevor G. Gates and Margery C. Saunders

See also LGBT Families; Sexual Minorities; Sexual Orientation, Attraction, and Identity

Further Readings

Gates, T. G., & Viggiani, P. A. (2014). Understanding lesbian, gay, and bisexual worker stigmatization: A review of the literature. *Journal of Sociology and Social Policy, 34*(5/6), 359–374.

Herek, G. M. (2004). Beyond "homophobia": Thinking about sexual prejudice and stigma in the twenty-first century. *Sexuality Research & Social Policy, 1*(2), 6–24.

Hines, J. M. (2012). Using an anti-oppressive framework in social work practice with lesbians. *Journal of Gay & Lesbian Social Services, 24*(1), 23–39.

SEXUAL RELATIONSHIPS WITH CLIENTS

Sexual relationships with clients include any boundary violation between counselor and client where sexual relations occur through coercion or active participation by both parties. Managing professional relationship boundaries in a client–therapist relationship is of paramount importance. The goal of any therapy process is to establish a connection between a therapist and client at a professional, yet intimate level to allow honest communications to assist the client in navigating the therapeutic change process. The therapist always holds an ascribed position of power and trust as the expert from whom the client is seeking assistance. Thus, the therapist is given the sole charge of managing the boundaries that comprise this power differential. Unfortunately, a small percentage of therapists take advantage of the intimate nature of the therapeutic process, using their power to coerce their clients into sexual relationships. This type of sexual violation causes great harm to clients and their families and is expressly prohibited by all major mental health ethical codes and occupational licensing laws. An increasing number of states have enacted legislation making such boundary violations a prosecutable criminal offense, underscoring the egregious nature of such infractions. This entry first discusses what constitutes a sexual relationship with clients, the frequency of these relationships, and the ethical guidelines and laws restricting them. It then discusses the damage sexual relationships can cause to clients and their families, how therapists can maintain boundaries and deal with attraction to their clients, and how potential boundary violations are identified and addressed.

Definition and Scope of Problem

Over the years, mental health practice ethical standards have established increasingly restrictive guidelines on what are referred to as dual or multiple relationships. Such diverging relationships exemplify situations in which the therapist holds one or more different types of relationship with a client aside from the relationship that defines the therapeutic process. These dual or secondary relationships exist on a continuum that might include friendships with clients, work relationships, sexual relationships, and so on. The most serious and detrimental of all dual relationships is that of a sexual relationship. Entering into a sexual relationship with a client violates the sanctity of the trust placed upon the therapist, takes advantage of the position of authority a therapist holds over a client, and almost always leads to detrimental outcomes to a client.

Over the past three decades a number of studies have examined the frequency with which sexual boundary violations in the therapeutic relationship occur. Findings from such studies are limited as many victims do not wish to come forward, and many clinicians likely underreport their incidence in studies relying on the anonymous self-report of such behaviors by therapists and their colleagues. Figures uncovered in such studies suggest that 7% to 12% of mental health professionals surveyed reported having sexual contact with a client at some point in their career. In a majority of these cases, the therapist was male, and the client was female. Also, the sexual violations tended to occur over an extended period of time, with many therapists perpetrating violations upon more than one client during their careers. The reader must keep in mind that such sexual boundary violations include other behaviors aside from vaginal or anal intercourse. Other examples include sexual looks, remarks, or humor; kissing, fondling, or nudity; and, oral sex or other sexual acts with clients.

Ethical and Legal Guidelines and Requirements

Prior to the findings of a landmark lawsuit in 1975, which determined that a psychiatrist who became sexually involved with a patient had caused harm, sexual relationships with mental health professionals were not publicly acknowledged as problematic. Over the years since this case, virtually all mental health specialties and their corresponding ethical codes have established prohibitions on sexual relationships with clients, their partners, and family members. Such codes also prohibit entering into a romantic relationship with a client with whom the mental health professional has had a prior therapeutic relationship, although some professionals believe that this is acceptable if a specified amount of time has elapsed since therapeutic contact. Therapists who engage in such behaviors are open to sanctions from (a) professional associations (expulsion and publication of names and violations), (b) licensing boards (suspension or revocation of practice licenses and publication of findings), (c) civil lawsuits for damages caused to victims, and, (d) criminal prosecution in an increasing number of states (misdemeanor or felony, depending on the jurisdiction). It is important to note that in each of these cases, purported "consent" by the client to engage in sexual relationships with their therapist is not accepted as a defense for such behaviors.

In the eighth edition of their groundbreaking book, *The Counselor and the Law: A Guide to Legal and Ethical Practice,* Anne Marie Wheeler and Burt Bertram provide an overview of the actual scope of issues surrounding therapist–patient sexual relationships including issues surrounding civil lawsuits and sample criminal penalties. With regard to civil lawsuits, the Healthcare Providers Service Organization and the American Casualty Company, a malpractice/liability insurance company endorsed by the

American Counseling Association, published data related to closed liability claims between the years 2003 and 2012. These data indicate that approximately 40% of all malpractice claims addressed during this time period involved inappropriate sexual or romantic relationships between therapists and their clients. During this time period, the total compensation paid in claims related to therapist sexual relationships with clients or family members of clients was $2.2 million, with an average claim payment amount of $89,177.

Criminal penalties associated with therapist–client sexual relationships exist in Florida and Minnesota along with several other states. In Florida, for example, a psychotherapist who commits an act of sexual misconduct with a client by means of therapeutic deception has committed a felony in the second degree with a term of imprisonment not to exceed 15 years (30 years in the case of a habitual offender) and a fine of up to $10,000. In Minnesota, therapist–patient sexual contact is recognized as a fourth-degree criminal offense with a prison sentence of up to 10 years and a fine not to exceed $20,000. Yet in several other states, therapist–client sex is not yet classified as a criminal act. A movement, however, exists among state legislatures to criminalize such acts as an increasing number of lawmakers become educated on the harm such behaviors may cause to clients and their families.

Along with prohibiting sexual boundary violations with current clients, most ethical codes and occupational licensing laws extend this prohibition from 2 years to a lifetime, depending on the mental health specialty, following the termination of the counseling process. For example, psychologists and marriage and family therapists are prohibited from posttermination sexual contact with former clients for a period of 2 years, professional counselors for 5 years, and social workers for a lifetime. Further, even though many therapists embrace a "once a client, always a client" doctrine, those who follow the established minimum time period requirements for their specialty and subsequently choose to enter into a sexual relationship with a former client carry the burden of demonstrating that a significant number of conditions have been met to ensure that exploitation of the former client does not occur in the posttherapeutic sexual relationship. Such conditions often include professional consultation, written documentation, or attending therapy with the former client to examine a number of potential client exploitation risk factors.

Damage Caused to Clients and Their Families

Numerous studies have examined the harm caused by therapist sexual boundary violations. Perhaps the preeminent researcher on the effects of sexual boundary violations in therapy is Kenneth Pope. Through his research, Pope has identified what he refers to as therapist–patient sex syndrome, in which he identified 10 common harmful effects on clients who are sexually victimized by their therapist. These effects include (1) feelings of ambivalence, wherein clients often fear separation from the therapist while also wanting to escape the power he or she holds over their lives; (2) unfounded feelings of guilt and self-blame; (3) a feeling of isolation and emptiness; (4) a profound confusion about sexuality, which may lead to traumatic memories affecting future sexual relationships in their lives; (5) feelings of great distrust, particularly of future therapists, due to the vulnerable nature of therapy and the violation that occurred; (6) a harmed sense of identity, ability to establish or maintain appropriate boundaries with others, and ability to assume non-self-destructive roles in life; (7) emotional liability involving a range of uncontrollable emotional reactions and displays, particularly related to feelings of depression and anxiety; (8) suppressed rage that is often blocked from awareness, acceptance, and expression; (9) an increased risk of suicide and self-destructiveness, which paired with the aforementioned guilt, isolation, and distrust places a client in a very lethal situation; and (10) impaired cognitive functioning, particularly related to attention and concentration. While this list is comprehensive, it is by no means an all-inclusive list of potential harms of therapist–client sexual boundary violations.

Numerous other studies have examined the impact of sexually exploitive therapeutic relationships on clients, none of which have uncovered any positive outcomes for the client, as often alluded to by the offending therapist. Further, publicity about therapist–client sex may lead future clients to avoid entering therapy out of fear. Such publicity may also harm mental health professionals' ability to persuade the public, lawmakers, and others of the benefits of therapy. This only serves to further hinder access to mental health care despite a dedicated campaign to decrease the stigma associated with seeking help with mental health, family, or relationship struggles.

Managing Boundaries and Normal Sexual Attraction

Due to the intimate nature of the therapist–client professional relationship, romantic attraction often occurs. Some schools of therapy, such as psychoanalysis, seek to create an environment wherein clients project feelings related to people from their past onto their therapist. For example, a client might be encouraged to respond to the therapist as he or she has to a parent or past romantic partner, a phenomenon known as transference. This is done in an attempt to address issues from a client's past in the present relationship between therapist and client. Such interventions require a great deal of objectivity on behalf of therapists to ensure they maintain the professional boundaries necessary for proper therapeutic healing. If, however, therapists allow themselves to act upon their own feelings or urges in response to their clients without maintaining professional objectivity, a phenomenon known as countertransference, boundary violations of varying severity may very well occur. It is of paramount importance that therapists have safeguards in place to acknowledge and address feelings of countertransference, such as sexual attraction toward their clients, through supervision, consultation, and other introspective mechanisms before such feelings result in harmful actions with regard to their clients, the most serious of which involves sexual boundary violations.

Some researchers have pointed to a lack of training related to the management of sexual attraction in therapy among mental health training programs. Such training should emphasize the development of strategies for managing boundaries related to feelings of attraction between therapists and their clients. It is therefore incumbent upon training programs to increase awareness and provide training in addressing this issue since the onus of boundary management lies solely with the therapist. An increased educational focus on this issue prior to its occurrence may serve as a preventative strategy to help protect vulnerable clients. It is also of paramount importance that therapists who discover they are having feelings of attraction toward clients or who suspect clients are attracted to them acknowledge what is occurring and take steps to prevent harm as quickly as possible.

Identifying and Addressing Potential Boundary Violations

Aside from incorporating additional training in mental health training programs focusing solely on the taboo and forbidden nature of sexual boundary violations, other more proactive safeguards may be put into place. Of very high importance is the willingness of therapists to seek supervision, consultation, or personal counseling throughout their careers to address any internal issues that may affect their ability to provide objective counseling. Such steps, however, are only as effective as the therapist is willing to be honest with such individuals. Specifically, when therapists are seeking supervision, consultation, or personal counseling, they must be willing to share feelings, thoughts, or behaviors that they would most likely keep secret, as these are the very issues that supervision, consultation, and personal counseling are designed to address. Thus, the supervisor, consultant, or personal counselor must create an environment wherein a vulnerable therapist will not fear judgment or censure if he or she openly discusses issues of countertransference before progressing to the point of harming clients.

Other experts caution that therapists not view other therapists who engage in sexual relationships with clients from a dichotomous, "us versus them" perspective. From this vantage point, it is postulated that virtually any therapist may become susceptible to sexual or nonsexual boundary violations if the right circumstances are present. Examining the issue from this perspective keeps the therapist in a vigilant mind-set, allowing the therapist to seek supervision, consultation, or personal counseling at any point during which the therapist's moral compass indicates that something is going or has gone awry in his or her work with clients. If such issues are addressed early in their development, it is much easier to reduce the possibility of client harm. Doing so may prevent a well-intentioned therapist from crossing the point of no return with regard to professional therapeutic boundaries.

*Daniel J. Weigel and
Kimberly A. Donovan*

See also Dual and Multiple Relationships; Ethical Codes; Self of the Therapist; Sexual Assault and Rape

Further Readings

American Association for Marriage and Family Therapy. (2012). *AAMFT code of ethics.* Alexandria, VA: Author.

American Counseling Association. (2014). *ACA code of ethics.* Alexandria, VA: Author.

American Psychological Association. (2010). *Ethical principles of psychologists and code of conduct.* Washington, DC: Author.

Gabbard, G. O. (1996). Lessons to be learned from the study of sexual boundary violations. *American Journal of Psychotherapy, 50,* 311–322.

Herlihy, B., & Corey, G. (2015). *Boundary issues in counseling: Multiple roles and responsibilities* (3rd ed.). Alexandria, VA: American Counseling Association.

National Association of Social Workers. (2008). *Code of ethics of the National Association of Social Workers.* Washington, DC: Author.

Pope, K. S. (1994). *Sexual involvement with therapists: Patient assessment, subsequent therapy, forensics.* Washington, DC: American Psychological Association.

Welfel, E. R. (2013). *Ethics in counseling and psychotherapy: Standards, research, and emerging issues* (5th ed.). Belmont, CA: Cengage.

Wheeler, A. M., & Bertram, B. (2015). *The counselor and the law: A guide to legal and ethical practice* (7th ed.). Alexandria, VA: American Counseling Association.

SEXUAL TOYS/SEXUAL AIDS

Sex toys, or what are sometimes referred to as "marital aids," is an umbrella term that incorporates objects, oils, herbs, videos, and other devices that are used to increase or enhance sexual pleasure. The term *sexual toys* tends to refer to objects, and *sexual/marital aids* encompasses a broader array of materials meant to enhance pleasure and eroticism. Sex toys are marketed for both male and female consumers, but tend to be more targeted toward helping women reach orgasm. With advancement of technology, digitally enabled sex toys are being manufactured. Sex toys have become acceptable aids for overcoming minor sex-related health problems such as vaginal dryness, foreplay anxiety, and premature ejaculation. In addition to help with sexual dysfunction, they are used for pleasure and eroticism. The idea of sex being for pleasure and incorporating eroticism is part of the World Health Organization's definition of sexual health, rather than sex just being for procreation. These toys increasingly are geared toward giving a holistic experience, pleasure, intimacy and a sense of physical and psychological wellness. They can be used by individuals for masturbation or as part of sexual activities for couples to increase their pleasure. This entry provides a brief history of sexual toys, and the impact of technology on sexual toys.

Brief History

Sex toys and sexual aids have a long history and have served many purposes in human sexuality; they were used as a tool to enhance chances of procreation and sexual experience. There is some evidence that the first dildo, made from stone, may have been used 28,000 years ago. Sexual toys and aids have been used to enhance sexual experience since the time of Aristotle. Many cultures believe that different herbs, oils, and fragrances increase libido and enhance sexual experiences. Examples of sexual toys and aids dating back to centuries ago include dildos and geisha balls (used in Japan). Vatsayana's *Kama Sutra,* an ancient book written during the 2nd century CE, alludes to sex as a spiritual and a holistic experience and use of aids to enhance pleasure. Vibrators were in use to treat women with what was referred to as hysteria during the Victorian era in England.

In the 1980s feminists advocated sexual freedom; sex toys such as vibrators became popular, and many were sold with a sex positive message. It has been estimated that over $15 billion a year is now spent on sex toys, and the number of "adult" items available on the popular Internet shopping site Amazon is in the thousands. One of the most popular sex toys purchased online is the vibrator. Although sex toys are sold worldwide, the highest number of Google searches for sex toys occurs in the United States.

Technology and Sexual Toys/Aids

Current technology has made sexual toys more sophisticated and safe from both a technical and aesthetic perspective. The acceptance of sexual toys and aids has resulted in a proliferation of different toys, oils, creams, and pictures and videos meant for sexual arousal (pornography) and for sexual education. In addition, virtual worlds have become a source of intimacy and have evolved into sexual subcultures. The Internet provides pictures, videos, chat rooms, virtual worlds, and real-time video experiences.

Significant and sustained growth in the field of human computer interaction (HCI) is increasing the possibilities of sexual toys. The newest innovations in HCI integrate subjective, emotional, aesthetic, and/or bodily experiences into technology. This can include moving computer experiences from a monitor out into the world and people's bodies. It has the potential to make "virtual sex" more realistic. It includes technologies such as body sensors, interactive cloth, and small computing devices. In the sexual realms it has the potential to increase the experience, pleasure, and eroticism of sexual interactions (both human and virtual) and make virtual interactions more "real." This technology has the potential to make sexual encounters more connecting or more socially disconnecting, depending on how they are used.

Veena Prasad

See also Compulsive Sexual Behavior; Sexual Abuse; Sexual Assessment/History; Sexual Enhancement, Sexual Toys; Sexual Health; Sexual Prejudice; Sexuality Education

Further Readings

Annini, E. A., Limoncin, E., Ciocca, G., Buehler, S., & Krychman, M. (2012). Ethical aspects of sexual medicine. Internet, vibrators, and other sex aids: Toys or therapeutic instruments? *Journal of Sexual Medicine, 9,* 2994–3001. doi:10.1111/jsm.12018

Bardzell, J., & Bardzell, S. (2011). Pleasure is your birthright: Digitally enabled designer sex toys as a case of third-wave HCI. In *Proceedings of the SIGCHI Conference on Human Factors in Computing Systems* (pp. 257–266). New York: Association for Computing Machinery.

Brody, S. (2010). The relative health benefits of different sexual activities. *The Journal of Sexual Medicine, 7,* 1336–1361.

Eaglin, A., & Bardzell, S. (2011). Sex toys and designing for sexual wellness. In *CHI'11, Extended Abstracts on Human Factors in Computing Systems* (pp. 1837–1842). New York: Association for Computing Machinery.

Fahs, B., & Swank, E. (2013). Adventures with the "plastic man": Sex toys, compulsory heterosexuality, and the politics of women's sexual pleasure. *Sexuality & Culture, 17*(4), 666–685. doi:10.1007/s12119-013-9167-4

Henry, S. (2009, February 15). Love potions across cultures. *Los Angeles Times.* Retrieved from http://articles.latimes.com/2009/feb/15/news/adna-aphrodisiacs15

Lindau, S. T., & Gavrilova, N. (2010). Sex, health, and years of sexually active life gained due to good health: evidence from two US population based cross sectional surveys of ageing. *BMJ, 340*.

M. M. (2013, January 11). *Sex toys with ridiculously ancient origins*. Retrieved from http://toptenbestandworst.com/?p=7779

Maines, R (1999). *The technology of orgasm: Hysteria, the vibrator, and women's sexual satisfaction*. Baltimore, MD: Johns Hopkins University Press.

Ntseane, P. G. (2004, March). *Cultural dimension of sexuality: Empowerment challenge for HIV/AIDs prevention in Botswana*. Paper presented at the International Seminar/Workshop on Learning and Empowerment: Key Issues in strategies for HIV/AIDS Prevention, Chiangmai, Thailand.

Pace, T., Bardzell, S., & Bardzell, J. (2010, April). The rogue in the lovely black dress: Intimacy in world of warcraft. In *CHI'10, Proceedings of the SIGCHI Conference on Human Factors in Computing Systems* (pp. 233–242). New York: ACM Press.

Sexuality and Religion

Sexuality, an individual's capacity for sexual feelings, sexual activity, or sexual orientation or preference, is often perceived through a moral lens, and for many this moral lens is developed based on religious beliefs. Thus, the views that are held about sexuality are often influenced by religious values and principles and are constantly shifting in order to accommodate cultural and societal changes. Sexuality and religion are both significant topics that arise during the therapeutic process and significantly contribute to the makeup of a client's identity. These topics influence the lives of clients and the way treatment is conceptualized, and have an impact on the self of the therapist (the way the therapist's experiences, values, and beliefs impact their reaction to clients), making it imperative that marriage and family therapists (MFTs) receive adequate training on issues related to sexuality and religion. Although MFTs are trained to remain objective and provide unbiased care while working with clients, the sensitive nature of sexuality and religion can trigger strong reactions. This entry provides an overview of how sexuality and religion have evolved in the field of MFT and why it is imperative for MFTs to understand how and why these issues are so significant in treatment.

Sexuality, Religion, and the Mental Health Field

Historically, perceptions of sexuality have been influenced by religious, legal, and medical factors with each of these factors being influenced by societal advancements and cultural shifts. Of these factors, religion tends to have the most significant impact on perceptions of sexuality. There are 12 classical world religions, and although each world religion differs in its beliefs and practices, the religions share many similarities, especially regarding sexuality. Different religions hold different beliefs about sexual issues, such as gender, contraception, abortion, sex during menstruation, sexual orientation, same-sex sexual behaviors or relationships, masturbation, premarital sex, and infidelity. Of these sexuality issues, one that has received a large amount of attention is sexual orientation.

Same-Sex Sexual Orientation and the Mental Health Field

Individuals who identify as a sexual minority (i.e., anyone other than those who identify as heterosexual) have a history of being discriminated against by various religious, medical, and mental health organizations. In the late 1800s medical and mental health providers changed their conceptualization of sexual minority sexual orientations from being religiously based to being psychologically based. What had been discussed as issues of morality shifted to being seen as symptoms of a mental health disorder. The American Psychiatric Association published the *Diagnostic and Statistical Manual of Mental Disorders* (DSM) to help mental health providers assess and diagnose their clients with mental health issues, such as major depression, general anxiety disorder, and schizophrenia. In the first edition of the DSM, published in 1952, homosexuality was classified as a sociopathic personality disturbance, which then changed to a sexual deviation in the second edition, published in 1968. It was not until 1987, over 37 years after the DSM's first publication, that homosexuality was completely removed from the DSM. The late 1980s also brought more advocacy from mental health organizations that focused on preventing both discrimination within the mental health field and societal discrimination based on sexual orientation. More recent and political decisions involving sexual orientation include the 2015 United States Supreme Court ruling that all states must recognize same-sex marriages, which may lead to policy modifications among mental health care services as well.

Similar shifts can be seen in the American Association of Marriage and Family Therapy (AAMFT), the governing body of the MFT field. The organization took a stance on sexual orientation–related issues in the late 1990s, indicating that therapists practicing under this agency must not discriminate based on sexual orientation. These guidelines suggest that no one should be turned away from therapy for identifying with a certain sexual orientation. AAMFT is also supportive of diverse religious beliefs and the organization supports privately operated religious schools in maintaining their belief system and training competent therapists that adhere to the appropriate guidelines. Other efforts made by AAMFT include a focus on ethical and competent training practices, which has included the accrediting body of the field (Commission on Accreditation for Marriage and Family Therapy Education [COAMFTE]) creating standards that ensure accredited training programs include education about working with issues concerning sexual orientation.

Sexual Behaviors and Religiosity

Marriage and family therapists are trained to work with people of all ages who present with a wide range of problems. Assessing for healthy sexual practices in all ages is important for client care. Clinicians typically have knowledge about human development, which encompasses age-appropriate sexual behaviors and physiological development. Many religious beliefs hold ideas surrounding issues such as abortion, contraception, and sex education. At times, clients may struggle with navigating their sexual practices and safety.

Premarital Sex

Religious values often influence dating relationships and sexual behaviors. From the perspective of many religions, sex is a practice that is supposed to be between two married individuals, of the opposite sex, who have committed themselves to one another through marriage. Because many religions do not condone premarital sex, those who choose to have premarital sex may experience feelings of shame and guilt because they have violated a core principle of their religion. Similar feelings may be evoked if an individual has physically intimate interactions with members of the same sex.

Infidelity

Infidelity, or extramarital sex, is a common problem that impacts many couples. Statistics on frequency of infidelity are controversial, with some studies indicating that it occurs in as many as 50% of couples, with the most reliable studies indicating that infidelity behaviors occur in 6% to 25% of relationships. Many religions strongly speak out against any form of extramarital involvement and support monogamous relationships. Although many religions discourage infidelity, it is a common presenting problem in therapy. This type of relational violation creates a variety of difficult emotions for both partners, including anger, depression, hurt, jealousy, and loss of trust, and the healing process in treatment can be extensive and challenging.

Contraception and Abortion

Most religions do not condone premarital sex and religious organizations' messages to youth about sex often call for abstinence while not discussing healthy sexual practices. Depending on the religion, even married couples may be discouraged from using means of contraception to prevent pregnancy. The Catholic Church is commonly recognized as condemning the use of contraception. Many religions oppose abortion, although often among these religions there are limited circumstances in which abortion is condoned. These issues may arise in a clinical setting, whether it is a couple struggling to decide on the use of contraception or whether to terminate an unwanted pregnancy. For those seeking counseling services, these decisions are complicated by their religious beliefs and will need nonjudgmental support in exploring their options. As mentioned earlier, issues surrounding intimacy or contraception presented by clients may not be consistent with the therapist's values or belief system, and it is the therapist's responsibility to manage his or her reactions in an appropriate way.

Implications for Marriage and Family Therapists

Marriage and family therapists will undoubtedly work with clients who seek services concerning issues related to sexuality, their religious beliefs, and the intersection of both identities. While not exhaustive, this may include working with clients on issues related to sexual orientation, such as the coming-out process; overcoming discrimination or homophobia from family, peers, and authority figures; depression and suicide; and working with related issues. This also could include addressing sexual behaviors, such as sexual dysfunctions, sex therapy, infidelity, abortion, and the use of contraception.

Part of training also requires understanding the expectations that individuals face due to their gender. For instance, women are more frequently shamed for sexual behaviors, being expected to be maternal, nurturing, and submissive, whereas men are expected to be void of emotional expression and the primary caretakers of the family. An MFT's ability to competently and ethically provide these services requires specific training related to how to address these concerns in therapy and how to provide ethical services. Individuals struggling with coming out as gay or lesbian often face challenges with how this sexual orientation ownership may impact their participation in religious practices and how it may challenge their or their family's belief system.

Treatment

Many struggle with issues surrounding sexuality in various ways. Clients may present to therapy with an array of issues related to sex, such as sexual dysfunction (e.g., premature ejaculation, erectile dysfunction, vaginismus) or sexual desire. Sexuality is a complex, multicausal issue that is impacted by many factors. When assessing for presenting problems related to sexuality, a therapist must gather information about medical history as well as the values and beliefs each individual has surrounding sexuality. Asking questions about how an individual learned about sex and sexuality and how his or her family discussed issues related to sexuality is a good place to start.

Most MFT training programs require coursework on basic sex therapy practices and interventions. Some programs encourage clinicians to conceptualize intimacy-related issues using a biopsychosocial-spiritual lens, which encompasses biological, psychological, social, and spiritual factors that can contribute to sexual issues. Of additional importance is to consider how different social locations (i.e., religion, race, socioeconomic status) impact the meaning of sexuality. For example, an individual struggling with coming out as gay or lesbian often faces challenges with how ownership of his or her sexual orientation will impact participation in religious practices and how it may challenge the belief system of individuals or their family. In sum, certain religious groups have strong values around sexuality, and the MFT field recommends that therapists work with clients with careful consideration of their values and beliefs.

Conversion or Reparative Therapy

A relevant area to sexuality, religion, and treatment is conversion or reparative therapy, which is the practice of attempting to stop an individual from being lesbian, gay, bisexual, or transgender, or to reduce same-sex attraction or alter gender identity. This practice is highly controversial, and some jurisdictions, including California, New Jersey, and the District of Columbia, have enacted laws prohibiting mental health professionals in those states from offering these services to those under the age of 18. Many mental health organizations have made statements that these services are contraindicated and can cause more harm than good and are not effective at achieving their intended goal. For example, AAMFT indicates that the organization itself does not consider sexual orientation to be a pathological condition and does not support practice involving changing one's sexual orientation. The AAMFT requires therapists who hold licenses in the field to provide the best practices for their clients, based on current research, and because the organization does not see same-sex relationships, same-sex attraction, or gender identity as a mental health care–related concern, it finds no use for these types of therapy.

Self of the Therapist

Because therapists are human beings with their own identities, beliefs, and values, clients with presenting problems related to religion and sexuality may trigger strong reactions in the therapist. It is important for therapists to be cognizant of their reactions toward clients struggling with sexual and religious identity development. Therapists in training programs are supervised by more experienced clinicians and can use this time to process the reactions that may occur as a result of discussing issues about religion and sexuality that are inconsistent with their own values and beliefs. Even more experienced clinicians are encouraged to process such feelings with colleagues and supervisors after their training is complete.

One important issue concerning work with those who hold different beliefs and values than the MFTs is upholding the AAMFT code of ethics. Despite differences in beliefs it is an ethical violation to discriminate against clients based on aspects of their identity, including religion and sexual orientation. Thus, an MFT cannot refuse treatment to a client due to his or her religious beliefs or sexual orientation alone. For example, if an MFT viewed same-sex relationships as being a sin based on his or her religious beliefs, it would be unethical to refuse services to clients who identify as gay solely based on their sexual orientation.

Sarah Schonian and Jaclyn D. Cravens

See also Beliefs and Values; Gender- and Culture-Sensitive Therapies; Individual and Family Development; Pregnancy and Sexuality; Sexual Assessment/History; Therapists' Values

Further Readings

Carlson, T. D., Kirkpatrick, D., Heckner, L., & Killmer, M. (2010). Religion, spirituality, and marriage and family therapy: A study of family therapists' beliefs about the appropriateness of addressing religious and spiritual issues in therapy. *The American Journal of Family Therapy, 30*(2), 157–171.

Edwards, L. L., Robertson, J. A., Smith, P. A., & O'Brien, N. B. (2014). Marriage and family therapy training programs and their integration of lesbian, gay, and bisexual identities. *Journal of Feminist Family Therapy, 26*(1), 3–27.

Erickson, M. J., & Carlson, T. (2014). *Spirituality and family therapy.* New York: Routledge.

Hertlein, K. M., Weeks, G. R., & Gambescia, N. (Eds.). (2015). *Systemic sex therapy.* New York: Routledge.

Weiler, L. M., Lyness, K. P., Haddock, S. A., & Zimmerman, T. S. (2015). Contextual issues in couple and family therapy: Gender, sexual orientation, culture, and spirituality. In J. L. Wetchler & L. L. Hecker (Eds.), *An introduction to marriage and family therapy* (pp. 65–116). New York: Routledge.

Sexuality Education

Sexuality education refers to both formal and informal processes by which individuals acquire knowledge about human sexuality. Sexual knowledge includes scientific and medical information about biological processes of the human body, such as sexual development, reproductive health, and disease. In addition to scientific and medical information, sexuality education, sometimes referred to as sex education, may include instruction related to specific skills that are used to navigate sexual experiences, such as emotional skills, body awareness, self-understanding, and interpersonal skills.

Because of the varied opinions, norms, and values associated with sexuality in general, sexuality education is a complex topic. Sexuality education is an ongoing process that occurs formally and informally across the life span. Sexuality education, whether formal or informal, influences beliefs, attitudes, and values and has the potential to shape sexual behaviors and experiences. Because sexuality education occurs across the life span, it is important that formal curricula be sequenced with developmental appropriateness in mind. For this reason, sexuality education has long been of great interest to many groups, including public health officials, school personnel, and counselors. A number of formal curricula have been developed over the past several decades for use in health care, faith-based, community, and educational-based settings with the intended primary purpose of improving health outcomes and influencing behavior. Informal sexuality education also occurs across the life span through direct and indirect communication with parents and caregivers, peers, teachers, and partners. In addition, informal sexuality education occurs through exposure to media with implicit or explicit sexual messaging. Informal sexuality education may or may not be developmentally sequenced, especially with regard to exposure to sexual messaging through media and marketing sources. This entry reviews the maturity of formal sexuality education and the components of the various formal curricula, while emphasizing their points of similarity and their differences. This entry also discusses the importance of sexuality education and directions for the future of sexuality education.

The History of Formal Sexuality Education

Throughout history, children have received informal sexual education messages about sexuality from birth onward through contact with caregivers, peers, and teachers. In modern society, young people also receive numerous messages from media sources, such as books, magazines, television, film, the Internet, and advertising media. These messages have the power to shape behaviors and yet may be scientifically inaccurate or promoting values that run contrary to positive health behaviors. Determining pathways for sharing scientifically accurate information and shaping behaviors to enhance overall wellness was a public health concern even long before various media outlets were influencing sexuality education.

Some of the earliest accounts of formal sexuality education in the United States date back to the late 1800s. From this period through the 1940s, sexuality education was primarily in response to outbreaks of sexually transmitted infections spreading through rapidly developing and newly industrial urban cities and among soldier populations. During the late 1800s various health care and hygiene projects were even introduced into some public school curricula, and there was federal funding to educate troops. The first major work on sexuality education was published in 1916, and is an example of how sexuality education was and continues to be influenced by the historical context of the times. In that work masturbation was discouraged because it was believed to be harmful to future marital relationships. After the 1940s, more curricula in sexuality education were developed, and they were based on a growing body of empirical examination of human sexual behavior and attitudes toward sexuality.

Sexuality education began to slowly occur in some school settings; however, opposition groups, primarily some parents and religious organizations, argued against inclusion of sexuality education in schools. Minimal progress was made to integrate sexuality education through the mid-20th century, even while sexuality researchers like

Alfred Kinsey and William Masters and Virginia Johnson made headlines. During this period, distinctions arose between instructional methods and curricula in sexuality education that still exist today. Most people agreed that some form of sexuality education needed to occur during adolescence, yet what should be taught was not agreed upon.

As the social climate and culture changed in the second half of the 20th century, so too did sexuality education. The Sex Information and Education Council of the United States (SIECUS) was founded in the 1960s on the belief that sexuality is an integral part of the overall human experience, not something shameful or dangerous. SIECUS continues to serve as a source for nonjudgmental information about sexuality education. In the 1970s the term *comprehensive sexuality education* was established with SIECUS supporting its tenets and its place in school curriculum. This model of sexuality education delivers information about sexual decision-making to reduce risky behaviors and includes information about contraception and disease prevention.

To guide educators in delivering developmentally appropriate curricula from this model, SIECUS established *Guidelines for Comprehensive Sexuality Education: Kindergarten–12th Grade* in the early 1990s. Also, sexuality education was influenced by the AIDS epidemic of the 1980s, and during this time the U.S. surgeon general voiced strong support for comprehensive sexuality education offered in schools beginning in early grades. However, there remained advocates for education focusing on abstinence from sex, and in 1981 the Adolescent Family Life Act (AFLA) was enacted to focus sexuality education on prevention of pregnancy through abstinence and the use of adoption, not abortion, in cases of unintended pregnancies. Funding under AFLA was eliminated in fiscal year 2010, but as of 2015 the federal government continued to fund abstinence education while also funding more comprehensive approaches to sex education.

The debate as to the role of sexuality education in the public schools is ongoing. While the federal government has an impact on federal spending for different curricula, individual states pass legislation regulating public school sexuality education in practice. Differences of opinion and perspective have emerged on fundamental issues of what to include in the curriculum, but also on pragmatic issues such as whether or not have gender-segregated instruction and where in the overall curriculum to incorporate sexuality education. Should sexuality education be a stand-alone course or part of physical education, health, physiology, and biology instruction, and who is best suited to teach sexuality education: the school nurse, classroom teacher, or an external medical professional?

Since the earliest days of formal sexuality education, some groups have feared that exposure to sexuality education would promote sexual behavior among young people; however, research continues to indicate that this does not occur. In fact, comprehensive sexuality education is associated with delayed onset of initial sexual activity. Despite outcomes-based research, differences of opinion and moral opinions continue to shape sexuality education.

Comprehensive Sexuality Education and Abstinence-Only Sexuality Education

Comprehensive sexuality education occurs across the duration of K–12 education, is developmentally sequenced, and provides information about a broad array of topics. The goals of comprehensive sexuality education are to provide scientifically accurate information about human sexuality, to promote self-understanding about sexuality, to develop relationship skills, and to assist young people in exercising responsibility for sexual decision-making and behaviors. As with abstinence-only education, a goal of comprehensive sexuality education is to avoid potential negative consequences of sexual activity among young people. Yet rather than just trying to prevent negative consequences, comprehensive sexuality education aims to inform students of how to enhance their decision-making skills for optimal health.

Over the last several decades, many research studies have been completed comparing the sexual behaviors of adults who received no sexuality education, those who received abstinence-only sexuality education, and those who received comprehensive sexuality education during their K–12 education. These studies seek to describe the effectiveness of various sexuality education curricula or group-level intervention programs. Effectiveness is generally defined in these studies as helping young people to delay sexual activity, particularly vaginal intercourse, or to use contraception and condoms when engaging in sexual activity so as to minimize risk of infection or unintended pregnancies. Specific actions, not just beliefs, are measured to verify efficacy of programs.

Research indicates that curricula, including accurate information about condoms and contraception, such as in comprehensive sexuality education, lead to reductions in risky behaviors. Sexuality education programs are effective in improving the use of contraception, not necessarily decreasing rates of sexual activity. Abstinence-only curriculum can vary in specific focus from program to program, but primarily emphasizes abstinence from sexual behaviors until marriage. Some abstinence-only programs do include affirmative information about sexual behaviors other than intercourse, but the main educational goals are to deliver information about the benefits of abstinence and the potential negative outcomes of sexual behavior, such as disease and unintended pregnancy. The exclusive purpose of abstinence education, as federally defined, is to teach about the positive gains resulting from abstaining from sexual activity. Sexual activity after marriage is taught as the expected standard for all school age youth, and this is taught as the only way to avoid possible negative consequences of sexual activity, such as sexually transmitted infections.

Research indicates that abstinence-only sexuality education does not help adolescents to delay sexual behavior. Based on meta-analyses, what makes comprehensive sexuality education curricula most effective include (a) a collaborative approach to developing and pilot testing curriculum that involves experts, needs assessments, and community input; (b) a focus on goals, specific behaviors, risk, and protective factors; (c) support of school and local leaders, trained educators, participants to carry out the curriculum as planned, and; (d) a safe, engaged teaching approach to sequential topics that involves active learning strategies.

The Future of Sexuality Education

As themes in the construction of sexuality have shifted over time, so too have the themes of sexuality education, and the controversy around sexuality education continues. Sexuality educators continue to make progress in clarifying the pedagogy of sexuality education in order to ensure that sexuality education curricula are based on academically rigorous guidelines. As sexuality education moves into the future, sexuality education will continue to be shaped by political and moral shifts in U.S. culture.

There is also growing interest in sexuality education worldwide. Expanding sexuality education beyond Western culture is exciting and broadens perspectives, but also presents challenges when developing education programs that incorporate diverse cultural norms and patterns. Responding to diverse needs is essential in order for sexuality education to be effective in promoting positive wellness outcomes, promoting sexual pleasure, and reducing risk and negative consequences. Sexuality education received formally and informally, implicitly and explicitly, is an important developmental and lifelong process.

Angela R. McDonald and
Kylie P. Dotson-Blake

See also Beliefs and Values; Certified Family Life Educator; Effectiveness Research; Schools, Family Involvement in; Sex Positivity; Sex Researchers; Sexual Health

Further Readings

Haffner, D. (2002). *Beyond the big talk: Every parent's guide to raising sexually healthy teens from middle school to high school and beyond.* New York: New Market Press.

Harris, R. (2010). *Let's talk about sex: Changing bodies, growing up, sex, and sexual health*. London: Walker Books.

Schroeder, E., & Kuriansky, J. (Eds.). (2009). *Sexuality education: Past, present, and future*. Westport, CT: Praeger Perspectives.

Sex Information and Education Council of the United States (SIECUS). (2004). *Guidelines for comprehensive sexuality education: Kindergarten through twelfth grade* (3rd ed.) Washington, DC: Author.

Sexually Transmitted Infections

Sexually transmitted infections (STIs) are infections and illnesses generally acquired by sexual contact. The microorganisms that cause STIs are transmitted from person to person through blood, semen, vaginal, and other bodily fluids. Some STIs are transmitted by a mother to her unborn child during pregnancy or during the birthing process. Many STIs are asymptomatic, and individuals may not even know they are infected. Individuals may in fact appear and feel healthy. It is important to the overall health of a client and to that of his or her partners for a therapist to inquire about an individual's sexual health, practice, actions, and health concerns. In addition, it is important to help individuals, couples, and parents gain knowledge on STIs and how to communicate about preventing them or disclosing when one has an STI. This entry first discusses the prevalence of STIs in the United States, the terminology used when discussing STIs, and how STIs are transmitted. It then discusses the types of STIs, risk factors for STIs, and the prevention and treatment of STIs.

Prevalence

There are more than 120 million STIs in the United States. Each year, approximately 20 million new STIs are diagnosed and treated. While anyone can acquire an STI, approximately half of all infections occur in young adults ages 15 to 24 years of age. Most STIs are passed through microorganisms that live on the genital area or through bodily fluids that are transmitted during vaginal, oral, or genital sex. While many STIs are curable with proper treatment, many are not. Symptoms vary by infection, and many STIs are asymptomatic. If left untreated, many STIs can develop into more serious health concerns, including certain types of cancers, severe reproductive health complications, infertility, and even death.

Terminology

Although STI and STD are sometimes used interchangeably, many clinicians and researchers now use the term STI instead of *sexually transmitted disease* (STD) or *venereal disease* (VD). The reason for the use of STI instead of STD is that while individuals may have an infection they acquired during sexual contact, they may not have visible symptoms. Infections are often contagious, carry the potential to become a disease, and precede STDs, but not all STIs result in the development of an STD. The term STD denotes that the person in fact has a disease, not just an infection.

Transmission

Anyone is susceptible to contracting an STI. STIs affect people of all races, sexual orientations, partner status, and ages. Certain individual risk behaviors, coupled with barriers to proper screening, prevention information, and treatment, can increase the risk of infection. In the United States, there are more than 25 known STIs. There are four main causal agents of STIs: bacterial, viral, protozoal, and ectoparasitic.

All STIs vary in whether or not they will produce symptoms and whether they are curable. For example, many viral STIs, including herpes simplex, hepatitis C, the human papillomavirus (HPV) (commonly known as genital warts) and the human immunodeficiency virus (HIV) cannot be cured. In the case of viral STIs, symptoms may be treated and alleviated, but the infection is still considered contagious. In contrast, STIs caused by bacteria, such as syphilis, chlamydia, and gonorrhea, are often curable when treated with antibiotics. Additionally, other STIs can be caused by tiny organisms, such as pubic lice and scabies, and protozoa (trichomoniasis). These STIs are curable with either topical creams or antibiotics.

Types of Sexually Transmitted Infections

STIs are often categorized by their causal agents, and these are defined by the Centers for Disease Control and Prevention (CDC). Common bacterial infections include bacterial vaginosis (BV), chancroid, chlamydia, gonorrhea, syphilis, lymphogranuloma venereum (LV), donovanosis mycoplasma, and genital treponematosis (endemic). Viral infections include hepatitis A, hepatitis B, hepatitis C, herpes simplex virus (HSV-1 and HSV-2), HIV, HPV cytomegalovirus, Epstein-Barr virus, hepatitis D, human T-cell lymphotropic virus (HTLV-1), and molluscum contagiosum. The third causal agent, protozoal infections, cause trichomoniasis, amebiasis, cryptosporidium, and giardiasis. The last causal agent, under the category of ectoparasitic agents, is responsible for STIs such as pubic lice, scabies, and candidiasis.

Risk Factors

Risk factors vary by type of infection. STIs cost the U.S. health care system more than $15 billion each year. It is important to note that this figure captures only a fraction of the actual occurrences of STIs each year due to many cases that go undiagnosed or unreported. Several STIs, including herpes simplex virus, trichomoniasis, and the human papillomavirus, are not often reported to the CDC.

As relayed previously, individuals ages 15 to 24 are at the greatest risk for contracting an STI. Reasons for this include that biologically, young women's bodies are more susceptible to infection, often this age group does not seek proper STI screening or testing, access to services is difficult due to financial or insurance restraints, it is common for individuals in this age bracket to have multiple sex partners, and health care providers do not always discuss STI-related services or issues as often as they should.

While multiple factors increase a young person's susceptibility to STIs, the health consequences of contracting an STI can be lifelong for many. Consequences of having an untreated STI include increased rates of infertility (gonorrhea or chlamydia), long-term complications such as brain and organ damage (syphilis), stillbirth or physical deformity of baby upon birth (syphilis), and even death (syphilis). Research suggests that individuals with syphilis, gonorrhea, or chlamydia are also at increased risk for HIV, specifically in communities of Black men who have sex with men.

Prevention and Treatment

Prevention is an ongoing concern in the United States health care system. Continued education and increased screening protocols aimed at highrisk populations such as adolescents and gay men are needed to diagnose STIs. In order to combat the growing number of STIs, therapists must first understand the difference between the types of prevention: primary, secondary, and tertiary. Primary prevention focuses on ways to prevent STIs at the individual level. This includes providing education to uninfected and infected persons alike. It also involves the identification and treatment of individuals who have an STI and may or may not be experiencing symptoms. Thus, by reducing the number of exposures or behaviors that can lead to an STI, or increasing the use of contraceptive barriers to prevent infection, the goal of primary prevention is to eliminate STIs in the population. Secondary prevention includes the proper diagnosis and treatment for individuals with STIs so that other complications, such as infertility or increasing the risk of contracting other more serious infections can be evaded. Tertiary prevention focuses on decreasing the effects of complications due to STIs and increasing an individual's quality of life.

Prevention Methods

Prevention methods vary by individual preference. Prevention methods the CDC suggests include abstinence, reducing the number of sex partners, obtaining vaccines when possible, using emergency contraception, obtaining screening on a regular basis, and notifying partners of infection. While abstinence is the only sure way to avoid contracting an STI, it is not always the preferred prevention method patients choose. A monogamous relationship between two people without exposure to STIs is also another way to prevent an STI. When one of these two options is not possible, one of the most common prevention methods health providers discuss with patients is the use of condoms to protect against contracting an STI. Correct and consistent use of male condoms is the recommended prevention method for those who do not choose abstinence or monogamy. Condoms are not 100% effective, though they do reduce the risk of transmitting a STI.

Partner Notification

Partner notification identifies sexual partners of individuals who are infected with an STI (or multiple infections) for assessment, diagnosis, education, counseling, and treatment if necessary. In many cases, an individual can be reinfected with the same STI after receiving treatment. Partner notification and partner services include a multitude of services for individuals infected with an STI.

Counseling and Education

Counseling is also a crucial part of STI treatment protocol and management. Counseling provides patients with support, education, and resources for understanding STI diagnosis, transmission, treatment, and prevention. Counseling can assist patients in learning about their own risk factors for contracting or transmitting STIs and aid in the best choice of prevention method possible. Prevention programming should take into consideration population-specific information, including developmental ages and stages of patients, access to care considerations, and ethnicity of patients.

Reporting and Confidentiality

In every state, health care providers are required to report some STIs, including syphilis, chancroid, gonorrhea, chlamydia, HIV, and AIDS. Specific requirements vary by state, and clinicians need to know these regulations. Reporting of STIs is an important aspect of identifying morbidity trends, allocating resources, and assisting health authorities with partner notification, not to mention targeting specific populations to decrease STI rates. Often, reporting is done by laboratory-based facilities and protocols. Clinicians are responsible for knowing their state's specific requirements for reporting. CDC suggests that all pregnant women (or women who desire to become pregnant), adolescents, children, incarcerated individuals, and men who have sex with men should be routinely screened for STIs. While all persons at risk or who have been exposed to a partner with an STI should be screened, the populations just listed are based on disease prevalence, severity, costs, and other considerations for practice. As mentioned previously, adolescents are at a greater risk for contracting a STI due to being biologically more susceptible to infection and multiple partners, and they often do not receive adequate health care unless warranted. Regardless of whether a person belongs to a specific population, all persons should be educated about prevention methods for STIs.

Elizabeth B. Russell

See also Intimacy, Specific Threats to; Marriage, First and Second; Pregnancy and Sexuality; Sex, Definition of; Sex Researchers; Sexual Assessment/History; Sexual Health; Sexual Intimacy; Sexuality Education

Further Readings

Annon, J. (1976). The PLISSIT model: A proposed conceptual scheme for the behavioral treatment of sexual problems. *Journal of Sex Education Therapy*, 2(2), 81–88.

Centers for Disease Control and Prevention. (2012). *Sexually transmitted diseases surveillance*, 22. Atlanta, GA: Department of Health and Human Services.

Centers for Disease Control and Prevention. (2013). *Incidence, prevalence, and cost of sexually transmitted infections in the United States- fact sheet.* Washington: DC: Author. Retrieved from http://www.cancer.gov/cancertopics/factsheet/Risk/HPV

Sales, J., & DiClemente, R. J. (2010). *Adolescent STI/HIV prevention programs: What works for teens? Research facts and findings.* Ithaca, NY: ACT for Youth Center of Excellence. Retrieved from http://www.actforyouth.net/resources/rf/rf_sti_0510.pdf

Sutton, A. L. (2013). *Sexually transmitted diseases sourcebook* (5th ed.). Aston, PA: Omnigraphics.

U.S. Preventive Services Task Force. (2014). *Final recommendation statement: Sexually transmitted infections: behavioral counseling.* Rockville, MD: Author. Retrieved from http://www.uspreventiveservicestaskforce.org/Page/Document/RecommendationStatementFinal/sexually-transmitted-infections-behavioral-counseling1

World Health Organization. (2006). *Definitions: World Health Organization.* Geneva, Switzerland: Author. Retrieved from http://www.who.int/

SIBLING RELATIONSHIPS

Sibling relationships reflect a significant bond between children growing up in close proximity to each other, sometimes biologically related and sometimes not. Understanding sibling relationships in the formative years and the factors that influence personality development can be a significant aid to marriage, family, and couple therapists. This entry begins with a brief overview of sibling relationships, followed by a description of how sibling relationships create a blueprint for personality. Next, the concept of psychological birth order—that is, how perceptions of place within the family influence sibling relationships—is explained. Finally, the concepts of sibling rivalry and competition are discussed.

Overview of Sibling Relationships

In the United States, the norm is to grow up with siblings, with over 80% of children having one or more brothers or sisters. Relationships with siblings can be hostile and intense or affectionate and supportive, but either way the relationships have a lifelong impact. In fact, relationships with siblings often have a longer duration than most other relationships throughout a lifetime. The characteristics of those relationships are largely set in childhood, as it is uncommon that siblings will suddenly become close as adults. Sibling relationships set a foundation for personality and future relationships, as these relationships become a place to practice how to provide comfort to others, to share, fight, and communicate. Siblings growing up in the same household share the same environment but may develop vastly different perceptions of those shared experiences.

Siblings and Personality Development

Sibling relationships largely influence personality development and contribute to formulating conclusions about self, others, and the world. Every individual in the formative years strives to find a unique place of significance, and this striving becomes a road map to follow as each child develops. For example, if one sibling is an exceptional athlete, the other sibling may either strive to become an even better athlete or give up and complain of stomachaches to gain the attention of his mother, a nurse. Children will find their place in relationship to their siblings and other members of their family.

Alfred Adler and Rudolf Dreikurs emphasized the desire to belong as a critical motivating factor. All individuals start as weak and helpless and strive to overcome. There can be extreme emotions, either positive or negative. How well the siblings know each other and their level of intimacy can lead to significant support for each other or result in the siblings undermining each other. There is extreme variability, as each sibling wants a unique position among all others. A discussion of psychological birth order is a good starting point for understanding this desire for uniqueness and the implications for sibling interactions.

Psychological Birth Order

Dreikurs listed five basic psychological birth order positions: only, oldest, second, middle, and youngest. Sibling interactions are strongly influenced by which role is assumed. The actual ordinal position is not important but rather the child's perceptions of his or her place. Even if a child grows up in a blended family, a foster home, or among many other children, such as in an orphanage, a child will still align with other children perceived as siblings. The child will find a position among others no matter the circumstances. In considering the influences of other siblings, those 6 years older or 6 years younger would be considered to have the most significant relationship. For example, consider the following ages of children in a family: 18, 17, 16, 9, 8, and 2. This scenario might reflect an older subgroup of an older, middle, and youngest child, a second subgroup of an older and a second child, and a third subgroup of an only child. The gender of siblings may further influence the creation of subgroups. Siblings too far out of sight are not deemed sibling influences. When siblings are more than 6 years apart, their interactions are more similar to adult–child interactions.

The following descriptions of the five basic psychological positions are based on the work of Adler and Dreikurs. Some more recent research has found a more limited influence of birth order on personality traits, and some psychologists argue that the influence of birth order on personality is overemphasized.

Only Child

An only child may not have other children in close proximity. This child likely grows up in an adult world. Such a child may strive to meet standards and expectations set by authority figures and become responsible and overly pleasing. Or, such a child may become disheartened, feeling unable to meet standards, and thus become more passive or discouraged. One might assume there are no sibling relationships here, but a counselor must dig deeper to ascertain if such a child is truly an only child. Some parents treat their children as friends and do not act as parental authority figures. Such a child may be strongly influenced by what is more like a peer or sibling interaction than an adult–child relationship. An only child in these circumstances may end up feeling entitled to get what is due or overly burdened to be responsible for others. If an only child grows up with cousins living in close proximity or with other children in an apartment building, these influences may resemble sibling relationships. This is especially true if such children are interacting daily with these other children and are consistently vying for significance among them.

Oldest

Once a second child is born, the only becomes an oldest. These children most likely want to remain first; they are motivated to be the responsible ones meeting up to parental standards. Pleasing the parents and doing what is expected are important. This may also carry over to pleasing adults at school. It is common for oldest children to let younger siblings know they are in a privileged place by taking over and demonstrating their own competence while pointing out failings in others. This may result in the older answering for the younger or constantly pointing out where the younger child is falling short. If the younger sibling is especially ambitious and overtakes the oldest, then the oldest might become dethroned and become discouraged. That could open the door for the younger sibling to take on the psychological position as the oldest or responsible one. This heightened competition can put these children at odds with each other and can lead to an intense and constant struggle between them.

Second

If the older child has the responsible position well established, most likely the second will go in a different direction. If the oldest strives to please the adults and is a good student, the second might be more of a rebel and more social than studious. There is a likelihood of competition, especially in Western countries. This can show up as constantly attempting to prove which sibling is the "best." Competition may be quite open, or it could be more subtle. For example, one child may perform well in math while the other may do better in English. Each child will not want to be a copy of the other but instead will want to have his or her own unique position.

Middle

When a third child is born, the second may become a middle child. This child may not have the responsibilities of the oldest or the privileged role as the youngest. Middle children may feel that they do not have a place within the family. These children are often concerned with fairness and justice. They may feel as if they are the black sheep of the family. In other circumstances, they might favorably use their emphasis on fairness, and become the arbiter in the family, trying to ascertain whether everyone else is OK. They may also strive to be popular in ways different from the oldest.

Youngest

Youngest children have the farthest to catch up. They may be either super ambitious, trying to surpass all of the other siblings, or they may accept the role as the pampered youngest and act cute or helpless. They may look to the parents or older siblings to take care of them and do things for them. Some older siblings may be glad to assume this role, as it reinforces their own place of significance within the family.

Special Sibling Circumstances

There are unique circumstances that must be explored to understand fully how siblings may develop a place of significance and interact with each other. A girl with only male siblings, or a boy with only female siblings, may have exaggerated expectations of what girls and boys are expected to do. A girl in this situation might decide to pursue traditionally male sports or other roles, and focus on being as good as or better than her brothers, or she might emphasize her "cuteness" and seek protection from her brothers. Children living in the shadow of a deceased child may give up, as they may feel they can never be as good as the one who is idolized in memory. There can be a constant struggle to prove they are as good as, if not better than, the one not there. This can lead to resentments and ambivalent feelings. A child with an illness, disability, or a physical deformity may get most of the attention in the family due to these special needs. The siblings may feel left out and in turn feel guilty for having such thoughts. Other siblings may take on an extremely protective role, or they may be so resentful of the missed attention or focus that they may just hold on to anger and resentment. A gifted child or a child prodigy may demand similar attention. Extreme competition, resentment, or feeling less important may cloud the sibling relationship.

Sibling Rivalry and Competition

Although most sibling relationships are reported to be close, often a strong feeling of competition and conflict can characterize the relationship. Sibling rivalry and competition often stems from a perception by one or more siblings of parents being unfair or perceiving the parent as having a favorite child. If children perceive that they are the favorite, they might be unaware that a competition exists. It is those who perceive that they are losing the game who become discouraged. The child perceived to be a less-favored sibling might develop lower self-esteem, and this may impact personality development.

Jay Colker and Sarah J. Moses

See also Gender Roles; Parental Stress: Effects on Children; Stepfamilies

Further Readings

Dreikurs, R., & Soltz, V. (1964). *Children: The challenge.* New York: Duell, Sloan & Pearce.

Dunn, J. (2007). Siblings and socialization. In J. E. Grusec & P. D. Hastings (Eds.), *Handbook of socialization* (pp. 309–327). New York: Guilford Press.

Hayden, D. H., & Croake, J. W. (1984). A comparison of brothers and non-brothers. *Individual Psychology: Journal of Adlerian Theory, Research & Practice, 40*(3), 290–294.

Kiracofe, N. M. (1992). Child-perceived parental favoritism and self-reported personal characteristics. *Individual Psychology: Journal of Adlerian Theory, Research & Practice, 48*(3), 349–356.

Kiracofe, N. M., & Kiracofe, H. N. (1990). Child-perceived parental favoritism and birth order. *Individual Psychology: Journal of Adlerian Theory, Research & Practice, 46,* 74–81.

Kramer, L., & Perozynski, L. (1999). Parental beliefs about managing sibling conflict. *Developmental Psychology, 35,* 489–499.

Kramer, L., & Radey, C. (1997). Improving sibling relationships among young children: A social skills training model. *Family Relations, 46,* 237–246.

McCay, G. (2012). Position in family constellation influences lifestyle. In J. Carlson & M. Maniacci (Eds.), *Alfred Adler revisited* (pp. 71–88). New York: Routledge, Taylor & Francis.

Paulhs, D. L. (2008). Birth order. In M. M. Haith & J. B. Benson (Eds.), *Encyclopedia of infant and early childhood development.* Oxford, UK: Elsevier.

Pulakos, J. (1987). The effects of birth order on perceived family roles. *Individual Psychology: Journal of Adlerian Theory, Research & Practice, 43*(3), 319–328.

Shebloski, B., Conger, K. J., & Widaman, K. F. (2005). Reciprocal links among differential parenting, perceived partiality, and self-worth: A three-wave longitudinal study. *Journal of Family Psychology, 19,* 633–642.

Shulman, B. H., & Mosak, H. H. (1977). Birth order and ordinal position: Two Adlerian views. *Journal of Individual Psychology, 33*(1), 114–121.

SINGLE-PARENT FAMILIES

Single-parent families is a general term used to describe a situation where one parent (rather than two) holds the primary parenting responsibility for a child or children without the help of the other partner or spouse. However, there are different aspects of single-parent families. Some single-parent families rely solely on the custodial parent, while shared custody and support exist with others. It is important to remember that every family's situation is unique and that not all families will be alike. For example, many single parents pressure themselves to conduct their families and function as nuclear families; however, in many cases that is not possible and might be unrealistic considering the stressors and obstacles single parents are tasked with overcoming. This entry briefly introduces single-parent research as it relates to reasons for single-parent families; absent mothers/fathers; extended family, stressors, and impact on children; and clinical implications.

Reasons for Single-Parent Families

Absent fathers, absent mothers, divorce rates, incarceration, and unemployment all impact single-parent families. Absent fathers have become more prevalent in society, and there are several well-researched theories and reasons related to absent fathers. While absent mothers are the exception, there are many cases where the father is the parent in the single-parent family. Several researches have attempted to explain the reasons for the phenomenon of absent fathers.

Naturally, as divorce rates increase the prevalence of single-parent homes increase. Historically, fathers have left the home, leaving the mother to be the sole provider for the children. However, divorce is not the sole factor related to the increase of single-parent homes. In the United States, imprisonment rates contribute to single-parent families. For example, a survey of state prisons conducted by the U.S. Department of Justice infers that Black non-Hispanic males had an incarceration rate of 4,749 inmates per 100,000 U.S. residents, White non-Hispanic males comprised 708 inmates per 100,000 U.S. residents, and Hispanic males made up 1,822 inmates per 100,000 U.S. residents. Thus, in order for these men to remain in their children's lives, they must participate from a distance, which results in numerous absent-father homes in today's society. While incarcerated fathers may participate in their children's lives from a distance, they are unable to provide financial resources and assistance to the custodial parent due to their incarceration. Unemployment also impacts absent-father homes and single-parent families. Imprisonment and unemployment also help to create a formula for poverty in absent-father homes; thus, some single parents must rely on government assistance for necessities. Death and chronic illness are other factors that sometimes result in single-parent homes. Finally, there are specific situations (e.g., military service, overseas employment, or the chronic illness of a parent or another child) that force one parent to spend an extended period of time away from home and thereby result in a single-parent situation.

There is little research on absent mothers, but they exist, and there are some single-parent families headed by fathers. Custodial fathers often also struggle with poverty and lack of social support. Unlike their female counterparts, they may experience difficulties securing support from government agencies because of the misconception that men should be able to care for their families.

Extended Families

The extended family has been traditionally defined as relatives and family beyond that of the nuclear family. However, the definition of extended family has evolved to include those without a genetic kinship. Extended family members are described as persons other than a parent or sibling who is either related or nonrelated. The extended family and support system consist of a larger family that plays a role in the well-being and care of a single-parent family. Thus, an extended family and support may consist of neighbors, friends, distant relatives, members of one's religious congregation, and people who have gained the family's trust. The extended family represents the main support system that assists single parents in the raising of their children. Single parents often rely on the support from extended family to assist with the daily functioning of their families. Extended family members may play the role of caretaker when the primary parent is working. They also serve as mentors or role models and can be emotionally supportive of the parent when needed. Maintaining relationships with extended family remains an important aspect of single parenting because the extended family provides support for the children in the home. Furthermore, extended family members create an added layer of emotional support that assists with the psychological and emotional well-being of the custodial parent.

Stressors

Communication and conflict management are key elements in relationships and parenting. However, single-parent families have the common stressors of any relationship along with several others. Visitation, custody, conflict between parents, effect on children, children feeling torn between two parents, and dating are some of the stressors that single-parent families face on a daily basis.

Visitation and custody issues are stressors for both parents and children. Some parents enter into conflict surrounding visitation, travel arrangements, and logistics of the actual visits. While visits can be exciting for the children, they also create stress. Many children feel that they have to choose between parents or not talk about their visits due to fear of upsetting or hurting the other parent's feelings. Custody issues often create stress because parents are mediating and negotiating the specifics of the custody agreement(s), and frequently, it becomes a fight as to who is the better or the best parent for the child. Needless to say, parents often wonder about the impact that the familial situation has on their children. This fact in turn, creates another stressor, specifically, with the children's emotional well-being, and these issues often become visible at school and through their educational experiences and interactions with peers.

Additionally, many single parents choose to continue with their social life and start dating. Managing the logistics of new partners and dating is often at the forefront of a single parent's mind. They struggle with discretion with intimate partners, finding time to date, and some eventually struggle with how and when to integrate their new partner into their families.

Impact on Children

Children are greatly impacted by the actions and decisions of their parents whether or not the parents are present. In single-parent families, this is no different. Children in single-parent families are often labeled as at-risk and are linked to crime and delinquency, premature sexuality, poor educational achievement, and poverty, and they might have issues with moral development. Children in single-parent families may struggle with expressing their emotions toward both parents without continually questioning themselves whether they are favoring one parent over the other.

Finding time to share with their parent is also a concern that children in single-parent families could face. The fear of losing their parent(s) to someone else or another family is a fear that children face on a daily basis. More specifically, some children are afraid of their parents abandoning them for their partners and partners' families. Discretion and careful introductions to partners are recommended with regard to dating partners of either parent. Children in these families may take advantage of the distance and separation (perceived or real) between parents by playing one parent against the other.

Although children who live in single-parent families have struggles, they can be successful and often have innate qualities of resilience that allow them to overcome adversity and adapt to life circumstances. Support-based intervention programs that emphasize the importance of early parent–child relationships are key to fostering the process of resilience in relation to children who some consider to be at-risk.

Clinical Implications

Clinicians working with single-parent families should work with the entire system and consider the fact that members of the system may also need individual counseling. When working with the system, it is important to remember that children often feel torn between parents. Using techniques and interventions to assist the child with communication and expression (i.e., play therapy) may be beneficial when working with young children. Clinicians working with families may also want to emphasize the importance of effective communication skills and best practices of coparenting.

Angie D. Wilson

See also Divorce and Separation; Divorce Therapy; Family Resilience; Healthy Marriage and Responsible Fatherhood; Legal Issues in Parenting; Marriage, First and Second; Nonresidential Fathers; Parenting; Parent–Child Communication; Poverty/Family Finances; Stepfamilies

Further Readings

Baskerville, S. (2004). Is there really a fatherhood crisis? *Independent Review, 8*, 485–508.

Brown, B. V. (2000). The single father family: Demographic, economic, and public transfer use characteristics. *Marriage & Family Review, 29*(2–3), 203–220. doi:10.1300/J002v29n02_12

Cherlin, A. J. (2006). On single mothers "doing" family. *Journal of Marriage and Family, 68*(4), 800–803. doi:10.1111/j.1741-3737.2006.00294.x

Hill, S. (2009). Why won't African Americans get (and stay) married? Why should they? In H. E. Peters & C. M. Kamp Dush (Eds.), *Marriage and family: Complexities and perspectives* (pp. 345–364). New York: Columbia University Press.

Hilton, J. M., & Desrochers, S. (2000). The influence of economic strain, coping with roles, and parental control on the parenting of custodial single mothers and custodial single fathers. *Journal of Divorce & Remarriage, 33*(3), 55–76.

Wilson, A. D. (2014). The lived experiences of resilient single mothers who raised successful Black males. *Adultspan Journal, 13*(2), 90–108. doi:10.1002/j.2161-0029.2014.00029.x

Wilson, A. D., & Henriksen, R. C., Jr. (2012). The lived experience of Black collegiate males with absent fathers: Another generation. *Journal of Professional Counseling: Practice, Theory, & Research, 39*(2), 29–39.

Social Constructionism

Social constructionism, or the social construction of reality, is a theory based on the sociological perspectives of Peter L. Berger and Thomas Luckmann about how reality and meaning are shaped relationally in society. That is, this theory challenges the notion of absolute truth or objective reality and posits that social knowledge and meaning is constructed through language and person-to-person interaction within the larger social context. Social constructionism has served as a foundational framework for the development of postmodern family therapy modalities, including narrative family therapy. This entry examines the key assumptions of social constructionism and discusses the influence that this theory has had on the field of family therapy.

Key Assumptions

Social constructionism is based on several key assumptions about knowledge, meaning, language, and reality.

Knowledge Is Relationally Constructed

Social constructionism assumes that knowledge is created rather than discovered. It attends to the ways in which people use language to negotiate ideas and how all socially held meanings emerge out of dialogues and interactions. Kenneth Gergen, one of the foremost social constructionist theorists, made the observation that words are inherently meaningless, which suggests that they gain their meaning only out of the person-to-person relationships in which they are used. Hence, all meaning is relational. For example, the word *tree* is essentially devoid of meaning until there is agreement between people about what the word *tree* represents in a given context and how the word will be used. The word *tree* in and of itself does not contain objective truth. Rather, it is a construct that facilitates understanding between groups that have a shared agreement about its referent idea. The word *tree* means something different for biologists, spiritualists, loggers, and a family on a hiking trip, and not one meaning of tree is more true or accurate than another. Instead, it is the group consensus of the meaning that prevents misunderstandings from arising within the group. Thus, people construct words to serve as conduits for bridging understanding in relational systems, and both words and meaning hold relevance only within the context of a system.

Language Serves a Dynamic Function

Continuing with the example of the word *tree,* what people apprehend to be a tree in the colloquial sense can just as likely have been called by any other name. Ludwig Wittgenstein, an Austrian-British philosopher, stated that words do not carry inherent meaning and do not accurately depict the entirety of any phenomena. He introduced the concept of "language games," which referred to the idea that there are certain rules that people need to follow in order for words to gain meaning. To facilitate this process of meaning construction, people create and maintain coordinated sets of social conventions. For instance, there is a socially accepted way that people verbally and physically greet one another based upon who is involved in the greeting and who they are in relation to one another. Even the commonly used word *hey* can make or break a relationship if not used correctly within context. If used between friends, this word would evoke friendliness, whereas it would represent disrespect or aloofness if one used the same word to greet a person in a position of authority.

People also create societal rules around the use of objects to help convey meanings in cultural rituals and traditions. For example, *diploma* is a word that has come to mean a certificate that symbolizes one's completion of an academic degree. Yet the word itself is an arbitrary construction, as is the certificate that was chosen to represent it. However, the word *diploma* has meaning only because of the function it serves: to represent an accomplishment of one's learnedness in the institution of academia. It is important to note that the piece of paper itself does not make the diploma. What makes a diploma a *diploma* is the meaning that is shared by a system of people who use it in a coordinated way to express the meaning that it represents (i.e., academic achievement). A diploma could have been represented by a coin, a necklace, a scepter, and so on and so forth. Therefore, in order for a diploma to be a diploma, there has to be a system of people that recognize it, that have an agreed-upon name for it, that have an agreed-upon referent for it, and that use it in a coordinated way to mean an agreed-upon thing.

Language Is Power

Social constructionist theory was also influenced by Jacques Derrida, a French literary theorist, and Michel Foucault, a French philosopher. Derrida stated that language is a system of binaries or differences, meaning that things are in part understood by what they are not. Such understanding creates categories of difference (i.e., man versus woman). He also highlighted that societies tend to value or privilege one side of a binary above the other. Foucault was interested in how language constitutes reality and noticed that the Western world created two overarching categories, normal and abnormal, to shape the beliefs, values, and behaviors of society. He viewed this process as a manifestation of societal power and believed that people have power proportionate to the extent that they are able to participate in shaping societal discourses about normality and abnormality.

Dominant discourses are social messages that are passed down to individuals and become part of the fabric of day-to-day life when they are taken to be presumed truths. Fascinated by how power is created and enacted, Foucault highlighted how societal discourses construct ideas that people internalize about what they should, must, ought, and should not, must not, and ought not do. He raised consciousness about the ethics of power and knowledge, and in particular how societies construct rules and labels to separate, objectify, dehumanize, sequester, and oppress people.

Constructing and Maintaining Social Constructions

Social constructs are concepts that are constructed and maintained by members of society through societal discourses, and in return, these reciprocally shape the dominant discourses in a given society. For example, similar to the concept about trees given earlier, immaterial phenomena such as gender are also given meaning through the ways that people in society come to discuss and define it. The dominant discourse on gender suggests that it is an aspect of one's identity that is based on a binary system that has been created to consist of two categories, masculinity and femininity, or man and woman. Over time, however, opposing ideas arose, and individuals who shared similar thinking came together in groups to challenge the taken-for-granted truth about the binary system of gender. Although the discourse on gender has broadened to include greater complexity and flexibility, normative ideas continue to be propagated within society with prescribed rules for how gender should be viewed, expressed, and performed.

Berger and Luckmann described four processes a system uses to construct and maintain its ideas about reality. Typification is the process of organizing one's perceptions into categories or types. This creates the notion of different groups. For example, there are socially constructed ideas about what a man is, and because of this, people prescribe ideas, behaviors, and expectations for how someone who fits in this category should look, walk, talk, work, marry, play, and live. Anyone who does not mirror societal expectations is not deemed a *man*. In practice, people tend to accept the typifications they learn from the people in their social systems because are taken to be accurate reflections of the world. In a sense, typifications become part of the perceived objective reality, and consequently, they become invisible. Institutionalization is the formalization of typifications, which is done by establishing institutions around them (i.e., social class, marriage, etc.). Legitimation is the process by which a society validates the typifications and institutions it creates. For example, the media portray racialized groups in certain ways to validate the notion of race as group based, biologically based, and inherently meaningful. Last, reification is the overarching process that combines typification, institutionalization, and legitimation in ways to perpetuate socially constructed ideas.

Influence on the Field of Family Therapy

The theory of social constructionism has had a significant influence on the development of family therapy theory, practice, and research. Until the 1990s, the field of family therapy was primarily informed by modern ideas based upon the notion of empiricism, measurable reality, and therapist expertise. However, the family therapy landscape experienced a significant shift with the introduction of postmodern and social constructionist theories. These epistemologies challenged the discipline's views about the nature of therapeutic problems and change. The therapists' role was also decentered as the idea of client expertise and local knowledge was introduced. These concepts were first brought onto the family therapy scene by the pioneering work of Michael White and his collaborations with David Epston.

Narrative Therapy

White and Epston developed narrative therapy out of the clinical work they did with clients who were facing issues such as eating disorders, schizophrenia, and trauma. Informed by social constructionist thinking, they saw how societal discourses often restricted and pathologized (labeled as abnormal) people who did not fit socially constructed norms. They believed that people come to hold stories about themselves based on events and experiences in their lives and what they hear others say about them. These stories or narratives can be problem dominated, and this affects how people see themselves, what they believe about themselves, and how they live their lives. Thus, they believed that problem-saturated stories had a totalizing effect that kept people from living in preferred ways.

They also saw people as separate from their problems, and as experts of their own lived experiences who had the skills, strength, resourcefulness, insight, and competencies to shift the relationships they had with the problems they faced. They assumed that there are always alternative stories that lie outside the problem-saturated narrative and when identified and brought forth, can be thickened or developed to help clients live in ways that are more congruent with their values, hopes, and desires. These assumptions lead therapists to work in intentional ways. Narrative therapists map the influence of the problem in order to understand how the problem exerts an influence on the person's life and evaluate its effects. They also help people deconstruct problem-saturated stories by considering the larger social context and how societal discourses influence one's ideas, beliefs, and actions in oppressive ways. Throughout this process, the therapist listens for clues about a person's skills and strengths that run counter to the problem-dominated story. They then ask questions that open up space for clients to identify unique outcomes that do not fit with the problem-saturated story. This collaborative process helps re-author the dominant narratives of a person's life.

By adopting the idea of humans as resourceful and inherently competent and seeing the influence of social constructionism on problem formation, this therapeutic approach represented a significant departure from therapy approaches that viewed psychopathology as intrinsic to a person, and change as a process that is reliant on therapeutic intervention. It challenged the authority that was bestowed upon therapists to define problems and delineate societal standards for normal versus abnormal affect, behavior, and individual and family functioning. In short, social constructionism paved the way for transformative ways of working therapeutically that built upon client strengths and local knowledge and that allowed people the opportunity to reject the totalizing social discourses that constrained and limited the ways that people lived their lives.

Lana Kim and Kirstee Williams

See also Epistemology in Family Therapy; Postmodern Therapies; Power Issues in Couples; Narrative Therapy

Further Readings

Berger, P. L., & Luckmann, T. (1966). *The social construction of reality: A treatise in the sociology of knowledge*. Garden City, NY: Anchor Books.

Freedman, J., & Combs, G. (1996). *Narrative therapy: The social construction of preferred realities*. New York: W. W. Norton.

Gergen, K. (2009). *An invitation to social construction* (2nd ed.). Thousand Oaks, CA: Sage.

SOCIAL SUPPORT

Because humans are relational beings, social support is an important element of individual and relationship health. Social support refers to how friends, romantic partners, and families respond to everyday opportunities to show positive caring behaviors toward each other in response to a variety of life situations that may arise. Many times, problems that occur are not relationship-specific, or in other words, arise from outside of the relationship. Social support within relationships plays an important role in helping individuals develop the resources to cope with adverse circumstances while also enhancing the relationship. In this manner, social support buffers individuals against the sometimes harmful effects of stress. When the support network is not readily available, it can be more difficult when problems arise, and individuals are left to access only their personal resources. This entry discusses the different forms of social support, optimizing factors of social support, and support during success.

Forms of Social Support

There are four different types of support: (1) informational support, (2) tangible or instrumental support, (3) emotional support, and (4) esteem support. Informational support refers to providing information that is directly relevant to understanding, coping with, or overcoming a problem. Tangible or instrumental support refers to practical attempts to make a problem better. These support attempts can be directly related to working on the problem or can be indirect and involve more peripheral things such as providing time or resources that help enhance the other person's ability to cope with the problem. Emotional support refers to those behaviors that help others feel heard, understood, and validated. Relatedly, esteem support includes those behaviors designed to help enhance the other person's confidence and self-efficacy in coping with the problem.

Optimizing Factors of Social Support

Because of the potential for social support to benefit individuals and relationships, research has looked at those factors that optimize the effects of social support. Support needs are subjective and unique to each person and context, making the type, quality, amount, and timing of support important considerations in understanding how to respond. Because support needs are so individualized, it is not surprising that perceptions of received support have been found to be more predictive of outcome than perceptions of provided support. Effective support typically depends on the interaction between the needs of the support receiver and the motivations and behaviors of the support provider. Whether the support is spontaneous or solicited, there needs to be a match between the support desired and the support received. This is known as support adequacy and has been identified as an important part of effective support. If the support is unwanted, or if the amount of support received does not match what is desired, there is a misalignment of social support that risks ineffective or possibly even negative outcomes. Overprovision of support appears to be even more detrimental to a relationship than underprovision of support.

Because support needs are so individualized, it is not surprising that perceptions of received support have been found to be more predictive of outcome than perceptions of provided support. However, some research has found that the most effective support is able to provide the benefits that accompany support without the costs of receiving it. One way that this is maximized is through the provision of invisible support; invisible support occurs when support is reported by the provider but not by the receiver. This dynamic may point toward the importance of social support not adversely affecting the self-concept of the receiver. In addition to invisible support, one other way to minimize the costs of social support and buffer against negative self-concept is for the person to also have the opportunity to provide support, thereby creating more balance in the give-and-take dynamic of relationships.

Supports During Success

Although this entry focuses on social support during times of distress, social support processes can also be evident during positive events. Members of a support network may actively and constructively respond when positive events occur for an individual, or their response can be more subdued or even negative. When an individual tells another person about a positive event and receives an active, constructive response, it is referred to as *capitalization*. Whether members of the support network can actively celebrate and encourage one another is an important part of relationships.

Overall, these findings point toward the importance of individuals developing a pattern of support and comfort in their close relationships, especially for times of distress but also for times of success. This support dynamic is created when individuals feel safe enough to make clear and accurate bids for support in order to maximize the possibility of receiving the appropriate amount, type, and timing of support. Members of the support network also need to be adequately attuned and sensitive to potential bids from others so they can respond appropriately. Therapy can be an effective venue for helping individuals develop and fine-tune these patterns in their relationships so that they can more appropriately have their needs met and meet the needs of others.

Ryan B. Seedall

See also Attunement, Clinician; Attunement in Relationships; Communication in Couples and Families; Coping; Empathy; Stress

Further Readings

Bolger, N., Zuckerman, A., & Kessler, R. C. (2000). Invisible support and adjustment to stress. *Journal of Personality and Social Psychology, 79,* 953–961.

Gable, S. L., Gonzaga, G., & Strachman, A. (2006). Will you be there for me when things go right? Social support for positive events. *Journal of Personality and Social Psychology, 9,* 904–917.

Pasch, L. A., Bradbury, T. N., & Sullivan, K. T. (1997). Social support in marriage: An analysis of intraindividual and interpersonal components. In G. R. Pierce, B. Lakey, I. G. Sarason, & B. R. Sarason (Eds.), *Sourcebook of social support and personality* (pp. 229–256). New York: Plenum Press.

Sullivan, K. T., & Davila, J. (2010). *Support processes in intimate relationships.* New York: Oxford University Press.

Sullivan, K. T., Pasch, L. A., Eldridge, K. A., & Bradbury, T. N. (1998). Social support in marriage: Translating research into practical applications for clinicians. *The Family Journal: Counseling and Therapy for Couples and Families, 6,* 263–271.

Uchino, B. N. (2006). Social support and health: A review of physiological processes potentially underlying links to disease outcomes. *Journal of Behavioral Medicine, 29,* 377–387.

Socioeconomic Status

Money, status, and power are important factors in the lives of families, not only in how family members interact in society, but also within the family itself. The family therapist should be aware that income and socioeconomic status (SES) impact the lives of individuals and families and that beliefs about SES and income may underlie presenting concerns. Because of the complicated relationship between SES and family functioning, it is particularly important that family therapists be aware of the family's SES.

SES refers to the social and economic status of individuals and families in regard to education, social position, experience, income, and occupation. It is a broad aspect of diversity that permeates the lived experiences of individuals and families in both visible and invisible ways. Society and family therapists alike often overlook dimensions of SES, resulting in misunderstanding, blame, and conflict. When family therapists acknowledge the impact of SES for all social strata, it is easier to consider family problems in context. Situating problems in context empowers families to more accurately identify the origins and dynamics of problematic patterns, rather than blame, shame, or give up in frustration.

As an invisible aspect of diversity, SES often eludes definition. SES is composed of a complex interaction of money, power, and social standing. Financial status and social status are viewed as distinct yet highly correlated, especially in American culture, where affluence is highly valued. Social status is often more challenging to define because it involves a number of aspects, including family connections, education, and career. It is the interaction of the two that produces the power and privilege to self-determine.

Due to a hyperfocus on money, Western society tends to focus mostly on poverty when discussing SES, assuming that those with financial means are exempt from psychological pain or family dysfunction. While it is true that those living in poverty experience significant hardship, stigma, and classism, it is important to note that SES impacts all families in both beneficial and challenging ways. Thus, SES is an aspect of diversity that always deserves a place in conceptualizing the challenges faced by families. This entry discusses why it is often difficult to talk about SES, the dimensions of SES that relate to the family, and particular family challenges tied to SES.

The Taboo of SES

In many ways, discussion of SES has long been taboo in U.S. culture and in family therapy. Discussion of SES can feel awkward or risky because of values around money and power. Many in the United States believe that meritocracy and social mobility prevail within its economic and social systems and that anyone can achieve financial or social standing no matter what sort of barriers they face. Meritocracy refers to a system in which people rise to higher positions based on achievement, intellect, or talent. Social mobility refers to the potential for anyone to rise to a higher level of SES.

Deep-seated beliefs in meritocracy and social mobility make it easy for families and family therapists to blame those who do not have the wherewithal to rise above their challenges. Indeed, those who are unable to achieve success according to the word's conventional definitions are very likely to experience internalized classism, believing that they are defective, lazy, and deserving of shame and disrespect. This arrangement also allows those with privilege to assume that their SES is earned rather than given. The taboo of SES is not limited to social situations; it extends to the therapy room as well.

Those in higher SES groups clearly experience privilege in numerous life dimensions; however, greater wealth does not immunize families against challenges or hardship. Likewise, less wealth does not necessarily lead to unhappiness or family discord. These stereotypes about wealth and happiness should be recognized and actively challenged, understanding that our own cultural definitions of success inevitably impact the values and goals of families.

Dimensions of SES and the Family

Socioeconomic status impacts the family in innumerable ways. In some cases, SES is simply one aspect of diversity that does not play a significant part in case conceptualization or family therapy. In other cases, SES plays a critical role in ways both seen and unseen, in family rules and rituals, and in basic physical and emotional needs. A number of the dimensions of SES that may impact family functioning are described in this section.

Personal control over daily activities and overall ability to self-determine increase as SES rises. Families may be able to engage in more leisure and enrichment activities because they can hire others to complete time-consuming household tasks. Freedom from the emotional, cognitive, and physical stressors of limited finances has positive effects on overall family functioning. Over time personal and social power increases due to a rise in SES; however, living in higher SES is no panacea. Working-class and middle-class families may have numerous strengths, including more community loyalty or social support and less pressure to reach high-status professions or wealth.

SES has a critical impact on environmental safety. Families in middle, upper-middle and higher SES levels typically have access to safe schools, neighborhoods, parks, and private clubs. However, those without financial means to escape high crime and blighted neighborhoods may be severely impacted. At the lowest end of the continuum, children may be unable to safely play outside or travel to community centers or other havens of safety.

Financial wealth in particular has a well-documented impact on physical and behavioral health. Families at the higher levels of SES have access to quality health insurance, are able to afford copays and deductibles, and may have special access to expert care providers via personal or business connections. Those in middle classes and below may be less able to participate in healthful activities such as exercise and recreation due to high costs of participation or time limitations. Families in lower classes may live in "food deserts," or areas where groceries may be purchased only locally in neighborhood bodegas. In general, increasing financial pressures take a toll on mental health and family functioning in the form of excessive anxiety, addiction, depression, or even suicidality. Impaired parental functioning or social withdrawal may then produce a host of serious problems in children, including oppositional or rebellious behaviors and other emotional problems.

The stress of housing instability or frequent moves is significant and well-documented. At all SES levels, families that move must cope with navigating new communities, social circles, and schools, while coping with the loss of prior communities and relationships. Families in lower classes are hit harder because financial distress often causes the move. However, for all families severing ties with one's community can severely impact the family safety net, which may include social or volunteer clubs, youth centers, senior centers, or religious institutions.

An obvious sign of SES is educational opportunity and its short- and long-term impacts. Families in higher SES have the means to supplement children's learning with a wide variety of extracurricular activities, thereby making their children more competitive for prestigious schools. These families may find that their lives center on their children's development, with little time for family bonding and leisure. In contrast, the struggle to make ends meet by working multiple jobs may make it impossible for some parents to engage with the school via parent–teacher meetings or extracurricular activities. Parents' own educational experiences may also cause them to feel intimidated by the educational system, resulting in less ability to be advocates for their children's needs. Pressures for either high educational achievement or mere educational survival inevitably impact the family's feelings of competence and hope for the vocational or higher education opportunities of young adulthood.

Family Challenges Tied to SES

In family therapy SES can be a relatively minor component of case conceptualization, as a factor in determining goals and methods for achieving goals, or it can be a focal point of treatment when there is an abrupt change in SES. These changes include "class jumping," partner discrepancy in SES, and SES-related differences in parenting, among others. A few of these examples are explored in this section.

Some of the impacts of SES are actual, while some are a matter of perception. For example, Western cultures may promote the idea that greater wealth leads to a better life. However, it has been suggested that levels of happiness are only slightly impacted when families move from middle-class to upper-middle-class SES. In this case, inaccurate perceptions may cause family members to believe that all family problems will be solved when the family has more income. Such inaccurate perceptions can be especially important in some cultures where partner differences in original SES play a significant role in the marital relationship.

Class jumpers are individuals or families who find that they have either risen or fallen in terms of SES. Societal values suggest that upward mobility is inextricably linked with improved well-being; however, this is not always the case. Upwardly mobile families may find that their social support system has weakened or grown complicated. For example, friends may believe that the family has "sold out" or that they abandoned the community by leaving behind long-standing relationships or failing to share their resources with those who need their help. Others may accuse the family of getting "above their raising," acting superior to the group they have left. The downwardly mobile may feel excessive shame related to perceived failure and disconnection from prior social supports. In either direction, there is also the discomfort of having arrived into an SES where there are subtle rules and power structures to navigate or, for some, financial hardship to endure or overcome.

Those who marry or partner with someone from a different social class may experience both benefits and costs. They may not feel comfortable or as though they belong in their new class. Couples may benefit from knowledge about how other social groups operate and awareness of their place in the world. On the other hand, conflict may erupt over differences in values about money, education, and career. Those from higher SES backgrounds may attribute success to internal characteristics and believe that anyone who works hard enough can achieve a goal. Therefore, failure to "succeed" in terms of material and social status may be viewed as a result of one's laziness. On the other hand, those from lower SES backgrounds may view overemphasis on career achievement as selfishly caring more about status than about family. In sum, efforts at developing shared values and goals are complicated because the very definition of success varies by SES.

Conflicting SES values may make parenting particularly difficult. For example, a lower-SES parent might prefer to see children engaged in more free or creative leisure time, preferably with family or close neighbors. In contrast, a higher-SES parent might want to see a child engaged in structured enrichment activities and might view family leisure as a waste of time. Choices about children's academics are also likely to cause friction, as one's career is quite often a vehicle of social mobility and social status. In spite of these challenges, children with exposure to different SES groups potentially have a better concept of how different groups live and thrive, therefore giving children themselves more options for determining how they wish to live their own lives.

Conflicts between the SES of families and the communities within which they live may have a number of outcomes. Subtle rules in social situations, religious organizations, and schools may cause those from lower SES to feel misunderstood or unwelcome around wealthier counterparts. For example, higher-SES parents may not send children to a particular family's home to play because their food is not organic. Birthday parties in the community may be elaborate and costly. Religious communities may call only upon the wealthy for leadership. Conversely, some in lower-SES communities will distrust those with higher education or class status, anticipating condescension or judgment.

Misunderstanding and feelings of rejection and isolation are not uncommon when SES collides. Like other aspects of diversity, assumptions and biases play a critical part in how families view particular situations and choose to live their lives. Variations in SES among family members and communities have potential desirable outcomes. Living alongside someone of a different SES can dispel negative judgments and introduce others to different ways of thinking and living. Awareness about SES can open one's eyes to the need to care for others with less financial privilege and social status, and thereby allow greater potential for shared empathy. Families and communities flourish when diversity of SES challenges them to consider and value different perspectives.

*Louisa Foss-Kelly and
Jessica A. Baycroft*

See also Cultural Issues in Families and Couples; Debt and Financial Strain; Poverty and Family Development

Further Readings

Appio, L., Chambers, D., & Mao, S. (2013). Listening to the voices of the poor and disrupting the silence about class issues in psychotherapy. *Journal of Clinical Psychology, 69*(2), 152–161.

Atwood, N. C. (2014). Experiencing inequality: Memoirs, hardship, and working class roots. *Smith College Studies in Social Work, 84*(4), 484–501.

Ballinger, L., & Wright, J. (2007). "Does class count?" Social class and counselling. *Counselling & Psychotherapy Research, 7*(3), 157–163.

Dearing, E. (2008). Psychological costs of growing up poor. *New York Academy of Sciences, 1136*, 324–332.

Foss, L. L., & Generali, M. (2012). The CARE model for working with people in poverty. In D. C. Sturm & D. M. Gibson (Eds.), *Social class and the helping professions: A clinician's guide to navigating the landscape of class in America* (pp. 185–200). New York: Routledge.

Holman, D. (2014). "What help can you get talking to somebody?" Explaining class differences in the use of talking treatments. *Sociology of Health & Illness, 36*(4), 531–548.

Hooks, B. (2000). *Where we stand: Class matters.* New York: Routledge.

Kim, S., & Cardemil, E. (2012). Effective psychotherapy with low-income clients: The importance of attending to social class. *Journal of Contemporary Psychotherapy, 42*(1), 27–35.

Liu, W. M. (2011). *Social class and classism in the helping professions: Research, theory, and practice.* Thousand Oaks, CA: Sage.

Liu, W. M., Estrada-Hernández, N. (2010). Counseling and advocacy for individuals living in poverty. In M. Ratts & J. Manivong (Eds.), *ACA advocacy competencies: A social justice framework for counselors* (pp. 43–53). Alexandria, VA: American Counseling Association.

McDowell, T., Brown, A. L., & Cullen, N. (2013). Social class in family therapy education: Experiences of low SES students. *Journal of Marital and Family Therapy, 39*(1), 72–86.

McDowell, T., Melendez-Rhodes, T., Althusius, E., Hergic, S., Sleeman, G., My Ton, N. K., & Zimpfer-Bak, A. J. (2013). Exploring social class: Voices of inter-class couples. *Journal of Marital and Family Therapy, 39*(1), 59–71.

Smith, L., Li, V., Dykema, S., Hamlet, D., & Shellman, A. (2013). "Honoring somebody that society doesn't honor": Therapists working in the context of poverty. *Journal of Clinical Psychology, 69*(2), 138–151.

Smith, L., Shellman, A., & Smith, R. (2013). Inequality, poverty, and counseling practice. In W. Ming Liu (Ed.), *The Oxford handbook of social class in counseling* (pp. 428–445). New York: Oxford University Press.

Solution-Focused Brief Therapy

Solution-focused brief therapy (SFBT) is a model of therapy that focuses on cocreating the client's preferred future through solution-building. Coconstructing goals with a client (individual, couple, or family), searching for evidence of exceptions to the current problem, and building on the client's small positive changes are important pieces of the model. SFBT is systemic (looking at the relationships between people) in nature, making it an excellent model to use in marriage and family therapy. This entry covers the basic components and application of SFBT when working with individuals, couples, and families.

History of SFBT

Steve de Shazer and Insoo Kim Berg, the originators of SFBT, studied at the Mental Research Institute (MRI) in Palo Alto, California. De Shazer and Berg were introduced to one another and eventually moved together to Milwaukee, founding the Brief Family Therapy Center (BFTC) in 1978. The SFBT model was born out of paying close attention to what the therapist did that helped clients improve.

SFBT was influenced by social constructionism (a sociological theory that shows how culture influences information and that reality is subjective), the work of psychiatrist and psychologist Milton Erickson, the philosopher Ludwig Wittgenstein, and the team of therapists at the MRI. These philosophical and theoretical underpinnings had an impact on Berg and de Shazer's assumptions about clients, change, and the process of therapy. De Shazer and Berg adopted notions that include the following: clients are competent and possess all of the resources they need to meet their goals; the problem and the solution are not always connected; small change leads to big change; clients are experts about their own lives and therapists are experts in asking useful questions; change is always occurring; if something does not work, do not continue doing it; if something works, do more of it; and "If it ain't broke, don't fix it."

Process of Therapy

The process of conducting SFBT interviews has three unique components, according to the Solution-Focused Brief Therapy Association's *Solution Focused Therapy Treatment Manual for Working With Individuals*. First, the process of change in SFBT involves what is occurring *between* the therapist and client in their dialogue, not what is happening *within* the client. While other approaches focus on internal processes within the client, SFBT focuses on the client and therapist's coconstruction of the client's goals. The second component is focusing on what is observable, what is really happening between the therapist and client, in dialogue. The process of observing therapist–client interactions was part of the inductive development of SFBT. Finally, SFBT developed from using communication research as a foundation to build a brief, solution-focused form of psychotherapy.

Solution-Building

Solution-building is a paradigm shift from the traditional problem-solving approach used in psychotherapy. Where problem-solving tries to identify the best possible solution to a client's problem, solution building involves a process of coconstructing a client's preferred future. The following are some helpful distinguishing factors between problem-solving and solution-building. In problem-solving it is important to understand the root of the problem, whereas in solution-building, the focus is on the client's preferred future despite the presence of a problem. In problem-solving, the problem is defined first and then one best possible solution is explored. In SFBT, the detailed description of the solution is of most importance. Lastly, problem-solving includes acquiring specific skills to reach the best solution, whereas in solution-building the assumption is that clients already possess everything they need to reach their preferred future.

Stages and Process of Solution-Building

Peter De Jong and Berg describe the stages of solution-building in five steps: (1) describing the problem, (2) developing well-formed goals, (3) looking for exceptions, (4) client feedback at the end of the session, and (5) evaluating the client's progress. In order to move through the stages of solution-building, it is important to adopt the process of *listen, select, and build* as described by De Jong and Berg. The therapist carefully listens for exceptions to the client's problem, as well as details about his or her preferred future. Once the details about the solution are heard, the therapist selects the client's specific description and builds toward goals, solutions, and preferred future.

Useful Questions and Techniques

One of the first stages in solution-building is defining well-formed goals. Goals in SFBT are defined by any cognitions, emotions, behaviors, and interactions that the client wants in his or her life and should (1) be realistic, (2) involve the client doing hard work, (3) have importance and be meaningful to the client, (4) be small, and (5) be concrete (specific and behavioral). Coconstructing well-formed client goals can be done at the beginning of an intake session by asking "So how can

I be helpful to you?" or "What needs to happen today, during our time together, that would move things in the right direction for you?" After the initial opening question about goals, therapists can ask questions such as "When your problem is not quite as bad as it is today, what will be different?" or "So, how will you know you no longer need to come see me for therapy?"

The Miracle Question. The most famous goal-formulating question is called the miracle question (MQ). It is asked once a clearly defined goal is formed. The therapist uses the MQ to help clients identify what they will notice when their preferred future occurs. There are slightly different variations to the MQ. The following is an example:

> Is it OK if I ask you a strange question? The strange question is [pause] Imagine that you leave here today, go home and do your regular routine for the rest of the day and evening. You eat dinner and eventually go to bed and fall asleep. While you are sleeping, something shifts, a miracle occurs and the problem that brought you here today is solved. You now are [insert the client's description of their preferred future here]. However, this miracle happens while you were sleeping so you have no way of knowing that it happened. So, when you wake up tomorrow, the day after this miracle occurs, what would be the first small thing that you would notice that would let you know, something incredible has happened?

Five main elements must be included in the miracle question: (1) the change needs to be significant to the client and unlikely to occur naturally, (2) the "miracle" must be defined using the client's words about their preferred future, (3) the miracle must have an element of immediacy (it happens tonight), (4) the client can't know that the miracle happened while sleeping, and (5) the client is asked to describe the first things noticeable upon awakening the next morning after the miracle has occurred.

Once any of the general or specific (miracle question) goal-formulating questions are asked during a session, it is important to continue the dialogue with one of the following: "Once your relationship with your partner has improved, what will you notice?" "So when you are feeling better, who will be the first to notice?" "What will your wife do when she notices that you are feeling better?" "What will you do next once you are happier?" The aim is to ask a variety of follow-up questions in order to better define the client's goal and the details of his or her preferred future.

Exception Questions. Exception questions are asked to gain more information about times in the client's life when things have been better (exceptions to the current problem). Questions such as "Tell me about a time when things were better, even just a little bit better?" or presession change questions like "What changes have you noticed since you called to make your appointment?" help the client to recall times when things were better. This type of questioning serves several purposes. First, it shows the client that things have not always been bad or difficult. It also highlights a belief of SFBT that the problem is not always occurring, or at least things are a little bit better at times. These types of questions also help the client remember what he or she was doing that made things better. Helping clients find exceptions to their problems is a key piece in solution-building.

Coping Questions. Coping questions are specific exception questions that inquire about how the client was able to cope during a difficult time. Sometimes clients will say that things have been bad for a long time and they struggle to come up with exceptions to their problem. This is an excellent time to ask questions about coping. A therapist can ask, "Wow, that sounds very hard. What did you do to cope during that difficult time?" Versions of this question are helpful when clients come to therapy with very difficult situations.

Relational Questions. Relational questions are helpful to ask once exceptions have been explored. Questions such as, "So how would that make a difference for your husband if you were more energetic?" or (asking a client's boyfriend) "What difference would that make for you if your girlfriend were happier?"

are relational questions that can be asked in couples sessions. Rephrasing the questions to "So what do you think your husband would say about how your increased energy would make a difference for him?" or "What do you think your girlfriend would say about how her happiness will make a difference for you?" can be used in individual sessions. It is interesting to note that most clients will be able to give more details about their preferred futures when they are asked to answer from someone else's perspective.

Scaling Questions. Once goal-formulating, exception, and relational questions are asked, scaling questions can be used to track progress. Questions such as "On a scale from 1 to 10, 10 being the most satisfied you can be in your relationship and 1 being farthest from that, where would you say you would rate yourself today?" or "On a scale from 0 to 10, where 10 is coping the best that you possibly can and 0 stands for not being able to cope at all, where would you rate your coping today?" are examples of scaling questions. The important parts to remember about scaling questions are: (a) that the 1 (or 0) and 10 need to be clearly defined, (b) 10 is always the client's desired behavior or goal and 1 or 0 is opposite of that, and (c) the meanings of the numbers on the scale have a unique connotation to the client (i.e., 5 isn't necessarily halfway to one's goal). Scaling can be used to measure progress toward the client's goal, the client's level of coping, the client's confidence in reaching the goal, and the client's motivation.

Taking a Break. During the development of SFBT, taking a break toward the end of the session gave the therapist a chance to gather compliments from the team of therapists to share with the client(s). Since having a team behind a one-way mirror is not always possible, the therapist can either take a short break and leave the room or remain in his or her chair, taking a few moments to compose some compliments for the client(s). This break also gives clients a chance to reflect on the session and on goals.

Compliments. After the break, compliments are given to the client. Solution-focused compliments are different from other forms of complimenting in life and therapy. They are not what the therapist or the team *likes* about the client but what the client has specifically mentioned (using the client's exact words) about liking himself or herself, or accomplishments that the client is proud of. For example, if a client says in the beginning of a session the following: "I had a pretty good week. I found out that I got an A on a test that was really hard, so that made me pretty excited." An SFBT compliment might then be "I was very impressed about the A that you received on your test. Given that the test was hard, it sounds like that was a real accomplishment!" If a team is watching the session, the therapist gathers compliments from the team during the break.

Experiments and Homework. At the end of the session, the therapist usually gives the client a homework task or asks the client to experiment with doing something different. Homework and experiments can be basic. They may be introduced to the client as the following: "Over the next week, I would like you to notice those times when things are a bit better in your relationship. During these times when things are better, notice what you and your partner are doing differently," or "Over the next few weeks I would like you to wake up every morning and pretend for the first 20 minutes of your day that your miracle has happened. What are you doing differently during the first 20 minutes, and who is noticing?" It is best if the homework comes from what the client wants to be working on. The client could have mentioned something earlier in the session such as "Some days I wake up and things are better, but it only lasts for a few moments. [pause] It only lasts until I get out of bed." In the homework task, the therapist is asking the client to make the exceptions to the problem his or her daily experience. Homework should be kept short and specific. At the follow-up session, the therapist should let the client report on the homework assignment instead of asking the client if the homework was completed. For SFBT therapists, it is OK if the client didn't complete the homework. Since the client is the expert of his or her life, the assumption is that the client found something else more useful to work on during the week.

Follow-Up Sessions. Follow-up sessions should begin by asking a version of the question "So what's been better since the last time we met?" The therapist should have clients give lots of details about their improvements. If "nothing was better" or "things were worse," the therapist can ask "So how did you keep things from getting worse (or much worse)?" or "What did you do to make it through the week?" Next, the therapist asks scaling questions. If things were better, the therapist asks the client about the positive change. If the client reports a lower number on the scale, the therapist can ask "So how did you manage to only drop 2 points on the scale and not 3?" Difference questions (e.g., "So what difference has that made that you were able to get up an hour earlier most days this week?") and "Who has noticed these changes?" questions (e.g., "So who in your life has noticed this change?") can be asked next. The next part of the session involves asking questions about how the client(s) can continue this positive change, what differences this change will make in their life, and what needs to happen next to move up on their scale. Finally, toward the end of the session the therapist will take a break, give compliments, and assign homework.

Couples and Families

For couples and families, the structure is very similar. Some therapists become overwhelmed when partners or family members want different things. The key is treating the couple or family as a unit and looking for themes in couple or family members' goals. For example, when asking "How can I be helpful?" one partner might answer "She needs to respect me" and the other might say "He needs to listen to me!" The therapist can follow with "So, when your wife is respecting you and your husband is listening, what difference will that make in your relationship?", "So how would that be helpful if you were respecting and listening to one another?"

or "So what would it look like if your wife was respecting you? And what would it look like for you if your husband was listening to you?" Coconstructing a joint couple or family goal is important.

Groups

Solution-focused group therapy (SFGT) has its own session format and is discussed in Teri Pichot and Yvonne Dolan's 2003 book *Solution-Focused Brief Therapy: Its Effective Use in Agency Settings.* Although it was originally adapted for substance abuse groups, the format can be used for any type of therapy group.

Evidence-Based Practice

SFBT has been shown to be both efficacious and effective with a variety of clinical issues. Alasdair Macdonald provides an online list of SFBT research studies. According to Macdonald, a review of data from 8,000 clients receiving SFBT found that 60% of these cases showed positive outcomes after 3 to 6.5 sessions. In addition, solution-focused group therapy is among the interventions listed as an evidence-based program and practice for the group treatment of substance use disorders in the National Registry of Evidence-Based Programs and Practices of the Substance Abuse and Mental Health Services Administration, an agency of the U.S. Department of Health and Human Services.

Sara Smock Jordan

See also Brief Family Therapy; Couples and Marriage Counseling; Evidence-Based Practice With Couples and Families; Family Strengths; Goals, Treatment

Further Readings

Bavelas, J., De Jong, P., Franklin, C., Froerer, A., Gingerich, W., Kim, J., Korman, H., Langer, S., Lee, M. Y., McCollum, E. E., Smock Jordan, S., & Trepper, T. S. (2013). *Solution focused therapy treatment manual for working with individuals: Revised 2013.* Santa Fe, NM: Solution-Focused Brief Therapy Association.

de Shazer, S. (1988). *Clues: Investigating solutions in brief therapy.* New York: W. W. Norton.

de Shazer, S. (1991). *Putting difference to work.* New York: W. W. Norton.

de Shazer, S. (1994). *Words were originally magic.* New York: Norton.

de Shazer, S., Dolan, Y., Korman, H., Trepper, T., McCullom, E., & Berg, I. K. (2007). *More than miracles: The state of the art of solution-focused brief therapy.* New York: Haworth.

DeJong, P., & Berg, I. K. (2013). *Interviewing for solutions* (4th ed.). Belmont, CA: Brooks/Cole.

Lipchik, E. (2011). *Beyond technique in solution-focused brief therapy: Working with emotions and the therapeutic relationship.* New York: Guilford Press.

MacDonald, A. (2015). *Solution-focused brief therapy evaluation list.* Retrieved from http://www.solutionsdoc.co.uk/sft.html

Pichot, T., & Dolan, Y. (2003). *Solution-focused brief therapy: Its effective use in agency settings.* Binghamton, NY: Haworth.

Ratner, H., George, E., Iveson, C. (2012). *Solution focused brief therapy: 100 key points and techniques.* New York: Routledge.

Somatic Symptom Disorder and Related Disorders in Adolescents

Somatic symptom disorder (SSD) and related disorders focus on psychiatric factors and physical symptoms that do not require a medical diagnosis and yet come to preoccupy an individual to the extent that they impact the individual's quality of life and functioning. Adolescents, like other people who experience SSD, may misinterpret somatic symptoms as signs of serious illness, and their intense reactions may impair day-to-day functioning. This entry addresses symptoms, treatment options, and the impact somatic symptom disorder in adolescents has on schoolwork, other activities, and relationships.

Somatic Symptom Disorder

With somatic symptom disorder, individuals are excessively preoccupied with one or more real physical symptoms that persist for a minimum of 6 months and are overwhelmed with distressing thoughts, feelings, and behaviors that are maladaptive and disproportionate to the severity of physical symptoms. Individuals are constantly searching the Internet to confirm fears that they have a severe medical illness. Somatic symptoms may co-occur with an actual serious medical illness, but the patient misinterprets the severity of common symptoms such as stomachaches, headaches, or nausea as evidence of a serious illness. In this case, the anxiety about having a serious medical illness is more intense than would be expected from the actual physical symptoms reported.

Symptoms typically begin in the 30s but can appear in adolescence, with prevalence higher in girls than in boys. Adolescents with a history of sexual abuse are more likely to report symptoms of somatic symptom disorder. Adolescents with symptoms are generally seen initially in medical settings (e.g., a pediatrician's office, primary care, emergency room) rather than psychiatric settings, and parents often take them to be evaluated by a number of physicians and specialists to find a cure for their child's pain. Treatment begins with a comprehensive examination to rule out medical problems or disorders. A consistent relationship with one physician is essential to building trust and protecting the adolescent from unnecessary or duplicate laboratory tests that may be ordered from multiple health providers. Maladaptive reactions could result when an adolescent's needs are not met or symptoms are not taken seriously. Prompt medical assessment and treatment can prevent exacerbation of symptoms and possible suicide ideation or attempt.

Diagnosis for somatic symptom disorder is made through assessment, interviews with the adolescent, parents, and other members in the household (e.g., grandparents, siblings, housekeeper, or nanny), and the therapist's clinical judgment. The excessiveness of the teenager's thoughts, feelings, and behaviors leads the physician to consider an emotional link to the somatic concerns. The diagnosis is specified with predominant pain or with persistent pain if symptoms continue for more than 6 months, causing significant impairment. One behavior is rated mild; two or more behaviors are rated moderate; and two or more behaviors with one or more serious symptoms are coded severe.

Concurrent with medical care, cognitive-behavioral therapy (CBT) is recommended for symptom reduction and relief, clarification of thoughts and elimination of faulty thinking, development of coping skills, and use of supportive relationships. CBT and solution-focused therapy approaches also help to identify what increases pain and when there are exceptions to the pain so that the adolescent can learn to cope. Adolescents who are significantly affected by their magnification of illness and preoccupation with symptoms benefit from understanding that their intense worries and thoughts are cognitive distortions and not evidence of illness.

Adolescents and School Issues

Adolescents diagnosed with somatic symptom disorder may not be aware that their extreme reactions impact school performance. With excessive consecutive absences, teenagers may be assigned to home instruction, which is a consequence of school attendance policies that may inadvertently provide students with an irrational confirmation that they have a serious illness. Home instruction or taking the teenager to medical or mental health appointments and laboratory tests can compromise parents' job attendance. Parents may arrange for a relative or a caregiver at considerable expense or may feel forced to quit their job to remain at home. Parents' and grandparents' time and attention are also often directed toward the ill teen at the expense of other children, resulting in tension and resentment in the family.

Teenagers may be reluctant to participate in physical education classes and athletic activities, fearing activity will increase their pain or exacerbate symptoms; thus engagement in classes and on teams is severely curtailed. It may be difficult for the adolescents' parents to verify a disability or impairment required for accommodations such as adaptive physical education. Increased family physical activities (e.g., bowling, table tennis, walking, hiking, or YMCA family day) may ameliorate worry, increase social contact, provide exercise, and promote a gradual return to normal activities.

Persistent worry about illness strains the teenager's relationships with friends, and chronic school absenteeism severely reduces opportunities to spend consistent time together with friends in classes, lunch, homeroom, and on the school bus. The student is often unable to attend parties and social events and may miss or delay important milestones in high school with classmates, including moving-up day, prom, college examinations, behind-the-wheel driver's education, and commencement. Family events, religious services, holidays, outings, and vacations are also affected. Family meetings and counseling sessions can help plan events and activities so that every member's concerns are heard and addressed.

Related Disorders

Factitious Disorder

The major difference between somatic symptom disorder and factitious disorder is the intent when individuals intentionally feign, create, falsify, or induce somatic symptoms and present themselves or another as ill or injured. There is no financial reward or other external incentive for this behavior that cannot be better identified by another disorder.

When individuals create or exacerbate their symptoms, factitious disorder imposed on self (formerly Munchausen syndrome) is specified. When victims show symptoms induced by another, they are coded with physical abuse, and the perpetrator is diagnosed with factitious disorder imposed on another (FDIA, formerly known as factitious disorder by proxy or Munchausen syndrome by proxy). Both types are specified as single or recurrent episodes (two or more episodes).

Multiple episodes are typically more intermittent than persistent; however, persistent, recurrent episodes can be a lifelong disorder.

Symptoms of factitious disorder appear early in life and are more prevalent in males, often following a hospitalization for a medical or psychiatric condition. Perpetrators may have a need to be ill, and that need is met by inducing sickness in victims. Although 4 years is the average age at diagnosis, adolescents are also victimized, showing symptoms frequently in childhood. Victim prevalence is equally male and female, and the perpetrator, primarily female and often the mother of the victim, generally selects one victim at a time. Fathers are often uninvolved, although some fathers collaborate with the perpetrator, who could be a grandmother, stepmother, guardian, or babysitter. Siblings can be victimized or at risk for becoming victims.

Induced or feigned symptoms are typically fever, asthma, vomiting, diarrhea, rash, loss of consciousness, seizure, respiratory arrest, electrolyte changes, bleeding, or failure to thrive. Victims may appear healthier than the symptoms present, and health professionals typically identify victims by an unusual clinical course, inconsistent lab results, or repeated visits to the emergency room. The perpetrator often has considerable medical knowledge and experience in a health setting, and may demonstrate pathological lying, showing no concern for the adolescent when observed without their knowledge (e.g., through a one-way mirror). If confronted, perpetrators may become angry, hostile, depressed, and even suicidal, and may try to remove the victim from the hospital and go to distant hospital where the victim and perpetrator are not known.

Adolescents presenting with factitious disorder visit the nurse's office frequently and are often absent from school, falling behind in coursework and learning. Students involved in sports, clubs, or band may struggle to meet attendance requirements out and the perpetrator may seek special treatment for the victim. The perpetrator may induce symptoms that appear at the beginning of the school day or during lunch that result in stomachaches and nausea with frequent bathroom visits. The adolescent is generally unaware of the perpetrator's intentions and shows normal behavior in between induced events. Teachers often notice different behavior patterns or symptoms at the same time each day. Teenagers may exhibit problems with concentration, attention, and behavior; emotional problems; or strict compliance with rules. The parent as perpetrator typically appears uninvolved in the victim's school; however, some perpetrators request accommodations or exemptions for tests, class work, and attendance because of the adolescent's induced illness. School personnel may have difficulty gaining the parent's permission to provide the student with counseling, or find the parent elated that the school is taking the student's illness seriously. With the perpetrator most likely living with the victim, interventions may include legal action, therapy, foster care, or medical treatment for injuries or damage from chemical or pharmacological ingested substances. A multidisciplinary treatment team with a medical professional, counselor, family therapist, child advocate, and other health providers is recommended.

Illness Anxiety Disorder

Illness anxiety disorder differs from somatic symptom disorder by a lack of physical symptoms and illness, with the central focus the patient's anxiety and worry about having a serious illness or disease. Individuals diagnosed with illness anxiety disorder (formerly known as hypochondriasis) are excessively fearful, anxious, and preoccupied about being sick despite having minimal or no medical symptoms. The disorder is specified care-seeking or care-avoidant type. Care-seeking adolescents become easily alarmed reading or hearing about serious illnesses and may go posthaste to the emergency room or physician's office, while care-avoidant types cope with intense anxiety by missing medical checkups and laboratory tests and avoiding hospitals.

Emotional symptoms generally begin in the 20s, but may surface earlier in adolescents. Duration is

6 months or more, with prevalence equal in males and females. Assessment and diagnosis begin with a comprehensive evaluation to deny major medical conditions or illnesses that would explain the excessive worry. While onset is typically after adolescence, teenagers who have been diagnosed with illness anxiety disorder may have been ill as children. Adolescents check themselves repeatedly in front of a mirror for signs of the illness and spend excessive time researching medical conditions on the Internet. They are frequently absent from school for medical appointments and lab tests, and their cumulative absences and diagnosis can lead to home instruction and the loss of social engagement with friends at school.

The preoccupation with symptoms and excessive worry about illness strains family relationships and creates tension among siblings. With chronic, extreme worries about being ill, adolescents can become dependent on painkillers and medication, and later become homebound, postponing college and work experiences. One consistent health provider is recommended to build trust and to avoid unnecessary medical tests and procedures. Counseling using CBT is helpful for addressing faulty thinking, identifying when distress increases, and developing coping skills.

Conversion Disorder

Symptoms of conversion disorder (formerly neurological symptom disorder) differ significantly from the common medical symptoms of somatic syndrome disorder such as headaches, stomachaches, joint pain, or nausea. Unusual changes in sensory and voluntary motor functioning are not consistent with medical or neurological conditions, have no known physical cause, and cannot be explained by cultural ritual or context. Patients with a lack of education and medical knowledge have a higher incidence of reporting unusual symptoms, but they do not generally appear concerned or worried about the symptoms. This indifference toward atypical symptoms is known as *la belle indifference,* and prevalence is higher in women and in younger patients.

Duration of less than 6 months is specified as an acute episode, and duration of longer than 6 months is specified as persistent. Conversion disorder can also be specified with a psychological stressor using the type of symptom: weakness or paralysis; abnormal movement (e.g., unusual gait, limb shaking or positioning); swallowing or speech symptoms (e.g., slurred speech); attacks or seizures; anesthesia or sensory loss (e.g., stocking anesthesia); special sensory symptoms (e.g., hallucinations or sensory disturbances); or mixed symptoms. Other symptoms can include syncope, coma, impaired consciousness, tunnel vision, tremor, or dissociation. Symptoms can lead to significant impairment and disability in school, as well as in personal, social, or work environments.

Psychological Factors Affecting Other Medical Conditions

In this category psychological factors exacerbate or negatively impact a medical condition, interfere with its treatment, or increase health risks for pain or death. Factors include lack of adherence to medical treatment, distress, coping, personality traits, or risky health behaviors, and must be differentiated from culturally accepted behaviors or practices. Counselors working with adolescent immigrants, refugees, and victims of war or terrorism should consult with medical and mental health professionals familiar with the country of origin so cultural factors are not confused with signs of the disorder. The severity of thoughts, feelings, or behaviors may not be excessive and is specified as mild, moderate, severe (requiring hospitalization), or extreme (life threatening). The diagnosis is more frequent than somatic symptom disorder and is considered when all criteria for a mental disorder are not met or explained by another disorder, such as posttraumatic stress disorder or panic disorder.

Other Specified Somatic Symptom and Related Disorder

In this category, symptoms of somatic symptom and related disorders are present but do not meet full criteria for a diagnosis. Other specified somatic symptom and related disorders include brief somatic symptom disorder with a duration of less than 6 months, brief illness anxiety disorder with a duration of less than 6 months, illness anxiety disorder without excessive health-related behaviors, and pseudocyesis, which is associated with the false belief of being pregnant and includes physical symptoms of being pregnant but without the presence of a fetus. Adolescent girls with signs of pseudocyesis may have a history of sexual abuse.

Unspecified Somatic Symptom and Related Disorder

This category is considered where there is significant functional impairment or distress but insufficient information to make a more specific diagnosis. This category is used only in highly unusual presentations with symptoms of somatic symptom and related disorders that do not meet all the required criteria.

*Jane M. Webber and
J. Barry Mascari*

See also Adolescent Behavior Problems; Adolescent Mental Health; Children With Chronic Illness; Health Issues; Parent–Adolescent Relations

Further Readings

Arnold, I. A., deWaal, M. W. M., Eekhof, J. A. H., & van Hemert, A. M. M. (2006). Somatoform disorders in primary care: Course and the need for cognitive-behavioral therapy. *Psychosomatics, 47*(6), 498–503.

Feinstein, R. E., & deGruy, F. V. (2011). Difficult patients: Personality disorders and somatoform complaints. In R. E. Rakel (Ed.), *Textbook of family medicine* (8th ed., pp. 1038–1059). Philadelphia: Elsevier Saunders.

Greenberg, D. B., Braun, I. M., & Cassem, N. H. (2008). Functional somatic symptoms and somatoform disorders. In T. A. Stern, J. F. Rosenbaum, M. Fava, M. J. Biederman, & S. L. Rauch (Eds.), *Massachusetts General Hospital comprehensive clinical psychiatry* (pp. 255–264). Philadelphia: Mosby Elsevier.

Hendricks-Matthews, M. K., & Hoy, D. M. (1993). Pseudocyesis in an adolescent incest survivor. *Journal of Family Practice, 36*(1), 97–104.

Huffman, J. C., & Stern, T. A. (2003). The diagnosis and treatment of Munchausen's syndrome. *General Hospital Psychiatry, 25,* 358–363.

Kellner, R. (1992). *Psychosomatic syndromes: Somatic symptoms.* Washington, DC: American Psychiatric Publishers.

Stirling, J. (2007). Beyond Munchausen syndrome by proxy: Identification and treatment of child abuse in a medical setting. *Pediatrics, 119,* 1026–1030. Retrieved from http://pediatrics.aappublications.org/content/119/5/1026.full

Witthoft, M. L., & Hiller, W. (2010). Psychological approaches to origins and treatments of somatoform disorders. *Annual Review of Clinical Psychology, 6,* 257–283. doi:10.1146/annurev.clinpsy.121208.131505

SPIRITUALITY

Differences between religiosity and spirituality have been well articulated, although there continues to be overlap in how the terms are sometimes used. Religion tends to be defined as set of organizing beliefs and practices legitimized by a group's established views. Spirituality tends to be defined more subjectively, often including the search for something sacred, a belief in something bigger than oneself, and experiences of self-transcendence. Spirituality is often but not always associated with an emotional and relational connection with the divine. Despite such definitional distinctions, there appears to be no universal agreement on the difference between religion and spirituality.

Spirituality appears to impact human experience not only emotionally and relationally but also biologically. Studies indicate that experiences of spiritual self-transcendence have been linked to increased binding potentials for the hormone serotonin in the hippocampal and neocortex areas of the brain. Such findings suggest a biological basis for spiritual experience and expand the definition of spirituality to include multiple aspects of the person. This entry first discusses the relationship between spirituality and mental health, research into spirituality, and spirituality as a factor in marital experience. It then discusses the interaction of gender and spirituality in couples' relationships and the need for clinicians to understand the role of spirituality in their clients' lives.

Spirituality and Mental Health

There appears to be a growing recognition of the importance of spirituality on health across multiple disciplines. For example, this is seen in the call to revise the World Health Organization's definition of health to include spirituality not only as an influence on health, but also as a dimension of health. Spirituality that focuses specifically on relational connection with the divine has been linked in a growing number of studies to health and wellbeing. Grounded within the larger body of literature on religion and spirituality, relational spirituality refers to the particular experience of an intimate relationship with God. Relational spirituality involves the ability to experience a sense of connection in this world that emerges from the divine–human relationship. Such terms as *connectedness, interconnectedness* and *relationship* underscore the concept of rationality as inherent in certain types of spirituality. Among relational spirtualties, different religious beliefs, traditions, and rituals uniquely contextualize how people connect with the divine. For example, Christian orthodoxy, New Age spirituality, Kabbalah or Jewish mysticism, and Islam's Sufi mystics practice forms of relational spirituality focusing on union or intimacy with the divine. Increasingly research is recognizing relational spirituality as a potential component of mental health, including marital health and general well-being.

Spirituality as a Research Topic

The study of spirituality tends to focus on how people relate to and experience the divine. Interestingly, how people relate to the divine seems linked to how couples relate to each other, with evidence that spirituality plays a significant role in the marital experience. Research on spirituality tends to reflect people's experiences and perceptions of the divine much more robustly than religiosity studies that determine frequency of prayer and worship or level of religious commitment. Yet spirituality studies on the quality of the divine–human relationship have traditionally been scarce to nonexistent. This conceptual difference between spirituality and religiosity is particularly of interest to those studying couple experience.

For example, when couples share similar degrees of religiosity, spirituality does not always seem to be experienced similarly between partners. Such findings suggest that spirituality and religiosity are related to each other but remain independent. Yet other findings suggest that some dimensions of spirituality are more closely related to religiousness than others. For example, having a strong sense of meaning and purpose in life seems to be a spiritual dimension more closely related to religiosity, while self-sacrifice, idealism, and awareness of pain appear less closely related to religiosity. Such differences make studying the impact of spirituality on couples potentially more challenging, as the concept of spirituality needs to be defined in a manner capturing both its more personal and individual aspects and its relational impact.

Research on spirituality has been increasing, as reflected by new research measures created to test spirituality. For example, the Spiritual Transformation Scale, Spirituality Index of Well-Being, and the Intrinsic Spirituality Scale all focus on different yet similar ways to measure spirituality. Some measures, such as the Dedication to the Sacred Scale and the Attachment to God Inventory, are based on a model of relational spirituality and directly measure the divine–human relationship. Other measures, like the Adult Attachment Interview, study relationships in general and have been used to study relational spirituality.

Despite all these innovations in ways of measuring spirituality, researching spirituality remains difficult and divisive. In particular, disagreements about how to define spirituality, how to measure spirituality, and how spirituality differs from religiosity make spirituality a challenging research subject. Yet even with such challenges, specific measures of spirituality continue to yield interesting findings. For example, the Dedication to the Sacred Scale focuses on the degree to which a person views the divine as a personal or impersonal being and supports that those who have a more relational view of the divine are able to be more successful in human relationships, specifically in the area of forgiveness.

Similarly, the Attachment to God Inventory tests different types of connection to the divine and has been used to support the theory that one's connection with the divine corresponds with one's primary connection with early caregivers. For example, Christian college students from very religious homes seemed to have relationships with the divine that corresponded with student–parent relationships. Students with authoritarian parents tended to fear abandonment by God, have high anxiety in their relationships with God, and have difficulty relying on and feeling intimate with God. Yet other studies indicate that one's connection with the divine can either correspond with or compensate for one's primary connection with early caregivers. With the compensation theory, a person's positive connection with the divine seems to compensate for negative connection with an early caregiver. Such conflicting findings demonstrate the complexity of studying spirituality and understanding the role of spirituality in human relationships. Despite the contradictions, the significance of the divine–human relationship on human relationships is becoming more visible.

Spirituality as a Factor in Marital Experience

As described earlier, studies investigating relational aspects of spirituality on couples and marriage appear more rarely in the literature than studies of religion and marriage. Nevertheless, spirituality, as distinct from religiosity, has been linked with positive marital experience. Evidence seems to suggest that some couples report having spiritual experiences within their marriages and even see their relationships as sacred expressions of their connection with the divine. Such findings highlight the pervasiveness of spirituality within the context of marriage and the daily experience of couple relationships.

Studies continue to find that spirituality is a factor in marital relationship outcomes. Such studies tend to use measures of spirituality as well as measures of marital well-being to demonstrate connections between spirituality and marriage outcomes. For example, ENRICH, a standardized marriage index, has been used with the Spiritual Experience Index, which measures spiritual maturity, to demonstrate a link between spirituality and positive marital experiences. Increasing examples of positive links between spirituality and marriage exist, such as findings that show spiritual beliefs have decreased the development and maintenance of couples' problems. Yet the link between spirituality and marriage does not always appear positive. Spirituality has been found to be closely tied to both positive and negative patterns of communication and problem-solving. These connections between more negative spiritual beliefs and poor marital experiences seem to suggest that certain forms of spirituality benefit marriages while other forms of spirituality can cause distress.

For example, what couples believe impacts both spiritual and marital experiences. For some Catholic couples who strongly believe in and practice natural family planning, spiritual beliefs about conception have been linked to increased relational closeness with God and with their spouses. Such studies reflect the positive impact that beliefs can have on spiritual and marital experience. However, there remains a need for future research to continue investigating the link between spirituality and marital experience, both experiences of couple distress and satisfaction. For example, research is needed to improve understanding of how specific behaviors such as prayer relate to experiences of spirituality and impact couple relationships. While an increasing number of studies reveal potential links, further research is necessary to better understand exactly how spirituality influences couple connectedness and satisfaction.

Couples, Spirituality, and Gender

As has been discussed, some spiritual practices have been linked to increased distress among couples. Researchers have found that some couples tend to engage in harmful patterns of triangulation with the divine. For example, a husband may evoke his "God-given" position as "head of the house" to justify unilateral, noncollaborative decision-making. Such findings suggest that a couple's relationship with the divine seems susceptible to distortion by traditional power and gender imbalances. Some research further suggests that spirituality can be used to widen the gendered-power gap, exacerbating relational practices of inequality already established between partners. On the other hand, studies have also shown that couples that tend to share power equally, for example being mutually impacted by one another's needs, seem to share more positive spiritual and relational connection.

While power is not inherently detrimental to relational intimacy, the way in which power is used has the potential to significantly impact the marital relationship either positively or negatively. Traditional gendered-power processes have been shown to disrupt the connection relational power helps build. Stereotypic gender differences, rooted in the traditional institutions of marriage and religion, have been shown to actually hurt couple relationships. Researchers and clinicians who support more egalitarian gender dynamics argue for relational experiences that foster couple equality: equal status, mutual accommodation, mutual attending, and mutual well-being. Interestingly, they suggest that helping couples deepen their spiritual awareness can foster these egalitarian relational criteria without some of the defensiveness inherent in addressing power imbalances due to religion and gender.

While spiritual awareness may benefit both husbands and wives, women tend to participate in spiritual practices and identify as spiritual more frequently than men. Interestingly, for some women, spirituality seems linked to identity and a more authentic sense of self. Women's spirituality, sometimes referred to as feminist spirituality, has been marked by a desire for healthy, connected, egalitarian relationships where authenticity and empowerment are shared. For married men, spirituality has been shown to relate more to their relationship with their wife than their own personal connection with the divine. Not only does how men and women experience spirituality seem to differ, but spirituality seems inherently linked to relationships and in particular to experiences of relational mutuality and equality. It remains to be seen exactly how couples can engage in spiritual practices that transcend gendered differences and the negative ways in which gender can organize couple interactions. Further research is needed to understand how to foster a spirituality leading to more connection and intimacy.

Clinicians and Understanding Spirituality

Increasingly researchers and mental health clinicians are recommending the importance of attending to couples' spirituality, including integrating spiritual strategies in couples therapy and highlighting the link between spirituality and marriage. Clinicians need to understand spirituality as another important identity intersecting with clients' multiple other identities. Clinicians also need to assess for spirituality as a possible coping resource and assess how spirituality is being used to support or hinder client growth. Because the research indicates a complex relationship between spirituality and mental health, clinicians need to assess for both positive and negative impacts of spirituality. As research indicates that spiritual struggles can be linked to psychological distress, it seems important for clinicians to address such struggles as a possible clinical issue. Integrating spirituality into mental health remains a current topic in the literature, as clinicians increasingly understand that a person's spirituality really matters and actually impacts mental health.

Elisabeth Esmiol Wilson

See also Beliefs and Values; Faith-Based Therapy; Religion

Further Readings

Anderson, D. A., & Worthen, D. (1997). Exploring a fourth dimension: Spirituality as a resource for the couple therapist. *Journal of Marital and Family Therapy, 23*(1), 3–12.

George, L. K., Larsons, D. B., Koeing, H. G., & McCullough, M. E. (2000). Spirituality and health: What we know, what we need to know. *Journal of Social and Clinical Psychology, 19*(1), 102–116.

Helmeke, K. B., & Bischof, G. H. (2007). Couple therapy and spirituality and religion: State of the art. *Journal of Couple & Relationship Therapy, 6*(1/2), 167–179.

Mahoney, A. (2010). Religion in families, 1999–2009: A relational spirituality framework. *Journal of Marriage & Family, 72*(4), 805–827.

Moreira-Almeida, A., Koenig, H. G., & Lucchetti, G. (2014). Clinical implications of spirituality to mental health: Review of the evidence and practical guidelines. *Revista brasileira de Psiquiatria, 36,* 176–182.

Prest, L. A., & Keller, J. F. (1993). Spirituality and family therapy: Spiritual beliefs, myths, and metaphors. *Journal of Marital and Family Therapy, 19*(2), 137–148.

Walsh, F. (2008). Religion, spirituality and the family: Multifaith perspectives. In F. Walsh (Ed.), *Spiritual resources in family therapy* (pp. 3–30). New York: Guilford Press.

STAGES OF FAMILY THERAPY

In each field of therapy, there has been a point in which stages have been introduced in order to clarify the therapeutic process. The therapeutic process is different given each context, and in the field of family therapy, there are other aspects that make it unique; for this reason, there is a body of literature focusing specifically on stages of family therapy. Each of the stage theories has unique aspects as well as significant similarities with the others. In order to understand the different stage theories commonly adopted in family therapy, this entry examines David Freeman's phases, Susan Schilling and Ellen Gross's stages, and Alan Carr's stages.

History of Family Therapy Stages

The concept of therapeutic stages was first introduced in the 1950s and 1960s in individual and group therapy. It was not until the 1970s that the family therapy field saw an introduction of the stages of family therapy. Freeman was the first to introduce a stage concept in family therapy and originally called them phases of family therapy in 1976. Then in 1979, Schilling and Gross introduced their own stages of family therapy. These two publications created an understanding of the therapeutic process with families. The discussion about the stages of family therapy has decreased over the last few decades, but the introduction of this concept presented the initial idea that families, just like individuals and groups, proceed through a slightly predictable sequence of stages in the course of their therapeutic treatment. Currently there are several phase or stage theories in the field of family therapy; some have concrete therapeutic techniques that fit with specific therapeutic theories, and others are much more abstract and applicable to many theories or techniques.

Freeman's Phases of Family Therapy

David Freeman, a Canadian social worker, was the first person to develop a theory about the stages of family therapy; he took the lead from individual and group stage theory. His theory was informed by his own work with families. His theory is very basic and involved three stages of family therapy: beginning, middle, and end. Notably, Freeman uses the concepts of phases and stages interchangeably. His theory is rooted in the relational nature of family therapy, as well as the unique therapeutic process that occurs only in family therapy.

Beginning

The beginning or first stage of family therapy involves the family coming to a clear definition of the problem. This often involves each family member discussing thoughts and feelings about the problem and allows each person to understand how the others are being affected by the problem. This also allows a shift in perspective that can open doors toward change. As the family begins to understand the problem, so too does the therapist. The struggle to fully understand the presenting problem as well as the family is the therapist's main priority. During this stage, the therapist is attentive to how family members present their concerns and how the problem is discussed. Initially, families tend to blame one person or discuss the problem with accusatory attitudes. Once the family has shifted toward the next phase, the language and discussion about the problem is no longer centered on blaming individuals but rather on understanding the problem within the context of family.

This phase of family therapy allows a relationship to be established between the therapist and family. It is imperative that during this stage each family member discuss his or her thoughts and feelings within the therapeutic setting, in order to establish that expectation through the therapeutic process. During this stage the therapist works thoughtfully at asking questions that allow the family to think differently about the problem while also seeking to understand the family and each of its members.

Middle

The middle phase in family therapy is the most productive and is often identified as the working stage. Individual family members begin to take more responsibility within the family unit. The conversations that take place in therapy are no longer focused on one facet of the problem and have likely evolved into collective discussion about different facets of the problems; other concerns are also beginning to surface. The therapist takes on a role of consultant in the therapy in order to talk openly about other issues of which the family may not be aware. Being very attentive to the family dynamics and discussions, the therapist uses directive techniques that encourage the family to think critically about various issues. Freeman also discusses outside resources as an important aspect of family growth; during this stage finding new resources is encouraged. At the end of this stage, the family will have a variety of strong outside resources to strengthen it.

The family likely spends the majority of therapeutic time in this phase, and the therapist is more directive during this stage, since this is the period in which the family unit begins to work toward lasting change. This phase is not only focused on fixing the identified problem but also on building awareness strategies that can help prevent future problems from creating undue stress in the family. Outside resource identification is a part of this preventative process.

Ending

During the ending stage, the family has made changes, established outside supports, and begun to think collectively about problems, and it is now time to terminate therapy. The family has been and will likely continue to be proactive with problems that arise. At this time the therapist encourages the family to acknowledge their growth and helps the family recognize the resources they have both within and outside of the unit. The family is equipped to confront new problems that may emerge with new insight. Termination is easier with a family unit than with an individual because of the relational attachments being less focused on the therapist; for this reason, termination may be brief.

This phase is often quickly accomplished, and the family and therapist come to acknowledge the progress made in the therapeutic process. The family is ready to work together without the support of the therapist. It is important that the family and therapist identify each area of growth made and the long-term implications of those changes. The therapist communicates his or her confidence in the family's future growth and happiness together.

Schilling and Gross's Stages of Family Therapy

Both Susan Schilling and Ellen Gross had a wealth of experience working with families in both inpatient and outpatient settings, and this combined experience informed and inspired their stage theory. This theory is a developmental model used to delineate the development of a family in therapy. It hypothesizes that therapy will be effective only if each of these stages is successfully completed. According to this theory, growth within a family is dependent on completion of this process with its many stages rather than on a specific therapeutic model's use. This theory places the utmost importance on the therapeutic alliance, which can be observed in the stages. This theory has four main stages: (1) preparation, (2) transition, (3) consolidation, and (4) termination. Each stage also has unique and detailed substages.

Preparation

This first stage places emphasis on the reduction of anxiety and preparing the family for the therapeutic journey. This stage is likely the most important because of the need to establish a safe space for the family to work together during therapy.

Substage 1. Mutual Acceptance by Family Members and Therapist. The family is likely feeling unsure about the therapist and whether he or she can be trusted. This is a time in which boundaries are established. It is necessary that the therapist develop trust with the family by acknowledging each person's pain and showing respect toward all members.

Substage 2. Definition of the Problem. It is during this substage that the family and therapist come to an agreed definition of the problem. Although the therapist may have different ways of perceiving the problem as it relates to his or her therapeutic orientation, it is imperative that an agreement be made about what exactly the problem is.

Substage 3. Formulation of Goals. After the problem has been defined, the next task is to establish mutually agreed-upon goals of therapy. These goals relate to not only the presenting problem but the format and content of the therapy as well; this information tends to naturally relieve stress because the family will feel more control. This substage establishes the expectations regarding the distribution of power for the remainder of the therapy.

Transition

The transition stage of the therapy is the point at which each member within the family begins to grapple with the coming changes. This pending change can cause anxiety that can become directed toward the therapist; it is during this stage that the family realizes that the therapeutic process is not simply the instillation of hope for change but rather the process of attempting to attain change.

Substage 1. Beginning Actualization. Family members begin to discuss the presenting problem(s) in more specific terms; this can often start to change the family dynamics. This stage can be characterized by family members seeking to alleviate stress caused by the acknowledgment of the problem by making promises of change that are likely not sustainable.

Substage 2. Crisis. In their quest toward change, the family begins to attempt to make changes that can often lead to chaos. The problem, which may have been considered simple at first, is now being understood as much more complex. This stage incites crisis but is pivotal in the change process.

Substage 3. Reformulation and Acceptance. In order to overcome the crisis, the family will now become more accepting of the problem and become more authentic in therapy. This transition allows the therapist to better understand the problem and develop a treatment plan.

Consolidation

It is during the consolidation stage in family therapy that family members bring a new and heightened level of commitment, which invigorates the family to work toward change. The family begins to communicate about solutions for the problem and starts to make long-lasting modifications to the family's behaviors.

Substage 1. Investment in the Therapeutic Work. At this point in the therapeutic process, families begin to focus on understanding one another and each other's perspectives. It is no longer about identifying problems but rather solutions; families begin to discuss their thoughts and feelings with more depth.

Substage 2. Working Through Alternatives. The family has now released most of their defensiveness and fear. Family members are seeking to understand one another and provide support in the journey toward lasting change. The therapist must continue to usher this change and ensure that the family continues to move forward.

Termination

Once a long-term solution to the problem has been achieved, the therapist begins the termination process. The therapist begins to encourage the family to be independent by identifying their strengths and the change that has occurred.

Substage 1. Defining the Duration and Format of the Ending. At this point the therapist begins to discuss the potential for termination. The family and therapist then develop a plan to terminate.

Substage 2. Termination Work. The therapist acknowledges the change that has occurred within therapy and discusses the family strengths. The discussion allows the family to understand and take ownership of their growth. The family discusses their future without the therapist and identifies if or when the therapist may be needed in the future.

Carr's Stages of Family Therapy

In his book about family therapy, Alan Carr identifies stages in family therapy that cover the entire therapeutic experience from the initial phone call through termination. With great detail, he identifies four distinct stages, with a number of tasks within each stage. A family's inability to complete a stage or task successfully may have negative effects on the therapeutic success. Each stage provides the family and therapist with the necessary information and skills to successfully proceed further.

Stage 1. Planning

The first stage begins with the initial therapist contact; at this point, the family has decided to pursue services for a problem. It is imperative that the therapist does his or her due diligence to identify during the initial phone call who may be an important contributor to the therapy. The therapist will need to decide who is invited to the first session; this can be accomplished by discussing the problem briefly over the phone and making that determination based on the information provided in that brief conversation, or the therapist may ask the family member to identify which people may be helpful to invite into the therapeutic process. More often than not, the immediate family members are part of the family counseling, but social workers, probation officers, extended family members, or legal guardians may be invited.

The next important task to be accomplished in the first stage is setting the agenda for the therapy. Family members can be anxious and unsure about what to share and expect from counseling, and for this reason the therapist must be methodical in the choice of questions. It is typical for therapists to come into the initial first session with a few hypotheses regarding the presenting problem based on the phone call and referral information. This initial session allows the therapist to make a more educated hypothesis and then discuss the future plan or agenda for the therapy with the family.

This stage is one of the briefest but also one of the most important. It is often during this stage that the family determines the therapist's ability to help them as well as whether the family can be helped. If the therapist is to proceed with intentionality when discussing the problem and the family, it is beneficial to ask the family thoughtful questions, using great empathy and sensitivity.

Stage 2. Assessment

The next stage in family therapy focuses on assessment of the family and the problem. At this time the therapist is expected to establish and commit to a treatment plan with the family that will allow for initial assessment. This may change as the therapy continues, but it is important that each family member commit to an initial assessment. For this reason, the therapist must skillfully manage any person's attempts to disengage in therapy. During this stage the therapist is further testing and developing hypotheses based on various possible assessment strategies, ranging from discussing the problem to creating genograms to administering questionnaires.

The final important component to the second stage is building rapport and a therapeutic alliance. When this task is not completed and rapport is not established, families are more likely to drop out or not achieve goals. The family must accept the therapist as a partner in the family growth process.

With the emphasis on assessment during this stage, the therapist must be present as a friendly and curious investigator. It is important for the therapist to proceed in a way that makes the family feel safe and encouraged rather than pathologized. When this stage has been successfully overcome, the family will feel fully understood and ready to work toward a solution that has become more clear to both the family and therapist.

Stage 3. Treatment

During the treatment stage the family is establishing goals and committing to a plan of action. The family therapist and family have done some initial work together and can decide to proceed together. The goals the family sets are an important step in the therapeutic process; they must be realistic and clear, and the goals that are initially established can set a family up for success or failure. The therapist must be patient and encouraging at this point, helping the family negotiate their priorities for treatment. Once the goals are established, the family and therapist can discuss their plans for treatment. While the therapist is using his or her best clinical judgment regarding the future treatment plans, decisions about who attends therapy and how often are openly discussed by the family and therapist in order to come to an agreement. The bulk of this stage is spent using interventions with the family that are congruent with the treatment plan and goals; these can change significantly depending upon a therapist's theoretical orientation.

This is the stage that change begins to occur and the family and therapist begin their journey together with a common understanding and purpose. This collaboration is imperative for progress to be made; the family looks to the therapist for guidance and hope. As progress is made, the therapist must help the family identify and celebrate their successes.

Stage 4. Disengagement or Recontracting

The final stage of family therapy is focused on disengaging and recontracting with the family. It is inevitable that therapy must come to an end. Carr believes that it important to increase the time between sessions as the family or therapist notices improvement. During this stage, the family and therapist also discuss the likelihood of the change made while in therapy lasting long-term. Discussion about making changes permanent is an important component at this stage in the therapy. It is also during this stage that families identify when and why additional therapy may be needed in the future. For some families, this stage of family counseling may conclude one part of the therapeutic process as individuals or subsystems seek additional therapy (recontracting for other treatment).

The final stage is one that is marked with a feeling of success and triumph, and it is important that the family identify their areas of growth and identify their strategies to ensure that growth remains. The therapist uses this time to discuss their thoughts regarding the family's future growth and challenges. It is often important that the family discuss future family counseling possibilities, understanding that this process is not a sign of failure but rather prudence and persistence.

Family therapy stage theories tend to be brief, having three or four stages that often involve rapport building, treatment planning, interventions, and termination. Although each of these theories is unique and brings insight to the therapeutic process with families, it is clear that families do tend to follow a typical process while in therapy. Over the past decade, stage theories have become less discussed in family therapy, but they are still relevant to understanding the process of family therapy.

Amanda A. Brookshear

See also Genograms; Group Family Therapy; Termination; Treatment Planning With Couples and Families

Further Readings

Carr, A. (2012). *Family therapy: concepts, process, and practice* (3rd ed.). Oxford: Wiley-Blackwell.

Freeman, D. S. (1976). Phases of family therapy. *Family Coordinator, 25*, 265–270.

Schilling, S. M., & Gross E. (1979). Stages of family therapy: A developmental model. *Clinical Social Worker, 7*, 105–114.

Statutory Rape

Statutory rape is defined as sexual intercourse by an adult with a person below a statutorily designated age. Generally, this encounter is not forced or coerced but involves two individuals, one of which because of the individual's age is not capable of making an informed decision regarding the sexual relationship. The basis for statutory rape laws is the idea that many minors are not capable of making a decision to engage in sexual intercourse and it is the state's responsibility to protect these children. An understanding of statutory rape is useful for families, as many may have to understand and deal with the consequences of this crime. It can impact a family in multiple ways: emotionally, mentally, financially, and physically. The concept of statutory rape may be difficult at times to understand because there are differences in laws across states. This entry first provides an overview of the topic, details the differences among states in laws and reporting requirements dealing with statutory rape, and discusses the impact of statutory rape on youths and families. The entry concludes with a look at concerns about research into statutory rape.

Background

In recent years the focus of statutory rape has changed slightly; some of the emphasis on it has been in order to address and reduce adolescent pregnancy. In 1996, Congress passed the Personal Responsibility and Work Opportunity Reconciliation Act, which discussed prosecuting more statutory rape crimes. The motivation to prosecute these crimes came from a desire by Congress to decrease teenage pregnancy in order to lower welfare costs. The lawmakers found that a large portion of teenage mothers were receiving federal financial support and that many teen pregnancies were a result of sexual intercourse with adult males.

Differences Among States

Each state determines the age of consent. Statutory rape that does not involve force is different from forcible rape because if the minor were of age, there would be no crime. Although the minor may have said "yes" to sexual contact, the law does not consider the minor able to give consent because of his or her age. The consequence of this crime varies in each state. It may be a felony or misdemeanor and may be punishable by incarceration, fine, probation, and/or registering as a sex offender depending on the state and specifics of the crime. Since laws differ from state to state, there is confusion, and many offenses go unreported. There are also incidents that in some states are not illegal but may be considered inappropriate, such as sexual intercourse between minors or sex between a 16-year-old and a 19-year-old.

Age of Consent

Each state has a designated age of consent for the minor; depending on the state, it is 16, 17, or 18. The age of consent determines whether a minor is able to consent to sexual intercourse with an adult. In some states, there are provisions that either prevent or reduce criminal charges when the two parties are close in age; in some states an individual can have lawful sex with someone below the age of consent if he or she is close in age to the younger partner. For instance, in New Jersey, the age of consent is 16 years old, but the law states that in most cases 13-year-olds can legally engage in sexual intercourse with anyone who is less than 4 years older. This would mean that a 13-year-old can engage in sexual intercourse with a 17-year-old without legal repercussions.

In some states, the age differential varies depending on the age of the minor. For example, in Washington, sexual intercourse with a minor between the ages of 14 and 16 is illegal if the individual is 4 or more years older than the minor. This changes if the victim is 13 years old, where the age differential reduces to 3 or more years older than the minor. It changes one final time if the younger partner is 12 years old, where the age differential is now 2 or more years older than the minor. In Ohio, sexual intercourse with a minor 13 and under is illegal regardless of the age of the other party. If the minor is between the ages of 13 and 16, it is illegal to engage in sexual intercourse only if the other party is over the age of 18. Some states do not have close-in-age exemptions to their statutory rape laws. In California, for instance, the age of consent is 18, and two individuals younger than 18 who have sex theoretically could each be prosecuted for statutory rape.

Legal Terms

Only five states have laws that use the term *statutory rape*. The other states include the definition of statutory rape in other sexual offenses and depending on the details of the sexual offense (e.g., age of both individuals, type of sexual activity) will vary in how the offending adult is charged. For example, the crime may be in the category of criminal sexual conduct, sexual assault, or aggravated sexual assault.

The codes and details of statutory rape may be included in crimes dealing with minors, children, and families. For those who are working with minors, it is important to understand the legal ramifications regarding this crime. A conviction may have implications for an individual who later becomes involved in the legal system and is charged with other crimes. The legal system may then view the individual as a recurring criminal, resulting in a more severe penalty for a subsequent conviction. Additionally, the minor involved in the statutory rape does not press charges against the individual with whom she or he is involved. The charges are generally spearheaded by the parents or guardians of the minor or by law enforcement officials based on the nature of the sexual act, details of the sexual incident, and the specific requirements via the state law.

Reporting Requirements

Each state varies regarding the requirements for professionals to report known or suspected cases of statutory rape. Professionals working with minors are advised to research their state's requirements regarding the reporting requirements and legal obligations of professionals working with minors. In some states reporting to law enforcement authorities is required, while in other states, reporting is to child protective services.

Impact on Youths and Families

The consequences of these sexual relationships or encounters are important for practitioners to understand when working with families. Adolescent females who become pregnant at 15 years old or younger are impregnated by adult males 60% to 80% of the time. This means that sexual intercourse between young girls and adult males often results in pregnancy. This has a long-term impact on the adolescent girl regardless of her decision about her pregnancy.

The emotional impact on many adolescent girls of a sexual relationship with an older man can be significant. Girls between the ages of 11 and 13 who are engaging in sexual relationships with men more than 5 years older are significantly more likely to attempt suicide. It has been found that girls who are targeted by older men become lifelong victims of sexually based crimes. When these girls are compared with girls the same age who engage in sexual activity with boys their own age, the girls engaging with older males were more likely to have multiple sex partners, engage in dangerous sexual behaviors, be lured into prostitution or pornography, become pregnant, drop out of school, or abuse drugs and alcohol. It has been reported that sexually transmitted diseases are highest among females 15 to 19 years old and that the majority of these females contracted the disease from their adult male sexual partner.

Research Concerns

While researchers are interested in understanding patterns to adolescents' sexual activity, there is still difficulty in ethically and scientifically gathering such information. In order to protect confidentiality, adolescents must trust researchers and be willing to share information regarding their sexual history. If adolescents share sexual experiences that involve an adult, where laws of statutory rape may be violated, a researcher can be placed in a difficult position because of mandatory reporter requirements. Due to this, adolescents need to be told that some information may not be confidential, which may then deter adolescents from participating in research or from being honest in their reporting of their sexual history. For researchers to engage in ethical research, informed consent forms must include specific language that addresses these areas of concern. It is imperative for researchers in this area to ensure that they understand the law explicitly so that they report the information required and are able to protect information that is nonreportable. For anyone engaging in research in this area, it would be useful to review suggestions for working with adolescents to obtain the necessary data without violating any laws or ethical guidelines.

While some adults who engage in this type of behavior are predatory and abusive toward minors, there are cases where the minors are not coerced and have engaged in a relationship willingly. Researchers are examining these incidents to understand what the attraction is for minors to engage in illicit relationships with adults, the type of relationship these individuals engage in, and the type of adult who engages in this type of relationship. It appears, based on the literature, that minors who engage in this type of relationship are in need of additional services (e.g., mental health services, child protective services), but it is unclear whether they are able to access these services. Researchers are also examining how to discourage this type of relationship before it starts in order to protect the minor. Research is lacking on sexual relationships between adults and minors and on the specific components of these relationships, such as attraction. Some of the research that has been done is flawed because it has combined minors who have wanted the sexual relationship and minors who may have been coerced into the sexual relationship. Additional research is needed to understand the risk associated with statutory rape, how to effectively report instances of statutory rape, and how to prevent these relationships from developing. This may involve studying current or recent relationships between minors and adults that fall within the definition of statutory rape.

Meredith Drew

See also Informed Consent for Research; Pregnancy; Prevention Research; Rule-Setting; Sex Researchers

Further Readings

Hines, D. A., & Finkelhor, D. (2007). Statutory sex crime relationships between juveniles and adults: A review of social scientific research. *Aggression and Violent Behavior, 12,* 300–314.

Hodgkinson, S., Lewin, A., Chang, B., Beers, L., & Silber, T. (2014). Informed consent and the implications for statutory rape reporting in research with adolescents.

The American Journal of Bioethics, 14(10), 54–55. doi:10.1080/15265161.2014.947818

Kandaki, T., Ding, K., Broomfield, T. S., & Iverson, S. V. (2013). Perceptions matter: Case studies of policing statutory rape. *Journal of Ethnographic & Qualitative Research, 7*(3), 155–168.

Koon-Magnin, S., & Rubak, R. B. (2013). The perceived legitimacy of statutory rape laws: The effects of victim age, perpetrator age, and age span. *Journal of Applied Social Psychology, 43*(9), 1978–1930. doi:10.1111/jasp.12131

Oudekerk, B. A., Farr, R. H., & Reppucci, N. D. (2013). Is it love or sexual abuse? Young adults' perceptions of statutory rape. *Journal of Child Sexual Abuse, 22*(7), 858–877. doi:10.1080/10538712.2013.830668

U.S. Department of Health & Human Services. (2004, Dec. 15). *Statutory rape: A guide to state laws and reporting requirements.* Retrieved from http://aspe.hhs.gov/hsp/08/sr/statelaws/summary.shtml

STEPFAMILIES

The term *stepfamily* generally refers to a family in which a couple is married or in a committed relationship and there is a child or children from one or more previous relationships. A parent entering a stepfamily may have children from a relationship that ended in a breakup or divorce, or because of the death of one partner. Stepfamilies are often very complex. Several factors impact the stepfamily unit, including the age of the child(ren), whether the other parent is in the picture, the stepparents' desire to be involved, and myths and stereotypes about stepparents. Stepfamilies use counseling services due to the complexity of the familial relationship combined with the stereotypes of society. Focusing on the developmental needs of each person within the family, a clinician and the stepfamily unit can work to achieve a positive family system. This entry first discusses the definition of stepfamilies and myths and stereotypes about stepparents. It then discusses the relationships between stepparents and stepchildren, challenges facing stepfamilies, and considerations in the counseling of stepfamilies.

Defining Stepfamilies

Stepfamilies are often defined as involving a couple that marries where one of the spouses has a child or children from a previous relationship. If both parents have children it is often referred to as a blended family. Many people associate stepfamilies with divorce or the end of a relationship.

However, stepfamilies are also formed after the death of a parent. Some things that may make a stepfamily different include the following:

- One of the partners may have experienced marriage before the other.
- Stepparents who are not biological parents may be unaccustomed to family life.
- The relationship between the adult partners involves children from the start.
- Stepparents may not have had time to bond with children before being responsible for them.
- Children may live in two homes with two sets of rules.
- When both parents have children, there may be children constantly coming and going.
- Members of the family may have to move, change jobs, or change schools as a result of the formation of the family.
- There may be unfinished business from previous relationships.
- There may be a lack of trust.
- Differences in children's surnames can create a sense of not belonging.
- There is no legal relationship between stepparent and stepchild.
- Sibling order may change.
- There is often less space for each person.

The living arrangements of a stepfamily vary. Some children may be present only during the week and others present only during the weekend. Some families' custody arrangements are one week on and one week off. There are also families with half-siblings, which can create questions for children.

Formation of Stepfamilies

It has been estimated that there are 15 million to 20 million stepfamilies in the United States.

According to the American Psychological Association, about 40% to 50% of married couples in the United States divorce; parents often begin dating shortly after separation and eventually remarry. As of 2010, 42% of American adults had a stepparent, step- or half sibling, or a stepchild, according to the Pew Research Center.

It can take 1 to 7 years for stepfamilies to adjust to their new lifestyle. The timing of a stepfamily's formation makes a difference in that adjustment. The formation of a stepfamily with adolescent children is the most difficult. There is an attempt at a new familial cohesion while at the same time the adolescents are trying to break free and find their own independence.

Family Cycle

Stepfamilies are constantly evolving, and it is believed that they have their own developmental cycle. The stepfamily cycle often contains five stages of growth. The first stage is the *fantasy stage*. In this stage all family members are excited about the joining of a family. The couple is excited to start the new stage of their relationship. The children may be excited to have a whole family again. In this stage everyone is on their best behavior. Not all stepfamilies start in this stage. The second stage is the *confusion stage*. In this stage the unrealistic expectations in the fantasy stage begin to fade. Tension begins to rise, and the romantic phase of the marriage begins to drift. There is fear that the family will not make it if issues are not resolved. The third stage is the *conflict stage*. In this stage anger and aggression begin to appear. Family members begin to be aware that their wants and needs are not being met. The success of the family is determined by how this stage is handled. The fourth stage is the *coming-together stage*. During this stage the family is beginning to resolve issues and learn how to function together. The final stage is the resolution stage. During this stage, family members are able to be themselves and accept other members of the family. The family has successfully learned how to manage conflict. Stepfamilies that reach this stage have a greater chance of success.

Myths and Stereotypes

Our society tends to have a negative view of stepfamilies. Children's fairy tales have been a major source of the negative representation of the stepfamily. According to Anne Jones, one out of every six children's fairy tales has an evil stepmother as a character. This viewpoint leads children to believe they can only have one loving parent and that a stepparent is dangerous and abusive. Shows like *The Brady Bunch* do not always help either. They depict the blending of a family that gets along almost perfectly. It may set unrealistic expectations of what a blended family should be. Common myths about stepfamilies include that step families function the same as first-time families, with time all members of the family will love each other, stepfamilies that result from death are easier than those that resulted from divorce, all the children will get along, stepfamilies are more successful because the parents learned from their mistakes, part-time stepfamilies have fewer problems than full-time families, and partners who truly love each other can easily deal with problems.

Stereotypes can also play a role in how stepmothers are depicted. Research suggests that being a stepmother is more difficult than being a stepfather due to myths, stereotypes, and negative media portrayals. Since stepmothers often do not live with their stepchildren, they must establish a positive relationship during visits that debunks negative stereotypes.

Stepparents and Stepchildren

Children living in a stepfamily sometimes struggle because they have gone through many family transitions. They need to successfully mourn the previous relationship before moving on to the next transition. They often have to adapt to multiple relationships before a marriage occurs. A key factor in the child–stepparent relationship is the age of the child when the relationship formed. The younger the child, the more likely he or she is to view a stepparent as a real parent. An attachment is a bond between a child and caregiver and is strongest in the first 2 years of the child's life and continues to be the most significant until age 5. It can be more difficult to obtain an attachment after age 5, and it is noted that the older the child the less likely he or she will have an attachment to the stepparent.

The roles of stepparent, stepchild, and stepsibling are not clearly defined in many societies, thus resulting in a group of people trying to define who they are. These definitions come with stress and conflict. A range of viewpoints is taken in terms of the stepparents' responsibility. On one end people believe stepparents should take a full parent role, while the other end has people who believe a stepparent should have no parenting authority.

Stepparents report that they receive many different messages about what they should and should not be doing. Often these messages are not helpful. Some stepparents are told not to be their stepchild's parent, but rather be their friend. The role a stepparent is going to play should be discussed between the couple early in a serious relationship to avoid a difference of opinion that leads to decisions being made by emotion. Stepparents are also told not to discipline their stepchildren. It is important for both parents to set firm, realistic boundaries for the children and to discuss how discipline will take place. Discipline should be dealt with in the moment and not have to wait for a parent to come home.

Stepparents are also told that stepchildren should be allowed to misbehave. This sends an inconsistent message to children in a family, especially if there are half-siblings (children born from both parents in the stepfamily unit). It is important to realize all children go through situations and all children misbehave. That being said, all children need love and discipline. Stepparents are told is that it is easier if the child's noncustodial parent is not involved in the child's life. While this may seem true, it is not in the best interests of the child. Stepparents should focus on the child's needs and not drama that can occur with past relationships. Lastly, stepparents are told that they will eventually grow to love their stepchildren and the child will grow to love them. This is not always the case, especially in stepfamilies where the children are older. Stepfamilies are not the same as families consisting of a mother, father, and the biological children they have together or children they adopt together.

Challenges Facing Stepfamilies

Stepfamilies face relationship troubles of triangulation (someone who plays a person against the person they are upset with), loyalty, parent–child conflict, and marital conflict. Marital problems in first marriages usually move downward from the couple to the children. In stepfamilies, marital problems typically come upward from parent–child conflict.

Factors that impact stepfamilies include sibling relationships. Children's age and gender also have an impact. Children who were able to voice their thoughts and opinions about their new family were more likely to have a successful transition.

A stepparent's role and function in a family is the number one predictor for the success of the marriage. Despite the increasing number of stepfamilies, social policy and law have been slow to adapt. Stepparents are seen as having no rights. They are not obligated to provide for a child, make an emergency medical decision, or sign school papers. Legal guardians or foster parents have more rights than stepparents do. The concern for this lack of acknowledgment is that it may lead stepparents to believe they do not need to care for a child at all, thus alienating the family unit. Some have written that there should be a policy that after 2 years of marriage stepparents would have the ability to obtain a "residence order," giving them the same authority as a biological parent.

Counseling for Stepfamilies

Clinicians often struggle with stepfamilies. Traditional family therapy does not always work for stepfamilies, and many variables impact the success of the family. From a counseling point of view, it is best to focus on the development of the family and each person's developmental level. By describing where each person is developmentally in the new family unit, the family is able to better adapt.

Myths and unrealistic expectations set unachievable standards for stepfamilies that counselors need to help debunk. There is a need to educate counselors in stepfamily therapy given that stepfamilies will at some point be part of their caseload. Enhancing the skills of counselors could prevent the remarriage cycle in both the client's current marriage and the children's possible future marriage and allow counselors to be advocates on behalf of stepfamilies in society, thus changing the viewpoint of the relationship. Stepfamily education can bring the family unit together. Often the education is focused on the couple, but evidence shows that including the children has lasting impacts on them.

Conclusion

Many factors impact the way people view stepfamilies. Stepfamily success is dependent on establishing roles and responsibilities that work within the new family. The expected roles of a nuclear family do not apply to stepparents. There is a need for clear, concrete roles for each person within the blended family; however, these do not exist based on social or legal norms.

Given that the United States has the highest remarriage rate in the world, the stepfamily structure merits the attention of clinicians. The therapeutic techniques from a traditional family do not work on stepfamilies. Focusing on the developmental cycles of the members of a stepfamily teach the members how to problem-solve while getting their needs met, thus resulting in a successful family unit.

Ashley R. Cosentino

See also Divorce and Separation; Marriage, First and Second; Multiple Family Therapy

Further Readings

Bray, J. H. (2001). Therapy with stepfamilies: A developmental systems approach. In S. H. McDaniel, D. Lusterman, C. L. Philpot (Eds.), *Casebook for integrating family therapy: An ecosystemic approach* (pp. 127–140). Washington, DC: American Psychological Association. doi:10.1037/10395-010

Browning, S., & Artelt, E. (2012). The evolution of the stepfamily field. In *Stepfamily therapy: A 10-step clinical approach* (pp. 13–34). Washington, DC: American Psychological Association. doi:10.1037/13089-001

Browning, S., & Artelt, E. (2012). The extended family in a stepfamily. In *Stepfamily therapy: A 10-step clinical approach* (pp. 205–223). Washington, DC: American Psychological Association. doi:10.1037/13089-007

Cherlin, A. J., & Furstenberg, F. F. (1994). Stepfamilies in the United States: A reconsideration. *Annual Review of Sociology, 20*, 359–381. doi:10.1146/annurev.so.20.080194.002043

Jones, A. C. (2003). Reconstructing the stepfamily: Old myths, new stories. *Social Work, 48*(2), 228–236. doi:10.1093/sw/48.2.228

Newman, M. (1994). *Stepfamily realities: How to overcome difficulties and have a happy family.* Oakland, CA: New Harbinger Publications.

Pew Research Center. (2011, January 13). *A portrait of stepfamilies.* Washington, DC: Author. Retrieved from http://www.pewsocialtrends.org/2011/01/13/a-portrait-of-stepfamilies/

Stillbirth and Miscarriage

The loss of a child at any stage of life, including stillbirths and miscarriages, can have devastating effects on a couple. With the death of an unborn child, there is a need for the mother to heal physically, emotionally, and mentally. Her significant other also experiences grief and needs to address the event and its emotional effects. This entry defines both stillbirth and miscarriages, provides further information about these occurrences, and discusses the counseling interventions that may be helpful for couples and families.

Stillbirth

A stillbirth occurs when the fetus dies in utero at or after 20 weeks gestational age. The statistics regarding the occurrence of stillbirths vary, but approximately 1 of every 160 pregnancies results in stillbirth. The majority of stillbirths occur in utero, and the pregnant woman may feel a change in the pregnancy, most notably a decrease in movement. There are a small number of stillbirths that occur during labor and delivery. If there is concern that a fetus is no longer moving in utero, an ultrasound can be performed, which is able to verify if a heart is still beating. If the heart is no longer beating, then it is clear that the fetus has died.

After the fetus has died, the health care provider will then discuss the options that the pregnant woman has in order to deliver the fetus. This decision is then made with the health care provider and the pregnant woman to determine the mode of delivery (i.e., natural delivery, medically assisted delivery, or cesarean section delivery). Women may choose to wait for labor to begin naturally, which generally happens within two weeks after the loss of the fetus. Generally, this does not pose a medical risk to the female. Many women choose instead to induce labor shortly after learning of the death of their fetus. If labor is induced, medical intervention is used to start labor for the woman and is done in a hospital or medical facility.

Causes of Stillbirth

After the birth of the fetus, medical tests are conducted to determine the cause of the death; for this purpose, the umbilical cord and placenta are sent to a laboratory for evaluation. Additionally, the health care provider will perform an autopsy and check for chromosome disorders and possible infections. Based on research, there have been a number of identified causes of stillbirth.

Birth Defects

Research shows that approximately 15% to 20% of stillbirths are due to one or more birth defects. At least 20% of these have chromosomal disorders, such as Down syndrome. The remaining stillbirths may have other birth defects as a result of genetic, environmental, or other unknown cases.

Placental Problems

Placental problems cause approximately 25% of stillbirths. Placental abruptions, where the placenta peels away from the uterine lining, cause complications to mother and baby, specifically a depletion of oxygen for the fetus, resulting in death, and heavy bleeding for the mother. Some women are at greater risk for these complications based on using cocaine throughout pregnancy or smoking cigarettes throughout pregnancy.

Poor Fetal Growth

Fetuses that grow too slowly are at risk for stillbirth; about 40% of stillborn fetuses had slow growth. Women who smoke cigarettes or have high blood pressure are at risk for slow growth in their fetuses, which then increases the risk for stillbirth. The use of ultrasound imaging assists health care providers in measuring the growth of the fetus and providing intervention if appropriate or required.

Infections

Infections cause about 10% to 25% of stillbirths and pose a risk to mother, fetus, and placenta. Infection plays a vital role in fetal death prior to 28 weeks. Some infections may go unnoticed in the woman and pose no threat to her. These include infections of the genitals, urinary tract, or certain viruses, such as fifth disease or erythema infectiosum (also known as parvovirus infection). These diseases or infections may go undiagnosed until they cause serious complication, such as fetal death or premature labor (labor prior to 37 weeks gestational age).

Chronic Health Conditions in Pregnant Women

Approximately 10% of stillbirths are related to chronic health conditions in the pregnant woman. These may include high blood pressure, kidney disease, diabetes, and thrombophilia (blood clotting disorders). These conditions may contribute to poor fetal growth or placental abruption. High blood pressure that is pregnancy induced (preeclampsia) may also increase the risk, especially when this occurs in second or later pregnancies.

Umbilical Cord Accidents

Accidents involving the umbilical cord may contribute to approximately 2% to 4% of stillbirths. These include a knot in the cord, the cord around the neck or lung area, or abnormal placement of the cord into the placenta. Any of these potential complications can cause lack of oxygen to the fetus, resulting in fetal death.

Other Causes of Stillbirth

There are other causes of stillbirth that are related to trauma (e.g., car accidents), pregnancy continuing beyond the 42 weeks gestational age, and a lack of oxygen during a difficult delivery (asphyxia). These occurrences are uncommon and rare. There are also additional risk factors associated with stillbirth, such as maternal age over 35, maternal obesity, multiple gestation (twins or more), and African American ancestry. African American women are 2 times more likely than White women to experience a stillbirth, although the reason for this is not known. For Hispanic women, the risk is similar to that for White women.

Further Risks

Overall, the risk of stillbirth has declined dramatically over the years. The lowered risk is believed to be because of better health care for pregnant women, especially early on in the pregnancy. While many stillbirths cannot be prevented, it is believed that regular prenatal visits will assist in preventing stillbirth. There are some women who fear repeated stillbirths, although there is no data or research to confirm that there is a higher risk of stillbirth in women who have experienced a previous stillbirth.

Miscarriage

A miscarriage occurs when a fetus dies in the womb prior to 20 weeks. An estimated 10% to 15% of recognized pregnancies end in miscarriage. In addition, many miscarriages happen prior to the woman knowing that she is pregnant. Most miscarriages occur in the first trimester of pregnancy, which is the first 13 weeks of pregnancy. Second-trimester miscarriages (13 through 19 weeks) occur in about 1 to 5 out of 100 pregnancies.

Causes of Miscarriages

There are a variety of causes for miscarriages. Some of the risks for miscarriage may affect multiple and recurrent pregnancies. Other risks may impact one pregnancy, and the woman will later have other healthy, normal pregnancies.

Chromosomes

When pregnancy occurs, the sperm and egg each contribute 23 chromosomes, which create the 46 chromosomes needed for a pregnancy to continue and develop. In some cases, the sperm or egg may not contain enough chromosomes or may contain too many chromosomes. If this happens, the fetus generally does not develop, and miscarriage is the result. This is the cause of more than half of the miscarriages in the first trimester of pregnancy.

Blighted Ovum

When a blighted ovum occurs, the fertilized egg does implant in the uterus, but the pregnancy does not develop and instead pregnancy symptoms fade and miscarriage occurs. The pregnancy is thought to end because of chromosomal issues.

Substances

Smoking may increase chances of miscarriage in pregnant women. Drug use and alcohol consumption also increase the risk of miscarriage.

Health Conditions

There are some health conditions that may contribute to health care concerns for women and have a negative effect on pregnancy. Hormone imbalances and infections affect pregnancy and may result in miscarriage. Thyroid disease may negatively impact pregnancy. The thyroid is a gland in the neck that makes hormones that help the body make and store energy from food. Lupus and other autoimmune disorders may impact pregnancy negatively. Immune disorders mean that the body isn't able to respond and fight off infection because immunity is compromised. Based on this, the body may not be able to protect the fetus, and the pregnancy may end in miscarriage.

Signs and Symptoms of Miscarriage

Since most miscarriages occur early in pregnancy, relying on the fetus's movement is not a reliable way to ensure a pregnancy is continuing. The signs of miscarriage are similar to the signs of a women's menstrual cycle. A woman may begin to feel cramping and abdominal pain along with spotting or bleeding. There are circumstances where some of these symptoms occur and the pregnancy continues to develop until full-term. There are other cases where this is the start of a miscarriage. Pregnant women who experience these symptoms should contact their health care provider. The health care provider may perform blood work, pelvic exam, and an ultrasound scan to determine the prognosis of the pregnancy. Recovery from miscarriage will vary between a few weeks to a few months, depending on how long it takes for the woman to miscarry and whether it occurs naturally or a medical procedure is performed. Some miscarriages will happen naturally, and other miscarriages may be diagnosed prior to the death of the fetus and will require medical intervention.

Medical Intervention

If it is diagnosed that a pregnancy will not continue for one of a variety of reasons (e.g., chromosomal issues, heart not developing) the health care provider may provide counseling to assist the pregnant woman in understanding the loss of the pregnancy. For many, the recommendation is to allow the body to miscarry on its own and in its own time. There are some occasions where this process may be risky or takes longer than medically deemed appropriate and assistance with the termination is needed. If this occurs, a physician performs a dilatation and evacuation, which aids in ending the pregnancy and removing the uterine wall. This then allows the body to further complete the miscarriage and prepare for the menstrual cycle to continue again as it normally would. Due to the surgical intervention, some health care providers may have pregnant women wait longer before trying to conceive a child again.

Grief Counseling and Process

The loss of a pregnancy by miscarriage or by stillbirth is a traumatic event. As with other types of loss, families, couples, parents, and the pregnant woman need to grieve the loss. This expression of grief can vary depending on the person and the experience of loss. Generally with many miscarriages, the reason is more difficult to determine than with a stillbirth. The pregnancy loss is often too early to enable an autopsy evaluation and therefore does not provide health care professionals or the couple with the answers to their questions. Sometimes the reason for the miscarriage is a chromosomal abnormality, and the fetus would not further develop, regardless of medical intervention. In some instances when a miscarriage occurs, a reason or possible reason can be found, and that can assist in the grief process. It can allow for the pregnant woman to create a plan for a potential next pregnancy and generally brings a level of comfort to planning for the future.

When multiple losses occur, it raises the question of potentially more counseling interventions needed to support the process and prepare the pregnant woman. In some cases, health care providers will strongly recommend that a couple (or individual) take a break from trying to conceive and enter into longer-term counseling to address issues of grief and other behaviors that may come with the process of conceiving and pregnancy. The loss of a pregnancy may require some individuals to process the loss and arrive at different conclusions. It is important to provide support to those experiencing the loss and to be aware of signs of depression and other mental health responses in women who experience pregnancy loss.

Related to the grief counseling may be individual or couples counseling. This is in response to the traumatic loss and the way each partner experiences and processes it. It may also be important for the couple, individually or together, to determine their continued desire to become pregnant. For some, the loss of a pregnancy may result in a shifting of their decision to have children, which may impact the relationship in many ways (e.g., a new disconnect between partners, a change in future plans for partners, separation, or divorce). Each of these effects on the relationship is important, and many medical providers will also recommend counseling to help support the couple in their decisions and determine the best way for them to proceed.

Meredith Drew

See also Adoption; Bereavement; Bereavement Counseling; Birth Control and Contraception; Childless Couples; Pregnancy

Further Readings

Capitulo, K. L., Huang, S., & Lu, X. (2014). Should parents and families of stillborn babies be encouraged to see, hold, and have funerals for the babies? *American Journal of Maternal Child Nursing, 39*(3), 146–147. doi:10.1097/NMC.0000000000000040

Daugirdaite, V., van den Akker, D., & Purewal, S. (2015). Posttraumatic stress and posttraumatic stress disorder after termination of pregnancy and reproductive loss: A systemic review. *Journal of Pregnancy,* 1–14. http://dx.doi.org/10.1155/2015/646345

Kolte, A. M., Olsen, L. R., Mikkelson, E. M., Christiansen, O. B., & Nielsen, H. S. (2015). Depression and emotional stress is highly prevalent among women with recurrent pregnancy loss. *Human Reproduction, 30*(3), 495–498. doi:10.1093/humrep/deu299

Musters, A. M., Koot, Y. E. M., van den Boogaard, N. M., Kaaijk, R., Macklon, N. S., van der Veen, F., Nieuwkerk, P. T., & Goddijn, M. (2013). Supportive care for women with recurrent miscarriages: A survey to quantify women's preferences. *Human Reproduction, 28*(2), 398–405. doi:10.1093/humrep/des374

Ockhuijsen, H. D. L., Boivin, J., van den Hoogen, A., & Macklon, N. S. (2013). Coping after recurrent miscarriage: Uncertainty and bracing for the worst. *Journal of Family Planning & Reproductive Health Care, 39,* 250–256. doi:10.1136/jfprhc-2012-100346

STRATEGIC FAMILY THERAPY

Strategic family therapy targets problematic behaviors within a family, using the interactions between its members as a means of creating change. Strategic practitioners accept responsibility for that change, customizing their interventions to meet the needs of clients. They emphasize the importance of therapeutic action, relying on a variety of directive techniques to expand a family's behavioral options. This entry first discusses the development of the strategic approach in family therapy and how, in strategic family therapy, practitioners view communication, the need to define or redefine the family hierarchy, and the role of symptoms. It then discusses the role of the therapist and strategic techniques in this approach to therapy.

The Strategic Approach

Throughout the first half of the 20th century, mental health practitioners perceived psychotherapy as an individual matter. Issues, problems, and pathologies existed *within* the individuals who came into the therapist's office, as—to some extent—did the cures. Treatment tended to take a Freudian form, with therapists passively guiding clients on journeys through their unconscious minds. The goal? To help clients gain insight and emotional release, a one-two therapeutic punch that would allegedly boost a client's character.

Strategic family therapy—rooted in communication theory and championed by master therapists Jay Haley and Cloé Madanes—considered much of so-called traditional psychotherapy counterintuitive. Strategic therapists recognized human beings as social creatures, men and women caught up in complex web of interpersonal relationships. That being so, the idea that mental health professionals would have to disconnect clients from the other people in their lives and sequester them from their social circles in order to therapeutically address their life challenges seemed unreasonable, if not downright illogical.

Therapists from the strategic school are much more relational in nature, shifting away from the internal, individual focus of traditional treatment styles in order to examine the social context in which people's behaviors exist and persist. Relationships, a strategic practitioner would say, provide clues to—even the basis for—people's thoughts and emotions, so paying attention to clients' social connections is essential to changing the way people think and feel. Strategic family therapy, then, sidesteps the need to find an inner "cause" for someone's pathology and attends to the pattern of behaviors they use to communicate with others—patterns that often appear as psychological "symptoms."

That focus on responding to symptoms has led to the depiction of the strategic approach as a problem-solving therapy. It examines client concerns (i.e., symptoms) within the framework of their familial relationships, and seeks to bring about change by taking action within that family system. As mentioned earlier, Freudian psychoanalysis presented personal awareness as *the* vehicle for transformation. The idea was that gaining insight into the reasons one engaged in a particular act would be enough to prompt a change in that behavior. To a strategic thinker, however, insight is insufficient. Change, they assert, comes about through action, by expanding or diversifying the ways people can respond to one another, changing their preexisting behavior patterns, or adding entirely new options so that clients don't need to rely upon their symptoms for aid in their relationships any longer.

The Nature of Communication

In strategic family therapy, communication and organization are constants. Whether it's in terms of conversation or silence, action or inaction, all human behaviors deliver a message (i.e., people cannot not communicate), and all messages contain information about the relationship of those involved in the exchange (i.e., they serve to define the connection and detail each person's relative level of status/power). Strategic family therapy addresses the interaction between those constants, suggesting that it is in the interplay that conflict/pathology may arise.

Defining a Relationship

Relationships, by their very nature, involve communication. All communication requires rules, whether explicit (e.g., "Raise your hand if you have a question") or implicit (e.g., Don't make jokes about bombs while waiting in the security line at the airport). By extension, all relationships involve a set of guidelines according to which communication will take place. That is, the participants need to identify what behaviors are acceptable in the relationship and determine how and to what extent those behaviors may be used. When the involved parties settle upon a standard operating procedure, it can be said they have arrived at a mutual definition of their relationship.

Any relational definition, however, is fluid. The parameters are always in flux, forever facing efforts at renegotiation. Sometimes, changes come about when participants try to modify—some might say "control"—the terms of the agreement. One person communicates a message intended to redefine the relationship, presenting the other with a choice: accept, thereby agreeing to a new mutual definition, or offer a counterproposal, continuing the process of renegotiation. In addition, the relational system may demand a redefinition on its own, either due to a change of environmental circumstances (e.g., long-distance relationship partners moving in together) or expansions/reductions to the system (e.g., birth of a child, loss of a family member).

Given that malleability, the constant back and forth, relationships tend to shift in their nature, existing along a spectrum between relational styles known as complementary and symmetrical. Complementary relationships involve an exchange of "balancing" behaviors. One partner may play the part of teacher, and the other, of learner. A protective person may be countered by a risk-taker, or an overpowering partner by a submissive one. Symmetrical relationships, on the other hand, tend to involve competitive interactions, often characterized by a cycle of "one-upmanship"-style behaviors. A joke by one partner is met with sarcasm from the other. The sarcasm escalates to direct criticism, which leads to verbal aggression.

Command, Report, and Congruence

Strategic family therapists recognize that, whatever the style of relationship, all forms of communication exist on multiple levels. Typically, messages can be said to involve both a report and a command. The former is a statement intended to pass along information; the latter is a suggestion of how the recipient of the message should respond in light of the specific context. For example, if a husband's voice emanates from the bathroom saying, "Honey, we're out of toilet paper," the report communicates the observed lack of a particular household item. The command states, "Bring me some toilet paper." Should the husband's partner deliver the supplies, she would be tacitly accepting his definition of the relationship. If the partner replies by saying, "Good thing you brought the newspaper in there with you," it becomes apparent the definition is still in flux.

In addition to their report and command functions, messages also involve qualification. People qualify their communications in any number of ways (e.g., tone of voice, volume, facial expressions, gestures, body positioning, context). These qualifications prompt the receiver to determine whether the message makes sense in light of the manner in which it was delivered. In the case of a mother returning home from a business trip, for example, the smiles and hugs from her children would match (i.e., be deemed congruent) with their enthusiastic "We're so excited you're home" statements. On the other hand, a lackadaisical embrace and dour, almost-bored "I'll miss you" message from a wife bidding her husband farewell at the airport could be considered confusing (i.e., incongruent). Incongruent messages—more popularly known as "mixed messages"—indicate something is amiss in the relational definition, and may lead to conflict within the relationship.

Determining a Hierarchy

Relational definitions help individuals organize the communications that take place between them. That is, the definitions lay the groundwork for the behavior of anyone involved. Given that all organizational structures involve some degree of inequality (i.e., no two members of a system have the same level of influence), the very act of communicating introduces the notion of power into a relationship—what strategic therapists call a hierarchy. Each person in a hierarchy typically has a particular set of expectations placed upon him or her, corresponding to status within the hierarchy. Those expectations are expressed through behaviors that are interactive; every family member's behavior impacts the others', which prompts the other family members to respond in kind.

In most cases, hierarchies are capable of self-regulation. However, when a pattern of behaviors within a family (i.e., repetitive interactive sequences) call into question the clarity of its hierarchy (e.g., when a teenager is uncertain about his or her place within the system or when a grandparent and young child form an alliance to take power away from a parent), the ensuing struggles for power may manifest as symptoms. At such times, intervention may become necessary.

A strategic family therapist seeks to define (or redefine) the social structure in order to change the context in which the behaviors are being acted out. By breaking up the pattern of interactions (Haley recommended modifying a minimum of behaviors within the problematic sequence), the therapist may bring about sufficient change to prevent the symptoms from continuing.

The Function of Symptoms

Within strategic family therapy, problematic behaviors are considered in terms of the system that contains them. They are viewed as adaptive, meaning they serve a particular role in communicating someone's response to a situation. Symptoms, in other words, are seen as serving an interpersonal function; an effect, perhaps, most apparent in the way they can be used to exert relational control.

One case was when a new couple sought a therapist's help with anxiety. After moving in together, the husband began having sudden and severe bouts of panic; incidents so intense that the wife feared for her partner's well-being. They explained the anxiety first arose after a discussion centered on the storage of condiments—the husband believed mustard belonged in the refrigerator, while the wife believed in the pantry. The conversation led to a back-and-forth game, with each moving the mustard to their preferred storage site. One day, the husband found the mustard in the pantry, and began experiencing shortness of breath and chest pains. Medical tests found nothing. After spending some time with the couple, the therapist hypothesized the issue to be one of power. The location of the mustard in the home, she realized, was irrelevant; it was control (i.e., who had the authority to make decisions about things in the household) that was the issue of consequence. The husband's anxiety tipped the scales in his favor, as the wife began to refrain from expressing her desires for fear of triggering an attack.

The symptom—or rather, the repetitive pattern of symptomatic behavior (i.e., the occurrence of an attack whenever the husband failed to get his way; the wife subsequently acceding to avoid discomfort)—effectively positioned the husband atop the hierarchy in the household, granting him say over the definition of the marriage. The husband's attacks were not consciously manipulative; they were painful and frightening, and both members of the couple perceived the behaviors as being outside of the husband's control. A case could be made, however, that the symptoms, no matter how unpleasant, enabled the couple to sidestep the often-difficult process of openly negotiating the parameters of their relationship. Living a relatively calm life in which anxiety attacks occasionally take place could be seen as preferable to living under the constant uncertainty present in a home in which no one knows who is in charge. Thus, the anxiety could actually be viewed as helpful, offering the relationship a measure of stability.

Symptoms and the systems in which they exist have an almost symbiotic relationship. The former reflects the latter, and vice versa. That connection enables the therapist to use the presenting problems in a family to inform their efforts to enact change. Once symptoms have been clearly defined, clinicians alter those symptoms to modify the hierarchy, then restructure the hierarchy to eliminate the symptoms. It may sound straightforward, but the change processes targeted by strategic family therapy require considerable innovation, as well as yet another divergence from traditional psychotherapeutic approaches.

The Role of the Therapist

To many, therapists are mental archaeologists: interviewers who dig into clients' pasts, dredge up emotional experiences, and offer elaborate interpretations to provide clients a deeper level of self-understanding. Strategic family therapists tend to be cut from a different cloth. They act as agents of change, assuming responsibility for devising unique transformational strategies to resolve clients' problems within the context of their social situations.

Recognizing that all behavior is communication and that all communication contains a level of command, strategic practitioners forgo the notion of being passively involved in the treatment process. They realize anything said in the presence of clients can be considered a command (of sorts) and use that to their advantage. They do so by taking charge of the therapeutic interaction and employing measures, commonly called "directives," to actively take control of a client's symptoms. It starts with the initial client contact, when the therapist begins gathering information on the client's current social circumstances and the relative function of his or her symptoms, emphasizing positive aspects (e.g., "How is the symptom helping the client adapt?"). Doing so enables the therapist to increase the client's level of investment in the therapy while simultaneously addressing the importance of taking action toward the ultimate goal: change.

The process of change in strategic family therapy is typically gradual; the counselor motivates clients to enact small modifications, which ultimately build toward larger alterations of the system. By making it clear that "standard family rules" do not apply within the therapy room, the counselor creates an alternative setting to the one family members are used to. By controlling how family members interact with the therapist, by asking them to actually demonstrate the behaviors that brought them to counseling (albeit with intentional, therapeutic modifications), the therapist models different ways for family members to deal with one another.

The therapist's modifications begin with the development of a hypothesis about the presenting problem: a theory that considers the roles each family member plays in its perpetuation. Building upon on that idea, the counselor devises an intervention, unique to the family, aimed at reorganizing the social structure surrounding the problem. Through that directive, the therapist challenges the family members to interact in ways different enough from their normal behaviors that they rob the symptom of its power and purpose. Should the strategy prove unsuccessful, the therapist revises the hypothesis and changes the approach.

As clients take it upon themselves to use the new methods of relating, the therapist shifts to more of a governing position, overseeing the new patterns while avoiding being provoked into reinforcing the old symptomatic behaviors. Such provocation can be seen in family members' efforts to persuade the therapist to take sides in arguments. Strategic practitioners recognize alignments in a family (e.g., a father allying with a daughter against her mother) can, at times, disrupt the hierarchy. Rather than simply point that out—action being more likely to foster change than insight—the strategic family therapist attempts to rearrange the overall system so the alignments prove unnecessary. This may involve temporarily aligning with family members to shift the behavioral sequences as needed, but the therapist endeavors to remain fair to, and open with, the family as a whole.

Strategic Techniques

Change requires action. Strategic practitioners, therefore, employ a highly directive, action-oriented approach. Therefore, it is essential for strategic practitioners to establish rapport with their clients. By displaying empathy, adopting a positive perspective, and demonstrating willingness to consider clients' behaviors adaptive to their situation, therapists can foster client motivation, eliciting their cooperation in the actions the therapist will inevitably require.

Directives

From a communication standpoint, any comment, cocked eyebrow, or quiet moment in counseling can be considered a directive (i.e., a message intended to stimulate a client response). Strategic therapists expand upon that notion, taking great care to design customized directives that encourage clients to actively modify both their symptoms and the family's interactive behavior patterns. In situations where clients bestow authority upon the therapist, those directives may be straightforward—the therapist may coach clients to interact in new, more functional ways. In situations where the therapist lacks such power, indirect directives (e.g., paradoxical interventions) may be required.

Paradox

A classic technique within strategic family therapy, paradoxes take full advantage of the communication theory at the heart of the approach. A paradox is, in short, a directive that qualifies another directive in a way designed to cause conflict between them. Traditionally, two forms of paradox exist. One restricts the client from altering the problematic behaviors. Given the lengths to which the therapist goes to establish therapy as a place of change-directed action, the command to stay the same creates a cognitive imbalance that motivates the family to resist the therapist's command. To resist, the family must change.

The second type of paradox evolves from the notion that symptoms represent clients' efforts to wrongly do the right thing. To correct the behavior, a strategic practitioner will direct clients, explicitly or subtly, to engage in their symptoms. Behaving symptomatically as a result of a command changes the nature of the symptom, granting the therapist authority over the behavior, power that can, in turn, be used to enact more substantive changes.

For example, a therapist may direct a family to have a daily argument, involving everyone in the household, that starts at 7 p.m. and lasts for no less than 20 minutes. Whether the family follows through with the directive or decides not to argue, they will be taking action that acknowledges they have control over the problem.

Christopher Lawrence and Verl T. Pope

See also Complementary and Symmetrical Relationships; Double-Bind Theory; Hierarchy; Paradoxes and Paradoxical Intervention; Systemic Family Therapy

Further Readings

Haley, J. (1963). *Strategies of psychotherapy.* New York: Grune & Stratton.

Haley, J. (1971). *Changing families: A family therapy reader.* New York: Grune & Stratton.

Haley, J. (1973). *Uncommon therapy: The psychiatric techniques of Milton H. Erickson, M.D.* New York: W. W. Norton.

Haley, J. (1981). *Reflections on therapy and other essays.* Chevy Chase, MD: Family Therapy Institute.

Haley, J. (1984). *Ordeal therapy: Unusual ways to change behavior.* San Francisco: Jossey-Bass.

Haley, J. (1987). *Problem-solving therapy* (2nd ed.). San Francisco: Jossey-Bass.

Haley, J. (1996). *Learning & teaching therapy.* New York: Guilford Press.

Haley, J., & Hoffman, L. (1967). *Techniques of family therapy.* New York: Basic Books.

Haley, J., & Richeport-Haley, M. (2003). *The art of strategic therapy.* New York: Brunner-Routledge.

Madanes, C. (1984). *Behind the one-way mirror: Advances in the practice of strategic therapy.* San Francisco: Jossey-Bass.

Madanes, C. (1990). *Strategic family therapy.* San Francisco: Jossey-Bass.

STRESS MANAGEMENT

Stress management can be defined as the set of methods and strategies individuals and families use to cope with painful emotions such as anxiety, feeling overwhelmed, worry, fear, burnout, and the like. Positive stress management strategies can be proactive and wellness oriented, or they can be reactive and healing oriented. Negative strategies leave the individual and family weak in the face of stressors, and may cause further damage when implemented following a stressful event. Healthy stress management strategies help both individuals and the families become more resilient, while unhealthy choices can cause harm to the individual, the family, or others. The family's response to stress establishes future responses to stress.

In this entry, stress management is discussed within the broader constructs of wellness and resilience. The entry focuses on individual and family stress management strategies, presents a theoretical base for family stress management, and lists behaviors that detract from healthy stress management.

Stressors and Their Impact on the Family

Every individual and every family will experience a variety of stressors over their lifetime. Stressors themselves do not cause negative responses from individuals or families. Rather, the *response* (or *management*) of the stressor and associated reactions are the focus of successful resolution to stressful situations.

Stress can be harmful to individuals in a number of ways. Scientific research has proven that overexposure to unresolved stress can lead to a suppressed immune system, sleep disturbance, and isolation from social support. When taken beyond this initial level, overexposure to stress can lead to a variety of depression or anxiety disorders, substance abuse, and even suicidality. Since families are systems within which one person's reaction to stressful events impacts others' reactions, individual stress management skills impact the broader family response to stress, and vice versa. Family stressors, therefore, include the internal and external stressors experienced by individual members of the family, along with many others, including but not limited to system stress, work–family balance, financial issues, dual careers, elderly parents, chronic illness, death in the family, manmade or natural disaster, divorce, blended families, disabilities, addiction, and trauma. Much of the scholarly literature addressing family stress management is focused on the stress associated with work–life balance and financial strain.

Models for Family Stress Management

Shortly after the separation and eventual reunion of families associated with World War II, the first family stress management model, which emphasized both risk and protective factors, was developed and named the ABC-X model. In the model, A is the stressor or stressful event; B refers to the resources available to the family (both internal and external, including social connectedness outside the family); C represents the perceptions of the family regarding the stressor (the degree to which they see the stressor as devastation or an opportunity), and X connotes the crisis that may ensue if proper balance is not restored to the family system.

For example, X (crisis) occurs when families are not well bonded to each other, have very few internal and external resources, are not connected socially, think of most stressors as highly threatening, and are then faced with an unexpected stressful event. On the other hand, a different family might avert the crisis associated with the same stressor (A) if they are strongly bonded to one another, have adequate internal and external resources including social connectedness, and think they can manage anything together. For example, consider the stress a family might experience when one member is in a serious car accident. Some families (those with more protective factors than risk factors) actually get closer to each other during times like this. They pull together to support one another by providing emotional support, and by making sacrifices for the good of the group. Other families (those with more risk factors than protective factors) facing the same event may experience more tension and pull away from one another.

Following the Vietnam War, the model was expanded to the double ABCX model, adding postcrisis coping mechanisms to explain how families achieve adaptation over time. In this model, the family that has been unsuccessful in restoring balance navigates and assesses existing resources and perceptions, and may make efforts to secure additional resources or change perceptions. Ultimately, these families achieve bonadaptation (balance between members and the whole family and balance between the family and the community), adaptation, or maladaptation (continued imbalance, including some sacrifice of integrity, development, or autonomy within the family). In the double ABCX model, the X (crisis) represented the family's inability to successfully adapt to a stressor or stressful event. Healthy families faced with crisis situations could work to restore harmony and balance in the midst of whatever changes needed to take place as a result of the crisis. Based on both the ABC-X and the double ABCX models, scholars and practitioners have developed ideas for families to increase their resiliency.

Preventative Stress Management for Families

Families may participate in a variety of behaviors to increase their resilience and strengthen their ability to successfully navigate unforeseen stressors. Helpful choices also contribute to good mental and physical health, better relationships, and overall improved quality of life among individual members. Healthy, preventive measures focus on bolstering positive family time together, thereby strengthening connectedness and internal resources. Simple activities, such as sharing meals together, going to the zoo or to the movies together, and creating simple family rituals together can improve family resilience. Further, families who volunteer in the community together develop a mutual commitment to social interest and become better connected among themselves and with the community. Families that are structured in a manner that supports the adults being regarded as "in charge" are also stronger. Other strategies for family stress management include laughing together, choosing a family mantra or song, working together, and creating time for regular family dialogue in which individual members can safely express their own feelings, reactions, and desires.

Parents can help children manage stress in a number of ways. This begins with parents taking good care of their own physical and mental wellness. Responses and consequences of previous stress episodes can strengthen or weaken a parent's ability to nurture resilience in children. Attachment theory supports the importance of adult emotional health in forming strong, healthy bonds with children.

Children should eat regular meals and snacks, not skip meals, and engage in vigorous exercise. This has become more of a challenge as children become attached to television, computer games, and tablets, but getting outside for a game of kickball or tennis can relieve tension, release endorphins, and allow for social interaction. Children become more resilient when there is consistency in their environment regarding rules, routines, and rituals. Rules should be clearly set and consistently enforced; therefore, parents should be mindful of how many rules they really want to set. Parents should genuinely listen to their children and be interested in their experiences and feelings. They should teach and model the value of a sincere apology in the presence of mistakes, and help their children see that mistakes can be fixed.

Individual family members may adopt certain strategies in efforts to increase their own resilience, thereby contributing to the resilience of the family. Committing to one's own self-care (social and relational boundaries, life–work–play balance, and time with loved ones), spirituality (meditation, spiritual/religious practices, alone time), physical wellness (healthy eating, sleeping, and exercise patterns), and vocational/avocational balance keeps individuals strong and healthy, both inside and out. Strong members contribute to strong families, and strong families strengthen their members. However, the reverse can also be true.

Individuals detract from their own emotional, spiritual, intellectual, and physical wellness by neglecting to take care of themselves. A sedentary lifestyle, the inability to maintain a healthy weight, smoking, addiction, and emotional dysregulation, including the inability to balance time alone and time with others, or establish and maintain appropriate boundaries with others, all lead to significantly reduced ability to manage stressors in a healthy manner. Inasmuch as stressors come in many forms, it's important to monitor all those aspects of the whole self. Likewise, families who neglect to spend time together or who don't take time to nurture and regard each other are in a weakened state to face the stressors that life will bring.

Responding to Stress in Real Time

The preventive measures described in the previous section help prepare individuals and families by focusing resilience, strength, and overall individual and family health. When stressful situations actually occur, individual and family reactions can also fall into helpful and unhelpful categories.

When individuals are faced with stress that is beyond their normal ability to cope, they should maintain keen attention to their own wellness strategies. Taking a walk, exercising, or phoning a friend to talk about it can be very helpful in terms of reducing the immediate fear, anger, or panic that might be experienced in the moment. These are powerful emotions that can quickly deplete overall energy and any ability to cope with a threatening situation. Behaviors that don't help a situation, and may in fact worsen it, include self-medicating with drugs or alcohol, lashing out at others, and withdrawing from important relationships.

These emotions and behaviors can carry over into the family system when the whole unit faces a stressful time. The family should be sure to discuss things in the open to facilitate problem-solving and avoid unresolved issues in the future. Families should honor the importance of stressors brought by an individual (e.g., loss of a job or death of a pet dog) and engage in supportive behaviors that facilitate healthy resolution. Likewise, in the case of any problem, getting on the same side of the problem and focusing on a solution are more productive and adaptive than finding fault or blaming. Respecting each other's privacy is another way families can support each other. But when secret-keeping might become divisive to the family, the truth should be brought into the open.

Stress management for families includes proactive strengthening of the family unit and choosing appropriate, helpful strategies when reacting to stress. Individual and family resilience impact each other in a dynamic manner that can predict future adjustment to stressors for both individuals and families. The family is the first social group that children encounter, and family of origin experiences can impact individuals long into their adulthood. Therefore, parents should be intentional about creating a healthy, strengths-focused family environment.

Anita A. Neuer Colburn

See also Anger Management; Attachment Theory; Chosen Families; Chronic Illness With Couples and Families; Conflict in Couples and Families; Crisis Intervention With Couples and Families; Depression, Couples and Families; Debt and Financial Strain; Family Resilience; Family Stress; Family Stress Adaptation Theory; Life Balance; Resilience

Further Readings

Boss, P. (2001). *Family stress management: A contextual approach* (2nd ed.). Thousand Oaks, CA: Sage.

Clark, M., Michel, J., Early, R., & Baltes, B. (2014). Strategies for coping with work stressors and family stressors: Scale development and validation. *Journal of Business & Psychology, 29*, 617–638.

Hall, J. C. (2015). Mother-daughter relationships, self-esteem, and problem-solving: Do socialization practices matter? *Journal of Human Behavior in the Social Environment, 25*, 137–146.

Hill, R. (1949). *Families under stress: Adjustment to the crisis of war separation and reunion.* New York: Harper & Brothers.

Laurent, H. K. (2014). Clarifying the contours of emotional regulation: Insights from parent-child stress research. *Child Development Perspectives, 8*(1), 30–35.

McCubbin, H. I., & Patterson, J. M. (1983). The family stress process: The double ABCX model of family adjustment and adaptation. In H. L. McCubbin, M. Sussman, & J. M. Patterson (Eds.), *Social stress and family: Advances and developments in family stress theory and research* (pp. 7–37). Binghamton, NY: Haworth.

Santiago, C. D., Etter, E. M., Wadsworth, M. E., & Raviv, T. (2012). Predictors of responses to stress among families coping with poverty-related stress. *Anxiety, Stress & Coping, 25*, 239–258.

Structural Determinism

Structural determinism reflects the view that there are structural elements or factors that deterministically affect outcomes, events, or processes. As a foundational concept within structural family therapy (SFT), structural determinism defines the potential range of change that a system can tolerate without a loss of identity. It is mechanistic in nature, and leads to ascribed behaviors and events that evolve into recursive interactions, or feedback loops. This entry addresses the concepts of structural determinism, family structure and its relationship to the environment, and structures and subsystems.

When applied within the context of a family, the concept of structure defines how a family should organize its relationships and functioning. Within the context of the family system, structure represents the pattern or style that a family uses to fulfill its goals of togetherness and preservation of the family unit. Specifically, the structure here consists of the rules, agreements, and assumptions that guide the family toward successfully achieving these goals. Each family member constructs his or her own view of reality based on these rules, and all biological, sociocultural, and intergenerational components are incorporated into the structure that helps support the family's interactions. These components are subject to change or alter perceptions upon interaction with the environment at any given time, and this is the key to helping the family restructure their behaviors based on the acceptance of this reality.

Recursive Interactions

Recursive interactions, based on an agreed-upon set of rules, shape the concept of structural determinism, which emphasizes structural change based on a cause-and-effect system of events. This concept assumes that a family is a living organism in which behaviors are predictable, and each behavior is a patterned response to the behavior that directly preceded it. This reciprocal continuity maintains balance in the family system due to its determined nature, and change is tolerated only within the context of this predictable system. Thus, the patterns of behavior are determined only until fundamental structural change occurs. For example, if a child feels ignored by her parents, she may misbehave in school. Her parents may become angry and will scold her; though the attention is punitive, the child learns that misbehavior will elicit attention from her otherwise inattentive parents. However, if a counselor asks the parents to praise the child positively when she does not misbehave instead of scolding her when she does, the predictable action and reaction are interrupted by introducing a different pattern.

Interactions With the Environment

The family structure is in constant transformation, always adapting to a dynamic social environment, and behaviors are a function of our reciprocal interactions with this environment. In the context of family therapy, the family creates a social environment that is a comprehensive system of predictable actions and reactions. Within the family environment, there are rules, roles, and boundaries that define each relationship within the greater family system. It is this system that comprises the environment. If this environment changes or, more simply, if one or more of the relationships is altered within this environment, the family is forced to adjust to the redefined environment.

Behaviors in family structures are determined insofar as the behaviors preserve the family's boundaries. More explicitly, when new environmental circumstances are encountered, the family is confronted with change opportunities, but a family with a dysfunctional structure sees these opportunities as nonviable options. When explained within the concept of structural determinism, the family has created a social environment in which all interactions can be predicted and expected. The family's behavior is designed to preserve this environment, but when the environment is challenged by circumstances (stress, new relationships, etc.), the family encounters a choice: adapt to the new circumstance or continue to react to one another in the established, predictable way. If the family chooses the latter, they find that the interactions do not fit within the new environmental framework, and the family subsequently falls into crisis. In terms of structural determinism, they are losing their identity and have no coping skills that would help them navigate new circumstances and adjust healthfully.

Within the environment of family counseling, the counselor is an active agent of change in the dysfunctional family structure. Intervening in existing patterns and interactions causes changes by interrupting negative and stagnant feedback loops and resolves dysfunction in the family. When the counselor interrupts the predictability in communication that has already been accepted as determined within the family, the family must now accommodate this change and establish a new structure. As the family learns to adjust to these new structures, new patterns of communication will be the family's new behavior determinants. When the family engages in these behaviors with repeated action, the structure of the system is stabilized with functional support, and former patterns disintegrate as they are no longer needed to predict, and determine, dysfunctional behavioral interactions and outcomes.

For example, if a family engages in an argument repeatedly, each family member has a set of rules that guides his or her behavior during these arguments. Although the topic of the argument may be different, the structure of the interaction dynamics is the same because they are determined by established and predictable patterns. When the counselor intervenes, the argument's structure is no longer determined, and the family must accommodate a new structure. To avoid this change process in everyday life, families will rigidly adhere to their structural boundaries, thereby preventing the exploration of alternative ways of communication and functioning. To make structural change within the family, the counselor must observe the family as they socialize; the whole structure cannot be assessed in parts.

Structure and Subsystems

The structure is stabilized by each family member's contributions within an organized hierarchy, consisting of three primary subsystems: a parental subsystem, a sibling subsystem, and a spousal subsystem. A parental subsystem is one where the relationships with parents are operational; a sibling subsystem is the relationship of the children in the family and their function within the system; and a spousal subsystem contains a couple relationship such as a marriage or close intimate relationship. Rigid boundaries demarcate these subsystems, and each subsystem interacts with the others using circular causality, or by reacting to a behavior and causing a subsequent reaction in another family member. These subsystems are hierarchical in nature, even if not functional, and are based on perceived power and set boundaries within the system. Subsystems arise due to differences between members in the family system, and are ideally complementary or accommodating, depending on each member's defined expectations and rules. These subsystems are resistant to change, and thus counselors can identify them as structural problems. Characteristics of problematic structures are evident as disengaged relationships in which there is distance based on the perception of unresolvable issues, or as enmeshed relationships, which are overcompensatory behaviors designed to maintain distance in one subsystem by indulging in excessive involvement in another one within the greater family system. In the context of counseling, the constellation of subsystems in a family, along with the boundaries that separate the various subsystems from each other, are collectively referred to as the *structure of the family*.

Structural subsystems in a dysfunctional family are seen as rigid or diffuse. While a healthy structure allows for varying flexibility regarding environmental change, dysfunctional structures work against inevitable change, resulting in an intolerance for differentiation. For example, a teenager may be ignored or treated with hostility for rejecting the advice of his parents or selecting friends his parents did not choose. This appears to a counselor as a determined pattern of behavior that reciprocally encourages each member of the subsystem and larger system to maintain closeness and a collective approach to problem-solving with active discouragement of individual uniqueness and contributions. Counselors will observe these patterns when families encounter a normative life-cycle transition, or an acute stressor that tests the family's coping skills and resolve. During such times, a family will develop behaviors that refuse accommodation to the transition or stressor and will instead strive to retain its identity as a definitive unit by preserving these behaviors through repeated cause-and-effect circumstances.

Adrianne L. Johnson

See also Ecosystems Perspective; Social Constructionism; Structural Family Therapy; Structural Maps

Further Readings

Durtschi, J. A., & Wetchler, J. L. (2015). *Structural family therapy*. In J. L. Wetchler & L. L. Hecker (Eds.), *An introduction to marriage and family therapy* (2nd ed., pp. 119–154). New York: Routledge.

Efran, J., & Blumberg, M. J. (2013). Emotion and family living: The perspective of structure determinism (pp. 172–206). In S. M. Johnson & L. S. Greenberg (Eds.), *The heart of the matter: Perspectives on emotion in marital therapy*. New York: Brunner/Mazel.

Parmanand, S. P., & Benoit, E. (2015). Structural theory: Approaches and applications. In D. Capuzzi & M. D. Stauffer (Eds.), *Foundations of couples, marriage, and family counseling* (pp. 215–237). Hoboken, NJ: Wiley.

Walsh, F. (2012). Clinical views of family normality, health, and dysfunction: From a deficits to a strengths perspective. In F. Walsh (Ed.), *Normal family processes: Growing diversity and complexity* (4th ed., pp. 27–54). New York: Guilford Press.

Structural Family Therapy

Structural family therapy (SFT) is one of the original models of family therapy that continue to influence the field of marriage and family therapy today. Although several theorists contributed to its development, including Braulio Montalvo, Charles Fishman, and George Simon, Salvador Minuchin is generally credited for the development of the model. In the 1960s, the focus of his therapy practice was working with delinquent adolescent boys in a residential setting called the Wiltwyck School for Boys in New York. At that time in history, many of the psychotherapy approaches were developed for high functioning, middle-class individuals. However, Minuchin observed that traditional psychotherapy approaches had a limited effect on his patients, and any improvements became short-lived once the patients returned home. This observation prompted him to explore interventions that expanded beyond the individual to include change within the family. During the time that Minuchin was practicing at the Wiltwyck School for Boys, Gregory Bateson and his colleagues were already conducting innovative research in Palo Alto, California, that examined the family as a system that creates a context for mental health symptoms. Minuchin eventually joined Bateson in his work with family systems to better understand the effect of family relationships on a person's behavior.

In the 1970s, Minuchin became the director of the Philadelphia Child Guidance Clinic, where he continued to develop and refine SFT. Therapy interventions were tested on a broader population of clients, and therapists were trained and closely supervised in the model. The research that was conducted at the Child Guidance Clinic resulted in a formally written description of SFT in 1972. SFT is essentially focused on a family's organization as a significant influence on personal and interpersonal distress. In other words, the difficulty that someone experiences is strongly affected by the organization of the family and vice versa. A structural therapist intervenes with the intention of challenging the family's organization to reduce the distress of the family members. This entry further elaborates on these tenets of structural family therapy, including the influence of family systems theory, the role a structural therapist plays in therapy, and specific interventions used in SFT. Finally, recent advancements of SFT for use in mental health treatment are discussed.

Family Systems Theory Influences

The initial development and evolution of SFT was greatly influenced by family systems theory (FST) and the research of Bateson, Minuchin, and their colleagues. The core assumptions of FST were innovative at the time, as they proposed families were living systems made of more than simply a group of individuals. FST assumptions challenged previous perspectives that mental health symptoms were an inherent pathology within the individual. Instead, symptoms were considered a natural product of dysfunctional family interaction patterns that made sense within the context. A cause-and-effect or linear understanding of human behavior was replaced with the idea of circular causality, which suggests there are reciprocal influences between family members that affect one's behavior. From this systemic stance, individuals' behavior cannot be understood as separate from their family relationships. Traditional individual psychotherapy approaches aimed to change the *intra*psychic influences affecting the client, such as modifying behavior or exploring the unconscious mind. On the other hand, systemically informed approaches are aimed at altering the cycle of family interactions that have become problematic to the family. It is then assumed that changes for the individual will naturally occur as a by-product of more functional family dynamics. Each model of therapy that is based on family systems theory has a unique approach to altering dysfunctional relational patterns; however, SFT is implemented with the overall goal of restructuring the family.

Goals of Structural Family Therapy

The overall goal of structural therapy is to alleviate the family's distress by interrupting the patterns of interaction that they continue to use to solve their problems even when it is no longer helpful. Patterns of interaction may include with whom, when, and how members of the family communicate with one another, which are determined by a set of unspoken rules and expectations that each person must follow. Observing and experiencing the ways that family members interact with one another in the session offers an initial understanding of the rules, roles, and expectations within the family. By altering those rules of interacting with one another (i.e., restructuring) during the session, family members are able to experience one another in new ways that are more appropriate for meeting the needs of each family member.

Healthy family functioning is conceptualized as the ability to adapt to changes in family circumstances to ensure the growth and development of its members. These changes create new or different needs within the family, which requires some or all of the family members to take on new roles and create new expectations. For example, a child who has entered into adolescence will have different needs in the family to continue to grow and develop. Families that are unable to adapt to changes often use the same patterns of interaction even after they are no longer appropriate. In other words, the family has outgrown the previous structure and is then unable to reorganize, which results in personal distress among the family members. The loss of a job, death of a family member, or transition into a new stage of development are just a few examples of changes that may require restructuring. Due to the various factors that influence family interactions, identifying the family structure over the course of therapy is a sophisticated process. The challenge to the structural therapist, however, is the fluid nature of the family structure, which is continually changing in response to circumstances.

The Structural Family Therapist

From a structural approach, the therapist holds a central role as a vital instrument and catalyst through which family change occurs. A structural therapist must be comfortable with challenge, resistance, intensity, and engagement in order to interrupt the existing patterns of interaction that may be maintaining the presenting problems. Metaphors that have been used to describe the structural therapist include director, sculptor, warrior, and helmsman. Each of these metaphors emphasizes the highly directive, expert stance of the therapist who accepts responsibility for facilitating interventions. In contrast to other therapy approaches that have bolstered a not-knowing stance, information that is shared by the family is organized into a structural framework. The therapist holds expertise in family intervention and adaptive family functioning and assumes a position of power in the therapy process. The therapist uses the position of power to realign family members, challenge the family's assumptions, and block maladaptive patterns of interaction. In order to assume this directive stance, it is necessary to consider the therapist's use of self in the therapy process.

An inherent assumption of SFS is that therapists have their own personal issues and emotional struggles. These issues are considered a reflection of their humanity, a natural result of their life experiences and social forces. Since the self influences therapeutic engagement with families, it is the obligation of the therapist to monitor and continually work through these issues. Contrary to other therapeutic approaches, the aim for the full resolution of personal issues or suspension of beliefs, biases, and values is not inherent within a structural approach. The therapist's internal responses and emotional struggles during interactions with clients can be used as a tool to affect the therapy process.

Assessment of Family Structure

The initial assessment of the family structure is based on a preliminary evaluation of family functioning, which is continually refined over the course of therapy. As family members share their view of the presenting problem, the focus is the process of the family's interactions: nonverbal responses, who speaks, who does not speak, who interacts with whom, or physical positioning in the room. Spatial indicators such as seating position in relation to others, proximity from the therapist, and body language are also used to assess family structure. These processes are used to determine structural qualities, such as family boundaries, subsystems, and hierarchy. A structural map is an assessment tool that may be used as a visual representation of these processes and guide the direction of therapy. As the therapist continues to become accepted by the family, particular themes begin to emerge that reveal the family's processes of interaction.

Boundaries

A family structure that supports the development and growth of its members are constructed with flexible boundaries. Flexible boundaries are defined by clear rules for interaction that allow for the growth and development of family members. On the other hand, maladaptive family functioning is characterized by inflexible boundaries that limit the ability to adapt to change. Specifically, the structure of families that have limited responses to accommodate change are constructed with rigid and/or diffuse boundaries. Diffuse boundaries are characteristic of enmeshment within family relationships that discourage autonomy and exploration in favor of family loyalty. Behaviors that may indicate diffuse boundaries in session are frequent interruptions during conversation or a family member speaking for another. Conversely, rigid boundaries result in family disengagement, which interferes with interdependence and support among family members. Infrequent verbal communication and proximity distance in the session are potential indicators of rigid boundaries.

One goal for the structural therapist is to alter rigid and or diffuse boundaries through various interventions over the therapy process.

Subsystems

Within the family system are subsystems that are a focus of assessment and intervention using a structural approach. Subsystems are formed for the purpose of contributing to family functioning based on a variety of individual characteristics of the family members, each with unique rules for interaction that establish the boundaries defining the relationship. Characteristics may include gender (e.g., mother–daughter), generation (e.g., siblings), or function (e.g., parental subsystem). It is important to note that family members participate in multiple subsystems and respond differently based on their role within each subsystem. Further, subsystems do not function independently, as they are also influenced by one another. For example, the sibling subsystem is affected by the functioning of the parental subsystem. Family functioning becomes maladaptive when members of the subsystems are no longer able to serve their function because the system is unable to adapt to changing circumstances. There is a dedicated focus on the family members who are serving the executive function in the family. In the event that the executive subsystem is not able to fulfill the family's need for direction and authority, the distribution of power, or hierarchy, is a priority in the goal of family restructuring.

Hierarchy

The subsystem that is responsible for implementing authority in the family structure is the hierarchical subsystem, which determines the distribution of power within the system. A maladaptive power distribution in the family systems is conceptualized as one or more family members who are responsible for asserting authority that they are not qualified to implement. Children and adolescents acting as authority figures are an example of ineffective hierarchical subsystems due to a lack of developmental skills and experiences. Multigenerational households are another example of potential ineffective authority when there is role confusion between the parent and grandparent. The focus of a structural therapist is to alter the family hierarchy by modifying the interactions to redistribute power within the family system. The power that is associated with the expert stance of the structural therapist is used as a means to redistribute power in such a way that authority becomes more adaptive to the needs of the family system.

Structural Interventions

Joining

A change in family organization, or restructuring, is achieved only by joining with the family, as change must come from within the family system. In order to deliver therapeutic interventions effectively, the therapist must first be accepted into the family system by following the simple rules of etiquette that are recognized by the family. The structural therapist accepts the family's organization and respects the rules of the system to understand the family in an experiential way. By joining with the system, the therapist is able to use the self as a vehicle for change. Mimesis is a method of joining that accommodates the family's language, emotional climate, and nonverbal postures. However, it is important to note that joining is more than simply being polite and conversational. Joining efforts should be implemented with intention and purpose of allowing intervention that the family will accept. Only through acceptance into the family is the structural therapist able to support and challenge the system toward change.

Challenging the View of the Problem

The foundation for structural change is to challenge the way the family views the problem and recognizing the relational nature of the problem in which everyone plays a role. As opposed to the behavior of one family member, a structural approach conceptualizes the presenting problem as the family members' interactions that are maintaining the problem. In other words, all family members are equally participating in the presenting problem. Families often hold a narrow, linear view of the problem that requires a cure for a particular family member, or symptom bearer. The family's current view limits the use of new rules and roles that are needed to adapt to changing circumstances. By challenging a linear view of the problem, families are able to reorganize the rules and roles that govern their interactions. Challenging is implemented through various means that may be described as explicit or implicit. Reframing the description of an individual's problematic behavior is an explicit measure to highlight the systemic nature of the problem. Including or excluding specific family members in conversation, blocking interruptions, or therapist alignment are implicit ways to redistribute power within the system, also known as unbalancing. Many structural interventions that are intended to accomplish restructuring, such as enactments and boundary-making, also serve the dual purpose of challenging the maladaptive view of the problem.

Enactments

The primary goal of a structural enactment is for family members to experience one another in a new way. Enactments are far more complex than simply directing family members to talk to one another about an issue of conflict to gain a deeper insight or improve communication skills. Change is expected to occur as a result of actively addressing the problems in the session, rather than simply talking about them. A carefully designed enactment introduces an appropriate level of emotional intensity into the session so the family reveals their typical response to emotional stress. Although family members can simply be asked how they respond to emotional stress, enactments allow the therapist to observe interactions that may be outside their awareness. The typical response pattern is then interrupted with an in-session directive that the therapist gives to facilitate an alternative way of adapting to the problem. Facilitating enactments requires a therapist who feels comfortable with an active role that may require interrupting and challenging clients when it becomes necessary. For example, a parent who responds passively to a child's misbehavior during the session may be specifically directed to independently construct and deliver a consequence for a defiant child's misbehavior. It is important to emphasize that the outcome of an enactment cannot be anticipated, so the therapist must also be comfortable accommodating the family's unpredictable responses.

Boundary-Making

Boundary-making interventions are intended to guide families toward reorganization by actively creating or altering the family's boundaries in the session. There are numerous means of implementing boundary-making interventions; however, the purpose is always to promote boundaries that allow healthier family functioning. The therapist modifies the patterns of interaction among family subsystems that exhibit enmeshment by actively creating boundaries during the session. Methods for strengthening diffuse boundaries may include blocking interruptions among enmeshed relationships or changing the physical proximity during the session to create a physical boundary. Family relationships that are characterized by rigid boundaries must be actively reengaged to alter the specific patterns that maintain the disengagement. The therapist may bring the members of the subsystem in closer physical proximity to one another and actively block interruption from other family members. Adjusting physical proximity and focusing attention to desired interactions while ignoring others provides the opportunity to support new, more adaptive transactions among family members.

Advancements in Structural Family Therapy

As the field of family therapy has evolved, so too has structural family therapy. Changing societal circumstances have resulted in advancements to the model to accommodate such changes. A major contributing factor to the changes in family therapy, and structural therapy in particular, is the emphasis on evidence-based practice, or the need for research that shows the practice is effective. These expectations have led to both advancements and limitations of structural therapy. For example, several therapy approaches that are shown to be effective in treating family distress have been highly informed by structural therapy, which allows a broader use of the model. The broader use of the model has resulted in further refinement to identify under what circumstances and with whom structural therapy is the most effective. There is now a notable trend in family therapy toward a collaborative, client-centered treatment that minimizes the role of the therapist as the expert.

On the other hand, one limitation of the movement toward effectiveness research is the focus on treating a mental health diagnosis and other presenting problems focused on the individual. A foundation of structural therapy is the presumption that presenting problems are a function of maladaptive family interactions that must be interrupted rather than the result of a dysfunctional quality that is inherent within the individual. A major concern of these changes is that structural therapy will be simplified into a group of interventions, as opposed to the focus on systemic functioning. The intent of making sure there is empirical support for the family therapy approach used offers the benefit of holding clinicians responsible for demonstrating successful outcomes. However, it is equally important to maintain the integrity of structural family therapy by adhering to the original theoretical principles that support successful family change.

M. L. Parker

See also Circularity and Linearity; Enactments; Hierarchy; Person of the Therapist; Structural Maps; Systems Theory

Further Readings

Colapinto, J. (1991). Structural family therapy. In A. S. Gurman & D. P. Kniskern (Eds.), *Handbook of family therapy* (pp. 417–443). New York: Brunner/Mazel.

Minuchin, S. (1974). *Families and family therapy*. Cambridge, MA: Harvard University Press.

Minuchin, S., & Fishman, H. C. (1981). *Family therapy techniques*. Cambridge, MA: Harvard University Press.

Minuchin, S., Lee, W., & Simon, G. (2006). *Mastering family therapy: Journeys of growth and transformation*. Hoboken, NJ: Wiley.

Minuchin, S., Nichols, M. P., & Lee, W. Y. (2007). *Assessing families and couples: From symptom to system*. New York: Pearson.

Minuchin, S., Reiter, M. D., & Borda, C. (2014). *The craft of family therapy: challenging certainties*. New York: Routledge.

STRUCTURAL MAPS

A structural map is an assessment tool that developed out the structural family therapy tradition in the mid- to late 20th century under the leadership of Salvador Minuchin. When creating a structural map, the therapist constructs a visual snapshot of a family at a particular point in time. Representing the therapist's working hypothesis of a family's recurring patterns of interaction, structural maps identify a family's relationships, subsystems, boundaries, hierarchy, and distribution of power. This entry describes how structural maps aid counselors in obtaining a clearer understanding of family dynamics and enhance treatment planning in family counseling.

Structural Mapping as a Systemic Assessment Tool

Structural maps assist family therapists in identifying repetitive patterns of interactions within families. This diagnostic tool helps inoculate the therapist from understanding the problem as being embedded within a particular family member. In structural family therapy, the counselor assumes that the presenting problem is in some way maintained by the family's current organization. By mapping the family's current structure, the therapist can better envision *how* the family can redefine their relationships in order to promote the growth of its members. Table 1 describes standard symbols used in structural maps.

Table 1 Structural Map Symbols

Father	F
Mother	M
Husband	H
Wife	W
Stepfather	SF
Stepmother	SM
Grandmother	GPA
Grandfather	GMA
Son (first-born son)	S1
Son (second-born son)	S2
Daughter (first-born daughter)	D1
Daughter (second-born daughter)	D2
Therapist	Th

Relationships

Mapping the relationships within a family yields essentially three relationship styles: (1) enmeshed, (2) disengaged, and (3) affiliation. High levels of conflict, dependency, and limited autonomy characterize enmeshed relationships. They provide an exaggerated sense of closeness and family loyalty but limit independence. In an enmeshed relationship, a counselor may notice that a father regularly speaks on behalf of his daughter despite her adolescent status. In disengaged relationships, family members have an underdeveloped sense of connection and belonging. While family members might enjoy a great degree of access to the outside world, they lack intimacy with each other.

When family members enjoy an affiliation, individuality and togetherness are well balanced. Individual differences are not seen as a threat to family bonding or coaction; rather, differences among family members are valued. It is crucial to note that all affiliations within families are not healthy. Similarly, all enmeshed or disengaged relationships are not dysfunctional. Relationships within a family must be understood within their unique cultural and developmental context for the functionality of current relationships to be effectively assessed.

Disengaged style relationships may be healthy in instances of a divorced couple relationship or in instances of child abuse. Enmeshed style relationships can be healthy in various nontraditional family types or at particular developmental phases, such as when parents deal with infants and toddlers. In structural maps, relational symbols are used to signify key relationship patterns, as shown in Figure 1. While many of the symbols are intuitive, the following symbols merit an explanation. A bracketing symbol can be used to highlight coalitions within families. Coalitions are secret alliances that organize a family into particular teams during conflict. Conflict lines can also be used as an alternative to the disengaged symbol. Conflict lines highlight relationship distress.

Subsystems and Boundaries

Families are complex living systems that comprise smaller subsystems. Subsystems form in families based on generational status, gender, and function. Common subsystems within families are the couple, parental/executive, sibling, and grandparental subsystems. Subsystems are also formed based on common interests or activities. For example, a subsystem in one family might consist of a stepfather and his three stepdaughters. Stepdad is the soccer coach for his girls. Whether it is strategizing for an upcoming match or commiserating over their favorite Major League Soccer team's poor performance, this particular subsystem membership is well defined.

Boundaries are the invisible rules that regulate the flow of communication within and between subsystems. These boundaries define "who's in" and "who's out" of each subsystem. Some families become symptomatic when their boundaries are overly restrictive in their structure. On the other hand, some families might lack the necessary organization for its members to flourish. In structural maps, there are three basic boundary styles: (1) diffuse, (2) rigid, and (3) clear, as shown in Figure 2.

Fences in residential neighborhoods provide a helpful metaphor for understanding interpersonal boundaries within families. Diffuse boundaries lack definition; it is not entirely clear who participates in what subsystem and how. When neighbors do not have a fence to separate their properties, it can be hard to know as a homeowner whose yard one is in at any given time. Clear boundaries can be likened to picket fences. Picket fences clarify property lines, and yet the space between the slats and lower fence height promotes connection and affiliation between neighbors. Both homeowners can see each other, and yet both are aware of the outer limits of their property. Privacy fences are symbolic of rigid boundaries in that they are impermeable. In rigid boundaries, family members are cut off from each other. While their "relational property" is clearly defined, the imposing nature of the fence prevents access and open communication between neighbors.

Just as boundaries are used to demarcate the relationships between subsystems within a family, boundaries are used in structural maps to

Figure 1 Relationship Symbols

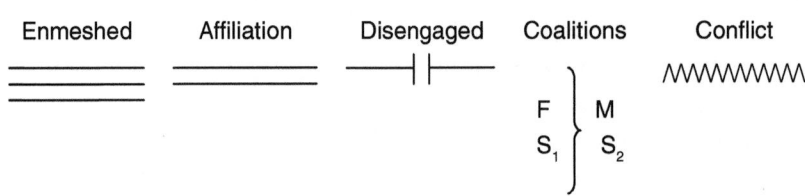

Figure 2 Boundary Styles

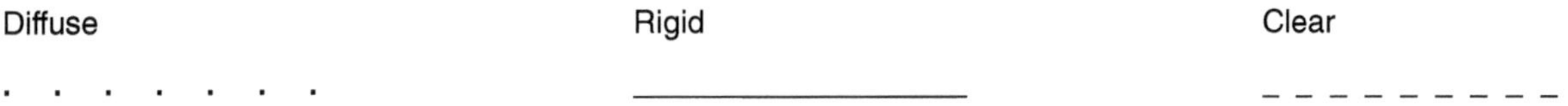

Diffuse   Rigid   Clear

. . . .   ─────────────   ─ ─ ─ ─ ─ ─ ─ ─

capture the relationship between the family and the outside world. These boundaries depict the family in relation to larger systems such as formal and informal supports, clubs and organizations, religious and spiritual communities, and extended family.

Hierarchy and Power

Each family has its own way of regulating power and influence over its members. A basic assumption in structural family therapy is that families should have clear leadership. This is accomplished by having a well-defined hierarchy or parental/executive subsystem that functions as a well-coordinated team. When members of a parental subsystem are not working together out of a shared plan of family governance, families are often stuck vying for power rather than facing life tasks with coordination, collaboration, and complementary roles. Hierarchy and power can be depicted in three primary ways in a structural map. One way to designate who is in charge is by positioning these family members within the executive subsystem, as shown in Figure 3.

A counselor can also designate which parent or family member has more power by placing that member in a vertically elevated position within the respective subsystem. A final way to designate power is by the size of the symbol of each family member. It is quite possible that a 10-year-old child has immense power within a family system. As a counselor, one might notice that much of the family's conversation is organized around their symptomatic child. While the child may not be functioning in a parental role, his relative power within the family warrants an oversized symbol to highlight the commanding role he plays within the family.

Figure 4 demonstrates one such family in which parents are struggling to work together as a team in response to their son's symptoms. Over the past year, their children have had limited access to their father, who has been overinvolved at work due to a restructuring of his job responsibilities. The firstborn son's grief over the absence of his father finds expression in his externalizing behaviors. Over time, Mom and Dad have become increasingly polarized over how best to help their son. The son unwittingly exploits his parents' dissension by

Figure 3 Subsystem Levels With Couple or With Grandparental Relationships

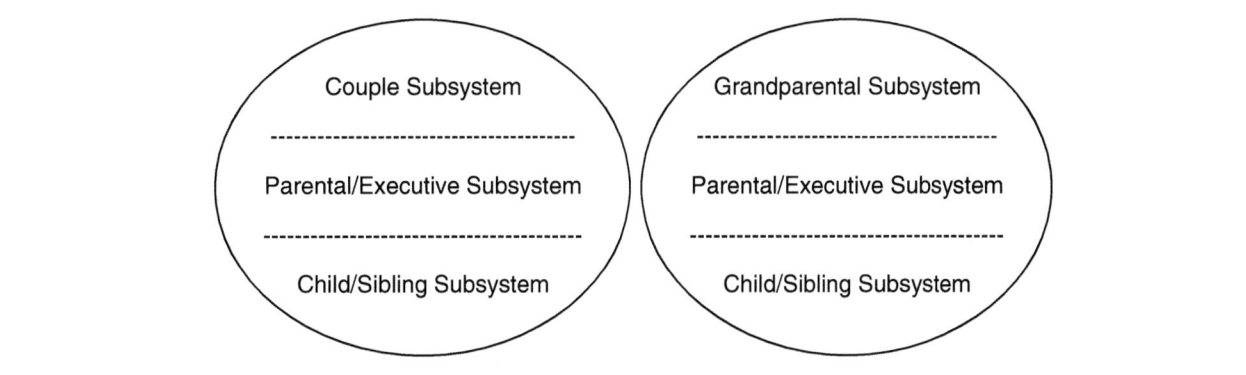

Figure 4 Map of a Family Presenting With Preadolescent Externalizing Behaviors

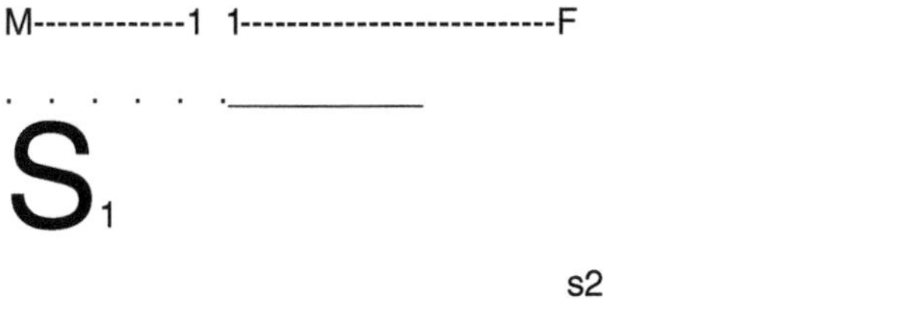

```
M------------1  1-------------------------F
 . . . . .    _____
S₁

                        s2
```

appealing to the sympathies of his mother, who also misses her husband. In the wake of this dynamic is a lost child (i.e., second-born son), whose internalized grief goes unnoticed in the family.

Family Life-Cycle Considerations

Consistent with structural family therapy's competency-based approach, structural maps often punctuate developmental themes. A family's current organization is often a product of a structure that has served the family well in years past. Due to the developmental changes that occur in families across time (e.g., shift from families with children to families with adolescents), it may be necessary for a family to renegotiate their relationships in order to accommodate the maturation of its members. In other words, families seeking help are not dysfunctional in the universal sense, but rather they are stuck in a relational structure that is no longer compatible with the family's current stage of development. Much of family counseling is about helping families navigate normal, developmental transitions.

Structural Mapping as Intervention

Ideal Structural Maps

Constructing ideal structural maps is a creative way of imagining family change. When making an ideal map, the counselor takes into consideration the family type, cultural context, developmental life stage, and specific goals of the family. The ideal map illustrates *how* various shifts in a family's structure might enhance family cohesiveness and promote the well-being of each person. Ideal maps help the therapist envision the family's solution state while taking into account current family challenges.

In Figure 5, a family is mapped at the start of treatment. Due to the high conflict and eroding intimacy in the couple relationship, a diffuse boundary was created between the wife and the outside world that increased the couple's vulnerability to an affair. The marital distress floods into their coparenting relationship, making coaction difficult as parents. This structural arrangement leaves Mom to shoulder much of the parental responsibilities and Dad deactivated in his parental role. With this fracturing in family leadership, the children are induced to pick sides, with one daughter clearly aligning with Dad but racked with anxiety and the other daughter stuck in the middle.

With this vision established, the ideal map provides a blueprint for family change. Ideal maps echo the advice from Minuchin that "Families always have alternatives." Ideal maps capture these alternatives. As shown in Figure 6, the family is reorganized in order to promote individual

Figure 5 Initial Structural Map: Adolescent Anxiety

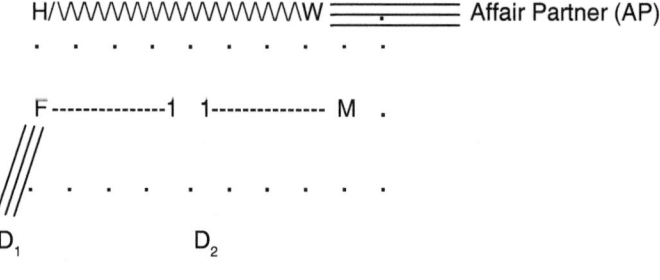

and family wellness. Assuming the husband and wife decide to stay married, a rigid boundary is established between mom and her affair partner. This rigid boundary is in part maintained by increased intimacy and closeness in the couple relationship. By establishing clearer boundaries between the couple and parenting subsystems, the couple is better positioned to block their marital conflict from spilling over into their parenting relationship. Given Mom and Dad's increased affiliation as coparents, the children are no longer drawn into teaming with either parent.

Locating the Position of the Therapist

Consistent with the postmodern tradition, the counselor is not a neutral, objective outsider to the family, but a participant who influences and is in turn influenced by the family. During treatment, the therapist joins the family system. The person of the therapist, rather than therapeutic technique, is the most potent instrument of change. Given the counselor's unique personal history, cultural identity, and life roles, the counselor has at his or her disposal a rich repertoire of roles to play with a family. It is not uncommon for a counselor to get induced by the family to play a particular role that meets a need for the family but interferes with their lasting change. By positioning the counselor on the family's map, counselors can reflect on the role they are playing with the family in order to evaluate how helpful their current position is with the family.

Generally, the therapist will prioritize joining with the executive subsystem as a way of honoring the family's hierarchy. If a counselor joins the family at the child subsystem, the powerbroker(s) of the family may be more inclined to reject the counselor's influence. While the counselor may initially start by aligning with the executive subsystem, the structural map will provide direction for what position(s) the counselor should take in order to promote structural change.

Jonathan Impellizzeri

See also Ecosystemic Structural Family Therapy; Structural Family Therapy; Systemic Family Therapy

Further Readings

Minuchin, S. (1974). *Families and family therapy.* Cambridge, MA: Harvard University Press.

Minuchin, S., Nichols, M., & Lee, W. Y. (2007). *Assessing families and couples: From symptom to system.* Boston: Allyn & Bacon.

Minuchin, S., Reiter, M., & Borda, C. (2013). *The craft of family therapy: Challenging certainties.* New York: Routledge.

Nichols, M. P. (2013). *Family therapy: Concepts and methods* (10th ed.). Upper Saddle River, NJ: Pearson.

Simon, G. M. (2008). Structural couple therapy. In A. Gurman (Ed.), *Clinical handbook of couple therapy* (4th ed., pp. 323–349). New York: Guilford Press.

Substance Use Disorders in Adolescence

Substance use disorder is the clinical designation for continued use of substances despite negative consequences in the biological, psychological, and social domains of one's life. Substance use, abuse, and dependence among youth are common and often co-occur with other disorders. Because adolescent brain development persists into the early to mid-20s, and because many substances of use and abuse are associated with brain tissue changes and brain damage, substance use disorders are one of the foremost risks to youth development. This entry describes the features of substance use disorders, discusses risk and protective factors associated with

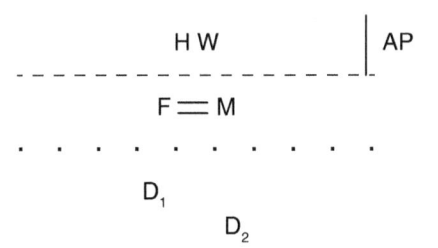

Figure 6 Ideal Structural Map for Family

substance use disorders, details the types of substances involved in substance use disorders, and reviews some of the more common treatment models for substance use disorders.

Features

Psychoactive substances are substances that are introduced into the body and that influence psychological aspects such as moods, perceptions, thoughts, or energy levels. Common substances of abuse and addiction include illicit, or illegal substances, such as methamphetamines and heroin; legal substances, such as alcohol, tobacco, caffeine; inhaled chemicals, such as cleaning products; and prescription drugs used outside of their intended purposes, such as opiate pain medications. The diagnosis of a substance use disorder is highly dependent on whether the use causes impairment, either in the short term or in the long term.

The *Diagnostic and Statistical Manual of Mental Disorders,* in its fifth edition (DSM-5), and the World Health Organization's *International Classification of Disorders* (ICD-10) each contain criteria for substance use disorders. The DSM-5 merged what were previously classified as two distinct but often overlapping disorders: substance abuse and substance dependence. Substance abuse is the use of a substance that yields negative physical, psychological, or social consequences. For instance, if a teenager takes a small drink of whiskey, the liquid makes its way through the digestive system, and its toxicity is mostly managed through the liver and kidney. If too much is ingested, however, the effects may be undesirable. Biologically, too much alcohol can put strain on the liver and kidneys, cause damage to the nervous and cardiopulmonary systems, and even interact with other drugs in the body. Psychologically, the alcohol use may bring about feelings of guilt, or be a response to the drinker's desire to escape the stresses of life. Socially, the intoxication (also known as drunkenness) may cause driving impairment or reduce the drinker's social inhibitions, causing awkward social situations in family, peer, or school settings. The disorder's severity is measurable through how many consequences are experienced, as well as a pattern of increased usage.

The DSM-5 establishes overall criteria for substance use disorders in categories. The first category is loss of control, and includes failure to self-correct troubling patterns of use, considerable time and effort devoted to use and recovery from using, structuring one's daily life around the substance, and obsession over the substance even when not using. The second category is social impairment, and it is marked by difficulties in family and peer relationships, hindered performance in school or work, withdrawal from other life interests and activities, and continued use, even despite perhaps being aware of social domain impairments. The third category is risky use of the substance, and may include awareness of physical or psychological problems that result from the substance's use, and continued usage despite that awareness. The final category involves what the DSM calls the pharmacological criteria of tolerance and withdrawal. Tolerance occurs as the user continues to use a substance in greater and greater amounts in order to achieve the same effect—this is due to the body's adjustment to the resultant changes the drug introduces. Body systems tend to self-regulate in order to maintain stability and health, a process sometimes referred to as homeostasis. When substance use is then reduced or stopped, the body reacts with withdrawal. Various substances have their own withdrawal symptoms, from the flu-like symptoms of heroin withdrawal to life-threatening seizures that sometimes accompany sudden alcohol cessation among chronic, heavy drinkers.

Risk and Protective Factors

A landmark study by the University of Michigan over a 30-year period called into question national efforts to control the supply of illicit drugs. Sometimes referred to as the drug war, criminalizing drug use and supply has been a controversial strategy. The University of Michigan study found that despite supply reduction efforts, drug availability has remained fairly level in the United States over the past three decades. The study found, however, that as knowledge of drug-use-related risks increases, adolescent drug use decreases.

Substance use disorders are related to a number of risk and protective factors. It is important when considering these associations that when variables are related, this does not mean that one causes the other. Some of the strongest risk factors, or variables, that predict adolescent drug use are environmental. Youth whose social groups use drugs are more likely to use drugs. Antisocial behavior is behavior that features cruelty and deprivation of others' rights—not introversion or preferring to be alone. Antisocial behaviors such as those found in conduct disorder are highly correlated with drug use. Impulsivity is also predictive of drug use. Male children tend to use more drugs than females. The earlier an adolescent begins experimenting with substances, the greater the likelihood for a substance use disorder; this association is seen particularly in the case of substance abuse disorders involving the illicit drugs that are considered most dangerous. There is a line of research that seeks to identify genetic predispositions to addiction.

One controversy in discussions of substance use disorders and risk factors is the concept of the gateway drug. A gateway drug is defined as a drug that most abusers of a more dangerous illicit drug have used in the past. Marijuana, for instance, is widely regarded as a gateway drug to drugs that are considered more dangerous, such as heroin and methamphetamines. The notion of the gateway drug is not universally accepted, as detractors of the theory point out that even if most users of a highly dangerous drug tried marijuana first, most marijuana users do not go on to more dangerous drugs.

Some factors, mostly environmental factors, are known to be protective against drug abuse. Higher education levels correlate with lower substance abuse. Parental involvement and high levels of parental acceptance are related inversely to substance use disorders. High engagement in extracurricular interests and academics are preventative factors among adolescents.

Substance Categories

Substances are often categorized based on their effects, although some can fit in multiple categories. Nicotine, for instance, raises central nervous system activity and heart rate, but also has an overall calming effect. Most emergency room visits involving substance use are related to the use of multiple drugs, typically from different categories. For example, heroin produces a euphoric effect, but also has a sedative effect; so many heroin users take the drug in conjunction with cocaine, a stimulant. Combining heroin and cocaine is often referred to as a speedball; the heroin also curtails withdrawal symptoms from the cocaine. Tolerance, or the need to take more of a drug to get the same effect, is so different from person to person that dosing toxicity can be unpredictable. The following are the main categories of drugs that tend to be abused.

Stimulants

Stimulants tend to raise energy levels as well as increase focus. Some stimulants, such as cocaine, also produce a sense of euphoria in the user. Other examples of stimulants include caffeine, the most used stimulant; and methylphenidate, otherwise known as the medication Ritalin. Ritalin and Adderall, a combination of the stimulants amphetamine and dextroamphetamine, are often prescribed for adolescents with attention deficit disorder. Adderall and Ritalin are often taken illegally to improve academic performance or to enhance wakefulness. Methamphetamine, also known as meth, crystal meth, or ice, induces intense feelings of euphoria in users. Methamphetamines can be fast-acting, and fast-acting drugs tend to build tolerance, and thus dependence, quickly. Some of the mild side effects of stimulants include insomnia and aggression. Stimulant overdoses can induce life-threatening hyperthermia, or overheating, as well as heart stroke or cardiac arrest and/or seizures. Other overdosing consequences, sometimes referred to by users as overamping, include paranoia, hypervigilance, hallucinations, and sudden fatigue.

Depressants

Depressants lower the heart rate and other central nervous system functions and have a sedative effect on the body. Benzodiazepines such as clonazepam (brand name Klonopin) and alprazolam (brand name Xanax) fall under this category. Sleeping pills are classified as barbiturate depressants. Some prescription antipsychotics such as haloperidol (Haldol) or quetiapine (Seroquel) are classified as depressants and prescribed for anxiety. A depressant overdose can threaten involuntary central nervous system respiratory and cardiac functioning as the user falls asleep.

Hallucinogens

Hallucinogens are typically sought for their effects on perceptual experiences, and sometimes the moods, of users. D-lysergic acid diethylamide, or LSD, and MDMA (popularly known as "ecstasy" or "Molly") are examples of commonly used hallucinogens. Peyote, often used in religious observances, is a cactus plant that contains mescaline, which has a similar structure to LSD. Another hallucinogen often used among adolescents is psilocybin, the active ingredient in hallucinogenic mushrooms.

Adolescents are likely to look to peers and Internet-based information sources as they explore hallucinogens. They potential for receiving misinformation from these sources is high, which may be especially dangerous in the case of hallucinogens because the potency of the average dose varies greatly from one type of hallucinogen to the next. Hallucinogen-induced persisting perceptual disorder is a risk most associated with LSD, in which a user experiences perceptual disruptions for a year or longer after the LSD usage. The perceptual experiences, which can include hallucinations, that the user has while under the effects of a hallucinogen are often referred to as a psychedelic experience or trip. In many cases, hallucinogen users find they must take more of the substance in order to achieve intoxication, which indicates tolerance. The main risks inherent in hallucinogen abuse are related to a loss of behavior control and decision-making, mood swings, and anxiety. The behaviors and choices made by someone hallucinating should not be underestimated, as the user may make a dangerous decision that puts self or others at risk.

Opioids

Opioids are mostly used for pain reduction, relief of anxiety, and euphoria. Opioids are common narcotics that are either derived from the poppy plant or produced synthetically with a similar chemical structure. Opium, heroin, codeine, and morphine are poppy plant products, while synthetic opioids include oxycodone and hydrocodone. Opioids are highly addictive, and users often rapidly develop tolerance to the drugs. People who are addicted to opioids are sometimes prescribed certain synthetic opioids such as methadone or naltrexone, sold under the brand name Vivitrol, since withdrawal from these drugs produces less pronounced symptoms. Replacing a drug with another drug is controversial, particularly among those who advocate abstinence. Proponents of drug replacement, or harm reduction therapies, argue that such techniques reduce the negative consequences of withdrawal, place the patient under closer supervision, reduce potential diseases transmitted through reusing syringes, and reduce crimes related to obtaining money to purchase heroin or other opioids. As with depressants, an opioid overdose can result in reduced or halted central nervous system functions such as breathing and heart rate. A user in overdose is asleep at the point that these dire conditions occur.

Marijuana

Marijuana, a product of the *Cannabis sativa, Cannabis indica,* and *Cannabis ruderalis* plants, is often categorized on its own, as it has depressant and hallucinogenic properties. Marijuana has been at the center of controversy in recent years as several states have legalized its use and many others have allowed its use for medical purposes, although it remains illegal for any purpose under federal law. Delta-9-tetrahydrocannabinol, or THC, is the active ingredient in marijuana. Marijuana is used medically for pain relief, nausea control, and anxiety, among other ailments. Proponents of marijuana's recreational use note that fatal overdose is not possible, although there is mixed research on whether chronic use leads to ongoing cognitive problems. Research has found associations between marijuana use and cognitive functioning to be mostly acute, or those related to recent use, rather than long-term results of chronic use. Acute effects include behavioral lethargy, fatigue, and short-term memory loss. Marijuana's frequent appearance in entertainment media may contribute to the relatively high levels of use of the drug among adolescents. Among high school seniors in the United States surveyed in 2014, 21% reported using marijuana in the past month, with nearly 6% reporting daily use.

Alcohol

Alcohol has both stimulant and depressant effects. Alcohol users experience reduced coordination of motor skills, reduced anxiety and inhibitions, and euphoria. Outside of the stimulant effects, alcohol serves as a depressant, similar to barbiturates. Alcohol is absorbed through the digestive system and makes its way into the blood before being metabolized through the liver. Alcohol is thus at its most toxic when it interacts with other drugs that also rely on the liver for metabolism. Tolerance is built as the liver becomes more accustomed to handling large amounts of alcohol.

The dangers of alcohol overuse include biological and behavioral risks. Biologically, an overworked liver and kidneys are possible from chronic heavy drinking, potentially resulting in permanent damage or failure. Central nervous system and cardiopulmonary issues, as well as gastrointestinal distress, are also prominent dangers. Alcohol overdose is potentially life threatening. An acute negative consequence of alcohol use is known as a hangover. Hangovers include flu-like symptoms such as stomachache, fatigue, headache, and dehydration. Withdrawal in cases where chronic heavy drinking is suddenly discontinued is sometimes called *abstinence syndrome*. It is potentially deadly, and includes tremors, delirium, hallucinations and seizures. In terms of behavioral risks of alcohol use, one of the most serious is driving under the influence. More than 10,000 people were killed in motor vehicle crashes involving alcohol in 2013, accounting for nearly one third of all traffic-related deaths in the United States, according to the Centers for Disease Control and Prevention.

Treatment Models

Substance use disorders are typically treated according to how each model views the etiology, or cause, for the condition. While there are many available treatments, some of the most frequent models are the abstinence or 12-step model, cognitive-behavior therapy, and motivational interviewing. Because substance use disorders co-occur frequently with other adolescent disorders, particularly with mood disorders and conduct disorder, treatments often address multiple issues together.

12-Step Model

The 12-step model was developed initially by Alcoholics Anonymous. The movement, which features local group meetings, also includes Narcotics Anonymous and has offshoots for various religions and situational settings. The underlying notions of substance use disorders in the 12-step model include that it is marked by loss of control over the substance, that the condition is incurable outside of complete and permanent abstinence, and that the addiction is the primary underlying disease. The mechanism of treatment consists of a structured regular meeting where mentoring and support are offered. Treatment follows an instructional book that is widely distributed. The 12-step model includes a focus on spirituality with the idea that a "higher power" is in control, introspection on past errors and efforts to make up for those errors, and mentoring new members. Every milestone of abstinence is celebrated. A person who is further along in terms of abstinence commonly mentors newer members, whose focus is often just to stay sober for the moment, or the day.

Cognitive-Behavioral Therapy

Cognitive-behavioral therapy (CBT) for substance use disorders focuses on identifying cognitions or thought patterns that result in the addictive behavior. Aaron Beck and David Burns are among the originators of CBT, which is based on social learning theory. Social learning theory posits that virtually all behaviors are learned. According to CBT, problematic behavior results from having been conditioned to approach a given situation ineffectively, and that thought pattern, or cognition, can be relearned. Behaviors, then, according to CBT, are a result of the thought patterns that occur prior to behaving.

Examining one's faulty thoughts and the situational triggers that occur to prompt those thoughts is sometimes taught by describing some of the cognitive distortions. For example, an adolescent who has positive interactions with everyone at school on a given day, except for one person who insulted her for her hairstyle, may arrive home focusing only on the insult and not on the more numerous positive interactions. To focus on the negative issue is called *filtering*. A teen who has decided to stop drinking alcohol makes it through most of the week, and then steals a beer from his grandparents' refrigerator. While the therapist affirms 6 days of sobriety, the teen decides he has failed—because he did not make it through the entire week—so the week was not a success. This is an example of all-or-nothing thinking. CBT is sometimes criticized for being highly prescriptive, in that the therapist tends to play a teaching role at times, and for a supposed assumption that simply knowing and thinking will lead to behavior change. Proponents of CBT tout its emphasis on empowering and reinforcing its participants with a greater sense of control over behaviors and feelings—a liberating state for the individual who previously believed feelings and behaviors were automatic.

Motivational Interviewing

Motivational interviewing, or MI, developed by William Miller and Stephen Rollnick, seeks to assist clients without using confrontation, absolute rules, or prescriptive programming. All client perspectives are fully accepted by the motivational interviewing therapist. Empathy is central to the therapist's role in MI. Intrinsic motivations are encouraged to help the client prioritize and plan personal goals. The overarching strategy followed by motivational interviewing is to continually assess the client's motivation to change, from precontemplation through action, and to acknowledge that relapse may occur. Relapse in MI is accepted, and, while not encouraged, it is acknowledged as a learning experience and a natural part of treatment.

An example of how motivational interviewing is used can be seen in the case of a client who has lost custody of his children because of chronic illicit drug use. The client would like visiting privileges and ultimately to win custody. The therapist collaborates with the client, without pushing or judging, to find out what the client holds most dear. If the client wants his children more than he wants to be intoxicated, then ambivalence has been identified: intoxication plays an important role in the client's life, but the children are more important. At this point, the client is in a position to weigh change versus no change—and this demonstrates motion. Simply considering change is considered progress. Above all, the client's autonomy is upheld, and the client decides when and how change will occur.

Treatment Outcomes

There are many types of treatment available for substance use disorders. In studies that compare multiple theoretical methods, it is often the characteristics of the therapist–client relationship that predict success. Also, among adolescents who experiment with substances and even those who experience substance use disorder symptoms, many of them simply mature out of the behaviors or stop using a substance to avoid its consequences. Focusing on career development, education, and strongly held interests among adolescents with substance use disorders is reported to be efficacious. Substance use disorders are also often tied to other mental health disorders in adolescence, and they may subside as treatment for another disorder succeeds.

Andrew M. Byrne

See also Adolescent Behavior Disorders; Adolescent Mental Health; Anxiety; Cognitive-Behavioral Family Therapy; Conduct Disorder; DSM and V-Codes; Empathy; Goals, Treatment; Mood Disorders in Adolescents; Psychoeducation; World Health Organization

Further Readings

Alcoholics Anonymous. (2001). *Alcoholics anonymous* (4th ed.). New York: A.A. World Services.

American Psychiatric Association. (2013). *Diagnostic and statistical manual of mental disorders* (5th ed.). Arlington VA: American Psychiatric Publishing.

Bachman, J. G., O'Malley, P. M., Schulenberg, J. E., Johnston, L. D., Freedman-Doan, P., & Messersmith, E. E. (2008). *The education-drug use connection: How successes and failures in school relate to adolescent smoking, drinking, drug use, and delinquency.* New York: Lawrence Erlbaum Associates/Taylor & Francis.

Beck, J. S. (2011). *Cognitive behavior therapy: Basics and beyond* (2nd ed.). New York: Guilford Press.

Hart, C., & Ksir, C. (2014). *Drugs, society, and human behavior* (16th ed.). Boston: McGraw-Hill Education.

Inaba, D. S., & Cohen, W. E. (2011). *Uppers, downers, all arounders* (7th ed.). Medford, OR: CNS Productions.

Johnston, L. D., O'Malley, P. M., Miech, R. A., Bachman, J. G., & Schulenberg, J. E. (2015). *Monitoring the future national survey results on drug use: 1975–2014: Overview, key findings on adolescent drug use.* Ann Arbor: Institute for Social Research, University of Michigan.

Miller, W. R., & Rollnick, S. (2012). *Motivational interviewing: helping people change* (3rd ed.). New York: Guilford Press.

Perkinson, R. R., Jongsma, A. E., & Bruce, T. J. (2014). *The addiction treatment planner* (5th ed.). Hoboken, NJ: Wiley.

SUICIDE

Suicide is the act of ending one's own life. In the United States, suicide is the 10th leading cause of death for all age groups, and is even higher among specific populations. Worldwide, it is reported that more than 800,000 people *die by suicide* (the more appropriate term than to "commit suicide") every year. True statistics for suicide may be even higher than those reported due to stigma surrounding the topic of suicide, which causes underreporting by families and medical professionals. This entry first discusses the spectrum of suicidality, the causes of suicide, and populations at higher risk for suicide. It then discusses methods of suicide, means of suicide prevention and intervention when people are considering suicide, and the effects on survivors of those who have died by suicide. Finally, information for counselors is presented, and directions for future research are examined.

Spectrum of Suicidality

Generally, statistics on suicide refer only to the completed act of death by suicide. When suicide is viewed on a spectrum of suicidality, including suicidal ideation (thoughts about suicide), suicidal behaviors, suicide attempts, and suicide completions, the issue becomes exponentially greater. Therefore, it may be impossible to estimate an accurate number of people affected by suicidality.

Suicidal ideation can be defined as thoughts of ending one's own life, which can be thoughts that do not reflect serious distress (e.g., "I wonder what it would be like if I weren't alive anymore," or "Would my problems go away if I just died?"), or can fall within the realm of psychological distress and psychopathology (e.g., "All I think about is ending my own life," or "I'm planning on hanging myself next Tuesday because my life is terrible.").

Suicidal behaviors are any actions an individual takes that place him or her in physical danger, with or without the specific intent to die. For example, a man might drive his car at 120 miles per hour on a narrow road, or a child might bang her head repeatedly on the ground. There is some debate in the literature on suicide as to whether some types of self-injurious behaviors, such as cutting, scratching, or burning oneself, or pulling out hair, are forms of suicidal behavior. It is important to take all self-injurious or unhealthy behaviors seriously and to seek professional help for those demonstrating suicidal behavior because it can lead to completed suicides, intended or unintended.

Suicide attempts are any actions taken to intentionally end one's life, but that do not successfully result in death. Suicide attempts may be aborted by the individual (they stopped the actions on their own before dying), interrupted by another person (e.g., a friend persuaded the individual not to take the bottle of pills, or a physician pumped the individual's stomach to save his life), or unsuccessful (e.g., the gun misfired, or the dose of pills taken turned out not to be lethal).

It may be helpful to visualize a pyramid, with suicidal ideation at the bottom and affecting the greatest number of people, suicidal behaviors and attempts in the middle, and completed suicides at the top—not rare, but affecting fewer individuals than those who had only considered suicide.

Causes

There are a variety of causes that lead people to consider suicide. Many turn to suicide due to hopelessness and difficulty coping after stressful life events. Common stressors related to suicidality include abuse (physical, emotional, or sexual) and neglect (including hunger); loss (of a special person by death, distance, or the end of a relationship; or loss of a job, power, or status position); physical illness (especially those involving chronic pain and terminal conditions); and incarceration. Others who consider suicide may struggle to manage mental illnesses (e.g., depression, posttraumatic stress disorder, schizophrenia, psychosis, anxiety disorders) or substance use disorders.

As individuals of any age can experience these stressors, it is logical to conclude that suicide is a life span issue that affects people from birth through older adulthood. While the highest suicide rates in the United States affect older adults (age groups 45 to 64, and 65 or older, with a dramatic increase over age 85), younger age groups are also affected by suicidality. Suicide is the second leading cause of death for 10- to 24-year-olds worldwide, second only to accidental injuries. Although much more rare in terms of completed suicides, infants and children under 10 years old can also experience the full spectrum of suicidality.

It is also important to remember that not everyone who faces adversity and significant life stressors will experience suicidality. Additional factors that may increase risk for suicidality include poor self-esteem, an insufficient support system, low socioeconomic status (including limited resources and limited access to services), poor or underdeveloped coping skills, a tendency to be impulsive, and having multiple stressors or holding multiple minority statuses.

Higher-Risk Populations

Certain populations are at greater risk than others for experiencing suicidality, as described in this section. Treatment providers should be diligent in screening for possible suicidality in all individuals, regardless of their group memberships.

Family History

Individuals who have a family history of suicide are at greater risk for suicidality. Individuals who have witnessed a family member's suicidality are considered to be at even higher risk, due to related trauma and possibly because they have witnessed suicidal behavior as a coping mechanism in the past.

Male Gender

Males die by suicide 4 times more frequently than females, although females attempt suicide more frequently than males do. The reason for this discrepancy is that males typically choose methods of suicide with a higher lethality (e.g., firearms, suffocation), than the methods that females choose (e.g., intentional poisoning or overdose), although women may be more outwardly expressive of emotional pain.

Racial Background

Individuals of American Indian/Alaskan Native backgrounds are at higher risk for completed suicides than individuals of any other racial background. Whites are the second most represented race in deaths by suicide. Although overall rates of completed suicide are lower among Hispanic, African American, and Asian populations, there are still within-group populations that remain at significant risk, such as Latina female adolescents.

LGBT Populations

Lesbian, gay, bisexual, and transgender (LBGT) individuals are reported to be at higher risk for suicide attempts than heterosexual individuals. The reason for this increased risk is not necessarily the identification with a minority sexuality or gender itself, but the discrimination, harassment, and rejection (and subsequent depression and related feelings) that comes from anti-LGBT sentiment.

Military Veterans

Recent research has found an elevated risk for suicide among military veterans compared to the civilian population, with one study of wartime veterans finding the highest rate among veterans who were not deployed to war zones. A U.S. Army-funded study in 2015 by Han Kang and colleagues found that previously deployed veterans had a 41% greater risk for suicide, while nondeployed veterans had a 61% greater risk.

Methods of Suicide

Methods of suicide vary slightly by age group, gender, and access to lethal means, but the three main methods of suicide by adults in the United States are firearms, suffocation (i.e., hanging), and poisoning (i.e., intentional overdose on a medication or other drug). Individuals with increased access to lethal means (e.g., residing in a household with firearms, or being easily able to obtain pills from relatives or friends) are significantly more at risk than individuals with limited or no access. Children who are suicidal may choose methods that are more accessible to them, such as running into traffic or jumping from a high place, and may use more common household or personal items for suffocation (e.g., shoelaces).

Prevention and Intervention

One primary way of preventing suicide is to build individuals' protective factors prior to the first suicidal ideation. This means that prevention should occur as early as possible in the life span. Some examples of protective factors are having a supportive family and community connections, holding cultural or religious values that exclude suicide, building positive problem-solving skills, and restricting access to lethal means. Another task of suicide prevention is to educate individuals and systems about suicide across the life span. Individuals should be proactive about seeking mental health and substance use treatment before additional stressors occur. Schools can incorporate suicide prevention training through character education in the classroom (including specific topics of suicide, building healthy social skills, and self-esteem), which has been shown to have long-term positive effects for young people. Health care professionals and law enforcement personnel may also need specific training on the risk factors and warning signs of suicidality in order to provide appropriate screening and referrals to at-risk individuals. Counties, regions, or states can make sure that all residents have access to appropriate treatment providers and medical care to address suicidality and other health problems.

Intervention strategies for suicidality range according to the immediacy of the suicidal individual's situation. All points of the suicidality spectrum should be taken seriously and acted on promptly, and in a calm fashion. In case of emergency, responders should call 911 or transport the suicidal individual to the nearest hospital. Suicidal individuals will need a full evaluation of risk across all areas of functioning. Responders should consider the safety of the suicidal individual and any family members who might also be at risk. For individuals who are not in immediate danger, there are multiple treatment options to consider. Suicidality can be considered a feeling, for which there are many causes. It is important that the treatment of suicidality match the underlying cause (for example, if the reason someone is feeling suicidal is related to a substance use disorder, then they should first seek drug or alcohol treatment), and it is essential for the individual to engage in decision-making regarding a course of treatment, if possible, to increase one's sense of empowerment and control. Some treatments may include counseling or psychotherapy (in individual, family, or group modalities), consultation with a medical doctor, psychotropic medication, or other age- and culturally appropriate interventions. In addition, the National Suicide Prevention Lifeline is a free telephone hotline at 1-800-273-TALK (8255), which provides crisis counseling and referrals to individuals considering suicide.

Survivors of Suicide

Suicide affects not only the individuals who have considered ending their lives or who have died by suicide, but all of the systems of which the individuals are or were a part as well. All family members, friends, and community members who have lost someone to suicide are considered survivors. Suicidality is an incredibly difficult matter to approach because of the taboo status that it holds in many communities and the stigma surrounding suicide. For some, mental illness and related issues are considered shameful or something to be kept secret. For others, suicide—similar to other end-of-life issues—is simply too painful to discuss. Not only do survivors face issues of grief and loss, but they also frequently have to deal with feelings of anger, doubt, guilt, and a lack of closure. In addition, the survivors are then, themselves, at increased risk for death by suicide. If not dealt with properly, suicide contagion, or the prompting of additional suicides, can result within a community.

Information for Counselors

Specific counseling approaches that have proven (through clinical trials) to be effective for treating individuals with suicidal ideation, behaviors, or attempts are cognitive-behavioral therapy (CBT) and dialectical behavior therapy (DBT). Both methods are aimed at having the individual connect feelings to behaviors, and when applied to suicidality, the individual learns to manage feelings of suicide to avoid suicidal behaviors and attempts.

Counselors are not immune from feeling the stigma and uncertainty regarding suicidality. It is important for counselors to receive comprehensive training before working with suicidal clients and to engage in clinical supervision or consultation when encountering suicidal clients on their caseload.

Research Directions

Suicide has been well-researched in the past, but there continue to be components of suicidality that have not been explored. For example, although much is known about suicide in adolescent and adult populations, little is known about suicidality in infancy through early childhood (up to age 10). Also, although certain populations have been identified as at-risk for suicidality, those populations have not yet been studied extensively to better understand the cause of the risk. Additional treatments for suicidality, such as creative therapies (art, dance, music) require additional research.

Katherine A. Shirley

See also Assessment, Suicide; Depression in Adolescents; Depression in Children; Depression in Couples and Families

Further Readings

American Foundation for Suicide Prevention. (2015). *Understanding suicide: Facts and figures.* Retrieved from https://www.afsp.org/understanding-suicide/facts-and-figures

Capuzzi, D. (Ed.). (2004) *Suicide across the life span: Implications for counselors.* Alexandria, VA: American Counseling Association.

Centers for Disease Control and Prevention. (2014, December 16). *National suicide statistics at a glance.* Retrieved from http://www.cdc.gov/violenceprevention/suicide/statistics/

Kang, H. K., Bullman, T. A., Smolenski, D. J., Skopp, N. A., Gahm, G. A., & Reger, M. A. (2015). Suicide risk among 1.3 million veterans who were on active duty during the Iraq and Afghanistan wars. *Annals of Epidemiology, 25,* 96–100. doi:http://dx.doi.org/10.1016/j.annepidem.2014.11.020

Movement Advancement Project. (2011). *Talking about suicide and LGBT individuals.* Retrieved from http://www.lgbtmap.org/effective-messaging/talking-about-suicide-and-lgbt-populations

SUPERVISION

Marriage and family therapists (MFT) in training, including those in master's or doctoral level programs and those with degrees who are working toward licensure, are required to obtain clinical supervision during their training period. Additionally, it is good practice for clinicians to seek consultation through supervision. Clinical supervision is provided by an experienced therapist, usually with an MFT license or equivalent. The supervisory relationship consists of oversight, teaching, and mentoring for a prolonged period of time. The time frame varies depending on the guidelines of the degree program or the state or province and country in which the therapist-in-training resides. This entry reviews the supervisor's training requirements, purpose of supervision, supervisory relationship, suggested formats, and common issues focused on in supervision for marriage and family therapists. The American Association for Marriage and Family Therapy (AAMFT) supervision guidelines are reviewed in detail in the entry. However, other organizations also provide guidelines for supervision, including the International Association of Marriage and Family Counselors, American Psychological Association, the American Family Therapy Academy, and the National Association of Social Workers.

Supervisor Training and Requirements

The specific training and requirements for marriage and family therapy (MFT) supervisors vary by state, province, and country. However, AAMFT provides guidelines that are nationally recognized, which include training, ethics, and maintenance of the AAMFT supervisor designation.

According to AAMFT, supervisors should complete a 30-hour supervision class focused on the fundamentals of supervision. Additionally, supervisors must provide supervision for at least 18 months while receiving mentoring (supervision of supervision) from an advanced supervisor. During this time, supervisors are required to complete a certain number of hours of supervision. As a therapist brings cases to his or her supervisor, a supervisor-in-training brings supervision cases to discuss with his or her mentor. As a part of their training, AAMFT approved supervisors write a philosophy of supervision paper outlining their model of supervision and how they focus on the supervisory relationship. Reading the philosophy of supervision paper, or requesting this information of potential supervisors, may help supervisees choose a supervisor who is a good fit for them.

In addition to receiving specific supervision training and mentorship, supervisors are required to follow local and AAMFT ethical guidelines. The AAMFT *Code of Ethics* Principle IV outlines seven ethical principles that apply specifically to supervisors. First, supervisors understand that they have influence over the supervisees and agree not to exploit them. Supervisors should discuss how they will manage this power imbalance and protect the supervisee's trust and dependency.

Second, supervisors are not allowed to provide therapy to supervisees. Third, supervisors should not engage in a sexual relationship with supervisees. Fourth, supervisors must help supervisees to understand their scope of practice and work within it. Fifth, supervisors make certain that supervisees provide professional services. Sixth, supervisees avoid supervision with people with whom they had a prior relationship. If this is unavoidable, the supervisor must work to remain objective. The seventh and final principle states that supervisors are required to maintain the supervisee's confidentiality. As in therapy, the supervisor cannot release information without written consent or if required by law. Both supervisors should review these, and local state or province ethical codes with their supervisees in an effort to be transparent and to protect the supervisee.

To renew the AAMFT supervisor designation, supervisors must reapply and take a refresher course every 5 years. In order to maintain an AAMFT supervisor designation, the supervisor must be licensed and follow the above mentioned code of ethics. It is important for supervisees to ask supervisors about their current supervisor approval to make sure they are receiving quality supervision.

Purpose of Supervision

The primary purposes for the MFT supervisory experience include mentoring, teaching, and gatekeeping or ensuring that MFTs are competent and well trained. The MFT supervisor assists the beginning therapist with his or her professional development. Supervisors and supervisees often discuss the supervisee's professional goals and how to obtain them. For example, the supervisee may talk with the supervisor about negotiating the specific licensure requirements of his or her state, province, and/or country. Furthermore, the supervisee may request help in how to talk with his or her internship site or place of employment about negotiating policies that affect work with clients.

Another goal of the supervisory relationship is to guide the supervisee in developing competence. As the supervisor reviews the supervisee's work, he or she will give suggestions, discuss theory, and help the supervisee identify additional techniques or interventions that the supervisee can use with clients. Over time, this will increase the supervisee's knowledge of and the application of MFT theory, which will increase competence as an MFT.

Last, the supervisor is responsible for monitoring the supervisee's work and acting as a gatekeeper for the profession, which makes the relationship hierarchical. The supervisor evaluates the supervisee's work informally during each supervision session and formally through completing evaluations and giving recommendations for graduation or licensure. According to the AAMFT *Code of Ethics*, the supervisor is responsible for monitoring the supervisee's professionalism and competence. Specifically, supervisors should not allow the supervisee to work beyond his or her competence, experience, or training. Additionally, they monitor and discuss the supervisee's understanding and how the supervisee is adhering to ethical guidelines. In these ways, the supervisor is responsible for monitoring the quality of the supervisee's work and thus, protecting clients.

Supervision Relationship

Because of this multilayered relationship, one in which the supervisor is a mentor, teacher, and evaluator, supervision should occur in a context that allows for open, respectful communication. Additionally, some researchers have suggested that the quality of the supervisor–supervisee relationship affects the supervisee's job satisfaction, work-related stress, and perception of effective supervision. Thus, the supervisor is responsible for helping the supervisee feel safe and respected so that the supervisee will feel comfortable discussing strengths and mistakes, trying new techniques, accepting feedback, and giving the supervisor feedback about their relationship. The supervisor and supervisee should discuss whether the supervisor's expectations and style are a good fit for that supervisee. Supervisors initiate this through negotiating a supervision contract with the supervisee. In the supervision contract, the supervisor should identify clear expectations of the supervisee, how they will be evaluated, and the consequences poor evaluations will have.

Format of Supervision

The different formats of supervision, individually or in group settings, each have advantages and disadvantages. Individual supervision allows the supervisor to focus on the supervisee without interruptions or other people to focus on. The supervisor is able to focus training on specific issues applicable to the supervisee's needs. Likewise, the supervisee is able to focus on one perspective and the client issues that feel most relevant without hearing opposing views or about other issues from the group. Additionally, having a private nurturing space may allow the supervisor to challenge the supervisee without group members observing. Similarly, the supervisee may feel more comfortable bringing up difficult issues without his or her group members present. While these may represent advantages for some, other supervisees may become too dependent on the supervisor and thus, benefit from a group supervision setting.

Group supervision allows supervisees to interact and learn from each other. Presenting cases and hearing their peers' encouragement may help the supervisee to gain confidence. Additionally, when other members are presenting, the supervisee may be exposed to other theoretical views and techniques, which promotes the supervision goal of teaching. Last, seeing multiple supervisees in a group allows supervisors to offer discounted rates to supervisees. While there are advantages and disadvantages of individual and group supervision, it is commonly thought that a combination of both leads to the best outcomes for the supervisee.

Another format that is becoming more common is electronic supervision, such as phone or online video conferencing. The AAMFT recently changed its requirements to allow electronic supervision. Additionally, many states allow supervisees to obtain a certain amount of supervision electronically. When doing supervision through any electronic means, the supervisor and supervisee must carefully follow their local laws and regulations regarding privacy and confidentiality.

Regardless of whether supervision is done individually or in a group setting, electronically or in person, supervision consists of viewing videotaped or live sessions, talking through scenarios, exploring different perspectives, and role-playing. There needs to be more research regarding the effectiveness of supervision, but the research that does exist indicates that all of the supervision activities just discussed may be effective and should be incorporated into both group and individual supervision.

Focus of Supervision

Supervisors commonly conduct supervision from a particular counseling theoretical perspective, such as solution-focused, psycho-dynamic, experiential, and feminist family therapy. For example, a solution-focused supervisor might focus on identifying the supervisee's strengths, listening for and highlighting concerns, and encouraging the supervisee to continue doing what is working. Regardless of the supervision theory used, there are common issues frequently focused on in supervision, such as cultural competency, countertransference, and isomorphism.

Cultural Competency

Discussing cultural issues in supervision helps supervisees to be more conscious of cultural issues, which increases their therapeutic competence, and enhances the supervision relationship. On the other hand, when supervisors are not culturally sensitive and do not discuss cultural issues in supervision, the supervisory relationship may be negatively impacted. For example, supervisees may not self-disclose as much, which may negatively impact therapy. Thus, it is important for supervisees to address cultural issues as they arise and set aside time for critical conversations about culture.

Countertransference

Countertransference is the therapist's reactions to the characteristics or experiences of his or her clients. This may be noticeable in the supervisee's attitudes, judgments, and feelings about his or her clients. It is important for the supervisee to listen for countertransference, as it may be something the supervisee is not aware of. When the supervisor suspects this may be an issue, he or she can point out the behavior or comments to the supervisee. The supervisee and supervisor should have an open conversation about what these behaviors or comments mean. Becoming aware of these issues can help the supervisee recognize personal issues to be addressed. Additionally, he or she can develop a plan with the supervisor about how to interact with and support clients. These conversations can help the supervisee assure that countertransference enhances rather than interferes with therapy.

Isomorphism

It is commonly believed that supervision is an isomorphic process to therapy—in other words, that there is a parallel or similar process between therapy and supervision. Thus, the dynamics that occur between the therapist and client may be replicated in the supervisor–supervisee relationship. It is important for both the supervisee and supervisor to be aware of how they are feeling and the dynamics between them. Discussing this awareness can give them insight into what is going on between the supervisee/therapist and client. For example, if the supervisor is feeling bored when the supervisee is discussing a particular client, it may be that the supervisee is also feeling bored in session. Talking about these issues may lead to invaluable discussions about what is going on in the therapy session and how to better help clients.

Vanieca I. Kraus

See also American Association for Marriage and Family Therapy; Isomorphism; Live Supervision; Supervision of Supervision; Supervision Theories

Further Readings

American Association for Marriage and Family Therapy. (2012, July). *Code of ethics.* Retrieved from http://www.aamft.org/iMIS15/AAMFT/Content/Legal_Ethics/Code_of_Ethics.aspx

American Association for Marriage and Family Therapy. (2014, January). *Approved supervision designation: Standards handbook.* Retrieved from http://www.aamft.org/iMIS15/AAMFT/Content/Supervision/AS_Designation.aspx

Celano, M. P., Smith, C. O., & Kaslow, N. (2010). A competency-based approach to couple and family therapy supervision. *Psychotherapy Theory, Research, Practice, Training, 47,* 35–44. doi:10.1037/a0018845

Falender, C. A., Shafranske, E. P., & Ofek, A. (2014). Competent clinical supervision: Emerging effective practices. *Counselling Psychology Quarterly, 27,* 393–408. doi:10.1080/09515070.2014.934785

Garcia, M., Kosutic, I., McDowell, T., & Anderson, S. A. (2009). Raising critical consciousness in family therapy supervision. *Journal of Feminist Family Therapy, 21,* 18–38. doi:10.1080/08952830802683673

Gehlert, K. M., Pinke, J., & Segal, R. (2013). A trainee's guide to conceptualizing countertransference in marriage and family therapy supervision. *The Family Journal, 22,* 7–16. doi:10.1177/1066480713504894

Lee, R. E., & Nelson, T. S. (2014). *The contemporary relational supervisor.* New York: Routledge.

Storm, C. L., Todd, T. C., Sprenkle, D. H., & Morgan, M. M. (2001). Gaps between MFT supervision assumptions and common practice: Suggested best practices. *Journal of Marital and Family Therapy, 27,* 227–239. doi:10.1111/j.1752-0606.2001.tb01159.x

Todd, T. C., & Storm, C. L. (Eds.). (1997). *The complete systemic supervisor: Context, philosophy, and pragmatics.* Needham Heights, MA: Allyn & Bacon.

Supervision, Approved Supervisor in Marriage and Family Therapy

The American Association of Marriage and Family Therapy (AAMFT) offers an approved supervisor designation. Supervision by a more experienced member of the mental health profession is often required by state licensing boards, but most other mental health professions do not have a separate process for achieving a specialized supervisor designation. AAMFT requires a professional identity as a marriage and family therapist (MFT), specialized training, and supervision experience. At the core of the MFT identity is being a systemic thinker (one who thinks in terms of relationships, patterns, and mutual influence) who practices therapy using systemic theories. Systemic theories incorporate the belief that the clinician perceives clients as part of a system, where they affect and are affected by all other persons in their systems, be that marital family, family of origin, school, friends, work, or general society. The best work occurs when the most influential people are involved in the therapy with an individual client; therefore change occurs in the system, which is longer lasting than behavioral change in the individual. In this entry the requirements for becoming an AAMFT approved supervisor are reviewed.

Prerequisites

There are many requirements that an MFT must abide by in order to become an AAMFT approved supervisor. Primarily, one must have a minimum of 3 years of experience as an MFT. To be an AAMFT approved supervisor, one must follow the AAMFT *Code of Ethics* and be an AAMFT clinical member or be offered membership by AAMFT due to qualifications that were met, to include 2 years of clinical experience as an MFT. In order to become eligible for the supervisor candidate designation, the MFT must have a master's degree in marriage and family therapy or a closely related mental health field, such as social work, mental health counseling, or psychology, or have completed 2 years of a doctoral degree in marriage and family therapy.

A supervision candidate must complete a 30-hour marriage and family supervision fundamentals course provided by AAMFT. The completion of this fundamentals course requires a philosophy of supervision paper, which is reviewed by the course instructor. As a supervisor candidate, one must have an AAMFT approved supervisor mentor, who provides 36 hours of supervision over a minimum of 18 months. During this supervision period, the supervision candidate provides 180 hours of supervision to at least two MFT interns, each for a time period of at least 9 months.

Throughout Supervision

Supervision with an approved supervisor mentor begins with a supervision contract. Supervision contracts are essential in providing expectations for supervision as well as an opportunity to inform supervisees about the supervisor's obligations and background. Contracts inform supervisees that the approved supervisor mentor is a systemic supervisor, bound by the AAMFT *Code of Ethics*, and the evaluation of performance would use the tenets of the systemic theories. This is also an example of isomorphism, as the approved supervisor mentors demonstrate for the supervision candidates the relationship and curiosity they should have for their supervisees.

During the supervision period, the approved supervisor mentor provides supervision to the supervisor candidate, at the same time the supervisor candidate supervises other MFT interns, who have a caseload of clients. It is important to clarify that the supervisor candidate is receiving the same level of supervision as the MFT Intern. To carry the concept of isomorphism further, any tension that occurs in the supervisor–supervisee relationship will also present itself in the counselor–client relationship. A difference to note is that the approved supervisor mentor is not providing therapy to the supervisor candidate, who in turn is not providing therapy to the MFT intern, or to the MFT intern's clients. However, the primary responsibility of the supervisor is the confidentiality and autonomy of the clients of the MFT intern.

Supervisor candidates present their cases to the approved supervisor in a variety of modalities. One type of modality is case presentation, which is a discussion of the cases that the supervisor candidate has reviewed with the MFT intern.

Another modality is video recorded supervision, where the supervisor candidate records sessions with the MFT intern and plays the clips during supervision with the approved supervisor in order to receive feedback. A third modality is the live supervision approach, in which the supervisor candidate invites the MFT intern to the supervision session with the approved supervisor. The approved supervisor then conducts supervision at the same time as the supervisor candidate provides supervision to the MFT intern.

The approved supervisor is responsible for taking notes of the supervision sessions; the supervisor candidates have the same responsibility with the MFT interns' supervision sessions. The MFT interns as well as the supervisor candidates have the responsibility of keeping a log of supervision hours, which their respective supervisors must sign, in order to submit the final paperwork to the state licensure board as well as AAMFT.

Conclusion of Supervision

At the end of the 36 hours of supervision, there is an evaluation process of the supervisor candidate. The approved supervisor evaluates many aspects of the supervisor candidate's growth. The supervisor candidate must be familiar with the major models of marriage and family therapy and supervision, and one must demonstrate a personal model of supervision. The supervisor candidate must facilitate the evolving therapist–client and supervisor–therapist–client relationships, as well as be able to evaluate and identify problems in those respective relationships. The supervisor candidate must demonstrate sensitivity to culture, gender, ethnicity, and economics, as well as ethical and legal issues of supervision. The approved supervisor determines whether the supervisor candidate has completed all of the necessary requirements of AAMFT as well as the state licensure board, and at the same time determines the readiness of the supervisor candidate to succeed in the MFT field as a supervisor. The final step for the supervisor candidate to become an AAMFT approved supervisor is to submit the application to AAMFT once the requirements have been met.

In order to remain current as an approved supervisor, one must maintain the MFT license. The AAMFT approved supervisor designation lasts for 5 years and must be updated each year when AAMFT dues are paid. At the end of the 5-year period, the approved supervisor may renew the designation by taking a 5-hour approved supervisor refresher course. If the approved supervisor remains current with state licensure requirements and continuing education, the designation of AAMFT approved supervisor may be sustained throughout one's career.

Julie Martin

See also Supervision, Developmental Model; Supervision, Gatekeeping; Supervision Contract; Supervision Philosophy Statement; Supervision Theories

Further Readings

American Association of Marriage and Family Therapy. (2015). *Code of ethics*. Alexandria, VA: Author.

Bernard, J., & Goodyear, R. (2004). *Fundamentals of clinical supervision* (3rd ed.). Boston: Pearson.

Corey, G. (2009). *Theory and practice of counseling and psychotherapy* (8th ed.). Belmont, CA: Thomson Brooks/Cole.

Council for Accreditation of Counseling and Related Educational Programs (CACREP). (2016). *2016 accreditation standards*. Retrieved from http://www.cacrep.org.

Lee, R. E., & Everett, C. A. (2004). *The integrative family therapy supervisor*. New York: Brunner-Routledge.

Nichols, M. P., & Schwartz, R. C. (2005). *The essentials of family therapy* (2nd ed.). Boston: Pearson.

Storm, C. L., & Todd, T. (2003). *The reasonably complete systemic supervisor resource guide*. Lincoln, NE: iUniverse.

Supervision, Developmental Model

The developmental model of supervision is based on the premise that supervisees follow a pattern of growth throughout the supervision process. As the supervisor provides feedback and support, the supervisee progresses from one level to the next. Therefore, the relationship between the supervisor and supervisee is paramount to the development of the supervisee. From among the various models of supervision, Cal Stoltenberg and Ursula Delworth's developmental model highlights how the supervisor guides the supervisee through the levels of supervision and eight growth areas. The developmental model of supervision is particularly relevant to counseling families because it outlines a growth process for both the supervisor and supervisee that can be used to facilitate the growth process for families as well. This entry focuses on the levels of supervision and the integrated processes that are essential to development, and provides a description of each of the eight growth areas in Stoltenberg and Delworth's model.

Levels of Supervision

According to Stoltenberg and Delworth, there are three levels of supervision: beginning, intermediate, and advanced. The beginning level is marked by the supervisee's dependence on the supervisor for support in diagnosing and developing treatment plans for clients. During this level of supervision, the supervisor gains an understanding of how best to support the supervisee through additional instruction. The supervisor may provide support to the supervisee through the role of counselor or teacher, helping the supervisee to process any discomfort or uncertainty about the work. The supervisor role is important, as the supervisee at this level is typically anxious about being a counselor, focused more on skills than on the client, and is anxious about receiving feedback from the supervisor. The beginning level of supervision lasts until the supervisee becomes more comfortable and confident providing services to clients.

In the intermediate level of supervision, the supervisee is less dependent on the supervisor to help with diagnosis and treatment planning. Although the supervisee may request guidance when working with clients who may be more challenging to support, the tendency of the supervisee at this level is to resist feedback from the supervisor about any other clients. As a result, it is during this intermediate level of supervision that conflict is most likely to occur between the supervisor and supervisee. The supervisee is typically more empathetic toward the client, yet struggling to balance self-awareness with how best to provide support. The supervisee may ask the supervisor for help, yet make more decisions independently. The role of the supervisor at this level is to help the supervisee work through any resistance to feedback by continuing to provide information that will help to build supervisee competence. Supervisor feedback to the supervisee also helps ensure that the clients receive quality mental health services. The intermediate level of supervision lasts until the supervisee can receive supervisor feedback without resistance and work with clients with less difficulty.

In the advanced and final level of supervision, the supervisee works more independently with clients. The supervisor remains available for support when needed, though the supervisee works with more confidence and takes more responsibility for decisions made. The supervisee is typically highly self-aware and is able to focus more on the needs of the client. It is important at this level of supervision that the supervisor review the supervision contract to determine if there are additional goals to meet. At the advanced level, the supervisee may ask the supervisee if additional supervision is needed. If more supervision sessions are required, the supervisor and supervisee would discuss the purpose and process of an ongoing relationship. Once it is agreed that the supervisee has met the goals outlined in the contract, the supervisory relationship may be terminated. At the conclusion of these levels of supervision, also known as integration, the supervisee demonstrates a high level of self-confidence, awareness, and a personal counseling style.

Growth Areas

Stoltenberg and Delworth highlighted eight growth areas as part of the developmental model of supervision. These growth areas are designed to help the supervisee self-identify strengths. The eight areas are interventions skill competence, assessment techniques, interpersonal assessment, client conceptualization, individual difference, theoretical orientation, treatment goals and plans, and professional ethics. While this list is not meant to be exhaustive of every strength that a supervisee may possess, it is representative of those strengths that are significant for the competent clinician. Ideally, if a supervisee develops strengths in all eight areas, there is an increased chance that quality mental health services will be provided.

Interventions Skills Competence

The clinical use of techniques to promote desirable change for a client promotes intervention skills competence. A supervisor may suggest an intervention such as role-playing, for example, in order to increase the proficiency of the supervisee. When a supervisee is able to demonstrate that the level of skill continues to increase, it is an indicator of competence as well as a progression toward termination of the supervisory relationship.

Assessment Techniques

Assessment techniques are strategies used to determine areas of capacity and competence. Whether used formally or informally, these strategies are designed for use by the supervisor who has been trained in the proper use of the techniques. The supervisee can use questioning, for example, to assess client preparedness to engage in the counseling process.

Interpersonal Assessment

Strategies used to analyze and understand the relationship between the counselor and client, or interpersonal assessments, can be useful in the counseling relationship. Though different theories approach the process of building the counselor–client relationship in different ways, most theories place high value on its importance. The supervisee who builds competence in using interpersonal assessments has an increased chance of strengthening the relationship with the client, therefore increasing the probability of change for the client.

Client Conceptualization

An integrative and comprehensive way of understanding the whole client is referred to as client conceptualization. In consideration of client wellness, it is imperative that the supervisee take into consideration several aspects of the client's complex world. Client social support, finances, morals/values, and education, for example, are all factors that help shape individual personality and therefore are critical to understanding client behavior.

Individual Differences

Knowledge and understanding that every client brings unique experiences (or individual differences) to the counseling relationship is an important factor in building supervisee competence. The supervisee who is aware that each client is different and who is careful to respect those differences will be better able to support client goals. Critical to the supervisory relationship is an open dialogue about any supervisee biases, assumptions, or prejudices that may impact the quality of treatment for the client.

Theoretical Orientation

The framework used to guide clinical intervention, or the theoretical orientation of the supervisee, may not be determined at the onset of supervision. Often it is during the supervisory relationship that the supervisee chooses a theoretical orientation that best aligns with beliefs about client problems and the process of change. In the developmental model of supervision, theory selection is a typical and expected part of the growth process for the supervisee. While it is not expected that the supervisee discuss theory with the client, some aspects of the theoretical orientation would be discussed in supervision for the purpose of guiding and supporting the supervisee.

Treatment Goals and Plans

Treatment goals or plans are detailed outlines for achieving client-driven outcomes in therapy. Treatment plans have been called the blueprint of the counseling relationship. Without a plan, it may be difficult to determine how best to support the client. Supervisees use treatment goals on an ongoing basis throughout the counseling relationship to determine client progress. Supervisors use client treatment plans during supervision to help support the work of the supervisee.

Professional Ethics

Standards for the provision of mental health services, including but not limited to the assessment and treatment of clients, are part of professional ethics. In the counseling field, these ethics are outlined by the American Counseling Association (ACA). The ACA created the *Code of Ethics* so that counselors have clear guidelines to govern clinical work. As the supervisee becomes more familiar with professional ethics, the need for supervisory support in that area may decrease.

Conclusion

Supervisee growth is an important part of the supervision process. According to the developmental model of supervision, the primary role of the supervisor is to provide support and feedback in order to help the supervisee move from one level of development to the next. The three levels of supervision (beginning, intermediate, and advanced) along with integrated processes are all part of Cal Stoltenberg and Ursula Delworth's developmental model. As the supervisee moves through the developmental process of supervision, there are eight areas in which growth should become evident: intervention skills competence, assessment techniques, interpersonal assessment, client conceptualization, individual difference, theoretical orientation, treatment goals and plans, and professional ethics. When a supervisee is able to accept feedback from the supervisor, move through the levels of supervision, and experience growth, the supervisee experiences a higher level of confidence that can have a profound impact on the quality of mental health services provided.

Camille Y. Humes

See also Supervision Theories; Supervision Contract; Supervision; Supervision, Approved Supervisor in MFT; Supervision Philosophy Statement; Supervision Gatekeeping

Further Readings

Bernard, J. M., & Goodyear, R. K. (2013). *Fundamentals of clinical supervision* (5th ed.). Boston: Pearson.

Falender, C. A., & Shafranske, E. P. (2004). *Clinical supervision: A competency-based approach*. Washington, DC: American Psychological Association.

Haynes, R., Corey, G., & Moulton, P. (2003). *Clinical supervision in the helping professions: A practical guide*. Pacific Grove, CA: Brooks/Cole.

Jensen, M. J., McAuliffe, G. J., & Seay, R. (2015). Developmental level as a predictor of counseling skills. *The Journal of Counselor Preparation and Supervision, 7*(1). doi.org/10.7729/71.1065

Ronnestad, M. H., & Skovholt, T. M. (2003). The journey of the counselor and therapist: Research findings and perspectives on professional development. *Journal of Career Development, 30,* 5–44.

Stoltenberg, C. D., McNeill, B., & Delworth, U. (1998). *IDM supervision: An integrated developmental model for supervising counselors and therapists*. San Francisco: Jossey-Bass.

SUPERVISION, GATEKEEPING

In the fields of couples and family therapy, counseling, and counselor education, gatekeeping is an essential ethical duty of site and faculty supervisors, licensure boards, and colleagues. This may include restricting access to training, licensure, and employment, dependent upon the degree to which the behaviors, attitudes, or beliefs of the counselor or counselor in training warrant concern. Gatekeeping strategies and duties may be employed at any point before or after counselor training, including during the training admissions process up through the point of licensure renewal for seasoned professionals.

There exists no specified standard regarding gatekeeping protocols and procedures in counseling and therapy, though there are some commonly used strategies that might be employed at different training and professional junctures. Ultimately, it is left up to training programs, employers and colleagues, professional organizations, and licensure boards to develop their own gatekeeping guidelines and procedures. This entry examines gatekeeping during the admissions, training, and posttraining periods and considers some of the challenges associated with gatekeeping across the profession.

Gatekeeping During Admissions

The application and admissions process in training programs often provides the first opportunity that educators have to engage in gatekeeping practices. This might be accomplished through rigorous interviews, academic standards, or essays. Generally, focusing on opportunities to measure the dispositions of potential trainees, as well as their likeliness for interpersonal and academic success in a counselor training program, are emphasized. Fields of counselor education, therapist education, and other similar mental health professions have engaged in lengthy discussion regarding the ethics of using personality assessments, such as the Minnesota Multiphasic Personality Inventory, as admissions screening tools. At the time of this publication, those instruments are not being widely used in counselor education or marriage and family therapy program admissions. Upon admission, programs may require potential students to sign retention documents that outline expectations regarding performance, behaviors, and traits that students are expected to maintain during the training program.

Gatekeeping During Training

Gatekeeping concerns arise not infrequently in counselor and therapist training programs. The concerns are often noted in relation to problematic behaviors, attitudes, or beliefs exhibited by counseling trainees, either in the academic setting or during field placement experiences. In defining those as "problematic," codes of ethics as well as other training standards may be used. Examples might include violation of the American Counseling Association (ACA), American Association for Marriage and Family Therapy (AAMFT), or other codes of ethics, negative reactions to feedback, inability or unwillingness to integrate feedback, ineffective or inconsistent application of core and advanced counseling skills, poor emotional regulation, interpersonal concerns with peers, faculty, or site supervisors, and more. Academic concerns may be more easily identified, and standards of academic performance are often set in place by the institution as well as by the program, and academic concerns may be more easily addressed than nonacademic ones.

Some programs develop minimum performance standards that are measured throughout the training program and are linked to retention protocols. Ultimately, gatekeeping concerns regarding student performance may result in remediation, suspension, or dismissal from the training program.

Gatekeeping Posttraining

Gatekeeping duties exist for professional counselors, and therapists, throughout their career. As supervisors, gatekeeping procedures may be more formal than between colleagues; whether supervision is linked to a training program or private (i.e., postgraduation) agreement, clarification of performance expectations between supervisor and supervisee is advised. From a collegial standpoint, it is the ethical duty of all counselors and marriage and family therapists to note when other professionals' traits or behaviors may warrant concern and to take action accordingly. Dependent upon the gravity of the situation, practitioners may address their colleagues' concerns directly or via reports to the appropriate ethical and licensure boards.

License and ethics boards also have a duty to gatekeep on behalf of the field of counseling and therapy. As with training programs, there is not a widely accepted standard of gatekeeping for licensure boards. Some boards require background checks and the signing of statements of professionalism while others require supervisors' endorsement. Many boards perform random audits to ensure that licensed professionals are keeping up with minimum continuing education standards as a requirement of continued licensure.

Ethics boards, such as those of the ACA and AAMFT, have procedures in place to address reported violations of ethics. Through these rigorous procedures, investigation of the reports, statements by the accused professional, and potentially statements of support will be gathered. If complaints are found warranted, this may result in remediation (e.g., specific education requirements), suspension, or permanent revocation of professional membership. As some licensing agencies require disclosure of ethical complaints, this may also have an impact on the professional's continued licensure eligibility. It is important to note that legal complaints against a professional do not automatically result in sanctions by the licensure board or ethics committees, or vice versa.

Gatekeeping Challenges

The lack of consensus regarding specific gatekeeping standards and measures may pose a challenge to gatekeepers, especially if they find themselves in uncharted waters with regard to gatekeeping concerns. In addition, the fear of legal retaliation may lead educators and supervisors to be overly cautious when it comes to gatekeeping—especially surrounding suspension or removal from training programs. Sensitivity to issues of discrimination and privacy rights have been impactful on the programs' decisions to forgo the use of clinical personality inventories in screening and selection of training candidates. Legal consultation is recommended, if not mandatory, in addressing significant gatekeeping concerns, regardless of the professional role of the gatekeeper.

Ann M. McCaughan

See also Supervision, Developmental Model; Supervision, Individual and Group; Supervision Contract

Further Readings

Frame, M. W., & Stevens-Smith, P. (1995). Out of harm's way: Enhancing monitoring and dismissal processes in counselor education programs. *Counselor Education & Supervision, 35*, 118–129.

Homrich, A. M., DeLorenzi, L. D., Bloom, Z. D., & Godbee, B. (2014). Making the case for standards of conduct in clinical training. *Counselor Education & Supervision, 53*(2), 126–144.

Lumadue, C., & Duffey, T. (1999). The role of graduate programs as gatekeepers: A model for evaluating student counselor competence. *Counselor Education & Supervision, 39,* 101–109.

McAdams, C.R., & Foster, V.A. (2007). A guide to just and fair remediation of counseling students with professional performance deficiencies. *Counselor Education & Supervision, 47,* 2–13.

McCaughan, A. M., & Hill, N. R. (2015). The gatekeeping imperative in counselor education admission protocols: The criticality of personal qualities. *International Journal for the Advancement of Counselling, 37*(1), 28–40.

Ziomek-Daigle, J., & Christensen, T. M. (2010). An emergent theory of gatekeeping practices in counselor education. *Journal of Counseling & Development, 88*(4), 407–415.

Supervision, Individual and Group

Supervision is a process that involves gatekeeping, mentoring, remediation, and training from an experienced professional with a clinician-in-training or a less experienced professional. The American Counseling Association (ACA) 2014 *Code of Ethics* provides a framework for ethical and legal practice for supervisors and supervisees with the intent to protect the client and ensure training and skill development for counseling trainees. The Council for Accreditation of Counseling and Related Programs (CACREP) and the Commission of Accreditation of Marriage and Family Therapy Education (COAMFTE) have standards outlining graduate program training requirements for those wanting to become marital, couple, and family counselors/therapists. As part of that training, students are required to work with clients under supervision. In addition, professional licensure requires continued supervision for a designated period of time or until certain requirements are met. Supervisors are trained professionals who are tasked with mentoring clinicians-in-training and serving as gatekeepers to the mental health profession. Two important formats that are used to prepare counselors-in-training include individual supervision and group supervision. Selecting one over the other format depends on the supervisor training, preference, accreditation requirements, and licensing requirements. This entry provides a brief overview of both individual and group supervision.

Individual Supervision

Individual supervision occurs when a supervisor meets with one (dyadic) or two (triadic) supervisees at a time. While in training students are required to meet with a supervisor once a week for 50 minutes. The supervisor will discuss a variety of topics with supervisees. This includes but is not limited to client cases, agency rules, ethical and legal issues, supervisee development, how to apply models and interventions to particular presenting problems, and documentation/paperwork.

As with working with clients, the first step is to build rapport between supervisor and supervisee and discuss expectations for the process of supervision. The expectations for supervision can be discussed informally or written up formally in a supervision contract. Part of the process of supervision may be influenced by the supervision model of the supervisor. Depending on the model, the supervisor may emphasize supervisee development, strengths, experiences and feelings, thoughts and behaviors, or psychoeducation.

The content of supervision may be based on various forms of content. In the field of marriage and family therapy, the content is generically divided into "live" and "dead" supervision. Live supervision is based on direct observation of supervisee/client sessions or video/audio recordings. Dead supervision is based on anything that is not live (e.g., supervisees' verbal description of cases, journaling, transcription of cases, case notes, or treatment plans). Case conceptualizations are used to identify client personal information history and presenting issues; audio/video recordings are used to evaluate the supervisees' counseling skills and provide feedback; journaling can serve as a reflective piece and provide insight to the supervisees' thoughts and processes; and transcriptions are self-evaluation tools that offer the supervisee another perspective into his or her counseling skills.

While supervision is meant to help safeguard the rights and needs of clients with clinicians-in-training, it is also meant to support and train the supervisee. When meeting individually with a supervisee, the thoughts, feelings, behaviors, and needs of the supervisee can take priority in supervision. If there is only supervisor and one supervisee in the session, then limited confidentiality can be maintained, helping create a safe and supportive environment for the supervisee. There are limitations to confidentiality if the supervisee reports doing something unethical, illegal, or has other issues that seem to impede his or her progress toward becoming a mental health professional.

Group Supervision

Group supervision is a method whereby one supervisor meets with three or more supervisees at the same time to discuss client cases, provide skills feedback, and share experiences and ideas. Group supervision typically includes between three and six supervisees and one supervisor and is usually 1.5 hours every week or 3 hours every other week. The supervisor is responsible for building rapport and developing a good working alliance with all of the supervisees. Because supervisees are in a group, they may not feel as comfortable sharing sensitive or private information. In addition, the supervisor cannot guarantee confidentiality when there is more than one supervisee present. While the supervisee may not be able to spend as much time with each supervisee in the group format, there are advantages to being in a group.

Group supervision allows the supervisor to provide information and feedback to individual supervisees, while also allowing the supervisor to facilitate a group process among the supervisees. The other supervisees can be another source of learning and support. They can empathize with one another, learn from each other's cases and experiences, and provide feedback to one another. They share and receive feedback from not only the supervisor but also their peers. As in individual supervision, group supervision can be live or dead. When a group does live supervision by watching a case as it is being conducted, they may work as a team on a case.

Using Technology With Individual and Group Supervision

Current trends in supervision include the use of technology for individual and group supervision. For example, supervisors can use a "bug-in-the-ear" to guide supervisees during live supervision. The supervisee has a small earpiece, and the supervisor can speak to the supervisee and offer directives while the supervisee is in session with clients. In addition, some graduate programs offer online supervision or online supervision courses. These online modes can be asynchronous and synchronous supervision. Supervisors can use web cameras to do individual supervision. In addition, supervisees can attend group supervision via a computer and participate in the session with their peers to process cases and give and receive feedback.

Belinda J. Lopez

See also Clinician-Directed, Solution-Focused Supervision; Supervision, Developmental Model; Supervision, Gatekeeping; Supervision Contract; Supervision of Supervision; Supervision Philosophy Statement

Further Readings

American Counseling Association. (2014). *ACA code of ethics.* Alexandria, VA: Author.

Bernard, J. M., & Goodyear, R. K. (2014). *Fundamentals of clinical supervision.* Upper Saddle River, NJ: Pearson.

Borders, L. D., Welfare, L. E., Greason, P. B., Paladino, D. A., Mobley, K., Villalba, J. A., & Wester, K. L. (2012). Individual and triadic and group: Supervisee and supervisor perceptions of each modality. *Counselor Education and Supervision, 51,* 281–295.

Coker, J. K., & Schooley, A. (2009). Investigating the effectiveness of a clinical supervision in a CACREP accredited online counseling program. In *Ideas and research you can use: VISTAS 2012.* Retrieved from https://www.counseling.org/resources/library/vistas/vistas12/Article_42.pdf

Council for Accreditation of Counseling and Related Educational Programs. (2009). *2009 standards.* Retrieved from http://www.cacrep.org/doc/2009%20Standards.pdf

SUPERVISION CONTRACT

Mental health fields require trainees and new professionals to see clients under the supervision of a more experienced professional or one who is specifically trained in supervision. A supervision contract is a document designed to establish the parameters of a supervisory relationship. It is created as an individualized learning plan for the supervisee. The contract is written by the supervisor and is typically presented to the supervisee before or during the first supervision meeting. It is during the first or second meeting that the contract is reviewed, discussed, and modified if necessary. The supervisee has the opportunity to ask questions and gain clarity about the contract before agreeing to the terms outlined in the document. When both the supervisor and supervisee are in agreement about the terms of the contract, it is signed by both parties, and they each receive a copy for their records. This entry provides a rationale for the use of a supervision contract and concludes with a general overview of the content of a supervision contract.

Rationale for a Supervision Contract

A supervision contract is a document that specifically outlines the components of the supervisory relationship. It is important that both the supervisor and supervisee agree to the terms of the relationship prior to beginning supervision. A supervision contract is useful to the supervisor because it establishes guidelines regarding communication and the nature of support to the supervisee. The contract makes clear to the supervisor some of the professional obligations of supervision that are guided by certain institutions, organizations, and licensing boards. The supervisee can use the supervision contract to gain clarity about the supervisory process and supervisor expectations. Like the supervisor, the supervisee can refer to the contract to learn about professional obligations when working with clients. Though the contents of a supervision contract can vary, there are standard components that establish a foundation for the supervisory relationship.

Content of a Supervision Contract

Supervision contracts cover several areas of the supervisory relationship. These areas include but are not limited to supervisor qualifications, goals of supervision, supervision schedule, supervisor and supervisee responsibilities, an evaluation plan, communication, and confidentiality. Each part of the contract is developed based on the supervisor's experience, the supervisee's needs, and the standards of the profession.

In a supervision contract, the qualifications of the supervisor are briefly defined, including any pertinent information about years of supervision experience, counseling licensure, and other credentials. While the qualifications section is not written like a biography, it should provide an overview of the supervisor's professional experiences and accomplishments. It is in the qualifications section that the supervisor may also list any current professional goals or projects.

The goals of supervision are summarized so that the supervisee is clear about the expected outcomes of the supervisory relationship. Typically, the goals of clinical supervision are twofold: to help develop the counseling skills of the supervisee and to ensure that the clients are protected. These goals can be modified to meet the needs of the supervisee and supervisor. The goals section of the supervision contract may also include a general statement about the supervisor's model or approach to supervision.

The supervision contract includes a schedule that is agreed upon by the supervisor and supervisee. The schedule outlines the meeting day, time, and location for supervision. This section of the contract may also include specifics about a cancellation or rescheduling policy.

The responsibilities of the supervisor and supervisee are listed in the supervision contract. The responsibilities of the supervisor may include but are not limited to completing required paperwork, meeting regularly with the supervisee, following all legal and ethical codes of conduct, and ensuring that the supervision goals are met. The responsibilities of the supervisee may include but are not limited to completing required paperwork, meeting regularly with the supervisor, following all legal and ethical codes of conduct, and meeting with the assigned client(s).

An evaluation plan for the supervisor is outlined so that the supervisee is clear about when and how the work will be assessed. In this section of the supervision contract, the method of evaluation is explained in detail. The supervisor may choose to provide verbal feedback, use a form of supervisee self-assessment, or any other method of evaluation that is deemed appropriate.

Specifics about how the supervisee can communicate with the supervisor are included in the supervision contract. The method of communication and appropriate time to communicate are defined. Emergency protocol and communication information is shared in this section as well. The supervision contract also specifies whom the supervisee can contact with any complaints about the supervisor or the supervision process.

The parameters of confidentiality are an essential part of the supervision contract. Confidentiality between the supervisor and supervisee is clearly defined according to the American Counseling Association (ACA) *Code of Ethics*. There are also clear guidelines regarding confidentiality of information between the supervisee and the clients. The supervision contract must address these guidelines, and the supervisor must ensure that the supervisee is clear about confidentiality in regard to all communication, including recordings (video and audio) and documentation.

The supervision contract is a brief but essential part of the supervisory relationship. It is critical to understanding the supervisor and supervisee roles and expectations. Though supervision contracts may vary in content, there is some basic information that should be included. As the supervision contract is the foundation of the supervisory relationship, its development is most important to supporting the learning process of the supervisee.

Camille Y. Humes

See also Supervision; Supervision, Approved Supervisor in Marriage and Family Therapy; Supervision of Supervision; Supervision Philosophy Statement; Supervision Theories

Further Readings

Bernard, J. M., & Goodyear, R. K. (2013). *Fundamentals of clinical supervision* (5th ed.). Boston: Pearson.

Campbell, J. M. (2006). *Essentials of clinical supervision.* Hoboken, NJ: Wiley.

Martin, F. A., & Cannon, W. C. (2010). *The necessity of a philosophy of clinical supervision.* Retrieved from http://counselingoutfitters.com/vistas/vistas10/Article_45.pdf

SUPERVISION OF SUPERVISION

The developmental process of a clinical supervisor has received much less attention in the field than the developmental process for mental health counselors. Supervisors tend to be viewed as competent in their ability to supervise counselors based upon their level of education, professional license, and years of experience as a counselor. The main factor that is commonly used to determine the competency of a supervisor tends to be the experience gained as a counselor. However, strong clinical skills do not equate to strong supervisory skills. Training in supervision has been shown to positively impact the competence and professional identity of supervisors. As the mental health field progresses, ethical mandates for clinical supervisors and educational training in supervision mandated by accrediting bodies will become the standard. This entry provides an introduction to the topic of supervision of clinical supervisors, as well as information on the current research in the field, identification of core skills of a supervisor, developmental stages of supervisor development, and the role of a supervisor's supervisor.

Supervision of Supervisors in Training

Current Research on Supervisor Development

Research on the supervision process of the supervisor in training (SIT) is highly limited, with much focus still on the developmental process of counselors. Many prominent researchers in the field have attempted to develop a theory of supervisor development but have fallen short in terms of empirical evidence to support the theory. Clifton Edward Watkins developed a model for supervisory development that was based on the counselor development work developed by R. A. Hogan and adopted by Cal Stoltenberg. Watkins's model identified four stages with five dimensions of supervisory growth: (1) role of supervisor, (1) affective focus of supervisor, (3) cognitive/skills focus of supervision, (4) dependency in supervision, and (5) role of support and confrontation.

Stage 1 of Watkins's model, role of the supervisor, is characterized by feelings of confusion on the supervisor's part regarding the boundaries of the supervisory role and how to exactly define what to do with supervisees. This confusion brings forth feelings of anxiety and insecurity, followed by either a withdrawal from the process or the implementation of rigid structure with supervisees.

Stage 2, role recovery and transition, allows for the regaining of realistic views of competency and the start of a sense of confidence in the supervisory role. The ambiguity that is common in supervision sessions becomes more tolerable, resulting in greater ability to work with supervisees. A Stage 2 supervisor is less anxious and more willing to take risks in supervision. This stage starts the process of supervisor identity development.

A Stage 3 supervisor has a broader concept of the supervision process, allowing for consistency and accuracy in thinking, resulting in consistent performance as a supervisor. At this stage, the supervisor views himself or herself as a competent, qualified supervisor. Progression into Stage 4 involves mastery of supervisory skills.

Identification of Core Skills of a SIT

The first step in understanding the training process of a SIT is to identify the core skills expected of a supervisor. First, supervisors are expected to know how to guide supervisees in the process of client treatment planning. This includes knowing how to conduct a diagnostic assessment, develop treatment goals and objectives, and identify how to determine the progress being made in client sessions. A large part of the treatment planning process will include a counselor's case conceptualization skills. Supervisors must have strong conceptualization skills in order foster the growth of the supervisees.

Second, SITs need to be able to help the supervisees develop a theoretical orientation. The development of a theoretical orientation includes helping the supervisees to understand who they are as a counselor and how their worldview fits in with their clinical skills. The process of learning how to guide supervisees in their own professional development is more than a "do as I do" mentality. It involves being able to identify key aspects of a supervisee's conceptualization skills and assist with aligning these perspectives to complementary theories. Often, it is necessary for a supervisor of the supervisor (SOS) to assist with the process of determining and integrating theory into practice.

It is not enough for supervisors to be effective counselors; supervisors must also be able to teach the supervisees what they know and how they know it. This developmental task can comprise a large part of the supervision process.

Another factor to consider when reviewing the supervision sessions is how to work with multicultural components of the supervisory relationship. It is critical for SITs to understand their own cultural identity and know how to discuss culture with their supervisees. This is a process of professional development as a counselor that can be a critical function of the supervisory environment. A SIT who is unable to demonstrate his or her own level of awareness and multicultural competency will struggle with this stage. An assessment of the SIT allows the SOS to assess how the SIT's cultural background may be impacting the supervisory relationships.

Furthermore, a SIT needs to understand the developmental process of becoming a competent counselor. Just because the SIT has moved through his or her own developmental process does not mean that the SIT has the awareness of the specific needs and tasks involved with counselor identity formation. SITs require psychoeducation on various developmental, social-role, and theoretically specific models pertaining to clinical supervision. This may or may not be an area of knowledge that the SIT currently possesses. As a result, an assessment of the current level of awareness that the SIT possesses regarding this area is necessary. SOSs can then work in their meetings to determine what level the SIT's supervisees are functioning at and what skills the SIT needs to integrate into his or her supervisory sessions.

It is also important to identify what characteristics beyond the demonstration of strong counseling skills are necessary for the SIT to develop. Four specific categories that can be used to determine the level of identify development and growth are competency/incompetency, autonomy/dependency, identity/identity diffusion, and self-awareness/ unawareness. The categories are complementary to Watkins's developmental theory discussed previously. SITs who possess traits such as dependency on their own supervisor show a novice level of supervisory skills and require more direction and structure. When SITs are more readily available to manage the lack of structure in their own supervision, it means a supervisor is demonstrating the movement toward a supervisor identity. The identity formation of a supervisor allows for the management of anxiety and uncertainty that is often characteristic of this role. SITs who can demonstrate the basic skills of supervision are more aware of their strengths and limitations and less likely to experience anxiety when in the role of a supervisor.

The Developmental Process of SIT

Developmental supervision models not only reference the development of a counselor, but also the development of a SIT. An example of this is Stoltenberg and Ursula Delworth's integrated developmental model (IDM) of supervision. The developmental process of a supervisor can help to identify potential areas of concern that the supervisor is encountering and provide a framework for a SIT to understand his or her current performance levels. Stoltenberg and Delworth have identified four stages of supervisory development. Level 1 SITs are characterized as dependent on their supervisors, highly motivated, mechanistic, and requiring moderate to high levels of structure. Level 2 SITs view supervision as a more complex environment and experience fluctuating motivation in their role. This level of supervisor may experience boundary issues due to the loss of objectivity with their supervisees. A Level 3 SIT is classified as having the following traits: functions autonomously, has self and supervisee awareness, differentiates boundaries and roles, is able to supervise at all times, prefers to work with Level 3 counselors. The final level is the Level 3 integrated supervisor, which is viewed as a supervisor's supervisor. After examining these levels, a SOS not only has information on what to expect of the SIT but also the skills that supervisors are expected to possess.

Specific Needs of SIT

The identification of core competencies of a supervisor and the application of identified developmental models still leaves gaps in the literature on how to effectively supervise a SIT. The reason for this gap is the continued lack of empirical evidence to support what exactly supervisors do and how they learn to do it. Much of the research in the field of training supervisors relies on research of counselor development. The question remains, "What do supervisors need?" Based on information collected in a study of supervisor development, a significant need was found in the ability for supervisors to learn how to shift from the role of a counselor to the role of a supervisor. This is best done when SITs are able to experience didactic training as well as experiential training with their own supervisees. This format allows SITs to address feelings of anxiety, lack of confidence, and skill confusion with their SOS, providing greater opportunity for skill growth.

Once a SIT is able to gain experience as a supervisor, the focus of the training sessions moves to the use of interventions in supervision. This includes the introduction to concepts such as parallel processing and developmental models. SITs also express difficulty understanding how to manage their own level of self-care and well-being. The infusion of theory into practice as a supervisor was also reported as a key task in a supervisor's development.

The Role of the SOS

The SOS acts as a supervisor and consultant to the SIT. This role is meant to be collaborative and supportive of the developmental process of the SIT. A role of a SOS is not intended to be directly involved in the process by telling the SIT what to do or giving directives on how to respond in supervision. The SOS provides the opportunity for self-reflection on the part of the SIT in order for the SIT to move along the continuum toward autonomy and increased self-confidence. The SOS provides opportunities for new ideas to be explored and also challenges the SIT to move beyond his or her comfort level, expanding the SIT's initial clinical impressions from a counselor perspective to include the dynamic of professional growth from a supervisory context.

Kimberly Duris

See also Supervision; Supervision, Developmental Model; Supervision, Individual and Group; Supervision Contract; Supervision Theories; Training and Licensure

Further Readings

Baker, S. B., Exum, H. A., & Tyler, R. E. (2002). The developmental process of clinical supervisors in training: An investigation of the supervisor complexity model. *Counselor Education and Supervision, 42,* 15–30. doi:10.1002/j.I556-6978.2002.tb01300.x

Bernard, J. M., & Goodyear, R. K. (2014). *Fundamentals of clinical supervision* (4th ed.). Upper Saddle River, NJ: Pearson.

De Stefano, J., Gazzola, N., Audet, C., & Thériault, A. (2014). Supervisors-in-training: The experience of group-format supervision-of-supervision. *Canadian Journal of Counselling and Psychotherapy, 48*(4), 409–424.

Falender, C. A., Cornish, J. A. E., Goodyear, R., Hatcher, R., Kaslow, N. J., Leventhal, G., . . . Grus, C. (2004). Defining competencies in psychology supervision: A consensus statement. *Journal of Clinical Psychology, 60*(7), 771–785. doi:10.1002/jclp.20013

Gosselin, J., Barker, K. K., Kogan, C. S., Pomerleau, M., & d'Ioro, M. P. (2015). Setting the stage for an evidence-based model of psychotherapy supervisor development in clinical psychology. *Canadian Psychology, 56*(4), 379–393.

Hogan, R. (1964). Issues and approaches in supervision. *Psychotherapy: Theory, Research, and Practice, 1,* 139–141.

Stoltenberg, C., & Delworth, U. (1987). *Supervising counselors and therapists: A developmental approach.* San Francisco: Jossey-Bass.

Watkins, C. E., Jr. (1993). Development of a psychotherapy supervisor: Concepts, assumptions, and hypotheses of the supervisor complexity model. *American Journal of Psychotherapy, 47,* 58–74.

Watkins, C. E., Jr., Schneider, L. J., Hayners, J., & Nieberding, R. (1995). Measuring psychotherapy supervisor development: An initial effort at scale development and validation. *Clinical Supervisor, 13*(1), 77–90.

Supervision Philosophy Statement

Clinical supervision is an intervention that is facilitated by a more experienced clinician to a counselor-in-training for the purpose of improving conceptualization and attending skills and building a counselor-in-training's knowledge base. A part of clinical supervision is having the supervisor possess a philosophy of supervision. The philosophy statement provides a framework by which the supervisor conducts himself or herself as a professional in and out of the supervision session. The statement contains the following elements: an articulated theoretical style, a list of professional interests, one's specific supervision style, and how feedback will be provided to the supervisee. These variables, which are discussed in further detail in the following paragraphs, act as a map to guide the supervisor.

A theoretical style assists the counselor with conceptualizing a client's problem and using techniques, within that model, to assist in moving the client toward wellness. However, counselors' theoretical styles typically flow from who they are as a person. Their values, personality traits, and the lens through which they see the world are a natural influencing factor for the theory of choice. Potential theories upon which supervisors can draw to guide their supervision process include psychotherapy models, developmental models, and social role models.

Some of the major models of psychotherapy include psychodynamic, person-centered, cognitive-behavioral, and systemic approaches. The psychodynamic school of thought believes that the therapist is the authority figure or expert. This concept transfers to the supervisor–supervisee relationship and thereby positions the supervisor as the source of knowledge. Regarding person-centered supervision, Carl Rogers indicated that the three elements of his model—genuineness, empathy, and warmth—were necessary for the client–therapist relationship as well as the supervisor–supervisee dynamic. Cognitive-behavioral supervision differs from the person-centered approach because it is concerned with the supervisee's ability to demonstrate technical mastery, while the systemic model takes into consideration the broader context of the family.

Developmental models view the supervisee as a counselor-in-training who is developing via distinct levels of professional growth. Under this model, a supervisor's philosophy would take into consideration where the supervisee may be on the growth continuum. Thus, variables such as motivation, autonomy, and awareness must be assessed to determine what specifically the supervisee needs. Motivation speaks to the supervisee's desire to develop as a professional while autonomy and awareness measure conceptualization skills, attending skills, and knowledge base.

The discrimination model is one of the social role models. One of the oldest models in supervision, it addresses three foci of supervision and three roles of the supervisor. Intervention, conceptualization, and personalization are the three foci of intervention. Intervention focuses on what the supervisee is doing within the session, conceptualization concerns itself with how the supervisee understands what is happening in the session, and personalization addresses how the supervisee creates an individual style of counseling without allowing personal issues to become a factor. Teacher, counselor, and consultant are the three roles of the supervisor. As a teacher, the supervisor passes along information the supervisee needs; as a counselor, the supervisor points out potential issues of countertransference; and as a consultant, the supervisor assists the supervisee in thinking about the client from a number of different models.

Professional interests also inform the supervisor–supervisee relationship. For instance, a supervisor with interests in spirituality, religion, group work, trauma, or recovery would evidently be a good fit for a supervisee who has similar professional interests. If a supervisee is seeking clinical training in a postgraduate context in order to work with trauma victims, choosing a supervisor with experience working with trauma victims is likewise important.

Supervision style is another component to the supervision philosophy statement. It is closely aligned with the theoretical persuasion of the supervisor. However, it also addresses areas such as personality characteristics, leadership style, work values, and learning style.

Providing feedback to supervisees is a main part of the supervision process. It enables supervisees to know what they are doing well and what areas of growth—namely, conceptualization skills, attending skills, and knowledge base—still require additional work.

Having a supervision philosophy statement is particularly important for the reasons stated previously. The philosophy statement helps a supervisee determine whether a particular supervisor is appropriate for him or her based on the professional goals set. Specifically, this is done by addressing what population the supervisee wishes to work with and who can provide that training, and how the supervisor sees the supervisor–supervisee relationship and how to best facilitate training. It is for these reasons that having a supervision philosophy statement is so crucial.

Jason K. Neill

See also Live Supervision; Supervision; Supervision, Developmental Model; Supervision, Gatekeeping; Supervision of Supervision; Supervision Contract; Supervision, Individual and Group

Further Readings

Bernard, J. M., & Goodyear, R. K. (2009). *Fundamentals of clinical supervision* (4th ed.). Upper Saddle River, NJ: Pearson.

Campbell, J. M. (2000). *Becoming an effective supervisor: A workbook for counselors and psychotherapists.* New York: Routledge.

Campbell, J. M. (2006). *Essentials of clinical supervision.* Hoboken, NJ: Wiley.

SUPERVISION THEORIES

Clinical supervision is a process in which mental health professionals engage in a collaborative relationship with their supervisors and work to improve the skills essential to being competent, effective, and ethical practitioners. This process simultaneously serves to enhance professional functioning, monitor the quality of professional services, and serve as a gatekeeper to the profession. More specifically, clinical supervision helps to (a) ensure that clients receive acceptable care, (b) minimize harm by therapists, (c) confirm that therapists possess sufficient skills to function as therapists, and (d) engage those lacking therapeutic skills with the opportunity for remediation. First popularized in the 1920s, participation in clinical supervision is said to be positively correlated with increased clinical knowledge, improved clinical skills, an enhanced therapeutic alliance, and positive therapeutic outcomes. Further, it provides the supervisee with acculturation to the profession while simultaneously limiting direct and vicarious liability. In this entry the purpose of clinical supervision and models of supervision are reviewed.

Purpose of Clinical Supervision

Many experts within the field of counseling assert that supervision is a key component of counselor training. In fact, numerous accreditation bodies and licensure boards require participation in clinical supervision as one element of counselor training and certification. Unlike in other fields, the practice of counseling does not seem to be one that an individual may master simply by observing more-skilled practitioners within the field. Instead, research suggests that to be an effective practitioner one must not only hone his or her clinical skills but also develop reflective skills regarding self, the process of counseling, and the dynamics included within a counseling relationship.

Over the years, the purpose of clinical supervision has been widely debated. One perspective asserts that the purpose of supervision should be to serve as therapy to the supervisee in an effort to facilitate greater insight into interpersonal dynamics and guarantee optimal functioning. The other major perspective regarding clinical supervision holds that the purpose of clinical supervision should be to educate the supervisee. Most clinicians concede that the most effective supervisory relationships likely serve in both capacities to some degree, as clinical supervision is a complex and dynamic process.

Clinical supervision allows for the supervisor and supervisee to engage in a prolonged relationship that facilitates formal evaluation and enhances professional functioning. There are two main styles of supervision: that which is active and that which is reactive. Active supervision involves the supervisor asking the supervisee direct questions regarding case conceptualization, intended treatment outcomes, and proposed interventions. Additionally, the supervisor may provide the supervisee with resources, examples, and detailed answers to his or her questions. The direct approach is aimed at assisting supervisees in interpreting case dynamics and devising specific solutions to client problems or needs. Indirect supervision, on the other hand, is less facilitative. Rather than provide supervisees with direct discussion regarding case interpretations and treatment interventions, supervisors facilitate opportunities for self-reflection during which supervisees may explore practitioner dynamics and discover how their own thought processes influence clinical outcomes.

Engaging in ongoing quality supervision is not only a matter of best practice but one benchmark of minimal ethical behavior in counseling. Supervision may take place in a number of formats, including individual supervision, group supervision, team supervision, or peer supervision.

Psychotherapy-Based Models

Supervisors' approaches within supervision are typically influenced by their general theoretical orientations. While they may certainly subscribe to one technique over others, competent clinical supervisors should be familiar with a variety of models available so that they may have the skills and knowledge to meet any supervisee's needs in an effective and ethical manner. Supervision models increase supervisors' knowledge and also provide a framework to guide the supervisor in how to organize the supervisory experience as well as a lens from which to view the supervisee's learning process. Regardless of the model used, the supervisor should always adhere to mandated ethical expectations and legal requirements pertaining to the profession. Additionally, he or she should demonstrate multicultural competence and a commitment to social justice. Psychotherapy-based models of supervision include the psychodynamic model, person-centered model, behavioral model, cognitive model, constructivist model, and systems model.

Psychodynamic Model

Psychodynamic models attend to the relational dynamics that occur within the supervisory session. Supervisors who ascribe to such models typically describe supervision as a parallel process to traditional therapy, meaning that the supervisor–supervisee relationship is likely reflective of the dynamics that occur between the supervisee and client. Interpersonal dynamics are of primary importance and provide opportunities for observation to discover cognitive routines and sensory processes. A primary assumption associated with psychoanalytic-based supervision is that learning occurs through internalization. With that, the exploration of countertransference is important. It is typical within psychodynamic supervision to explore and confront the supervisee's unconscious materials, as permitted by the supervisee. Given the particularly obvious power differential within the psychodynamic supervisory relationship, it is important that the supervisee address only unconscious materials for the purpose of teaching. This is often referred to the "teach-treat" boundary.

Person-Centered Model

The person-centered supervision model recognizes the growth potential of the supervisee. The methods used by supervisors who subscribe to this model are similar to those demonstrated by those within the humanist tradition. An emphasis on facilitative conditions, including genuineness, warmth, empathy, and positive regard is said to encourage the supervisee's willingness to be open to personal discovery within the supervisory process. Carl Rogers, often referred to as the father of humanistic psychology, suggested that there should be "no clean way" to differentiate between supervision and personal therapy, as they are likely part of the same continuum. He suggested that supervision, in many ways, is likely best conceptualized as a modified clinical interview. The supervisor's role within this relationship is to (a) trust the supervisee's ability to grow and explore and (b) promote such a process. In addition to providing facilitative conditions, the person-centered supervision model also empowers the supervisee by encouraging the individual to review the transcripts of his or her work to determine patterns to address in the future.

Behavioral Model

The behavioral model of supervision holds that a counselor's functioning is the direct result of his or her learned skills. Thus, the purpose of supervision is to assess current skills, identify the need for additional skills, and to apply to the principles of conditioning to increase those skills. Typically, supervisors using this model will allow the supervisee the opportunity to engage in self-assessment and then combine peer supervision, modeling, role-play, self-management, and positive reinforcement as strategies to increase skills.

Cognitive Model

The cognitive framework of supervision suggests that perceptions, affect, and behaviors are based in one's cognitive conceptualization of the world. In this model, the purpose of supervision is to monitor interpersonal processes and to facilitate self-awareness. Cognitive supervisors tend to observe entire sessions of their supervisees with clients so that they may evaluate the structure of the session and also assess the likely accuracy of the supervisee's conceptualization of the client's case. This technique allows the supervisor insight into the supervisee's strengths and weaknesses. Using many of the techniques found in traditional cognitive-behavioral therapy, including direct instruction, guided discovery, role-playing, and responding to automatic thoughts, cognitive models of supervision allow the supervisee the opportunity to have his or her cognitive misperceptions regarding the process of counseling and specific clients challenged in a structured and supportive environment.

Cognitive supervision sessions are typically structured in a similar manner to a traditional cognitive therapy session, with a check-in, setting of an agenda, a bridge, prioritizing the agenda, discussion of difficult cases or problems, homework, a concluding summary, and the provision of feedback. Within this framework, the supervisor and supervisee collaborate to examine the supervisee's core beliefs, conditional assumptions, and coping strategies. The supervisee is provided homework to continue to build upon or increase his or her skills between sessions. When using this model, a supervisor must engage in an ongoing assessment of his or her supervisee involving conceptualizing and planning for supervision on two levels. First, the supervisor must detect and focus on client difficulties and then conceptualize and instruct in response to supervisee challenges, addressing the noted client difficulties.

Constructivist Model

Constructivist, or solution-based, supervision focuses on a supervisee's strengths and successes rather than failures. Constructivist supervision may be best described as a respectful and collaborative process between the supervisor and supervisee in which the supervisee is encouraged to be curious and increasingly autonomous. Within this framework, knowledge is cocreated within the supervisory interactions. In this role, the supervisor serves primarily as a consultant as he or she highlights the supervisee's competencies and notable achievements while simultaneously discouraging the supervisee's negative self-talk. In line with the techniques implicit in solution-based therapies, constructivist supervision makes use of scales, focused questions, constructive feedback, and looking for exceptions to aid the supervisee in discovering what is possible. Additionally, the supervisor guides the supervisee in making small achievable changes that increase competence and confidence.

Systemic Model

Systemic supervision attends to interlocking systems dynamics. Specifically, it attends to family and therapist–family interactions and repetitive interaction patterns, and focuses on stories that families tell themselves that maintain or perpetuate dysfunction. Systemic therapy supervision is unique in that it focuses on strengths and resources rather than pathology. A primary assumption of this model is that people are both capable of and invested in change. Within the systemic framework, the supervisory relationship is said to serve as a parallel process or isomorphism to therapy. Accordingly, there is an experiential focus on the here-and-now in which the therapist uses himself or herself to affect interactions as the social agent of change within the therapeutic relationship. This is replicated again within the supervision environment. The role of the supervisor is to work on multiple levels: first attending to the needs of the client while also providing parallel interventions with the counselor in an effort to encourage new behaviors while constructing new or evolving stories. One technique that is especially prominent within systemic therapy and therefore also plays an integral role within systemic supervision is that of structural mapping. This pictorial method allows supervisees to recognize the interaction patterns affecting their behaviors, including clinical work. Specifically, the use of structural mapping within supervision allows supervisees to examine the effects of their place in family of origin, previous training, and culture (including gender, age, and economic status) on their current clinical work.

Developmental Models

Psychotherapy-based models are often commended for the fact that they allow the supervisee an in-depth exposure to a single therapeutic model, which may facilitate future understanding of clients' reactions to techniques associated with that model. At the same time, however, this method of supervision may be limited in that it requires the supervisee to commit to a particular therapeutic model when he or she may not be developmentally ready to do so. Further, the divide between therapy and supervision is often unclear within these supervision strategies.

Developmental supervision models assume that supervisees' knowledge and capabilities will evolve over time as the result of experiences and reflection. Two main assumptions drive the developmental supervision models, including the understanding that supervisees move through qualitatively different stages and that each stage requires a different environment to facilitate the progression of development. Some supervisors believe the most effective supervisory relationships are those in which the supervisor's behaviors align with the supervisee's developmental needs. They suggest that as the supervisee gains experience and confidence, he or she will become less dependent on the supervisor. Accordingly, the supervisor should react by shifting from providing concrete direction to facilitating the supervisee's autonomy by allowing opportunities for self-monitoring and increased reflection.

A general view of supervisee development can be conceptualized in three stages: the stagnation stage, the confusion stage, and the integration stage. At the time of stagnation, the supervisee is unaware of his or her thinking, tends to engage in black-and-white thinking, lacks motivation, and is dependent on the supervisor. During the confusion stage, the supervisee is released from his or her previously rigid perceptions of the counseling process and may be described as more cognitively aware of the nuances associated with interpersonal interactions than in the stagnation stage. Finally, during the integration stage, the supervisee maintains a more realistic understanding of his or her skills as well as the abilities of the supervisors. This increased understanding is secondary to amplified self-awareness and results in the supervisee taking more responsibility for his or her clinical actions. Within each of these stages, there are eight professional areas to be addressed, including the following: competence, emotional awareness, autonomy, professional identity, respect for individual differences, purpose and direction, personal motivation, and ethics. It is incumbent on the supervisor to properly assess the supervisee's status on each of these main issues and to then attempt to facilitate the supervisee's progression to the next stage of development.

Integrated Developmental Model

The integrated developmental model suggests that there are three domains of development change: awareness, motivation, and autonomy. These accompany eight growth dimensions: intervention skills, assessment techniques, interpersonal assessment, client conceptualization, individual differences, theoretical orientation, treatment plans and goals, and professional ethics. Within this framework, there are three distinct levels of counselor development, where one transitions from a high level of dependence to conditional dependency. Level 1 counselors are those who are just entering the field and require the highest amount of direct observation, skills training, and assistance with case conceptualization. Level 2 supervisees typically have 1 to 2 years of postgraduate experience. Those classified at this level typically have solid technical and case conceptualization. Consequently, most supervisory efforts are aimed at addressing personal issues pertaining to self-awareness, defensiveness, transference, countertransference, and the immediate dynamics within the supervisory relationship. Level 3 supervisees are the most autonomous. They retain technical skills, conceptual abilities, and a high level of personal insight. As such, they are able to effectively identify clients' needs and aid them via clinical interventions. The supervisory relationship with a Level 3 supervisee is one best described as collegial rather than dependent. The integrated developmental model is both descriptive and prescriptive, as it describes the supervisee behaviors typical at each level of development and also suggests a number of specific interventions to help the supervisee progress to the next level. Supervisors can enable such advancement via facilitative interventions (such as the use of open-ended questions), authoritative interventions (giving advice, providing information, pointing out discrepancies, etc.), and conceptual interventions (helping to link theory to practice).

Systemic Cognitive-Developmental Model of Supervision

The systemic cognitive-developmental model of supervision states that supervisees hold one of four orientations. These orientations are (1) the sensorimotor, in which the supervisee relies on emotion or what "feels right" rather than strict clinical strategies to direct his or her work, (2) the concrete, in which supervisees tend to conceptualize the client's behavior as the consequence of a cause-and-effect interaction, (3) the formal, in which supervisees tend to consider the application of theories and are therefore very analytical, and (4) the dialectic, in which supervisees consider things broadly, but may become easily overwhelmed by challenging themselves to think further. These orientations should not be viewed as hierarchical in nature, and therefore it is not the goal to promote a supervisee from one orientation to another. Instead, the purpose of supervision is to increase the supervisee's level of flexibility, or ability to see the world from the standpoint of other orientations. That being so, the main supervisory task is to identify the supervisee's primary orientation and then mismatch it via supervisory actions to promote growth through challenge.

While developmental supervision strategies are somewhat varied in their conception of supervisee growth, the ultimate goal of all is to facilitate a change in professional identity in which the supervisee gains a sense of competence and confidence in his or her clinical abilities. The domains of autonomy, self–other awareness, and a motivation to develop skills must be addressed within each stage in a manner that allows for supervisee development.

Processed-Based Models

Process-based approaches, or social role supervision models, suggest that supervisors must assume different roles with their supervisees to facilitate clinical proficiency and professional development. The supervisor's designated role at any particular time is influenced by the supervisee's developmental stage and theoretical orientation, as well as the specific issue to be addressed within the supervisory session.

Discrimination Model

One of the most widely adopted social role models is Janine Bernard's discrimination model. The discrimination model indicates that the supervisor is to take on three complementary roles within the context of the supervisory relationship: teacher, counselor, and consultant. Within these roles, the supervisor has four main areas of focus with which he or she aids the supervisee: instruction, personalization, conceptualization, and professional behavior. In the role of teacher, the supervisor must determine what information must be known and then offer instruction regarding the same. In the role of counselor, the supervisor aids the supervisee in attending to interpersonal and intrapersonal functioning. Finally, within the consultant role, the supervisor acts as the supervisee's peer, and the two engage in an exchange of ideas regarding conceptualizations, interventions, and treatment modalities. Bernard calls on supervisors to remain flexible and attentive to the supervisee's style, ability, understanding, and goals while adapting to the same.

Systems Approach

Another process-based approach is Elizabeth Holloway's systems approach. This approach emphasizes the learning alliance between supervisor and supervisee and recognizes that the dynamics of this relationship are dependent on a number of factors, including supervisory expectations, power differentials, and the institution in which the supervision occurs. Emphasis within Holloway's model is placed on the developmental needs of the supervisee within the context of the supervisory relationship specifically. As with traditional two-person psychology, much of focus within the supervisory session becomes about attending to the dynamics present between the supervisor and supervisee. By attending to specific tasks, bonds, and goals, the supervisee and his or her supervisor are able to interact in a manner that provides opportunities for self-reflection, relational insight, and professional development.

An Integrated Approach

Research suggests that most supervisors describe themselves as "eclectic" in their approach to supervision, relying on techniques based in several models of supervision. Typically, such supervisors do not subscribe to one particular approach to supervision but, rather, integrate their knowledge from several perspectives into one comprehensive approach. Regardless of the supervisory model used, however, research indicates that it is the supervisory alliance in particular, rather than the specific technique applied, that serves as most robust predictor of supervisory outcome.

Sara Bender

See also Clinical Practice; Ethical Codes; Licensure and Certification; Postdoctoral Training; Supervision; Supervision, Developmental Model

Further Readings

Bernard, J. M. (1979). Supervisor training: A discrimination model. *Counselor Education and Supervision, 19*, 60–68.

Campbell, J. M. (2006). *Essentials of clinical supervision.* Hoboken, NJ: Wiley.

Holloway, E. (1995). *Clinical supervision: A systems approach.* Thousand Oaks, CA: Sage.

Littrell, J. M., Lee-Borden, N., & Lorenz, J. A. (1979). A developmental framework for counseling supervision. *Counselor Education and Supervision, 19*, 119–136.

Loganbill, C., Hardy, E., & Delworth, U. (1982). Supervision: A conceptual model. *Counseling Psychologist, 10*, 3–42.

O'Connell, B., & Jones, C. (1997). Solution-focused supervision. *Counselling, 8*(4), 289–292.

Rigazio-Digilio, S. A. (1996). Systemic cognitive-developmental therapy: A counselling model and an integrative classification schema for working with partners and families. *International Journal for the Advancement of Counselling, 19*(2), 143–165.

Skovolt, T. M., & Ronnestad, M. H. (1992). *The evolving professional self: Stages and themes in therapist and counselor development.* Chichester, UK: Wiley.

Stoltenberg, C. D., McNeill, B., & Delworth, U. (1998). *IDM supervision: An integrated developmental model for supervising counselors and therapists.* San Francisco: Jossey-Bass.

Watkins, C. E. (Ed.). (1997). *Handbook of psychotherapy supervision.* Hoboken, NJ: Wiley.

Support Groups

Support groups provide a venue for promoting positive therapeutic outcomes and decreasing social isolation across diverse populations and presenting issues. This entry begins by reviewing the purpose of support groups, as well as the process by which individuals select and participate in these groups. The entry then explores types of support groups and common therapeutic factors among them, the role of the group facilitator and the structure of group sessions, potential outcomes of participation, and major criticisms of support groups. It concludes by describing the benefits and challenges associated with online support groups and communities.

Overview of Support Groups

Support groups represent the most commonly functioning group when compared to other therapeutic or counseling groups. The Association for Specialists in Group Work (ASGW) indicates that support groups' goals can range from coping with and managing unalterable situations and circumstances to enhancing individual life skills and competencies and correcting existing challenges. Support group referrals can come from a variety of different sources, including but not limited to hospitals, nursing homes, mental health agencies, religious and spiritual organizations, schools, and community centers, as well as state and national organizations that focus on outreach, information sharing, or advocacy.

Depending on the group setting and population, group facilitators' level of expertise, experience, and educational level can vary dramatically from a trained mental health professional to a voluntary unpaid leader who shares experiences similar to those of group members but does not have formal training or a mental health background. Support groups are not to be confused with psychotherapy groups. The American Group Psychotherapy Association differentiates support groups from psychotherapy groups by indicating that support groups are usually facilitated by professionals who focus on coping with and alleviating symptoms, as opposed to psychotherapy groups, which focus on change and growth. Sources of funding for support groups vary, but typically rely on donations or fundraising efforts of the facilitator, members, community organizations or grants. In some cases, there may be a sponsoring agency for the group, which is most commonly a mental health agency.

Types of Support Groups

There are numerous types of support groups, and therefore it is beyond the scope of this entry to offer an exhaustive list. However, this section attempts to share the diversity of populations and individuals that support groups serve. A very commonly known support group is Alcoholics Anonymous (A.A.), which has a total reported membership of over 2 million. The organization was founded in 1935 and solidified its basic principles in the publication *Twelve Traditions of Alcoholics Anonymous*. Offshoots of A.A. that also focus on 12-step recovery have emerged over time, including Narcotics Anonymous and Al-Anon Family Group.

In addition to these well-known networks of support groups, there are a multitude of other types. There are medical support groups for individuals with various health conditions, including cancer, diabetes, fibromyalgia, eating disorders, lupus, Crohn's disease, and many others. Mental health support groups help individuals with conditions such as generalized anxiety disorder, bipolar disorder, and schizophrenia. Trauma survivors, including those who have survived domestic violence, sexual abuse, rape, and assault, often rely on support groups as well. Caregiver support groups exist for those caring for an elderly parent or loved one, as well as for single parents of infants and young children. Women and their partners who are struggling with infertility or who have experienced infant loss and miscarriage may also benefit from support groups. There are support groups for recent immigrants and refugees struggling to transition to living in a new country. There are support groups for youth and adults who are lesbian, gay, bisexual, transgender, and queer. Other groups exist to support military personnel, veterans, and their families, as they cope with their own unique experiences and challenges.

Common Therapeutic Factors

As outlined in the previous section of this entry, support groups serve the purpose of gathering individuals who are all struggling with or challenged by a similar issue or concern. Many support groups serve as supplemental support for primary therapy treatments. For example, an individual struggling with clinical depression and anxiety could be a member of a support group focused on decreasing social isolation and increasing a sense of belonging and understanding. However, that individual would ideally also be a client engaged in therapy. This therapy may be individual, family, or group therapy or some combination of these types of therapy taking place in an inpatient or outpatient setting. An individual may use a support group as the only form of intervention (e.g., participation in an Al-Anon group for family members of alcoholics or addicts, or a Weight Watchers group). There is evidence that a multilayered, comprehensive treatment focused on alleviating symptoms if possible, increasing coping strategies, and enhancing support is most beneficial to individuals. Given the overall diversity of support groups, it can be challenging to identify commonalities; however, there are still several shared themes and factors that these groups all share.

Across these various populations and group settings, the primary focus of most of these groups is on social support, which hinges on the development of close-knit relationships among members. In addition to social support, many groups provide education and impart information. This education typically comes in the form of facts and information about an issue or topic such as a diagnosis, symptoms, coping strategies, evidence-based interventions, learning strategies, wellness tips, and behavior modification. The educational component can play a critical role in the perception of the support that members feel, but there are also certain therapeutic factors that should emerge from all types of support groups and the populations they serve.

First, support groups tend to use a systemic perspective; facilitators will emphasize that the challenges and struggles of the individual are not necessarily the fault of the individual, but are more significantly a feature of society and social norms. Second, support groups, like other therapeutic groups, can promote core therapeutic conditions. Irvin Yalom, a leading expert in group therapy, noted the role of specific therapeutic factors that enhance the positive outcomes of group participation, including instillation of hope, universality, imparting information, development of socializing techniques, and altruism. The promotion of universality and hope is essential to the success of support groups. As a sense of social isolation decreases, group members begin to understand not only that they are not alone in their struggle but also that others have had growth and positive outcomes. This recognition of the success of others "like me" can significantly increase an individual's sense of hope for the future. The altruistic caring for others and the ability to demonstrate empathy through communication and social skills increase the level of group cohesion. Support group members learn over time that the benefit of attending group is not only to receive support from others but also to give it to other members. Given the emphasis on group cohesiveness, members' sense of community builds over time, which leads to greater therapeutic outcomes.

Structure and Facilitation of a Group Session

The structure of a support group session can vary greatly depending on the population it serves, the setting and topic or presenting issue, and the style and background of the facilitator. However, generally, support groups tend to follow a loose structure that focuses on sharing, imparting information, normalizing, and promoting universality among group members. Many groups will begin with an opening statement, which sets the tone for the session and builds a sense of community; this could be accomplished by sharing a poignant quote, a relevant reading, or establishing and describing a theme for that particular week. Facilitators will then typically summarize the purpose of the group and the overarching mutualistic goals, which serves to welcome new members and to establish continuity between sessions. The majority of the session is devoted to open sharing, where all members are given an opportunity to tell their story. The purpose of this entry is to focus on the support aspect of the group and provide a normalizing quality to the experience. Additionally, as previously mentioned, there may be a psychoeducational component to the group where members receive information and resources relevant to the issue or challenge. Facilitators will typically conclude the group session by summarizing the major themes and issues presented during their time together.

The role of the group facilitator will vary depending on his or her style and expertise of leadership; this may range from directive to nondirective. Despite the group facilitator's level of direct input, he or she should use a variety of essential skills in order to increase therapeutic outcomes and enhance the effectiveness of the support group. There are a multitude of facilitation skills that leaders should use throughout the group process, starting during the first group meeting, continuing into the working stage of the group, and culminating in the final group session. There are numerous texts on group leadership and facilitation skills that offer in-depth information, but this entry highlights some of the essential facilitation skills.

Effective group facilitators tend to be actively engaged in the group process, and demonstrate active listening through supportive, nonverbal cues (e.g., head nods, eye contact, open posture) and words of encouragement (e.g., "mmhmm", "tell us more," "thank you for sharing"). Furthermore, group facilitators will model appropriate forms of social support and provide feedback for group members, as needed. Groups are most successful when facilitators are able to increase group cohesiveness by linking the statements and common themes of the various group members; promoting engagement and interaction among members is more essential than increasing communication between a leader and a member of a group. At times, a group leader might choose to block certain behaviors, such as one member harassing another or lengthy and dominating storytelling. This type of blocking skill must be direct, while also respectful and sensitive to the needs of the individual. Group facilitators must be able to deal constructively with conflict as it arises through a variety of tactics, including working out compromises, forming new solutions, or helping the group to move on or suppress the conflict. Strong group facilitation skills coupled with a clear purpose and structure increase the chances that a support group will enhance the positive outcomes of its members.

Participation Outcomes

Due to the variety of support groups available for individuals, it is challenging to address specific outcomes attributable to participation. However, as many group members are also in another form of mental health therapy or treatment, support groups can enhance or increase treatment efficacy. Support groups can provide consistent social reinforcement when members work with one another and reiterate the importance of engaging in self-care and mental health therapy and counseling. Broadly, given the focus on interpersonal support, groups may also serve to decrease social isolation of members. Given that groups are centered on a specific topic or issue (e.g., living with bipolar disorder, coping with type 2 diabetes), members will typically feel less isolated and alone and will recognize that there are other people struggling with similar concerns. Most support groups offer access to important information about the topic or issue; a support group for new parents, for example, may share a variety of relevant information, including postpartum depression, breastfeeding challenges and support, and signs of sleep deprivation. Furthermore, support groups can help members set personal goals and may help facilitate and provide the knowledge and skills necessary for goal attainment. Group members can encourage their fellow members to meet their goals and provide necessary accountability. Members are likely to develop coping strategies, enhanced emotional regulation abilities, communication, and social skills. Although this is not an exhaustive list, it is clear that there are numerous positive outcomes associated with participation in a support group.

Criticism of Support Groups

Despite the significant positive outcomes that may result from participation in a support group, there have been criticisms regarding the effectiveness and therapeutic value of these groups. One of the primary criticisms relates to the lack of research determining the effectiveness of these types of groups. Part of the challenge with conducting research on support group outcomes is that individuals tend to participate in these groups in conjunction with other forms of therapy or treatment. Furthermore, membership is often anonymous, and identifying participants for research can be a challenge. Another criticism relates to the lack of training that support group facilitators, as opposed to other types of group facilitators, may have; Alcoholics Anonymous and Narcotics Anonymous are examples of this, as facilitators are typically recovered addicts or alcoholics who have not received formal training in group facilitation and are not mental health professionals. A final criticism of note is the lack of consistency across support group structure and processes. Given the diversity of groups and group facilitators, an individual may have very different experiences in terms of level of support and sharing opportunities, accurate information, and learning and mental health outcomes.

Online Support Groups and Communities

Alternative to traditional face-to-face support groups are online support groups or communities. The abundance of technological possibilities now available to individuals ranges from computer-based Internet access to multiple social media options to smartphones and numerous "apps." With this substantial increase and variation in technological access, the way that people support and connect with one another has also diversified. Thousands of online support groups exist across a variety of different presenting issues and populations. Some larger online support group websites such as DailyStrength offer multiple groups including, but not limited to, those focusing on miscarriage, depression, hepatitis C, bipolar disorder, and many more. Many online boards or groups choose to stay private, and individuals must receive an invitation to participate. Other groups offer open access to all but are still managed and visited almost exclusively by individuals who have a personal connection to the identified issue or concern. For example, using an empowered, slightly ironic tone, CrazyBoards.org offers a supportive environment for individuals struggling with mental illness or mental health concerns, including obsessive-compulsive disorder, depression, and schizophrenia.

There are many benefits to offering or participating in online support groups. Individuals who have physical limitations or live in remote areas can access this type of support group as an alternative to a traditional group that may not exist where they live or that they are unable to access. The guarantee of anonymity is much stronger because individuals can choose the extent to which they share personal or confidential information with other members in the group. It may be easier for individuals to take initiative in their own treatment and feel a sense of empowerment as they explore and select online support groups that best fit their needs. However, more effective than solely participating in an online support group is a multilayered and regulated approach that includes consistently high participation in the online group rather than infrequent or inconsistent participation. Furthermore, individuals who have access to and take advantage of information through online readings and modules are more likely to experience decreased negative symptoms and enhanced coping skills. Regardless of modality, traditional and online support groups can provide many important benefits across diverse issues, interests, and challenges, including decreased social isolation and symptoms, as well as increased interpersonal support and coping strategies.

Marte Ostvik-de Wilde

See also Group Family Therapy; Group Parenting Classes; Marital Group Therapy; Self-Help; Social Support

Further Readings

Cerel, J., Padgett, J. H., & Reed, G. A. (2009). Support groups for suicide survivors: Results of a survey of group leaders. *Suicide and Life-Threatening Behavior, 39*(6), 588–598.

Corey, M. S., & Corey, G. (2013). *Groups: Process and practice* (9th ed.). Monterey, CA: Brooks/Cole.

Gladding, S. T. (2012). *Groups: A counseling specialty* (6th ed.). Upper Saddle River, NJ: Pearson.

Griffiths, K. M., Mackinnon, A. J., Crisp, D. A., Christensen, H., Bennett, K., & Farrer, L. (2012). The effectiveness of an online support group for members of the community with depression: A randomized controlled trial. *PLOS ONE, 7*(12). doi.org/10.1371/journal.pone.0053244

Kelly, J. F., & Yeterian, J. D. (2011). The role of mutual-help groups in extending the framework of treatment. *Alcohol Research & Health, 33*(4), 350–355.

Metel, M., & Barnes, J. (2011). Peer-group support for bereaved children: A qualitative interview study. *Child and Adolescent Mental Health, 16*(4), 201–207.

Yalom, I. D., & Leszcz, M. (2005). *The theory and practice of group psychotherapy* (5th ed.). New York: Basic Books.

Symbolic Interactionism

Symbolic interactionism (SI) is a principal family theory that originated in the 1920s and 1930s. This theory describes how symbols are created through human interactions and how those symbols then influence other human interactions. This theory also explains the idea that families are social groups comprising interacting selves and identities. This entry explores the history and the key assumptions and concepts of SI.

Historical Background

While SI has evolved over the years, with certain generations using concepts and ideas that were pertinent to the social issues of their era, SI does have a strong conceptual and research background. It drew from ideas put forth by moralists and idealists, the most critical contributors being American pragmatists Josiah Royce, Charles Peirce, William James, and John Dewey. These moralists, idealists, and pragmatists influenced Charles Horton Cooley, George Herbert Mead, and W.I. Thomas, the predominant pioneers who laid the groundwork for SI.

There is not one specific founder of SI theory; rather it was the result of a collaboration of a number of people. Along with Cooley, Mead, and Thomas, those who contributed to the core of the theory included Robert E. Park, Ernest W. Burgess, Willard Waller, Reuben Hill, and Herbert Blumer.

The 1800s were a time of rapid change and growth in the United States. The transition from living in isolated rural conditions to living in towns and cities and from working the family farm to working in industry happened fairly quickly. The scholars of the time were anxious to explain the societal changes based on their respective fields and opinions. A group of sociology scholars from the University of Chicago made great headway in providing a unique explanation, different from the prevailing biological and economic determinism of the time. This new perspective asserted that human beings have control over social changes and can create the societies in which they live. This was a more favorable and empowering explanation than the conventional deterministic perspective, and it afforded people a greater sense of control over their destiny and direction.

Themes and Assumptions of Symbolic Interaction

The three themes of SI address the importance of meanings, self-concept, and the interactional exchange between individuals within society.

The first theme targets the importance of the meanings humans assign to things and how these meanings impact their behavior. Three assumptions support the first theme, starting with the assumption that individual human behavior is based on the meanings those individuals assign to certain events and phenomena. SI theorists argue that as part of the progression from stimulus to response to feelings and actions, there is conscious thought and cognitive meaning assigned to the stimulus. This assigned meaning is what determines how an individual responds to the stimulus, be it an event, object, or person.

The next assumption emphasizes the interactions between people. It is in these interactions that meaning arises. Symbols are the shared meanings that two or more people construct around a certain stimulus.

The last assumption is that each person modifies the shared meaning as he or she interprets the meaning based on personal experiences. SI argues that individuals interpret reality through the shared meanings and symbols of their culture. From this interpretation, humans then construct meanings of self, others, and social settings.

The second theme focuses on the development and importance of self-concept, and takes the nondeterministic view that an individual has a thoroughly social and active self. The two assumptions that support this theme begin with the idea that individuals are not born with a self-concept; rather it is through social interactions that the self-concept is developed. SI argues that it is only through interactions that a child learns concepts such as "mine" and "me" within a social context in the case of social norms and values.

The other supporting assumption asserts that once self-concept is developed, an individual now has a motive for behavior. This is an important aspect of SI as this is how behavior is explained. A person develops a sense of self, including self-values, beliefs, and feelings. This sense of self in itself does not directly explain behavior. Rather, motivations emanate out of the developed sense of self, which, in turn, influences behavior.

The third and final theme of SI targets the interactional exchange between individuals and society. There are two assumptions that undergird that interactional exchange, and those two assumptions distinguish between humans' involvement in creating the foundational social structure of society and how that social structure becomes embedded into the society to influence human behavior within the society. First of all, individuals have the ability to choose and with the freedom to use that ability, humans can create the foundational social structure of beliefs, values, and norms within a society.

The second assumption then depicts the process of how those societal beliefs, values, and norms have influence on individuals and small groups such as families. Individuals obtain an understanding of the social structure of society through everyday social interactions with other individuals. This assumption differentiates the creation of the social structure from the adoption of the structure. The integration of a society's social structure occurs through making sense of the social beliefs, values, and norms by interaction among humans within the society.

Concepts

The four primary concepts of SI are identity, roles, interactions, and context. Identity is used in reference to the self-meaning a person has in a role. For example, the role of a grandparent can vary based on the meaning that role has for that individual. One grandparent may feel that her identity is to continue to parent her grandchild, while a different grandparent may view his identity as being the person to spoil the grandchildren. It is the same role (grandparent), but two different individuals have a different self-meaning for the role.

A person has multiple identities and will assign an importance or a hierarchy to these identities. The process or the probability that a person uses an identity is called *salience*. The concept of salience is the explanation for why some roles are more prominent than others. Individuals each have roles that they feel are a more prominent part of their identity, so they will strive to do well in these roles. For example, a father might continue to seek higher-paying employment in order to excel in his identity as the primary financial provider for his family.

An individual's identities and salience determine behavior. One's commitment to an identity and the importance of an identity are what guide a person to make decisions about how and where to spend time and efforts. The more important or salient a role is, the more time and energy a person will invest in the identity. An individual assumes the more salient identities with greater frequency, will talk about these identities more, and the more salient identities will have greater influence on their self-esteem. SI theorists posit that an individual's desire to have positive self-esteem is a motivation for behavior. Individuals want to feel good about themselves and therefore will seek to excel in their identities in order to increase self-esteem.

The next concept of SI is roles. A person creates an identity for the different roles to fill. These roles are defined by the social norms and expectations for that role. Different roles include mother, father, daughter, son, grandparents, and so on. Each of these roles has a societal norm associated with it. The norms for the role establish expectations for individual behavior in that role. For example, a social norm might be that a son should obey his father, so the expectation is that when the father asks his son to do something, his son will comply. An individual's knowledge, ability, and emotions about that role also include expectations from critical players related to that role.

Roles become most pertinent when they are considered in relation to another individual. For example, a mother is a mother because she has children; a spouse is a spouse because of the existence of a marital partner. Roles can be formal and recognized by society or informal. A formal role is one that is understood by most of society: mother, father, student, store clerk. An informal role is more ambiguous, and outsiders may not understand the role. Roles also change over time, being informed by the past, as well as influenced by the current situation. Role-taking, the action of fitting into a role as defined by others, and role-making, the action of making or creating a role, are also key concepts.

Interactions are crucial to SI. An individual creates meanings and shares the meanings and symbols with others through social interactions. Individuals continually present themselves to others and constantly receive feedback on their presentation and their performance in their roles. Both nonverbal and verbal cues in interactions help a person to know what is expected, what is acceptable behavior in a role and what is not, and help a person create an identity.

Every social interaction does not have the same impact. Some people are more important to us than others. Different people in an individual's life have more authority and influence; thus interactions with these people are more impactful. Because family is so central to most people's lives, it is a primary influence in an individual's development of self, meanings, and roles.

Finally, context refers to the society and culture that influences the individual. Symbolic interactionists argue that humans are not preprogrammed to behave the same way in every situation; rather, humans understand that different contexts call for different behavior.

Natasha Bell

See also Cultural Issues in Couples and Families; Family of Origin; Family Values; Gender Roles; Narrative Therapy; Postmodern Therapies; Social Constructionism

Further Readings

Boss, P. G., Doherty, W. J., LaRossa, R., Schumm, W. R., & Steinmetz, S. K. (1993). *Sourcebook of family theories and methods: A contextual approach.* New York: Plenum.

SYSTEMIC FAMILY THERAPY

Systemic family therapy is an approach that conceptualizes people in terms of their relationships and tends to view problems and solutions to problems as related to the family system, rather than in terms of individual behavior. Systemic family therapy looks at the relationships in the family, how people relate to each other and to themselves, and how their perceptions of others influence that interaction. In the field of family therapy, similar terms such as *systems theory* and *systems thinking* are also used. Systems theory is transdisciplinary study of groups of interrelated parts (systems). Early family therapists adapted and applied these principles to work with families. Systems thinking refers to the idea that family therapists conceptualize families in terms of repetitive patterns, communication, relationships, and circular causality (all parts of a system influence one another rather than one person "causing" something to happen).

The term *systemic family therapy* is often used to refer to all different types of family therapy models because they all share principles of systems theory. It is also used to refer to early pioneers in the field of family therapy who first applied systems theory to work with families. Many of the early pioneers went on to create a particular model of family therapy called *strategic therapy*. This entry first discusses the influence of systems theory on family therapy and the development of systemic family therapy. It then further explores systemic family therapy by looking at the processes that occur in therapy, the interventions systemic family therapists use, the approach to assessment, and recent therapeutic approaches and modifications.

Systems Theory in Family Therapy

Early influences on systems theory in family therapy included cybernetics and general systems theory. Cybernetics is a theory of living and nonliving systems that explains how the system's behavior provides information (feedback) to the system on whether to change or stay the same. Since the system both creates and is influenced by its own information, it is called a *feedback loop*. In addition to using ideas from cybernetics to describe and understand family systems' behavior, general systems theory influenced early family therapists. In this theory, the difference between "closed systems" and "open systems" was emphasized. Closed systems do not have interaction with the surrounding environment, but open systems do. Families are open systems, and open systems behave differently than closed systems. Concepts from both cybernetics and general systems theory are integrated into the systems thinking used by family therapists.

From a systems thinking perspective, therapists identify patterns of communication that are no longer functional (that is, they do not meet the needs of the system) and address those problems directly, rather than attribute a diagnosis, or focus on the past causes of the behavior. The family is seen as including circular interactions of communication repeated over time, and attempted solutions to problems. Communication in this context includes behavior, verbal and nonverbal communication, and formal and informal rules. The family is also seen as a unit acting socially with its environment. In other words, the family system is influenced by the larger systems in which it is embedded. Systems theory and systems thinking is too comprehensive to cover in this entry; however, some basic principles common to most models of family therapy are as follows:

- Families (systems) are more than the sum of their parts.
- Systems are governed by general rules.
- Systems have boundaries. These are rules about communication and contact between subsystems within the family and between the family and other systems.
- Family systems tend to gravitate toward a stable state called *homeostasis*. However, living systems cannot always stay the same. Systems must be capable of growth and change.
- Communication and feedback, or feedback loops, are important to the functioning of the system. Negative feedback tends to maintain the status quo of the system, and positive feedback tends to elicit change in the system.
- Circular causality is more helpful in understanding family systems than linear causality. In linear causality, things happen as cause and effect. One thing causes another to happen, and the influence happens in one direction, from *A* to *B*. In circular causality, influence is multidirectional and recursive. *A* affects *B*, but *B* also affects *A*.

Development of Systemic Family Therapy

Many of the early ideas of systemic family therapy were influenced by two groups: the Mental Research Institute (MRI) and the Milan Group. MRI evolved from a group of professionals working together in the 1950s and 1960s in Palo Alto, California. Later some of these people formed MRI. The Palo Alto group, which included Gregory Bateson, Donald Jackson, John Weakland, William Fry, Virginia Satir, Paul Watzlawick, and others, studied ideas from anthropology, social psychology, cybernetics, and general systems theory. Based on some work they were doing related to schizophrenia, they become particularly interested in communication in all forms and its influence in family functioning. The history of systemic family therapy, later to become strategic therapy, is associated with the work of Watzlawick, Weakland, and Richard Fisch and their interactional model of change. Based on much of their work, Steve de Shazer created the solution-focused model, which is used to disrupt interactional patterns in order to explore future potential solutions. In addition, Salvador Minuchin and Jay Haley added to their work with the idea that systems can be interrupted through process and structural changes, often with the involvement and direction of the therapist.

Milan family therapy practitioners Luigi Boscolo, Gianfranco Cecchin, and Giuliana Prata, led by Mara Selvini Palazzoli at The Institute for Family Study, contributed greatly to the development of systemic family therapy. Their ideas evolved through conversations about the families that they had worked with over the years. Eventually the Milan Group's conversations gravitated to the idea that problems in the family were the result of faulty interactional patterns that violated family rules. Drawing from Bateson's concept of homeostasis, equilibrium is maintained in the family by following the rules of interaction. Families tend to like to maintain their status quo (equilibrium), but families must also be flexible enough to change and evolve when needed. Families evolve naturally when the equilibrium is unbalanced, and they either return to the previous patterns or make changes to a new, evolved pattern. The power of the family resides in the rules, and how the rules either serve the needs of the family and evolve when needed, or stay the same, even when the family needs them to change.

The Milan Group's focus in systemic family therapy evolved from the idea that the problem keeps the family stuck in unhealthy patterns. Initially their focus was on resistance, where clients and therapists are opposed to each other or clients are opposed to change. Therapists began looking for secretive ways (interventions outside the family's awareness) in order not to elicit resistance and to defeat the family's unhealthy behavior. They de-emphasized the problem focus and considered family problems a result of faulty family beliefs that maintain the family system.

Early assumptions about intervening with a family were that the homeostasis was maintained by unaddressed epistemological issues (ways the family viewed the world), but as the Milan Group's views evolved, interventions surrounded the family's beliefs about each other and the rules in the family that support those beliefs. Since families would evolve during the course of treatment, it meant that the therapist's interventions must also evolve during the course of treatment. Boscolo, Cecchin, Lynn Hoffman, and Peggy Penn suggested it was better to do away with the idea of a family unit and instead think of the treatment unit as meaningful. Because the therapist and the family are the treatment unit, they would not say that the system creates the problem but would reverse the sentence: the problem creates the system. The idea of seeing the therapist as part of the treatment system, rather than just the family, is sometimes referred to as *second-order cybernetics, cybernetics of cybernetics,* or the *second wave* in family therapy.

Processes in Systemic Family Therapy

In 1978 in *Paradox and Counterparadox* by Selvini Palazzoli, Boscolo, Cecchin, and Prata, the Milan Group established the overall framework of a family therapy session as having five parts: (1) the presession where the therapists receive information about the family, (2) the session where the therapists ask questions through hypothesis and observe the nature of the responses, (3) the discussion of the session where the therapists involved meet separately from the family, (4) the conclusion of the session where the therapists return and report to the family what comments or out-of-session work they would like the family to consider, and (5) the discussion of the family's reaction, which is the postmeeting conversation among the therapists as to how the family reacted to the feedback.

Within the context of the session three processes occur: therapist hypothesis, circularity of questions, and neutrality of the therapist's position with the family. Hypothesis is the way in which the therapist organizes information in order to generate the questions needed to be asked of the family. The information can be organized around connecting patterns, which then generate questions for the family about such patterns and how they are each impacted. Hypothesizing is the therapist's developing theories about how the family functions in preparation to test those theories with the family. Even if the therapist suggests a view of the family's behavior that is different from the family's view, it allows the therapist to be seen as an outside entity and introduces new information into the family discussion. According to Boscolo and Cecchin, all hypotheses should be considered, including those the family suggests.

Circularity is the concept that is foundational to systemic family therapy. Circularity is a mindset systemic family therapists hold that permits them to explore the experience and feedback that they get from the family. The family drives the direction of the therapist and, in turn, the therapist gives feedback to the family. In return, a therapist's hypothesis about a family may change as a reflection of the responses from the family. A new hypothesis is generated, identifying new questions, which may lead to new perspectives by the family. The new perspectives generated from the use of circularity could provide the family with enough information to unbalance the homeostasis and provoke change.

Two techniques that model circularity in the counseling process are using questions of differences and triadic questioning. Questions of differences are questions used in order to learn more about differences in the family by comparing and contrasting issues between family members. This process further develops hypotheses about family beliefs. Triadic questioning involves asking family members to comment on the relationship of two other family members. The comments from one member provide another viewpoint of the relationship. When the systemic family therapist has multiple members' triadic responses, he or she gains added layers of perspective around one symptom. Further pathways to differences among family members can come from asking about differences in behavior, changes in behavior before and after events, and ranking family members by the degree to which they exhibit certain behaviors. The questioning provides new data to the family and leads the family and the therapist to additional questions and an ever-evolving hypothesis.

This circular questioning is a derivative of Bateson's work. Bateson noticed that knowledge acquired is always filtered through mechanisms where it is compared with existing knowledge and scanned for difference. Circular questioning addresses the natural tendency for living things to form loops of information instead of linear causal thinking. Circular questions occur when a systemic family therapist finds "openings" or clues dropped by family members during the course of the interview that indicate a theme. Circular questions would explore the implications of the theme by addressing it with each family member.

Neutrality is the third process that occurs within the context of a systemic family therapy session. Neutrality is the therapist's active avoidance of hierarchy in the session. The therapist avoids seizing power or taking sides with family members and instead, remains open to see how the hypotheses play out and see how the family reacts and responds together. The therapist can generate hypotheses and share them with the family without assuming the family is accepting or rejecting the hypotheses in response to the role of the therapist.

Cecchin suggested that "curiosity" may be a better descriptor for neutrality, since neutrality, to many therapists, represents an uninvolved disengagement. Curiosity can be seen as an active interest in exploring with the family the possibilities that exist for change. Instead of the systemic therapist having to actively avoid overinvestment in one solution, or even believing that he or she must be the agent of change, the therapist is free to remain curious and generate new hypotheses alongside the family. Karl Tomm, in 1984, asserted that the goal is to change the family's ability to change.

In systemic family therapy, sessions are typically held with longer breaks between sessions than in other models of family therapy. Systemic family therapists believe that change, even incremental change, takes time for families to achieve, and families need more time between the typical weekly sessions to see the changes that occur. One month or more between sessions may be the norm for some systemic family therapists.

Interventions in Systemic Family Therapy

Paradoxical Interventions

If families remain stuck in their interactional patterns and want change without changing, then systemic therapists often use paradoxical interventions to deal with resistance. Paradoxes include contradictory instructions, and in order to follow through on the instructions people must change their view or change the rules of the situation. Paradoxical interventions are directives or suggestions that are formed in a way not to elicit family resistance, but to still help them change. There are different types of paradoxical interventions: positive connotation, symptom prescription, symptom exaggeration, and predicting/prescribing a relapse.

Positive connotation occurs when a systemic family therapist describes positively the symptomatic behavior and ties the symptomatic behavior to the whole family interaction. Positive connotation is not directed to family members but instead addresses the family system that is self-maintaining as a whole. Rather than blaming an individual member, problems are seen in the context of whole family/system interactions. Symptom prescription and symptom exaggeration involves having individuals or the family engage in the problematic behavior or engage in it to an extreme, rather than trying to end the behavior. Often the clients learn they have more control over the problematic behavior than they thought if they can engage in it purposely. When the symptom is exaggerated, it often becomes more burdensome to maintain the problematic behavior than to change it. Finally, predicting or prescribing a relapse can help relieve the pressure to maintain change. The family will either not have a relapse, or, if they do, then they can view it as "normal" and not a failure.

Family Rituals

In *Paradox and Counterparadox* the Milan Group provides examples of the between-session interventions expected of families. Much of the work could be characterized as family rituals. Selvini Palazzoli, Boscolo, Cecchin, and Prata distinguish between rituals that can be performed for effect only once, and ritualized behavior, which can be performed many times in many different scenarios. Ritualized behavior generally has a set script, set rules, and defined enactment; however, because the action is being done regularly and is not a singular event, families can make adjustments as the situation calls for and as they have new data from the experience.

Ritualized behavior was used in early systemic family therapy as platform for addressing paradoxical interventions. Paradoxical interventions, drawn from Bateson's work on double-bind communication patterns, are incorporated into rituals so a typical family communication pattern is revealed and the double bind forces them to behave differently. Double binds arise when an individual or group is faced with two conflicting messages: one message negates the other, the messages create emotional distress, and the individual or group cannot comment on or leave the situation.

Invariant Prescription

In 1979, Selvini Palazzoli, looking for a repeated intervention to use with families, developed over the course of working with families the invariant prescription. This became the basis of her research and work. The invariant prescription is a response to the six-stage model of a psychotic family game that plays out in families with psychotic children. These six stages are explained in her book *Family Games*. In the first stage of the model there is a marital stalemate with regard to the problems. The second stage involves the child aligning with the parent whom he or she perceives as the loser in the stalemate. The third stage involves the child escalating symptoms for the winner to show the loser how to cope. In the fourth stage, the loser aligns with the winner to disapprove of the child's escalated behavior. Next, in the fifth stage, the child feels misunderstood by the parents and continues the game. The sixth stage arise when the family concludes that the child is crazy and will always be crazy. When applied to this situation, invariant prescription calls for parents to spend increasing time alone together and separate from the family and without the children's knowledge. Initially the parents will have a few confidential therapy sessions to progress to secret outings, and then to periods of time together extending into days without the children's knowledge or contact. These secret outings disrupt the symptom structure in the family and help develop a parental alliance that is resistant to the coercion from other members.

Systemic Family Assessment

The systemic family therapy approach challenges traditional methods of diagnosis as they lead to negative connotation and labels that hinder the progression toward health. The traditional diagnosis process attributes causality to the client. With that attribution comes feelings of guilt and blame that reinforce the problems they are attempting to correct. Diagnostic barriers and clinical labels create even more resistance for the family entering treatment. Because of this, Boscolo, Cecchin, Hoffman, and Penn suggest that systemic family therapists consider the impact of the traditional diagnosis schema on the family.

Assessment also means understanding, which family beliefs offer the most opportunity for new information. Some family beliefs hold with them more of the problem behavior than other beliefs. Prioritizing the beliefs and their connection to problem behavior can be done only through carefully observing the family and assessing the feedback given to the therapist.

David Campbell, Rosalind Draper, and Elaine Crutchley extend some of the ideas of the Milan approach into practical aspects of assessment. In their approach, the fit between family and therapist determines the success of the treatment unit. Does the therapeutic fit permit the family to take in new information, increase awareness of their beliefs and values, and assist them in solving their own problems? In order for the relationship to be therapeutic, five elements should occur: family members must feel that they have been heard, the family and therapist must feel that there is some risk of change, the family's responses should stimulate the therapist's curiosity, the information being exchanged must be perceived to have been covering new territory, and the interview must connect problem behavior to wider issues. Throughout this process "stuckness" is not attributed to the family's reluctance to share information, but to the therapist's inadequacy in asking the correct questions.

Recent Approaches to Systemic Family Therapy

Boscolo and Cecchin continued to work on the ideas established in *Paradox and Counterparadox* and extended them with *Milan Systemic Family Therapy* in 1987. Modifications to the Milan method of strategic family therapy over the years included a reduction of intentional strategic homework such as rituals and ritualistic behavior. To Boscolo and Cecchin, paradoxical interventions, such as telling the family to amplify negative behavior, could cause the family to rebel in anger. Symptoms would vanish but families would concurrently terminate treatment.

Boscolo and Cecchin rethought the idea of positive connotation, concerned that it implies that negative thought is somehow a natural condition needed by the family, and that positive connotation is the response. With this, they considered renaming positive connotation as logical connotation. Instead of implying that the problem is useful to the family (as the need for positive connotation does), they thought that it would be more affirming of the family to say that the problem is something that the family has gotten accustomed to or has become a habit. Other reconsiderations for the systemic family therapy model include a preference for ritualistic behavior that has alternating-day scenarios, where family members alternate roles on a daily basis. The Milan team also reduced a judgmental reaction to families who are ignoring a directive, no longer seeing the refusal to follow the direction as a manipulation, but rather as new data regarding communication patterns in the family.

Marty Jencius

See also Circularity and Linearity; Cybernetics; Family Rituals; Hypothesis, Systemic; Milan Team; Neutrality and Curiosity

Further Readings

Boscolo, L., Cecchin, G., Hoffman, L., & Penn, P. (1987). *Milan systemic family therapy: Conversations in theory and practice.* New York: Basic Books.

Campbell, D., Draper, R., & Crutchley, E. (1991). The Milan systemic approach to family therapy. In A. S. Gruman & D. P. Kniskern (Eds.), *Handbook of family therapy* (Vol. 2, pp. 325–362). New York: Brunner/Mazel.

Cecchin, G. (1987). Hypothesizing, circularity, and neutrality revisited: An invitation to curiosity, *Family Process, 26*(4), 405–413.

Selvini Palazzoli, M. (1989). *Family games: General models of psychotic processes in the family.* New York: W. W. Norton.

Selvini Palazzoli, M., Boscolo, L., Cecchin, G., & Prata, G. (1974). The treatment of children through brief therapy of their parents. *Family Process, 13*(4), 429–442.

Selvini Palazzoli, M., Boscolo, L., Cecchin, G., & Prata, G. (1979). *Paradox and counterparadox: A new model in the therapy of the family in schizophrenic transaction.* Lanham, MD: Jason Aronson.

Selvini Palazzoli, M., Boscolo, L., Cecchin, G., & Prata, G. (1980). Hypothesizing—circularity—neutrality: Three guidelines for the conductor of the session. *Family Process, 19*(1), 3–12.

Systems, Subsystems, and Metasystems

A family is a system of individuals who are intricately connected through one or more of the following: biology, legal circumstances, cultural history, emotional context, or implied future goals. Within the context of family therapy, the family is defined as a unit, or system. The counselor assesses system health by collecting diagnostic information from initial interviews with family members to identify which family subsystems are functioning maladaptively by identifying system properties, roles, and rules. Examples of system properties are values, identity, priorities, developmental stage, communication styles, nurturance level, location, and system status (growing, stuck, or decaying).

A family functions, even when behaving in a dysfunctional manner, because it is a unified living entity, which features many interrelated dynamics and communication patterns. This entry first describes the family system and the qualities that make up a healthy system before going into more detail about the defining characteristics of family systems. The entry then defines metasystems and subsystems in the family context.

As complex interactive systems, families are seen as being goal oriented. Families strive to reach certain objectives and goals together, and dissuade any member from derailing the intent of the whole system to achieve these goals (which is often simply to maintain homeostasis). Through patterns of interactions, such as negative and positive feedback loops, the achievement of the goals becomes more or less attainable.

A family system consists of at least one primary caretaker (parent or guardian), and at least one child. Other definitions of family system compositions include a nuclear family, consisting of a father, a mother, and their biological children; and a blended family, or stepfamily, which is a family formed by the marriage or long-term cohabitation of two individuals, where one or both have at least one child from a previous relationship living part-time or full-time in the household, and in which the individual who is not the biological parent of the child or children is referred to as the stepparent. Within these relationships, there is the expectation of reciprocity; the influence of one system is evident in all other systems, and thus affects the functioning of the whole system.

The Healthy System

A healthy family system has several identifiable qualities, including the ability to make adaptive changes in its structure relative to the family's circumstances and the developmental stages of its family members. Because individual problems arise when family structures are inflexible, the counselor strives to help the family learn to rebuild a healthier system in which each member accommodates, nurtures, and supports the autonomy of every other member in the family. Counselors help the family members refine their communication skills, and learn how to negotiate needs, recognize complementary and reciprocal behavior, accommodate change, and adjust to changing circumstances that cannot be avoided or events that cannot be altered. Sibling relationships should feature security and strength, and caretaker dyads should rely on support and cooperation. All subsystems should be distinctly defined, and ideally these healthy, balanced subsystems should scaffold the whole system.

Systems

Family systems are identifiable by a number of defining characteristics. Systems are defined by external and internal family boundaries, the rules of the family, role organization, power distribution among family members, and the communication process. The family system encounters normative and nonnormative changes throughout the life span of the system, and the system reacts in predictable ways. Normative events can be anticipated and planned for, while nonnormative events cannot be anticipated, and result in unexpected change. These events are more likely to be experienced as crises, and are more likely to result in the family life course being changed. When this occurs, the family system in crisis engages in predictably dysfunctional behaviors to regain its balance.

Structure and Boundaries in a System

Family systems also have notable interrelated elements and structure. Elements are the individuals within the system, and these individuals share relationships within the general system. These relationships, or subsystems, within the system function on an interdependent basis, which create the structure of the whole system. Every family member plays an essential role in this system; every family member is connected to each other through a system of overlapping and intertwining relationships. These relationships may be dyadic, involving two family members, or triadic, involving three. Three members create a triangle; this triangular relationship results whenever two members in the family system have problems with each other, and subsequently involve a third member as a way of stabilizing their own relationship.

Within the boundaries of the system, patterns develop as certain family members' behavior is influenced by, and subsequently has a direct influence on, other family members' behaviors in predictable ways. Maintaining the same pattern of behaviors within a system may lead to balance in the family system, but also to dysfunction due to lacking flexibility which accommodates growth. Four relationship patterns define where problems may develop in a family system: marital conflict, dysfunction in one spouse, impairment of one or more children, and emotional distance. Many families under stress elect divorce as the means of distancing themselves from the problems caused by a dysfunctional system. While divorce is often used as a remedy for seemingly irreconcilable problems, unless the divorcing parties resolve their own contributions to the failed relationship, there is strong likelihood that old and destructive behaviors will reemerge in subsequent relationships.

Open and Closed Systems

The structure within systems is established on a continuum from open to closed. Every system has specific and unique ways of including and excluding elements so that the line between those within the system and those outside of the system is clear to every member within the family system. If a family has permeable and vague boundaries, it is considered open. Open boundary systems allow elements and situations outside the family to influence them. Characteristics of open systems are little privacy, spontaneity, high value on uniqueness, little emotional regulation, and structural chaos. Alternatively, closed, or impermeable, boundary systems isolate its members from the environment, and will appear isolated, insular, and self-contained.

Closed systems value the suppression of the expression of emotion, a high degree of privacy, rigidly controlled connections to extended family or friends, closely monitored activities, and a strong emphasis on discipline. In a closed system, an attempt by a family member outside of a subsystem or an individual outside of the family system who attempts to decrease negative patterns of communication is interpreted as threatening the equilibrium and homeostasis of the family, since this action will be attempting to change the boundaries of the relationship.

Rules and Messages in a System

Every family system has rules of which each family member is aware, either knowingly or unknowingly. Family rules are defined as an invisible set of functional demands that persistently organizes the interaction of the family. In a system context, messages and rules are in place and observed by family members to maintain boundaries. Messages and rules are relationship agreements which define what is acceptable behavior within the system, and limit the behaviors of family members that threaten the boundaries. Members of the system are consistently expected to respond to each other in a certain way according to their role, which is determined by these relationship agreements. Rules are clear in open and closed systems, but may become unclear if the family structure is redefined at any point through disruption, trauma, or the addition or subtraction of family members.

Messages exchanged between members in the system are repetitive and redundant, and it is important to note that both rules and messages are rarely literally communicated; they are usually not explicitly written, and the meaning of the messages is implied rather than definitively articulated. Rules are reinforced by messages; rules allow family members to define their perceived power in the system, and messages serve to remind other members of the limits of these rules and define the contexts and circumstances in which these rules apply. Messages also reinforce the strength of the family system; when a family member breaks an implicit rule, that member may experience guilt, denial, or shame as a result of compromising the understood and expected homeostasis of the system. For example, a closed system may not allow a child to have friends of differing cultures due to a perceived conflict of values within the family system.

Boundaries in a System

Boundaries in a family system are invisible barriers that regulate the amount, direction, and style of contact between family members. These serve to protect the autonomy of the family, and guide the family system toward goal accomplishment. There are three categories of boundaries: clear, rigid, and diffuse. Clear boundaries are firm but flexible, and allow for permeable degrees of autonomy for family members and the system as a whole. Rigid boundaries are characterized by disengagement within and between systems; family members are isolated from one another, and subsystems are resistant to all change.

Diffuse boundaries are those that define an enmeshed family; indicators of this type of boundary setting include extreme hovering and oversupporting. Enmeshment is a component of systemic cohesion, or the emotional bonding that family members have with one another. The level of cohesion within a system is identified on a spectrum that ranges from low to high: disengaged, separated, connected, and enmeshed. The extremes (disengaged or enmeshed) are considered to be problematic. Families falling in the middle of the dimension (separated or connected) are healthy, because family members can be both independent of, and connected to, their families. Cohesion is directly affected by family boundary flexibility, or the amount of change that the system is willing to accommodate regarding leadership and rules.

The most healthy system is one in which boundaries are both clear and semidiffuse, allowing the caretakers to interact with one another with apparent respect and authority when negotiating family goals and parenting strategies if children are members of the family system. Interactions between caretakers, children, and siblings should follow socialization patterns that emphasize support, nurturance, and guidance. There should not be evident disengagement, rigidity, or aloofness when indicating or responding to needs of family members. Dysfunctional family systems often exhibit inappropriate and ineffective hierarchies and unclear boundaries; for example, a parent may involve a child in a conflict with an emotionally absent or neglectful spouse, a process known as triangulation. This may also represent a degree of enmeshment, or a diffusion of personal boundaries in a system with undefined roles. An enmeshed family allows individual members little to no autonomy or personal boundaries.

Family Roles in a Dysfunctional System

The roles among family members within a system can be very rigid, and rules are clear, though unhealthy and often resembling codependence. Roles are assumed by each member in the system, and each has a specific task or set of tasks that maintains homeostasis and reduces problematic tension that arises from poor communication. There are six roles that appear in a dysfunctional, enmeshed family, roles that comprise a model of addictive behavior in families described by Sharon Wegscheider-Cruse. These roles are not explicitly assigned, but each role actively discourages other members within the system from developing their own feelings and preferences, thereby maintaining equilibrium within the system. Each individual assumes the role that assists in the continuity of communication stagnation, and although they are often unaware of their behaviors, the family members play these roles to perpetuate the family dysfunction.

The caretaker, or enabler, is one of the most powerful roles in the system hierarchy; the individual who assumes this role enables the other members to engage in their roles without challenge, and to indulge dysfunctional patterns without redirection. They nurture poor communication patterns by excusing ineffective ones. Enabling is a behavior that inadvertently supports the addictive behaviors of the addict, by helping an alcoholic or addict avoid the natural consequences of irresponsible behavior. By doing so, the caretaker/enabler has successfully achieved the primary family goal of reducing tension in the family system.

The addict is the center of attention, and all roles are secondary; this individual behaves incapably and requires constant care. This person is dependent and self-deleterious.

The hero is many times the oldest child, and is sometimes referred to as the golden child. This individual strives to maintain the facade of normality through overachievement and success. These individuals often feel isolated, as their task is to mask the dysfunction of the family at the expense of healthy social engagement.

The scapegoat is the diametric opposite of the hero/golden child; he or she appears hostile or troubled, and competes for the attention received by the addict or the hero in the family system. This individual engages in behaviors that may appear deviant or defiant, and the system will readily assign blame to this person to avoid addressing other subsystems and unhealthy dynamics. Some scapegoats enter into the trap of trying fervently to redeem themselves in the eyes of their family so they can finally be respected and appreciated for who they really are, but a dysfunctional family system will reject this attempt to revise their role.

The mascot, or clown, is usually the youngest member of the family, and invests most of his or her energy in distracting the other family members from their own roles to defuse tension. The mascot has difficulty accepting and expressing difficult feelings, and will joke the way out of serious circumstances, avoiding the real issue that needs to be addressed. This individual helps maintain family homeostasis by bringing laughter and fun into the home; this person brightens the family atmosphere, becoming a natural counterbalance against the tension that is so prevalent and oppressive in dysfunctional family systems. The mascot is generally the one member of the family system that the other members have few, if any, complaints about.

The lost child is indeed lost within the family structure; this individual is quiet and shy and often feels ignored. The primary goal of the individual in this role is to avoid conflict at all costs. This person handles tension within the system by withdrawing from it and avoiding interaction with the other members of the family.

Feedback Loops

The concept of feedback loops is used to describe the patterns or channels of interaction and communication that facilitate movement toward morphogenesis or morphostasis. Negative feedback loops are those patterns of interaction that maintain stability or constancy while minimizing change. Negative feedback loops help to maintain homeostasis. Positive feedback loops, in contrast, are patterns of interaction that facilitate change or movement toward either growth or dissolution. Negative feedback loops are associated with patterns of interaction and communication that keep the family system functioning in its current way. Positive feedback loops are patterns of interaction and communication that emerge as a result of the need for change.

Morphostasis

Morphostasis is the ability of a system to maintain its structure while sustaining a changing environment. As a system, the family exists in paradox; stability provides continuity over time, but a healthy family system needs to be able to adapt to the changes in and among family members. For a family with dysfunctional patterns, their goal will be to retain the subsystems in place and the predictable dysfunction of the whole system, and reduce boundary ambiguity when their basic structure is challenged. Alternatively, morphogenesis describes the ability of a system to grow as a systemic unit over time to adapt to the changing needs of the family. In all families there is an ongoing dynamic tension between trying to maintain stability and introducing change; dysfunctional family systems strive to maintain this dynamic tension by contradicting change or trying to deter it.

Metasystems

When the counselor enters the system to intervene, the system evolves from a system into a metasystem, or the expansion of the system to include other systems to resolve dysfunction and problematic patterns of communication within the primary system. These metasystems include the family, and any one or combination of service sectors such as social workers, court-appointed representatives, schools, pediatric health centers, hospital personnel, specialty mental health systems, juvenile justice systems, child protection services, and substance use treatment systems. Metasystems are influenced by culturally defined values, normative developmental processes, and the resiliency skills, coping skills, and commitment of each entity.

Subsystems

Each subsystem has its own rules, boundaries, and unique characteristics. Membership in subsystems can change over time. Subsystems are groups of members with their own special roles, rules, boundaries, and alliances. Typical subsystems include living and dead grandparents, parenting adults, siblings, relatives, and in-laws. Subsystems can be detached or bonded, harmonious to conflictual, and dominant or dominated. Examples of subsystems include caretaker and child, other caretaker and child, two or more caretakers, or a child with siblings. The subsystems resemble hierarchies, and often are organized by gender or generation.

The structure of the subsystems is defined by the boundary that each individual in the relationship agrees upon through role definition. For example, a mother and teenager may argue about household chores. The elements in this subsystem are the mother and the teenager, and each believes she or he is entitled to certain rights based on the definitions of these roles within their family. These beliefs and adherence to their perceived roles will influence their communication patterns and exchanged expectations, which create the structure of the relationship. This is a dyadic subsystem, and roles are maintained through consistent communication patterns and style. This is predictable and unchanged, and maintains the family system's equilibrium through cyclic repetition.

Adrianne L. Johnson

See also General Systems Theory; Individual Versus Family Therapy; Mental Health, Systemic Perspective; Structural Family Therapy; Systemic Family Therapy; Systems Theory

Further Readings

Criss, M. M., Henry, C. S., Harrist, A. W., & Larzelere, R. E. (2015). Interdisciplinary and innovative approaches to strengthening family and individual resilience: An introduction to the special issue. *Family Relations, 64*(1), 1–4.

Erdman, P., & Caffery, T. (Eds.). (2003). *Attachment and family systems: Conceptual, empirical, and therapeutic relatedness*. New York: Brunner-Routledge.

Gurman, A. S., & Kniskern, D. P. (Eds.). (2014). *Handbook of family therapy*. New York: Routledge.

Swartz, R. (2013). *Family therapy review: Contrasting contemporary models*. New York: Routledge/Taylor & Francis Group.

Wetchler, J., & Heckler, L. L. (Eds.). (2015). *An introduction to marriage and family therapy* (2nd ed.). New York: Routledge/Taylor & Francis Group.

Systems Theory

Systems theory is a way of thinking about how the world is organized. It is a theoretical move away from a focus on "stuff"—material, matter, substance, content—and a move toward a focus on relationship—process, organization, form, pattern, and context. Since the early 1900s, many fields and disciplines, such as physics, biology, architecture, and family therapy, have adopted a systemic orientation, understanding phenomena in terms of relationship rather than "things." This entry offers a definition and description of systems theory and the role it plays in family therapists' thinking. It then moves to a discussion of the relationship between change and systemic practice. The purpose of this entry is to give the reader an idea of what a systemically oriented therapy might look like.

From the time of Isaac Newton, science has been preoccupied with notions of cause and effect. This orientation required that scientists think of the world as a vast collection of things: objects that impacted other objects. Given this orientation, scientists viewed change as occurring by forces and impacts. Systems theory proposes a radical departure from such a material notion, suggesting instead that the world and all its phenomena are interrelated and interdependent. Relationship, rather than "stuff," is primary. Rather than a vast collection of separate entities, each operating individually and independently of all others, interrelatedness suggests that the nature of reality is less like a mechanical clock, as René Descartes proposed, and more like music—a complex system of wholes and parts, interweaving with other complex systems of wholes and parts. Descartes's mechanistic (also called atomistic or reductionistic), clocklike view of the world, which has underpinned scientific thinking since the 1600s, assumes that wholes—a family, for example—can be understood by analyzing the properties of their parts. Systems theory, on the other hand, proposes that the sum of the whole is greater than its parts. Fritjof Capra, a physicist, offers the sugar molecule as an illustration: Individually, the carbon, oxygen, and hydrogen atoms that make up a sugar molecule have no sweetness. The taste of sweetness emerges only in the special interactive relationship between (a) the combination of atoms in the specific arrangement that constitutes a sugar molecule and (b) human taste buds. Sweetness cannot be located. It is not "in a thing" or "at a place," but instead arises in relationship.

For family therapists, who view the world systemically, the family cannot be understood by decomposing it down to its individual members. Like the sugar molecule, a family has properties that are not found in its parts. Individual family members, the "parts," are best understood within the context of the whole family. Without looking at the larger context of family relationships, sense cannot be made of behavior—like sweetness, behavior occurs in context, in relationship to others. While it comes from a person, it is not located inside a person. Therapists, therefore, cannot make sense of a person's behavior without looking at the web of family or social relationships within which the individual is embedded.

Change

Family therapists are trained in the art and science of facilitating change, because change is family therapy's raison d'être. People who see therapists want to change something in their lives, usually something they don't like or that is causing pain. Clients want to change someone (this may include themselves), something (perhaps a circumstance, an irritating habit, or an emotion, such as anger), or perhaps a state of mind or a mood (such as depression or anxiety).

The phenomenon "change" can be rather complex, and helping someone change, even when they want to, can be difficult to do. Over their lifetimes, people come to learn how difficult it can be to change something in their own lives, even something they desperately want to be different. Anxious people work desperately to calm themselves, procrastinators try to break the habit, and the sleepless, finding themselves still wide awake at 3 a.m., struggle to make sleep come.

How Systemic Therapy Facilitates Change

While change may be at the heart of the matter for all therapies, systems thinking is at the heart of the matter for many family therapists. In the mid-1940s and early 1950s, important ideas about systems were being developed in different places around the world. In Europe, these ideas tended to go by the name *cybernetics,* while in the United States, the preferred term was *systems theory,* following the writings of biologist Ludwig von Bertalanffy, generally known as a founder of general systems theory. Whether called systems theory or cybernetics, all of these ideas dealt with variations of the same subject: how systems are organized and patterned and how communication works in systems. It was Gregory Bateson, a social scientist, linguist, and semiotician, and his groundbreaking work on systems and communication theory, who garnered the attention of those people who would later be thought of as family therapy founders. Bateson's systems theoretical ideas were at that time, and continue to be today, the foundation from which many new family therapy ideas and innovations have sprung. Though not a family therapist himself, Bateson's work continues to be highly regarded and stands as a cornerstone of family therapy.

Systems theory and cybernetics embrace a view of the world as an interconnected web of relationships, rather than a collection of disparate and disconnected objects. Systems of any sort, whether social (the relationships between the ants in an anthill, between members of a human family, or members of a flock of migrating birds), ecological (the relationship between plants, animals, and environment), or societal (relationships between different societies or within societal systems such as financial, educational, and religious systems) are all examples of information traveling in circuit, connecting with information traveling in circuits of other systems, which interconnect with yet other systems to create a web of interconnected, information-processing systems Bateson called "mental systems" or "mind."

In contrast, nonsystemic therapies think in straight lines of unidirectional causality: The alcoholic father is the cause of his son's alcoholism; the depressed mother causes depression in her child. *A causes B.* These therapies assume that problems have root causes, so treatment concerns itself with tracing back and finding these causes. Imagine a man comes to see a therapist and tells her that he wants to stop thinking about his wife who left him a few years ago. Seen from a causal point of view, the man will be said to be suffering from a mental illness caused by obsessive thoughts, which were, in their turn, caused by the circumstance of his wife's departure. He will likely be diagnosed as having some sort of thought disorder and medication may be prescribed. The man's "thought disorder" will be seen as located inside him as an internal, individual pathology.

Systems thinking, with its view of interconnectedness is, on the other hand, circular. *A* gives rise to *B and B* gives rise to *A*—a multidirectional interactional sequence. A systemic family therapist will see a pattern of interaction, not only between the man and his wife but between the man and his own thoughts. Because the man doesn't want to have thoughts of his wife, his thoughts become "something-to-be-gotten-rid-of." Consequently, a context of opposition is established, and the man's efforts to stop his own thoughts generate a neverending feedback loop: The more he (A) tries to *not* think of his wife, the more he (B) thinks of her, and the more he (B) thinks of her, the more he (A) tries not to. *A* generates *B* and *B* generates *A*. Rather than join the man in a fruitless effort to purposefully stop his thoughts (because the therapist knows that thoughts are not removable, physical objects), the therapist will, instead, help the man change his relationship to his thought-stopping efforts.

The single tool therapists have available to them to facilitate change is language. But words are not "things" and cannot be wielded like hammers, pliers, or knives to pound, pluck, or cut a problem away. Implements belong to the category of objects; language belongs to the category of relationship. Therapists who throw words at their clients as if they were objects, therapists who cajole, plead, threaten, preach, sell, shame, convince, praise, or lecture their clients as a means of provoking change, will find that no matter how brilliant their logic, no matter how silver-tongued, fierce, or gentle their persuasion, the problem remains, unmoved and unchanged.

This raises the question of how a therapist "sees" relationship, given that relationships are abstractions, not objects that can actually be seen with the human eye. Bateson tells us that to "see" relationship, we must look with binocular vision. We must "see double." By viewing the man's dilemma as a complementary relationship (think thoughts/stop thinking thoughts), we are able to see pattern—efforts to stop thoughts about his wife provoke those very thoughts, which call on further effort to stop the thoughts, provoking more thoughts about his wife, and so on. By seeing double, we are able to see his dilemma as the product of an interaction with himself that is set within a context of opposition. Thus seen, we avoid putting him in the wrong or localizing the problem as residing inside him as some sort of pathology. We don't regard him as a psychiatric patient or an "obsessive thinker," but rather a person caught in an escalating interaction. By applying systemic principles, by viewing problems as changeable in the here-and-now, and by assuming client strength and resiliency, family therapists are able to focus on possibilities for real change and give clients what they are asking for, which is to feel better in the future.

The relational thinking described here is unique to family therapy, the new kid on the therapy block and a relatively recent addition to the arena of psychotherapy. Beginning in the 1940s and 1950s, a number of therapists, who recognized how difficult it is to facilitate lasting change, adopted systemic ideas and began researching and experimenting with new ways of thinking about change and doing therapy. This began a move away from strict analysis of the individual patient, which had been *de rigueur* since Sigmund Freud's theories gave birth to modern psychotherapy in the 1890s. However, as is the case in many fields, not all family therapy theorists agreed on exactly how change best comes about. As a result, family therapy has a number of theoretical models and philosophical schools, each with its own theorists, each proposing a different lens through which to view the way problems are formulated and resolved.

Murray Bowen, a psychiatrist deeply committed to systems theory, theorized that humans seek a balance between togetherness and individuality, a struggle informed by not just the nuclear family, but multigenerational family relationships. Don Jackson, psychiatrist turned family therapist who worked closely with Bateson for many years, was intensely drawn to Bateson's ideas and based his own numerous groundbreaking theoretical concepts and developments on them. Carl Whitaker, also a psychiatrist, developed an experiential model of family therapy designed to get people in touch with their deeper, authentic selves through an experience with a therapist able to be his or her true self.

Paul Watzlawick, an Austrian-born psychiatrist, and his colleagues, proposed that when attempts to solve a problem don't work, people often simply reapply the same solution over and over, each time with more intensity or frequency. For example, when one finds oneself still awake in the middle of the night, one has probably already spent several hours trying to force sleep upon oneself. As the night wears on one gets more frantic for sleep and continues attempts to force sleep, which makes it more difficult to go to sleep. Round and round the frantic cycle goes until the forced efforts become, themselves, the problem.

The students and protégés of these pioneering family therapists came behind their teachers with new ideas that strengthened and expanded their teachers' theoretical models. Philip Guerin, a student of Bowen's, developed a number of distinctive therapeutic techniques designed to address specific Bowenian concepts. Betty Carter, a Bowen devotee, expanded and popularized Bowen's concept of the family life cycle and added gender equality concepts to the Bowenian model. Karl Tomm, a Canadian psychiatrist, deeply interested in the application of systems theory to therapy, refined circular questioning, a technique that sought to operationalize Bateson's notion of binocular vision.

The work of these family therapy pioneers included whole families in treatment and was informed by systems theory, which, although just a small blip on the radar screen at the time, was to grow into a full-blown paradigm shift in the field of family therapy. Systems theory became the foundational theory with which the field of family therapy grew to be identified.

Martha Laughlin

See also Circularity and Linearity; Cybernetics; Ecosystemic Structural Family Therapy; Ecosystems Perspective; General Systems Theory; Hypothesis, Systemic; Questions: Open, Closed, and Circular; Systemic Family Therapy

Further Readings

Bateson, G. (2000). *Steps to an ecology of mind.* Chicago: University of Chicago Press.

Bertalanffy, L. von. (1968). *General system theory.* New York: George Braziller.

Fisch, R., Weakland, J. H., & Segal, L. (1982). *The tactics of change: Doing therapy briefly.* San Francisco: Jossey-Bass.

Flemons, D. (1991). *Completing distinctions.* Boston: Shambhala.

Flemons, D. (2002). *Of one mind: The logic of hypnosis, the practice of therapy.* New York: W. W. Norton.

Keeney, B. P. (1983). *Aesthetics of change.* New York: Guilford Press.

Watzlawick, P., Beavin, J. H., & Jackson, D. D. (1967). *Pragmatics of human communication: A study of interactional patterns, pathologies, and paradoxes.* New York: W. W. Norton.

Watzlawick, P., Weakland, J., & Fisch, R. (1974). *Change: Principles of problem formation and problem resolution.* New York: W. W. Norton.

TECHNOLOGY AND FAMILIES/MARRIAGE

There are several issues that emerge in couples and families related to technology. Common technology issues that emerge in couples counseling include any issue that creates some impairment in intimacy, how intimacy is expressed online, how it is constructed using the Internet, and how the Internet and new information technologies affect the development of intimacy. Online intimacy problems disrupt a couple's level of self-disclosure and partner responsiveness. This includes, but is not limited to, cybersex, online infidelity, online pornography usage, and online addiction (in some cases specific to sex addiction fueled by the Internet). Other issues experienced by couples include a limited amount of shared time together, issues concerning video gaming, the emergence of suspicion and jealousy in a relationship, accountability, and monitoring of one another's online interactions and offline behaviors. In addition, in families, the issues raised most frequently include the monitoring of a youth's behavior and online interactions, the experience of being cyberstalked or cyberbullied, complaints of one parent over the other parent's communications with their child over electronic text (specifically in cases where the parents are separated), rules concerning cell phone usage, and responsiveness to parents through these technologies. This entry examines cybersex, as well as some of the broader impacts of new technologies on the lives of couples and families.

Definition of Cybersex

Cybersex is a general term used to describe a collection of sexual activities facilitated by an Internet connection and can have a pronounced effect on couples and children. For couples, cybersex can be a form of infidelity and can interfere with a couple's intimacy and relational satisfaction. For children and adolescents, engaging in inappropriate sexual communication or other sexual activities may expose them to emotional harm and may provide a predator with future physical access to an unsuspecting child or adolescent.

For couples, online communications can constitute sexual and/or emotional infidelity. Online infidelity is defined as occurring when one person communicates outside the primary relationship to the exclusion of the primary partner, is secret, and takes resources (e.g., time or money) away from the primary relationship. This communication can be sexual in nature (thus, it can have a cybersex component) or can be solely emotional. The determination as to whether it constitutes an affair is the extent to which the activities and exchanges are maintained in secret and exclude the primary partner. Online infidelity differs from an Internet sex addiction in that the focus in online infidelity tends to be on one person rather than focusing on sexual gratification.

Theories Explaining the Involvement of Technology in Couple and Family Life

There are several key theories that explain the involvement of technology in couple and family life. Many of the theories focusing on technology specifically relate to motivations for its usage such as the *technology adaptation model* (TAM) or the *uses and gratifications model*. There are two theories that address technology impact as it relates to families: domestication theory and the couple and family technology framework. Domestication theory attends to the recursive nature of the role of technology in couples and families. Specifically, it explores the role that technology has in one's home life, how the individuals in the environment adapt to the technology, and how the technology then changes and evolves in response to the ways in which individuals have adapted to it. Yet, this theory is limited in its interpretation of the direct impact of technology on the process within relationships themselves. In response to the limitations, the couple and family technology framework was developed to more specifically attend to the implications technology has on couple and family life.

The Couple and Family Technology Framework

The couple and family technology (CFT) framework was developed to understand the impact of technology on couples and families. It is comprised of three main elements interacting with one another; one relates to the characteristics of technology itself and the remaining two are concerned with relational systems. The first area, ecological elements, refers to the seven qualities of the Internet and technology that have a specific impact on relationships. These characteristics include anonymity, accessibility, affordability, acceptability, approximation, accommodation, and ambiguity. *Anonymity* refers to the quality of the Internet that allows users to present themselves in any way they choose. This means one can put out as much information as one wants about oneself and hold back other characteristics one might view as unfavorable. This differs from face-to-face interactions, because there are certain elements about face-to-face interactions that cannot be hidden (i.e., facial expressions, the way one looks, and location). *Accessibility* means the Internet is readily available on both small to large devices and from virtually any location; this increases one's ability to gain access to information and other people at any time. *Affordability* refers to the quality of the Internet that allows many people across a variety of socioeconomic statuses to access digital technologies, either in their personal residences or in public places that offer a free connection. Having such access and using devices is highly acceptable across many demographic groups. Today's technologies also allow one to approximate real-time interactions in a variety of ways (e.g., through advanced visual graphics, synchronous communication methods, and video conferencing). This may be related to the next element, *accommodation,* which describes the user's ability to use the computer or Internet to accommodate behavior one would not have the ability to perform in one's offline life. Finally, rules around engagement in the computer and the extent to which one's behavior can be considered problematic are often *ambiguous* and open to interpretation, specifically in the case of texts and e-mails, which are sent often without the accompaniment of nonverbal signs and symbols.

Implications for Relational Structure

As a collective set, the ecological elements have an impact on the structure and process of relational systems. There are three primary ways in which these ecological elements have an impact on the structure of relationships. First, existing rules in couples and families are now challenged. The introduction of such technologies may result in the creation of new rules. In some cases, the new rules can be adaptive; in other ways, they may be constrictive. Second, the integration of the Internet into couples and families introduces a new perspective in how boundaries are established and managed in the relational system. For example, due to the accessibility of the Internet, it is often easy to locate someone or have someone locate you. The Internet and new technology provide ways to be contacted by people who know you as well as people who do not, thus compromising boundaries. In other ways, the Internet can help relationships establish certain boundaries that were not present before. In social media, for example, users can set what they want others in their social network to see, setting a series of boundaries around what is shared. Third, roles in relationships are also affected by the ecological elements. For example, teens who have been raised with technology (i.e., it has been accessible to them throughout their development) may be more proficient in its usage and exhibit a higher level of technological literacy. In such cases, the hierarchical roles in families may be flipped due to the difference in knowledge with regard to some topics.

In addition, the roles of parents and partners have changed with the accessibility, anonymity, and affordability of technologies. Parents can track their children's whereabouts and monitor their contacts; partners can do the same. In addition, the anonymity, approximation, and ambiguity contribute to the dilemma as to whether it is appropriate to request one's password for various websites or devices. In some ways, the request of a password could be interpreted as a demonstration of trust; in other cases, it could be interpreted as a challenge to the trust ostensibly present in the relationship. Parents' roles change with the decision to monitor their children's online activities and are further impacted by the decision to engage in this monitoring overtly or covertly.

Implications for Relational Processes

These ecological elements and changes to roles, rules, and boundaries also have implications for the processes of relationships in three key ways; specifically, they have changed how relationships are initiated, maintained, and terminated. For example, the accessibility and affordability of the Internet allows relatives who are distant to initially find one another or to reconnect despite great geographical distance and the passage of time. Additionally, computer users also now have a number of possibilities in front of them to locate options for adoption in other countries. There is also a body of research dedicated to the initiation of romantic relationships in which the Internet, phone applications, and other new technologies play a major part; again, to some degree, this is fueled by the affordability, accessibility, acceptability, and anonymity provided by digital technologies. Maintaining couple and family relationships is also influenced by ecological elements. Research in the field of communication studies indicates that text-based messages and electronic communication puts a heavier reliance on self-disclosure than physical appearance, contributing to higher degrees of commitment, connection, and intimacy. On the other hand, the experience of intimacy may be mitigated if one or both partners are using the anonymity inherent in electronic communication (whatever the medium) to mislead the individual on the other end of the communication. In addition, technologies may speed up intimacy, since one may engage in behaviors with someone online more quickly than one would offline, thus solidifying the unique relationship between the two people. Also, ambiguous statements offered over text and through e-mail can be interpreted in ways that sustain intimacy or interfere with it, depending on how the receiver interprets the message and its context. Maintenance of relationships is also impacted by the timing and tempo changes in relationships with the accessibility and acceptability of technology. Research shows that couples communicate more frequently over the course of the day but those interactions are shorter, which may have implications for the ways in which couples communicate and the type of information that is shared.

Relationship termination is also influenced by technology's qualities. Accessibility makes it easy for users to post status changes in their relationships. Users may also attempt to lessen the impact of a break-up by texting and e-mailing rather than breaking up face-to-face. In addition, families can easily and affordably create legacy pages or tributes to loved ones who have passed away. Finally, social networking pages are often maintained as a way for others to post statements and recollections about a loved one who has passed away, giving them a permanent online presence.

Unique Characteristics of the CFT Framework

One of the principles of the couple and family technology framework is that it is not a prescriptive model. In other words, the model describes the areas in which couples and families are affected by technology, but this is not to say that couples and families are affected in one particular direction. For example, some families may be affected by experiencing fewer boundaries as a result of the use of technology. In other families, the effect may be the opposite (e.g., they may feel that their lives are more restricted). In addition, there is not a value judgment placed on the effect of technology on a family system. For example, having boundaries in a system as the result of technology is not viewed as exclusively having a negative effect on the relational system. Instead, the effect of technology on the system is interpreted only in context with the relational system itself. In this way, the framework can be applied to couples and families from diverse backgrounds. Another unique element to the CFT framework is the notion of the technological genogram. The technological genogram (a visual representation of a family and their relationships) describes the relationship of couples and family to technology as if the technology was another person in their home with whom each member of the family has a relationship and with whom each member interacts. From this frame, technology grows and changes with the family as the family grows and changes with the technology.

Katherine M. Hertlein

See also Communication in Couples and Families; Parent–Adolescent Relations; Systems Theory

Further Readings

Blumer, M., Hertlein, K. M., Smith, J., & Allen, H. (2014). How many bytes does it take? A content analysis of cyber issues in couple and family therapy journals. *Journal of Marital and Family Therapy, 40*(1), 34–48.

Hawkins, B. P., & Hertlein, K. M. (2013). Treatment strategies for online role-playing gaming problems in couples. *Journal of Couple and Relationship Therapy, 12*(2), 150–167.

Hertlein, K. M. (2012). Digital dwelling: Technology in couple and family relationships. *Family Relations, 61*(3), 374–387.

Hertlein, K. M., & Ancheta, K. (2014). Clinical application of the pros and cons of technology in couple and family therapy. *American Journal of Family Therapy, 42*(4), 313–324.

Hertlein, K. M., & Blumer, M. L. C. (2013). *The couple and family technology framework: Intimate relationships in a digital age.* New York, NY: Routledge.

TEEN PARENTING

Teen parenting is a term applied to those who conceive during their adolescent years. Some studies define teen parents as those who are between the ages of 13 and 19, or who are not legally considered adults. Teen parenting is seen as a social issue that affects the child as well as the parents. State-funded programs focus on the prevention of adolescent pregnancy, as well as assistance for adolescent parents and their children. As adolescents are developing into adulthood, educational, psychosocial, and environmental factors may influence their ability to parent. In order to compensate for these influences, multigenerational families adapt to take care of the adolescent, as well as the child. In this entry common issues for adolescent mothers, the involvement of adolescent fathers, and sociocultural factors that influence the occurrence and outcomes of teen parenting are discussed.

Social Support

Multigenerational Families

It is common for adolescent mothers and their children to live in a multigenerational family for financial, emotional, and practical support. The parents themselves are often finishing high school and may need help from kin to raise the child. Such multigenerational families have been found to be helpful in attaining positive outcomes for the child, especially during the earliest years. As the adolescent mother is developing her competency in parenting, the multigenerational family serves as a protective factor in coping with the child's externalizing behaviors—negative actions directed at the people or things in one's environment—until the child is of preschool age. At that point, the children's ability to develop socially is strongly influenced by their parents being competent in their parenting abilities. Within the multigenerational family, the maternal grandmother has been found to play a gatekeeping role in relation to the biological father's involvement in his child's life. Her approval of him has been found to be indicative of the time he spends with the child.

Coparenting

The adolescent mother is more likely than the father to have custody of the child; however, the negative stereotype of adolescent fathers being uninvolved is not supported by research. In one study, most adolescent fathers, when questioned at the hospital of their baby's delivery, voiced interest in their child's well-being and willingness to be involved in their children's lives. Notwithstanding, financial circumstances and low education often lead to dependence on the multigenerational family structure and may prevent teen fathers from giving the financial support that is often associated with being involved in their child's life.

It must be acknowledged, however, that adolescent fathers are not well represented in research. Their participation in research tends to be limited because they are less easy to access than adolescent mothers. The fathers that researchers are more likely to include are those who are more involved in their children's lives through parenting programs or at the hospital during the birth. Accordingly, there is still much to be learned about the adolescent father. Nevertheless, some things about fathers can be learned from mothers. For mothers who were questioned, the adolescent father's involvement was hindered by lack of income, lack of parental knowledge, or a poor relationship with the mother. Adolescent father involvement is more likely when the adolescent parents are cohabiting, or if the mother–father relationship is amicable.

Peers

During pregnancy, many adolescent mothers experience social isolation. The same is not the case for adolescent fathers, perhaps due to a lack of physical change during expectation of the child. Adolescent mothers have been found to have a lack of peer support from their nonparenting peers due to a lack of a common struggle—unless, of course, they have a friend who is pregnant or a parenting adolescent as well. A parenting teen friend has proven helpful for both parent and child outcomes.

Marriage

Adolescent parents are significantly more likely to marry during their teen years when compared with their peers; however, most adolescent parents in the United States do not marry. This leaves the parent and child vulnerable because the limited education of the adolescent leads to restricted career opportunities. Circumstances often entail a multigenerational family in which the adolescent mother lives with her extended family, typically including the child's maternal grandmother, as noted earlier, and the biological father is involved.

Cyclical Issues

Multiple Children

An estimated 40% of adolescent pregnancies are not first pregnancies. Adolescent mothers are likely to have other pregnancies during their adolescence. This implies there are recurring factors that influence the likelihood of adolescent parenthood. In the United States in 2009, adolescent pregnancies were found to have resulted in live births (57%), abortions (27%), or miscarriage/fetal loss (16%).

Generational

Adolescent parents are more likely to have children who themselves become adolescent parents. This is a cyclical issue that may be due to factors associated with adolescent parenthood, such as single-parent households, less permissive parenting styles, and low income.

Child Outcomes

Perhaps due to the stigmatization of adolescent parenthood or fear of parental reaction, adolescent mothers tend to seek prenatal care later in pregnancy than do older mothers. This, as well as other factors, may be a determinant of the child's being at greater risk for infant fatality or sudden infant death syndrome (SIDS). Babies of adolescent parents tend to be of lower birth weight. Early prenatal care is important in helping with these issues and ensuring that the unborn fetus receives the best chances of survival and healthy development.

Children of adolescent mothers also experience psychosocial issues, including intellectual, language, and socioemotional deficiencies. As early as early childhood, the offspring of adolescent mothers have been found to have poorer testing scores, negative externalized behaviors, and higher association with later substance abuse in comparison with children of adult parents. Efforts looking to moderate these associations have included parenting programs, as well as programs focused on helping with the parents' outcomes. This, in turn, affects the child's outcomes.

Maternal Outcomes

Adolescent mothers have been found to be more likely to depend on government assistance later in life, which may be due to an association of teen parenting with failure in school and fewer subsequent opportunities. This stigmatized expectation can lead to a lack of expectations by adolescent mothers, inevitably resulting in mental health effects. Adolescent mothers have been found more likely to be depressed than their adolescent nonparenting peers, as well as adult parents. Adolescent mothers have also been found to have more stress and to use more permissive parenting styles.

Disparities

Although the number of teen parents has been declining for the past few decades, the United States' numbers are still high compared with those of other Western countries. Minorities generally are more likely to experience adolescent parenting, but minorities are also more likely to be in the low-income population. It has been found that income level is more indicative of adolescent parenting than are race and ethnicity.

When it comes to the environment in which the mother raises the child, African American families have been seen to have less stress in response to the new baby. Latin American multigenerational homes have been found to be second in terms of stress. White multigenerational families with adolescent parenting have been found to have the highest stress in response to the circumstance. This is important as stress is related to maternal depression, and maternal depression is related to the child's outcomes.

Causes

Cause of adolescent pregnancy can be a controversial topic. A lack of sexual education or birth control can contribute to adolescent pregnancy. Studies have found an association between adolescent pregnancy and drug use, especially alcohol, marijuana, and ecstasy. Opiate use has been found to have a negative correlation with adolescent impregnation. Age difference of the partners has also been found to be associated with adolescent pregnancy; adolescents are more likely to become impregnated by their older partners than are adolescents who date boys their own age. Girls who experienced sexual abuse as children are also significantly more likely to become adolescent mothers when compared with girls who were not abused as children.

Prevention

Adolescents may be apprehensive about seeking birth control because of discomfort in speaking to their parents about being sexually active. Adolescent pregnancy can be prevented through sexuality education, as well as the improvement of access to birth control. Sexual education consisting solely of a sexual abstinence message has been found to be ineffective.

Katharine Melyssa Murphy-Edmunds

See also Parenting; Parenting Education; Pregnancy; Pregnancy and Sexuality; Sexual Abuse

Further Readings

Clear, E. R., Williams, C. M., & Crosby, R. A. (2012). Female perceptions of male versus female intendedness at the time of teenage pregnancy. *Maternal and Child Health Journal, 16*(9), 1862–1869.

Ellis, B. J., Bates, J. E., Dodge, K. A., Fergusson, D. M., Horwood, L. J., Pettit, G. S., & Woodward, L. (2003). Does father absence place daughters at special risk for early sexual activity and teenage pregnancy? *Child Development, 74*(3), 801–821.

Gomez Scott, J., & Cooney, T. M. (2014). Young women's education and behavioral risk trajectories: Clarifying their association with unintended pregnancy resolution. *Culture, Health & Sexuality, 16*(6), 648–665.

Rose, I., Prince, M., Flynn, S., Kershner, S., & Taylor, D. (2014). Parental support for teenage pregnancy prevention programs in South Carolina public middle schools. *Sex Education, 14*(5), 510–524.

TERMINATION

There is a saying associated with Geoffrey Chaucer that "All good things must come to an end." This is true of counseling—eventually all counseling relationships must come to an end. The ending of a counseling relationship is called termination. While a more traditional, dictionary definition of termination refers to the act of something ending, termination in counseling refers to the termination of a counseling relationship as a process. It is not simply one act (the final session) but rather a stage or transition that occurs over time, and which affects both clients and counselor. It is such an important component that termination is a topic that should be discussed with clients as early as the first session and revisited throughout the course of the counseling relationship; it should also be recognized as the ultimate goal for therapy. Although the process of termination is similar for all clients, special consideration may need to be made for younger clients whether one is working with individual children or families. In this entry several important aspects of termination in counseling are examined, including the ways in which termination might occur, the ethical obligations counselors face with regard to termination, and some common termination rituals.

Ethical Considerations and Termination

Counseling is a time-limited professional relationship in which counselors engage with clients and assist them in identifying life issues, resolving their concerns, and ultimately ending therapy in a way that allows the clients to function independently of the counselor. The length of the counseling relationship often relies on the number and extent of the client issues presented, the motivation of the client to explore those issues, and the client's ability to develop and deploy the resources necessary to resolve his or her concerns. Ethically and professionally, the expectation of all counselors is that at some point the counseling relationship will end. Because counseling creates a setting where clients ultimately reveal intimate details of their lives to the counselor, special care must be taken to ensure that termination is carefully and effectively addressed.

The American Counseling Association (ACA) Code of Ethics (2014) addresses the topic of termination and outlines certain obligations that counselors have when it comes to termination with a client. According to the code, counselors are obligated to avoid entering or continuing counseling relationships in which the counselor lacks the competence to be of assistance to the client. The code also stipulates that counselors must properly terminate with clients when it is clear that the client no longer needs assistance, the client is no longer benefiting from counseling, or when the client may actually be harmed by continuing counseling. Counselors are ethically required to provide clients with referrals and can never simply refer clients based solely on the fact that the counselor's personal views or beliefs are inconsistent with those of the client. Part of a counselor's ethical obligation is to make sure that clients receive proper care when the time comes to terminate.

How Termination Occurs

Termination can occur under a number of circumstances. Under ideal conditions, counseling ends after the client and counselor determine together that the client's goals have been met or the presenting issue can now be managed effectively by the client independently. At other times, clients and counselors may disagree that counseling has reached an appropriate end point and ultimately make an independent decision that termination is the best course of action. Clients may initiate termination because they feel that their goals have been met, the counselor is no longer helpful (and in some cases is actually harmful), they are frustrated with the process of counseling, they are financially unable to continue, they are relocating, or more pressing things in life have taken place and the issue for which they originally sought counseling no longer seems important.

Sometimes termination is counselor driven. Examples of this are when the counselor recognizes that goals have been accomplished by the client, the counselor has exhausted all resources and gone as far as he or she can with the client, or the client issues that surface in counseling require more extensive work in an area in which the counselor is not as familiar or competent. Counselors sometimes move, retire, or become ill and are unable to continue the counseling relationship. Additionally, in the case of a student intern, the counseling relationship may need to be terminated simply because the student is graduating or moving to a different field placement site. The unpredictability of life further stresses the importance of properly preparing clients for the inevitable reality of termination.

The process of termination, although it may be very difficult for some clients, gives counselor and client an opportunity to review the goals made by the client for therapy, identify strengths and growth seen in therapy, recap the journey and process of counseling, and ultimately achieve a healthy closure of the counseling relationship. This process can sometimes be challenging for clients who do not have healthy or positive models in their own lives for ending relationships. As with *any* relationship that ends, there are certain emotions that accompany the end of a counseling relationship for both the client and the counselor. Clients can feel happy, sad, confused, proud, or overwhelmed. Although termination is the goal of counseling and it often signals the point when goals have been achieved, clients may paradoxically resist termination. For some clients, this counseling relationship may be the first or only time in their life in which they are fully attended to, given unconditional positive regard, encouraged and recognized for their accomplishments, and not judged or shamed for what they reveal in session. They may have come to enjoy meeting with their counselor and feel truly accepted by him or her.

Some clients feel completely overwhelmed with the idea of terminating the counseling relationship, fearful that they cannot succeed without the help of the counselor, and driven to convince the counselor that they are not ready to terminate. In an attempt to keep the relationship "active" and to avoid termination, clients may, either consciously or subconsciously, find additional concerns or create new goals for themselves. It is not uncommon for the thought of termination to cause some clients to experience a temporary crisis or to find new issues to present to the counselor. Clients who lack good models for appropriate and healthy endings to relationships may actively avoid coming to the final session in order to avoid the reality that the relationship is drawing to a close; they are unsure of how to end this relationship that has been stable, predictable, and positive, in a healthy way. Sometimes they do not want to face the "end," so they stop coming in anticipation of what they see as a very difficult process. They may also find ways to have a conflict with the counselor, so ending the relationship is not so painful. On the other hand, some clients may also feel more comfortable sharing aspects and issues with the counselor, knowing that the end is soon coming and that they will have little or no time to explore those issues. In essence, they have a sense a relief that they will not have to address these issues with the counselor. Each of these pretermination issues can become opportunities for the counselor to demonstrate healthy ways to correctly manage the end of the clinical relationship and by extension other important relationships in the life of the client.

The process of termination is so important that the way in which termination is managed determines how clients will view counseling overall and how they will implement what they learned in the counseling process. Most professional counselors agree that a sudden or unexpected termination often traumatizes clients. As previously noted, the unpredictability of life demands that client and counselor address termination from the outset of the clinical relationship. Once it has been decided by the client, counselor, or both that the relationship is at a place where ending is appropriate and most beneficial, the counselor often decreases the frequency of the sessions to biweekly or even once per month. Once it has been determined how many sessions remain, the counselor should look to the client to decide how he or she wants to spend their last few sessions. What do they want to focus on? Is there any unfinished business? As the last session approaches, it will be important to process the growth and accomplishments that the client has made, review any skills he or she has learned, discuss any challenges that might surface after termination and the plan for addressing them (which should include using the skills learned in counseling), and process any feelings about termination that might surface.

While youthful clients (children and adolescents) should process termination in the same way as adults, there are some differences. Children view time differently than adults, so the use of a countdown calendar is particularly helpful for them. Each week the counselor has the child check off the day and count the remaining days so the child has a clearer picture of the time left in their work together. Children also tend to see weekly meetings as a pattern to which they quickly acclimate. Following termination, they will remark that they missed counseling because they "always" go to counseling. Care and attention to detail regarding termination is particularly important when working with children and adolescents.

Effect of Termination on Counselors

Sometimes counselors are affected by the process of termination. Like the client who has enjoyed the relationship, they too can find a sense of joy in their work with a particular client over an extended period of time. They may find the client humorous or insightful and enjoy watching the client make strides toward his or her goals. Additionally, the counselor may have feelings of wanting to be needed or appreciated and may—although it is not psychologically healthy to do so—wish for that relationship to continue. The counselor who feels that the client has some "unfinished" business or sees some additional growth potential will sometimes not feel ready for the relationship to end. A counselor who is not ready to terminate may, consciously or subconsciously, find reasons that the client should not terminate and may encourage the client to continue therapy. Just as the client might have unhealthy models of a relationship ending, termination with a client might uncover some painful or unresolved feelings of loss for the counselor. However, an ethical and psychologically healthy counselor will correctly identify these needs to continue the relationship as a problem best addressed through consultation with colleagues or a supervisor, or by working through those issues with their own personal counselor.

Termination Rituals

Often counselors and clients find a way to bring meaning to their experience and put an end to their time together. As previously mentioned, many clients begin to taper the frequency of their counseling session from once per week, to every other week, to eventually once per month. At this point, many clients consider this an opportunity to check in with the counselor and process any small issues that might have come up since the last session. The ultimate goal in counseling is for clients to be able to gain the skills and insight to recognize and address challenges on their own. Counseling at that point becomes more like consultation. There are many resources that can be found in the literature that suggest helpful activities for termination. Some counselors have clients create something that represents their "journey" in counseling. The representation can be anything clients would like to make that shows the place in which they started therapy, the movement through therapy (including positive strides and occasional setbacks), where they feel they are now, and what they anticipate for the future.

Christine H. Ebrahim

See also Clinical Practice; Group Family Therapy; Support Groups; Therapists' Values

Further Readings

Lanning, W., & Carey, J. (2011). Systematic termination in counseling. *Counselor Education and Supervision, 27*(2), 168–173.

Ward, D. (2011). Termination of individual counseling: Concepts and strategies. *Journal of Counseling & Development, 63*(1), 21–25.

Therapeutic Alliance

Therapeutic alliance is defined as the strong emotional bond that is created between therapists and clients, and it is considered the cornerstone of healing as clients engage with the therapy process and enact change. The strength of the alliance is characterized by a sense of trust between clients and therapists, the belief that the process is collaborative, mutual agreement on tasks and goals, and the clients' perception that the therapist is personally invested in helping the clients meet their goals in therapy. Research has shown that the quality of the therapeutic relationship is the greatest predictor of outcome in individual therapy and also predicts outcome in therapy with couples even when different models are used in treatment. The necessary and sufficient conditions for creating a therapeutic alliance, the complexity of creating multiple alliances with couples and families, therapeutic alliance within the context of specific family therapy models, and how to repair an alliance are presented below.

Necessary and Sufficient Conditions

Carl Rogers was one of the founders of the humanistic approach (client-centered approach) to working with clients, and his views on the six core conditions necessary for therapeutic personality change are accepted by therapists around the world. According to Rogers, change only occurs within a relationship. Therefore, the first condition for change is that two persons must be in psychological contact with one another. What Rogers meant by this is that both persons must be connected enough to have a shared experience of one another. The second condition is that the client is in a state of incongruence, that is, a discrepancy between the client's perception of the self and the client's desired experience of the self. The next three conditions define the characteristics that the therapist brings to the relationship with the client: congruence, unconditional positive regard, and an empathic understanding of the client's frame of reference. Finally, the therapist must be able to communicate empathic understanding and unconditional positive regard so that it becomes part of the client's experience in the relationship.

These conditions are considered to be so important and fundamental that they are part of relationship training for most helping professionals. Rogers arrived at the six conditions necessary for personality change through his observation of what was effective in his own work as well as what research had reported as important. Although Rogers referred to the simplicity of these conditions, putting them into action in sessions is not easy, as clients bring their own personalities to therapy and therapists themselves have personal and emotional responses to what is presented in sessions.

It is important to note that Rogers stated that these conditions are enough to *initiate* personality change. Since Rogers identified these basic conditions, researchers and practitioners have added to them to develop what is now known as *therapeutic alliance*. Aside from the therapeutic skills and behaviors unique to different theoretical approaches, there are common beliefs regarding the ways of thinking and behaving that are crucial to establishing a therapeutic alliance. For example, the ability to create a therapeutic alliance requires an understanding and appreciation of the influence of culture on clients, a willingness on the part of the therapist to shed stereotypes, and awareness of how culture impacts the therapeutic relationship. As part of a congruent relationship, therapists should be aware of their own defenses or facades and use self-disclosure as appropriate while still maintaining healthy boundaries. Therapists should have effective interpersonal and communication skills, utilize humor when appropriate, accept and acknowledge when mistakes are made, and maintain a passion for the profession and a commitment to social justice.

Therapeutic Alliance in Couples and Family Therapy

If establishing a therapeutic alliance in individual therapy has its challenges, these challenges are compounded when therapists have to establish multiple alliances with members of a couple or family group in therapy. Therapists must be able to encourage and manage communication from all members, many of whom are involuntary clients. Members come to therapy with different personalities, complaints, motivations, beliefs, goals, and levels of commitment.

Therapeutic alliance with multiple clients is a reciprocal process. A therapeutic alliance with one member influences the alliance with other members. Therefore, the therapist must develop alliances at the individual, subsystem, and family levels. Depending on the intervention in process, the therapist may seem to shift alliance to meet the goal in process. For example, a structural family therapist may physically move his seat next to a client to support a hierarchical change that needs to occur in a family.

The perception of safety is a consideration in the degree to which clients are able to ally with therapists. Clients are vulnerable in session and the information shared in therapy is not neatly packaged and left in the therapist's files at the end of sessions. As part of the therapeutic alliance the therapist must establish boundaries so that what is discussed in session is not used to harm others in between sessions. Safety considerations evolve as members engage and disengage in therapy and as new secrets or problems are revealed. The perception that the therapeutic environment is not safe or supportive can greatly undermine trust in the therapist and in the process. Family members who feel safe in therapy are likely to be more comfortable in expressing emotion, encourage communication from other members, and look for feedback on the family's progress.

Another factor to consider in building a therapeutic alliance with a couple or family is that whatever occurs in session, and out of session as well, involves the therapist. The therapist becomes a part of at least one triangle, and possibly more than one triangle when working with families. The therapist must shift alliance from one person to another and must be able to ally with the couple or family as an entity itself. In couples or family therapy, there is no way that the therapist can avoid being pulled into the system, regardless of the therapist's efforts to maintain boundaries. The therapist becomes the expert, the person responsible for the success or failure of the relationship, and the person who is accountable for initiating change. As a result, the family may resist interventions and alliance in an effort to maintain the system's accustomed way of functioning. The struggle for leadership and power offers an opportunity for corrective interventions but also requires a challenge for the alliance.

Model-Driven Therapeutic Alliance

The ability to build a therapeutic alliance with couples and families is influenced by each individual's conflicts, emotions, issues, and commitment to change. This creates a unique challenge for the therapist, who must create an alliance with each person. Having a conceptual framework or guiding theory helps to organize therapists' thinking and understanding of the interactions within the system and provides methods of working with the system to develop alliance while also working toward systemic change. The means of creating therapeutic alliance is specific to the tasks, goals, and bonds that are unique to the model adopted by the therapist. The concept of *tasks* refers to the agreement of the process and structure of therapy and is agreed upon by therapist and clients. *Goals* are the outcomes of therapy that are also formed in collaboration between therapist and clients. The term *bonds* incorporates the empathic connection Rogers described as necessary for therapeutic change. Because of the collaborative nature and agreement in creating the tasks, goals, and bonds, alliances are likely to be strong.

Although there is agreement that a therapeutic alliance is necessary to facilitate change, there is less agreement on what therapist behaviors are desirable. Therapist behaviors will vary depending on client and family personality, developmental level, areas of concern, and the model that guides the therapist's work. The reciprocal relationship between therapist and family members is influenced by the varying degrees in which members bond with the therapist and whether they agree with tasks and goals. The ability to form an alliance is also confounded by the awareness members have of the therapist's interaction with other members and how the family is responding to what is happening in therapy.

When evaluating therapeutic outcomes, therapists would be wise to remember that many studies have reported that the quality of the therapeutic alliance is the greatest predictor of successful therapy. While therapists should not neglect their focus on improving techniques, they might also improve therapeutic outcomes by evaluating their interpersonal skills and adapting to meet the criteria identified by the literature that supports the development and maintenance of a strong therapeutic alliance.

Creating therapeutic alliance is not prescriptive. What alliance actually looks like in therapy is influenced by the therapist's personality, individual characteristics, therapeutic style, model, intention, and what interventions match the personalities of the couple or family being served. The process of therapeutic alliance is as creative as the therapists themselves. Following are examples of three pioneers in family therapy whose different styles of creating therapeutic alliance represent their very different ways of approaching family therapy.

Virginia Satir

Virginia Satir was known for her warmth, genuineness, and creativity. Her model of working with families was based on instinctive interventions rather than a prescriptive set of therapeutic behaviors or techniques. Satir believed that the therapeutic alliance occurred in a relationship in which people felt free to take risks. Therapy was not hierarchical; therapists and clients were expected to be equal partners in the process and in the learning that occurred as a result of therapy. Satir's role of therapist was as a facilitator, which allowed for her to work spontaneously and flexibly so that she could take advantage of what was happening in the moment and use it to influence change. She was an active participant in therapy, using herself in whatever role was useful in the moment to set an example for the family, or detaching when it was more appropriate to observe the process rather than actively participate in it.

Satir believed that it was the suppression of feelings that resulted in the loss of autonomy or intimacy in the family. Therefore, the goal of therapy was to help clients let down their guards and become interactive and playful so they would be more likely to reach deeper levels of emotion. As a result, clients were expected to develop heightened sensitivity to others, to recognize and act on their freedom to make choices, and to share feelings.

Murray Bowen

Murray Bowen believed that therapists should act as coaches and catalysts for change. Paradoxically, Bowen's model of therapeutic alliance was somewhat driven by the need to remain detached and to avoid becoming engaged in the emotionally driven automatic responses inherent in family therapy. Bowen saw the role of therapist as being objective and differentiated from the family's process. His goal was to maintain a neutral position. He created a therapeutic alliance by clients feeling understood by him, but not feeling like he was taking anyone's particular "side." Bowen believed that decreasing anxiety and increasing the focus on the self and one's role in interpersonal process were the key to change. Therefore, the role of the therapist was to minimize emotion and ask questions to individuals rather than encourage family dialogue. Bowen avoided becoming a target of the family's transference (projecting emotions from the past or current relationships onto the therapist) and getting involved in their emotional process, thus controlling his own reaction and avoiding triangulation (being pulled into arguments and having to "side" with someone).

Bowen disliked the idea of being technique driven, though he did utilize the concept of the process question to slow people down and help them understand their contributions to the interpersonal patterns in their families. Although Bowen initially worked with families, he eventually directed his focus to individuals because family dialogues became emotional and he felt that more effective work could be done in individual sessions. However, he still maintained an awareness of the family system, and the goal of therapy was to increase differentiation, to improve communication, and to help individuals gain self-awareness regarding their roles in problems rather than blame the family system for their problems.

Salvador Minuchin

Salvador Minuchin's structural family therapy includes three main phases: (1) taking the leadership position while *joining* with the family, (2) mapping the family structure, and (3) intervening to change the structure. Within this process the quality of the interaction between the therapist and family is considered to be critically important. Therapeutic alliance is facilitated through the process of joining with the family. This process begins by disarming the family's resistance through offering understanding and acceptance to every member.

As therapy continues, the therapist takes on a creative, active role as the expert, using interventions that will change the underlying structure of the family and patterns of interaction so problems are not maintained. Therapists may occasionally create alliances with subsystems, with a goal of changing the relationship between the members in the subsystem. While this may seem detrimental to therapeutic alliance, the ultimate result of this intervention is a realignment of a healthier system. The goals of therapy are to bring problematic behaviors and patterns of thought to the awareness of the family so the family can examine them, make changes, and solve their own problems.

Alliance Rupture and Repair

Therapeutic alliance problems can occur at the beginning of a therapy with difficulty in joining with clients, or later when there is a negative shift in the relationship. Because clients come to therapy with their own perceptions of what is likely to occur, client resistance may influence the therapist's ability to form an alliance with the couple or family. Ruptures can be due to misunderstandings and resolved quickly or can create a long-standing problem that leads to hostility, noncompliance, treatment failure, and dropout.

Understanding the purpose of resistance from family members can help therapists understand what needs to happen to initiate or repair the alliance. For example, despite the therapist's best efforts, a family may not comply with homework assignments or engage in therapeutic work while in session. As a result, the therapist feels and exhibits frustration with the family and the family's resistance increases in response to the therapist's behavior. Because the alliance is influenced by mutual agreement on tasks and goals as well as the bond with the family, the therapist might approach the rupture by exploring goals. Goals should originate with the clients and should be specific, behavioral, and measurable. For example, a goal that family members will respect one another is ambiguous and hard to put into action. The therapist needs to take the time to concretize the goal so all members know specifically what respect looks like and can recognize respectful behavior when it occurs.

Another way to assess or repair bonds and alliance is to ask clients for feedback about the process. This can be as simple as scheduling time at the beginning or end of sessions for clients to share what they feel is going well in sessions and what they would like to see done differently. Asking for this feedback gives the therapist useful information about the process that will guide future sessions, but it will also encourage client participation as the therapist can remind clients that the sessions are driven by what they said they wanted. As an alternative to impromptu feedback, therapists can schedule interview sessions in which the focus is to formally assess the effectiveness of the therapy and to get feedback on alternative direction.

Finally, it is important for therapists to assess their own responses to couples or families. It is not always easy to like clients or even to want to make connections with them. In this case, therapists should seek supervision to work through the issues that are interfering with their cases. Therapists should be introspective about their own processes, looking for the source of their own emotional responses, assessing personal issues that arise when working with certain clients, and exploring countertransference.

Patricia A. Robey

See also Clinical Practice; Couples and Marriage Counseling; Couples Therapy Research; Empathy; Humanistic Family Therapy; Joining; Self of the Therapist

Further Readings

Blow, A. J., & Sprenkle, D. H. (2001). Common factors across theories of marriage and family therapy: A modified Delphi study. *Journal of Marital and Family Therapy, 27*(3), 385–401.

Bordin, E. S. (1979). The generalizability of the psychoanalytic concept of the working alliance. *Psychotherapy: Theory, Research, and Practice, 16*, 252–260.

Friedlander, M. L., Escudero, V., Heatherington, L., & Diamond, G. M. (2011). Alliance in couple and family therapy. *Psychotherapy, 28*(1), 25–33.

Karam, E. A., Sprenkle, D. H., & Davis, S. D. (2015). Targeting threats to the therapeutic alliance: A primer for marriage and family therapy training. *Journal of Marital and Family Therapy, 41*(4), 389–400.

Knerr, M., Bartle-Haring, S., McDowell, T., Adkins, K., Delaney, R. O., Gangamma, R., Giebova, T., Grafsky, E., & Meyer, K. (2011). The impact of initial factors on therapeutic alliance in individual and couples therapy. *Journal of Marital and Family Therapy, 37*(2), 182–199.

Knobloch-Fedders, L. M., Pinsof, W. M., & Mann, B. J. (2007). Therapeutic alliance and treatment progress in couple psychotherapy. *Journal of Marital and Family Therapy, 33*(2), 245–257.

Minuchin, S. M., & Nichols, M. P. (1993). *Family healing: Strategies for hope and understanding.* New York, NY: The Free Press.

Nichols, M. P., & Schwartz, R. C. (2012). *Family therapy: Concepts and methods* (8th ed.). Needham Heights, MA: Pearson.

Rait, D. S. (2000). The therapeutic alliance in couples and family therapy. *JCLP/In Session: Psychotherapy in Practice, 56*(2), 211–224.

Rogers, C. R. (2007). The necessary and sufficient conditions of therapeutic personality change. *Psychotherapy: Theory, Research, Practice, Training, 44*(3), 240–248.

Safran, J. E., Muran, J. C., & Eubanks-Carter, C. (2011). Repairing alliance ruptures. *Psychotherapy, 48*(1), 80–87.

Slone, N. C., & Owen, J. (2015). Therapist alliance activity, therapist comfort, and systematic alliance on individual psychotherapy outcome. *Journal of Psychotherapy Integration, 25*(4), 275–288.

Snow, K., Crethar, H. C., Robey, P., & Carlson, J. (2005). Theories of family therapy (Part I & Part II). In R. H. Coombs (Ed.), *Family therapy review: Preparing for comprehensive and licensing examinations* (pp. 117–168). Mahwah, NJ: Erlbaum.

THERAPEUTIC ASSESSMENT

The term *Therapeutic Assessment* was first applied to a specific model of assessment by Stephen Finn in 1993. Finn was influenced by Constance Fischer, Leonard Handler, and Caroline Purves, other influential clinical psychologists who were developing and working within collaborative assessment methods. He further developed the Therapeutic Assessment model through his work with Mary Tonsager and conducted several clinical trials to provide evidence of the efficacy of this method of assessment. Currently, Therapeutic Assessment is a respected model that has been incorporated into many training programs and postgraduate trainings. Therapeutic Assessment as a model is different from the more generic term *therapeutic assessment,* and certainly not to be confused with transactional analysis. Generic therapeutic assessment is a broad term applied to the process of providing assessments for use in therapy to gather initial data, whereas Therapeutic Assessment is a model of assessment administration, scoring, and interpretation that is grounded in philosophical and theoretical roots.

This entry defines Therapeutic Assessment and examines its core values, process, and application.

Defining Therapeutic Assessment

A therapist can become certified to provide with a series of training programs offered through the Center for Therapeutic Assessment in Austin, Texas, where Stephen Finn is in residence. In the most simplistic terms, Therapeutic Assessment is a method of psychological testing in which the therapist works with clients to understand their difficulties and to answer the questions they may have about themselves. It is a method of working with clients on their psychological difficulties that is empowering for clients and leads to higher rates of positive outcomes; it can even be used as a method of intervention. As a method of clinical work, Therapeutic Assessment falls in line with postmodern constructivist approaches to psychotherapy, since the model is influenced by collaborative processes of client–therapist agreement and the philosophical underpinnings of personal truth versus absolute truth.

Core Values

There are several core values associated with Therapeutic Assessment that serve as the underlying basis for this approach to evaluation. They include collaboration, respect for the client, humility, compassion, openness, and curiosity. Many therapists already practice these beliefs in their everyday sessions with their clients. What makes Therapeutic Assessment unique is that these components are added to, and focused around, the psychological evaluation process. This method of evaluation deconstructs the traditional hierarchy of therapist-as-expert and reconstructs the process by allowing clients to be seen as cocreators of their own reality and allows them the opportunity to assign meaning to things they find important.

Process of Therapeutic Assessment

Typically, a Therapeutic Assessment will be comprised of several "steps." They include the initial session(s), standardized testing session(s), assessment intervention session(s), summary and discussion session(s), written feedback, and any follow-up session(s) a client system may request. These different steps, in addition to the core values of Therapeutic Assessment, are what sets this approach apart from traditional evaluation.

Initial Session

The initial session consists of interviewing and getting to know the client(s). This is one of the most important steps in the whole process. This is where the collaborative stance and relationship with the client is first established. This may take the form of a typical therapy session, in which a therapist engages in discussing presenting problems and difficulties of the client, but also includes a thorough examination of what the client wants to get out of the testing process, including identifying the exact questions for which the client wishes to find answers. For people who are referred by another helping professional, the integration of their concerns are brought into the discussion. It is also during this time that the therapist proposes the different assessments for clients to take that will be able to answer their questions. Obviously, the therapist must be very familiar with a wide range of instruments in order to be able to select only the appropriate questionnaires that will be able to fully answer the client's and referring provider's questions.

Standardized Testing Session(s)

The next part of the process is the standardized testing session, where the client returns to complete the assigned tests. Depending on the number of instruments and length of time required to complete them, the testing sessions may be extended beyond one visit. This is especially true if there are cognitive or memory tests, which are usually more taxing. One of the main concerns during this time is to make sure that clients are able to adhere to the published standardized norms for the instrument. After the completion of the testing sessions, clients are invited to speak with the therapist about what the experience was like, and how they felt about the tests and instruments, including items on the test, and whether or not they felt as though the instrument was going to be able to help them or not.

Assessment Interview Session(s)

During the assessment interview sessions a therapist engages in discussions and other nonstandard methods of assessment that are more subjective in nature, but which can be incredibly enlightening for the assessment process. These include the administration of nonobjective tests and/or interpretive tests, such as the Thematic Appperception Test or Rorschach, interviews, and role-plays among other types of interpretive tests. The therapist is required to make an interpretation of the information gleaned from the tests; during the fourth stage of Therapeutic Assessment the results are corroborated with the perceptions of the client. All of this information is also included in the report and influenced by the questions that the client would like answered from step one.

Summary Discussion Session(s)

Step four is called the summary/discussion session and is focused on a verbal review of the results of the assessments and how those results are able to answer the questions posed from step one. It is very important to carefully plan how the results are given to the client; the therapist should focus on a strengths-positive perspective within a collaborative framework. This allows clients to see the results not as absolute truth that is being given to them, but instead allows them the opportunity to create a sense of meaning from the results with the therapist. These collaborative answers to the client's questions are incorporated into any and all reports from the assessment sessions.

Written Feedback and Follow-Up

After the summary/discussion session, written feedback is provided to the clients. This usually takes the form of a letter or narrative that is addressed specifically to the clients themselves. If a formal report is required for a referral agency or other professional, a similar report can be provided that is addressed to them (with copies given to the client as well). This is an important component of the Therapeutic Assessment process as it highlights one of the major underlying assumptions of this approach—namely, that the client is a full partner in the evaluation process. Once the feedback is provided, follow-up sessions may take place to utilize the information from the Therapeutic Assessment sessions to incorporate changes into the client's life.

One of the unique contributions of Therapeutic Assessment to the evaluation process is the integration of providing written feedback to the client and gathering the client's feedback before the final report is distributed/written. The report itself is different from a traditional psychological evaluation report in that it includes the actual questions of the client and is written from the point of view of helping the client to better understand him- or herself. Therefore, it is often written in the first person and is written for the client as opposed to about the client. This is a distinct difference that creates a different atmosphere and reading experience. That is not to say that the report does not contain significant information related to the testing procedures and interpretation; it is just written at a level that most people who are untrained in clinical work can understand.

Breadth and Use of Therapeutic Assessment

Some may argue that Therapeutic Assessment is not an appropriate method of evaluation for more high-risk referrals, such as those in which child custody, forensic psychological investigation, or cognitive abilities are being tested. However, research has shown that Therapeutic Assessment is a valuable and valid method of evaluation regardless of the presenting problem. As such, there is no reason not to incorporate methods of Therapeutic Assessment throughout a psychological evaluation.

Any mental health professional who engages in evaluation or testing can utilize Therapeutic Assessment. As well, research has shown that referrals to a provider who practices from a Therapeutic Assessment approach will foster a larger systemic change than simply referring to traditional forms of evaluation. Couples and family therapists are uniquely suited to providing Therapeutic Assessment to clients. As a field, they often embrace a collaborative, client-centered, systemic view that is nestled in a strengths-based paradigm.

Christopher K. Belous

See also Adult Attachment Assessments; Assessment, Biopsychosocial; Assessment, Suicide; Family Assessment, Models of; Functional Assessment and Children; Scales, Children; Scales, Couple and Marital; Scales, Family; Sexual Assessment/History

Further Readings

Finn, S. E. (2007). *In our clients' shoes: Theory and techniques of Therapeutic Assessment*. Mahwah, NJ: Erlbaum.

Finn, S. E. (2008). The many faces of empathy in experiential, person-centered, collaborative assessment. *Journal of Personality Assessment, 91*, 20–23.

Finn, S. E., & Martin, H. (1997). Therapeutic assessment with the MMPI-2 in managed health care. In J. N. Butcher (Ed.), *Personality assessment in managed health care: Using the MMPI-2 in treatment planning*. New York, NY: Oxford University Press.

Finn, S. E., & Tonsager, S. E. (1992). The therapeutic effects of providing MMPI-2 test feedback to college students awaiting psychotherapy. *Psychological Assessment, 4*, 278–287.

Finn, S. E., & Tonsager, M. E. (1997). Information-gathering and therapeutic models of assessment: Complementary paradigms. *Psychological Assessment, 9*, 374–385.

Finn, S. E., & Tonsager, M. E. (2002). How Therapeutic Assessment became humanistic. *The Humanistic Psychologist, 30*, 10–22.

Handler, L. (2007). The use of therapeutic assessment with children and adolescents. In S. R. Smith & L. Handler (Eds.), *The clinical assessment of children and adolescents: A practitioner's handbook.* Mahwah, NJ: Erlbaum.

Hopwood, C. J., & Bornstein, R. F. (Eds.). (2014). *Multimethod clinical assessment.* New York, NY: Guilford Press.

Morey, L. C., Lowmaster, S. E., & Hopwood, C. J. (2010). A pilot study of manual-assisted cognitive therapy with a therapeutic assessment augmentation for borderline personality disorder. *Psychiatry Research, 178,* 531–535. doi:10.1016/j.pyschres.2010.04.055

Therapeutic Contract

A foundational element of effective, ethical, and legal counseling services is the use of a therapeutic contract. Similar to other forms of contracts, the therapeutic contract is a formal agreement between two parties. If you are a counselor in private practice, for example, your clients contract services with your practice. Within the contract, clear responsibilities, roles, and expectations are outlined for both the client and the counselor. In contemporary counseling practice, ethical and legal challenges are inevitable. The therapeutic contract in counseling evolved out of a desire to minimize those challenges and provide a transparent and well-documented process for all parties involved.

In addition to mitigating potential legal and ethical concerns, the therapeutic contract puts into practice the ethical concepts of beneficence and autonomy that serve as a foundation for the therapy profession. Because the therapeutic contract begins the process of helping the client, it comes from a place of beneficence. The therapeutic contract contains the client's rights and responsibilities, which empowers the client and fosters accountability to the process. Thus, the contract implements the ethical principle of autonomy. This entry examines the general terms of therapeutic contracts, theoretical perspectives on therapeutic contracts, and how these contracts are shaped by specific presenting concerns (e.g., suicidal tendencies). Specific attention is given to the use of therapeutic contracts in couples and family therapy. The concluding section considers some of the ways in which therapeutic contracts can circulate.

General Contract

A general therapeutic contract contains a number of standard elements. These elements were born out of the legal system and case law precedents to serve as the standard of practice for counselors. Suggested elements include, but are not limited to, the following:

- The counselor's name, title, training, and experience. Licenses and certifications are included here as well. It is prudent to include areas of special expertise or any areas in which the counselor is not adequately trained to provide services to clients.
- An explanation of, and limitations to, confidentiality.
- How records are maintained and stored as well as the policies on client access to records.
- Anticipated length of services.
- Benefits and risks associated with the treatment approach.
- Alternatives to the services planned.
- Fees for services, billing, and insurance information. This includes a discussion of stigma related to diagnosis typically required for insurance use.
- The rights of the client if he or she proceeds with services.
- The rights of the client if he or she chooses not to proceed with services.
- Emergency and crisis procedures, including after-hours contact.

How a Therapeutic Contract Differs From Informed Consent

Much of the information presented in the general contract may be similar to informed consent. Informed consent provides the client with the expectations of counseling and ensures that the client is able to make an appropriate choice to proceed or not proceed with services. It is quite similar to the therapeutic contract, but the therapeutic contract takes informed consent one step further to include the rights and responsibilities of the client and counselor. In addition, the therapeutic contract addresses rights and responsibilities of the counselor and client in relation to the specific theoretical approach of the counselor or presenting concern of the client.

Therapeutic Contracts Specific to Marriage, Couples, and Family Counseling

In marriage, couples, and family counseling, the therapeutic contract is slightly different than when working with individual adult or minor clients. In marriage, couples, and family counseling, the counselor must address the therapeutic approach to a system, rather than an individual. As such, the contract must incorporate the context of family interactions in the concept of change. In other words, therapeutic success is not measured by a change in one person but a change in the system.

Therapeutic Contracts Based on Theoretical Approach

When developing a therapeutic contract, counselors will determine if it is a contract based on an issue or the counselor's theoretical approach. For example, counselors who practice from a dialectical behavior therapy (DBT) perspective or who use transactional analysis may develop theory-specific contracts.

Dialectical Behavior Therapy

Outside of the general areas of therapeutic agreement, a therapeutic contract rooted in DBT will also include elements specific to that theory. For example, a commitment to engage in DBT skills training will likely be part of that contract. Some therapists teach these skills in group sessions, which would also be indicated in the therapeutic contract. In addition, the contract may include DBT target behaviors for therapy such as mindfulness, interpersonal effectiveness, emotional regulation, and distress tolerance. These behaviors are taught and measured in DBT. Accordingly, a DBT-specific contract outlines the responsibilities of the client and the counselor who would come from that particular theoretical perspective.

Transactional Analysis

Transactional analysis is often used in marriage and family counseling to address relational issues. Because transactional analysis is an active therapeutic stance, a contract is often employed to establish client commitment to the work of therapy. The contract might state specifically that in order to adhere to the tenets of transactional analysis, the client will avoid a passive role in therapy and the counselor will avoid a rescuer role. Articulating these expectations early in the therapeutic relationship commits both parties to an active, participatory role that benefits the client.

Therapeutic Contracts Based on Client Presenting Concern

In addition to therapeutic contracts that stem from the counselor's theoretical orientation, counselors and clients may find themselves entering into a contract specific to a particular presenting problem, such as suicide or self-harm.

Suicide

Some counselors employ the use of a no-suicide contract or suicide prevention contract when they have a client who is suicidal. In this case, the word "contract" can be misleading. To be clear, these contracts are not legal documents but are simple agreements between a client and counselor to prevent the client from attempting or committing suicide.

A no-suicide contract contains the following elements: an explicit statement in which the client agrees not to attempt or commit suicide, a time limit for the duration of the agreement, a contingency plan outlining what the client should do if the commitment to a no-suicide plan changes (e.g., client becomes suicidal), and the specific responsibilities that apply to the client and the counselor within the contract.

Proponents of such contracts find that they create a climate of suicide prevention. These contracts contain specific steps that the client is to follow if he or she becomes suicidal. Counselors who choose to use these contracts want their clients to have clear, written instructions during a time in which they are likely emotional, frightened, and not thinking clearly. Because of these concerns for their clients, counselors recommend signing the contracts and having the client keep a copy of the contract somewhere easily accessible.

This type of therapeutic contract is not universally supported in the profession. While many counselors find them to be helpful to particular clients, there is a lack of empirical support as to their clinical usefulness. Some counselors, instead, choose to use a commitment-to-treatment statement, which is a form of a contract that focuses on contracting for treatment, rather than avoiding suicide.

Self-Harm

In addition to contracts related to suicide, many counselors choose to address self-harm, also known as self-injury, using a therapeutic contract. Self-harm generally refers to intentional injury to one's person, such as to body tissue, typically without any suicidal intent. Common forms of self-harm include cutting or burning of the skin but can also include bruising of tissue, breaking bones, scratching, or interfering with wound healing. Although these behaviors are not generally associated with suicide, they may reflect a variety of motivations. For example, self-harm is often associated with clinical diagnoses such as depression, anxiety, and borderline personality disorder, and it may also be found in those with a history of trauma or abuse. In addition, self-harm is also seen in clients with autism spectrum disorder, developmental delays, or neurological disorders.

Not surprisingly, counselors often want to reduce episodes of self-harm as they work with underlying concerns that may lead to this behavior. This is where therapeutic contracts come into play. Counselors may find that engaging the client in a contract related to the behavior may be helpful. A self-harm therapeutic contract will often focus on options to use instead of self-harm, such as phoning or texting a friend, exercising, journaling, or listening to music. In addition to these distractions, the contract may also contain alternative replacement behaviors such as writing on the skin instead of cutting it. Ultimately, the goal of a therapeutic contract for self-harm is to reduce or replace the undesirable behavior.

Contingency Contracting

Another form of therapeutic contract that works to reduce or replace undesirable behavior is the contingency contract. A contingency contract can also be used to increase desirable behaviors. Contingency contracts describe what behaviors are expected and what behavioral reinforcers or rewards will follow. They specify a target behavior, the conditions under which the behavior should occur or not occur, and the consequences for engaging in or avoiding the behavior. These contracts should involve one behavior and have only one goal.

Determining the behavior to address in the contingency contract is part of the therapeutic process and typically involves establishing a baseline. For example, if a client wants to reduce critical comments directed at his partner, it is important to know how many critical comments the client makes each day. Then a target can be set, along with reinforcers. Reinforcers are rewards for being successful with the contract and must be individualized to the client. In the example provided, the client may want to try a new restaurant but won't be able to go until he has reached an agreed-upon goal that reduces the negative comments over a period of time. These therapeutic contracts are written in advance; the exact conditions that must be met to earn the reward are outlined and agreed upon with the client's involvement.

Therapeutic Contracts in Marriage, Couples, and Family Counseling

Among the more widely recommended uses of therapeutic contracts in marriage, couples, and family counseling is in addressing challenging interpersonal behaviors. Typically, these contracts are not established immediately; effective communication strategies must be implemented first. However, once couples are communicating well, they are ready to begin contracting for specific behavior changes. Some areas of change include role responsibilities, conflict management, and interpersonal trust.

Role Responsibilities

Couples and families tend to create patterns of behavior through which each member fulfills a family function. These roles may be instrumental and include such things as providing or maintaining the household, food, and other tangible resources. Other roles include those that provide emotional support and resources. Certainly each member can fulfill, at least partially, more than one role. However, there are times when only one family member serves a particular function and another family member may need to be involved. In this case, a role or responsibilities therapeutic contract can be helpful. For example, if one parent is primarily in charge of putting children to bed, the couple may contract for the other parent to share this activity. The parent who had been the exclusive provider of the role can then contract to fulfill other roles in the household or family.

Conflict Management

Couples and families routinely enter counseling due to excessive conflict. Perhaps the family has taken on an aging relative for caregiving or is having financial difficulties due to a job loss. Whatever the reason for the conflict, addressing the manner of conflict can be helpful in counseling. Therapeutic contracts for conflict management do not solve the root problem of a financial crisis or a sick loved one, but they can make life more pleasurable while living with these challenges. A central theme that must be stressed by the counselor is that no family, regardless of how healthy, is free from conflict. As such, reducing conflict is critical to setting the stage for marriage, couples, or family counseling.

A sample therapeutic contract for a couple experiencing conflict may include items such as the following:

- We agree that even when disagreeing or fighting that we are allies; that is, partners who love each other and will therefore treat each other with respect and kindness.
- We agree not to threaten, intimidate, attack, insult, or harm each other physically, psychologically, or emotionally.
- We will maintain civil tones and reasonable volume when having a disagreement or a difficult conversation. We will avoid raised voices, offensive or insulting language, yelling, aggression, hitting, kicking, or throwing objects.
- We agree to identify the issue that needs discussion and to keep the conversation about the issue at hand.
- We agree we will not name-call, shame, use offensive language, or blame our partner.
- We will use "I" statements when addressing how the other person makes us feel.
- We agree to limit discussions of loaded topics to 20 minutes. A timer can be used if either partner wishes. When the time is up we will either agree to continue or reschedule a time to complete the conversation.
- We agree not to attempt to discuss loaded topics before 9:00 a.m. or after 9:00 p.m.
- We also agree not to attempt to resolve conflict while in public or around family members.
- We agree that if one of us needs to leave the situation and cool off we will not use it as leverage or a threat. We will phrase the departure as a need to calm down, and we will provide a reasonable time that we can be expected to return.

Counselors can work with the couple or family to generate a therapeutic contract that addresses their unique style and specific needs for conflict management.

Interpersonal Trust

Couples and families generally desire and value the ability to rely on one another. Increasing interpersonal trust is one way to boost family members' ability to rely on each other. Some counselors like to have families and couples initiate caring days to help build trust. To start this therapeutic contract with a couple, each partner would list those activities or behaviors that show expressions of love. These behaviors need to involve both parties (solitary time doesn't count) and be small behaviors that can be done daily. The behaviors can also be things that the partner does already but that one partner has a desire or need to increase. For example, making coffee for one's partner, giving a hug upon arrival home, or sending loving text messages could be included in the contract. These are discrete behaviors that can be objectively assessed as either occurring or not occurring.

Partners exchange lists and work with the counselor to determine how many behaviors can and should occur daily, weekly, and so on. The partners are responsible for keeping up with the fulfillment of the contract and reporting back in counseling. The counselor can use the success, or failure, of the contract as an assessment point in therapy.

What to Do With the Therapy Contract

After creating a therapy contract, counselors may wonder what they should do with the document besides giving it to new clients. Many counselors, especially those in private practice, use their websites to post their general therapeutic contracts and those based on their theoretical approach. Doing so serves as a form of pre-informed consent for clients. In contemporary counseling practice, clients are apt to window-shop for providers. A sample therapeutic contract can help them clearly see the benefits of working with a specific counselor. Still other counselors individualize their contracts in such a way that posting a general example is not feasible. These practitioners cover the therapy contract during the initial intake session.

Ultimately, the therapeutic contract is a tool for marriage, couples, and family counselors to benefit clients and provide clear expectations for all parties involved. From a best-practice perspective, it is preferred that clients sign the contract. Overall, it is suggested that the language be clear, user-friendly, and not legalistic in nature. For the counselor, it is imperative to keep the client's welfare in mind and make the therapeutic contract something that will benefit the process and not simply help to avoid potential legal and ethical conflicts. By using this tool, marriage, couples, and family counselors have an opportunity to begin the process of communication about treatment goals and expectations early on and can return to the document as needed to benefit the therapeutic experience.

Donna S. Sheperis

See also Informed Consent in Clinical Work; No-Secrets Contracts; Practice Management; Self-Injury; Suicide; Treatment Planning With Couples and Families

Further Readings

Hyldahl, R. S., & Richardson, B. (2011). Key considerations for using no-harm contracts with clients who self-injure. *Journal of Counseling & Development, 89*(1), 121–127.

Luscombe, B. (2010). Week-on, week-off parenting. *Time, 176*(16), 67–68.

Rentz, P. A. (2014). Transactional analysis (TA). In *Salem Press encyclopedia of health*. Ipswich, MA: Research Starters.

Rudd, M. D., Mandrusiak, M., & Joiner, T. E. (2006). The case against no-suicide contracts: The commitment to treatment statement as a practice alternative. *Journal of Clinical Psychology: In Session, 62*(2), 243–251.

THERAPEUTIC IMPASSES

In couples and family therapy, impasses refer to difficult encounters involving both the therapist and clients that stall therapeutic progress. When this occurs, the therapeutic process itself is at an impasse. An impasse can occur following several unsuccessful interventions, resulting in the therapist being at a loss and unsure of how to proceed.

The therapist might assess therapy as going in circles, while producing only minimal results. At this point the clients, as well as the therapist, may experience despair, including loss of hope. On a micro level, clients frequently experience impasses in their relationships. An impasse in a couple relationship occurs when the couple believes they have tried everything and are seeing little progress in their therapy. These micro impasses in a couple's relationship can occur multiple times during the course of therapy. These non-core impasses, however, can provide opportunities for couples to work through a series of life challenges. When working through these challenges, accompanied by subsequent impasses, the couple relationship is often strengthened as they learn new ways of coping with problems. This entry examines impasses during couples therapy, the reasons underlying impasse occurrences, and the effects on the therapist. Included are suggestions for addressing therapeutic impasses, and a case study of one couple at an impasse.

Impasses in Couples Therapy

What couples bring to therapy influences the course of therapy as well as the nature of an impasse that might occur. A number of factors can ignite an impasse when working with couples, including poor relationship skills, ineffective communication skills, family-of-origin issues, traumatic experiences, high stress levels, health problems, loneliness, power struggles, abandonment issues, fear, anxiety, anger issues, and loss. Additional factors enhancing the presence of an impasse during couples therapy include high levels of rigidity by one or both partners, lack of empathy toward one's partner, high levels of defensiveness, blaming, criticizing, contempt, withdrawal, irrationality, secretive behavior, lying, game playing, one-upmanship, lack of commitment, infidelity, dependent personality characteristics, mental health disorders, peer and family influences, priorities, and substance and/or process addictions. One should not presume that a presence of one or more of the above traits by a couple will automatically lead to an impasse.

However, the probability of an impasse occurring is significantly enhanced when the aforementioned factors are brought into the therapeutic setting.

Effects on the Therapist

A therapeutic impasse affects the therapist, the couple, and the direction of therapy. During an impasse the therapist, along with the couple, can become frustrated. When beginning work with a couple, most therapists believe in the counseling approach in which they were trained and have subsequently implemented with success. However, when therapy is stuck and an impasse occurs, self-doubt can begin to surface. The therapist might begin questioning whether therapy will be successful, particularly if the impasse is prolonged over several sessions. Effects on the therapist of a long-lasting impasse can include loss of trust in the process, hopelessness, anger, feelings of negativity, discomfort, emotionality, feelings of being trapped, failure feelings, self-doubt, and fear.

The duration of an impasse and the personal traits of the couple and therapist will determine the degree to which the impasse will affect therapy and the therapist. Impasses continued for lengthy periods of time can demoralize the therapist, causing him or her to question approaches used and interventions attempted. Carried to the extreme, the therapist's discomfort in working with the couple during an impasse could lead to negative feelings, anger, and loss of hope.

Addressing the Therapeutic Impasse

It is important to think systemically to effectively address an impasse. One needs to examine interrelated parts of the dilemma, including the therapist, the couple relationship, characteristics of individuals in the relationship, the context of the couple (e.g., family, friends, finances, history, stress, health issues), and the therapeutic model. The therapist would be wise to review his or her own role regarding the impasse, including perceptions he or she may have of the couple and their relationship, as well as personal meanings attributed to impasses in general. If the therapist blames the couple by labeling them as resistant or obstinate, it is not likely the impasse will be resolved. It is more probable the couple will terminate therapy. The therapist's view of an impasse should therefore be examined, particularly if the therapist rigidly believes it is always necessary to personally fix the couple and the impasse. If the therapist is inclined to have this view, it is quite probable that when faced with an intense, emotionally laden impasse one's frustration and anxiety will lead to burnout. Self-examination and consultation with colleagues are steps the therapist can take when initially addressing an impasse.

There are a number of possible actions available to the therapist when addressing a "stuck situation" in couples therapy. A basic but important approach one can use resides at the core of counseling and psychotherapy—providing a safe, trusting environment. During an impasse, it is important to assure the couple of a safe, trusting environment, as emphasized by Carl Rogers and others. The therapeutic relationship established with the couple will influence their perception of safety. The couple should be able to provide affirmative answers to the following questions:

- Is it safe to freely express myself in therapy?
- Does the therapist care about me, us as a couple, and our safety?
- Can I trust the therapist?
- Does the therapist understand me?
- Is the therapist genuine with me and us as a couple?

The therapeutic presence is worth reviewing when attempting to address an impasse. The "therapeutic presence" involves being open to what is presented during the course of therapy and involves listening, accepting difficult emotional states, and being in the moment with the couple. In addition to therapeutic presence, efforts should be made to re-create a sense of hope starting with small steps that will gradually rebuild the couple relationship. Instillation of hope, emphasized by Irvin Yalom and Victor Frankel, is considered essential for all therapies and is particularly germane when working with couples.

Several concepts aligned with modern therapeutic approaches can further help address an impasse. Michael White, from a narrative therapy perspective, emphasized examining problems by looking at them from the outside. By externalizing the impasse as something outside of each individual person and influencing them all, the therapist can help couples work together as a team to overcome the impasse that is influencing everyone in the room. Interventions associated with solution-focused therapy, an approach closely related to narrative therapy, are also recommended to mitigate an impasse during couples therapy. These strengths-based interventions include focusing on exceptions to the problem (when the impasse did not exist), scaling questions (assessing the impasse and discussing gradual change), and the miracle question (imagining a time when all problems have disappeared). In addition, research by John and Julie Gottman provides direction to overcoming impasses. In their model, the Gottman method couples therapy, they suggest examining four patterns that may lead to couples getting stuck: criticism, contempt, defensiveness, and stonewalling.

Strategic family therapy emphasizes setting goals and focusing on behaviors that lead to resistance and stalls in therapeutic progress. Strategic therapists use both direct and indirect interventions. The therapist and couple can track sequences of behavior before and after the impasse, looking for triggers that initiate an impasse. Once triggers are identified, it is recommended that the therapist and couple develop plans to interrupt triggers and identify behavioral patterns that ineffectively respond to triggers. If directly intervening with triggers does not work, a therapist might find indirect ways to help the couple avoid triggers. He or she will assign homework assignments that help clients bypass impasses without a client being overtly aware of what the point of the intervention is.

Addictions counselors, like strategic therapists, tend to examine patterns that may contribute to problems in therapy. They also look for triggers through examining outside influences of peers, relatives, and coworkers. In addition, to combat impasses they may tap spirituality as a resource, emphasize using mentors as support, stress personal responsibility, and confront denial.

Sometimes therapy is at an impasse owing to past, childhood life experiences. These experiences, often traumatic, can deter progress in therapy. Family-of-origin experiences can deter one's ability to establish healthy relationships. By examining each partner's family of origin, the couple can become more insightful about their own relationship and reasons for being emotionally stuck. In addition, through the sharing of family-of-origin experiences, the couple can increase their level of empathy for each other.

Case Study

To further illustrate what form an impasse might take and possible methods of intervention, consider the following scenario. Anne and Douglas have been married for 11 years. Anne is a devoted Christian and stayed home to take care of her family; Douglas is a soon-to-be-retired professor who describes himself as more spiritual than religious. They have been coming to couples therapy for the past 6 months because, as Douglas prepares to retire, arguing and disagreements have increased between the couple. Additionally, the couple revealed that they had not had sex for more than 2 years. While in session they are often critical of each other, making frequent attempts to prove the other wrong. The couple engages in a repetitious pattern of nitpicking, criticizing, defensiveness, and contempt. The therapist tried for several months to interrupt this pattern. At times improvements have been made; however, the couple soon relapses into familiar communication habits. Anne often refuses to acknowledge her resentment and anger toward Douglas because she believes as a Christian she must practice forgiveness. Douglas, who sees himself as a true investigative academic, engages in fault finding and is critical.

As the sessions progressed, the therapist noted that Douglas became less willing to participate. Over time Douglas became less focused on enhancing his relationship and more focused on correcting Anne and defending himself. When Anne voices her discontent with Douglas he responds in a detached and uncooperative manner, similar to that experienced at home. Disappointed, frustrated, and irritated with the lack of progress in sessions, the therapist worries about the impasse that has been reached.

In this case, the therapist decided to take a risk by using immediacy (commenting on what is going on in the moment), stating, "I noticed that I am not being as effective as I would like to be; you both seem to be stagnating. I feel as though Anne is very angry with Douglas even though she really wants to be forgiving. I also notice that Douglas is responding very defensively to me even though I feel very accepting of him." Immediacy involves inviting the client to examine the immediate, prominent dynamics of the session. Through invoking immediacy, the therapist offers the couple the opportunity to work as a team and process the impasse. Douglas and Anne struggled with these observations. Anne stated it is difficult to be a forgiving Christian, and she is actively working on "forgiving Douglas for his transgressions against her." Douglas responded that he finds it difficult because he often feels attacked in session and that he feels the therapist is not on his side. Following these revelations the therapist used scaling questions to discuss gradual change the couple would like to see in session.

Robert L. Smith and
Shanice N. Armstrong

See also American Association for Marriage and Family Therapy; Couples and Marriage Counseling; Gottman Method Couples Therapy; Hope-Focused Approach to Couple Enrichment in Counseling; International Association of Marriage and Family Counselors; Resistance; Solution-Focused Brief Therapy

Further Readings

Geller, S. M., & Greenberg, L. S. (2002). Therapeutic presence: Therapists' experience of presence in the psychotherapy encounter. *Person-Centered and Experiential Psychotherapies, 1,* 71–86.

Johnson, S. M., Makinen, J. A., & Millikin, J. W. (2001). Attachment injuries in couple relationships: A new perspective on impasses in couples therapy. *Journal of Marital and Family Therapy, 27*, 145–155.

Moltu, C., Binder, P., & Nielsen, G. H. (2010). Commitment under pressure: Experienced therapists' inner work during difficult therapeutic impasses. *Psychotherapy Research, 20*, 309–320.

Rogers, C. R. (1957). The necessary and sufficient conditions of therapeutic personality change. *Journal of Consulting Psychology, 21*, 95–103.

Scheinkman, M., & Fishbane, M. D. (2004). The vulnerability cycle: Working with impasses in couple therapy. *Family Process, 43*, 279–299.

Strean, H. S. (1999). Resolving some therapeutic impasses by disclosing countertransference. *Clinical Social Work Journal, 27*, 123–140.

THERAPISTS' VALUES

Values are standards and principles that guide decision-making and influence human behavior. In this sense, values provide criteria by which information can be assessed, judgments are determined, and actions are taken. Everyone has values, whether acknowledged or not; it is impossible to be "valueless." Therapists are sometimes directed to be neutral and "leave their values at the therapy door" when working with clients, but this is not feasible. Instead, therapists should work to identify and understand their own values, and they should consider how their values may intentionally or unintentionally influence the therapy process. For example, values about what helps create change (i.e., behavior, emotions, thoughts, relationships) are a part of the therapy process for every therapist; however, there are other values that, if imposed on clients, can harm or violate those clients' rights. The specific values that therapists hold can, and often do, conflict with those held by their clients, but it's when the therapist lets those values influence clients' lives in negative ways that they may cause ethical problems. The complexity of value conflicts is often magnified when working with couples and families, particularly when competing values are represented by various members within the family system. Understanding the role of values in the family beliefs and communication is an important task when treating couples and families. Therapists have an ethical responsibility to maintain a balance between knowledge and awareness of held values and competing value systems (e.g., cultural, religious, family, personal). This entry provides a definition of values, identifies the nature of bias embedded in values and value systems, outlines the roles values can play in therapy, and provides an overview of how therapists should manage values in therapy.

Values Defined

The term *values* has many different meanings ascribed to it, and there are many types of values, including personal values, family values, social values, cultural values, moral values, and so on. In brief, values are principles and standards that guide the relative weight (worth or significance) attributed to various types of information including ideas or concepts, beliefs, and experiences. Values influence both cognitive and emotional processing of information, which ultimately shapes attitudes. Cognitive and emotional processing utilizes values systems, including sociocultural beliefs, for decision-making and for determining behavioral responses. Therefore, values are not neutral in terms of processing information. Values can be thought of as one's source of information that contains certain biases, and subsequently influences how information is processed and ultimately how decisions are made—particularly therapeutic decisions, including choice of therapeutic interventions. For example, on the basis of their therapeutic knowledge and guiding value system, therapists apply certain techniques and interventions according to what they believe is in the best interest of the client.

Two related constructs are sometimes used interchangeably: *values* and *morals*. However, they are not the same constructs. Although values shape the relative weight therapists apply to morals, morals are the socially accepted standard that societies (groups) acknowledge and adopt in various ways, such as codification in law and by other social institutions and practices. Therapists apply their values to social morals, which in turn determine the relative weight (importance) they hold. For example, "freedom" is a value held by most democratic societies; however, there is no specific moral of freedom; whereas there is a universally accepted moral code not to murder. How societies legitimize this moral code varies widely according to practices of law and other social mechanisms. More simply put, values tend to be individual standards about what is a priority, important, or valuable. Morals tend to describe the "goodness" or "badness" of decisions or actions and are typically based on larger group views.

Therapists' Values: A Source of Bias

Values are, of course, not neutral. All values contain bias of various sorts—sociocultural bias, political bias, religious bias, racial bias, gender bias, age bias, and so forth. Although therapists subscribe to the principle that "values are left at the therapist's door," the reality is that this is impossible to do 100% of the time, or even to be aware of one's values all of the time. Values may be so thoroughly internalized that they may be difficult to discern. Necessarily, therefore, therapists' values do influence the therapeutic process. Since therapists' values are principles and standards by which all sources of information are assessed, therapists must understand how values influence thinking and decision-making. As a component of the process of assessing information, therapists' values guide therapeutic decision-making processes. Therapists' values influence the manner in which client information is processed and the manner in which therapeutic intent and decisions are derived. Therefore, therapists' values are a significant moderator in the therapeutic process. Therapists' values not only shape opinions and attitudes about information but also shape how the therapist feels about certain topics. Therapists' values can influence the therapeutic process in any number of ways and can be problematic (antitherapeutic) and have unintended consequences. Imposition of values can affect the therapeutic process from a small rupture in the therapeutic relationship to an ethical violation.

Ethics

Counseling ethics are a principled set of standards and practices that counseling organizations have codified in order to help guide clinical practice. Because therapists hold to differing sets of morals and values, counseling ethics are designed to provide an accepted set of professional standards and practices. Depending on individual values and morals, therapists may not fully agree with every ethical standard and practice set forth by an organization but will agree to abide by them as a member of the organization.

There are core principles embedded in each code of ethics in major mental health professions. Although each code may not be exactly the same, they usually share major ideas. These typically include honoring diversity, supporting the dignity of clients, respecting clients' rights to make their own decisions, and protecting the therapist–client relationship. For example, the American Counseling Association's (ACA) Code of Ethics states that "the primary responsibility of counselors is to respect the dignity and promote the welfare of clients." This mandate outweighs any specific values the counselor may have about the actions, views, or attitudes of the client. In addition, the ACA's Code of Ethics specifically warns counselors to be aware of their own values and avoid imposing their own values on clients, students, or research participants. If they find their values are getting in the way of providing ethical services, then counselors are required to get extra training and/or supervision in areas where they are at risk of imposing their values. Other examples include the American Association of Marriage and Family Therapy (AAMFT) Code of Ethics, which prohibits "discrimination on the basis of race, age, ethnicity, socioeconomic status, disability, gender, health status, religion, national origin, sexual orientation, gender identity or relationship status."

Regardless of the particular profession, the primary goal of all health professionals is to advance the welfare of their clients.

Shannon Smith

See also American Association for Marriage and Family Therapy; Beliefs and Values; Competency-Based Standards for Marriage, Couple, and Family Counseling; Council for Accreditation of Counseling and Related Educational Programs; Diversity; Ethical Codes; International Association of Marriage and Family Counselors

Further Readings

Doherty, W. J. (1985). Values and ethics in family therapy. *Counseling and Values, 30*(1), 3–8.

Gladding, S. T., Remley, T. P., & Huber, C. H. (2001). *Ethical, legal, and professional issues in the practice of marriage and family therapy.* Upper Saddle River, NJ: Merrill-Prentice Hall.

Jensen, J. P., & Bergin, A. E. (1988). Mental health values of professional therapists: A national interdisciplinary survey. *Professional Psychology: Research and Practice, 19*(3), 290.

Patterson, C. H. (1958). The place of values in counseling and psychotherapy. *Journal of Counseling Psychology, 5*(3), 216.

TIME PROGRAM

See Training in Marriage Enrichment (TIME) Program

TORTURE TREATMENT

Torture occurs across both international (e.g., interrogating political prisoners for intelligence) and domestic (e.g., unlawful detention, police brutality) contexts. It is estimated that 1.5 million survivors of such practice(s) currently reside in the United States alone. Many of these survivors require mental health care. Service providers, however, are often not familiar with legal definitions of torture (and implications of these definitions for care access) and/or best practices in torture treatment across individual, dyadic, and familial levels. This entry introduces important international and domestic legal definitions of torture. It then outlines recent global torture practices, alongside how these practices' effects most commonly present in later clinical work. In addition, guiding therapeutic principles and steps for effectively engaging torture survivors are described.

International and Domestic Legal Definitions of Torture

The most widely accepted international legal definition of torture originates from the United Nations (UN) Convention Against Torture (CAT) and Other Cruel, Inhumane or Degrading Treatment or Punishment (1984). The CAT defines *torture* as follows:

> Any act by which severe pain or suffering, whether physical or mental, is intentionally inflicted on a person for such purposes as obtaining from him or a third person information or a confession, punishing him for any act he committed, or intimidating or coercing him or a third person, or for any reason based on discrimination of any kind, when such pain or suffering is inflicted by or at the instigation of or with the consent or acquiescence of a public official or other person acting in an official capacity. (pp. 1986–1987)

The legal domestic definition, however, originates from the Torture Victims Relief Act (TVRA, 1988, 2014), which defines torture as "an act committed by a person acting under the color of law specifically intended to inflict severe physical or mental pain or suffering … other than pain or suffering incidental to lawful sanctions" (1988, pp. 73–74).

Differences Between International and Domestic Legal Definitions of Torture

The differences between the international and domestic definition of torture impact the ability to provide mental health, medical, social, and legal services to immigrants and refugees. The first difference is that in the international definition of torture, there must be a specific intent to induce severe pain or suffering. A general intent to commit torture—as outlined in the international definition—is inadequate to meet the definition of torture. But survivors who experience threats of torture, even without being physically hurt per se, can still be traumatized. This overlaps with the second difference. While the domestic definition includes "custody or physical control," the international definition does not; this is important because it does not recognize psychological torture, which can also be debilitating. The third difference is that the domestic definition does not require torture to be committed for purposes like obtaining information or a confession, punishing for an act committed or suspicion thereof, intimidation or coercion, and/or discrimination. These differences matter because the domestic definition is used to determine whether a person is eligible to receive rehabilitative services in the United States.

Effects of Torture

Research has demonstrated that the infliction of torture by people or institutions is particularly devastating to victims. The effects can be long-lasting and multifaceted. While physical wounds fade over time, psychological scars can endure indefinitely. These lead to ineffective coping mechanisms (e.g., smoking, excessive alcohol use, drug abuse) that may not only prevent personal and professional success but also lead to dysfunctional interpersonal relationships. Posttraumatic stress disorder (PTSD) symptoms as a result of torture, for example, often manifest as anger outbursts and violence. When directed toward family and friends, these behaviors cause conflict. The psychological effects of torture (e.g., re-experiencing or "flashbacks," avoidance, general anxiety) also lead to withdrawal and as a result, social isolation. Furthermore, these stressors are compounded by anxiety related to navigating various legal processes (e.g., being granted asylum in the United States).

Physical Effects

The majority of torture survivors experience persistent physical pain as a result of multiple and frequent assaults. Research has shown that the most reported regions of physical pain are in the back and neck (60–90%), chest and thorax (20–40%), joints (20–40%), feet (30–70%), and pelvis (up to 20%). These estimates may be biased because they originate from specialized torture treatment settings where providers have been trained to recognize the physical effects of torture. In primary and secondary care settings, it is estimated that nearly half of physical torture effects go unrecognized because providers have not been trained to effectively inquire or assess for torture's effects. It has been noted that immigrants and refugees, particularly those from cultures that stigmatize mental health problems, may instead present with stress-related somatic complaints. It is beneficial to either screen persecuted minorities with complaints of persistent physical pain for torture (i.e., whether they have been tortured) or refer them to specialized treatment centers.

Psychological Effects

An estimated 60% of torture survivors experience PTSD symptoms and 80% experience anxiety symptoms. The most reported psychological symptoms reported by survivors of torture are re-experiencing (e.g., nightmares, flashbacks); avoidance (e.g., preventing exposure to stimuli that reminds them of torture experiences); and increased general anxiety (e.g., racing thoughts, worry/rumination, sense of feeling "on edge" or hypervigilance). Despite a high prevalence of psychological symptoms, torture survivors' complaints may fall outside of a simple PTSD or major depressive disorder (MDD) diagnosis.

Psychosocial Effects

The psychosocial effects of torture are grounded in boundary violations, which are critical to identity formation. Boundaries determine a person's sense of belonging and separateness. When boundaries are flexible, a person is able to explore alternative solutions to a problem. This allows the person to separate his or her thoughts, feelings, and actions from those of others. But when boundaries are inflexible, a person is unable to explore alternative solutions to a problem. She or he becomes stuck in perpetual crises. As the experience of torture is destructive to one's sense of trust in others, she or he develops rigid interpersonal boundaries as a defense mechanism. The separateness serves as protection from further psychological harm. While this prevents the person from getting hurt, it also prevents others from getting close. In turn, this makes survivors of torture feel lonely and socially isolated. Beyond these types of interpersonal effects, torture survivors also struggle with preparing for, adjusting to, and functioning in the social world. This includes, but is not limited to, learning a new language, regaining their social status (e.g., through education or employment), and reuniting with their families.

Guiding Clinical Principles of Working With Torture Survivors

Torture survivors are often reluctant to discuss their experiences as a result of being unfamiliar with, or distrustful of, providers and organizations. This makes establishing a therapeutic relationship difficult, which can be frustrating to both the client and provider. Caring for torture survivors requires providers to be patient and take a position of advocacy. While the range of personal backgrounds that these clients bring may require an individual focus, field leaders emphasize the importance of interpersonal relationships in recovering from trauma. Cognitive-behavioral conjoint therapy for posttraumatic stress disorder (CBCT for PTSD) takes a relational approach by sequentially organizing 15 sessions of 75 minutes each into three phases.

Phase 1

The focus of the first phase, which is organized into two sessions, is to establish a sense of safety and stability. This is accomplished through psychoeducation about torture-related symptoms (e.g., nightmares, racing thoughts, worry/rumination), how they develop, and their relationship effects. The first phase includes addressing how avoidance of negative feelings or thoughts maintains and may even exacerbate relationship problems. In such cases, stress management techniques, such as deep breathing and guided imagery, should then be introduced. The introduction of stress management techniques is important because it helps interrupt the "Fight, Flight, or Freeze" (sympathetic arousal) response. This enables the couple and/or family to discuss how the torture has affected their relationship. Research has demonstrated that stress management techniques are also effective in decreasing pain perception.

Phase 2

The second phase, which is organized into five sessions, focuses on increasing relationship satisfaction while decreasing negative feelings or thoughts. This is accomplished through communication skills such as active listening and channel checking. These skills are essential not only in managing conflict but also in rebuilding trust and a sense of safety in the relationship. In combination with stress management techniques, communication skills provide a foundation for addressing how torture-related symptoms maintain but can also improve relationship problems. They also help torture survivors regain their sense of control when they feel overwhelmed.

Phase 3

The focus of the third phase, which is organized into eight sessions, is on further applying stress management techniques and communication skills. Instead of avoiding torture-related beliefs that contribute to relationship problems, each partner is encouraged to discuss core beliefs that have been severely impacted by his or her experiences. It is important to emphasize that torture survivors are not required to disclose details of their experiences in CBCT for PTSD. Instead, treatment focuses on discussing emotions and meaning surrounding memories. The formation of new meaning in a safe context is what enables each person to feel less afraid, guilty, and ashamed. This sets the foundation for increased trust, control, and closeness. It also helps torture survivors acculturate in their host country (e.g., the United States) through social engagement.

Important Considerations for Treatment

Some have argued that there is little value in providing couples and/or family therapy to torture survivors before they regain their skills in interpersonal functioning (e.g., being aware of and able to effectively manage feelings). The problem with this assumption, however, is that it may take months or even years for a torture survivor to regain his or her interpersonal functioning. A relational approach to treatment is a more effective option because it is grounded in the family systems principle that individuals cannot be understood in isolation. This is especially relevant when working with torture survivors because meaning, for them, is organized around the survivors' experience of the violation of basic trust and safety.

The exclusion criteria in cognitive-behavioral conjoint therapy for PTSD are limited but important. They include substance dependence, uncontrolled severe mental health problems, severe cognitive impairment, and suicidal or homicidal ideation. Although working with torture survivors may be difficult, healing is nevertheless possible. And healing through a relational approach enables survivors to rebuild their lives.

*Damir S. Utržan and
Tai J. Mendenhall*

See also Grief Counseling; Immigrant Families; Intergenerational Trauma; Loss; Trauma and Children; Trauma and Families; Trauma-Focused Cognitive-Behavioral Therapy; Trust

Further Readings

Birrell, P., & Freyd, J. (2006). Betrayal trauma: Relational models of harm and healing. *Journal of Trauma Practice, 5*(1), 49–63. doi:10.1300/J189v05n01_04

Cleveland, J., Rousseau, C., & Guzder, J. (Eds.). (2015). *Cultural consultation: Encountering the other in mental health care.* New York, NY: Springer.

Gorman, W. (2001). Refugee survivors of torture: Trauma and treatment. *Professional Psychology: Research and Practice, 32*(5), 443–451. doi:10.1037/0735-7028.32.5.443

Jaranson, J., & Popkin, M. (Eds.). (1998). *Caring for victims of torture.* Washington, DC: American Psychiatric Association Press.

Levine, P. A. (2010). *In an unspoken voice: How the body releases trauma and restores goodness.* Berkeley, CA: North Atlantic Books.

Monson, C., & Fredman, S. (2012). *Cognitive-behavioral conjoint therapy for PTSD.* New York, NY: Guilford Press.

Torture Victims Relief Act of 1998, H.R. 4309, 105th Cong. (1998). Retrieved from http://www.congress.gov/105/plaws/publ320/PLAW-105publ320.pdf

Torture Victims Relief Reauthorization Act of 2014. H.R. 4987, 113th Cong. (2014). Retrieved from http://www.congress.gov/113/bills/hr4987/BILLS-113hr4987ih.pdf

United Nations. (1984). *Convention against torture and other cruel, inhumane or degrading treatment or punishment.* Retrieved from http://legal.un.org/avl/ha/catcidtp/catcidtp.html

Williams, A., & Amris, K. (2007). Pain from torture. *Journal of Pain, 133,* 5–8. doi:10.1016/j.pain.2007.10.001

TRAINING AND LICENSURE

Training and licensure refers to the process by which an individual becomes educationally qualified and registered to legally practice as a marriage and family therapist. This entry covers the training requirements common in the field of marriage and family therapy, including a review of some of the requirements set forth by the Commission on Accreditation for Marriage and Family Therapy Education. This entry will also address some of the general requirements for licensure outlined by those states and provinces that regulate marriage and family therapy.

Training

There are a number of avenues for being trained to work with couples and families; however, the Commission on Accreditation for Marriage and Family Therapy Education (COAMFTE) is generally recognized by state and provincial governments as *the* body responsible for overseeing the education of marriage and family therapists (MFTs). One notable exception to this is the state of California, which has its own codified requirements for marriage and family therapy education and does not recognize the hegemony of a COAMFTE-accredited education. As of 2015 there were more than 100 programs that have been accredited by COAMFTE throughout the United States and Canada. COAMFTE provides specific guidance on the curriculum, structure, and outcomes for accredited programs.

Students graduating from a program based on the COAMFTE educational model can expect to be exposed to various professional marriage and family therapy principles, which include the American Association for Marriage and Family Therapy (AAMFT) Code of Ethics, the AAMFT Core Competencies, the Association of Marital and Family Therapy Regulatory Boards (AMFTRB) Guidelines, and state licensure regulations. The AAMFT Core Competencies include 128 statements concerning the knowledge, skills, and abilities individuals should possess before becoming fully licensed to practice marriage and family therapy. However, it is not usually expected that a student in a training program will demonstrate competence in all 128 areas at the time of graduation. Marriage and family therapy training programs often target a subset of the AAMFT Core Competencies and train their students in such a manner that they are able to demonstrate achievement in those areas. Individuals are expected to continue developing their knowledge, skills, and abilities as therapists during the training period after graduation.

Similar to the AAMFT Core Competencies, the AAMFT Code of Ethics includes a series of statements MFTs are expected to know and abide by in the treatment of individuals, couples, and families. The Code of Ethics is usually taught as part of a course in the program's curriculum and applied during contact with clients as part of the program's direct client contact requirements. The AMFTRB Guidelines concern the areas of the Examination in Marital and Family Therapy (usually taken after graduation) about which students are expected to be knowledgeable.

The COAMFTE also provides educational guidelines for programs to follow in constructing the curriculum students complete as part of their studies in marriage and family therapy. The curriculum of MFT programs is generally centered on theory, clinical knowledge, ethics, research, and human development. Students in an MFT program can expect to take several courses that explicitly teach systems theory and the major models of marriage and family therapy. Among the major models of marriage and family therapy are structural family therapy, cognitive-behavioral therapy, strategic family therapy, solution-focused brief family therapy, and experiential therapies, such as emotionally focused therapy. Students also take at least one course on ethics and research at the master's level.

In addition to the coursework, MFT programs require a practicum experience wherein the student is responsible for applying the models taught in the program. This is accomplished through the provision of treatment to individuals, couples, and families. The clinical experience requirements are usually completed concurrently with the course work, and typically consistent of up to 500 hours of direct client contact. Some MFT training programs have an on-site clinic associated with the university where students can see clients, while other programs rely on placements in the surrounding communities. Other programs offer a combination of these two types of practicum experiences. Regardless of the setting, MFT students in practicum are responsible for assessing the client system and providing a diagnosis, designing a treatment plan and delivering the therapy services outlined therein, and evaluating the progress of treatment and determining when the client is ready for termination. Students in practicum are also responsible for learning how to manage client crises and deliver services in an ethical manner. Because of their status as novice therapists, students are closely supervised by more experienced therapists throughout the practicum experience.

Although a master's degree is considered the terminal degree in marriage and family therapy (meaning you can practice independently at this level), there are several doctoral-level programs offering degrees in this field as well. Doctoral programs are most often tailored toward those who are interested in academics and usually have a heavy focus on original research and teaching. Doctoral programs also offer advanced clinical training beyond what is available in a master's-level program and usually have at least one course designed to help individuals become marriage and family therapy supervisors. As is true for master's-level programs, doctoral-level programs can also be accredited by COAMFTE.

Another type of training opportunity is a postdegree program, which offers specialized training in specific areas of marriage and family therapy. These programs are responsible for determining that a candidate has a foundation in marriage and family therapy and sufficient experiences with MFT services before admittance to the program. An example of this type of program is available at the University of Rochester, which offers a postdegree certificate in medical family therapy. Another example is the Philadelphia Child & Family Therapy Training Center, which provides advanced training in structural family therapy.

As noted above, there are a number of methods for obtaining quality training in marriage and family therapy outside of COAMFTE-accredited programs. While AAMFT created the core competencies for MFTs, other professions (e.g., counselors, social workers, and psychologists) are able to receive training in the provision of these services. One of the most notable of these is training offered in programs accredited by the Council for Accreditation of Counseling and Related Educational Programs (CACREP). Although CACREP offers accreditation for a number of different fields within mental health (e.g., school counseling and counselor education/supervision), one of the options for programs is to have a marriage, couples, and family therapy specialization. Some states even consider graduation from a CACREP program with this specialty as equivalent to graduating from a COAMFTE-accredited program for the purpose of licensure. In addition to CACREP programs, the International Association of Marriage and Family Counselors, which is linked to the American Counseling Association, has a process for certification in family therapy. Likewise, Division 43 of the American Psychological Association is dedicated to research and clinical practice related to marriage and family therapy and offers board certification through the American Board of Couple and Family Psychology.

Licensure

Licensure is state specific, with each state having its own rules and qualifications. Usually, after completing the minimum educational requirements (i.e., a master's degree), marriage and family therapists enter into a training period before they are eligible for full licensure as MFTs. Some states have a provisional license that can be granted to an MFT during this training period. Whether or not this is required depends on the way the state laws were constructed. For example, in Iowa marriage and family therapists can apply for a temporary license during the training period, but it is not required. MFTs in this state can also opt to work for an agency under the supervision of a state-approved supervisor without the temporary license during the training period, and apply for full licensure after meeting the experience requirements the same as if they had obtained a temporary license. The motivation for obtaining a temporary license in this state is that many employers require one before they will consider hiring a newly graduated therapist.

During the training period MFTs are required to accumulate direct client contact hours, supervision, and related work experience. Supervision is required during the training period and can usually be a combination of individual supervision and group supervision; however, many states require that at least half of the supervision be provided as individual supervision to prevent individuals from obtaining supervision entirely in a group format, wherein the supervisee may not be the focus on the supervision session. Some states even allow a portion of the supervision to be provided electronically.

The related work experience includes sundry activities that are associated with the provision of therapy services, such as participating in trainings, staff meetings, case documentation, and phone consultations. The amount of required related experience can range anywhere from 1,500 to 3,000 additional hours. The amount of direct client contact hours varies by state, though it is usually between 1,000 and 1,500 hours, and must take place over a period of at least two years. Most states also require that a certain portion of the direct client contact hours be obtained through provision of services to couples and/or families.

During the training period, MFTs are also required to take and pass a comprehensive exam to test their knowledge of professional MFT principles. Most often this is the Examination in Marital and Family Therapy, which is constructed and administered by the AMFTRB. As is true with the educational requirements, California serves as an exception to the rule. In California, MFTs are required to pass a written exam administered by the state, as well as an oral exam, which is administered by the state board. However, the Examination in Marital and Family Therapy is used by most states and, accordingly, will be given more attention here. This exam has a total of 200 questions, each with four answers, of which there is only one correct answer. Test-takers are given a total of four hours to complete the exam. The exam includes six domains, which cover (1) the practice of systemic therapy, (2) assessment and diagnosis, (3) designing and conducting treatment, (4) evaluating treatment and readiness for termination, (5) managing crises, and (6) ethical, legal, and professional standards (e.g., HIPAA). Each state licensing board determines the number of questions that must be answered correctly to pass the test, though usually answering more than 70% of the questions correctly is sufficient.

Comparison With Other Professions

Like other mental health professionals, MFTs are currently eligible for licensure in all 50 states of the United States. In addition, there are two provinces in Canada that regulate marriage and family therapy as a profession. However, in contrast with other professions, marriage and family therapists are required to complete a substantial amount of course work and clinical experience directly related to the treatment of couples and families. D. Russell Crane and his associates reviewed licensure laws and training requirements for the major mental health professions in the United States and found that the only other profession that requires any training in marriage and family therapy is mental health counseling. This is in spite of the recognition that most of the other mental health professions are known to provide couples and family therapy services. In fact, MFTs are required to complete three times more relational course work and 16 times more direct relational client contact hours than any other mental health profession. MFTs are the only profession with training requirements and licensure laws that specifically identify conjoint treatment as a prominent modality. The high training standards required of marriage and family therapists are intended to provide the public with assurance that the services they receive are offered by qualified individuals.

Jacob D. Christenson

See also American Association for Marriage and Family Therapy; Clinical Practice; Competency-Based Standards for Marriage, Couple, and Family Counseling; Council for Accreditation of Counseling and Related Educational Programs; DSM and V-Codes; Ethical Codes; HIPAA Standards; International Association of Marriage and Family Counselors; Medical Family Therapy; Postdoctoral Training

Further Readings

Caldwell, B. E., Kunker, S. A., Brown, S. W., & Saiki, D. Y. (2011). COAMFTE accreditation and California MFT licensing exam success. *Journal of Marital and Family Therapy, 37*(4), 468–478.

Crane, D. R., Shaw, A. L., Christenson, J. D., Larson, J. H., Harper, J. M., & Feinauer, L. L. (2010). Comparison of the family therapy educational and experience requirements for licensure or certification in six mental health disciplines. *The American Journal of Family Therapy, 38*(5), 357–373.

Nelson, T. S., Chenail, R. J., Alexander, J. F., Crane, D. R., Johnson, S. M., & Schwallie, L. (2007). The development of core competencies for the practice of marriage and family therapy. *Journal of Marital and Family Therapy, 33*(4), 417–438.

Nelson, T. S., & Smock, S. A. (2005). Challenges of an outcome-based perspective for marriage and family therapy education. *Family Process, 44*(3), 355–362.

Northey, W. F., Jr. (2009). The legitimization of marriage and family therapy in the United States: Implications for international recognition. *Journal of Family Psychotherapy, 20*(4), 303–318.

Sprenkle, D. H. (2010). The present and future of MFT doctoral education in research-focused universities. *Journal of Marital and Family Therapy, 36*(3), 270–281.

West, C., Hinton, W. J., Grames, H., & Adams, M. A. (2013). Marriage and family therapy: Examining the impact of licensure on an evolving profession. *Journal of Marital and Family Therapy, 39*(1), 112–126.

Woolley, S. R. (2010). Purposes, diversities, and futures in MFT doctoral education. *Journal of Marital and Family Therapy, 36*(3), 282–290.

Training in Marriage Enrichment (TIME) Program

The Training in Marriage Enrichment (TIME) program was created by Don Dinkmeyer Sr. (1924–2001) and Jon Carlson as a psychoeducational program to assist couples in learning the skills needed to create a satisfying partnership. The TIME program is a skill-based intervention that supplements or replaces therapy by showing couples healthier ways in which to interact in order to achieve a more loving, supportive, and enriching relationship. This program has been empirically validated and was created for counselors, therapists, or clergy to help any couple motivated to grow and strengthen their relationship, not necessarily just for couples experiencing extreme marriage challenges. The TIME program can be modified and used with couples in a variety of settings. It can be conducted in a weekly group meeting (10 weeks), a weekend workshop, or a couples' retreat, individual sessions, or as a supportive intervention for use by marriage and family therapists. This entry provides an overview of the principles of the program and details as to how it can be used.

The TIME program is outlined in detail in the form of a workbook for participants, with various readings and exercises intended to assist each partner in learning the skills presented. The TIME program is theoretically based in the psychological theory of Alfred Adler or individual psychology, and is a sociopsychological approach to interpersonal relationships. The intention of the TIME program is to help couples understand and take responsibility for the behaviors each exhibits toward the other in the relationship.

TIME Program Principles

There are five guiding principles upon which the TIME program is based. The first principle is the assertion that the couple must make the relationship a priority in order to develop and sustain it. The second principle implies that the skills needed for a strong marriage can be learned, and this newfound knowledge can help all couples understand more fully how the marriage operates as well as skills that are needed. The third principle is the contention that change begins with each partner and that changes may not happen as quickly as hoped, so patience is key. The fourth basic principle is that when changes in behavior occur, positive feelings between the couple that may have not been present for some time will return to the relationship. The final principle recognizes how smaller changes in the relationship can act as a catalyst for bigger changes in the relationship to occur. The intention is that many small changes will occur over time, leading to a more fulfilled relationship within the couple.

TIME Program

The TIME program follows the 10 chapters of the *Time for a Better Marriage* workbook. Participants in the TIME program have assigned readings from the workbook to complete prior to each session (one chapter in the workbook per week). In the session, couples participate in activities designed to build skills (i.e., communication, encouragement) with each other, discuss activities and readings, and learn by practicing a new skill taught in the session. At the end of the session each participant engages in a written exercise, assessing his or her progress over the week as well as identifying any post-session concerns. To conclude the session, the facilitator summarizes the events of the meeting and highlights what participants can expect at the next session.

Each of the 10 sessions of the psychoeducational model has a specific focus for the participants. The first session focuses on the participants accepting responsibility for their own choices and behavior, as well as for the potential success (or not) of the marriage. Participants are taught how to identify both positive goals (supporting, helping, etc.) and goals that have a strong negative impact on the relationship (blaming, demanding, etc.). The second session focuses on encouragement, both within the marriage and of themselves as individuals. The third session centers on priorities and values that impact the relationship. An emphasis is placed on helping the couple avoid games with one another and focus on understanding and decreasing potential rigidity with one another. In the fourth session, couples learn how to verbally express their internal feelings in the moment, while maintaining sensitivity toward each other. The fifth session focuses on the couple's ability to listen and respond to what is being communicated to them while maintaining empathy. The importance of being solely responsible for your own feelings is stressed. The sixth session targets communication skills while session seven focuses on choice-making skills, which are helpful to the health of the relationship. Sessions eight and nine revolve around conflict resolution and present coping skills to help offset anger when it arises when the couple is attempting to communicate with one another. The final session allows couples an opportunity to process what has been learned throughout the TIME program and establish future goals to keep the skills acquired and help "divorceproof" the marriage.

The TIME program offers couples skills and allows for insight to develop not only their relationship but also on an individual level. This insight can ultimately strengthen each individual in the couple personally and collectively moving forward. The TIME program can be used by therapists, counselors, and clergy and can be easily adapted to fit the needs of couples motivated to improve their relationship. The program can be used independently, or as a follow-up program for couples who have completed another marriage enrichment program in the past.

Sharon Silverberg

See also Couple Development; Couples and Marriage Counseling; Marital Distress; Marriage Enrichment

Further Readings

Carlson, J., & Dinkmeyer, D. (1985). Time for a better marriage. *Individual Psychology: The Journal of Adlerian Theory, Research & Practice, 41*(4), 444.

Carlson, J., & Dinkmeyer, D. (2003). *Time for a better marriage*. Atascadero, CA: Impact Publishers.

Dinkmeyer, D. (2007). A systematic approach to marriage education. *Journal of Individual Psychology, 63*(3), 315–321.

Dinkmeyer, D., & Carlson, D. (1986). A systematic approach to marital enrichment. *American Journal of Family Therapy, 14*(2), 139–153.

Huber, C. H., & Dinkmeyer, D. (1987). Premarital counseling using Time for a Better Marriage. *Individual Psychology: The Journal of Adlerian Theory, Research & Practice, 43*(2), 202–205.

TRANSGENDER FAMILIES

As more people openly identify as transgender, there is a growing need for family therapists to understand the specific needs and stressors facing transgender individuals and their families. This entry examines the experience of transgender individuals, the relevance of the minority stress model for understanding the experience of transgender individuals, especially in the context of the family, and approaches to clinical work with transgender individuals and their families.

Defining Transgender

Transgender is often used as an umbrella term to represent people who are gender diverse, but in reality this term most accurately applies to individuals whose internal sense of self differs from the societally based expectations of their anatomical makeup. Transgender individuals may be considering, be in the process of, or have completed a body-based transition of gender through gender reassignment surgeries, but physical transition is not a necessity for identifying as transgender. For many individuals, adjustments in gender expression may feel sufficient for consolidating their gender identity. Subtleties in transgender identity include *trans-women,* who were assigned a male sex at birth but who identify internally as female, and *trans-men,* who were assigned a female sex at birth and identify internally as male. Terms used to reference individuals who are in the process of transition may include FTM (female to male) and MTF (male to female). Subgroups of individuals generally included under the blanket term transgender are persons identifying as *bi-gendered* or *two-spirited,* who experience themselves as having both male and female genders, persons identifying as *cross-dressers,* who cross-dress for relaxation and/or pleasure but who have no desire to alter their gender expression permanently, and those who are *intersex,* with both male and female genitalia or undefined genitalia. Often individuals identifying as *gender nonconforming* are included under the broader term *transgender,* although this is a uniquely identifying subgroup of individuals. This group includes individuals who do not identify within the male/female gender binary, identify as neither female nor male, or identify as none or both. *Gender fluid, genderqueer, gender bender,* and *pangender* are identities that challenge a dichotomous view of gender and are characterized by fluid gender expressions and presentations. Most gender nonconforming individuals do not feel the same impetus for physical transformation that trans men and trans women might. One final identity important to note for understanding the experiences of transgender families is the *cisgender* gender identity. Persons identifying as cisgender experience their internal sense of self as aligned with their assigned sex and conform to the societally based expectations of their anatomical makeup. Drawing these descriptions together, *transgender families* are those in which at least one family member does not identify with or conform to a cisgender identity.

Experiences of Transgender Individuals

Population-based estimates for the prevalence of transgender identifying adults are virtually nonexistent, but a report from the Williams Institute published in 2011 combined data sources to estimate that there are nearly 700,000 (0.3%) transgender-identifying individuals in the United States. Researchers' inability to calculate demographic data for the transgender population stems from a few primary challenges. First, the United States Census does not include options for gender identity outside of the gender binary "male" or "female," requiring transgender individuals to misidentify or to omit their response completely. Second, for research that includes flexible gender options, there is a great deal of difficulty defining who is included in the "transgender" community. With the many variations of gender identity and expression as well as the common misapplication of the term *transgender* to gender nonconforming individuals, miscommunication between survey respondents and researchers is common. Finally, individuals identifying as transgender may fear disclosing their minority gender identity, even within the confines of a confidential survey. This fear is a function of the daily anti-transgender bias faced by transgender people in their immediate and macro-level social contexts. Anti-transgender bias can occur directly through overt acts of discrimination, but also covertly through structural inequities and marginalization. The National Transgender Discrimination Survey (NTDS) report from 2011 showed that 63% of their 6,456 transgender-identifying participants had experienced a serious act of discrimination that directly influenced their quality of life, their financial stability, or their emotional well-being. These acts of discrimination ranged from the loss of their job, eviction from their home, school bullying with subsequent dropout, physical and sexual assault, the loss of a partner and/or children, denial of medical services, and incarceration due to gender identity or expression. Less obvious sources of anti-transgender bias included barriers to obtaining new identification documents with a cross-gender identity, facing arrest, harassment, violence for entering gendered public restrooms, and the threat or experience of being forcibly housed according to biological sex rather than gender identity when incarcerated.

Applying the Minority Stress Model

The minority stress model describes how individuals with marginalized and stigmatized identities experience chronic stress associated with holding minority status. According to this model, transgender individuals may experience this stress by way of three processes. The first process is through an individual's environment and any external events, including immediate and/or distal experiences of discrimination as well as threats to a person's well-being. Examples of this source of minority stress can be found in the National Transgender Discrimination Survey (NTDS, 2011) findings that showed participants were refused housing (19%) and evicted (11%) because of their gender identity or expression. Furthermore, participants reported extremely high rates of harassment and mistreatment in work contexts (90%). Those experiencing these direct forms of discrimination were at a substantially greater risk for poor mental health, with 55% of those who had experienced a job loss reporting they had attempted suicide.

A second process by which marginalization manifests as stress for minority individuals is through the anticipation or expectation of an external stressful event like discrimination, which for many people is accompanied by hypervigilance and chronic anxiety. For individuals within the National Transgender Discrimination Survey, this emerged in the participants' decisions to hide their gender identity or expression (71%), to delay transition in order to keep a job (57%), or deciding not to pursue a promotion or a raise in pay (30%). Additionally, for transgender individuals there exists a unique and very real physical health outcome for having to anticipate and avoid discrimination in public restrooms. In her 2013 study, Jody Herman reported that 54% of her transgender participants had some type of physical problem resulting from avoiding gendered public restrooms. These physical problems included dehydration, urinary tract infections, kidney infections, and other kidney-related problems.

Finally, individuals may experience stress as a result of having internalized transphobic messages. Internalizing society's negative messages often means believing one's personhood is of less value than that of others; this would understandably influence a person's mental health and well-being. Essentially, what the minority stress model suggests is that, by virtue of living in a transphobic sociopolitical context, transgender individuals experience chronic stress above and beyond the stress of daily living and that this additional stress helps to explain the disproportionately poor mental and physical health that exists within the community.

Clinical Work With Transgender Individuals and Families

Families with members who identify as transgender are at the nexus for understanding resiliency and adaptation within family contexts. These families face significant distress associated with living in a prejudiced cultural context and, in the face of these challenges, these families organize their roles and identities in flexible and adaptive ways. For this reason, clinicians working with transgender families must be aware of the effects of anti-transgender bias and the many ways minority stress can impact and organize transgender individuals' experiences, but they must also understand that not all individuals identifying within the transgender community utilize therapy solely for the purposes of addressing gender-based concerns. Work with transgender families must begin with a culturally competent assessment focused on determining whether the concerns expressed by clients are generic relationship-based concerns, concerns unique to the experiences of transgender individuals and families, or a blend of both. For many transgender families, issues raised in therapy reflect relationship distress not specifically related to gender identity. In situations such as these, clinicians would be misguided focusing on a client's gender identity and could possibly be operating from a place of bias.

While many transgender families do not come to therapy explicitly to address gender-based concerns, there are a number of clinical concerns that emerge consistently in work with transgender individuals and families. These issues are often a function of living in a transphobic and cisnormative environment. For many transgender individuals, therapy is the first place safe enough to disclose a minority gender identity or even to question their gender identity. Although not always the case, those in therapy disproportionately report that they do not have the support of immediate family members and often come to therapy alone. For these situations, clinicians should focus on normalizing diverse gender identities and encouraging clients to explore their internal sense of self and the possibility of transitioning. It is important to note that transgender individuals' desire for transition exists on a continuum and is a blend of both social and internal influences. For many it is a process of balancing gains and losses, essentially deciding whether what will be gained through transition will outweigh what might be lost. Those with a strong need for transition often describe feelings as though they were born in the wrong body and that the pain of living in the wrong body is unbearable. For these individuals, the gains of transition far outweigh the costs. Other individuals feel less wedded to the physical component of gender and are comfortable living in their cross-gender identity without changing their bodies. Although many factors contribute to an individual's desire for transition, some reported reasons include the amelioration of extreme discomfort with genitalia, the ability to engage sexually in current or future romantic partnerships as one's true gender identity, and feeling integrated in terms of internal sense of self and physical presentation. Clinicians might consider using a diagnosis of gender dysphoria for persons describing these experiences in order to help them utilize medical interventions for a body-based transition.

For those interested in a physical transition, the process often begins with a social transition that includes shifts in gender presentation to a cross-gender expression. This typically includes experimentation with cross-dressing and starting a course of hormone replacement therapy (HRT) to alter secondary sex characteristics. It is commonly the case that transgender individuals come to therapy with family members during these early stages of transition. Shifts in gender expression often require disclosure of minority gender identity within and beyond the core family unit. It is during this period that experiences of discrimination and transphobia become increasingly salient, and families often come to therapy for help in processing and dealing with the effects of these oppressive systems. For partners and loved ones who are not transitioning, the focus is often on helping them understand the experiences of the transitioning family member and providing psychoeducation about the differences in gender orientation, gender identity, gender expression, and anatomy. Often from the dominant community, partners vary in terms of their support for the transition, but even the most supportive partners talk of a grief process resulting from having to "let go of the person they knew." Clinical efforts at this point should focus on helping transitioning partners explore their emerging gender identity while also honoring the feelings of loss felt by nontransitioning family members. For some families, simply helping them process shifting family roles is a useful objective. It is often during this work that the resiliency unique to transgender families emerges. Adapting to shifting roles within the family system, transgender families often experience a reorganization of priorities that emphasizes the health of and connection among family members. The resilience of these families is most pronounced, however, as the family members focus on embracing each other as their authentic selves.

Lindsay L. Edwards

See also Gender- and Culture-Sensitive Therapies; Gender Orientation, Gender Identity, and Gender Expression; LGBT Families

Further Readings

Blumer, M. C., Ansara, Y. G., & Watson, C. M. (2013). Cisgenderism in family therapy: How everyday clinical practices can delegitimize people's gender self-designations. *Journal of Family Psychotherapy,* 24(4), 267–285. doi:10.1080/08975353.2013.849551

Coolhart, D., Baker, A., Farmer, S., Malaney, M., & Shipman, D. (2013). Therapy with transsexual youth and their families: A clinical tool for assessing youth's readiness for gender transition. *Journal of Marital and Family Therapy,* 39(2), 223–243. doi:10.1111/j.1752-0606.2011.00283.x

Gates, G. J. (2011). *How many people are lesbian, gay, bisexual and transgender?* Los Angeles, CA: UCLA, The Williams Institute.

Grant, J. M., Mottet, L., Tanis, A. J., Harrison, J., Herman, J. L., & Keisling, M. (2011). *Injustice at every turn: A report of the national transgender discrimination survey.* Washington, DC: National Center for Transgender Equality and National Gay and Lesbian Task Force.

Lev, A. I. (2004). *Transgender emergence: Therapeutic guidelines for working with gender-variant people and their families.* Binghamton, NY: Haworth.

Nagoshi, J. L., Nagoshi, C. T., Brzuzy, S., Filip-Crawford, G., Varley, A., & Hess, R. I. (2014). *Gender and sexual identity: Transcending feminist and queer theory.* New York, NY: Springer Science + Business Media. doi:10.1007/978-1-4614-8966-5

TRANSGENERATIONAL FAMILY THERAPY

Family therapy involves a complex system of connections, changes, and multiple relation patterns that can make an air traffic controller's screen at an international airport seem simplistic. By comparison, when one airplane moves even slightly off course, other planes nearby must take quick action to respond to the change. The action of one plane affects the function of the entire system. The transgenerational family system is similar insofar as the actions and reactions of each generation influence the family as a whole, which in turn seeks a functional balance in this newly formed, complex unit. This entry examines several key conceptualizations of the family, including those developed by Murray Bowen (1913–1990), Ivan Boszormenyi-Nagy (1902–2007), and James Framo (1922–2001).

Since Murray Bowen pioneered the concept of family as a complex, interworking system, therapists have gained a broader view of the family as both the whole and the sum of its parts. As the life span increases in the United States, more families are becoming multigenerational units with three, four, and five generations living together and dealing with caregiving responsibilities for longer periods. This lifestyle trend prompts therapists to become more familiar with theories and approaches to transgenerational family therapy.

When a family brings in one or more older adults, the family system must shift to meet caregiving needs and rebalance the relationships. Murray Bowen pioneered the concept of the family as a unique system. In dealing with the family rather than the person identified as the "problem" from a Bowenian viewpoint, the transgenerational family therapist looks at how the family functions as an integrated system whose life and beliefs are interwoven in ways that change the interactions of that family, for better or worse.

The eight concepts that constitute Bowen's framework for his family theory are triangles, differentiation of self, the nuclear family emotional system, family projection process, multigenerational transmission process, emotional cutoff, sibling position, and societal emotional process; all of these elements have application to the transgenerational family system. Of particular importance is what Bowen saw as the long-range impact of "multigenerational transmission," which he graphically displayed using the family genogram. Notably, the genogram is a diagram of the family system similar to an organizational chart in business, which offers a visual representation of relationships, interaction patterns, and levels of connection.

Even when individuals insist that they are different from their parents or grandparents, the patterns with a family system persist and may be repeated in younger generations. Family members may ascribe to a child the personality or behavior of a parent or grandparent, as if to suggest that these connections are transmitted across generations similar to the way that biological similarities are transmitted. Family therapists working with the transgenerational family can observe these similarities or connections across generations, which may also be modeling or exhibit a strong identification with another family member.

Ivan Boszormenyi-Nagy's contextual family therapy, which focuses on transgenerational solidarity, would apply effectively to today's three and four generations living as a newly formed transgenerational family unit. Nagy also identified the ways in which families keep score and transmit memories of past hurts or expectations that occurred between or among family members from prior generations. These positive and negative recollections are part of the family history that can be used to solidify or block transgenerational connections. In working with transgenerational families, the family therapist needs to identify how items on the score card from the past can set up alliances or block connections in the present family unit. The importance of revising the impact of past events on current family system beliefs was also a major part of Virginia Satir's family reconstruction therapy.

The family is more than a collection of related persons who live together. As the generations merge into the new transgenerational family unit, the elder generation brings the family legends and history. These legends and the incorporation of elders with a different worldview begin to influence the emotional aspects of the family system. When the older adults coming into this family system are from different families (for example, the mother of one partner and spouse and father of the other partner or spouse), there is an added complexity of merging three families: the family of origin of each partner and the family that this couple (or single adult) has formed. The potential for triangulation involving the adult child, his or her spouse, and the older adult parent is high as the elder seeks to find a role within the family. If there are existing patterns of triangulation from the family of origin, this behavior may persist and add stressors to the couple's relationship.

James Framo was a passionate advocate of transgenerational family therapy and the potential it held to create positive interaction patterns, which he believed would become the new norm for succeeding generations. The stresses of elder caregiving within a multigenerational family typically fall on the female, who may also have children or grandchildren in the home and be struggling to maintain employment outside the home. The time and emotional demands of caregiving added to the expected demands of child-rearing and work often become a divisive issue for the couple relationship. As the issues brought into marriage or couples therapy are explored, the therapist may find that transgenerational family therapy can better serve the needs of this couple as well as the family system. By widening the perspective from individual or couples therapy to transgenerational family therapy, the therapeutic potential increases.

Transgenerational family therapy has encountered the same conundrum as other specialties within the family therapy arena due to the pressure to deliver evidence-based therapy. Families are complex, representing many variables. The influences of culture, ethnicity, lifestyle, and experiences are often more suited to case studies, which have been the historical foundation of family therapy. The pioneers of family therapy were practitioners and not from the pure research camp. The worldwide trend of larger aging adult populations who are living longer is the driving force behind the increase in multiple generations living under one roof as a transgenerational family unit. With greater longevity comes increased years of caregiving, an added financial burden, and the emotional stressors of caregiving associated with what is often described as the "sandwich generation" (post–World War II baby boomers or Gen X adults). These stressors on the caregiving family have become a focus of research that can yield more information to help therapists understand the dynamics of multiple generations living together with the common task of caregiving. As family therapists contribute more on treatment processes, case studies, and mixed methods research, the body of knowledge for working with the 21st-century transgenerational family system will refine ways to meet evidence-based practice standards. The complexity of the family unit with three, four, or five generations living together is ripe for research and redefinition, as are the ways therapists apply traditional family systems approaches to this larger system.

Kathie Erwin

See also Bowen Family Systems Theory; Differentiation; Family Resilience; Functional Family Therapy; Nuclear Family; Triangulation

Further Readings

Boszormenyi-Nagy, I. (1986). Transgenerational solidarity: The expanding context of therapy and prevention. *American Journal of Family Therapy, 14*(3), 195–212.

Bowen, M. (2004). *Family therapy in clinical practice.* Lanham, MD: Rowman & Littlefield. (Originally published 1978)

Framo, J. L. (1992). *Family of origin: An intergenerational approach.* New York, NY: Brunner-Routledge.

Klever, P. (2005). The multigenerational transmission of family unit functioning. *American Journal of Family Therapy, 33,* 253–264.

TRANSRACIAL ADOPTION

Transracial adoption, also known as transcultural adoption, is defined by Rita Simon and Howard Alstein as the process by which a parent or couple from one racial, ethnic, or cultural group adopts a child from a differing racial, ethnic, or cultural group. A White couple adopting a Hispanic child is an example of a transracial adoption due to their differences in racial and cultural backgrounds. These adoptions can be domestic (e.g., foster care, private adoption, or stepchildren in an interracial marriage) or international (adopting children from another country). A 2009 report from the U.S. Department of State indicated that U.S. parents had adopted close to 500,000 children from other countries since 1971. These children were primarily from Asia, Africa, and South America. Additionally, 40% of the domestic adoptions in the United States are transracial. Transracial adoption is considered to be the most visible form of adoption because of the distinct racial/ethnic differences between the adoptive parents and the adoptee. This entry provides an overview of the issues facing transracially adopted children and their families as well as implications for therapists in their work with these families.

While transracial adoption is a common form of adoption, it is also controversial. One reason is that most commonly these adoptions involve White and U.S.-born individuals adopting children of color or children from other nationalities. Some groups that oppose transracial adoption assert that White and U.S.-born individuals are not adequately prepared to raise children of racially and culturally differing backgrounds. J. Toni Oliver, vice president of the National Association of Black Social Workers, emphasizes that families considering transracial adoption should be prepared by their agencies to understand the pervasive impact of race on achievement, self-esteem, self-concept, and mental health. Alternately, groups that support transracial adoption affirm that what is most important is placing children in available adoptive families regardless of ethnicity, race, or culture as opposed to delaying adoptions to place children in families that are of similar ethnic, racial, or cultural backgrounds.

Transracial Adopted Families' Experiences

Maria Vidal de Haynes and Shirley Simon report that the experiences of families involved in the adoption of children who vary in racial background from the adoptive family's dominant culture are different across various cultures and racial groups. However, there are some similarities among these families regardless of the differences between adopter and adoptee culture groups, which are not shared by families who adopt within their own culture/racial group. The differences include the perceptions of outsiders, increased visibility of the adoption to outsiders, lack of support from extended families and the larger community, and increased pressure to include others from the adopted child's race or ethnic background.

Many of these families come to recognize that outsiders often perceive them as having rescued their adopted children rather than as a family unit (parents and children), which is how they see themselves. This perception is exacerbated by visible differences in racial aspects (e.g., skin color, facial features). Families who adopt transracially often also feel defensive in the face of those who do not hold similar perceptions of their families.

Families with a transracially adopted child experience varying degrees of support from extended family members. Families may have very supportive extended families; however, some experience alienation and an absence of backing. The families who experience a lack of support may not be prepared for the backlash from their extended family, whom they may have found supportive of other endeavors throughout their lives. Also, these families may experience less support from the community at large. Some families of transracial adoption have difficulty engaging with the public due to the increased visibility of their family adoption and the perceptions of those from the adopter's dominant culture and adoptee's culture. This can cause families of transracial adoption to withdraw from community engagement, which leads to decreased sources of support for the family unit.

However, even though there may be motivation to withdraw from the community due to perceptions of insufficient support, adopters want their children to have experiences from within their own culture or racial group. It can sometimes be difficult for families to find outlets for their transracially adopted children owing to a lack of racial and/or cultural diversity within the adopted parents' own social group. These families often look for outlets to increase diversity within their own social network in order to increase their transracially adopted children's exposure to a culture and/or race similar to their own.

All of these experiences are similar among transracially adopted families; however, this list is not exhaustive of the experiences that families who choose to adopt across racial barriers encounter. A counselor/family therapist will need to be open and discuss the family's own unique experiences with transracial adoption.

Implications and Recommendations for Counselors/Family Therapists

Prior to engaging in a therapeutic relationship with families with transracial adoptees, counselors need to consider their level of interpersonal awareness and understanding of research and interventions for families of transracial adoption. A counselor may best serve a family by being aware of his or her own competence to work with a family in this context.

A heightened awareness of personal bias is especially important when working with families that involve multiple cultural and racial backgrounds. Krista Malott and Christopher Schmidt summarize findings across various research journals that encourage multicultural competency of counselors who work with families of transracial adoption. These biases and beliefs are held specifically by the counselor and can be multifaceted. For example, a counselor's personal beliefs regarding the ability of White families to raise children from a different race or culture, along with a bias that children should look like their parents, will affect the counselor's perception and conceptualization of the family and, in turn, impact his or her goals and objectives working with the family. It is imperative that counselors question their own beliefs and biases and how they may affect their work with these families prior to engaging in a therapeutic relationship.

There is a certain area of knowledge that needs to be attained and understood by a counselor working with a transracially adopted family. These areas of knowledge will help the counselor better understand the special circumstances of the family and intervene in an appropriate manner. Some families continue to report difficulty and lack of encouragement from social programs during their transracial adoption process. Counselors should also be aware of the personal experiences of the family they are working with. For instance, some families may have experienced aggressions or microaggressions while other families don't have those experiences or aren't even aware that their family dynamic involving an adopted child from a different race could be viewed by others as controversial. Counselors should be aware of the racial identity development process of transracial adoptees and the differences in several different models. Malott and Schmidt conclude that parental involvement with transracially adopted individuals has been shown to have a direct effect on identity development. Finally, a counselor should be aware of the effects that the transracial adoption process has on the overall development of the adoptee. For example, internationally adopted children can show a delay in verbal and physical development, which is a direct effect of their adoption and not necessarily an issue of concern requiring specific intervention by specialists.

Lastly, counselors should develop specific skills in working with transracially adoptive families. These skills encompass many of the knowledge fields discussed above but with specific action and intentionality. Therefore, since there is history and controversy encompassing transracial adoption, counselors should advocate and develop advocacy skills for the families who may experience racism. These skills are important since the parents in these families may have never experienced controversy or racial aggressions themselves. The counselor should also include psychological education and even family support groups or multifamily sessions to encourage development of a support network. Counselors should also be prepared to help families along the entire process of adoption along with developing skills specific to combating negative perceptions and stereotypes, which the family may never have experienced before.

Blake Sandusky and Kristine Ramsay

See also Adoption; Adoptive Families; Cultural Issues in Couples and Families

Further Readings

Baden, A., Gibbons, J., Wilson, S., & McGinnis, H. (2013). International adoption: Counseling and the adoption triad. *Adoption Quarterly, 16,* 218–237.

Baden, A., Treweeke, L., & Ahluwalia, M. (2012). Reclaiming culture: Reculturation of transracial and international adoptees. *Journal of Counseling and Development, 90,* 387–399.

Bradley, C., & Hawkins-León, C. (2002). The transracial adoption debate: Counseling and legal implications. *Journal of Counseling and Development, 80,* 433–440.

Corbin Dwyer, S., & Gidluck, L. (2012). Talking about adoption: Considerations for multicultural counsellors when working with transracial families. *Asia Pacific Journal of Counseling and Psychology, 3*(1), 61–71.

Jacobson, C., Nielsen, L., & Hardeman, A. (2012). Family trends and transracial adoption in the United States. *Adoption Quarterly, 15*(2), 73–87.

Lindgren, C., & Zetterqvist Nelson, K. (2014). Here and now—there and then: Narrative time and space in intercountry adoptees' stories about background, origin and roots. *Qualitative Social Work, 13*(4), 539–554.

Malott, K., & Schmidt, C. (2012). Counseling families formed by transracial adoption: Bridging the gap in the multicultural counseling competencies. *The Family Journal, 20*(4), 384–391.

San Roman, B. (2013). "I am white . . . even if I am racially black" "I am afro-spanish": Confronting belonging paradoxes in transracial adoptions. *Journal of Intercultural Studies, 34*(3), 229–245.

Vidal de Haymes, M., & Simon, S. (2003). Transracial adoption: Families identify issues and needed support. *Child Welfare League of America, 82*(2), 251–272.

Trauma and Children

Childhood trauma is a growing mental health and public health concern. In the United States, the average proportion of children experiencing trauma is one in four. Approximately 20% of these children will later develop symptoms of posttraumatic stress disorder. This entry briefly introduces trauma and discusses trauma as it relates to children from birth to 16 years of age. It is important to note that children 6 years and under display different symptoms post-trauma than other age-groups.

Defining Trauma

Trauma refers to a single incident or set of incidents that are extremely stressful, threaten life, or eradicate one's sense of safety and security. What qualifies as a traumatic experience is subjective based on an individual's emotional experience and response to the event; among these are sexual trauma, physical trauma, emotional trauma, neglect, violence, and war. Thus, trauma is a broad term used to identify a negative experience that leaves an individual with psychological or emotional impact. These experiences can also occur indirectly, through exposure in the form of being told that a close friend or family member experienced trauma, as well as from prolonged exposure to the details of a traumatic event. Although trauma is determined individually, an event is most likely to result in trauma if it happens unexpectedly, if it occurs repeatedly, if an individual feels powerless to prevent or end it, and if it happens in childhood.

Types of Trauma

Trauma among children occurs when they are exposed to an intense event that threatens or causes harm emotionally or physically. Trauma can be the result of experiencing or witnessing violence, serious injury, or abuse. Trauma can also occur when a child is exposed to terrorism, war, natural disaster, or the loss of a loved one. Chronic traumatic events occur repeatedly over a long period and typically include physical, emotional, or sexual abuse, and feelings of being in danger due to ongoing war or violence occurring in one's surroundings. Acute traumatic events tend to leave children feeling helpless and afraid. Chronic traumatic events generally result in children feeling shame, guilt, and a loss of trust in others.

Each traumatic event can vary in the degree that a child's life feels threatened or violated. Each child may experience different thoughts, feelings, and responses to a traumatic event. A child's level of development must be taken into consideration when looking at the complex layers of exposure to trauma. Each child's response to trauma will be influenced by internal and external factors specific to that child. Internal factors may include previous exposure to trauma, prior health and mental health concerns, natural temperament, and development. External factors may include family support, community and school support, and cultural dynamics.

Trauma Outcomes in Children

Experiencing trauma as a child can have long-lasting biological, emotional, and cognitive effects.

Children may differ in the way they respond to and cope with witnessing or experiencing a traumatic event, and the most recent psychological approaches emphasize respecting each child's style of coping and not labeling one coping method as more appropriate than another. Considerations are also made for the age and development of each child when assessing traumatic impact.

Children who have witnessed or experienced a traumatic event will have initial reactions and delayed emotional, physical, cognitive, and behavioral responses. Initial emotional reactions may include denial, helplessness, guilt, anger, anxiety, fear, and numbness. Initial physical responses may include high blood pressure, increased heart rate, and nausea. Memory lapses, distortion of time and space perception, racing thoughts, and difficulty concentrating are examples of initial cognitive responses. Children may also become more argumentative and demonstrate difficulties in communicating thoughts and feelings. Delayed emotional responses include irritability, depression, and emotional instability. Delayed physical responses of children include increased levels of cortisol (a hormone secreted as a response to stress) that, unless followed by a physical release of fight or flight, can have long-term harmful effects on the organs.

Ongoing outcomes for children who experience trauma include insensitivity to pain or hypersensitivity to physical contact. They often experience interrupted sleep patterns due to ongoing dreams that reference their traumatic experience, and may suffer from psychosomatic bodily reactions including upset stomach and increased heart rates. Trauma can also adversely affect brain development, resulting in cognitive and language acquisition delays. Children who experience trauma often view the world as untrustworthy and unpredictable and therefore demonstrate strong emotional responses with the onset or potential onset of relationships, including problems with boundaries, trust, social cues, and difficulty empathizing.

Children who have experienced trauma can have diverse responses on a continuum ranging from withdrawal to trauma-induced hallucinations. Children who withdraw tend to be very quiet and passive, are easily alarmed by noise or sudden movement around them, and are extremely fearful of new surroundings. In some cases, especially in younger children, they regress to toddler-like behaviors to include thumb sucking, bed-wetting, and unprovoked crying. Children who display intense emotionality often have difficulty regulating their mood, which is demonstrated by strong mood swings and an inability to identify or describe their feelings. They also tend to display poor impulse control, aggression toward others, and self-destructive behavior. Child traumatic stress can also result in diminished self-concept, body image issues, risk-taking behaviors, and the use of drugs or alcohol to cope with the lasting effects of trauma. One of the most impactful outcomes of trauma in children is their developed expectation of abandonment and maltreatment.

Children may face these symptoms and outcomes on a continual basis, with some children responding through self-injurious behavior or thoughts of suicide. It is important to note that although children face these symptoms, this does not routinely result in a psychiatric diagnosis of posttraumatic stress disorder (PTSD) or another diagnosis. Child trauma refers only to the stress of any child who has experienced a traumatic event and is having difficulty coping with its effects. Children can receive ongoing therapeutic support for experiencing trauma without having a psychiatric diagnosis.

Treatment of Trauma for Children

With specialized training, mental health professionals identify trauma-exposed children and take careful considerations in providing culturally and developmentally appropriate support and treatment. The first responsibility of a mental health professional is to assess the risk for imminent danger to self or others, imminent danger imposed on the child, and the possible need to involve emergency services to include medical, social services, or law enforcement. The second responsibility is to ensure that the child's basic needs are being met. These basic needs may include supportive family or community, shelter, and ongoing safety. A key element in responding to child trauma is providing education and information to the child and the caregivers. Mental health providers must also assess the child's psychological state and begin providing therapeutic services based on the individual child's needs and current response symptoms to the traumatic event.

Cognitive-behavioral therapy (CBT) has been shown to be highly effective for treating children who have experienced trauma. Trauma-focused CBT includes the child discussing the exposure to a trauma and the mental health provider educating the child on effective anxiety management techniques to include relaxation, correction of distorted thoughts, and assertiveness training, teaching individuals how to communicate and advocate on their own behalf. Children and caregivers also receive psychoeducation where they learn about the symptoms and effects of trauma exposure.

Play therapy is a developmentally appropriate form of treatment often used with young children. Play therapy gives children the opportunity to express their thoughts and feelings through the use of self-guided writings, drawing, and games.

Psychological first aid is generally used as a part of crisis intervention when a school-aged child or adolescent has been exposed, for example, to a natural disaster, a school shooting, or community violence. The goal is to create a safe environment, provide emotional support to the child and caregiver, teach calming techniques, and assess to determine whether there is a need for additional treatment.

The overall goal of therapeutic interventions for children who have experienced or witnessed trauma is to reduce ongoing exposure to stressors, reduce the risk of secondary trauma, and teach skills that will assist the child in becoming aware of his or her emotions, while providing coping skills and replacement behaviors to help manage emotions.

Dialectical behavior therapy (DBT) is a cognitive-behavioral treatment that is also shown to be effective in treating older children who have experienced or witnessed trauma. DBT provides children with behavioral skills training in a counseling group format and individual therapy where the focus in on increasing the child's ability to apply the skills learned in behavioral skills training. Children also receive DBT coaching, where a therapist can use in-the-moment assistance via telephone as difficult situations occur outside of the therapeutic environment. This provides the opportunity for children to seek direct help before responding to a perceived negative situation. The goal of DBT is to increase mindfulness, being fully aware and present in the moment, and increase distress tolerance, referring to the ability to tolerate uncomfortable and difficult situations that cannot be changed. DBT also aims to have children develop open communication, establish or maintain self-respect, and create healthy boundaries with others. Emotion regulation is also a key concept of DBT, working to help children change the emotions that they want to change. Overall, DBT works to help children balance the idea of acceptance and change, as they need to do both successfully in varying aspects of their lives after experiencing a traumatic event.

Current knowledge of trauma events experienced by children demonstrates a great need for early awareness and impactful treatment. Although trauma experienced by children can have long-lasting negative effects, if children receive treatment as soon as possible following the occurrence of a traumatic event, the risk of lifelong effects decreases. In cases of infant and early childhood trauma (birth to age 6), barriers to effective communication have been identified; current research efforts in this area are focusing on identification and assessment of trauma, as well as effective treatment.

Sarah N. Brant-Rajahn

See also Depression in Children; Mindfulness and Children; Posttraumatic Stress Disorder in Children; Somatic Symptom Disorder and Related Disorders in Adolescents

Further Readings

Allen, B., & Kronenberg, M. (2014). *Treating traumatized children: A casebook of evidence-based therapies.* New York, NY: Guilford Press.

Center for Substance Abuse Treatment. (2014). Understanding the impact of trauma. In *Trauma-informed care in behavioral health services* (Treatment Improvement Protocol [TIP] Series, No. 57, pp. 59–89). Rockville, MD: Substance Abuse and Mental Health Services Administration. Retrieved from http://www.ncbi.nlm.nih.gov/books/NBK207191/

Nader, K. (2007). *Understanding and assessing trauma in children and adolescents: Measures, methods, and youth in context.* New York, NY: Routledge.

U.S. Department of Health and Human Services, Administration for Children and Families, Administration on Children, Youth and Families, Children's Bureau. (2012). *Child maltreatment 2011.* Available from http://www.acf.hhs.gov

Trauma and Families

Psychologically speaking, traumatic experiences are defined as events that overwhelm an individual's (or groups') resources and abilities to cope physically, psychologically, and spiritually, resulting in a period of psychological suffering. The history of humankind has included war, interpersonal violence, natural disasters, and other events—both natural and human—resulting in lasting psychological distress, physical injury, and spiritual pain for affected individuals. The impact of these events is disruptive to the psychological and relational functioning of individuals, interpersonal relationships, and families. Therefore, therapeutically exploring the meaning and impact of traumatic events is often involved directly or indirectly in the therapeutic work of family therapy. In this entry, the rationale for using family therapy with trauma, the diagnosis of trauma, the intersection of trauma and development, trauma within interpersonal relationships, and family therapy approaches for trauma are discussed.

Family Therapy and Trauma

Due to the universal nature of trauma exposure, trauma therapy is a common theme in family therapy models across cultures. Family therapy for traumatic events can be couples focused, child focused, child incorporative, or provided for adult members of an extended family. The incorporation of family members may be influenced by the nature of the traumatic event, the ages of family members, and the culturally informed practices of the therapist providing services.

Family therapy for traumatic events can be trauma informed or trauma focused. Trauma-informed therapeutic care occurs when a clinician incorporates an understanding of present symptoms and coping reactions in respect to a past trauma when addressing a presenting concern. A clinician using a trauma-informed perspective would incorporate clinical conceptualization and treatment planning to accommodate the trauma experience while focusing on the more pressing presenting concern, such as marital difficulties or parenting concerns. Trauma-focused therapeutic care is the implementation of theory, technique, and evidence-based practices that are specifically tailored to reduce trauma-related symptoms and to aid the client(s) in achieving psychological resolution in regard to the traumatic experience.

Diagnosis and Trauma

While not all individuals who experience a traumatic event will receive a mental health diagnosis, the experience of a traumatic event can contribute to the development of or exacerbate existing mood, anxiety, psychosis, substance abuse, and personality disorders, which must be properly diagnosed and treated. The use of diagnostic labels to conceptualize traumatic response has been a controversial topic for much of the 20th century. While American mental health professionals began to write about and discuss the impact of traumatic events on the individual and family as early as World War I, there was little scholarly agreement on the factors that resulted from traumatic events. In the field of family therapy, there was little therapeutic attention to the physiological and relational changes that are caused by traumatic experiences beyond early childhood attachment disruptions until the modern period of traumatic stress studies.

The modern study of traumatic stress and related traumatic responses became a strong movement in the 1970s and 1980s following the Vietnam conflict. Following Vietnam, veterans groups and mental health professionals began to observe that many soldiers returning from combat experience were displaying a syndrome of symptoms that were thematically linked to combat experience. This syndrome included the experience of nightmares, flashbacks, depressed mood, emotional dysregulation, and destructive behaviors such as increased suicidality and substance misuse. Simultaneously, women's groups and mental health professionals were also recognizing that women and children who had experienced domestic abuse and sexual assault were also being observed to have a syndrome with similar symptoms labeled "battered women's syndrome" or "rape crisis syndrome."

The efforts to lobby for diagnostic recognition of this syndrome pattern resulted in the incorporation of posttraumatic stress disorder in the "Anxiety Disorders" chapter in the third edition of the *Diagnostic and Statistical Manual* (1980) (DSM-III). In that version of the manual the definition of trauma was in reference to events considered outside of the realm of normal human experience. Additional population-based research across multiple populations suggested that approximately 50% to 80% of individuals worldwide are exposed to potentially traumatic events in their lifetime; therefore, the definition was modified in the publication of the fourth edition of the *Diagnostic and Statistical Manual* (1995) (DSM-IV). DSM-IV changed the diagnostic features from focusing on event exposure to the reaction of the individual in helplessness and horror. Subsequent to the incorporation of the posttraumatic stress disorder (PTSD) diagnosis, research in the 1990s and 2000s focused on the existence of a spectrum of posttrauma exposure responses, since the vast majority of trauma-exposed individuals do not develop PTSD but display a range of other symptoms.

It has been well documented that individuals exposed to trauma may respond with a wide variation of mood, anxiety, relational, substance related, and behavioral symptoms, such as eating disorders as well as dissociative and psychotic symptoms in addition to the cluster of symptoms identified as PTSD. Mental health clinicians and researchers further recognize that even in the absence of a diagnostic label such as PTSD or major depression, those who have experienced traumatic events may adapt their personality and relational patterns as a result of the traumatic experience. Therefore, even in the absence of a presentation resulting in a diagnostic label, trauma-informed therapy may be beneficial to the personal and relational life of individuals and families impacted by traumatic experiences.

Trauma and Development

The developmental age of an individual at the time he or she is exposed to a traumatic event is an important mediating factor that shapes the individual's experience of the event, his or her coping resources, development of resilience, and his or her trajectory of symptoms later in life. Early childhood experiences shape attachment patterns, which in turn shape relating patterns throughout the life span. When trauma occurs during sensitive developmental periods, such as childhood and adolescence, attachment patterns may be disrupted, and permanent neurological changes can occur and impact the brain's emotional regulation and executive functioning structures. These changes in turn shape an individual's emotional regulation and anxiety response in later life situations.

Adults exposed to early-life traumatic events in childhood have been demonstrated to have higher risk of anxiety and stress-related health disorders after additional adult exposure to traumatic events. Research has consistently documented that these long-term effects are moderated by interpersonal relationships. The presence of secure parental relationships, strong sibling relationships, and safe environmental factors has been demonstrated to both protect against and reduce severity of childhood stress responses. For this reason, early intervention is heavily emphasized in the family therapy and mental health literature and is thought to potentially prevent the development of lifelong psychological consequences if protective family processes are set in place. One such model of trauma-focused therapy is the evidence-based trauma-focused cognitive-behavioral therapy (TF-CBT). TF-CBT, when used with children and adolescents, specifically integrates family education and incorporates the presence of the child's parents during sessions in which the child discusses the most stressful aspects of the traumatic experience. TF-CBT was specifically designed as a family-incorporative trauma therapy for the purpose of reducing child distress and to build resilience.

Trauma Within the Interpersonal Relationship

The interpersonal context and impact of trauma can have lasting effects on individuals, couples, and families. Much of the trauma perpetrated on victims around the world occurs within an interpersonal context. Experiences of interpersonal violence can impact an individual's ability to build trusting relationships, to experience vulnerability, and to express and understand emotional communication, as well as impact sexual and occupational functioning. Interpartner violence and sexual abuse are two of the most common causes of traumatic stress reactions, but other relational traumas, including experiences of caregiver abandonment or death, verbal abuse, stalking, bullying, and criminal victimization by a family member or friend, also are interpersonal traumas.

The goal of family or couples therapy after relational trauma is to rebuild trust, reestablish outlets for regulated emotional expression, and establish health communication patterns. In distinct contrast to more individual models of intervention, family therapy may involve therapeutic care of one or more family members who have been victims of another family member's abusive behavior. Therefore, careful attention must be given to determining the safety of family members and the potential power/control dynamics that are present when victim and perpetrator of abuse are present simultaneously. In situations of physical or sexual violence, it is recommended that family therapy not include the perpetrator as it is possible to create dynamics of abuse within the therapy and to endanger the victims if they confront or disobey the abuser. One evidence-based therapy that addresses the interpersonal communication difficulties that often result from interpersonal trauma is emotion-focused couples therapy (EFT). EFT is based on attachment theory and works to help partners engage in expressing and receiving vulnerable emotional expressions in healthier ways.

Family Therapy

When providing family-based trauma-informed or trauma-focused therapy, it is important that family therapists remain aware of the family dynamics that may influence the effectiveness of therapeutic intervention. While the intergenerational effects of trauma are just being explored, it is understood that the children of trauma-exposed parents are often at higher risk for experiencing trauma in their lifetime, potentially resulting in multiple trauma experiences within one family. Traumatic events can be experienced individually, simultaneously with other family members, and vicariously as family members experience the events through the perspective of their loved ones. Family members influence one another reciprocally in both direct and indirect ways. Exposure to traumatic events can result in interpartner stress and parenting stress, creating additional tension within family systems. Parental responses to stress and disaster influence the psychological reaction of other family members. Studies after natural disasters and interpersonal violence have found that parents' responses to traumatic events strongly influence the emotional disturbance and emergence of subsequent disorders in their children. In contrast, strong attachment bonds and positive family relationships have been demonstrated to reduce risk of children developing traumatic stress symptoms.

In her definitive 1993 book *Trauma and Recovery*, Judith Herman proposed that trauma therapy must occur in three stages. The first stage involves crisis stabilization and establishment of rudimentary self-care skills. The second stage involves building a narrative of the traumatic experience and its subsequent impact on the individual and his or her family so that they can mourn the event. The final stage is rebuilding their life goals and dreams in a way that incorporates the loss from the traumatic event. While this model was initially established in regard to individual trauma therapy, it is a meaningful framework for understanding the stages of therapy when working with families as well. The growing movement of evidence-based therapy has resulted in the development of several trauma-informed treatments including TF-CBT, EFT, and functional family therapy. Efforts have also been made to develop culturally targeted therapies, such as helping and understanding grieving suicide survivors (HUGSS), which is a culturally responsive therapy for African American families who have lost a member to suicide.

Tara C. Samples

See also Evidence-Based Practice With Couples and Families; Intergenerational Trauma; Self-Care Practices for the Trauma-Informed Couple and Family Counselor; Trauma and Children; Trauma-Focused Cognitive-Behavioral Therapy

Further Readings

Briere, J. N., & Scott, C. (2014). *Principles of trauma therapy: A guide to symptoms, evaluation, and treatment*. Thousand Oaks, CA: Sage.

Cohen, J. A., Mannarino, A. P., Kliethermes, M., & Murray, L. A. (2012). Trauma-focused CBT for youth with complex trauma. *Child Abuse & Neglect, 36*(6), 528–541.

Foroughe, M., & Muller, R. (2014). Attachment-based intervention strategies in family therapy with survivors of intra-familial trauma: A case study. *Journal of Family Violence, 29*(5), 539–548. doi:10.1007/s10896-014-9607-4

Foster, J. M. (2014). Supporting child victims of sexual abuse: Implementation of a trauma narrative family intervention. *Family Journal, 23*(3), 332–338.

Herman, J. L. (1997). *Trauma and recovery*. New York, NY: Basic Books.

Johnson, S. M. (2002). *Emotionally focused couple therapy with trauma survivors: Strengthening attachment bonds*. New York, NY: Guilford Press.

Kaslow, N. J., Samples, T. C., Rhodes, M., & Gantt, S. (2011). A family-oriented and culturally sensitive postvention approach with suicide survivors (pp. 301–323). In J. R. Jordan & J. L. McIntosh (Eds.), *Grief after suicide: Understanding the consequences and caring for the survivors*. New York, NY: Routledge.

MacIntosh, H. B., & Johnson, S. (2008). Emotionally focused therapy for couples and childhood sexual abuse survivors. *Journal of Marital and Family Therapy, 34*(3), 298–315.

McGoldrick, M., Giordano, J., & Garcia-Preto, N. (2005). *Ethnicity and family therapy*. New York, NY: Guilford Press.

Nygaard, E., Jensen, T. K., & Dyb, G. (2010). Posttraumatic stress reactions in siblings after mutual disaster: Relevance of family factors. *Journal of Traumatic Stress, 23*(2), 278–281.

Siegel, J. P. (2013). Breaking the links in intergenerational violence: An emotional regulation perspective. *Family Process, 52*(2), 163–178.

Sprang, G., Staton-Tindall, M., Gustman, B., Freer, B., Clark, J. J., Dye, H., & Sprang, K. (2013). The impact of trauma exposure on parenting stress in rural America. *Journal of Child & Adolescent Trauma, 6*(4), 287–300.

Trauma-Focused Cognitive-Behavioral Therapy

Trauma-focused cognitive-behavioral therapy (TF-CBT) is an evidence-based treatment for families affected by childhood trauma. It adapts elements of cognitive-behavioral therapy to address the unique mental health needs of traumatized children and adolescents. Represented by the acronym PRACTICE, TF-CBT includes the following core treatment components: Psychoeducation and parenting skills training, Relaxation and stress management, Affective expression and modulation, Cognitive coping and processing, Trauma narration, In vivo exposure, Conjoint parent–child sessions, and Enriching future safety and development. This entry provides an overview of TF-CBT, focusing especially on the clinical application of the core treatment components.

Overview of TF-CBT

Many families are affected by experiences of childhood trauma. The prevalence of childhood physical and sexual abuse, for example, is alarmingly high. The consequences of childhood trauma can be devastating. Early exposure to traumatic events has been empirically linked to higher incidence of serious physical and mental health problems. Children and adolescents with a history of trauma may be at greater risk for developing posttraumatic stress disorder as well as various other mental health disorders and behavior problems. Common symptoms of childhood trauma include intrusive troubling memories of the traumatic event, efforts to avoid being reminded of the traumatic event, emotional distress and compensatory numbing, and heightened physical and emotional arousal. TF-CBT was designed to address the most common adverse effects of childhood trauma and enhance mental health and well-being among children, adolescents, and families.

Developed by Judith Cohen, Esther Deblinger, and Anthony Mannarino at Allegheny General Hospital's Center for Traumatic Stress in Children and Adolescents, TF-CBT was originally intended to treat posttraumatic stress resulting from childhood sexual abuse. It has since been adapted for use with children and adolescents exposed to a wide variety of traumatic experiences, including physical abuse, domestic violence, natural disasters, terrorism and war, and trauma-related grief and loss. Notably, TF-CBT has also been utilized in the treatment of children and adolescents who have endured multiple traumatic events over an extended period of time.

Regardless of the nature of the traumatic event, the effectiveness of TF-CBT has been well documented. Indeed, this treatment is one of the most empirically supported treatments for posttraumatic stress among children and adolescents. In numerous carefully controlled scientific studies (e.g., randomized clinical trials), TF-CBT was found to relieve symptoms of posttraumatic stress as well as depression, anxiety, and other mental health symptoms. It has also been found to increase the quality of interpersonal relationships and reduce the severity of behavior problems. These results were consistent among children and adolescents from diverse social and cultural backgrounds.

TF-CBT is a short-term, structured, components-based treatment for children, adolescents, and families affected by childhood trauma. Length of treatment typically lasts between 12 and 16 weeks, with one 50- to 90-minute counseling session per week. Sessions are highly structured, guided by a treatment manual, and organized into modules that correspond to each of the core treatment components. Despite its structured framework, the practice of TF-CBT is flexible and adaptive. Counselors are encouraged to exercise clinical judgment and creativity when deciding how best to implement each treatment component. They must, therefore, consider the unique needs of each child, adolescent, and family and respond to them accordingly, prioritizing their needs over strict adherence to the treatment manual. Knowing that experiences of childhood trauma affect entire families, children and parents participate in treatment together whenever possible. Both participate in separate individual sessions as well as conjoint child–parent sessions.

The practice of TF-CBT begins with a comprehensive clinical assessment of child or adolescent clients. A complete trauma history must also be taken in which detailed information is gathered about all past traumatic experiences and their impact on clients' mental health. This information is obtained through separate interviews with children and adolescents and their parents. In some cases, formal assessment tools may be utilized. It is important to note that this assessment does not focus solely on clients' problems; information is also gathered about their personal strengths and resources. Clients' social and cultural backgrounds must be examined and taken into account when planning treatment. The initial assessment will determine if children and adolescents are a good fit for this treatment. TF-CBT is not suitable for those with severe depression, suicidal ideation, or significant behavior problems. Appropriate interventions should be utilized to resolve these particular difficulties before initiating TF-CBT.

Core Treatment Components

The core components of TF-CBT are represented by the acronym PRACTICE, which stands for Psychoeducation and parenting skills, Relaxation and stress management, Affective expression and modulation, Cognitive coping and processing, Trauma narration, In vivo mastery of trauma triggers, Conjoint parent–child sessions, and Enriching future safety and development. Below, each of these components is described and applied to clinical practice.

Psychoeducation and Parenting Skills Training

TF-CBT begins with psychoeducation and parenting skills training. In these first modules, counselors take an educative role and provide families with general information about traumatic stress and its impact on child and adolescent development and mental health. This information should be communicated sensitively, directly, and in ways that children, adolescents, and parents can easily understand. Common trauma symptoms should be described, which can help children and adolescents understand their own symptoms, however distressing, as normal reactions to traumatic events, rather than indicators that something is "wrong" with them. To reduce feelings of stigma and shame, statistics about the prevalence of childhood trauma may be shared as well. To further orient families to treatment, counselors explain what TF-CBT entails and briefly describe the core treatment components. It is important for families to know what to expect before engaging in treatment. To increase positive expectations and confidence in treatment, information about the effectiveness of TF-CBT might also be shared. Also, results of the initial assessment are discussed, and any diagnostic considerations are carefully explained.

In addition to providing psychoeducation, parents are given information about specific parenting skills that have been shown to support trauma recovery. They are taught strategies for enhancing children's and adolescents' sense of safety and security within the home. Methods for improving communication among family members are discussed as well. Because children's and adolescents' behavior sometimes changes dramatically following experiences of trauma, parents are taught how to implement a number of trauma-sensitive (e.g., they avoid exacerbating the adverse effects of trauma) behavior management strategies. These parenting skills are not only intended to promote positive behavior; they also improve the overall quality of family relationships.

Relaxation and Stress Management

The next module focuses on developing relaxation and stress management skills. Counselors teach families to utilize a number of cognitive-behavioral techniques that have been found to decrease stress and promote relaxation. These techniques include controlled breathing, relaxation training, and thought-stopping exercises. Controlled breathing involves focused attention on breathing while taking slow, deep breaths. This exercise may incorporate a relaxing word or image on which to meditate. Relaxation training involves deliberately tensing and then relaxing various muscle groups. Thought-stopping exercises involve disrupting distressing thoughts or memories through use of a verbal cue (e.g., "Stop!") and, instead, directing attention to pleasant thoughts or memories.

When counseling children, it is important to describe these techniques in ways they can understand. Creativity, therefore, is a definite asset. For example, while practicing deep breathing exercises, children may be asked to imagine themselves slowly blowing up a large balloon. While practicing muscle relaxation, they may be instructed to tense their muscles as if they were tin soldiers and then relax them as if they were rag dolls. To make thought-stopping techniques more concrete, children might snap a rubber band around their wrists upon identifying a distressing thought, a signal to shift attention from the distressing thought to a more positive thought. These creative descriptions may or may not be helpful when counseling adolescents. In addition to buffering the impact of stress and promoting relaxation, these techniques also help children and adolescents recognize their ability to effectively cope with unwanted thoughts and feelings, which can boost their sense of self-efficacy.

Along with these specific cognitive-behavioral techniques, children and adolescents are also encouraged to develop their own personal practices for relieving stress. For example, some may benefit from meditation or prayer, mindfulness practices, listening to music, making art, talking to friends, going for walks, or any number of other activities. Whatever practices children and adolescents identify for managing their stress should be practiced regularly. They can (and should) be used to prevent stress as well as to relieve it when it builds up.

Affective Expression and Modulation

This component deals with affective (i.e., emotional) expression and modulation. It aims to help children and adolescents to identify a wide range of emotions and learn to express them appropriately, a difficult task for many children and adolescents with a history of trauma. Because traumatic events provoke such intense emotional reactions, children's and adolescents' capacity for appropriate affective expression and modulation can be compromised. They often struggle to regulate emotional arousal, especially when confronted with reminders of traumatic events.

Counselors work with children and adolescents to identity and differentiate among a wide variety of emotions. This increases their emotional vocabulary, thus expanding their range of emotional expression. Interventions can involve direct discussions about emotion, where children and adolescents describe what it feels like for them to be happy, sad, angry, or afraid. Working with feelings flashcards can help children and adolescents learn to label and define different emotional states. In the same way, using feelings wheels can help clients differentiate among emotions as well as rate the intensity of their emotions. Counselors might also use expressive techniques, such as drawing or writing, to engage clients in this module. Simply being able to identify and acknowledge feelings, especially distressing feelings, can go a long way in assisting children and adolescents to regulate emotional arousal.

Cognitive Coping

This component focuses on the relationship among thoughts, feelings, and behaviors. How children and adolescents think about and interpret experiences influences how they feel and behave. Inaccurate thoughts or interpretations of experiences can lead to significant emotional and behavioral problems. To help children and adolescents grasp these principles, counselors pose ambiguous social situations and ask them to interpret them in various ways, identifying the thoughts, feelings, and behaviors associated with each interpretation. In this way, children and adolescents begin to recognize how experiences can be interpreted differently, and how different interpretations can lead to different feelings and subsequent behaviors. The differences between accurate/inaccurate and helpful/unhelpful interpretations are also explained and applied to hypothetical scenarios as well as children's and adolescents' own lives. They are encouraged to question their own interpretations of memories and experiences and ensure that they are accurate and helpful.

Traumatic Narration and Processing

The traumatic narration and processing module involves direct discussion of traumatic experiences.

Children and adolescents are asked to "tell their trauma story," recalling what took place before, during, and after the traumatic event. Gradually, they are encouraged to describe their experiences in as much detail as they can, including what they were thinking and feeling during the trauma itself. Children may write about their traumatic experiences or choose to depict them in some expressive way.

Beyond helping children and adolescents overcome avoidance of traumatic memories, constructing a trauma narrative also helps them to integrate these memories into a larger life narrative. It is important that children and adolescents realize that their entire lives are not defined by their traumatic experiences. The trauma narrative can also be utilized to facilitate cognitive coping by helping to identify and replace inaccurate or unhelpful thoughts about the trauma. In particular, counselors help children and adolescents to process any interpretations of traumatic events that lead to feelings of guilt, shame, and self-blame.

Families must be informed about what this module entails and why it is necessary. The importance of not shying away from talking about the trauma must be emphasized. All family members must be prepared emotionally to engage in trauma narration and processing, as this can be an especially difficult task. Counselors must pace clients as they tell their trauma stories, careful that their narratives unfold gradually. This module must not cause too much emotional discomfort for families, as this could re-traumatize them and undermine treatment altogether.

In Vivo Exposure

In vivo exposure aims to reduce problematic avoidance behaviors associated with a traumatic event. Avoidance is a common response to traumatic experiences. Children and adolescents who have experienced a traumatic event often avoid people, places, things, and memories that remind them of that event. Reminders of the trauma are associated with danger, and the threat of danger evokes avoidant behaviors. Not all avoidance behaviors are problematic, of course. Some are functional and promote safety and security in the face of legitimate threats, such as an adolescent exposed to community violence who avoids dark alleys at night. Others, however, are dysfunctional and need to be overcome, especially if they are generalized to nonthreatening stimuli. For example, a child who suffered severe burns after being in a terrible car accident may become terrified of riding in cars altogether and avoid them whenever possible.

Overcoming these problematic avoidance behaviors is achieved by systematic desensitization, a technique that gradually exposes clients to reminders of their traumatic event while implementing relaxation and stress management techniques. Children and adolescents are asked to make a list of their most-feared trauma reminders, rank-ordering them from least to most feared. Beginning with the least feared, children and adolescents are exposed to these trauma reminders while, at the same time, incorporating relaxation and stress management techniques in order to regulate their emotional response.

Conjoint Parent–Child Sessions

Conjoint parent–child sessions are intended to open lines of communication between children and parents (or other adult caregivers). Conversations that once were avoided finally take place. In these sessions, trauma narratives are shared with parents and processed together. As children share more openly and honestly about their traumatic experiences, parents can respond with greater sensitivity and care, thus enhancing the overall quality of their relationships. In addition to providing parents with opportunities to provide validation and encouragement, conjoint sessions also allow them to model effective coping skills. As children and adolescents see their parents demonstrate these skills, they may be more likely to look to them for continued support after treatment ends.

Enhancing Safety and Future Development

Enhancing safety and future development involves helping children and adolescents take practical steps to protect themselves from future harm. It is important that children and adolescents feel empowered to make important decisions about their safety. Clients are helped to recognize and cultivate their own strengths and resources.

In addition to helping children and adolescents identify warning signs that might alert them to potential threats, they also develop individualized personal safety plans. Working collaboratively, children and adolescents plan and rehearse what actions to take if and when they find themselves in another unsafe situation. While much of this module focuses on physical safety, enhancing relational safety is also a priority. Dynamics of safe and healthy relationships may also be discussed. This module is intended to ensure that clients take responsibility for their continued trauma recovery and future well-being.

Stanley C. Hoover

See also Adolescent Mental Health; Child Maltreatment; Crisis Intervention With Couples and Families; Domestic Violence; Evidence-Based Practice With Couples and Families; Interpersonal Violence; Sexual Abuse; Sexual Assault and Rape; Trauma and Families

Further Readings

Black, P. J., Woodworth, M., Tremblay, M., & Carpenter, T. (2012). A review of trauma-informed treatment for adolescents. *Canadian Psychology, 53*(3), 192–203.

Cary, C. E., & McMillen, J. C. (2012). The data behind the dissemination: A systematic review of trauma-focused cognitive behavioral therapy for use with children and youth. *Children and Youth Services Review, 34*(4), 748–757.

Child Sexual Abuse Task Force and Research & Practice Core, National Child Traumatic Stress Network. (2004/2008). *How to implement trauma-focused cognitive behavioral therapy.* Durham, NC, and Los Angeles, CA: National Center for Child Traumatic Stress. Available at http://www.NCTSN.org

Cohen, J. A., Deblinger, E., Mannarino, A. P., & Steer, R. A. (2004). A multi-site, randomized controlled trial for sexually abused children with PTSD symptoms. *Journal of the American Academy of Child and Adolescent Psychiatry, 43,* 393–402.

Cohen, J. A., & Mannarino, A. P. (2012). *Trauma-focused CBT for children and adolescents: Treatment applications.* New York, NY: Guilford Press.

Cohen, J. A., Mannarino, A. P., & Deblinger, E. (2006). *Treating trauma and traumatic grief in children and adolescents.* New York, NY: Guilford Press.

Cohen, J. A., Mannarino, A. P., & Knudsen, K. (2005). Treating sexually abused children: One year follow-up of a randomized controlled trial. *Child Abuse & Neglect, 29,* 135–145.

Medical University of South Carolina. (2015, February 6). *TF-CBTWeb: A web-based learning course for trauma-focused cognitive-behavioral therapy.* Available at https://tfcbt.musc.edu

Runyon, M. K., & Deblinger, E. (2014). *Combined parent-child cognitive behavioral therapy (CPC-CBT): An approach to empower families at-risk for child physical abuse.* New York, NY: Oxford University Press.

TREATMENT PLANNING WITH COUPLES AND FAMILIES

As the term implies, a treatment plan outlines the expected course of treatment to address a client's presenting concerns. Although few examples can be found in the formal professional literature, treatment planning is one of the commonly used written documents in 21st-century couples and family therapy. Widely regarded as standard practice in the field, treatment planning is arguably an ethical obligation in contemporary practice and is a central component to most licensing exams and agency documentation.

Treatment Plan Formats

Clinicians have several options for developing treatment plans in couples and family therapy, each serving different needs. Broadly speaking, treatment plans can be categorized as those used primarily for third-party reimbursement and those used for conceptualizing clinical interventions. Most clinicians will need to become skilled at both types of treatment plans to meet the demands of employers, supervisors, third-party payers, and competent care.

Symptom-Based Treatment Plans

Treatment plans used for reimbursement are closely modeled after treatment plans used by other health professionals, such as doctors and physical therapists, and generally focus on psychiatric diagnoses and symptoms. These plans are symptom focused and use almost exclusively behavioral and psychiatric terminology so that they are in a similar format to those of other health care professions. Treatment goals in these plans target specific symptoms, such as anxious behavior, depressed mood, hallucinations, compulsive behavior, and so on. Typically, they must identify an observable, measurable behavior and have a measurable target, such as to reduce food bingeing episodes to no more than one per month. Most often, these plans also include clinical interventions to achieve each goal. When working for government agencies, these plans are the standard.

Examples of symptom-based treatment plan goals include the following:

- Increase engagement in social activities to at least one outing per week.
- Decrease visual hallucinations to no more than one mild episode per month.
- Reduce panic attacks to no more than one mild episode per month.
- Reduce couple conflict to no more than one mild episode per week.

Clinically Focused Treatment Plans

Symptom-based treatment plans are often problematic when working with couples and families because—as required by third-party payers—these plans target a single person's mental health symptoms. However, when working with couples and families, rarely is treatment conceptualized in terms of a single person's psychopathology. Instead, couples and family therapists typically view individual pathology as part of a larger systemic dynamic, both influencing and being influenced by the system. Thus, most couples and family therapists find clinical treatment plans philosophically more appropriate as well as more clinically practical.

Clinically focused treatment plans are grounded in therapeutic theories rather than psychiatric language. So rather than a behavioral goal such as "reduce compulsive hand washing," a clinically informed goal would address the underlying dynamic believed to be related to the psychiatric symptom: "Reduce enmeshment with mother in order to reduce compulsive hand washing." For goals to be clinically relevant in couples and family therapy, the plan needs to describe *how* the practitioner plans to achieve symptom reduction. These plans are grounded in the therapist's theory-informed case conceptualization of the client's presenting concern; thus, these plans directly reveal the theoretical orientation the therapist plans to use for the case.

Below are some examples of clinical treatment goals:

- Increase parental hierarchy to reduce child's tantrums. (Structural theory)
- Increase secure attachment between husband and wife to reduce conflict. (Emotionally focused therapy)
- Interrupt and reduce negative interaction cycle between father and son to reduce conflict. (Systemic theory)
- Reduce triangulation of mother-in-law to reduce couple conflict. (Bowen intergenerational theory)

Elements of Treatment Plans

Although there are endless possibilities for outlining treatment plans in couples and family therapy, most have the same key elements, which include a multipart organization, goals, and interventions; some plans also include treatment tasks.

Organization of Plans

Rather than a single list of goals, most treatment plans are divided into phases of treatment.

For example, the more symptom-based plans developed by Arthur E. Jongsma and colleagues include (a) long-term goals and (b) short-term objectives. The more clinically oriented plans by Diane Gehart include (a) early, (b) working, and (c) closing phase goals. This phase-based organization helps outline the expected progression of therapy and helps clinicians identify when and where to intervene.

Goals

Goals are the key element of any treatment plan. An effective goal should clearly define how the symptom or problem dynamic will *change*, such as "increase self-confidence," "reduce conflict," and "improve congruent communication." In addition, many agencies and third-party payers prefer that goals be behavioral and measurable. A behavioral and measurable goal requires stating the goal in such a way that a clearly identifiable behavior is targeted. Some examples of behavioral and measurable goals include the following:

- Reduce parent–child conflict to no more than one mild episode per week.
- Increase son's cooperative behaviors to be measured by no more than one mild incident of disobedience per week.
- Increase secure emotional bond between mother and son to be measured by no more than one emotionally reactive outburst when mother makes requests per week.
- Reduce enmeshment between partners in couple to be measured by no more than one mild argument stemming from boundary issues per month.

Interventions

Most treatment plans also include interventions or techniques that will be used to achieve the stated goal. Virtually all interventions or techniques are derived from the therapist's theory of choice. Examples of commonly used interventions in couple and family therapy include the following:

Theory	*Interventions*
Structural Therapy	Enactments
	Boundary making
	Challenging worldview
	Intensity and crisis inductions
	Unbalancing
	Expanding family truths
	Shaping competence
Systemic and Strategic	Reframing
	Therapeutic double bind
	Directives
	Circular questions
	Ordeal therapy
	Pretend techniques
Emotionally Focused Couples Therapy	Validation
	Reflecting primary and secondary emotions
	Tracking interaction patterns and cycles
	Evocative responding
	Empathetic conjecture and interpretation
	Heightening
	Reframing in context of cycle and attachment needs
	Enactments
	Softening emotions
Solution-Focused Therapy	Formula first session task
	Scaling questions
	Coping questions
	Compliments
	Miracle question

Treatment Tasks

Treatment plans can also be written to convey all tasks-related treatment, including various elements of case management and case planning. These treatment tasks can include

- establishing a therapeutic relationship using a specific therapeutic approach;
- assessment and case conceptualization;
- setting goals for treatment;
- referrals for psychiatric assessment, medical evaluation, group therapy, support groups, and so on;
- monitoring for progress using clinical assessment tools such as the Session Rating Scale, Outcome Rating Scale, and Symptom Checklist; and
- developing after-care plans.

Treatment Plans for Couples and Families

Treatment plans for couples and families typically require a more sophisticated process of theory-based case conceptualization than working with an individual with a single issue, such as depression or anxiety. Typically, couples and families present with very similar presenting problems: conflict between couples, conflict between parents and child, loss of affection with couples, or simply "we don't communicate well." However, there are multiple and numerous potential causes to these similar-sounding

Table 1 Sample Emotionally Focused Treatment Plan for a Couple

Initial Phase of Treatment

1. Increase couple's awareness of negative interaction cycle and the primary emotions for each.
   a. Identify the negative interaction cycle with both secondary and primary emotions for each partner.
   b. Reframe their conflict in the broader systemic context of the negative cycle to help create a greater sense of unity and understanding.

Working Phase of Treatment

2. Increase emotional engagement and expression of withdrawn partner to reduce avoidance.
   a. Use empathy, validation, and conjecture to help withdrawn partner express attachment needs and primary emotions.
   b. Facilitate enactments to allow couple to directly communicate about attachment needs and to facilitate acceptance by partner.

3. Reduce criticism by pursuing partner and replace with increased nonblaming expression of underlying attachment needs.
   a. Heighten pursuer's primary emotions to help facilitate softening of critical position.
   b. Facilitate enactments to promote acceptance and prompt new healing interaction cycles.

4. Increase the ability of both partners to respond to each other and create a sense of relational safety.
   a. Track interaction cycle to help couple develop new interaction patterns.
   b. Use enactments to help couple develop new ways of responding to each other.

Closing Phase

5. Increase couple's ability to effectively respond to new stressors in the relationship.
   a. Track positive interaction cycles to identify what worked and how they affected each person's sense of emotional safety.

6. Solidify secure bond by increasing the consistency of the positive interactions.
   a. Facilitate enactments that highlight how safety is created for each partner.
   b. Heighten new emotional responses.

issues. For example, using a structural therapy conceptualization, family conflict can arise with both enmeshed and disengaged boundaries; thus, the therapist must first conceptualize the reason for conflict in order to determine how the boundaries need to shift to reduce conflict—or whether the issue is more closely related to an ineffective or overly rigid parental hierarchy. Table 1 shows a sample clinical treatment plan for a couple with pursuit/withdrawal as the primary relational dynamic; note how the goals are based in the theoretical assumptions and language of the approach.

Diversity and Treatment Planning

When developing treatment plans, couples and family therapists should design goals that are appropriate for a client's sociocultural context, which requires assessing diversity factors such as race, ethnicity, gender, sexual/gender orientation, religion, socioeconomic status, language, education, and immigration status. Often a client's cultural or religious background informs particular forms of couple and family relationships; in such cases, each member's level of acculturation plays a significant role in defining appropriate goals for the couple or family. When using theories that have predefined norms and theories of health—such as humanistic, psychodynamic, and cognitive-behavioral approaches—couples and family therapists need to take particular care to ensure that the long-term goals in these approaches are appropriate for the client's particular sociocultural context. For example, when using a humanistic approach with an East Asian immigrant family, such as the Satir model that emphasizes direct and congruent expression of emotion, the therapist must carefully assess cultural norms, level of acculturation, and family preferences to set culturally appropriate and relevant goals. Similarly, couples and families from communal cultures will often have different norms for healthy boundaries, parental hierarchy, and the role of the first-born child than may be typical in more individualistic cultures, such as the dominant culture of the United States. Additionally, the concept family may include "family of choice" for gay, lesbian, bisexual, and transgendered clients, thus requiring treatment plans that include this expanded definition of family.

Do Plans Make a Difference?

Finally, some may wonder whether treatment plans are worth the effort because so often things seem to change in clients' lives. In truth, therapy rarely goes according to plan: new problems arise, a crisis occurs, or a sudden positive turn of events changes relational dynamics drastically. However, even when therapy does not go according to plan, treatment plans are exceedingly valuable to clients and therapists. Creating a treatment plan helps a therapist to carefully think about how to help a particular client, which should help the therapist convey a sense of confidence and hope to clients. Common-factors research indicates that conveying such a sense of hope is significantly correlated with positive outcomes in therapy. Furthermore, having a clear plan can make it clearer when things are off course and can help the therapist determine the next steps when circumstances change. Additionally, a well-crafted treatment plan requires the therapist to prioritize and sequence therapy to maximize positive outcomes. Thus, treatment plans do make a significant difference for therapists and clients alike, even when therapy does not go exactly according to plan.

Diane Gehart

See also Goals, Treatment; Practice Management; Progress Notes for Couples and Families; Stages of Family Therapy; Therapeutic Contract

Further Readings

Datillio, F. M., & Jongsma, A. E. (2014). *The family therapy treatment planner* (2nd ed.). New York, NY: Wiley.

Gehart, D. (2014). *Mastering competencies in family therapy: A practical approach to theory and clinical case documentation* (2nd ed.). Pacific Grove, CA: Brooks/Cole.

Gehart, D. (2015). *Theory and treatment planning in family therapy: A competencies-based approach.* Pacific Grove, CA: Brooks/Cole.

Johnson, S. M. (2004). *The practice of emotionally focused marital therapy: Creating connection* (2nd ed.). New York, NY: Brunner/Routledge.

Jongsma, A. E., & Peterson, L. M. (2014). *The complete adult psychotherapy treatment planner* (5th ed.). New York, NY: Wiley.

McGoldrick, M., Giordano, J., & Garcia-Preto, N. (Eds.). (2005). *Ethnicity and family therapy* (3rd ed.). New York, NY: Guilford Press.

O'Leary, K. D., Heyman, R. E., & Jongsma, A. E. (2015). *The couples psychotherapy treatment planner* (2nd ed.). New York, NY: Brunner/Routledge.

TRIANGULATION

If two people lived in a vacuum, their communication and interactions would involve only the other person. If one person were to have a conversation, it would be with the other, without interference from a third party. If one person were to get in a fight, it would be with the other. A dyad (two people) is the most basic relationship possible. However, this situation is not realistic since most people do not live in isolation. The most basic interpersonal relationship involves two individuals and the interactions and communications connecting them, but there are typically others who influence their communication. Triangulation occurs when these interactions and communications involve or go through another person or thing. The notion of triangulation was introduced in 1971 by Ernest Abelin, when he used the term to describe how one might act as a third party pulling young children away from the mother–child relationship and into a larger world. In family therapy, Murray Bowen's family systems theory and Salvador Minuchin's structural therapy both incorporate the idea of triangles into their approach. Bowen focused on emotional triangles and drawing in a third person into a relationship in order to stabilize it. Minuchin focused on how people "detour" their problems through a third person or form cross-generational coalitions (e.g., a parent engages a child into a relationship against the other parent). In this entry, triangulation will be primarily discussed in relation to couples, though triangulation can occur in any relationship no matter how intimate or platonic. Specifically, triangulation will be considered in three forms: first, as a mechanism to keep relationships stable; second, as a mechanism to avoid responsibility; and third, as a mixture of the two and as a useful tool in therapy.

Stability Through Triangulation

Dyads are more efficient forms of relationships, but triads are more stable. Three wheels make a tricycle more stable, but it is not necessarily the most efficient form of cycle. Tricycles are significantly more stable while standing still and while moving slowly. This is because of the fact that there are three wheels involved in the system. While learning to ride a bicycle or how to have relationships, it is very common to include other wheels or persons in the system to make it more stable. However, as speed and difficulty of terrain increases it becomes more difficult to adapt and change direction with three wheels than with two. This is not to suggest that support networks during times of trouble and distress are not helpful but rather to point out that these supports, which can and do become a part of a relationship, can have a significant impact. When a system is confronted with an unsolvable chronic issue, or a partner who is unwilling to change, venting through this sort of triangulation may be all that can be done.

Having a "three-wheeled" relationship is an important concept in Bowen's family systems theory, and he called this triadic relationship a triangle. Bowen looked at how families manage emotional anxiety within and between generations of families. He thought the way to improve relationships was to make sure people had direct, nonreactive communication with one another and maintain a balance of closeness and distance. When a dyad pulls a third party into its relationship, it is called triangulation. Bowen believed that using triangulation as a way to manage relationships keeps people reactive in the long run and keeps them from learning how to directly communicate with one another. Triangulation allows a relationship to have greater stability because it allows for tension to be diffused (to the third party) outside of the relationship. Think of a relationship as a large balloon. A balloon needs at least a minimal amount of air in it to be viable as a balloon. One can change the shape of a balloon by adding air or letting air out. Any time people experience anxiety more air is blown into a balloon. When people work through the emotional anxiety, air is let out of the balloon. The balloon gets larger and smaller throughout the relationship, and the elasticity of the balloon allows this. However, if there is a lot of emotional anxiety, more and more air is blown into the balloon until it is on the verge of exploding. Couples can keep their balloon from exploding either by letting air out through direct communication or by avoiding putting air into the balloon (diffusing). People avoid putting air into the balloon by letting some of their anxiety go through discussing problems with other people (rather than with each other directly). While either method keeps the balloon from exploding, avoiding putting air into their balloon by venting to others is not an effective way to manage a relationship, and in the long run it may totally deflate the couple's balloon.

In the short run, it is often easier to avoid emotional anxiety in a relationship, and this makes the relationship, like a tricycle, more stable. Though stability does mean the relationship is less likely to dissolve, it means it is less likely to improve and be satisfying. The ability to process emotional anxiety and emotions—both good and bad—is required to help a relationship improve.

Avoiding Responsibility Through Triangulation

Another reason triangulated relationships are more stable than dyadic relationships is the potential for responsibility to be diffused from within the dyad to a third party. Children sometimes try to intervene in their parents' problems, or parents can avoid focusing on their problems by focusing on a problematic child. Oftentimes parents bring in their children to be "fixed," but do not see or take responsibility for their own part in the pattern that keeps their child misbehaving. In systemic therapy (therapeutic approaches where the therapist tends to look at the patterned behavior of a group of people and how they influence one another), the misbehavior of one family member often serves as a stabilizing function for the larger system (family).

One type of family pattern, called the *drama triangle,* was proposed by Stephen Karpman. The three actors of the drama triangle are the persecutor, the rescuer, and the victim. These roles are examples of triangulation because the actors are performing their respective roles to avoid actually dealing with the issue at hand. Each of the roles in the triangle exhibits some sort of control or coercion to maintain the role and pattern of drama rather than to accept its own responsibility. People playing the victim—it is worth noting that this does not apply to people who are actually victimized—feel helpless or fearful of making decisions and will often seek rescuers to care for them, or even persecutors to blame for keeping them down. People playing the role of persecutor refuse to accept their own responsibility and actively push blame onto others, especially victims. People playing the role of rescuer often experience anxiety or discomfort when drama exists and do what they can to help fix the situation, which often involves taking on more responsibility themselves. This rescuer role is extremely important to the therapeutic process because it can be easily mistaken for care and loving efforts to help others.

The rescuer's actions, while helpful to others, are actually about the rescuer avoiding his or her own issues. It is very easy for therapists to fall into this pattern and need their clients to have problems for the therapist to fix. In this situation, the therapist plays the role of rescuer and circumvents the therapeutic process by making the process about his or her own needs instead of about the client's needs. This triangulation formed through avoiding responsibility and creating roles for others in the system can be addressed through understanding the underlying motivations for each actor's behavior and addressing this process of diffusing responsibility rather than the content that is brought forward in session.

Utilizing Triangulation in Therapy

It is unrealistic to expect triangulation to be entirely absent, and some triangulation is normal. Learning when triangulation can be used as a stabilizing force, as a method of avoiding responsibility, and using both of these as a therapeutic tool is an essential part of systemic intervention. As previously mentioned, in situations of chronic disease or when another person is unwilling to change, one of the realistic outcomes for therapy is being able to cope with the problems rather than solve them. This is an essential therapeutic task. Allowing clients to avoid responsibility and diffuse some of the tension surrounding their emotions—especially in higher volatility cases—can also be transformed from a harmful pattern into a useful tool.

Although it is important for couples to communicate directly, during session Bowen sometimes used a therapeutic triangle. In order to keep reactivity low, a therapist sometimes has a couple speak to each other through the therapist. The point of couples and family therapy is for the therapist to be brought into the system and then to help to change the system. In many respects, the therapist is triangulated while in session. When this triangulation is purposeful and planned, it will serve to further treatment goals. There are times when therapists will be triangulated without purpose, but as long as the therapist is aware of the function this triangulation is serving it need not be a barrier to treatment. However, when this triangulation happens and the therapist is unaware of it, the treatment process will be slowed.

At its extreme, triangulation means that the couple does not communicate with one another except through the third party. Many couples come to therapy at or near this extreme point and as such, triangulation may be very functional. Essentially, it is the purpose of a therapist to encourage the triangulation in order to encourage each party to communicate and also to engage in the therapy process. In the initial stages, clients will speak to each other only through the therapist. The therapist can help clients to soften their responses to their partners and also to soften the way they communicate. By doing this, the therapist creates triangulation that serves a therapeutic purpose. After the clients have de-escalated and felt heard, the therapist can then help the clients speak to one another without the therapist as a go-between.

The point of utilizing triangulation in therapy is to help clients process their feelings and uncover the underlying motivations and meanings about what is occurring in their family system. It is often not possible for partners or families to share their deepest and scariest feelings with each other due to the barriers they have built. Therapeutic triangulation allows the therapist to hold a client's emotions and help the client to more deeply understand what he or she is experiencing and then give this clearer message to the other members of the family. Once understanding begins to happen on both sides of the triangle, it is the therapist's job to then help the clients begin to exclude the therapist from the triangle and strengthen their dyad.

Quintin A. Hunt

See also Bowen Family Systems Theory; Double Bind Theory; Paradoxes and Paradoxical Intervention; Scapegoating; Second-Order Change; Self of the Therapist; Stages of Family Therapy; Systems Theory; Therapeutic Alliance

Further Readings

Abelin, E. (1971). The role of the father in the separation-individuation process. In J. B. McDevitt & C. F. Settlage (Eds.), *Separation-individuation* (pp. 229–252). New York, NY: International Universities Press.

Bell, L. G. (2001). Triangulation and adolescent development in the U.S. and Japan. *Family Process, 40*(2), 173–186. doi:10.1111/j.1545-5300.2001.4020100173.x

Bowen, M. (1985). *Family therapy in clinical practice.* New York, NY: Rowman & Littlefield.

Chan, S. T.-M. (2013). The manifestation of family triangulation in Asian-Chinese families and its relevance to father-son conflict. *Journal of Social Work Practice, 27*(4), 393–406. doi:10.1080/02650533.2012.753516

Dallos, R. (2012). Systems theory, family attachments and processes of triangulation: Does the concept of triangulation offer a useful bridge? *Journal of Family Therapy, 34*(2), 117–137. doi:10.1111/j.1467-6427.2011.00554.x

L'Abate, L. (2009). The drama triangle: An attempt to resurrect a neglected pathogenic model in family therapy theory and practice. *American Journal of Family Therapy, 37*(1), 1–11. doi:10.1080/01926180701870163

Long, L. L., & Young, M. E. (2007). *Counseling and therapy for couples.* Belmont, CA: Thomson Brooks/Cole.

Karpman, S. B. (1968). Fairy tales and script drama analysis. *Transactional Analysis Bulletin, 7,* 39–43.

Keval, N. (2003). Triangulation or strangulation: Managing the suicidal patient. *Psychoanalytic Psychotherapy, 17*(1), 35–51. doi:10.1080/0266873031000096063

Rupprecht-Schampera, U. (1995). The concept of "early triangulation" as a key to a unified model of hysteria. *International Journal of Psychoanalysis, 76*(3), 457–473.

Venkatesan, S. (2011). Blame game triangulation between parents, teachers and children with academic problems. *Psychological Studies, 56*(2), 206–215. doi:10.1007/s12646-011-0082-1

Weeks, G. R., & Treat, S. R. (2009). *Couples in treatment.* New York, NY: Routledge.

Trust

Trust is an important construct in human social interactions. Trust can be defined as the belief that someone or something is good. Here, "good" may include a number of positive qualities such as honesty, truthfulness, and trustworthiness. In intimate relationships, trust takes on a special meaning and is at the cornerstone of healthy family and long-term, committed relationships. It means that one has confidence that the other will be attuned to one's needs, has one's best interests at heart, and will follow through on promises. Overall, social interactions and trust can be analyzed at the micro and macro levels. On a micro level, trust impacts relationships in the home, at school, at work, and in the community. On a macro level, trust may impact the role and function of major religious, political, economic, and social institutions and groups within society. Therefore, religious institutions seek the trust of members, political parties seek the trust of electorates, and businesses seek the trust of consumers. At varying levels, individuals continually make decisions regarding who or what is worthy or unworthy of their trust. From a systemic perspective, trust is important from the smallest systems to the largest ones. This entry explores the significance of trust in human social interactions at both a micro and macro level, with a specific focus on the role of trust in family, marriage, and couple relationships.

Trust, Social Interaction, and Goal Attainment

If given a choice, most human beings would choose social interaction over isolation. This idea is central to the understanding of the concept of trust. Human beings rely on each other to achieve many goals that are critical for survival. Human cooperation supports practical goals such as providing for food, clothing, shelter, and protection. In early societies, there were advantages to collectively hunting, gathering, and sharing food.

Human cooperation often aims at achieving various objectives. There is usually a shared purpose for working together. In this sense, the utilitarian and reciprocal purpose of trust is highlighted. Trust is important because it is *useful* to human beings; it provides mutual and reciprocal benefits. Trust is a critical factor in families prospering and in counties working together for defeating common enemies, peace, mutual economic development, humanitarian efforts, and other international endeavors. Political scientist and political economist Francis Fukuyama, in his book titled *Trust:*

The Social Virtues and the Creation of Prosperity, highlighted the importance of family and kinship relationships in creating economic wealth. He identified trust as the critical factor in determining family success in businesses and other economic activities. Furthermore, in 2005, the Institute for American Values published a report titled *Why Marriage Matters: Twenty-Six Conclusions From the Social Sciences.* This report highlighted important social, economic, and health benefits for spouses, children, and the wider society that are associated with marriage. A critical factor that determines whether or not these benefits are realized is often the level of trust between spouses and the family as a whole. While there are other important factors at play in all relationships, trust may be the factor that determines success or failure.

Trust and Survival

The need to survive is regarded as a critical factor that forces human beings into trusting relationships. There is often a shared understanding that survival can be best achieved through collective efforts. Trust and reciprocity become useful factors in human efforts to interact as a cohesive unit. Indeed, human beings often enter trusting relationships because of their mutual dependence on each other for survival. This dependence begins quite early in life. The human child, for example, cannot survive without the care of an adult. As such, infancy is a critical period of life and one when a child's survival is heavily dependent on his or her mother and other adult caregivers. Noted developmental psychologist John Bowlby identified this period as critical in the child's development of trust and attachment. He also noted that disruptions in the mother–child relationship could be detrimental to the child's ability to trust in later years.

The Value and Desirability of Trust

Trust is a highly valued and desired construct in human social interactions. Significant efforts are often directed at improving the levels of trust among the parties involved in a relationship, with the understanding that higher levels of trust support goal attainment. For example, premarital counseling may involve a counselor assessing the degree of trust that exists between couples. In another instance, a family counselor may work with a couple to rebuild trust after infidelity. In these instances trust becomes a desirable commodity; it is seen as critical for the survival of marriage relationships. Parents may lose trust in their adolescent child after they discover that he or she has been sneaking out of the house to attend unsupervised parties with friends. If the problem intensifies, they may need the help of a counselor to assist in repairing trust in the parent–child relationship.

Trust may not always be desirable depending on the intent of the individuals, group, or institutions involved in the relationship. Inasmuch as one may seek to promote trust, there may be others intent on promoting distrust. A political campaign, for example, may seek to create messages that result in electorates distrusting an opponent. Therefore, while trust may be highly desired in relationships, desirability ultimately resides in the intentions of those directly or indirectly involved in the relationship.

Measuring Trust

Researchers Douglas Creed and Raymond Miles identified three important determinants of trust in human relationships: (1) individuals' predisposition to trust, (2) their characteristic similarities, and (3) their experience of reciprocity. Based on these factors, some individuals are more likely to trust than others, individuals are more likely to trust those with whom they share similar characteristics, and trust is strengthened when individuals have mutually positive experiences with each other. It may also be important to consider the subjective ways in which individuals and groups often seek to measure trust in their relationships. Statements such as "I gave him all my trust" or "I trusted her 100%" can be seen as efforts to measure the levels of trust in relationships. Feelings of trust may therefore be experienced at varying levels and intensities. In a relationship there may be high levels of trust, low levels of trust, a lack of trust, mistrust, or a growth or decline in trust. With varying levels of awareness, individuals are often involved in a process of assessing the role of trust in their relationships. Life events such as births, deaths, or the loss of employment may impact trust in relationships. Tragedies, for example, often serve to intensify trust and social cohesion in family systems while destroying trust in others.

Measuring trust may also involve comparing the levels of trust that each party brings to a relationship. One party may bring more trust to a relationship, resulting in an imbalance in trust. Deciding how much trust to put in a relationship or if someone is worthy of your trust may be factors that are considered. The awareness that our assessment of others may be inaccurate and that trust can be misplaced are factors to be considered. After several years of a failed marriage, it is not unusual for one partner to declare that he or she once placed too much trust in the other. Such declarations may be accompanied by feelings of betrayal and loss.

This brings into focus ideas of mutual trust and reciprocity, which are often seen as desirable for relationships to succeed. Mutual trust assumes that all parties in the relationship are more or less equally trusting of each other. However, levels of mutual trust can be viewed as dynamic in nature, since they are susceptible to change as a relationship progresses. Mutual trust may be consistent with shared objectives and goals of all members in the relationship. Unequal levels of trust or mistrust may pose a number of challenges for goal attainment and the relationship in general.

In an effort to measure trust in a relationship, the idea of trusting too much is an important area of focus. It implies that a partner in a relationship has miscalculated the level of trust or the intentions of the other partner(s) in the formative or later stages of the relationship. Trusting too much may also result in questioning the original intention of the other partner. There may be questions and speculations regarding a partner's ill intent or preconceived agenda prior to entering into the relationship. In the measurement of trust, knowing whom to trust, what to trust, and the amount of trust to give may become critical. The words "inexperienced" or "naive" may be used to describe an individual who failed to accurately measure the levels of trust in his or her relationships.

At a personal level, people may come across individuals who struggle with trusting others. These struggles may be specific to their romantic relationships or may be more generalized to most individuals they come across. Psychologists often point to deeper psychological issues that may be impacting such an individual's struggles with trusting others. Early experiences in the context of family and trauma may be explored as causative factors. This discussion also brings into focus the concept of intrapersonal trust, which relates to the ability of individuals to trust themselves to achieve general or specific objectives. After three failed marriages, a divorcée may declare that she has lost trust or confidence in her own ability to pursue a successful relationship. Intrapersonal trust assumes that a person possesses the confidence in him- or herself to pursue successful social connections.

Capacity to Trust

Trust may be desirable, but it is not always easily attained. There may be complex human psychological factors that impact one's capacity to trust. It is possible to meet individuals who declare that they trust no one and have no desire to be trusted by anyone. Similarly, it is possible for one to experience difficulties in his or her effort to establish trust. Individuals have varying capacities to trust, and these capacities impact the relationships they enter. A partner in a romantic relationship may find it difficult to trust because of his or her prior relationships and experiences.

Trust remains an important factor in all human social interactions. Human relationships of all kinds rely on trust in order to achieve many different objectives. Reliance on each other for social, economic, political, and psychological survival necessitates entry into trusting relationships. Marriage, family, and coupling relationships rely heavily on trust to survive and thrive. The desirability of trust does not guarantee its attainability. Understanding the nature of trust in a relationship can be difficult given the multiple social factors involved. Measuring the levels and intensity of trust, assessing one's capacity to trust, and evaluating a party's worthiness of trust are among the factors to consider.

Charles C. Edwards

See also Attachment; Beliefs and Values; Decision-Making; Fidelity; Respect

Further Readings

Berg, J., Dickhaut, J., & McCabe, K. (1995). Trust, reciprocity, and social history. *Games and Economic Behavior, 10*(1), 122–142.

Creed, W. D., & Miles, R. E. (1996). Trust in organizations. A conceptual framework linking organizational forms, managerial philosophies and opportunity cost controls. In R. M. Kramer & T. R. Tyler (Eds.), *Trust in organizations: Frontiers of theory and research* (pp. 16–38). London, England: Sage.

Frith, U., & Frith, C. (2001). The biological basis of social interaction. *Current Directions in Psychological Science, 10*(5), 151–155.

Fukuyama, F. (1995). *Trust: The social virtues and the creation of prosperity*. New York, NY: Free Press.

Hosking, G. (2014). *Trust: A history*. New York, NY: Oxford University Press.

Ingold, T. (1994). From trust to domination: An alternative history of human-animal relations. In A. Manning & J. Serpell (Eds.), *Animals and human society: Changing perspectives* (pp. 1–22). London, England: Routledge.

Institute for American Values. (2005). *Why marriage matters: Twenty-six conclusions from the social sciences* (2nd ed.). New York, NY: Author.

Urban Families

The vast majority of families in the United States reside in an urban environment: those densely developed residential and commercial centers with a population density at or greater than 2,500 people per square mile. Beginning with a more detailed look at the demographics of urban families, this entry highlights the psychosocial forces that are salient for this population and discusses the importance of multicultural competence and a social justice approach for those who do counseling work with urban families.

Demographics

The 2010 national census for the United States identified 486 urban centers containing 249,253,271 people, representing 80.7% of the population. The number of urban centers is on the rise: 36 more were added between the 2000 and the 2010 census. While the recent increase in newly defined urban areas has been the result of mostly White, domestic migration (Nashville, Tennessee, and Charlotte, North Carolina, for example) the majority of the 486 urban areas in the United States continue to represent highly diverse populations that are growing as a result of immigration. Approximately 1 million persons immigrate to the United States each year, and most choose to settle in urban areas. Persons of Latina/o decent represent the majority of new Americans, followed by an influx of persons from South Asia, East Asia, the Caribbean, the Middle East, and sub-Saharan Africa. A higher concentration of demographic heterogeneity within urban centers is not limited to race and ethnicity. Gay, lesbian, bisexual, transgender, and genderqueer populations have been able to more freely establish LGBT-friendly "gay villages" and neighborhood enclaves within many metropolitan areas. Also, large communities of faith that are non-Christian—Judaism, Islam, Hindu, Sikhism, Baha'i faith, Jainism—are more likely to be found within urban areas.

Multicultural Competence

Because family counselors working with urban families are far more likely to engage with families that do not represent dominant U.S. culture—rather than with those smaller, two-generation nuclear families who identify as White, heterosexual, cisgender, and Christian—it is paramount that family counselors and therapists practice with a high degree of multicultural competence. For more than 30 years, multicultural competence has been operationalized as the possession of the awareness, knowledge, and skills to provide effective counseling services to individuals and families who occupy diverse and nondominant social locations: clients of color, multiracial couples and families, lesbian, gay, bisexual, pansexual, transgender, or gender-queer clients, new Americans, clients from nondominant traditions of faith, families with (dis)abilities, and clients with lower socioeconomic status. The following sections address the relevance of each domain of multicultural competence with regard to counseling urban families.

Awareness

Multicultural awareness pertains to exploring one's assumptions and beliefs about families that occupy different social locations from one's own. This includes awareness of how deeply one has internalized dominant cultural values, one's level of appreciation for cultural variability, and perhaps most important, awareness of one's own biases, prejudices, and stereotypes. A substantial body of literature has documented that well-intentioned, well-meaning, beneficent counselors nevertheless hold and express racial, sexual orientation, gender, class, (dis)ability, and religious bias and prejudice. More often than not, such bias is implicit and outside of the awareness of the counselor. Family counselors working in highly diverse urban settings should be actively and intentionally engaged in the lifelong work of identifying and interrupting internalized prejudices and stereotypes toward families who occupy nondominant social locations. For example, the dominant culture has positioned urban families within a deficit narrative that fosters the following stereotype: Owing to indifferent and inept parents and community leaders, urban families are usually impoverished, distressed, highly unstable, disadvantaged minorities who make up the urban underclass by choosing to be stuck in the "ghetto" with bad schools and unsafe parks and playgrounds. More on this widespread deficit narrative will be discussed subsequently, but for greater multicultural awareness it is vital that family counselors interrogate the various stereotypes of urban families that they have internalized.

Knowledge

Multicultural knowledge encompasses knowledge of culturally distinct norms, mores, and practices of specific social groups, as well as knowledge of the historical and political factors that have influenced these and other diverse social and cultural groups. For example, counselors working with a new American urban family should have knowledge of the family's culturally distinct interaction patterns, values regarding the balance between open and closed family boundaries, as well as culturally specific messages and rules that may shape family members very differently from what is practiced by the dominant culture. Counselors need to also have knowledge of concepts such as assimilation stress and levels of acculturation; the distinct pressures experienced by interracial, interethnic, and interreligious couples and families; the role of a positive ethnic and racial identity in promoting healthy family systems; and the unique strengths and challenges of three- and four-generational family systems.

Skills

Finally, possessing multicultural skills means that family counselors are able to develop goals and engage in interventions that are consistent with the family's experience and cultural values. Moreover, the skilled counselor is able to implement such interventions with cultural humility and sensitivity. Multiculturally attuned skill sets may include, but are not limited to, using cultural genograms with families, broaching conversations regarding experiences of microaggressions, marginalization, and prejudice without hesitancy or fear, creating family sculptures that attempt to capture differing generational experiences of acculturation, and being advocates for families from traditionally marginalized groups who are experiencing psychosocial oppression at the community and political levels. Multiculturally skilled counselors also take an intersectional approach to their work with urban families. Working from an intersectional lens means that counselors work with the understanding that every family, and each member within the family unit, has multiple social identities that are connected to either social privileges or social oppression. For example, for a family of color, the entire family occupies a nondominant, marginalized social location with regard to race. However, the males in the family also possess privilege with regard to their gender identity, while gay, lesbian, or bisexual members of family will need to negotiate additional prejudice and stigma owing to their nondominant social identity as nonheterosexual.

Deficit Narrative

While there is great economic and social class diversity within urban areas, many urban families do indeed exist within concentrated areas of stark poverty. The vast array of potential risk factors faced by these diverse urban families is well-documented. Social risk factors such as unemployment, underresourced schools, poverty, and drug abuse are just some of the challenges that are overrepresented in low-income, urban communities of color. In addition to multicultural competence, it is imperative for family counselors to consider the impact of sociocultural and sociopolitical factors such as racism, classism, and other forms of systemic, institutionalized discrimination on the well-being of families who live in urban contexts. Much of the extant research in the field of family counseling and therapy related to those who live in urban communities has focused on familial deficits. The pathologizing of this population within the mental health literatures reinforces the larger societal narrative that diverse urban families experience adverse psychosocial outcomes as the natural consequence of cultural deficiencies like negligent parenting, problematic values, and poor decision-making. This societal myth is otherwise known as the "culture of poverty." By this view, urban families, especially those of color, have no one to blame but themselves.

This microscopic and distorted view of diverse urban families ignores the very real sociohistorical forces that continue to plague high-poverty communities. For most of the 20th century, residents in urban neighborhoods have struggled to survive the devastating effects of widespread urban decay. As critics have noted, as a result of various federal, state, and municipal policies and legislation, many city neighborhoods were devastated by the loss of businesses, leaving behind a trail of families living in poverty with insufficient resources and opportunities to thrive. But again, the overwhelming deficit narrative of diverse urban families makes it difficult to disentangle the real effects of poverty and historical discrimination from the continuation of systemic oppression. It is important to note that there have always been counternarratives, which emphasize the strengths and resiliency of these devalued and marginalized groups.

Challenging the pervasive deficit narrative of diverse urban families is important, but one must be careful to avoid oversimplifying the issue by claiming that *all* families within these contexts function well. Further, well-intended research that is meant to identify important familial factors that correlate with certain poor psychosocial outcomes is not the problem per se. It is simply the overproduction of such scholarship within the literature that fuels discriminatory stereotypes and limits the range of interventions that family counselors and therapists consider when setting out to improve the well-being of diverse families living in low-income environments. Undoubtedly, the stresses and strains that come with living in high-poverty environments clearly have the potential for preventing high levels of functioning within a family. Poverty itself forces adults into exhausting situations, such as juggling multiple low-wage jobs, identifying affordable child care, and navigating time-consuming and unwelcoming bureaucracies. With respect to children, research has shown that lower socioeconomic status can detrimentally affect not only their general happiness but also their cognitive development. Therefore, family counselors working with diverse urban families will often need to intervene at the microlevel to facilitate change. However, we also encourage counselors and therapists who work with diverse urban families to consider integrating macrolevel interventions as well.

Social Justice Lens

The multicultural counseling competencies framework provides an excellent foundation for working with diverse, urban families. However, it is also important to consider the limitations of microlevel family counseling interventions regardless of how culturally sensitive they may be. In recent years, counseling professionals have been criticized for overrelying on traditional individual-level interventions like family therapy over efforts to dismantle the macrolevel problems that continue to plague our society. Social justice scholars in the field of family counseling and therapy have been at the forefront in encouraging mental health professionals to incorporate a stronger focus on the systemic forces that contribute to the poor psychosocial outcomes experienced by many families living in high poverty, underresourced communities. Social justice is defined as the fundamental valuing of fairness and equity in resources, rights, and treatment for marginalized families who do not share equal power in society. Therefore, social justice–oriented family counseling entails the work of transforming the systems and institutions that prevent an equitable distribution of resources and opportunities.

Adopting an advocacy based social justice approach could not be more relevant for working with diverse urban families. The challenges faced by this population are clearly not limited to intrapersonal or familial dysfunction. Many children and families who reside in low-income urban neighborhoods are exposed to various stressors like exposure to drugs and violence, substandard housing, food deserts, and lack of safe recreational spaces. Research has shown that chronic exposure to these specific types of environmental stressors are associated with various negative psychosocial outcomes among urban youth like anxiety, poor academic performance, and delinquency. Therefore, counselors and therapists who rely solely on family-level interventions are essentially colluding with larger systemic injustices. A social justice perspective moves the field of family therapy away from endlessly trying to "fix" the damage done by oppressive forces to devalued and marginalized families.

Although it is essential to always consider institutional inequities when working with diverse urban families, it is just as important for family counselors and therapists who work with these populations to remember that many families who reside in underresourced communities thrive despite the numerous environmental challenges they face. Resiliency research has clearly demonstrated that youth and adults who live in these contexts have individual and contextual resources that allow them to overcome challenging circumstances. Therefore, working with diverse families in low-income neighborhoods should include prevention programs aimed at enhancing the strengths and resiliency factors that are already present among this population. There is now a large body of empirical studies demonstrating that preventive interventions can reduce the incidence of negative psychological outcomes as well as promote the positive development of children and adults. Social justice preventive interventions should also be aimed at the various forms of systemic discrimination that interfere with the well-being of diverse urban families.

*Lance Christian Smith and
Richard Q. Shin*

See also Multicultural Counseling Competence; Multiculturalism; Poverty and Family Development

Further Readings

Aldarondo, E. (Ed.). (2007). *Advancing social justice through clinical practice*. New York, NY: Routledge.

Furstenberg, F. F. (Ed.). (1999). *Managing to make it: Urban families and adolescent success*. Chicago, IL: University of Chicago Press.

Goodman, R., & Gorski, P. (Eds.). (2014). *Decolonizing "multicultural" counseling and psychology: Visions for social justice theory and practice*. New York, NY: Springer-Verlag.

Horowitz, K., McKay, M., & Marshall, R. (2005). Community violence and urban families: Experiences, effects, and directions for intervention. *American Journal of Orthopsychiatry, 75*, 356–368.

Knight, M. G., Norton, N. E., Bentley, C. C., & Dixon, I. R. (2004). The power of Black and Latina/o counterstories: Urban families and college going processes. *Anthropology & Education Quarterly, 35*(1), 99–120.

McGoldrick, M., Giordano, J., & Garcia-Preto, N. (Eds.). (2005). *Ethnicity and family therapy*. New York, NY: Guilford Press.

Skowron, E. A. (2005). Parent differentiation of self and child competence in low-income urban families. *Journal of Counseling Psychology, 52*(3), 337.

Sue, D. W. (2010). *Microaggressions in everyday life: Race, gender, and sexual orientation*. Hoboken, NJ: Wiley.

Virginia Satir Model

In the field of marriage and family therapy, there are several theoretical approaches inextricably linked with their creators, therapeutic perspectives rooted in the worldview of the individuals who served as their greatest champions. The Virginia Satir Model epitomizes that phenomenon. Virginia Satir (1916–1998) was both a humanist and a systems thinker. She believed everyone had a potential toward which they could grow, and that the context of their lives played an important role in their development. To Satir, growth involved more than simply gaining information or accumulating facts; it also involved the experiences, interpersonal connections, and perceptions that impact people at an emotional level. In her work, she tried to foster such connections with her clients—as she once said, "How can I use me, any me, to make a change in people?" This was the foundation of the concept of selfless respect for others that permeated all she did, and the basis for her family therapy model, one of the preeminent humanistic/experiential approaches in the field's history.

Major Concepts

At the base of the Virginia Satir Model is Satir's hope and desire that every individual who walked into her counseling office, herself included, could be his or her best possible self. This belief emanated from a deeply spiritual connection and the idea that all individuals can experience a productive existence by tapping into a life energy that is both unique to the individual and shared with all. As one remains connected with this energy, his or her human potential is more fully realized. While connection brings growth, disconnection brings loss and pain. This affects how one experiences, perceives, and interprets feelings, thoughts, relationships and, sometimes most importantly, expectations. Further, there is a natural process for individuals to seek out others who, through real connections, can invite him or her to learn about self and live a more productive life. Satir invited therapists to join her in delving into the lives of clients to access the potential within. She believed all people can connect in a positive, loving, and accepting way, since they all draw upon the same life energy or universal life force. Accordingly, each individual, at his or her core, is good. Each person's connection with that positive core constitutes a validation of one's own self-worth.

In terms of interpersonal interactions, Satir was convinced people share the same human processes—that all human beings think, do, feel, expect, want, and connect with self and others in fundamentally the same way. As such, connection can transcend individual circumstances, environment, and culture. While the experience and conclusions may be different, the processes of human connection are the same. Given that all people have the capacity for substantial growth and the ability to handle life circumstances, the shared human processes provide individuals with the internal resources one needs to deal with whatever situation with which one is confronted.

According to Satir, the primary issue that brings people to counseling centers is the misinterpretation of problems. A "problem" can be viewed as a symptom that, in various ways, temporarily provides relief for an underlying issue. For example, an employee who quits his job because he cannot get along with his coworkers is temporally relieved by not having to deal with people, only to find that the coworkers at his next job are just as difficult to work with. Or a couple having relationship problems decides to have a child to "save their marriage" only to find the underlying marital problems remain and the solution, the child, actually complicates the problem.

Therapists operating in the Satir model focus their attention on the ways clients cope or deal with a problem, rather than the "problem" itself. How seriously one experiences a problem and how one attaches meaning to a particular issue has a direct impact on how a person handles, copes with, or grows from or through a problem. Therapy, then, aims to address long-term, productive ways of addressing issues, accessing an individual's potential for positive personal and relational growth.

At the heart of the model is the belief a person can *always* change. Even if the world remains the same, one can alter one's response to it. People often hold to the idea that it is the external world that is in control, an idea that helps them protect their internal thoughts or feelings. For example, a woman expresses intense pain associated with being trapped in a loveless marriage. Satir would encourage the woman to tap into her positive core to love herself. As a greater connection to this core was made, the woman would have an increased ability to communicate her needs to both herself and her partner, thus enabling her to either find greater love in her marriage or connect to her strength and get out of the marriage. This provides her a way to accept responsibility for how she perceives the marriage on the inside, even as she struggles to change it on the outside.

Each individual's past impacts their present and future. However, the degree and direction of influence past events have on the individual's current view of self can be addressed. Helping the client connect with his or her strong, caring, loving core enables past slights, negative messages and interpretations, hurts, fears, and relationships to be seen in a more productive context. That said, Satir believed everyone has the right to feel the way he or she wants. Feelings belong to the individual. While the process of feeling is universal, the way one feels in any given situation is personal and must be respected. It is not productive to tell others how to feel. For example, saying "You shouldn't feel that way because . . ." denies or invalidates the emotional experience.

Building on that notion, Satir made it a professional point to "cut people slack," believing that from moment to moment, each person was doing the best he or she could. This level of functioning was a reflection of one's current understanding and acceptance of self-worth. Satir did not blame the client for past mistakes or failures yet would encourage the client to learn and grow from these to both improve self-concept (how one thinks about self) and self-esteem (how one feels about self) and make new, more functional choices in the future.

The concepts of balance and wholeness are internal to the therapeutic process. This is reminiscent of psychologist Abraham Maslow's (1908–1970) concept of self-actualization. Individuals are drawn to natural growth and positive change and are becoming more true to one's potential self (as opposed to reacting to perceived outside forces). As one gains greater self-awareness and connects with the strength of their internal self, one becomes more balanced and whole.

Change, then, comes from the client, aided by the therapist's use of self. Like the client, the therapist is also a person who has his or her own interconnection with self and the collective life force and common processes that bind all people together. When a therapist makes a real connection with the client, there is a blending of strength.

Both the client(s) and the therapist can achieve a therapeutic benefit through that connection.

Fostering such a bond requires what Satir termed *hope,* a personal belief that change can take place. The therapist must see the client as a positive, good, and whole individual and treat the client that way. As the therapist makes contact with the client as a person, this hope is transferred to the client in a positive and healing way that comes from all authentic, genuine, and caring contact between people. This becomes the foundation that guides the client through the therapeutic process toward lasting change.

The Family

Satir believed that the family was the "factory" where all people were made, and it is in the family where people develop either the patterns of successful and effective personal interactions or ineffective patterns of interrelating with self and others. There are four primary issues that have their roots in the family of origin.

The first is *self-worth.* This is the amalgamation of one's beliefs, ideas, and feelings about oneself. The hope is to have a positive self-worth that results from positive beliefs and ideas about oneself and productive feelings.

The second is *effective communication.* People develop patterns of communication that help them work out meaning with each other. The more flexible and respectful this interaction, the more effective the communication.

The third involves *rules.* The family of origin establishes foundational rules that most follow throughout their lives. These rules run the gamut of how to act and feel to what to think and how to connect with others.

The fourth entails a *link to society.* All people relate to others and institutions outside the family. This link to society will many times reflect the self-worth, rules, and communication that people develop in their respective families.

In recognizing the family as a people factory, Satir also recognized the complexity of the relations, rules, and societal links and their ultimate impact on self-worth. Many of her interventions addressed these family interactions.

Tools and Techniques

Because Satir asserted that the most fundamental aspect of the human experience is one's ability to connect with others, the only technique that matters is the use of self to make an authentic, genuine, and congruent connection with the client or the family. This relationship serves as the conduit for change. Once the connection is made, the opportunities to provide corrective emotional experiences for the client become almost endless. To develop that relationship, Satir often relied upon a number of tools.

Personal connection, including eye contact, touch, and handholding, was Satir's hallmark. She would physically connect with all of her clients. This was an extension of who she was and was simply congruent with her. Others who follow her theory are quick to note that they only use touch when it is congruent for them and appropriate for the client.

She conducted a family life chronology, an understanding of significant events that happened within the family over a corresponding time frame. These were created to both help connect with the client or family and to get a clear picture of the interactions they have, the rules they follow, and the roles they accept.

Satir's Self-Esteem Maintenance Tool Kit is a set of symbolic "tools" that are used to remind an individual of changes that can be made to facilitate healthy self-esteem. While Satir recognized there were many things that could go in the tool kit, she included a wishing wand to remind one of wishes and hopes, a courage stick to foster risk taking, a detective hat to help to analyze thoughts, a heart to help connect with compassion and feelings, a golden key to open new possibilities, a yes–no medallion to help with establishing boundaries, and a wisdom box to find inner truth.

The most well-known of Satir's techniques is family sculpting, a process where a human sculpture of the family is developed. In working with families,

Satir would carefully listen to the "structure" that the family was forming and the roles individuals were playing. Many times, she would use a family sculpture to exaggerate and represent family interactions. For a sculpture, Satir would ask family members to create a "moving statue" of sorts that captures the way the family members interact. There were a number of forms (i.e., roles) family members might play. Some of the more common sculpture forms are represented in the blamer, who would be a family member pointing at another; the placater, who would many times be kneeling down being pointed at by the blamer; the super-reasonable, who maintains a distant, thoughtful pose; and the irrelevant, who does his or her own thing, disconnected from the family. Satir might also ask a member of the family to act out in the sculpture, such as two children pulling on mom's arms, fighting for her attention.

Satir would also use sculpting to encourage change. One common way of doing so was through the use of leveling. In many cases, the heights of individuals in a family are different, with parents taller than children and husbands taller than wives. Satir would take a box, a step, or a stool that would bring the two people to the same height so they could see each other in the eyes as a way of "leveling" the interaction.

Satir had her early training as a teacher and, at times, when she was connected to the client or family, she would teach new concepts and new ideas to help provide a context for different ways of interacting. Some common lessons include the iceberg metaphor, in which she would explain that behaviors are what one sees above the surface. Underneath, one goes through thoughts, feelings, expectations, values, and yearnings before ultimately getting to the true self. She might also teach them about the Five Freedoms. These are (1) the freedom to see and hear what is there instead of what should be, was, or will be; (2) the freedom to say what one feels and thinks instead of what one should feel or think; (3) the freedom to feel what one feels instead of what one ought to feel; (4) the freedom to ask for what one wants instead of always waiting for permission; and (5) the freedom to take risks on one's behalf instead of choosing to be only "secure" and not rocking the boat.

Satir also made use of a variety of communication games, designed specifically to challenge the established patterns of communication and rules of interaction. Sometimes, for example, Satir might ask one member to always agree with others no matter what was said or how one felt. Other times, she might ask a member to disagree with everyone. She would also use techniques to address verbal (overt) messages and nonverbal (covert) messages as well as double-bind messages (statements that are by their nature traps or paradoxes that cannot be resolved). The point was always to be encouraging the family members to change their meta-communication (the rules or messages about the messages) so that they would avoid being locked into one way of interacting.

The roots of her approach are linked to a model known as human validation process.

The Human Validation Process Model

The human validation process model has several different iterations, which is consistent with Satir adjusting the message to fit the need of the clients or students to whom she was presenting. Generally there are three stages to the model.

Making Contact

This starts when the therapist meets with the individual or family and ends when the therapist has determined that he or she has enough information and both the therapist and the clients have trust in each other to begin working together. In this stage, the therapist must make contact with each member individually and the family as a whole. This is done by showing genuine interest in each member and the family. This is only possible if the therapist *does* have a genuine interest in the family. At this point, the therapist must help to instill the idea that change and improvement is possible, helping the family find hope.

Chaos

The status quo is maintained in the initial stage. While in the chaos stage, however, communication patterns, rules, and interaction patterns are disrupted and confusion and disorder abound. This is done by requiring one or more of the members to leave the comfort of the known and try out new ways of interaction. All other members must adjust, compensate, and change the way they interact with the others. As members move into unknown territory, change and improvement now become possible. The therapist helps members "try on" new ways of interacting and encourages experimentation of these new behaviors with the family.

Integration

This stage is characterized by hopefulness and a desire and willingness to try new ways of interacting. Not only does it create a new status quo, it also incorporates the confidence of dealing with the chaos stage, thus changing the metacommunication rules that allow for more independent improvement if additional problems arise. This concept is parallel with the overall direction of therapy where new emergent needs are addressed along the way with a "hope" for continuous improvement.

Satir's warmth and caring evidenced her natural tendency to be compassionate in every therapeutic interaction she had. Because of this, at least according to those around her, virtually every interaction she had was therapeutic. Although Virginia Satir passed away in 1988, her voice in support of the importance of acceptance, caring, congruence, genuineness, hope, and love as indispensable in the process of therapy will echo for many years to come.

Verl T. Pope and Christopher Lawrence

See also Strategic Family Therapy

Further Readings

Satir, V. (1972/1990). *Peoplemaking.* London, England: Souvenir Press.
Satir, V. (1976). *Making contact.* Millbrae, CA: Celestial Arts.
Satir, V. (1978). *Your many faces.* Millbrae, CA: Celestial Arts.
Satir, V. (1983). *Conjoint family therapy.* Palo Alto, CA: Science and Behavior Books.
Satir, V. (1988). *The new peoplemaking.* Palo Alto, CA: Science and Behavior Books.
Satir, V. (2001). *Self esteem.* Millbrae, CA: Celestial Arts.
Satir, V., & Baldwin, M. (1983). *Satir step by step: A guide to creating change in families.* Palo Alto, CA: Science and Behavior Books.
Satir, V., Bandler, R., & Grinder, J. (1976). *Changing with families.* Palo Alto, CA: Science and Behavior Books.
Satir, V., Gomori, M., Banmen, J., & Gerber, J. S. (1991). *The Satir model: Family therapy and beyond.* Palo Alto, CA: Science and Behavior Books.
Satir, V., Stachowiak, J., & Taschman, H. A. (1994). *Helping families to change.* Northvale, NJ: Jason Aronson.

WOMEN'S PROJECT, THE

The Women's Project in Family Therapy was formed in 1977 by Betty Carter, Peggy Papp, Olga Silverstein, and Marianne Walters. The project was created to examine gender biases in the theory and practice of systemic family therapy, as well as to create a model of family therapy that included gender awareness principles in its practice. This model was a precursor to the practice of feminist family therapy, which examines the impact of race, class, and gender on the personal problems of individual families. Carter, Papp, Silverstein, and Walters collaborated on issues regarding women in families and family therapy, initially presenting their ideas and encouraging dialogue in workshops about feminist theory in family work. The work culminated in the publication of *The Invisible Web: Gender Patterns in Family Relationships*, which was the first book to focus on women's relationships in the family and integrated feminist insights into clinical practice.

History

In the 1970s, U.S. culture had begun to shift to an increased awareness of women's concerns. Women were challenging old assumptions about gender and society's definition of what it means to be a woman. Women were experiencing new rights across a number of arenas (i.e., personal, political, professional), and the Equal Rights Amendment, which affirmed the equal application of the U.S. Constitution to both males and females, was an active cause. Similarly, the field of mental health and psychology was beginning to acknowledge the experiences of women as being different from those of men. There was a burgeoning awareness that developmental theory was based primarily on the experiences of men, yet the majority of mental health clients were women. The definitions of gender-based pathology were being questioned, and there was a recognition of the impact of females growing up in a male-dominated society. The presence of a male paradigm, from which the female body and mind were considered different, reduced many experiences, beliefs, and feelings of women as atypical. For example, the value of autonomy appears to be more closely aligned with masculinity. Therefore, a women's desire for connection may have been seen as pathological and labeled as such.

Hitherto, the acknowledgment of a feminist perspective within the family therapy field had been limited. The family system can be considered gender based, as both a social and an economic system. However, the leaders within the family therapy field had not yet accepted the changing role of women within society, and the subsequent impact on the family system. Walters attributed the ignorance of sex role stereotyping and gender socialization to the theoretical foundations of systems theory. By definition, systems theory allows the family to be considered self-contained, with having a unique set of laws that govern the system itself. Perhaps it was this very definition, which defined how a system functions, that created a sense of isolation from the external forces that impact the system itself.

Contributors

Peggy Papp was one of the first women to achieve status in the field of family therapy. She worked at the Ackerman Institute for much of her career and began the Brief Therapy Project at the Ackerman Institute with one of her students, Olga Silverstein, in 1974. Papp also cofounded the Center for Family Learning in New York with Betty Carter, Tom Fogarty, and Phil Guerin in 1973. After a split at the Center for Family Learning, Carter became the first woman in the country to found and direct a family training institute, the Family Institute of Westchester, in 1977. In 1980, Walters founded the Family Therapy Practice in Washington, D.C.

In their leadership roles within the family therapy field, Papp, Walters, Carter, and Silverstein were opening a space for dialogue regarding the struggles of being a woman in a field that was dominated by men. The four met together for the first time in the summer of 1977 with the intention to talk about ways in which feminist consciousness and women's issues might be brought into family therapy. In the course of this initial meeting, the women recognized the impact of the women's movement on their own development and begin a process of self-examination regarding their own gender beliefs. In December 1978, the group presented their first workshop, titled "Women as Family Therapists." The workshop was met with enthusiasm by the participants, who shared a general consensus that the voice of women in the mental health field had not been heard. It was after this initial workshop that the group agreed to formally call themselves The Women's Project. There was agreement among the members that they wanted to pursue another workshop and to collaborate on issues related to women in families. The group also agreed that Walters would take the lead and that her practice, the Family Therapy Practice Center, in Washington, D.C., would house the administration of the project.

Recognition

The members of The Women's Project traveled internationally, giving workshops, writing monographs, and prompting change in theory, practice, and leadership. The presentations of the project resonated with women across the country and internationally because it gave voice to the unrecognized dilemmas that women face in family relationships. The workshop series in 1979, "The Dilemma of Women in Families," led the group to recognize a need to narrow their focus on the roles and relationships of women. The next public presentation, "Mothers and Daughters," held in 1980, was well received in New York and led to repeated workshops in the United States and abroad from 1981 to 1983. In 1984, the group presented workshops on "Mothers and Sons, Fathers and Daughters," and published two monographs on the topic. The Women's Project served as a "think tank" to debate gender issues but also as a consultation group to offer support and mentoring to other women.

The work concluded in the book *The Invisible Web: Gender Patterns in Family Relationships*, which began in 1984 and was published in 1988. The process in writing the volume was collaborative, with the women each writing their own chapters and meeting frequently to read aloud and review each other's work. The meetings were just as much personal as professional, with the group often sharing family stories and providing relational support before moving into the writing. In 1986, The Women's Project was presented with the American Family Therapy Academy Award for distinguished contribution to family therapy. The Women's Project ended after 20 years, with the members extending the discourse on gender in their own clinical and writing projects.

Melissa K. Smothers

See also Feminist Family Therapy; Gender Issues; Gender Roles; Systemic Family Therapy; Systems Theory

Further Readings

Imber-Black, E. (2007). Celebrating Peggy Papp and Olga Silverstein. *Family Process, 46*(3), 271–277.

Papp, P. (2006). In loving memory of Marianne Walters. *Family Process, 45*(2), 139–142.

Walters, M. (1988). Prologue: Our experiences. In M. Walters, B. Carter, P. Papp, & O. Silverstein (Eds.), *The invisible web: Gender patterns in family relationships* (pp. 1–12). New York, NY: Guilford Press.

Wylie, M. S. (2006, May/June). Larger than life: Marianne Walters was family therapy's foremost feminist. *Psychotherapy Networker, 30*(3). Retrieved from http://www.psychotherapynetworker.org/help/magazine/item/529-larger-than-life

Work Relationships

Full-time employees spend the majority of their waking hours at work or completing work-related tasks. As such, most individuals have numerous work relationships, or influential connections and affiliations within the workplace. These work relationships are impacted by a myriad of variables including individual characteristics (e.g., gender, personality, attitude, personal life), job-related responsibilities and stress, work environment, other employees' personal characteristics, and duration at one's current position, among others. Work relationships can impact an individual's satisfaction within the workplace, the home environment, and familial relationships. Clinically, therapists will benefit from an awareness and acknowledgment of the influence of work relationships on home and family life. A clinical approach to addressing work relationships should focus on each individual's experience both inside and outside of the workplace. Increasing communication skills, creating personal boundaries, and fostering spousal understanding can facilitate ongoing professional and personal life satisfaction. This entry briefly introduces work relationships as a construct and discusses possible implications of work relationships on couples and family functioning. In addition, methods for counseling individuals, couples, and families regarding work relationships will be presented.

Work Life and Family Life

A synergetic relationship exists between work and family relationships. Four constructs are commonly used to depict the reciprocal relationship between work life and family life: work–family conflict, family–work conflict, spillover, and crossover. The work–family conflict, the extent to which stressors and demands from work negatively influence an individual's ability to manage or engage in responsibilities at home, has most specifically been demonstrated to have a negative effect on an individual's overall well-being. The family–work conflict is the reverse of this construct; it describes the negative influence of home stressors and demands on one's ability to manage work responsibilities. *Spillover* describes the interaction between positive and negative work or family influences onto other aspects of life. These issues "spill over" into multiple aspects of one's life. The *crossover* effect is when the partner of the working individual absorbs the emotional manifestations of the other's work stress. The negative crossover of work stress between partners is primarily related to lack of support and problematic interpersonal relationships at work.

Factors such as job satisfaction and level of contentment with one's job are a crucial influence on overall individual well-being and fulfillment impact on one's family life. One important component of job satisfaction is the quality of relationships with others within the work environment. In fact, people who report having a good friend at work are more likely to be satisfied, creative, productive, and engaged with their work. These individuals also report experiencing their jobs as more fun, enjoyable, worthwhile, and satisfying. Additionally, individuals who report having positive work relationships are less stressed, experience less burnout, and are less likely to quit their jobs.

Conversely, work stress can increase as a result of negative or lacking work relationships. Work stress has been linked to a decline in physical and psychological health, including increased risk for heart disease, depression, anxiety, insomnia, and psychological burnout.

Similarly, the work environment can negatively impact family life and couples' interactions. Often, professionals experience coworker enmeshment (lack of appropriate boundaries), which can adversely influence family functioning through the creation of spousal jealousy and disconnection. A close work friend, sometimes deemed a "work spouse," can celebrate or commiserate in an intimate way due to shared knowledge of the idiosyncratic work environment. While these close relationships can increase feelings of support at work, they can also leave spouses feeling removed, uninformed, emotionally abandoned, and jealous.

Clinical Practice

A healthy work–life balance is individually defined, complex, and influential on both job and life satisfaction. As such, a therapist will benefit from awareness of the multiple influences of these relationships. Clinical focus will depend on client personal characteristics and the therapeutic modality (e.g., individual, couples, or family therapy).

When working with an individual client, assessing job satisfaction and work relationships is important for a holistic understanding of the person. If work relationships appear to be strained, a clinical focus on communication skills and boundaries may be pertinent. Psychoeducation on the use of "I" statements, speaking from a first-person perspective, can be helpful in transforming communication skills. Developing healthy boundaries and self-protective personal limitations within work relationships is a crucial skill. When an individual has a clear understanding of his or her personal comfort level prior to engaging in relationships, he or she is less likely to feel taken advantage of, or pressured into undesirable situations. Finally, active listening skills should be fostered within the counseling environment, as individuals need to be adept at genuinely hearing and appropriately responding to others in the workplace. Clinicians can focus on helping clients learn strong active-listening skills, which will benefit them in both work and family environments.

When a couple presents for counseling, the influence of workplace relationships on each partner's life can be an area of assessment. Clinicians can work with couples on reaching a mutual understanding of the other's work experiences, stressors, and relationships with coworkers. These conversations can help increase transparency and support within the relationship. Discussions may foster an understanding of one another's insecurity, jealousy, or assumptions about work relationships. Increasing transparency regarding the nature and scope of work relationships can increase partners' awareness, empathy, and support as well as decrease the amount of negative emotional crossover.

Courtney M. Holmes and Katherine M. Hermann

See also Debt and Financial Strain; Dual-Earner Families; Job Loss; Life Balance; Retirement

Further Readings

Crossfield, S., Kinman, G., & Jones, F. (2005). Crossover of occupational stress in dual career couples. *Community, Work and Family,* 8(2), 211–232.

Gallup, Inc. (2013). *The state of the American workplace: Employee engagement insights for U.S. business leaders.* Retrieved from http://employeeengagement.com/wpcontent/uploads/2013/06/Gallup-2013-State-of-the-American-Workplace-Report.pdf

Gao, Y., Shi, J., Niu, Q., & Wang, L. (2012). Work-family conflict and job satisfaction: Emotional intelligence as a moderator. *Stress Health,* 29(3), 222–228.

Tatman, A. W., Hovestadt, Y. P., Fenell, D. L., & Canfield, B. S. (2006). Work and family conflict: An overlooked issue in couple and family therapy. *Contemporary Family Therapy,* 28(1), 39–51.

Wheatley, D. (2012). Work-life balance, travel-to-work, and the dual career household. *Personnel Review,* 41(6), 813–831.

World Association for Sexual Health

The World Association for Sexual Health (WAS) is a global organization that addresses sexual health and advocates for the sexual rights of all people around the world. Founded in 1978, WAS, originally named the World Association of Sexology, is composed of multiple sexological societies and members from various disciplines globally. Membership in the organization is awarded at three levels: organizational, individual, and student. Maintained through contributions from corporations, foundations, governmental agencies, and individuals, WAS is able to sustain and continue working toward the goals of good sexual health and sexual rights for all. The aim of the organization is to help develop and support sexology professionals from all nations around the world. The objectives of providing information and bringing awareness are achieved through research and scholarship shared by professionals throughout the field.

The WAS biennial congress (conference) is an opportunity to share new research and scholarship with other professionals and newcomers to the field. The congress is a comprehensive program covering all aspects of sexual health and sexual rights through lectures, instructional courses, open discussions, symposiums, debates, and poster sessions. Discussions of the latest information, new developments within the profession, and ways to become more efficient (and thus more successful) are introduced.

In 2010, WAS also instituted an annual World Sexual Health Day, celebrated on September 4 globally. Furthermore, the day is used to promote the fact that true sexual health is attained through sexual rights. Celebrated in 35 countries around the world, on this day many initiate festivities that are inclusive of disease testing, conferences, roundtable discussions, demonstrations, and exhibits. A wide variety of subjects regarding basic human rights, sexuality, and sexual health are discussed. Concerns and issues, for both men and women of all sexual identities and sexual orientations, are explored. In addition to the congress and the World Sexual Health Day, WAS produces the *International Journal of Sexual Health*, the official journal of WAS.

Sexual Health and Sexual Rights

Sexuality is an essential part of human development. When looking at sexuality one must also consider sexual health. Within sexual health, the mental, emotional, physical, and social well-being of an individual are all factors to be considered. Although the definition of sexual health varies, according to WAS it is defined as a state of physical, emotional, mental, and social well-being in relation to sexuality; it is not merely the absence of disease, dysfunction, or infirmity. The definition continues by stating sexual health requires a positive and respectful approach to sexuality and sexual relationships, as well as the possibility of having pleasurable and safe sexual experiences, free of coercion, discrimination, and violence. Additionally, for sexual health to be attained and maintained, the sexual rights of all persons must be respected, protected, and fulfilled.

World Association for Sexual Health: Resources

Among its resources, WAS has set standards of practice for multiple disciplines engaging in sexology, a millennium declaration, declaration of sexual rights, international standards of practice for sexuality educators and sexual health promotion, definitions of professional specialties, and international standards of practice for sexual counselors and sexual psychotherapists. Because sexual health and sexual rights can be complicated, education and practice vary across the globe. WAS seeks to change varying activities, practices, and education through the developed set of core standards. As sexual health and sexual rights vary from an educational, legal, psychological, and psychosocial perspective, the goal of WAS is to close this gap and reduce the variance for all professionals around the world. Additionally, the intent is to supply educators, professionals, and other governing bodies around the world with standard tools to use in the formation of curriculum, educational objectives, and assessments.

Millennium Declaration

WAS states that sexual health is key in contributing to overall wellness. To encourage ethical, equitable, and socially responsible behavior, WAS provides a declaration that it urges all academic institutions, local and international government agencies, the private sector, members of WAS, and the greater society to adhere to. The declaration identifies eight goals: (1) Recognize, promote, ensure, and protect sexual rights for all; (2) Advance toward gender equality and equity; (3) Condemn, combat, and reduce all forms of sexuality-related violence; (4) Provide universal access to comprehensive sexuality education and information; (5) Ensure that reproductive health programs recognize the centrality of sexual health; (6) Halt and reverse the spread of HIV/AIDS and other sexually transmitted infections (STIs); (7) Identify, address, and treat sexual concerns, dysfunctions, and disorders; and (8) Achieve recognition of sexual pleasure as a component of holistic health and well-being.

International Standards for Practice

Each area identified by WAS for specialized practice in sexology has specified standards. The purpose of this is to promote high standards for ethical and professional practice when delivering services to clients or providing education regarding sexual health and sexual rights. These standards of practice ensure that practitioners are aware of and commit to upholding important standards of practice for various areas of the profession. The standards outline what the profession expects from its members and promote guidelines for professional practice. Designed to provide a general framework for all sexology professionals, the standards measure behavioral outcomes and encourage professionals to continue seeking educational opportunities to meet the standards of the profession. In addition, the standards allow for important reflection of practice, self-assessment, and evaluation of practice by colleagues, employers, and clients. Even more, the standards assist with understanding the various roles of those within the profession. Also, standards help individuals or agencies not associated with practice, such as clients, other health care professionals, and governmental officials, to understand the duties and responsibilities of those within the profession. Furthermore, as education on sexuality is intended to foster human development and encourage sexually healthy practices, the use of applications, exercises, and interventions in clinical practice must strive toward achieving and preserving good sexual health overall. A core set of standards supports this goal.

Jahaan R. Abdullah

See also Compulsive Sexual Behavior; Human Sexual Response; Sexual Health; Sexual History; Sexual Intimacy

Further Readings

Coleman, E. (2008). Sexual health for the millennium: An introduction. *International Journal of Sexual Health, 20*(1–2), 1–6. doi:10.1080/19317610802156954

Giami, A., Assalian, P., Levin, R., & Wylie, K. (2011). Scientific research at the World Association for Sexual Health. *Journal of Sexual Medicine, 8*(Suppl. 3), 82–83. doi:10.1111/j.1743-6109.2011.02324_4.x

World Association for Sexual Health: http://www.worldsexology.org/

World Association for Sexual Health. (2013). *Millennium declaration.* Retrieved from http://176.32.230.27/worldsexology.org/wp-content/uploads/2013/08/millennium-declaration-english.pdf

World Association for Sexual Health. (2014). *Declaration of sexual rights.* Retrieved from http://www.worldsexology.org/wp-content/uploads/2013/08/declaration_of_sexual_rights_sep03_2014.pdf

World Association for Sexual Health. (n.d.). *Professional ethics.* Retrieved from http://www.worldsexology.org/resources/professional-ethics/

World Association for Sexual Health (WAS) guiding ethical principles. (2009). *Sexuality education: Past, present, and future: Vol. 1. History and foundations* (pp. 272–278). Westport, CT: Praeger/Greenwood.

WORLD HEALTH ORGANIZATION

The World Health Organization is dedicated to global health education and the prevention, intervention, treatment, and eradication of international public health concerns. The organization was established in 1948 and is a specialized agency of the United Nations. Today, the World Health Organization (WHO), with headquarters in Geneva, Switzerland, has offices in more than 150 countries and employs more than 7,000 medical and health-related professionals. WHO is responsible for the foremost international publications on health: the *World Health Report, World Health Survey*; it is also the sponsor of the international World Health Day. WHO is governed by the World Health Assembly, which is made up of 194 member states and is the main decision-making body for WHO. The World Health Assembly meets annually each year in Geneva, Switzerland. The Health Assembly appoints the director-general, supervises the financial policies of WHO, and reviews and approves the program budget.

History

The World Health Organization's inception was based on an international need for disease control, prevention, and eradication. WHO became the first specialized agency of the United Nations. Its constitution formally came into force on the first World Health Day, held April 7, 1948. In the course of the 1945 United Nations Conference, Dr. Szeming Sze deliberated with two ambassadors from Norway and Brazil. Together these ambassadors formulated an international health organization under the auspices of the United Nations. After failing to get a resolution accepted at this meeting in 1945, Alger Hiss, the secretary general of the conference, suggested using a declaration to establish such an organization. Consequently, Dr. Sze and the other ambassadors petitioned and a declaration passed calling for an international conference on health. As a result of this, the constitution of the World Health Organization was signed by all of the member states of the United Nations (51 countries). WHO's first legislative action was the collecting of accurate statistics on the spread and morbidity of disease. The first priority of WHO was to control the spread of malaria, tuberculosis, and sexually transmitted infections. Also, WHO initially was tasked with improving maternal and child health, nutrition, and environmental sanitization.

World Health Organization Professionals

As noted earlier, WHO employs more than 7,000 people and works with more than 150 countries. In addition to medical doctors, public health specialists, scientists, and epidemiologists, WHO's staff includes people trained to manage administrative, financial, and information systems, as well as experts in the fields of health statistics, economics, and emergency relief. These various professionals are employed on fixed-term appointments, working in WHO's Geneva headquarters, its six regional offices, and in the many local offices that are housed in more than 150 countries.

Governance

The World Health Organization is governed by The World Health Assembly, which is composed of 194 member states and is the organization's main decision-making body. The World Health Assembly, which meets annually each year in Geneva, appoints the director-general, supervises WHO's financial policies, and reviews and approves the program budget. The World Health Assembly is made up of an executive board that currently has 34 members who are all highly qualified health care professionals. Members of the executive board are elected for 3-year terms.

Constitution

The constitution of the World Health Organization was signed by 61 countries on July 22, 1946. Following is a statement of its constitutional principles:

- Health is a state of complete physical, mental and social well-being and not merely the absence of disease or infirmity.
- The enjoyment of the highest attainable standard of health is one of the fundamental rights of every human being without distinction of race, religion, and political belief, economic or social condition.
- The health of all peoples is fundamental to the attainment of peace and security and is dependent on the fullest co-operation of individuals and States.
- The achievement of any State in the promotion and protection of health is of value to all.
- Unequal development in different countries in the promotion of health and control of diseases, especially communicable disease, is a common danger.
- Healthy development of the child is of basic importance; the ability to live harmoniously in a changing total environment is essential to such development.
- The extension to all peoples of the benefits of medical, psychological and related knowledge is essential to the fullest attainment of health.
- Informed opinion and active co-operation on the part of the public are of the utmost importance in the improvement of the health of the people.
- Governments have a responsibility for the health of their peoples which can be fulfilled only by the provision of adequate health and social measures.

Primary Focus

The World Health Organization supports countries as they coordinate the efforts of multiple divisions of their governments and partners to achieve a wide range of health objectives and support national health policies and strategies. WHO's primary focus is to direct and coordinate international health within the United Nations system. Since its inception, WHO has been a leader and is consistently at the forefront in the treatment and containment of a plethora of communicable diseases including, but not limited to, smallpox, HIV/AIDS, Ebola, malaria, and tuberculosis. Other areas of focus are noncommunicable diseases; sexual/reproductive health; life span development/aging; nutrition, food safety, and healthy eating habits; work-related health; and substance abuse and addiction.

Elizabeth Suzanne Thraen

See also International Association of Marriage and Family Counselors; International Family Therapy; *International Classification of Diseases* (ICD); World Association for Sexual Health

Further Readings

World Health Organization: http://www.who.int/en/
World Health Organization. (n.d.). In *Encyclopædia Britannica online*. Retrieved from http://www.britannica.com/topic/World-Health-Organization
World Health Organization. (n.d.). In *Encyclopædia online*. Retrieved from http://www.encyclopedia.com/topic/World_Health_Organization.aspx

Appendix A

The History of Marriage, Family, and Couples Therapy

The history of family therapy can be divided artificially into four periods. These periods are by no means discrete. Indeed, overlap between the periods is the rule rather than the exception.

The first period begins in the early 20th century and extends into the 1970s. This is when the early pioneers of family practice began to integrate a systemic perspective into clinical work and develop the language of family therapy. Included in this period is the work of Alfred Adler, Nathan Ackerman, Ivan Boszormenyi-Nagy, Murray Bowen, Virginia Satir, Carl Whitaker, and their associates. The second period gains prominence in the 1970s when the structural and strategic models dominate the field of family practice. The stories of Salvador Minuchin and Jay Haley briefly coincide in Philadelphia at the Child Guidance Center, but their models diverge, and the strategic approach diversifies into centers in Palo Alto, California (Mental Research Institute [MRI]); Washington, D.C. (Haley and Cloe Madanes); and Milan, Italy (Mara Selvini Palazzoli and associates). The third period is a postmodern, social constructivist era. It develops in the late 1980s as a reaction to the directiveness and dominance of the structural–strategic models. Emerging from the philosophical orientations of Michel Foucault, Jerome Bruner, and Kenneth Gergen, the work of Steve de Shazer and Insoo Kim Berg; Karl Tomm; Michael White and David Epston; Harold Goolishian and Harlene Anderson; and the reflecting teams of Tom Andersen turned the structural–strategic models upside down. Through social constructivism, the client became the expert, and narratives were the avenues for restoring or creating preferred life stories. Concurrent with the postmodern period, a focus on managed care and brief therapy led to the emergence of evidence-based practice (EBP) where models like cognitive-behavioral family therapy and solution-focused therapy thrive. It is in this fourth and present period that models of couples and family therapy take on a decidedly scientific orientation, as is evident in the work of John and Julie Gottman, Susan Johnson, and others. The development of the field is intimately linked to the stories of those who have led the field. These are the stories of family therapy. These are the stories of the profession, its development, and the people who mastered the art and science of family practice.

The First Period: The Pioneers

Freud, Adler, and Their Professional Offspring

Sigmund Freud is often credited as the father of modern psychology; however, modern psychology has more in common with Alfred Adler. The history of family therapy, like most approaches to psychotherapy, starts with Freud, at least as a point of departure. Many of the pioneers of family therapy were psychoanalytically trained. Nathan Ackerman and Ivan Boszormenyi-Nagy, for example, both started out as psychoanalysts before going on to develop distinctive models of family therapy in the United States. While Freud himself did not work with families nor did he develop what would be considered a systemic model, he did coach a father on how to help his son therapeutically in a case called "Little Hans." Still, Freud's main focus was on individuals and the intrapsychic.

One of Freud's contemporaries was Alfred Adler. Unlike Freud, Adler developed an approach that was both systemic (initiating such concepts as family atmosphere, family constellation, and birth order) and teleological (or grounded in purposeful behavior and goals). Because purposes and goals intend and are enacted relationally (with the family being the first and primary setting for growth and development), Adler actually engaged in family therapy sessions in open community settings.

Rudolf Dreikurs was one of Adler's many colleagues; he immigrated to the United States before the Nazis took over Germany. After Adler's death in 1937, Dreikurs organized and structured the process of Adlerian family counseling around identifiable goals in children; he also developed the child-rearing models that would become the foundation for most parenting programs in the United States. Still, this family model went mostly underground until the 1950s.

By the 1940s, the neo-Freudians began to take center stage with multiple models of child development that focused on the relationship between the infant and the mother. Prominent among these scholar–practitioners were Erik Erikson, W. R. D. Fairbairn, Edith Jacobson, Melanie Klein, Heinz Kohut, and Margaret Mahler, to name a few. More than just expanding Freud's original drive or structural psychology, these theorists created increasingly precise theories of development emphasizing early attachment to mothers (object relations) that would lay a foundation for modern attachment theory and parenting. Harry Stack Sullivan seems to have been the first neo-Adlerian to emphasize interpersonal relations in psychotherapy; he also laid the philosophical foundation for what would come to be known as participant observation (which later morphed into second-order cybernetics).

Nathan Ackerman was psychoanalytically trained, and he began his career at the Menninger Clinic in Topeka, Kansas. He published one of the first American articles on family therapy in the *Bulletin of the Kansas Mental Hygiene Society*. Noting that the family was a social–emotional unit, he began to work with nonpsychotic children who nonetheless exhibited disturbing behaviors within the family. He was also the first to send therapists into homes to study families in their natural environment. In the 1950s, he became an organizer, sponsoring panels and meetings on family therapy at professional conferences.

New York City's Ackerman Institute opened in 1960; it still serves as a training center for family therapists even though the models taught today are vastly different from the one used when the institute first began. Together with Don Jackson and Jay Haley of MRI, Ackerman cofounded *Family Process*. This journal was the first devoted to family practice, and it is still published today. Ackerman focused on family roles and the impact that the family unit had on its members. He could be direct, even confrontational, but his use of psychoanalytic interpretations with troubled families often provided a new understanding and an impetus for change.

Peggy Papp and Lynn Hoffman both taught and trained at the Ackerman Institute. Papp was one of several Bowen therapists who would transform our understanding of the role of women in families. Hoffman, who started out training with Haley, brought strategic interventions to the work at Ackerman, later evolving into more social constructivist approaches.

Born in Hungary, Ivan Boszormenyi-Nagy came to the United States in 1948. He partnered with Geraldine Spark, a psychoanalytic social worker, in the 1950s, and together they would create a multigenerational approach to family therapy based on reciprocal roles and the generation of ethical commitments of family members to each other. Boszormenyi-Nagy started the first Family Therapy Department at Eastern Pennsylvania Psychiatric Institute in 1957, and he succeeded in recruiting pioneers like Ray Birdwhistell, who introduced kinesics (body language) to the field; Gerald Zuk, who developed triadic family therapy; and James Framo, who was one of the first to work with multiple generations.

Boszormenyi-Nagy worked to create balance in families based on mutual *trust* and *loyalty*. He saw these attributes as part of a necessary family exchange that every member could count on, sometimes needing more, sometimes giving more.

James Framo's approach was very similar to the model Murray Bowen eventually established. Bowen would occupy the East Coast, while Framo settled in Southern California. Framo was an early proponent of family-of-origin work in the training of therapists, and his ability to create safety in therapy would eventually become essential in object relations family therapy.

Other psychoanalytically trained family practitioners included Theodore Lidz at Yale University, who studied and worked with fathers of schizophrenic patients, and Lyman Wynne from Harvard, who would eventually head the National Institute of Mental Health (NIMH) in the early 1950s. Wynne was one of the first to focus on communication in families. His concepts included *pseudomutuality* (or a façade that faked cooperation and masked conflict), *pseudohostility* (or playing at bickering and fighting to mask a deeper hostility), and the *rubber fence* (or the tendency of tightly controlled families to pull members back into family isolation when an individual did more than go to school or work). And then there was John Elderkin Bell, who used his understanding of John Bowlby's work with families in England as a foundation for family group therapy, which he started at Clark University in Massachusetts.

Bowlby's attachment theories combined with the models and processes of the object relations theorists (Klein, Fairbairn, Donald Winnicott, Mahler, Jacobson, Otto Kernberg, and Kohut, among others) would lay the foundation for a number of later developing (fourth period) models, including the couples therapy of Susan Johnson and the neuropsychology of Allan Schore. But perhaps the greatest use of the psychoanalytic-attachment models is in the work of David Scharff and Jill Savege Scharff, who developed object relations family therapy and provided training for their approach in Chevy Chase, Maryland.

In the 1920s, Alfred Adler established more than 30 public Child Guidance Clinics in Vienna, Austria. He and his associates would work with parents, teachers, and children in weekly public forums where Adler would help whole communities understand the goals and purposes of children's misbehavior. Rudolf Dreikurs systematized Adler's approach and brought it to the United States. In 1940, Dreikurs introduced the four goals of children's misbehavior and along with an investigation of family constellation (or the family system), interactions during a typical day, and a process for goal disclosure with children, he began to develop family education centers in Chicago and beyond.

Dreikurs founded Chicago's Alfred Adler Institute (now Adler University) in 1954 and taught courses at Northwestern University; two of his first students were Ray Lowe and Manford Sonstegard. Lowe took up residence at the University of Oregon in Eugene where he would run family counseling programs on Saturday, known as the Family Circus. In Oregon, Dreikurs met Oscar Christensen, who would later leave to teach family counseling at the University of Arizona for more than 30 years. More than any other person, Christensen was the prime ambassador for Adlerian family counseling, training people around the world. Two of his students, Bill Nicoll and Clair Hawes, would be cofounders (along with James Bitter) of Adlerian brief therapy with couples and families. Similarly, Sonstegard brought Dreikurs to Iowa, where "Sonste" had started his own family education centers. When Sonste moved to West Virginia University, he used that university as a base for setting up family education centers throughout the eastern part of the United States as well as in Europe. In 1974, James Bitter joined Sonste in West Virginia: Together, they would train Adlerian family counselors for more than 30 years.

Don Dinkmeyer was another of Dreikurs's students. He and his son, Don Dinkmeyer Jr., were among the first to differentiate Adlerian family therapy from Adlerian counseling. Don Sr. was a prolific writer who heavily influenced Adlerian leaders like Len Sperry and Jon Carlson. The Dinkmeyers would also bring Dreikurs's parenting model to video. For years, Systematic Training for Effective Parenting (STEP) was the major parent training program in the country. Dreikurs's parenting model would eventually be the foundation for other learning programs including Active Parenting, Positive Parenting, and Cooperative Discipline. While hundreds of people across the world have contributed to the development of Adlerian couples and family therapy, the two people who have most clearly articulated the Adlerian approach to couples and families are Len Sperry and Jon Carlson.

Murray Bowen

In the mid-1950s, Murray Bowen went to work at the NIMH. Bowen was there for only 5 years, but during that time, he began the development of what would be the most comprehensive family systems theory (FST) of its day, and he experimented with interventions that included hospitalizing entire families with schizophrenic members. This latter intervention was not altogether new to Bowen. Like Ackerman, he had trained as a psychoanalyst at the Menninger Clinic in the late 1940s, and while there, he began to work on relational family processes. It was at Menninger that Bowen experimented with having mothers and children live in cottages at the clinic. In 1959, Bowen left NIMH for the Department of Psychiatry at Georgetown University. At Georgetown, he was able to more fully articulate the processes that made up his multigenerational model. More than any other model in family systems therapy, Bowen's work depended on a theory-driven practice.

Bowen's theory starts with the belief that problems in families can be (and often are) transmitted across generations. The most common process in family dysfunction is called *triangulation*, where conflict between two family members is defused by incorporating a third person into the relationship. Triangulation is triggered by recurrent interactions designed to push the buttons of various family members, resulting in *emotional reactivity*. Because emotional reactivity was so common and so overpowering, Bowen sought to strengthen rational thought as a means of controlling the emotions. He referred to this process as *differentiation* and would coach the strongest family member in developing a *differentiation of self*.

For Bowen, a family system is often stronger at maintaining dysfunction (the *undifferentiated family ego mass*) than the therapist is at facilitating change. At Georgetown, Bowen emphasized the importance of trainees doing their own family-of-origin work, of being able to recognize and control their own emotional reactivity. He wanted his therapists to be able to walk into emotional family situations and become observers rather than unwilling participants. Bowen trained Philip Guerin and Tom Fogarty, who would more fully develop work with triangles, describing a five-step process for detriangulation in both individuals and families.

Betty Carter and Monica McGoldrick were also Bowen trainees before they transformed family therapy with the development of the *family life cycle*, a systemic developmental model that complemented individual developmental theory. Monica McGoldrick is responsible for the development of *genogram*s, melding the family mapping processes of Bowen, Satir, Minuchin, Haley, and others into a single paradigm. She would also lead family therapy to include race, culture, and gender in family practice.

Carl Whitaker

Carl Whitaker and John Warkentin worked together at Oak Ridge Hospital in Tennessee from 1944 to 1946; it was there that they started seeing families. In 1946, they left Oak Ridge for the Department of Psychiatry at Emory University. Not long after that, Thomas Malone joined them at Emory just to work with Whitaker. Out of that collaboration, Whitaker and Malone wrote *The Roots of Psychotherapy* in 1953, a book that laid the foundation for their work.

At about this same time, Whitaker began to hold conferences twice a year in which family therapists from Pennsylvania to California would join his staff to watch demonstrations behind one-way screens, the first known use of this method in the field. Whitaker spent 9 years in private practice in Atlanta before moving to the University of Wisconsin at Madison in 1965. While in Wisconsin, he teamed up with Gus Napier to write a family therapy masterpiece, *The Family Crucible*. Whitaker always favored working in therapeutic teams, and both David Keith and William Bumberry were cotherapists and scholars in Whitaker's later efforts.

Whitaker avoided theory in favor of developing the spontaneity of the therapist. Whitaker's symbolic-experiential approach to family therapy, however, was not without structure. Whitaker's approach to family therapy was essentially existential in nature. He believed that families lose the ability to live fully, often getting stuck in routines, fixed rules, and repetitive responses; these processes stagnate the growth of both the family system and the family members. Family members come to therapy when the stress and anxiety within the system can no longer be controlled. It is this anxiety that makes change possible. Rather than alleviate family anxiety, Whitaker and colleagues would increase the anxiety, seed the unconscious, and stimulate action: The goal of therapy was to increase flexibility in the family system and to engage the authenticity of family members, leading to real intimacy within the family.

In the later years of Whitaker's life, he and Salvador Minuchin became both personal and professional friends. They would often make presentations to professional audiences together and appear to spar over therapeutic process and interventions. Each was clearly influenced by the other. Carl Whitaker died in April 1995. He was one of the most revered practitioners in the field.

Women Pioneers

Up until this point in the history of family therapy, the field seemed to have been dominated by men—and for the most part, it was. There were two women pioneers, however, one of whom transformed family therapy with nurturance, touch, and caring as well as an emphasis on self-esteem, emotional honesty, and congruent communication. That woman started out life as Virginia Pagenkopf, a daughter of German American farming parents from the Midwest. We know her as Virginia Satir. The other woman would literally transverse the field of family therapy, starting at MRI in Palo Alto with its strategic orientation and moving to the East Coast with Jay Haley, before setting up practice with other formidable women at the Ackerman Institute. Toward the end of her career, she came to appreciate the reflecting teams of Tom Andersen and adopted the more collaborative approaches of the postmodern social constructionists. This woman was Lynn Hoffman.

Virginia Satir

Satir was born and raised on a farm in Wisconsin. She often noted that even in her childhood she was fascinated by the power and behavior of parents; at the age of 5, she decided to be a children's detective on parents.

Her education started in a one-room schoolhouse; after high school and college, she became a teacher and then a principal for a short while. Eventually, she entered graduate school in social work at Northwestern University, completing her degree at the University of Chicago.

Satir started seeing young adolescents in private practice after she received her master's degree. Her work with adolescents quickly evolved into seeing whole families, where she would carefully watch the communication patterns that governed family life and impacted the self-esteem of her young clients. It was out of these experiences that Satir's focus on nurturing triads and congruent communication emerged. In time, Satir would meet with Murray Bowen in Washington, D.C., and later join Don Jackson, Jay Haley, Jules Riskin, and others at MRI in Palo Alto, California.

During her time at MRI, Satir completed a rough draft of her book *Conjoint Family Therapy*. Lynn Hoffman was also at MRI in those days, and she was asked to help Satir polish and complete her book, which she did. Hoffman's first impressions of Satir were not significantly different from similar impressions late in Satir's life. She seemed to Lynn Hoffman to be physically imposing, colorful, sexy, warm, almost like an earth mother, and sympathetic to and caring for her patients.

For a while, after leaving MRI, Satir became the first director of training at the Esalen Institute in Big Sur, California. Esalen was a place in which she could experiment and develop her work with other creative people. In 1972, she published *Peoplemaking*; the book was eventually published in 27 languages, and Virginia Satir became an international star. Her emphasis on the process of change, communication stances, the transformation of family rules, nurturing triads, self-esteem, and human validation drew followers from all over the world.

By the late 1970s, Satir formed a training group then called AVANTA, and she would run monthlong process communities in Crested Butte, Colorado. Each of these process communities brought together more than 100 people. A follow-up process community was led by Satir, John Banmen, Jane Gerber, and Maria Gomori. In 1989, Satir had just returned from Russia when she was diagnosed with cancer. She named Jean McLendon as director of training for AVANTA. Today, McLendon is the director of the Satir Institute of the Southeast and one of the leading practitioners of the Satir model.

Satir often developed interventions for working with families and groups on the spot; she would use whatever she had at her disposal, from people to rope to bedsheets. Just a few of her interventions include *sculpting, ropes, parts parties, family reconstruction, ingredients of an interaction,* and *the human mandala.* The process of sculpting was more fully developed by Bunny Duhl, a cofounder of the Boston Family Therapy Institute: Bunny was an early member of Satir's AVANTA Network.

Lynn Hoffman

Lynn Hoffman was born in New York City, the daughter of Ruth Reeves, an artist whose work in fabric design was well known. Lynn went to progressive schools and lived in a family that was fully engaged in art, music, literature, and politics. She wanted to be a writer. She attended Radcliffe University, graduating summa cum laude in English literature.

Lynn's marriage to Ted Hoffman was initially an adventure. He was a professor of theater who began his career at Bard College. In a rather constant search for new or better positions, the Hoffmans would move first to Oxford, England; then to Berkeley, California; then to Pittsburgh, Pennsylvania, at Carnegie Mellon; and back again to California at Stanford University. Ted was at Stanford for only a year before he won a grant to travel the country setting up regional theaters. Lynn stayed at home with her children, and their marriage suffered from the distance, ending in divorce.

While living in Palo Alto, Lynn met Jay Haley and joined him at MRI. They were both interested in writing, both fascinated with families, and both turned practice into scholarship. When Haley moved to the East Coast, Hoffman followed. Haley and Minuchin worked together for a while in Philadelphia, but eventually, he and his wife, Cloe Madanes, would open their own institute in Washington, D.C.

Hoffman's interest in therapy took her back to New York where she completed an MSW and joined the Ackerman Institute. There she joined Peggy Papp and Olga Silverstein in the Brief Therapy Project, a family model that used strategic interventions based on paradoxes. What these women added to a strategic model was a focus on language and metaphor. This process of paying attention to language and metaphor gradually evolved into the adoption of postmodern approaches to family therapy. In later years, she reinterviewed families from her strategic period, and sadly discovered that most of them simply chose to ignore the paradoxical directives that her team had used.

Lynn's postmodern work was heavily influenced by Harold Goolishian and Harlene Anderson's linguistic therapy. Lynn's work retained its team approach but morphed into the reflecting practices developed by Tom Andersen in Norway. Her life and career spanned the breadth and depth of family therapy from her initial meetings with Satir, then her work with Haley, to the team processes at Ackerman, and finally, a full transformation into postmodern work. Throughout her life, she did not just practice family therapy; she wrote about it and developed its language, philosophy, and orientations.

In a field dominated by men, Virginia Satir and Lynn Hoffman were two women who made a mark on the field; to paraphrase Gregory Bateson, they made a difference that actually made a difference. They received little or no support from the powerful in the field, and they were too often belittled in their efforts, but they took advantage of the opportunities that presented themselves. In so many ways, the early history of family therapy was their lived experiences.

The Second Period: Structural–Strategic Therapy to Solution-Focused Treatment

Starting in 1958, two models of family therapy emerged that dominated the field for two decades. Based on his early work with families while working in New York at the Wiltwyck School, Salvador Minuchin created the foundation for structural family therapy (SFT) and discussed its application in the book *Families of the Slums: An Exploration of Their Structure and Treatment* (written with Braulio Montalvo). The other model was the MRI version of strategic family therapy, based on an epistemology provided by Gregory Bateson and a practice developed through the observation of actual families by Don Jackson, Jules Riskin, Jay Haley, and John Weakland. Haley was also influenced by the hypnotic treatments of Milton Erickson. He was a prolific writer, and assisted by his first wife, Elizabeth, he would be a founding editor (with Nathan Ackerman and Don Jackson) of *Family Process*, the first family therapy journal. Haley left MRI in the mid-1960s, joining Minuchin, the director, and Montalvo at the Philadelphia Child Guidance Center. Haley was influenced by the structural approach and contributed greatly to its development, especially the supervision model that became standard practice there. In 1976, Haley and his second wife, Cloe Madanes, left Philadelphia for Washington, D.C., where they would open the Family Therapy Institute of Washington, D.C. Haley's strategic model relied heavily on Ericksonian hypnosis and paradoxical interventions. His many books spread the influence of strategic therapy worldwide. In Milan, Italy, a team headed by Mara Selvini Palazzoli would expand the use of paradox and counter-paradox; focus on family games; and invent an interviewing process based on *circular questioning*, or questions about the influence that other members of the family might be having on various family interactions.

In 1978 two therapists, spouses and partners, started the Brief Family Therapy Center in Milwaukee, Wisconsin. Insoo Kim Berg was a social worker, studying at MRI when she was introduced by her mentor John Weakland to her future husband, Steve de Shazer. While the MRI model always treated the problem in the family as the real problem and set about developing strategies to solve it, de Shazer and Berg became convinced that family solutions did not have to be related to the problems at all. Indeed, de Shazer often felt that he could help families develop solutions without ever knowing what the problem was. This is the philosophy behind their model of solution-focused therapy. The actual practice of this model is family driven and family centered, rather than therapist directed, turning the MRI model inside out. Over the past 40 years, this model has been further developed by Eve Lipchik, John Walter, Jane Peller, and Michele Weiner-Davis. In 1989, Weiner-Davis joined Bill O'Hanlon in proposing a modification of solution-focused therapy that is now called *solution-oriented therapy*. These solution models are the bridge from the structural–strategic period to the postmodern, social constructivist period.

Salvador Minuchin

Salvador Minuchin was born in Argentina to Russian Jewish immigrants. After he completed his medical degree, he immigrated to Israel in

1948 and volunteered for service in the army. Following the war with the Arabs, he moved to the United States to train in psychoanalysis and child psychiatry with Nathan Ackerman. Minuchin did a second tour of duty in Israel in 1952, working with displaced children and their families.

Minuchin returned to New York in 1954; completed his training in psychoanalysis; and in 1960, went to work at the Wiltwyck School for Boys in New York. It was there that Minuchin and his associates worked with inner-city delinquent children, most of whom were Black or Puerto Rican kids from low-income families. This is where Minuchin first introduced the concept of structure to family therapy, defining the function of systems and subsystems within families.

From this period, we get the concepts of the overly involved (enmeshed) or detached (disengaged) parents, structures that eroded effective leadership. Minuchin also identified *subsystems*, each with tasks, processes, and interactions that were appropriate to and specific to that subsystem. With subsystems came the concept of *boundaries*—boundaries that were either diffuse or too rigid led to dysfunction.

Minuchin became the director of the Philadelphia Child Guidance Clinic in 1965. By 1967, he had recruited Jay Haley. Minuchin taught his model by doing demonstrations with real families. He would initiate therapy by *joining* with families, initially adopting the family's language and ways of operating. He would use family maps and directives to define coalitions and structural difficulties. When he wanted to restructure the family, he would engage the members in enactments or experiments that could be used for both assessment and change. By the 1970s, joining, assessment, and enactment became standard practice for the majority of family therapists.

Minuchin's interest in working with the poor continued in Philadelphia where other social activists became trained in the structural model. People like Harry Aponte, Jorge Colapinto, and Charles Fishman all worked in this model. Aponte's classic book *Bread and Spirit* offers an eco-structural model for working with the poor.

In 1981, Minuchin returned to New York City. Jorge Colapinto now directs the Minuchin Center for the Family there. In recent years, at this writing, Minuchin is the last of the family therapy masters and pioneers still alive.

Family Systems, Cybernetics, Bateson, and the Mental Research Institute

Looking at the family as a systemic unit rather than a collection of individuals was the revolution that launched family therapy. Understanding and evaluating individuals became so much less important than understanding interaction or even interactional sequences. When viewing a system, the therapist can never really know what causes it to be the way it is. The system can be described, interactions can be tracked, and even purposes can be suggested, but causation remains elusive. If a family is made up of members A, B, and C, each one impacts and is impacted by the others. This is true even when the sequences of interaction are repetitive, as in routines. Even in a routine, if we replace any person in the interaction with someone new, the interaction will change.

In a similar way, family communication (language) is often a sequence of messages. There is, of course, the content of what is said, the actual words that form the more or less flat message of what is said. There is, however, in any communication a set of messages about the content; these come in the form of body language or movements, tone of voice, history of interaction, and so on. *Meta-messages* are directions about how the content is to be taken. "That really depresses me" changes in meaning if the tone of voice is sarcastic rather than sad or lonely in tone. People within an ongoing system tend to respond to messages and meta-messages in relatively fixed and repetitive ways, and given a choice between responding to the content or the meta-message, the meta message almost always carries the weight of the meaning.

Anthropologist Gregory Bateson appropriated the concept of cybernetics from Norbert Wiener. Wiener was a mathematician who applied his ideas to machines and computers. In treating these functional machines as systems, he was able to build feedback into the system that could correct or guide the work of the machine in different contexts. Cybernetics is a way of thinking and conceptualizing how systems work, how they self-regulate and remain stable.

Every time a family enacts its normal routines, follows family rules, or communicates information, it is engaged in feedback. The actions or communications of one family member affect other people in the family; in turn, their responses affect that individual. In family cybernetics, the system is maintained through circular causality and feedback loops.

Applied to machines, cybernetics is highly predictable, because a machine is a closed system; the ignition of gasoline may cause pistons to pump, which generates power for a host of other mechanical parts to move in line with directions received from shifting gears. A breakdown in any part of a machine's system generally shuts down the whole system. Families, however, are living systems, growing and changing systems, often open systems, where adaptation, rather than predictability, is the rule.

In families, a feedback loop is defined in terms of its function within the system. Feedback that exists to initiate or promote change is called a *positive feedback loop*; those interactions that deter change are said to have a *negative feedback loop*. Positive and negative, in this sense, are not about good and bad or right and wrong; these concepts refer only to whether family communications or processes promote change (positive) or not (negative).

These are the original systemic concepts that Gregory Bateson brought to understanding how families function. Bateson noted that superficial changes, now called *first-order changes*, were just ways for the family system to stay the same and maintain homeostasis or balance within the system. The early practitioners at MRI were interested in what is now called *second-order change*, or changes in the ongoing functioning and functionality of the family. Bateson never practiced family therapy, but he influenced his colleagues, MRI practitioners Don Jackson, Jay Haley, and John Weakland, the cofounders of MRI.

The first clients of MRI included families with schizophrenic members. Watching the families interact, these scholar–practitioners began to view schizophrenic families as locked in no-win–no-escape interactions called *double binds*. Double binds only exist if an individual feels trapped in a relationship from which there is no escape, and she or he is compelled to respond to both the message and the contradictory meta-message at the same time. In 1956, Bateson, Jackson, Haley, and Weakland published their first paper on the cybernetic communication that they believed was the foundation of schizophrenia.

As it turned out, double-bind theory was an inadequate description of schizophrenia, but their first paper helped to launch the field of family therapy, refocusing the helping professions on an understanding of symptoms as mechanisms within systems that support and maintain family patterns.

As already noted, living systems are different than closed, mechanical systems. Living systems grow. They evolve and become rather than merely exist. In this sense, every living system is comprised of subsystems, and every system is a subsystem to larger systems. As living systems and subsystems grow and change, they develop the capacity for what systems theorist Ludwig von Bertalanffy calls *equifinality*, the ability to get to a desired end in different ways.

The therapy offered at MRI continued the strategic, paradox-centered interventions that started with the original research team. Therapy often involved therapists taking a one-down position to empower families, giving directives for change, and using paradoxical interventions to bypass resistance. These interventions were believed to produce results in a short period of time, and the MRI model increasingly became associated with brief therapy. In later years, the center would be led by scholar–practitioners such as Paul Watzlawick and Lynn Segal. From the late 1980s until March 31, 2007, when he died, Watzlawick was the main spokesperson for the MRI model.

Jay Haley

Jay Haley spent the first four years of his life in Montana and Wyoming before his family moved to California. He received a bachelor's degree from UCLA in theater and a master's degree in communication from Stanford University. Haley met Gregory Bateson while he was at Stanford, and based on a single conversation, Bateson invited Haley to be part of a group he was starting to investigate families as systems. What Bateson recognized in Haley was an ability to take very complicated ideas and present them clearly, which he would do for the Bateson team's first article on schizophrenia and family double binds, published in 1956.

In the early 1950s, both Haley and Weakland became fascinated with Milton Erickson and hypnosis, and they taped interviews with Erickson that would become the basis for several of Haley's first books. Haley brought *paradox*, *directives*, and *ordeals* from Ericksonian work into family practice. Erickson also taught them how to bypass resistance through the use of indirect interventions.

In 1959, Don Jackson formed MRI and Jay was named director of research. In 1963, Haley published *Strategies of Psychotherapy*. He was already collaborating with Lynn Hoffman; based on a set of interviews with family therapists about their first sessions, they published *Techniques of Family Therapy* in 1967. That same year, Haley left MRI to become part of Salvador Minuchin's team at the Philadelphia Child Guidance Clinic. In Philadelphia, Haley created a model for providing live supervision at the clinic, a model that is still in practice.

Haley met Cloe Madanes, who would become his second wife, at the Philadelphia Child Guidance Clinic. In 1976, they departed Philadelphia for Washington, D.C., where they opened their own family therapy and training center. The collaboration with Madanes led to Haley's most significant work, including therapeutic interventions aimed at effective problem-solving and family developmental processes. For her part, Madanes incorporated a humanistic-spiritual orientation to her strategic interventions. Both Haley and Madanes believed that therapy was about solving the problems that families brought to them. The problem was the problem, and when the problem was solved, therapy was finished.

Structural family therapy dominated the 1970s, and strategic family therapy took hold in the 1980s. By the mid-1980s, most of the new family practitioners were blending the structural and strategic models. Haley and Madanes eventually divorced. Haley moved back to Southern California, working with his third wife, Madeleine Richeport-Haley, on films related to anthropology and psychotherapy. Richeport-Haley helped Haley to publish the last two books of his career, *The Art of Strategic Therapy* and *Directive Family Therapy*. Haley died on February 13, 2007.

The Milan Model

In addition to the two strategic family therapy centers in the United States, a third center opened in Milan, Italy. Again influenced by the work of Bateson and Haley, the team of Mara Selvini Palazzoli, Luigi Boscolo, Gianfranco Cecchin, and Giuliana Prata developed a model in which a single therapist would interview a family at length, using *circular* or relational questions while other team members observed behind glass windows. Circular questions ask family members to comment on the relationships that others in the family have: When the two of you fight, which of your children is most upset? Palazzoli emphasized that families engage in games, rituals, and transactions that are designed to keep things just the same. For the Milan group, the great paradox was that family came to change while doing everything possible to maintain the status quo. *Counterparadoxes* were interventions that promoted change by insisting that the family stay the same. To this foundation, the Milan group added hypothesizing and reframing through positive connotations to facilitate change.

In 1980, the Milan group broke up, with Boscolo and Cecchin continuing to work with the model they had all developed. Palazzoli and Prata started a new group, experimenting with what came to be called the invariant prescription. This prescription was given to all families regardless of what the presenting problem was: The team would say that they would like the couple to go out for the evening, not telling their children where they were going or when they would be back, leaving the children to handle their own lives while the parents had a good time. This directive was designed to strengthen the bond between the parents while breaking up the parent–child coalitions that typically maintained family games. Only two years into the project, Palazzoli gave up on the invariant prescription, and she and Prata split up. For the last 10 years of her career, Palazzoli returned to working with clients in long-term, insight-oriented therapy. She died in 1999.

Solution-Focused/ Solution-Oriented Therapies

The brief model initiated in Milwaukee by Steve de Shazer and his partner Insoo Kim Berg eventually became known as solution-focused therapy. It is the bridge between the strategic models of the 1980s and the beginning of the postmodern, social constructionist period of the 1990s.

While there is no evidence that de Shazer ever studied at MRI, he was a close friend of John Weakland. Weakland was the mentor of Insoo Kim Berg, and he is credited with introducing them while she was still at MRI. In 1978, de Shazer and Berg moved to Milwaukee, Wisconsin, working in a community mental health center for a year before starting their own center, the Brief Family Therapy Center. Jim Derks and Eve Lipchick were part of the first therapy team at the center. Over the years, the center would train students who would come into prominence in their own right, including Michele Weiner-Davis, Yvonne Dolan, Scott Miller, John Walter, and Jane Peller.

While de Shazer was the grand design master focused on developing solution-focused therapy and its underlying theory, Berg was the more practical of the two, concentrating on training and the application of solutions to the most pressing family problems. The departure of de Shazer from the MRI model constituted a 180-degree turn: He believed that the negative language of problems actually held change back. Solutions generated hope, used positive language, and focused on possibilities and the future. He also believed that clients knew what they needed in terms of help and even to engage in change; *the client is the expert* is a postmodern position designed to undermine the power often granted to and assumed by the therapist. MRI directives were replaced by questions and human inquiry. Resistance was no longer an issue, because solution-focused therapists believed that people really wanted to change if they chose to come to therapy, and if a goal for that change could be concretely articulated, people and families would move in a positive direction.

A focus on solutions in therapy was facilitated by interventions like the miracle question, scaling questions, exceptions, coping questions, and compliments. Curiosity coupled with strategic questions helped families to construct solutions out of the system's ongoing lived experiences. Insoo Kim Berg would occasionally bring paradoxes into the process too but always in the service of creating solutions. She teamed up with Scott Miller in the early 1990s, applying solution-focused therapy to the problem of alcoholism and substance abuse. She also offered couples therapy and family therapy to the poor.

Many other people helped develop the solution-focused model. One of Eve Lipchick's contributions was a focus on emotions. John Walter and Jane Peller, from their center in Chicago, developed the use of exception questions and wrote two highly regarded books on solution-focused therapy. Yvonne Dolan was one of de Shazer's closest partners, applying the model to the experience of trauma or abuse. Dolan also coauthored de Shazer's last book in 2007.

Michele Weiner-Davis was one of the first students at the Brief Family Therapy Institute. She had a particular interest in working with couples and came to fame with popular books like *Divorce Busting*. Weiner-Davis and Bill O'Hanlon also created a variation on solution-focused therapy that, as noted earlier, is now referred to as solution-oriented therapy. The main difference in the two models is that solution-oriented therapy does not totally avoid talking about the problems that families bring to therapy. Indeed, Weiner-Davis and O'Hanlon believe that solutions often evolve out of the actual doing of problems. For some time now, these two models of solution work have coexisted. O'Hanlon and Weiner-Davis's partnership ended with O'Hanlon moving to New Mexico and calling his work *possibility therapy*.

Steve de Shazer died in 2005. Insoo Kim Berg died 2 years later, in 2007.

The Third Period: Postmodern Social Constructionism and Feminism

Postmodernism

Beginning in the 17th century, the Scientific Revolution and the Enlightenment changed everything. Up until that time, knowledge and truth were positions asserted by either the state or the Church—and often as not, these were the same. Several developments spurred the Enlightenment along: the printing press; the emergence of science, rather than religion, as a new source of knowledge; the scientific method itself; and the growth of universities. Within these universities, disciplines were named, and categories of knowledge were created. Inevitably, standards for credentials would be established. This new world of knowledge, and indeed truth itself, could now be known by everyone using reason, observation, and science. There arose a *modern*, new world in which the essence of things and the truth of any matter could be known.

The control and power of church and state were gradually replaced with the control and power of disciplines or knowledge positions, as Michel Foucault, a 20th-century French social scientist, called them. Certain knowledge positions gain power depending on the number and prominence of people who hold and support these positions. These positions become dominant and are often referred to as *the truth*.

Dominant knowledge positions maintain power through two functions: (1) They control the mechanisms by which they can constantly reinforce and reassert themselves, and (2) they eliminate or minimize alternative positions and explanations. To change dominant knowledge positions, Foucault used the skills of the historian, the archaeologist, and the cultural anthropologist, *deconstructing* the widely accepted positions and looking for alternative stories.

Dominant knowledge positions privilege those in charge—those with power—and they are used to maintain that power. In Western civilization, dominant knowledge positions privilege those who are male, White, heterosexual, rich, Christian, abled, professional, and mature without being old. Like history written by the victors, the stories that maintain privileged positions are ubiquitous, and they get absorbed even by those people who are most hurt by them. Dominant narratives on racism, sexism, and heterosexism are so strong that they often become part of the lived experience *within* marginalized communities.

As one of the most referenced political scientists of the postmodern era, Michel Foucault urged people to take a stand against the power of these dominant stories, to learn how to deconstruct them, and to reconstruct the alternative stories that made a difference in human life. In the 1980s and 1990s, Foucault's postmodern position was joined to the epistemology of Jerome Bruner and the social constructionism of Kenneth Gergen. Gergen, especially, emphasized that stories, perspectives, and knowledge are constructed narratives that are formed in relational interactions. What is known is highly dependent on who the knower is and with whom the knower is interacting at a moment in time. Knowing is a recursive experience. Knowledge is coconstructed and affects our views of everything from self-concept to family stories and rules to societal narratives about right and wrong and national values.

When children are little or feel helpless, overwhelmed, and in need of support, dominant knowledge positions provide a sense of security: These stories are absorbed. To the child, the parents embody the dominant knowledge position of the family. They have the power, and they seem to represent the perspectives of larger systems—society, religion, and culture. The child absorbs the dominant story of the family but often does not realize that the entry of the child into the family has already changed the story. In turn, families absorb the dominant power positions of the community or culture in which they live—just as the community absorbs the privileged positions of society. Schools are a major player in promoting the privileged stories of society. The larger systems, the macrosystems, foster normative behavior in subsystems and maintain powerful positions through the pervasion of social conformity.

As subsystems of society, individuals and families absorb both the useful and useless. The more closely associated one is with the dominant culture, the easier it is take advantage of the opportunities that culture controls. So, if you are male, White, heterosexual, abled, educated, and financially stable, life is clearly easier for you. Racism, patriarchy, and homophobia may not even seem real or important within this society. The privileges of the dominant culture just seem normal; everything else is abnormal. In psychology and psychiatry, less-than-normal has been extensively codified in the fifth edition of the *Diagnostic and Statistical Manual of Mental Disorders* (DSM-5; American Psychiatric Association [APA]) and the 10th revision of the *International Classification of Diseases* (ICD-10; World Health Organization [WHO]). For those engaged in postmodern social constructionist therapies, psychopathology is just a set of labels, narratives of unhappiness just as damaging as racism, sexism, or heterosexism—and just as easily absorbed.

Harlene Anderson, Harold Goolishian, and Karl Tomm

The interventions of the structural–strategic period were directive and authoritative as well as generated by the therapist who made an assessment and then decided what the family needed in order to solve their problems. To invert the power imbalance of this earlier period, Harlene Anderson and Harold Goolishian adopted a *not-knowing position* in therapy, an orientation to clients characterized by curiosity and exploration. They treated clients as experts in their own lives and used the next-most-interesting question kept to help evolve new and preferred stories. Their orientation to therapy is similar to what narrative therapists call a *decentered position*. In the 1990s, Anderson and Goolishian were part of the Houston Galveston Institute. Harold Goolishian died in 1991. Harlene Anderson continues her work as a private practitioner and a scholar.

In Norway, Tom Andersen, a therapist from the northern part of the country, created another form of deconstructing the power of therapists. His work had been an extension of the Milan style of strategic therapy complete with a team of therapists watching families from behind a one-way mirror. Northern Norway is a part of the world where half the year there is sunlight for 22 plus hours per day, and for the other half of the year, there is mostly darkness. Andersen realized that the use of the one-way mirror paralleled the affective experiences of his clients: They were in the light, and the team was in the dark.

In the early 1990s, Andersen reported on his use of *reflecting teams*. By bringing the therapy team out from behind the mirror, the family could see and listen to multiple perspectives that introduced a real sense of choice into understanding their lives and experiences. Further, Andersen discovered that when therapists spoke of the family in the light, they used more human terms and relied on metaphors to communicate perspective and meaning. The alternative perspectives of the reflecting team members offered another way to deconstruct the power of problem-oriented stories.

Tom Andersen, like Harlene Anderson and Harold Goolishian, was an influence on the later work of Lynn Hoffman and Peggy Papp at the Ackerman Institute. Hoffman and Papp adopted the use of reflecting teams, and their process evolved, like Andersen's, from a strategic orientation to a conversational one that privileged the client as expert. This latter orientation is at the heart of all postmodern therapies, including linguistic family therapy (Anderson and Goolishian), reflecting teams (Andersen), solution-focused/ solution-oriented therapy (de Shazer, Berg, Weiner-Davis), and narrative therapy (White and Epston).

In narrative therapy, social constructionism is intimately connected to social justice issues. Part of taking a stand against the dominant culture is addressing the psychological impact of racism, patriarchy, and heterosexism. In this regard, Karl Tomm was one of the key spokespersons for the causes of social justice. His approach to therapy, too, had evolved from an MRI strategic therapy model into a more decentered, narrative orientation. Tomm was among the first male therapists to embrace and address the many social justice critiques from feminists.

Michael White and David Epston

The early conversations between Michael White and David Epston included a consideration of the work of Gregory Bateson, Milton Erickson, and the emerging field of cybernetics. Both men were from Down Under. White lived in Adelaide, South Australia, and Epston had a private practice in Auckland, New Zealand. Epston introduced the concept of narratives to White, and over the next two decades, they would conceive their clients as people living within problem-saturated stories—stories fused with detrimental parts of the dominant culture. Sometimes, those detrimental parts were psychiatric labels; sometimes they were the manifestation of larger issues such as racism or sexism. White and Epston took on family stories dominated by problems like anorexia, encopresis, delinquency, and even schizophrenia. Similar to the not-knowing position, they adopted what White called a decentered position, which privileged the stories of their clients and investigated the development of problems with curiosity and interest. They also developed externalizing questions that addressed family problems as outside of the people, outside of the system, carefully exploring and mapping the relation of the problem to those affected by it. In essence, they applied the deconstruction methods of Foucault to family systems.

This deconstruction inevitably led to a discovery of unique events or exceptions to the dominant story. These events seemed to suggest a preferred stand that either the person or the family wished to take in relation to the problem. In coconstructing these latter stories, White and Epston sought to develop alternative narratives for the lives of their clients. These preferred stories could then be broadcast to a wide range of supportive communities, including extended family, friends, and outside witnesses, and even within processes that White called definitional ceremonies. Epston also developed an assortment of forms and certificates, letters, and ceremonies to celebrate the initiation of preferred stories and triumphs over problem-saturated stories. The similarity to solution-oriented work was not lost on Bill O'Hanlon, who incorporated some of White's approach into his own work.

Michael White was married to Cheryl, who helped to develop and manage Dulwich Centre, in Adelaide, South Australia, a therapy and training center from which much of narrative therapy was disseminated. In the United States, Jill Freedman and Gene Combs opened a training center in Evanston, Illinois; their book, *Narrative Therapy*, is considered one of the most comprehensive texts for this model. Jeffrey Zimmerman and Vicki Dickerson established the Bay Area Family Therapy Training Associates, working with adolescents, people with addictions, and couples. Their book *If Problems Talked,* like the book by Freedman and Combs, contributed to North American scholarship in narrative therapy. In fact, Zimmerman and Dickerson taught narrative therapy at MRI. Stephen Madigan lives in Vancouver, British Columbia, Canada, and at his center, he works with troubled youth and eating disorders. In addition to hosting numerous narrative therapy conferences in Vancouver, he is also a featured master therapist in videos and texts. In the past 25 years, no orientation to or model for family therapy has grown faster than narrative therapy.

In 2008, Michael White died of heart failure while having dinner with friends in San Diego, California. David Epston continues to write and practice in New Zealand.

The Feminist Critique and Feminist Family Therapy

The oldest and most pervasive discrimination in the world is the oppression of women. Patriarchy is so universal that it is treated as normal and goes almost unnoticed in everyday life. It permeates every culture and every part of the world. The very few societies that were matriarchal disappeared a long time ago. There was a period in 1970s America when the consciousness of women (and men) was focused on women's inequality. This was the time in which consciousness-raising groups were formed, the fight for the Equal Rights Amendment was joined, and stereotypical roles were challenged. Following on the heels of the civil rights movement and the antiwar movement, the women's movement seemed to be the next transformative step. The prominence of the women's movement in American thought was, however, short-lived—and after that, it progressively moved underground.

The pioneers in the field of family therapy included one woman, Rachel Hare-Mustin, who sometimes called herself the Christopher Columbus of family therapy, and very few other women who contributed to the various models. Existing models for family therapy, themselves, delineated elegant theories about structure and cybernetics, transactional sequences, and multigenerational interactive patterns. Yet such models all but eschewed the larger contexts of history, society, economics, culture, and politics. The people within families and their experiences in life were not nearly as important as the resolution of problems.

In 1978, Hare-Mustin published an article that was the first to name and expose the sexism in family systems models. For two decades, feminists took up Hare-Mustin's call, arguing that family therapy models had to consider the sociopolitical contexts in which families lived. Feminists challenged the belief that all people in a system contributed equally to the problem; this was especially true when *the problem* included assault against women by men. Women demanded that the implicit or explicit blaming of women as the source of pathology in families come to an end. Most importantly, feminist women made it clear that family therapists must abandon their neutral stances when the lives of women were negatively affected by the system.

Feminists pointed out that the *normal* family was not such a great experience for women. Stay-at-home mothers are often underappreciated, and too often, they were one heart attack away from poverty. Women who had careers outside of the home—at 75% of the pay that men in the same position earned—generally came home to a second career, cleaning the house, taking care of a spouse, and raising the children and volunteering in the community and at schools. The stress in women's lives was more than double that of their spouses—and so was the amount of anxiety and depression that they experienced. It would be a decade before gender issues were incorporated into our understanding of families and into the interventions that sought to help families heal. The models that feminist family therapists espoused cut across the field of psychotherapy, but the relative constant conceptualization of therapy as collaborative, mutually respectful, privileging the voice of women and others who have been marginalized clearly places them in the postmodern tradition.

This acknowledgment did not come without strong resistance, especially from those who had pioneered family systems models, but the persistence of feminist voices won out, and today, as Michael P. Nichols (2010) notes, these issues are no longer even debated.

Feminist therapy, in general, began during the second wave of feminism in the late 1960s; it was almost a decade later that Hare-Mustin critiqued the field of family therapy. In 1984, three women—Monica McGoldrick, Carol Anderson, and Froma Walsh—organized the Stonehenge Conference, a meeting of 50 prominent women in the field of family therapy. Four of the women at that meeting, namely Marianne Walters, Betty Carter, Peggy Papp, and Olga Silverstein, started The Women's Project.

Each of these women was a leading practitioner in family therapy; they were different from each other in many ways, but they found a way to work collaboratively without losing their individuality. The Women's Project made patriarchy central to all future discussions related to the development of family therapy.

In the early part of the 21st century, feminist family therapy became a fully developed model, thoroughly articulated by Louise Silverstein and Thelma Goodrich. Feminist principles and perspectives have recently been incorporated into many different models of therapy and family practice, but there are also family practitioners who have adopted feminism as a way of life; it permeates every part of their work with families. This latter group focuses therapy on the development of egalitarian relationships, a belief in the personal as political, a valuing of women's perspectives and women's voices in therapy, and a willingness to challenge gender stereotypes expressed and lived in the families they see.

An awareness of the oppression of women has led most feminists to support the competencies of multiculturalism; unfortunately, multicultural therapists do not always embrace feminism and support women's issues. In an effort to respect the diversity of multiple cultures, many multicultural therapists have chosen to stay neutral when confronting patriarchal cultural practices. Still, there is no place left in the world that does not have feminist voices in it.

The Fourth Period: Emphasizing Evidence-Based Practice

EBP seeks to answer this question: What works with the different problems that humans and families have? The question is really modernist in nature; it assumes that there is a single answer or a small set of similar and correct answers—and that science can be used to identify skills and interventions that will actually solve identified individual psychopathologies or dysfunctional family interactions. EBP requires that tactics for change be rigorously and continuously investigated and have a proven record of effectiveness.

Because insurance companies in the United States now pay for treatment, the emphasis on solving problems with evidence-based treatment has never been stronger. Some models, such as cognitive-behavioral therapy (CBT), have always laid claim to scientifically based practices, and such models have a head start in certifying their evidence base. Frank Dattilio's cognitive-behavioral family therapy certainly falls within the evidence-based therapy group. Solution-focused approaches also lay claim to EBPs. A number of other models are scrambling to catch up.

Couples therapy has for the most part been the stepchild of family therapy. Some of the early pioneers (e.g., Adler, Bowen, Satir, Napier, David Scharff, and Jill Savege Scharff) integrated couples work when needed in their family practices, and in some cases, they offered direct service to couples in distress. This was also true for those who practiced structural–strategic models and for the solution-focused therapists (e.g., Berg) and the solution-oriented therapists (e.g., Weiner-Davis). With the advent of John Gottman's marriage clinics and Susan Johnson's emotionally focused couple therapy (EFCT), EBP for couples took a giant leap forward.

In 2009, Salvador Minuchin was on a panel with John and Julie Schwartz Gottman: All of them were asked about EBP. When Minuchin responded, his position was diametrically opposed to the Gottmans' stance. Minuchin believed that the therapist and the couple or family had to find a common language within which they could engage in the creation of change. For him, therapy was still a creative art form. The Gottmans were actually spokespersons for a return to the certainty of science. In everything they proposed, they were precise about the interventions to be used and the endpoints to be achieved. Their work was a blend of medical efficiency and behavioral principles that had their foundation in the efforts of the first behaviorists 100 years earlier.

Ivan Pavlov, John B. Watson, and B. F. Skinner: The Development of Behavioral Approaches

In 1904, the Nobel Prize was awarded to Ivan Pavlov, a Russian physiologist, whose study of salivation in dogs led to the discovery of conditioned reflexes. His model for learning and behavioral control, later called classical conditioning, launched the science of human behavior. Sixteen years later, in 1920, John B. Watson and his assistant Rosalie Rayner applied classical conditioning principles in an experiment on a child, "Little Albert," demonstrating that a phobia could be learned and even generalized to other stimuli in life. There is no evidence that Little Albert ever had the phobia reversed, but in 1924, Mary Cover Jones demonstrated that she could reverse a conditioned phobia with a little boy named Peter. She paired successive approximations of the phobia with responses that were incompatible with fear. Her method was called *desensitization*, a method more fully developed by Joseph Wolpe and now called *systematic desensitization*. Desensitization processes also became a prominent factor in William H. Masters and Virginia E. Johnson's approach to healing human sexual dysfunction in couples. The scientific experiments that were carried out in the name of behaviorism occurred before the creation of professional ethical codes, and much like the medical science of that day, personal suffering in research clients and the lack of informed consent were simply part of the process. The fact that clients might be treated badly could not be a deterrent to the advancement of science.

This new science of behaviorism appealed to the American sensibility. It focused on pragmatic issues and concerns, and it used the freedom of inquiry to explain life and problems in a manner that almost anyone could understand. Behaviorism was also a model that Watson thought could explain everything; he literally gave it away to the general public in the form of popular books on everything from infant care to mental disease to parenting.

B. F. Skinner went to graduate school at Harvard University, getting a Ph.D. in 1931. His degree was in psychology, and he had studied the work of Pavlov and Watson. After graduating, he stayed at Harvard as a graduate assistant in both the physiology and psychology departments. He was given complete freedom to experiment in a Harvard laboratory, and that he did. His invention of a cumulative recorder, a device that measured each movement of rats in a box, allowed him to collect data that would lead to the creation of a model of behavior that inverted everything that was then known about behavior. He discovered that rats adopted specific behaviors based on the consequences of the rats' actions. For any given rat, those actions that were rewarded, or reinforced, continued; those that were not reinforced stopped or were extinguished. Skinner's model is known as *operant conditioning*.

Social learning theory is the formal name for Albert Bandura's application of operant conditioning to human, social interaction. Learning in Bandura's approach is shaped when one person watches the cues from another (modeling) and approximations of the modeled behavior are reinforced. This model applies to individual activity as well as human interaction. A whole host of behaviorists have applied social learning theory and behavioral principles to couples and family therapy. The roll call includes innovators like Gerald Patterson, Marion Forgatch, and Richard Stuart.

Albert Ellis, Aaron Beck, and the Development of Cognitive Approaches

Albert Ellis was raised in a family with parents who were quite often irrational. An oldest child, he was parentified very early and is credited with having raised his younger siblings.

Eventually, Ellis went to Columbia University, where he earned a master's degree and a doctorate in clinical psychology. He actually trained with Hermann Rorschach, the developer of the projective test by the same name, and for a while he practiced psychoanalysis. By 1955, he began to conceive of a rational therapy that would substitute rational thoughts for irrational ideas. In actual therapy, however, clients did not come to discuss their thinking. What motivated them were extreme feelings of unhappiness, like anxiety, depression, fear, panic, worry, and anger. When Ellis asked people why they felt anxious or depressed or angry, they would often associate it with an activating event, claiming that the event caused their feelings. Ellis's model challenged this assertion. By examining the thought processes between events and emotional reactions, Ellis found that there was always a choice between a rational belief and an irrational one. Challenging, even disputing, the irrational belief and supporting the rational belief became the basis for rational-emotive therapy.

Another cognitive therapist, Aaron Beck, graduated from Yale Medical School at about the same time that Ellis earned his doctorate in clinical psychology. Beck also completed training in psychoanalysis. His first studies of clients with anxiety and depression led him away from psychoanalytic theory and into an identification of automatic thoughts, essentially negative, pessimistic thoughts that people have about themselves, the world, or their future. Automatic thoughts were ones that people had held for most if not all of their lives; they were treated as normal and absolute. Like Ellis, Beck asked his patients to evaluate their thoughts and to challenge them with more realistic thinking. By focusing on the emotional disorders, Beck was able to identify and name multiple cognitive distortions, along with the negative effects these distortions had on behavior and human experience. Ellis and Beck really provide the foundation for what is now called CBT.

In the late 1980s, Beck identified the cognitive schema that most often accounted for marital discord. Beck's book *Love Is Never Enough* popularized his cognitive-behavioral approach for couples seeking help with their relationships.

In the field of psychotherapy, Beck's cognitive-behavioral approach is now the most researched method of therapy. It is the model to which most people refer when they are concerned about EBP.

Cognitive-Behavioral Family Therapy

Frank Dattilio is a former student of both Joseph Wolpe and Aaron Beck. No other person has applied CBT to couples and families with the thoroughness of Dattilio. To be sure there are other CBT therapists who engage in couples and family work, like Norman Epstein, Donald Baucom, and Terence Patterson, but it is really Dattilio who brings a systemic focus to couple and family interventions. Dattilio's assessment of cognitive schema in families of origin acknowledges the importance of attachment theory and the neurobiology of the mind and brings cognitive-behavioral interventions into mutually sustainable interactions and family patterns. Couples and family members use emotions to either connect with or distance themselves from others. Understanding the survival schema that activate either connecting or distancing emotions is at the heart of Dattilio's couple and family work. Andrew Christensen, Donald Baucom, and Mark Whisman are among those who are developing and researching CBT-based applications with couples.

Couples Therapy and Evidence-Based Practice

Couples therapy is fundamentally different from family practice. Couples therapy centers its work on intimacy and the intense energy that occurs when two people interact within a binding relationship. Family therapy is often about sequential actions and interaction—and literally a diffusion of energy within a multilayered system. Still, all of the family therapy models chronicled previously have practitioners who work with couples, and all of them have adapted the family model to address issues and concerns within intimate relationships.

Object-relations couples therapists, especially David Scharff and Jill Savege Scharff, focus on providing a holding space for couples in distress. They closely track the emotional states and reactions in the same way that a good enough parent attunes to the emotional needs of a child. In helping couples to develop this same attunement to each other, relational healing takes place.

Much of this stance is echoed in Adlerian interventions that focus on both social and emotional equality in intimate relationships. Adler noted that a quality marriage was one in which each person was more concerned about the well-being of the other than they were about themselves. It is this attitude that helps couples feel like a unit and to place value on the relationship while still respecting the individuality of each partner. Clair Hawes developed the first couples enrichment program from an Adlerian perspective, followed closely by Don Dinkmeyer and Jon Carlson's training in marriage enrichment (TIME) program. Adlerians Carlson and Len Sperry work with the meaning that individuals have assigned to their lives, trace it back to its emotional roots, and reconsider and reconfigure connection and communication in ways that support growth and change. More recently, Paul Rasmussen's adaptive reorientation therapy has blended the evolutionary psychology of Theodore Millon with Adlerian lifestyle assessment to help couples connect the adaptive processes of their childhood to current relationships.

A similar, but more structured approach to healing individuals within a coupled relationship is Harville Hendrix's imago relationship therapy. Imago therapy is based on the premise that the nature of everything in the universe is interconnectedness and that every being in the universe seeks connection. Coupling starts in the family when young children depend on parents for survival. When children feel wounded in these early connections, they seek to heal in later relationships. The task for couples is to identify and heal the wounds of childhood and forge a new connection based on clear communication and an appreciation for the needs of the other.

Virginia Satir's work focused on the power of congruent communication and emotional honesty to bring couples back together. It is Jean McLendon, however, who recognized in dysfunctional communication the reenactment of negative family-of-origin trance states. Those who coupled all too often found partners with whom the painful communication of childhood could be maintained in interactions that Bunny Duhl had called "negative Velcro loops." In every person, however, there are also positive family-of-origin trance states that can be triggered when people, again, are attuned to one another. The Satir couples therapy model presages the work of Susan Johnson's emotionally focused therapy (EFT) with couples.

Whitaker's symbolic-experiential model of therapy was most effectively translated into couples work by Gus Napier and his wife, Margaret. They see coupling as a fragile bond that must be nurtured to stay vital and enlivened. Here, the need to express one's attachment and relational needs from the heart as well as the mind leads to real intimacy. David Carson and Montserrat Casado-Kehoe extend this model by integrating detriangulation, fantasy, play, and provocation into their creative or experiential model.

Even the structural model in the form of ecosystemic structural couples therapy now integrates attachment theory, emotional regulation, cultural influences, and both individual and family developmental theory into the process of helping couples to change behaviors, emotions, and beliefs that keep people stuck in recurring and often damaging interactional patterns. Marion Lindblad-Goldberg has led the development of this structural model with couples. Of all the family therapy models, the one that has remained relatively constant in the transition from family work to couples work is the strategic model developed at MRI. As in family work, they see couples as being part of a system that maintains the problem, and therapy aims at changing the doing of the problem.

What almost all of these models have in common is a belief that current couple experience is intimately connected to the emotional unfinished business of childhood and early family life. Identifying old wounds, learning to appreciate the emotional meaning individuals have attached to their experiences, and seeking to support the relationship with care and attunement are essential ingredients to couples work. Recently, Allan Schore and Daniel Siegel have integrated the science of neurobiology with relational therapies and have provided a strong evidence base for this kind of work.

No one has accessed science in the development of couples therapy more than John Gottman and his associates. In 1992, Gottman published the first of seven studies on newlyweds and their relationships. These studies included physical measures as well as relational coding and behavioral analysis. The results of his investigations indicated that four relational processes were predictive of divorce; these processes, often called the "four horsemen," are criticism of the spouse's personality, contemptuous superiority, defensiveness, and stonewalling in the form of emotional withdrawal. Of the four, Gottman considered contempt to be the most damaging. His longitudinal studies looked at couples' emotional interactions in relation to stability versus divorce outcomes, which led to his claim that the four horsemen would predict divorce more than 90% of the time. His work has been criticized for making claims to prediction based on data outcomes that were already known. To be truly predictive, his critics argue, he would have to be able to assess couples and predict in advance whether they would actually divorce.

Still, beyond the ability to predict divorce, his research led to new understandings about couples that have dominated the field ever since. His studies demonstrated that anger and fighting were not necessarily going to destroy a marriage. His physical assessments did indicate that couples should not try to problem-solve when they are angry or fighting; he recommends a 20-minute cooldown period before trying to resolve conflict. His behavioral analysis noted that couples who turn toward each other rather than withdraw or turn away were more likely to have stable marriages. Further, healthy couples make or offer more invitations for connection when in each other's presence than troubled couples—and the more bids for connection that are made, the more stable the couple is likely to be. While early divorce is more likely to be caused by four horsemen communication, divorce later in marriage tends to result from a low amount of positive affect between the couple. Couples do not generally move from negative emotional experiences directly into positive ones. There is a space in between where they are simply in a neutral state. The ability to make positive use of the neutral state is also a sign of a healthy relationship. In the end, satisfied-to-happy couples often have the same issues 10 years into their relationship that existed at the beginning, but they have learned not to get locked into repetitive, damaging interactions around these issues.

Gottman's scientific therapy model supports and is supported by the studies by Schore, Siegel, and the reporting of Daniel Goleman, among others. All of these researchers have demonstrated that emotional intelligence is required in the neurobiology of the brain. Its purpose is to create interconnectedness, and this, in turn, is intimately linked to our survival. Therapy that focuses on the healing and understanding of emotional wounds and helps couples build emotional safe zones within their relationship is more likely to have positive results.

In 2015, John and Julie Schwartz Gottman outlined 10 principles for conducting couples therapy based on their research. These principles include needing therapy to be consistent with scientific research; assessing a couple before planning treatment; focusing on each person's subjective world and experience; mapping where you want to go with a couple and going there calmly with the couple; facing past problems, but not living in them; replacing the four horsemen with kind and caring conflict resolution skills; strengthening friendship and intimacy; appreciating and building on dreams; and creating shared meaning.

Susan Johnson started focusing on couple emotional interactions when everyone else was focused on teaching effective communication, problem-solving, and applying various theories to treatment. Perhaps because her work was not initially treated with a great deal of respect, Johnson set out to demonstrate its efficacy. In the early stages, she would assess her work and then interview couples about what parts of the session were helpful and what were not. Through this investigation, she determined that couples often engaged in negative interactions caused by undisclosed and often painful emotions. Her EFT with couples now follows a pattern of identifying and defusing the negative cycles and processes; reconnecting the couple through positive emotional bonding; and then consolidating the couple's relationship by supporting the deepening of the emotional bond.

Like the Gottmans, Susan Johnson believes that her work is evidence-based and scientifically supported. Indeed, as of 2008, there are more than two dozen outcome studies that support the effectiveness of EFT with couples.

The movement toward EBPs in couples and family therapy has supporters within the field as well as detractors. Clearly, scientists will continue to explore the neurobiology of relationships and the relationship of attachment and early family experiences to adult connections. Mindfulness and other processes for calming emotional processes in the brain will be tested and more specifically applied. History tells us that many different models can share the couple and family therapy stage during different periods of development. Because the field has been so dominated by the personalities of its masters, it will take time for new innovators to claim their space. Sometimes, history can tell us what to expect. In this case, we are not sure it can.

James Robert Bitter and Jon Carlson

Further Readings

Becvar, D. S., & Becvar, R. J. (2012). *Family therapy: A systemic integration* (8th ed.). Boston, MA: Pearson.

Bitter, J. R. (2014). *The theory and practice of family therapy and counseling* (2nd ed.). Belmont, CA: Brooks/Cole.

Braverman, L. (Ed.). (1988). *Women, feminism, and family therapy*. New York, NY: Haworth Press.

Carson, D. K., & Casado-Kehoe, M. (2011). *Case studies in couples therapy: Theory-based approaches*. New York, NY: Routledge.

Goldenberg, H., & Goldenberg, I. (2016). *Family therapy: An overview* (9th ed.). Belmont, CA: Brooks/Cole.

Hoffman, L. (2002). *Family therapy: An intimate history*. New York, NY: W. W. Norton.

Luepnitz, D. A. (2002). *The family interpreted: Psychoanalysis, feminism, and family therapy*. New York, NY: Basic Books. (Original work published 1988)

Nichols, M. (2010). *Family therapy: Concepts and methods* (9th ed.). Boston, MA: Pearson.

Appendix B

Resource Guide

Professional Associations and Organizations

The following is a listing of professional associations and organizations that focus on marriage, family, and couples counseling. Most offer publications, national conferences, and other services.

American Association for Marriage and Family Therapy (AAMFT)

https://www.aamft.org/iMIS15/AAMFT/

AAMFT is the professional association for the marriage and family therapy field. AAMFT represents the professional interests of more than 50,000 marriage and family therapists throughout the United States, Canada, and abroad.

American Association of Sexuality Educators, Counselors and Therapists (AASECT)

https://www.aasect.org/

AASECT, founded in 1967, is devoted to the promotion of sexual health. Through the development and advancement of the fields of sexual therapy, counseling, and education, AASECT's mission is the advancement of the highest standards of professional practice for educators, counselors, and therapists.

American Counseling Association (ACA)

https://www.counseling.org/

ACA is a not-for-profit, educational and professional organization. ACA is committed to the growth and enhancement of the counseling profession. Founded in 1952, ACA is the world's largest association exclusively representing professional counselors in a variety of practice settings.

American Family Therapy Academy (AFTA)

http://www.afta.org/about

AFTA offers an annual conference that focuses on relevant topics and knowledge that is intellectually stimulating, while addressing personal and professional growth in accessible and peer exchange formats. The conference generates and nurtures new ideas, and challenges itself to advance systemic family-centered perspectives on mental health, social constructionist, and next generation thinking.

Association of Marital and Family Therapy Regulatory Boards (AMFTRB)

https://www.amftrb.org/

AMFTRB is the association of statutorily constituted bodies, including administrative agencies, and is legally responsible for the regulation of marital and family therapists in their respective jurisdictions. AMFTRB is organized to facilitate communication among its member boards concerning the regulation of marital and family therapists; to sponsor collaboration among the member boards in developing compatible standards and family therapy services to other marital and family therapy organizations, as well as to legislative, judicial, regulatory, and executive governmental bodies, and to other groups or associations whose areas of interest may coincide with those of its membership; to aid its member boards in fulfilling statutory, professional, public, and ethical obligations; and to engage in and encourage research on matters related to the legal regulation of marital and family therapists.

Association for Play Therapy (APT)
http://www.a4pt.org/

APT is a national professional society, established in 1982 to foster contact among mental health professionals interested in exploring and applying the therapeutic power of play to communicate with and treat clients, particularly children.

Council for Accreditation of Counseling and Other Related Programs (CACREP)
http://www.cacrep.org/

CACREP accredits master's and doctoral degree programs in counseling and its related specialties offered by colleges and universities in the United States and throughout the world.

Commission on Accreditation for Marriage and Family Therapy Education (COAMFTE)
http://www.coamfte.org/iMIS15/coamfte/

COAMFTE works cooperatively with its parent organization, the American Association for Marriage and Family Therapy (AAMFT), state licensing and certification boards, and the Association of Marital and Family Therapy Regulatory Boards (AMFTRB). The accreditation process is a voluntary one that requires self-study by the program, an on-site review by a selected group of peers, and a review and decision by the COAMFTE to determine if compliance with accreditation standards has occurred. The COAMFTE program educational standards often serve as the foundation for the development of individual credentialing requirements. Once a program has become accredited, it is required to submit annual reports demonstrating continued compliance with standards, and accredited programs are reviewed at least every 6 years.

European Family Therapy Association (EFTA)
http://www.europeanfamilytherapy.eu/

EFTA is an international association dedicated to scientific purposes. The organization exists to promote family therapy and systemic practice across Europe.

International Association of Marriage and Family Counselors (IAMFC)
http://www.iamfconline.org/

IAMFC is a division of the American Counseling Association (ACA) that was chartered in 1989. IAMFC embraces a multicultural approach in support of the worth, dignity, potential, and uniqueness of all of the families served.

International Family Therapy Association (IFTA)
http://www.ifta-familytherapy.org/

With the support of its members, IFTA provides international conferences to encourage, promote, strengthen, and improve the quality of family therapy and the quality of relationships within families, and to promote overall well-being and peace within our world. IFTA, working in a collaborative fashion with other professionals and organizations around the world, also promotes continuing education in the development of quality standards for marriage and family therapy for professionals performing family therapy so that they may better assist families in the communities that they serve.

National Board for Certified Counselors (NBCC)
http://www.nbcc.org/

NBCC, established in 1982, is an independent, not-for-profit certification organization. NBCC's original and primary purposes are to establish and monitor a national certification system, to identify counselors who have voluntarily sought and obtained certification, and to maintain a register of those counselors. NBCC and its divisions and affiliates also work to advance the counseling profession and enhance mental health worldwide.

National Council on Family Relations (NCFR)
https://www.ncfr.org/

NCFR, founded in 1938, is the oldest nonprofit, nonpartisan, multidisciplinary professional association focused solely on family research, practice, and education. NCFR members are professionals committed to understanding and strengthening families around the world. NCFR members come from more than 35 countries and all 50 U.S. states. NCFR members include researchers, demographers, marriage and family therapists, parent/family educators, university faculty, students, social workers, public health workers, extension specialists and faculty, ECFE teachers, clergy, counselors, K-12 teachers, and more.

National Credentialing Academy (NCA)

http://nationalcredentialingacademy.com/

NCA was initiated in 1994 as a result of efforts by the International Association of Marriage and Family Counselors (IAMFC) in the area of credentialing. After requests from members and several years of surveying professionals, it was determined that a national certification process for family therapists was needed. NCA was incorporated with the primary purpose to create and monitor a national certification system, to identify professionals who have electively sought and obtained certification, and to maintain the certification process. This process grants recognition to professionals who have met predetermined NCA standards in their training and experience, and who meet ethical standards in the field.

Publications

American Journal of Family Therapy

http://www.tandfonline.com/toc/uaft20/current

The American Journal of Family Therapy is an incisive, authoritative, independent voice in an ever-changing field. Contents of the journal include the latest techniques for assessing and treating couples and families, as well as issues and research on a variety of topics including the following: normal and dysfunctional family relationships, sexuality, intimacy, divorce and premarital counseling, traditional and alternative family styles and parenting styles, family measurement techniques, family legal issues, school and community approaches to family intervention, child and family custody evaluations, couple and family therapy training and continuing education, family spirituality and religious issues, medical family therapy and family behavioral medicine, family therapy in integrated primary care, and evidence-based practice in family therapy. *The American Journal of Family Therapy* appeals to a wide readership, including marriage and family therapists, family counselors, psychiatrists, psychologists, various health practitioners, professional counselors, clinical social workers, clergy, physicians, and nurses.

Australian and New Zealand Journal of Family Therapy

https://www.aaft.asn.au/resources/the-australian-and-new-zealand-journal-of-family-therapy

Australian and New Zealand Journal of Family Therapy (ANZJFT) aims to represent family therapy, as well as other therapy approaches that can broadly be described as relational, systemic, or contextual. ANZJFT continues to publish on topics of research, practice, and theory, with special focus to showcase accessible and relevant information to all family-sensitive practice.

Contemporary Family Therapy

http://www.springer.com/psychology/journal/10591

Contemporary Family Therapy (COFT) is an international, quarterly, peer-reviewed publication that presents the latest developments in practice, theory, research, and training in the field of family and couples therapy. COFT embraces international and multidisciplinary perspectives and publishes applied and basic research with implications for theory, treatment, and policy. The overall goal of COFT is to understand couple and family functioning within their broader, systemic social contexts and throughout a multiplicity of forms. The journal's content is relevant to a variety of professionals including family practitioners, educators, marriage and family therapists, family psychologists, clinical social workers, researchers, and social policy specialists.

Couple and Family Psychology: Research and Practice

http://www.apa.org/pubs/journals/cfp/

Couple and Family Psychology: Research and Practice (CFP) is a scholarly journal that publishes peer-reviewed papers representing the science and practice of family psychology. CFP is the official publication of American Psychological Association (APA) Division 43 (Society for Couple and Family Psychology) and is intended to be a forum for scholarly discussion regarding the most pivotal emerging issues in the field. It is a primary outlet for research particularly as it impacts practice and for papers regarding education, public policy, and the identity of the profession of family psychology.

The Family Journal

https://us.sagepub.com/en-us/nam/the-family-journal/journal200924

The Family Journal is a professional publication based at Mississippi College promoting research, theory, and practice of marriage counseling and therapy. The journal covers a vast amount of information across the field, encouraging professionals to use the journal when working on research endeavors.

Family Relations: Interdisciplinary Journal of Applied Family Studies

https://www.ncfr.org/fr

Family Relations: Interdisciplinary Journal of Applied Family Studies, established in 1951, is a publication of the National Council on Family Relations (NCFR). The journal publishes basic and applied articles that are original, innovative, and interdisciplinary with a focus on diverse family forms and issues. Readers include educators in academic and community settings, researchers with an applied or evaluation focus, family practitioners, and family policy specialists. Articles included in the journal are empirically based applied research, educational philosophies or practices, critical syntheses of relevant substantive areas, program evaluations, curriculum development and assessment, issues in the discipline, professional development, and basic research with clearly articulated implications for practice and policy.

Human Systems Journal

http://www.humansystemsjournal.eu/

Human Systems Journal provides a platform for ideas, experiences, and rigorous leading-edge study of developments in systemic thinking and practice. *Human Systems Journal* plays a role in encouraging, developing, coordinating, and disseminating those developments for use by practitioners, trainers, and other scientists in the field. The journal intends to become a fully interactive part of the system, exemplifying in its operation the principles it supports through interactions with authors, commentaries, replies, and more.

Journal of Couples & Relationships Therapy

http://www.tandfonline.com/toc/wcrt20/current

The Journal of Couple & Relationship Therapy strives to promote a better understanding of what contributes to healthy adult relationships and how therapy facilitates the process. Experts address critical treatment issues for all types of adult relationships. Journal articles explore couples therapy through the lens of theory, research, and practice, as well as issues related to the supervision and personal growth of practicing clinicians. The journal includes special thematic issues that address a single topic for the entire issue, allowing a more specialized focus on that particular topic.

Journal of Family Psychology

http://www.apa.org/pubs/journals/fam/

The *Journal of Family Psychology* (JFP) consistently publishes strong empirical studies on what keeps couples together, what makes for strong parent–child relationships, and the subtle nuances in predicting healthy relationships over time. JFP provides an outlet for studies that test the effects of family- or couples-based therapy or prevention programs. Especially significant are reports that include couple or family characteristics as potential mediators and moderators of program effects.

Journal of Family Theory & Review
https://www.ncfr.org/jftr

The *Journal of Family Theory & Review* seeks to encourage integration and growth in the multidisciplinary and international domains of inquiry that define modern family studies. The journal publishes original contributions in all areas of family theory, including new advances in theory development, reviews of existing theory, and analyses of the interface of theory and method, as well as integrative and theory-based reviews of content areas and book reviews. The journal pulls from a broad range of social sciences, although scholarship based within the fields of family science, sociology and allied disciplines, developmental and social psychology, communications, and health and allied fields is favored. Families are viewed broadly and inclusively to include individuals of varying ages, genders, sexual orientations, ethnicities, and nationalities.

Journal of Marital and Family Therapy
http://onlinelibrary.wiley.com/journal/10.1111/%28ISSN%291752-0606

The *Journal of Marital and Family Therapy* is a well-regarded publication helping to make the field of family therapy stronger as a whole. The *Journal of Marital and Family Therapy* is a quarterly publication that helps to make sure all therapists working in the field have the best material on hand to refine their skills on the job.

Journal of Marriage and Family
https://www.ncfr.org/jmf

The *Journal of Marriage and Family* (JMF), published by the National Council on Family Relations, has been a leading research journal in the family field for more than 70 years. JMF features original research and theory using a variety of methods reflective of the full range of social sciences. Research and methods presented include quantitative, qualitative, and multimethod designs; research interpretation; integrative review; reports on methodological and statistical advances; and critical discussion concerning all aspects of marriage, other forms of close relationships, and families. JMF also publishes brief reports.

Journal of Sex and Marital Therapy
http://www.tandfonline.com/toc/usmt20/current

The *Journal of Sex and Marital Therapy* (JSMT) is an independent journal, providing an active and contemporary forum reflecting the most viable developments originating from the United States and abroad. JSMT strives to break new ground with innovative research, clinical writing, and presenting the most expansive traditional and contemporary thinking from all sources. The journal provides information on therapeutic techniques, outcome, special clinical and medical problems, and the theoretical parameters of sexual functioning and marital relationships.

Journal of Systemic Therapies
http://www.guilford.com/journals/Journal-of-Systemic-Therapies/Jim-Duvall,-MEd,-RSW/11954396

The *Journal of Systemic Therapies* is a practice-oriented journal presenting ideas that are provocative and methods that work with families, individuals, and groups. *Journal of Systemic Therapies* explores relevant and recent concepts in such areas as the brief therapies, solution-focused models, relational therapy, therapeutic conversations, and narrative therapy. This journal is an appropriate teaching tool, clearly and accessibly written with a significant focus on techniques.

Sexual and Relationship Therapy
http://www.tandfonline.com/toc/csmt20/current

Sexual and Relationship Therapy is a leading independent journal in the field and is well established and internationally recognized. *Sexual and Relationship Therapy* offers an active, multidisciplinary platform for review and debate across the spectrum of sexual and relationship dysfunctions and therapies. The journal presents original research and best practices, and is a vehicle for new theory and methodology, and application. Contributions from all concerned with the field of clinical sexuality and sexual medicine in its broadest sense are welcomed.

Appendix C

Selected Readings

Fundamentals and History of Marriage and Family Counseling

American Counseling Association. (2014). *20/20: Consensus definition of counseling*. Retrieved from http://www.counseling.org/knowledge-center/20-20-a-vision-for-the-future-of-counseling/consensus-definition-of-counseling

Becvar, D. S., & Becvar, R. J. (2012). *Family therapy: A systemic integration* (8th ed.). Boston: Pearson.

Bitter, J. R. (2014). *The theory and practice of family therapy and counseling* (2nd ed.). Belmont, CA: Brooks/Cole.

Goldenberg, H., & Goldenberg, I. (2016). *Family therapy: An overview* (9th ed.). Belmont, CA: Brooks/Cole.

Hoffman, L. (2002). *Family therapy: An intimate history*. New York, NY: W. W. Norton.

McGeorge, C. R., Carlson, T. S., & Wetchler, J. L. (2015). The history of marriage and family therapy. In J. L. Wetchler, L. L. Hecker, J. L. Wetchler, & L. L. Hecker (Eds.), *An introduction to marriage and family therapy* (2nd ed., pp. 3–42). New York, NY: Routledge.

Nichols, M. (2010). *Family therapy: Concepts and methods* (9th ed.). Boston: Pearson.

Wetchler, J. L., & Hecker, L. L. (2015). *An introduction to marriage and family therapy* (2nd ed.). New York, NY: Routledge.

Training, Licensure, and Accreditation

American Association for Marriage and Family Therapy. (2014). *Accreditation resources*. Retrieved from https://www.aamft.org/iMIS15/AAMFT/Content/COAMFTE/Accreditation_Resources.aspx

American Association for Marriage and Family Therapy: http://www.aamft.org

American Association for Marriage and Family Therapy. (2015). *Code of ethics*. Retrieved from http://www.aamft.org/imis15/Documents/Legal%20Ethics/AAMFT-code-of-ethics.pdf

American Association of State Counseling Boards: http://www.aascb.org

Bobbie, C. L. (1993, Winter). News and views: COPA officially recognizes CACREP's inclusion of marriage and family counseling/therapy programs. *CACREP Connection*. Retrieved from http://www.cacrep.org/wp-content/uploads/2013/03/Winter-1993.pdf

Caldwell, B. E., Kunker, S. A., Brown, S. W., & Saiki, D. Y. (2011). COAMFTE accreditation and California MFT licensing exam success. *Journal of Marital and Family Therapy, 37*(4), 468–478.

Council for Accreditation of Counseling & Related Educational Programs: http://www.cacrep.org/

Council for Higher Education Accreditation: http://www.chea.org/

Crane, D. R., Shaw, A. L., Christenson, J. D., Larson, J. H., Harper, J. M., & Feinauer, L. L. (2010). Comparison of the family therapy educational and experience requirements for licensure or certification in six mental health disciplines. *American Journal of Family Therapy, 38*(5), 357–373.

Lee, C. C. (2013). The CACREP site visit process. *Journal of Counseling & Development, 91*, 50–54.

National Board for Certified Counselors: http://nbcc.org/

Urofsky, R. I. (2013). The Council for Accreditation of Counseling and Related Educational Programs: Promoting quality in counselor education. *Journal of Counseling & Development, 91,* 6–14.

West, C., Hinton, W. J., Grames, H., & Adams, M. A. (2013). Marriage and family therapy: Examining the impact of licensure on an evolving profession. *Journal of Marital and Family Therapy, 39*(1), 112–126.

Woolley, S. R. (2010). Purposes, diversities, and futures in MFT doctoral education. *Journal of Marital and Family Therapy, 36*(3), 282–290.

Supervision

American Association for Marriage and Family Therapy. (2014, January). *Approved supervision designation: Standards handbook.* Retrieved from http://www.aamft.org/iMIS15/AAMFT/Content/Supervision/AS_Designation.aspx

Boyle, R., & McDowell-Burns, M. (2016). Modalities of marriage and family therapy supervision. In K. Jordan & K. Jordan (Eds.), *Couple, marriage, and family therapy supervision* (pp. 51–69). New York, NY: Springer.

Bursky, S. A., & Cook, R. M. (2016). Training the structural therapist. In K. Jordan & K. Jordan (Eds.), *Couple, marriage, and family therapy supervision* (pp. 151–168). New York, NY: Springer.

Caldwell, B. E. (2016). Ethics and supervision. In K. Jordan & K. Jordan (Eds.), *Couple, marriage, and family therapy supervision* (pp. 105–120). New York, NY: Springer.

Celano, M. P., Smith, C. O., & Kaslow, N. (2010). A competency-based approach to couple and family therapy supervision. *Psychotherapy Theory, Research, Practice, Training, 47,* 35–44. doi:10.1037/a0018845

Jordan, K. (2016). *Couple, marriage, and family therapy supervision.* New York, NY: Springer.

Jordan, K., & Fisher, U. (2016). History and future trends. In K. Jordan & K. Jordan (Eds.), *Couple, marriage, and family therapy supervision* (pp. 3–21). New York, NY: Springer.

Littrell, J. M., Lee-Borden, N., & Lorenz, J. A. (1979). A developmental framework for counseling supervision. *Counselor Education and Supervision, 19,* 119–136.

O'Connell, B., & Jones, C. (1997). Solution-focused supervision. *Counselling, 8*(4), 289–292.

Rigazio-DiGilio, S. A. (2016). MFT supervision: An overview. In K. Jordan & K. Jordan (Eds.), *Couple, marriage, and family therapy supervision* (pp. 25–49). New York, NY: Springer.

Todd, T. C., & Storm, C. L. (Eds.). (1997). *The complete systemic supervisor: Context, philosophy, and pragmatics.* Needham Heights, MA: Allyn & Bacon.

Pioneers and Theories

Bertalanffy, L. von. (1968). *General system theory.* New York, NY: George Braziller.

Bloch, D. A. (1974). Nathan W. Ackerman: The first family paper. In L. R. Wolberg, M. L. Aronson, L. R. Wolberg, & M. L. Aronson (Eds.), *Group therapy 1974: An overview.* Oxford, England: Stratton Intercontinental.

Boscolo, L., Cecchin, G., Hoffman, L., & Penn, P. (1987). *Milan systemic family therapy: Conversations in theory and practice.* New York, NY: Basic Books.

Boszormenyi-Nagy, I. (1987). *Foundations of contextual therapy: Collected papers of Ivan Boszormenyi-Nagy, M.D.* Philadelphia, PA: Brunner/Mazel.

Bowen, M. (1985). *Family therapy in clinical practice.* New York, NY: Rowman & Littlefield.

Bowlby J. (1988). *A secure base: Parent-child attachment and healthy human development.* London, England: Routledge.

Braverman, L. (1988). *A guide to feminist family therapy.* New York, NY: Harrington Park Press.

Connell, G., Mitten, T., & Bumberry, W. (1998). *Reshaping family relationships: The symbolic therapy of Carl Whitaker.* London, England: Routledge.

Diamond, G. M., Diamond, G. S., & Hogue, A. (2007). Attachment-based family therapy: Adherence and differentiation. *Journal of Marital and Family therapy, 33*(2), 177–191.

Framo, J. L. (1992). *Family-of-origin therapy: An intergenerational approach.* Philadelphia, PA: Brunner/Mazel.

Glick, I. D., & Clarkin, J. C. (1985). Review of *The Strength of Family Therapy: Selected Papers of Nathan W. Ackerman. Journal of Marital and Family Therapy, 11*(3), 329–330.

Goldner, V. (1985). Feminism and family therapy. *Family Process, 24,* 31–47.

Greenberg, L. S. (2004). Emotion-focused therapy. *Clinical Psychology & Psychotherapy, 11*(1), 3–16.

Greenberg, L. S., & Johnson, S. M. (1988). *Emotionally focused therapy for couples*. New York, NY: Guilford Press.

Guterman, J. T., & Leite, N. (2006). Solution-focused counseling for clients with religious and spiritual concerns. *Counseling and Values, 51*(1), 39–52.

Hecker, L. L., Mims, G. A., & Boughner, S. R. (2015). General systems theory, cybernetics, and family therapy. In J. L. Wetchler, L. L. Hecker, J. L. Wetchler, & L. L. Hecker (Eds.), *An introduction to marriage and family therapy* (2nd ed., pp. 43–64). New York, NY: Routledge/Taylor & Francis Group.

Hodge, D. R. (2006). Spiritually modified cognitive therapy: A review of the literature. *Social Work, 51*(2), 157–166.

Kempler, W. (1981). *Experiential psychotherapy with families*. New York, NY: Brunner/Mazel.

Satir, V. (1972). *Peoplemaking*. Palo Alto, CA: Science and Behavior Books.

Satir, V. (1983). *Conjoint family therapy* (3rd ed.). Palo Alto, CA: Science and Behavior Books.

Satir, V., & Baldwin, M. (1983). *Satir step-by-step*. Palo Alto, CA: Science and Behavior Books.

Satir, V., Bandler, R., & Grinder, J. (1976). *Changing with families*. Palo Alto, CA: Science and Behavior Books.

Satir, V., Gomori, M., Banmen, J., & Gerber, J. S. (1991). *The Satir model: Family therapy and beyond*. Palo Alto, CA: Science and Behavior Books.

Silverstein, L. B., & Goodrich, T. J. (2005). *Feminist family therapy: Empowerment in social context*. Washington, DC: American Psychological Association.

Stagner, B. H. (2012). Salvador Minuchin, family therapy pioneer. *Psyccritiques, 57*(39). doi:10.1037/a0030078

Stagoll, B. (2006). Gregory Bateson at 100. *Australian and New Zealand Journal of Family Therapy, 27*(3), 121–134. doi:10.1002/j.1467-8438.2006.tb00710.x

Whitaker, C. (1989). *Midnight musings of a family therapist*. New York, NY: W. W. Norton.

Whitaker, C., & Keith, D. (1982). Symbolic-experiential family therapy. In A. Gurman & D. Kniskern (Eds.), *Handbook of family therapy* (pp. 187–225). New York, NY: Brunner/Mazel.

Index

Note: Main topics and their page numbers are in **bold**.

Abandonment, **2**:510
ABCDE model, **3**:1425
ABC-X model, **2**:643–644, 646, 649–650, **3**:1400, **4**:1609
Abelin, Ernest, **4**:1739
ABFT. *See* **Attachment-based family therapy (ABFT)**
Abortion, **1**:165, **3**:1293, 1294, **4**:1552–1553
Abstinence syndrome, **4**:1627
Abuse
 child maltreatment, **1**:208–209
 elder abuse, **2**:508–511
 emotional abuse, **1**:209, 468, **2**:509, 908, 912
 forensics, **1**:370
 sexual abuse, **4**:1512–1515
ACA. *See* American Counseling Association (ACA)
Acceptance, **3**:1405
Acceptance and commitment therapy (ACT), 1:1–5
 acceptance, **1**:2–3
 content areas for certification, **2**:615
 defusion, **1**:4, **2**:621
 faith-based therapy, **2**:593
 goals, **1**:1
 method, **1**:5
 mindfulness, **1**:2
 origins, **1**:1
 principles, **1**:4–5
 relational frame theory, **1**:1–2
 values-based living, **1**:3–4
Accommodation
 commitment and, **1**:294
 joining and, **2**:931
 Piaget's theory of development, **2**:676
 respect, **3**:1405
Accreditation
 benefits, **1**:367
 CACREP standards, **1**:366–367
 competency-based standards, **1**:312–315
 learning environment, **1**:366
 professional counseling identity, **1**:366
 professional practice, **1**:366–367

Acculturation, 1:5–8
 Asian American families, **1**:77
 cultural identity, **1**:6–7
 culturally sensitive therapies, **2**:712
 defined, **1**:5
 generation gap, **1**:7–8
 levels of, **1**:6
 mental health, **1**:8
 stress associated with, **1**:7, 8
Ackerman, Nathan, **1**:248, 265, **2**:551, 558, **3**:1250, **4**:1446, 1767, 1768, 1773, 1774
Ackerman Institute, **4**:1760, 1768, 1779
ACT. *See* **Acceptance and commitment therapy**
Active listening. *See* **Listening, empathic**
Active Parenting, **3**:1209–1210, **4**:1770
Active Parenting, 1:9–10
Active Parenting program, **2**:757
Activity theory, **2**:840
Acute stress disorder (ASD), **1**:12
Adaptive grieving styles, **1**:151
Adderall, **4**:1625
Addiction, family resource management and, **2**:638
 See also **Alcohol and substance abuse; Compulsive sexual behavior; Gambling, compulsive; Hoarding**
ADHD. *See* Attention-deficit hyperactivity disorder (ADHD)
Adjustment disorder in adolescents, 1:11–14
 diagnostic issues, **1**:11, 12, 14
 overview, **1**:11–12
 symptoms, **1**:12–13
 treatment, **1**:13–14
Adler, Alfred, **1**:9, 15, 176–177, 332, 347, **2**:777–779, 795, 815, 839, 863, **3**:1033, 1191, 1208–1209, **4**:1480, 1561, 1713, 1767–1768, 1769, 1782, 1784
Adlerian family therapy, 1:14–20
 constructivism, **1**:350
 family atmosphere, **1**:16–17
 family constellation, **1**:17–18

individual psychology, **1:**15
initial considerations, **1:**16
mistaken goals, **1:**18–20
open-forum family counseling, **1:**20–23
reorientation, **1:**20
role-playing, **3:**1420
subjective and objective interviews, **1:**16
therapeutic process and assessments, **1:**16–20
typical day assessment, **1:**20, 22
See also **Brief Adlerian couples therapy**
Adlerian open-forum family counseling, 1:20–23
history of, **1:**21
limitations, **1:**23
stages, **1:**22–23
structure, **1:**22
Administration for Children and Families, **2:**771, **3:**1138
Administration for Community Living, **1:**308
Adolescent behavior disorders, 1:23–27, 33
adjustment disorder, **1:**11–14
anxiety disorders, **1:**24
disruptive disorders, **1:**25–26
eating disorders, **1:**26
mood disorders, **1:**24–25
psychotic disorders, **1:**26–27
Adolescent behavior problems, 1:27–30
brain development, **1:**29
conduct disorder, **1:**321–325
environmental context, **1:**30
externalizing behaviors, **2:**582–583
externalizing vs. internalizing, **1:**28
oppositional defiant disorder, **3:**1183–1186
prevention and intervention, **1:**30
theories of behavior development, **1:**28–29
variables affecting behavior, **1:**29–30
Adolescent development
depression, **1:**432–434
parent–adolescent relations, **3:**1210–1211
role-playing, **3:**1420
theories, **1:**28–29
Adolescent Family Life Act, **4:**1556
Adolescent mental health, 1:31–34
brain development, **1:**32
disorders, **1:**33
environmental context, **1:**32
healthy habits, **1:**33
storm-and-stress view, **1:**31
treatment, **1:**33–34
Adolescents
anxiety disorders, **1:**72–75
attachment, **1:**100–102
body dysmorphic disorder, **1:**166–167
brain development, **1:**29, 32
confidentiality in counseling settings, **1:**329

court-mandated clients, **1:**389
defined, **1:**31, 100
depression, **1:**431–432
evidence-based practice, **2:**575
family life cycle stage, **2:**612
family rituals, **2:**640
firesetting, **2:**933–936
friendship, **2:**691
health issues, **2:**759–760
homelessness, **2:**787–790
informed consent, **2:**857–858
intermittent explosive disorder, **2:**882–883
life transitions, **3:**963
mood disorders, **3:**1087–1091
parent–adolescent relations, **3:**1210–1214
pornography, **3:**1260–1261
pregnancy, **3:**1293
prevention research, **3:**1317
school issues, **4:**1581
somatic symptom and related disorders, **4:**1580–1584
statutory rape, **4:**1593–1595
substance use disorders, **4:**1623–1629
teen parenting, **4:**1682–1685
Adoption, 1:34–37
adoptive families, **1:**42–45
birth family issues, **1:**44–45
childless couples, **1:**228
cross-cultural and interracial, **1:**37–41, **4:**1720–1722
history of, **1:**34–35
LGBT, **1:**241
motivations, **1:**36, 43
preparations and adjustments, **1:**36–37, 43–45
same-sex couples, **1:**229
types, **1:**35–36, 43
"upbringing away from parents" as diagnosis, **3:**1382
See also **Foster children; Kinship care**
Adoption, cross-cultural and interracial, 1:37–41, **4:**1720–1722
clinical implications, **1:**41
counseling considerations, **4:**1721–1722
cultural socialization, **1:**39–40
families' experiences, **4:**1721
historical context, **1:**38
overview, **1:**37–38
research findings, **1:**38–39
Adoption and Safe Families Act, **2:**686, 687
Adoptive families, 1:42–45
adoption, **1:**34–37
birth family issues, **1:**44–45
child parent relationship theory, **1:**212
cross-cultural and interracial adoption, **1:**37–41
overview, **1:**42

preparations and adjustments, 1:43–45
resources, 1:45
statistics, 1:42
types, 1:43
Adorno, Theodor, 1:395
ADRESSING model, 1:379
Adult attachment assessments, 1:45–47
Adult Attachment Interview (AAI), 1:46
Adult Attachment Scale (AAS), 1:45–46
Adult Children of Alcoholics, 1:306, 3:1246
Adult development, 1:47–50
  ADHD, 1:118
  attachment, 1:98–99
  attachment and, 1:102–107
  future research, 1:50
  phases, 1:48–50
  theories, 1:47–48
  See also **Individual and family development**
Adult Protective Services, 3:1005
Adults
  family life cycle stage, 2:612
  health issues, 2:760–761
  life transitions, 3:963
  See also Middle adulthood; Older adults; Young adulthood
Affect
  chronic illness with couples and families, 1:244
  integrative couples therapy, 2:868–869
  marriage and family therapy assessment, 1:86
  See also Emotions
Affect regulation, 1:51–54
  biofeedback, 1:53
  cognitive-behavioral therapy, 1:53
  defined, 1:51–52
  dialectical behavior therapy, 1:52–53
  eye movement desensitization and reprocessing, 1:53
  general techniques, 1:54
  process model, 1:52
  regulation theory, 1:52
  See also Emotional regulation
Affective disorders. *See* **Mood disorders in adolescents; Mood disorders in children**
Affective involvement, in families, 2:606
Affective proximity, 2:500
Affective responsiveness, in families, 2:606
Affirmation, words of, 3:995–996
Affordable Care Act, 1:164, 3:1345
African American families, 1:54–57
  socialization, 1:57
  statistics, 1:55
  strengths, 1:55–57
  theories, 1:54
African American Healthy Marriage Initiative, 3:1138

African Americans
  adoption of, 1:38
  child-rearing practices, 3:1362–1363
  education, 1:56
  foster children, 1:56, 3:1361–1364
  kinship bonds, 1:55–56, 2:938
  marriage enrichment, 3:1030
  poverty, 3:1362
  racism, 3:1365–1368
  religion, 1:56
  resilience, 1:55
  teen pregnancy, 3:1293
Age of consent, for sexual intercourse, 4:1594
Ageism, 2:510–511, 3:1412
Agency, of clients, 3:1052
Agency for Healthcare Research and Quality, 2:574
Aggressiveness, 1:80, 2:883
Aging
  process of aging, 1:58
Aging and caregiving, 1:57–60
  benefits of aging, 1:58
  cultural factors, 1:59–60
  hospice, 2:808–811
  kinship care, 1:58–60, 2:938
  need for, 1:59
  See also **Kinship care**
Agoraphobia, 1:70, 73–74
Aholou, Tiffany, 3:1306
AIDS. *See* HIV/AIDS
Ainsworth, Mary, 1:97–98, 104–105, 108, 110–111, 123, 2:523, 897, 3:1233, 1322, 1424
Al-Anon/Alateen, 1:306, 3:1246, 4:1658
Alcohol, 4:1627
Alcohol and substance abuse, 1:61–63
  adolescents, 4:1623–1629
  child maltreatment, 1:210
  dependence vs. abuse, 1:62
  family assessments, 1:61–62
  family dynamics and patterns, 1:62–63, 4:1451–1452
  family of origin, 2:627
  peer counseling, 3:1246
  relationships affected by, 1:63
  reportable offenses, 1:62
  scales, 4:1442
  screening for, 1:381
  12-step programs, 1:306
  See also **Families and substance abuse**
Alcoholic families, 4:1451–1452
Alcoholics Anonymous, 1:306, 3:1246, 4:1627, 1658, 1660
Alexander, James F., 2:697, 3:1188
Allen, Tammy, 1:481
All-or-nothing thinking, 1:278

Allred, G. Hugh, **1**:180
Almeida, Rhea, **2**:664
Alprazolam, **4**:1626
Alprostadil, 2:556
Altruism, **3**:1010
Ambiguous loss, theory of, **2**:749
Ambivalent/resistant attachment, **1**:98, 101, 109, 111
American Academy of Pediatrics, **1**:225
American Association for Marriage and Family Therapy (AAMFT), 1:63–65, 4:1789
   accreditation powers, **1**:314
   Approved Supervisor credential, **1**:271
   approved supervisor designation, **4**:1636–1638
   code of ethics, **1**:266, **3**:1163, 1326, 1394, **4**:1511, 1633–1634, 1636–1638, 1642, 1643, 1705, 1710
   confidentiality guidelines, **1**:328, 485
   core competencies, **1**:356–359, **4**:1710
   duty to warn, **1**:482
   homosexuality policy, **3**:1039, **4**:1544, 1552, 1554
   membership, **1**:64
   multiculturalism, **3**:1116
   professional contributions, **1**:65
   resources and benefits, **1**:64–65
   supervisory guidelines, **4**:1633–1635
American Association for Sex Educators, Counselors, and Therapists, **3**:953
American Association of Christian Counselors, **3**:1030
American Association of Counseling and Development, **1**:313
American Association of Sexuality Educators, Counselors and Therapists (AASECT), **2**:557, **4**:1507, 1509, 1789
American Association of Suicidology, **3**:1150
American Board of Couple and Family Psychology, **4**:1711
American Casualty Company, **4**:1546
American Congress of Obstetricians and Gynecologists, **1**:163
American Counseling Association (ACA), **1**:266, 313, 314, 326, 327, 366, **2**:710, 888, **3**:1116, 1394, **4**:1435, 1544, 1547, 1789
   code of ethics, **2**:564, 568, **3**:1326, **4**:1641–1644, 1646, 1686, 1705
American Family Therapy Academy (AFTA), **4**:1633, 1789
American Group Psychotherapy Association, **4**:1658
American Indians. *See* Native Americans
American Journal of Family Therapy, **4**:1791
American Medical Association, **1**:224
American Mental Health Counselors Association, **3**:1326
American Personnel and Guidance Association (APGA), **1**:313, 366

American Psychiatric Association, **1**:239, 472, **2**:891, **3**:978, 1278–1279, **4**:1435
American Psychological Association, **1**:485, **2**:564, **3**:1266, 1394, **4**:1435, 1633, 1711
   Task Force on Evidence-Based Practices in Psychology, **2**:533
American Society of Group Psychotherapy and Psychodrama, **3**:1421
Amygdala, **2**:898, **3**:1078
Analytic functionalism, **2**:703
Ancient Egyptian culture, **3**:1170
Ancient Greco-Roman culture, **3**:954–955, 1170
Ancient Indian culture, **3**:1170
Andersen, Tom, **3**:969, 1378–1379, **4**:1772, 1779
Anderson, Carol, **2**:661, **4**:1781
Anderson, Harlene, **1**:291, **3**:1268, **4**:1772, 1779
Anger, relationships affected by, **1**:65–67
Anger management, 1:65–68
   complications attending, **1**:68
   strategies, **1**:68
   therapy models, **1**:67–68
Animal-assisted therapy, **2**:552–554
Animals
   filicide, **2**:802–803
   hoarding of, **2**:776
   homosexuality, **4**:1433
Anorexia nervosa, **1**:26, **2**:489, 490
Anorexics and Bulimics Anonymous, **1**:307
Antidepressants, **1**:204, **3**:1090, 1276
Antisocial personality disorder, **1**:321
Anxiety, 1:69–71
   anxiety disorder vs., **1**:69
   causes and risk factors, **1**:69–70
   childhood, **1**:220–222
   defined, **1**:69
   symptoms, **1**:69
   treatment, **1**:71
   types of disorders, **1**:70
Anxiety disorders in adolescents, 1:24, 72–75
   agoraphobia, **1**:73–74
   body dysmorphic disorder, **1**:166–167
   generalized anxiety disorder, **1**:74
   panic disorder, **1**:72
   separation anxiety disorder, **1**:74
   social anxiety disorder, **1**:73
   specific phobia, **1**:72–73
   symptoms, **1**:72
   treatment, **1**:75
   types, **1**:220–222
Anxious attachment. *See* Insecure-anxious attachment
Anxious-avoidant attachment, **1**:111
Anxious-resistant attachment, **1**:111–112, 339, **2**:921
Aponte, Harry, **2**:592–593, **4**:1473, 1774

Appetite, **1:**436
Applied behavior analysis, **1:**132
Appraisal respect, **3:**1404–1405
Appraisal theory of emotion, 2:530–531
Apsche, Jack, **2:**620–621
Aristotle, **2:**702, **3:**954–955
Arnett, Jeffrey Jensen, **1:**48, **3:**963
Arousal regulation, **2:**902
Arredondo, Patricia, **1:**456
Arson. *See* **Juvenile firesetter interventions**
Art, in play family therapy, **3:**1252–1253
Artificial consequences, **1:**323
Artificial insemination, **1:**229, **3:**1291
Asexual Visibility Education Network, **4:**1538
Asexuality, **4:**1538, 1542
Asian American families, 1:76–79
   acculturation, **1:**5–8, 77
   diversity of, **1:**76
   family values, **1:**78
   immigration, **1:**76–77
   intergenerational relationships, **1:**77–78
   model minority myth, **1:**78
   strengths of, **1:**78
   subgroups, **1:**76
   See also **Bilingual families**
Asian and Pacific Islander Healthy Marriage and Family Strengthening Initiative, **3:**1138
Asperger's disorder, **1:**129, 134, **2:**873
Assagioli, Robert, **2:**885
Assertiveness, 1:79–83
   assertiveness training, **1:**81, 144, 284
   clinical applications, **1:**81
   cognitive-behavioral therapy, **1:**80–81
   definition and explanation, **1:**80
   feminist therapy, **1:**81
   techniques, **1:**82–83
   therapeutic approaches, **1:**80–81
Assessment
   adult attachment, **1:**45–47
   family, **2:**602–609
   functional, **2:**692–697
   presentation of problems in, **3:**1312–1313
   procedures, **3:**1313–1314
   See also **Presenting problems**
Assessment, biopsychosocial, 1:83–89, 3:1051
   biological component, **1:**84–86
   components of model, **1:**84
   health behaviors, **1:**85
   immigrants and refugees, **1:**95–96
   psychological component, **1:**86–87
   sexual assessment, **4:**1520
   social component, **1:**87–88
   spiritual component, **1:**88–89

Assessment, suicide, 1:90–93, 3:1150–1151
   action options, **1:**92–93
   considerations in, **1:**91–93
   myths, **1:**90–91
   skills, **1:**90
Assessment system of narrative change, **3:**1137
Assimilation
   acculturation stage of, **1:**6
   cross-cultural and interracial adoption, **1:**39
   Piaget's theory of development, **2:**676
   processes, **1:**94–95
Assimilation: immigrants and refugees, 1:93–96
   clinical principles, **1:**95–96
   defined, **1:**93
   processes, **1:**94–95
Association for Counselor Education and Supervision (ACES), **1:**313, 366
Association for Couples in Marriage Enrichment (ACME), **3:**1028, 1029, 1031–1032, 1033
Association for Death Education and Counseling, **2:**751
Association for Play Therapy (APT), **3:**1326, **4:**1790
Association for Specialists in Group Work, **4:**1657
Association of Marital and Family Therapy Regulatory Board (AMFTRB), **3:**953, **4:**1710, 1789–1790
Assumption of malintent, **1:**364
Asylum-seekers, **1:**94
Atkinson, Brent, **3:**1081
At-risk youth, **1:**308
Attachment, 1:97–100
   adoption, **1:**44
   adult relationships, **1:**45–47
   adulthood, **1:**98–99, 102–107
   Ainsworth's contributions, **1:**97–98, 108
   attunement in relationships, **1:**123
   Bowlby's contributions, **1:**97, 108
   brain and, **1:**115
   changes in, **1:**99, 113
   defined, **1:**97, 102
   evolutionary perspective, **3:**990
   features, **1:**112
   fidelity, **2:**674
   forming, **1:**112
   interpersonal neurobiology, **2:**896–899, 902
   intervention programs, **1:**99–100
   neural development, **2:**898–899
   parenting, **3:**1232–1233
   psychobiology, **3:**1337–1338
   reactive attachment disorder, **2:**897, **3:**1368
   See also **Bonding**
Attachment and adolescents, 1:100–102
Attachment and health, 1:102–104
   interventions, **1:**103–104
   mental health, **1:**103

physical health, **1:**103
social support, **1:**104
Attachment and romantic love, 1:104–107, 113
Attachment anxiety, **1:**98, 106–107
   See also Anxious-resistant attachment; Insecure-anxious attachment
Attachment avoidance, **1:**98, 106–107
   See also Avoidant attachment
Attachment security, **1:**98, 106–107, 116–117
   See also Secure attachment
Attachment styles, 1:108–109
   adult relationships, **1:**45–46
   affect regulation, **1:**51–52
   conflict styles, **1:**339–341
   emotional intelligence, **2:**519–520
   intimacy, **2:**921
   persistence of, **1:**109
   secret-keeping, **4:**1469
   sexual intimacy, **4:**1536
   types, **1:**98, 101, 102, 108–109, 110–112
Attachment theory, 1:110–113
   caregiving, **1:**191
   clinical treatment, **1:**107
   couples and marriage counseling, **1:**381–382
   custody evaluations, **1:**404
   disinhibited social engagement disorder, **1:**453–454
   emotionally focused couples therapy, **2:**523–524
   emotionally focused therapy, **1:**383
   grief, **1:**152
   historical context, **1:**110–111
   interpersonal neurobiology, **2:**897–898, 901, 904
   love, **3:**986
   mother-blaming, **3:**1105
   overview, **1:**104–105, 108
   regulation theory, **1:**52
   restoration therapy, **3:**1406
   romance, **3:**1424
   sex therapy, **4:**1510
   therapy models, **1:**113
Attachment to God Inventory, **4:**1585–1586
Attachment-based family therapy (ABFT), 1:113, **114**–117
   adolescent depression, **1:**443
   attachment intervention, **1:**99–100
   child parent relationship theory, **1:**211–213
   interdependence, **1:**115–116
   intersubjectivity theory, **1:**114
   PACE approach, **1:**116
   safety and security, **1:**115
   secure attachment as goal of, **1:**116–117
   working models of self and others, **1:**116
Attending behaviors, **3:**1157–1158
Attention training, **3:**1082

Attention-deficit and disruptive behavior disorders, 1:117–119
Attention-deficit hyperactivity disorder (ADHD)
   characteristics, **1:**25
   disinhibited social engagement disorder, **1:**454
   externalizing behaviors, **1:**28
   mistaken for behavioral problems, **1:**202
   overview, **1:**118
   prevalence, **1:**117
   symptoms, **1:**118
   treatment, **1:**118
Attention-getting, **1:**19, 22
Attneave, Carolyn, **3:**1142
Attractors, **1:**198
Attributions, **3:**1390
Attunement, clinician, 1:120–122
Attunement in relationships, 1:122–124, **2:**738–739, 905
Australian and New Zealand Journal of Family Therapy, **4:**1791
Authenticity, **3:**1387
Authoritarian parenting
   characteristics, **1:**126, **3:**1236
   child adjustment, **3:**1237–1238
   child-centered parenting, **1:**217
   effectiveness, **1:**127
   emotional intelligence, **2:**520
   parent–adolescent relations, **3:**1213–1214
Authoritarian personality theory, **3:**1367
Authoritative parenting, 1:124–128
   benefits of, **1:**125
   characteristics, **1:**125–126, **3:**1236
   child adjustment, **3:**1237
   child-centered parenting, **1:**217
   effectiveness, **1:**127–128
   emotional intelligence, **2:**520
   family functioning, **1:**124–125
   parent–adolescent relations, **3:**1214
   parenting styles, **1:**125–128
Authority, in worker-client relationship, **1:**390
Autism and children, 1:129–133
   assessment and diagnosis, **1:**131
   causes, **1:**131–132, **3:**1104
   clinical features, **1:**129–130
   defined, **1:**129
   pathophysiology, **1:**132
   related disorders, **1:**130–131
   treatments, **1:**132–133
Autism Diagnostic Interview-Revised (ADI-R), **1:**131
Autism Diagnostic Observation Schedule, Second Edition (ADOS-2), **1:**131
Autism spectrum disorder, 1:129, **134**–137, **2:**873
   background, **1:**134
   causes, **1:**134

communication disorders, 1:298
diagnosis and treatment, 1:136–137
social challenges, 1:233–234
symptoms, 1:134–136
Autobiographies, 2:797
Automatic thoughts, 1:282
Autonomy, as ethical principle, 2:566
Avanafil, 2:556
AVANTA, 4:1772
Aversion therapy, 1:144, 239
Avoidance, 1:137–139
avoidant personality disorder, 1:139
reinforcement theory, 1:139
social and behavioral concepts, 1:137–139
Avoidance contingency, 1:138
Avoidance learning, 1:139
Avoidance of intimacy, 1:138
Avoidant attachment, 1:98, 101, 105, 109, 111, 339, 2:674, 4:1536
See also Attachment avoidance; Fearful attachment
Avoidant couples, 1:139
Avoidant personality disorder, 1:139
Awe, 1:89
Axline, Virginia, 3:1250

Baby blues, 3:1275
Baglivi, Giorgio, 2:489
Balance. *See* Life balance
Balanced bilinguals, 1:159
Bánáthy, Béla, 3:1350
Bandler, Richard, 3:1143–1145
Bandura, Albert, 1:29, 2:536, 795, 815, 840, 3:1211, 4:1783
Banmen, John, 4:1772
Bartholomew, Kim, 2:897
Barton, Allen, 3:1306
Basic self, 1:174
Basson, Rosemary, 2:812, 813, 4:1536
Bateson, Gregory, 1:181–183, 248, 249, 406, 471–472, 2:549, 551, 792, 863, 3:1061, 1067–1068, 1098, 1143, 1346, 1350, 1376, 1379, 4:1463, 1614, 1665–1668, 1676–1678, 1773–1776, 1780
Bateson, Lois, 1:182
Battered person syndrome, 1:199–201
Batterer intervention programs, 1:470
Baucom, D. H., 2:533, 587, 4:1784
Baumrind, Diana, 1:124–127, 3:1209, 1213, 1222, 1236–1238
Bay Area Family Therapy Training Associates, 4:1780
Bayley Scales of Infant and Toddler Development, 4:1438
Beacon Hill Sanitarium, 3:1421
Beall, Anne, 3:987
Bears (sexual identity), 4:1541

Beavers, W. Robert, 4:1443
Beavers Interactional Competence Scale, 2:605
Beavers Interactional Style Scales, 2:605
Beavers systems model, 2:604–605, 4:1443–1445
Beavin, Janet, 1:248
Beck, Aaron T., 1:67, 277, 282, 2:491, 620, 795, 4:1628, 1784
Bedwetting. *See* Enuresis
Behavior, 2:692–693
Behavior Assessment System for Children, 4:1438
Behavior control, in families, 2:606
Behavior modification, 1:204, 323
Behavior therapy, 1:393
Behavior window, 3:1199–1200
Behavioral addictions, 1:318
Behavioral coding, 3:1322–1323
Behavioral couples therapy, 1:277, 386–387, 2:576
Behavioral exchange agreements, 1:284
Behavioral family therapy (BFT), 1:141–145
contracts, 1:144–145
diversity of, 1:145
goals, 1:142
overview, 1:141
resistance to change, 1:145
stages, 1:142–143
substance abuse, 2:600
techniques, 1:143–144
tenets and assumptions, 1:141–142
See also **Cognitive-behavioral family therapy**
Behavioral marital therapy, 2:533
Behavioral scales, 4:1438
Behavioral theory, 3:1105
Behavioral therapy
autism spectrum disorder, 1:136
functional assessment, 2:692–697
supervision theories, 4:1653
See also Cognitive-behavioral therapy (CBT)
Beier-Sternberg Discord Questionnaire, 4:1441
Beliefs and values, 1:146–148
complexity of, 1:146–147
culture, 1:147, 148
death and dying, 2:810
decision-making, 1:427
ethics, 2:566
family culture, 2:845
family of origin, 2:627–628
importance of, 1:147
individual behavior related to, 1:147–148
Latino families, 3:941–942, 943–944
marriage-friendly, 3:1042
multicultural competence, 3:1110–1113
nature of, 1:146
neutrality, 3:1145–1147
personal, 1:148

quality time, **1:**376–377
rural families, **3:**1431
socioeconomic status, **4:**1574
values defined, **4:**1704–1705
See also **Family values; Religion; Spirituality; Therapists' values**
Bell, John, **1:**265, **4:**1769
Belonging, **1:**237
Beneficence, as ethical principle, **2:**566
Benjamin Standards of Care, **2:**718
Bennett, Linda, **3:**1415, 1417
Benzodiazepines, **1:**71, **3:**1090
Bereavement, 1:148–151
 coping, **1:**150–151
 factors in, **1:**148–149
 family impact, **1:**151
 reactions, **1:**149
 theories of grief and mourning, **1:**149–150
 See also **Loss**
Bereavement counseling, 1:152–156
 complicated grief, **2:**750
 conceptual approaches, **1:**152–153
 dual process model, **2:**749
 family systems, **1:**155–156
 multicultural aspects, **1:**152
 Rando's phase theory, **1:**153–154
 Whiting's developmental approach, **1:**154–155
 Worden's tasks of grief, **1:**154, **2:**749
 See also **Grief counseling**
Berg, Cynthia, **1:**244
Berg, Insoo Kim, **1:**181, 271, **3:**969, 1086, 1268, **4:**1448, 1575–1576, 1773, 1777–1778, 1782
Berger, Peter L., **4:**1567, 1568
Bergh, Henry, **1:**214
Bernard, Janine, **4:**1656
Bernet, William, **3:**1220
Berry, John, **1:**6
Bertalanffy, Ludwig von, **1:**248, **2:**503, 727, 791, 840–841, **3:**1059, 1098, 1262, 1350, **4:**1463, 1676, 1775
Bertillon, Jacques, **2:**891
Bertillon Classification of Causes of Death, **2:**891
Best interests of the child, 1:156–158, 404, **3:**945
BFT. *See* **Behavioral family therapy (BFT)**
Bias, therapist's, **4:**1705
Bibliotherapy, **2:**797, **4:**1487, 1488–1489
Bien, Thomas, **1:**311
Big Brothers Big Sisters, **1:**308
Bigamy, **3:**1258
Bilingual families, 1:159–161
 benefits and barriers, **1:**160–161
 characteristics, **1:**159–160
 forms of bilingualism, **1:**159
 implications for therapists, **1:**161

 Latino families, **3:**942
 multicultural considerations, **1:**161
 parentification, **3:**1229–1230
 socialization, **1:**160
Binet, Alfred, **4:**1436–1437
Binge eating disorder, **2:**489, 490
Bioecological systems theory, **2:**492–495
Biofeedback, **1:**53
Biopsychosocial model. *See* **Assessment, biopsychosocial**
Biopsychosocial-spiritual sensitivity, **1:**83–89, **3:**1051–1052, 1053–1054
Bipolar disorder, **3:**1089, 1090, 1093
Birchler, Timothy, **2:**598
Bird, Mark, **2:**587
Birdwhistell, Ray, **4:**1768
Birth, rituals associated with, **3:**994
Birth control and contraception, 1:162–165
 history of, **1:**162–163
 politics, **1:**163–164
 relationship issues, **1:**165
 religious/moral issues, **1:**163, **4:**1552–1553
 types, **1:**164–165
Birth order, **1:**17–18, 175, 178, 332, **2:**608, 842, **4:**1562–1563
Bisexuals, **4:**1542
 See also **LGBT community; LGBT families**
Bitter, J. R., **1:**19, **4:**1769
Black, Leora, **2:**664
Blaming, **1:**278, 301, **2:**817, **3:**1104–1107
Blatner, Adam, **3:**1422
Blatt, Sidney J., **1:**296
Blended families. *See* **Stepfamilies**
Blumer, Herbert, **4:**1662
Blustein, David L., **1:**190
Board Certified Art Therapists, **3:**953
Body
 Gestalt family therapy, **2:**740
 love, **3:**979–984
 nudity, **3:**1168–1171
 physiological data, **3:**1323–1324
 somatic symptom and related disorders, **4:**1580–1584
Body dysmorphic disorder in adolescents, 1:166–167
Body language, **3:**966, 1158
Bondage, discipline, sadism, masochism (BDSM) and dominance/submission practices, **2:**670, 671
Bonding, 1:168–170
 See also **Attachment**
Borge, Victor, **1:**377–378
Boscolo, Luigi, **3:**1068, 1071, 1359, 1376, **4:**1666–1669, 1776
Boss, Pauline, **1:**422, **2:**646, 749
Bossard, James H. S., **3:**1047

Bossard's Law, 3:1046–1047
Boszormenyi-Nagy, Ivan, 1:351, 354, 355, 2:546, 548, 878–879, 3:1059, 1334, 1373, 4:1718, 1719, 1767, 1768–1769
Boundaries, 1:171–172
   boundary-making interventions, 4:1618
   confrontation, 1:344
   family system, 2:766, 3:1099, 1102, 4:1616
   nudity, 3:1169
   respect, 3:1405
   sexual relationships with clients, 4:1545–1549
   systems theory, 2:729, 4:1671–1673
   torture, 4:1707–1708
   types, 2:766
Boundaryless career paths, 1:190
Bowen, Murray, 1:18, 63, 125, 172–177, 248, 265, 332, 382, 421–422, 448–449, 2:558, 704–705, 734, 841, 868, 3:1059, 1064, 1251, 1334, 4:1457, 1471–1472, 1537, 1677, 1691, 1718–1719, 1741, 1769, 1770, 1772, 1782
Bowen family systems theory, 1:172–176, 4:1770
   couples and marriage counseling, 1:382
   differentiation, 1:448–449
   family assessment, 2:608–609
   family of origin, 2:628–629
   genograms, 1:176, 2:734
   individual and family development, 2:841–843
   interventions, 1:175–176
   major concepts, 1:174–175
   metaphors used in, 3:1064
   psychoanalytic roots, 3:1334
   school settings, 4:1457
   sex therapy, 4:1510
   theoretical foundations, 1:173–174
   transgenerational family therapy, 4:1718–1719
   triangulation, 4:1739
Bowen intergenerational therapy
   case conceptualization, 1:258
Bowers v. Hardwick, 3:1038
Bowlby, John, 1:97, 101, 104–105, 108, 110–113, 114, 123, 152, 169, 381, 383, 421, 2:523, 580, 868, 897, 3:986, 1105, 1173, 1208, 1211, 1232, 1337, 1424, 4:1536, 1743, 1769
Brademas, John, 1:208
Brain
   adolescent development, 1:29, 32, 3:1212
   aging and, 1:58
   attachment and, 1:115
   holism, 2:779
   imago relationship therapy, 2:827–828
   interpersonal neurobiology, 2:896–907
   love, 3:979–983, 989–990
   mind distinguished from, 2:901, 905
   mindfulness, 3:1078

   plasticity, 1:274, 275, 2:897, 901, 905, 3:979
   regulation theory, 1:52
   triune model of, 1:173–174
   See also Neuroscience
Brain fog, 1:149
Branden, Nathaniel, 4:1480
Braverman, Lois, 2:661
Breakups. *See* **Dating relationship dissolution**
Brehm, Jack, 3:1192
Brief Adlerian couples therapy, 1:176–181
   basic tenets, 1:177–179
   interventions, 1:180
   stages, 1:179–180
   See also **Adlerian family therapy**
Brief family therapy, 1:181–186
   history, 1:181–182
   hypnosis, 2:822
   number of sessions, 1:184
   organizing principles, 1:182–183
   therapeutic practices, 1:183–186
Brief Family Therapy Center, 4:1773, 1777
Brief strategic family therapy, 2:575
Brief Therapy Project, 4:1760, 1772
Briere, John, 3:1280
Brodzinsky, David, 1:44
Brok, Albert, 1:274
Broken-record technique, 1:82
Bronfenbrenner, Urie, 1:124, 248–249, 389, 2:492–494, 504, 840
Brown, Elliot C., 2:779
Brumberg, Joan Jacobs, 2:489
Brüne, Martin, 2:779
Bruner, Jerome, 4:1778
Brunner, Heidi, 2:807
Bryan, Julia, 1:307
Buber, Martin, 1:354, 2:591, 827, 878
Buddha (Siddhartha Gautama), 1:347
Buddhism, 2:593, 3:955, 1076–1077, 1080, 1083
Buhler, Charlotte, 2:839
Building metaphors, 3:1066
Bulimia nervosa, 1:26, 2:489, 490
Bullying, 2:691, 911
Bumberry, William, 4:1771
Burdette, Amy, 3:1397
Burgess, Ernest, 1:193, 4:1662
Burns, David, 4:1628
Burton, Mark, 2:849
Busby, Dean, 4:1533
Bush, George W., 1:163, 2:939, 3:1138
Business cards, 3:1289
Business plan, 3:1288
Butch lesbians, 4:1434, 1540
Butler, Christopher C., 3:1109
Butler, Mark, 2:587

Butler, Robert, 2:510
Butterfly effect, 1:196, 197–198, 201
Byng-Hall, John, 2:623–624
Byrne, Donn, 3:1046

CACREP. See Council for Accreditation for Counseling and Related Educational Programs (CACREP)
Caffeine, 4:1625
Caldera, Yvonne, 2:764
Calvo, Gabriel, 3:1025, 1028
Campbell, David, 4:1669
Cancian, Francesca, 3:987
Cantril, Hadley, 4:1448
Caplan, Paula, 3:1105
Capra, Fritjof, 4:1675
CAPTA Reauthorization Act, 1:208
Career construction, 1:190
Career paths, 1:190
Career planning and couples/families, 1:187–190
    career construction and transition, 1:189
    meaning of work, 1:189–190
    work stressors, 1:187–189
Caregivers, 1:191–192
    cultural considerations, 1:192
    hospice, 2:809–810
    marriage and family therapy considerations, 1:192
    primary, 1:101
    stressors, 1:191–192
    transitions of, 1:191
Caregiving
    aging and, 1:58–60, 2:938
    bonding, 1:170
    workforce engaged in, 1:58
Carkhuff, Robert, 1:9
Carlson, Jon, 1:180, 3:1033, 4:1461, 1713, 1770, 1785
Carnes, Patrick, 1:319
Carolina Abecedarian Project, 3:1401
Carr, Alan, 4:1588, 1591–1593
Carroll, Lewis, *Alice in Wonderland*, 1:295
Carson, David, 4:1785
Carter, Betty, 2:611, 661, 662, 664, 916, 3:942, 1211, 4:1678, 1759–1760, 1770, 1781
Carter, Nick, 3:1234
Casado-Kehoe, Montserrat, 4:1785
Case conceptualization. *See* Clinical case conceptualization with couples and families
Cass identity model, 3:947
Catastrophizing, 1:278
Catharsis, 3:1010
Catherine of Siena, Saint, 2:489
Catholic Church
    birth control, 1:162, 163, 4:1553
    Latino families, 3:942–943
    marriage, 3:1037
    marriage education, 3:1025, 1028
Causal exclusion problem, 2:704
Cause and effect
    circular, 1:142, 2:602, 3:1100, 1102–1103, 1376, 4:1465–1466
    circularity, 1:248, 406–407
    reciprocal, 2:598
Caverject, 2:556
CBT. *See* **Cognitive-behavioral therapy (CBT)**
CD. *See* **Conduct disorder (CD)**
Cecchin, Gianfranco, 3:1068, 1071, 1359, 1376, 4:1666–1669, 1776
Center for Children, Families and the Law, Hofstra University School of Law, 1:466
Center for Family Learning, 4:1760
Center for Therapeutic Assessment, 4:1693
Centering, 1:89
Centers for Disease Control and Prevention, 1:208, 224, 307, 3:1314
Centers for Medicare and Medicaid Services, 2:892
Certification. *See* **Licensure and certification**
Certified Emotionally Focused Therapists, 3:953
Certified family life educator, 1:193–196
    certification requirements, 1:193–194, 2:614–615
    code of ethics, 1:195–196
    content area, 2:615
    differentiation, 2:608
    employment settings, 1:194–195
    history and purpose, 1:193
    research, 1:196
    See also **Family life educators**
Chamberlain, Patricia, 2:688
Change. *See* **First-order change**
Chaos family therapy, 1:196–201
    applications of chaos theory, 1:200–201
    battered person syndrome, 1:199–201
    butterfly effect, 1:201
    chaos theory principles, 1:196–199
Chaos theory, 1:196–199
Chapman, Gary, 3:995
Charity, 3:989
Chaucer, Geoffrey, 4:1685
Chemistry, of love, 3:982–984
Chen, Ji-Kang, 3:1224
Child abuse. *See* **Child maltreatment**
Child Abuse and Prevention Act, 2:687
Child Abuse Prevention and Treatment Act (CAPTA), 1:208, 215
Child and Youth Resilience Measure, 3:1401
Child Behavior Checklist, 4:1438
Child behavior problems, 1:202–205
    assessment, 1:203–204
    behavior modification, 1:204

conduct disorder, **1**:321–325
family systems approaches, **1**:204
natural and logical consequences, **1**:205
oppositional defiant disorder, **3**:1183–1186
overview, **1**:202–203
pharmacological interventions, **1**:204–205
risk factors, **1**:203
treatment, **1**:203–205
Child care, **1**:481
Child custody
evaluations, **1**:403–406
forensics, **1**:369–370, **3**:945–946
legal vs. physical, **3**:945
parental alienation syndrome, **3**:1218–1221
rights and responsibilities, **3**:945–946
single-parent families, **4**:1565
types, **1**:405
Child development
parental stress, **3**:1224–1225
posttraumatic stress disorder, **3**:1280
reactive attachment disorder, **3**:1370
research, **1**:206–207
role-playing, **3**:1420
self-esteem, **4**:1480, 1483–1484
Child FIRST program, **2**:782
Child Guidance Clinics, **1**:207, **4**:1614, 1769
Child guidance movement, 1:205–207
Child maltreatment, 1:207–210
Child Protective Services, **1**:213–216
Children's Bureau, **1**:207–208
defined, **1**:208
effects of, **1**:210
family preservation, **1**:389
incest, **2**:835–838
laws, **1**:208
mandates for reporting, **3**:1004–1006
overview, **1**:207
reactive attachment disorder, **3**:1369
risk factors, **1**:209–210, **3**:1006
sexual abuse, **4**:1514
treatment, **2**:910
types, **1**:208–209, **2**:908–910
unreported, **1**:210
Child parent relationship theory, 1:211–213
Child Protective Services, 1:208, 213–216, 3:1004
Child Welfare League of America, **1**:38
Childbirth, bonding after, **1**:169–170
Child-centered parenting, 1:216–219
characteristics, **1**:218–219
child parent relationship theory, **1**:211–213
criticisms of, **1**:219
parenting styles, **1**:217–218
Child-centered play therapy, **1**:211–213, **3**:1250–1254

Childhood anxiety, 1:220–222
overview, **1**:220
treatment, **1**:222
types, **1**:220–222
Childhood Autism Rating Scale, Second Edition (CARS-2), **1**:131
Childhood disintegrative disorder, **1**:134, **2**:873
Childhood obesity, prevention and treatment of, 1:223–226
consequences, **1**:223
family systems, **1**:225
measurement of, **1**:224
medical family therapy, **1**:225–226
prevalence, **1**:223–224
prevention and treatment, **1**:224
Childhood-onset fluency disorder, **1**:298
Childless couples, 1:227–229
infertility, **2**:850–854
involuntarily, **1**:227–228
voluntarily, **1**:228–229
Children
acculturation, **1**:7–8
Active Parenting, **1**:9
adoption, **1**:34–37, **4**:1720–1722
African Americans, **1**:57
autism, **1**:129–133
boundary development, **1**:171
confidentiality in counseling settings, **1**:329
deceased, parents of, **1**:417–420
depression, **1**:435–438
disinhibited social engagement disorder, **1**:452–454
divorce and separation, **1**:465
elimination disorders, **2**:511–513
emotional intelligence, **2**:517–520
externalizing behaviors, **2**:582–583
family life cycle stage, **2**:611–612
family rituals, **2**:640, 641
family substance abuse effects on, **1**:63
firesetting, **2**:933–936
foster children, **2**:686–689
functional assessment, **2**:692–697
health issues, **2**:759–760
homicide, **2**:801–803
immigrant families, **2**:833
informed consent, **2**:857–858
intergenerational relationships, **1**:77–78
kinship care, **2**:937–939
life transitions, **3**:962–963, 964
military families, **3**:1074
mindfulness, **3**:1080–1081
mood disorders, **3**:1091–1094
non–rapid eye movement sleep arousal disorders, **3**:1153–1155
nonresidential fathers, **3**:1156–1157

nudity, 3:1169
parent–child communication, 3:1226–1227
parentified, 1:63, 354, 3:1227–1231
pedophilic disorder, 3:1195
postpartum depression's impact, 3:1276
posttraumatic stress disorder, 3:1277–1281
poverty, 2:595
prevention research, 3:1317
psychoeducation, 3:1343
reactive attachment disorder, 1:453–454, 2:897, 3:1368–1371
resilience, 3:1401
rights, 3:946
rule-setting, 3:1426–1429
scales, 4:1436–1439
self-esteem, 4:1482–1486
single-parent families, 4:1566
stress management, 4:1610
trauma, 4:1723–1725
See also Adolescents; Birth order; Special-needs children; Stepchildren

Children with chronic illness, 1:229–232, 2:760
causes, 1:230
common illnesses, 1:229–230
emotional challenges, 1:233
family considerations, 1:230–231
parental stress, 3:1224
psychological and developmental impact, 1:230
treatment, 1:231–232

Children with special needs in family therapy, 1:232–235
administrative challenges, 1:234–235
counseling considerations, 1:235
definitions, 1:232
education, 1:234–235
emotional challenges, 1:233
social challenges, 1:233–234
types of families, 1:233

Children's Bureau, 1:207–208, 214
Children's Healthcare of Atlanta, 1:307
Chimpanzees, 3:1373
China
in-law relationships, 2:860
kinship care, 2:938

Choice theory and reality therapy, 1:236–238
faith-based therapy, 2:592
integrative approach, 2:865–866
quality time, 1:374–376
relationship habits, 1:236
WDEP system, 1:375–376

Chosen families, 1:239–242
conceptions of the family, 1:241–242
response to LGBT stigma, 1:239–241
See also **Adoptive families**

Christensen, Andrew, 4:1784
Christensen, Oscar, 1:21, 4:1769
Christianity
emotionally focused therapy, 1:68
hope-focused approach, 2:805

Chronic illness with couples and families, 1:242–245
clinician guidelines, 1:243–245
prevalence, 1:242
responses to, 1:242–243
shared character of, 1:244–245
See also **Children with chronic illness**

Chronosystem, 2:494–495, 497
Church of Jesus Christ of Latter-Day Saints, 3:1259
Cialis, 2:556, 4:1511
Cinematherapy, 1:245–247
Circular causality
behavioral family therapy, 1:142
cybernetics, 1:406–407, 3:1376
family assessment models, 2:602
morphogenesis, 3:1100
morphostasis, 3:1102–1103
second-order family therapy, 4:1465–1466
systems theory, 1:248
Circular questions, 1:252, 263–264, 3:1071, 1146, 1359, 1377, 4:1667

Circularity and linearity, 1:247–252
both/and approach, 1:250–251
complementary relationships, 1:250
couples and family therapy applications, 1:252
defining, 1:247
eco-maps, 2:496
feminist critiques, 1:250
first- and second-order family therapy, 4:1464, 1465–1466
general systems theory, 1:248–249
limitations, 1:251
Milan systemic approaches, 3:1070
recursiveness vs. circularity, 3:1375
symmetrical relationships, 1:249
systemic family therapy, 4:1667
systems theory, 4:1676–1677
See also Circular causality

Circumcision, 3:994
Circumplex model, 1:253–255
clinical applications, 1:255
cohesion, 1:253–254, 287–288
components, 1:253–254, 303, 2:603
couple and family maps, 3:1308
family assessment, 2:602–604
family stress, 2:647–648
research applications, 1:254–255
scales, 4:1441, 1445–1446
strengths-based approach, 2:644

Cisgender, 2:723, 4:1715
Civil unions, 3:1036–1040
Clarification, 2:622
Class. *See* Socioeconomic status
Class jumpers, 4:1573–1574
Classical conditioning, 2:528, 3:1204, 4:1783
Client-centered therapy, 2:577, 3:1199, 4:1688
Clinical case conceptualization with couples and families, 1:256–260
   diagnosis, 1:259–260
   diversity of, 1:259
   interaction patterns, 1:256–259
   overview, 1:256
   practice contexts, 1:260
   theory-specific, 1:257–258
Clinical interviews with couples and families, 1:260–264
   clinical applications, 1:263
   initial session, 1:262–263
   key concepts, 1:261
   questions, 1:263–264
   scale selection, 4:1438
   telephone interviews, 1:262
   theoretical considerations, 1:261–262
   value of, 1:260
Clinical practice, 1:264–267
   assessment and diagnosis, 1:266
   education, 1:265–266
   elements of, 1:266–267
   ethics, 1:266
   history and development, 1:264–265
   licensure, 1:265–266
   major concepts and theories, 1:265
   professional issues, 1:265–266
   therapy process, 1:266–267
Clinical Rating Scale (CRS), 2:603–604, 4:1441
Clinical versus statistical significance, 1:267–270
   history and importance of clinical significance, 1:269
   psychotherapy discipline, 1:267–268
   research recommendations, 1:269–270
   types of statistical significance, 1:268–269
Clinician attunement. *See* Attunement, clinician
Clinician-directed, solution-focused supervision, 1:270–273
   clinician needs, 1:271–272
   deconstructive meaning-making, 1:272–273
   self-supervision, 1:273
   strengths-based approach, 1:272
   supervision process, 1:272
Clinton, Bill, 2:600, 3:1038, 1138
Clonazepam, 4:1626
Clore, Gerald L., 3:1046
Closed adoptions, 1:35, 43, 45

Closed questions, 3:1358
Closeness, in couple/family relationships, 3:1309
Coalition for Marriage, Family and Couples Education, 3:1027, 1029, 1030, 1033
Co-Anon, 1:307
Cocaine, 4:1625
Cochrane, Archibald, 2:573
Code of Federal Regulations, Title 42, 3:1394
Codeine, 4:1626
Codependence, 2:599
Codes of ethics. *See* Ethical codes
Cognitive defusion, 1:4–5
Cognitive development, 1:29
Cognitive distortions, 1:278, 279
Cognitive maps and couples, 1:274–276
   neuroscience, 1:274
   pain and peace cycles, 1:274–276
   therapeutic applications, 1:276
Cognitive processing therapy, 4:1518
Cognitive therapy, 1:282
Cognitive-behavioral conjoint therapy for posttraumatic stress disorder, 4:1708–1709
Cognitive-behavioral couples therapy (CBCT), 1:258, 277–281
   applications, 1:277–279
   couples and marriage counseling, 1:382
   evidence-based practice, 2:576
   example, 1:280–281
   history of, 1:277
   interventions, 1:280
   limitations, 1:281
   overview, 1:277
   process of, 1:279–280
   therapist role, 1:280
Cognitive-behavioral family therapy (CBFT), 1:281–285
   assessment methods, 1:283
   diversity, 1:285
   goals and treatment planning, 1:284
   history, 1:282, 4:1784
   key concepts, 1:282–283
   overview, 1:261, 281
   process, 1:283
   techniques and interventions, 1:284–285
   therapist role, 1:285
   See also Behavioral family therapy
Cognitive-behavioral therapy (CBT)
   adjustment disorder, 1:13
   adolescent anxiety disorders, 1:24
   affect regulation, 1:53
   anger management, 1:67
   anxiety, 1:71

assertiveness, 1:80–81
child sexual abuse, 2:910
conduct disorder, 1:323–324
crisis intervention, 1:393
depression in couples and families, 1:443
eating disorders, 2:491
empirically validated models, 2:533
evidence-based practice, 2:575, 4:1782
faith-based therapy, 2:591–593
female orgasmic disorder, 2:656
historical development, 4:1783–1784
homework assignments, 2:795
integrative approach, 2:864–865
intermittent explosive disorder, 2:883
life events, 3:960
mindfulness, 3:1083
mood disorders, 3:1090
overview, 1:282, 4:1650–1651
postpartum depression, 3:1276
posttraumatic stress disorder, 3:1281
relational frame theory vs, 1:1
sexual dysfunction, 4:1523
somatic symptom disorder, 4:1581
substance use disorders, 4:1628
suicide, 4:1632
supervision theories, 4:1653–1654
trauma, 4:1725, 1728, 1731–1734
Cognitive-processing therapy, 4:1515
Cohabitation, 3:1020
See also Civil unions
Cohen, Judith, 4:1730
Cohesion, 1:286–288
circumplex model, 1:253–254, 287–288, 2:603, 4:1445
defining, 1:286–287
enmeshment as distinct from, 1:288
family, and schizophrenia, 4:1454
family systems perspective, 1:286–288
overview, 1:286
See also Social cohesion
Colapinto, Jorge, 4:1774
Collaborative couples therapy, 1:289–290
Collaborative divorce, 1:406, 466
Collaborative language systems, 1:291–293
overview and concepts, 1:291
therapist role, 1:292
therapy process, 1:292
uses, 1:292–293
Colleagues, 1:87–88
Collectivistic cultures, 2:651–653
Collins, Nancy L., 1:46
Combs, Gene, 4:1780
Coming of age, 3:994
Coming out, 3:947–948

Commission on Accreditation for Marriage and Family Therapy Education (COAMFTE), 1:65, 314, 2:688, 889–890, 3:950–954, 1116, 4:1643–1644, 1709–1712, 1790
Commitment, 1:293–294
commitment framework, 1:294
common behaviors, 1:294
intimacy, 2:920–921
investment model, 1:294
love, 3:984, 987
relationship enhancement, 3:1391
social exchange theory, 1:293–294
See also **Acceptance and commitment therapy**
Common factors, 1:295–296, 2:534, 3:1354
Commonwealth Fund, 1:207
Communication
autism, 1:129
circumplex model, 1:254, 288, 2:603
components, 2:603
cybernetics, 3:1376
dysfunctional stances, 1:300–301, 2:580, 817
experiential family therapy, 2:580
history and culture, 2:812–814
humanistic family therapy, 2:817
intimacy, 2:920
listening, 3:965–968
marital distress, 3:1007–1008
McMaster model of family functioning, 2:605–606
nonverbal, 3:1157–1161
parent–child, 3:1226–1227
power issues, 3:1286
premarital counseling, 3:1297–1298
privileged, therapist-client, 2:567–568
punctuation, 3:1346
relationship enhancement, 3:1392
respect, 3:1405
skills, 2:540
spatial relations in, 3:1159
strategic family therapy, 4:1604–1605
styles, 3:1297–1298
systems theory, 2:728
Communication disorders, 1:297–298
types, 1:297–298
Communication errors/problems in couples and families, 1:299–301
collaborative language systems, 1:292
communication styles, 1:299
family atmosphere, 1:17
Gottman's flawed patterns, 1:300
nonverbal, 1:301
premarital counseling, 3:1297–1298
Satir's communication stances, 1:300–301
verbal, 1:300–301

Communication in couples and families,
    1:302–305
  chronic illness with couples and families, 1:244
  cohesion model, 1:254
  conflict resolution, 1:332–333
  cultural influences, 1:304–305
  effective and supportive, 1:303–304
  factors affecting, 1:304
  family life cycle, 1:305
  family systems perspective, 1:302–304
  solution-focused therapy, 1:333
  sources of differences, 1:303
  transactional perspective, 1:302–303
  types, 1:302–303
Communication normalization, 3:1120
Communication stances, 1:300–301, 2:580, 817
Community
  adolescent development, 1:30
  marriage and family therapy assessment, 1:88
  school-family-community partnerships,
    4:1457–1459
Community development programs, 1:307
Community feeling, 1:21
Community Fund, 1:207
Community Mental Health Act, 1:305
Community programs, 1:305–308
  rationale, 1:305–306
  types, 1:306–308
Community reinforcement approach, 2:789
Community systems model, 1:393
Companioning, 2:751
Compassion, 1:309–312
  compassion fatigue, 1:312
  counselors, 1:311–312
  defined, 1:309
  empathy, 1:310–311
  for oneself, 1:310
  insight, 1:310
  mindfulness, 1:310, 3:1082–1083, 1085–1086
  opposite of, 1:311
  overview, 1:309
  understanding distress, 1:309–310
Compassion fatigue, 4:1476
Compersion, 3:1180
Competency-based standards for marriage, couple,
    and family counseling, 1:312–315
  accreditation, certification, and licensure
    compared, 1:315
  accreditation options, 1:313–314
  history of CACREP, 1:312–313
  programs, 1:314–315
  standards and core content areas, 1:314–315
  See also **Core competencies for marriage and family
    therapists**

Complementary and symmetrical relationships,
    1:249–250, **316–317**, 4:1604
Complicated grief, 2:750
Complicated loss, 3:978
Compulsive Eaters Anonymous, 1:307
Compulsive sexual behavior, 1:317–320
  characteristics, 1:318
  diagnosis and treatment, 1:318–320
Comstock Act, 1:162
Concentration meditation, 3:1077
Concurrent therapy, 1:362–363
Conduct disorder (CD), 1:118–119, **321–325**
  characteristics, 1:25, 321
  classification of, 1:118
  diagnosis, 1:321
  externalizing behaviors, 1:28
  manifestation, 1:321–322
  oppositional defiant disorder compared to,
    1:321, 322, 3:1184
  parent management training, 3:1203
  risk factors, 1:322
  treatments, 1:322–325
Confidentiality, 1:325–329
  breaches, 1:327, 483
  couple and family counseling, 1:327–328, 2:567
  duty to warn, 1:482–485
  ethical considerations, 2:567–568
  exceptions, 1:326–327, 3:1004
  forensics, 1:371
  group family therapy, 2:755–756
  group settings, 1:328–329
  home-based therapy, 2:783
  information qualifying for, 1:326
  minors, 1:329
  no-secrets contracts, 3:1163
  overview, 1:325
  progress notes, 1:329
  release of information, 3:1393–1395
  research, 1:329
  supervision contracts, 4:1646–1647
  therapist's knowledge concerning, 1:482–484
  See also **No-secrets contracts; Secrets**
Conflict in couples and families, 1:330–333
  communication, 1:332–333
  contracts, 4:1699
  family dynamics, 1:330
  good, 3:1387
  models for understanding and resolving, 1:331–333
  sources, 1:334
  stages, 1:332
  transitions, 1:331
Conflict resolution, 1:334–338
  conflict styles, 1:334–335
  interpersonal skills, 1:336–338

intrapersonal skills, 1:335–336
premarital counseling, 3:1299
sources of conflict, 1:334
Conflict styles, 1:338–341
anxious, 1:339, 341
attachment theory, 1:339–341
avoidant, 1:339–340, 341
conflict resolution, 1:334–335
overview, 1:338–339
Conflicts of interest, 1:478
Conformity
cultural identity development, 1:6
family culture, 2:846
Confrontation, 1:342–344
boundary setting, 1:344
common discrepancies, 1:342–343
crucible situations, 1:399
ethical considerations, 1:344
immediacy, 1:343–344
importance of, 1:342
process of, 1:343
resistance, 1:344
Confucianism, 3:955
Congruent communication, 2:817
Conjoint family therapy, 1:345–346, 3:965
Conjugal Relationship Enhancement program, 3:1028
Connectedness, 1:287
Connolly, Mary McCormack, 1:214
Connor-Davidson Resilience Scale, 3:1401
Consensual nonexclusive relationships. *See* Nonmonogamy
Conservation of resources theory, 2:521
Constructive entitlement, 2:547
Constructivism, 1:346–351
clinical techniques, 1:350–351
counseling considerations, 1:349–351
epistemology, 3:1375
epistemology in family therapy, 2:550
family therapy, 3:1347
foundations, 1:347–348
overview, 1:346–347
Piaget's theory, 2:840
postmodern therapies, 2:550, 3:1270
radical, 3:1144
supervision theories, 4:1654
theoretical assumptions, 1:348–349
See also **Social constructionism**
Containment, 3:1175
Contemporary Family Therapy (journal), 4:1791
Contempt, 1:300, 331, 2:746
Contextual family therapy, 1:351–355
conceptualization and major constructs, 1:352–354
contemporary applications, 1:355
entitlement, 2:546–548

first-order family therapy, 4:1464
foundations, 1:351–352
horizontal and vertical relationships, 2:546
intergenerational loyalty, 2:878
interventions, 1:354–355
psychoanalytic roots, 3:1334–1335
transgenerational family therapy, 4:1719
Contingency contracting, 1:145, 284, 4:1698
Continuing bonds theory, 1:150
Contraception. *See* **Birth control and contraception**
Contracts
behavioral family therapy, 1:144–145
contingency, 1:145, 284, 4:1698
divorce and separation counseling, 1:460
no-harm, 1:93, 3:1148–1153, 4:1698
no-secrets, 3:1162–1165
prenuptial agreements, 3:1303–1305
supervision, 4:1645–1647
therapeutic, 4:1696–1700
Control system theory, 2:865
Conversion disorder, 4:1583
Conversion therapy, 4:1039, 1435, 1544, 1553–1554
Cooking metaphors, 3:1066
Cooley, Charles Horton, 4:1662
Cooperative Discipline, 4:1770
Coparenting, 1:370, 2:764, 4:1683
Coping
bereavement, 1:150–151
loss, 3:978
parental acceptance-rejection theory, 3:1216–1217
reactive, 1:275
sexual assault, 4:1516
trauma-focused cognitive-behavioral therapy, 4:1732
Core competencies for marriage and family therapists, 1:356–359
admission to treatment, 1:357
clinical assessment and diagnosis, 1:357–358
legal issues, ethics, and standards, 1:358–359
overview, 1:356–357
research and program evaluation, 1:359
therapeutic interventions, 1:358
treatment planning and case management, 1:358
See also **Competency-based standards for marriage, couple, and family counseling**
Corey, Gerald, 2:752, 754
Corporal punishment, 2:909
Correlational designs, 2:532
Corsini, Ray, 1:21
Cost allocation, 1:360
Cost-benefit analysis, 1:359–362
commitment, 1:293–294
components, 1:361
cost allocation, 1:360
cost-effectiveness, 1:360–361

criticisms of, **1:**362
overview, **1:**359
uses, **1:**361–362
See also **Outcome research**
Cost-effectiveness, **1:**360–361
Cotherapy team, 1:362–365
challenges, **1:**363–364
rationale, **1:**363
supervision process, **3:**970, 971
techniques and practice issues, **1:**364–365
Council for Accreditation of Counseling and Related Educational Programs (CACREP), **1:**365–367, **4:**1790
accreditation standards, **1:**366–367
benefits of accreditation, **1:**367
competency-based standards, **1:**312–315
establishment of, **1:**366
foster care, **2:**688
licensure and certification, **2:**889–890, **3:**950–954
programs offered, **4:**1711
supervision, **4:**1643–1644
Council for Higher Education Accreditation (CHEA), **1:**366
Council on Rehabilitation Education (CORE), **1:**313
Council on Social Work Education, **2:**688
Counselor role. *See* **Therapist role**
Countertransference, **1:**399, **2:**837–838, 922, 931, **3:**1175, 1336, **4:**1547, 1636
Couple and family counseling
determining the client, **2:**565, 567
history, **4:**1767–1787
informed consent, **2:**858–859
treatment planning, **4:**1734–1738
Couple and family forensics, 1:368–371
abuse cases, **1:**370
child custody, **1:**369–370
coparenting, **1:**370
divorce, **1:**369
overview, **1:**368–369
parental alienation syndrome, **3:**1218–1221
Couple and Family Psychology: Research and Practice (journal), **4:**1792
Couple and technology framework, **4:**1680–1682
Couple CARE, **3:**1031
Couple Communication Program, **3:**1028, 1030, 1031
Couple Coping Enhancement Training, **3:**1031, 1032
Couple development, 1:371–374
connection, **1:**373–374
discovery, **1:**373
infatuation, **1:**371–372
post-rapture, **1:**372–373
Couple Handbook for Effective Communication (Allred and Graff), **1:**180

Couples, dual-earner, **1:**187–188
Couples, quality time, 1:374–378
characteristics, **1:**376–378
theory of, **1:**375
WDEP system, **1:**375–376
Couples and marriage counseling, 1:378–384
counselor attitudes, **3:**1041
counselor traits, **1:**379–380
defining couple and marriage relationships, **1:**378–379
determining suitability, **1:**380–381
discernment counseling, **1:**449–452
female orgasmic disorder, **2:**656
first and second marriages, **3:**1019
history, **4:**1767–1787, 1784–1786
hope-focused approach, **2:**805–808
individualistic approach, **3:**1041–1042
integrative approach, **2:**867–872
interpersonal neurobiology, **2:**900–903
key concepts, **1:**378
legal and ethical considerations, **1:**370–371
marital group therapy vs., **3:**1011
mindfulness, **3:**1081–1083
morphogenesis, **3:**1100
morphostasis, **3:**1103
multicultural considerations, **1:**379
postpartum depression, **3:**1276–1277
power issues, **3:**1285–1287
professionalism, **1:**380
relationship enhancement, **3:**1390–1392
research, **1:**383–384
rural families, **3:**1431–1432
scales, **4:**1440–1442
solution-focused brief therapy, **4:**1579
spirituality, **4:**1587
theories and models, **1:**381–382
therapeutic impasses, **4:**1701
trauma, **4:**1728
Couples Dialogue, **2:**830
Couples Growing Together, **1:**180
Couples Interaction Coding System, **3:**1323
Couples therapy research, 1:384–387
comparative approach, **1:**387
cultural factors, 1–385
defining, **1:**384
historical overview, **1:**384
past and future of, **1:**385
power issues, **3:**1287
treatment efficacy, **1:**385–387
Coupling, **2:**611
Court-mandated clients, 1:388–391
domestic violence, **1:**390
ethical considerations, **1:**390–391

history of family preservation, **1:**388–389
overview, **1:**388
substance abuse, **1:**389–390
Coworkers, **1:**87–88
Cozolino, Louis, **1:**121
Crane, D. Russell, 4:1712
Creed, Douglas, **4:**1743
Crisis incident stress management, **1:**393
Crisis intervention with couples and families, 1:391–394
history of, **1:**393
outcomes of crisis, **1:**392
overview, **1:**391–392
theoretical models, **1:**393–394
Crisis management, **3:**1120
Critical ethnography, **1:**397
Critical humanism, **1:**395–396
Critical inquiry, **2:**794, **3:**1271
Critical theory, 1:395–397
deficiency theory vs., **1:**396
definition and historical development, **1:**395
implications for counseling, **1:**397
overview, **1:**395
philosophical underpinnings, **1:**395–396
research strategies, **1:**397
role of voice, **1:**396–397
Criticism, **1:**300, 331, **2:**745
Cross, William, **1:**40
Cross-cultural adoption, **1:**37–41
Cross-cultural mental health, **2:**711
Cross-dressing, **3:**1197–1198, **4:**1715
Cross-sectional research, **3:**1353
Crouter, Ann, **1:**481
Crucible, 1:398–400
Crutchley, Elaine, **4:**1669
Cultural awareness, **1:**456
Cultural competence. *See* **Multicultural counseling competences, 3:**943–944
Cultural diversity, **3:**1115
Cultural humility, **3:**1116–1117
Cultural identity
acculturation, **1:**6–7
couples and family counseling, **1:**400
cross-cultural adoption, **1:**40–41
ethnicity, race, and, **2:**569–570
racial identity compared to, **1:**40
Cultural issues in couples and families, 1:400–403
clinician-family relations, **1:**401
cross-cultural and interracial adoption, **1:**37–41, **4:**1720–1722
family-culture relationships, **1:**400–402
intercultural marriage and family, **2:**875–877
intersectionality, **1:**400
Cultural knowledge, **1:**456

Cultural sensitivity, **3:**1115, 1131
Culture
aging and caregiving, **1:**59–60
beliefs and values, **1:**147, 148
case conceptualization, **1:**259
communication in couples and families, **1:**304–305
couples and marriage counseling, **1:**379
couples therapy research, 1–385
cross-cultural adoption, **1:**37–41, **4:**1720–1722
cultural differences, **2:**710–712, **3:**1112–1113
empathic listening, **3:**966–968
family of origin, **2:**627–628
family resource management, **2:**638–639
family rituals, **2:**640
family values, **2:**652–653
feminization of poverty, **2:**666
gender- and culture-sensitive therapies, **2:**710–715
individualistic, **2:**652–653
infidelity, **2:**586
in-law relationships, **2:**860–861
intercultural marriage and family, **2:**875–877
life balance, **3:**956
marriage and family therapy assessment, **1:**88
mate selection, **3:**1044
nonverbal communication, **3:**1160
parental stress, **3:**1224
parenting, **3:**1233
polyamory, **3:**1257
postmodern therapies, **3:**1268, 1271–1272
relational-cultural therapy, **2:**713, **3:**967, 1384–1388
retirement, **3:**1411–1412
See also **Multiculturalism**
Culture of poverty, **4:**1749
Curiosity. *See* **Neutrality and curiosity**
Current Relationship Interview (CRI), **1:**46–47
Custodial rights and responsibilities, **3:**945–946
Custody, child. *See* Child custody
Custody evaluations, 1:403–406
best interests of the child, **1:**157–158
ethical considerations, **1:**405
parental alienation syndrome, **3:**1218–1221
person conducting, **1:**404–405
proceedings, **1:**405
purpose, **1:**404
types of custody, **1:**405
Cutting. *See* **Self-injury**
Cybernetics, **1:**406–409, **4:**1774–1775, 1780
choice theory, **2:**865
circularity principle, **1:**249, 406–407
epistemology in family therapy, **2:**549
feedback, **1:**408–409, **3:**1262–1263
general systems theory, **2:**727
homeostasis, **2:**792–793
morphogenesis, **3:**1098

morphostasis, 3:1101
positive and negative feedback loops, 1:408–409
recursiveness, 3:1375–1376
second-order, 2:792, 3:1376, 4:1666
second-order family therapy influenced by, 4:1463
systemic family therapy, 4:1665
See also **Systems theory**
Czikszentmihalyi, Mihaly, 2:820

Dance of intimacy, 1:372, 2:524
Dare, Christopher, 2:491
Darwin, Charles, 2:777
Date rape, 2:911
Dating
  online, 3:1176–1179
  self-esteem, 4:1482
  See also **Romance**
Dating coaching, 1:411–414
  appropriateness, 1:412
  benefits, 1:412–413
  components, 1:412
  delivery methods, 1:413
  overview, 1:411
  recommendations, 1:414
  skills and topics offered, 1:413
  stigmas associated with, 1:413
Dating relationship dissolution, 1:414–416
  approaches to, 1:416
  cognitive and behavioral approaches, 1:416
  dynamics conductive to, 1:415–416
  process, 1:415
Dattilio, Frank, 1:283, 4:1782, 1784
David, Daniel, 1:67
Davis, Keith, 3:1047
Davis, Michele Weiner, *The Divorce Remedy*, 1:451
Davis, Thomas, 3:1096
DBT. *See* Dialectical behavior therapy (DBT)
De Jong, Peter, 4:1576
De Shazer, Steve, 1:181, 182, 185–186, 271, 333, 2:866, 3:969, 1086, 1087, 1268, 4:1448, 1457, 1575–1576, 1665, 1773, 1777–1778
De Waal, Frans B. M., 2:529, 3:1372–1373
Death, parents of deceased children, 1:417–420
Death and dying, 1:420–423
  avoidance of confronting, 1:421–422
  beliefs and values, 2:810
  bereavement, 1:148–151
  changing context, 1:420
  cultural responses, 1:152
  family context, 1:421–422
  family therapy, 1:422–423
  hospice, 2:808–811
  Kübler-Ross's stages of dying, 1:421
  loss, 3:976–977
  older adults, 2:762
  rituals associated with, 3:994
  stillbirth and miscarriage, 4:1599–1603
Deblinger, Esther, 4:1730
Debt and financial strain, 1:423–426, 3:1223
  power issues, 3:1286
  premarital counseling, 3:1299
  socioeconomic status, 4:1573
  See also **Family resource management**
Decentered position, 4:1779, 1780
DeChillo, Neal, 2:537
Decision-making, 1:426–429
  counseling, 1:428–429
  ethical considerations, 1:429, 3:1096
  gender roles, 1:428
  moral, 3:1097
  process, 1:428
  stress, 1:426–427
  theories, 1:426
  values, 1:427
Deconstruction, 3:1134, 4:1780
Dedication to the Sacred Scale, 4:1585–1586
De-escalation, 1:337–338
Defense of Marriage Act (DOMA), 2:875, 3:948, 1038, 1039
Defensiveness, 1:300, 331, 2:745–746
Deficiency theory, 1:396
Deficit hypothesis, 1:396, 4:1749–1750
Deficit Reduction Act, 3:1022, 1138
DeFrain, John, 2:643
Defusion, 1:4, 2:621
Deinstitutionalization, 3:1339, 4:1453
Delgado-Gaitan, Concha, 1:397
Delphi research method, 1:429–431
Delworth, Ursula, 4:1639–1641, 1649
Demonstration family counseling. *See* **Adlerian open-forum family counseling**
Demonstration of inadequacy, 1:19, 22
Denial
  debt and financial strain, 1:423–424
  divorce, 1:464
  domestic violence, 1:469
Denton, Frank, 3:1410
DEOR model, 2:813
Depakote, 3:1090
Department of Child and Family Services, 2:782
Depressants, 4:1626
Depression in adolescents, 1:431–435
  description, 1:431
  developmental influences, 1:432–434
  diagnosis, 1:431–432
  family engagement, 1:434–435
  family impact, 1:441

risk factors, **1**:432
treatment, **1**:443
Depression in children, 1:435–438
  causes, **1**:436–437
  family impact, **1**:440–442
  symptoms, **1**:435–436
  treatment, **1**:437–438, 443
  See also **Mood disorders in children**
Depression in couples and families, 1:439–444
  childhood depression, **1**:440–442
  impact on couples, **1**:439–440
  impact on families, **1**:440–441
  treatment, **1**:442–444
  types of depression, **1**:439
Derks, Jim, **4**:1777
Derogatis Interview for Sexual Functioning, **4**:1441
Derrida, Jacques, **4**:1568
Descartes, René, **4**:1675
Descriptive research, **3**:1353
Desensitization. *See* Eye movement desensitization and reprocessing (EMDR); Systematic desensitization
Despair, in late adulthood, **1**:50
Destructive entitlement, **2**:547–548, **3**:1335, 1374
Detect, direct, protect, and connect frameworks, **1**:393
Deutsch, Danica, **1**:177
Developmental disabilities, **2**:872
Developmental model of marriage, 1:444–447
  assumptions, **1**:445
  etiology, **1**:445
  markers of, **1**:444–445
  stage model, **1**:445–447
  therapeutic applications, **1**:447
Developmental scales, **4**:1438
Dewey, John, **1**:347, **2**:777, **3**:1201, **4**:1662
Diabetes mellitus, **1**:231
Diagnosis process, **1**:475–476
  See also **Relational diagnoses**
Diagnostic and Statistical Manual of Mental Disorders (DSM-I), homosexuality in, **4**:1551–1552
Diagnostic and Statistical Manual of Mental Disorders (DSM-II), homosexuality in, **1**:239, **3**:1039, **4**:1434, 1538, 1544, 1552
Diagnostic and Statistical Manual of Mental Disorders (DSM-III)
  eating disorders, **2**:489
  inhibited sexual desire, **3**:999
  intermittent explosive disorder, **2**:882
  posttraumatic stress disorder, **4**:1727
Diagnostic and Statistical Manual of Mental Disorders (DSM-III-R), hypoactive sexual desire disorder in, **3**:999
Diagnostic and Statistical Manual of Mental Disorders (DSM-IV), posttraumatic stress disorder in, **4**:1727

Diagnostic and Statistical Manual of Mental Disorders (DSM-IV-TR)
  autism, **1**:129
  behavior disorders, **1**:117
  conduct disorder, **1**:118
  hypoactive sexual desire disorder, **3**:999
  intermittent explosive disorder, **1**:118
  mental retardation, **2**:873
  oppositional defiant disorder, **1**:118
  sexual pain disorders, **2**:731
Diagnostic and Statistical Manual of Mental Disorders (DSM-5)
  adjustment disorder, **1**:11
  adult ADHD, **1**:118
  agoraphobia, **1**:73
  anxiety, **1**:70
  autism, **1**:129
  autism spectrum disorder, **1**:134, 135, **2**:873
  avoidant personality disorder, **1**:139
  behavior disorders, **1**:117
  binge eating disorder, **2**:489
  communication disorders, **1**:297–298
  complicated grief, **2**:750
  compulsive sexual behavior, **1**:319
  conduct disorder, **1**:118, 321, **3**:1203
  cross-cultural formulation, **1**:259
  diagnosis using, **3**:1313, 1380–1381, **4**:1779
  disinhibited social engagement disorder, **1**:453
  erectile disorder, **2**:554
  externalizing behaviors, **1**:28
  female orgasmic disorder, **2**:654
  female sexual interest/arousal disorder, **2**:657, 814, **4**:1523
  gambling disorder, **2**:708
  gender dysphoria, **2**:715
  generalized anxiety disorder, **1**:221–222
  genito-pelvic pain/penetration disorder, **2**:731
  hoarding, **2**:772
  ICD in relation to, **1**:473, **2**:891–893
  intellectual disability, **2**:873
  intermittent explosive disorder, **2**:882
  male hypoactive sexual desire disorder, **3**:999
  non–rapid eye movement sleep arousal disorders, **3**:1154
  panic disorder, **1**:222
  paraphilic disorders, **3**:1194
  parental alienation syndrome, **3**:1220
  postpartum depression, **3**:1274
  posttraumatic stress disorder, **4**:1516
  reactive attachment disorder, **1**:453, **2**:897, **3**:1368
  scales, **4**:1439
  selective mutism, **1**:221
  self-injury, **4**:1492
  separation anxiety disorder, **1**:74, 221

sex therapy and, 4:1509
sexual dysfunction, 2:814, 4:1530
sexual fetishes, 2:669, 670
specific phobia, 1:73
substance abuse and dependence, 1:62
substance use disorders, 4:1624
See also **DSM and V-codes**
Dialectical behavior therapy (DBT)
   acceptance, 1:3
   adolescent mood disorders, 1:24
   affect regulation, 1:52–53
   eating disorders, 2:491
   postmodern therapies, 3:1276
   suicide, 4:1632
   therapeutic contracts, 4:1697
   trauma and children, 4:1725
Dickerson, Vicki, 4:1780
Dicks, Henry V., 3:1175
DiClemente, Carlo, 1:62, 388, 3:1244
Diener, Ed, 3:1265
Diet, 1:85
Differential diagnosis, 1:475–476
Differentiation, 1:448–449
   Bowen family systems theory, 1:173, 174, 2:841, 3:1334, 4:1770
   family assessment, 2:608
   feminist perspective, 2:663
   integrative couples therapy, 2:869
   marital satisfaction, 3:1017, 4:1537
   psychoanalytic concept, 3:1334
   reconciliation, 3:1372
   sex therapy, 4:1510
Dignity therapy, 2:810
Dildos, 4:1526, 1550
Dinkmeyer, Don, 1:180, 3:1033, 1209, 4:1490, 1713, 1769–1770, 1785
Dinkmeyer, Don, Jr., 4:1769
Diogenes syndrome, 2:510
Direct association, 2:528–529
Direct masturbation training, 2:656
Direct observation, 2:695–696
Directives, 2:560, 4:1607–1608
Disabilities
   caregiving, 1:60
   developmental, 2:872–874
   hoarding, 2:775–776
   normalization, 3:1161–1162
   sexual enhancement, 4:1527–1528
   See also **Children with special needs in family therapy**
Discernment counseling, 1:449–452, 465
Discipline, 3:1236–1237
   child-centered parenting, 1:219
Disclosure, of sexual abuse, 4:1513–1514

Disconnection, 3:1384
Discrimination
   acculturative stress, 1:7
   cross-cultural and interracial adoption, 1:39–40
   institutional, 3:1366
   racial, 3:1366, 1367
   therapeutic settings, 3:1367
Discrimination model, of supervision, 4:1651, 1656
Disengaged parenting. *See* Rejecting-neglecting/ disengaged parenting
Disengagement
   emotional, 2:515–517
   family system, 1:171, 286, 287
Disengagement theory, 2:840
Disequilibrium, 2:792
Disinhibited social engagement disorder in children, 1:452–454
   diagnosis, 1:454
   reactive attachment disorder, 1:453–454
   risk factors, 1:454
   treatment, 1:454
Dismissing attachment, 1:98–99, 2:674, 921
Disorganized attachment, 1:98, 101–102, 109, 112
Disruptive disorders, 1:25–26, 117–119
Disruptive mood dysregulation disorder, 1:432, 3:1088, 1093
Dissonance, 1:6
Distraction, in communication, 1:301, 2:817
Distress prevention. *See* **Prevention research**
Divalproex sodium, 3:1090
Diversity, 1:455–457
   behavioral family therapy, 1:145
   case conceptualization, 1:259
   cognitive-behavioral family therapy, 1:285
   counselor awareness, 1:456
   cultural, 3:1115
   cultural knowledge, 1:456
   family mediation, 2:619
   interventions, 1:456–457
   Latino families, 3:941
   multicultural counseling competence, 1:455–456
   multisystemic therapy, 3:1123
   overview, 1:455
   postmodern therapies, 3:1272
   treatment planning, 4:1738
   See also **Multiculturalism**
Divorce and separation, 1:458–462
   assessment, 1:458–459
   children, 1:465
   collaborative divorce, 1:406, 466
   custody evaluations, 1:403–406
   family of origin, 2:627
   forensics, 1:369
   grief and loss, 1:461–462

interventions, **1:**459–462
nonresidential fathers, **3:**1155–1157
overview, **1:**458
parental alienation syndrome, **3:**1218–1221
prevention research, **3:**1316–1317
recovery, **1:**463–464
relational diagnosis, **3:**1383
relationship patterns, **1:**458–459
rituals associated with, **3:**993
spirituality, **1:**464–465
stages, **1:**459
See also **Marriage, first and second**
Divorce Care, **1:**464
Divorce therapy, 1:462–467
children, **1:**465
discernment counseling, **1:**449–452, 465
mediation, **1:**460, 466
overview, **1:**462–463
pre- vs. post-, **1:**463–464
recovery, **1:**463–464
resources, **1:**466
spirituality, **1:**464–465
Divorced families
communication, **1:**304
divorce therapy, **1:**465
parentification, **3:**1228–1229
"Do no harm" principle, **2:**566
Doctoral programs, **4:**1711
Documentation, **3:**1290
Dodo bird hypothesis, **1:**295
Doherty, William, **1:**243, 449, 465, **3:**1051
Dolan, Yvonne, **4:**1777
Domestic violence, 1:467–470
assessment, **1:**469–470, **2:**913
asymmetrical relationships, **1:**250
child maltreatment, **1:**209–210
child's witnessing of, **2:**908
costs, **1:**469
duty to warn, **1:**482–483
elder abuse vs., **2:**509
empowerment, **2:**537–538
family of origin, **2:**626–627
forensics, **1:**370
homicide, **2:**800–804
overview, **1:**467–468
poverty, **2:**595–596
prevention research, **3:**1316–1317
risk factors, **1:**468–469
same-sex couples, **4:**1434–1435
scales, **4:**1441
screening for, **1:**380
treatment, **1:**469–470, **2:**913–914
types and patterns, **1:**468, **2:**912–913
See also **Interpersonal violence**

Domestic violence-focused couple therapy, **2:**913–914
Domestication theory, **4:**1680
Dominant discourse, **3:**1133–1134
Dominant voices technique, **2:**713
Dopamine, **2:**673, **3:**982–983, 990, 1090, 1338
Double ABCX model, **2:**646, 649–650, **4:**1609
Double bind theory, 1:471–472, 2:560, 3:1061, 4:1668, 1775
See also **Paradoxes and paradoxical interventions**
Double binds, **1:**182
Dowbiggin, Ian, **3:**1040–1041
Down syndrome, **2:**872
Drama therapy, **3:**1420
Drama triangle, **4:**1740
Draper, Rosalind, **4:**1669
Draw-a-Person, **4:**1438
Dreikurs, Rudolf, **1:**9, 15, 16, 19, 21, 22, 177, 178, **3:**1209, **4:**1561, 1768, 1769
Children: The Challenge, **3:**1209
Drexel University, **4:**1473
Droste effect, **3:**1375
Drug replacement therapy, **4:**1626
DSM and V-codes, 1:472–476
components of DSM, **1:**473–474
diagnosis process, **1:**475–476
history and development, **1:**473
risks and benefits of diagnosis, **1:**475
Dual and multiple relationships, 1:476–479
benefits, **1:**478–479
ethical considerations, **2:**563–564, **3:**1288
important considerations, **1:**479
overview, **1:**476–477
risks, **1:**478
settings conducive to, **1:**477
types, **1:**477–478
See also **Sexual relationships with clients**
Dual-earner families, 1:479–482
child care, **1:**481
concerns, **1:**480–481
family impact, **1:**480–481
gender issues, **1:**481
historical development, **1:**480
rationales, **1:**480
same-sex couples, **1:**481
therapy, **1:**481–482
work stressors, **1:**187–188
Dual-process model, of coping, **1:**151
Ducommun-Nagy, Catherine, **1:**351, 354
Duhl, Bunny, **4:**1772, 1785
Dulwich Centre, **4:**1780
Durkheim, Émile, **2:**536, 839

Duty to warn and protect, 1:482–485
confidentiality considerations, 1:326, 483–485, 2:756
couple and family counseling, 2:565
elder abuse, 2:511
ethical considerations, 1:478–479, 2:563
group family therapy, 2:756
homicidal clients, 2:803
implications for therapy, 1:484–485
release of information, 3:1393–1395
sexual abuse, 4:1514
sexually transmitted infections, 4:1560
therapist role, 1:483–484
See also **Mandated reporter**
Dweck, Carol, 4:1485
Dyadic Adjustment Scale, 4:1440
Dyadic data analysis, 3:1355
Dyadic relationships, 1:174
Dynamic systems theory, 2:518, 521
Dysfunctional families, 1:16
Dysfunctional thought record, 1:285
Dysthymia. *See* Persistent depressive disorder

Earned attachment, 2:487–488
Earned secure attachments, 1:109, 113, 341, 2:487
Eating Addictions Anonymous, 1:307
Eating disorders, 2:488–491
adolescent behavior disorders, 1:26
family therapy, 2:491
history, 2:489
overview, 2:488
treatment, 2:490–491
12-step programs, 1:307
types, 2:490
See also **Unusual eating behaviors**
Ecograms, 2:593
Ecological systems, 2:492–495
eco-maps, 2:496–499
historical context, 2:492–493
major concepts, 2:493
overview, 2:492
theoretical underpinnings, 2:493
therapeutic applications, 2:495
See also **Ecosystems perspective**
Ecological systems theory, 1:248
Ecologically based family therapy, 2:495
Eco-map, 2:496–499
assessment and treatment using, 2:497–498, 505
ecosystemic structural family therapy, 2:502
elements of, 2:496–497
illustration, 2:498
research on, 2:498–499
systems theory, 2:496

Economic development programs, 1:307
Ecosystemic structural family therapy, 2:499–502
assessment tools, 2:502
constructs, 2:500
overview, 2:499, 506
process, 2:500–501
techniques, 2:502
therapeutic sequence, 2:501–502
Ecosystems perspective, 2:503–506
applications, 2:505–506
eco-maps, 2:496–499
ecosystemic structural family therapy model, 2:506
family resilience, 2:632
historical development, 2:503–504
human ecosystem, 2:504–505
major concepts, 2:504–505
overview, 2:503
societal systems, 2:505
transactional perspective, 2:505
See also **Ecological systems**
Ecstasy (drug), 4:1626
Education
adolescent school issues, 4:1581
African Americans, 1:56
autistic children, 1:132
clinical practice, 1:265–266
continuing education, 3:1288
family involvement, 4:1456–1459
licensure, 3:952
marriage education, 3:1023–1024
Parent Effectiveness Training, 3:1198–1202
parenting, 3:1234–1235
patriarchy, 3:1240
peer counseling, 3:1244–1245
premarital counseling, 3:1300
relationship education, 3:960, 1389–1390
rural families, 3:1430
self-help books, 4:1486–1490
sexuality education, 4:1554–1557
socioeconomic status, 4:1573
special needs children, 1:234–235
See also **Family psychoeducation; Psychoeducation; Training and licensure**
Education level, poverty linked to, 2:668
Effectiveness research, 2:506–508
clinical versus statistical significance, 1:267–270
common factors, 1:295–296
couples therapy, 1:385–387
postmodern therapies, 3:1272–1273
psychotherapy, 1:267–270, 295–296
quantitative research, 3:1354
See also **Empirically validated models; Evidence-based practice; Outcome research**

Elder abuse, 2:508–511, 914
  domestic violence vs., 2:509
  duty to protect, 2:511
  mandates for reporting, 3:1005
  overview, 2:508
  prevalence, 2:508–509
  risk factors, 2:509
  societal attitudes, 2:510–511
  types, 2:509–510
Elder Abuse Victims Act, 3:1005
Elder Justice Act, 3:1005
Elderly. *See* Older adults
Electro-stimulation, erotic, 4:1526
Elimination disorders in children, 2:511–513
Ellis, Albert, 1:67, 282, 2:620, 795, 4:1480, 1783–1784
Ellis, Henry Havelock, 4:1505
Ellison, Christopher, 3:1397
Embodiment. *See* Body
Emmons, Robert, 3:1265
Emotional abuse, 4:1512–1515
  child maltreatment, 1:209, 2:908
  domestic violence, 1:468, 2:912
  elder abuse, 2:509
Emotional and Social Competence Inventory, 2:519
Emotional cutoff, 1:175, 2:608, 705
Emotional disengagement, 2:513–517
  background on emotions, 2:514–516
  concept of disengagement, 2:515–516
  consequences, 2:516–517
Emotional expressiveness training, 1:280
Emotional fusion, 2:608, 663
Emotional intelligence, children, 2:517–520
  attachment styles, 2:519–520
  background, 2:517
  dynamic systems theory, 2:518
  functionalist theory, 2:518–519
  measurement, 2:519–520
  overview, 2:517
  parenting styles, 2:520
  trait emotional intelligence, 2:518
Emotional intelligence, families, 2:521–522
  background, 2:521
  conservation of resources theory, 2:521
  dynamic systems theory, 2:521
Emotional matching, 2:530–531
Emotional reasoning, 1:278
Emotional regulation, 2:898–899, 3:1078, 1319, 1408, 4:1732
  See also **Affect regulation**
Emotional triangles, 1:174
Emotional units, 2:608

Emotionally focused couple therapy (EFCT)
  attachment intervention, 1:104, 105, 113
  attunement in relationships, 1:123
  experiential family therapy, 2:580–581
  overview, 1:386–387
Emotionally focused therapy (EFT)
  anger management, 1:67–68
  attachment intervention, 1:99–100, 113
  couples and marriage counseling, 1:383
  depression in couples and families, 1:443
  empirically validated models, 2:533
  evidence-based practice, 2:576
  primary and secondary emotions, 3:1321
  process research, 3:1324
Emotionally focused therapy for couples, 2:522–527
  evidence-based practice, 4:1782
  overview, 2:522–523, 4:1786–1787
  sexual abuse, 4:1515
  stages and steps, 2:524–527
  trauma, 4:1728
  treatment plan, 4:1737
Emotions
  adolescent development, 1:433
  categorization, 2:514
  child-centered parenting, 1:218
  components, 2:515
  enhancing function of, 3:1320–1321
  expressed, 3:1383, 4:1454, 1732
  instrumental, 3:1320
  men and, 3:1058
  meta-emotional styles, 3:1007
  naming, 1:122
  overview, 3:1318
  primary, 2:524, 3:1318–1321
  processes, 3:1318–1319
  reptilian brain, 1:173
  secondary, 2:524, 3:1318–1321
  socialization and dysregulation, 2:514
  threats to intimacy, 2:919
  12-step groups, 1:307
  See also Affect
Emotions Anonymous, 1:307
Empathic curiosity, 3:1147
Empathy, 2:527–531
  attunement and, 1:122, 2:738–739
  behavioral perspective, 2:528–529
  chronic illness with couples and families, 1:245
  compassion, 1:310–311
  defined, 3:965
  developmental perspective, 2:528
  failures of, 2:530–531
  listening, 3:965–968
  metaphors and, 3:1063
  motivational interviewing, 3:1109

mutual, 3:1384, 1386–1387
neuropsychological perspective, 2:529–530
origin and definition of term, 1:290, 2:527–528
social learning perspective, 2:530–531
suicide assessment, 1:91
Empirically validated models, 2:531–534
  common factors, 2:534
  criticisms of, 2:534
  effective models, 2:533–534
  empirical research, 2:532
  evidence-based practice, 2:532–533
  See also Evidence-based practice
Empiricism, 2:549–550
Employment. *See* **Job loss;** Work
Empowerment, mutual, 3:1384
Empowerment in families, 2:535–538
  assessment tools, 2:536–537
  components, 2:536
  domestic violence, 2:537–538
  family support movement, 2:537
  family systems, 2:535
  overview, 2:535
  postmodern therapies, 3:1270–1271
  social cohesion, 2:536
  societal context, 2:537
Empty chair therapy, 3:1420
Enabling, 2:599
Enactments, 2:538–542
  behavioral, skill-based models, 2:539–540
  communication, 2:540
  developmental model, 2:541–542
  elements of successful, 2:542
  emotionally focused therapy, 2:540–541
  rationale, 2:539
  structural family therapy, 2:502, 539,
    4:1617–1618
Encopresis, 2:512
End-of-life care certificate programs, 2:811
Engagement, 2:622
Engel, George, 1:95, 243
Engendering hope, 2:543–545
Engle, George, 1:83
English-as-a-second-language, 3:1229–1230
Enmeshment
  family system, 1:171–172, 286–288
  feminist perspective, 2:663
  fusion, 2:706
  love, 1:104
ENRICH index, 4:1586
  See also **PREPARE/ENRICH**
Enright, Robert, 2:682, 684
Entitlement, 2:546–548
  constructive, 2:547
  contextual family therapy, 1:354

destructive, 2:547–548, 3:1335, 1374
horizontal and vertical relationships, 2:546
Enuresis, 2:512–513
Epistemology, 3:1375, 4:1567, 1778
Epistemology in family therapy, 2:549–552
  approaches, 2:549–550
  constructivism, 2:550
  empiricism, 2:549–550
  family systems therapy, 2:550–552
  overview, 2:549
  rationalism, 2:550
EPOR model, 2:812
Epstein, Nathan, 4:1446
Epstein, Norman, 4:1784
Epston, David, 3:969, 1064, 1133, 1268, 4:1569, 1780
Equifinality, 2:729, 4:1775
Equine Assisted Growth and Learning Association,
  2:553–554
Equine-assisted family therapy, 2:552–554
Erectile disorder, 2:554–557
  causes, 2:555
  consequences, 2:555–556
  diagnosis and description, 2:554–555
  medication, 2:556–557, 4:1524
  physical issues, 2:555
  psychological and relationship issues, 2:555
  risk factors, 2:555
  treatment considerations, 2:556–557
  See also Premature ejaculation
Erickson, Elizabeth, 4:1773
Erickson, Milton, 1:182, 2:557–562, 819, 821, 822,
  3:1087, 1143–1145, 1191, 1403, 4:1576, 1773,
  1776, 1780
Ericksonian family therapy, 2:557–562
  background, 2:558
  basic tenets, 2:558–559
  criticisms of, 2:561–562
  strategies and techniques, 2:559–561
Erikson, Erik, 1:28, 48, 432–433, 2:839–840, 3:1211,
  4:1480, 1768
Esalen Institute, 4:1772
Escape, 1:138
Essentialism, 2:550
Estradiol, 4:1529
Estrogen, 3:990, 1276, 4:1501
Ethical codes, 2:562–565
  American Counseling Association, 2:568
  certified family life educators, 1:195–196
  clinical practice, 1:266
  counselors' core competencies, 1:358–359, 4:1710
  couple and family counseling, 2:564
  discretionary, 2:564
  ethical decision-making, 2:568
  mandatory, 2:563–564

obligatory, 2:563–564
overview, 2:562–563
professional associations, 3:1326
prohibitive or restrictive, 2:563–564
purpose, 2:563, 3:1095–1096
structure of, 2:563–564
supervisor training, 4:1633–1634, 1641–1643, 1646
termination, 4:1686
Ethical decision-making, 2:566–569
components, 2:568–569
couple and family counseling, 2:567–568
overview, 2:566
Ethics
confidentiality, 1:325–329
confrontation, 1:344
court-mandated clients, 1:390–391
custody evaluations, 1:405
decision-making, 1:429, 3:1096
defining, 3:1094–1095
forensics, 1:370–371
group family therapy, 2:755–756
hoarding, 2:774–775
identified patient, 2:826
individual vs. family therapy, 2:849–850
informed consent, 2:854–859
isomorphism, 2:923–924
no-harm contracts, 3:1149
no-secrets contracts, 3:1164–1165
practice management, 3:1288
prenuptial agreements, 3:1305
principle ethics, 2:566
process research, 3:1324
progress notes, 3:1329
relational, 1:352, 353
release of information, 3:1393–1395
research considerations, 2:854–856
respect, 3:1404
self-care practices of counselors, 4:1477
sex therapy, 4:1511
termination, 4:1685–1686
therapist-client relationships, 1:478–479, 4:1546–1547
therapists' values, 3:1146, 4:1705–1706
values, 2:566
virtue ethics, 2:566
Ethnicity, 2:569–573
caregiving, 1:59
cross-cultural and interracial adoption, 1:37–40, 4:1720–1722
family counseling implications, 2:572
feminization of poverty, 2:666–668
identity, 2:569–572
overview, 2:569
parenting styles, 3:1238

Phinney's model of identity development, 2:571–572
race compared to, 2:571, 915
religion, 3:1397
transmission, 2:570
See also Minorities; Race
Ethnography of empowerment, 1:397
European Family Therapy Association (EFTA), 4:1790
Evidence-based practice, 4:1782
ecosystems perspective, 2:506
effectiveness research, 2:507–508
empirically validated models, 2:532–533
historical development, 2:533
solution-focused brief therapy, 4:1579
structural family therapy, 4:1618
See also **Empirically validated models**
Evidence-based practice with couples and families, 2:573–576
applications, 2:575–576
background, 2:573–574
children and adolescents, 2:575–576
clinical versus statistical significance, 1:267–270
components, 2:574–575
couples, 2:576
mental disorders, 2:576
overview, 2:573
Evolution, love's role in, 3:980–984, 989, 993
Evolution of Psychotherapy conferences, 1:23
Examination in Marital and Family Therapy, 4:1712
Exception talk, 4:1449
Executive functioning, 1:130
Exercise, 1:85
Ex-gay therapy, 3:1039, 4:1435, 1544, 1553–1554
Exhibitionistic disorder, 3:1195–1196
Existential therapy, 2:579, 591, 816, 3:960, 1064
Exosystem, 2:494, 496
Experiential avoidance, 1:137, 2:621
Experiential family therapy, 2:577–581
clinical practice context, 1:265
concepts, 2:577–578
conjoint family therapy, 1:346
current status of, 2:581
emotionally focused couples therapy, 2:523
faith-based therapy, 2:591
interventions, 2:581
leading figures, 2:578–581
metaphors used in, 3:1064
outcome research, 3:1188
overview, 2:577
role-playing, 3:1419–1420
therapist role, 3:1249
Experimental research, 3:1353
Exposure therapy, 4:1515
Expressed emotion, 3:1383, 4:1454
Expression, in attunement, 1:121–122

Extended families, 4:1565, 1721
Externalization, as therapeutic technique, 3:1065, 1135, 1272, 4:1702
Externalizing behaviors, 2:582–583
   adolescents, 2:582–583
   children, 2:582–583
   defined, 2:582
   developmental context, 2:583
   gender, 2:582–583
Externalizing disorders, 2:582
Extramarital affairs and infidelity, 2:584–587
   assessment, 2:587
   cultural and contextual factors, 2:586
   defined, 2:584
   impacts, 2:585–586
   Internet infidelity, 2:587, 4:1679
   marital distress, 3:1008
   prevalence, 2:585
   religion, 4:1552
   systemic perspective, 3:1060
   treatment, 2:587
   types, 2:584–585
   See also **Fidelity**
Eye contact and movement, 3:1159
Eye movement desensitization and reprocessing (EMDR), 1:53, 2:910, 3:1281, 4:1515
Ezpeleta, Lourdes, 3:1184

Facial expressions, 3:1159
Factitious disorder, 4:1581–1582
Fair Housing Act, 2:775
Fairbairn, Ronald, 3:1173, 4:1768, 1769
Faith-based therapy, 2:589–593
   general considerations, 2:590–593
   hope, 2:589
   overview, 2:589
   therapeutic relationship, 2:590
   therapy process, 2:589–590
   types, 2:591–593
Faithfulness, 2:673–674
Falicov, Celia, 3:1116–1117
Familicide, 2:801
Families
   acculturation gap, 1:7–8
   Adlerian family therapy, 1:14–20
   adolescent development, 1:30
   adoption, 1:34–37
   bereavement, 1:151, 155–156
   changing conceptions of, 1:241–242
   childhood chronic illness, 1:230–231
   depression's impact on, 1:440–442
   dysfunctional, 1:16
   marriage and family therapy assessment, 1:87
   morphostasis, 3:1101–1102
   parenting and, 1:124–125
   projection process, 1:175
   recursiveness, 3:1376
   schizophrenia, 4:1452–1455
   school involvement, 4:1456–1459
   self-esteem, 4:1481
   Virginia Satir model, 4:1755
   See also **African American families; Asian American families; Bilingual families; Chosen families; Immigrant families; Latino families; LGBT families; Nuclear family; Parenting; Single-parent families; Urban families**
Families and poverty, 2:594–596
Families and Schools Together, 3:1401
Families and substance abuse, 2:597–600
   child maltreatment, 1:210
   comorbidity, 2:598
   interrelationship, 2:598–599
   overview, 2:597–598
   therapeutic approaches, 2:599–600
   See also **Alcohol and substance abuse**
Family Adaptability and Cohesion Evaluation scales (FACES), 1:254–255, 2:603–604, 644, 4:1441, 1445
Family and individual emotional regulation, 2:500
Family and Medical Leave Act of 1993, 2:600–602
Family and Youth Services Bureau, 2:790
Family Assessment Device (FAD), 2:606, 4:1446–1447
Family Assessment Measure (FAM-III), 2:607
Family assessment, models of, 2:602–609
   Beavers systems model, 2:604–605
   circumplex model, 2:602–604
   genograms, 2:608–609
   McMaster model of family functioning, 2:605–607
   overview, 2:602
   process model of family functioning, 2:607–608
Family atmosphere, 1:16–17
Family Centered Treatment, 3:1317
Family Circus, 4:1769
Family class model, 3:1121
Family cohesion, 4:1454
Family constellation, 1:17–18, 178
Family culture, 2:844–847
Family development, 2:500, 3:1211–1212, 1282–1285
Family Digest, The, 2:889
Family disease approach, 2:599
Family drama, 2:818
Family Dynamics Institute, 3:1030
Family Empowerment Scale, 2:537
Family group conference, 1:216
Family Institute of Westchester, 4:1760
Family Journal, The, 2:889, 4:1792
Family Life, 3:1030

Family life cycle, 2:610–613
    childlessness, 1:228
    communication, 1:305
    criticisms of, 2:612–613
    individual and family development, 2:610–611
    interracial marriage and families, 2:916
    life transitions, 3:964–965
    overview, 2:610, 4:1770
    rituals, 3:1414
    stages, 2:611–612
    structural maps, 4:1622
    usefulness of concept, 2:613
    See also **Life transitions**
Family Life Education, 3:1024
Family life educators, 2:613–616
    career opportunities, 2:615–616
    certified, 1:193–196, 2:614–615
    guiding principles, 2:614
    history and purpose, 1:193
    objectives, 2:614
    overview, 2:613–614
    services provided by, 2:614
    skills and characteristics, 2:614
Family Life Project, 2:596
Family mediation, 2:616–619
    basic tenets, 2:617
    beneficiaries, 2:617–618
    counseling vs., 2:617
    counselor competencies, 2:619
    diversity, 2:619
    forms, 2:618
    history, 2:616
    issues addressed in, 2:617
    methods, 2:617
    overview, 2:616
    principles, 2:618
    steps, 2:618–619
Family metaphors, 3:1066
Family mode deactivation therapy, 2:620–622
    core concepts, 2:621–622
    effectiveness, 2:620–621
    schemas and modes, 2:620
    theoretical basis, 2:620
    validation, clarification, and redirection, 2:622
Family myth, 2:578, 623, 623–625
Family of origin, 2:625–629
    assessment, 2:626
    Bowen family systems theory, 2:628–629
    family therapy, 2:626–629
    integrative couples therapy, 2:868
    marital group therapy, 3:1013
    overview, 2:625–626
    solution-focused therapy, 2:629

    therapists,' 3:1248
    Virginia Satir model, 4:1755
Family organizational culture, 2:844–845
Family Preservation and Support Services Program Act, 2:780, 781
Family Process (journal), 4:1768, 1773
Family projection process, 2:842
Family psychoeducation
    evidence-based practice, 2:576
    multiple family therapy, 3:1122
    premarital counseling, 3:1300
    schizophrenia, 4:1454–1455
    traditional family therapy vs., 3:1341–1342
Family reconstruction, 2:580, 629–631, 818, 4:1719
Family Relational Communication Control, 3:1323
Family Relations: Interdisciplinary Journal of Applied Family Studies, 4:1792
Family resilience, 2:631–635
    assessing, 2:633
    concept of, 2:632–633
    developmental perspective, 2:632–633
    ecosystemic perspective, 2:632
    key processes, 2:633–635
    overview, 2:631–632
    practice applications, 2:635
    strengths-based approach, 2:644–645
Family resource management, 2:636–639
    addictions, 2:638
    benefits of counseling, 2:636–637
    blended families, 2:637–638
    components, 2:636
    cultural considerations, 2:638–639
    overview, 2:636
    poverty, 2:638
    single parents, 2:637
    technology use, 2:639
    See also **Debt and financial strain**
Family resources approach, 2:644
Family Ritual Questionnaire, 3:1415–1416
Family rituals, 2:639–641
    cultural, 2:640
    designing, 3:1416
    examples, 3:994–995
    family culture, 2:845–846
    historical perspective, 3:992
    importance of, 2:641
    life cycle, 3:1414
    love, 3:991–995
    Milan systemic approaches, 3:1070
    overview, 2:639–640, 3:1413–1414
    purposes, 3:1414–1415
    religious, 2:640
    routines vs., 2:640–641, 3:1414
    systemic family therapy, 4:1668

togetherness, 3:993–995
types, 3:1415
See also **Rituals in family therapy**
Family roles, in McMaster model of family functioning, 2:606
Family Satisfaction Scale, 4:1445
Family sculpting. *See* Sculpting
Family Solidarity Scale, 3:1401
Family Strength Research Project, 2:643
Family strengths, 2:642–645
 basic tenets, 2:642
 challenges, 2:642–643
 family research models, 2:643–644
 frameworks and approaches, 2:644–645
Family stress, 2:645–648
 autism, 1:130
 childhood chronic illness, 1:231
 overview, 2:645–646
 stress management, 2:647–648
 theories and models, 2:646–647
 See also **Parental stress: effects on children**
Family stress adaptation theory, 2:643–644, 648–650
 ABC-X model, 2:649–650
 double ABCX model, 2:649–650
 overview, 2:648–649
Family stress ballet, 2:818
Family structure
 Adlerian family therapy, 1:18
 defined, 2:929
 multiple family therapy, 3:1119
 nuclear family, 3:1166–1168
 parentification, 3:1227
 patriarchy, 3:1241
 poverty, 2:594
 recent trends, 3:1167–1168
 retirement, 3:1410–1411
 structural determinism, 4:1611–1613
 See also **Structural family therapy (SFT)**
Family support movement, 2:537
Family systems
 bereavement, 1:155–156
 chaotic nature of, 1:197
 child behavior problems, 1:204
 childhood obesity, 1:225
 circularity principle, 1:249
 cohesion, 1:286–288
 communication, 1:302–304
 couples and marriage counseling, 1:378
 dysfunctional, 4:1673–1674
 empowerment, 2:535
 epistemology in family therapy, 2:550–552
 family reconstruction, 2:629–631
 Internal Family Systems model, 2:884–888

 job loss, 2:926–927
 life events, 3:959
 morphogenesis, 3:1098–1099
 morphostasis, 3:1102–1103
 nudity, 3:1168–1170
 parentification, 3:1227–1231
 resilience, 3:1400–1401
 roles, 4:1673–1674
 school settings, 4:1456–1457
 substance abuse, 2:599–600
Family systems theory
 adolescent development, 3:1212
 Bowen family systems theory, 1:172–176
 development of, 3:1059
 parenting styles, 1:128
 second-order change, 4:1460–1462
 structural family therapy, 4:1614–1615
 systemic hypothesis, 2:822–824
Family therapy
 circularity principle, 1:248
 diagnosis of psychiatric disorders, 2:826
 functional family therapy, 2:697–701
 group family therapy, 2:752–756
 history, 4:1767–1787
 homeless youth, 2:789
 individual vs., 2:847–850
 international, 2:894–896
 metaphors used in, 3:1063–1065
 Milan team, 3:1067–1071
 mood disorders, 3:1090
 morphogenesis, 3:1100
 morphostasis, 3:1103
 multiple family therapy, 3:1117–1122
 paradox, 3:1191–1194
 play family therapy, 3:1250–1254
 psychoanalytic, 3:1332–1337
 qualitative research, 3:1350–1352
 rituals, 3:1413–1417
 rural families, 3:1431–1432
 scales, 4:1443–1447
 scapegoating, 4:1450–1452
 second-order, 4:1463–1467
 self-esteem, 4:1480
 self-help books, 4:1490
 sexual abuse, 4:1514–1515
 social constructionism, 4:1569
 special needs children, 1:232–235
 stage theories, 4:1588–1593
 systemic, 4:1664–1669
 transgenerational, 4:1718–1720
 trauma, 4:1726, 1728–1729
Family Therapy Practice Center, 4:1760
Family traditions. *See* **Family rituals**

Family values, 2:651–654
　Adlerian family therapy, 1:17
　collectivistic cultures, 2:651–653
　cultural comparisons, 2:652–653
　dynamic interplay of, 2:653
　individualistic cultures, 2:652–653
　overview, 2:651
　research recommendations, 2:653–654
　See also **Individual family culture**
Family violence, 2:907
Family-assisted modalities, 2:533
Farr, William, 2:891, 3:1020
Fatherhood
　involvement with children, 3:1155–1156
　love, 3:981
　nonresidential fathers, 3:1155–1157
　responsible fatherhood, 2:763–765
Fear, of intimacy, 2:919
Fearful attachment, 2:674, 921
　See also Avoidant attachment
Feedback
　biofeedback, 1:53
　cybernetics, 1:408–409
　family therapy, 4:1775
　homeostasis, 2:793
　morphostasis, 3:1101–1102
　systems theory, 2:729, 4:1674
　See also **Positive and negative feedback**
Feelings
　child-centered parenting, 1:218
　mammalian brain, 1:173
　See also Emotion
Fees, 3:1290
Felt security, 1:101
Female headship, 2:666
Female orgasmic disorder, 2:654–657
　causes, 2:655
　prevalence, 2:655
　symptoms and diagnosis, 2:654–655
　treatment, 2:655–657
Female sexual interest/arousal disorder, 2:657–660, 814
　causes, 2:658–659
　overview, 2:657
　prevalence, 2:658
　symptoms and diagnosis, 2:657–658
　treatment, 2:659–660
Female-supported households, 2:666
Feminism, 4:1781–1782
　analysis of self-help books, 4:1489–1490
　critique of circularity, 1:250
　love, 3:987
　multiculturalism and, 4:1782
　second-wave, 2:662
　third-wave, 2:662
　Women's Project, 4:1759–1760, 1781–1782
Feminist family therapy, 2:661–664
　applications, 2:663–664
　gender as organizing construct, 2:662–663
　history, 2:661–662, 4:1781–1782
　overview, 2:661
Feminist therapy
　assertiveness, 1:81
　critical stance of, 2:794
　gender-sensitive therapy, 2:714–715
　postmodern therapies, 3:1270
Feminization of love, 3:987
Feminization of poverty, 2:595
　causes and risk factors, 2:666–668
　global considerations, 2:668–669
　history, **2:665–669**
　key concepts, 2:665
　social and cultural influences, 2:666
Femme lesbians, 4:1434, 1541
Fetal alcohol syndrome, 2:872
Fetishes, 2:669–672, 3:1197
　classification of, 2:670
　development, 2:670
　gender, 2:671
　overview, 2:669–670
　relationship implications, 2:672
　social and legal implications, 2:671–672
　treatment, 2:671
Fidelity, 2:672–675
　attachment, 2:674
　ethical principle, 2:566
　faithfulness, 2:673–674
　intimacy, 2:675
　loyalty, 2:673
　overcoming infidelity, 2:675
　overview, 2:672–673
　reliability, 2:674–675
　trust, 2:674
　See also **Extramarital affairs and infidelity**
Fiese, Barbara, 3:1415
Fife, Stephen, 2:587
Figley, Charles, 1:312
Filial therapy model, 1:211, 3:1250
Filicide, 2:801–803
Filter theory, 3:1047
Finances, retirement and, 3:1411
　See also **Debt and financial strain**
Financial abuse, 2:510
Financial metaphors, 3:1066
Finkelstein, Lisa, 1:481
Finn, Stephen, 4:1693
Firesetting, 2:933–936

First-born children. *See* Oldest children
First-order change, 2:676–678, 4:1775
    feedback, 3:1264
    homeostasis, 2:793
    morphogenesis, 3:1099
    second vs., 2:676–678, 4:1460
First-order family therapy, 4:1463–1465
Fisch, Richard, 1:182, 2:676, 4:1461, 1665
Fischer, Constance, 4:1693
Fisher, Philip, 2:688
Fishman, Charles, 4:1614, 1774
Fitzgerald, John "Honey Fitz," 3:1060
Flattum, Colleen, 1:307
Flexibility
    acceptance and commitment therapy, 1:1–3
    affect regulation, 1:51
    circumplex model, 1:254, 287–288, 2:603, 4:1445
    couple/family relationships, 3:1309
    Ericksonian family therapy, 2:558–559
Flooding, 1:144, 336, 338
Flow, 2:820, 4:1535
Fluency disorder, 1:298
Fluoxetine, 2:883, 3:1303
Focal family therapy, 2:679–682
    applications, 2:681
    focal hypothesis, 2:681
    focal plan, 2:681–682
    theory, 2:679
    therapeutic relationship, 2:679–681
FOCUS (Families OverComing Under Stress), 3:1401
Fogarty, Tom, 4:1760, 1770
Fogging, 1:82
Ford, William, 2:601
Forensics, 1:368–371
Forester-Miller, Holly, 3:1096
Forgatch, Marion, 4:1783
Forgiveness, 2:682–685
    benefits, 2:683–684
    definition and conceptualization, 2:682–683
    intervention, 2:684–685
    misunderstandings, 2:683
    overview, 2:682
    process, 2:684
    pseudo-, 2:683
    See also **Reconciliation**
Forgiveness and Reconciliation through Experiencing Empathy, 3:1373
Forms, 3:1290, 1330
Fortune teller, as cognitive distortion, 1:278
42 CFR, 3:1394
Foster children, 1:36, 2:686–689
    African Americans, 1:56, 3:1361–1364
    counselor role, 2:688–689
    demographics, 2:686

    effectiveness research, 3:1354
    foster system challenges and regulations, 2:687–688
    key issues, 2:686
    overview, 2:686
    "upbringing away from parents" as diagnosis, 3:1382
    vulnerability of, 3:1363
Fostering Connections to Success and Increasing Adoptions Act, 2:687, 939
Foucault, Michel, 3:1133–1134, 1347, 4:1568, 1778, 1780
Fourteenth Amendment, 4:1434, 1435
Fourth force, 2:841, 3:1115
Fowers, Blaine, 3:1316
Fox, George, 2:616
Fox, Robin, 2:836
Framing, 1:183
Framo, James, 1:381, 2:868, 3:1010–1013, 1174, 4:1718, 1719, 1769
Frank, Jerome, 1:295–296
Frankl, Viktor, 1:418, 2:815, 4:1702
Fredrickson, Barbara, 3:1265
Free information, 1:82
Freedman, Jill, 4:1780
Freedom, 1:237
Freeman, Arthur, 1:280, 2:931
Freeman, David, 4:1588–1589
Freire, Paulo, 1:348
Freud, Anna, 3:1250
Freud, Sigmund, 1:149, 176, 381, 2:670, 839, 863, 868, 3:1104, 1145, 1147, 1173, 1175, 1333–1335, 1403, 4:1471, 1505, 1523, 1677, 1767–1768
Friends, 1:87
Friends with benefits, 3:1180, 4:1531
Friendship, 2:689–692
    adolescents, 2:691
    benefits, 2:692
    early childhood, 2:690
    early school, 2:690
    love, 3:989
    middle adulthood, 2:691
    middle school, 2:690–691
    older adults, 2:691–692
    overview, 2:689
    young adulthood, 2:691
Friesen, Barbara J., 2:537
Fromm-Reichmann, Frieda, 2:551, 3:1104
Frotteuristic disorder, 3:1196
Fry, Richard, 1:55
Fry, William, 1:181–182, 4:1665
Fukuyama, Francis, 4:1742–1743
Full-Service Community Schools Program, 1:308
Fulton, Paul, 1:311
Fun, 1:237, 377–378, 3:1391

Functional assessment and children, 2:692–697
    behavior and function, 2:692–694
    conducting, 2:694–696
    family, 2:696–697
    overview, 2:692
Functional bilingualism, 1:159
Functional family therapy (FFT), 2:697–701
    attention-deficit and disruptive behavior disorders, 1:119
    case conceptualization, 1:259
    characteristics, 2:698
    evidence-based practice, 2:575
    home-based therapy, 2:781
    outcome research, 3:1188
    outcomes, 2:700
    overview, 2:697–698
    phases, 2:699–700
    principles, 2:698–699
    training model, 2:700–701
Functionalism, 2:701–704
    arguments for, 2:703
    critiques of, 2:703–704
    defining, 2:702
    early theories, 2:702
    emotional intelligence, 2:518–519
    overview, 2:701
    types, 2:702–703
Fundamental attribution error, 2:744
Fusion, 1:173, 2:704–706
Futris, Ted, 3:1306

Gable, Shelly, 3:1264–1265
Gale, Alexandria, 3:1011–1012
Galinsky, Ellen, 3:1234
Gallagher, Chuck, 3:1025
Gambescia, Nancy, 2:587
Gamblers Anonymous, 2:709
Gambling, compulsive, 2:707–710
    characteristics, 2:707–708
    diagnosis, 2:708
    overview, 2:707
    treatment, 2:708–710
Garcia-Preto, Nydia, 1:95
Gardner, Howard, 2:517
Gardner, Richard A., 3:1219
Gateway drugs, 4:1625
Gays. *See* LGBT community; LGBT families
Gebhard, Paul, 4:1506
Gehart, Diane R., 1:283, 4:1736
Gemeinschaftsgefühl (sense of relatedness), 2:777–779
Gender- and culture-sensitive therapies, 2:710–715
    acculturation, 2:712
    cultural differences, 2:710–712
    culturally sensitive therapies, 2:712–713
    feminist therapy, 2:714–715
    gender differences, 2:713–714
    gender roles, 2:714
    male-sensitive therapy, 2:715
Gender dysphoria, 2:715–718
    gender nonconformity, 2:715–716
    overview, 2:715
    sexual orientation, 2:716–717
    treatment, 2:717–718
Gender empowerment measure, 2:665
Gender identity, 2:719
Gender identity disorder, 2:716
Gender issues, 2:718–721
    birth control, 1:163–164
    caregiving, 1:59
    cotherapy, 1:363
    counseling considerations, 2:720–721
    decision-making, 1:428
    depression, 1:439
    domestic violence, 1:468–469
    dual-earner families, 1:481
    externalizing behaviors, 2:582–583
    father-child relationship, 2:764
    feminist family therapy, 2:662–663
    feminization of poverty, 2:665–669
    gender differences, 2:713–714
    gender identity, 2:719
    gender nonconformity, 2:720
    gender presentation, 2:719
    immigrant couples, 2:833–834
    life balance, 3:956
    love, 3:987
    men in counseling, 2:720
    mother-blaming, 3:1106
    overview, 2:718–719
    parental stress, 3:1224
    poverty, 2:595–596
    power, 2:663, 664, 3:1286, 4:1587
    religion, 3:1398
    roles, 2:714
    sex in relation to gender, 4:1501
    sexual fetishes, 2:671
    sexual intimacy, 4:1535–1536
    social construction of gender, 2:722, 3:1239–1240
    socialization (see also **Gender roles**), 2:663, 713–714, 719
    spirituality, 4:1587
    suicide, 4:1630–1631
    women in counseling, 2:719–720
    Women's Project, 4:1760
    See also Men; Women
Gender nonconforming, 2:715–718, 720, 723, 3:1240, 4:1715

Gender orientation, gender identity, and gender
    expression, 2:719, 722–723, 725
Gender presentation, 2:719
Gender roles, 2:724–726
    conflicts, 2:725–726
    decision-making, 1:428
    education, 3:1240
    gender-sensitive therapy, 2:714
    identity formation, 2:725
    Latino families, 3:942
    mate selection, 3:1045
    men in counseling, 3:1057
    Muslim Americans, 3:1129–1130
    nuclear family, 3:1166–1167
    patriarchy, 3:1239–1242
    rural families, 3:1431
    same-sex couples, 4:1434
    workplace, 3:1240–1241
Gender-bender, 2:723
Gender-fluid, 2:723
Gender-queer, 2:723
Gender-related development index, 2:665
General systems theory, 2:727–729
    assumptions, 2:727–728
    circularity, 1:248–249
    concepts, 2:728–729
    cybernetics, 2:727
    feminist family therapy, 2:662–663
    homeostasis, 2:792
    overview, 2:727, 791–792
    system levels, 2:728
    See also Systems theory
Generalized anxiety disorder, 1:70, 74, 221–222
Generativity, in middle adulthood, 1:50
Generosity, 3:989
Genetics
    autism, 1:131
    basic needs and, 1:236
    childhood depression, 1:437
    mood disorders, 3:1092
Genital mutilation, 3:994
Genitals, 4:1502–1503
Genito-pelvic pain/penetration disorder, 2:730–733
    assessment, 2:732
    comorbidity, 2:732
    diagnosis, 2:731
    etiology, 2:731–732
    overview, 2:730
    relationship impact, 2:732
    treatment, 2:732–733
Genograms, 2:733–737
    Adlerian family therapy, 1:18
    Bowen family systems theory, 1:176, 2:734
    circularity principle, 1:252

clinical practice context, 1:265
clinical uses, 2:734–735
conflict, 1:332
considerations when using, 2:736–737
construction of, 2:735–736
couples and marriage counseling, 1:382
ecosystemic structural family therapy, 2:502
faith-based therapy, 2:593
family assessment, 2:608–609
family myths, 2:625
family of origin, 2:626
family resilience, 2:633
history, 2:733–734, 4:1770
illustration, 2:736
integrative couples therapy, 2:868
metaphoric function of, 3:1064
play family therapy, 3:1254
relationship characteristics, 2:735–736
Genos Emotional Intelligence Inventory, 2:519
Gerber, Jane, 4:1772
Gergen, Kenneth, 4:1567, 1778
Geriatric interdisciplinary team training, 2:811
Gerson, Randy, 1:252
Gestalt family therapy, 2:737–741
    experiential family therapy, 2:577, 578
    experimental attitude, 2:739–740
    family reconstruction, 2:629
    field/relational model, 2:738
    phenomenological stance, 2:740–741
    principles, 2:737–738
    therapist role, 2:738–739
Gestalt psychology, 2:591
Gestalt therapy, 3:1144, 1420
Gestational carriers, 1:227
Giedd, Jay, 3:1212
Gifts
    counselors' acceptance of, 2:564
    receiving, as indication of love, 3:996
Gil, Eliana, 3:1251, 1253
Gilbert, Kathleen, 3:977
Gilliam Autism Rating Scale, Third Edition
    (GARS-3), 1:131
Gilligan, Carol, 2:661
Giordano, Joe, 1:95
Glasser, William, 1:237, 375, 418, 2:865–866
Globalization, and feminization of poverty, 2:668–669
Goal attainment scaling, 4:1448
Goals, treatment, 2:741–743
Gobrogge, Kyle L., 3:1047
Goldenthal, Peter, 1:355
Goldstein, Sidney E., 1:193
Goleman, Daniel, 2:517, 4:1786
Gomori, Maria, 4:1772
Good conflict, 3:1387

Goodrich, Thelma Jean, 2:662, 663, 664, 4:1782
Goodridge v. Department of Public Health, 3:1039
Goolishian, Harry, 1:291, 3:1268, 4:1772, 1779
Gordon, Kristina, 2:587
Gordon, Thomas, 3:1198–1202, 1209, 4:1490
Gottman, John, 1:123, 300, 331, 334–336, 382, 407, 427, 460, 2:743–748, 912, 3:1007, 1082, 1299, 1322, 1324, 1373, 1390, 1391, 1404, 4:1489, 1497–1500, 1702, 1782, 1785–1786
Gottman, Julie, 1:123, 334, 336, 3:1082, 4:1702, 1782, 1786
Gottman Institute, 3:1404
Gottman method couples therapy, 2:743–748
  conflict, 1:331
  core triad of balance, 2:744–745
  couples and marriage counseling, 1:382
  evidence-based practice, 2:576
  "four horsemen of the apocalypse," 1:300, 382, 2:745–747, 3:1299, 4:1500, 1786
  interventions, 2:748
  overview, 2:743–744
  sound relationship house, 2:747–748
  techniques of repair, 2:747
Gottman-Rapoport exercise, 1:337
Graff, Thomas, 1:180
Grandfamilies, 2:937–939
Graunt, John, 2:890–891
Gray, John, *Men Are From Mars, Women Are From Venus*, 4:1487, 1489
Green, Robert-Jay, 3:948
Greenberg, Bernard, 1:243
Greenberg, Leslie (Les), 1:67, 104, 113, 123, 2:522, 3:1188, 1321, 1373
Greenberg Jay, 3:1333
Gridlocked problems, 1:427
Grief
  adoption, 1:44
  bereavement, 1:149–150, 152–155
  complicated, 2:750
  divorce and separation, 1:461–462
  families of children with special needs, 1:233, 235
  normative and nonnormative, 2:750
  parents of deceased children, 1:417–420
  symptoms, 2:750
  theories, 2:749–750
  See also **Loss**
Grief counseling, 2:748–751
  assessment, 2:751
  interventions, 2:751
  overview, 2:748–749
  stillbirth and miscarriage, 4:1602–1603
  symptoms of grief, 2:750
  theories, 2:749–750

  therapist role, 2:749–750
  See also **Bereavement counseling**
Grinder, John, 3:1143–1145
Gross, Ellen, 4:1588–1591
Gross, James J., 1:52
Group counseling
  confidentiality, 1:328–329
  postpartum depression, 3:1277
Group family therapy, 2:752–756
  ethical considerations, 2:755–756
  group therapy compared to, 2:752–754
  multiple family therapy, 3:1117–1122
  open-forum family counseling, 1:20–23
  overview, 2:752
  processes, 2:755
  stages, 2:754–755
  therapist role, 2:755
  See also **Marital group therapy**
Group parenting classes, 2:756–758
Group therapy, vs. group family therapy, 2:752–754
Guerin, Philip, 4:1678, 1760, 1770
Guerney, Bernard and Louise, 1:211, 3:1250, 1389–1390
Guided behavior change, 1:280
Guided discovery, 1:280
Guided imagery, 2:621
Guided meditation, 3:1084–1086
Gull, William, 2:489
Gurman, Alan, 2:849, 3:1189
Gurman, J. L., 2:533
Guttentag, Marcia, 3:1046
Guttmacher Institute, 4:1507

Haddock, Shelley, 2:664
Haeckel, Ernest, 2:503
Hage, Sally, 3:1315
Haldol, 4:1626
Haley, Jay, 1:181–182, 252, 262, 265, 333, 471, 2:558, 820, 863, 3:969, 1059, 1067–1068, 1191, 1376, 4:1463, 1603, 1665, 1768, 1771, 1773–1776
Halford, W. Kim, 3:1308
Hall, G. Stanley, 1:31
Hall-McCorquodale, Ian, 3:1105
Hallucinogens, 4:1626
Haloperidol, 4:1626
Handler, Leonard, 4:1693
Hardy, Ken, 2:547
Hare-Mustin, Rachel, 2:661, 4:1781
Hargrave, Terry, 1:274, 355, 3:1406
Harm reduction therapy, 4:1626
Hate crimes, 1:240
Hatfield, Elaine, 3:986
Havighurst, Robert, 2:840
Hawes, Clair, 1:180, 4:1769, 1785

Hayes, Steven C., **1:**1, 4, 5
Hays, Pamela, **1:**379
Hazan, Cindy, **1:**105, 113, 339, **2:**897
Health
 attachment and, **1:**102–104
 community programs, **1:**307
 marriage and, **3:**1020–1022
 marriage and family therapy assessment, **1:**84–85
 public, **3:**1344–1346
 religion, **3:**1395–1396
 retirement, **3:**1411
 rural families, **3:**1430
 sexual assault consequences, **4:**1517–1518
 sexual assessment, **4:**1520–1521
 sexual health, **4:**1502, 1528–1530
 sexually transmitted infections, **4:**1558–1560
 somatic symptom and related disorders, **4:**1580–1584
 spirituality as factor, **4:**1585
 World Health Organization (WHO), **4:**1765–1766
Health care settings, peer counseling in, **3:**1245–1246
Health Information Technology for Economic and Clinical Health, **2:**769–770
Health insurance, **3:**953
Health Insurance Portability and Accountability Act (HIPAA). *See* **HIPAA standards**
Health issues, 2:759–763
 adolescents, **2:**759–760
 adults, **2:**760–761
 children, **2:**759–760
 older adults, **2:**761–763
 overview, **2:**759
Health Resources and Services Administration, **1:**224
Healthcare Providers Service Organization, **4:**1546
Healthy Marriage and Responsible Fatherhood, 2:763–765, **3:**1027, 1138
Healthy marriage community programs, **1:**306
Healthy Marriage Initiative, **3:**1137–1138
Healthy relationships, **1:**179
Heartbeat, **3:**982
Helms, Janet, **2:**571
Helpful factors, **3:**1354
Helping and understanding grieving suicide survivors (HUGSS), **4:**1729
Help-seeking, by men, **3:**1056
Hendrick Sexual Attitude Scale, **4:**1441
Hendrix, Harville, **2:**827, **4:**1785
Henggeler, Scott, **1:**361, **2:**495, **3:**1123
Henry, Lynette, **1:**307
Henry, O., *The Gift of the Magi*, **1:**249
Hepworth, Jeri, **1:**243, **3:**1051
Herek, Gregory, **4:**1543
Herman, Jody, **4:**1716
Herman, Judith, **4:**1475, 1729

Hernandez, Almeida and Pilar, **2:**664
Heroin, **4:**1625, 1626
Hertlein, Katherine, **2:**585, 587
Heston, Jerry, **3:**1417
Hibbs, Janet, **1:**355
Hierarchy, 2:765–767
 strategic family therapy, **2:**765–766, **4:**1605
 structural family therapy, **2:**765–766, **4:**1616–1617
 structural maps, **4:**1621–1622
 systems theory, **2:**729
Higher education, peer counseling in, **3:**1245
Hill, Reuben, **2:**646, 649, 650, **3:**1400, **4:**1662
HIPAA standards, 1:329, 473, **2:**767–770
 administrative safeguards, **2:**769
 enforcement rule, **2:**769–770
 ICD, **2:**890
 physical safeguards, **2:**769
 privacy rule, **2:**767–769
 progress notes influenced by, **3:**1329–1330
 release of information, **3:**1394
 security rule, **2:**769–770
 technical safeguards, **2:**769–770
Hippocampus, **2:**898, **3:**1078
Hirschfeld, Magnus, **4:**1506
Hispanic families. *See* **Latino families**
Hispanic Healthy Marriage Initiative, 2:771–772, **3:**1138
Hispanics. *See* Latinos/as
Hiss, Alger, **4:**1765
Hitler, Adolf, **1:**15, 395
HIV/AIDS, **1:**240–241, **2:**789, **4:**1529
Hoarding, 2:772–776
 animal, **2:**776
 etiology, **2:**773–774
 legal and ethical considerations, **2:**774–775
 overview, **2:**772–773
 special populations, **2:**775–776
 treatment, **2:**774
Hobbes, Thomas, **2:**702
Hodgson, Jennifer, **3:**1051, 1053
Hof, Larry, **3:**1028
Hoffman, Lynn, **4:**1666, 1669, 1768, 1771–1773, 1776, 1779
Hoffman, Martin L., **2:**528
Hoffman, Ted, **4:**1772
Hogan, R. A., **4:**1647
Holidays, **3:**994
Holism, 2:776–779
 Adler's individual psychology, **2:**777–779
 concept of, **2:**776–777
 counseling considerations, **2:**778–779
 individual and family development, **2:**840–841
 overview, **2:**776

spirituality, 2:778
theories, 2:777
Holland, John L., 1:189, 3:1412
Holloway, Elizabeth, 4:1656
Holtzworth-Munroe, Amy, 2:912
Home-based therapy, 2:780–784
    approaches, 2:781–782
    basic tenets, 2:780
    benefits, 2:782–783
    concerns and challenges, 2:783–784
    history, 2:780
    hoarding, 2:775
    overview, 2:780
    therapists and, 2:781
Homelessness, 2:784–787
    advocacy, 2:786–787
    defined, 2:785
    interventions, 2:785–786
    overview, 2:784
    statistics, 2:785
Homelessness and youth, 2:787–790
    advocacy, 2:790
    categories, 2:788
    housing, 2:790
    interventions, 2:788–790
    overview, 2:787–788
    statistics, 2:788
Homeostasis, 2:791–794
    criticisms of, 2:794
    cybernetics, 1:408, 2:792–793
    family therapy, 3:1335
    feedback, 2:793, 3:1262–1263
    first- and second-order change, 2:793
    morphostasis, 3:1102
    overview, 2:791
    reconciliation, 3:1373
    scapegoating, 4:1450–1451
    systemic family therapy, 4:1666
    systems theory, 2:729, 791–792
    therapeutic applications, 2:793–794
Homestead services, 1:390
Homework assignments in therapy, 2:795–799
    benefits, 2:798
    brief family therapy, 1:184
    choosing and implementing, 2:795–796
    Milan systemic approaches, 3:1071
    noncompliance, 2:799
    overview, 2:795
    review of, 2:798–799
    scheduling, 2:796
    sensate focus, 4:1494–1495
    solution-focused brief therapy, 4:1578
    theory, 2:795
    types, 2:796–798

Homicide, 2:800–804
    assessment, 2:803
    counseling considerations, 2:803–804
    couples and families, 2:800–803
    risk factors, 2:803
Hooking up, 4:1531
hooks, bell, 2:662
Hooper, Lisa M., 3:1228
Hope
    faith-based therapy, 2:589
    instillation of, 3:1010
    marriage and family therapy assessment, 1:86
    poverty and family development, 3:1284–1285
    strategies for engendering, 2:544–545
    theories of, 2:543–544
    therapeutic impasses, 4:1702
    Virginia Satir model, 4:1755
Hope-focused approach to couple enrichment in counseling, 2:805–808
    basic tenets, 2:806
    conceptualization, 2:806–807
    historical development, 2:805–806
    interventions, 2:807–808
    overview, 2:805
    research outcomes, 2:807
Horizontal relationships, 2:546
Horizontal stressors, 2:647
Horkheimer, Max, 1:395
Hormone therapy, 3:1276
Hormones, and sexual health, 4:1529
Horney, Karen, 2:795, 815, 839, 4:1480
Horowitz, Leonard, 2:897
Horses. *See* Equine-assisted family therapy
Hospice, 2:802, 808–811
    advantages, 2:808–809
    approaches, 2:810–811
    caregivers, 2:809–810
    counselors' role, 2:810
    eligibility, 2:809
    overview, 2:809
Housing
    homeless youth, 2:790
    socioeconomic status, 4:1573
Houston Galveston Institute, 4:1779
Human Development Study Group, 2:682, 684
Human growth model, 1:258
Human poverty index, 2:665
Human rights, 4:1502
Human sexual response, 2:812–815
    models, 2:812–814
    overview, 2:812
    sensory pathways, 2:813–814
    sexual dysfunction, 2:814–815, 3:1000–1001
Human Systems Journal, 4:1792

Human validation process model, 2:818, 3:1064, 4:1756–1757
Humanistic family therapy, 2:579, 815–818
 basic tenets, 2:816–817
 family roles and communication, 2:817–818
 humanistic principles, 2:816
 overview, 2:815
 techniques, 2:818
Humanistic psychotherapy, 3:1029, 4:1688
Humor, 2:560, 818, 3:1388
Hunt, Helen, 2:827
Hydrocodone, 4:1626
Hynie, Michaela, 3:1224
Hyperactivity, 1:118
Hypnosis, 2:819–822
 brief family therapy, 2:822
 clinical applications, 2:821–822
 Ericksonian family therapy, 2:560, 561, 819, 821, 822
 family reconstruction, 2:629
 flow model, 2:820
 inductions, 2:820–821
 miracle question, 3:1087
 overview, 2:819
Hypochondriasis. *See* Illness anxiety disorder
Hypothesis, systemic, 2:822–824
Hysteria, 4:1525, 1550

"I" statements
 criticism of, 1:300
 divorce and separation counseling, 1:460
 focal family therapy, 2:680
 Gottman method, 2:745, 746
 solution-focused therapy, 1:333
 work relationships, 4:1762
IAMFC. *See* **International Association of Marriage and Family Counselors (IAMFC)**
ICD. *See* **International Classification of Diseases (ICD)**
Identified patient, 2:825–826
Identity
 adolescent development, 1:28
 cross-cultural and interracial adoption, 1:38, 40–41
 online dating, 3:1178
 symbolic interactionism, 4:1663
 See also Cultural identity
Identity development, 2:571–572
Illness anxiety disorder, 4:1582–1583
Illness narratives, 1:243
Imago relationship therapy, 2:827–831, 4:1785
 applications, 2:831
 case conceptualization, 2:829–830
 defined, 2:819–820
 marriage enrichment, 3:1031, 1032
 overview, 2:827

 process, 2:829–831
 relationship stages, 2:828–829
 techniques, 2:830–831
 theoretical basis, 2:827–829
 therapist role, 2:831
Imber-Black, Evan, 3:1414–1415
I-messages, 3:1201
Immediacy, 1:343–344
Immersion, 1:6
Immigrant families, 2:832–835
 Asian Americans, 1:76–77
 assimilation, 1:93–96
 children, 2:833
 couples, 2:833–834
 mental health, 2:834–835
 migration experience, 2:832–833, 3:943, 944
 undocumented immigrants, 2:834
Immigrants and refugees
 acculturation, 1:5–8
 assimilation, 1:93–96
 comparison of immigrants and refugees, 1:94
 definitions, 1:94
 historical overview, 1:94
 stress experienced by, 1:7, 8
 undocumented, 2:834
 See also **Immigrant families**
Immigration and Nationality Act, 1:77, 94, 2:832
Impotence. *See* **Erectile disorder**
Impulsivity, 1:118
In vitro fertilization (IVF), 1:227, 3:1291
In vivo exposure, 4:1518, 1733
Inattention, 1:118
Incest, 2:835–838
Incredible Years training program, 3:1203
Independent living programs, for homeless youth, 2:790
Indian Adoption Project, 1:38
Indian Child Welfare Act, 1:38
Individual and family development, 2:838–843
 Bowen family systems theory, 2:841–843
 family life cycle, 2:610–611
 holistic models, 2:840–841
 life events, 3:958–961
 multidimensional models, 2:840
 nature of development, 2:838–839
 ontogenic models, 2:839–840
 overview, 2:838
 sociogenic models, 2:840
 theories of development, 2:839
 transpersonal models, 2:841
 See also **Adult development**
Individual differences, 2:500
Individual family culture, 2:844–847
 elements, 2:845–846
 family organizational culture, 2:844–845

overview, 2:844
types, 2:846
See also **Family values**
Individual psychology, 1:176, 177, 2:777, 3:1033
Individual versus family therapy, 2:847–850
   ethical considerations, 2:849–850
   identified patient, 2:825–826
   overview, 2:847
   participation perspective, 2:847–848
   research, 2:848–849
   theoretical perspective, 2:848
   See also **Integrating systemic and individual theories**
Individualistic cultures, 2:652–653
Individualized education program (IEP), 1:234, 2:874
Individualized family service plan (IFSP), 1:234
Individuals with Disabilities Education Act, 1:234
Inductions, hypnotic, 2:820–821
Indulgent parenting. *See* Permissive-overprotective parenting
Inequality, 2:665
Infancy, and child-centered parenting, 1:218
Infanticide Act (Britain), 2:802
Infatuation, 1:371–372
Inferiority, 1:15, 178
Infertility, 2:850–854
   biological aspect, 2:851
   childless couples, 1:227
   collaborative treatment, 2:853–854
   meaning-making, 2:853
   overview, 2:850–851
   psychological aspect, 2:851–852
   social aspect, 2:852–853
Infidelity. *See* Extramarital affairs and infidelity; Fidelity
Informed consent for research, 2:567, 854–856
Informed consent in clinical work, 2:857–859, 4:1696–1697
In-Home Child and Adolescent Psychiatric Services, 2:782
In-law relationships, 2:860–862
Insecure-anxious attachment, 1:105, 109, 111–112
   See also **Attachment anxiety**
Insecure-avoidant attachment, 1:109
Insight, 1:310
Institute for American Values, 4:1743
Institute for Social Research, Frankfurt, Germany, 1:395
Institute of Medicine, 3:1315
Institutional review boards (IRBs), 2:856
Institutionalization, 4:1568
Intact family. *See* **Nuclear family**
Integrated developmental model, of supervision, 4:1649, 1655–1656
Integrated Family Violence program, 2:782

Integrating systemic and individual theories, 2:862–867
   overview, 2:862–863
   See also **Individual versus family therapy**
Integration
   cultural, 1:6
Integrative awareness, in cultural identity development, 1:7
Integrative behavioral couples therapy, 1:279, 386–387, 2:576
Integrative couples therapy, 2:867–872
   common counseling concerns, 2:868–870
   couples and marriage counseling, 1:383
   overview, 2:867
   pros and cons, 2:867–868
   stages of model, 2:870–872
Integrity, in late adulthood, 1:50
Intellectual disability and autism, 2:872–874, 3:1161–1162
Intellectual scales, 4:1438
Interaction patterns
   basic structure, 1:257
   conceptualizing, 1:256–259
   maps of, 1:252
Intercultural marriage and family, 2:875–877
   cross-cultural and interracial adoption, 1:37–41
   current challenges, 2:876
   historical and legal influences, 2:875–876
   interventions, 2:876–877
   overview, 2:875
   parenting and child-rearing, 2:876
   See also **Cultural issues in couples and families; Interracial marriages and families**
Interdependence, 1:115–116
Interethnic Adoption Provisions Act, 1:38
Intergenerational loyalty, 2:877–879
Intergenerational relationships
   Asian American families, 1:77–78
   couples and marriage counseling, 1:382
   in-law relationships, 2:862
   poverty, 2:596
   sexual assessment, 4:1521
   teen parenting, 4:1683
   transgenerational family therapy, 4:1718–1720
   transmission of violence, 2:910
   transmission process, 1:175, 2:608, 626–628, 842
Intergenerational trauma, 2:879–881
Intermittent explosive disorder, 1:118, 119
Intermittent explosive disorder in adolescents, 2:882–883
Internal Family Systems model, 2:884–888
   child sexual abuse, 2:910
   couples therapy, 2:887–888
   development of, 2:884–885

exiles, 2:885–886
experiential family therapy, 2:581
firefighters, 2:886
managers, 2:886
overview, 2:884
parts concept, 2:885
Self, 2:887
Internal working model, 2:524
International Academy of Sex Research, 4:1507
International adoptions, 1:35–36, 43
International Association of Group Psychotherapy, 3:1421
International Association of Marriage and Family Counselors (IAMFC), 1:266, 2:888–890, 3:1326, 4:1633, 1711, 1790
International Classification of Causes of Sickness and Death, 2:891
International Classification of Diseases (ICD), 1:12, 321, 473–474, 2:890–893, 2:897
  challenges and concerns, 2:892–893
  DSM in relation to, 1:473, 2:891–893
  future directions, 2:893
  history, 2:890–891
  oppositional defiant disorder, 3:1183
  overview, 2:890
  substance use disorders, 4:1624
  updates, 2:892
  V- and Z-codes, 3:1381
International Classification of Functioning, Disability and Health (ICF), 2:777
International family therapy, 2:894–896
International Family Therapy Association (IFTA), 2:895, 4:1790
International List of Causes of Death, 2:891
International Organization for Migration, 1:94
Internet dating. *See* Online dating
Internet infidelity, 2:584–585, 587, 4:1679
Interpersonal neurobiology, attachment and, 2:896–899
  affect regulation, 1:52
  attachment theory, 2:897–898
  background, 2:896–897
  love, 3:979
  neural development, 2:898–899
  therapeutic applications, 2:899
Interpersonal neurobiology, couples and, 2:900–903
  history, 2:900
  love, 3:979
  overview, 2:900
  theories and assumptions, 2:900–901
  therapeutic applications, 2:901–903
Interpersonal neurobiology, parenting and, 2:903–907
  basic tenets, 2:905
  criticisms of, 2:906–907

history, 2:904
overview, 2:903–904
theories and assumptions, 2:904–905
therapeutic applications, 2:905–906
Interpersonal skills, 1:336–338
Interpersonal violence, 2:907–914
  bullying, 2:911
  child maltreatment, 2:907–910
  domestic violence, 2:912–914
  elder abuse, 2:914
  family violence, 2:907
  neurobiology, 2:901
  overview, 2:907
  rape, 2:911
  sibling abuse, 2:910–911
  stalking, 2:911–912
  See also **Domestic violence**
Interracial marriages and families, 2:915–918
  challenges, 2:916
  considerations for children, 2:916–917
  cross-cultural and interracial adoption, 1:37–41
  prevalence, 2:915
  public opinion, 2:916
  racism and prejudice, 2:917–918
  socialization practices, 2:917
  See also **Intercultural marriage and family**
Intersectionality, 1:400
Intersex, 4:1501, 1715
Intersubjectivity theory, 1:114
Interviews. *See* Clinical interviews with couples and families; Motivational interviewing
Intimacy
  counselor attitudes, 1:379
  decline of, 3:1008
  love, 3:980–983, 987
  nudity, 3:1170
  physiology of, 3:980–983
  young adulthood, 1:49
Intimacy, specific threats to, 2:912, 918–921
  attachment styles, 2:921
  commitment, 2:920–921
  communication, 2:920
  fear, 2:919
  neglect, 2:919–920
  overview, 2:918
  types of intimacy, 2:918–919
Intimate partner homicide, 2:800–801
Intimate partner violence. *See* **Domestic violence**
Intimate relationships
  biopsychosocial assessment, 1:87
  complementary and symmetrical relationships, 1:316–317
  depression's impact on, 1:439–440
  imago relationship, 2:827

love, 3:985–986
   open relationships, 3:1180–1183
   relationship enhancement, 3:1389–1392
   See also **Friendship**; **Love**; **Romance**
Intimate terrorism, 1:468, 2:912
Intrapersonal skills, 1:335–336
Intrinsic Spirituality Scale, 4:1585
Introspection, 1:6–7
Invariant prescription, 4:1668–1669
Invisible loyalty, 1:353
Involuntary clients. *See* **Court-mandated clients**
Iowa Family Interaction Rating Scale (IFIRS), 2:607
Isolation, in young adulthood, 1:49
Isomorphism, 2:727, 922–924
   clinical relevance, 2:923
   ethical considerations, 2:923–924
   overview, 2:922
   parallel process compared to, 2:922–923
   supervisory context, 2:923–924, 4:1636
I-Thou relationship, 1:354, 2:591, 827

Jackson, Don, 1:181–182, 248, 265, 345, 471, 2:863, 3:1059, 1263, 1376, 4:1463, 1665, 1677–1678, 1768, 1772, 1773, 1775–1776
Jacobson, Edith, 4:1768, 1769
Jacobson, Neil, 1:277, 2:912
Jakubowski, Scott F., 2:807
James, William, 4:1662
Jarrott, S. E., 1:60
Jealousy, 3:1181–1182
Jeffries, Vincent, 3:987
Job loss, 2:925–927
Johnson, Michael, 2:912
Johnson, Susan (Sue), 1:67, 104, 105, 113, 123, 383, 407, 2:522–525, 580–581, 3:1188, 1321, 4:1536, 1769, 1782, 1785, 1786–1787
Johnson, Virginia, 2:812, 813, 3:1000, 4:1494, 1506, 1507, 1509, 1536, 1556, 1783
Joiner, Thomas, 1:90
Joining, 2:928–932
   accommodating, 2:931
   attunement, 1:122
   history of SFT, 2:929–930
   multiple family therapy, 3:1120
   overview, 2:928
   process, 2:930
   rapport building, 2:928
   structural family therapy, 4:1617
   therapeutic alliance, 2:929
   therapist role, 2:931–932
Joint Commission on Accreditation of Healthcare Organizations, 2:597
Joint custody, 1:405
Jones, Anne, 4:1597

Jones, Mary Cover, 4:1783
Jongsma, Arthur E., 4:1736
Jordan, Judith, 3:1384
Journal of Couples & Relationships Therapy, 4:1792
Journal of Family Psychology, 4:1792
Journal of Family Theory & Review, 4:1793
Journal of Feminist Family Therapy, 2:661
Journal of Marital and Family Therapy, 1:64, 2:575, 4:1793
Journal of Marriage and Family, 2:532, 4:1793
Journal of Sex and Marital Therapy, 4:1793
Journal of Systemic Therapies, 4:1793
Journal of the American Medical Association, 1:215
Journal writing, 2:713, 797
Jumping to conclusions, 1:278
Jung, Carl, 2:815, 839, 885, 4:1480
Jurkovic, Greg, 3:1229
Justice, as ethical principle, 2:566
Juvenile firesetter interventions, 2:933–936
Juvenile justice reform, 1:206

Kabat-Zinn, John, 3:1080
Kahn, Lauren, 3:1234
Kaleidoscope career paths, 1:190
Kam, Jennifer, 3:1229
Kanner, Leo, 3:1104
Kansas Marital Conflict Scale, 4:1441
Kant, Immanuel, 1:347
Kaplan, Helen Singer, 2:812, 813, 4:1494
Kardiner, Abram, 1:393
Karpel, Mark, 2:642, 644
Karpman, Stephen, 4:1740
Kass, Anne, 1:463
Kazdin, Alan, 3:1206, 1207
Kazdin Method, 3:1207
Keeney, Brad, 3:1347
Keith, David, 4:1771
Kelly, George, 1:347, 349, 3:1421–1422
Kempler, Walter, 2:578–579
Kennedy, Anthony, 4:1435
Kennedy, John F., 1:305, 3:1060
Kennedy, Joseph, Sr., 3:1060
Kerckoff, Alan, 3:1047
Kernberg, Otto, 4:1769
Ketamine, 3:1090
Key informants, 2:695
Keyes, Corey, 3:1265
Kieffer, Charles H., 2:536
Kilmann, Ralph, 1:339
Kim, B. K., 1:78
Kinsey, Alfred Charles, 2:812, 4:1506, 1556
Kinship bonds, of African Americans, 1:55–56

Kinship care, 2:937–939
  African Americans, 1:55–56, 2:938
  informal vs. formal, 2:937–938
  Latinos/as, 2:938
  orphans, 1:213
  overview, 2:937
  reasons for, 2:938
  rewards and benefits, 2:939
  "upbringing away from parents" as diagnosis, 3:1382
  See also **Aging and caregiving**
Kiser, Laurel, 3:1417
Kitchner, K. S., 3:1095, 1096
Klass, Dennis, 1:150
Klein, Melanie, 1:381, 3:1173, 1175, 1250, 1336, 4:1768, 1769
Kleptomania, 1:119
Kline, Christine, 3:1415
Klonopin, 4:1626
Knell, Susan, 3:1250
Knopf, Olga, 1:177
Knowledge. *See* Epistemology
Knudson-Martin, Carmen, 2:663
Knutson, Luke, 3:1306, 1308
Kohut, Heinz, 4:1768, 1769
Koren, Paul E., 2:537
Korlym, 3:1293
Kottman, Terry, 3:1250
Krasner, Barbara, 1:351, 355
Kübler-Ross, Elisabeth, 1:149–150, 152, 421, 464, 2:749
Kuhn, Thomas, 1:147, 3:1349

Labeling, 1:278
Lacroix, François Bossier de, 2:890–891
Lambert, Michael, 1:269, 270, 296
Lamson, Angela, 3:1051, 1053
Landreth, Garry, 1:211
Language
  collaborative language systems, 1:291–293
  conflict resolution, 1:332–333
  Latino families, 3:942
  love languages, 3:995–997
  narrative therapy, 3:1136
  neuro-linguistic programming, 3:1143–1145
  postmodern therapies, 3:1269–1270
  power, 4:1568
  relational frame theory, 1:1–2
  social constructionism, 4:1567–1568
  See also **Bilingual families**
Language disorder, 1:297
Laqueur, H. Peter, 3:1118–1119, 1121
Lasègue, Charles, 2:489
Laszloffy, Tracey, 2:547

Late appraisal model, 2:530
Latino families, 3:941–944
  counseling considerations, 3:943–944
  cultural values and scripts, 3:941–942, 943–944
  diversity of, 3:941
  kinship care, 2:938
  migration experience, 3:943, 944
  religion, 3:942–943
  social factors, 3:942–943
  See also **Bilingual families**
Latinos/as
  population size, 2:771
  teen pregnancy, 3:1293
Law
  best interests of the child, 1:156–158
  birth control, 1:162–164
  child maltreatment, 1:208, 213–216
  counselors' core competencies, 1:358
  court-mandated clients, 1:388–391
  duty to warn, 1:482–485
  ethical decision-making, 2:568, 3:1096
  filicide, 2:802
  firesetting, 2:935
  forensics, 1:368–371
  hoarding, 2:774–775
  identified patient, 2:826
  informed consent, 2:856
  intercultural marriage and family, 2:875–876
  interracial marriage, 2:915
  kinship care, 2:939
  mandated reporters, 3:1003–1006
  marriage equality, 3:948, 1038–1039, 4:1433–1434, 1435
  marriage vs. civil unions, 3:1036–1040
  no-secrets contracts, 3:1164–1165
  parental alienation syndrome, 3:1221
  parenting, 3:944–946, 949
  polygamy, 3:1259
  practice management, 3:1287–1288
  prenuptial agreements, 3:1303–1305
  release of information, 3:1394–1395
  sexual abuse counseling, 4:1514
  sexual fetishes, 2:671–672
  statutory rape, 4:1593–1595
  STI reporting, 4:1560
  therapist-client relationships, 4:1546–1547
  torture, 4:1706–1707
  See also **Legal issues in parenting**
Lawrence v. Texas, 3:1038
Lazarsfeld, Sophie, 1:177
Lazarus, Arnold, 1:80
Le Grange, Daniel, 2:491
League of the Iroquois, 3:1141
Lebow, A. S., 2:533

Lebow, Jay, 3:1043
Lee, Courtland C., 3:1111, 1115
Lee, John Alan, 3:986
Lee, Richard, 1:39
Leeds Alliance in Supervision Scale, 1:272
Legal issues in parenting, 3:944–946
   child rights, 3:946
   custodial rights and responsibilities, 3:945–946
   custody evaluations, 1:403–406
   defining parenthood, 3:944–945
   LGBT parents, 3:949
   See also Law
Legitimation, 4:1568
Lehman, James and Janet, 3:1210
Lesbians. *See* LGBT community; **LGBT families**
Letter-writing, 2:592
Leve, Leslie, 2:688
Levine, Peter, 4:1474
Levinger, G., 3:1425
Levinson, Daniel, 1:47, 2:839
Levitra, 2:556
Lewin, Kurt, 2:493
LGBT affirmative therapy, 4:1435–1436
LGBT community
   caregiving, 1:59–60
   coming out, 3:947–948
   couples therapy research, 1:385
   gender nonconformity, 2:716–717
   mate selection, 3:1047
   rights, 4:1435
   sexual minorities, 4:1538–1539
   sexual prejudice, 4:1543–1545
   social stigma, 1:239–241
   suicide, 4:1631
LGBT families, 3:947–950
   best practices, 3:949–950
   chosen families, 1:239–242
   coming out, 3:947–948
   counseling considerations, 3:949–950
   key issues, 3:947
   marriage equality, 3:948, 1038–1039
   overview, 3:947
   parental options and child-rearing, 3:948–949
   resources and recommendations, 3:950
   transgender, 3:949
   See also **Same-sex couples**
LGBT Families (organization), 3:950
LGBTQ+ individuals, 4:1539
   See also LGBT community; **LGBT families**
Li, L. C., 1:78
Licensure and certification, 3:950–954
   certification requirements, 1:315, 3:953–954
   clinical practice, 1:265–266
   defined, 1:315

   education, 3:952
   examination, 3:952–953
   exemptions, 3:952
   IAMFC, 2:889
   overview, 3:950–951
   practice laws, 3:951–952
   regulation of, 3:951, 953
   title laws, 3:951
   See also **Training and licensure**
Liddle, Howard A., 2:923, 3:1188
Lidz, Theodore, 4:1769
Lie-Bet tool, 2:709
Life balance, 3:952, 954–957
   counseling considerations, 3:957
   culture, 3:956
   developmental perspective, 3:956
   gender, 3:956
   goal, 3:955
   history, 3:954–955
   mental attitude, 3:955–956
   overview, 3:954
   process, 3:955
   wellness, 3:956–957
   work relationships, 4:1761–1762
Life career approach, 1:188
Life course theory
   poverty, 2:596
Life cycle. *See* Family life cycle
Life design paradigm, 1:190
Life events, 3:953, 958–961
   counseling considerations, 3:960–961
   couple and family counseling, 3:960–961
   death and dying, 1:420–423
   factors affecting, 3:959–960
   mental illness, 3:959
   overview, 3:958
   theoretical approaches, 3:960
   types, 3:958–959
Life tasks, 1:47–48, 179
Life transitions, 3:961–965
   bereavement, 1:148–151
   Ericksonian family therapy, 2:559
   family life cycle, 3:964–965
   overview, 3:961–962
   phases of adulthood, 1:48–50
   retirement, 3:1409–1412
   types, 3:962–964
   See also **Family life cycle; Life events**
Life-span theory, 3:1412
Lifestyles, 1:177–178
Liking, 3:985–986
Limbic system, 2:898, 3:982
Lindblad-Goldberg, Marion, 2:499, 4:1785

Lindemann, Erich, **1:**149, 393
Lindsey, Eric, **2:**764
Linearity. *See* **Circularity and linearity**
Linehan, Marsha M., **1:**3, 52
Link Crew, **3:**1245
Lipchik, Eve, **1:**186, **4:**1773, 1777
Listening, empathic, 3:965–968
 cultural competence, **3:**966–968
 mindfulness, **3:**968
 motivational interviewing, **3:**1110
 overview, **3:**965
 Parent Effectiveness Training, **3:**1200–1201
 relationship enhancement, **3:**1392
 skills, **3:**966
 therapeutic origins of, **3:**965
 See also **Life transitions**
Lithium, **3:**1090
Live supervision, 3:969–972
 advantages, **3:**970
 approaches, **3:**969–970
 challenges, **3:**970–971
 defining, **3:**969
 overview, **3:**969
 suggestions for practice, **3:**971–972
Lock, James, **2:**491
Locke-Wallace Marital Adjustment Test, **4:**1441
Logical consequences, **1:**205
Logotherapy, **3:**960
Loneliness, 3:972–975
 causes, **3:**974–975
 consequences, **3:**974
 manifestations, **3:**973–974
 overview, **3:**972
 positive aspects, **3:**975
 prevalence, **3:**973
 related constructs, **3:**972–973
 research, **3:**973–974
 research directions, **3:**975
 treatment, **3:**975
Long, Lynn, **1:**332, 383, **2:**870–871
Longitudinal research, **3:**1353
Lopez, Shane, **3:**1265
Lorenz, Edward, **1:**197
Loss, 3:976–978
 complicated, **3:**978
 coping, **3:**978
 death, **3:**976–977
 divorce and separation, **1:**461–462
 job loss, **2:**295–297
 non-death, **3:**977
 older adults, **2:**762
 overview, **3:**976
 parents of deceased children, **1:**417–420
 stillbirth and miscarriage, **4:**1599–1603

 traumatic, **3:**977
 See also **Bereavement;** Grief
Love
 affectionate, **3:**989
 attachment, **1:**104–107, 113
 charitable, **3:**989
 choice theory, **1:**237
 commitment, **3:**984
 conflict, **3:**991
 connection, **1:**373–374
 couple development, **1:**371–374
 discovery, **1:**373
 erotic, **3:**989, 1423
 gender, **3:**987
 infatuation, **1:**371–372
 maternal and paternal, **3:**981
 measuring, **3:**985
 money, **1:**424
 passionate, **3:**980–981, 986
 post-rapture, **1:**372–373
 relationship components, **1:**373
 Sternberg's triangular theory, **2:**675, **3:**1424
 types, **3:**1423, 1424–1425
 unconditional, **3:**981
 See also **Intimate relationships; Romance**
Love, Patricia, **1:**371–373
Love, physiology of, 3:979–984
 brain, **3:**979–983, 989–990
 chemistry, **3:**982–984
 lovemaking, **3:**983–984
 maternal and paternal love, **3:**981
 neurobiology, **3:**979–981, 989–990
 neurohormonal basis, **3:**981
 overview, **3:**979
 passionate love, **3:**980
 reproduction, **3:**981–982, 983
 self-preservation, **3:**981–982
 unconditional love, **3:**981
Love, theories of, 3:984–988
 attachment theory, **3:**986
 complementarity, **3:**985
 feminization, **3:**987
 liking and loving, **3:**985–986
 love styles, **3:**986
 marital quality and stability, **3:**987
 measurement of love, **3:**985
 overview, **3:**984–985
 passionate love, **3:**986
 social constructionism, **3:**987–988
 triangular, **3:**987
Love, types of, 3:988–991
 dynamics, **3:**990–991
 experiences, **3:**988–989

overview, 3:988
processes, 3:989–990
Love and rituals, 3:991–995
   examples, 3:994–995
   historical perspective, 3:992–993
   overview, 3:991–992
   togetherness, 3:993–995
Love attitudes scale, 3:986
Love languages, 3:995–997
   acts of service, 3:996–997
   learning, 3:997
   physical touch, 3:997
   quality time, 3:996
   receiving gifts, 3:996
   words of affirmation, 3:995–996
Love styles, 3:986
Loving kindness meditation, 3:1077, 1079
Loving v. Virginia, 2:915
Lowe, Ray, 1:21, 4:1769
Loyalty, 1:353–354, 2:673, 877–879, 4:1769
Loyer-Carlson, Vicki L., 1:416
LSD, 4:1626
Luckmann, Thomas, 4:1567, 1568
Luepnitz, Deborah, 2:661
Lust, 3:981
Luteinizing hormone, 4:1529
Lyubomirsky, Sonja, 3:1265

Macdonald, Alasdair, 4:1579
Mace, David and Vera, 3:1028, 1029
Machine state functionalism, 2:702–703
MacLean, Paul D., 1:173
MacPhee, David, 2:664
Macrosystem, 2:494, 496–497
Macy conferences, 4:1463
Madanes, Cloé, 1:262, 3:1068, 1191, 4:1603, 1772, 1773, 1776
Madigan, Stephen, 4:1780
Magnanimity, 3:989
Magnification, 1:278
Mahler, Margaret, 1:445, 4:1768, 1769
Mahoney, Michael, 1:347
Major depressive disorder, 1:431–432, 2:773, 3:1088, 1093
Malcolm, Wanda, 3:1373
Male hypoactive sexual desire disorder, 3:999–1002
   arousal in relation to, 3:1000–1001
   associated features, 3:1000
   counseling considerations, 3:1001–1002
   definition and diagnostic criteria, 3:999
   factors affecting, 3:1001
   prevalence, 3:1000
   treatment, 3:1001

Male-sensitive therapy, 2:715
Malia, Julia, 2:645
Malone, Thomas, 4:1770
Malott, Krista, 4:1722
Mandated reporter, 3:1003–1006
   acceptable evidence, 3:1006
   descriptions of, 3:1003–1004
   mandates for reporting abuse, 3:1004–1006
   need for, 3:1003
   overview, 3:1003
   penalties for failure to report, 3:1005
   reportable offenses, 3:1005–1006
   See also **Duty to warn and protect**
Mania, 3:1089
Manipulative feelings, 3:1320
Mannarino, Anthony, 4:1730
Maps
   couple and family, 3:1308–1310
   ecosystemic structural family therapy, 2:502
   family reconstruction, 2:631
   interaction patterns, 1:252
   neuro-linguistic programming, 3:1144
   structural, 4:1619–1623
   See also **Cognitive maps and couples; Eco-map**
Marcé, Louis-Victor, 2:489
Marcuse, Herbert, 1:395
Marginalization
   cultural, 1:6
   minority stress model, 4:1716
Margolin, Gayla, 1:277
Marijuana, 4:1626–1627
Marital distress, 3:1007–1008
   parental stress, 3:1223–1224
   prevention research, 3:1316–1317
   relational diagnosis, 3:1382–1383
   scales, 4:1441
Marital group therapy, 3:1009–1013
   benefits, 3:1009–1010
   couples therapy vs., 3:1011
   group criteria, 3:1011
   historical development, 3:1010–1011
   overview, 3:1009
   phases, 3:1011–1012
   therapeutic factors, 3:1010
   types of groups, 3:1012–1013
Marital Interaction Coding System, 3:1323
Marital satisfaction, 3:1014, 1017, 4:1536–1537
Marital Satisfaction Inventory, Revised, 4:1441
Mariticide, 2:800
Marlborough Family Services, 3:1121
Marriage
   cohabitation vs., 3:1020
   developmental model
   healthy, 2:763–765

Hispanic Healthy, 2:771–772
hope-focused approach, 2:805–808
intercultural, 2:875–877
interracial, 2:915–918
marital distress, 3:1007–1008
Muslim Americans, 3:1128–1129
national marriage initiative, 3:1137–1139
prenuptial agreements, 3:1303–1305
quality and stability, theory of, 3:987
religion as factor, 3:1397
rituals associated with, 3:993, 994
same-sex, 3:948, 4:1435
spirituality as factor, 4:1586

Marriage, arranged, 3:1013–1016
decline in, 3:1015–1016
marital satisfaction, 3:1014
Muslim Americans, 3:1128–1129
overview, 3:1013–1014
prevalence, 3:1014
United States, 3:1016
variations, 3:1015

Marriage, first and second, 1:461, 3:1017–1019
See also Divorce and separation
Marriage and family therapy (MFT), 4:1636–1638
Marriage and health, 3:1020–1022
Marriage Communication Labs, 3:1028
Marriage counseling. *See* Couples and marriage counseling
Marriage education, 3:1023–1024
marriage enrichment, 3:1027–1033
Marriage encounter, 3:1025–1027, 1028
Marriage Encounter program, 3:1031, 1032
Marriage enrichment, 3:1027–1033
effectiveness, 3:1030–1033
facilitator role, 3:1029–1030
history, 3:1028–1029
participant characteristics, 3:1030
theoretical basis, 3:1029
See also Relationship enhancement
Marriage equality, 3:948, 1038–1039, 4:1433–1434, 1435
Marriage market, 3:1045
Marriage myths, 3:1034–1036
Marriage Review, 2:532
Marriage versus civil unions, 3:1036–1040
counseling considerations, 3:1039–1040
history, 3:1037–1038
overview, 3:1036–1037
Marriage-friendly therapy, 3:1040–1044
core practices, 3:1042–1043
counselor attitudes, 3:1041
current status of, 3:1043–1044
historical background, 3:1040–1041

marriage-friendly values, 3:1042
overview, 3:1040–1041
Martin, Clyde, 4:1506
Masculine protest, 1:178
Masculinity, 3:1055–1058, 1239–1242
Maslow, Abraham, 1:417–418, 2:839, 841, 867, 3:1022, 4:1754
Masochism. *See* Sexual masochism disorder
Massachusetts Department of Mental Health, 3:1142
Masters, William, 2:812, 813, 3:1000, 4:1494, 1506, 1507, 1509, 1536, 1556, 1783
Masturbation, 2:656, 4:1526

Mate selection
concept of, 3:1044–1045
cultural differences, 3:1044
historical perspective, 3:1045
overview, 3:1044
theories, 3:1045–1047

Maturana, Humberto, 3:1350, 1379
Maudsley family therapy, 2:491
May, Rollo, 2:532
Mayer, John D., 2:517
McCarthy, Barry, 4:1534–1535
McCay, Elizabeth, 2:789
McCollum, Eric E., 2:913
McCubbin, Hamilton, 2:632, 643–644, 647, 649
McCullough, Michael, 3:1265
McDaniel, Susan, 1:231–232, 243, 3:1051
McFarlane, William, 3:1119
McGlothlin, Jason, 3:1150
McGoldrick, Monica, 1:95, 252, 2:611, 661, 664, 916, 3:942, 1211, 4:1770, 1781
McHale, Susan, 1:481
McKay, Gary, 3:1209, 4:1490
McKinney-Vento Homeless Assistance Act, 2:785, 790
McLendon, Jean, 4:1772, 1785
McMaster Clinical Rating Scale (MCRS), 2:606–607, 4:1446–1447
McMaster model of family functioning (MMFF), 2:605–607, 4:1446–1447
McMaster Structured Interview of Family Functioning (McSiff), 2:606
McWilliams, Nancy, 3:1333
MDMA, 4:1626
Mead, George Herbert, 4:1662
Meals on Wheels, 1:308
Mealtime Interaction Coding System (MICS), 2:607
Meaning reconstruction, 1:150
Meaning-making
biopsychosocial assessment, 1:89
collaborative language systems, 1:291
Gestalt family therapy, 2:739–740
infertility, 2:853

Measurement metaphors, 3:1066
Media
   military couples and families, 3:1074–1075
   polygamy, 3:1259
Media in family therapy, 3:1048–1049
   benefits, 3:1048
   clinical resources, 3:1049
   overview, 3:1048
   risks, 3:1048
   social media, 3:1048–1049
   See also Technology
Mediated association, 2:529
Mediation
   counseling vs., 2:617
   divorce and separation counseling, 1:460, 466
   family mediation, 2:616–619
   pregnancy termination, 3:1293
Medical family therapy (MFT), 3:1044–1047, 1050–1054
   agency, 3:1052
   childhood obesity, 1:225–226
   chronic illness, 1:243
   collaboration, 3:1052
   communion, 3:1052
   future directions, 3:1054
   historical development, 3:1050–1051
   levels of skill application, 3:1053–1054
   overview, 3:1050
   principles, 3:1051–1053
   systems theory, 3:1051
   three-world view of health care, 3:1052–1053
Medicare, 1:59, 2:809
Medication
   anxiety treatment, 1:71
   autism, 1:133
   autism spectrum disorder, 1:136
   child behavior problems, 1:204–205
   childhood depression, 1:437–438
   erectile disorder, 2:556–557
   gender dysphoria, 2:717
   intermittent explosive disorder, 2:883
   mood disorders in adolescents, 3:1090
   sexual dysfunction, 4:1523–1524
   See also Pharmacology
Meditation, 3:1077, 1080, 1084–1086
Megahead, Hamido, 2:687
Meissner, William, 3:1175
Memory, 2:898, 3:1374
Men
   erectile disorder, 2:554–557, 4:1523
   gender socialization, 2:713–714, 724–726
   hypoactive sexual desire disorder, 3:999–1002
   male-sensitive therapy, 2:715
   patriarchy, 3:1239–1242
   postpartum depression, 3:1275
   premature ejaculation, 3:1301–1303, 4:1523
   responsible fatherhood, 2:763–765
   sexual cycle, 2:554–555
   sexual intimacy, 4:1535–1536
   See also **Gender issues**
Men in counseling, 2:720, 3:1055–1058
   counseling considerations, 3:1056–1058
   help-seeking, 3:1056
   overview, 3:1055
   patriarchy, 3:1241–1242
   presenting concerns, 3:1055
Mencher, Samuel, 1:390
Mendenhall, Tai, 3:1051, 1060
Mental filter, 1:278
Mental health
   acculturation, 1:8
   adult attachment, 1:103
   Asian American families, 1:79
   community centers, 1:305
   court-mandated clients, 1:390
   cross-cultural, 2:711
   deinstitutionalization, 3:1339, 4:1453
   evidence-based practice, 2:576
   family of origin, 2:627
   immigrant families, 2:834–835
   life events, 3:959
   marriage and family therapy assessment, 1:86
   maternal, 1:170
   mother-blaming, 3:1107
   Muslim Americans, 3:1130–1131
   postdoctoral fellowships, 3:1266–1267
   public health and, 3:1345
   religion, 3:1395–1396
   screening for, 1:381
   sexual assault consequences, 4:1516–1517
   sexuality and religion, 4:1551–1552
   spirituality, 4:1585
   stigma associated with, 3:1345
Mental Health Centers Act, 3:1339
Mental health, systemic perspective, 3:1059–1060
Mental Research Institute (MRI), 1:181–182, 257, 345, 2:822, 866, 3:1068, 1376, 1379, 4:1463, 1471, 1575–1576, 1665, 1771, 1775–1776
Meritocracy, 4:1572
Mesosystem, 2:494, 496
Meta-analysis, 3:1353–1354
Metacommunication, 3:1060–1062
   applications, 3:1061–1062
   Bateson's research on, 3:1061
   enactments, 2:540
   humanistic family therapy, 2:817

Metaphors, 3:1062–1067
 appropriate, 3:1063
 architectural, 3:1066
 consistency of, 3:1066–1067
 constructivism, 1:350
 culinary, 3:1066
 empathy conveyed by, 3:1063
 Ericksonian family therapy, 2:561
 family therapy applications, 3:1063–1065
 family-based, 3:1066
 financial, 3:1066
 humanistic family therapy, 2:818
 linguistic role, 3:1062–1063
 measurement-based, 3:1066
 nature-based, 3:1066
 overview, 3:1062
 play family therapy, 3:1252
 sport-based, 3:1065
 types, 3:1065–1066
 war-based, 3:1066
 weather-based, 3:1066
 work-based, 3:1065
Metasystems. See Systems, subsystems, and metasystems
Methadone, 4:1626
Methamphetamine, 4:1625
Methylphenidate, 1:204, 4:1625
Metz, Michael, 4:1534–1535
Microaggressions, 2:711–712, 3:1140, 1367–1368
Microsystem, 2:493, 496
Middle adulthood, friendship in, 2:691
Middle children, 1:17–18, 178, 332, 4:1563
Midlife, family life cycle stage, 2:612
Mifepristone, 3:1293
Milan team, 3:1067–1071
 circular questions, 3:1359
 empirically validated models, 2:533
 guidelines, 3:1070–1071
 history, 3:1067–1068, 4:1471, 1773, 1776–1777
 joining, 2:928
 narrative therapy, 3:1133
 neutrality, 3:1146
 recursiveness, 3:1376–1377
 systemic family therapy, 4:1665–1666, 1668
 team approach, 3:1379
 techniques, 3:1069–1070
 therapy process, 3:1068–1069
Milburn, Norweeta, 2:789
Miles, Raymond, 4:1743
Military couples and families, 1:188, 3:1072–1076
 challenges of military lifestyle, 3:1072–1073
 changes in military, 3:1076
 counseling process, 3:1075
 counselor role, 3:1072
 history of military family counselors, 3:1073–1074
 key elements of therapy, 3:1075–1076
 media role, 3:1074–1075
 military cultures, 3:1072
 parentification, 3:1229
 posttraumatic stress disorder, 3:1074
Military reservists, 3:1073
Military veterans, 1:188, 4:1631
Miller, Jean Baker, 3:1384
Miller, Richard B., 2:807
Miller, Scott, 4:1777
Miller, William, 3:1028, 1107–1109, 4:1628
Millon, Theodore, 4:1785
Milne, Eric P., 2:807
Milton H. Erickson Institute, 1:23
Mimicry, 2:528
Mind, brain distinguished from, 2:901, 905
Mind–brain identity theory, 2:703
Mindfulness, 3:1076–1079
 acceptance and commitment therapy, 1:2
 compassion, 1:310
 conflict resolution, 1:336
 effectiveness, 3:1078
 emotional regulation, 3:1078
 faith-based therapy, 2:593
 family mode deactivation therapy, 2:621–622
 family relations, 2:905–906
 listening, 3:968
 marriage and family therapy assessment, 1:89
 overview, 3:1076–1077
 restoration therapy, 3:1409
 theoretical basis, 3:1077
 therapeutic applications, 3:1078–1079
 types of practice, 3:1077–1078
Mindfulness and children, 3:1080–1081
Mindfulness and couples, 3:1081–1083
Mindfulness and sex, 3:1083–1086
 hypnosis and guided meditation, 3:1084–1086
 overview, 3:1083
 sexual dysfunction, 3:1083–1084
Mind-reading, 1:278
Mindsight Institute, 2:899
Minimization, 1:278
Minimized emotions, 1:280
Minnesota Couples Communication program, 3:1028, 1316
Minnesota Family Investment Project, 3:1401
Minnesota Multiphasic Personality Inventory-2, 4:1442
Minorities
 acculturation, 1:5–8
 cross-cultural and interracial adoption, 1:37–41, 4:1720–1722
 See also African Americans; Asian Americans; Ethnicity; Latinos/as; Race

Minority stress model, 4:1716
Minuchin, Salvador, 1:122, 125, 265, 330, 2:491, 499, 539, 706, 729, 928, 929, 931, 3:969, 1103, 1133, 1227, 1251, 4:1451, 1457, 1471–1472, 1614, 1619, 1622, 1665, 1691, 1739, 1771, 1773–1774, 1782
Minuchin Center for the Family, 4:1774
Minuhi, 3:1059
Miracle question, 2:742, **3:1086–1087**, 4:1449, 1577
Mirror neurons, 2:529, 900, 904, 3:1078
Mirroring, 3:965
Miscarriage, 4:1599–1603
Mistaken goals, 1:178
Mitchell, Stephen, 3:1333
Mize, Jacquelyn, 2:764
Mode deactivation therapy, 2:620
Model minority myth, 1:78
Modeling, 1:144
Modulated disenmeshment, 3:1120
Molly (drug), 4:1626
Mondale, Walter, 1:208
Money, 1:424
Money, John, 4:1507
Monoamine oxidase inhibitors, 3:1090
Monroe, Marilyn, 3:1060
Monshi, Bardia, 1:484
Montalvo, Braulio, 4:1614, 1773
Montel, Kelly, 3:1316
Mood, marriage and family therapy assessment of, 1:86
Mood disorders, 1:24–25
Mood disorders in adolescents, 3:1087–1091
　overview, 3:1087–1088
　risk factors, 3:1088
　symptoms, 3:1088–1089
　treatment, 3:1089–1091
Mood disorders in children, 3:1091–1094
　assessment, 3:1093–1094
　causes, 3:1091
　overview, 3:1091
　resilience, 3:1093
　risk factors, 3:1092–1093
　symptoms, 3:1091–1092
　treatment, 3:1093–1094
　types, 3:1093
　See also **Depression in children**
Moral dimensions of therapy, 3:1094–1097
　counseling considerations, 3:1096–1097
　decision-making, 3:1097
　models and theories, 3:1095
　moral principles, 3:1095
　overview, 3:1094–1095
　role of voice, 3:1095–1096

Morals and morality, 1:163, 4:1704–1705
　See also Ethics
Moreno, Jacob, 2:629, 3:1418, 1421
Mormon Church, 3:1259
Morphine, 4:1626
Morphogenesis, 3:1098–1100
Morphostasis, 3:1101–1104, 4:1674
　See also **Homeostasis**
Morrison, Todd Graham, 3:1258
Morton, Richard, 2:489
Moses, 4:1449
Moss, Bleema, 2:561
Mother-blaming, 3:1104–1107
　gender, 3:1106
　mental health, 3:1107
　overview, 3:1104
　research on, 3:1105–1106
　social context, 3:1106
　theories, 3:1104–1105
Motherhood, love in, 3:981
Motivational interviewing, 3:1107–1110
　development of, 3:1107–1108
　overview, 3:1107
　principles, 3:1109–1110
　spirit of, 3:1108
　substance use disorders, 4:1628
　youth homelessness, 2:790
Mourning, 1:149–150
Moustakas, Clark E., 3:975
Movies, 1:245–247
MRI. See Mental Research Institute (MRI)
MRI model, 1:182, 185–186, 3:1379, 4:1773, 1775, 1777
Multicultural and Social Justice Counseling Competencies, 1:456–457
Multicultural counseling competences, 3:1104, 1110–1113
　components, 3:1111–1112
　counseling considerations, 3:1113
　cultural differences, 3:1112–1113
　diversity, 1:455–456
　Latino families, 3:943–944
　listening, 3:966–968
　men in counseling, 3:1055–1058
　Muslim American families, 3:1131
　Native American families, 3:1140–1141
　overview, 3:1110–1111
　practice management, 3:1288
　principles, 3:1111
　standards, 3:1115–1116
　strategies and techniques, 3:1112
　supervision, 4:1635
　training, 3:1116–1117
　urban families, 4:1747–1749

Multiculturalism, 3:1114–1117
  bereavement counseling, 1:152
  bilingual families, 1:161
  counseling competencies, 1:455–456
  couples and marriage counseling, 1:379
  feminism and, 4:1782
  historical and theoretical development, 3:1114–1116
  intercultural marriage and family, 2:875–877
  oppositional defiant disorder, 3:1186
  skills associated with, 1:457
  training, 3:1116–1117
  See also **Diversity**
Multidimensional family therapy
  evidence-based practice, 2:575
  home-based therapy, 2:781–782
  individual and family development, 2:840
  outcome research, 3:1188
Multidirected partiality, 1:355
Multiethnic Placement Act, 1:38
Multigenerational relationships. *See* Intergenerational relationships
Multiple family therapy, 3:1117–1122
  children and adolescents, 3:1122
  components, 3:1120–1121
  concepts, 3:1118
  history, 3:1118–1120
  marital group therapy, 3:1013
  models, 3:1121–1122
  overview, 3:1117–1118
  structure of, 3:1119
Multiple impact therapy, 1:393–394
Multiple relationships. *See* **Dual and multiple relationships**
Multiracial individuals, 2:916–917
Multisystemic ecological comparative approach, 3:1117
Multisystemic Therapy (MST), 3:1123–1127
  attention-deficit and disruptive behavior disorders, 1:119
  challenges and criticisms, 3:1126–1127
  core principles, 3:1124
  diversity, 3:1123
  ecological perspective, 2:495
  evidence-based practice, 2:575
  goals, 3:1123–1124
  interventions, 3:1124–1125
  outcomes, 3:1125–1126
  overview, 3:1123
  therapist role, 3:1124
  training and supervision, 3:1126
Multisystemic Therapy (MST) for Juvenile Offenders, 3:1317
Munchausen syndrome, 2:802, 4:1581–1582
Munkvold, L. H., 3:1186

Murder. *See* **Homicide**
Murray-Garcia, Jann, 3:1116
Murstein, Bernard, 3:1045
Muse, 2:556
Muslim American families, 3:1128–1131
  diversity of, 3:1128
  gender expectations, 3:1129–1130
  marriage, 3:1128–1129
  mental health services, 3:1130–1131
  overview, 3:1128
Mutual influence, 2:728–729
Mutuality, 3:1384, 1405
Myers-Briggs Type Indicator, 1:339, 4:1442
Myths, 2:623–624

Naltrexone, 4:1626
Naming emotions, 1:122
Napier, Augustus, 1:398–399, 4:1771, 1782, 1785
Napier, Margaret, 4:1785
Narada, Bhikku, 1:311
Narcotics Anonymous, 1:306, 4:1627, 1658, 1660
Narrative career counseling, 1:190
Narrative therapy, 3:1133–1137
  counseling process, 3:1134–1135
  faith-based therapy, 2:592
  interventions and techniques, 3:1135–1137
  metaphors used in, 3:1064–1065
  overview, 3:1133, 4:1780
  postmodern therapies, 3:1133–1134, 1271–1272
  research, 3:1137
  resilience, 3:1401
  second-order family therapy, 4:1464
  sex therapy, 4:1510
  social constructionism, 4:1569
  therapist role, 3:1134
Narratives
  clinical interviews, 1:261
  deficit, 4:1749–1750
  emotional regulation, 2:899
  Ericksonian family therapy, 2:561
  family myths, 2:578, 623–625
  illness, 1:243
  postmodern therapies, 3:1268, 1271–1272
  rituals linked to, 3:992
  trauma-focused cognitive-behavioral therapy, 4:1732–1733
National Alliance on Mental Illness (NAMI), 1:435, 2:758
National Association of Black Social Workers (NABSW), 1:38
National Association of Parents, 3:1210
National Association of Social Workers, 3:1115, 1394, 4:1435, 1544, 1633

National Board of Certified Counselors (NBCC), **1:**313, 367, **2:**889, **4:**1790
National Center for Family and Marriage Research, **3:**1022
National Center on Child Abuse and Neglect, **1:**208
National Child Abuse Prevention and Treatment Act, **3:**1004–1006
National Child Traumatic Stress Network, **3:**1279
National Clinical Mental Health Counseling Exam, **3:**953
National Council on Family Relations (NCFR), **1:**193–196, **2:**613, 614–615, **3:**1024, **4:**1507, 1790–1791
National Counseling Exam, **3:**953
National Credentialing Academy (NCA), **2:**889, **4:**1791
National Family Caregiver Support Program, **2:**939
National Guard, **3:**1073
National Healthy Marriage Resource Center, **3:**1022, 1027
National Institute on Drug Abuse, **3:**1267
National Institute on Mental Retardation (Canada), **3:**1161
National Institutes of Health, **3:**1267, 1314
National Marriage Encounter, **3:**1025
National marriage initiative, 3:1137–1139
National Parenting Center, **3:**1210
National Registry of Evidence-based Programs and Practices (NREPP), **1:**10, **3:**1245, 1316
Native American Church, **3:**1140
Native American families, 3:1139–1141
   common characteristics, **3:**1140
   counseling considerations, **3:**1140–1141
   cultural trauma, **3:**1140–1141
   history, **3:**1139–1140
   overview, **3:**1139
Native American Healthy Marriage Initiative, **3:**1138
Native Americans
   adoption of, **1:**38
   balance and harmony, **3:**955
   gender nonconformity, **2:**716
   suicide, **4:**1631
Natural consequences, **1:**205, 323
Nature metaphors, **3:**1066
Naturism, **3:**1170–1171
Nazi Party, **1:**15, 21, 395
Negative affect reciprocity, **2:**744
Negative assertion, **1:**82
Negative feedback. *See* **Positive and negative feedback**
Negative inquiry, **1:**82
Negative reinforcement, **1:**138, 141, 323, **2:**693–694, **3:**1204

Neglect
   child maltreatment, **1:**209, **2:**908
   elder abuse, **2:**510
   intimacy, **2:**919–920
Neglectful parenting. *See* Rejecting-neglecting/disengaged parenting
Neimeyer, Robert, **1:**347
Nelsen, Jane, **3:**1210
Neocortical system, **1:**173, 274
Neomammalian brain, **1:**173
Neopragmatism, **2:**550
Netherlands, **4:**1504
Network therapy, 3:1142–1143
Networking, **3:**1289, 1325–1326
Neugarten, Bernice, **1:**48, **2:**840
Neumiller, S., **2:**786
Neural loops, **2:**621
Neurobiology
   adolescent development, **3:**1212
   cognitive maps, **1:**274
   empathy, **2:**529–530
   interpersonal neurobiology, **2:**896–907
   love, **3:**979–981, 989–990
   mindfulness, **3:**1076–1078
   regulation theory, **1:**52
   See also Brain
Neuro-linguistic programming, 3:1143–1145
Neuroplasticity, **1:**274, 275, **2:**897, 905, **3:**979
Neutrality and curiosity, 3:1145–1148
   systemic family therapy, **4:**1667
New York Society for the Prevention of Cruelty to Children, **1:**214
News releases, **3:**1289
Newsletters, **3:**1289
Ng, G. F., **1:**78
Nichols, Michael, **1:**471, **2:**581, **3:**1333–1336, **4:**1781
Nickman, Steven, **1:**150
Nicolaisen, Magnhild, **3:**974
Nicoll, Bill, **4:**1769
Niemeyer, Robert, **1:**150
Nietzsche, Friedrich, **2:**839
Night terrors, **3:**1154
Nixon, Richard, **1:**208
No-harm contracts, 1:93, 3:1148–1153, 4:1698
   assessment, **3:**1150–1151
   developing safety plan, **3:**1151–1152
   essential elements, **3:**1152
   ethical considerations, **3:**1149
   objectives, **3:**1149–1150
   overview, **3:**1148
   special considerations and populations, **3:**1152–1153
   therapeutic relationship, **3:**1149

Nonmaleficence, as ethical principle, 2:566
Nonmatching emotional responses, 2:530–531
Nonmonogamy, 3:1180–1181, 1255–1258, 1259
Nonprofessional relationships. *See* Dual and multiple relationships
Non–rapid eye movement sleep arousal disorders in children, 3:1153–1155
   causes, 3:1154
   counseling considerations, 3:1154–1155
   risks, 3:1154
   sleep stages, 3:1153
   symptoms, 3:1154
   treatment, 3:1154
Nonresidential fathers, 3:1155–1157
Nonverbal communication, 3:1157–1161
   best practices, 3:1148–1149
   cultural variations, 3:1160
   defined, 1:302
   errors/problems, 1:301
   overview, 3:1157–1158
   premarital counseling, 3:1298
   therapists' use of, 3:1160–1161
   types, 3:1158–1160
Norcross, J. C., 2:532
Norepinephrine, 3:982–983, 1090
Normalizing, 3:1161–1162
No-secrets contracts, 1:328, 2:565, 3:1162–1165
   confidentiality considerations, 3:1163
   content, 3:1164
   determining the client, 3:1163
   ethical and legal implications, 3:1164–1165
   limitations, 3:1165
   overview, 3:1162–1163
   types, 3:1163–1164
   See also Confidentiality; Secrets
Not-knowing position, 4:1779
Nouwen, Henri, 4:1473
Nuclear family, 3:1166–1168
   communication, 1:304
   defined, 3:1166
   emotional process, 1:174–175, 2:608, 842
   normative character of, 3:1166–1168
   prevalence of, 1:242
   societal changes affecting, 3:1167–1168
   traditional concept, 3:1166–1167
Nudism, 3:1170–1171
Nudity: beliefs and values, 3:1168–1171
Nuremberg Code, 2:856
Nurse Home Visitation Program, 3:1401
Nurturing Parent program, 2:757

Oaklander, Violet, 3:1250
Obama, Barack, 1:164, 3:948, 1005, 1039
Obergefell v. Hodges, 3:948, 1039, 4:1435

Obesity. *See* Childhood obesity, prevention and treatment of
Object relations family therapy, 4:1769
Object relations theory, 3:1173–1176
   conflict, 1:331–332
   couples and family counseling, 3:1175–1176
   couples and marriage counseling, 1:381
   Freudian theory in relation to, 3:1333–1334
   individual psychology, 3:1173–1174
   key theorists, 3:1173, 4:1768
   overview, 3:1173
   partner relationships, 3:1174–1175
   therapist role, 3:1175–1176
Observation. *See* Direct observation
Observational coding, 3:1323–1325
Obsessive-compulsive disorder (OCD), 2:773
ODD. *See* Oppositional defiant disorder (ODD)
O'Farrell, Gary, 2:598
Offer, Daniel, 1:31
Office for Human Research Protections, 2:854
Office of Family Assistance, 3:1138
Office of Juvenile Justice and Delinquency Prevention, 1:26
Office of the Assistant Secretary for Planning and Evaluation, 2:771
Office space, 3:1289
Ogles, Benjamin, 1:269, 270
O'Hanlon, Bill, 4:1511, 1773, 1777–1778, 1780
Olanzapine, 1:133
Older adults
   community programs, 1:308
   family life cycle stage, 2:612
   feminization of poverty, 2:667
   friendship, 2:691–692
   health issues, 2:761–763
   hoarding, 2:775
   life transitions, 3:963–964
   peer counseling, 3:1246
   retirement, 3:1409–1412
Older Americans Act, 1:308
Oldest children, 1:17, 178, 332, 4:1562
Oliver, J. Toni, 4:1720–1721
Olson, David, 1:253, 2:644, 3:1306, 1308, 1316, 4:1445
Online dating, 3:1176–1179
   counseling considerations, 3:1179
   history, 3:1177
   Internet infidelity, 2:584–585, 587
   overview, 3:1176
   process, 3:1177
   research directions, 3:1179
   risks, 3:1178–1179
   typical online dater, 3:1177–1178

Online support groups and communities, 4:1661
Only children, 1:17, 178, 4:1562
Open adoptions, 1:35, 43, 44–45
Open monitoring, 3:1082
Open questions, 3:1357–1358
Open relationships, 3:1180–1183
    client implications, 3:1181–1182
    counseling considerations, 3:1182–1183
    overview, 3:1180
    rule management, 3:1182
    terminology, 3:1180
    See also **Polyamory**
Open space awareness, 3:1078
Open-forum family counseling. *See* **Adlerian open-forum family counseling**
Operant conditioning, 1:141–142, 2:693, 3:1204, 4:1783
    See also Reinforcement
Opioids, 4:1626
Opium, 4:1626
Opportunity gap, 3:1283
Oppositional defiant disorder (ODD), 3:1183–1186
    case conceptualization, 3:1184–1185
    causes, 3:1185
    characteristics, 1:25, 119
    classification of, 1:118
    comorbidity, 3:1186
    conduct disorder compared to, 1:321, 322, 3:1184
    externalizing behaviors, 1:28
    future research, 3:1186
    multicultural perspective, 3:1186
    overview, 3:1183–1184
    parent management training, 3:1203
    prevalence, 3:1185
    symptoms, 3:1184
    treatment and management, 3:1185–1186
Orphan trains, 1:214
Orphans, 1:213–214
Other specified anxiety disorder, 1:75
Outcome research, 3:1187–1190
    See also **Cost-benefit analysis; Effectiveness research**
Overeaters Anonymous, 1:307
Overgeneralization, 1:278
Oxford Group, 1:306
Oxycodone, 4:1626
Oxytocin, 2:673, 3:981, 982, 983, 990, 1338

Paavola, Marilyn, 3:1417
PACE approach, 1:116
Paik, Anthony, 4:1532
Pain, acceptance and commitment therapy for, 1:1–4
Pain cycles, 1:275, 3:1407–1408
Pairing Enrichment Program, 3:1033
PAIRS curriculum, 3:1012, 1030

Palazzoli, Mara Selvini, 4:1666
Paleomammalian brain, 1:173
Palo Alto group, 3:1068, 4:1463, 1665
Pangendered, 2:723
Panic attacks, 1:72–73
Panic disorder, 1:70, 72, 222
Pansexuality, 4:1538–1539, 1542
Papp, Peggy, 2:661, 662, 4:1759–1760, 1768, 1772, 1779, 1781
Paradoxes and paradoxical interventions, 3:1191–1194
    brief family therapy, 1:182
    case example, 3:1193–1194
    conceptual basis, 3:1191–1192
    indications and contraindications, 3:1192–1193
    Milan systemic approaches, 3:1069
    reactance theory, 3:1192
    resistance, 3:1403
    strategic family therapy, 4:1607–1608
    systemic family therapy, 4:1668, 1669
    value of, 3:1193
    See also **Double bind theory**
Paralanguage, 3:1159
Parallel play, 2:690
Parallel process, 2:922–923
Paraphilic disorders, 3:1194–1198
    exhibitionistic disorder, 3:1195–1196
    fetishistic disorder, 3:1197
    frotteuristic disorder, 3:1196
    overview, 3:1194–1195
    pedophilic disorder, 3:1195
    sexual masochism disorder, 3:1196–1197
    sexual sadism disorder, 3:1196–1197
    transvestic disorder, 3:1197–1198
    voyeuristic disorder, 3:1196
Parens patriae, 1:213
Parent Effectiveness Training (P.E.T.), 3:1198–1202, 4:1490
    components, 3:1200–1202
    core competencies, 3:1202
    foundations, 3:1199–1200
    history, 3:1198–1199, 1209
    instructor training, 3:1202
    overview, 3:1198
Parent Encouragement Program, 3:1210
Parent management training, 3:1203–1207
    basics, 3:1205–1206
    behavioral parent training, 3:1207
    evidence-based practice, 2:576
    history, 3:1203–1204
    Kazdin Method, 3:1207
    Oregon Model, 3:1206–1207
    overview, 3:1203
    principles and concepts, 3:1204–1205

problem-solving skills training, 3:1206
Yale Program, 3:1205–1206
Parent Project, 2:758
Parent study groups, 3:1208–1210
Parent–adolescent relations, 3:1210–1214
   adolescent development, 3:1210–1211
   family development theories, 3:1211–1212
   parenting, 3:1213–1214
   theories of adolescence, 3:1211
Parental acceptance-rejection theory, 3:1215–1218
   coping subtheory, 3:1216–1217
   overview, 3:1215
   personality subtheory, 3:1216
   sociocultural subtheory, 3:1217–1218
   warmth dimension, 3:1215–1216
Parental alienation syndrome, 3:1218–1221
   controversy over, 3:1220–1221
   defined, 3:1218–1219
   DSM-5 and, 3:1220
   legal interventions, 3:1221
   overview, 3:1218
   research on, 3:1219–1220
   therapeutic interventions, 3:1221
Parental stress: effects on children, 3:1222–1225
   child development, 3:1224–1225
   child maltreatment, 1:210
   childhood chronic illness, 1:231
   clinical practice implications, 3:1225
   cultural factors, 3:1224
   finances, 1:425
   financial and occupational stress, 3:1223
   gender as factor, 3:1224
   love, 3:982
   marital stress, 3:1223–1224
   medical stress, 3:1224
   overview, 3:1222
   parenting styles, 3:1222–1223
   relational diagnosis, 3:1382
   single-parent families, 4:1565
   symptomatology, 3:1223
   See also **Family stress**
Parent–child communication, 3:1226–1227, 4:1733
Parent–child interaction therapy, 2:576, 3:1203, 1400
Parent–child relationship
   depression's impact on, 1:441–442
   intergenerational trauma, 2:880–881
   relational diagnosis, 3:1381–1382
Parentification and diverse family systems, 3:1227–1231
   alcohol and substance abuse, 1:63
   consequences, 3:1230–1231
   contextual family therapy, 1:354
   defined, 3:1227–1228
   divorced families, 3:1228–1229

   English-as-a-second-language families, 3:1229–1230
   lower SES families, 3:1228
   military families, 3:1229
   overview, 3:1227
   typical family systems, 3:1228–1230
Parenting, 3:1231–1234
   Active Parenting, 1:9–10
   acculturation gap, 1:7–8
   adolescent-parent relations, 3:1213–1214
   adoption, 1:34–37
   African Americans, 1:57
   attachment, 3:1232–1233
   best interests of the child, 1:157
   bonding, 1:168–170
   challenges, 3:1233
   child adjustment, 3:1237–1238
   child parent relationship theory, 1:211–213
   child-centered, 1:216–219
   coparenting, 1:370, 2:764
   cultural factors, 3:1233
   defining parenthood, 3:944–945
   family functioning, 1:124–125
   information and models available, 3:1233–1234
   intercultural marriage and family, 2:876
   interpersonal neurobiology, 2:903–907
   legal issues, 3:944–946, 949
   LGBT, 1:241
   life transitions, 3:964
   nonresidential fathers, 3:1155–1157
   overview, 3:1231–1232
   Parent Effectiveness Training, 3:1198–1202
   parent management training, 3:1203–1207
   premarital counseling, 3:1299–1300
   reparenting, 3:1408
   rule-setting, 3:1427
   self-esteem, 4:1481
   societal changes affecting, 3:1232
   stages, 3:1234–1235
   study groups, 3:1208–1210
   teen parenting, 4:1682–1685
Parenting education, 3:1234–1235
   characteristics and objectives, 3:1235
   group classes, 2:756–758
   trauma-focused cognitive-behavioral therapy, 4:1731
Parenting styles, 3:1236–1239
   discipline techniques, 3:1236–1237
   emotional intelligence, 2:520
   impact, 3:1238
   influence of stress on, 3:1222–1223
   parent–adolescent relations, 3:1213–1214
   race and ethnicity, 3:1238
   socioeconomic status, 3:1238
   types, 1:125–128, 217–218, 3:1236–1238

Parents
    deceased children, 1:417–420
    depression, 1:441–444
    family atmosphere grounded in, 1:16–17
    intergenerational relationships, 1:77–78
    role models, 1:219
Parents' Evaluation of Developmental Status, 4:1438
Park, Robert E., 4:1662
Parker, Lynn, 2:664
Paroxetine, 2:883
Partner-assisted modalities, 2:533
Partnerships to Improve Community Health, 1:307
Passion, 3:980–981, 986, 987
Passivity, 1:80
Patient-focused research, 1:269
Patriarchy, 3:1239–1242
    implications for therapy, 3:1241–1242
    overview, 3:1239
    social settings, 3:1239–1241
Patterson, Gerald, 3:1203–1206, 4:1783
Patterson, Joan, 2:643–644, 647, 649
Patterson, Terence, 4:1784
Paulson, Friedrich, 3:1095
Pavlov, Ivan, 1:382, 4:1782–1783
Paxil, 2:883
Peace cycles, 1:275, 3:1408–1409
Pearce, Diane, 2:665
Pedersen, Paul, 3:1115
Pedophilic disorder, 3:1195
Peer counseling, 3:1242–1246
    counselor training, 3:1243–1244
    overview, 3:1242
    rationale, 3:1243
    settings, 3:1244–1246
Peer relationships, 1:100–101, 3:1212
Peirce, Charles, 4:1662
Peller, Jane, 4:1773, 1777
Penn, Peggy, 4:1666, 1669
Peplau, Letitia, 3:974–975
Perception-action models, 2:529–530
Pereira, Jennifer, 3:1419
Perel, Esther, 4:1537
Perlman, Daniel, 3:974–975
Perls, Fritz, 3:1011, 1143, 1144
Permission, limited information, specific suggestions, and intensive therapy (PLISSIT) model, 4:1520
Permissive-overprotective parenting, 1:217
    characteristics, 1:127, 3:1236–1237
    child adjustment, 3:1238
    effectiveness, 1:127–128
    emotional intelligence, 2:520
    parent–adolescent relations, 3:1214
Perrone, Kristin, 1:481
Persistent complex bereavement disorder, 3:978

Persistent depressive disorder, 1:432, 3:1088–1089, 1093
Person of the therapist, 3:1247–1249
    clinical approaches, 3:1249
    family of origin, 3:1248
    overview, 3:1247, 4:1470–1471
    personal context, 3:1247–1248
    person-of-the-therapist training model, 4:1473–1474
    self-examination and self-awareness, 3:1248–1249
    structural family therapy, 4:1615
    termination, 4:1687–1688
    therapeutic impasses, 4:1701
    See also **Self of the therapist**
Personal Growth in Marriage, 3:1033
Personal Responsibility and Work Opportunity Reconciliation Act, 3:1138, 4:1593
Personality
    marriage and family therapy assessment, 1:86
    sibling relationships, 4:1561
Personality Inventory for Children, 4:1438
Personality scales, 4:1438, 1442
Personalization, 1:278
Person-centered therapy, 1:322–323, 2:816, 3:1199, 1250, 4:1650, 1653
Pervasive developmental disorder-not otherwise specified, 1:129, 2:873
Pervasive developmental disorders, 1:134, 2:873
Peterson, Christopher, 3:1265
Peyote, 4:1626
Pfitzer, Franz, 3:1406
PFLGA, 3:950
Pharmacology. *See* Medication
Phenomenology, and Gestalt family therapy, 2:740–741
Philadelphia Child Guidance Clinic, 4:1773, 1774, 1776
Phinney, Jane, and model of ethnic identity development, 2:571–572
Phosphodiesterase-5 (PDE5) inhibitors, 3:1303, 4:1524
Physical abuse
    child maltreatment, 1:208–209, 2:908–909
    domestic violence, 2:912–913
Physical touch, 3:997
Physiological data, 3:1323–1324
Piaget, Jean, 1:29, 347–348, 2:676, 840
Pichot, Teri, 4:1579
Piercy, Fred, 2:587, 664
Pinsof, W. M., 2:532, 533
Placating, 1:300–301, 2:817
Planned Parenthood Federation of America, 4:1507
Plato, 3:954–955
Play, fathers' style of, 2:764

Play family therapy, 3:1250–1254
   assessment, 3:1252
   child parent relationship theory, 1:211–213
   history, 3:1250–1251
   interventions, 3:1252–1254
   rationale and benefits, 3:1251–1252
   role-playing, 3:1420–1421
   tenets, 3:1251
Play therapy
   child assessment and diagnosis, 4:1438–1439
   childhood anxiety, 1:222
   disinhibited social engagement disorder, 1:454
   posttraumatic stress disorder, 3:1281
   trauma, 4:1725
Poddar, Prosenjit, 1:326, 483
Pokorny, Jennifer, 3:1372–1373
Politics, of birth control, 1:163–164
   See also Sociopolitical environment
Polster, Erving, 1:23
Polyamory, 3:1180–1181, 1255–1258
   challenges and rewards, 3:1257–1258
   defining, 3:1255
   forms of, 3:1256
   historical and multicultural perspectives, 3:1257
   orientation, practice, or identity, 3:1256–1257
   overview, 3:1255
   See also **Open relationships**
Polyandry, 3:1258
Polyfidelity, 3:1256
Polygamy, 3:1258–1260
   counseling considerations, 3:1259–1260
   defining, 3:1258–1259
   media representations, 3:1259
   overview, 3:1258
   religion, 3:1259
Polygyny, 3:1258
Pomeroy, Wardell, 4:1506
Pope, Kenneth, 4:1547
Popkin, Michael, 3:1209
Popper, Karl, 3:1349
Porder, Michael, 3:1175
Pornography, 3:1260–1261
Positive and negative feedback, 3:1262–1264
   cybernetics, 1:408–409, 3:1262–1263
   family system, 4:1775
   feedback loops, 3:1263–1264
   homeostasis, 2:793
   overview, 3:1262
   systems theory, 3:1262–1263
Positive connotation, 3:1069–1070, 4:1668, 1669
Positive Discipline, 3:1210
Positive Parenting, 4:1770
Positive psychology, 3:1264–1265, 1399
Positive reinforcement, 1:141, 323, 2:693, 3:1204

Positive self-care, 3:978
Positivism, 3:1375
Possibility therapy, 4:1511, 1778
Postdoctoral training, 3:1266–1267, 4:1711
Postmodern therapies, 3:1267–1273
   basic tenets, 3:1269–1272, 4:1779–1780
   collaborative couples therapy, 1:289–290
   constructivism, 2:550
   contextual perspective, 3:1269
   critical stance of, 2:794, 3:1271
   cultural perspective, 3:1268, 1271–1272
   diagnostic practices, 3:1269
   diversity, 3:1272
   effectiveness, 3:1272–1273
   empowerment, 3:1270–1271
   faith-based therapy, 2:592
   gender- and culture-sensitive therapies, 2:712–713
   interventions, 3:1272
   key theorists, 3:1268
   language, 3:1269–1270
   metaphors used in, 3:1064–1065
   narrative therapy, 3:1133–1137
   narratives, 3:1268, 1271–1272
   overview, 3:1267–1268
   qualitative research, 3:1351
   research directions, 3:1272–1273
   second-order family therapy, 4:1463, 1466–1467
   sex therapy, 4:1510
   social change, 3:1270–1271
   therapist role, 3:1270–1271
Postmodernism, 4:1778–1779
Postpartum depression, 1:170, 3:1274–1277, 1294
   counseling considerations, 3:1276–1277
   emotional changes, 3:1275
   factors affecting, 3:1274–1275
   impact on children, 3:1276
   lifestyle changes, 3:1275
   men, 3:1275–1276
   overview, 3:1274
   physical changes, 3:1274–1275
   symptoms, 3:1275
   treatment, 3:1276–1277
Postpositivism, 3:1349, 1375
Post-rapture, 1:372–373
Posttraumatic stress disorder in children, 3:1277–1281
   diagnosis, 3:1278–1279
   overview, 3:1277
   risk and protective factors, 3:1281
   treatment, 3:1281
   understanding, 3:1279–1280
Posttraumatic stress disorder (PTSD)
   adjustment disorder vs., 1:12
   adolescents, 1:24
   diagnosis, 4:1727

military couples and families, 3:1074
sexual assault, 4:1516, 1518
torture, 4:1707–1709
Poverty
African Americans, 3:1362
childhood depression, 1:437
defined, 2:594
effects of, 2:594–595
family resource management, 2:638
family structure, 2:594
feminization of, 2:665–669
gender, 2:595–596
intergenerational, 2:596
opportunity gap, 3:1283
parentification, 3:1228
prevalence, 2:594
risk factors, 2:594
rural, 2:596, 3:1430–1431
stress, 2:595
urban, 2:596
urban families, 4:1749
women, 2:595–596, 665–669
See also Socioeconomic status
Poverty and family development, 3:1282–1285
challenges, 3:1282–1283
family development states, 3:1283–1284
overview, 3:1282
strength and hope, 3:1284–1285
Power
choice theory, 1:237
empowerment in families, 2:535–538
gender, 2:663, 664, 3:1286, 4:1587
language, 4:1568
postmodern therapies, 3:1270–1271
race, 3:1365
relations of, 1:250–251
structural maps, 4:1621–1622
supervision process, 3:971
vertical relationships, 2:546
Power Equity Guide, 2:664
Power issues in couples, 3:1285–1287
gender, 3:1286
overview, 3:1285–1286
related issues, 3:1286–1287
research, 3:1287
Power struggle, 1:19, 22
Powers, William, 2:865
Practical Application of Intimate Relationship Skills (PAIRS), 3:1031, 1032
Practice management, 3:1287–1291
business aspects, 3:1288–1290
business plan, 3:1288
ethical aspects, 3:1288
legal aspects, 3:1287–1288

marketing, 3:1289
office procedures, 3:1289–1290
personal aspects, 3:1290–1291
Practice-based evidence, 2:499, 3:1273
Prata, Giuliana, 3:1068, 1359, 1376, 4:1666, 1668, 1776
Praxis, 1:396, 397
Predicting/prescribing a relapse, 4:1668
Prefrontal cortex, 2:898, 902, 906, 3:982
Pregnancy, 3:1291–1294
abortion, 1:165, 3:1293, 1294
assisted, 1:227–229, 3:1291
birth rituals, 3:994
bonding, 1:169
Family and Medical Leave Act of 1993, 2:600–602
fetal experience, 3:982
infertility, 1:227, 2:850–854
legal issues, 3:945
mental health after, 1:170, 3:1274–1277, 1294
overview, 3:1291
relationship impact, 3:1293–1294
statistics, 3:1292–1293
stillbirth and miscarriage, 4:1599–1603
teen pregnancy, 3:1293, 4:1593
trimesters, 3:1291–1292
Pregnancy and sexuality, 3:1294–1296
birth control and conception, 1:162–165
Premarital contracts. *See* Prenuptial agreements
Premarital counseling, 3:1296–1301
child-rearing, 3:1299–1300
communication, 3:1297–1298
conflict resolution, 3:1299
expectations, 3:1297
finances, 3:1299
finding a counselor, 3:1300
goals, 3:1300–1301
overview, 3:1296
partner roles, 3:1298
prevention research, 3:1316
relationship education, 3:1300
sex, 3:1298–1299
Premarital Preparation and Relationship Enhancement (PREPARE), 3:1031
Premarital Relationship Enhancement Program (PREP), 3:1316–1317
Premarital sex, 4:1552
Premature ejaculation, 3:1301–1303
See also Erectile disorder
Premenstrual dysphoric disorder, 1:432, 3:1089, 1093
Prenuptial agreements, 3:1303–1305
Preoccupied attachment, 1:98, 2:674
PREP. *See* Premarital Relationship Enhancement Program (PREP)
PREP 7.0 curriculum, 3:1012

PREPARE/ENRICH, 2:604, 3:1012, 1030, **1306–1311**
   couple and family maps, 3:1308–1310
   effectiveness, 3:1306
   foundations and components, 3:1307–1308
   goals, 3:1308
   overview, 3:1306
   scales, 4:1440, 1445
   training, 3:1311
   types of married couples, 3:1308, 1309
   value of, 3:1310–1311
Prescribing the symptom, 2:561
Presenting problems, 3:1311–1314
   assessment, 3:1312–1313
   client expectations, 3:1313
   overview, 3:1311
   procedures in assessment, 3:1313–1314
   typical, 3:1313
   See also Assessment
Preston, Stephanie D., 2:529
Prevention and Relationship Enhancement Program (PREP), 3:1030, 1031
Prevention research, 3:1314–1317
   areas covered, 3:1314–1315
   categorizing prevention, 3:1315
   children/youth, 3:1317
   distress, divorce, and domestic violence, 3:1316–1317
   importance and limitations, 3:1317
   matrix for, 3:1315–1316
   overview, 3:1314
   premarital intervention, 3:1316
Prigogine, Ilya, 3:1350
Primary and secondary emotions, 2:524, 3:1318–1321
   adaptive vs. maladaptive, 3:1319–1320
   emotional processes, 3:1318–1319
   enhancing emotional functioning, 3:1320–1321
   overview, 3:1318
Primary caregivers, 1:101
Primary Communication Inventory, 4:1441
Primary survival triad, 2:580
Principle ethics, 2:566
Private logic, 1:19, 177–178
Privileged communication, 2:567–568
Privileged position technique, 2:713
Problem-solving
   cognitive-behavioral family therapy, 1:284
   conduct disorder, 1:323
   McMaster model of family functioning, 2:605
   parent management training, 3:1206
Problem-solving skills training, 3:1206
Process addictions, 1:307
Process model of emotional regulation, 1:52
Process model of family functioning, 2:607–608

Process research, 3:1321–1325
   behavioral coding, 3:1322–1323
   clinical relevance, 3:1324
   ethical considerations, 3:1324
   limitations, 3:1324–1325
   overview, 3:1321–1322
   physiological data, 3:1323–1324
   research findings, 3:1324
   research-practice gap, 3:1322
   task analysis, 3:1323
Process theories, of mate selection, 3:1047
Process-oriented model, 1:426
Prochaska, James O., 1:62, 3:1244
Productive bilinguals, 1:159
Professional Association for Therapeutic Riding, International, 2:554
Professional associations, 3:1325–1326
   ethical standards, 3:1326
   networking, 3:1325–1326
   resources, 3:1326
Professionalism
   accreditation, 1:366–367
   associations and organizations, 4:1789–1791
   clinical practice, 1:265–266
   comparison with other professions, 4:1712
   couples and marriage counseling, 1:380
   dual and multiple relationships, 1:476–479
   journals, 4:1791–1793
   licensure and certification, 3:950–954
Progesterone, 4:1501, 1529
Progress notes, 1:329
Progress notes for couples and families, 3:1327–1332
   best practices and standards, 3:1330–1332
   ethical considerations, 3:1329
   form and content, 3:1327–1328
   HIPAA influence on, 3:1329–1330
   importance of, 3:1328–1329
   overview, 3:1327
   templates and formats, 3:1330
   treatment file information, 3:1328
Project for Strong African American Marriages, 3:1030
Projective identification, 3:1174–1175, 1336
Prolactin, 3:982
Prolonged exposure, 4:1518
Promoting Safe and Stable Families Act, 2:687
Propagative parenting. *See* **Authoritative parenting**
Protean career paths, 1:190
Protected health information, 2:767–770
Proximity-seeking, 1:101
Prozac, 2:883, 3:1303
Pseudohostility, 4:1769
Pseudomutuality, 4:1769
Pseudo-self, 1:174

Psilocybin, 4:1626
Psychiatrists, 1:474
Psychoanalytic family therapy, 3:1332–1337
   countertransference, 3:1336
   development of, 3:1333–1334
   Freud's drive model, 3:1333
   overview, 3:1332–1333
   psychoanalysis–family therapy link, 3:1334–1335
   resistance, 3:1335
   transference, 3:1335–1336
   value of, 3:1336–1337
Psychoanalytic theory
   mother-blaming, 3:1104–1105
   object relations theory, 3:1173–1176
   sexual dysfunction, 4:1523
   therapist role, 3:1145
Psychobiology of attachment, 3:1337–1338
Psychodrama, 2:629, 903, 3:1418–1419, 1421
   See also Role-playing
Psychodynamic family therapy, 1:265
Psychodynamic model, 4:1650, 1653
Psychoeducation, 3:1339–1343
   children, 3:1343
   cognitive-behavioral family therapy, 1:284
   couples and family counseling, 3:1342–1343
   family psychoeducation, 3:1341–1342
   group family therapy, 3:1012
   groups, 3:1340–1341
   historical background, 3:1339–1340
   marriage enrichment, 3:1029
   modality and settings, 3:1340
   overview, 3:1339
   reactive attachment disorder, 3:1371
   risks and benefits, 3:1343
   schizophrenia, 4:1454–1455
   school settings, 3:1341
   self-injury, 4:1493
   trauma-focused cognitive-behavioral therapy, 4:1731
   See also Family psychoeducation
Psychofunctionalism, 2:703
Psychological abuse. *See* Emotional abuse
Psychological flexibility. *See* Flexibility
Psychologists, 1:474, 3:952
Psychology
   marriage and family therapy assessment, 1:86–87
Psychometrics, 3:1354–1355
Psychosocial stage theory, 1:48
Psychotherapy
   anxiety treatment, 1:71
   common factors, 1:295–296
   couples and marriage counseling, 1:381
   effectiveness measures, 1:267–270
   supervision theories, 4:1652–1654
Psychotherapy notes, 3:1330
Psychotic disorders, 1:26–27
PTSD. *See* Posttraumatic stress disorder (PTSD)
Public health code, 3:1344–1346
Public speaking, 3:1289
Punctuation, 3:1346–1347
Punishment, 1:141, 2:693–694, 3:1428
   See also Corporal punishment
Puppets, in play family therapy, 3:1254, 1419
Purves, Caroline, 4:1693
Pyromania. *See* **Juvenile firesetter interventions**, 1:119

Quakers, 2:616, 3:1028
Qualitative research, 3:1349–1352
   data collection and analysis, 3:1351
   Delphi research method, 1:429–431
   emergent character of, 3:1350
   empirically validated models, 2:532
   family therapy, 3:1350–1352
   outcome research, 3:1188
   postmodern perspective, 3:1351
   premises, 3:1350
   systems theory, 3:1350
   therapist role, 3:1351
Quality of life, 3:1430
Quality time, 1:374–378, 3:996
Quality world, 1:237–238
Quantitative research, 3:1352–1355
   Delphi research method, 1:429–431
   empirically validated models, 2:532
   evaluation of, 3:1355
   family research, 3:1354–1355
   overview, 3:1352–1353
   premises, 3:1352
   types, 3:1353
Quasiexperimental designs, 2:532
Queer, 4:1539, 1542
Questioning, of one's sexual orientation, 4:1539
Questionnaires, 1:430–431
Questions: open, closed, and circular, 3:1356–1360
   circular, 1:252, 263–264, 3:1071, 1146, 1359, 1377, 4:1667
   clinician attunement, 1:121
   closed, 3:1358
   constructivist approaches, 1:350
   counseling process, 3:1356
   formation of questions, 3:1356–1357
   listening skills, 3:966
   open, 3:1357–1358
   overview, 3:1356
   See also **Miracle question**; **Scaling questions**
Quetiapine, 4:1626

Race
  caregiving, 1:59
  ethnicity compared to, 2:571, 915
  feminization of poverty, 2:666–668
  identity, 2:569–571
  interracial adoption, 1:37–41
  interracial marriage and families, 2:915–918
  parenting styles, 3:1238
  power, 3:1365
  religion, 3:1397
  transracial adoption, 1:37–40, 4:1720–1722
  See also **Ethnicity**; Minorities
Racial disparities in foster care, 3:1361–1364
Racial identity
  cultural identity compared to, 1:40
  interracial adoption, 1:40–41
Racism, 3:1364–1368
  African Americans, 1:57
  clinical applications, 3:1367–1368
  discrimination, 3:1366
  history, 3:1365–1366
  interracial adoption, 1:39–40
  interracial marriage and families, 2:917–918
  Native Americans, 3:1141
  overview, 3:1364–1365
  theories, 3:1366–1367
Raczynski, Katherine, 3:1315
Radical constructivism, 3:1144
RAND Corporation, 1:429
Rando, Therese, 1:150, 152–154
Randomized clinical trials (RCTs), 2:507, 508, 3:1188, 1354
Rape. *See* **Sexual assault and rape**; **Statutory rape**
Rappaport, Roy, 3:1414
Rapport, 2:928
Rasmussen, Paul, 4:1785
Rational choice theory, 3:1046
Rational emotive behavior therapy (REBT), 1:67, 2:593
Rational emotive therapy, 2:620
Rationalism, 2:550
Reactance theory, 3:1192
Reactive attachment disorder in children, 3:1368–1371
  developmental considerations, 3:1370
  diagnosis, 3:1368–1369
  disinhibited social engagement disorder, 1:453–454
  interpersonal neurobiology, 2:897
  overview, 3:1368
  risk factors, 3:1369–1370
  treatment, 3:1370–1371
Read, Stephen J., 1:46

Reality therapy. *See* **Choice theory and reality therapy**
Reauthorization of the Older Americans Act, 2:939
Recapitulation of the family, 3:1010, 1013
Receptive bilinguals, 1:159
Reciprocal causality, 2:598
Reciprocity, 3:1405
Recognition reflex, 1:21, 22
Recognition respect, 3:1404–1405
Reconciliation, 3:1372–1374
  barriers, 3:1374
  inner resources supporting, 3:1372
  models, 3:1372–1373
  overview, 3:1372
  process, 3:1373–1374
  See also **Forgiveness**
Recursiveness, 3:1374–1377, 4:1612
Redirection, 2:622
Reductionism, 3:1375
Redundancy principle, 2:792
Reeves, Ruth, 4:1772
Referrals, 3:1288
Reflecting, 1:121
Reflecting team, 3:1378–1380, 4:1779
Reflective listening. *See* **Listening, empathic**
Reframing, 1:183, 184–185, 2:794, 818, 3:1069
Refrigerator mother, 1:131, 3:1104
Refugee Act, 1:94
Refugees. *See* **Immigrants and refugees**
Registered Play Therapists, 3:953
Regulation theory, 1:52
Reich, Wilhelm, 3:1219
Reification, 4:1568
Reik, Theodor, 3:985
Reimbursements, from health insurance companies, 3:953
Reinforcement
  avoidance, 1:139
  functional assessment, 2:693–694
  rule-setting, 3:1428
  See also **Negative reinforcement**; **Operant conditioning**; **Positive reinforcement**
Reinforcement schedule, 2:694
Reiss, Ira, 4:1506
Reiss Motivation Profile for Children, 4:1438
Rejecting-neglecting/disengaged parenting
  characteristics, 1:127, 3:1237
  child adjustment, 3:1238
  child-centered parenting, 1:217–218
  effectiveness, 1:128
  emotional intelligence, 2:520
  parent–adolescent relations, 3:1214
RELATE couple inventory, 3:1308
Relational aggression, 2:883

Relational diagnoses, 3:1380–1383
   counseling considerations, 3:1381–1383
   Diagnostic and Statistical Manual of Mental Disorders (DSM-5), 3:1380–1381
   V- and Z-codes, 3:1381
Relational ethics, 1:352, 353
Relational Ethics Scale, 1:355
Relational frame theory, 1:1–2
Relational-cultural therapy, 3:1384–1388
   assessment, 3:1385–1386
   empathic listening, 3:967
   gender- and culture-sensitive therapies, 2:713
   history, 3:1384
   key concepts, 3:1384–1385
   overview, 3:1384
   therapeutic process, 3:1385–1388
   working with couples, 3:1386–1388
Relationship education, 3:960
Relationship enhancement, 3:1389–1392
   couples counseling, 3:1390–1392
   overview, 3:1389
   relationship education, 3:1389–1390
   See also **Marriage enrichment**
Relationship Enhancement Program, 3:1028, 1030, 1031, 1316, 1389–1391
Relationship habits, effective and ineffective, 1:236
Relationship stage theory, 3:1425
Relationships. *See* Intimate relationships; Love; Romance
Relativism, 2:550
Relaxation
   anger management, 1:68
   conflict resolution, 1:336
   family stress, 2:648
   hypnosis, 2:820
   sexual pain disorders, 2:733
   systematic desensitization, 2:656–657
   trauma-focused cognitive-behavioral therapy, 4:1731–1732
Release of information for couples and families, 3:1393–1395
Reliability, 2:674–675
Religion, 3:1395–1398
   African Americans, 1:56
   birth control, 1:163, 4:1552–1553
   defining, 3:1395
   faith-based therapy, 2:589–593
   family culture, 2:846
   family rituals, 2:640
   forgiveness, 2:683
   gender, 3:1398
   health and well-being, 3:1395–1396
   Latino families, 3:942–943
   marital experience, 3:1397–1398
   marriage encounter, 3:1025–1027
   motivations, intrinsic and extrinsic, 3:1396
   polygamy, 3:1259
   race and ethnicity, 3:1397
   religious clients, 3:1398
   same-sex marriage, 4:1435
   sexuality, 4:1551–1554
   spirituality compared to, 4:1584–1585
   See also **Spirituality**
Religiosity, 3:1396
Remarriage. *See* Marriage, first and second
Reparative/reorientation therapy, 3:1039, 4:1435, 1544, 1553–1554
Reparenting, 3:1408
Repetitive behaviors, 1:129–130
Reproduction, 3:981–982, 983
Reptilian brain, 1:173
Research
   couples therapy, 1:384–387
   Delphi method, 1:429–431
   effectiveness, 2:506–508
   ethical considerations for, 2:854–856
   informed consent for, 2:854–856
   outcome, 3:1187–1190
   prevention, 3:1314–1317
   process, 3:1321–1325
Research design, 1:430–431
Resilience, 3:1399–1401
   African American families, 1:55
   characteristics, 3:1399–1400
   chronic illness with couples and families, 1:245
   concept of, 3:1399
   development of, 3:1399–1400
   family resilience, 2:631–635
   family systems, 3:1400–1401
   mood disorders in children, 3:1093
   overview, 3:1399
   relational-cultural therapy, 3:1388
   vicarious, 3:1401
Resilience Scale, 3:1401
Resiliency Scale, 3:1401
Resistance, 3:1402–1403
   behavioral family therapy, 1:145
   cultural identity development, 1:6
   Ericksonian family therapy, 2:560
   motivational interviewing, 3:1109
   multiple family therapy, 3:1121
   overview, 3:1402
   psychoanalytic therapy, 3:1335
   recognizing, 3:1402–1403
   therapeutic alliance, 4:1692
   therapy setting, 1:344
   treatment, 3:1403

Resistant attachment. *See* Ambivalent/resistant attachment
Resocialization, 3:1119
Resonance, 1:122
Resource theory, 1:426
Respect, 3:1404–1406
 benefits, 3:1406
 child-centered parenting, 1:218
 key elements, 3:1405–1406
 overview, 3:1404
 relational-cultural therapy, 3:1387
 types, 3:1404–1405
Responsible authenticity, 3:1387
Restoration therapy, 1:274, 3:1406–1409
Restricted emotions, 1:280
Retirement, 3:1409–1412
 conceptualizations, 3:1409–1410
 determinants, 3:1410–1412
 overview, 3:1409
 process perspective on, 3:1410
 theories, 3:1412
Retrouvaille, 3:1027
Revenge, 1:19, 22
Reverse sexual imprinting, 2:835
Revised Conflict Tactics Scale, 4:1441
Reynolds Intellectual Assessment Scales, 4:1438
Richards, Ellen Swallow, 2:503
Richeport-Haley, Madeleine, 4:1776
Rickert, Eve, 3:1182
Riessman, Frank, 3:1140
Ripley, Jennifer S., 2:806–807
Riskin, Jules, 4:1772, 1773
Risperidone (Risperdal), 1:133, 204
Ritalin, 1:204, 4:1625
Rituals. *See* **Family rituals**
Rituals in family therapy, 3:1413–1417
 applications, 3:1416–1417
 assessment, 3:1415–1416
 designing rituals, 3:1416
 overview, 3:1413–1414
 purposes of rituals, 3:1414–1415
 research recommendations, 3:1417
 types of rituals, 3:1415
 See also **Family rituals**
Roberto, K. A., 1:60
Roberts, Janine, 3:1414–1415
Roberts's seven-stage crisis intervention model, 1:393
Robinson, Margaret, 3:1257
Robinson, Paul, 2:813
Rogers, Carl, 1:9, 2:580, 3:965, 1010, 1029, 1109, 1199, 1200, 1208, 1250, 4:1471, 1480, 1650, 1653, 1688–1689, 1702
Role models, parents as, 1:219

Role reversal, 1:144
Role theory, 1:426
Role-playing, 3:1418–1422
 Adlerian psychology, 3:1420
 behavioral family therapy, 1:144
 classical psychodrama, 3:1418–1419
 experiential family therapy, 3:1419–1420
 family reconstruction, 2:629, 630
 key theorists, 3:1421–1422
 overview, 3:1418
 play therapy, 3:1420–1421
 social and developmental needs of children and adolescents, 3:1420
 therapeutic techniques, 3:1419
 See also Psychodrama
Roles
 family systems, 4:1673–1674
 symbolic interactionism, 4:1663
Role-taking, 2:529
Rollnick, Stephen, 3:1107–1109, 4:1628
Romance, 3:1422–1425
 concept of, 3:1423
 dating coaching, 1:411–414
 dating relationship dissolution, 1:414–416
 importance of, 3:1425
 online dating, 3:1176–1179
 overview, 3:1423
 passionate love, 3:980
 theories, 3:1424–1425
 See also Intimate relationships; Love
Roosevelt, Franklin D., 1:214
Roosevelt, Theodore, 1:214
Ropes (therapeutic technique), 2:818
Rorschach, Hermann, 4:1783
Rosenzweig, Saul, 1:295
Rowntree, Seebohm, 2:596
Royce, Josiah, 4:1662
RU-486, 3:1293
Rubber fence, 4:1769
Rubin, Zick, 3:985
Rule-setting, 3:1426–1429
 administration of, 3:1427
 enforcement, 3:1428–1429
 home setting, 3:1426–1427
 parenting issues, 3:1427
 punishment, 3:1428
 reinforcement, 3:1428
Runaway and Homeless Youth Act, 2:790
Rural families, 3:1429–1432
 counseling considerations, 3:1431–1432
 education, employment, and poverty, 3:1430–1431
 family composition, structure, and values, 3:1431
 well-being and quality of life, 3:1430

Russell, Candyce, 1:253, 3:1308
Russell, Gerald, 2:489
Ryan, Elizabeth "Toodles," 3:1060

Sadism. *See* Sexual sadism disorder
Sadness, 1:436
SAFE Children, 3:1317
Safe School Ambassadors, 3:1245
Safe-haven behavior, 1:101
Safety. *See* Security
Safety plans, 3:1148–1149, 1151–1152
Salmon, Thomas W., 1:393
Salovey, Peter, 2:517
Same-sex couples, 4:1433–1436
   adoption, 1:229
   affirmative therapy, 4:1435–1436
   childless, 1:229
   chosen families, 1:241
   dual-career/earner, 1:188–189, 481
   gender roles, 4:1434
   history, 4:1433–1434
   intimate partner violence, 4:1434–1435
   marriage equality, 3:948, 1038–1039
   overview, 4:1433
   right and marriage equality, 4:1435
   trends, 4:1434
   See also **LGBT families**
Sand tray, in play family therapy, 3:1253
Sanger, Margaret, 1:162
Sapolsky, Robert, 2:645
Sargent, George, 2:561
Satir, Virginia, 1:125, 182, 258, 265,
   300–301, 345–346, 2:580, 591, 629–631,
   815, 816–818, 3:965, 1064, 1143–1145, 1251,
   1422, 4:1471–1472, 1480–1481, 1665,
   1690–1691, 1719, 1753–1757, 1771–1773,
   1782, 1785
   See also **Virginia Satir model**
Satir Institute of the Southeast, 4:1772
Savickas, Mark, 1:190
Saving Your Marriage Before It Starts,
   3:1031, 1032
Sayre, Paul, 1:193
Scaffolding, 3:1137
Scales, children, 4:1436–1439
   categories and types, 4:1438–1439
   clinical use, 4:1437–1438
   history, 4:1436–1437
   importance of, 4:1439
   play therapy, 4:1438–1439
Scales, couple and marital, 4:1440–1442
   special considerations, 4:1440
   types, 4:1440–1441
   useful individual scales, 4:1442

Scales, family, 4:1443–1447
   Beavers systems model, 4:1443–1445
   circumplex model, 4:1445–1446
   limitations, 4:1447
   McMaster model of family functioning,
      4:1446–1447
   overview, 4:1443
Scaling questions, 4:1448–1449, 1578
Scapegoating, 4:1449–1452
   alcoholic families, 4:1451–1452
   families, 4:1450–1452
   groups, 4:1450
   overview, 4:1449–1450
   racism, 3:1366
   triangulation, 4:1451
Schaefer, Charles, 3:1251
Scharff, David, 4:1769, 1782, 1784
Scharff, Jill Savege, 4:1769, 1782, 1784
Schechter, Marshall, 1:44
Scheduling appointments, 3:1290
Schilling, Susan, 4:1588–1591
Schizophrenia and families, 4:1452–1455
   adolescents, 1:26–27
   double bind theory, 1:471, 3:1061
   expressed emotion, 4:1454
   family cohesion, 4:1454
   history, 4:1453
   history of, 1:264, 3:1059, 1339–1340
   overview, 4:1452–1453
   psychoeducation, 4:1454–1455
   symptoms, 4:1452–1453
   treatment and recovery, 4:1453–1455
Schizophrenogenic mother, 3:1104–1105
Schlossberg, Nancy K., 1:189
Schmidt, Christopher, 4:1722
Schnarch, David, 3:1265, 4:1510, 1537
School
   adolescent development, 1:30, 32
   adolescent issues, 4:1581
   See also Education
School-based community programs, 1:307–308
Schools, family involvement in, 4:1456–1459
   challenges, 4:1457
   family systems perspective, 4:1456–1457
   overview, 4:1456
   partnerships, 4:1457–1459
   theories, 4:1457
   wraparound plans, 4:1459
Schopenhauer, Arthur, 2:839
Schore, Allan N., 1:52, 2:896, 900, 904,
   4:1769, 1785
Schramski, Tom, 1:21
Schut, Henk, 2:749
Schwartz, Jonathan, 3:1315

Schwartz, Richard, **1:**330, 471, **2:**581, 884–887, **3:**1333–1336
Schwartz, Shalom H., **1:**146
SCOPE personality assessment, **3:**1307
Sculpting, **2:**580, 629, 630, 818, **4:**1755–1756
Seasons of life theory, **1:**47
Second children, **4:**1562–1563
Second Vatican Council, **3:**1025
Second-order change, 4:1460–1462, 1775
   feedback, **3:**1264
   first- vs., **2:**676–678, **4:**1460
   homeostasis, **2:**793
   implications for therapy, **4:**1461–1462
   morphogenesis, **3:**1099
   overview, **4:**1460
   techniques, **4:**1462
   theoretical basis, **4:**1460–1461
Second-order family therapy, 4:1463–1467
   circular causality, **4:**1465–1466
   first-order vs., **4:**1463–1465
   overview, **4:**1463
   practice considerations, **4:**1466–1467
Secord, Paul F., **3:**1046
Secrets, 4:1467–1470
   outcomes, **4:**1470
   reasons for, **4:**1468–1470
   sexual assessment, **4:**1521
   types, **4:**1467
   See also **Confidentiality; No-secrets contracts**
Secure attachment, **1:**98, 101, 105, 108–109, 111, 116–117, **2:**674, **3:**1372, **4:**1536
   See also **Attachment security**
Secure-base behavior, **1:**101
Security
   attachment theory, **1:**115
   choice theory, **1:**236
Segal, Lynn, **4:**1775
Selective mutism, **1:**70, 221, 233–234
Selective reuptake inhibitors, **3:**1090
Selective serotonin reuptake inhibitors (SSRIs), **1:**71, 222, **2:**710, **3:**1302–1303, **4:**1493
Self
   basic, **1:**174
   differentiation, **1:**173, 174, 448–449, **3:**1017, **4:**1510, 1770
   imago relationship therapy, **2:**827–828
   Internal Family Systems model, **2:**884–887
   pseudo-, **1:**174
Self of the therapist, 4:1470–1474
   contextual family therapy, **1:**355
   crucible situations, **1:**399
   family systems therapy, **2:**824
   historical background, **4:**1471–1472
   imago relationship therapy, **2:**831
   joining, **2:**931–932
   obstacles to developing, **4:**1472
   personal care, **3:**1291
   person-of-the-therapist training model, **4:**1473–1474
   role of the self, **4:**1471
   sexuality and religion, **4:**1554
   training therapists in self-development, **4:**1472–1473
   See also **Person of the therapist; Therapist role**
Self-care, after loss, **3:**978
Self-care practices for the trauma-informed couple and family counselor, 4:1474–1477
   consequences of exposure to client trauma, **4:**1476
   ethical considerations, **4:**1477
   overview, **4:**1474–1475
   therapist role, **4:**1475–1476
   trauma, **4:**1475
   trauma characteristics, **4:**1476
   trauma resolution guidelines, **4:**1477
   trauma resolution models, **4:**1477
Self-concept, **4:**1662–1663
Self-disclosure, **1:**82
Self-efficacy
   family empowerment, **2:**536
   human sexual response, **2:**814–815
   motivational interviewing, **3:**1108, 1109
Self-esteem, 4:1478–1482
   counseling considerations, **4:**1482
   dating, **4:**1482
   family's effect on, **4:**1481
   overview, **4:**1478–1480
   significance of, **4:**1479
   theories, **4:**1480–1481
   Virginia Satir model, **4:**1755
Self-esteem in children, 4:1482–1486
   developmental perspective, **4:**1483–1484
   factors affecting, **4:**1484
   importance of, **4:**1483
   limitations of construct, **4:**1485–1486
   methods of enhancing, **4:**1484–1485
   overview, **4:**1482–1483
Self-help, 4:1486–1490
   benefits, **4:**1487–1488
   bibliotherapy, **4:**1488–1489
   cautions, **4:**1488
   family counseling, **4:**1490
   feminist analysis of, **4:**1489–1490
   market for books, **4:**1486–1487
   overview, **4:**1486
   practice applications, **4:**1489
   social context, **4:**1487
Self-injury, 4:1491–1493
   assessment, **3:**1150–1151
   characteristics of superficial, **4:**1491–1492
   contracts, **3:**1148–1153, **4:**1698

cycles, 4:1493
forms of, 4:1491
individuals undertaking, 4:1492–1493
onset, 4:1492
overview, 4:1491
physiological response, 4:1493
suicidal behaviors, 4:1630
Self-in-relation theory, 3:1384
Self-mutilation, 4:1491
  See also **Self-injury**
Self-neglect, 2:510
Self-preservation, 3:981–982
Self-reflexiveness, 2:728
Self-regulation, 2:898
Self-reliance, 1:115–116
Self-Report Family Inventory, 2:605, 4:1443–1444
Self-serving bias, 1:335
Self-worth. *See* **Self-esteem; Self-esteem in children**
Seligman, Martin, 3:1264–1265
Selvini Palazzoli, Mara, 1:265, 3:1068, 1359, 1376, 1413, 4:1666, 1668, 1773, 1776–1777
Sensate focus, 4:1494–1496
  benefits, 4:1496
  concept of, 4:1494
  effectiveness, 4:1496
  female orgasmic disorder, 2:656
  origin, 4:1494
  overview, 4:1494, 1509
  premature ejaculation, 3:1302
  stages, 4:1495–1496
  therapeutic use, 4:1494–1496
Sensitive dependence on initial conditions.
  See **Butterfly effect**
Sensory processing disorder, 1:130
Sentiment override, positive and negative, 4:1497–1500
  couples counseling, 3:1390
  "four horsemen of the apocalypse," 4:1500
  negative, 4:1497
  overview, 4:1497
  perception of relationship, 4:1498–1499
  positive, 4:1498
  sound relationship house, 4:1499–1500
Separateness, 1:287
Separation. *See* **Divorce and separation**
Separation anxiety disorder, 1:70, 74, 220–221
Seponski, Desiree, 3:1306
September 11, 2001 terrorist attacks, 3:1072–1073, 4:1487
Seroquel, 4:1626
Serotonin, 3:982, 1090, 4:1493
Serotonin-norepinephrine reuptake inhibitors (SNRIs), 1:71
Sertraline, 1:204, 3:1303

Service, acts of, 3:996–997
Sex, definition of, 4:1500–1503
  activity, 4:1501–1502
  biology, 4:1501
  genitals, 4:1502–1503
Sex education. *See* **Sexuality education**
Sex Educators, 3:953
Sex Information and Education Council of the United
  States, 4:1556
Sex negativity, 4:1503–1504
Sex positivity, 4:1503–1505
Sex researchers, 4:1505–1508
  marriage, couples, and family counseling, 4:1507–1508
  modern sex research, 4:1507
  pioneers, 4:1505–1507
  See also **Sex therapy**
Sex therapy, 4:1509–1512
  approaches, 4:1509–1511
  erectile disorder, 2:557
  ethical considerations, 4:1511
  female orgasmic disorder, 2:656–657
  hypnosis and guided meditation, 3:1084–1086
  issues addressed in, 4:1509
  overview, 4:1509
  referrals, 4:1511–1512
  sensate focus, 4:1494–1496, 1509
  See also **Sex researchers**
Sex toys. *See* **Sexual enhancement, sexual toys; Sexual toys/sexual aids**
Sexual abuse, 4:1512–1515
  child maltreatment, 1:209, 2:909–910
  disclosure, 4:1513–1514
  effects of, 4:1512
  elder abuse, 2:509–510
  family therapy, 4:1514–1515
  incest, 2:835–838
  intimate partners, 2:913
  overview, 4:1512–1513
  prevalence, 4:1512
  research, 4:1514
Sexual Addiction Screening Test, 1:320
Sexual and Relationship Therapy, 4:1793
Sexual assault and rape, 4:1515–1518
  coping strategies, 4:1516
  date rape, 2:911
  defined, 4:1513
  disclosure, 4:1516–1517
  impact on health and health-risk behaviors, 4:1517–1518
  interventions, 4:1518
  mental health consequences, 4:1516–1517
  overview, 4:1515

statistics, 4:1515–1516
statutory rape, 4:1593–1595
Sexual assessment/history, 4:1519–1522
   biopsychosocial approach, 4:1520
   comfort with sexuality, 4:1521–1522
   intersystem approach, 4:1520–1522
   models, 4:1520–1522
   overview, 4:1520
   therapist role, 4:1521–1522
   timing of, 4:1521
   See also **Sexual history**
Sexual attraction, 4:1540
Sexual coercion, 2:911
Sexual compulsivity. *See* **Compulsive sexual behavior**
Sexual dysfunction, 4:1522–1525
   barriers to treatment, 4:1524–1525
   categories, 2:814
   causes, 4:1522
   erectile disorder, 2:554–557
   female orgasmic disorder, 2:654–657
   female sexual interest/arousal disorder, 2:657–660
   fetishes, 2:669–672
   gender, 4:1522–1523
   genito-pelvic pain/penetration disorder, 2:730–733
   human sexual response, 2:814–815
   male hypoactive sexual desire disorder, 3:999–1002
   mindfulness, 3:1083–1084
   overview, 4:1522
   premature ejaculation, 3:1301–1303
   sensate focus, 4:1494–1496
   sex toys, 4:1527
   treatment, 4:1523–1524
Sexual enhancement, sexual toys, 4:1525–1528
   cautions, 4:1528
   health concerns, 4:1526–1527, 1550
   overview, 4:1525, 1549
   persons with disabilities, 4:1527–1528
   products and their use, 4:1525–1526, 1549–1550
   sexual dysfunction, 4:1527
   technology, 4:1550
Sexual health, 4:1502, 1528–1530
   World Association for Sexual Health, 4:1763–1764
   See also **Sexuality education**
Sexual history, 4:1530–1534
   counseling considerations, 4:1533–1534
   importance of, 4:1533
   overview, 4:1530–1531
   relationship issues, 4:1531–1532
   research on, 4:1531
   See also **Sexual assessment/history**
Sexual identity, 4:1540
Sexual intimacy, 4:1534–1537
   attachment styles, 4:1536
   attitudes, 4:1532–1533
   controversies, 4:1536–1537
   decline of, 3:1008
   defining, 4:1534
   Ericksonian family therapy, 2:558
   fidelity, 2:675
   gender, 4:1535–1536
   mindfulness, 3:1083–1086
   motivations/purposes, 4:1534–1535
   neurohormonal basis, 3:981
   open relationships, 3:1180–1183
   personal history, 4:1530–1534
   physiology of, 3:983–984
   power issues, 3:1286–1287
   pregnancy and, 3:1294–1296
   premarital counseling, 3:1298–1299
   scales, 4:1441
   sensate focus, 4:1494–1496
   sexual satisfaction, 4:1536–1537
   therapist-client relationships, 1:477–478, 2:563, 564, 4:1511, 1545–1549
   threats to, 2:919
   See also **Intimacy, specific threats to; Sex therapy; Sexual dysfunction**
Sexual masochism disorder, 3:1196–1197
Sexual minorities, 4:1538–1539, 1551–1552
   See also **Sexual prejudice**
Sexual orientation, attraction, and identity, 4:1540–1543
   female-associated, 4:1540–1541
   flow model, 4:1535
   gender dysphoria, 2:716–717
   gender fluid or nonspecific, 4:1542
   male-associated, 4:1541
   overview, 4:1540
   polyamory, 3:1256–1257
   prejudice, 4:1543–1545
   sexual activity–specific, 4:1542–1543
   sexual minorities, 4:1538–1539
Sexual pain disorders, 2:730–733
Sexual prejudice, 4:1543–1545
   See also **Sexual minorities**
Sexual reassignment surgery, 2:717
Sexual relationships with clients, 4:1511, 1545–1549
   boundary violations, 4:1548–1549
   definition and scope, 4:1546
   effects on clients and families, 4:1547–1548
   ethical and legal issues, 4:1546–1547
   managing attractions and boundaries, 4:1548
   overview, 4:1545–1546
   See also **Dual and multiple relationships**
Sexual rights, 4:1763–1764
Sexual sadism disorder, 3:1196–1197
Sexual satisfaction, 4:1536–1537

Sexual surrogacy, 4:1511
Sexual toys/sexual aids, 4:1549–1550
   See also **Sexual enhancement, sexual toys**
Sexuality
   attachment theory, 1:107
   comfort with, 4:1521–1522
   compulsive behavior, 1:317–320
   counselor attitudes, 1:379
   cybersex, 4:1679
   human sexual response, 2:812–815
   male sexual cycle, 2:554–555
   mindfulness, 3:1083–1086
   overview, 4:1502
   paraphilic disorders, 3:1194–1198
   pornography, 3:1260–1261
   religion, 4:1551–1554
   scales, 4:1441
   sex negativity, 4:1503–1504
   sex positivity, 4:1503–1505
   social reframing, 4:1504
   See also **Pregnancy and sexuality**
Sexuality and religion, 4:1551–1554
   counseling considerations, 4:1553–1554
   mental health, 4:1551–1552
   overview, 4:1551
   sexual behaviors, 4:1552–1553
Sexuality Counselors, 3:953
Sexuality education, 4:1554–1557
   abstinence-only, 4:1557
   comprehensive, 4:1556–1557
   effectiveness, 4:1557
   female orgasmic disorder, 2:656
   future of, 4:1557
   history, 4:1555–1556
   overview, 4:1554–1555
Sexuality Information and Education Council of the United States, 4:1507
Sexually transmitted infections (STI), 4:1529, 1558–1560
   overview, 4:1558
   prevalence, 4:1558
   prevention and treatment, 4:1559–1560
   reporting, 4:1560
   risk factors, 4:1559
   transmission, 4:1558
   types, 4:1559
SFT. *See* **Structural family therapy (SFT)**
Shame, 4:1469
Shapiro, Francine, 1:53
Shared parenting, 1:405
Shaver, Phillip, 1:105, 113, 339, 2:897
"Should" statements, 1:278
Shrodes, Caroline, 4:1488
Shulman, Julie, 3:948

Shuttling, 1:121
Sibling abuse, 2:910–911
Sibling position. *See* Birth order
Sibling relational problem, 3:1382
Sibling relationships, 4:1561–1563
   and self-esteem, 4:1481
   birth order, 4:1562–1563
   overview, 4:1561
   personality development, 4:1561
   rivalry and competition, 4:1563
   special circumstances, 4:1563
Siegel, Daniel, 1:122, 123–124, 2:885, 896, 899, 900–901, 904–906, 4:1785
Significance. *See* **Clinical versus statistical significance**
Sildenafil, 2:556, 4:1524
Silverman, Phyllis, 1:150
Silverstein, Louise, 2:662, 664, 4:1782
Silverstein, Olga, 2:661, 662, 4:1759–1760, 1772, 1781
Simon, George, 4:1614
Simon, Shirley, 4:1721
Simpson, Jeffrey A., 1:46
Simulated family, 2:818
Simultaneous bilingualism, 1:159
Single motherhood, 2:667
Single-parent families, 4:1564–1566
   counseling considerations, 4:1566
   extended families, 4:1565
   family resource management, 2:637–638
   impact on children, 4:1566
   overview, 4:1564
   reasons for, 4:1564–1565
   stressors, 4:1565
Situational couple violence, 1:468, 2:912
Skills-based interventions, 1:280
Skinner, B. F., 1:139, 2:693, 3:1059, 1204, 1208, 4:1783
Skinner box, 1:139
Slavery, 3:1365
Sleep
   childhood depression, 1:436
   marriage and family therapy assessment, 1:85
   non–rapid eye movement sleep arousal disorders, 3:1153–1155
   stages, 3:1153
Sleep terrors, 3:1154
Sleepwalking, 3:1154
Sluzki, Carlos, 3:1347
SMART goals, 1:225
Smart Marriages, 3:1030
Smith, Adam, 2:531
Smith, Manuel, 1:82
Smuts, Jan, 2:776–777
Snyder, Douglas, 2:587

Snyder, Richard, 2:543–544
Social (pragmatic) communication disorder, 1:298
Social anxiety disorder, 1:24, 70, 73, 221
Social change, postmodern therapies and, 3:1270–1271
Social clock theory, 1:48
Social cohesion, 2:536, 3:992–995
Social constructionism, 4:1566–1569
   assumptions, 4:1567–1568
   collaborative language systems, 1:291
   family therapy, 4:1569
   gender, 2:722
   language, 4:1567–1568
   love, 3:987–988
   narrative therapy, 4:1569
   overview, 4:1566–1567
   postmodern therapies, 3:1270
   processes, 4:1568
   solution-focused brief therapy, 4:1576
   See also **Constructivism**
Social development
   adolescents, 1:433–434
   disinhibited social engagement disorder, 1:452–454
   role-playing, 3:1420
Social exchange theory
   cognitive-behavioral couples therapy, 1:278
   commitment, 1:293–294, 2:920
   decision-making, 1:426
Social isolation, 3:972–973
Social justice, 3:1112, 1116, 1368, 4:1750, 1780
Social learning theory, 1:29, 278, 2:530–531, 840, 4:1783
Social media, 3:1048–1049, 1289
Social mobility, 4:1572–1574
Social phobias, 1:24
Social reinforcement, 1:144
Social reward, 2:920–921
Social Security, 1:59
Social Security Act, 1:214
Social support, 4:1570–1571
   autism, 1:133
   forms, 4:1570
   in-law relationships, 2:861
   marriage and family therapy assessment, 1:87
   multiple family therapy, 3:1119
   peer counseling, 3:1242–1246
   positive events, 4:1571
   support groups, 4:1657–1661
Social threat, 2:920–921
Sociality, 1:177, 3:981
Socialization
   African Americans, 1:57
   cross-cultural and interracial adoption, 1:39–40
   defined, 1:39

   emotions, 2:514
   ethnicity, 2:570, 571
   family myths, 2:623
   gender, 2:663, 713–714, 719
   interracial marriage and families, 2:917
   parental acceptance-rejection theory, 3:1215–1218
   racism, 3:1367
   See also **Gender roles**
Society
   challenges for children with special needs, 1:233–234
   emotional process, 1:175, 2:608
Society for Free Psychoanalytic Study, 1:177
Society for Sex Therapy and Research, 4:1507
Society for the Scientific Study of Sexuality, 4:1507
Society of Friends, 2:616
Socioeconomic status, 4:1571–1575
   dimensions of, 4:1572–1573
   family challenges, 4:1573–1575
   overview, 4:1571–1572
   parentification, 3:1228
   parenting styles, 3:1238
   taboo status, 4:1572
   urban families, 4:1749–1750
   See also Poverty
Sociopolitical environment, 1:88
   See also Politics
Socratic questioning, 1:280
Soliday, Elizabeth, 2:687
Sollee, Diane, 3:1029
Solomon, Richard, 1:139
Soltz, Vicki, 3:1209
Solution-focused brief family therapy, 4:1575–1579
   clinician-directed, solution-focused supervision, 1:271
   couples and families, 4:1579
   evidence-based practice, 4:1579
   groups, 4:1579
   history, 1:181, 4:1471, 1575–1576, 1773
   miracle question, 3:1086–1087
   overview, 4:1575
   process, 4:1576–1579
   question-asking, 4:1577–1578
   scaling questions, 4:1448–1449
   second-order family therapy, 4:1464
   sexual abuse, 4:1515
   therapeutic practices, 1:185–186
Solution-focused family therapy
   case conceptualization, 1:258–259
   clinician-directed, solution-focused supervision, 1:270–273
   overview, 1:262
   school settings, 4:1457

Solution-focused therapy, 4:1777–1778
   conflict resolution, 1:333
   crisis intervention, 1:393
   faith-based therapy, 2:592
   family of origin, 2:629
   integrative approach, 2:866
   process research, 3:1324
   sex therapy, 4:1511
   therapeutic impasses, 4:1702
Solution-oriented therapy, 4:1773, 1777–1778
Somatic symptom disorder and related disorders in adolescents, 4:1580–1584
   conversion disorder, 4:1583
   diagnosis, 4:1580–1581
   factitious disorder, 4:1581–1582
   illness anxiety disorder, 4:1582–1583
   overview, 4:1580
   symptoms, 4:1580
Sonstegard, Manford, 1:21, 4:1769
Sound relationship house, 2:747–748, 4:1499–1500
South Korea, in-law relationships, 2:860–861
South Oaks Gambling Screen, 2:709
Spanish language, 3:942
Spark, Geraldine, 1:351, 4:1768
Spatial relations, in communication, 3:1159
Speaker-listener technique, 1:337
Special needs children
   adoption, 1:36
   See also **Children with special needs in family therapy**
Specific Affect Coding System, 3:1323
Specific phobias, 1:70, 72–73, 221
Speck, Ross, 3:1142
Speech sound disorder, 1:297–298
Spencer, Byron, 3:1410
Sperry, Len, 4:1461, 1770, 1785
Spiegel, Herbert, 1:393
Spillover/crossover stressors, 2:647, 4:1761
Spiritual Experience Index, 4:1586
Spiritual Transformation Scale, 4:1585
Spirituality, 4:1584–1587
   adolescent development, 1:434
   awe and wonder, 1:89
   connection with society/humanity, 1:89
   counseling considerations, 4:1587
   couples counseling, 4:1587
   defining, 2:590–591
   divorce, 1:464–465
   faith-based therapy, 2:590–593
   gender, 4:1587
   health, 4:1585
   holism, 2:778
   infertility, 2:853
   marital experience, 4:1586
   marriage and family therapy assessment, 1:88
   meaning-making, 1:89
   mental health, 4:1585
   overview, 4:1584–1585
   practices, 1:88–89
   religion compared to, 4:1584–1585
   research, 4:1585–1586
   See also **Religion**
Spirituality Index of Well-Being, 4:1585
Splinter skills, 1:130
Split loyalty, 1:353
Sport metaphors, 3:1065
Sprecher, Susan, 3:986
Sprenkle, Douglas, 1:253, 3:1308
SSRIs, 1:222
Stages of Change model, 1:62
Stages of family therapy, 4:1588–1593
   Carr's theory, 4:1591–1593
   Freeman's theory, 4:1588–1589
   history, 4:1588
   Schilling and Gross's theory, 4:1589–1591
Stagnation, in middle adulthood, 1:50
Stalking, 2:911–912
Standards of Care for the Health of Transsexual, Transgender, and Gender Nonconforming People, 2:717–718
Star, in family reconstruction, 2:630
Statistical significance. *See* **Clinical versus statistical significance**
Statutory rape, 4:1593–1595
Stellate ganglion block, 3:1371
Stendra, 2:556
Stepchildren
   adoption, 1:36
   stepparent relations with, 4:1597–1598
Stepfamilies, 4:1596–1599
   challenges, 4:1598
   communication, 1:304
   counseling considerations, 4:1598–1599
   defining, 4:1596–1597
   family cycle, 4:1597
   family resource management, 2:637–638
   formation of, 4:1596–1597
   myths and stereotypes, 4:1597
   overview, 4:1596
   self-help books, 4:1490
   stepparent–stepchild relations, 4:1597–1598
Stereotypic self-mutilation, 4:1491
Sternberg, Robert, 1:379, 2:675, 3:987
Stevenson, Armeda, 2:585
Stewart B. McKinney Homeless Assistance Act Amendments, 1:208
STI. *See* **Sexually transmitted infections (STI)**
Stigma reversal, 3:1119–1120

Stillbirth and miscarriage, 4:1599–1603
Stimulant medications, 1:204, 4:1625
Stinnett, Nick, 2:643
Stith, Sandra M., 2:913
Stiver, Irene, 3:1384
Stoltenberg, Cal, 4:1639–1641, 1647, 1649
Stone Center theory, 3:1384
Stonehenge Conference, 4:1781
Stonewall Rebellion, 3:1038
Stonewalling, 1:300, 331, 2:746–747
Stop Anger and Violence Escalation (SAVE), 3:1317
Storytelling. *See* Narratives
Strange attractors, 1:198
Strange situation, 1:97–98, 108, 110–111, 220
Strategic family therapy, 4:1603–1608
    clinical practice context, 1:265
    communication, 4:1604–1605
    double bind theory, 1:471–472
    evidence-based practice, 2:575
    function of symptoms, 4:1605–1606
    hierarchy, 2:765–766, 4:1605
    history, 4:1603–1604, 1664, 1773
    metaphors used in, 3:1064
    overview, 1:262, 4:1603
    paradox, 3:1191
    techniques, 4:1607–1608
    therapeutic impasses, 4:1702
    therapist role, 4:1606–1607
Strategic Hope-Focused Enrichment, 3:1030, 1031
Strategic therapy
    brief family therapy, 1:181
    case conceptualization, 1:257–258
    resistance, 3:1403
Strategies to Enhance Positive Parenting (STEPP), 3:1207
Street Outreach Program, 2:790
Strength-based perspective, 3:1058
Strengthening Families Program, 3:1317
Stress and stressors
    caregiving, 1:191–192
    decision-making, 1:426–427
    family stress, 2:645–648, 4:1608–1609
    horizontal, 2:647
    life events, 3:959
    marriage and family therapy assessment, 1:87
    minority stress model, 4:1716
    poverty, 2:595
    spillover/crossover, 2:647
    vertical, 2:647
    work, 1:187–189
    See also **Parental stress: effects on children**
Stress management, 4:1608–1611
    family impact of stress, 4:1608–1609
    family models, 4:1609

    family stress, 2:647–648
    overview, 4:1608
    preventative, for families, 4:1609–1610
    responding in real time, 4:1610–1611
    trauma-focused cognitive-behavioral therapy, 4:1731–1732
Stroebe, Margaret, 2:749
Strong4Life, 1:307
Structural determinism, 4:1611–1613
Structural family therapy (SFT), 4:1614–1618
    advancements, 4:1618
    assessment, 4:1616–1617
    boundaries, 1:171–172
    case conceptualization, 1:258
    clinical practice context, 1:265
    eating disorders, 2:491
    ecosystemic, 2:499–502
    enactments, 2:539
    evidence-based practice, 2:575
    family systems theory, 4:1614–1615
    first-order family therapy, 4:1464
    goals, 4:1615
    hierarchy, 2:765–766
    history, 2:929–930, 3:1251, 4:1471–1472, 1773, 1774
    interventions, 4:1617–1618
    joining, 2:928–932
    metaphors used in, 3:1064
    morphostasis, 3:1103
    overview, 1:261, 346, 4:1614
    process research, 3:1324
    scapegoating, 4:1451
    school settings, 4:1457
    structural determinism, 4:1611–1613
    structural maps, 4:1619–1623
    therapeutic alliance, 4:1691
    therapist role, 4:1615
    triangulation, 4:1739
    See also **Family structure**
Structural maps, 4:1619–1623
    assessment tool, 4:1619–1620
    family life cycle, 4:1622
    hierarchy, 4:1621–1622
    ideal, 4:1622–1623
    interventions, 4:1622–1623
    power, 4:1621–1622
    subsystems, 4:1613
    subsystems and boundaries, 4:1620–1621
    systemic supervision, 4:1654
    therapist position, 4:1623
Structured Enrichment program, 3:1028, 1031, 1032
Stuart, Richard, 1:277, 4:1783
Stunkard, Albert, 2:489
Stuttering, 1:298

Su, Chang, 3:1224
Subjective Units of Distress Scale, 4:1448
Substance Abuse and Mental Health Services Administration (SAMHSA), 1:10, 61, 3:1245, 1267, 1316
Substance Abuse Subtle Screening Inventory-3, 4:1442
Substance use
  marriage and family therapy assessment, 1:85–86
  See also **Alcohol and substance abuse; Families and substance abuse**
Substance use disorders in adolescence, 4:1623–1629
  alcohol, 4:1627
  depressants, 4:1626
  features, 4:1624
  marijuana, 4:1626–1627
  opioids, 4:1626
  overview, 4:1623–1624
  risk and protective factors, 4:1624–1625
  stimulants, 4:1625
  substance categories, 4:1625–1627
  treatment models, 4:1627–1628
  treatment outcomes, 4:1628–1629
Substance-induced mood disorder, 3:1089, 1093
Subsystems. *See* **Systems, subsystems, and metasystems**
  ecological perspective, 2:493
Successive bilingualism, 1:159
Sudden unexplained deaths in infancy (SUDI), 2:802
Sue, David, 1:6
Sue, Derald Wing, 1:6
Suffering, vs. pain, 1:4
Suicide, 4:1629–1632
  adolescent depression, 1:431
  assessment, 1:90–93, 3:1150–1151
  causes, 4:1630
  childhood depression, 1:436
  contracts and safety plans, 1:93, 3:1148–1153, 4:1697–1698
  counselor training, 4:1632
  high-risk populations, 4:1630–1631
  ideation, 4:1629
  methods, 4:1631
  myths, 1:90–91
  overview, 4:1629
  prevention and intervention, 4:1631–1632
  research directions, 4:1632
  spectrum of suicidality, 4:1629–1630
  survivors, 4:1632, 1729
Suitcase of behavior, 1:375
Sullivan, Harry Stack, 4:1768
Super, Donald, 1:188, 3:1412
Superficial self-mutilation. *See* **Self-injury**
Superiority, 1:178
Super-reasonableness, 1:301, 2:817

Supervision, 3:971, 4:1633–1636
  clinician-directed, 1:270–273
  cotherapy, 3:970
  countertransference, 4:1636
  cultural competence, 4:1635
  format, 4:1635
  growth areas, 4:1639–1641
  isomorphism, 2:923–924, 4:1636
  levels, 4:1639
  live vs. dead, 3:969–972, 4:1644
  overview, 4:1633
  peer counselors, 3:1244
  purpose, 4:1634, 1652
  supervisory relationship, 4:1634–1635
  training and requirements, 4:1633–1634
Supervision, approved supervisor in marriage and family therapy, 4:1636–1638
Supervision, developmental model, 4:1638–1641
Supervision, gatekeeping, 4:1641–1643
Supervision, individual and group, 4:1635, 1643–1645, 1712
Supervision contract, 4:1645–1647
Supervision of supervision, 4:1647–1650
Supervision philosophy statement, 4:1650–1651
Supervision theories, 4:1651–1657
  developmental models, 4:1654–1656
  overview, 4:1651–1652
  processed-based models, 4:1656–1657
  psychotherapy-based models, 4:1652–1654
  purpose of supervision and, 4:1652
Support groups, 4:1657–1661
  common factors, 4:1658–1659
  criticisms, 4:1660–1661
  online, 4:1661
  overview, 4:1657–1658
  participation outcomes, 4:1660
  structure and facilitation of sessions, 4:1659–1660
  types, 4:1658–1659
Surrey, Janet, 3:1384
Surrogacy, 1:227, 229
Survival, 1:236
Survivors, 2:907
Survivors of Incest Anonymous, 1:307
Swanson, Gloria, 3:1060
Swinging (sexuality), 3:1181
Symbolic interactionism, 4:1662–1664
Symmetrical relationships. *See* **Complementary and symmetrical relationships**
Symptom exaggeration, 4:1668
Symptom prescription, 1:185, 4:1668
Synaptic dysfunction, 1:131
Systematic desensitization, 1:71, 2:656–657, 4:1783
Systematic Training for Effective Parenting (STEP), 3:1209, 4:1490, 1770

Systemic cognitive-developmental model, of supervision, 4:1656
Systemic family therapy, 4:1664–1669
    assessment, 4:1669
    historical development, 4:1665–1666
    interventions, 4:1668–1669
    overview, 4:1664
    processes, 4:1666–1667
    recent approaches, 4:1669
    systems theory, 4:1665
Systems, subsystems, and metasystems, 4:1670–1675
    boundaries, 4:1671–1673
    family roles, 4:1673–1674
    family structure, 4:1613, 1616
    family system, 4:1670
    healthy system, 4:1670–1671
    hierarchy, 2:765–767
    joining, 2:932
    metasystems, 4:1674
    open and closed, 4:1671–1672
    rules and messages, 4:1672
    structural maps, 4:1620–1621
    structure and boundaries, 4:1671
    subsystems, 4:1674–1675
    systems theory, 2:728
Systems perspective, 4:1774
    case conceptualization, 1:257–258
    clinical practice context, 1:265
    conjoint family therapy, 1:345–346
    court-mandated clients, 1:392
    depression in couples and families, 1:442–444
    ecological systems, 2:492–495
    mental health, 3:1059–1060
    neutrality, 3:1146
    qualitative research, 3:1350
    supervision theories, 4:1654, 1656–1657
    supervisor philosophy, 4:1651
Systems theory, 4:1675–1678
    change, 4:1676
    chaos family therapy, 1:196–201
    circular causality, 4:1676–1677
    eco-maps, 2:496
    epistemology in family therapy, 2:549
    feedback, 3:1262–1263
    first-order change, 2:676–678
    integrating individual and, 2:862–867
    medical family therapy, 3:1051
    morphogenesis, 3:1098
    morphostasis, 3:1101–1104
    See also **Cybernetics; General systems theory**
Sze, Szeming, 4:1765

Tadalafil, 2:556
Taft, William Howard, 1:207
Tansley, Arthur, 2:503
Tarasoff, Tatiana, 1:326, 482–483, 483
Tarasoff v. Board of Regents of the University of California, 1:326
Task analysis, 3:1323
Technology
    artificial insemination and in vitro fertilization, 1:227, 229, 3:1291
    HIPAA standards, 2:769–770
    Internet infidelity, 2:587
    online dating, 3:1176–1179
    online support groups and communities, 4:1661
    sexual toys/aids, 4:1550
    supervisor training, 4:1635, 1645
Technology adaptation model, 4:1680
Technology and families/marriage, 4:1679–1682
    couple and family technology framework, 4:1680–1682
    cybersex, 4:1679
    family resource management, 2:639
    family therapy, 3:1048–1049
    Internet infidelity, 2:584–585
    overview, 4:1679
    relationship changes, 4:1680–1682
    theories, 4:1680
Teen parenting, 4:1682–1685
    causes, 4:1684–1685
    cyclical issues, 4:1684
    overview, 4:1682
    preventing, 4:1685
    social support, 4:1683
Teen pregnancy, 3:1293, 4:1593
Telephone interviews, 1:262
Terminal illness. *See* **Death and dying**
Termination, 4:1685–1688
    effect on counselors, 4:1687–1688
    ethical considerations, 4:1685–1686
    overview, 4:1685
    process, 4:1686–1687
    rituals, 4:1688
Tervalon, Melanie, 3:1116
Testimony, court, 1:368
Testosterone, 3:981, 990, 4:1501, 1529
Thanatologists, 2:751
Therapeutic alliance, 4:1688–1692
    Adlerian family therapy, 1:16
    cognitive-behavioral family therapy, 1:285
    collaborative language systems, 1:292
    common factors, 1:296
    confrontation, 1:342
    couples and family therapy, 4:1689–1690
    dual and multiple relationships, 1:478–479
    ecosystemic structural family therapy, 2:501
    emotionally focused couples therapy, 2:525

forensics, **1:**369
immigrant/refugee counseling, **1:**96
individual vs. couples/family therapy, **3:**1163
Internet infidelity, **2:**584–585
joining and, **2:**929
key theorists, **4:**1688–1691
models, **4:**1690
overview, **4:**1688
Rogers's six conditions, **4:**1688–1689
rupture and repair, **4:**1691–1692
See also Therapist role

Therapeutic assessment, 4:1693–1695
biopsychosocial, **1:**83–89
play-based, **4:**1439
suicide, **1:**90–93

Therapeutic contract, 4:1696–1700
client presenting concerns, **4:**1697–1698
conflict management, **4:**1699
informed consent compared to, **4:**1696–1697
marriage, couples, and family counseling, **4:**1698–1700
overview, **4:**1696
role responsibilities, **4:**1699
standard elements, **4:**1696
theory-specific, **4:**1697
uses, **4:**1700
See also Contracts

Therapeutic factors, **3:**1010

Therapeutic impasses, 4:1700–1703
addressing, **4:**1701–1703
case study, **4:**1703
couples therapy, **4:**1701
effects on therapist, **4:**1701
overview, **4:**1700–1701

Therapist role
cognitive-behavioral couples therapy, **1:**280
cognitive-behavioral family therapy, **1:**285
collaborative couples therapy, **1:**289–290
collaborative language systems, **1:**291–293
confrontation, **1:**343
contextual family therapy, **1:**355
couples and marriage counseling, **1:**379–380
crucible situations, **1:**399–400
divorce and separation counseling, **1:**460
duty to warn, **1:**483–484
enactments, **2:**538–542
experiential family therapy, **2:**577–579
faith-based therapy, **2:**590
focal family therapy, **2:**679–680
Gestalt family therapy, **2:**738–739
goal setting, **2:**742
grief counseling, **2:**749–750

group family therapy, **2:**755
hospice, **2:**810
joining, **2:**928–932
Milan systemic approaches, **3:**1070–1071
moral dimensions of therapy, **3:**1096–1097
motivational interviewing, **3:**1107–1108
multisystemic therapy, **3:**1124
narrative therapy, **3:**1134
neutrality and curiosity, **3:**1145–1148
no-harm contracts, **3:**1149
nonverbal communication, **3:**1160–1161
object relations theory, **3:**1175–1176
postmodern therapies, **3:**1270–1271
qualitative research, **3:**1351
religion in counseling, **3:**1398
sexual assessment, **4:**1521–1522
strategic family therapy, **4:**1606–1607
structural family therapy, **4:**1615
structural maps, **4:**1623
traumatized clients, **4:**1475–1476
Virginia Satir model, **4:**1755
See also **Dual and multiple relationships; Person of the therapist; Self of the therapist; Sexual relationships with clients; Therapeutic alliance**

Therapist Use-of-Self Orientations Questionnaire, **4:**1472–1473

Therapists' values, 4:1704–1706
bias resulting from, **4:**1705
ethical considerations, **4:**1705–1706
marriage, **3:**1041
morality, **3:**1096–1097
multicultural competence, **3:**1111
neutrality and curiosity, **3:**1145–1148
open relationships, **3:**1182
self-examination of, **3:**1248
sexuality and religion, **4:**1554

Third-order change, **4:**1461
Thomas, Kenneth, **1:**339
Thomas, W. I., **4:**1662
Thorndike, E. L., **2:**517, **3:**1204
Thorndike's law of effect, **1:**139, **3:**1204
Thorsen, Kristin, **3:**974
Thought records, **2:**797
Ticker to Work and Work Incentive Act, **3:**1345
Time lines
ecosystemic structural family therapy, **2:**502
family resilience, **2:**633
Titchener, Edward B., **2:**527–528
Togetherness, **3:**993–995
Token economy, **1:**144
Tolman, Edward, **1:**274
Toman, Walter, **1:**18, 175, **2:**608
Tomm, Karl, **4:**1667, 1678, 1780
Tonsager, Mary, **4:**1693

Torture treatment, 4:1706–1709
  counseling considerations, 4:1708–1709
  effects of torture, 4:1707–1708
  legal definitions, 4:1706–1707
  overview, 4:1706
  treatment considerations, 4:1709
Torture Victims Relief Act, 4:1706
Total behavior, 1:238, 375
Total Transformation Program, 3:1210
Touch, 3:997, 1159, 4:1755
Touching hands, 2:818
Tracking, in attunement, 1:121
Traditional behavioral couple therapy, 1:386–387
Training and licensure, 4:1709–1712
  comparison with other professions, 4:1712
  continuing education, 3:1288
  education, 4:1710–1711
  licensure, 4:1711–1712
  multicultural competence, 3:1116–1117
  peer counselors, 3:1243–1244
  postdoctoral fellowships, 3:1266–1267
  training, 4:1710–1711
  See also Licensure and certification
Training in Marriage Enrichment,
  1:180, 3:1031, 1033
Training in Marriage Enrichment (TIME) Program,
  4:1713–1714, 1785
Trait emotional intelligence, 2:518
Trait Emotional Intelligence Questionnaire, 2:519
Traits of a Happy Couple, 3:1031, 1032
Tranquilizers, 1:204
Transactional analysis, 2:816, 4:1697
Transcutaneous electrical nerve stimulation (TENS)
  machines, 4:1526
Transference, 1:399, 2:922, 3:1175, 1335–1336,
  4:1547
Transgender families, 3:949, 4:1715–1718
  counseling considerations, 4:1716–1718
  experiences of transgender individuals,
    4:1715–1716
  minority stress model, 4:1716
  terminology, 4:1715
  See also LGBT community; LGBT families
Transgenerational family therapy, 4:1718–1720
Transgenerational model. See Bowen family systems
  theory; Intergenerational relationships
Transient situational disturbance. See Adjustment
  disorder in adolescents
Transitions and palliative care therapy model,
  2:810–811
Transpersonalism, 2:841
Transracial adoption, 1:37–41, 4:1720–1722
Transsexual Road Map, 3:950
Transvestic disorder, 3:1197–1198

Trauma
  common factors, 4:1476
  defining, 4:1723
  developmental perspective, 4:1727–1728
  diagnosis, 4:1726–1727
  overview, 4:1475
  types, 3:1279–1280, 4:1723
  vicarious, 4:1476
  See also Intergenerational trauma; Posttraumatic
    stress disorder in children; Posttraumatic stress
    disorder (PTSD)
Trauma and children, 4:1723–1725
  developmental perspective, 4:1727–1728
  outcomes, 4:1723–1724
  treatment, 4:1724–1725
  types, 4:1723
Trauma and families, 4:1726–1729
  developmental perspective, 4:1727–1728
  diagnosis, 4:1726–1727
  family therapy, 4:1726, 1728–1729
  interpersonal relationships, 4:1728
Trauma recovery, 3:1371
Trauma-focused cognitive-behavioral therapy,
  4:1728, 1729–1734
  overview, 4:1729–1731
  treatment components, 4:1731–1734
Traumatic loss, 3:977
Treatment planning with couples and families,
  4:1734–1738
  clinically focused, 4:1735
  diversity, 4:1738
  plan elements, 4:1735–1738
  plan formats, 4:1734–1735
  symptom-based, 4:1735
  value of, 4:1738
Triangulation, 4:1739–1741
  avoiding responsibility, 4:1740–1741
  Bowen family systems theory, 1:63, 174,
    2:841–842, 4:1770
  family assessment, 2:608
  feminist perspective, 2:663
  love, 2:675, 3:987, 1424
  scapegoating, 4:1451
  stability, 4:1739–1740
  therapeutic applications, 4:1741
TRICARE, 3:953
Tricyclic antidepressants, 1:71, 3:1090
Triple-P Positive Parenting Program, 3:1203
True experimental designs, 2:532
Trueba, Henry T., 1:397
Trust, 4:1742–1745
  capacity for, 4:1744–1745
  contextual family therapy, 1:353
  fidelity, 2:674

measuring, 4:1743–1744
overview, 4:1742
relationship components, 1:373
social interaction, 4:1742–1743
survival, 4:1743
therapeutic contracts, 4:1699–1700
value of, 4:1743, 1769
Turbulence, 1:198
Turing, Alan M., 2:702
Turner, Patrice, 2:806–807
12-step community programs, 1:306–307
12-step models, 4:1627–1628
Twinks (sexual identity), 4:1541
Two-spirit people, 2:716, 723, 4:1715
Tyndall, Lisa, 3:1053
Type A personality, 1:70
Typification, 4:1568

Unconscious mind, 2:559
Underlying anger, 1:66
Undocumented immigrants, 2:834
Uniform Child Custody Jurisdiction Enforcement Act, 1:158
Uniform Premarital Agreement Act, 3:1304
Uninvolved parenting. *See* Rejecting-neglecting/disengaged parenting
United Nations, 2:665, 3:1246
  Convention Against Torture and Other Cruel, Inhuman or Degrading Treatment or Punishment, 4:1706
United Nations Development Fund for Women, 2:666
United States v. Windsor, 3:1039
Unresolved attachment, 1:99
Unspecified anxiety disorder, 1:75
Unusual eating behaviors, 1:130
  See also Eating disorders
Upbringing away from parents, 3:1382
Upchurch, Renn, 1:244
Urban families, 4:1747–1750
  deficit narratives, 4:1749–1750
  demographics, 4:1747
  multicultural competence, 4:1747–1749
  social justice, 4:1750
U.S. Bureau of Indian Affairs, 1:38, 3:1139
U.S. Constitution, 3:1038, 1039, 4:1435
U.S. Department of Defense, 3:953, 1076
U.S. Department of Education, 1:308
U.S. Department of Health and Human Services, 1:308, 2:771
U.S. Department of Veterans Affairs, 3:953, 1266
Uses and gratifications model, 4:1680
Uxoricide, 2:800

Vaillant, George, 1:47–48
Validation, 1:121, 2:622
Values. *See* **Beliefs and values**
Values-based living, 1:3–4
Van Deurzen, Emmy, 3:1097
Vardenafil hydrochloride, 2:556
Vasopressin, 3:981, 982, 990
Vatican II, 3:1025
V-codes. *See* **DSM and V-codes**, 3:1381
Veaux, Franklin, 3:1182
Venereal disease. *See* **Sexually transmitted infections** (STI)
Veracity, as ethical principle, 2:566
Verbal communication
  defined, 1:302
  errors/problems, 1:300–301
Vertical relationships, 2:546
Vertical stressors, 2:647
Veterans. *See* Military veterans
Veterans Administration (VA), 1:188
Viagra, 2:556, 4:1511, 1524
Vibrators, 4:1525–1526, 1550
Vicarious Resilience Scale, 3:1401
Vicarious trauma, 4:1476
Victims. *See* Survivors
Vidal de Haynes, Maria, 4:1721
Violence. *See* **Domestic violence; Interpersonal violence**
Virginia Satir model, 4:1753–1757
  family setting, 4:1755
  human validation process model, 4:1756–1757
  key concepts, 4:1753–1755
  techniques, 4:1755–1756
Virtue ethics, 2:566
Visser, Coert, 4:1448
Vivitrol, 4:1626
Vocal qualities, 3:1159
Voice, 1:396–397
Voyeuristic disorder, 3:1196
Vygotsky, Lev, 1:348, 2:493, 3:1137

Wade, Nathaniel G., 2:806
Wainwright, Nigel, 1:272
Waldo, Michael, 3:1315
Walker, Alex J., 1:416
Wall, John, 3:1041
Waller, Willard, 3:1045, 4:1662
Walsh, Froma, 2:592, 632, 642, 644–645, 661, 4:1781
Walsh family resilience framework, 2:633–635
Walter, H., 3:1186
Walter, John, 4:1773, 1777
Walters, Marianne, 2:661, 662, 4:1759, 1781
Wampold, B. E., 2:534
Wants, 1:375

War metaphors, 3:1066
Ward, David B., 2:544
Warkentin, Joh, 4:1770
Watkins, Clifton Edward, 4:1647
Watson, John B., 2:840, 3:1105, 1208, 4:1783
Watzlawick, Paul, 1:182, 248, 2:676, 3:1068, 1346, 4:1460–1461, 1463, 1665, 1678, 1775
WDEP system, 1:375–376
Weakland, John, 1:181–182, 186, 471, 2:558, 676, 863, 3:1376, 4:1460–1461, 1463, 1665, 1773, 1775–1776
Weather metaphors, 3:1066
Weber, Scott, 3:1280
Websites, professional, 3:1289
Wechsler, David, 4:1437
Wechsler Adult Intelligence Scale, 4:1437
Wechsler Intelligence Scale for Children, 4:1437, 1438
Wechsler Preschool and Primary Scale of Intelligence, 4:1437
Weddings, 3:994
Weeks, Gerald, 2:587
Wegscheider-Cruse, Sharon, 4:1451–1452, 1673
Wei, Ha-Sheng, 3:1224
Weiner-Davis, Michele, 4:1773, 1777–1778, 1782
Weiss, Paul A., 3:1350
Weiss, Robert, 4:1497, 1498
Wellness, 2:840, 3:956–957
We-ness, 3:1387
Westermarck, Edvard, 2:835–836
Weston, Kath, 1:239
Wheeler, Anne Marie, 4:1546
Wheeler, Etta, 1:214
Whisman, Mark, 4:1784
Whitaker, Carl, 1:265, 398–399, 2:551, 558, 578, 579, 3:969, 1060, 1064, 1251, 1419, 4:1471–1472, 1678, 1770–1771, 1785
White, Cheryl, 4:1780
White, Kerr, 1:243
White, Michael, 3:969, 1064, 1133, 1137, 1268, 4:1484–1485, 1569, 1702, 1780
White House Conference on the Care of Dependent Children, 1:214
Whiting, Peggy, 1:153, 154–155
Whiting, Richard, 3:1414–1415
Whytt, Robert, 2:489
Wicks, Jared, 3:1026
Wieling, Elizabeth, 1:95
Wiener, Norbert, 1:406, 2:549, 865, 3:1098, 1101, 1262, 4:1463, 1774
Wilcox, W. Bradford, 3:1397
Wile, Daniel B., 1:289–290
Williams, Franklin, 1:243
Williams syndrome, 1:454
Wilson, Mary Ellen, 1:214

Wiltwyck School for Boys, 2:929, 4:1614, 1773, 1774
Winch, Robert, 3:1046
Winnicott, Donald, 1:121, 4:1769
Wittgenstein, Ludwig, 4:1567, 1576
Wolfelt, Alan, 2:751
Wolfensberger, Wolf, 3:1161, 1162
Wolin, Steven, 3:1415
Wolpe, Joseph, 1:80, 4:1448, 1783, 1784
Women
  careers, 1:187–188
  counseling considerations, 2:719–720
  Family and Medical Leave Act of 1993, 2:601
  feminist family therapy, 2:661–664
  feminist therapy, 2:714–715
  gender socialization, 2:713–714, 724–726
  hypoactive sexual desire disorder, 4:1523
  orgasmic disorder, 2:654–657, 4:1523
  poverty, 2:595–596, 665–669
  relational-cultural therapy, 3:1384
  sexual interest/arousal disorder, 2:657–660, 4:1523
  sexual intimacy, 4:1535–1536
  sexual pain disorders, 2:730–733
  See also Feminism; Gender issues
Women's Project, 4:1781–1782
Women's Project, The, 2:661, **4:1759–1760**
Wonder, 1:89
Worden, William, 1:150, 153, 154, 2:749
Work
  Family and Medical Leave Act of 1993, 2:600–602
  job loss, 2:925–927
  meaning of, 1:189–190
  parental stress, 3:1223
  patriarchy, 3:1240–1241
  retirement, 3:1409–1412
  rural families, 3:1430
Work metaphors, 3:1065
Work relationships, 4:1761–1762
Workable compromise, 1:82
Work-life balance. See Life balance
Worksheets, 2:797
World Association for Sexual Health, 4:1763–1764
World Health Organization Disability Assessment Scale, 1:473
World Health Organization (WHO), 1:207, 208, 321, 473, 2:594, 891, 3:1314, 4:1501–1502, 1549, 1585, **1765–1766**
World Professional Association for Transgender Health, 2:718
Worldwide Marriage Encounter, 3:1025
Worthington, Everett L., 2:805–807, 3:1373
Wraparound plans, 4:1459
Wrap-Around services, 1:390
Wundt, Wilhelm, 2:527
Wynne, L. C., 2:532, 533, 4:1769

Xanax, **4:**1626

Yalom, Irvin, **2:**752, 755, **3:**1010, **4:**1659, 1702
Young, Mark, **1:**332, 383, **2:**870–871, **3:**1300
Young adulthood, **2:**611
   friendship, **2:**691
Youngest children, **1:**18, 178, 332, **4:**1563
Youth. *See* Adolescents

Z-codes, **1:**473, **3:**1381
Zeig, Jeff, **1:**23

Zero-order change, **4:**1461
Zieglmayer, Verena, **1:**484
Zimmerman, Jeffrey, **4:**1780
Zimmerman, Marc A., **2:**536
Zimmerman, Toni, **2:**664
Zoloft, **1:**204, **3:**1303
Zone of proximal development, **1:**348, **3:**1137
Zuccarini, Dino, **4:**1536
Zuckerman, Edward L., *The Paper Office*, **3:**1290
Zuk, Gerald, **4:**1769
Zyprexa, **1:**133

The Mystery of the Magi's Treasure

THREE COUSINS DETECTIVE CLUB®

#1 / The Mystery of the White Elephant
#2 / The Mystery of the Silent Nightingale
#3 / The Mystery of the Wrong Dog
#4 / The Mystery of the Dancing Angels
#5 / The Mystery of the Hobo's Message
#6 / The Mystery of the Magi's Treasure
#7 / The Mystery of the Haunted Lighthouse
#8 / The Mystery of the Dolphin Detective
#9 / The Mystery of the Eagle Feather
#10 / The Mystery of the Silly Goose
#11 / The Mystery of the Copycat Clown
#12 / The Mystery of the Honeybees' Secret
#13 / The Mystery of the Gingerbread House
#14 / The Mystery of the Zoo Camp
#15 / The Mystery of the Goldfish Pond
#16 / The Mystery of the Traveling Button
#17 / The Mystery of the Birthday Party
#18 / The Mystery of the Lost Island

THREE COUSINS 6 DETECTIVE CLUB

The Mystery of the Magi's Treasure

Elspeth Campbell Murphy
Illustrated by Joe Nordstrom

BETHANY HOUSE PUBLISHERS
MINNEAPOLIS, MINNESOTA 55438

Cover and story illustrations by Joe Nordstrom

Three Cousins Detective Club® and TCDC® are registered trademark of Elspeth Campbell Murphy

Copyright © 1995
Elspeth Campbell Murphy

All rights reserved. No part of this publication may be reproduced, stored in a retrieval system, or transmitted in any form or by any means electronic, mechanical, photocopying, recording, or otherwise without the prior written permission of the publisher and copyright owners.

Published by Bethany House Publishers
A Ministry of Bethany Fellowship, Inc.
11300 Hampshire Avenue South
Minneapolis, Minnesota 55438

Printed in the United States of America.

Library of Congress Cataloging-in-Publication Data

Murphy, Elspeth Campbell.
    The mystery of the Magi's treasure / Elspeth Campbell Murphy ; [illustrated by Joe Nordstrom].
        p.   cm. — (Three Cousins Detective Club® ; bk. 6)
    Summary: While celebrating "Christmas in July," the three cousins come into some stolen art works and discover that even bad boys can be good.

    [1. Mystery and detective stories. 2. Cousins—Fiction.
3. Conduct of life—Fiction.] I. Nordstrom, Joe, ill. II. Title.
III. Series: Murphy, Elspeth Campbell. Three Cousins Detective Club® ; 6.
PZ7.M95316Mydd   1995
[Fic]—dc20   95–7097
ISBN 1–55661–410–1   CIP
                                                                   AC

In loving memory of my father-in-law,
Howard R. Murphy,
whose life was filled with
love, joy, peace,
patience, kindness, goodness,
faithfulness, gentleness, and self-control.

ELSPETH CAMPBELL MURPHY has been a familiar name in Christian publishing for over fifteen years, with more than seventy-five books to her credit and sales reaching five million worldwide. She is the author of the best-selling series *David and I Talk to God* and *The Kids From Apple Street Church*, as well as the 1990 Gold Medallion winner *Do You See Me, God?* A graduate of Trinity College and Moody Bible Institute, Elspeth and her husband, Mike, make their home in Chicago, where she writes full time.

Contents

1. The Kevins 9
2. Christmas in July 11
3. Bragging Grandma 15
4. Something Odd 19
5. Gold, Frankincense, and Myrrh 22
6. Beautiful Boxes 26
7. Missing 29
8. The T.C.D.C. 32
9. Sylvia 35
10. The Perfect Hiding Place 38
11. Stuffed Animals 42
12. Decoys 45
13. Back on the Horse 49
14. Help! Police! 53
15. Heroes 56

1

The Kevins

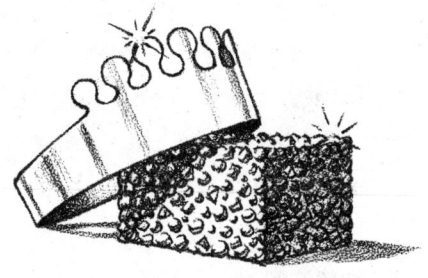

*T*imothy Dawson sometimes wondered what it would be like to be really, really bad.

Not the kind of bad where you beat up on people or steal things. But just the kind of bad where you were always acting up and goofing off and no one ever expected you to behave yourself.

Timothy sometimes wondered what it would be like to be one of the Kevins.

The Kevins were three boys who went to the church where Timothy's grandfather was the pastor. Timothy and his cousins Sarah-Jane Cooper and Titus McKay knew the Kevins slightly from being in the same Sunday school class with them when the cousins visited. But it was more like they knew *of* the Kevins.

But then—everybody knew *of* the Kevins. The three boys had met when they had all toddled into the same nursery Sunday school class on the same day. They had been together ever since. Every teacher they'd ever known had declared, "Those three boys should be separated!"

But somehow Kevin O'Connell, Kevin Jones, and Kevin Weston had managed to stay together. Always acting up and goofing off. And no one ever expected them to behave themselves.

And that's how—on the hottest day of the summer so far—Timothy, Titus, and Sarah-Jane came to be wearing long, flowing robes and fancy crowns.

They were supposed to be the Three Wise Men.

They were not too happy about it.

And it was all because of the Kevins.

2

Christmas in July

*I*t had happened like this:

The resort town where the cousins' grandparents lived got a lot of tourists in the summertime. And there were a lot of artists who lived there all year round.

So every summer the town sponsored a sidewalk art fair. This year the theme was "Christmas in July," and everyone was going all out.

Even the churches had gotten involved. They had joined together for a free outdoor concert and carol sing-along, complete with peppermint ice cream and Christmas cookies.

The problem was making sure that visitors knew about the concert. The churches had put up posters, of course.

But then someone thought it would be a good idea to have church people go among the crowds to hand out leaflets.

And then someone else said that this sounded like a good job for the kids.

And then someone else said it would be cute to have the kids dressed as angels and shepherds.

And then someone else said not to forget the Three Wise Men.

So it was decided that a few kids from each church would go around in costumes handing out leaflets about the concert. All the other kids would be in the choir.

The trouble came when someone, who didn't know of the Kevins, picked *them* to be the Three Wise Men.

When Timothy heard about this, he couldn't wait to see what would happen. At Christmastime, whichever kids played the Wise Men walked in single file slowly and solemnly down the center aisle as the choir sang, "We Three Kings of Orient Are."

It would be a change to see the Three Kings knocking one another's crowns off and rolling around in the dirt.

And that's exactly what happened at rehearsal.

"No, no, no, no, no!" said the choir director, who *did* know of the Kevins. "This will never do. We need three completely dependable children to be the Wise Men."

The cousins should have seen what was coming. But they didn't.

As the Kevins scrambled out of their costumes, the choir director scanned the choir for

replacements. He found them.

"Timothy! Titus! Sarah-Jane! Get down here. On the double."

The Kevins were put in the choir—as far apart as the director could get them without knocking people off the risers.

The cousins slumped into the Wise Men costumes and picked up their leaflets.

The robes were hot.

The crowns were heavy.

Timothy caught sight of the Kevins. They were grinning.

He doubted the Kevins were anywhere near as dumb as they pretended to be.

3

Bragging Grandma

The choir director came over to check on the cousins. "There now," he said heartily. "You know what to do? Good. Then we're all set. I know you'll do a great job. Your grandmother is always telling us how intelligent and responsible and polite you three are."

It's a good thing for him we're so polite, thought Timothy. *Too polite to say what we think of being pulled out of the choir to dress up as the Wise Men in the middle of July. Those lucky kids in the choir don't even have to wear their robes until dress rehearsal.*

The director went back to the choir, and the cousins were left to themselves.

"Well, you guys," said Sarah-Jane. "Looks like Grandma strikes again."

The Mystery of the Magi's Treasure

The boys knew right away what she meant. It was a standing joke in the family how much Grandma BRAGGED about her grandchildren.

"It's our own fault, really," said Titus with a dramatic sigh. "If only we weren't such *wonderful* children!"

Timothy laughed. But he saw the serious side of it, too. The problem with everybody thinking you were a good kid was that you couldn't exactly complain about it. It wasn't as if people were calling you names or anything. . . .

Just then some tourists passed by. He heard one of them say, "Oh, look, honey! The Three Magi! Aren't they just *adorable*?"

"That does it," Timothy muttered to his cousins. "We have *got* to tell Grandma to stop bragging about us. Look where it's gotten us. Let's ask her to make them get some other kids to be the Wise Men."

Titus and Sarah-Jane nodded. But they didn't have time to say anything.

It just so happened Grandma was coming by at the same time. And she had overheard

Bragging Grandma

what the lady had said about the adorable Wise Men.

"They're my grandchildren, you know," she announced to this complete stranger.

"Oh, are they *really*?" cried the lady. "You must be very proud."

"Oh, I am!" said Grandma. "They're just as good as gold. The three of them are visiting their grandpa and me. And they never give us a minute's trouble."

The cousins glanced at one another. How could they make a stink about being the adorable Magi now?

After chatting for a while, the people moved on, and Grandma turned back to the cousins.

"I'm glad I ran into you," she said. "I was just coming to tell you I'm going out for a while. Grandpa's in his study with Gubbio if you need anything."

Gubbio was Titus's little dog. For once the cousins were glad he wasn't trotting along at their heels. It was bad enough being the Three Wise Men without being the Three Wise Men and a Yorkshire terrier.

"Where are you going?" Sarah-Jane asked Grandma.

"Did I ever mention my young friend Sylvia?"

"The artist?" asked Timothy.

"That's right," said Grandma. "She's what you might call a 'folk artist.' She hasn't been to art school. And I think she feels inferior to some of the artists around here. Anyway, I heard that one of the gallery owners, Mr. Fitzgerald, is very open to showing new folk art. I want to encourage Sylvia to take a few pieces to show him."

Grandma hurried off, and Timothy wished that he could go with her.

This past year at school, art had become his all-time favorite subject. And he loved putzing around at home, just making stuff. He wondered what sort of art Sylvia made.

But for now, he had a job to do.

4

Something Odd

The job of handing out leaflets wasn't nearly as bad as Timothy had thought it was going to be. People were delighted to hear about the concert. And everyone was very nice.

Sure, it was annoying the way people kept telling them how cute they looked in their costumes. But the cousins made themselves get over it.

So everything was going fine.

Until something odd happened.

A frazzled-looking lady came rushing up to them.

"There you are!" she cried. "I've been looking all over for you!"

The cousins blinked. As far as they knew,

The Mystery of the Magi's Treasure

they had never met this person before in their lives.

"Us?" asked Timothy. "You were looking for us?"

"You're the Three Wise Men, aren't you?" replied the lady.

The cousins glanced at one another. In these getups, who else would they be?

But before they could answer, the lady thrust three boxes into their hands.

"Here. The Wise Men are supposed to have gifts for Baby Jesus, aren't they? Your costumes aren't complete without them. So here's the gold. And that incense stuff. And the um—"

Something Odd

"Myrrh?" said Titus.

"Right, right. The . . . myrrh. OK. Now, you hold on to those boxes, you hear me?

"Whatever you do, don't lose them. And don't give them to anyone else but me. I'm the one in charge of the um—"

"Props?" said Titus.

"Right, right. The . . . props."

The woman turned to leave.

"Wait a minute," said Sarah-Jane, looking anxiously at the throngs of people. "How will we find you when we're done handing out leaflets?"

"Don't worry about that," said the lady briskly. "I'll find you. In those costumes, it will be easy to find you in the crowd."

"Wait a minute," said Timothy. He could hear his voice getting whiny. But the grown-ups kept making this job harder and harder. "How are we supposed to hold on to these boxes and hand out leaflets at the same time?"

Apparently the lady didn't want to hear any complaints, because she hurried away without answering.

5

Gold, Frankincense, and Myrrh

"This is a nuisance," said Sarah-Jane, trying to hold on to her box with one hand and her leaflets with the other.

Titus agreed. "I don't see why we need to carry the presents at all. Why can't we just be the Wise Men *after* they found Jesus? They wouldn't have the presents with them then."

Sarah-Jane and Timothy had to agree that this made perfect sense. But what could they do?

Titus paused for a moment. Then he said, "You know what's funny?"

"Funny ha-ha? Or funny weird?" asked Sarah-Jane.

"Funny weird," said Titus.

"What is?" asked Sarah-Jane.

"OK," said Titus. "We already agreed that it's funny weird that we have to pass out leaflets *and* carry boxes at the same time. But why are we getting the boxes *now*? Why weren't they with the costumes?"

Sarah-Jane thought about that for a minute. "Well, all the churches are going together on this, right? So maybe someone from one church made the costumes. And maybe someone from another church made the props."

"Makes sense," said Titus. "And the prop lady was just running late. That's why she didn't give us the boxes till now. Right?"

"Right . . ." said Sarah-Jane. But she didn't sound as if she were buying her own explanation.

"So what's bothering you about it?" asked Titus.

The three cousins often talked things through like this. They had a detective club, and they always perked up when they came upon something odd.

Sometimes something that seemed odd at

first turned out later to have a logical explanation.

But sometimes something just seemed out of whack, and you couldn't explain it away.

The cousins had solved a lot of mysteries, and they had developed a kind of sense about these things. A feeling that something is wrong. But you don't know what. Or what it means.

That's what it felt like now.

The cousins had also discovered that talking about the mystery could help to solve it.

"OK," said Sarah-Jane slowly, thinking out loud. "This lady is in charge of the Christmas-story props. Right? But she doesn't even know the names of the Wise Men's gifts. The only one she got right was gold. I mean, doesn't that strike you as odd?"

"Yes, now that you mention it," said Titus. "Gold. Frankincense. And myrrh. I didn't know what frankincense and myrrh were until my Sunday school teacher told us. They're like rare, expensive perfume that you would bring to honor someone very important.

"But even before I knew what the words *meant*, I knew what the words *were*. This lady didn't even know what the words were. And she's the one in charge of the boxes."

"Speaking of the boxes . . ." said Timothy. He had been following his cousins' conversation and thinking his own thoughts all at the same time. "There's something wrong with them, too."

Titus and Sarah-Jane took a good look at their boxes for the first time. Then they looked at Timothy in surprise.

"What's wrong with them, Tim?" asked Titus. "They're EXcellent!"

"Absolutely beautiful!" agreed Sarah-Jane.

"My point exactly," said Timothy.

6

Beautiful Boxes

As detectives, the cousins had trained themselves to notice things. But Timothy was an artist as well as a detective. And that was why he noticed something odd about the boxes: They were *too* beautiful.

Timothy had once made a jewelry box as a present for his mother. First, he had emptied his rock collection out of his best cigar box. Then he had taken a bunch of macaroni in all kinds of different shapes and glued them close together, all over the lid. Finally, he had asked his father to help him spray-paint the whole box gold.

His mother had said it was the most beautiful box she had ever seen. She had even lent the box to the church for the Christmas pageant.

But Timothy knew his beautiful box was nowhere near as beautiful as these.

"Think about it," he said to his cousins. "When have you ever seen Christmas pageant props that look this good? What do the Wise Men carry at your church?"

Titus and Sarah-Jane closed their eyes, trying to picture it.

"An empty bubble-bath jar sprinkled with glitter," said Titus.

"Something like that," said Sarah-Jane.

"Same here," said Timothy. "But now look at these boxes."

The cousins looked at them again. The boxes had started out as plain old wooden boxes, probably. But someone had painted them with gorgeous colors—so shiny and luscious you just wanted to lick them. And then, on top of that, little objects had been glued in beautiful patterns.

When you looked very closely, you could see that the objects were common, everyday things. Colored glass. Buttons. Keys. Bottle caps. Even little plastic gumball machine toys.

Junk. The kind of things people throw away. But on these boxes the junk was all part of a master design.

Where most people saw junk, the person who made these boxes saw good stuff to work with.

It was then that Titus and Sarah-Jane realized what Timothy had noticed first.

They were looking at good, good work. Whoever had made these boxes was a real artist.

"But why are they using such special boxes as props?" asked Sarah-Jane.

Timothy shrugged. "I have no idea."

"Whatever the reason," said Titus, "the prop lady isn't taking any chance on something happening to them. She's over there behind you. Watching us."

7

Missing

Sarah-Jane and Timothy knew better than to whirl around yelling, "Where? Where?" when Titus said they were being watched.

Rather, they just looked around very, very casually. And when they spotted the prop lady, they gave no sign at all that they had noticed her.

They just turned back casually to face Titus.

"Why is she watching us?" muttered Sarah-Jane. "To make sure we don't lose the boxes? If she's that worried, why did she give them to us in the first place? Or why doesn't she just come get them back?"

Without knowing exactly why, the cousins held on to the boxes a little tighter.

Then—when Titus said, "It's all right; she's going away now"—all three of them gave a little sigh of relief.

"What's wrong with us?" asked Timothy. "What are we so jumpy about?"

None of them had an answer for that.

But at least they figured out what to do with their leaflets.

They went up to the booth of an artist they knew and set their beautiful boxes on the ground. It felt good to give their hands a rest. But they still guarded the boxes with their feet.

The artist let them put the leaflets on a corner of his table. They didn't have all that many left. So they put them in a pile. They weighted the leaflets down with a rock so they wouldn't blow away.

Then they borrowed a marking pen and some masking tape. On the back of one leaflet they printed in big letters: FREE! PLEASE TAKE ONE! HELP YOURSELF! They taped the sign to the awning pole right beside the pile of leaflets. This way, the leaflets could sort of pass themselves out.

The cousins were just wondering what to do next when another artist hurried up to the

booth with a warning for his friend.

"Keep an eye on your stuff," he said. "Some art pieces are missing, and no one has any idea where they could be."

8

The T.C.D.C.

"What happened?" asked Timothy, instantly tuning in to a mystery.

"Well, it was the strangest thing," said the artist's friend, whose name tag said *Bob*. "I heard that some artist—I didn't recognize the name—had stopped in at a gallery to show some of her pieces to the owner.

"The person who told me about it didn't know what the work looked like. I got the impression it was something offbeat and unusual.

"Anyway, the gallery hadn't opened for the day, yet. But the artist met a woman just outside the front door of the gallery. The woman said she was the owner's assistant."

"But was she really?" asked Titus.

The T.C.D.C.

Both artists looked at the cousins in surprise.

"You kids are pretty quick, aren't you?" said the artist they knew, whose name was John.

The cousins gave embarrassed little shrugs. What could you say to that? Well, yes, we are?

Sarah-Jane said, "It's just that we're the members of the T.C.D.C. So we're interested in these things."

"What's a 'teesy-deesy'?" asked John.

"It's letters," explained Timothy. "Capital T. Capital C. Capital D. Capital C. It stands for the Three Cousins Detective Club."

"Oh," said Bob. "Then this will be right up your alley."

He went on with the story. "It turns out this woman was *not* the gallery assistant. But the artist didn't know that at the time. And she had no reason to be suspicious. The 'assistant' was very friendly and helpful. She told the artist that the gallery owner was away—but that she would see that he got the artwork. She even wrote the artist a receipt."

"Then what happened?" asked Sarah-Jane.

"How did the artist find out something was wrong?"

"Good question," said Bob. "A little bit later, the artist thought of something she wanted to ask. So she went back to the gallery. It was open by then. The owner, Mr. Fitzgerald, was there. But his assistant—his *real* assistant—was on a trip. A thousand miles away! The so-called assistant was nowhere to be seen. And neither was the artwork. I wish I could remember the artist's name. I'm not familiar with her work at all."

The cousins looked at one another. They had a sinking feeling that they were all guessing the same thing.

Timothy said, "Her name wouldn't be Sylvia, would it?"

9

Sylvia

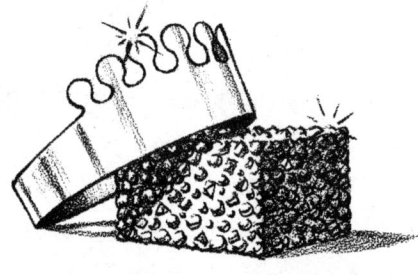

"That's it!" cried Bob. "Sylvia! That was the name. Sylvia. But how in the world did you kids know that?"

"Well, we're not positive," said Timothy. "But our grandmother has an artist friend named Sylvia who does really good work. Only Sylvia's really shy about it. So our grandmother told her to show some of her work to Mr. Fitzgerald."

John said, "What kind of stuff does Sylvia do? Painting? Pottery?"

Timothy shrugged. "We haven't actually seen it ourselves. Grandma just called it 'folk art.' That's why she told Sylvia to talk to Mr. Fitzgerald. She heard he likes that kind of thing."

Bob and John nodded. Bob said, "Sounds like your grandmother gave Sylvia some good advice."

"Yes," said Titus. "But it sure didn't work out very well! Poor Grandma. I know it's not her fault. But, knowing Grandma, she'll feel terrible about it."

"And poor Sylvia!" said Sarah-Jane. "The stuff must be long gone by now."

"Not necessarily," said Bob. "That's what I meant when I said that no one knows where the art could be."

The cousins looked at him eagerly.

He explained. "Well, it's possible, of course, that the thief got clean away—and, as Sarah-Jane said, the artwork is long gone.

"But getting away would be tricky. It's hard to move in these crowds. And how could the thief be sure Sylvia wouldn't see her walking off with the artwork? It would be safer to hide it and just lay low for a while. So it's just possible the thief stashed the pieces somewhere. And that she's planning to come back for them later."

The cousins and John agreed with Bob that it was just possible the art was still hidden somewhere.

But where?

Bob went on. "The problem is, hiding the stuff would be tricky, too. Where could the thief hide the art without anyone seeing her do it? And how could she hide it where no one else could get it? It would have to be a place where no one would think to look. Where would you find such a good hiding place in such a hurry?"

"Beats me," said John. "This sounds like a job for the T.C.D.C."

"I'm afraid it beats the T.C.D.C., too," said Sarah-Jane with a sigh.

There was nothing more to say.

Bob had to get back to his own booth.

John had to wait on a customer.

And the cousins had to walk around looking wise.

They picked up their boxes and wandered off.

They hadn't gone all that far before they stopped dead in their tracks.

They knew what Sylvia's artwork looked like.

They knew who had taken it.

And they knew exactly where it was hidden.

10

The Perfect Hiding Place

"I saw this movie once," said Timothy to his cousins as they set off through the crowds for their grandparents' house.

"In the movie, everybody was going crazy trying to find this really big diamond. An old man had hidden it in his house. Only he died before he could tell anybody where it was. The relatives tore the place up looking for a secret hiding place. But the diamond was right out in the open the whole time. People passed it a dozen times a day. But they didn't even see it."

"Where was it?" cried Sarah-Jane and Titus, dying of curiosity.

Timothy paused, making the most of the moment. "In the crystal chandelier," he said.

"Aha!" cried Sarah-Jane. "That was the

The Perfect Hiding Place

perfect hiding place—because the diamond blended right in with the cut glass!"

"EXcellent!" agreed Titus. "What do they call it when that happens?"

Timothy and Sarah-Jane waited to see if Titus would come up with the answer to his own question. He often did that. It was his way of thinking out loud.

"Got it!" said Titus. "'Hidden in plain sight.' That's what they call it when something is right out in the open. But people don't see it, because it's—what's that word? Camouflaged."

"And it's like Grandpa says," added Sarah-Jane. "People see what they expect to see. And they don't see what they don't expect to see."

Timothy and Titus knew exactly what Sarah-Jane was talking about.

Of course, no one would expect to see stolen art being carried around out in the open by three kids.

But what if it were Christmas in July?

And what if those three kids were dressed as the Magi in long, flowing robes and fancy crowns?

The Mystery of the Magi's Treasure

And what if the missing art pieces were boxes?

Well then.

The boxes would blend right in with the costumes. Who would look twice at Wise Men carrying gold, frankincense, and myrrh? You would expect to see *that*.

Even the Wise Men themselves had been fooled.

For a while.

But, as Timothy had said, the boxes were just too beautiful to be props.

And after they'd heard Bob's story about stolen art, it all fell into place.

The cousins were almost positive that the boxes were Sylvia's stolen artwork and that they themselves had been the perfect hiding place.

But they had to check it out to see if they were right.

Checking things out. It was all part of the detective work. They would take the boxes to their grandmother and ask if they were Sylvia's. Then they would know for sure.

"I still can't believe that odd woman," muttered Sarah-Jane. "First she pretended to

Sylvia that she was Mr. Fitzgerald's assistant so she could steal the boxes. Then she pretended to us that she was some kind of prop lady so she could hide the boxes. On us! She hid them on us!"

"But at least the boxes are safe," said Timothy.

"Don't be so sure," murmured Titus. "She's watching us."

11

Stuffed Animals

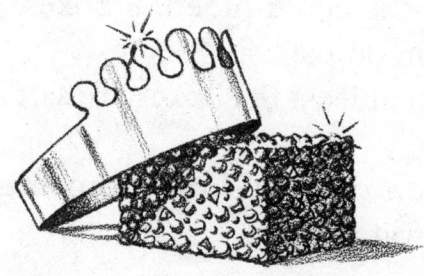

The cousins knew better than to make any sudden moves.

Very, very casually they ambled over to a booth filled with homemade stuffed animals. They wanted it to seem as if they were picking out a present for Timothy's baby sister, Priscilla.

"Ooo, here's a cute bunny rabbit, Tim," said Sarah-Jane in a perfectly normal voice, in case the woman came close enough to hear them.

Under her breath she said to the boys, "What are we going to do? If we run, she'll know we're on to her. Then she's sure to come after the boxes."

"But the baby hippo is more unusual," said Titus, making conversation.

Then he murmured, "We just have to act

casual and get home as soon as we can, I guess. The problem is these costumes. We're sitting ducks in them. She can spot us anywhere in the crowd."

"I think I'll come back later and get the piglet," said Timothy. "Priscilla is crazy about pigs."

Titus and Sarah-Jane didn't know if he was making that up. But they realized it didn't really matter.

Timothy whispered, "We could maybe ditch the costumes in that alleyway over there. We can always come back for them later. But

that still doesn't solve the problem. She knows what we look like. And if she sees us without the robes and still carrying the boxes, she'll know something's up."

Suddenly Timothy grabbed his cousins and said urgently, though still whispering, "You guys! Look! Look over there! Do you see what I see?"

Titus and Sarah-Jane scanned the crowds to see what had caught Timothy's attention like that.

They saw the three Kevins, dawdling on their way to dress rehearsal.

The Kevins were wearing choir robes.

12

Decoys

The woman's back was safely turned. The cousins scooted across, grabbed the Kevins, and hauled them into the alley.

"OK, here's the deal," said Timothy quickly before the Kevins could get over their surprise. "We're in big trouble, and we need your help. See that woman over there? The one looking around? Just peek out. Don't let her see you!"

"What about her?" asked Kevin O'Connell.

"She's an art thief, and she's after us," said Timothy.

The Kevins looked at them with interest. "Cool," they said.

So far, so good.

Timothy rushed on. "She's actually after these boxes. It's a long story. But we have to get

The Mystery of the Magi's Treasure

the boxes back to the artist. Only that woman—the thief—keeps following us. So we need you to change robes with us. We need you to throw her off track so that we can get the boxes away."

"Like a decoy, you mean," said Kevin Jones.

"Exactly!" said Titus. "Will you do it?"

The cousins held their breath.

The Kevins looked at one another and shrugged. "Sure. Why not?" they said.

Timothy could hardly believe his ears. Who would have thought the Kevins would be so helpful?

Quickly, the Kevins and the cousins changed robes.

"OK," said Timothy. "All you have to do is walk around and get her to follow you. But don't let her get a good look at you."

Then Sarah-Jane thought of something important. "But always make it look like you're carrying something. Otherwise, she'll get suspicious. Maybe you could hold your hands together in front of you with the sleeves covering them."

"OK," said Kevin Weston. "Except—maybe we should *really* be carrying something.

That way, we won't forget and accidentally put our hands down."

"Good thinking," said Titus. And Timothy agreed. The Kevins were really getting into this.

They all scouted around the alley and found three good-sized rocks about the same size as the boxes. If the Kevins stayed far enough away from the woman and let their sleeves cover their hands, the plan might just work.

"Is that it?" asked Kevin O'Connell.

"That's it," said Timothy. "We don't think she's in any hurry. In fact, we think she might be waiting until the crowds thin out a little be-

fore she comes to get the boxes back and make her getaway. It's a long story."

But the Kevins looked so interested that Timothy quickly filled them in on how they came to have the boxes in the first place. He finished by saying, "So, if she comes up to you to get the boxes, just play dumb."

The Kevins looked at one another and grinned. "We can handle that," they said.

When the woman wasn't looking, the Kevins slipped out of the alley and wandered away among the booths. They kept their backs to the woman. Then—sure enough—the woman spotted them and followed at a safe distance.

The cousins made themselves count to ten to let the Kevins lead the thief farther away.

Then Timothy, Titus, and Sarah-Jane hid the beautiful boxes in the sleeves of their choir robes.

They slipped out of the alley.

And walked quickly away in the opposite direction.

13

Back on the Horse

The cousins hid themselves in a group of choir kids on their way to rehearsal.

"Hey!" said one of the choir kids. "What are you guys doing here? Aren't you supposed to be the Three Wise Men?"

"It's a long story," said Timothy. He said this in a way that meant he wasn't going to tell it. He had already explained everything to the Kevins. And he knew he was soon going to have to explain everything to his grandmother. So he didn't feel like explaining it all another time in between.

At the house, the cousins found their grandmother in the kitchen, talking to a young woman. They guessed she was Sylvia.

Both ladies looked pretty discouraged.

The Mystery of the Magi's Treasure

The cousins' grandparents had fairly strict rules about not interrupting. But Timothy figured this was an emergency.

"Excuse us, Grandma," he said. "But we have two questions. Number one: Is this Sylvia?"

Grandma and the lady looked at them in surprise and said that it was.

"OK," said Timothy. "Question number two is for Sylvia: Do these boxes belong to you?"

Grandma and Sylvia jumped up with exclamations of astonishment and joy.

It took a while—quite a while—to explain how it was that Timothy, Titus, and Sarah-Jane came to have the boxes. And how it came to be that they weren't in costume.

"Well, now, young lady," Grandma said to Sylvia, sounding friendly and firm all at the same time. "I think it's time you got back on the horse."

The cousins knew there wasn't really any horse. It was just an expression. A way of speaking. They knew that if you fell off a horse, you were supposed to get right back on. Otherwise, if you waited, you might get too scared to go riding again.

That was the way it was with any hard thing you had to do. If something bad or discouraging happened, you had to try again right away. Otherwise, if you waited, you might get too scared to try again.

"What do you mean?" Sylvia asked Grandma. Of course, Sylvia probably knew there wasn't really any horse, either.

"I mean," said Grandma, "that you're going to go right back to Mr. Fitzgerald's gallery and show him these lovely boxes."

"Oh, no—I don't know, Mrs. Gordon . . ." Sylvia began.

Timothy thought of something important, so he figured it was all right to interrupt again.

"Look at it this way," he said to Sylvia. "Somebody liked your boxes enough to steal them."

Everyone laughed. And Timothy had to admit that it had come out sounding funny.

"No, I mean it, Sylvia," he said earnestly, one artist to another. "That woman took one look at your work, and she knew it was really good. What she did was really bad. But what she did should tell you your work is good. And

The Mystery of the Magi's Treasure

if you at least show it to Mr. Fitzgerald, that would be good."

Sylvia stood up straight and picked up her boxes. "OK, I'll do it! On one condition—that all of you come with me."

They stopped on the way to explain to the choir director why the Kevins weren't at rehearsal yet.

The cousins didn't want the Kevins to get in trouble. Of course, the Kevins were almost always in trouble. But it didn't seem fair for them to be in trouble for doing something good.

"Speaking of the Kevins," said Titus. "I wonder if that phony-assistant-prop-lady-thief has spotted the switch yet?"

"I wouldn't be surprised," said Timothy. "She must have come back for the boxes by now."

Sarah-Jane said, "And once she saw that *we* were gone, and the *boxes* were gone . . ."

Timothy and Titus knew what Sarah-Jane meant. And they had to agree. The boxes were safe. But the *thief* was probably long gone.

That's where they hadn't counted on the Kevins.

14

Help! Police!

The cousins and Grandma and Sylvia walked back to the center of town to visit Mr. Fitzgerald's gallery.

They had expected to run into the Christmas-in-July crowds, of course.

But they suddenly realized that something strange was happening.

Rather than wandering here and there, the crowds were gathering in a big circle.

The cousins spotted Bob and John and hurried over to them.

"What's going on?" they asked.

"Beats me," said John. "I just got here. I heard all the commotion and came to see what was going on."

Commotion was right.

From the center of the circle came the sound of shouting.

It sounded like—

It sounded like—

For a split second the cousins just stared at one another.

The Kevins?!?!

Without another word, they rushed through a gap in the crowd, with Grandma and Sylvia following close behind.

No wonder people were staring!

At the center of the circle stood a furious-looking woman—the thief—with the Three Wise Men running in circles around her, yelling, "Help! Police! Help! Police!" at the top of their lungs.

At that very moment, a couple of police officers cleared a way through the crowd to see what all the ruckus was about.

And then Sylvia—who hardly ever spoke above a whisper—stormed into the circle, yelling, "That's her! That's her! She's the one who stole my boxes!"

And the Kevins kept running around yell-

ing, "Help! Police! Help! Police!" until the policemen made them stop.

Everyone said it was the best art festival the town had ever had.

15

Heroes

*I*t turned out that the phony-assistant-prop-lady-thief was already wanted by the police for a string of art thefts.

So the cousins and the Kevins were Big Heroes that day.

The police made them go over the whole story from the beginning.

And this time, Timothy didn't mind telling it.

In the meantime, Grandma told anyone and everyone that three of these wonderful children were her grandchildren and that the other three wonderful children were well-known boys who went to her church.

"I always wondered what that would be like," Kevin O'Connell said to Timothy.

"What what would be like?" asked Timothy.

"You should know," said Kevin. "What it would be like to have people saying how smart you are. How brave you are. How *good* you are. I always wondered what it would feel like to be really, really good."

"So how does it feel?" asked Timothy.

Kevin grinned. "Good."

It also turned out that Mr. Fitzgerald *loved* Sylvia's boxes.

But people were so interested in them because they had been stolen by a notorious art thief that the boxes were bought up before they could even reach the gallery.

Mr. Fitzgerald asked Sylvia to bring him some more of her work.

Grandma told Sylvia it was high time she thought of herself as an artist and met some other artists in town. The cousins got Sylvia started on that by introducing her to Bob and John.

And finally, it turned out that the Christmas concert was a wonderful success.

Apparently the screaming Wise Men had been great publicity.

"Come to my workshop," Sylvia told the cousins and the Kevins after the concert. "I have something for each of you."

What Sylvia had for them were tiny handmade Nativity sets from the collection of her artwork.

The Nativity sets were like Sylvia's boxes. All made from everyday objects with great care. All beautiful and good.

"Wise Men for the Wise Men," Sylvia said. "To thank you for all you've done."

Timothy looked at his tiny Magi, bringing their rich gifts to an even tinier Baby Jesus.

It was amazing when you stopped to think about it, Timothy thought to himself. Wisdom and Goodness showed up in the most unexpected places.

Who would have expected the Kevins to come through like that?

Who would have expected Sylvia could make such beautiful art out of ordinary junk?

Who would have expected to find a King in a stable?

The Wise Men certainly deserved to be called wise, Timothy decided. They found an ordinary-looking child in a humble little place.

But the Wise Men never wondered if they'd made a mistake. They knew Goodness when they saw it. So they bowed down before Jesus and gave Him their treasures.

"Thank you, Sylvia!" said Timothy.

And so did all the others.

But just as they were leaving, Timothy thought of something else he wanted to say. He told the others he would catch up to them. Then he went running back to Sylvia.

"Sylvia, can I come watch how you work sometime? Because . . . I like art. And . . . well, you're an artist."

"Sure," said Sylvia. "I'd like that very much. And as for being an artist—I have a feeling you're one, too."

The End

The Mystery of the Hobo's Message

THREE COUSINS DETECTIVE CLUB®

#1 / The Mystery of the White Elephant
#2 / The Mystery of the Silent Nightingale
#3 / The Mystery of the Wrong Dog
#4 / The Mystery of the Dancing Angels
#5 / The Mystery of the Hobo's Message
#6 / The Mystery of the Magi's Treasure
#7 / The Mystery of the Haunted Lighthouse
#8 / The Mystery of the Dolphin Detective
#9 / The Mystery of the Eagle Feather
#10 / The Mystery of the Silly Goose
#11 / The Mystery of the Copycat Clown
#12 / The Mystery of the Honeybees' Secret
#13 / The Mystery of the Gingerbread House
#14 / The Mystery of the Zoo Camp
#15 / The Mystery of the Goldfish Pond

THREE COUSINS 5 DETECTIVE CLUB

The Mystery of the Hobo's Message

Elspeth Campbell Murphy
Illustrated by Joe Nordstrom

BETHANY HOUSE PUBLISHERS
MINNEAPOLIS, MINNESOTA 55438

Cover and story illustrations by Joe Nordstrom

Three Cousins Detective Club® and TCDC® are registered trademarks of Elspeth Campbell Murphy

Copyright © 1995
Elspeth Campbell Murphy

All rights reserved. No part of this publication may be reproduced, stored in a retrieval system, or transmitted in any form or by any means electronic, mechanical, photocopying, recording, or otherwise without the prior written permission of the publisher and copyright owners.

Published by Bethany House Publishers
A Ministry of Bethany Fellowship, Inc.
11300 Hampshire Avenue South
Minneapolis, Minnesota 55438

Printed in the United States of America.

Library of Congress Cataloging-in-Publication Data
Murphy, Elspeth Campbell.
　The mystery of the hobo's message / Elspeth Campbell Murphy.
　　p.　cm. — (Three Cousins Detective Club® ; bk.5)
　Summary: When the three cousins find some strange symbols carved in an old tree, they start learning about hobo code and in the process learn about the importance of kindness as well.

　[1. Mystery and detective stories.　2. Tramps—Fiction.
3. Cousins—Fiction.　4. Twins—Fiction.　5. Christian life—Fiction.]
I. Title.　II. Series: Murphy, Elspeth Campbell. Three Cousins Detective Club™ ; 5.
PZ7.M95316Mych　　　1995
[Fic]—dc20　　　　　　　　　　　　　　　　　　　　94–49224
ISBN 1–55661–409–8　　　　　　　　　　　　　　　　　CIP
　　　　　　　　　　　　　　　　　　　　　　　　　　　AC

In loving memory of my father-in-law,
Howard R. Murphy,
whose life was filled with
love, joy, peace,
patience, kindness, goodness,
faithfulness, gentleness, and self-control.

ELSPETH CAMPBELL MURPHY has been a familiar name in Christian publishing for over fifteen years, with more than seventy-five books to her credit and sales reaching five million worldwide. She is the author of the best-selling series *David and I Talk to God* and *The Kids From Apple Street Church*, as well as the 1990 Gold Medallion winner *Do You See Me, God?* A graduate of Trinity College and Moody Bible Institute, Elspeth and her husband, Mike, make their home in Chicago, where she writes full time.

Contents

1. Cat Man 9
2. The Sweetest House 13
3. A Job for Cat Man 18
4. Tree Pictures 22
5. The Hobo Code 25
6. The Willowbys 28
7. Warning Signs 32
8. Chalk Talk 36
9. No Twins 40
10. The Accident 44
11. Fast Help 47
12. The Secret Hideout 50
13. The Sign of the Dagger 55
14. A Problem Solved 58
15. Home 61

1

Cat Man

Much as he loved animals, Titus McKay was not too crazy about cats. That was probably why cats were so crazy about him. Titus had noticed something about cats. They always seemed to go to the people who didn't particularly want them.

At least that was true of his grandparents' two cats. Whenever Titus and his cousins sat down to work on their code books or something, the cats came running. They loved to drape themselves across Titus's shoulders. Titus kept peeling them off. But they always came back.

Titus's cousin, Timothy Dawson, thought this was hilarious. He called Titus "Cat Man."

Titus's other cousin, Sarah-Jane Cooper,

thought it was unfair. No matter how much she pleaded, "Here, kitty, kitty," the cats climbed all over Titus.

Titus's Yorkshire terrier, Gubbio, thought it was outrageous. Titus was *his* boy, after all. At first, Gubbio had tried to chase the cats away. But they had just looked at him as if they were looking at air. If he barked at them, they just meowed sweetly as if to say, "Dog? What dog? We don't see a dog."

Finally, Gubbio gave up trying to get rid of the cats. But whenever they jumped on Titus's shoulders, he jumped on Titus's lap.

Titus was the first to admit that nothing made a house look more homey than pets— even cats. But having them around made it hard to get stuff done. Granted, Titus and his cousins were on vacation at their grandparents' house. But they still wanted to get stuff done. Their code books, for example.

The cousins had a detective club. And they wanted to be able to pass secret messages to one another.

They were working on this—or trying to— when their grandfather came by. He was a pastor, and he was on his way to his study in the church next door.

He said with a straight face, "Rather hot to be wearing a fur coat, isn't it, Titus?"

"Grandpa, will you please take them with you?" Titus pleaded.

Grandpa laughed. *Sometimes* the cats would come when he called.

But before he could try it, the phone rang.

Grandpa sighed. "I hope it's not those developers again," he said. "They've been calling every day and sometimes twice a day. I don't know what I'm going to do."

The cousins looked at one another in surprise. It was not often that their grandfather didn't know what to do. What was going on?

2

The Sweetest House

The cousins knew it was impolite to listen in on other people's conversations. But their grandfather *had* taken the call in the kitchen. And he *hadn't* asked them to leave. Besides, there might be some way they could help. You never could tell.

"No, I haven't reached a decision yet," said Grandpa, sounding weary but firm. "No, the house isn't listed with a real estate agent.... Yes, it will be a private sale.... No, I'm not at liberty to quote you a price.... Yes, the terms were very specific.... No, I can't tell you what they were. That's confidential.... Yes, I will let you know when I've made up my mind.... No, there's really no need for you to call again tomorrow.... Yes, I will let you know...."

Yes. . . . Yes, I will. . . . No, that won't be necessary. . . . Yes. . . . Goodbye."

"Arrrghh!" said Grandpa when he had hung up the phone. "They say the squeaky wheel gets the grease. But these people really are impossible!"

"Grandpa!" cried Sarah-Jane, looking wide-eyed with alarm. "You're not selling the house, are you?"

"Oh, no, sweetheart," Grandpa assured her. "I'm not selling *our* house. I'm selling *a* house."

"Huh?" said Timothy.

"Come again?" said Titus.

"It's a cottage, really," explained Grandpa. "And it belonged to old Mrs. Willowby. You remember Mrs. Willowby, don't you? She was a member of the church for longer than anyone."

The cousins nodded. Just thinking of old Mrs. Willowby made them smile. She had always been so kind to them. To everyone. But thinking about her made them feel sad, too, because they knew she had died not that long ago.

"Anyway," said Grandpa. "Mrs. Willowby had no family. She asked me to find just the

The Sweetest House

right people and sell them her cottage. It's all in her will, and I have to honor her wishes. But her house sits on a lovely piece of property. A lot of people would love to get their hands on it."

"Is there anything we can do to help?" asked Titus. He didn't really think there was. It didn't sound like the kind of thing a kid could do.

Grandpa smiled. "Thanks for the offer. I'll keep it in mind. Right now, you can help by keeping me company. I want to ride over and check on the cottage."

When most grown-ups said "ride," they meant in a car. When Grandpa said "ride," he meant on his bicycle.

The cousins had brought their bikes with them. And soon all four of them were pedaling along through the little resort town where Pastor and Mrs. Gordon lived.

The cousins had never seen Mrs. Willowby's cottage. They stopped their bikes and looked down on it from a little hill.

Titus said the first thing that popped into his head. "The cottage looks like her."

Everybody laughed. But it was the kind of laugh you give when someone says something odd that you know is absolutely true.

Titus was right. The house *did* look like Mrs. Willowby. Small and trim and peaceful. As if having a person like Mrs. Willowby live inside it all those years had somehow rubbed off on the house itself.

"It's just the *sweetest* house!" declared Sarah-Jane. And although they might not have put it that way, the men had to agree.

It was only when they got closer that they noticed the two kids sitting on the porch. A boy and a girl, who looked to be the same age as the cousins. And who looked almost exactly like each other. Twins?

They were staring anxiously up into a tree.

3

A Job for Cat Man

"What seems to be the trouble here?" Grandpa asked them kindly.

The boy and girl jumped. Apparently they had been so intent on the tree that they hadn't heard Grandpa and the cousins ride up.

For a moment the two kids just stared at them in alarm. In fact, Titus thought they were about to run away. But they didn't seem to want to leave the tree.

"It's our cat," said the girl at last. "He climbed up there. And now he can't get down."

They all peered up into the branches at the pretty little orange-striped cat. He was bigger than a kitten, but not quite full-grown. He meowed piteously down at them.

Titus stood back, rubbed his chin, and studied the situation. He had seen this type of thing before.

"What's his name?" Sarah-Jane asked the girl.

"He doesn't have one yet," she replied. "We just got him yesterday."

"Actually, he's not exactly ours," the boy corrected. "He's a stray that just sort of adopted us."

"That means *he* thinks he's ours," persisted the girl. "Or that we're his. And either way, we can't just leave him up there." She sounded on the verge of tears.

"Here, kitty, kitty," said Sarah-Jane, wanting to help. But her track record of getting cats to come to her was not very good. And even she didn't sound very hopeful.

Timothy stepped forward and said boldly, "Obviously, somebody has to go up there and bring the cat down." He paused. "I nominate Cat Man."

"I second the motion!" cried Sarah-Jane joyously.

Grandpa said, "It has been moved and seconded that Titus Gordon McKay—otherwise known as Cat Man—be given the task of getting the cat in question down from said tree. All in favor, say 'aye.' "

"Aye!" yelled everyone, including the boy and girl, who laughed in spite of themselves.

Titus nodded. He had expected as much. In fact, he had already worked out in his head the best way up.

Cat Man was a good nickname for him not just because cats adored him. It was also a good nickname because he could climb as well as any cat. Better. At least *he* knew how to get down. He had rescued a few cats in his day, and he had even worked out a system.

His method was to climb up slowly and casually. He would get as close to the cat as possible. And completely ignore it. It never failed. All he had to do was wait, and the cat would come to him. Once the cat was holding on to him, Titus could climb down for both of them.

Grandpa gave him a boost, and Titus swung himself onto the lowest branch. From there he began to climb according to the route he had mapped out down below.

He got to the branch he was aiming for.

Then he settled down to wait without so much as a glance at the cat.

It was nice up there, Titus thought. The sunlight played tag with the leaves, and little bugs ran up and down the trunk.

But suddenly Titus noticed something. Something very, very odd.

4

Tree Pictures

Carved into the trunk of the tree was a little group of pictures.

There was a top hat:

A smiling cat:

A kind of tent:

And a little circle inside a circle:

What in the world? Titus had seen initials carved on a tree, but never anything like this. So he held on to the branch with one hand and dug into his pocket with the other. He pulled out the little notebook and pencil stub he al-

Tree Pictures

ways carried. Balancing carefully, he copied the pictures exactly as they appeared on the tree.

The pictures weren't hard to copy. They were just simple little drawings. But Titus didn't think they were just meaningless doodles, either. He didn't know *what* they were.

He was so busy thinking about the pictures that he forgot all about the cat. He didn't have to pretend to ignore it. It just worked out that way.

But the cat couldn't ignore Titus.

It landed with a little "thwup!" on his shoulder. Titus almost fell off his branch in surprise.

He shoved the notebook and pencil stub in his pocket and started carefully down. He didn't want to startle the cat with any sudden noise or movement. So he acted like: Cat? What cat? I don't see a cat.

By the time they were safely down, the cat was sick and tired of being ignored. So when Sarah-Jane and the other girl rushed over, calling it a poor, sweet baby, the cat just ate it up. And to Sarah-Jane's great delight, the cat let her cuddle him.

"Oh, were you scared way up there in that great big tree?" she cooed.

"No," said Titus. "But thanks for asking."

The others, who had gotten acquainted while Titus was up in the tree, all laughed and burst into applause while Titus took a bow.

Titus found out that his first guess was right. The boy and girl were twins. He learned their names were Matthew and Amanda Jennings and that they were just visiting.

Sarah-Jane and Amanda were still fussing over the cat. And that reminded Titus of the smiling cat and the other drawings on the tree. He pulled out his notebook.

None of the kids knew what to make of them, either. But Grandpa looked long and hard at the drawings.

"Well, I'll be!" he said softly, more to himself than to anyone else. "I haven't seen the likes of these in more than fifty years."

5

The Hobo Code

The kids all stared at him.

Timothy said, "You mean you've seen pictures like these before? In some other place?"

"Oh, yes," said Grandpa with a faraway look in his eyes. "What we have here is a hobo code."

The cousins looked a question at one another. They knew what a code was. And they sort of knew what a hobo was. But what was a hobo code?

Grandpa sat down on the porch. And from the way he settled in, the cousins knew he was about to Explain Something. Timothy, Titus, and Sarah-Jane settled in around him. And—with an uncertain glance at each other—Matthew and Amanda sat down, too. Their cat, of course, sat on Titus.

"Now," said Grandpa. "The first thing you have to understand about a hobo is that he didn't want to be called a tramp or a bum. Tramps and bums were not honest people, and they didn't want to work. A hobo, on the other hand, thought of himself as an honest, wandering worker. Some hoboes wandered because there was no work back home. Other hoboes wandered because they liked the adventure of moving from place to place."

"Sounds like it could be kind of fun, I guess," said Titus.

"That's what my father thought," said Grandpa with a twinkle in his eye.

The cousins stared at him. "You mean our great-grandfather was a *hobo*?" Sarah-Jane squeaked. It sounded kind of unreal.

Grandpa laughed. "For a while, yes. When he was a teenager. This was long before I was born."

"Did he carry his stuff in a bandanna on a stick?" asked Timothy.

"It was called a bindle," said Grandpa. "Like bundle. And a worker was called a stiff.

The Hobo Code

So another name for a wandering worker was a 'bindle stiff.' "

Titus loved the sound of that. He said thoughtfully, "Our great-grandfather was a bindle stiff. . . . But, Grandpa, what do the little pictures have to do with hoboes?"

"Well," said Grandpa. "The life of a hobo might have been fun in some ways. But it could be pretty lonely. And it could also be very dangerous. You never knew what to expect when you came to a new place.

"So the hoboes figured out a way to help one another—a secret code of pictures. When a hobo passed through a place, he would kindly leave a message for the hoboes who would come after him. The message was in the form of a little picture that told them what to expect. My father taught the code to me."

Titus pointed to his notebook. "So what do these pictures mean?"

6

The Willowbys

*E*veryone crowded around eagerly.

"Well, let's see if I can remember," said Grandpa. "The top hat stood for a gentleman. The Willowbys lived in this house for about as long as anyone can remember. So this hat must have stood for Mr. Willowby. And if anyone could be called a gentleman, it was Mr. Willowby. What a kind and generous person he was!

"Now, the smiling cat—that stood for a kindhearted woman."

"Mrs. Willowby!" cried Sarah-Jane.

"It would certainly fit her, wouldn't it?" said Grandpa. "If a hungry hobo, down on his luck, saw a drawing like this little smiling cat, he knew a kindhearted woman lived there.

The Willowbys

And she would give him something to eat.

"The next picture of a little tentlike thing meant it was a good jungle, and you could make yourself at home."

"A jungle?" asked Timothy.

"Another word for a hobo camp," said Grandpa. "The Willowbys must have let the hoboes camp on their land. Not everyone would have done that.

"And, if I remember correctly, the little circle inside the bigger circle meant 'very good.'"

Grandpa was quiet for a moment. Then he said thoughtfully. "You know, I never knew this about the Willowbys—that they gave a helping hand to the hoboes. But given Mrs. Willowby's concern for the homeless, it certainly fits."

The Mystery of the Hobo's Message

Matthew and Amanda shifted restlessly. And then they all seemed to realize that they had been sitting in one position too long.

As Titus stretched, he looked up at the tree. "Why put the code up so high?" he asked. "Who in the world would see it up there?"

"It wasn't up that high when it was carved," said Grandpa. "Remember, the days of the hoboes died out with the passing of the railroad. There are still trains, of course, but not as many as there once were. And hoboes depended on the freight trains for hitching rides."

Titus thought about that for a minute. "Oh, I see what you're saying! Hobo days were a long time ago, right? So the tree grew. And the pictures got carried up high."

"Exactly right," said Grandpa.

Timothy said, "So probably no one has even seen those pictures in years and years. Not until Titus came along."

"And Hobo," said Amanda.

She and Matthew had been listening so quietly that now it was almost as if the tree had said something.

"Who's Hobo?" asked Sarah-Jane. "Oh, the *cat*! Right? *Cute name!*"

"Wait a minute," said Matthew to his sister. "Don't I get a vote on what to call him?"

"Nope," said Amanda. "He likes the name Hobo."

Matthew shrugged. He seemed to know when it was useless to argue. "OK. Hobo it is. It *is* a good name, I guess. Well, we'd better get going."

He picked up Hobo, who had climbed on Titus's head and was trying to knock his glasses off. "Thanks for getting our cat, Titus!"

Titus gladly handed Hobo over. "That's OK. No problem."

"See you around," said Matthew.

"Yes, see you," said Amanda a little wistfully.

The twins got on their bikes and rode off. They were already well down the road when the cousins remembered something they wanted to ask them.

"Wait a minute," called Timothy. "Where are you staying?"

But the twins must not have heard him.

7

Warning Signs

"But what if some people weren't kind like the Willowbys?" asked Timothy, getting back to the subject of the hobo code when they were back home. "What if some people were mean? How would a hobo know that?"

"There were signs in the hobo code for that, too," said Grandpa. "For example, a dagger meant a dishonest man. Watch out. Not a good place to ask for work. Or there might be a picture of a comb."

"A *comb*?!" said Timothy, Titus, and Sarah-Jane all together.

"What did *that* mean?" asked Timothy. "Beware of neat hair?"

"No," said Grandpa, laughing. "But think about it. A comb has teeth. The sign warned the hobo to beware of something else with teeth."

"A dog!" cried Titus. "Beware of the dog. Right?"

"Right," said Grandpa.

"Woof!" said Gubbio happily. He knew a few key words—like dog—but he couldn't always follow a conversation.

"You're back," said Grandma, coming into the kitchen. "Those developers called again while you were out."

"Arrrghh!" said Grandpa and the cousins.

Grandma laughed. "They said they were afraid they hadn't been clear enough about their plans. They said they wanted to use the house and land for low-cost housing and that they'd like to talk to you about that."

"Really?" said Grandpa. "That's the first I've heard about that. Well, I guess I should at least hear what they have to say. Then I can see if it's in keeping with Mrs. Willowby's wishes. Would you call them back for me? Tell them I can meet them at the cottage later this afternoon."

"Will do," said Grandma.

Grandpa headed for his study, and the

cousins went along with him. He said he had an old book that might have some more of the hobo code in it.

Of all the places on earth, Grandpa's study was one of Titus's favorites. He loved the worn leather chairs. He loved the big, wooden desk. He loved the rows and rows and rows of books. Most of all he loved a little plaque on the wall, because it seemed exactly right for his grandfather. He wasn't sure what it all meant. But he had loved it ever since he had learned to read.

> *Life is short*
> *and we have never too much time*
> *for gladdening the hearts*
> *of those who are traveling*
> *the dark journey with us.*
> *Oh, be swift to love,*
> *make haste to be kind.*
>
> *–Henri Frederick Amiel*

Grandpa had once explained that "dark journey" was another way of saying "life." He said that sometimes life seems dark because we're sad and lonely. And sometimes life seems dark just because we never know what lies ahead. Grandpa had explained that life is like a journey for everyone and that we all need to be kind to one another because we are all fellow travelers.

Today the little plaque reminded Titus of the hoboes and how they left helpful signs for one another.

The cousins found a page of hobo signs in the book. Grandpa said they could borrow it to copy the signs into their code books.

Grandpa looked tired, Titus thought. He looked as if he had a lot on his mind, like keeping his promise to Mrs. Willowby.

Titus saw something in the book. He copied it onto a piece of scratch paper and held it out for his grandfather to see. It was a picture of two overlapping circles:

Grandpa studied the drawing for a moment, trying to recall what it meant. Suddenly he smiled.

The sign meant, "Don't give up."

8

Chalk Talk

The cousins loved the junk drawer in their grandparents' kitchen. It was the best place in the world to hunt for little treasures.

When the cousins were little, they had never questioned how it was that exactly the right treat showed up at exactly the right time. And in the junk drawer, of all places.

But now they were older and wiser. And they were getting suspicious. Like today, when they found exactly what they needed there.

First they had finished copying the hobo signs into their code books. (The cats had left them alone, because Grandma was making a little quilt for a baby shower. And if there was one thing the cats loved more than climbing on

Chalk Talk

Titus, it was climbing on Grandma when she was sewing.)

And then the cousins had wanted to practice the code by drawing on the sidewalk. And what should they find in the junk drawer but washable chalk for drawing on the sidewalk.

"Hmmm," said Titus. "Very in-ter-es-ting."

"Downright weird, if you ask me," said Timothy.

"How does she *know*?" asked Sarah-Jane.

They decided there were some things not even detectives could find out. So they just left their own mysterious thank-you note. A chalk drawing on the front of the drawer. A picture of a smiling cat.

Then they took the chalk outside to practice. With practice, they got really good at using the code.

They learned how to tell one another the direction in which they were traveling:

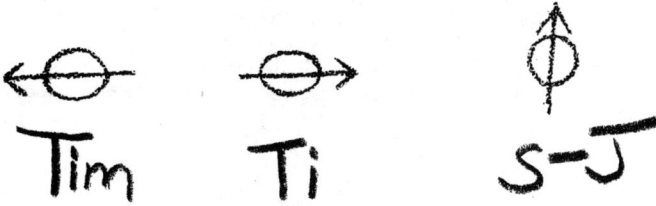

They learned how to warn about bad water:

And how to show which people would help you if you were sick:

They could show that a good place was all right:

    $+$

And they could tell you where you would get nothing:

    $\bigcirc$

They even knew how to say with pictures "Keep quiet":

And "Danger":

Granted, it was hard to say how any of this would come in handy. But one thing the cousins knew from experience: you never could tell.

9

No Twins

*I*t was something Titus had noticed—whenever you learned something new and exciting, you wanted to teach it to someone else.

Also, as much as he and his cousins liked playing together, they liked playing with other kids, too.

So it seemed as if all three of them got the same good idea at the same time: Show the hobo code to Matthew and Amanda!

This made sense, because Matthew and Amanda had been as fascinated as the cousins were with the little pictures Titus had found on the tree. They had hung on Grandpa's every word when he was telling about hoboes. And they had even named their cat Hobo.

There was just one problem with Matthew

and Amanda: Where were they?

"You know what's kind of funny?" Titus began.

"Funny ha-ha? Or funny weird?" asked Timothy.

"Funny weird."

"What is?"

"The way Matthew and Amanda just sort of took off like that," said Titus.

"Yes, now that you mention it," agreed Sarah-Jane. "I mean, I think they liked us and everything. But they didn't hang around long enough for us to invite them over."

"And they didn't invite us to their place, either," said Timothy.

"Maybe it's not their house," said Sarah-Jane. "They said they were just visiting. But still . . ."

Titus said, "Well, if they're visiting friends, I don't see how we can find out who they're staying with.

"But if they're staying at a bed and breakfast or a motel, we could maybe find them. We could call and see if any place has a family named Jennings with twins staying there."

Timothy and Sarah-Jane thought this was

as good an idea as any. So they asked their grandmother if they could use the phone. And they started calling. There were about a bazillion motels in the resort town.

At first it was fun. They took turns. They started with the places that were closest to the cottage and sort of worked their way out.

Then, after a while, the calling got pretty tedious. But the cousins knew that detective work could be that way sometimes. And it was worth it when you finally found what you were looking for.

Except sometimes you *didn't* find what you were looking for. They found a couple of families named Jennings all right.

But none with ten-year-old twins.

10

The Accident

*A*ll in all it had been a very frustrating experience. So the cousins felt the need to get out and move around. They were allowed to go off on their bikes by themselves as long as they wore their helmets, and stayed together, and got back by a certain time.

Without exactly planning to, they rode back over to the cottage. It looked so cozy and peaceful. What would happen to it, Titus wondered. Who would live there?

The cousins got off their bikes and walked around the cottage, peeking in the windows.

Then they found a way to get under the high front porch. As detectives, they were always looking for good hiding places. If you didn't mind a little dirt—which the cousins

The Accident

didn't—this was a wonderful hiding place.

It was especially good because you had to pull out a loose latticework board to get through. Then once you were in, you could pull the board back in place. You could easily see out through the holes. But it made it almost impossible for people on the other side to see the hiders.

"This is EXcellent!" said Titus.

"Neat-O!" agreed Timothy.

"So cool!" said Sarah-Jane.

But there wasn't a lot to do once they had found the place. And there wasn't actually anything to hide from. And after a while they needed sunlight and air.

So they crawled out and got back on their bikes. They rode off in the direction Matthew and Amanda had taken earlier, down a gravel road.

Everything was going fine until Timothy suddenly hit a bump. His bike skidded on the gravel, Timothy lost his balance, and before he could stop himself, he was thrown to the ground.

"Tim! Tim! Are you all right?" cried Sarah-Jane and Titus, rushing to his side.

Timothy sat up carefully. Nothing seemed to be broken.

"But what about your chin?" asked Titus. "You must have cut it on something. It's bleeding like crazy!"

Fortunately, Timothy had a clean handkerchief, and he held it to his chin. But the cousins knew they had to get help fast.

The problem was, they seemed to be out in the middle of nowhere. There were no houses or stores that they could see. And they desperately needed to get to a phone.

They were just trying to stay calm and *think* when suddenly something else happened.

Something leaped out of the bushes at the side of the road. It landed with a "thwup!" on Titus's shoulder.

11

Fast Help

*H*obo!

Titus knew a cat wasn't like a dog. You couldn't say, "Hobo, get help!" and expect anything to happen.

But he also realized that Hobo's being there might be a good sign. It might mean that help was nearby.

Titus jumped up and yelled, "Matthew! Amanda! Are you there? We need help!"

Sarah-Jane caught on right away. "Amanda!" she yelled. "Matthew! If you're there, come help us!"

Timothy caught on right away, too, but he couldn't yell because of his chin.

Almost immediately the cousins heard pounding footsteps. Matthew and Amanda appeared over a little ridge. With them was a lady who looked so much like them she had to be their mother.

Mrs. Jennings rushed to Timothy and took a look at the cut. She murmured something that sounded to Titus like "poor little guy." But it didn't sound babyish. It just sounded nice. It sounded like someone who was sorry for you but who knew everything was going to be all right.

The words from his grandfather's plaque popped into Titus's head—make haste to be kind. He also thought of the picture signs for a kindhearted woman and people who would help you if you were sick.

"I don't think it's too bad," Mrs. Jennings said. "But it will probably need stitches. We move our chins so much talking and eating that it's a hard place for a cut to heal. Let's get you to the campground. It's just over the ridge. We'll wash off the cut and I'll drive—Timothy, is it?—to the hospital. You can call your parents to meet us there."

"We're visiting our grandparents," explained Sarah-Jane. "Our grandfather is a pastor here. Pastor Gordon."

Fast Help

Mrs. Jennings nodded. "That's good. That means they probably know him at the hospital, right? You can use the phone at the campground office to call him."

Even with his cut chin, Timothy seemed to still have his mind on detective work. He mumbled to Titus and Sarah-Jane, "Why didn't we think of looking for Matthew and Amanda at the campground? The one place we didn't think to look is the place we found them."

All this time Matthew and Amanda had been looking worried about Timothy. But now they looked embarrassed—and kind of mad about looking embarrassed.

When Titus saw their station wagon, he realized why. The backseat was fixed up almost like an extra room.

Matthew and Amanda weren't camping for the fun of it. This was where they lived.

12

The Secret Hideout

"It's not so bad," said Matthew with a careless little shrug. "Rainy days are the worst, of course. And we don't know what will happen after Labor Day."

"That's when the campground closes for the season," explained Amanda. "We'll have to move for sure. We just don't know where. Daddy is looking for a job all the time. He makes some money with odd jobs. But not enough to—"

"We get by," Matthew interrupted gruffly.

Amanda sighed wistfully. "I just love this little house."

The five of them were gathered again on the front porch of Mrs. Willowby's cottage. No one knew what to say to Amanda. Titus had

The Secret Hideout

the feeling that she came over here a lot to play and that Matthew just trailed along behind her. Matthew probably loved the house every bit as much as Amanda did. But Titus had the feeling that Matthew didn't see the point of hanging around something you wanted with all your heart if you could never have it.

At the hospital, Titus had managed to pull Grandpa aside and explain privately about where Matthew and Amanda lived. Titus knew he was explaining things especially well. And even though Grandpa hadn't said a lot, he had listened intently, as if he were thinking hard about something.

At the hospital, Grandma and Grandpa had thanked Mrs. Jennings over and over for her kindness to Timothy, who had gotten three stitches in his chin.

Grandma had wanted Timothy to go home and lie down. But she knew as well as Titus and Sarah-Jane did that getting Timothy to take a nap would be like getting him to eat pineapple or coconut. It just wasn't going to happen.

So the five kids had been allowed to ride over to the cottage on the condition that Timothy didn't "overdo it."

The Mystery of the Hobo's Message

They had left their bikes in the trees behind the cottage. And now they were just hanging out on the porch in the shade of what they called "The Hobo Tree."

No one knew what to say when Amanda said she loved the house. To break the silence, Titus said, "We can show you something interesting we found...."

He looked at Sarah-Jane and Timothy before he said any more. He didn't want to say anything about the secret hideout without their permission. They nodded, giving him the go-ahead. So Titus explained to the twins about the way to get under the porch.

"It's so cool," said Sarah-Jane. "We're always on the lookout for good hiding places because of being the T.C.D.C."

"What's a 'teesy-deesy'?" asked Amanda.

"It's letters," explained Timothy.

"Capital T. Capital C. Capital D. Capital C. It stands for the Three Cousins Detective Club."

Matthew and Amanda were clearly impressed with all this detective stuff. They had already learned some more of the hobo code

52

The Secret Hideout

from the cousins, and now they wanted to see the hideout.

There was plenty of room for all five kids. Make that five kids and a cat. Hobo had found them at the cottage, and now he insisted on exploring the hideout with them.

They had just gotten settled with the latticework in place when they heard something. A car pulled up in front, and three men got out. They came and stood just a few inches from where the cousins and the twins were hiding.

The Mystery of the Hobo's Message

Titus couldn't help thinking it would look kind of stupid if they all crawled out now. Apparently the others were thinking the same thing, because nobody moved. They would just have to wait till the men went away.

Then one of the men said to the others, "OK. Let's get our story straight before the good pastor gets here. It's not going to be easy to put something over on Rev. Gordon."

Quickly Titus drew something in the dirt. There was just enough light for the others to see. They took one look and nodded silently.

For Titus had drawn: ◇

And: ▭

Keep Quiet.
Danger.

13

The Sign of the Dagger

"OK, here's the deal," said the first man. "We know that Old Lady Willowby left some kind of wacky instructions in her will. And Rev. Gordon feels 'duty-bound to honor her wishes,' as he puts it. Give me a break. He won't even say what the old lady wanted."

Titus bit down hard on his lip. It was hard not to go charging out and say, "For your information, Buster, Mrs. Willowby was *not* 'wacky.' She was one of the kindest people I ever met. And furthermore—my grandfather keeps his promises. What else would you expect? And furthermore—my grandfather does *not* go blabbing stuff that people tell him in private. Not to you or anybody else. It's called honor. Look it up."

Titus doubted he could really have gotten all that out.

Besides, something told him it was wiser to keep quiet. He felt the tiniest ripple of angry movement on either side of him. And he guessed that Timothy and Sarah-Jane were itching to do the same thing he wanted to.

But they kept still. They had trained themselves to do that. Matthew and Amanda copied them and kept quiet, too. Even Hobo was still. He was curled up sound asleep under Titus's chin.

"So where does that leave us?" asked the second man. "We don't know what the old lady wanted. So how can we offer something Rev. Gordon will take?"

"We can't tell him what we're really planning," said the third man. "To tear down the cottage and build another luxury motel on the land."

Under the porch, Amanda clapped her hand over her mouth. Other than that, no one moved.

"No, of course we can't tell him that," said the first man impatiently. "That's why we're going to talk to Rev. Gordon about the need for low-income housing. Lead him to believe we're going to put up a small apartment building for the poor or something like that."

"Right," said the second man. "If he thinks it's going for such a good cause, he'll probably be willing to sell us the place—no matter what the will says."

"How can he say no?" asked the third man. "And by the time he finds out what we're really building, it will be too late."

"Just follow my lead and everything will be all right," said the first man. "We have to be careful not to lay it on too thick. We don't want him to get suspicious."

The men walked off toward the road to wait for Pastor Gordon.

But no way was Pastor Gordon going to fall for their scam.

That was because just as he rode up, Titus crept out from under the porch. He took a piece of washable chalk from his pocket and drew a big picture on the door of the house:

A dagger. A hobo warning.
Beware of dishonest men.

14

A Problem Solved

The men turned to see what Grandpa was looking at.

Titus thought—with a certain amount of satisfaction—that they looked alarmed to see him there. He could almost hear them wondering: Where did that kid come from? Did he overhear what we said? Does Rev. Gordon know him? Why is he drawing on the door?

If the men were surprised to see Titus, they were flabbergasted to see four other kids crawl out from under the porch. Make that four kids and a crabby cat. Hobo didn't take kindly to being wakened from a nap—no matter what the reason.

Grandpa hurried over. "What's all this about?" he asked.

A Problem Solved

It took a while—quite a while—to explain what they were doing under the porch and what they had overheard when they were under there.

Grandpa turned to confront the men, who had been planning to lie to him. But their car was already skidding out of the driveway.

"Well, Grandpa," said Timothy. "I don't think you'll be getting any more calls from them."

"That's right," agreed Sarah-Jane. "But it still doesn't solve Grandpa's problem of what to do with Mrs. Willowby's house."

"On the contrary," said Grandpa. "I have just about solved that problem. Thanks to you three."

"Us!" said Titus. "What did *we* do?"

"We'll talk about it at dinner," said Grandpa.

And the cousins knew from experience they wouldn't get another word out of him till then.

"By the way," said Grandpa, turning to Matthew and Amanda. "Tell your parents that Mrs. Gordon and I would like to invite them to dinner tonight. There's something I need to talk to them about. You come, too, of course. You can even bring Hobo." He paused and added with a straight face, "It's like Titus always says. You can never have too many cats."

15

Home

Gubbio usually loved it when company came to dinner. But when he saw that these people had brought a cat with them, he looked at Titus as if to say, "How could you do this to me?"

So when Titus showed Mr. and Mrs. Jennings into Grandpa's study before supper, Gubbio went along. In the study he could be safely away from all those annoying cats.

That meant that Gubbio heard all that Grandpa and Mr. and Mrs. Jennings talked about. But no one else did.

All that the cousins and the twins knew was that something wonderful must have happened—even though both Mr. and Mrs. Jennings looked as if they had been crying.

"What's going on?" asked Amanda a little anxiously as they sat down to dinner.

"Oh, not much," said her father. "We just bought a house. That's all."

"A house!" cried Matthew. "What house? Where did we get the money to buy a house?"

Grandpa smiled. "It's like this. Mrs. Willowby made me promise I would find the right people and sell them her cottage."

Amanda gasped.

Everyone laughed. Grandpa went on. "Mrs. Willowby wanted her cottage to go to people who really needed it. She wanted people who would love it and take care of it. And she wanted people who would in turn be kind to others. Well, I found just such people in the Jennings family. Or rather—my grandchildren found them. And Mrs. Willowby said when I found these people I was to sell them her cottage for the grand sum of one dollar."

"A *dollar*?" cried Matthew. "Mrs. Willowby sold us her house for a *dollar*?!"

"That's just the kind of person she was," said Grandma with a gentle, remembering smile.

"Oh!" cried Amanda and Sarah-Jane to-

Home

gether. "It's just the *sweetest house!*"

And, though he might not have put it that way, Titus had to agree.

He wished everyone in the whole world who needed a house could have one just like it.

But Mrs. Willowby had done what she could. And that's all anyone could do, Titus thought. It was what the plaque in his grandfather's study meant when it said:

> *Life is short*
> *and we have never too much time*
> *for gladdening the hearts*
> *of those who are traveling*
> *the dark journey with us.*
> *Oh, be swift to love,*
> *make haste to be kind.*

The End

The Mystery of the Dancing Angels

THREE COUSINS DETECTIVE CLUB®

#1 / The Mystery of the White Elephant
#2 / The Mystery of the Silent Nightingale
#3 / The Mystery of the Wrong Dog
#4 / The Mystery of the Dancing Angels
#5 / The Mystery of the Hobo's Message
#6 / The Mystery of the Magi's Treasure
#7 / The Mystery of the Haunted Lighthouse
#8 / The Mystery of the Dolphin Detective
#9 / The Mystery of the Eagle Feather
#10 / The Mystery of the Silly Goose
#11 / The Mystery of the Copycat Clown
#12 / The Mystery of the Honeybees' Secret
#13 / The Mystery of the Gingerbread House
#14 / The Mystery of the Zoo Camp
#15 / The Mystery of the Goldfish Pond
#16 / The Mystery of the Traveling Button
#17 / The Mystery of the Birthday Party
#18 / The Mystery of the Lost Island

THREE COUSINS 4 DETECTIVE CLUB

The Mystery of the Dancing Angels

Elspeth Campbell Murphy
Illustrated by Joe Nordstrom

BETHANY HOUSE PUBLISHERS
MINNEAPOLIS, MINNESOTA 55438

Cover and story illustrations by Joe Nordstrom

Three Cousins Detective Club® and TCDC® are registered trademarks of Elspeth Campbell Murphy.

Copyright © 1995
Elspeth Campbell Murphy

All rights reserved. No part of this publication may be reproduced, stored in a retrieval system, or transmitted in any form or by any means electronic, mechanical, photocopying, recording, or otherwise without the prior written permission of the publisher and copyright owners.

Published by Bethany House Publishers
A Ministry of Bethany Fellowship, Inc.
11300 Hampshire Avenue South
Minneapolis, Minnesota 55438

Printed in the United States of America.

Library of Congress Cataloging-in-Publication Data
Murphy, Elspeth Campbell.
    The mystery of the dancing angels / Elspeth Campbell Murphy.
       p. cm. — (The Three Cousins Detective Club® ; bk. 4)
    Summary: The three cousins are stuck babysitting their bratty third-cousin Patience and when she disappears while they are visiting an old mansion, they must investigate.

    [1. Mystery and detective stories. 2. Cousins—Fiction. 3. Christian life—Fiction.] I. Title. II. Series: Murphy, Elspeth Campbell. Three Cousins Detective Club® ; 4.
PZ7.M95316Myad   1994
[Fic]—dc20   94–49223
ISBN 1–55661–408–X   CIP
                                                          AC

In loving memory of my father-in-law,
Howard R. Murphy,
whose life was filled with
love, joy, peace,
patience, kindness, goodness,
faithfulness, gentleness, and self-control.

ELSPETH CAMPBELL MURPHY has been a familiar name in Christian publishing for over fifteen years, with more than seventy-five books to her credit and sales reaching five million worldwide. She is the author of the bestselling series *David and I Talk to God* and *The Kids From Apple Street Church*, as well as the 1990 Gold Medallion winner *Do You See Me, God?* A graduate of Trinity College and Moody Bible Institute, Elspeth and her husband, Mike, make their home in Chicago, where she writes full time.

Contents

1. A Family Riddle 9
2. Visitors 12
3. Patience 17
4. The Family Tree 20
5. The Woodcarver 24
6. A Little Name 28
7. Tall Tales 31
8. Hiding 36
9. The Hundred-Year-Old House 40
10. Upstairs Alone 44
11. Missing 47
12. The Dancing Angels 51
13. The Angels' Secret 54
14. The Discovery 57
15. Penny 60

1

A Family Riddle

The way Sarah-Jane Cooper saw it, there was good-boring and bad-boring.

Bad-boring was when you got stuck doing something you didn't want to do.

Good-boring was when you had all the time in the world, but there was nothing you *had* to do. You could make plans if you wanted to. But you didn't have to.

If all you wanted to do was to lie on the grass and look up at the clouds, that was OK. In fact, this was one of Sarah-Jane's favorite things to do. She especially loved it when the clouds looked like angels. It always reminded her of a nursery rhyme her grandmother had taught her:

Grasp the clouds by will or chance,
And you shall see the angels dance.

Sarah-Jane loved the sound of that, but she had no idea what it meant. How could anyone grasp the clouds? Even if you could reach them, how could you hold on to them? And even if you could—why would that let you see dancing angels? It didn't make sense.

Sarah-Jane and her cousins Timothy Dawson and Titus McKay had once asked their grandmother what it meant. But all she knew was that she had learned it from *her* grandmother.

Grandma said the rhyme might be just pretty-sounding words that didn't mean anything. Or it could be a family riddle that would never be solved.

The cousins didn't like the idea of a riddle that would never be solved. They liked solving mysteries and finding things out. That's why they had a club called the Three Cousins Detective Club.

Sarah-Jane lay awake in the little bed in her grandmother's sewing room. Just taking her time getting up. Good-boring was waking up at your grandparents' house on a beautiful

A Family Riddle

summer morning—the first day of your vacation there. Timothy and Titus were there, too. Timothy's baby sister, Priscilla, was too young to be away from her parents. But Titus had brought his Yorkshire terrier, Gubbio. Gubbio had never been there before and was very excited about having "grandparents" to spoil him.

The cousins' mothers, who were sisters, had told them a thousand times to be good and not to wear out Grandma's patience.

The cousins' grandmother, who was one of the most patient people in the world, had just laughed and said they'd be fine.

Sarah-Jane felt so grown-up and happy that she sang "Oh, What a Beautiful Morning" to herself as she got dressed.

On such a beautiful morning, what could possibly go wrong?

2

Visitors

When it came to their grandparents, the cousins were sort of spoiled and sort of not.

At least, that's how Sarah-Jane saw it.

Take breakfast, for example. Their grandmother would buy them any kind of cereal they wanted. But after breakfast, they had to rinse their own dishes and put them in the dishwasher.

Today they were extra spoiled. Donuts for breakfast! But there was also a note from their grandmother that put them on the honor system. Only two donuts each, and they had to have milk and juice, too.

They were on the honor system because their grandparents had already gone out.

Grandpa, who was a pastor, had gone to his

Visitors

study in the church next door. That wasn't unusual. But it was kind of unusual for Grandma to be out so early.

She had left a note with the breakfast instructions. And at the bottom it said:

Will be back soon. Have gone to the train station to pick up Patience.

Grandpa always joked that Timothy woke up "bright-eyed and bushy-tailed." And that Titus "woke up slow."

Titus just blinked at the note. He said groggily, "I thought patience was something you got after all sorts of rotten stuff happened to you. So how can you pick up some patience at the train station?"

Timothy was already awake enough to think about it. "It's not *some* patience," he explained. "It's Patience with a capital P. That means it's somebody's name."

Titus blinked again. "Patience? That's somebody's name? Patience?"

"Patience can be a name," said Sarah-Jane. "In fact, there was somebody a long time ago in our family named that. I know because my mother told me she almost named *me* Patience."

The Mystery of the Dancing Angels

At the thought of Sarah-Jane being named Patience, Timothy and Titus laughed so hard they almost fell on the floor.

Sarah-Jane would have gotten mad at them. But she could understand why it was so funny. She was *not* the most patient person in the world. Anyway, she liked being named after both her aunts—Timothy's mother, Sarah, and Titus's mother, Jane.

Sarah-Jane said sternly, "OK, so it's funny. But it's not *that* funny."

"Sorry, S-J," mumbled Timothy.

"Yeah, sorry, S-J," agreed Titus.

Sarah-Jane could tell they were about to burst out laughing again. But just then there was the sound of a car pulling up, and all three of them ran to the living room window.

Grandma and a lady about her same age got out of the front seat. Was this Patience?

Who was she, anyway?

The lady opened the back door and helped out a little girl. Sarah-Jane wasn't that good at guessing ages. But she thought the little girl looked smaller than a kindergartner.

She also looked a lot like Sarah-Jane. They both had red hair exactly the color of a shiny

new penny. Sarah-Jane didn't have a little sister. But if she had, this is probably what she would have looked like.

Timothy and Titus looked back and forth between the little girl and Sarah-Jane. "What's going on here?" muttered Timothy.

The cousins, feeling oddly shy, came out on the front porch.

The little girl didn't seem the least bit shy. She stood squarely in the middle of the sidewalk with her hands on her hips. First she looked the house over as if she were thinking of buying the place. Then she pointed at the cousins and demanded loudly, "Do they belong to me?"

3

Patience

To the cousins' amazement, their grandmother just laughed. This was puzzling, because—with *them*—Grandma was a stickler for politeness. And this kid was downright rude.

Even more surprising was Grandma's answer. "Well, yes, dear. I suppose they *do* belong to you."

To everyone Grandma said, "Let's all go inside and get introduced."

The cousins hung back a bit and went in after the others. Timothy muttered again, "What is going *on* here?"

"I don't know," replied Titus. "But I've got a bad feeling about this kid."

His little dog, Gubbio, seemed to agree. He made a funny whining noise—as if he just knew he was going to get his tail grabbed.

The cousins found the others in the kitchen. The ladies were having coffee. Grandpa had popped in to say hello. And the little redhead was scarfing down a donut. Gubbio took one look at her, made a beeline to Grandpa, and hid behind his feet.

"Now then," said Grandma happily. She rested her hand on the other lady's shoulder. "This is Patience. And she's my—"

"*I'm* Patience!" interrupted the little girl.

"Yes, darling," said the lady. "We're both named Patience. You were named after me. And I was named after *my* grandmother."

The cousins glanced at one another. So it seemed the little girl was the lady's granddaughter. But that still didn't explain who they were or what they were doing here.

But before anyone *could* explain, the little girl spoke up again. Loudly. "My name is Patience Elizabeth North. I live at 1535 Grand Avenue. My phone number is 555–1602. And I'm four years old."

It was on the tip of Sarah-Jane's tongue to say, "Who cares?" But from the way the grown-ups were beaming at Little Patience,

Patience

she didn't think that would go over too well.

Grandma said, "It's wonderful how she knows her address and phone number."

Little Patience nodded as if she agreed that she had done something wonderful. She reached for another donut. The cousins watched her carefully. She'd better not try for more than two. . . .

Grandma Patience smiled fondly at her and looked over at the cousins. "You know, Grace," she said to their grandmother. "I just can't get over the resemblance between my Patience and your Sarah-Jane!"

"Isn't it something?" agreed Grandma. "You can certainly tell they're related!"

4

The Family Tree

*R*elated? To *Patience*? Say it wasn't so!

But it was so, of course. Grandma Patience had even brought along a little chart to prove it.

"I didn't put *everyone* on our family tree," she explained. "That would get kind of confusing and take up too much room."

Grandpa, who was not going to be on Grandma's family tree, pretended to be mad and went back to work. Gubbio, who was not on the family tree either, trotted along at his heels. The cousins watched them go. So Gubbio had figured out how to get away from Little Patience. Lucky dog.

Grandma Patience said, "Let me show you how all the rest of us fit together. Family his-

The Family Tree

tory—it's called genealogy—is a hobby of mine. I just love it! In fact, that's why I'm here today. Because of something I just learned about your great-great-great-grandfather, Daniel. I'll get to that in a minute."

She spread out the chart on the kitchen table, and the cousins bent to study it.

Grandma Patience said, "Your grandmother Grace and I are first cousins. Our children—my son, Tom, and your mothers—are second cousins. Our grandchildren—you

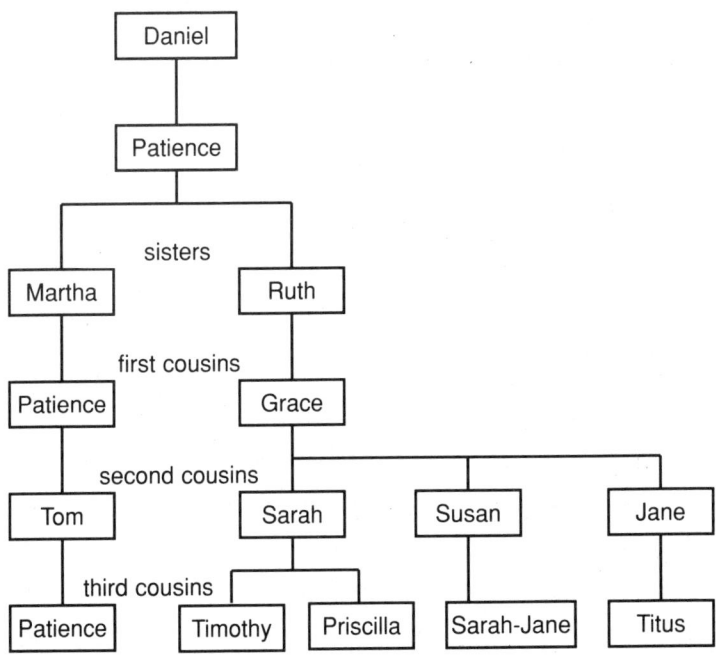

The Mystery of the Dancing Angels

three and Patience—are third cousins."

So that was it. Patience was their third cousin.

"You mean . . ." Sarah-Jane spoke slowly, thinking it through. "That when Tim and Ti and I have children, our kids will be second cousins. And that when Tim and Ti and I have grandchildren, our grandchildren will be third cousins."

"Exactly," said Grandma Patience.

Titus pointed to the second name on the chart. "You were right, S-J. There was someone a long time ago in our family named Patience."

"I'M PATIENCE!"

"Yes, dear," said her grandmother. "But that was also the name of your great-great-grandmother. We can call her Long-ago Patience. That's how you and Timothy, Titus, and Sarah-Jane are related. You all have the same great-great-grandmother."

Maybe Patience didn't like the idea of that any more than the cousins did. Or maybe she just felt like being bratty. Whatever the reason, she waited until the grown-ups weren't looking. Then she turned to the cousins and stuck out her tongue.

Sarah-Jane hadn't done that in years and years. But Patience made her so mad she did it right back.

"Nonnie!" Patience wailed. "Sarah-Jane stuck her tongue out at me!"

5

The Woodcarver

The cousins' own grandmother looked startled—as if she couldn't quite believe what she had heard.

"She started it," Sarah-Jane mumbled.

Even though Timothy and Titus backed her up on that, Sarah-Jane felt her face grow hot. She knew what her grandmother must be thinking: A ten-year-old acting like a four-year-old.

No one expected what happened next.

Grandma Patience stuck out her tongue at Little Patience.

"Nonnie!" Patience gasped in a voice so shocked it made everyone laugh.

But her grandmother spoke seriously to her. "We've talked about this before, young

The Woodcarver

lady. You don't like it when people do that to you, so you shouldn't do it to them. Now, where were we?"

"You were going to tell us about our great-great-great-grandfather," said Sarah-Jane, glad for a change of subject.

"Ah, yes!" said Grandma Patience. "Daniel was a master woodcarver. In a town not far from here, there's a beautiful 100-year-old house. It's being restored by the Historical Society. Well, in my research, I discovered that Daniel had worked on it! So I wrote to the historian in charge of the project. And what do you think! He invited us to come see the

house—even before it's open to the public. He said he can't wait to compare notes. And since it's so close to your grandmother, I just had to call her. We'll all go together. Isn't that wonderful?"

Sarah-Jane nodded politely. Who knew? It might be wonderful. Or it might be bad-boring. You never could tell.

"That must be such an interesting job," said Grandma. "Restoring old houses, I mean."

"Oh, absolutely," said Grandma Patience. "I even said that to the historian, Professor Brown. I said, 'If only old houses could talk. What stories they could tell.' And he said that he wished the house they're working on could tell them what happened to the ruby necklace."

The cousins perked up at that.

"What necklace?" asked Titus.

Grandma Patience explained. "There's a portrait of the first owners. And in it, the wife is wearing a beautiful ruby necklace that once belonged to a queen. The necklace should be in a museum."

"Why isn't it?" asked Timothy.

"Because no one knows where it is," said Grandma Patience. "It was never reported lost or stolen. It was never given away. It has never turned up anywhere. It's just gone. Professor Brown wonders if it could still be somewhere in the house. But, if so, they haven't found it."

"Aha!" cried Grandma with a laugh. "This sounds like a job for the T.C.D.C.!"

"What's a 'teesy-deesy'?" asked Grandma Patience.

"It's letters," explained Sarah-Jane. "Capital T. Capital C. Capital D. Capital C. It stands for the Three Cousins Detective Club. Tim and Ti and I are the only members."

It was at this point that Little Patience—who had been quietly watching her third cousins for a while—suddenly burst into noisy sobs.

6

A Little Name

"We didn't do anything!" cried Timothy, Titus, and Sarah-Jane all together.

"Sweetie, sweetie, what's the matter?" asked Grandma Patience.

It was a while before Patience could talk. And when she finally gulped out some words, they didn't make any sense.

"I want a little name! Nonnie, make them give me a little name!"

"Sweetie, Nonnie wants to make it all better. But she doesn't know what you mean."

Neither did anyone else.

Patience buried her head in her grandmother's shoulder. She settled down to just sniffles while her grandmother rocked her. "I want a little name," she mumbled to herself.

A Little Name

"She's had a big day already," said her grandmother. "Getting up early and riding on the train. Her grandfather and I are living at her house while her mommy and daddy are away. They got a wonderful chance to go to—"

"YURP!"

At first Sarah-Jane thought Patience had hiccupped. But then she realized she was trying to tell them something again.

"What did you say?" Sarah-Jane asked her.

"Yurp," repeated Patience. She seemed pleased that Sarah-Jane was still speaking to her after the whole tongue thing. "That's where my mommy and daddy went. To Yurp."

Sarah-Jane still didn't get it.

Then suddenly—she did.

"Oh, to *Europe*!"

"Very good, Sarah-Jane!" Grandma Patience smiled at her like one grown-up to another over the head of the little one. "Not everyone would have gotten that."

Sarah-Jane felt pretty pleased with herself. Talking to Patience was a lot like figuring out a riddle.

Grandma Patience said, "You know, I just realized that Long-ago Patience would have been about ten years old when the house her father worked on was built. She might even have gone there to see his work. So you three will enjoy it. Patience is a little too young, I'm afraid. But the chance to see the house came up so quickly, I couldn't get a sitter."

"Oh, don't worry about that," said Grandma. "Look how well Sarah-Jane understands Patience. Sarah-Jane and the boys will look after her."

Talk about mixed feelings. Here was Grandma, practically bragging about how grown-up Sarah-Jane was. Even after the whole tongue thing. That was good. But having to look after Patience? That was bad. Very, very bad. Boring. Bad-bad-boring.

7

Tall Tales

The cousins went out to the backyard for a breath of air.

Titus tipped an imaginary hat to Sarah-Jane. He said in an innocent drawl, "Well, now, ma'am. It looks like you're the one in charge around here."

"Yup," said Timothy. "We're just the hired hands. Around these parts they call us 'The Boys.' "

The cousins weren't supposed to say 'shut up.' But Sarah-Jane said it now anyway. She said it quietly, but with a lot of feeling. "Shut up, shut up, shut up!"

Timothy and Titus just laughed.

And Titus said in a whiny little voice, "Nonnie! Sarah-Jane said 'shut up!' "

The Mystery of the Dancing Angels

Not even Sarah-Jane could keep from laughing then. But she still managed to sound fierce. "I mean it, you two. You'd better help me with that kid."

Timothy and Titus solemnly promised.

And just in time, too.

The screen door squeaked open and banged shut. Patience came running over to them.

"HEY, YOU GUYS!"

"Hey, Patience."

"Your grandma and Nonnie said you have to play with me."

"OK."

"And you know what? You're not supposed to let me get dirty for a few little whiles."

Titus and Timothy looked to Sarah-Jane for a translation.

"She means, we're leaving in a few minutes or a little while. And we're supposed to stay clean for when we go to the house, right?"

Patience nodded. "So what are we playing?"

Again Timothy and Titus looked to Sarah-Jane.

"We're going to spread a blanket on the

grass and look for shapes in the clouds," said Sarah-Jane. She used a voice that didn't allow for argument from anyone. In a way, she hated to use her favorite, private, good-boring thing to do. But she had to keep Patience clean and out of trouble for a few little whiles. And Patience seemed to like it.

After a while, Sarah-Jane relaxed a bit and said dreamily,

"Grasp the clouds by will or chance."

She half-expected Timothy or Titus to finish the riddle-rhyme.

The last thing she expected was to hear Patience say,

"And you shall see the angels dance."

The cousins sat up straight and stared at Patience.

"How did you know that rhyme?" Sarah-Jane asked her.

Patience shrugged. "My Nonnie teached me. How can you touch the clouds?"

"You can't really," said Sarah-Jane.

"I can."

"No, you can't."

"Yes, I can! Because you know how? That boy in the story is a *giant* boy. And he picked me up. And I was way up high. And I grabbed the clouds."

"What boy in the story?" asked Titus.

"Will."

"Oh!" cried Sarah-Jane, suddenly understanding. "Will is not a boy." When Patience started to protest, Sarah-Jane went on quickly. "Your *will* is when you *want* to do something. When the rhyme says, 'Grasp the clouds by will,' it means on purpose. When it says 'by chance,' it means you grasp them by accident."

Sarah-Jane was feeling pretty pleased with the way she had explained all that.

Patience nodded thoughtfully. "That's what Will says, too. He told me to pull on the clouds. And the angels danced. I danced with them. But Will didn't want to. Because you know why? He's a giant and when he dances everything shakes. He breaks things."

"Patience," said Timothy. "That is a tall tale."

"It is *not!*" cried Patience. "What's a tall tale? I don't have a long tail. I'm telling!"

And before anyone could stop her, Patience was up and running toward the house.

Sarah-Jane covered her face with her hands

and flopped back on the blanket. "Ohhh," she groaned. "Where will it all end?"

"It's going to be a long day," agreed Timothy.

"Come on," sighed Titus. "Let's go explain what really happened. Again."

Just then Grandma called cheerfully from behind the screen door. "Timothy! Titus! Sarah-Jane! Patience! Come on, kids! It's time to go."

The cousins struggled to their feet and folded up the blanket.

Then the same thought seemed to strike each of them at the same time. If Patience had gone inside to tell on them, why was Grandma calling her?

8

Hiding

"Oh, no!" cried Sarah-Jane. "We were supposed to be watching her, and now she's gone!"

"She can't have gotten far," said Titus. "Let's just think a minute. She didn't go in the back door or Grandma would have seen her. So she's probably somewhere in the yard."

"Or maybe she snuck around to the front and went in the house that way," said Timothy. "Or maybe she went in the church."

"Or maybe she wandered off," said Sarah-Jane. She couldn't keep the fear out of her voice. "Oh, please tell me she didn't wander off!"

At that moment, Grandma came to the door again to see what was taking them so

Hiding

long. The cousins ran over to the back porch. Grandma took one look at their faces and said, "What's wrong? Where's Patience?"

"She said she was going in the house," said Timothy. "A couple of minutes ago."

"We didn't actually *see* her go in the house, though," said Titus.

"Patience!" called Sarah-Jane. "Patience, where are you?"

Something crawled out from behind the big bush by the back porch.

It grabbed Sarah-Jane's ankle.

Sarah-Jane knew perfectly well that there were no boa constrictors in her grandparents' backyard. But to her shattered nerves, that's just what it felt like.

She screamed and tried to kick whatever it was away.

"Ow!" yelled the boa constrictor, sliding back behind the bush. "Nonnie! Sarah-Jane kicked me."

Grandma Patience had come out when she first heard the commotion. Now she looked into the bush. "Patience Elizabeth North. Are you hiding again?"

"I like to hide," said the bush.

"I know you do. But you come out of there right now. We talked about this before, young lady. It's wrong to make people worry about

Hiding

you. Now, come out of there and apologize to everyone."

To the others Grandma Patience said, "She's done this at home. Once we found her curled up in the kneehole of a desk. I thought I would lose my mind."

Patience did as she was told.

Then to Sarah-Jane she said, "You know, it would be easier to call me if I had a little name."

9

The Hundred-Year-Old House

*I*t was not the best car trip they had ever been on.

For one thing, they were late getting started. And that made the grandmothers a little nervous.

They were late because of Patience hiding, of course. And because she got so dirty hiding it took forever to get her cleaned up.

On the way they stopped for lunch. That was good. But because they were running late, they had to skip dessert. That was bad. And it was all because of Patience.

But when Sarah-Jane saw the house, all other thoughts went clean out of her head.

The Hundred-Year-Old House

"EXcellent!" said Titus beside her.
"Neat-O!" agreed Timothy.
"So cool!" said Sarah-Jane.

It was the biggest, fanciest house she had ever seen. It was the kind of house that made you want to wear long dresses and ruby necklaces and to ride in horse-drawn carriages.

She was dying to see inside, but she also felt a little scared.

Someone else must have been feeling the same way, because Sarah-Jane felt a little hand slide into hers.

Sarah-Jane looked down at the penny-red hair. Well, you couldn't stay mad forever. She gave the hand a little squeeze.

For once, Patience seemed at a loss for words.

But the grandmothers were not at a loss for words. They closed in for a little talk.

"All right, now. We're counting on you to be on your Best Behavior."

"Don't touch anything."

"And no running around."

"No loud noises."

"Patience, you stay with Sarah-Jane."

"Sarah-Jane, you *watch* her."

The Mystery of the Dancing Angels

"Timothy and Titus, you help Sarah-Jane."

"Don't touch anything. Let's all just have a nice time."

Titus raised his hand as if he were in school. When Grandma called on him he said, "Does this mean we can't turn the place upside down looking for the ruby necklace?"

"We were looking forward to that," added Timothy wistfully.

"Oh, you guys," said Grandma with a laugh. "I can't take you anywhere." But she sounded kind of proud when she said it. Because she knew she really *could* take them anywhere.

Professor Brown greeted them at the front door. He seemed delighted to hear them gasp when they stepped into the hall.

Sarah-Jane had never seen anything like it. It was more like being in a church than a house.

The hall was paneled in rich, glowing wood. And high up in the corners were carved flowers and fruit and ribbons and birds. All carved by her own great-great-great-grandfather.

"Step into the library," said Professor Brown. "And I'll give you the guided tour. We haven't completed the entire house, yet. Some of the upstairs rooms are still empty. We'll finish them when we've raised more funds. Note the beautiful carving on the mantelpiece. Such workmanship. And over the mantelpiece you'll see a portrait of the original owners, who . . ."

"The ruby necklace!" cried Sarah-Jane before she could stop herself.

Professor Brown was delighted to repeat the story of the lost necklace that he had told Grandma Patience. But he was interrupted again. This time by Patience, who seemed to have gotten over her shyness.

"I HAVE TO GO POTTY!"

10

Upstairs Alone

"Oh, dear," murmured Grandma Patience. "I was afraid of this."

"I'll take her," volunteered Sarah-Jane.

"Oh, would you, dear?" said Grandma Patience. "That would be so helpful."

Professor Brown directed them to the staff room up the stairs and all the way down to the last room on the right.

"Come on, Patience," said Sarah-Jane. She felt incredibly grown-up. Doing a favor for the grandmothers. Being trusted to walk through the house on her own. Handling Patience without any trouble.

They found the washroom all right. But it seemed strange being up there all by themselves. The others seemed so far away. Rooms

Upstairs Alone

and rooms and rooms away.

Patience didn't want Sarah-Jane to come in with her. So Sarah-Jane waited outside in the hallway.

"Don't lock the door," she said.

"Why?"

"Because sometimes little kids lock themselves in and then they can't figure out how to unlock the door."

"I know," said Patience from the other side. "Because you know what? Once when I was little, we were at these people's house. And I locked myself in the bathroom. And you know what? The firemens had to come get me."

It sounded like another tall tale. But knowing Patience, it was probably true.

A sudden thought struck Sarah-Jane. "Patience Elizabeth North. Did you really have to go potty? Or did you just want to see the bathroom?"

"No, Sarah-Jane. I really have to go."

"Well, all right then. Just don't forget to wash your hands. And don't take all day."

"OK."

While she was waiting for Patience, Sarah-

The Mystery of the Dancing Angels

Jane couldn't resist peeking in the rooms around her. Most of the rooms at this end of the hall were unfurnished.

Sarah-Jane tiptoed back toward the stairway. Here the rooms were all decorated. The beds were so high you needed a little stepstool to climb into them. And a couple of them even had a canopy. Sarah-Jane had always wanted a canopy. It would make you feel like a princess. Wait till Patience saw this.

Patience!

Sarah-Jane had actually forgotten why she was up there. Patience should have been out of the washroom by now.

Sarah-Jane turned and hurried back to the end of the hall. She tapped on the washroom door.

"Come on, Patience. I said not to take all day. They'll be wondering where we are."

There was no answer.

11

Missing

"Patience?"

Sarah-Jane opened the door and stepped into the washroom.

There was no one there.

The little bar of soap on the sink was all wet. And the paper towel in the waste paper basket was damp. So Patience had washed her hands as she had been told.

But where was she?

Then Sarah-Jane saw something she hadn't noticed before. There was another door in the washroom. And this door led to the staff room on the other side.

It had a kitchenette and a table and chairs. But no people today.

"Patience?"

Sarah-Jane was about to turn back when she noticed a door on the other side of the staff room. This door led to an empty bedroom beyond. Sarah-Jane glanced in. This room had a door that led to yet *another* room.

"Patience!"

Sarah-Jane looked around in dismay. Was Patience hiding again? Or had she just wandered off to peek in rooms as Sarah-Jane herself had? Either way, how would she ever find her? Sarah-Jane knew she had to get help.

She turned and fled back to the hallway, then down the hallway to the grand staircase. Even though she was worried about Patience, one part of her mind was imagining something else. Lady Sarah-Jane with her long dress billowing gracefully as she swept around the landing—

And slammed smack into Timothy and Titus.

"Ow!" said Timothy. "My cousin the linebacker. You know you're not supposed to be running, S-J."

"Shh!" said Sarah-Jane. "Just shut up and listen."

"You know you're not supposed to tell us to shut up, S-J," said Titus solemnly.

"Tim! Ti! Please! Quit kidding around! I need you to help me."

"OK, OK. What's up?"

Sarah-Jane took a deep breath. "I lost her."

"What?!"

"Patience. She's gone. She could be anywhere. You've got to help me find her. What's

The Mystery of the Dancing Angels

Grandma going to say? I'm supposed to be watching her."

"It's all right, S-J," said Titus. "Grandma isn't worried or anything. The grown-ups are just talking and talking. Grandma just sent us to see if you'd gotten lost or something."

"Let's split up," suggested Timothy. "Don't worry, S-J. Wherever that kid can hide, the T.C.D.C. can find her."

But as it turned out, they didn't have to look very far.

They had just reached the top of the stairs when the washroom door burst open. Patience came running toward them.

She was grubby from head to toe. But her eyes were shining with excitement.

Before Sarah-Jane could scold her for running off and getting dirty, Patience spoke all in a rush. "You guys! You guys! Come see! Come see! The angels danced. I made them do it. I pulled on the clouds. And the angels danced!"

12

The Dancing Angels

"What's she talking about, S-J?" asked Timothy.

"Oh, who knows?" muttered Sarah-Jane. She was feeling relieved that Patience was safe but annoyed with her for running off. "We'd better go along with her. Otherwise we'll never get her back downstairs."

To Patience she said, "All right. Show us what you have to show us. But this had better not be another tall tale."

"It's not. I seed them with my own eyes, Sarah-Jane," said Patience earnestly.

"How did you get so sooty anyway?" Titus asked her. "What were you doing? Crawling around in a fireplace or something?"

"Yep," said Patience happily. As if this were

something people did all the time for fun.

Patience led them through the washroom, through the staff room, through the bedroom, and into the little room beyond.

The Dancing Angels

"TAA-DAA!" she said. "See? I told you. Angels!"

The cousins stood and stared. They hadn't been expecting to see anything. Certainly not angels. But there they were. Beautiful, graceful angels. Carved all in a row into the mantelpiece. Carved by their own great-great-great-grandfather. It gave Sarah-Jane shivers—good shivers—just to think about it.

"Now, watch!" commanded Patience. "Watch me make them dance."

And before anyone could stop her, she darted into the fireplace. She was small enough to stand up under the mantel. She reached up and pulled on something.

And with a soft, scraping noise, the angels glided apart in a stately dance.

They left a dark open space in the middle of the mantel. Patience pulled on something again. With the same gentle dance, the angels glided together.

And it was as if the empty space had never been there.

13

The Angels' Secret

"Patience! How did you *do* that?" cried Timothy, Titus, and Sarah-Jane all together.

They rushed over to the fireplace and scooched down to look under the mantelpiece.

No one would have expected carvings under there where no one could see them. But their great-great-great-grandfather had taken the time to carve beautiful, puffy clouds there. If you looked really hard, you could see that one band of clouds stood out from the rest. They made a kind of handle or lever. And when you grasped it and pulled, the angel panel opened and closed.

A grown-up, who knew about the lever, could just reach under the mantel and pull it. Otherwise, you would never, ever guess.

The Angels' Secret

So how had Patience found it?

She must have known what they were thinking, because she explained. "I finded it when I was hiding." She must have caught a look on Sarah-Jane's face, because she hurried on. "Then I saw all the pretty clouds. And I saw a cloud I could pull on. And I did. Because I wanted to see the angels dance."

As if on cue, all four of them said the rhyme together.

"Grasp the clouds by will or chance,
And you shall see the angels dance."

"Do you know what?" said Sarah-Jane. "Grandma always said she learned that rhyme from her grandmother."

"That's what Nonnie says, too," said Patience.

"Right," said Sarah-Jane. "Grandma and Nonnie had the same grandmother. And who was that? Long-ago Patience. I think Long-ago Patience made up the rhyme to tell about the mantelpiece. We didn't think you could *really* grasp a cloud. But Patience did. And she was right. We didn't think you could *really* see angels dance. But Patience did. And what do you know? She was right."

Patience nodded. "What do you know? I was right."

Of course, they each had to have a turn grasping the clouds to make the angels dance.

"A secret compartment!" said Titus. "This is just so incredibly excellent."

"You know what, though?" said Timothy. "We were so busy working the panel, we didn't even look inside."

14

The Discovery

"It's dark in that hole," said Patience.

"Never fear. Timothy's here!" said Timothy, and he pulled a tiny flashlight out of his pocket.

Titus ran to get a chair from the staff room.

"Me, me, me! Let *me* look!" said Patience.

The cousins glanced at one another. She *had* been the one to find the secret space. . . .

Titus put the chair in front of the fireplace for her to stand on. Sarah-Jane helped her to climb up. And Timothy held the flashlight.

"I see something!" cried Patience.

And without giving a thought to the dark or dirt or cobwebs, Patience reached into the hole.

Honestly! thought Sarah-Jane. *The kid has no fear.*

"I feel something!" cried Patience.

The Discovery

And she pulled out a metal box.

They knew the rule was: Don't touch anything.

But they couldn't help it.

The box wasn't locked. Inside the box there was another box. And inside that box was a soft velvet bag. And inside the bag was a ruby necklace.

They knew the rules were: Don't run. Don't yell.

But they couldn't help it.

15

Penny

*I*t took a while—quite a while—to explain to the grown-ups just what had happened.

But when they understood it, they were absolutely thrilled.

"Imagine that, Grace!" exclaimed Grandma Patience. "We learned that little nursery rhyme, and we never knew that it meant anything. We just passed it along to our own grandchildren because we liked the sound of it. I think Sarah-Jane is right. I think Longago Patience made it up when she saw the work her father, Daniel, did on the mantelpiece. But maybe even she forgot what it was about."

Professor Brown said, "No one had any idea this secret compartment was there. Probably the only ones who ever knew about it were

Patience and her father and the original owners. And the owners were probably the only ones who knew that this is where they would hide the necklace. Until these children came along."

He looked at the cousins and Little Patience with amazement.

"Oh, you can depend on the T.C.D.C. all right," said Grandma Patience.

Professor Brown looked puzzled. "What's a 'teesy-deesy'?" he asked.

"It's letters," piped up Patience before anyone else could answer. "Capital B. Capital P. Capital V. Capital G. It stands for the Three Cousins Detective Club."

She tugged on Sarah-Jane's hand and looked up with big, pleading eyes. "Sarah-Jane. I helped find the necklace. Can't I please have a little name?"

All of a sudden, Sarah-Jane knew what she meant.

"Yes, Patience," she said. "I think it's time we gave you a little name."

Everyone looked to Sarah-Jane for an explanation.

"Patience wants a nickname. Just like when

we cousins call one another Tim, Ti, and S-J. Isn't that right, Patience?"

Patience nodded so hard they thought her head would fall off.

Sarah-Jane went on, "Patience wants a nickname to show she belongs to us cousins and to show that we belong to her."

Again Patience nodded.

"What's short for Patience?" asked Titus. "Pat?"

But Patience shook her head. "Pat is my teddy bear's name." She sounded surprised that he didn't already know that.

"How about initials?" suggested Timothy. "Patience Elizabeth North. P.E.N. Pen."

"A pen is something you write with," said Patience doubtfully.

"But not if you turn it into a girl's name," said Sarah-Jane. "Especially if the girl has hair the same color as a . . ."

"Penny!" said Timothy and Titus.

"Penny," repeated Patience. "Penny. Penny. Penny. Penny. Penny. *I'm* Penny!"

Later that day the grandmothers pulled

Sarah-Jane aside and thanked her for taking care of Patience.

"You are so patient with her!" exclaimed Grandma Patience.

Sarah-Jane couldn't believe her ears. "*Me? Patient?* Are you kidding?"

"Oh, you were wonderful," said Grandma Patience. "I love that child with all my heart. But she does drive me crazy sometimes."

"Me, too," said Sarah-Jane in a small voice.

The grandmothers laughed and hugged her.

Grandma said, "Being patient with people doesn't mean that they don't drive us crazy sometimes. It means treating people well even so."

Grandma Patience said, "I just hope looking after my little pumpkin wasn't too boring for you."

Sarah-Jane shook her head. "Nope! That's one thing you can say about Patience. She's *not* boring!"

The End

Series for Young Readers*
From Bethany House Publishers

★ ★ ★

THE ADVENTURES OF CALLIE ANN
by Shannon Mason Leppard

Readers will giggle their way through the true-to-life escapades of Callie Ann Davies and her many North Carolina friends.

★ ★ ★

BACKPACK MYSTERIES
by Mary Carpenter Reid

This excitement-filled mystery series follows the mishaps and adventures of Steff and Paulie Larson as they strive to help often-eccentric relatives crack their toughest cases.

★ ★ ★

THE CUL-DE-SAC KIDS
by Beverly Lewis

Each story in this lighthearted series features the hilarious antics and predicaments of nine endearing boys and girls who live on Blossom Hill Lane.

★ ★ ★

RUBY SLIPPERS SCHOOL
by Stacy Towle Morgan

Join the fun as home-schoolers Hope and Annie Brown visit fascinating countries and meet inspiring Christians from around the world!

★ ★ ★

THREE COUSINS DETECTIVE CLUB®
by Elspeth Campbell Murphy

Famous detective cousins Timothy, Titus, and Sarah-Jane learn compelling Scripture-based truths while finding—and solving—intriguing mysteries.

* (ages 7–10)

The Mystery of the Silent Nightingale

"Start from the beginning," said Sarah-Jane.

So they started with pictures of when they were newborn babies.

The cousins had all been born right about the same time. Sarah-Jane was the oldest. She was a month older than Timothy. Timothy was a month older than Titus.

Sarah-Jane came upon a picture of a young girl sitting on a couch, holding a baby. Sarah-Jane looked more closely.

"That's Kelly!" she exclaimed.

"That's right," said her mother. "And the baby is you. Kelly would have been about eight years old when you were born. She was too young to sit for you then. But she used to stop by after school to play with you. She used to love to read to you. When you got a little older—about the age your cousin Priscilla is now—you used to wait for Kelly. As soon as you saw her coming, you would grab a book. And you would yell, 'Weed tory! Weed tory!'"

In the old days when Timothy and Titus came to visit, Sarah-Jane's mother got out a special stroller she had found at a garage sale. It was made for triplets. When the cousins

7

Photographs

"Speaking of Janice—" said Sarah-Jane. "Kelly said Janice lived in Fairfield about five years ago. Maybe she knew us when we were little before she moved away."

"Yes, but five years ago we were only five years old," said Titus. "We would have looked really different then. Kelly would have looked really different, too."

Thinking about how they would have looked five years ago made the cousins want to get out the photograph albums.

Sarah-Jane's mother took a break from her work and sat down with them.

"We don't think she had a chance to," said Sarah-Jane. "We think Dorothy scared her."

"Ah," said her mother. "That I can believe. I know Dorothy. She doesn't suffer fools gladly."

"What does *that* mean?" exclaimed Titus.

Aunt Sue laughed. "It means she doesn't have much patience with people. In this case, the word 'suffer' means to allow. Dorothy doesn't allow or put up with any foolishness. And that's all right, to a certain extent. But Dorothy carries it a little too far. She doesn't allow for any mistakes."

"We all make mistakes," said Timothy.

"That's right," said his aunt. "The point is to learn what we can from them and keep trying."

"So, if Dorothy is the office manager, that means she's Janice's boss, right?" asked Sarah-Jane.

"That's right," said her mother.

Titus said, "I can see why Janice looked so nervous."

Questions

Jane said they saw something strange, they saw something strange.

"I suppose we could just go back in and ask her," said Kelly doubtfully.

But the cousins knew that asking questions wasn't *always* the best thing to do. At least you had to pick the right time. Janice had been so flustered when Dorothy looked over at her. And now Dorothy was explaining something to Janice.

This was not the right time.

But the detective-cousins were still in the mood to ask questions. So after they dropped Kelly off, they went home and talked to Sarah-Jane's mother.

"Aunt Sue," began Titus. "Do you know a lady at Mr. Donovan's office named Janice?"

"I don't think so, Titus. Why?"

Timothy said, "Because when we stopped by there with Kelly, this lady—Janice—looked like she recognized us."

"*Really* recognized us," added Sarah-Jane. "Like we were special and she knew us from someplace."

"Did she say anything to you?" asked Sarah-Jane's mother.

The Mystery of the Silent Nightingale

Kelly gave a puzzled little laugh. "Well, of course she recognized me. She works for my dad."

"No," said Sarah-Jane. "We mean that she *really* recognized you. Like she knows you from somewhere."

"I don't see how," said Kelly. "Janice used to live in Fairfield. But my dad said she moved away about five years ago. She's only been back for a couple of months. Besides, if she knows me from somewhere, why hasn't she said anything?"

"That's just it," said Sarah-Jane. "It was like she just recognized you for the first time today. And how could that be when she's seen you before? And if she did, why not say something to you today?"

"Yes," said Timothy. "And it doesn't explain why it looked like she recognized *us* too."

"You, too?" asked Kelly. "But you don't know her, do you?"

The cousins shook their heads. They knew Kelly wouldn't ask them if they were imagining things. And she didn't. She knew they were detectives, who noticed what was going on around them. If Timothy, Titus, and Sarah-

6

Questions

When Kelly came out, the cousins were waiting for her—with questions. That's one thing detectives do. They ask questions.

Sarah-Jane said, "Kelly, who was that lady in there? Not Dorothy. The other one."

"That's Janice," said Kelly.

"Do you know her really well?" asked Titus.

"No," replied Kelly. "Hardly at all. I'm not even sure I know her last name. She's new. I've only seen her a few times. Why?"

"She looked like she recognized you," said Timothy.

The Mystery of the Silent Nightingale

ther were so busy talking they didn't notice. But when Dorothy turned around, the young woman turned bright pink. She snatched up some papers and turned away to the filing cabinets.

Sarah-Jane looked quickly at Timothy and Titus. She could tell by the way they looked back at her that they had noticed something, too.

"What was all that about?" muttered Timothy.

They stepped outside so they could talk better. They weren't sure why they didn't want to be overheard. It was just a feeling they had that something mysterious was going on.

Sarah-Jane said, "I don't get it. Why was that lady so surprised to see Kelly? She works for Kelly's dad. Kelly stops by the office a lot. They must have seen each other lots of times before."

Timothy added, "And if she was so glad to see Kelly, why didn't she say anything to her? Why did she just turn away like that?"

"But it wasn't just Kelly," said Titus. "It was *us*. I'm sure that lady recognized *us*."

"But how could she?" asked Sarah-Jane. "We've never seen her before in our lives."

5
Something Strange

A young woman came out of a back room and sat down at her desk. She glanced over at Kelly, Mr. Donovan, and Dorothy with a polite smile.

Then she saw the cousins.

Instantly her expression changed. Her eyes opened wide, and her mouth dropped open. Sarah-Jane didn't know when she had ever seen anyone look so surprised. But there was something else. It took Sarah-Jane a moment to figure it out. It was a look of pure joy.

The young woman looked back at Kelly as if she were seeing an angel. Kelly and her fa-

would believe she was a senior no matter which side the tassel was on.

Of course, Kelly *was* a senior, and she was even more excited about the cap and gown than Sarah-Jane. (If that was possible.) She wanted to stop by her father's office to show him. So the cousins went along.

Mr. Donovan came out to the reception area to greet them. He looked so proud of Kelly, Sarah-Jane thought he was going to burst. Even Dorothy, the stern-looking office manager, smiled.

The cousins hung back by the door, feeling a little shy.

Then something strange happened.

The Mystery of the Silent Nightingale

Or ever *be* as big as the seniors they saw all around them.

Kelly's friends were very nice to them. But Kelly was the nicest one of all. She even let them try on her cap. It was called a mortarboard.

"The tassel goes on the right-hand side of your face," Kelly explained. "Then, after you get your diploma, you move it to the left-hand side."

They each practiced a few times.

Sarah-Jane liked the mortarboard so much she hated to give it back. But she knew no one

4

Seniors

Kelly was just coming out of the library as the cousins hurried up.

"I hope we're not late," said Sarah-Jane.

"Nope, right on time," said Kelly with a smile. "This is fun having you guys come along."

The cousins chatted with Kelly all the way to the high school. But when they got there, they didn't say much. They were too busy looking around at the wide hallways and rows and rows of lockers. It seemed impossible to believe they would ever go to a school that big.

tive club. And they had even solved quite a few real mysteries themselves.

Kelly used to take Sarah-Jane, Titus, and Timothy to the library. In fact, she had been with them when Sarah-Jane got her first library card years ago.

And now Kelly was leaving. She wouldn't even be here for the summer. She was going away to attend special classes right after graduation.

Yes, things were changing. And Sarah-Jane didn't know how a person was supposed to feel joyful with all that change going on.

The Mystery of the Silent Nightingale

"Yes," said Timothy. "I'm glad you showed us the locket, S-J. It would have been a great thing to get for Kelly. That is, if we hadn't already gotten her what we got her."

"Which was also great," added Titus.

Sarah-Jane smiled. It was nice of her cousins to say so. But she wasn't sad because there were no nightingales nearby. (Although that *was* kind of sad when you stopped to think about it.) No, Sarah-Jane was sad because Kelly was going away.

Kelly Donovan had been Sarah-Jane's baby-sitter ever since Sarah-Jane could remember. When the boys came to visit—which was often—Kelly had been their baby-sitter, too.

As baby-sitters went, Kelly was pretty strict. But she was never mean. And you always had the feeling she knew what she was doing.

But best of all, Kelly always read to the cousins—even after they had learned to read for themselves. You never got too old to like hearing stories read aloud. The cousins especially liked mystery stories. They had a detec-

3

The Best Baby-Sitter

Timothy said, "We have some cardinals in our backyard. But I don't think I've ever seen a nightingale."

"Or heard one, either," agreed Titus. "We have a lot of birds in the city. But mostly they're sparrows and pigeons."

Sarah-Jane shook her head. "That's because there are no nightingales in America. Mr. Robinson told me."

She sounded so sad the boys wanted to cheer her up.

"Well, at least you can see a picture of a nightingale on the locket," said Titus.

The Mystery of the Silent Nightingale

nightingale was so sweet and happy sounding that it made people feel joyful and full of hope just to hear it.

This was true even when times were bad. And times were very bad for the early Christians. They were punished and even killed for believing in Jesus. They had to hide in underground cemetery tunnels. But even then they felt joy. They knew that no matter how bad things were, God was in charge. And that gave them hope.

To show how hopeful they felt, they drew pictures on the walls. They drew pictures of flowers and birds—nightingales.

Sarah-Jane said, "So ever since that time—almost two thousand years ago—the nightingale has been a Christian sign of joy."

2

The Silver Locket

They were looking at a beautiful silver locket that was almost a hundred years old. It was decorated with flowers around the edge. And right in the center there was a sweet little bird.

"It's a nightingale," said Sarah-Jane proudly. "Read the card beside it."

The card said that the nightingale was an early Christian symbol for joy. Mr. Robinson had explained it to Sarah-Jane, and now she explained it to Timothy and Titus.

Most birds went to sleep at nightfall. But the nightingale woke up in the early evening and sang through the night. The song of the

In the Store Window

Timothy and Titus thought.

But even they had to admit that Sarah-Jane had picked out the perfect gift for Kelly, who was going away to college. It was a beautiful wooden bookstand for holding a book open so you could study better. Kelly loved books. She was going to be either a teacher or a librarian.

Sarah-Jane gave an exasperated sigh. "I didn't say this thing I want to show you is what we're *going* to get Kelly. I said this thing is what I *wish* we could get her—if we hadn't already gotten her what we got her."

Titus looked at Timothy. "Are you following any of this?"

Timothy groaned and shook his head. Then he said to Sarah-Jane, "What's wrong with what we already got her?"

Sarah-Jane stared at the boys in alarm. "Nothing! I *love* what we got her! Why? Don't you?"

Timothy and Titus knew when they were licked. So they quit arguing and let Sarah-Jane drag them over to the store window.

And they had to admit that what Sarah-Jane wanted to show them was worth seeing.

"EXcellent," declared Titus.

"Neat-O," agreed Timothy.

The Mystery of the Silent Nightingale

She dragged the boys over to the crowded window of Mr. Robinson's antiques store. "I want to show you what I wish we could get Kelly for graduation. It's so cool!"

"I thought you already got Kelly's graduation present. It's supposed to be from all of us," said Timothy.

"Yes," said Titus. "I thought your mom let you pick Kelly's gift out of the catalog all by yourself."

No one could spend more time looking at catalogs than Sarah-Jane. At least that's what

1

In the Store Window

No one could spend more time looking in store windows than Sarah-Jane Cooper. At least that's what her cousins Timothy Dawson and Titus McKay thought. And now they said so. Loudly.

"Come *on*, S-J!" said Timothy. "We're supposed to meet Kelly at the library when she gets off work. We don't want to be late."

Titus added, "If we're late, we can't go over to the high school with Kelly to pick up her cap and gown."

But Sarah-Jane stood firm. "No, no. *Wait.* This is *about* Kelly.

Contents

 1. In the Store Window 9
 2. The Silver Locket 13
 3. The Best Babysitter 15
 4. Seniors 19
 5. Something Strange 23
 6. Questions 25
 7. Photographs 29
 8. Another Mystery 33
 9. The Graduation Present 35
10. Joy! 39
11. At the Antiques Store 43
12. More Questions 47
13. The T.C.D.C. 51
14. The Nightingale's Story 55
15. One More Mystery 59

ELSPETH CAMPBELL MURPHY has been a familiar name in Christian publishing for over fifteen years, with more than seventy-five books to her credit and sales reaching five million worldwide. She is the author of the bestselling series *David and I Talk to God* and *The Kids From Apple Street Church*, as well as the 1990 Gold Medallion winner *Do You See Me, God?* A graduate of Trinity College and Moody Bible Institute, Elspeth and her husband, Mike, make their home in Chicago, where she writes full time.

In loving memory of my father-in-law,

Howard R. Murphy,

whose life was filled with
love, joy, peace,
patience, kindness, goodness,
faithfulness, gentleness, and self-control.

Copyright © 1994
Elspeth Campbell Murphy
All Rights Reserved

THREE COUSINS DETECTIVE CLUB® and TCDC® are
registered trademarks of Elspeth Campbell Murphy.

Cover and story illustrations by Joe Nordstrom

Published by Bethany House Publishers
A Ministry of Bethany Fellowship, Inc.
11300 Hampshire Avenue South
Minneapolis, Minnesota 55438

Printed in the United States of America

Library of Congress Cataloging-in-Publication Data

Murphy, Elspeth Campbell.
   The mystery of the silent nightingale / Elspeth Campbell Murphy.
       p.   cm. — (The Three Cousins Detective Club® ; 2)
   Summary: Sarah-Jane and her two cousins solve a mystery involving an antique locket they plan to give their favorite baby-sitter.
   [1. Mystery and detective stories. 2. Babysitters—Fiction. 3. Cousins—Fiction. 4. Christian life—Fiction.] I. Title. II.Series: Murphy, Elspeth Campbell. Three Cousins Detective Club® ; 2.
PZ7.M95316Myhf   1994
[Fic]—dc20   94–16718
                                                                CIP
ISBN 1–55661–406–3   AC

THREE COUSINS 2 DETECTIVE CLUB

The Mystery of the Silent Nightingale

Elspeth Campbell Murphy
Illustrated by Joe Nordstrom

BETHANY HOUSE PUBLISHERS
MINNEAPOLIS, MINNESOTA 55438

THREE COUSINS DETECTIVE CLUB®

#1 / The Mystery of the White Elephant
#2 / The Mystery of the Silent Nightingale
#3 / The Mystery of the Wrong Dog
#4 / The Mystery of the Dancing Angels
#5 / The Mystery of the Hobo's Message
#6 / The Mystery of the Magi's Treasure
#7 / The Mystery of the Haunted Lighthouse
#8 / The Mystery of the Dolphin Detective
#9 / The Mystery of the Eagle Feather
#10 / The Mystery of the Silly Goose
#11 / The Mystery of the Copycat Clown
#12 / The Mystery of the Honeybees' Secret
#13 / The Mystery of the Gingerbread House
#14 / The Mystery of the Zoo Camp
#15 / The Mystery of the Goldfish Pond
#16 / The Mystery of the Traveling Button
#17 / The Mystery of the Birthday Party
#18 / The Mystery of the Lost Island

# The Mystery of the Silent Nightingale

The Mystery of the Wrong Dog

THREE COUSINS DETECTIVE CLUB®

#1 / The Mystery of the White Elephant
#2 / The Mystery of the Silent Nightingale
#3 / The Mystery of the Wrong Dog
#4 / The Mystery of the Dancing Angels
#5 / The Mystery of the Hobo's Message
#6 / The Mystery of the Magi's Treasure
#7 / The Mystery of the Haunted Lighthouse
#8 / The Mystery of the Dolphin Detective
#9 / The Mystery of the Eagle Feather
#10 / The Mystery of the Silly Goose
#11 / The Mystery of the Copycat Clown
#12 / The Mystery of the Honeybees' Secret
#13 / The Mystery of the Gingerbread House
#14 / The Mystery of the Zoo Camp
#15 / The Mystery of the Goldfish Pond
#16 / The Mystery of the Traveling Button
#17 / The Mystery of the Birthday Party
#18 / The Mystery of the Lost Island

THREE COUSINS 3 DETECTIVE CLUB

The Mystery of the Wrong Dog

Elspeth Campbell Murphy
Illustrated by Joe Nordstrom

BETHANY HOUSE PUBLISHERS
MINNEAPOLIS, MINNESOTA 55438

Copyright © 1994
Elspeth Campbell Murphy
All Rights Reserved

THREE COUSINS DETECTIVE CLUB® and TCDC® are
registered trademarks of Elspeth Campbell Murphy.

Cover and story illustrations by Joe Nordstrom

Published by Bethany House Publishers
A Ministry of Bethany Fellowship, Inc.
11300 Hampshire Avenue South
Minneapolis, Minnesota 55438

Printed in the United States of America

Library of Congress Cataloging-in-Publication Data
Murphy, Elspeth Campbell.
 The mystery of the wrong dog / Elspeth Campbell Murphy.
   p. cm. — (The Three Cousins Detective Club® ; 3)
 Summary: Titus and his cousins are taking care of their
neighbors' crabby Yorkshire terrier when the dog suddenly becomes
sweet-tempered and the cousins have a mystery on their hands.

 [1. Mystery and detective stories. 2. Dogs—Fiction.
3. Cousins—Fiction. 4. Christian life—Fiction.] I.Title.
II. Series: Murphy, Elspeth Campbell. Three Cousins Detective
Club® ; 3.
PZ7.M95315Myr   1994
[Fic]—dc20   94-16716
ISBN 1–55661–407–1   CIP
                                                                 AC

In loving memory of my father-in-law,

Howard R. Murphy,

whose life was filled with
love, joy, peace,
patience, kindness, goodness,
faithfulness, gentleness, and self-control.

ELSPETH CAMPBELL MURPHY has been a familiar name in Christian publishing for over fifteen years, with more than seventy-five books to her credit and sales reaching five million worldwide. She is the author of the best-selling series *David and I Talk to God* and *The Kids From Apple Street Church*, as well as the 1990 Gold Medallion winner *Do You See Me, God?* A graduate of Trinity College and Moody Bible Institute, Elspeth and her husband, Mike, make their home in Chicago, where she writes full time.

Contents

1. A Peculiar Feeling 9
2. Saint Francis of Assisi 12
3. Crabby Old Kingsley 15
4. At the Bakery 17
5. The Sweetest Dog 22
6. An Emergency Meeting 25
7. Questions 28
8. "The Curious Incident of the Dog in the Night-time" 31
9. A Face at the Window 34
10. Doggy Doubles 37
11. *Now* What Do We Do? 41
12. Peacemaking 45
13. Gubbio 50
14. Saint Francis and the Wolf 52
15. Home 57

1

A Peculiar Feeling

*T*itus McKay couldn't shake the feeling that he was being watched.

It happened lately whenever he took his neighbor's dog—a scrappy little Yorkshire terrier named Kingsley—for a walk.

Today, even Kingsley seemed to notice that there was something odd. He stopped growling at small children long enough to lift his head and sniff the air.

"Woof?!" he said to Titus, as if demanding an explanation.

"I don't know, boy," Titus said. "It's strange, isn't it?"

The really strange part was that Titus didn't feel afraid. A little uneasy maybe. And definitely puzzled. But not scared.

Titus was a city kid, and he prided himself

on being as streetwise as the next guy. He knew how to play it safe and how to stay alert. Some inner sense told him that he was being watched. But at the same time, he didn't sense danger.

Titus shook his head. "I don't know, Kingsley. It's a peculiar feeling. But we have to go home now anyway. My cousins are coming for a visit. The girl is called Sarah-Jane Cooper. And the boy is called Timothy Dawson. You'll like them."

Actually, Titus doubted that. Kingsley didn't like anybody.

Kingsley belonged to Titus's elderly neighbors, Sam and George. They were two brothers who shared an apartment down the hall from Titus. That is, they *used* to share an apartment until a few days ago when George moved out.

Sam and George were always bickering about one thing or another. But this time George had stomped off to live with his sister, Marie, a few blocks away. Then Sam had gone into the hospital.

So Kingsley had moved in with Titus for a while.

For Titus, having Kingsley live in his own apartment was a kind of test to prove how well

A Peculiar Feeling

he could handle a dog of his own.

More than anything else in the world, Titus wanted a dog of his own. His parents were just about convinced. The way Titus saw it, saying they would think about it was just one small step away from saying yes.

Titus was good with animals. He held a job in his building feeding fish and birds and cats when the owners were away. He was also a good dog walker. That's how he had gotten to know Kingsley in the first place.

Kingsley. What a dog. Titus called him "good dog" whenever he could. But that was stretching things a bit. Kingsley was never actually "good." But with Titus he was "less bad" most of the time. Titus was just about the only person besides Sam and George who could handle him. Titus's father said that was because Kingsley thought Titus was the "top dog," the "leader of the pack."

And Titus had pointed out that if he could handle Kingsley, he could certainly handle a dog of his own.

His parents were just about convinced.

2

Saint Francis of Assisi

At the side of Titus's building there was a peaceful little courtyard. At the center of the courtyard, there was a gently splashing fountain. It was called the Saint Francis fountain. On the edge of the fountain stood a statue of a man in a long robe. He was Saint Francis of Assisi. And Titus thought he had one of the nicest faces he had ever seen. Carved birds sat peacefully on his shoulders, and small animals gathered at his feet.

Titus was good with animals. But he wasn't *that* good. No one he knew could get wild animals to come close like that.

Most amazing of all was that Saint Francis's hand rested on the head of a big wolf. Not a big dog. A wolf. Not everyone could tell the difference between, say, an Alaskan malamute

Saint Francis of Assisi

or a Siberian husky and a wolf. But Titus could. And this was a wolf. Titus was sure of it. But what it was doing there with Saint Francis, he had no idea.

Around the edge of the basin were carved the words: *Lord, make me an instrument of Thy peace.*

Whenever Titus passed the fountain, he wondered about those words. Although, if Kingsley was with him, he didn't have much time to wonder about anything.

Kingsley seemed to think it was his job to clear the courtyard of every living thing—except himself. He dashed about, barking his little head off. Pigeons rose in a noisy flapping of wings. Sparrows scattered, chattering, to the streetlights. Squirrels dashed to the nearest trees.

"Kingsley, you are the most UNpeaceful animal on the face of the earth," Titus scolded. "Do you notice that not even Saint Francis of Assisi has a Yorkshire terrier? He'd rather have a wolf."

Kingsley muttered something under his breath that Titus couldn't quite catch and headed for the building.

The Mystery of the Wrong Dog

But just at that moment, the side door burst open, and Timothy and Sarah-Jane tumbled out.

"We got here early, Ti," Timothy said. "Aunt Jane said you were out walking the dog, so we came to meet you."

"Oh, look at the sweet little dog!" cried Sarah-Jane. "Oh, Ti! He's so cute I can't stand it!"

And before Titus could stop her, Sarah-Jane reached out to cuddle Kingsley.

3

Crabby Old Kingsley

Sarah-Jane screamed and jumped back.

"What happened?" cried Timothy. "Did he bite you?"

Sarah-Jane shook her head.

"Scared you, though," said Titus.

Sarah-Jane nodded.

To give Kingsley credit, he never actually bit anyone. But he was always threatening to. And that was almost as bad.

"Bad dog!" said Titus sternly. "Bad, bad, bad, bad dog. Sarah-Jane was just trying to be nice to you. Why do you have to go and embarrass me in front of my cousins? Now, *be good*."

In all the commotion, Titus had dropped the leash. Timothy picked it up. Kingsley twisted around and got his end of the leash in

The Mystery of the Wrong Dog

his mouth. He jerked the leash right out of Timothy's hand.

"Ow!" yelled Timothy. But it was so funny he and Titus started to laugh. "That dog is a menace to society," added Timothy cheerfully.

But Sarah-Jane wasn't quite over her hurt feelings yet. "It's not fair! Dogs that horrible shouldn't be allowed to look so cute. How's a person supposed to know you can't pick them up and cuddle them?"

By now Titus had a firm hold on the leash and had even gotten Kingsley to heel.

"Don't tell on him, OK, you guys?" Titus pleaded. "I'm trying to prove to my mom and dad that I can handle a dog of my own. And they might change their minds if they find out how bad Kingsley was today. I don't want to take any chances."

Timothy said, "What are the chances any other dog would be that crabby?"

"Crabby old Kingsley," muttered Sarah-Jane.

"Woof!" said Kingsley.

"Who asked you?" said Sarah-Jane.

But Kingsley hadn't actually done any harm. So both Sarah-Jane and Timothy promised not to tell on him.

4

At the Bakery

"Oh, I almost forgot," said Timothy. "Your mom gave us some money. She said you should take us to Petersen's Bakery. She said we can pick out whatever we want for dessert tonight."

"Oh, wow," said Titus. "You guys are not going to believe this place. It has the most EXcellent stuff."

They set off for the bakery with Kingsley. He behaved pretty well except for putting up a little bit of a fuss when they came to a busy intersection and Titus picked him up.

Titus explained, "His owners, Sam and George, say it's safer this way. You don't have much time to get across. Besides, Kingsley is so short, his face is close to the car exhaust pipes. It's not good for you to breathe in all those fumes, is it, boy?"

Kingsley couldn't really argue with that. So he stopped fussing, and they hurried across the street.

In all that had happened, the feeling never left Titus that he was being watched.

He put Kingsley down on the other side of the street and told his cousins about it.

Timothy and Sarah-Jane were fascinated. They loved mysteries, and so did Titus. In fact, the three of them even had a club called the Three Cousins Detective Club. They had solved quite a few mysteries. But they didn't know what to make of this one.

"Do you feel like you're being watched, too?" asked Titus.

"Yes, now that you mention it," said Sarah-Jane. "But maybe it's just my imagination *because* you mentioned it."

Timothy stopped and sniffed the air, much as Kingsley had done earlier. He said, "I don't think we're imagining things. Something's odd. But I don't know what."

They were almost at the bakery. And when they got there, one look in the window made it

At the Bakery

hard to think of anything but dessert.

"Neat-O!" said Timothy.

"So cool!" agreed Sarah-Jane.

"Didn't I tell you it was EXcellent?" asked Titus, feeling very pleased.

Dogs weren't allowed in the store, of course. But that was all right. City dogs were used to waiting patiently out on the sidewalk while their owners shopped. Even Kingsley.

Titus tied Kingsley's leash to a "No Parking" sign and told him to be good. Fortunately, there were no other dogs that day for Kingsley to argue with.

The Mystery of the Wrong Dog

The three cousins stepped into the bakery and just about passed out from all the delicious smells.

It took a while to pick out what they wanted. But finally they came out with a pink cardboard box tied up with string.

Kingsley did a little doggy dance of joy when they came over to him.

"What's gotten into Kingsley?" asked Timothy. "Does he want dessert?"

"He never has before," said Titus. "I tried giving him a piece of cake once. But he wouldn't eat it."

"Well, something sure put him in a good mood," said Timothy. "Let me try taking the leash again."

This time Kingsley didn't jerk the leash out of Timothy's hand. Instead, he trotted along contentedly with no complaints at all.

When they got to the intersection, Titus went to pick him up. But Sarah-Jane's arms were aching for the feel of fur. So she said bravely, "Let me try."

Kingsley didn't squirm and he didn't fuss. Instead he nestled down peacefully in Sarah-Jane's arms, to her great delight.

At the Bakery

She said, "You just needed time to get used to us, didn't you, Kingsley? Oh, you're just the sweetest, cutest, cuddliest little dog in the whole world!"

"S-J!" wailed Titus. "That's enough to make anyone want to bite you."

But Kingsley didn't bite. He didn't even threaten to. He just looked at them all with eyes full of love and licked Sarah-Jane on the chin.

Titus was so puzzled by all of this that it took him a while to notice something else.

The feeling of being watched was completely gone.

5

The Sweetest Dog

Dogs weren't allowed in the people elevator. So the cousins and Kingsley went in the back way and rode the freight elevator to the nineteenth floor.

They walked down the hall. That is, the cousins walked. Kingsley was still getting a free ride. Sarah-Jane hadn't wanted to set him down after she'd carried him across the intersection. So she had carried him all the way home. And—to Titus's surprise—Kingsley had seemed to enjoy every minute of it.

They passed Sam and George's apartment. At least, it *used* to belong to both of them—until the big argument when George had moved out.

Usually Titus had a hard time with Kingsley at this spot. Kingsley would whine and paw

The Sweetest Dog

at the door, wanting to go home to his two owners. And Titus couldn't really blame him. Homesick was a lousy feeling.

But today Kingsley just ignored his own apartment and went happily to Titus's at the end of the hall.

When the cousins and Kingsley came in, Titus's father looked up from the super-duper spaghetti sauce that he was making for dinner.

"Well, I'll be! Looks like you made a friend, Sarah-Jane."

"Oh, Uncle Richard, he's just the *sweetest dog*!"

"Who's the sweetest dog?" asked Titus's mother, coming into the kitchen.

"Kingsley," said Titus's father, waiting to see the astonished look on his wife's face. He was not disappointed.

"*Kingsley!?*" exclaimed Titus's mother. "That dog is more ornery than any cat I ever saw. If we're even a few minutes late with his supper, he kicks his dish across the floor."

"Well, look at him now," her husband replied.

Sarah-Jane's arms were getting tired. Reluctantly she set Kingsley down. He went right

The Mystery of the Wrong Dog

to his water dish and got a drink. But—to the McKays' surprise—he didn't sit barking at the cabinet where the dog biscuits were kept. That's what he usually did when he came in from a walk.

Titus got him a dog biscuit anyway. Kingsley seemed delighted, not demanding.

"Good dog!" said Titus. It felt strange to say that to Kingsley and really mean it.

Titus's mother shook her head as if she couldn't quite believe what she was seeing. "Well, I must say, you've done wonders with Kingsley. He's like a different dog."

"Good work, Son," said his father. "I'm really impressed with the way you handle him."

Timothy and Sarah-Jane nudged Titus excitedly. Things were going great. If this kept up, Titus would soon have a dog of his own.

But Titus didn't feel excited. And he didn't feel peaceful about how things were going. Something was seriously out of order. And he knew that until he faced up to it, he wouldn't have any peace.

He called an emergency meeting of the Three Cousins Detective Club.

6

An Emergency Meeting

*I*n his room Titus had a big poster that showed all the different breeds of dog. It was not everyone who knew the difference between a greyhound and a whippet. But Titus did.

Titus used to think that when it came to dogs, bigger was better. He spent hours trying to decide between a Great Dane and an Irish wolfhound. Dogs didn't come any bigger than that. But he knew this was just an imaginary decision. Just like his imaginary way of getting to school in the winter. By dog sled.

But Titus knew that a little dog who was real was better than any big dog who was imaginary. Titus looked over at the little Yorkshire terrier, who was sniffing at the dog bed as if he had never seen it before. And Titus realized with a pang that of all the dogs on his poster, of all the dogs in the world, he wanted *this* dog.

But there was a problem.

Timothy and Sarah-Jane looked expectantly at him, waiting to hear what this emergency meeting was all about.

Titus cleared his throat and got right to the point.

"You guys? This dog isn't Kingsley."

"*What?!*" cried Timothy and Sarah-Jane together.

Titus held up his hand. "No, don't say anything yet. Just listen a minute."

He ticked off the points with his fingers.

"One: Kingsley doesn't like anybody. But when we came out of the bakery, he was delighted to see us.

"Two: When you first saw Kingsley, back in the courtyard, he grabbed the leash out of Tim's hands. But when we came out of the bakery, he let Tim take the leash—no problem.

"Three: When Sarah-Jane first tried to pet Kingsley, he practically scared her to death. When we came out of the bakery, he let her carry him across the intersection. He let her carry him all the way home.

"Four: When we came back, Kingsley

didn't whine at his own apartment. Why? Because this dog has never been here before. It's not his apartment. And he's not Kingsley.

"Five: This dog didn't bark at the cabinet where we keep Kingsley's dog biscuits. Why? Because this dog has never been in my kitchen before. He didn't even know there *were* dog biscuits—let alone where we keep them."

Sarah-Jane and Timothy had listened seriously. But Titus could tell they had some doubts about what he was saying.

Sarah-Jane asked, "But doesn't all that just prove that you know how to handle Kingsley and make him be good? Even your parents said that."

Titus shook his head. "They haven't spent as much time with Kingsley as I have. Believe me, *no* one could make Kingsley be this good. Saint Francis of Assisi couldn't make Kingsley be this good."

"So what you're saying—" began Timothy carefully, "is that someone *switched* dogs with us?"

"That's exactly what I'm saying," replied Titus.

7

Questions

"That doesn't make sense, Ti," said Sarah-Jane. "Why would anyone switch dogs? Why would anyone want crabby old Kingsley when they could have this dog? He's the sweetest dog in the world."

"S-J!" exclaimed Titus. "Listen to what you just said. You *know* this isn't Kingsley."

Sarah-Jane and Timothy looked again at the Yorkshire terrier, curled up on the floor beside Titus with his chin resting on Titus's ankle. (Was there any cozier feeling in the world?) Suddenly his cousins saw what Titus meant.

Titus stroked the dog's silky fur. "We went to the bakery with Kingsley. And we came back with this little guy." He added softly, sadly, "I don't even know his name."

Titus's mind was whirling with questions,

which he put to his cousins. "Who took Kingsley? Why? Where is he now? And how in the world am I going to get him back?"

Sarah-Jane gave an awkward little cough, as if she were embarrassed to be asking. "Do you absolutely *have* to get Kingsley back? I mean, this little dog is so wonderful. And Kingsley is so—"

"Of course I have to get Kingsley back," Titus moaned. "Sam will know right away that this isn't his dog. How is that going to look? He goes into the hospital. He trusts me with his dog. He comes back and discovers I put another dog in

The Mystery of the Wrong Dog

his place. He's going to want to know what I did with Kingsley."

"You didn't do anything with Kingsley," said Sarah-Jane. "Someone took him."

"Who's going to believe that?" asked Titus. "It all sounds so crazy." The questions came rushing back: "Who took Kingsley? Why? Where is he now?"

"I have another question," said Timothy. Gently he picked up the dog and set him on his lap. "See? He's wearing Kingsley's dog tag. That means whoever switched dogs had to switch collars, too. Right? And my question is: How? I can see getting the collar off this little guy. But think of the Kingsley we all know and love. Can you imagine him letting *anyone* get close enough to take his collar off? Why didn't we hear anything? Kingsley would have barked his fool head off."

As soon as Timothy said that, Titus felt as if a light bulb had switched on in his head. Just like in the comics.

He knew who took Kingsley.

He knew why.

And he had a pretty good idea of where Kingsley was.

He jumped up and said, "Listen, you guys! I want to read you something."

8

"The Curious Incident of the Dog in the Night-time"

His cousins stared at him open-mouthed. "You want to *read* us something?" asked Sarah-Jane, as if she couldn't be hearing right. "What about Kingsley?"

"This is about Kingsley," said Titus.

He went to his bookshelf and pulled down a very large, very well-worn book. It was called *The Complete Sherlock Holmes.*

Titus said, "My Grand-uncle Frank gave this book to my dad when he was a kid. Then my dad gave it to me."

The stories were kind of long and hard for Titus to get through on his own. So he and his father had read them together.

The Mystery of the Wrong Dog

Timothy and Sarah-Jane waited patiently while Titus hunted for the page he wanted.

"OK," said Titus. "Here it is. This story is called 'Silver Blaze.' That's the name of this really valuable racehorse that gets stolen. So Sherlock Holmes and his friend Dr. Watson get called out to the farm to see what happened. And the policeman—the inspector—is there, too. And he knows Sherlock Holmes is this great detective. So the inspector asks Sherlock Holmes for advice. OK? Here it is. The inspector says:

" 'Is there any point to which you would wish to draw my attention?'

" 'To the curious incident of the dog in the night-time.' That's Sherlock Holmes talking. Then the inspector says—

" 'The dog did nothing in the night-time.'

" 'That was the curious incident,' remarked Sherlock Holmes."

Timothy said, "The dog did *nothing*? That *is* weird. *Very* curious. A horse gets stolen right out from under his nose, and he doesn't even bark or anything? He's not much of a watchdog if he lets strangers come in and steal like that."

"That's exactly what Sherlock Holmes was getting at," said Titus.

"Unless—" said Sarah-Jane, thinking out loud. "Unless it wasn't a stranger. What if it was an inside job? What if the horse was taken by someone the dog knew? He wouldn't bark then!"

"Bingo!" said Titus. "That's just what happened in the story."

"And that's what you think happened with Kingsley!" said Timothy. "He didn't bark when somebody took him. Because *he was taken by somebody he knew!*"

By this time, Titus was pacing around his small room. It was hard not to trip over the Yorkshire terrier, who was trotting along at his heels.

Titus said, "As far as I know, there are only three people on earth who could have gotten Kingsley's collar off and taken him away—without World War III breaking out. I'm one of them. Sam's in the hospital. So that leaves just one."

9

A Face at the Window

Titus's parents had a rule that he always had to tell them where he was going. And if something came up while he was out, he always had to call home.

"Mom, Tim and Sarah-Jane and I are going over to see George at his sister Marie's house, OK?"

"Oh, I think that would be very nice," said his mother. "I'm sure George is lonely without Sam. And I know Sam misses George. I wish those two would patch up their differences and make peace with each other. This building is George's home, after all. He's lived here forever. And Sam is going to need someone around when he comes home from the hospital. You're taking Kingsley, aren't you? I'm sure George would love to see him."

A Face at the Window

The excitement of Titus's hunch was beginning to wear off for him. In fact, he was beginning to wonder if the "great dog switch" was all his imagination. He didn't want to say any more about it until he had checked it out.

"Uh, right. We're taking the dog. Come on, boy."

It seemed the Yorkie couldn't believe his good luck at getting another walk so soon with his favorite people. Titus had to wait to put the leash on until the terrier had done another little doggy dance of joy.

At the Saint Francis fountain the Yorkie couldn't resist chasing the pigeons for the sheer fun of it. He didn't seem to take the pigeons as seriously as Kingsley had.

Titus led his cousins down some quiet, peaceful side streets, lined with tall, narrow houses. But Titus didn't feel peaceful. His mind kept doing flip-flops. One minute he was positive he was right. The next minute he was sure he was wrong. And if it turned out he was wrong, he knew he was going to feel pretty stupid. But he also knew that sometimes you have to risk feeling stupid if you want to find something out.

The Mystery of the Wrong Dog

When they came to Marie's house, Titus hesitated. He was having one of his "sure-he-was-wrong moments" right then. He glanced at his cousins. Somehow he could sense that Timothy and Sarah-Jane were feeling pretty tense, too. Titus was so glad that he could count on his cousins not to make fun of him if this turned out to be a wild-goose chase.

The three of them stood there, looking up at the house. Suddenly a face appeared at the window. A fierce face.

A fierce, furry, yapping, little face.

The cousins burst out laughing.

Kingsley!

10

Doggy Doubles

As soon as Titus's dog saw Kingsley, he started barking, too.

That made Kingsley bark all the more.

Stereo Yorkies yapping their furry little heads off. Not a pretty sound.

The door opened and George looked out. "Ah, Titus," he said. "I should have known you would catch on. Give me a minute. Let me put Kingsley in the backyard."

The cousins stood waiting on the small front porch. They could hear George leading a furious Kingsley down the hall and out the back door.

Marie bustled to the front door. "George!" she called over her shoulder. "Why did you leave these children standing on the front porch? I'm telling you, that dog of yours will

The Mystery of the Wrong Dog

have to go. We can't even have visitors with him around!" To the cousins she said, "Come in, darlings. Come in. Come in."

She led them into a small living room crammed with old-fashioned but beautiful furniture. Titus knew the Yorkie wouldn't chew it. But Titus picked him up and put him on his lap anyway.

Marie was surprised to see another Yorkshire terrier. "Am I seeing double?" she asked. "Now *that* is a nice dog. I told my brother I don't mind having a nice dog. But that other one!" She cocked her head toward the backyard.

The cousins glanced at one another. Kingsley—the real Kingsley—had not exactly made friends with Marie.

Marie said, "I'm a cat person myself. I used to have a cat. But she died."

"Oh, I'm sorry," said Sarah-Jane.

"It's very sweet of you to say so, my dear. My cat was very old. I had her for a long time. I didn't want to get another cat for a while. But then I felt ready to get another kitten. That's when my brother George wanted to move in with his dog. And I thought, 'A cute little dog. How bad could that be?' "

The cousins glanced at one another again. Knowing Kingsley, pretty bad.

Marie said, "I didn't know what Kingsley was like. Whenever I had my brothers over for dinner, they had to leave the dog at home. Because of my cat, you see.

"So anyway, George moves in with his dog. And at first everything was fine. He was the sweetest dog you ever saw. Just like yours. Then my brother took him for a walk today. And the dog comes back mean and crabby. Almost like a different dog. Do you know what he did? Stood barking for a dog biscuit. And when I didn't get it for him right away, he kicked his supper dish across the floor. Have you ever heard of such a thing?"

The cousins glanced at one another yet again. Yes, actually. They had heard of a dog doing that.

Just then George came back. It had taken him a while to get Kingsley calmed down.

Titus realized that in all the fuss with Kingsley, he hadn't introduced his cousins to George and Marie. Everyone said, "How are you?" "Pleased to meet you."

And then Marie asked, "And what's your dog's name, Titus?"

"He's not exactly my dog," said Titus wistfully. "And—I don't know his name."

"His name is Gubbio," said George. "It's spelled G-U-B-B-I-O, and it's pronounced GOO—bee—oh."

Marie was suspicious as she turned to her brother. "How is it you know Titus's dog's name—and Titus doesn't?"

George sighed. "It's a long story."

"Let's hear it," said his sister.

11

Now What Do We Do?

George said, "Gubbio belonged to friends of mine who moved overseas. It would have been too complicated to take a dog with them. Much as they hated to give him up! Anyway, they knew I didn't have a dog anymore. And they knew I liked Yorkies. So they asked if I would like to have Gubbio. And I said I would be delighted. It seemed like the perfect arrangement. I even thought if I renamed him Kingsley, it would be like old times. Except—except that I missed the *real* Kingsley."

Marie and the cousins stared at him in disbelief.

Timothy said, "You mean to tell us you had Gubbio, but you missed *Kingsley*?"

"That Kingsley—he doesn't like women," said Marie.

The Mystery of the Wrong Dog

"Tell me about it!" said Sarah-Jane.

"Kingsley doesn't like anybody," said Titus.

"Woof!" said Gubbio.

George didn't argue with them. "I know. I know. Kingsley is a crabby old thing. But then—so am I. And he's my *dog*, you know?"

"Yours and Sam's," Marie corrected him.

George sighed. "I know. You're right, of course. I knew Sam would never give me Kingsley. So I—I took him. I tried to convince myself that I was doing Sam a favor. I told myself I didn't just take Kingsley and leave him without a dog. I told myself it would be *better* for Sam to have a nice, quiet, well-behaved dog when he came home from the hospital. So I hung around whenever I knew Titus was due to take Kingsley for a walk."

"Which is why I had the feeling I was being watched," said Titus.

"Did you really?" asked George. "I hope I didn't scare you, Titus. I didn't mean to."

"No," said Titus. "I wasn't scared. But it was still weird. Then after we came out of the bakery I noticed the feeling was gone. That's

Now What Do We Do?

because you weren't watching anymore. You had Kingsley back."

George nodded. "Yes, that's exactly how it was. I figured one of these days you'd stop at a store and leave Kingsley outside. And that happened today."

Titus was quiet for a minute. He was trying to remember something he'd heard his father say once. It was when his dad was having a polite argument with someone on the phone. Titus remembered what it was and said it to George. "George, 'you put me in an awkward position.' I mean, *I* could have gotten blamed for what *you* did. Sam would have known right away that wonderful little Gubbio wasn't Kingsley. Sam might have thought I lost Kingsley—and then tried to fool him by putting another Yorkshire terrier in Kingsley's place."

George looked at Titus in alarm. "Oh, I'm so sorry! I never even thought of that! I was just so desperate to get Kingsley back! Please forgive me, Titus. Peace?"

"I forgive you," said Titus. "But things still aren't very peaceful. Sam is going to be pretty mad at you for taking Kingsley. He's still going to want him back. And Sam is even going to be mad at me for not watching Kingsley closely enough. So *now* what do we do?"

12

Peacemaking

"I'll tell you one thing," said Marie. "That Kingsley—he's not staying here."

"What!" cried George.

"No, I mean it," said Marie. "I'm putting my foot down. It's one thing to have a good dog around—" She pointed at Gubbio. "But that other one! That Kingsley—he drives me crazy. Besides, all this talk about pets has made me lonely for a cat. I want to get a cat."

Titus spoke up quickly. "There *is* one way George could keep Kingsley."

They all looked at him, waiting.

"He could move back home with Sam," Titus said.

"That old coot!" snorted George.

"But he needs you," said Titus. "He would probably never admit it. But he does need you.

The Mystery of the Wrong Dog

Especially now when he's coming home from the hospital. For one thing, he needs you to help take care of Kingsley."

"Well," said George, weakening. "I suppose you've got a point there."

"Why don't you call him?" asked Titus.

When George didn't answer, Titus said, "Would it be OK if I called him for you?"

"I guess I can't stop you," said George. But he didn't sound at all as if he wanted to stop Titus from calling.

The phone was in the kitchen. Titus went

off to call Sam. Gubbio trotted along at his heels.

Through the kitchen window Titus could see Kingsley busily digging holes in the yard. Marie would love that.

The hospital number was already jotted down on Marie's pad on the wall.

"How's Kingsley?" was the first thing Sam asked.

"He's fine," replied Titus. "He misses you." He paused. "George misses you, too."

"That old coot!" snorted Sam.

"I think George would like to come home," said Titus carefully.

"Huh!" said Sam. "Did he say so?"

"Not exactly. He would probably never admit he's homesick. But he did wonder who would be there to help you when you got home from the hospital. Who's going to help you take care of Kingsley?"

"Well," said Sam, weakening. "I suppose you've got a point there."

Titus made himself sound casual. "I'm calling from Marie's house. I think George would like to talk to you."

"Oh, all right," muttered Sam.

The Mystery of the Wrong Dog

"Hold on," said Titus. "Don't hang up."

He and Gubbio dashed to the living room door. Then Titus remembered to slow down and sound casual.

"George, Sam wants to talk to you."

"He *does*?"

"He's on the line now—waiting for you."

"Go!" Marie said to George. "Go make peace with your brother."

When George came back a little later, he was smiling.

"It's all set," he told them. "I'm going to move back home today."

"And you can take that Kingsley with you," said Marie.

"Oh, yes," said George happily. "Kingsley and I are going home to stay."

This was wonderful news.

But suddenly Titus had an awful thought.

Kingsley would never let another dog live in his apartment. And Marie really wanted a cat. So where did that leave Gubbio? Where was Gubbio going to live?

He put the question to George and Marie, Timothy and Sarah-Jane. But no one had an answer. His cousins sat up straight, though, their eyes sparkling with excitement.

"Marie," said Titus. "Can I use your phone again?"

The rule was if something came up, he had to call home. Well, something had certainly come up. And to Titus, this felt like the most important phone call of his life.

13

Gubbio

Sarah-Jane and Timothy went with Titus into the kitchen, guessing what he was going to do. And, of course, Gubbio trotted along.

Titus took a deep breath and dialed his own number.

It took a while—quite a while—to explain that the nice Kingsley his parents had liked so much wasn't Kingsley at all but rather a wonderful dog named Gubbio who had no place to live.

"So—" said Titus, hardly daring to breathe, "Can I keep him?"

When he heard the answer, he burst into his own little doggy dance of joy.

George and Marie were delighted to hear that Gubbio would have a home with Titus.

George said, "I'll write to my friends and

tell them the good news. I have Kingsley back. And Gubbio has the perfect new owner—someone who's *very* good with dogs."

"And very good at figuring things out," said Marie. "All of you—such smart children!"

Timothy grinned. "It's all in a day's work for the T.C.D.C."

"What's a 'teesy-deesy'?" asked George and Marie together.

"It's letters," explained Sarah-Jane. "Capital T. Capital C. Capital D. Capital C. It stands for the Three Cousins Detective Club."

"Well, the T.C.D.C. certainly figured everything out," said George.

"There's just one more thing I need to know," replied Titus. "Where in the world did your friends get the name Gubbio?"

14

Saint Francis and the Wolf

George laughed and repeated the question: "Where in the world did my friends get the name Gubbio? You asked that question the right way, Titus. That's because Gubbio is a *place*. Gubbio is a town in the country of Italy. Something special once happened there hundreds of years ago. And even now when people think of Gubbio, they think of peace and friendship between animals and people. My friends told me their Yorkie was such a peaceful, friendly little dog that the name just seemed to fit him."

"What special thing happened at Gubbio?" asked Timothy.

"Ah," said George. "That was where Saint Francis met the wolf."

Titus sat up straight. "Like on the Saint

Saint Francis and the Wolf

Francis fountain by our building!"

"Exactly," said George.

Marie got up and took a drawing off the wall. "Here is a picture of Saint Francis and the wolf of Gubbio," she said.

The cousins clustered round to see. The picture showed a gentle-faced man in a long brown robe. Next to him sat a huge, dark wolf. He looked like the big, bad wolf from fairy tales. But the look on his face was positively sweet. And, most amazing of all, he rested one of his paws in the man's hand.

"Once there was a fierce and hungry wolf," George began. "He attacked the animals of Gubbio—the livestock and pets—and even some of the people. The townspeople were terrified.

"Saint Francis came from the town of Assisi to help them. The people were glad to see him. But they didn't think anyone could help. They begged Saint Francis not to go outside the town for fear of the wolf. But Saint Francis was not afraid. He went out of the town to find the wolf.

" 'Brother Wolf,' called Saint Francis, 'Come out here to me.'

The Mystery of the Wrong Dog

"Suddenly the wolf came rushing out of his lair, fierce and hungry.

"But Saint Francis said, 'Brother Wolf, I must talk to you in the name of the Lord.'

"When the wolf heard that, he lay down at the man's feet like a big, gentle dog.

" 'Brother Wolf,' said Saint Francis. 'I have heard bad things about you. You make war with your fellow creatures—the animals and people of Gubbio. This must stop.'

"The wolf hung his head. Saint Francis understood why the wolf had been attacking the town. It was because he was too old and frail to hunt with the pack. And the wolf was hungry.

"So Saint Francis said, 'Come with me, Brother Wolf, and I will make a bargain with you and the people.'

"The townspeople were amazed that the wolf hadn't eaten Saint Francis right on the spot. But they were even *more* amazed—not to mention alarmed—when Saint Francis led the wolf right into the town square.

" 'Good people,' said Saint Francis. 'If you will promise to feed the wolf and care for him, there can be peace in Gubbio. The wolf will

Saint Francis and the Wolf

not attack you. Will you agree to do this?'

"And the people all agreed that they would.

"Then Saint Francis turned to the wolf in front of all the people. He said, 'Brother Wolf, if you will promise not to attack the people and animals, there can be peace in Gubbio. The people will feed you. Will you agree to this?'

"Of course, the wolf couldn't speak as the townspeople had. But he could make a sign of his promise. He lifted his paw and laid it peacefully in the hand of Saint Francis.

"So the townspeople took turns feeding the wolf, and he lived among them as everyone's pet until two years later when he died of old age. And everyone missed him, for they had come to love their Brother Wolf."

"EXcellent story!" said Titus.

"Neat-O," agreed Timothy.

"So cool," murmured Sarah-Jane, sniffing a little.

"And I love this picture," added Titus.

"It's yours," said Marie.

"Oh, no, I couldn't . . ." Titus began, thinking that was the polite thing to say. But he couldn't help adding, "*Really?* Really can I have it?"

Marie smiled. "I *insist* that you have it!"

"Then, thank you so much!" said Titus.

"It's a picture of peace," said Marie. "Today you have brought peace to my brothers. And because Kingsley is going home, you have brought peace to my house."

Titus didn't say what he was thinking—that he hoped Kingsley would be long gone before Marie saw her backyard. . . .

15

*H*ome

*T*itus was always glad to have his cousins with him. But he was especially glad now, when there was so much to carry. For a little dog, Gubbio sure had a lot of stuff. So did Kingsley, for that matter. George said he would stop by Titus's apartment later to get Kingsley's things.

Sarah-Jane gathered up Gubbio's toys and put them in his bed. She carried that.

Timothy collected Gubbio's dog food and dishes and put them in a grocery bag. He carried that.

Titus had the best job of all. He put Gubbio's real collar on him. (George had to get it off Kingsley first.) Then he snapped on the leash. With his picture of Saint Francis and the wolf in one hand, and his dog's leash in the

The Mystery of the Wrong Dog

other, Titus was ready to go home.

When they came to the courtyard, all four of them stopped to look at the Saint Francis fountain.

Timothy read the words aloud: "*Lord, make me an instrument of Thy peace.* That's like what you were, Ti."

"I know what Tim means," said Sarah-Jane. "It's like Marie said. You brought peace. You were like the tool that put George and

Sam and Kingsley back together again."

"Oh," said Titus. "I never thought of it like that."

It was nice to hear. But he wasn't sure what else he should say.

It had been quite a day. Sometimes when the cousins had had a big day, they couldn't stop talking. But now as they rode the freight elevator to the nineteenth floor, they were all thinking.

They were thinking about Saint Francis and his Brother Wolf. They were thinking about peace. And joy.

And Titus's thoughts especially were filled with love. Love for his new . . . his very own . . . his just-the-right . . . *dog*!

The End

Photographs

rode in it, they looked like they were riding in a little train. And there was a picture of Kelly, proudly pushing them.

"You three were the cutest babies!" exclaimed Sarah-Jane's mother. "Everyone stopped to admire you. You didn't look that much alike. But everyone thought you were triplets until they found out you were actually cousins."

Later, of course, the cousins had gotten too big for the stroller.

When they were five and Kelly was thirteen, she had watched them by herself as her first baby-sitting job with all three of them. She had taken them to the library for story time. That had been an extra-special day for Sarah-Jane. She had learned to print her name well enough to get her very own library card. There was even a cute picture in the album of Kelly and the cousins when they came home that day. Sarah-Jane was holding the books she had checked out all by herself.

Timothy, Titus, and Sarah-Jane had a wonderful time looking at old pictures of themselves. It wasn't until they closed the photograph albums and put them away that they remembered something.

Janice.

There had been nothing in the albums to give them a clue as to who she was.

Yet the cousins were sure of two things:

Janice knew them.

And they didn't know her.

8

Another Mystery

It was just after lunch that another mystery popped up.

Kelly called and asked the cousins to come over and help her look for something. Something, she said, that should be there—but wasn't.

Kelly lived only a couple of houses away from Sarah-Jane. The cousins hurried over. They found Kelly searching around the bushes in her front yard.

"What are you looking for?" asked Titus. "What did you lose?"

"I didn't exactly lose it," said Kelly. "I

never actually had it. See, someone left a graduation present on the porch. But there's no card to say who it's from. I'm thinking the card must have blown away. And I know you guys are great at finding things...."

"Say no more," said Timothy.

"You've come to the right place," said Titus.

"Absolutely," said Sarah-Jane. Then she added, "There's not much wind today. It can't have blown far."

So they searched all around Kelly's house. Front yard. Backyard. Side of the house. Nothing.

They searched up and down the street. Across the street. And even all along the alley. Nothing.

"I feel terrible about this," said Kelly. "Someone went to all the trouble of getting me this *beautiful* graduation present that I just *love*. And now I can't even say thank you. How embarrassing! What is this person going to think?"

Sarah-Jane said, "It's possible the person just forgot to put the card on it. And so maybe that person will remember and tell you who the present was from."

"Unless..." said Timothy.

—— 9 ——

The Graduation Present

They all looked at Timothy, waiting for him to go on.

"Unless what?" asked Titus.

"Unless there never was a card in the first place," said Timothy. "Maybe whoever left the present doesn't want you to know who did it."

"You mean like a 'secret pal'?" asked Kelly.

"Sort of," said Timothy. "Sometimes the secret is just for fun. Or sometimes there's a good reason for someone—" He paused, trying to remember the right phrase. "Wishing to remain anonymous."

Titus said, "That happened to our grand-

The Mystery of the Silent Nightingale

father once. Someone left a birthday present for him."

"Did he ever find out who left it?" Kelly asked.

The cousins looked at one another. They couldn't help smiling and feeling kind of pleased with themselves.

"We solved the mystery," said Sarah-Jane. "We found out who left the present, and why, and it all worked out fine."

"It sounds like you need the T.C.D.C.," said Titus.

Kelly's mother had just come out to see how it was going. She heard what Titus said, but she didn't understand it.

"What's a 'teesy-deesy'?" she asked.

"It's letters," explained Sarah-Jane. "Capital T. Capital C. Capital D. Capital C. It stands for the Three Cousins Detective Club."

Kelly sighed. "Well, I agree that I need detective help right now. I hate the thought of going away without knowing who gave me such a great present."

At the thought of Kelly going away, Sarah-Jane's stomach gave a little lurch. But all she said was, "Let's see what we can do. Why don't

The Graduation Present

you show us the present. Maybe it will give us some idea of who left it."

It was a long shot, but the cousins knew they had to start somewhere.

Kelly led them inside. First she showed them the wrapping paper. It was decorated with rolled-up diplomas and mortarboards and words that said, *Congratulations, Graduate!*

"Nothing unusual here," said Titus. "You can buy this kind of paper just about anywhere this time of year."

They examined it carefully front and back for any kind of handmade notes or marks. There weren't any.

Then Kelly showed them the little box. Again, nothing unusual. It was when Kelly opened the box that the cousins gasped.

They were looking at a beautiful silver locket. It was decorated with flowers all around the edge. And right in the center there was a sweet little bird.

A nightingale.

10

Joy!

Timothy, Titus, and Sarah-Jane were too surprised to say a word.

"See? It's a locket," said Kelly, opening it up. She seemed surprised at how quiet the cousins were. "Nothing inside, of course. I thought there might be a clue in there. Maybe a picture of the person who sent it. But there wasn't. And there's nothing engraved on the back. But there is maybe *one* clue. See? This little information card tells about it. It tells how the nightingale is a Christian symbol for joy."

The cousins recognized the card as the one

The Mystery of the Silent Nightingale

from Mr. Robinson's store window. They leaned forward and read the card again.

Timothy said, "It looks like someone took a red pen and drew a circle around the word *joy*."

"And put an exclamation point beside it," added Titus.

"I noticed that," said Kelly. "What do you suppose it means? That graduation is a joyful time? I mean, I guess it is. But sometimes I don't feel so joyful about it."

Sarah-Jane looked up quickly.

Kelly must have guessed that Sarah-Jane wasn't feeling very joyful, either. She reached out and squeezed her hand.

"I'm sad about leaving home and all my friends. And—can I tell you a secret? I'm scared. Really scared about going away to college. I'm worried about finding my way around. And about fitting in. And about doing the work. But at the same time, I really want to go. I feel hopeful. And excited. Even though I'm sad and scared at the same time."

The cousins nodded. They knew what it was like to have all sorts of mixed-up feelings all at the same time. But it had never occurred

Joy!

to them that seniors would be afraid of anything. Especially not Kelly.

"So, anyway," said Kelly. "I think this locket will help me. It will remind me that I can be hopeful no matter what's going on around me. Sarah-Jane, are you OK?"

Sarah-Jane forced herself to smile. "I'm fine," she said. But actually she felt very jealous. Who had sent 'her' present to 'her' Kelly? Sarah-Jane knew she wasn't being exactly fair. The locket was in the store window for anyone to buy. And Kelly wasn't just Sarah-Jane's

The Mystery of the Silent Nightingale

friend. Sarah-Jane knew that. But she felt more than ever that she wanted to get to the bottom of this.

And she suddenly had an idea of how to do it.

11

At the Antiques Store

Sarah-Jane said, "We don't know who bought the locket. But we know where it came from because we saw it ourselves. It was in the window of Mr. Robinson's antiques store just this morning."

"It was?" exclaimed Kelly. "So that means someone bought it only a little while ago."

"Right," said Sarah-Jane. "So here's the plan: Mr. Robinson is a friend of ours. He likes to talk to the people who come in his store. So he must have talked to the person who bought the locket for you. We'll just go over there and ask him who it was."

The Mystery of the Silent Nightingale

Timothy and Titus stared at her as if to say, "Why didn't *we* think of that?"

But the detective-cousins had been around enough mysteries to know that things weren't always as simple as they seemed. Still, it was a good idea. So Timothy, Titus, and Sarah-Jane—plus Kelly—hurried off to the antiques store to get to the bottom of things.

But Mr. Robinson wasn't there.

"You just missed him," said his assistant, Bill. "He left on a buying trip. Won't be back for a couple of weeks."

Kelly groaned. "I'll be gone by then."

When she said that, Sarah-Jane's stomach gave another little lurch.

"Something I can help you with?" asked Bill.

"Maybe so," said Titus. "We're trying to find out who bought a silver locket today."

"Oh, right. The nightingale," Bill replied.

"Yes! Yes! Yes!" the cousins practically shouted together.

Bill took a step back, and that made them all laugh. Maybe they were getting a little carried away. It was just that they were so close to solving the mystery, they could hardly stand it.

At the Antiques Store

Kelly took a deep breath and explained, "See—the locket was a graduation present for me. But I don't know who it's from. If there was a card, it got separated from the box. And now I don't know who to thank. So can you tell me who bought it?"

"I'm sorry. I can't help you there," said Bill.

12

More Questions

Kelly looked at Bill in dismay.

Timothy said, "Do you mean it was a secret? Did the person swear you to secrecy? Is that why you can't tell us?"

"No, nothing like that," said Bill. "I can't tell you who bought the locket because I don't know. I was working in the back room when this lady came in. Mr. Robinson waited on her."

A lady. Well, that narrowed it down.

A little. Not much. The cousins went into their questioning routine.

The Mystery of the Silent Nightingale

"So you never actually saw her at all?" asked Sarah-Jane.

"That's right," said Bill.

"And you didn't recognize her voice?" asked Timothy.

Bill shook his head.

"Well, what about the voice?" asked Titus. "Young? Old? Accent?"

"She wasn't a kid," said Bill. "And not an old lady. Somewhere in between. No accent."

The cousins glanced at one another.

This wasn't getting them very far.

Timothy had a sudden thought. "What about a credit card receipt? Could you get the name off of that?"

They all perked up until Bill shook his head apologetically. "Cash."

They had turned to leave when Sarah-Jane remembered the thing she knew about her friend Mr. Robinson. She remembered that he liked to chat with his customers.

She asked, "Did the lady and Mr. Robinson talk about anything?"

Bill frowned, thinking hard. The cousins could tell he was trying. He really was. But

More Questions

they knew not everyone noticed things as much as they did.

"They talked about the locket," said Bill slowly. "About how beautiful it was. About how the nightingale stood for joy. And Mr. Robinson asked her if she wanted a gift box. And she said yes, because it was a present. She said it was the perfect present, because it was for someone who had once brought her a lot of joy. Oh! And she said she had just run into that person today. This person had once helped her several years ago. She said the locket was her way of saying thank you all these years later."

Bill beamed at them, clearly pleased with himself.

"Well!" said Titus. "That certainly ties in with the little information card. I mean—the way the word *joy* had a circle around it and even an exclamation point."

"Now we're getting somewhere," said Timothy, sounding pretty joyful himself. "Who was it you helped so much, Kelly?"

But Kelly wasn't looking at all joyful. She looked flabbergasted. And she sounded as if she might start crying. "That's just it! I don't know! I don't *know*!"

Sarah-Jane didn't say anything for a moment. She was remembering the look of joy on someone's face. Joy when that person had looked at Kelly.

"Let's go," she said.

13
The T.C.D.C.

Janice was alone in the office when Kelly and the cousins came in. The time was right for asking some questions.

Janice looked startled—as if she knew that was what they had come for. Her eyes went right to the nightingale locket. Kelly had taken it out of her pocket and hung it around her neck.

Kelly said gently, "Janice, are you the person I should thank for this beautiful graduation present?"

At first Janice gave a little shake of her head. Then she turned pink and nodded.

The Mystery of the Silent Nightingale

"How did you know?" she asked softly.

Kelly said, "You have the T.C.D.C. to thank for that."

Janice looked confused. "What's a 'teesy-deesy'?" she asked.

"It's letters," explained Sarah-Jane for the second time that day.

"Capital T. Capital C. Capital D. Capital C. It stands for the Three Cousins Detective Club."

"Oh," said Janice, sounding as if that cleared things up a little. But only a little.

Timothy explained some more. "Well, see, it all started when S-J—Sarah-Jane—wanted to show us this neat-o present that she wished we could get Kelly for graduation."

"Oh, you guys!" interrupted Kelly, sounding again as if she was going to start crying. "I didn't know that! No wonder you were so quiet when I showed you the locket. Oh, you are just so sweet!"

She reached out and hugged Sarah-Jane, who happily hugged her back. Kelly would have hugged Timothy and Titus, too, but they were able to hop out of the way just in time.

"Anyway," said Titus. "We already had an

The T.C.D.C.

excellent present for Kelly, so we didn't think any more about it. But then the locket showed up with no name. And we knew it came from Mr. Robinson's store. So we went there to see who bought it. Only Mr. Robinson wasn't there. And all Bill could tell us was that it was a lady that Kelly helped once."

"But how did you know that was me?" asked Janice.

Sarah-Jane said, "Because of the way you looked at Kelly and us when we came in earlier today. It was like you recognized us. *Really* recognized us."

"You're exactly right," said Janice. "I *did* recognize you."

"But how?" asked Timothy. "We don't know you, do we?"

"And what did Kelly do to help you that made you remember her all these years?" asked Titus.

It had just occurred to the detective-cousins that they had come in to ask some questions. But so far all they had done was answer them.

It was time to hear from Janice.

14

The Nightingale's Story

Janice took a deep breath. "It all happened about five years ago. I—well, this is hard for me to admit. But, well, you see—I was all grown up before I learned how to read."

The cousins stared at her. They had never heard of such a thing. A grown-up who didn't know how to read? How could that be? They were too polite to say any of this. But Janice must have guessed what they were thinking. She said, "Oh, yes. There are lots of people like me. We try not to let anyone know. We're so embarrassed. We just sort of fake our way along. And it's not easy, believe me! In my case

The Mystery of the Silent Nightingale

I dropped out of school, which only made things worse.

"Then one day I overheard some people talking about special classes starting that afternoon at the library. The classes were for people like me. Grown-ups who had missed out somehow on learning to read, and who had to start at the beginning.

"I knew where the library was, so I got up my courage and went over there. But when I got there, I couldn't tell where the class was being held. And, of course, I couldn't read the signs. I couldn't ask the librarian, because there were some people I knew by her desk. I was just too embarrassed.

"I was all set to run out of there. But then I saw this young girl come in with three absolutely adorable children, two boys and a girl."

It took the cousins a moment to realize Janice was talking about them.

Janice smiled right at Sarah-Jane and said, "The little girl was getting her very own library card that day. And the look of joy on her face—well, you never saw anything like it! And I thought to myself, 'I want that, too. I want to learn how to read and check out books.'

The Nightingale's Story

"Well, the older girl—you, Kelly—was so good with the little ones that I thought, 'Here's someone I can trust.' I went up to you and asked if you could tell me where the class was. It was a moment that changed my life."

Kelly shook her head sadly. "I'm so sorry, Janice. I don't remember that."

But Janice just smiled. "It's all right. I think we all go through life, trying the best we can. And we don't always know the joy we bring to other people.

"Anyway, you told me to hold on a minute while you got the little ones settled in the story circle. Then you didn't just tell me where the class was. You went with me. And you said you could tell I was embarrassed about needing this class. But you said I shouldn't be. That it took courage to do what I was doing. And that I was doing the best thing in the world for myself.

"Well, you were right! I learned to read. And when I moved away I kept on studying until I got my diploma.

"I never forgot you, Kelly. But I just never made the connection between my boss's daughter and the young girl who helped me

The Mystery of the Silent Nightingale

five years ago. You're all grown up now. It wasn't until you came in with those same three adorable kids—who are also pretty grown up—that I realized who you were! And then—well, I just wanted to get you something as a way of saying thank you. And the joy of the nightingale seemed just right."

"But this is *so cool*!." cried Sarah-Jane. "Why didn't you tell us before? Why did you want to keep the locket a secret?"

Janice looked down at her lap. "I guess you could call me a silent nightingale. I had all this joy, but I didn't want to sing out about it. To tell you the truth, not everyone is as understanding as you people are. I want so much to do a good job here. I just thought it might be harder if—if Dorothy found out I hadn't even learned to read until a few years ago."

Titus nodded. "Dorothy doesn't suffer fools gladly. Not that you're a fool," he added quickly. "I didn't mean that—"

Janice laughed. "I know exactly what you mean."

It was at that moment that the door opened and Mr. Donovan and Dorothy came in.

15

One More Mystery

Mr. Donovan looked pleased but surprised to see them. He said, "Back again? What's up? Kelly, where did you get that gorgeous locket?"

Kelly didn't lie. But she didn't give away Janice's secret. Rather she said, "It's a graduation present, Daddy. But, as Timothy once put it, the giver wishes to remain anonymous."

The cousins were impressed. But before anyone could reply, Janice spoke up. "It's all right, Kelly. You once told me I had nothing to be embarrassed about. And I think I need to remember that now."

Just as before, she took a deep breath. Quickly she repeated to Mr. Donovan what she had just told Kelly and the cousins.

It seemed to Sarah-Jane that if Mr. Donovan had been bursting with pride before, he was about to explode with pride now. He grinned at Kelly and said over and over, "That's my girl. That's my girl."

Even the cousins couldn't resist a little cheer when Janice got to the part about the three absolutely adorable children.

"So anyway," Janice finished. "I suddenly realized as I was telling Kelly about how she helped me that I want to help, too. I want to tutor people who don't know how to read. But how can I help them not be embarrassed—if I'm still embarrassed myself? Now, maybe if they know I did it, they'll believe they can do it, too."

"Humph!" said the gruff voice of Dorothy. Everyone jumped, even Mr. Donovan.

"If you want to tutor someone," she said, "how about starting with my grandson? He's having an awful time in school. I've tried to help him, goodness knows. But no, he doesn't want any help from Grandma Dorothy."

One More Mystery

The cousins glanced at one another. They were too polite to say what they were thinking, which was: "Who would?"

But Kelly stepped in smoothly. "Well, sometimes it's easier to accept that kind of help from a stranger than from a relative."

Sarah-Jane didn't know when she had heard any kid sound so grown up. Not even a senior.

"Fair enough," replied Dorothy. "I'll pay for the lessons. I just want to help him. It doesn't matter how I do it. And I know Janice here is as smart as they come. Now, don't we all have work to do?"

With that she marched back to her desk, as though she was afraid she might say something else nice if she wasn't careful.

When the cousins got home later they got out the photograph albums again.

They especially wanted to see the picture of when they had come home from the library that day long ago. There was Sarah-Jane, with her arms full of books and her face full of joy.

When they got to the end of the album the

The Mystery of the Silent Nightingale

cousins saw something strange.

The most recent photograph was missing.

"Where's the picture of us?" cried Sarah-Jane.

"It's a mystery," answered her mother.

And that's all she would say.

But solving mysteries was what the cousins did for fun.

"Let's think this through," said Titus. "You take a picture out of the album. Where do you put it?"

"In a picture frame?" suggested Timothy. "In a wallet?"

Sarah-Jane gasped. You would have to cut the picture down to get it to fit, of course. But—yes!—there was one other place she could think of where you could put a photograph.

And she was right.

That evening after graduation she asked Kelly if she could see inside the locket.

Kelly laughed and said, "You three don't miss much, do you? I didn't think it would take you long to figure it out. See? The nightingale on the outside will remind me of the joy I was able to bring to Janice. And the pictures on the

62

One More Mystery

inside will remind me of some people who have brought a whole lot of joy to me."

She opened the locket and showed them. On the one side there was a picture of Timothy and Titus together. On the other side there was a picture of Sarah-Jane.

Kelly reached out and caught Sarah-Jane in a big, happy hug.

Timothy and Titus tried to hop out of the way.

They didn't make it.

The End

was the most loving place she'd ever been in? I mean, things didn't turn out so great for her. She got caught. And she didn't get to keep the cookie jar she wanted so much."

Timothy's father said, "Love doesn't mean that we get to do whatever we want. Love means that God wants what's best for us. And that's what we should want for other people—whatever's best for them. Stealing is not the best thing for anyone. Mrs. Foster's friend must have felt that the people at church really cared about her. Even when she didn't get her own way. She must have felt that she was valuable to them."

"She didn't feel like a white elephant," said Sarah-Jane.

"God doesn't have any white elephants," said Titus.

"Speaking of white elephants . . ." said Timothy's mother.

"Say no more," said Timothy, picking up the mirror.

And for the second time that day, he and his cousins went up to the attic.

The End

"Not even Mrs. Foster wanted two of them," said Titus.

"Poor Mrs. Foster," said Sarah-Jane. "It must be so awful to have a friend trick you like that. Even though her friend cried and said she was sorry."

They were all quiet, remembering how it had been. The cousins had just shown Pastor Parry the elephant in the tote bag. Then Mrs. Foster had come up, dragging her friend behind her. Her friend didn't want to make a fuss, Mrs. Foster had said. But her tote bag was missing. And wasn't that awful—on top of the missing cookie jar? And Pastor Parry had replied that what was even more awful was that the two things had been found in the same place.

That's when Mrs. Foster's friend had started crying. The cousins had gladly left Pastor Parry to sort that one out.

He must have done a good job, because Mrs. Foster had come over to thank them, and to tell them everything was going to be all right.

Timothy asked, "What did Mrs. Foster mean when she said her friend felt our church

15

Back to the Attic

"How is it possible that there could be two mirrors like that in the world?" exclaimed Timothy's father.

The swap meet was over. The cousins and Timothy's parents were back at home. They all sat around the kitchen table with the mirror in the middle. It wasn't the same mirror they had taken to the white elephant swap meet. But it was one just like it. Someone else had brought it and put it on the table at the last minute. But no one would admit bringing it. And Timothy's family had ended up with it because no one else would take it.

They all let out a sigh of relief. Now all they had to do was put Priscilla in the stroller and whisk the whole thing off to Pastor Parry.

But Priscilla had other ideas. "Me me me me me me me me!"

"Oh, puh-leese!" groaned Titus. "Don't tell me that means what I think it means."

"It means she wants to push," said Timothy. "And take it from someone who knows. There's not a thing we can do about it."

So they made their way toward Pastor Parry, with Priscilla happily pushing her stroller. They were walking so slowly they thought they were going to topple over.

They walked right by Mrs. Foster and her friend. Fortunately, they were talking to some other people about Canada.

Not much farther.

Pastor Parry looked up and saw them coming. Even though they weren't rushing, he must have been able to guess something from their faces. "You found it!" he said, just as he had before.

And this time Timothy was able to say, "Exactly!"

Titus said, "There's a sweater on top. And something underneath wrapped in newspapers."

"Maybe I can tear a little bit off," said Timothy. "And see if—yes!"

"Yes?" asked Sarah-Jane. *"Yes?"*

"Yes," said Timothy. "We found the jar!"

But how to get it to Pastor Parry without being seen?

"Quick," said Titus. "Put it in the pouch in back of Priscilla's stroller."

Sarah-Jane turned the stroller around, and the boys got the tote bag safely hidden.

14

Exactly

Timothy scooped up Priscilla, and the four cousins practically flew to the bench.

Yes. There—hidden in plain sight among the other tote bags—was one with a telltale maple leaf.

While Sarah-Jane fumbled with Priscilla's stroller, Timothy and Titus fumbled with the tote bag.

"Hurry! *Hurry!*" Sarah-Jane muttered to the boys. To Priscilla she said, "Come over here, and be a good little baby detective. Sarah-Jane needs Priscilla to help block the boys while they're digging in a lady's tote bag." To the boys she said, "Is it there? Is it there?"

Baby-Sitters and Detectives

"There you are!" he said. "Where have you guys been?"

But before they could even begin to explain, he went on. "Listen, Priscilla's been asking for you constantly. 'Ware Timmy go? Ware Sayway-Zane? Ware Tidus?'"

The cousins couldn't help laughing. It sounded so funny to hear Timothy's father talking like Priscilla. Priscilla laughed, too—even though she had no idea what was so funny. And that made them laugh harder.

"So how about it, kids?" said Timothy's father. "Spend a little time with her, OK? After all, she's a cousin, too."

How could they say no to that? So they took Priscilla with them. Even though it meant they had to be baby-sitters *and* detectives. All at the same time.

Next to cookies and her blankie, Priscilla loved her stroller most of all. Sometimes she rode in it. Sometimes she insisted on pushing it herself. The cousins knew the stroller would keep her happy and quiet. And with Priscilla in the stroller, they could move around faster. So they walked her over to get it.

The Mystery of the White Elephant

The stroller was propped up against a bench with a lot of other stuff that people had set down. Things like: Other strollers. Umbrellas. Jackets. Tote bags.

13

Baby-Sitters and Detectives

*T*he cousins felt like three balloons with all the air let out of them.

"Don't tell me she *hid* the tote bag somewhere," groaned Titus. "Oh, please—not another search. I feel like I've been hunting elephants my whole life."

Sarah-Jane shrugged helplessly. "What else can we do?"

"Let's get started then," said Timothy.

They were just about to go off on another search when Timothy's father came up to them. He was carrying Priscilla.

Coincidence?

place to ditch the disguise. She could just hang around downstairs for a while—maybe in the social hall or the washroom. And then she could go find Mrs. Foster and pretend she just got here."

"Is she here now?" asked Titus, scanning the crowd.

But, of course, neither Titus nor Sarah-Jane could tell who was a visitor when they didn't know most of the people anyway.

But Timothy could. And he took a good look around.

"There she is!" he said, trying not to talk too loudly. "There's a lady with Mrs. Foster now. She's nobody I recognize from church. So that must be her."

The cousins could hardly stand still. It was so exciting, so satisfying, to figure things out like that. It took them a moment to realize that the lady wasn't carrying anything.

Where was the tote bag?

Where was the cookie jar?

The Mystery of the White Elephant

Timothy said, "So she told Mrs. Foster she would come over later. But actually she came over early."

"Wearing an old rain poncho and a sun hat," said Sarah-Jane. "That was in case Mrs. Foster saw her. She didn't want to be recognized. Anyway, she just strolled over to the table when the coast was clear. And she just slipped the cookie jar into the tote bag. Even though we were watching her, we didn't see her do that. Maybe she used the rain poncho as a cover for what she was doing."

"But it wasn't all that easy for her," said Titus. "Because Pastor Parry started to come over to say hello. She couldn't let him see her up close. Because she knew Mrs. Foster would want to introduce them later. And what if Pastor Parry said, 'Weren't you the lady I saw earlier?' No, that would look too suspicious."

"So she had to get away," said Timothy. "Without looking suspicious. And the only place to go was the church. Maybe she wanted to look like she was going to help in the kitchen or use the washroom. She probably noticed the Lost-and-Found closet when she was down there. And she figured that was the perfect

Coincidence?

lady. Anybody can go to Canada and buy a tote bag...."

Titus shook his head. "Is that too much of a coincidence? Because not just anybody knew Mrs. Foster was going to bring the cookie jar to the swap meet. Only Mrs. Foster's houseguest knew that. And she even tried to stop her by buying it herself, remember? She just made up the part about the white elephant being embarrassing."

Timothy said, "She tried to buy it for a few dollars. What a cheat."

Sarah-Jane said, "It would have been cheating if she had bid only a few dollars on it at the auction, too. But she knew guests couldn't bid on things their hosts had brought."

"And besides," added Titus. "What if someone came to the auction who *knew* the cookie jar was worth a lot? And what if that person was willing to pay full price? She couldn't get it cheap then. As it turned out, that's exactly what happened—with Mr. Ramsey. So Mrs. Foster's houseguest knew she really *had* to get her hands on the cookie jar before the sale."

12

Coincidence?

They wanted to tell Pastor Parry what they were thinking. But before they could say anything, a group of people came over and began talking to him.

So the cousins went off and told themselves what they were thinking.

Sarah-Jane said, "The red maple leaf on the tote bag was just like the one on the Canadian flag. OK. So. A person could probably buy a tote bag like that as a souvenir in Canada. And we know Mrs. Foster's houseguest just got back from Canada." She frowned. "Of course, that doesn't prove she was the poncho-

A Red Leaf

member? A red flower, maybe?"

"No," said Titus, suddenly remembering. "Not a flower—a leaf."

"A red leaf," said Sarah-Jane. "Like from a maple tree in the fall."

"A red maple leaf," repeated Pastor Parry. "Like the one on the Canadian flag? Is that what you mean?"

The cousins looked at one another. But this time they didn't feel like grinning. Yes, a Canadian maple leaf was exactly what they meant.

The Mystery of the White Elephant

Pastor Parry patted each of them on the back. "Great! When you find it, report back to me. I'll have a talk with the owner. I don't know what I'll say exactly. I'll have to play it by ear. The things they don't tell you in seminary!"

He started to walk off. Then he turned back. "Now tell me again what we're looking for. Just a plain beige tote bag?"

"No, not quite plain," said Timothy, thinking hard. He appealed to his cousins. "The tote bag had some sort of red design on it, re-kind. Kids have book bags. Even Priscilla has a diaper bag. The poncho-lady just had an ordinary beige tote bag."

Pastor Parry sighed. "That's where it gets sticky. There could be a lot of beige tote bags here today. And we can't just demand that people show us what's in them. That really would ruin everyone's day! And I don't know what I'm going to tell Mrs. Foster. She was thrilled to find out the jar was worth that much. She insisted the money should all go to the church building fund."

They were all quiet for a moment, wondering what to do next.

Pastor Parry said, "Tell you what. You kids have done such a fantastic job, I'm going to ask you to keep at it, all right?"

The cousins looked at one another. It was hard to keep from grinning. More detective work was always all right with them.

Pastor Parry said, "I'll try to keep an eye out for this tote bag. But right now I have to help with the picnic. So I want you three to keep looking around. Will you do that?"

"Yes, we will," said Timothy. "And don't worry. If the bag is still here, we'll find it."

11

A Red Leaf

Timothy said, "We started off thinking that the thief might have hidden the cookie jar somewhere in the church. But probably the poncho-lady thought that would make it too hard to get the cookie jar back at the end of the picnic. She didn't care if she couldn't get the clothes back. They're pretty old anyway. But it was different with the cookie jar. So then we thought that she would want to keep the cookie jar nearby. But it had to be in a place that didn't look suspicious."

Titus said, "A bag wouldn't look suspicious. Just about everyone has a bag of some

"No," replied Pastor Parry, thinking back. "Of course, I couldn't see her face because of that big hat. But it didn't *seem* like anyone I knew. Do you know what I mean? I didn't think to myself, 'Oh, that's Mrs. So-and-So, wearing a big hat.' It was more like, 'I wonder who that could be?' I thought maybe she was a guest. But then I wondered why a guest would be here so early." He looked at the clothes. "But how do you come to have her things?"

"They were hanging in the Lost-and-Found," said Timothy.

Pastor Parry gave a low whistle. "That *is* unusual! You mean she just left them there? Does that mean she's long gone? Or does that mean she's still at the picnic—'disguised' as herself?"

"We don't know," said Timothy. "But what's really weird is what we *didn't* find. When we first saw her, she was carrying a beige tote bag. The tote bag was *not* in the Lost-and-Found."

Pastor Parry saw right away what they were getting at. He said, "Find the tote bag, and you'll find the cookie jar. Is that it?"

The cousins nodded. That was about the size of it.

Lost-and-Found

tion. OK. Let's say the poncho-lady came prepared with a disguise because she wanted to steal the cookie jar. How did she know the cookie jar would be here at the swap meet? And we're still stuck with the most important question of all: Where is the cookie jar *now*?"

All during this conversation with his cousins, Timothy had the strange feeling that his brain was trying to remember something. But what?

What?

He didn't know what.

Timothy sighed. "We don't even know *for sure* if the clothes have anything to do with the cookie jar at all."

"No, we don't," agreed Sarah-Jane. "But Pastor Parry said he was going to ask people if they had seen anything unusual. Well, we saw something unusual. There's no doubt about *that*!"

They bundled up the hat and poncho and went to find Pastor Parry. Sarah-Jane and Titus said that Timothy should be the one to carry the things since it was his church.

As they scurried up the stairs and across the yard, Timothy still had the strange feeling of not being able to remember something. But he also had the feeling that it was coming closer.

"Something's missing," he said to his cousins. "There's something that should have been in the closet with the poncho and the hat. But it wasn't there."

"What? What?" cried Sarah-Jane and Titus together.

Timothy groaned. "That's the problem. I don't know what. I can't remember!"

Then suddenly—he did.

When he told his cousins, they stopped dead in their tracks and stared at him.

10

Something Unusual

When Pastor Parry saw the cousins rushing toward him, he came to meet them.

"You found it!" he exclaimed.

"Not exactly," gasped Timothy. "But we're close. Very close."

It was hard to calm down and explain. But if the cousins had learned anything about telling exciting things to grown-ups, it was that you had to take it slow. Otherwise, grown-ups would just make you take a deep breath and start over. And that was an even bigger waste of time than going slowly in the first place.

So Sarah-Jane started off with a deep

breath. "Pastor Parry, you said you were going to ask people if they had seen anything unusual."

He nodded. "I did ask the people on the picnic committee. But unfortunately, no one remembered seeing anything out of the ordinary. Maybe they were just too busy."

Sarah-Jane nodded back and took another deep breath. "Well, we saw something *very* unusual. And so did you."

"I did?" exclaimed Pastor Parry.

"Yes," said Titus. "Remember before most of the people got here? There was this lady? She was wearing these things here. Remember?"

Timothy held up the hat and the poncho and picked up on the story. "You started to come over to say hello to her. But she hurried away."

"Ah!" said Pastor Parry, remembering. "Now that you mention it, I *did* think that was odd. Most people get upset if the pastor *doesn't* say hello to them."

"We think she didn't want you to recognize her," said Timothy.

"Did you recognize her?" asked Titus.

The Mystery of the White Elephant

all covered up. Because you didn't want anyone to see who you were. The poncho and the hat were a disguise!"

"That's what I think," said Sarah-Jane.

"So what are you saying?" asked Titus thoughtfully. "That somebody decided to wear a disguise and came looking in the Lost-and-Found for something to wear? Usually the Lost-and-Found just has little things—like scarves and stuff."

Timothy said, "These things weren't in the Lost-and-Found before. At least they weren't in here last Sunday when I came looking for Priscilla's shoes. I think somebody wore the disguise to church and then ditched the stuff in the closet when she didn't need it anymore."

"OK, I'll buy that," said Titus. "But why would anyone wear a disguise to a church picnic in the first place?"

Sarah-Jane raised her eyebrows and said what they were all thinking. "Because she was planning to steal a valuable cookie jar?"

Titus shrugged. "You guys? Is it just me? Or is this just about the most exasperating case we've ever had? I mean, every time we come up with an answer, we just get a harder ques-

Lost-and-Found

from head to toe. Yes, they're too big for me. But these clothes are even big enough to hide a grown-up. Do you see what I'm getting at?"

The cousins often found that when they came up against something they didn't understand, it helped to talk things out.

Sarah-Jane continued. "When we saw that strange-looking lady by the tree, Tim said—"

Timothy jumped in. "I said: 'Why would you wear a rain poncho and a sun hat at the same time? Especially when you didn't need either one.' Answer: Because you wanted to be

9

Lost-and-Found

*F*or a moment they just stared at the clothes as if they couldn't take in what they were seeing.

Then on impulse, Sarah-Jane grabbed the poncho and hat and put them on.

"How do I look?" she asked the boys.

"Ridiculous!" said Titus.

"Come on, S-J. Quit fooling around," said Timothy.

"Gentlemen. I am trying to make a point here."

"Which is?" asked Titus, super politely.

"Which is: That these clothes cover me up

Another Search

Timothy turned back to a door tucked away under the stairs. A sign on the door said "Lost-and-Found."

Timothy said, "It wouldn't hurt to look in here. Besides, I should check on a pair of shoes Priscilla lost a couple of weeks ago."

Timothy pulled open the door. The Lost-and-Found closet was actually a tiny room. Just big enough for the three detective-cousins to step inside. The room was filled with all sorts of odds and ends.

They didn't find the cookie jar.

They didn't find Priscilla's shoes.

What they *did* find was a rain poncho and a big, floppy sun hat.

The Mystery of the White Elephant

The cousins went downstairs, Timothy leading the way.

They peeked into the church kitchen. People scurried here and there, heating up food and making coffee.

"I don't think anyone could have hidden the cookie jar in the kitchen," Timothy said softly to his cousins. "There are just too many people around. It would have looked too suspicious if anyone had tried to hide anything."

They decided to skip the kitchen for now. They could always come back later.

They checked out the washrooms. Again, there were just too many people around.

Next they checked the social hall. With the picnic being held outside, the social hall was dim, cool, and quiet. The cousins tiptoed in and looked all through it. But there were hardly any hiding places. Not for something as big as a cookie jar. They checked the door to the storage room. Locked.

Timothy sighed. "Well, that's it for the inside. There's a lot of ground outside that we haven't covered yet. The bushes. The flower beds. The parking lot. Let's get started."

They were about to head upstairs when

Another Search

said Sarah-Jane. "Maybe whoever stole it took it home already."

"Let's hope not!" said Timothy. "Let's hope whoever took it thought it would look suspicious to leave before the picnic even got started."

They all agreed that there was still a good chance the cookie jar was hidden somewhere around the church. And they knew they had to do their level-headed best to track it down.

Since they had already looked outside around the tables, they decided to try something different and look inside the church.

All the doors were locked except the side door, so there was a lot of coming and going through there. Just inside there was a landing and stairs leading down to the basement. From below they could hear voices and laughter and the clatter of pots and pans.

"What's downstairs?" asked Titus. "Just the kitchen?"

Timothy counted off on his fingers. "The kitchen. The washrooms. The social hall. The storage room. The Lost-and-Found closet. That's about it."

8

Another Search

"What on earth are we going to do?" asked Timothy. "We already looked everywhere."

Titus said slowly, "Well, not exactly. We didn't look *everywhere*. We just looked all around the tables. That was when we thought someone misplaced the cookie jar by accident. But what if somebody hid the cookie jar on purpose?"

"You mean so they could get it later?" asked Sarah-Jane. "After the picnic when there weren't a lot of people around?"

"Exactly," said Titus.

"And maybe it's not even here anymore,"

A Collector's Item

"Oh, dear," sighed Pastor Parry. "I'd better have a quiet word with her. I'll also talk to the people in charge of the picnic. Maybe one of them set the cookie jar aside for some reason. Or maybe one of them saw something unusual. I really don't want to make a general announcement and ruin everyone's day unless I absolutely have to. Maybe we can track the cookie jar down ourselves."

Mr. Ramsey unhappily agreed that this was the right thing to do.

Pastor Parry smiled at the cousins. "We sure could use the T.C.D.C. right now."

"What's a 'teesy-deesy'?" asked Mr. Ramsey.

"It's letters," Timothy explained. "Capital T. Capital C. Capital D. Capital C. It stands for the Three Cousins Detective Club."

Mr. Ramsey looked a little doubtful. But Pastor Parry had seen firsthand how the cousins had solved mysteries before.

Pastor Parry and Mr. Ramsey went off to talk to Mrs. Foster. The cousins looked at one another. They had a mystery on their hands all right. And one thing was sure: This was no game.

The Mystery of the White Elephant

I'm sure she had no idea how valuable it was when she donated it."

The cousins gulped.

"You're talking about the baby elephant cookie jar, aren't you?" asked Titus.

"Yes," said Mr. Ramsey. "How did you know?"

"Because we wanted to buy it ourselves," replied Sarah-Jane. "Except we had no idea it could cost so much money!"

Timothy said, "But there's a problem. A BIG problem. The cookie jar is gone."

"What!?" cried Mr. Ramsey and Pastor Parry together. "What do you mean, *gone?*"

Timothy shook his head. "All I know is that we wanted to show it to my mom. But when we got to the table it was gone. We think somebody stole it."

"Maybe it was just misplaced," suggested Pastor Parry.

"We thought so, at first," Timothy said.

"But we can't find it," said Titus. "And we looked everywhere."

"Everywhere," said Sarah-Jane. "We even asked Mrs. Foster. She didn't know it was gone. And she wasn't the least bit worried when we told her. So I'm sure she doesn't know how much the cookie jar is worth."

7

A Collector's Item

Timothy's parents went off to help with lunch. Timothy, Titus, and Sarah-Jane went to go look for Pastor Parry. But just as they did, they saw Pastor Parry heading in their direction. With him was Mr. Ramsey from the choir. Both men looked happy and excited.

"The most amazing thing!" said Pastor Parry to the cousins. "Mr. Ramsey tells me something quite valuable has shown up at our little swap meet. He's a collector, and he says a similar item recently sold for $350.00. He's offering the same amount. Isn't that wonderful? Now, we'd better set it aside so it doesn't get broken. And I need to talk to Mrs. Foster.

The Mystery of the White Elephant

Sarah-Jane joined in, thinking things through. "But why steal it? The cookie jar was for sale. Why not just bid on it at the auction?"

Titus added, "And it wouldn't even cost that much. It's just a cookie jar. It's not like it was really valuable or anything."

Timothy's mother sighed. "I don't know what to tell you. I agree that it doesn't make sense for someone to take it. I hate to think anyone would. It would be like taking money from the church. Even if the jar wasn't worth much, it's still wrong. But let's not jump to conclusions. Why don't you talk to Pastor Parry about it?"

The cousins agreed that this was a good idea. And it gave them something to do. There was nothing worse than having a problem and not being able to do anything to solve it.

Stolen?

"Never mind, sweetie," said Timothy's mother when they reported back. "Why don't you pick out something else?"

"No!" cried Timothy. "I wanted you to have the cookie jar! Besides—it doesn't make sense."

Sarah-Jane and Titus nodded. They knew Timothy hated it when things didn't make sense. They felt the same way.

Timothy went on. "I mean, the cookie jar didn't just *walk* away. Does that mean somebody *stole* it?"

The Mystery of the White Elephant

Foster if she had changed her mind about selling it.

But Mrs. Foster was just as puzzled as they were.

"No, I left the cookie jar right there. What in the world could have happened to it?

"It's no great loss, but I *do* hope nothing else is missing. I'd better go keep an eye on that gorgeous mirror! Excuse me."

And she hurried off. Timothy's parents stared after her. Then they turned to the cousins.

"Don't ask," said Titus.

"But it's true," said Sarah-Jane. "Mrs. Foster loved our mirror. And we loved her cookie jar."

And now the cookie jar was missing. The cousins decided to look around. Maybe someone *had* set the cookie jar down in the wrong place. It was time for another search. But this one wasn't for fun.

The cousins did a quick check of all the tables. Quick but careful. They looked everywhere. On the tables. Even under the tables. The baby elephant cookie jar was nowhere to be seen.

6

Stolen?

"But it was right here!" cried Timothy.

He pointed to the empty spot on the table where the cookie jar should have been.

Sarah-Jane said, "No one else could have bought it already. The auction isn't until after the picnic."

Titus said, "Maybe somebody else was looking at it and set it down in the wrong place."

Timothy knew his cousins were trying to make him feel better. But they sounded as puzzled—and worried—as he was.

Sarah-Jane had the idea of asking Mrs.

pull his hair out. "Why do I try?"

But seeing a baby with a cookie had suddenly reminded him of something.

The cousins had been so interested in the mysterious poncho-lady that they had almost forgotten about the baby elephant cookie jar.

Now the three cousins dragged Timothy's mother—laughing—to see the white elephant that *really was* a white elephant.

But when they got to the table, the baby elephant cookie jar was gone.

Pastor Parry glanced her way. He started over as if to say hello. But the lady didn't wait. Instead, she turned and hurried away. The cousins got a last glimpse of her as she slipped through the side door of the church.

The cousins glanced at one another. Should they keep up the detective game and follow her?

But at that moment Timothy's parents and baby sister found them.

Priscilla squealed with delight when she saw Timothy, Titus, and Sarah-Jane—even though she had seen them only a little while ago.

"Kee-coo!" she said, proudly holding out one of the cookies her mother had baked for the picnic. Usually they weren't allowed to have dessert first. But Priscilla was something of a "cookie monster." It would have been impossible to bring a tray of cookies and Priscilla to the same place without giving her one.

Timothy said, "No, not kee-*coo*. You have it backwards again, Baby Girl. It's cookie. *Cook*-ee."

Priscilla nodded happily. "Kee-coo!"

"Arghh!" cried Timothy, pretending to

The Mystery of the White Elephant

tree," said Titus. "She's got a beige tote bag with some kind of red leaf design in the corner of it. And she's wearing a rain poncho. Why would you wear a rain poncho when it looks like the rain is going to hold off?"

"And the sun hat," added Sarah-Jane. "Why would you wear a big, floppy hat on a cloudy day?"

Timothy said, "That's what I mean. Why would you wear a rain poncho and a sun hat *at the same time*. Especially when you don't need either one."

This was exactly the kind of detective game the cousins loved to play. They would notice what was going on around them and ask themselves questions about it. They especially noticed things that seemed somehow odd or out of place. Sometimes, of course, they actually stumbled onto a real mystery. Sometimes not. But the cousins' motto was: *Keep alert. Pay attention.*

As they watched, the lady moved away from the tree. They couldn't see her in the mirror anymore. But by turning a little bit, they could watch her out of the corner of their eyes.

She wandered casually up to the tables.

5

The Stranger in the Mirror

Usually when someone says "don't turn around," the first thing you do is turn around. But the cousins had trained themselves not to do that. Good detectives don't give themselves away.

"What is it?" murmured Titus.

Timothy said softly, "Look in the mirror. Pretend like you're interested in buying it. But use it to see what's going on behind you. Do you see anything strange?"

Very, *very* casually the cousins took turns looking in the mirror.

"I see a lady hanging around by that big

That mirror is the most beautiful thing I've ever seen!"

Could they have been wrong about the mirror?

After Mrs. Foster left them, the cousins went back to take another look at it.

Nope.

It was still as perfectly awful as ever.

They were just about to go see if Timothy's parents were there yet when Timothy froze.

"Don't turn around," he whispered to Titus and Sarah-Jane.

Another Person's Treasure

Sarah-Jane asked, "Your friend won't mind if Aunt Sarah buys it, will she? Because I don't think guests can bid on what their friends brought."

"That's right, they can't," agreed Mrs. Foster. "But my friend isn't interested in the swap meet. And I didn't ask her to come early to help set up. She's been on vacation in Canada. And I think she's rather tired from the trip. But she said she'd walk over later for the picnic. She just offered to buy the elephant to be nice."

"Well, I don't think you should be embarrassed about it at all," said Titus.

"Your white elephant is the *only* thing I saw that I liked," said Timothy.

"There *are* some rather unusual things here," agreed Mrs. Foster. "Did you see that really fancy mirror? Do you know who brought that?"

The cousins glanced at one another—then stared at their shoes. Now who was embarrassed?

But before they could say anything, Mrs. Foster went on. "That's what *I* want to buy.

The Mystery of the White Elephant

then," said Mrs. Foster. "I've had that cookie jar for ages. But I never bake anything. It was just taking up room in the cupboard. I thought it would be funny to bring a white elephant to a white elephant sale."

"I think it's a great idea," said Timothy. "A white elephant that *really is* a white elephant!"

"Well, I'm glad to hear that," said Mrs. Foster. "Because my houseguest thought I was crazy. She even offered to buy the cookie jar herself for a few dollars so that I would bring something else and not be embarrassed."

4

Another Person's Treasure

A lady Timothy knew from church came up to them. Her name was Mrs. Foster. Mrs. Foster was wearing a funny little kind of smile herself—as if maybe she was embarrassed.

"What do you think of my white elephant?" she asked.

"It's neat-O!" said Timothy.

Mrs. Foster looked as if she couldn't quite believe her ears. "Really? Really, do you like it? You don't think it was a silly thing to bring?"

"No!" said Timothy. "My mom will love it. She likes to bake cookies."

"Well, I hope she gets it at the auction

The Mystery of the White Elephant

Today, Timothy didn't see anything he liked. Until he spotted the baby elephant.

"Look, you guys!" he said to his cousins. "Somebody actually brought a white elephant to the white elephant sale!"

"EXcellent!" said Titus.

"So cool!" said Sarah-Jane.

The baby elephant was actually a china cookie jar. It was sitting up like a teddy bear. It wore a ruffly bonnet and held an ice cream cone in its trunk. It had such a funny little smile on its face that it made you want to smile right back.

Baby Elephant

you'd like your family to bid on. We're starting to fill up the display tables, I see. It should be a great day. It's not a sunny day. But at least it looks as if the rain is going to hold off."

The cousins took Pastor Parry's advice and wandered around by the tables. They were searching again. But this time they were searching for a white elephant they'd like to buy. It was really up to Timothy's parents to decide what to bid on, of course. But the cousins thought it wouldn't hurt to give them some ideas. And even that was mostly up to Timothy.

They saw lots of lamps.

And lots of vases.

And lots and lots of knickknacks.

Sarah-Jane thought there were quite a few possibilities. But Timothy and Titus didn't see eye to eye with Sarah-Jane on the subject of knickknacks. Once, at a flea market, Sarah-Jane had bought a china cat that looked as if it were laughing. The boys had thought she was crazy at the time. But now they had to admit that the laughing cat had led to quite an adventure. And that was the start of their detective club.

The Mystery of the White Elephant

the mirror as a wedding present."

Sarah-Jane explained, "Aunt Sarah said it's nicely made. But it's much too glitzy for their house."

Titus said, "That's because it's the glitziest mirror in the whole history of the world."

"Could be," said Pastor Parry. "But probably someone will think it's just wonderful."

Timothy agreed. "My mom says one person's white elephant is another person's treasure."

"And she said only *things* can be white elephants. Not people," added Sarah-Jane. "Aunt Sarah says God doesn't have any white elephants."

"She's right," said Pastor Parry. "No matter how bad someone might look to us, God looks at that person and sees something to treasure."

Titus said, "If God came to a swap meet, and all the things were people, he would want all of them."

Pastor Parry laughed. "Exactly so. But I'm not sure I would want to take home all the things on *these* tables. As long as you're here early, you should look around for something

3

Baby Elephant

The cousins agreed that they were each going to keep a straight face when they showed the mirror to Pastor Parry. They had come over to church early because they couldn't wait to put the perfectly awful mirror on display.

Pastor Parry kept a straight face, too. "Well, now, Timothy," he said. "That is a mirror. Yes. That certainly is a mirror."

But they couldn't keep it up. All four of them burst out laughing.

Timothy said, "I never saw it before. My dad said that's because it's been up in the attic since way before I was born. My parents got

The Mystery of the White Elephant

with fake pearls and jewels and china flowers and chubby baby angels. One of the cherubs even had a bunch of grapes on his head.

Titus and Sarah-Jane just stared at it for a minute as if they couldn't think of a thing to say.

Finally Sarah-Jane said, "Where in the world did that come from?"

"I have no idea," said Timothy. "I never saw it before in my life. What do you think?"

"What do I think?" said Sarah-Jane. "I think it's *perfect*."

"Perfectly awful, you mean," said Titus, nodding his head with satisfaction.

Timothy agreed. "Perfectly, perfectly, perfectly awful. Lady and Gentleman, we have our white elephant."

"Yes," said Timothy. "But it's just plain ugly. You know what I mean? We want something weirder. Something funnier. Let's keep looking."

So they kept looking.

And looking.

In a way, this was the perfect job for them. That's because searching is a big part of detective work. And the cousins were used to detective work. They even had a club for it called the Three Cousins Detective Club. In fact, they had solved a lot of mysteries. But even when they didn't have an actual mystery to solve, they liked to play detective games to keep in practice.

So they kept on looking and looking for the perfect white elephant to take to the church swap meet. And finally all that looking paid off.

Dusty, but grinning from ear to ear, Timothy pulled something out of the corner and held it up.

"Ti! S-J! I think I found it!"

Timothy unwrapped the clear plastic it was wrapped in. It was a mirror. It had a fancy frame all around it. The frame was covered

The Mystery of the White Elephant

work, searching for the perfect white elephant. They didn't know exactly what they were searching for. But they knew they would know it when they found it. It couldn't be anything broken. And it couldn't be anything junky. And they knew that it didn't actually have to be an elephant.

"How about this, Tim?" Titus asked, sounding a little doubtful. He held up a clunky, boring lamp.

"It's very ugly, Tim," said Sarah-Jane, super politely, as if it were a compliment.

2
Perfectly Awful

Timothy had never been in his attic without a grown-up before. Sarah-Jane and Titus had never been in Timothy's attic at all.

But this morning Timothy's mother was super busy. Especially since she had stopped to answer so many questions about white elephants. And Timothy's father had taken Timothy's baby sister, Priscilla, grocery shopping with him. So it was up to Timothy—with the help of his cousins, of course—to find the family's white elephant.

Timothy divided the attic into three sections, and they each took one part. They set to

The Mystery of the White Elephant

picnic, we'll have an auction to sell the white elephants. The money will go to the church building fund."

"Let me get this straight," said Titus. "We take something we want to get rid of—so someone can buy it. But then we have to buy something that someone else wants to get rid of?"

His aunt laughed. "That's about the size of it. Sounds crazy, I know. But we might actually find something we like at the swap meet. One person's white elephant is another person's treasure."

Sarah-Jane said, "What if we take something we like—and we don't see anything at the swap meet that we like better? Can we bid on our own elephant?"

Aunt Sarah shook her head. "No, that's one of the rules. No one in the family—or the family's guests—can go home with the same thing they brought. And I think you guys slipped in a couple of extra questions. So get to work!"

An Elephant in the Attic?

considered so special it couldn't be used for work. It just ate and ate and got in the way. The owner went broke just feeding it! But since it was a present from the king, the owner couldn't give it away. So he was stuck with a white elephant he didn't want or need."

Titus said, "It makes you feel sorry for the guy. I mean, I know he was obnoxious and everything, but still . . ."

"I feel sorry for the elephant!" declared Sarah-Jane. "I wouldn't want to be a white elephant and just get in the way."

Her aunt laughed. "That's something you don't have to worry about, Sarah-Jane. God doesn't have any white elephants. He doesn't want any of us to stand around thinking we're better than everybody else. And He doesn't want any of us to feel useless, either. He loves us so much He wants the best for us. That's why it's OK to call a *thing* a 'white elephant,' but not a person."

"One more question," said Timothy. "Why are we taking *this* white-elephant thing to church?"

"Each family has to bring something for the swap meet," replied his mother. "After the

The Mystery of the White Elephant

"Ex*cuse* me?" said Timothy. "Did you just tell us to get a white elephant out of the attic?"

Timothy's mother looked up from what she was doing and laughed. "The term 'white elephant' is just a way of speaking. It means something you have that you don't like or need. Something that's more trouble than it's worth. It just gets in the way, but somehow you can't bring yourself to throw it out."

The cousins thought about this for a minute.

Sarah-Jane said, "So—this thing doesn't actually have to be like a china elephant or something?"

"That's right," said her Aunt Sarah. "A 'white elephant' is just what it's called."

"Why is it called that?" asked Titus.

Timothy's mother explained. "It comes from a story about a country that used to be called Siam. When the king of Siam had a proud and bossy person at court, he had a way to deal with him. The king would give that obnoxious person a very special present. A rare white elephant. A real one. Now, this *seemed* like a great honor. But actually it was a punishment. That's because a white elephant was

1

An Elephant in the Attic?

"*T*imothy, do me a favor," said his mother, all in a rush. "I have to finish baking these cookies for the church picnic. Take your cousins up to the attic and see if you can find a white elephant. We need to take it to the church picnic with us. Everyone is supposed to bring a white elephant."

Timothy Dawson looked across the kitchen table at his cousins Sarah-Jane Cooper and Titus McKay. They looked back at him. They all looked at Timothy's mother.

Had she really said what they thought she said?

Contents

1. An Elephant in the Attic? 9
2. Perfectly Awful 13
3. Baby Elephant 17
4. Another Person's Treasure 21
5. The Stranger in the Mirror 25
6. Stolen? 29
7. A Collector's Item 33
8. Another Search 36
9. Lost-and-Found 40
10. Something Unusual 45
11. A Red Leaf 48
12. Coincidence? 52
13. Baby-Sitters *and* Detectives 56
14. Exactly 59
15. Back to the Attic 62

ELSPETH CAMPBELL MURPHY has been a familiar name in Christian publishing for over fifteen years, with more than seventy-five books to her credit and sales reaching five million worldwide. She is the author of the bestselling series *David and I Talk to God* and *The Kids From Apple Street Church*, as well as the 1990 Gold Medallion winner *Do You See Me, God?* A graduate of Trinity College and Moody Bible Institute, Elspeth and her husband, Mike, make their home in Chicago, where she writes full time.

In loving memory of my father-in-law,
Howard R. Murphy,
whose life was filled with
love, joy, peace,
patience, kindness, goodness,
faithfulness, gentleness, and self-control.

Copyright © 1994
Elspeth Campbell Murphy
All Rights Reserved

Three Cousins Detective Club® and TCDC® are registered trademarks of Elspeth Campbell Murphy

Cover and story illustrations by Joe Nordstrom

Published by Bethany House Publishers
A Ministry of Bethany Fellowship, Inc.
11300 Hampshire Avenue South
Minneapolis, Minnesota 55438

Printed in the United States of America

Library of Congress Cataloging-in-Publication Data

Murphy, Elspeth Campbell.
    The mystery of the white elephant / Elspeth Campbell Murphy.
       p.   cm. — (The Three Cousins Detective Club® ; 1)
    Summary: When Timothy and his cousins go to the church swap meet, they discover a thief has stolen the white elephant they plan to buy, and it's up to them to find the culprit.
    [1. Mystery and detective stories. 2. Rummage sales—Fiction. 3. Cousins—Fiction. 4. Christian life—Fiction.] I. Title. II. Series: Murphy, Elspeth Campbell. Three Cousins Detective Club® ; 1.
PZ7.M95316Myp   1994
[Fic]—dc20   94–16719
                                                                  CIP
ISBN 1–55661–405–5   AC

THREE COUSINS **1** DETECTIVE CLUB

The Mystery of the White Elephant

Elspeth Campbell Murphy
Illustrated by Joe Nordstrom

BETHANY HOUSE PUBLISHERS
MINNEAPOLIS, MINNESOTA 55438

THREE COUSINS DETECTIVE CLUB®

#1 / The Mystery of the White Elephant
#2 / The Mystery of the Silent Nightingale
#3 / The Mystery of the Wrong Dog
#4 / The Mystery of the Dancing Angels
#5 / The Mystery of the Hobo's Message
#6 / The Mystery of the Magi's Treasure
#7 / The Mystery of the Haunted Lighthouse
#8 / The Mystery of the Dolphin Detective
#9 / The Mystery of the Eagle Feather
#10 / The Mystery of the Silly Goose
#11 / The Mystery of the Copycat Clown
#12 / The Mystery of the Honeybees' Secret
#13 / The Mystery of the Gingerbread House
#14 / The Mystery of the Zoo Camp
#15 / The Mystery of the Goldfish Pond
#16 / The Mystery of the Traveling Button
#17 / The Mystery of the Birthday Party
#18 / The Mystery of the Lost Island

The Mystery of the White Elephant